Australian
Constitutional
Law and Theory

Australian Constitutional Law and Theory

Commentary and Materials

Fourth Edition

Tony Blackshield

Emeritus Professor, Macquarie University
Visiting Professor, University of New South Wales
Barrister of the Supreme Court of New South Wales and of the High Court

George Williams

Anthony Mason Professor
Director, Gilbert + Tobin Centre of Public Law
University of New South Wales
Barrister of the Supreme Court of New South Wales and of the High Court

THE FEDERATION PRESS
2006

Published in Sydney by
The Federation Press
PO Box 45, Annandale, NSW, 2038.
71 John St, Leichhardt, NSW, 2040.
Ph (02) 9552 2200. Fax (02) 9552 1681.

First edition   1996 Blackshield, Williams, Fitzgerald
Second Edition   1998 Blackshield, Williams
Third Edition   2002 Blackshield, Williams
Fourth Edition   2006 Blackshield, Williams
                   Reprinted 2007

National Library of Australia
Cataloguing-in-Publication entry
    Blackshield, AR (Anthony Roland)
        Australian constitutional law and theory: commentary and materials

    4th ed.
    Includes index.
    ISBN 1 86287 585 5

    1. Constitutional law – Australia. 2. Constitutional law – Australia – Cases. I. Williams, George.
    II. Title.

342.9402

Typeset by The Federation Press, Leichhardt, NSW.
    Printed by Ligare Pty Ltd, Riverwood, NSW.

Preface to the Fourth Edition

[I]n what we generally refer to as commentary, the difference between primary text and secondary text plays two interdependent roles. On the one hand, it permits us to create new discourses ad infinitum: the top-heaviness of the original text, its permanence, its status as discourse ever capable of being brought up to date, the multiple or hidden meanings with which it is credited, the reticence and wealth it is believed to contain, all this creates an open possibility for discussion. On the other hand, whatever the techniques employed, commentary's only role is to say *finally*, what has silently been articulated *deep down*. It must . . . say, for the first time, what has already been said, and repeat tirelessly what was, nevertheless, never said . . . [I]t gives us the opportunity to say something other than the text itself, but on condition that it is the text itself which is uttered and, in some ways, finalised . . . The novelty lies no longer in what is said, but in its reappearance.

Michel Foucault, *The Archaeology of Knowledge*
(transl AM Sheridan Smith, Pantheon Books, 1972), 221

This book was first published in 1996, and thus this edition marks its 10th anniversary. In that time, the High Court has been transformed, with only Gummow J remaining on the bench from the time of the first edition. The Court's case mix and judicial approach has seen an equivalent shift. Gone are the days when the Court under Sir Anthony Mason first implied a freedom of political communication and even considered the idea of a guarantee of legal equality. Such implications are now more likely to be narrowly construed, or indeed bypassed due to the use of principles of statutory construction that enable the Court to avoid the need for constitutional analysis at all.

To reflect these and other changes, this book has continued to evolve from how we conceived it a decade ago. It is certainly a larger work (though thankfully only a little bigger than the 3rd edition). It has also been restructured and rewritten to account for the shifting focus of the Court, with greater attention paid to issues such as the separation of judicial power. This edition even has a whole chapter devoted to the idea of judicial and non-judicial detention, an essential addition given developments since the 3rd edition in the fields of immigration and terrorism law as well as in the law and order debate. This edition takes account of all such developments in the law up to the retirement of Justice Michael McHugh and the swearing in of Justice Susan Crennan on 8 November 2005. We have also been able to accommodate some significant developments that took place after that time.

The fourth edition has involved a thorough rewrite. Each chapter has been looked at again from beginning to end, with fresh choices made for extracts to bring the book up to date for new materials and scholarship, and commentary often rewritten to provide clearer explanation and to account for new developments. While all chapters contain important changes, some required more fundamental revision. For example, the chapters on the executive, and on characterisation and the trade and commerce power, have been rewritten to provide a more straightforward structure and to provide greater clarity and contemporary relevance. Other changes have been made in order to restructure the book and to provide room for the substantial new material. This has involved rethinking the placement of some material. For example, the appropriations and grants powers of the Commonwealth are now grouped together, while the "nationhood" power is treated primarily as an aspect of executive power.

Major cases added since the last edition include *Al-Kateb, Ame, APLA, Austin, Baker, Behrooz, Coleman, Colonel Aird, Combet, Fardon, Lam, Marquet, McBain, Mulholland, Permanent Trustee, Plaintiff S157, Re Woolley, Roberts v Bass, Ruhani, Shaw, Singh* and *Yorta Yorta*. Some of the other changes are: new sections on the separation between church and state, remedies in constitutional law and the Bill of Rights debate in light of the *Human Rights Act 2004* (ACT); a rewritten first chapter to provide a more accessible introduction; new material explaining the power to enter into international treaties, as well as material dealing with international law and constitutional interpretation; and expanding the appendix to include more information on the justices of the High Court.

In writing this edition we have benefited greatly from the suggestions and insights of many people. In particular, we would like to thank those who reviewed the last edition as well as the people who sent us ideas for change. They include Emma Armson, Keven Booker, Sean Brennan, Michael Coper, Freya Dawson, Carolyn Evans, Simon Evans, Elizabeth Handsley, Rosemary Huisman, Helen Irving, Sarah Joseph, Andrew Lynch, Alex Reilly, Gary Rumble, Greg Taylor, Steven Tudor and Kristen Walker. We also thank Anna Saulwick for her research assistance. As with the last three editions, we owe an enormous debt of gratitude to the team at Federation Press for their support of and dedication to this project.

Tony Blackshield would also like to thank Rosemary Huisman, and George Williams would like to thank Emma Armson, both for their positive support and for their forbearance.

As between the two of us, this book has again been a fully collaborative effort, and we take joint responsibility for all chapters.

Tony Blackshield
George Williams

11 November 2005

Table of Contents

Acknowledgments

The authors and publishers thank these organisations for permission to reproduce the following material:

ACT Government for extracts from: Report of the ACT Bill of Rights Consultative Committee, *Towards an ACT Human Rights Act* (May 2003).

Adelaide Law Review for extracts from: the *Adelaide Law Review*.

Allen and Unwin for extracts from: R Smith (ed), *Politics in Australia* (2nd ed 1993).

American Political Science Association for extracts from: the *American Political Science Review*.

Australian Archaeology for extracts from: *Australian Archaeology*.

Australian Bar Review for extracts from: the *Australian Bar Review*.

Australian Government Publishing Service for extracts from: Constitutional Commission, *Final Report of the Constitutional Commission* (1988); Council for Aboriginal Reconciliation, *Recognising Aboriginal and Torres Strait Islander Rights* (2000); I Harris (ed), *House of Representatives Practice* (AGPS, 5th ed 2005); P Keating, *An Australian Republic: The Way Forward* (7 June 1995); JA Pettifer (ed), *House of Representatives Practice* (1st ed 1981); Republic Advisory Committee, *An Australian Republic: The Options* (1993); G Sawer, *The Australian Constitution* (2nd ed 1988).

Bar News (NSW) for extracts from: *Bar News*.

Blackwell for extracts from: the *Australian Journal of Politics & History* 510; *Ratio Juris*; A Vincent, *Theories of the State* (1987).

Boston College Law Review for extracts from: the *Boston College Law Review*.

Cambridge University Press for extracts from: J Locke, *Two Treatises of Government* (1690; critical ed by P Laslett, 2nd ed 1967); A Ortony (ed), *Metaphor and Thought* (1979).

Canada Government Publishing Centre for extracts from: *The Supreme Court Reports*.

Cape York Institute for Policy and Leadership for extracts from: N Pearson, "The High Court's Abandonment of 'The Time-Honoured Methodology of the Common Law' in its interpretation of Native Title in *Mirriuwung Gajerrong* and *Yorta Yorta*" (2003) 7 *Newcastle Law Review* 1.

Centre for Continuing Education, ANU, for extracts from: AR Blackshield, "The Law" in *Power in Australia: Directions of Change* (1981).

Centre for Independent Studies for extracts from: C Kukathas (ed), *Multicultural Citizens: The Philosophy and Politics of Identity* (1993).

Centre for Research on Federal Financial Relations, ANU, for extracts from: RL Mathews, *Revenue Sharing in Federal Systems* (Research Monograph No 31, 1980).

Columbia Law Review for extracts from: the *Columbia Law Review*.

Columbia University Press for extracts from: L Henkin, *The Age of Rights* (1990); J Rawls, *Political Liberalism* (1993).

Commonwealth Parliament for extracts from: S Bennett, *The Politics of Constitutional Amendment* (Research Paper No 11 2002-03); Senate Legal and Constitutional References Committee, *The Road to a Republic* (2004).

Council for Law Reporting for New South Wales for extracts from: *The New South Wales Law Reports*.

Dorset Press for extracts from: G Smith, *A Constitutional and Legal History of England* (1990).

Drummond Publishing for extracts from: P Weller and D Jaensch (eds), *Responsible Government in Australia* (1980).

Duncker & Humblot for extracts from: W Krawietz et al (eds), *Theorie der Normen: Festgabe für Ota Weinberger zum 65. Geburtstag* (1984).

Federal Law Review for extracts from: the *Federal Law Review*.

Hale & Iremonger for extracts from: M Bevege, M James & C Shute (eds), *Worth Her Salt: Women at Work in Australia* (1982).

Harper & Brothers for extracts from: FG Marcham, *A Constitutional History of Modern England, 1485 to the Present* (1960).

Harvard University Press for extracts from: J Shklar, *Legalism: Law, Morals, and Political Trials* (1964, reissued 1986).

Harvester Press for extracts from: M Foucault, *Power/Knowledge* (1980).

Human Rights and Equal Opportunity Commission for extracts from: Aboriginal and Torres Strait Islander Social Justice Commissioner, *Native Title Report 2002* (2003).

Ideology and Consciousness for extracts from: M Foucault, "Politics and the Study of Discourse" (1978) 4 *Ideology and Consciousness* 7.

Incorporated Council of Law Reporting of England and Wales for extracts from: *The Law Reports*.

Juta Legal & Academic Publishers for extracts from: LJ Boulle, *South Africa and the Consociational Option* (1984).

Law Quarterly Review for extracts from: the *Law Quarterly Review*.

Law Reform Commission of Canada for extracts from: *The Legal Status of the Federal Administration* (1985).

Lawyers Cooperative Publishing for extracts from: *The Supreme Court Reports*.

Legislative Studies for extracts from: G Carney, "Separation of Powers in the Westminster System", Vol 8, No 2, Autumn 1994.

LexisNexis for extracts from: L Zines, *The High Court and the Constitution* (4th ed 1997); *Law Reports of the Commonwealth; The Australian Law Reports*.

Macmillan (UK) for extracts from: AV Dicey, *Introduction to the Study of the Law of the Constitution* (10th ed 1959); J Alder, *Constitutional and Administrative Law* (2nd ed 1994).

MacMillan Education Australia for extracts from: J Brett, J Gillespie and M Goot (eds), *Developments in Australian Politics* (1994).

Macmillan Publishing Co and The Free Press for extracts from: P Edwards (ed), *The Encyclopaedia of Philosophy* (1967), Vol 4.

McCulloch Publishing for extracts from: J Scutt (ed), *Lionel Murphy: A Radical Judge* (1987).

Melbourne University Law Review for extracts from: the *Melbourne University Law Review*.

Melbourne University Press for extracts from: G Craven (ed), *Australian Federation* (1992); G de Q Walker, *The Rule of Law* (1988).

Michigan Law Review for extracts from: the *Michigan Law Review*.

New York Review of Books for extracts from: the *New York Review of Books*.

Northwestern University Law Review for extracts from: the *Northwestern University Law Review*.

Oxford University Press for extracts from: S Avieneri and A De-Shalit (eds), *Communitarianism and Individualism* (1992); TRS Allan, *Law, Liberty and Justice: The Legal Foundations of British Constitutionalism* (1993); RTE Latham, *The Law and the Commonwealth* (1949 reprint); JR Lucas, *The Principles of Politics* (1966); VP Luthera, *The Secular State and India* (1964).

Palgrave Macmillan for extracts from: H Emy and O Hughes, *Australian Politics: Realities in Conflict* (2nd ed, 1991).

Public Law for extracts from: *Public Law*.

Reconciliation Australia for extracts from: Council for Aboriginal Reconciliation, *Australian Declaration towards Reconciliation*.

Routledge for extracts from: R Beardsworth, *Derrida & the Political* (1996); D Cornell, M Rosenfeld and D Carlson (eds), *Deconstruction and the Possibility of Justice* (1992), 152.

Russell and Russell for extracts from: H Kelsen, *General Theory of Law and State* (1945).

Sweet and Maxwell Ltd for extracts from: PP Craig, *Administrative Law* (3rd ed 1994); O Hood Phillips and P Jackson, *O Hood Phillips' Constitutional and Administrative Law* (7th ed 1987).

Sydney Law Review for extracts from: the *Sydney Law Review*.

Taylor & Francis for extracts from: the *Australian Journal of Political Science*; J Derrida, *Acts of Religion* (ed G Anidjar, Routledge, 2001).

Thomson Legal & Regulatory Limited for extracts from: A Castles, *An Australian Legal History* (1982); P Parkinson, *Tradition and Change in Australian Law* (3rd ed 2005); PA Joseph, *Constitutional and Administrative Law in New Zealand* (1993); *Australian Law Journal*; *Commonwealth Law Reports*; *Public Law Review*.

Transnational Law and Contemporary Problems for extracts from: *Transnational Law and Contemporary Problems*.

University of California Press for extracts from: H Kelsen, *Pure Theory of Law* (1967).

University of Chicago Press for extracts from: J Derrida, *Positions* (transl A Bass, 1981); G Burchell, C Gordon and P Miller (eds), *The Foucault Effect: Studies in Governmentality* (1991).

University of London Press for extracts from: WI Jennings, *The Law and the Constitution* (5th ed 1959).

University of New South Wales Law Journal for extracts from: the *University of New South Wales Law Journal*.

University of Queensland Press for extracts from: B Galligan, *Politics of the High Court* (1987).

University of Tasmania for extracts from: M Sornarajah (ed), *The South West Dam Dispute: The Legal and Political Issues* (1983).

University of Toronto Press for extracts from: the *University of Toronto Law Journal*; JS Mill, *On Liberty* in *Collected Works of John Stuart Mill*, vol 18, 1977.

Virginia Law Review for extracts from: the *Virginia Law Review*.

Table of Cases

(References in **bold** type are to extracts of cases)

Table of Legislation

United States

Chapter 1

Foundations

1. Constitutionalism

The Commonwealth of Australia came into being at the stroke of midnight on 1 January 1901 when the *Commonwealth of Australia Constitution Act 1900* (Imp) entered into force. The Australian Constitution is a hybrid of ideas and models. From the United Kingdom, Australia took the fundamentals of the Westminster system of representative and responsible government, while from other nations with written constitutions, especially the United States, it adopted the concepts of federalism, the separation of powers and judicial review.

The symbolic façade of the Australian system can mask its substance. The façade is that of monarchical government. The Queen, as represented in Australia by the Governor-General, is Australia's Head of State. While the Constitution does not mention offices such as the Prime Minister or bodies like Cabinet, it does specify that the Queen and her representative possess a range of important powers. Under s 59, for example, the Queen is able to disallow, or annul, laws made by the federal Parliament. However, that provision is obsolete and, in reality, the Queen and the Governor-General have little scope to act independently of advice. By convention, they normally act on the advice of the Prime Minister and other Ministers.

Representative government means government by the people (sometimes identified as "citizens") through their elected representatives, while responsible government means that the executive arm of government is responsible to Parliament for its actions. In the British version of these ideas still dominant in Australia, the Parliament is the central institution through which all the disparate elements of the system of government, from "the people" through to "the Crown", are welded into one consolidated chain of command. The power of the Crown is controlled by the ministry; the ministry is controlled by the Parliament; and the Parliament is controlled by the electorate. By this means, the power wielded by the institutions of government is conceptualised as an expression of the power of the people themselves.

In the elements borrowed from the United States, the unifying theme is the need to protect the people *against* the power of government, by distributing and dismembering that power in ways that ensure there is no single consolidated chain of command. The powers of government are divided by a "separation of powers", which allocates legislative, executive and judicial functions to distinct institutions at least partially independent of one another, and by "federalism", which allocates all governmental powers (and especially legislative powers) among different political and territorial units. These allocations are themselves subject to checks and balances, including the ability of the courts to exercise a power of judicial review to strike down laws and governmental action found to be inconsistent with the Constitution.

It would be a mistake, however, to assume that the British inheritance is *simply* concerned with establishing a strong governmental chain of command, while the American borrowings are *simply* concerned with limiting its power. It would be more accurate to assume that, in every system of government, the basic rules of constitutional law must have both of these functions. Indeed, when the British system is conventionally described as one of "constitutional monarchy", what is meant is that the *power* embodied in the idea of "monarchy" is *limited* by the ideals and principles of "constitutionalism".

Giovanni Sartori, "Constitutionalism: A Preliminary Discussion"
(1962) 56 *American Political Science Review* 853

[854] [I]n the 19th century, all over Europe as well as in the United States, a general agreement prevailed as to the basic meaning of the term "constitution" …

[855] What really matters is the end, the *telos*. And the purpose, the *telos*, of English, American and European constitutionalism was, from the outset, identical … [T]his common purpose could be expressed and synthesized by just one word: the French (and Italian) term *garantisme*. In other terms, all over the Western area people requested, or cherished, "the constitution," because this term meant to them a fundamental law, or a fundamental set of principles, and a correlative institutional arrangement, which would restrict arbitrary power and ensure a "limited government" …

[856] [I]n the terminology of the Constitution of Pennsylvania of September 28, 1776, a constitution contains two basic elements: a "plan (or frame) of government," and a "bill of rights." For the framers of the 18th century charters it was self-evident that the two component parts could not be separated: both were needed for a constitution to be a constitution. They did not mean in the least that *any* plan of government amounted to a constitution: they meant that this was the case only when a frame of government provided for a bill of rights and the institutional devices that would secure its observance. Continental jurists, however, were anxious to put their rationalistically trained juridical consciences at ease by finding a "universal" definition of constitution. And for this purpose they found it expedient to separate the universal trait (the "plan of government" meaning) from the *garantiste* component. Therefore, often enough, they did come to say – *qua* pure jurists – that any "frame of government" amounted to a constitution. They said it, but – let me stress this point – they immediately denied it. For they went on to say that "it had become customary" to use the term constitution in a more specific *garantiste* sense; and therefore that, according to this practice, it was improper to hold that every state was a constitutional state. *Every* state had a "constitution," but only *some* states were "constitutional." …

It was an uneasy equilibrium … But one can have an Achilles heel and nevertheless survive. So, despite this weakness, I believe … (i) that for almost 150 years "constitution" has been associated with *garantisme*; and (ii) that the primary agent of change cannot be located in the inner logic of development of the European juristic tradition … What started the new trend was the impact of the political atmosphere of the 1920's …

I have said "political atmosphere." It is fair to add that in some countries it was not only a question of atmosphere. In Italy, and in the 1930's in Germany, jurists were somehow compelled to adopt a merely formal, "organizational," neutral definition of constitution … What is surprising is that in the meantime the British, too, had come to adopt very much the same position.

Let me refer again to Wheare's definition, according to which the English constitution is "the collection of legal rules and non-legal rules which govern the government in Britain." Or allow me to quote, as another instance, Jennings' definition, according to which a constitution is "the document in which are set out the rules governing the composition, powers and methods of operation of the main institutions of government." The peculiar feature of these definitions is … the silence which covers the *telos* of constitutionalism. Actually they are purely "formal" definitions, in the sense that they can be filled with any content whatever. We are thus faced, **[857]** nowadays, with this puzzling situation: that the very inventors of the constitutional solution provide us with a definition which amounts to saying that any instrument of government, any "traffic rule," is a constitution … It is not astonishing, therefore, if the Continental theory of constitutionalism has shown, since World War II, very little evidence of recovery. For whenever somebody claims … that *garantisme* remains the core of constitutionalism, one is likely to be confronted with this reply: why should we be concerned with this problem more than the English? …

[I]f a constitution is defined as "any way of giving form to any State whatever," then the question "What is the role of a constitution in a political system?" either cannot be answered, or can be answered only country by country, and even then in a very uninteresting and banal way. For in this case the answer is that the constitution plays no role, properly speaking: It is only a short-hand report which may describe … the formalization of the power structure of the given country …

[We need] a convincing answer to the question, "What is a constitution?" …

[861] Basically we are confronted with three possibilities: (i) *garantiste* constitution (constitution, proper); (ii) nominal constitution; (iii) façade constitution (or fake constitution).

I call "nominal" the constitutions that Loewenstein labels "semantic" … [Otherwise] I entirely underwrite his description of the specimen: "The constitution is fully applied and activated, but its ontological reality is nothing but the formalization of the existing location of political power for the exclusive benefit of the actual power holders". Nominal constitutions are therefore "nominal" in the very simple sense that they bear the "name" constitution. This amounts to saying that nominal constitutions are merely organizational constitutions, *ie*, the collection of rules which organize but do not restrain the exercise of political power in a given polity. Actually, nominal constitutions do not really pretend to be "real constitutions." They frankly describe a system of limitless, unchecked power …

The façade constitutions are different from the nominal ones in that they take the appearance of "true constitutions." What makes them untrue is that they are disregarded (at least in their essential *garantiste* features). Actually they are "trap-constitutions." As far as the techniques of liberty and the rights of the power addressees are concerned, they are a dead letter …

There is often a considerable overlapping between nominal and façade constitutions. The distinction is nevertheless basic, for the two cases are indeed very different. Nominal constitutions actually describe the working of the political system (they do not abide by the *telos* of constitutionalism, but they are sincere reports), while the façade constitutions give us no reliable information about the real governmental process. In most cases one can clearly perceive … which is the prevalent aspect: I mean, whether a constitution is basically nominal or basically a disguise.

Sartori's contrast of "*garantiste* constitutions" with "nominal" or "façade" constitutions is not meant to suggest that any actual constitutional system conforms precisely to any one of these descriptions. We should not ask whether a constitutional system is appropriately labelled "*garantiste*" or "nominal" or "façade". Instead, in any functioning political system, we should expect to find elements of all of these. We should ask: to what extent, and in what respects, does this constitutional system achieve or aspire to *garantism*? To what extent, and in what respects, is the constitution merely nominal, or merely a façade? Fundamental doctrines – such as federalism, responsible government, the separation of powers and judicial review – are all explained by conventional political theory as having a *garantiste* function. Yet in any functioning political system one needs to be aware that some of its institutional safeguards may be merely nominal, and some may be merely a façade.

Similar questions should be borne in mind in analysing the constitutional developments traced in this book. For example, would Australian constitutionalism be enhanced by proposals to change the structural foundation of Australian government from that of a monarchy to that of a republic (see Chapter 30, §3)? If so, why? If not, why not? Under s 128 of the Constitution, the document can only be amended by a process which includes approval at a referendum by a majority of electors and a majority of electors in a majority of States. Is that sufficient immediately to identify the Constitution as *garantiste*? Was the *garantiste* nature of the Constitution enhanced by the apparent judicial tendency in the early 1990s to find limitations on law-making power *implied* in the Constitution? Or did that degree of judicial initiative entail a further departure from constitutionalism?

In its British usage the term "constitutional law" has been used "**[22]** to describe rules which directly or indirectly affect the distribution of the sovereign power in the state" (AV Dicey, *Introduction to the Study of the Law of the Constitution*, Macmillan, 1st ed 1885, 10th ed 1959). Constitutional law thus describes that body of rules according to which a state is constituted or governed, the way in which the organs of government are structured and defined, and the way in which those organs relate to one another and to citizens. Note that this definition does not *exclude* the point made by Sartori that one purpose of the rules is to protect the citizens against the excessive use of government power. Sartori's criticism of the conventional British definitions is only that they typically fail to mention this purpose.

Owen Hood Phillips and Paul Jackson, *Constitutional and Administrative Law*
(Sweet and Maxwell, 7th ed 1987)

[5] A constitution is said to be "written" when the most important constitutional laws are specifically *enacted*. Probably all civilised states, except the United Kingdom, New Zealand and Israel now have mainly written or enacted constitutions. Those who attain power in a state, whether as a result of revolution (*eg* France), war of independence (*eg* United States), federation or confederation of existing units (*eg* Switzerland), or emergence of a new independent nation (*eg* former British colonies and protectorates), put into the form of legislative enactment the manner in which the state is to be organised, government carried on and justice administered, and this arrangement is commonly approved by a referendum of the electorate. The most important [6] laws constituting the basis of the state are specified in one formal document or a series of formal documents which are binding on the courts and all persons concerned.

It is not practicable for a written constitution to contain more than a selection of constitutional laws. It is invariably supplemented, within the limits prescribed in the constitution, by amendments passed in the prescribed manner; by organic laws, and other legislation passed in the ordinary way from time to time to fill in gaps; usually also by judicial decisions interpreting the written documents; and by customs and conventions regulating the working of the machinery of government ...

A more significant classification of the types of constitution is that into "flexible" and "rigid," metaphors given currency by Bryce. A *flexible* constitution was defined by Dicey as "one under which every law of every description can legally be changed with the same ease and in the same manner by one and the same body." Dicey defined a *rigid* constitution as "one under which certain laws generally known as constitutional or fundamental laws cannot be changed in the same manner as ordinary laws." The distinction is of great importance in relation to constitutional amendment.

Where the constitution is rigid, certain provisions are distinguished from others in that some *special procedure* is necessary for their alteration, if they are legally alterable at all. Most European and American constitutions are rigid. The method of amending "fundamental" or "constitutional" laws varies in different constitutions: it may be the legislature sitting in a special way (as in France) or with a prescribed majority or a prescribed quorum (as in Belgium), the convention of a special constituent body (as in the United States), the consultation of the component members of a composite state (as in the United States and Swiss Federations), or a referendum of the electorate (as in Switzerland and Australia). Amendment of the United States Constitution, for example, requires either initiation by two-thirds of both Houses of [7] Congress and ratification by the legislatures of three-fourths of the states (the usual method), or initiation by two-thirds of the states and ratification by conventions in three-fourths of the states ...

Sometimes a constitution or part of it may not be legally alterable at all, as certain articles of the Constitution of the German Federal Republic (1949), the "basic articles" of the Constitution of the Republic of Cyprus (1960) and the representation of a state in the United States Senate (unless that state consents) ... In such cases any alteration would legally amount to revolution.

Unwritten constitutions are in practice flexible, but written constitutions are not necessarily rigid. The Constitution of Singapore is written but entirely flexible, while the constitutions of the Australian states are written and largely flexible.

Australian constitutional law is both written and unwritten. The written document known as "the Constitution" is set out in s 9 of the *Commonwealth of Australia Constitution Act*. This rigid Constitution is complemented by the *Statute of Westminster 1931* (Imp) and the *Australia Act 1986* (Cth) and is supplemented by the common law and unwritten conventions. Each of the Australian States has a written (but largely flexible) constitution that is also supplemented by conventions and the common law.

2. Power and Norm

For lawyers, one main function of a constitution is to establish the institutions that serve as authoritative sources of law and endow them with legislative power. Sometimes the grant of power is accompanied by explicit *limitations* on power. Always there is an implied limitation, namely that the power can only be exercised by the institutions to which the power is given, and according to the procedures which the constitution prescribes. Whether these and other more explicit limitations on law-making power are judicially enforceable depends in part on funda-mental issues of legal theory, and in part on the text and structure of the particular constitution.

The theories of "legal positivism" that came to dominate legal theory during the 19th century have greatly influenced the development of Australian constitutional law. Their central thesis is that the validity of any legal rule depends solely on questions about power: that is, on whether the authority issuing the rule had the *legal* power to do so. Since the grant of *legal* power must itself be conferred by a legal rule, the object is to show that the legal order is a self-contained universe of discourse, within which any legal question can be given a purely legal answer. The most elegant expression of this idea was the *Stufentheorie* ("steps and stairs theory") of the legal philosopher Hans Kelsen (1881-1973), who portrayed the entire legal order as a pyramid of norms derived (through successive levels of derivation) from the norm-creating powers conferred by the Constitution, which itself derived its validity from any earlier constitutional arrangements pursuant to which it was adopted, and ultimately from a *Grundnorm* or "basic norm" embodying the axiomatic assumption or postulate that the legal order was to be obeyed.

According to Kelsen, this analysis merely elicits the underlying structure of the way that lawyers actually think. Suppose, for example, that a local council inspector orders you to cut down a tree. If you instruct your lawyer to contest this order, he or she will do so by asking whether the inspector had *power* to issue such an order. The answer will depend on the terms of the council ordinance pursuant to which the inspector was acting. If, by that test, the inspector's order is valid, the next step will be to ask whether the council had power to issue the ordinance. Again, this will depend on a scrutiny of the powers given to the council by the relevant *Local Government Act*. If the grant of power at that level is clear, the next step will be to ask whether the parliament had power under the Constitution to enact the relevant provisions of the *Local Government Act*. Logically the next step would be to ask whether the Constitution is valid; but in fact lawyers never do ask this (though political theorists may do so). All the other operations lawyers perform are explained by the fact that they simply *assume* that the Constitution is binding. The "basic norm" is Kelsen's name for this assumption.

In this analysis the question of legal validity is always a question of power. Kelsen concedes that in some normative systems (for instance those of morals or of "natural law") the *content* of each derivative norm can be *logically* derived from the *content* of the immediate higher norm. (He calls this "static" derivation.) By contrast, he insists that in every system of positive law, the downwards derivation of legal validity flows exclusively through successive acts of *authorisation* or *empowerment*. (He calls this "dynamic" derivation.)

Hans Kelsen, *Pure Theory of Law*
(transl by Max Knight, University of California Press, 1967)

[198] *The Reason for the Validity of a Legal Order*
The norm system that presents itself as a legal order has essentially a dynamic character. A legal norm is not valid because it has a certain content, that is, because its content is logically deducible from a presupposed basic norm, but because it is created in a certain way – ultimately in a way determined by a presupposed basic norm. For this reason alone does the legal norm belong to the legal order whose norms are created according to this basic norm. Therefore any kind of content might be law … The validity of a legal norm may not be denied for being (in its content) in conflict with that of another norm which does not belong to the legal order whose basic norm is the reason for the validity of the norm in question. The basic norm of a legal order is not a material norm

5

which, because its content is regarded as immediately self-evident, is presupposed as the highest norm and from which norms for human behavior are logically deduced. The norms of a legal order must be created by a specific process. They are posited, that is, positive, norms, elements of a positive order. If by the constitution of a legal community is understood the norm or norms that determine how (that is, by what organs and by what procedure – through legislation or custom) the general norms of the legal order that constitute the community are to [199] be created, then the basic norm is that norm which is presupposed when the custom through which the constitution has come into existence, or the constitution-creating act consciously performed by certain human beings, is objectively interpreted as a norm-creating fact; if, in the latter case, the individual or the assembly of individuals who created the constitution … , are looked upon as norm-creating authorities. In this sense, the basic norm determines the basic fact of law creation and may in this respect be described as the constitution in a logical sense of the word (which will be explained later) in contradistinction to the constitution in the meaning of positive law. The basic norm is the presupposed starting point of a procedure: the procedure of positive law creation. It is itself not a norm created by custom or by the act of a legal organ; it is not a positive but a presupposed norm so far as the constitution-establishing authority is looked upon as the highest authority and can therefore not be regarded as authorized by the norm of a higher authority.

If the question as to the reason for the validity of a certain legal order is raised, then the answer can only consist in the reduction to the basic norm of this legal order, that is, in the assertion that the norm was created – in the last instance – according to the basic norm …

The question of the reason for the validity of a legal norm belonging to a specific national legal order may arise on the occasion of a coercive act; for example, when one individual deprives another of his life by hanging, and now the question is asked why this act is legal, namely the execution of a punishment, and not murder. This act can be interpreted as being legal only if it was prescribed by an individual legal norm, namely as an act that "ought" to be performed, by a norm that presents itself as a judicial decision. This raises the questions: Under what conditions is such an interpretation possible, why is a judicial decision present in this case, why is the individual norm created thereby a legal [200] norm belonging to a valid legal order and therefore ought to be applied? The answer is: Because this individual norm was created in applying a criminal law that contains a general norm according to which (under conditions present in the case concerned) the death penalty ought to be inflicted. If we ask for the reason for the validity of this criminal law, then the answer is: the criminal law is valid because it was created by the legislature, and the legislature, in turn, is authorized by the constitution to create general norms. If we ask for the reason of the validity of the constitution, that is, for the reason of the validity of the norms regulating the creation of the general norms, we may, perhaps, discover an older constitution; that means the validity of the existing constitution is justified by the fact that it was created according to the rules of an earlier constitution by way of a constitutional amendment. In this way we eventually arrive at a historically first constitution that cannot have been created in this way and whose validity, therefore, cannot be traced back to a positive norm created by a legal authority; we arrive, instead, at a constitution that became valid in a revolutionary way, that is, either by breach of a former constitution or for a territory that formerly was not the sphere of validity of a constitution and of a national legal order based on it … [I]f we ask for the reason of the validity of the historically first constitution, then the answer can only be (if we leave aside God or "nature") that the validity of this constitution – the assumption that it is a binding norm – must be *presupposed* if we want to interpret (1) the acts performed according to it as the creation and application of valid general legal norms; and (2) the acts performed in application of these general norms as the creation or application of valid individual legal norms. Since the reason for the validity of a norm can only be another norm, the presupposition must be a norm: not one posited (ie, created) by a legal authority, but a presupposed norm … formulated as follows: [201] Coercive acts [ ]ought to be performed under the conditions and in the manner which the historically first constitution, and the norms created according to it, prescribe. (In short: One ought to behave as the constitution prescribes.) The norms of a legal order, whose common reason for their validity is this basic norm are not a complex of valid norms standing coordinatedly side by side, but form a hierarchical structure of super- and subordinate norms …

The Basic Norm as Transcendental-logical Presupposition
To understand the nature of the basic norm it must be kept in mind that it refers directly to a specific constitution, actually established by custom or statutory creation, by and large effective, and indirectly to the coercive order created according to this constitution and by and large effective; the basic norm thereby furnishes the reason for the validity of this constitution and of the coercive order created in accordance with it. The basic norm, therefore, is not the product of free invention. It is not presupposed arbitrarily in the sense that there is a choice between different basic norms … Only if this basic norm, referring to a specific constitution, is presupposed, that is, only if it is presupposed that one ought to behave according to this specific constitution – only then can the subjective meaning of a constitution-creating act and of the acts created according to this constitution be interpreted as their objective meaning, that is, as objectively valid legal norms …

In presupposing the basic norm referring to a specific constitution, the contents of this constitution and of the national legal order created according to it is irrelevant – it may be a just or unjust order; it may or may not guarantee a relative condition of peace … The presupposition of the basic norm does not approve any value transcending positive law …

[203] Since a positivistic science of law regards the creator of the his-[204]-torically first constitution as the highest legal authority and therefore cannot maintain that the norm to obey the commands of the creator of the constitution is the subjective meaning of the act of will of an authority higher than the creator of the constitution – such as God's or nature's – so therefore, the science of law cannot base the validity of this norm on a syllogistic procedure. A positivistic science of law can only state that this norm is presupposed as a basic norm in the foundation of the objective validity of the legal norms, and therefore presupposed in the interpretation of an effective coercive order as a system of objectively valid legal norms. Since this basic norm cannot be the meaning of an act of will; and since this norm (rather: the statement about it) is logically indispensable for the foundation of the objective validity of positive legal norms, it can only be the meaning of an act of thinking; the science of law can state no more than: the subjective meaning of the acts by which legal norms are created can be interpreted as their objective meaning only if we presuppose in our juristic thinking the norm: "One ought to obey the prescriptions of the historically first constitution."

The science of law does not prescribe that one ought to obey the commands of the creator of the constitution. The science of law remains a merely cognitive discipline even in its epistemological statement that the basic norm is the condition under which the subjective meaning of the constitution-creating act, and the subjective meaning of the acts performed in accordance with the constitution, are interpreted as their objective meaning, as valid norms, even if the meaning of these acts is so interpreted by the legal science itself.

By offering this theory of the basic norm, the Pure Theory of Law does not inaugurate a new method of legal cognition. It merely makes conscious what most legal scientists do, at least un-[205]-consciously, when they understand the mentioned facts not as causally determined, but instead interpret their subjective meaning as objectively valid norms, that is, as a normative legal order, without basing the validity of this order upon a higher, meta-legal norm, that is, upon a norm enacted by an authority superior to the legal authority; in other words, when they consider as law exclusively positive law. The theory of the basic norm is merely the result of an analysis of the procedure which a positivistic science of law has always applied.

[221] THE HIERARCHICAL STRUCTURE OF THE LEGAL ORDER …
The peculiarity of the law that it regulates its own creation, has been pointed out before in these pages. This can be done by a norm determining merely the procedure by which another norm is to be created. But it can be done also by a norm determining, to a certain extent, the content of the norm to be created. Since, because of the dynamic character of law, a norm is valid because, and to the extent that, it had been created in a certain way, that is, in a way determined by another norm, therefore that other norm is the immediate reason for the validity of the new norm. The relationship between the norm that regulates the creation of another norm and the norm created in conformity with the former can be metaphorically presented as a relationship of super- and subordination. The norm which regulates the creation of another norm is the higher, the norm created in conformity with the former is the lower one. The legal order is not a system of coordinated norms of equal

7

level, but a hierarchy of different levels of legal norms. Its unity is brought about by the connection that results from the fact that the validity of a norm, created according **[222]** to another norm, rests on that other norm, whose creation in turn, is determined by a third one. This is a regression that ultimately ends up in the presupposed basic norm. This basic norm, therefore, is the highest reason for the validity of the norms, one created in conformity with another, thus forming a legal order in its hierarchical structure.

Throughout the past half-century, variants of Kelsen's theory have remained influential (see, for example, HLA Hart, *The Concept of Law* (Clarendon Press, 2nd ed 1994)). However, there have also been radical challenges to the kind of scholarly project such a theory pursues.

Michel Foucault, "Politics and the Study of Discourse"
(1978) 4 *Ideology and Consciousness* 7

[8] I am a pluralist: the problem which I have set myself is that of the *individualization* of discourses …

[10] Nothing … is more foreign to me than the quest for a sovereign, unique and constraining form. I do not seek to detect … the unitary spirit of an epoch, the general form of its consciousness: something like a *Weltanschauung*. Nor have I described either the emergence and eclipse of a formal structure which might reign for a time over all the manifestations of thought: I have not written the history of a syncopated transcendental. Nor, finally, have I described thoughts or century-old sensitivities coming to life, stuttering, struggling and dying out like great phantoms – ghosts playing out their shadow theatre against the backdrop of history. I have studied, one after another, ensembles of discourse; I have characterized them; I have **[11]** defined the play of rules, of transformations, of thresholds, of remanences. I have established and I have described their clusters of relations. Wherever I have deemed it necessary I have allowed the *systems* to proliferate …

My problem is to substitute the analysis of *different types of transformation* for the abstract, general and monotonous form of "change" in which one so willingly thinks in terms of succession. This implies two things: setting aside the old forms of weak continuity through which one ordinarily attenuates the raw fact of change (tradition, influences, habits of thought, broad mental forms, constraints of the human mind), and stubbornly stressing instead the lively intensity of difference … Replacing, in short, the theme of *becoming* (general form, abstract element, primary cause and universal effect, a confused mixture of the identical and the new) by the analysis of the *transformations* in their specificity …

What is important to me is to show that there are not on the one hand inert discourses, already more than half dead, and then, on the other hand, an all-powerful subject which manipulates them, upsets them, renews them; but that the discoursing subjects are part of the discursive field – they have their place there (and the possibilities of their displacements), their function (and their possibilities of functional mutation). The discourse is not the place where pure subjectivity irrupts; it is a space of positions and of differentiated functions for subjects …

[14] The question which I ask is not that of codes but of events … : the conditions of their singular emergence; their correlation with other previous or simultaneous events … This question, however, I try to answer without referring to the consciousness, obscure or explicit, of speaking subjects …

[17] [For] the opposition between periods of stability or of universal convergence and moments of effervescence when minds enter into crisis, when sensibilities are metamorphosed, when all notions are revised, overturned, revivified, or for an indefinite time, fall into disuse … I would like to substitute the analysis of the field of simultaneous differences (which define at a given period the possible dispersal of knowledge) and of successive differences (which define the set of transformations, their hierarchy, their dependence, their level). Whereas one used to relate the history of traditions and of invention, of the old and the new, of the dead and the living, of the closed and the open, of the static and the dynamic, I undertake to relate the history of perpetual difference …

[23] I am anxious to show you just one thing: how what I am attempting to bring out through my analysis – the *positivity* of discourses, their conditions of existence, the systems which regulate their emergence, their functioning and their transformations – can concern political practice; to show you what this practice can do with it; to convince you that by outlining this theory … I am not just amusing myself by making the game more complicated for a few lively minds. I am trying to define in what way, to what extent, to what level discourses, and particularly scientific discourses, can be objects of a political practice, and in what system of dependency they can be in relation to it.

What Foucault describes here is his approach to the exploration of history through what he initially called "archaeology" (that is, the study of cultural "archives"), but later came to call "genealogy" (since the archaeological metaphor still implied the uncovering of structures that were already there). His approach is characterised by flux, inconsistency, discontinuity and change, and an unremitting rejection of analyses that purport to uncover objective "structures". Thus the approaches of Foucault and Kelsen reflect very different conceptions of what intellectual discourse can be. What Kelsen seeks to do is to construct (or perhaps to educe) a systematic framework for a pure theory of law, characterised by hierarchy and unity. His approach is essentially ahistorical and apolitical. He acknowledges the need to trace legal validity to "the historically first constitution". He also expounds the hierarchy of norms as if it is amenable to observation, narration and description – as if he is giving a magisterial account of how law comes about. But, although he approaches his system as if it is real, it is abstracted from the material world. Ultimately for him the purity of the pure theory of law is a defence against the turmoil of politics. By contrast, Foucault insists that discourse can only ever be inconsistent and ruptured, and that only out of such a discourse can ideas originate.

For Kelsen the law-creator is a "subject", whose meaning is initially "subjective". It becomes a legal norm when legal cognition, by reference to the basic norm, endows it with objectivity. But this implies a dichotomy between the objective product of law-creation, and the person by whom it is created. For Foucault there is no such dichotomy: "[11] there are not on the one hand inert discourses … and then, on the other hand, an all-powerful subject which manipulates them". Despite Kelsen's emphasis on the "dynamics" of law, his hierarchy of norms would seem to Foucault "foreign" and "inert".

3. The State

If the ideals of "constitutionalism" give expression to the need of a human society for limits on the power of government, the need for a society to pursue its collective goals through effective concentration of organised governmental power is encapsulated in the idea of "the State". If this idea has been less influential in the British political tradition than in other Western countries, it is partly because the concentration of power has been symbolised instead by "the Crown" (see Chapter 12, §1). Nevertheless the idea of the State is fundamental.

Andrew Vincent, *Theories of the State*
(Blackwell, 1987)

[19] A State will usually claim hegemony or predominance within a given territory over all other associations, organizations or groups within it. The motto 'thou shalt have no other association but me' is the conventional approach to group/State relations. However this supremacy is *legal* – it is based on rules which have some degree of universal recognition within the territory. In other words, the rules are not just the whims of the ruler. Thus exclusive power to determine rights and duties within a territorial limit is both *de facto* [20] and *de jure*. Such an idea runs up against a multitude of problems. Since the advent of international legal, political, economic, military and cultural organizations – for example, the existence of international law and courts, the United Nations, the EEC, GATT, NATO and the Warsaw Pact, as well as multinational companies and so on – it is less easy to speak of the dominance of a State even within its own territory. Despite this point there is still a formal acknowledgment that States have legal supremacy within their territory and that they are independent of external powers.

In comparison to groups within the State, it is generally true that the State has the maximal control over resources and force. At the same time it is not simply a power system. The forces of the State are regulated by rules, which of course can be distorted. However, the monopoly of force is tied to specific ends, namely the maintenance of internal order and external defence … [These notions] are open to interpretation. The idea of legitimacy is important here since force exercised by the State is usually recognized by the population as distinct from other types of force. The State possesses authority to carry out actions. Its monopoly is recognized formally as necessary and *de jure*.

The State as supreme authority claims sole *imperium* within a territory. It is sovereign. This is an extremely problematic concept … [W]hat is meant here is two things: first, within a territory, the State has no rivals – it is predominant; second, externally, a State is sovereign if it is recognized by other States as a separate unit. This often boils down to the somewhat fuzzy notion of territorial integrity.

The State is the source of law or at least its very nature is tied up with the existence of law. Law originates with the State. The most extreme version of this [idea] is the school of legal positivism. The State is recognized as the only source of compulsory rules … [T]here are other traditions, such as natural law and customary law, which do not identify the State as the source of law. The whole point of the natural law approach is to argue that the State is subject to law or law pre-dates the State … [E]ven within legal positivism there is some recognition of different types of legal rule, some of which are not so susceptible to change by the State …

The State tends to have wider or more comprehensive aims than most associations or groups. Its fundamental aim, in traditional **[21]** terminology, is to promote the commonwealth or common good although these terms are equally open to considerable interpretation. Furthermore, whereas most groups have a voluntary nature, the State in seeking its broad aims claims compulsion. No one can usually choose not to abide by traffic laws. Yet the voluntary and limited character of some groups is in doubt. No one can choose to be a member of a family. Many groups have complex rules which demand conformity and can, if disobeyed, result in punishment. If one were a member of the Catholic Church or the Mafia such punishments could have mortal significance. Moreover, it is an approximate truth that States usually have broader and more comprehensive aims.

The really crucial formal feature of the State … is that it is a continuous public power. This public power is formally distinct from both ruler and ruled. Its acts have legal authority and are distinct from the intentions of individual agents or groups. Thus the State, as public power, embodies offices and roles which carry the authority of the State. Since this appears to give the State an autonomy apart from private individuals many theorists have been led to accord the State a personality.

For Kelsen, the concept of "the state" is subsumed within that of "the legal order".

Hans Kelsen, *General Theory of Law and State*
(Russell & Russell, 1945)

[188] The legal order furnishes that scheme according to which the individuals themselves, acting as subjects and organs of the State, interpret their behavior and according to which, therefore, a sociology that wishes to grasp the "State" has to interpret its object. It is rather misleading to say that this object is the State, the "sociological" State. The State is not identical with any of those actions which form the object of sociology, nor with the sum of them all. The State is not an action or a number of actions, any more than it is a human being or a number of human beings. The State is that order of human behavior that we call the legal order, the order to which certain human actions are oriented, the idea to which the individuals adapt their behavior. If human behavior oriented to this order forms the object of sociology, then its object is not the State. There is no sociological concept of the State besides the juristic concept. Such a double concept [189] of the State is logically impossible, if for no other reason because there cannot be more than one concept of the same object. There is only a juristic concept of the State: the State as – centralized – legal order. The sociological concept of an actual pattern of behavior, oriented to the legal order, is not a concept of the State, it presupposes the concept of the State, which is a juristic concept …

It is the juristic concept of the State that sociologists apply when they describe the relations of domination within the State. The properties they ascribe to the State are conceivable only as properties of a normative order or of a community constituted by such an order. Sociologists also consider an essential quality of the State to be an authority superior to the individuals, obligating the individuals. Only as a normative order can the State be an obligating authority, especially if that authority is considered to be sovereign. Sovereignty is … conceivable only within the realm of the normative.

That the State must be a normative order is obvious also from the "conflict" between State and individual, which is a specific problem not only of social philosophy but also of sociology. If the State were an actual fact, just as the individual is, then there could not exist any such "conflict," since facts of nature never are in "conflict" with each other. But if the State is a system of norms, then the will and the behavior of the individual can conflict with these norms, and so can arise the antagonism between the "is" and the "ought" which is a fundamental problem of all social theory and practice …

The identity of State and legal order is apparent from the fact that even sociologists characterize the State as "politically" organized society. Since society – as a unit – is constituted by organization, it is **[190]** more correct to define the State as "political organization." An organization is an order. But in what does the "political" character of this order lie? In the fact that it is a coercive order. The State is a political organization because it is an order regulating the use of force, because it monopolizes the use of force. This, however … is one of the essential characters of law. The State is a politically organized society because it is a community constituted by a coercive order, and this coercive order is the law.

The State is sometimes said to be a political organization on the ground that it has, or is, "power." The State is described as the power that lies back of law, that enforces law. Insofar as such a power exists, it is nothing but the fact that law itself is effective, that the idea of legal norms providing for sanctions motivates the behavior of individuals, exercises psychic compulsion upon individuals. The fact that an individual has social power over another individual manifests itself in that the former is able to induce the latter to the behavior which the former desires. But power in a social sense is possible only within the framework of a normative order regulating human behavior. For the existence of such a power, it does not suffice that one individual is actually stronger than another and can force him to a certain behavior – as one forces an animal into submission or makes a tree fall. Power in a social or political sense implies authority and a relation of superior to inferior.

Such a relation is possible only on the basis of an order by which the one is empowered to command and the other is obligated to obey. Social power is essentially correlative to social obligation, and social obligation presupposes social order or, what amounts to the same, social organization. Social power is possible only within social organization. This is particularly evident when the power does not rest with a single individual but – as is usually the case in social life – with a group of individuals. Social power is always a power which in some way or other is organized. The power of the State is the power organized by positive law – is the power of law; that is, the efficacy of positive law.

Speaking of the power of the State, one usually thinks of prisons and electric chairs, machine guns and cannons. But one should not forget that these are all dead things which become instruments of power only when used by human beings, and that human beings are generally moved to use them for a given purpose only by commands they regard as norms. The phenomenon of political power manifests itself in the fact that the norms regulating the use of these instruments become efficacious. "Power" is not prisons and electric chairs, machine guns and cannons; "power" is not any kind of substance or entity hidden behind the social order. Political power is the efficacy of the coercive order recognized as **[191]** law. To describe the State as "the power behind the law" is incorrect, since it suggests the existence of two separate entities where there is only one: the legal order. The dualism of law and State is a superfluous doubling or duplication of the object of our cognition; a result of our tendency to personify and then to hypostatize our personifications. A typical example of this tendency … [is] the animistic interpretation of nature, that is, primitive man's idea that nature is animated, that behind everything there is a soul, a spirit, a god of this thing: behind a tree, a dryas, behind a river, a nymph, behind the moon, a moon-goddess, behind the sun, a sun-god. Thus, we imagine behind the law, its hypostatized personification, the State, the god of the law. The dualism of law and State is an animistic superstition. The only legitimate dualism here is that between the validity and the efficacy of the legal order …

The necessary unity of State and law can be seen also through the following considerations. Even exponents of the organic theory recognize that the State is not an object that can be apprehended by the senses. Even if, in some sense, the State were formed out of human beings, it could not be a body composed of individual human bodies as a natural organism is composed of cells. The State is not a visible or tangible body. But, then, how does the invisible and intangible State manifest itself in social life? Certain actions of individual human beings are considered as actions of the State. Under what conditions do we attribute a human action to the State? Not every individual is capable of performing actions which have the character of acts of the State; and not every action of an individual capable of performing acts of the State has this character. How can we distinguish human actions which are, from human actions which are not, acts of the State? The judgment by which we refer a human action to the State, as to an invisible person, means an imputation of a human action to the State … The State is, so to speak, a common point into which various human actions are projected, a common point of imputation for different human actions. The individuals whose actions are considered to be acts of the State, whose actions are imputed to the State, are designated as "organs" of the State …

[192] An analysis shows that we impute a human action to the State only when the human action in question corresponds in a specific way to the presupposed legal order. The imputation of a human action to the State is possible only on the condition that this action is determined in a specific way by a normative order; and this order is the legal order. Though, in reality, it is always a definite individual who executes the punishment against a criminal, we say that the criminal is punished "by the State" because the punishment is stipulated in the legal order. The same State is said to exact a fine from a negligent tax-payer since it is the same legal order that stipulates the fine. An action is an act of the State insofar as it is an execution of the legal order. The actions by which the legal order is most directly executed are the coercive acts provided as sanctions by the legal order. But, in a wider sense, the legal order is executed by all those actions which serve as a preparation for a sanction, in particular actions by which sanction-stipulating norms are created. Acts of State are not only human actions by which the legal order is executed but also human actions by which the legal order is created, not only executive but also legislative acts. To impute a human action to the State, as to an invisible person, is to relate a human action as the action of a State organ to the unity of the order which stipulates this action. The State as a person is nothing but the personification of this unity. An "organ of the State" is tantamount to an "organ of the law."

The result … is that there is no sociological concept of the State different from the concept of the legal order; and that means, that we can describe the social reality without using the term "State."

Though this concept of the unity of State and law is presented from the viewpoint of Kelsen's "pure theory of law", he seeks also to establish his "juristic concept" as a "sociological concept" by which "[192] we can describe the social reality". Again, Foucault's conception of social reality is very different. By assimilating the State to the hierarchy of norms, Kelsen seeks to reduce it almost to a metaphysical conception: not a natural organism, nor a physical or tangible body. His dilemma then is that, just as "the State" can act only through human agents, one can apprehend it only through their actions. For Kelsen it is the hierarchy of norms that endows those actions of subjective human agents with objective meaning; for Foucault it is action and inter-action that create the subjectivity of the agent.

Michel Foucault, *Power/Knowledge*
(Harvester Press, 1980)

[93] What I mean is this: in a society such as ours, but basically in any society, there are manifold relations of power which permeate, characterise and constitute the social body, and these relations of power cannot themselves be established, consolidated nor implemented without the production, accumulation, circulation and functioning of a discourse … We are subjected to the production of

truth through power and we cannot exercise power except through the production of truth. This is the case for every society, but I believe that in ours the relationship between power, right and truth is organised in a highly specific fashion ... Power never ceases its interrogation, its inquisition, its registration of truth: it institutionalises, professionalises and rewards its pursuit. In the last analysis, we must produce truth as we must produce wealth, indeed we must produce truth in order to produce **[94]** wealth in the first place ...

So, it is the rules of right, the mechanisms of power, the effects of truth or if you like, the rules of power and the powers of true discourses, that can be said more or less to have formed the general terrain of my concern ... As regards the general principle involved in a study of the relations between right and power, it seems to me that in Western societies since Medieval times it has been royal power that has provided the essential focus around which legal thought has been elaborated. It is in response to the demands of royal power, for its profit and to serve as its instrument or justification, that the juridical edifice of our own society has been developed. Right in the West is the King's right. Naturally everyone is familiar with the famous, celebrated, repeatedly emphasised role of the jurists in the organisation of royal power ... And when this legal edifice escapes in later centuries from the control of the monarch, when, more accurately, it is turned against that control, it is always the limits of this sovereign power that are put in question, its prerogatives that are challenged. In other words, I believe that the King remains the central personage in the whole legal edifice of the West. **[95]** When it comes to the general organisation of the legal system in the West, it is essentially with the King, his rights, his power and its eventual limitations, that one is dealing. Whether the jurists were the King's henchmen or his adversaries, it is of royal power that we are speaking in every case when we speak of these grandiose edifices of legal thought and knowledge.

There are two ways in which we do so speak. Either we do so in order to show the nature of the juridical armoury that invested royal power, to reveal the monarch as the effective embodiment of sovereignty, to demonstrate that his power, for all that it was absolute, was exactly that which befitted his fundamental right. Or, by contrast, we do so in order to show the necessity of imposing limits upon this sovereign power, of submitting it to certain rules of right, within whose confines it had to be exercised in order for it to remain legitimate. The essential role of the theory of right, from medieval times onwards, was to fix the legitimacy of power; that is the major problem around which the whole theory of right and sovereignty is organised ...

My general project over the past few years has been, in essence, to reverse the mode of analysis followed by the entire discourse of right from the time of the Middle Ages. My aim, therefore, was to invert it, to give due weight ... to the fact of domination, to expose both its latent nature and its brutality. I then wanted to show not only how right is, in a general way, the instrument of this domination – which scarcely needs saying – but also to show the extent to which, and the forms in which, right (not simply the laws but the whole complex of apparatuses, institutions and regulations responsible for their application) transmits and **[96]** puts in motion relations that are not relations of sovereignty, but of domination. Moreover, in speaking of domination I do not have in mind that solid and global kind of domination that one person exercises over others, or one group over another, but the manifold forms of domination that can be exercised within society. Not the domination of the King in his central position, therefore, but that of his subjects in their mutual relations: not the uniform edifice of sovereignty, but the multiple forms of subjugation that have a place and function within the social organism.

The system of right, the domain of the law, are permanent agents of these relations of domination, these polymorphous techniques of subjugation. Right should be viewed, I believe, not in terms of a legitimacy to be established, but in terms of the methods of subjugation that it instigates.

The problem for me is how to avoid this question, central to the theme of right, regarding sovereignty and the obedience of individual subjects in order that I may substitute the problem of domination and subjugation for that of sovereignty and obedience. Given that this was to be the general line of my analysis, there were a certain number of methodological precautions that seemed requisite to its pursuit. In the very first place, it seemed important to accept that the analysis in question should not concern itself with the regulated and legitimate forms of power in their central locations, with the general mechanisms through which they operate, and the continual effects of these. On the contrary, it should be concerned with power at its extremities, in its ultimate destinations, with those points where it becomes capillary, that is, in its more regional and local forms and institutions. Its paramount concern, in fact, should be with the point where power surmounts the rules of right which organise and delimit it and extends itself beyond them, invests itself in institutions, becomes embodied in techniques, and equips itself with instruments and eventually even violent means of material intervention. To give an example: rather than try to discover where and how the right of punishment is founded on sovereignty, how it is presented in the theory of monarchical right or in that of democratic right, I have tried to see in what ways punishment and the power of punishment are effectively embodied **[97]** in a certain number of local, regional, material institutions, which are concerned with torture or imprisonment, and to place these in the climate – at once institutional and physical, regulated and violent – of the effective apparatuses of punishment. In other words, one should try to locate power at the extreme points of its exercise, where it is always less legal in character.

A second methodological precaution urged that the analysis should not concern itself with power at the level of conscious intention or decision; that it should not attempt to consider power from its internal point of view and that it should refrain from posing the labyrinthine and unanswerable question: 'Who then has power and what has he in mind? What is the aim of someone who possesses power?' Instead, it is a case of studying power at the point where its intention, if it has one, is completely invested in its real and effective practices. What is needed is a study of power in its external visage, at the point where it is in direct and immediate relationship with that which we can provisionally call its object, its target, its field of application, there – that is to say – where it installs itself and produces its real effects.

Let us not, therefore, ask why certain people want to dominate, what they seek, what is their overall strategy. Let us ask, instead, how things work at the level of on-going subjugation, at the level of those continuous and uninterrupted processes which subject our bodies, govern our gestures, dictate our behaviours etc. In other words, rather than ask ourselves how the sovereign appears to us in his lofty isolation, we should try to discover how it is that subjects are gradually, progressively, really and materially constituted through a multiplicity of organisms, forces, energies, materials, desires, thoughts etc. We should try to grasp subjection in its material instance as a constitution of subjects. This would be the exact opposite of Hobbes' project in *Leviathan*, and of that, I believe, of all jurists for whom the problem is the distillation of a single will – or rather, the constitution of a unitary, singular body animated by the spirit of sovereignty – from the particular wills of a multiplicity of individuals. Think of the scheme of Leviathan: insofar as he is a fabricated man, Leviathan is no other than the amalgamation of a certain number of separate in-**[98]**-dividualities, who find themselves reunited by the complex of elements that go to compose the State; but at the heart of the State, or rather, at its head, there exists something which constitutes it as such, and this is sovereignty, which Hobbes says is precisely the spirit of Leviathan. Well, rather than worry about the problem of the central spirit, I believe that we must attempt to study the myriad of bodies which are constituted as peripheral *subjects* as a result of the effects of power.

A third methodological precaution relates to the fact that power is not to be taken to be a phenomenon of one individual's consolidated and homogeneous domination over others, or that of one group or class over others. What, by contrast, should always be kept in mind is that power, if we do not take too distant a view of it, is not that which makes the difference between those who exclusively possess and retain it, and those who do not have it and submit to it. Power must [be] analysed as something which circulates, or rather as something which only functions in the form of a chain. It is never localised here or there, never in anybody's hands, never appropriated as a commodity or piece of wealth. Power is employed and exercised through a net-like organisation. And not only do individuals circulate between its threads; they are always in the position of simultaneously undergoing and exercising this power. They are not only its inert or consenting target; they are always also the elements of its articulation. In other words, individuals are the vehicles of power, not its points of application.

The individual is not to be conceived as a sort of elementary nucleus, a primitive atom, a multiple and inert material on which power comes to fasten or against which it happens to strike, and in so doing subdues or crushes individuals. In fact, it is already one of the prime effects of power that certain bodies, certain gestures, certain discourses, certain desires, come to be identified and constituted as individuals. The individual, that is, is not the *vis-à-vis* of power; it is, I believe, one of its prime effects. The individual is an effect of power, and at the same time, or precisely to the extent to which it is that effect, it is the element of its articulation. The individual which power has constituted is at the same time its vehicle …

[99] [W]hen I say that power establishes a network through which it freely circulates, this is true only up to a certain point … We are not dealing with a sort of democratic or anarchic distribution of power through bodies … [T]he important thing is not to attempt some kind of deduction of power starting from its centre and aimed at the discovery of the extent to which it permeates into the base, of the degree to which it reproduces itself down to and including the most molecular elements of society. One must rather conduct an *ascending* analysis of power, starting, that is, from its infinitesimal mechanisms, which each have their own history, their own trajectory, their own techniques and tactics, and then see how these mechanisms of power have been – and continue to be – invested, colonised, utilised, involuted, transformed, displaced, extended etc, by ever more general mechanisms and by forms of global domination …

[102] [W]e should direct our researches on the nature of power not towards the juridical edifice of sovereignty, the State apparatuses and the ideologies which accompany them, but towards domination and the material operators of power, towards forms of subjection and the inflections and utilisations of their localised systems, and towards strategic apparatuses. We must eschew the model of Leviathan in the study of power. We must escape from the limited field of juridical sovereignty and State institutions, and instead base our analysis of power on the study of the techniques and tactics of domination.

For both Kelsen and Foucault, the action of an executioner in carrying out a sentence of death is a focal point for analysis; and for both of them it is significant that the executioner acts as an agent of "the State". But where Kelsen focuses on the executioner's action in order to explain its legitimacy, Foucault approaches it as an instance of social subjugation and "discipline". For Kelsen the executioner is *merely* an agent of the State. In Foucault's analysis, the agent in whom power is invested is constructed as a product of the effects of power, even while he exercises power. "[98] The individual is not … a sort of elementary nucleus … The individual is an effect of power, and at the same time … its vehicle". Their differing approaches illustrate their different conceptions of power. Where power for Kelsen is hierarchical, a relation of superior to inferior, for Foucault it circulates through a multiplicity of social relationships.

In his lectures at the Collège de France in the 1970s, Foucault's focus on apparatuses of domination and subjugation, rather than on "[102] the juridical edifice of sovereignty", led him to describe the functions of contemporary governments in terms of an increasing managerial focus on control of the national economy, and also of the population. He noted that the word "statistics" had come into use in the 18th century to refer to the systematic gathering of "facts of a state" (from Latin *statisticus*, "concerning state affairs"). He saw these developments as the culmination of a new political mindset that emerged in Europe with the rise of the modern nation state, for which he coined the term "governmentality". He traced its origins to a "[87] notable series of political treatises" on the theme of "the art of government" written from the 16th century onwards in response to Niccolò Machiavelli's *The Prince* (1513), and particularly including Guillaume de La Perrière's *Miroir Politique* (1567).

Michel Foucault, "Governmentality"
in Graham Burchell, Colin Gordon and Peter Miller (eds),
The Foucault Effect: Studies in Governmentality (University of Chicago Press, 1991), 87

[90] *The Prince* … is essentially a treatise about the prince's ability to keep his principality. And it is this *savoir-faire* that the anti-Machiavellian literature wants to replace by something else and new, namely the art of government. Having the ability to retain one's principality is not at all the same thing as possessing the art of governing. But what does this latter ability comprise? …

[Writers like La Perrière] constantly recall that one speaks also of 'governing' a household, souls, children, a province, a convent, a religious order, a family …

[92] The art of government, as becomes apparent in this literature, is essentially concerned with answering the question of how to introduce economy – that is to say, the correct manner of managing individuals, goods and wealth within the family (which a good father is expected to do in relation to his wife, children and servants) and of making the family fortunes prosper – how to introduce this meticulous attention of the father towards his family into the management of the state.

This, I believe, is the essential issue in the establishment of the art of government: introduction of economy into political practice … In Rousseau's *Encyclopedia* article on 'Political economy' [in 1755] the problem is still posed in the same terms. What he says … is that the word 'economy' can only properly be used to signify the wise government of the family for the common welfare of all …; the problem, writes Rousseau, is how to introduce it … into the general running of the state. To govern a state will therefore mean to apply economy, to set up an economy at the level of the entire state, which means exercising towards its inhabitants, and the wealth and behaviour of each and all, a form of surveillance and control as attentive as that of the head of a family over his household and his goods.

An expression which was important in the eighteenth century captures this very well: [François] Quesnay speaks of good government as 'economic government'. This latter notion becomes tautological, given that the art of government is just the art of exercising power in the form and according to the model of the economy. But the reason why Quesnay speaks of 'economic government' is that the word 'economy', for reasons that I will explain later, is in the process of acquiring a modern meaning, and it is at this moment becoming apparent that the very essence of government … is to have as its main objective that which we are today accustomed to call 'the economy'. …

[93] [According to Guillaume de La Perrière] 'government is the right disposition of things, arranged so as to lead to a convenient end' …

I would like to pause over this word 'things' … I do not think this is a matter of opposing things to men, but rather of showing that what government has to do with is not territory but rather a sort of complex composed of men and things. The things with which in this sense government is to be concerned are in fact men, but men in their relations, their links, their imbrication with those other things which are wealth, resources, means of subsistence, the territory with its specific qualities, climate, irrigation, fertility, etc; men in their relation to that other kind of things, customs, habits, ways of acting and thinking, etc; lastly, men in their relation to that other kind of things, accidents and misfortunes such as famine, epidemics, death, etc … [This understanding is] readily confirmed by the metaphor which is inevitably invoked in these treatises on government, namely that of the ship. What does it mean to govern a ship? It means clearly to take charge of the sailors, but also of the boat and its cargo; to take care of a ship means also to reckon with winds, rocks and storms; and it consists in that activity of establishing a relation between the sailors who are to be taken care of and the ship [94] which is to be taken care of, and the cargo which is to be brought safely to port, and all those eventualities like winds, rocks, storms and so on … The same goes for the running of a household …

[95] [With this definition] I believe we can see emerging a new kind of finality. Government is defined as a right manner of disposing things so as to lead not to the form of the common good, as the jurists' texts would have said, but to an end which is 'convenient' for each of the things that are to be governed. This implies a plurality of specific aims: for instance, government will have to ensure that the greatest possible quantity of wealth is produced, that the people are provided with sufficient means of subsistence, that the population is enabled to multiply, etc. There is a whole series of specific finalities, then, which become the objective of government as such … [W]ith sovereignty the instrument that allowed it to achieve its aim – that is to say, obedience to the laws – was the law itself; law and sovereignty were absolutely inseparable. On the contrary, with government it is a question not of imposing law on men, but of disposing things: that is to say, of employing tactics rather than laws, and even of using laws themselves as tactics …

I believe we are at an important turning point here: whereas the end of sovereignty is internal to itself and possesses its own intrinsic instruments in the shape of its laws, the finality of government resides in the things it manages and in the pursuit of the perfection and intensification of the processes which it directs; and the instruments of government, instead of being laws, now come to be a range of multiform tactics. Within the perspective of government, law is not what is important ...

[96] The theory of the art of government was linked, from the sixteenth century, to the whole development of the administrative apparatus of the territorial monarchies, the emergence of governmental apparatuses; it was also connected to a set of analyses and forms of knowledge which began to develop in the late sixteenth century and grew in importance during the seventeenth, and which were essentially to do with knowledge of the state, in all its different elements, dimensions and factors of power, questions which were termed precisely 'statistics', meaning the science of the state ...

[I]n the late sixteenth century and early seventeenth century, the art of government ... [97] [is] organized around the theme of reason of state ...; the state, like nature, has its own proper form of rationality, albeit of a different sort ... [But] right until the early eighteenth century, this form of 'reason of state' acted as a sort of obstacle to the development of the art of government.

This is for a number of reasons. Firstly, there are the strictly historical ones, the series of great crises of the seventeenth century: first the Thirty Years War with its ruin and devastation; then in the mid-century the peasant and urban rebellions; and finally the financial crisis, the crisis of revenues which affected all Western monarchies at the end of the century ... [It was also impeded] by a series of other factors which I might term, to use expressions which I do not much care for, mental and institutional structures ... So long as the institutions of sovereignty were the basic political institutions and the exercise of power was conceived as an exercise of sovereignty, the art of government could not be developed in a specific and autonomous manner ...

[98] How then was the art of government able to outflank these obstacles? Here again a number of general processes played their part: the demographic expansion of the eighteenth century, connected with an increasing abundance of money, which in turn was linked to the expansion of agricultural production ... If this is the general picture, then we can say more precisely that the art of government found fresh [99] outlets through the emergence of the problem of population ...

It was through the development of the science of government that the notion of economy came to be recentred on to that different plane of reality which we characterize today as the 'economic', and it was also through this science that it became possible to identify problems specific to the population; but conversely we can say as well that it was thanks to the perception of the specific problems of the population, and thanks to the isolation of that area of reality that we call the economy, that the problem of government finally came to be thought, reflected and calculated outside of the juridical framework of sovereignty. And that 'statistics' ... now becomes the major technical factor, or one of the major technical factors, of this new technology ...

The perspective of population, the reality accorded to specific phenomena of population, render possible the final elimination of the model of the family and the recentring of the notion of economy. Whereas statistics had previously worked within the administrative frame and thus in terms of the functioning of sovereignty, it now gradually reveals that population has its own regularities, its own rate of deaths and diseases, its cycles of scarcity, etc; statistics shows also that the domain of population involves a range of intrinsic, aggregate effects, phenomena that are irreducible to those of the family, such as epidemics, endemic levels of mortality, ascending spirals of labour and wealth; lastly it shows that, through its shifts, customs, activities, etc, population has specific economic effects: statistics, by making it possible to quantify these specific phenomena of population, also shows that this specificity is irreducible to the dimension of the family. The latter now disappears as the model of government, except for a certain number of residual themes of a religious or moral nature. What, on the other hand, now emerges into prominence is the family considered as an element internal to population, and as a fundamental instrument in its government.

In other words, prior to the emergence of population, it was impossible to conceive the art of government except on the model of the family, in terms of economy conceived as the management of a family; from the moment when ... population appears absolutely irreducible to the family, the latter becomes of secondary importance ... [100] [T]he family becomes an instrument rather than a model: the privileged instrument for the government of the population and not the chimerical model of good government. This shift from the level of the model to that of an instrument is, I believe, absolutely fundamental, and it is from the middle of the eighteenth century that the family appears in this dimension of instrumentality relative to the population, with the institution of campaigns to reduce mortality, and to promote marriages, vaccinations, etc. Thus, what makes it possible for the theme of population to unblock the field of the art of government is this elimination of the family as model.

In the second place, population comes to appear above all else as the ultimate end of government. In contrast to sovereignty, government has as its purpose not the act of government itself, but the welfare of the population, the improvement of its condition, the increase of its wealth, longevity, health, etc; and the means that the government uses to attain these ends are themselves all in some sense immanent to the population; it is the population itself on which government will act either directly through large-scale campaigns, or indirectly through techniques that will make possible, without the full awareness of the people, the stimulation of birth rates, the directing of the flow of population into certain regions or activities, etc. The population now represents more the end of government than the power of the sovereign; the population is the subject of needs, of aspirations, but it is also the object in the hands of the government, aware, *vis-à-vis* the government, of what it wants, but ignorant of what is being done to it ...

[101] The new science called political economy arises out of the perception of new networks of continuous and multiple relations between population, territory and wealth; and this is accompanied by the formation of a type of intervention characteristic of government, namely intervention in the field of economy and population. In other words, the transition which takes place in the eighteenth century from an art of government to a political science, from a regime dominated by structures of sovereignty to one ruled by techniques of government, turns on the theme of population ...

This is not to say that sovereignty ceases to play a role ... [O]n the contrary, the problem of sovereignty was never posed with greater force than at this time, because it no longer involved ... an attempt to derive an art of government from a theory of sovereignty, but instead, given that such an art now existed and was spreading, involved an attempt to see what juridical and institutional form, what foundation in the law, could be given to the sovereignty that characterizes a state ...

As for discipline, this is not eliminated either; clearly its modes of organization, all the institutions within which it had developed in the **[102]** seventeenth and eighteenth centuries – schools, manufactories, armies, etc – ... [began with] the great administrative monarchies, but nevertheless, discipline was never more important or more valorized than at the moment when it became important to manage a population; the managing of a population not only concerns the collective mass of phenomena, the level of its aggregate effects, it also implies the management of population in its depths and its details ...

[By 'governmentality'] I mean three things:

1. The ensemble formed by the institutions, procedures, analyses and reflections, the calculations and tactics that allow the exercise of this very specific albeit complex form of power, which has as its target population, as its principal form of knowledge political economy, and as its essential technical means apparatuses of security.

2. The tendency which, over a long period and throughout the West, has steadily led towards the pre-eminence over all other forms (sovereignty, discipline, etc) of this type of power which may be termed **[103]** government, resulting, on the one hand, in the formation of a whole series of specific governmental apparatuses, and, on the other, in the development of a whole complex of *savoirs*.

3. The process, or rather the result of the process, through which the state of justice of the Middle Ages, transformed into the administrative state during the fifteenth and sixteenth centuries, gradually becomes 'governmentalized'.

We all know the fascination which the love, or horror, of the state exercises today; we know how much attention is paid to the genesis of the state, its history, its advance, its power and abuses, etc. The excessive value attributed to the problem of the state is expressed, basically, in two ways: the one form, immediate, affective and tragic, is the lyricism of the *monstre froid* we see confronting us; but there is a second way of overvaluing the problem of the state, one which is paradoxical because apparently reductionist: it is the form of analysis that consists in reducing the state to a certain number of functions, such as the development of productive forces and the reproduction of relations of production, and yet this reductionist vision of the relative importance of the state's role nevertheless invariably renders it absolutely essential as a target needing to be attacked and a privileged position needing to be occupied. But the state ... does not have this unity, this individuality, this rigorous functionality, nor, to speak frankly, this importance; maybe, after all, the state is no more than a composite reality and a mythicized abstraction, whose importance is a lot more limited than many of us think. Maybe what is really important for our modernity – that is, for our present – is not so much the *étatisation* of society, as the 'governmentalization' of the state.

4. Separation of Powers

The idea of a differentiation between the three different functions of government, legislative, judicial and executive, is as old as Isaiah 33.22 ("The Lord is our judge; the Lord is our lawgiver; the Lord is our King"). The idea that these different functions should be vested in different institutions has its origins in the writings of Aristotle, but became influential in the 18th century through the observations of Charles Louis de Secondat, Baron de Montesquieu. In England from 1729 to 1731, Montesquieu absorbed the Whig ideology of a separation of powers (although he failed to see that it bore little resemblance to English political practice).

Baron de Montesquieu, *The Spirit of the Laws*
(transl Thomas Nugent, Hafner Press, 1949)

[150] Political liberty is to be found ... only where there is no abuse of power. But constant experience shows us that every man invested with power is apt to abuse it, and to carry his authority as far as it will go. Is it not strange, though true, to say that virtue itself has need of limits?

To prevent this abuse, it is necessary from the very nature of things that power should be a check to power ...

[151] In every government there are three sorts of power: the legislative; the executive in respect to things dependent on the law of nations, and the executive in regard to matters that depend on the civil law.

By virtue of the first, the prince or magistrate enacts temporary or perpetual laws, and amends or abrogates those that have already been enacted. By the second, he makes peace or war, sends or receives embassies, establishes the public security, and provides against invasions. By the third, he punishes criminals, or determines the disputes that arise between individuals. The latter we shall call the judiciary power, and the other simply the executive power of the state ...

When the legislative and executive powers are united in the same person, or in the same body of magistrates, there can be no liberty; because apprehensions may arise, lest the same [152] monarch or senate should enact tyrannical laws, to execute them in a tyrannical manner.

Again, there is no liberty, if the judiciary power be not separated from the legislative and executive. Were it joined with the legislative, the life and liberty of the subject would be exposed to arbitrary control; for the judge would be then the legislator. Were it joined to the executive power, the judge might behave with violence and oppression.

There would be an end of everything, were the same man or the same body, whether of the nobles or of the people, to exercise those three powers, that of enacting laws, that of executing the public resolutions, and of trying the causes of individuals.

Owen Hood Phillips and Paul Jackson, *Constitutional and Administrative Law*
(Sweet and Maxwell, 7th ed 1987)

[11] Montesquieu in *L'Esprit des Lois* (1748), following attempts by Aristotle and Locke, divided the powers of government into: (i) the legislative power; (ii) the executive power in matters pertaining to the law of nations, and (iii) the power of judging; and so we get the first statement of the modern classification to which we are now accustomed, viz: (i) legislative, (ii) executive, and (iii) judicial ...

(i) *The legislative function* is the making of new law, and the alteration or repeal of existing law. Legislation is the formulation of law by the appropriate organ of the state, in such a manner that the actual words used are themselves part of the law: the words not only contain the law, but in a sense they constitute the law. Legislation may take the form of the decree of a personal ruler, whether king or dictator; or it may be issued by an autocratic body or by a democratic assembly wholly or partly elected by the people. Without a legislative body of some sort a state could not provide law readily enough to meet modern conditions ...

[12] (ii) *The executive or administrative function* is the general and detailed carrying on of government according to law, including the framing of policy and the choice of the manner in which the law may be made to render that policy possible. In recent times, especially since the industrialisation of most civilised countries, the scope of this function has become extremely wide. It now involves the provision and administration or regulation of a vast system of social services – public health, housing, assistance for the sick and unemployed, welfare of individual workers, education, transport and so on – as well as the supervision of defence, order and justice, and the finance required therefore, which were the original tasks of organised government.

(iii) *The judicial function* consists in the interpretation of the law and its application by rule or discretion to the facts of particular cases. This involves the ascertainment of facts in dispute according to the law of evidence ...

Although the above classification of the functions and corresponding powers of government, based on a material or functional analysis, may be useful in helping to arrange the facts and to think about the problems of government, the categories are inclined to become blurred when it is attempted to apply them to the details of a particular constitution. Some hold that the true distinction lies not in the nature of the powers themselves, but rather in the procedure by which they are exercised. Thus legislation involves a formal and instantaneous act designed to establish general rules by which all disputes shall be settled; administration is a continuing and mainly informal process aimed at preventing disputes in classes of cases and does not create rights by establishing precedents; adjudication pre-supposes an existing dispute in a particular case, is governed by strict rules of procedure and evidence and tends to create rights by establishing precedents.

Others hold that the distinction is organic or formal. Thus administration consists of the operations, whatever their intrinsic nature may be, which are performed by administrators; and administrators are all state officials who are neither legislators nor judges. This last doctrine seems to be as difficult to apply as the functional or material conception of governmental functions. Thus in the Constitution of the Fifth French Republic not only has the Parliament other powers than the strictly **[13]** legislative, but the law-making power is divided between the Parliament (*loi*) and the government (*règlement*), so that the Parliament may only make laws dealing with matters enumerated in article 34, while all others matters fall within the province of ministerial regulation ...

A complete separation of powers, in the sense of a distribution of the three functions of government among three independent sets of organs with no overlapping or co-ordination, would (even if theoretically possible) bring government to a standstill. What the doctrine must be taken to advocate is the prevention of tyranny by the conferment of too much power on any one person or body, and the check of one power by another. There is an echo of this in Blackstone's *Commentaries* (1765): "In all tyrannical Governments ... the right of making and of enforcing the laws is vested in one and the same man, or the same body of men; and wheresoever these two powers are united together there can be no liberty"; and this doctrine was taken over by the fathers of the American Constitution.

Gerard Carney, "Separation of Powers in the Westminster System"
Legislative Studies (Vol 8, No 2, Autumn 1994), 59

[60] [T]he basic control adopted [by a separation of powers] is to vest the three types of governmental power, legislative, executive and judicial in three separate and independent institutions, the legislature, the executive and the courts, with the personnel of each being different and independent of each other. There is a complete separation as regards powers, institutions and personnel. Yet, there seems to be no current constitutional system which adopts this complete separation of powers. Some of the early American States and the French constitution of 1791 tried strictly to give effect to this doctrine but failed. The strict doctrine is only a theory and it has to give way to the realities of government where some overlap is inevitable. But while permitting this overlap to occur, a system of checks and balances has developed (and needs to continue to develop).

The **United States Constitution of 1787** incorporates the doctrine of separation of powers with a system of checks and balances as Table 1 illustrates:

Table 1:

Institution	Power	Personnel	Control
Congress	Power to make laws	Elected representatives	Presidential veto; Supreme Court review of validity
President	Executive power	Elected. Cannot be a member of Congress	Senate ratification necessary for cabinet and diplomatic appointments, and treaties; Judicial review; Impeachment by removal by Congress
Supreme Court	Judicial power including review of legislative and executive activity	Appointed by President with Senate ratification	Impeachment by Congress

The **Westminster system** (see Table 2) effects only a *partial* separation of powers:

[61] Table 2:

Institution	Power	Personnel	Control
Parliament	Make Laws	Representatives elected to lower house. Elected or appointed to upper house	(Royal Assent) Supervision and/or expulsion by the House
Executive Council (Cabinet)	Executive power	Ministers appointed by the Crown with the support of the lower House. Must be Members of the Parliament.	Maintain support of the lower House. Parliamentary and Judicial Review
The Courts	Judicial Power	Judges appointed by the Executive	Superior Court justices removal by the Crown on an address from both Houses on certain grounds.

The first three chapters of the Australian Constitution are headed respectively "The Parliament", "The Executive Government", and "The Judicature". Each of these chapters begins with a section (ss 1, 61, 71) by which the relevant "power of the Commonwealth" (legislative, executive or judicial) is "vested" in the appropriate persons or bodies. Evidently, at least in this formal sense, the framers of the Australian Constitution were influenced by the American version of the "separation of powers". However, they were also influenced by the Westminster system and the doctrine of responsible government. Accordingly, a strict separation is not maintained between Parliament and the executive (s 64 provides that federal Ministers – members of the executive – must sit in Parliament).

In any event, what Foucault describes as the growth of "governmentality" has put the traditional separation of powers under increasing strain.

Julius Stone, *Social Dimensions of Law and Justice*
(Maitland Publications, 1966)

[696] In the nineteenth century, even when the separation of powers was not a constitutional imperative, it was deemed to be a moral and political imperative for the preservation of liberty. The precise boundaries between the powers were assumed to be fixed and discoverable, for without this the imperative would be brought to naught. So that what was not for the judicial power must be

either for the legislature or the executive; and if the subject-matter was also not within precon-ceived legislative power, it must fall to the executive. The allocation of subject-matters thus tended to begin not from the subject-**[697]**-matter itself, as a basis for asking which kind of organ was functionally most apt for just and efficient handling of this. It began rather from the ambit of power of each kind of organ, as this was assumed to be pre-set. No doubt the preconceived ambits thus assigned were built in part on the functions traditionally performed by each branch of government. But they were also built on abstract notions of what it is "right" or "legitimate" for each branch by its nature to do ...

Obviously the executive power insofar as it executes rules laid down by the legislator has always had "administrative" functions in a broad sense. In origins the Barons of the Exchequer were engaged in the administration of the taxation laws. Yet even this example is eloquent also that administration and adjudication are not strangers to each other. For this administrative task raised questions of whether the tax was due, or why though due it was not forthcoming. And as this happened the administrators were led to decide such questions and with them the rights of the subjects. The Exchequer gradually turned into a judicial court which acquired and exercised for centuries a substantial jurisdiction in civil matters. So, too, modern problems of administration are raised by the rapid and unremitting extension of administrative tasks beyond mere execution of statutes to the tasks of deciding questions and making rules ancillary to legislative activity, under powers delegated by the legislature.

This extension has been so dramatic since the industrial revolution, and has since 1900 followed so steadily on the growth of legislative intervention in new areas of economic and social relations, that the traditional separation of powers has seemed threatened at its foundations. So that much of the work on public law of the [twentieth] century has been concerned either with the defence of the separation of powers doctrine, or with attempts to find room within it to accom-modate the administrative arm. Either administration was sought to be held within a matrix which would allow it to fit into one of the three traditional divisions, or the doctrine of separation of powers was reinterpreted so as to accommodate what actually goes on in administration. The most important effort of this last kind has been, of course, the translation of the doctrine from one *prescribing separation* of *powers*, into one *describing distribution* of *functions* according to *time* and *structure* and *aptitudes* available ...

[702] It now seems clear that modern administrative power ... must be seen as a distinct and largely new constellation of functions. To try to accommodate this reality thinkers have succes-sively sought to redefine the executive function, or to separate the **[703]** "administrative" from the executive function and attach it to Congress, or have come to the view that administration must be seen finally as neither of these. The version of this last view which comes nearest to the present position is that the administrative function has developed within the space left under modern exigencies by the three traditionally separated powers. Though in a sense administration subverts this tripartite system, it does so only by becoming a distinct kind of focus of power necessary to keep that system going. For without it, the balance presupposed by the tripartite system would disappear in face of the extended functions of government. It could be formally preserved only by so vast an expansion of executive authority that no countervailing power could in fact be set against it. Administration, then, is rather a fourth group of functions, not sharply and clearly distinguished from the traditional three, but interstitial and supplementary to these.

President's Committee on Administrative Management,
Administrative Management in the Government of the United States
(United States Government Printing Office, 1937)

[36] Beginning with the Interstate Commerce Commission in 1887, the Congress has set up more than a dozen independent regulatory commissions to exercise the control over commerce and business necessary to the orderly conduct of the Nation's economic life. These commissions have been the result of legislative groping rather than the pursuit of a consistent policy. This is shown by the wide variety in their structure and functions and also by the fact that just as frequently the Congress has given regulatory functions of the same kind to the regular executive departments.

These independent commissions have been given broad powers to explore, formulate, and administer policies of regulation; they have been given the task of investigating and prosecuting business misconduct; they have been given powers, similar to those exercised by courts of law, to pass in concrete cases upon the rights and liabilities of individuals under the statutes. They are in reality miniature independent governments set up to deal with the railroad problem, the banking problem, or the radio problem. They constitute a headless "fourth branch" of the Government, a haphazard deposit of irresponsible agencies and uncoordinated powers. They do violence to the basic theory of the American Constitution that there should be three major branches of the Government and only three …

[38] We have watched the growth of boards and commissions transform the executive branches of our State governments into grotesque agglomerations of independent and irresponsible units, bogged by the weight and confusion of the whole crazy structure. The same tendency in national administration will bring the same disastrous results. That tendency should be stopped.

On the other hand, James Landis, *The Administrative Process* (Yale University Press, 1938), thought that this report had used the term "fourth branch" "[47] [s]omewhat hysterically … upon the mystical hypothesis that the number 'four' bespeaks evil or waste as contrasted with some beneficence emanating from the number 'three'." He added: "The desirability of four, five, or six 'branches' of government would seem to be a problem determinable not in the light of numerology but rather against a background of what we now expect government to do".

5. Judicial Review

The Australian Constitution assumes that, where a statute is enacted by an Australian parliament that exceeds the powers recognised or conferred by the Constitution or infringes some express or implied constitutional limitation, the courts (and in practice especially the High Court) have the power to declare the enactment to be unconstitutional and therefore invalid. This power of judicial review is a crucial means of ensuring that, where parliaments are invested with power, they operate within constitutional limits.

Whether a similar assumption was made when the United States Constitution was adopted is historically unclear. However, the idea that such a judicial power was entailed in that constitutional scheme was successfully advanced by the United States Supreme Court itself in its famous decision in *Marbury v Madison*, 5 US (1 Cranch) 137 (1803).

The background to the case was intensely political. In 1800 John Adams was nearing the end of his term as second President of the United States and John Marshall was his Secretary of State. Adams and the majority of Congress belonged to the Federalist Party, but at the November election the Republican Party gained control of both Congress and the Presidency. The inauguration of Thomas Jefferson as the new President was scheduled for 4 March 1801. In December, Chief Justice Oliver Ellsworth retired, and Adams nominated Marshall to replace him. The outgoing Congress confirmed the appointment, though Marshall agreed to stay on as acting Secretary of State for the balance of Adams' term of office. In February 1801, the Congress passed the *Organic Act*, creating 42 new justices of the peace, and the *Circuit Court Act*, which doubled the size of the federal judiciary (thus enabling Adams to appoint a large number of Federalist judges). The outgoing Congress also reduced the size of the Supreme Court, eliminating a vacancy which Jefferson would have been able to fill.

Throughout February 1801, President Adams nominated many new Federalist judges, with Congressional advice and consent. On 2-3 March, Adams and Marshall (as the outgoing President and Secretary of State) worked frantically to issue, seal and deliver the commissions to the new "midnight judges". They managed to deliver commissions to all but four of the newly confirmed justices of the peace. One of the four was William Marbury.

On 4 March, Jefferson was inaugurated and James Madison became his Secretary of State. When the four Federalist justices of the peace asked for their commissions, Jefferson refused, calling them "nullities". They then applied to the Supreme Court (now presided over by Marshall) for a writ of mandamus to compel the issue of their commissions. Marshall's response was "[129] a Solomonic blend of diplomacy and defiance" (AR Blackshield, "The Courts and Judicial Review", in S Encel, D Horne and E Thompson (eds), *Change the Rules! Towards a Democratic Constitution* (Penguin Books, 1977), 118). He held that the appointees were entitled to their commissions, and hence to a writ of mandamus; but that the Court could not grant such a writ because the *Judiciary Act* of 1789, which empowered it to do so, was unconstitutional. Writs of mandamus pertained to a court's *original* jurisdiction; and, under the Constitution, Congress could invest the Supreme Court only with *appellate* jurisdiction.

Marbury v Madison
5 US (1 Cranch) 137 (1803)

Marshall CJ: [176] The question, whether an act, repugnant to the constitution, can become the law of the land, is a question deeply interesting to the United States; but, happily, not of an intricacy proportioned to its interest. It seems only necessary to recognise certain principles, supposed to have been long and well established, to decide it.

That the people have an original right to establish, for their future government, such principles as, in their opinion, shall most conduce to their own happiness, is the basis, on which the whole American fabric has been erected. The exercise of this original right is a very great exertion; nor can it, nor ought it to be frequently repeated. The principles, therefore, so established, are deemed fundamental. And as the authority, from which they proceed, is supreme, and can seldom act, they are designed to be permanent.

This original and supreme will organizes the government, and assigns, to different departments, their respective powers. It may either stop here; or establish certain limits not to be transcended by those departments.

The government of the United States is of the latter description. The powers of the legislature are defined, and limited; and that those limits may not be mistaken, or forgotten, the constitution is written. To what purpose are powers limited, and to what purpose is that limitation committed to writing, if these limits may, at any time, be passed by those intended to be restrained? The distinction, between a government with limited and unlimited powers, is abolished, if those limits do not confine the persons on whom they are imposed, and if acts pro-[177]-hibited and acts allowed, are of equal obligation. It is a proposition too plain to be contested, that the constitution controls any legislative act repugnant to it; or, that the legislature may alter the constitution by an ordinary act.

Between these alternatives there is no middle ground. The constitution is either a superior, paramount law, unchangeable by ordinary means, or it is on a level with ordinary legislative acts, and like other acts, is alterable when the legislature shall please to alter it.

If the former part of the alternative be true, then a legislative act contrary to the constitution is not law: if the latter part be true, then written constitutions are absurd attempts, on the part of the people, to limit a power, in its own nature illimitable.

Certainly all those who have framed written constitutions contemplate them as forming the fundamental and paramount law of the nation, and consequently the theory of every such government must be, that an act of the legislature, repugnant to the constitution, is void.

This theory is essentially attached to a written constitution, and is consequently to be considered, by this court, as one of the fundamental principles of our society …

If an act of the legislature, repugnant to the constitution, is void, does it, notwithstanding its invalidity, bind the courts, and oblige them to give it effect? Or, in other words, though it be not law, does it constitute a rule as operative as if it was a law? …

It is emphatically the province and duty of the judicial department to say what the law is. Those who apply the rule to particular cases, must of necessity expound and interpret that rule. If two laws conflict with each other, the courts must decide on the operation of each.

[178] So if a law be in opposition to the constitution; if both the law and the constitution apply to a particular case, so that the court must either decide that case conformably to the law, disregarding the constitution; or conformably to the constitution, disregarding the law; the court must determine which of these conflicting rules governs the case. This is of the very essence of judicial duty.

If then the courts are to regard the constitution; and the constitution is superior to any ordinary act of the legislature; the constitution, and not such ordinary act, must govern the case to which they both apply.

Those then who controvert the principle that the constitution is to be considered, in court, as a paramount law, are reduced to the necessity of maintaining that courts must close their eyes on the constitution, and see only the law.

This doctrine would subvert the very foundation of all written constitutions. It would declare that an act, which, according to the principles and theory of our government, is entirely void, is yet, in practice, completely obligatory. It would declare, that if the legislature shall do what is expressly forbidden, such act, notwithstanding the express prohibition, is in reality effectual. It would be giving to the legislature a practical and real omnipotence, with the same breath which professes to restrict their powers within narrow limits. It is prescribing limits, and declaring that those limits may be passed at pleasure.

That it thus reduces to nothing what we have deemed the greatest improvement on political institutions – a written constitution – would of itself be sufficient, in America, where written constitutions have been viewed with so much reverence, for rejecting the construction. But the peculiar expressions of the constitution of the United States furnish additional arguments in favour of its rejection.

The judicial power of the United States is extended to all cases arising under the constitution.

[179] Could it be the intention of those who gave this power, to say that, in using it, the constitution should not be looked into? That a case arising under the constitution should be decided without examining the instrument under which it arises?

This is too extravagant to be maintained.

In some cases then, the constitution must be looked into by the judges. And if they can open it at all, what part of it are they forbidden to read, or to obey?

There are many other parts of the constitution which serve to illustrate this subject.

It is declared that "no tax or duty shall be laid on articles exported from any state." Suppose a duty on the export of cotton, of tobacco, or of flour; and a suit instituted to recover it. Ought judgment to be rendered in such a case? ought the judges to close their eyes on the constitution, and only see the law.

The constitution declares that "no bill of attainder or *ex post facto* law shall be passed."

If, however, such a bill should be passed and a person should be prosecuted under it; must the court condemn to death those victims whom the constitution endeavours to preserve?

"No person," says the constitution, "shall be convicted of treason unless on the testimony of two witnesses to the same overt act, or on confession in open court."

Here the language of the constitution is addressed especially to the courts. It prescribes, directly for them, a rule of evidence not to be departed from. If the legislature should change that rule, and declare *one* witness, or a confession *out* of court, sufficient for conviction, must the constitutional principle yield to the legislative act?

From these, and many other selections which might be made, it is apparent, that the framers of the consti-**[180]**-tution contemplated that instrument, as a rule for the government of *courts*, as well as of the legislature.

Why otherwise does it direct the judges to take an oath to support it? This oath certainly applies, in an especial manner, to their conduct in their official character. How immoral to impose it on them, if they were to be used as the instruments, and the knowing instruments, for violating what they swear to support!

The oath of office, too, imposed by the legislature, is completely demonstrative of the legislative opinion on this subject. It is in these words, "I do solemnly swear that I will administer justice without respect to persons, and do equal right to the poor and to the rich; and that I will faithfully and impartially discharge all the duties incumbent on me as according to the best of my abilities and understanding, agreeably to *the constitution*, and laws of the United States."

Why does a judge swear to discharge his duties agreeably to the constitution of the United States, if that constitution forms no rule for his government? if it is closed upon him, and cannot be inspected by him?

If such be the real state of things, this is worse than solemn mockery. To prescribe, or to take this oath, becomes equally a crime.

It is also not entirely unworthy of observation, that in declaring what shall be the *supreme* law of the land, the *constitution* itself is first mentioned; and not the laws of the United States generally, but those only which shall be made in *pursuance* of the constitution, have that rank.

Thus, the particular phraseology of the constitution of the United States confirms and strengthens the principle, supposed to be essential to all written constitutions, that a law repugnant to the constitution is void; and that *courts*, as well as other departments, are bound by that instrument.

The rule must be discharged.

JR Lucas, *The Principles of Politics*
(Clarendon Press, 1966)

[39] The Constitution [of the United States] … includes enough statements of general principle to communicate to any reader the spirit of the Constitution, while ensuring, by means of judicial review, that the other organs of government cannot disregard the general principles it has set out. In this way, the Constitution lays down limits, which are clear enough in normal circumstances, but which, if a new situation does arise where the application is not clear, can be given an authoritative interpretation.

The combination of Constitution and Supreme Court has proved in practice an effective check upon the powers of the other organs of government in America. The question then arises about the role of the Supreme Court: if the Supreme Court is the sole authoritative interpreter of the Constitution, it will be argued by proponents of the various doctrines of sovereignty that in the United States sovereignty is vested in the Supreme Court. So far as lawyers are concerned, the Constitution is what the Supreme Court says it is. It, and it alone, is guardian of the Constitution; *quis custodiet ipsos custodes?* [Who watches the watchmen?]…

[40] [T]wo points must be conceded: the interpretation placed by the Supreme Court on the Constitution goes beyond, and in some cases is clearly contrary to, what the framers of the Constitution had in mind when they formulated it in words; that is to say, the Supreme Court takes a generous view of its interpretative powers, and does not feel restricted to determining the semi-historical question of what the words of the Constitution were meant to mean when they were adopted: and secondly, the decisions of the Supreme Court are effective; not since Andrew Jackson has any organ of the Federal government dared to ignore the Supreme Court's ruling.

In spite of these arguments, it does not follow that the Supreme Court is the Sovereign Body of the United States. To make a minor point first, the Supreme Court can only adjudicate disputed cases, and cannot promulgate laws in general application on their own initiative. The restriction to particular cases does not matter, since all inferior courts must follow the Supreme Court's ruling in all similar cases, but the restriction on initiative does confine the Supreme Court's powers to those questions on which the citizens of the United States are not all agreed …

The Supreme Court is restrained not only by its formal procedures as a court from acting arbitrarily. It is also subject to the substantial check that it derives all its authority from its *rôle* as interpreter of the Constitution, and the Constitution can be read by any American citizen. Its powers of interpretation may be wide, but are not infinitely wide, and if the Supreme Court were thought to be abusing its position as interpreter it would lose respect and cease to be effective.

The reference to President Andrew Jackson is to the aftermath of *Worcester v Georgia*, 31 US (6 Peters) 515 (1832), where Chief Justice Marshall, speaking for the United States Supreme Court, held that Georgia legislation providing for removal of the Cherokee Nation from their lands was unconstitutional (see Chapter 5, §6). Jackson responded: "John Marshall has made his decision; now let him enforce it if he can", and the Cherokee were driven from their lands. In the 1950s there were similar reactions in several southern States when the Supreme Court ruled in *Brown v Board of Education*, 347 US 483 (1954) that "[493] segregation of children in public schools solely on the basis of race" was unconstitutional, and followed that up with the directive in *Brown v Board of Education*, 349 US 294 (1955) that the public schools be desegregated "[301] on a racially nondiscriminatory basis with all deliberate speed". On that occasion, however, President Dwight Eisenhower ensured that the Supreme Court's decision was enforced by backing it with military force, despatching federal troops and National Guardsmen to the high school in Little Rock, Arkansas to supervise the enrolment and attendance of African American children.

The crisis in Arkansas had been heightened by the public defiance of the Supreme Court expressed by the State's Governor Orville Faubus and by its legislature, in particular through a 1956 amendment to the Arkansas State Constitution that required the legislature to oppose "in every Constitutional manner the Un-constitutional desegregation decisions of May 17, 1954 and May 31, 1955 of the United States Supreme Court". Against that background, the Little Rock School Board petitioned the courts for a moratorium on further implementation of its school desegregation plan. The Supreme Court held that the petition must be dismissed.

Cooper v Aaron
358 US 1 (1958)

The Court: [15] One may well sympathize with the position of the Board in the face of the frustrating conditions which have confronted it, but, regardless of the Board's good faith, the actions of the other state agencies responsible for those conditions compel us to reject the Board's legal position ...

[16] The constitutional rights of respondents are not to be sacrificed or yielded to the violence and disorder which have followed upon the actions of the Governor and Legislature ... [L]aw and order are not here to be preserved by depriving the Negro children of their constitutional rights. The record before us clearly establishes that the growth of the Board's difficulties to a magnitude beyond its unaided power to control is the product of state action ...

[17] What has been said, in the light of the facts developed, is enough to dispose of the case. However, we should answer the premise of the actions of the Governor and Legislature that they are not bound by our holding in [*Brown v Board of Education*, 347 US 483 (1954)] ... It is necessary only to recall some basic constitutional propositions which are settled doctrine.

[18] Article VI of the Constitution makes the Constitution the "supreme Law of the Land." In 1803, Chief Justice Marshall, speaking for a unanimous Court, referring to the Constitution as "the fundamental and paramount law of the nation," declared in the notable case of *Marbury v Madison* [5 US (1 Cranch) 137 at 177], that "It is emphatically the province and duty of the judicial department to say what the law is." This decision declared the basic principle that the federal judiciary is supreme in the exposition of the law of the Constitution, and that principle has ever since been respected by this Court and the Country as a permanent and indispensable feature of our constitutional system. It follows that the interpretation of the Fourteenth Amendment enunciated by this Court in the *Brown* case is the supreme law of the land, and Art VI of the Constitution makes it of binding effect on the States "any Thing in the Constitution or Laws of any State to the Contrary notwithstanding." Every state legislator and executive and judicial officer is solemnly committed by oath taken pursuant to Art VI, cl 3, "to support this Constitution." Chief Justice Taney, speaking for a unanimous Court in 1859, said that this requirement reflected the framers' "anxiety to preserve it [the Constitution] in full force, in all its powers, and to guard against resistance to or evasion of its authority, on the part of a State ..." *Ableman v Booth* [62 US (21 How) 506 at 524 (1859)].

No state legislator or executive or judicial officer can war against the Constitution without violating his undertaking to support it. Chief Justice Marshall spoke for a unanimous Court in saying that: "If the legislatures of the several states may, at will, annul the judgments of the courts of the United States, and destroy the rights acquired under those judgments, the constitution itself becomes a solemn mockery ..." *United States v Peters* [9 US (5 Cranch) 115 at 136 (1809)]. A Governor who asserts a [19] power to nullify a federal court order is similarly restrained. If he had such power, said Chief Justice Hughes, in 1932, also for a unanimous Court, "it is manifest that the fiat of a state Governor, and not the Constitution of the United States, would be the supreme law of the land; that the restrictions of the Federal Constitution upon the exercise of state power would be but impotent phrases ..." *Sterling v Constantin* [287 US 378 at 397-8 (1932)] ...

The principles announced in [*Brown*] ... and the obedience of the States to them, according to the command of the Constitution, **[20]** are indispensable for the protection of the freedoms guaranteed by our fundamental charter for all of us. Our constitutional ideal of equal justice under law is thus made a living truth.

Both President Jackson's refusal to enforce the Court's decision in 1832, and President Eisenhower's willingness to do so in 1957, are vivid illustrations of a prediction made in 1788 about the likely power of the Court.

Alexander Hamilton, *The Federalist (No 78)*
in Isaac Kramnick (ed), *The Federalist Papers* (Penguin Books, 1987), 436

[437] Whoever attentively considers the different departments of power must perceive that, in a government in which they are separated from each other, the judiciary, from the nature of its functions, will always be the least dangerous to the political rights of the Constitution; because it will be least in capacity to annoy or injure them ... The judiciary ... has no influence over either the sword or the purse; no direction either of the strength or of the wealth of the society; and can take no active resolution whatever. It may truly be said to have neither FORCE nor WILL but merely judgment; and must ultimately depend upon the aid of the executive arm even for the efficacy of its judgments.

While the Australian Constitution does not expressly confer a power of judicial review, the delegates to the 1890s Conventions were aware of the way that the system had evolved in the United States, and evidently assumed that the High Court would exercise a similar role. As Fullagar J stated in *Australian Communist Party v Commonwealth* (*Communist Party Case*) (1951) 83 CLR 1, "**[262]** in our system the principle of *Marbury v Madison* is accepted as axiomatic". This is reflected in s 30 of the *Judiciary Act 1903* (Cth), which, in accordance with s 76 of the Constitution, provides that "the High Court shall have original jurisdiction: ... (a) in all matters arising under the Constitution or involving its interpretation".

6. *Grundnorm* and *Coup d'Etat*

If the whole enterprise of judicial review should be understood as appealing to the basic norm that the Constitution should be obeyed, more radical disruptions of political consensus can result in doubt as to what the basic norm is. In particular, the overthrow of a legal order through revolution or *coup d'état* can pose a genuine dilemma for domestic courts. A court formed before the coup and not overthrown by it may be faced with proceedings that require a decision on whether the new regime should be given judicial recognition. On the one hand, the court should uphold the rule of law as embodied in the prior legal order; on the other hand it may be faced with a *fait accompli*, such that any order it makes in support of the displaced legal system would not only be futile but might prolong community distress and uncertainty.

FM Brookfield, *Waitangi & Indigenous Rights: Revolution, Law and Legitimation*
(Auckland University Press, 1999)

[23] Where a court is called upon to decide whether a new revolutionary regime has become lawful, has it the jurisdiction to do so? There are two possible views.

First, there is the older constitutionalist view that a court created under the pre-revolutionary constitution has no jurisdiction to recognise a revolutionary regime as lawful but is bound to the constitution which created it (even though it may give limited recognition to the regime's day-to-day acts of government under the de facto doctrine). Similarly, if created by a new revolutionary constitution, it has no jurisdiction to do otherwise than recognise its creator ... The essence of this view is that the rule that judges cannot inquire into the validity of the constitution under which they hold office, clearly applicable in circumstances that are not revolutionary, applies also in circumstances that are. They are precluded from recognising a new revolutionary regime as lawful, even if it is firmly and certainly established. They must maintain this non-recognition as long as the revolutionaries permit the court to function or until the judges themselves resign or are driven from office. Similarly the revolutionaries are assured of full recognition by a court [24] which *they* set up and which indeed may be a means of securing the revolution and claiming the allegiance of citizens.

The view has good theoretical or jurisprudential support. In Kelsen's terms, the basic norm of the legal order may be destroyed by revolution. But the courts of that order, their jurisdiction being necessarily founded ultimately on the basic norm, cannot adjudicate upon the revolutionary change in the other (that is, the executive and legislative) branches of government by holding the new regime to be lawful. If the revolutionaries want full legal recognition (as distinct from the limited recognition of their day-to-day acts of government allowed by the de facto doctrine), they must complete the usurpation by appointing a new judiciary bound by their oaths of office to uphold the new revolutionary order. Of course, individual judges from the pre-revolutionary order may be willing to accept (or continue) office under the new, but that is quite a different matter from their adjudicating upon the revolutionary change.

A certain Judge Magrath in the United States Federal Court in Charleston, South Carolina, made the point dramatically in 1860, when that state seceded from the Union. He stepped down from the bench, declaring the 'Temple of Justice closed'. A few months later, the Confederacy having been formed, he re-opened the 'Temple' as the Confederate District Court for South Carolina. Clearly, he did not claim a supra-constitutional jurisdiction to give legal recognition to the new (short-lived) Confederate legal order. Rather the (pre-revolutionary) Federal Court had ceased to exist and the (revolutionary) Confederate Court took its place.

But, secondly, there is a newer view, more difficult to explain theoretically, which has found favour with the courts of a number of countries and has the powerful support of the majority judgment of the Privy Council in *Madzimbamuto v Lardner-Burke* [[1969] 1 AC 645]. This view is that courts, including those created by a written constitution, are authorised and required to decide when and if a revolutionary regime has become lawful …

[25] That is a question which a municipal court (that is, a court of the country in which the revolution occurred) 'must decide'. It is assumed that the court does have a supra-constitutional jurisdiction, exercisable in the extreme revolutionary circumstances visualised …

There have been other instances, notably in Uganda, Pakistan, Grenada, Lesotho and Bophuthatswana, where a court has assumed a supra-constitutional jurisdiction to decide whether or not a revolutionary regime has become lawful, and has not regarded the issue as conclusively determined by the constitutional source of the court's jurisdiction. But we are left with two questions: first, how one is to explain the basis for the supra-constitutional jurisdiction and, secondly, what the principles are upon which that supra-constitutional jurisdiction should be exercised.

The first question is not an easy one … Judges in Pakistan, Uganda and Southern Rhodesia thought to find the explanation in Kelsen's theory of revolutionary change in the basic norm, in effect seeing the theory as one which judges, qua judges, can apply. But this seems to be a mistake. For Kelsen it is not the judge but the jurist or legal scientist who presupposes the basic norm and who, when a new legal order replaces it by becoming by and large effective in its stead, will presuppose the basic norm of the new order. A person who is a judge may assume and function in that other role; but it appears that he or she, *as judge*, may function only within the legal order founded on the basic norm and cannot step outside that order to determine whether by a revolution a new legal order has replaced it … Seemingly, the supra-constitutional jurisdiction which a court necessarily claims if, as the Privy Council says it 'must', it accepts the role of deciding whether the revolution has succeeded, is based 'on some principle of law independent of any particular system [which] authorises a judge, simply by virtue of his [or her] office, and irrespective of the source of … jurisdiction, to recognise the revolutionary regime'. Judges in Pakistan, for example, have, explained their jurisdiction in terms of their Islamic faith, seeing themselves as judges holding office in a legal order whose basic norm is the sovereignty of Allah. That explanation may be generalised (in a de-mythologised form, for the secularist) to mean [26] that, in any particular legal order in which the judiciary is separated from the other branches of government, there may be behind Kelsen's 'basic' norm a norm or principle more basic still upon which the judges' supra-constitutional jurisdiction is founded.

Secondly, what principle or principles must the court apply in exercising the supra-constitutional jurisdiction? We may accept that the matter can be dealt with judicially, by the application of relevant principle and apart from a judge's personal politics. The Privy Council in *Madzimbamuto v Lardner-Burke* certainly thought so.

There is no doubt that one of the principles – it may be the only principle – is that of by-and-large effectiveness. The revolution must be practically successful. If that is the only principle, then of course the test based on it is in effect in accordance with Kelsen's theory of revolutionary change; except that, because a judge applies the test in adjudicating upon the change, the basic norm is not after all basic. In doubting the reasoning but accepting the results of Pakistan and Ugandan cases where Kelsen was purportedly applied, the Privy Council in *Madzimbamuto* appears to have accepted the effectiveness test but without needing to define it further.

While Kelsen's purpose in postulating the *Grundnorm* or "basic norm" is to establish the framework for a realm of pure "legal science", the conditions under which such a postulate is possible are political rather than legal. The crisis in Southern Rhodesia (now Zimbabwe) in the 1960s was a striking example. On 11 November 1965, the white supremacist regime of Ian Smith issued a "Unilateral Declaration of Independence" proclaiming that a new "Constitution of Rhodesia, 1965" had "superseded" the *Southern Rhodesia (Constitution) Order in Council* 1961, made under the *Southern Rhodesia (Constitution) Act 1961* (Imp). The United Kingdom Parliament responded by passing the *Southern Rhodesia Act 1965* (Imp). Under that Act, the *Southern Rhodesia (Constitution) Order* was issued, declaring "for the avoidance of doubt that any instrument made or other act done in purported promulgation of any Constitution for Southern Rhodesia except as authorised by Act of Parliament is void and of no effect".

In *Madzimbamuto v Lardner-Burke*, 1968 2 SA 284, a majority of the High Court of Southern Rhodesia held that only the 1961 Constitution, and the laws flowing from it, had any legal validity. But they also held that, for public safety, the *de facto* effectiveness of the Smith regime required that its day-to-day "law and order" directives should be enforced. Although the Rhodesian judges quoted at length from Kelsen's writings, they concluded that no appeal to a "basic norm" could resolve their dilemma. The competition between two Constitutions was also a competition between two "basic norms"; and while the concept of a "basic norm" might help to clarify the nature of the problem, it could not provide a solution. Another way of putting it might be that there was *no* "basic norm": that when Kelsen asks us to *assume* that the Constitution is binding, the making of such an assumption as a basis for legal cognition is possible only when it is in fact assumed by most of the population (or at least by most lawyers) as a matter of unambiguous and unquestioned consensus.

On appeal, Lord Reid writing for a majority of the Privy Council held that the compromise reached by the High Court was not possible: that the only valid legal system for Rhodesia, and the only one that any court could recognise or enforce in any way, was that flowing from the 1961 Constitution. After finding that "**[723]** conceptions of international law" on the recognition of revolutionary governments were "quite inappropriate in dealing with the legal position of a usurper within the territory of which he has acquired control", he continued:

Madzimbamuto v Lardner-Burke
[1969] 1 AC 645

Lord Reid: [724] But the position is quite different where a court sitting in a particular territory has to determine the status of a new régime which has usurped power and acquired control of that territory. It must decide. And it is not possible to decide that there are two lawful governments at the same time while each is seeking to prevail over the other.

It is an historical fact that in many countries – and indeed in many countries which are or have been under British Sovereignty – there are now régimes which are universally recognised as lawful but which derive their origins from revolutions or coups d'état. The law must take account of that fact. So there may be a question how or at what stage the new régime became lawful ...

[725] The Chief Justice of Uganda (Sir Udo Udoma CJ) said [in *Uganda v Commissioner of Prisons* [1966] EA 514 at 533]: 'The Government of Uganda is well established and has no rival.'

The court accepted the new Constitution and regarded itself as sitting under it. The Chief Justice of Pakistan (Sir Muhammed Munir CJ) said [in *State v Dosso* [1958] 2 PSCR 180 at 185]: 'Thus the essential condition to determine whether a Constitution has been annulled is the efficacy of the change.' It would be very different if there had been still two rivals contending for power. If the legitimate Government had been driven out but was trying to regain control it would be impossible to hold that the usurper who is in control is the lawful ruler, because that would mean that by striving to assert its lawful right the ousted legitimate Government was opposing the lawful ruler.

[726] In their Lordships' judgment that is the present position in Southern Rhodesia. The British Government acting for the lawful Sovereign is taking steps to regain control and it is impossible to predict with certainty whether or not it will succeed. Both the judges in the General Division and the majority in the Appellate Division rightly still regard the 'revolution' as illegal and consider themselves sitting as courts of the lawful Sovereign and not under the revolutionary Constitution of 1965. Their Lordships are therefore of opinion that the usurping Government now in control of Southern Rhodesia cannot be regarded as a lawful government.

One result of the Privy Council decision was that most of the Rhodesian judges resigned, since the compromise that they had sought to maintain had been dismissed as impossible.

The American case of Andrew G Magrath, referred to by Brookfield, is different. As a prominent southern secessionist, he resigned from the United States Federal District Court in 1860 because he could no longer sit as a judge of a regime which he had repudiated. He then purported to sit afresh to constitute a "Confederate District Court", and in 1864 became the Confederate Governor of South Carolina. Ironically, in that capacity, he issued a proclamation in 1865 advising submission to the Union authorities. Magrath was one of 13 federal judges who resigned at the time of secession. One Supreme Court Justice from Alabama, John Campbell, also resigned, although he had previously done his best to avert secession. Only one federal judge, West H Humphreys of Tennessee, purported to sit as a Confederate judge *without* having first resigned from the federal judiciary of the United States. In 1862 he was impeached and removed from federal judicial office by the United States Senate.

In *Madzimbamuto v Lardner-Burke*, Lord Reid accepted that the test is one of effective control, and that it is not made out when a former government is still striving for power. A more elaborate test was set out by Cullinan CJ of the High Court of Lesotho.

Mokotso v HM King Moshoeshoe II
[1989] LRC (Const) 24

Cullinan CJ: [133] A court may hold a revolutionary government to be lawful, and its acts to have been legitimated ab initio, where it is satisfied that (a) the government is firmly established, there being no other government in opposition thereto; and (b) the government's administration is effective, in that the majority of the people are behaving, by and large, in conformity therewith.

Earlier, in *Mitchell v Director of Public Prosecutions* [1986] LRC (Const) 35, Haynes P of the Court of Appeal of Grenada had included two further elements: "**[72]** (c) such conformity and obedience [must be] due to popular acceptance and support and ... not mere tacit submission to coercion or fear of force; and (d) it must not appear that the regime was oppressive and undemocratic". This attempt to add to the test proved controversial. It was rejected in *Mokotso* because "**[130]** [t]hroughout the course of history there have been regimes, indeed dynasties, holding sway for many years, indeed centuries, whose rule could not be said by any manner of means to be popular and could even be described as oppressive: but who is there to say that a new legal order was not created with their coming and going?"

The scope of the effectiveness test arose during the 2000 coup in Fiji. On 19 May 2000, a year into the term of Fiji's first Indo-Fijian Prime Minister Mahendra Chaudhry, a group of armed men led by George Speight seized Parliament and took the Prime Minister and members of Parliament hostage. Ten days later, the Commander of the Fiji Military Forces imposed martial law and issued Interim Military Government Decree No 1, *Fiji Constitution Revocation Decree*

2000, which stated: "Notwithstanding the provisions of any law existing … the Fiji Constitution Amendment Act 1997 is with effect from 29th Day of May 2000, wholly removed". On 4 July, further Military Decrees established an Interim Civilian Government with the power to make laws for the peace, order and good government of Fiji. When the last of the hostages were released by Speight on 14 July, despite the arrest of Speight, no attempt was made by the military to restore the 1997 Constitution or Parliament.

An action was filed in the High Court of Fiji by Chandrika Prasad, who with his family had been forced off his land in the wake of the Speight coup attempt, seeking a declaration that the 1997 Constitution remained in force and that the elected government of Fiji had not been lawfully dismissed. He was successful in *Prasad v Republic of Fiji* [2001] 1 LRC 665, with Gates J ruling that "**[692]** The 1997 Constitution is the supreme and extant law of Fiji today" and that "Parliament should be summoned by the President at his discretion but as soon as practicable". The Interim Civilian Government then lodged an appeal, but the Court of Appeal, composed of two judges from New Zealand and one judge each from Australia, Papua New Guinea and Tonga, again found for Prasad. The case is the only example of refusal by a domestic court to give legal recognition to a usurper controlling the apparatus of government.

Republic of Fiji v Prasad
[2001] 2 LRC 743

The Court: [759] We resist the temptation to discuss the theoretical basis for exercising this supra-constitutional jurisdiction. It is sufficient to observe that such a jurisdiction has been exercised by judges in other cases. We consider that not only is it appropriate for us to consider the seminal issues raised by this appeal, but that it is our duty as judges of Fiji to do so …

[763] Various formulations are given in the cases of what must be proved to validate a new legal order in place of the previous one. None of the authorities is binding on this court. Some seem over-influenced by the writings of the Austrian jurist Hans Kelsen, whose theories, on one view, might too readily reward a usurper … Many of the authorities were decided before the modern shift towards insistence on basic human rights in a raft of international treaties and, more importantly for present purposes, the 1997 Fiji Constitution …

[768] *Mokotso* [[1989] LRC (Const) 24] is valuable but we consider that the Chief Justice's formulation of the efficacy test is too narrowly expressed. Haynes P's 'extra conditions' in *Mitchell v DPP* [[1986] LRC (Const) 35] have been criticised as unable to be 'reconciled with the facts of history': see *Makenete v Lekhanya* [1993] 3 LRC 13 at 63 per Ackerman JA. It may be that Haynes P went too far in his condition (d) (ie it must not appear that the regime was oppressive and undemocratic) because, as *Brookfield* opined, the condition goes to the legitimacy of a regime and not its legality. The distinction does not always appear to have been fully understood in some of the authorities cited to us …

[769] Mr Robertson urged us to add to our formulation of the efficacy test an additional criterion to those of Haynes P, namely whether the new regime acknowledges basic human rights as evidenced by international obligations assumed by the nation. We do not think it necessary to include a requirement that a usurping regime has to show adherence to international human rights treaties. The 1997 Constitution was made in Fiji for Fiji by the Parliament and people of Fiji. It contains many of the rights and freedoms mandated by international instruments. It protects the rights of the indigenous people and entrenches some of those rights as we have detailed earlier. The extensive consultation undertaken by the Reeves Commission that preceded its adoption **[770]** in Parliament provides strong evidence that the 1997 Constitution reflected the will of the great majority of the people of Fiji. It is permissible when assessing the test for efficacy in this context to take into account the evidence which suggests contentment with or acceptance of the 1997 Constitution by the population at large. Such acceptance militates against the proposition that there has been general acquiescence in its abrogation.

In formulating our understanding of the common law of Fiji on the efficacy question, we are conscious that we are sitting as judges of a Fiji court. Consequently, statements by judges which may have been appropriate for other countries where a 'revolution' may have come about in a variety of ways need not be adopted here ... [T]his case is unique in that it is the interim civilian government itself that seeks a ruling on the legality of its regime, only some seven months after it was established. Nor is Mr Prasad like the appellants in the Seychelles and Grenada cases who sought to manipulate the legal aftermath of a coup to avoid, in one case, payment of tax and, in the other, a trial for murder. By contrast, Mr Prasad is just an ordinary citizen seeking a return to normality.

We see the 'efficacy' test, in the context of the common law of Fiji, as follows. (a) The burden of proof of efficacy lies on the de facto government seeking to establish that it is firmly in control of the country with the agreement (tacit or express) of the population as a whole. (b) Such proof must be to a high civil standard because of the importance and seriousness of the claim. (c) The overthrow of the Constitution must be successful in the sense that the de facto government is established administratively and there is no rival government. (d) In considering whether a rival government exists, the inquiry is not limited to a rival wishing to eliminate the de facto government by force of arms. It is relevant in this case that the elected government is willing to resume power, should the Constitution be affirmed. (e) The people must be proved to be behaving in conformity with the dictates of the de facto government. In this context, it is relevant to note that a de facto government (as occurred here) frequently re-affirms many of the laws of the previous constitutional government (eg criminal, commercial and family laws) so that the population would notice little difference in many aspects of daily life between the two regimes. It is usually electoral rights and personal freedoms that are targeted. As one of the deponents said, civil servants such as tax and land titles officials worked normally throughout the coup and its aftermath. Their functions were established and needed no ministerial direction. We derive little proof of acquiescence from facts of that nature. (f) Such conformity and obedience to the new regime by the populace as can be proved by the de facto government must stem from popular acceptance and support as distinct from tacit submission to coercion or fear of force. (g) The length of time in which the de facto government has been in control is relevant. Obviously, the longer the time, the greater the likelihood of acceptance. (h) Elections are powerful evidence of efficacy. It follows that a regime where the people have no elected representatives in government and no right to vote is less likely to establish acquiescence. (i) Efficacy is to be assessed at the time of the hearing by the court making the decision ...

[771] In relation to the first requirement of control, the violence and lawlessness that ensued in the country following the events of May 19 took the country to the verge of anarchy. The interim military government successfully undertook the task of restoring order. On 2 November, an attempt by elements of the army to take control was effectively put down. There is no evidence of an effective organised resistance or an attempt to displace the interim civilian government by force. That does not mean that there is not a 'rival government'.

Affidavits filed by the former Prime Minister, Mahendra Chaudhry and former members of his Cabinet claim that the Peoples Coalition is ready and willing to resume office under the 1997 Constitution. Adi Kuini Speed in her affidavit said that the coalition still has the support of least 44 out of the 71 seats in the House of Representatives and thus a comfortable majority, enough to form a government. In addition to this, two proceedings have been instituted in the High Court by members of the coalition challenging the abrogation of the 1997 Constitution ...

This is evidence that demonstrates that there is a rival government seeking through the courts to assert its authority to govern.

So far as the second requirement, that of acquiescence, is concerned, counsel for the interim coalition government relied on the continuing functioning of the administration of government throughout the attempted coup and its aftermath, for inferring acquiescence of the people in the interim civilian government and the abrogation of the 1997 Constitution. We consider that this factor affords little proof of acquiescence ...

[772] Five volumes of affidavits were filed on behalf of Mr Prasad to prove that people in Fiji by and large do not support the interim civilian government ...

[773] Undoubtedly most people will have noticed little difference between this and the former constitutional regime in many aspects of their daily lives which they carry on as before, but such passive compliance is hardly a persuasive indication of true acquiescence in a government which has been in power for only about seven months and severely restricts public protest. The affidavits produced on behalf of Mr Prasad ... demonstrate that substantial sections of the community do not

accept the legitimacy of the present government or acquiesce in it. It should also be remembered that the elected government has said it will await the outcome of this appeal before taking any further steps.

In the absence of any convincing evidence of real acquiescence, we must hold that the interim civilian government has not discharged the burden of proving acquiescence and has accordingly failed to establish that it is the legal government of Fiji. The purported abrogation of the 1997 Constitution has not been justified and it remains in place.

The Prime Minister of the Interim Civilian Government Laisenia Qarase then announced that the nation would be returned to democratic rule under the 1997 Constitution. However, Parliament was not recalled. Instead, it was dissolved by the President who called a general election under the 1997 Constitution that returned a coalition government led by Qarase.

After the election, a fresh controversy arose in regard to s 99(5) of the 1997 Constitution, which provides: "In establishing the Cabinet, the Prime Minister must invite all parties whose membership in the House of Representatives comprises at least 10% of the total membership of the House to be represented in the Cabinet in proportion to their numbers in the House". The Fijian Labor Party ("FLP"), led by former Prime Minister Chaudhry, had won 28 of the 71 seats (about 38 per cent). Qarase invited the party to join the Cabinet, but later withdrew the invitation amid disagreement on the conventions to govern a multi-party Cabinet. Thereupon, further legal proceedings ensued. A declaration that the Prime Minister was required to appoint to the Cabinet a proportionate number of FLP members was upheld by the Supreme Court of Fiji in *Qarase v Chaudhry* [2003] FJSC 1. The President then referred to the Supreme Court a request for clarification of how the "proportion" was to be computed. The answer given in *Qarase v Chaudhry* [2004] FJSC 1 was that the proportion should correspond to "the number of places which each party, including the Government Prime Minister's party, ... bears to the membership of that party in the House of Representatives".

7. Further References

Agamben, G, *Homo Sacer: Sovereign Power and Bare Life* (Stanford University Press, 1998).

Agamben, G, *State of Exception* (University of Chicago Press, 2005).

Barry, A, Osborne, T, and Rose, N, *Foucault and Political Reason: Liberalism, Neo-Liberalism and Rationalities of Government* (University of Chicago Press, 1996).

Beck, A, "Foucault and Law: The Collapse of Law's Empire" (1996) 16 *Oxford Journal of Legal Studies* 489.

Das, C, "Governments and Crisis Powers" [1996] *Malaysian Current Law Journal* 1.

Foucault, M, "Power and Norm: Notes" (transl by Suchting, W) in Morris, M, and Patton, P (eds), *Michel Foucault: Power, Truth, Strategy* (Feral Publications, 1979).

Handley, KR, "The Constitutional Crisis in Fiji" (2001) 75 *Australian Law Journal* 688.

Head, M, "A Victory for Democracy? An Alternative Assessment of *Republic of Fiji v Prasad*" (2001) 2 *Melbourne Journal of International Law* 535.

Hindess, B, *Discourses of Power: From Hobbes to Foucault* (Blackwell, 1996).

Hunt, A, "Foucault's Expulsion of Law: Toward a Retrieval" (1992) 17 *Law and Social Inquiry* 1.

Loewenstein, K, *Political Power and the Governmental Process* (University of Chicago Press, 1957).

Loughlin, M, *Public Law and Political Theory* (Oxford University Press, 1992).

Mahmud, T, "Jurisprudence of Successful Treason: Coup d'Etat and Common Law" (1994) 27 *Cornell International Law Journal* 49.

Newman, S, *Power and Politics in Poststructuralist Thought: New Theories of the Political* (Routledge, 2005).

Symposium, "Changing Images of the State" (1994) 107 *Harvard Law Review* 1179.

Vincent, A, *Nationalism and Particularity* (Cambridge University Press, 2002).

Walzer, M, "The Politics of Michel Foucault" in Hoy, DC (ed), *Foucault: A Critical Reader* (Blackwell, 1986).

Williams, G, "The Case that Stopped a Coup? The Rule of Law and Constitutionalism in Fiji" (2001) 1 *Oxford University Commonwealth Law Journal* 73.

Chapter 2

Political Liberalism

1. The Liberal Tradition

The growth of modern Western democracies was shaped by a dominant constitutional tradition of civil and political "liberalism". This is an ideological position that values the liberty of individuals to engage in activities considered to be important for self-expression or political participation, and supports constitutional arrangements to protect those activities from excessive state intervention. However, this broad orientation was compatible with a very wide range of political theories and practices. In particular, in the fluctuations of history, it seemed that "civil and political liberalism" might or might not go hand in hand with "economic liberalism", which postulates a similar resistance to state interference with the free market economy. Hence, while the association of "political" and "economic" liberalism (thereby matching freedom of spirit with freedom of enterprise) was common in England in the 1840s, this might either be defended as a natural correlation, or condemned as an erroneous transference.

Maurice Cranston, "Liberalism"
in Paul Edwards (ed), *The Encyclopaedia of Philosophy*
(Macmillan Publishing Co and The Free Press, 1967), vol 4

[458] **English liberalism.** Traditional English liberalism has rested on a fairly simple concept of liberty – namely, that of freedom from the constraints of the state. In Hobbes's memorable phrase, "The liberties of subjects depend on the silence of the law." In general, however, English liberals have always been careful not to press this notion to anarchist extremes. They have regarded the state as a necessary institution, ensuring law and order at home, defense against foreign powers, and security of possessions – the three principles Locke summarized as "life, liberty and property." English liberals have also maintained that the law can be used to extend the liberties of subjects insofar as the law is made to curb and limit the activities of the executive government. Thus, for example, the English laws of habeas corpus, of bail, and of police entry and arrest all constrain or restrain the executive and, in so doing, increase the freedom of the people …

The traditional form of English political liberalism naturally went hand in hand with the classical economic doctrine of laissez-faire. Toward the end of the nineteenth century, however, certain radical movements and certain English liberal theorists, such as Matthew Arnold and TH Green, developed, partly under foreign, left-wing influences, a different – as they claimed, a broader – concept of freedom, which was, to a large extent, to prove more popular in the twentieth century than traditional English liberalism with its economic gospel of laissez-faire. The central aim of this new school was utilitarian – namely, freeing men from misery and ignorance. Its exponents believed that the state must be the instrument by which this end was to be achieved. Hence, English liberal opinion entered the twentieth century in a highly paradoxical condition, urging, on the one hand, a freedom which was understood as freedom from the constraints of the state and, on the other, an enlargement of the state's power and control in order to liberate the poor from the oppressive burdens of poverty. In the political sphere this contradiction in the liberal ideology ended in the disintegration of the British Liberal party … , the right-wing, or laissez-faire, element joining forces with conservatism and the radical, *étatiste* element merging with socialism. Only a "rump" remained.

French liberalism. The ambiguity of the word "liberalism" is more marked in French than in any other European language. Some writers hold that as a result of events in France since the time of Louis XIV, the French people **[459]** have been divided into two political camps: one which supports the Roman Catholic church, traditional social patterns, and the Syllabus of Pius IX (1864) and one which opposes the church and favors parliament, progress, and the rights of man. Historians who see France in these terms call one side *conservateur*, the other *libéral* … [Other historians] see not two, but at least three, continuing traditions in French political thought: on the right, royalism and conservatism; on the left, socialism, anarchism, syndicalism, and communism; in the center, liberalism. In the first of these two analyses, *libéralisme* is understood to embrace all the creeds of the left; according to the second analysis, *libéralisme* is a political doctrine at variance with the creeds of the left.

Again, one can distinguish two distinct – indeed, opposing – schools among French theorists who claim to be liberal. One is the Lockean liberalism of Voltaire, Montesquieu, and Benjamin Constant … the liberalism of the minimal state, individualism, and laissez-faire. But there is a second liberalism, represented by the masters of the French Revolution and by the youthful Napoleon, which is democratic, Rousseauesque, and *étatiste*. Whereas Lockean liberalism understands freedom as being left alone by the state, the other liberalism sees freedom as ruling oneself through the medium of a state which one has made one's own.

Both these schools of *libéralisme* contributed something to the ideology of the French Revolution, and the often unperceived contradiction between them may also be said to have contributed to the intellectual confusion of those times. The fall of Napoleon was the signal for a return to the more purely Lockean style of liberalism. Benjamin Constant not only insisted that Rousseau's concept of liberty was an illusory one but also maintained that "*Du Contrat Social* [1762] so often invoked in favour of liberty, is the most formidable ally of all despotisms." Constant and his friends desired only to reproduce in France the Lockean Glorious Revolution of 1688. In 1830 they believed they had succeeded; Louis Philippe was enthroned on the basis of an understanding very like that on which William and Mary had been crowned in England. Politicians like Guizot, who called themselves Libéraux, were put in charge of the kingdom. The result was not inspiring. A new bourgeoisie basked in the liberty the Lockean state introduced; the great were diminished, but the poor were not elevated. A rebellion came from the left in 1848, and the right replied with Napoleon III. Henceforth, there were few self-styled Libéraux of any importance in French politics and no liberal party. When new parties were formed later in the century, the name chosen by the center was Republicain rather than Libéral. This is not to say that liberalism died in France in 1848; rather, the word *libéralisme* thereafter ceased to call to the minds of French-speaking people any clear or distinct idea …

German liberalism. The word "liberal" was first heard in Germany in 1812, going there, as it went to England, from Spain. But the last years of Napoleon's power marked the decline of one tradition of German liberalism and the beginning of a new one. For in Germany, as elsewhere, we may discern not a single doctrine of liberalism but at least two main, conflicting schools, which again may be classified as the Lockean and the *étatiste*. The older German tradition was not merely derivatively Lockean; it also had contributed much to the formulation of Locke's own thought. In the sixteenth century it was a German philosopher, Johannes Althusius, who proclaimed that sovereignty derived from the people, and it was the German *Naturrechts* school of jurists which provided the bridge between the Stoic concept of *jus naturale* and the Lockean doctrine of the rights of man. But Locke, in turn, influenced the eighteenth-century German liberals, among whom Wilhelm von Humboldt was perhaps the most conspicuous. The very title of his book *Ideen zu einem Versuch, die Grenzen der Wirksamkeit des Staates zu bestimmen* ("Ideas towards an Investigation to Determine the Proper Limits of the Activity of the State," 1792), reveals his preoccupation with limited sovereignty and the minimal state. In this work Humboldt argued that the function of the state is not to do good but to ward off evil, notably the evil which springs from man's disregard for his neighbors' rights. The state, he said, "must not proceed a step further than is necessary for the mutual security of citizens and protection against foreign enemies; for no other object should it impose restrictions on freedom." Eighteenth-century Germany also had several liberal economists, including Christian Kraus, who considered that Smith's *Wealth of Nations* (1776) was the most important book after the Bible.

In the nineteenth century a new school of liberalism, which was first and foremost nationalistic, arose in Germany. The freedom it stood for was the freedom of Germany, and the condition of the realization of this national **[460]** freedom was the unification of Germany. Thus, whereas the old Lockean liberals were against the state, the new nationalist liberals wanted to create a greater state. The French declaration of 1789 proclaimed the rights of *man*; the German liberals inspired in 1848 a declaration of the rights of the German people. The new German liberals thought in terms of collective, rather than individual, rights. Thus, the *étatiste* German liberals saw nothing incongruous in sending a mission in 1849 from the Frankfurt parliament to Berlin to offer the crown of all Germany to a Prussian monarch, Friedrich Wilhelm, who detested democracy and who, in any event, grandly announced that he did not take crowns from commoners.

The difficulty of understanding in what sense this new German liberalism rested on a principle of freedom is that of understanding what it was that its votaries were demanding freedom from. Indeed, for many German liberals it was not a question of freedom from anything. German metaphysics of the same period was working out a concept of freedom which had nothing to do with resisting constraint. Guido de Ruggiero, a sympathetic Italian historian of German liberalism wrote:

> The eternal glory of Kant is to have demonstrated that obedience to the moral law is freedom … It was the great merit of Hegel to have extracted from the Kantian identification of freedom with mind, the idea of an organic development of freedom, coinciding with the organisation of society in its progressively higher and more spiritual forms … The State, the organ of coercion *par excellence*, has become the highest expression of liberty. (*History of European Liberalism* [1925]).

The idea that true freedom is to be found in obedience to the morally perfected state gave a theoretical justification (of a highly abstract kind) to the nineteenth-century German liberals' pursuit of liberty in submission to a strong and unified nation-state. But these high-thinking theorists never recovered from Friedrich Wilhelm's snub in 1849. Germany got its unity, but it was the imperialists, not the new liberals, who achieved it, and it was Bismarck, rather than Kant, who gave the unified nation its political ethos. After the defeat of the Nazi regime in 1945, however, there was some revival of the Lockean type of liberalism in Germany.

American liberalism. In the United States the word "liberal" has never enjoyed the prestige it has in the United Kingdom, for in America there has never been, as there has been in England, a national liberal party. The short-lived Liberal Republican party of the 1870s was without a coherent program. Horace Greeley, its presidential candidate, was at once a socialist, spiritualist, vegetarian, and total abstainer; his personality led many Americans of his time to associate the word "liberal" with a visionary crank, and some still do …

Just as in France the word "liberal" had been used by some writers for almost any kind of left-wing opinion, so in America the word "liberal" was widely adopted after the depression as a soubriquet for "socialist." In *The Liberal Imagination*, Lionel Trilling defined liberalism as meaning, among other things, "a belief in planning and international co-operation, especially where Russia is in question." This definition may not have been wholly authorized by common usage, but there can be no doubt that the word "liberal" has come to be associated in the American public's mind with *étatiste* and left-wing ideologies rather than with the Lockean notions of laissez-faire and mistrust of organized power.

Indeed, it was one of Parrington's arguments in *Main Currents in American Thought* that American liberalism, as he called it, had always been concerned with democracy in a way that Locke and his English followers had not. Yet even before the emergence of twentieth-century left-wing liberalism, two rival creeds, both of which could reasonably be called liberal, contended for political supremacy. The first, as Parrington pointed out, was close to the "English philosophy of *laissez-faire*, based on the assured universality of the acquisitive instinct and postulating a social order answering the needs of the abstract 'economic man' in which the state should function in the interests of trade." The second liberalism was Rousseauesque rather than Lockean. It was "based on the conception of human perfectibility" and looked towards an egalitarian democracy "in which the political state should function as the servant to the common well-being."

The dominant political sentiment of the American tradition derives something from both these kinds of liberalism, for it has combined a Lockean attachment to liberty from the state with a Rousseauesque belief in democracy and equality. Nevertheless, perhaps it is still not quite respectable to be an avowed liberal in America. This may be partly because there has been no traditional support for a liberal party. It is also partly because not only socialists, but also communists and communist sympathizers, have not ceased to assume the title "liberal" rather than a more explicit expression of their political commitment.

A remarkable variety of political structures has been thought by different philosophers to embody liberty, and a correspondingly mixed company has shared the name "liberal." In singling out certain main streams or schools of liberal thought, one has to be mindful of the divergencies that exist even among those which can be usefully grouped together … [O]ne might divide liberals into those who see freedom as something which belongs to the individual, to be defended against the encroachments of the state, and those who see freedom as something which belongs to society and which the state, as the central instrument of social betterment, can be made **[461]** to enlarge and improve. It remains to be said that some of the greatest names in the history of liberal thought, including John Stuart Mill himself, are strangely poised between these two positions.

In the closing decades of the 20th century, "liberalism" assumed a new kind of significance in theoretical debate. The underlying ideas were reconstructed, by critics and defenders alike, as a more schematic theoretical position, supposedly unifying the development of Western political systems into a plan of unilinear growth unfolding from the 17th century onwards.

In part, this was a conservative reaction to the "legitimation crisis" afflicting advanced capitalist societies in the 1960s and 1970s (see Jürgen Habermas, *Legitimation Crisis* (1973; transl Thomas McCarthy, Heinemann, 1976)). The challenge was to devise a new legitimating framework appropriate to the needs of the "post-modern" age that appeared to be dawning. Instead, a generation of writers anxious to preserve the status quo reacted "**[125]** by dusting off the underpinnings of the age we were moving away from" (AR Blackshield, "The Pious Editor's Creed" in AR Blackshield (ed), *Legal Change: Essays in Honour of Julius Stone* (Butterworths, 1983), 123). The result was a resurgence of long-outmoded "social contract" theories. More generally, there was a reintegration of "liberalism" into a resurrection of its 17th-century origins in the theories of Thomas Hobbes and John Locke.

Yet the theories of Hobbes and Locke, however effective they may have been as strategies to meet the historical exigencies of their own time and place, were distinctively responsive to that time and place. Even if we credit them with having laid the foundations of "modern" political institutions, it is only by an anachronism that they could be thought of as solutions to the "legitimation crisis" arising from the apparent breakdown of those institutions. Hobbes, writing in 1651 from virtual exile in Paris, was seeking a formula for the political stability which, amid the upheavals of the time, neither King nor Parliament seemed able to provide. Locke, writing in 1689, one year after the English "Glorious" or "Bloodless" Revolution (see Chapter 3, §2(d)), sought to ground political legitimacy in concepts of "rights" and "trust". If Hobbes was an ambiguous apologist for the King, Locke was an undoubted apologist for the Revolution.

Thomas Hobbes, *Leviathan, Or the Matter, Forme and Power of a Commonwealth Ecclesiasticall and Civil*
(1651; Everyman's Library, 1914)

[64] [I]n the nature of man, we find three principall causes of quarrell. First, Competition; Secondly, Diffidence; Thirdly, Glory.

The first, maketh men invade for Gain; the second, for Safety; and the third, for Reputation. The first use Violence, to make themselves Masters of other mens persons, wives, children, and cattell; the second, to defend them; the third, for trifles, as a word, a smile, a different opinion, and any other signe of undervalue, either direct in their Persons, or by reflexion in their Kindred, their Friends, their Nation, their Profession, or their Name.

Hereby it is manifest, that during the time men live without a common Power to keep them all in awe, they are in that condition which is called Warre; and such a warre, as is of every man against every man. For WARRE, consisteth not in Battell onely, or the act of fighting; but in a tract of time, wherein the Will to contend by Battell is sufficiently known: and therefore the notion of *Time*, is to be considered in the nature of Warre; as it is in the nature of Weather. For as the nature of Foule weather, lyeth not in a showre or two of rain; but in an inclination thereto of many dayes together; So the nature of War, consisteth not in actual fighting; but in the known disposition thereto, during all the time there is no assurance to the contrary. All other time is PEACE.

Whatsoever therefore is consequent to a time of Warre, where every man is Enemy to every man; the same is consequent to the time, wherein men live without other security, than what their own strength, and their own invention shall furnish them withall. In such condition, there is no place for Industry; because the fruit **[65]** thereof is uncertain: and consequently no Culture of the Earth; no Navigation, nor use of the commodities that may be imported by Sea; no commodious Building; no Instruments of moving, and removing such things as require much force; no Knowledge of the face of the Earth; no account of Time; no Arts; no Letters; no Society; and which is worst of all, continuall feare, and danger of violent death; And the life of man, solitary, poore, nasty, brutish, and short …

[66] To this warre of every man against every man, this also is consequent; that nothing can be Unjust. The notions of Right and Wrong, Justice and Injustice have there no place. Where there is no common Power, there is no Law: where no Law, no Injustice. Force, and Fraud, are in warre the two Cardinall vertues. Justice, and Injustice are none of the Faculties neither of the Body, nor Mind. If they were, they might be in a man that were alone in the world, as well as his Senses, and Passions. They are Qualities, that relate to men in Society, not in Solitude. It is consequent also to the same condition, that there be no Propriety, no Dominion, no *Mine* and *Thine* distinct; but onely that to be every mans, that he can get; and for so long, as he can keep it. And thus much for the ill condition, which man by meer Nature is actually placed in; though with a possibility to come out of it, consisting partly in the Passions, partly in his Reason …

[87] The finall Cause, End, or Designe of men, (who naturally love Liberty, and Dominion over others,) in the introduction of that restraint upon themselves, (in which wee see them live in Commonwealths), is the foresight of their own preservation, and of a more contented li[f]e thereby; that is to say, of getting themselves out from that miserable condition of Warre, which is necessarily consequent … to the naturall Passions of men, when there is no visible Power to keep them in awe, and tye them by feare of punishment to the performance of their Covenants …

For the Lawes of Nature (as *Justice, Equity, Modesty, Mercy*, and (in summe) *doing to others, as wee would be done to*,) of themselves, without the terrour of some Power, to cause them to be observed, are contrary to our naturall Passions, that carry us to Partiality, Pride, Revenge, and the like. And Covenants, without the Sword, are but Words, and of no strength to secure a man at all. Therefore notwithstanding the Lawes of Nature, … if there be no Power erected, or not great enough for our security; every man will, and may lawfully rely on his own strength and art, for caution against all other men …

[88] It is true, that certain living creatures, as Bees, and Ants, live sociably one with another, (which are therefore by *Aristotle* numbred amongst Politicall creatures;) and yet have no other direction, than their particular judgments and appetites; nor speech, whereby one of them can signifie to another, what he thinks expedient for the common benefit: and therefore some man may perhaps desire to know, why Mankind cannot do the same …

[89] [But] the agreement of these creatures is Naturall; that of men, is by Covenant only, which is Artificiall: and therefore it is no wonder if there be somewhat else required (besides Covenant) to make their Agreement constant and lasting; which is a Common Power, to keep them in awe, and to direct their actions to the Common Benefit.

The only way to erect such a Common Power, as may be able to defend them from the invasion of Forraigners, and the injuries of one another, and thereby to secure them in such sort, as that by their owne industrie, and by the fruites of the Earth, they may nourish themselves and live contentedly; is, to conferre all their power and strength upon one Man, or upon one Assembly of men, that may reduce all their Wills, by plurality of voices, unto one Will: which is as much as to say, to appoint one Man, or Assembly of men, to beare their Person; and every one to owne, and acknowledge himselfe to be Author of whatsoever he that so beareth their Person, shall Act, or cause to be Acted, in those things which concerne the Common Peace and Safetie; and therein to submit their Wills, every one to his Will, and their Judgements, to his Judgement. This is more than Consent, or Concord; it is a reall unitie of them all, in one and the same Person, made by Covenant of every man with every man, in such manner, as if every man should say to every man, *I Authorise and give up my Right of Governing my selfe, to this Man, or to this Assembly of men, on this condition, that thou give up thy Right to him, and Authorise all his Actions in like manner*. This done, the Multitude so united in one Person, is called a COMMON-WEALTH, in latine CIVITAS. This is the Generation of that great LEVIATHAN, or rather (to speake more reverently) of that *Mortall God*, to which wee owe under the *Immortall God*, our peace and defence. For by this Authoritie, given him by every particular man in the Common-Wealth, he hath the use of so much Power and Strength conferred on him, that by terror thereof, he is **[90]** inabled to forme the wills of them all, to Peace at home, and mutuall ayd against their enemies abroad. And in him consisteth the Essence of the Common-wealth; which (to define it) is *One Person, of whose Acts a great Multitude, by mutuall Covenants one with another, have made themselves every one the Author, to the end he may use the strength and means of them all, as he shall think expedient, for their Peace and Common Defence*.

And he that carryeth this Person, is called SOVERAIGNE, and said to have *Soveraigne Power*; and every one besides, his SUBJECT …

A *Common-wealth* is said to be *Instituted*, when a *Multitude* of men do Agree, and *Covenant, every one, with every one*, that to whatsoever *Man*, or *Assembly of Men*, shall be given by the major part, the *Right* to *Present* the Person of them all, (that is to say, to be their *Representative*;) every one, as well he that *Voted for it*, as he that *Voted against it*, shall *Authorise* all the Actions and Judgements, of that Man, or Assembly of men, in the same manner, as if they were his own, to the end, to live peaceably amongst themselves, and be protected against other men …

[91] Because the Right of bearing the Person of them all, is given to him they make Soveraigne, by Covenant onely of one to another, and not of him to any of them; there can happen no breach of Covenant on the part of the Soveraigne; and consequently none of his Subjects, by any pretence of forfeiture, can be freed from his Subjection. That he which is made Soveraigne maketh no Covenant with his Subjects before-hand, is manifest; because either he must make it with the whole multitude, as one party to the Covenant; or he must make a severall Covenant with every man. With the whole, as one party, it is impossible; because as yet they are not one Person: and if he make so many severall Covenants as there be men, those Covenants after he hath the Soveraignty are voyd, because what act soever can be pretended by any one of them for breach thereof, is the act both of himselfe, and of all the rest, because done in the Person, and by the Right of every one of them in particular. Besides, if any one, or more of them, pretend a breach of the Covenant made by the Soveraigne at his Institution; and others, or one other of his Subjects, or himself alone, pretend there was no such breach, there is in this case, no Judge to decide the controversie: it returns therefore to the Sword again; and every man recovereth the right of Protecting himselfe by his own strength, contrary to the designe they had in the Institution. It is therefore in vain to grant Soveraignty by way of precedent Covenant. The opinion that any Monarch receiveth his Power by Covenant, that is to say on Condition, proceedeth from want of understanding this easie truth, that Covenants being but words, and breath, have no force to oblige, contain, constrain, or protect any man, but what it has from the publique Sword; that is, from the untyed hands of **[92]** that man, or Assembly of men that hath the Soveraignty, and whose actions are avouched by them all, and performed by the strength of them all, in him united.

John Locke, *Two Treatises of Government*
(1690; critical edition by Peter Laslett, Cambridge University Press, 2nd ed 1967)

[288] 6. But though this [State of Nature] be a State of Liberty, yet it is not a State of Licence, though Man in that State have an uncontroleable Liberty, **[289]** to dispose of his Person or Possessions, yet he has not Liberty to destroy himself, or so much as any Creature in his Possession, but where some nobler use than its bare Preservation calls for it. The State of Nature has a Law of Nature to govern it, which obliges every one, and Reason, which is that Law, teaches all Mankind, who will but consult it, that being all equal and independent, no one ought to harm another in his Life, Health, Liberty or Possessions. For Men being all the Workmanship of one Omnipotent, and infinitely wise Maker; All the Servants of one Sovereign Master, sent into the World by his order and about his business, they are his Property, whose Workmanship they are, made to last during his, not one anothers Pleasure. And being furnished with like Faculties, sharing all in one Community of Nature, there cannot be supposed any such *Subordination* among us, that may Authorize us to destroy one another, as if we were made for one anothers uses, as the inferior ranks of Creatures are for ours. Every one as he is *bound to preserve himself*, and not to quit his Station wilfully, so by the like reason when his own Preservation comes not in competition, ought he, as much as he can, *to preserve the rest of Mankind*, and may not unless it be to do Justice on an Offender, take away, or impair the life, or what tends to the Preservation of the Life, the Liberty, Health, Limb or Goods of another.

7. And that all Men may be restrained from invading others Rights, and from doing hurt to one another, and the Law of Nature be observed, which willeth the Peace and *Preservation of all Mankind*, the *Execution* of the Law of Nature is in that State, put into every Mans hands, whereby every one has a right to punish the transgressors of that Law to such a Degree, as may hinder its Violation. For the *Law of Nature* would, as all other Laws that concern Men in this World, be in vain, if there were no body that in the State of Nature, had a *Power to Execute* that Law, and thereby preserve the innocent and restrain offenders, and if **[290]** any one in the State of Nature may punish another, for any evil he has done, every one may do so. For in that *State of perfect Equality*, where naturally there is no superiority or jurisdiction of one, over another, what any may do in Prosecution of that Law, every one must needs have a Right to do.

8. And thus in the State of Nature, *one Man comes by a Power over another*; but yet no Absolute or Arbitrary Power, to use a Criminal when he has got him in his hands, according to the passionate heats, or boundless extravagancy of his own Will, but only to retribute to him, so far as calm reason and conscience dictates, what is proportionate to his Transgression, which is so much as may serve for *Reparation* and *Restraint*. For these two are the only reasons, why one Man may lawfully do harm to another, which is that we call *punishment*. In transgressing the Law of Nature, the Offender declares himself to live by another Rule, than that of *reason* and common Equity, which is that measure God has set to the actions of Men, for their mutual security: and so he becomes dangerous to Mankind, the tye, which is to secure them from injury and violence, being slighted and broken by him. Which being a trespass against the whole Species, and the Peace and Safety of it, provided for by the Law of Nature, every man upon this score, by the Right he hath to preserve Mankind in general, may restrain, or where it is necessary, destroy things noxious to them, and so may bring such evil on any one, who hath transgressed that Law, as may make him repent the doing of it, and thereby deter him, and by his Example others, from doing the like mischief. And in this case, and upon this ground, every *Man hath a Right to punish the Offender, and be Executioner of the Law of Nature* …

[341] 87. Man being born, as has been proved, with a Title to perfect Freedom, and an uncontrouled enjoyment of all the Rights and Priviledges of the Law of Nature, equally with any other Man, or Number of Men in the World, hath by Nature a Power, not only to preserve his Property, that is, his Life, Liberty, and Estate, against the Injuries and Attempts of other Men; but to judge of, **[342]** and punish the breaches of that Law in others, as he is perswaded the Offence deserves, even with Death it self, in Crimes where the heinousness of the Fact, in his Opinion, requires it. But because no *Political Society* can be, nor subsist without having in it self the Power to preserve the Property, and in order thereunto punish the Offences of all those of that Society; there, and there only is *Political Society*, where every one of the Members hath quitted this natural

Power, resign'd it up into the hands of the Community in all cases that exclude him not from appealing for Protection to the Law established by it. And thus all private judgement of every particular Member being excluded, the Community comes to be Umpire, by settled standing Rules, indifferent, and the same to all Parties; and by Men having Authority from the Community, for the execution of those Rules, decides all the differences that may happen between any Members of that Society, concerning any matter of right; and punishes those Offences, which any Member hath committed against the Society, with such Penalties as the Law has established: Whereby it is easie to discern who are, and are not, in *Political Society* together. Those who are united into one Body, and have a common establish'd Law and Judicature to appeal to, with Authority to decide Controversies between them, and punish Offenders, *are in Civil Society* one with another: but those who have no such common Appeal, I mean on Earth, are still in the state of Nature, each being, where there is no other, Judge for himself, and Executioner; which is, as I have before shew'd it, the perfect *state of Nature* …

[375] 135. Though the *Legislative*, whether placed in one or more, whether it be always in being or only by intervals, tho' it be the *Supream* Power in every Commonwealth; yet,

First, It is *not*, nor can possibly be absolutely *Arbitrary* over the Lives and Fortunes of the People. For it being but the joynt power of every Member of the Society given up to that Person, or Assembly, which is Legislator, it can be no more than those persons had in a State of Nature before they enter'd into Society, and gave up to the Community. For no Body can transfer to another more power than he has in himself; and no Body has an absolute Arbitrary Power over himself, or over any other, to destroy his own Life, or take away the Life or Property of another. A Man, as has been proved, cannot subject himself to the Arbitrary Power of another; and having in the State of Nature no Arbitrary Power over the Life, Liberty, or Possession of another, but only so much as the Law of Nature gave him for the preservation of himself, and the rest of Mankind; this is all he doth, or can give up to the Commonwealth, and by it to the *Legislative Power*, so that the Legislative can have no more than this. Their Power in the utmost Bounds of it, is *limited to the publick good* of the Society. It is a Power, that hath no other end but preservation, and therefore can never have a right to destroy, enslave, or designedly to impoverish the Subjects. The Obligations of the Law of Nature, [376] cease not in Society, but only in many Cases are drawn closer, and have by Humane Laws known Penalties annexed to them, to inforce their observation. Thus the Law of Nature stands as an Eternal Rule to all Men, *Legislators* as well as others. The *Rules* that they make for other Mens Actions, must, as well as their own and other Mens Actions, be conformable to the Law of Nature, *ie* to the Will of God, of which that is a Declaration, and the *fundamental Law of Nature* being *the preservation of Mankind*, no Humane Sanction can be good, or valid against it.

Both Hobbes and Locke influenced the later development of British constitutionalism and its consensual, liberal and individualistic outlook; and Locke's influence strongly carried through into the framing of the American Constitution a century later.

From the early 1970s onwards, "liberalism", bolstered by some version of a metaphorical "social contract" or "compact", became the unifying framework around which orthodox legal theories tended to converge in defence of the status quo. Conversely, the more radical challenges to orthodoxy were united in their rejection of that version of "liberalism". While the primary focus of that debate was on civil and political theory, a similar debate came to characterise the "law and economics" movement, since many of the more influential analyses of "law and economics" have been predicated on a model of economic liberalism – that is, on the model of a free market and individual freedom of contract.

This market-oriented version of "law and economics" has focused in particular on the law of torts and contracts. Its application to the law of tort is not confined to the so-called "economic torts", but seeks rather to re-orient decision-making in tort litigation in order to replicate the economically efficient solutions that a hypothetical market transaction would arrive at (allowing for, and where possible eliminating, transaction costs). Typically, this has involved the modelling of a hypothetical market transaction according to "the Coase theorem" – which postulates that if transaction costs are eliminated, parties pursuing conflicting goals will always arrive through negotiation at the most efficient outcome, regardless of who has the stronger legal claim. This "theorem" was supposedly derived from a study of the law of nuisance by Ronald Coase, though in fact Coase did not there propose any "theorem" at all (see RH Coase, "The Problem of Social Cost" (1960) 3 *Journal of Law and Economics* 1).

The application of this approach to constitutional theory has been labelled "public choice theory". It takes the techniques developed by the "law and economics" movement for modelling efficient solutions to private interactions, and seeks to adapt those techniques to the analysis of "public" choices. It treats government policy and decision-making as open to capture by interest groups who will use the political process to buy "wealth transfers" ("rent") from others less powerful. The market generates wealth and the state transfers it in accordance with what the "rent-seeking" groups want and what they can offer in exchange. The process is represented as a giant bribe. Those who pay the bribe will get their policies implemented, and "rent" (or wealth) will flow to them from the less well-organised or powerful (see Jonathan R Macey, "Transaction Costs and the Normative Elements of the Public Choice Model: An Application to Constitutional Theory" (1988) 74 *Virginia Law Review* 471). For "public choices", as for "private choices", the market is assumed to be the generator of economic efficiency and consequently state intervention is assumed to be inefficient.

Stephen Bottomley and Stephen Parker, *Law In Context*
(Federation Press, 2nd ed 1997)

[298] [T]here are close links between mainstream economic analysis of law and many of the central tenets of liberalism. Indeed ... , classical liberalism is commonly identified with classical economics, and neo-classical economics today (within which almost all the literature on economic analysis of law is located) retains strong associations with 18th and 19th-century liberalism. As Lawrence H Tribe has pointed out,

> many of the tools and concepts of economics, and its underlying assumptions, are already engineered, whether intentionally or not, to serve a specific agenda. The intellectual and social heritage of these ideas, as well as their natural tendency, lies in the classical eighteenth and nineteenth century economics of unfettered contract, consumer sovereignty, social Darwinism, and perfect markets ... This brings those ideas within a paradigm of actions guided by a preexisting set of personal preferences – a paradigm inclined toward the exaltation of possessive individualism, "efficient" resource allocation, and maximum productivity, as against respect for distributive justice, procedural fairness, and the irreducible and sometimes inalienable values associated with personal rights and public goods ...

Neo-classical economics ... treats the individual as the basic unit of analysis. It assumes that individuals act rationally to maximise their own self-interest, and that individuals are the best judges of their own welfare ... Chicago school economics, in particular, has expressed a strong preference for the market mechanism (especially freedom of contract) over state intervention and, where the market malfunctions, for common law (which "mimics" the market) over statute law.

Again, its analysis of political and regulatory decision-making ... is characterised by methodological individualism, by the theory of social contract, and by arguments for holding the "Leviathan-like proclivities of government in check".

In summary, as Gary Minda has pointed out:

> **[299]** Law and economics can be understood to be a liberal movement which is seeking to build on the vision of the liberal state. Indeed, many of the arguments which these scholars advance are in reality a justification for the existing institutional practices of the modern liberal state such as the allocation of functions between the legislature and the judiciary as well as the doctrinal legal categories which support the notion of what is public and what is private, and so forth ...

[359] Beginning in the 1960s, a group of economists began to extend the behavioural model which they had used to understand private markets and applied this model to those who participate in political roles as voters, politicians, bureaucrats, planners and party leaders. This enterprise has become known as "public choice" theory (or "the economic theory of regulation"). It is, in essence, the economic analysis of political (or non-market) decision making. Thus we can say that while traditional economics is "the science of the private choice of private goods on the market", the economic theory of regulation is "the science of the public choice of public goods through government" ...

Public choice theory approaches its task by taking the tools and methods of economic theory and applying them to government and collective political action. As in neo-classical (Chicago school) economics generally, the basic behavioural postulate is that individuals are egoistic, rational, utility maximisers. Thus people are assumed to behave in political decision-making processes very much as they are assumed to behave in the market place:

> [F]irms seek to maximise profits, consumers seek to maximise utility, and policy makers seek to maximise political support ... Public policy makers are not benevolent maximisers of social welfare ... but are instead motivated by their own self-interests.

In both contexts, individuals seek to maximise their utility by trading with each other, but whereas in the market they trade goods and commodities, in the political sphere they trade votes and other units of political exchange ...

[360] At a positive level, it offers an understanding of "the complex institutional interactions that go on in the political sector" and it [361] attempts to *explain and predict* political outcomes. At a normative level, it attempts to prescribe what political institutions *should* be adopted, suggesting a range of constitutional and deregulatory mechanisms to minimise "inefficient" state intervention ...

Conventional public choice theory, in particular the Virginia school, analyses the behaviour of voters, politicians, members of political parties and bureaucrats, and attempts to model their behaviour on an economic basis. It seeks to develop a "theory of political institutions" which incorporates theories of voting, theories of electoral and party competition and theories of bureaucracy. For example, the behaviour of parliaments and bureaucracies has been modelled to generate propositions about political behaviour. There has been particular emphasis on why voters vote and what leads them to vote as they do, on the importance of electoral competition and majority rule, and on a variety of alternatives to majority rule. Research has also sought to understand the importance of legislative procedural rules, such as committee structures and amending procedures, in affecting the ultimate legislative outcome.

In each case, it is postulated that individual legislators, voters, leaders and members of political parties and bureaucrats act primarily out of self-interest (as rational maximisers of utility) and that legislative and bureaucratic outcomes can be understood ... in terms of "the rational behaviour of those engaged in legislative and bureaucratic choice under prevailing political rules".

Thus it is argued that various self-interested strategies are adopted by participants in the political process to achieve their own ends. Elected representatives make political decisions that maximise votes so that the representative or her political party wins elections. Legislators can be expected to engage in such activities as "log-rolling" – trading votes on one issue for desired votes on another issue ("you vote for my port, I'll vote for your dam"). Individuals [362] or groups affected by government action (and with sufficient self-interest) engage in "rent-seeking", that is, they "devote scarce resources to the pursuit of a degree of monopoly rights granted by government". Thus at one time, butter producers virtually suppressed the use of margarine by obtaining laws that forbade colouring it to look like butter. Other examples would be an industry which lobbies government to receive protection from import competition or a group which "seeks government aid in monopolising what would otherwise remain a competitive industry, in order to transfer consumer surplus to the producer group." The problem with rent-seeking is that it involves the expenditure of resources on things such as lobbyists, lawyers, accountants, and press agents rather than on more economically productive activities.

Bureaucratic behaviour is viewed with equal scepticism. Because they are in charge of actually implementing government policy, bureaucrats play a crucial role in the political arena. William Niskanen, who is responsible for the most developed model of bureaucratic behaviour within a public choice perspective, has argued that the goal of bureaucratic decision makers is to maximise their own "satisfaction". This includes variables such as salary, job security, office space, working conditions, power, patronage and public recognition. Niskanen argues that the bureaucracy can manipulate the policy debate through its information advantage over the legislature, thereby distorting legislation in favour of its own interests, and that their need to maximise budgets (which "satisfaction" requires) leads bureaucrats to engage in excessive (sub-optimal) regulation ...

[368] Unsurprisingly, public choice theorists (of whatever school) conclude that representative democracy gives disproportionate emphasis to the interests of small groups who have most to gain from legislation, and that this is commonly at the expense of the larger public, who pay the price of higher taxes and higher prices for goods and services. This is consistent with empirical evidence which suggests that many regulatory programmes have "large social costs, small public benefits and **[369]** (often) substantial transfers from the public to some discrete group, typically the industry ostensibly controlled by the regulatory program". On this view, government regulation, far from correcting market failure in the public interest, instead provides a means by which special interests profit at the public expense ...

At a normative level, the conclusion that government regulation does not serve the public interest has led to a variety of recommendations for constitutional, legal and political reform, consistent with achieving the particular liberal values which underpin the public choice tradition. Thus public choice theorists argue that appropriate political institutions can and should be designed to enhance individual liberty and freedom, to constrain the scope of government spending (and thereby reduce taxation) and to build barricades against affirmative government action ...

[370] In the Chicago-school strand of public choice, emphasis is placed on rolling back the state by deregulation, an enterprise in respect of which it has had considerable success. Public choice arguments in favour of deregulation were embraced with enthusiasm by the Reagan and Thatcher administrations during the 1980s. In a more modest way, some of the recent deregulatory initiatives in Australia can be attributed to the same source.

James Gillespie, "New Federalisms"
in Judith Brett, James Gillespie and Murray Goot (eds), *Developments in Australian Politics* (MacMillan, 1994), 60

[66] [Economists and political scientists associated with the New Right] have drawn on American arguments that the unrestrained growth of government provides the main threat to the survival of private property and individual liberty. Much of their work has concentrated on the design of constitutional barriers to increased government spending and revenue raising. Federal government is seen as a further refinement of these restrictions on the power of government. Working with the metaphor of marketplace competition, Ostrom argues that 'the monopoly position of any one government is ameliorated by the availability of alternative governments'. The overlapping jurisdictions and fragmentation of authority of a federal system become major safeguards against mighty central government.

This public choice model starts from the behavioural assumptions of neo-classical economics. Political processes are explained as expressions of the self-interested motivation of individuals. The market performs this function in economic life; in the more artificial world of politics, institutions must be consciously created to steer behaviour. The work of Buchanan, Brennan (the leading Australian exponent), Tullock and other public choice theorists concentrates on these problems of institutional and constitutional design, of constitutional engineering to set rules, and institutional structures that inhibit the growth of government. Starting with the assumption that market forms of allocation of goods are more efficient than centralised control, public choice theorists have been strong advocates of federal forms of dispersed authority, decentralising to introduce 'market-like alternatives into the political process'. Popular sovereignty is exercised through individuals shifting jurisdictions in order to find a mix of taxation and service levels that best suit them, 'the more closely **[67]** political institutions resemble the economic institutions of the competitive market, the more responsive they will be. And the more restricted the scope of a political decision, that is, the more localised the political unit, the more it will approximate that arrangement. Thus, [ ]the level of government becomes more important than its type'. Where classical models of democratic participation see the vote, or 'voice', as the key moment in citizen participation, these models add 'exit' – voting with the feet.

There have been problems in applying this approach in Australia. Competition requires a multiplicity of units of governments, and Australia's six states and two territories hardly offer the range of choice expected by American federal theorists. Mobility has also been limited by cost, distance and the structure of Australian labour markets. The one practical example of the widespread use of the exit option to reduce state taxation levels was the abolition of death duties. After Queensland abolished them in 1977, the other states were forced to follow suit. More seriously, the Australian experience of competitive federalism has not been a happy one. Bidding between the states for industrial and mining development has often degenerated into a competition in laxity: lowering standards of environmental protection, or scrambling over one another to offer cheap energy resources and other concessions to attract industries, accentuating the fragmented structure and low economies of scale that have inhibited the formation of a national market and stultified Australian industrial development.

2. Pluralism

The 19th-century liberal conception of individualism left no room for a conception of groups or bodies existing at an intermediate level between individuals and their government. In the 20th century, attempts to remedy this omission came through pluralist and corporatist writings that explored the relationship between groups and the exercise of sovereign power.

Political pluralism embraces two different views. The use of the term in the English tradition is very different from its use in American political science.

LJ Boulle, *South Africa and the Consociational Option*
(Juta, 1984)

[25] (*a*) **English political pluralism**
English political pluralism emerged in the early decades of the present century and was promoted by writers such as JN Figgis, Harold Laski, and [26] GD Cole, most of whom had strong socialist leanings. The theory rested on three basic principles:

(i) The first was that liberty is the most important political value and is best preserved by the dispersal of power in society. The fear of concentrated power was a pervasive feature of pluralist thought.

(ii) The second principle was that groups should not be depicted merely as collections of individuals but as having a real personality. The English pluralists argued that groups could not adequately be understood simply in terms of the lives of their individual members, and that both political and legal theory should take more seriously their substantive personality and consequent rights. Maitland was one of the first pluralist writers to assert that groups were real entities in society, and he drew on the work of Otto van Gierke who, although writing on German nationalism and not himself a pluralist thinker, emphasised the significance of groups and their claim to legally recognised rights and privileges.

(iii) The third principle involved a denial of the theory that in every state there must be a sovereign. As far as legal sovereignty was concerned pluralism took issue with the view that law is simply the will of the sovereign irrespective of its content or character. This involved a rejection of Bentham's sovereign legislator and Austin's positive law, as well as the model of the state as a legal order in which a determinate authority acts as the ultimate source of power. The pluralists also criticised the notion of political sovereignty, which held that in every society there is an ultimate authority which can resolve disputes and demand obedience, as being of doubtful factual correctness and having dangerous moral consequences.

In developing their doctrine the English pluralists were reacting against nineteenth century liberalism and utilitarianism, which had placed the individual in a social vacuum and focused exclusively on the relationship between the individual citizen and the sovereign state. By drawing on the evidence of man's interest in, and loyalty to, a plurality of groups, they emphasised the group nature of politics. The view that the individual's relationship with the state was mediated by groups and associations was averse to the classical liberal tradition, which was based on an individualistic or atomistic model of politics and society and viewed politics in terms of a basic opposition between the individual and the state. In the pluralist view the groups and associations in society were characterised by voluntary (and hence at times overlapping) memberships, were equal in status with one another, and possessed autonomy in deciding on their own rules of behaviour.

The function of the state, according to this tradition, was to provide and maintain the framework within which groups interacted and pursued their substantive purposes, and to guarantee the continued existence of the groups. The state's authority was limited by other powers in society, exercised by different non-state organisations, with whose autonomy it ought not to interfere. Political action was perceived not as the exercise of sovereign power, but as the interplay of a variety of plural associations [27] resulting at times in a conflict of wills arising from the complex network of group relationships. Freedom was formulated not negatively, in terms of the limitations on governmental powers, but positively, as the equal opportunity for self-realisation by individuals in their groups or social structures. By spreading power according to the diversity of [its] functions ... the state could maximise the opportunities for freedom and development. In this view of politics the participatory role of the citizen became crucial – he had a duty to become involved both in the state and in the society as a whole, and participated through his membership in a plurality of groups. Moreover, as the state created areas of freedom in which groups could operate, the groups and their members shared responsibility for the society's conditions – pluralism of responsibility became a feature of the pluralist model. Finally, in so far as the citizen was faced with a choice between conflicting loyalties, to the state and organisations in competition to it, he might at times be compelled to give his loyalty to a non-state group and resort to civil disobedience.

The English pluralist view implied more complex institutional arrangements than the direct democracy of Rousseau, or the simple representative mechanisms described by Locke. Nicholls refers to various institutional embodiments of pluralism, such as the guilds envisaged by the guild socialists, as well as to various forms of corporativism and functionalism which it advocated. The pluralist model could be described as essentially 'federal' in so far as it implied a functional division of power among corporate groups. Laski observed that for a proper understanding of any society it should be regarded as essentially 'federal' in nature. By this he meant that general activities which interested all members of society belonged to the state, while activities which were primarily specific in their incidence should be administered by those most directly affected by them; the latter activities interested the state only in so far as they affected the rest of the community, in which event it might ultimately exercise its reserve power. The criterion for the functional devolution of power was social utility. However, although functional federalism was an essential doctrine of English pluralism its constitutional principles remained largely undefined.

The influence of English political pluralism had begun to wane before the emergence of its American counterpart. It had tended to be more normative than empirical, and it was criticised because it ignored the complex reality of group life and the possibility of the groups becoming oligarchical and unscrupulous, it incorrectly presupposed the individual's interest and rationality in politics, and it tended to overlook the dangers of deadlock and stalemate in the political system. Even its proponents began to perceive the need for something beyond a vigorous group life, such as national leadership and a more purposeful role for the state. The tradition's opposition to state absolutism, and its emphasis on the dispersal of power and the group nature of politics, constituted its main contributions to political theory.

(b) American political pluralism

Pluralism has been the dominant tradition within American political sociology for several decades. It has purported to be an explanation of, [28] and justification for, the United States' political system, although, as the critics observe, the system has been viewed at times in a rather romantic light. The tradition may be traced back to De Tocqueville, with his reflections on self-governing 'intermediate bodies' capable of countervailing both an atomistic society and a totalitarian state, and Arthur Bentley, who portrayed the political arena as comprising a large number of groups each attempting to promote a particular interest. These themes were developed by subsequent American theorists who came to associate democracy with pluralism; far from viewing differences in social and political positions as being incompatible with democratic ideals the pluralists saw in their balanced adjustment the essential conditions for democracy. In pluralist theory policy outcomes were perceived as the result of group processes, and not individual rational choices as envisaged by classical democratic theory.

In the 1950s American pluralist theory began to take on the role of an ideology and to be applied in a descriptive and prescriptive manner. A free society was said to be characterised by a multiplicity of semi-autonomous groups whose leaders compete for political power. The groups are characterised by cross-cutting cleavages, and the multiple affiliations of individuals prevent the emergence of exclusive loyalties which would exacerbate conflict. The existence of multiple affiliations, together with a commitment to common values and a competitive balance of power, leads to the integration and stability of such a society. The political structure is also plural, in that equal political rights are exercised by its citizens in a constitutional system embodying a separation of legislative, executive and judicial powers, a justiciable bill of rights, and a federal or quasi-federal division of competence. Not only is political power fragmented among the branches of government, but it is shared between the state and a number of private groups and individuals. As far as the relationship between the groups and state is concerned Wolff distinguishes between two different theories in the pluralist tradition: the 'vector-sum' version in which the different groups are seen to exert pressures on government agencies which formulate a compromise, and the 'referee' version, in which the state is perceived as a passive co-ordinating authority which upholds the rules for competition and conflict resolution. In the latter theory groups achieve their goals directly, and in the former indirectly through organising as pressure groups. Both theories emphasise the value of a plurality of interest groups in society and a decentralisation of public power.

In opposition to the pluralist writers of the fifties other theorists began to emphasise the élitist nature of the American polity, and while this criticism was to stimulate a vigorous defence of the orthodox pluralist position it led ultimately to a redefinition of the concept – whereas historically pluralism had implied active citizen participation in group and public affairs (and a reasonable equality of bargaining power among interest groups), it began to mean competition among élites and organised groups, irrespective of whether decision-making within the groups was dominated by the few. American pluralism's emphasis on group behaviour led to the decline of individualism and to élitist theories of democracy.

[29] It is beyond the scope of this work to provide a detailed critique of the pluralist political model. One of the most persistent criticisms is that, while purporting to be empirical, it ignores the realities of the American political process which has been blatantly undemocratic vis-à-vis groups which have shown the greatest degree of cultural or social pluralism. This can be expatiated in terms of Wolff's three-point criticism. The first is that existing groups are in practice always favoured over groups in the process of formation, thereby inhibiting social change. The second is that in the case of intergroup conflicts the system consistently favours the stronger over the weaker party, and legitimate interests which are unorganised find their disadvantaged position perpetuated. These two criticisms are based on the empirical evidence of the American system. The third is based on an alternative philosophy of society which rejects the pluralist notion that there is no such thing as the public interest or the common good in the modern state. While the pluralist emphasis on public competition among groups might be appropriate for solving some problems of distributive justice it is inadequate for solving problems relating to the common good or for reorganising society on a large scale. This requires the broader vision of 'community' which Wolff attempts to formulate as an alternative to the pluralist model. From the class perspective Szymanski advances two primary criticisms of pluralism. The first concerns its assumption that American society is composed of a diversity of equally powerful groups reflecting the interests of most people, when in fact only half the population belongs to voluntary associations, most of which have only a peripheral interest in politics. The second concerns the function of the state, which in the pluralist model is that of reconciling the various group influences and converting them into state policies; this approach fails to recognise the limited number of policies which the state can follow without causing socio-economic disruption of the society, and the fact the state's main purpose might be to defend the predominance of a particular class.

PP Craig, *Administrative Law*
(Sweet and Maxwell, 3rd ed 1994)

[24] [T]he traditional view of administrative law was itself premised upon a particular view as to how our democracy functioned. This was termed unitary democracy, to express the idea that all public power was and should be channelled through Parliament, which body possessed a legislative monopoly. When practical necessity required the delegation of power to a minister or agency the purpose of administrative law was to ensure that the agency remained within its assigned area and therefore did not trespass upon the legislative monopoly of Parliament by [25] exercising power outside of this sphere. This Diceyan view of administrative law (and indeed of constitutional law) was expressly challenged on the grounds that his vision of unitary democracy was both descriptively flawed and prescriptively questionable. Three strands of this challenge should be distinguished.

The *first strand* was composed of writers in the late nineteenth and early twentieth centuries who advanced an explicitly pluralist vision of democracy to replace the unitary view espoused by Dicey. The views of the pluralists differed, but central themes ... can nonetheless be delineated.

They began by revealing the historical foundations of the unitary view of the state. The idea that sovereignty was indivisible appeared initially in the writings of, among others, Hobbes as a defence against anarchy. Only if the state was all powerful could a breakdown in society be prevented. If groups or associations were rivals to the state then chaos would ensue. This political justification for the unitary state was unsurprising given the turmoil that occurred in the English civil war. This reasoning was reinforced in the nineteenth century by jurists like Austin, who argued in a more analytical vein, that it was simply not possible to have a sovereign who was limited in any way. Dicey then built on Austin. In a democracy where the people elected MPs who represented their views and controlled the executive, it was "right" that this central power should be all embracing. The democratically elected Parliament did have and should have all public power.

Having revealed the foundations of the unitary view, the pluralists then proceeded to challenge them. They presented both descriptive and prescriptive arguments.

In *descriptive terms*, they contested the idea that all public power was in fact wielded by the state. They pointed to pressure groups which shaped and constrained state action. Religious, economic and social associations exercised authority, and took part in decisions of a public character. "Legislative" decisions would often be reached by the executive, after negotiation with such groups, and would then be forced through the actual legislature.

In *prescriptive terms*, group power was applauded rather than condemned. The all powerful unitary state was dangerous. Liberty was best preserved by the presence of groups within the state to which the individual could owe allegiance. Decentralisation and the preservation of group autonomy were to be valued.

This vision of political pluralism was complemented by a concern with ... social and economic conditions ... There was a strong belief that political liberty was closely linked with social and economic equality. This influenced the pluralists' approach to the emergent regulatory welfare legislation which was passed in the early decades of the twentieth century. Such legislation was viewed in a favourable light, being [26] one step in the alleviation of social and economic hardship and therefore of central importance to the effective operation of a pluralist democracy.

A *second strand* of the challenge to the unitary vision of democracy has assumed a slightly different form. Its thrust is implicitly, rather than explicitly, pluralist. The essence of this argument is as follows. The unitary vision of democracy is flawed not just because public power is exercised by groups outside of the parliamentary process. It is also misleading because even those rules which are formally legitimated by Parliament are not really properly scrutinised by them. Pressures of time, and executive dominance of the legislature combine to ensure that legislative control over, for example, secondary legislation is minimal. In addition, departmental policy choices which are made pursuant to the implementation of legislation may be inadequately thought through, with the consequence that there is no proper consideration of differing ways to attain legislative goals. Accountability is reduced to a minimum because there is no realistic method of testing the departmental policy choice, ministerial responsibility itself being ineffective.

How then does this type of argument have pluralist implications? The answer, in outline at least, is simple. If Parliament cannot effectively control such matters, and if the parliamentary legitimation is really just formal, then we might need to think of other additional ways in which to legitimate and control the use of public power in society. One such way is to think of legitimation and control through citizen participation in the process of making agency rules. Whereas the unitary vision of democracy sees all public power as being legitimated through participation by MPs in Parliament, the pluralist vision carries the implication that power can be legitimated and constrained in more diverse ways, such as by citizen participation.

3. Corporatism

A focus on group activity also underpins corporatism, a descriptive theory that develops some themes of political pluralism to suggest that some large and powerful interest groups not only influence policy outcomes, but actually become parties to the policy-making and implementation process. In this sense, corporatism redefines the constituent parts of the state.

PP Craig, *Administrative Law*
(Sweet and Maxwell, 3rd ed 1994)

[26] A *third strand* in the challenge to the unitary state is that of "corporatism." Now corporatism is one of those terms which has assumed a wide variety of meanings, not all of which are mutually consistent. The central thrust of this idea can nonetheless be conveyed in a straightforward manner. Corporatism provides an explanation both of the form which pressure group action will assume, and also the reasons for its existence.

The *form* of interest group pressure under corporatist theory is best viewed as a modification of pluralism. The latter depicts the political process as one in which a relatively wide range of different groups will affect political decision-making. Such groups will compete between themselves for political influence and no particular group will enjoy a monopoly of representational status with the government. Corporatist theory depicts the form of interest group pressure differently. The principal [27] distinction is that a particular group or groups will be accorded a privileged representational status with the government; that the government will "license" such a group to represent the interests of other less powerful groups within the same area; and that the privileged status accorded to the dominant group carries a "price", in the sense that such a group will then accept certain controls or constraints on the range of demands which it advances.

What then are the *reasons* for the existence of this type of pressure group action? The modern state is required to undertake a wide range of activities in order to correct defects in, or problems arising from, the capitalist system. Governments are forced to juggle with goals such as full employment, economic growth, the resolution of labour conflicts, inflation and the provision of protection for consumers and workers. The pursuit of these objectives necessitates discussion and collaboration with major interest groups. Such groups help to shape governmental policy and their own objectives are fashioned or constrained by the same process. Major power groups achieve their dominant representational status for a number of reasons. The government perceives obvious benefits in dealing with one bargaining agent. A relationship of trust can be built up, an understanding of the rules of the game and an assuredness that the organisation will promote an agreed policy among the relevant "constituency". Industrial concentration and economies of scale further the impetus towards the emergence of a particular interest group which will bargain and speak for the whole.

It is readily apparent from the preceding discussion that the corporatist theory is to some extent at odds with classical pluralist doctrine, insofar as the latter assumes the existence of a more multiple, competitive structure amongst pressure groups. What is more relevant for our present purposes is the fundamental conflict between corporatism and the unitary view of the state which provided the basis of the traditional model. Corporatism undermines the unitary thesis in two complementary ways. On the one hand, it postulates the existence of groups which wield public power outside of the normal parliamentary process. On the other hand, it helps us to understand how the alliance between such groups and the executive can bypass Parliament. This can happen in a variety of ways. A policy may be agreed between a dominant group and the executive, which is then forced through Parliament with little opportunity for comment. Or the executive and the relevant group may simply arrive at an understanding which never sees the parliamentary light of day at all, but remains in non-statutory form.

Alan Cawson, *Corporatism and Political Theory*
(Basil Blackwell, 1986)

[35] [P]luralism is premised on a separation between public and private: between the sphere of government, and the private groups of civil society. By contrast the stress within corporatist writing has been on the growing interpenetration of the public and the private spheres. The crucial concept is that of public policy as the outcome of a bargaining process between state agencies and those organised interests whose power in the political marketplace means that their co-operation is indispensable if agreed policies are to be implemented. The state is not sufficiently powerful for officials to dictate policies and impose them unilaterally, but at the same time it is sufficiently powerful to resist capture by those interests. This notion is clearly implicit in the concept of bargaining: each party must have resources to bargain with; otherwise the relationship is one of subservience or submission.

In spite of assertions to the contrary ... , this idea of bargaining is not inconsistent with the relative absence of competition in the political marketplace. The corporatist idea does not imply that there is no competition within the bargaining process, ie between state and organised interests, but it does pre-suppose the parties to the process are each free of any effective challenge to their own right to bargain. For the state this issue is less problematic than it is for [36] interest groups: by definition the concept of the state involves unchallengeable monopoly powers in fields such as law-making, taxation, and most importantly, the ultimate sanction of the legitimate use of force. But for interest groups, there is, at least in the longer term, the effect of changes in economic structure and consequent power potential which can erode the value of their bargaining counters. The ideal type of corporatism assumes that specialisation is complete and monopoly effective: the application of the idea to actual cases and historical trends must involve the analysis of observed discrepancies from such stringent conditions.

The role of the state is thus central to the concept of corporatism: the state is the arena in which the process of corporatist politics takes place. This rules out of the concept processes which take place wholly in civil society without the intervention of public authority or the presence of state actors. Bargaining in which compromises are reached between conflicting class interests, for example in collective bargaining between employers and unions, is not corporatism unless there is a significant state presence. But equally the concept should not be restricted to those instances alone where bargaining takes place within a tripartite structure of business, labour and state. But if we suggest that corporatism can comprise bipartite bargaining between organised interests and state agencies, how are we to define bargaining so as to sift out the important relationships from the myriad of contacts between modern states and interest groups?

The answer I propose concerns the nature of bargaining itself, which in turn is restricted to the particular organisational capacities of corporatist groups, which differ in kind from the voluntary and fluid structures of pluralist groups. It is this feature which get[s] us to the heart of the concept of corporatism itself. Corporatist bargains are those which are negotiated between monopolistic interest organisations and implemented through the self-regulatory actions of those organisations. This stipulation is crucial, and allows us to reject instances where bargaining involves, for example, the content of legislation before parliament, which is then implemented through bureaucratic or legal structures. The bargaining of the welfare lobby over the content of social security legislation is not corporatism: it is quite properly to be seen as part of those pluralist processes which remain an important part of the political life of liberal democracies. What would turn such bargaining from pluralism to corporatism would be if the welfare lobby comprised an interest organisation (or a number with specifically limited domains) with a monopoly representative capacity, and the political cohesion required to itself act as the administrative partner of [37] the state, disciplining and controlling its membership to accept the compromises worked out in negotiation with state agencies.

In some Scandinavian countries the trade union movement has developed its welfare concerns to such an extent that it does bargain social policy in a corporatist fashion, and does implement public policy, as for example in Sweden …

Corporatist bargaining is thus qualitatively different from pluralism, where the stress is on interest representation and lobbying, access and influence. The corporatist relationship between state agencies and organised interests is two-way; the pluralist relationship is one-way – from the group to the state – in that policy implementation is the preserve of the state. Under a corporatist arrangement interest organisations are an integral part of administration; they are not merely consulted over the implementation of policy.

The nature of corporate groups

From the remarks in the two foregoing sections, we can draw out the implications of the argument for the nature of what we shall henceforth call 'corporate groups', as distinct from 'preference groups' which exist in a mutually competitive political environment.

The basis for the organisation of the corporate group is its function. Groups constituted on the basis of a shared value position cannot become corporate groups in the sense used here; they will always remain preference groups, and will always exist within the pluralist sphere of the polity. This does not mean that they can never become powerful, but it does mean that they can never become self-regulating agents of policy implementation.

If our focus is on the sphere of production, then the major differentiating structural characteristic with respect to function will be class. Corporate groups in production represent class interests. This of course does not deny that under certain circumstances, for example in tripartite bargaining, corporatism represents a process of class collaboration. For some … corporatism *is* class collaboration, but this seems unduly restrictive in that it excludes from the corporatist net [those] processes which involve policy formation and implementation of a bipartite character.

Class seen as relationship to the means of production, or the means of administration, does not however comprise the only structural basis **[38]** upon which corporate groups form. As Parkin convincingly argues, following Weber, social closure can take place around skills as well as property ownership so long as the control over the validation of those skills is enforceable. The process of social closure is a part of the concentrative dynamic argued here to be the essential independent variable in the development of corporatism. The most important examples of closure around skills in contemporary politics are the professions, which distinguish themselves by erecting monopolistic barriers to entry to their ranks, and developing effective procedures for self-regulation.

The existence of powerful professional groups controlling specific occupations, as with the legal and medical professions, provides fertile ground for the development of bipartite corporatist processes. The administration of legal aid in Britain; the administration of the National Health Service, at least until the triumph of managerialism in the 1960s, and the administration of public land drainage policy provide good examples of corporatist policy-making.

The chief characteristic then, is monopoly, and with this goes the capacity for self-regulation and the possibility of delivering negotiated agreements through the disciplined co-operation of members. But a wholly private self-regulating body would not come within the present definition of a corporate group. The intervention of the state in the process of closure, and the existence of negotiated agreements between state agencies and groups is crucial …[Here again], the presence of the state is a defining characteristic of corporatism. It may be possible to conceive of corporatism without labour, or even without capital, as in the Social Contract phase of British economic management in the 1970s, but it is not possible to conceive of corporatism without the state.

A conceptual definition of corporatism

We can summarise this discussion … by suggesting the following as a concise definition …:

> *Corporatism is a specific socio-political process in which organisations representing monopolistic functional interests engage in political exchange with state agencies over public policy outputs which involves those organisations in a role which combines interest representation and policy implementation through delegated self-enforcement.*

[39] What must be emphasised is that corporatism is not a phenomenon of the group process (but concentration within that process is a precondition for its development), nor is it a phenomenon of state form (although an interventionist state is also a precondition). What makes corporatism distinctive is the fusion of representation and intervention in the *relationship* between groups and the state ...

A continuum between pluralism and corporatism

So far we have for the purposes of analytical clarity distinguished between pluralism and corporatism in terms of ideal types, and suggested that the existence of corporatist processes within liberal democratic polities weakens the claim of pluralist models to provide an adequate description of those polities. In some of the corporatist literature it is suggested that there is an evolutionary process which is transforming once pluralist societies into corporate ones, and that pluralism as a concept should be abandoned in favour of corporatism.

The view taken here is, however, rather different, and involves seeing pluralism and corporatism as distinctive processes *co-existing* in any given society, so that one can speak of a corporate and a competitive sphere of politics ... Once it is recognised that pluralism and corporatism are not rival contenders as explanatory models of whole societies, it is possible to give more attention to specifying the relationship between them. One way of doing this is through the idea of a continuum in which the end points are defined in relation to a particular variable. A recent exchange in *Political Studies* between Ross Martin and Colin Crouch helps to clarify ... the appropriate variable ...

Martin suggests a continuum 'focused on the access and role that groups are accorded by government office-holders' so that the appropriate variable is the degree of importance of interest organisation in public policy-making. The corporatist end would be where 'groups have a formalized and substantial share in formulating and administering government policy'; the pluralist end would be where 'parliamentary channels provide the only means of contact between office-holders and organized interest groups'.

Such theories challenge our traditional thinking about constitutional law. To the extent that corporatism now exists in Australia, any faith in the effectiveness of notions such as representative government and the rule of law must be called into question.

4. Communitarianism

The focus of classic liberal theory was the individual. Notions of the community and common good were eschewed. However, there has been a revival in theoretical approaches that argue from the premise that people exist primarily as members of a community. Communitarianism mounts at least two basic claims. First, that an individual can only be understood in context: that is, within the community he or she inhabits. Secondly, communitarians claim that community is desirable and that people can only flourish in communities. This allows the communitarian to justify community obligations that are imposed rather than accepted.

Shlomo Avineri and Avner De-Shalit (eds), *Communitarianism and Individualism*
(Oxford University Press, 1992)

[2] Communitarianism is put forward in two spheres. One is methodological, the communitarians arguing that the premises of individualism such as the rational individual who chooses freely are wrong or false, and that the only way to understand human behaviour is to refer to individuals in their social, cultural, and historical contexts. That is to say, in order to discuss individuals one must look first at their communities and their communal relationships. The second sphere is the normative one, communitarians asserting that the premises of individualism give rise to morally unsatisfactory consequences. Among them are the impossibility of achieving a genuine community, the neglect of some ideas of the good life that should be sustained by the state, or others that should be dismissed, or – as [3] some communitarians argue – an unjust distribution of goods. In other words, the community is a good that people should seek for several reasons and should not be dismissed ...

Both communitarian and individualist theories begin with the image of the individual. But the former claims that there are social attachments which determine the self and thus individuals are constituted by the community of which they are a part. In that sense the individualist image of the self is ontologically false. Individualists also fail to see that this community is not necessarily a voluntary one, and that the social attachments which determine the self are not necessarily chosen ones ...

[4] A new image of the individual implies a new conception of community. The 'communitarian' community is more than a mere association; it is a unity in which the individuals are members. This membership is neither artificial nor instrumental, but rather has its own intrinsic value. This is in contrast to the individualist conception of community, which communitarians hold to be superficial, even obnoxious. The free person conceived of by the individualists, Sandel argues, is someone who is freed, as it were, from 'the dictates of nature and the sanction of the social roles', but this does not make any sense of our social life ...

[6] But the communitarian argument and the individualist response go beyond the issue of methodology to include the normative discourse. From the ontological argument communitarians conclude that, in order to justify the special obligations that we hold to members of our communities – families, nations, and so forth – one must attach some intrinsic (ie non-instrumental) value to the community itself and to our relations with other members of the community. That these obligations are not always voluntary does not detract from the fact that they are taken for granted by most people. On the other hand, communitarians argue, how can an individualist theory justify an obligation to fight for the state in the case of war? The communitarian contention is that their theory better justifies obligations that are not universal but rather specific and particular, because these obligations are part of what constitutes the self. For such a self, which is constituted by its relations to others in the community and which wishes to sustain the community, it is only natural to hold these obligations. The individualist self, on the other hand, is determined by its distance from others or by instrumental attachments alone. Thus for the individualist, the communitarians argue, it is more difficult, indeed virtually impossible, to justify such obligations, with which our lives are replete.

Indeed, the term 'community' as used in contemporary political thought is a normative concept, ... [describing] a desired level of human relationships. The community, as a body with some common values, norms, and goals, [7] in which each member regards the common goals as her own, is a good in itself. Communitarians argue that it is morally good that the self be constituted by its communal ties ...

[10] [C]ommunitarianism has been reproached for being conservative in its implications. If the communitarians are right in saying that we are not free to choose but rather that our values are determined by our community, the individualists say, then there is no reason to criticize the values of one's society.

But such criticism is far too hasty, firstly because many communitarian philosophers are quite radical in their social demands and in the way they would like society to change. Walzer's egalitarianism, Miller's market-socialism, Friedman's feminism, and Gutmann's readiness to renew liberal thought are only four examples. Secondly, communitarians do think in terms of 'reflection', 'critical scrutiny', and 'corrections of beliefs' in communities which are engaged in a process of a public debate and self-criticism. Moreover, communitarians believe that the roots of totalitarianism do not lie in their own premisses, but in limiting the political sphere, in alienating people from public debate and public activity. This constitutes their main argument in favour of extending political participation. And, thirdly, the modern conception of community is less deterministic and holistic than is sometimes believed. Contemporary communitarians leave room for non-communitarian relationships in society, the market being the most common example.

Liberals and communitarians diverge over whether the individual or the community has formative priority. As Richard Beardsworth puts it (*Derrida & the Political* (Routledge, 1996)): "[51] For the liberals, rights are the very condition of community. For the communitarians, community is the very condition of rights". The liberal conception of the individual contracting, through a real or postulated consent, into a very limited type of community brought about by that process, is at odds with the communitarian conception of individuals constituted by the web of community relationships. Does either model explain what happened when the Australian Constitution was adopted? Were we a collection of atomic individuals who achieved "community" through federation? Were we already a community who through the Constitution were able to agree on a vision of the common good? Or was it something else?

Insofar as ours is a communitarian culture, does the judicial explication of implied constitutional "rights" give expression to community values? Or does the very process of judicial explication of "rights" offend the communitarian idea? In any event, are the supposedly opposing claims for "rights" and "the common good" as incompatible as communitarians and liberals think they are? In an article published after his death, the Argentinean writer Carlos Santiago Nino (1943-93), drawing on the political history of his country, dealt with some of these questions by exploring parallels between communitarianism and legal positivism.

Carlos Santiago Nino, "Positivism and Communitarianism: Between Human Rights and Democracy"
(1994) 7 *Ratio Juris* 14

[21] One of the contributions of the communitarian trend consists in giving a picture of liberalism which is sometimes clearer than that provided by liberals themselves. In this way, MacIntyre, for instance, puts forward the following distinguishing features of liberalism, mainly in the Kantian variant. First, the idea that morality is mainly composed of rules which would be accepted by any rational individual under ideal circumstances. Second, the requirement that these rules should be neutral with regard to the interests of individuals. Third, the demand that moral rules should be also neutral with regard to conceptions of the good individuals may hold. Finally, the requirement that moral rules should be applied equally to all individual human beings regardless of their social context.

Communitarianism objects to each one of these assumptions of liberalism and it does so after proposing a diagnosis of the common source of so many philosophical mistakes. Charles Taylor, for instance, locates that source in an "atomist" conception of individuals according to which they are self-sufficient regardless of their social environment. Sandel expands the argument maintaining that Kantian liberalism assumes an outlook of moral agents as constant along time, disconnected thus from their own varying desires and interests, free from the causal flux which affects those desires and interests, mutually separated, and isolated from the social context. MacIntyre in his turn maintains that the abandonment of a teleological conception of human nature seriously disrupted moral discourse, since it now lacks the element which constituted the bridge between factual propositions about actual human behavior and moral rules which have a normative character.

These authors maintain that only an impoverished conception of the moral person, such as that referred to above, allows liberalism to sustain its distinctive thesis about the independence of justice and human right from a conception of what is good in life. Liberal neutrality about the ideals of virtue or of human excellence is achieved at the expense of adhering to a view of human agents as noumenal entities which not only lack a distinctive telos, but also possess an identity which is not dependent on ... [22] their relationship with other individuals, and on their insertion in a specific social environment.

Therefore, liberals are being accused of endorsing a social morality centered on human rights without realizing that they require a conception of the good, as is shown in cases like conflicts of rights which can only be solved by resorting to such a conception. Alternatively, liberals are also being accused of smuggling in a hidden conception of the good despite their pretence of neutrality. The conception of the good which liberals are said to endorse implicitly is the same as that of utilitarianism in the prevailing version: The satisfaction of desires or preferences of individuals whatever their content. This conception of the good is, in its turn, put into question by communitarians ...

Charles Taylor intends to show, in almost syllogistic fashion, how liberal thinking contradicts itself when it assumes there is a set of individual rights which have primacy over other normative relations ... Taylor's reasoning runs as follows: (1) The ascription of rights depends on the recognition of certain capacities, like expressing opinions, developing a spiritual life, feeling pleasure and pain, etc … (2) It is not enough for ascribing rights to recognize certain capacities. These should be considered *valuable* so as to be differentiated from others which are not the grounds of rights; (3) If something is valuable there is a duty to preserve and to expand it, materializing the conditions on which that materialization or expansion depends; (4) The majority if not all the capacities on which the ascription of rights depends are conditioned to membership in a society; they require tools like language, conceptual schemes and institutions which are inherently social …

[23] The conclusion of this reasoning is, of course, that the ascription of the rights presupposes the duty to preserve the links of community which make possible the development of the valuable capacities which underlie rights. Liberalism would contradict itself when it gives to rights primacy over the duties related to the preservation of society which makes the former possible.

MacIntyre arrives at the same conclusion with light variations in the premises: The rules which ascribe rights are justified on the basis of certain goods; these goods are internal to changing social practices. Thus, moral evaluation is subject to the traditions and practices of each society … [T]his may be dangerous, since it restricts the capacity [for] criticism of social institutions and practices; but he contends that the dissociation between morality and social practices which underlies liberalism is also dangerous since it neutralizes all motivation to be moral.

This allows us to distinguish the following aspects of the communitarian program: In the first place, the derivation of the principles of justice and rights from a certain conception of the good. Second, a conception of the good in which the social dimension is central and even dominant. Third, a relativization of the rights and duties of individuals to their particular attachments to other individuals and to the particular features and traditions of their society. Finally, a dependency of moral *criticism* on moral *practice* as it is manifested in the traditions, conventions and institutions of each society …

[25] The first association which I want to establish between [positivism and communitarianism] is that … [despite] quite amiable faces, both … may also show us quite frightful countenances.

In the case of ideological positivism, all of us know how the doctrine that whoever has the coercive power to make a social group obey certain prescriptions acquires legitimacy to issue them and is the recipient of the [26] corresponding duty to abide by them of the people was used to justify extreme authoritarian regimes, like the Nazi or Fascist ones … Of course, this does not mean that only ideological positivism is used to legitimize authoritarian regimes like Nazism. Different varieties of natural law theory … have been used for the same ignoble purpose. But it is clear that the doctrine that positive law whatever its content provides reasons for justifying actions and decisions constitutes the most direct and easy way conceivable to justify an authoritarian regime while it is in force …

[L]et me illustrate the grim face of ideological positivism with the case of Argentina. Since 1865, and especially since 1930 on until 1984, each time that there was a *coup d'etat* in Argentina the Supreme Court recognized the power of the *de facto* regime to issue valid laws and the obligation of the population and officials to obey and to apply them on the basis that that regime had acquired the control of the coercive power of the State and was able to impose order on society. This recognition of legitimacy was at the beginning quite restricted, mostly to issuing executive decrees, but with time the power to enact legislation and even to modify and to suspend the Constitution was recognized on the mere basis of the *factum* of positive law … In 1984, the Argentine Supreme Court changed its doctrine on the basis that the validity of the law was a normative predicate which could only be applied to those enacted democratically, so that only when the *de facto* laws were explicitly or implicitly ratified or not rejected by democratic bodies could they acquire validity. But the Supreme Court … went back in 1990 to its old doctrine of clearly positivist inspiration (it said that whatever are our "affective or ideological attitudes" concerning military regimes we must recognize as a fact that they are able to enact valid laws …).

Communitariarism may also develop in a quite unattractive way, even though none of the authors mentioned promotes that development. Despite the appeal of its realist vision of man, of the value of family and social links as grounds for special rights and duties, of the connection between values and social practices, each one of the distinguishing marks of communitarianism [27] may generate, when it is developed in all its implications, a different aspect of a totalitarian vision of society.

The primacy of the good over individual rights allows for the justification of perfectionist policies which intend[ ] to impose ideals of excellence or personal virtue, even when individuals do not perceive them and thus do not subscribe to them. In effect, if rights are ... only means to satisfy a certain conception of the good, why not prescind from them when that conception of the good may be more efficaciously materialized through other routes? Here it is also possible to allude to the example of Argentina, where military governments, backed by conservative sectors of the Catholic Church, had the invariable policy of coercing citizens into supposed ideals of virtue even with regard to private life. Thus, films and publications were censored even for adult exhibitions, deviant sexual behavior was persecuted, and even the ways in which people dressed or had their hair cut were overseen.

The idea that the social dimension is dominant in the conception of the good may lead one to justify sacrifices of individuals for the sake of promoting the well-being of society or the State conceived of in holistic terms. The glorification of particular links with social groups, like the family or the Nation, may serve as ground for collectivist, tribalist or nationalist attitudes which underlie many of the conflicts that humanity must endure ... Here it is also useful to allude to the example of Argentina during military regimes: The so-called "dirty war against subversion," which led to the disappearance, death and torture of thousands of people, often unrelated to left-wing subversion, was carried out under the "doctrine of national security," which is a holistic conception based on the good of the "national being", the interests of whom were held to prevail over those of individuals, and were interpreted in a privileged way by certain groups like the armed forces or the Church ...

Lastly, the dependence of criticism on moral practice which is also one of the main aspects of communitarianism may lead to a conservative relativism that, on the one hand, is inept for solving conflicts among those who appeal to different traditions or conventions, and, on the other hand, does not permit the evaluation[ ] of those traditions and conventions ... To give an extreme example again taken from the last dictatorship in Argentina: The military authorities of the Province of Cordoba prohibited the teaching [28] of modern mathematics in schools, under the idea that it would train students in a degree of abstraction which could later on be expanded in other fields of thought, and thus, when applied to the political and moral realm, would create the risk of making people prone to criticize the traditions and conventions which define the national being ...

Consequently, these two ugly faces which ideological positivism and communitarianism may present ... may combine together to legitimize abhorrent regimes: Ideological positivism may justify their authoritarian origin, and communitarianism their totalitarian content ...

The second connection between the two positions which I want to mention ... has to do with some coincidence between vague but legitimate preoccupations which make plausible both legal positivism and communitarianism in their best versions. I mentioned earlier what are those preoccupations of positivism: The subjectivity and arbitrariness of decisions which affect social relationships if the factum of positive law were not held to bind those decisions ... The terror of ideological positivists materializes in the image of a judge who leaves aside a clear text of the law and takes a decision which cannot be derived from a reasonable interpretation of it, either alleging that a decision against the law is as good as one according to it or invoking *his* moral values to disqualify the law and to decide directly according to those values. This is the terror of moralism.

If one digs deep into the concerns of many communitarians, I think that *some* of [their concerns] ... are of a similar tenor. They think that liberalism, mainly in its Kantian variety, lends itself to subjective and arbitrary moral conclusions ... [and implies] [29] an individualist moral epistemology in which some "enlightened" individuals may come to the conclusion of what morality requires on the basis of assumptions of practical reasoning ... without regard to the collective practices of the people concerned themselves which result from their own experiences and struggles.

Thus, one strand of communitarianism is distinctively worried about the epistemic elitism which it perceives in liberalism. For instance, Michael Walzer (1981) inveighs against the new "philosopher-kings" who try to influence mainly judges and mainly in the exercise of judicial review about what is the true set of rights enshrined in the Constitution whatever the experience of the people in their political practices. This concern about elitism is not necessarily shared by ideological legal positivism. But elitism presupposes the wider phenomenon of subjectivism and arbitrariness and here is where the minds of one and the others meet. Therefore, when a typical morally inspired judge of the North American Supreme Court nullifies a statute on the basis that it violates the right of privacy – as in [*Griswold v Connecticut*, 381 US 479 (1965)] – the positivist and the communitarian may both complain in chorus: The positivist because she does not see that right consecrated within the four corners of the Constitution, the communitarians because they do not see that right … as derived from a conception of the good embedded in the social practice of the relevant community. But they coincide not only in their complaints but in the fear that Justices are imposing arbitrarily their own subjective views of social morality on the rest of the community …

What I would like to argue next is that, though this concern of both ideological positivists and communitarians about the subjectivity and arbitrariness involved in liberal moralism is quite justified, they give to it two different wrong solutions because of another feature they have in common. This time what they share is a serious philosophical misconception.

Nino argues that positivism attempts to justify legal propositions by recourse to the mere fact of what a legislature has decreed. However, he says, that justification is logically incomplete unless we supply some evaluative reason why the legislature *ought* to be obeyed.

[32] The dependence of legal discourse on wider moral discourse manifests itself in many ways. Mainly it emerges in critical cases in which the authority of the issuer of a legal prescription is put in question, like, for instance, in the case of usurpation of who was normally taken to be the ultimate authority, or when there is a conflict between different basic sources, or when a conflict between international law and domestic law ensues, or when there are problems of interpretation which cannot be settled by legal standards since they are themselves affected by problems of interpretation …

[33] To summarize, ideological positivism misconceives legal discourse, because it sees it as autonomous and insular, when in fact it is dependent on and it is part of a wider moral discourse … Curiously … , positivism which seems to be so respectful of the *facta* behind some norms ignores the very basic fact of how normative discourse is constituted in our culture …

I believe that communitarianism incurs … essentially the same mistake …

One of the aspects of our social practice of moral discussion is that it allows us to criticize any social institution or practice, including, of course, itself – as is done by the very communitarian authors. This is because … arguments of authority religious, legal or *conventional* are never final and conclusive within our practice of giving reasons to each other. All authority should be justified on the basis of principles which are not themselves accepted on the basis of authority. This, of course, applies to traditions and conventions. Therefore, communitarians are wrong in thinking that some social traditions or conventions may be exempted from moral criticism …

Secondly, it is not true that the post-Enlightenment practice of moral discussion, the assumptions of which we all, including communitarians, share, pretends to allow for the derivation of rights without a previous conception of the good … [T]he practice of giving reasons to each other presupposes the value of acting on the basis of reasons freely accepted and this constitutes the value of autonomy, in the Kantian sense … [34] Therefore, the liberalism implicit in our practice of moral discussion is not entirely neutral towards conceptions of the good, as communitarians object, but it presupposes the good of autonomy … Communitarians are wrong in asserting that liberals who rely on assumptions of our practice of moral discussion intend to derive rights out of the blue without any conception of the good, and are doubly wrong when they introduce, contravening those assumptions, supposed goods which preclude that of autonomy. Of course, autonomy requires some pre-conditions … [including] the membership of social groups: But if that membership is valued just because it is an instrument of autonomy, it should be made as voluntary as possible in order not to frustrate the good which it serves.

Of course, our practice of moral discourse … also assumes the requirement of impartiality … When we discuss with each other we try to determine which is the principle which an ideal arbiter would accept in order to solve the conflict. This includes the requirements of generality and universality, since we do not think that impartial principles may make differences on the basis of circumstances identified by proper names or definite descriptions or those which are applied differently to cases which do not differ in properties taken into account by those very principles …

[W]e do not think that the mere fact of living in Africa, for instance, gives somebody a different moral status, though some circumstances like starvation, ignorance, illness, etc. may make a difference to the implications of general and universal principles. Communitarians are never clear about what are the principles of their traditions that they refuse to apply to others and why …

[35] Of course, the assumptions of autonomy and impartiality implicit in the social practice of moral discourse lead to a certain conception of the person, according to which … the identity of each person is separable from that of each other, and that identity is not affected by her membership of one or other social group. It is no use for communitarians to make fun of this conception as unrealistic …, since this conception is not anthropological but normative: It is just an abstraction of the normative requirements of autonomy and impartiality and determines what sort of reasons we can give to others are valid and what are not. For instance, the idea of separation of persons involved in this conception does not deny that persons are deeply attached to each other and the good of others may be central for the interests of each of us; it only implies that we cannot give as sole reason for harming the autonomy of somebody that this serves to grant greater autonomy to others.

In sum, like ideological positivists, communitarians contradict their own main tenet: In this case, that main tenet is to take into account social practices in the derivation of moral principles. But they do not consider the assumptions of the very practice of moral discussion that we all share. It is not logically possible both to criticize our culture for features of its practice of moral discussion … and to advocate taking into account cultural specificity. It just happens that the specificity of our culture is not to take into account cultural specificities in making basic moral judgements!

Nino also considers the theoretical issues arising from the acceptance, in some non-European communities, of traditional or religious practices which, from the viewpoint of European liberalism, are perceived as inhumane. Such practices present a challenge to communitarian theories, since those theories may seem to legitimate practices that their proponents might not wish to support. On the other hand, they also present a challenge to liberalism, since they sharply remind us that conceptions of fundamental human rights are not necessarily universal. Perhaps optimistically, Nino concludes that, within his preferred framework of democratic deliberation by a particular community, there may be some opportunity to accommodate the accepted practices of that community; and that, in any event, the more troubling practices are unlikely to survive increasing democratisation.

5. Church and State

Perhaps the most important stimulus for the growth, from the 17th century onwards, of liberalism as a doctrine of personal freedom was the demand for freedom of religion, and hence for tolerance among different religions. As Locke developed these demands in his famous *Letter Concerning Toleration*, written in 1689, they could only be achieved through a reciprocal withdrawal by political authorities from religious affairs and by religious bodies from any role in the politics of the state.

John Locke, *A Letter Concerning Toleration* (1689)
(transl William Popple, 1689; retransl JW Gough and ed R Klibansky, Clarendon Press, 1968)

[65] I regard it as necessary above all to distinguish between the business of civil government and that of religion, and to mark the true bounds between the church and the commonwealth …

The commonwealth seems to me to be a society of men constituted only for preserving and advancing their civil goods.

[67] What I call civil goods are life, liberty, bodily health and freedom from pain, and the possession of outward things, such as lands, money, furniture, and the like.

It is the duty of the civil magistrate, by impartially enacted equal laws, to preserve and secure for all the people in general, and for every one of his subjects in particular, the just possession of these things that belong to this life. If anyone presumes to violate these laws, contrary to justice and right, his presumption is to be checked by the fear of punishment …

Now, that the whole jurisdiction of the magistrate is concerned only with these civil goods, and that all the right and dominion of the civil power is bounded and confined solely to the care and advancement of these goods; and that it neither can nor ought in any way to be extended to the salvation of souls, the following considerations seem to me to prove.

First, because the care of souls is not committed to the civil magistrate, any more than to other men. It is not committed to him by God; because it does not appear that God ever gave any such authority to one man over another as to compel other men to embrace his religion. Nor can any such power be vested in the magistrate by men, because no man can so far abandon the care of his own eternal salvation as to embrace under compulsion a worship or faith prescribed by someone else ...

[69] In the second place, the care of souls cannot belong to the civil magistrate, because his power consists wholly in compulsion. But true and saving religion consists in the inward persuasion of the mind, without which nothing has any value with God ... [T]he civil power ought not to prescribe articles of faith, or doctrines, or forms of worshipping God, by civil law. For if no penalties are attached to them, the force of laws vanishes, while if penalties are applied they are obviously futile and inappropriate for convincing the mind. If anyone wishes to adopt some doctrine or form of worship for the salvation of his soul, he must firmly believe that the doctrine is true, and that the form of worship will be pleasing and acceptable to God; but penalties are in no way capable of producing such belief ...

[71] In the third place ... even if the authority of laws and the force of penalties were capable of converting men's minds, yet this would not help at all in the salvation of their souls. For there being but one true religion, one way to heaven, what hope is there that most men would reach it, if mortals were obliged to ignore the dictates of their own reason and conscience, and blindly accept the doctrines imposed by their prince, and worship God in the manner laid down by the laws of their country? ...

These considerations, among many others that might have been urged ... seem to me sufficient for us to conclude that the whole power of civil government is concerned only with men's civil goods, is confined to the care of the things of this world, and has nothing whatever to do with the world to come.

Let us now consider what a church is. A church seems to me to be a free society of men, joining together of their own accord for the public worship of God in such manner as they believe will be acceptable to the Deity for the salvation of their souls.

I say it is a *free and voluntary society*. Nobody is born a member of any church; otherwise a man's religion, along with his estate, would descend to him by the law of inheritance from his father and his ancestors, and he would owe his faith to his parentage; than which nothing more absurd can be imagined ... No man is bound by nature to any [73] church or assigned to any sect, but he voluntarily joins that society in which he believes he has found true religion and the form of worship that is acceptable to God. The hope of salvation that he finds there, as it was the only cause of his entering that church, so it can be the only reason for his staying there. If afterwards he discovers anything either erroneous in the doctrine or incongruous in the worship, he must always have the same liberty to go out as he had to enter ... A church, then, is formed of members uniting voluntarily and for this end ...

Since no society can hold together ... if it is entirely without laws; so also a church must have its laws, to settle the times and places of meeting, to prescribe conditions for admitting or excluding members, to regulate differences of function, the orderly conduct of its affairs, and so on. But since this union is spontaneous, as has been shown, and free from all coercive force, it necessarily follows that the right of making its laws can belong to none but the society itself; or at least, which comes to the same thing, to those whom the society has authorised by consent ...

[77] The end of a religious society ... is the public worship of God, and, by that means, the gaining of eternal life. All discipline ought therefore to aim at this end, and all ecclesiastical laws to be confined within these limits. In this society nothing is or can be done that relates to the possession of civil or earthly goods: no force is to be employed here for any reason whatever. For force belongs wholly to the civil magistrate, and the possession and use of outward goods is subject to his jurisdiction ...

[79] This being so, let us inquire, in the next place, what everyone's duty is in regard to toleration.

First, I say that no church is bound in the name of toleration to cherish in her bosom a man who, after admonition, continues obstinately to offend against the laws established in that society … Nevertheless, care must be taken that the sentence of excommunication carry with it no insulting words or rough treatment, whereby the ejected person may be injured in any way, in body or estate. For all force, as I have said, belongs to the magistrate, and no private person is allowed to use it, except only in self-defence. Excommunication neither does nor can deprive the excommunicated person of any of his civil goods or private possessions. They all concern his position as a citizen, and are under the magistrate's protection …

Secondly, no private person ought in any way to attack or damage another person's civil goods because he professes another religion or form of worship. All the rights that belong to him as a man, or as a citizen, are inviolably to be preserved to him. These are not the business of religion; all violence and injury must be avoided, whether he be Christian or Pagan. Nor must we be content with the standard of bare justice; benevolence and charity must be added to it. This the Gospel enjoins, this reason directs, and this the natural fellowship of common humanity requires of us. If any man errs from the [81] right way, it is his own misfortune, and no injury to you; nor are you called upon to punish him in the things of this life because you believe that he will perish in the life to come.

What I have said about the mutual toleration of private persons differing from one another in religion, I understand also of particular churches, which stand in the same kind of relation to one another as private persons: nor has any one of them any jurisdiction over any other, not even when the civil magistrate, as may sometimes happen, belongs to this or that church; for the civil government can give no new right to a church, nor a church to the civil government. So that whether the magistrate joins any church or leaves it, the church always remains the same as it was before, a free and voluntary society. It neither acquires the power of the sword by the magistrate's coming to it, nor by his going from it does it lose the authority to teach and excommunicate which it previously possessed …. Therefore peace, equity, and friendship are always mutually to be observed by different churches, as by private persons, without any claim to jurisdiction over one another.

To explain the matter by an example, let us suppose two churches at Constantinople, one of Remonstrants, the other of Anti-remonstrants. Will anyone say that either of these churches has a right to deprive the members of the other of their liberty or property … because they are dissenters …? But if one of these churches has a power to illtreat the other, I ask which of the two it is, and by what right? No doubt it will be answered that it is the orthodox church which has this power over the erroneous or heretical. This is to use great and specious words to say nothing at all. For every church is orthodox to itself and [83] erroneous or heretical to others … Thus the controversy between these churches about the truth of their doctrines and the purity of their worship is equal on both sides; nor is there any judge, either at Constantinople or elsewhere upon earth, by whose sentence it can be determined …

Further, if it could be made clear which of those who disagree held the right religious opinions, that would not confer upon the orthodox church any right of destroying the others. For churches have no jurisdiction in earthly matters, nor are sword and fire proper instruments for refuting errors or instructing and converting men's minds …

[85] None, therefore, neither individuals, nor churches, nor even commonwealths, have any just title to invade civil rights and rob each other of worldly goods on the plea of religion. Those who think otherwise I would ask to consider with themselves what limitless occasions for discords and wars, how powerful a provocation to rapines, slaughters, and endless hatreds they furnish to mankind …

This is not the place to inquire into the origin either of the power or of the dignity of the clergy. But this I say, that from whatever source their authority springs, since it is ecclesiastical, it ought to be confined within the bounds of the church, nor can it in any way be extended to civil affairs, because the church itself is absolutely separate and distinct from the commonwealth and civil affairs. The boundaries on both sides are fixed and immovable. He mixes heaven and [87] earth together, things most remote and opposite, who confuses these two societies, which in their origin, their end, and their whole substance are utterly and completely different …

[I]t is not enough that churchmen abstain from violence and rapine and all manner of persecution. One who professes to be a successor of the Apostles, and has taken upon himself the office of teaching, is obliged also to warn his hearers of the duties of peace and good will towards all men, towards the erroneous as well as the orthodox; towards those who differ from him in faith and worship as well as towards those who agree with him. And he should exhort all men … to charity, meekness, and toleration, and allay and temper all that heat and antipathy of mind which either a man's fiery zeal for his own religion and sect, or the craft of others has kindled against dissenters. I will not presume to describe the quality and abundance of the fruit that would be gathered, both in church and state, if the pulpits everywhere sounded with the doctrine of peace and toleration … But this I say, that … if anyone who professes himself to be a minister of the word of God, and a preacher of the gospel of peace, teaches otherwise, he either does not understand or neglects the business of his calling, and one day will have to account for it to the Prince of peace …

[103] The sole business of the church is the salvation of souls, and it in no way concerns the neighbourhood or the commonwealth that this or that ceremony is practised. Neither the observance nor the omission of any ceremonies in religious assemblies either does or can damage the life, liberty, or property of others. For example, grant that the washing of a new-born infant with water is in itself an indifferent thing. Grant also that it is lawful for the magistrate to order this by law, provided that he knows such washing to be useful for **[105]** curing or preventing some disease to which infants are liable … Will anyone therefore say that a magistrate has the same right to ordain by law that all children shall be baptized by priests in the sacred font for the purification of their souls? Or that they shall be initiated by any sacred rites at all? Who does not see at a glance that these two cases are totally different? Suppose it were the child of a Jew, and the case speaks for itself … If you admit that such an injury may not be done to a Jew as to compel him, against his own conviction, to practise in his religion a thing which is in its own nature indifferent, do you maintain that this may be done to a Christian? …

[117] [T]here is absolutely no such thing under the Gospel as a Christian commonwealth. I admit that there are many kingdoms and cities which have been converted to the Christian faith, but they have retained and preserved their ancient form of government, on which Christ enjoined nothing in his law. He taught the faith and conduct by which individuals might obtain eternal life; but he instituted no commonwealth, he introduced no new form of government, peculiar to his own people, nor did he arm any magistrate with a sword with which to force men into the faith or worship he prescribed for his people, or prevent them from practising another religion …

[121] [T]he magistrate ought not to forbid the holding or teaching of any speculative opinions in any church, because they have no bearing on the civil rights of his subjects. If a Papist believes that what another man calls bread is really the body of Christ, he does no injury to his neighbour. If a Jew does not believe the New Testament to be the word of God, he **[123]** does not alter any civil rights. If a heathen has doubts about both Testaments, he is not therefore to be punished as a dishonest citizen. The power of the magistrate and the property of citizens may be equally secure whether any man believes these things or not. I readily grant that these opinions are false and absurd. But laws are not concerned with the truth of opinions, but with the security and safety of the commonwealth and of each man's goods …

[149] God Almighty grant that the gospel of peace may at length be preached, and that civil magistrates, becoming more anxious to conform their own consciences to the law of God than to bind other men's by human laws, may, like fathers of their country, direct all their counsels and endeavours to promote the general civil welfare of their children, except such as are shameless, malicious, and wicked; and that all churchmen, who proclaim themselves to be the successors of the Apostles, walking in the Apostles' footsteps and not meddling in politics, may peaceably and modestly apply themselves wholly to promote the salvation of souls. Farewell.

Although Locke's argument was a response to the hostilities convulsing Christendom in his own lifetime, it built on older Christian foundations.

VP Luthera, *The Secular State and India*
(Oxford University Press, 1964)

[15] The concept [of the secular state] originated during the days of the Roman Empire when the Caesars demanded allegiance from their Christian subjects in all walks of … life including the religious. Those Christians who refused to render their religious allegiance to the Caesars were subjected to severe persecution. It was at that time that its philosophical foundations were laid in a sermon of Christ, recorded in St Mark's Gospel (xiii.7), 'Render to Caesar the things that are Caesar's and to God the things that are God's'.

The sermon had far-reaching implications. It meant a break with the system of ideas prevalent in the Greek and the Roman city-states. Neither in the Greek *polis* nor in the Roman *civitas* was any distinction made, or even known, between the things that were Caesar's and the things that were God's. Both these states were omnicompetent, all-inclusive 'Society-States' in which human life was not differentiated but was unified in a 'single embracing and compelling community' under the control of a single authority which was the state. The state exercised authority over all aspects of human life including the religious. The Greek city-state was itself of a religious origin and grew up around some famous temple. Each city-state was the city of a god. Thus, Athena was the god of Athens … [16] Similarly, the Roman emperor was the God himself. His worship was a condition precedent to the citizenship of the state. 'For the pagan', says [George Sabine], 'the highest duties of morality and religion met in the state, symbolically in the person of the emperor, who was at once the supreme civil authority and a divinity.'

But Christ in his sermon distinguished the religious aspect of human life from its other aspects. He distinguished the relationship between man and God from that between man and state and asserted that Caesar had no jurisdiction over the former relationship and that Christians owed their religious allegiance to God alone. Christ's sermon sought to place a limit upon the authority of Caesar because it set apart the religious sphere … [as one] over which Caesar had no jurisdiction. In the words of Professor Barker, it involved 'the sundering of the sphere of Society from the sphere of the State …'.

This novel Christian position implied many new things. It implied a doctrine of two ends of human life, the secular end which belonged to Caesar and the religious or eternal end which belonged to God. It further implied a corresponding doctrine of 'two powers', pursuing their respective ends. It involved the delimitation of jurisdiction which had hitherto been vested in one agency, Caesar (state), into two jurisdictions to be vested in two agencies, Caesar (state) and God (church). It further meant that the two institutions were to remain distinct and their [17] respective jurisdictions inviolate. It thus stipulated the creation of two spheres of authority, one pertaining to the state and the other to the church in which both were independent of each other. The theoretical delimitation of their respective spheres was later developed by the Christian Fathers and the Popes. It received its authoritative statement at the close of the fifth century by Pope Gelasius I and is known after him as the Gelasian theory of 'two swords' or two authorities, the secular authority and the religious authority. Each authority 'has its own sphere of action, with which the other must not interfere' …

While the theoretical foundations of the separation of the state and the church were thus laid, its implementation in practice was hardly yet begun. In the times that followed, that is, the Patristic Age, the Carolingian Age and the Middle Ages the theory of a distinction between the secular and religious powers and their independence of each other, was recognized as an ideal and appeal was made to it again and again both by the Fathers and the Popes on the one hand and [by] the emperors and kings on the other hand. But in practice the relations between the church and the state 'tended at once towards the secularization of the former and the clericalization of the latter'. Thus, in the Carolingian Age, on the one hand the state continually interfered in purely ecclesiastical matters. On the other hand, the church played a significant role in the administration of the affairs of the state. Similarly, during the Middle Ages the state and the church continued to be intertwined. The church was involved in numerous functions of the state and the state, in turn, was involved in many matters relating to the church. [18] 'The church was a state church and the state was a church state ….' The citizenship of the state was connected with the membership of the church. Membership of the one involved membership of the other. The basis of political homogeneity was Roman

Catholicism. Those who dissented from it were severely crushed by the state as was indicated by the Inquisition. Roman Catholicism embraced all aspects of human life and consequently all human activity was conducted in terms of its dictates … The political institutions had religious sanctions. All economic activity had to fall in line with [the church's] teachings. The code of social morality was based upon its doctrines. In brief the Roman Catholic Church was involved in almost all the functions of the state.

The situation outlined above began to undergo a radical change in the sixteenth century … New forces emerged which made it impossible for Roman Catholicism and, thus, for the Roman Catholic Church to command the unquestioned loyalty of people to its tenets and teachings. Renaissance and Humanism by laying emphasis on secular values weakened the Church. Explorers and navigators were returning home and narrating stories of their exploits which contradicted the teachings of Roman Catholicism. Men who had hitherto been taught that Roman Catholicism was the only 'true' religion and that outside the Christian Commonwealth there existed no other human beings were discovering people who professed religions different from Roman Catholicism. The rise of international commerce necessitated 'such a state of spiritual neutrality' as would enable Catholics and Jews, Chinese and Protestants, to do business at the trading centres. All these factors joined together to deal a blow to the Roman Catholic Church from without. From within, there was a revolt against the Church, the Reformation, which undermined [19] the strength of the Church and accelerated the pace of the forces set in motion by the Renaissance, Humanism, discoveries and international trade.

The Reformation, as the word itself indicates, was primarily directed towards securing the reform of the Roman Catholic Church. The secularization of the state or its separation from the church, was not even remotely among its avowed purposes. Yet the Reformation made a tremendous contribution by creating, as we shall see, a situation conducive to the establishment of a secular state.

One immediate consequence of the Reformation was the breakdown of the medieval *Respublica Christiana* and the emergence from the ruins of several separate independent prince-states. The rise of the prince-states was, however, in no way a step forward towards the birth of a secular state. Rather … in these states, 'a return was made to the classical unity of the Greek city-state and the Roman Empire, with their integration of human life in a single embracing and compelling community. The state now becomes, at any rate in the area of the Anglican and Lutheran reformation … a church as well as a state … the one and total organization of human life.' … *Cuius regio, eius religio*, was the prevalent rule. The emerging states were religious, some of them Protestant, others Roman Catholic.

In matters of church-state relations internally the Protestant states were not much different from the Catholic states. The state and the church still remained intertwined. Religious uniformity as the basis of political homogeneity was enforced in these states as [vehemently] as in the *Respublica Christiana*, although the religion in this case was Protestantism. 'During the Middle Ages', [20] writes [Henrik Van Loon], 'there had been one universal and intellectual prison-house. The Protestant rebellion had ruined the old building, and out of part of the available material it had constructed a gaol of its own. After the year 1517 there are therefore two dungeons, one reserved exclusively for the Catholics, the other for the Protestants.'

But this situation could not continue for long. Christendom was not to remain divided into two confessions. The forces let loose by the Reformation were too strong and they overflowed into a 'thousand channels of heresy'. Soon the people of Christendom were divided into numerous sects professing different faiths and mutually antagonistic. The havoc caused by the resulting religious wars which overtook Europe and wrecked the peace and order of the society … [is] well known …

The coming into being of a multiplicity of … religious sects in the body-politic of the states gave rise to an entirely different situation than had thitherto prevailed. While the people of a state professed but one religion, the state had no difficulty in identifying its interests with those of the church. But now the people were divided into a multitude of sects. The state, therefore, could now no longer be a Protestant or a Catholic one … Nor could the state enforce any one religion because in many of the states the various denominations had become very well balanced and the enforcement of any one creed would have led to the disruption of the peace and order of the society. Under these circumstances there was, of necessity, a tendency towards mutual toleration. Thus we find that the contemporary European philosophers argued against the enforcement by the state of any religion on its subjects. The opposition to such an enforcement did not stem, in some cases, from any genuine belief in religious freedom but was merely the making of a virtue out of a necessity. [21] While recognizing the need to prevent the rise of new sects, Bodin argued that 'where two or more religions already existed in a state ... it was useless and worse than useless for the state to seek to impose religious uniformity. To do so would merely lead to civil war and thus weaken the state.' The Politiques, while accepting the desirability of the unity of faith and [even of] persecution, insisted that the 'civil society must not perish for conscience's sake. The interests of peace come first; the religious interest is a secondary consideration'. The state, confronted by the multiplicity of sects, was compelled in varying degrees gradually to separate its own interests from those of any one sect as distinct from others. It was compelled to do so to avoid incurring the hostility of the sects and to prevent a religious crisis precipitating a civil war.

The new situation necessitated a search for new patterns of state-church relations. Consequently, in Europe two distinct patterns were evolved. First, there was the system of establishment of a particular church which was recognized as the religion of the state. The other churches were granted freedom the degree of which differed from country to country. The established church enjoyed certain benefits and privileges which were denied to the other churches. The state subsidized it and, at the same time, controlled and regulated its affairs. As an example of this pattern may be quoted the case of the United Kingdom where the Church of England is established. The Church receives certain privileges and benefits from the state. The state, on the other hand, controls and regulates the Church. For instance, it makes appointments to the offices of the Church of England. The British Parliament is vested with the ultimate authority to determine the forms of worship, to decide what changes are necessary in the organization of the Church and to deal, as it deems right, with its finances and property. A second pattern evolved was based on the principle of equality of churches and was known as Jurisdictionalism. Under Jurisdictionalism 'the state aims to [22] maintain equal status for the confessions within its domain ...'. It aims at giving freedom to all religious groups and 'equal liberty of conscience and worship' to all citizens. But the 'jurisdictionalist states' are not separated from the churches. Instead, they are intertwined with them. They 'do not divest themselves entirely of their responsibility for the historic churches, exercising a considerable measure of control over them, and continuing in some cases to grant them subsidies'. They exercise a 'vigilant supervision of their [churches'] activities'. However, 'Jurisdictionalism does not necessarily prevent one religious body from having special forms of recognition from a state where its membership is in the large majority, but it does assure that the state shows its fostering care for and equal protection to all important religious bodies which it believes loyal to its higher interests'.

These two patterns of state-church relations became popular in Europe and one or the other was adopted by many of the European states. The patterns are still prevalent in most of the European states ... [Some] have established churches while others, for example, Holland follow ... Jurisdictionalism.

But the state under both of these systems was not secular. It was not so because it was not separate from religion. In the case of the establishment of a single church it was intertwined with one church and controlled and regulated the affairs of one church. In the case of jurisdictionalist states, the state was intertwined with all churches and controlled and regulated the affairs of all churches. In the latter case, therefore, there was a more comprehensive application of the principle underlying the establishment of a single church. In a jurisdictionalist state there existed what has been [23] called 'multiple establishments' ie the establishment of many churches.

It was left to the American people ... to establish a state which was *constitutionally* secular and separate from the church. Before the founding of the United States of America, the patterns of state-church relations as established in various colonies followed the European patterns. The Pilgrim Fathers had inherited European traditions. Initially, therefore, they adhered to the European tradition of a close union of the state and the church and planted this principle in every colony except [Rhode Island]. But the 'American environment' was not favourable to the union of the state and the church and there developed in due course a trend towards their separation. A generation arose in whose thinking the traditional union of the state and the church and the concomitant admixture of religion and politics did not find a place. Men like Roger Williams took a 'radically secular view of the state …'. Many of the ideas contained in Madison's *Memorial* echoed the implications of Christ's sermon, 'Render to Caesar the things that are Caesar's and to God the things that are God's'. The *Memorial* said: 'Religion is wholly exempt from the cognizance of Civil Society … whose authority is necessarily subordinate to the individual's allegiance to the Universal sovereign … Since religion is exempt from the authority of the Society at large, still less can it be subject to that of the Legislative Body whose jurisdiction is both derivative and limited … Since religion is not within the cognizance of Civil Government … its legal establishment cannot be said to be necessary to civil Government.'

James Madison's *Memorial and Remonstrance against Religious Assessments* was written in 1785 in opposition to a proposal before the Virginia Legislature for a residence tax to pay the salaries of "teachers of the Christian Religion", with taxpayers designating the church and minister of their choice. Madison's argument succeeded: the Bill was abandoned, and a few months later the Virginia Legislature adopted instead the *Virginia Act for Establishing Religious Freedom* (1786), essentially in the form drafted by Thomas Jefferson in 1779.

The efforts of Madison and Jefferson laid the foundation for the First Amendment to the United States Constitution, which prohibits any law "respecting an establishment of religion, or prohibiting the free exercise thereof". The widest interpretation of these prohibitions was given by Jefferson in the first year of his presidency. In a letter to a congregation of Baptists at Danbury, Connecticut, written on 1 January 1802, he referred to the First Amendment as "building a wall of separation between church and state" (AA Lipscomb and Albert E Bergh (eds), *The Writings of Thomas Jefferson* (Thomas Jefferson Memorial Association, 1905), vol 16, 281-2).

The "wall" metaphor encapsulates both sides of Locke's equation: no political interference in religious affairs, and no religious intrusion into politics. In the liberal tradition, religious toleration is achieved by exploiting the liberal dichotomy between "public" and "private". The religious beliefs and practices of each individual are consigned to the "private" sphere, towards which the state and law should maintain respectful non-interference. However, the corollary is that groups or individuals ought not to obtrude their "private" religious preoccupations into the "public" sphere. In a fully developed liberal democracy, the maintenance of law and politics depends upon a public consensus; and the only public consensus compatible with habits of religious tolerance is that in religious matters there is no consensus.

John Rawls, *Political Liberalism*
(Columbia University Press, 1993)

[9] [The aim is] a conception of justice that may be shared by citizens as a basis of a reasoned, informed, and willing political agreement. It expresses their shared and public political reason. But to attain such a shared reason, the conception of justice should be, as far as possible, independent of the opposing and conflicting philosophical and religious doctrines that citizens affirm. In formulat-[10]-ing such a conception, political liberalism applies the principle of toleration to philosophy itself. The religious doctrines that in previous centuries were the professed basis of society have gradually given way to principles of constitutional government that all citizens, whatever their religious view, can endorse. Comprehensive philosophical and moral doctrines likewise cannot be endorsed by citizens generally, and they also no longer can, if they ever could, serve as the professed basis of society.

Thus, political liberalism looks for a political conception of justice that we hope can gain the support of an overlapping consensus of reasonable religious, philosophical, and moral doctrines in a society regulated by it. Gaining this support of reasonable doctrines lays the basis for answering … [the question of] how citizens, who remain deeply divided on religious, philosophical, and moral doctrines, can still maintain a just and stable democratic society. To this end, it is normally desirable that the comprehensive philosophical and moral views we are wont to use in debating fundamental political issues should give way in public life. Public reasoning – citizens' reasoning in the public forum about constitutional essentials and basic questions of justice – is now best guided by a political conception the principles and values of which all citizens can endorse ... That political conception is to be, so to speak, political and not metaphysical.

Political liberalism, then, aims for a political conception of justice as a freestanding view. It offers no specific metaphysical or epistemological doctrine beyond what is implied by the political conception itself ... [It] does not deny there being other values that apply, say, to the personal, the familial, and the associational; nor does it say that political values are separate from, or discontinuous with, other values ... **[11]** [The aim] is to specify the political domain and its conception of justice in such a way that its institutions can gain the support of an overlapping consensus.

Clearly, these ideals have never fully been realised in practice. As the great sociologist Max Weber (1864-1920) wrote in *Economy and Society* (G Roth and C Wittich (eds), University of California Press, 1968, vol 2): "**[1207]** The formula of the separation of church and state is feasible only if either of the two powers has in fact abandoned its claim to control completely those areas of life that are in principle accessible to it". In the United States, judicial decisions interpreting the religion clauses of the First Amendment have been perennially controversial (see, for example, the series of cases culminating in *City of Boerne v Flores*, 521 US 507 (1997) – see Chapter 18, §6). In England, the basic demand for tolerance of religious diversity was achieved only gradually, and even the landmark 19th-century statutes seem nowadays extraordinarily grudging both in formal enactment (see, for example, the *Roman Catholic Relief Act 1829* (UK) (10 Geo IV c 7) and the *Jewish Relief Act 1858* (UK) (21 & 22 Vict c 49)), and in practical implementation (see, for example, the history of the *Oaths Act 1858* (UK) (21 & 22 Vict c 48), as reflected in cases like *Bradlaugh v Gossett* (1994) 12 QBD 271 – see Chapter 3, §3). Lord Eldon's dictum in *Re Masters &c of the Bedford Charity* (1819) 2 Swans 470, 36 ER 696, that "**[527]** Christianity is part of the law of England", was not abandoned until *Bowman v Secular Society* [1917] AC 406, while in 2004 and 2005 a United Kingdom proposal to legislate against religious vilification resulted in heated controversy.

Nor has it ever been true in practice that religious communities or individuals have refrained from political intervention. On the contrary, the gradual process by which religious discrimination was slowly removed from the English statute book was the product of intense political lobbying by the Protestant Dissenter congregations, initially on their own behalf and later on behalf of Roman Catholics and Jews as well. Moreover, their lobbying was a crucial factor in other landmark developments of the 19th century, including the abolition of slavery and the repeal of the artificially high prices maintained by the Corn Laws (see Raymond Cowherd, *The Politics of English Dissent* (New York University Press, 1956)).

Nevertheless, at the national elections of October and November 2004, in both the United States and Australia, many commentators were surprised by the apparently strong electoral influence of fundamentalist Christian beliefs, including the emergence (and success) of candidates explicitly representing evangelical Christian constituencies. Viewed against the background of what some have interpreted as the re-emergence of a global conflict between Christendom and Islam, such developments have been seen as a radical challenge to the settled liberal understanding of constitutionalism. In particular, any attempt to impose upon the general culture the communal values of a particular religious community displays both the strengths and the dangers of communitarianism.

6. Further References

Barber, BR, *Strong Democracy: Participatory Politics for a New Age* (University of California Press, 1984).

Breslin, B, *The Communitarian Constitution* (Johns Hopkins University Press, 2004).

Carens, JH, *Culture, Citizenship, and Community: A Contextual Exploration of Justice as Evenhandedness* (Oxford University Press, 2000).

Christodoulidis, EA (ed), *Communitarianism and Citizenship* (Ashgate, 1998).

Etzioni, A, *The New Golden Rule: Community and Morality in a Democratic Society* (Basic Books, 1996).

Etzioni, A, *The Spirit of Community* (Simon & Schuster, 1994).

Gunningham, N, "Public Choice: The Economic Analysis of Public Law" (1992) 21 *Federal Law Review* 117.

Held, D, *Models of Democracy* (Cambridge, 2nd ed 1996).

Hindess, B, *Discourses of Power: From Hobbes to Foucault* (Blackwell, 1996).

Kim, N, "Towards a Feminist Theory of Human Rights: Straddling the Fence between Western Imperialism and Uncritical Absolutism" (1993) 25 *Columbia Human Rights Law Review* 49.

Loughlin, M, *Public Law and Political Theory* (Oxford University Press, 1992).

Nethercote, JR (ed), *Liberalism and the Australian Federation* (Federation Press, 2001).

Nino, CS, *The Constitution of Deliberative Democracy* (Yale University Press, 1996).

Powell, JP, "The Other Double Standard: Communitarianism, Federalism, and American Constitutional Law" (1996) 7 *Seton Hall Law School Constitutional Law Journal* 69.

Powell, JA, "The Multiple Self: Exploring between and beyond Modernity and Postmodernity" (1997) 81 *Minnesota Law Review* 1481.

Sandel, MJ, *Liberalism and the Limits of Justice* (Cambridge University Press, 1982).

Tam, H, *Communitarianism: A New Agenda for Politics and Citizenship* (Macmillan Press, 1998).

Vincent, A, *Nationalism and Particularity* (Cambridge University Press, 2002).

Young, IM, "The Ideal of Community and the Politics of Difference" in Nicholson, LJ (ed), *Feminism/Postmodernism* (Routledge, 1990), 300.

Chapter 3

The Westminster Constitution

1. Introduction

Constitutional law has a twofold function. It is invoked by those who seek a stable and secure basis for the exercise of government power, but also by those who seek to limit that power. It is thus both a supportive and a constraining framework. The way in which these competing functions were gradually developed and reconciled through the institutions, traditions and practices of constitutional government in Britain (and especially in England, since "Britain" did not exist as a political entity until the Union with Scotland in 1707) has continued to provide the historical framework for much of Australia's constitutional law.

2. English Constitutional History

(a)   Magna Carta

The significance of Magna Carta (the Great Charter) lies in what came to be seen as its symbolic role in limiting the arbitrary exercise of monarchical power, not only through its original acceptance by King John in 1215 but even more importantly through its solemn reaffirmation by each of the monarchs who succeeded him. For this reason, it is seen as a precursor of the principle now known as the rule of law.

Geoffrey de Q Walker, *The Rule of Law: Foundation of Constitutional Democracy*
(Melbourne University Press, 1988)

[95] Magna Carta and its forty-five later confirmations were an important restatement of the notion of government under law, as well as of the ideas of constitutional monarchy and limited government.

There has been a tendency among commentators influenced by New Whig, positivist or Marxist ideas to denigrate Magna Carta, to stigmatize it as a purely feudal document, as a deal struck between the kings and the barons for the benefit of the nobility, and even as an obstacle in the path of freedom and democracy. These views cannot be supported. As the more recent studies have emphasized, what was distinctive about the Charter was precisely that, owing to a peculiar conjunction of events and alliances, its provisions were not purely for the benefit of the barons. The group that drew it up was not composed solely of the nobility and the clergy, but also included the merchants, the townsmen, the inhabitants of the forests and freemen generally. The Charter's most important general provisions were expressly worded so as to apply to all these groups, and even to the unfree classes as well. Chapter 39 declared that 'No free man' might be imprisoned, **[96]** exiled or in any way destroyed 'except by the lawful judgment of his peers [and] by the law of the land'. While this wording necessarily extended to free women, there were also specific protections for women, as in Chapter 8: 'No widow shall be compelled to marry, so long as she prefers to live without a husband'.

How far Chapter 39's provisions for free men operated for the benefit of the large villein class, who were partly free and partly bonded, is disputed. By the time of Magna Carta villeinage was largely a matter between the lord and the villein and had little legal significance for outsiders. At all events, Chapter 40 then went on to declare that 'To no-one [*no-one*] will we sell, to no one will we refuse or delay, right or justice'. Following immediately the declaration relating to 'free men' in Chapter 39, this language must surely have been intended to cover *all* persons in the realm, whether free or not. Sir Edward Coke certainly read it so: 'And therefore, every subject of this realme, for injury done to him in [goods, land or person], by any other subject, be he ecclesiasticall or temporall, free, or bond, man, or woman, old, or young, or be he outlawed, excommunicated, or any other without exception, may take his remedy by the course of the laws and have justice, and right for the injury done to him …'.

In *Ex parte Walsh and Johnson; In re Yates* (1925) 37 CLR 36, Isaacs J referred to Magna Carta as the "**[79]** great confirmatory instrument … which is the groundwork of all our Constitutions". In what is now Chapter 29 of the Charter he detected "three basic principles, namely 1) … every free person has an inherent individual right to his life, liberty, property and citizenship; 2) his individual rights must always yield to the necessities of the general welfare at the will of the State; 3) the law of the land is the only mode by which the State can so declare its will". His enthusiastic endorsement of Magna Carta has not always been shared.

John Alder, *Constitutional and Administrative Law*
(Macmillan, 2nd ed 1994)

[39] Magna Carta is sometimes regarded as Britain's closest equivalent to a written constitution. In fact, Magna Carta is an ordinary piece of legislation dealing mainly with specific grievances between the king on the one hand and the feudal claims of the king's tenants-in-chief on the other. Although concessions were made by the king, these were wrung from him by force. Other groups including the Church, the cities, and the boroughs also obtained a measure of protection. Nevertheless, Magna Carta is of symbolic interest revealing as it does the subservience of the king to ideas of law, and also setting up rudimentary enforcement machinery against the king (legalised rebellion).

The original Magna Carta was signed in 1215 at Runnymede. It has since been confirmed many times. The version set out below dates from 1297, the reign of Edward I. This is the Magna Carta most often cited. In the original 1215 document the due process and justice clauses were numbered 39 and 40 respectively, while in the following document they were combined and numbered clause 29. This occurred because some clauses of the original charter were deleted from the 1297 confirming document (see M Evans and R Ian Jack, *Sources of English Legal and Constitutional History* (Butterworths, 1984), 55-6).

Magna Carta *(The Great Charter)*
(9 Hen III (1225), as confirmed in 25 Edw I (1297))

EDWARD by the grace of God king of England, lord of Ireland and duke of Aquitaine, to all to whom these present letters come, greeting. We have inspected the great charter of the lord Henry, sometime king of England, our father, concerning the liberties of England in these words:

Henry by the grace of God king of England, lord of Ireland, duke of Normandy and Aquitaine, and count of Anjou, to the archbishops, bishops, abbots, priors, earls, barons, sheriffs, reeves, ministers and all his officials and faithful subjects, greeting. Know you that we, from reverence for God and for the salvation of our soul and the souls of our ancestors and successors, for the exaltation of holy church and the reform of our realm, of our spontaneous and good will, have given and granted to the archbishops, bishops, abbots, priors, earls, barons and all freemen of our realm, these liberties following, to be held in our realm of England for ever.

1. In the first place we have granted to God and by this our present charter have confirmed, for us and our heirs in perpetuity, that the English church shall be free, and shall have its rights undiminished and its liberties unimpaired. We have also granted and given to all the free men of our realm for ourselves and our heirs for ever, all the liberties written below, to have and to hold, to them and their heirs from us and our heirs.

2. If any of our earls or barons, or others holding of us in chief by knight service shall die, and at his death his heir be of full age and owe relief, he shall have his inheritance on payment of the ancient relief, namely the heir or heirs of an earl £100 for a whole earl's barony, the heir or heirs of a baron £100 for a whole barony, the heir or heirs of a knight 100 shillings at most for a whole knight's fee; and anyone who owes less shall give less according to the ancient usage of fiefs.

3. If, however, the heir of any such person has been under age, his lordship shall not have the wardship of him nor of his land, before he had taken his homage; and after such an heir has been in wardship, when he comes of age, namely twenty-one years, he shall have his inheritance without relief and without fine, so that, if he is made a knight while he is under age, his land shall nevertheless remain in the wardship of his lords to the aforesaid date.

4. The guardian of the land of such an heir who is under age shall not take from the land more than the reasonable revenues, customary dues and services, and that without destruction and waste of men or goods. And if we entrust the wardship of the land of such a one to a sheriff, or to any other who is answerable to us for its revenues, and he destroys or wastes the land in his charge, we will take amends of him, and the land shall be entrusted to two lawful and prudent men of that fief who will be answerable to us for the revenues or to him to whom we have assigned them. And if we give or sell to anyone the wardship of any such land and he causes destruction or waste, he shall lose the wardship and it shall be transferred to two lawful and prudent men of the fief who shall be answerable to us as is aforesaid.

5. Moreover so long as the guardian has the wardship of the land, he shall maintain the houses, parks, preserves, fishponds, mills and the other things pertaining to the land from its revenues; and he shall restore to the heir when he comes of age all his land stocked with ploughs and all other things at the least as he received the land. All these things shall be observed in the wardships of archbishops, bishoprics, abbacies, priories, churches and vacant dignities, which pertain to us except that such wardship shall not be sold.

6. Heirs shall be given in marriage without disparagement.

7. After her husband's death, a widow shall have her marriage portion and her inheritance at once and without any hindrance; nor shall she pay anything for her dower, her marriage portion, or her inheritance which she and her husband held on the day of her husband's death; and she may stay in her husband's house for forty days after his death, within which period her dower shall be assigned to her, unless it were not assigned to her before or unless the house be a castle. And if she leave the castle, then a suitable house shall be provided for her at once in which she may honourably live until her dower is assigned to her as aforesaid; and in the meantime she shall have her reasonable estover. And a third part of all her husband's land which was his during his life, shall be assigned for her dower, unless she was endowed of less at the door of the church. No widow shall be compelled to marry so long as she wishes to live without a husband, provided that she gives security that she will not marry without our consent if she holds of us, or without the consent of the lord of whom she holds, if she holds of another.

8. Neither we nor our bailiffs will seize any land or rent in payment of a debt so long as the chattels of the debtor are sufficient to repay the debt; nor shall the sureties of the debtor be distrained so long as the debtor himself is capable of paying the debt; and if the principal debtor defaults in the payment of the debt, having nothing wherewith to pay it, the sureties shall be

answerable for the debt; and, if they wish, they may have the lands and revenues of the debtor until they have received satisfaction for the debt they paid on his behalf, unless the principal debtor shows that he has discharged his obligations to the sureties.

9. And the city of London is to have all its ancient liberties and free customs both by land and water. Furthermore, we will and grant that all other cities, boroughs, towns and the barons of the Cinq Ports and all ports shall have all their liberties and free customs.

10. No man shall be compelled to perform more service for a knight's fee or for any other free tenement than is due therefrom.

11. Common pleas shall not follow our court but shall be held in some fixed place.

12. Recognisances of novel disseisin and mort d'ancestor, shall not be held elsewhere than in the court of the county in which they occur, and in this manner: we, or if we are out of the realm our chief justiciar, shall send our justices through each county once a year who, with the knights of the shire, shall hold the said assizes in the county court. And those things which at the coming of our said justices into the counties, sent to take the said assizes, cannot be determined, shall be determined by the same justices elsewhere on their itinerary. And those things which because of the difficulty of some articles cannot be determined shall be referred to our justices of the bench and there determined.

13. Assizes of darrein presentment shall always be taken before the justices of the bench and there determined.

14. A free man shall not be amerced for a trivial offence, except in accordance with the degree of the offence; and for a serious offence he shall be amerced according to its gravity, saving his livelihood; and a merchant likewise, saving his merchandise; in the same way a villein shall be amerced saving his wainage; if they fall into our mercy. And none of the aforesaid amercements shall be imposed except by the testimony of reputable men of the neighbourhood. Earls and barons shall not be amerced except by their peers and only in accordance with the nature of the offence. No clerk shall be amerced on his lay tenement except in the manner of the others aforesaid and without reference to the size of his ecclesiastical benefice.

15. No vill or man shall be forced to build bridges at river banks, except those who ought to do so by custom and law.

16. No river banks shall henceforth be enclosed unless they were enclosed in the time of King Henry our grandfather [Henry II], for the same places and boundaries as they were accustomed to be in his time.

17. No sheriff, constable, coroner or other of our bailiffs may hold pleas of our Crown.

18. If anyone holding a lay fief of us dies and our sheriff or bailiff shows our letters patent of summons for a debt which the deceased owed us, it shall be lawful for the sheriff or our bailiff to attach and list the chattels of the deceased found in lay fee to the value of that debt, by the view of lawful men, so that nothing is removed until the evident debt is paid to us, and the residue shall be relinquished to the executors to carry out the will of the deceased. And if he owes us nothing, all the chattels shall be accounted as the deceased's, saving their reasonable shares to his wife and children.

19. No constable or his bailiff shall take the corn or other chattels of any man who is not of the town where the castle is located, unless he pays cash for them at once or can delay payment with the seller's agreement. If, however, he is of the same town, he shall hand over the price within 40 days.

20. No constable is to compel any knight to give money for castle guard, if he is willing to perform that guard in his own person or by another reliable man, if for some good reason he is unable to do it himself; and if we take or send him on military service, he shall be excused the guard in proportion to the period of his service, in fee by which he did service in the army.

21. No sheriff or bailiff of ours or anyone else is to take the horses or carts of anyone for carting unless he pays the price decreed, namely for one cart with two horses 10d a day, and for a cart with three horses 14d a day. No demesne cart of any ecclesiastic or knight or any lord shall be taken by our bailiffs. Neither we nor our bailiffs nor anyone else shall take anyone's wood for castles or other works of ours, without the agreement of the owner.

22. We will not hold the lands of convicted felons for more than a year and a day, when the lands shall be returned to the lords of the fiefs.

23. Henceforth all fish-weirs shall be completely removed from the Thames and the Medway and throughout all England, except on the sea coast.

24. The writ called *precipe* shall not, in future, be issued to anyone in respect of any holding whereby a free man may lose his court.

25. Let there be one measure of wine throughout our kingdom and one measure of ale and one measure of corn, namely the London quarter, and one width of cloth whether dyed, russet or halberjet, namely two ells within the selvedges. Let it be the same with weights as with measures.

26. Henceforth nothing shall be given or taken for the writ of inquisition of life or limb, but it shall be given freely and not refused.

27. If anyone holds of us by fee farm, by socage or by burgage, and holds land of someone else by knight service, we will not, by virtue of that fee farm, socage or burgage, have wardship of his heir or of land of his that belongs to the fief of another; nor will we have custody of that fee farm or socage or burgage unless such fee farm owes knight service. We will not have custody of the heir or land of anyone who holds of another by knight service, by virtue of any petty sergeanty which he holds of us by the service of rendering to us knives or arrows or the like.

28. Henceforth no bailiff shall put anyone on trial by his own unsupported allegation, without bringing credible witnesses to the charge.

29. No free man shall be taken or imprisoned or disseised of his freehold, liberties or free customs or outlawed or exiled or in any way ruined, nor will we go or send against him, except by the lawful judgment of his peers or by the law of the land. To no one will we sell, to no one will we deny or delay right or justice.

30. All merchants, if not previously prohibited publicly, are to be safe and secure in leaving and entering England, and in staying and travelling in England, both by land and by water, to buy and sell free from all maletotes by the ancient and rightful customs, except, in time of war, such as come from an enemy country. And if such are found in our land at the outbreak of war they shall be detained without damage to their persons or goods, until we or our chief justiciar know how the merchants of our land are treated in the enemy country; and if ours are safe there, the others shall be safe in our land.

31. If anyone dies who holds of some escheat such as the honours of Wallingford, Boulogne, Nottingham or Lancaster, or of other escheats which are in our hands and are baronies, his heir shall not give any relief or do any service to us other than what he would have done to the baron if that barony had been in a baron's hands; and we shall hold it in the same manner as the baron held it. Neither shall we have any escheat or wardship of any of our men because of any barony or escheat, unless the holder of the barony or escheat otherwise held of us in chief.

32. No free man shall henceforth give or sell to anyone any more of his land than such that from the remainder of his land the lord of the fee may have the due service which belongs to that fee.

33. All patrons of abbeys who have charters of advowson of the kings of England, or ancient tenure, shall have custody thereof during vacancies, as they ought to have, and as it is declared above.

34. No one shall be taken or imprisoned upon the appeal of a woman for the death of anyone except her husband.

35. Henceforth no county court shall be held except from month to month and where a longer period has been usual let it be longer. No sheriff or his bailiff shall make his tourn in the hundred except twice a year and only in the due and accustomed place, namely once after Easter and again after Michaelmas, and view of frankpledge shall be then done at that Michaelmas, without hindrance; so that every man shall have his liberties, which he had or used to have in the time of King Henry our grandfather or which he has acquired later. View of frankpledge shall be done in this way, namely that our peace shall be maintained and that the tithing shall be kept intact as it was wont to be; and that the sheriff shall not make difficulties and that he shall be content with what the sheriff was accustomed to have for the making of his view in the time of King Henry our grandfather.

36. From now on no one shall be allowed to give his land to a religious house in such a way that he takes the land back to be held of the same house; nor shall any religious house be allowed to take anyone's land and lease it to the person from which the house received it. If any henceforth

thus give his land to any religious house and be convicted on this count, his gift shall be entirely void and the land shall return to the lord of the fee.

37. Scutage shall henceforth be taken as it used to be in the time of King Henry our grandfather. Saving to the archbishops, bishops, abbots, priors, templars, hospitallers, earls, barons and all others, both ecclesiastics and laymen, all liberties and free customs which they have had in time past. All men of our realm, both clerks and laymen, shall, as far as it pertains to them, observe towards their own men all the aforesaid customs and liberties, which we have granted to be held in our realm as far as it pertains to us and ours. For this gift and grant of liberties and others contained in our charter of liberties of the forest, the archbishops, bishops, abbots, priors, earls, barons, knights, free tenants and all men of our realm, have given us a fifteenth part of all their moveables. We have granted them, for us and our heirs, that neither we nor our heirs shall procure or do anything by which the liberties in this charter shall be infringed or broken. And if anything shall be procured by any one contrary to this grant, it shall be of no force and void.

We, ratifying and approving these gifts and grants aforesaid, confirm and make strong all the same for us and our heirs perpetually, and, by the tenor of these presents, do renew the same; willing and granting for us and our heirs, that this Charter, and all and singular its articles, forever shall be steadfastly, firmly, and inviolably observed.

(b)   Parliament

CF Padfield, *British Constitution Made Simple*
(WH Allen, 4th ed 1977)

[17] The word 'Parliament' meant a talk, and was originally applied in the thirteenth century to the after-dinner gossip of monks in their cloisters, which incidentally, was condemned as unedifying. The word was also used to describe solemn conferences such as that in 1245 between Louis IX of France and Pope Innocent IV. It then came into use for the national assemblies in England after the middle of the thirteenth century.

The Kings of England were once powerful figures who claimed to rule their lands by divine right. A Monarch cannot, however, rule a kingdom by himself. [18] The Anglo-Saxon kings were assisted by the Witenagemot, an assembly of the wisest of men in the kingdom, to give counsel (rede) to the Monarch. Even in those times it was an English custom that in important matters such as the interpretation of laws, the King ought not to act alone but should first obtain the advice and consent of the wisest of his people. Custom also required that he hold 'deep speech' with the Witan, or council of wise men, two or three times a year. After listening to the speeches of the leaders, the assembly gave a vote for or against a proposition by clashing their arms against their shields.

The Anglo-Saxon Witan appears to have been a small aristocratic body of variable composition with great powers. FW Maitland stated:

> It can elect Kings and depose them; the King and Witan legislate; it is with the counsel and consent of the Witan that the King publishes laws; the King and Witan nominate the ealdormen and bishops, make grants of the public lands, impose taxes, decide on peace and war and form a tribunal of last resort for causes criminal and civil. It is a supreme legislative, governmental and judicial assembly.

Here ... was a free assembly of men who, though not elected, were representative of all parts of the country. They came from the shires (later called 'counties') and smaller units into which the country was divided. The ealdormen were important local figures; the sheriff was the King's outpost officer who represented the King's interests and presided in the shire court to do justice and administer the laws. The sheriff was an important powerful figure and his office survived the Conquest ...

The Witan disappeared with the Anglo-Saxon Kings. William I and his successors held Great Councils instead. These were assemblies of the King's tenants in chief (ie the nobles and others who held their lands directly from the King). 'Thrice a year,' we are told, 'King William wore his crown every year he was in England; at Easter he wore it at Winchester, at Pentecost at

Westminster, and at Christmas at Gloucester, and at these times all the men of England were with him – archbishops, bishops and abbots, earls, thegns, and knights.'

During the thirteenth century the 'Councils' began to be called 'Parliaments'. The barons were thus, on occasion, summoned by the King to attend a 'Parliament'. They were the aristocracy and did not represent all the classes of England. The knights and the burgesses (ie citizens) in the medieval [19] boroughs were not represented, and these were growing wealthier and more important.

In 1265 Simon De Montfort summoned representatives of the commons, ie the commoners, which included the Knights from the counties and two elected burgesses from the independent towns or boroughs with Royal Charters. In 1295 the so-called Model Parliament of Edward I was summoned which included barons (the nobility), knights, burgesses, senior clergy, and lower clergy. All were summoned on the principle "that what touches all should be approved by all".

These groups of people, comprising the three estates of the Realm (the Lords Spiritual, the Lords Temporal and the Commons) were summoned by the King to Westminster to some of the Parliaments, particularly when the King required extra money to carry on government or to engage in wars or crusades.

The foregathering of all classes in the country was a big step forward. In the first half of the fourteenth century the practice developed whereby the Lords and the Commons met separately from each other in private assemblies or gatherings to discuss their answers to the King who called them to his presence. These answers were given to the King *in Parliament*.

Most of the discussions or debates took place in these private meetings of the Lords and the Commons. From some time in the middle of the fourteenth century the Commons elected a speaker who presided over the meetings. He acted also as a channel of communication with the King. When the King demanded money from the Commons, the latter began submitting to the King petitions or bills requesting a change in the law of the land. During this time the vital principle of grievances before supply was established. When the King asked for financial aid from his people, the Commons chose the moment to strike a bargain with him regarding the redress of grievances which were brought to his notice in Parliament in the form of petitions.

From the time of Henry V (1413-22) a Bill so presented was enacted in the form the Commons desired. Nevertheless for some time afterwards both the [20] Sovereign and the Lords considered they could tamper with or alter the text extensively without obtaining the approval of the Commons. It was not until the reign of Henry VII (1485-1509) that the practice was established of sending up petitions (apart from Private Bills) to the King in the form of statutes to which the King could either assent or dissent.

The Tudor and Stuart Period

The sixteenth and seventeenth centuries witnessed a great constitutional struggle between the Monarchs on the one hand and Parliament on the other. Henry VIII was the most absolute of Monarchs; Elizabeth I, his daughter, avoided a head-on conflict and ruled through Parliament for her own purposes. Charles I was aristocratic and wished to claim prerogative rights which Parliament and, eventually, the common law judges opposed. These prerogative powers included the right to issue ordinances and proclamations, the right to tax, and the right to exercise dispensing and suspending powers, ie the right to grant immunity or dispensation to any person he liked or to suspend the operation of laws which had properly been enacted.

James II (1685-8) claimed to rule the country by divine right, used arbitrary methods which alienated the Crown's supporters and openly defied Parliament itself. In the Bloodless Revolution (or Glorious Revolution as it is sometimes called) Parliament finally resisted the King in 1688, and James II thereupon fled to France. William III and Mary (1689-1702) were invited to accede to the throne of England, and Parliament thereupon secured the passing of the Bill of Rights in 1689, one of the most important constitutional documents. The Bill at long last ensured the ultimate supremacy of Parliament. One of its most important effects was that henceforward the King would be definitely below Parliament and, indeed, owed his position to Parliamentary vote. Executive government depended upon Parliament for the laws it administered and the funds of money which the Executive required for the purpose of government. We must remember that the Monarch continued to play a leading part for some time as head of the Executive, until the emergence of a Prime Minister and a Cabinet.

The Tudor period (1485-1603) marked a crucial time of development for Parliament. The body became the foremost consultative assembly in England.

Frederick Marcham, *A Constitutional History of Modern England, 1485 to the Present*
(Harper & Brothers, 1960)

[59] THE position of Parliament in English government was in some respects well established at the beginning of the Tudor period. Parliament had been in existence for about 200 years, had met frequently – on occasions annually – and at one time or another had played a prominent part in giving effect to the wishes of the king and of the nobles and of the merchants and lesser land-owners. Law had been declared in Parliament, new kings had had their titles recognized there, taxes had been made legal; Parliament had sentenced great men to death. Two centuries of varied activity had made Parliament one of the great central institutions of government ...

While the work of Parliament grew more varied, the qualifications associated with membership of Parliament gradually gained definition. The king was a part of Parliament; his participation was vital to its formal actions; he attended its opening and closing and was free to attend its other meetings. His principal officers attended Parliament; the chancellor served as presiding officer of the assembly of nobles and leading churchmen who came to be called the House of Lords, while judges and other officials attended to give technical advice. At the beginning of Henry VII's reign, the king summoned twenty-nine noblemen to Parliament. Henry and his Tudor successors gradually increased the number until by the end of Elizabeth's reign it had reached sixty. During the same period there was a decline in the number of spiritual peers ...

[60] This increase in membership was accompanied by a change in the relationship between the members and the constituencies they represented. Until almost the end of the Middle Ages, the traditional practice had been that members were residents of the constituencies they represented and, in the case of those who represented boroughs and cities, were men who were thought of as performing a service for their fellows and who were entitled to be paid for their work. During the Tudor period the rule regarding residence fell into disuse, and candidates from among the country gentry and professional classes offered to serve as members without pay. Thus the composition of the House of Commons underwent important change. In the later Tudor period, almost all the members came from the lesser aristocracy and the professional classes ...

[61] Parliamentary elections were uncommon events in the Tudor period, because the monarch summoned new Parliaments at infrequent intervals – on the average, about three years apart. There was an interval of seven years in Henry VIII's reign and one of four and one-half years in Elizabeth's reign. On a few occasions a Parliament when once assembled was, after a short session, adjourned and reassembled later. The Parliament assembled by Henry VIII in 1529 – the so-called Reformation Parliament – was in this way kept alive from one annual session to the next until 1536. All but a few sessions of Parliament in the Tudor period were short, lasting two or three months. In consequence, in Elizabeth's reign of forty-five years there were ten parliaments and the total period of their sessions was only thirty-five months. The powers of the monarchs, as exercised by the council and individual administrators and by the courts, ordinarily kept English government in motion. The monarch called Parliament only when the government had special functions to perform.

The functions performed by Parliament in the Tudor period may in general be described as the exercise of jurisdiction, the granting of taxes, and the declaring of law; to be more precise, while other agencies of the government had the power to tax, to legislate, and to do justice, Parliament also was competent to perform these functions – though, in fact, it did so for special purposes and on special occasions. For example, the judicial function of Parliament arose from its power to hear cases concerning peers who were charged with treason or felony, to hear impeachments, to declare acts of attainder and to reverse attainders, and to hear cases which had been before the ordinary central courts of justice but had been disputed on the ground that there had been error in the statement of facts concerning the case. In addition, in all these matters, except attainders and reversals, the judicial power of Parliament was the judicial power of the king in Parliament, which meant, in this connection, the House of Lords. The participation of the House of Commons in attainders and reversals arose from the fact that these actions took the form of acts of Parliament. Each house had power to decide cases concerning its own privileges.

The power of Parliament to tax must be related to the concept that in ordinary circumstances the king should live of his own. To do so, he had **[62]** many sources of income: his rents, fines, fees, and forfeitures, his feudal dues, and the proceeds of traditional customs duties. Parliament granted him tonnage and poundage for life at the beginning of his reign, and this revenue became an important and continuing part of his income. Otherwise, grants made by Parliament were intended to meet financial emergencies; such, for example, as might arise when the king decided to go to war or, when in the course of a war, his expenses came to be more than he had estimated. In circumstances such as these the king appealed to Parliament for money, and the lords and commons took such action as they deemed appropriate. For these purposes each house was competent to initiate taxation, though, as in the case of other parliamentary legislation, the agreement of both houses was necessary before an act granting taxes to the king became legal ...

In the field of legislation, Parliament – the king in Parliament – shared authority with the king himself – the king in council – because the judges gave full legal force to the products of both lawmaking bodies: the acts of Parliament and the royal proclamations. By the opening years of the Tudor period, Parliament was already showing a considerable degree of technical development in its work as lawmaker. Bills dealing with matters of general interest came before Parliament in draft form, ready for discussion and action there. Bills of this kind, as distinct from private bills – the bills dealing with the affairs of individuals or special communities – were in most instances based on drafts which had been prepared by royal officials, or, if they were drawn up in the House of Commons, were scrutinised by royal judges before being considered by the House of Lords. The king or his agent might present a bill for first consideration to either house of Parliament; wherever introduced, the bill had three readings in each house and required acceptance by both houses before being passed on to the king for his approval. The control of the king over public – as opposed to private – parliamentary legislation was therefore almost complete, particularly because of his role as prin-**[63]**-cipal initiator of legislation. If a bill proved unsatisfactory to him while it was under discussion, he could kill it; and, in any case, he could veto it after it had passed both houses. Evidence of the completeness of royal control of parliamentary legislation in the early Tudor period lies in the fact that, of the more than a hundred public – as distinct from private – bills which passed through the Parliaments of Henry VII, he vetoed none.

The limits to the range and authority of parliamentary legislation were still in question. At the beginning of the Tudor period, the accepted notion was that acts of Parliament applied or declared the law as did the decisions or judgements of other courts. The law was conceived of as a body of rules founded on God's will; as He had declared it in the Scriptures and had applied it in nature, and as it could be found in traditional patterns of public life. In consequence, men could not create law, in the sense of devising rules contrary to God's will, though they might make new applications of the law when new circumstances forced them to do so. However, during the Tudor period the conditions and demands of English public life changed rapidly and the policies of the monarchs called forth important new statements regarding the law. Fundamental changes in religious, political, and social life caused the monarchs ... to frame new rules regarding the government of the church, the nature of treason, and the order of the succession.

These decisions became official actions in the forms of statutes. Certainly from the time of Henry VIII's so-called Reformation Parliament until the end of the Tudor period, Parliament made law in the sense of substantially changing the patterns of English public life. The immediate needs of the monarch or of the state became one of the reasons for new laws; and in consequence, Parliament acquired a wider range of authority as a lawmaker. The variety, force and number of Tudor statutes might well have raised the question whether there was a limit to what could be done by act of Parliament; whether, that is, the authority of a statute was so high that its validity could not be challenged by appealing to what had hitherto been regarded as the rules of public life, grounded on God's will. The Tudor monarchs, who were the principal initiators of parliamentary legislation, had no cause to ask such a far-reaching question. Though an occasional member of Parliament asserted that the monarch was under the law – meaning thereby that he ought to govern in accordance with the law – Tudor Parliaments in general took pains to act in such a way that they affirmed traditional rights of the crown and applied them to new situations, and did not restrict them or give them entirely new meaning. Such rights, no less than the rights of Parliament, were deemed to be part of the acknowledged laws of the land …

[66] [T]he most important … privilege to become a cause of discussion and action in the Tudor period was the right of free speech in Parliament. During the later Middle Ages the Speaker had asked for this right in terms suggesting that he was not interested in the advantages of free discussion but in protecting members from attack for what they had said; he wished to insure, in particular, that members of the House of Commons would not be punished for uttering words offensive to the monarch. When in 1523, Sir Thomas More, who was then the Speaker, made the same plea, he put the request differently. Having asked that each member have freedom "to discharge his conscience and boldly … declare his advice" he asked the king "to take all in good part" and to interpret what was said as coming "of a good zeal towards the profit of your realm and honour of your royal person." For More, free speech had a positive value. In the ensuing generation, the Speaker continued to ask for this privilege. The house meanwhile made itself a judge of the appropriateness of a member's speech, and on two occasions dealt out punishment to members whose speeches were deemed to be extravagant. By the opening of Elizabeth's reign, the request had become formal in tone; and the record refers to the Speaker as making his requests "in the usual form." His words were "that they might have liberty and freedom of speech in whatsoever they treated of, or had occasion to propound and debate in the house." To this the Lord Keeper, replying for the queen, said that she was "right well contented" with the liberty, "but so as [the members] be neither unmindful or uncareful of their duties, reverence, and obedience to the sovereign."

In the Parliaments of Elizabeth's reign, the House of Commons often discussed the right of free speech, sometimes when the queen intervened to stop the consideration of bills introduced by members and sometimes when members themselves directly gave their views on the nature and purpose of free speech in Parliament. Elizabeth asserted almost continuously through-[67]-out her reign that certain topics were beyond the range of independent action by the House of Commons. Discussions or action could take place only if she had given her permission. A member who introduced a bill on one of these subjects, or who in any other way brought about independent action by the house, provoked a vigorous response from the queen or from someone acting in her behalf. The offender's action would be countermanded; he might be taken to prison; the house might be forbidden to meddle in the matter. Questions concerning religion and the succession to the throne were chief among the forbidden topics.

(c)   Star Chamber and Common Law Courts

The Tudor period, particularly during the reign of Henry VII, also saw the real beginnings of the modern English state, with the emergence of recognisable modern forms of bureaucratic administration and statute law. It was during this period that England came closest to having a "state" apparatus. The ecclesiastical Court of High Commission and the Court of Star Chamber were Tudor inventions. The latter, in particular, has entered into common law folklore as a symbol of oppression and tyranny, despite its popularity with Elizabethan litigants.

Frederick Marcham, *A Constitutional History of Modern England, 1485 to the Present*
(Harper & Brothers, 1960)

[35] [T]he Court of Star Chamber, took its form (though not its origin) from early Tudor legislation. In origin it belonged to the later Middle Ages, when meetings of the king's council were held from time to time in the Star Chamber, a room in the old royal palace at Westminster, overlooking the Thames. These meetings were for the discharge of council business, judicial and otherwise; and in this sense, a Court of Star Chamber existed before the passage of the act of 1487, later known as the Star Chamber Act. This act and the Statute of Liveries of 1504 spoke of special reasons for action by [36] the council meeting in the Star Chamber and described how it should act; they set forth the need for suppressing certain offences, the minimum number of councilors and

others who would constitute a court for the trial of these offences, the procedure to be followed, and the punishment to be meted out. The Court of Star Chamber, as it developed during the sixteenth century, was therefore the council meeting in the Star Chamber to carry out a specific purpose in a definite manner ...

In describing the personnel of the Court of Star Chamber, early Tudor legislation named specifically the chancellor, the treasurer, the keeper of the privy seal, and the president of the council; and it gave them authority to call in as colleagues two other councilors, one a bishop and the other a temporal lord, as well as the two chief justices of the King's Bench and Common Pleas or two other justices. These persons formed a court whose purpose was to aid in suppressing certain specified offences, notably riots and attempts to obstruct the working of the ordinary courts and the execution of justice. These offences, the statutes declared, had already been branded as crimes, but little "is or hath been done for the punishment of the offenders in that behalf." The purpose of the Court of Star Chamber was therefore to remedy a defect in the working of the established judicial system. To this end the legislation gave the court powers in the gathering of evidence, in the examination of the parties involved, and in dealing out punishments; and these powers were more appropriate to an administrative body than to an English court. There was no confrontation of accuser and accused; instead, they made their charges and rebuttals in written statements. The examination of witnesses took place in secret, and the only occasion when the case emerged into public view was when the court met in the Star Chamber to announce a decision to the accused. The court was free to award punishment according to the penalties provided in existing statutes, or at its discretion. In brief, the court had almost complete freedom as to the procedure it followed, the evidence it considered, and the punishment it meted out. Armed with these powers, the Court of Star Chamber made short work of the particular group of offenders it was empowered to suppress – the so-called "overmighty subjects."

Wolsey put an end to this problem during the time when, as Lord Chancellor, he was presiding officer in the Court of Star Chamber. But by then the court had proved to be a useful aid to the administration and no less useful to the subject, who approved the speed and vigour of its actions. At least, suits continued to pour in, the complainant always stretching his case [37] in such a way as to make his opponent's actions appear to have been riotous. On the government's side there was stretching of another kind: that is, readiness to enlarge the range of the court's jurisdiction, and naturally so during the middle years of the Tudor period when many of the policy changes then taking place might have been difficult to administer without the swift and vigorous support of the Court of Star Chamber. Thus by the middle of the sixteenth century the Court of Star Chamber remained in close association with the council; it continued to do much business and to use the procedure developed by the court during the early Tudor period. The principal change was in the topics with which it dealt. In association with the busy Privy Council of the later Tudor period, the Court of Star Chamber became a powerful influence in enforcing the policies of the government.

During Elizabeth's reign, the Court of Star Chamber adhered to a relatively fixed pattern as to procedure, the frequency of meetings, and the range of jurisdiction. Meetings took place twice a week during the normal law court terms; they were held in the Star Chamber, were open to the public, and were presided over by one or more privy councilors and two judges. From time to time the Privy Council held its own private meetings in the Star Chamber before or after sessions of the court. The court had its own clerk and records. The attorney general attended to present a case for the government when that was necessary. The court still listened to complaints of alleged riots and the other major offences assigned to the court in the early Tudor period. In addition, the jurisdiction included acts of defiance against Privy Council proclamations and certain other offences not directly punishable under existing laws, notably fraud, perjury, libel, conspiracy, threats of violence to important officials, and challenges to duels. The Court of Star Chamber continued to examine witnesses and otherwise to search out the truth by means of agents, who made their inquiries in private and put those whom they questioned, including the defendant, under oath.

In awarding punishment, the court refrained, as it had done previously, from use of the death penalty. It imprisoned the guilty; sometimes it also fined them and required them to pay damages to the person they had injured. In many instances, the court caused the guilty person to perform a humiliating task in public, or to suffer mutilation so as to advertise his offence and make plain its enormity. As the lightest penalty of this kind, the court might order an offender to ride through the streets bearing a paper with a description of his offence. He might be publicly whipped, have his ears or a hand cut off in public, or be branded on the face with a letter signifying his offence. Whenever there was opportunity, the court made a public spectacle of the man's conviction and punishment, as though to drive home [38] to all Englishmen the gravity of certain illegal acts and the determination of the court to stamp them out. In brief, the Court of Star Chamber was not merely a court where certain crimes were inquired into and, if necessary, punished; it was also an agency of propaganda, enabling the Privy Council to make plain its intention vigorously to enforce the government's policies and the government's concept of public peace and order. Yet despite the decisiveness of its acts and the heavy, often cruel, punishments imposed, the Court of Star Chamber was not an unpopular institution in Tudor times. The thousands who presented complaints to it thought no other court would remedy their grievances; they welcomed the speed and finality of the court's actions; and in general they accepted the standards of right and wrong on which the court based its decisions.

JR Tanner, *Tudor Constitutional Documents AD 1485-1603 with an Historical Commentary*
(Cambridge University Press, 2nd ed 1930)

[257] The Star Chamber not only made a special business of punishing offenders against royal proclamations, but also claimed the right of issuing decrees, some of them of a very comprehensive character, and enforcing them by penalties. These are scarcely distinguishable from Orders in Council, and may be regarded as an exercise of the original authority of the King in Council from which the Court derived so large a part of its powers. There are decrees concerning trading companies, as for instance a decree of 29 January, 1577, deciding a controversy between the Company of Haberdashers and the hat and feltmakers in or near the City of London, and placing the feltmakers under the control of the Haberdashers' Company under penalty of contempt of court. The most important of these decrees were those regulating printing, and so establishing a censorship of the press.

Although the Star Chamber was a judicial tribunal, it never quite lost its political character as a council of state, and ambassadors were sometimes [258] received there and speeches made before the Lords on occasions of special solemnity. For instance, on 28 November, 1567, the Lord Keeper gave an address in the Star Chamber 'before the Council and others' touching seditious books; and a letter of 1600 gives an account of 'a very grave speech' on various matters delivered in the Star Chamber by the Lord Keeper, apparently to the judges of assize about to proceed on circuit.

The Star Chamber was tyrannical, because it tended to become 'a court of politicians enforcing a policy, not a court of judges administering the law'; but there can be little doubt that in the Tudor period, at any rate, its jurisdiction was on the whole beneficial. It had two functions of high importance to perform which no tribunal [composed and proceeding otherwise] ... could have discharged efficiently. It had to put down anarchy, baronial and other, and to supplement the defects of the common law. The work was well done and the earlier writers are loud in their praise of the Court.

Under the Stuart kings, the jurisdictional rivalries between common law courts and the newer tribunals were absorbed into wider issues about the scope of the royal prerogative (see Chapter 12, §2(a)). The chief defender of the common law was Sir Edward Coke (pronounced Cook).

Goldwin A Smith, *A Constitutional and Legal History of England*
(Scribners, 1955; repr Dorset Press, 1990)

[304] James I believed in what is usually described as "the divine right of kings." According to this theory, a king was appointed by God and responsible only to Him. His subjects might not resist the king's commands, for resistance was a sin. The people were a "headless multitude" who owed active obedience to the king who conferred organization, at God's command, upon the nation. Under such a theory the king, as deputy of God, was above Parliament, above the laws of England,

above the people. It was his duty to see to the welfare of his subjects, for God would one day hold him accountable for his stewardship ... Whatever privileges Parliament possessed, the law courts possessed, or any individual possessed, were theirs by grace of the king, and were not held by any right ...

[305] From the common law courts James I and Charles I encountered strong resistance. One of the greatest foes of the Stuart concept of sovereignty was Sir Edward Coke, famous author of the *Institutes,* Chief Justice of the Court of Common Pleas, later Chief Justice of the Court of King's Bench (1613) and, later still, a member of Parliament (1621). Coke and his supporters among the judges and lawyers insisted that the common law controlled the province of the royal prerogative power. They asserted that the rights of both king and Parliament were derived from and defined by precedent. They were usually determined to enforce these views quite sturdily. Coke himself was an obstinate fighter. To him the peculiar wisdom of the common law determined the goods and liberties of the people. The wisdom of the king, asserted Coke, could not do that. The king, Coke held, was legally limited by the common law. The law was greater than the Crown ...

[306] Several judicial cases are of special interest. In 1606 John Bate[s], an English merchant trading with the East, refused to pay on some currants a duty of five shillings a hundredweight imposed by James I in addition to the import levy established by Parliament. Bate[s] was brought to trial before the Court of Exchequer [*Bates' Case* (1606) 2 St Tr 371]. The court upheld the legality of the king's duties, arguing that impositions on foreign goods and all foreign relations were matters of state and belonged in the province of the king's "absolute" power ("The king's power is double, ordinary and absolute"). Because the king must have revenues, said Chief Baron Fleming and Baron Clark, he must and can take them when he has need to do so. In such affairs, the king governed by his "absolute," indisputable, private prerogative and this might not be disputed in the courts. The "ordinary" prerogative, on the other hand, was subject to the courts' rulings ...

[309] There were several other judicial problems ... For instance, Sir Edward Coke frequently directed a jealous and jaundiced eye towards the rival Chancery and the prerogative courts. He weakened the church courts by ruling that they had no right to imprison individuals charged with adultery. He also laid down the principle that if the common law courts provided a remedy the ecclesiastical tribunals should not have jurisdiction. Sir Edward Coke was always anxious to preserve and extend the jurisdiction of the common law courts. One way of doing [310] this was to multiply the writs of prohibition issuing out of the Court of King's Bench on matters of disputed jurisdiction.

Church officials frequently complained that the ecclesiastical courts were being unjustly bombarded by these writs of prohibition. In Fuller's Case (1607) [12 Co Rep 41; 77 ER 1322] the issue was raised directly. Fuller was a Puritan lawyer who insulted the Court of High Commission, whereupon he was locked up. Fuller thereupon appealed to the Court of King's Bench for a writ of prohibition, asserting that the Court of High Commission had no right to imprison for contempt. The writ was issued and the case was referred to the Court of Exchequer Chamber. When Archbishop Bancroft appealed directly to the king, Sir Edward Coke intervened [*Prohibitions del Roy* (1607) 12 Co Rep 63; 77 ER 1342] ... In the end the king agreed with the judges of Exchequer Chamber that King's Bench should continue to issue writs of prohibition, although with discrimination and sound sense.

In the Case of Proclamations [(1611) 12 Co Rep 74; 77 ER 1352] Sir Edward Coke and his fellow justices took issue with the Lord Chancellor who said that "every precedent had first a commencement and that he would advise the judges to maintain the power and prerogative of the king, and in cases in which there is no authority and precedent to leave the king to order in it, according to his wisdom and for the good of his subjects." Sir Edward and his colleagues decided "that the king by his proclamation cannot create any offence that was not an offence before; for then he may alter the law of the land by his proclamation ... For, if he may create an offence where none is, upon that ensues fine and imprisonment. Also the law of England is divided into three parts: common law, statute law, and custom. But the king's proclamation is none of them ... Also it was resolved that the king hath no prerogative but that which the law of the land allows him." In the specific case at issue Sir Edward ruled that a man could not be brought to trial for building a house in a particular spot in defiance of a royal proclama-[311]-tion. Coke said simply that a royal proclamation was not a law.

Prohibitions del Roy
(1607) 12 Co Rep 63; 77 ER 1342

Coke CJ: [63] Note, upon Sunday the 10th of November in this same term, the King, upon complaint made to him by Bancroft, Archbishop of Canterbury, concerning prohibitions, the King was informed, that when the question was made of what matters the Ecclesiastical judges have cognizance, either upon the exposition of the statutes concerning tithes, or any other thing ecclesiastical, or upon the statute 1 El concerning the high commission or in any other case in which there is not express authority in law, the King himself may decide it in his Royal person; and that the judges are but the delegates of the King, and that the King may take what causes he shall please to determine, from the determination of the Judges, and may determine them himself. And the Archbishop said, that this was clear in divinity, that such authority belongs to the King by the word of God in the Scripture. To which it was answered by me, in the presence, and with the clear consent of all the Judges of England, and Barons of the Exchequer, that the King in his own **[64]** person cannot adjudge any case, either criminal, as treason, felony, &c or betwixt party and party, concerning his inheritance, chattels, or goods &c but this ought to be determined and adjudged in some Court of Justice, according to the law and custom of England ... And the Judges informed the King, that no King after the Conquest assumed to himself to give any judgment in any cause whatsoever, which concerned the administration of justice within this realm, but these were solely determined in the Courts of Justice ... [T]hen the King said, that he thought the **[65]** law was founded upon reason, and that he and others had reason, as well as the Judges: to which it was answered by me, that true it was, that God had endowed His Majesty with excellent science, and great endowments of nature; but His Majesty was not learned in the laws of his realm of England, and causes which concern the life ... of his subjects, are not to be decided by natural reason but by the artificial reason and judgment of law, which law is an act which requires long study and experience, before that a man can attain to the cognizance of it: that the law was the golden metwand and measure to try the causes of the subjects; and which protected His Majesty in safety and peace: with which the King was greatly offended, and said, that then he should be under the law, which was treason to affirm, as he said; to which I said, that Bracton saith, *quod Rex non debet esse sub homine, sed sub Deo et lege* [the King should not be under man, but under God and the Law].

The report of *Prohibitions del Roy* was written by Coke himself. In his *History of English Law* (Methuen & Co, 3rd ed 1945), vol 5, Sir William Holdsworth suggested that Coke may not have "**[430]** come off **[431]** with such flying colours as his *ex post facto* narrative suggests". Holdsworth quotes another account as stating that "**[431 n 2]** his Majestie fell into that high indignation as the like was never knowne in him, looking and speaking fiercely with bended fist, offering to strike him etc, which the lo Cooke perceaving fell flatt on all fower".

In all these cases, Coke challenged the prerogative powers of the King. But in *James Bagg's Case* (1615) 11 Co Rep 93b, 77 ER 1271, he extended the writ of mandamus to judicial control of local government bodies as well; and in a famous passage in *Dr Bonham's Case* (1610) 8 Co Rep 113b, 77 ER 646, he appeared to challenge the authority of Parliament itself.

AD Boyer, "'Understanding, Authority, and Will':
Sir Edward Coke and the Elizabethan Origins of Judicial Review"
(1997) 39 *Boston College Law Review* 43

[82] Thomas Bonham was a medical practitioner in London. He held a bachelor's degree from Cambridge, and seems to have held an MD from that university as well. As early as 1602, he was associated with surgeons who practiced in the capital, and as early as 1605, he had begun to have trouble with the Royal College of Physicians. The College was authorized, by statutes passed under Henry VIII, to fine any person who practiced medicine in London without being licensed by the College. The College was also authorized to govern the medical community of London. A second clause in the statute allowed it to punish malpractice with powers including the ability to fine and imprison.

In 1605 and 1606, the College denied Bonham's application for membership and then fined him when he continued to practice. In November 1606, after Bonham defiantly told the College's *comitia censorum* that the body had no authority to regulate medical practice by university graduates, the College jailed him. Within a week, however, Bonham was released. His attorney had obtained a writ of *habeas corpus* from the Common Pleas, over which Chief Justice Coke presided.

In May 1607, at an informal conference held at the house of Thomas Egerton, Lord Chancellor Ellesmere, six judges agreed that the College had the right to govern all medical practitioners in London, even those holding university degrees. Thus encouraged, in early 1608, the College sued Bonham in the Court of King's Bench, seeking **[83]** a fine of sixty pounds. Bonham then countersued in the Common Pleas (in his turn, seeking one hundred pounds damages for false imprisonment). In early 1609, the King's Bench found Bonham guilty of illicit practice. In 1610, however, the Common Pleas ruled that the College lacked the power to punish Bonham – setting Bonham free, and levying a forty-pound fine against the College.

Coke offered five reasons for freeing Bonham. One drew on the *lex talionis*. Coke suggested that only the doctor whose malpractice harmed his patient should himself be punished "in his body", ie, be jailed; the physician whose sole fault was unauthorized practice might be punished in some other way, but not through imprisonment. Three other reasons were essentially technical, close readings of the two relevant statutory clauses: Coke found that the first clause, the one under which Bonham had been prosecuted, did not authorize the College to imprison him (a power available only for prosecutions under the second clause).

The last reason (fourth of the five, as Coke marshaled them) was the one holding the gunpowder. Referring expressly to the first clause, authorizing action by the College, Coke struck this down because it allowed the College to retain half of the fines it imposed on unauthorized practitioners:

> The censors cannot be judges, ministers, and parties: judges to give sentence or judgment; ministers to make summons; and parties to have the moiety of the forfeiture, *quia aliquis non debet esse Judex in propria causa, imo iniquum est aliquem suae rei esse judicem* … And it appears in our books, that in many cases, the common law will control acts of Parliament, and sometimes adjudge them to be utterly void; for when an act of Parliament is against common right and reason, or repugnant, or impossible to be performed, the common law will control it, and adjudge such act to be void [8 Co Rep at 118a; 77 ER at 652].

To support his conclusion, Coke cited four cases, precedents which were less than truly compelling. In one, *Tregor's Case* [(1335) YB 8 Edw 3, Pasch 26], Coke elabo-**[84]**-rately misquoted the text; only what he added suggested that the common law might override a statute. In another, the court had considered, but not actually ruled on, the conflict caused when statute law and canon law prescribed different rules for custody of monastery seals. In the third decision, *Stroude's Case* [(1575) 1 Anderson 45; 123 ER 345], the court did nothing more than clarify that the statutory phrase *rent service* also meant *rent charge*.

Only one precedent squarely supported Coke: a Year Book case, dating back more than three centuries, in which the court had refused to allow a plaintiff to maintain an action allowed by statute. In this decision (and some closely related cases, also decided under the Plantagenets), common-law judges had refused to give effect to the text of statutes. Nonetheless, as TFT Plucknett noted:

> The courts in these cases did undoubtedly "disregard the plain meaning of an Act of Parliament"; but in telling the story Lord Coke has made the important addition of the words "because it would be against common right and reason, the common law adjudges the said act of parliament as to that point void". There is no [such] judgment as this in the report; the statute is not held void; it is just ignored. *To this fact Coke has really added an explanation and a theory all his own.*

If the theory and the explanation were Coke's own, so too was the reading of the case law … In voiding a statute, Coke was breaking new ground. **[85]** Rather than rely on the judges' power to construe a statute, he reached out to assert that they held this fundamental authority.

It cannot be denied, in the end, that Coke acted in the belief that courts could strike down statutes which offended the common law – that is, which the judges in their wisdom found unreasonable. Nor can it be denied that Coke understood fully what he was doing. He wrote out the relevant passage from *Bonham's Case*, in two different manuscripts, in his own hand – a fact that suggests he understood what his words might unleash.

Any doubts as to Coke's intentions were dispersed in 1612, when the Common Pleas decided *Rowles v Mason* [(1612) 2 Brownlow 192; 123 ER 892]. Without citing *Bonham's Case*, Coke used *Rowles* to reiterate that the common law "corrects, allows, and disallows both statute law and custom, for if there be repugnancy in a statute; or unreasonableness in custom, the common law disallows and rejects it." ...

[86] *Bonham's Case* was controversial in its day, possibly as controversial as any other case in which judges have invalidated any law. Coke's decision drew criticism from his opponents and displeasure from his king. Where there is pressure, there is resistance. Coke steadfastly refused to take back what he had written. His refusal to recant followed through on what he had held; he had asserted the superiority of the judges' wisdom, and now he maintained that. His steadfast assertion of judicial independence bore witness to his assertion of judicial supremacy.

After *Bonham's Case* was published, Coke came under fire for its holding. Coke's rivals saw very clearly what the decision meant. Lord Chancellor Ellesmere noted the decision with special emphasis in his criticism of Coke's *Reports*. Ellesmere wrote that *Bonham's Case*

derogateth much from the wisdom and power of the parliament, that when the three estates – the King, the Lords and the Commons – have spent their labors in making a law, then shall three judges on the bench destroy and frustrate all their points because the act agreeth not in their particular sense with common right and reason, whereby [Coke] advanceth the reason of a particular court above the judgment of all the realm ... For it is *Magis Congruum* that acts of parliament should be corrected by the same pen that drew them, rather than to be dashed to pieces by the opinion of a few judges.

Nor can it be said that Coke held back from the dispute. When he published *Bonham's Case*, he added what might have seemed an innocuous postscript. The case was one of first impression; he wrote, **[87]** "the first judgment on the said branch concerning fine and imprisonment which has been given since the making of the said charter and Acts of Parliament, and therefore I thought it worthy to be reported and published."

To those who knew Coke well, this postscript was not innocuous. When Coke took a controversial stance, he typically offered a transparently disingenuous explanation ... He was not printing the case because it was the first to explicate the statute – as everyone knew. He was printing the case because it struck down the statute – as everyone knew.

The dispute over *Bonham's Case* was only one of the factors which cost Coke his sovereign's confidence. He had carried on a lifelong feud with Sir Francis Bacon, who now served as Attorney-General ... He had simultaneously pressed a second feud with Ellesmere, a dying lion who roused himself for one final battle. Between them, Bacon and Ellesmere brought Coke down ...

Goldwin A Smith, *A Constitutional and Legal History of England*
(Scribners, 1955; repr Dorset Press, 1990)

[311] One other case of high importance was the occasion of further dispute before Sir Edward Coke was dismissed from the Court of King's Bench. This was the Case of Commendams (Neile's Case, 1616) [Hobart 140; 80 ER 290]. Neile was a clergyman who was appointed Bishop of Coventry and Lichfield in 1614. He obtained the king's permission to hold two other ecclesiastical livings temporarily *(in commendam)*. There were two objections to holding livings in this way. In the first place, canon law stated that no bishop should have any position involving pastoral duties. Secondly, these livings were technically advowsons and their owners were actually deprived of their right of appointment by the fact that Neile occupied and profited from them.

The owners of one of the advowsons sued Neile in the Court of Common Pleas for interfering with their rights. The case came before Sir Edward Coke and the other judges in the Court of Exchequer Chamber. At this point Sir Francis Bacon, the attorney general, summoned the judges before the king. James I wanted to have a delay in the case in order to survey the whole problem ...

When the summons from the king came before Exchequer Chamber, Sir Edward Coke apparently persuaded his fellow judges that the **[312]** order of Sir Francis Bacon was illegal because all judges were bound by their oaths to delay no case … The summons of the attorney general was therefore ignored and the Exchequer Chamber continued to hear arguments …

James I at once ordered the twelve judges to appear before him in the council. He then compelled them to listen to his arguments. They were asked a question: "Whether if, at any time in a case depending before the judges which his majesty conceived to concern him either in power or profit, and therefore required to consult with them and that they should stay proceedings in the meantime, they ought not to stay accordingly?" Eleven judges agreed that they would halt proceedings and acknowledged it to be their duty to do so. The twelfth judge was Sir Edward Coke and he said "that when that case should be, he would do what should be fit for a judge to do." All the judges but Coke yielded to James.

Shortly afterwards the council, at the request of the king, began proceedings against Sir Edward Coke. He was charged with failing to pay an installment on a debt owed to Sir Christopher Hatton, with "speeches of high contempt, uttered as he sat in the seat of justice, touching the overthrow of the common law," with failing to give a satisfactory answer "to excuse his uncivil and indiscreet carriage before his majesty …" Coke was suspended from the council and the summer circuit of assize and ordered to review his "book of reports, wherein (as his majesty is informed) there be many exorbitant and extravagant opinions set down and published for positive and good law."

Sir Edward Coke refused to alter the sections of his manuscript that seemed adversely critical of the royal prerogative. In November, 1616, he was dismissed from all offices under the Crown … Nevertheless, the voice of Coke was not stilled. His acute defense of the common law provided an arsenal of ideas for the men of Parliament as they battled with the first two Stuarts. Coke **[313]** himself was soon elected to Parliament and he was not idle there. His legal writings were studied long after the head of Charles I had rolled.

The suggestion in *Dr Bonham's Case* that a statute perceived as contrary to "common right and reason" might judicially be held invalid was deeply influential in the later development of American constitutional law, but in England was largely abandoned, if indeed it was ever an accurate reading of the earlier judicial practice. The inconclusive precedents on which Coke relied are discussed in TFT Plucknett, *Statutes & Their Interpretation in the First Half of the Fourteenth Century* (Cambridge University Press, 1922), 66-71 and TFT Plucknett, "Bonham's Case and Judicial Review" (1926) 40 *Harvard Law Review* 30. The Year Book case referred to by Boyer as "**[84]** squarely support[ing]" Coke" was a later reaffirmation of *Copper v Gederings* (1310) YB Pasch 3 Edw II 105 (Selden Society Year Book Series vol III, Case 25).

The Year Book reports on which Coke relied had begun to appear in printed form towards the end of the 15th century; but originally they were circulated in manuscript form, and most lawyers of Coke's generation still had their own jealously guarded library of Year Book manuscripts. Written in Law French, and apparently originating simply as students' notes of the arguments they had heard in court, they are often obscure, unreliable, and frustratingly incomplete. How far Coke's precedents actually supported his argument is thus controversial. Nevertheless, as scholarly editions of the Year Books continue to appear, new evidence sometimes comes to light. For example, the publication in 1996 of Volume II of the Ames Foundation series drew attention to the case of *Re Fawsley* (1382) Mich 6 Rich II (Ames Foundation Year Book Series Vol II, Case No 20), involving a counterclaim based on the document known as *De Praerogativa Regis*, then at least 60 years old. We now know that *De Praerogativa Regis* was probably not a statute at all (see Chapter 12, §2(a)); but it was certainly supposed to be one in 1382, and the Year Book report refers to it as "lestatut de Prerogativa Regis". It recounts that on hearing a counterclaim based on cap 5 of the supposed statute, Belknap CJ left the Chancery and went to his brethren on the Common Bench to ask their advice on the matter, observing that if cap 5 had really been law, it surely would have been applied by Thorpe CJ and other earlier judges. Skipwith J responded to the Chief Justice's inquiry by assuring him bluntly: "It has never been law, nor shall it ever be" ("il ne fut ia ley ne ia serra"), and Asty J agreed. Thereupon Belknap CJ referred to two other provisions in *De Praerogativa Regis* (caps 10 and 18), and observed that they too were examples of statutory provisions "which are not held to be law" ("qe ne sount pas tenuz pur ley").

In any event, the modern consensus has been not only that any evidence of an older judicial practice supporting Coke's claim is at best inconclusive and ambiguous, but that Coke himself may have intended a more limited claim than is sometimes supposed.

Goldwin A Smith, *A Constitutional and Legal History of England*
(Scribners, 1955; repr Dorset Press, 1990)

[308] The orthodox interpretation of *Bonham's Case* is that Coke stated the doctrine of judicial review – later so important to the United States – **[309]** which maintains the principle that acts of the executive and legislative branches of government might be reviewed by the judges and overthrown if the courts found those acts in contravention of a higher law. This interpretation has been challenged by several authorities. Professor FD Wormuth, for example, has pointed out that Coke was really denying the right of the College of Physicians to be a judge in its own case against Bonham and if Coke's dictum is taken to apply *only to this or similar situations* the limitation upon the legislative power is one of procedural due process, not substantive due process. There may be no reference to the constitutional question consciously raised. It is probable, indeed, that Coke's appeals to a higher law were often seen more clearly by later commentators than by Coke himself.

By 1885 AV Dicey was able to relegate *Dr Bonham's Case* to a footnote as "obsolete" (*Introduction to the Study of the Law of the Constitution* (Macmillan, 1st ed 1885, 10th ed 1959), 61-2 n). Occasional dicta in recent years have suggested that such a doctrine might be revived (see Chapter 11, §2(a)); but the general response has not been encouraging.

On 20 June 1616, as the proceedings for Coke's removal from the Bench began, James I lectured an audience of judges in the Court of Star Chamber on the evils of jurisdictional rivalry. He also enjoined them, in language foreshadowing many future debates, to confine their role to "applying" rather than "making" the law.

James I, "A Speach in the Starre-Chamber"
in CH McIlwain (ed), *The Political Works of James I* (Harvard University Press, 1918), 326

[331] Now my Lords the Judges for your parts, the Charge I have to give you, consists … in three parts.

First in generall, that you doe Justice uprightly, as you shall answere to GOD and mee: For as I have only GOD to answere to, and to expect punishment at his hands, if I offend; So you are to answere both to GOD and to mee, and expect punishment at GODS hands and mine, if you be found in fault.

Secondly, to doe Iustice indifferently betweene Subject and Subject, betweene King and Subject, without delay, partialitie, feare or bribery, with stout and upright hearts …

[332] When I bid you doe Justice boldly, yet I bid you doe it fearefully; fearefully in this, to utter your owne conceites, and not the trew meaning of the Law: And remember you are no makers of Law, but Interpretours of Law, according to the trew sence thereof; for your Office is *Ius dicere*, and not *Ius dare*: And that you are so farre from making Law, that even in the higher house of Parliament, you have no voyce in making of a Law, but onely to give your advice when you are required.

And though the Laws be in many places obscure, and not so wel knowen to the multitude as to you; and that there are many parts that come not into ordinary practice, which are knowen to you, because you can finde out the reason thereof by bookes and [precedents]; yet know this, that your interpretations must be alwayes subject to common sense and reason.

For I will never trust any Interpretation, that agreeth not with my common sense and reason, and trew Logicke: for *Ratio est anima Legis* in all humane Lawes, without exception; it must not be Sophistrie or straines of wit that must interprete, but either cleare Law, or solide reason.

But in Countreys where the formalitie of Law hath no place, as in *Denmarke*, which I may trewly report, as having my selfe beene an eye-witnesse thereof; all their State is governed only by a written Law; there is no Advocate or Proctour admitted to plead, only the parties themselves plead their owne cause, and then a man stands up and reads the Law, and there is an end, for the very Law-booke it selfe is their onely Judge. Happy were all Kingdomes if they could be so: But heere, curious wits, various conceits, different actions, and varietie of examples breed questions in Law: And therefore when you heare the questions if they be plaine, there is a plaine way in it selfe; if they be such as are not plaine (for mens inventions dayly abound) then you are to interprete according to common sense, and draw a good and certaine *Minor* of naturall reason, out of the *Major* of direct Lawe, and thereupon to make a right and trew *Conclusion*.

For though the Common Law be a mystery and skill best knowen unto your selves, yet if your interpretation be such, as other men which have Logicke and common sense understand not the reason, I will never trust such an Interpretation.

Remember also you are Judges, and not a Judge, and divided into Benches, which sheweth that what you doe, that you should doe with advice and deliberation, not hastily and rashly, before you well study the case, and conferre together; debating it duely, not giving single opinions, *per emendicata suffragia*; and so to give your Judgement, as you will answer to God and me.

Now having spoken of your Office in generall, I am next to come to the limits wherein you are to bound your selves ... First, Incroach not upon the Prerogative of the Crowne: If there fall out a question that concernes my Prerogative or mystery of State, deale not with it, till you consult with the King or his Councell, or both: for they are transcendent matters, and must not be sliberely caried with over-rash wilfulnesse; for so may you wound the King [333] through the sides of a private person: and this I commend unto your speciall care, as some of you of late have done very well, to blunt the sharpe edge and vaine popular humour of some Lawyers at the Barre, that thinke they are not eloquent and bold spirited enough, except they meddle with the Kings Prerogative: But doe not you suffer this; for certainely if this liberty be suffered, the Kings Prerogative, the Crowne, and I, shall bee as much wounded by their pleading, as if you resolved what they disputed: That which concernes the mysterie of the Kings power, is not lawfull to be disputed; for that is to wade into the weaknesse of Princes, and to take away the mysticall reverence, that belongs unto them that sit in the Throne of God.

Secondly, That you keepe your selves within your owne Benches, not to invade other Juris-dictions, which is unfit, and an unlawful thing ... Besides the Courts of Common Law, there is the Court of Requests; the Admiraltie Court; the Court of the President and Councell of Wales, the President and Councell of the North; High Commission courts, every Bishop in his owne Court.

These Courts ought to keepe their owne limits and boundes of their Commission and Instructions, according to the ancient [Precedents]: And like as I declare that my pleasure is, that every of these shall keepe their owne limits and boundes; So the Courts of Common Lawe are not to encroach upon them, no more then it is my pleasure that they should encroach upon the Common Law ...

Keep you therefore all in your owne bounds, and for my part, I desire you to give me no more right in my private Prerogative, then you give to any Subject; and therein I will be acquiescent: As for the absolute Prerogative of the Crowne, that is no Subject for the tongue of a Lawyer, nor is lawfull to be disputed.

It is Atheisme and blasphemie to dispute what God can doe: good Christians content themselves with his will revealed in his word. So, it is presumption and high contempt in a Subject, to dispute what a King can doe, or say that a King cannot doe this, or that; but rest in that which is the Kings revealed will in his Law ...

[335] Remember therefore, that hereafter you keepe within your limits and Jurisdictions. It is a speciall point of my Office to procure and command, that amongst Courts there bee a concordance, and musicall accord; and it is your parts to obey, and see this kept: And, as you are to observe the ancient Lawes and customes of England; so are you to keepe your selves within the bound of direct Law, or [Precedents]; and of those, not every snatched [Precedent], carped now here, now there, as it were running by the way; but such as have never beene controverted, but by the contrary, approved by common usage, in times of best Kings, and by most learned Judges ...

[336] Remember now how I have taught you brotherly love one toward another: For you know well, that as you are Judges, you are all brethren, and your Courts are sisters. I pray you therefore, labour to keepe that sweete harmonie, which is amongst those sisters the *Muses*. What greater miserie can there bee to the Law, then contempt of the Law? and what readier way to contempt,

then when questions come, what shall bee determined in this Court, and what in that? Whereupon two evils doe arise; The one, that men come not now to Courts of justice, to heare matters of right pleaded, and Decrees given accordingly, but onely out of a curiositie, to heare questions of the Jurisdiction of Courts disputed, and to see the event, what Court is like to prevaile above the other; And the other is, that the Pleas are turned from Court to Court in an endlesse circular motion, as upon *Ixions* wheele: And this was the reason why I found just fault with that multitude of Prohibitions: For when a poore Minister had with long labour, and great expence of charge and time, gotten a sentence for his Tithes, then comes a Prohibition, and turnes him round from Court to Court, and so makes his cause immortall and endlesse: for by this uncertaintie of Jurisdiction amongst Courts, causes are scourged from Court to Court, and this makes the fruit of Suits like *Tantalus* fruite, still neere the Suiters lips, but can never come to taste it. And this in deed is a great delay of Justice, and makes causes endlesse: Therefore the onely way to avoyd this, is for you to keepe your owne bounds, and nourish not the people in contempt of other Courts, but teach them reverence to Courts in your publique speaches, both in your Benches, and in your Circuits; so shall you bring them to a reverence, both of GOD, and of the King.

Keepe therefore your owne limits towards the King, towards other Courts, and towards other Lawes, bounding your selves within your owne Law, and make not new Law. Remember, as I said before, that you are Judges, to declare, and not to make Law: For when you make a Decree never heard of before, you are Law-givers, and not Law-tellers.

(d) The Bloodless Revolution

The 1628 Petition of Right, in response to which Charles I yielded to the demand of Parliament for control of taxation, was also drafted by Coke. However, by that time the competing demands for supremacy by King and Parliament were irreconcilable. The republican "Commonwealth" or "Interregnum" that followed the Civil War of the 1640s and the execution of Charles I in 1649 failed to produce a stable parliamentary alternative to monarchical rule, and in 1660 the monarchy was restored with Charles II. The eventual compromise, with Parliament as the supreme law-making body governing through a monarch of its own choice, came about through the "bloodless" or "glorious" revolution of 1688.

PA Joseph, *Constitutional and Administrative Law in New Zealand*
(Law Book Co, 1993)

[174] The Bill of Rights 1688 (Eng) ended the Stuart claims to rule by prerogative right. In December 1688, James II cast the Great Seal of the Realm into the Thames and fled the country. The Convention Parliament met and resolved that James II had abdicated, "having endeavoured to subvert the Constitution of the kingdom by breaking the original contract between the King and people … and having violated the fundamental laws". A declaration of the Lords and Commons affirmed the rights and liberties of the people and settled the Crown on William and Mary of Orange. William and Mary accepted the declaration which was proclaimed to the nation and enacted as the *Bill of Rights* 1688. This document was given force of law by the *Crown and Parliament Recognition Act* 1688 (Eng) which ratified and confirmed the Acts of the Convention Parliament …

[175] The austere clarity of the *Bill of Rights 1688* gives the document a timeless relevance. It was more of a political compact for the subject's protection than a legal statute; it established the supremacy or rule of law in a way no ordinary statute could have done. The abolition of the Court of Star Chamber in 1640 left public as well as private acts subject to the common law, except as altered from time to time by Act of Parliament. Only executive discretions remained with the Crown. The King was compelled to govern through Parliament and to accept the independence of his judges under the *Act of Settlement* 1700 (Eng). The judges conceded the supremacy of statute over common law but turned their attention to securing the individual from official interference.

The operative provisions of the *Bill of Rights 1688* are set out below.

Bill of Rights 1688
(I Will & Mary, Sess 2 c 2)

[T]he said Lords Spiritual and Temporal and Commons, pursuant to their respective Letters and Elections, being now assembled in a full and free Representative of this Nation, taking into their most serious Consideration the best Means for attaining the Ends aforesaid, do in the first Place (as their Ancestors in like Case have usually done) for the vindicating and asserting their ancient Rights and Liberties, declare:

1. That the pretended Power of suspending of Laws, or the Execution of Laws, by regal Authority, without consent of Parliament, is illegal.
2. That the pretended Power of dispensing with Laws, or the Execution of Laws, by regal Authority, as it hath been assumed and exercised of late, is illegal.
3. That the Commission for erecting the late Court of Commissioners for Ecclesiastical Causes, and all other Commissions and Courts of like Nature, are illegal and pernicious.
4. That levying Money for or to the Use of the Crown, by Pretence of Prerogative, without Grant of Parliament, for longer Time, or in other Manner than the same is or shall be granted, is illegal.
5. That it is the Right of the Subjects to petition the King, and all Commitments and Prosecutions for such petitioning are illegal.
6. That the raising or keeping a standing Army within the Kingdom in Time of Peace, unless it be with Consent of Parliament, is against Law.
7. That the Subjects which are Protestants, may have Arms for their Defence suitable to their conditions, and as allowed by Law.
8. That Election of Members of Parliament ought to be free.
9. That the Freedom of speech, and Debates or Proceedings in Parliament, ought not to be impeached or questioned in any Court or Place out of Parliament.
10. That excessive Bail ought not to be required, nor excessive Fines imposed; nor cruel and unusual Punishments inflicted.
11. That Jurors ought to be duly impanelled and returned, and Jurors which pass upon Men in Trials for High Treason ought to be Freeholders.
12. That all Grants and Promises of Fines and Forfeitures of particular Persons before Conviction, are illegal and void.
13. And that for Redress of all Grievances, and for the amending, strengthening and preserving of the Laws, Parliaments ought to be held frequently.

Both Magna Carta and the *Bill of Rights* have continuing legal relevance in Australia through the reception of English law (see Chapter 4, §2(b)). For example, s 6 of the *Imperial Acts Application Act 1969* (NSW) declares that the *Bill of Rights* and Magna Carta remain in force in New South Wales to the extent that they are not "affected by" other State or Imperial enactments. Today, Australian parliaments can limit the operation of the instruments or even repeal them. As Wilson J observed in *Re Cusack* (1985) 66 ALR 93: "**[95]** The validity of laws enacted by the Commonwealth Parliament falls to be determined by reference to the proper construction of the Australian Constitution. It is not open to base an argument for invalidity by reference to alleged inconsistencies between laws of the Commonwealth and either Magna Carta or the Bill of Rights". On the other hand, the *Bill of Rights* has been invoked for its historical importance as an affirmation of parliamentary privilege (for example, in *Egan v Willis* (1998) 195 CLR 224). In taxation cases, its insistence on parliamentary consent to taxation has been invoked as excluding tax liabilities based on executive discretion rather than statutory criteria (*Commissioner of Stamps (SA) v Telegraph Investment Co Pty Ltd* (1995) 184 CLR 453), while also underpinning the broader constitutional importance of parliamentary control of taxation (*Northern Suburbs General Cemetery Reserve Trust v Commonwealth* (1993) 176 CLR 555). Its insistence on parliamentary consent to the maintenance of armed forces in peacetime was also relied on by Brennan and Toohey JJ in *Re Tracey; Ex parte Ryan* (1989) 166 CLR 518 as supporting the view that military law could not oust the ordinary criminal law, while its enjoinder against "cruel and unusual Punishments" was powerfully invoked by Murphy J in *Sillery v The Queen* (1981) 180 CLR 353.

The new compact between the Parliament and the king was cemented by a series of further enactments. Chief among these was the *Act of Settlement 1701* (12 & 13 Will 3 c 2).

Goldwin A Smith, *A Constitutional and Legal History of England*
(Scribners, 1955; repr Dorset Press, 1990)

[369] The last important part of the Revolution arrangements was the Act of Settlement of 1701, passed to make legally clear the nature of the succession, to guard against the restoration of the old Stuart line, and to make a series of specific rules upon other matters shortly to be described. After Mary died (1694) without issue the heir to the throne upon the death of William (1701) was Mary's sister Anne. By 1700 the last of Anne's thirteen children had died and this event meant that the direct Protestant line of the Stuarts would end with the passing of Anne. The Act of Settlement declared that Anne should succeed William and that if she died without direct heirs the throne should pass to the Electress Sophia of Hanover and her issue. Sophia was the daughter of James' daughter Elizabeth and Frederick the Elector Palatine. The succession of the Hanoverians thus seemed assured.

The Act of Settlement also ... provided that the king's pardon under the Great Seal would not be a bar to an impeachment by Parliament. By another important provision judges were to hold office during good behavior instead of at the king's pleasure. They were to be removed or have their salary altered only upon an address by both houses of Parliament as a result of charges of misconduct proved in Parliament. The Act of Settlement further provided that the sovereign must be a member of the Church of England; that if he were a foreigner England was not obligated to defend his foreign possessions; that he might not leave England without the permission of Parliament ... [370] Finally, the Act of Settlement provided that "no person who has an office or other place of profit under the king or receives a pension from the crown shall be capable of serving as a member of the House of Commons." This clause in the Act of Settlement was extended in the Place Act of 1707.

Together, the *Bill of Rights* and the *Act of Settlement* signified that Parliament, and not the monarch, was the supreme law-making body of England. The *Act of Settlement* continues to govern the succession to the British throne (and therefore also to the position of King or Queen of Australia). Even today, the Act provides that "every person and persons that then were, or afterwards should be reconciled to, or shall hold communion with the see or Church of Rome, or should profess the popish religion, or marry a papist, should be excluded, and are by that Act made for ever incapable to inherit, possess, or enjoy the Crown and government of this realm".

(e)   Limited Government

The theory of limited government that underlay the constitutional settlement of 1688-89 was articulated in its most enduring form by John Locke (see Chapter 2, §1). Locke based his conception of the purpose (and therefore the limits) of government on a theory of "natural rights", chief among which he counted the right to property. The Lockean conception of the sanctity of private property was the key to *Entick v Carrington* (1765) 19 St Tr 1030, a decision that has been perceived as reinforcing the supremacy of Parliament, the rule of law and the separation of powers.

Two King's messengers, under the authority of a warrant issued by the Secretary of State, had broken and entered Entick's house and taken away his papers. Entick was alleged to be the author of seditious writings. When the messengers were sued by Entick for trespass to his house and goods, it was argued that the warrant was legal, as the power to issue such warrants was essential to government as "the only means of quieting clamours and sedition".

Entick v Carrington
(1765) 19 St Tr 1030

Lord Camden CJ: [1064] This power, so claimed by the secretary of state, is not supported by one single citation from any law book extant. It is claimed by no other magistrate in this kingdom but himself …

Before I state the question, it will be necessary to describe the power claimed by this warrant in its full extent.

If honestly exerted, it is a power to seize that man's papers, who is charged upon oath to be the author or publisher of a seditious libel; if oppressively, it acts against every man, who is so described in the warrant, though he be innocent …

[1065] Such is the power, and therefore one should **[1066]** naturally expect that the law to warrant it should be clear in proportion as the power is exorbitant.

If it is law, it will be found in our books. If it is not to be found there, it is not law.

The great end, for which men entered into society, was to secure their property. That right is preserved sacred and incommunicable in all instances, where it has not been taken away or abridged by some public law for the good of the whole. The cases where this right of property is set aside by positive law, are various. Distresses, executions, forfeitures, taxes, &c are all of this description; wherein every man by common consent gives up that right, for the sake of justice and the general good.

By the laws of England, every invasion of private property, be it ever so minute, is a trespass. No man can set his foot upon my ground without my licence, but he is liable to an action, though the damage be nothing … If he admits the fact, he is bound to shew by way of justification, that some positive law has empowered or excused him. The justification is submitted to the judges, who are to look into the books; and see if such a justification can be maintained by the text of the statute law, or by the principles of common law. If no such excuse can be found or produced, the silence of the books is an authority against the defendant, and the plaintiff must have judgment.

According to this reasoning, it is now incumbent upon the defendants to shew the law, by which this seizure is warranted. If that cannot be done, it is a trespass.

Papers are the owner's goods and chattels: they are his dearest property; and are so far from enduring a seizure, that they will hardly bear an inspection; and though the eye cannot by the laws of England be guilty of a trespass, yet where private papers are removed and carried away, the secret nature of those goods will be an aggravation of the trespass, and demand more considerable damages in that respect. Where is the written law that gives any magistrate such a power? I can safely answer, there is none; and therefore it is too much for us without such authority to pronounce a practice legal, which would be subversive of all the comforts of society …

[1067] I come now to the practice since the Revolution, which has been strongly urged, with this emphatical addition, that an usage tolerated from the aera of liberty, and continued downwards to this time through the best ages of the constitution, must necessarily have a legal commencement …

If the practice began then, it began too late to be law now. If it was more ancient, the Revolution is not to answer for it; and I could **[1068]** have wished, that upon this occasion the Revolution had not been considered as the only basis of our liberty …

With respect to the practice itself, if it goes no higher, every lawyer will tell you, it is much too modern to be evidence of the common law …

This is the first instance I have met with, where the ancient immemorable law of the land, in a public matter, was attempted to be proved by the practice of a private office.

The names and rights of public magistrates, their power and forms of proceeding as they are settled by law, have been long since written, and are to be found in books and records. Private customs indeed are still to be sought from private tradition. But whoever conceived a notion, that any part of public law could be buried in the obscure practice of a particular person?

To search, seize, and carry away all the papers of the subject upon the first warrant: that such a right should have existed from the time whereof the memory of man runneth not to the contrary, and never yet have found a place in any book of law; is incredible. But if so strange a thing could be supposed, I do not see, how we could declare the law upon such evidence.

But still it is insisted, that there has been a general submission, and no action brought to try the right.

I answer, there has been a submission of guilt and poverty to power and the terror of punishment. But it would be strange doctrine to assert that all the people of this land are bound to acknowledge that to be universal law, which a few criminal booksellers have been afraid to dispute ...

[1073] It is then said, that it is necessary for the ends of government to lodge such a power with a state officer; and that it is better to prevent the publication before than to punish the offender afterwards ... [W]ith respect to the argument of State necessity, or a distinction that has been aimed at between State offences and others, the common law does not understand that kind of reasoning, nor do our books take notice of any such distinctions ...

Lastly, it is urged as an argument of utility, that such a search is a means of detecting offenders by discovering evidence ...

In the criminal law such a proceeding was never heard of; and yet there are some crimes, such for instance as murder, rape, robbery, and house-breaking, to say nothing of forgery and perjury, that are more atrocious than libelling. But our law has provided no paper-search in these cases ...

[1074] If, however, a right of search for the sake of discovering evidence ought in any case to be allowed, this crime above all others ought to be excepted, as wanting such a discovery less than any other. It is committed in open day-light, and in the face of the world; every act of publication makes new proof; and the solicitor of the treasury, if he pleases, may be the witness himself ...

I have now taken notice of everything that has been urged upon the present point; and upon the whole we are all of opinion, that the warrant to seize and carry away the party's papers in the case of a seditious libel, is illegal and void.

Another landmark in the symbolic narrative of common law solicitude for individual liberty was *Sommersett's Case* (1772) 20 St Tr 1. According to the evidence "James Sommersett, a negro, was confined in irons on board a ship called the Ann and Mary ... , lying in the Thames, and bound for Jamaica". At the suit of the English Anti-Slavery League, Lord Mansfield issued a writ of habeas corpus addressed to the ship's commander. The return to the writ asserted that Sommersett was a runaway slave who had been recaptured by his master, Charles Steuart, and was held in irons at Steuart's request. The Court held that this was not a sufficient return, and ordered that Sommersett be released.

Sommersett's Case
(1772) 20 St Tr 1

Serjeant Davy (in argument): [78] [To] make a slave of a negro, who is one, by his complexion; is a cruelty and absurdity that I trust will never take place here: such as, if promulged, would make England a disgrace to all the nations under heaven: for the reducing a man, guiltless of any offence against the laws, to the condition of slavery, the worst and most abject state. Mr Dunning has mentioned, what he is pleased to term philosophical and moral grounds, I think, or something to that effect, of slavery; and would not by any means have us think disrespectfully of those nations, whom we mistakenly call barbarians, merely for carrying on that trade: for my part, we may be warranted, I believe, in affirming the morality or propriety of the practice does not **[79]** enter their heads; they make slaves of whom they think fit. For the air of England; I think, however, it has been gradually purifying ever since the reign of Elizabeth. Mr Dunning seems to have discovered so much, as he finds it changes a slave into a servant; though unhappily he does not think it of efficacy enough to prevent that pestilent disease reviving, the instant the poor man is obliged to quit ... this happy country. However, it has been asserted, and is now repeated by me, this air is too pure for a slave to breathe in: I trust, I shall not quit this court without certain conviction of the truth of that assertion.

Lord Mansfield: [81] We are so well agreed, that we think there is no occasion of having it argued (as I intimated an intention at first,) **[82]** before all the judges, as is usual, for obvious reasons, on a return to a Habeas Corpus. The only question before us is, whether the cause on the return is sufficient? If it is, the negro must be remanded; if it is not, he must be discharged. Accordingly, the return states, that the slave departed and refused to serve; whereupon he was kept, to be sold abroad. So high an act of dominion must be recognized by the law of the country where it is used. The power of a master over his slave has been extremely different, in different countries. The state of slavery is of such a nature, that it is incapable of being introduced on any reasons, moral or political, but only by positive law, which preserves its force long after the reasons, occasion, and time itself from whence it was created, is erased from memory. It is so odious, that nothing can be suffered to support it, but positive law. Whatever inconveniences, therefore, may follow from the decision, I cannot say this case is allowed or approved by the law of England; and therefore the black must be discharged.

In the version of this case that entered the oral tradition of the common law, it was said that Lord Mansfield had ended his judgment by declaiming: "The air of England is too pure for a slave to breathe in. Let the black go free". It appears that this was an embroidery, based in part on Serjeant Davy's argument. Indeed, a similar line had earlier been used by counsel for the ship's commander, *denying* that "[74] the air of England is too pure for a slave to breathe in". Presumably both he and Serjeant Davy were quoting a saying already in current use.

(f)　　Responsible and Representative Government

After the revolutionary settlement of 1688, Parliament gradually began to take on a more representative character.

Patrick Parkinson, *Tradition and Change in Australian Law*
(LBC Information Services, 3rd ed 2005)

[101] Through the rest of the 18th century, English government continued its progress from a monarchical system wielding direct governmental authority, to a system of parliamentary democracy. The evolution was a slow one. Throughout most of the century, the monarchs retained a personal involvement in government in the sense that ministers were in office by royal choice and owed their position to that link with the Crown, rather than with each other or with their political party. George I (1714-1727) and George II (1727-1760) chose ministers from the Whig party throughout their reigns, and managed to secure compliant Parliaments. This favouritism towards the Whigs was because they had supported the Hanoverian succession. The power and influence of royal ministers increased with the succession of the Hanovers. George I knew as little about his new kingdom as he did of its language and, therefore, was content to leave decisions to his ministers. George II was similarly uninvolved in the day-to-day work of government, and both of them rarely attended cabinet meetings.

George III, who came to the throne in 1760, took a more active role in government, but continued the practice of his predecessors in leaving cabinet meetings to his ministers. The Privy Council continued to decline in practical significance, and by the middle of the century it was possible to identify one minister, usually, but not always, the First Lord of the Treasury, who was the leader of the government. At the same time, the practical power of the king to choose his own ministers declined. Ministers needed to have [102] the support of Parliament in order to govern effectively, and there were times when the king was forced to accept ministers whom he disliked, because their political position was so strong in the country.

From this, in due course, the system of party political government emerged. However, it needed a fundamental reform of the franchise before the personal power of the monarch was displaced. Under the 18th century political system, in which the right to vote was strictly limited and the size of electorates in each constituency varied markedly, royal patronage and influence could usually ensure that elections brought about a desirable composition of Parliament. It was in this way that the Whigs were able to dominate between 1714 and 1760, and the Tories for a half century thereafter.

In 1832, a *Reform Act* was passed which effected the abolition of various constituencies which no longer had sizeable populations to support them, and which created new constituencies, especially in London and the north of England. The franchise was also enlarged. Further reform took place by the *Reform Act 1867*. While these enlarged the franchise, [they] did so only for men. Universal adult suffrage of both men and women had to wait until the 20th century.

The effect of these reforms was to make it impossible for the Crown to retain its influence over the Parliament in quite the way it had done hitherto. The power of the monarch to choose her or his own ministry, which had waned throughout the 18th century, was extinguished by 1867. Thenceforward, Parliamentarians had to be responsive to electorates in a way which had not been true of the 18th century … [M]inisters needed the confidence of Parliament, and from that time on, party political government was firmly established. Furthermore, it was clear that the monarch had a very limited role constitutionally. Walter Bagehot, in his famous work, *The English Constitution* (1867) wrote:

> "To state the matter shortly, the sovereign has, under a constitutional monarchy such as ours, three rights, the right to be consulted, the right to encourage, the right to warn."

As representative government developed so did responsible government (see Chapter 12, §4(a)). Increasingly the monarch was reduced to a ceremonial role. By the end of the 19th century, British constitutionalism had reached a point where a representative Parliament had emerged as the sovereign power; and the notion of rule according to the law, rather than according to the arbitrary wishes of the monarch, was firmly entrenched.

3. Parliament versus the Courts

In Britain, the battle for supremacy between Parliament and the courts was a stand-off, with each institution respecting the other's autonomy up to a point and neither forcing to a final confrontation the unresolved tensions between them. The nearest approach to a showdown was the series of cases beginning with *Stockdale v Hansard* (1837) 2 M & Rob 9; 174 ER 196.

Luke Hansard and his family held the contract for printing House of Commons parliamentary papers from 1774 onwards. In 1803, they began to print, and eventually to publish, complete reports of parliamentary debates. To this day, the official reports of debates in most Parliaments conducted on the Westminster model are still referred to as "Hansard". It was in relation to the routine printing of parliamentary papers that the Hansard family faced a series of actions for defamation.

JJ Stockdale was a bookseller and publisher. In the 1836 Report of the Inspectors of Prisons, a parliamentary paper printed by the Hansard family, the Inspectors complained that a book published by Stockdale had been circulating in Newgate prison. The book was said to be "**[9]** of the most disgusting nature, and the plates … obscene and indecent in the extreme". Stockdale contended that it was a serious textbook on the physiology and anatomy of the human reproductive system, illustrated by anatomical plates. He sued the Hansards for libel. The jury found that the words complained of, "disgusting" and "obscene and indecent", were true. This was enough to dispose of Stockdale's action. The jury also found that, because the report was published by authority of the House of Commons, it was protected by parliamentary privilege. Lord Denman CJ, who presided at the trial, remarked from the bench that he was not aware of any such privilege. It appears that parliamentary indignation at this unnecessary obiter dictum was the motivation for subsequent events.

In August 1836, the Inspectors of Prisons made a written reply to criticisms of their Report. This too was printed by the Hansards so that it could be tabled in Parliament. In it the imputations concerning Stockdale's book were repeated. Stockdale then brought a second libel action (*Stockdale v Hansard* (1839) 9 Ad & E 1; 112 ER 1112). This time, before the case came on for hearing, the House of Commons resolved:

House of Commons Journals
(31 May 1837), Vol 92

[419] *Resolved*, That the power of publishing such of its Reports, Votes, and Proceedings as it shall deem necessary or conducive to the public interests, is an essential incident to the constitutional functions of Parliament ...

Resolved, That by the law and privilege of Parliament, this House has the sole and exclusive jurisdiction to determine upon the existence and extent of its privileges, and that the institution or prosecution of any action, suit or other proceeding, for the purpose of bringing them into discussion or decision before any court or tribunal elsewhere than in Parliament, is a high breach of such privilege, and renders all parties concerned therein amenable to its just displeasure, and to the punishment consequent thereon ...

Resolved, That for any court or tribunal to assume to decide upon matters of Privilege inconsistent with the determination of either House of Parliament thereon, is contrary to the law of Parliament, and is a breach and contempt of the Privileges of Parliament.

The House of Commons instructed the Hansards not to raise a defence of truth, but to base their defence solely on the fact that the publication had been authorised by the House of Commons. The Hansards pleaded their defence on that basis. However, the Court of Queen's Bench held that their claim to parliamentary privilege was no defence to an action for libel.

Stockdale v Hansard
(1839) 9 Ad & E 1; 112 ER 1112

Lord Denman: [107] The plea, it is contended, establishes a good defence to the action on various grounds.

1. The grievance complained of appears to be an act done by order of the House of Commons, a Court superior to any Court of Law, and none of whose proceedings are to be questioned in any way.

This principle the learned counsel for the defendant repeatedly avowed in his long and laboured argument; but it does not appear to be put forward in its simple terms in the report that was published by a former House of Commons.

It is a claim for an arbitrary power to authorise the commission of any act whatever, on behalf of a body [108] which in the same argument is admitted not to be the supreme power in the State.

The supremacy of Parliament, the foundation on which the claim is made to rest, appears to me completely to overturn it, because the House of Commons is not the Parliament, but only a co-ordinate and component part of the Parliament. That sovereign power can make and unmake the laws; but the concurrence of the three legislative estates is necessary; the resolution of any one of them cannot alter the law, or place any one beyond its control. The proposition is therefore wholly untenable, and abhorrent to the first principles of the Constitution of England.

The next defence involved in this plea is, that the defendant committed the grievance by order of the House of Commons in a case of privilege, and that each House of Parliament is the sole judge of its own privileges. This last proposition requires to be first considered. For, if the Attorney-General was right in contending, as he did more than once in express terms, that the House of Commons, by claiming any thing as its privilege, thereby makes it a matter of privilege, and also that its own decision upon its own claim is binding and conclusive, then plainly this Court cannot proceed in any enquiry into the matter, and has nothing else to do but declare the claim well founded because it has been made.

This is the form in which I understand the committee of a late House of Commons to have asserted the privileges of both Houses of Parliament: and we are informed that a large majority of that House adopted the assertion. It is not without the utmost respect and [109] deference that I proceed to examine what has been promulgated by such high authority ... But, when one of my fellow subjects presents himself before me in this Court, demanding justice for an injury, it is not at my option to grant or withhold redress; I am bound to afford it if the law declares him entitled to it. I must then ascertain how the law stands ...

Parliament is said to be supreme; I most fully acknowledge its supremacy. It follows, then, as before observed, that neither branch of it is supreme when acting by itself. It is also said that the privilege of each House is the privilege of the whole Parliament. In one sense I agree to this; because whatever impedes the proper action of either impedes those functions which are necessary for the performance of their joint duties. All the essential parts of a machine must be in order before it can work at all. But it by no means follows that the opinion that either House may entertain of the extent of its own privileges is correct, or its declaration of them binding ...

[110] I am far from believing that the Judges ever had, or ought to have, by law, the smallest power over Parliament or either House of Parliament. The independence of Parliament is the corner stone of our free [111] Constitution. The Judges who invaded it in the reign of James the First and his son have justly shared with those who betrayed the rights of the people in the case of ship money the abhorrence of all enlightened men. But a mean submissiveness to power has not been always confined to the Judges ... When we remember the sentence pronounced against an unfortunate gentlem[a]n of the name of Floyde, for a slight offence, if it were one, against King James the First, in speaking of his daughter and son in law, we shall allow that the two Houses had as little sense of independence as of justice. The Commons resolved, declared, and adjudged that his fortune should be confiscated, and his body tortured, his name degraded, and himself imprisoned for life. The Lords rebuked the invasion of their privileges of punishing, for which the Commons humbly apologised; but the sentence was carried into full effect: and can any one believe that these two Houses, thus vying in obsequiousness and cruelty, could entertain good views on the constitutional independence of Parliament? ...

[113] [T]he privilege of having their debates unquestioned, though denied when the members began to speak their minds freely in the time of Queen Elizabeth, [114] and punished in its exercise both by that princess and her two successors, was soon clearly perceived to be indispensable and universally acknowledged. By consequence, whatever is done within the walls of either assembly must pass without question in any other place. For speeches made in Parliament by a member to the prejudice of any other person, or hazardous to the public peace, that member enjoys complete impunity. For any paper signed by the Speaker by order of the House, though to the last degree calumnious, or even if it brought personal suffering upon individuals, the Speaker cannot be arraigned in a Court of Justice. But, if the calumnious or inflammatory speeches should be reported and published, the law will attach responsibility on the publisher. So, if the Speaker, by authority of the House, order an illegal Act, though that authority shall exempt him from question, his order shall no more justify the person who executed it than King Charles's warrant for levying ship-money could justify his revenue officer ...

[148] I come at length to consider whether this privilege of publication exists. The plea states the resolution of the House that all Parliamentary reports printed for the use of the House should be sold to the public, and that these several papers were ordered to be printed, not however stating that they were printed for the use of the House. It then sets forth the resolution and adjudication before set out. We know, by looking at the documents referred to at the Bar, that this resolution and adjudication could not justify the libel complained of, because it was not in fact passed till after action brought. But, passing over all minor objections, I assume that the defendant has properly pleaded a claim, on the part of the House, to authorise the indiscriminate publication and sale of all such papers as the House may order to be printed for the use of its members.

The Attorney-General would preclude us from commencing this enquiry. He protests against our taking any other step than that of recording the judgment already given in the Superior Court, and registering the edict which Mr Hansard brings to our knowledge. But, having convinced myself that the mere order of the House will not justify an act otherwise illegal, and that the simple declaration that that order is made in exer-[149]-cise of a privilege does not prove the privilege, it is no longer optional with me to decline or accept the office of deciding whether this privilege exist in law. If it does, the defendant's prayer must be granted and judgment awarded in his favour; or, if it does not, the plaintiff, under whatever disadvantage he may appear before us, has a right to obtain at our hands, as an English subject, the establishment of his lawful rights and the means of enforcing them ...

[155] The practice of a ruling power in the State is but a feeble proof of its legality. I know not how long the practice of raising ship-money had prevailed before the right was denied by

Hampden; general warrants had been issued and enforced for centuries before they were questioned in actions by Wilkes and his associates, who, by bringing them to the test of law, procured their condemnation and abandonment. I apprehend that acquiescence on this subject proves, in the first place, too much; for the admitted and grossest abuses of privilege have never been questioned by suits in Westminster Hall. The most obvious reason is, that none could have commenced a suit of any kind for the purpose, without **[156]** incurring the displeasure of the offended House, instantly enforced, if it happened to be sitting, and visiting all who had been concerned. During the session, it must be remembered that privilege is more formidable than prerogative, which must avenge itself by indictment or information, involving the tedious process of law, while privilege, with one voice, accuses, condemns, and executes. And the order to "take him," addressed to the serjeant at arms, may condemn the offenders to persecution and ruin. Who can wonder that early acquiescence was deemed the lesser evil, or gravely argue that it evinced a general persuasion that the privilege existed in point of law? ...

[161] I am of opinion, upon the whole case, that the defence pleaded is no defence in law, and that our judgment must be for the plaintiff on this demurrer.

In August 1839, Parliament was prorogued until the following January. Thereupon Stockdale brought a third action against the Hansards for libel. This time, the Hansards offered no defence and the jury awarded damages of £600. Stockdale applied to the Sheriff of Middlesex for a writ of *fieri facias*, that is, a writ of execution under which the Sheriff would seize the defendants' goods and sell them in satisfaction of judgment. The Sheriff's officers duly seized and sold goods belonging to the Hansards, but deferred any payment of the money to Stockdale until the legality of such a payment could be tested by further court proceedings.

On 16 January 1840, while those proceedings were still pending, Parliament reconvened. On 21 January 1840, the House of Commons resolved that the seizure and sale of the goods had been in contempt of the House, and ordered the Sheriff to refund the money. The office of Sheriff of Middlesex was held by two men, William Evans and John Wheelton, and they were summoned before the House of Commons. The House resolved that they be committed to the custody of the serjeant-at-arms and that the Speaker issue a warrant accordingly.

On 22 January 1840, while Evans and Wheelton were being held in custody by the serjeant-at-arms, the Court of Queen's Bench heard argument on the return of a summons obtained by Stockdale, calling on Evans and Wheelton to show cause why they should not now hand over to Stockdale the proceeds of the execution. The Court ordered them to do so.

Stockdale v Hansard
(1840) 11 Ad & E 253; 113 ER 411

Lord Denman: [263] The plaintiff has recovered damages in an action, and has sued out process of execution in due course of law. What is to prevent him from obtaining the fruits of that execution? Nothing that I am able to perceive. I infer, from the resolutions brought before us, that the House of Commons disapprove of our judgment in the former case between these parties, and I deeply lament it; but the opinion of that House on a legal point, in whatever manner communicated, is no ground for arresting the course of law, or preventing the operation of the Queen's writs in behalf of every one of her subjects who sues in her Courts.

Meanwhile, Evans and Wheelton, still held in custody by the serjeant-at-arms, obtained a writ of habeas corpus returnable before the Court of Queen's Bench. The warrant for the arrest had not stated the grounds on which the House of Commons had adjudged them guilty of contempt. The Court of Queen's Bench therefore held that the two men had to remain in custody.

The Case of the Sheriff of Middlesex
(1840) 11 Ad & E 273; 113 ER 419

Lord Denman: [285] I think it necessary to declare that the judgment delivered by this Court last Trinity term, in the case of *Stockdale v Hansard* ([(1839)] 9 A & E 1), appears to me in all respects correct. The Court decided that there was no power in this country above being questioned by law. The House of Commons there **[286]** attempted to place its privilege on the footing of an unquestionable and unlimited power ... I endeavoured to establish that the claim advanced in that case tended to a despotic power which could not be recognised or exist in this country, and that the privilege of publication, as there asserted, had no legal foundation. To all these positions I, on farther consideration, adhere; all of them I believe in my conscience to be true. And if this were not so, it is strange that the case should not have been brought before the other ten Judges by writ of error. The House could have suffered no loss of dignity by submitting to them the question which it had already laid before us ...

[291] On the motion for a **[292]** habeas corpus, there must be an affidavit from the party applying; but the return, if it discloses a sufficient answer, puts an end to the case: and I think the production of a good warrant is a sufficient answer. Seeing that, we cannot go into the question of contempt on affidavit, nor discuss the motives which may be alleged. Indeed (as the Courts have said in some of the cases) it would be unseemly to suspect that a body, acting under such sanctions as a House of Parliament, would, in making its warrant, suppress facts which, if discussed, might entitle the person committed to his liberty. If they ever did so act, I am persuaded that, on further consideration, they would repudiate such a course of proceeding. What injustice might not have been committed by the ordinary Courts in past times, if such a course had been recognised! as, for instance, if the recorder of London, in *Bushell's case* [(1670) Vaugh 135; 124 ER 1006], had, in the warrant of commitment, suppressed the fact that the jurymen were imprisoned for returning a verdict of acquittal. I am certain that such will never become the practice of any body of men amenable to public opinion.

In the present case, I am obliged to say that I find no authority under which we are entitled to discharge these gentlemen from their imprisonment.

Although, on 22 January 1840, Stockdale had obtained an order requiring Evans and Wheelton to pay him the proceeds of the execution, they did not comply with that order, as they were still held in custody by the serjeant-at-arms. Accordingly, on 27 January 1840, Stockdale returned to the Court of Queen's Bench to apply for a writ of attachment against them. The two men replied by affidavits stating that they were still in custody; but the writ was granted.

Wheelton was released from House of Commons custody on compassionate grounds on 11 February 1840, and Evans on 7 March 1840. The end of the story came when the *Parliamentary Papers Act 1840* (Imp) received the Royal Assent. That Act gave statutory protection to reports, papers, votes or proceedings published on the authority of the House of Commons. A similar Act has been adopted in other parliamentary systems patterned on the Westminster model (see *Parliamentary Papers Act 1908* (Cth)).

On the larger issue, the result was a stand-off. By persistently upholding Stockdale's rights, the Court of Queen's Bench was defying the Parliament. By persistently resisting any enforcement of Stockdale's rights, the House of Commons was defying the court. Yet neither institution directly confronted the other. Instead, Wheelton and Evans bore the brunt of their mutual unwillingness to do so.

Both the courts' jurisdiction over questions of law and their ultimate deference to the power of Parliament to control its own affairs were reaffirmed in a series of cases beginning with *Clarke v Bradlaugh* (1881) 7 QBD 38. Charles Bradlaugh was a self-proclaimed atheist who was elected to Parliament in 1880. Under the *Parliamentary Oaths Act 1866* (Imp), every new member was required to swear an oath of allegiance, subject only to an exception for "Quakers and every other person for the time being permitted by law to make a solemn affirmation". Bradlaugh was not a Quaker, nor otherwise legally permitted to affirm, yet given his professed beliefs he could not in conscience swear a religious oath. The plaintiff in *Clarke v Bradlaugh* sued as a common informer, complaining that Bradlaugh had not complied with the *Parliamentary Oaths Act* and was therefore not entitled to sit in the House of Commons. The Court of Appeal accepted that argument and Bradlaugh's seat was vacated. The result was upheld on appeal to the House of Lords (*Bradlaugh v Clarke* (1883) 8 App Cas 354).

Thereafter, Bradlaugh was repeatedly re-elected, but repeatedly expelled from the House. Finally, in July 1883 the House of Commons resolved that he be excluded from the House until he undertook to disturb it no longer. He sued for a declaration that this resolution was invalid and an injunction to restrain the serjeant-at-arms from carrying it out. His action failed.

Bradlaugh v Gossett
(1884) 12 QBD 271

Stephen J: [277] Taken by itself, the order of the 9th of July states nothing except that the House had by resolution excluded a member, who in the judgment of the House had disturbed its proceedings, till he undertook not [278] further to disturb it. It is obvious that we could not interfere with what might be a mere measure of internal discipline. The order as it stands is consistent with the supposition that Mr Bradlaugh, on presenting himself to take the oath, had in some way misconducted himself, and that the House had ordered him to be excluded till he promised not to repeat his misconduct. With such a measure of internal discipline we obviously could not interfere. The correspondence with the Speaker certainly sets the matter in a different light …

The legal question which … appears to me to [arise] for our decision is this:– Suppose that the House of Commons forbids one of its members to do that which an Act of Parliament requires him to do, and, in order to enforce its prohibition, directs its executive officer to exclude him from the House by force if necessary, is such an order one which we can declare to be void and restrain the executive officer of the House from carrying out? In my opinion, we have no such power. I think that the House of Commons is not subject to the control of Her Majesty's Courts in its administration of that part of the statute-law which has relation to its own internal proceedings, and that the use of such actual force as may be necessary to carry into effect such a resolution as the one before us is justifiable.

Many authorities might be cited for this principle; but I will quote two only. The number might be enlarged with ease by reference to several well-known cases. Blackstone says: "The whole of the law and custom of Parliament has its original from this one maxim, 'that whatever matter arises concerning either House of Parliament ought to be examined, discussed, and adjudged in that House to which it relates, and not elsewhere.'" This principle is re-stated nearly in Blackstone's words by each of the judges in the case of *Stockdale v Hansard* [(1839) 9 Ad & E 1; 112 ER 1112] …

[284] It is certainly true that a resolution of the House of Commons cannot alter the law. If it were ever necessary to do so, this Court would assert this doctrine to the full extent to which it was asserted in *Stockdale v Hansard*. The statement that the resolution of the House of Commons was illegal, must I think, be assumed to be true, for the purposes of the present case. The demurrer for those purposes admits it. We decide nothing unless we decide that, even if it is illegal in the sense of being opposed to the Parliamentary Oaths Act, it does not entitle the plaintiff to the relief sought. This admission, however, must be regarded as being made for the purposes of argument only. It would, as I have already said, be wrong for us to suggest or assume that the House acted otherwise than in accordance with its own view of the law; and, as we know not what that view is, nor by what arguments it is supported, we can give no opinion [285] upon it. I do not say that the resolution of the House is the judgment of a Court not subject to our revision; but it has much in common with such a judgment. The House of Commons is not a Court of Justice; but the effect of its privilege to regulate its own internal concerns practically invests it with a judicial character when it has to apply to particular cases the provisions of Acts of Parliament. We must presume that it discharges this function properly and with due regard to the laws, in the making of which it has so great a share. If its determination is not in accordance with law, this resembles the case of an error by a judge whose decision is not subject to appeal. There is nothing startling in the recognition of the fact that such an error is possible. If, for instance, a jury in a criminal case give a perverse verdict, the law has provided no remedy. The maxim that there is no wrong without a remedy does not mean, as it is sometimes supposed, that there is a legal remedy for every moral or political wrong. If this were its meaning, it would be manifestly untrue. There is no legal remedy for the breach of a solemn promise not under seal and made without consideration; nor for many kinds of

verbal slander, though each may involve utter ruin: nor for oppressive legislation, though it may reduce men practically to slavery; nor for the worst damage to person and property inflicted by the most unjust and cruel war. The maxim means only that legal wrong and legal remedy are correlative terms; and it would be more intelligibly and correctly stated, if it were reversed, so as to stand, "Where there is no legal remedy, there is no legal wrong." ...

[286] We ought not to try to make new laws, under the pretence of declaring the existing law. But I must add that this is not a case in which I at least feel tempted to do so. It seems to me that, if we were to attempt to erect ourselves into a Court of Appeal from the House of Commons, we should consult neither the public interest, nor the interests of parliament and the constitution, nor our own dignity. We should provoke a conflict between the House of Commons and this Court, which in itself [287] would be a great evil; and, even upon the most improbable supposition of their acquiescence in our adverse decision, an appeal would lie ... to the Court of Appeal, and thence to the House of Lords, which would thus become the judge in the last resort of the powers and privileges of the House of Commons.

4. The Westminster Constitution

The picture of British constitutionalism presented in the late 19th century by AV Dicey (1835-1922) proved tremendously influential both in the United Kingdom and Australia. In the 1890s, Dicey's writings clearly influenced the framers of the Australian Constitution, and helped to shape its drafting. Dicey argued that the fundamental principles of British constitutional law were representative democracy, parliamentary sovereignty and the rule of law.

(a)   Parliamentary Sovereignty

AV Dicey, *Introduction to the Study of the Law of the Constitution*
(Macmillan, 1st ed 1885, 10th ed 1959)

[39] THE NATURE OF PARLIAMENTARY SOVEREIGNTY
The sovereignty of Parliament is (from a legal point of view) the dominant characteristic of our political institutions.

My aim in this chapter is, in the first place, to explain the nature of Parliamentary sovereignty and to show that its existence is a legal fact, fully recognised by the law of England; in the next place, to prove that none of the alleged legal limitations on the sovereignty of Parliament have any existence; and, lastly, to state and meet certain speculative difficulties which hinder the ready admission of the doctrine that Parliament is, under the British constitution, an absolutely sovereign legislature.

A. *Nature of Parliamentary Sovereignty.* – Parliament means, in the mouth of a lawyer (though the word has often a different sense in ordinary conversation), the Queen, the House of Lords, and the House of Commons; these three bodies acting together may be aptly described as the "Queen in Parliament," and constitute Parliament.

The principle of Parliamentary sovereignty means neither more nor less than this, namely, that Parliament thus defined has, under the English constitu-[40]-tion, the right to make or unmake any law whatever; and, further, that no person or body is recognised by the law of England as having a right to override or set aside the legislation of Parliament.

A law may, for our present purpose, be defined as "any rule which will be enforced by the courts." The principle then of Parliamentary sovereignty may, looked at from its positive side, be thus described: Any Act of Parliament, or any part of an Act of Parliament, which makes a new law, or repeals or modifies an existing law, will be obeyed by the courts.

The same principle, looked at from its negative side, may be thus stated: There is no person or body of persons who can, under the English constitution, make rules which override or derogate from an Act of Parliament, or which (to express the same thing in other words) will be enforced by the courts in contravention of an Act of Parliament ...

[59] *The Vote of Parliamentary Electors.* – Expressions are constantly used in the course of political discussions which imply that the body of persons entitled to choose members of Parliament possess under the English constitution some kind of legislative authority. Such language is, as we shall see, not without a real meaning; it points to the important consideration that the wishes of the constituencies influence the action of Parliament. But any expressions which attribute to Parliamentary electors a legal part in the process of law-making are quite inconsistent with the view taken by the law of the position of an elector. The sole legal right of electors under the English constitution is to elect members of Parliament. Electors have no legal means of initiating, of sanctioning, or of repealing the legislation of Parliament. No court will consider for a moment the argument that a law is invalid as being opposed to the opinion of the electorate; their opinion can be legally expressed through Parliament, and through Parliament alone …

[60] *The Law Courts.* – A large proportion of English law is in reality made by the judges, and whoever wishes to understand the nature and the extent of judicial legislation in England, should read Pollock's admirable essay on the *Science of Case Law* … All that we need note [here] is that the adhesion by our judges to precedent, that is, their habit of deciding one case in accordance with the principle, or supposed principle, which governed a former case, leads inevitably to the gradual formation by the courts of fixed rules for decision, which are in effect laws. This judicial legislation might appear, at first sight, inconsistent with the supremacy of Parliament. But this is not so. English judges do not claim or exercise any power to repeal a Statute, whilst Acts of Parliament may override and constantly do override the law of the judges. Judicial legislation is, in short, subordinate legislation, carried on with the assent and subject to the supervision of Parliament …

[75] Nothing is more certain than that no English judge ever conceded, or, under the present constitution, can concede, that Parliament is in any legal sense a "trustee" for the electors. Of such a feigned "trust" the courts know nothing. The plain truth is that as a matter of law Parliament is the sovereign power in the state, and that the "supposition" [to that effect] treated by Austin as inaccurate is the correct statement of a legal fact which forms the basis of our whole legislative and judicial system. It is, however, equally true that in a political sense the electors are **[76]** the most important part of, we may even say are actually, the sovereign power, since their will is under the present constitution sure to obtain ultimate obedience. The language therefore of Austin is as correct in regard to "political" sovereignty as it is erroneous in regard to what we may term "legal" sovereignty. The electors are a part of and the predominant part of the politically sovereign power. But the legally sovereign power is assuredly, as maintained by all the best writers on the constitution, nothing but Parliament …

As to the actual limitations on the sovereign power of Parliament. – The actual exercise of authority by any sovereign whatever, and notably by Parliament, is bounded or controlled by two limitations. Of these the one is an external, the other is an internal limitation.

The external limit to the real power of a sovereign consists in the possibility or certainty that his subjects, **[77]** or a large number of them, will disobey or resist his laws …

[80] The internal limit to the exercise of sovereignty arises from the nature of the sovereign power itself. Even a despot exercises his powers in accordance with his character, which is itself moulded by the circumstances under which he lives, including under that head the moral feelings of the time and the society to which he belongs … The combined influence both of the external and of the internal limitation on legislative **[81]** sovereignty is admirably stated in Leslie Stephen's *Science of Ethics*, whose chapter on "Law and Custom" contains one of the best statements to be met with of the limits placed by the nature of things on the theoretical omnipotence of sovereign legislatures.

> "Lawyers are apt to speak as though the legislature were omnipotent, as they do not require to go beyond its decisions. It is, of course, omnipotent in the sense that it can make whatever laws it pleases, inasmuch as a law means any rule which has been made by the legislature. But from the scientific point of view, the power of the legislature is of course strictly limited. It is limited, so to speak, both from within and from without; from within, because the legislature is the product of a certain social condition, and determined by whatever determines the society; and from without, because the power of imposing laws is dependent upon the instinct of subordination, which is itself limited. If a legislature decided that all blue-eyed babies should be murdered, the preservation of blue-eyed babies would be illegal; but legis-

lators must go mad before they could pass such a law, and subjects be idiotic before they could submit to it."

Despite its apparent dominance, the doctrine of parliamentary sovereignty has been subject to recurrent questioning. According to RFV Heuston, *Essays in Constitutional Law* (Stevens, 2nd ed 1964), the doctrine is "[1] almost entirely the work of Oxford men". The Oxford men he had in mind were Thomas Hobbes, William Blackstone and Dicey.

Geoffrey de Q Walker, "Dicey's Dubious Dogma of Parliamentary Sovereignty"
(1985) 59 *Australian Law Journal* 276

[276] According to Professor Dicey's theory of sovereignty, Parliament had absolute power. By way of legislation it could ... do anything at all, and there was no person or body in the kingdom with power to set its Acts aside. No matter that a purported statute trampled on ancient constitutional principles or flew in the face of the most deep-rooted customs and moral values of the people. No matter that Parliament could therefore validly pass retroactive criminal statutes or ... command that all blue-eyed babies be killed ...

Dicey could not cite a single case in support of his absolutist and unbalanced view of the Constitution, nor could he point to any reference to it in any statute or constitutional instrument. To use AWB Simpson's succinct words, "Dicey announced that it was the law that Parliament was omnicompetent, explained what this meant, and never devoted so much as a line to fulfilling the promise he made to demonstrate that this was so". His argument ... consisted of: (i) references to a number of far-reaching statutes passed by Parliament which had never been tested in court; (ii) the rejection of three possible limitations (morality and international law, the prerogative and the binding of following Parliaments – and on this subsidiary point he did cite some cases); and (iii) references to the writings of Blackstone ...

[278] The legal foundations of the theory are far less secure than Dicey revealed, however. In recent years the doctrine has been increasingly questioned. Professor Philip Allott has argued that the views that have grown up around Dicey's theory "fly in the face of 1,000 years of talk about 'fundamental law' by Kings, judges, political men and commentators". "If there is one thread which runs through the whole turbulent story of British constitutional development", he continues, "it is the belief that we are the servants of fundamental constitutional rules which were there before us and will be there after we are gone." He asks whether the development since 1689 of cabinet government, the party system and executive control of Parliament amounts to a factual and political change so fundamental as to unsettle the accepted basis of the Constitution. "It would be a painful irony if we had to conclude that the most fundamental principles of our constitution had led inevitably and unquestionably to 'elective dictatorship' in law as well as in fact, because those principles confer absolute and unlimited power on a body which, in conformity with accepted conventions of the constitution, is now in the grasp of 'the King outside Parliament'." ...

[279] [B]y dint of sheer repetition, academic preaching of the absolutist theory of sovereignty has diverted the attention of bench and bar away from the more limited and balanced principle developed by the common lawyers during the seventeenth century. This principle is one of parliamentary *supremacy*, not sovereignty, for as Sir Edward Coke declared in the debates on the liberty of the subject and the Petition of Right in 1628, "*'sovereign power' is no parliamentary word* ... Magna Charta is such a fellow that he will have no sovereign". Sir Thomas Wentworth continued, "our laws are not acquainted with sovereign power". Perhaps Pym's words are the clearest: "All our Petition is for the Laws of England and this power [the sovereign power claimed by the King] seems to be another distinct power from the power of the law ... *And we cannot leave to him a sovereign power when we never were possessed of it.*"

The debate was, of course, about the King's claim to reserve to *himself* a sovereign power. But the repeated assertions that the very notion of sovereign power was unknown to Parliament or to the law ... make it clear that what Parliament had in mind was a government of laws and not of men. Neither the Civil Wars nor the Restoration altered the picture ...

[283] It seems that Dicey's theory is like some huge, ugly Victorian monument that dominates the legal and constitutional landscape and exerts a hypnotic [284] effect on legal perception.

Professor Nevil Johnson has observed that it has in Britain become a serious obstacle to any fruitful constitutional development. But its foundations are weak and it has never clearly and formally, least of all democratically, been made part of our Constitutions.

Jeffrey Goldsworthy, *The Sovereignty of Parliament: History and Philosophy*
(Clarendon Press, 1999)

[233] If the doctrine of parliamentary sovereignty was a dogma, it was not Dicey's dogma, but that of the political nation as a whole.

But of course, the doctrine never was a dogma, in the sense of an unreasoned article of faith. The lawyers, statesmen, and political theorists, whose ideas [234] contributed to its evolution over many centuries, were not fools. They accepted the doctrine for many reasons, not all compatible with one another. These include the ideas that:

1. as a matter of either logical or practical necessity, there had to be a single, ultimate, and unlimited law-making power in the kingdom;
2. with the consent of his subjects in Parliament, the King exercised an absolute power to make law, conferred by and subject only to God;
3. Parliament was the highest court in the land, the authority of last resort from which no appeal was possible, which could make new laws as well as interpret and apply old ones;
4. if its authority were limited, Parliament might be unable to take extraordinary measures needed to protect the community in emergencies;
5. every generation must be equally free to make and change its law, as contemporary circumstances might require;
6. all subjects were represented in Parliament, and were therefore deemed to consent to its acts and to be estopped from disputing them;
7. Parliament's decisions reflected the collective wisdom of the entire community, which, if not infallible, was far superior to that of any other agency in the state;
8. the ability of the King, Lords, and Commons to check and balance one another was the best possible safeguard against tyranny;
9. judges could not be trusted with authority to nullify Parliament's judgments; and
10. to limit Parliament's powers to prevent it from abusing them would be to adopt a cure much more dangerous than the highly improbable disease of parliamentary tyranny.

Among Dicey's most constructive critics was W Ivor Jennings (1903-65).

WI Jennings, *The Law and the Constitution*
(University of London Press, 5th ed 1959)

[144] THE dominant characteristic of the British Constitution is, as has previously been emphasised, and as Dicey pointed out, the supremacy or sovereignty of Parliament. This means, in Dicey's words, that Parliament has the right to make or unmake any law whatever, and that no person or body is recognised by the law of England as having a right to override or set aside the legislation of Parliament.

The consequence is that not only the courts but everybody in the United Kingdom regard that as binding law which Parliament has enacted. It is not possible for any person to refuse to obey the orders of Parliament because they are not law, though it is possible for him to disobey on the ground that they ought not to be law. Nor is it possible, as it is in some countries such as the United States and most Commonwealth countries, for the courts to declare that an Act of Parliament need not be obeyed because it is *ultra vires* or beyond the powers of Parliament. These two assertions, it should be noted, are not the same. For though in most countries the powers of the legislature are limited, it is not necessarily the prerogative of the courts to refuse to obey legislation. The notion that a court of law could determine the legality of legislation [145] comes from the United States, where the Supreme Court assumed the power of declaring the statutes of Congress to be not applicable because they did not conform with the Constitution. The same power has either been assumed by the courts or provided by the constitutions in Canada, Australia, India, Pakistan, Ceylon, Ghana, and the Federation of Malaya. But many continental countries continue to follow the old principle that excess of legislative authority is a matter between the legislature and the electors. Consequently, the fact that the *courts* do not regard themselves as competent to restrict the exercise of the legislative power is not in itself conclusive of the extent of that power …

[147] Parliament may remodel the British Constitution, prolong its own life, legislate *ex post facto*, legalise illegalities, provide for individual cases, interfere with contracts and authorise the seizure of property, give dictatorial powers to the Government, dissolve the United Kingdom or the British Empire, introduce communism or socialism or individualism or fascism, entirely without legal restriction.

SOVEREIGNTY

Dicey has called this enormous legal power the "sovereignty" of Parliament. But this is a word of quasi-theological origin which may easily lead us into difficulties. Sovereignty was a doctrine developed at the close of the Middle Ages to advance the cause of the secular State against the claims of the Church. "Sovereignty," said Bodin in 1576, "is supreme power over citizens and subjects unrestrained by the laws." Though the sovereign was bound by divine law and the [148] law of nature, he could within these limits make what laws he liked: and in every community there must be such a sovereign. Developed by Hobbes, Bentham, and Austin, this theory has passed into the current legal theory of England. It appears particularly appropriate to us because it seems to fit the facts of English political institutions.

Yet if sovereignty is supreme power, Parliament is not sovereign. For there are many things, as Dicey and Laski both point out, which Parliament cannot do. "No Parliament," says Professor Laski, "would dare to disfranchise the Roman Catholics or to prohibit the existence of trade unions." Parliament is not the permanent and personal sovereign contemplated by Bodin. It consists of two groups of men, of which the members of one will within five years at most cease to have anything to do with Parliament, and who, if they wish to join "the best club in Europe" once again, must offer themselves through a complicated political organisation for re-election by a heterogeneous group of their fellow citizens. Since, if they wish for re-election, they may be called upon to give an account of their actions, they must consider in their actions what the general opinion about them may be. Parliament passes many laws which many people do not want. But it never passes any laws which any substantial section of the population violently dislikes.

[149] LEGAL AND POLITICAL SOVEREIGNTY

These considerations made Austin a little doubtful about the seat of sovereignty in England. Dicey felt compelled to draw a distinction between legal sovereignty and political sovereignty. "Legal sovereignty," he said, "is a merely legal conception, and means simply the power of law-making unrestricted by any legal limit." Whereas "that body is politically sovereign or supreme in a State the will of which is ultimately obeyed by the citizens of the State." Thus Parliament is the legal sovereign and the electors the political sovereign.

If this is so, legal sovereignty is not sovereignty at all. It is not supreme power. It is a legal concept, a form of expression which lawyers use to express the relations between Parliament and the courts. It means that the courts will always recognise as law the rules which Parliament makes by legislation; that is, rules made in the customary manner and expressed in the customary form. Unfortunately, Dicey does not use it in this sense when he proceeds to discuss the consequences of the sovereignty of Parliament. He draws two conclusions which are not necessarily true. In the first place, he assimilates all legislative authorities which are not "sovereign" and assumes that the same principles must apply to them, whether they are Dominion legislatures or town councils. And, in the [150] second place, he asserts the principle that, because of its sovereignty, Parliament cannot bind its future action.

"NON-SOVEREIGN" LEGISLATURES

The basis of the first of these assertions is a clear distinction between sovereign and non-sovereign legislatures. If sovereignty is supreme power, the fundamental problem of constitutional law is to determine its seat. Any legislative powers which are not vested in the "sovereign" must be derived from it. If, therefore, Parliament is truly a "sovereign," it is very different from any legislative body which is not. In this way a town council or a railway company with power to make byelaws may be likened to the United States Congress or the Dominion Parliament of Canada.

But we have seen that Parliament has not supreme power in this sense. It has powers derived from the law. So have the United States Congress, the Dominion Parliament of Canada, the London County Council, and the Southern Railway Company. The question then becomes one of the variety of legislative powers which these bodies possess. And we find that the law treats these bodies very differently. Parliament may pass laws on any subject. The Congress may pass laws of any sort on any subject within the ambit of its powers, and so may every legislature in the British Commonwealth. The only function of the courts is to determine whether legislation is within the limits of the powers, and these powers are wide general powers, which may be called powers of government.

[151] Indeed, in modern constitutional law it is frequently said that a legislature is "sovereign within its powers." This is, of course, pure nonsense if sovereignty is supreme power, for there are no "powers" of a sovereign body; there is only the unlimited power which sovereignty implies. But if sovereignty is merely a legal phrase for legal authority to pass any sort of laws, it is not entirely ridiculous to say that a legislature is sovereign in respect of certain subjects, for it may then pass any sort of laws on those subjects, but not on any other subjects.

No such phrase is used of local authorities or public utility corporations. They have the strictly limited powers set out in statutes. They have no general law-making powers on certain wide aspects of government. And in interpreting the powers the courts adopt a very different attitude. They are far more ready to declare an exercise of a power void: they regard as void any exercise of a power which they consider "unreasonable": and there are other rules of interpretation which rigidly limit the law-making capacity of the authority. In law there is no comparison between the Parliament of Canada and the London County Council. Decisions applying to the one cannot be used to explain the law applying to the other. Dicey's comparison is, as a matter of law, entirely beside the point.

LIMITATION OF A SOVEREIGN POWER

The same cause produces the second principle. "A sovereign power cannot, while retaining its sovereign character, restrict its own powers by any particular [152] enactment," says Dicey, repeating the sense of a proposition which Bodin himself had laid down. This is a perfectly correct deduction from the nature of a supreme power. If a prince has supreme power, and continues to have supreme power, he can do anything, even to the extent of undoing the things which he had previously done. If he grants a constitution, binding himself not to make laws except with the consent of an elected legislature, he has power immediately afterwards to abolish the legislature without its consent and to continue legislating by his personal decree.

But if the prince has not supreme power, but the rule is that the courts accept as law that which is made in the proper legal form, the result is different. For when the prince enacts that henceforth no rule shall be law unless it is enacted by him with the consent of the legislature, the law has been altered, and the courts will not admit as law any rule which is not made in that form. Consequently a rule subsequently made by the prince alone abolishing the legislature is not law, for the legislature has not consented to it, and the rule has not been enacted according to the manner and form required by the law for the time being.

The difference is this. In the one case there is sovereignty. In the other, the courts have no concern with sovereignty, but only with the established law. "Legal sovereignty" is merely a name indicating that the legislature has for the time being power to make [153] laws of any kind in the manner required by the law. That is, a rule expressed to be made by the Queen, "with the advice and consent of the Lords spiritual and temporal, and Commons in this present Parliament assembled, and by the authority of the same," will be recognised by the courts, *including a rule which alters this law itself*. If this is so, the "legal sovereign" may impose legal limitations upon itself, because its power to change the law includes the power to change the law affecting itself.

In recent times, there has been a search for a more principled approach to the power of Parliament. Trevor Allan has sought a solution in a reinterpretation of Diceyan theory. For Allan, parliamentary sovereignty is a concept that is intricately linked to representative democracy and thus cannot be exercised in an undemocratic manner.

TRS Allan, *Law, Liberty, and Justice:*
The Legal Foundations of British Constitutionalism
(Oxford University Press, 1993)

[282] *The limits of parliamentary sovereignty*

The legal doctrine of legislative supremacy expresses the courts' commitment to British parliamentary democracy. It provides for the exercise of the political will of the electorate through the medium of its parliamentary representatives. If an appropriate conception of the boundaries of the political community provides the framework for the doctrine's application, some conception of democracy must provide its substantive political content. In other words, the courts' continuing adherence to the legal doctrine of sovereignty must entail commitment to some irreducible, minimum concept of the democratic principle. In almost all likely circumstances, that political commitment will demand respect for the legislative measures adopted by Parliament as the representative assembly.

That respect, however, clearly cannot be a limitless one. A parliamentary enactment whose effect would be the destruction of any recognizable form of democracy – for example, a measure purporting to deprive a substantial section of the population of the vote on the grounds of their hostility to government policies – could not consistently be applied by the courts as law. Judicial obedience to the statute in such (unlikely) circumstances could not coherently be justified in terms of the doctrine of parliamentary sovereignty, since the statute would violate the political principle which the doctrine itself enshrines. The practice of judicial obedience to statute obviously cannot itself be based on the authority of statute: it can only reflect judicial understanding of what (in contemporary conditions) political morality demands. The limits of that practice of obedience must therefore be constituted by the boundaries of that morality. An enactment which threatened the essential elements of any plausible conception of democratic government would lie beyond those boundaries. It would forfeit, by the same token, any claim to be recognized as law.

Although, therefore, the familiar distinction between the application and interpretation of statute suffices for most practical purposes, it ultimately breaks down in the face of changing views of the contours of the political community – Britain or Europe? – or serious threats to the central tenets of liberal democracy. Presumptions of legislative intent, which draw their strength from the requirements of justice, as these are presently understood, cannot in normal circumstances override the explicit terms of an Act of Parliament. This is because a commitment to representative government and loyalty to democratic institutions are themselves basic constituents of political morality. Judicial percep-**[283]**-tions of justice must generally give way to the results of Parliament's deliberations, where they are plainly inconsistent. The legal authority of statute depends in the final analysis, however, on its compatibility with the central core of that morality which constitutes the rule of law.

If Parliament ceased to be a representative assembly, in any genuine sense of that idea, or if it proceeded to enact legislation undermining the democratic basis of our institutions, political morality might direct judicial resistance rather than obedience. No comfortable distinction between legal doctrine and political principle can ultimately be sustained. Such questions about the proper relationship between the courts and Parliament cannot be settled by resort to competing formulations of some supposed pre-existing legal rule: it is the scope and content of that rule – its meaning and application – which are themselves in issue. Answers can only be supplied as a matter of political theory – in terms of the values which we regard as fundamental to the constitutional order …

[290] These conclusions suggest how the apparent conflict between Dicey's 'guiding principles' of legislative sovereignty and the rule of law might finally be resolved. I have suggested that a statute which threatened fundamentally the central tenets of our democracy could derive no authority from the doctrine of sovereignty, properly understood. Implicit in Dicey's conception of the rule of law is a view of the rights of the individual as basic to the political order. The protection of the individual in civil society is guaranteed by his freedom from arbitrary rule, uncontrolled by law. Government officials are answerable to the courts for their treatment of him – [because of] the equal subjection of all classes to the ordinary law …

The limits of legislative supremacy are to be discovered, then, in that deeper constitutional morality from which the rule of law derives its strength and virtue.

(b)   The Rule of Law

AV Dicey, *Introduction to the Study of the Law of the Constitution*
(Macmillan, 1st ed 1885, 10th ed 1959)

[183] THE RULE OF LAW: ITS NATURE AND GENERAL APPLICATIONS

Two features have at all times since the Norman Conquest characterised the political institutions of England.

The first of these features is the omnipotence or undisputed supremacy throughout the whole country of the central government. This authority of the state or the nation was during the earlier periods of our history represented by the power of the Crown. The King was the source of law and the maintainer of order ... This royal supremacy has now passed into that sovereignty of Parliament which has formed the main subject of the foregoing chapters.

[184] The second of these features, which is closely connected with the first, is the rule or supremacy of law ...

[194] An Englishman naturally imagines that the rule of law (in the sense in which we are now using the term) is a trait common to all civilised societies. But this supposition is erroneous. Most European nations had indeed, by the end of the eighteenth century, passed through that stage of development (from which England emerged before the end of the sixteenth century) when nobles, priests, and others could defy the law. But it is even now far from universally true that in continental countries all persons are subject to one and the same law, or that the courts are supreme throughout the state. If we take **[195]** France as the type of a continental state, we may assert, with substantial accuracy, that officials – under which word should be included all persons employed in the service of the state – are, or have been, in their official capacity, to some extent exempted from the ordinary law of the land, protected from the jurisdiction of the ordinary tribunals, and subject in certain respects only to official law administered by official bodies.

There remains yet a third and a different sense in which the "rule of law" or the predominance of the legal spirit may be described as a special attribute of English institutions. We may say that the constitution is pervaded by the rule of law on the ground that the general principles of the constitution (as for example the right to personal liberty, or the right of public meeting) are with us the result of judicial decisions determining the rights of private persons in particular cases brought before the courts; whereas under many foreign constitutions the security (such **[196]** as it is) given to the rights of individuals results, or appears to result, from the general principles of the constitution ...

[202] That "rule of law," then, which forms a fundamental principle of the constitution, has three meanings, or may be regarded from three different points of view.

It means, in the first place, the absolute supremacy or predominance of regular law as opposed to the influence of arbitrary power, and excludes the existence of arbitrariness, of prerogative, or even of wide discretionary authority on the part of the government. Englishmen are ruled by the law, and by the law alone; a man may with us be punished for a breach of law, but he can be punished for nothing else.

It means, again, equality before the law, or the equal subjection of all classes to the ordinary law of the land administered by the ordinary law courts; the "rule of law" in this sense excludes the idea of any exemption of officials or others from the duty of **[203]** obedience to the law which governs other citizens or from the jurisdiction of the ordinary tribunals; there can be with us nothing really corresponding to the "administrative law" (*droit administratif*) or the "administrative tribunals" (*tribunaux administratifs*) of France. The notion which lies at the bottom of the "administrative law" known to foreign countries is, that affairs or disputes in which the government or its servants are concerned are beyond the sphere of the civil courts and must be dealt with by special and more or less official bodies. This idea is utterly unknown to the law of England, and indeed is fundamentally inconsistent with our traditions and customs.

The "rule of law," lastly, may be used as a formula for expressing the fact that with us the law of the constitution, the rules which in foreign countries naturally form part of a constitutional code, are not the source but the consequence of the rights of individuals, as defined and enforced by the courts; that, in short, the principles of private law have with us been by the action of the courts and

Parliament so extended as to determine the position of the Crown and of its servants; thus the constitution is the result of the ordinary law of the land.

WI Jennings, *The Law and the Constitution*
(University of London Press, 5th ed 1959)

[45] THE RULE OF LAW AND THE LIBERAL TRADITION

If the rule of law is a synonym for law and order, most States have achieved it, and it is a universally recognised principle. The degree of obedience varies from country to country; but, to use traditional English phrases, the king's peace exists over the whole country and the king's writ runs everywhere. For later generations, however, this was not necessarily enough. An all-powerful monarch or dictator may be as dangerous to the liberty and happiness of the people as a collection of bandits. He may be, in other words, no more than a bigger and better bandit. Louis XIV could claim that he maintained order in his own dominions because he was the State; but some of his subjects escaped with relief across the Channel and discovered with gratitude the comparative liberty that existed on English soil. The rise of liberalism and the burden of despotic rule created popular leaders prepared to rebel. As the liberal tradition developed on English principles and by French methods, many monarchs shared the fate of Louis XVI or were urged unceremoniously into retirement. It was considered necessary to extend the notion and ambit of the rule of law. It ceased to be **[46]** only a rule among citizens and became also a rule among rulers.

This development results essentially from liberal or liberal-democratic principles, and therefore the rule of law in this sense is not universally accepted. If it is believed that the individual finds his greatest happiness, or best develops his soul, in a strong and powerful State, and that government implies not the chaos of competing interests stimulated by self-seeking demagogues but the unity of the nation behind a wise and beneficent leader, the rule of law is a pernicious doctrine. Or, even if it is believed that there are no universal principles of government, and that each nation must achieve its destiny by the methods which suit the spirit and the ethos of its history, the rule of law, which may perhaps be regarded as suitable for Anglo-Saxons and Frenchmen, is not a product capable of export. Like good wine, it does not travel.

BRITISH EXPERIENCE

The peculiarity of English history is that absolutism, except for a short time under the Common-wealth, and then only in a mild form (for Cromwell and his army were honest and God-fearing men), has never developed. The king's authority was limited by his barons. They compelled John, for instance, to seal Magna Carta, an instrument which, though intended primarily to safeguard the liberties of lords, was regarded as a safeguard for the liberties of the people by generations that knew not lords and feared only the king. Later kings had to fight the great landowners; and though they often won they sometimes lost. When lords dis-**[47]**-appeared there was in existence a Parliament strong enough to curb the royal authority, to partake of the royal power, to contest its limits, and finally to destroy the king whose ideas and actions went beyond the bounds of what Parliament thought reasonable. The Revolution of 1642 was not a great social upheaval designed, like the French Revolution, to overthrow a system of despotic government and the society on which it was based, but a mere contest between king and Parliament. Since the final victory of Parliament in 1689, therefore, the rule of law in this liberal sense has existed in England. Indeed, it was an English Parliamentary lawyer, Sir John Fortescue, who first drew attention to its characteristics, and the theorist of the English Revolution, John Locke, who laid down the doctrine of the liberal State.

Expressed in English terms, the rule of law in this liberal sense requires that the powers of the Crown and of its servants shall be derived from and limited by either legislation enacted by Parliament, or judicial decisions taken by independent courts. It is not enough to say with Dicey that "Englishmen are ruled by the law, and by the law alone" or, in other words, that the powers of the Crown and its servants are derived from the law; for that is true even of the most despotic State. The powers of Louis XIV, of Napoleon I, of Hitler, and of Mussolini were derived **[48]** from the law, even if that law be only "The Leader may do and order what he pleases." The doctrine involves some considerable limitation on the powers of every political authority, except possibly (for this is open to dispute) those of a representative legislature. Indeed it contains, as we shall see, something more, though it is not capable of precise definition. It is an attitude, an expression of liberal and democratic principles, in themselves vague when it is sought to analyse them, but clear enough in their results. There are many facets to free government, and it is easier to recognise it than to define it. It is clear, however, that it involves the notion that all governmental powers, save those of the representative legislature, shall be distributed and determined by reasonably precise laws. Accordingly a king or any other person acting on behalf of the State cannot exercise a power unless he can point to some specific rule of law which authorises his act. The State as a whole is regulated by law. For this reason, the doctrine is expressed in continental legal theory by saying that the State is a "legal State" – *Rechtsstaat, état de droit, stato di diritto* – and it has been the subject of a vast literature. It must be confessed that attempts to analyse its contents have not been very successful. Since fundamentally it requires a limitation of powers, most States have sought to attain it by written constitutions, for such a constitution is fundamental law which limits by express rules the powers of the various governing bodies and thus **[49]** substitutes constitutional government (in large part a synonym for the rule of law) for absolutism. It implies also a separation of powers, since the confusion of powers in one authority is dictatorship or absolutism, which, according to liberal ideas, is potential tyranny.

It contains also the notion of equality, a notion whose scope, however, is as imprecise as the notion of the rule of law itself. It was developed primarily as a principle to be used for criticism of the unequal distribution of property, and was so used in England in the Peasants' Revolt and by some of the sects in the Commonwealth. In the England of the eighteenth century, property did not in itself imply powers of government, though of course government was in fact in the hands of the landed interest; but elsewhere property and governmental privileges went together, and those who attacked property attacked privilege also. In the nineteenth century, the liberal tradition **[50]** ignored economic equality and concentrated upon what has been called "equality before the law." This concept does not imply that property should be distributed equally, nor that the same laws should apply to all persons in the same State. Indeed, the modern differentiation of economic and social functions, together with the growing intervention of the State in economic and social life, makes the latter principle, at least, impossible of attainment. Three-fourths of modern legislation is of no general interest, because it applies to special classes. Nor, apparently, does equality before the law necessarily imply political equality: it is only since 1928 that the British Parliamentary system has been based upon complete adult suffrage, and even now it is not proposed that the vote should be given to little children, however much they are doomed to lead us. The notion is really much more limited. It assumes that among equals the laws should be equal and should be equally administered, that like should be treated alike. The right to sue and be sued, to prosecute and be prosecuted, for the same kind of action should be the same for all citizens of full age and understanding, and without distinction of race, religion, wealth, social status, or political influence. There are certain parts of the law, including the ordinary law of contracts, torts, and crimes, which are of general application, which in other words apply to every person who is not incapacitated physically or mentally. Even here, however, a qualification is introduced, particularly in respect of the criminal law: for though the law usually creates crimes for all citizens of full age and understanding, it leaves a very large discretion in **[51]** its application. Not only is there a large discretion left in practice to the police as to whether they shall or shall not prosecute, but also the courts are expected to inflict punishment, if at all, not merely according to the nature of the crime, but according to the particular circumstances of the criminal. The primary purpose of judicial administration is not to punish crime but to prevent it.

In the criminal law, indeed, the rule of law implies a combination of the notion of equality before the law with the notion that the limits of police powers should be rigidly defined. The rule of law in this sense is expressed in the maxim, derived from nineteenth-century liberalism, *nulla poena sine lege*. Professor Jerome Hall has pointed out that this includes at least four notions. First, it means that the category of crimes should be determined by general rules of a more or less fixed character. Secondly, it implies that a person should not be punished except for a crime which falls within these general rules; or, as Dicey put it admirably (if his statement be taken to relate only to the criminal law, which in fact it did not) that "no man is punishable … except for a distinct breach of law established in the ordinary legal manner before the ordinary courts." Thirdly, it may mean that penal statutes should be strictly construed, so that no act may be made criminal which is not clearly covered by the statutes. Fourthly, it may mean that penal laws should never have retrospective effect …

[53] Above all, the rule of law implies the even less precise notion of liberty. Liberty and equality are of course closely associated, as in the slogan of the French Revolution, "Liberty, equality, fraternity." Liberty, like equality, was regarded as a fundamental or natural right which had in many States been destroyed by the development of absolute government. "Man is born free; and everywhere he is in chains," began Rousseau in the *Social Contract*. It was in the cause of liberty that Parliament raised an army against Charles I, and that the Paris crowd captured the Bastille … Indeed, the reaction to absolutism went very far. Largely through the influence of Kant it was assumed that the alternative to the despotic or police State (*Polizeistaat*) was the State which did nothing save maintain order and conduct external relations, and the latter kind of State has sometimes been called the *Rechtsstaat*. The same assumption was made by many in Great Britain during the first half of the nineteenth century. Under the influence of Adam Smith and Ricardo trade was freed from the shackles of mercantilism; and generally the Liberal Party, or the Whig wing of the Liberal Party, adopted the principles of *laissez-faire* or individualism, until after the second Reform Act in 1867 the notion of a free State exercising considerable functions on collect-ivist principles began to develop under the influence of the Radical wing of the Party. The writer who studied the nature of the rule of law in England in this kind of background was AV Dicey, whose exposition proved **[54]** to be so acceptable that until recently it was generally assumed that the rule of law and Dicey's exposition of it were the same.

In recent times, the rule of law has been subjected to strong criticism. Critics have argued that the formalism and neutrality which the rule of law claims to engender mask the hegemonic, economic and political underpinnings of law (see Roberto Unger, "The Critical Legal Studies Movement" (1983) 90 *Harvard Law Review* 561). There have also been strong feminist critiques of the rule of law (see Ngaire Naffine, *Law and the Sexes: Explorations in Feminist Jurisprudence* (Allen and Unwin, 1990), Chapters 2-3). Julius Stone has argued that the rule of law may be understood as an ethical, rather than merely a legal, doctrine.

Julius Stone, *Social Dimensions of Law and Justice*
(Maitland Publications, 1966)

[619] [I]nsofar as democracy is achieved, men appear to conform to legal rules not only under coercion but with a sense of ethical obligation, both the elements of coercion and of ethical conviction being vital. And those who exercise power in democratic societies also generally recognise the rules they apply and enforce as ethically binding on themselves. This is spectacularly seen in the English constitutional conventions, the restraints of which are accepted by the power-holders additionally to the rules of law themselves …

Recognition of this ethical component in democratic law is also an important corrective to misunderstandings of the doctrine of "the rule of law" made famous by Dicey. The heart of the doctrine seems rather to lie in the recognition by those in power that their **[620]** power is wielded and tolerated only subject to the restraints of shared socio-ethical convictions. The central *legal* point, that state officials and ideally state organs themselves must be answerable in the courts like all other persons and bodies, seems but a concrete application of this. But this *legal* point is not the main point about "the rule of law" for our present more general purpose.

Several important truths follow from the ethical import of the rule of law notion. One is that it is artificial and confused to juxtapose "the rule of law" and the sanctity of "human rights", as if these were competing ideals. A second is that, whatever its history, the rule of law notion is not a mere national legal doctrine, Anglo-Saxon or other. A third is that precepts as to "equal application" and organisational and procedural safeguards, such as the existence of an independent judiciary and bar, the opportunity to be heard by officials not involved in day-to-day adminis-tration, the right to a reasoned decision, and the right of appeal at least on points of law, express only part of the ideal. No less important are the substantive contents of law, and the existence of a responsible legislature, pre-supposing equality in the franchise and respect for the dignity of all individuals by legislative as well as judicial and administrative action. This substantive reference imports both a minimal justness of rules, and a dynamic responsiveness of substantive law to the needs of social and economic development.

"The rule of law" in any case, does *not* demand a uniform rule on all matters for every person in society, regardless of the merits of varying **[621]** situations. It does not make "the rule of the road" the model for all law, and condemn all laws aiming at a substantive ideal of justice. We have seen elsewhere that such a meaning raises insuperable philosophical and practical difficulties, and would condemn as violative of the "rule of law" great segments of traditional common law and equity, as well as of more recent legislation. They would mostly be segments which almost all thoughtful people regard as expressions of elementary social justice; and to the more traditional of them even Dicey himself took no exception. We have amply shown that equality as a value constantly has to compete, adjust and combine with other values. It is well to recognise, moreover, that if all this were not so, there would arise unbridgeable gaps between the ethical convictions of the community, and the use of power in that community. Historically the identification of "the rule of law" with mere *uniformity* of rules of law represented the dominant conviction of a particular important period. Its actual ambit even then never approached what was claimed for it. To infer from this an identification for all time, regardless of changes in men's convictions as to justice, would divorce the principles on which power is exercised from the values cherished by those subject to the power. This, by hypothesis, would strip power of all but domination. It would impair "the rule of law" in the more intelligible sense.

Another vital insight from this analysis is that mere conformity to law *in the lawyer's sense* is not sufficient for conformity to a meaningful ideal of "the rule of law". In *merely* the lawyer's sense it is not inconceivable that the unitary and supreme English Parliament might enact a law for the liquidation of opposition leaders. Such a law would obviously contradict an important part of whatever we can mean by "the rule of law". So far as restraints *by lawyer's law* are concerned, in short, the power even of a democratic legislature can be as naked as its members for the time being are willing to make it. This seems subject in the English unitary system only to the legal check of a general election, the *de facto* check of the ruler's anticipation of the people's reactions, and the extra-legal check of revolution. Under rigid constitutions like the Australian, Canadian and the American, it may, of course, also be subject to constitutional limitations by the separation of powers, bills of rights and the like.

Thus understood, "the rule of law" cannot be limited to the three rather formal propositions articulated by Dicey. By reducing it to those three propositions Dicey was trying to demonstrate that "the rule of law" is itself a rule of law (or more accurately three rules of law). Today it is much more.

International Commission of Jurists, *The Rule of Law in a Free Society* – Report of the International Congress of Jurists, New Delhi 1959
(Geneva, 1959)

[313] 1. The Rule of Law is a convenient term to summarize a combination of ideals and practical legal experience concerning which there is over a wide part of the world, although in embryonic and to some extent inarticulate form, a consensus of opinion among the legal profession.

2. Two ideals underlie this conception of the Rule of Law. In the first place, it implies without regard to the content of the law, that all power in the State should be derived from and exercised in accordance with the law. Secondly, it assumes that the law itself is based on respect for the supreme value of human personality.

3. The practical experience of lawyers in many countries suggests that certain principles, institutions and procedures are important safeguards of the ideals underlying the Rule of Law. Lawyers do not however claim that such principles, institutions and procedures are the only safeguards of these ideals and they recognize that in different countries different weight will be attached to particular principles, institutions and procedures.

4. The Rule of Law … may therefore be characterized as: 'The principles, institutions and procedures, not always identical, but broadly similar, which the experience and traditions of

lawyers in different countries of the world, often having themselves varying political structures and economic backgrounds, have shown to be important to protect the individual from arbitrary government and to enable him to enjoy the dignity of men'.

High Court judges have acknowledged the rule of law as an implicit, but undefined, part of Australia's constitutional system (for more explicit use in Canada, see *Re Manitoba Language Rights* [1985] 1 SCR 721, (1985) 19 DLR (4th) 1). In *Australian Communist Party v Commonwealth* (*Communist Party Case*) (1951) 83 CLR 1, Dixon J stated that the Constitution "[193] is an instrument framed in accordance with many traditional conceptions, to some of which it gives effect, as, for example, in separating the judicial power from other functions of government, others of which are simply assumed". He went on to say: "Among these I think that it may fairly be said that the rule of law forms an assumption". This cryptic statement has often been quoted, but, as Gummow and Hayne JJ stated in *Kartinyeri v Commonwealth* (*Hindmarsh Island Bridge Case*) (1998) 195 CLR 337, "[381] the occasion has yet to arise for consideration of all that may follow from [it]" (see also *Plaintiff S157/2002 v Commonwealth* (2003) 211 CLR 476 in Chapter 12, §4(b)).

(c)   Reconciling Parliamentary Sovereignty and the Rule of Law

AV Dicey, *Introduction to the Study of the Law of the Constitution*
(Macmillan, 1st ed 1885, 10th ed 1959)

[406] RELATION BETWEEN PARLIAMENTARY SOVEREIGNTY AND THE RULE OF LAW

The sovereignty of Parliament and the supremacy of the law of the land – the two principles which pervade the whole of the English constitution – may appear to stand in opposition to each other, or to be at best only counterbalancing forces. But this appearance is delusive; the sovereignty of Parliament, as contrasted with other forms of sovereign power, favours the supremacy of the law, whilst the predominance of rigid legality throughout our institutions evokes the exercise, and thus increases the authority, of Parliamentary sovereignty.

The sovereignty of Parliament favours the supremacy of the law of the land.

That this should be so arises in the main from two [407] characteristics or peculiarities which distinguish the English Parliament from other sovereign Powers.

The first of these characteristics is that the commands of Parliament (consisting as it does of the Queen, the House of Lords, and the House of Commons) can be uttered only through the combined action of its three constituent parts, and must, therefore always take the shape of formal and deliberate legislation. The will of Parliament can be expressed only through an Act of Parliament … The principle that Parliament speaks only through an Act of Parliament greatly increases the authority of the judges. A Bill which has passed into statute immediately becomes subject to judicial interpretation, and the English Bench have always refused, in principle at least, to interpret an Act of Parliament otherwise than by reference to the words of the enactment …

[408] The second of these characteristics is that the English Parliament as such has never, except at periods of revolution, exercised direct executive power or appointed the officials of the executive government.

Dicey's reconciliation of his two primary principles has been seen as unpersuasive. The idea of the rule of law is to prevent arbitrary government; but if Parliament can legislate anything it pleases, it cannot be bound by the rule of law, and thus can exercise its power arbitrarily.

WI Jennings, *The Law and the Constitution*
(University of London Press, 5th ed 1959)

[54] The particular principle of the individualist or *laissez-faire* school was that any substantial discretionary power was a danger to liberty. The fact that he held such a principle was not explicitly avowed by Dicey, because he assumed that he was analysing not his own subjective

notions (shared, of course, by many of his contemporaries), but the firm and unalterable principles of English constitutional law. It will be convenient to analyse his notion on that basis.

"No man," he said, "is punishable or can be lawfully made to suffer in body or goods except for a distinct breach of law established in the ordinary legal manner before the ordinary courts of the land. In this sense the rule of law is contrasted with every system of government based on the exercise by persons in authority of wide, arbitrary, or discretionary powers of constraint." ...

[55] If we look around us, we cannot fail to be aware that public authorities do in fact possess wide discretionary powers. Many of them formed part of the law even when Dicey wrote in 1885. Any court can punish me for contempt of court by imprisoning me for an indefinite period. If I am convicted of manslaughter, I may be released at once or imprisoned for life. If I am an alien, my naturalisation is entirely within the discretion of the Home Secretary. If the Queen declares war against the rest of the world, I am prohibited from having dealings abroad. If the country is in danger, my property can be taken, perhaps without compensation. If a public health authority wants to flood my land in order to build a reservoir it can take it from me compulsorily. I can be compelled to leave my work for a month or more, in order to serve on a jury. All these powers, and many more, were possessed by public authorities in 1885, and can still be exercised.

Dicey did not mention all these, because nowhere in his book did he consider the *powers* of authorities. He seemed to think that the British Constitution was concerned almost entirely with the *rights of individuals*. He was imagining a constitution dominated by the doctrine of *laissez-faire*. The function of government, as he unconsciously assumed, was to protect the individual against internal and external aggression. Given such protection, each individual was allowed to live his life almost as he pleased, so long as he did not interfere with the similar liberty of others. He re-[56]-garded this as desirable, and therefore tended to minimise the extent to which public authorities could interfere with private action ...

Nevertheless, the argument need not be placed entirely on this narrow ground. For the main discretionary power is placed in England not in the executive but in Parliament. Parliament, as has [57] already been emphasised, can pass what legislation it pleases. It is not limited by any written constitution. Its powers are not only wide, but unlimited. In most countries, not only the administrative authorities but also the legislature have powers limited by the constitution. This, one would think, is the most effective rule of law. In England, the administration has powers limited by legislation, but the powers of the legislature are not limited at all. There is still, it may be argued, a rule of law, but the law is that the law may at any moment be changed.

Dicey attempts to meet this argument in two ways. "The commands of Parliament," he said, "can be uttered only through the combined action of its three constituent parts, and must, therefore, always take the shape of formal and deliberate legislation." Formal it may be; it may not be deliberate. We saw – Dicey saw before he died in 1922 – how the Defence of the Realm Act was passed in 1914. The Cabinet decided that it wanted drastic powers. The majority which it commanded in the House of Commons supported its motion to suspend the Standing Orders. The Bill was passed through at one sitting. The House of Lords did the same. Thus at one stroke, without any long deliberation, the Cabinet acquired the powers it needed. The "gold standard" was similarly swept away in 1931. The Cabinet ordered the Bank of England not to exchange notes into gold. The next day Parliament met and the necessary legislation was passed through not only to make paper currency inconvertible, but also to ratify the illegal acts of the [58] Cabinet and of the Bank before the Act was passed. Here was arbitrary power indeed, but it was by no means as arbitrary as the power exercised by Parliament in 1939 and 1940.

Moreover, Parliament is not limited to the enunciation of general rules. It can give orders which are not strictly legislative. "The will of Parliament can be expressed only through an Act of Parliament," said Dicey; but it can express anything whatever. It can condemn a man to death as it condemned the Earl of Strafford. It can release an individual from compliance with the law, as it has done in many statutes. It can enable a landlord to enclose the common land on which his poor neighbours subsist, as it did in the host of Enclosure Acts. It can declare a marriage void or dissolve a marriage, as it frequently did before the Divorce Court was set up. It can enable one person to take the property of another, as it does in nearly every local Act. It can authorise the building of a power station which will be a nuisance to all those who live in the neighbourhood, as it does in some local Acts. It can place persons and property at the disposal of Her Majesty's Government.

"A Bill which has passed into a statute," said Dicey, "immediately becomes subject to judicial interpretation": but not if Parliament provides otherwise. And if Parliament does not like the interpretation given by the judges, it can always reverse the interpretation.

Dicey's view was that individual rights were adequately protected by the ordinary common law, and did not need special protection through a judicially enforceable Bill of Rights or any other mechanism specifically directed to the exercise of legislative and governmental power.

AV Dicey, *Introduction to the Study of the Law of the Constitution*
(Macmillan, 1st ed 1885, 10th ed 1959)

[197] In England the right to individual liberty is part of the constitution, because it is secured by the decisions of the courts, extended or confirmed as they are by the Habeas Corpus Acts ...

[198] Liberty is as well secured in Belgium as in England, and as long as this is so it matters nothing whether we say that individuals are free from all risk of arbitrary arrest, because liberty of person is guaranteed by the constitution, or that the right to personal freedom ... forms part of the constitution because it is secured by the ordinary law of the land.

[199] The Habeas Corpus Acts declare no principle and define no rights, but they are for practical purposes worth a hundred constitutional articles guaranteeing individual liberty. Nor let it be supposed that this connection between rights and remedies which depends on the spirit of law pervading English [200] institutions is inconsistent with the existence of a written constitution, or even with the existence of constitutional declarations of rights ...

The fact, again, that in many foreign countries the rights of individuals, *eg* to personal freedom, depend upon the constitution, whilst in England the law of the constitution is little else than a generalisation of the rights which the courts secure to individuals, has this important result. The general rights guaranteed by the constitution may be, and in foreign countries constantly are, suspended. They are something extraneous to and independent of the ordinary course of [201] the law ... Freedom from arbitrary arrest, the right to express one's opinion on all matters subject to the liability to pay compensation for libellous or to suffer punishment for seditious or blasphemous statements, and the right to enjoy one's own property, seem to Englishmen all to rest upon the same basis, namely on the law of the land. To say that the "constitution guaranteed" one class of rights more than the other would be to an Englishman an unnatural or a senseless form of speech ... Where, on the other hand, the right to individual freedom is part of the constitution because it is inherent in the ordinary law of the land, the right is one which can hardly be destroyed without a thorough revolution in the institutions and manners of the nation. The so-called "suspension of Habeas Corpus Act" bears, it is true, a certain similarity to what is called in foreign [202] countries "suspending the constitutional guarantees".

Eric Barendt, "Dicey and Civil Liberties"
[1985] *Public Law* 596

[599] The principal implication of [Dicey's approach], as Sir Ivor Jennings pointed out, is that Englishmen are free simply to do whatever the law does not prohibit. In other words, civil liberties are residual. There are no special laws protecting them, though there may be particular remedies fashioned by the judges or provided by statutes, as with the Habeas Corpus Acts. So, there is personal freedom from arbitrary arrest or invasion of property rights because the courts have not recognised the existence of those wide powers which would effectively curtail the freedoms. Here, of course, the third tenet of Dicey's "rule of law" only has substance because one or other, or both, of the other two principles are applicable ... *Entick v Carrington* [(1765) 19 St Tr 1030] ... shows perhaps all three principles of the rule of law: the courts' hostility to arbitrary powers, the subjection of everyone including government officials to the common law, and the formulation of freedoms through concrete litigation. It also evinces a judicial enthusiasm for general principles, markedly lacking in most English judges today. Would modern English judgments contain a sentiment such as: "The great end, for which men entered into society, was to secure their property.

That right is preserved sacred and incommunicable in all instances, where it has not been taken away or abridged by some public law for the good of the whole." Never mind the substance of this opinion: this type of approach would not now be adopted in a case involving freedom of speech, religion or any other fundamental right ...

But even judged from a contemporary perspective, the thesis – and in particular this third tenet of the rule of law – seems peculiar. The contrast drawn between the formulation of rights in a written constitution or Bill of Rights and judge-made or common law is surely overstated. At the least it needs refinement. Constitutions have to be interpreted and applied by the courts, so **[600]** that in a sense freedom of speech and personal freedom are as much judge-made law, say, in the United States as they are in Britain. Indeed, in the present day, when the role of the judiciary here is so much constrained by tightly-drawn statutes, judge-made law is much more significant in the USA, Germany and all other jurisdictions where the courts construe a constitution or Bill of Rights ...

Both judge-made law and statute are in various places in his constitutional writing contrasted with the broad declarations of principle found in written constitutions and Bills of Rights. Constitutional constraints on legislation are criticised for weakening the role of public opinion in developing **[601]** the law ... Dicey then might well have identified the protection of individual freedoms by concrete common law and legislative rules as one feature of the rule of law in England, a formulation which would incidentally have been perfectly compatible with the other tenets of the doctrine. Arthur Goodhart has pointed out that Anglo-American concepts of the rule of law usually exaggerate [the role of] the judicial process ... [since the rule of law] is also the responsibility of the legislative and executive branches of government. Moreover, Dicey would not have had so much difficulty in reconciling Parliamentary Sovereignty and the rule of law – surely one of the least happy chapters of his book – had he seen the latter as a legislative principle as well as a statement about the judicial role.

Is there any explanation for this aspect of Dicey's rule of law doctrine? I suspect the correct answer is rather dull and obvious. Even in the *Relation between Law and Public Opinion*, Dicey made no attempt to disguise his preference for the "judicial legislation" of the common law and equity. It is more concerned than statute law with the general symmetry of the law, with the requirements of certainty and consistency and generally with the requirements of justice. Acts of Parliament are frequently the work of "legislators who are much influenced by the immediate opinion of the moment, who make laws with little regard either to general principles or to logical consistency, and who are deficient in the skill and knowledge of experts." Moreover, the areas of civil liberties chosen by Dicey for discussion in the earlier work were at that time more or less entirely governed by common law decisions, as will shortly be seen in the context of freedom of speech and freedom to hold meetings. The Habeas Corpus Acts ... were regarded as meeting the deficiencies of the common law writ rather than establishing new principles. The thesis that the general principles of the Constitution rested on judicial decisions was, as Sir Ivor Jennings has said, a partial presentation of the true position; but it was then much more accurate than it would be now ...

[604] Dicey's account of these rights was and remains accurate as a statement of the law, but its tone trivialises the issues which ought to be discussed: should there be positive rights to hold public meetings? Should there at least be equal rights of access for all political parties and groups to use public premises for meetings? What powers should the police enjoy to prevent outbreaks of violence at such gatherings? The rule of law does not provide an adequate framework for tackling these problems. But the same is true of civil liberties generally. I shall now explain why Dicey's account of this subject is so defective for the present day ...

The press ... was in Dicey's view governed simply by the ordinary law of the land, and for him that meant the common law of criminal and civil libel. Statutory restrictions on speech and the exercise of other liberties were barely discussed, largely because they were then of relatively little significance. The absence of arbitrary power made so much of in *The Law of the Constitution* was an absence of autonomous executive or prerogative power; what we are more concerned with nowadays is the risk of governments abusing their powers through their de facto control of the legislature. Dicey appreciated that governments would from time to time need to acquire wider discretionary powers under Acts of Parliament, but he did not foresee that some of these, for example, the Official Secrets legislation and the Incitement to Disaffection Act, would remain permanent features of the statute book. And in the last page of his chapter dealing with the relation between the rule of law and sovereignty, he seems to have **[605]** exaggerated the extent to which the courts are prepared to limit the scope of legislation by the application of liberal common law principles.

The rule of law is a quite valueless doctrine these days unless it is accepted as a rule which binds the legislature, either as a matter of constitutional law or at least as a general political principle or convention. There is little evidence for its general acceptance by modern British legislators. Might may not be right, but a parliamentary majority is. This is shown by the ease with which governments have secured the passage of such legislation as the Immigration Acts, and the rules made under them, which to some extent have retrospective effects; other rules have recently been held by the European Court of Human Rights to discriminate against women. Moreover, governments of recent decades have proved reluctant to clarify or reform civil liberties law until there has been an adverse ruling of the European Court ... Where there has been no such impetus from abroad, British administrations prefer to remain idle ...

If Dicey more or less ignored the role of Parliament in safeguarding the values implicit in the rule of law, he surely exaggerated the willingness and ability of the judiciary to perform this task. Although one or two judges have been keen to protect fundamental freedoms, wherever possible, and to shape the common law accordingly, many more give them inadequate weight or refuse to recognise the presence of a civil liberties question ... **[606]** Major cases on the scope of contempt of court have paid little or no regard to free speech implications. And in some recent decisions, the courts have extended police powers of arrest and of seizure of property, before the Police and Criminal Evidence Act 1984 rendered further judicial innovation on this subject unnecessary. Of course, this is only a partial picture of judge-made law in the civil liberties field, but it is perhaps enough to show that Dicey's reliance on the judiciary fully to protect these freedoms was excessive.

Moreover, there is an inevitable drawback to the conclusion that in England freedoms are residual, in that everyone is free to do whatever the law does not prohibit. For this proposition is as true for the Government and other public authorities as it is for the ordinary citizen, an equality required by the rule of law itself. In *Malone v Metropolitan Police Commissioner* [[1979] Ch 344], the plaintiff claimed an injunction to restrain telephone tapping by the Post Office under the warrant of the Home Secretary and on behalf of the police who suspected that Malone had handled some stolen property. Sir Robert Megarry V-C refused to grant the remedy because the Post Office had committed no wrong; there was no trespass and English law does not recognise a cause of action for invasion of privacy. "If the tapping of telephones by the Post Office at the request of the police can be carried out without any breach of the law, it does not require any statutory or common law power to justify it: it can lawfully be done simply because there is nothing to make it unlawful." [[1979] Ch at 367] The same principles applied incidentally to prevent the common law developing any rules against discrimination; an employer, for example, was free to discriminate against blacks because this did not amount to any tort or wrong before the introduction of the Race Relations legislation.

Had the judge been a bold eighteenth century innovator, it is conceivable that he might have formulated a new tort of invasion of privacy, at least in this context, for it was clear that there was an injustice in the case which needed correction. But it is apparently no longer appropriate for the judiciary in England to create new rights; they and the citizen must wait for Parliament – or more **[607]** likely, the European Court of Human Rights. This surely shows the advantage of a positive statement of fundamental freedoms and rights in some constitutional document or other. In the absence of such a statement and of a well-recognised cause of action (for trespass or assault, for instance), the courts cannot protect interstitial residual freedoms. Dicey's obsession with remedies made him oblivious to the importance of rights ...

[608] Dicey's treatment of civil liberties, therefore, seems inadequate now, first, because it leaves out of account the serious erosion that may be made on the exercise of the freedoms through legislation enacted in disregard of the rule of law principles, secondly, in view of the change in character of the judiciary and their attitude to development of the common law, and thirdly and perhaps most importantly, because residual freedoms can never provide a firm support for judicial innovation.

Dicey's view that the common law is a sufficient protector of civil liberties has been superseded in the United Kingdom by the enactment of a statutory Bill of Rights – the *Human Rights Act 1998* (UK), which incorporates the European Convention for the Protection of Human Rights and Fundamental Freedoms 1950 into United Kingdom law. However, the Act still incorporates a significant degree of deference to parliamentary sovereignty: where a statute is found to infringe the European Convention, the only judicial remedy is a "declaration of incompatibility", which may then trigger a statutory amendment (or, in an extreme case, an interim amendment by executive order, without waiting for Parliament's approval).

Although it is true that the meaning judicially ascribed to a statute can always be over-ridden by statute, in practice this rarely happens; and the judges' power of interpreting statutes (and, indeed, the necessity of their doing so before a statute can be applied) is probably the most frequent and effective means by which parliamentary sovereignty is reconciled with the rule of law. It is aided by the related presumptions that statutes are not intended to alter the common law, and that they are not intended to impair civil liberties or fundamental human rights. The latter presumption, in particular, has frequently been applied by the High Court.

An early example is *Potter v Minahan* (1908) 7 CLR 277, where the Court held by 3:2 that an Australian-born person returning from overseas could not be regarded as an "immigrant" (see Chapter 20, §2). O'Connor J treated this as purely a question of construction under the *Immigration Restriction Act 1901* (Cth), and proceeded to apply the presumption.

Potter v Minahan
(1908) 7 CLR 277

O'Connor J: [303] Mr Bryant on behalf of the appellant boldly contended that the legislature had used the word "immigrant" in a sense much wider than its ordinary meaning; that, in order to give full effect to the enactment, "immigrating" into Australia must be taken to mean "entering" Australia, and that every person entering Australia is primâ facie an immigrant. There is nothing in the Act to justify the interpretation of the word in a sense so different from its ordinary meaning. To do so would lead to the consequence that an Australian-born, whose actual permanent residence was in Australia, might be made subject to the dictation test on his return home after a month's stay in New Zealand. It is hardly necessary to say that an **[304]** interpretation which would impute to the legislature an intention to bring about that result stands condemned on the face of it. So far from extending the operation of the Act beyond the ordinary meaning of the words which the legislature has used, it is always necessary, in cases such as this where a Statute affects civil rights, to keep in view the principle of construction stated in Maxwell on Statutes, 4th ed, p 121:– "There are certain objects which the legislature is presumed not to intend; and a construction which would lead to any of them is therefore to be avoided." After dealing with other matters … the learned author continues (at page 122):– "One of these presumptions is that the legislature does not intend to make any alteration in the law beyond what it explicitly declares, either in express terms or by implication; or, in other words, beyond the immediate scope and object of the Statute. In all general matters beyond, the law remains undisturbed. It is in the last degree improbable that the legislature would overthrow fundamental principles, infringe rights, or depart from the general system of law, without expressing its intention with irresistible clearness; and to give any such effect to general words, simply because they have that meaning in their widest, or usual, or natural sense, would be to give them a meaning in which they were not really used."

Mr Duffy relied strongly on this principle, and urged that there was one right which it would not be assumed the legislature intended to take away except by express words or necessary implication. That is the right of every British subject born in Australia, and whose home is in Australia, to remain in, depart from, or re-enter Australia as and when he thought fit, unless there was in force in Australia a positive law to the contrary. The existence of that right is, to my mind, beyond serious controversy … **[305]** It cannot be denied that, subject to the Constitution, the Commonwealth may make such laws as it may deem necessary affecting the going and coming of members of the Australian community. But in the interpretation of those laws it must, I think, be assumed that the legislature did not intend to deprive any Australian-born member of the Australian community of the right after absence to re-enter Australia unless it has so enacted by express terms or necessary implication.

Isaacs J (who dissented) found it "**[310]** difficult to see what application that rule has to the present case", since "[t]he words of the Statute taken literally are the broadest and most comprehensive that could be used". However, in *Waterside Workers' Federation of Australia v Gilchrist, Watt & Sanderson Ltd* (1924) 34 CLR 482 he too invoked the presumption in a judgment delivered jointly with Rich J: "**[522]** [E]ven where Parliament confessedly possesses plenary power within its own territory, the full literal intention will not ordinarily be ascribed to general words where that would conflict with recognized principles that Parliament would be prima facie expected to respect. Something unequivocal must be found, either in the context or the circumstances, to overcome the presumption".

There were similar statements by O'Connor J in *Sargood Bros v Commonwealth* (1910) 11 CLR 258 at 279, and by Higgins J in *Melbourne Corporation v Barry* (1922) 31 CLR 174 at 206. Perhaps the fullest exposition was given by Higgins J in *R v Macfarlane; Ex parte O'Flanagan and O'Kelly* (*Irish Envoys Case*) (1923) 32 CLR 518 (see Chapter 20, §2). However, his judgment was also a chastening reminder that the presumption is sometimes unavailing.

In order to secure the deportation from Australia of Father Michael O'Flanagan and JJ O'Kelly, the Commonwealth had not only charged them with sedition, but had summoned them before a Board established under s 8A of the *Immigration Act 1901* (Cth) to show cause why they should not be deported. One issue for the High Court was whether the Board was amenable to prohibition. The whole Court held that it was not because its proceedings were not "judicial"; but Higgins J wrestled with the issue at length.

R v Macfarlane; Ex parte O'Flanagan and O'Kelly (*Irish Envoys Case*)
(1923) 32 CLR 518

Higgins J: [568] There are many cases that could be cited as showing the lengths to which Courts have gone in their endeavours to construe Acts in such a way as will make them consistent with the first principles of justice, and as will leave fundamental, time-honoured, practices standing; but I shall refer to one case only. In *Cox v Hakes* [(1890) 15 App Cas 506] the *Judicature Act* 1873 had provided that the Court of Appeal might entertain an appeal "from *any* judgment or order" of the Queen's Bench. There had existed, however, for centuries a principle that if the Queen's Bench had once discharged a prisoner from custody under a habeas corpus there could be no appeal; and it was held in the House of Lords that the unqualified words of the *Judicature Act* must be read with a qualified meaning, must be treated as confined to *appealable* cases. There is the highest authority, therefore, for approaching this case with the prepossession that our Parliament did not intend to violate constitutional liberties, and must have intended that the Board should be a judicial tribunal. As *Marshall* CJ said in *United States v Fisher* [6 US (2 Cranch) 358 at 390 (1804)], "where rights are infringed, where fundamental principles are overthrown, where the general system of the laws is departed from, the legislative intention must be expressed with irresistible clearness to induce a Court of justice to suppose a design to effect such objects" …

[569] It is not for those who exercise the judicial power of the Commonwealth to condemn what is done by those who exercise the legislative power. That is not our business. But it is my right, and my duty, to act on this presumption, and to state it where expedient. The presumption itself is based on respect for Parliament, and to ignore it would be disrespectful to Parliament.

I have therefore anxiously sought to find in these provisions of sec 8A, or in the rest of the Act, something which would justify me in holding that this Board of inquiry has the essential qualities of a judicial tribunal, and that these men cannot be ejected from Australia without a trial of some sort. The test, however, put by *Brett* LJ of a judicial tribunal is, has it "the power of imposing an obligation upon individuals" (*R v Local Government Board* [(1882) 10 QBD 309 at 321]) … The mere facts that there is an inquiry upon which evidence can be taken to which witnesses can be summoned, and that the decision involves certain discretion, are not enough … Here, the Board merely recommends or refuses to recommend; and if it recommends deportation the Minister may refuse to act on the recommendation. Proceedings which can end in a mere recommendation are not judicial proceedings … I am compelled to say that this **[570]** Board is not a judicial tribunal to try these men in any sense for the offence; and in my opinion, therefore, the rules nisi for prohibition must be discharged.

The same presumption has frequently been invoked (though not always applied) in more recent Australian cases, including those involving the effect of statutes on the privilege against self-incrimination (see, for example, Kirby J in *Accident Insurance Mutual Holdings Ltd v McFadden* (1993) 31 NSWLR 412) or on the related doctrine protecting legal professional privilege (see, for example, *Daniels Corporation International Pty Ltd v Australian Competition and Consumer Commission* (2002) 213 CLR 543). In *Re Minister for Immigration and Multicultural and Indigenous Affairs; Ex parte Ame* (2005) 218 ALR 483, Kirby J was willing to invoke it again as offering a potential protection against arbitrary deprivation of citizenship, though in that case he agreed that no relevant principle had in fact been infringed.

In *Coco v The Queen* (1994) 179 CLR 427, the conviction of Santo Coco for attempted bribery of Commonwealth police was quashed. The conviction had been secured by evidence of private conversations, obtained through a listening device secretly installed at Coco's Queensland factory by Commonwealth police disguised as Telecom employees. The installation had purportedly been authorised under s 43(2)(c) of the *Invasion of Privacy Act 1971* (Qld), and the need for such authorisation was purportedly negated by s 12 of the *Australian Federal Police Act 1979* (Cth); but the Court held that neither of these provisions could legitimate the unlawful entry by means of which the device had been installed.

Coco v The Queen
(1994) 179 CLR 427

Mason, Brennan, Gaudron and McHugh JJ: [436] Statutory authority to engage in what otherwise would be tortious conduct must be clearly expressed in unmistakable and unambiguous language. Indeed, it has been said that the presumption is that, in the absence of express provision to the contrary, the legislature did not intend to authorize what would otherwise have been tortious conduct. But the presumption is rebuttable and will be displaced if there is a clear implication that authority to enter or remain upon private property was intended. Such an implication may be made, in some circumstances, if it is necessary to prevent the statutory provisions from becoming inoperative or meaningless. However, as Gaudron and McHugh JJ observed in *Plenty v Dillon* [(1991) 171 CLR 635 at 654]:

> "[I]nconvenience in carrying out an object authorized by legislation is not a ground for eroding fundamental common law rights." …

[437] The insistence on express authorization of an abrogation or curtailment of a fundamental right, freedom or immunity must be understood as a requirement for some manifestation or indication that the legislature has not only directed its attention to the question of the abrogation or curtailment of such basic rights, freedoms or immunities but has also determined upon abrogation or curtailment of them. The courts should not impute to the legislature an intention to interfere with fundamental rights. Such an intention must be clearly manifested by unmistakable and unambiguous language. General words will rarely be sufficient for that purpose if they do not specifically deal with the question because, in the context in which they appear, they will often be ambiguous on the aspect of interference with fundamental rights.

So long as the requirement for express statutory authorization is understood in the sense explained above, we would accept the requirement as a correct statement of principle. At the same time, in our view, the principle was expressed more simply by Brennan J in *Re Bolton; Ex parte Beane* [(1987) 162 CLR 514 at 523] in these terms:

> "Unless the Parliament makes unmistakably clear its intention to abrogate or suspend a fundamental freedom, the courts will not construe a statute as having that operation."

In *Bropho v Western Australia* [(1990) 171 CLR 1 at 18, quoting *Potter v Minahan*, 7 CLR at 304], Mason CJ, Deane, Dawson, Toohey, Gaudron and McHugh JJ pointed out that the rationale against the presumption against the modification or abrogation of fundamental rights is to be found in the assumption that it is:

> "'in the last degree improbable that the legislature would overthrow fundamental principles, infringe rights, or depart from the general system of law, without expressing its intention with irresistible clearness; and to give any such effect to general words, simply because they have that meaning in their widest, or usual, or natural sense, would be to give them a meaning in which they were not really used'."

At the same time, curial insistence on a clear expression of an unmistakable and unambiguous intention to abrogate or curtail a fundamental freedom will enhance the parliamentary process by **[438]** securing a greater measure of attention to the impact of legislative proposals on fundamental rights.

The need for a clear expression of an unmistakable and unambiguous intention does not exclude the possibility that the presumption against statutory interference with fundamental rights may be displaced by implication. Sometimes it is said that a presumption about legislative intention can be displaced only by necessary implication but that statement does little more than emphasize that the test is a very stringent one. As we remarked earlier, in some circumstances the presumption may be displaced by an implication if it is necessary to prevent the statutory provisions from becoming inoperative or meaningless. However, it would be very rare for general words in a statute to be rendered inoperative or meaningless if no implication of interference with fundamental rights were made, as general words will almost always be able to be given some operation, even if that operation is limited in scope.

In short, judicial reconciliation of parliamentary sovereignty with the rule of law is effective only where the legislative utterance permits it. At a pinch, parliamentary sovereignty prevails. Even the disingenuous rationale accepted by Higgins J in the *Irish Envoys Case*, that the imputation of benevolent intentions to Parliament is a matter of "respect" for Parliament, imports (insofar as it is not merely specious) a significant degree of judicial deference.

Allan has attempted a reconciliation at a more theoretical level. He argues that parliamentary sovereignty is a principle given life by democracy: it is supported and encouraged because it facilitates democracy, that is, political resolution of communal issues through representative and elected government. However, he suggests that if the Parliament were to legislate for the demise of democracy it would be using its sovereignty in an unacceptable way. At this point the rule of law becomes a substantive – not merely procedural – principle, given definition by the political morality of the community. For Allan, the rule of law acts to restrict parliamentary sovereignty to its purpose of facilitating democracy.

TRS Allan, *Law, Liberty, and Justice:*
The Legal Foundations of British Constitutional Law
(Oxford University Press, 1993)

[12] At the heart of the rule of law ideal is a conception of adjudication which treats legislation as the outcome of a democratic process whose legitimacy is ultimately dependent on its respecting minimum standards of justice. A judge defers to the popular will, as represented by statutes duly enacted, because his conception of political morality includes (we may reasonably suppose) a commitment to democracy. But it is necessarily a qualified commitment. He would be unlikely, for example, to accept that the (existing) legal rights of individual litigants could be **[13]** determined, in cases of dispute, by popular opinion. And the virtues of democracy will not persuade a judge – if he is rational – of the necessity to give automatic and unqualified allegiance to every parliamentary enactment, whatever its content. A wise judge will be reluctant to accept at face value legislation which violates important civil rights and will strive to interpret it consistently with traditional (common law) values of individual liberty and autonomy …

[15] It is, of course, often suggested that the traditional precedence given to common law values is inconsistent with a modern, progressive legal order, in which legislation deserves enhanced respect. I shall argue, none the less, that the common law is a constantly evolving apparatus for protecting basic values. It is inherently open to changing perceptions of the requirements of justice and the demands of basic principle. It follows that the content of the common law is ultimately a matter of reason. If the common law is primarily constituted by general principles, moreover, it follows that lawyers' perceptions of justice have no unique authority. Principles cannot be imposed by authority but must be **[16]** argued for and *understood*. The common law constitution therefore enshrines a 'protestant' conception of the rule of law, which might usefully be understood as a continuing process of argument about the requirements of justice and reason – a process in which every citizen should be encouraged to participate as an integral part of conscientious citizenship …

Dicey's failure to provide a consistent and coherent theory of the constitution was mainly attributable to his adherence to Austinian legal positivism. It was ultimately impossible to reconcile his emphasis on the rule of law with the unlimited sovereignty of Parliament. If there are truly no limits to legislative supremacy, common law rights and liberties can always be overridden. An insistence on there being a source of ultimate political authority, which is free from all legal restraint and from which every legal rule derives its validity, is incompatible with constitutionalism. It envisages the legitimate exercise of absolute power, albeit according to constitutional forms, regardless of its consequences for established rights or settled expectations …

Dicey's conception of legislative supremacy has become so ingrained amongst English lawyers – Scots lawyers have wisely been more cautious – that it is hard to question his doctrine without appearing to lose touch with practical reality. Until very recently, it was almost unthinkable that the courts would ever refuse to apply an Act of Parliament; and attempts to indicate necessary exceptions to the doctrine were understandably thought to be somewhat unreal, addressing 'improbable extremes'. But Dicey's positivist assumptions – and those of his adherents – have skewed our wider constitutional vision and the confused condition of contemporary theory seems to be the consequence.

It is a question of the nature of public law and the legitimacy of the judicial function. If all authority ultimately derives from Parliament, on the ground of its connections to the electorate, even the interpretative function must be seriously constrained. If judicial review must be **[17]** understood – as standard explanations would have it – as essentially a means of ensuring compliance with the legislative will, the traditional role of the courts in defence of individual rights is undermined. Inevitably, it comes to appear an illegitimate usurpation of political power, because individual rights – if they are genuine – necessarily inhibit the freedom of majorities or governments to enforce their will.

The truth seems to be that there is no straightforward or objective distinction between the *application* of statutes and their *interpretation*. The restrictive interpretation of statute, in defence of individual rights, necessarily limits the field of its operation; and the *most* restrictive construction may reduce it to practical impotence. The *legitimacy* of such interpretative approaches to duly enacted legislation is obviously a question of great importance and lively controversy. The point remains, however, that the traditional role of the common law in defence of justice and liberty – as those ideals have been understood – is radically inconsistent with a notion of unlimited legislative supremacy. The interpretative function itself denies that the only source of legal authority is Parliament, even in respect of statute; or at least entails that, in the course of applying statutory injunctions to particular cases, the legislative will must be tempered with (judicial) reason …

[18] It follows that the court's adherence to legislative supremacy must, if rational, be a qualified one. On some questions Parliament must have full authority. It is not the courts' function to formulate conceptions of the public interest in opposition to legislative requirements. In supervising the execution of public policy in particular cases, however, the judicial function must rely on constitutional principles which are accepted for their intrinsic value, and not because they have legislative approval – unless such approval is purely notional, and therefore mainly fictitious. It is therefore worth contesting the scope of parliamentary sovereignty, not merely on account of the ultimate contradiction between unlimited legislative supremacy and constitutional government, but also because by taking Dicey's doctrine literally public lawyers have confused the nature of public law.

(d)   *Constitutional Conventions*

AV Dicey, *Introduction to the Study of the Law of the Constitution*
(Macmillan, 1st ed 1885, 10th ed 1959)

[23] The one set of rules are in the strictest sense "laws", since they are rules which (whether written or unwritten, whether enacted by statute or derived from the **[24]** mass of custom, tradition, or judge-made maxims known as the common law) are enforced by the courts; these rules constitute "constitutional law" in the proper sense of that term, and may for the sake of distinction be called collectively "the law of the constitution."

The other set of rules consist of conventions, understandings, habits, or practices which, though they may regulate the conduct of the several members of the sovereign power, of the Ministry, or of other officials, are not in reality laws at all since they are not enforced by the courts. This portion of constitutional law may, for the sake of distinction, be termed the "conventions of the constitution," or constitutional morality.

To put the same thing in a somewhat different shape, "constitutional law", as the expression is used in England, both by the public and by authoritative writers, consists of two elements. The one element, here called the "law of the constitution," is a body of undoubted law; the other element, here called the "conventions of the constitution," consists of maxims or practices which, though they regulate the ordinary conduct of the Crown, of Ministers, and of other persons under the constitution, are not in strictness laws at all.

Are conventions law or not? Is it possible to label conventions as "principles of law"? Although they are not directly enforceable, they can be judicially noticed and may influence the interpretation of statutes, for example through a presumption that parliament would not intend a breach of convention (see *Copyright Owners Reproduction Society Ltd v EMI (Australia) Pty Ltd* (1958) 100 CLR 597 at 612 per Dixon CJ).

The legal status of conventions was considered by the Supreme Court of Canada in *Re Resolution to Amend the Constitution* [1981] 1 SCR 753; (1981) 125 DLR (3d) 1. In 1981, both Houses of the Canadian Parliament adopted a resolution requesting that the British Parliament pass legislation amending the Canadian Constitution, then titled the *British North America Act 1867* (Imp). This was part of a successful federal plan to "patriate" the Constitution and to obtain a domestic amending procedure and the Canadian Charter of Rights and Freedoms. The governments of several Canadian Provinces opposed the resolution. By 6:3, the Supreme Court held that a constitutional convention existed that the federal Parliament would not request amendments to the Canadian Constitution affecting the powers, rights or privileges of the Provinces without first obtaining a "**[905]** substantial degree of provincial consent". However, the Court also held, this time by 7:2, that this convention did not impose a legal requirement and accordingly that this degree of consent was not constitutionally required.

Re Resolution to Amend the Constitution
[1981] 1 SCR 753; (1981) 125 DLR (3d) 1

Martland, Ritchie, Dickson, Beetz, Chouinard and Lamer JJ: [877] Those parts of the Constitution of Canada which are composed of statutory rules and common law rules are generically referred to as the law of the constitution. In cases of doubt or dispute, it is the function of the courts to declare what the law is and since the law is sometimes breached, it is generally the function of the courts to ascertain whether it has in fact been breached in specific instances and, if so, to apply such sanctions as are contemplated by the law, whether they be punitive sanctions or civil sanctions such as a declaration of nullity. Thus, when a federal or a provincial statute is found by the courts to be in excess of the legislative competence of the legislature which has enacted it, it is declared null and void and the courts refuse to give effect to it. In this sense it can be said that the law of the constitution is administered or enforced by the courts.

But many Canadians would perhaps be surprised to learn that important parts of the constitution of Canada, with which they are the most familiar because they are directly involved when **[878]** they exercise their right to vote at federal and provincial elections, are nowhere to be found in the law of the constitution. For instance it is a fundamental requirement of the constitution that if the opposition obtains the majority at the polls, the government must tender its resignation forthwith. But fundamental as it is, this requirement of the constitution does not form part of the law of the constitution.

It is also a constitutional requirement that the person who is appointed prime minister or premier by the Crown and who is the effective head of the government should have the support of the elected branch of the legislature; in practice this means in most cases the leader of the political party which has won a majority of seats at a general election. Other ministers are appointed by the Crown on the advice of the prime minister or premier when he forms or reshuffles his cabinet. Ministers must continuously have the confidence of the elected branch of the legislature, individually and collectively. Should they lose it, they must either resign or ask the Crown for a dissolution of the legislature and the holding of a general election. Most of the powers of the Crown under the prerogative are exercised only upon the advice of the prime minister o[r] the cabinet which means that they are effectively exercised by the latter, together with the innumerable statutory powers delegated to the Crown in council.

Yet none of these essential rules of the constitution can be said to be a law of the constitution. It was apparently Dicey who, in the first edition of his *Law of the Constitution*, in 1885, called them the "conventions of the constitution", (see WS Holdsworth, "The Conventions of the Eighteenth Century Constitution" (1932), 17 Iowa Law Rev 161), an expression which quickly became current. What Dicey described under these terms are the principles and rules of responsible government, several of which are stated above and which regulate the relations between the Crown, the prime minister, the cabinet and the two Houses of Parliament. These rules developed in Great Britain by way of custom and precedent during the nineteenth century and were exported to such British colonies as were granted self-government …

[880] The main purpose of constitutional conventions is to ensure that the legal framework of the constitution will be operated in accordance with the prevailing constitutional values or principles of the period. For example, the constitutional value which is the pivot of the conventions stated above and relating to responsible government is the democratic principle: the powers of the state must be exercised in accordance with the wishes of the electorate; and the constitutional value or principle which anchors the conventions regulating the relationship between the members of the Commonwealth is the independence of the former British colonies.

Being based on custom and precedent, constitutional conventions are usually unwritten rules. Some of them, however, may be reduced to writing and expressed in the proceedings and documents of Imperial conferences, or in the preamble of statutes such as the *Statute of Westminster, 1931*, or in the proceedings and documents of federal-provincial conferences. They are often referred to and recognized in statements made by members of governments.

The conventional rules of the constitution present one striking peculiarity. In contradistinction to the laws of the constitution, they are not enforced by the courts. One reason for this situation is that, unlike common law rules, conventions are not judge-made rules. They are not based on judicial precedents but on precedents established by the institutions of government themselves. Nor are they in the nature of statutory commands which it is the function and duty of the courts to obey and enforce. Furthermore, to enforce them would mean to administer some formal sanction when they are breached. But the legal system from which they are distinct does not contemplate formal sanctions for their breach.

Perhaps the main reason why conventional rules cannot be enforced by the courts is that they are **[881]** generally in conflict with the legal rules which they postulate and the courts are bound to enforce the legal rules. The conflict is not of a type which would entail the commission of any illegality. It results from the fact that legal rules create wide powers, discretions and rights which conventions prescribe should be exercised only in a certain limited manner, if at all …

[883] It should be borne in mind however that, while they are not laws, some conventions may be more important than some laws. Their importance depends on that of the value or principle which they are meant to safeguard. Also they form an integral part of the constitution and of the constitutional system. They come within the meaning of the word "Constitution" in the preamble of the *British North America Act, 1867*:

> Whereas the Provinces of Canada, Nova Scotia, and New Brunswick have expressed their Desire to be federally united ... with a Constitution similar in Principle to that of the United Kingdom:

That is why it is perfectly appropriate to say that to violate a convention is to do something which is unconstitutional although it entails no direct legal consequence. But the words "constitutional" and "unconstitutional" may also be used in a strict legal sense, for instance with respect to a statute which is found *ultra vires* or unconstitutional. The foregoing may perhaps be summarized in an equation: constitutional conventions plus con-[884]-stitutional law equal the total constitution of the country.

Conventions also underpin the day-to-day operation of the Australian Constitution. For example, the Constitution does not mention the office or powers of Prime Minister, these being left to convention. Moreover, it provides that the executive power of the Commonwealth "is exercisable by the Governor-General as the Queen's representative" (s 61); that ministers may be appointed by the Governor-General (s 64); and that the Governor-General is the commander in chief of the Commonwealth's military forces (s 68). These sections apparently vest considerable power in the Governor-General. However, convention based upon the doctrine of responsible government (see Chapter 12, §4(a)) means that the Governor-General's powers are largely illusory. By convention, the Governor-General, except in very limited circumstances, exercises his or her powers on the advice of the parliamentary leader of the majority party in the House of Representatives.

Colin Hughes, "Conventions: Dicey Revisited"
in Patrick Weller and Dean Jaensch (eds), *Responsible Government in Australia*
(Drummond Publishing, 1980)

[41] To indicate their role two 'definitions' of constitutional conventions may be selected from the many available:

> The short explanation of the constitutional conventions is that they provide the flesh which clothes the dry bones of the law; they make the legal constitution work; they keep it in touch with the growth of ideas. A constitution does not work itself; it has to be worked by men. It is an instrument of national co-operation, and the spirit of co-operation is as necessary as the instrument. The constitutional conventions are the rules elaborated for effecting that co-operation. Also, the effects of a constitution must change with the changing circumstances of national life. New needs demand a new emphasis and a new orientation even when the law remains fixed. Men have to work the old law in order to satisfy the new needs. Constitutional conventions are the rules which they elaborate (Jennings 1943: 80-81).
>
> They are rules of political conduct or binding usages, most of which are capable of being varied or simply disappearing as political conditions and ideas change ... If one can borrow from the vocabulary of HLA Hart, constitutional conventions are primary rules of obligation unaccompanied by an adequate apparatus of secondary rules of recognition, interpretation (or adjudication) and change. And the tests for the ascertainment of conventions are neither universally agreed nor, when agreed, easily applied in a large number of marginal cases. Some conventions are clear-cut; some are flexible; some are so elusive that one is left wondering whether the 'convention' is an ethereal will-o'-the-wisp. It is often particularly hard to say whether a political practice has crystallized into a constitutional convention and, if so, what is its scope (de Smith 1971: 37, 59).

Three characteristics emerge. Conventions expand and render workable the letter of the law; [42] they appear, change and disappear, reflecting new circumstances; they are often uncertain in content. One of the pitfalls in discussing the place of constitutional conventions in Australian government is that so much of the commentary derives from Britain where the absence of a written constitution has given them a more prominent role. On the other hand, a richer constitutional history makes British experience, and writing thereon, an essential source of ideas for any work on the place of constitutional conventions in Australia. Moreover, Australian politicians, when they talk about the matters which are affected by conventions, are quite ready to cite British precedents and conventions as immediately applicable to the Australian situation – or at least when such precedents or conventions are favourable for the course they wish to follow …

The flow of authority established by convention reverses the formal allocation by the royal prerogative and the letter of the written constitution. The governor-general acts on the advice of his ministers; the ministers exercise their power to advise only so long as they retain the confidence of parliament; the parliament represents and reflects the will of the nation to which it submits at regular intervals and also when special circumstances require. Those conventions which concern the key points of linkage are the ones which warrant the label of 'fundamental' to distinguish them from others which, for example, concern intercameral relations within the parliament without having implications for the flow of authority. (But a convention subordinating the non-elected House of Lords to the elected House of Commons would best be termed 'fundamental' because it recognised that in most circumstances the Commons represent the nation and the Lords do not.) Even if one accepts Dicey's view that the ultimate objective of **[43]** most conventions relates to the maintenance of the flow, it is still possible to distinguish among them on the basis of relative importance in maintaining the direction in which authority moves at the key points. Even if space permitted, it would be pointless to attempt to list the 'fundamental' conventions for no two authors would agree on a list …

Explanations of why constitutional conventions are obeyed fill an inordinate number of pages in books on constitutional law. The debate began with Dicey who rejected fear of impeachment, then examined the force of public opinion and wrote in a famous passage:

> it is difficult not to suspect that, in England at least, the conventions of the constitution are supported and enforced by something beyond or in addition to the public approval.
>
> What then is this 'something'? My answer is, that it is nothing else than the force of law. The dread of impeachment may have established, and public opinion certainty adds influence to, the prevailing dogma of political ethics. But the sanction which constrains the boldest political adventurer to obey the fundamental principles of the constitution and the conventions in which these principles are expressed, is the fact that the breach of these principles and of these conventions will almost immediately bring the offender into conflict with the courts and the law of the land (Dicey 1948: 445-46).

Using the convention that there must be an annual assembling of parliament (in Australia a requirement of the Constitution, s 6) as the illustration, he contended that the need to pass annually the Army (Annual) Act and the Finance Act ensured that a ministry which did not convene parliament for a year would find itself unable to maintain discipline in the army and to raise and expend revenue. Similarly, should the ministry disregard the convention that it must retire on a vote which showed that it no longer possessed the confidence of the House of Commons, the House would have the means of ultimately forcing the ministry 'either to respect the constitution or to violate the law' when the time for the necessary annual legislation came round (Dicey 1948: 449-50). Among the body of conventions meant to secure the essential principle of the constitution of 'obedience by all persons to the deliberately expressed will of the House of Commons in the first instance, and ultimately to the will of the nation expressed through Parliament', some, such as the requirement of annual parliaments,

> are so closely connected with the respect due to Parliamentary or national authority, that they will never be neglected by anyone who is not prepared to play the part of a revolutionist; such rules have received the undoubted stamp of national approval, and their observance is secured by the fact that whoever breaks or aids in breaking them will almost immediately find himself involved in a breach of law. Other constitutional maxims stand in a very different position. Their maintenance up to a certain point tends to secure the supremacy of Parliament, but they are themselves vague, and no one can say to what extent the will of Parliament or the nation requires their rigid observance; they themselves obtain only a varying and indefinite amount of obedience (Dicey 1948: 456).

Thus a second characteristic of the 'fundamental' conventions: they are more certain to lead to an ultimate breach of law.

The status and existence of conventions, particularly in regard to responsible government, was a significant issue in the controversial dismissal of the Whitlam Government by Governor-General Sir John Kerr, on 11 November 1975 (see Chapter 12, §3).

5. Further References

Allan, TRS, *Constitutional Justice: A Liberal Theory of the Rule of Law* (Oxford University Press, 2003).

Allan, TRS, "Legislative Supremacy and the Rule of Law: Democracy and Constitutionalism" (1985) 44 *Cambridge Law Journal* 111.

Cooray, LJM, *Conventions, The Australian Constitution and the Future* (Legal Books, 1979).

Craig, P, "Dicey: Unitary, Self Correcting Democracy and Public Law" (1990) 106 *Law Quarterly Review* 105.

Craig, P, "Prerogative, Precedent and Power" in Forsyth, C, and Hare, I (eds), *The Golden Metwand and the Crooked Cord* (Clarendon Press, 1998).

Dike, C, "The Case against Parliamentary Sovereignty" [1976] *Public Law* 283.

Dyzenhaus, D (ed), *Recrafting the Rule of Law: The Limits of Legal Order* (Hart Publishing, 1999).

Elton, GR, *The Tudor Constitution: Documents and Commentary* (Cambridge University Press, 2nd ed 1982).

Goodman, E, *The Origins of the Western Legal Tradition: From Thales to the Tudors* (Federation Press, 1995).

Gough, J, *Fundamental Law in English Constitutional History* (Oxford University Press, 1955).

Hanham, HJ, *The Nineteenth Century Constitution 1815-1914: Documents and Commentary* (Cambridge University Press, 1969).

Hutchinson, AC, and Monahan, P (eds), *The Rule of Law: Ideal or Ideology* (Carswell, 1987).

Jaconelli, J, "Do Constitutional Conventions Bind?" (2005) 64 *Cambridge Law Journal* 149.

Kenyon, JP, *The Stuart Constitution 1603-1688: Documents and Commentary* (Cambridge University Press, 1966).

Kinley, D, "Constitutional Brokerage in Australia: Constitutions and the Doctrines of Parliamentary Supremacy and the Rule of Law" (1994) 22 *Federal Law Review* 194.

Mason, K, "The Rule of Law" in Finn, PD (ed), *Essays on Law and Government: Principles and Values* (Law Book Co, 1995) vol 1, 114.

McIlwain, CH, *Constitutionalism: Ancient and Modern* (Cornell University Press, 1947).

McKechnie, WS, *Magna Carta* (Burt Franklin, 2nd ed 1914).

Munro, CR, "Laws and Conventions Distinguished" (1975) 91 *Law Quarterly Review* 218.

Sampford, C, "'Recognise and Declare': An Australian Experiment in Codifying Constitutional Conventions" (1987) 7 *Oxford Journal of Legal Studies* 369.

Sampford, C, and Wood, D, "Codification of Constitutional Conventions in Australia" [1987] *Public Law* 231.

Saunders, C, and Le Roy, K (eds), *The Rule of Law* (Federation Press, 2003).

Spigelman, JJ, "Principle of Legality and the Clear Statement Principle" (2005) 79 *Australian Law Journal* 769.

Stephenson, C, and Marcham, FG, *Sources of English Constitutional History* (Harper & Row, 1937, 2nd ed in 2 volumes by FG Marcham, 1972).

Stuckey, M, "The Evolution of the 'Star Chamber'" (1994) 68 *Australian Law Journal* 670.

Tomkins, A, *Our Republican Constitution* (Hart Publishing, 2005), Ch 3.

Trowbridge, HF, *Albert Venn Dicey: The Man and His Times* (Barry Rose, 1985).

Walker, G de Q, *The Rule of Law: Foundation of Constitutional Democracy* (Melbourne University Press, 1988).

Williams, EN, *The Eighteenth Century Constitution 1688-1815: Documents and Commentary* (Cambridge University Press, 1960).

Winterton, G, "The British Grundnorm: Parliamentary Supremacy Re-examined" (1976) 92 *Law Quarterly Review* 591.

Chapter 4

Penal Colony to Popular Sovereignty

1. Colonisation and the Law

The organised system of law and government now in force in Australia is historically dependent on a series of British statutes, notably including the *Commonwealth of Australia Constitution Act 1900* (Imp). Looked at from an Imperial point of view, the legal authority of the United Kingdom Parliament to enact those statutes depended on the acquisition of the Australian continent as a territorial possession of the British Crown. At common law the acquisition and sometimes the governance of overseas territories were functions of the royal prerogative, an aspect of executive power (see Chapter 12, §2(a)); but as political power in the United Kingdom shifted from the Crown to Parliament, many of those functions came to be exercised by "the Queen in Parliament" (see Chapter 3, §2).

In colonies where the common law applied, it operated to limit the extent of the Crown's prerogative power, though whether this was so in the early years of the New South Wales colony was not clear. Indeed, although the foundational rules of colonial law and government are now regarded as settled, their evolution was often confused and contradictory. Some of the clearest formulations arose from cases involving the British "plantations" in the West Indies.

Blankard v Galdy
(1692) 2 Salkeld 411; 91 ER 356

Per Holt CJ & Cur: [411] 1st, In case of an uninhabited country newly found out by English subjects, all laws in force in England are in force there; so it seemed to be agreed.

2dly, Jamaica being conquered, and not pleaded to be parcel of the kingdom of England, but part of the possessions and revenue of the Crown of England, the laws of England did not take place there, until declared so by the conqueror or his successors. The Isle of Man and Ireland are part of the possessions of the Crown of England; yet retain their ancient laws: **[412]** That in Davis 36, it is not pretended, that the custom of *tanistry* was determined by the conquest of Ireland, but by the new settlement made there after the conquest: that it was impossible the laws of this nation, by mere conquest, without more, should take place in a conquered country; because, for a time, there must want officers, without which our laws can have no force: that if our law did take place, yet they in Jamaica having power to make new laws, our general laws may be altered by theirs in parti-culars; also they held, that in the case of an infidel country, their laws by conquest do not entirely cease, but only such as are against the law of God; and that in such cases where the laws are rejected or silent, the conquered country shall be governed according to the rule of natural equity.

Anonymous
(1722) 2 Peere Williams 75; 24 ER 646

[75] Memorandum, 9th of *August* 1722, it was said by the Master of the Rolls to have been determined by the Lords of the privy council, upon an appeal to the King in council from the foreign plantations,

1*st*, That if there be a new and uninhabited country found out by *English* subjects, as the law is the birthright of every subject, so, wherever they go, they carry their laws with them, and therefore such new found country is to be governed by the laws of *England*; though, after such country is inhabited by the *English*, acts of parliament made in *England*, without naming the foreign plantations, will not bind them; for which reason, it has been determined that the statute of *frauds and perjuries*, which requires three witnesses, and that these should subscribe in the testator's presence, in the case of a devise of land, does not bind *Barbadoes*; but that,

2*dly*, Where the King of *England* conquers a country, it is a different consideration: for there the conqueror, by saving the lives of the people conquered, gains a right and property in such people; in consequence [76] of which he may impose upon them what laws he pleases. But,

3*rdly*, Until such laws given by the conquering prince, the laws and customs of the conquered country shall hold place; unless where these are contrary to our religion, or enact any thing that is *malum in se*, or are silent; for in all such cases the laws of the conquering country shall prevail.

The argument in *Blankard v Galdy* that English law could not immediately be enforced in a conquered country for want of "officers" seems equally applicable to an uninhabited country. Nevertheless, these distinctions gained general acceptance – primarily through a classic passage in Blackstone's *Commentaries on the Laws of England*, first published in 1765. By the time of the fifth edition, Blackstone had added the qualifications printed in italics below.

William Blackstone, *Commentaries on the Laws of England*
(Clarendon Press, 5th ed 1773), Volume I, Introduction, sect 4

[106] Plantations, or colonies in distant [107] countries, are either such where the lands are claimed by right of occupancy only, by finding them desart and uncultivated, and peopling them from the mother country; or where, when already cultivated, they have been either gained by conquest, or ceded to us by treaties. And both these rights are founded upon the law of nature, or at least upon that of nations. But there is a difference between these two species of colonies, with respect to the laws by which they are bound. For it hath been held, that if an uninhabited country be discovered and planted by English subjects, all the English laws then in being, which are the birthright of every subject, are immediately there in force. *But this must be understood with very many and very great restrictions. Such colonists carry with them only so much of the English law, as is applicable to their own situation and the condition of an infant colony; such, for instance, as the general rules of inheritance, and of protection from personal injuries. The artificial refinements and distinctions incident to the property of a great and commercial people, the laws of police and revenue, (such especially as are inforced by penalties) the mode of maintenance for the established clergy, the jurisdiction of spiritual courts, and a multitude of other provisions, are neither necessary nor convenient for them, and therefore are not in force. What shall be admitted and what rejected, at what times, and under what restrictions, must, in cases of dispute, be decided in the first instance by their own provincial judicature, subject to the revision and control of the king in council: the whole of their constitution being also liable to be new-modelled and reformed by the general super-intending power of the legislature in the mother country.* But in conquered or ceded countries, that have already laws of their own, the king may indeed alter and change those laws; but, till he does

actually change them, the antient laws of the country remain, unless such as are against the law of God, as in the case of an infidel country. Our American plantations are principally of this latter sort, being obtained in the last century either by right of con-[108]-quest and driving out the natives (with what natural justice I shall not at present enquire) or by treaties. And therefore the common law of England, as such, has no allowance or authority there; they being no part of the mother country, but distinct (though dependent) dominions. They are subject, however, to the control of the parliament.

According to the accepted understanding of this passage as it applied to New South Wales, both the common law and the statute law of England were immediately in force in the new colony as from 26 January 1788. They were part of the "[107] birthright" that the settlers carried with them – but only to the extent that the rules thus transplanted were "applicable to … the condition of an infant colony". At the same time, the United Kingdom Parliament retained an overriding power to legislate specifically for the new colony, or generically for all British colonies. In the 19th century such legislation was said to operate by "paramount force".

If, in Blackstone's terms, the Australian colonies had been regarded as "conquered" by Great Britain, or as "ceded" to Great Britain by an Indigenous sovereign or by consent of the Indigenous peoples, then the pre-existing laws of the Indigenous sovereign or Indigenous peoples would have remained in force, subject to modification or replacement by the Crown or by the British Parliament. By contrast, to conceive of the new territory as "settled" implied an absence of pre-existing law, and the legal vacuum thus postulated was immediately filled by the English common law. The common law as thus "received" could be altered by legislation, but not by prerogative power, since that power was itself dependent on the common law.

That the British colonisation of Australia would be conceptualised as "settlement", rather than "conquest" or "cession", was determined virtually from the moment of Captain James Cook's "discovery" of the continent in 1770.

Alex Castles, *An Australian Legal History*
(Law Book Co, 1982)

[20] From the time of Cook's journey up the eastern coast in 1770 the entire continent was treated by Britain as territorium nullius under International Law. As a consequence, Australia became "one of the rare examples of a large tract of inhabited territory acquired peaceably by occupation without any consent from the native population". Essentially, along the lines suggested by Vattel, the Aborigines were treated as peoples who lacked effective possession of the lands over which they roamed. All land in the country came to be treated as belonging to the British Crown which could dispose of it as it wished …

[21] The exploration of the eastern coast of mainland Australia by James Cook and his company in the *Endeavour* in 1770 provided an important starting point for the later policies adopted by Britain in treating the continent as a place for settlement. Cook's instructions followed the principles of International Law in laying down two ways in which a southern continent might be acquired for Britain. They acknowledged that territory might be acquired "with the Consent of the Natives", thus creating a situation in which such a new acquisition would be treated as a conquest. On the other hand, it was prescribed that "if you find [22] the Country uninhabited Take Possession for His Majesty by setting up Proper Marks and Inscriptions as first discoverers and possessors".

As the *Endeavour* made its way northwards along the coast it seems to have become clear that there was no real possibility of acquiring territory with the consent of the Aborigines. The members of the expedition had only fleeting contacts with the Aborigines when they were ashore. As Cook summed up some of his impressions of the Aborigines in his journal they seemed to be in the position of peoples like those described by Vattel who had not taken possession of the lands over which they roamed. As Cook wrote, the Aborigines seemed "to have no fix'd habitation but move on from place to place like Wild Beasts in search of food …". He noted also that they lived "wholy by fishing and hunting, but mostly by the former for we never saw one Inch of Cultivated Land in the Whole Country".

Almost of necessity in the circumstances, Cook proceeded to lay claim to the eastern seaboard of the continent on the basis that it was to be treated as uninhabited territory. When the *Endeavour* was anchored in Botany Bay the British colours were symbolically displayed on the shore. An inscription was cut into a tree recording the details of the arrival of the ship. More solemnly on 22nd August, 1770 at Possession Island, off Cape York, the British navigator followed the appropriate forms of the day to claim possession of an "uninhabited land". As the ship's log recorded: "At six possession was taken of this country in his Majesty's name and under his colours, fired several volleys of small arms on the occasion, and cheer'd three times, which was answer'd from the ship." Through this formal ceremony and supported by the other occasions when the British flag was hoisted on shore Cook purported to take possession of the eastern coast of the Australian continent for the British Crown.

[23] In 1786 as the first detailed planning was contemplated for the establishment of New South Wales it was assumed that the new colony would be treated as one being carved out of unclaimed territory. The "Heads of a Plan" prepared by the Pitt government declared that the "whole regulation and management of the settlement would be committed to the care of a discreet officer, and provision made in all cases, both civil and military, by special instructions under the Great Seal, or otherwise as may be thought proper". Governor Phillip's first, brief commission, issued in 1786, arbitrarily determined the limits of the new colony as far as the British claim was concerned. Phillip's second, much more detailed commission, issued in 1787, provided even stronger evidence that the colony would be treated as a place of settlement. Unequivocally, it assumed that all lands in the colony were vested in the Crown and could be disposed of under the Governor's directions. As far as the Aborigines were concerned, no provision was made for preserving their lands or their customs. Phillip's Instructions enjoined him simply to "endeavour by every possible means to open an intercourse with the natives and to conciliate their affections, enjoining all our subjects to live in amity and kindness with them". The Instructions also laid it down that "if any of our subjects shall wantonly destroy them, or give them unnecessary interruption in the exercise of their several occupations, it is our will and pleasure that you do cause such offenders to be brought to punishment according to the degree of the offence".

There is evidence … [that] Phillip himself, even before his departure for Australia, assumed that the new colony would be treated as a place for settlement. Commenting on the conduct of affairs after his arrival he wrote that "the laws of this country will, of course, be introduced in [New] South Wales". Phillip seems to have been particularly concerned at the possibility that some form of slavery might be established in the colony. On the assumption that English law would apply, as in the mother [24] country, he asserted that "there can be no slavery in a free land, and, consequently no slaves".

The ceremonies which followed the arrival of the First Fleet at Port Jackson confirmed that a new legal regime was being created in an area being regarded as otherwise unclaimed territory. On 26th January, 1788 a simple, symbolic ceremony took place on the site of what is now the Customs House, opposite Circular Quay in Sydney. In the traditional fashion, the Governor and his officials affirmed that the British Crown was asserting an independent right to control New South Wales. A British flag was unfurled. The Governor joined with his fellow officers in toasting the success of the new colonial venture. A feu de joie was fired by a detachment of marines. Phillip Gidley King, who was later to become a Governor of the colony, noted in his journal that with this ceremony possession of New South Wales "was taken for His Majesty". On 7th February, 1788 a more elaborate ceremony was carried out with all of the pomp and circumstance which could be mustered in the infant settlement. Convicts and marines assembled in a clearing near Sydney Cove. The Governor and his chief officials marched to the centre of the clearing to strains of music from a marine band. Phillip's Commission was read out. The Act of Parliament and the First Charter of Justice which created the first courts were broadcast to the convicts and their gaolers …

[25] Officially, Phillip's commission proclaimed that his colonial demesne extended from Cape York in the north to the southern tip of Van Diemen's Land. It extended to the west to the 135th degree of longitude which took in all of the continent from just west of the Gulf of Carpentaria in the north to a point on the southern coast, west of Spencer's Gulf, in what is now South Australia. This area was considerably larger than the region claimed by Cook.

Mabo v Queensland (No 2)
(1992) 175 CLR 1

Brennan J: [35] According to Blackstone, English law would become the law of a country outside England either upon first settlement by English colonists of a "desert uninhabited" country or by the exercise of the Sovereign's legislative power over a conquered or ceded country. Blackstone did not contemplate other ways by which sovereignty might be acquired. In the case of a conquered country, the general rule was that the laws of the country continued after the conquest until those laws were altered by the conqueror. The Crown had a prerogative power to make new laws for a conquered country although that power was subject to laws enacted by the Imperial Parliament. The same rule applied to ceded colonies, though the prerogative may have been limited by the treaty of cession. When "desert uninhabited countries" were colonized by English settlers, however, they brought with them "so much of the English law as [was] applicable to their own situation and the condition of an infant colony". English colonists were, in the eye of the common law, entitled to live under the common law of England which Blackstone described as their "birthright". That law was not amenable to alteration by exercise of the prerogative. The tender concern of the common law of England for British settlers in foreign parts led to the recognition that such settlers should be regarded as living under the law of England if the local law was unsuitable for Christian Europeans. This rule was applied even **[36]** to English residents in Eastern countries which were not under British sovereignty.

When British colonists went out to other inhabited parts of the world, including New South Wales, and settled there under the protection of the forces of the Crown, so that the Crown acquired sovereignty recognized by the European family of nations under the enlarged notion of terra nullius, it was necessary for the common law to prescribe a doctrine relating to the law to be applied in such colonies, for sovereignty imports supreme internal legal authority. The view was taken that, when sovereignty of a territory could be acquired under the enlarged notion of terra nullius, for the purposes of the municipal law that territory (though inhabited) could be treated as a "desert uninhabited" country. The hypothesis being that there was no local law already in existence in the territory, the law of England became the law of the territory (and not merely the personal law of the colonists). Colonies of this kind were called "settled colonies". Ex hypothesi, the indigenous inhabitants of a settled colony had no recognized sovereign, else the territory could have been acquired only by conquest or cession. The indigenous people of a settled colony were thus taken to be without laws, without a sovereign and primitive in their social organization. In *Advocate-General (Bengal) v Ranee Surnomoye Dossee* [(1863) 2 Moo NS 22 at 59; 15 ER 811 at 824; 9 Moo Ind App 391 at 428; 19 ER 786 at 800] Lord Kingsdown used the term "barbarous" to describe the native state of a settled colony:

> "Where Englishmen establish themselves in an uninhabited or barbarous country, they carry with them not only the laws, but the sovereignty of their own State; and those who live amongst them and become members of their community become also partakers of, and subject to the same laws." ...

In *Cooper v Stuart* [(1889) 14 App Cas 286 at 291] Lord Watson proffered the absence of "settled inhabitants" and "settled law" as a **[37]** criterion for determining whether inhabited territory had been acquired by "settlement" under English law ... As the settlement of an inhabited territory is equated with settlement of an uninhabited territory in ascertaining the law of the territory on colonization, the common law which the English settlers brought with them to New South Wales could not have been altered or amended by the prerogative – only by the Imperial Parliament or by the local legislature. (This principle raises some doubts about the validity of the exercise of legislative power by the Governor of New South Wales before a Legislative Council was established in 1823, but we need not pause to consider that question.) In a settled colony in inhabited territory, the law of England was not merely the personal law of the English colonists; it became the law of the land, protecting and binding colonists and indigenous inhabitants alike and equally. Thus the theory which underpins the application of English law to the Colony of New South Wales is that English settlers brought with them the law of England and that, as the indigenous inhabitants were regarded as **[38]** barbarous or unsettled and without a settled law, the law of England including the common law became the law of the Colony (so far as it was locally applicable) as though New South Wales were "an uninhabited country ... discovered and planted by English subjects".

The legal situation in the first turbulent decades of the New South Wales colony was unclear. For one thing, the practicalities of government in a penal colony seemed closer to an exercise of prerogative power than the settled rules for reception of the common law would allow.

HV Evatt, "The Legal Foundations of New South Wales"
(1938) 11 *Australian Law Journal* 409

[415] One of our ablest historians has said that every Australian should "recognize with pride and gratitude the precision and foresight whereby the founders laid the keystones for all the diverse interests which now form the fabric of civilization in this young nation."

Now this theory argues an elaborate plan of colonial development. It may be admitted that one or two individuals, such as Sir Joseph Banks, [James] Matra, and even Governor Phillip, during his rare moments of optimism, looked forward to the evolution of the penal settlement into a colony or plantation proper. But the legal instruments which embodied the policy of the English Government ... were not concerned with, and did not contemplate, such an evolution. On the contrary, the early Governors were plagued with doubts and difficulties which could and must have been avoided if the theory I have mentioned were sound. The sounder inference is that the English Government was concerned with the removal of convicts, and so long as there was a *de facto* occupation of New South Wales which might incidentally foil any coup on the part of France, the development of colonial status could look after itself. This view finds support in the great emphasis which, from the very first, was laid upon the administration of criminal justice in the Colony. By contrast, the basis of the administration of civil law was left insecure ...

The New South Wales Statute 27 Geo III c 2, not only defined the jurisdiction and regulated the composition of the Criminal Court but also ascertained the law to be applied by the Court. The jurisdiction extended to "all such outrages and misbehaviours as, if committed within this realm, would be deemed and taken, according to the laws of this realm, to be treason or misprision thereof, felony or misdemeanour." ... [This] test involved the continuous and automatic application to the Colony of the Criminal Law for the time being in force in England. Of course, such application did not avoid every possible difficulty. For one thing, the actual definition either of the crime created or [of] the punishment imposed by English law might be difficult or even impossible of application in New South Wales. For instance, during Bligh's governorship, a question arose whether a criminal statute passed in 1795 for the personal protection of George III could be applied in the colony so as to punish seditious conduct aimed at the annihilation of Bligh's authority as the supreme executive of the colony. Further, there was often great practical difficulty [416] in discovering the criminal statutes which were in force in England. Law books were scarce. For some time during Bligh's regime the best law library in the colony belonged to a layman – Simeon Lord – and to an emancipated convict, one Crossley ... Thus we find that in 1808 Bligh's advisers were compelled to resort to Simeon Lord for a loan of an edition of Blackstone's Commentaries in order to see what was provided by the English Act of 1795. Curiously enough the editor of the then current edition of Blackstone was Edward Christian, Downing Professor of Law and brother of the leader of the Bounty mutiny against Bligh ...

[417] The inevitable result of the growing complexity in the social and economic life of New South Wales was that a mere slavish following of the civil law in force in England became impossible. Hence the issue by the Governors of orders and regulations. In August, 1789, Governor Phillip promulgated watch or police regulations for Sydney. The number of orders and regulations increased enormously under subsequent administrations. Thus, in 1796, we find a government regulation fixing the price of wheat at ten shillings per bushel. Regulations are made for the owners of firearms to be registered, the distillation of spirits is prohibited, the use as currency of store receipts for grain supplied to Government Stores is forbidden. Governor Hunter invariably transmitted copies of his orders and regulations to the Secretary of State. As Dr Watson notes:–

"When received in England, no comment or criticism was made. This system was commenced under the patriarchal government of Phillip, who issued orders for the regulation of the small community under his control. It was continued and extended, until the Governor exercised the power of issuing proclamations, controlling the jurisdiction of magistrates, regulating the validity of deeds relating to land transfers, etc, imposing [418] penalties for crimes, ordering the minutest details of civil life, deporting undesirables, creating a coinage, imposing taxation, etc. In fact, the Governor assumed powers of legislation, uncontrolled and entirely on his own initiative, as great as those which are the prerogative of Parliament and greater than those of the King." ...

Governor King ... dismissed the contention that the laws of England were of themselves sufficient for the government of New South Wales. He agreed that, if the inhabitants resembled those of an English town or country, the reasoning would be good; and then added:

"But when it is considered that three-fourths of the inhabitants have been spared from an ignominious death by the humanity of the laws of England, and that the greater part of that number are so rooted in wickedness and vice, which can never be changed by any time or place (at least as far as respects the present generation), joined to the very little amendment that is seen in those who have either expiated their crimes, either by having served their terms or become emancipated – the necessity of these restrictive Regulations must be visible to everyone who is, or ever has been acquainted with the depravity of those which they govern." ...

In 1803, Bentham published what he called "A Plea for the Constitution, shewing the enormities committed, to the oppression of British subjects, innocent as well as guilty in breach of Magna Charta, the Petition of Right, the Habeas Corpus Act, and the Bill of Rights ... in and by the Design, Foundation and Government of the Penal Colony of New South Wales." ...

He contended that the power of making regulations was essentially legislative in character and that, in relation to New South Wales, it had never been lawfully vested in any authority other than the Parliament at Westminster. He said:–

"From one source or another – from within or without – from intrinsic authority or from extrinsic – who ever heard of the foundation of a state, dependent or independent, without a power to make laws?"

He did not blame the Governors for passing regulations which were thought necessary, saying:

"This assumption of power, how shall it be accounted for? On the part of the Governor, there can be little difficulty. Whatsoever were given to him for law, by his superiors at the [419] Council Board, or the Secretary of State's Office, would naturally enough, one might almost say, unavoidably be taken by this *sea Captain* for law. By this sea Captain: for such has been the profession and rank of every gentleman who has ever as yet been invested with this important office." ...

[420] The solution of the constitutional problem is, I think, to be found, not in general reasoning from the condition of an ordinary settled English Colony, certainly not in the curious view of Webb that, until 1823, no laws, save only the criminal law of England, were in force – I suggest that is a fair statement of his view – but in a recognition of the fact that, in point of legal intendment, New South Wales at its commencement was a penitentiary, situated, not in England, but at the other end of the world ... As late as 1806, Governor King emphasised the enormous practical significance still attaching to the penal aspect of the life of the Colony. Bentham went further and seemed to admit that, in respect of the officers and privates of the King's forces and of all convicts in a state of legal bondage, the Governor possessed a very ample degree of authority. From Bentham certainly Bladen derived his argument that the [421] free settlers "at least" were free of the Governor's orders. But such a legal differentiation could not be applied without absurdity. If the price of wheat was fixed by the Governor's regulation, if his order required a free settler to provide a fixed scale of rations to a convict labourer, such regulations and orders were either valid and binding upon all parties concerned, or they were entirely unlawful. It was impossible for them to be good in part only ... The proper conclusion is that, at the first stage of the settlement, the Governor, as the King's officer, was exercising absolute control of an unusually extended penitentiary, most of the members of which were compelled by law to remain within it, and the remainder of whom had to be regarded as choosing to remain within it. If that is true of the first stage, nothing could alter the legal position except an Imperial Act terminating the Royal power, or Royal instructions countermanding the authority given to the earlier governors. Therefore the basis,

and the only legal basis of the absolute dictatorship of the Governor was that he was in law to be regarded as the Superintendent-General or Head Gaoler. His power to make orders and regulations was an essential part of a disciplinary jurisdiction without which, at the foundation of the settlement, every person connected with it might have perished.

Evatt concedes that the *New South Wales Act 1787* (Imp) (27 Geo III c 2) had at least made clear provision for the reception of English *criminal* law. Other constituent documents were ambiguous: in particular, an implication or at least an assumption that English law was applicable can be found in the Warrant for the first Charter of Justice (2 April 1787); and the Letters Patent for the second Charter of Justice (4 February 1814) (*Historical Records of Australia*, Series IV, vol 1, at 6 and 77 respectively). But however those documents are construed, the ambiguities were only resolved, as Evatt argues, by the *New South Wales Act 1823* (Imp) (4 Geo IV c 96) and the *Australian Courts Act 1828* (Imp) (9 Geo IV c 83).

Alex Castles, "The Reception and Status of English Law in Australia"
(1963) 2 *Adelaide Law Review* 1

[2] For some years after its settlement it was not clear whether New South Wales was to be treated on the same basis as a "settled colony" for the purposes of applying English law. As New South Wales was founded as a penal settlement, with the early Governors exercising almost plenary powers over all of the inhabitants, it could be argued that the colony could not be treated as ["settled"] … The situation was [3] finally cleared up when the British Parliament passed "an Act to Provide for the Administration of Justice in New South Wales and Van Diemen's Land" in 1828. Section 24 of this enactment stated: "That all Laws and Statutes in force within the Realm of England at the Time of the passing of this Act … shall be applied in the Administration of Justice In the Courts of New South Wales and Van Diemen's Land respectively, so far as the same can be applied within the said Colonies." This provision made it clear that New South Wales and Tasmania, which had been separated from the "mother colony" in 1825, were to be placed on the same footing as settled colonies, as at July 28, 1828.

This Act also provides a starting point for the application of English law to Victoria, which was separated from New South Wales in 1851. Queensland, too, dates its reception of English law back to July 25, 1828, following that State's separation from New South Wales in 1859. As far as South Australia is concerned, this State was originally part of New South Wales. But subsequent enactments and decisions … have confirmed that the application of English law to that State is to be considered "as if this province never had any association with the mother colony". The application of English law to South Australia applies as at December 28, 1836, which has been legislatively defined as the State's date of settlement. The Interpretation Act of Western Australia provides that June 1, 1829, is the date on which that State "shall be deemed to have been established", for the purpose of determining the application of English statutory law.

As South Australia and Western Australia were "settled colonies" within the meaning of the common law and New South Wales and Tasmania were virtually treated as such in the 1828 Act, each of the Australian States directly inherited a vast body of English law. This included statutes which had been passed by the English Parliament [4] up to the creation of the British Parliament, and subsequent enactments passed by the Parliament at Westminster, following the Act of Union with Scotland in 1703. In addition, the general principles of unenacted law, which had been developed by English courts over the centuries, were also received as part of the law of the colonies.

2. Reception of English Law

(a)　　Common Law

The main function of the *Australian Courts Act* in its application to the common law was to validate retrospectively the assumption that all of its principles and precedents had been "received" at the moment of settlement. Whereas statutes explicitly *change* the law (and so normally operate prospectively from the date of commencement), common law decisions have traditionally been conceived of as merely declaring what has always been the law (and so normally operate retrospectively). For the common law, therefore, the date of settlement remains the critical date.

Sir Victor Windeyer, "'A Birthright and Inheritance' – The Establishment of the Rule of Law in Australia"
(1962) 1 *Tasmanian University Law Review* 635

[635] [A]ny reference to the introduction of law into Australia makes most Australian lawyers think at once of section 24 of the Australian Courts Act, 9 Geo IV, c 83, an Act of the British Parliament passed in the year 1828. It provided that all laws and statutes in force within the realm of England on 25th July 1828 should be applied … in the courts of New South Wales and Van Diemen's Land 'so far as the same can be applied within the said colonies'. English law – both the common law and statute law – as it stood in 1828 was thus declared to be the law of the two eastern colonies, New South Wales (then including what is now Victoria and Queensland) and Tasmania. And, except so far as it has been altered since then by our own Parliaments in Australia, and by such Acts of the British Parliament as have [636] been made to apply here, it is still the law. So that today lawyers look to the Statute of 1828 as the good root of title of our inheritance of the law of England. But we must not think of it as the source of that inheritance. The source is the common law itself. The law of England had come to Australia with the First Fleet, forty years before 1828. Section 24 was inserted into the Act 9 Geo IV, c 83 to get over a particular difficulty. It fixes a date. It does not originate a doctrine.

Blackstone's insistence that only those laws "applicable to the condition of an infant Colony" were to be received applied to both common and statute law; but as to the common law its practical operation was limited. A belief in the underlying unity of the common law (itself a Blackstonian notion) gave rise from the outset to a strong presumption that whatever was the common law of England must also be the common law of Australia. This conception of a unified common law was aided by the colonists' tendency to see their new world through English eyes – and also by the assumed homogenous unity, for all of the Australian colonies, of the body of common law principles which all of them had received. To this day (by contrast with the position in the United States, where each State is conceived of as having its own common law, not necessarily coincident with that of other States), the Australian conception is that the common law is the same in every State. The same wine, it is said, was poured into six separate bottles. The Australian conception was spelled out by Griffith CJ in 1915.

R v Kidman
(1915) 20 CLR 425

Griffith CJ: [435] The laws … brought to Australia undoubtedly included all the common law relating to the rights and prerogatives of the [436] Sovereign in his capacity as head of the Realm and the protection of his officers in enforcing them, including so much of the common law as imposed loss of life or liberty for infraction of it. When the several Australian Colonies were erected this law was not abrogated, but continued in force as law of the respective Colonies applicable to the Sovereign as their head. It did not, however, become disintegrated into six separate codes of law, although it became part of an identical law applicable to six separate political entities … In so far as any part of this law was afterwards repealed in any Colony, it, no doubt, ceased to have effect in that Colony, but in all other respects it continued as before. When in 1901 the Australian Commonwealth was formed, this law continued to be the law applicable to the rights and prerogatives of the Sovereign as head of the States as before, subject to any such local repeal. But, so far as regards the Sovereign as head of the Commonwealth, the current which had been temporarily diverted into six parallel streams coalesced, and in that capacity he succeeded as head of the Commonwealth to the rights which he had had as head of the Colonies.

Despite occasional criticisms of this conception (notably by LJ Priestley, "A Federal Common Law in Australia?" (1995) 6 *Public Law Review* 221), it was strongly reaffirmed by the High Court in *Lipohar v The Queen* (1999) 200 CLR 485 and in *John Pfeiffer Pty Ltd v Rogerson* (2000) 203 CLR 503 (see Chapter 6, §6).

As time went on, this conception was reinforced by the unifying effect of a common hierarchy of appeals to the High Court or Privy Council. The notion of unity with English law was further reinforced by the overlapping membership of the Judicial Committee of the Privy Council with that of the (judicial) House of Lords. Moreover, from the very beginning, the assumption of unity within Australia was aided by the fact that, for the four eastern colonies, the "reception" of common law had happened at the same historical moment. At least for those four colonies, the "received" common law was necessarily the same. In this context, it is not surprising that attempts to negate the application of common law doctrines by appeal to local conditions have usually been unsuccessful.

Alex Castles, "The Reception and Status of English Law in Australia"
(1963) 2 *Adelaide Law Review* 1

[7] Under the common law principles on the reception of English law it is clear that the general principles of unenacted English law were received by settled colonies. These included the vast bulk of the unenacted law of inheritance, torts, criminal law, mercantile law, private international law, real and personal property and equity. Where the unenacted law on such subjects was not related to artificial requirements peculiar to England [it] became part of the English law received by the Australian States.

If the cases reported in Legge's selection of New South Wales Supreme Court decisions are a true indication, little difficulty was experienced in applying the English common law. Almost all of the cases on the application of English law in these reports relate to the reception of English statutory law under the 1828 Act. It was assumed, virtually without question, that the unenacted law of libel and real property, for example, was part of the law of New South Wales. It is clear, too, that it was generally accepted that no inquiry need be made to ascertain if common law principles were suitable to the conditions of the colony at the time English law was made applicable. The case of *Fitzgerald v Luck* [(1839) 1 Legge 118] seems to be decisive authority on this point, at least as far as New South Wales is concerned. Three judges of the Court unanimously agreed that the mercantile law principles relating to sales in market overt were part of the common law which had been received into the colony under the 1828 Act. In 1839, when this case was decided, however, no public markets had been established where the doctrine could operate. [The Chief Justice] indicated that when public markets were established in the colony the doctrine of [8] market overt would become relevant ...

[9] [T]here seems to have been a general disinclination on the part of Australian courts to take into account special local conditions in deciding whether the general principles of unenacted law should apply. On some occasions no doubt, as exemplified by the majority decision of the Supreme Court of New South Wales in *R v Farrell* [(1831) 1 Legge 5], judges felt constrained to look to special local conditions and were influenced by them in reaching their conclusions on the application of English law. In that case Stephen and Dowling JJ held that a "convict attaint" could be a competent witness in the colony although this was not strictly in accord with the English common law on the subject. Dowling J pointed out [1 Legge at 17] that in applying the laws of evidence to ex-convicts who had been transported to the colony reference must be made "to their peculiar condition, and to the necessities of the place in which they were inhabiting, arising from the gradual emancipation of individuals from penal restraint". Apart from such limited exceptions, it would seem that by the second half of the nineteenth century it was generally accepted that little judicial encouragement was given to attempts to make unenacted law yield to special conditions in a colony. Sir Harrison Moore in his examination of a "Century of Victorian Law", lists several important instances in which a good case could have been made out for modifying or refusing to apply English unenacted law in Victoria. On each occasion, however, the courts rejected the contention that local con-[10]-ditions could limit the application of the general principles of English law.

Cooper v Stuart (1889) 14 App Cas 286 is nowadays best known for its obiter dicta endorsing the legal fiction that, before European settlement, the Australian continent was *terra nullius* (see Chapter 5, §3). Its actual focus was much narrower. A proclamation in the New South Wales *Government Gazette* on 14 November 1882 had created what is now Alexandria Park (on the corner of Buckland and Wyndham Streets in the Sydney suburb of Waterloo). In 1823 the original grant of "the Waterloo estate" (comprising 1400 acres) had contained a clause "reserving to His Majesty … any quantity of land, not exceeding ten acres, in any part of the said grant, as may be required for public purposes". The proclamation in November 1882 was expressed to be pursuant to that reservation. William Cooper, the successor in title of the original grantee William Hutchinson, challenged the proclamation, inter alia, on the ground that the original reservation in 1823 was invalid, as contrary to the rule against perpetuities. The question was whether the rule against perpetuities was a part of New South Wales law. The Privy Council held that it was, but that its alleged application to a reservation in a Crown grant was not.

Cooper v Stuart
(1889) 14 App Cas 286

Lord Watson (for their Lordships): [290] It does not appear to their Lordships to be necessary, for the purposes of the present case, to decide whether the Crown, in attaching such reservations to grants of land in England, would be affected by the rule against perpetuities. In order to succeed in this appeal, it is not enough for the appellant to establish that the Crown would be within the rule here; he must also shew that the rule, in so far as it affects the Crown, was operative in **[291]** the Colony of New South Wales at the time when his land was originally granted to William Hutchinson; and that, in the opinion of their Lordships, he has failed to do.

The extent to which English law is introduced into a British Colony, and the manner of its introduction, must necessarily vary according to circumstances. There is a great difference between the case of a Colony acquired by conquest or cession, in which there is an established system of law, and that of a Colony which consisted of a tract of territory practically unoccupied, without settled inhabitants or settled law, at the time when it was peacefully annexed to the British dominions. The Colony of New South Wales belongs to the latter class. In the case of such a Colony the Crown may by ordinance, and the Imperial Parliament, or its own legislature when it comes to possess one, may by statute declare what parts of the common and statute law of England shall have effect within its limits. But, when that is not done, the law of England must (subject to well-established exceptions) become from the outset the law of the Colony, and be administered by its tribunals. In so far as it is reasonably applicable to the circumstances of the Colony, the law of England must prevail, until it is abrogated or modified, either by ordinance or statute. The often-quoted observations of Sir William Blackstone (1 Comm 107) appear to their Lordships to have a direct bearing upon the present case …

[292] Blackstone, in that passage, was setting right an opinion attributed to Lord Holt, that all laws in force in England must apply to an infant Colony of that kind. If the learned author had written at a later date he would probably have added that, as the population, wealth, and commerce of the Colony increase, many rules and principles of English law, which were unsuitable to its infancy, will gradually be attracted to it; and that the power of remodelling its laws belongs also to the colonial legislature.

Their Lordships have not been referred to any Act or Ordinance declaring that the laws of England, or any portion of them, are applicable to New South Wales. There was no land law or tenure existing in the Colony at the time of its annexation to the Crown; and, in that condition of matters, the conclusion appears to their Lordships to be inevitable that, as soon as colonial land became the subject of settlement and commerce, all transactions in relation to it were governed by English law, in so far as that law could be justly and conveniently applied to them …

Their Lordships have recently had occasion to consider, in *Jex v McKinney* [(1889) 14 App Cas 77], the authorities bearing upon the question of the suitability of English law to colonial circum-**[293]**-stances. That case differed from the present in this respect, that there the law of England was introduced into the Colony by statute, and not by the silent operation of constitutional principles;

but its introduction was qualified by words which excluded the application of laws prevailing here which were unsuitable in their nature to the needs of the Colony.

The rule against perpetuities, as applied to persons and gifts of a private character, ... [is] an important feature of the common law of England. To that extent it appears to be founded upon plain considerations of policy, and, in some shape or other, finds a place in most, if not in all, complete systems of jurisprudence. Their Lordships see no reason to suppose that the rule, so limited, is not required in New South Wales by the same considerations which have led to its introduction here, or that its operation in that Colony would be less beneficial than in England. The learned judges of the Supreme Court of the Colony, in deciding this case, proceeded on the assumption that the rule applies there as between subject and subject; and their Lordships are of opinion that the assumption is well founded.

Assuming next (but for the purposes of this argument only) that the rule has, in England, been extended to the Crown, its suitability, when so applied, to the necessities of a young Colony raises a very different question. The object of the Government, in giving off public lands to settlers, is not so much to dispose of the land to pecuniary profit as to attract other colonists. It is simply impossible to foresee what land will be required for public uses before the immigrants arrive who are to constitute the public. Their prospective wants can only be provided for in two ways, either by reserving from settlement portions of land, which may prove to be useless for the purpose for which they are reserved, or by making grants of land in settlement, retaining the right to resume such parts as may be found necessary for the uses of an increased population. To adopt the first of these methods might tend to defeat the very objects which it is the duty of a colonial governor to promote; and a rule which rests on considerations of public policy cannot be said to be reason- [294]-ably applied when its application may probably lead to that result.

Their Lordships have, accordingly, come to the conclusion that, assuming the Crown to be affected by the rule against perpetuities in England, it was nevertheless inapplicable, in the year 1823, to Crown grants of land in the Colony of New South Wales.

One remarkable feature of *Cooper v Stuart* is Lord Watson's remark that their Lordships had "[292] not been referred to any Act or Ordinance" relating to the reception of English law in New South Wales. Their decision is based on "[293] the silent operation of constitutional principles", relied upon in apparent ignorance of the *Australian Courts Act*, and of any earlier instruments. To be sure, if the *Australian Courts Act* is understood as effecting, on 25 July 1828, a reception of English law into what had previously been a legal vacuum, it could have no bearing on whether the rule against perpetuities was in force in 1823. But the *Australian Courts Act* has not usually been understood in that way. Their Lordships had been referred to the Royal Commission to Governor Brisbane in 1821, "[292] but it gives no indication of the law which was to be in force in the Colony". In the contrasting case of *Jex v McKinney* (1889) 14 App Cas 77, to which Lord Watson refers, the colonial legislature of British Honduras (now Belize) had itself passed an Act in 1856 making English laws applicable "in so far as they are applicable or can be applied to this Settlement and the inhabitants thereof, and are not at variance with or qualified by any local law or recognised custom thereof".

Their Lordships' refusal to apply the rule against perpetuities to a Crown grant was based on their assessment of whether such a rule would be "beneficial" and consonant with "public policy" in a developing colony. Australian courts have taken a more limited view of the test to be applied. In 1904 the High Court rejected an argument that, at the critical date, the common law doctrine of "ancient lights" had been inapplicable in New South Wales. According to that doctrine one may, by prescription, acquire an easement for uninterrupted access of air and light to one's windows. For Sir Thomas Littleton in the 1480s, the proof of such an easement had depended on continuous usage from time immemorial, but by the time of Lord Mansfield in 1786, 20 years' continuous usage was enough. Even that 20-year period would have been impossible for any of the settler population to comply with in 1788, but by 1828 it was of course possible. For Griffith CJ the issue was whether the law relating to "ancient lights" had been "[297] introduced into New South Wales, either upon the settlement of that colony, or by the Statute, 9 Geo IV c 83 (passed in 1828)". His answer can only be understood as asserting that the doctrine, though not originally "received" in 1788, was "received" by the operation of the *Australian Courts Act* on 25 July 1828. On that basis the judgment given by Griffith CJ included an elaborate review of the English authorities on "ancient lights" up to 1828.

Delohery v Permanent Trustee Co of NSW
(1904) 1 CLR 283

Griffith CJ: [310] [I]t is clear that before 1828 the law of England was clearly settled so far as judicial decision could settle it.

Was then this law part of the common law introduced into New South Wales on settlement? Or, if not, was it, in the words of the Act of 9 Geo IV, a law "which can be applied" in the administration of justice in New South Wales?

In *Attorney-General v Stewart* ([(1817)] 2 Mer, 143 [35 ER 895]), a case in which the question was whether the English *Statute of Mortmain* had been introduced into the colony of Granada, *Sir W Grant*, MR, said [2 Mer at 160-1]: "Whether the Statute be in force in the Island of Granada will, as it seems to me, depend on this consideration, whether it be a law of local policy adapted solely to the country in which it was made, or a general regulation of property equally applicable to any country in which it is by the rules of English law that property is governed." Applying this test, which has been generally accepted, we think that the law of prescription, which is, in various forms, part of the law of most civilized countries, cannot be regarded as a law of local policy adapted solely to the locality in which it was made, but must be regarded as a general regulation of property. In this regard we are unable to draw any distinction in principle between prescription at common law and prescription by Statute. It has never been doubted that the *Statute of Limitations* of 1623 (21 Jac I, c 16) applied to New South Wales (*Devine v Holloway*, [(1861)] 14 Moo PC, 290 [15 ER 314]), and it was expressly decided in *Attorney-General v Love*, [[1898] AC 679], that the *Nullum Tempus Act* (9 Geo III, c 16) is in force there. The learned Chief Judge appears to have thought that, in determining whether any particular part of the law of England was introduced into New South Wales by the Statute of 1828, the test to be applied is to consider whether the law is beneficial, by which we understand him to mean suitable to the existing conditions of Australia. But whether a law is suitable or beneficial to a country or not is a question for the legislature, and not for a Court of law. Moreover, the test prescribed by the Statute is **[311]** not whether the law is suitable or beneficial, but whether it can be applied. It is plain that a law may be applicable in the sense that it can be administered, although it may, as a matter of opinion, be considered not "applicable," in the sense of being suitable or beneficial. The Statute does not, indeed, itself use the term "applicable," from the use of which in a double sense confusion has arisen ...

We cannot see that there would be any difficulty in administering the law of prescription, so far as it regards ancient lights, in a new country, so soon as occupation had proceeded to such an extent as to allow of a continued enjoyment for 20 years. Possibly in determining whether the enjoyment was unexplained, some different, and, indeed, novel considerations might arise, but this would not render impracticable the administration or application of the law itself.

This approach depends on focusing strictly on the words of s 24 of the *Australian Courts Act* ("shall be applied ... so far as the same can be applied"). A more flexible approach may be better attuned to the nature of the unwritten common law principles to be received.

Skelton v Collins
(1966) 115 CLR 94

Windeyer J: [134] Our ancestors brought the common law of England to this land. Its doctrines and principles are the inheritance of the British race, and as such they became the common law of Australia. To suppose that this was a body of rules waiting always to be declared and applied may be for some people satisfying as an abstract theory. But it is simply not true in fact. It overlooks the creative element in the work of courts. It would mean for example, that the principle of *Donoghue v Stevenson* [[1932] AC 562], decided in the House of Lords in 1932 by a majority of three to two, became law in Sydney Cove on 26th January 1788 or was in 1828 made part of the law of New South Wales by 9 Geo IV c 83, s 25. In a system based, as ours is, on case law and precedent there is both an inductive and a deductive element in judicial reasoning, especially in a court of final appeal for a particular realm or territory.

It is, of course, impossible for anyone to say that a decision of the House of Lords is wrong in the sense of not a correct decision according to the law of England prevailing in England. But how far the reasoning of judgments in a particular case in England accords with common law principles that are Australia's inheritance is a matter that this Court may have sometimes to consider for itself. This Court is the guardian for all Australia of the corpus iuris committed to its care by the Imperial Parliament. The Constitution makes its judgments in its appellate jurisdiction final and conclusive ...

[135] This is not the place for an essay on jurisprudence or a full consideration of the theoretical problem of reconciling a common heritage of doctrine with the development of differing doctrines. It is enough I think to say that our inheritance of the law of England does not consist of a number of specific legacies selected from time to time for us by English courts. We have inherited a body of law. We take it as a universal legatee. We take its method and its spirit as well as its particular rules. A narrower view than this would put a sad strain upon allegiance. Here, as it is in England, the common law is a body of principles capable of application to new situations, and in some degree of change by development. Lord Reid recently said in the House of Lords: "I have never taken a narrow view of the functions of this House as an appellate tribunal. The common law must be developed to meet changing economic conditions and habits of thought, and I would not be deterred by expressions of opinion in this House in old cases": *Myers v Director of Public Prosecutions* [[1965] AC 1001 at 1021]. And we, in this Court, need not, in exercising our functions as an appellate tribunal, be deterred by expressions of opinion in their Lordships' House in old cases or new cases. Nevertheless I believe that we must not only give respectful attention to whatever is said there, but that the decision of the majority of their Lordships on questions of common law will ordinarily be followed in this Court, leaving it to the Australian legislatures to correct the result if they think fit. But all judgments of the House of Lords are not equally persuasive and all statements in all speeches of their Lordships are not equally acceptable. This Court must consider the question for itself; and all the more so, it seems to me, if the decision in England was reached after reference only to English decisions, not to the state of the law elsewhere, and seemingly to meet only economic and social conditions prevailing in England. And too what is said is less persuasive when law is as it were fluid and when the conditions which it is being developed to meet are not the same in England and Australia. The law of damages, especially damages or personal injuries, is of that kind. It is a branch of the law in which further developments and fresh refinements in the application of principles are still going on: and the backgrounds against which it operates are not the same in England and in Australia ... **[136]** Uniformity and solidarity of law throughout the countries inhabited by British peoples may up to a point be a good in themselves. But too much store can be set upon uniformity of law when it operates in conditions that are not uniform.

In two remarkable decisions in the late 1970s, the High Court held that two common law rules – one very ancient, one quite recent – were in force in Australia. The ancient doctrine was that of "civil death" – the idea that, once a person convicted of a felony has been sentenced to death, the resulting attainder or "corruption of the blood" renders that person incapable of suing in the civil courts. Darcy Dugan was sentenced to death in 1950, but the sentence was commuted to life imprisonment. In the 1970s he sued a newspaper for defamation; but the High Court majority accepted a defence that the notion of civil death had been received in Australia in 1788, and was still in force. It followed that Dugan was attainted as "civilly dead" and could not sue (*Dugan v Mirror Newspapers Ltd* (1978) 142 CLR 583).

The more recent doctrine, also held to have been "received", was the rule in *Searle v Wallbank* [1947] AC 341 in which the House of Lords held, by way of exception to the general principles of negligence, that a landowner has no duty to prevent animals straying onto a highway. That rule was invoked in *State Government Insurance Commission v Trigwell* (1979) 142 CLR 617, where the plaintiffs (members of the Trigwell family) had been injured when their vehicle collided with another vehicle driven by Christine Rooke (who had been killed in the accident). It appeared that Rooke had collided with two sheep on the highway and that, as a result of that collision or in an attempt to avoid it, she had collided with the Trigwells. The owners of the sheep (the Kerins) were joined as defendants in the action. It was alleged that the presence of the sheep on the highway was the result of their negligence, or alternatively that it constituted a nuisance which they had failed to prevent. A majority of the High Court held that *Searle v Wallbank* had been received into South Australian law upon settlement in 1836, and absolved the Kerins of any liability for the straying sheep. Mason J observed that the legislative abolition of the rule in the United Kingdom "**[636]** has no relevance for us, except to confirm my opinion that the question should be left to Parliament". The rule has now been abolished by legislation in all Australian jurisdictions except Queensland and the Northern Territory; and in *Commissioner of Main Roads v Jones* (2005) 215 ALR 418, an argument that a roads authority should have posted signs warning motorists of straying animals was unanimously dismissed.

(b) Statute Law

The statutory "cut-off dates" (25 July 1828 for the four eastern States; 1 June 1829 for Western Australia and 28 December 1836 for South Australia) were important primarily as determining the "reception" of English statute law. English statutes passed before the specified date were automatically "received" (unless clearly unsuitable for colonial conditions), and remain in force today unless validly repealed by a competent legislature. Those passed after the specified date did not apply unless, expressly or by clear implication, they were intended to apply to the colonies through the exercise of the continuing power of the Imperial Parliament to make law for all or any parts of the British Empire by "paramount force".

Alex Castles, "The Reception and Status of English Law in Australia"
(1963) 2 Adelaide Law Review 1

[14] The difficulties which arose in Australia on the application of English statutory law mainly occurred in the context of applying those statutes which were received under the common law and did not apply by paramount force. As far as the statutes which applied by paramount force were concerned, it was beyond dispute that the British Parliament had an inherent right to make and unmake law in British overseas possessions.

Under the common law principles relating to the reception of English statutory law, which did not apply in a settled colony by paramount force, particular importance was attached to the date of settlement. Only those British statutes in force on the date of settlement, deemed to be applicable to the "situation and condition of the infant colony", were received under the common law. Amendments to such statutes or even their repeal by the British Parliament, subsequent to the date of settlement, did not affect their operation in a colony unless the British Parliament made special provision to incorporate these changes in the law of the overseas possession. Similarly, new legislative enactments of the British Parliament after a colony's settlement did not apply to it unless the British legislation operated in the colony by paramount force …

[16] The date set for the reception of British statutes is not only important because it delimits the class of enactments, which can be applied under the common law, to those in force in Britain at that time. The same date looms large in the practical application of the common law principles to concrete situations. Unlike the reception of the common law, British statutes in force at the date of settlement could not be subsequently attracted if they were unsuitable to the circumstances and condition of a colony at the time English law was received …

[17] In determining the applicability of British statutes … two main considerations had to be taken into account. Firstly, the courts had to examine a particular British statute to ascertain its general suitability to overseas possessions. Secondly, even if such a statute might generally be suitable for overseas possessions the question still remained whether such a statute was suitable to the circumstances and conditions prevailing in a colony at the time of the reception of English law.

As Blackstone had recognised in his Commentaries, not all British statutes could become part of the "birthright" law of a settled colony. Statutes which contained "artificial distinctions and refinements", specifically referring to British conditions, such as the "laws of police and revenue, the mode of maintenance for the established clergy, the jurisdiction of spiritual courts" might well be neither "necessary nor convenient" for a settled colony. In such instances the statutes could not be received into a colony under the common law ...

[19] As the cases on this issue have demonstrated, however, problems on the applicability of British statutes can arise if the Statutes contain general provisions as well as others which are particularly related to special British conditions. The weight of judicial opinion would seem to favour the view that the whole of a British enactment need not be applicable before it can become part of the received statutory law of an overseas possession. The situation ... was perhaps best summed up by Chief Justice Griffith in the High Court cases of *Quan Yi[c]k v Hinds* [(1905) 2 CLR 345 at 364] and *Mitchell v Scales* [(1907) 5 CLR 405]. In the first of these cases the Chief Justice stated that if the general provisions of a British statute were not unsuitable to the conditions of the Colony, "the mere fact that some minor or several provisions could not come into operation owing to local circumstances is not sufficient reason for denying the applicability of the Statute as a whole. On the other hand if the general provisions of a Statute were inapplicable it would seem to follow that it is not competent to select a particular provision of the Statute which if it stood alone might be applicable and to say that it is therefore applicable."

Quan Yick v Hinds (1905) 2 CLR 345 was one of a series of cases in which Chinese Australians were prosecuted under the *Lotteries Act 1823* (UK) for selling tickets in a Chinese lottery. In *Anderson v Ah Nam* (1904) 4 SR (NSW) 492, the Supreme Court of New South Wales had held that the 1823 Act *was* in force, relying on the first limb of the proposition stated by Griffith CJ above, and quoting (at 499) from Manning J in *R v Colan* (1878) 1 SCR (NSW) (NS) 1: "[4] We are to apply the laws of England as far as we can, and ought not to hold a whole Act inoperative, because some of its minor provisions cannot, under our local circumstances, be complied with". However, the decision on the *Lotteries Act* was overruled in *Quan Yick v Hinds*, which held that the relevant provision would not have been enforceable since its enforcement would have depended on s 41 of the *Vagrancy Act 1824* (UK) ("An Act for the Punishment of idle and disorderly Persons, and Rogues and Vagabonds, in that Part of *Great Britain* called *England*"). It was, said Griffith CJ, impossible to pick out s 41 from an Act whose more general provisions were clearly not applicable in New South Wales. It was in that context that he formulated the second limb of the proposition quoted above. In *Mitchell v Scales* (1907) 5 CLR 405, he repeated the point: "[411] You cannot select one isolated provision and say that that alone is such as might have been made law in New South Wales".

One factor in the apparent reluctance to treat English statutes as "received" may have been a belief that the emergent local legislatures should be free to make their own laws. It was thought at one stage that, once received, an English statute could not be repealed by a local legislature (see §5 below). Indeed, Stephen J suggested as much in the New South Wales Supreme Court in *Ex parte Lyons – In re Wilson* (1939) 1 Legge 140: "[153] I take it to be clear, that, if this Court shall once determine any given statute to be in force, the Colonial Legislature can have no power to repeal, even if they had to amend it". In that case the Court was asked to determine whether the *Bankruptcy Amendment Act 1825* (UK) was in force in New South Wales (so as to give the Court a bankruptcy jurisdiction). The draft of a New South Wales bankruptcy law had already been circulated. In an interesting clash of colonial attitudes Stephen J thought the local draft far superior to the English model; Willis J thought quite the reverse. But they both agreed with Dowling CJ that the English model was not "applicable".

Ex parte Lyons – In re Wilson
(1839) 1 Legge 140

Dowling CJ: [142] [I]t is quite obvious from every clause in it, that the English Bankrupt Law could not be carried out into practical operation in this Colony. It contemplates a state of things that does not exist here. The initiatory jurisdiction is given to the Lord Chancellor alone; it authorises the appointment of Commissioners and other officers ... by that high functionary only; provides for the publication of proceedings in the *London Gazette*, and English newspapers; … it imposes penalties on different parties, says what shall be done with bankrupts having privilege of Parliament, points out the course to be taken in seizing the effects of a bankrupt in Ireland and Scotland, prescribes the duties of Masters in Chancery and Masters Extraordinary, points out the course to be taken with the bankrupt's estates abroad and in colonies, regulates the mode of enrolling the proceedings under the Commission, makes provision as to copy-hold lands, exempts proceedings from stamp and auction duties, – in short, every clause of the Act contemplates a vast variety of matters and things unknown in this Colony; and we could no more fit the law, as it is thus enacted, to the state of this young country, than we could apply the English Marriage Act, the **[143]** English Poor Laws, Tithe Laws, Usury Laws, Revenue Laws, and many other laws not necessary nor convenient for this part of the world. It may be, and I think it is absolutely necessary for this Colony to have some Law of Bankruptcy, but it is neither convenient nor practicable to adopt the English Bankrupt Law, even if it were undeniably the best system ever enacted for a commercial people. One irresistible objection, if no other existed, … would be the frightful expense involved, in order to carry it into operation.

The status of received Imperial laws is now dealt with by statute. The Imperial Acts received in the Australian States are listed in, for example, the *Imperial Acts Application Acts* passed in New South Wales in 1969, in Victoria in 1980, and in Queensland in 1984.

3. Powers of Colonial Legislatures

The bicameral legislatures established in the Australian colonies under 19th-century British rule did not have the theoretical omnicompetence of the Parliament at Westminster. Nor did they have the same history of gradual organic evolution. Each had achieved its legal and institutional presence at a precise historical moment by the operation of a "higher law", that is, an Act of the British Parliament which took effect by virtue of British "parliamentary sovereignty" (see Chapter 3, §4(a)). In that sense they were subordinate legislatures.

Nevertheless, by the 1850s, the political slogan of "responsible government" was powerful enough to ensure that the colonies received real powers of local self-government (see, for example, *Constitution Act 1854* (Tas); *Constitution Act 1855* (NSW)). Moreover, their very derivation from the British Parliament gave them a kind of continuity with its organic traditions. Accordingly, the theory was that within their limits of subject and area, the colonial legislatures had the same omnicompetence as their legislative creator (see Chapter 11, §§1-2). After all, they had been made in its image.

This theory was expressed by the Privy Council in a series of cases beginning with *R v Burah* (1878) 3 App Cas 889. An Indian statute in 1869, passed after repeated outbreaks of political violence amongst the Himalayan hill tribes to the north of Bengal, authorised the Lieutenant-Governor of Bengal to issue notifications removing the hill areas from the jurisdiction of the courts, in effect subjecting them to martial law. Under that regime, Burah and his accomplice Book Singh were convicted of murder. They sought to appeal to the Calcutta High Court, which held that it did have jurisdiction. The Crown appealed to the Privy Council.

The first question was whether the Act of 1869 had purported to take away the right of appeal to the High Court. As a matter of construction, their Lordships held that it had. The next issue was whether the Indian legislature could validly do this. In part, this depended on whether the Act was inconsistent with the *Indian High Courts Act 1861* (Imp). Their Lordships held that there was no inconsistency, finding on the contrary that "**[903]** such an exercise of legislative authority … is expressly contemplated and authorized both by those [Imperial] statutes and by the letters patent themselves".

The final argument was that the power given to the Lieutenant-Governor to determine by notification in the *Gazette* the areas in which the Act of 1869 would operate, involved a delegation to him of legislative power, thus violating the maxim *delegatus non potest delegare* ("a delegate may not itself delegate"). Their Lordships held that there was no delegation of legislative power. The legislature had devised a change in the criminal justice system, leaving it to the Lieutenant-Governor to say at what time that change would take place. In any event, their Lordships held that the maxim *delegatus non potest delegare* was irrelevant since the Indian Legislature was not in any sense a "delegate".

R v Burah
(1878) 3 App Cas 889

Lord Selborne (for their Lordships): [904] The Indian Legislature has powers expressly limited by the Act of the Imperial Parliament which created it, and it can, of course, do nothing beyond the limits which circumscribe these powers. But, when acting within those limits, it is not in any sense an agent or delegate of the Imperial Parliament, but has, and was intended to have, plenary powers of legislation, as large, and of the same nature, as those of Parliament itself. The established Courts of Justice, when a question arises whether the prescribed limits have been exceeded, must of necessity determine that question; and the only way in which they can properly do so, is by looking to the terms of the instrument by which, affirmatively, the legislative powers [905] were created, and by which, negatively, they are restricted. If what has been done is legislation, within the general scope of the affirmative words which give the power, and if it violates no express condition or restriction by which that power is limited (in which category would, of course, be included any Act of the Imperial Parliament at variance with it), it is not for any Court of Justice to inquire further, or to enlarge constructively those conditions and restrictions.

The reference in this passage to limitations arising from any "[905] express condition or restriction", including those imposed by "Act[s] of the Imperial Parliament", was a reminder that a colonial legislature was still a subordinate institution, dependent at least initially on the will of the Imperial Parliament and unable to override that will. The extent of this constraint was unclear. At the least, however, it meant that the Imperial Parliament, which had created the colonial legislature, could make and re-make the rules controlling its degree of subordination.

Their Lordships repeated these doctrines in *Hodge v The Queen* (1883) 9 App Cas 117. Under the *Liquor License Act 1877* (Ontario), the License Commissioners had prohibited the playing of billiards in taverns. The first question involved the federal distribution of powers in Canada under the *British North America Act 1867* (Imp). Did liquor licensing come within the list of Dominion powers in s 91 (as "Regulation of Trade and Commerce"), or within the list of Provincial powers in s 92 (as "Property and Civil Rights in the Province")? Their Lordships held that it came within both. Finally, the maxim *delegatus non potest delegare* was relied on. Again their Lordships held that reliance on that maxim was misconceived.

Hodge v The Queen
(1883) 9 App Cas 117

Sir Barnes Peacock (for their Lordships): [132] It appears to their Lordships, however, that the objection thus raised by the appellants is founded on an entire misconception of the true character and position of the provincial legislatures. They are in no sense delegates of or acting under any mandate from the Imperial Parliament. When the British North America Act enacted that there should be a legislature for Ontario, and that its legislative assembly should have exclusive authority to make laws for the Province and for provincial purposes in relation to the matters enumerated in sect 92, it conferred powers not in any sense to be exercised by delegation from or as agents of the Imperial Parliament, but authority as plenary and as ample within the limits prescribed by sect 92 as the Imperial Parliament in the plenitude of its power possessed and could bestow. Within these limits of subjects and area the local legislature is supreme, and has the same authority as the Imperial Parliament, or the Parliament of the Dominion, would have had under like circumstances to confide to a municipal institution or body of its own creation authority to make by-laws or resolutions as to subjects specified in the enactment, and with the object of carrying the enactment into operation and effect.

It is obvious that such an authority is ancillary to legislation, and without it an attempt to provide for varying details and machinery to carry them out might become oppressive, or absolutely fail. The very full and very elaborate judgment of the Court of Appeal contains abundance of precedents for this legislation, entrusting a limited discretionary authority to others, and has many illustrations of its necessity and convenience. It was argued at the bar that a legislature committing important regulations to agents or delegates effaces itself. That is not so. It retains its powers intact, and can, whenever it pleases, destroy the agency it has created and set up another, or take the matter directly into [its] own hands. How far it shall seek the aid of subordinate agencies, and how long it shall continue them, are matters for each legislature, and not for Courts of Law, to decide.

R v Burah and *Hodge v The Queen* were reviewed and applied in *Powell v Apollo Candle Company* (1885) 10 App Cas 282. The *Customs Regulation Act 1879* (NSW), as well as prescribing customs duties for a long list of dutiable articles, authorised the Governor to fix additional duties. Again, the Privy Council held that the New South Wales Legislature "**[290]** is a Legislature restricted in the area of its powers, but within that area unrestricted, and not acting as an agent or a delegate".

The degree of colonial independence proclaimed by these cases had seemed far less clear in the Australian colonies earlier in the 19th century. Even in the *Apollo Candle Case*, the Supreme Court of New South Wales had initially taken the opposite view to that finally taken by the Privy Council (see *Apollo Candle Coy (Ltd) v Powell* (1883) 4 NSWR 160). It had seemed clear that in some sense the local legislatures must be subordinate to the Imperial Parliament. They had been created by it, exercised powers devolved upon them by it and were bound by the laws which it laid down. How then could these subordinate bodies legislate contrary to the law imposed by the sovereign Parliament? If British statutes applied in the colonies through the colonising power of paramount force, how could a local body legislate inconsistently with those statutes? Indeed, if even the common law was part of the fundamental law which the colonists had brought with them, and which the Imperial Parliament through statutes like the *Australian Courts Act* had declared to apply in Australia, how could a local legislature alter the common law?

In South Australia, these questions were brought to a head by Benjamin Boothby, a judge of that colony's Supreme Court from 1853 to 1867. In a series of cases he held that enactments of the local colonial legislature were invalid by reason of "repugnancy" to the laws of England, including both common and statute law. "Repugnancy" in this context meant simply "inconsistency", and the "inconsistencies" which Boothby J found were often elusively slight.

Alex Castles, "The Reception and Status of English Law in Australia"
(1963) 2 *Adelaide Law Review* 1

[23] By the end of 1858 responsible government, with bicameral Parliaments, vested with ostensibly wide legislative powers, had been created in New South Wales, South Australia, Victoria and Tasmania. As a result of events in South Australia, soon after the attainment of responsible government in that State, the question whether the new legislatures could enact laws contrary to the Statutes and unenacted law which had been received in Australia became a pressing issue.

The focal of the controversy was Judge Benjamin Boothby who had been appointed to the Supreme Court of South Australia by the British government in 1853. It was said that when Boothby's appointment was placed before Queen Victoria for approval she asked: "Why on earth does he want to go to South Australia?" To which the Duke of Newcastle replied: "Ma'm he has nine sons to provide for." A biographer has summed up Boothby J in the following way: "Mr Boothby's career at the bar, although in no way exceptional, had been meritorious, and he had attained a respectable standing. His learning, if it was neither as deep as a well, nor as wide as a Church door, was at least as extensive as that of the average barrister who was a candidate for a colonial judgeship."

For almost ten years the judgments of Boothby J threatened to frustrate many of the legislative endeavours of the South Australian Parliament. Although frequently opposed by Chief Justice Hanson, Boothby J was often joined by Gwynne J, the other judge on the Supreme Court Bench, in striking down local enactments. Three separate grounds were called in aid to test the validity of South Australian legislation. Firstly, Boothby J sometimes claimed that the [24] South Australian Parliament had exceeded its specific powers under its own Constitution and British statutes which applied in the Province by paramount force. Secondly, he argued that some Acts were void because the Governor had failed to reserve the local legislation to England to obtain the Royal Assent. Thirdly, he often asserted that legislation was repugnant to the law of England, and should be struck down on this ground.

To be fair to Boothby, there was substance in the claim that each of these three grounds were recognised as possible ways in which colonial legislation could be struck down. Indeed, there are occasions even today when these grounds may be used to nullify State enactments. But even after taking into account the vituperative partisanship of his critics, who were many, it is hard to deny that Boothby J went considerably further than his contemporaries in denying power to a colonial legislature. His concept of repugnancy in particular, sometimes meant that local laws would be struck down even if there were only minor technical differences between South Australian enactments and the received statutory and unenacted law ...

[25] By 1863, "there seemed no limit to the laws declared invalid through careless drafting or through repugnancy". Governor Daly wrote despairingly to the British government in 1865 that "no one can tell under what laws he is living or what will, in any given instance, be the decision of the Supreme Court." But relief was in sight. Communications passed between South Australia and the British government on the need for remedial legislation to clarify the situation and finally a bill, which became the Colonial Laws Validity Act 1865, was sent from London to Adelaide. The bill was approved by the South Australian government and was returned to England where it was enacted by the British Parliament.

Although the Colonial Laws Validity Act was passed because of the controversial situation that had developed in South Australia in the preceding decade, this Statute was made expressly applicable to all "colonial laws" with the exception of those made in the Channel Islands, the Isle of Man and "such territories as may for the time being [be] vested in Her Majesty under or by virtue of any Act of Parliament for the Government of India". The judicial interpretation of sections 2 and 3 of this Statute soon made it clear that colonial legislatures, such as the South Australian Parliament, were to have much more extensive powers of amending or repealing received English law than Boothby J would have been prepared to accord to them ...

[26] The interpretation placed on sections 2 and 3 of the Colonial Laws Validity Act ensured that colonial legislatures were henceforward only to be bound by British statutes which applied to them by paramount force ...

In *Phillips v Eyre* [(1870) LR 6 QB 1], which was decided soon after the Act came into force, Willes J detailed the meaning to be ascribed to "repugnancy" under the Colonial Laws Validity Act. He said "... it is clear that the repugnancy to English law, which avoids a colonial act, means repugnancy to an Imperial Statute or order made by authority of such statute, applicable to the colony by express words or necessary intend-[27]-ment". As a result of this and other decisions which have interpreted sections 2 and 3 of the Act, "repugnancy" can only arise as a ground for invalidating a "colonial statute" when the local statute is "repugnant" to British laws which apply to the overseas possession by express words or necessary intendment. Subject to two provisoes, this meant that [those] statutes which could apply to South Australia and Western Australia at their dates of settlement, and those Statutes which were made applicable to the other States under the 1828 Act, could be freely amended or repealed by State Parliaments. The first proviso was that local legislation could not exceed the powers vested in a State Parliament under its own Constitution. Secondly, under the Colonial Laws Validity Act, local laws were void if they were repugnant to English statutes which applied to a State by paramount force. A good example of a statute which expressly applied to the Australian States is, of course, the Colonial Laws Validity Act itself. State legislatures were not permitted under the terms of the Act to pass laws "repugnant to the laws of England", and they were also subject to the limitation of "manner and form" contained in section 5, relating to the local alteration of their own constitutions ...

Following the enactment of the Colonial Laws Validity Act the [28] status of English law in Australia could be defined with reasonable clarity. On the one hand, subject to their own consti-tutions and the 1865 British Statute, the Australian states could repeal or amend the British statutes and unenacted English law which had been received under the common law constitutional principles. On the other hand, the States were still bound by British statutes, passed before or after 1865, which applied to them by paramount force.

The *Colonial Laws Validity Act* (see Appendix) confirmed that statutes passed by the colonial legislatures could override received English statutes and common law. However, it also made clear that this power did *not* extend to colonial laws whose effect would be "repugnant to" (that is, inconsistent with) those British statutes applicable by paramount force (that is, those "made applicable to such Colony by ... express Words or necessary Intendment"). Its effect on the authority of the State constitutions (and on the power of the State Parliaments to amend their constitutions) is considered in Chapter 11, §§2(b) and 3; the later operation of the "repugnancy" doctrine is considered in §7(b) below. One example of a legislative instrument made applicable by paramount force is, of course, the Australian Constitution.

4. The Path to Federation

As LF Crisp wrote in *Australian National Government* (Longman Cheshire, 5th ed 1983): "**[1]** There was no Damascus Road miracle about Australia's federal conversion. It took sixty years of spasmodic official effort and fluctuating public interest to bring the Commonwealth into being". The 1890s was the crucial decade. After two Conventions (see *Official Record of the Debates of the Australasian Federal Convention* (1891-98, reprinted Legal Books 1986)), the Constitution was approved by the people of the Australian colonies in referenda from 1898 to 1900. Subject to a negotiated compromise as to the future of appeals to the Privy Council, the approved draft was enacted by the British Parliament as the *Commonwealth of Australia Constitution Act 1900* (Imp). The Act completed its passage through that Parliament on 5 July 1900, was assented to by Queen Victoria on 9 July 1900 and came into force on 1 January 1901.

Patrick Parkinson, *Tradition and Change in Australian Law*
(LBC Information Services, 3rd ed 2005)

[135] From 1788-1855, the development of constitutional law in Australia had progressed to a stage where out of the original penal colony of New South Wales, there had emerged a number of colonies each of which had a bicameral legislature and responsible government ... Already, by 1847, there was some discussion of a federal structure, but the impetus for this came from Britain rather than the Australian colonies. Earl Grey, as Colonial Secretary, had tried to introduce such a structure in the Bill which later became the *Australian Constitutions Act 1850*, in order to promote inter-colonial co-operation, especially over such matters as tariffs. However, 1850 was too early for the colonies to consider federation. Port Phillip had only then been conceded a separate existence as its own colony of Victoria. South Australia prided itself on its differences as a colony with only free settlers, and Western Australia was just beginning to become a place for transportation of convicts at the very time when this was ceasing in Van Diemen's Land, and had already ceased in New South Wales.

It was another 50 years before the Australian colonies were to become a federation. For much of this period, the various colonies were consumed by internal political problems such as land policy and electoral reform. There were, however, numerous issues on which inter-colonial co-operation was necessary or desirable. Chief amongst the problems was that of customs tariffs at colony borders. These were resolved to a certain extent by compacts and compromises, but they were likely to continue as a source of friction between the colonies for as long as protectionist ideas flourished in other parts of the world – as they did in the late 19th century. Victoria, in particular, adopted a protectionist policy from the middle of the 1860s, in order to protect its local industries which were suffering from a severe downturn following the end of the gold-mining boom. By contrast, there was a strong ideological commitment in New South Wales to free trade. The problem of customs duties thus represented both a reason for federation, and an obstacle to it.

Federation had the potential to ensure that throughout the continent, trade and commerce would be unaffected by customs tariffs imposed between the colonies. However, a federated Commonwealth would need to determine whether its tariff policy with regard to imports from overseas would be protectionist or free trade. Complicating the picture was the fact that customs tariffs were not only a means of protecting local industry, but also the main source of income for the colonial governments. Thus, while Victoria and New South Wales were opposed to one another in their philosophy about **[136]** trade, both in fact had tariffs; one was designed to protect local industry, while in the other, customs duties were fixed as a source of governmental revenue.

These were not the only tensions which inhibited federation. The colonies also had to be persuaded that federation was in their interests. For those colonies which were smaller in population, there was the potential for losing their identity in the larger mass, and being dominated by New South Wales. For the larger colonies there was the possibility that they could be required to subsidise the struggling economies of Tasmania and South Australia, and, if it joined, Western Australia. Furthermore, the experience of other federations in the second half of the 19th century was less than inspiring. In particular, the United States had experienced a traumatic civil war.

If there were reasons to be cautious about federation, there were other factors which drew the colonies closer together. Fear of common enemies was one cause of co-operation ... The expansion of German interests in the South Pacific, and the activities of the French, led to the formation of a body to represent the affairs of the Australasian colonies in their relations with the South Pacific islands. Formally established in 1885, the founding members of the Federal Council of Australasia were Victoria, Tasmania, Queensland, Western Australia and Fiji. South Australia joined later, for a short period, but New South Wales and New Zealand were not involved. The Federal Council had the power to pass Bills in relation to such matters as the exclusion of criminals, extradition, the enforcement of judgments beyond the borders of a colony and the regulation of fisheries. It was the first major form of inter-colonial co-operation, and a movement towards closer ties was encouraged by an increasing nationalism amongst Australians, the great majority of whom were native born. However, for as long as New South Wales remained outside of the Council, it could not be an effective federal voice; New South Wales preferred to deal with its problems alone and was large enough to do so ...

It was in the course of the 1890s that serious proposals were developed for a federation ... Henry Parkes, the Premier of New South Wales, was instrumental in encouraging this further discussion. He involved leaders of the other colonies in attending a conference in Melbourne in 1890, which led to the National Australasian Convention, meeting in Sydney in 1891. New Zealand was represented at both the conference and the Convention, although there was no great likelihood that it would want to enter into the proposed federation, and its delegates realised that their participation was mainly as interested observers.

A basic question for the delegates to these assemblies was how to structure a federation within the Westminster tradition of government. Britain, of course, could provide **[137]** no experience with federation, since the Scots, the Welsh and the Irish were part of a United Kingdom, not a federated one ... Canada did offer an example of federation within a Westminster system of government. The *British North America Act 1867*, which had formed the Canadian provinces into a federation, provided a model with respect to the relations between the federation and the Crown within the context of the Empire. However, there was less enthusiasm for other aspects of the Canadian approach. In particular, it was considered by the smaller Australian colonies that the Canadian Constitution gave far too much power to the central government. In its division of legislative powers between the provinces and the federal government, it had enumerated a list of powers given to the centre and a list of powers retained by the provinces. All other powers were to be exercised centrally. Parkes put forward as a central proposition at Sydney that "the powers and privileges and territorial rights of the several existing Colonies shall remain intact, except in respect to such surrenders as may be agreed upon as necessary and incidental to the power and authority of the National Federal government".

Although Switzerland provided another example of a federation, it was inevitable that the delegates should look to the Constitution of the United States as the other major model of a federation within the English-speaking world. The American Constitution provided an example for the protection of States' rights. It gave just a few powers to the federal government and left the majority of matters within the legislative competence of the States. It also provided that the Senate should consist of an equal number of members from each State while the House of Representatives should reflect the national distribution of population. It was early perceived that a suitable constitution for Australia would marry the American concept of a Senate representing each State equally with the Westminster system of government by which the government of the day, with its ministers drawn from the ranks of the Parliament, would be required to maintain the confidence of a popularly elected lower House ...

[138] [T]here was much in the way of detail which had to be resolved before the various colonies could agree to enter into a federation. There would be strong resistance to the federation in New South Wales unless its politicians could be satisfied that the federation's tariff policy would not be protectionist. One former Victorian premier described this as "the lion in the way" of federation. A further fundamental issue was how to distribute the excess customs duties from the central government to the States. Sir Samuel Griffith, sometime premier of Queensland, and later the first Chief Justice of the High Court of Australia, identified with great clarity at the Sydney Convention perhaps the greatest problem of all: how to structure the relationship between the lower and upper houses within the federal Parliament. How were they to reconcile government by a majority of the people with government by a majority of the States? If the latter consideration was important, then the Senate must be given a power of veto over Bills emanating from the lower house, including money Bills. Otherwise, the most populated States, Victoria and New South Wales, with their dominance in the lower house, would have effective control over the country. The smaller colonies, by and large, thus favoured a powerful Senate. In Victoria and New South Wales, however, there was great nervousness about the potential which this would create for serious conflict between the upper and lower houses ...

The 1891 Convention attempted answers to some of these questions. It produced a draft Constitution, under the guidance of Griffith ...

The Convention agreed that this draft constitution should be submitted to the colonial Parliaments. However, the enthusiasm of some of its proponents was not matched by widespread support in the various colonies. The Convention had been attended only by parliamentary representatives. It had not galvanised popular support. Furthermore, opponents pointed out the areas in which the draft Constitution had [139] avoided the difficult issues. The Bill lapsed in New South Wales, and the other colonies were unwilling to proceed unless and until New South Wales signalled its commitment ...

It was not until 1895 that the federation movement gained a major fresh impetus. A proposal was accepted by the premiers of the six Australian colonies to establish a new Convention by popular vote, with the resulting draft of the constitution being submitted to the electors in each colony in a referendum. The enabling Bill was to be submitted to the New South Wales Parliament first, to ensure that the largest colony was committed to the process. The Convention finally met in 1897. Internal political disputes in Queensland meant that it was not represented, and the Western Australian delegation was appointed by the State Parliament rather than elected by popular vote, since it did not pass an enabling Bill in the same terms as the other colonies. New Zealand, which had shown no interest in federation since 1891, was not involved.

The Convention held meetings over the course of a year, beginning first in Adelaide in 1897, later meeting in Sydney and culminating in Melbourne in March 1898. After the Adelaide meeting, the colonial Parliaments took the opportunity to debate the emerging Bill and to suggest changes. The draft Constitution Bill which emerged from this process was in many respects quite similar to the Bill of 1891. The basic principles which had been agreed upon in 1891 were once again adopted in 1898 ...

[An] issue which aroused considerable debate was the question of appeals from the High Court to the Privy Council. A degree of lobbying between the Adelaide and Melbourne sessions, together with indications from London that it wished to retain the possibility of Privy Council appeals in all cases, led to the adoption of a provision that the High Court should be the final court of appeal in matters of constitutional interpretation unless the public interests of another part of Her Majesty's Dominions were involved. While allowing for other appeals from the High Court to the Privy Council, it empowered the federal Parliament to limit the matters upon which such an appeal might lie.

In the Convention, the larger colonies (Victoria and New South Wales) were outnumbered by the smaller ones, since each delegation had an equal number of members. However, before being submitted to London, the draft constitution needed to be ratified by the electorate in each colony, and this referendum allowed the opportunity for these issues to be debated afresh in the public arena. Although the 1898 Bill was a great improvement on its predecessor, still it had features about it which were disturbing **[140]** to New South Wales in particular. One area of concern was about customs duties. At the insistence of the smaller colonies, a section had been inserted into the draft Constitution which provided that three quarters of the customs dues would be paid to the States. This was acceptable to New South Wales as an interim measure in order to help the smaller States put their budgets on a sound financial basis, but it was unacceptable in the longer term because a high tariff would be necessary to meet the growing financial needs of the federal government as it expanded. A second area of concern, not surprisingly, was the question of the powers of the upper house and the way in which deadlocks should be resolved. By allowing deadlocks to be resolved by a three fifths majority in a joint sitting of the Houses, it was realised that this gave disproportionate power to the smaller States to assert their will over that of the House of Representatives, which was taken to reflect the will of a majority of the population.

The referendum in June 1898 saw large majorities in favour of the Bill in Victoria, South Australia and Tasmania. In Western Australia, no referendum was held, although the Bill was considered again by Parliament. Queensland remained outside the process. In New South Wales, the Bill was passed by a small majority of those who voted, but the affirmative vote did not reach the minimum number of those eligible to vote which had been specified by the New South Wales Parliament in its enabling legislation.

The result was that further negotiations took place between the premiers, including the premier of Queensland. They agreed to amend the deadlock provision so that, following a dissolution of both Houses, only an overall majority in a joint sitting of the Houses was required to resolve the deadlock. Further, they agreed that the provision which stipulated that three quarters of the customs revenues would be given back to the States should be limited to the first ten years of federation, unless federal Parliament provided for its continuance. They added to this a seemingly innocuous proviso that the Parliament might grant financial assistance to any State on such terms and conditions as it saw fit … Other difficulties were also resolved by the premiers' conference, including the location of the seat of government within the territory of New South Wales, at least 100 miles from Sydney.

In its amended form, the draft constitution was submitted afresh to a referendum in every colony except Western Australia. This included Queensland, despite its absence from the Convention. It secured the approval of the electors, and the legislatures of each colony formally passed an Address requesting the Queen to enact the Bill in the Westminster Parliament. This was necessary, for only by an Act of the imperial Parliament could there be any legal basis for the federation of a group of colonies. Western Australia held back at that stage. The Bill as accepted by the five colonies went to Britain where a final opportunity presented itself for those who were dissatisfied with any aspect of the Bill to seek changes by lobbying the Colonial Office. The instructions given to the delegates from the Australian colonies by their governments were that they should endeavour to maintain the text as it had been put to the electors, and that they should oppose any changes suggested by the government in Britain. Nonetheless, they were reliant on the Westminster Parliament to pass the relevant legislation, and eventually, changes were forced on them.

The issue was the question of Privy Council appeals. There was disquiet among the Chief Justices of some of the colonies at the prospect that the federal Parliament could pass legislation severely curtailing the right to appeal from the High Court to the Privy Council. The result of this lobbying was that the imperial government insisted upon alterations to the relevant clause. It provided, as enacted, that on constitutional matters concerning the limits of the powers of the Commonwealth or States, no appeal should **[141]** be taken to the Privy Council unless the High Court first certified that the matter should be determined by the Council. The power of the federal Parliament to curtail appeals from the High Court in other matters was retained, but any such Bills should be reserved for "Her Majesty's Pleasure".

Finally, the *Commonwealth of Australia Constitution Act* was passed by the British Parliament in 1900. Western Australia agreed to join the Commonwealth in time for it to be an original member at the beginning of the Federation on January 1st 1901. The Commonwealth of Australia thus came into being nearly ten years after the Convention meeting in Sydney had approved for the first time, a draft Bill for a federal constitution.

The framers of the Constitution were mainly concerned with the financial and trade issues arising from Federation and how best to weigh the interests of the small States against those of the more populous States in the new federal Parliament. In these and other areas they adapted provisions from the United States Constitution. However, they did not include a Bill of Rights.

The Tasmanian Attorney-General, Andrew Inglis Clark (1848-1907) argued at the 1891 Convention for inclusion of a range of provisions protecting human rights. His efforts are reflected in ss 80 and 116 of the Constitution, which respectively guarantee (so far as Commonwealth law is concerned) the right to a jury trial for indictable offences, and freedom of religion. However, he was unable to gain support for a clause based on the Fourteenth Amendment to the United States Constitution, which would have provided:

110 The citizens of each state, and all other persons owing allegiance to the Queen and residing in any territory of the Commonwealth, shall be citizens of the Commonwealth, and shall be entitled to all privileges and immunities of citizens of the Commonwealth in the several states; and a state shall not make or enforce any law abridging any privilege or immunity of citizens of the Commonwealth; nor shall a state deprive any person of life, liberty, or property without due process of law, or deny to any person within its jurisdiction the equal protection of its laws.

The delegates to the 1897-98 Convention rejected this clause. Instead, they inserted what became s 117 of the Constitution, which is limited to laws that impose a disability or discrimination on the basis of State residence. The rejection of Clark's clause 110 reveals some important themes in the drafting of the Australian Constitution.

George Williams, *Human Rights under the Australian Constitution*
(Oxford University Press, 1999)

[39] Many of the framers were clearly influenced by the works of two nineteenth-century English constitutional commentators, J Bryce (*The American Commonwealth*) and AV Dicey (*Introduction to the Study of the Law of the Constitution*). Both authors were sceptical of the need to expressly guarantee rights in written constitutions. Writing within a scheme of responsible government, Dicey argued that civil liberties can be adequately protected through the common law and political processes without the incorporation of guarantees of rights in a written constitution. He saw this as one aspect of the rule of law. The failure to include a Bill of Rights in the Australian Constitution was consistent with the Diceyean notion of parliamentary sovereignty, which Dicey described as the 'dominant characteristic of our political institutions'. By parliamentary sovereignty, Dicey meant 'that Parliament ... has ... the right to make or unmake any law whatever; and, further, that no person or body is recognised by the law of England as having a right to override or set aside the legislation of Parliament'. This found expression in a diluted form in the Australian Constitution, in the grant of plenary power to the Commonwealth in the specified areas listed mainly in sections 51 and 52, but subject to the adoption of the United States notion of judicial review, under which the High Court can invalidate legislation inconsistent with the Constitution. Parliamentary sovereignty found clearer expression in the unwillingness of the Convention delegates to place fetters on the power of the new federal and state Parliaments to abrogate human rights.

The desire of the delegates that the Australian Constitution reflect their British inheritance was clearly manifested in the Convention debates. Several delegates suggested that the Australian Constitution did not need to incorporate express rights as the rule of law would provide adequate protection: 'Like anyone else within the English tradition, they must have felt that the protections to individual rights provided by the traditions of acting as honourable men were quite sufficient for a civilised society'. [40] Thus, in Melbourne in 1898, in the debate over Clark's clause 110, Dr Alexander Cockburn, former Premier of South Australia, argued that it would 'be a reflection on our civilization' if the Australian Constitution protected Australians from laws that would 'deprive any person of life, liberty, or property without due process of law'. He argued that such constitutional protection would mean that 'People would say – "Pretty things these States of Australia; they have to be prevented by a provision in the Constitution from doing the grossest injustice"'. Here, in the words of Sir Owen Dixon, former Chief Justice of the High Court, Cockburn was asking why 'should doubt be thrown on the wisdom and safety of entrusting to the chosen representatives of the people … all legislative power, substantially without fetter or restriction?'

This position did not go entirely unchallenged. O'Connor replied strongly that protection was needed as a right attaching to the citizenship of the Australian people:

> We are making a Constitution which is to endure, practically speaking, for all time. We do not know when some wave of popular feeling may lead a majority in the Parliament of a state to commit an injustice by passing a law that would deprive citizens of life, liberty, or property without due process of law.

After interjections by Isaacs and Cockburn, and a suggestion by John Gordon of South Australia that 'might you not as well say that the states should not legalize murder', O'Connor continued: 'We need not go far back in history to find cases in which the community, seized with a sort of madness with regard to particular offences, have set aside all principles of justice' … After Sir Edward Braddon of Tasmania pointed out that the clause 'is calculated to do harm rather than good' and would also interfere with the 'rights of the several states', the guarantee that no person be deprived of life, liberty, or property except with due process of law was rejected by 23 votes to 19 …

[41] Clause 110 was also rejected because the delegates were concerned to maintain the power of colonies, once they became the Australian states, to discriminate between people on the ground of their race. Cockburn argued that the Fourteenth Amendment to the United States Constitution had been inserted 'to inflict the grossest outrage which could be inflicted on the Southern planters, by saying – "You shall not forbid the negro inhabitants to vote. We insist on their being placed on an equal footing in regard to the exercise of the franchise with yourselves"'. Cockburn's position is clear from his focus on the 'outrage' committed on the southern American states rather than on any prior abrogation of the rights of black Americans. In Cockburn's view, there was no need for clause 110 because 'We are not going to have a civil war here over a racial question'.

The debate on clause 110 undermined any pretence that the framers were generally concerned to foster human rights or that they viewed responsible government as being appropriate because of its scope to protect minority rights. Their intention was in fact the opposite: to ensure that the Australian Constitution did not prevent the colonies, once they became states, from continuing to enact racially discriminatory legislation. After Isaacs had pointed out that clause 110 would prevent the colonies discriminating against people on the basis of their race, Higgins interjected: 'It protects Chinamen too, I suppose, as well as negroes?' Isaacs answered this by arguing that clause 110 should be deleted because it might otherwise override racially discriminatory factory legislation in the colonies. He supported this by reference to the decision of the United States Supreme Court in *Yik Wo v Hopkins* 118 US 356 (1886). That case, on the Fourteenth Amendment to the United States Constitution, showed, Isaacs said, how that amendment operated 'in several cases in a way quite unexpected'. The result in *Yik Wo v Hopkins* was that a 'Chinese established his right in spite of the state legislation to have the same laundry licence as the Caucasians have'. Clause 110 might thus have made it more difficult to gain the support of the 'workers of this colony [Victoria] or of any other colony'.

There were also concerns that clause 110 would override Western Australian laws under which 'no Asiatic or African alien can get a miner's right or go mining on a gold-field'. Sir John Forrest, Premier of Western Australia, summed up the mood of the 1897-98 Convention when he stated:

> It is of no use for us to shut our eyes to the fact that there is a great feeling all over Australia against the introduction of coloured persons. It goes without saying that we do not like to [42] talk about it, but still it is so. I do not want this clause to pass in a shape which would undo what is about to be done in most of the colonies, and what has already been done in Western Australia, in regard to that class of persons.

In formulating the words of s 117 of the Constitution, which replaced Clark's clause 110, Higgins argued that … the new provision 'would allow Sir John Forrest … to have his law with regard to Asiatics not being able to obtain miners' rights in Western Australia. There is no discrimination there based on residence or citizenship; it is simply based on colour and race'.

5. The Colonial Legacy: The Commonwealth

The birth of the Commonwealth of Australia on 1 January 1901 might have been seen as a catalyst for independence from Britain. Legally, however, the Commonwealth was created by the Imperial Parliament's enactment of the Constitution as contained in s 9 of the *Commonwealth of Australia Constitution Act*, that is, by virtue of a British statute applying to Australia by paramount force. Furthermore, the new Commonwealth of Australia was not itself considered to be free from legislation passed with paramount force by the British Parliament. The *Colonial Laws Validity Act* was treated as continuing to apply, through the notion of repugnancy, to limit the legislative power of the Commonwealth as well as the States.

The new federal Commonwealth did not receive British statute law, since it was not subject to the *Australian Courts Act 1828* (Imp). It might therefore have been argued that the Commonwealth Parliament was not limited by the repugnancy doctrine. Moreover, the *Commonwealth of Australia Constitution Act*, as a later enactment of the British Parliament, might have been regarded as impliedly repealing the *Colonial Laws Validity Act* to the extent of any inconsistency. Thus, each grant of legislative power to the Commonwealth in s 51 of the Constitution – as incorporated in s 9 of the *Commonwealth of Australia Constitution Act* – might have been regarded, within its own definitional limits, as freeing the new Parliament from the repugnancy doctrine. However, this was not how it was seen at the time.

In *Union Steamship Co of New Zealand Ltd v Commonwealth* (1925) 36 CLR 130, the High Court held that the repugnancy doctrine continued to apply to the Commonwealth. The Court held that provisions of the *Navigation Act 1912* (Cth) were invalid by reason of "repugnancy" to the *Merchant Shipping Act 1894* (Imp). This conclusion was reached despite s 98 of the Constitution, which reads: "The power of the Parliament to make laws with respect to trade and commerce extends to navigation and shipping".

Yet barely six months earlier the Court had taken a different view. By s 39(2) of the *Judiciary Act 1903* (Cth), the Commonwealth had sought to exclude the possibility of appeals to the Privy Council from State Supreme Courts in constitutional cases. In *Commonwealth v Limerick Steamship Co Ltd* (1924) 35 CLR 69, the High Court held that this provision was valid. It was not repugnant to the specific provision for Privy Council appeals in s 15 of the *Australian Courts Act*, nor to the more general provisions in the *Judicial Committee Act 1844* (Imp), for the simple reason that the power to enact s 39(2) was conferred by the *Commonwealth of Australia Constitution Act*, itself an Imperial statute, and "**[96]** assuming two Imperial enactments conflict, the later must prevail". Note that the argument was not that the Australian Constitution overrode the *Colonial Laws Validity Act*, but only that it overrode the particular Imperial laws that might otherwise have given rise to repugnancy. Those laws, to the extent of their inconsistency with the grants of power in the Commonwealth Constitution, would impliedly be repealed; and there would then be nothing left on which the repugnancy doctrine could operate. Why then did this reasoning not apply in the *Union Steamship Case* to the *Merchant Shipping Act*? In *Commonwealth v Kreglinger & Fernau Ltd* (*Skin Wool Case*) (1926) 37 CLR 393, Isaacs J attempted an explanation. Once again the question was whether s 39(2) of the *Judiciary Act* was repugnant to the Order in Council regulating Privy Council appeals, as authorised by the *Judicial Committee Act*.

Commonwealth v Kreglinger & Fernau Ltd (*Skin Wool Case*)
(1926) 37 CLR 393

Isaacs J: [406] It is true that in each case there is an Imperial Act dealing with a matter from an Empire point of view. But still there are inherent and obvious distinctions. The first is that the shipping regulations dealt with in the *Merchant Shipping Act* 1894 and held to prevail concerned themselves with non-Australian ships, and the substantive rights of other parts of the Empire were involved. The Order in Council in question here is wholly concerned with Australian affairs, the local administration of justice. This is a vital distinction, and is a material factor in attracting an opposite conclusion.

He also relied on the development of responsible government throughout the Empire.

Isaacs J: [414] In relation to the present matter the Australian Constitution is not subordinate to, but is *pro tanto* superior to, the earlier Act, the *Judicial Committee Act*, passed at an earlier stage of constitutional development. The significance of that fact is apprehended when it is remembered that the *Order in Council is an Executive act* to which statutory force is given by the Act under which it is made. But it is an Executive act on the advice of Imperial Ministers responsible only to the Imperial Parliament and yet controlling the civil rights of Australian citizens in Australia to appeal on (assumedly) Federal questions. Though the Order in Council is, for purposes of repugnancy to colonial Acts and consequent invalidity, placed on the same footing as the Act under which it is made, yet it is not on the same footing for all purposes. It is not, for instance, in the same position as the direct regulative provisions of Parliament in the *Merchant Shipping Act* 1894. It needs the intermediate operation of responsible administration; and when that is a factor, it may entirely alter the emphasis to be placed on the later instrument of self-government. That instrument in this case must, in my opinion, be read as modifying the earlier enactment, at least to the extent of leaving the will of the Australian national Parliament on the subject of civil rights in Australia, in relation to Federal matters specifically **[415]** enumerated in the Constitution, free from the control of Imperial ministerial discretion.

Of course, the need for these rather strained distinctions might have been avoided if the High Court had consistently taken the view that the express grants of power to the Commonwealth Parliament in the *Commonwealth of Australia Constitution Act* overrode the repugnancy doctrine of the *Colonial Laws Validity Act*. However, even before the *Commonwealth of Australia Constitution Act* was enacted, the Australian delegates had assured the British government that the new Australian legislature would still be subject to the *Colonial Laws Validity Act* (see Stephen J in *China Ocean Shipping Co v South Australia* (1979) 145 CLR 172 in §7(b) below).

The new Commonwealth and its constituent States were also regarded as limited by the doctrine of extraterritoriality. According to the moderate version of this doctrine, an exercise of colonial legislative power was invalid unless its operation had a sufficient connection with the geographical area of the legislating colony. On a more extreme version, a colony's laws could have no operation outside its territorial borders at all. Despite the uncertainty as to its scope, some version of this doctrine was thought to be applicable to the Commonwealth Parliament until its "adoption" (as from 1939) of s 3 of the *Statute of Westminster 1931* (UK), and to the States until s 2(1) of the *Australia Act 1986* (Cth) came into force in 1986.

It seems clear that the extraterritorial limits on the colonies were overstated. The orthodox Imperial view of colonial legislative competence was consistently that of *Hodge v The Queen* (1883) 9 App Cas 117 (see §3 above) – namely that "**[132]** within [its] limits of subjects and area the local legislature is supreme", with "authority as plenary and as ample … as the Imperial Parliament in the plenitude of its power possessed and could bestow". The question raised by the reference to "limits of … area" was how far the law-making power of a self-governing polity can extend beyond the geographical borders of its own territory.

Obviously, both the actual and the intended operation of any exercise of government power – legislative, executive or judicial – will primarily be upon persons and events within the territorial borders. However, under international law a sovereign state can sometimes legislate extra-territorially – for example, by making laws to regulate not only behaviour on its ships and aircraft anywhere in the world, but also the conduct of its citizens anywhere in the world. A contemporary example is the *Crimes (Child Sex Tourism) Amendment Act 1994* (Cth), which amended the *Crimes Act 1914* (Cth) to permit the prosecution of Australian citizens or residents in respect of offences committed outside Australia (see also *Re Colonel Aird; Ex parte Alpert* (2004) 220 CLR 308, discussed in Chapter 18, §5).

In British law, the "sovereignty" or "supremacy" of the British Parliament would seem to imply that its law-making power has no territorial limit. A British law attempting to regulate the litter problem in the streets of Paris would obviously be ineffective, but, on the basis of Dicey's view of "parliamentary sovereignty", it would seem to be legally valid from the viewpoint of the

British legal system. Yet, so long as the British colonies were conceived of as parts of an Empire, at least some authorities on Imperial law were prepared to insist that those colonies had no extraterritorial power at all. However "ample" or "plenary" the legislative power given to them by the Imperial Parliament might be, it could only be exercised by each colony within its own territorial borders. The high point of this doctrine was *Macleod v A-G (NSW)* [1891] AC 455. Macleod had married his first wife in Sydney in 1872. While his first wife was still alive, he had married a second wife in the United States. The Privy Council held that he could not be prosecuted for bigamy under New South Wales law since the second marriage, the allegedly bigamous one, had taken place outside the territorial limits of New South Wales.

So far as the Commonwealth Parliament was concerned, the grants of legislative power in s 51 of the Constitution were sometimes of such a nature (or expressed in such language) as almost necessarily to have an extraterritorial operation: for example, the power in s 51(i) to legislate with respect to "trade and commerce with other countries" necessarily extends to the regulation of activities outside Australia (see *Crowe v Commonwealth* (1935) 54 CLR 69). The same reasoning applies to s 51(xxix) (the external affairs power) and to other grants of power with an obvious international operation. In the "fisheries" power (s 51(x)), for example, the fact that the legislation is to operate "beyond territorial limits" is explicit.

In other instances, however, the extraterritoriality doctrine was initially thought to apply to the Commonwealth as well as to the States. In *Merchant Service Guild of Australasia v Commonwealth Steamship Owners' Association (No 3)* (1920) 28 CLR 495, the High Court held that Commonwealth legislative power with respect to "industrial disputes" (s 51(xxxv)) was confined to industrial disputes within Australian territorial limits, and did not extend to disputes on Australian ships outside Australian waters. Eventually in *R v Foster; Ex parte Eastern and Australian Steamship Co Ltd* (1959) 103 CLR 256 a wider view prevailed. That view has now been extended, in *Re Maritime Union of Australia; Ex parte CSL Pacific Shipping Inc* (2003) 214 CLR 397, to a case where the shipowner was incorporated in Barbados and ultimately owned by a Canadian company, and the crew were "[408] foreign seafarers, not resident in Australia, not engaged in Australia and not members of any relevant Australian industrial organisation".

6. The *Statute of Westminster*

The *Statute of Westminster 1931* (Imp) (see Appendix) freed the Dominions, including the Commonwealth, from Imperial restrictions by excluding the operation of the *Colonial Laws Validity Act* and thereby the repugnancy doctrine. The Statute also removed any restrictions upon Commonwealth legislative power arising under the extraterritoriality doctrine.

The *Statute of Westminster* was a major landmark in the shift from the notion of the "British Empire" to the "British Commonwealth of Nations", and, at least for the major Dominions such as Canada and Australia, from the status of colonial dependency to that of national independence. World War I had wrought major changes to the British Empire. From Canada, South Africa, India, Australia and New Zealand, contingents of "colonial" military forces had contributed to the British war effort in a manner expressive both of loyalty to the Empire and of an emerging national identity.

From 1917 onwards, a series of "Imperial Conferences" met in London to redefine the relationships among the major centres of British settlement. Canada, South Africa and the Irish Free State persistently demanded greater autonomy and independence. Australia was far less vocal, and even reluctant; but even in Australia the need for a shift from colonial to Dominion status was clear. As the Report of the 1926 Imperial Conference ("the Balfour Report", *Cmd* 2768) proclaimed: "[14] We refer to the group of self-governing communities composed of Great Britain and the Dominions. Their position and mutual relation may be readily defined. *They are autonomous Communities within the British Empire, equal in status, in no way subordinate one to another in any aspect of their domestic or external affairs, though united by a common allegiance to the Crown, and freely associated as members of the British Commonwealth of Nations*". However, this proclamation did not match the existing law and practices.

Geoffrey Sawer, *The Australian Constitution*
(AGPS, 2nd ed 1988)

[71] The [Balfour] report identified five matters in which there appeared to be conflict between the status so defined and existing British legal powers or practices. First, the royal style and titles. (In 1927 legislation was passed, since amended, to make it clear that the monarch was directly related to Dominion governments, and not indirectly through the British Government.) Second, the position of governors-general. (A resolution of 1917 had already established that they were to be regarded solely as the representatives of the Crown, and not in any sense representatives of or answerable to the British Government.) Third, the operation of Dominion legislation (in particular reservation and disallowance powers of the Crown, the effect of the *Colonial Laws Validity Act* 1865, and extraterritorial operation). Fourth, British merchant shipping legislation. Fifth, Privy Council judicial appeals. The four last points were left for expert attention, but the report recorded as an accepted conventional rule, already applicable, that all surviving British legislative and executive powers directly bearing on Dominion affairs were to be used only as requested by the relevant Dominion governments.

Constitutional arrangements and understandings within the United Kingdom itself had always depended heavily on "conventions" (see Chapter 3, §4(d)). Frequently, a convention may preclude the exercise of a power still available at law (see, for example, Constitution, s 59). Relations among the Dominions after World War I evolved along a similar pattern. In particular, though the British Parliament still had power to legislate for the Dominions through paramount force, it came to be assumed that this power would never be exercised unless such legislation was requested and consented to by the Parliament of the relevant Dominion.

Great Britain and Australia might have been content to allow this new pattern to evolve merely at the level of unwritten "convention". However, for different reasons, Canada, South Africa and the Irish Free State wanted more tangible guarantees. They pressed, first, for clear statements by Imperial Conferences of the new "conventions" and then, from 1926 onwards, for translation of "convention" into "law". The result was the *Statute of Westminster*.

Section 2 of the *Statute of Westminster* provided that the *Colonial Laws Validity Act*, and thus the doctrine of repugnancy, did not apply to the Dominions (including Australia). Under s 4 the British Parliament could still legislate for Australia, but only with the "request and consent" of the Commonwealth Parliament. The Statute marked an important step in Australian legal independence. The Commonwealth Parliament could now enact laws inconsistent with British legislation (except that, under s 8, it could not alter or repeal the Australian Constitution); while any territorial limit on its legislative powers was brought to an end by s 3. Yet Australia's reluctance to accept this new freedom was manifested in two remarkable ways:

1. The crucial provisions of the *Statute of Westminster* did not automatically apply to Australia, nor to New Zealand or Newfoundland. At the request of those Dominions, it was left to them to "adopt" these provisions under s 10 of the Act. This Australia did in the *Statute of Westminster Adoption Act 1942* (Cth), which backdated the adoption to 3 September 1939 (that is, to the outbreak of World War II).

2. The implications for the federal structures of Canada and Australia were quite different. For Canada, s 7(2) of the *Statute of Westminster* ensured that the liberating effect of the Act extended to the Provinces as well as the Dominion Parliament. There was no such provision for the Australian States. On the contrary, s 9 preserved the existing legal position.

Under s 2 of the *Statute of Westminster*, it was clear, at least once Australia had "adopted" the *Statute of Westminster*, that neither the repugnancy doctrine nor the *Colonial Laws Validity Act* could restrict the powers of the Commonwealth Parliament. Section 2 was applied in *Copyright Owners Reproduction Society Ltd v EMI (Australia) Pty Ltd* (1958) 100 CLR 597. The *Copyright Act 1911* (Imp) applied to Australia by "paramount force". However, in the United Kingdom, that Act had been repealed and replaced by the *Copyright Act 1956* (UK). The High Court held that this 1956 Act did not extend to Australia since it did not comply with the "request and consent" requirement of s 4 of the *Statute of Westminster*. It was not necessarily that the British Parliament *could not* legislate contrary to the *Statute of Westminster*, but rather that, as a matter of construction, it could not be interpreted as having *intended* to do so unless such an intention had been made unmistakably clear.

The Court also had to consider whether certain amendments to the *Copyright Act*, made in the United Kingdom by the *Copyright (Mechanical Instruments: Royalties) Act 1928* (UK), had taken effect in Australia. The 1928 Act had been passed before the *Statute of Westminster*, but the Court gave this question a similar answer on the basis that by 1928 the effect of s 4 of the *Statute of Westminster* was already clearly established as a matter of inter-Imperial convention. Again, the point was not that the British Parliament could not in 1928 have legislated with effect for Australia, but only that it should be interpreted as not having intended to legislate in breach of convention.

7. The Colonial Legacy: The States

The *Statute of Westminster* left two impediments to full Australian legal independence. First, under s 4, the United Kingdom could still legislate for the Commonwealth, albeit at the Commonwealth's "request and consent". Secondly, the States were still bound by the doctrines of repugnancy (under the *Colonial Laws Validity Act*) and extraterritoriality. Both of these came to be seen as incongruous. The incongruity was not dispelled until the *Australia Act*.

(a)   Extraterritoriality

The idea that the colonies could not legislate extraterritorially had always been controversial. For the Empire in general, the doctrine was finally overthrown in *Croft v Dunphy* [1933] AC 156. The schooner *Dorothy M Smart* was seized by Canadian customs officers 11½ miles off the coast of Nova Scotia. She was carrying a cargo of rum and other liquors from the French island of St Pierre, and was apparently attempting to avoid customs duty. The ship was seized under s 151 of the *Customs Act 1927* (Canada). The *Dorothy M Smart* was registered in Nova Scotia. The question was whether, in a case like this involving a Canadian vessel, the Dominion could legislate to extend its jurisdiction outwards to a 12-mile limit, that is, extraterritorially. The Privy Council held that it could.

Croft v Dunphy
[1933] AC 156

Lord Macmillan (for their Lordships): [162] It may be accepted as a general principle that states can legislate effectively only for their own territories. To what distance seaward the territory of a state is to be taken as extending is a question of international law upon which their Lordships do not deem it necessary or proper to pronounce. But whatever be the limits of territorial waters in the international sense, it has long been recognized that for certain purposes, notably those of police, revenue, public health and fisheries, a state may enact laws affecting the seas surrounding its coasts to a distance seaward which exceeds the ordinary limits of its territory ...

[163] But while the Imperial Parliament may be conceded to possess such powers of legislation under international law and usage, the respondent contends that the Parliament of Canada has no such powers. It is not contested that under the British North America Act the Dominion legislature has full power to enact customs laws for Canada, but it is maintained that it is debarred from introducing into such legislation any provisions designed to operate beyond its shores or at any rate beyond a marine league from the coast.

In their Lordships' opinion the Parliament of Canada is not under any such disability. Once it is found that a particular topic of legislation is among those upon which the Dominion Parliament may competently legislate as being for the peace, order and good government of Canada or as being one of the specific subjects enumerated in s 91 of the British North America Act, their Lord-ships see no reason to restrict the permitted scope of such legislation by any other consideration than is applicable to the legislation of a fully Sovereign State.

Although the decision in *Croft v Dunphy* removed or relaxed the supposed rule, and was clearly meant to apply throughout the Empire, Australian courts and Parliaments were reluctant to take the benefit of the relaxation, at least in cases where the legislative powers of the States were concerned. Sometimes it was said that *Croft v Dunphy* was inapplicable to the Australian States because it depended on the *Statute of Westminster*. At other times, it was said to depend on the grant by the Imperial Parliament of an enumerated list of specified powers, so that in Canada the reasoning extended to the Dominion and to the Provinces, but in Australia only to the Common-wealth. The result was a confusing series of cases in which the power of the Australian States to legislate with extraterritorial effect was sometimes read permissively and sometimes restrictively (see, for example, *Millar v Commissioner of Stamp Duties* (1932) 48 CLR 618; *Broken Hill South Ltd v Commissioner of Taxation (NSW)* (1937) 56 CLR 337; *Ex parte Iskra* [1963] SR (NSW) 538; *Welker v Hewlett* (1969) 120 CLR 503). These cases insisted that any attempted out-of-State operation must have *some* connexion with the legislating State, but the rigour with which the necessary connexion was defined varied widely. Among the more generous formulations was that of Dixon J in *Broken Hill South*.

Broken Hill South Ltd v Commissioner of Taxation (NSW)
(1937) 56 CLR 337

Dixon J: [375] The power to make laws for the peace, order and good government of a State does not enable the State Parliament to impose by reference to some act, matter or thing occurring outside the State a liability upon a person unconnected with the State whether by domicil, residence or otherwise. But it is within the competence of the State legislature to make any fact, circum-stance, occurrence or thing in or connected with the territory the occasion of the imposition upon any person concerned therein of a liability to taxation or of any other liability. It is also within the competence of the legislature to base the imposition of liability on no more than the relation of the person to the territory. The relation may consist in presence within the territory, residence, domicil, carrying on business there, or even remoter connections. If a connection exists, it is for the legislature to decide how far it should go in the exercise of its powers. As in other matters of jurisdiction or authority courts must be exact in distinguishing between ascertaining that the circumstances over which the power extends exist and examining the mode in which the power has been exercised. No doubt there must be some relevance to the circumstances in the exercise of the power. But it is of no importance upon the question of validity that the liability imposed is, or may be, altogether disproportionate to the territorial connection or that it includes many cases that cannot have been foreseen.

It was not until 1976 that a more relaxed view based on *Croft v Dunphy* was finally established. John Florenca was charged with an offence under s 24 of the *Fisheries Act 1905* (WA). The alleged offence, possession of undersized rock lobsters, had been detected 12 miles off the coast of Western Australia. The Act had been drafted on the assumption that each State had legislative power over its own territorial sea, but in *New South Wales v Commonwealth (Seas and Submerged Lands Case)* (1975) 135 CLR 337 that assumption was held to be wrong. The seaward territorial boundaries of the States were to be drawn at low-water mark. Beyond that point, the territorial sea was controlled by the Commonwealth and not by the States. Accordingly, the Western Australian law had to be assessed on the basis that it related to activities outside the State's territory. The High Court held that the law was valid. The decision was unanimous, except for Barwick CJ who saw no need to resolve the issue.

Pearce v Florenca
(1976) 135 CLR 507

Gibbs J: [514] During the course of the nineteenth century the advisers to the Colonial Office formulated a principle that a colonial legislature has no power to enact laws having effect beyond the limits of the colony, and this view came to be accepted by the colonial courts (*Ray v M'Mackin* [(1875) 1 VLR (L) 274]; *R v Barton* [(1879) 1 QLJ (Supp) 16]). In *Macleod v Attorney-General (NSW)* [[1891] AC 455] the support of the Judicial Committee was given to the opinion that the jurisdiction of colonial legislatures is "confined within their own territories", but the decision of that case turned on a question of construction, rather than a question of power, and the remarks on the latter question were obiter dicta ... **[515]** Another explanation of the principle that colonial legislatures are subject to limitations in respect of their power of enacting legislation which has an extra-territorial effect is that it derives from the fact that a colonial legislature is empowered only to legislate for the "peace, order and good government" of the colony and that those words themselves import a territorial connexion. This explanation has been so often repeated in judgments of this Court and in the Judicial Committee that it seems necessary to regard it as correct. However, to accept it raises certain logical difficulties. By s 5 of the *Colonial Laws Validity Act*, 1865 (Imp) every representative legislature was given "full power to make laws respecting the constitution, powers and procedure of such legislature" and it is difficult to see why, if the suggested limitation arises from the words of the constitution of a State, that limitation might not simply be removed, nowadays at least, by the State legislature itself amending its constitution and increasing its own powers. Moreover, the same words appear in s 51 of the Commonwealth Constitution and they do not there appear to have a similarly restrictive effect, at any rate since the passage of the **[516]** Statute of Westminster ...

The doctrine as to the limitation on the power of colonial legislatures to legislate with extra-territorial effect, as originally enunciated, proved to be too widely stated. It is misleading to refer to it as a "doctrine forbidding extra-territorial legislation"; in *British Coal Corporation v The King* [[1935] AC 500 at 580], their Lordships so described it but went on immediately to say that it is "a doctrine of somewhat obscure extent". The power of a subordinate legislature (as colonial, State and Dominion legislatures have sometimes been called) to enact legislation that takes effect beyond territorial limits was firmly established by the decision in *Croft v Dunphy* [[1933] AC 156] ... It has been pointed out on a number of occasions in this Court that the decision in no way depended on the effect of s 3 of the Statute of Westminster and is just as much applicable to the legislation of a colony or a State as to that of a Dominion. That case has constantly been followed. This Court, in *O'Sullivan v Dejneko* [(1964) 110 CLR 498], upheld the validity of a New South Wales statute which imposed liabilities on a person resident in South Australia who had never been in New South Wales ... [T]he operation of the legislation held to be valid was clearly not confined within the territory of New South Wales. It is in my opinion now right to say, as Lord Uthwatt said in *Wallace Brothers and Co Ltd v Commissioner of Income Tax, Bombay* [(1948) LR 75 Ind App 86 at 98]: "There is no rule of law that the territorial limits of a subordinate legislature define the possible scope of its legislative enactments or mark the field open to its vision."

After quoting the reasoning in *Croft v Dunphy*, Gibbs J went on:

Gibbs J: [517] In accordance with those reasons, it is now often said that the test of validity of a State statute is simply whether it is legislation for the peace, order and good government of the State (*R v Foster; Ex parte Eastern and Australian Steamship Co Ltd* [(1959) 103 CLR 256 at 307]), and that no additional restriction placed upon mere territorial considerations should be placed upon the constitutional powers of a State ... However, the test whether a law is one for the peace, order and good government of the State is, as so stated, exceedingly vague and imprecise, and a rather more specific test has been adopted; it has become settled that a law is valid if it is connected, not too remotely, with the State which enacted it, or, in other words, if it operates on some circumstance which really appertains to the State.

The passage from Dixon J in *Broken Hill South* had been quoted in part by the Privy Council in *Thompson v Commissioner of Stamp Duties* [1969] 1 AC 320 at 335-6. Gibbs J also quoted it in that form, and concluded:

Gibbs J: [518] Even in its modern form, the rule requiring a relevant connexion between the persons or circumstances on which the legislation operates and the State is still capable of giving rise to that practical inconvenience and uncertainty to which the report of the 1929 Conference on the Operation of Dominion Legislation alluded ... For that reason it is obviously in the public interest that the test should be liberally applied, and that legislation should be held valid if there is any real connexion – even a remote or general connexion – between the subject matter of the legislation and the State. And it has been established by a series of well-known decisions ... that within their limits the legislatures of the States have powers "as plenary and as ample" as those of the Imperial Legislature itself. It would seem anomalous and unfitting that the enactments of such a legislature should be held invalid on narrow or technical grounds.

The general approach of *Pearce v Florenca* is now regarded as settled. In *Robinson v Western Australian Museum* (1977) 138 CLR 283, Gibbs and Mason JJ took that approach, and in *Union Steamship Co of Australia Pty Ltd v King* (1988) 166 CLR 1 it was reaffirmed in a joint unanimous judgment. By the time that the latter case was decided, the *Australia Act* was in force, and s 2(1) of that Act had done for the States what s 3 of the *Statute of Westminster* had done for the Commonwealth: that is, it had given the States the power to pass laws with an extraterritorial operation. However, the joint unanimous judgment in *Union Steamship* was at pains to point out that, in this respect, the *Australia Act* did no more than had already been achieved judicially through the series of cases culminating in *Pearce v Florenca*.

Sydney King was employed by the Union Steamship Co as a crew attendant on its ship, the *Seaway Princess*, a ship registered in New South Wales. He claimed to have been afflicted by boilermakers' deafness while working on the ship outside New South Wales, and brought a claim in the New South Wales Compensation Court under ss 7 and 46 of the *Workers Compensation Act 1926* (NSW). That Act allowed worker's compensation claims for injury occurring anywhere in the world on a ship registered in New South Wales. Section 5 of the *Constitution Act 1902* (NSW) empowered the New South Wales Parliament to legislate for the "peace, welfare, and good government of New South Wales". The appellant argued that the *Workers Compensation Act* was not a law for the "peace, welfare, and good government of New South Wales" because it lacked a sufficient territorial nexus. This argument was rejected on the basis that s 5 was a grant of "plenary power" (see Chapter 11, §2(a)).

Union Steamship Co of Australia Pty Ltd v King
(1988) 166 CLR 1

The Court: [12] It might have been possible to confine the authority of *Croft v Dunphy* [[1933] AC 156] to the legislatures of the Dominions as distinct from those of the colonies and States, on the footing that, following the Balfour Declaration of 1929, self-governing Dominions had achieved fully independent and sovereign status. But that is not how things have turned out. It is now accepted beyond any question that colonial legislatures had power to make laws which operate extraterritorially ...

The same comment applies with equal force to the Parliaments of the Australian States. Immediately following *Croft v Dunphy*, Evatt J in *Trustees Executors & Agency Co Ltd v Federal Commissioner of Taxation* [(1933) 49 CLR 220 at 235] stated that the supposed territorial restrictions on State Parliaments were confined to "a very small compass indeed". It has been said that the words "peace, order and good government" are now the source of whatever territorial limitations exist in relation to the Parliaments of the States: *R v Foster; Ex parte Eastern & Australian Steamship Co Ltd* [(1959) 103 CLR 256 at 307]; *Johnson v Commissioner of Stamp Duties (NSW)* [[1956] AC 331]. As Windeyer J noted in *Foster* [103 CLR at 308], the words simply express the fact that in "a general and remote sense the purpose and design of every law is to promote the welfare of the community", to use the words **[13]** of Professor W Harrison Moore in *Commonwealth of Australia*, 2nd ed (1910), pp 274-275.

After quoting the passage from Dixon J in *Broken Hill South*, the Court said:

The Court: [13] The Solicitor-General for New South Wales, appearing for the Attorney-General for that State as intervener, submitted that even the statement of Dixon J is too restrictive an interpretation of the Parliament's legislative authority. The nineteenth century Privy Council decisions, he submitted, recognize that the grant of power is as large and ample as that enjoyed by the Imperial Parliament itself. As that Parliament is not subject to any territorial restraint, so the Parliament of New South Wales is likewise free from such a restraint. The short answer to this contention is that the nineteenth century decisions, in comparing the scope and extent of the grant of legislative power to colonial legislatures with the power of the Imperial Parliament, explicitly qualified that comparison by reference to the limits of the grant itself ... Accordingly, the nineteenth **[14]** century decisions do not deny that the words "peace, order and good government" may be a source of territorial limitation, however slight that limitation may be. And, as each State Parliament in the Australian federation has power to enact laws for its State, it is appropriate to maintain the need for some territorial limitation in conformity with the terms of the grant, notwithstanding the recent recognition in the constitutional rearrangements for Australia made in 1986 that State Parliaments have power to enact laws having an extraterritorial operation: see *Australia Act 1986* (Cth), s 2(1); *Australia Act 1986* (UK), s 2(1). That new dispensation is, of course, subject to the provisions of the Constitution (see s 5(a) of each Act) and cannot affect territorial limitations of State legislative powers inter se which are expressed or implied in the Constitution. That being so, the new dispensation may do no more than recognize what has already been achieved in the course of judicial decisions. Be this as it may, it is sufficient for present purposes to express our agreement with the comments of Gibbs J in *Pearce* [(1976) 135 CLR 507 at 518] where his Honour stated that the requirement for a relevant connexion between the circumstances on which the legislation operates and the State should be liberally applied and that even a remote and general connexion between the subject-matter of the legislation and the State will suffice.

Note particularly in this passage: (1) the suggestion that s 2(1) of the *Australia Act* merely duplicated what had already been achieved judicially; and (2) that there may still be some territorial limits on State legislative power arising in part from the federal nature of the Constitution and in part from the fact that the plenary grant of State power refers to the "peace, order and good government" *of the State*. The way in which any such continuing limits might be grounded in the "text and structure" of the Constitution, or in implications therefrom, was discussed inconclusively in *Mobil Oil Australia Pty Ltd v Victoria* (2002) 211 CLR 1 (in relation to Pt 4A of the *Supreme Court Act 1986* (Vic), inserted in 2000 to invest the Supreme Court with a jurisdiction in "group proceedings", often involving parties from other States); and again inconclusively in *BHP Billiton Ltd v Schultz* (2004) 211 ALR 523 (in relation to s 13 of the *Dust Diseases Tribunal Act 1989* (NSW), which permitted the Tribunal to direct that hearings may "take place outside New South Wales"). In both cases it was held that the legislative powers of the State had not been exceeded. The suggested constitutional bases for a territorial limit on power included the ideas that matters properly within the legislative ambit of a particular State might be "withdrawn" from the Parliaments of other States by s 107 of the Constitution; that intrusive legislation might be inhibited by the need under s 118 to give "full faith and credit" to the laws of other States; that limits on State power are presupposed by the reference in s 74 to questions "as to the limits inter se of the Constitutional powers of any two or more States"; and that there might be as between different States an implied immunity similar to that established as between the Commonwealth and its component States in *Melbourne Corporation v Commonwealth* (1947) 74 CLR 31 (see Chapter 25, §2).

In *Port MacDonnell Professional Fishermen's Assn Inc v South Australia* (1989) 168 CLR 340, the High Court, in a joint judgment, stated that *Union Steamship* had established that "**[372]** what is essential to the extraterritorial operation of a State law is a connexion between the enacting State and the extra-territorial persons, things or events on which the law operates". The Court also noted Gibbs J's statement in *Pearce v Florenca* that the test should be "**[518]** liberally applied" and that even a "remote or general connexion" would suffice. That formula was again reaffirmed in *Mobil Oil Australia Pty Ltd v Victoria* (2002) 211 CLR 1, which in *APLA Ltd v Legal Services Commissioner (NSW)* (2005) 219 ALR 403 was treated as authoritative on the point.

(b) Repugnancy

In the 1970s and 1980s, a series of High Court cases showed that the legislative powers of the States were still limited by the repugnancy doctrine enshrined in s 2 of the *Colonial Laws Validity Act*. All of the cases involved the same issue: namely, the continued operation in Australia of the *Merchant Shipping Act 1894* (Imp).

In *Bistricic v Rokov* (1976) 135 CLR 552, the plaintiff was a crew member aboard the *John Dory*, a boat registered in New South Wales. While the ship was moored in Sydney Harbour, Bistricic fell and caught his hands in a motor. He sued his employers for damages. Part VIII of the *Merchant Shipping Act* imposed strict limitations on the amount of damages payable by shipowners for loss or injury sustained on board a ship or through its "improper navigation". In particular, s 503(1) fixed a maximum level of damages by reference to the ship's tonnage. For death or personal injury, the maximum payable was £15 per ton, and for property damage the maximum was £8 per ton. The practical effect, if s 503(1) were still applicable in New South Wales, was that Bistricic's damages were limited to $1489.75.

The limits in s 503(1) of the *Merchant Shipping Act* had been modified for the United Kingdom by s 2(4) of the *Merchant Shipping (Liability of Shipowners and Others) Act 1958* (UK). If Bistricic was entitled to the benefit of that modification, his damages would be much larger. He did not dispute that the 1894 Act was applicable in Australia, but he argued that the 1958 Act was also applicable. The 1958 Act did not expressly advert to that issue, but it did provide in s 10 that its provisions should extend to Northern Ireland, and also, in s 11(1)(c), that the Queen, by Order in Council, might extend its provisions, with modifications, to "any colony, or any country or place outside Her Majesty's dominions in which for the time being Her Majesty has jurisdiction, or any territory consisting partly of one or more colonies and partly of one or more such countries or places". The High Court unanimously held that the 1958 provisions did not apply in Australia, and thus that Bistricic's damages were limited to $1489.75. Mason J quoted ss 10 and 11 of the 1958 Act, stressing that s 11(1)(c) could not extend to New South Wales since, in light of s 11 of the *Statute of Westminster*, New South Wales was neither a "colony" nor a "country or place outside Her Majesty's Dominions".

Bistricic v Rokov
(1976) 135 CLR 552

Mason J: [557] The legislative policy which underlies s 11 of the Statute of Westminster is as important as the language of the section. This policy, which has evolved over the long history of constitutional development leading to responsible government, legislative autonomy and Australian nationhood, is that a statute of the United Kingdom Parliament, if it is intended to apply to an Australian State, will be expressed to apply to that State. The case might be disposed of on the simple ground that the 1958 Act makes no mention of the Australian States but, as it happens, the presence of s 10 and more particularly of s 11 in the 1958 Act makes it perfectly plain that its operation is confined to Britain except in so far as provision is otherwise made by ss 10 and 11 for a more extended operation. There may be ... special reasons which made it necessary or expedient to state specifically that the statute was to apply to Northern Ireland, the Channel Islands and the Isle of Man, but this in itself furnishes no reason for thinking that the 1958 Act was to have an operation wider than its provisions explicitly claimed for it. Moreover, the presence of s 11, applying as it does to colonies generally, cannot be explained, as the appellant would have it, by a desire to overcome difficulties that might otherwise arise in the application of the Act to colonies governed in the exercise of the prerogative.

The appellant's case ... chiefly rests on the proposition that because the 1894 Act enunciated the law for **[558]** New South Wales any amendment to that Act should be approached on the footing that it was intended to amend the law wherever the 1894 Act applied in 1958. If we were to turn our backs on the long history of constitutional development which has taken place since 1894 and on the provisions of the 1958 Act which delimit with some particularity its spheres of operation, this would be an attractive argument. But in the light of all that has happened since 1894 and all that is provided by the 1958 Act the argument is quite unacceptable.

Jacobs J reached the same result by a more cautious route. He was reluctant to exclude the possibility of Imperial legislation completely, for fear of creating a legislative vacuum. Barwick CJ agreed with Mason J, and Stephen J agreed with both Mason and Jacobs JJ. Murphy J took a far more radical view in reaching the same result.

Murphy J: [565] The United Kingdom Parliament has no power (and had none in 1958) to make a law having force in any part of Australia ...

[P]aramount force and the Imperial Parliament no longer exist for Australia. Australia is an independent and equal member of the community of nations. Its relationship with the United Kingdom has long ceased to be imperial-colonial and is now international. The change in relationship was not brought about by the Statute of Westminster 1931, which was adopted by the Australian Parliament as a practical measure "to remove doubts [566] as to the validity of certain Commonwealth legislation, to obviate delays occurring in its passage, and to effect certain related purposes" during wartime (see long title and preamble, *Statute of Westminster Adoption Act* 1942). The *Statute of Westminster* dealt with constitutional forms, not substance, as was well recognized at the time.

The United Kingdom has no legislative or executive authority over Australia (or any part of it). Any authority over the people of a State would be incompatible with the integrity of the Australian nation which is an indissoluble union of the people of the Commonwealth. The Constitutions of the States now have their source in s 106 and the following sections of the *Commonwealth of Australia Constitution Act* ... There is no proper constitutional relationship between the governments of the States of Australia and the government of any other country (including the United Kingdom) and therefore any State government which deals with the Queen through the United Kingdom government is acting unconstitutionally. This does not exclude the concept of the indivisible personal link of the Crown which joins the United Kingdom, Australia and other independent nations, nor the participation of the Crown (although nominal) in the legislatures or executive governments of the States ...

The original authority for our Constitution was the United Kingdom Parliament, but the existing authority is its continuing acceptance by the Australian people. In *British Coal Corporation v The King* [[1935] AC 500 at 520], the Privy Council said:

"It is doubtless true that the power of the Imperial Parliament to pass on its own initiative any legislation that it thought fit extending to Canada remains in theory unimpaired: indeed, the Imperial Parliament could, as a matter of abstract law, repeal or disregard s 4 of the Statute. But that is theory and has no relation to realities."

[567] Any theory which has no relation to realities is suspect. The United Kingdom Parliament could of course repeal the Statute of Westminster. It could repeal the *Commonwealth of Australia Constitution Act*. But such repeals would have no effect in Australia. Their effect, if any, would be confined to the municipal law of the United Kingdom (including the residual Imperial-colonial system). If the members of the Privy Council [in *Oteri v The Queen* [1976] 1 WLR 1272] thought otherwise (as I think they did), they were wrong. The United Kingdom can have no power to make laws for an independent nation which was a former colony unless its paramount force is restored ...

In my opinion (notwithstanding many statements to the contrary) Australia's independence and freedom from United Kingdom legislative authority should be taken as dating from 1901. The United Kingdom Parliament ceased to be an Imperial Parliament in relation to Australia at the inauguration of the Commonwealth. Provisions of statutes directed towards regulating the Imperial-colonial relations (eg, those in the *Colonial Laws Validity Act* 1865) then ceased to be applicable. There are strong grounds for considering that cases which held Commonwealth legislation ultra vires because of inconsistency with any law other than the Constitution (eg, *Union Steamship Co of New Zealand Ltd v Commonwealth*) were wrongly decided.

In any event, Australia was independent before 1958. The *Merchant Shipping (Liability of Shipowners and Others) Act*, 1958 (whatever its interpretation) is therefore not part of the laws of Australia. The question of the continuing operation of the *Merchant Shipping Act*, 1894 (Imp) has not been directly raised.

Apart from a hint by Murphy J in the last paragraph above, no one in *Bistricic v Rokov* questioned the assumption that the *Merchant Shipping Act* itself was still applicable in Australia.

That issue was raised in *China Ocean Shipping Co v South Australia* (1979) 145 CLR 172. The *Wuzhou*, a ship owned by the China Ocean Shipping Co, had collided with a jetty at Wallaroo that was owned by the South Australian government. The State claimed damages. The shipowners sought to limit their liability by relying on s 503 of the *Merchant Shipping Act*. By a 4:1 majority, with Murphy J dissenting, the High Court held that the Act was still applicable in Australia. Barwick CJ also held that the Act applied in this case. Gibbs, Stephen and Aickin JJ on the other hand held that the shipowners could not invoke s 503, since, as a matter of construction, the limitations it imposed did not avail against the Crown and hence not against a State government. They based this conclusion on the general presumption that a statute does not bind the Crown unless it is expressly or by clear implication intended to do so.

On the major question of the applicability of the *Merchant Shipping Act*, South Australia sought squarely to test the validity of the views put by Murphy J in *Bistricic v Rokov*. Predictably, Murphy J took the opportunity to reaffirm his position, but no other member of the Court took a similar stand. Barwick CJ, Gibbs, Stephen and Aickin JJ, for reasons most fully stated by Stephen J, all adhered to the traditional view that British statutes continued to apply in the States through paramount force.

China Ocean Shipping Co v South Australia
(1979) 145 CLR 172

Stephen J: [209] The history of the Constitutional Conventions leading to Federation is, I think, consistent only with a contemplation by those who were, in the last decade of the nineteenth century, concerned to bring about Federation that the establishment of the Commonwealth would not of itself involve either the ending of the application to Australia of existing Imperial laws or the denial to the Parliament at Westminster of continued competence to legislate for Australia. One instance will serve to make the point. When that decade's endeavours culminated in the Australian delegates' negotiations with the Imperial authorities in London in 1900 the form of covering cl 5 of the delegates' proposed Commonwealth of Australia Constitution Bill was a point of contention, the matter in issue being whether the clause made it sufficiently clear that laws enacted by the Commonwealth Parliament would be "colonial laws" subject to the provisions of the *Colonial Laws Validity Act*, 1865 (Imp). The Imperial Government wished to leave no "room for doubt as to the paramount authority of Imperial legislation", while, as Quick and Garran observe at p 350 of their *Annotated Constitution*, the Australian framers of the Commonwealth Bill had not "thought **[210]** necessary to declare that the Constitution should be read in conjunction with the *Colonial Laws Validity Act*. It was assumed, as a matter of course, that that would be done". The Australian delegates, determined to avoid any change, even to the covering clauses, of a document so long debated in Australia and which had just been approved by referendum of the Australian people, contended that the Bill in fact left no room for doubt: "The Commonwealth appears to the Delegates to be clearly a 'Colony' and the Federal Parliament to be a 'Legislature' within the meaning of the *Colonial Laws Validity Act*" they observed in their memorandum to the Colonial Office and of this they succeeded finally in convincing the Imperial Crown Law Officers. As Quick and Garran observe, at p 352, "It may be assumed, therefore, that the Crown Law Officers were satisfied that the *Colonial Laws Validity Act* is applicable to the Constitution as it stands".

Here, then, was the expression of a common understanding. There had been occasional individual doubts, the expression of which may be found in the course of Constitutional Convention debates, and these were reflected in the reposte of the Australian delegates, towards the close of their protracted London negotiations, that it was scarcely appropriate that the Act of 1865 should apply to a great self-governing community. Nevertheless, the outcome was an express recognition, by those most closely concerned with Federation, of the continuing application of Imperial laws to federated Australia. That what was expressly in issue was the *Colonial Laws Validity Act* is particularly significant, since its continued application ensured the supremacy of Imperial laws expressed to apply to Australia over any legislation enacted by the Parliament of the Commonwealth repugnant to those Imperial laws. As Professor Castles observes in his article, "Reception and Status of English Law in Australia", in *Adelaide Law Review*, vol 2 (1963) 1, at p 27, viewed in the perspective of the nineteenth and of the early part of the twentieth century that Act, and with it the preservation of the residual legislative power of the Imperial Parliament, was still acceptable to the peoples of many British possessions.

This being the state of political realities affecting relations between Australia and the United Kingdom at the inception of the Commonwealth, it long continued to be the basis of the relationship between Imperial and Australian governments, regardless of their respective, and fluctuating, political complexions, as is shown by the course of subsequent events.

After dealing with the Balfour Report and the *Statute of Westminster*, Stephen J continued:

Stephen J: [212] It is, then, not the rejection of the legislative power of the Parliament at Westminster to make laws in the future for Australia, still less the abrogation of existing Imperial laws, that has marked, in this century, the progressive development of the constitutional relationship between Australia and the United Kingdom. Instead, the realities of the relationship have involved the continued application of existing Imperial laws, but subject now to the power of repeal or amendment by Commonwealth legislation.

Had it been otherwise and had Imperial law in fact ceased to be law for Australia in 1901 or at some later date, as the defendant's **[213]** submission would have it, there would have thenceforth been revealed some areas of law, formerly regulated by Imperial statute, in which no law existed. One instance among many is that of copyright. The considerable extent to which, until 1907, copyright protection in Australia depended upon Imperial legislation, and the inadequacy of the protection otherwise afforded by legislation of the various Australian colonies, later States, is succinctly described in Ch VIII of the fourth edition of Scrutton's *Law of Copyright*. Only with the proclamation, in 1907, of the commencement of the *Copyright Act* 1905 did Commonwealth legislation enter the field ...

[214] It is for these reasons that I would reject the defendant's submission ... Both the *Merchant Shipping Act*, 1894 and the amending Act of 1900, have, at all material times, been law in Australia. In so concluding I am not unaware of the unsatisfactory situation which has long been recognized as existing in relation to the law governing merchant shipping in Australia, itself a situation largely attributable to the very proposition which the defendant's submission would deny, the continued operation in Australia of Imperial laws. As long ago as 1929 JG Latham, then Commonwealth Attorney-General, spoke of the position as "confused, obscure and radically unsatisfactory": *Australia and the British Commonwealth*, (1929), p 103. It is a situation which has remained substantially unaltered through the lives of many successive governments ... It no doubt calls for radical reform but it is by legislative initiative, possible ever since the adoption of the *Statute of Westminster*, that it must be achieved and not, at least in my view, by the adoption of the defendant's present submission.

Even while *China Ocean* was being argued in the High Court, the Commonwealth was conducting a sweeping review of the *Navigation Act 1912* (Cth), in part because it had been decided to ratify the 1957 International Convention relating to the Limitation of the Liability of Owners of Sea-going Ships. The result was the *Navigation Amendment Act 1979* (Cth). Section 104(3) of that Act provided: "Part VIII of the Merchant Shipping Act is repealed". It came into force on 31 January 1981. The British limitation provisions in s 503(1) of the *Merchant Shipping Act* therefore ceased to apply in Australian waters from that date.

On 9 August 1981, Shawar Kirmani was a passenger on the *Captain Cook II*, a ferry operating from Circular Quay in Sydney and carrying passengers on pleasure cruises around Sydney Harbour, when she was injured in a fall. She sued the owners of the ferry for negligence. The defendants filed a defence in which they sought to limit their liability under s 503(1) of the *Merchant Shipping Act*. The plaintiff sought to strike out this defence on the ground that that Act had been repealed. The defendants answered that:

1. the repeal by the Commonwealth did not affect the *Merchant Shipping Act* as a part of the law of New South Wales; and

2. the Commonwealth had no power to repeal that Act in its New South Wales operation.

By 4:3, Gibbs CJ, Wilson and Dawson JJ dissenting, the Court held that the *Navigation Amendment Act* had successfully repealed Pt VIII of the *Merchant Shipping Act*. However, while the result was clear, there was no majority agreement on the reasons for that result.

Brennan J identified the relevant Commonwealth power as arising from s 2(2) of the *Statute of Westminster*. He concluded that "**[405]** Section 2 conferred on Dominion Parliaments a new power to repeal an Imperial law which extended expressly or by necessary intendment to the Dominion". There were, however, two difficulties with a simple reliance on s 2(2).

The first was a suggestion by Sir Owen Dixon ("The Statute of Westminster 1931" (1936) 10 *Australian Law Journal* (Supp) 96) that the power to repeal or amend Imperial statutes conferred on the Dominion Parliaments by s 2(2) might be merely a corollary of their liberation from the "repugnancy" doctrine. On that basis, the power might arise only in cases of repugnancy between Imperial and Dominion statutes; it would extend only so far as to eliminate the repugnancy, and could arise only in areas which in any event fell within the Dominion's existing legislative powers. Brennan J rejected this possibility in part by relying on the very broad language used in s 2(2), and in part on the basis of the Privy Council's decision, in *Moore v Attorney-General (Irish Free State)* [1935] AC 484, that the *Statute of Westminster* had freed the Irish Free State to amend its own Constitution by abolishing Privy Council appeals. Brennan J found in their Lordships' reasoning a conclusive answer to the argument that the "power to repeal or amend" should be given a limited construction. On the contrary, the Statute was "**[409]** an organic law ... [conferring] the full measure of powers needed to make the Dominion Parliaments wholly independent".

The second difficulty was that, in the case of Australia, the powers conferred by the *Statute of Westminster* were expressly limited by s 9(1) of the Statute, so as not to permit Commonwealth legislation "on any matter within the authority of the States of Australia, not being a matter within the authority of the Parliament or Government of the Commonwealth". As Brennan J construed this provision, it meant that a matter *excluded* from the Commonwealth's power to repeal or amend British legislation must satisfy two qualifications: it must be a matter within State legislative power, and it must not be a matter within Commonwealth legislative power. The absence of either one of these qualifications would be enough to exclude the operation of s 9(1) of the Statute, thereby permitting unrestricted recourse to the power conferred by s 2(2). Concluding that the repeal or amendment of the British *Merchant Shipping Act* was not "a matter within the authority of the States of Australia", Brennan J held that this was sufficient to take the matter outside the scope of s 9(1). It was therefore unnecessary for him to determine whether the matter was independently within Commonwealth legislative power under s 51 of the Constitution.

Murphy J reached the same result on very different grounds. His central theme in *Bistricic v Rokov* had been that Australia's sovereign independence was not an emanation from the *Statute of Westminster*, nor from a slow process of evolution, but had come into full-blown existence on 1 January 1901. For him, the source of Commonwealth power to repeal the *Merchant Shipping Act* did not lie in the *Statute of Westminster*, but in the Constitution itself. He found it in s 51(xxix), which grants legislative power to the Commonwealth with respect to "external affairs" (see Chapter 19). He held that the repeal of Pt VIII of the *Merchant Shipping Act* was itself an "external affair" involving Australia's relations with other countries.

In order to hold that the repeal was valid, Brennan J relied on the *Statute of Westminster* and Murphy J on the Commonwealth's "external affairs" power. Mason and Deane JJ, who also held that the repeal was valid, used a combination of both these grounds. Like Brennan J, they approached the issue primarily on the basis of exegesis of the *Statute of Westminster*, and agreed with him that the power conferred by s 2(2) must be broadly construed. As to s 9(1) of the Statute, however, Mason J, in particular, was inclined to accept an argument on which the dissenting judges relied. This was that, under s 735 of the *Merchant Shipping Act*, the matter was "within the authority of the States of Australia", so that the first qualification for the operation of s 9(1) would be satisfied. Although Mason J found it "**[378]** unnecessary to decide", he had "little doubt" that this argument was valid. However, he saw no need to pursue it because in any event, on his view, the matter was brought within Commonwealth authority by the "external affairs" power.

Deane J took a similar view. Both he and Mason J agreed with Murphy J that the matter was within the "external affairs" power. But where Murphy J relied on the "external affairs" power as the sole basis for the validity of the Commonwealth repeal, Mason and Deane JJ relied on it only to exclude the operation of s 9(1) of the *Statute of Westminster*, and thus to give unrestricted play to the power conferred by s 2(2) of the Statute. In closing, however, Deane J echoed some of the earlier dicta of Murphy J.

Kirmani v Captain Cook Cruises Pty Ltd (No 1)
(1985) 159 CLR 351

Deane J: [441] Some statements in this judgment have contained the qualification "according to traditional legal theory". That is because the case was, in accordance with the approach long accepted in this Court, argued on the basis that the authority of the provisions of the Australian Constitution and the *Statute of Westminster* rests, as a matter of legal theory, wholly upon their enactment by the Imperial Parliament as distinct from resting upon a wider foundation which also encompasses the social compact and the international agree-**[442]**-ments which the Constitution and the Statute respectively embodied. That is not to suggest that there may be grounds for questioning the rejection by this Court of the general proposition that Imperial statutes which applied to Australia have somehow automatically ceased so to apply: see, eg, *China Ocean Shipping Co v South Australia* [(1979) 145 CLR 172]. It may, however, be necessary at some future time to consider whether traditional legal theory can properly be regarded as providing an adequate explanation of the process which culminated in the acquisition by Australia of full "independence and Sovereignty". Plainly, there is something to be said for the view that any explanation of the legal nature of that process is incomplete if it fails to acknowledge and examine the relevance and importance, under both international law and internal law, of that social compact, of those inter-national agreements, of the "established constitutional position" to which the *Statute of Westminster* expressly refers and of international recognition of Australia as an independent and sovereign State whose only de jure government is that which is locally based: cf *Buck v Attorney-General* [[1965] 1 Ch 745 at 770]; *Ibralebbe v The Queen* [[1964] AC 900 at 924-5]. Those questions could become of some practical importance if the Parliament of the United Kingdom were, for example, to purport on its own initiative to repeal the provisions of the Constitution or the provisions of the Statute or otherwise to legislate for Australia. Apart from such far-fetched examples however, they lie largely in the realm of theory by reason of the scope of the power to amend the Constitution by the process which it itself contains (s 128) and, at least since the *Statute of Westminster*, of the full ambit of the power under the Constitution to make laws, however extra- territorial be their operation and however repugnant they be to the law of another country, with respect to external affairs. The practical effects of that power to amend the Constitution and of that legislative power which the Constitution confers are that, whatever be the theoretical explanation, ultimate authority in this country lies with the Australian people and that, subject to the Constitution and to the State Constitutions which it protects, the Commonwealth Parliament possesses legislative competence to preclude or exclude from Australia and from Australian law the direct operation of the laws, executive actions and judicial decisions of any other country including the United Kingdom.

The central point on which Gibbs CJ, Wilson and Dawson JJ dissented was that, in their view, the repeal of the *Merchant Shipping Act* was a "matter within the authority of the States of Australia" within the meaning of s 9(1) of the *Statute of Westminster*. This conclusion was based upon s 735 of the *Merchant Shipping Act*, which provided that a colonial legislature, including that of an Australian State, could repeal any provision of the Act subject to confirmation by Her Majesty in Council. Of course, in order to bring the matter within s 9(1) of the *Statute of Westminster*, it was necessary to show both that it fell within State authority, *and* that it did not fall within Com-monwealth authority. This the dissenters did by holding that the matter was not within the Commonwealth's power over "external affairs".

8. The *Australia Act*

The *Australia Act 1986* (Cth) (see Appendix) was assented to on 4 December 1985 and came into operation on 3 March 1986 when it was proclaimed by Elizabeth II, who travelled to Canberra for that purpose to make it clear that she was acting in her capacity as Queen of Australia. The Act brought to an end the continued application and paramountcy of Imperial laws in the Australian States. The passing of the Act also signalled the end of the power of the British Parliament to legislate for Australia (s 1) and removed the doctrines of extraterritoriality (s 2) and repugnancy (s 3) insofar as they applied to the States.

Substantially identical versions of the *Australia Act* were enacted by the United Kingdom and Commonwealth Parliaments. The United Kingdom version was enacted, as the *Statute of Westminster* required, with the Commonwealth's request and consent, as expressed by the *Australia (Request and Consent) Act 1986* (Cth). Both the United Kingdom Act and the Australian version of the *Australia Act* had also been requested by the Parliament of each State (see, for example, *Australia Acts Request Act 1985* (NSW)). Thus, whatever doubt there may have been about the capacity of any one of the participating Parliaments to terminate the States' residual links with Britain, the doubt was eradicated by legislation at every possible level.

The *Australia Act* was the final step in the severing of legal (as opposed to symbolic) ties with the United Kingdom. This was made clear by Gleeson CJ, Gaudron, Gummow and Hayne JJ in *Sue v Hill* (1999) 199 CLR 462, where they held that the United Kingdom is now "a foreign power" for the purposes of s 44(i) of the Constitution. The consequence was that Heather Hill, who stood for the Senate in Queensland in the 1998 federal election, was disqualified because she had not renounced her United Kingdom citizenship (see Chapter 10, §5).

The argument that the United Kingdom is "a foreign power" was resisted by Hill on the basis that, so long as the United Kingdom retained any residual influence upon legislative, executive or judicial processes in Australia, it could not be regarded as "foreign" to Australia. Gleeson CJ, Gummow and Hayne JJ responded by showing that, since the *Australia Act*, the United Kingdom retains no such influence. Moreover, that result was sufficiently achieved by the *Australia Act* in its Australian version, since that version was validly enacted under s 51(xxxviii) of the Constitution. In explaining that basis for its validity, they also explored the effect of s 1 of the Act, denying the power of the British Parliament to legislate for Australia.

Sue v Hill
(1999) 199 CLR 462

Gleeson CJ, Gummow and Hayne JJ: [491] The *Australia Act* was enacted before s 51(xxxviii) had been construed in *Port MacDonnell Professional Fishermen's Assn Inc v South Australia* [(1989) 168 CLR 340]. Apparently out of a perceived need for abundant caution, legislation of the Westminster Parliament was sought and passed as the 1986 UK Act.

The effect of s 51(xxxviii) is to empower the Parliament "to make laws with respect to the local exercise of any legislative power which, before federation, could not be exercised by the legislatures of the former Australian colonies" [168 CLR at 378]. It represents an actual enhancement of the legislative powers of the States because "it confers, by implication, power upon the Parliament of a State to participate in the legislative process which the paragraph requires, namely request (or concurrence) by a State Parliament and enactment by the Commonwealth Parliament" [168 CLR at 379]. There is a potential enhancement of State legislative powers because the Parliaments of the States are the potential recipients of legislative power under a law made pursuant to the paragraph. Any room for an inhibition against giving to the grant in s 51(xxxviii) its full scope and effect by reason of what was once the status of the Commonwealth itself within the British Empire no longer applies.

Section 1 of the *Australia Act* does not purport to exclude, as a matter of the law of the United Kingdom, the effect of statutes thereafter enacted at Westminster. Rather, it denies their efficacy as part of the law of the Commonwealth, the States and the Territories. Section 51(xxxviii) extends to the actual execution within this country of a power of the sort described in that paragraph. The scope of the phrase "within the Commonwealth" in s 51(xxxviii) includes the exercise of legislative power with effect upon the political structures **[492]** with authority over the geographical area of the Commonwealth, the States and the Territories and the areas provided for in the *Seas and Submerged Lands Act* 1973 (Cth). It follows that s 1 of the Australia Act was validly enacted under that paragraph.

The expression in s 1 of the 1986 UK Act "[n]o Act of the Parliament of the United Kingdom passed … shall extend, or be deemed to extend" was used in s 4 of the *Statute of Westminster* 1931 (UK). Provisions such as s 1 may present doctrinal questions for the constitutional law of the United Kingdom, in particular for the dogma associated with Dicey's views as to the sovereignty of the Parliament at Westminster. Professor Sir William Wade pointed out more than forty years ago that Dicey never explained how he reconciled his assertions that Westminster could destroy or transfer sovereignty and the proposition that it could not bind future Parliaments. The effect in the United Kingdom of any amendment or repeal by the United Kingdom Parliament of s 1 would be for those adjudicating upon the constitutional law of that country. But whatever effect the courts of the United Kingdom may give to an amendment or repeal of the 1986 UK Act, Australian courts would be obliged to give their obedience to s 1 of the statute passed by the Parliament of the Commonwealth.

Similarly, they noted that, by terminating any remaining appeals from Australian courts to the Privy Council, the Act had ensured that "**[493]** no institutions of government of the United Kingdom exercise any judicial powers with respect to this country". The same conclusion was reached in respect of executive power.

Gleeson CJ, Gummow and Hayne JJ: [495] It has been accepted, at least since the time of the appointment of Sir Isaac Isaacs in 1931, that in making the appointment of a Governor-General [under s 2 of the Constitution] the monarch acts on the advice of the Australian Prime Minister. The same is true of the exercise of the power vested by s 4 of the Constitution in the monarch to appoint a person to administer the government of the Commonwealth and the power given to the monarch by s 126 to authorise the Governor-General to appoint deputies within any part of the Commonwealth.

Section 58 makes provision for the Governor-General to reserve a "proposed law passed by both Houses of the Parliament" for the Queen's pleasure, in which event the law shall not have any force unless and until, in the manner prescribed by s 60, the Governor-General makes known the receipt of the Queen's assent. Further, s 59 provides for disallowance by the Queen of any law within one year of the Governor-General's assent. The text of the Constitution is silent as to the identity of the Ministers upon whose advice the monarch is to act in these respects.

As indicated when dealing earlier in these reasons with the former position of the States, provisions in colonial constitutional arrange-**[496]**-ments for reservation and disallowance had been designed to ensure surveillance of colonial legislatures by the Imperial Government. The convention in 1900 was that the monarch, in relation to such matters, would act on the advice of a British Minister. That advice frequently was given after consultation between the Colonial Office and the Ministry in the colony in question. With respect to the Commonwealth, the whole convention, like that respecting the appointment of Governors-General, changed after the Imperial Conference of 1926.

As early as 1929, it was stated in the *Report of the Royal Commission on the Constitution* with reference to the provisions of ss 58 and 59 of the Constitution that "in virtue of the equality of status which, from a constitutional as distinct from a legal point of view, now exists between Great Britain and the self-governing Dominions as members of the British Commonwealth of Nations, and on the principles which are set out in the Report submitted by the Inter-Imperial Relations Committee to the Imperial Conference in 1926", for "British Ministers to tender advice to the Crown against the views of Australian Ministers in any matter appertaining to the affairs of the Commonwealth" would "not be in accordance with constitutional practice".

Whilst the text of the Constitution has not changed, its operation has. This reflects the changed identity of those upon whose advice the sovereign accepts that he or she is bound to act in Australian matters by reason, among other things, of the attitude taken since 1926 by the sovereign's advisers in the United Kingdom. The Constitution speaks to the present and its interpretation takes account of and moves with these developments.

After analysing the place of "the Crown" in Australian constitutional practice, they concluded:

Gleeson CJ, Gummow and Hayne JJ: [503] Almost a century has passed since the enactment of the Constitution Act in the last year of the reign of Queen Victoria. In 1922, the Lord Chancellor observed that doctrines respecting the Crown often represented the results of a constitutional struggle in past centuries, rather than statements of a legal doctrine. The state of affairs identified in … these reasons is to the contrary. It is, as Gibbs J put it, "the result of an orderly development – not … the result of a revolution" [*Southern Centre of Theosophy Inc v South Australia* (1979) 145 CLR 246 at 261]. Further, the development culminating in the enactment of the *Australia Act* (the operation of which commenced on 3 March 1986) has followed paths understood by constitutional scholars writing at the time of the establishment of the Commonwealth.

The point of immediate significance is that the circumstance that the same monarch exercises regal functions under the constitutional arrangements in the United Kingdom and Australia does not deny the proposition that the United Kingdom is a foreign power within the meaning of s 44(i) of the Constitution. Australia and the United Kingdom have their own laws as to nationality so that their citizens owe different allegiances. The United Kingdom has a distinct legal personality and its exercises of sovereignty, for example in entering military alliances, participating in armed conflicts and acceding to treaties such as the Treaty of Rome, themselves have no legal consequences for this country.

There was no dissent from this conclusion, although McHugh and Kirby JJ did not express a final opinion and Callinan J indicated that, if necessary, he might have been inclined to dissent.

Callinan J: [571] The evolutionary theory is, with respect, a theory to be regarded with great caution. In propounding it, neither the petitioners nor the Commonwealth identify a date upon which the evolution became complete, in the sense that, as and from it, the United Kingdom was a foreign power. Nor could they point to any statute, historical occurrence or event which necessarily concluded the process. There were, they asserted, a series of milestones, for example, Federation itself, the *Statute of Westminster Adoption Act* 1942 (Cth), the *Royal Style and Titles Act* 1973 (Cth) and the *Australia Acts* but neither the last of these nor any other enactment was said to be the destination marker of the evolution.

The great concern about an evolutionary theory of this kind is the doubt to which it gives rise with respect to peoples' rights, status and **[572]** obligations as this case shows. The truth is that the defining event in practice will, and can only be a decision of this Court ruling that the evolutionary process is complete, and here, as the petitioners and the Commonwealth accept, has been complete for some unascertained and unascertainable time in the past. In reality, a decision of this Court upon that basis would change the law by holding that, notwithstanding that the Constitution did not treat the United Kingdom as a foreign power at Federation and for some time thereafter, it may and should do so now …

[573] I would therefore be inclined to hold that the evolutionary theory which has been advanced in this case, having as it does the defect of uncertainty as to events and conclusion, should not be accepted or applied here. However on neither that nor the other arguments relied on by the parties and the Commonwealth is it necessary for me to express any concluded opinion.

However, in the later cases of *Attorney-General (WA) v Marquet* (2003) 217 CLR 545 and *Shaw v Minister for Immigration and Multicultural Affairs* (2003) 218 CLR 28, Callinan J appears to have abandoned these doubts (see below).

Section 15 of the *Australia Act* allows the Commonwealth, "at the request or with the concurrence of the Parliaments of all the States", to repeal or amend both the *Statute of Westminster* (in its Australian applications) and the *Australia Act* itself. It has been suggested that this would allow s 8 of the *Statute of Westminster* to be amended or repealed so as to clear the way for amendment or repeal – without a referendum – of the Constitution, and in particular of s 128 (see, for example, Christopher Gilbert, "Section 15 of the Australia Acts: Constitutional Change by the Back Door?" (1989) 5 *Queensland University of Technology Law Journal* 55). This reading, while superficially plausible, runs counter to the emerging notion of popular sovereignty. Moreover, the "request and consent" procedure referred to in s 15 of the Act is presumably the procedure referred to in s 51(xxxviii) of the Constitution, which is expressed to be "subject to this Constitution". In any event, if the *Australia Act* did have the effect that such arguments envisage, neither the *Australia Act 1986* (Cth) nor the *Australia (Request and Consent) Act 1986* (Cth) would be constitutional, since they would infringe s 128, which insists that: "This Constitution shall not be altered except in the following manner …".

A variant on these suggestions was accepted by Kirby J in *Marquet*. At issue was the attempted repeal of the *Electoral Distribution Act 1947* (WA), with a view to replacing the State electoral distribution under that Act with a new and more equal distribution (see Chapter 10, §4(c)). The majority of the High Court held that the attempted repeal was blocked by s 13 of the 1947 Act, which effectively provided that "any Bill to amend this Act" must be passed by an absolute majority in both Houses of the State Parliament. The restraint thus imposed by s 13 was said to be rendered effective by s 6 of the *Australia Act*, which effectively reduplicates, for laws "made after the commencement of this Act", the "manner and form" requirements formerly imposed by s 5 of the *Colonial Laws Validity Act* (see Chapter 11, §3).

Kirby J, in sole dissent, held that, at least to that extent, the *Australia Act* was unconstitutional. He reasoned that, because s 6 purported to impose a new restraint on the legislative power of State Parliaments, it impliedly amended ss 106 and 107 of the Commonwealth Constitution by introducing into the State Constitutions a new element which had not been envisaged by those provisions. Yet, as Kirby J pointed out, no amendment of ss 106 and 107 could be valid unless effected by referendum pursuant to s 128 of the federal Constitution.

Attorney-General (WA) v Marquet
(2003) 217 CLR 545

Kirby J: [614] [Section 128] reserves to the Australian people, as electors of the Commonwealth, the power to make formal changes affecting the basic law of the nation. Any change to the basic constitutional powers of the Parliaments of the States of Australia, and to the Constitution of each State, limiting or controlling the constituent powers of those legislatures (as the *Australia Act 1986* (Cth) purports to introduce) amounts to an attempt at a formal alteration to ss 106 and 107 of the Constitution. As such, it can only be effected if it is passed in accordance with s 128 of the federal Constitution. Otherwise, any such purported imposition of new limitations by federal law (or by the laws of other States) is invalid and ineffective. In accordance with s 106 of the federal Constitution, the Constitution of each State would remain as it was in 1901 until altered "in accordance with the Constitution of the State", not as purportedly altered by a federal Act, such as the *Australia Act 1986* (Cth).

However desirable particular provisions of the *Australia Act 1986* (Cth) may seem to be, it is a statute of one constituent part of the Commonwealth purporting to alter the Constitutions of other constituent parts of the Commonwealth made without the one essential and undoubted "entrenched" requirement for such alterations, namely the participation of the electors of the Commonwealth in an amendment approved by them in accordance with s 128.

Convenience may ultimately overwhelm these legal and logical difficulties. The "march of history" [*Bonser v La Macchia* (1969) 122 CLR 177 at 223] may pass by my concerns. The passage of time may accord constitutional legitimacy and respectability to what has happened. Constitutional law is often dragged by the chariot of political realities, at the end of a long chain. The legislative and governmental unanimity, and the generally advantageous nature of the purported changes in the *Australia Acts*, may reward those measures with perceived effectiveness that becomes unquestioned law with the passing years. However, in case a similar attempt is made in the future to circumvent s 128 of the Constitution in such a way, by intergovernmental agreement and legislation without the participation of the people of Australia as electors, I lift my voice in protest.

In the view that I take, nothing in s 6 of the *Australia Acts* or either **[615]** of them (nor the *Australia Acts (Request) Act 1985* of each State) validly authorised the imposition on a Parliament of a State by federal or foreign law of a restriction not otherwise existing at the time of the federal Constitution concerning the power of the Parliament of that State to enact laws respecting the "constitution, powers or procedure of the Parliament of the State". On this basis, the supposed foundation in s 6 of the *Australia Act*, whether of the United Kingdom or of the Federal Parliament, for the effectiveness of s 13 of the 1947 Act, is unavailing. Subject to what follows, deprived of the support of s 6 of the *Australia Acts*, the supposed new source for the binding force of s 13 … is knocked away …

The joint reasons complain that the parties, interveners and *amici* did not challenge the validity of the *Australia Acts*. But that has been the problem – that governmental and political parties have not contested the validity of that legislation. They represent the very class who devised and enacted it. The constitutional arrangements of this country do not belong to them but to the people as electors for whom this Court stands guardian. It is not for parties, interveners or *amici*, by their agreements or silence, to oblige this Court to misapply the law – least of all constitutional law, concerned as it is with the fundamentals of government. The question of validity was repeatedly raised by me during argument in these applications, as it has been in other cases. Justices of this Court owe a higher duty to the Constitution and the law. They are not hostages to the arguments of the parties. Nor are they mere arbitrators of the disputes that parties choose to define and propound.

No other judge accepted this argument. The joint judgment of Gleeson CJ, Gummow, Hayne and Heydon JJ denied that any such contention had been raised during oral argument, and in any event rebutted it by invoking the unanimous affirmation in *Port MacDonnell Professional Fishermen's Assn Inc v South Australia* (1989) 168 CLR 340 that "**[381]** the continuance of the Constitution of a State pursuant to s 106 is subject to any Commonwealth law enacted pursuant to the grant of legislative power in par (xxxviii)" of s 51. Thus (as in *Sue v Hill*) the majority based their reasoning solely on the Australian version of the *Australia Act*; assumed that the Australian version was valid (that is, that in 1986 the Commonwealth Parliament had the power to sever all the remaining links of Australian State laws and institutions with those of the United Kingdom); and based this assumption (as in *Sue v Hill*) on s 51(xxxviii).

It is true that the Australian version of the *Australia Act* was passed in reliance on s 51(xxxviii); that was the point of the various *Australia Acts Request Acts* passed by the Australian States. It was only after that mechanism had already been set in train, however, that the High Court handed down its decision in *Kirmani v Captain Cook Cruises Pty Ltd (No 1)* (1985) 159 CLR 351. Although that decision had no clear ratio decidendi, Murphy J held that the severing of residual legal links with Britain fell within the external affairs power, and Mason and Deane JJ relied on that view as establishing that the matter was one "within the authority of the Parliament or Government of the Commonwealth" for the purposes of s 9(1) of the *Statute of Westminster*. On that basis, the Australian version of the *Australia Act* may be valid even without reliance on s 51(xxxviii).

Callinan J perhaps hinted at this in *Marquet* when he stated that "**[636]** The Australia Acts may have been in part at least passed pursuant to s 51(xxxviii) of the Constitution, but there is more that can be said of them than that. All of the relevant Acts (federal and State) as **[637]** well as the *Australia Act 1986* (UK) represent a final and indubitable recognition, a settlement between the United Kingdom, Australia and its States, and an ultimate legitimization of the respective constitutions, the sovereignty and the plenitude of the powers of the respective Australian polities. They also represent a remarkable and rare consensus of polities which requires that their terms be given full effect". Similarly, in *Shaw v Minister for Immigration and Multicultural Affairs* (2003) 218 CLR 28, Callinan J extolled the Australian version of the *Australia Act* as the "**[85]** overt legislative act, mirroring simultaneous legislation in the United Kingdom, that gave voice to the completion of Australia's evolutionary independence. It was a formal declaration that the Commonwealth of Australia and the Australian states were completely constitutionally independent of the United Kingdom. Nothing can serve so well to give legitimacy to a nation and its constitutional integrity as a rare and complete consensus of governments of the kind that the enactment of the *Australia Acts* represents".

The problem that Callinan J was addressing in *Shaw* was that of identifying the "**[82]** magic date" at which Australian independence became so complete that the former status of "British subject" had finally ceased to have any Australian significance (see Chapter 20, §3(b)). He concluded that "**[84]** the correct date ... **[85]** can be no earlier than the coming into force of the *Australia Acts*: 3 March 1986". McHugh and Kirby JJ also accepted this view, the latter stressing that the Royal Assent had been "**[67]** signified by Her Majesty personally in Canberra on that day". Moreover, noting that his view in *Marquet* "**[66]** was not adopted by the majority of this Court", Kirby J also announced in *Shaw* that: "Pending a greater enlightenment, I must accept this Court's holding that the *Australia Acts* are valid laws".

9. Popular Sovereignty

The Constitution of India begins: "We, the People of India ... , do hereby adopt, enact, and give to ourselves this Constitution". The United States Constitution begins: "We the People of the United States, in Order to ... secure the Blessings of Liberty to ourselves and our Posterity, do ordain and establish this Constitution for the United States of America". By contrast, the *Commonwealth of Australia Constitution Act 1900* (Imp) was enacted by the Imperial Parliament, though it does begin with the recital: "Whereas the people of [the colonies] ... have agreed to unite in one indissoluble Federal Commonwealth ...". Formally, therefore, the Australian Constitution derives its validity from an exercise of British sovereignty.

Sir Owen Dixon, "The Law and the Constitution"
(1935) 51 *Law Quarterly Review* 590

[597] The framers of our own federal Commonwealth Constitution (who were for the most part lawyers) found the American instrument of government an incomparable model. They could not escape from its fascination. Its contemplation damped the smouldering fires of their originality. But, although they copied it in many respects with great fidelity, in one respect the Constitution of our Commonwealth was bound to depart altogether from its prototype. It is not a supreme law purporting to obtain its force from the direct expression of a people's inherent authority to constitute a government. It is a statute of the British Parliament enacted in the exercise of its legal sovereignty over the law everywhere in the King's Dominions. In the interpretation of our Constitution this distinction has many important consequences. We treat our organs of government simply as institutions established by law, and we interpret their powers simply as authorities belonging to them by law. American doctrine treats them as agents for the people who are the source of power and their powers as authorities committed to them by a principal. From this arises the theory that powers may not be delegated; that the agent selected by the principal to exercise a function of government may not transfer any part of his authority to some other person or body, a theory which finds no place in our system.

While Australia has attained full legal independence, the Constitution remains in the form of an Imperial statute. However, now that the *Australia Act* has diminished – and perhaps extinguished – the continuing legal relevance of Imperial legislation, the opening recital "Whereas the people ..." has assumed a deeper significance. It may supply a persuasive explanation of why the Constitution is binding.

Geoffrey Lindell, "Why is Australia's Constitution Binding? – The Reasons in 1900 and Now, and the Effect of Independence"
(1986) 16 *Federal Law Review* 29

[30] *The Answer in 1900*
An examination of the Constitution Act supplies an obvious starting point ... The Constitution is itself part of an Act passed by the British Imperial Parliament by virtue of covering clause 9 of the same Act. Covering clause 5 makes clear that the Constitution was intended to "be binding on the courts, judges and people of every State and of every part of the Commonwealth" ... Two features of the Constitution would have been important in explaining its character at the time of its enactment. First its *legal* status was derived from the fact that it was contained in an enactment of

the British Imperial Parliament. Secondly, its *political* legitimacy or authority was based on the words contained in the preamble to that enactment which refer to the people of the Australian colonies having agreed to unite in a "Federal Commonwealth". Whatever the legal position, these words draw attention to the political reason for its enactment, the document having been in large measure approved by the people of Australia even if the number of persons who actually voted was only 60% of the eligible voters. The importance of the role played by the Australian people was to be further underlined by the ability given to them to amend the Constitution in accordance with proposals initiated by the Federal Parliament under s 128 ...

[32] In conclusion, as regards the explanation which would have been given in 1900, the Constitution was legally binding because of the status accorded to British statutes as an original source of law in Australia and also because of the supremacy accorded to such statutes. Local legislation was only [33] recognised so far as it complied with British statutes which applied by paramount force including those which authorised or made provision for the enactment of legislation by the local parliaments. It will be noticed that this explanation does not treat as legally relevant the agreement of the Australian people to federate however important such a factor may have been in explaining the political reason for the adoption of the Constitution. This was in effect the approach which Sir Owen Dixon adopted ... – an approach which as he himself was concerned to emphasise, contrasted with that adopted in the United States where the supremacy of that country's constitution is normally attributed to "the people's inherent authority to constitute a government".

"Independence", the Statute of Westminster and the Australia Acts
A number of important changes have taken place in relation to the constitutional and international status of the Australian nation since the enactment of the Constitution Act in 1900. Those changes include:

1. the development of Australia's independence in the eyes of the international community;
2. the inability of the British Parliament to legislate for Australia; and
3. the ability of both Commonwealth and State Parliaments to alter or repeal British statutes of any kind other than the Commonwealth Constitution and the Australia Acts (otherwise than in accordance with the procedure set out in s 128 of the Commonwealth Constitution, as regards the alteration of that Constitution, and also the procedures set out in the Australia Acts, as regards the alteration of those Acts).

The first of these developments was of course evolutionary in character and was largely the result of the operation of constitutional practices and conventions such as the well known Balfour Declaration. Formal legal declarations to symbolise the attainment of independence have in the main been absent except for such enactments as the Statute of Westminster. On the other hand, the Australia Acts can now be seen to evidence a more explicit declaration of that independence since they do not leave the remaining residual links between the United Kingdom and the Australian States to be terminated by the operation of constitutional conventions ...

[37] *The Answer in 1986*
The question can now be addressed as to whether the changes that have occurred to the constitutional status of Australia since 1900 affect the explanation which should be given for the legally binding and fundamental character of the Australian Constitution. The attainment of complete constitutional independence need not affect the nature of that explanation according to what may be termed an historical approach to the problem. This approach would stress the essential continuity in the chain of legislative authority. The Federal and State legislatures were entrusted with certain grants of legislative powers which were not enlarged as a result of developments since 1900 except as regards the ability to override the enactments of the British Parliament other than, *inter alia*, the Constitution. The fundamental nature of the Constitution can then be explained in 1986 by reference to the fact that *nothing has happened to change the pre-existing inability of the Parliaments of the Commonwealth and the States to legislate inconsistently with the Constitution* whatever changes may have occurred in relation to the ability of those Parliaments to enact legislation which is inconsistent with *other* British Acts of Parliament.

In the view of the writer, the historical explanation is constitutionally and legally sound. However its necessary reliance on Australia's colonial past may, understandably, lead to a search for an additional, although not necessarily alternative, way of explaining the reason for the legally binding and fundamental character of the Constitution. In short that explanation can be found in the words of the preamble to the Constitution Act referred to earlier, namely, the agreement of the people to federate, supported by the role given to them in approving proposals for constitutional alteration under s 128 of the Constitution, as well as their acquiescence in the continued operation of the Constitution as a fundamental law. According to this approach the Constitution now enjoys its character as a higher law because of the will and authority of the people. Such an explanation more closely conforms to the present social and political reality and has the advantage of ensuring that the legal explanation for the binding character of the Constitution coincides with popular understanding.

Even before the passage of the *Australia Act*, Murphy J had argued in *Bistricic v Rokov* that the Constitution was binding because of "[566] its continuing acceptance by the Australian people". For other judges, the *Australia Act* was decisive. As Mason CJ put it in *Australian Capital Television Pty Ltd v Commonwealth* (1992) 177 CLR 106, the *Australia Act* "[138] marked the end of the legal sovereignty of the Imperial Parliament and recognised that ultimate sovereignty resided in the Australian people". And in *Theophanous v Herald & Weekly Times Ltd* (1994) 182 CLR 104, Deane J argued that the present legitimacy of the Constitution "[171] lies exclusively in the original adoption (by referenda) and subsequent maintenance (by acquiescence) of its provisions by the people". The sovereignty of the people is thus conceived of as expressed by their acquiescence in the constitutional system established by the *Commonwealth of Australia Constitution Act 1900* (Imp). Yet the hierarchies thereby established may not be acquiesced in by all people, nor is Australia's constitutionalism strictly limited to that Act. Reliance upon the successful referenda of 1898-1900 is also problematic.

George Williams, "The High Court and the People"
in Hugh Selby (ed), *Tomorrow's Law* (Federation Press, 1995), 271

[286] There remain significant conceptual and practical difficulties with the basis upon which the Australian people are said to underpin the sovereignty of the Constitution. Both of the bases suggested by Deane J may be questioned.

Approval by referenda
The Australian Constitution was supported by the people at referenda as follows (the figures in brackets are for the first referenda of 1898):

Colony	For	Against	Majority
New South Wales (1899)	107,420 (71,595)	82,741 (66,228)	24,679 (5.367)
Victoria (1899)	152,653 (100,520)	9,805 (22,099)	142,848 (78,421)
South Australia (1899)	65,990 (35,800)	17,053 (17,320)	48,937 (18,480)
Tasmania (1899)	13,437 (11,797)	791 (2,716)	12,646 (9,081)
Queensland (1899)	38,488	30,996	7,492
Western Australia (1900)	44,800	19,691	25,109
Totals	422,788 (219,712)	161,077 (108,363)	261,711 (111,349)

Only 52% of persons eligible to vote at the referenda did so, with the Constitution receiving only narrow support in New [287] South Wales (56% in 1899, 52% in 1898) and Queensland (55% in 1899). In any event, most women and many of Australia's Aboriginal people (Queensland did not grant voting rights to its Aboriginal people until 1965) were excluded from voting.

Women were only able to vote for the Constitution in South Australia and Western Australia. Not one of the delegates that met and drafted the Constitution was female.

Australia's Aboriginal people were also not involved in the discussions that led to the drafting of the Australian Constitution. As a result, until the Constitution was amended in 1967, Aboriginal people could not be included under section 127 of the Constitution in "reckoning the numbers of the people of the Commonwealth, or of a State or other part of the Commonwealth".

These statistics demonstrate that, while the Constitution was supported by a majority of the people who actually voted, large sections of the community were excluded from voting and many people who were entitled to vote did not do so. In these circumstances, the Constitution cannot be said to be the people's document because of their support in the referenda at the turn of the century. Popular support for the Constitution must therefore be sought from other avenues or from future referenda.

Approval by acquiescence

Deane J's novel idea in *Theophanous* was that the supremacy of the Constitution is not only based upon the will of the people as expressed in referenda but also in the continuing acquiescence of the people to the operation of the Constitution ...

There are significant difficulties with Deane J's argument. Australians do not go about deciding whether to continue to acquiesce to the existing constitutional structure. It is true that popular support in referenda has frequently demonstrated, as recently as 1988, that the people are reluctant to **[288]** amend the Constitution. However, it cannot be assumed from this that the people continue to support, or even tacitly approve of, the Constitution.

A further, and deeper, problem with the notion that the legitimacy of the Constitution is upheld by the acquiescence of the people is that the people are largely ignorant of the Constitution. Australians possess an appalling lack of knowledge about their system of government. This was found by the 1994 report on citizenship by the Civics Expert Group.

The Civics Expert Group found that only 18% of Australians have some understanding of what their Constitution contains, while only 40% can correctly name both Houses of the Federal Parliament. More than a quarter of those surveyed nominated the Supreme Court, rather than the High Court, as the "top" court in Australia. Some Australians, particularly younger Australians, even demonstrated a greater awareness of the United States Constitution than the Australian Constitution. These results should come as no surprise. A 1987 survey conducted for the Australian Constitutional Commission found that 47% of Australians were unaware that Australia has a written Constitution.

The lack of civics education in schools and the prevailing apathy in the community towards our politicians and political processes are largely responsible for the ignorance of the Australian people about the Constitution. The Constitution is also, at least at face value, an uninspiring document. There are only meagre rewards available for any non-lawyer willing to engage in a cover-to-cover read. As stated by Lois O'Donoghue, Chairperson of the Aboriginal and Torres Strait Islander Commission:

It says very little about what it is to be Australian. It says practically nothing about how we find ourselves here – save being an amalgamation of former colonies. It says nothing of how we should behave towards each other as human beings and as Australians ...

[289] In these circumstances it is hardly surprising that Australians are largely unaware of the terms of the Constitution. At most, it might be said that just under one in five Australians have some idea of what the Constitution contains while just over one in two Australians are aware that we have a written Constitution at all. This cannot amount to maintenance of the Constitution by the acquiescence of the people. Ignorance cannot provide a foundation for the popular legitimacy of the Australian Constitution.

Helen Irving has argued that, despite the low number of votes actually cast for the new Constitution, Federation can still be regarded as a "popular" process.

Helen Irving, "The People and their Conventions"
in Michael Coper and George Williams (eds), *Power, Parliament and the People*
(Federation Press, 1997), 113

[121] How can Federation be considered "popular", or the Constitution to have received the approval of the people, it might be asked, if a total numerical majority did not vote "yes"?

We do not know, and cannot take account of the reasons for the failure of numbers of people to turn up to vote: their absence may be taken as rejection, even alienation from the processes. It may just as well be read as complaisance, even approval and acceptance. But considering those who did vote, the claim that Federation was not a "popular" process because the percentage of "yes" votes in the referendums fell in some (although not **[122]** the majority) of the colonies below 50 percent of the eligible voters is problematic. The idea that "popular" and "democratic" can only be demonstrated where very large majorities of the total population participated, positively rules out probably most historical claims to a mandate, and effectively also obscures any difference between participatory processes where such a majority was not achieved, and processes in which no participation at all was permitted. But there can scarcely have been a significant historical change of any sort in which an overwhelming, even literal majority of the people participated positively. Many, if not most, governments in Australia are elected as the product of tiny majorities, and in some cases, of statistical minorities.

What matters is less the statistics, and more the mechanism. "The people" is a shifting, contested concept in any case. It is more a mechanism than a literal count of heads. What was "popular" about the federation process of the second half of the 1890s, and about conventions that debated and wrote the Constitution, was that they required participation. They opened up a field in which public debate, petitions, letters to the press, and scrutiny of official processes were not only accepted, they were central. Once the vote was to be counted, "the people's" interests had to be acknowledged, their power to make or break the result, taken into account.

Although women did not have the vote in four colonies, we must not underestimate the significance of their franchise at that time in two. Women's enfranchisement in South Australia (where they voted both for the convention and in the referendums) and in Western Australia (where they were enfranchised just before that colony's referendum) was important in inspiring women to take part elsewhere in the campaigns, stimulating them to press harder for the suffrage where they had not achieved it, and drawing the attention of male politicians to women as a political constituency. Once a public, participatory process began, women were able to think of themselves, in many cases for the first time, *as* political, and able to comment and agitate with legitimacy. The women themselves recognised this as an important change in the political culture, and the politically active among them began to take advantage of it.

The situation was far from ideal by today's standards. It might well have been better had conservative Upper Houses in New South Wales, Tasmania and Victoria not rejected Bills coming from their Lower Houses, **[123]** which would have given women the right to join their South Australian and West Australian counterparts in voting directly at the 1898 and 1899 referendums. But, it *was* much worse elsewhere in the world, and it had been worse in the early 1890s, at the time of the first convention, where the draft Constitution was written with reference only to the colonial parliaments.

At best, in the absence of a reformed Constitution and a better informed electorate, words like "acquiescence" and "complaisance" must have the meaning assigned to them by the "ticket cases" in 19th-century contract law (see, for example, *Parker v South Eastern Railway* (1877) 2 CPD 416). These cases suggest that so long as people are aware – or have had a reasonable opportunity to become aware – of the existence of predetermined rules that may affect their behaviour, then if such people do not bother to find out what the rules are they must be taken to have given their implied consent to whatever the rules turn out to be.

10. Further References

Bennett, JM, and Castles, A (eds), *A Source Book of Australian Legal History* (Law Book Co, 1979).

Craven, G, "A Few Fragments of State Constitutional Law" (1990) 20 *University of Western Australia Law Review* 353.

Davidson, A, *The Invisible State: The Formation of the Australian State 1788-1901* (Cambridge University Press, 2002).

Deakin, A, *The Federal Story: The Inner History of the Federal Cause, 1880-1900* (Melbourne University Press, 2nd ed 1963).

Dixon, O, "The Statute of Westminster 1931" (1936) 10 *Australian Law Journal* (Supplement) 96.

Evans, S, "Why is the Constitution Binding?: Authority, Obligation and the Role of the People" (2004) 25 *Adelaide Law Review* 103.

Finn, PD, "A Sovereign People, A Public Trust" in Finn, PD (ed), *Essays on Law and Government: Principles and Values* (Law Book Co, 1995), vol 1, 1.

Goldring, J, "The Australia Act 1986 and the Formal Independence of Australia" [1986] *Public Law* 192.

Irving, H (ed), *A Woman's Constitution? Gender and History in the Australian Commonwealth* (Hale & Iremonger, 1996).

Irving, H (ed), *The Centenary Companion to Australian Federation* (Cambridge University Press, 1999).

Irving, H, *To Constitute a Nation: A Cultural History of Australia's Constitution* (Cambridge University Press, 1997).

Kercher, B, *An Unruly Child: A History of Law in Australia* (Allen & Unwin, 1995).

Kirby, M, "Deakin: Popular Sovereignty and the True Foundation of the Australian Constitution" (1996) 3 *Deakin Law Review* 129.

La Nauze, JA, *No Ordinary Act: Essays on Federation and the Constitution* (Melbourne University Press, 2001).

La Nauze, JA, *The Making of the Australian Constitution* (Melbourne University Press, 1972).

Lindell, G, "Further Reflections on the Date of the Acquisition of Australia's Independence", in French, R, Lindell, G, and Saunders, C (eds), *Reflections on the Australian Constitution* (Federation Press, 2003), 51.

McPherson, BH, "The Mystery of Anonymous (1722)" (2001) 75 *Australian Law Journal* 169.

Moshinsky, M, "State Extraterritorial Legislation and the Australia Acts 1986" (1987) 61 *Australian Law Journal* 779.

Moshinsky, M, "State Extraterritorial Legislation – Further Developments" (1990) 64 *Australian Law Journal* 42.

Neal, D, *The Rule of Law in a Penal Colony: Law and Power in Early New South Wales* (Cambridge University Press, 1991).

The New Federalist: The Journal of Australian Federation History (University of Adelaide, 1998-2001).

Quick, J, and Garran, R, *The Annotated Constitution of the Australian Commonwealth* (Legal Angus & Robertson, 1901; repr Legal Books, 1995).

Salmond, JW, "The Limitations of Colonial Legislative Power" (1917) 33 *Law Quarterly Review* 117.

Thomson, JA, "The Australia Acts 1986: A State Constitutional Law Perspective" (1990) 20 *University of Western Australia Law Review* 409.

Thomson, JA, "The Australian Constitution: Statute, Fundamental Document or Compact?" (1985) 59 *Law Institute Journal* 1199.

Twomey, A, *The Constitution of New South Wales* (Federation Press, 2004), Ch 2.

Twomey, A, "*Sue v Hill* – The Evolution of Australian Independence" in Stone, A, and Williams, G (eds), *The High Court at the Crossroads: Essays in Constitutional Law* (Federation Press, 2000), 1.

Wait, M, "The Slumbering Sovereign: Sir Owen Dixon's Common Law Constitution Revisited" (2001) 29 *Federal Law Review* 57.

Williams, JM, "'With Eyes Open': Andrew Inglis Clark and Our Republican Tradition" (1995) 23 *Federal Law Review* 149.

Williams, JM, "Race, Citizenship and the Formation of the Australian Constitution: Andrew Inglis Clark and the '14th Amendment'" (1996) 42 *Australian Journal of Politics and History* 10.

Williams, JM, *The Australian Constitution: A Documentary History* (Melbourne University Press, 2005).

Winterton, G, "Popular Sovereignty and Constitutional Continuity" (1998) 26 *Federal Law Review* 1.

Winterton, G, "The Acquisition of Independence", in French, R, Lindell, G, and Saunders, C (eds), *Reflections on the Australian Constitution* (Federation Press, 2003), 31.

Zines L, "The Growth of Australian Nationhood and its Effect on the Powers of the Commonwealth" in Zines, L (ed), *Commentaries on the Australian Constitution* (Butterworths, 1977), 1.

Zines, L, "The Sovereignty of the People" in Coper, M, and Williams, G (eds), *Power, Parliament and the People* (Federation Press, 1997), 91.

Chapter 5

Indigenous Peoples and Sovereignty

1. Introduction

The structures of government in Australia were originally seen as deriving their legitimacy from the sovereignty of the British Parliament and the Imperial Crown. Since the *Australia Act 1986* (Cth), some members of the High Court have put forward as an alternative the concept of popular sovereignty (see Chapter 4, §9). Yet the pattern of colonial settlement and expansion unfolded against the background of an older and perhaps competing source of potential authority: namely, the diverse patterns of belief and power expressed through the traditions and practices of Indigenous peoples.

In *Mabo v Queensland (No 2)* (1992) 175 CLR 1 the High Court did not accord to this antecedent normative foundation any legal force of its own. Through recognition by the common law, this older tradition was acknowledged as an embodiment of inherent and judicially cognisable bonds between Indigenous peoples and their ancestral lands. However, by formulating it as "native title" depending on common law recognition, the Court avoided any suggestion of Indigenous "sovereignty".

By contrast, the governmental structures established by the United States Constitution have been able to accommodate recognition of the governmental structures of the native American tribes, which are conceived of as "domestic dependent nations". Whether such an accommodation could ever be possible in Australia, and whether "reconciliation" between Indigenous and non-Indigenous Australians is possible without it, are questions of fundamental importance for the theory and the practical politics of Australian constitutionalism.

In *Mabo (No 2)* the High Court took care to avoid undermining the formal constituent structures of Australian governance. The Court recognised the customary laws and entitlements of Indigenous peoples only to the extent that they saw this as consistent with existing constitutional norms. Moreover, both in that decision and in *Wik Peoples v Queensland* (1996) 187 CLR 1, native title was said to continue only when not extinguished. Any valid legislative or executive action of the Commonwealth or of its constituent States, or their predecessors in Imperial or colonial power, will suffice to extinguish it. Even the controversial decision in the *Wik Case*, that "[133] there was no necessary extinguishment of those rights by reason of the grant of pastoral leases", was qualified by a reminder that in cases of inconsistency "the rights and interests conferred by native title … must yield … to the rights of the grantees".

For other aspects of the laws of Indigenous peoples, even this degree of accommodation-on-sufferance may not be achieved. Thus, in *Walker v New South Wales* (1994) 182 CLR 45, Mason CJ, sitting alone, insisted that in criminal law an inherent and imperative need for uniformity and equality of application meant that the constitutionally established law must operate to the exclusion of any other law. Yet, given a federal system of government that already encompasses different laws co-existing at different levels, we may need to ask whether such an exclusive monistic conception is necessary, or even possible.

2. Voting Rights and the Constitution

In Queensland, Aborigines other than freeholders were excluded from the franchise by a proviso to s 6 of the *Elections Act 1885* (Qld) ("No aboriginal native of Australia, India, China, or of the South Sea Islands ..."). In Western Australia a similar disqualification was imposed by a proviso to s 12 of the *Constitution Amendment Act 1893* (WA) ("No aboriginal native of Australia, Asia or Africa ..."). The other four States imposed no such disqualification, and accordingly Aborigines in those States were legally entitled to vote for the first federal Parliament in 1901. Before Federation, women had also been entitled to vote in South Australia and Western Australia; and, in order to preserve the rights of women, particularly in South Australia, s 41 of the Constitution provided that "no adult person" entitled to vote at State elections should be prevented from voting at federal elections "by any law of the Commonwealth" (see Chapter 26, §2). Clearly, at the first federal election in 1901, this provision operated to ensure that women in South Australia and Western Australia could vote, and also that Aborigines in all States except Queensland and Western Australia could do so.

Soon after Federation, the *Commonwealth Franchise Act 1902* (Cth) extended the federal franchise to women, so that as to women s 41 had no further work to do. The Franchise Bill had also proposed to extend the franchise to Aborigines; but that proposal was strongly resisted and was finally defeated (*Hansard*, House of Representatives, 24 April 1902, 11975-80). Among its opponents were Isaac Isaacs, who thought Aborigines "**[11979]** have not the intelligence, interest or capacity" to vote; and HB Higgins, who thought it "**[11977]** utterly inappropriate ... [to] ask them to exercise an intelligent vote". As finally enacted, s 4 of the 1902 Act specifically denied the voting rights of "aboriginal native[s] of Australia ... unless so entitled under Section 41 of the Constitution". It took until 1962 to amend the *Commonwealth Electoral Act 1918* (Cth) to extend universal adult suffrage to Aboriginal people. Even then, full equality at federal elections did not occur until 1983, when the Act was amended to make enrolment for and voting in federal elections compulsory for Indigenous people as it is for other Australians.

On one reading of s 41, as other States extended the franchise to Aborigines, they would automatically have become entitled to vote in federal elections as well. Murphy J favoured this reading, in dissent, in *R v Pearson; Ex parte Sipka* (1983) 152 CLR 254. He argued that the operation of s 41, thus construed, had in fact ensured that Aborigines in all States except Queensland and Western Australia had been able to exercise guaranteed voting rights at federal elections before 1962. In that way, s 41 had not been, as the majority thought, a dead letter after 1902. On the contrary, s 41 had had an important practical impact.

In fact Murphy J's view of the practical impact of s 41 was wrong. The narrow meaning of s 41, as accepted by the majority in *R v Pearson; Ex parte Sipka*, had in fact been proposed as the preferable meaning by John Quick and Robert Garran, *The Annotated Constitution of the Australian Commonwealth* (Angus & Robertson, 1901; repr Legal Books, 1995), 486-7. On that interpretation, s 41 was a transitional provision operating only to regulate the franchise at the very first federal election in 1901. Once the first Commonwealth Parliament had passed the *Commonwealth Franchise Act*, the transitional arrangements made by s 41 were exhausted. However, even on this narrow view s 41 had operated in 1901 for the benefit of Aborigines in New South Wales, South Australia, Tasmania and Victoria as well as women in South Australia and Western Australia; and, even on that narrow view, the persons who thereby acquired a constitutional right to vote at the 1901 election retained that right forever after.

Sir Robert Garran, the co-author of this transitional interpretation of s 41, was the Secretary to the Commonwealth Attorney-General's Department until 1916, and thereafter served as Solicitor-General until 1932. In that capacity, when issues arose of possible entitlements to vote under s 41, Garran consistently gave advice based on the narrow interpretation. The Electoral

Commission, relying on that advice, consistently denied federal enrolment to any person not entitled to vote in a State election before 1902. Thus, far from a broad view of s 41 achieving the Aboriginal enfranchisement that Murphy J extolled in *R v Pearson; Ex parte Sipka*, the reality was that a narrow view of s 41, adopted at the administrative level, had effectively disenfranchised even those Aborigines entitled to vote in their own home States. Moreover, in 1912 Garran amended the Electoral Handbook to state: "It has been held that a right under Section 41 ... does not entitle any person to vote whose name is not on a Commonwealth Electoral Roll". On that basis, even Aborigines who were clearly entitled to vote under s 41 (that is, Aborigines in New South Wales, South Australia, Tasmania and Victoria enrolled before 1902) began to have their voting rights taken away from them (see Pat Stretton and Christine Finnimore, "Black Fellow Citizens: Aborigines and the Commonwealth Franchise" (1993) 25 *Australian Historical Studies* 521).

The statutory change to the *Commonwealth Electoral Act* in 1962 was followed by changes to the Constitution in 1967. Neither of the 1890s Conventions that debated the Constitution had included Indigenous people: cast as a "dying race", they played no meaningful role in its drafting. It is not surprising then that the Constitution as enacted in 1901 did not reflect their interests or aspirations. While the preamble to the Constitution suggests that "the people ... have agreed to unite", it makes no mention of Aboriginal people or their prior occupation of the lands upon which the new nation was formed. The operative provisions of the Constitution were also premised upon exclusion and even discrimination. It made two references to them (although in neither case were they referred to as "people"). Section 51(xxvi) empowered Parliament to make laws with respect to: "The people of any race, *other than the aboriginal race in any State,* for whom it is deemed necessary to make special laws". The 1967 referendum deleted the words in italics. It also repealed s 127 of the Constitution, which provided: "In reckoning the numbers of the people of the Commonwealth, or of a State or other part of the Commonwealth, aboriginal natives shall not be counted".

The 1967 amendments were carried by the largest "Yes" vote ever recorded (see Appendix). However, the amendments deleted text from the Constitution without inserting anything in its place. They therefore left the Constitution silent with respect to Aboriginal people. While the objective of the 1967 referendum was to remove discriminatory references and to allow the Commonwealth to take over responsibility for Indigenous welfare, it may also be that the failure to reflect this benevolent intention by explicit words in the Constitution has enabled the Commonwealth to pass laws that impose a disadvantage. This is because the open words of s 51(xxvi), and the racially discriminatory intentions behind it, were extended to Aboriginal people without any indication that the power can be applied only for their benefit (see Chapter 21, §4).

Many federal enactments rely upon the expanded scope of the races power. In February 1973, the Whitlam government appointed Justice Woodward to report on Aboriginal land rights. Although his terms of reference were limited to the Northern Territory, it was thought his report would establish principles to be implemented throughout Australia. His first report was delivered in July 1973. In his second report, in April 1974, he explained the broad objectives of the legislative program he thought should follow.

Aboriginal Land Rights Commission: Second Report
(Parliamentary Paper No 69 of 1974, Session 1974, Vol 1, 1)

[2] **3.** In order to achieve recognition of land rights for Aborigines in the best possible form, it is necessary first to be clear as to the aims underlying such recognition. I have assumed these to be:

    (i) the doing of simple justice to a people who have been deprived of their land without their consent and without compensation,

    (ii) the promotion of social harmony and stability within the wider Australian community by removing, so far as possible, the legitimate causes of complaint of an important minority group within that community,

(iii) the provision of land holdings as a first essential for people who are economically depressed and who have at present no real opportunity of achieving a normal Australian standard of living,

(iv) the preservation, where possible, of the spiritual link with his own land which gives each Aboriginal his sense of identity and which lies at the heart of his spiritual beliefs, and

(v) the maintenance and, perhaps, improvement of Australia's standing among the nations of the world by demonstrably fair treatment of an ethnic minority.

4. I believe that these aims can best be achieved by:

(a) preserving and strengthening all Aboriginal interests in land and rights over land which exist today, particularly all those having spiritual importance;

(b) ensuring that none of these interests or rights are further whittled away without consent, except in those cases where the national interest positively demands it – and then only on terms of just compensation,

(c) the provision of some basic compensation in the form of land for those Aborigines who have been irrevocably deprived of the rights and interests which they would otherwise have inherited from their ancestors, and who have obtained no sufficient compensating benefits from white society, and

(d) the further provision of land, to the limit which the wider community can afford, in those places where it will do most good, particularly in economic terms, to the largest number of Aborigines.

From 1974 onwards, the recommendations of the Woodward Report were the basis of the Whitlam government's legislative program, as continued by the Fraser government in 1976. The first round of laws included the *Aboriginal Land Fund Act 1974* (Cth), *Aboriginal Land Rights (Northern Territory) Act 1976* (Cth) and *Aboriginal Councils and Associations Act 1976* (Cth). Later enactments include the *Aboriginal and Torres Strait Islander Heritage Protection Act 1984* (Cth) and *Council for Aboriginal Reconciliation Act 1991* (Cth).

3. *Mabo* and Indigenous Law

The High Court decision in *Mabo v Queensland (No 2)* (1992) 175 CLR 1 was handed down on 3 June 1992. The argument which the majority accepted had been pending since 1982. In that year Eddie Mabo, James Rice and David Passi brought an action, on their own behalf and that of the Meriam people, asserting that traditional Meriam title to the Murray Islands in the Torres Strait was unimpaired by Queensland's annexation of the islands in 1879 or by any later developments. In February 1986, Gibbs CJ remitted the issues of fact to the Supreme Court of Queensland, where Moynihan J began taking evidence in October 1986. The hearings were suspended while the High Court reviewed the validity of Queensland legislation purporting to defeat the claim. That legislation was held invalid by 4:3 in *Mabo v Queensland (No 1)* (1988) 166 CLR 186 (see Chapter 9, §6). The hearings by Moynihan J then resumed. He handed down three volumes of findings on 16 November 1990.

With the benefit of these findings of fact, the High Court held by 6:1 that the common law as received into New South Wales, and thereby applicable in the Murray Islands, recognised the continuance of "traditional native title" after the British acquisition of sovereignty. It was held that, on the new foundation of the "radical" title taken by the Crown, existing rights survive unless expressly extinguished. The dissenting judgment of Dawson J held that native title had been extinguished upon settlement or annexation.

The majority judges accepted many of the findings favourable to Aboriginal plaintiffs made by Blackburn J in *Milirrpum v Nabalco Pty Ltd* (*Gove Land Rights Case*) (1971) 17 FLR 141. However, they rejected the conclusions that had ultimately led Blackburn J to find that the Aboriginal plaintiffs in that case must fail. The most important of those adverse conclusions related to the application, in Australia, of the common law rules regulating the consequences of British acquisition of sovereignty over overseas colonies, as expounded, barely five years before

Cook raised the British flag in Australia, in William Blackstone's *Commentaries on the Laws of England* (1765, University of Chicago Press reprint, 1979), Volume I, Introduction, sect 4 (see Chapter 4, §1). If, in Blackstone's terminology, Australia had been "conquered" (by British acts of force) or "ceded" (by Indigenous acts of submission), then Indigenous legal traditions, and entitlements thereunder, would have survived under the new British sovereign (though subject to future extinguishment). By contrast, the governing assumption that Australia was "settled" implied a legal vacuum that was filled immediately with English law to the exclusion of any other laws or entitlements. According to Blackstone, this was the appropriate analysis where the newly occupied territory was "**[104]** desart and uncultivated". In the *Gove Land Rights Case* Blackburn J noted that while these words "**[201]** are Blackstone's own", they "have always been taken to include territory in which live uncivilized inhabitants in a primitive state of society".

On this basis, the assumption that the Australian colonies were "settled" did not deny the physical existence of the Aboriginal tribes inhabiting the continent at the time of the British arrival. However, it did imply that, as the Privy Council put it in *In re Southern Rhodesia* [1919] AC 211: "**[233]** Some tribes are so low in the scale of social organization that their usages and conceptions of rights and duties are not to be reconciled with the institutions or the legal ideas of civilized society. Such a gulf cannot be bridged". Blackburn J did not accept in the *Gove Land Rights Case* that this was an appropriate estimation of the level of "social organization" attained by the Australian Aboriginals. Instead, he took a strongly contrary view, finding that "**[267]** The evidence shows a subtle and elaborate system highly adapted to the country in which the people led their lives, which provided a stable order of society and was remarkably free from the vagaries of personal whim or influence. If ever a system could be called 'a government of laws, and not of men', it is that shown in the evidence before me".

Despite this, Blackburn J adhered to what he saw as the traditional view. This was that the assumption that Australia was "settled" had itself been settled *as a matter of law*: "**[202]** [T]he attribution of a colony to a parti-**[203]**-cular class [for example, 'settled'] is a matter of law, which becomes settled and is not to be questioned upon a reconsideration of the historical facts". On this basis, Blackburn J held that he was bound by a series of obiter dicta in which, for purposes of analysing the foundations of Australian property law, earlier courts had assumed that the Australian colonies were "settled". In addition to the Privy Council's observations in *Cooper v Stuart* (1889) 14 App Cas 286, there were similar dicta in *Attorney-General v Brown* (1847) 1 Legge 312, 2 SCR (NSW) App 30; *Williams v Attorney-General (NSW)* (1913) 16 CLR 404 and *Randwick Municipal Council v Rutledge* (1959) 102 CLR 54. However, all these cases arose within the context of the transplanted British system of Crown grants, reservations and dedications of land. The relationship of that transplanted system to any Indigenous system or scheme of interests was never in issue.

Even if the Privy Council's pronouncement in *Cooper v Stuart* was merely obiter, it may be understandable that Blackburn J, in 1971, regarded himself as bound to follow it. But clearly, in 1992, the High Court was not so bound. Without overruling any actual decisions, it was open to the Court to hold that the classification of the Australian colonies as "settled" was a misapplication of Blackstone's categories, and had never been an accurate statement of the common law. Instead, however, the majority judges agonised over whether it was open to them to *change* the common law (see especially Brennan J at 43-7). The supposed "change" involved the acceptance of two propositions:

1. that in 1788 Australia, and more particularly New South Wales, was not terra nullius (that is, land belonging to no-one); and

2. that the Crown upon acquisition of Australia in 1788 did not immediately and automatically assume full beneficial ownership of all land in Australia.

In *Mabo (No 2)*, Blackstone's concept of "desart and uncultivated" land was assimilated to the concept of terra nullius in international law. The unreality of that description, as applied to the Australian continent before the British arrival, was emphatically asserted. This entailed a rejection of the proposition from which Blackburn J took comfort in the *Gove Land Rights Case*, namely that assessments on such an issue are assessments of law, not open to correction or modification by reference to historical facts. Instead, the *Mabo (No 2)* majority reformulated the legal conceptualisation of events in such a way as to bring it more closely into line with historical reality. The result was to restate the consequences of British sovereignty over Australia in the terms that Blackstone considered appropriate for a "conquered" colony. This recognised that the Indigenous population had a pre-existing system of law, which, along with all rights subsisting thereunder, would remain in force under the new sovereign except where specifically modified or extinguished by legislative or executive action. The Court purported to achieve all this without altering the traditional assumption that the Australian land mass was "settled". Instead, the rules for a "settled" colony, *where there was an existing population*, were said to be assimilated to the rules for a "conquered" colony.

In correcting the terra nullius error without fully working out the consequences for the "conquered"/"settled" distinction, the Court may have left its historical re-analysis incomplete. Indeed, Toohey J noted that: "**[182]** The plaintiffs accept[ed] that the Islands were settled by Britain rather than conquered or ceded". If this aspect of *Mabo (No 2)* depends only on a concession by the parties, it may be that the issue should not be regarded as having been decided.

Mabo v Queensland (No 2)
(1992) 175 CLR 1

Brennan J: [38] It is one thing for our contemporary law to accept that the laws of England, so far as applicable, became the laws of New South Wales and of the other Australian colonies. It is another thing for our contemporary law to accept that, when the common law of England became the common law of the several colonies, the theory which was advanced to support the introduction of the common law of England accords with our present knowledge and appreciation of the facts ...

[39] The facts as we know them today do not fit the "absence of law" or "barbarian" theory underpinning the colonial reception of the common law of England. That being so, there is no warrant for applying in these times rules of the English common law which were the product of that theory. It would be a curious doctrine to propound today that, when the benefit of the common law was first extended to Her Majesty's indigenous subjects in the Antipodes, its first fruits were to strip them of their right to occupy their ancestral lands. Yet the supposedly barbarian nature of indigenous people provided the common law of England with the justification for denying them their traditional rights and interests in land ... As the indigenous inhabitants of a settled colony were regarded as "low in the scale of social organization" [*In re Southern Rhodesia* [1919] AC 211 at 233], they and their occupancy of colonial land were ignored ... **[40]** Ignoring those rights and interests, the Crown's sovereignty over a territory which had been acquired under the enlarged notion of terra nullius was equated with Crown ownership of the lands therein, because, as Stephen CJ said, there was "no *other* proprietor of such lands". Thus, a Select Committee on Aborigines reported in 1837 to the House of Commons that the state of Australian Aborigines was "barbarous" and "so entirely destitute ... of the rudest forms of civil polity, that their claims, whether as sovereigns or proprietors of the soil, have been utterly disregarded". The theory that the indigenous inhabitants of a "settled" colony had no proprietary interest in the land thus depended on a discriminatory denigration of indigenous inhabitants, their social organization and customs. As the basis of the theory is false in fact and unacceptable in our society, there is a choice of legal principle to be made in the present case. This Court can either apply the existing authorities and proceed to inquire whether the Meriam people are higher "in the scale of social organization" than the Australian Aborigines whose claims were "utterly disregarded" by the existing authorities or the Court can overrule the existing authorities, discarding the distinction between inhabited colonies that were terra nullius and those which were not.

Brennan J went on to examine the decision of the International Court of Justice in its *Advisory Opinion on Western Sahara* (1975) ICJR 12 at 39, after which he continued:

Brennan J: [41] If the international law notion that inhabited land may be classified as terra nullius no longer commands general support, the doctrines of the common law which depend on the notion that native peoples may be "so low in the scale of social organization" that it is "idle to impute to such people some shadow of the rights known to our law" [[1919] AC at 233-4] can hardly be retained. If it were permissible in past centuries to keep the common law in step with international law, it is imperative in today's world that the common law should **[42]** neither be nor be seen to be frozen in an age of racial discrimination.

The fiction by which the rights and interests of indigenous inhabitants in land were treated as non-existent was justified by a policy which has no place in the contemporary law of this country ... Whatever the justification advanced in earlier days for refusing to recognize the rights and interests in land of the indigenous inhabitants of settled colonies, an unjust and discriminatory doctrine of that kind can no longer be accepted. The expectations of the international community accord in this respect with the contemporary values of the Australian people. The opening up of international remedies to individuals pursuant to Australia's accession to the Optional Protocol to the International Covenant on Civil and Political Rights brings to bear on the common law the powerful influence of the Covenant and the international standards it imports. The common law does not necessarily conform with international law, but international law is a legitimate and important influence on the development of the common law, especially when international law declares the existence of universal human rights. A common law doctrine founded on unjust discrimination in the enjoyment of civil and political rights demands reconsideration. It is contrary both to international standards and to the fundamental values of our common law to entrench a discriminatory rule which, because of the supposed position on the scale of social organization of the indigenous inhabitants of a settled colony, denies them a right to occupy their traditional lands.

The majority in *Mabo (No 2)* also rejected the proposition put in cases like *Attorney-General v Brown* that, immediately upon the acquisition of sovereignty, full legal and beneficial ownership of all the lands of the Colony vested in the Crown. That proposition would only be appropriate in relation to territory which was literally terra nullius. In other cases, including Australia, the new property law which the British Crown brought with it for British settlers presupposed that property interests were to be held on tenure from the Crown; but that only made it necessary, as Brennan J expressed the point, to ascribe to the Crown

Brennan J: [48] a title, adapted from feudal theory, that was called a radical, ultimate or final title ... The radical title is a postulate of the doctrine of tenure and a concomitant of sovereignty. As a sovereign enjoys supreme legal authority in and over a territory, the sovereign has power to prescribe what parcels of land and what interests in those parcels should be enjoyed by others and what parcels of land should be kept as the sovereign's beneficial demesne ...

But it is not a corollary of the Crown's acquisition of a radical title to land in an occupied territory that the Crown acquired absolute beneficial ownership of that land to the exclusion of the indigenous inhabitants. If the land were desert and uninhabited, truly a terra nullius, the Crown would take an absolute beneficial title ... for the reason given by Stephen CJ in *Attorney-General (NSW) v Brown* [(1847) 1 Legge 312 at 317-18]: there would be no *other* proprietor. But if the land were occupied by the indigenous inhabitants and their rights and interests in the land are recognized by the common law, the radical title which is acquired with the acquisition of sovereignty cannot itself be taken to confer an absolute beneficial title to the occupied land ...

[50] [T]he radical title, without more, is merely a logical postulate required to support the doctrine of tenure (when the Crown has exercised its sovereign power to grant an interest in land) and to support the plenary title of the Crown (when the Crown has exercised its sovereign power to appropriate to itself ownership of parcels of land within the Crown's territory). Unless the sovereign power is exercised in one or other of those ways, there is no reason why land within the Crown's territory **[51]** should not continue to be subject to native title.

Coupled with this "radical title" was an absolute sovereign power to determine the disposition of all land held under the Crown, including that of Indigenous owners. It followed that any surviving native title is liable to be extinguished by express action of the Crown at any time, and also to be extinguished by any legislative or executive disposition of the land which is inconsistent with the continuance of the Indigenous claim. Yet this combination of "radical title" with sovereign power over native title did not add up to "full beneficial ownership":

Brennan J: [51] It is only the fallacy of equating sovereignty and beneficial ownership of land that gives rise to the notion that native title is extinguished by the acquisition of sovereignty.

If it be necessary to categorize an interest in land as proprietary in order that it survive a change in sovereignty, the interest possessed by a community that is in exclusive possession of land falls into that category. Whether or not land is owned by individual members of a community, a community which asserts and asserts effectively that none but its members has any right to occupy or use the land has an interest in the land that must be proprietary in nature: there is no other proprietor. It would be wrong, in my opinion, to point to the inalienability of land by that community and, by importing definitions of "property" which require alienability under the municipal laws of our society, to deny that the indigenous people owned their land. The ownership of land within a territory in the exclusive occupation of a people must be vested in that people: land is susceptible of ownership, and there are no other owners. True it is that land in exclusive possession of an indigenous people is not, in any private law sense, alienable property for the laws and customs of an indigenous people do not generally contemplate the alienation of the people's traditional land. But the common law has asserted that, if the Crown should acquire sovereignty over that land, the new sovereign may extinguish the indigenous people's interest in the land and create proprietary rights in its place and it would be curious if, in place of interests that were classified as non-proprietary, proprietary rights could be created. Where a proprietary title capable of recognition by the common law is found to have been possessed by a community in occupation of a territory, there is no reason why that title should not be recognized as a burden on the Crown's radical title when the Crown acquires sovereignty over that territory. The fact that individual members of the community, like the individual plaintiff Aborigines in *Milirrpum* [(1971) 17 FLR 141 at 272], enjoy only usufructuary rights that are not proprietary in nature is no impediment to the recognition of a proprietary community title. Indeed, it is not possible to admit traditional usufructuary rights without admitting a traditional proprietary community title. There may be difficulties of proof of boundaries or of membership of the community or of representatives of the community which was in exclusive possession, but those difficulties afford no reason for denying the existence of a **[52]** proprietary community title capable of recognition by the common law ...

Once it is accepted that indigenous inhabitants in occupation of a territory when sovereignty is acquired by the Crown are capable of enjoying – whether in community, as a group or as individuals – proprietary interests in land, the rights and interests in the land which they had theretofore enjoyed under the customs of their community are seen to be a burden on the radical title which the Crown acquires. The notion that feudal principle dictates that the land in a settled colony be taken to be a royal demesne upon the Crown's acquisition of sovereignty is mistaken.

Consistently with these observations, the High Court subsequently held that native title was not extinguished by the mere settlement of Western Australia (*Western Australia v Commonwealth* (*Native Title Act Case*) (1995) 183 CLR 373 at 432-3).

In the *Gove Land Rights Case* Blackburn J had accepted the practices and beliefs of the Rirratjingu clan as disclosing a system of "law", but concluded that the clan's relationship to its land under that system could not be recognised at common law because it did not conform to the notion of "property" as understood by European systems of law. By contrast, *Mabo (No 2)* assumed that, if the common law is to recognise claims derived from an Indigenous legal tradition, the nature and incidents of those claims must be defined *by that tradition*.

Brennan J: [58] Native title has its origin in and is given its content by the traditional laws acknowledged by and the traditional customs observed by the indigenous inhabitants of a territory. The nature and incidents of native title must be ascertained as a matter of fact by reference to those laws and customs. The ascertainment may present a problem of considerable difficulty, as Moynihan J perceived in the present case. It is a problem that did not arise in the case of a settled colony so long as the fictions were maintained that customary rights could not be reconciled "with the institutions or the legal ideas of civilized society", [and] that there was no law before the arrival of the British colonists ... But once it is acknowledged that an inhabited territory which became a settled colony was no more a legal desert than it was "desert uninhabited" in fact, it is necessary to ascertain by evidence the nature and incidents of native title ...

[59] Of course, since European settlement of Australia, many clans or groups of indigenous people have been physically separated from their traditional land and have lost their connexion with it. But that is not the universal position ... Where a clan or group has continued to acknowledge the laws and (so far as practicable) to observe the customs based on the traditions of that clan or group, whereby their traditional connexion with the land has been substantially maintained, the traditional community title of that clan or group can [60] be said to remain in existence. The common law can, by reference to the traditional laws and customs of an indigenous people, identify and protect the native rights and interests to which they give rise. However, when the tide of history has washed away any real acknowledgment of traditional law and any real observance of traditional customs, the foundation of native title has disappeared. A native title which has ceased with the abandoning of laws and customs based on tradition cannot be revived for contemporary recognition. Australian law can protect the interests of members of an indigenous clan or group, whether communally or individually, only in conformity with the traditional laws and customs of the people to whom the clan or group belongs and only where members of the clan or group acknowledge those laws and observe those customs (so far as it is practicable to do so) ...

[61] The incidents of a particular native title relating to inheritance, the transmission or acquisition of rights and interests on death or marriage, the transfer of rights and interests in land and the grouping of persons to possess rights and interests in land are matters to be determined by the laws and customs of the indigenous inhabitants, provided those laws and customs are not so repugnant to natural justice, equity and good conscience that judicial sanctions under the new regime must be withheld. Of course in time the laws and customs of any people will change and the rights and interests of the members of the people among themselves will change too. But so long as the people remain as an identifiable community, the members of whom are identified by one another as members of that community living under its laws and customs, the communal native title survives to be enjoyed by the members according to the rights and interests to which they are respectively entitled under the traditionally based laws and customs, as currently acknowledged and observed.

The metaphorical reference by Brennan J to "[60] the tide of history ... wash[ing] away ... the foundation of native title" has been important in later cases, notably in *Yorta Yorta Aboriginal Community v Victoria* (2002) 214 CLR 422. However, the true significance of the metaphor has been disputed. See, for example, Ann Genovese and Alexander Reilly, "Turning the Tide of History: Metaphor in Native Title Extinguishment" (2003) 2 *Griffith Review* 209.

As the "tide of history" metaphor acknowledged, and as all the majority judges in *Mabo (No 2)* accepted, to say that full beneficial ownership did not immediately vest in the Crown is not to deny the historical process by which the Aboriginal peoples were dispossessed of most of their lands. It merely clarifies the juristic basis on which that dispossession occurred. It happened piecemeal, through successive legislative and executive actions of the colonial governments and their successors. It did not happen all at once as an automatic corollary of British sovereignty. And in any case where nothing has happened inconsistent with the continuance of native title, that title subsists to this day, though still subject to extinguishment by State or Commonwealth legislative or executive acts. As Brennan J summarised his conclusions:

Brennan J: [69] 1. The Crown's acquisition of sovereignty over the several parts of Australia cannot be challenged in an Australian municipal court.

2. On acquisition of sovereignty over a particular part of Australia, the Crown acquired a radical title to the land in that part.

3. Native title to land survived the Crown's acquisition of sovereignty and radical title. The rights and privileges conferred by native title were unaffected by the Crown's acquisition of radical title but the acquisition of sovereignty exposed native title to extinguishment by a valid exercise of sovereign power inconsistent with the continued right to enjoy native title.

4. Where the Crown has validly alienated land by granting an interest that is wholly or partially inconsistent with a continuing right to enjoy native title, native title is extinguished to the extent of

the inconsistency. Thus native title has been extinguished by grants of estates of freehold or of leases but not necessarily by the grant of lesser interests (eg, authorities to prospect for minerals).

5. Where the Crown has validly and effectively appropriated land [70] to itself and the appropriation is wholly or partially inconsistent with a continuing right to enjoy native title, native title is extinguished to the extent of the inconsistency. Thus native title has been extinguished to parcels of the waste lands of the Crown that have been validly appropriated for use (whether by dedication, setting aside, reservation or other valid means) and used for roads, railways, post offices and other permanent public works which preclude the continuing concurrent enjoyment of native title. Native title continues where the waste lands of the Crown have not been so appropriated or used or where the appropriation and use is consistent with the continuing concurrent enjoyment of native title over the land (eg, land set aside as a national park).

6. Native title to particular land (whether classified by the common law as proprietary, usufructuary or otherwise), its incidents and the persons entitled thereto are ascertained according to the laws and customs of the indigenous people who, by those laws and customs, have a connection with the land. It is immaterial that the laws and customs have undergone some change since the Crown acquired sovereignty provided the general nature of the connection between the indigenous people and the land remains. Membership of the indigenous people depends on biological descent from the indigenous people and on mutual recognition of a particular person's membership by that person and by the elders or other persons enjoying traditional authority among those people.

7. Native title to an area of land which a clan or group is entitled to enjoy under the laws and customs of an indigenous people is extinguished if the clan or group, by ceasing to acknowledge those laws, and (so far as practicable) observe those customs, loses its connection with the land or on the death of the last of the members of the group or clan.

8. Native title over any parcel of land can be surrendered to the Crown voluntarily by all those clans or groups who, by the traditional laws and customs of the indigenous people, have a relevant connection with the land but the rights and privileges conferred by native title are otherwise inalienable to persons who are not members of the indigenous people to whom alienation is permitted by the traditional laws and customs.

9. If native title to any parcel of the waste lands of the Crown is extinguished, the Crown becomes the absolute beneficial owner.

Note, in paras 3, 4 and 5, the use of the words "valid" and "validly". Brennan J was prepared to concede that any Crown action affecting Indigenous title could be scrutinised according to the conventional standards of legal validity (for example, to require that it be within a clearly delegated power), and also to insist that it must evince a clear and plain intention to extinguish the traditional title. Beyond this, he was not willing to go.

Brennan J: [63] Sovereignty carries the power to create and to extinguish private rights and interests in land within the Sovereign's territory. It follows that, on a change of sovereignty, rights and interests in land that may have been indefeasible under the old regime become liable to extinction by exercise of the new sovereign power. The sovereign power may or may not be exercised with solicitude for the welfare of indigenous inhabitants but, in the case of common law countries, the courts cannot review the merits, as distinct from the legality, of the exercise of sovereign power.

Deane and Gaudron JJ also held that native title could be extinguished by clear and unambiguous legislative action. But they added that "[111] wrongful" extinguishment might incur liability in damages, or might be prevented by injunction; and that the power to extinguish might be subject to other limitations.

Deane and Gaudron JJ: [110] The personal rights conferred by common law native title do not constitute an estate or interest in the land itself. They are extinguished by an unqualified grant of an inconsistent estate in the land by the Crown, such as a grant in fee or a lease conferring the right to exclusive possession. They can also be terminated by other inconsistent dealings with the land by the Crown ... The personal rights of use and occupation conferred by common law native title are not, however, illusory. They are legal rights which are infringed if they are extinguished, against the wishes of the native title-holders, by inconsistent grant, dedication or reservation and which, subject only to their susceptibility to being wrongfully so extinguished, are binding on the Crown and a burden on its title ...

[111] [T]he rights are not entrenched in the sense that they are ... beyond the reach of legislative power. The ordinary rules of statutory interpretation require, however, that clear and unambiguous words be used before there will be imputed to the legislature an intent to expropriate or extinguish valuable rights relating to property without fair compensation. Thus, general waste lands (or Crown lands) legislation is not to be construed, in the absence of clear and unambiguous words, as intended to apply in a way which will extinguish or diminish rights under common law native title. If lands in relation to which such title exists are clearly included within the ambit of such legislation, the legislative provisions conferring executive powers will, in the absence of clear and unambiguous words, be construed so as not to increase the capacity of the Crown to extinguish or diminish the native title. That is to say, the power of the Crown wrongfully to extinguish the native title by inconsistent grant will remain but any liability of the Crown to pay compensatory damages for such wrongful extinguishment will be unaffected ...

There are, however, some important constraints on the legislative power of Commonwealth, State or Territory Parliaments to extinguish or diminish the common law native titles which survive in this country. In so far as the Commonwealth is concerned, there is the requirement of s 51(xxxi) of the Constitution that a law with respect to the acquisition of property provide "just terms". Our conclusion that rights under common law native title are true legal rights which are recognised and protected by the law would, we think, have the consequence that any legislative extinguishment of those rights would constitute an expropriation of property, to the benefit of the underlying estate, for the purposes of s 51(xxxi). An even more important restriction upon legislative powers to ex-[112]-tinguish or diminish common law native title flows from the paramountcy of valid legislation of the Commonwealth Parliament over what would otherwise be valid State or Territory legislation. In particular, as *Mabo v Queensland* [(1988) 166 CLR 186] has demonstrated, the provisions of the *Racial Discrimination Act* 1975 (Cth) represent an important restraint upon State or Territory legislative power to extinguish or diminish common law native title ...

[C]ommon law native title-holders in an eighteenth century British Colony were in an essentially helpless position ... [T]he vulnerability of the rights under native title resulted in part from the fact that they were personal rights susceptible to extinguishment by inconsistent grant by the Crown and in part from the immunity of the Crown from court proceedings. The vulnerability persists to the extent that it flows from the nature of the rights as personal. On the other hand, as legislative reforms increasingly subjected the Crown ... to the jurisdiction of the courts and to liability for compensatory damages for a wrong done to a subject, the ability of native title-holders to protect and vindicate the personal rights under common law native title significantly increased. If common law native title is wrongfully extinguished by the Crown, the effect of those legislative reforms is that compensatory damages can be recovered provided the proceedings for recovery are instituted within the period allowed by applicable limitations provisions. If the common law native title has not been extinguished, the fact that the rights under it are true legal rights means that they can be vindicated, protected and enforced by proceedings in the ordinary courts.

In a case where the Crown or a trustee appointed by the Crown wrongly denies the existence or the extent of an existing common [113] law native title or threatens to infringe the rights thereunder (eg by an inconsistent grant), the appropriate relief ... will ordinarily be declaratory only since it will be apparent that the Crown or the trustee, being bound by any [judicial] declaration, will faithfully observe its terms. Further relief is, however, available where it is necessary to protect the rights of the title-holders. One example of such further relief is relief by way of injunction. Notwithstanding their personal nature and their special vulnerability to wrongful extinguishment by the Crown, the rights of occupation or use under common law native title can themselves constitute valuable property. Actual or threatened interference with their enjoyment can, in appropriate circumstances, attract the protection of equitable remedies. Indeed, the circumstances of a case may be such that, in a modern context, the appropriate form of relief is the imposition of a remedial constructive trust framed to reflect the incidents and limitations of the rights under the common law native title. The principle of the common law that pre-existing native rights are respected and protected will, in a case where the imposition of such a constructive trust is warranted, prevail over other equitable principles or rules to the extent that they would preclude the appropriate protection of the native title in the same way as that principle prevailed over legal rules which would otherwise have prevented the preservation of the title under the common law. In particular, rules relating to requirements of certainty and present entitlement or precluding remoteness of vesting may need to be adapted or excluded to the extent necessary to enable the protection of the rights under the native title.

Toohey J similarly concluded that, at least at the State level, any future attempt to dispossess Indigenous title holders might be made inoperative by s 109 by reason of inconsistency with the *Racial Discrimination Act 1975* (Cth) (see Chapter 9, §6); and also that "[196] where an executive act is relied upon to extinguish traditional title, the intention of the legislature that executive power should extend this far must … appear plainly and with clarity". In one respect, Toohey J went further than any other member of the Court. An argument put by the plaintiffs was that the Crown in right of Queensland "[199] is under a fiduciary duty, or alternatively bound as a trustee, to the Meriam People … , to recognize and protect their rights and interests in the Murray Islands". Toohey J held that, precisely because the Crown has such absolute power over the holders of native title, it is under a fiduciary duty in respect of that power. He concluded that the "[205] fiduciary obligation on the Crown does not limit the legislative power of the Queensland Parliament, but legislation will be a breach of that obligation if its effect is adverse to the interests of the titleholders, or if the process it establishes does not take account of those interests".

Brennan J was willing to consider the legal validity, but not the merits, of interferences with Indigenous title. In case this was ambiguous, the implications were spelled out by Mason CJ and McHugh J, who largely confined themselves to agreeing with Brennan J, but added:

> **Mason CJ and McHugh JJ: [15]** In the result, six members of the court (Dawson J dissenting) are in agreement that the common law of this country recognises a form of native title which, in the cases where it has not been extinguished, reflects the entitlement of the indigenous inhabitants, in accordance with their laws or customs, to their traditional lands and that, subject to the effect of some particular Crown leases, the land entitlement of the Murray Islanders in accordance with their laws or customs is preserved, as native title, under the law of Queensland. The main difference between those members of the Court who constitute the majority is that, subject to the operation of the *Racial Discrimination Act* 1975 (Cth), neither of us nor Brennan J agrees with the conclusion to be drawn from the judgments of Deane, Toohey and Gaudron JJ that, at least in the absence of clear and unambiguous statutory provision to the contrary, extinguishment of native title by the Crown by inconsistent grant is wrongful and gives rise to a claim for compensatory damages. We note that the judgment of Dawson J supports the conclusion of Brennan J and ourselves on that aspect of the case since his Honour considers that native title, where it exists, is a form of permissive occupancy at the will of the Crown.
>
> We are authorized to say that the other members of the Court [16] agree with what is said in the preceding paragraph about the outcome of the case.

Note the attempt to use Dawson J's *dissenting* judgment, treating native title as extinguished on settlement, to make up a 4:3 majority against any remedy for wrongful extinguishment.

An attempt to build upon the notion of fiduciary duty as developed by Toohey J in *Mabo (No 2)* was unsuccessful in *Wik Peoples v Queensland* (1996) 187 CLR 1. While that result depended on a particular statutory context, in the earlier case of *Coe v Commonwealth (No 2)* (1993) 118 ALR 193, Mason CJ, sitting alone, was similarly unreceptive to an assertion of a "trust" or "fiduciary duty". In *Bodney v Westralia Airports Corporation Pty Ltd* (2000) 180 ALR 91, Lehane J, after a full review of the authorities, concluded that decisions in Canada and elsewhere supporting the imputation of a fiduciary duty "[116] do not provide a firm basis for the assertion of a fiduciary duty of the kind for which [the native title claimants] contend"; and that "the tendency of authority in the High Court … is against the existence of such a duty". In this respect he relied in particular on the analysis in *Breen v Williams* (1996) 186 CLR 71 of the duty relationship between doctor and patient. However, none of these cases can be taken to have decided whether the power of the Crown to extinguish native title gives rise to a fiduciary obligation owed by the Crown to the Indigenous peoples of Australia. Hence, in *Western Australia v Ward* (*Miriuwung-Gajerrong Case*) (2002) 213 CLR 1, Gleeson CJ, Gaudron, Gummow and Hayne JJ observed: "**[67]** [T]he statement in *Mabo (No 2)* that native title 'may be protected by such legal or equitable remedies as are appropriate to the particular rights and interests established by the evidence' [175 CLR at 61] is yet to be developed by decisions indicating what is involved in the notion of 'appropriate' remedies".

4. *Wik* and *Ward*

The most important, and most controversial, aspect of *Wik Peoples v Queensland* (1996) 187 CLR 1 was its resolution of whether native title is extinguished by the grant of something less than a full freehold interest. That question had not been resolved in *Mabo (No 2)*. The formal order of the Court, declaring the Meriam people entitled "**[217]** to possession, occupation, use and enjoyment of the lands of the Murray Islands", was made subject to an express reservation: "putting to one side the Islands of Dauer and Waier and the parcel of land leased to the Trustees of the Australian Board of Missions". The two islands referred to had been the subject of a lease for purposes of a sardine factory in 1931, and the mission site had originally been leased to the London Missionary Society in 1882. The Court left unresolved whether the granting of those leases had extinguished native title. Thus, the actual decision in *Mabo (No 2)* made it clear that the mere grant of something less than a full freehold interest did not necessarily extinguish native title. On the other hand, a passage in the judgment of Brennan J suggested that the granting of a leasehold interest did have that effect.

Mabo v Queensland (No 2)
(1992) 175 CLR 1

Brennan J: [68] A Crown grant which vests in the grantee an interest in land which is inconsistent with the continued right to enjoy a native title in respect of the same land necessarily extinguishes the native title. The extinguishing of native title does not depend on the actual intention of the Governor in Council (who may not have adverted to the rights and interests of the indigenous inhabitants or their descendants), but on the effect which the grant has on the right to enjoy the native title. If a lease be granted, the lessee acquires possession and the Crown acquires the reversion expectant on the expiry of the term. The Crown's title is thus expanded from the mere radical title and, on the expiry of the term, becomes a plenum dominium. Where the Crown grants land in trust or reserves and dedicates land for a public purpose, the question whether the Crown has revealed a clear and plain intention to extinguish native title will sometimes be a question of fact, sometimes a question of law and sometimes a mixed question of fact and law. Thus, if a reservation is made for a public purpose other than for the benefit of the indigenous inhabitants, a right to continued enjoyment of native title may be consistent with the specified purpose – at least for a time – and native title will not be extinguished. But if the land is used and occupied for the public purpose and the manner of occupation is inconsistent with the continued enjoyment of native title, native title will be extinguished. A reservation of land for future use as a school, a courthouse or a public office will not by itself extinguish native title: construction of the building, however, would be inconsistent with the continued enjoyment of native title which would thereby be extinguished. But where the Crown has not granted interests in land or reserved and dedicated land inconsistently with the right to continued enjoyment of native title by the Indigenous inhabitants, native title survives and is legally enforceable.

In *Western Australia v Ward* (*Miriuwung-Gajerrong Case*) (2002) 213 CLR 1, the references in this passage to the "use" of land were impliedly criticised by Gleeson CJ, Gaudron, Gummow and Hayne JJ as liable to "**[136]** distract attention from the relevant inquiries: namely, whether rights have been created in others that are rights inconsistent with native title rights and interests, and whether the Crown has asserted rights over the land that are inconsistent with native title rights and interests. Use of the land may suggest, it may even demonstrate, that such rights have been created or asserted, but the basic inquiry is about inconsistency of *rights*, not inconsistency of *use* ... **[142]** [W]e consider that looking to the use that has actually been made of land distracts attention from the central inquiry which is an inquiry about rights created in others or asserted by the executive, not the way in which they may have been exercised at any **[143]** time". Callinan J agreed with these observations (at 398, n 1101).

As it stood at the time of the *Wik Case*, however, the passage set out above was equivocal. Its broad thrust was consistent with that of all the majority judgments in *Mabo (No 2)*: namely, that native title survives unless and until the land is dealt with in a manner clearly inconsistent with its continuance. On the other hand, the two sentences relating to the effect of a lease reflected an analysis in terms of "possession" and "reversion", the combined effect of which would necessarily be inconsistent with any continuing native title. Assuming that this accurately stated the effect of a standard lease, it was still an open question whether the same analysis would apply to the pastoral leases that had widely been used to implement colonial land policy, or whether such leases were rather to be governed by the final sentence quoted above.

In *North Ganalanja Aboriginal Corp v Queensland* (*Waanyi Case*) (1995) 132 ALR 565, a Full Court of the Federal Court divided 2:1 on the issue. Jenkinson and Hill JJ held that native title was automatically extinguished by the grant of such leases, but the dissent of Lee J indicated that the issue was still unresolved. An appeal to the High Court in that case was expected to settle the issue, but succeeded on a different ground: the Court held that the initial reference to the Federal Court had so miscarried that there was no properly constituted proceeding in which it was possible to rule on the question of pastoral leases (*North Ganalanja Aboriginal Corporation v Queensland* (*Waanyi Case*) (1996) 185 CLR 595).

The issue in the *Wik Case* was whether claims to continuing rights over land advanced by the Wik and Thayorre Peoples had been extinguished by the granting of pastoral leases under the *Land Act 1910* (Qld) and *Land Act 1962* (Qld). The Thayorre claim related primarily to the Mitchellton Holding (535 square miles), for which a first pastoral lease (issued in 1915) had been forfeited for non-payment of rent in 1918, and a second (issued in 1918) had been surrendered in 1921. The lessee never entered into possession under either lease, and in 1922 the land was reserved for Aboriginal use. The Wik claim related primarily to the Holroyd River Holding (1120 square miles), for which a first pastoral lease (issued in 1945) had been surrendered in 1973, and a second (still current) lease was issued on 27 March 1975. In response to a question about improvements under the first lease the lessees had answered: "Nil at present". To a question about land "cultivable or suitable for ... pasture", they had also answered: "Nil". The 1975 lease had included conditions requiring certain improvements, but as at 1988 some of the required improvements had not been made and others had already fallen into disuse.

In separate judgments, Toohey, Gaudron, Gummow and Kirby JJ held that the mere granting of the pastoral leases had not necessarily extinguished any claim that the plaintiffs might now be able to establish. Brennan CJ, Dawson and McHugh JJ dissented.

Wik Peoples v Queensland
(1996) 187 CLR 1

Toohey J: [115] At the forefront of the respondents' case was the argument that an essential feature of a lease is that it confers exclusive possession on the lessee. In their submission, it followed that the instruments, being pastoral leases, conferred on the lessees exclusive possession of the land. To pose the issue in that way is to focus unduly on leasehold interests as known to the common law and to give insufficient recognition to the fact that the pastoral lease is a creature of statute. Accordingly, the rights it confers and the obligations it imposes must **[116]** be determined by reference to the applicable statutory provisions. That is not to say that reference to leasehold interests at common law does not aid an understanding of these rights and obligations. But it must not be allowed to obscure the particular nature of a pastoral lease under the relevant legislation.

And it must not divert attention from the basic question whether the grant of a pastoral lease was so inconsistent with the existence of native title rights that those rights must be regarded as having been extinguished ...

[118] Certainly, the authorities point to exclusive possession as a normal incident of a lease. They do not exclude, however, an inquiry whether exclusive possession is in truth an incident of every arrangement which bears the title of lease. Furthermore, those authorities, which are directed to commercial transactions between individual persons or corporations, are not concerned whether something that is underpinned by common law recognition, namely, native title rights, are excluded by the grant by the Crown of what is described as a pastoral lease over land to which those rights attach.

Toohey J noted that historically, both in England and in Australia, there had been "**[119]** almost constant" expressions of concern "that the grant of pastoral **[120]** leases should not be used to prevent Aborigines from using the land for subsistence purposes". He went on to say:

Toohey J: [120] Against this background, it is unlikely that the intention of the legislature in authorising the grant of pastoral leases was to confer possession on the lessees to the exclusion of Aboriginal people even for their traditional rights of hunting and gathering. Nevertheless, "intention" in this context is not a reference to the state of mind of the Crown or of the Crown's officers ... What is to be ascertained is the operation of the statute and the "intention" to be discerned from it ...

[122] As has been seen, each lease contained a number of reservations of rights of entry, both specific and general. The lessee's right to possession must yield to those reservations. There is nothing in the statute which authorised the lease, or in the lease itself, which conferred on the grantee rights to exclusive possession, in particular possession exclusive of all rights and interests of the indigenous inhabitants whose occupation derived from their traditional title ... That is not to say the legislature gave conscious recognition to native title ... It is simply that there is nothing in the statute or grant that should be taken as a total exclusion of the indigenous people from the land ...

[126] Inconsistency can only be determined, in the present context, by identifying what native title rights ... are asserted in relation to the land contained in the pastoral leases. This cannot be done by some general statement; it must "focus specifically on the traditions, customs and practices of the particular aboriginal group claiming the right" [*R v Van der Peet* [1996] 2 SCR 507 at 559; (1996) 137 DLR (4th) 289 at 318]. Those rights are then measured against the rights conferred on the grantees of the pastoral leases; to the extent of any inconsistency the latter prevail. It is apparent that at one end of the spectrum native title rights may "approach the rights flowing from full ownership at **[127]** common law" [*Mabo v Queensland (No 2)* (1992) 175 CLR 1 at 89]. On the other hand they may be an entitlement "to come on to land for ceremonial purposes, all other rights in the land belonging to another group" [175 CLR at 190]. Clearly there are activities authorised, indeed in some cases required, by the grant of a pastoral lease which are inconsistent with native title rights that answer the description in the penultimate sentence. They may or may not be inconsistent with some more limited right.

Kirby J stressed that it was "**[218]** common ground that this Court should confine its attention to the particular leases in question in this case" – with no assumption that these leases "were necessarily typical or representative of Queensland pastoral leases generally", let alone those in other jurisdictions. He also said that the *Mabo* principles were part of "the Australian legal system": that is, of the legal order deriving its initial validity from British sovereignty.

Kirby J: [213] This Court, established by the Constitution, operates within the Australian legal system. It draws its legitimacy from that system. Self-evidently, it is not an institution of Aboriginal customary law. To the extent that native title is recognised and enforced in Australia by Australian law, this occurs because, although not of the common law, native title is recognised by the common law as not inconsistent with its precepts. This does not mean that, within its own world, native title (or any other incidents of the customary laws of Australia's indigenous peoples) depends upon the common law for its legitimacy or content. To the extent that the tide of history has not washed away traditional laws and real observance of traditional customs, their legitimacy and content rest upon the activities and will of the indigenous people themselves ... **[214]** But no dual system of law, as such, is created by *Mabo (No 2)*. The source of the enforceability of native title in this or in any other Australian court is, and is only, as an applicable law or statute provides. Different considerations may arise in different societies where indigenous peoples have been recognised, in effect, as nations with inherent powers of a limited sovereignty that have never been extinguished. This is not the relationship which the indigenous people of Australia enjoy with the legal system of Australia. For Aboriginal legal rights ... to be enforceable in an Australian court, a foundation must be found within the Australian legal system.

Further, Kirby J stressed that, in spite of the leases, the Wik and Thayorre peoples had never in fact been excluded from their lands. Instead, there had been consistent adherence to the policy expressed in 1903 by the Northern Protector of Aboriginals: namely, "**[217]** that the aboriginals have as much a right to exist as the Europeans, and certainly a greater right, not only to collect the native fruits, but also to hunt and dispose of the game upon which they have been vitally dependent from time immemorial". Thus the question "was not whether in fact the Wik and the Thayorre had physically remained on their traditional lands. It was simply whether in *law* they did so in pursuance of the native title rights which the common law recognised and which the common law and the *Native Title Act* 1993 (Cth) would now protect". Against this background, he identified "**[221]** three possible doctrinal solutions":

Kirby J: [221] (1) *The exercise of sovereignty test*: That once the Crown proceeded in any way to convert its ultimate or radical title into some other estate or interest in land, it exercised its sovereignty. In doing so, necessarily and without anything more, it extinguished any fragile native title interests in the land affected.

(2) *The inconsistency of incidence test*: That once the Crown's ultimate or radical title was converted, by the exercise of sovereignty into an estate or interest in land, the question became whether that estate or interest, of its legal character, was inconsistent with the continuance of native title in the land. The question was not whether the estate or interest had been exercised, in fact, in a way that was incompatible with the exercise of native title rights, but whether it was legally capable of being so exercised. The issue was one of legal theory, not detailed evidence.

(3) *The factual conflict test*: That the issue is in every case one of actual or practical inconsistency between the estate or interest conferred in the land ... and the actual exercise of surviving native title rights. If, in actuality, the two may be reconciled, the native title rights are not extinguished. They survive as a continuing burden on the Crown's radical title.

He noted that the passage relied on from the judgment of Brennan J in *Mabo (No 2)* "**[224]** contains the seeds of each of the three theories stated above". However, he rejected the first hypothesis because the overall reasoning of the *Mabo* judgments, and the actual orders of the Court – in particular, the abstention from any decision on the effect of the sardine factory lease and the missionary lease – seemed inconsistent with such a theory. He also rejected the third theory – namely, that extinguishment depends merely on the compatibility or otherwise of competing *uses* of land in each individual case, and is therefore merely a question of fact. Accordingly, Kirby J adopted the second of the three hypotheses.

Brennan CJ dissented, since in his view the grant of a pastoral lease gave a right to exclusive possession inconsistent with the continuance of any other rights. He added, however:

Brennan CJ: [87] The submission that inconsistency in the practical enjoyment of the respective rights of the native title holders and of the pastoral lessees, not inconsistency between the rights themselves, determines whether native title has been extinguished is founded on the notion that the 1910 Act and pastoral leases should be given a restrictive operation so as to permit, as far as possible, the continued existence of native title. If that notion is not applied, there is "a significant moral shortcoming in the principles by which native title is recognised," to adopt a dictum of French J [*Re Waanyi People's Native Title Application* (1995) 129 ALR 118 at 166].

So much can be admitted. The position of the traditional Aboriginal inhabitants of the land demised by the Mitchellton leases is a good illustration. If it be right to hold that the mere grant of those leases **[88]** extinguished the native title of the traditional Aboriginal inhabitants, the law will be held to destroy the legal entitlement of the inhabitants to possess and enjoy the land on which they are living and on which their forebears have lived since time immemorial. That would be a significant moral shortcoming. But the shortcoming cannot be remedied by denying the true legal effect of the 1910 Act and pastoral leases issued thereunder ... For the reasons stated, the lessees had the right of exclusive possession and that right was inconsistent with native title (except for non-accessory rights, if any) and, as the right of exclusive possession was conferred on the lessees by the Crown as the sovereign power, that right prevailed and the rights of the holders of native title were extinguished.

That does not mean that the holders of native title became trespassers. Their continued presence on the land would have been expected and probably known by the lessees. Unless the lessees took some action to eject them, their presence on the land would have been impliedly consented to ... Nevertheless ..., the inhabitants of the land demised became liable to exclusion by the lessee once the lease issued. From this it follows that native title could not co-exist with the leasehold estate ...

[97] The principles of the law may thus be thought **[98]** to reveal "a significant moral shortcoming" which can be rectified only by legislation or by the acquisition of an estate which would allow the traditions and customs of the Wik and Thayorre Peoples to be preserved and observed. Those avenues of satisfaction draw on the certainty of proprietary rights created by the sovereign power. Such rights, unlike the rights of the holders of native title, are not liable to extinguishment by subsequent executive action.

The 4:3 decision in the High Court meant that the native title claims in the *Wik* case were able to proceed. On 3 October 2000, an interim determination, made by consent, recognised the existence of native title rights to more than 6000 square kilometres of land; and on 13 October 2004 (more than a decade after the claim was first made in 1993), in a special sitting of the Federal Court held at Aurukun, Cooper J formally recognised the claimants' native title rights and interests to more than 12,500 square kilometres of land.

In *Fejo v Northern Territory* (1998) 195 CLR 96, the native title claimants were less successful. Predictably, a unanimous Court reaffirmed the basic principle of *Mabo (No 2)* that native title is extinguished by the grant of an estate in fee simple. In *Commonwealth v Yarmirr* (*Croker Island Case*) (2001) 208 CLR 1, the central issue was the application of the *Native Title Act* to offshore waters. The joint judgment of Gleeson CJ, Gaudron, Gummow and Hayne JJ held that, under the Act, native title rights could be asserted over such waters, but that in the instant case the claimants had failed, as a matter of evidence, to establish a tradition of "exclusive" possession and use of the waters they claimed. The joint judgment added that, in any event, as a matter of law, any claim to *exclusive* use of coastal waters would necessarily be extinguished by inconsistency with international rights of innocent passage, and common law rights of fishing and public access. Kirby J dissented because he held that these rights of passage, fishing and access could coexist with a qualified claim to "exclusive" Indigenous possession; McHugh and Callinan JJ dissented because in their view the common law could not accommodate the possibility of native title rights in coastal waters at all. When the central holding in *Yarmirr* was reaffirmed in *Western Australia v Ward* (*Miriuwung-Gajerrong Case*) (2002) 213 CLR 1, at 187, Kirby J (at 251-2) reluctantly acquiesced.

In any event, from *Yarmirr* onwards, issues of native title were increasingly entangled in a labyrinth of statutory provisions, including the extensive 1998 amendments to the *Native Title Act* made in response to the *Wik Case*. In *Ward,* the joint majority judgment explained why this must necessarily be the case. *Mabo (No 2)*, *Wik* and *Fejo* had been decided on the basis of "**[60]** the general law" (that is to say, the common law); but this was no longer possible.

Western Australia v Ward (*Miriuwung-Gajerrong Case*)
(2002) 213 CLR 1

Gleeson CJ, Gaudron, Gummow and Hayne JJ: [60] [The issues in these appeals] were framed in the abstract. The supposition appeared to be that the answer to them is to be found by an examination of the general law as revealed in previous decisions of this Court. The supposition cannot be supported ...

In the present litigation, the determination provisions of the [*Native Title Act 1993* (Cth)] are directly engaged. Thus, statute lies at the core of this litigation ...

[65] Much of the argument in the courts below, as in this Court, took as its starting point consideration of what was said in *Mabo (No 2)* [*Mabo v Queensland (No 2)* (1992) 175 CLR 1]. No doubt account may be taken of what was decided and what was said in that case when considering the meaning and effect of the [*Native Title Act*] ... It is, however, of the very first importance to recognise ... that the claims that gave rise to the present appeals are claims made under the [*Native Title Act*] for rights that **[66]** are defined in that statute ...

[69] [I]t must be emphasised that it is to the terms of the [*Native Title Act*] that primary regard must be had, and not the decisions in *Mabo (No 2)* or *Wik* [(1996) 187 CLR 1]. The only present relevance of those decisions is for whatever light they cast on the [*Native Title Act*].

The Miriuwung and Gajerrong People claimed native title over land and waters in the Kimberley region, extending from the north of Western Australia into the Northern Territory. The Federal Court had made a determination in their favour; but the High Court majority decision set that determination aside, remitting the matter to the Federal Court with extensive rulings on how the statutory framework was to be construed and applied. That framework included not only the 1998 amendments to the *Native Title Act*, but also State legislation enacted in reliance on those amendments – notably the *Titles Validation Amendment Act 1999* (WA) and the *Titles (Validation) and Native Title (Effect of Past Acts) Amendment Act 1999* (WA). (This was so although those Acts had come into force *after* the original hearing in the *Ward* case. Federal Court decisions holding that such legislation could not be taken into account, relying on s 24 of the *Federal Court of Australia Act 1976* (Cth), were overruled.) It was partly because of this emphasis on the State legislation that references in *Mabo (No 2)* to the "use" of land were dismissed as misleading:

> **Gleeson CJ, Gaudron, Gummow and Hayne JJ: [137]** Because the disposition of Crown lands in Western Australia is now, and, since the coming of representative government, has been, *wholly* regulated by statute it is to the applicable statutes that attention must be directed. If the land is used in some way, there will be some statutory warrant for that use. In some cases that statutory authority will be a *Land Act*; in others it will be found in some other statute. The question of extinguishment ... requires attention to the rights that are asserted rather than the use that is made of the land.

The contrast with the earlier cases was overstated. In *Wik*, too, the question of extinguishment was said to depend on inconsistent rights rather than inconsistent usage; and in *Wik*, too, the decision that Queensland pastoral leases did not automatically extinguish native title was based on painstaking analysis of the relevant State legislation, as well as on the terms and conditions of the actual leases. Indeed, despite the above disclaimers, the joint majority judgment in *Ward* essentially followed *Wik* – holding that in Western Australia, too, the mere grant of a pastoral lease did not necessarily extinguish all aspects of native title. "**[123]** The rights obtained under a pastoral lease were limited ... The interest obtained was precarious ... **[126]** [It] was very different, in many respects, from the interest that a lessee would obtain under a lease for a term of years granted to the lessee by the freehold owner of the land".

On the other hand, in *Wilson v Anderson* (2002) 213 CLR 401 – decided on the same day as *Ward* – it was held by a majority of 6:1 (Kirby J dissenting) that a "lease in perpetuity" under s 23 of the *Western Lands Act 1901* (NSW) *did* confer a right to exclusive possession, and was therefore inconsistent with the continuance of any native title rights and interests. And even in *Ward* itself, while denying that the Western Australian leases had wholly extinguished native title, the joint judgment also held that the mere grant of such leases was inconsistent with any Indigenous claim "**[131]** for control of access to the land the subject of the grants".

> **Gleeson CJ, Gaudron, Gummow and Hayne JJ: [209]** The grant of a pastoral lease in Western Australia extinguished the native title right to control access to, or the use to be made of, the land. The grant of a pastoral lease did not give a right of exclusive possession. Native title rights and

interests, other than the right just mentioned, probably continued unaffected by the grant, but to what extent we cannot say from the present findings of fact. To the extent that rights and interests granted by a pastoral lease were not inconsistent with native title rights and **[210]** interests, the rights and interests under the lease prevailed over, but did not extinguish, native title rights.

The joint majority judgment reached a similar conclusion (at 190-8) for pastoral leases in the Northern Territory. Again, however, the conclusion was qualified: the pastoral leases "**[196]** were inconsistent with the continued existence of the native title right to control access to and make decisions about the land", but "not necessarily inconsistent with the continued existence of all native title rights and interests". There were similar conclusions (at 138) in respect of the reservation of land for public purposes, and (at 157-70) in respect of mining leases. On all these issues Kirby J generally agreed, while McHugh and Callinan JJ dissented.

The pattern of reasoning in all these instances – concluding that the various instruments referred to had extinguished Indigenous control of the land, without necessarily extinguishing all aspects of native title – depended initially on acceptance of the statutory distinction between acts that "have completely extinguished native title", and acts that have extinguished it "partially" or "to the extent of any inconsistency" (*Native Title Act*, s 23A). But it also depended on a corollary attached to this distinction: namely that, in order to apply the statutory provisions, native title claims must be disaggregated into a series of more specific claims, for each of which the question of extinguishment or non-extinguishment will be determined independently. This involved an endorsement of the approach of Beaumont and von Doussa JJ in the Federal Court (*Western Australia v Ward* (2000) 170 ALR 159), and a corresponding rejection of the approach taken at first instance by Lee J, who had held (in *Ward v Western Australia* (1998) 159 ALR 483) that "**[508]** [n]ative title at common law is a communal 'right to land' arising from the significant connection of an indigenous society with land under its customs and culture. It is not a mere 'bundle of rights'."

> **Gleeson CJ, Gaudron, Gummow and Hayne JJ: [89]** There was much debate in the Full Court as to whether native title rights and interests are properly to be seen as a bundle of rights, the separate components of which may be extinguished separately. The [*Native Title Act*], particularly in the distinction now drawn in s 23A ... between complete extinguishment and extinguishment "to the extent of any inconsistency", mandates the correctness of the approach taken by the Full Court ...
>
> **[95]** The metaphor of "bundle of rights" ... is useful in two respects. It draws attention first to the fact that there may more than one right or interest and secondly to the fact that there may be several *kinds* of rights and interests in relation to land that exist under traditional law and custom. Not all of those rights and interests may be capable of full or accurate expression as rights to control what others may do on or with the land.

From a functional viewpoint, the reduction of native title to a "bundle of rights" is double-edged. On the one hand, it may tend to confine the effect of extinguishment to one limited aspect of an Indigenous claim, thus allowing other aspects of the claim to be quarantined against what might otherwise have been a wholesale extinguishment. (Thus, in *Ward*, the extinguishment of rights of "control" did not necessarily extinguish other Indigenous rights and interests in the subject land.) On the other hand, it may allow different aspects of the claim to be picked off one by one. Thus, in *Ward*, the majority (with McHugh and Callinan JJ concurring and Kirby J dissenting) upheld the Federal Court's decision (*Western Australia v Ward* (2000) 170 ALR 159) that "**[321]** a right to maintain, protect and prevent the misuse of cultural knowledge ... [cannot] be the subject of a determination of native title".

A passage in the judgment of Callinan J (at 273), contrasting the effect of a "bundle of rights" with the amplitude of an estate in fee simple, suggests that the "rights" comprised in such a bundle must necessarily be limited rights. In any event, as the Aboriginal and Torres Strait Islander Social Justice Commissioner, Dr William Jonas, put it in his *Native Title Report 2002* (Parliamentary Paper No 41 of 2003): "**[29]** A bundle of rights approach to recognition creates an inherently weak title that is able to be eroded, piece by piece".

The ideological effect of such a piecemeal approach is not so equivocal. As Dr Jonas also observed: "**[27]** The construction of native title as a bundle of rights and interests, confirmed in the *Miriuwung Gajerrong* decision, ... reflects the failure of the common law and the [*Native Title Act*] to recognise Indigenous people as a people with a system of laws based on a profound relationship to land. Native title as a bundle of separate and unrelated rights with no uniting foundation is a construction which epitomises the disintegration of a culture when its law-making capacity, that is its sovereignty, is neatly extracted from it". Indeed, the joint judgment itself appeared to concede the incongruity of such an approach.

Gleeson CJ, Gaudron, Gummow and Hayne JJ: [64] As is now well recognised, the connection which Aboriginal peoples have with "country" is essentially spiritual. In *Milirrpum v Nabalco Pty Ltd* [(1971) 17 FLR 141 at 167], Blackburn J said that: "the fundamental truth about the aboriginals' relationship to the land is that whatever else it is, it is a religious relationship ... There is an unquestioned scheme of things in which the spirit ancestors, the people of the clan, particular land and everything that exists on and in it, are organic parts of one indissoluble whole". It is a relationship which sometimes is spoken of as having to care for, and being able to "speak for", country. "Speaking for" country is bound up with the idea that, at least in some circumstances, others should ask for permission to enter upon country or use it or enjoy its resources, but to focus only on the requirement that others seek permission for some activities would oversimplify the nature of **[65]** the connection that the phrase seeks to capture. The difficulty of expressing a relationship between a community or group of Aboriginal people and the land in terms of rights and interests is evident. Yet that is required by the [*Native Title Act*]. The spiritual or religious is translated into the legal. This requires the fragmentation of an integrated view of the ordering of affairs into rights and interests which are considered apart from the duties and obligations which go with them.

Kirby J, who generally agreed with the joint judgment, accepted the need for "**[243]** a list of activities and uses recognised as 'native title rights and interests'", but warned that "recognition of native title rights and interests" might thereby be "unduly narrowed": "The object ... is the recognition of 'native *title*', rather than the provision of a list of activities permitted on, or in relation to, areas of land or waters the subject of a claim to native title". McHugh and Callinan JJ dissented. In their view the various instruments referred to had wholly extinguished native title, and both of them mounted a sustained attack on the majority judgments in *Wik*.

McHugh J: [213] Professor Maitland famously said that the "forms of action we have buried, but they still rule us from their graves". The reasoning of Gleeson CJ, Gaudron, Gummow and Hayne JJ in these cases indicates a similar truth about *Wik Peoples v Queensland* ...

Wik is one of the most controversial decisions given by this Court. It subjected the Court to unprecedented criticism and abuse, though the criticism and abuse were mild compared to that directed to the United States Supreme Court after its two decisions in *Brown v Board of Education of Topeka* [347 US 483 (1954); 349 US 294 (1955)]. No doubt the decision in *Wik* was controversial because to most people it was unexpected. There were at least three matters that led people to believe that the grant of a pastoral lease extinguished any native title ... First, statements by the majority Justices in *Mabo v* **[214]** *Queensland (No 2)* had indicated that the grant of a lease extinguished native title. Second, the preamble to the *Native Title Act* 1993 (Cth) had declared that this Court had "held that native title is extinguished by valid government acts that are inconsistent with the continued existence of native title rights and interests, such as the grant of freehold or leasehold estates". Third, the *Land Act* 1910 (Q) and the *Land Act* 1962 (Q) described pastoral leases as leases and were perceived as vesting in the lessee an estate or interest in the land. And, if that was not enough, for 126 years Queensland lawyers had taken the view that a pastoral lease gave a legal right of exclusive possession to the land.

But to the surprise of most people who had thought about the matter, a narrow majority ... held in *Wik* that the claims of pastoral lessees and native-title holders could be reconciled. Despite the description of pastoral leases as leases in the *Land Act* 1910 (Q) and the *Land Act* 1962 (Q) and the long held professional opinion as to their legal effect and nature, the majority Justices held that pastoral leases were not in fact leases, as lawyers understood that term. The majority held that the rights given by the "leases" and the rights of native title were not necessarily inconsistent. Whether or not the grant of a pastoral lease extinguished native title rights depended upon the particular rights conferred by the lease and the incidents of the relevant native title. In *Mabo (No 2)*, Brennan J had said that the Australian Aborigines had been "dispossessed of their land parcel by parcel, to make way for expanding colonial settlement" [175 CLR at 69]. *Wik* held that henceforth Aborigines could only be dispossessed of their land, the subject of a Queensland pastoral lease, metre by metre. They could be dispossessed only after a federal court had held that a native title right claimed in relation to a particular place was necessarily inconsistent with the rights of the pastoral lessee.

The Federal Parliament responded to *Wik* by enacting Act No 97 of 1998 (Cth) … [so that] the reasoning in the *Wik* decision would henceforth be confined to narrow areas. But as the reasons of the majority Justices in this case show, the ideas that generated that decision still haunt the corridors of native title law. In particular, they have survived its burial in relation to pastoral and mining leases …

Brennan CJ, Dawson J and I dissented in *Wik* … I thought then, and I think now, that the reasoning of Brennan CJ was correct. But that does not mean that I think that *Wik* should be overruled or not followed in Queensland cases … As Brandeis J pointed out in *Burnet v Coronado Oil & Gas Co* [285 US 393 at 406 (1932)], "[s]tare decisis is usually the wise policy, because in most matters it is more important that the applicable rule of law be **[216]** settled than that it be settled right". It does not follow, however, that either *Wik* or its reasoning governs these appeals.

As the judgment of Callinan J shows, *Wik* has no ratio decidendi. The lack of a ratio decidendi makes the case of limited precedent value. But even if his Honour's analysis of the reasons of the majority in *Wik* was not correct, *Wik* could only have limited value as a precedent when construing the legislation of another jurisdiction. Judicial decisions on statutory terms can never give more than guidance as to the meaning of the same terms in different statutes unless the statutes are not materially different in context, history and purpose …

A judicial decision on a statute is likely to be of even less assistance in construing another statute when the judicial decision turned on an inference or inferences drawn from the statute as a whole. That was the case in *Wik*. Because the structure, terms and history of the statutes involved in the present cases are materially different from those of the *Land Act* 1910 (Q) and the *Land Act* 1962 (Q), *Wik* does not govern their construction.

The conclusion of Kirby J in *Wik*, that the Queensland Parliament would not have intended to drive Indigenous people from their lands, was dismissed as "**[230]** no more than speculation":

McHugh J: [230] In seeking explanations of the terms and purposes of the Queensland legislation, it is impossible to overlook the racist nature of Australian society at the relevant times. It was a society that championed a White Australia policy, carefully chose the words of s 117 of the Constitution so that Chinese and other aliens could not receive its protection and drafted its Constitution so that the Aboriginal people were treated as non-persons.

A more likely explanation, or speculation, … is that the majority of the legislature simply ignored or turned a blind eye to the position of the Aboriginal people. Given the racist nature of Australian society at material times, it would not surprise me that, if the Aboriginal people had complained of the injustice of their treatment, the legislature would have replied as the **[231]** Athenian representatives cynically replied to the Melians from whom they were demanding tribute:

"[Y]ou know as well as we do that, when these matters are discussed by practical people, the standard of justice depends on the equality of power to compel and that in fact the strong do what they have the power to do and the weak accept what they have to accept."

Marx thought that law was a body of rules that upheld what the dominant class in a particular society called its rights. But you do not have to be a Marxist to recognise that at least on occasions the dominant class in a society will use its power to disregard the rights of a class or classes with less power. On any view, that is what the dominant classes in Australian society did – and in the eyes of many still do – to the Aboriginal people.

Within the framework of the common law and the widespread issue of Crown grants of land, this Court in *Mabo (No 2)* did what it could to remedy one of the injustices that the Aboriginal people had suffered – the dispossession of their lands. But consistent with the proposition that the grant of an estate in fee simple or a lease extinguishes native title rights, the grant of the ordinary pastoral lease before the enactment of the *Racial Discrimination Act* 1975 (Cth) must be taken to have extinguished native title rights ... *Wik* held that in Queensland pastoral leases did not have that effect. And that holding must be followed. But the decision in *Wik* does not control the outcome of these cases ...

[240] The dispossession of the Aboriginal peoples from their lands was a great wrong. Many people believe that those of us who are the beneficiaries of that wrong have a moral responsibility to redress it to the extent that it can be redressed. But it is becoming increasingly clear – to me, at all events – that redress can not be achieved by a system that depends on evaluating the competing legal rights of landholders and native-title holders. The deck is stacked against the [241] native-title holders whose fragile rights must give way to the superior rights of the landholders whenever the two classes of rights conflict. And it is a system that is costly and time-consuming. At present the chief beneficiaries of the system are the legal representatives of the parties. It may be that the time has come to think of abandoning the present system, a system that simply seeks to declare and enforce the legal rights of the parties, irrespective of their merits. A better system may be an arbitral system that declares what the rights of the parties *ought to be* according to the justice and circumstances of the individual case.

Callinan J argued that, despite a common conclusion, the four majority judgments in *Wik* had each relied on a different concatenation of factors to support that conclusion. Accordingly, the decision had no clear ratio decidendi, and was binding as a precedent only for precisely similar facts (see Chapter 13, §7). He took this to mean that the decision was applicable "[311] only to leases of approximately the same size, in the same districts, in the same form, and issued under the same Act". However, like McHugh J, he too offered some more general observations:

Callinan J: [395] I add this. The first non-indigenous people who occupied this [396] country brought with them their common and statutory law which had long included a doctrine of adverse possession and settled notions about the use and occupation of land. These were closely connected ideas: land was to be used and enjoyed, and those who possessed, used and enjoyed the land should own it ...

Those early non-indigenous settlers also brought with them a knowledge of agriculture and husbandry, and of domestic, commercial and official construction of a kind completely different from that of the indigenous peoples. To the undiscriminating, and perhaps insensitive and unimaginative eyes of the former it must have appeared that much of this large continent was not in fact being used or enjoyed, or certainly not so in a way that was familiar. After discussing the use and occupation of Crown lands by reference to the Old Testament, Blackstone says [*Commentaries on the Laws of England* (Clarendon Press, 5th ed 1773), Volume 2, ch 1, at 7] ...:

> "Upon the same principle was founded the right of migration, or sending colonies to find out new habitations, when the mother-country was over-charged with inhabitants; which was practised as well by the Phoenicians and Greeks, as the Germans, Scythians, and other northern people. And, so long as it was confined to the stocking and cultivation of desert uninhabited countries, it kept strictly within the limits of the law of nature. But how far the seising on countries already peopled, and driving out or massacring the innocent and defenceless natives, merely because they differed from their invaders in language, in religion, in customs, [in]government, or in colour; how far such a conduct was consonant to nature, to reason, or to christianity, deserved well to be considered by those, who have rendered their names immortal by thus civilizing mankind."

Activities of this kind undoubtedly occurred in Australia. Some were utterly indefensible. It is possible to understand, again without condoning, that others of them might have occurred, in part because of different conceptions about land and how it might be possessed, used or owned. The different conceptions held by the new settlers, much the [397] stronger of the peoples, were bound to prevail. This was inevitable when those who were more powerful had a well settled, long-standing body of property law in written texts, statutes and cases, and those whom they dispossessed depended for the assertions of their rights to occupy and use the land upon traditional oral customs and practices. Perhaps it was equally significant that the new settlers brought with them a transparent system of legal enforcement and courts to give effect to the resolution of disputes over property. To these new settlers, it might also have appeared, whether it was true or not, that the country was so sparsely populated that disputes did not arise between competing indigenous people over land.

The problems for the indigenous people were compounded by the difficulty of finding any conceptual common ground between the common and statutory law of real property and Aboriginal law with respect to land. It seems likely that the first settlers would have regarded the two as incompatible, that whatever the Aboriginal peoples possessed by way of title to land was too foreign, fragile and elusive to withstand and survive the common law. *Mabo (No 2)* was a brave judicial attempt to redress the wrongs of dispossession. But its "recognition" of native title has involved the courts in categorising and charting the bounds of something that, being sui generis, really has no parallel in the common law. The Court has endeavoured to find a way of recognising, and to a degree protecting, that anomalous interest without unduly disturbing the law of Australian property. The results of this enterprise can hardly be described as satisfactory. The decisions of this Court and of lower courts have resulted in something that is not strictly property, as common lawyers would understand it, being regarded as a burden on the Crown's radical title. Long settled understandings about land law relating to exclusive possession and leases have been questioned. Parliament has been compelled to intervene, repeatedly, to secure the validity of acts that were never before thought to be problematic. And we now have a body of law that is so **[398]** complicated, shifting and abstruse that it continues to require the intervention of this Court to resolve even the most basic issues, such as the effect of freehold or leases on native title. Judging from the submissions to this Court and the native title legislation that we have had to consider, few people, if any, have been able to thread this labyrinth of Minos unscathed. To these drawbacks flowing from the recognition of native title may be added others: considerable uncertainty has been created; commercial activity and therefore national prosperity has been inhibited; much time and money have been expended on litigation; and, I fear, the expectations of the indigenous people have been raised and dashed.

I do not disparage the importance to the Aboriginal people of their native title rights, including those that have symbolic significance. I fear, however, that in many cases because of the chasm between the common law and native title rights, the latter, when recognised, will **[399]** amount to little more than symbols. It might have been better to redress the wrongs of dispossession by a true and unqualified settlement of lands or money than by an ultimately futile or unsatisfactory, in my respectful opinion, attempt to fold native title rights into the common law.

5. Yorta Yorta

The traditional Yorta Yorta "country" comprised some 5000 square kilometres on either side of the Murray River, including significant areas of Victoria and New South Wales and towns including Shepparton, Echuca, Yarrawonga and Wangaratta. In the Federal Court on 18 December 1998, the claim of the Yorta Yorta people to continuing native title was rejected by Olney J (*Yorta Yorta Aboriginal Community v Victoria* [1998] FCA 1606). He found "**[129]** that before the end of the 19th century the ancestors through whom the claimants claim title had ceased to occupy their traditional lands in accordance with their traditional laws and customs. The tide of history has indeed washed away any real acknowledgement of their traditional laws and any real observance of their traditional customs". The "tide of history" metaphor, which Brennan J had used in *Mabo (No 2)*, was invoked in Olney J's judgment four times.

He relied particularly on a petition signed in 1881 by 42 Indigenous natives of the area (including several of the identified "ancestors" from whom the Yorta Yorta claimants had sought to establish their descent). The petition – set out in para **[119]** of Olney J's judgment – recited "That all the land within our tribal boundaries has been taken possession of by the Government and white settlers". On this basis Olney J concluded: "**[121]** It is clear that by 1881 those through whom the claimant group now seeks to establish native title were no longer in possession of their tribal lands and had, by force of the circumstances in which they found themselves, ceased to observe those laws and customs based on tradition which might otherwise have provided a basis for the present native title claim; and the dispossession of the original inhabitants and their descendants has continued through to the present time".

On 8 February 2001 an appeal to the Full Court of the Federal Court was dismissed by 2:1 (Black CJ dissenting). The majority judgment resumed an ongoing debate in that Court as to the effect of the definition in s 223(1) of the *Native Title Act 1993* (Cth), as amended in 1998:

Native Title Act 1993 (Cth)

223 (1) The expression *native title* or *native title rights and interests* means the communal, group or individual rights and interests of Aboriginal peoples or Torres Strait Islanders in relation to land or waters, where:

   (a)   the rights and interests are possessed under the traditional laws acknowledged, and the traditional customs observed, by the Aboriginal peoples or Torres Strait Islanders; and

   (b)   the Aboriginal peoples or Torres Strait Islanders, by those laws and customs, have a connection with the land or waters; and

   (c)   the rights and interests are recognised by the common law of Australia.

Focusing on s 223(1)(c), and recalling an earlier discussion of that paragraph in *Commonwealth v Yarmirr* (*Croker Island Case*) (1999) 168 ALR 426, Branson and Katz JJ said:

Members of the Yorta Yorta Aboriginal Community v Victoria
(2001) 180 ALR 655

Branson and Katz JJ: [684] The preferable view, in our opinion, is that s 223(1)(c) is not concerned only with the kinds of rights and interests which may found a determination of native title under s 225 ... Rather, it seems to us, s 223(1)(c) incorporates into the statutory definition of native title the requirement that, in the **[685]** case of a claimed communal title, the holders of the native title are members of an identifiable community "the members of whom are identified by one another as members of that community living under its laws and customs" (*Mabo v Queensland (No 2)* 175 CLR at 61 ...) and that that community has continuously since the acquisition of sovereignty by the Crown been an identifiable community the members of which, under its traditional laws observed and traditional customs practised, possessed interests in the relevant land ... The paragraph also, in our view, incorporates into the statutory definition ... [the] refusal of the common law to recognise rights and interests ... repugnant to natural justice, equity and good conscience. In addition, in our view, the paragraph incorporates the notion of extinguishment – whether by a positive exercise of sovereign power ... or by reason of the native title having expired so as to allow the Crown's radical title to expand to a full beneficial title ... Under the common law, the native title to any area of land or waters will have so expired if, at any time since the Crown acquired the radical title to the land, the traditional laws and customs, the acknowledgment and observance of which provided the foundation of native title, ceased to be acknowledged and observed, or (which may factually amount to the same thing) the Aboriginal people or Torres Strait Islanders who by those laws and customs had a connection with the land or waters, whether as a community, a group or as individuals, ceased to have that connection.

Given Olney J's findings of fact (which Branson and Katz JJ declined to disturb), the requirement of a community continuously identifiable since 1788 was enough to defeat the claimants' case. Their appeal was therefore dismissed. However, the reference to continued "acknowledgment and observance" of laws and customs raised issues that were not finally resolved. Branson and Katz JJ *rejected* the idea that Olney J had adopted a "frozen in time" approach (that is, a requirement that the laws and customs must remain exactly as they were in 1788); and in any event they acknowledged that such an approach would be inconsistent with "**[116]** the evolving nature of traditional laws and customs" as repeatedly recognised in *Mabo (No 2)*.

Branson and Katz JJ: [688] The test of whether a law acknowledged, or a custom observed, is a traditional law or custom is, in our view, principally an objective test. The primary issue is whether the law or custom has in substance been handed down **[689]** from generation to generation; that is, whether it can be shown to have its roots in the tradition of the relevant community. However, for the reasons so persuasively articulated by Toohey J in *Mabo (No 2)* [175 CLR at 192] ..., it cannot be accepted that the fact that an indigenous society has adopted certain aspects of the now dominant culture means that the society has necessarily abandoned its traditional connection with land or waters. To take an example raised during argument on this appeal, the purchasing by members of an indigenous community of food from a supermarket does not, of itself, demonstrate a loss by that community of traditional connection with land or waters ...

Where an indigenous people possessed rights and interests in particular areas ... under the traditional laws and customs observed by them at the time of the acquisition of sovereignty by the Crown, the radical title of the Crown was burdened, not by those traditional laws and customs, but by the native title of the indigenous people possessed by them under their traditional laws and customs ...

[T]raditional laws and customs can evolve and change over time. It may be assumed that in many instances traditional laws and customs evolved and changed over time without necessarily impacting on the native title rights and interests possessed thereunder. For example, a right to enter upon land to hunt for game would, at the time of the acquisition of sovereignty by the Crown, have been exercised by the hunting of native animals. However, if the numbers of native animals to be found on the land thereafter diminished so that rabbits became the most common animal hunted by the native title holders, the native title right to enter upon the land to hunt for game would be unaffected.

The claimants appealed to the High Court, where by 5:2 their claim was again dismissed. Again there was inconclusive discussion of the extent to which traditional laws and customs might acceptably be modified over time; but again the finding by Olney J that the Yorta Yorta community had not existed continuously since 1788 was treated as decisive. The joint judgment of Gleeson CJ, Gummow and Hayne JJ did not, however, accept the emphasis hitherto placed on the reference in para (c) of s 223(1) to recognition by "the common law".

Members of the Yorta Yorta Aboriginal Community v Victoria
(2002) 214 CLR 422

Gleeson CJ, Gummow and Hayne JJ: [434] [T]he questions which arise in this matter turn more on a proper understanding of par (a) of the definition of native title, and in particular what is meant by "are possessed under the traditional laws acknowledged, and the traditional customs observed" by the relevant peoples, than [they do] on par (c) of the definition. But, of course, it will be necessary to consider all elements of the definition ...

[440] It is necessary ... to begin consideration of a claim for determination of native title by examination and consideration of the provisions of the *Native Title Act*. As has been pointed out above, what the claimants sought was a determination that is a creature of that Act, not the common law.

In undertaking that task, all elements of the definition of native title must be given effect. "Native title" means certain rights and interests of indigenous peoples. Those rights and interests may be communal, group or individual rights and interests, but they must be "in relation to" land or waters. The rights and interests must have three characteristics. The first is that they are possessed under the traditional laws acknowledged and the traditional customs observed by the peoples concerned. That is, they must find their source in traditional law and custom, not in the common law ...

Secondly, the rights and interests must have the characteristic that, by the traditional laws acknowledged and the traditional customs observed by the relevant peoples, those peoples have "a connection with" the land or waters. Again, the connection to be identified is one whose source is traditional law and custom, not the common law.

Thirdly, the rights and interests in relation to land must be "recognised" by the common law of Australia and it was … upon the operation of this requirement that much of the debate on the hearing of this appeal centred. Three separate strands of argument about this element of the definition … will require consideration. First, does this element of the definition permit, even require, consideration of any aspect of the general law as it stood after the decision in *Mabo v Queensland (No 2)* [(1992) 175 CLR 1] but before the enactment of the *Native Title Act*? Secondly, does this element of the definition carry within itself any rule or principle relating to extinguishment, abandonment, or loss of native title rights, by which it can be decided whether native title rights which existed at sovereignty may no longer be the subject of a determination of native title under the *Native Title Act*? Thirdly, what, if anything, does this element of the definition … say about the significance that is to be attached to the identification of what traditional law or custom may have said, *at the time sovereignty was first asserted*, about the rights **[441]** and interests of peoples in the land or waters in which native title is now claimed?

None of these questions can be answered without an understanding of the operation of *all* of the elements of the definition of native title. Most especially is that the case in connection with the third of the strands we have identified. In order to understand the work that is to be done by par (c) of the definition of native title, with its reference to recognition by the common law of Australia, it is necessary to understand the operation of par (a), and what is meant by "possessed under the traditional laws acknowledged, and the traditional customs observed".

The joint judgment proceeded to gloss the wording of para (a) by a jurisprudential analysis, concluding that the words required an inquiry "**[447]** about the relationship between the laws and customs now acknowledged and observed, and those that were acknowledged and observed before sovereignty", which in turn involved a consideration of "whether the laws and customs can be said to be the laws and customs of the society whose laws and customs are properly described as traditional laws and customs". Since these requirements were to be deduced from the words of para (a), it followed that there was no need for an importation of common law principles through the gateway of para (c).

Gleeson, Gummow and Hayne JJ: [453] To speak of the "common law requirements" of native title is to invite fundamental error. Native title is not a creature of the common law, whether the Imperial common law as that existed at the time of sovereignty and first settlement, or the Australian common law as it exists today. Native title, for present purposes, is what is defined and described in s 223(1) of the *Native Title Act*. *Mabo (No 2)* decided that certain rights and interests relating to land, and rooted in traditional law and custom, survived the Crown's acquisition of sovereignty and radical title in Australia. It was *this* native title that was then "recognised, and protected" in accordance with the *Native Title Act* and which, thereafter, was not able to be extinguished contrary to that Act.

The *Native Title Act*, when read as a whole, does not seek to create some new species of right or interest in relation to land or waters which it then calls native title. Rather, the Act has as one of its main objects "to provide for the *recognition* and *protection* of native title" (emphasis added), which is to say those rights and interests in relation to land or waters with which the Act deals, but which are rights and interests finding their origin in traditional law and custom, not the Act. It follows that the reference in par (c) of s 223(1) to the rights or interests being *recognised* by the common law of Australia cannot be understood as a form of drafting by incorporation, by which some pre-existing body of the common law of Australia defining the rights or interests known as native title is brought into the Act. To understand par (c) as a drafting device of that kind would be to treat native title as owing its origins to the common law when it does not. And to speak of there being common law elements for the *establishment* of native title is to commit the same error. It is, therefore, wrong to read par (c) of the definition of native title as requiring reference to any such body of common law, for there is none to which reference could be made.

The reference to recognition by the common law serves a different purpose … [It] emphasises the fact that there is an intersection between legal systems and that the **[454]** intersection occurred at the time of sovereignty. The native title rights and interests which are the subject of the Act are those which existed at sovereignty, survived that fundamental change in legal regime, and now, by resort to the processes of the new legal order, can be enforced and protected. It is those rights and interests which are "recognised" in the common law.

The reasoning by which para (a) was made to yield up an analysis effectively eliding the need for any reference to para (c) began by focusing on the concept of "rights and interests ... possessed under ... traditional laws". It assumed (perhaps debatably) that the "rights" referred to must be *legal* rights, and perhaps (more debatably) that the "interests" referred to must be *legal* interests. This in turn imported the further assumption that validly created legal rights (and interests?) must depend on the operation of a valid and effective system of law. For this proposition, in turn, the joint judgment supplied two further presuppositions. One was that a valid legal system presupposes "sovereignty"; the other was that an effective legal system presupposes an existing "society". While these two propositions do not necessarily entail each other, the joint judgment apparently assumed that they did so.

The "sovereignty" postulate was important because the sovereignty from which Indigenous legal systems derived their validity must necessarily have been that which inhered in Indigenous communities before 1788. But in 1788 *that* sovereignty had been displaced or extinguished. It followed that from 1788 onwards a legal system derived from *that* sovereignty could no longer validly operate to generate new rights (or interests). Hence the "rights" (and interests?) derived from that legal system must be those to which it had given rise before 1788.

Gleeson CJ, Gummow and Hayne JJ: [441] First, it follows from *Mabo (No 2)* that the Crown's acquisition of sovereignty over the several parts of Australia cannot be challenged in an Australian municipal court. Secondly, upon acquisition of sovereignty over a particular part of Australia, the Crown acquired a radical title to the land in that part, but native title to that land survived the Crown's acquisition of sovereignty and radical title. What survived were rights and interests in relation to land or waters. Those rights and interests owed their origin to a normative system other than the legal system of the new sovereign power; they owed their origin to the traditional laws acknowledged and the traditional customs observed by the indigenous peoples concerned.

When it is recognised that the subject matter of the inquiry is rights and interests ... it is clear that the laws or customs in which those rights or interests find their origins must be laws or customs having a normative content and deriving, therefore, from a body of norms or normative system – the body of norms or normative system that existed before sovereignty ...

[442] [T]he fundamental premise from which the decision in *Mabo (No 2)* proceeded is that the laws and customs of the indigenous peoples of this country constituted bodies of normative rules which could give rise to, and had in fact given rise to, rights and interests in relation to land or waters. And of more immediate significance, the fundamental premise from which the *Native Title Act* proceeds is that the rights and interests with which it deals (and to which it refers as "native title") can be possessed under traditional laws and customs. Of course, those rights and interests may not, and often will not, correspond with rights and interests in land familiar to the Anglo-Australian property lawyer. The rights and interests under traditional laws and customs will often reflect a different conception of "property" or "belonging". But none of those considerations denies the normative quality of the laws and customs of the indigenous societies. It is only if the rich complexity of indigenous societies is denied that reference to traditional laws and customs as a normative system jars the ear of the listener.

To speak of such rights and interests being possessed under, or rooted in, traditional law and traditional custom might provoke much jurisprudential debate about the difference between what HLA Hart referred to as "merely convergent habitual behaviour in a social group" and legal rules. The reference to traditional customs might invite debate about the difference between "moral obligation" and legal rules. A search for parallels between traditional law and traditional customs on the one hand and Austin's conception of a system of laws, as a body of commands or general orders backed by threats which are issued by a sovereign or subordinate in obedience to the sovereign, may or may not be fruitful. Likewise, to search in **[443]** traditional law and traditional customs for an identified, even an identifiable, rule of recognition which would distinguish between law on the one hand, and moral obligation or mere habitual behaviour on the other, may or may not be productive.

This last question may, however, be put aside when it is recalled that the *Native Title Act* refers to traditional laws acknowledged *and* traditional customs observed. Taken as a whole, that expression, with its use of "and" rather than "or", obviates any need to distinguish between what is a matter of traditional *law* and what is a matter of traditional *custom*. Nonetheless, because the subject of consideration is rights or interests, the rules which together constitute the traditional laws acknowledged and traditional customs observed, and under which the rights or interests are said to be possessed, must be rules having normative content. Without that quality, there may be observable patterns of behaviour but not rights or interests in relation to land or waters.

The consequences of sovereignty for the pre-sovereignty normative system
What is important for present purposes, however, is not the jurisprudential questions that we have identified. It is important to recognise that the rights and interests concerned originate in a *normative* system, and to recognise some consequences that follow from the Crown's assertion of sovereignty. Upon the Crown acquiring sovereignty, the normative or law-making system which [previously] existed could not thereafter validly create new rights, duties or interests. Rights or interests in land created after sovereignty and which owed their origin and continued existence *only* to a normative system other than that of the new sovereign power, would not and will not be given effect by the legal order of the new sovereign.

That is not to deny ... the efficacy of rules of transmission of rights and interests under traditional laws and traditional customs which existed at sovereignty, where those native title rights continue to be recognised by the legal order of the new sovereign. The rights and interests in land which the new sovereign order recognised included the rules of traditional law and custom which dealt with the transmission of those interests. Nor is it to say that account could never be taken of any alteration to, or development of, that traditional law and custom that occurred after sovereignty. Account may have to be taken of developments at least of a kind contemplated by that traditional law and custom. Indeed, in this matter, both the claimants and respondents accepted that there could be "significant adaptations". But what the assertion of sover-[444]-eignty by the British Crown necessarily entailed was that there could thereafter be no parallel law-making system in the territory over which it asserted sovereignty. To hold otherwise would be to deny the acquisition of sovereignty and as has been pointed out earlier, that is not permissible. Because there could be no parallel law-making system after the assertion of sovereignty it also follows that the only rights or interests in relation to land or waters, originating otherwise than in the new sovereign order, which will be recognised after the assertion of that new sovereignty are those that find their origin in pre-sovereignty law and custom.

Consequences for construction of "native title"
Construction of the definition of native title must take account of these considerations. The first level of inquiry is whether, on the proper construction of the *Native Title Act* and the definition of native title, the Act is to be understood as creating new rights and interests in land which it calls "native title". Putting the same question another way, does an application for determination of native title seek the determination of rights and interests which find their origin in the *new* sovereign order, or is it seeking a determination of the existence of rights and interests which, recognised after the assertion of that new sovereignty, nonetheless find their origin in pre-sovereignty law and custom? Hitherto it has been accepted, and the contrary was not contended in this appeal, that the native title rights and interests to which the *Native Title Act* refers are rights and interests finding their origin in pre-sovereignty law and custom, not rights or interests which are a creature of that Act.

That being so, the references, in pars (a) and (b) of the definition of native title, to "traditional" law or custom must be understood in the light of the considerations that have been mentioned. As the claimants submitted, "traditional" is a word apt to refer to a means of transmission of law or custom. A traditional law or custom is one which has been passed from generation to generation of a society, usually by word of mouth and common practice. But in the context of the *Native Title Act*, "traditional" carries with it two other elements ... First, it conveys an understanding of the age of the traditions: the origins of the content of the law or custom concerned are to be found in the normative rules of the Aboriginal and Torres Strait Islander societies that existed before the assertion of sovereignty by the British Crown. It is only those normative rules that are "traditional" laws and customs.

Secondly, and no less importantly, the reference to rights or interests in land or waters being *possessed* under traditional laws acknowledged and traditional customs observed by the peoples concerned, requires that the normative system under which the rights and interests are possessed (the traditional laws and customs) is a system that has had a continuous existence and vitality since sovereignty. If that normative system has not existed throughout that period, the rights and interests **[445]** which owe their existence to that system will have ceased to exist.

As to the postulate of a continuing "society", the joint judgment said:

Gleeson CJ, Gummow and Hayne JJ: [445] Laws and customs do not exist in a vacuum. They are, in Professor Julius Stone's words, "socially derivative and non-autonomous". As Professor Honoré has pointed out, it is axiomatic that "all laws are laws of a society or group". Or as was said earlier, in Paton's *Jurisprudence* [(Clarendon Press, 1946), 34], "law is but a result of all the forces that go to make society". Law and custom arise out of and, in important respects, go to define a particular society. In this context, "society" is to be understood as a body of persons united in and by its acknowledgment and observance of a body of law and customs. Some of these issues were considered in *Milirrpum v Nabalco Pty Ltd* [(1971) 17 FLR 141 at 165-76] where there appears to have been detailed evidence about the social organisation of the Aboriginal peoples concerned ...

To speak of rights and interests possessed under an identified body of laws and customs is, therefore, to speak of rights and interests that are the creatures of the laws and customs of a particular society that exists as a group which acknowledges and observes those laws and customs. And if the society out of which the body of laws and customs arises ceases to exist as a group which acknowledges and observes those laws and customs, those laws and customs cease to have continued existence and vitality. Their content may be known but if **[446]** there is no society which acknowledges and observes them, it ceases to be useful, even meaningful, to speak of them as a body of laws and customs acknowledged and observed, or productive of existing rights or interests, whether in relation to land or waters or otherwise.

What is the position if, as is said to be the case here, the content of the laws and customs is passed on from individual to individual, despite the dispersal of the society which once acknowledged and observed them, and the descendants of those who used to acknowledge and observe these laws and customs take them up again? Are the laws and customs which those descendants acknowledge and observe "traditional laws" and "traditional customs" as those expressions are used in the *Native Title Act*, and are the rights and interests in land to which those laws and customs give rise possessed under traditional laws acknowledged and traditional customs observed?

Again, it is necessary to consider the several elements of the issues that thus arise. Has the society ceased to exist? Does not the survival of knowledge of the traditional ways suggest that it has not? Or is it shown that, although there is knowledge, there has been or is no observance or acknowledgment? These may be very difficult questions to resolve. Identifying a society that can be said to continue to acknowledge and observe customs will, in many cases, be very difficult. In the end, however, because laws and customs do not exist in a vacuum, because they are socially derivative and non-autonomous, if the society (the body of persons united in and by its observance and acknowledgment of a body of law and customs) ceases to acknowledge and observe them, the questions posed earlier must be answered, no.

When the society whose laws or customs existed at sovereignty ceases to exist, the rights and interests in land to which these laws and customs gave rise, cease to exist. If the content of the former laws and customs is later adopted by some new society, those laws and customs will then owe their new life to that other, later, society and they are the laws acknowledged by, and customs observed by, *that later society*, they are not laws and customs which can now properly be described as being the existing laws and customs of the earlier society. The rights and interests in land to which the re-adopted laws and customs give rise are rights and interests which are not rooted in pre-sovereignty traditional law and custom but in the laws and customs of the new society.

The joint judgment went on to make it clear that the "sovereignty" postulate and the "society" postulate were conceived of as interdependent:

Gleeson CJ, Gummow and Hayne JJ: [446] In so far as it is useful to analyse the problem in the jurisprudential terms of the legal positivist, the relevant rule of recognition of a traditional law or custom is a rule of recognition found in the social structures of the relevant indigenous society as those structures existed at sovereignty. It is not some later created rule of recognition rooted in the social structures of a society, even an indigenous society, if those structures were structures newly created after, or even because of, the change in sovereignty. So much necessarily follows as a consequence of the assertion of sovereignty and it finds reflection in the definition **[447]** of native title and its reference to possession of rights and interests under traditional law and custom ...

[A]ny analysis of the traditional laws and customs of societies having no well-developed written language by using analytical tools developed in connection with very differently organised societies is fraught with evident difficulty. The difficulty of that analytical task should not be understood, however, as denying the importance of recognising two cardinal facts. First, laws and customs and the society which acknowledges and observes them are inextricably interlinked. Secondly, one of the uncontestable consequences of the change in sovereignty was that the only native title rights or interests in relation to land or waters which the new sovereign order recognised were those that existed at the time of change in sovereignty. Although *those* rights survived the change in sovereignty, if *new* rights or interests were to arise, those new rights and interests must find their roots in the legal order of the new sovereign power ...

[454] For the reasons given earlier, "traditional" does not mean only that which is transferred by word of mouth from generation to generation, it reflects the fundamental nature of the native title rights and interests with which the Act deals as rights and interests rooted in pre-sovereignty traditional laws and customs.

Note that the only conceptions of "sovereignty" referred to are those of English analytical positivism: either the model proposed by John Austin (1790-1859) of law as the commands of a determinate sovereign habitually commanding obedience, or its modification by HLA Hart (1907-92), ascribing the validity of "primary rules" to an institutional "rule of recognition". This is so despite an implied concession that "**[446]** the jurisprudential terms of the legal positivist" may not provide the only possible way of understanding "sovereignty" (let alone "validity"), and despite the express concessions that the search for an Austinian model of sovereignty "**[442]** may or may not be fruitful"; that the search for a rule of recognition "**[443]** may or may not be productive"; and that the application of such conceptions to traditional systems of law "**[447]** is fraught with evident difficulty". It is so despite the fact that Hart's "rule of recognition", like Kelsen's "basic norm" (see Chapter 1, §2), far from establishing an alternative version of "sovereignty", is intended as a device for analysing legal systems *without* importing unnecessary notions of "sovereignty" or of "the State" (see Chapter 1, §3); and despite the fact that, in *The Concept of Law* (Clarendon Press, 1961), Hart's analysis of "secondary rules" (rules of adjudication, rules of change, and "**[92]** a rule of recognition") was developed out of speculation on the elements that do *not* occur in the kind of legal system which is "**[89]** always found in the primitive societies of which we have knowledge". (The fact that Hart's speculations had no empirical foundation is beside the point, as is his own admission in a footnote that in reality "**[244n]** few societies have existed" in which his three kinds of secondary rules "were all entirely lacking".) And, of course, the joint judgment wholly ignores the phenomenon of Jewish law, which persisted for many centuries although Hebrew "sovereignty" had long been destroyed, and Hebrew "society" fragmented by the diaspora into hundreds of precarious ghettoes.

As for the issue debated in the courts below, of how far the recognition of native title could accommodate change in traditional laws and customs, the joint judgment said:

Gleeson CJ, Gummow and Hayne JJ: [455] [D]emonstrating the content of pre-sovereignty traditional laws and customs may be especially difficult in cases, like this, where it is recognised that the laws or customs now said to be acknowledged and observed are laws and customs that have been adapted in response to the impact of European settlement. In such cases, difficult questions of fact and degree may emerge, not only in assessing what, if any, significance should be attached to the fact of change or adaptation but also in deciding what it was that was changed or adapted. It is not possible to offer any single bright line test for deciding what inferences may be drawn or when they may be drawn, any more than it is possible to offer such a test for deciding what changes or adaptations are significant. Indeed, so far as the second of those issues is concerned, it would be wrong to attempt to reformulate the statutory language when it is the words of the definition to which effect must be given.

What is clear, however, is that demonstrating some change to, or adaptation of, traditional law or custom or some interruption of enjoyment or exercise of native title rights or interests in the period between the Crown asserting sovereignty and the present will not *necessarily* be fatal to a native title claim. Yet both change, and interruption in exercise, may, in a particular case, take on considerable significance in deciding the issues presented by an application for determination of native title ... The key question is whether the law and custom can still be seen to be traditional law and traditional custom. Is the change or adaptation of such a kind that it can no longer be said that the rights or interests asserted are possessed under the traditional laws acknowledged and the traditional customs observed by the relevant peoples when that expression is understood in the sense earlier identified?

However, the problem of adaptation did not need to be further explored, since what Olney J had found was not a mere "adaptation" of traditional custom, but a radical discontinuity. The joint judgment conceded that some degree of "interruption" to the actual exercise of traditional rights might not always be fatal, since the relevant questions "[455] are directed to possession of the rights or interests, not their exercise", and relate to "[456] *present* possession of rights or interests and *present* connection of claimants with the land or waters". Nevertheless, the jurisprudential analysis earlier in the judgment meant that Olney J's findings must be decisive:

Gleeson CJ, Gummow and Hayne JJ: [456] [I]t is important to bear steadily in mind that the rights and interests which are said now to be possessed must nonetheless be rights and interests possessed under the traditional laws acknowledged and the traditional customs observed by the peoples in question. Further, the connection which the peoples concerned have with the land or waters must be shown to be a connection by their traditional laws and customs. For the reasons given earlier, "traditional" in this context must be understood to refer to the body of law and customs acknowledged and observed by the ancestors of the claimants at the time of sovereignty.

For exactly the same reasons, acknowledgment and observance of those laws and customs must have continued substantially uninterrupted since sovereignty. Were that not so, the laws and customs acknowledged and observed *now* could not properly be described as the *traditional* laws and customs of the peoples concerned. That would be so because they would not have been transmitted from generation to generation of the society for which they constituted a normative system ... as the body of laws and customs which, for each of those generations of that society, was the body of laws and customs which in fact regulated and defined the rights and interests which those peoples had and could exercise ... They would be a body of laws and customs originating in the common acceptance by or agreement of a new society of indigenous peoples to acknowledge and observe laws and customs of content similar to, perhaps even identical with, those of an earlier and different society.

To return to a jurisprudential analysis, continuity in acknowledgment and observance of the normative rules in which the claimed rights and interests are said to find their foundations before sovereignty is essential because it is the normative quality of those rules which rendered the Crown's radical title acquired at sovereignty subject to the rights and interests then existing and which now are identified as native title.

In the proposition that acknowledgment and observance must have continued substantially uninterrupted, the qualification "substantially" is not unimportant. It is a qualification that must be made in order to recognise that proof of continuous acknowledgment and observance, over the many years that have elapsed since sovereignty, of traditions that are oral traditions is very difficult. It is a qualification that must be made to recognise that European settlement has had the most profound effects on Aboriginal societies and that it is, therefore, inevitable that the structures and practices of those societies, and their members, will have undergone great change since European settlement. Nonetheless, **[457]** because what must be identified is possession of rights and interests under traditional laws and customs, it is necessary to demonstrate that the normative system out of which the claimed rights and interests arise is the normative system of the society which came under a new sovereign order when the British Crown asserted sovereignty, not a normative system rooted in some other, different, society. To that end it must be shown that the society, under whose laws and customs the native title rights and interests are said to be possessed, has continued to exist throughout that period as a body united by its acknowledgment and observance of the laws and customs ...

[458] [T]he primary judge's critical findings of fact ... were findings about *interruption* in observance of traditional law and custom not about the content of or changes in that law or custom. They were findings rejecting one of the key elements of the case which the claimants sought to make at trial, namely, that they continued to observe laws and customs which they, and their ancestors, had continuously observed since sovereignty. More fundamentally than that, they were findings that the society which had once observed traditional laws and customs had ceased to do so and, by ceasing to do so, no longer constituted the society out of which the traditional laws and customs sprang ...

[T]he findings we have identified are more radical than is acknowledged by arguments about the particular content of laws and traditions at particular times. They are findings that the forebears of the claimants had ceased to occupy their lands in accordance with traditional laws and customs and that there was no evidence that they continued to acknowledge and observe those laws and customs. Upon those findings, the claimants must fail.

In *Commonwealth v Yarmirr* (*Croker Island Case*) (2001) 208 CLR 1 and in *Western Australia v Ward*, Gaudron J had participated in a joint majority judgment along with Gleeson CJ, Gummow and Hayne JJ. In *Yorta Yorta*, however, she joined Kirby J in dissent. Conversely, McHugh and Callinan JJ agreed that the appeal must be dismissed, though McHugh J challenged the interpretation given by the joint judgment to s 223(1) of the Act. He conceded that it was required by the Court's decisions in *Yarmirr* and *Ward*; but insisted that it represented a sharp departure from legislative intention:

McHugh J [467]: I remain unconvinced that the construction that this Court has placed on s 223 accords with what the Parliament intended. In *Yarmirr*, I cited statements from the Ministers in charge of the Act when it was enacted in 1993 and when it was amended in 1997. They showed that the Parliament believed that, under the *Native Title Act*, the content of native title would depend on the developing common law. Thus, Senator Evans told the Senate in 1993:

"We are not attempting to define with precision the extent and incidence of native title. That will be a matter still for case by case determination through tribunal processes and so on. *The crucial element of the common law is the fact that native title as such, as a proprietary right capable of being recognised and enjoyed, and excluding other competing forms of proprietary claim, is recognised as part of the common law of the country.*" (emphasis added)

Similarly, Senator Minchin told the Senate in 1997:

"I repeat that our [A]ct preserves the fact of common law; who **[468]** holds native title, what it consists of, is entirely a matter for the courts of Australia. *It is a common law right.*" (emphasis added)

Section 12 of the *Native Title Act* 1993 also made it clear that the content of native title under that Act was to be determined in accordance with the developing common law. Section 12 provided:

"Subject to this Act, the common law of Australia in respect of native title has, after 30 June 1993, the force of a law of the Commonwealth."

In *Western Australia v Commonwealth* (*Native Title Act Case*) [(1995) 183 CLR 373 at 486-7], however, this Court held that s 12 was invalid ... But its enactment in the 1993 Act shows that the Parliament intended native title to be determined by the common law principles laid down in *Mabo v Queensland (No 2)*, particularly those formulated by Brennan J in his judgment in that case. When s 223(1)(c) of the 1993 Act referred to the rights and interests "recognised by the common law of Australia", it was, in my view, referring to the principles expounded by Brennan J in *Mabo (No 2)*.

Compare the observations of Callinan J in *Yarmirr* that the statutory language "**[151]** is a restatement, practically verbatim, of a passage from the judgment of Brennan J in *Mabo*", and in

Western Australia v Ward "**[269]** that the legislature was not intending to create some sort of special statutory title for Indigenous people, but was adopting the characteristics of, and limitations on, native title so far revealed in the case law".

The decision in *Yorta Yorta* has been widely criticised. In March 2003, Aboriginal leader Noel Pearson delivered the Sir Ninian Stephen Annual Lecture at the University of Newcastle. He began by quoting what he had said four months earlier in the Bob Hawke Memorial Lecture at the University of South Australia, where he had summarised *Mabo (No 2)* as having proposed a historical compromise.

Noel Pearson, "The High Court's Abandonment of 'The Time-Honoured Methodology of the Common Law' in its Interpretation of Native Title in Mirriuwung Gajerrong and Yorta Yorta"
(2003) 7 *Newcastle Law Review* 1

[2] The first part of that compromise, if we are truthful, was the most unequivocal. The first part of the compromise said that the titles accumulated over the last two centuries inhering in the settlers and their descendants, could not now be disturbed. Those titles were now indefeasible. Even if those titles were gained in circumstances of regret and denial of right, the Court said that the **[3]** accumulation of these many millions of titles over two centuries could not now be disturbed ...

The second principle of native title law articulated by the Court is very simple also. It proposed that all of those lands that remained after 204 years, unalienated, was the legal right of the traditional owners ... [I]n the most settled parts of the country, these lands are few and far between indeed. If you want to find unalienated Crown land on the east coast of Australia you would need to go down near the mangroves and find a block of unallocated state land or down near the dump or some inhospitable wedge of land in some remote corner of the countryside and of course most generously, in the most deserted regions of our continent.

That was what was proposed by the High Court in the Mabo decision. Let me put it colloquially: the whitefellas get to keep everything they have accumulated, the blackfellas should now belatedly be entitled to whatever is left over. The imperative flowing from the Mabo decision in 1992 was the swiftest unambiguous and ungrudging delivery of that remainder to the indigenous peoples entitled to that belated recognition. In some of our states we have yet to get one hectare, we are yet to get one acre, we are yet to get one square metre of land under a Native Title determination after 10 years.

The third part ... of the compromise was put forward by the High Court in 1996 in the *Wik* decision. It said that there are some large areas of land covered by pastoral leases and national parks where Native Title may co-exist with the Crown Title. The Court ruled by a majority of four to three that in that co-existence, the Crown Title prevails over the Native Title if there is any inconsistency.

So those are the three limbs of Native Title Law as articulated by our High Court in this country. The whitefellas keep all that is now theirs, the blackfellas get whatever is left over and there are some categories of land where there is co-existence and in the co-existence the Crown Title always prevails over the Native Title.

After thus quoting what he had said in November 2002, Pearson went on in March 2003:

[4] Then the High Court delivered its judgment in *Yorta Yorta* in December 2002 and put the lie to my interpretation of the meaning of native title. The three principles of native title law are not that the whitefellas get to keep all that they have accumulated, that the blackfellas get what is left over and they share some larger categories of land titles with the granted titles prevailing over the native title. Rather the three principles of native title are that the whitefellas do not only get to keep all that they have accumulated, but the blacks only get a fraction of what is left over and only get to share a coexisting and subservient title where they are able to surmount the most unreasonable and unyielding barriers of proof – and indeed only where they prove that they meet white Australia's cultural and legal prejudices about what constitutes "real Aborigines". To the Australian courts charged with the responsibility of administering the historic compromise set out in *Mabo*, the Yorta Yorta Peoples were not sufficiently Aboriginal to get one square metre of what was left over after the whites had taken all that they wanted …

The present High Court does not know what it is doing with the responsibility which their predecessors assumed with *Mabo*. They have rendered a great disservice to indigenous Australians and to our past and future as a nation. For in their flawed and discriminatory conceptualisation of native title and in their egregious misinterpretation of fundamental provisions of the *Native Title Act,* they are destroying the opportunity for native title to finally settle the outstanding question of indigenous land justice in Australia.

As to the joint judgment's interpretation of s 223(1) of the *Native Title Act*, Pearson said:

[4] The enactment of native title legislation in the wake of the High Court's 1992 decision in *Mabo* was the subject of an intense national political and legislative debate during 1993, in which Aboriginal advocates participated vigorously.

What were we defending in that process and what did we think that we had achieved with the Commonwealth government under Prime Minister Paul Keating?

We thought, and I am sure all members of Parliament and all Australians who followed the proceedings thought, that the whole exercise was about preserving the rights declared under the common law of Australia. In other words we thought that the *Mabo* decision, and the [5] rights and interests that flowed from that decision, [were] being recognised and protected in Commonwealth legislation …

So we thought that the *Native Title Act* preserved the *Mabo* decision. And we thought that all claims for native title that would be made under the framework of the new legislation would be adjudicated according to principles of the High Court's decision in *Mabo* and the body of common law of which it forms a part.

But this is not what the High Court has determined in the cases leading up to, and now settled in, *Yorta Yorta*. Whilst the High Court denies that it is approaching native title as a creature of the *Native Title Act*, nevertheless it has given an independent role to the definition of native title set out in section 223(1). Indeed the High Court has taken the legislation as the starting point and the ending point for interpreting native title.

Indeed the relevance of the *Mabo* decision … is almost rejected by the court. In their joint judgment Gleeson CJ and Gummow and Hayne JJ remarked [214 CLR at 451] …: "It may be that undue emphasis was given in the reasons to what was said in *Mabo (No 2)*, at the expense of recognising the principal, indeed determinative, place that should be given to the *Native Title Act*."

Pearson argued that the definition of "native title" in s 223(1) of the Act could only be understood in one of two ways: either it "[6] did not in any way alter the common law meaning of native title", or it did alter that meaning. He suggested, however, that no alteration could be constitutionally valid, in view of the requirement of "just terms" imposed by s 51(xxxi) on any "acquisition of property". Either an alteration would *increase* the common law entitlements of native title holders (in which case it would involve a taking of property from the non-indigenous settler population), or it would *reduce* those entitlements (in which case it would involve a taking of property from the native title holders). Besides, there were "[7] even more compelling reasons why the approach of the High Court … is wrong":

[7] The High Court's interpretation is patently at odds with the intention of Parliament, both during the time of the Keating government in 1993 and at the time the *Native Title Amendment Act 1998* (Cth) was passed by the Howard government in 1998. Both Parliaments understood that their respective laws were preserving the common law rights articulated in the *Mabo* decision …

[8] Justice McHugh's understanding of what section 223(1) meant is my understanding of what was meant. It is Paul Keating and Gareth Evans' understanding of what was meant. It is John Howard's and Nick Minchin's understanding of what was meant.

Amazingly, despite McHugh J's clear statement that his colleagues had settled upon what was a "narrower" interpretation of section 223 – contrary to Parliament's intention – he capitulated to this narrower interpretation and was prepared to accept it as settled law. This in itself is instructive.

Justice McHugh was dealing here with a profound question of fundamental property rights of Australian citizens entitled to rigorous application of the rules of law when they bring their claims before the **[9]** courts for adjudication. It is hard to imagine any other area of law where a judge would so lightly abandon his or her conviction about an interpretation of a statutory provision which is pivotal not just to the instant case, but to all future cases to come before the courts ...

[11] The judgments in both *Mirriuwung Gajerrong* and *Yorta Yorta* run to hundreds of pages. And all of these pages of discussion concern statutory interpretation – rather than any discussion of cases. **[12]** Astoundingly there is absolutely no reference whatsoever to the Supreme Court of Canada's 1997 decision in [*Delgamuukw v British Columbia* [1997] 3 SCR 1010; (1997) 153 DLR(4th) 193]. This is the leading Canadian case in native title – their equivalent of *Mabo* which was substantially informed by the Australian High Court's decision. And the only reference in *Mirriuwung Gajerrong* to *Delgamuukw* is a reference to Lambert J's decision in the British Columbia Court of Appeal.

Despite the fact that in *Delgamuukw* Lamer CJ discussed the very issues concerning the concept and proof of native title which are at fundamental issue in these Australian cases – there was no reference to the emerging Canadian law. There was no reference to any other cases either. *Mabo* itself is not discussed and only mentioned for historical and contextual purposes.

There is no discussion of important questions that have hitherto been unresolved and uncertain in the common law of Australia and Canada – many of them still under development – by reference to cases. Meanings are attributed to key concepts such as "continuity", "connection", "tradition", "suspension", "extinguishment", "expiry" ..., "possessed under", and so on – without any reference to case law. These important concepts are treated as part of a statutory interpretation exercise, in an area of statutory interpretation which is conveniently without precedent.

What the High Court has decided is that it will draw a line between the Australian law on native title after the enactment of the *Native Title Act* and the body of North American and British colonial case law which has dealt with native title over the past two centuries, and which informed and underpinned the decision in *Mabo*.

This case law, upon which Brennan J and other members of the court drew in their judgments in *Mabo* concerning colonies in the subcontinent and West Africa, the United States and Canada – as well as cases concerning Wales and Ireland – has been conveniently disposed of. Rather than developing the fledgling Australian law by grappling with this considerable body of law, with which – as *Mabo* showed – there are more areas of common principle than there are differences, the High Court has taken the easy road of interpreting and developing native title under the rubric of statutory interpretation.

By treating native title as defined by section 223(1) the High Court is ruling on important questions and principles on the basis of bare assertion, rather than through what McLachlin J [*R v Van der Peet* [1996] 2 SCR 507 at 641; (1996) 137 DLR(4th) 289 at 377] called "the time-honoured methodology of the common law".

Pearson argued that in order to redress the Court's misinterpretation of s 223(1), the definition should be amended to stipulate simply that "'native title' and 'native title rights and interests' are those rights and interests which are recognised by the common law". He also argued that the common law principles that such an amendment would restore should themselves be restated, so that what is said to continue after the British acquisition of sovereignty "**[10]** is the right to occupy and possess the land under one's traditional law and custom ... **[11]** [I]t is the entitlement to occupy the land which continues after sovereignty, not the incidents of rights and interests that are established by reference to arcane traditional laws and customs". He found support in what Toohey J had said in *Mabo (No 2)*: "**[188]** It is presence amounting to occupancy which is the foundation of the title and which attracts protection, and it is that which must be proved to establish title ... Thus traditional title is rooted in physical presence".

The criticisms mounted by Dr William Jonas, Aboriginal and Torres Strait Islander Social Justice Commissioner from 1999 to 2004, have been equally forceful. He has suggested that the underlying problem can be traced back to *Mabo (No 2)*:

Aboriginal and Torres Strait Islander Social Justice Commissioner, *Native Title Report 2002*
(Human Rights and Equal Opportunity Commission, 2003)
(Parliamentary Paper No 41 of 2003)

[23] [T]here is a troubling disjuncture in the reasoning of the High Court in *Mabo*. On the one hand terra nullius was overturned because it failed to recognise the social and political constitution of Indigenous people. Yet the recognition of native title was premised on the supreme power of the state to the exclusion of any other sovereign people. Thus the characteristics of Indigenous sovereignty, the political, social and economic systems that unite and distinguish Indigenous people as a people were erased from the developing law of native title ...

[24] The assertion in *Mabo* of supreme and exclusive sovereign power residing in the State has been confirmed in the *Miriuwung Gajerrong* and *Yorta Yorta* decisions ... It can be seen in the *Miriuwung Gajerrong* decision, as in the *Mabo* decision, that the construction of native title at common law as an inherently fragile and inferior interest in land, originates from an assumption that the nature of the power asserted by the colonizing state is singular, total and all-encompassing ... The implications of the *Mabo* decision, that native title does not give recognition to the economic political and legal systems of Indigenous people, as a people, are fully realised in the *Yorta Yorta* decision.

> [W]hat the assertion of sovereignty by the British Crown necessarily entailed was that there could thereafter be no parallel law-making system in the territory over which it asserted sovereignty [214 CLR at 443-4].

The basis for limiting native title to the recognition of rights and interests and not the laws and customs from which these emanate can be found in this paragraph. The monopoly on law-making held by the new sovereign renders [25] the law-making capacity of the Indigenous legal system defunct upon sovereignty being acquired. For this reason the recognition of native title rights and interests is limited to those created prior to the acquisition of sovereignty ...

In fastening the recognition of native title to a pre-sovereign system of laws, every claimant group must satisfy a court that the contemporary expression of their culture and their religion, does not emanate from Indigenous laws or customs that were created after sovereignty. Whenever present beliefs or practices appear in any way to differ from past beliefs and practices, the issue of whether these differences can be seen as evidence of a new set of laws and customs or adaptations of the pre-sovereign set of laws is raised and subject to proof. The difficulties of proving this distinction are discussed below. What is important to note here is the concept of sovereignty on which this distinction is based and how this concept limits the recognition of contemporary expressions of Indigenous culture.

Yet the assumption of exclusive sovereignty by a colonial power over Indigenous people is not shared in the world view of Indigenous people nor at international law. The evolution of the principle of self-determination at international law challenges the notion that the non-Indigenous state has exclusive jurisdiction over traditional land, not by replacing it with exclusive Indigenous jurisdiction, but by challenging the foundations on which the assertion of paramount control by one group to the exclusion of all others rests.

6. Sovereignty and Self-Determination

Indigenous peoples have sought in various ways to build upon the partial recognition of their rights in *Mabo (No 2)*, sometimes by calling for a recognition of Indigenous "sovereignty". However, in two separate cases where Indigenous statements of claim were struck out, Mason CJ, sitting alone, made it clear that no such recognition can be expected in Australia, at least judicially, in the near future.

Coe v Commonwealth (No 2)
(1993) 118 ALR 193

Mason CJ: [194] The plaintiff claims to sue on behalf of the Wiradjuri tribe, being Aboriginal people, and seeks declarations of various kinds and consequential relief. They include declarations to the effect that the Wiradjuri are the owners of lands constituting a very large part of southern and central New South Wales. In her statement of claim, the plaintiff puts the claim to relief on a variety of grounds ...

[195] The first ground, described as "the sovereignty claim", is pleaded ... as follows:

6.   The Wiradjuri are a sovereign nation of people.

7.   In the alternative to paragraph 6 herein, the Wiradjuri are a domestic dependent nation, entitled to self government and full rights over their traditional lands, save only the right to alienate them to whoever they please.

8.   In the further alternative to paragraphs 6 and 7 herein, the Wiradjuri are a free and independent people entitled to the possession of those rights and interests (including rights and interests in land) which as such are valuable to them ...

[199] *Coe* [(1979) 24 ALR 118] lends no support whatsoever to a subsisting Aboriginal claim to sovereignty. That claim was rejected by all four justices. Gibbs J stated that the annexation of the east coast of Australia by Captain Cook and the subsequent acts by which the whole of the Australian continent became part of the Dominions of the Crown were acts of state whose validity could not be challenged. His Honour continued [24 ALR at 128-9]:

> If the amended statement of claim intends to suggest either that the legal foundation of the Commonwealth is insecure, or that the powers of the Parliament are more limited than is provided in the Constitution, or that there is an Aboriginal nation which has sovereignty over Australia, it cannot be supported. In fact, we were told in argument, it is intended to claim that there is an Aboriginal nation which has sovereignty over its own people, notwithstanding that they remain citizens of the Commonwealth; in other words, it is sought to treat the Aboriginal people of Australia as a domestic dependent nation, to use the expression which Marshall CJ applied to the Cherokee Nation of Indians: *Cherokee Nation v State of Georgia* [30 US (5 Pet) 1 (1831)]. However, the history of the relationships between the white settlers and the Aboriginal peoples has not been the same in Australia and in the United States, and it is not possible to say, as was said by Marshall CJ of the Cherokee Nation, that the Aboriginal people of Australia are organized as a "distinct political society separated from others", or that they have been uniformly treated as a state ... The Aboriginal people are subject to the laws of the Commonwealth and of the States or Territories in which they respectively reside. They have no legislative, executive or judicial organs by which sovereignty might be exercised. If such organs existed, they would have no powers, except such as the law of the Commonwealth, or of a State or Territory, might confer upon them. The contention that there is in Australia an Aboriginal nation exercising sovereignty, even of a limited kind, is quite impossible in law to maintain.

Jacobs J described the first part of the proposed amended statement of claim as being:

> **[200]** ... apparently intended to dispute the validity of the British Crown's and now the Commonwealth of Australia's claim to sovereignty over the continent of Australia in the face of sovereignty alleged to be possessed by the Aboriginal nation [24 ALR at 132].

Jacobs J refused to allow the first part of the proposed statement of claim "because generally it is formulated as a claim based on a sovereignty adverse to the Crown" [24 ALR at 133]. His Honour said of paras 2A and 3A, which disputed the validity of the Crown's claim of sovereignty and sovereign possession, that they were "not matters of municipal law but of the law of nations and are not cognisable in a court exercising jurisdiction under that sovereignty which is sought to be challenged".

Although Murphy J did not deal specifically with the sovereignty claim, his Honour agreed generally with Jacobs J and with the order proposed by him. Murphy J was of opinion that the plaintiff was entitled to argue that the sovereignty acquired by the British Crown did not extinguish "ownership rights" in the Aboriginals. But his Honour agreed with the order refusing leave to amend in the form of the first part of the proposed amended statement of claim.

Mabo (No 2) is entirely at odds with the notion that sovereignty adverse to the Crown resides in the Aboriginal people of Australia. The decision is equally at odds with the notion that there resides in the Aboriginal people a limited kind of sovereignty embraced in the notion that they are "a domestic dependent nation" entitled to self-government and full rights (save the right of alienation) or that as a free and independent people they are entitled to any rights and interests other than those created or recognised by the laws of the Commonwealth, the State of New South Wales and the common law. *Mabo (No 2)* denied that the Crown's acquisition of sovereignty over Australia can be challenged in the municipal courts of this country. *Mabo (No 2)* recognised that land in the Murray Islands was held by means of native title under the paramount sovereignty of the Crown. The principles of law which led to that result apply to the Australian mainland as the judgments make clear. The consequence is that paras 6, 7 and 8 which are the core of the plaintiff's claim do not disclose a reasonable ground for relief.

Walker v New South Wales
(1994) 182 CLR 45

Mason CJ: [47] The defendant's case is that the statement of claim does not plead a reasonable cause of action. By that statement of claim, the plaintiff accepts that he has **[48]** been charged with an offence against the laws of New South Wales which allegedly occurred at Nimbin, a place said to be within the area of the Bandjalung "nation" of Aboriginal people. The plaintiff himself is said to be a member of the Noonuccal "nation" of Aboriginal people. The statement of claim alleges that the common law is only valid in its application to Aboriginal people to the extent to which it has been accepted by them. Concerning statute law the statement of claim then alleges:

"10. The Parliaments of the Commonwealth of Australia and of the States lack the power to legislate in a manner affecting aboriginal people without the request and consent of the aboriginal people.

11. Further and in the alternative, if the Parliament of the Commonwealth or of a State legislates in a manner affecting aboriginal people the law in so far as it relates to aboriginal people is of no effect until it is adopted by the aboriginal people whom, or whose land, it purports to effect [*sic*]."

Couched as they are in terms of the legislative incapacity of the Commonwealth and State Parliaments, those pleadings are untenable. The legislature of New South Wales has power to make laws for the peace, welfare and good government of New South Wales in all cases whatsoever. The proposition that those laws could not apply to particular inhabitants or particular conduct occurring within the State must be rejected. As Gibbs J (with whom Aickin J agreed) said in *Coe v Commonwealth* [(1979) 24 ALR 118 at 129]: "The Aboriginal people are subject to the laws of the Commonwealth and of the States or Territories in which they respectively reside." In that case all the justices on appeal upheld the view which I had taken at first instance rejecting the plaintiff's claim that sovereignty resided in the Aboriginal people. There is nothing in the recent decision in *Mabo v Queensland (No 2)* [(1992) 175 CLR 1] to support the notion that the Parliaments of the Commonwealth and New South Wales lack legislative competence to regulate or affect the rights of Aboriginal people, or the notion that the application of Commonwealth or State laws to Aboriginal people is in any way subject to their acceptance, adoption, request or consent. Such notions amount to the contention that a new source of sovereignty resides in the Aboriginal people. Indeed, *Mabo (No 2)* rejected that suggestion ...

[49] In so far as it is based on the proposition that the legislatures lacked power to legislate over Aboriginal peoples, the statement of claim discloses no reasonable cause of action.

However, counsel for the plaintiff in his oral submissions put the matter somewhat differently. He submitted that the question which arose was whether customary Aboriginal criminal law is something which has been recognized by the common law and which continues to this day, in the same way that *Mabo (No 2)* decided that the customary law of the Meriam people relating to land tenure continues to exist. Counsel relied on a passage in Blackstone's *Commentaries* on the introduction of English law into a country that had been outside the King's dominions:

"Such colonists carry with them only so much of the English law, as is applicable to their own situation and the condition of an infant colony." ...

It was submitted that statutes must be construed so as to accord with what was said to be the common law principle set out by Blackstone, with the consequence that the criminal statutes of New South Wales did not apply to people of Aboriginal descent.

That proposition must be rejected. It is a basic principle that all people should stand equal before the law. A construction which results in different criminal sanctions applying to different persons for the same conduct offends that basic principle. The general rule is that an enactment applies to all persons and matters within the territory to which it extends, but not to any other persons and matters. The rule extends not only to all persons ordinarily **[50]** resident within the country, but also to foreigners temporarily visiting. And just as all persons in the country enjoy the benefits of domestic laws from which they are not expressly excluded, so also must they accept the burdens those laws impose. The presumption applies with added force in the case of the criminal law, which is inherently universal in its operation, and whose aims would otherwise be frustrated ...

Even if it be assumed that the customary criminal law of Aboriginal people survived British settlement, it was extinguished by the passage of criminal statutes of general application. In *Mabo (No 2)*, the Court held that there was no inconsistency between native title being held by people of Aboriginal descent and the underlying radical title being vested in the Crown. There is no analogy with the criminal law. English criminal law did not, and Australian criminal law does not, accommodate an alternative body of law operating alongside it. There is nothing in *Mabo (No 2)* to provide any support at all for the proposition that criminal laws of general application do not apply to Aboriginal people.

These judgments suggest that recognition of an independent sovereignty of Aboriginal peoples is unlikely to be accepted by the courts. Yet whether that position can be maintained may be doubted. In *Coe v Commonwealth (No 2)*, Mason CJ relied heavily upon what was said by Gibbs J in *Coe v Commonwealth (No 1)* (1979) 24 ALR 118 to distinguish the history of European settlement in America from that in Australia. However, after *Mabo (No 2)* it is clear that the distinctions drawn by Gibbs J are either factually incorrect or irrelevant. For example, Gibbs J contrasts the American pattern of a continent populated by a diversity of Indigenous "peoples" or "nations", with the postulate of one supposedly homogenous race, "the Aboriginal people of Australia". Yet in the wake of *Mabo (No 2)*, non-Indigenous Australians have discovered that this concept of a single homogenous "Aboriginal people" is as much of a historical fiction as the notion of terra nullius itself. It is clear that Australia's Indigenous "peoples" have *severally* the kind of cultural identity that might entitle them, under emerging norms of international law, to rights of self-determination.

Erica-Irene Daes, "Some Considerations on the Right of Indigenous Peoples to Self-Determination"
(1993) 3 *Transnational Law and Contemporary Problems* 1

[2] The adoption of the General Assembly resolution containing the important Declaration on the Granting of Independence to Colonial Countries and Peoples [14 December 1960] was clearly the beginning of a revolutionary process within the United Nations ... [The Declaration] expressly provides that "all peoples have the right to self-determination; by virtue of that right they freely determine their political status and freely pursue their economic, social and cultural development." The declaration is essentially a political document with questionable legal authority, but it has formed the cornerstone of what may be called the new UN law of **[3]** self-determination. That such law exists is taken for granted by a majority of UN members, especially as evidenced in UN practice ...

However, the exact content of the aforementioned law is frequently debated. Upon whom is the right to self-determination conferred, according to the new UN law regulating the subject? The answer, given in identical terms in the Declaration ... and in the two International Covenants on

Human Rights, is as simple in formulation as it is chimerical in fact. All three international instruments stipulate that "[a]ll peoples have the right to self-determination." Nevertheless, the context in which the universal goal is declared demonstrates an intention to confine the right to [4] peoples who are still "dependent," and those subjected to "alien subjugation, domination and exploitation." Unfortunately, no specific reference has been made to indigenous peoples ...

In theory, *external* self-determination – the act by which a people determines its future international status and liberates itself from alien rule – may be distinguished from *internal* self-determination, which includes the selection of both the desired system of government and the substantive nature (democratic, socialist, or other) of the regime selected. However, the nature of the link between these components of self-determination is postulated differently by each group of states ...

The right to self-determination is best viewed as entitling a people to choose its political allegiance, to influence the political order under which it lives, and to preserve its cultural, ethnic, historical, [5] or territorial identity. Here again, this broader view of self-determination does not resolve the question of what constitutes a "people" for the purposes of self-determination. Governments often have sought to narrow the definition of "peoples" in order to limit the number of groups entitled to exercise a self-determination claim. By contrast, groups making such claims, and in particular indigenous groups, have pressed for a broader application of the term ...

Whether a group is a people for the purposes of self-determination depends in my view on the extent to which the group making a claim shares ethnic, linguistic, religious or cultural bonds, although the absence or weakness of one of these bonds or elements need not invalidate a claim. The subjective standard should weigh the extent to which members within the group perceive the group's identity as distinct from the identities of other groups ...

[6] Indigenous peoples are unquestionably "peoples" in every social, cultural, and ethnological meaning of this term. They have their own specific languages, laws, values, and traditions; their own long histories as distinct societies and nations; and a unique economic, religious, and spiritual relationship with the territories in which they have so long lived. It is neither logical nor scientific to treat them as the same "peoples" as their neighbours, who obviously have different languages, histories, and cultures, and who often have been their oppressors. The United Nations should not pretend, for the sake of a convenient legal fiction, that those differences do not exist.

Living side-by-side as neighbours under one State may gradually blend the characteristics of different peoples, reducing their original differences. If history is any judge of such matters, however, the most important differences between peoples can be subtle, and very resistant to change. Recent events in the former Yugoslavia are instructive in this regard. Moreover, a people cannot lose its most fundamental human rights simply by changing, as all peoples do, over time. The African colonies of France surely retained their languages, habits, and institutions. The proper legal issue is not the amount of difference that exists today, but the fact that two peoples have had, for millen[n]ia, separate histories which touched each other very little or not at all.

In eastern Europe, peoples that were joined together in states more than fifty years ago have re-emerged as separate states with the full recognition and protection of the United Nations. Other indigenous peoples were only absorbed by States, in all but the most theoretical terms, within the past fifty years or less. Many were also incorporated into their present-day states under formal agreements of union, like, for example, the republics which were part of the former Soviet Union. It would be strange, and arguably racist, for the United Nations to recognize the break-up of a historical union of European peoples, but to condemn the break-up of a union elsewhere in the world simply because indigenous peoples were involved.

This recognition does not mean, however, that every people has the right to secede and form a separate State. Some limitations on the exercise of this universal right exist, which are expressed best and most fully in the Declaration on Principles of International Law Concerning Friendly Relations and Co-operation Among States in Accordance with the Charter of the United Nations [24 October 1970]. It states in relevant part that:

[7] States enjoying full sovereignty and independence, and possessed of a government effectively representing the whole of their population, shall be considered to be conducting themselves in conformity with the principle of equal rights and self-determination of peoples as regards that population. Nothing in the foregoing paragraphs shall be construed as

authorizing any action which would impair, totally or in part, the territorial integrity, or political unity, of such States.

The meaning of this is plain: once an independent State has been established and recognized, its constituent peoples must express their aspirations through the national political system and not through the creation of new States, unless the national political system becomes so exclusive and non-democratic that it no longer can be said to represent the whole of the population. At that point, and if all reasonable international legal and diplomatic measures fail to protect the peoples concerned from the State, a people may perhaps be justified in exercising the right to self-determination to the extent of creating a new State for their safety and security. Indeed, in such a situation, legal arguments cease to have any real meaning, since peoples will defend themselves by whatever means they can ...

[8] With few exceptions, indigenous peoples were never part of state-building. They did not have an opportunity to participate in designing the modern constitution of the states in which they live, or to share, in any meaningful way, in national decision-making. In some countries they have been excluded by law or by force, but in many countries they have been separated by language, poverty, and the prejudices of their non-indigenous neighbours. Whatever the reason, indigenous peoples in most countries have never been, and are not **[9]** now, full partners in the political process, and lack others' ability to use democratic means to defend their fundamental rights.

What, then, should the response of the international community be to the situation of indigenous peoples who lack effective partnership in governing the States in which they live? It would be inadmissible and discriminatory to argue that these peoples lack the right to self-determination merely because of their indigenousness. Moreover, such an argument would imply not only that they lack the right to secede, but also that they lack the right to demand full democratic partnership. A more logical and useful approach would be to agree, in keeping with the Declaration on Friendly Relations, that indigenous peoples do have the right to self-determination, and that the existing State has a duty to accommodate the aspirations of indigenous peoples through constitutional reforms designed to share power democratically. This approach also would mean that indigenous peoples have the duty to try to reach an agreement, in good faith, on sharing power within the existing State, and, to the extent possible, to exercise their right to self-determination by this means.

With regard to indigenous peoples, then, I believe that the right of self-determination should ordinarily be interpreted as the right of these peoples to negotiate freely their political status and representation in the States in which they live. This process might best be described as a kind of belated State-building, through which indigenous peoples are able to join with all the other peoples that make up the State on mutually-agreed upon and just terms, after many years of isolation and exclusion. This process does not require the assimilation of individuals, as citizens like all others, but the recognition and incorporation of distinct peoples in the fabric of the State, on agreed terms.

The United States' recognition of "Indian tribes" as "domestic dependent nations", rejected as an analogy in *Coe v Commonwealth (No 1)* and *Coe v Commonwealth (No 2)*, has itself had an uneven history. The phrase "**[17]** domestic dependent nations" was coined by Chief Justice John Marshall in *Cherokee Nation v Georgia*, 30 US (5 Peters) 1 (1831); but he used it to contrast the status of the tribes with that of "foreign States". It followed from this contrast that the Cherokees' action against the State of Georgia, in which they sought to resist the State's acquisition of their remaining lands, was not a case "between a State ... and foreign States" for purposes of Supreme Court jurisdiction under Article III, §2 of the United States Constitution. The action was accordingly dismissed – though the Cherokees were said to be "**[16]** a distinct political society, separated from others, capable of managing its own affairs and governing itself", with "**[17]** an unquestionable, and heretofore unquestioned right to the lands they occupy, until that right shall be extinguished by a voluntary cession".

A year later, when the same Georgia laws were challenged at the suit of an individual (a missionary named Samuel Worcester), Chief Justice Marshall held them invalid. The political aftermath of the decision was tragic: President Andrew Jackson refused to enforce the decision (see Chapter 1, §5) and the Cherokees were driven from their lands. Legally, however, the case remained of fundamental importance.

Worcester v Georgia
31 US (6 Peters) 515 (1832)

Marshall CJ: [542] America, separated from Europe by a wide ocean, was inhabited by a distinct people, divided into separate nations, independent of each other and of the rest of the world, having institutions of their own, and governing themselves by their **[543]** own laws. It is difficult to comprehend the proposition, that the inhabitants of either quarter of the globe could have rightful original claims of dominion over the inhabitants of the other, or over the lands they occupied; or that the discovery of either by the other should give the discoverer rights in the country discovered, which annulled the pre-existing rights of its ancient possessors ...

Did [the European] adventurers, by sailing along the coast, and occasionally landing on it, acquire for the several governments to whom they belonged, or by whom they were commissioned, a rightful property in the soil, from the Atlantic to the Pacific; or rightful dominion over the numerous people who occupied it? Or has nature, or the great Creator of all things, conferred these rights over hunters and fishermen, on agriculturists and manufacturers? ...

The great maritime powers of Europe discovered and visited different parts of this continent at nearly the same time. The object was too immense for any one of them to grasp the whole, and the claimants were too powerful to submit to the exclusive or unreasonable pretensions of any single potentate. To avoid bloody conflicts, which might terminate disastrously to all, it was necessary for the nations of Europe to establish some principle which all would acknowledge, and which should decide their respective rights as between themselves. This principle ... was, "that discovery gave title to the government by whose subjects or by whose authority it was made, against all other European **[544]** governments, which title might be consummated by possession [*Johnson v McIntosh*, 21 US (8 Wheat) 543 at 573 (1823)].

This principle, acknowledged by all Europeans, because it was the interest of all to acknowledge it, gave to the nation making the discovery, as its inevitable consequence, the sole right of acquiring the soil and of making settlements on it. It was an exclusive principle which shut out the right of competition among those who had agreed to it; not one which could annul the previous rights of those who had not agreed to it. It regulated the right given by discovery among the European discoverers; but could not affect the rights of those already in possession ... It gave the exclusive right to purchase, but did not found that right on a denial of the right of the possessor to sell.

The relation between the Europeans and the natives was determined in each case by the particular government which asserted and could maintain this pre-emptive privilege in the particular place. The United States succeeded to all the claims of Great Britain, both territorial and political; but no attempt, so far as is known, has been made to enlarge them ...

Soon after Great Britain determined on planting colonies in America, the King granted charters to companies of his subjects who associated for the purpose of carrying the views of the crown into effect, and of enriching themselves. The first of these charters was made before possession was taken of any part of the country. They purport, generally, to convey the soil, from the Atlantic to the South Sea. This soil was occupied by numerous and warlike nations, equally willing and able to defend their possessions. The extravagant and absurd idea, that the feeble settlements made on the sea coast, or the companies under whom they were made, acquired legitimate power by them to govern the people, or occupy the lands from **[545]** sea to sea, did not enter the mind of any man. They were well understood to convey the title which, according to the common law of European sovereigns respecting America, they might rightfully convey, and no more. This was the exclusive right of purchasing such lands as the natives were willing to sell. The crown could not be understood to grant what the crown did not affect to claim; nor was it so understood ...

[547] Certain it is, that our history furnishes no example, from the first settlement of our country, of any attempt on the part of the crown to interfere with the internal affairs of the Indians, farther than to keep out the agents of foreign powers, who, as traders or otherwise, might seduce them into foreign alliances. The king purchased their lands when they were willing to sell, at a price they were willing to take; but never coerced a surrender of them. He also purchased their alliance and dependence by subsidies; but never intruded into the interior of their affairs, or interfered with their self-government, so far as respected themselves only ...

[556] From the commencement of our government, congress has passed acts to regulate trade and intercourse with the Indians; which treat them as nations, respect their rights, and manifest [557] a firm purpose to afford that protection which treaties stipulate. All these acts, and especially that of 1802, which is still in force, manifestly consider the several Indian nations as distinct political communities, having territorial boundaries, within which their authority is exclusive, and having a right to all the lands within those boundaries, which is not only acknowledged, but guarantied by the United States ...

[559] The Indian nations had always been considered as distinct, independent political communities, retaining their original natural rights, as the undisputed possessors of the soil, from time immemorial, with the single exception of that imposed by irresistible power, which excluded them from intercourse with any other European potentate than the first discoverer of the coast of the particular region claimed: and this was a restriction which those European potentates imposed on themselves, as well as on the Indians. The very term "nation," so generally applied to them, means "a people distinct from others." The constitution, by declaring treaties already made, as well as those to be made, to be the supreme law of the land, has adopted and sanctioned the previous treaties with the Indian nations, and consequently admits their rank among those powers who are capable of making treaties. The words "treaty" and "nation" are words of our own language, selected in our diplomatic and legislative proceedings, by ourselves, having each a definite and well understood meaning. We [560] have applied them to Indians, as we have applied them to the other nations of the earth. They are applied to all in the same sense ...

[561] The Cherokee Nation ... is a distinct community occupying its own territory, with boundaries accurately described, in which the laws of Georgia can have no force, and which the citizens of Georgia have no right to enter, but with the assent of the Cherokees themselves, or in conformity with treaties, and with the acts of congress.

Half a century later, in *Ex parte Crow Dog*, 109 US 556 (1883), it was held that the jurisdiction of United States courts could not extend to criminal offences committed by tribal Indians on reservation land. In such cases, jurisdiction could be exercised by tribal courts only, since otherwise the persons accused would be tried "[571] not by their peers ... [but by] a different race, according to the law of a social state of which they have an imperfect conception". Thereafter, such doctrines were progressively drained of significance until, by the time of *Tee-Hit-Ton Indians v United States*, 348 US 272 (1955), only a feeble remnant remained. However, by the 1970s the influence of *Worcester v Georgia* appeared to have undergone a resurgence.

In *McClanahan v Arizona Tax Commission*, 411 US 164 (1973), a Navajo woman successfully sued the State of Arizona for a refund of State income tax. The Court held that "[165] reservation Indian[s] with income derived wholly from reservation sources" were not liable to State income tax, since the tax would interfere "with matters which the relevant treaty and statutes leave to the exclusive province of the Federal Government and the Indians themselves". In part the issue was treated as one of two-tiered federalism: the State had exceeded its powers because relations with tribal Indians were a matter exclusively for the federal government. The Court noted a trend "[172] away from the idea of inherent Indian sovereignty as a bar to state jurisdiction", and instead "toward reliance on [the doctrine of] federal pre-emption". It preferred "to avoid reliance on platonic notions of Indian sovereignty and to look instead to the applicable treaties and statutes". The Court emphasised, however, that "[170] it would vastly oversimplify the problem to say that nothing remains of the notion that reservation Indians are a separate people to whom state jurisdiction ... may not extend". As had been said in *United States v Kagama*, 118 US 375 (1886), the tribes remained "[381] semi-independent" – not "possessed of the full attributes of sovereignty", but "a separate people, with the power of regulating their internal and social relations" and to that extent immune from the operation of State or federal laws.

The tension between conceptions of tribal sovereignty as "inherent", and the view that it was derived from (and dependent on) treaties and statutes, was central to two cases decided in March 1978. In *Oliphant v Suquamish Indian Tribe*, 435 US 191 (1978), the Supreme Court held that the criminal jurisdiction of tribal courts did not extend to offences committed by non-Indians, even though the offences were committed on the reservation and were subversive of tribal law enforcement. (One case involved assault on a tribal policeman; another a drag race on reservation roads, ending in a collision with a tribal police car.) In dissent, Justice Marshall (joined by Chief Justice Burger) held "[212] that Indian tribes enjoy as a necessary aspect of their retained sovereignty the right to try and punish all persons who commit offenses against tribal law within the reservation". By contrast, the majority held that any historical instances of tribal jurisdiction over non-Indians had depended on "[197] a congressional statute or treaty provision to that effect", and that on *a priori* grounds this must necessarily be so: "[210] By submitting to the overriding sovereignty of the United States, Indian tribes ... necessarily give up their power to try non-Indian citizens ... except in a manner acceptable to Congress".

Two weeks later, in *United States v Wheeler*, 435 US 313 (1978), it was held that a conviction validly obtained in a Navajo Tribal Court did not preclude a subsequent prosecution for the same offence in a United States District Court – not because the Navajo conviction was in any way inferior, but precisely because its validity depended on inherent sovereignty. The double jeopardy clause of the Fifth Amendment does not apply to successive prosecutions by separate sovereigns; and that principle was applicable because "[328] the power to punish offenses against tribal law committed by Tribe members ... was part of the Navajos' primeval sovereignty". As such it had "never been taken away from them, either explicitly or implicitly, and is attributable in no way to any delegation to them of federal authority. It follows that when the Navajo Tribe exercises this power, it does so as part of its retained sovereignty and not as an arm of the Federal Government". Admittedly, the criminal jurisdiction of Indian courts had been *regulated* by federal legislation from time to time. "But none of these laws *created* the Indians' power to govern themselves and their right to punish crimes committed by tribal offenders ... That Congress has in certain ways regulated the manner and extent of the tribal power of self-government does not mean that Congress is the source of that power".

Santa Clara Pueblo v Martinez, 436 US 49 (1978), was a parallel to the Canadian case of *Attorney General of Canada v Lavell* [1974] SCR 1349, (1973) 38 DLR(3d) 481. A female member of the Santa Clara Pueblo tribe had challenged the validity of a tribal ordinance denying membership of the tribe to the children of women who married outside it. She based her claim on the *Indian Civil Rights Act 1968* (US), which subjected tribal powers of self-government to selected provisions of the Bill of Rights, including an "equal protection" clause modelled on that in the Fourteenth Amendment. The Bill of Rights itself could not apply directly: "[56] As separate sovereigns pre-existing the Constitution, tribes have historically been regarded as unconstrained by those constitutional provisions framed specifically as limitations on federal or state authority". Equally, the Supreme Court held that enforcement action under the *Indian Civil Rights Act* was barred by the tribe's sovereign immunity from suit. "[58] Indian tribes have long been recognized as possessing the common-law immunity from suit traditionally enjoyed by sovereign powers ... This aspect of tribal sovereignty, like all others, is subject to the superior and plenary control of Congress ... [59] [But in the absence] of any unequivocal expression of contrary legislative intent, we conclude that suits against the tribe under the [*Indian Civil Rights Act*] are barred by its sovereign immunity from suit". Similarly, the Court refused to find that the Act had impliedly created a cause of action against individual tribal officers, since this would "[64] undermine the authority of tribal forums", and "plainly ... be at odds with the congressional goal of protecting tribal self-government".

The assumption in *Oliphant* that the tribes' sovereignty is subject to inherent limitations, especially as against non-Indians, has since been developed in ways that have led some commentators to suggest that the principle of tribal sovereignty has again been significantly eroded (see, for example, Joseph Singer, "Canons of Conquest: The Supreme Court's Attack on Tribal Sovereignty" (2003) 37 *New England Law Review* 641). *Oliphant* dealt with the tribal courts' criminal jurisdiction; but later cases have set similar limits to the tribes' civil authority as well. Thus, in *Montana v United States*, 450 US 544 (1981), the Court held that the Crow Tribe of Montana had no power to regulate hunting and fishing by non-Indians on land owned by non-Indians, even when the land lay within the boundaries of the reservation. *Oliphant* was said to support "[565] the general proposition that the inherent sovereign powers of an Indian tribe do not extend to the activities of nonmembers of the tribe". The Court added, however, that the tribes' "inherent sovereign power" extended to "some forms of civil jurisdiction over non-Indians on their reservations", for example where the non-Indians concerned have "consensual relationships with the tribe or its members, through commercial dealing, contracts, leases, or other arrangements ... [566] A tribe may also retain inherent power to exercise civil authority over the conduct of non-Indians on fee lands within its reservation when that conduct threatens or has some direct effect on the political integrity, the economic security, or the health or welfare of the tribe".

In *Brendale v Confederated Tribes of Yakima Nation*, 492 US 408 (1989), it was held that a tribe has no power to impose its zoning laws on land owned by non-Indians, even when the land lies within the boundaries of the reservation and even though its exclusion from zoning makes coherent policies of land use impossible. The exception acknowledged in *Montana v United States* was now limited to extreme cases: "[431] The impact must be *demonstrably serious* and must *imperil* the political integrity, the economic security, or the health and welfare of the tribe" (emphasis added). In *Atkinson Trading Co v Shirley*, 532 US 645 (2001), it was held that the Navajo Nation could not impose a hotel occupancy tax on tourist rooms at a trading post whose owner was not an Indian, even though the trading post was located within the boundaries of the reservation, was dependent on Navajo police, fire and medical services, and employed about a hundred Navajo. The effect of *Montana v United States* was said to be that "[650] Indian tribe power over nonmembers on non-Indian fee land is sharply circumscribed ... [653] An Indian tribe's sovereign power to tax – whatever its derivation – reaches no further than tribal land". In *Strate v A-1 Contractors*, 520 US 438 (1997), the *Montana* approach to "regulatory authority" was extended to tribal court jurisdiction as well: "[453] As to nonmembers ... a tribe's adjudicative jurisdiction does not exceed its legislative jurisdiction". It was held that tribal law could not govern – and hence tribal courts could not determine – tort liability for a collision between non-Indian drivers on a state-owned road, although the road lay within the reservation and the tribe had an admitted interest in maintaining road safety there.

In all these cases, the fact that the tribe was not the owner of the land involved was treated as decisive; but in *Nevada v Hicks*, 533 US 353 (2001), that factor was effectively discarded. Three judges (Justices Souter, Kennedy and Thomas) read *Montana v United States* as laying down a general proposition "[377] that, at least as a presumptive matter, tribal courts lack civil jurisdiction over nonmembers", even when the actions complained of occurred on tribal land. That is, they thought that what was said in *Oliphant v Suquamish Indian Tribe* as to criminal jurisdiction should apply to civil jurisdiction as well. The formal Opinion of the Court took a narrower ground, confined to the particular facts of the case – a tort claim against State game wardens who had entered the reservation to conduct a search (with a search warrant from the tribal court) for evidence that a tribal Indian had been killing protected sheep. However, that opinion (written by Justice Scalia) also treated *Montana v United States* and *Strate v A-1 Contractors* as potentially excluding tribal jurisdiction even when activity on tribally owned land is involved: "[360] the existence of tribal ownership is not alone enough to support regulatory jurisdiction over non-members". Chief Justice Rehnquist joined in that opinion; Justice Ginsburg concurred in its result while emphasising that it left the general issues of tribal court jurisdiction unresolved; and three judges (Justices O'Connor, Stevens and Breyer) protested against a "[387] sweeping opinion [which], without cause, undermines the authority of tribes to 'make their own laws and be ruled by them'." They joined in the unanimous result on the ground that the lower courts had failed to consider whether the defendant game wardens were protected by official or qualified immunity.

The language used in these cases was equivocal: sometimes the persons held to lie beyond the reach of tribal sovereignty were referred to as "non-Indians", sometimes as "nonmembers of the tribe". For criminal cases the ambiguity was resolved by *Duro v Reina*, 495 US 676 (1990). Albert Duro was accused of killing a teenage boy on the Salt River Reservation in Arizona, the home of the Pima-Maricopa Indian Community. Duro was living on the reservation at the time, cohabiting with a Pima-Maricopa woman and working for a Pima-Maricopa construction company; but he was not a member of the tribe. He was an Indian, but came from California and belonged to a different tribe. When a federal indictment for murder was abandoned, he was brought before the Pima-Maricopa tribal court on a lesser charge (illegally firing a weapon on the reservation); but the Supreme Court held that the tribal jurisdiction was limited to members of the tribe. It was said that Indian tribes no longer possess "**[685]** full territorial sovereignty" ("the power to enforce laws against all who come within the sovereign's territory, whether citizens or aliens"), but only that degree of sovereignty that is "needed to control their own internal relations, and to preserve their own **[686]** unique customs and social order". The Court reaffirmed its recognition of "**[687]** broader retained tribal powers outside the criminal context", but thought that criminal jurisdiction should be more tightly controlled, since it "**[688]** involves a far more direct intrusion on personal liberties". Jurisdiction over tribal members was "**[694]** justified by the voluntary character of tribal membership and the concomitant right of participation in a tribal government, the authority of which rests on consent".

The result in *Duro v Reina* was immediately reversed by legislation. The statutory definition of tribal "powers of self-government" (United States Code Title 25, §1301(2)) was amended to include "the inherent power of Indian tribes, hereby recognized and affirmed, to exercise criminal jurisdiction over all Indians". In *United States v Lara*, 541 US 193 (2004), the Court accepted this amendment as valid. The legislation had been accompanied by repeated assertions that it did not confer a new power but merely recognised an inherent power. For example, Congressman George Miller (California) stated that the amendment "is not a delegation of authority", but "an affirmation that tribes retain all rights not expressly taken away"; it "recognizes an inherent tribal right which always existed" (137 *Congressional Record* 10712-14 (1991)). In *Lara*, however, the Court preferred to ascribe its validity to the legislative power of removing "judicially made" restrictions on the tribes' inherent authority.

The legislative response to *Duro v Reina* demonstrates that, whatever the fluctuations in judicial opinion, the recognition of tribal sovereignty has broad political acceptance. In April 1994, this was reaffirmed by a memorandum by President Bill Clinton.

Government-to-Government Relations with Native American Tribal Governments
(Presidential Memorandum for the Heads of Executive Departments and Agencies,
29 April 1994)

The United States Government has a unique legal relationship with Native American tribal governments as set forth in the Constitution of the United States, treaties, statutes, and court decisions. As executive departments and agencies undertake activities affecting Native American tribal rights or trust resources, such activities should be implemented in a knowledgeable, sensitive manner respectful of tribal sovereignty. Today ... I am outlining principles that executive departments and agencies, including every component bureau and office, are to follow in their interactions with Native American tribal governments. The purpose of these principles is to clarify our responsibility to ensure that the Federal Government operates within a government-to-government relationship with federally recognized Native American tribes. I am strongly committed to building a more effective day-to-day working relationship reflecting respect for the rights of self-government due the sovereign tribal governments.

In order to ensure that the rights of sovereign tribal governments are fully respected, executive branch activities shall be guided by the following:
(a) The head of each executive department and agency shall be responsible for ensuring that the department or agency operates within a government-to-government relationship with federally recognized tribal governments.
(b) Each executive department and agency shall consult, to the greatest extent practicable and to the extent permitted by law, with tribal governments prior to taking actions that affect federally recognized tribal governments. All such consultations are to be open and candid so

that all interested parties may evaluate for themselves the potential impact of relevant proposals.

(c)   Each executive department and agency shall assess the impact of Federal Government plans, projects, programs, and activities on tribal trust resources and assure that tribal government rights and concerns are considered during the development of such plans, projects, programs, and activities.

(d)   Each executive department and agency shall take appropriate steps to remove any procedural impediments to working directly and effectively with tribal governments on activities that affect the trust property and/ or governmental rights of the tribes.

(e)   Each executive department and agency shall work cooperatively with other Federal departments and agencies to enlist their interest and support in cooperative efforts, where appropriate, to accomplish the goals of this memorandum.

(f)   Each executive department and agency shall apply the requirements of Executive Orders Nos. 12875 ("Enhancing the Intergovernmental Partnership") and 12866 ("Regulatory Planning and Review") to design solutions and tailor Federal programs, in appropriate circumstances, to address specific or unique needs of tribal communities.

The head of each executive department and agency shall ensure that the department or agency's bureaus and components are fully aware of this memorandum, through publication or other means, and that they are in compliance with its requirements ...

THE WHITE HOUSE   William J Clinton

This policy is bipartisan. On 12 November 2001, in proclaiming the month of November as "National American Indian Heritage Month", President George W Bush affirmed that: "My Administration will continue to work with tribal governments on a sovereign to sovereign basis ... We will protect and honor tribal sovereignty and help to stimulate economic development in reservation communities. We will work with the American Indians and Alaska Natives to preserve their freedoms, as they practice their religion and culture".

Contemporary moves in Australia for some form of self-government to be granted to Indigenous peoples are unlikely to involve "government-to-government relations" on the United States model. Still less would they involve a return to what *McClanahan v Arizona Tax Commission* called "[172] platonic notions of ... sovereignty". As Larissa Behrendt has shown, demands for "sovereignty" have multiple meanings in Australian Indigenous discourse.

Larissa Behrendt, *Achieving Social Justice: Indigenous Rights and Australia's Future*
(Federation Press, 2003)

[87] Indigenous communities are diverse in culture and circumstance and therefore their needs are very different. Communities that are enclaves within urban areas, finding themselves a sub-group of a larger, non-Indigenous political unit, have different needs and strategies to those of Indigenous communities living in remote and distinct geographical areas where they may already be engaged in initiatives that can be categorised as decentralised self-governing actions. Aspirations will be specific to small communities – the need for a medical centre or a doctor, a school – but there is also a broader vision of the relationship that is sought within Australian society and its institutions ...

[94] One obstacle in the debate has been the confusion that surrounds the use of the word 'sovereignty'. It is a term that has become a [95] catch-phrase for indigenous people in expressing their vision for the future but a phrase that is met with confusion and suspicion from non-Indigenous people who understand the word only in its context under international law. They see the claim as radical, subversive and dangerous and they therefore strongly oppose it ...

This reminds me of something my father wrote [Paul Behrendt, "Aboriginal Sovereignty: Australian Republic: A Catalogue of Questions and Answers" in Irene Moores (ed), *The Voices of Aboriginal Australia: Past, Present, Future* (Butterfly Books, 1995) 399]:

It is an historical fact that from the very inception of British colonisation, the indigenous people of this country have been treated as a separate society. However, when we project this fact in our aim of achieving sovereignty and of our struggle for compensation for dispossession and for economic independence that will allow us to run our own affairs, people say 'You can't do that – it's divisive'.

[96] Very few activists have claimed that sovereignty embraces notions of statehood and succession … Others have put forward the notion of sovereignty as an option, stating quite clearly that it is but one option open to the Indigenous people …

Kevin Gilbert, the Aboriginal poet, artist and activist, was one of the strongest and most passionate advocates of sovereignty. In a draft treaty written in consultation with Aboriginal Members of the Sovereign Aboriginal Coalition at Alice Springs in 1987, Gilbert wrote the following points …:

    1.1.3 Our Sovereign Aboriginal Ownership, Possession and Sovereign Root Title to these our Land and our People have never been lost, removed or ceded in any form or manner by any *legal* act or claim …

    1.1.5 We are free to manage our own affairs both internally and externally to the fullest possible extent, in the proper exercise of our Sovereign Right as a Nation …

    1.1.7 Our Sovereign Aboriginal Nation, fulfilling the criteria of Statehood, having Inherent Possessory Root Title to Lands, a permanent population and a representative governing body according to our indigenous traditions, having the ability to enter relations with other States, possesses the right to autonomy in self-determination of our political status, to freely pursue our economic, social and cultural development and to retain our rights in religious matters, tradition and traditional practice.

[97] 1.1.8 We, the Sovereign Aboriginal People are to be accorded our right and proper recognition as a People and a Nation State, subjects of international law.

Gilbert and his co-authors envisaged a single Indigenous nation with the same status as other nations …

[98] [O]ther Indigenous people have used the concept … at a grass-roots community level …

Kerry Reed-Gilbert, activist and writer, describes with great passion the way in which the refusal to sign a treaty and the continual attempts, overt and subversive, by Indigenous people to resist the institutions of the dominant culture combine to show that the sovereignty of Indigenous Australians that existed in 1788 has not been eroded:

Sovereignty is us as a people being the prior owners of this country and never losing our sovereign rights as that people. Our own self-determination as black people has been going on 205 years after invasion. When Cook landed here as the first boat people he tried to [99] take our sovereign rights as the people of this country. But he never did. We have never lost our sovereign rights. And we've never lost our own need for self-determination … When you talk about self-determination and sovereignty, you are talking about our human rights, our rights as the owners of this land. Our sovereignty needs to be recognised. When it becomes recognised, people will start acknowledging that we have had, in our own way, self-determination for 205 years … When you see sovereignty, self-determination, equal rights, human rights, they are all empowered into that one thing. I see them as our basic needs. As the needs we have been fighting for.

Human rights, basic needs, decision-making processes, recognition of past injustice, sovereignty and self-determination all weave into Ms Reed-Gilbert's vision of sovereignty. Importantly, she believes that the recognition of sovereignty is a device by which other rights can be achieved. Rather than being the *aim* of political advocacy, it is a *starting point* for recognition of rights and inclusion in democratic processes. It is seen as a footing, a recognition, from which to demand those rights and transference of power from the Australian state, not a footing from which to separate from it …

[101] Through language that is as moral as it is political and legal, Indigenous people are attaching a unique interpretation to the term [102] sovereignty. It includes concepts such as representative government and democracy, the recognition of cultural distinctiveness and notions of the freedom of the individual that are embodied in liberalism …

What is most striking is the use of the word sovereignty amongst Indigenous people who have adopted the term devoid of its implications under international law ... In this popular appropriation of the word, political aspirations to the recognition of sovereignty include an aspiration to greater community autonomy but this falls short of advocating a separation from the Australian state ... It is acknowledged by members of the Indigenous community that their communities do not have the resources, infrastructure or desire to be separated from the Australian state. Instead, they need to be empowered to build that independence within pockets of Australia ...

[103] The use of the term sovereignty in Indigenous rights advocacy illustrates how a technical legal term can leak into the political rhetoric of a disadvantaged and alienated group, become a catch-phrase for political goals and transform into a word with a different meaning. In this way, language can actually confine a debate in the absence of a clear understanding by both parties as to what is meant by the lexicon of political terms being used. This highlights how a semantic block can occur when two sides in a debate have different understandings of the vocabulary they are using.

Elsewhere, Behrendt has written ("The Power We Bring: Indigenous Sovereignty and Self-Determination in the Treaty Process" (2002) 5 *Balayi* 1) "[4] that the right to self-determination includes the right not to be discriminated against, the rights to enjoy language, culture and heritage, our rights to land, seas, waters and natural resources, the right to be educated and to work, the right to be economically self sufficient, the right to be involved in decision-making processes that impact upon our lives and the right to govern and manage our own affairs in our own communities". The acceptance of these demands might involve a judicious drawing of lines, on the basis of negotiation between the governments and Indigenous peoples, between those matters appropriately regulated by State and Commonwealth laws, and those left to regulation by Indigenous customary law and self-government.

Such issues have been raised as part of the Australian "reconciliation" movement. The Council for Aboriginal Reconciliation was established in 1991 (by the *Council for Aboriginal Reconciliation Act 1991* (Cth)). The Council's vision for "[a] united Australia which respects this land of ours; values the Aboriginal and Torres Strait Islander heritage; and provides justice and equity for all" was expressed at its last major event "Corroborree 2000", a ceremony held at the Sydney Opera House on 27 May 2000. The following day an estimated 250,000 people walked across the Sydney Harbour Bridge in support of reconciliation, with similar bridge walks taking place around the nation. At the ceremony on 27 May, the Council released a "Roadmap for Reconciliation" and a draft Australian Declaration Towards Reconciliation, which all levels of Australian government were urged to adopt:

Draft Australian Declaration Towards Reconciliation

We, the peoples of Australia, of many origins as we are, make a commitment to go on together in a spirit of reconciliation.

We value the unique status of Aboriginal and Torres Strait Islander peoples as the original owners and custodians of lands and waters.

We recognise this land and its waters were settled as colonies without treaty or consent.

Reaffirming the human rights of all Australians, we respect and recognise continuing customary laws, beliefs and traditions.

Through understanding the spiritual relationship between the land and its first peoples, we share our future and live in harmony.

Our nation must have the courage to own the truth, to heal the wounds of its past so that we can move on together at peace with ourselves.

Reconciliation must live in the hearts and minds of all Australians. Many steps have been taken, many steps remain as we learn our shared histories.

As we walk the journey of healing, one part of the nation apologises and expresses its sorrow and sincere regret for the injustices of the past, so the other part accepts the apologies and forgives.

We desire a future where all Australians enjoy their rights, accept their responsibilities, and have the opportunity to achieve their full potential.

And so, we pledge ourselves to stop injustice, overcome disadvantage, and respect that Aboriginal and Torres Strait Islander peoples have the right to self-determination within the life of the nation.

Our hope is for a united Australia that respects this land of ours; values the Aboriginal and Torres Strait Islander heritage; and provides justice and equity for all.

However, in a press release on 11 May, some two weeks before "Corroborree 2000", Prime Minister John Howard indicated that despite "significant agreement ..., in several areas it has not been possible for the government to give its full support" to the draft of the Australian Declaration. Instead he released an alternative draft "to which the government would have given its full support". This involved the following changes:

First version	*Second version*
(Council for Aboriginal Reconciliation)	*(Australian government)*
Reaffirming the human rights of all Australians, we respect and recognise continuing customary laws, beliefs and traditions ...	Reaffirming the human rights of all Australians, we respect the cultures and beliefs of the nation's first people and recognise the place of traditional laws within these cultures ...
As we walk the journey of healing, one part of the nation apologises and expresses its sorrow and sincere regret for the injustices of the past, so the other part accepts the apologies and forgives.	As we walk the journey of healing, Australians express their sorrow and profoundly regret the injustices of the past and recognise the continuing trauma and hurt still suffered by many Aboriginals and Torres Strait Islanders.
We desire a future where all Australians enjoy their rights, accept their responsibilities, and have the opportunity to achieve their full potential.	We desire a future where all Australians enjoy equal rights, live under the same laws and share opportunities and responsibilities according to their aspirations.
And so, we pledge ourselves to stop injustice, overcome disadvantage, and respect that Aboriginal and Torres Strait Islander peoples have the right to self-determination within the life of the nation.	And so, we pledge ourselves to stop injustice, overcome disadvantage and respect the right of Aboriginal and Torres Strait Islander peoples, along with all Australians to determine their own destiny.
Our hope is for a united Australia that respects this land of ours; values the Aboriginal and Torres Strait Islander heritage; and provides justice and equity for all.	*(Final paragraph omitted)*

The Prime Minister's press release explained that: "The areas of difference relate to customary law, the general application of the laws of Australia to all citizens, self determination and a national apology as distinct from an expression of sorrow and sincere regret". It emphasised that, despite these differences, "there is common ground ... on most of the sentiments contained in the document", and a "common commitment to the process of reconciliation".

The Council's Roadmap for Reconciliation comprised four "National Strategies": Overcoming Disadvantage; Achieving Economic Independence; Sustaining the Reconciliation Process; and Recognising Aboriginal and Torres Strait Islander Rights. In the last of these, the Council reaffirmed its view of Aboriginal self-determination.

Council for Aboriginal Reconciliation, *Recognising Aboriginal and Torres Strait Islander Rights*
(AGPS, 2000)

[14] When Australia was colonised, Aboriginal and Torres Strait Islander peoples occupied the entire continent, with their own political and legal and social systems. Yet, Aboriginal and Torres Strait Islander peoples never had the opportunity to participate in the nation-building surrounding

federation. For Aboriginal and Torres Strait Islander peoples, however, the need to negotiate this relationship is central to their aspirations. It is often referred to in terms of self-determination.

The meaning of self-determination is often confused by references to secession and separate statehood, but such references are unfairly inflammatory and do not reflect Aboriginal and Torres Strait Islander aspirations. Self-determination is much more about the process of decision-making. It reflects the need for Aboriginal and Torres Strait Islander peoples to negotiate a relationship with the Australian government, which may lead to many outcomes that have the potential to enhance rather th[a]n undermine our sense of national unity. It also reflects the kind of autonomy and decision-making that is already being exercised by communities who take responsibility for the delivery of services or programs. That is, self-determination is reflected in the recognition by governments of Aboriginal and Torres Strait Islander peoples['] right to exercise a sphere of authority and responsibility and the communities' exercise of that right.

In international law self-determination is 'the right of all peoples to freely determine their political status and to pursue their own economic, social and cultural development'. It has its origins in the theory of self-government – that a society should be able to determine for themselves how they are to be governed and to make the decisions that directly affect them.

The right to self-determination is a fundamental principle of international human rights and is included as the first Article of both the United Nations International Covenants on Civil and Political Rights and Economic, Social and Cultural Rights (the ICCPR and ICESCR). It is often associated with the relationship between states in the international sphere but it also has many other facets that operate within nation states, particularly where countries are made up of a number of different peoples. In recent years, it has been specifically acknowledged that Aboriginal and Torres Strait Islander peoples should freely exercise this right.

Australia has a sophisticated approach to the division of authority and responsibility to various levels of government in our federal structure as well as through our system of local government. With respect to Aboriginal and [15] Torres Strait Islander peoples, too, there are some models of self-determination and empowerment already existing in Australia, for example in the Torres Strait or in the system of Local Aboriginal Councils, where regional self-government is evolving.

The Council supports self-determination as the guiding principle for government policy on Aboriginal and Torres Strait Islander affairs at all levels.

Actions for implementation

A. Governments at all levels acknowledge Aboriginal and Torres Strait Islander peoples' right to self-determination as the basis for policy on Aboriginal and Torres Strait Islander affairs.

B. Governments at all levels enter into negotiations with Aboriginal and Torres Strait Islander peoples in order to realise self-determination goals.

C. Commonwealth government, ATSIC and Reconciliation Australia work together to promote discussion and education on the meaning of self-determination in the context of Aboriginal and Torres Strait Islander peoples.

The Council's final report dealt mainly with the need for education and community awareness. It made the following final recommendations.

Council for Aboriginal Reconciliation, *Reconciliation: Australia's Challenge*
(AGPS, 2000)

[105] **1.** The Council of Australian Governments (COAG) agree to implement and monitor a national framework whereby all governments and the Aboriginal and Torres Strait Islander Commission (ATSIC) work to overcome Aboriginal and Torres Strait Islander peoples' disadvantage through setting program performance benchmarks that are measurable (including timelines), are agreed in partnership with Aboriginal and Torres Strait Islander peoples and communities, and are publicly reported.

2. All parliaments and local governments pass formal motions of support for the Australian Declaration Towards Reconciliation and the Roadmap for Reconciliation, enshrine their basic principles in appropriate legislation, and determine how their key recommendations can best be implemented in their jurisdictions.

3. The Commonwealth Parliament prepare legislation for a referendum which seeks to:

- recognise Aboriginal and Torres Strait Islander peoples as the first peoples of Australia in a new preamble to the Constitution; and
- remove section 25 of the Constitution and introduce a new section making it unlawful to adversely discriminate against any people on the grounds of race.

[106] 4. Recognising that the formal reconciliation process over the last decade has achieved much and has helped bring Australians together, all levels of government, non-government, business, peak bodies, communities and individuals commit themselves to continuing the process and sustaining it by:

- affirming the Australian Declaration Towards Reconciliation and actioning the Roadmap for Reconciliation;
- providing resources for reconciliation activities and involving Aboriginal and Torres Strait Islander peoples in their work;
- undertaking educational and public-awareness activities to help improve understanding and relations between Aboriginal and Torres Strait Islander peoples and the wider community; and
- supporting Reconciliation Australia, the foundation which has been established to maintain a national leadership focus for reconciliation, report on progress, provide information and raise funds to promote and support reconciliation.

5. Each government and parliament:

- recognise that this land and its waters were settled as colonies without treaty or consent and that to advance reconciliation it would be most desirable if there were agreements or treaties; and
- negotiate a process through which this might be achieved that protects the political, legal, cultural and economic position of Aboriginal and Torres Strait Islander peoples.

6. That the Commonwealth Parliament enact legislation (for which the Council has provided a draft in this report) to put in place a process which will unite all Australians by way of an agreement, or treaty, through which unresolved issues of reconciliation can be resolved.

In January 2001 a non-government, non-profit foundation was established under the name Reconciliation Australia to provide a continuing national focus for reconciliation. On 27 May 2004 – the fourth anniversary of "Corroborree 2000" – a ceremony was held on the Sydney Harbour Bridge to lay a plaque commemorating the bridge walks of May 2000, and to launch a new program under the title "Pathways to Reconciliation". This was designed to encourage the laying of local "pathways" by local councils, schools, workplaces and community groups, building up to a National Reconciliation Pathway in Reconciliation Place on Ngunnawal land in Canberra. The laying of the National Pathway began a year later on 29 May 2005.

Most of the recommendations of the Council for Aboriginal Reconciliation have yet to be implemented. The lack of action was the subject of an inquiry by the Senate Legal and Consti-tutional References Committee, which in its final report, *Reconciliation: Off Track* (Parliamentary Paper No 207 of 2003), urged governments to implement the recommendations in full. However, events have moved on. Most significantly, ATSIC, a national body of elected Indigenous representatives with a major role in policy-making and service delivery, was abolished in March 2005 by the *Aboriginal and Torres Strait Islander Commission Amendment Act 2005* (Cth). Its functions were transferred to other government departments, and ATSIC itself was replaced by the National Indigenous Council, an advisory body composed of government appointees.

On the other hand, in 2004 an acknowledgment of Indigenous peoples was added to the Victorian Constitution. After a preamble that gives an account of the creation of self-government in Victoria, the Constitution provides:

Constitution Act 1975 (Vic)

1A Recognition of Aboriginal people

(1) The Parliament acknowledges that the events described in the preamble to this Act occurred without proper consultation, recognition or involvement of the Aboriginal people of Victoria.

(2) The Parliament recognises that Victoria's Aboriginal people, as the original custodians of the land on which the Colony of Victoria was established—

    (a)   have a unique status as the descendants of Australia's first people; and

    (b)   have a spiritual, social, cultural and economic relationship with their traditional lands and waters within Victoria; and

    (c)   have made a unique and irreplaceable contribution to the identity and well-being of Victoria.

(3) The Parliament does not intend by this section—

    (a)   to create in any person any legal right or give rise to any civil cause of action; or

    (b)   to affect in any way the interpretation of this Act or of any other law in force in Victoria.

Similarly, the new preamble to the Australian Constitution proposed at the 1999 referendum spoke of "honouring Aborigines and Torres Strait Islanders, the nation's first people, for their deep kinship with their lands and for their ancient and continuing cultures which enrich the life of our country". However, the preamble was rejected along with the proposal for an Australian republic (see Chapter 30, §3).

Attention has also focused on the Council's recommendation for an "agreement, or treaty, through which unresolved issues of reconciliation can be resolved". Australia is the only Commonwealth nation that does not have a treaty with its Indigenous peoples. New Zealand, for example, has the *Te Tiriti o Waitangi* (the Treaty of Waitangi), an agreement signed in 1840 between the British Crown and over 500 Maori chiefs, while Canada and the United States have hundreds of treaties dating back as far as the 1600s. In the United States, the Indian tribes entered into treaty relationships for "as long as the rivers run and grass shall grow", and many still seek to hold governments to those agreements. In Canada, the *Constitution Act 1982* (Can) grants protection to similar agreements. Section 35(1) provides that: "The existing aboriginal and treaty rights of the aboriginal peoples of Canada are hereby recognized and affirmed", while ("for greater certainty") s 35(3) stipulates that "'treaty rights' includes rights that now exist by way of land claims agreements or may be so acquired".

Canada also has a contemporary record of treaty-making between First Nations and governments. For example, after a 25-year process the Nisga'a Agreement came into effect in 2000. It involved a substantial cash settlement (C$190 million) and established the Nisga'a Lisims government, with ownership of over 1900 square kilometres of land and entitlements to fish stocks and wildlife harvests. By comparison, in 1999 the new self-governing Territory of Nunavut was created in the far north of Canada, where 85 per cent of the population is Inuit. In that case, agreement was reached upon a more open public model of government rather than an exclusively Indigenous form of self-government. It is likely that more treaties will be concluded in the coming years, particularly in the western Province of British Columbia where few treaties were made during the early years of colonisation.

Sean Brennan, Larissa Behrendt, Lisa Strelein and George Williams, *Treaty*
(Federation Press, 2005)

[98] The experiences of the United States, Canada and New Zealand with treaty-making might lead a person to reject the idea of a treaty **[99]** for Australia because in each case Indigenous peoples continue to suffer from deep-seated socio-economic problems and their rights and interests have often not been protected. These are valid concerns that reflect the limits of what a treaty might achieve. Certainly, a treaty is not an easy answer to the wide range of problems that continue to beset Indigenous peoples in post-colonial countries around the world. These are issues that no legal instrument, by itself, can remedy.

Despite the limitations of a treaty, these countries do show that such instruments can have a subtle and profoundly important impact. They can introduce notions of rights and sovereignty into the dialogue between Indigenous and non-Indigenous people in a way that can affect the outcomes of that discussion. The denial of inherent Indigenous rights was more vehement and long-standing in Australia. Rights have also been seen in a more holistic way in those countries as a result of treaties. Thus, when native title was found to exist as part of the common law in Canada, its extension to hunting and fishing rights was readily accepted because treaties had always emphasised the inter-relationship between land and the livelihood of Indigenous people. Similar understandings of rights to fish in New Zealand and rights to water in the United States show how treaties can promote an appreciation of the connection between land and aspirations to self-government and economic self-sufficiency.

In each of the three countries, the idea of treaty-making continues to shape contemporary relationships. With processes in each country that allow for the enforcement and, in Canada, the negotiation and re-negotiation of treaties, there is more accountability by governments for the promises made in treaty documents (even where such treaties have been ignored in the past). This has provided opportunities for economic activity such as through the protection of rights to hunt and fish, exemptions from State or provincial taxes and an ability to engage in commercial activity on Aboriginal land ...

[100] What specific lessons then can Australia learn from these countries and their history? First, each of these countries has accommodated some notion of shared sovereignty, fundamental relationship or government-to-government dealings within a constitutional structure that has many similarities to our own. Each has achieved this without undermining that structure. In each case this reflects a recognition of the special status of Indigenous peoples as the first peoples of a country. Although there are debates about the rights that flow from that status, there is at least recognition of an agreement to co-exist.

Second, we should not romanticise the treaty experience of these other countries. The contemporary treaty-making process in Canada is slow, complex and expensive. In many earlier instances, treaties were negotiated in circumstances of duress and their provisions have been breached repeatedly. Criticisms of the content and implementation of treaties come from all sides of the debate in each country. In these circumstances, the treaties themselves provide more a means of managing conflict than removing disagreement altogether. Adopting a treaty approach in Australia involves acceptance that it brings its own problems and shortcomings. It underlines the need for public debate and a hard-headed assessment of both treaty-making and the alternatives.

Third, a treaty is only as good as the underlying relationship and the preparedness of each side to honour its commitments. Without this, there is a risk that treaties can become a dead letter, or worse give a false impression of the true state of affairs.

Fourth, each country shows that treaties can have enduring political, legal and cultural significance. Indigenous peoples in the United States, Canada and New Zealand typically regard treaties as important continuing agreements negotiated and entered into in good faith. They are agreements embodying principles, rights and responsibilities they can seek to hold governments to. For the Indigenous nations that signed them, they remain documents negotiated in the exercise of their sovereignty. In this context, a treaty can be seen as an attempt to express in legal terms the unique relationship between the coloniser and the colonised. History shows that even if the quality and mutuality of the relationship has deteriorated over decades, even centuries, the relationship can be revisited and its health restored. Treaties new or old can play a role in that renaissance.

Fifth, a modern treaty-making process, especially in a federation like Australia, will require the resolution of a range of technical and procedural issues. These include:

[101] • Who will be parties to the negotiations?
   • What processes will be adopted?
   • Will there be an umpire and enforceable rules while the parties are negotiating?
   • What legal effect will the outcome have? and
   • How will it all be financed?

Sixth, principles of interpretation are needed to help give legal force to treaty provisions. The experience of all three countries suggests that such principles can and should take account of how each side understands the terms of the agreement.

Seventh, treaties are only ever one part of the picture. In Canada, the United States and New Zealand the legal position of Indigenous peoples within the state continues to be shaped by constitutions, bills of rights, legislation, court decisions and government action. Treaties are an important way, but only one way, by which Indigenous peoples can seek to assert their rights and to define their place in modern Western states.

Finally, treaties can play a positive role in promoting economic development and tackling social problems in Indigenous communities. For example, as Canadians have become more comfortable with comprehensive agreement-making, they have come to see the value of incorporating self-government provisions that recognise Indigenous jurisdiction. Empirical research into successful social and economic development within Indigenous communities supports the wisdom of this approach.

It should be kept in mind that, just as the dispossession of Indigenous peoples has been a long and drawn-out historical process, so their struggle for redress may need to be seen in a similarly long-term perspective, with *Mabo (No 2)* merely the first tentative step. Consider, for example, the history of the Sioux claim to the Black Hills of Dakota in the United States. The Fort Laramie Treaty of 1868 had recognised the claim, and an area including the Black Hills had been set aside for the absolute and undisturbed use and occupation of the Sioux. But in 1876 the Sioux were called upon to accept a new treaty relinquishing their rights to the Black Hills in exchange for subsistence rations; and, although only 10 per cent of adult male Sioux were persuaded to sign the treaty, in 1877 Congress enacted it into law.

In 1920, the Sioux lodged a claim for compensation in the Court of Claims after special legislation was enacted enabling them to do so. In 1942, the claim was dismissed: the Court held that it could not question the adequacy of the compensation provided by Congress in 1877, and that the compensation clause of the Fifth Amendment to the United States Constitution had no application. In 1946, Congress created an Indian Claims Commission, which reheard and upheld the Sioux claim; but on appeal the Court of Claims held that compensation was barred by the operation (as *res judicata*) of its own 1942 decision. In 1978, Congress legislated again to authorise a further hearing; and on that basis, in 1980, the Court of Claims finally upheld the claim (*United States v Sioux Nation of Indians*, 65 L Ed 2d 844 (1980)), and awarded compensation of $17.1 million, with interest to run from 1877. This brought the total sum awarded to $106 million.

At this stage, however, the Sioux refused to accept the award, since they recognised that acceptance of the money would permanently extinguish their title. Instead, they resolved to go on fighting for the return of their lands. Already, before the case was decided, six of the eight Sioux tribes had informed the Court that they no longer wanted a monetary settlement; and when the award was nonetheless made, the six tribes unsuccessfully appealed. Since 1980, the interest on the judgment fund has continued to accrue, bringing the current total to over $600 million. Meanwhile, the Sioux continue to fight for the return of their lands.

7. Further References

Anaya, J, *Indigenous Peoples in International Law* (Oxford University Press, 2nd ed 2004).

Attwood, B, and Markus, A, *The 1967 Referendum, or When Aborigines Didn't Get the Vote* (Australian Institute of Aboriginal and Torres Strait Islander Studies, 1997).

Behrendt, L, "Mind, Body and Spirit: Pathways Forward for Reconciliation" (2001) 5 *Newcastle Law Review* 38.

Brennan, F, "The Indigenous People" in Finn, PD, *Essays on Law and Government: Principles and Values* (Law Book Co, 1995) vol 1, 33.

Brennan, F, *Securing a Bountiful Place for Aborigines and Torres Strait Islanders in a Modern, Free and Tolerant Australia* (Constitutional Centenary Foundation, 1994).

Brennan, S, "Native Title in the High Court of Australia a Decade after Mabo" (2003) 14 *Public Law Review* 209.

Brennan, S, "Reconciliation in Australia: The Relationship between Indigenous Peoples and the Wider Community" (2004) 11 *Brown Journal of World Affairs* 149.

Brennan, S, Gunn, B, and Williams, G, "'Sovereignty' and its Relevance to Treaty-Making between Indigenous Peoples and Australian Governments" (2004) 26 *Sydney Law Review* 307.

Brookfield, FM, *Waitangi and Indigenous Rights: Revolution, Law and Legitimation* (Auckland University Press, 1999).

Chesterman, J, and Philips, D (eds), *Selective Democracy: Race, Gender and the Australian Vote* (Melbourne Publishing Group, 2003).

Dodson, M, and Strelein, L, "Australia's Nation-Building: Renegotiating the Relationship between Indigenous Peoples and the State" (2001) 24 *University of New South Wales Law Journal* 826.

Hannum, H, *Autonomy, Sovereignty, and Self Determination* (University of Pennsylvania Press, 1990).

Hookey, J, "The Gove Lands Rights Case: A Judicial Dispensation for the Taking of Aboriginal Lands in Australia?" (1972) 5 *Federal Law Review* 85.

Jonas, W, "Unfinished Business – The Recognition of Aboriginal and Torres Strait Islander Rights" (2001) 5 *Newcastle Law Review* 53.

Jull, P, and Kajlich, H, "First Peoples, Late Admissions: Recognising Indigenous Rights" in Sampford, C, and Round, T (eds), *Beyond the Republic: Meeting the Global Challenges to Constitutionalism* (Federation Press, 2001), 257.

Keon-Cohen, BA, "The Mabo Litigation: A Personal and Procedural Account" (2000) 24 *Melbourne University Law Review* 893.

Langton, M, Tehan, M, Palmer, L, and Shain, K (eds), *Honour among Nations? Treaties and Agreements with Indigenous People* (Melbourne University Press, 2004).

Mansell, M, "Australians and Aborigines and the Mabo Decision: Just Who Needs Whom the Most?" in *Essays on the Mabo Decision* (Law Book Co, 1993), 48.

McIntyre, G, and Doohan, K, "Labels, Language and Native Title Groups: The Miriuwung-Gajerrong Case" in Henderson, J, and Nash, D (eds), *Language in Native Title* (Australian Institute of Aboriginal and Torres Strait Islander Studies, 2002), 187.

McNeil, K, *Common Law Aboriginal Title* (Clarendon Press, 1989).

McNeil, K, "The Vulnerability of Indigenous Land Rights in Australia and Canada" (2004) 42 *Osgoode Hall Law Journal* 271.

Nettheim, G, "Indigenous Australian Constitutions" (2001) 24 *University of New South Wales Law Journal* 840.

Nettheim, G, "Making a Difference: Reconciling Our Differences" (2001) 5 *Newcastle Law Review* 3.

Patapan, H, *Judging Democracy: The New Politics of the High Court of Australia* (Cambridge University Press, 2000), Ch 5.

Reynolds, H, *Aboriginal Sovereignty: Reflections on Race, State and Nation* (Allen & Unwin, 1996).

Reynolds, H, *The Law of the Land* (Penguin, 2004).

Russell, PH, *Recognizing Aboriginal Title: The Mabo Case and Indigenous Resistance to English-Settler Colonialism* (University of Toronto Press, 2005).

Sawer, G, "The Australian Constitution and the Australian Aborigine" (1966) 2 *Federal Law Review* 17.

Stephenson, MA, and Ratnapala, S (eds), *Mabo: A Judicial Revolution* (University of Queensland Press, 1993).

Sutton, P, *Native Title in Australia: An Ethnographic Perspective* (Cambridge University Press, 2003).

Tehan, M, "A Hope Disillusioned, an Opportunity Lost? Reflections on Common Law Native Title and Ten Years of the *Native Title Act*" (2003) 27 *Melbourne University Law Review* 253.

"Treaty: Let's Get it Right", Special Edition (2002) 4 *Balayi: Culture Law and Colonialism*.

Williams, G, "Race and the Australian Constitution: From Federation to Reconciliation" (2000) 38 *Osgoode Hall Law Journal* 643.

Chapter 6

The Federal System

1. Federalism

Federalism is a two-tiered system of government in which power is divided between the central and the state or regional governments. Australian federalism adheres closely to the American model. However, in their understanding of that model, the Australian framers were heavily influenced by the writings of two British observers – Albert Dicey (1835-1922) and his friend and protégé James Bryce (1838-1922), who first visited the United States together in 1870.

AV Dicey, *Introduction to the Study of the Law of the Constitution*
(Macmillan, 1st ed 1885, 10th ed 1959)

[140] A federal state requires for its formation two conditions.

[141] There must exist, in the first place, a body of countries such as the Cantons of Switzerland, the Colonies of America, or the Provinces of Canada, so closely connected by locality, by history, by race, or the like, as to be capable of bearing, in the eyes of their inhabitants, an impress of common nationality. It will also be generally found (if we appeal to experience) that lands which now form part of a federal state were at some stage of their existence bound together by close alliance or by subjection to a common sovereign ... [We cannot] assert that this earlier connection is essential to the formation of a federal state. But it is certain that where federalism flourishes it is in general the slowly-matured fruit of some earlier and looser connection.

A second condition absolutely essential to the founding of a federal system is the existence of a very peculiar state of sentiment among the inhabitants of the countries which it is proposed to unite. They must desire union, and must not desire unity ... **[142]** The phase of sentiment, in short, which forms a necessary condition for the formation of a federal state is that the people of the proposed state should wish to form for many purposes a single nation, yet should not wish to surrender the individual existence of each man's State or Canton. We may perhaps go a little farther, and say, that a federal government will hardly be formed unless many of the inhabitants of the separate States feel stronger allegiance to their own State than to the federal state represented by the common government. This was certainly the case in America towards the end of the eighteenth century, and in Switzerland at the middle of the nineteenth century. In 1787 a Virginian or a citizen of Massachusetts felt a far stronger attachment to Virginia or to Massachusetts than to the body of the confederated States ... The sentiment therefore which creates a federal state is the prevalence throughout the citizens of more or less allied countries of two feelings which are to a certain extent inconsistent – **[143]** the desire for national unity and the determination to maintain the independence of each man's separate State. The aim of federalism is to give effect as far as possible to both these sentiments.

A federal state is a political contrivance intended to reconcile national unity and power with the maintenance of "state rights." The end aimed at fixes the essential character of federalism. For the method by which Federalism attempts to reconcile the apparently inconsistent claims of national sovereignty and of state sovereignty consists of the formation of a constitution under which the ordinary powers of sovereignty are elaborately divided between the common or national government and the separate states. The details of this division vary under every different federal constitution, but the general principle on which it should rest is obvious. Whatever concerns the nation as a whole should be placed under the control of the national government. All matters which are not primarily of common interest should remain in the hands of the several States …

[144] A federal state derives its existence from the constitution, just as a corporation derives its existence from the grant by which it is created. Hence, every power, executive, legislative, or judicial, whether it belong to the nation or to the individual States, is subordinate to and controlled by the constitution. Neither the President of the United States nor the Houses of Congress, nor the Governor of Massachusetts, nor the Legislature or General Court of Massachusetts, can legally exercise a single power which is inconsistent with the articles of the constitution. This doctrine of the supremacy of the constitution is familiar to every American, but in England even trained lawyers find a difficulty in following it out to its legitimate consequences. The difficulty arises from the fact that under the English constitution no principle is recognised which bears any real resemblance to the doctrine (essential to federalism) that the Constitution constitutes the "supreme law of the land." …

[146] In the supremacy of the constitution are involved three consequences:–

The constitution must almost necessarily be a "written" constitution.

The foundations of a federal state are a complicated contract. This compact contains a variety of terms which have been agreed to, and generally after mature deliberation, by the States which make up the confederacy. To base an arrangement of this kind upon understandings or conventions would be certain to generate misunderstandings and disagreements. The articles of the treaty, or in other words of the constitution, must therefore be reduced to writing. The constitution must be a written document, and, if possible, a written document of which the terms are open to no misapprehension …

The constitution must be what I have termed a "rigid" or "inexpansive" constitution.

The law of the constitution must be either legally immutable, or else capable of being changed only by [147] some authority above and beyond the ordinary legislative bodies, whether federal or state legislatures, existing under the constitution …

It is, at any rate, certain that whenever the founders of a federal government hold the maintenance of a federal system to be of primary importance, supreme [148] legislative power cannot be safely vested in any ordinary legislature acting under the constitution. For so to vest legislative sovereignty would be inconsistent with the aim of federalism … If Congress could legally change the constitution, New York and Massachusetts would have no legal guarantee for the amount of independence reserved to them under the constitution, and would be as subject to the sovereign power of Congress as is Scotland to the sovereignty of Parliament; the Union would cease to be a federal state, and would become a unitarian republic. If, on the other hand, the legislature of South Carolina could of its own will amend the constitution, the authority of the central government would (from a legal point of view) be illusory; the United States would sink from a nation into a collection of independent countries united by the bond of a more or less permanent alliance. Hence the power of amending the constitution has been placed, so to speak, outside the constitution, and one may say, with sufficient accuracy for our present purpose, that the legal sovereignty of the United States resides in the States' governments as forming one aggregate body [149] represented by three-fourths of the several States at any time belonging to the Union … A federal constitution is capable of change, but for all that a federal constitution is apt to be unchangeable.

Every legislative assembly existing under a federal [150] constitution is merely a subordinate law-making body, whose laws are of the nature of by-laws, valid whilst within the authority conferred upon it by the constitution, but invalid or unconstitutional if they go beyond the limits of such authority …

[151] The distribution of powers is an essential feature of federalism. The object for which a federal state is formed involves a division of authority between the national government and the separate States. The powers given to the nation form in effect so many limitations upon the authority of the separate States, and as it is not intended that the central government should have

the opportunity of encroaching upon the rights retained by the States, its sphere of action necessarily becomes the object of rigorous definition. The constitution, for instance, of the United States delegates special and closely defined powers to the executive, to the legislature, and to the judiciary of the Union, or in effect to the Union itself, whilst it **[152]** provides that the powers "not delegated to the United States by the constitution nor prohibited by it to the States are reserved to the States respectively or to the people." ...

[158] The legal supremacy of the constitution is essential to the existence of the state; the glory of the founders of the United States is to have devised or adopted arrangements under which the constitution became in reality as well as name the supreme law of the land. This end they attained by ... a very obvious principle, and by the invention of appropriate machinery for carrying this principle into effect.

The principle is clearly expressed in the Constitution of the United States. "This constitution," runs article 6, "and the laws of the United States which shall be made in pursuance thereof ... shall be the supreme law of the land, and the judges in every State shall be bound thereby, anything in the constitution or laws of any State to the contrary notwithstanding." The import of these expressions is unmistakable. "Every Act of Congress," writes Chancellor Kent, "and every Act of the legislatures of the States, and every part of the constitution of any State, which are repugnant to the Constitution of the United States, are necessarily void. This is a clear and settled principle of [our] constitutional jurisprudence." The legal duty therefore of every judge, whether he act as a judge of the State of New York or as a judge of the Supreme Court of the United States, is clear. He is bound to treat as void every legislative act, whether proceeding from Congress or from the state legis-**[159]**-latures, which is inconsistent with the Constitution of the United States ...

To have laid down the principle with distinctness is much, but the great problem was how to ensure that the principle should be obeyed; for there existed a danger that judges depending on the federal government should wrest the constitution in favour of the central power, and that judges created by the States should wrest it in favour of State rights or interests. This problem has been solved by the creation of the Supreme Court and of the Federal Judiciary ...

[171] Our survey from a legal point of view of the characteristics common to all federal governments forcibly suggests conclusions of more than merely legal interest, as to the comparative merits of federal government, and the system of Parliamentary sovereignty.

Federal government means weak government.

The distribution of all the powers of the state among co-ordinate authorities necessarily leads to the **[172]** result that no one authority can wield the same amount of power as under a unitarian constitution is possessed by the sovereign. A scheme again of checks and balances in which the strength of the common government is so to speak pitted against that of the state governments leads, on the face of it, to a certain waste of energy. A federation therefore will always be at a disadvantage in a contest with unitarian states of equal resources ... **[173]** Hence a federal government can hardly render services to the nation by undertaking for the national benefit functions which may be performed by individuals. This may be a merit of the federal system; it is, however, a merit which does not commend itself to modern democrats, and no more curious instance can be found of the inconsistent currents of popular opinion which may at the same time pervade a nation or a generation than the coincidence in England of a vague admiration for federalism alongside with a far more decided feeling against the doctrines of so-called *laissez faire*. A system meant to maintain the *status quo* in politics is incompatible with schemes for wide social innovation.

Federalism tends to produce conservatism.

This tendency is due to several causes. The constitution of a Federal state must, as we have seen, generally be not only a written but a rigid constitution, that is, a constitution which cannot be changed by any ordinary process of legislation. Now this essential rigidity of federal institutions is almost certain to impress on the minds of citizens the idea that any provision included in the constitution is immutable and, so to speak, sacred. The least observation of American politics shows how deeply the notion **[174]** that the constitution is something placed beyond the reach of amendment has impressed popular imagination. The difficulty of altering the constitution produces conservative sentiment, and national conservatism doubles the difficulty of altering the constitution ...

[175] Federalism, lastly, means legalism – the predominance of the judiciary in the constitution – the prevalence of a spirit of legality among the people.

That in a confederation like the United States the courts become the pivot on which the constitutional arrangements of the country turn is obvious. Sovereignty is lodged in a body which rarely exerts its authority and has (so to speak) only a potential existence; no legislature throughout the land is more than a subordinate law-making body capable in strictness of enacting nothing but by-laws; the powers of the executive are again limited by the constitution; the interpreters of the constitution are the judges. The Bench therefore can and must determine the limits to the authority both of the government and of the legislature; its decision is without appeal; the consequence follows that the Bench of judges is not only the guardian but also at a given moment the master of the constitution.

James Bryce, *The American Commonwealth*
(Macmillan, 1st ed 1888, 3rd ed 1908)

[312] The contests in the Convention of 1787 over the framing of the Constitution, and in the country over its adoption, turned upon two points: the extent to which the several States should be recognized as independent and separate factors in the construction of the National government, and the quantity and nature of the powers which should be withdrawn from the States to be vested in that government ... [S]ince 1791 there has been practically no dispute as to the former point, and little as to the propriety of the provisions which define the latter. On the interpretation of these provisions there has, however, been endless debate, some deeming the Constitution to have taken more from the States, some less; while still warmer controversies have raged as to ... whether the States retain their sovereignty, and with it the right of nullify-**[313]**-ing or refusing to be bound by certain acts of the national government, and in the last resort of withdrawing from the Union. As these latter questions ... have now been settled by the Civil War, we may say that in the America of today there exists a general agreement –

That every State on entering the Union finally renounced its sovereignty, and is now for ever subject to the Federal authority as defined by the Constitution.

That the functions of the States as factors of the national government are satisfactory, *ie* sufficiently secure its strength and the dignity of these communities.

That the delimitation of powers between the national government and the States, contained in the Constitution, is convenient, and needs no fundamental alteration ...

I. The distribution of powers between the National and the State governments is effected in two ways – Positively, by conferring certain powers on the National government; Negatively, by imposing certain restrictions on the States. It would have been superfluous to confer any powers on the States, because they retain all powers not actually taken from them. A lawyer may think that it was equally unnecessary and, so to speak, inartistic, to lay any prohibitions on the National government, because it could *ex hypothesi* exercise no powers not expressly granted. However, the anxiety of the States to fetter the master they were giving themselves caused the introduction of provisions qualifying the grant of express powers, and interdicting the National government from various kinds of action on which it might otherwise have been tempted to enter. **[314]** The matter is further complicated by the fact that the grant of power to the National government is not in all cases an exclusive grant: *ie* there are matters which both, or either, the States and the National government may deal with ...

[315] II. The powers vested in the National government alone are such as relate to the conduct of the foreign relations of the country and to such common national purposes as the army and navy, internal commerce, currency, weights and measures, and **[316]** the post-office, with provisions for the management of the machinery, legislative, executive, and judicial, charged with these purposes.

The powers which remain vested in the States alone are all the other ordinary powers of internal government, such as legislation on private law, civil and criminal, the maintenance of law and order, the creation of local institutions, the provision for education and the relief of the poor, together with taxation for the above purposes ...

[318] VI. The powers vested in each State are all of them original and inherent powers, which belonged to the State before it entered the Union. Hence they are *prima facie* unlimited, and if a question arises as to any particular power, it is presumed to be enjoyed by the State, unless it can be shown to have been taken away by the Federal Constitution; or, in other words, a State is not deemed to be subject to any restriction which the Constitution has not distinctly imposed.

The powers granted to the National government are delegated powers, enumerated in and defined by the instrument [319] which has created the Union. Hence the rule that when a question arises whether the National government possesses a particular power, proof must be given that the power was positively granted. If not granted, it is not possessed, because the Union is an artificial creation, whose government can have nothing but what the people have by the Constitution conferred. The presumption is therefore against the National government in such a case, just as it is for the State in a like case.

VII. The authority of the National government over the citizens of every State is direct and immediate, not exerted through the State organization, and not requiring the co-operation of the State government. For most purposes the National government ignores the States; and it treats the citizens of different States as being simply its own citizens, equally bound by its laws. The Federal courts, revenue officers, and post-office draw no help from any State officials, but depend directly on Washington ...

On the other hand, the State in no wise depends on the National government for its organization or its effective working. It is the creation of its own inhabitants ... It goes its own way, touching the National government at but few points. That the two should touch at the fewest possible points was the intent of those who framed the Federal Constitution ... Their aim was to keep the two mechanisms as distinct and independent of each other as was compatible with the still higher need of subordinating, for national purposes, the State to the Central government ...

[322] X. There are several remarkable omissions in the constitution of the American federation.

One is that there is no grant of power to the National government to coerce a recalcitrant or rebellious State. Another is that nothing is said as to the right of secession. Any one can understand why this right should not have been granted. But neither is it mentioned to be negatived.

The Constitution was an instrument of compromises; and these were questions which it would have been unwise to raise.

There is no abstract or theoretic declaration regarding the nature of the federation and its government, nothing as to the ultimate supremacy of the central authority outside the particular sphere allotted to it, nothing as to the so-called sovereign rights of the States. As if with a prescience of the dangers to follow, the wise men of 1787 resolved to give no opening for abstract inquiry and metaphysical dialectic. But in vain. The human mind is not to be so restrained ... The drily legal and practical character of the Constitution did not prevent the growth of a mass of subtle and, so to speak, scholastic metaphysics regarding the nature of the government it created. The inextricable knots which American lawyers and publicists went on tying, down until 1861, were cut by the sword of the North in the Civil War, and need concern us no longer. It is now admitted that the Union is not a mere compact between commonwealths, dissoluble at pleasure, but an instrument of perpetual efficacy, emanating from the whole people, [323] and alterable by them only in the manner which its own terms prescribe. It is 'an indestructible Union of indestructible States'.

It follows from the recognition of the indestructibility of the Union that there must somewhere exist a force capable of preserving it. The National government is now admitted to be such a force. 'It can exercise all powers essential to preserve and protect its own existence and that of the States, and the constitutional relation of the States to itself, and to one another.'

'May it not', some one will ask, 'abuse these powers, abuse them so as to extinguish the States themselves, and turn the [324] federation into a unified government? What is there but the Federal judiciary to prevent this catastrophe? and the Federal judiciary has only moral and not also physical force at its command.'

No doubt it may, but not until public opinion supports it in so doing – that is to say, not until the mass of the nation which now maintains, because it values, the Federal system, is possessed by a desire to overthrow that system. Such a desire may express itself in proper legal form by carrying amendments to the Constitution which will entirely change the nature of the government. Or if the minority be numerous enough to prevent the passing of such amendments, and if the desire of the majority be sufficiently vehement, the majority which sways the National government may disregard legal sanctions and effect its object by a revolution. In either event – and both are improbable – the change which will have passed upon the sentiments of the American people will be a sign that Federalism has done its work, and that the time has arrived for new forms of political life.

The American federation was conceived of as "a more perfect Union" superseding the earlier "confederacy" of 1781, by which the original 13 States had entered into "a firm league of friendship with each other for their common defence, the security of their liberties, and their mutual and general welfare". Under the Articles of Confederation the capacity to enforce the obligations of member States was obscure, with disputes resolved by an ad hoc panel of judges appointed by the confederate Congress and acceptable to the disputants. Only member States were bound by the Articles; the Congress had no capacity to make laws binding on individuals. The absence, in that sense, of a national government, was seen as a crucial weakness, which the 1789 Constitution was to solve. The issue was explained by James Madison in *The Federalist (No 39)*. *The Federalist* – a series of letters and essays written in 1787-88 by Madison, Alexander Hamilton and John Jay to convince the people of New York to join the new federation – is widely used as a guide to the intended operation of the 1789 Constitution.

James Madison, *The Federalist (No 39)*
in Isaac Kramnick (ed), *The Federalist Papers* (Penguin Books, 1987)

[256] [I]t appears, on one hand, that the Constitution is to be founded on the assent and ratification of the people of America, given by deputies elected for the special purpose; but, on the other, that this assent and ratification is to be given by the people, not as [257] individuals composing one entire nation, but as composing the distinct and independent States to which they respectively belong. It is to be the assent and ratification of the several States, derived from the supreme authority in each State – the authority of the people themselves. The act, therefore, establishing the Constitution will not be a *national* but a *federal* act.

That it will be a federal and not a national act, ... the act of the people, as forming so many independent States, not as forming one aggregate nation – is obvious from this single consideration: that it is to result neither from the decision of a *majority* of the people of the Union, nor from that of a *majority* of the States ... Each State, in ratifying the Constitution, is considered as a sovereign body independent of all others, and only to be bound by its own voluntary act. In this relation, then, the new Constitution will, if established, be a *federal*, and not a *national* constitution.

The next relation is to the sources from which the ordinary powers of government are to be derived. The House of Representatives will derive its powers from the people of America; and the people will be represented in the same proportion and on the same principle as they are in the legislature of a particular State. So far the government is *national*, not *federal*. The Senate, on the other hand, will derive its powers from the States as political and coequal societies; and these will be represented on the principle of equality in the Senate, as they now are in the existing Congress. So far the government is *federal*, not *national*. The executive power will be derived from a very compound source. The immediate election of the President is to be made by the States in their political characters. The votes allotted to them are in a compound ratio, which considers them partly as distinct and coequal societies, partly as unequal members of the same society. The eventual election ... is to be made by that branch of the legislature which consists of the national representatives; but in this particular act they are to be thrown into the form of individual delegations from so many distinct and coequal bodies politic. From this aspect of the government it [258] appears to be of a mixed character, presenting at least as many *federal* as *national* features.

The difference between a federal and national government, as it relates to the *operation of the government*, is by the adversaries of the plan of the convention supposed to consist in this, that in the former the powers operate on the political bodies composing the Confederacy in their political capacities; in the latter, on the individual citizens composing the nation in their individual capacities. On trying the Constitution by this criterion, it falls under the *national* not the *federal* character; though perhaps not so completely as has been understood. In several cases, and particularly in the trial of controversies to which States may be parties, they must be viewed and proceeded against in their collective and political capacities only. But the operation of the government on the people in their individual capacities, in its ordinary and most essential proceedings, will, in the sense of its opponents, on the whole, designate it, in this relation, a *national* government.

But if the government be national with regard to the *operation* of its powers, it changes its aspect again when we contemplate it in relation to the extent of its powers. The idea of a national government involves in it not only an authority over the individual citizens, but an indefinite supremacy over all persons and things, so far as they are objects of lawful government. Among a people consolidated into one nation, this supremacy is completely vested in the national legislature. Among communities united for particular purposes, it is vested partly in the general and partly in the municipal legislatures ... In this relation, then, the proposed government cannot be deemed a *national* one; since its jurisdiction extends to certain enumerated objects only, and leaves to the several States a residuary and inviolable sovereignty over all other objects. It is true that in controversies relating to the boundary between the two jurisdictions, the tribunal which is ultimately to decide is to be established under the general government. But this does not change the principle of the case ... Some such tribunal is clearly essential to prevent ... a dissolution of the compact; and that it ought to be established under the general rather than under the **[259]** local governments ... is a position not likely to be combated.

If we try the Constitution by its last relation to the authority by which amendments are to be made, we find it neither wholly *national* nor wholly *federal*. Were it wholly national, the supreme and ultimate authority would reside in the *majority* of the people of the Union; and this authority would be competent at all times, like that of a majority of every national society, to alter or abolish its established government. Were it wholly federal, on the other hand, the concurrence of each State in the Union would be essential to every alteration that would be binding on all. The mode provided by the plan of the convention is not founded on either of these principles. In requiring more than a majority, and particularly in computing the proportion by *States*, not by *citizens*, it departs from the *national* and advances towards the *federal* character; in rendering the concurrence of less than the whole number of States sufficient, it loses again the *federal* and partakes of the *national* character.

The proposed Constitution, therefore, ... is, in strictness, neither a national nor a federal Constitution, but a composition of both.

2. Australian Federalism

On 1 January 1901 the Australian nation was created as a federation. As stated in the preamble to the Constitution, the colonies agreed to "unite in one indissoluble Federal Commonwealth".

Constitutional Commission, *Final Report of the Constitutional Commission* (AGPS, 1988), Vol 1

[53] Federal features in the Australian Constitution

2.15 In the nineteenth century, the Constitution of the United States was seen by many as the pre-eminent model of federal government. Our Framers looked mainly to it as a guide to the sort of governmental system they were seeking to establish. While they rejected the presidential system of government and a comprehensive Bill of Rights, in other respects they found, in the American system, what Sir Owen Dixon described as 'an incomparable model.' The federal features of that country's Constitution that we followed were:

   (a) the establishment of a central (or Federal) Government and State Governments, each with its own governmental institutions;
   (b) a distribution of authority between the Federal and State Governments that confined the former to express enumerated subjects, while leaving the undefined residue to the States;
   (c) a judicial authority, appointed by the Federal Government, to determine whether either level of government had exceeded its legislative, executive or judicial powers;
   (d) the supremacy of federal laws over State laws in cases of inconsistency; and
   (e) an entrenchment of these features by a rigid constitutional framework that is difficult to alter.

2.16 It would seem that the minimal essential features of a federal system as it has come to be understood in Australia are a high degree of autonomy for the governmental institutions of the Commonwealth and the States, a division of power between these organisations, and a judicial 'umpire'.

2.17 There are other aspects of the Constitution which, while not creating a federal state, reflect its federal nature. Some of these are concerned with ensuring that the Commonwealth behaves fairly to each State as compared with other States. These include section 51(ii) which restricts the taxation power 'so as not to discriminate between States or parts of States'; section 51(iii) and section 88 which require bounties and customs duties, respectively, to be 'uniform throughout the Commonwealth'; and section 99 which **[54]** provides that 'the Commonwealth shall not, by any law or regulation of trade, commerce, or revenue give preference to one State or any part thereof over another State or any part thereof.'

2.18 Similarly there are provisions relating to the respect and fairness owed by a State to the Government and people of other States. Section 117 is aimed at preventing a State (and perhaps the Commonwealth) from discriminating against non-alien residents of other States. Section 118 requires that 'full faith and credit' be given throughout the Commonwealth to 'the laws, the public Acts and records and the judicial proceedings of every State.' Discrimination against the trade and commerce of another State is prohibited, and the entry of its people is protected, by section 92, guaranteeing that 'trade, commerce and intercourse among the States shall be absolutely free', and by section 102 dealing with State railway rates which are 'undue and unreasonable or unjust to any State.'

2.19 Another feature of the Constitution which has, in the courts and in public political debate, been closely associated with the federal principle in Australia is representation in the Senate. The people of the Original States are guaranteed equal representation (section 7). The founding fathers were divided on the desirability of an upper House of this nature (usually depending on whether they came from the larger or smaller colonies). Many of the delegates seem to have approved the adoption of this principle on the practical ground that otherwise union would have been impossible, rather than on the basis of federal principle. This is perhaps borne out by the fact that the right of equal representation in the Senate was not granted to any new State which might be admitted to the Commonwealth, but was, in section 121, made to depend on the will of the Federal Parliament.

Brian Galligan and Cliff Walsh, "Australian Federalism Yes or No?"
in Gregory Craven (ed), *Australian Federation* (Melbourne University Press, 1992), 193

[195] For the most part ... the Australian founders focused on the practicalities of devising an appropriate scheme of federal government that would be accepted by the people of the Australian colonies. Although the theoretical **[196]** exposition of federalism and its advantages was virtually absent from the Australian debates, that does not mean that Australian federalism is devoid of both as some have assumed – only that we have to look elsewhere for their articulation. The appropriate place is not to Bryce who had a rigid view of federalism as a co-ordinate system of parallel machinery of government, nor to his intellectual successor KC Wheare who continued this arid tradition of defining federalism in terms of co-ordinate institutions. The 'federal principle', according to Wheare, was the 'method of dividing powers so that the general and regional governments are each, within a sphere, co-ordinate and independent'.

The theory of federalism ... was best articulated ... in the *Federalist Papers*. Surprisingly this definitive exposition of federalism by its United States inventors was not well known to the Australian founders, and only in recent times has become a primary source for exposition of Australian federalism ... The case for federalism follows directly from the key attributes of federal theory. These are: that federalism provides a robust constitutional system that anchors pluralist democracy, and that it enhances democratic participation through providing dual citizenship in a compound republic. If one values these two things, one ought to favour federalism. Australian critics who reject federalism usually do so because they prefer more direct and unrestrained democracy at the national level, and have little respect for the more localised democracy that State governments provide ...

[197] Liberal constitutionalism generally and Federalist theory in particular are not about prescribing substantive outcomes but rather enshrining institutional processes. Their purpose is to guarantee citizens and groups the right to pursue their own happiness, and to restrict governments from legislating happiness schemes. No public good is presupposed, but rather a multiplicity of private goods; or put another way, the public good lies in ensuring toleration and pluralism. Hence Hamilton's claim that the United States Constitution, because of its elaborate system of checks and balances, was 'itself, in every rational sense, and to every useful purpose, A BILL OF RIGHTS' ...

[198] The resilience of Australian federalism derives from its second main attribute of enhanced democratic participation that was also an important part of the original Federalist design. Federalism preserves the States as small democratic polities and establishes a system of dual citizenship or double democracy. Federalism enables the national strength of a large nation to be added to the enhanced participatory qualities of small democratic States: in Tocqueville's summing up, federalism combines the 'different advantages which result from the magnitude and the littleness of nations.' ...

[199] Because they are quasi-independent political communities, the States can and do play a major political and policy role. The character of the States' policy role varies among policy areas, depending on whether the States have primary jurisdiction, or have a shared input along with the Commonwealth, or are involved in a mediating role of delivering Commonwealth programmes, or have an indirect impact through their control over related programmes. As one might expect given the cultural homogeneity of the Australian people and the fiscal dominance of the Commonwealth, there are striking similarities in the policies of the various States. But there are also notable and persistent differences. While the policy differences are obvious manifestations of the independent character of the States as distinct political communities, the more pervasive similarities are not evidence to the contrary.

For even if the States produced identical policy outcomes, that would not constitute a good reason for not having them as some might think. The justification for States does not depend on their producing differential policy outcomes. It might simply be that all the State political communities have similar policy preferences. In no way does that derogate from the inherent value of enhanced democratic participation in the political and policy processes of small polities. In the same way, just because individuals or groups choose the same thing, this does not imply that they should not be allowed to choose. The justification for democracy at any level has to be primarily in terms of process rather than outcome. Democracy itself is defined and justified not in terms of policy results but in terms of the basic values embodied in its political processes. Since federalism both increases popular participation in politics and allows public goods to be more finely tailored to popular preferences, it can be said to enhance democracy. This enhancement of democratic participation through dual citizenship and multiple governments in a compound republic is undoubtedly federalism's most positive quality and largely explains its strength and resilience in Australia.

The argument that federalism can secure democracy and human rights has been bolstered under contemporary "public choice" theories (see Chapter 2, §1) by the notions of "voice" and "exit". The former term means that, in the smaller political units that make up the federation, individuals can participate more directly than in a monolithic unitary government. The latter means that individuals dissatisfied with conditions in one State have the option of moving to another. As Robert Bork puts it for the United States (*The Tempting of America: The Political Seduction of the Law* (Macmillan, 1990)), the federal system is an important protector of human rights because "**[53]** if another state allows the liberty you value, you can move there, and the choice of what freedom you value is yours alone, not dependent on those who made the Constitution. In this sense, federalism is the constitutional guarantee most protective of the individual's freedom to make his own choices". Of course, such arguments assume that a freedom of movement between States is necessarily secured by a federal system. In any event, the capacity of a federal system to protect civil liberties has been disputed.

James Gillespie, "New Federalisms"

in Judith Brett, James Gillespie and Murray Goot (eds), *Developments in Australian Politics*
(MacMillan, 1994), 60

[69] Does federalism have the potential to limit the oppressive powers of government? The demand for a more coherent defence of federalism has led to a new interest in divided sovereignty as a limitation on the power of central executive government. One of the oldest arguments for a federal system is based on the belief that the division of powers between levels of government is a guarantee that the state will not become too large or oppressive. The classic statement of this position came in the debates around the adoption of the United States Constitution. *The Federalist*, a series of papers written to win support for a stronger national government in the American federation, reassured opponents who worried about a rebirth of aristocratic tyranny that the limits set by the new Constitution on the powers of the central government would provide a major 'check and balance'. If sovereignty were divided between rival levels of government, each with its own democratic franchise, it would set a major barrier to the concentration of political power in too few hands. First, federalism can limit government power to infringe rights, since it creates the possibility that a legislature wishing to restrict liberties will lack the constitutional power, while the level of government that possesses the power lacks the desire. Second, the tortuous and legalistic decision making processes characteristic of federal systems limit the speed with which governments can act – even if their actions prove to be constitutional. Federalism helps enshrine the principle of 'due process', limiting arbitrary action by the state.

The late nineteenth century British liberal tradition, with which the Australian founding fathers were familiar, showed increasing interest in institutional measures to restrict the powers of government. The strength of demands for political democracy – and the potential tyranny of democratic majorities – with the growing size of the imperial state **[70]** seemed to threaten the liberal traditions of British politics. Divided sovereignty was seen as an important measure of protection of the rights of minorities. Federalism could be a solution to the dilemma of the preservation of liberty in large political units, a bulwark against the majoritarian tide. The British political theorist Harold Laski developed this pluralist defence of federalism, arguing that 'There can be no servility in a State that divides its effective governance. The necessity of balancing interests, the need for combining opinions, results in a wealth of political thought such as no state where the real authority is single can attain'.

Galligan, Knopff and Uhr have recently developed similar arguments in the Australian context. They have suggested that the vitality of Australian federalism removes the need for a Bill of Rights to entrench the protection of individual civil liberties in the Constitution. They suggest that 'a federal constitution is itself a bill of rights' as the division of authority between different spheres of government 'guarantees due process in government'; in turn this promotes what they term 'rights-oriented citizenship'. The complications, overlapping jurisdictions and administrative inefficiencies of a federal system are transformed into virtues. The citizens of a federal state have more remedies and political resources to draw upon. Equally, in the face of an oppressive state, at least they have the possibility of sheltering from its excesses beneath the sovereign powers of other levels of government. Galligan pushes this further by arguing that the 'enhancement of democratic participation through dual citizenship and multiple governments is undoubtedly federalism's most positive quality that largely explains its strength and resilience in Australia'. The inefficiencies that the planners of past decades deplored, become a guarantee against government becoming too oppressive, a fragmentation of the 'revenue-maximising Leviathan' state.

This is more than a revamped theory of competitive federalism – a celebration of the creativity and diversity that can result from maintaining a multiplicity of centres of government. Three major criticisms can be levelled at this attempt to place federal theory on a libertarian basis. First, its authors have been long on general assertions of principle, but rather short on explaining what they mean by 'liberty' and on the presentation of empirical evidence. It is difficult to detect any federal component to the protection of individual rights in Australia. Galligan, Knopff and Uhr manage to present their civil libertarian defence without citing a single case.

Instances of the coincidence of states' rights and individual liberties have been rare. The division of powers between federal and state levels [has] left many of the key areas affecting minority rights in state hands: the regulation of morals, including medical and mental health, land law [71] and control of indigenous populations, even after the 1967 referendum ... The defence of states' rights has hardly provided a theme for those concerned with the rights of Aboriginal communities. Recent discussions of potential statehood for the Northern Territory have been dominated by fears for the future of Aboriginal organisations stripped of the limited protection offered by Canberra. Rowse has criticised the Northern Territory's moves to impose the standard model of Australian federalism – a strong state government dominating local government – to eliminate the nascent model of 'dispersed governance' that might enable Aboriginal self-determination.

Second, they confuse the rights of individuals with those of states. In Australia some of the major intergovernmental conflicts in recent decades have been the direct result of federal intervention to secure the rights of minority groups, and required limitations on the powers of state governments. It is also essential to avoid confusion between the constraints set by judicial review, the constitutional power of the courts to overrule Parliament, and federalism itself. The 'parliamentary despotism' of undivided sovereignty has come under strong attack in contemporary Britain. The key problem has been identified as the lack of a written constitution. This could be remedied without introducing federal arrangements – although these are also receiving serious discussion. Finally, their position is based on a very narrow notion of liberty. They see freedom as a negative condition, as the absence of external constraints on action. Government intervention may be a source of freedom – for example by liberating individuals from the crushing dictates of the market by providing social security benefits and health insurance.

Galligan and Walsh refer to the "[196] arid" definition of "co-ordinate federalism" advanced by the Australian-born scholar KC Wheare (1907-79). In *Federal Government* (Oxford University Press, 4th ed 1963), Wheare defined "the federal principle" as "[10] the method of dividing powers so that the general and regional governments are each, within a sphere, co-ordinate and independent". He insisted that "[12] [t]he essential point" is that "neither general nor regional government is subordinate to the other".

Wheare was sensitive to criticisms of his approach as "[15] too academic". He protested that he did *not* regard his "federal principle" as "[34] a kind of end or good in itself", or believe "that any deviation from it in law or in practice is a weakness or defect ... [W]hile I have maintained that it is necessary to define the federal principle dogmatically, I do not maintain that it is necessary to apply it religiously". He conceded that particular constitutions (such as that of Australia) might be classified as "federal constitutions" in spite of "modifications in the application of the federal principle"; and even in cases where he thought that the written constitution could no longer be classified as "federal", he was still prepared to concede that in practice there might be a "federal government".

More recent studies of federalism are less preoccupied with such schematic taxonomies. It is clear, however, that Australia's first three High Court judges – Griffith CJ, Barton and O'Connor JJ – believed in "co-ordinate federalism" in Wheare's rigid sense (see Chapter 7, §2). Indeed, as the economist Russell Mathews (1921-2000) observed ("The Development of Australian Federalism" in RL Mathews (ed), *Federalism in Australia and the Federal Republic of Germany: A Comparative Study* (Australian National University Press, 1980), 3): "[4] The original Australian federal system was ... a co-ordinate federal system in the classical mould, the Commonwealth and the States each being co-ordinate and independent in their own fields of responsibility". Mathews went on to identify four evolutionary phases in Australian federalism. These were (1) a period of "*co-ordinate federalism*", brought to an end in 1920 by the *Engineers' Case* (see Chapter 7, §2); (2) a period of "*co-operative federalism*" in the 1920s and 1930s, culminating in developments such as the 1927 Financial Agreement and the establishment in 1933 of the Commonwealth Grants Commission; (3) a centralising period of "*coercive federalism*" ushered in by the wartime uniform tax scheme (see Chapter 24, §2(b)); and (4) a period of "*co-ordinative federalism*" characterised by recognition of "[12] the need for intergovernmental policy co-ordination" – initiated by the Premier's Conference of May 1975, and carried through into the "new federalism" of the Fraser Government.

More recently, the economic developments of the 1990s have led Martin Painter to offer a model of "collaborative federalism" (*Collaborative Federalism: Economic Reform in Australia in the 1990s* (Cambridge University Press, 1998)): that is, "**[25]** a system of interlocking *executive* federalism", in which "[t]he institutions of collaboration – ministerial councils, officials' committees and joint administrative bodies – are executive bodies, and the lines of authority and accountability are based on consultation, clearance and agreement by ministers" through "highly formalized structures and procedures". Painter attributes this model to the "managerialist perspective" of recent Commonwealth governments, and plays it off against a model of "competitive federalism" – which "**[28]** has entered the public realm as part of a rhetoric in defence of the states against the Commonwealth", but which "has its origins in an economic analysis of systems of decentralized government, in which multiple jurisdictions offer distinctive bundles of services and policies, each attracting different firms and residents and, in the process, competing with each other".

It is sometimes said that all federations are subject to centripetal and centrifugal tendencies, with political power moving either towards the centre and away from the component States (centripetal, seeking out the centre), or in the converse direction (centrifugal, running away from the centre). While these should be regarded as countervailing tendencies rather than inexorable forces, it is fair to say that the evolution of Australian federalism has generally been centripetal. While constitutional amendment has had some influence in this regard (see, for example, the special status conferred on the 1927 Financial Agreement by the insertion of s 105A), the primary catalysts for change have been the High Court's interpretation of the Constitution and political pressures for the Commonwealth to meet national needs, particularly during times of war.

3. Co-operative Federalism

A persistent theme running through the above variations is the recognition of the need for some version of "co-operative federalism", in which State and national governments work together for the attainment of common objectives. Particularly in areas where the federal Parliament lacks the power to enact comprehensive laws, State and federal governments have worked together to establish national regulatory regimes, for instance to facilitate the marketing of agricultural products or to implement competition policy. The High Court has generally upheld such co-operation. In *R v Duncan; Ex parte Australian Iron and Steel Pty Ltd* (1983) 158 CLR 535, Deane J described Commonwealth-State co-operation as "**[589]** a positive objective of the Constitution". In that case, the Court held that the Commonwealth and the States could jointly create a body, the Coal Industry Tribunal, invested with both Commonwealth and State power. Moreover, the Court held that this could be achieved without incurring problems of inconsistency between laws under s 109 of the Constitution.

R v Duncan; Ex parte Australian Iron and Steel Pty Ltd
(1983) 158 CLR 535

Gibbs CJ: [552] In the argument on behalf of the prosecutor a challenge was made to the legislative competence of the Commonwealth to create an authority jointly with a State, or at least an authority which derives from a State power which the Commonwealth itself could not confer upon it. It does not seem to me to matter whether the effect of the statutes of the Commonwealth and the State was to create one tribunal which derived power from two sources, or two tribunals, deriving power from different sources, but constituted by one person. In my opinion, it was within the power of the Commonwealth Parliament to follow either course. The Constitution effects a division of powers between the Commonwealth and the States but it nowhere forbids the Commonwealth and the States to exercise their respective powers in such a way that each is complementary to the other. There is no express provision in the Constitution, and no principle of constitutional law, that would prevent the Commonwealth and the States from acting in cooperation, so that each, acting in its own field, supplies the deficiencies in the power of the other, and so that together they may achieve, subject to such limitations as those provided by s 92 of the Constitution, a uniform and complete legislative scheme ... Further, no reason is provided by constitutional **[553]** enactment or constitutional principle why the Commonwealth and a State or States should not simultaneously confer powers on one person and empower that person to exercise any or all of those powers alone or in conjunction. In one instance the Constitution has expressly recognized the possibility of co-operation of that kind when it enables the Parliament to invest a court of a State with federal jurisdiction: Constitution, ss 71, 77(iii). It would be an absurd result, for example, if the Commonwealth and a State were unable, by complementary legislation, to empower an officer of police to enforce both the laws of the Commonwealth and the laws of the State, or to give power to a fisheries inspector to act in Australian waters both within and beyond territorial limits, or to authorize a public servant to collect State taxes as well as Commonwealth taxes. There is nothing in the decisions of this Court to provide authority for such a restrictive view of constitutional power. The position of an administrative body such as the Tribunal is no different; legislation of the Commonwealth Parliament, otherwise within power, is not invalid because it establishes, jointly with a State, one body which derives its powers from the State as well as from the Commonwealth.

As at present advised, I can see no reason why a body which derives power from two sources cannot exercise whichever power appears available and appropriate in any particular case. If, in settlement of an interstate dispute, the Tribunal made an award under powers which it derived from the Commonwealth Coal **[554]** Industry Act, the Tribunal might later amend that award in the exercise of powers which derived from the State Coal Industry Act for the purpose of settling a purely intrastate dispute. The inconsistency between the original award and the amendment would be resolved in favour of the amendment, since that would be later in time. Section 109 of the Constitution would have no operation, because, on the view which I am suggesting, the relevant law of the Commonwealth, ie, the Commonwealth Coal Industry Act, reveals the intention that the Tribunal may use powers given to it by the State Coal Industry Act for the purpose of varying an award which it has made in the exercise of power given by the Commonwealth Coal Industry Act.

In the 1990s, the Corporations Law was viewed as an important example of Commonwealth-State co-operation. The scheme was a response to the High Court's decision, in *New South Wales v Commonwealth* (*Incorporation Case*) (1990) 169 CLR 482, that the Commonwealth could not use its corporations power (s 51(xx)) to regulate the incorporation of companies. In that case sections of the *Corporations Act 1989* (Cth), the Commonwealth's unilateral attempt to regulate the area, were held to be invalid. Instead, under Heads of Agreement signed by the Commonwealth and the States at Alice Springs on 29 June 1990, the Commonwealth legislated under its Territories power (s 122) to amend the 1989 Act so that it enacted a corporations law scheme for the Australian Capital Territory. This scheme was then adopted by legislation passed by the Parliaments of each State and of the Northern Territory (for example, by the *Corporations* (*South Australia*) *Act 1990* (SA)). These enactments brought the Corporations Law into force nationally from 1 January 1991.

The Corporations Law included elements of another important co-operative venture, the "cross-vesting" scheme. The creation of the Federal Court of Australia had given rise to jurisdictional problems in cases where the same substantive dispute had elements of federal jurisdiction (for example, under the *Trade Practices Act 1974* (Cth)), but also had elements of State jurisdiction (for example, as to a common law action for passing off). Some of these problems were solved by s 32 of the *Federal Court of Australia Act 1976* (Cth), which allowed the Federal Court to exercise "associated jurisdiction" – that is, to decide federal matters related to a claim within its jurisdiction despite the absence of any specific statutory grant of jurisdiction in those matters. Others were solved by judicial endorsement of the notion of "accrued jurisdiction", enabling the Federal Court to decide matters arising at common law, or otherwise within State jurisdiction, that were sufficiently related to a federal matter (see especially *Stack v Coast Securities (No 9) Pty Ltd* (1983) 154 CLR 261). However, these concepts of associated and accrued jurisdiction themselves gave rise to difficulties of analysis.

At the same time, a series of High Court decisions on the scope of the Commonwealth's constitutional powers with respect to marriage and matrimonial causes (s 51(xxi) and (xxii)) gave rise to jurisdictional problems in cases involving matrimonial property, and (particularly) the custody of children. Where issues in these categories were held not to be within federal constitutional power, it followed that the Family Court of Australia had no jurisdiction and thus that the issues had instead to be decided by the State Supreme Courts.

From 1986 onwards the particular problem relating to the custody of children was solved by a State referral to the Commonwealth, pursuant to s 51(xxxvii) of the Constitution (see below) of a very broad power to legislate with respect to the maintenance and custody of children (see, for example, the *Commonwealth Powers (Family Law – Children Act) 1990* (Qld)). On that basis, the Commonwealth was able to enact a new Pt VII of the *Family Law Act 1975* (Cth) relating to children. At the same time, as a more comprehensive solution to the wider range of jurisdictional problems referred to above, the "cross-vesting" scheme was adopted – enacted by the *Jurisdiction of Courts (Cross-vesting) Act 1987* (Cth) and the similarly titled Acts of each of the States, and coming into force on 1 July 1988.

The scheme was designed to enable every aspect of a dispute to be heard by a single court, and to that end to enable proceedings commenced in any Australian court to be transferred to any other Australian court. While the scheme also operated as between the courts of different States, its primary purpose was to overcome the jurisdictional questions that had arisen between State and federal courts. To this end the legislation purported to vest State judicial power in federal courts, and vice versa. The resulting arrangement was hailed as a model co-operative regime, with strong support from all State and federal governments.

Under the Alice Springs Agreement, the *Corporations Act* and the State Acts adopting it established their own "cross-vesting" scheme – parallel to the general scheme, but intended to preserve the Corporations Law as a self-contained code. However, just as the Corporations Law was created in response to a High Court decision, its unravelling was also brought about by the Court, with the incidental effect of demolishing the general "cross-vesting" scheme as well.

Section 77(iii) of the Constitution states that the federal Parliament "may make laws ... [i]nvesting any court of a State with federal jurisdiction". But the Constitution is silent on the converse issue of whether a federal court can be invested with State jurisdiction. In *Gould v Brown* (1998) 193 CLR 346, a High Court of six was evenly divided on this question. Brennan CJ, Toohey and Kirby JJ upheld the legislation, while Gaudron, McHugh and Gummow JJ held that the vesting of jurisdiction in the Federal Court was unconstitutional. The scheme survived because, under s 23(2)(a) of the *Judiciary Act 1903* (Cth), in the event of an equally divided High Court the decision of the court below (in this case the Full Court of the Federal Court, which upheld the legislation) is affirmed. Inevitably, however, the matter came before the Court again. In the meantime, two of the judges (Brennan CJ and Toohey J) who upheld the legislation in *Gould v Brown* had retired and been replaced by Gleeson CJ and Callinan J. In addition, Dawson J, who had retired before *Gould v Brown*, had been replaced by Hayne J. In *Re Wakim; Ex parte McNally (Cross-vesting Case)* (1999) 198 CLR 511, the three new judges joined Gaudron, McHugh and Gummow JJ in holding that State jurisdiction could not be vested in a federal court. Kirby J was in sole dissent.

While Gleeson CJ noted that the "**[540]** legislation has been commended as an example of co-operation between the Parliaments of the Federation", he went on to say: "Approval of the legislative policy is irrelevant to a judgment as to constitutional validity; just as disapproval of the policy would be irrelevant". McHugh J also rejected the attempt to use co-operative federalism as a constitutional principle that could shape the interpretation of the Constitution.

Re Wakim; Ex parte McNally (Cross-vesting Case)
(1999) 198 CLR 511

McHugh J: [548] It would be very convenient and usually less expensive and time-consuming for litigants in the federal courts if those courts could deal with all litigious issues arising between the litigants, irrespective of whether those issues have any connection with federal law. From the litigant's point of view that is saying a great deal. But unfortunately, from a constitutional point of view, it says nothing. The deficiencies and complexities of federal jurisdiction have been pointed out many [549] times before, never more powerfully than by Mr Owen Dixon KC in giving evidence before the Royal Commission on the Constitution in 1928. The inability of the federal courts to exercise cross-vested State jurisdiction in the manner provided for under the present legislation simply shows another deficiency in the system. I do not think that it can be seriously doubted that, if Australia is to have a system of federal courts, the public interest requires that these courts should have jurisdiction to deal with all existing controversies between litigants in those courts ...

[550] Change to the terms and structure of the Constitution can be carried out only with the approval of the people in accordance with the procedures laid down in s 128 of the Constitution. Until change is made, the function of the judiciary is to give effect to the present terms and structure of the Constitution. We must, of course, never forget Marshall CJ's words "that it is a *constitution* we are expounding" [*McCulloch v Maryland*, 17 US (4 Wheat) 159 at 200 (1819)]. As the Chief Justice said in that case in speaking of incidental powers [17 US at 206], "Let the end be legitimate, let it be within the scope of the constitution, and all means which are appropriate, which are [551] plainly adapted to that end, which are not prohibited, but consist with the letter and spirit of the constitution, are constitutional." In the present case, however, I think that the Constitution does prohibit the States from vesting State jurisdiction in federal courts and prohibits the Commonwealth consenting to the vesting of State jurisdiction in those courts ...

[556] [I]t is clear that the Parliament of the Commonwealth cannot give a federal court jurisdiction to exercise State judicial power ... I did not understand this proposition to be challenged in the present proceedings.

How then can a State Parliament invest a federal court with a jurisdiction which the Parliament of the Commonwealth, which has created the court, cannot invest in that court? Co-operative federalism is the chief answer given by the parties and the interveners supporting the validity of the legislation. But co-operative federalism is not a constitutional term. It is a political slogan, not a criterion of constitutional validity or power. It records a result reached as the result of a State and the Commonwealth legislating *within the powers* conferred on them by the Constitution. Behind its invocation in the present cases lies a good deal of loose thinking.

There is no doubt that, as a result of co-operation between a State and the Commonwealth, the Commonwealth may achieve objects that are beyond the constitutional competence of the Commonwealth. Similarly, as the result of joint legislation, a State and the Commonwealth may achieve an object that neither could achieve by its own legislation. But that is because each political entity has the constitutional power to do what is jointly necessary to achieve the object. Where constitutional power does not exist, no cry of co-operative federalism can supply it. If the object lies outside the reach or the effect of what a State or the Commonwealth can constitutionally do, the subject matter is beyond the reach of the legislatures of Australia ... In such cases, "the totality of legislative power in Australia [proves] to be less than the totality of power in other civilized countries." But that is the price and consequence of federalism. [557] As Professor Dicey pointed out long ago: "Federal government means weak government."

Co-operative federalism does not assist those supporting the validity of the present legislation. That is because the legislatures of the States have no power, with or without the consent of the Parliament of the Commonwealth, to invest State jurisdiction or judicial power in federal courts. There is not a word in Ch III which indicates expressly or by implication that it authorises the Parliament of the Commonwealth to create federal courts to exercise State jurisdiction or State judicial power. Nor is there a word in Ch III which indicates that the States can invest such jurisdiction or power in the federal courts. That is hardly surprising. "In a dual political system you do not expect to find either government legislating for the other" or its courts [*In re Foreman & Sons Pty Ltd; Uther v Federal Commissioner of Taxation* (1947) 74 CLR 508 at 529]. Because that is so, s 77(iii) of the Constitution expressly empowers the Parliament of the Commonwealth to invest "any court of a State with federal jurisdiction". Given the presence of s 77(iii), the absence of any express power in the States to invest State jurisdiction in federal courts is itself enough to indicate that the States lack the power to do so ...

[559] One of the remarkable aspects of the argument of those supporting the validity of the legislation is that they contend that the States can invest only *judicial* power in the federal courts

and that they cannot do so without the consent of the Commonwealth. Why do they contend that the States cannot invest non-judicial power in the federal courts? It is because they accept that Ch III impliedly forbids it. That is to say, they accept that the terms of ss 71, 75 and 76 contain an implication that the general powers of the States, saved and continued by ss 106 and 107 of the Constitution, do not extend to investing non-judicial power in the federal courts. Yet those supporting validity deny that those same sections contain an implication that the States cannot invest judicial power in the federal courts ...

[560] Chapter III either forbids the States conferring jurisdiction on the federal courts or it does not. If the States can confer judicial power on federal courts, they can confer non-judicial powers on them, at all events non-judicial power that is not incompatible with the exercise of State judicial power. There is nothing in Ch III that would permit the conferral of one class of State jurisdiction but totally prevent the conferral of the other. If the general powers of the States enable them to legislate for the federal courts, they must be able to legislate generally for those courts. If Ch III does not prevent them doing so in respect of State judicial power, there is no logical basis for holding, for example, that it withdraws from a State the power to invest the federal courts with the jurisdiction of its Supreme Court which may well require the exercise ... of non-judicial power as that term is understood in Ch III.

Gummow and Hayne JJ, with whom Gaudron J agreed, took a similar view.

Gummow and Hayne JJ: [571] Considerable emphasis was given in the arguments of those supporting the validity of the cross-vesting arrangements to the facts **[572]** that both the general cross-vesting arrangements and the similar arrangements made under the Corporations Act have operated for some years and have the support of the Commonwealth and all of the States and mainland Territories... But neither the time for which the provisions have stood without challenge nor the support of all governments in Australia can relieve the Court of deciding what it is that the Constitution permits or requires.

It was suggested in argument that, in considering the validity of the legislation, significance should be attached to the statement in the preamble as to the legislative purpose of ameliorating what is identified as inconvenience and expense occasionally caused to litigants by jurisdictional limitations in federal, State and Territory courts. However, the purposes, motives or intentions of the relevant legislatures and their members do not provide a criterion by which validity is to be determined. Rather, it is the operation and effect of the law in question which defines its constitutional character ...

[576] [I]t was held in *Duncan* [(1983) 158 CLR 535] that the Coal Industry Tribunal could exercise both Commonwealth and State powers ... But what is of note is that the combined operation is limited according to the constitutional validity which each respective parliament can give. In *Duncan* there was no doubt that both the Commonwealth and the States had power to give some authority to the Tribunal. The effect of the decision was that the limited power of each was joined to form a body with power greater than any one of the polities, acting alone, [577] could have conferred. It is a case about the complementing of existing powers, not the creation of new powers. In the present cases the immediate question is whether the Commonwealth Parliament has any power either to consent to States conferring jurisdiction on federal courts or itself to confer State judicial power on federal courts. If there is no power for the Commonwealth to take those steps, the fact that all the States wish that it could do so or seek to have it do so, does not supply that absent power. *Duncan* recognises (as had long been recognised) that the Constitution not only does not forbid Commonwealth-State co-operation, it expressly provides in some respects for such co-operation ... But no amount of co-operation can supply power where none exists. To hold to the contrary would be to hold that the Parliaments of the Commonwealth and the States could, by co-operative legislation, effectively amend the Constitution by giving to the Commonwealth power that the Constitution does not give it ...

[579] The reliance on an incidental power (whether the express power in s 51(xxxix) to legislate with respect to "matters incidental to the execution of any power vested by this Constitution ... in the Federal Judicature" or an implied incidental power in s 71) must fail. The laws now in question cannot be described as being laws with respect to matters incidental to the execution of a power vested by the Constitution in the federal judicature. And although as was noted by the

majority in *Boilermakers* [(1956) 94 CLR 254 at 278] "[t]he judicial power, like all other constitutional powers, extends to every authority or capacity which is necessary or proper to render it effective" it cannot be said that these laws are necessary or proper to render effective the judicial power that is given by Ch III.

These incidental powers give no support to the laws now in question because Ch III, and the federal judicature with which it deals, are concerned with the judicial power of the Commonwealth. The judicial power that is conferred by these Acts (whether that is by the operation of the States' laws or the Commonwealth's laws) is not part of the judicial power of the Commonwealth, it is the judicial power of the States. In the case of the general cross-vesting arrangements, it is said to be conferred on the federal judicature to avoid "inconvenience and expense ... occasionally [being] caused to litigants by jurisdictional limitations in federal, State and Territory courts". That is, it is conferred in aid of what is thought to be the more efficient disposition of matters that fall within the *States'* judicial power ...

The fact that there is a power to invest State courts with federal jurisdiction does not mean that there must be some capacity to make a reciprocal arrangement ... [M]ore importantly, the only connection between the investing of State judicial power on federal courts and the judicial power of the Commonwealth is that it is said that it would be "convenient" or "more efficient" if federal courts could exercise State judicial power. These assertions of "convenience" and "efficiency" may well be open to question. It is, perhaps, significant in that regard that the Cross-vesting Acts refer to inconvenience and expense as having been **[580]** encountered only "occasionally". Further, what is meant in this context by "convenience" and "efficiency" may require rather more analysis than an unthinking resort to the slogan that "arid jurisdictional disputes" are thus avoided; it would be necessary, at least, to test the unstated premises of the assertion that these disputes occur often enough to constitute a real problem and that the cross-vesting arrangements are the *only* way or the best way of avoiding them. But if it is accepted that the cross-vesting arrangements *are* convenient and more efficient, the question becomes convenient in what sense, or for whom, and more efficient than what?

No single formula will describe the relationship that must exist between a power or group of powers and some exercise of power that is said to be incidental to the execution of the principal power or is necessary or proper to render the main grant of power effective ... The first focus of inquiry must therefore be on the subject matter of the power to which the step in question is said to be incidental. In the present matters, that is the Commonwealth's power with respect to the judicial power of the Commonwealth. Once it is recognised that this is the main power, it can be seen that it is not necessary to the exercise of *that* power, and it is not reasonably necessary to carry it into effect, that State judicial power is conferred on federal courts. To put the matter in another way, it is not conducive to the success of the legislation that establishes the federal courts or defines their jurisdiction that State judicial power is conferred upon them. In truth, **[581]** what is sought to be done by the legislation that now is in question is to supplement the power that the Commonwealth is given by the Constitution with respect to the federal judicature, not to complement it.

Kirby J: [600] The Constitution, and in particular Ch III, does not impose Laocoönian constraints on this Court. The proper approach to Ch III, applicable to these proceedings, is that recently stated by Gleeson CJ and McHugh J in *Abebe v Commonwealth* [(1999) 197 CLR 510 at 532]. Rigid and impractical outcomes are justified only by "the clearest constitutional language" which "compel them". As their Honours concluded in that case, so do I here ...

[601] On the face of things ... , there would not seem to be any reason of constitutional principle or policy to forbid the kind of legislative cooperative scheme between all of the governments and legislatures of the Commonwealth instanced by the two legislative systems of cross-vesting. A negative implication will only arise where it is manifest from the language used in the provisions within Ch III or is logically or practically necessary for the preservation of the integrity and structure of the Judicature envisaged in that Chapter. The governments involved have maintained their support for the legislation under consideration despite many changes of political complexion. Over more than a decade, none of the legislatures has evidenced a desire to withdraw from either of the cross-vesting systems. It is not as if the polities constituting the Australian Commonwealth are, in relation to each other, foreign states. All of them are parts of an integrated federal nation which the Constitution itself summoned forth ...

In Australia, the courts of the States and Territories are not subordinate in independence, integrity or professional skills to the federal courts provided for in Ch III. There is movement between, and overlap within, their personnel. The Constitution, the legal tradition of the nation and decisions of this Court help to ensure high common standards ... **[602]** [T]here is nothing obviously offensive in the adoption of sensible cooperative arrangements between the courts and the executive governments of the Commonwealth, the States and the Territories to achieve objectives such as those stated in the preambles adopted in common form in the cross-vesting laws ...

A legislature cannot, by preambular assertions, recite itself into constitutional power where none exists. Yet the agreement of all the democratically elected legislatures of Australia that a system of cross-vesting is necessary to help avoid inconvenience and expense, and to remove injustices and uncertainties occasioned by jurisdictional conflict, provides at least persuasive evidence that the legislation serves a practical national purpose. Everyday experience in the courts **[603]** would probably establish that fact in any case. Some lawyers enjoy the intricate intellectual problems which can arise where there is a conflict or disparity of jurisdiction. Occasionally, a party may take advantage of them. But few ordinary citizens see their merits. Most parties discern no beauty or value in conflicts of this kind. If this amounts to an "unthinking resort to" slogans about "arid jurisdictional disputes", I must bear that label. However, I also invite attention to the complex and disputable legal points (about which differences persist) that will be necessary to resolve some of these cases once the cross-vesting laws are struck down. They illustrate what the future now holds for Australian courts and those who use them.

The need for a system such as the cross-vesting legislation within the Australian Commonwealth can therefore scarcely be doubted. Statistical and other material was provided to this Court about the use made of the legislation challenged in these proceedings ... Yet such statistics, significant as they are, seriously understate the utilisation of the legislation. They concentrate on matters transferred to and from the jurisdiction of the Federal Court of Australia. They do not quantify other inter-jurisdictional transfers. They do not measure the matters commenced in a jurisdiction which, but for the cross-vesting legislation, would have been impermissible ...

[604] There is ... nothing inherent in the Australian Constitution which forbids the co-operative sharing and combination of governmental powers within the federation. On the contrary, the constitutional text expressly contemplates various forms of inter-governmental co-operation and co-operation between the Parliaments of the Commonwealth and of the States. This, then, is the constitutional setting in which the suggested negative implications of Ch III must be evaluated. If some forms of inter-governmental and inter-legislative co-operation are permissible, and have been achieved, the question is immediately posed as to why, within the Australian judiciary, similar inter-jurisdictional co-operation must be regarded as totally forbidden. This is just another way of saying, once again, that **[605]** in the context of the Australian Constitution, very clear language in Ch III would be required to produce such an unyielding and rigid outcome.

The first step of the challengers' argument latches onto the express provision in s 77(iii) of the Constitution. By that paragraph the federal Parliament may make laws "investing any court of a State with federal jurisdiction". By an appeal to the expressio unius principle of construction, it is claimed that the Australian Constitution envisages, in the case of the judiciary, a one-way street of inter-jurisdictional conferral of judicial power. It would only flow from the Commonwealth to a State. It could not flow in the opposite direction. This argument is completely unconvincing. This probably explains why the challengers in these proceedings advanced it in muted tones.

The expressio unius rule must always be used with caution. It is especially perilous in construing a constitution written in sparse language, such as ours. There are many reasons why s 77(iii) provides as it does. Most of them are historical. The State (formerly colonial) courts were well established at the time of federation. There were no federal courts at that time. Indeed, there were few federal courts in Australia until the 1970s ... The provision of a power compulsorily to invest the established State courts with federal jurisdiction was therefore an urgent necessity. It was so if the new Commonwealth, with its limited resources, were to avoid the burdensome obligation of creating immediately a parallel federal judiciary such as had been established in the United States of America. In that country, the uneven quality and varying methods of appointment of the judiciary of the States had resulted in the growth of a substantial and separate federal judiciary. By way of contrast, the Australian colonial (and later State) judiciaries exhibited uniformly high standards of integrity and ability rendering the "autochthonous expedient" [*R v Kirby; Ex parte Boilermakers' Society of Australia* (1956) 94 CLR 254 at 268] particularly suitable to Australia's initial federal judicial arrangements.

Far from giving rise to an implication that a reverse conferral of State jurisdiction on federal courts is impermissible, the history of almost a century during which federal jurisdiction has frequently been invested by federal laws in the courts of the States established a constitutional environment in which reciprocal laws of the States were both a natural and permissible development. The lack of express **[606]** provision in Ch III for that to happen can also be explained by reference to the text. Ch III is concerned with the judicial power of the Commonwealth. It is addressed, substantially, to the establishment of this Court and provision for the creation of other federal courts, exercising the jurisdiction there specified. Although the continued existence of the courts of the States, and specifically the Supreme Courts, is clearly contemplated by Ch III, provision for them, and for the exercise of the judicial power of the States, is properly reserved to the constitutions of each State … The failure to deal with that power in Ch III is therefore no indication of a constitutional prohibition. It is simply a reflection of the respective functions of the federal and State constitutions …

[609] [The majority view] would appear to consign those seeking to restore the benefits of cross-vesting legislation, enjoyed these past dozen years, to the highly **[610]** problematic and expensive task of proposing and securing a formal amendment to the Australian Constitution. The inconvenience of such a rigid construction of Ch III is then shown in sharp relief. The amendment would be necessary not to delete offending words nor to overcome an expressly stated prohibition. It would be needed to reverse an implication which this Court (in my view needlessly) reads into the Chapter. It would require the most compelling arguments of constitutional authority, principle and policy to persuade me that the combined Parliaments of the Commonwealth of Australia cannot, after nearly a century of federation, do together (with all the travail that such a course involves) what the Imperial Parliament might readily have done in 1901 on a relatively straightforward machinery matter of this kind.

Kirby J went on to hold that the powers of the federal Parliament under ss 71 and 77 to create federal courts and define their jurisdiction, combined with the incidental powers, enabled the Commonwealth to consent to a State conferral of jurisdiction on a federal court. In conclusion he quoted Barton J in *Duncan v Queensland* (1916) 22 CLR 556 at 605: "**[619]** 'To say that one regrets to differ from one's learned brethren is a formula that often begins a judgment. I end mine by expressing heavy sorrow that their decision is as it is'." To this Kirby J added: "So, in this case, do I".

Re Wakim meant that almost all corporate law matters must be heard by the State Supreme Courts and not by the Federal Court, despite its significant expertise in the area. The effect on the workload of the Federal Court was dramatic. While 1946 corporate law matters were filed in that Court in 1995-96, the number dropped to six for 1999-2000 (Federal Court of Australia, *Annual Report 1999/00* (AGPS, 2000), 135). In order to preserve the practical effect of past decisions and orders by the Federal Court in cases heard by it under the two cross-vesting schemes, each State passed an Act entitled the *Federal Courts (State Jurisdiction) Act 1999*, declaring that the "rights and liabilities" of the persons affected were the same as if the Federal Court judgments had been State Supreme Court judgments. The validity of that legislation was upheld in *Residual Assco Group Ltd v Spalvins* (2000) 202 CLR 629 and *Re Macks; Ex parte Saint* (2000) 204 CLR 158.

Re Wakim had dealt a major blow both to the general scheme of cross-vesting, and to the co-operative scheme underpinning the Corporations Law. A further blow to the latter scheme was dealt by *Byrnes v The Queen* (1999) 199 CLR 1 and *Bond v The Queen* (2000) 201 CLR 213, quashing sentences imposed by the Supreme Courts of South Australia and Western Australia respectively for offences committed under the Corporations Law. The sentences had been imposed as a result of appeals by the Commonwealth Director of Public Prosecutions against the original lower sentences, but the High Court held that the provisions of the State and Commonwealth laws enabling the Commonwealth's prosecution authorities to exercise "enforcement powers" under State law did not extend to such appeals. On one view, the decisions merely identified a lacuna in the legislation that might have been cured by amendment. But, two months after *Bond*, another case posed a more fundamental threat.

R v Hughes (2000) 202 CLR 535 was a challenge to the power of the Commonwealth Director of Public Prosecutions to prosecute breaches of the Corporations Law. Offences under that Law were created by a State Act, in this case the *Corporations (Western Australia) Act 1990* (WA). Section 29 established that a breach of the State law is "taken to be" an offence against the laws of the Commonwealth and not "an offence against the laws of" the State. Section 45 of the *Corporations Act 1989* (Cth) then required such offences to be "taken to be" offences against the "laws of the Commonwealth", while s 46 conferred on the federal Attorney-General, as a matter of Commonwealth law, "such functions and powers as are expressed to be conferred on him or her by or under [the State Act]". Thus, Commonwealth law empowered the federal Attorney-General, and Commonwealth agencies such as the Director of Public Prosecutions, to prosecute offences created by State law. Section 47 of the *Corporations Act* and reg 3(1)(d) of the *Corporations (Commonwealth Authorities and Officers) Regulations* (Cth), in particular, specified that the Director of Public Prosecutions had the functions and powers conferred by the State Act. Further, the regime removed the responsibility of enforcement from the relevant State authorities: s 33 of the State Act provided that where a function or power is conferred on an officer or authority of the Commonwealth it may not be performed or exercised by an officer or authority of the State.

When the validity of this elaborate conferral and acceptance of enforcement power was challenged, the Court unanimously upheld the validity of the prosecution by federal authorities in this particular instance, but did so in a way that cast doubt upon the capacity of federal authorities to enforce other parts of the Corporations Law.

R v Hughes
(2000) 202 CLR 535

Gleeson CJ, Gaudron, McHugh, Gummow, Hayne and Callinan JJ: [553] It may be accepted that, subject to what may be the operation of negative implications arising from the Constitution, for example Ch III, in the exercise of the incidental power the Parliament may permit officers of the Commonwealth holding appointments by or under statute to perform functions and accept appointments in addition to their Commonwealth appointments. Provisions such as s 46 and s 47 [of the *Corporations Act 1989* (Cth)] illustrate two further propositions. The first is that a State by its laws cannot unilaterally invest functions under that law in officers of the Commonwealth; the second is that a State law which purported to grant a wider power or authority than that the acceptance of which was prescribed by Commonwealth law would, to that extent, be inconsistent with the Commonwealth law and invalid under s 109 of the Constitution.

However, those propositions do not exhaust the operation of s 47 in the present matter; nor do they explain the operation of s 46. In particular, they do not provide a basis for the imposition by federal law upon Commonwealth officers of duties to perform functions or exercise powers created and conferred by State law. Such a federal law must be supported by a head of power … [T]he effect of the national scheme was to substitute the Commonwealth prosecution apparatus for that of the relevant State. State functionaries were directed by State law, in this case by s 33 of the WA Corporations Act, not to perform or exercise functions or powers conferred by the State legislation upon an officer or authority of the Commonwealth.

It is submitted, principally by the DPP and the Attorney-General who intervened in his support, that reg 3(1)(d) of the Regulations and the federal laws which support it involve no more than an approval or consent to the exercise of State functions and powers by the DPP. It is said that the State provisions simply purport to confer powers upon the DPP, whose exercise may be the subject of general directions by the Attorney-General under s 8 of the DPP Act. However, what is involved in the federal legislation is more than consent or permission by the Commonwealth to the exercise by its officers of additional functions and powers derived entirely from State law. These additional functions and powers are imposed by federal law as a matter of duty or obligation, lest there be an abdication of State authority with no certainty of its effective replacement.

We have stated above our acceptance of a proposition as to permissive provisions respecting the exercise of additional functions by Commonwealth officers. Whether the further step taken here of imposing duties by Commonwealth law was necessary not merely to implement the agreement between the respective Executive Govern-[554]-ments, but as a constitutional imperative, we need not stay to consider. The immediate point is that, the step having been taken, the federal law taking it required support by an available head of power.

The joint judgment held that in this instance the prosecution could be supported by a head of Commonwealth power. The case involved investment funds being channelled through a United States securities house and returning (with profit) to the investors in Australia. It therefore related to trade and commerce with other countries (s 51(i)), and to matters territorially outside Australia (s 51(xxix)). To the extent that the scheme might enable the Commonwealth to initiate other prosecutions not supported by a head of power, the joint judgment held that the conferral of authority could be "read down" under s 15A of the *Acts Interpretation Act 1901* (Cth). The judgment then discussed the implications of its decision for the earlier case of *R v Duncan*.

Gleeson CJ, Gaudron, McHugh, Gummow, Hayne and Callinan JJ: [557] Reference was made in argument to what was decided in *Duncan* [(1983) 158 CLR 535]. The Attorney-General submits that the legislation whose validity was at issue in *Duncan* may have impliedly imposed duties upon the tribunal and not merely conferred powers. The Attorney-General for the State of Victoria goes further and says that the tribunal plainly had a duty to exercise the powers or jurisdiction conferred on it. That may well be so, but would not undermine the decision in *Duncan*. This is because the several judgments of Mason, Murphy, Brennan and Deane JJ in that case support the proposition that the powers in s 51(xxxv) and s 51(xxxix) support legislation to establish a tribunal to exercise federal and State powers where this may better achieve the object of preventing and settling interstate disputes in the coal industry. What has been said above respecting the powers and functions of the DPP which derive from State law is consistent with that approach.

Duncan is one of a number of decisions which recognise that [558] co-operation on the part of the Commonwealth and States may well achieve objects that could be achieved by neither acting alone. Nothing in these reasons denies that general proposition. The present case emphasises that for the Commonwealth to impose on an officer or instrumentality of the Commonwealth powers coupled with duties adversely to affect the rights of individuals, where no such power is directly conferred on that officer or instrumentality by the Constitution itself, requires a law of the Commonwealth supported by an appropriate head of power.

Kirby J reached the same conclusion.

Kirby J: [583] In the present matter, the "actual operation of the law in question" undoubtedly affects rights, duties, powers and privileges in relation to activities falling within established heads of federal constitutional power, namely s 51(i) and (xxix). Although the text of the law is silent about these propounded paragraphs of the Constitution, the law is as valid as it would have been if they had been expressly mentioned in the text and called in aid of the claim to constitutional validity. The absence of an explicit reference to the constitutional source is certainly unusual. It invites challenges such as the present. However, upon analysis, it is not fatal in this particular instance.

Obviously, to the extent that federal law purports to authorise an officer or authority of the Commonwealth to perform functions conferred by State law which seriously affect the liberty and property rights of individuals, it may be expected that, when challenged, those who propound the constitutional validity of such authorisation will be able to demonstrate that validity exists. The more drastic the consequences for those affected, the more vigilant will be the scrutiny of the impugned law, measured against the constitutional warrant. The proposition that serious and burdensome consequences of criminal proceedings may be sustained by reference to nothing more than the creation of the office of the Commonwealth DPP and incidents thereto in the context of the joint cooperative scheme (or this with the execution of the Executive power of the Commonwealth or the implied nationhood power) is highly doubtful. For such outcomes a firm foundation of constitutional authority would appear to be necessary. Under our Constitution, criminal liability and punishment, when provided in a federal law, must be supported by demonstrable constitutional authority. Convenience and desirability are not enough if the constitutional foundation is missing.

[584] In the peculiar circumstances of this case that foundation exists. It might also exist in some other circumstances where the practical operation of the law (substance), as well as the legal operation (form), are held to fall within an established head of federal legislative power. Obviously, the search for a constitutional source is not helped by the absence of any relevant expression by the Federal Parliament of the propounded constitutional bases of its enactment. It remains to be seen whether, in other factual circumstances, such defects will prove fatal to other prosecutions. Clearly, it is a fragile foundation for a highly important national law. The present accused fails in his challenge. But the next case may not present circumstances sufficient to attract the essential constitutional support. Early attention to the "novel legislative device" would appear to be prudent.

The prosecution in *R v Hughes* involved overseas transactions, and was therefore held to be supported by a head of Commonwealth power. However, it was not clear that prosecutions could be brought in other areas of the Corporations Law where such support might be lacking. For example, the *Incorporation Case* decided that the corporations power does not enable the Commonwealth to regulate the process of incorporation. Did this mean that offences relating to the formation of companies could not be prosecuted?

Many options emerged for remedial action after *Re Wakim* and *R v Hughes*, including amendment of the Constitution to provide that federal courts can be invested with State jurisdiction. Instead, the federal government pressed the States for a "referral" of legislative power under s 51(xxxvii) of the Constitution. After lengthy negotiations, all States agreed (see, for example, the *Corporations (Commonwealth Powers) Act 2001* (NSW)). What they have referred to the Commonwealth is not a general power over corporations and securities, but only a specific power to enact the Corporations Bill 2001 and the Australian Securities and Investments Commission Bill 2001 – along with a limited power of amendment confined to "the formation of corporations, corporate regulation and the regulation of financial products and services", and not extending to laws on those matters made otherwise than by amendment of the principal legislation. Under s 5 of each Act, the referral terminates after five years. The Acts allow this period to be extended by proclamation, except in South Australia where any extension of the referral would require an amendment of the *Corporations (Commonwealth Powers) Act 2001* (SA).

Acting on the referrals, the Commonwealth Parliament enacted the *Corporations Act 2001* (Cth) and the *Australian Securities and Investments Commission Act 2001* (Cth), which came into effect on 15 July 2001. The constitutional basis of the *Corporations Act* is made clear in s 3. It provides that the Act is based so far as possible on the Commonwealth's existing powers under ss 51 and 122 of the Constitution. As a consequence, the Act relies upon power referred by the States only to the extent that those existing powers do not support it. This means that should one or more States withdraw the referral, as was threatened by Western Australia and Queensland in 2005 in negotiations over the distribution of GST revenue, the Act will continue to operate across Australia so far as possible on the basis of existing Commonwealth powers. Moreover, because of transitional provisions like s 1400, the provisions of the Act can operate in relation to events and liabilities arising *before* 2001. The validity of this operation as falling within the States' referral was upheld by a Full Court of the Federal Court in *Kennedy v Australian Securities and Investments Commission* (*Offset Alpine Printing Case*) (2005) 218 ALR 224: the referral legislation "[240] deals with the period *in which* the Commonwealth Parliament may legislate. It does not deal with the period *for which* it may legislate".

The referral mechanism in s 51(xxxvii) of the Constitution, on which the above arrangements rely, has often been used in the past. Prominent examples include the 1996 referral by Victoria of wide-ranging power over industrial relations (*Commonwealth Powers (Industrial Relations) Act 1996* (Vic)) and the 2002 referral by each State of power over terrorism (see, for example, *Terrorism (Commonwealth Powers) Act 2002* (Tas) and the acceptance of those referrals in the *Criminal Code Amendment (Terrorism) Act 2003* (Cth)). Over the first century of the Australian federation, 38 referral Acts were passed by State Parliaments, of which 17 remain in force. One factor that may have alleviated State concern about such referrals is the recognition by the High Court that a referral does not necessarily transfer power to the Commonwealth once and for all.

R v Public Vehicles Licensing Appeal Tribunal (Tas); Ex parte Australian National Airways Pty Ltd
(1964) 113 CLR 207

The Court: [225] A great deal of discussion has taken place as to the true meaning and operation of par (xxxvii) … The simplest approach, however, to the problem is simply to read the paragraph and to apply it without making implications or imposing limitations which are not found in the express words. We must remember that it is part of the Constitution and go back to the general counsel to remember that it is a constitution we are construing and it should be construed with all the generality which the words used admit. **[226]** See per *O'Connor* J in the *Jumbunna Case* [(1908) 6 CLR 309 at 367, 368]. So reading it, why should there be found in the words "matters referred to the Parliament of the Commonwealth by the Parliament or Parliaments of any State or States" any implications concerning the period of reference? It is plain enough that the Parliament of the State must express its will and it must express its will by enactment. How long the enactment is to remain in force as a reference may be expressed in the enactment. It none the less refers the matter. Indeed the matter itself may involve some limitation of time or be defined in terms which involve a limitation of time. In the argument before us there seemed to be an assumption that to include the Tasmanian Act No 46 of 1952 within par (xxxvii) there must be implications in the words the paragraph employs. But this seems to be an error. There is no reason to suppose that the words "matters referred" cannot cover matters referred for a time which is specified or which may depend on a future event even if that event involves the will of the State Governor-in-Council and consists in the fixing of a date by proclamation. The question which was discussed at length before us as to whether when the Parliament of a State has made a reference it may repeal the reference does not directly arise in this case. It forms only a subsidiary matter which if decided might throw light on the whole ambit or operation of the paragraph. We do not therefore discuss it or express any final opinion upon it … But it must be remembered that the paragraph is concerned with the reference by the Parliament or Parliaments of a State or States. The will of a Parliament is expressed in a statute or Act of Parliament and it is the general conception of English law that what Parliament may enact it may repeal.

Another significant mechanism for the redistribution of legislative power is s 51(xxxviii) of the Constitution, which enables the Commonwealth, "at the request or with the concurrence of the Parliaments of all the States directly concerned", to exercise any power that was formerly exercisable only by the Imperial Parliament or by the Federal Council of Australasia. For example, as a result of Commonwealth-State negotiations following the High Court decision in *New South Wales v Commonwealth* (*Seas and Submerged Lands Case*) (1975) 135 CLR 337), the States were given the power to legislate over the territorial sea, or at least that part of it extending three nautical miles from the coast. This was achieved through complementary legislation by the State and Commonwealth Parliaments. The Commonwealth, pursuant to its power under s 51(xxxviii), and in response to a request by the Parliament of each of the States, enacted the *Coastal Waters (State Title) Act 1980* (Cth) and the *Coastal Waters (State Powers) Act 1980* (Cth), providing for the exercise of legislative power by the States.

Coastal Waters (State Powers) Act 1980 (Cth)

5 The legislative powers exercisable from time to time under the constitution of each State extend to the making of – …

  (c) laws of the State with respect to fisheries in Australian waters beyond the outer limits of the coastal waters of the State, being laws applying to or in relation to those fisheries only to the extent to which those fisheries are, under an arrangement to which the Commonwealth and the State are parties, to be managed in accordance with the laws of the State.

In 1989, the validity of s 5(c) was upheld by the High Court.

Port MacDonnell Professional Fishermen's Assn Inc v South Australia
(1989) 168 CLR 340

The Court: [378] [T]he primary subject to which par (xxxviii) was addressed was the perceived need to ensure that legislative powers necessary for the purposes of the new nation could be exercised locally notwithstanding that, prior to federation, they were beyond the competence of local legislatures. In that context, there is no valid reason why the words "within the Commonwealth" should be given a more constrictive operation than that which flows from their ordinary grammatical construction. On that ordinary grammatical construction, the words refer to the location of the exercise of legislative power of the designated kind and not to the area of operation of the laws made by the exercise of such power ...

As the references to the United Kingdom Parliament and the Federal Council of Australasia make plain, the "power" to which the paragraph refers is legislative power. Shortly stated, the effect of s 51(xxxviii) is to empower the Commonwealth Parliament to make laws with respect to the local exercise of any legislative power which, before federation, could not be exercised by the legislatures of the former Australian colonies. In the early days of the Constitution, there may well have been some inhibition against giving that grant of legislative power its full scope and effect in that it could have been seen as controlled by the then status of the Commonwealth itself within the British Empire. Today, any room for such inhibition has long been denied by "the silent operation of constitutional principles" in the context of complete independence and international sovereignty (see *Commonwealth v Kreglinger & Fernau Ltd and Bardsley* [(1926) 37 CLR 393 at 413] ...). That being so, there is no extrinsic reason why s 51(xxxviii) should not be given the broad interpretation which befits it as a constitutional provision with a national purpose of a fundamental kind. Indeed, the reasons justifying [that] approach ... **[379]** are applicable with more than ordinary force to par (xxxviii) for two reasons. First, that it is clear that one of the functions which par (xxxviii) was intended to serve was that of plugging gaps which might otherwise exist in the overall plenitude of the legislative powers exercisable by Commonwealth and State Parliaments under the Constitution. Secondly, the grant of power contained in par (xxxviii) does not represent the enhancement of Commonwealth legislative power at the cost of the diminution or potential diminution of the effectiveness of State legislative power. Indeed, the contrary is the case since one of the more obvious examples of a law with respect to the exercise within the Commonwealth of a legislative power of the kind described in par (xxxviii) is a law providing that a particular legislative power of that kind may be exercised by a designated local legislature such as the Commonwealth Parliament itself or the Parliament (or Parliaments) of a State (or States). That being so, par (xxxviii) can properly be seen as representing both actual and potential enhancement of State legislative powers – actual in that it confers, by implication, power upon the Parliament of a State to participate in the legislative process which the paragraph requires, namely request (or concurrence) by a State Parliament and enactment by the Commonwealth Parliament; potential in that the State Parliaments are potential recipients of legislative power under a law made pursuant to the paragraph ...

Section 5(c) of the *Coastal Waters (State Powers) Act* does not in terms confer legislative power. It provides that the legislative powers exercisable by the States extend to the making of laws of the designated category. Its purported operation is to confirm the existence of the legislative power to make that category of law to the extent that it already existed and to confer that particular legislative power if, and to the extent that, it did not already exist. One possible broad characterization of s 5(c) is as a law with respect to the power to make laws of the designated category. If that were the only permissible characterization of a law which, like s 5(c), provides that a State Parliament possesses power to make laws of a designated category, the requirements of par (xxxviii) would be satisfied only if the power to make laws of the designated **[380]** category could, at the establishment of the Constitution, have been exercised only by the Parliament of the United Kingdom. To the extent that a colonial parliament had power, the power of the Parliament of the United Kingdom would not have been exclusive. That would mean that par (xxxviii) was partially ineffective to serve its intended function of providing for the local exercise of "any" power which was previously exercisable only by the United Kingdom Parliament since it would not extend to a law which confirmed, as distinct from conferred, State legislative power. The result would be that a law enacted in accordance with the procedural requirement of par (xxxviii) to remove doubts about the existence of a particular State legislative power could only be within that paragraph if it were first found that the particular State legislative power did not previously exist at all ...

A law can, however, ordinarily be properly characterized in a number of different ways. In determining characterization for the purposes of par (xxxviii), we may take as a starting point some relevant legislative power which could, at the establishment of the Constitution, be exercised only by the United Kingdom Parliament. If no such relevant legislative power can be identified, that will be the end of the matter. If such a relevant legislative power can be identified, the question will then arise whether the particular law can properly be characterized as a law with respect to the exercise of that legislative power. In the case of s 5(c), there is an obviously relevant legislative power which could, at the establishment of the Constitution, be exercised only by the United Kingdom Parliament. That power is the power to control by external (in the sense of external to the relevant State Constitution) legislation the extent of the legislative powers of the States (then Colonies) under their respective Constitutions ... Some of the provisions of the Imperial Statutes 13 & 14 Vict c 59 (*An Act for the better Government of Her Majesty's* Australian *Colonies*) and 28 & 29 Vict c 63 (*An Act to remove Doubts as to the Validity of Colonial Laws*) provide **[381]** ready examples of the exercise by the United Kingdom Parliament of that formerly exclusive legislative power ... That being so and in the context of the settled broad interpretation of the words "with respect to" in s 51, s 5(c) can properly be characterized, for the purposes of par (xxxviii), as a law with respect to the exercise of that formerly exclusive legislative power of the United Kingdom Parliament. It follows that s 5(c) satisfies the requirement of s 51(xxxviii) that it be a law "with respect to ... [t]he exercise within the Commonwealth, at the request ... of the Parliaments of all the States directly concerned, of [a] power which can at the establishment of this Constitution be exercised only by the Parliament of the United Kingdom ...".

In *Sue v Hill* (1999) 199 CLR 462, the joint judgment of Gleeson CJ, Gummow and Hayne JJ treated the enactment of the *Australia Act 1986* (Cth) as depending on an exercise of power under s 51(xxxviii) (see Chapter 4, §8).

4. Equal Treatment of States

Sections 51(ii) and 99 of the Constitution have much in common with each other and also perhaps with ss 117 and 92. Ultimately, all these provisions reflect the aspiration that Australia should be "one country", at least in the sense that Australians should not be treated unequally simply because they happen to live in different States.

Sections 51(ii) and 99 are also sometimes linked with other provisions like ss 80 and 116 as potentially important guarantees of fundamental human rights. As with those other provisions, however, the practical operation of ss 51(ii) and 99 has been drastically limited. For one thing, the latter sections have been held not to apply to the indirect implementation of Commonwealth policy through grants to the States under s 96 (*Deputy Federal Commissioner of Taxation (NSW) v WR Moran Pty Ltd* (1939) 61 CLR 735; [1940] AC 838).

A more general limitation has been the emphasis by the High Court on form rather than substance. For example, a law imposing a tax on the mining of gold at the rate of 20 per cent in Western Australia and at the rate of 30 per cent in Tasmania would be invalid for discriminating between the States (*Cameron v Deputy Federal Commissioner of Taxation* (1923) 32 CLR 68). However, a tax at the rate of 25 per cent in both States would not infringe s 51(ii), despite its dramatically greater impact in Western Australia because of that State's larger gold mining industry (*Colonial Sugar Refining Company Limited v Irving* [1906] AC 360). As Higgins J put it in *James v Commonwealth* (1928) 41 CLR 442: "**[462]** [W]here the rule laid down is general, applicable to all the States alike, but it is found to operate unequally in the several States, not from anything done by the Commonwealth Parliament, but from the inequality in the conditions existing in … the States themselves … the Commonwealth Parliament has not been guilty of discrimination or preference between States".

The operation of s 99 has been further limited as follows:

1. The section is expressed to apply to a "law or regulation of trade, commerce, or revenue". As to "trade" and "commerce", the High Court has restricted the provision even further by holding that it applies only to laws capable of being made under s 51(i) (*Morgan v Commonwealth* (1947) 74 CLR 421). However, in *Permanent Trustee Australia Ltd v Commissioner of State Revenue (Vic)* (2004) 220 CLR 388, the Court was unanimous in refusing to draw a similar inference limiting laws or regulations of "revenue" to those made under s 51(ii). Specifically, the Court held that s 99 applies to "revenue" laws enacted under s 52(i) as well as under s 51(ii). As to *Morgan v Commonwealth* the joint majority judgment said only: "[426] The present case concerns a law or regulation of 'revenue' not of trade or commerce. *Morgan* may be put to one side".

2. The word "preference" has been interpreted as referring only to trading or commercial preference. The mere fact that a law is discriminatory does not amount to a "preference". There must be a grant of some commercial advantage before s 99 can apply.

3. Mere geographical preference that favours a particular locality, and in that sense favours a State or part of a State, is not enough to infringe s 99. The locality must be singled out for differential treatment *because* it is a State or part of a State.

The main authority on points 2 and 3 is *Elliott v Commonwealth* (1936) 54 CLR 657. In that case, the *Transport Workers (Seamen) Regulations* (Cth) imposed a system of licensing for seamen. Certain "prescribed ports" had licensing officers, and at those ports no seaman could be signed on for a voyage without a licence. The only "prescribed ports" were Sydney, Melbourne, Brisbane, Newcastle and Port Adelaide. Eliot Elliott, a seaman whose home port was Sydney, complained that seamen at the "prescribed ports" were disadvantaged as compared with seamen at other ports. The issue was whether this was a "preference", and if so whether it operated as between "States or parts of States". Latham CJ, Rich, Starke and McTiernan JJ held that s 99 was not infringed. Dixon and Evatt JJ dissented.

Elliott v Commonwealth
(1936) 54 CLR 657

Latham CJ: [668] What sec 99 prohibits is giving *preference* "*to* one State or any part thereof *over* another State or any part thereof." In order to apply this section it is necessary to determine that there is preference: it is necessary also to ascertain what the preference is, and to identify the State or part of a State to which the preference is given and the other State or part of another State over which the preference is given. The Constitution appears to be based upon the view that differentiation in some laws or regulations of trade and commerce (namely, those which do not relate to taxation, including customs duties, or bounties) may be proper and desirable or at least permissible, even as between different States, but that such differentiation must not amount to the giving of preference to one State or any part thereof over another State or any part thereof.

In the case now before the Court there is no doubt that the law which applies in, for example, Sydney, does not apply in Fremantle. **[669]** The result of the legislation is to make a difference in the law applicable in these two places. It does not, in my opinion, follow from this fact that the law gives preference to one place over the other place. In the case of a law or regulation of trade and commerce the difference between the two places under consideration (whether they be States or parts of States) must be such as to amount to a trading or commercial preference which is definitely given to one State or part thereof over another State or part thereof. This is the view expressed in the case of *Crowe v Commonwealth* [(1935) 54 CLR 69] …

I proceed to inquire whether any such preference is to be found in the *Transport Workers Act* or in the regulations in question. The Act itself was not attacked in argument … When I consider the regulations I at once find a divergence of outlook in the definition of the "advantage" said to be given or conferred by the regulations …, and also a difficulty in determining which State or part of a State is to be regarded by a Court as receiving the advantage. One view is … that Fremantle was preferred to Sydney because the seamen in Fremantle were free from regulations **[670]** to which they were subject in Sydney. This proposition adopted the point of view of certain seamen. A second view would be that of other seamen, who are equally entitled to consider that the regulations give them an advantage in Sydney over seamen in Fremantle, where the licensing system is not in operation. According to this view Sydney is preferred over Fremantle. A third view which is put forward is that it is Sydney and not Fremantle that obtains preference – but for the different reason that employers of seamen in Sydney are regarded as receiving an advantage over employers of seamen in Fremantle. At the same time the argument is accepted that, from the point of view of certain seamen, Fremantle is given a preference over Sydney. I can understand that one legislative provision may give preference to State A or a part of State A over State B or a part of State B within the meaning of sec 99, and that another provision in the same statute or in the same statutory rule may give preference within the meaning of the same section to State B or part of B over State A or part of State A. But I have difficulty in understanding how one and the same legislative provision can, within the meaning of sec 99, at once give preference to State A over State B and also preference to State B over State A …

Thus there is difficulty in ascertaining satisfactorily what the alleged preference is and what State or part of a State receives it. It is, I think, entirely a question of opinion, which cannot be settled upon legal grounds, whether all or some only of the seamen of Sydney or the seamen of Fremantle or the employers of seamen in Sydney or the employers of seamen in Fremantle receive an advantage by reason of the legislation in question.

Where there is such vagueness as to the nature of the preference and the recipients of the preference I find myself unable to hold that there is here any tangible commercial advantage.

By contrast, Evatt J held that because the licensing system strengthened the hand of shipowners against the trade unions, it did give "**[700]** a definite material and economic advantage" to those ports, like Sydney, where it was in force over those, like Fremantle, where it was not. Dixon J also found a "preference".

Dixon J: [682] It is in the words "give preference over" that the crux of the case appears to me to lie. They express a conception necessarily indefinite. Their meaning cannot be considered apart from the words "law or regulation of trade, commerce, or revenue." By limiting the class of law or regulation which may not be used as a means of giving preference, those words necessarily determine the kind of preference prohibited.

[683] In *Crowe v Commonwealth* [54 CLR at 92] I said that in relation to trade and commerce, as distinguished from revenue, the preference referred to by sec 99 is evidently some tangible advantage obtainable in the course of trading or commercial operations, or, at least, some material or sensible benefit of a commercial or trading character. I intended the expression "trading or commercial operations" to bear a very wide and general meaning. It includes the activities which attend carriage by sea or land. Further consideration has confirmed me in the view which I then expressed. I repeat that the preference may consist in a greater tendency to promote trade, in furnishing some incentive or facility, or in relieving from some burden or impediment. But it is, perhaps, desirable to notice that the phrase is not "give a preference" but "give preference." The difference may be slight, but the latter expression seems to bring out the element of priority of treatment, while the former has more suggestion of definite and actual advantage in the treatment. What is forbidden by sec 99 is, in a matter of advantage to trade or commerce, the putting of one State or part of a State before another State or part thereof. But the section does not call upon the Court to estimate the total amount of economic or commercial advantage which does or will actually ensue … It is enough that the law or regulation is designed to produce some tangible advantage obtainable in the course of trading or commercial operations, or some material or sensible benefit of a commercial or trading character. To give preference to one State over another State discrimination or differentiation is necessary. Without discrimination between States or parts of respective States, it is difficult to see how one could be given preference over the other. But I agree that it does not follow that every discrimination between States is a preference of one over the other. The expressions are not identical in meaning. More nearly, if not exactly, the same in meaning, is the expression "discrimination against." If sec 99 had been expressed to forbid the Commonwealth by a law or regulation of trade, commerce, or revenue to discriminate against a State or part of a State, I do not think its effect would have been substantially varied.

[684] The present regulations are restrictive and regulative. But the restrictions and regulations are directed at the disciplined and orderly conduct of a vocation or pursuit the work of which is essential to the carriage of goods or persons by sea. Ports in reference to which the system is applied enjoy its advantages whatever they may be. It is a system designed to promote the ease, convenience and orderliness of operations forming part of trade and commerce. The degree to which in practice it may do so, the manner in which it may be actually regarded by seamen, on the one hand, and shipmasters, on the other, and generally the merits or demerits of the system are, I think, beside the true question, which, in my opinion, is whether in a matter directed at commercial advantage one or more States have been put before another or others. That, in my opinion, has been done by giving to the sea commerce of four States a means devised for the enlistment and control of seamen and for maintaining order and discipline among them and by withholding it from the remaining two States.

If the regulation had shown upon its face an intention that the system should be applied as a remedy for a particular inconvenience or evil which might be found at one place and not at another, if the Minister were authorized to prescribe ports only when he found a given state of facts to prevail there, it might, perhaps, have been open to us to decide that the facts and not the "law or regulation of commerce" made the discrimination. I had some doubt whether, even without such limitation of the discretion conferred upon the Minister, the Court might not, for the purpose of ascertaining whether preference was given, examine the actual grounds upon which the specification of ports proceeded. But I think that sec 99 does not allow such a course. No doubt it does not require the Court to consider a law or regulation of commerce *in abstracto*. Preference and trade and commerce are conceptions which relate entirely to practical affairs. But sec 99 does establish a standard of validity which is concerned with the character of the law or regulation of commerce and not with the particular trading or economic consequences which may or may not in fact ensue from it at a particular place and time.

Behind the treatment in *Elliott v Commonwealth* of the expression "States or parts of States", as found in both ss 51(ii) and 99, lay the dissent of Isaacs J in *R v Barger* (1908) 6 CLR 41. In that case, manufacturers offering "fair and reasonable" labour conditions had been exempted from excise duties. What was "fair and reasonable" was to be determined, inter alia, "by a Judge of the Supreme Court of a State or … a State Industrial Authority". There was thus a possibility that determinations might differ from State to State. The majority held that, simply because a statutory reference to "a State" was involved, s 51(ii) was infringed. Isaacs J argued in dissent that s 51(ii) only operates where there is discrimination against a State or part of a State "as such": "[108] [T]he pervading idea is the preference of locality merely because it is locality, and because it is a particular part of a particular State. It does not include a differentiation based on other considerations, which are dependent on natural or business circumstances, and may operate with more or less force in different localities".

In the aftermath of *Amalgamated Society of Engineers v Adelaide Steamship Co Ltd* (*Engineers' Case*) (1920) 28 CLR 129 (see Chapter 7, §4), Isaacs J's dissent in *R v Barger* was followed by the whole Court in *Cameron v Deputy Federal Commissioner of Taxation* (1923) 32 CLR 68. In that case, regulations made under the *Income Tax Assessment Act 1915* (Cth) were held to infringe s 51(ii) by reason of discrimination "between States or parts of States". The regulations had provided that, for taxation purposes, "the value of live stock on hand" should be assessed where possible at cost price and in other cases "at the fair average value set forth in Table III in the Schedule". The values set forth in the Schedule varied from State to State: for example, a cow in Queensland was valued at £3 and a cow in New South Wales at £6. In holding that this infringed s 51(ii), the whole Court followed what Isaacs J had said in *R v Barger*. Isaacs J quoted a passage from his earlier judgment in which he had said that "discrimination" involves a person or property being "[110] treated differently" because of locality, "regardless of any other circumstance". After quoting that passage, Isaacs J went on:

Cameron v Deputy Federal Commissioner of Taxation
(1923) 32 CLR 68

Isaacs J: [76] It was said by Sir *Edward Mitchell* that as a "fair average value" was applied in each State, that was not "regardless of any other circumstance" than State situation. But that is an error. Stock in Queensland and stock in New South Wales are, by reason solely of their State situation, "treated differently," by the mere fact that different standards are applied to them respectively. It does not matter whether those legal standards are arbitrary or measured, whether dictated by a desire to benefit or to injure, the simple fact is they are "different," **[77]** and those different legal standards being applied simply because the subject of taxation finds itself in one State or the other there arises the discrimination by law between States which is forbidden by the Constitution.

On this basis, the majority in *Elliott v Commonwealth* held that the limitation of the seamen's licensing system to specified ports did not operate by reference to "States or parts of States".

Elliott v Commonwealth
(1936) 54 CLR 657

Latham CJ: [675] [T]he *discrimen* which sec 99 forbids the Commonwealth to select is not merely locality as such, but localities which for the purpose of applying the *discrimen* are taken as States or parts of States. In the regulations in question the application of the regulations depends upon the selection of ports as ports and not of States or parts of States as such. In my opinion sec 99 does not prohibit such differentiation …

I am aware that it may be thought that the result is to make the protection of the section largely illusory. The operation of the section can be excluded by avoiding the adoption of reference to States or parts of States as such as a *discrimen*. It is however, some relief to me to find that the opposite view is open, from all practical points of view, to substantially the same objection. The opposite view concedes that sec 99 is not infringed if the preferential treatment is based not upon locality alone but also upon other circumstances. Thus, upon that view, the operation of the section can be excluded by including among the conditions even of avowedly preferential treatment a condition referring to some circumstance other than locality, possibly to any such circumstance, **[676]** but certainly to any other circumstance which is itself relevant to or an aspect of inter-State or foreign trade or commerce.

Dixon and Evatt JJ dissented. Dixon J thought that "**[682]** even if, in prescribing a port in one State, the Minister cannot be considered to have adopted 'part of a State' … as the basis of his differentiation", nevertheless the specified ports were so crucial to the interstate and overseas commerce of their respective States that "in specifying the chief ports in each of four States a course was taken which must be considered as affecting each of those States as a whole".

Evatt J: [689] An analysis of sec 99 shows that it forbids four distinct types of preference laws, that is to say:–
   (1) Laws giving preference to a State over another State;
   (2) Laws giving preference to a State over any part of another State;
   (3) Laws giving preference to any part of a State over another State;
   (4) Laws giving preference to any part of a State over any part of another State.
   It is evident that commercial or revenue regulations which are not geographically uniform and which confer advantages based solely upon the discrimen of locality in any State will usually find ready inclusion in one or more of the four categories set out above. Of **[690]** course an enactment which merely preferred one part of a State (eg Sydney) over another part of the same State (eg Bathurst) would be unaffected by sec 99. But, in practice, it would be almost impossible to pass such an enactment, because the States other than New South Wales would either be treated in the same way as Sydney or not; in the first case, the enactment would give preference to the other States over part of New South Wales (Bathurst); and in the latter case the enactment would give preference to part of New South Wales (Sydney) over the other States.

Accordingly, there was a very solid foundation for the conclusion reached in *Barger's Case* [(1908) 6 CLR 41] by the majority of the Court – that sec 99 forbids all preferences which arise solely as a legal consequence of association with or reference to any locality in "Australia," ie, "one or more of the States of Australia." The opposing view of *Isaacs* J – that the only preference forbidden by sec 99 is preference to a State or a part of a State "considered as" such – involves the proposition that sec 99 is not infringed if (say) a Commonwealth enactment exempts from taxation "all persons carrying on business or resident at Brisbane." On *Isaacs* J's view, presumably, such an enactment would not give a preference to a part of Queensland "considered as" a part of Queensland. But it is indisputable that such an enactment would give a preference to Brisbane, and, as Brisbane is part of the State of Queensland, the enactment would give a preference to a part of a State over the five remaining States of the Commonwealth. Similar examples may be multiplied indefinitely – eg, preferences might be given to persons associated with an electoral division, a municipal or shire area, and so forth; in all such cases a careful analysis of the enactment would reveal an infringement of sec 99. In truth, the extension of the prohibition in sec 99 to "part of" a State, whether it is a large part or only a small part, makes it impossible to apply the view, advanced by *Isaacs* J in *Barger's Case*, but rejected by the majority.

In his able argument, Mr *Pat[t]erson* gave a further illustration of a law of revenue which offends against sec 99. He supposed that a Commonwealth law provided that persons resident in, and carrying on business at, Sydney, Newcastle, Melbourne, Brisbane, Port **[691]** Adelaide and Townsville (the six places specified in the present regulations) should be exempt from taxation if their incomes exceeded £500. In such a case, he said, first, that there would be an infringement of sec 51(II), because the law of taxation would "discriminate between States or parts of States." This view is obviously sound, because it is preposterous to suggest that, before the prohibitions of sec 51(II) or sec 99 of the Constitution can apply, the name of one or more States must be branded upon the face of the offending legislation. If this view is correct, it also shows that the word "because" as used by *Isaacs* J in *Barger's Case* [(1905) 6 CLR 41 at 110] in the phrase "*because one man or his property is in one locality*" … cannot be taken as a reference to the Legislature's or Executive's *reason* for giving a preference arising from mere locality. For, in the example mentioned, the reason for the preference would not be apparent from the Act or regulation, and it is not easy to imagine how otherwise that reason could ever be ascertained. The word "because" in the phrase defining locality preferences must mean that the particular legislation operates solely *as a consequence* of geographical situation within a State of the Commonwealth …

The illustration given by counsel should be followed a little further. Does such an Act as he envisaged confer a preference contrary to sec 99 as well as to sec 51(II)? He contended, and his contention has not, and I think cannot, be answered, that such a law would give preference to those residing or carrying on business in any of the six localities specified over all persons residing or carrying on business in any locality within Western Australia and Tasmania, as well as over all such persons in all localities in the four States except the localities preferred.

In *Commissioner of Taxation v Clyne* (1958) 100 CLR 246, the challenge was to a scheme of allowable deductions based on residence in "Zone A" or "Zone B". Each Zone comprised parts of several States and no part of Victoria fell in either Zone. Whether the scheme infringed either s 51(ii) or s 99 was not finally decided. However, Dixon CJ took the opportunity to reassert what he and Evatt J had said in *Elliott v Commonwealth* and, especially, what Evatt J had said in a similar dissent in *Deputy Federal Commissioner of Taxation (NSW) v WR Moran Pty Ltd* (1939) 61 CLR 735. Dixon CJ cast doubt on the helpfulness of the formula laid down by Isaacs J in *R v Barger* and *Cameron v Federal Commissioner of Taxation*.

Commissioner of Taxation v Clyne
(1958) 100 CLR 246

Dixon CJ: [266] For myself I have the greatest difficulty in grasping what exactly is the requirement that the selection of an area shall be as part of the State. No doubt it may be expressed in various ways, eg "in virtue of its character as part of the State" or "*qua* part of the State" or "because it is part of a State" or "as such". However it may be expressed I find myself unable to appreciate the distinction between the selection by an enactment of an area in fact forming part of a State for the bestowal of a preference upon the area and the selection of the same area for the same purpose "as part of the State".

The issue did not need to be resolved in this case, since the Court held that, even if the 1945 amendments adding the "zoning" scheme were invalid, that did not affect the validity of the Act as a whole, which was in fact the matter under challenge. Only Webb J gave a full judgment. He held that the "zoning" scheme did not infringe s 51(ii) or s 99. The other judges expressed their agreement with Dixon CJ, though McTiernan J stated: "**[268]** But I would affirm the decision of the majority in *Elliott's Case*".

In *Conroy v Carter* (1968) 118 CLR 90, the *Poultry Industry Levy Act 1965* (Cth) had authorised the Commonwealth to make "arrangements" for State Egg Boards to collect a poultry levy on its behalf. Building on what Isaacs J had said in *R v Barger* and *Cameron v Federal Commissioner of Taxation*, the whole Court held that the "arrangements" were valid under s 51(ii), even if they operated unequally from State to State. As Anthony Mason QC put it in argument, the provision for "arrangements" "**[93]** is a general law applicable throughout the Commonwealth, but any difference in its application to individual taxpayers springs from different conditions arising from the existence or absence of arrangements between the Commonwealth and State or States. It does not spring from any provision of the section itself".

The legislation considered in *Conroy v Carter* had also provided that, where an "arrangement" had been made for a State Egg Board to collect the poultry levy, the relevant Board could deduct the amount of the levy from any payments it made to the taxpayer. Although the Court had unanimously held that the differential "arrangements" for collecting the levy did not involve any "preference" for purposes of s 99, its members divided 3:3 on whether the provision for automatic deductions in States where "arrangements" had been made constituted "discrimination" for the purposes of s 51(ii).

Only two full judgments were delivered. Menzies J, with whom Barwick CJ and McTiernan J agreed, held that, as between a State with an "arrangement" for an Egg Board and a State with no such arrangement, poultry farmers in the former State were exposed to "**[103]** a particular disadvantage at **[104]** law ... , namely the retention of the levy out of moneys owing by a State Egg Board to the taxpayer". Taylor J, with whom Kitto and Windeyer JJ agreed, held that mere differential provision "**[102]** for the manner in which a liability for the levy may be discharged" was no more discriminating than "**[101]** a law which provided that levies due in New South Wales should be paid to the Deputy Commissioner of Taxation in New South Wales, and that those due in Western Australia should be paid to the Deputy Commissioner of Taxation in that State", or a law that provided that the levies should be payable "**[102]** at any branch of the Commonwealth Bank even if in one State the Commonwealth Bank should have no branches". The Court being evenly divided, the Chief Justice's view prevailed under s 23 of the *Judiciary Act 1903* (Cth) and the legislation was held to infringe s 51(ii). Neither judgment referred to the issues raised by Dixon CJ in *Federal Commissioner of Taxation v Clyne*.

The third edition of this book suggested (at 998, 1004) that judicial tendencies in the 1990s had been moving towards an emphasis on substance rather than on form in a way that might provoke a reinterpretation of ss 51(ii) and 99. However, when the issue arose again in *Permanent Trustee Australia Ltd v Commissioner of State Revenue (Vic)* (2004) 220 CLR 388, the joint majority judgment noted that "**[423]** this is not the occasion to seek to disentangle the reasoning in all the disparate authorities [on s 99] in the first fifty years of the Court". Instead, it proceeded to add a further conceptual level by using the theory of "discrimination" developed by Gaudron J in cases like *Street v Queensland Bar Association* (1989) 168 CLR 461 (see Chapter 26, §5) to illuminate the meaning of "preference" in s 99. Indeed, it suggested that a similar analysis was implicit in the judgments of Rich and Starke JJ in *Elliott v Commonwealth* (1936) 54 CLR 657: for example, Starke J had said in that case that the licensing system there in issue fell within a class of "**[680]** discriminations [which] are often desirable", and hence that it "is not a preference of one locality over another, or of one State or part of a State over another: it is a regulation required for the circumstances of particular ports and the labour conditions of those ports".

Permanent Trustee arose as a sequel to *Allders International Pty Ltd v Commissioner of State Revenue (Vic)* (1996) 186 CLR 630, which had held that Victorian stamp duty could not be levied on a lease at Tullamarine airport, since the airport was a place "acquired by the Commonwealth for public purposes" and hence subject (under s 52(i)) to exclusive Commonwealth legislative power. *Allders* had followed *Worthing v Rowell and Muston Pty Ltd* (1970) 123 CLR 89, which established that no State law could operate in any "Commonwealth place". The effect of *Worthing* had been overcome by the *Commonwealth Places (Application of Laws) Act 1970* (Cth), but that legislation contained an exception for State laws imposing taxes. The legislative response to the *Allders* decision did not remove that exception, but enacted parallel legislation – the *Commonwealth Places (Mirror Taxes) Act 1998* (Cth) – designed to pick up and apply, in any "Commonwealth place", any State taxing law which had been rendered "inapplicable by reason only of the operation of section 52 of the Constitution in relation to Commonwealth places". Since the taxes thus reinstated now applied by virtue of the exercise of Commonwealth legislative power, it was argued in *Permanent Trustee* "**[39]** that the Mirror Taxes Act has an effect of preferring one State over another State because different rates of taxation and exemptions from taxation apply depending solely on whether the relevant Commonwealth place is in one State rather than another". (At issue once again was the stamp duty on a lease at Tullamarine airport, this time for a hotel.)

The whole Court held that the *Mirror Taxes Act* was a law of "revenue" within the meaning of s 99. However, by 5:2 the Court declined to find a "preference". Invoking the approach to "discrimination" in *Street v Queensland Bar Association*, the joint majority judgment said:

Permanent Trustee Australia Ltd v Commissioner of State Revenue
(2004) 211 ALR 18

Gleeson CJ, Gummow, Hayne, Callinan and Heydon JJ: [41] Where then in the Mirror Taxes Act is there to be found the necessary element of discrimination between one State or any part thereof and another State or any part thereof? The scheme of the Mirror Taxes Act is to treat as relevantly of the same character the whole of the geographic area of each State, including those portions which are Commonwealth places; the taxation laws applying in the Commonwealth places are assimilated with those laws in the surrounding State. The scheme of the Mirror Taxes Act may produce differences in revenue outcomes between States, but that mirrors the differences that exist between the different taxation regimes from State to State. The differential treatment and unequal outcome that is involved here is the product of distinctions that are appropriate and adapted to a proper objective. There is no benefit or advantage enjoyed in or in relation to a Commonwealth place that is not shared by the remainder of the State in which it is located ...

The appellant resisted these conclusions by reliance in particular upon *Cameron v Deputy Federal Commissioner of Taxation* [(1923) 32 CLR 68]. In that case, the valuation placed by regulations made under the *Income Tax Assessment Act 1915* (Cth) upon livestock differed according to the particular State in which the livestock was found and regardless of any other circumstances. The effect was held to discriminate between States or parts of States within the meaning of s 51(ii) of the Constitution. The appellant submits that, as with the regulations under challenge in *Cameron*, the criterion which gives rise to differential treatment here is location of the proposed hotel at Tullamarine Airport.

That involves several oversimplifications. The application of the Mirror Taxes Act produces the same revenue outcome as if the site were elsewhere in the State of Victoria. It is true that if the site were a Commonwealth place in another **[42]** State the Mirror Taxes Act could produce a result differing from that obtained at Tullamarine Airport. However, this would be a product of the assimilation of the other Commonwealth place to the situation of other localities in the other State in question ... Even if all Commonwealth places, whatever their State location, are to be considered as relevantly "equal", their differential treatment to assimilate them in this way is a proper objective ...

The joint judgment explained this objective by reference to s 8(4) of the Act, which permitted State Treasurers to prescribe "modifications" of State revenue laws as applied in Commonwealth places, for the purpose of ensuring that a taxpayer's liability is "as nearly as possible the same" as it would be under the State law if no Commonwealth place were involved.

Both McHugh and Kirby JJ, who dissented, were critical of the majority slippage between "preference" and "discrimination". McHugh J accepted the invitation to review the earlier cases, expressing his own preference for the dissenting views of Dixon and Evatt JJ in *Elliott v Commonwealth*. After reviewing other cases, he said:

McHugh J: [57] The purpose of this extended discussion of the cases ... is to show that, apart possibly from a dictum [58] by Starke J in *Elliott* [(1936) 54 CLR 657 at 680], there is nothing in the case law that supports the claim that the Mirror Taxes Act does not contravene s 99. To the contrary, the decisions in *Cameron* [*v Deputy Federal Commissioner of Taxation* (1923) 32 CLR 68] and *James* [*v Commonwealth* (1928) 41 CLR 442] show that the Act does breach s 99. And, properly understood, I do not think that Starke J intended any more than that licensing systems do not necessarily constitute preference. Despite the considerable division of judicial opinion in the cases to which I have referred, one proposition appears uncontentious: a law of the Parliament that imposes different rates of taxes by reference to State boundaries breaches s 99 of the Constitution. That view is supported by all Justices of the Court including Starke J. My own view is that the construction that Dixon and Evatt JJ have placed on s 99 is the correct construction of that constitutional provision. But even if the view of Isaacs J as expressed in *Barger* [(1908) 6 CLR 41] is accepted, the Mirror Taxes Act breaches s 99 of the Constitution. It is a law of the Parliament that imposes differential rates of stamp duty in respect of instruments by reference to their locality in a particular State ... [B]y operation of laws of the respective States the lessee of land in New South Wales, Queensland and Western Australia pays less duty than a person who leases land in Victoria, South Australia, Tasmania or in the case of duty on premiums, Western Australia. By the Mirror Taxes Act, the federal Parliament maintains this distinction in respect of Commonwealth places. The lessee of land in a Commonwealth place in New South Wales pays less duty than the lessee of such a place in Victoria. The federal legislation gives a clear preference to residents of New South Wales who must pay stamp duty on instruments concerned with Commonwealth places over those who reside in other States and must pay stamp duty on such instruments. This is done by a law of the Parliament by reference to the *State* in which the land is located.

Questions of preference under s 99 of the Constitution are not synonymous with the legal notion of discrimination although no doubt preference involves discrimination in one sense in treating one State or part differently from another State or part. The correct meaning and application of s 99 is not informed by the jurisprudence that has developed in respect of discrimination in equal opportunity law in the last 50 years. In s 99, "give preference" means no more than give advantage or priority. It is not concerned with the objective or motive of the giver. The differential treatment of States or parts of States cannot be justified by saying that the difference is the product of a distinction which is appropriate and adapted to the attainment of some proper objective of the Parliament of the Commonwealth. The mischief to which s 99 is directed is not the fairness or unfairness of the effect of any preference given in a particular case. The section is contravened by the mere giving of a preference referable to the State or part of a State to which the law applies. Under the Mirror Taxes Act, two identical transactions, occurring in Commonwealth places, may be assessed for different amounts of stamp duty, solely by reference to the State in which the Commonwealth place is located. The relevant "equals" to compare for the purpose of identifying a preference in this case are those transacting in [59] Commonwealth places, not those transacting in each State. That is because s 99 is concerned with preferences given *by the federal Parliament*. The federal law cannot prefer one Commonwealth place over another by reference to the State in which it is located. And yet that is what the Mirror Taxes Act purports to do. Consistently with s 99, the Parliament of the Commonwealth cannot levy an income tax of 65 cents in the dollar on all residents of Australia except those residing in the Kimberley or Cape York regions although the law has the worthy objective of encouraging development in remote areas of Australia. What s 99 says is that the Commonwealth "shall not ... give preference". It must not prefer one State or part of a State over another State or any part thereof.

Those who made the Constitution were well aware of the distinction between preference and discrimination, as they made plain in enacting s 102. They were also well aware that, in some cases, preference or discrimination might operate unduly, unreasonably or unjustly. That is why in s 102 the Parliament was empowered to make laws forbidding any preference or discrimination as to railways that was "undue and unreasonable, or unjust to any State; due regard being had to the financial responsibilities incurred by any State in connexion with the construction and maintenance of its railways". They made no such qualification in s 99.

Nor is the application of s 99 determined by reference to whether any benefit or advantage enjoyed in relation to a Commonwealth place is not shared by the remainder of the State in which it is located. According to four Justices of this Court in *Morgan v The Commonwealth* [(1947) 74 CLR 421 at 452], s 99 "does not purport to deal with preferences within a single State". The issue is not whether the Mirror Taxes Act produces the same revenue outcome as would be the case if the Commonwealth place was not a Commonwealth place. It is whether a law of the Parliament lays down a rule for Victoria that is different from the rule that it lays down in the same Act for other States and that rule benefits Victoria or the other States. If it does, it is invalid whatever its objectives or motives. Section 99 is concerned with the character of the law or regulation raising revenue and not with the objects of that law. As Isaacs J pointed out in *Cameron* [32 CLR at 76-7]:

> "It does not matter whether those legal standards are arbitrary or measured, *whether dictated by a desire to benefit or to injure*, the simple fact is they are 'different', and those different legal standards being applied simply because the subject of taxation finds itself in one State or the other there arises the discrimination by law between States which is forbidden by the Constitution." (emphasis added)

Regardless of the legislative objective, if, from a federal perspective, the application of those different legal standards results in a preference, as it does in this case, the Constitution forbids the federal law.

5. The Territories

The place of the Australian Territories within the federal system has been controversial. Indeed, the controversy has extended to whether they have any place in that system at all. The power to "make laws for the government" of the Territories, assigned to the Commonwealth by s 122 of the Constitution, is not confined by words of limitation. The diversity of territorial circumstances to which the power extends makes it necessary for it to be broad and flexible.

Re Governor, Goulburn Correctional Centre; Ex parte Eastman
(1999) 200 CLR 322

Gleeson CJ, McHugh and Callinan JJ: [331] One of the reasons for the difficulty in giving the relevant provisions a meaning which achieves internal consistency, and at the same time accommodates the realities of government and administration with which the Constitution must deal, is the disparate nature of territories. Some (such as the ACT, the Northern Territory, and the Jervis Bay Territory) are internal. Others (such as Norfolk Island, the Coral Sea Islands, the Australian Antarctic Territory, the Ashmore and Cartier Islands, the Cocos (Keeling) Islands, Christmas Island, and the Heard and McDonald Islands) are external ... The territories have been, still are, and will probably continue to be, greatly different in si[z]e, population, and development. Yet they are all dealt with, compendiously and briefly, in s 122.

The diversity is extensive. Self-government through a local Legislative Assembly has been granted to the principal internal Territories (by the *Northern Territory (Self-Government) Act 1978* (Cth) and the *Australian Capital Territory (Self-Government) Act 1988* (Cth)), and to Norfolk Island (by the *Norfolk Island Act 1979* (Cth)). The people of the Northern Territory have been represented in the House of Representatives since 1922, and those of the Australian Capital Territory (ACT) since 1948. Both have been represented in the Senate since 1975 (see Chapter

10, §4(b)). Eligible residents of Norfolk Island have been able to vote in federal elections since 1992, though they must enrol in a State subdivision or in the Division of Canberra.

The people of the Cocos (Keeling) Islands, in an Act of Self Determination supervised by the United Nations on 6 April 1984, also voted overwhelmingly to integrate with Australia. The impasse reflected in *Clunies-Ross v Commonwealth* (1984) 155 CLR 193 was resolved in 1993, when the Commonwealth purchased the last remaining property of the Clunies-Ross family, which had formerly controlled the islands. However, the islands remain heavily dependent on Commonwealth support. Christmas Island is governed by an administrator appointed under the *Christmas Island Act 1958* (Cth), though since 1992 it has had a Shire Council exercising powers of local government, and for purposes of federal elections it is treated as a subdivision of the Northern Territory. By contrast, the Ashmore and Cartier Islands and the Coral Sea Islands Territory are largely uninhabited, while the Australian Antarctic Territory and the Territory of Heard Island and McDonald Islands are separately administered and, despite the common assumption, should perhaps be regarded as falling within s 51(xxix), the external affairs power, and not within s 122 at all, especially having regard to the terms of the 1959 Antarctic Treaty.

The legislative power that has been conferred on the self-governing Territories is plenary. Like the self-governing colonies of the 19th century, they are not mere delegates of the superior Parliament by which their powers were granted. To that extent, their powers are assimilated to those of the States. However, the four judges (Brennan, Deane, Toohey and Gaudron JJ) who took that view in *Capital Duplicators Pty Ltd v Australian Capital Territory (No 1)* (1992) 177 CLR 248 held also, as a necessary corollary, that the exclusive Commonwealth power to levy duties of excise under s 90 of the Constitution excludes the self-governing Territories just as it excludes the States – whereas, if their powers had been "delegated", they might have claimed to exercise the same powers as the Commonwealth itself. Given that the creation of legislatures for the Territories was contemplated by s 122, the "[279] exclusivity of power" contemplated by s 90 could only be ensured if it was taken to operate "to the exclusion of the legislatures of both States and internal territories".

Like the 19th-century colonies, the self-governing Territories are subject to the "para-mountcy" of the superior Parliament (in this case the Commonwealth Parliament), which retains the power to override their laws and circumscribe or withdraw their powers. The *Euthanasia Laws Act 1997* (Cth) did both: it overrode the *Rights of the Terminally Ill Act 1995* (NT), "except as regards the lawfulness or validity" of actions already taken; and it withdrew from the legisla-tures of the ACT, the Northern Territory and Norfolk Island the power to make laws "which permit or have the effect of permitting (whether subject to conditions or not) the form of inten-tional killing of another called euthanasia … or the assisting of a person to terminate his or her life".

The self-governing Territories are also subject to the equivalent of s 109 of the Constitution, which provides that in the event of inconsistency between a State and Commonwealth law, the latter shall prevail. For the ACT, s 109 is substantially replicated in s 28 of the *Australian Capital Territory (Self-Government) Act*. The *Northern Territory (Self-Government) Act* is silent on the issue; but a similar result would probably follow from covering clause 5 of the Constitution, which extends the binding effect of Commonwealth laws to the "people … of every part of the Commonwealth". In any event, the result has been held to follow from the doctrine of "para-mountcy". According to Lockhart J in *Attorney-General (NT) v Minister for Aboriginal Affairs* (1989) 90 ALR 59: "[75] It is not a question of inconsistency between the two sets of laws which may otherwise be valid, rather it is a question going to the competency of the subordinate legislature to enact laws or to cause laws to operate in a manner inconsistent with or repugnant to laws of the paramount legislature".

As Gummow J explained in *Newcrest Mining (WA) Ltd v Commonwealth* (1997) 190 CLR 513 at 604-5, the description of a power as "plenary" does not necessarily mean that it is subject to no limitations. However, in the case of the Commonwealth's power under s 122, that has often been assumed to follow. The express and implied limitations that apply when the Parliament legislates under s 51 have been thought to have no application when it legislates under s 122. Section 51 is expressed to be "subject to this Constitution"; s 122 is not. The enumerated powers in s 51 are part of a careful distribution of State and Commonwealth powers within a federal system, whereas the functions of the Commonwealth Parliament in relation to the Territories lie outside that system. If the federal arrangement is conceived of as a "compact" with the States, the Territories are not parties to that compact. As the Privy Council put it in *Attorney-General (Commonwealth) v The Queen (Boilermakers' Case)* [1957] AC 288: "**[320]** The legislative power in respect of the territories is a disparate non-federal matter".

The first hint that the power in s 122 might be radically disjoined from those in s 51 came in *Buchanan v Commonwealth* (1913) 16 CLR 315, where it was held that the restrictions on taxation laws imposed by s 55 apply only to taxation laws passed under s 51(ii), not to those under s 122. If s 55 had applied, it would have meant that, when South Australia surrendered the Northern Territory to the Commonwealth, or when New South Wales surrendered "the Territory for the seat of government", the Commonwealth's administration and acceptance Acts could not have dealt with taxation, which would have needed to be the subject of separate legislation. Barton ACJ could not believe that the framers of the Constitution could have intended such "**[327]** evils ... dangers and disabilities". He argued that "they avoided the evils by the structure of the Constitution", since ss 51 and 122 are "separated by four chapters". He also argued that "sec 122, by itself, contains all the necessary power to legislate for a Territory, including the imposition or continuance of any kind of taxation. It does not need any assistance from sec 51 in respect either of taxation, or of anything else. It would suffice for all its purposes if there were no sec 51 at all".

In the context of contemporary reappraisals of the constitutional status of the self-governing Territories, it is probable that *Buchanan* is no longer good law. The discussion in *Permanent Trustee Australia Ltd v Commissioner of State Revenue (Vic)* (2004) 220 CLR 388 stopped short of overruling it, but the joint majority judgment pointed out that "**[406]** [t]hings have changed since *Buchanan* was decided", and that Barton ACJ had based his reasoning on assumptions that no longer apply (for example, that the people of the Territories were not represented in the federal Parliament). Nevertheless, *Buchanan* laid the foundation for a separatist view of the Territories that prevailed well into the 20th century.

If *Buchanan v Commonwealth* was specifically directed to the transfer to the Commonwealth of responsibility for the Northern Territory, the next case was specifically directed to circumstances in Papua (then an Australian territory and now part of the nation Papua New Guinea). The Central Court of Papua had convicted George Bernasconi of assault and sentenced him to 12 months' imprisonment. He appealed on the ground that, under s 80 of the Constitution, he should have been tried by a jury. Isaacs J observed that since s 80 applies only to trials "on indictment", its provisions are irrelevant if an offence "**[637]** is not made triable on indictment at all". But the whole Court also held that, in any event, s 80 had no application.

R v Bernasconi
(1915) 19 CLR 629

Griffith CJ: [635] In my judgment, Chapter III is limited in its application to the exercise of the judicial power of the Commonwealth in respect of those functions of government as to which it stands in the place of the States, and has no application to territories. Sec 80, therefore, relates only to offences created by the Parliament by Statutes passed in the execution of those functions, which are aptly described as "laws of the Commonwealth". The same term is used in that sense in sec 5 of the *Constitution Act* itself, and in secs 41, 61 and 109 of the Constitution. In the last mentioned section it is used in contradistinction to the law of a State. I do not think that in this respect the law of a territory can be put on any different footing from that of a law of a State.

The power conferred by sec 122, although conferred by the same instrument, stands on a different footing ... In my opinion, the power conferred by sec 122 is not restricted by the provisions of Chapter III of the Constitution, whether the power is exercised directly or through a subordinate legislature.

Isaacs J: [637] [Section 80] is one of the *fasciculus* of sections collected in one Chapter and united and inter-related as members of a distinct group under the title of "The Judicature". The "judicial power of the Commonwealth" – that is, the whole judicial power of the Commonwealth proper – is there dealt with ...

When the Constitution, however, reaches a new consideration, namely, the government of territories, not as constituent parts of the self-governing body, not "fused with it" as I expressed it in *Buchanan's Case* [(1913) 16 CLR 315], but rather as parts annexed to the Commonwealth and subordinate to it, then sec 122 provides the appropriate grant of power.

It is plain that that section does not consist merely of additional legislative power over territories beyond the powers already conferred upon Parliament in relation to the Commonwealth itself, for its language is unrestricted and covers many of the subjects already specified in sec 51. It is an unqualified grant complete in itself, and implies that a "territory" is not yet in a condition to enter into the full participation of Commonwealth constitutional rights and powers. It is in a state of dependency or tutelage, and the special regulations proper for its **[638]** government until, if ever, it shall be admitted as a member of the family of States, are left to the discretion of the Commonwealth Parliament. If, for instance, any of the recently conquered territories were attached to Australia by act of the King and acceptance by the Commonwealth, the population there, whether German or Polynesian, would come within sec 122, and not within sec 80. Parliament's sense of justice and fair dealing is sufficient to protect them, without fencing them round with what would be in the vast majority of instances an entirely inappropriate requirement of the British jury system.

Although the specific issue related only to s 80, Griffith CJ extended his opinion to the whole of Ch III. In *Porter v The King; Ex parte Chin Man Yee* (1926) 37 CLR 432, a similar extension led Knox CJ and Gavan Duffy J, in dissent, to hold that the Territories also lay outside the High Court's appellate jurisdiction under s 73 of the Constitution. However, the majority in *Porter* rejected that conclusion, holding that for appellate purposes the Northern Territory Supreme Court was a "federal court" because of (or in spite of) its dependence on s 122. That involved a tortured explanation by Isaacs J of his earlier judgments in *R v Bernasconi* and in *Mainka v Custodian of Expropriated Property* (1922) 34 CLR 297, which appeared to suggest that a Territory court both was and was not a "federal court" for Ch III purposes.

From the holding in *R v Bernasconi* as to s 80 and the holding in *Buchanan* as to s 55, there developed the further generalisation that none of the express or implied limitations found elsewhere in the Constitution is applicable to laws made for the Territories under s 122. One difficulty with this generalisation is that, while some constitutional limitations can be seen to have a particular significance or function in a federal context, most of them can also be seen as informing a broader conception of the kind of government we wish to have. From that point of view, there is no apparent reason why the limitations should not apply to the Commonwealth's role under s 122 as much as to its role as a national government within a federation.

Ironically, much of the subsequent case law has developed in relation to two Territories which arguably should never have been regarded as falling within s 122 at all. One of these was the former Territory of Papua and New Guinea (now independent). The former Crown Colony of Papua fell clearly within s 122, since it was "placed by the [King] under the authority of and accepted by the Commonwealth" by virtue of a British Order in Council made in 1902. What was less clear was the status of the former German colony in north-eastern New Guinea. From 1920 onwards it was administered by Australia under a League of Nations Mandate; in 1946 that was replaced by a Trusteeship Agreement with the United Nations. The original authority to accept the League of Nations Mandate was given to the Governor-General by the *New Guinea Act 1920* (Cth), while a similar authority was given to the King by the *Treaty of Peace Act 1919* (UK). Apparently relying primarily on the British legislation, and on the King's acceptance of the Mandate, Isaacs J held in *Mainka v Custodian of Expropriated Property* (1922) 34 CLR 297 that the mandated Territory came within s 122 (as he had already asserted in anticipation in *R v*

Bernasconi). However, in *Jolley v Mainka* (1933) 49 CLR 242, Evatt J argued forcefully that the power to legislate for the mandated Territory was located not in s 122, but in s 51(xxix). He insisted that the language of s 122 simply had no application.

Jolley v Mainka
(1933) 49 CLR 242

Evatt J: [278] [T]he Mandated Territory was never "placed by the King under the authority of and accepted by the Commonwealth". The documents … negative any such action on the part of His Majesty or of the Commonwealth. The sources to which alone the exercise of Commonwealth control must be referred are recited both in the *New Guinea Act* 1920 and in the mandate itself. They consist of (1) Germany's renunciation of all her rights in favour of the principal and associated Powers, (2) the agreement of the principal Allied and associated Powers that the Commonwealth of Australia should be the mandatory, (3) the issue under art 22 of the mandate for the control of the territory, and (4) the acceptance of such mandate by the Commonwealth. These sources completely exclude any "placing by the King" of New Guinea under Commonwealth authority. And there are no other sources.

Nor is it possible to regard the mandated area as ever having been "acquired" by the Commonwealth. The area is not, in law or in fact, so "acquired". No legal title has been vested in the Commonwealth … The mandated territory is not part of, but outside, His Majesty's Dominions. Very strong, if not conclusive, evidence of that fact is furnished by two Imperial Orders in Council – No 648 of 1923 and No 1030 of 1928. The first was made under sec 737 of the *Merchant Shipping Act* 1894, the second under sec 30 of the *Fugitive Offenders Act* 1881. Each not only recites, but is expressly based upon the position that, in law and in fact, the Mandated Territory of New **[279]** Guinea is a place "outside" or "out of" His Majesty's Dominions.

Further, sec 122 not only looks to the "acquisition" of territory, but to the possibility of the representation of every such territory in the Commonwealth Parliament itself. The process envisaged is one of a gradual approach of the acquired territory towards inclusion within the existing organization of the Commonwealth. In the Mandated Territory, the process envisaged by art 22 is exactly the reverse. It is to be controlled as if it were, contrary to the fact, an integral portion of the Commonwealth; but its development is to be not towards, but away from, absorption by the Commonwealth. "It is never," as *Corbett* says, "to be incorporated in the territory of the mandatory" unless, of course, by further international action (*British Year Book of International Law* (1924), at p 135).

It is improbable that sec 122 would ever have been regarded as relevant but for the fact that the word "territory" is used in that section and in the mandate alike.

Evatt J repeated and expanded his analysis in *Ffrost v Stevenson* (1937) 58 CLR 528. He did so with some support from Latham CJ, at least as to the initial steps bringing New Guinea under Australia's governmental authority and as to the application (with which *Ffrost v Stevenson* was concerned) of the *Service and Execution of Process Act 1901* (Cth). In other respects, however, Latham CJ continued to insist that the relevant source of legislative power must be s 122. Dixon J did not need to decide the point. He acknowledged the arguments of Evatt J as "**[566]** showing clearly the difficulties" in treating the Territory as part of the British Dominions, and as giving rise to unresolved problems related to the different possible sources of legislative power. For example, given the decisions in cases like *Buchanan*, *R v Bernasconi* and *Porter*, to say that legislation for the mandated Territory did *not* fall under s 122 might lead to "different consequences". Further, if s 122 was the source of power, it might be the *only* source of power, and might therefore exclude any possible resort to powers contained in s 51 such as the defence power (s 51(vi)) or the external affairs power (s 51(xxix)). Despite these difficulties, Dixon CJ continued to think as late as *Fishwick v Cleland* (1960) 106 CLR 186 that although s 122 was "**[197]** framed in terms perhaps not altogether appropriate in expression to the mandatory or trusteeship system … [o]n the whole it seems preferable to refer the source of power over New Guinea to s 122 rather than to s 51(xxix)".

Similarly, in *Re Minister for Immigration and Multicultural and Indigenous Affairs; Ex parte Ame* (2005) 218 ALR 483, where the Court upheld the validity of Australian regulations made in 1975 to facilitate the transfer of sovereignty and citizenship to the newly independent Papua New Guinea, the whole Court treated the issue as turning on s 122, with no reference to the external affairs power, *Ffrost v Stevenson* or *Jolley v Mainka*. The joint majority judgment found it "[494] unnecessary to consider whether the legislation was also supported by s 51(xxx) (relations with islands of the Pacific)", but offered not even this degree of acknowledgment to the possible relevance of s 51(xxix). The separate judgment of Kirby J also treated this aspect of the case as turning solely on s 122. He emphasised, however, that the language of s 122 establishes a clear disjunction between Territories "surrendered by any State to and accepted by the Commonwealth" (and thus necessarily "[512] within the continental description of Australia"), and Territories "placed by the Queen under the authority of and accepted by the Commonwealth" or "otherwise acquired by the Commonwealth" (which are necessarily external to Australia); and that the powers conferred by s 122 must necessarily operate differently for these two classes of case. Similarly, the reasoning in the joint judgment was confined to legislation affecting "[495] the inhabitants of external territories".

By contrast, for Commonwealth legislation relating to Nauru it seems always to have been assumed that the relevant source of power was the external affairs power (s 51(xxix), or perhaps the power with respect to "the relations of the Commonwealth with the islands of the Pacific" (s 51(xxx)). That assumption was spelled out by Attorney-General Robert Ellicott as the basis for the *Nauru (High Court Appeals) Act 1976* (Cth) (*Hansard*, House of Representatives, 7 October 1976, p 1647) and confirmed by the High Court when it upheld the validity of that legislation in *Ruhani v Director of Police* (2005) 219 ALR 199. Australia's responsibility for Nauru, as for New Guinea, had arisen initially under the League of Nations mandate system and then under the United Nations Trusteeship system; and although, in the case of Nauru, the responsibility was more fully shared with New Zealand and the United Kingdom, it is difficult to see any distinction in principle between the two cases.

The other Territory whose place within s 122 has sometimes been questioned is the ACT (or, as it was called until 1938, "the Territory for the Seat of Government"). Both the *Seat of Government Surrender Act 1909* (NSW) and the *Seat of Government Acceptance Act 1909* (Cth), by using the language of "surrender" and "acceptance", disclosed an intention to use the mechanism of surrender and acceptance provided for in s 111 of the Constitution; and, clearly, any Territory thus surrendered and accepted becomes subject to s 122. On the other hand, s 125, which provides for the Commonwealth seat of government, envisages that once the Commonwealth has "determined" its location, the relevant Territory will then be "granted to or acquired by the Commonwealth, and shall be vested in and belong to the Commonwealth". If the ACT were thought of as "granted" or "acquired" and "vested" under s 125, rather than "surrendered" and "accepted" under s 111, the relevant legislative power would be found not in s 122, but in s 52(i) – which expressly includes laws with respect to "[t]he seat of government of the Commonwealth". Yet the legislative power given by s 52(i) is "subject to this Constitution", so that the normal express and implied limitations on power apply (see JQ Ewens, "Where is the Seat of Government?: An Examination of the Sources of Legislative Power for the Australian Capital Territory" (1951) 25 *Australian Law Journal* 532; Bernard Sugerman, "Letter to the Editor" (1973) 47 *Australian Law Journal* 344).

The initial assumption, made for example by Dixon J in *Federal Capital Commission v Laristan Building & Investment Co Pty Ltd* (1929) 42 CLR 582 and by Evatt J in *Davies v Ryan* (1933) 50 CLR 379, was that all legislation for the ACT had its source in s 52(i). What led to a departure from this early assumption was the issue of whether judicial appointments in the ACT must satisfy the requirements in Ch III of the Constitution, specifically s 72. If the ultimate source of the appointments lay in s 52(i), they would be "subject to this Constitution", and s 72 would apply. But in *Spratt v Hermes* (1965) 114 CLR 226, and more recently when that decision was affirmed in *Re Governor, Goulburn Correction Centre; Ex parte Eastman* (1999) 200 CLR 322, it was held that the relevant source of power was s 122. It followed that the appointments need not comply with s 72.

In *Spratt v Hermes*, Kitto and Taylor JJ held that the whole of Ch III was inapplicable to judicial power conferred under s 122. Other members of the Court were more cautious. In particular, Barwick CJ and Menzies J, while holding that s 72 did not apply to judicial appointments in the Territories, denied that this meant that Ch III as a whole had no application.

Spratt v Hermes
(1965) 114 CLR 226

Barwick CJ: [243] Some would support [this] result upon the fundamental view that Chap III as a whole is inapplicable to or in respect of territories. The consequences of such a view are, in my opinion, so far-reaching and my respect for those who have entertained and do entertain it so great, that I feel bound to indicate the reasons for my inability to accept it ...

The conclusion that this Court may not exercise the powers given it by s 75 of the Constitution to prohibit a wrongful act or compel a lawful act whatever the source of the unlawfulness or of the duty by a Minister of the Crown done or to be done at the seat of government, which by the Constitution must be within a territory of the Commonwealth (s 125), is, to my mind, so disturbing that one must immediately doubt the validity of the course of reasoning which appears to lead to it, and, however time honoured it may be, re-examine it ...

[244] [T]he decision in *R v Bernasconi* [(1915) 19 CLR 629] may be supported upon the ground that upon the proper construction of s 80 ..., the offences to which it refers are offences created ... pursuant to legislative powers derived from s 51 of the Constitution ... [This] might be derived from the unlikelihood that it could have been thought that juries would be found in such potential territories ... as might have been within contemplation at the foundation of the Commonwealth; and perhaps from the circumstance that the section appears to be in some sense related to ss 71 and 72.

But, whatever reason is found for so con[s]truing it, in my respectful opinion, it is because of the construction of s 80 itself, as distinct from any reasoning affecting Chap III as a whole, that the decision in *R v Bernasconi* should be supported ...

[245] There does not seem to me to be any single theme running throughout Chap III which requires it to be treated so much all of one piece that if any part of it relates only to federal matters, every part of it must likewise be restrained. Thus the mere presence of s 80 in Chap III does not, in my respectful opinion, require that it be inapplicable to territories and therefore to non-federal offences.

Also, in my opinion, parts of Chap III are clearly "applicable to the territories" ...

[Section 75] must, in my opinion, apply no matter where the act upon which the proceedings before the court are founded has been or ought to be done and whether the cause of action derives from an exercise of legislative power given by s 51 or by s 122. Again, s 78 is **[246]** not limited to the making of laws to proceed against the Commonwealth in federal matters ...

Further, it seems to me, with the utmost respect, to be an error to compartmentalize the Constitution, merely because for drafting convenience it has been divided into chapters. No doubt on some occasions some assistance may be obtained from the place in the layout of the Constitution which a particular provision occupies when resolving ambiguities in language. But this does not call for disjoining a part of the Constitution from the rest ...

Obviously some of the provisions found in Chap I of the Constitution are "applicable to the territories" ... Sections 43, 44, 45, and 46 must apply to a member for whom provision is made pursuant to s 122. Section 49 must, as *Dixon* CJ pointed out in *Lamshed v Lake* [(1958) 99 CLR 132 at 143], apply when laws made pursuant to s 122 are passing through the House. There would seem to be no reason why a double dissolution should not result from a disagreement of the House and the Senate upon a proposed law to be made under the powers derived from s 122.

Again, the duty to execute laws made for territories is surely no less under Chap II than it is in respect of laws made under s 51. Nor is there any reason to think that a Department of Territories may not be created under s 64; and so it may be shown that much of Chap II must be "applicable to the territories".

It seems to me therefore, with the utmost respect, that whilst s 122 does give a complete and, as opposed to those given by s 51, a different power – there is no warrant for segregating that power from the rest of the Constitution or for taking any global view of any chapter of the Constitution and regarding it as wholly inapplicable ...

It may be granted ... **[247]** that the powers which were given to the Commonwealth were of different orders, some federal, limited by subject matter, some complete and given expressly, and some no doubt derived by implication from the very creation or existence of the body politic. Consequently, the need to observe the nature of the powers sought to be exercised at any time by the Commonwealth is ever present. But, the Constitution brought into existence but one Commonwealth which was, in turn, destined to become the nation. The difference in the quality and extent of the powers given to it introduced no duality in the Commonwealth itself. The undoubted fact that the Commonwealth emerged from a federal compact or that that compact is reflected in the limitations placed upon some of the powers of the Commonwealth or that the new political entity derived from a union of the peoples of the former colonies does not deny the essential unity and singleness of the Commonwealth.

Consequently, in my opinion, the expression "law of the Commonwealth" embraces every law made by the Parliament whatever the constitutional power under or by reference to which that law is made or supported ...

Although the territories may not be included in the federal system in the sense that the powers of the Commonwealth with respect to them are not federally circumscribed, they are, in my opinion, clearly included in the expression "The Commonwealth", eg throughout Chap I of the Constitution. I see no occasion for contrasting a Commonwealth which contains or embraces only the constituent elements of a federation with a Commonwealth which includes all the areas over which it can by one power or another legislate. If the fundamental concept of a single Commonwealth is accepted, there would seem to be no need to entertain any distinction between territories which originally contained people who were members of a colony at the point of federation and other territories or to seek to find significance in the presence within a territory of the seat of government.

No doubt some of the powers of the Commonwealth are appropriate to the rule of non self-governing possessions whilst others, though federally disposed, are truly those of a self-governing people. But this neither means that the Constitution is divisible into two parts without any mutual interaction nor that the power **[248]** to govern dependent territories is in no respect controlled by any other part of the Constitution ...

Though the abandonment of a doctrine of interpretation of the Constitution is something not lightly and but rarely to be done, I feel compelled after deep consideration, because of the logical consequences of doing so, to express the view that the Constitution ought not to be interpreted as if Chap III as a whole were "inapplicable to territories".

Menzies J: [269] There are ... in some cases statements that would indicate that s 122 relates only to territories which do not form part of what has been referred to as "the Federal System" ... It appears to me that the Australian Capital Territory cannot be regarded as outside "the Federal System", notwithstanding that the territory is not within the legislative competence of any State legislature. As was said in *Federal Capital Commission v Laristan Building and Investment Co Pty Ltd* [(1929) 42 CLR 582 at 585]: "The seat of government is an integral part of the Federal System ..." If, therefore, s 122 were to be regarded as merely authorizing the making of laws for territories outside "the Federal System", it would not authorize the making of laws applicable to the Australian Capital Territory. I am not able, however, to accept the suggested limitation upon s 122. The notion that there are territories which do not form part of "the Federal System" has been put forward to explain why it is that constitutional limitations such as those which are to be found in s 55 and Chap III of the Constitution do not apply to laws made under s 122 and also how the High Court can, by a law made under s 122, be given jurisdiction to hear appeals from non-federal courts ... For my part, I am prepared to accept as binding decisions such as *Bernasconi, Buchanan* [(1913) 16 CLR 315] and *Yee* [(1926) 37 CLR 432] without accepting the particular rationalization that [270] has been offered for them, viz that territories of the Commonwealth are outside "the Federal System". To me, it seems inescapable that territories of the Commonwealth are parts of the Commonwealth of Australia and I find myself unable to grasp how what is part of the Commonwealth is not part of "the Federal System" … If there be room for doubt as to this in so far as territories outside Australia are concerned, I think the terms of s 122 itself preclude doubt in the case of territories within Australia. That section contemplates that an area which is part of a State and so within "the Federal System" will be accepted by the Commonwealth and may be represented in either House of the Parliament. I do not understand how the surrender and acceptance authorized by s 111 of the Constitution can take the area affected outside "the Federal System". To my mind, the notion that an area which is geographically within Australia and is part of the Commonwealth of Australia is outside "the Federal System" should be given no further countenance. Surely, if the phrase "the Federal System" is to be used to define some legal concept, it can but mean the system of government established by the Constitution itself: if it be understood to mean the system of dual government by the Commonwealth and a State so that an area not so subject is outside the system, then, of course, the seat of government of the Commonwealth for which the Constitution expressly provides is nevertheless outside "the Federal System" – a conclusion that would suggest to me a misuse of language. It seems to me that s 122, which subjects territories to the legislative power of the Parliament and makes provision for the representation of those territories in Parliament, itself cannot be regarded as dealing with non-federal matters. Particularly is this so when laws made under that section are laws of the Commonwealth which may operate throughout the Commonwealth, States and territories alike … Moreover, it has to be remembered that s 122 is not the only source of power to make laws for the government of the territories. A law of the Commonwealth made under s 51 may operate within the territories simply because they are parts of the Commonwealth. [271] It cannot, therefore, be said that the territories are governed by "territorial laws" as distinct from laws of the Commonwealth.

It appears that the only basis for regarding s 122 as inapplicable to the Australian Capital Territory is by treating the power conferred upon the Parliament by that section as limited to territories outside "the Federal System" and then finding – as I would – that the Australian Capital Territory is within that system. For the reason I have given, however, I do not accept the limitation which it has been sought to impose upon s 122 and my conclusion is that the section does confer upon the Parliament power to authorize the making of a law such as the *Court of Petty Sessions Ordinance* (No 2) so that the attack upon its validity fails.

Spratt v Hermes decided that the requirements of s 72 were not applicable to the appointment of an ACT magistrate. In *Capital TV and Appliances Pty Ltd v Falconer* (1971) 125 CLR 591, that decision was reaffirmed and extended to the appointment of judges of the ACT Supreme Court. However, Menzies J took the opportunity to add s 76(ii) to the earlier catalogue of provisions in Ch III that should be regarded as applying to the Territories.

Despite the doubts expressed by Barwick CJ in *Spratt v Hermes* about the supposed wholesale exclusion of the Territories from the requirements of Ch III, he did not hesitate to hold that for other purposes the Territories were outside the federal system. In *Teori Tau v Commonwealth* (1969) 119 CLR 564, he spoke for the whole Court in dismissing *ex tempore* an Indigenous claim to land occupied by the Bougainville copper mine, on the ground that s 51(xxxi) of the Constitution (requiring "just terms" for any "acquisition of property" for Commonwealth purposes) had no application to lands acquired under s 122.

Teori Tau v Commonwealth
(1969) 119 CLR 564

Barwick CJ (for the Court): [570] [T]his submission [that s 122 is subject to s 51(xxxi)] is clearly insupportable. Section 51 is concerned with what may be called federal legislative powers as part of the distribution of legislative power between the Commonwealth and the constituent States. Section 122 is concerned with the legislative power for the government of Commonwealth territories in respect of which there is no such division of legislative power. The grant of legislative power by s 122 is plenary in quality and unlimited and unqualified in point of subject matter. In particular, it is not limited or qualified by s 51(xxxi) or, for that matter, by any other paragraph of that section.

While the Constitution must be read as a whole and as a consequence, s 122 be subject to other appropriate provisions of it as, for example, s 116, we have no doubt whatever that the power to make laws providing for the acquisition of property in the territory of the Commonwealth is not limited to the making of laws which provide just terms of acquisition.

What we decide in this respect is not, of course, limited to the Territory of Papua and New Guinea, although it happens that the question has first arisen expressly for decision in connexion with that territory. Our decision applies to all the territories, those **[571]** on the mainland of Australia as well as those external to the continent of Australia.

Well before *Spratt v Hermes*, however, Dixon CJ in *Lamshed v Lake* (1958) 99 CLR 132 had expressed more fundamental doubts. In that case the High Court held by majority (McTiernan and Williams JJ dissenting) that laws made under s 122 were enforceable throughout the Commonwealth. Dixon CJ made the converse point that many of the laws made under s 51 of the Constitution must necessarily apply to the Territories, and in that sense s 51 itself must so apply. For example, he instanced the powers relating to postal services (s 51(v)), naval and military defence (s 51(vi)) and naturalisation and aliens (s 51(xix)), and "the relations of the Commonwealth with the islands of the Pacific" (s 51(xxx)).

The immediate point of Dixon CJ's catalogue (which could readily be extended) was to demonstrate that, conversely, a law made with respect to the Territories must be enforceable in the rest of Australia. However, the catalogue has a wider significance. Rhetorically, it invites the question: if the *powers* conferred by the "federal" parts of the Constitution are "applicable to the Territories", why should the *limitations* on those powers not be equally applicable? It also invites a more practical question: if a law that can be characterised as a law with respect to the government of a Territory can also be characterised as a law with respect to a head of power contained in s 51, why is it not *in that latter aspect* subject to the ordinary constitutional limitations on power? Most obviously, this question might arise in relation to the external Territories, at least some of which might readily be characterised as falling within the "external affairs" power as well as within s 122.

It is only in relation to an internal Territory that the implications of dual characterisation (see Chapter 16, §5) have thus far been accepted as a basis for decision. From 1987 onwards, by proclamations under the *National Parks and Wildlife Conservation Act 1975* (Cth), and by legislative provisions inserted by the *National Parks and Wildlife Conservation Amendment Act 1987* (Cth), the Commonwealth had effectively prohibited mining in Kakadu National Park. In *Newcrest Mining (WA) Ltd v Commonwealth* (1997) 190 CLR 513, Toohey, Gaudron, Gummow and Kirby JJ held that, although the legislation could be characterised as being for the government of the Northern Territory under s 122, it could also be characterised as legislation with respect to external affairs under s 51(xxix), since a purpose of the 1975 Act was to implement Australia's obligations under the 1972 Convention for the Protection of the World Cultural and Natural Heritage. Viewed in this latter aspect, it could be regarded as effecting, within the meaning of s 51(xxxi), an acquisition of property "for any purpose in respect of which the Parliament has power to make laws", and thus as invalid for want of "just terms" (see Chapter 27, §2). Brennan CJ, Dawson and McHugh JJ dissented. While the main point is sufficiently made in terms of "dual characterisation" – that is, the recognition that a law might be characterised by reference *both* to s 122 *and* to one of the heads of power in s 51 – Gaudron J went further, suggesting that the alternative characterisation might wholly displace any characterisation by reference to s 122: "**[567]** It is unlikely that an Act of general application throughout the Commonwealth will also be a law passed pursuant to s 122".

In a different respect, three of the majority judges in *Newcrest* went further again. Although Dixon CJ, in *Lamshed v Lake*, had assumed that what s 122 conferred was a "subject matter" power, Gaudron, Gummow and Kirby JJ viewed it as a purposive power. They held that, even when characterised as legislation under s 122, the measures relating to Kakadu could be seen (for purposes of s 51(xxxi)) as being "for [a] purpose in respect of which the Parliament has power to make laws". On that basis they were prepared to overrule *Teori Tau*.

The dissenting judges in *Newcrest*, Brennan CJ, Dawson and McHugh JJ, were not prepared to do so, while the fourth majority judge, Toohey J, also stopped short of overruling. However, his willingness to allow *Teori Tau* to stand was conditioned on his perception that it "**[561]** seems almost inevitable that any acquisition of property by the Commonwealth will now attract the operation of s 51(xxxi) because it will be in pursuit of a purpose in respect of which the Parliament has power to make laws, even if that acquisition takes place within a Territory". Accordingly, "any implications overruling *Teori Tau* would have would likely be for the past rather than the future".

The willingness of Gaudron, Gummow and Kirby JJ to see the power given by s 122 as a purposive power may have broader implications (although, of course, what constitutes a legislative "purpose" in the context of s 51(xxxi) may not necessarily be regarded as a "purpose" in other contexts). Suppose that the power in s 122 were conceived of more generally as a "purposive" power, rather than a "subject matter" power. There might then be room for judicial assessment of whether any particular enactment was appropriate and adapted to that purpose – that is, for a proportionality test (see Chapter 16, §8). Moreover, just as Brennan and Deane JJ in *Commonwealth v Tasmania (Tasmanian Dam Case)* (1983) 158 CLR 1 applied their proportionality test not by asking whether the legislative measures adopted were appropriate and adapted to the global purpose of protecting the world's cultural and natural heritage, but rather by asking whether they were appropriate and adapted to the needs of each particular heritage item, so in the context of s 122 a proportionality test could be tailored to the needs of each particular Territory. On such an approach, there would still, of course, be a need for a very high degree of deference to legislative judgment. Nevertheless, within such a context, any impairment of express or implied constitutional limitations could be assessed, not by abstract assessment of whether or not the limitation in question was "applicable to the Territories", but by asking whether, in the specific context, the impairment of the relevant limitation was reasonable, in light of the circumstances of that particular Territory, as a way of achieving for that Territory the legislative purpose in issue. In this way, the Court might at last be able to break through the two globalising tendencies to generalisation that have so bedevilled decisions in this area: the tendency to suppose that, if *some* express or implied limitations are not "applicable to the Territories", *none* of them can be applicable; and the tendency to assume that, whatever answer is given to such questions, it must apply to *all* the Territories as one undifferentiated class.

Although the precise decision in *Newcrest* was limited to the application of s 51(xxxi), much of the reasoning in the majority judgments had implications for other aspects of the supposed "disjoinder" of s 122 from the rest of the Constitution. For example, both Gummow and Kirby JJ emphasised that no significance should be attached to the absence, from s 122, of the words "subject to this Constitution".

Newcrest Mining (WA) Ltd v Commonwealth
(1997) 190 CLR 513

Gummow J: [606] The phrase "subject to this Constitution" also serves in s 51 to emphasise that the subject matter with respect to which the Parliament otherwise may make laws under s 51 is restrained by provisions such as ss 92, 99, 100 and 116 of the Constitution. But the same result would follow from the operation of the prohibitions in which those sections are expressed without the confirmatory warning in s 51 itself. No particular conclusion follows in this respect from the presence (in s 51) or the absence (from s 122) of the phrase "subject to this Constitution". It can hardly be suggested that s 122 operates other than subject to the Constitution, and, in particular, that it is not to be read with the Constitution as a whole.

The issue of whether the legislative power given by s 122 is subject to the various guarantees of religious freedom contained in s 116 of the Constitution divided the Court in *Kruger v Commonwealth* (*Stolen Generations Case*) (1997) 190 CLR 1, handed down just two weeks before *Newcrest*. Before *Kruger*, the dicta on the point had been typically unclear. In *Lamshed v Lake*, Dixon CJ saw no reason "**[143]** why s 116 should not apply to laws made under s 122"; and even in *Teori Tau*, Barwick CJ conceded that s 122 must be subject to "**[570]** appropriate provisions ... as, for example, s 116". By contrast, in *Attorney-General (Vic); Ex rel Black v Commonwealth* (*DOGS Case*) (1981) 146 CLR 559, Gibbs CJ found such dicta "**[593]** very difficult to **[594]** reconcile" with the general assumption that laws made under s 122 stand outside the normal constitutional framework.

Reviewing these dicta in *Kruger*, Gaudron J held that s 116 does apply as a limit on Territory laws, though she added that "**[123]** s 116 is directed to laws made by the Commonwealth, not laws enacted by the legislature of a self-governing Territory". Toohey and Gummow JJ were strongly inclined to agree. Dawson J, with whom McHugh J agreed, expressed a contrary view: for him, the decision in *R v Bernasconi* was a barrier against the extension to the Territories of *any* express or implied constitutional limitations on power. He concluded: "**[60]** I do not think that it is possible while *R v Bernasconi* stands to hold that s 116 restricts s 122. Nor do I think that the reasoning in *Lamshed v Lake* is necessarily to be preferred to that in *R v Bernasconi*". Contrary to the common assumption that the place of s 116 in Ch V of the Constitution ("The States") is anomalous, he argued that the limit it imposes on Commonwealth laws affecting religion was part of "the division of legislative power between the Commonwealth and the States within the federation", and hence should have no application to laws under s 122. Clearly, the opinions expressed in *Kruger* in relation to s 116 by Gaudron, Toohey and Gummow JJ on one hand, and by Dawson and McHugh JJ on the other, were consistent with their subsequent views in *Newcrest* in relation to s 51(xxxi).

Equally divisive in *Kruger* was the application of Ch III. Dawson J, with whom McHugh J agreed, held simply that "**[62]** Courts created under s 122 are not federal courts", and accordingly that the doctrine of separate and independent judicial power "has no application in the territories". Brennan CJ applied "**[44]** the accepted doctrine" to that effect. On the other hand Toohey, Gaudron and Gummow JJ all expressed support for the opposite view, though none of them finally decided the issue. (Gummow J held that in order to do so it would be necessary to reconsider "**[170]** at least" the decisions in *Spratt v Hermes* and *Capital TV & Appliances Pty Ltd v Falconer*.) In substance, therefore, the Court in *Kruger* was evenly divided on the issue. However, later decisions have confirmed the insistence of Barwick CJ in *Spratt v Hermes* that the issue must be fragmented: that is, that not *all* provisions in Ch III can be put aside as not "applicable to the Territories".

In *Northern Territory v GPAO* (1999) 196 CLR 553, the High Court held that confidentiality provisions in the *Community Welfare Act 1983* (NT) were an effective answer to a subpoena issued by the Family Court of Australia. In order to arrive at that decision, it was necessary to clarify the basis on which, in the Northern Territory, the Family Court exercises its powers under Pt VII of the *Family Law Act 1975* (Cth) in relation to children. Part VII was added in 1987, and in 1995 its operation was extended by a new Subdiv F, providing in part, by s 69ZG: "This Part applies in and in relation to the Territories". In *GPAO* it was assumed that, despite its insertion in a general law operating throughout the Commonwealth, s 69ZG is a law made under s 122 for the government of the Territories. It was nevertheless held that the jurisdiction exercised pursuant to s 69ZG is federal jurisdiction, and that Pt VII as applied by s 69ZG is "a law of the Commonwealth" for the purposes of s 76(ii) of the Constitution. In that sense, s 76(ii) is "applicable in the Territories". However, it also followed that, when the Family Court sits in the Northern Territory, s 79 of the *Judiciary Act 1903* (Cth) operates to "pick up" the restrictive provisions of the *Community Welfare Act*.

As to the applicability of s 76(ii), Gleeson CJ and Gummow J, with whom Hayne J agreed, accepted the reasoning of Menzies J in *Capital TV and Appliances Pty Ltd v Falconer*. Gaudron

J, while more sharply critical of the line of decisions excluding laws made under s 122 from the operation of Ch III, reached the same result. She conceded that the decisions relating specifically to s 72 "**[603]** should stand". On the other hand, she saw "**[604]** no reason in principle" why federal jurisdiction might not be conferred on "a non-federal court created pursuant to s 122". It followed, in her view, that such courts are included in the words of s 71 ("such other courts as it invests with federal jurisdiction"), and that laws relating to such courts are included in the words of s 76(ii) ("any laws made by the Parliament"). McHugh and Callinan JJ agreed that the *Community Welfare Act* was applicable, but dissented from the majority view of the relationship between s 122 and Ch III of the Constitution. Instead, they mounted a strong defence of the traditional doctrine.

Northern Territory v GPAO
(1999) 196 CLR 553

McHugh and Callinan JJ: [616] Although these decisions have attracted criticism in subsequent cases, the terms of Ch III, read in the light of the Convention Debates, give much support for the view that s 122 is not affected by the operation of Ch III. Considerations supporting that view include: (1) Ch III makes frequent reference to "federal", "Commonwealth" and "State" but there is no mention of "territory". (2) The use of the term "federal" is more consistent with Ch III being concerned with the allocation of power between the Commonwealth and the States than with the exercise of judicial power in the Commonwealth, the States *and any territory*. (3) It is settled that territory courts are not federal courts for the purpose of Ch III. That being so, ss 75, 76 and 77 of the Constitution – which deal with the jurisdiction of Ch III courts – are concerned with this Court, federal courts and the State courts, not territory courts. There is no reason, therefore, for thinking that Ch III generally is concerned with the territories. (4) The carefully worked out provisions of Ch III, defining the powers and securing the independence of federal courts, were necessary to ensure the maintenance of the federal structure ... Nothing in the relationship between the Commonwealth and the territories, however, requires that the jurisdiction of courts exercising jurisdiction under territorial law should be subject to the inhibitions imposed by Ch III including the appointment, removal and tenure of territory judges. Ch III imposes no obligations on the **[617]** States in respect of their courts except to the extent that *Kable v Director of Public Prosecutions (NSW)* [(1996) 189 CLR 51] applies to them. There is no reason why the Commonwealth, in legislating for its territories and their courts, should be subject to constitutional burdens which do not apply to the States when they legislate for their courts. (5) If Ch III applies to the territories when the Commonwealth is creating courts or investing judicial power in the territories, then it must apply to territorial legislatures, which have been given self-government, when they do those things. The Commonwealth could no more escape the operation of Ch III by setting up self-governing legislatures than it could escape its operation by giving the Governor-General in Council power to create courts under a regulation. In contrast, s 121 permits the Parliament to admit new States into the federation upon "such terms and conditions, including the extent of representation in either House of the Parliament, as it thinks fit." Under s 121, the Parliament could make it a term or condition that Ch III should not apply at all or in some amended form to a new entrant. It is difficult to see why the Constitution should require the Parliament legislating for a territory, or a self-governing territory, to comply with Ch III when the Parliament could admit the territory as a State with no obligation to comply with Ch III. (6) If "federal jurisdiction" in Ch III includes jurisdiction over "matters" arising under laws made under s 122, s 77(iii) of the Constitution would authorise the conscription of State courts to determine matters arising under territory laws, matters which have nothing to do with the federal nature of the Constitution. (7) At Federation, it was assumed that the Commonwealth would have a number of sparsely populated territories under its control including territories outside Australia. To require the Commonwealth to comply with such provisions of Ch III as ss 72 and 80 and to prevent it from giving non-judicial functions to a territory court would have been inconvenient to say the least. (8) One of the reasons that the Constitutional Convention rejected Sir Edward Braddon's suggestion that territorial representation in the Parliament should be "in accordance with the ratio of representation provided in the Constitution" was that it would be "a great mistake" to bring the territories into line with the States.

Indeed, the only powerful argument in support of applying Ch III to s 122 is that s 76(ii) refers to the conferral of jurisdiction "arising under any laws made by the Parliament". But given the many considerations which point in the opposite direction, this seems too weak a foundation for applying Ch III as a whole to the territories or to hold that the exercise of judicial power under a law, enacted under s 122, is an exercise of "federal jurisdiction".

Kirby J – in sole dissent – held that the relevant provision of the *Community Welfare Act* was rendered inoperative by inconsistency with the *Family Law Act*. This enabled him also to reject the argument that the Territory provision was "picked up" by s 79 of the *Judiciary Act*.

The decision in *GPAO*, if not the reasoning of Barwick CJ in *Spratt v Hermes*, made it impossible to maintain the simple proposition accepted by Kitto J in *Spratt v Hermes* "[257] that the power of Parliament under s 122 … [is] unrestricted by anything expressed or implied in Chap III". Nevertheless, in *Re Governor, Goulburn Correctional Centre; Ex parte Eastman* (1999) 200 CLR 322, where the issue again arose of whether judicial appointments in the ACT should comply with s 72 of the Constitution, the High Court held by a 6:1 majority that s 72 had no application, thus reaffirming *Spratt v Hermes* and *Capital TV and Appliances v Falconer*. Kirby J was again the only dissenter. Moreover, the whole Court (including Kirby J) reaffirmed that the ultimate source of legislation for the ACT was s 122, not s 52(i).

What Gleeson CJ, McHugh and Callinan JJ endorsed in *Ex parte Eastman* was the limited proposition accepted by Barwick CJ in *Spratt v Hermes*, "[332] which gives a negative answer, not to a wide question as to the relationship between Ch III and s 122, but to a particular question as to whether s 72 addresses the position of courts created pursuant to s 122". They held that this "produces a sensible result, which pays due regard to the practical considerations arising from the varied nature and circumstances of territories". They added that if s 72 were read as applicable to the Territories, it would in fact apply to some Territories and not to others, since in any case where a self-governing territorial legislature had legislated in respect of its own courts, they would no longer be "courts created by the Parliament".

Consistently with her judgment in *GPAO*, Gaudron J would have given leave to reopen *Spratt v Hermes* and *Capital TV and Appliances v Falconer*, and would indeed have overruled them except that, by a more elaborate route, she was able to establish that the approach of Barwick CJ in *Spratt v Hermes* was a plausible one. She added that if a Territory court is not to be held to the requirements of s 72, "[340] a question could arise as to whether, in accordance with the principles recognised in *Kable v Director of Public Prosecutions (NSW)*, there is not some implicit requirement in Ch III with respect to the nature of the matters that may be dealt with by it and perhaps, also, with respect to the manner in which it is constituted before federal jurisdiction can be vested in it".

In preliminary obiter dicta, Gummow and Hayne JJ accepted an analysis similar to that of Gaudron J. They stressed that "[344] the judicial power of the Commonwealth referred to in s 71 is not segmented in some fashion to reflect geographic divisions", any more than the legislative power invested by s 1, or the executive power invested by s 61, could be limited so as to exclude the Territories. As to executive power they noted that, in *Johnson v Kent* (1975) 132 CLR 164, it was accepted that the erection of the Black Mountain telecommunications tower in the ACT was an exercise of Commonwealth executive power. Adopting what Gaudron J had said in *GPAO*, they held that: "[348] The preferable construction is that a court created by the Parliament for the government of a territory is not a federal court created under ss 71 and 72 but may answer the description of one of the 'other courts' which are invested by laws made by the Parliament with federal jurisdiction within the meaning of s 71 and thus are recipients of the judicial power of the Commonwealth. The investment of federal jurisdiction in such a non-federal Territory court would be by a law supported not by s 77 but by s 122".

Gummow and Hayne JJ based their rejection of the applicant's submission on a narrower ground – namely, that the effect of the *Australian Capital Territory (Self-Government) Act* and the *Capital Territory Supreme Court (Transfer) Act 1992* (Cth) was that the Supreme Court of the ACT should now be regarded as a court created by a law of the ACT Legislative Assembly. It could therefore not be regarded as one of the "courts created by the Parliament" within the meaning of s 72. They noted that in *Kruger* "**[349]** Gaudron J observed that, whatever view be taken of the decisions in *Spratt v Hermes* and *Capital TV*, it may be that different considerations apply to laws enacted by the legislature of a self-governing territory. The present case bears out the point".

The traditional view that s 72 does not apply to judicial appointments in the Territories was cemented in place by *Ex parte Eastman*. In *North Australian Aboriginal Legal Aid Service Inc v Bradley* (2004) 218 CLR 146, Gleeson CJ tacitly assumed, and the other six judges expressly held, that "**[164]** for these proceedings the point should be taken as settled". However, the joint judgment also endorsed the suggestion made by Gaudron J (in *GPAO*) that the courts of the Territories may be invested with federal jurisdiction, and her further suggestion (in *Ex parte Eastman*) that they thereupon become subject to the principles enounced in *Kable v Director of Public Prosecutions (NSW)* (1996) 189 CLR 51 (see Chapter 15, §2). In *Bradley*, the joint judgment accepted, on the basis of these suggestions, "**[163]** that it is implicit in the terms of Ch III of the Constitution, and necessary for the preservation of that structure, that a court capable of exercising the judicial power of the Commonwealth be and appear to be an independent and impartial tribunal", and that this requirement extends to courts in the Territories as it does to other courts that exercise federal jurisdiction.

It followed that the continued exclusion of judicial appointments in the Territories from s 72 is now of diminished importance. On the other hand, the standard of judicial independence derived from *Kable* remains less rigorous than that of s 72. Hence, in *Bradley* the appointment of Hugh Bradley as Chief Magistrate of the Northern Territory was held to satisfy the *Kable* standard, even though it would not have satisfied the requirements of s 72.

6. The Common Law

When litigation in the courts of one State or Territory involves persons or events in another State or Territory, which is the law to be applied? The rules on this topic were once referred to as "private international law", later as "conflicts of laws", and nowadays (see *John Pfeiffer Pty Ltd v Rogerson* (2000) 203 CLR 503 at 527) as "choice of law" rules. The problem occurs most frequently in tort litigation, and the principal choice is between the law of the court hearing the action (*lex fori*, the law of the forum) and that of the place where the tort was committed (*lex loci delicti*). Running through High Court judgments on this issue are two recurring though perhaps antinomic themes: that so far as possible the applicable law should always be that of the State or Territory where the relevant events occurred, and that throughout the whole of Australia one uniform common law applies.

The latter proposition is further evidence that the balance between "national" and "federal" conceptions (see *The Federalist (No 39)* in §1 above) has worked out very differently in Australia and in the United States. The American view, established by *Erie Railroad Co v Tompkins*, 304 US 64 (1938), is that although the law of most States is derived from the English common law, the development of that law by the courts of each State has proceeded separately, so that even in the federal courts "**[78]** the law to be applied in any case is the law of the State ... There is no federal general common law". That decision overruled the earlier doctrine of *Swift v Tyson*, 41 US (16 Peters) 1 (1842), which had held that, in a commercial dispute between a plaintiff from Maine and a defendant from New York, a federal court need not apply the law of either Maine or New York, but was free to develop its own conception of a federal common law, whose "**[19]** true interpretation and effect ... [was] to be sought, not in the decisions of the local tribunals, but in the general principles and doctrines of commercial jurisprudence". In place of that doctrine, *Erie Railroad Co v Tompkins* gave effect to an earlier famous dissent by Oliver Wendell Holmes.

Black and White Taxicab Co v Brown and Yellow Taxicab Co
276 US 518 (1928)

Holmes J: [533] Books written about any branch of the common law treat it as a unit, cite cases from this Court [the Supreme Court], from the Circuit Court of Appeals, from the State Courts, from England and the Colonies of England indiscriminately, and criticize them as right or wrong according to the writer's notions of a single theory. It is very hard to resist the impression that there is one august corpus, to understand which clearly is the only task of any Court concerned. If there were such a transcendental body of law outside of any particular State but obligatory within it unless and until changed by statute, the Courts of the United States might be right in using their independent judgment as to what it was. But there is no such body of law. The fallacy and illusion that I think exist consist in supposing that there is this outside thing to be found ... The common law so far as it is enforced in a State, whether called common law or not, is not the common law generally but the law of that State existing by the authority of that State without regard to what it **[534]** may have been in England or anywhere else ...

If within the limits of the Constitution a State should declare one of the disputed rules of general law by statute there would be no doubt of the duty of all Courts to bow, whatever their private opinions might be ... I see no reason why it should have less effect when it speaks by its other voice ... If a state constitution should declare that on all matters of general law the decisions of the highest Court [of that State] should establish the law until modified by statute or by a later decision of the same Court, I do not perceive how it would be possible for a Court of the United States to refuse to follow what the State Court decided in that domain. But when the constitution of a State establishes a Supreme Court it by implication does make that declaration as clearly as if it had said it in express words, so **[535]** far as it is not interfered with by the superior power of the United States. The Supreme Court of a State does something more than make a scientific inquiry into a fact outside of and independent of it. It says with an authority that no one denies, except when a citizen of another State is able to invoke an exceptional jurisdiction, that thus the law is and shall be. Whether it be said to make or to declare the law, it deals with the law of the State with equal authority however its function may be described.

In this reasoning, Holmes gave effect to his famous epigram in *Southern Pacific Co v Jensen*, 244 US 205 (1917): "**[222]** The common law is not a brooding omnipresence in the sky but the articulate voice of some sovereign or quasi-sovereign that can be identified".

In his *Black and White Taxicab* dissent, Holmes took care to acknowledge that his concept of separate development of the law by State courts could operate only "**[534]** within the limits of the Constitution", and "so **[535]** far as it is not interfered with by the superior power of the United States". One crucial difference between the Australian and United States Constitutions is the one that underlay the dilemma in *Theophanous v Herald & Weekly Times Ltd* (1994) 182 CLR 104 (see Chapter 28, §4): namely, that the High Court of Australia is, while the Supreme Court of the United States is not, a general court of appeal from the States in matters of general law. Thus the High Court does exercise an overall supervision of the development of the common law in each State, correcting it when necessary; and when it does so, its pronouncements apply to all States and Territories, since all of them are subject to the same appellate supervision. Accordingly, since *Viro v The Queen* (1978) 141 CLR 88, the Court has recognized that its principal function, in its appellate jurisdiction, is (as Gibbs J expressed it) "**[120]** to expound and develop the law for Australia". Even when State courts take differing views of the common law, the differences are only transitional: sooner or later, they will be resolved by a High Court pronouncement which is binding on all Australian courts.

Before *Viro*, the High Court had shared this role with the Privy Council (see Chapter 13, §4), whose decisions were an equally powerful source of uniformity not just among the Australian jurisdictions, but of all of them with the common law of England. The early conception of a uniform Australian (and English) common law had been sentimental as well as practical: the Australian colonies that federated in 1901 conceived of themselves as integral parts of the British Empire, and as having a shared inheritance of the English common law. For New South Wales,

Victoria, Queensland and Tasmania, that inheritance was necessarily uniform: the "reception" of English law under s 24 of the *Australian Courts Act 1828* (Imp) (see Chapter 4, §2) applied equally to New South Wales and Tasmania, and at that time Queensland and Victoria were still parts of New South Wales. Though South Australia and Western Australia had later reception dates, their commitment to a shared British inheritance was equally strong.

Griffith CJ had appeared to accept the idea of a single Australian common law as early as *R v Kidman* (1915) 20 CLR 425 (see Chapter 4, §2(a)). The received common law did not, he said, "**[436]** become disintegrated into six separate codes of law", but "became part of an identical law applicable to six separate political entities"; and at Federation "the current which had been temporarily diverted into six parallel streams coalesced". However, his immediate concern in that case was only to demonstrate that the common law offence of conspiracy to defraud the Crown could apply to the Crown in right of the Commonwealth; and his judgment in *R v Snow* (1915) 20 CLR 315, handed down on the same day as *R v Kidman*, declared that "**[325]** whatever power the High Court may have to entertain an appeal from a judgment of the Supreme Court of a State, it must give judgment according to the law of that State".

In any event, for Griffith CJ and other judges of his generation, "the common law" meant the English common law, and the "choice of law" rules to be applied were those of English law. Those rules had been developed not in a federal but an international context; the different legal systems which they presupposed were those of sovereign nation states. The earliest High Court judges saw no incongruity in applying those laws to the Australian States, since their conception of federalism treated each of the States as an independent sovereign power (see Chapter 7, §§1-3). For example, in *Potter v Broken Hill Pty Co Ltd* (1906) 3 CLR 479, where the High Court held that the validity of a patent issued in New South Wales could not be examined in the courts of Victoria, Griffith CJ refused to hold that "**[494]** the Australian States are not Sovereign States in the full sense of the term, *ie*, as between themselves and foreign Powers", and insisted that the case must be considered "**[495]** on precisely the same basis as if the patent ... had been granted by the Government of the French Republic or of the United States of America". Not only were the Australian "choice of law" rules a replication of those developed in England, but their application as between States proceeded as if the relationship among the States was the same as that of foreign countries. As Windeyer J put it in *Pedersen v Young* (1964) 110 CLR 162: "**[170]** The States are separate countries in private international law, and are to be so regarded in relation to one another".

Under the English "choice of law" rules, the deference that was often accorded to foreign executive governments did not extend to their laws. Consistently, when the question was one of the law to be applied by an English court to a foreign tort, the English rules leant towards the *lex fori*: that is, they tended to produce the result that English law should apply. The leading case on the subject, *Phillips v Eyre* (1870) 6 QB 1, had purported to effect a compromise, giving some weight to the *lex fori* and some to the *lex loci delicti*: "**[28]** As a general rule, in order to found a suit in England for a wrong alleged to have been committed abroad, two conditions must be fulfilled. First, the wrong must be of such a character that it would have been actionable if committed **[29]** in England ... Secondly, the act must not have been justifiable by the law of the place where it was done". But exactly what limited role was accorded to the *lex loci delicti* by the second limb of this rule was notoriously unclear (see J Stone, *Legal System and Lawyers' Reasonings* (Maitland Publications, 1964), 248).

In *Koop v Bebb* (1951) 84 CLR 629, the High Court applied *Phillips v Eyre* to hold that Victorian plaintiffs, suing a New South Wales defendant in respect of their father's death in a New South Wales accident, could sue in the Supreme Court of Victoria. For Dixon, Williams, Fullagar and Kitto JJ the applicable law was the *Wrongs Act 1928* (Vic); for McTiernan J it was the *Compensation to Relatives Act 1897* (NSW). In that case there was no material difference between the two statutes; but in *Anderson v Eric Anderson Radio & TV Ltd* (1965) 114 CLR 20, the "choice of law" was crucial. The *lex loci delicti* was that of the Australian Capital Territory (ACT), where the old rule treating a plaintiff's contributory negligence as a complete defence had already been abolished by the *Law Reform (Miscellaneous Provisions) Ordinance 1955* (Cth). The *lex fori* was that of New South Wales, where the rule had not yet been abolished. Citing *Phillips v Eyre*, the High Court held that the *lex fori* applied.

The first serious questioning of the common law rules came in *Breavington v Godleman* (1988) 169 CLR 41. Anthony Breavington, a Telecom employee, was a passenger in a Telecom vehicle (driven by a fellow employee, Charles Piercy) that was travelling along the Stuart Highway in the Northern Territory when it was hit by a car driven by Rodney Godleman. Breavington was injured and sued Godleman, Piercy and Telecom. He sued in the Supreme Court of Victoria: Godleman was a Northern Territory resident at the time of the accident but had later moved to Victoria, and Victorian law allowed unlimited common law damages, whereas under the *Motor Accidents (Compensation) Act 1979* (NT), damages in road accident cases were limited to pain and suffering and loss of amenities of life.

The Full Supreme Court of Victoria, reversing the decision of O'Bryan J, held that the *lex loci delicti* applied, so that Breavington could claim only the heads of damage allowed in the Northern Territory (*Godleman v Breavington* [1987] VR 645). Breavington then appealed to the High Court. At a hearing before a five-judge bench, Deane J suggested that s 118 of the Constitution was relevant; and Gaudron J asked whether the involvement of Telecom might attract s 56(1)(b) of the *Judiciary Act 1903* (Cth), which requires that claims against the Commonwealth in a State or Territory must be brought in the courts "of that State or Territory". Accordingly, the matter was reargued before a seven-judge bench.

The whole Court held that the Northern Territory's restrictions on damages applied. However, Deane J reached that result by using s 118 of the Constitution and the concept of a "[123] national system of law" to conclude that, throughout the Commonwealth, the substantive law of the locus State should *always* be applied. Adopting the language of Jacobs J when in the Supreme Court of New South Wales in *Anderson v Eric Anderson Radio & TV Ltd* (1964) 65 SR (NSW) 279 at 288, Deane J argued that, when viewed in a constitutional context, the traditional choice of law rules were "[125] incongruous and unsatisfactory".

Breavington v Godleman
(1988) 169 CLR 41

Deane J: [120] [T]he Constitution must be construed in the general context that, while the Federation was intended to preserve the existence of the former Colonies as States, the compact between the people of those Colonies was to unite in one indissoluble Commonwealth under a new system of law to which all within its territory ("courts, judges, and people of every State and of every part": covering cl 5 of the *Constitution of Australia Act* 1901 (Cth)) were thenceforth to be subject. The compact itself was that new system of law, incorporating by assumption the substratum of the common law upon which it was built. Under it, the **[121]** constitutions and the laws (both inherited and statutory) of the States continued to the extent to which the Constitution and valid Commonwealth laws enacted pursuant to it allowed (see, in particular, ss 106, 107 and 108). To that extent, the constitutions and the laws of the States were not diminished. They were enhanced as part of a new national structure.

It is in that context that an important question … falls to be determined. That question, stated in deceptively simple terms …, is whether the Commonwealth and State constitutions and laws comprise a unitary system of law. By "a unitary system of law", I mean a comprehensive legal system in which the substantive law applicable to govern particular facts or circumstances is objectively ascertainable or predictable and internally consistent or reconcilable. It is not essential … that identical rules regulate conduct, property or status and define its consequences or attributes regardless of where in the jurisdictional territory it may occur or exist: a single system of law may well incorporate State or other local rules applying to persons, acts and things within the relevant State or other locality. What is essential is that the substantive rule or rules applicable to determine the lawfulness and the legal consequences or attributes of conduct, property or status at a particular time in a particular part of the national territory will be the same regardless of whereabouts in that territory questions concerning those matters or their legal consequences may arise. In a federation such as Australia where there are a number of legislatures and a number of distinct court systems, such unity cannot exist unless the legal principles for determining legislative competence and for resolving conflicts between different laws in a particular case will operate with identical results in any of the different court systems ...

[I]t appears to me to be manifest that the comprehensive system of law which the Constitution established was intended to be a unitary one in the above sense. The fundamental provisions of that system of law were the terms of the Constitution itself. The purpose of those fundamental provisions [122] was to federate the former Colonies into a single nation. They subjected Colonial legislative powers and Colonial laws, which they continued and incorporated as State legislative powers and State laws, completely to their terms ... It is reasonable to infer that it was intended that valid Commonwealth and State substantive laws, made or continued under the authority of the federal compact, would be integrated in the sense that they were internally consistent or reconcilable.

As evidence of this intention he pointed to the vesting in State and federal courts of federal jurisdiction, particularly "between residents of different States" under s 75(iv); and also to the mechanism provided by s 109 for the resolution of inconsistencies between State and Commonwealth laws. More broadly, he relied on the establishment by Ch III of independent federal judicial power as assuming an ascertainable "[122] national law, with Commonwealth and State ingredients". In particular, he relied on the High Court's appellate jurisdiction under s 73, which Sir Owen Dixon in *Jesting Pilate* (Law Book Company, 1965) saw as expressing "[201] an instinctive faith in the unity of the system and in the consequent need of uniform interpretations". In addition, Deane J pointed to Dixon's conception in *Jesting Pilate* of "[199] Australian law as a unit", encompassing in particular "the anterior operation of the common law", and "the duty of all courts to recognize that it is one system which should receive a uniform interpretation and application". These conceptions, said Dixon, made it "[201] possible for an Australian to regard his country as governed by a single legal system".

Within this national system, as Deane J conceived it, legislative power is divided vertically between States and Commonwealth, and horizontally among the States. The vertical division is effected by s 51 (which allocates to the Commonwealth legislative power on specified subject-matters or for specified purposes) and by s 109 (which ensures that within those areas of power the Commonwealth law shall prevail). The horizontal division is effected on a territorial basis: each State has primary legislative responsibility for matters arising within its own territory. Accordingly, problems of conflict or competition between the laws of different States should similarly be resolved on a territorial basis by ensuring that, for matters arising within a State, the laws of that State are decisive. He read the requirement in s 118 of "full faith and credit" for the laws of the States as intended to ensure this resolution. He denied that the common law "choice of law" rules could be an acceptable alternative, since they might mean "[127] that the substantive law applicable to a particular accident in one part of this country" could vary from State to State. Explaining his view of the operation of s 118, he said:

Deane J: [129] [T]hat constitutional provision is relevant in two distinct ways. First, it serves to confirm, if confirmation be necessary, the national character ("throughout the Commonwealth") of the system of law which the Constitution established. Second, it requires and ensures that, within that national system of law, full faith and credit be given to the laws and public Acts of each State.

To give full faith and credit to something does not, as a matter of ordinary language, mean merely to acknowledge the fact that it exists. Thus, to give full faith and credit to a person's word does not mean merely to accept the fact that the person says something. It means to accept and act upon the content of what he says. To give full faith and credit to a judgment means, as a matter of ordinary language, not only to recognize its existence but, while it stands, to accept and abide by its contents ... Likewise, the [130] directive of s 118 to give full faith and credit "throughout the Commonwealth" to the laws and Acts of a State ... does not, as a matter of ordinary language, mean merely to accept that such laws or Acts exist or have been made. It decrees that those laws must be accepted *throughout the Commonwealth* as the national law applicable to regulate, and define the consequences or attributes of, conduct, property or status within that particular part of the national territory ...

[134] The effect of the Constitution was to establish a comprehensive and truly unitary system of substantive law. That national law [135] applies throughout the territory of the nation. It encompasses: the Constitution itself; the constitutions of the States to the extent to which they are continued under the Constitution; the laws made by, and under the authority of, the Parliament; the laws made by, and under the authority of, the Parliaments of the States; and the common law. Within that unitary system of national law there is no room for the direct application of private international law principles to resolve competition or inconsistency between a law of the Commonwealth and a law of a State or between the laws of different States. The Constitution itself resolves such competition or inconsistency: by s 109 (in the case of inconsistency between a law of the Commonwealth and a law of a State); by the confinement of the operation of State laws by reference to territorial (or predominant territorial) nexus under the constitutional structure and the mandatory directive of s 118 (in the case of competition or conflict between the laws of different States). Under the constitutional structure, State laws are essentially territorial in the sense that they apply to regulate (or to define the consequences or attributes of) conduct, property or status within, or having a sufficient relevant nexus with, that part of the nation which constitutes the territory of the particular State ...

[I]t would be to substitute the bedlam of a Babel for an ordered system of law to recognize the right of each of the country's court systems, notwithstanding the place of this Court in all of them, to speak at the same time but in conflicting terms about the lawfulness, consequences or attributes of a particular act or thing in a particular place at a particular time.

Deane J conceded that it is "[135] necessary to draw a distinction between substantive laws ... and procedural or adjectival laws". As to matters of the latter kind the *lex fori* could apply, since a law "[136] directed to regulating court proceedings will have its territorial operation in the territory in which those court proceedings take place". He also conceded that, to the extent that "[137] the common law rules of private international law are traditionally based on notions of territoriality", they might sometimes be relevant "by way of analogy".

The joint judgment of Wilson and Gaudron JJ took a broadly similar view. They too held that the question "[93] must be resolved by reference to the federal compact embodied in the Constitution, including by reference to s 118 of the Constitution", which they read as requiring "[98] that the one set of facts occurring in a State would be adjudged by only one body of law and thus give rise to only one legal consequence, regardless of where in the Commonwealth the matter fell for adjudication". They held that this conception could be made effective "only by the adoption of an inflexible rule that questions of liability in tort be determined by the substantive law that would be applied if the matter were adjudicated in a court exercising the judicial power of the State in which the events occurred".

Brennan and Dawson JJ reached the same result by holding that since Breavington's claim to general damages would not be recognised by Northern Territory law, it did not satisfy the second limb of *Phillips v Eyre*. Toohey J reached the same result by applying the "[162] flexible" restatement of *Phillips v Eyre* by the House of Lords in *Chaplin v Boys* [1971] AC 356. He did not appear unsympathetic to reliance on s 118, but held that, since it refers only to the laws "of every State", it could not apply in a case involving the laws of a Territory. "[164] The consequences it may have for choice of law rules when a statute of one State is considered by the court of another State is something which may await another day". Mason CJ proposed a "[76] qualified or flexible application of the law of the place of the wrong" – reflecting his approach in *Pozniak v Smith* (1982) 151 CLR 38 to the somewhat analogous problem of deciding which of two competing States should receive the remitter of an action commenced in the High Court. His approach in *Breavington v Godleman* was influenced by his recognition that "[78] Australia is one country and one nation"; but he firmly rejected any attempt to "[83] spell out a rigid and inflexible approach from the language of s 118".

Although all judges in *Breavington v Godleman* reached the same result, the underlying issue remained unsettled; and in *McKain v RW Miller & Co (SA) Pty Ltd* (1991) 174 CLR 1 the pendulum swung the other way. William McKain, a marine steward from Sydney, was injured while serving on the motor vessel *Troubridge* in South Australia. Almost six years later he filed a statement of claim against the charterers of the *Troubridge* in the Supreme Court of New South Wales. The *Limitation Act 1969* (NSW) prescribed a six-year limitation period for actions in tort: if the *lex fori* applied, McKain had sued in time. The *Limitation of Actions Act 1936* (SA) and the *Workers Compensation Act 1971* (SA) prescribed three-year limitation periods: if the *lex loci delicti* applied, the claim was statute-barred. The argument in the High Court assumed that the applicable *substantive* law was that of South Australia, but that the applicable *procedural* law was that of New South Wales. Thus the immediate practical issue was whether a limitation period is a matter of procedure or of substance. Brennan, Dawson, Toohey and McHugh JJ took the former view; hence the New South Wales law applied and the claim was not statute-barred. Mason CJ, Deane and Gaudron JJ dissented.

The dissenting judgments of Deane and Gaudron JJ again relied on s 118; the dissenting judgment of Mason CJ again rejected its relevance, except to a limited extent. To apply the *lex loci delicti* meant, he thought, not only that the New South Wales Court must apply South Australia's three-year limitation period, but also that it could exercise the discretion given by s 48 of the South Australian Act to grant an extension of time. On his analysis, s 118 cannot solve a "choice of law" problem; but once an interstate law has been chosen, s 118 then applies to ensure that it receives "full" faith and credit. By contrast, the joint majority judgment emphatically rejected the use of s 118 to "constitutionalise" the issue.

McKain v RW Miller & Co (SA) Pty Ltd
(1991) 174 CLR 1

Brennan, Dawson, Toohey and McHugh JJ: [36] To describe the States, as Windeyer J once described them [*Pedersen v Young* (1964) 110 CLR 162 at 170], as "separate countries in private international law" may sound anachronistic. Yet it is of the nature of the federation created by the Constitution that the States be distinct law areas whose laws may govern any subject matter subject to constitutional restrictions and qualifications. The laws of the States, though recognized throughout Australia, are therefore capable of creating disparities in the legal consequences attached in the respective States to the same set of facts unless a valid law of the Commonwealth overrides the relevant State laws and prescribes a uniform legal consequence. That may or may not be thought to be desirable, but it is the hallmark of a federation as distinct from a union. Far from eliminating the differential operation of State laws, s 118 commands that all the laws of all the States be given full faith and credit: the laws of the forum are to be recognized as fully as the laws of the place where the set of facts occurred. Section 118 would not be obeyed by refusing recognition to the laws of a forum State and by applying only the laws of the part of Australia in which the set of facts occurred. A disparity in legal consequences attached to a set of facts cannot be eliminated by refusing recognition to laws of the forum which create the disparity. In our respectful opinion, **[37]** s 118 does not prescribe the selection of the lex loci delicti or other extraterritorial body of law as the exclusive body of law governing liability for extraterritorial torts. The selection of the applicable rules governing liability is the function of the common law.

When the issue arose again in *Stevens v Head* (1993) 176 CLR 433, Deane and Gaudron JJ again dissented, and again the majority applied the traditional common law rules. However, the conclusions in *Kable v Director of Public Prosecutions (NSW)* (1996) 189 CLR 51 (see Chapter 15, §2) were linked by several of the judges in that case (notably by McHugh J at 111-15) to the underlying conception of an integrated national system of law; and in 1997 the issue drew fresh life from the unanimous pronouncements in *Lange v Australian Broadcasting Corporation* (1997) 189 CLR 520 that "**[563]** [t]here is but one common law in Australia" and that "**[566]** [o]f necessity, the common law must conform with the Constitution".

The first significant shift came in *Lipohar v The Queen* (1999) 200 CLR 485. As in *R v Kidman*, the issue arose from a prosecution for the common law offence of conspiracy to defraud.

Edward Lipohar and Mark Winfield were convicted of that offence at a trial in South Australia. The conviction was based on representations made at a meeting in Brisbane, relating to a proposed tenancy of commercial premises in Melbourne. The representations related in part to supposed business links with Indonesia and Thailand. The company to which the representations were made, Collins Street Properties Pty Ltd, was the owner of the Melbourne premises, but was incorporated and managed in South Australia as a wholly owned subsidiary of another company also incorporated in South Australia and owned by its State Government Insurance Commission (SGIC). Dismissing an appeal against conviction, the High Court held that South Australia's assertion of jurisdiction was valid.

The principal majority judgment was that of Gaudron, Gummow and Hayne JJ. They explained South Australia's exercise of jurisdiction on the basis that the offence arose under "the common law of Australia", and that what the South Australian court was doing was to enforce that national common law as part of the law of the State.

Lipohar v The Queen
(1999) 200 CLR 485

Gaudron, Gummow and Hayne JJ: [505] The common law ... is a body of law created and defined by the courts. Whatever may once have been the case in England the doctrine of precedent is now central to any understanding of the common law in Australia. To assert that there is more than one common law in Australia or that there is a common law of individual States is to ignore the central place which precedent has in both understanding the common law and explaining its basis.

This Court is placed by s 73 of the Constitution at the apex of a judicial hierarchy to give decisions upon the common law which are binding on all courts, federal, State and territorial. Different intermediate appellate courts within that hierarchy may give inconsistent rulings upon questions of common law. This disagreement will indicate that not all of these courts will have correctly applied or declared the common law. But it does not follow that there are as many bodies of common law as there are intermediate courts of appeal ...

[507] This Court is the final appellate court for the nation. When an appeal is dealt with in this Court, and its reasons are published, those reasons will form part of the common law of Australia and will bind all courts in the country. The Court never has [sought] and never should seek to identify some common law rule that is peculiar to one or more of the States. And yet that is the role which would be assigned to it if there were more than a single common law of Australia.

The federal system operates with what is now the common law of Australia. One consequence is that there do not arise in Australia, as once might have been thought, difficulties with the notion of a distinct "federal common law" which still are encountered in the United States after the over-ruling of *Swift v Tyson* [41 US (16 Peters) 1 (1842)] by *Erie Railroad Company v Tompkins* [304 US 64 (1938)] ...

[508] The liability of the Commonwealth in tort and contract is created by the common law; s 75(iii) of the Constitution denies operation of what otherwise might be doctrines of Crown or executive immunity in these fields. The "common law" here is that of Australia, rather than a "federal common law" distinct from the common law of each of the other bodies politic in Australia.

The activities of the executive government of the Commonwealth which give rise to liabilities in contract and tort will, to a very significant degree, be conducted outside the seat of government and in the States. If the common law were fragmented, it would be necessary to spell out of the Australian constitutional structure principles to resolve conflicts or variances between, in particular, "federal common law" and that of the particular State in which the executive government of the Commonwealth conducted its activities ... However, any conundrum is avoided once it is seen that there is but one common law, not as many as there are bodies politic.

It is true ..., that the common law of England was received at different times and in different circumstances in various parts of what is now Australia ... The common law of England was received into what were then colonies, not what are now States. Nonetheless, as Griffith CJ emphasized [*R v Kidman* (1915) 20 CLR 425 at 436], the common law did not thereby "become disintegrated into six separate codes of law", one for each colony. Rather, in *Skelton v Collins* [(1966) 115 CLR 94 at 134-5], Windeyer J spoke of what was inherited as **[509]** both a body of doctrines and principles, and "its method and its spirit", including "the creative element in the work of courts". His Honour there identified this as having become the common law of Australia …

As was emphasised in *Lange v Australian Broadcasting Corporation* [(1997) 189 CLR 520 at 566], the development of the common law in Australia must conform with the Constitution because "[t]he common law and the requirements of the Constitution cannot be at odds". The recognition of an Australian common law was essential to the reasoning in that case, particularly for the putting to one side of any question of adoption from the United States of a "constitutional privilege" against enforcement of the distinct common laws of the several States of the Union. However, within their respective spheres of competence, the common law may be abrogated or amended by the federal Parliament and the Parliaments of the States and legislatures of certain Territories. Laws so made may be repealed and the common law revived. The result at any given time may be that **[510]** the operation of the common law upon a particular subject may vary according to the circumstances of litigation, including the identity of the forum and of the lex causae.

In this case, while the prosecution and conviction in South Australia were to be understood as enforcing "the common law of Australia", Gaudron, Gummow and Hayne JJ did not contend that this in itself was sufficient to give South Australia jurisdiction, since "**[532]** territorial nexus with the nation as a whole is not sufficient". The question "**[534]** whether a particular court in Australia has jurisdiction to try an offence against the common law of Australia" must still depend on a more precise finding of territorial nexus at the State or Territory level. These three judges held, however, that such a nexus had been established.

Gaudron, Gummow and Hayne JJ: [534] The requirement of nexus should be liberally applied. A real **[535]** connection with the jurisdiction will suffice. The object of the conspiracy was to cheat Collins Street out of a particular receipt. In that sense the immediate victim in prospect was Collins Street. The company was incorporated in South Australia. Its legal advisers with respect to the proposed transaction were in Adelaide.

[A] conclusion as to the sufficiency of the connection … [is also] to be reached by having regard to the commercial realities of the situation … Given the corporate structure which we have indicated, it would, for present purposes, be artificial to quarantine the effect sought to be obtained through the conspiracy by ignoring the real and practical consequences for SGIC, and thus for the South Australian body politic. A connection of this character will suffice.

Gleeson CJ also found a sufficient nexus. He held that, in deciding that issue, the Court should not be constrained by the old idea that a crime must have a single geographical location: "**[500]** The common law offence of conspiracy which, by its nature, is capable of having trans-jurisdictional operation and effect, has not been subjected to a rigid, single-situs, rule of territoriality". Accordingly, the question "**[501]** should be approached without any preconception" that an alleged conspiracy must have "only a single situs". For offences other than conspiracy, he acknowledged that the idea of a crime having "**[498]** but a single location" might sometimes reflect "practical necessity" (see, for example, *Ward v The Queen* (1980) 142 CLR 308); but even then he thought that "**[499]** [t]he general common law requirement of a single situs has never been absolute, and there is no reason, either in principle or in practical necessity, why it should be". However, he did not think that anything said in *Lange* had changed the situation. It was wholly consistent with the recognition of a uniform national common law to assert that it "**[500]** recognises the States as separate jurisdictions, or law areas, where to do so is appropriate in the application of common law principles".

Kirby and Callinan JJ each dissented in part. Callinan J agreed that there was a sufficient nexus with South Australia, but rejected the idea of a uniform Australian common law. Kirby J dissented from the view that a sufficient nexus with South Australia had been established, but agreed with the majority view that the issue must be approached in light of "**[553]** the integrated character of the Australian federation".

Kirby J: [551] There are some express provisions of the Australian Constitution that may be mentioned in this connection. By covering cl 5, the Constitution is binding on the courts, judges and people of every State and of every part of the Commonwealth. By s 51(xxiv) the Federal Parliament is empowered to make laws with respect to the service and execution throughout the Commonwealth of the civil and criminal process and the judgments of the courts of the States. It is pursuant to that power that the *Service and Execution of Process Act* 1992 (Cth) has been enacted ... By s 51(xxv) of the Constitution provision is made for the Federal Parliament to make laws for the recognition throughout the Commonwealth of the laws and judicial proceedings of the States. By s 51(xxviii) the Parliament is empowered to make laws with respect to the influx of criminals. In Ch 3 of the Constitution an integrated Judicature is established. Appeals ultimately lie from courts, federal and State, to this Court.

It is the last-mentioned feature of the Australian Constitution which gives this Court functions in relation to the content of the common law in Australia which are different from the functions of the Supreme Court of the United States of America. It is a reason why, in Australia, there can ultimately be but one unified common law. It is a common law that is constantly in the process of definition and refinement by the judges of the several courts of Australia. In its evolution, it is **[552]** necessarily affected by the different statutory contexts in which the common law grows and develops in different States and Territories. It is inevitable that different statements of the common law will be made from time to time in different courts. Diversity of opinion about the content of the common law is one of the grounds upon which special leave to appeal to this Court may be, and commonly is, given. However, the fundamental postulate of the Constitution is of a unified Australian common law ...

Finally, there is the command of s 118 of the Constitution that full faith and credit be given throughout the Commonwealth to the laws and the judicial proceedings of every State ... The inferences drawn by Deane J in *Breavington v Godleman* [(1988) 169 CLR 41] from the language and purpose of s 118 of the Constitution have not yet attracted a majority in this Court ... However, the foregoing provisions of the Constitution, its structure and purpose, the institutions which it creates and the federal nation which it establishes, are clearly relevant to the content of the applicable common law rule ...

To treat **[553]** the several jurisdictions of the Australian Commonwealth, in relation to each other, as foreign states is erroneous, even absurd. It ignores the provisions and purposes of the Constitution and the federal nation which it brought into existence. Yet equally absurd, and alien to the Constitution, would be the mistake of ignoring the territorial divisions of the Commonwealth and the limited law-making responsibilities established for each "law area". No rule of the common law dealing with the definition of State offences or the jurisdiction of State courts could be inconsistent with the assumptions inherent in the division of Australia into territorial units called States or Territories. Nor could any such rule ignore the provision to each such State or a self-governing Territory of its own legislature with law-making powers expressed as being "for the peace, welfare, and good government of" or "in and for" the State in question or for the "peace, order and good government" of the self-governing Territory concerned ...

[557] It is ... suggested that the solution lies in deriving from the proposition that there is but one unified common law within Australia the consequence that a common law offence is committed in every jurisdiction of Australia and so may be prosecuted in any. In *Lange v Australian Broadcasting Corporation* this Court concluded that there was but one common law in Australia, namely the law declared by this Court. However, I do not believe that this proposition sustains the invocation of the common law as a foundation for a new nationwide criminal jurisdiction capable of prosecution, trial, conviction and punishment of common law offences anywhere in Australia.

In *Lange*, this Court emphasized that the common law in Australia may not contradict constitutional imperatives. If the provisions of a supposed common law rule are inconsistent with the Constitution, they must yield to the constitutional norm. A cardinal feature of the Australian Constitution is its federal character. The existence of a single or unified common law, ultimately discoverable from the decisions of this Court, affords a norm that must be applied by a court whose jurisdiction is lawfully invoked when it is invited to apply common law principles in relation to its territorial boundaries. But it may not deny the constitutional provisions which divide Australia into federal, State and Territory law areas, including for criminal law purposes. I do not believe that the ultimate unity of the common law in Australia affords a new legal foundation to hold that the constitutional divisions of Australia inherent in its federal character, can for this purpose be disregarded. Or that common law offences may ... be prosecuted anywhere in Australia, no matter how tenuous, remote or even nonexistent are the connections between the forum and the elements of the offence.

Callinan J: [574] On the question whether the common law of South Australia is part of, or in all respects necessarily identical with the common law everywhere else in or of Australia, or that the only common law in Australia is a, and the, common law of Australia, I am of the opinion that it is not for a number of reasons.

The first reason is that each State is beyond doubt a polity well capable of, and frequently legislating separately and to different effect from time to time. It would be anomalous that although the law according to statute may differ from state to state, the common law (to the extent that it is unaffected by statute) must necessarily, and in respect of all matters, be the same. Secondly, the colonies which were to become the States received the common law into their jurisdictions at different times. The landscapes and conditions in the different colonies varied greatly and still do in many respects. It is not unthinkable, for example, that over time, in a state which is largely a desert state, the common law in relation to water usage and rights might evolve differently from a state in which water is much more plentiful. In other words, the creative element in the work of Supreme courts in moulding the common law may operate to provide a different result in a different state ...

[575] Thirdly, I would, with respect, find it difficult to accept that a common law offence may not be committed in Australia against a State community or a State community interest rather than the broader Australian society. And whilst it must be accepted that the common law and the requirements of the Constitution cannot be at odds, that proposition holds true whether there is one common law, or as many common laws as there are polities in Australia ...

[576] This nation remains a federal nation. Power, legislative, executive and judicial is divided among Federal, State and Territory parliaments. The executive of each manages, appoints and controls those who are to be responsible for law enforcement within the polities. Enforcement is not the sole province of police forces. Many other arms of the executive may be involved. For example, environmental, mining, industrial, health and emergency authorities will usually have an enforcement role to play. In so doing their rights and obligations need to be clear and defined by reference to the polity to which they are accountable. It is not an opinion universally held in this country that power and authority should inexorably accrue in all, or indeed, most matters to the central organs of government ...

[582] In *Lange v Australian Broadcasting Corporation* there are several unequivocal statements by this Court that there is one common law for the whole of Australia. If I were convinced that remarks to that effect so understood were necessary for that decision, I would of course have to apply them accordingly. I am bound on any view to accord them great weight and respect which I do. However, I do not think that their Honours' remarks were necessary for the decision in *Lange*. Once the Court said, as it did [189 CLR at 566], that, "[O]f necessity, the common law must conform with the Constitution" and that [they] cannot be at odds, it becomes apparent that this was so, no matter whether there might be one, or six or more, common laws of defamation in Australia. None of them could prevail over the Constitution ...

The Privy Council as a final court of appeal from the Australian colonies had before federation inevitably exerted a strong, unifying influence on the common law in this country. There were not, so far as **[583]** the administration of justice was concerned, the same difficulties and unevenness ... as between the respective colonies and their citizens, as existed in North America at the time of the establishment of the United States. Any differences that exist or may emerge in the common law of the States in this country are likely to be extremely rare and slight, but in my view it is not appropriate and there is no constitutional imperative to foreclose the possibility of such differences ...

[I]t is important that the autonomy (subject to the Constitution) of the States not be eroded. The people of a State look to that polity for the enforcement of the law. The police force is part of the executive of each State. It falls to the police force of each State to be the primary law enforcer of, and within the boundaries of a State. It is, in my opinion well settled that "all offences are local and territorial" [*Grannall v C Geo Kellaway & Sons Pty Ltd* (1955) 93 CLR 36 at 52]. The locality and territory for Australian purposes should be taken to be the State (except of course with respect to offences enacted to be such by Commonwealth legislation within power). The people have, and are entitled to have an expectation that breaches of the law within the State, or having a sufficient connexion with it, will be checked and punished by the polity of the State. It is important that there be, close at hand a sovereign authority, empowered so to act and with the means of doing so …

[589] It is unnecessary to consider the argument … based on s 118 of the Constitution.

In *John Pfeiffer Pty Ltd v Rogerson* (2000) 203 CLR 503, the conceptions emerging from the joint judgment in *Lipohar* were applied directly to the "choice of law" issues that had divided the High Court in *McKain v Miller* and *Stevens v Head*, and both cases were overruled.

David Rogerson suffered a fall at work and sued his employers, the appellants. Their place of business was in the ACT but at the time of the injury he was working in Queanbeyan in New South Wales. Under ACT law (the *lex fori*) his damages were assessed at $30,000. Under New South Wales law (the *lex locus delicti*) his damages would have been much lower because of the statutory "cap" imposed by the *Workers Compensation Act 1987* (NSW). By 6:1, Callinan J dissenting, the High Court held that in all such cases throughout Australia the *lex locus delicti* should always be applied. The joint judgment in *Lipohar* had been delivered by Gaudron, Gummow and Hayne JJ. They were joined now by Gleeson CJ, as well as by McHugh J (who did not sit in *Lipohar*). The joint judgment of these five judges again affirmed the existence of "[630] a single common law of Australia", citing in support of that proposition not only *Lange* and *Lipohar* but *Mabo v Queensland (No 2)* (1992) 175 CLR 1 at 15, and *Environment Protection Authority v Caltex Refining Co Pty Ltd* (1993) 178 CLR 477 at 556.

Moreover, the joint judgment also affirmed the general principle "[524] that the common law of Australia must adapt to the Constitution", as authoritatively laid down in *Lange v Australian Broadcasting Corporation* (1997) 189 CLR 520 (see Chapter 28, §5). It followed that the reasoning in the earlier cases "can only be accepted if it is consistent with the Constitution"; and hence that those cases "must be examined to determine whether they are consistent with Ch III of the Constitution and the integrated judicial system which it mandates". Indeed, the common law rules in this area needed to be "[534] developed to take into account various matters arising from the Australian constitutional text and structure".

The joint judgment distilled these matters into a series of dot points: they included the provision in Ch III for the exercise of a federal jurisdiction, and particularly for its exercise by State courts; the special position of the High Court as the ultimate court of appeal for every Australian jurisdiction; the effect of ss 117 and 118 of the Constitution; the distribution of jurisdiction between States and Territories on a territorial basis; and "[535] more generally, the nature of the federal compact". The relevance of some of these matters had been spelled out in the earlier cases, notably *Breavington v Godleman*; but for the most part these cases were not specifically acknowledged, nor was the reasoning further explained.

The resulting "[544] [d]evelopment of the common law to reflect the fact of federal jurisdiction and, also, the nature of the Australian federation" was said to require "[540] a single choice of law rule [to be applied] consistently in both federal and non-federal jurisdiction in all courts", so as to "recognise and give effect to the predominant territorial concern of the statutes of State and Territory legislatures". The joint judgment held that this single rule should be one that dictated the application of the *lex loci delicti*. Accordingly, the rule in *Phillips v Eyre*, which had sought to allow for some operation of both the *lex loci delicti* and the *lex fori*, should no longer be followed; and its Australian development in *McKain v Miller* and *Stevens v Head* should no longer be followed either. (The joint judgment emphasised that those were "[535] decisions which pre-date *Lange*".)

The joint judgment noted that "[535] the constitutional imperative" that was said to require the modification of the common law in *Lange* was there treated also as an "imperative [that] 'operates as a restriction on legislative power' so that '[s]tatutory regimes cannot trespass upon the constitutionally required freedom' [189 CLR at 566]". Whether that would apply in this case was treated as an open question: that is, the judgment left the possibility open that the constitutional considerations which had pointed to a new choice of law rule might also "operate constitutionally to entrench that rule ... If so, the result would be to restrict legislative power to abrogate or vary that common law rule".

The joint judgment also took the first steps towards a redefinition of the traditional distinction between questions of substance (governed by the choice of law rule) and questions of procedure (governed by the *lex fori*). Without fully resolving the issues involved, it laid down two specific rulings which effectively reversed the actual results in *McKain v Miller* and *Stevens v Head*. "**[544]** First, the application of any limitation period, whether barring the remedy or extinguishing the right, would be taken to be a question of substance not procedure ... [and] would, therefore, continue to be governed ... by the lex loci delicti. Secondly, *all* questions about the kinds of damage, or amount of damages that may be recovered, would likewise be treated as substantive issues governed by the lex loci delicti".

Kirby J agreed with these holdings. Callinan J, for his part, would not have abandoned the general choice of law rule developed in *McKain v Miller* and *Stevens v Head*. He did, however, agree that the traditional rule assigning procedural matters to the *lex fori* needed to be more narrowly limited. He would have confined "procedural" matters to those "**[574]** which are reasonable and necessary, in the lex fori for the conduct of the action only; that is to say the laws and rules relating to procedures such as the initiation, preparation, and the prosecution of the case, the recovery processes following any judgment and the rules of evidence". By contrast, "[i]n any realistic and practical sense the application of a statute of limitations will have the most profound of impacts upon the rights of the parties. With almost equal force the same may be said of provisions limiting either heads of damage or measures of damages, particularly in tort cases". He therefore agreed that laws on these topics should be assigned to the category of "substance" rather than "procedure". On that basis, he joined in the overruling of *McKain v Miller* and *Stevens v Head*, and in holding that, in the present case, the "cap" imposed on damages by New South Wales law should be applied by the ACT Supreme Court.

The end result appears to be that the Constitution and the common law are in symbiosis, or (to borrow another conception of the older private international law) in a state of perpetual *renvoi*. The Constitution provides the context within which, and in consonance with which, the common law must be developed, whether or not its influence is expressed through a definite limitation on what legislators and judges can do. At the same time, the common law provides the context within which and in consonance with which the Constitution must be construed.

7. Further References

Aroney, N, "Imagining a Federal Commonwealth: Australian Conceptions of Federalism, 1890-1901" (2002) 30 *Federal Law Review* 265.

Booker, K, "Section 51(xxxviii) of the Constitution" (1981) 4 *University of New South Wales Law Journal* 91.

Brown, AJ, "After the Party: Public Attitudes to Australian Federalism, Regionalism and Reform in the 21st Century" (2002) 13 *Public Law Review* 171.

Craven, G, *Conversations with the Constitution: Not Just a Piece of Paper* (University of New South Wales Press, 2004).

Crommelin, M, "Federalism" in Finn, PD (ed), *Essays on Law and Government: Principles and Values* (Law Book Co, 1995), vol 1, 168.

Filippov, M, Ordeshook, P, and Shvetsova, O, *Designing Federalism: A Theory of Self-Sustainable Political Institutions* (Cambridge University Press, 2003).

Fletcher, C, "Rediscovering Australian Federalism by Resurrecting Old Ideas" in Lovell, D, McAllister, I, Maley, W, and Kukathas, C (eds), *The Australian Political System* (Longmans, 2nd ed 1998).

Foley, K, "The Australian Constitution's Influence on the Common Law" (2003) 31 *Federal Law Review* 131.

French, RS, "The Referral of State Powers" (2003) 31 *University of Western Australia Law Review* 19.

Galligan, B (ed), *Australian Federalism* (Longman Cheshire, 1989).

Galligan, B, *A Federal Republic: Australia's Constitutional System of Government* (Cambridge University Press, 1995), Chs 2, 8, 9.

Gummow, WMC, "The Constitution: Ultimate Foundation of Australian Law?" (2005) 79 *Australian law Journal* 167.

Gummow, WMC, "Full Faith and Credit in Three Federations" (1995) 46 *South Carolina Law Review* 979.

Harvey, MNC, "James Bryce, 'the American Commonwealth', and the Australian Constitution" (2002) 76 *Australian Law Journal* 362.

Herzfeld, P, "Constitutional Limitations on State Choice of Law Statutes" (2005) 16 *Public Law Review* 188.

Hill, G, "Revisiting *Wakim* and *Hughes*: The Distinct Demands of Federalism" (2002) 13 *Public Law Review* 205.

Hill, G, "Will the High Court '*Wakim*' Chapter II of the Constitution?" (2003) 31 *Federal Law Review* 445.

Horan, C, "Section 122 of the Constitution: A 'Disparate and Non-federal' Power?" (1997) 25 *Federal Law Review* 97.

Keyzer, P, "The 'Federal Compact', the Territories and Chapter III of the Constitution" (2001) 75 *Australian Law Journal* 124.

Keyzer, P, "Judicial Independence in the Northern Territory: Are Undisclosed Remuneration Arrangements Repugnant to Chapter III of the Constitution?" (2004) 32 *University of Western Australia Law Review* 30.

Kirk, J, "Conflicts and Choice of Law within the Australian Constitutional Context" (2003) 31 *Federal Law Review* 247.

McDonald, S, "Territory Courts and Federal Jurisdiction" (2005) 33 *Federal Law Review* 57.

McNab, P, "'Snaking Through': Territories and Chapter III of the Constitution" (2000) 20 *Australian Bar Review* 293.

Mossop, D, "The Constitutional Basis for the Government of the Australian Capital Territory" (1999) 6 *Canberra Law Review* 5.

Mossop, D, "The Judicial Power of the Australian Capital Territory" (1999) 27 *Federal Law Review* 19.

Nicholson, G, "The Constitutional Status of the Self-Governing Northern Territory" (1985) 59 *Australian Law Journal* 698.

Priestley, LJ, "A Federal Common Law in Australia?" (1995) 6 *Public Law Review* 221.

Rose, D, "Discrimination, Uniformity and Preference" in Zines, L (ed), *Commentaries on the Australian Constitution* (Butterworths, 1977), 191.

Rose, D, "The Bizarre Destruction of Cross-Vesting" in Stone, A, and Williams, G (eds), *The High Court at the Crossroads: Essays in Constitutional Law* (Federation Press, 2000), 186.

Saunders, C, "Collaborative Federalism" (2002) 61 *Australian Journal of Public Administration* 69.

Saunders, C, "Concepts of Equality in the Australian Constitution" in Lindell, G (ed), *Future Directions in Australian Constitutional Law* (Federation Press, 1994), 209.

Sawer, G, *Modern Federalism* (Pitman, 2nd ed 1976).

Selway, B, "The Australian 'Single Law Area'" (2003) 29 *Monash University Law Review* 30.

Selway, BM, "The *Hughes* Case and the Referral of Powers" (2001) 12 *Public Law Review* 288.

Stone, A, "Choice of Law Rules, the Constitution and the Common Law" (2001) 12 *Public Law Review* 9.

Stellios, J, "Choice of Law and the Australian Constitution: Locating the Debate" (2005) 33 *Federal Law Review* 7.

Thompson, E (ed), *Keeping the Show Together: The "Federalism Forums" 2001* (NSW Centenary of Federation Committee, 2002).

Walker, G de Q, *Ten Advantages of a Federal Constitution: And How to Make the Most of Them* (Centre for Independent Studies, 2001).

Williams, G, "Co-operative Federalism and the Revival of the Corporations Law: *Wakim* and Beyond" (2002) 20 *Company & Securities Law Journal* 160.

Williams, G, and Darke, M, "Euthanasia Laws and the Australian Constitution" (1997) 20 *University of New South Wales Law Journal* 647.

Zines, L, "Changing Attitudes to Federalism and its Purpose" in French, R, Lindell, G, and Saunders, C (eds), *Reflections on the Australian Constitution* (Federation Press, 2003), 86.

Zines, L, *The Common Law in Australia: Its Nature and Constitutional Significance* (Law and Policy Paper 13, Federation Press and Centre for International and Public Law, 1999).

Chapter 7

The *Engineers' Case*

1. Introduction

The Australian Constitution assigns to the Commonwealth Parliament a specified list of powers relating to a range of subjects and purposes – primarily in the 40 numbered paragraphs, or placita, of s 51. Powers not thus assigned are left to be exercised by the States. This follows the model of the United States Constitution, but differs from the plan adopted for Canada by the *British North America Act 1867* (Imp) (renamed the *Constitution Act* in 1982). The latter assigns one list of specific powers to the central or Dominion Parliament (s 91), and a separate list of exclusive powers to the Provinces (s 92, now supplemented by s 92A), with a prefatory statement in s 91 that the central or Dominion Parliament has residual power in "all Matters not coming within the Classes of Subjects by this Act assigned exclusively to the Legislatures of the Provinces".

Other distributions are possible. For example, in the Seventh Schedule to the Constitution of India, one list of powers is assigned exclusively to the national Parliament (List I, "the Union List"); another list is assigned exclusively to the States (List II, "the State List"); and a third list enumerates powers which may be exercised at both levels (List III, "the Concurrent List"). The Union List includes "[a]ny other matter not enumerated in List II or List III". Thus, in both the Canadian and the Indian models, the central legislature has residual powers.

By contrast, in Australia it is the unspecified fund of legislative power left to the States, and declared by s 107 to "continue", that is referred to as "residual" power. This, however, can be misleading. It is true that in any area not specifically assigned to the Commonwealth, legislative power remains with the States. However, the normal arrangement is one of *concurrent* powers: that is, even in an area where the Commonwealth has a clear grant of law-making power, the State Parliaments will still normally have power in that area too. It is because of this assumption of concurrent law-making power that the possibility arises of conflict between State and Commonwealth laws. That possibility is acknowledged by s 109 of the Constitution, which provides that in a case of conflict the Commonwealth law shall prevail.

There are some exceptions to this pattern of concurrent power. In some areas, the Constitution gives to the Commonwealth *exclusive* law-making power. In these exceptional areas, such as those set out in s 52 of the Constitution, the grant of power to the Commonwealth deprives the States of any power to enact valid laws. Of the sections conferring exclusive power, the one with the most practical impact is s 90, which provides that excise duties may only be imposed by the Commonwealth Parliament.

The wide extent of concurrent power might seem to imply that, within areas of Commonwealth power, the Commonwealth can make laws binding on the State governments, and conversely that the States, within their spheres of power, can make laws binding on the Commonwealth government. Initially, however, the High Court denied this possibility. If federalism means that each level of government is sovereign, then, it was thought, it must follow that no government at either level could be told by any other government or parliament what it might or might not do. Hence, far from being bound by each other's laws, the "implied immunity of instrumentalities" doctrine meant that both the States and the Commonwealth were normally to be immune from each other's laws. This reasoning was used to protect the States and their agencies from Commonwealth interference.

In this early line of thinking, the States were protected in another way as well. Supposedly with some support from the language of s 107 of the Constitution, it was said that State legislative power was "residual" in the sense that any legislative powers not specifically assigned to the Commonwealth were reserved to the States. The "reserved State powers" doctrine meant that Commonwealth grants of power were to be interpreted so as to ensure that they did not encroach too far upon the "residual" powers of the States.

The High Court as appointed in October 1903 consisted of only three judges, Griffith CJ, Barton and O'Connor JJ. In formulating the doctrines outlined above, they saw themselves as developing a model of balanced federalism. However, from 1906 onwards, when Isaacs and Higgins JJ joined the Court, the early doctrines began to be eroded. In 1920, the doctrines of "implied immunity of instrumentalities" and "reserved State powers" were swept away by the landmark decision in *Amalgamated Society of Engineers v Adelaide Steamship Co Ltd* (*Engineers' Case*) (1920) 28 CLR 129. That decision not only transformed the structural frame-work of Commonwealth-State relations, but also enjoined a distinctive approach to constitutional interpretation that dominated the Court's work for many years thereafter.

2. Implied Immunity of Instrumentalities

The "implied immunities" doctrine asserted that, given two levels of government in the same geographical territory, the governments must normally be immune from each other's laws. This was not because the Constitution said so, although it does incorporate some aspects of the notion in sections such as s 114, but because reciprocal immunity was thought to be necessarily implied in the very idea of federalism.

In *D'Emden v Pedder* (1904) 1 CLR 91, Henry D'Emden, the Commonwealth's Deputy Postmaster-General for Tasmania, gave a receipt for his Commonwealth salary to a Commonwealth officer without paying the 2d stamp duty required by Tasmanian law. It was held that the State law could not apply because Commonwealth officers and procedures were neces-sarily immune from State laws.

D'Emden v Pedder
(1904) 1 CLR 91

Griffith CJ (for the Court): [109] In considering the respective powers of the Commonwealth and of the States it is essential to bear in mind that each is, within the ambit of its authority, a sovereign State, subject only to the restrictions imposed by the Imperial connection and to the provisions of the Constitution, either expressed or necessarily implied …

[110] [T]he Commonwealth has, with respect to all matters enumerated in the Constitution as within the ambit of its authority, sovereign power, subject only to the limitations already men-tioned. But a right of sovereignty subject to extrinsic control is a contradiction in terms. It must, therefore, be taken to be of the essence of the Constitution that the Commonwealth is entitled, with-in the ambit of its authority, to exercise its legislative and executive powers in absolute freedom, and without any interference or control whatever except that prescribed by the **[111]** Constitution itself … It follows that when a State attempts to give its legislative or executive authority an operation which, if valid, would fetter, control, or interfere with, the free exercise of the legislative or executive power of the Commonwealth, the attempt, unless expressly authorized by the Constitution, is to that extent invalid and inoperative.

In *Deakin v Webb* (1904) 1 CLR 585, the High Court applied the "immunities" doctrine to hold that a Commonwealth cabinet minister, Alfred Deakin, was not liable to State income tax.

Deakin v Webb
(1904) 1 CLR 585

Griffith CJ (for the Court): [616] [T]he argument ... has especial force when regard is had to the circumstances of Australia. The income taxes in the several States are unequal in their incidence. They may be of any amount which the State thinks fit to impose. In order, therefore, to give effect to the provisions of the federal laws regulating ... salaries ... , it would be necessary to make special provision for adjusting their incomes when transferred from one State to another. State taxation of federal salaries is open then to two objections: (1) It in effect diminishes the recompense allotted by the Commonwealth to its officers, and so interferes with its agencies; and (2) It interferes with the freedom of action of the Commonwealth in the transfer of its officers from State to State.

In both cases, Griffith CJ quoted at length from decisions of the United States Supreme Court: in *D'Emden v Pedder* from *McCulloch v Maryland*, 17 US (4 Wheat) 316 (1819), which held that the States could not tax a national bank established by the United States Congress, and in *Deakin v Webb* from *Dobbins v Commissioners of Erie County*, 41 US (16 Peters) 435 (1842), which held that a State could not tax the salary of a United States customs officer (the captain of a "revenue cutter"). While *Deakin v Webb*, like the American cases, was specifically concerned with taxation, the principle enunciated in *D'Emden v Pedder* was much wider.

Although taxation was also involved in *Municipal Council of Sydney v Commonwealth* (*Municipal Rates Case*) (1904) 1 CLR 208, the constitutional issue was different. At Federation a number of buildings in Sydney, including the Customs House at Circular Quay and the General Post Office in Martin Place, had been transferred to the Commonwealth. Previously, when owned by the New South Wales government, these buildings had been liable to municipal rates; the question was whether they were still so liable once they were vested in the Commonwealth. The decision that they were not liable did not depend on "implied immunities", but on the express immunity from State taxation conferred by s 114 of the Constitution on "property of any kind belonging to the Commonwealth". Nevertheless, it was in this context that O'Connor J gave a fuller explanation of the "implied immunities" doctrine.

Municipal Council of Sydney v Commonwealth (*Municipal Rates Case*)
(1904) 1 CLR 208

O'Connor J: [239] Before examining the words of [s 114], it will be useful to advert to the circumstances which the Convention had in view in framing this section, and their purpose and object in relation to those circumstances.

From the very nature of the Constitution, and the relation of States and Commonwealth, in the distribution of powers, it became necessary to provide that the sovereignty of each within its sphere should be absolute, and that no conflict of authority within the same sphere should be possible. The principles laid down by *Marshall*, CJ, in his historic judgment in *McCulloch v Maryland* (4 Wheat, ([17] US), p 316 [(1819)]), are as applicable to the Australian Commonwealth Constitution as to the United States Constitution, and it must be taken that those principles and the controversies which had arisen in the United States in reference to their appli-**[240]**-cation, were within the knowledge of the Convention. In laying down these principles the Courts of the United States, in the absence of express provision, rested their reasoning upon the underlying principles of the Constitution, and on what was necessarily involved in the grant of sovereign powers.

In *Webb v Outtrim* [1907] AC 81 (wrongly reported as *Webb v Outrim*) the Privy Council held that *D'Emden v Pedder* and *Deakin v Webb* had been wrongly decided. The matter had reached the Privy Council directly, bypassing the High Court and circumventing s 39 of the *Judiciary Act*

1903 (Cth), which had been designed to block such appeals. The manoeuvres involved are summarised in Chapter 13, §4. The Privy Council dealt with that problem by treating s 39 as invalid; but in *Baxter v Commissioners of Taxation (NSW)* (1907) 4 CLR 1087 a majority of the High Court responded that their Lordships had spoken without jurisdiction, so that their decision could have no binding force as a precedent. Accordingly, in *Baxter*, the Court reaffirmed the "implied immunities" doctrine, this time holding that a Commonwealth customs officer did not have to pay State income tax. Higgins J dissented on the ground that the Privy Council's decision was binding. Isaacs J dissented on the ground that, although the basic principle in *D'Emden v Pedder* was right, the State income tax did not interfere with the Commonwealth's constitutional functions.

Baxter v Commissioners of Taxation (NSW)
(1907) 4 CLR 1087

Isaacs J: [1161] [T]he State Act touches no function of the officer, it intrudes its operations into no public act that he performs, it affixes no condition and imposes no qualification upon the discharge of his duties, it makes no demand upon his public time, and seeks no service at his hands; it merely requires of him his just share of the ordinary burden of his fellow citizens in return for the protection and benefits the State affords him.

The controversy as to State taxation of federal salaries was finally settled when the Commonwealth Parliament enacted the *Commonwealth Salaries Act 1907* (Cth), which made the salaries of federal officers taxable by the States. In *Chaplin v Commissioner of Taxes for South Australia* (1911) 12 CLR 375, the High Court held that this Act was valid. If tax immunity for federal salaries was a Commonwealth privilege, the Commonwealth could give it up.

Meanwhile, the doctrine of "implied immunities" had taken a different turn. In all the above cases, *Commonwealth* agencies and personnel were held to be immune from *State* laws. However, Griffith CJ had consistently hinted that a similar principle might be applied to insulate State agencies from Commonwealth laws. A holding to that effect came in *Federated Amalgamated Government Railway and Tramway Service Association v New South Wales Railway Traffic Employees Association* (*Railway Servants' Case*) (1906) 4 CLR 488. The case was decided 11 days after the Privy Council decision in *Webb v Outtrim*, and after the news of it had reached Australia. Yet the High Court not only reaffirmed the "implied immunities" doctrine, but ruled that it worked both ways. The Court held that a New South Wales union representing employees of a State government agency could not be registered under the *Commonwealth Conciliation and Arbitration Act 1904* (Cth) because this would be incompatible with the reciprocal immunities of the Commonwealth and the States. Insofar as the Act had authorised such interference, it was unconstitutional. Isaacs (as Commonwealth Attorney-General) and HB Higgins (for the respondent union) had both appeared as counsel to argue that the legislation was valid. Higgins' argument laid the foundation for later developments.

Federated Amalgamated Government Railway and Tramway Service Association v New South Wales Railway Traffic Employees Association
(Railway Servants' Case)
(1906) 4 CLR 488

Higgins KC (in argument): [506] There is also a distinction between the immunities which belong to a sovereign State by virtue of its sovereignty, and those immunities which belong to it in respect of its commercial undertakings. A sovereign power entering into a contract is liable to the incidents of contracts ... In all the American cases it is recognized that the doctrine of the non-interference with State instrumentalities does not extend to instrumentalities which are used for the purpose of commerce. "The exemption of State agencies and instrumentalities from National taxation is limited to those which are of a strictly governmental character, and does not extend to those which are used by the State in the carrying on of an ordinary private business:" *South Carolina v United States* [199 US 437 at 461 (1905)] …

The main attributes of sovereignty are three, viz, legislative, executive, and judicial functions. With regard to the business of railways, one can conceive of them being given up by the States. If there is a function which is essential to government that is an **[507]** attribute of sovereignty. The whole tendency of recent decisions in the United States has been to limit the doctrine of the immunity of State instrumentalities …

Griffith CJ: It is important to remember that State railways were recognized functions of government at the time of the inauguration of the Commonwealth, and that they are recognized as such by the Constitution.

Higgins KC: At that time there were State industries in all the States and the tendency was for them to increase in number. Can it reasonably be supposed that, when the Commonwealth was given power to legislate as to conciliation and arbitration, State enterprises were to be excluded? Although the Constitution recognizes railways as being carried on by the States, there is nothing in the Constitution which lifts railways out of the ordinary category of business undertakings up into the domain of strictly governmental functions … The governmental functions are those functions which cannot be contemplated as being intended to be delegated to private persons.

Griffith CJ gave judgment on behalf of the Court. He emphasised the many references to State railways in the Constitution: s 51(xxxii), (xxxiii) and (xxxiv), and ss 101, 102 and 104. He quoted from what he had said in *D'Emden v Pedder*, and also from what the United States Supreme Court had said in *Collector v Day*, 78 US (11 Wall) 113 (1870), in holding that the federal government could not tax a State judge's salary. As to *D'Emden v Pedder* he said:

Griffith CJ (for the Court): [537] In that case the question was as to an attempted invasion of the ambit of Commonwealth authority by a State authority. The present case is the converse, but the doctrine is equally applicable …

[538] The argument [in *Collector v Day* 78 US (11 Wall) 113 (1870)] is to our minds incontrovertible. It was answered that the doctrine applies only to taxation. But taxation is only an instance of interference and control. The foundation of the argument is the necessity for freedom from control, and taxation is only forbidden because it is an interference. In our opinion any authority which can lawfully say to another "Thou shalt" or "Thou shalt not" exercises control over that other in the sense in which that term is used in this argument. It is nothing to the purpose to say that the exercise of the power would be, or was intended to be, beneficial or remedial. Such an intention may, and perhaps ought to, be attributed to all legislative action …

But it is said that a State railway is not a State instrumentality within the meaning of the rule, and the case of *South Carolina v United States* was referred to … Whether the majority judgment would or would not commend itself to this Court in a similar case, we are of opinion that it has no application in the present case. The argument as presented to us is that State instrumentalities for the purposes of the doctrine in question are limited to those which are, strictly speaking, of what was called in argument a "governmental" character, and that the business of common carriers is not a part of any of the recognized branches of government, legislative, judicial and executive. We appre-**[539]**-hend, however, that the execution or administration of the laws of the State is in the strictest sense a governmental function, and that no rule can be formulated, because there is no authority competent to formulate it, which shall prescribe what functions the State shall undertake in the supposed exercise of its duty to promote the well being of its people. There is high authority, both ancient and modern, for holding that the construction and maintenance of roads and means of communication is one of the most important, as it is necessarily one of the first, of the functions of government. It cannot be denied in this twentieth century that railways are a most important means of communication, or that they are in substance highways, however their use may be restricted or controlled by the conditions of the particular franchises granted in respect of them. Apart, however, from this general consideration, we are of opinion that in the year 1900, when the Constitution was adopted, the construction and maintenance of railways was in fact generally regarded as a govern- mental function in all the Australian Colonies, and that they are expressly recognized as such in the sections of the Constitution above quoted. We think, therefore, that the doctrine of mutual freedom from interference as between the Commonwealth and State Governments would be sufficient to exclude any implication that sec 51(xxxv) was intended to extend to State railways. And, having regard to the careful enumeration of specific matters in respect of which express powers were conferred upon the Commonwealth Parliament to interfere with or control these railways, we think that the notion of such an implied extension is absolutely negatived.

By the time this judgment was given, both Isaacs and Higgins had been appointed to the Court. In *Baxter's Case* both of them dissented. Thereafter, the "immunities" cases produced a steady series of dissents and distinctions, and increasingly awkward concessions by the majority.

In 1907 the New South Wales government imported from England a shipment of wire netting, and a separate shipment of lengths of steel railway line. The Commonwealth customs duty on the shipments was disputed on the ground that the *Customs Act 1901* (Cth) should be construed as not intended to bind the Crown (*R v Sutton* (*Wire Netting Case*) (1908) 5 CLR 789), and also on the ground of the "implied immunities" doctrine (*Attorney-General of NSW v Collector of Customs for NSW* (*Steel Rails Case*) (1908) 5 CLR 818). Both arguments failed. As to the "immunities" doctrine, Griffith CJ pointed out that the doctrine depended on an implication, and therefore could not override the express provisions of the Constitution.

Attorney-General of NSW v Collector of Customs for NSW (*Steel Rails Case*)
(1908) 5 CLR 818

Griffith CJ: [833] If a power conferred upon the Commonwealth in express terms is of such a nature that its effective exercise manifestly involves a control of some operation of a State Government the doctrine has no application to that operation. Sec 51 of the Constitution confers upon the Parliament many powers of this nature, *eg*, the power to control quarantine (IX), weights and measures (XV), immigration (XXVII). The power to make laws respecting trade and commerce with other countries and among the States (I) is of the same kind, and necessarily involves the power to interfere with the operations of the State Governments so far as to make effectual any condition or prohibition imposed by the Commonwealth upon importation. Taxation by means of Customs duties is in law, as well as in fact, a mode of regulating trade with other countries. It follows that it was the intention of the legislature that the right of State Governments to import goods should be subject to the control of the Commonwealth, so that the rule in *D'Emden v Pedder* [(1904) 1 CLR 91] has no application.

Barton J pointed out that s 90 of the Constitution makes the Commonwealth power of imposing customs duties exclusive. Moreover, the power to regulate trade and commerce with other countries under s 51(i), though not expressly exclusive, is inherently exclusive in the sense that no one State can claim to speak internationally for Australia as a whole. To this he added (at 835) a quotation from *D'Emden v Pedder*: "**[111]** With respect, however, to matters within the exclusive competence of the Federal Parliament no question of conflict can arise, inasmuch as from the point at which the quality of exclusiveness attaches to the federal power the competency of the States is altogether extinguished". Thus, said Barton J, where the Commonwealth has exclusive power, the doctrine of implied State immunities cannot apply. It is only when the States and the Commonwealth both have functions to perform that the exercise of those functions is reciprocally immune. O'Connor and Higgins JJ broadly agreed, but Isaacs J was not satisfied.

R v Sutton (*Wire Netting Case*)
(1908) 5 CLR 789

Isaacs J: [813] The Constitution, in apportioning and distributing political powers, rights and duties, between Commonwealth and States, regards them as distinct and separate organisms for their several functions. This was necessary to the scheme of government it introduced, for operating as these several authorities do, at the same time, on the same territory, the same persons, and the same property, any other conception would produce confusion. No doctrine of law, however applicable to the purely unitary form of [814] government, can, if inconsistent with the great, essential and dominant purpose of the Federal Constitution, be allowed to prevail.

Any theory, therefore, is inadmissible which would permit the States ... to claim entire exemption from the general operation of a federal law, regulating a matter of national concern, and made by virtue of a granted power of such a nature that the exemption would or might either utterly frustrate the legislation or render it practically ineffective.

A more significant erosion of the "immunities" doctrine flowed from Higgins' argument in the *Railway Servants' Case*. Although Griffith CJ had rejected Higgins' distinction between commercial undertakings and governmental functions, he had also held that the construction and maintenance of railways *was* a governmental function, thus providing a foothold for the distinction that Higgins had sought to establish. The distinction was accepted as a legitimate basis for distinguishing the "immunities" doctrine in *Federated Engine-Drivers and Firemen's Association of Australasia v Broken Hill Pty Co Ltd* (*Engine-Drivers' Case*), reported at (1911) 12 CLR 398 and again in (1913) 16 CLR 245. Again, the issue was one concerning the scope of the federal arbitration system: in this case, whether the Melbourne City Council, as an employer making use of "land engines", could be made a party to a federal award. The Council's "land engines" were used in connection with the supply of electricity, the sale of manure, and the maintenance of public refrigeration space for hire. The High Court held that none of these was a governmental function, and hence that the Council was properly joined as a party to the arbitration proceedings. Assuming that a municipal council could be a State instrumentality, any immunity it might then have from Commonwealth interference could only extend to its governmental functions, not to mere trading functions.

This inroad into the "immunities" doctrine was carried further in *Federated Municipal and Shire Council Employees' Union of Australia v Melbourne Corporation* (*Municipalities Case*) (1919) 26 CLR 508. In that case, it was held, again for purposes of industrial arbitration, that municipal councils had no "immunity" from Commonwealth interference in "the making, maintenance, control and lighting of public streets".

The only issue in the *Engineers' Case* was whether Commonwealth arbitration power could extend to engineers employed by State instrumentalities in Western Australia: the State Sawmills, the State Implement and Engineering Works, and the Minister for Trading Concerns. On the basis of the *Engine-Drivers* and *Municipalities* cases, it would have been easy to argue that the functions of these three instrumentalities were not governmental functions. When the young Robert Menzies, aged 25, argued the matter before the High Court, he initially relied on that ground. In later years, Menzies was fond of recalling how his more radical attack on the whole "immunities" doctrine had been invited by the High Court itself.

RG Menzies, *Central Power in the Australian Commonwealth*
(Cassell, 1967)

[38] [A]n hour or so after I had begun by developing this argument, distinguishing the *Railway Servants' Case*, doing lip service to the Doctrine, Mr Justice Starke, ... whose blunt habits of expression made no exception in favour of a very young man, looking at me in a grumbling way, said, 'This argument is a lot of nonsense!' ... [I] replied: 'Sir, I quite agree.' 'Well', intervened the Chief Justice, Chief Justice Knox ..., 'why are you putting an argument which you admit is nonsense?' 'Because', said the young Menzies (the old Menzies would not have dared to do this) 'I am compelled by the earlier decisions of this [39] Court. If your Honours will permit me to question all or any of these earlier decisions, I will undertake to advance a sensible argument.' I waited for the heavens to fall. Instead, the Chief Justice said: 'The Court will retire for a few minutes.' And when they came back, he said, 'This case will be adjourned for argument at Sydney. Each government will be notified so that it may apply to intervene. Counsel will be at liberty to challenge any earlier decision of this Court!'

Menzies may have been indulging his fondness for a good anecdote here. In 1995, on the 75th anniversary of the *Engineers' Case*, research by Sir Gerard Brennan into the original notebooks kept by the members of the *Engineers* bench disclosed that the argument against any reciprocal immunity had already been clearly stated by Menzies during his initial argument at the Melbourne hearings, and that at the Sydney hearings the fuller version of the argument was put by Leverrier KC, not by Menzies ("Three Cheers for *Engineers*" in Michael Coper and George Williams (eds), *How Many Cheers for* Engineers? (Federation Press, 1997), 145 at 146-8). In any event, the argument was accepted and the doctrine was overruled.

3. Reserved State Powers

The "reserved State powers" doctrine was primarily directed to the interpretation of Commonwealth grants of legislative power. The idea was that the Constitution had impliedly "reserved" to the States their traditional areas of law-making power; and hence that the grants of law-making power to the Commonwealth must be narrowly construed so as not to encroach on these traditional powers of the States. The underlying argument was first foreshadowed in *Peterswald v Bartley* (1904) 1 CLR 497. In that case, by taking a narrow view of the Commonwealth's exclusive power to levy excise duties in s 90 of the Constitution, the Court was able to leave intact the New South Wales brewers' licensing system.

R v Barger (1908) 6 CLR 41 was an "excise" case that took the simple ideas of *Peterswald v Bartley* much further. Section 2 of the *Excise Tariff Act 1906* (Cth) imposed excise duties at scheduled rates on various agricultural implements. The section went on to provide that the excise did not apply to goods manufactured under conditions where the remuneration of labour was, for example, "declared by resolution of both Houses of Parliament to be fair and reasonable" or was "in accordance with an industrial award under the *Commonwealth Conciliation and Arbitration Act* 1904". The issue before the Court was whether s 2 was a law with respect to "taxation" under s 51(ii) of the Constitution.

By 3:2, Isaacs and Higgins JJ dissenting, the Court held that s 2 could not be supported by s 51(ii). The essential majority argument of Griffith CJ, Barton and O'Connor JJ was that "**[73]** [i]t is clear that the power to pass such an Act must be vested *either* in the Parliament *or* in the State legislatures" (emphasis added). Because the subject-matter lay within State legislative power, it therefore could not lie within the Commonwealth's taxation power.

R v Barger
(1908) 6 CLR 41

Griffith CJ, Barton and O'Connor JJ: [67] The scheme of the Australian Constitution, like that of the United States of America, is to confer certain definite powers upon the Commonwealth, and to reserve to the States, whose powers before the establishment of the Commonwealth were plenary, all powers not expressly conferred upon the Commonwealth ...

[69] The grant of the power of taxation is a separate and independent grant. This is the accepted law in the United States. In interpreting the grant it must be considered not only with reference to other separate and independent grants, such as the power to regulate external and inter-state trade and commerce, but also with reference to the powers reserved to the States.

It was not contested in argument that regulation of the conditions of labour is a matter relating to the internal affairs of the States, and is therefore reserved to the States and denied to the Commonwealth, except so far as it can be brought within one of the thirty-nine powers enumerated in sec 51 ...

[T]he power of taxation, whatever it may include, was intended to be something entirely distinct from a power to directly regulate the domestic affairs of the States, which was denied to the Parliament ...

[73] We propose now to inquire what is the true nature and character of the Act before us, and in this connection it will be convenient to inquire whether it is such an Act as could be passed by a State legislature with regard to domestic matters. It is clear that the power to pass such an Act must be vested either in the Parliament or in the State legislatures. If the tax is an Excise duty within the meaning of sec 90, the power of the Parliament is exclusive, and the State could not impose it ...

[74] [I]t is clearly within the competence of a State legislature to regulate the conditions of labour employed in the manufacture of agricultural implements. It is equally clear that a State legislature, having prescribed such conditions, could impose a pecuniary burden upon everyone who did not conform to them, and that the payment might be made proportionate to the number of articles produced. Yet, if such payment were a duty of Excise, the State could not impose it, for the power of the Parliament to impose duties of Excise is exclusive. Such an Act might be framed in several different ways. It might be prescribed that certain conditions as to the remuneration of labour should be observed in the manufacture, and that any manufacturer who failed to comply should be liable to a penalty of so much for every article manufactured. Or, without formally prescribing any such condition, it might provide that any manufacturer who did not observe certain conditions should be liable to a penalty of so much per article. Or it might, instead of using the word penalty, say that the manufacturer who did not comply with certain conditions should be bound to pay a licence fee, the amount of which should be computed at so much for every article manufactured. Or it might provide that every manufacturer should at his option either comply with certain prescribed conditions or pay to the State Treasurer a sum computed &c, and in default should be liable to a penalty of &c. Or, finally, it might provide that any manufacturer who did not comply with certain specified conditions should pay a tax at a specified rate. In all the cases supposed the substance would be the same, [75] though the form would differ. And, in every case, the substance would be a regulation of the conditions of labour in the industry in question. Attention has already been drawn to the immateriality, as far as regards the validity of an Act, of the motives or indirect results in contemplation of the legislature ...

[77] In our opinion the exclusive power of the Parliament to impose duties of Excise cannot be construed as depriving the States of the exclusive power to make such enactments as we have suggested above. The substantial nature and character of the legislation is the same whether it is passed by one legislature or the other. It follows that such an Act would not be in substance an Act imposing duties of Excise within the meaning of sec 90 of the Constitution. If, then, the Act in question is not, in substance, an Act imposing duties of Excise, what is it? We think that it is an Act to regulate the conditions of manufacture of agricultural implements, and not an exercise of the power of taxation conferred by the Constitution.

The dissenting judgments of Isaacs and Higgins JJ depended on an analogy, which both of them were to use repeatedly in their attack on the "reserved State powers" doctrine, with the way in which a will is interpreted when distributing a testator's estate. They argued that one cannot construe a will by first determining the scope of the residuary legacy and then, in the light of that, by determining the content of the specific bequests. To give effect first to the specific bequests is the only possible course. Similarly, in construing the Australian Constitution, one must first give full effect to the specific grants of Commonwealth power. Any concept of a residue retained by the States can only meaningfully refer to what is left over after the Commonwealth's powers are determined.

The majority argument in R v Barger was not applied to save a State law, as in Peterswald v Bartley, but to strike down a Commonwealth law; and not only to limit the Commonwealth's exclusive power as to "excise duties", but also to limit the Commonwealth's general power as to "taxation". Most remarkably, it was used to slide from an exclusive power of the Commonwealth as to excise duties, to an exclusive power of the States to regulate labour conditions.

Where might this last mentioned exclusive power come from? One possible answer is s 51(xxxv) of the Constitution, which gives the Commonwealth legislative power with respect to "Conciliation and arbitration for the prevention and settlement of industrial disputes extending beyond the limits of any one State". Insofar as this wording does not include industrial disputes confined wholly within one State, it might be said to exclude such disputes from the scope of the

Commonwealth power, and in that sense to make them a subject of exclusive State power. A similar argument can be made as to Commonwealth power under s 51(i) with respect to "Trade and commerce with other countries, and among the States". Again, this wording has the effect of excluding trade and commerce conducted wholly within one State. Yet even if these exclusions are given full weight as limitations on Commonwealth power, why should they result in a narrow reading of *other* heads of Commonwealth power? For this is what the "reserved State powers" doctrine ultimately entailed.

This basis of the "reserved State powers" doctrine was not made clear in *Peterswald v Bartley*, nor even in *R v Barger*. It emerged through a series of later judgments written by Griffith CJ, beginning with his judgment in *Attorney-General (NSW) v Brewery Employees Union of NSW* (*Union Label Case*) (1908) 6 CLR 469 and including his judgment in *Huddart, Parker & Co Pty Ltd v Moorehead* (1909) 8 CLR 330. In the latter case, Griffith CJ held that the Commonwealth could not, under its corporations power (s 51(xx) of the Constitution), enact legislation regulating intrastate trade practices. He stated that the provision "[354] ought not to be construed as authorising the Commonwealth to invade the field of State law as to domestic trade". The reasoning that led to this conclusion is analysed below.

AR Blackshield, "Damadam to Infinities! The Tourneyold of the Wattarfalls"
in M Sornarajah (ed), *The South West Dam Dispute: The Legal and Political Issues* (University of Tasmania, 1983), 37

[45] In the *Union Label Case* [(1908) 6 CLR 469] the majority struck down Part VII of the Trade Marks Act 1905, which provided for the registration as "trade marks" of statements that a product was made by an individual worker, or by members of a [46] specified union. Such marks had been accepted as "trade marks" by the English Trade Marks Act 1905; but the High Court majority declined to treat them as "trade marks" within the meaning of s 51(xviii), by confining those words to their technical meaning as at 1900. Griffith CJ and O'Connor J had an additional reason for this: ... they in effect read down the grant of power in s 51(xviii) so that what remained could be treated as an appropriate means of implementing the 1883 Convention for the Protection of Industrial Property.

In *Huddart Parker & Co Pty Ltd v Moorehead* [(1909) 8 CLR 330] the usual majority (joined this time by Higgins J, though only on "characterisation" grounds) struck down ss 5 and 8 of the Australian Industries Preservation Act 1906 – which applied to the classes of "corporation" mentioned in s 51(xx) of the Constitution the same prohibitions of combinations in restraint of trade, and of monopolies, as ss 4 and 7 of the Act had already applied to all persons engaged in interstate or overseas commerce ...

Finally, in the *Woodworkers' Case* [(1909) 8 CLR 465], a statutory majority comprising Griffith CJ and O'Connor J held that where a minimum wage determination by a State Wages Board involved "the making of a general law by a law-making authority constituted by Statute for that purpose", the State determination was "binding on the federal tribunal", and that "any direction in a [federal] award inconsistent with its provisions would be invalid". To that extent the two majority judges read down the grant of Commonwealth power in s 51(xxxv).

As Griffith CJ explained his position from *Union Label* onwards, these results flowed from three distinct steps. The first ... was a "literal" reading of s 51(i). The grant of power spoke only of interstate and overseas trade and commerce; it therefore impliedly withheld from the Commonwealth any power of regulating purely intrastate trade. In other words, s 51(i) must be read "as if it contained an express declaration" that power to regulate purely intrastate trade "is reserved to the States".

The second step was a conjoint reading of s 51(i) (as thus construed) with s 107 (as construed in *Deakin v Webb* [(1904) 1 CLR 585]). Since the power to regulate intrastate trade was not, by s 51(i), in any sense "withdrawn from" the States, it must remain unimpaired.

The third step extended these conclusions beyond s 51(i) itself to every other head of power which might involve an "invasion" of purely intrastate commerce and trade. If other heads of power *expressly* authorised such invasions, they must of course be given effect: to that extent, s 107 would recognise a *pro tanto* "withdrawal" of power from the States. But, except where *expressly* so required, all other placita must be read down so as not to authorise indirect trespasses behind the iron curtain surrounding intrastate trade and commerce. Indeed, this reading down was to govern the process of ascertaining exactly what "invasions" any given placitum did expressly require. Placitum (ii) was so read down in *Barger* [(1908) 6 CLR 41], placitum (xviii) in *Union Label,* placitum (xx) in *Huddart Parker,* and placitum (xxxv) in *Woodworkers.*

Isaacs and Higgins JJ did not necessarily dissent from the first of these steps; certainly they agreed that the grant of power in s 51(i) did not itself extend to purely intrastate trade. From the beginning they launched a swingeing attack on the second step, rejecting it finally in *Engineers* [(1920) 28 CLR 129 at 154] as "a fundamental and fatal error"; but Isaacs J, at least, was not above using the language of "reserved powers" when it suited his purpose.

[47] What neither of them could countenance was the third step. As Higgins J explained in *Huddart Parker,* he accepted the "exclusionary" meaning of s 51(i) as prohibiting Commonwealth sorties into "the forbidden area" of intrastate trade; but he nevertheless thought that other placita must be given their natural meaning, even if "the forbidden area" was progressively narrowed thereby. In the *Engineers' Case* the second step, based on s 107, was abolished (as it were) by a sideswipe; the actual decision was only that the limits of s 51(i) could not be imposed to restrict the scope of s 51(xxxv). It seems clear that in pressing for such a conclusion Isaacs and Higgins JJ were prompted especially by their concern for the Commonwealth's arbitration power; but, of course, if placitum (i) does not control placitum (xxxv), it follows that it does not control any other placitum, either ...

[I]t is nowadays clear that *each* of the three steps outlined above was a "fundamental and fatal error"; and their interdependence renders the reasoning vulnerable at three separate points. The first step is fallacious because the "mere language" of s 51(i) does *not* imply a prohibition of Commonwealth incursions into the domain of intrastate trade. It does what it purports to do, no more and no less: it grants the Commonwealth power over interstate and overseas commerce, but as to intrastate commerce it neither authorises nor prohibits Commonwealth laws. Such a law cannot be supported by s 51(i); but if it is authorised by some other provision, s 51(i) is no barrier. "Section 51(i) contains no explicit or implicit prohibition and does not reserve the subject of intra-State trade to the States" [*Strickland v Rocla Concrete Pipes Ltd* [(1971) 124 CLR 468 at 488] ...

The second of the three steps identified above is also fallacious. Section 107 *cannot* be read as setting up any "reservation" of pre-existing State powers, nor even as bolstering any "reservation" created elsewhere. What it does is very simple. It sets aside two classes of powers (which appear indeed to be a single class under two alternative descriptions): powers "exclusively vested" in the Commonwealth, and those "withdrawn from" the States. With these exceptions, it says only that existing State powers shall "continue": that is, that the States still have power. It is when we lay this continued State power alongside the Commonwealth powers listed in s 51 that the notion of "concurrent powers" arises. But, as to these, the position can only be what Quick and Garran stated it to be in 1901:

[48] Concurrent powers ... may be exercised by the State Parliaments simultaneously with the Federal Parliament subject to the condition that, if there is any conflict or repugnancy between the Federal law and the State law ... , the Federal law prevails, and the State law to the extent of its inconsistency is invalid ...

[Thus] it does not matter which reading [of s 107] we adopt. As soon as any facts or activities have consequences or characteristics which attract a Commonwealth power under s 51, they must to that extent be brought within "concurrent" power, and s 109 must apply.

The third step in the reasoning of Griffith CJ in *Barger* and *Union Label* – reading down other heads of power by reference to the supposed "reservation" in s 51(i) – is also inherently fallacious. Instead of treating the various placita in s 51(i) as independent grants of power, each demanding primarily to be construed on its own terms, it assumes that all of them must be read together as a comprehensive and internally consistent code of powers, so that any limitation arising from the terms of one grant of power must extend to all others as well. As Latham CJ pointed out in *Pidoto v Victoria* [(1943) 68 CLR 87 at 101], such an approach is simply unworkable ...

[51] [A]fter 1913 the decline of the doctrine was evident. In the *Sugar Commission Case* [*A-G (Commonwealth) v Colonial Sugar Refining Co Ltd* [1914] AC 237], "reserved powers" were

wielded more zealously by the Privy Council than by anyone in the High Court. Their Lordships not only bungled their brief, but lent their authority to the idea that "reserved powers" could displace the normal presumption of validity by reversing the onus of proof ... In *Australian Steamships Ltd v Malcolm* [(1914) 19 CLR 298] the Court's new alignment was clear. Gavan Duffy, Powers and Rich JJ all joined Isaacs J in upholding the Seamen's Compensation Act 1911 – thereby spurring him on to one of his most vigorous onslaughts on "reserved State powers", with only Griffith CJ and Barton J in dissent ... **[52]** In *Farey v Burvett* [(1916) 21 CLR 433] the main protagonists partly switched roles. On the one hand, even Griffith CJ treated Commonwealth defence power as "paramount", so that "if it comes into a conflict with any reserved State rights the latter must give way"; on the other hand, in the midst of some of his most impassioned rhetoric, even Isaacs J conceded that the Commonwealth is not "at liberty wantonly and with manifest caprice to enter upon the domain ordinarily reserved to the States" ... Both here and in *Stemp v Australian Glass Manufacturers Co Ltd* [(1917) 23 CLR 226] Gavan Duffy and Rich JJ dissented, but not on "reserved powers" grounds. In *Stemp* ..., the argument for "reserved powers" met with little support from the bench. Like *Malcolm*, the case is remarkable mainly for the opportunity it gave to Isaacs J to renew his attack on the doctrine. Three years later, in *Engineers*, he finally had the opportunity to write his views into law.

The rejection of the "reserved State powers" doctrine in the *Engineers' Case* means that many of these early cases (or at least the reasonings on which they depended) are no longer good law. Thus, *Huddart Parker v Moorehead* was overruled in *Strickland v Rocla Concrete Pipes Ltd* (*Concrete Pipes Case*) (1971) 124 CLR 468 (though partially revived in *New South Wales v Commonwealth* (*Incorporation Case*) (1990) 169 CLR 482: see Chapter 17, §4). The more general implications of the departure from *R v Barger* are considered in Chapter 16.

4. Engineers' Case

Although the principal judgment in the *Engineers' Case* was joined in by Knox CJ, Rich and Starke JJ, it was delivered by Isaacs J and evidently written by him. Geoffrey Sawer has criticised the judgment as being "**[130]** one of the worst written and organized in Australian judicial history. Isaacs was given to rhetoric and repetition, and here he gave those habits full rein" (*Australian Federalism in the Courts* (Melbourne University Press, 1967). Its overthrow of the "implied immunities" and "reserved State powers" doctrines was decisive and of lasting effect. Moreover, the rhetoric by which Isaacs J supported that result spelled out principles of constitutional interpretation that were to be deeply influential. Nowadays, these principles are more controversial, and even at the time they may have somewhat overstated Isaacs J's own judicial practices and beliefs.

The *Engineers' Case* arose from a claim by a union of engineers in the Commonwealth Court of Conciliation and Arbitration for an award relating to 843 employers across Australia. In Western Australia, the employers included three governmental employers. The question was whether a Commonwealth law made under the "conciliation and arbitration" power (s 51(xxxv) of the Constitution) could authorise the making of an award binding those three employers.

Amalgamated Society of Engineers v Adelaide Steamship Co Ltd (Engineers' Case)
(1920) 28 CLR 129

Knox CJ, Isaacs, Rich and Starke JJ: [141] The question presented is of the highest importance to the people of Australia, grouped nationally or sectionally, and it has necessitated a survey not merely of the Constitution itself, but also of many of the decisions of this Court on various points more or less closely related to the question we have directly to determine. The more the decisions are examined, and compared with each other and with the Constitution itself, the more evident it becomes that no clear principle can account for them. They are sometimes at variance **[142]** with the natural meaning of the text of the Constitution; some are irreconcilable with others, and some are individually rested on reasons not founded on the words of the Constitution or on any recognized principle of the common law underlying the expressed terms of the Constitution, but on implication drawn from what is called the principle of "necessity," that being itself referable to no more definite standard than the personal opinion of the Judge who declares it. The attempt to deduce any consistent rule from them has not only failed, but has disclosed an increasing entanglement and uncertainty, and a conflict both with the text of the Constitution and with distinct and clear declarations of law by the Privy Council.

It is therefore, in the circumstances, the manifest duty of this Court to turn its earnest attention to the provisions of the Constitution itself. That instrument is the political compact of the whole of the people of Australia, enacted into binding law by the Imperial Parliament, and it is the chief and special duty of this Court faithfully to expound and give effect to it according to its own terms, finding the intention from the words of the compact, and upholding it throughout precisely as framed. In doing this, we follow, not merely previous instances in this Court and other Courts in Australia, but also the precedent of the Privy Council in *Read v Bishop of Lincoln* [[1892] AC 644], where the Lord Chancellor, speaking for the Judicial Committee in relation to reviewing its own prior decisions, said: "Whilst fully sensible of the weight to be attached to such decisions, their Lordships are at the same time bound to examine the reasons upon which the decisions rest, and to give effect to their own view of the law." The grounds upon which the Privy Council came to that conclusion we refer to, but need not repeat, adding, however, that as the Commonwealth and State Parliaments and Executives are themselves bound by the declarations of this Court as to their powers *inter se*, our responsibility is so much the greater to give the true effect to the relevant constitutional provisions. In doing this, to use the language of Lord *Macnaghten* in *Vacher & Sons Ltd v London Society of Compositors* [[1913] AC 107 at 118], "a judicial tribunal has nothing to do with the policy of any Act which it may be called upon to interpret. That may be a matter for private judgment. The duty of the **[143]** Court, and its only duty, is to expound the language of the Act in accordance with the settled rules of construction" ...

[144] The chief contention on the part of the States is that what has been called the rule of *D'Emden v Pedder* [(1904) 1 CLR 91] justifies their immunity from Commonwealth control in respect of State trading. The rule referred to is in these terms: "When a State attempts to give to its legislative or executive authority an operation which, if valid, would fetter, control, or interfere with, the free exercise of the legislative or executive power of the Commonwealth, the attempt, unless expressly authorized by the Constitution, is to that extent invalid and inoperative." So far from that rule supporting the position taken up on behalf of the States, its language, strictly applied, is destructive of it. An authority has been set up by a State which is claimed to be an executive authority and which, if exempt from Commonwealth legislation, does fetter or interfere with free exercise of the legislative power of the Commonwealth under pl XXXV of sec 51, unless that placitum is not as complete as its words in their natural meaning indicate, or, since sec 107 applies to State concurrent powers equally with its exclusive powers, unless every Commonwealth legislative power, however complete in itself, is subject to the unrestricted operation of *every* State Act. It is said that the rule above stated **[145]** must be read as reciprocal, because some of the reasoning in *D'Emden v Pedder* indicates a reciprocal invalidity of Commonwealth law where the State is concerned. It is somewhat difficult to extract such a statement from the judgment; it would be *obiter* if found. It is said, however, that the later cases regard *D'Emden v Pedder* as supporting that view, and ultimately the doctrine of mutual non-interference finds its most distinct formulation in *Attorney-General for Queensland v Attorney-General for the Commonwealth* [(1915) 20 CLR 148]. There *Griffith* CJ, assuming the implication of non-interference to arise *primâ facie* from necessity *in all cases*, and then to be subject to *exclusion* where the necessity ended, proceeded to say: "It is manifest that, since the rule is founded upon the necessity of the implication, the implication is excluded if it appears upon consideration of the whole Constitution that the Commonwealth, or, conversely, the State, was intended to have power to do the act the validity of which is impeached." Then, how is that *intention* to be ascertained? The learned Chief Justice proceeds to ascertain it by reference to outside circumstances, not of law or constitutional practice, but of fact, such as the expectations and hopes of persons undefined that Crown lands then leased would become private property. It is an interpretation of the Constitution depending on an implication which is formed on a vague, individual conception of the spirit of the compact, which is not the result of interpreting any specific language to be quoted, nor referable to any recognized principle of the common law of the Constitution, and which, when started, is rebuttable by an intention of exclusion equally not referable to any language of the instrument or acknowledged common law constitutional principle, but arrived at by the Court on the opinions of Judges as to hopes and expectations respecting vague external conditions. This method of interpretation cannot, we think, provide any secure foundation for Commonwealth or State action, and must inevitably lead – and in fact has already led – to divergencies and inconsistencies more and more pronounced as the decisions accumulate. Those who rely on American authorities for limiting pl xxxv in the way suggested, would find in the celebrated judgment of *Marshall* CJ in *Gibbons* **[146]** *v Ogden* [22 US (9 Wheat) 1 (1824)] two passages militating strongly against their contention. One is at p 189 in these words: "We know of no rule for construing the extent of such powers, other than is given by the language of the instrument which confers them, taken in connection with the purposes for which they were conferred." The other is at p 196, where, speaking of the commerce power, the learned Chief Justice says: "This power, like all others vested in Congress, is complete in itself, may be exercised to its utmost extent, and acknowledges no limitations, other than are prescribed in the Constitution."

However, the joint judgment went on to argue that American cases were irrelevant.

Knox CJ, Isaacs, Rich and Starke JJ: [146] But we conceive that American authorities, however illustrious the tribunals may be, are not a secure basis on which to build fundamentally with respect to our own Constitution. While in secondary and subsidiary matters they may, and sometimes do, afford considerable light and assistance, they cannot, for reasons we are about to state, be recognized as standards whereby to measure the respective rights of the Commonwealth and States under the Australian Constitution. For the proper construction of the Australian Constitution it is essential to bear in mind two cardinal features of our political system which are interwoven in its texture and, notwithstanding considerable similarity of structural design, including the depositary of the residual powers, radically distinguish it from the American Constitution. Pervading the instrument, they must be taken into account in determining the meaning of its language. One is the common sovereignty of all parts of the British Empire; the other is the principle of responsible government. The combined effect of these features is that the expression "State" and the expression "Commonwealth" comprehend both the strictly legal conception of the King in right of a designated territory, and the **[147]** people of that territory considered as a political organism. The indivisibility of the Crown will be presently considered in its bearing on the specific argument in this case. The general influence of the principle of responsible government in the Constitution may be more appropriately referred to now.

In the words of a distinguished lawyer and statesman, Lord *Haldane*, when a member of the House of Commons, delivered on the motion for leave to introduce the bill for the Act which we are considering:– "The difference between the Constitution which this bill proposes to set up and the Constitution of the United States is enormous and fundamental. This bill is permeated through and through with the spirit of the greatest institution which exists in the Empire, and which pertains to every Constitution established within the Empire – I mean the institution of responsible government, a government under which the Executive is directly responsible to – nay, is almost the creature of – the Legislature. This is not so in America, but it is so with all the Constitutions we have granted to our self-governing colonies. On this occasion we establish a Constitution modelled on our own model, pregnant with the same spirit, and permeated with the principle of responsible government. Therefore, what you have here is nothing akin to the Constitution of the United States except in its most superficial features." With these expressions we entirely agree ... **[148]** But it is plain that, in view of the two features of common and indivisible sovereignty and responsible government, no more profound error could be made than to endeavour to find our way through our own Constitution by the borrowed light of the decisions, and sometimes the dicta, that American institutions and circumstances have drawn from the distinguished tribunals of that country. See also the observations of Sir *Henry Jenkyns* in *British Rule and Jurisdiction Beyond the Seas*, at p 90. We therefore look to the judicial authorities which are part of our own development, which have grown up beside our political system, have guided it, have been influenced by it and are consistent with it, and which, so far as they existed in 1900, we must regard as in the contemplation of those who, whether in the Convention or in the Imperial Parliament, brought our Constitution into being, and which, so far as they are of later date, we are bound to look to as authoritative for us.

Accordingly, the joint judgment applied "**[143]** the settled rules of construction".

Knox CJ, Isaacs, Rich and Starke JJ: [148] The settled rules of construction which we have to apply have been very distinctly enunciated by the highest tribunals of the Empire. To those we must conform ourselves; for, whatever finality the law gives to our decisions on questions like the present, it is as incumbent upon this Court in arriving at its conclusions to adhere to principles so established as it is admittedly incumbent upon the House of Lords or Privy Council in cases arising before those ultimately final tribunals.

What, then, are the settled rules of construction? The first, and "golden rule" or "universal rule" as it has been variously termed, has been settled in *Grey v Pearson* [(1857) 6 HLC 61; 10 ER 1216] and the *Sussex Peerage Case* [(1844) 11 Cl & Fin 85; 8 ER 1034], in well-known passages which are quoted by Lord *Macnaghten* in *Vacher's Case* [[1913] AC 107 at 117-8]. Lord *Haldane* LC, in the same case [[1913] AC 107 at 113], made some observations very pertinent to the present occasion. His Lordship, after stating that speculation on the motives of the Legislature was a topic which Judges cannot profitably or properly **[149]** enter upon, said:– "Their province is the very different one of construing the language in which the Legislature has finally expressed its conclusions, and if they undertake the other province which belongs to those who, in making the laws, have to endeavour to interpret the desire of the country, they are in danger of going astray in a labyrinth to the character of which they have no sufficient guide. In endeavouring to place the proper interpretation on the sections of the statute before this House sitting in its judicial capacity, I propose, therefore, to exclude consideration of everything excepting the state of the law as it was when the statute was passed, and the light to be got by reading it as a whole, before attempting to construe any particular section. Subject to this consideration, I think that the only safe course is to read the language of the statute in what seems to be its natural sense." In the case of *Inland Revenue Commissioners v Herbert* [[1913] AC 326 at 332] Lord *Haldane* reaffirms the principle, with special reference to legislation of a novel kind. Other cases, of equal authority, could be cited, but it is not necessary.

With respect to the interpretation of a written Constitution, the Privy Council has in several cases laid down principles which should be observed by Courts of law, and these principles have been stated in the clearest terms. In *R v Burah* [(1878) 3 App Cas 889 at 904-5] Lord *Selborne*, in speaking of the case where a question arises as to whether any given legislation exceeds the power granted, says: – "The established Courts of Justice, when a question arises whether the prescribed limits have been exceeded, must of necessity determine that question; and the only way in which they can properly do so, is by looking to the terms of the instrument by which, affirmatively, the legislative powers were created, and by which, negatively, they are restricted. If what has been done is legislation, within the general scope of the affirmative words which give the power, and if it violates no express condition or restriction by which that power is limited (in which category would, of course, be included any Act of the Imperial Parliament at variance with it), it is not for any Court of Justice to inquire further, or to enlarge constructively those conditions and restrictions." In *Attorney-General for Ontario v* **[150]** *Attorney-General for Canada* [[1912] AC 571 at 583] Lord *Loreburn* LC, for the Judicial Committee, said:– "In the interpretation of a completely self-governing Constitution founded upon a written organic instrument, such as the *British North America Act, if the text is explicit the text is conclusive, alike in what it directs and what it forbids*. When the text is *ambiguous*, as, for example, when the words establishing two mutually exclusive jurisdictions are wide enough to bring a particular power within either, recourse must be had to the context and scheme of the Act."

In two decisions the Judicial Committee has applied these principles to the interpretation of this Constitution, namely, *Webb v Outrim* [[1907] AC 81] and the *Colonial Sugar Refining Co's Case* [[1914] AC 237]. In the first mentioned case, quite independently of any observations as to the meaning of the word "unconstitutional," it is clear that their Lordships proceeded on the ordinary lines of statutory construction. In the second case the Judicial Committee considered the nature of the instrument itself in order to determine the more satisfactorily the depository of residual powers, and having arrived at the conclusion, as to which this Court has never faltered, that the Commonwealth is a government of enumerated or selected legislative powers, their Lordships examined the language of sec 51 to ascertain from its words whether the suggested power could be deduced. The method of arriving at the conclusion is all that is relevant here. We therefore are bound to follow the course of judicial investigation which those two august tribunals of the Empire have marked out as required by law.

Before approaching, for this purpose, the consideration of the provisions of the Constitution itself, we should state explicitly that the doctrine of "implied prohibition" against the exercise of a power once ascertained in accordance with ordinary rules of construction, was definitely rejected by the Privy Council in *Webb v Outrim*. Though subsequently reaffirmed by three members of this Court, it has as often been rejected by two other members of the Court, and has never been unreservedly accepted and applied. From its nature, it is incapable of consistent application, because **[151]** "necessity" in the sense employed – a political sense – must vary in relation to various powers and various States, and, indeed, various periods and circumstances. Not only is the judicial branch of the Government inappropriate to determine political necessities, but experience, both in Australia and America, evidenced by discordant decisions, has proved both the elusiveness and the inaccuracy of the doctrine as a legal standard. Its inaccuracy is perhaps the more thoroughly perceived when it is considered what the doctrine of "necessity" in a political sense means. It means the necessity of protection against the aggression of some outside and possibly hostile body. It is based on distrust, lest powers, if once conceded to the least degree, might be abused to the point of destruction. But possible abuse of powers is no reason in British law for limiting the natural force of the language creating them. It may be taken into account by the parties when creating the powers, and they, by omission of suggested powers or by safeguards introduced by them into the compact, may delimit the powers created. But, once the parties have by the terms they employ defined the permitted limits, no Court has any right to narrow those limits by reason of any fear that the powers as actually circumscribed by the language naturally understood may be abused. This has been pointed out by the Privy Council on several occasions, including the case of the *Bank of Toronto v Lambe* [(1887) 12 App Cas 575]. The ordinary meaning of the terms employed in one place may be restricted by terms used elsewhere: that is pure legal construction. But, once their true meaning is so ascertained, they cannot be further limited by the fear of abuse. The non-granting of powers, the expressed qualifications of powers granted, the expressed retention of powers, are all to be taken into account by a Court. But the extravagant use of the granted powers in the actual working of the Constitution is a matter to be guarded against by the constituencies and not by the Courts. When the people of Australia, to use the words of the Constitution itself, "united in a Federal Commonwealth," they took power to control by ordinary constitutional means any attempt on the part of the national Parliament to misuse its powers. If it be conceivable that the representatives of the people of Australia as a whole would ever proceed **[152]** to use their national powers to injure the people of Australia considered sectionally, it is certainly within the power of the people themselves to resent and reverse what may be done. No protection of this Court in such a case is necessary or proper. Therefore, the doctrine of political necessity, as means of interpretation, is indefensible on any ground. The one clear line of judicial inquiry as to the meaning of the Constitution must be to read it naturally in the light of the circumstances in which it was made, with knowledge of the combined fabric of the common law, and the statute law which preceded it, and then *lucet ipsa per se* ...

[154] Applying these principles to the present case, the matter stands thus:– Sec 51(XXXV) is in terms so general that it extends to all industrial disputes in fact extending beyond the limits of any one State, no exception being expressed as to industrial disputes in which States are concerned; but subject to any special provision to the contrary elsewhere in the Constitution. The respondents suggest only section 107 as containing by implication a provision to the contrary. The answer is that sec 107 contains nothing which in any way either cuts down the meaning of the expression "industrial disputes" in sec 51(XXXV) or exempts the Crown in right of a State, when party to an industrial dispute in fact, from the operation of Commonwealth legislation under sec 51(XXXV). Sec 107 continues the previously existing powers of every State Parliament to legislate with respect to (1) State exclusive powers and (2) State powers which are concurrent with Commonwealth powers. But it is a fundamental and fatal error to read sec 107 as reserving any power from the Commonwealth that falls fairly within the explicit terms of an express grant in sec 51, as that grant is reasonably construed, unless that reservation is as explicitly stated. The effect of State legislation, though fully within the powers preserved by sec 107, may in a given case depend on sec 109.

However valid and binding on the people of the State where no relevant Commonwealth legislation exists, the moment it encounters repugnant Commonwealth legislation operating on the same field the State legislation must give way. This is the true foundation of the doctrine stated in *D'Emden v Pedder* [(1904) 1 CLR 91] in the so-called rule quoted, which is after all only a paraphrase of sec 109 of the Constitution. The supremacy thus established by express **[155]** words of the Constitution has been recognized by the Privy Council without express provision in the case of the Canadian Constitution (see, *eg*, *La Compagnie Hydraulique v Continental Heat and Light Co* [[1909] AC 194]). The doctrine of "implied prohibition" finds no place where the ordinary principles of construction are applied so as to discover in the actual terms of the instrument their expressed or necessarily implied meaning. The principle we apply to the Commonwealth we apply also to the States, leaving their respective acts of legislation full operation within their respective areas and subject matters, but, in case of conflict, giving to valid Commonwealth legislation the supremacy expressly declared by the Constitution, measuring that supremacy according to the very words of sec 109. That section, which says "When *a law* of a State is inconsistent with *a law* of the Commonwealth, the latter shall prevail, and the former shall, to the extent of the inconsistency, be invalid," gives supremacy, not to any particular class of Commonwealth Acts but to *every* Commonwealth Act, over not merely State Acts passed under concurrent powers but *all* State Acts, though passed under an exclusive power, if any provisions of the two conflict; as they may – if they do not, then *cadit quaestio*.

We therefore hold that States, and persons natural or artificial representing States, when parties to industrial disputes in fact, are subject to Commonwealth legislation under pl XXXV of sec 51 of the Constitution, if such legislation on its true construction applies to them.

Higgins J delivered a separate judgment in which he, too, overruled the *Railway Servants' Case*. Gavan Duffy J dissented. The effect of the *Engineers' Case* was that many of the earlier High Court cases, notably *Railway Servants*, were overruled. In others, notably *D'Emden v Pedder*, the actual decision was reaffirmed, but was now explained as depending on s 109 of the Constitution (see Chapter 9). The status as precedents of other cases was left unclear.

The historical impact of the *Engineers' Case* was assessed by Windeyer J in *Victoria v Commonwealth* (*Payroll Tax Case*) (1971) 122 CLR 353, where he noted "**[394]** some distant echoes and muffled undertones" of a conflict between assertions of "centralism" and claims to "State rights" and observed: "In federations of all kinds this has been a perennial controversy".

Victoria v Commonwealth (*Payroll Tax Case*)
(1971) 122 CLR 353

Windeyer J: [395] The Commonwealth Constitution was enacted at Westminster in 1900 as a product of the assent and agreement of the peoples of the Australian Colonies. It was sought by Australians, not imposed upon them. The *Constitution Act* itself was carefully worded so as not to be coercive. Section 3 provided that Western Australia should not become part of the new Commonwealth unless Her Majesty was satisfied that the people of that Colony had agreed thereto. As an agreement of peoples, British subjects in British Colonies, and the enactment thereafter by the sovereign legislature of the British Empire of a law to give effect to their wishes, the Australian federation can be described as springing from an agreement or compact. But agreement became merged in law. The word "compact" is still appropriate but strictly only if used in a different sense – not as meaning a pact between independent parties, but as describing a compaction, a putting of separate things firmly together by force of law. The Colonies which in 1901 became States in the new Commonwealth were not before then sovereign bodies in any strict legal sense; and certainly the Constitution did not make them so. They were self-governing colonies which, when the **[396]** Commonwealth came into existence as a new Dominion of the Crown, lost some of their former powers and gained no new powers. They became components of a federation, the Commonwealth of Australia. It became a nation. Its nationhood was in the course of time to be consolidated in war, by economic and commercial integration, by the unifying force of federal law, by the decline of dependence upon British naval and military power and by a recognition and acceptance of external interests and obligations. With these developments the position of the Commonwealth, the federal government, has waxed; and that of the States has waned. In law that is a result of the paramount position of the Commonwealth Parliament in matters of concurrent power. And this legal supremacy has been reinforced in fact by financial dominance. That the Commonwealth would, as time went on, enter progressively, directly or indirectly, into fields that had formerly been occupied by the States, was from an early date seen as likely to occur. This was greatly aided after the decision in the *Engineers' Case* [(1920) 28 CLR 129], which diverted the flow of constitutional law into new channels. I have never thought it right to regard the discarding of the doctrine of the implied immunity of the States and other results of the *Engineers' Case* as the correction of antecedent errors or as the uprooting of heresy. To return today to the discarded theories would indeed be an error and the adoption of a heresy. But that is because in 1920 the Constitution was read in a new light, a light reflected from events that had, over twenty years, led to a growing realization that Australians were now one people and Australia one country and that national laws might meet national needs. For lawyers the abandonment of old interpretations of the limits of constitutional powers was readily acceptable. It meant only insistence on rules of statutory interpretation to which they were well accustomed. But reading the instrument in this light does not to my mind mean that the original judges of the High Court were wrong in their understanding of what at the time of federation was believed to be the effect of the Constitution and in reading it accordingly. As I see it the *Engineers' Case*, looked at as an event in legal and constitutional history, was a consequence of developments that had occurred outside the law courts as well as a cause of further developments there. That is not surprising for the Constitution is not an ordinary statute: it is a fundamental law. In any country where the spirit of the common law holds sway the enunciation by courts of constitutional principles based on the interpretation of a written constitution [397] may vary and develop in response to changing circumstances. This does not mean that courts have transgressed lawful boundaries: or that they may do so.

Another famous appraisal of the *Engineers' Case* was published in 1937 by Richard Latham, the son of Chief Justice Latham. A lecturer at the University of London, Latham was killed in the Battle of Britain. This brilliant essay was his only publication.

RTE Latham, "The Law and the Commonwealth"
in WK Hancock, *Survey of British Commonwealth Affairs: Problems of Nationality 1918-1936*
(Oxford University Press, 1937), vol 1, 510

[563] The original bench of the High Court of Australia, maturely wise without excess of cleverness, treated the constitution as a federal compact, and saved as far as possible the integrity of both States and Commonwealth by applying the American doctrine of the immunity of federal and state instrumentalities, a sort of rule of mutual tolerance. A brilliant minority, appointed to the bench in 1906, broke British judicial tradition by persisting in consistent dissent. They repeatedly refused to recognize previous majority decisions *in pari materia* as binding in subsequent cases, and elaborated an heretical doctrine in exhaustive dissenting judgments. As the older judges left the bench, and new appointments were made, this solid minority became the majority. The revolutionary *Engineers' Case* [(1920) 28 CLR 129] in 1921 marks the point at which their heterodoxy became the new orthodoxy. The reasoning of this decision is open to all sorts of criticism. The case was decided on high constitutional ground, when a much simpler argument would have sufficed. It cut off Australian constitutional law from American precedents, a copious source of thoroughly relevant learning, in favour of the crabbed English rules of statutory interpretation, which are one of the sorriest features of English law, and are, as we have seen, particularly unsuited to the interpretation of a rigid constitution. The majority judgment was, further, self-contradictory in two ways. It declared that the Constitution was [564] to be interpreted by its words alone; yet the court, in reaching that very proposition, took notice of responsible government, a matter far more extrinsic to strict law, and far less admissible by the English rules of statutory construction themselves, than the close verbal correspondence with the United States Constitution upon which the early High Court had relied to bring American authorities in point. And this very judgment which abandoned American precedents would not have been possible if the majority had not followed the

loose American rather than the strict English view of the binding authority of precedent. The fundamental criticism of the decision is that its real ground is nowhere stated in the majority judgment. This real ground was the view held by the majority that the Constitution had been intended to create a nation, and that it had succeeded; that in the Great War the nation had in fact advanced in status while the States stood still, and (as was a patent fact) that the peace had not brought a relapse into the *status quo ante bellum*; that a merely contractual view of the Constitution was therefore out of date, and its persistence in the law was stultifying the Commonwealth industrial power, which they believed to be a real and vital power; and finally, that the words of the Constitution permitted the view of the federal relationship which the times demanded. A judgment on these lines would have made the *Engineers' Case* frankly a quasi-political decision, based on a far-sighted view of ultimate constitutional policy, of the type with which the Supreme Court of the United States in its greatest periods has made us familiar. It would have been no more political than several of Sir Isaac Isaacs' most notable judgments.

5. Literalism and Legalism

The judicial tug-of-war that culminated in the *Engineers' Case* was not merely concerned with questions of the power relationships between State and Commonwealth governments, but also with the judicial methodology by which the High Court should resolve such questions. On that issue, the *Engineers' Case* is generally regarded as consummating a triumph of legalism, which is then perceived as having dominated the High Court's approach ever since. Of course, this avowedly apolitical approach may itself serve highly political purposes (see Brian Galligan, *Politics of the High Court* (University of Queensland Press, 1987)).

Part of the impact of the *Engineers' Case* arises from the emphasis of Isaacs J on the words of the Constitution, that is, on a literal interpretation (though in fact throughout the judgment Isaacs J took care to stress that he was not advocating *mere* literalism, but literalism within a context of traditional legal principles and techniques). This facet of the case is sometimes conflated with the famous declaration made by Sir Owen Dixon when, after 23 years on the High Court bench, he finally became Chief Justice in 1952.

Swearing in of Sir Owen Dixon as Chief Justice
(1952) 85 CLR xi

[xiii] Federalism means a demarcation of powers and this casts upon the court a responsibility of deciding whether legislation is within the boundaries of allotted powers. Unfortunately that responsibility is very widely misunderstood, misunderstood, largely by the popular use and misuse of terms which are not applicable, and it is not sufficiently recognised that the court's sole function is to interpret [xiv] a constitutional description of power or restraint upon power and say whether a given measure falls on one side of a line consequently drawn or on the other, and that it has nothing whatever to do with the merits or demerits of the measure.

Such a function has led us all I think to believe that close adherence to legal reasoning is the only way to maintain the confidence of all parties in Federal conflicts. It may be that the court is thought to be excessively legalistic. I should be sorry to think that it is anything else. There is no other safe guide to judicial decisions in great conflicts than a strict and complete legalism.

In 1981 Sir Garfield Barwick ascribed his own approach more directly to the *Engineers' Case*.

Retirement of Sir Garfield Barwick as Chief Justice
(1981) 148 CLR v

[ix] This Court, under the Constitution, has to decide the meaning of the words in which it is expressed. When the court deals with a matter of common law, the general law, where there is no text, the Court has a little more room to perhaps re-express the law in terms that are more

conformable to the needs of the day. We have done so. That requires, of course, both courage and a great deal of proper knowledge. When we have a statute to interpret, we have a text. The legislature has expressed itself in words, and those words bind. They cannot be side-stepped and the Court's task is to say what the words mean and there are quite distinct and understandable rules by which courts interpret statutory provisions. In the case of a constitution, it is so, but even to a greater degree. There is no room for the Court to change the Constitution. There is a means of doing that – difficult maybe – but there is a means. When the Court has to decide what the Constitution means, it has to assign a meaning to language. The Constitution gives to the Commonwealth certain powers, legislative powers. It describes those powers briefly in words by reference to subjects. It gives to the States the residue of power after the Commonwealth power is defined and exercised. So the problem for the Court always, is to decide on the extent of Commonwealth power. The Constitution decides the State power by providing it to have the residue. Why I mention that is this. There seems a growing tendency to want to put a brand on a constitutional lawyer or a judge that he either favours the Commonwealth or he favours the State. But the truth is he has no choice. His task is to decide on Commonwealth power and after that the Constitution works itself out. To talk of him as a centralist or a centrist is quite inapt, but I hear it.

[x] Earlier, the first judges thought the way to interpret the words was to say you interpret them against powers reserved to the States. But in the *Engineers' Case* that was departed from and it was pointed out – and we have always followed the same plan since – you take the words, you decide on the Commonwealth power and you do not decide on the Commonwealth power looking over your shoulder as to what effect your decision will have on State power. The Constitution will take care of that.

Of course, because attention is focused on the Commonwealth power, the tendency is to think that the Court is advancing Commonwealth power, whereas, in fact, it is only inducing it, bringing it out and making it plain. I thought it right to say that, on an occasion like this, because I notice occasionally little echoes of the old doctrine, as if the reserve powers doctrine that was exploded so long ago still had legs.

I think all of us who work in constitutional work, whether it be at the Bar or on the Bench, or in academia, need to be very wary that the triumph of the *Engineers' Case* is never tarnished and that we maintain stoutly that [n]otion, that the function of the Court is to give to the words their full and fair meaning and leave the Constitution which places the residue of the states to work itself out.

For Barwick CJ in 1981 (with far less equivocation than for Isaacs J in 1920) the emphasis was on the words of the Constitution, that is, on "literalism". Although the distinction is often blurred, Sir Owen Dixon's emphasis on "legalism" has a different focus – pointing not so much to the words as to the technique by which they should be interpreted. Although Barwick CJ acknowledged that the Court must "[ix] assign a meaning to language" (that is, the Court must *supply* a meaning not necessarily – or at least not self-evidently – contained in or umbilically attached to the words), he also spoke as if the Court must "[x] give to the words their full and fair meaning" (that is, the meaning they already have). His specific reaffirmation of the refusal, in the *Engineers' Case*, to interpret the words by reference to a presupposed context of reserved State powers seems intended to exemplify a more general rejection of reference to any interpretive context: the words, as they are, are to speak for themselves. This would be very different from the willingness of Isaacs J in the *Engineers' Case* to consider not only "[142] the words of the Constitution ... [but also] any recognized principle of the common law underlying the expressed terms of the Constitution"; not only "[152] to read it naturally" but to do so "in the light of the circumstances in which it was made, with knowledge of the combined fabric of the common law, and the statute law which preceded it".

The additional aids to interpretation emphasised in the *Engineers' Case* as qualifications to "literalism" lie outside the constitutional text; but they all involve reference to authoritative legal materials, and therefore still fall within Sir Owen Dixon's conception of "legalism". "Legalism" does not insist that interpretive or justificatory reasoning be limited to any one source, but only that all its sources be located within a self-contained autonomous body of law.

Judith Shklar, *Legalism: Law, Morals, and Political Trials*
(Harvard University Press, 1964, reissued 1986)

[8] To say that [legalism] is an ideology is to criticize only those of its traditional adherents who, in their determination to preserve law from politics, fail to recognize that they too have made a choice among political values … As a social ethos which gives rise to the political climate in which judicial and other legal institutions flourish, legalism is beyond reproach. It is the rigidity of legalistic categories of thought, especially in appraising the relationships of law to the political environment within which it functions, that is so deleterious. This is the source of the artificiality of almost all legal theories …

Legalism as an ideology … is what gives legal thinking its distinctive flavor on a vast variety of social occasions, in all kinds of discourse … Legalism is, above all, the operative outlook of the legal profession, both bench and bar. Moreover, [9] most legal theory … depends on categories of thought derived from this shared professional outlook. The tendency to think of law as "there" as a discrete entity, discernibly different from morals and politics, has its deepest roots in the legal profession's views of its own functions, and forms the very basis of most of our judicial institutions and procedures. That lawyers have particularly pronounced intellectual habits peculiar to them has often been noticed, especially by historians and other students of society whose views differ sharply from those of the legal profession. As one English lawyer [JAG Griffith] has put it, "A lawyer is *bound* by certain habits of belief … by which lawyers, however dissimilar otherwise, are more closely linked than they are separated … A man who has had legal training is never quite the same again … is never able to look at institutions or administrative practices or even social or political policies, free from his legal habits or beliefs. It is not easy for a lawyer to become a political scientist. It is very difficult for him to become a sociologist or a historian … He is interested in relationships, in rights in something and against somebody, in relation to others … This is what is meant by the legalistic approach … [A lawyer] will fight to the death to defend legal rights against persuasive arguments based on expediency or the public interest or the social good … He distrusts them … He believes, as part of his mental habits, that they are dangerous and too easily used as cloaks for arbitrary action." …

[10] The dislike of vague generalities, the preference for case-by-case treatment of all social issues, the structuring of all possible human relations into the form of claims and counter-claims under established rules, and the belief that the rules are "there" – these combine to make up legalism as a social outlook. When it becomes self-conscious, when it challenges other views, it is a full-blown ideology … As law serves ideally to promote the security of established expectations, so legalism with its concentration on specific cases and rules is, essentially, conservative. It is not, however, a matter of "masking" a specific class and economic interest … [L]egalism is no mask for anything. It is an openly, intrinsically, and quite specifically conservative view, because law is itself a conservatizing ideal and institution. In its epitome, the judicial ethos, it becomes clear that this is the conservatism of consensus. It relies on what appears already to have been established and accepted. When constitutional and social changes have become inevitable and settled, the judiciary adapts itself to the new order …

[12] If many lawyers, in America especially, do recognize that the courts do legislate and make basic social choices, this is less true and even less accepted in other countries. Even in the United States, … the public at large and important sections of the bar do not perceive their functions thus. The courts are expected to interpret the law, not to alter it. Professional ideology and public expectations, in fact, do mold the conduct of the judiciary and its perception of its role. To seek rules, or at least a public consensus that can serve in place of a rule, must be the judge's constant preoccupation, and it affects his choices in ways that are unknown to less constrained political agents. To avoid the appearance of arbitrariness is a deep inner necessity for him. The trouble is that the possibility of aloofness does not depend on the judge's behavior alone, but also on the public responses to it …

[N]o basic social decision, whether made by court or legislature, can ever meet with unanimous approval in a heterogeneous society. Without consensus the appearance of [13] neutrality evaporates. Every offended party characteristically responds to a decision by accusing the judges of "legislating." It is not the law, which is clearly far from self-evident, but the judge, who is at fault, and an erring judge is a legislating judge, since the losing party begins its case by presenting its version of the true law. The result is that, as denunciations of "lawmaking" multiply, the legalistic ethos is reinforced and the likelihood of judges satisfying it becomes increasingly rare. As long as substantial interests and expectations are disappointed by judicial decisions, there can be no realization of legalistic hopes for a neutral judicial process ... The easiest resort, under such circumstances, is for judges to escape into formalism when they can. For American judges this is frequently not possible. In England it is. As for analytical legal theory, it is more than anything an effort to enhance the formalism that is already a built-in feature of legal discourse. Modern legal theory would be incomprehensible if it were forgotten that its creators are themselves lawyers and that professional habits of mind exercise a real influence upon them as they strive to extract the formal essence of law from the confusion of its historical reality.

The fundamental difficulty encountered by any "legalistic" conception of the judge's role is also the very element that allows such conceptions to appear plausible. This is that, on any comprehensive view of the authoritative legal materials, those materials themselves require the judge to draw upon sources that cannot be confined to an autonomous discourse of purely legal considerations. The following summary draws on articles published by Roscoe Pound in the first half of the 20th century, including "Juristic Science and Law" (1918) 31 *Harvard Law Review* 1047; "The Theory of Judicial Decision" (1923) 36 *Harvard Law Review* 641; "The Ideal Element in American Judicial Decision" (1932) 45 *Harvard Law Review* 136; and "Hierarchy of Sources and Forms in Different Systems of Law" (1933) 7 *Tulane Law Review* 475.

AR Blackshield, "The Law"
in *Power in Australia: Directions of Change*
(Centre for Continuing Education, Australian National University, 1981)

[174] [I]f the authoritative legal materials with which judges must work are "restrictive" (in the sense that each judge is *limited*, in his dialectical and decisional tasks, to what he can do with these given materials), they are also an inexhaustible source of rhetorical and interpretive potential. In recent years jurisprudential debate has focused on the inadequacy of attempts to understand the legal system merely in terms of "rules": the judge (it is said) must take account not only of the clear and specific directives supposedly embodied in authoritative "rules", but also of "principles" and "policies". Yet these modern attempts to go beyond the "restrictive" component of legal materials are still themselves too restrictive, proceeding as they do from anaemic analytical premises which they strive in vain to surmount. A far richer and more fully descriptive appraisal of the diverse resources available in the authoritative legal materials was given over half a century ago by Roscoe Pound. "Rules", he said, were only one kind of "precepts" found in legal materials; in addition, "the precept element in law" included "principles", [precepts defining] "conceptions", and [precepts defining] "standards" ...

A "rule", in Pound's usage, is "a definite detailed provision" which prescribes "a fixed and definite result for a fixed and definite situation of fact". The task of judicial application is reduced to "ascertaining whether that state of facts exists" ...

Rules are "especially important" in property and commercial law, and in criminal law. But even there, their function is not to resolve the "hard cases" with which appellate judicial decision is concerned; rather, their function is to minimise the occasions on which such "hard cases" arise. The "hard cases" which reach appellate courts, almost by definition, are characterised by the *absence* of any "fixed and definite" rules precisely in point. In this situation a court is likely to fall back on "principles":

> that is premises for juristic deduction, to which we turn to supply new rules, to interpret old ones, to meet new situations, to measure the scope and application of rules and **[175]** standards, and to reconcile them when they conflict. These principles are the living part of the legal system and are its most significant institution ...

What is clear from Pound's account is that "principles", as compared with "rules", are formulated at a higher level of generality; are in every sense more equivocal and open to debate; and reflect a creative judicial choice, in which value preferences reflecting the judges' ideal pictures of the legal and social order play a formative role. In formulating a "principle", a court "lays down a sweeping generalisation as an authoritative premise for judicial and juristic reasoning where rules of law are wanting or inapplicable or inconvenient". Although a principle is thought of as an "authoritative starting point",

> Very often these authoritative starting points compete. There is often a choice of such starting points from which to proceed and no precepts are at hand to determine which is to be chosen. Here usually choice is made by referring the result of the respective starting points to the received ideals and following the lines leading to decisions in accord therewith ... Where [principles] come into play choice of starting points is the decisive consideration, and this choice is seldom authoritatively fixed ... [A] principle is likely to be chosen, consciously or unconsciously to the measure of a received ideal.

Clearly, the value-based "principles" envisaged by Roscoe Pound ... are very different from the "neutral principles" advocated by Herbert Wechsler ... But perhaps the real secret of the rhetorical power of the concept of "principles" lies in its ability to accommodate *both* these contrasting views. Principles have about them an aura *both* of commitment to fundamental values, *and* of impartial resort to lofty points of vantage or leverage, transcending the hurly-burly of conflicting interests.

"Conceptions" (which tend in practice to be associated with "rules") are shorthand "counters" which lump together all fact situations of a common type, along with the entire bundle of rules, principles and legal consequences pertaining to fact situations of that type. The result is "an authoritative category into which cases may be fitted so that, when **[176]** placed in the proper pigeonhole, a series of rules and principles and standards become applicable." Finally, "standards" (which tend in practice to be associated with "principles") are "measures of conduct" embedded in rules and principles and requiring an *evaluation* (by criteria only allusively and connotatively defined) of the facts at issue: "due care", "harsh and unconscionable", "the ordinary prudent purchaser", and above all "the reasonable man" ...

Clearly, the many statutory schemes which lay down criteria for case-by-case application by administrative agencies are heavily reliant on "standards". But in addition (as Pound long ago predicted) the history of *judicial* decision in the twentieth century has been one of increasing resort to "standards", with all the indeterminacy of degree and of substantive value-criteria which that resort entails.

All this, then, makes up what Pound called "the precept element in law". But this was only one of three elements embedded in his conception of "the authoritative legal materials". In order to apply "the precept element" it was necessary for judges to have recourse (secondly) to "the technique element" and (thirdly) to "the ideal element".

By "the technique element in law" Pound meant

> a body of traditional ideas as to how legal precepts should be interpreted and applied and causes decided, and a traditional technique of developing and applying legal precepts whereby these precepts are eked out, extended, restricted, and adapted to the exigencies of administration of justice ... [These ideas] are not legal precepts; they are modes of looking at and handling and shaping legal precepts. They are mental habits governing judicial and juristic craftsmanship ... The doctrine of precedents [for example] ... is not something to be developed by analogy. It is not an authoritative premise from which to deduce grounds of decision. It is by no means anything so simple as a rule or a principle. It is not a legal precept at all. It is a traditional art of judicial decision; a traditional **[177]** technique of deciding with reference to judicial decision in the past; a traditional technique of developing the grounds of decision of particular cases on the basis of reported judicial experience ... "To know rules of law", says the Digest, "is not merely to understand the words, but as well their force and operation." This force and operation are determined largely by the traditional technique of decision and traditional rules of art that determine how legal materials shall be looked at and how they shall be developed and applied. An account of law that overlooks this element, by confounding it with the aggregate of received legal precepts for the time being, gives an untrue picture of the actual phenomena.

In particular, he thought, each legal system has its own distinctive way of handling judicial precedents; its own habitual preferences as between specific and substituted remedies; and its own approach to statutes. In each of these three respects "the modes of thought are wholly unlike, and these modes of thought have decisive effect upon the administration of justice" ...

The third ingredient is perhaps the most fundamental ... By "the ideal element in law" Pound meant

> a body of traditional or received ideals as to the nature of politically organised society and the purpose of the legal ordering of human relations, and hence as to what legal precepts should obtain, what the content of precepts should be, and how they should be applied. Whether these ideals are received and held consciously or unconsciously, they form the background of all judicial action and of juristic writing. Legal precepts are continually moulded and reshaped by them and thus in time given new content and new application. This element in law changes slowly. But it does change with social, economic and political development. One has only to read English decisions of the seventeenth century in comparison with those of today to see that the ideals of the relationally organised society of the Middle Ages, and the ideals of the seventeenth and eighteenth-century era of absolute government, gave way to a new set of ideals for the era of the classical economics with its theory of justice as requiring a maximum of abstract individual free self-assertion. Indeed one cause of judicial vacillation and divided courts is that the nineteenth-century ideal is gradually giving way before a new conception of justice which has yet to be formulated. Nowhere are such ideals more controlling than in the application of legal standards.

It is clear that Pound was talking here of intra-systemic ideals: not those *Weltanschauungen* which judges as human beings have brought with them to the study, practice and exegesis of law, but those which they have imbibed unconsciously from years of working with the authoritative legal materials themselves. He spoke of ideal "pictures of the social and political order" which have "acquired a certain fixity in the judicial and professional tradition", and "are part of 'the law' quite as much as legal precepts"; of "the traditional or reasonably fixed **[178]** professional pictures for the time being of the legal and social order and of the end of law" which are "part of the law"; of "broader idealised pictures of the social order and of the end of law, the main lines of which, in any given time and place, are as well fixed as those of the body of legal precepts and of the traditional rules of art and techniques of decision". His argument was that these "ideal pictures", secreted in the authoritative legal materials themselves, were one main channel through which those materials controlled the course of judicial decision, and were thus a major source of stability and continuity in legal systems ... Yet ... he also thought that these ideal pictures were subject to change, and not always to glacial change. "Modification of the current ideal picture of the social order by which judges are governed in choosing analogies, in developing principles, and in applying rules, may change the law in action profoundly within a generation while the outward forms remain the same." And in his own sweeping impressionistic surveys of changes in legal ideals, it was clear that the intra-systemic changes reflected extra-systemic cultural changes – in social attitudes, economic pressures, intellectual fashions and "period style" – and thus reflected the inarticulate major premises of judges not merely as judges, but as human beings of their time.

The truth is that, at the level of generality and impressionism involved when we try to diagnose "the ideal element in law", it is impossible to disentangle the ideals embedded *within* the authoritative legal materials from those extra-systemic ideals which each judge brings with him to those materials. Even those "ideal pictures" most clearly embedded within the legal materials will be interpreted and internalised differently by different minds. But this is only to confirm Pound's point that the presence of an "ideal element" within the received legal materials is yet another reason why those materials both circumscribe, and constantly stimulate, the interpretive role of the judge. To think of the authoritative legal materials as merely *restrictive* of what judges can do is to settle for "an ideal picture of the legal order" which is simply illusory.

6. *Jumbunna Coal Case*

Look again at what is said in the above extract about the characteristics of "principles", and consider the extent to which an identical set of characteristics can be attributed to a Constitution. Also consider the extent to which the Constitution itself, quite apart from any semantic content it may have as a text, is made to stand as the supreme symbol of "an ideal picture of the legal order". Indeed, this symbolic aspect of the Constitution may sometimes influence the interpretation of its semantic content. Hence, when Isaacs J emphasised in *Australasian Temperance and General Mutual Life Assurance Society Ltd v Howe* (1922) 31 CLR 290 that the Court was called upon to interpret "**[306]** a great instrument of government", he was drawing on a rival tradition of constitutional interpretation that has always interacted with "literalism", sometimes as a reinforcement of close and authoritative textual reading and sometimes as its most powerful alternative.

In United States constitutional law, the source of this alternative approach is the judgment of Chief Justice John Marshall in *McCulloch v Maryland*, 17 US (4 Wheat) 316 (1819). In that case, the United States Supreme Court held that the United States Congress *did* have constitutional power to establish a national bank, and that the State of Maryland *did not* have power to tax such a bank. The negative holding, restricting the power of the State to tax an agency of the federal government, was to be an important source of the Australian doctrine of "implied immunities"; but the positive holding as to the breadth of congressional power was equally important. That holding rested partly on Art I, § 8, cl 18 of the United States Constitution, which gives Congress the power "To make all Laws which shall be necessary and proper for carrying into Execution" its other enumerated powers.

McCulloch v Maryland
17 US (4 Wheat) 316 (1819)

Marshall CJ: [406] Among the enumerated powers, we do not find that of establishing a bank or creating a corporation. But there is no phrase in the instrument which, like the articles of confederation, excludes incidental or implied powers; and which requires that every thing granted shall be expressly and minutely described. Even the 10th amendment ... declares only that the powers "not delegated to the United States, nor prohibited to the States, are reserved to the States or to the people;" thus leaving the question, whether the particular power which may become the subject of contest has been delegated to the one government, or prohibited to the other, to depend on a fair construction of the whole instrument ... **[407]** A constitution, to contain an accurate detail of all the subdivisions of which its great powers will admit, and of all the means by which they may be carried into execution, would partake of the prolixity of a legal code, and could scarcely be embraced by the human mind. It would probably never be understood by the public. Its nature, therefore, requires, that only its great outlines should be marked, its important objects designated, and the minor ingredients which compose those objects be deduced from the nature of the objects themselves ... In considering this question, then, we must never forget, that it is *a constitution* we are expounding.

Although, among the enumerated powers of government, we do not find the word "bank" or "incorporation," we find the great powers to lay and collect taxes; to borrow money; to regulate commerce; to declare and conduct a war; and to raise and support armies and navies. The sword and the purse, all the external relations, and no inconsiderable portion of the industry of the nation, are entrusted to its government. It can never be pretended **[408]** that these vast powers draw after them others of inferior importance, merely because they are inferior. Such an idea can never be advanced. But it may with great reason be contended, that a government, entrusted with such ample powers, on the due execution of which the happiness and prosperity of the nation so vitally depends, must also be entrusted with ample means for their execution. The power being given, it is the interest of the nation to facilitate its execution. It can never be their interest, and cannot be presumed to have been their intention, to clog and embarrass its execution by withholding the most appropriate means. Throughout this vast republic, from the St Croix to the Gulph of Mexico, from the Atlantic to the Pacific, revenue is to be collected and expended, armies are to be marched and supported. The exigencies of the nation may require that the treasure raised in the north should be transported to the south, *that* raised in the east conveyed to the west, or that this order should be reversed. Is that construction of the constitution to be preferred which would render these operations difficult, hazardous, and expensive? Can we adopt that construction, (unless the words imperiously require it,) which would impute to the framers of that instrument, when granting these powers for the public good, the intention of impeding their exercise by withholding a choice of means? If, indeed, such be the mandate of the constitution, we have only to obey; but that instrument does not profess to enumerate the means by which the powers it confers may be executed; nor does it prohibit the creation of a corpo-**[409]**-ration, if the existence of such a being be essential to the beneficial exercise of those powers. It is, then, the subject of fair inquiry, how far such means may be employed ...

The government which has a right to do an act, and has imposed on it the duty of performing that act, must, according to the dictates of reason, be al-**[410]**-lowed to select the means; and those who contend that it may not select any appropriate means, that one particular mode of effecting the object is excepted, take upon themselves the burden of establishing that exception ...

Ironically, in the midst of this appeal to the "great outlines" of the Constitution, Marshall CJ turned to a textual argument dependent on close semantic analysis. He pointed out that, in the "necessary and proper" clause (Art I, §8, cl 18), the word "necessary" need not "**[413]** import an absolute physical necessity", but might extend to other shades of meaning: "**[414]** A thing may be necessary, very necessary, absolutely or indispensably necessary". He clinched the argument by pointing to Art I, §10, cl 2: "No State shall, without the consent of the congress, lay any Imposts or Duties on Imports or Exports, except what may be *absolutely necessary* for executing its inspection Laws" (emphasis added). In other words, when the founders meant "absolutely necessary", they said so. He concluded that: "**[415]** This word, then, like others, is used in various senses; and, in its construction, the subject, the context, the intention of the person using them, are all to be taken into view". This brought him back to his larger theme.

Marshall CJ: [415] The subject is the execution of those great powers on which the welfare of a nation essentially depends. It must have been the intention of those who gave these powers, to insure, as far as human prudence could insure, their beneficial execution ... This provision is made in a constitution intended to endure for ages to come, and, consequently, to be adapted to the various *crises* of human affairs. To have prescribed the means by which government should, in all future time, execute its powers, would have been to change, entirely, the character of the instrument, and give it the properties of a legal code. It would have been an unwise attempt to provide, by immutable rules, for exigencies which, if foreseen at all, must have been seen dimly, and which can be best provided for as they occur. To have declared that the best means shall not be used, but those alone without which the power given would be nugatory, would have been to deprive the legislature of the capacity to avail itself of experience, to exercise its reason, and to accommodate its legislation to circum-**[416]**-stances ...

[418] In ascertaining the sense in which the word "necessary" is used in this clause of the constitution, we may derive some aid from that with which it is associated. Congress shall have power "to make all laws which shall be necessary and *proper* to carry into execution" the powers of the government. If the word "necessary" was used in that strict and rigorous sense for which the counsel for the State of **[419]** Maryland contend, it would be an extraordinary departure from the usual course of the human mind, as exhibited in composition, to add a word, the only possible effect of which is to qualify that strict and rigorous meaning; to present to the mind the idea of some choice of means of legislation not straitened and compressed within the narrow limits for which gentlemen contend.

But the argument which most conclusively demonstrates the error of the construction contended for by the counsel for the State of Maryland, is founded on the intention of the Convention, as manifested in the whole clause. To waste time and argument in proving that, without it, Congress might carry its powers into execution, would be not much less idle than to hold a lighted taper to the sun. As little can it be required to prove, that in the absence of this clause, Congress would have some choice of means. That it might employ those which, in its judgment, would most advantageously effect the object to be accomplished. That any means adapted to the end, any means which tended directly to the execution of the constitutional powers of the government, were in themselves constitutional. This clause, as construed by the State of Maryland, would abridge, and almost annihilate this useful and necessary right of the legislature to select its means. That this could not be intended, is, we should think, had it not been already controverted, too apparent for controversy. We think so for the following reasons:

1st. The clause is placed among the powers of Congress, not among the limitations on those powers.

[420] 2nd. Its terms purport to enlarge, not to diminish the powers vested in the government ... Had the intention been to make this clause restrictive, it would unquestionably have been so in form as well as in effect ...

If no other motive for its insertion can be suggested, a sufficient one is found in the desire to remove all doubts respecting [421] the right to legislate on that vast mass of incidental powers which must be involved in the constitution, if that instrument be not a splendid bauble.

We admit, as all must admit, that the powers of the government are limited, and that its limits are not to be transcended. But we think the sound construction of the constitution must allow to the national legislature that discretion, with respect to the means by which the powers it confers are to be carried into execution, which will enable that body to perform the high duties assigned to it, in the manner most beneficial to the people. Let the end be legitimate, let it be within the scope of the constitution, and all means which are appropriate, which are plainly adapted to that end, which are not prohibited, but consist with the letter and spirit of the constitution, are constitutional.

A similar broad approach to constitutional interpretation was unanimously adopted by the High Court in *Jumbunna Coal Mine NL v Victorian Coal Miners' Association* (1908) 6 CLR 309 – where the final sentence set out above from *McCulloch v Maryland* was quoted by Higgins J (at first instance, sitting as the President of the Commonwealth Court of Conciliation and Arbitration) and also by Barton and O'Connor JJ (on appeal to the High Court). Through most of the High Court's history, the "legalism" or "literalism" supposedly derived from the *Engineers' Case* has vied with the alternative approach symbolised in the United States by *McCulloch v Maryland*, and in Australia by *Jumbunna Coal*.

The *Commonwealth Conciliation and Arbitration Act 1904* (Cth) had been challenged as lacking validity under s 51(xxxv) – (1) because s 55 of the Act permitted registration of "any association of not less than one hundred employés in or in connection with any industry" (and therefore permitted registration of a union whose membership was confined to one State); and (2) because s 58 effectively recognised registered associations as corporate entities. The High Court held that in both respects the legislation was valid. Just as the result in *McCulloch v Maryland* turned in part on the "necessary and proper" clause (US Constitution Art I, § 8, cl 18), so the result in *Jumbunna Coal* turned in part on the "incidental" power (see Chapter 16, §7). On another issue raised by the *Jumbunna Coal Case*, however, the judgment of O'Connor J was a classic example of interpretive technique supported partly by "literalism", partly by appeal to established legislative usage, and partly by the broad maieutic approach symbolised by *McCulloch v Maryland*. The statutory definition of "industry" was wide enough to extend to such occupational groups as cooks, waiters and hairdressers. The appellants argued that this was too wide, since the phrase "industrial disputes" in s 51(xxxv) of the Constitution must be construed according to a narrower definition of "industry". O'Connor J rejected that argument. He held that "industrial dispute" [365] was not, when the Constitution was framed, a technical or legal expression", but "meant just what the two English words in their ordinary meaning conveyed to ordinary persons". To illustrate this "ordinary meaning" he quoted extensively from *Webster's International Dictionary* (1892 edition), the *Standard Dictionary* (1893), and the *Oxford English Dictionary* ("*Murray's New English Dictionary*"). He also reviewed the usages and definitions of the words "industry" and "industrial" in the colonial legislation of the 1890s, and in reports of the British Commission of Labour. He concluded, however, that on the issue before him all of this evidence was equivocal.

Jumbunna Coal Mine NL v Victorian Coal Miners' Association
(1908) 6 CLR 309

O'Connor J: [367] After an examination of all these sources of information as to the sense in which the word "industrial" in connection with labour disputes was used at the time of the passing of the Constitution, I have come to the conclusion that it was used in two senses – in the narrower sense contended for by the appellants, and in the broader sense contended for by the respondents. There is nothing in the Constitution to show that the word was intended to be used in the narrower sense. On the contrary, the scope and purpose of sub-sec xxxv would lead to an opposite conclusion. The use of the word in its wider sense does not offend against any prohibition of the Constitution, nor is it inconsistent with any of its provisions …

It was to remedy the evils of industrial disturbances extending beyond the territorial limits of any one State that the power in question was conferred. It must have been well known to the framers of the Constitution that such disturbances are not confined to industries connected directly or indirectly with manufacture or production. The case of cooks, stewards, waiters, hairdressers, are instances of trades which would not come within the narrower sense of the term "industry." Yet it is well known that unions existed in those trades long before the enactment of the Constitution. There seems to be nothing in the Constitution itself to indicate that the power conferred was intended to cover part only of the evils aimed at. The words used are large enough to cover all of them, and where it becomes a question of construing words used in conferring a power of that kind on the Commonwealth Parliament, it must always be remembered that we are interpreting a Constitution broad and **[368]** general in its terms, intended to apply to the varying conditions which the development of our community must involve.

For that reason, where the question is whether the Constitution has used an expression in the wider or in the narrower sense, the Court should, in my opinion, always lean to the broader interpretation unless there is something in the context or in the rest of the Constitution to indicate that the narrower interpretation will best carry out its object and purpose.

As to the definition of "industry" the judgments in the *Jumbunna Coal Case* were not unanimous: Isaacs J agreed with O'Connor J, but Griffith CJ (and perhaps Barton J) did not. In 1983, however, after a long historical detour, the approach of O'Connor J finally prevailed in *R v Coldham; Ex parte Australian Social Welfare Union (CYSS Case)* (1983) 153 CLR 297.

In other contexts, the judgment of O'Connor J in *Jumbunna Coal* has often been cited as a classic statement of the broad and constructive approach that constitutional interpretation requires. Another frequently cited passage is in *R v Public Vehicles Licensing Appeal Tribunal (Tas); Ex parte Australian National Airways Pty Ltd* (1964) 113 CLR 207, where the dictum of O'Connor J enabled the Court to say that powers vested in the Commonwealth by s 51 of the Constitution should be "**[225]** construed with all the generality which the words used admit".

None of the judgments quoted above is a neat unequivocal illustration of any one approach to constitutional interpretation: literalism, legalism and constitutionalism jostle one another indiscriminately as each judge tries to marshal arguments that give persuasive support to the conclusion at which he or she has arrived. Consider again the famous sentence from *McCulloch v Maryland* relied on in the *Jumbunna Coal Case*: "**[421]** Let the end be legitimate, let it be within the scope of the Constitution, and all means which are appropriate, which are plainly adapted to that end, which are not prohibited, but consist with the letter and spirit of the Constitution, are constitutional". Although this sentence is intended, as are the habitual quotations of it by later judges, to justify a broad view of constitutional power, the words "appropriate" and "adapted" might suggest quite a different judicial approach – that even when a law is clearly "within the scope of the Constitution", it may still be invalid if it is not sufficiently proportionate (that is, "appropriate" and "adapted") to its legislative purpose. While this may be an unorthodox reading of the passage from *McCulloch v Maryland*, it is a reading which in recent years has loomed large in Australian constitutional law, especially in relation to express or implied constitutional limits on legislative power (see Chapter 16, §8).

Another way of subverting the conventional rhetorical use of the passage in *McCulloch v Maryland* is to emphasise the word "spirit". In *Garcia v San Antonio Metropolitan Transit Authority*, 469 US 528 (1985), for example, Justice O'Connor quoted the famous sentence but italicised the words "and spirit", adding: "**[585]** It is not enough that the 'end be legitimate'; the means to that end chosen by Congress must not contravene the spirit of the Constitution". This reference to the "spirit" of the Constitution is itself double-edged. What Sandra O'Connor was arguing in the United States was very much what Richard O'Connor had argued in Australia 80 years earlier: namely, that the express grants of federal legislative power must be subject to an implied limitation protecting the integrity of the States. In short, she was invoking the "spirit" of the Constitution to *limit* what the national legislature could do. More frequently, the reference to "spirit" will be used to reinforce the more obvious rhetorical emphasis of *McCulloch v Maryland* and *Jumbunna Coal* – that is, to justify a broad view of national power in the interests of national government and of flexible adjustment over time. Ironically, that is how the "legalistic" approach of the *Engineers' Case* has also been used.

7. Further References

Booker, K, and Glass, A, "The *Engineers* Case" in Lee, HP, and Winterton, G (eds), *Australian Constitutional Landmarks* (Cambridge University Press, 2003), 34.

Cooray, LJM, and Ratnapala, S, "The High Court and the Constitution – Literalism and Beyond" in Craven, G (ed), *The Convention Debates: Commentaries, Indices and Guide* (Legal Books, 1986), 203.

Coper, M, and Williams, G (eds), *How Many Cheers for* Engineers? (Federation Press, 1997).

Craven, G, "The Crisis of Constitutional Literalism in Australia" in Lee, HP and Winterton, G, (eds), *Australian Constitutional Perspectives* (Law Book Co, 1992), 1.

Gageler, S, "Foundations of Australian Federalism and the Role of Judicial Review" (1987) 17 *Federal Law Review* 162.

Lindell, G, "Recent Developments in the Judicial Interpretation of the Australian Constitution" in Lindell, G (ed), *Future Directions in Australian Constitutional Law* (Federation Press, 1994), 1.

Parkinson, C, "The Early High Court and the Doctrine of Immunity of Instrumentalities" (2002) 13 *Public Law Review* 26.

Walker, G De Q, "The Seven Pillars of Centralism: *Engineer's* Case and Federalism" (2002) 76 *Australian Law Journal* 678.

Williams, G, "*Engineers* is Dead, Long Live the Engineers!" (1995) 17 *Sydney Law Review* 62.

Zines, L, *The High Court and the Constitution* (Butterworths, 4th ed 1997), Chapters 1, 17.

Chapter 8

Constitutional Interpretation

1. The Conduit Metaphor

In an influential analysis in 1979, Michael Reddy suggested that the common expressions we use to talk about meaning and communication import a misleading metaphor that he labelled "the conduit metaphor". To say that writing "is a way of conveying meaning", or to talk about "getting ideas across", or "capturing" or "packaging" ideas in words, implies that "**[287]** language transfers thought to others" using words as the "container, or conveyer". Difficulties in communication arise from defective packaging or from defective extraction, but typically the conduit metaphor leads us to blame the former: "**[289]** After all, receiving and unwrapping a package is so passive and so simple ... A package can be difficult or impossible to open. But, if it is undamaged, and successfully opened, who can fail to find the right things in it?"

Similarly, our common expressions import a powerful condemnation of those who "read things into" the text: "We must see the reader as having surreptitiously made use of his power to insert thoughts into words when he should have restricted himself purely to extraction. He sneaked those thoughts into the words himself, and then turned around and pretended that he found them there". To illustrate the fallacies involved, Reddy proposes an alternative metaphor.

Michael Reddy, "The Conduit Metaphor – A Case of Frame Conflict in Our Language about Language"
in Andrew Ortony (ed), *Metaphor and Thought* (Cambridge University Press, 1979), 284

[290] [T]he core expressions ... which constitute the "major framework" of the conduit metaphor ... imply, respectively, that: (1) language functions like a conduit, transferring thoughts bodily from one person to another; (2) in writing and speaking, people insert their thoughts or feelings in the words; (3) words accomplish the transfer by containing the thoughts or feelings and conveying them to others; and (4) in listening or reading, people extract the thoughts and feelings once again from the words ...

[292] In order to investigate the effect of the conduit metaphor on the thought processes of speakers of English, we need some alternate way of conceiving of human communication. We require another story to tell, another model, so that the deeper implications of the conduit metaphor can be drawn out by means of contrast ...

Imagine, if you will, for sake of the story, a huge compound, shaped like a wagon wheel ... Each pie-shaped sector of the wheel is an environment, with two spokes and part of the circumference forming the walls. The environments all have much in common with one another – water, trees, small plants, rocks, and the like – yet no two are exactly alike. They contain different kinds of trees, plants, terrain, and so on. Dwelling in each sector is one person who must survive in his own special environment. At the hub of the wheel there is some machinery which can deliver small sheets of paper from one environment to another. Let us suppose that the people in these environments have learned how to use this machinery to exchange crude sets of instructions with one another – instructions for making things helpful in surviving, such as tools, perhaps, or shelters, or foods, and the like. But there is, in this story, absolutely no way for the people to visit each other's environments, or even to exchange samples of the things they construct. This is crucial. The people can only exchange these crude sets of instructions – odd looking blueprints scratched on special sheets of paper that appear from a slot in the hub and can be deposited in another slot – and nothing more. Indeed, since there is no way to shout across the walls of the sectors, the people only know of one another's existence indirectly, by a cumulative series of inferences. This part of the story, the no visiting and no exchange of indigenous materials rule, we shall call the postulate of "radical subjectivity." ...

[293] Suppose that person A has discovered an implement that is very useful to him. Say he has learned to build a rake and finds he can use it to clear dead leaves and other debris without damaging the living plants. One day person A goes to the hub and draws as best he can three identical sets of instructions for fashioning this rake and drops these sets in the slots for persons B, C, and D. As a result, three people struggling along in slightly different environments now receive these curious sheets of paper, and each one goes to work to try to construct what he can from them. Person A's environment has a lot of wood in it, which is probably why he has leaves to rake in the first place. Sector B, on the other hand, runs more to rock, and person B uses a lot of rock in his constructions. He finds a piece of wood for the handle, but begins to make the head of the rake out of stone. A's original rake [294] head was wood. But since it never occurred to him that anything but wood would be available or appropriate, he did not try to specify wood for the head in his instructions. When B is about halfway finished with the stone rake head, he connects it experimentally to the handle and realizes with a jolt that this thing, whatever it is, is certainly going to be heavy and [unwieldy]. He ponders its possible uses for a time, and then decides that it must be a tool for digging up small rocks when you clear a field for planting. He marvels at how large and strong person A must be, and also at what small rocks A has to deal with. B then decides that two large prongs will make the rake both lighter and better suited to unearthing large rocks.

Quite happy with both his double-bladed rock-pick and his new ideas about what this fellow A must be like, person B makes three identical sets of instructions himself, for his rock-pick, and inserts them in the slots for A, C, and D. Person A, of course, now assembles a rock-pick following B's instructions, except that he makes it entirely of wood and has to change the design a little if a wooden, two-pronged head is to be strong enough. Still, in his largely rockless environment, he cannot see much use for the thing, and worries that person B has misunderstood his rake. So he draws a second set of more detailed instructions for the rake head, and sends them out to everyone. Meanwhile, over in another sector, person C, who is particularly interested in clearing out a certain swamp, has created, on the basis of these multiple sets of instructions – the hoe. After all, when you are dealing with swamp grass and muck, you need something that will slice cleanly through the roots ...

[T]he primary heroes of this story are persons A and B. We return now to them for the climax of the great rake conversation, in which, to everyone's surprise, some real communication takes place. A and B, who have had profitable interchanges in the past, and thus do not mind working quite hard at their communications, have been caught up in this rake problem for some time now. Their instructions simply will not agree. B has even had to abandon his original hypothesis that A is a huge man who has only small rocks to deal with. It just does not fit the instructions he is getting. A, on his side, is getting so frustrated that he is ready to quit. He sits down near the hub and, in a kind of absent-minded display of anger, grinds two pebbles together. Suddenly he stops. He holds these rocks up in front of his eyes and seems to be thinking furiously. Then he runs to the hub and starts scribbling new instructions as fast as he can, this time using clever iconic symbols for [295] rock and wood, which he hopes B will understand. Soon A and B are both ecstatic. All sorts of previous sets of instructions, not just about rakes, but about other things as well, now make perfect sense. They have raised themselves to a new plateau of inference about each other and each other's environments ...

[296] I do not want to argue too strongly either for or against either of these models in this paper … For the real question here is to what extent language can influence thought processes. To me, from my vantage point now, it seems that the toolmakers paradigm and radical subjectivism simply form a coherent, common-sense view of what happens when we talk … But if my major claim is true – that the conduit metaphor is a real and powerful semantic structure in English, which can influence our thinking – then it follows that "common sense" about language may be confused …

[308] [T]he conduit metaphor … objectifies meaning in a misleading and dehumanising fashion. It influences us to talk and think about thoughts as if they had the same kind of external, intersubjective reality as lamps and tables. Then, when this presumption proves dramatically false in operation, there seems to be nothing to blame except our own stupidity or malice …

[T]o the extent that the conduit metaphor does see communication as requiring some slight expenditure of energy, it localizes this expenditure almost totally in the speaker or writer. The function of the reader or listener is trivialized. The radical subjectivist paradigm, on the other hand, makes it clear that readers and listeners face a difficult and highly crea-**[309]**-tive task of reconstruction and hypothesis testing. Doing this work well probably requires considerably more energy than the conduit metaphor would lead us to expect.

Finally, Reddy considers expressions like: "You'll *find* better *ideas* than that *in the library*". These, he says, are "**[309]** derived from the conduit metaphor by a chain of metonymies".

[309] That is, we think of the ideas as existing in the words, which are clearly there on the pages. So the ideas are "there on the pages" by metonymy. Now the pages are in the books – and again, by metonymy, so are the ideas. But the books are in the libraries, with the final result that the ideas, too, are "in the libraries". The effect of this … is to suggest that the libraries, with their books, and tapes, and films, and photographs, are the real repositories of our culture …

Suppose now that we drop the conduit metaphor and think of this same situation in terms of the toolmakers paradigm. From this point of view, there are of course no ideas in the words, and therefore none in any books, nor on any tapes or records. There are no ideas whatsoever in any libraries. All that is stored in any of these places are odd little patterns of marks or bumps or magnetized particles capable of creating odd patterns of noise. Now, if a human being comes along who is capable of using these marks or sounds as instructions, then this human being may assemble within his head some patterns of thought or feeling or perception which resemble those of intelligent humans no longer living. But this is a difficult task, for these ones no longer living saw a different world from ours, and used slightly different language instructions. Thus, if this human who enters the library has not been schooled in the art of language …, and if he does not have a rather full and flexible repertoire of thoughts and feelings to draw from, then it is not likely that he will reconstruct in his head anything that deserves to be called "his cultural heritage."

Quite obviously, the toolmakers paradigm makes it plain that there is no culture in books or libraries, that, indeed, there is no culture at all unless it is reconstructed carefully and painstakingly in the living brains of each new generation. All that is preserved in libraries is the **[310]** mere opportunity to perform this reconstruction. But if the language skills and the habit of engaging in reconstruction are not similarly preserved, then there will be no culture, no matter how large and complete the libraries may become … The only way to preserve culture is to train people to rebuild it, to "regrow" it, as the word "culture" itself suggests, in the only place it can grow – within themselves.

The conduit metaphor has been pervasive in approaches to legal interpretation, including the interpretation of the Constitution. Theories that seek fidelity to the intentions of the framers, such as the various versions of "originalism", presuppose that a fixed and objective meaning has been packed into the text by those who wrote it, and that the task of the reader is to unpack that meaning. But many other approaches also assume that a predetermined meaning is buried in the text, and has simply to be disinterred. This includes the approach of Isaacs J in *Amalgamated Society of Engineers v Adelaide Steamship Co Ltd* (*Engineers Case*) (1920) 28 CLR 129, with its focus on the "**[151]** true meaning" of language. However, in his emphasis on reading the text "**[152]** in the light of the circumstances in which it was made, with knowledge of the combined fabric of the common law, and the statute law which preceded it", Isaacs J did acknowledge an environment which could infuse the text with meaning, and assist us to decipher its meaning. That environment was the shared tradition of the common law.

2. Legalism and Judicial Choice

"Legalism", at least in its narrower versions, perpetuates the simplistic idea that the pre-existing body of authoritative legal materials (in particular, the constitutional text and its encrustation with interpretive precedents) already contains a uniquely predetermined "right answer" to any legal problem; and that the task of the judge is to ascertain that uniquely predetermined answer by an essentially mechanical process. That idea is no longer tenable. Contemporary theories of constitutional interpretation that appeal to the intention of the framers ("originalism", "intentionalism" or "noninterpretivism"), at least in their more moderate versions, do not make such a claim. On the contrary, they recognise that the application of an old text to new problems may yield contradictory, inconclusive or indeterminate meanings from amongst which the judge must *choose*. Precisely because of that unavoidable need for judicial choice, they argue that the better choice (because it is the most nearly objective choice) will be that which proceeds from an attempt to discover the intention of the framers.

The curious combination of legal positivism and analytical jurisprudence that grew up around John Austin's *Lectures on Jurisprudence* after they were published posthumously by his widow in 1863 did not necessarily entail a denial of the creative or choice-making character of judicial decision-making. On the contrary, if the core idea of legal positivism is that law is that which is "posited" – that is, laid down by determinate human beings on determinate historical occasions – then such a doctrine should be receptive to the idea that propositions of "law", when announced in the course of a judge's decision, are necessarily fashioned by the judge as part of the creative process of making that decision. Austin's published lectures were littered with incomplete notes in which he tried to develop an adequate theory of "judicial legislation". Even in the lectures themselves, he complained of the tunnel vision that had trapped *Blackstone's Commentaries* in "[634] the childish fiction employed by our judges, that judiciary or common law is not made by them, but is a miraculous something made by nobody, existing, I suppose, from eternity, and merely *declared* from time to time by the judges". He insisted that judge-made law was in the fullest sense "law"; and that any doubts as to its democratic legitimacy could be overcome by vesting the appointment of judges "[643] in some party [644] or another whose interests do not conflict with those of the community at large". He also denied "that judicial legislators legislate arbitrarily".

John Austin, *Lectures on Jurisprudence*
(John Murray, 5th ed by Robert Campbell, 1885)

[645] Where subordinate judges subvert existing law, they commonly are doing that which the opinion of the community requires; to which the sovereign legislature expressly or tacitly consents; and which the sovereign legislature would do directly, if it cared sufficiently for the general interests, or were competent to the business of legislation …

[646] The truth is, that too great a respect for established rules, and too great a regard for consequence and analogy, has generally been shewn by the authors of judiciary law. Where the introduction of a new rule would interfere with interests and expectations which have grown out of established ones, it is clearly [647] incumbent on the Judge *stare decisis*; since it is not in his power to indemnify the injured parties. But it is much to be regretted that Judges of capacity, experience and weight, have not seized every opportunity of introducing a new rule (a rule beneficial for the future), whenever its introduction would have no such effect …

A striking example of this backwardness of Judges to innovate, is to be found in the origin of the distinction between law and equity; which arose because the Judges of the Common Law

Courts would not do what they ought to have done, namely to model their rules of law and of procedure to the growing exigencies of society, instead of stupidly and sulkily adhering to the old and barbarous usages.

For all this, given the ideological needs of lawyers and judges in the 1860s – and for several decades thereafter – what was attractive about Austin's attempt to locate the study of law in a systematic intellectual framework was precisely the hope it appeared to offer that the legal materials to be deployed as the basis for judicial decision might be reduced to a schematic body of expert "knowledge", from which predeterminate "correct" solutions to particular problems might be derived in a mechanical way. Legal problems were to have "single right answers"; and the task of judges was to *discover* those answers, not to *invent* them.

In Australia, the unusually early move to the teaching of law as a university discipline intensified these aspirations. By contrast, in the United States, the mythology of the judicial process as a value-free application of determinate pre-existing legal rules never had quite the same impact. Even the Austinian approach worked out differently. Thus John Chipman Gray, despairing of finding in the United States an Austinian "sovereign" whose commands would constitute "law", defined "law" instead by reference to the pronouncements of the judges.

John Chipman Gray, *The Nature and Sources of the Law*
(1909; 2nd ed by R Gray, Macmillan, 1921)

[121] [W]e have seen that the Law is made up of the rules for decision which the courts lay down; that all such rules are Law; that rules for conduct which the courts do not apply are not Law; that the fact that courts apply rules is what makes them Law; that there is no mysterious entity called "The Law" apart from these rules; and that the judges are rather the creators than the discoverers of the Law …

[125] It has been sometimes said that the Law is composed of two parts,– legislative law and judge-made law, but, in truth, all the Law is judge-made law. The shape in which a statute is imposed on the community as a guide for conduct is that statute as interpreted by the courts. The courts put life into the dead words of the statute. To quote again from Bishop Hoadly … : "Nay, whoever hath an *absolute authority* to *interpret* any written or spoken laws, it is *he* who is truly the *Law-giver* to all intents and purposes, and not the person who first wrote or spoke them."

Other factors in American legal history contributed to the relatively candid acceptance of the judges' responsibility for the shaping of social and legal policy. Not least among these factors was the flexible adaptation of the system of precedent to frontier conditions (see FG Kempin, "Precedent and Stare Decisis: The Critical Years, 1800 to 1850" (1959) 3 *American Journal of Legal History* 28). By 1908 Roscoe Pound had launched his famous attack on mechanical jurisprudence in "Mechanical Jurisprudence" (1908) 8 *Columbia Law Review* 605. By 1923 he had delivered his series of lectures on "The Theory of Judicial Decision" (1923) 36 *Harvard Law Review* 641, 802, 940, ending with a rallying call for greater judicial self-awareness as a step towards more adequate judicial performance: "[959] Much will be gained when courts have perceived what it is that they are doing, and are thus enabled to address themselves consciously to doing it the best that they may". By the 1930s "American legal realism" was in unrestrained ferment, particularly at the Law Schools of Columbia and Yale Universities (see William Twining, *Karl Llewellyn and the Realist Movement* (Weidenfeld & Nicolson, 1973)).

At the University of Sydney from 1942 to 1972, and thereafter at the University of New South Wales until 1985, Julius Stone translated these American perspectives into a systematic demonstration of the pervasive indeterminacy of legal materials (see *The Province and Function of Law* (Maitland Publications, 1946)). Stone's method was to demonstrate that the orthodox legalistic use of authoritative legal materials depends on "categories of illusory reference", the effect of which is that the judge's resort to legal doctrine *cannot* provide predetermined solutions to the problems of evaluative choice by which litigious outcomes must be determined, since what the legal materials do is precisely to confront the judge with the inescapable need for choice. Through ambiguities, indeterminate terms, logical circularities and contradictions, and above all through the constant presentation of alternative starting points, the judge is *required* to make personal choices in order to apply "the law". The central point is that, wherever a judge is driven to make a choice between two versions of "the law", that choice itself cannot be controlled or determined by "the law", but must ultimately depend on the judge's own sense of what "the law" *ought* to be. By mid-century, even in British countries, this kind of understanding of the judicial process had gained widespread academic and judicial acceptance. In Australia, the Sydney graduates who carried these teachings with them onto the High Court bench included Justices Mason, Jacobs, Murphy, Deane and Kirby (see Michael Kirby, "Julius Stone and the High Court of Australia" (1997) 20 *University of New South Wales Law Journal* 239 – and compare Dyson Heydon, "Judicial Activism and the Death of the Rule of Law", 47 *Quadrant* No 1 (January-February 2003) 9, with Michael Kirby, "Beyond the Judicial Fairy Tales", 48 *Quadrant* Nos 1-2 (January-February 2004) 26).

Yet even while that generation of judicial appointees was working out how a more candid acceptance of judicial responsibility for choice could be made operational, legal theory was taking a different turn. For lawyers clinging to the belief that certainty and objectivity might be attained through impersonal and rational law, the orthodox theories of the 1960s and 1970s offered a way of avoiding the full significance of "judicial discretion", or at least of relegating that significance (and that discretion) to occasional areas of "penumbral" uncertainty, or to "hard cases". The former kind of relegation was associated particularly with the work of HLA Hart (*The Concept of Law* (Clarendon Press, 1961, 2nd ed 1994)), the latter with the work of Ronald Dworkin ("The Model of Rules" (1967) 35 *University of Chicago Law Review* 14, reprinted in *Taking Rights Seriously* (Duckworth, 1977), 14-45).

Meanwhile, in the United States, the theoretical debate about the nature of the judicial process had increasingly been embroiled with political controversies surrounding the role of the United States Supreme Court, often under the opposing banners of "judicial activism" and "judicial self-restraint". Although the word "activism" had a respectable philosophical history, the use of it to characterise a particular type of judicial approach seems first to have become current in the 1940s, in response to the apparent judicial conflicts that emerged as the conservative Supreme Court majority of Franklin Roosevelt's first term as President (1932-36) was replaced during his second term (1936-40) by new appointees drawn largely from among the architects of President Roosevelt's "New Deal". In an influential magazine article published in 1947 ("The Supreme Court: 1947", *Fortune*, January 1947, Vol 35, No 1, 73, 201), historian Arthur M Schlesinger Jr contrasted "the judicial activists" with the "champions of self-restraint". He concluded: "[212] The conflict on the Court, if it can be restrained from intellectual and personal extremes, may lead to a debate in the most fruitful tradition of American political thought. The tension between self-denial and activism is a historic element in our judicial system. Its wise resolution could easily make this Court, with its remarkable abilities and its agreement on a wide range of constitutional fundamentals, one of the great creative Courts of history". (See also CH Pritchett, *The Roosevelt Court: A Study in Judicial Politics and Values, 1937-1947* (Macmillan, 1948), 277-87.)

The Supreme Court's "activism" in the 1950s in matters of civil and political rights led to new calls for judicial decisions based on "neutral principles" (see Herbert Wechsler, "Towards Neutral Principles of Constitutional Law" (1959) 73 *Harvard Law Review* 1). In 1963 Martin Golding replied that what was needed was not the discovery of some mother-lode of objective "principles", but the practice of an intellectual method of "principled decision-making".

Martin Golding, "Principled Decision-Making and the Supreme Court"
(1963) 63 *Columbia Law Review* 35

[42] Principled legal judgment is not so much a matter of content as it is of form. Neutrality and generality are to be found not in the content of the law but in its application or administration ...

[43] A legal system, then, may broadly fix the starting-points of deliberation and the criteria of relevant distinctions. It is the lesson of American jurisprudence that this fixity has its limits and that

a degree of discretion is inevitable. But we still demand that, so far as possible, courts be principled in their exercises of this discretion. This applies with greatest force to the Supreme Court when it has constitutional questions before it. Lower courts often have no choice once the higher courts have spoken ... But the Supreme Court, when ruling on constitutional issues, has no higher guide than the Constitution itself. Of course, there are times when "the relative compulsion of the language of the Constitution, of history and precedent" do combine to make the answer clear; but frequently they do not. Professor Wechsler maintains, and I agree, that the due process clauses ought to be read as "a compendious affirmation of the basic values of a free society ..." Furthermore, it is possible to overstate the specificity of other provisions of the Bill of Rights ... They, too, must be read as "an affirmation of the special values they embody rather than as statements of a finite rule of law ...". Constitutional interpretation by the Supreme Court, then, most closely approximates moral decision-making; and when it is principled it will rest "on reasons with respect to all the issues in the case, reasons that in their generality and neutrality transcend any immediate result that is involved".

The "neutral principles" debate, and others that have followed it, have not necessarily sought to deny the inevitable reality of "judicial legislation", nor even to deny that the vigorous exploitation of that reality through judicial "activism" may sometimes be appropriate. Rather, precisely because of the broad recognition that judging invariably *does* and *must* involve an element of personal choice (and responsibility for choice), the more thoughtful contributions have sought to develop criteria and guidelines helping judges to think self-consciously about when or whether or how or how far, in what circumstances and with what justification, the impact of creative judicial decision should be maximised, and when it should rather be minimised. Such contributions have recognised that the choice between "activism" and "judicial self-restraint" is itself one of the inescapable policy choices that a judge must make. For some judges, it may even be the decisive choice by which more particular value-judgments on individual cases will be overshadowed or predetermined. For others, competing value-conceptions of the judicial role will merely play their part among all the values that must somehow be taken into account in seeking the most appropriate solution for any particular case.

When contemporary theories of judicial decision-making seek to influence this aspect of judgment, they do so in many different ways and at many different levels. They may seek to establish persuasive arguments for judicial self-restraint, or suggest strategies by which to achieve it; or they may seek principled justifications for judicial activism – so that, within the limits thus indicated, "activism" will be legitimate, while elsewhere it will be eschewed.

The different versions of "originalism" discussed in §3 below are essentially strategies of this kind: at least in their more moderate forms, they seek to *acknowledge* but also to *limit* the interpretive role of the judge. Another group of popular strategies is clustered around the idea of "proceduralism": the argument is that, in a democracy, judicial "activism" *cannot* legitimately be deployed in the service of substantive social and political values, but *can* legitimately be deployed in defence of the social and political procedures by which our conflicts over substantive values are managed. The immediate source for most versions of "proceduralism" is the work of John Hart Ely (1938-2003), especially in his book *Democracy and Distrust* (Harvard University Press, 1980). Its roots go back to Paul Freund's conception of "representative self-government" (*The Supreme Court of the United States* (World Publishing Co, 6th ed 1967), 81-2), or before that to the second paragraph of a "famous footnote" initially appended to a United States Supreme Court opinion in 1938, and later sometimes invoked as a checklist of three different types of case which might justify judicial "activism".

United States v Carolene Products Co
304 US 144 (1938)

Stone J: [152 n 4] There may be narrower scope for operation of the presumption of constitutionality when legislation appears on its face to be within a specific prohibition of the Constitution, such as those of the first ten amendments ...

It is unnecessary to consider now whether legislation which restricts those political processes which can ordinarily be expected to bring about repeal of undesirable legislation, is to be subjected to more exacting judicial scrutiny ... than are most other types of legislation ...

Nor need we inquire whether similar considerations enter into the review of statutes directed at particular religions ... or national ... or racial minorities ...: whether prejudice against discrete and insular minorities may be a special condition, which tends seriously to curtail the operation of those political processes ordinarily to be relied upon to protect minorities, and which may call for a correspondingly more searching judicial inquiry.

A recurrent objection to "proceduralism" is that its essential distinction between substantive and procedural values cannot in fact be sustained. A recurrent objection to "originalism" is that the "original intention" it seeks may not be historically recoverable, and may never have existed in any unequivocal form. Moreover, while "originalism" is proposed as a way of ensuring objectivity, its critics contend that it sometimes masks a conservative political agenda. In 1987 this perception contributed both to the nomination of the leading "originalist" Robert Bork to the United States Supreme Court, and to the defeat of the nomination by a hostile Senate Committee.

Stripped of their particular resonance in American political debates, these and other contemporary "isms" can usefully remind us of factors that judges faced with the difficult exercise of judicial power may sometimes properly take into account, or strategies they may sometimes usefully follow. Yet their presentation as "isms" should be treated with caution. Just as the authoritative legal materials can never provide a reliable algorithm by which to be sure of discovering "correct" responses to judicial problems, so no single theory or "ism" can yield such an algorithm either. In the end the difficulties of judgment must simply be met head on.

Daniel Farber, "The Originalism Debate: A Guide for the Perplexed"
(1989) 49 *Ohio State Law Journal* 1085

[1103] The real problem may be that both sides have demanded too much. We may have to be content with an approach to constitutional law that leaves some room for judicial discretion while attempting to channel that discretion. In other words, the real problem may not be that originalism is less desirable than some other global theory of constitutional law, but that no global theory can work. If so, we might do better to abandon the attempt to create a theory of constitutional interpretation, and get on with the business of actually interpreting the Constitution. Perhaps, in other words, constitutional interpretation is best thought of as an activity that one can do well or poorly, rather than as an application of some explicit general theory.

3. The Intention of the Framers

Insofar as the "legalism" of the *Engineers' Case* depended on treating the Constitution as an Act of the Imperial Parliament, to be interpreted like any other statute, it was merely reiterating the basic approach that had dominated the High Court's work from the outset. The earliest formulation concerned the transitional arrangements surrounding the Commonwealth's assumption of exclusive responsibility for customs and excise duties under s 90.

Section 89 provided that *before* the new uniform Commonwealth customs duties were introduced, the Commonwealth should make monthly payments to each State of all "revenues collected therein by the Commonwealth" (after deduction of specified Commonwealth expenditures in or for the State, calculated in part on a population basis). Section 93 provided that for five years *after* the imposition of uniform duties of customs ("and thereafter until the Parliament otherwise provides"), the same monthly payments should continue – provided that, for goods taxed in one State but "afterwards passing into another State for consumption", the relevant customs or excise duty "shall be taken to have been collected not in the former but in the latter State". Goods which *before* the imposition of uniform duties of customs were imported into Victoria or manufactured there had attracted customs and excise duties (respectively) which were duly collected by the Commonwealth (using the old Victorian tariff) and credited to Victoria under s 89. But *after* the imposition of uniform duties of customs, goods imported into or manufactured in Victoria (involving a total credit in respect of customs and excise duties of £12,000) were shipped to Tasmania. Tasmania argued that it was now entitled to the relevant credits, on the basis that s 93 was intended to continue the colonial system of "drawbacks" – by which, when goods imported into one colony were subsequently shipped to another colony and attracted customs duty there, the customs duty incurred in the former colony was remitted. The argument was put to the Court by Patrick Glynn, himself a member of the judiciary committee at the 1897 Convention that drafted the Constitution. The argument failed, as did his attempt to rely on the records of debate at the Convention.

Tasmania v Commonwealth and Victoria
(1904) 1 CLR 329

PM Glynn (in argument): [333] The principle contemplated by the Constitution is that duties should be credited to the State of consumption of the goods on which the duties were paid. The object of secs 89-93 was to carry out that principle with the least loss of revenue, and the least disturbance of the old conditions, under which that result was brought about by the system of drawbacks … An examination of the draft bills prepared by the different conventions supports the contention of the plaintiff.

EF Mitchell KC (for Victoria): Is the plaintiff entitled to refer to those drafts for the purpose of interpreting the Constitution?

Griffith CJ: We think that as matter of history of legislation the draft bills which were prepared under the authority of the Parliaments of the several States may be referred to. That will cover the draft bills of 1891, 1897, and 1898. But the expressions of opinion of members of the Conventions should not be referred to …

PM Glynn: [334] Admitting for argument that there is an ambiguity, it may be solved by reference to existing usage, to other constitutions, to every one of the draft bills, and to other parts of the Constitution itself … The policy carried out under the system of drawbacks must be assumed to have been intended to be continued … **[335]** There is no break in the policy of drawbacks, and there should be none in crediting duties to the States of consumption.

Griffith CJ: That would be all very well if the Constitution had said so.

PM Glynn: If the Constitution has said the contrary, it is departure from previous policy or a *casus omissus*. On constitutional principles there should be no injustice done. The Constitution is only a declaration of principles for guidance. The draft bill of 1891, clauses 4 and 9, gave all that Tasmania claims here. So does clause 91(3) of the draft bill of 1897.

Barton J: That was abandoned before being put into form by the draftsmen.

PM Glynn: It was the deliberate judgment of the Convention as to that for which the plaintiff now contends.

Griffith CJ: We have to decide what the legislature means by what it has now said. There has been a change in the language, and therefore the argument from the draft bill of 1891 is against the plaintiffs. These tentative drafts do not affect the construction of the final form.

PM Glynn: As to the principles applicable to the interpretation of a Constitution, see *Black's Constitutional Law*, 2nd ed, p 67. The construction of sec 93 contended for is a possible one, and, if more than one construction is possible, Tasmania is entitled to that which is more liberal and will carry out the intention of the framers of the Constitution.

The Court held that the opening words of s 93 ("During the first five years after the imposition of uniform duties of customs …") governed the whole of the section, so that the reference to customs duties "chargeable" in the State of first importation applied only to duties that became so "chargeable" *after* the critical date. All three judges also elaborated on the above exchange.

Griffith CJ: [338] We were invited by Mr Glynn to apply, in construing the Constitution, some higher rule of construction; to look beyond the letter of the Constitution; to adopt something which would commend itself to our minds as being a principle of abstract justice, and if possible to read the Constitution in conformity with that principle. Before stating the reasons which to my mind entirely dispose of the matter, I will refer to some rules which have been laid down for the interpretation of Acts of Parliament, for this Constitution is an Act of Parliament. It is said that the ordinary rules for construing Acts of Parliament do not apply to the Constitution. That proposition may be true in one sense, viz, that the Constitution is not a code going into minute details of the means by which the federation is to be carried into effect by the sovereign power created by it. There are many powers necessary to that end which are conferred – and one would expect them to be conferred – by necessary implication rather than in express words. It is, however, always a question of construction, whether we are called upon to construe the terms of a section, or to decide whether powers are necessarily to be implied in addition to those which are expressed. The same rules of interpretation apply that apply to any other written document …

[339] I propose to refer to two authorities only as to the rules of construction. The first is a passage in the opinion of the Judges given to the House of Lords in the *Sussex Peerage Case*, (1844) 11 Cl & F 85, at p 143 [8 ER 1034 at 1057]. Lord Chief Justice *Tindal*, delivering the opinion of the Judges, says:– "My Lords, the only rule for the construction of Acts of Parliament is, that they should be construed according to the intent of the Parliament which passed the Act. If the words of the Statute are in themselves precise and unambiguous, then no more can be necessary than to expound those words in their natural and ordinary sense. The words themselves alone do in such a case best declare the intention of the law-giver." The other passage I will read from the speech of Lord Selborne in *Hardy v Fothergill*, (1888) 13 App Cas, 351, at p 358:– "It is not, I conceive, for your Lordships, or for any other Court, to decide such a question as this under the influence of considerations of policy, except so far as that policy may be apparent from, or at least consistent with, the language of the legislature in the Statute or Statutes upon which the question depends." …

Mr Glynn referred to the proposal made in 1891, which, if adopted, would have given Tasmania exactly what he says his clients claim in this case. After that, other schemes were proposed, and finally the scheme was adopted which is found in the Constitution. It is manifest that whatever scheme was adopted was a purely arbitrary rule. One was finally adopted, and what that is is is to be ascertained from the language [340] of the Constitution, and all we have to do is to interpret that language. Some other scheme might have been adopted which some persons might think fairer, but that is a matter of opinion. The judges as to what was the fairest and best scheme were the people, by whom the Constitution was adopted, and the question is not one for our decision. We have merely to ascertain from the language used what was the scheme adopted, and to give effect to it.

Barton J: [358] I have nothing to add except that I can understand the hardship which Tasmania thinks she has suffered, and I can sympathise with her. There is no Act of Parliament for the displacement of old conditions and the substitution of new ones, which can be so applied as to prevent hardship. The Constitution does not differ from other Statutes in that respect. It cannot go further than to lay down broad principles. Hardship must arise, and if the Constitution had attempted to deal with details, the result would possibly have been to create more hardships. We have no right, however, in this Court to submit our judgment to be influenced by any such consideration. We have to declare what seems to us to be the proper meaning of the language, and we are to arrive at that meaning by reference to the words themselves and to the history of the law.

O'Connor J: [358] I concur in the judgments which have just been delivered. I do not think it can be too strongly stated that our duty in interpreting a Statute is to declare and administer the law according to the intention expressed in the Statute itself. In this respect the Constitution differs in no way from any Statute of the Commonwealth or of a State. In his very able argument for Tasmania, Mr Glynn seemed to me rather to [359] reverse the position in which considerations in the interpretation of a Statute are to be applied. He laid down some general principles of what he described as ethics – international or inter-State ethics – and he asked us to say that the interpretation of the Constitution must be based on those principles. It appears to me the only safe rule is to look at the Statute itself, and to gather from it what is its intention. If we depart from that rule we are apt to run the risk of the danger described by *Pollock*, CB, in *Miller v Salomons*, (1852) 7 Ex, 475, at p 560. "If," he says, "the meaning of the language be plain and clear, we have nothing to do but to obey it – to administer it as we find it; and, I think, to take a different course is to abandon the office of Judge, and to assume the province of legislation." Some passages were cited by Mr Glynn from *Black on the Interpretation of Laws* [*sic*], which seem to imply that there might be a difference in the rules of interpretation to be applied to the Constitution and those to be applied to any other Act of Parliament, but there is no foundation for any such distinction. The intention of the enactment is to be gathered from its words. If the words are plain, effect must be given to them; if they are doubtful, the intention of the legislature is to be gathered from the other provisions of the Statute aided by a consideration of surrounding circumstances. In all cases in order to discover the intention you may have recourse to contemporaneous circumstances – to the history of the law, and you may gather from the instrument itself the object of the legislature in passing it. In considering the history of the law, you may look into previous legislation, you must have regard to the historical facts surrounding the bringing the law into existence. In the case of a Federal Constitution the field of inquiry is naturally more extended than in the case of a State Statute, but the principles to be applied are the same. You may deduce the intention of the legislature from a consideration of the instrument itself in the light of these facts and circumstances, but you cannot go beyond it. If that limitation is to be applied in the interpretation of an ordinary Act of Parliament, it should at least be as stringently applied in the interpretation of an instrument of this kind, which not only is a statutory enactment, but also embodies **[360]** the compact by which the people of the several colonies of Australia agreed to enter into an indissoluble union.

While these judgments permitted limited recourse to the "legislative history" of the Constitution (in the form of the earlier drafts considered by the Conventions of the 1890s), they did not permit any reference to what had been said in the Convention Debates (see also *Municipal Council of Sydney v Commonwealth* (1904) 1 CLR 208 at 213). That continued to be the position until 1988. Thus, in *Attorney-General (Cth); Ex Rel McKinlay v Commonwealth* (1975) 135 CLR 1, Barwick CJ spoke of the "**[17]** settled doctrine in Australia that the records of the discussions in the Conventions and in the legislatures of the colonies will not be used as an aid to the construction of the Constitution".

Despite the strict embargo on reference to the Convention Debates, the High Court did allow the use of other historical material, such as the drafts of the Constitution. It also permitted reference to John Quick and Robert Garran, *The Annotated Constitution of the Australian Commonwealth* (Angus & Robertson, 1901; repr Legal Books, 1995), a detailed contemporary commentary on the drafting of the Constitution that makes extensive use of the Convention Debates. Hence, the Court was prepared to use secondary material – the accuracy of which has sometimes been questioned – but not the primary material upon which the secondary material itself relied. At the hearing of *Strickland v Rocla Concrete Pipes Ltd* (*Concrete Pipes Case*) (1971) 124 CLR 468, a case on the interpretation of s 51(xx) of the Constitution, the denial of use of the Convention Debates led to the following exchange (as extracted in Leslie Zines, "Book Review" (1972) 5 *Federal Law Review* 158 at 159-60).

Strickland v Rocla Concrete Pipes Ltd (*Concrete Pipes Case*)
(Transcript of Argument, High Court of Australia)

JF Lyons (in argument): Your Honour, with respect, I know we are not permitted to construe para (xx) by reference to what is in the convention debates, but the convention debates show – this is the only way I can answer your Honour's question – that it was not so much that the framers thought that special problems arose out of trading and financial corporations, but that they originally had all corporations and they wished to exclude special kinds …
Windeyer J: Then it was made trading, I think, and then financial was added at one of the conventions.
Mr Lyons: Yes, they were; those words were inserted, your Honour, and "financial", because …
Walsh J: If you were looking at this ground which you say is probably impermissible, this historical thing …
Mr Lyons: I did not say historical is impermissible, your Honour, I …

Walsh J: You get that the earlier form of it was that it related to status, then they changed it.

Mr Lyons: Yes. I said it was impermissible to look at the convention debates, your Honour, but not impermissible to look at surrounding statutory history which ...

Owen J: What if they change the status quo? I suppose that is an impermissible question.

Mr Lyons: Certainly it is the fact, your Honour, that it is first said ...

Owen J: Do not answer it; it is quite irrelevant ...

RJ Ellicott QC: My friend Mr Lyons did refer to the convention debates as if they might support the view for which he contended. That reference, of course, was not permissible; but all I want to say is that if they were looked at, one would find the contrary.

Menzies J: That, too, is impermissible.

Mr Ellicott: No doubt your Honours will not look at them.

Similarly, in *Brown v The Queen* (1986) 160 CLR 171, Dawson J used the formula: "**[214]** It is apparent even without reference to the Convention Debates ..." (which he then proceeded to cite). On the other hand, Wilson J at 189 referred to the Debates directly.

The unanimous decision in *Cole v Whitfield* (1988) 165 CLR 360 marked a break from this restrictive tradition. Although a full record of the Convention Debates had always been available, it may not be a coincidence that in 1986 a fully re-edited and indexed version of the Debates had been published (see Gregory Craven (ed), *The Convention Debates 1891-1898: Commentaries, Indices and Guide* (Legal Books, 1986), 6 vols). In *Cole v Whitfield*, the Court reinterpreted s 92 of the Constitution with the aid of the Convention Debates (see also *New South Wales v Commonwealth* (*Incorporation Case*) (1990) 169 CLR 482). The Court held that regard could be had to the history of a section of the Constitution, including the relevant Convention Debates, "**[385]** for the purpose of identifying the contemporary meaning of language used, the subject to which that language was directed and the nature and objectives of the movement toward federation"; but not "for the purpose of substituting for the meaning of the words used the scope and effect – if such could be established – which the founding fathers subjectively intended the section to have".

To that limited extent, the High Court has opened the way to the interpretive approach much debated in the United States in recent years under the name of "originalism" – that is, the attempt to discover the meaning of the constitutional text, not by looking exclusively to the "intention" to be gathered *from the text itself* by traditional methods of statutory interpretation, but by looking to historical evidence of what was in fact the intention of the framers.

Greg Craven, "Original Intent and the Australian Constitution – Coming Soon to a Court Near You?"
(1990) 1 *Public Law Review* 166

[167] The term "original intent" is one much bandied about in the United States, but it is also one which is difficult to define satisfactorily ... However, the kernel of the theory undeniably lies in that mystic incantation "fidelity to the framers". At least in its purer forms, a theory of original intent takes as its starting point the proposition that, in interpreting a written constitution, the sacred and supreme duty of the judiciary is to ascertain the intentions of those who wrote that document, and to give effect faithfully to those intentions. Regardless of such questions as the level of generality at which the relevant intent is to be ascertained, it is ultimately the notion that the wishes of the Founders are paramount that lies at the heart of original intent. This "pure" expression **[168]** of originalism might conveniently be referred to as "overriding originalism" ...

[T]he ultimate duty of a fundamentally "originalist" court will be to find the intention of the framers of the Constitution. This duty will transcend any lesser question of judicial or interpretative methodology. Accordingly, a judge who is genuinely committed to a theory of original intent – or at least to a position of what has been described here as overriding originalism – is unlikely to view the bare words of the constitution which he or she is applying as ultimately controlling. To such a judge, the intention of the founders is the grail: the words of the constitution will be an indispensable tool in discerning that intention, but they will not be the only tool, and in the event that a judge is satisfied (for whatever reason and by whatever process) that the words in question do not truly reflect the intentions of the Framers, then that judge will be duty-bound to give effect to the intention over the words …

[I]t is clear that there is room for shades of originalism, and for degrees of judicial commitment to originalism. While overriding originalism undoubtedly represents the theory in its purest and least compromising form, more timid constitutional souls might well attach themselves to some less unyielding version. For example, one might adopt the stance that, where the words of a constitution are absolutely plain, originalism has no role to play, or, to put the matter more accurately, that in such circumstances the intent of the Framers is conclusively conveyed by those words, but that in the case of "ambiguity" the extrinsically ascertained original intent is controlling. Lest it be thought that such a position varies little from more traditional notions of constitutional construction, it should be stressed that anyone prepared to go so far along the road of original intent would be unlikely to hesitate in discerning ambiguity in broad constitutional provisions, and so bringing the intention of the Framers into play. The plain truth is that many, if not most, constitutional provisions are sufficiently ambiguous as to admit of the requisite degree of doubt, and generations of Australian High Court Judges who could not imagine how their brethren could be so mistaken on the meaning of this or that provision bear eloquent testimony to this fact. Thus, even what may be referred to as "modified originalism" has a profound tendency to dethrone the bare words of the Constitution.

[169] It may be conceded at the outset that any debate over original intent is unlikely to be quite as fierce in Australia as it has been – and doubtless will continue to be – in the United States. The reason for this is clear. The originalism debate in the United States has largely been fought over the interpretation of the Bill of Rights, with its broad, sweeping guarantees of fundamental human rights. It is in this highly emotive context, the stalking-ground of rights to abortion and freedom from racial discrimination, that the performance of the Supreme Court has been vilified or defended according to the stance of commentators upon the question of original intent. The Australian Constitution does not include a bill of rights, and so the High Court has not been called upon to deploy its interpretive armoury in so controversial a field …

This is not to say that the High Court's constitutional methodology has been entirely free from controversy. However, such controversy as has arisen has generally concerned the effect of the Court's interpretative techniques upon the comparatively dry and arcane subject of federalism, rather than upon human rights which are the object of intense and widespread popular and political concern. Yet even within the confines of this comparatively restrained constitutional debate there have been commentators who have levelled harsh criticisms at the Court, accusing it of adopting methods of constitutional interpretation which have subverted the intentions of the Founding Fathers for a strongly federal nation, and instead delivered the States bound hand and foot into the crushing embrace of the Commonwealth …

[177] [A] basic case for original intent … would begin something along these lines: words, including the words of a constitution, are mere tools of communication to convey the intentions of those from whom they emanate. Naturally, words are imperfect, and therefore may imperfectly convey intention. When this occurs in a constitutional context, as in any other, the imperfect words should not prevail over the intention: rather, the intention, however it is to be discovered, should overcome the deficient words. Words are the servants of intention, not the other way around …

Those who framed the Constitution were the elected representatives of the Australian colonies and their peoples chosen for the specific purpose of drawing up a federal constitution. These men were the authors of the Constitution, its words are their words, and those words were selected by them for the sole purpose of conveying their intentions concerning the federal compact which they were drafting. Their debates and deliberations were public and published. Their [178] wider activities were heavily publicised, and were followed and discussed by the public at large. Finally, with full knowledge, the populations of the colonies ratified the acts of their agents and adopted the Constitution which they had drafted, a Constitution which (as stated above) consists of nothing more than words chosen by the Framers to reflect their intentions. Accordingly, it is the duty of the courts to give effect to the intentions of the Founders, as these intentions are ultimately backed by the last authentic democratic expression of the will of the Australian people on the subject of their constitutional dispositions. Of course, some of these dispositions may be overtaken by time, and may be in need of change. But, in this eventuality, that change will also be democratically achieved in accordance with the vision of the Founders themselves, under s 128, and not pursuant to some ukase from the Court …

[182] [T]here are at least three reasons why original intent is a more plausible theory in relation to the Australian Constitution than the American.

First, both the process by which the Australian Founders were appointed, and the process by which the result of their labours was ratified, were far more founded in democratic principle than were their equivalents in the United States. The constitutional legitimacy of the intentions of our Founders is correspondingly strengthened. Secondly, it is far easier to determine the intentions of Framers operating 90 years ago than it is in the case of those whose views are almost two centuries old. The record of the framing of the Australian Constitution is far more accessible than that of the United States Constitution; it is also considerably easier for us to place ourselves in the position of our own great-grandparents than it is to stand in the shoes of their great-grandparents.

Thirdly, and on a purely pragmatic level, the ends to which literalism and progressivism have been put by the High Court are far less attractive than those to which the expansive interpretation of the United States Constitution has been directed by the Supreme Court … The most spectacularly non-originalist interpretations of the Supreme Court (at least in recent times) have been aimed at securing fundamental human rights, so that however much one might deplore the methodology one may still be very much inclined to applaud the practical results. In Australia, the High Court has, in the main, departed from the intentions of the Framers merely for the purpose of reallocating power from the regions to the centre, and has been extremely timid in using its powers of interpretation to "recognise" human rights. Indeed, the willingness of the Court to interpret the Constitution broadly in the interest of extending Commonwealth power stands in stark and even disturbing contrast to its nervous unwillingness to apply the same free-wheeling standards of interpretation for the purpose of implying fundamental freedoms …

[183] In all probability, original intent will appeal most to those who wish to turn back the tide of judicial interpretation favouring the enlargement of Commonwealth power. In contrast to most American originalists, such persons are not necessarily activated by social conservatism: federalism as a political concept may be conservative, radical, or anything in between. Since *Engineers* [(1920) 28 CLR 129], judges, counsel and commentators of this persuasion have been playing a losing constitutional hand, seeing themselves as being forced to operate within the literalist construct for fear of being labelled as adherents of "reserved powers", when the very acceptance of literalism virtually concludes the issue against them in advance. To such constitutional lawyers, original intent would present the possibility of a new game with new rules, one in which they may not win, but might at least break even.

Jeffrey Goldsworthy has argued for a form of "moderate" originalism – which would look to the founders' intentions only insofar as they are ascertainable from publicly available evidence; would give primacy to the founders' conception of the principles and purposes adopted, but not necessarily of their application to particular factual contexts; and would recognise that, where evidence of their intentions is ambiguous or inconclusive, there may still be a legitimate role for the creative judicial process.

Jeffrey Goldsworthy, "Originalism in Constitutional Interpretation"
(1997) 25 *Federal Law Review* 1

[20] Moderate originalism differs from, and is superior to, extreme versions of originalism for three important reasons. First, it holds that the meaning of the Constitution depends on evidence of the founders' intentions which in 1900 was readily available to their intended audience, but not on other evidence of their intentions … The meaning of a law, like that of any other utterance, is something public, not hidden …

Second, moderate originalism holds that only the founders' "enactment intentions" are relevant to the meaning of the Constitution, and not their "application intentions". The object is to clarify the meaning of the provisions which they enacted, and not to discover their beliefs about how those provisions ought to be applied. Those beliefs are not part of the Constitution and have no legal status. Our system of government is based on the principle of the separation of powers, including the independence of the judiciary: law-makers enact the law, and judges apply it according to its true meaning, regardless of the law-makers' opinions or preferences. In addition, the law-makers' beliefs about how their law ought to be applied may be erroneous: they are not infallible authorities when it comes to interpreting and applying their own laws ... Lord Halsbury went so far as to assert that the worst person to construe a statute is the person who drafted it, because "he is very much disposed to confuse what he intended to do with the effect of the language which in fact has been employed" [*Hilder v Dexter* [1902] AC 474 at 477].

Third, moderate originalism concedes that resort to the founders' intentions cannot answer all, or probably even most, interpretative disputes of the kind which appellate courts are required to resolve. It holds that interpretation begins with an examination of all relevant evidence of the law-makers' intentions, but not that, in difficult cases, it very often ends there. If relevant evidence of those intentions does not resolve a dispute, then judges may be forced to act creatively, and after considering matters such as consistency with general legal doctrines and principles, public policy, and justice, stipulate what the disputed provision should thenceforth be taken to mean. They must [21] settle the dispute: they cannot wash their hands of it and leave the parties to fight it out in the street. Furthermore, when judges act creatively in this way, they are free to take into account contemporary concepts and values. Some of the traditional maxims and presumptions of statutory interpretation can possibly be understood as contributing to this creative process, rather than to the logically prior cognitive process of discovering a statute's pre-existing meaning ...

[T]he most persuasive arguments ... against originalism are either aimed at what I call extreme originalism, rather than moderate originalism, or are inapplicable to the Australian context ...

[25] Some of the arguments made against originalism in the United States are applicable in Australia, but these tend to be weak. One is that the very idea of a collective legislative intention is incoherent or fictional. This argument is surely impossible to sustain. The idea of a collective intention is not, of course, that there can exist an ontologically queer "group mind", which somehow transcends the individual minds of the members of the group. It is simply that people collectively engaged in a co-operative enterprise can knowingly hold the same or interrelated intentions with respect to it. As the eminent American philosopher John Searle recently put it, "[I]t seems obvious that there really is collective intentional behaviour as distinct from individual intentional behaviour. You can see this by watching a football team execute a pass play or hear it by listening to an orchestra" ...

The enactment of the Constitution does raise special difficulties. What group of people are we talking about? Who were "the founders" whose intentions are relevant: the members of the various Conventions which drafted it, the voters who endorsed it in referendums as a condition precedent to its enactment, the members of the Imperial Parliament which enacted it, or all of them? Without attempting a comprehensive analysis, I would suggest the following. The Imperial Parliament played a purely formal role, enacting the Constitution as it had been drafted and endorsed by voters in Australia (except for amendments to s 74 dealing with Privy Council appeals ...). Its role was analogous to that of the monarch in assenting to Bills: to rubber stamp proposed laws prepared by other people to serve their purposes, and therefore embodying their intentions.

[26] As for choosing between those who drafted and debated the Constitution, and the voters who approved it, very often no choice is necessary, because our evidence of the original intention applies equally to both: for example, evidence concerning the meaning of words in 1900, or beliefs and values which were widely shared at the time ... As Richard Kay puts it:

> [I]t will be enough in most cases to learn what people, at the time, *generally* meant when they used certain language and what people involved in the process of enactment thought was at issue. A presumption that the majority adopting a measure shared that intention is reasonable unless evidence to the contrary is adduced.

Moreover, even if it is not possible ... to choose between two alternative meanings, it will *always* be possible to rule out at least some other meanings, which might otherwise be logically open, on the ground that it is inconceivable that they would have been generally entertained in 1900 ...

[27] Another superficially plausible argument against originalism is that no good reason can be given for today's generation being ruled by "the dead hand of the past", rather than by its own principles and values. The argument loses its plausibility when it is realised that it is really an argument against having a constitution, or indeed any law, at all, since it is of the essence of law that decisions are governed by norms laid down in the past. Taken to its logical extreme, it is an argument not only that judges should ignore the law, but also that everyone else should ignore the judges, who owe their authority to laws laid down by "the dead hand of the past". This would, of course, be a disaster. A constitution laid down by a founding generation empowers as well as restricts subsequent generations, by providing them with the incalculable benefits of an established and accepted set of procedures for making collective decisions binding on all their members. The empowerment conferred by such procedures is inseparable from the restrictions which they impose: they are two sides of the same coin. If some attempt to evade the restrictions, others may be tempted to follow suit, leading eventually to the collapse of the constitution and the loss of the empowerment it provided.

Today's generation of Australians is not restricted by the dead hand of the past in any invidious sense, because the Constitution can be altered by popular referendum pursuant to s 128. Those who are really restricted by the referendum requirement are government officials, whether legislative, executive or judicial, who might otherwise have had power to alter the Constitution without first having to obtain the consent of the people. Those who argue that "we", or "today's generation", should not be bound by the dead hand of the past, usually mean that the High Court should not be bound by it. They want to defend the "discovery" of principles in the Constitution which the founders never intended to put there. The "dead hand" argument then amounts to this: that the judges should not be deterred from over-riding decisions of our elected representatives by the failure of "the dead hand of the past" to give them the power to do so. But since the authority of our elected representatives, as well as that of the judges, derives from the Constitution, created by the "dead hand of the past", this is a dangerous argument. It could just as plausibly be used by our representatives to claim powers which were not given to them by "the dead hand of the past". Why should they be bound by that hand if the judges are not? And if neither is, why should our representatives be bound by decisions of the judges rather than *vice versa*?

Goldsworthy identifies two High Court pronouncements that in his view are not compatible with any principled version of "originalism". One is the suggestion by Toohey and Gaudron JJ in *McGinty v Western Australia* (1996) 136 CLR 140 that "representative government", as envisaged by the voting provisions in the Constitution, must now be expanded or adapted to encompass what would now be regarded as essential features of that conception, even though they would not have been so regarded in 1900. For instance, though in 1900 the right of women to vote was still controversial, the constitutional commitment to "representative government" must now include that right. The other example is the suggestion in *Cheatle v The Queen* (1993) 177 CLR 541 that the conception of "trial by jury" embodied in s 80 of the Constitution must now include the empanelment of women jurors, even though that was not a feature of trial by jury in 1900. As to the former example, Toohey J had said in *McGinty* that "**[201]** while the essence of representative democracy remains unchanged, the method of giving expression to the concept varies over time and according to changes in society". To the same effect Gaudron J thought it necessary "**[221]** that the content and application of the words 'chosen by the people' be determined in the light of developments in democratic standards and not by reference to circumstances as they existed at Federation". For Goldsworthy, the degree of flexibility envisaged here is judicially impermissible. He concedes that any attempt to deny the right of women to vote or to sit on juries would be "**[48]** so outrageous … that were the High Court ever confronted with such an attempt, it should do everything in its power to defeat it"; but for that very reason he thinks that such an attempt "**[49]** is not even a remote possibility". These are therefore "**[48]** horror hypotheticals" that should not distort normal principles of legal interpretation. In support of this argument he invokes the "profound meditation on judicial review" of a Pennsylvania judge who argued in 1825 that while laws infringing the Constitution of the United States should be struck down by the courts, those infringing the Constitution of Pennsylvania should not.

Eakin v Raub

12 *Sergeant & Rawles* 330 (Pa 1825)

Gibson J: [355] I am of opinion that it rests with the people, in whom full and absolute sovereign power resides, to correct abuses in legislation, by instructing their representatives to repeal the obnoxious act. What is wanting to plenary power in the government, is reserved by the people for their own immediate use; and to redress an infringement of their rights in this respect, would seem to be an accessory of the power thus reserved. It might, perhaps, have been better to vest the power in the judiciary; as it might be expected that its habits of deliberation, and the aid derived from the arguments of counsel, would more frequently lead to accurate conclusions. On the other hand, the judiciary is not infallible; and an error by it would admit of no remedy but a more distinct expression of the public will, through the extraordinary medium of a convention; whereas, an error by the legislature admits of a remedy by an exertion of the same public will, in the ordinary exercise of the right of suffrage, – a mode better calculated to attain the end, without popular excitement. It may be said, the people would probably not notice an error of their representatives. But they would as probably do so, as notice an error of the judiciary; and, beside, it is a *postulate* in the theory of our government, and the very basis of the superstructure, that the people are wise, virtuous, and competent to manage their own affairs: and if they are not so, in fact, still every question of this sort must be determined according to the principles of the constitution, as it came from the hands of its framers ... [A]lthough this power has all along been claimed by the state judiciary, it has never been exercised. *Austin v The University of Pennsylvania*, (1 *Yeates*, 260, [(Pa 1793)]) is the only case even apparently to the **[356]** contrary; but there the act of assembly had been previously repealed. In *Vanhorne v Dorrance* [2 US (2 Dallas) 304 at 309 (1795)], decided by the Circuit Court of the *United States* under similar circumstances, the right is peremptorily asserted and examples of monstrous violations of the constitution are put in a strong light by way of example; such as taking away the trial by jury, the elective franchise, or subverting religious liberty. But any of these would be such a usurpation of the political rights of the citizens, as would work a change in the very structure of the government; or, to speak more properly, it would itself be a revolution, which, to counteract, would justify even insurrection; consequently, a judge might lawfully employ every instrument of official resistance within his reach. By this I mean, that while the citizen should resist with pike and gun, the judge might co-operate with *habeas corpus* and *mandamus*. It would be his duty, as a citizen, to throw himself into the breach, and, if it should be necessary, perish there; but this is far from proving the judiciary to be a *peculiar organ* under the constitution, to prevent legislative encroachment on the powers reserved by the people; and this is all that I contend it is not.

Goldsworthy's use of *Eakin v Raub*, repeated in his book *The Sovereignty of Parliament: History and Philosophy* (Clarendon Press, 1999), 269, has been criticised by one reviewer.

Douglas Edlin, "Rule Britannia"

(2002) 52 *University of Toronto Law Journal* 313

[327] Goldsworthy's citation of Mr Justice Gibson's opinion is problematic for two reasons. First, Mr Justice Gibson wrote in dissent in *Eakin*. Contrary to Mr Justice Gibson's opinion, *Eakin* stands for the proposition that judges may, and must, invalidate legislation that violates American constitutional principles. As the Supreme Court of Pennsylvania has explained [in *Hertz Drivurself Stations, Inc v Siggins*, 359 Pa 25 at 33 (1948)], '[t]he rule [is] that a law repugnant to the Constitution is void and that it is not only the right but the duty of a court so to declare when the violation unequivocally appears.' Consequently ..., Goldsworthy's mention of Mr Justice Gibson's dissenting opinion in *Eakin* seems somewhat dubious.

Second, Gibson CJ was writing in a country that had already rejected English parliamentary sovereignty in favour of judicial review. Judicial review was established in federal law by ... *Marbury v Madison* [5 US (1 Cranch) 137 (1803)], over twenty years before the *Eakin* decision. The federal principle articulated in **[328]** *Marbury* is identical to its Pennsylvania analogue, discussed by the majority in *Eakin*. As a result, Mr Justice Gibson's dissent in *Eakin* provides scant support for Goldsworthy's defence of England's continued adherence to its doctrine of absolute parliamentary sovereignty.

However, Goldsworthy concedes that there are some legitimate techniques by which the Constitution can be adapted to changing circumstances consistently with "moderate" originalism.

Jeffrey Goldsworthy, "Originalism in Constitutional Interpretation"
(1997) 25 *Federal Law Review* 1

[28] The usual statements about constitutions being "broad and general", and requiring flexible interpretation, are … vague, and their ritual incantation generally [29] unhelpful. There must be limits beyond which flexibility cannot be called interpretation in any real sense of the term: everyone agrees that judges are not entitled to amend statutes or constitutions as they see fit. The problem is to find the boundary between legitimate interpretative flexibility, and illegitimate judicial amendment; to identify the ways in which the meaning or application of a statute or constitution can in some sense change, consistently with the fundamental principle of original, intended meaning. As Sir Daryl Dawson put it, "[T]he metaphor of a living tree does nothing to tell the judge where he should allow growth to take place or where he should apply the pruning knife".

We are not forced to choose between two starkly opposed metaphors of constitutional law, the "living tree" versus the "dead hand of the past". The metaphor of the "living tree" does not imply that everything is subject to change: indeed, the very possibility of growth depends on the trunk and roots remaining firmly in place. The tree was designed and planted by the founders, and must not … be uprooted and planted elsewhere; nor should the judges, in allowing for growth, lop off branches or graft the branches of other trees onto it. Radical tree surgery must be authorised by s 128. On the other hand, no-one believes that constitutional law today is or should be exactly the same as that which the founders created in 1900. Clearly they did create something capable of growth.

There are many ways in which constitutions not only can but should be given a flexible interpretation, according to contemporary circumstances or values, which are consistent with moderate originalism and the principle of original, intended meaning … [One is] the principle of *stare decisis*, which may require an erroneous interpretation to be followed in the future, in effect changing the Constitution. The second is the enormous scope for legitimate judicial creativity when the Constitution is ambiguous, vague or internally inconsistent. A large part of what is called "constitutional law" consists of general doctrines, methodological principles, and interpretations of specific provisions which are consistent with, but not required by, the text of the Constitution and the intentions of the founders. This perfectly legitimate, and indeed necessary, part of constitutional law … is the creation of the judges, who may continue to develop it as they deem the good government of the nation to require …

There are three more "methods" … by which the Constitution can be given a flexible operation …

[30] Method 1. Application and enactment intentions
In deciding what a statutory or constitutional provision means, the law-makers' enactment intentions may be critical. But once its meaning has been determined, and the question is how it applies in a particular case, their further intentions are irrelevant. The law consists of the provision which the law-makers actually enacted, and not their possibly mistaken beliefs about its meaning or proper application. The rule of law and the separation of powers require that judges decide for themselves how a law should be applied, according to its meaning, rather than slavishly deferring to whatever the law-makers may have expected or wanted …

[C]onsider the 1952 law which prohibited the entry into the United States of any person with a "psychopathic personality". When this law was enacted, Congress believed that homosexuality was a pathological condition, and expected that the law would result in the exclusion of homosexuals. And indeed it did, for a considerable time. But today, because the scientific community rejects that understanding of homosexuality, judges would rightly refuse to exclude homosexuals. In doing so, they might be flouting Congress's application intention, but not its enactment intention …

For the same reason, to properly apply a provision incorporating a moral or other evaluative principle judges must decide what the principle requires, rather than what the law-makers may have believed it requires. There are many cases involving statutory interpretation which are best explained on this basis. Statutory terms such as "obscene", "indecent", "the public interest", "exceptional depravity", "necessary" and "the interests of science, literature, art or learning", have been applied according to current understandings, rather than those of the law-makers.

The United States Constitution arguably includes many moral principles, such as that there shall be no cruel or unusual punishment. Flogging is now unusual, although it was not in the founders' era. But is it also cruel? The founders may not have believed that it was, but arguably they enacted a moral principle forbidding cruelty, not their own beliefs about the application of the principle in particular instances. If so, then to apply that principle, judges today must make a moral judgment about cruelty, and not a factual judgment about the founders' beliefs …

[31] In the United States, this kind of argument is often thought to refute "originalism". But it refutes only an extreme and implausible version of originalism, which holds that judges must defer to the founders' application intentions as well as their enactment intentions. The argument actually depends on moderate originalism, because it depends on whether the founders intended to enact a moral principle: it depends on their enactment intention …

It must be conceded that enactment and application intentions are not mutually exclusive, and the distinction between them may be very difficult to apply, and perhaps in some cases illusory. Well known application intentions also serve as enactment intentions when they clarify the meaning of a law. For example, they may clarify what would otherwise be an ambiguity, or make it obvious that a word or phrase has been used in a non-literal or special sense. Or they might justify holding general terms to be subject to an implied qualification, because they make it obvious that the law-makers expressed themselves ineptly or, quite reasonably, took something for granted. The latter possibility is plausible only in limited situations, and subject to stringent conditions …

Method 2. Connotation and denotation

The High Court has often said that the "connotation" of a constitutional provision must stay the same, although its "denotation" can change. The distinction between connotation and denotation derives from the philosophy of John Stuart Mill, and is similar if not equivalent to the modern distinctions between sense and reference, and intension and extension. The denotation, reference or extension of a term is comprised of all the things in the world which the word refers to; its connotation, sense or intension consists of the criteria which define it, and thereby determine its denotation.

It is undeniable that the denotation of a constitutional term can change. The denotations of terms are constantly changing: for example, every time an old lighthouse is demolished, or a new one is built, the denotation of the term "lighthouse" changes. The Constitution was obviously not intended to give the Commonwealth power only over those lighthouses which existed when it came into force on January 1, 1901. When a new lighthouse is built, the question is simply whether it is a "lighthouse" according to the meaning, or connotation, of the word as it appears in the Constitution …

[32] For an example of the way in which this distinction can explain quite dramatic changes in the operation of the Constitution, consider the Commonwealth Parliament's external affairs power, and assume that the connotation of the words conferring the power is such that it originally included power to legislate to implement international treaties which the Crown has entered into. In the early part of this century that treaty implementing power was very modest, because the number of treaties entered into was small, and the kinds of subject-matters with which they dealt were very limited. Because of a massive increase in both respects, the power is now a very broad and important one. Yet although the denotation of the words conferring the power has changed, their connotation has not.

The connotation/denotation distinction can be invoked in this fashion to justify many changes in the practical operation of the Constitution. In 1900, when juries included only men, was the connotation of the word "jury", in s 80 of the Constitution, more like "a panel of men convened to decide questions of fact", or "a panel representing the community convened to decide questions of fact"? If the former, then women cannot even today serve on juries in trials involving indictable Commonwealth offences, but if the latter, they can. The High Court has rightly chosen the latter interpretation: there is no good reason to believe that, at a time when women's civil rights were being debated and reformed, juries were regarded as an essentially and permanently male preserve. But in many cases the connotation/ denotation distinction can be very difficult, and perhaps in some cases impossible, to apply. In 1900, when only those over 21 years of age were recognised by law as adults, was the connotation of the words "adult person", in s 41 of the Constitution, "person over 21 years of age", or "person recognised by law as of mature age"? If the former, the words cannot even today apply to persons between 18 and 21 years of age, despite legal reforms according them adult status for other purposes; but if the latter, they can. In answering these kinds of questions, and also when it cannot answer them, the Court should choose the connotation which best reflects the purpose behind the provision in question.

[33] Method 3. Non-literal, purposive interpretation

The United States Constitution provides that Congress has power to raise "Armies" and "a Navy", and to regulate "the land and naval Forces" (Art I Sect 8). There is no mention of air forces, which were unknown when the Constitution was created. When technological change later made it possible to raise air forces, did Congress have power to do so? The connotation/denotation distinction does not help if air forces do not come within the connotation of the words "Armies" or "Navy". But the founders' underlying purpose is quite clear: to give Congress power to raise and regulate all the military forces of the United States. Unless the nation is to be forced to formally amend the Constitution, which is a time-consuming and expensive business, the only way to reach the result which is obviously consistent with the founders' clearly expressed purpose is to interpret the words according to their spirit rather than their letter.

There are a few cases of statutory interpretation involving the same principle, although apparently not many. For example, the words "bankers books" have been interpreted to include microfilms; and "document" to include a computer database. In Australian constitutional law, cases in which the connotation/denotation distinction has been used in a strained and artificial fashion may be examples.

This principle is not necessarily inconsistent with the principle of original, intended meaning, because that meaning may not be the same as the original, literal meaning. Immediately after the enactment of a statute, a court can interpret it "flexibly", departing from the literal meaning of its words in order to avoid absurdity and give effect to its obviously intended purpose. There may be little difference in principle between new and very old statutes with respect to this kind of treatment, although the latter may require it more often.

But how far can this kind of purposive interpretation be taken? La[w]rence Lessig has recently proposed a theory of interpretation as "translation", according to which it can be taken very far indeed. According to Lessig, the courts ought to interpret the American Constitution so that the founders' purposes can be faithfully put into effect in today's much changed world, even if that requires radical departures from the words of the Constitution, involving in effect substantial judicial re-drafting. Courts in the common law tradition have always been averse to engaging in such a process, regarding any necessary up-dating of statutes, for example, as the responsibility of the legislature. There is a difficult problem here. No-one would regard it as sensible for the [34] courts to refuse to permit Congress to raise an air force until such time as the Constitution should have been formally amended. But if the courts can engage in re-drafting to that extent, how and where is the line to be drawn? It is clearly a question of degree. I would expect Australian judges to take a "flexible" approach only when the words of the Constitution can be expanded or contracted in a simple and obvious way, and according to a very clear underlying purpose.

As to Goldsworthy's example of the prohibition of "cruel and unusual punishments" in the Eighth Amendment to the United States Constitution, see *Atkins v Virginia*, 536 US 304 (2002), holding by 6:3 that that clause prevents the execution of mentally retarded persons, and *Roper v Simmons*, 543 US 551 (2005), holding by 5:4 that it also prevents the execution of persons who were under 18 years of age when their crimes were committed. Writing for the Court in the latter case, Justice Kennedy explained that: "[560] The prohibition against 'cruel and unusual punishments', like other expansive language in the Constitution, must be interpreted according to its text, by considering history, tradition, and precedent, and with due regard for its purpose and function in the constitutional design. To implement this [561] framework we have established the propriety and affirmed the necessity of referring to 'the evolving standards of decency that mark the progress of a maturing society' [*Trop v Dulles*, 356 US 86 at 101 (1958)] to determine which punishments are so disproportionate as to be cruel and unusual".

Greg Craven, too, has made some concessions towards Goldsworthy's attempt at striking a balance among three different interpretive "methods", albeit in his own more polemical style.

Greg Craven, *Conversations with the Constitution*
(University of New South Wales Press, 2004)

[156] There are three methods by which a court can interpret a Constitution. The High Court has tried all three, and still flits promiscuously between them according to taste and exigency. The first is intentionalism: the court could interpret the Constitution according to the intentions of those who wrote it, a dull but faithful calling for judicial basset [157] hounds, all jowls and fidelity. The second is literalism, where the court simply gives literal effect to the Constitution's written words, an approach appealing to chartered accountants and cataloguing librarians. The last is progressivism, which sees the court constantly updating the Constitution to accord with the contemporary needs of the Australian people. This method casts the judges less in robes and wigs than slinky jackets and leather pants …

[159] The real question is which of these three methods should be used by the Court as a universal spanner on the rusty nut of the Constitution? Each has its attractions. Intentionalism's charms are rooted in democratic theory. The Constitution was written by delegates elected by the people. They drafted, debated and digested each word of the [160] document, before it was itself endorsed at referendum. Its meaning is their meaning, and the correct method of interpretation is to ask what these representatives of the people thought. This is consistent with the idea, astonishingly widespread outside universities, that writing actually is a way of conveying meaning. Clearly, intentionalism will produce a judiciary as constitutionally athletic as Uluru.

It is therefore feverishly attacked by those favouring inspired judicial hyperactivity, on the familiar grounds that the founders and their drafting process were indifferently democratic, that we will be ruled by the skeletal claw of Samuel Griffith, and that the founders never in any event expected to be taken seriously … [N]one of this is particularly convincing in the context of a popularly ratified Constitution, drafted by elected representatives, and amendable by referendum.

A further argument is that even if we want to abide by the founders' intentions we cannot, because it is impossible to ascertain what they were. The founders, however, left behind them five fat volumes of transcribed debates, and while inevitably there are moments of ambiguity, on the big issues – like the powers of the states, the existence of exotic rights and the right of the High Court to creative control – they speak with the diffidence of an air-raid siren. Far more likely to provoke genuine angst are the profound practical implications of intentionalism. The powers of the states would shoot like the dormant thistle seeds, the opportunity to invent rights would burst like an information technology boom, and the High Court would be off the lecture circuit.

The appeal of literalism for many Australian lawyers resembles the marketing pitch for dishwashing liquids … [L]iteralism is simple, certain and, in its addiction to dictionary definition, warranted not to provoke political or intellectual argument. This is ironic, given that literalism has for eighty years achieved the highly political outcome of centralising power. This delicious irony is literalism's strongest point: it is both objective and [161] programmed, appealing simultaneously to legal pedants and pro-commonwealth judicial politicians. With literalism, no-one can reasonably object to the court's decision: like a judicial poker player, it simply points to the words, and intones: 'Read 'em and weep'.

The standard justification for constitutional literalism turns on the simple and reassuring idea that the safest way to understand a document is to read its words. Below this lurks the assumption that it is the words of a document that are the best guide to its authors' intentions, not their assumed preferences, books, letters, watercolours or psychological conditions. In this sense, literalism is a very narrow version of intentionalism. It accepts that the High Court is trying to find the founders' intention, but argues that the written words are the only one safe source of that commodity.

Like socialism and Sydney, literalism has surface appeal but little depth. Its most obvious problem is ambiguity. Literalism assumes that each term of the Constitution has a more or less clear meaning, waiting only to be extracted by a judge with a dictionary. Yet even a nodding acquaintance with reality suggests that constitutions contain more ambiguity than most documents, and once a provision has been identified as genuinely ambiguous, a literal approach will be as much help as an umbrella in an oil fire. For example, were some literal lunatic to assert that the commonwealth's power over external affairs gave it competence over extramarital relationships openly maintained, as opposed to the conduct of foreign relations, how could they be gainsaid simply by use of a dictionary, and without the deployment of wider historical material, or possibly a cudgel? This fundamental deficiency means that disagreements between literalist judges can resemble spats between eight-year olds with dictionaries, neither side having anywhere to go once they have asserted that their semantic meaning is correct ...

[162] Progressivism is the Marilyn Monroe of the Constitution: its attractions are obvious, if a little over-ripe. To those who want radical (or any) change to the Constitution, it offers a way of achieving this without the distressing necessity of asking the Australian people, who give the wrong answer as often as a two-bob watch. For judges and lawyers, progressivism takes them from a life as chewers of quills and spongers of blots to a new eminence as touch-judges of the national psyche.

Obviously enough, the arguments for progressivism are a constitutional adaptation of those generally supporting judicial activism. Progressivism is justified on the broad ground that democracy must involve more than majority rule, by which is meant that it should involve nothing of the sort. Particularly in the context of human rights, the court must save democracy from itself by ... restraining the people and politicians from their animal appetites. The judges have always made law, and there is nothing special about the Constitution. In any event, the founders never intended the Constitution as a straitjacket for the court, but rather as a loose-fitting lounging robe – probably silk – to be altered as taste requires ...

This case is formidable in its appeal to contemporary demands and contemporary self-congratulation. It has little sense of humour, and reacts to counter-arguments with hurt resentment. Inevitably, these start and finish with democracy. The High Court is not elected, and has no more claim to popular legitimacy than a road repair gang: on what [163] basis is it to determine that the Constitution must be varied in the interests of the Australian people? Australian democracy may well need friends, but it will hardly be saved by seven unelected judges acting out a fantasy as judicial men on horseback. The idea that the founders spent eight years, forests of paper and buckets of sweat to produce a Constitution that is merely a broad hint to the High Court resembles the self-refuting puffery of television investment advisors. Finally, the dead hand of the past does not grip. If we want the Constitution changed, we ask the people, and our only fear will be their answer, typically rude and two-fingered as it so often is.

There is a further, very pointed rejoinder to progressivism. Like fascism and football, progressivism is intrinsically result-oriented. Its ultimate justification is that it produces desired constitutional outcomes: human rights, more centralised power and so forth. Yet even lawyers can concede that constitutional interpretation involves more than the 'right' answer: it should at least be honest. The court should be able to identify, explain and defend its method. The problem with progressivism is that it is the method that only half-dares speak its name.

Judges are understandably nervous about telling the Australian people that when the Constitution says it is alterable only by referendum, this is a polite way of saying that the High Court can do pretty much as it likes. Consequently, while judges talk progressivism in heroic speeches and toy with it in turgid articles, their temptation is to think progressively but act cowardly. In other words, when conforming the meaning of the Constitution to some direct policy choice, judges are tempted to dress up the grisly fact of progressivism as some implausible literal interpretation, or even a grotesque distortion of the founders' intentions. All too often, the High Court has produced judgements that conceal rather than expose its reasoning.

As with every religion, all the constitutional isms have their good bits. Everyone would like a constitution that could be read as literally as a television program guide. Everyone likes the idea of a permanent psy-[164]-chic relay between Deakin and the current chief justice. Everyone is excited by the prospect of a constitution as sensitive to the demands of the day as a party pollster. A case can be made for all the league teams of constitutional interpretation, but the ultimate test is which is most consistent with the basic character of the Australian Constitution.

Predictably, by this criterion, Craven ultimately comes down in favour of a preference for "intentionalism". Yet it may be neither necessary nor possible to make this final choice. There appears to be some degree of consensus that at least three factors can legitimately be taken into account: (1) the literal meaning of the words, or what to a common sense view would appear to be their literal meaning; (2) extrinsic evidence of the framers' intentions; and (3) an element of judicial creativity, in the sense of "flexible" or "purposive" interpretation. Other points remain contentious. One is whether all three factors can be (as they often are) weighed together, or whether it is possible or desirable to prescribe a priority rule, such that a judge may only proceed to (2) if (1) yields no clear result, and may only proceed to (3) if both (1) and (2) are inconclusive. Other areas of disagreement relate to the scope and frequency of the judicial discretion acknowledged by (3); and to the claim made by some "originalists" that even the exercise of that discretion is controlled by "originalism", in the sense that the purposes and values to which the judge seeks to give effect must still be those of the framers.

Among the most forthright judicial refusals to be bound by "the dead hand of the past" – or at least to allow an "[171] unexpressed intention of the framers of the Constitution" to override "the natural implications" to be drawn from "its express provisions or fundamental doctrines" – was the judgment of Deane J in *Theophanous v Herald & Weekly Times Ltd* (1994) 182 CLR 104. Invoking the idea that the Constitution now derives its authority from its "acceptance by the people", that is, from popular sovereignty (see Chapter 4, §9), he saw this as a reason for refusing "to construe the Constitution on the basis that the dead hands of those who framed it reached from their graves to … deprive what was intended to be a living instrument of its vitality and its adaptability to serve succeeding generations". To counter the "errors of such a dead hands theory of construction", he invoked the authority of Andrew Inglis Clark, describing him as "[172] the primary architect of our Constitution". (That is, he invoked original intent to counter the search for original intent!)

Andrew Inglis Clark, *Studies in Australian Constitutional Law*
(Charles Maxwell, 1901; Legal Books, 1997 reprint)

[21] [T]he Constitution was not made to serve a temporary and restricted purpose, but was framed and adopted as a permanent and comprehensive code of law, by which the exercise of the governmental powers conferred by it should be regulated as long as the institutions which it created to exercise the powers should exist. But the social conditions and the political exigencies of the succeeding generations of every civilized and progressive community will inevitably produce new governmental problems to which the language of the Constitution must be applied, and hence it must be read and construed, not as containing a declaration of the will and intentions of men long since dead, and who cannot have anticipated the problems that would arise for solution by future generations, but as declaring the will and intentions of the present inheritors and possessors of sovereign power, who maintain the Constitution and have the power to alter it, and who are in the immediate presence of the problems to be solved. It is they who enforce the provisions of the Constitution and make a living force of that which would otherwise be a silent and lifeless document. Every community of men is governed by present possessors of sovereignty and not by the commands of men who have ceased to exist. But so long as the present possessors of sovereignty convey their commands in the language of their predecessors, that language must be interpreted by the judiciary consistently with a proper use of it as an intelligible vehicle of the conceptions and intentions of the human mind, and consistently with the historical associations from which particular words and phrases derive the whole of their meaning in juxtaposition with their context. If the present possessors [22] of sovereignty discover that the result so produced is contrary in particular cases to their will in regard to future cases of a like character, they will amend the language which they previously retained as the expression of their will. If they do not

amend it they must be presumed to accept the interpretation put upon it by the judiciary as the correct announcement of their present commands.

The same passage was cited by Kirby J in *Eastman v The Queen* (2000) 203 CLR 1 at 79-80. Indeed, in this respect Kirby J appears to have inherited the mantle of Deane J. See, for example, his judgments in *Gould v Brown* (1998) 193 CLR 346 at 476-7; *Abebe v Commonwealth* (1999) 197 CLR 510 at 581-2; *Re Colina; Ex parte Torney* (1999) 200 CLR 386 at 422-4; and *Grain Pool of Western Australia v Commonwealth* (2000) 202 CLR 479 at 522-5. In June 2001 he summarised his approach as follows:

Brownlee v The Queen
(2001) 207 CLR 278

Kirby J: [314] If constitutional interpretation in Australia were nothing more than a search for the "intentions" of the framers of the document in 1900, doubtless a single answer would, theoretically, be available as to the meaning of every word of the Constitution. Such meaning would be found in history books; not by legal analysis. But if, as I would hold, the text of the Constitution must be given meaning as its words are perceived by succeeding generations of Australians, reflected in this Court, it is imperative to keep the mind open to the possibility that a new context, presenting different needs and circumstances and fresh insights, may convince the Court, in later times and of later composition, that its predecessors had adopted an erroneous view of the Constitution …

[320] [M]y own approach … holds that constitutional expressions must be given contemporary meaning, as befits the character of a national basic law, which is extremely resistant to formal amendment, but which must, of necessity, apply to new, unforeseen and possibly unforeseeable circumstances …

[321] Because, by definition, the world of the framers was not that of today's Australians, it is misleading, and prone to result in serious error, to accept as the applicable principle of constitutional interpretation the "intention" of those who framed it. One thing the framers certainly knew was that they were creating a new polity to be governed indefinitely by a fundamental written law. That document [322] appears in statutory form. Its meaning is therefore uncovered by the general techniques of statutory construction. However, because the Constitution is a special statute of a peculiar kind for particular purposes and unique operation, the rules of construction applicable to it include some that are special, particular and unique. Even with ordinary legislation, expected to have an extended operation, it is increasingly accepted that language lives and meaning adapts to changed circumstances. Words are not necessarily confined to the meaning that would subjectively have been ascribed to them by the Parliament that enacted them. This is even more true of constitutional words and phrases. A recognition of this fact does not render wholly irrelevant the consideration of history – as in the debates that preceded adoption of the Constitution. But it does limit the utility of such searches when the real consideration is what those words and phrases mean in their contemporary institutional setting and as they must operate in accordance with the "accepted standards of a modern democratic society", such as the Constitution was adopted to provide.

The siren song of 1900 does not therefore become more attractive by embracing the fiction … that an "intention" of the framers of the Constitution in 1900 can be "objectively" discovered. Some such fictitious reification of the ideas of 1900 would certainly be necessary if countless instances by which this court has adapted constitutional language to contemporary circumstances [were] to be explained …

[327] It will take time for the search for constitutional meaning by reference to the imputed "intention of the framers" in 1900 to be abandoned in favour of a search for the essential characteristics of words and phrases having enduring constitutional operation. But, as this court embarks on the second century of the Constitution, it may be expected that the unreliability of the past criterion, and the demonstrated ambivalence of past practice, will indicate ever more clearly the error inherent in "faint-hearted originalism". It will show the need for a different principle of interpretation, one appropriate to the task of giving effect to the nation's fundamental law. Without

a clear principle, consistently applied, the outcomes of constitutional disputes are bound to evidence inconsistency and to elicit deserved criticism.

In counterpoint to these judgments by Kirby J, McHugh J has defended the view that the judges' responsibility is to give effect to the "intention" of the text, as ascertained by traditional methods of legal interpretation. Indeed, Kirby J's ironic use of the expression "faint-hearted originalism" was a riposte to McHugh J's observations on the use of that phrase by Justice Antonin Scalia of the United States Supreme Court.

Eastman v The Queen
(2000) 203 CLR 1

McHugh J: [44] Probably, most Australian judges have been in substance what Scalia J of the United States Supreme Court once called himself – a faint-hearted originalist. Speaking of the United States situation, Scalia J said that he was a member of "a small but hardy group of judges and academics ... [who] believe that the Constitution has a fixed meaning, which does not change: it means today what it meant when it was adopted, nothing more and nothing less".

It is, however, too simplistic to view even "faint-hearted originalism" as meaning that a word or phrase in the Constitution only applies in circumstances envisaged by the makers of the Constitution. Scalia J himself acknowledges that old constitutional principles may be applied to new physical realities. Nevertheless, he emphasises that "acknowledging the need for projection of old constitutional principles upon new physical realities is a far cry from saying what the non-originalists say: that the Constitution changes; that the very act **[45]** which it once prohibited it now permits, and which it once permitted it now forbids" ...

In one very important respect, judicial practice in Australia has departed from Scalia J's view of constitutional interpretation and the notion that the meaning of constitutional provisions is fixed as at 1900. Even taking the most favourable view of the Court's interpretation of some constitutional provisions, it is difficult to reconcile some judicial decisions as to their meaning with the theory that the meaning of each constitutional provision is that which it had in 1900 ...

[46] The reason for the Court's interpretation is that the relevant intention of constitutional provisions is that expressed in the Constitution itself, not the subjective intentions of its framers or makers. It is an intention that is determined objectively. Indeed until *Cole v Whitfield* [(1988) 165 CLR 360] the Court would not even look at the Convention Debates. No doubt the notion of constitutional intent, like that of legislative intent, is fictitious. But it serves a useful purpose, as Professor Popkin has recently pointed out:

> "The simple act of thinking about the meaning of statutory language in this broader context – which the judge must do – requires judgment about how the text should interact with its past and future. That is why, despite its being an obvious fiction, the judge when engaged in statutory interpretation is unable to do without the concept of legislative intent. Intent is matched with text as an essential aspect of statutory meaning, not because the judge has any confidence that legislative intent is knowable, but because 'intent' (or 'will') captures the idea that choices *must* be made in order to apply a text to facts. Legislative intent is a useful judicial construct because the judge is required to make the choices that best express the statutory text's meaning."

Because the intention of the makers of the Constitution is one to be determined objectively, the present generation may see that the provisions of the Constitution have a meaning that escaped the *actual understandings or intentions* of the founders or other persons in 1900. If asked in that year what an industrial dispute extending beyond the limits of any one State meant, most people would probably have said that it meant strikes in more than one State by workers in the same industry. They would have had in mind the maritime and shearers strikes of the 1890s. But we now perceive that "industrial disputes", in their context, easily cover paper disputes arising out of the service of logs of claims on employers in more than one State for wages and conditions for numerous categories of employment in disparate **[47]** industries. The makers of the Constitution intended the Parliament to have legislative powers in respect of "industrial disputes" of a certain kind. If those words cover "paper disputes" about wages and conditions, it is irrelevant that those who framed and enacted the Constitution had something else in mind ... It is therefore true to say, as Windeyer J said in the *Payroll Tax Case* [(1971) 122 CLR 353 at 396-7], that the meaning of the Constitution is not necessarily the same as that which it had for an earlier, or I would add a later, generation.

The traditional approach to constitutional interpretation in Australia is probably best described as textualism or semantic intentionalism. It is not literalism, if by literalism is meant no more than [that] a statute is to be interpreted by reference to its words according to their natural sense and in the context of the document. As many cases show, the Court has frequently taken into account the consequences of particular interpretations in determining the meaning of constitutional provisions, as well as the history and circumstances of their making.

It has often been suggested that *Amalgamated Society of Engineers v Adelaide Steamship Co Ltd* (the *Engineers' Case*) [(1920) 28 CLR 129] committed the High Court to a regime of literalism. Although the majority justices in the *Engineers' Case* emphasised the necessity to construe the words of the Constitution, their approach is probably better regarded as one of legalism with textualism the instrument of that legalism. The majority justices in the *Engineers' Case* emphatically rejected the use of external political principles or policies to interpret the Constitution, and thereby committed the Court to the strict legalism of which Sir Owen Dixon became the leading proponent. However, the *Engineers' Case* did not rule out the history or background of the Constitution as interpretative aids. The majority justices in that case expressly said that the Constitution was to be read in the light of the circumstances in which it was made with knowledge of the combined fabric of the common law and the pre-Constitution statute law ...

[49] Nevertheless, even when we see meaning in a constitutional provision which our predecessors did not see, the search is always for the objective intention of the makers of the Constitution. [50] A commitment to discerning the intention of the makers of the Constitution, in the same way as a court searches for the intention of the legislature in enacting an ordinary statute, does not equate with a Constitution suspended in time. Our Constitution is constructed in such a way that most of its concepts and purposes are stated at a sufficient level of abstraction or generality to enable it to be infused with the *current* understanding of those concepts and purposes. This is consistent with the notion that our Constitution was intended to be an enduring document able to apply to emerging circumstances while retaining its essential integrity. The Constitution was addressed to posterity as well as to those living at the time of its enactment. Those who framed and enacted the Constitution knew that the meaning of the document would have to be deduced by later generations as well as their contemporaries. This Court has not accepted that the makers' actual intentions are decisive, and I see no reason why we should regard the understandings of the immediate audience as decisive.

The fact that the meaning attributed to a particular provision now may not be the same as the meaning understood by the makers of the Constitution or their 1901 audience does not make constitutional adjudication a web of judicial legislation. They may not have envisaged that freedom of political communication was part of the system of representative government. They may not have understood that the Commonwealth power with respect to industrial disputes could be invoked by the serving of a log of claims. The participants at the Constitutional Conventions may not have understood that juries would include women or those without property or that "the people of the Commonwealth" might include Aboriginal people. But to deny that the events following federation and the experiences of the nation can be used to see more than the Constitutional Convention participants or the 1901 audience saw in particular words and combinations of words is to leave us slaves to the mental images and understandings of the founding fathers and their 1901 audience, a prospect which they almost certainly did not intend.

The application, and sometimes the meaning, of a constitutional provision may therefore be informed by an appreciation of "contemporary circumstances". This approach recognises that those who made and enacted the Constitution intended it to endure, to be responsive and relevant to the community in which it would operate, and to be sufficiently malleable to account for circumstances and conditions that they could not have foreseen. According to this view, the Constitution is not "a rigid blueprint" but rather "an outline or broad framework for national government capable of adjusting to changing conditions and circumstances." Such a view enjoys [51] some heritage in Australian constitutional thinking. Justice Dixon advocated it in *Australian National Airways Pty Ltd v Commonwealth* [(1945) 71 CLR 29 at 81] when he said that "it is a Constitution we are interpreting, an instrument of government meant to endure and conferring powers expressed in general propositions wide enough to be capable of flexible application to changing circumstances."

Thus, one of the chief proponents of legalism and textualism in Australia saw no inconsistency between textualism and an evolving approach to the Constitution.

Re Wakim; Ex parte McNally (Cross-vesting Case)
(1999) 198 CLR 511

McHugh J: [549] [T]he judiciary has no power to amend or modernize the Constitution to give effect to what the judges think is in the public interest. The function of the judiciary, including the function of this Court, is to give effect to the intention of the makers of the Constitution as evinced by the terms in which they expressed that intention. That necessarily means that decisions, taken almost a century ago by people long dead, bind the people of Australia today even in cases where most people agree that those decisions are out of touch with the present needs of Australian society. Judge Easterbrook has pointed out that a written constitution "is designed to be an anchor in the past. It creates rules that bind until a supermajority of the living changes them." In the same article, he pointed out that a person cannot logically deny the power of the past to rule today's affairs and at the same time assert that Art III of the United States Constitution (the equivalent of our Ch III) still binds. Judicial review of the constitutional validity of legislation "depends on the belief that decisions taken long ago" still bind today's society …

[551] The starting point for a principled interpretation of the Constitution is the search for the intention of its makers. That does not mean a search for their subjective beliefs, hopes or expectations. Constitutional interpretation is not a search for the mental states of those who made, or for that matter approved or enacted, the Constitution. The intention of its makers can only be deduced from the words that they used in the historical context in which they used them. In a paper on constitutional interpretation, presented at Fordham University in 1996, Professor Ronald Dworkin argued, correctly in my opinion:

"We must begin, in my view, by asking what – on the best evidence available – the authors of the text in question intended to say. That is an exercise in what I have called constructive interpretation. It does not mean peeking inside the skulls of people dead for centuries. It means trying to make the best sense we can of an historical event – someone, or a social group with particular responsibilities, speaking or writing in a particular way on a particular occasion."

The application which this Court has given to some words and phrases of the Constitution would almost certainly have surprised most of those who participated in the making of the Constitution. Most of them could not have foreseen the extent to which the application of those words and phrases would enable the Commonwealth to dominate the federation and reduce the power of the States to control their domestic affairs. But that does not mean that this Court's interpretation of our Constitution has lacked fidelity to the intentions of those who made the Constitution …

[552] [M]any words and phrases of the Constitution are expressed at such a level of generality that the most sensible conclusion to be drawn from their use in a Constitution is that the makers of the Constitution intended that they should apply to whatever facts and circumstances succeeding generations thought they covered. Examples can be found in the powers conferred on the Parliament of the Commonwealth to make laws with respect to "trade and commerce with other countries, and among the States", "trading or **[553]** financial corporations formed within the limits of the Commonwealth", "external affairs" and "conciliation and arbitration for the prevention and settlement of industrial disputes extending beyond the limits of any one State". In these and other cases, the test is simply: what do these words mean to us as late twentieth century Australians? Such an approach accords with the recognition of Isaacs J in *Commonwealth v Kreglinger & Fernau Ltd and Bardsley* [(1926) 37 CLR 393 at 413] that our Constitution was "made, not for a single occasion, but for the continued life and progress of the community".

The level of abstraction for some terms of the Constitution is, however, much harder to identify than that of those set out above. Thus, in 1901 "marriage" was seen as meaning a voluntary union for life between one man and one woman to the exclusion of all others. If that level of abstraction were now accepted, it would deny the Parliament of the Commonwealth the power to legislate for same sex marriages, although arguably "marriage" now means, or in the near future may mean, a voluntary union for life between two *people* to the exclusion of others.

But even if we continue to hold, as Windeyer J asserted in *R v Commonwealth Conciliation and Arbitration Commission; Ex parte Professional Engineers' Association* [(1959) 107 CLR 208 at 267], that the meanings of the words in the Constitution do not change as language changes, the meanings that we now place on the Constitution may not entirely coincide with the meanings placed on it by those who drafted, approved or enacted that document. That is because a Constitution contains implications, inferences and propositions as well as words, phrases and clauses. Experience derived from the events that have occurred since its enactment may enable us to see more in the combination of particular words, phrases or clauses or in the document as a whole than would have occurred to those who participated in the making of the Constitution. Thus we now see, although it was not seen in 1901, that freedom of communication on matters of government and politics is an indispensable incident of the system of government created by the Constitution and that the law of defamation must not be inconsistent with that freedom. Similarly, we now see, although it was probably not seen in 1901, that "industrial **[554]** disputes" can be manifested by unions serving logs of claim on employers who reject them.

As to McHugh J's last two examples, see respectively Chapters 28-29 and Chapter 22, §§5-7. As to the example of same-sex marriages, the House of Lords has since held in *Fitzpatrick v Sterling Housing Association Ltd* [2001] 1 AC 27 that, although the word "spouse" in the context of the *Rent Act 1977* (UK) must mean only "wife or husband", the phrase "member of the original tenant's family" could include the survivor of a same-sex partnership. In that context, McHugh J's observation was used by Lord Slynn to make the point that "**[34]** in other contexts, the words may have a wider or a narrower meaning than here", since "changes in attitudes and perceptions may require a wider meaning to be given to a word such as 'marriage'." In *Grain Pool of Western Australia*, Kirby J saw this as "**[529]** a particularly vivid illustration of the way that words in statutes are not fixed for their meaning by reference to the understanding of that meaning at the time of enactment", and added: "What is true of an ordinary statute is much more applicable to a constitutional text which may not be so easily changed and … is intended to operate indefinitely as a source for future legislation".

4. Coherence, Integrity and Fidelity

Those writers who acknowledge a wider scope for the legitimate exercise of creative judicial development and adaptation of textual meanings still seek to articulate standards by which such an exercise can be rationally guided or confined. Michael Coper has suggested that one criterion of acceptable judicial performance is that, over a series of cases, the principles and reasoning strategies adopted by any one judge should at least maintain a consistency from one case to another ("Interpreting the Constitution: A Handbook for Judges and Commentators", in AR Blackshield (ed), *Legal Change: Essays in Honour of Julius Stone* (Butterworths, 1983), 52). Kirby J has taken that idea further. In *Eastman v The Queen* (2000) 203 CLR 1, he protested that: "**[81]** This court should adopt a single approach to the construction of the basic document placed in its care. Constitutional elaboration, above all, should be approached in a consistent way, lest the inconsistencies of an *originalist* approach here and a *contemporary* approach there be ascribed to the selection of whichever approach produces a desired outcome". Similarly, in *Brownlee v The Queen* (2001) 207 CLR 278, he stressed the need for constitutional interpretation to be based on "**[320]** a theory", since "[o]therwise, the result will inevitably be inconsistent decisions reflecting no more than the intuitive responses to the text of the Constitution by different justices (or of the same justices at different times)". He added that: "**[322]** Either this court should adhere to construing the words of the Constitution according to the understandings of 1900, or **[323]** it should accept another approach, such as I favour. In my respectful opinion, a hybrid approach is intellectually incoherent".

Indeed, Neil MacCormick has suggested that since the criterion of "consistency" is satisfied merely by an absence of self-contradiction, "coherence" might be a better criterion. He distinguishes between "narrative coherence" (which in legal contexts would be a criterion for findings of fact and the drawing of inferences from evidence) and "normative coherence".

Neil MacCormick, "Coherence in Legal Justification"
in W Krawietz et al (eds), *Theorie der Normen: Festgabe für Ota Weinberger zum 65. Geburtstag* (Duncker & Humblot, 1984), 37

[37] [A] lack of coherence in what is said involves a failure to make sense. An incoherent set of norms might be such that each could be fulfilled without infringing any other, yet the whole seems to make no sense as constituting or mapping out a reasonable order of conduct – imagine a house within which all inhabitants are to make their rooms as untidy as possible on Mondays, Wednesdays and Fridays, then tidy them up to the highest perfection on Tuesdays, Thursdays and Saturdays, Sundays being strictly observed as a day of rest. To have, and to observe, such house rules is possible – but what sense does it make? …

[40] [A]t least one aspect of normative coherence is … the common subservience by a set of laws to a relevant value or values; and an absence of avoidable conflict with other relevant values …

Are there then other aspects of coherence? One candidate which comes to mind has to do with principles. We might say that a set of rules is coherent if they all satisfy or are instances of a single more general principle …

The … question [is] whether appeal to 'values' is different in substance from appealing to principles, or only different in grammatical form. 'Safety on the roads' is a noun phrase; 'safety on the roads' conceived as a *value* is the state of affairs signified by the noun phrase conceived as being a state of affairs which is a good or worthy purpose of human endeavour. 'That human life ought not to be unduly endangered by motor traffic on the roads' is a normative sentence which in virtue of its very general scope can be considered as a possible principle …

[41] [T]here appears to be an extensional equivalence as between 'values' and 'principles'. For any value V there is a principle according to which V either may be, or ought in the absence of countervailing considerations to be, or ought normally to be, or must in the absence of overriding considerations be, pursued or realised …

I conclude that the coherence of norms is a matter of their 'making sense' by being rationally related as a set, instrumentally or intrinsic-[42]-ally, *either* to the realisation of some common value or values; *or* to the fulfilment of some common principle or principles. At the level of the highest-order principles or values there is a further requirement of coherence: that, after allowance for the fulfilment of priority rankings of principles and/or values we consider that in their totality they express a satisfactory form of life, and one which it would be possible for human beings, as human beings are, to live. In short, the coherence of a set of norms is a function of its justifiability under higher order principles or values … ; provided that the higher or highest-order principles and values seem acceptable as delineating a satisfactory form of life, when taken together.

In Ronald Dworkin's earlier writings, including *Taking Rights Seriously* (Duckworth, 1977), his emphasis on "principles" was apparently intended to *control* judicial discretion, suggesting that for any interpretive problem there must still be a single right answer. His later writings seem to acknowledge a greater leeway for legitimate divergence among judges as to what, all things considered, is the most appropriate reading of the legal materials. In *Law's Empire* (Fontana Press, 1986), he argues for a model of "law as integrity". This is contrasted on the one hand with "conventionalism" (the belief that "[95] a right or responsibility flows from past decisions only if it is explicit within them or can be made explicit through methods or techniques conventionally accepted by the legal profession as a whole"). It is contrasted on the other hand with "legal pragmatism" (which postulates "that judges do and should make whatever decisions seem to them best for the community's future"). "Conventionalism", says Dworkin, is "[225] backward-looking"; "pragmatism" is "forward-looking". His own model of "law as integrity" seeks to "combine backward- and forward-looking elements", and "interpret contemporary legal practice

... as an unfolding political narrative". The "integrity" which it seeks is that of the entire (and continuously expanding) body of authoritative legal materials, viewed as if "they were all created by a single author – the community personified". In this way the judge seeks to arrive at "a coherent conception of justice and fairness", which provides "the best constructive interpretation of the community's legal practice".

The process is an ongoing one because each judge continually "[229] adds to the tradition he interprets". Accordingly, as a supplement (but not an alternative) to the postulate of a single notional author, Dworkin develops the metaphor of a "chain novel", in which each novelist "interprets the chapters he has been given in order to write a new chapter, which is then added to what the next novelist receives, and so on. Each has the job of writing his chapter so as to make the novel being constructed the best it can be", so that the cumulative work "can be construed as the work of a single author rather than, as is the fact, the product of many different hands". The interpretation of chapters already written is guided by a "[230] dimension of fit", so that as far as possible all the components can be seen as part of one coherent whole; but also by "[231] more substantive aesthetic judgments, about the importance or insight or realism or beauty of different ideas the novel might be taken to express". These judgments determine the choice between different interpretations, either of which would satisfy the criterion of "fit", by indicating "which of these eligible readings makes the work in progress the best, all things considered".

The aim of successive judges in adding their chapters to the juristic "chain novel" is not merely to rationalise the content of the existing legal materials, but to read them as an expression of "[255] some coherent set of principles about people's rights and duties, the best constructive interpretation of the political structure and legal doctrine of their community". Ultimately, each judge "[256] must choose between eligible interpretations by asking which shows the community's structure of institutions and decisions ... in a better light from the standpoint of political morality".

Applying this model of "law as integrity" to constitutional interpretation, Dworkin rejects "historicism" (by which he means originalism) and also "passivism" (defined by reference to its opposition to "activism"). But this does not mean that he endorses "activism", either. Indeed, he denounces it as "[378] a virulent form of legal pragmatism". Judges must "enforce the Constitution through interpretation, not fiat, meaning that their decisions must fit constitutional practice, not ignore it". Their sense of justice is relevant to their judgments of legal "integrity", but only as one among "many political virtues", including their "[257] convictions about fit" and their "commitment to integrity" itself. Ultimately, a Justice of the United States Supreme Court must be guided by a belief "[398] that the American Constitution consists in the best available interpretation of American constitutional text and practice as a whole, and his judgment about which interpretation is best is sensitive to the great complexity of political virtues bearing on that issue".

McHugh J has frequently referred to Dworkin's writings. For example, in Re Wakim; Ex parte McNally (Cross-vesting Case) (1999) 198 CLR 511 at 554, he agreed with Dworkin ("The Arduous Virtue of Fidelity: Originalism, Scalia, Tribe, and Nerve" (1997) 65 Fordham Law Review 1249) that: "[1249] Lawyers and judges faced with a contemporary constitutional issue must try to construct a coherent, principled, and persua-[1250]-sive interpretation of the text of particular clauses, the structure of the Constitution as a whole, and our history under the Constitution – an interpretation that both unifies these distinct sources, so far as this is possible, and directs future adjudication. They must seek, that is, constitutional *integrity*".

For Dworkin's analogy with a chain novel, Lawrence Lessig ("Fidelity in Translation" (1993) 71 *Texas Law Review* 1165; "Understanding Changed Readings: Fidelity and Theory" (1995) 47 *Stanford Law Review* 395) has substituted an analogy with translation from a foreign language; and for Dworkin's "integrity" Lessig substitutes a standard of "fidelity" to the original source. His argument is that, just as the translator has to adapt the original text in a way that will be appropriate to a different language, so the judge in interpreting an authoritative text must adapt it to a new context. Moreover, the contextual changes may arise not only because of new factual circumstances, but at a deeper level because our underlying presuppositions and values have changed. At the same time, in adapting the original text to its altered setting, the translator-judge must still observe the requirements of fidelity to the original. In this as in other currently debated accounts of what happens or should happen in the interpretation of authoritative legal texts, the objective is to combine recognition of the need for judicial renovation with a way of keeping the renovation within rational constraints.

5. Traces and Connotations

In "Some Fundamental Legal Conceptions as Applied in Judicial Reasoning" (1913) 23 *Yale Law Journal* 16, Wesley Hohfeld (1879-1918) proposed that legal interpretation would be clarified by attention to the interrelations among eight elementary concepts. At the level of positive legal entitlements an enforceable legal *right* was to be distinguished from a mere *privilege*; from a *power* to regulate the legal rights and privileges of others; and from an *immunity* against the possibility of such regulation of one's own legal situation by others. Each of the four terms was to be understood not only by its difference from each of the other three, but also by its relations of correlation and opposition with other legal imputations importing subordination or detriment. Most obviously, a "right" was the correlative of a *duty*: in Hohfeld's view it was only possible to speak of a person having a legal "right" in the context of a relationship with some other person on whom the law imposed a correlative "duty". But "duty" was also the opposite of "privilege": that is, the situation of being legally obliged to perform an action was contrasted with the situation of being legally free to perform the action or not. Similarly, the correlative of A's "power" over the legal situation of B was the *liability* of B to the exercise of that power, "liability" being the opposite of "immunity". In turn, the correlative of B's "immunity" from the exercise of power by A was A's *disability* to affect B's position, "disability" being the opposite of "power". To complete this pattern of "jural opposites" and "jural correlatives", Hohfeld proposed that we speak of a *no-right* to denote the opposite of a "right" and the correlative of a "privilege".

A common criticism of Hohfeld's scheme (sometimes attributed to Albert Kocourek) was that, logically, the opposite of "a right" is everything in the world that is not "a right", including an elephant, a star and an angel. Although the point was vividly made, it may not have been especially relevant. Our apprehension of what is meant by "a right" is not significantly assisted by our conscious or unconscious awareness of its difference from an elephant, a star or an angel. It may well be significantly assisted by our conscious or unconscious awareness that it is different from a privilege, an immunity or a duty.

In fact the conscious or unconscious awareness of such differences informs our practice of reading at a very elementary level. In this respect contemporary interpretations of our practice build on the work of Ferdinand de Saussure (*Course in General Linguistics* (transl Roy Harris, Duckworth, 1983)), who argued that "[118] in a language there are only differences, *and no positive terms*". At the alphabetical level "[t]he one essential thing [for a writer] is that his *t* should be distinct from his *l*, his *d*, etc". For the reader what is essential is that "[116] two signs are never grasped as such by our linguistic consciousness, but only the difference between *a* and *b*". Thus, for example, it is only our understanding of the difference between *c* and *b* that enables us to distinguish between the words "cat" and "bat". For words, and for more complex linguistic constructions, Saussure makes the same point: "[114] In a given language, all the words which express neighbouring ideas help define one another's meaning. Each of a set of synonyms … has its particular value only because they stand in contrast with one another … [T]he value of any given word is determined by what other words there are in that particular area of the vocabulary … No word has a value that can be identified independently of what else there is in its vicinity". The *différances* that Jacques Derrida employs as a device for the deconstruction of texts build directly on this idea.

Jacques Derrida, *Positions*
(transl Alan Bass, University of Chicago Press, 1981)

[26] The play of differences supposes, in effect, syntheses and referrals which forbid at any moment, or in any sense, that a simple element be *present* in and of itself, referring only to itself. Whether in the order of spoken or written discourse, no element can function as a sign without referring to another element which itself is not simply present. This interweaving results in each "element" – phoneme or grapheme – being constituted on the basis of the trace within it of the other elements of the chain or system. This interweaving, this textile, is the *text* produced only in the transformation of another text. Nothing, neither among the elements nor within the system, is anywhere simply present or absent. There are only, everywhere, differences and traces of traces.

The analytical philosopher John Searle, in a critical review of a book by Jonathan Culler on deconstruction, has accepted the basic Saussurean point but rejected Derrida's gloss on it, and hence the entire notion of "traces".

JR Searle, "The Word Turned Upside Down"
in *New York Review of Books*, Vol 30, No 16, 27 October 1983, 74

[76] [T]his involves an important shift from Saussure's insight. The correct claim that the elements of the language only function as elements because of the differences they have from one another is converted into the false claim that the elements "consist of" (Culler) or are "constituted on" (Derrida) the *traces* of these other elements. "There are only, everywhere, differences and traces of traces." But the second thesis is not equivalent to the first, nor does it follow from it. From the fact that the elements function the way they do because of their relations to other elements, it simply does not follow that "nothing, neither among the elements nor within the system, is anywhere ever simply present or absent. There are only, everywhere, differences and traces of traces." ...

Consider an example. I understand the sentence "the cat is on the mat" the way I do because I know how it would relate to an indefinite – indeed infinite – set of other sentences, "the dog is on the mat", "the cat is on the couch," etc. But I understand the differences between the two sentences "the cat is on the mat" and "the dog is on the mat" in precisely the way I do because the word "cat" is present in the first while absent from the second, and the word "dog" is present in the second, while absent from the first. The system of differences does nothing whatever to undermine the distinction between presence and absence; on the contrary the system of differences is precisely a system of presences and absences.

Although Searle may have missed Derrida's metaphysical intentions, the practices of legal interpretation may offer some support for both views. The application of the maxim *expressio unius exclusio alterius* ("express reference to one example excludes other examples") depends precisely on presences and absences: the *presence* of what is stipulated draws attention to the *absence* of what is not. Again, in the High Court's interpretation of s 51(i) of the Constitution, the *presence* of a Commonwealth power with respect to overseas and interstate trade is used to draw attention to the *absence* of any power with respect to intrastate trade.

On the other hand, the High Court's practice before 1920 of interpreting grants of Commonwealth legislative power in the light of what were thought to be the States' "reserved powers" (see Chapter 7, §3) seems better accounted for by Derrida's analysis. The express grants of power to the Commonwealth were confined by the "traces" of the presupposed powers of the States: what was there in the constitutional text was read in the light of a background understanding of what was not there. And even today, more than 80 years after the doctrine was abandoned, it has sometimes seemed possible to detect "traces" of the doctrine of reserved State powers. Even more pervasively, the *omission* of any systematic Bill of Rights leaves a deeply equivocal "trace" whose ambiguous meaning affects virtually every debate about constitutional interpretation.

If the "traces" of possible alternatives are one source of multilevelled complexity in constitutional interpretation, the conventional literary use of the concepts of "connotation" and "denotation" might be another source. According to that conventional use, the meaning of a word is instantiated by the total number of concrete examples to which it directly refers, and which give it a precise denotative meaning or content; but the word also has wider associative or emotional connotations that will often provide its rhetorical effect. In that usage, though the denotation of a word may be fixed, its connotation may be more flexible and indeterminate. In the High Court, however, the connotation/denotation distinction tends to be used the other way round. The *connotation* of words in the Constitution is fixed as at 1900; its *denotation* may be subject to change as new instances, or different kinds of instances, arise. In fact, as Dawson J explained in *Street v Queensland Bar Association* (1989) 168 CLR 461, the High Court usage conforms to a technical usage proposed by John Stuart Mill.

Street v Queensland Bar Association
(1989) 168 CLR 461

Dawson J: [537] The essential meaning of the Constitution must remain the same, although with the passage of time its words must be applied to situations which were not envisaged at federation. Expressed in the technical language of the logician, the words have a fixed connotation but their denotation may differ from time to time. That is to say, the attributes which the words signify will not vary, but as time passes new and different things may be seen to possess those attributes sufficiently to justify the application of the words to them.

This technical use of the words "connotation" and "denotation" was adopted by John Stuart Mill and is described in his *A System of Logic: Ratiocinative and Inductive* (1875), pp 31-42. It is almost the converse of the popular or etymological use of those words in which "to denote" merely means to signify and "to connote" means to signify in addition. In *Commonwealth v Tasmania; Tasmanian Dam Case* [(1983) 158 CLR 1 at 302-3], I intentionally used the two words in their popular sense, preferring that to the way in which they are used by the logician. I now doubt the wisdom of having done so. Previous judgments had used the terms in their technical sense **[538]** more or less consistently for many years and, upon reflection, that usage seems to offer a precision which the popular usage does not.

The distinction between a fixed "connotation" and a varying "denotation" has repeatedly been applied to achieve a measure of flexibility. The contrast between "connotation" and "denotation" is used to argue that the meaning, or core characteristics, of an expression should be ascertained as if fixed at 1900, but that once so ascertained it may come to include new things over time (see Windeyer J in *Ex parte Professional Engineers' Association* (1959) 107 CLR 208 at 267). In a passage in *Re Wakim; Ex parte McNally (Cross-vesting Case)* (1999) 198 CLR 511, repeated in *Airservices Australia v Canadian Airlines International Ltd* (1999) 202 CLR 133 at 238, McHugh J assimilated the distinction to that drawn by Ronald Dworkin (*Taking Rights Seriously* (Duckworth, 1977), 134) between "concepts" and "conceptions".

Re Wakim; Ex parte McNally (Cross-vesting Case)
(1999) 198 CLR 511

McHugh J: [551] Where the interpretation of individual words or phrases of the Constitution is in issue, the current doctrine of the Court draws a distinction between connotation and denotation or, in other words, between meaning and application ...

[552] Philosophers are now said to regard the distinction between connotation and denotation as outdated ... But whether criticism of the distinction is or is not valid should not be seen as decisive. What is decisive is that, with perhaps only two exceptions, the Court has never hesitated to apply particular words and phrases to facts and circumstances that were or may have been outside the contemplation of the makers of the Constitution. That is because, with the striking exception of s 92 – which has an historical meaning – the words of the Constitution, for the most part, describe concepts and purposes that are stated at a sufficiently high level of abstraction to enable events and matters falling within the current understanding of those concepts and purposes to be taken into account ... That being so, once we have identified the concepts, express and implied, that the makers of our Constitution intended to apply, we can give effect to the present day conceptions of those concepts.

The "**[551]** two exceptions" that McHugh J referred to were *King v Jones* (1972) 128 CLR 221 (as to the meaning of the word "adult" in s 41), and *Attorney-General for NSW v Brewery Employees Union of NSW* (*Union Label Case*) (1908) 6 CLR 469, where Griffith CJ declared that "**[501]** [t]he meaning of terms used in [the Constitution] must be ascertained by their signification in 1900". Yet even Griffith CJ added that "with advancing civilization new developments, now unthought of, may arise with respect to many subject matters"; and that "[s]o long as those new developments relate to the same subject matter the powers of the Parliament will continue to extend to them". In that case, a majority of the High Court held that workers' trade marks, that is, marks indicating that goods had been produced using union labour, did not come within the connotation of "trade marks" as at 1900 and were thus not trade marks under s 51(xviii). Griffith CJ, O'Connor and Barton JJ held that an essential requirement of a trade mark is a trade or business connection between its owner and the goods to which the mark is affixed, with the mark being used in business to distinguish those goods from other goods. Griffith CJ relied on the now defunct "reserved powers" doctrine. Isaacs and Higgins JJ, in dissent, argued that workers' trade marks did come within the connotation of trade marks, since they had all the relevant characteristics of a trade mark as at 1900.

It may be compatible with this to say that, although the "connotation" or "concept" of "trade marks" remains fixed as at 1900, it might over time have come to include new things such as "service marks" that did not exist in 1900 (see *Davis v Commonwealth* (1988) 166 CLR 79 at 96). In any event, when s 51(xviii) was considered again in *Grain Pool of Western Australia v Commonwealth* (2000) 202 CLR 479, the joint judgment of Gleeson CJ, Gaudron, McHugh, Gummow, Hayne and Callinan JJ essentially adopted the dissenting judgment of Higgins J in the *Union Label Case*. In a separate judgment Kirby J agreed. The joint judgment rejected "**[495]** any notion that the boundaries of the power conferred by s 51(xviii) are to be ascertained solely by identifying what in 1900 would have been treated as a copyright, patent, design or **[496]** trade mark", as making "insufficient allowance for the dynamism which, even in 1900, was inherent in any understanding of the terms used in s 51(xviii)". Emphasising the "**[501]** cross-currents and uncertainties in the common law and statute at the time of federation", the joint judgment held that it was plainly within power for Parliament to resolve them, and indeed "to determine that there be fresh rights in the nature of copyright, patents of inventions and designs and trade marks". The *Circuit Layouts Act 1989* (Cth), considered in *Nintendo Co Ltd v Centronics Systems Pty Ltd* (1994) 181 CLR 134, was adduced as an example; and dicta in *Nintendo* extending the power to "**[160]** laws which create, confer, and provide for the enforcement of, intellectual property rights in original compositions, inventions, designs, trade marks and other products of intellectual effort" were approved.

One other feature of *Nintendo* emphasised in the joint judgment was its reference to *R v Brislan; Ex parte Williams* (1935) 54 CLR 262 – often cited as a classic example of adapting the words of the Constitution to later developments in a way that (it is said) could not have been foreseen. In that case the power under s 51(v) to make laws with respect to "Postal, telegraphic, telephonic, and other like services" was treated as extending to radio, since it fell within the words "other like services". Thirty years later it then became easy to read the same words as extending to television (*Jones v Commonwealth (No 2)* (1965) 112 CLR 206). And in 2004, in *Bayside City Council v Telstra Corporation Ltd* (2004) 216 CLR 595, it was held that the power extended not only to telecommunications services, but to "**[624]** laws regulating the terms and conditions upon which such services may be provided, the licensing of carriers, their conduct as licensees, and the conferring upon them of powers and immunities [including immunities from municipal charges] in connection with the activities undertaken by them pursuant to the chosen regulatory framework".

There is evidence that the words "other like services" were added to s 51(v) precisely because some new communications technology in the nature of radio *was* foreseen (see JA La Nauze, *The Making of the Australian Constitution* (Melbourne University Press, 1972), 69). On that basis, in *Grain Pool of Western Australia*, the joint judgment emphasised that the decisions on radio and television had demonstrated "**[493]** the inherent scope for expansion" of the power in s 51(v), thereby showing that: "Later developments in scientific methods for the provision of telegraphic and telephonic services were contemplated by s 51(v). Likewise, it would be expected that what might answer the description of an invention for the purpose of s 51(xviii) would change to reflect developments in technology".

6. "Different Voices"

In Carol Gilligan's book *In a Different Voice* (Harvard University Press, 1982) she argued that men and women typically have distinctive patterns of normative perception and moral development. She stressed that "**[2]** this association is not absolute". Her purpose was "to highlight a distinction between two modes of thought ... rather than to represent a generalisation about either sex"; and she argued that mature moral development involved a "convergence" or "interplay" of these voices "within each sex". The female world involved "**[32]** a web of relationships ... sustained by a process of communication", giving rise to a morality of care; the male world was one of "hierarchical ordering", giving rise to a morality of justice. Whether this distinction is valid, or is valid beyond a particular class and ethnicity, remains controversial, but it poses the question whether modes of constitutional reasoning which emphasise hierarchical power may not reflect excessively "masculine" perceptions. That in turn opens up a range of questions about how constitutional thought might be enriched or modified by "convergence" or "interplay" of male and female voices.

Earlier, Suzanna Sherry had conflated Gilligan's distinction between the "web" and the "ladder", as images of ethical perception, with her own distinction between "modern" and "classical" paradigms of political theory. The former "**[547]** reflects an infrastructure of independent, autonomous individuals, tied together by nothing more than the necessity of society". The "classical" paradigm focuses on "connection rather than autonomy ... Relations among individuals are more important than the discrete, abstract individuals themselves".

Suzanna Sherry, "Civic Virtue and the Feminine Voice in Constitutional Adjudication"
(1986) 72 *Virginia Law Review* 543

[580] *A. Introduction*

New studies in a variety of academic disciplines suggest that women in fact may have a unique perspective, a world-view that differs in significant respects from that of men. Feminist scholars in such diverse fields as philosophy, history, sociology, art, and anthropology have identified peculiarly feminine perspectives in those disciplines. Recent work in psychology and in literary theory is particularly illuminating. Psychological studies suggest that women's moral development and concept of self may differ from those of men. Feminist literary theory suggests that women's writing differs from men's in ways that reflect a radically different perspective. Despite the independence of the research and the differences in both topics of investigation and terms of description, the feminine perspective identified in each of these fields is, at its core, a single, common approach. That approach is captured in the tension between women's primary concern with intimacy or connection and men's primary focus on separation or autonomy.

[581] This difference between men and women may influence the manner in which they think about, write about, and practice their disciplines. Thus, it is probable that women's unique perspective on law and jurisprudence, as a function of their different world-view, extends well beyond areas traditionally seen as affecting women, and in fact encompasses all legal issues. Just as women's writing on all subjects – not just on intimacy, domesticity, or women's place in society – reflects a different cast, women's views on the law in general may provide insights and approaches that are less natural to, and therefore less available to, male lawyers and judges.

This different approach to the law makes women a potentially innovative force in the legal community. Because women have been excluded from the mainstream of legal authority and legal change, the legal system, like moral, political, and philosophical discourse, has become "a set of cultural and symbolic forms that view human experience from the distorted and one-sided perspective of a single gender." This is not to suggest merely that the legal structure [582] ignores or minimizes significant gender differences, but rather that because women have been excluded from shaping our legal structure in general, that structure reflects a distorted view of the tension between autonomy and connection and between the individual and society.

What sort of distortion has the masculine paradigm introduced into our legal system? Feminist scholars identify three primary dichotomies between men's and women's thinking: while women emphasize connection, subjectivity, and responsibility, men emphasize autonomy, objectivity, and rights. Although the parallels between the feminine perspective and classical paradigm, or between the masculine perspective and modern paradigm, are not precisely congruent, the similarities are too strong to ignore …

A brief caveat is in order. First, I am not contending that gender-based differences are universal, only that they are likely enough that the historical exclusion of women from the shaping of [583] the legal system has had a profound impact, which cannot be reversed – or, to a large extent, even recognized – until women begin to participate in that enterprise. Second, I am not limiting my analysis to a feminist perspective: feminists have a particular political agenda that may or may not be shared by all women (and is shared by some men) … Finally, I am not suggesting that the feminine perspective [584] is any better than the masculine perspective, just that it is different. The incorporation of a new perspective need not imply a hierarchical ranking; I am arguing merely that the law has been distorted by its one-sided focus and that the feminine perspective described here represents a move toward correcting that distortion. In particular, the feminine perspective is a natural reflection of the classical paradigm, and its integration is likely to remove the particular distortions of modern liberalism.

B. Connection and Autonomy

Like the classical paradigm, the feminine perspective views individuals primarily as interconnected members of a community. Nancy Chodorow and Carol Gilligan, in groundbreaking studies on the development of self and morality, have concluded that women tend to have a more intersubjective sense of self than men and that the feminine perspective is therefore more other-directed. Other studies tend to confirm this finding. The essential difference between the male and female perspectives mirrors the fundamental difference between the modern and classical paradigms: "[t]he basic feminine sense of self is connected to the world, the [585] basic masculine sense of self is separate." Women thus tend to see others as extensions of themselves rather than as outsiders or competitors.

Gilligan suggests that Kohlberg's description of a morally mature person – a "rational individual aware of values and rights prior to social contracts" who adopts "universal principles of justice," including "respect for the dignity of human beings as individual persons" – instead describes a masculine morality. That masculine perspective embodies the individualism inherent in the modern paradigm. The parallel between the classical paradigm and feminine morality, by contrast, is clearly illustrated by Gilligan's quotation of a typical female response to a moral dilemma:

> By yourself, there is little sense to things. It is like the sound of one hand clapping, the sound of one man or one woman, there is something lacking. *It is the collective that is important to me*, and that collective is based on certain guiding principles, one of which is that *everybody belongs to it*, and that you all come from it. You have to love someone else, because while you may not like them, you are inseparable from them. In a way, it is like loving your right hand. *They are part of you; that other person is part of that giant collection of people that you are connected to.*

Women's emphasis on connection also suggests that the cliche that women are more cooperative and less competitive than men may have some basis in fact. Historically, women have tended to **[586]** achieve their goals communally; from quilting bees to consciousness-raising sessions, women have banded together rather than striving individually. There are analogous differences between the organization and ideology underlying women's traditional dominion, the family, and men's traditional arena, the marketplace: as Frances Olsen notes, the market is based on an individualist ethic and the family on an altruistic ethic ...

[587] *C. Contextuality and Abstraction*

Scholarship in literature and psychology also suggests that women are more contextual and men more abstract. Piaget, for example, found that girls playing children's games tend to treat the rules of the game as less fixed and more flexible than do boys and that girls are more likely to stop a game altogether – thus preserving friendships – if a dispute arises. For boys, development and application of fixed, abstract rules is almost as important as the object of the game itself. Again, Kohlberg's description of moral development (ie, the development of the masculine perspective) stresses a progression from context-bound judgments to abstract moral principles. Women, on the other hand, in responding to moral dilemmas, tend instead to look to circumstances rather than to abstractions: the right moral response depends on the context.

[588] This concept of feminine reliance on context is borne out in some empirical experiments. For example, the greater familiarity of even young boys with universal principles is well illustrated by a simple experiment in which boys and girls were shown pictures of everyday objects and asked to group related objects:

> [B]oys tend to bracket together objects (or pictures of objects) whose intrinsic characteristics are similar, whereas girls weight more heavily the functional and relational characteristics of the entities to be compared. For instance, boys frequently bracketed together such entities as a truck, a car, and an ambulance, while girls bracketed such entities as a doctor, a hospital bed, and an ambulance.

The boys focused on the abstraction of "locomotion," seeing the objects as independent units, while the girls emphasized instead the concrete relationships among objects. Other studies confirm that males of all ages are better able to separate discrete objects from their backgrounds and relationships than are females. Males are said to be less field-dependent; that is, they have a greater "ability to overcome the influence of an embedding context." ...

[590] *D. Responsibility and Rights*

Until recently, the archetypal developmental continuum of individual moral sensibility was believed to be an orderly progression from self-centeredness through other-centeredness to the development of logical, independent, universal principles – rights – that depend neither on one's own needs nor on what others believe is right. Although this progression mirrors male moral development, it fails to reflect the moral growth pattern of women.

Gender-based differences in moral structure, long seen as evidence of women's moral immaturity, may in fact be evidence of a feminine morality that differs in its emphasis from that of males. In her study of moral development, Carol Gilligan found that women tend to view a moral problem as "a problem of care and responsibility in relationships rather than as one of rights and rules." When faced with the moral dilemma of whether a man should steal a drug he cannot afford to save his dying wife, Gilligan found that, while men struggle with the conflicting rights of the parties, women focus on the druggist's "moral obligation to show compassion," "not on the conflict of rights but on the failure of response." Although men and women may agree that the man ought to steal the drug, men justify it in terms of a resolution be-**[591]**-tween conflicting rights of husband and druggist, and women in terms of the need for more compassion by the druggist in the face of the husband's compassion for his wife. Whether personal or political, the moral structure of "mature" males reflects a paradigm of independent rights, while that of females emphasizes relational responsibilities.

In the same spirit David McKnight (*Beyond Right and Left: New Politics and the Culture Wars* (Allen & Unwin, Sydney, 2005)), also building (at 195) on Gilligan's work, has called for a "new moral framework" built around "**[259]** the centrality of caring and caring values", so that "**[196]** the values embodied in nurturing and caring" could be made to "imbue [our] social structures, politics and ... culture".

Whether or not it is helpful to perceive it as "gendered", there is a pervasive difference between those styles of judicial interpretation that focus on the precise analysis of discrete propositions, each isolated from any broader context, and those which seek a broader and more syncretic view – which will usually prove to be a more dynamic view – by a sensitivity to the interdependence of legal propositions, so that the overall fabric of ideas and arguments becomes itself the context by which the meaning of its component parts is enhanced. A particularly stark example, with pivotal consequences for Commonwealth-State relations, was the Court's insistence in *South Australia v Commonwealth* (*First Uniform Tax Case*) (1942) 65 CLR 373 (see Chapter 24, §2(b)) on reviewing the four challenged enactments in that case separately, thus excluding any consideration of their effect as an interlocking "scheme". Similar contrasts – at several different levels – run through the shifting judicial approaches to *Melbourne Corporation v Commonwealth* (1947) 74 CLR 31 (see Chapter 25, §2). One example is the shift from *Re Australian Education Union; Ex parte Victoria* (1995) 184 CLR 188 (with its broad impressionistic evocations of State "integrity" and "autonomy") to *Victoria v Commonwealth* (*Industrial Relations Act Case*) (1996) 187 CLR 416 (with its rigid factual categories). A very different example is the shift from the judgment of Mason J in *Queensland Electricity Commission v Commonwealth* (1985) 159 CLR 192 (with its precise enumeration of "two elements" in the *Melbourne Corporation* principle) to the judgment of Gaudron, Gummow and Hayne JJ in *Austin v Commonwealth* (2003) 215 CLR 185 (with its insistence on "**[249]** but one limitation ... [which] turns upon matters of evaluation and degree and of 'constitutional facts' ... not readily established by objective methods in curial proceedings").

More striking than these Australian examples is the cumulative shift since 1950 in the approach of the Supreme Court of India to the interpretation of that country's Constitution, and particularly of the "Fundamental Rights" and "Directive Principles" spelled out in Pts III and IV. Initially the Court took a technical and legalistic view, construing each Article as a discrete and narrowly confined provision (notably in *AK Gopalan v Union of India*, AIR 1950 SC 27). But increasingly the Court has woven different provisions together (especially the guarantee of equality in Art 14, the specific freedoms in Art 19, and the protection against arbitrary interference with the "right to life" in Art 21) to project a far-reaching vision of judicially enforceable rights in which each provision is read in the heuristic context supplied by the others. In this steady development the decision of a seven-judge bench in *Maneka Gandhi v Union of India*, AIR 1978 SC 597, was a major landmark. In *TV Vatheeswaran v State of Tamil Nadu*, AIR 1983 SC 361, Chinnappa Reddy J summed up the effect of *Maneka Gandhi* by saying "**[364]** that the various articles of the Constitution in Chapter III (Fundamental Rights) are not several, isolated walled fortresses, each not reacting on the other", but were "parts of a great scheme to secure certain basic rights to the citizens of the country, each article designed to expand but never to curtail the content of ... the other". The separate provisions "**[366]** are not mutually exclusive ... [but] sustain, strengthen and nourish each other".

In other legal cultures, the tendency persists to isolate the analysis of legal problems within doctrinal "walled fortresses", both by categorising areas of legal doctrine and by reducing broad statements of principle within each doctrinal area to concrete "categories" taken as independent starting-points for legal analysis. Whether or not this predilection for the isolation of "categories" reflects a distinctively masculine mode of perception, many feminists have argued that it inhibits an adequate legal response to the problems of women's lives. In branches of the law such as tort and contract, or criminal law and family law, for example, Regina Graycar has argued ("Legal Categories and Women's Work: Explorations for a Cross-Doctrinal Feminist Jurisprudence" (1994) 7 *Canadian Journal of Women and Law* 34) that conventional legal categories and definitions – including the doctrinal boundaries between tort and contract, or criminal law and family law – are often not readily receptive to "**[39]** the concrete reality of women's lives". The problem is not merely that the categories "**[36]** have been fashioned by men, about men, and constructed by reference to men's experiences", but that some of the legal problems most commonly experienced by women "**[37]** may cut across a number of different doctrinal categories", while others "do not fall into [any] recognized class of action", and hence are "most likely to disappear through the cracks".

The problem in constitutional law may be of the latter kind, involving not so much an overlap as an *absence* of relevant categories. One agenda for feminist constitutional law would be to reflect on where women's "rights" can be *found* in the Constitution. An interpretation of s 51(xxix), the "external affairs" power, makes it possible for Parliament to enact the *Sex Discrimination Act 1984* (Cth). An interpretation of the "marriage" power in s 51(xxi) makes the power a mechanism that can be used to privilege those relationships that the interpreter considers legitimate, and can then be used to regulate their incidents as broadly or as narrowly as the interpreter determines. And despite the Court's unsympathetic response to the "**[486]** general doctrine of legal equality" suggested in *Leeth v Commonwealth* (1992) 174 CLR 455, it seems clear that the Court will continue to educe more limited protections of individual liberty and equal justice from Ch III of the Constitution, conceived of as an insulated, self-contained universe of Commonwealth judicial power (see Chapter 14, §8).

These interpretive approaches illustrate both the limitations and the potentialities of law. The reliance on the external affairs power shows how limited and artificial are the constitutional avenues for recognising the "rights" of women: legislation is dependent on the availability of a relevant international treaty, and is limited to what the treaty provides for. Nonetheless, to identify such strategies is to move beyond merely criticising the law to expanding the legal resources through which the law itself may be reformed. Moreover, these examples suggest that once we adopt a woman-centred approach, the boundaries of discussion shift and the *categories* of law, of which "constitutional law" is one, are broken down. In this way, "asking the 'woman' question" becomes a strategy not only for challenging the hegemony of legal formalism, but for stretching the boundaries of feminist inquiry.

In any event, the feminist argument is but one illustration of the wider point that the structuring of a field of discourse by means of "categories" will invariably have an ideological base, and will often be quite artificial. Faced with a particularly elaborate example, the Argentinian poet Jorge Luis Borges (1899-1986) ("The Analytical Language of John Wilkins", in *Other Inquisitions 1936-1952* (transl R Simms, University of Texas Press, 1993), 101) was reminded of "**[103]** a certain Chinese encyclopaedia entitled *Celestial Emporium of Benevolent Knowledge*", in which "animals are divided into (a) those that belong to the Emperor, (b) embalmed ones, (c) those that are trained, (d) suckling pigs, (e) mermaids, (f) fabulous ones, (g) stray dogs, (h) those that are included in this classification, (i) those that tremble as if they were mad, (j) innumerable ones, (k) those drawn with a very fine camel's hair brush, (l) others, (m) those that have just broken a flower vase, (n) those that resemble flies from a distance". (See also the Preface to Michel Foucault, *The Order of Things: An Archaeology of the Human Sciences* (Tavistock Publications, 1970), using the "**[xv]** stark impossibility" of this classification to explore the contrast between "**[xxi]** order in its primary state", and the way in which "**[xx]** the fundamental codes of a culture" shape the "**[xix]** grid of identities, similitudes, analogies, [that we] become accustomed to" in "establishing an order among things".)

7. Postmodernity and Postmodernism

The increasing pace and far-reaching effects of technological change as the world approached the 21st century led some to argue that human civilisation was entering a new kind of era, and with it a new cultural context to which judicial techniques must adapt – not merely because theories of "postmodernism" must influence interpretive methods, but because the surrounding technological and cultural context to which law must adapt is one of "postmodernity".

JM Balkin, "What is a Postmodern Constitutionalism?"

(1992) 90 *Michigan Law Review* 1966

[1976] What, then, is a postmodern constitutionalism? It should be quite clear from what I have said above that I do not think that the greatest relevance of postmodernism to American constitutional law lies in methods of interpreting the Constitution. Rather, I think constitutional lawyers need to understand postmodernism because they need to understand the cultural changes that have taken place around them **[1977]** in art, politics, technology, and economics. Just as one cannot understand modernism without understanding the Industrial Revolution and the spurt of technological and cultural change that accompanied it, one cannot understand postmodernism without understanding the particular technological and cultural changes in society that have accompanied it. Postmodernity is the era in which the industrial model of mass production is applied to the creation and distribution of symbolic forms. Therefore, we might approach the question of postmodern constitutionalism in the following way: How have changes in technology, communication, and the organization of living and working changed the public's understandings and practice of law, the Constitution, human rights and democracy? How should the various social actors concerned with the Constitution (lawyers, judges, academics, legislators, citizens) understand the forms and practices of democratic self-government in light of the cultural changes occurring during the postmodern period, and what should they do in response to these changes? ...

[1978] A postmodern constitutionalism, in my view, must ask how postmodern culture and technology have affected law as an institution: the way that the courts, Congress, and the executive interact with each other, and the way that law is understood, promulgated, argued about, experienced, and assimilated. How is information about constitutional rights distributed and spread? What changes have occurred in the ways in which politics is organized, and in the ways in which laws are debated publicly or within government institutions? How have advances in technology changed the possible forms of power, control, and surveillance? What effect has mediazation wrought on the practice of American democracy? These are the key questions for a postmodern constitutionalist.

If "postmodernity" is loosely used as a label for our contemporary civilisation and its discontents, "postmodernism" is an even looser label for a range of theoretical challenges to the objectivity of commonplace perceptions of "truth" – insisting that what we regard as knowledge is also ideology, and that both knowledge and ideology are contextually formed.

From the viewpoint of most postmodernist theorists, "originalism" suffers from three interrelated fallacies. *First*, it perpetuates "the myth of origin", that is, the belief that a body of doctrine can be endowed with authority by tracing it back to a foundational "beginning" or "origin". In some versions of this belief the "origins" relied on may themselves be mythical (see, for example, Peter Goodrich, *Oedipus Lex: Psychoanalysis, History, Law* (University of California Press, 1995), 26-30 and following, suggesting that for English common law and constitutionalism the "**[99]** conception of legitimacy depended upon an indefinite time of origin, an originary presence that was never present and so could be neither sensed nor touched"). If, on the other hand, the claim to authority is based on a unique foundational event, itself supposedly independent of earlier foundations (compare Kelsen's search for a historically first constitution in Chapter 1, §2), then the "myth" is one of circularity: the "origin" relied upon to endow a system of beliefs with authority can do so only if the "origin" is itself endowed with authority by the system of beliefs. *Secondly*, at the conceptual level, "originalism" entails a reduction of history to the kind of dichotomy rejected by Foucault ("Politics and the Study of Discourse" (1978) 4 *Ideology and Consciousness* 7 – see the extract in Chapter 1, §2) between (on the one hand) long continuous "**[17]** periods of stability or of universal convergence" and (on the other hand) sudden historical "moments of effervescence" or revolution in which a new tradition springs up. *Thirdly*, at a more pragmatic level, by seeking to approach the problems of the present historical moment exclusively by reference to the "originating" meaning of the text at a specific past historical moment, "originalism" effects an *erasure* of all the interpretations that may have accumulated in between. Conversely, some versions of "originalism" appear to be a specific response to the claims of postmodernism. For example, it would seem that for an "originalist" judge like Justice Scalia of the United States Supreme Court, his "originalism" is a strategy in the "[652] culture war" over issues of sexuality about which he spoke in *Romer v Evans*, 517 US 620 (1996).

The "deconstruction" of texts that serves as a central methodological strategy of post-modernist theory is associated particularly with the work of Jacques Derrida (1930-2004). In several contexts where a text has been signed as a mark of authorship or solemnisation, Derrida has sought to deconstruct the text by deconstructing the signature. At the University of Virginia in 1976, he did this in a public lecture on the occasion of the bicentennial of the signing of the Declaration of Independence. He had been invited to undertake "[7] a 'textual' analysis ... of the Declaration of Independence and the Declaration of the Rights of Man".

Jacques Derrida, "Declarations of Independence"
(1986) 15 *New Political Science* 7

[7] At first, I was astonished. An intimidating proposition. Nothing had prepared me for it. No previous work had led me along the path of such analyses ... On reflection, I said to myself that if I had the time and the strength to do it, I'd like to try the experiment ... I would have liked, if not to try a juridico-political study of the two texts and the two events which are marked there – a task inaccessible to me – then at least to sharpen, in a preliminary way and using these texts as an example, some questions which have been elaborated elsewhere ... [O]ut of all these questions, the only one I will retain for the occasion ... [8] is this one: *who signs, and with what so-called proper name, the declarative act which founds an institution*?

Such an act does not come back to a constative or descriptive discourse. It performs, it accomplishes, it does what it says it does: that at least would be its intentional structure ... The declaration which founds an institution, a constitution or a State requires that a signer engage him- or herself. The signature maintains a link with the instituting act, as an act of language and of writing, a link which has absolutely nothing of the empirical accident about it ... Although in principle an institution – in its history and in its tradition, in its offices [*permanence*] and thus in its very institutionality – has to render itself independent of the empirical individuals who have taken part in its production, although it has in a certain way to mourn them or resign itself to their loss [*faire son deuil*], even and especially if it commemorates them, it turns out, precisely by reason of the structure of instituting language, that the founding act of an institution – the act as archive as well as the act as performance – *has to maintain within itself the signature.*

But just whose signature exactly? Who is the actual signer of such acts? And what does actual [*effectif*] mean? ...

Take, for example, Jefferson, the "draftsman [*rédacteur*]" of the project or draft [*projet*] of the Declaration ... No one would take him for the true signer of the Declaration. *By right*, he writes but he does not sign. Jefferson represents the representatives who have delegated to him the task of drawing up [*rédiger*] what they knew *they* wanted to say. He was not responsible for *writing*, in the productive or initiating sense of the term, only for *drawing up*, as one says of a secretary that he or she draws up a *letter* of which the spirit has been breathed into him [9] or her, or even the content dictated. Moreover, after having thus drawn up a project or a draft, a sketch, Jefferson had to submit it to those whom for a time, he *represented* and who are themselves *representatives*, namely the "representatives of the United States in General Congress assembled." These "representatives," of whom Jefferson represents a sort of advance-pen, will have the right to revise, to correct and to ratify the project or draft of the Declaration ...

As for the "representatives" themselves, they don't sign either ... [or] at least ... the right is divided here. In fact, they sign; by right, they sign for themselves but also "for" others. They have been delegated the proxies, the power of attorney, for signing [*Ils on délégation or procuration de signature*]. They speak, "declare,", declare themselves and sign "in the name of ...": "We, therefore, the representatives of the United States of America in General Congress assembled, do in the name and by the authority of the good people of these [...] that as free and independ[e]nt states ...".

By right, the signer is thus the people, the "good" people (a decisive detail because it guarantees the value of the intention and of the signature, but we will see ... on what and on whom such a guarantee is founded or founds itself). It is the "good people" who declare themselves free and independent by the relay of their representatives and of their representatives of representatives. One cannot decide – and that's the interesting thing, the force and the coup of force of such a declarative act – whether independence is stated or produced by this utterance … Is it that the good people have already freed themselves in fact and are only stating the fact of this emancipation in [*par*] the Declaration? Or is it rather that they free themselves at the instant of and by [*par*] the signature of this Declaration? It is not a question here of an obscurity or of a difficulty of interpretation, of a problematic on the way to its (re)solution … This obscurity, this undecidability between, let's say, a performative structure and a constative structure, is *required* in order to produce the sought-after effect …

[10] Here then is the "good people" who engage themselves and engage only themselves in signing, in having their own declaration signed. The "we" of the declaration speaks "in the name of the people."

But this people does not exist. They do *not* exist as an entity, it does *not* exist, *before* this declaration, not *as such*. If it gives birth to itself, as free and independent subject, as possible signer, this can hold only in the act of the signature. The signature invents the signer. This signer can only authorize him- or herself to sign once he or she has come to the end [*parvenu au vout*], if one can say this, of his or her own signature, in a sort of fabulous retroactivity. That first signature authorizes him or her to sign …

There was no signer, by right, before the text of the Declaration which itself remains the producer and guarantor of its own signature. By this fabulous event, by this fable which implies the structure of the trace and is only in truth possible thanks to [*par*] the inadequation to itself of a present, a signature gives itself a name. It opens *for itself* a line of credit, *its* own credit, for itself *to* itself. The *self* surges up here in all cases (nominative, dative, accusative) as soon as a signature gives or extends credit to itself, in a single coup of force, which is also a coup of writing, as the right to writing. The coup of force makes right, founds right or the law, gives right, *brings the law to the light of day, gives both birth and day to the law* [donne le jour à la loi] …

That this unheard-of thing should also be an everyday occurrence should [11] not make us forget the singular context of this act. In this case, another state signature had to be effaced in "dissolving" the links of colonial paternity or maternity. One will confirm it in reading: this "dissolution" too involves both constation and performance, indissociably mixed. The signature of every American citizen today depends, in fact and by right, on this indispensable confusion. The constitution and the laws of your country somehow guarantee the signature, as they guarantee your passport …

And yet. And yet another instance still holds itself back behind the scenes. Another "subjectivity" is still coming to sign, in order to guarantee it, this production of signature. In short, there are only countersignatures in this process. There is a differential process here because there is a countersignature, but everything should concentrate itself in the *simulacrum of the instant*. It is still "in the name of" that the "good people" of America call *themselves* and declare *themselves* independent, at the instant in which they invent (for) themselves as a signing identity. They sign in the name of the laws of nature and in the name of God. They *pose* or *posit* their institutional laws on the foundation of natural laws and by the same coup (the interpretive coup of force) in the name of God, creator of nature. He comes, in effect, to guarantee the rectitude of popular intentions, the unity and goodness of the people. He founds natural laws and thus the whole game which tends to present performative utterances *as* constative utterances …

[The Declaration states:] "We therefore the Representatives of the United States of America, in General Congress assembled, appealing to the Supreme Judge of the world for the rectitude of our intentions, do in the Name and by the authority of the good People of these Colonies solemnly *publish* and *declare*, that these united Colonies are and of right ought to be *free and independ[e]nt states* […]."

"Are and ought to be"; the "and" articulates and conjoins here the two discursive modalities, the to be and the ought to be, the constation and the prescription, the fact and the right. *And* is God: at once the creator of nature and [12] judge, supreme judge of what is (the state of the world) and of what relates to what ought to be (the rectitude of our intentions). The instance of judgment, at the level of the supreme judge, is the last instance for saying the fact *and* the law. One can understand this Declaration as a vibrant act of faith, as a hypocrisy indispensable to a politico-military-economic, etc coup of force, or, more simply, more economically, as the analytic and consequential deployment of a tautology: for this Declaration to have a meaning *and* an effect, there must be a last instance. God is the name, the best one, for this last instance and this ultimate signature. Not only the best one in a determined context (such and such a nation, such and such a religion, etc), but the name of the best name in general ...

Someone, let's call him Jefferson (but why not God?), desired that the institution of the American people should be, by the same coup, the erection of his proper name. A name of State.

Did he succeed? I would not venture to decide ...

[13] The question remains. How is a State made or founded, how does a State make or found itself? And an independence? And the autonomy of one which both gives itself, and signs, its own law? Who signs all these authorizations to sign?

I won't, in spite of my promise, engage myself on this path, today.

Despite Derrida's willingness to "deconstruct" the authority of the founders (and hence of "originalism"), his attitude to the authority of the law is more ambiguous. In "Before the Law", in *Acts of Literature* (D Attridge (ed), Routledge, 1992), 181, he suggested that our inability to gain access to the foundations of law is precisely what gives it authority: "[192] What remains concealed and invisible in each law is ... the law itself, that which makes laws of these laws, the being-law of these laws ... [204] We must remain ignorant of who or what or where the law is, we must not know who it is or what it is, where and how it presents itself, whence it comes and whence it speaks. This is what *must* be before the *must* of the law".

Although contemporary deconstructionist and hermeneutic theories have varied widely in their approach to the interpretation of texts, they agree in rejecting "foundationalism" (that is, the belief that a text has a predetermined meaning which rests upon some objective foundation). In this sense, of course, "originalism" is a form of "foundationalism".

Stephen Feldman, "Diagnosing Power: Postmodernism in Legal Scholarship and Judicial Practice"
(1994) 88 *Northwestern University Law Review* 1046

[1060] Philosophical hermeneutics is most easily understood in opposition to foundationalist views of understanding and interpretation. Foundationalists hold that the meaning of a text rests on some firm ground or foundation – an object that is separate and independent from, yet somehow accessible to, a perceiving subject. To understand a text correctly, the subject implements a mechanical technique or method that either bridges the gap to the objective meaning of the text or, at least, mirrors in consciousness the content of the text. To take an example familiar to attorneys, some constitutional foundationalists maintain that a reader of the Constitution must somehow reconstruct in his or her own consciousness the intentions of the Framers, as memorialized in the constitutional text.

Philosophical hermeneutics, contrary to foundationalism, maintains that no matter what we do, we are always and already interpreting. All experience, perception, and understanding are interpretive. Thus, the text (or a text-analogue) is not an object in the foundationalist sense; no uninterpreted source of meaning stands outside of or prior to an interpretive act. And since the text does not exist in an independent [1061] and uninterpreted state, its meaning cannot be derived through some mechanical technique or method. As Hans-Georg Gadamer, one of the foremost interpretivist philosophers, writes: "[O]ur perception is never a simple reflection of what is given to the senses."

Nonetheless, according to philosophical hermeneutics, this rejection of objectivity does not mean that understanding or interpretation is purely subjective or capricious. The reader (or interpreter) is never an independent and autonomous subject who freely or arbitrarily imposes meaning on a text (or text-analogue). To the contrary, the interpreter is always situated in a "tradition" or, in Stanley Fish's words, in an "interpretive community," from which we inherit prejudices and interests that constrain and direct our understandings of texts. One's life within [1062] a community and its traditions necessarily limits one's range of vision – what one can possibly see or understand in a text. As Gadamer says, the traditions of one's community help to shape the interpreter's "horizon": "the range of vision that includes everything that can be seen from a particular vantage point." Furthermore, the notion of an interpretive *community* underscores that we are historical beings who *live* in tradition: "[W]e are always situated within traditions ... [which are] always part of us ..." . Thus, tradition is not a thing of the past; rather it is something in which we constantly participate. As Gadamer notes: "Tradition is not simply a permanent precondition; rather, we produce it ourselves inasmuch as we understand, participate in the evolution of tradition, and hence further determine it ourselves."

A crucial element of philosophical hermeneutics is the recognition that although communal traditions and the concomitant prejudices constrain our possibilities for understanding, they simultaneously *enable* us to communicate and to understand. Our traditions, prejudices, and interests actually open us to meaning, understanding, and truth. Gadamer writes:

> This formulation certainly does not mean that we are enclosed within a wall of prejudices and only let through the narrow portals those things that can produce a pass saying, 'Nothing new will be said here.' Instead we welcome just that guest who promises something new to our curiosity. But how do we know the guest whom we admit is one who has something new to say to us? Is not our expectation and our readiness to hear the new also necessar-**[1063]**-ily determined by the old that has already taken possession of us?

Hence, truth, knowledge, and understanding are possible only *because* we participate in the tradition of an interpretive community.

Because we always live within the traditions of interpretive communities, philosophical hermeneutics further holds that we never approach any text or text-analogue without some "fore-understanding" derived from our traditions and prejudices. One's fore-understanding, however, does not undermine the interpretive process by pre-determining meaning: rather interpretation consists of a dialogical "play" between the interpreter and the text in which the meaning of the text dialectically comes into being. Interpretation requires one to question the text, to probe for its meaning, to ask new questions, to listen to the answers, and to continue in this dialogical process as if in a conversation. One's fore-understanding "is constantly revised in terms of what emerges as [the interpreter] penetrates into the meaning [of the text]." Thus, the dialogical process of understanding assures that one's answer often changes as meaning emerges even though one already expects a certain answer as soon as interpretation begins ...

[1064] Gadamer emphasizes that the hermeneutic act is "one unified process." Others have insisted that understanding, interpretation, and application are separate events: we understand the meaning of a text directly; we interpret a text only when we self-consciously reflect upon its meaning (for example, when we attempt to resolve a textual ambiguity); and we apply our understanding or interpretation of the meaning of the text when we attempt to transfer it to a new situation. Gadamer, however, maintains that understanding, interpretation, and application are not distinct events; rather they constitute the components of a unified hermeneutic act. We understand (or fore-understand) a text only insofar as we open to its meaning because of our prejudices derived from communal traditions; we develop prejudices only as we simultaneously accept and reconstruct – or interpret – communal traditions; and we understand and interpret texts as well as traditions only insofar as we apply them to practical problems within our current horizon. We cannot extract any one component of this hermeneutic process, such as an understanding of a text, and treat it as an uncontested, stable, or non-contingent starting point.

Finally, according to Gadamer, the "medium" of tradition and un-**[1065]**-derstanding is language. Tradition exists and is handed down to us in and through language, and therefore understanding, which is possible only because of tradition, must itself be linguistic in character. To Gadamer, then, language is not simply a tool or a possession of humanity; rather one experiences the world linguistically. Each person, in short, "lives in a language." Gadamer writes: "Language is the fundamental mode of operation of our being-in-the-world and the all embracing form of the constitution of the world."

In sum, philosophical hermeneutics rejects the foundationalist opposition of subject and object yet resurrects the possibility of truth and knowledge. An interpreter is never a radically free subject who arbitrarily imposes meaning on a text; we are always limited by the prejudices that we inherit from our interpretive community and its traditions. Furthermore, truth never exists as an object or brute datum that can be grasped or mirrored somehow in consciousness. Instead, truth is possible only because we live within communal traditions that open us to the possibility of understanding and knowledge.

Michel Rosenfeld, "Deconstruction and Legal Interpretation: Conflict, Indeterminacy and the Temptations of the New Legal Formalism"
in Drucilla Cornell, Michel Rosenfeld and David Carlson (eds), *Deconstruction and the Possibility of Justice* (Routledge, 1992), 152

[152] The practice of legal interpretation is mired in a deep and persistent crisis …

In the broadest terms, the crisis reflects a loss of faith concerning the availability of objective criteria permitting the ascription of distinct and transparent meanings to legal texts. Moreover, this loss of faith manifests itself in the intensification of the conflict among the community of legal actors, the dissolution of any genuine consensus over important values, the seemingly inescapable indeterminacy of legal rules, and the belief that all the dispositions of legal issues are ultimately political and subjective. The roots of the crisis affecting legal interpretation can be traced back to the Legal Realists' critique of legal formalism …

Deconstruction appears to buttress the proposition that application of legal rules and legal doctrine is ultimately bound to lead to conflict, contradiction and indeterminacy. Any attempt at defining deconstruction is hazardous at best as there is disagreement over whether deconstruction is a method, a technique or a process based on a particular ontological and ethical vision. Nevertheless … , it seems fair to assert that deconstruction postulates that writing precedes speech instead of operating as a mere supple-[153]-ment to speech, stresses that every text refers to other texts, and emphasizes that discontinuities between the logic and rhetoric of texts create inevitable disparities between what the author of a text "*means to say*" and what the text is "nonetheless *constrained to mean*". In other words, in the context of deconstruction, all texts (whether oral or written) are writings that refer to other writings. A text is not a pure presence that immediately and transparently reveals a distinct meaning intended by its author. Instead, from the standpoint of deconstruction, every writing embodies a failed attempt at reconciling identity and difference, unity and diversity and self and other. A writing may give the impression of having achieved the desired reconciliation, but such impression can only be the product of ideological distortion, suppression of difference or subordination of the other. Consistent with these observations, legal discourse – and particularly modern legal discourse with its universalist aspirations – cannot achieve coherence and reconciliation so long as it produces writings that cannot eliminate from their margins ideological distortions, unaccounted differences or the lack of full recognition of any subordinated other.

For those who take the challenge posed by deconstruction seriously, there can be no easy solution to the crisis affecting legal interpretation. Thus, for example, there cannot be a return to the narrowly circumscribed and simpler jurisprudence of original intent where the meaning of legal texts can be precisely framed by reference to some transparent, self-present intent of the framer of a constitution, a legislator or a party to a private contract … [E]ven divinely prescribed law involves multiple writings, erasure and intersubjective collaboration. Accordingly, in light of deconstruction, resort to the jurisprudence of original intent can only lead to a paralyzing idolatry that forecloses any genuine intertextual elucidation of legal relationships. In other words, by isolating a particular writing and by elevating it above all other writings in such a way as to sever the intertextual links that constitute an indispensable precondition to the generation of meaning, the jurisprudence of original intent both promotes blind worship of the arbitrary and the unintelligible and blocks discovery of the intertextual connections necessary to endow legal acts with meaning.

Other attempts at overcoming the crisis affecting legal interpretation do not fare significantly better in the face of the challenge posed by deconstruction. For example, the claim that an adequate standard of legal interpretation can be fashioned by reference to the intersub-[154]-jective perspective of an "interpretive community," can only prevail through the suppression of difference and the subordination of the dissenting other. Indeed, as evidenced by the very crisis sought to be overcome, legal interpretation becomes manifestly problematic *because* of conflict and fragmentation *within* the interpretive community. Therefore, unless appeal to the interpretive community comes on the heels of a genuine resolution of the aforementioned conflict and fragmentation, such an appeal would only make sense if it were accompanied by suppression of some of the clashing voices found in the interpretive community ...

There is a different kind of approach to the crisis of legal interpretation which may initially seem particularly attractive because it does not apparently rely on a concrete definition of the object of legal interpretation or on contested extra-legal values. This kind of approach stresses the *process* of interpretation above the object of interpretation or the substantive values espoused by the interpreter. It is a procedural approach in so far as it suggests that so long as legitimate interpretive procedures are followed, the interpretive outcome will be justified regardless of actual substantive disagreements concerning the object of interpretation or extra-legal values held by members of the community of legal actors.

A prime example of the approach under consideration is provided by Ronald Dworkin's theory of law as integrity ... [He] maintains that legal interpretation does not take place in a vacuum, but **[155]** that it is an historically situated practice. An interpreter confronted with the task of determining what the law requires in a particular case must refer to relevant past instances of legal interpretation in order to be in a position to provide the best possible interpretation of the law in the case at hand ...

Dworkin's approach is intertextual, and while formal and procedural, it is not purely abstract. The substantive values of the community of legal actors do not directly figure in legal decisions but they are not simply severed from the process of legal interpretation. Traces of these substantive values are embedded in the legal precedents that confront the legal interpreter and must therefore be implicitly taken into account by the latter in his or her formulation of an interpretation that is compatible with precedent while preserving the integrity of the legal process.

Under closer scrutiny, Dworkin's theory of law as integrity fails to provide an acceptable solution to the crisis affecting legal interpretation. The principal reason for this failure is ... that the criterion of fit is too indeterminate to endow Dworkin's principle of integrity with a sufficiently concrete meaning. Indeed, Dworkin's requirement of fit and integrity is reducible to an appeal to coherence made in an interpretive universe that has been stripped of intelligible criteria of coherence. Either the measure of fit and integrity is based on some set of substantive values such as those embedded in certain relevant judicial precedents, or it is reducible to a purely formal and abstract notion that cannot be given any non-arbitrary concrete instantiation. If fit and integrity depend on particular substantive values – even if these values have been filtered through the interpretive process involved in the attempted reconcilia-**[156]**-tion of judicial precedents – then Dworkin's theory is ultimately subject to the same criticisms as those theories which select one set of contested substantive extra-legal values as dominant and the remainder as subordinate. On the other hand, if fit and integrity are to be understood in purely formal and abstract terms, cut off from all extra-legal substantive values, then the coherence which they seek is a mere transcendent ideal devoid of any particular concrete purchase.

Although Dworkin's principle of integrity fails to deliver the means to overcome the challenge posed by deconstruction, the notion of integrity should not be discarded altogether. Indeed, integrity may play a useful, if more modest, role than that reserved for it by Dworkin, in the quest for a satisfactory solution to the crisis affecting legal interpretation. That role is a critical one, and it consists in serving as a constant reminder against the acceptability of a conception of law that tolerates the reduction of law to mere politics ... Even if no concrete embodiment of law as integrity is presently attainable, drawing attention to the absence of integrity may foster resistance against abandoning law to politics. In short, while legal interpreters may lack a positive conception of integrity, integrity can nevertheless still play the important negative role of standing in for the coherence and the principles that law that is reducible to politics lacks.

Postmodernism presents the judge with a dilemma and an opportunity. The dilemma arises because, if there is nothing behind the text – no solid referential meaning or original intent – then interpretation becomes impossible. As Richard Beardsworth puts it (*Derrida & the Political* (Routledge, 1996)): "**[7]** On the one hand, the sign dominates the horizon of contemporary thinking because it is no longer regarded ... as a secondary instance which represents or communicates a prior entity ...; on the other hand, just when it assumes this primary position, it moves into crisis. Since language is largely defined as a *medium* conveying an instance prior to it, the moment this instance withdraws, the very identity of language does as well. The sign becomes at one and the same time both a privileged object of reflection and a volatile object unsure of its vocation". The opportunity arises because, the more we acknowledge the ultimate indeterminacy of textual meanings, the greater is the possibility that the judicial *construction* of authoritative texts can be morally or socially *constructive*. Richard Rorty ("The Banality of Pragmatism and the Poetry of Justice" (1990) 63 *Southern California Law Review* 1811) has suggested that path-breaking decisions such as *Brown v Board of Education*, 347 US 483 (1954) (on the racial desegregation of schools) and *Roe v Wade*, 410 US 113 (1973) (on abortion rights) are made possible only by the kind of "**[1816]** vision that [cannot] be successfully backed up by ... argument about the presuppositions of rational discourse. But visions do not really need backup. To put forth a vision is always one of **[1817]** Fitzjames Stephen's 'leaps in the dark'." (The reference is to James Fitzjames Stephen, *Liberty, Equality, Fraternity* (Smith, Elder & Co, 1873, 2nd ed 1874): "**[353]** In nearly all the important transactions of life, indeed in all transactions whatever which have relation to the future, we have to take a leap in the dark".)

More fundamentally, at a 1989 symposium on "Deconstruction and the Possibility of Justice", Jacques Derrida argued that just decision-making is a possibility only because the very act of decision-making necessarily encounters "aporias".

Richard Beardsworth, *Derrida & the Political*
(Routledge, 1996)

[32] Aporia comes from the Greek *aporos*, which means 'without passage' or 'without issue'. An aporia is something that is impracticable. A route which is impractical is one that cannot be traversed, it is an uncrossable path. Without passage, not treadable. For the Eleatic Zeno, who ... was the first to use the term consistently, aporia implied the suspension (*epokhe*) of judgement. At the point where the path of thinking stopped, judgement was suspended. This definition of aporia was inherited by the presocratic sophists who called an aporia two contradictory sayings of equal value. The suspension of judgement was a mode of perplexity before the inability to ground either saying ...

[I]f Derrida uses the concept of aporia, it is *not* within traditional sitings of the term ... For example, aporia, for Derrida, is not, as it was for the presocratics, an oscillation between two contradictory sayings ... [T]he 'contradiction' applies to one and the same entity, not to two different entities.

A common example of an aporia in legal reasoning is what Julius Stone (*The Province and Function of Law* (Maitland Publications, 1946)) called "categories of competing reference": that is, the situation "**[176]** where two or more legal categories, or their respective logical consequences, each prescribing different rules, overlap in their application to a particular situation". The situation referred to above by Beardsworth, where "**[32]** the 'contradiction' applies to one and the same entity, not to two different entities", was analysed by Stone as involving "**[179]** the single legal category with competing versions of reference ... **[180]** 'Competing versions' of a legal category are a normal feature of the authoritative materials: and wherever they exist, a set of facts will sooner or later arise which stands between the competing versions, and can only be dealt with by a fresh creative decision". However, where Stone's examples referred to aporias that arise *within* the enterprise of legal reasoning, Derrida sought to articulate the aporias that underlie the very attempt to embark on that enterprise at all.

Jacques Derrida, "Force of Law"
in Jacques Derrida, *Acts of Religion* (ed G Anidjar, Routledge, 2002), 230

[241] The very emergence of justice and law, the instituting, founding, and justifying moment of law implies a performative force, that is to say always an interpretative force and a call to faith: not in the sense ... that law would be *in the service* of force, its docile instrument, servile and thus exterior to the dominant power, but rather in the sense of law that would maintain a more internal, more complex relation to what one calls force, power or violence. Justice – in the sense of *droit* (right or law) – would not simply be put in the service of a social force or power ... Yet, the operation that amounts to founding, inaugurating, justifying law, to *making law*, would consist of a *coup de force*, of a performative and therefore interpretative violence that in itself is neither just nor unjust and that no justice and no earlier and previously founding law, no preexisting foundation, could, by definition, guarantee or contradict or invalidate ...

[242] Since the origin of authority, the founding or grounding, the positing of the law cannot by definition rest on anything but themselves, they are themselves a violence without ground. This is not to say that they are in themselves unjust, in the sense of "illegal" or "illegitimate." They are neither legal nor illegal in their founding moment. They exceed the opposition between founded and unfounded, or between any foundationalism or antifoundationalism. Even if [their] success presupposes earlier conditions and conventions ..., the same "mystical" limit will reemerge at the supposed origin of said conditions, rules or conventions, and [also] at the origin of their dominant interpretation ...

In the structure I am here describing here, law is essentially *deconstructible,* whether because it is founded, that is to say constructed, upon interpretable and transformable textual strata (and that is the history of law, its possible and necessary transformation, sometimes its amelioration), or because its ultimate foundation is by definition unfounded. The fact that law is deconstructible is not bad news. One may even find in this the political chance of all historical progress. But [243] the paradox that I would like to submit for discussion is the following: it is this deconstructible structure of law or, if you prefer, of justice as law, that also ensures the possibility of decon-struction. Justice in itself, if such a thing exist, outside or beyond law, is not deconstructible. No more than deconstruction itself, if such a thing exist. *Deconstruction is justice.* It is perhaps because law (which I will therefore consistently try to distinguish from justice) is constructible ... [that it is] deconstructible and, better yet, that it makes deconstruction possible ... Whence these three propositions:

1. The deconstructibility of law (for example) makes deconstruction possible.
2. The undeconstructibility of justice also makes deconstruction possible, indeed is inseparable from it.
3. *Consequence:* Deconstruction takes place in the interval that separates the undecon-structibility of justice from the deconstructibility of law. Deconstruction is possible as an experience of the impossible, there where, even if it does not exist, if it is not *present,* not yet or never, *there is* justice ...

In other words, the hypothesis and propositions toward which I am tentatively moving here would rather call for the subtitle: justice as the possibility of deconstruction, the structure of right or of the law, the founding or the self-authorizing of law as the possibility of the exercise of deconstruction ...

[244] [There are] infinite problems, infinite in their number, infinite in their history, infinite in their structure, covered by the title *Deconstruction and the Possibility of Justice.* But we already know that these problems are not infinite simply [because] they are infinitely numerous ... They are infinite, if one may say so, *in themselves,* because they require the very experience of the aporia that is not unrelated to what we just called the *mystical.*

By saying that they even require the *experience of aporia,* one can understand two things that are already quite complicated:

1. As its name indicates, an *experience* is a traversal ... and travels toward a destination for which it finds a passage. The experience finds its way, its passage, it is possible. Yet, in this sense there cannot be a full experience of aporia, that is, of something that does not allow passage. *Aporia* is a nonpath ... [Thus] justice would be the experience of what we are unable to experience ...
2. But I believe that there is no justice without this experience, however impossible it may be, of aporia. Justice is an experience of the impossible: a will, a desire, a demand for justice the structure of which would not be an experience of aporia, would have no chance to be what it is – namely, a just *call* for justice. Every time ... that we placidly [but mechanically] apply a

good rule to a particular case, to a correctly subsumed example, according to a determinant judgment, law perhaps [can] sometimes finds itself accounted for, but one can be sure that justice does not.

Law is not justice. Law is the element of calculation, and it is just that there be law, but justice is incalculable, it demands that one calculate with the incalculable; and aporetic experiences are the experiences, as improbable as they are necessary, of justice, that is to say of moments in which the *decision* between just and unjust is never insured by a rule ...

[245] [J]ustice, as law, seems always to suppose the generality of a rule, a norm or a universal imperative. How to reconcile the act of justice that must always concern singularity, individuals, groups, irreplaceable existences, the other or myself *as* other, in a unique situation, with rule, norm, value, or the imperative of justice that necessarily have a general form, even if this generality prescribes a singular application in each case? If I were content to apply a just rule, without a spirit of justice and without in some way and each time inventing the rule and the example, I might be sheltered from criticism, under the protection of law, my action conforming to objective law, but I would not be just. I would act, Kant would say, *in conformity* with duty but not *through* duty or *out of respect* for the law. Is it ever possible to say that an action is not only legal, but just? ...

[248] One must be *juste* with justice, and the first justice to be done is to hear it, to try to understand where it comes from, what it wants from us ... One must know that this justice always addresses itself to singularity ..., despite or even because it pretends to universality. Consequently, never to yield on this point, constantly to maintain a questioning of the origin, grounds and limits of our conceptual, theoretical or normative apparatus surrounding justice – this is, from the point of view of a rigorous deconstruction, anything but a neutralization of the interest in justice, an insensitivity toward injustice. On the contrary, it hyperbolically raises the stakes in the demand for justice.

Against this background Derrida gave three examples of aporias – or, rather, three versions of the same example, since "[250] [i]n fact, there is only one aporetic potential that infinitely distributes itself", arising from the "difficult and unstable distinction between justice and law, between justice (infinite, incalculable, rebellious to rule and foreign to symmetry, heterogeneous and heterotropic) on the one hand, and, on the other, the exercise of justice as law, legitimacy or legality, a stabilizable, statutory and calculable apparatus". For our purposes, the most pertinent example is the first. It postulates that any judge who merely applies a rule mechanically cannot be described as "just", since justice, like other moral virtues, presupposes personal responsibility and freedom of action. On the other hand, a judge who makes no reference to rules at all would not be acting justly, either:

[251] To be just, the decision of a judge, for example, must not only follow a rule of law or a general law but must also assume it, approve it, confirm its value, by a reinstituting act of interpretation, as if ... the law did not exist previously – as if the judge himself invented it in each case. Each exercise of justice as law can be just only if it is a "fresh judgment" ... This new freshness, the initiality of this inaugural judgment can very well – better yet, must very well – conform to a preexisting law, but the reinstituting, reinventive and freely deciding interpretation of the responsible judge requires that his "justice" not consist only in conformity, in the conservative and reproductive activity of judgment. In short, for a decision to be just and responsible, it must, in its proper moment, if there is one, be both regulated and without regulation, it must preserve the law and also destroy or suspend it enough to have to reinvent it in each case, rejustify it, reinvent it at least in the reaffirmation and the new and free confirmation of its principle.

The underlying point of all three examples is that "[251] law claims to exercise itself in the name of justice", while "justice demands for itself that it be established in the name of a law ... Deconstruction always finds itself and moves itself between these two poles".

8. Further References

Baines, B, and Rubio-Marin, R, *The Gender of Constitutional Jurisprudence* (Cambridge University Press, 2005).

Balkin, J, "Transcendental Deconstruction, Transcendent Justice" (1994) 92 *Michigan Law Review* 1131.

Barker, I, "Judicial Activism in Australia: A Perspective" (2005) 79 *Australian Law Journal* 783.

Birch, C, "Mill, Frege and the High Court: The Connotation/Denotation Distinction in Constitutional Interpretation" (2003) 13 *Australian Bar Review* 296.

Chin, G, "Technological Change and the *Australian Constitution*" (2000) 24 *Melbourne University Law Review* 609.

Craven, G (ed), *The Convention Debates: Commentaries, Indices and Guide* (Legal Books, 1986), vol 6.

Dawson, D, "Intention and the Constitution – Whose Intention?" (1990) 6 *Australian Bar Review* 93.

Goldsworthy, J, "Interpreting the *Constitution* in its Second Century" (2000) 24 *Melbourne University Law Review* 677.

Kirby, M, "Constitutional Interpretation and Original Intent: A Form of Ancestor Worship?" (2000) 24 *Melbourne University Law Review* 1.

Kirk, J, "Constitutional Interpretation and a Theory of Evolutionary Originalism" (1999) 27 *Federal Law Review* 323.

Machor, JL, "The Object of Interpretation and Interpretive Change" (1998) 113 *MLN* 1126 (formerly *Modern Language Notes*).

Mason, K, "What's Wrong with Top-Down Legal Reasoning?" (2004) 7 *Judicial Review* 9.

McCamish, C, "The Use of Historical Materials in Interpreting the Commonwealth Constitution" (1996) 70 *Australian Law Journal* 638.

McHugh, M, "The Law-making Function of the Judicial Process" (1988) 62 *Australian Law Journal* 15 (Pt I) and 116 (Pt II).

Meagher, D, "Guided by Voices? Constitutional Interpretation on the Gleeson Court" (2002) 7 *Deakin Law Review* 261.

Nerhot, P (ed), *Law, Interpretation and Reality: Essays in Epistemology, Hermeneutics and Jurisprudence* (Kluwer Academic Publishers, 1990).

Norris, C, *Deconstruction: Theory and Practice* (Methuen, 1982).

Ortiz, D, "The Price of Metaphysics: Deadlock in Constitutional Theory" in Brint, M, and Weaver, W (eds), *Pragmatism in Law and Society* (Westview Press, 1991), 311.

Patapan, H, "The Dead Hands of the Founders? Original Intent and the Constitutional Protection of Rights and Freedoms in Australia" (1997) 25 *Federal Law Review* 211.

Ricoeur, P, *The Conflict of Interpretations: Essays in Hermeneutics* (Ihde, D (ed), Northwestern University Press, 1974).

Ricoeur, P, *From Text to Action: Essays in Hermeneutics, II* (transl Blamey, K, and Thompson, JB, Northwestern University Press, 1991).

Roach, K, *The Supreme Court on Trial: Judicial Activism or Democratic Dialogue* (Irwin Law, 2001).

Sampford, C, and Preston, K (eds), *Interpreting Constitutions: Theories, Principles and Institutions* (Federation Press, 1996).

Schlag, P, "The Problem of Subject" (1991) 69 *University of Texas Law Review* 1627.

Schoff, P, "The High Court and History: It Still Hasn't Found[ed] What It's Looking For" (1994) 5 *Public Law Review* 253.

Selway, BM, "Methodologies of Constitutional Interpretation in the High Court of Australia" (2003) 14 *Public Law Review* 234.

Selway, BM, "The Use of History and other Facts in the Reasoning of the High Court of Australia" (2002) 20 *University of Tasmania Law Review* 129.

Thomson, JA, "Principles and Theories of Constitutional Interpretation and Adjudication: Some Preliminary Notes" (1982) 13 *Melbourne University Law Review* 597.

Ward, KD, and Castillo, CR (eds), *The Judiciary in American Democracy: Alexander Bickel, the Counter-Majoritarian Difficulty, and Contemporary Constitutional Theory* (State University of New York Press, 2005).

Zines, L, "The Present State of Constitutional Interpretation" in Stone, A, and Williams, G (eds), *The High Court at the Crossroads: Essays in Constitutional Law* (Federation Press, 2000), 224.

Chapter 9

Inconsistency

1. The Meaning of "Invalid"

Where the power to legislate on one or more topics is concurrently held by the Commonwealth and the States, as in most of the powers listed in s 51 of the Constitution, some method must exist for resolving conflicts between the laws of the different Parliaments. Section 109 achieves this by providing that the laws of the Commonwealth shall prevail over those of a State to the extent of any inconsistency. In the absence of s 109, this function might have been fulfilled by covering clause 5 of the Constitution, which makes Commonwealth laws "binding on the courts, judges and people ... of every part of the Commonwealth".

In order for s 109 to apply, there must be a valid State law and a valid Commonwealth law. If either is invalid in the positivist sense of being beyond power, no conflict of "laws" arises. Hence, in many s 109 cases, an initial step is to determine whether the Commonwealth and State laws are "valid", that is, whether the respective Parliaments had the power to enact them. It follows that the final word in s 109, "invalid", can be misleading as to the effect of s 109. The generally accepted analysis is that when a State law fails because of s 109, it is *not* "invalid" in the positivist sense that the State Parliament lacks power to pass it. The State law, though enacted with full validity, merely ceases to operate.

For practical or "operative" purposes the State law thus yields to the Commonwealth law, but remains a valid law of the Parliament which enacted it. The practical significance of this will become apparent if, at some later date, the overriding Commonwealth law ceases to operate. For example, suppose that a Commonwealth law was enacted in 2000 and repealed in 2005. An inconsistent State law lying dormant from 2000 will automatically be reactivated in 2005. Throughout the period of its ouster by an overriding Commonwealth law it has remained valid, though inoperative. Once the bar to its practical operation is removed, there is no reason why it should not resume its normal legislative effect.

Carter v Egg and Egg Pulp Marketing Board (Vic)
(1942) 66 CLR 557

Latham CJ: [573] [Section 109] applies only in cases where, apart from the operation of the section, both the Commonwealth and the State laws which are in question would be valid. If either is invalid *ab initio* by reason of lack of power, no question can arise under the section. The word "invalid" in this section cannot be interpreted as meaning that a State law which is affected by the section becomes *ultra vires* in whole or in part. If the Commonwealth law were repealed, the State law would again become operative ... Thus the word "invalid" should be interpreted as meaning "inoperative." This is, I think, made clear by the provision that the Commonwealth law "shall prevail" – that is, the Commonwealth law has superior authority and takes effect to the exclusion of the inconsistent State law.

2. The Tests of Inconsistency

The evolution of High Court doctrine in s 109 cases has led to three broad approaches to "inconsistency" (for a further, idiosyncratic, approach see the "sponge and fibre" test of Higgins J in *Clyde Engineering Co Ltd v Cowburn* (1926) 37 CLR 466 at 500). According to these tests, "inconsistency" is present, and the Commonwealth law prevails:

1. If it is impossible to obey both laws (the reference is to a logical impossibility: one law requires that you *must* do X, the other that you *must not* do X). A classic example is *R v Brisbane Licensing Court; Ex parte Daniell* (1920) 28 CLR 23. A State referendum on liquor trading hours was fixed by State law for the same day as a federal Senate election. The Commonwealth law provided that a State referendum could not be held on that day.

2. If one law purports to confer a legal right, privilege or entitlement that the other law purports to take away or diminish (one law says that you *can* do X, the other that you *cannot* do X). For example, the Commonwealth provision in *Colvin v Bradley Brothers Pty Ltd* (1943) 68 CLR 151 affirmed that employers in certain industries could employ women to work on certain machines; the State provision made it an offence to do so. It was possible to obey both laws, since nothing in the Commonwealth law *required* the employment of females. This type of inconsistency may require a more subtle analysis than test 1. For one thing, test 1 is more likely to be apparent on the face of the laws, whereas the reasoning involved in test 2 may require a working-out of the actual effect of both laws in an individual case. But once test 2 is found to be applicable, it too can be reduced to a contradiction ("X is lawful" versus "X is not lawful"; or "Y has legal permission or authority to do X" versus "Y does not have legal permission or authority to do X").

3. If the Commonwealth law evinces a legislative intention to "cover the field". In such a case there need not be any direct contradiction between the two enactments. It may even happen that both require the same conduct, or pursue the same legislative purpose. What is imputed to the Commonwealth Parliament is a legislative intention that its law shall be all the law there is on that topic. In that event, what is "inconsistent" with the Commonwealth law is the existence of any State law at all on that topic. This involves two questions:

    (a) Is the Commonwealth law intended to be exclusive, that is, the only law on the topic?

    (b) Does the State law operate in the same field as the Commonwealth law?

Inconsistency arises where the answer is "yes" to both questions. Question (a) is straightforward in those cases where the Commonwealth law evinces an express intention that it is to be exclusive within its field. In other cases, the Court will look to a variety of factors, such as the subject-matter of the law and whether for the law to achieve its purpose it is necessary that it be a complete statement of the law on that topic. Question (b) can be problematic, since it may require a subjective assessment of the scope and operation of the State and Commonwealth laws. The cases outlined below illustrate this, as well as the resulting difficulty in predicting how the Court will approach a particular statutory situation.

Tests 1 and 2, although sometimes only test 1, are said to involve "direct" inconsistency. Test 3 involves a more indirect form of inconsistency. It makes s 109 a much more powerful instrument for ensuring the supremacy of Commonwealth law.

Both the "rights" test of inconsistency (test 2), and the "cover the field" test (test 3), received their first clear formulation in *Clyde Engineering Co Ltd v Cowburn* – the former test by Knox CJ and Gavan Duffy J and the latter test by Isaacs J. For Isaacs J, this was the culmination of a long battle with Griffith CJ, Barton and O'Connor JJ over the supremacy of the Commonwealth industrial arbitration system.

The early High Court had held that when a State Wages Board or industrial tribunal had specific statutory wage-fixing powers, its awards had statutory force and became part of the "general law" of the State legal regime. The Court further held that when the Commonwealth entered that regime, in the person of an industrial arbitrator, it must be subject to that "general law". In other words, the wage levels set by State tribunals would operate as a constraint on what the Commonwealth arbitration system could do. Isaacs and Higgins JJ dissented from this doctrine from the beginning, and gradually sought to minimise or neutralise its effects. For them, it was fundamental that the Commonwealth wage-fixing system should prevail over those of the States.

In *Clyde Engineering v Cowburn*, by proclaiming the "cover the field" test, Isaacs J was able to ensure the supremacy of the Commonwealth system. The test had first been suggested by Starke J as counsel in *Australian Boot Trade Employees Federation v Whybrow* (1910) 10 CLR 266. Ironically, his argument was that, because the State wages regime had "covered the field", the Commonwealth must accept that regime. Isaacs J simply adopted Starke's idea, but applied it the other way round. Dixon J, as counsel in *Commonwealth v Queensland* (1920) 29 CLR 1, had foreshadowed a similar test: "[5] The Federal Parliament has appropriated the particular field of legislation". As Starke J himself expressed the idea in *Clyde Engineering v Cowburn*: "[525] The question is whether there is inconsistency, contrariety, repugnancy ... between the State law and the scope and purpose of the law of the Commonwealth".

The case was one in which the State law prescribed "ordinary working hours" of 44 hours a week (with overtime entitlements thereafter), whereas the relevant federal award fixed "ordinary hours of duty" (without overtime) of 48 hours a week. John Cowburn, relying on the State Act, worked a 44-hour week. His employer, relying on the federal award, then deducted 9s 4d from his wages. By adopting a 44-hour working week it was possible to comply with both laws: but the rights of the employer under the federal award were denied by the State law, while the rights of the worker under State law were denied by the federal award.

Clyde Engineering Co Ltd v Cowburn
(1926) 37 CLR 466

Isaacs J: [479] [T]he question for this Court ... [is] whether the Commonwealth as a whole is empowered to deal with its most momentous social problem on its own broad scale unimpeded by the sectional policies of particular States, or whether its legal adjustments of the reciprocal claims and moral rights of organized labour on the one hand, and organized capital on the other, so as to secure their peaceful collaboration in the interests and on the uniform basis of the larger Australian citizenship and the larger Australian community, are to be in the first place prevented or afterwards antagonized, and in effect undone, by additions, qualifications or negations dictated by the more limited objects of a State and that in actual working vitally alter, or neutralize or even destroy them ...

[480] The appellant contends for the first alternative I have stated, that is, for the full and free operation of every Commonwealth adjustment of an inter-State industrial dispute, leaving it to the Commonwealth authority to make, as it is at liberty, quite as amply as any State, to make, from time to time all corrections or modifications shown to be just. The respondent contends that that adjustment can never be full or free of any assured permanency, but is always and every moment subject in each State to be either annulled or weighted with whatever additional complications any State Parliament may see fit to enact. The arguments of Mr *Piddington* and Mr *Flannery* with great candour, force and consistency asserted this power of every State ... It follows, however, that, if that view be correct, then the industries of Australia and the rights and obligations of employers and employees alike, where they are prescribed by a Federal award, instead of being referable to that award alone as the Australian law on the subject so that he who runs may read, must always be in an utter state of uncertainty and confusion. They will be constantly liable to disintegration of industrial forces and to such distracting inequalities and distortions dictated by warring sectional policies as to make true inter-State free trade impossible. This would certainly give much justification for Bacon's aphorism that **[481]** "there is no worse torture than the torture of laws." In my opinion, however, that view is not correct, and the first alternative should prevail. Applying the principle of that alternative, there is little room for serious doubt that this appeal must succeed ...

[489] There arises on the threshold a question as to the proper test of inconsistency. It is said that the State Act concedes to the Federal award its full operation, since it says nothing about the deduction for hours not worked, and merely creates a new and independent right to a further payment for the hours actually worked. The infallible test of whether in so providing there is inconsistency is said for the respondent to be whether the two provisions of deduction on the one hand and extra payment on the other could both be obeyed. No doubt the employer *could* obey both, that is physically. So he *could* if the State Act required him after deducting the 9s 4d to return it immediately. That, it is gravely argued, avoids inconsistency. If an Act of Parliament, for instance, prescribed 25 lashes for robbery under arms and a later Act prescribed that such an offender should be punished with 20 lashes, it could, of course, with equal truth be said that both provisions *could* be obeyed, and therefore, applying the suggested test, the offender must receive 45 lashes. But surely the vital question would be: Was the second Act on its true construction intended to cover the whole ground and, therefore, to supersede the first? If it was so intended, then the inconsistency would consist in giving any operative effect at all to the first Act, because the second was intended entirely to exclude it. The suggested test, however useful a working guide it may be in some cases or, in other words, however it may for some cases prove *a* test, cannot be recognized as *the* standard measuring rod of inconsistency. If, however, a competent legislature expressly or impliedly evinces its intention to cover the whole field, that is a conclusive test of inconsistency where another legislature assumes to enter to any extent upon the same field ... **[490]** If such a position ... be in fact established, the inconsistency is demonstrated, not by comparison of detailed provisions, but by the mere existence of the two sets of provisions. Where that wholesale inconsistency does not occur, but the field is partly open, then it is necessary to inquire further and possibly to examine and contrast particular provisions. If one enactment makes or acts upon as lawful that which the other makes unlawful, or if one enactment makes unlawful that which the other makes or acts upon as lawful, the two are to that extent inconsistent. It is plain that it may be quite possible to obey both simply by not doing what is declared by either to be unlawful and yet there is palpable inconsistency. In the present case there is inconsistency in both of the senses I have described.

Knox CJ and Gavan Duffy J also agreed that a simple test of logical contradiction (test 1) was "**[478]** not sufficient or even appropriate in every case", and enunciated test 2: "Two enactments may be inconsistent although obedience to each of them may be possible without disobeying the other. Statutes may do more than impose duties: they may, for instance, confer rights; and one statute is inconsistent with another when it takes away a right conferred by that other even though the right be one which might be waived or abandoned without disobeying the statute which conferred it".

The "cover the field" test became fully authoritative when Dixon J, himself the successful counsel in *Clyde Engineering v Cowburn*, adopted it in *Ex parte McLean* (1930) 43 CLR 472. By s 44 of the *Conciliation and Arbitration Act 1904* (Cth), a person in breach of an award was liable to a penalty not exceeding a maximum to be fixed by the Court of Conciliation and Arbitration or by a Conciliation Commissioner. By s 4 of the *Masters and Servants Act 1902* (NSW), any person who "absents himself from" or "neglects to fulfil" a contract of service was liable to a penalty not exceeding £10. Frederick Firth, a grazier, alleged that James McLean, an itinerant shearer, had "neglected to fulfil" his contract through incompetence. McLean argued that, because both he and Firth were bound by a 1927 award made under the Commonwealth Act, the State Act was thereby rendered "invalid" by s 109. An "inconsistency" was held to arise because the same acts or omissions were made subject to the penal sanctions of a Commonwealth enactment as well as to the different penal sanctions of a State enactment.

Ex parte McLean
(1930) 43 CLR 472

Dixon J: [483] Sec 44 of the *Commonwealth Conciliation and Arbitration Act* 1904-1928 penalizes any breach or non-observance of an award, and, inasmuch as the award in this case commanded performance of the applicant's contract, his neglect to fulfil it would constitute an offence under this provision. The same acts or omissions were therefore made subject to the penal sanctions of the Federal enactment and the somewhat different penal sanctions of the State enactment.

When the Parliament of the Commonwealth and the Parliament of a State each legislate upon the same subject and prescribe what the rule of conduct shall be, they make laws which are inconsistent, notwithstanding that the rule of conduct is identical which each prescribes, and sec 109 applies. That this is so is settled, at least when the sanctions they impose are diverse (*Hume v Palmer* [(1926) 38 CLR 441]). But the reason is that, by prescribing the rule to be observed, the Federal statute shows an intention to cover the subject matter and provide what the law upon it shall be. If it appeared that the Federal law was intended to be supplementary to or cumulative upon State law, then no inconsistency would be exhibited in imposing the same duties or in inflicting different penalties. The inconsistency does not lie in the mere coexistence of two laws which are susceptible of simultaneous obedience. It depends upon the intention of the paramount Legislature to express by its enactment, completely, exhaustively, or exclusively, what shall be the law governing the particular conduct or matter to which its attention is directed. When a Federal statute discloses such an intention, it is inconsistent with it for the law of a State to govern the same conduct or matter.

Clearly, the "cover the field" test may reveal inconsistency even where no inconsistency arises under either of the "direct" tests 1 and 2; and conversely, a "direct" inconsistency will bring s 109 into play even where there is no evidence of a Commonwealth intention to "cover the field". In *Telstra Corporation Ltd v Worthing* (1997) 197 CLR 61, Allan Worthing made a claim under the *Workers Compensation Act 1987* (NSW) in respect of injuries he sustained while working as a Telecom linesman in 1986 and 1988, and a further injury in 1993 (by which time the name of his employer had been changed to "Telstra"). However, it was held that none of the three injuries was compensable under the State legislation. At the time of the earlier injuries the State law in force was the *Workers Compensation Act 1926* (NSW); but that law was not binding on the Commonwealth, and by s 21(3) of the *Telecommunications Act 1975* (Cth), Telecom and its successors were not subject to any obligation or liability under a law of a State to which the Commonwealth was not subject. As for the 1993 injury, it was covered by the workers compensation regime for Commonwealth employees introduced by the *Safety, Rehabilitation and Compensation Act 1988* (Cth); and because the compensation available under that Act was different from that available under the State Act, the State Act would have the effect of qualifying or impairing the Commonwealth Act, and to some extent directly negating it. Hence an inconsistency arose under test 2 (and perhaps under test 1).

Telstra Corporation Ltd v Worthing
(1997) 197 CLR 61

The Court: [76] In *Victoria v Commonwealth* [(1937) 58 CLR 618 at 630], Dixon J stated two propositions which are presently material. The first was:

"When a State law, if valid, would alter, impair or detract from the operation of a law of the Commonwealth Parliament, then to that extent it is invalid."

The second, which followed immediately in the same passage, was:

"Moreover, if it appears from the terms, the nature or the subject matter of a Federal enactment that it was intended as a complete statement of the law governing a particular matter or set of rights and duties, then for a State law to regulate or apply to the same matter or relation is regarded as a detraction from the full operation of the Commonwealth law and so as inconsistent."

The second proposition may apply in a given case where the first does not, yet, contrary to the approach taken in the Court of Appeal, if the [77] first proposition applies, then s 109 of the Constitution operates even if, and without the occasion to consider whether, the second proposition applies.

After reviewing the differences between the 1987 State Act and the 1988 Commonwealth Act that had been identified in the New South Wales Court of Appeal, the Court continued:

The Court: [78] From that analysis, it follows that to apply the State law to the claim made by Mr Worthing would qualify, impair and, in some respects, negate the application of federal law, with the consequence that, to the extent of the inconsistency thereby made out, the State law was invalid. That conclusion means that Telstra should have succeeded on its motion that the application to the Compensation Court be struck out.

It would be no answer that the subject-matters of the two laws are not co-incident. Rather, the State law, by granting certain rights, would deny or vary a right, power or privilege conferred by the federal law. Indeed, in the Court of Appeal, Cole JA, having completed the comparative legislative analysis to which we have referred, concluded that there were "gross inconsistencies" between the two sets of provisions.

Nevertheless, the Court of Appeal proceeded as if it was not the inevitable consequence of such a view of the matter that s 109 operated and went on to consider whether the federal law "covered the field". The Court of Appeal then decided that, because there were provisions in the federal law which provided strong indications that the field was not covered, the whole case with respect to inconsistency failed. Having reached [that] point ..., it was unnecessary for the Court of Appeal to proceed further ...

What has been said above is sufficient to bring about the result that the appeals to this Court must be allowed.

In practice, the three tests sometimes overlap. For example, in *Commercial Radio Coffs Harbour v Fuller* (1986) 161 CLR 47 the finding that there was no inconsistency depended on all three tests. A Commonwealth licence for a new commercial radio station in Coffs Harbour had been given under the *Broadcasting and Television Act 1942* (Cth). A condition of the licence required the erection of two antennae each 170 metres high. A local "Save Our Scenery" committee took proceedings in the New South Wales Land and Environment Court, seeking a further environmental impact assessment under the *Environmental Planning and Assessment Act 1979* (NSW). The question thus arising of inconsistency between the State and Commonwealth laws was removed into the High Court, which held that there was no inconsistency. The two laws were directed to different purposes, and therefore occupied different fields: one concerned with the technical requirements of broadcasting, the other with the environment. Accordingly, there was no inconsistency under test 3. The licence condition *requiring* the company to erect the two antennae was construed as stopping short of giving an *authority* to do so; hence there was no inconsistency under test 2. By s 132(1) of the Commonwealth Act, "Any person who ... fails to comply with ... any condition of a licence ... is guilty of an offence" (punishable by fine); but the duty thus imposed was construed as impliedly stopping short of requiring a licensee to disobey any relevant law of a State; hence there was no inconsistency under test 1.

Commercial Radio Coffs Harbour v Fuller
(1986) 161 CLR 47

Gibbs CJ and Brennan J: [50] Ordinarily, a provision which imposes a duty under penalty to do a thing specified in the provision would be construed as conferring on the person on whom the duty is imposed a power or authority to do that thing ... But an alternative construction may be warranted. If it is impossible to do the thing specified in the provision without contravening another law, the provision may be construed either as authorizing the doing of that thing (so that it is inconsistent with the other law) or as imposing a qualified duty which stops short of requiring contravention of the other law. It would be erroneous to construe s 132(1) – a general offence-creating provision – as conferring authority to do the many and diverse things which fall within its scope if the doing of those things is prohibited by other laws. The better construction is to read s 132(1) as not applying to a failure to comply with a condition ... where compliance is impossible without contravening another law (provided, of course, that the other law is not inconsistent with the more specific provisions of the Act).

Wilson, Deane and Dawson JJ: [56] [O]ur construction of the Commonwealth Act leads us to conclude that it does not purport to state exclusively or exhaustively the law with which the operation of a commercial broadcasting station must comply ... The licence confers on the grantee a permission to broadcast. There is nothing in the Act which suggests that it confers an absolute right or positive authority to broadcast so that the grantee, because he has a licence, is immune or exempt from compliance with State laws. On the contrary, in concentrating on the technical efficiency and quality of broadcasting **[57]** services, the Act leaves room for the operation of laws, both State and Commonwealth, dealing with other matters relevant to the operation of such services. For example, the applicant was required to obtain, as it in fact did before the issue of the licence, the consent of the Department of Aviation to the erection of two radio antennas, subject to conditions relating to marking and lighting under reg 92 of the Air Navigation Regulations. Another example is the purchase or lease of the land, upon which the broadcasting station is to be built, in accordance with State property laws ... The intention of the Commonwealth Act is to maintain the provision of high quality and technically efficient broadcasting services which are commercially viable and receptive to the needs of the community. It does so by the prohibition of broadcasting except under licence granted subject to certain conditions. But the relaxation of the prohibition by the granting of a licence does not confer an immunity from other laws, Commonwealth or State. The Act does not purport to lay down the whole legislative framework within which the activity of broadcasting is to be carried on. It is intended to operate within the setting of other laws with which the grantee of **[58]** a licence will be required to comply ... In the words of Dixon J in *Ex parte McLean* [(1930) 43 CLR 472 at 483], the Act was intended to be "supplementary to or cumulative upon State law."

Conversely, the conclusion that there is an inconsistency may depend on more than one test. In *Wallis v Downard-Pickford (North Queensland) Pty Ltd* (1994) 179 CLR 388, s 6(1) of the *Carriage of Goods by Land (Carriers' Liabilities) Act 1967* (Qld), which limited the liability of carriers for loss or injury to goods, was held to be inconsistent with the warranties implied by s 74(1) of the *Trade Practices Act 1974* (Cth). Toohey and Gaudron JJ explained that "**[396]** the warranty created by s 74 carries with it full contractual liability for breach. Section 6(1) of the Queensland Act purports to limit that liability. The consequence is that there is a conflict between the two statutes, a conflict which amounts to a direct inconsistency in the sense that the Queensland Act detracts from the full operation of a right granted by the *Trade Practices Act*". Accordingly, they thought it "**[397]** unnecessary to consider" an argument involving the operation of the "cover the field" test. They added, however, that there was also a conflict under test 1: the effect of ss 6 and 9 of the Queensland Act was to imply the limit on liability into every contract of carriage as a term of the contract, whereas s 68(1) of the Commonwealth Act declared any such contractual term to be void. Thus the Queensland Act "**[398]** purports to imply into contracts exactly those terms that s 68 [of the *Trade Practices Act*] forbids".

The overlapping effect of the different tests was strikingly illustrated by the divergent reasoning employed in *Ansett Transport Industries (Operations) Pty Ltd v Wardley* (1980) 142 CLR 237. That case arose out of the fight by Deborah Wardley to become Australia's first female commercial airline pilot. By way of explanation of the decision not to employ her, the General Manager of Ansett Airlines wrote in a letter to the Women's Electoral Lobby (extracted in *Wardley v Ansett Transport Industries (Operations) Pty Ltd* [1984] EOC ¶92-002 at 75,260): "We ... have adopted a policy of only employing men as pilots. This does not mean that women cannot be good pilots, but we are concerned with the provision of the safest and most efficient air service possible. In this regard we feel that an all male pilot crew is safer than one in which the sexes are mixed". The letter ended: "I am sure you will be pleased to know that I have met Mrs

Wardley and find her a very nice person, highly intelligent and undoubtedly a good pilot, but that is not quite what we are talking about".

The Victorian Equal Opportunity Board found that Ansett had refused to employ her because of her sex. On the basis of s 18 of the *Equal Opportunity Act 1977* (Vic), which made sex discrimination in employment or dismissal unlawful, the Board ordered that Ansett employ her as a pilot. Ansett argued that s 18 was inconsistent with cl 6B of the Airline Pilots Agreement 1978. That Agreement had been certified under s 28 of the *Conciliation and Arbitration Act 1904* (Cth) and was therefore deemed to be an award. Clause 6B provided that Ansett could dismiss pilots of less than six months' service by giving seven days' notice in writing. A majority, with Barwick CJ and Aickin J dissenting, dismissed Ansett's challenge.

Ansett Transport Industries (Operations) Pty Ltd v Wardley
(1980) 142 CLR 237

Stephen J: [246] In my view there is in this case no inconsistency within the meaning of s 109 of the Constitution. I regard the right of termination of the contract of employment which cl 6 of the Agreement confers as no absolute right, such as that for which Ansett contends. The right which it confers is not one which is capable of exercise regardless of the unlawfulness under State law of the ground for its exercise. On the contrary it is a right the nature of which is to be understood against the background to its operation which general laws of the land, whether State or federal in origin, provide.

The Agreement is not, I think, to be read as if creating a partial vacuum, within which the relationship between Ansett and its pilots lies wholly withdrawn from the operation of those general laws of the land which are applicable to other members of the **[247]** community. To take an example which s 6 itself affords, when par A of that clause requires pilots "to serve the employer in any part of the world" it is not for a moment to be understood as seeking to ignore, even were it able to do so, such restrictions upon travel by Australians, say to countries with which Australia is at war, as the Commonwealth Government may at any time impose. Resort to context would, simply as a matter of construction, readily resolve such a suggested conflict. It happens that in this example it would be with Commonwealth not State law that, until properly construed, the Agreement might seem to conflict, and an award cannot, in any event prevail over Commonwealth law: *Federated Seamen's Union of Australasia v Commonwealth Steamship Owners' Association* [(1922) 30 CLR 144]. However, at the level of construction, as distinct from power, the illustration is apt. The present industrial agreement, made in settlement of an industrial dispute, is concerned with industrial matters and its terms should be construed accordingly; they should not be regarded as trespassing upon alien areas remote from its purpose and subject matter, whether those areas concern the nation's foreign affairs or social evils such as discrimination upon the ground of sex.

When the power of termination which cl 6B confers upon the parties to the contract of employment comes to be construed it can be seen to contain nothing in its quite unexceptional wording to suggest that it should stand inviolate, unresponsive to a general law applicable to the community at large and directed to the prevention of some evil practice which, of its nature, may manifest itself in a variety of ways, including the exercise by an employer of his power of dismissal. The concern of the Agreement is, after all, entirely unremarkable, being exclusively devoted to the settlement of an industrial dispute. This is an inherently improbable source in which to discover, in the form of a simple power to bring their contract to an end conferred upon both parties to a contract of employment, a right on the employer's part to practise discrimination upon the grounds of sex, contrary to, and immune from the prohibition of, State law ...

[252] I cannot regard the effect of the State Act as in any way destroying or varying "the adjustment of industrial relations established" by the Agreement. Moreover the respective natures of those two measures are such that collision is not likely to occur between them, and this because they are laws on different subjects ... Discrimination is not simply an item separate from other subject matters within the area of industrial relations, it itself forms no part of that area. Where the ground for dismissal with which a State law deals is unrelated to industrial considerations and instead relates to discrimination, whether upon the grounds of sex, race or religion, the existence of a federal award or industrial agreement will present no situation of inconsistency ...

[253] Concluding, as I have, that there is here no question of direct collision between Agreement and Act, there is, a fortiori, no such inconsistency arising under the doctrine of "covering the field", and this very much for the reasons which I have stated in dealing with direct collision. Whatever field the Agreement may cover, the question of dismissal upon the discriminatory ground that the pilot is a woman is in my view no part of it.

I have sought in the foregoing to give effect to what I regard as important factors in this case: the contrast between the Agreement, in itself an unremarkable instrument serving the useful but quite limited purpose of settling a particular dispute between one employer and a class of its employees, and the Act, a measure of general application giving effect to far-reaching social reforms: the comparable contrast which may be drawn between cl 6B of the Agreement, which deals in the most general and unemphatic way with rights of termination of the contract of service, and the clear and specific terms of s 18(2)(b) of the Act: the preoccupation of the Agreement with no more than the narrow area of industrial relations and the absence of any attempted usurpation of that area by the Act: the way in which the Agreement operates against the background of the general law while the Act provides a part of that same background. It is, in essence, these factors which, in construing these two measures, have led me to conclude that no inconsistency exists between Agreement and Act. What seems to me to be wholly absent is any inconsistency, whether by direct collision of laws or by some federal covering of a particular field, which calls for the exercise of the puissant power of s 109 ...

Mason J: [259] I should point out that the major thrust of Ansett's case is to establish the existence of what has been called "direct inconsistency", that is, the disconformity which is created by the presence of an absolute right to dismiss for any reason whatsoever, which Ansett finds in the Agreement, and the presence in the State Act of a prohibition against dismissal for the prescribed reasons. "Direct inconsistency" is a description which has always been applied to cases in which it is impossible to obey both laws (*R v Licensing Court* **[260]** *of Brisbane; Ex parte Daniell* [(1920) 28 CLR 23]; *Blackley v Devondale Cream (Vic) Pty Ltd* [(1968) 117 CLR 253 at 258]). It is also a description which has been applied to cases in which the Commonwealth law grants a permission or a right and the State law prohibits that which is permitted or prohibits the exercise of the right (*Colvin v Bradley Brothers Pty Ltd* [(1943) 68 CLR 151]). Cases of this kind have sometimes been treated as a separate head of inconsistency (*O'Sullivan v Noarlunga Meat Ltd* [(1954) 92 CLR 565 at 592]), though even when so treated they have generally been related to the "cover the field" test (*O'Sullivan v Noarlunga Meat Ltd* [(1956) 95 CLR 177 at 182, 185]; *Swift Australian Co (Pty) Ltd v Boyd Parkinson* [(1962) 108 CLR 189 at 207]), apparently on the ground that direct inconsistency is confined to a situation in which simultaneous obedience to both laws is impossible.

As the various tests which have been applied by the Court are all designed to elucidate the issue of inconsistency it is not surprising that they are interrelated and that in a given case more than one test is capable of being applied so as to establish inconsistency. Especially is this so when it is the giving of a permission or the grant of a right by Commonwealth law that is the foundation of a claim of inconsistency. If, according to the true construction of the Commonwealth law, the right is absolute, then it inevitably follows that the right is intended to prevail to the exclusion of any other law. A State law which takes away the right is inconsistent because it is in conflict with the absolute right and because the Commonwealth law relevantly occupies the field. So also with a Commonwealth law that grants a permission by way of positive authority. The Commonwealth legislative intention which sustains the conclusion that the permission is granted by way of positive authority also sustains the conclusion that the positive authority was to take effect to the exclusion of any other law. Again it produces inconsistency on both grounds: *cf Airlines of New South Wales Pty Ltd v New South Wales* [(1965) 113 CLR 54], where the permission for which Commonwealth law provided was neither absolute nor comprehensive ...

[262] From my examination of the Agreement as a whole, I conclude that it should not be viewed as a general industry award which seeks to determine exhaustively the respective rights of employer and employee. Although the Agreement does deal with many of the matters usually found in an award, such as pay, hours of work and leave, its emphasis is on setting out in exact

detail the manner and procedure governing the advancement of a pilot in terms of seniority and rights dependent thereon. Clause 6B does not deal with the substantive right of dismissal. Instead, its opening words assume the right of the employer under the general law to terminate the employment of a pilot and the import of the clause as laid down in pars 1, 2, 3 and 4 is to prescribe the procedure and regulate the means whereby the right to terminate may be effected ...

[263] Consequently, I do not find any direct inconsistency between cl 6B and the State Act. The Agreement does not confer on Ansett a substantive right of dismissal; it merely assumes the right of dismissal for which the general law provides. The right of an employer under the general law to dismiss an employee has [264] been altered in Victoria by the State Act in that an employer may not discriminate against an employee on the ground of sex in offering employment, refusing to offer employment or in the terms on which employment is offered (s 18(1)) or by dismissing an employee by reason of sex (s 18(2)(b)). The Agreement is to be read in the light of this alteration in the general law. The grounds on which I have reached the conclusion that there is no direct inconsistency also require the conclusion that cl 6B of the Agreement does not seek to cover the field of the employer's substantive right to dismiss.

Aickin J: [274] Inconsistency under s 109 is usually described as taking one of two forms, ie it may arise from "direct conflict" or from a Commonwealth legislative intent to cover a particular legislative "field" and to make its law ... exclusive in that particular field. These tests have never been regarded as mutually exclusive ...

The argument in this case was primarily directed to the question whether the Agreement was intended to cover the field of the terms of employment of airline pilots by Ansett, including the terms upon which such employment might be terminated, to the exclusion of any State regulation of any aspect of such employment, including the termination of the employment of an [275] individual employee, ie [to whether] there was inconsistency in the sense in which the expression "cover the field" has been used since *Ex parte McLean* [(1930) 43 CLR 472] ... The present case may however provide an example of "direct conflict" between the provisions of a federal law and a State law. Such a conflict is not confined to a situation where it is impossible to obey both laws, but may occur also when a State law prohibits conduct permitted expressly or impliedly by a federal law ...

In relation to dismissal at least the present case may be regarded as an example of "direct conflict" in that the Agreement appears to permit the dismissal without review of a pilot during his first six months of service on either the giving of notice of seven days, or upon payment of seven days' salary, upon any ground whatever, whereas the State Act prohibits dismissal on specified grounds. It is therefore convenient to consider first the question of direct conflict ...

The Agreement makes an express provision for dismissal of such a pilot, or termination of his employment without restricting [276] in any way the grounds upon which such termination may be given. The State Act would enable such a decision to be set at nought by the Board ordering reinstatement or re-employment, and apparently payment in respect of any period between the termination and the reinstatement. This appears to me to involve inconsistency in the sense that the State Act would if valid "impair alter or detract from the operation of" the Agreement ...

[280] The two different aspects of inconsistency are no more than a reflection of different ways in which the Parliament may manifest its intention that the federal law, whether wide or narrow in its operation, should be the exclusive regulation of the relevant conduct. Whether it be right or not to say that there are two kinds of inconsistency, the central question is the intention of a particular federal law. The field of its operation may be regarded as wide or narrow and produce inconsistency because of the intention to cover a particular field exclusively or because of an intention to regulate specific conduct so that any other regulation of that conduct is inconsistent because the attempt to regulate the identical conduct in a different manner, or perhaps at all, necessarily impairs the operation of the federal regulation of that conduct.

The laws considered in *Wardley's Case* were held not to be inconsistent because they occupied different fields. On the other hand, in *Australian Mutual Provident Society v Goulden* (1986) 160 CLR 330, the High Court unanimously held that the *Anti-Discrimination Act 1977* (NSW) was inconsistent with the *Life Insurance Act 1945* (Cth).

Evan Goulden, who had been blind since birth, took out a life insurance policy with the AMP. Later he sought to vary the policy by adding a "waiver of premium benefit" – a provision that, if he suffered total disablement through illness, accident or injury, the AMP would waive payment of premiums during the period of disablement. The AMP refused to add such a provision because of his blindness. The matter came before the New South Wales Equal Opportunity Tribunal under s 49K(1) of the *Anti-Discrimination Act*, which provided: "It is unlawful for a person who provides, for payment or not, goods or services to discriminate against a physically handicapped person on the ground of his physical impairment ... by refusing to provide him with those goods or services; or ... in the terms on which he provides him with those goods or services". Section 78(1) of the *Life Insurance Act* provided: "A company shall not issue any policy unless the rate of premium chargeable under the policy is a rate which has been approved by an actuary as suitable for the class of policy to which that policy belongs".

Australian Mutual Provident Society v Goulden
(1986) 160 CLR 330

The Court: [336] [The *Life Insurance Act* is] directed towards ensuring adequate supervision and regulation of the insurance practices of life insurance companies to protect policy holders in respect of, among other things, the financial soundness of such companies, their statutory funds and the financial viability of the rates of premium charged for particular classes of insurance. Central to the practices of the insurance companies which the provisions of the Act are designed to regulate and control are the classification of risks and the setting of premiums. They are the essence of life insurance business ... [T]he Act proceeds on the underlying legislative assumption that, subject to some qualifications for which the Act provides, the life insurance business of such a company is more likely to prosper and the interests of its policy holders are more likely to be protected, if it is permitted to classify risks and fix rates of premium in that business in accordance with its own judgment founded upon the advice of actuaries and the practice of prudent insurers ...

[337] [T]he Act should be understood as giving expression to a legislative policy that the protection of the interests of policy holders is to be achieved by allowing a registered life insurance company to classify risks and fix rates of premium in its life insurance business in accordance with its own judgment founded upon the advice of actuaries and the practice of prudent insurers. In the words of Dixon J in *Victoria v Commonwealth* [(1937) 58 CLR 618 at 630], it "would alter, impair or detract from" the Commonwealth scheme of regulation established by the Act if a registered life insurance company was effectively precluded by the legislation of a State from classifying different risks differently, from setting different premiums for different risks or from refusing to insure risks which were outside the class of risk in respect of which it wished to offer insurance. In particular, State legislation which, either absolutely or subject to qualifications and exceptions, made it generally unlawful for a life insurance company to take account of physical impairment in determining whether it would or would not accept a particular proposal or the terms upon which it would grant insurance cover would be inconsistent with the essential scheme of the provisions of the Act regulating the issue of policies and the fixing of premiums. Indeed, such legislation would undermine and, to a significant extent, negate the legislative assumption of the underlying ability of a registered life insurance company to classify risks and fix rates of premium in accordance with its own judgment based upon actuarial advice and prudent insurance practice upon which, as has been mentioned, the stringent controls and requirements which the Act imposes in respect of life insurance business of registered life insurance companies are predicated.

The proposition accepted in *Goulden* – that a State law is rendered inconsistent if it "would alter, impair or detract from" the operation of a Commonwealth law – was invoked in *APLA Ltd v Legal Services Commissioner (NSW)* (2005) 219 ALR 403 as one of several unsuccessful grounds of challenge to the *Legal Profession Amendment (Personal Injury Advertising) Regulation* (NSW). That Regulation prohibited any advertisement for legal services referring to personal injury, to compensation for personal injury, or to "any circumstance in which personal injury might occur, or any activity, event or circumstance that suggests or could suggest the possibility of personal injury, or any connection to or association with personal injury or a cause of personal injury". The alleged "impairment" was of Commonwealth laws establishing rights to compensation for victims of personal injury (including the *Trade Practices Act 1974* (Cth), the *Safety, Rehabilitation and Compensation Act 1988* (Cth) and the *Superannuation (Resolution of Complaints) Act 1993* (Cth)); and also of Commonwealth laws establishing rights of appearance in federal courts (including the *Judiciary Act 1903* (Cth) and the *Federal Court of Australia Act 1976* (Cth)). Only Kirby J found a relevant impairment.

APLA Ltd v Legal Services Commissioner (NSW)
(2005) 219 ALR 403

Kirby J: [477] No doubt, as the plaintiffs conceded, the federal provisions, and causes of action, were "intended to operate within the setting of other laws", including State **[478]** laws. However, the recognition of this fact is only the beginning of the constitutional analysis. The question remains whether any State law, enacted or made, is inconsistent with the federal provisions because its operation would "alter, impair or detract from the operation of a law of the Commonwealth Parliament" …

The federal causes of action provided for in ss 52, 75AD and 82 of the [*Trade Practices Act 1974* (Cth)] are, and are intended to be, enforceable in the specified federal and State courts. Clearly, the Federal Parliament's purpose was to create new rights, remedies, duties and powers in order to carry into effect the objectives identified in the [*Trade Practices Act*]. Those objectives were, relevantly, twofold: to modify conduct of the specified corporations judged to be antisocial and to provide remedies to individuals harmed as a consequence of any breach. It cannot be imagined that the Parliament, in enacting such federal laws, regarded it as sufficient to put them on the federal statute book as a pure symbol or hollow injunction to good conduct … [I]t is clear that the Federal Parliament intended that persons falling within the class of those injured by the breach of the [*Trade Practices Act*] were intended to have "the exercise or enjoyment" of those rights, not the "vain thing" of "a right without a remedy" [*Ashby v White* (1703) 2 Ld Raym 938 at 953, 92 ER 126 at 136].

Unless persons affected may be informed about the existence of such rights, and how they may go about enforcing them, the rights will in many cases be entirely theoretical. They will be unknown or, if known, unenforced because **[479]** of ignorance, uncertainty or fear of the costs and other difficulties of attempting to turn the rights into remedies. Adapting the words of Dixon J in *Stock Motor Ploughs Ltd v Forsyth* [(1932) 48 CLR 128 at 136], a State law purporting to impede the provision of information supportive of those affected in some cases, useful in others and essential in still others for enforcement of the law, would "impair the enjoyment of that right" afforded by the Federal Parliament …

I agree with the plaintiffs' submission that many non-lawyers have little, if any, detailed knowledge of what their legal rights, privileges and remedies may be; of what courts (or tribunals) may provide a forum for the pursuit of such rights, privileges and remedies; and of the consequences, risks and costs which may accompany their pursuit. This assertion is borne out by common experience of any member of the legal profession who has had dealings with poor and disadvantaged clients. Typically, their legal needs are quite different from those of corporations, the wealthy, or criminal accused and others entitled to public legal aid …

[481] In some ways the position in the present case is akin to that which arose in *Australian Mutual Provident Society v Goulden* [(1986) 160 CLR 330]. There, a State law purported to prohibit discrimination on the basis of physical disability. However, that State law was held inconsistent with "the essential scheme" of the *Life Insurance Act 1945* (Cth) which contemplated differential premium rates, including by reference to the criterion nominated in the State law … If such an intersection of a particular State law and a general federal law was inconsistent with the Constitution in a defined and well-intentioned field of **[482]** State lawmaking, it is difficult, with respect, for this Court, acting consistently, to uphold the present blunderbuss of State prohibitions when they directly impinge upon the effectiveness of rights conferred by remedial federal legislation. This Court should be as vigilant to protect the rights of vulnerable people like Mr Darcy [a client of one of the plaintiffs, in litigation under the *Trade Practices Act* relating to faulty heart pacemakers], as it proved to be in *Goulden*, in protecting the rights and interests of a large insurance corporation.

Inherent in the oft-repeated references of this Court to notions of "operational inconsistency" for the purposes of s 109 of the Constitution is a search for something more than verbal or theoretical intersection of laws. It is an inquiry into the practical operation of the State law that is impugned and whether, if it operates as its language provides and its purpose appears to intend, it would alter, impair or detract from the operation of the federal law. In the present case, the answer to that question is ... made easier because of the undiscriminating overreach of the Regulation and the muzzling effect it seeks to impose on all communications of the kind that might otherwise occur in our society to inform those affected of the legal rights, privileges and remedies they enjoy, or might enjoy.

McHugh J did not find it necessary to consider this argument, while all of the other judges rejected it. Accordingly, they held that s 109 did not apply.

Gleeson CJ and Heydon J: [416] The Court noted [in *Goulden*] that the *Life Insurance Act* was framed on the basis that it would operate in the context of local laws in the various States and Territories ... The same may be said of the federal laws relied on in this case in relation to the structure and regulation of the legal profession. However, the Court also pointed out that the *Life Insurance Act* made detailed provision for supervising and regulating the statutory funds of life insurers, such supervision and regulation being aimed at protecting policy holders ... It would alter, impair or detract from the Commonwealth scheme of regulation if a registered life insurance company was prevented by State legislation from classifying different risks differently or from setting different premiums for different risks. Discrimination in that sense is of the essence of life insurance. If State anti-discrimination legislation prevented life insurers from differentiating between sick or disabled persons and others, then the federal scheme of regulation would be set at naught. That was the context in which reference was made to impairment of a federal scheme of legislation.

Preventing lawyers from advertising does not impair the federal legislation referred to in the case stated. Indeed, most of the legislation was originally enacted at a time when restriction on advertising by lawyers was the generally accepted professional standard. None of the federal legislation depends for its efficacy upon the unrestricted promotion of legal services. The rights, powers, and jurisdictions created have full legal effect and operation regardless of whether, at any given time, the States or Territories permit or restrict advertising by lawyers.

Callinan J: [527] The notion that a restriction upon advertising by solicitors soliciting personally injured or other clients, alters, impairs or detracts from the pursuit of remedies made available under federal legislation is, I think, far-fetched. People pursuing them are in no way impeded from doing so because lawyers may be subject to State rules about the way in which they may promote themselves or offer their services. Indeed, a restrictive rule about advertising is much less likely to have an obstructive effect upon the making of federal claims, than a rule that the plaintiff must pay a filing fee, or that a plaintiff in a remote area must file his or her process in a metropolitan registry, or that in an action in a State court exercising federal jurisdiction, the rules of court may impose more onerous procedural obligations on plaintiffs than in a federal court.

The Commonwealth may well be able to legislate partially, or exhaustively if it wishes, for the advertising of federal causes of action, rights to pursue them, and rules relating to, legal practice in federal courts, and, arguably, in State courts exercising federal jurisdiction, but it has not done so here.

The provisions of the [*Trade Practices Act*] to which the plaintiffs point create causes of action. A rule about non-advertising cannot defeat, or indeed in any way even impinge upon those causes of action or remedies. And ss 39(2) and 39B(1A)(c) of the *Judiciary Act*, which do no more than invest federal jurisdiction in State **[528]** courts and confer jurisdiction upon federal courts are similarly unaffected ...

Whether lawyers can or cannot communicate that they wish to **[529]** undertake the pursuit of claims under these enactments does not alter, impair or detract from the operation or objects of them, or the pursuit of federal claims or rights to which they give rise ... [A] slight or marginal or insignificant impact of a State law upon a federal law will not give rise to a constitutional inconsistency. The impact must be one of some significance and such as would have the effect, if the State law were valid, of precluding, overriding or rendering ineffective an actual exercise of federal jurisdiction. But as I have said, I do not think that even a marginal impact is made here by the contested provisions.

The concept of "operational inconsistency" referred to by Kirby J above initially emerged as no more than a gloss on the "cover the field" test. On the one hand, it is potentially more far reaching than "cover the field", since it may arise even when two laws are addressed to completely different fields. On the other hand, it is potentially narrower in the sense that what it would render inoperative is not the whole of the State law, but only those particular applications of it which impact on the Commonwealth law. The idea is mostly invoked in a negative or hypothetical way (see, for example, Brennan CJ in *Project Blue Sky Inc v Australian Broadcasting Authority* (1998) 194 CLR 355 at 372; Gaudron J in *Re Tracey; Ex parte Ryan* (1989) 166 CLR 518 at 599-600 and *Re Macks; Ex parte Saint* (2000) 204 CLR 158 at 186). The origin of the concept is usually traced to *Victoria v Commonwealth* (*The Kakariki*) (1937) 58 CLR 618, where the High Court held that there was no inconsistency between State and Commonwealth provisions for the removal of sunken ships from coastal waters. However, the Court envisaged that, if the Commonwealth authorities were to take steps for removal of a wreck, the State legislation might then become inapplicable to that particular wreck. Dixon J expressed this by saying that the Commonwealth authorities might be entitled to proceed "[631] without interference from any other public authority". He stressed, however, that in such a case the impact on the State law would "extend no further than the application which its general language might otherwise have" to that particular wreck.

In *Commonwealth v Western Australia* (*Mining Act Case*) (1999) 196 CLR 392, it was held that, with one qualification, the *Mining Act 1978* (WA) did not authorise the granting of exploration licences over certain lands used by the Commonwealth as a defence practice area – primarily because, as a matter of construction, the *Mining Act* simply had no application to the relevant lands. The qualification arose because, unlike the practice area, a "perimeter area" was potentially subject to the *Mining Act*. The question therefore arose whether, in respect of the "perimeter area", the operation of the *Mining Act* would be inconsistent with Commonwealth regulations made under the *Defence Act 1903* (Cth). The majority (Kirby and Callinan JJ dissenting) rejected an argument that the regulations had "covered the field", and held that any inconsistency that might emerge would be "operational" only.

Commonwealth v Western Australia (*Mining Act Case*)
(1999) 196 CLR 392

Gleeson CJ and Gaudron J: [416] It is clear that the regulations ... constitute an exhaustive statement of the Commonwealth's rights and obligations with respect to private land in a defence practice area. However, they make limited provision as to the rights and obligations of other persons. Save to that limited extent, their rights and [417] obligations are left to the general law. Accordingly, it cannot be said that the Defence Regulations manifest an intention to "cover the field" with respect to the rights and obligations of persons other than those acting for or on behalf of the Commonwealth in relation to the perimeter area.

Nor, in our view, can it be said that any provision of the *Mining Act* would, if valid, alter, impair or detract from the operation of the Defence Regulations or that the Act is otherwise inconsistent with the Regulations because, for example, the Act and the Regulations cannot be obeyed simultaneously or one takes away what the other confers. That is because the *Mining Act* does not confer rights to enter upon or use land in the perimeter area. Rather, it simply allows that authority may be granted to persons to enter or conduct mining operations on that land.

The Defence Regulations do not operate to prevent entry or activity on the perimeter area, except if a defence operation or practice has been authorised by a chief of staff pursuant to reg 51(1). It would seem clear that, were authority to be granted pursuant to the *Mining Act* to enter upon or conduct mining activities on land in the perimeter area at a time or times specified in an authorisation under reg 51(1) for the conduct of a defence operation or practice, there would be direct inconsistency between that authorisation and the authority granted under the *Mining Act*. That inconsistency would result from the inconsistent operation in the particular circumstances of the *Mining Act* and the Defence Regulations – "operational inconsistency", as it is called.

Section 109 of the Constitution operates to render a State law inoperative only to the extent of its inconsistency with a law of the Commonwealth and only for so long as the inconsistency remains. Although there may be "operational inconsistency" between the *Mining Act* and the Defence Regulations in the event and to the extent that authority is conferred pursuant to the former to enter upon or engage in activities on land in the perimeter area at a time when a defence operation or practice is authorised under reg 51(1) of the Defence Regulations, that situation has not yet arisen. Thus, at the present time, there is no inconsistency.

Other suggestions that "operational inconsistency" might arise have usually been hypothetical, and have usually been rejected. In *Mobil Oil Australia Pty Ltd v Victoria* (2002) 211 CLR 1, the suggestion was that Victorian legislation permitting class actions in Victoria might give rise to "operational inconsistency" with the laws of other States. Only Kirby found it necessary to consider this possibility, and he rejected it. "**[61]** [T]he occasion to consider such cases of inconsistency would be one where the concrete facts required that the issue be addressed … **[62]** It will be time enough for this Court to consider the constitutional rule for dealing with operational conflict between competing State laws if and when a demonstrated instance of conflict of that kind arises".

3. Self-executing Machine?

In the area of industrial relations between employers and employees, the ultimate paramountcy of the Commonwealth regulatory system over those of the States has traditionally depended on the operation of s 109; and despite the sweeping changes to the Commonwealth system effected by the *Workplace Relations Amendment (Work Choices) Act 2005* (Cth), it seems inevitable that this dependence on s 109 will continue. The operation of s 109 in that context is considered in §4 below.

Under the older regime displaced by those changes, the Commonwealth's control of industrial relations depended primarily on awards obtained by compulsory arbitration of industrial disputes (see Chapter 22, §§4-5). The use of s 109 in that context, however, was troubled by an analytical puzzle that until the decision in *Ex parte McLean* had never been fully resolved. What is to prevail under s 109 is a Commonwealth "law"; and an industrial award is not a "law" because arbitration is not legislation. Yet repeatedly the practical question was whether a Commonwealth award should prevail over a State law. In *Ex parte McLean* Dixon J worked out an elaborate analysis of how this can be. It was the *Commonwealth Conciliation and Arbitration Act 1904* (Cth) that prevailed over conflicting State law. That Act empowered arbitrators to make awards; and this statutory empowerment, rather than the award, was the "law" upon which s 109 operated to override the State law.

The Commonwealth Parliament had attempted to ensure the supremacy of its awards by inserting into the *Conciliation and Arbitration Act* a section duplicating in statutory form the effect of s 109: originally s 30 of the Act; later s 51; later again s 65. When the legislation was recast as the *Industrial Relations Act 1988* (Cth), the provision, without any further change, was re-enacted as s 152 of that Act. Section 152 was recast as s 152(1) – with some exceptions, for example, as to termination of employment – when the *Industrial Relations Act* was amended to become the *Workplace Relations Act 1996* (Cth).

Workplace Relations Act 1996 (Cth)

152 (1) Subject to this section, if a State law or a State award is inconsistent with, or deals with a matter dealt with in, an award, the latter prevails and the former, to the extent of the inconsistency or in relation to the matter dealt with, is invalid.

The further amendments in 2005 do not entirely exclude this provision. Though the old s 152 is repealed, it lingers on in residual form in sub-s (1) of the new s 15 (initially introduced as s 7D): "An award or workplace agreement prevails over a law of a State or Territory, a State award or a State employment agreement, to the extent of any inconsistency". Again, the effect of this provision is subject to stated exceptions, this time for the benefit of State laws on such matters as workers compensation, apprenticeship, and occupational health and safety.

The reasoning of Dixon J in *Ex parte McLean* did not depend on this kind of provision. Indeed, the early High Court took the view that the original provision was invalid (see, for example, Isaacs J in *Federated Saw Mill &c Employees of Australasia v James Moore & Son Pty Ltd* (*Woodworkers' Case*) (1909) 8 CLR 465 at 538). There has been a strong judicial tendency to view s 109 as having a unique "supremacy" of its own, as a kind of automatic logical machine operating of its own inexorable force. Either it operates, or it does not. Parliament cannot make it do so. If s 109 does operate, a statutory recital to that effect is unnecessary. If s 109 does not operate, such a recital is ineffectual.

In the 1950s, the High Court appeared to soften its earlier strictures on the *Conciliation and Arbitration Act* provision. It tended now to be seen as harmless, and possibly even as helping to show an intention that industrial awards should "cover the field". But the Court still allowed no real effect to the provision. If s 109 applied, it did so of its own force (see, for example, *Collins v Charles Marshall Pty Ltd* (1955) 92 CLR 529 at 548-9). Dixon J's analysis in *Ex parte McLean* of the operation of s 109 on statutory provisions giving effect to industrial awards was restated in *TA Robinson & Sons Pty Ltd v Haylor* (1957) 97 CLR 177 at 182-3.

In 1983, the High Court took a different view again. The same *Conciliation and Arbitration Act* provision (now s 65) was seen in *Metal Trades Industry Association v Amalgamated Metal Workers' and Shipwrights' Union* (1983) 152 CLR 632 as being "**[648]** of paramount importance". It was this provision, rather than the empowering or effectuating provisions relied on in *Ex parte McLean* or in *TA Robinson v Haylor*, that enabled s 109 to operate on arbitral awards. It did so by evincing a legislative intention that such awards were to "cover the field". In *Dao v Australian Postal Commission* (1987) 162 CLR 317 the joint judgment of Mason CJ, Wilson, Deane, Dawson and Toohey JJ went even further. They referred to the 1983 *Metal Trades Case* and other cases arising under the *Conciliation and Arbitration Act* and stated: "**[337]** it must be remembered that in those circumstances the question of inconsistency can arise only because of the provisions of s 65 of that Act".

The view taken in the *Metal Trades Case* and in *Dao's Case* is questionable. The early view that a statutory provision of this kind is invalid may be excessively severe, but the later view that s 109 applies to industrial awards only because the Act contains such a provision may overstate its importance. The better analysis seems to be that of Dixon CJ in *Ex parte McLean* and in *TA Robinson v Haylor*: that in arbitration cases s 109 operates on the empowering or authorising provisions of the Act, and hence not on an award as such, but on the "law" by which it is so empowered or authorised. The better view of the statutory recital appears to be the middle view. It is ineffective, but harmless, and may merely assist the Court in ascertaining whether the law is intended to cover the field. Whether on that view it is competent for Parliament to carve out exceptions from the field to be covered (as it has done in the most recent versions) may be a more difficult question.

Of course, a provision in an arbitral award attempting to claim supremacy over State law will get little judicial sympathy (see *R v Members of the Railways Appeals Board and Commissioner for Railways (NSW); Ex parte Davis* (1957) 96 CLR 429). This is because an award is not legislation or even delegated legislation. If an award triggers s 109, it can only do so in the parasitic way explained by Dixon J in *Ex parte McLean*.

Part of the problem with statutory provisions like the former s 152(1) of the *Workplace Relations Act* is the idea that the Commonwealth might seek to control the operation of s 109. The Commonwealth, both as a political entity and as a legislative body, is a creature of the Constitution. It can only exercise those powers that the Constitution gives it, and every aspect of its behaviour is controlled by the document in which it finds its source. It cannot therefore, through Parliament or otherwise, reach up above its own defining instrument and control the operation of the provisions by which it is itself controlled. This is one aspect of the mantra referred to by Fullagar J in *Australian Communist Party v Commonwealth* (*Communist Party Case*) (1951) 83 CLR 1 that "[258] a stream cannot rise higher than its source". Moreover, this might be one intelligible sense in which s 109 might be thought of as an impersonal self-executing machine. Either there is an inconsistency or there is not, but the Commonwealth cannot be permitted to "create" or to "fabricate" an inconsistency.

On the other hand, in this context as elsewhere, it may be true that once we move away from the varieties of "direct" inconsistency (tests 1 and 2 above), the depiction of s 109 as self-executing is no longer workable. If the presence or absence of "inconsistency" depends upon the Commonwealth's intention that its law shall be the supreme or exclusive law on the topic, how is that intention to be expressed except through legislation? If the Commonwealth is constitutionally entitled to form such an intention, how can it not be entitled to express it?

4. Manufacturing Inconsistency

The idea that Commonwealth legislation cannot be permitted to "create" or "manufacture" an inconsistency was articulated most clearly by Evatt J, in a development of ideas that he had first expressed in *Stock Motor Ploughs Ltd v Forsyth* (1932) 48 CLR 128. That case concerned the *Moratorium Act 1930* (NSW), by which the New South Wales Parliament sought to defer or control the enforcement of debts under mortgages and hire-purchase agreements during the Great Depression. It was argued that the provisions relating to hire-purchase agreements were inoperable by reason of inconsistency with the *Bills of Exchange Act 1909* (Cth). The Court, with Dixon J dissenting, held that there was no inconsistency.

Evatt J argued that, even when in a particular case the two laws converged on the same transaction, they approached it from different viewpoints and for different purposes and therefore related to different legislative topics. More generally, he sought to argue that in spite of the expanding "cover the field" test, the area within which Commonwealth laws could suppress or supplant State legislation was a limited one. The limitations, as he tried to explain them, depended on the different kinds of subject-matter assigned to the Commonwealth Parliament by s 51. On some topics, such as "aliens" and "taxation", he found it almost inconceivable that any valid Commonwealth enactment could "cover the field" so as to squeeze out ordinary State legislation. As to "aliens", this was because the power conferred by s 51(xix) is a "person" power: it indicates "[148] a class of persons who may enter into an innumerable number of relations with the States and their citizens". It was therefore difficult to see how a Commonwealth law imposing duties on aliens could exclude "State laws imposing separate and additional duties, even upon aliens alone". On other topics, such as conciliation and arbitration, the enactment of a Commonwealth law might almost necessarily "cover the field", with "little or no room left for any action by other persons or authorities having the effect of adding to, much less altering, the duties laid down in the Commonwealth code".

Evatt J developed this analysis further in *West v Commissioner of Taxation (NSW)* (1937) 56 CLR 657. He denied that s 109 "[686] gives the Commonwealth some general 'supremacy' over the States" and insisted that "it is not possible for the Commonwealth to force its salary or pensions legislation into direct conflict with the income taxation laws of a State without destroying the validity of its own legislation".

West v Commissioner of Taxation (NSW)
(1937) 56 CLR 657

Evatt J: [707] [A]s I endeavoured to illustrate in the case of *Stock Motor Ploughs Ltd v Forsyth* [(1932) 48 CLR 128], attempts by the Commonwealth Parliament to manufacture "inconsistency" between its own legislation and that of the States will often be essayed only at the price of making the Commonwealth legislation *ultra vires*. Of course, lawful attempts by the Commonwealth may occur, as in *R v Brisbane Licensing Court; Ex parte Daniell* [(1920) 28 CLR 23], where State referenda and general elections were forbidden to be held on the same day as Commonwealth elections. No doubt, the State's legislation, actual and prospective, was avoided *pro tanto*. But the Commonwealth's legislative power over its own electoral system was deemed sufficient to enable it to prevent the awkwardness and confusion which might well result from a simultaneous Commonwealth and State election. In fact, the State was not impeded in its constitutional functions, for 364 other days in the year were left for it to choose from. On the other hand, a Commonwealth electoral law which forbade the holding of State elections for six months prior to a Commonwealth election would obviously be invalid.

Later attempts to apply Evatt J's reasoning have failed. An important test case was *Wenn v Attorney-General (Vic)* (1948) 77 CLR 84. The general issue was whether a Commonwealth scheme for preferential employment of ex-service personnel after World War II overrode a similar State scheme. The more precise issue was whether s 27 of the *Re-establishment and Employment Act 1945* (Cth), which made no provision for preference to ex-service personnel in promotions, could override the aspect of the *Discharged Servicemen's Preference Act 1943* (Vic) that did provide for preference in promotions. The crucial provision in the Commonwealth Act was s 24(2).

Re-establishment and Employment Act 1945 (Cth)

24 (2) The provisions of this Division shall apply to the exclusion of any provisions, providing for preference in any matter relating to the employment of discharged members of the Forces, of any law of a State, or of any industrial award, order, determination or agreement made or filed under or in pursuance of any such law, and whether the law, award, order, determination or agreement was enacted, made or filed before or after the commencement of this section.

Lionel Wenn was a member of the Victorian Public Service, who claimed that he was entitled to promotion to a position as Senior Warder at Pentridge Prison. He was not a discharged serviceman within the meaning of the Victorian Act, but would have been entitled to be promoted to the position unless the Public Service Board of Victoria was bound by the State Act to promote a discharged serviceman in priority to him.

The Court held that the State Act was overridden by the Commonwealth Act. Section 24(2) was especially important for Latham CJ, with whom McTiernan J agreed, because for these two judges the substantive provisions in s 27 of the Commonwealth Act, silent as they were on the precise question of preferential promotion, would not have been enough to override the Victorian provision on that question. On this view, the inconsistency that brought s 109 into play, thereby excluding the Victorian Act, depended on s 24(2).

Wenn v Attorney-General (Vic)
(1948) 77 CLR 84

Latham CJ: [110] In a series of cases (to several of which I have referred) it has been held that it may be ascertained by inference from the nature and scope of the provisions of a Commonwealth statute that it was the intention of the Parliament that the provisions of the statute should be the only law to be applied to the subject, so that it can be seen that the Commonwealth Parliament intended that there should be no State law dealing with the particular subject matter in question.

Where such an inference can properly be drawn the Commonwealth legislation prevails over any State law by virtue of s 109 of the Constitution. In the Commonwealth Act now under consideration, however, the Commonwealth Parliament has not left this matter to be determined by an inference (possibly disputable) from the nature and scope of the statute. The Parliament has most expressly stated an intention which in the other cases mentioned was discovered only by a process of inference. If such a parliamentary intention is effective when it is ascertained by inference only, there can be no reason why it should not be equally effective when the intention is expressly stated ...

[111] It is argued for the defendant that s 24(2) is really an attempt to prevent State Parliaments legislating upon the subject with which it deals (whether the Commonwealth Parliament passes legislation upon that subject or not) and that s 24(2) is invalid because it is a law with respect to State legislative powers and not with respect to the subject of the restoration of discharged servicemen to civil life. The "rehabilitation" – the restoration to and re-establishment in civilian life – of discharged members of the forces is a matter which falls within the legislative power of the Commonwealth Parliament: see *Attorney-General (Commonwealth) v Balding* [(1920) 27 CLR 395]. The statutory provision under consideration in that case was part of a provision "for the re-establishment in civil life of persons who have served in the defence forces of the Commonwealth when they are discharged from such service." It was held that "that is a matter so intimately connected with the defence of the Commonwealth as manifestly to be included within the scope of the power" – ie the defence power: see also *Real Estate Institute of NSW v Blair* [(1946) 73 CLR 213]. Section 24(2) is a provision prescribing the area within which Federal law, as enacted in the Act, is to apply to the exclusion of State law in respect of a subject as to which the Commonwealth Parliament has full legislative power. All valid Federal laws prevail over State laws which are inconsistent with them – Constitution, s 109. But the Federal laws which so prevail do not therefore become laws invalidly attempting to limit the powers of State Parliaments.

For Dixon J, with whom Rich J agreed, s 24(2) was merely part of the material on which he based an overall judgment that the Commonwealth Act had "covered the field".

Dixon J: [119] There are in my opinion two independent reasons why this argument cannot be maintained. The first is that the Federal Act discloses a legislative determination by the Federal Parliament of the question what shall be the extent of the legal obligation to give preference in matters of employment; and the decision embodied in the Act is that the legal obligation shall not apply where the employer appoints a person already employed by him. Between s 10 of the State Act, providing as it does for preference to discharged servicemen in promotion, and the Federal legislation there is consequently an inconsistency which must be fatal to the section under s 109 of the Constitution ... It is not necessary to say much in support of the first reason I have assigned. Section 24 and s 27, the effect of which I have already described, appear to me to justify the conclusion that, on the one hand, the Federal Parliament intended to define the extent to which the duty to give preference should go and to do it so as to exclude promotion, and, that on the other hand, it intended to provide in this and other respects what would be the only rule upon the subject and so would operate uniformly and without differentiation based on locality or other conditions. In this Court it is far too late to contend that s 109 does not invalidate State law which in **[120]** such a state of affairs carries the regulation of the same matter further than the Federal legislation has decided to go. This is a case where the Federal legislation undertakes a regulation or statutory determination of the very subject and then goes on to express an intention that it shall be an exhaustive declaration of the law on that particular subject.

To legislate upon a subject exhaustively to the intent that the areas of liberty designedly left should not be closed up is, I think, an exercise of legislative authority different in kind from a bare attempt to exclude State concurrent power from a subject the Federal legislature has not effectively dealt with by regulation, control or otherwise. It is still more widely different from an attempt to limit the exercise of State legislative power so that the Commonwealth should not be consequentially affected in the ends it is pursuing. This is not a case which, in my opinion, falls within the description of legislation so powerfully attacked by *Evatt* J in *West v Commissioner of Taxation (NSW)* [(1937) 56 CLR 657].

There is no doubt great difficulty in satisfactorily defining the limits of the power to legislate upon a subject exhaustively so that s 109 will of its own force make inoperative State legislation which otherwise would add liabilities, duties, immunities, liberties, powers or rights to those which the Federal law had decided to be sufficient. But within such limits an enactment does not seem to me to be open to the objection that it is not legislation with respect to the Federal subject matter but with respect to the exercise of State legislative powers or that it trenches upon State functions. Beyond those limits no doubt there lies a debatable area where Federal laws may be found that seem to be aimed rather at preventing State legislative action than dealing with a subject matter assigned to the Commonwealth Parliament.

Neither Latham CJ nor Dixon J excluded the possibility that Evatt J had envisaged of a Commonwealth legislative attempt to "manufacture" inconsistency which would for that very reason be invalid. However, both of them agreed that s 24(2) was not such a case.

The reasoning of Evatt J was rejected again in *Australian Coastal Shipping Commission v O'Reilly* (1962) 107 CLR 46. In that case the Court upheld the validity of s 36(1) of the *Australian Coastal Shipping Commission Act 1956* (Cth), which provided that the Commission "is subject to taxation under the laws of the Commonwealth, but is not subject to taxation under a law of a State or Territory of the Commonwealth to which the Commonwealth is not subject". Essentially the question was treated as one of characterisation: the legislative power under s 51(i) of the Constitution with respect to interstate trade enabled the Commonwealth to establish a Commission which would itself engage in such trade, and the question whether it should be liable to State taxation was an obvious policy matter appropriately dealt with as part of the Commission's establishment. This was so although Evatt J had said in *West v Commissioner of Taxation (NSW)* that the Commonwealth had no power to create "[684] an immunity from the general or non-discriminatory taxation legislation … [of] a State".

The only decision that seems arguably to lend itself to the kind of analysis suggested by Evatt J is *Airlines of NSW Pty Ltd v New South Wales (No 2)* (*Second Airlines Case*) (1965) 113 CLR 54. A confrontation between New South Wales and the Commonwealth over intra-State air routes in New South Wales arose in the early 1960s. The Commonwealth government was using its licensing of air navigation to favour Airlines of NSW Pty Ltd, while the State government licensing scheme favoured East-West Airlines Pty Ltd. In *Airlines of NSW Pty Ltd v New South Wales* (*First Airlines Case*) (1964) 113 CLR 1, the High Court treated this as a political deadlock which involved no legal inconsistency, and accordingly refused to interfere. Following that decision, the State Labor government had a change of leadership. The new administration not only maintained its support for East-West Airlines, but enacted stronger legislation in the form of the *Air Transport Act 1964* (NSW). Meanwhile, the Commonwealth also strengthened its position by amending the *Air Navigation Regulations* (Cth) (made under the *Air Navigation Act 1920* (Cth)).

On this basis Airlines of NSW again took action in the High Court. The Court found that the State and the Commonwealth had enacted valid laws to which different policy objectives could be ascribed, so that there was no inconsistency between them. Once again, any deadlock had to be resolved by negotiation. According to Menzies J: "[144] The answer to stalemate or deadlock in such circumstances is co-operation".

Airlines of New South Wales Pty Ltd v NSW (No 2) (Second Airlines Case)
(1965) 113 CLR 54

Kitto J: [120] The question remains whether the State legislation contained in the *Air Transport Act*, 1964 (NSW) is inconsistent with regs 198, 199, 320A and 320B, so as to be by force of s 109 of the Constitution invalid to the extent of the inconsistency. There is no actual contrariety … for the prohibitions of both the federal and the State provisions can of course operate side by side. The submission is that the apparent intention of the federal provision is to provide "completely, exhaustively or exclusively" what shall be the law governing the particular conduct or matters to which its attention is directed, and that the provisions of the State Acts nevertheless affect to govern the same conduct or matters. If this be true, there is inconsistency in the constitutional sense: *Ex parte McLean* [(1930) 43 CLR 472 at 483]; *O'Sullivan v Noarlunga Meat Ltd* [[1957] AC 1 at 28].

As regards regs 320A and 320B it seems to me beyond question that the suggested inconsistency does not exist. These regulations are directed, the one to landing at and taking off from aerodromes, airstrips or the like which have been acquired by the Commonwealth for public purposes, and the other to the control of flying in controlled air space, in the interests of the safety of persons and aircraft engaged in air navigation of certain kinds to which federal legislative power extends. The *Air Transport Act* of the State is not directed to either topic. It provides for a licensing system for the intra-State carrying of passengers or goods by aircraft, the purpose of the system being broadly, as appears from s 6, to regulate such carrying by reference to public needs, particularly as regards routes, the allocations of routes between licensees so as to foster the existence of competition between airlines and discourage monopoly of public air transport services within the State, the character, suitability and fitness of an applicant to hold the licence applied for, the extent to which areas, districts or routes are or are likely to be served by other forms of public transport, and the effect the air services may have upon other forms of transport. These matters are altogether different from those to which regs 320A and 320B relate. It is true that as a practical result of the co-existence of these regulations and the State Act a person who desires to operate a regular public air transport service which is wholly intra-State must possess and **[121]** conform to Commonwealth licences under regs 320 and 320B in order that he may use Commonwealth aerodromes or airstrips and fly aircraft in controlled air space, and must also possess and conform to a State licence for his aircraft extending to the route he wishes to adopt. If either the federal licences or the State licence be refused him the result may be that a particular intra-State route is without an air service. In the plaintiff's argument this situation was described as one of deadlock, and it is said that thereby the inconsistency of the two sets of provisions is demonstrated. In truth all that is demonstrated is that unless and until the federal and State authorities grant their respective licences to the one operator a degree of public inconvenience will exist. While this may be regretted, it leads to no legal conclusion.

The position as to regs 198 and 199 is perhaps not so clear, and it is for that reason that I have left it to the last. But I cannot say that I feel real doubt about it. The deadlock argument is used once more, but with no greater claim to acceptance. The topic and the only topic to which regs 198 and 199 direct their attention, so far as they apply to intra-State operations, is the safety, regularity and efficiency of air navigation. Regulation 199(4) makes that clear. The State Act, on the other hand, does not concern itself with that topic in any way. The fact that each piece of legislation sets up a licensing system operating independently of the licensing system established by the other may from time to time lead to a situation in which A, though holding a licence under the State Act for a proposed service, may be unable to obtain a licence for that service under reg 199, while B, though holding a licence for the service under reg 199, may be unable to obtain a licence for it under the State Act. But any ground for suggesting inconsistency disappears if the situation is more fully described, as by saying that consideration of matters concerning the safety, regularity and efficiency of air navigation has led the federal Director-General of Civil Aviation to conclude that A, though not B, should be debarred from conducting the service, while consideration of matters concerning public needs in relation to air transport services or concerning other topics mentioned in s 6(3) of the State Act has led the State Commissioner for Motor Transport to conclude that B, though not A, should be debarred from conducting the service. The federal Regulations and the State Act each employ a licensing system to serve a particular end; but the ends are different, and that means that the two sets of provisions are directed to different subjects **[122]** of legislative attention. In my opinion there is no mutual inconsistency in any relevant sense.

Regulation 200B of the Commonwealth *Air Navigation Regulations* provided that "an airline licence authorizes the conduct of operations in accordance with the provisions of the licence subject to the Act and these Regulations and to the other laws of the Commonwealth". It thereby sought to give the holder of a Commonwealth licence a positive authority to fly the specified intra-State air route, irrespective of any State law. Thus, had reg 200B been valid, it would have broken the deadlock. Yet it was for this very reason that the regulation was held invalid. Kitto J expressed this conclusion in language that seemed to bear directly on the issue of "manufactured" inconsistency.

Kitto J: [118] I turn next to reg 200B. It provides that an airline licence (as well as licences of certain other kinds) "authorizes the conduct of operations in accordance with the provisions of the licences but subject to the Act and these Regulations and to the other laws of the Commonwealth". The plain meaning is that such conduct of operations is not unlawful by reason of anything in the laws of a State. By the new paragraph (f) of reg 6(1) this provision is applied even to wholly intra-State air navigation.

[119] The argument in support of the provision in its application to wholly intra-State operations is that regs 198 and 199 set up a licensing system enabling the Director-General to select the persons who shall be entitled to use aircraft in regular public transport operations, even intra-State, and that reg 200B gives effect to the choice by excluding the application of any State law which in any instance would render the choice nugatory. It is only a loose use of terms, however, which makes the proposition appear plausible. What reg 199 provides for is not a selection of persons to be "entitled" to use aircraft in regular public transport operations, but a determination as to which of the persons who apply for licences ought, and which ought not, to remain forbidden, absolutely or conditionally, to use aircraft in such operations, having regard to matters concerned with the safety, regularity and efficiency of air navigation. I can see no escape from recognizing that the operation which reg 200B purports to have is, not to protect from State interference a "right" acquired under federal law, but to supplement the grant of an exemption from a particular prohibition under federal law by conferring in addition an immunity from any prohibition which State law may impose. The character of the regulation in its application to intra-State operations is therefore not that of a law with respect to a matter within federal power, but is that of a law with respect to the application of State laws – a matter not within federal legislative competence. By no line of reasoning that I have found it possible to accept can reg 200B be supported as valid federal legislation.

While the whole Court agreed that reg 200B was invalid, no other judge adopted reasoning similar to that of Kitto J. Instead, all the other judges treated the issue as one of characterisation under the relevant heads of power. Regulation 200B was not authorised by s 51(i) of the Constitution (see Chapter 16, §6), nor by s 51(xxix) (see Chapter 19, §4(a)). Accordingly, it was invalid. In a preamble to his judgment, Windeyer J seemed to reject the approach of Kitto J as harking back to the days of "reserved State powers" put to rest in *Amalgamated Society of Engineers v Adelaide Steamship Co Ltd (Engineers' Case)* (1920) 28 CLR 129 (see Chapter 7, §3).

Windeyer J: [148] The central point of the case is reg 200B of the *Air Navigation Regulations* recently made under the *Air Navigation Act* 1920-1963 (Cth). In the written case submitted for the State of New South Wales this is called a "transparent attempt on the part of the Commonwealth to usurp State legislative power". That indicates a wrong approach to the question. It reveals a misconception of the same sort as lies in the description that one sometimes hears of the State as a "sovereign State". A valid **[149]** Commonwealth law will override any State law inconsistent with it, for the Constitution so provides. A Commonwealth law is valid if it be a law with respect to some subject matter with respect to which the Commonwealth Parliament has power to make laws for the peace, order and good government of the Commonwealth. This is trite; but listening to the argument for the defendant State I caught some echoes of doctrine long discarded. This is not to say that there are no implications in the Constitution arising from its federal structure; in particular from s 107.

A similar issue of "manufactured" inconsistency arose in *Botany Municipal Council v Federal Airports Corporation* (1992) 175 CLR 453. The idea of a third runway at Sydney (Kingsford-Smith) Airport extending into Botany Bay was adopted by the Hawke Labor government in 1989 after years of controversy. An environmental impact statement under the *Environment Protection (Impact of Proposals) Act 1974* (Cth) found no major problems; but two Sydney councils sought an injunction in the New South Wales Land and Environment Court, arguing that the dredging of the bay floor required an additional environmental impact statement under the *Environmental Planning and Assessment Act 1979* (NSW).

Before the matter could be heard by the Land and Environment Court, the Commonwealth made regulations under the *Federal Airports Corporation Act 1986* (Cth) and the matter was removed to the High Court. The regulations unmistakably evinced an intention on the part of the Commonwealth to "cover the field". Thus, the only real prospect for success was to argue that the regulations were invalid. Regulations 7 and 8 established a system by which "works" would be undertaken and "rights" exercised by licensees. Regulation 9(1) provided that "a person who is not a licensee" must not carry out any part of the "works" or exercise any of the "rights". By reg 9(2): "A licensee is authorised to carry out the part of the works ... referred to in the licence in spite of a law, or a provision of a law, of the State of New South Wales ...". There then followed a long list of New South Wales laws specifically overridden, including the *Environmental Planning and Assessment Act*. In a joint unanimous judgment, the Court held that the regulations, including reg 9(2), were valid.

Botany Municipal Council v Federal Airports Corporation
(1992) 175 CLR 453

The Court: [463] The applicant's principal challenge to the validity of the Regulations rests on the submission that the sole object of the making of the Regulations was to displace the operation of State law upon the dredging and construction activities involved in the proposal for the extension to the airport. The applicant points to the fact that it is s 109 of the Constitution, not the particular Commonwealth statute or regulation which is inconsistent with State legislation, that renders that State legislation inoperative. Consequently, the applicant argues, if all the Regulations seek to do is to render the State legislation inoperative, they are invalid.

The most obvious answer to this argument is that the Regulations have a wider purpose. They establish a licensing regime regulating the engagement of contractors who are to carry out any part of the works or exercise any of the rights within or over either or both the airport or the dredging site. The objects of the Regulations are (reg 5):

"(a) to ensure that the works are carried out and the rights are exercised in accordance with the environmental standards; and

(b) to remove doubt about the extent to which the laws of the State of New South Wales apply to the carrying out of the works or the exercise of the rights; and

(c) to remove doubt about the extent to which the provisions of laws of the State of New South Wales applied in and in relation to Commonwealth places in that State under the *Commonwealth Places (Application of Laws) Act* 1970 apply to the carrying out of the works or the exercise of the rights." ...

[464] Regulation 9(2) is designed to ensure that the carrying out of the works and the exercise of the rights is governed by, and is in accordance with, the environmental standards as defined by the Regulations, that is, the Commonwealth standards, and to ensure that the work authorized by Commonwealth law is neither prevented nor hindered by State law. To attain those two objects, reg 9(2) confers upon a contractor an immunity from liability under State law in respect of what he or she does in accordance with a licence granted by the Chief Executive Officer. Legislation which attains those objects and confers that immunity is necessarily inconsistent with State law and therefore becomes inoperative by operation of s 109 of the Constitution. Viewed in this way, reg 9(2) is plainly valid. This is not a case in which the Commonwealth law is aimed at preventing or controlling State legislative action rather than dealing with a subject matter assigned to the Commonwealth **[465]** Parliament. Nor is it a case in which the Commonwealth law invalidly seeks to displace or expand the operation of s 109.

There can be no objection to a Commonwealth law on a subject which falls within a head of Commonwealth legislative power providing that a person is authorized to undertake an activity despite a State law prohibiting, restricting, qualifying or regulating that activity. Indeed, unless the law expresses itself directly in that way, there is the possibility that it may not be understood as manifesting an intention to occupy the relevant field to the exclusion of State law. It is sufficient to refer to the remarks of Dixon CJ in *Australian Coastal Shipping Commission v O'Reilly* [(1962) 107 CLR 46 at 56-7] where his Honour said:

"The argument that under a legislative power of the Commonwealth the operation of State laws cannot be directly and expressly excluded has been used without effect in a succession of cases beginning with *Commonwealth v Queensland* [(1920) 29 CLR 1] … The Court has interpreted s 109 as operating to exclude State law not only when there is a more direct collision between federal and State law but also when there is found in federal law the manifestation of an intention on the part of the federal Parliament to 'occupy the field': see *Hume v Palmer* [(1926) 38 CLR 441]; *Ex parte Nelson (No 2)* [(1929) 42 CLR 258]; *Ex parte McLean* [(1930) 43 CLR 472]. Surely, consistency with that doctrine demands that a legislative power, such as that given by s 51(i) together with s 98, must extend to a direct enactment which expressly excludes the operation of State law provided the enactment is within the subject matter of the federal power. Indeed there can really be no other way of expressing the intention and accomplishing the federal legislative purpose."

The drafting strategies upheld in this judgment have now been further developed by ss 14-16 of the *Workplace Relations Act 1996* (Cth), introduced (initially as ss 7C to 7E) by the *Workplace Relations Amendment (Work Choices) Act 2005*. The crucial provision is s 14(1):

Workplace Relations Act 1996 (Cth)

Act excludes some State and Territory laws

14(1) This Act is intended to apply to the exclusion of all the following laws of a State or Territory so far as they would otherwise apply in relation to an employee or employer:

  (a) a State or Territory industrial law;

  (b) a law that applies to employment generally and deals with leave other than long service leave;

  (c) a law providing for a court or tribunal constituted by a law of the State or Territory to make an order in relation to equal remuneration for work of equal value …;

  (d) a law providing for the variation or setting aside of rights and obligations arising under a contract of employment, or another arrangement for employment, that a court or tribunal finds is unfair;

  (e) a law that entitles a representative of a trade union to enter premises for a purpose other than a purpose connected with occupational health and safety.

The expression "a State or Territory industrial law", as used in para (a), is defined by s 4. It specifically includes the *Industrial Relations Acts* of New South Wales, Queensland, Tasmania and Western Australia and the *Fair Work Act 1994* (SA). It also includes:

  (b) an Act of a State or Territory that applies to employment generally and has one or more of the following as its main purpose or one or more of its main purposes:

   (i) regulating workplace relations (including industrial matters, industrial disputes and industrial action, within the ordinary meaning of those expressions);

   (ii) providing for the determination of terms and conditions of employment;

   (iii) providing for the making and enforcement of agreements determining terms and conditions of employment;

   (iv) providing for rights and remedies connected with the termination of employment;

   (v) prohibiting conduct that relates to the fact that a person either is, or is not, a member of an industrial association …

The definition also extends to subordinate legislation under any such Acts, and to other State or Territory laws that may be prescribed. However, s 14(2) and (3) then provide that the intended exclusion does *not* apply to State or Territory laws dealing with anti-discrimination, equal opportunity and other "non-excluded matters" (such as superannuation, workers compensation, child labour, long service leave and industrial action affecting essential services). On the other hand, the supremacy of federal awards or workplace agreements over inconsistent State and Territory provisions is provided for by s 15 (see §3 above); while s 16 leaves room for additional operations of s 109 by stipulating that the preceding sections "are not a complete statement of the circumstances in which this Act and instruments made under it are intended to apply to the exclusion of, or prevail over, laws of the States and Territories or instruments made under those laws".

Ironically, the objective sought by these provisions is the same as that sought by Isaacs J in *Clyde Engineering Co Ltd v Cowburn* (1926) 37 CLR 466: namely, to ensure that the Commonwealth regime for the regulation of industrial relations can operate without any impediment from State or Territory regimes. For Isaacs J that objective was quite independent of any policy preference as between Commonwealth and State regimes: one regime "**[479]** may be more or may be less generous or humane" than the other, but "that is not a question for this Court". Accordingly, even apart from the judgments in the *Botany Council* case, an attack on the above provisions on grounds of "manufactured" inconsistency may now seem unlikely to succeed.

On the other hand, the "simplified national system of workplace relations" which these provisions are designed to protect is primarily dependent for its validity on the "corporations" power (s 51(xx)); and the question whether the above provisions are sufficiently related to that head of power may appear open to debate. Thus, in *CFMEU v Newcrest Mining Ltd* (2005) 139 IR 50, the New South Wales Industrial Commission held (on the basis of the 1996 provisions) that "**[64]** there are limits to the extent to which the corporations power can be used to support a law to exclude a State award or State agreement ... **[67]** The corporations power is not a power that authorises laws the effect of which would be to extinguish the power of a State Industrial Authority ... to resolve an industrial dispute". There may also be an analogy with Evatt J's suggestion in *Stock Motor Ploughs Ltd v Forsyth* that no law relating to "aliens" could completely "cover the field", since the power over "aliens" is a "person power" and the States must always be able to make other laws with respect to that class of persons. A view of the "corporations" power as a "person power" might provide the basis for a similar argument.

Such an argument would be assisted by the Court's apparent tendency to treat issues about the extent of the "corporations" power primarily as issues of characterisation (see Chapter 17, §3). It would further be assisted by cases like *Bayside City Council v Telstra Corporation Ltd* (2004) 216 CLR 595, which suggest that arguments about "manufactured inconsistency" are also to be treated primarily as depending on characterisation. At issue in that case was the protection given to the broadband coaxial cables installed by telecommunications providers by cl 44(1) of Div 8 of Pt I of Sch 3 to the *Telecommunications Act 1997* (Cth):

Telecommunications Act 1997 (Cth)
Schedule 3, Part I, Division 8

44(1) The following provisions have effect:

(a) a law of a State or Territory has no effect to the extent to which the law discriminates, or would have the effect (whether direct or indirect) of discriminating, against a particular carrier, against a particular class of carriers, or against carriers generally;

(b) without limiting paragraph (a), a person is not entitled to a right, privilege, immunity or benefit, and must not exercise a power, under a law of a State or Territory to the extent to which the law discriminates, or would have the effect (whether direct or indirect) of discriminating, against a particular carrier, against a particular class of carriers, or against carriers generally;

(c) without limiting paragraph (a), a person is not required to comply with a law of a State or Territory to the extent to which the law discriminates, or would have the effect (whether direct or indirect) of discriminating, against a particular carrier, against a particular class of carriers, or against carriers generally.

Subclause (2) conferred a similar protection on "eligible users" of the cables.

In response to community concerns about the possible damage to the environment and to human health arising from the use of coaxial cables, a number of municipal councils in both New South Wales and Victoria exercised the powers given to them respectively by the *Local*

Government Act 1993 (NSW) and the *Local Government Act 1989* (Vic) to impose annual charges for the cables installed by corporate arms of both Telstra and Optus. Typically, the charges applied to both underground and aerial cables, though often at a significantly higher rate for the latter. By actions instituted in the Federal Court, both Telstra and Optus challenged the councils' power to impose the charges. They argued that, by comparison with the treatment of other public utilities, the charges were "discriminatory" within the meaning of cl 44, which prevailed over the empowering provisions in the State *Local Government Acts* by virtue of s 109. At first instance, Wilcox J rejected these claims (*Telstra Corporation Ltd v Hurstville City Council* (2000) 181 ALR 406); but the Full Federal Court reversed his decision (*Telstra Corporation Ltd v Hurstville City Council* (2002) 189 ALR 737), and on appeal the High Court affirmed the decision of the Full Federal Court (*Bayside City Council v Telstra Corporation Ltd* (2004) 216 CLR 595).

Notice that, in its application to rates and charges, cl 44(1) excludes only those that "discriminate" against one or more carriers of telecommunications. It was thus an exception to an earlier provision (cl 36) which provided that the activities of carriers were not generally exempt from State or Territory laws. In *West v Commissioner of Taxation (NSW)* Evatt J had suggested only that the Commonwealth had no power to create "[684] an immunity from the *general or non-discriminatory* taxation legislation ... [of] a State" (emphasis added) – so that, even if his approach were adopted, it would not necessarily exclude the power to give protection against a discriminatory tax. However, in the *Telstra* litigation nothing turned on this distinction. Indeed, at first instance Wilcox J came close to drawing a distinction the other way: he held that the Commonwealth could have brought s 109 into play by providing "[449] that telecommunications carriers, as entities carrying out a function subject to regulation by Commonwealth law, should be relieved of the burden of State taxation", since the operation of such a law would have been precisely defined. However, he held that "[d]iscrimination is an inappropriate concept to act as a trigger for the operation of s 109". Since such a concept requires "[451] a value judgment about factual situations", in a manner "[450] far removed from the simple test embodied in s 109", it is not amenable to the simple self-executing operation which s 109 should have. Moreover, the necessary value judgment was a judgment about the effect of the relevant State law; thus the operation of cl 44 "is made to depend, not upon the Commonwealth law itself, but upon the law of the State". However, neither of the appellate benches accepted this analysis.

Note also that in earlier cases such as *Australian Coastal Shipping Commission v O'Reilly* (1962) 107 CLR 46, the relevant immunity from State taxation was primarily claimed by the Commonwealth itself, and extended to its instrumentalities. By contrast, Optus had always been a private corporate enterprise, and by legislation in 1991 and 1993 Telstra, too, had been privatised and corporatised as a public company limited by shares (although, as the joint judgment in the High Court coyly noted, "[624] at the relevant times a majority of the shares was held by the Commonwealth"). However, no judge treated this distinction as making any difference. For example, Wilcox J accepted that the Commonwealth "[448] might exercise its constitutional legislative power in respect of a particular topic by authorising a privately owned entity to take particular action", and would then "have the competence to prescribe the legal regime that was to apply", including "exemption from a liability under State law".

As in *Australian Coastal Shipping Commission v O'Reilly*, the High Court majority treated the matter primarily as one of characterisation:

Bayside City Council v Telstra Corporation Ltd
(2004) 216 CLR 595

Gleeson CJ, Gummow, Kirby, Hayne and Heydon JJ: [624] The power conferred by s 51(v) of the Constitution, to make laws with respect to postal, telegraphic, telephonic and other like services, includes a power to make laws with respect to telecommunications services. So far as presently relevant, it extends to making laws regulating the terms and conditions upon which such services may be provided, the licensing of carriers, their conduct as licensees, and the conferring upon them of powers and immunities in connection with the activities undertaken by them pursuant to the chosen regulatory framework. The federal object of promoting the development of the telecommunications industry, and ensuring that telecommunications services would be provided to meet the needs of the Australian community, falls within a head of the legislative power of the Parliament of the Commonwealth. Conferring upon carriers an immunity from discriminatory burdens imposed upon them by State or Territory laws in their capacity as carriers has a direct and substantial connection with the power ...

[627] Telstra and Optus contend that, if and to the extent to which the provisions of the Local Government Acts of New South Wales and Victoria, pursuant to which the charges and rates in question were imposed or levied, fall within the description of laws which discriminate, or would have the effect (whether direct or indirect) of discriminating, against carriers generally, then they are inconsistent with the Telco Act and invalid.

In *Commonwealth v Queensland* [(1920) 29 CLR 1], this court held that a provision in the *Commonwealth Inscribed Stock Act 1911* (Cth) that "interest derived from stock or Treasury bonds shall not be liable to income tax under any law of the Commonwealth or a State" unless a certain condition was satisfied was a law supported by the power in s 51(iv) of the Constitution to make laws with respect to "[b]orrowing money on the public credit of the Commonwealth", and declared that Queensland legislation which made interest derived from Commonwealth stock or Treasury bonds liable to State income tax was to that extent invalid. That decision was referred to by Dixon CJ, in *Australian Coastal Shipping Commission v O'Reilly* [(1962) 107 CLR 46 at 56], as the first in a line of cases in which "[t]he argument that under a legislative power of the Commonwealth the operation of State laws cannot be directly and expressly excluded has been used without effect" ...

[628] The argument for the appellants invoked the idea, expressed by Evatt J in *West v Commissioner of Taxation (NSW)* [(1936) 56 CLR 657 at 707], that attempts by the Parliament of the Commonwealth to manufacture inconsistency between its own legislation and that of the States could result in a law of the Commonwealth which is itself ultra vires. A description of inconsistency as "manufactured" may beg the question ...

It is inconsistency between a valid law of the Commonwealth and a law of a State that is involved, and, to be valid, the federal law must be a law with respect to a subject of federal legislative power. This case does not enter upon what Dixon J in *Wenn* [*v Attorney-General (Vic)* (1948) 77 CLR 84 at 120] described as "a [629] debatable area" in the law of the Constitution and so does not require consideration of the existence of such an area. The concern indicated by Dixon J appears to arise where a law on its face made in exercise of a head of concurrent legislative power in s 51 of the Constitution is "aimed at" preventing the exercise of State legislative power and accordingly is not "a law of the Commonwealth" for the purposes of s 109 of the Constitution and cannot prevail over legislation of a State passed in exercise of its concurrent power.

It appeared to Wilcox J that, in the application of s 109, there is a material difference between a federal law which provides, for example, that a carrier shall not be liable to any State tax, and a law which provides that a carrier shall not be liable to any discriminatory State tax. If the difference is thought to be that a law of the second kind is a law with respect to discrimination and not a law within s 51(v), then the answer to that is given above. Beyond that, the difference is elusive. If protecting carriers against the imposition of burdens, such as taxation, by State law has a sufficient connection with the power confined by s 51(v), then it is difficult to understand why protecting carriers against discriminatory burdens does not have the same connection with the power. Nor does such a limited protection become a bare attempt to exclude State power upon a subject as to which the parliament has not chosen to legislate exhaustively.

In cl 39, the parliament declared an intention not to protect carriers from State taxes of general application, but the scheme of powers and immunities created by Sch 3, which was to govern the operations of the carriers, was to include (by virtue of cl 44) a protection from discriminatory State taxes and charges. The reasons of policy underlying the distinction are a matter for the legislature, although the responses of local authorities to what Wilcox J described as community concern at the cabling may indicate some of the policy considerations at work. The legislative history shows that an attempt to impose discriminatory taxes or charges, perhaps in order to discourage cabling, or at least overhead cabling, or perhaps simply to raise revenue, was foreseen. As a matter of power, the narrower immunity is as easily sustained as a wider immunity. The enactment of a valid federal law pursuant to the power engages s 109.

Notice how this judgment keeps open the "debatable area" acknowledged by Dixon J in *Wenn v Attorney-General* by contrasting a law which is properly characterised by reference to a head of Commonwealth power with one that is "aimed at" preventing the exercise of State legislative power. It may be for this reason that while the new objectives inserted by the 2005 amendments into s 3 of the *Workplaces Relations Act* include "(b) establishing and maintaining a simplified national system of workplace relations", they avoid any reference to an objective of excluding the concurrent operation of State and Territory laws.

In *Bayside City Council* only Callinan J dissented from the above conclusions; and he did so on the ground that, in his view, the effect of cl 44 in restricting the regulatory choices available to the States (and to their municipal instrumentalities) infringed the *Melbourne Corporation* principle (see Chapter 25, §2). He therefore did not find it necessary to consider the effect of s 109.

5. Clearing the Field

Whatever doubt may remain about whether the Commonwealth can "cover the field" by an express provision declaring its legislative intention to do so, there appears to be no doubt that it can avoid covering a legislative "field" by an express provision declaring its intention not to do so. Such a declaration will be accepted by the High Court as a virtually conclusive indication. This means in practice that the Commonwealth can control the operation of s 109 in a negative way by making it clear that related State laws are to operate concurrently with the Commonwealth law. The leading case is *R v Credit Tribunal; Ex parte General Motors Acceptance Corporation* (1977) 137 CLR 545, where the following provision was held to be valid:

Trade Practices Act 1974 (Cth)

75 (1) Except as provided by sub-section (2), this Part is not intended to exclude or limit the concurrent operation of any law of a State or Territory.

(2) Where an act or omission of a person is both an offence against section 79 and an offence under the law of a State or Territory and that person is convicted of either of those offences, he is not liable to be convicted of the other of those offences.

(3) Except as expressly provided by this Part, nothing in this Part shall be taken to limit, restrict or otherwise affect any right or remedy a person would have had if this Part had not been enacted.

R v Credit Tribunal; Ex parte General Motors Acceptance Corporation (*GMAC Case*)
(1977) 137 CLR 545

Mason J: [563] [A] Commonwealth law may provide that it is not intended to make exhaustive or exclusive provision with respect to the subject with which it deals, thereby enabling State laws, not inconsistent with Commonwealth law, to have an operation. Here again the Commonwealth law does not of its own force give State law a valid operation. All that it does is to make it clear that the Commonwealth law is not intended to cover the field, thereby leaving room for the operation of such State laws as do not conflict with Commonwealth law.

It is of course by now well established that a provision in a Commonwealth statute evincing an intention that the statute is not intended to cover the field cannot avoid or eliminate a case of direct inconsistency or collision, of the kind which arises, for example, when Commonwealth and State laws make contradictory provision upon the same topic, making it impossible for both laws to be obeyed. In *R v Loewenthal; Ex parte Blacklock* [(1974) 131 CLR 338 at 346-7], I pointed out that such a provision in a Commonwealth law cannot displace the operation of s 109 in rendering the State law inoperative. But where there is no direct inconsistency, where inconsistency can only arise if the Commonwealth law is **[564]** intended to be an exhaustive and exclusive law, a provision of the kind under consideration will be effective to avoid inconsistency by making it clear that the law is not intended to be exhaustive or exclusive.

It is against this background of settled constitutional interpretation that s 75 is to be construed. In the light of what has already been said, the terms of s 75(1) are open to the objection that they refer to the concurrent operation of State laws; they do not speak of the extent of the intended operation of the Commonwealth law. None the less, there is to be gathered from the sub-section a very clear expression of intention that the *Trade Practices Act* is not an exhaustive enactment on the topics with which it deals and that it is not intended to operate to the exclusion of State laws on those topics. As such it does not avoid any instance of direct inconsistency which may occur between the *Trade Practices Act* and the two South Australian Acts, but in accordance with all that I have said, it eliminates any suggestion of inconsistency otherwise arising.

Note the stipulation that the Commonwealth "**[563]** cannot avoid or eliminate a case of direct inconsistency". In cases involving direct inconsistency (tests 1 and 2), s 109 will operate of its own force and no statutory assertion to the contrary can prevent it from doing so. In such a case, no question under the "cover the field" test arises (see *Telstra Corporation Ltd v Worthing* (1997) 197 CLR 61 in §2 above). Accordingly, the effect of the *GMAC Case* is only this: where the question is whether the Commonwealth enactment "covers the field", a provision for the concurrent operation of State laws will be accepted as a clear indication that the Commonwealth enactment is not intended to "cover the field".

6. Inconsistency and Racial Discrimination

The basic principles applied by the High Court to determine how s 109 operates were established in the context of the old regime of industrial arbitration. When the same principles have been applied in the field of human rights, the results have arguably been anomalous. This has been particularly true in cases involving anti-discrimination legislation, such as *Australian Mutual Provident Society v Goulden* and *Dao v Australian Postal Commission* (1987) 162 CLR 317.

George and Stella Viskauskas had a hotel in Kempsey, New South Wales. On 27 November 1980, three Aborigines said that they had been refused service on the ground of their race. A complaint about the incident was made on their behalf to the Commissioner for Community Relations under the *Racial Discrimination Act 1975* (Cth), who immediately commenced an inquiry. Five days later the three complainants themselves wrote to the Counsellor for Equal Opportunity under the *Anti-Discrimination Act 1977* (NSW), who also began an inquiry. Immediately after this second complaint, the hotel owners brought an action seeking a declaration that the New South Wales Act was invalid by reason of inconsistency with the Commonwealth Act. The Commonwealth Act was passed under the "external affairs" power (s 51(xxix)) to implement Australian obligations under the 1966 International Convention on the Elimination of All Forms of Racial Discrimination. In *Viskauskas v Niland* (1983) 153 CLR 280, the High Court held the New South Wales Act to be inoperative because the Commonwealth Act had "covered the field".

Viskauskas v Niland
(1983) 153 CLR 280

The Court: [292] Sometimes it may be difficult to ascertain the precise limits of the field which the Commonwealth legislation reveals an intention to cover, but that is not so in the present case. The Commonwealth Act deals with the subject of racial discrimination. It is true that it does so for the purpose of giving effect to the Convention, but the parties to the Convention "undertake to prohibit and to eliminate racial discrimination in all its forms": Art 5; see also Art 2. Parties to the

Convention are to "assure to everyone within their jurisdiction effective protection and remedies": art 6. The Commonwealth Parliament has chosen the course of itself legislating to prohibit racial discrimination, and having done so it can only fulfil the obligation cast upon it by the Convention if its enactment operates equally and without discrimination in all the States of the Commonwealth. It could not, for example, admit the possibility that a State law might allow exceptions to the prohibition of racial discrimination or might otherwise detract from the efficacy of the Commonwealth law. The subject matter of the Commonwealth Act suggests that it is intended to be exhaustive and exclusive, and this conclusion is supported by the fact that the provisions of Pt II (and especially those of s 9) are expressed with complete generality, and by the further fact that s 6 reveals an intention to bind the Crown in right of each State as well as the Crown in right of the Commonwealth. It appears from both the terms and the subject matter of the Commonwealth Act that it is intended as a complete statement of the law for Australia relating to racial discrimination.

Even if that were not so, the provisions of s 19 of the State Act deal with the subject of racial discrimination in relation to the provision of goods and services in terms substantially similar to those of s 13 of the Commonwealth Act. The consequences provided by the respective Acts for breaches of the sections, although in some respects similar, are not the same. Under the Commonwealth Act the powers to make orders against a person who has committed an act of discrimination are vested in a court, in proceedings which can only be instituted upon a certificate under s 24(3). Under the State Act, the powers are entrusted to a tribunal. Under the Commonwealth Act the court may award damages in respect of, inter alia, loss of dignity, humiliation and injury to feelings, and no limit is provided to the amount of damages [293] that may be awarded. Under the State Act the damages that may be awarded are "for any loss or damage suffered by reason of the respondent's conduct" and there is a pecuniary limit. There are other differences in relation to powers and procedure, as the sections already mentioned reveal. At least with regard to the subject matter of racial discrimination in relation to the provision of goods and services, the test as stated in *Ex parte McLean* [(1930) 43 CLR 472] applies exactly – the two legislatures have legislated upon the same subject, and have prescribed what the rules of conduct will be and (if it matters) the sanctions imposed are diverse. Clearly in respect of that subject matter there is an inconsistency.

One month after the *Viskauskas* decision, the *Racial Discrimination Act* was amended to make it clear that it was intended to operate concurrently with State or Territory legislation. Further, the amendment sought to vacate retrospectively the field identified in *Viskauskas* and thereby retrospectively to revive the New South Wales law.

Racial Discrimination Act 1975 (Cth)

6A (1) This Act is not intended, and shall be deemed never to have been intended, to exclude or limit the operation of a law of a State or Territory that furthers the objects of the Convention and is capable of operating concurrently with this Act.

The retrospective operation of s 6A was considered by the High Court in *University of Wollongong v Metwally* (1984) 158 CLR 447, again with a disconcerting result. Mohamed Metwally was an Egyptian postgraduate student at Wollongong University. In March 1981, some time before s 6A(1) was passed, but within the period of its intended retrospective operation, Metwally lodged complaints against the University under the *Anti-Discrimination Act*. He was successful in his complaints and was awarded damages by the New South Wales Equal Opportunity Tribunal. The University challenged the finding, arguing that s 6A was invalid insofar as it purported to have any retrospective operation.

Gibbs CJ, Murphy, Brennan and Deane JJ held that s 6A could not retrospectively revive the New South Wales *Anti-Discrimination Act*. Mason, Wilson and Dawson JJ dissented. To complicate matters, while Murphy and Deane JJ held that the original State law could not be revived by retrospective Commonwealth legislation, they also found that a retrospective Commonwealth law could, in the words of Murphy J, "[469] clear the way for the State Parliament to make a fresh State Act to apply retrospectively in the same terms".

University of Wollongong v Metwally
(1984) 158 CLR 447

Gibbs CJ: [456] It is said in *Butler v Attorney-General (Vic)* [(1961) 106 CLR 268] that "invalid" in s 109 of the Constitution means, not void, but "inoperative", so that if a State law, which was inconsistent with a law of the Commonwealth, was not repealed by the State legislature and remained on the statute book, the expiration or repeal of the Commonwealth law would have the result that the State law would come into force; in those circumstances the State law would have remained in abeyance during the time when the inconsistency existed and, when the inconsistency no longer existed, would cease to be inoperative. It follows that if a Commonwealth statute which, on its proper construction, had revealed an intention to cover exclusively and exhaustively the subject-matter with which it dealt, so that in consequence a State statute dealing with the same subject-matter was rendered inoperative, were subsequently amended in such a way as to manifest an intention that it was not intended to exclude the operation of the State law, the operation of the State statute would thereupon revive. There is therefore no reason to doubt (assuming the correctness of the assumptions to which I have referred) that after 19 June 1983, when the Amendment Act came into force, the *Anti-Discrimination Act* again became operative in New South Wales.

It was submitted that since the Commonwealth Parliament has power to make its enactments retrospective, it could retrospectively amend the Commonwealth Act, so as to indicate an intention not to [457] exclude the operation of the State law, and thereby cause the *Anti-Discrimination Act* to have a valid operation from its inception, notwithstanding that in truth it was inconsistent with the Commonwealth Act at all times before the Amendment Act was passed. The acceptance of this argument would mean that the Commonwealth Parliament could enact a law which would retrospectively deprive s 109 of the Constitution of its operation. If, at a particular time, a State law was inconsistent with a law of the Commonwealth, s 109, applied at that time, would have resulted in the invalidity of the State law. If, on the other hand, the State law was not inconsistent with that law of the Commonwealth, s 109 would not render it invalid. If the respondent's argument were correct, the Commonwealth Parliament could retrospectively reveal that the Commonwealth law had an intention, which it lacked at the earlier time, either to cover, or not to cover, the whole field, with the result that the State law would be retrospectively invalidated or validated. In other words, the Commonwealth law itself could vary the effect which s 109 had produced at the relevant time; it could give to a State law a valid operation as at a time when s 109 had rendered it invalid. But Commonwealth statutes cannot prevail over the Constitution. The deeming provisions in sub-ss (1) and (2) of s 6A do not state the effect which the *Anti-Discrimination Act* in truth had before the Amendment Act was passed; what they do is to create a "statutory fiction", to use the well-known words to which reference was made by Windeyer J in *Hunter Douglas Australia Pty Ltd v Perma Blinds* [(1970) 122 CLR 49 at 65]. Before the Amendment Act came into effect, the Commonwealth Act, on its proper construction, was intended to be a complete and exclusive statement of the law of Australia with regard to racial discrimination, and Pt II of the *Anti-Discrimination Act* was inconsistent with that law and therefore invalid by force of s 109. What the Amendment Act in effect provides is that the Commonwealth Act should now be understood as though it did not have that intention and that Pt II of the *Anti-Discrimination Act* was therefore not inconsistent with it. In other words, the Parliament has attempted to exclude the operation of s 109 by means of a fiction. The short answer to the submissions of the respondents is that the Parliament cannot exclude the operation of s 109 by providing that the intention of the Parliament shall be deemed to have been different from what it actually was and that what was in truth an inconsistency shall be deemed to have not existed. Section 109 deals with "a matter of prime importance" in the constitutional framework (see *Butler v Attorney-General* **[458]** *(Vic)* [(1961) 106 CLR 268 at 282]), namely the effect of an inconsistency between the enactments of two legislatures both of which operate in the same territory. Its provisions are not only critical in adjusting the relations between the legislatures of the Commonwealth and the States, but of great importance for the ordinary citizen, who is entitled to know which of two inconsistent laws he is required to observe. With all respect, I do not agree with the remark of Evatt J in *Victoria v Commonwealth* [(1937) 58 CLR 618 at 634], that the section does "no more than declare a rule of last resort". If there is an inconsistency between a law of a State and a law of the Commonwealth there is no other rule than that laid down by s 109 by which the inconsistency may be resolved. In the present case, since an inconsistency in fact existed, the provisions of s 109 were called into play and their effect cannot later be excluded by retrospectively declaring that the truth was other than it was.

Deane J: [476] In the course of argument on behalf of the respondents, the submission was made that s 109 of the Constitution was designed to ensure supremacy of valid Commonwealth laws and that it would be anomalous if such a provision were to be interpreted in a way which would detract from the parliamentary sovereignty of the Commonwealth. Even if that were the sole function served by s 109, that assertion would have little force since, on any approach, s 109 enhances the supremacy of Commonwealth laws by directly invalidating State laws to the extent of any inconsistency. More important, the submission fails adequately to acknowledge that the Australian federation was and is a union of people and that, **[477]** whatever may be their immediate operation, the provisions of the Constitution should properly be viewed as ultimately concerned with the governance and protection of the people from whom the artificial entities called Commonwealth and States derive their authority. So viewed, s 109 is not concerned merely to resolve disputes between the Commonwealth and a State as to the validity of their competing claims to govern the conduct of individuals in a particular area of legislative power. It serves the equally important function of protecting the individual from the injustice of being subjected to the requirements of valid and inconsistent laws of Commonwealth and State Parliaments on the same subject. The section expressly provides that, in such a case, the law of the Commonwealth "shall prevail" and that the law of the State "shall, to the extent of the inconsistency, be invalid". In its express stipulation of invalidity, the section has no parallel in the Constitutions of the United States or Canada and there is little point in looking to decisions of the Supreme Courts of those countries for assistance in the resolution of the question involved in the present case. In cases in this Court, it has been established that the word "invalid" in s 109 should be read in the limited sense of "inoperative" and that, when inconsistency ends, the State law again becomes operative. The decisions to that effect, while perhaps making the ascertainment of the law sometimes more difficult, leave intact the essential protection which s 109 affords a person faced with the competing, and conceivably impossible, demands of inconsistent Commonwealth and State laws. In that predicament, he or she cannot be subjected to the ordeal of being legally required to comply with both. For as long as inconsistency exists, s 109 of the Constitution deprives the State law of its validity with the consequence that he or she has the constitutional right to ignore it ...

[478] A parliament may legislate that, for the purposes of the law which it controls, past facts or past laws are to be deemed and treated as having been different to what they were. It cannot, however[,] objectively[ ] expunge the past or "alter the facts of history": cf *Akar v Attorney-General (Sierra Leone)* [[1970] AC 853 at 870]. If the fact was that its Emperor wore no clothes, it is powerless either to reverse that fact outside the fields in which it is master or objectively to convert into falsehood the truth which a small child saw. That position is, of course, a fortiori in the case of a parliament whose powers are limited even within the territorial area for which they exist. For the purposes of an organic law, such as the Constitution, which lies above the law which such a parliament may make, it may be a relevant fact that that parliament has enacted that some fact or law which in truth existed is to be deemed never to have been. If, however, that organic law is framed so as to act upon the reality, the retrospective fictions of the subordinate law will be unavailing. It is only if the organic law is framed to act upon any fictions that might subsequently be introduced into that subordinate law that the parliament which has power over that subordinate law can control the operation of the organic law by the retrospective introduction of such fictions.

Section 109 of the Constitution is not concerned with legal fictions. It is concerned with the reality of contemporaneous inconsistency between a valid law of the Commonwealth and an otherwise valid law of a State. According to its terms, its operation is immediate. Its terms are unqualified and self-executing. If there *is* inconsistency between an otherwise valid law of a State and a valid law of the Commonwealth the State law *shall* be, to the extent of the inconsistency, invalid. It is not the Commonwealth law which operates to make the State law invalid, it is the Constitution itself: see *Federated Saw Mill &c Employés of Australasia v James Moore & Son Pty Ltd* [(1909) 8 CLR 465 at 536]; *Wenn v Attorney-General (Vic)* [(1948) 77 CLR 84 at 120]. It is the

Constitution and not the Commonwealth Parliament which tells the citizen faced with the dilemma of inconsistent Commonwealth [479] and State laws which both, according to their terms, apply to him or her that the State law is invalid and can be disregarded. If, at some subsequent time, the Commonwealth repeals or amends its law to remove the inconsistency, the State law will then become again valid or operative not from some prior date but from the time when there was, in fact, no longer inconsistency. The fact that the Commonwealth Parliament legislates retrospectively to introduce the fiction that, for the purposes of its law, its inconsistent law never existed or had a different operation to that which it in fact had cannot alter the objective fact that at the previous time when s 109 operated that inconsistency did exist. Nor can it alter the fact that the immediate and self-executing provisions of s 109 have already operated upon that inconsistency to invalidate the State law not for the period in which the Commonwealth Parliament, by the introduction of a fiction for its purposes, has subsequently said that its law had a different operation to that which it in fact had but for the period in which the fact of that inconsistency existed. So to say is not to construe s 109 of the Constitution as imposing a restriction on Commonwealth legislative power. It is simply to recognize that while the Commonwealth can retrospectively legislate for itself it cannot retrospectively impose *as State law* the provisions of a law which the Constitution has said was invalid because of contemporaneous inconsistency which has subsequently been removed. That is something which, if it is to be done, must be done retrospectively by the relevant State.

It follows that the Commonwealth Parliament, being subordinate to the Constitution, could not, by its 1983 Amending Act, reverse the past operation of s 109 of the Constitution which had rendered invalid or inoperative the relevant provisions of the NSW Act. The Commonwealth Parliament possessed no power unilaterally to override that operation of the Constitution either by amending the terms of s 109 or by creating a legally effective illusion that the section had never operated at all by the introduction of a retrospective fiction into its law. That being so, the position remains that the relevant provisions of the NSW Act were not operative at the time the acts complained of in the present case were committed and the conduct for which the appellant has been held responsible was not unlawful under the provisions of the NSW Act.

Mason J: [460] The effect of [s 109], like that of other provisions of the Constitution, is to inhibit the Commonwealth Parliament from enacting contradictory legislation. The Parliament could not, for example, either prospectively or retrospectively provide that a State law which was inconsistent with a Commonwealth law should have, or have had, full force and effect, notwithstanding that inconsistency. This is because the invalidity of the inconsistent State law is brought about by the operation of s 109; the Commonwealth law does not operate of its own inherent force to invalidate the State enactment …

But there is no objection to the enactment of Commonwealth legislation whose effect is not to contradict s 109 of the Constitution but to remove the inconsistency which attracts the operation of that section. So, where inconsistency between Commonwealth and State laws arises, as it did in *Viskauskas* [(1983) CLR 280], because the Commonwealth law, according to its true construction, is intended to regulate the subject-matter exhaustively or exclusively, the Commonwealth [461] Parliament may legislate to remove that inconsistency by providing that the Commonwealth law is not intended to regulate the subject-matter exhaustively or exclusively, thereby opening the way to the concurrent operation of a State law on the subject-matter. It is, of course, well settled that: "a Commonwealth statute may provide that it is not intended to make exhaustive or exclusive provision with respect to the subject with which it deals thereby enabling State laws, not in direct conflict with a Commonwealth law, to have an operation": *Palmdale-AGCI Ltd v Workers' Compensation Commission (NSW)* [(1977) 140 CLR 236 at 243].

What the Parliament can enact prospectively in the exercise of its legislative powers it can also enact retrospectively: *R v Kidman* [(1915) 20 CLR 475]. Just as a Commonwealth law can validly provide that it is not intended to operate as an exhaustive or exclusive regulation of the subject-matter so it may validly provide that it never was intended to so operate: *Strickland v Rocla Concrete Pipes Ltd* [(1971) 124 CLR 468 at 492]. Indeed, as I understand the argument, this is not disputed.

The point of departure is reached when and only when the retrospective operation of the Commonwealth statute displaces an inconsistency or cause of inconsistency with a State law which has previously arisen. According to the argument, this is because the Commonwealth statute is attempting to give a valid operation to a State statute which was rendered inoperative by s 109. This analysis misstates the legal operation of s 6A. It says nothing about the State Act; it amends the Commonwealth Act by altering its prospective and retrospective operation. In so doing … , it removes the inconsistency with the State Act. And in removing the inconsistency, s 6A does not attempt to contradict the operation of s 109. What the statutory provision does is to eliminate the basis on which s 109 can operate.

As to the claim by Deane J that the majority view was a vindication of the rights of individual citizens, Mason J observed:

Mason J: [463] [Section 109] is not a source of individual rights and immunities except in so far as individual rights and immunities are necessarily affected because the section renders inoperative a State law which is inconsistent with a Commonwealth law. Nor is the section a source of protection to the individual against the unfairness and injustice of a retrospective law. That is a matter which lies quite outside the focus of the provision … [T]o distil from s 109 an unexpressed fetter upon Commonwealth legislative power is to twist the section from its true meaning and stand it upon its head.

Ever since the action in *Viskauskas v Niland* had been commenced in the High Court, other complaints of racial discrimination awaiting hearing by the NSW Equal Opportunity Tribunal had been put on hold. One of these was *Dao v Australian Postal Commission* (1987) 162 CLR 317, in which two Vietnamese women, Dao Thi Nguyet Thanh and Nguyen Thi Dieu Ahn, complained that the Postal Commission had first refused to appoint them as mail sorters, and then dismissed them from temporary employment in that capacity after a medical examination found them to be below the minimum weight for persons of their height and sex. Both women were of average weight and height for Vietnamese women, but below the average weight of women born in Australia. Once *Metwally* had been decided by the High Court, the Tribunal accepted that it had no power to investigate the *Dao* case as one of racial discrimination, but proposed to consider it instead as possibly involving discrimination on grounds of sex.

The Supreme Court of New South Wales granted prohibition on the ground that, once the postal service had been transferred to the Commonwealth under s 69 of the Constitution, it became a subject of exclusive Commonwealth legislative power under s 52(ii) (*Australian Postal Commission v Dao* (1985) 3 NSWLR 565). The High Court, though unanimously dismissing an appeal, did not consider that issue and relied instead on s 109.

Section 42(2) of the *Postal Services Act 1975* (Cth) directed that a person "shall not be appointed as an officer" unless "the Commission is satisfied, after … a medical examination required by the Commission, as to [the applicant's] health and physical fitness". The High Court saw this as "**[334]** a duty which the Commission may not disregard". The prospect that the Tribunal might find the Commission's decision unlawful, and even order it to grant the women's applications for permanent appointment, was seen as "**[335]** a clear usurpation by the Tribunal, under the authority of the State Act, of the responsibility resting on the Commission under the Commonwealth Act". Thus the State Act was "clearly in collision with s 42 of the Common-wealth Act and must therefore, by force of s 109 of the Constitution, give way".

The two women had sought to avoid this result by relying on *Maguire v Simpson* (1977) 139 CLR 362, which had held that s 64 of the *Judiciary Act 1903* (Cth) may sometimes render the Commonwealth liable to be sued under State law. However, the Court held that, whatever effect s 64 might otherwise have had, "**[331]** the constitutional provision, as the basic law, must receive prior consideration". The *Judiciary Act* provision could not be used "to finesse or sidestep that prior question of constitutional invalidity". Its purpose was "to fill what would otherwise be lacunae or gaps in the law of the Commonwealth. It is not to be understood as intended to have the practical effect of overriding s 109 of the Constitution".

Another kind of possible inconsistency with the Commonwealth *Racial Discrimination Act* was considered in *Mabo v Queensland (No 1)* (1988) 166 CLR 186, a skirmish in the 10 years of litigation culminating in the landmark decision in *Mabo v Queensland (No 2)* (1992) 175 CLR 1.

In *Mabo (No 2)* the High Court held by 6:1, with Dawson J dissenting, that when in 1879 the State of Queensland annexed the Murray Islands in Torres Strait the traditional inhabitants of the islands had a "traditional native title" recognised by the common law. It was further held that this title had survived under the sovereignty of successive colonial, State and Commonwealth governments as a "burden" on the "radical" title of the Crown and had never been extinguished (though the Crown in right of Queensland had the power to do so).

Throughout the litigation the State of Queensland denied that any such title existed. But it also attempted to pre-empt the issue by enacting the *Queensland Coast Islands Declaratory Act 1985* (Qld), which purported to extinguish any traditional rights that the plaintiffs might be held to have had. The State then pleaded this Act as a defence to the plaintiffs' claim. The issue in *Mabo (No 1)* was whether the Queensland Act was "invalid" under s 109 by reason of inconsistency with the *Racial Discrimination Act*.

Racial Discrimination Act 1975 (Cth)

10 (1) If, by reason of, or of a provision of, a law of the Commonwealth or of a State or Territory, persons of a particular race, colour or national or ethnic origin do not enjoy a right that is enjoyed by persons of another race, colour or national or ethnic origin, or enjoy a right to a more limited extent than persons of another race, colour or national or ethnic origin, then, notwithstanding anything in that law, persons of the first-mentioned race, colour or national or ethnic origin shall, by force of this section, enjoy that right to the same extent as persons of that other race, colour or national or ethnic origin.

(2) A reference in sub-section (1) to a right includes a reference to a right of a kind referred to in Article 5 of the Convention [on the Elimination of All Forms of Racial Discrimination].

The rights to be enjoyed "without distinction as to race, colour, or national or ethnic origin" under Art 5(d) of the Convention included "(v) The right to own property alone as well as in association with others", and "(vi) The right to inherit".

Mabo v Queensland (No 1)
(1988) 166 CLR 186

Brennan, Toohey and Gaudron JJ: [217] Although the human right to own and inherit property (including a human right to be immune from arbitrary deprivation of property) is not itself necessarily a legal right, it is a human right the enjoyment of which is peculiarly dependent upon the provisions and administration of municipal law. Inequality in the enjoyment of that human right may occur by discrimination in the provisions of the municipal law or by discrimination in the administration of the municipal law or by both. When inequality in enjoyment of a human right exists between persons of different races, colours or national or ethnic origins under Australian law, s 10 operates by enhancing the enjoyment of the human right by the disadvantaged persons to the extent necessary to eliminate the inequality. As the inequality with which s 10 is concerned exists "by reason of" a municipal law, the operation of the municipal law is nullified by s 10 to the extent necessary to eliminate the inequality.

The question which s 10 poses in the present case is whether, under our municipal law, the Miriam people enjoy the human right to own and inherit property – a right which includes an immunity from arbitrary deprivation of property – to a more limited extent than other members of the community. ("Property" in this context must embrace rights of any kind in or over the Murray Islands.) In respect of property rights arising under the Crown lands legislation, the answer must be no. A person who is a member of the Miriam people is entitled to own and inherit those property rights in the same way and to the same extent as any other Australian. **[218]** Section 10(3) was enacted to override laws which might have restricted the capacity of Aboriginals and Torres Strait Islanders to manage their own property.

But the 1985 Act destroys the traditional legal rights in and over the Murray Islands possessed by the Miriam people (and particularly by the plaintiffs) and, by an arbitrary deprivation of that property, limits their enjoyment of the human right to own and inherit it. If the assumption be made that traditional rights survived the annexation of the islands and were thereafter recognized by the common law, and if the effect of the 1985 Act be left aside, the general law of Queensland would now recognize two categories of legal rights to be enjoyed under the Crown in and over the Murray Islands: traditional rights and rights granted in pursuance of Crown lands legislation. Traditional rights are characteristically vested in members of the Miriam people; rights under Crown lands legislation are vested in grantees who may be of any race, colour or national or ethnic origin. However, it is not the source or history of legal rights which is material but their existence. It is the arbitrary deprivation of an existing legal right which constitutes an impairment of the human rights of a person in whom the existing legal right is vested. Leaving aside the 1985 Act, the general law leaves unimpaired the immunity of each person in whom any legal right in or over the Murray Islands is vested from arbitrary deprivation of that person's legal right. The relevant human right is immunity from arbitrary deprivation of legal rights in or over the Murray Islands. The 1985 Act operates in this context.

By extinguishing the traditional legal rights characteristically vested in the Miriam people, the 1985 Act abrogated the immunity of the Miriam people from arbitrary deprivation of their legal rights in and over the Murray Islands. The Act thus impaired their human rights while leaving unimpaired the corresponding human rights of those whose rights in and over the Murray Islands did not take their origin from the laws and customs of the Miriam people. If we accord to the traditional rights of the Miriam people the status of recognized legal rights under Queensland law (as we must in conformity with the assumption earlier made), the 1985 Act has the effect of precluding the Miriam people from enjoying some, if not all, of their legal rights in and over the Murray Islands while leaving all other persons unaffected in the enjoyment of their legal rights in and over the Murray Islands. Accordingly, the Miriam people enjoy their human right of the ownership and inheritance of property to a "more limited" extent than others who enjoy the same human right.

In practical terms, this means that if traditional native title was not extinguished before the *Racial Discrimination Act* came into [219] force, a State law which seeks to extinguish it now will fail. It will fail because s 10(1) of the *Racial Discrimination Act* clothes the holders of traditional native title who are of the native ethnic group with the same immunity from legislative interference with their enjoyment of their human right to own and inherit property as it clothes other persons in the community. A State law which, by purporting to extinguish native title, would limit that immunity in the case of the native group cannot prevail over s 10(1) of the *Racial Discrimination Act* which restores the immunity to the extent enjoyed by the general community. The attempt by the 1985 Act to extinguish the traditional legal rights of the Miriam people therefore fails.

Deane J concurred on a slightly different basis. Mason CJ did not reach a conclusion since he held that, at this preliminary stage of the litigation, the issues could only be considered in the abstract by making assumptions as to matters of fact. Wilson and Dawson JJ dissented.

Wilson J: [205] [T]here is no suggestion in the statement of claim that there are any persons of another race who enjoy the same rights of which the plaintiffs have been deprived by the Queensland [206] Act. In those circumstances there is nothing to attract the operation of s 10. It may be accepted that the Queensland Act purports, on the assumption that underlies the hearing of the demurrer, to deprive the plaintiffs of certain of the human rights and fundamental freedoms which are referred to in Art 5(d) of the Convention. But the practical effect of that deprivation is not to create an inequality between them and persons of another race which is then removed by the operation of s 10 of the Commonwealth Act. On the contrary, its effect is to remove a source of inequality formerly existing between the plaintiffs and persons of another race because, on the facts as disclosed in the statement of claim, the plaintiffs were alone in the enjoyment of traditional rights. Henceforth, by virtue of the assumed operation of the Queensland Act, the plaintiffs will enjoy the same rights with respect to the ownership of property and rights of inheritance as every other person in Queensland of whatever race. There will be equality before the law.

The Commonwealth's response to *Mabo (No 2)* was the *Native Title Act 1993* (Cth). Although that Act validated existing non-Indigenous titles, and also enabled the States to do so, it purported to do this without disturbing the *Racial Discrimination Act*. This meant that, for State legislation purporting to respond to *Mabo (No 2)*, potential problems under s 109 arose in at least two ways. First, there was the problem of whether the State legislation might infringe the *Racial Discrimination Act* by dealing with the land rights of Indigenous Australians less favourably than with the comparable rights of non-Indigenous Australians. Secondly, there was the problem of consistency with the Commonwealth *Native Title Act*. However, the latter Act did not attempt to "cover the field"; any such attempt was disavowed by s 8, which provided: "This Act is not intended to affect the operation of any law of a State or a Territory that is capable of operating concurrently with this Act".

The Western Australian response to *Mabo (No 2)* was the *Land (Titles and Traditional Usage) Act 1993* (WA) (assented to on 2 December 1993, some three weeks before the Commonwealth Act). That Act purported to extinguish all native titles subsisting in Western Australia, thus wholly negating the common law as declared in *Mabo (No 2)*. Such titles were then replaced with statutory "rights of traditional usage" equivalent in principle to those recognised by *Mabo (No 2)*, but subject to specific modifications by other provisions of the Act.

Land (Titles and Traditional Usage) Act 1993 (WA)

7 (1) On the commencement of, and by operation of, this section –
(a) any native title to land that existed immediately before that commencement is extinguished; and
(b) the members of an Aboriginal group who held native title to land immediately before that commencement become entitled to exercise rights of traditional usage in relation to that land under and subject to this Act.
(2) Rights of traditional usage created by subsection (1) (b) in relation to land replace the rights and entitlements that were incidents of the native title to that land extinguished by subsection (1) (a) and, unless this Act provides otherwise, are equivalent in extent to the rights and entitlements that they replace.

Section 28(1) precluded any compensation for the extinguishment of native title under s 7.

The Western Australian Act also had a retrospective application. Section 5 confirmed the validity of non-Indigenous titles granted between 31 October 1975 (the day the *Racial Discrimination Act* commenced operation) and 2 December 1993 (the day Parts 2 and 3 of the Western Australian Act came into operation). If the effect of that confirmation was to extinguish or impair native title, a claim for compensation could be made under s 28.

The Commonwealth *Native Title Act* also worked by statutory modification of the common law as enunciated in *Mabo (No 2)*. It did so on the basis stated in ss 10 and 11.

Native Title Act 1993 (Cth)

10 Native title is recognised, and protected, in accordance with this Act.

11 (1) Native title is not able to be extinguished contrary to this Act.
(2) An act that consists of the making, amendment or repeal of legislation on or after 1 July 1993 by the Commonwealth, a State or a Territory is only able to extinguish native title:
(a) in accordance with Division 3 of Part 2 (which deals with future acts and native title); or
(b) by validating past acts in relation to the native title.

Although the Western Australian Act had received the Royal assent before the Commonwealth Act, s 11(2) was expressed to operate retrospectively on and from 1 July 1993. Moreover, the mechanism in s 7 of the Western Australian Act was also dealt with more directly. For the purposes of the Commonwealth Act, the expressions "native title" and "native title rights and interests" were defined by s 223.

223 (3) Subject to subsection (4), if native title rights and interests as defined by subsection (1) are, or have been at any time in the past, compulsorily converted into, or replaced by, statutory rights and interests in relation to the same land or waters that are held by or on behalf of Aboriginal peoples or Torres Strait Islanders, those statutory rights and interests are also covered by the expression **"native title"** or **"native title rights and interests"**.

Thus, even if s 7 of the Western Australian Act was effective in removing native title from the umbrella of the Commonwealth law, s 223(3) of the Commonwealth law would simply bring such titles back beneath that umbrella by means of redefinition.

The High Court considered the effect of s 109 on these provisions in *Western Australia v Commonwealth* (*Native Title Act Case*) (1995) 183 CLR 373. The Court unanimously held, with Dawson J concurring in a separate judgment, that the Western Australian Act was wholly inoperative as inconsistent with both the *Racial Discrimination Act* and the *Native Title Act*.

Western Australia v Commonwealth (*Native Title Act Case*)
(1995) 183 CLR 373

Mason CJ, Brennan, Deane, Toohey, Gaudron and McHugh JJ: [435] [T]he critical consideration is whether there was inconsistency with the *Racial Discrimination Act*. If there was supervening inconsistency between the WA Act and the *Racial Discrimination Act*, native title to land in Western Australia may have survived so that the *Native Title Act* can operate upon it. The WA Act is said to discriminate against the Aborigines (who, but for the operation of s 5 or s 7 of the WA Act, would be holders of native title) in comparison with the holders of other forms of title. The WA Act is said to discriminate against those Aborigines by denying them equal enjoyment of certain human rights appearing in Art 5 of the International Convention on the Elimination of All Forms of Racial Discrimination scheduled to the *Racial Discrimination Act* ...

[437] By the operation of s 10(1) of the *Racial Discrimination Act*, equality of enjoyment of the human rights to own and inherit property is conferred on the "persons of a particular race". The *Racial Discrimination Act* does not alter the characteristics of native title, but it confers on protected persons rights or immunities which ... allow protected persons security in the enjoyment of their title to property to the same extent as the holders of titles granted by the Crown are secure in the enjoyment of their titles. "Property" in the context of the human rights with which we are concerned includes land and chattels as well as interests therein. Where, under the general law, the indigenous "persons of a particular race" uniquely have a right to own or to inherit property within Australia arising from indigenous law and custom but the security of enjoyment of that property is more limited than the security enjoyed by others who have a right to own or to inherit other property, the persons of the particular race are given, by s 10(1), security in the enjoyment of their property "to the same extent" as persons generally have security in the enjoyment of their property. Security in the right to own property carries immunity from arbitrary deprivation of the property. Section 10(1) thus protects the enjoyment of traditional interests in land recognised by the common law. However, it has a further operation.

If a law of a State provides that property held by members of the community generally may not be expropriated except for prescribed purposes or on prescribed conditions (including the payment of compensation), a State law which purports to authorise expropriation of property characteristically held by the "persons of a particular race" for purposes additional to those generally justifying expropriation or on less stringent conditions (including lesser compensation) is inconsistent with s 10(1) of the *Racial Discrimination Act*.

[438] The two-fold operation of s 10(1) ensures that Aborigines who are holders of native title have the same security of enjoyment of their traditional rights over or in respect of land as others who are holders of title granted by the Crown and that a State law which purports to diminish that security of enjoyment is, by virtue of s 109 of the Constitution, inoperative. The security of enjoyment of what the WA Act includes in "title" by the holders thereof is the benchmark by which to determine whether, for the purposes of the *Racial Discrimination Act*, the Aborigines who hold native title enjoy their human rights in relation to land to a more limited extent than do persons of other races.

To determine whether the prospective provisions of the WA Act are inconsistent with s 10(1) of the *Racial Discrimination Act*, it is necessary to compare the position of the Aborigines who hold s 7 rights with the position of the holders of forms of title other than native title. Or, as s 10(1) of the *Racial Discrimination Act* confers on the Aborigines who hold native title security of enjoyment to the same extent as the holders of other forms of title have security of enjoyment, it is equally valid to compare the position of the Aborigines who hold s 7 rights with the position in which those Aborigines would be if the WA Act had not purported to extinguish their native title and substitute s 7 rights in its place. If, by virtue of the WA Act, Aborigines on whom s 7 rights are conferred do not enjoy the same security of enjoyment of those rights as do the holders of "title", there is an inconsistency between the WA Act and s 10(1) of the *Racial Discrimination Act* … On the other hand, if the WA Act were to ensure to Aborigines the same security of possession and enjoyment of s 7 rights as the *Racial Discrimination Act* confers on the Aboriginal holders of native title, there would be no inconsistency in respect of security of title between the WA Act and the *Racial Discrimination Act*.

The joint judgment then reviewed the comparative positions of native title holders and the holders of other titles under various enactments amended by the West Australian *Land (Titles and Traditional Usage) Act*, such as the *Land Act 1933* (WA) and the *Mining Act 1978* (WA). The review showed that, as a result of the amendments, Aboriginal holders of native title did not enjoy the same security as the holders of other titles. Accordingly, the joint judgment held "**[450]** that the qualification of s 7 rights effected by the various provisions of the WA Act is inconsistent with s 10(1) of the *Racial Discrimination Act*. The prospective operation of the WA Act, based on s 7, is destroyed by that inconsistency".

In argument before the High Court, Western Australia conceded that the *Land (Titles and Traditional Usage) Act* would be inconsistent with the *Native Title Act* if the latter Act was valid. However, the joint judgment held that in all material respects the *Native Title Act* was valid under s 51(xxvi) of the Constitution, the "races power". It was further argued that certain specific sections of the *Native Title Act* were invalid, and hence could not prevail over the State legislation, because they "**[464]** purport to control the exercise by the State of its legislative power or purport directly to render State laws invalid". This argument was also rejected.

The effect of these decisions, particularly *Mabo (No 1)* and the *Native Title Act Case*, in working out the operation of s 109 in the context of the Commonwealth regime established by the *Racial Discrimination Act* and the *Native Title Act*, has since been elaborately restated: see *Western Australia v Ward* (*Miriuwung-Gajerrong Case*) (2002) 213 CLR 1 at 99-109, 153, 201-2, 278-88. The joint majority judgment in that case emphasised, however, that analysis of the operation of s 10 of the *Racial Discrimination Act* in the context of native title "**[102]** should not … be understood as enlarging accepted principles about the operation of s 109".

7. Further References

Coper, M, *Encounters with the Australian Constitution* (CCH, 1988), Chs 1, 4.

Hanks, P, "'Inconsistent' Commonwealth and State Laws: Centralising Government Power in the Australian Federation" (1986) 16 *Federal Law Review* 107.

Hill, G, "Resolving a True Conflict between State Laws: A Minimalist Approach" (2005) 29 *Melbourne University Law Review* 39.

Katz, L, "*Ex parte Daniell* and the Operation of Inoperative Laws" (1976) 7 *Federal Law Review* 66.

Lee, HP, "Retrospective Amendment of Federal Laws and the Inconsistency Doctrine in Australia" (1985) 15 *Federal Law Review* 335.

McCarry, G, "Landmines among the Landmarks: Constitutional Aspects of Anti-Discrimination Laws" (1989) 63 *Australian Law Journal* 327.

Morabito, V, and Strain, H, "The Section 109 'Cover the Field' Test of Inconsistency: An Undesirable Legal Fiction" (1993) 12 *University of Tasmania Law Review* 182.

Murray-Jones, A, "The Tests for Inconsistency under Section 109 of the Constitution" (1979) 10 *Federal Law Review* 25.

Rumble, GA, "The Nature of Inconsistency under Section 109 of the Constitution" (1980) 11 *Federal Law Review* 40.

Sawer, G, "Substance and Form in the Relations between Federal and State Legislation in Australia" in Tammelo, I, Blackshield, A, and Campbell, E (eds), *Australian Studies in Legal Philosophy* (*Archiv für Rechts- und Sozialphilosophie*, Beiheft No 39, 1963), 61.

Tammelo, I, "The Tests of Inconsistency between Commonwealth and State laws" (1956) 30 *Australian Law Journal* 496.

Tarrant, S, "Using the Commonwealth Sex Discrimination Act and s109 of the Constitution to Challenge State Abortion Laws" (1998) 20 *Adelaide Law Review* 207.

Williams, G, "The Return of State Awards – Section 109 of the Constitution and the Workplace Relations Act 1996 (Cth)" (1997) 10 *Australian Journal of Labour Law* 170.

Chapter 10

The Federal Parliament

1. Introduction

Chapter I of the Constitution ("The Parliament") comprises 60 sections. Section 1 provides that the legislative power of the Commonwealth shall be vested in a federal Parliament consisting of the Queen, a Senate (the upper House) and a House of Representatives (the lower House). Section 7 permits legislation to increase or decrease the number of senators – provided that, because the Senate was conceived of as a "States' House", the six original States must still be represented by equal numbers of senators, regardless of differences in population size.

Section 24 requires that the number of members in the House of Representatives "shall be, as nearly as practicable, twice the number of Senators". This "nexus" between the two Houses means that any increase in the size of one House must entail an increase in the other. When the first Commonwealth Parliament met on 9 May 1901, the House of Representatives had 75 members and the Senate had 36. Today, the House has 150 members and the Senate has 76 (12 for each State, plus two each for the Northern Territory and the Australian Capital Territory). The formula in s 24 for computing the ratio between the two Houses is applicable only "until the Parliament otherwise provides"; but in *A-G (NSW); Ex rel McKellar v Commonwealth* (1977) 139 CLR 527, a statutory variation on the formula was held to be invalid because the formula used *before* the change gave a closer approximation of a 2:1 ratio than the new formula could do.

Except for the list of Commonwealth legislative powers in s 51, most sections in Chapter I attracted little judicial attention until the 1970s. Insofar as these sections regulate the composition and procedure of the Parliament, they are unlikely to be invoked in litigation. Even when they are invoked, the High Court has been reluctant to embark on the inquiries or judgments involved. The general rule-of-thumb has been that Parliament is entitled to control its own affairs and that the courts should not interfere. This has reflected a carrying over into Australia of judicial attitudes formed by the British conception of "parliamentary sovereignty".

2. Parliamentary Privilege

Section 49 of the Constitution gives the federal Parliament the power to declare its own "powers, privileges, and immunities". It also establishes that, until such "powers, privileges, and immunities" are declared, they shall be those that were held by the House of Commons in the United

Kingdom as at the establishment of the Commonwealth. The power in s 49 was not exercised until 1987. Thus, when an issue of contempt of Parliament arose in 1955, it was assumed that the relevant rules and procedures were those of the House of Commons.

Frank Browne, a freelance political journalist and the author of a newsletter called *Things I Hear*, was the editor of the *Bankstown Observer*, owned by Raymond Fitzpatrick, a Bankstown blue metal contractor. In it he published an article accusing the local member, Charles Morgan of the Australian Labor Party, of trafficking in entry permits for refugee migrants. Morgan complained to a newly established Committee on Privileges, which reported to the House of Representatives that a breach of privilege had occurred. Browne and Fitzpatrick were called before the Bar of the House and sentenced to six months' imprisonment. When the two men applied to the High Court for writs of habeas corpus, the answer given was that, if the warrant for their arrest had specified a particular allegation against them, the Court could have adjudicated on that allegation; but because the warrant was in general terms, it was conclusive.

R v Richards; Ex parte Fitzpatrick & Browne
(1955) 92 CLR 157

Dixon CJ (for the Court): [162] It is unnecessary to discuss at length the situation in England; it has been made clear by judicial authority. Stated shortly, it is this: it is for the courts to judge of the existence in either House of Parliament of a privilege, but, given an undoubted privilege, it is for the House to judge of the occasion and of the manner of its exercise. The judgment of the House is expressed by its resolution and by the warrant of the Speaker. If the warrant specifies the ground of the commitment, the court may, it would seem, determine whether it is sufficient in law as a ground to amount to a breach of privilege, but if the warrant is upon its face consistent with a breach of an acknowledged privilege it is conclusive and it is no objection that the breach of privilege is stated in general terms. This statement of law appears to be in accordance with cases by which it was finally established, namely, the *Case of the Sheriff of Middlesex* [(1840) 11 Ad & E 273; 113 ER 419] ...

[164] In the present case the warrant would clearly be sufficient if it had been issued by the Speaker of the House of Commons in pursuance of the resolution of that House ...

[I]f, under the law which we have attempted to describe, that warrant were produced to a court sitting in London, as we are here, as a warrant of the House of Commons, it would be regarded by the court as conclusive of what it states, namely, that a breach of privilege had been committed and that the House, acting upon that view, had directed that the two persons concerned should be committed and the Speaker, accordingly, had issued his warrant. In the ordinary phrase current in the law courts, it would not be possible to go behind that warrant. It states a contempt or breach of privilege in general terms, and not in particular terms, but it is completely consistent with a breach having occurred and it states that one did occur.

The question in the case is whether that state of the law applies under s 49 of the Constitution to the House of Representatives. If you take the language of the latter part of s 49 and read it apart from any other considerations, it is difficult in the extreme to see how any other answer could be given to the question than that that law is applicable in Australia to the House of Representatives ... The language is such as to be apt to transfer to the House the full powers, privileges and immunities of the House of Commons. As Lord *Cairns* has said, an essential ingredient, not a **[165]** mere accident, in those powers, is the protection from the examination of the conclusion of the House expressed by the warrant. There are, however, other considerations in this Constitution which have been availed of by counsel for the two men concerned as grounds upon which to urge that a restrictive construction should be given to those words, giving them less operation than their terms seem to require ...

It is convenient, first, to go to the important argument that this Constitution of Australia is a rigid federal Constitution under which it is the duty of the courts of the Commonwealth, and, indeed, the courts of law generally, to consider whether any act done in pursuance of the powers given by the Constitution, whether by the legislature or by the executive, is beyond the power which the Constitution assigns to that body.

As a general proposition, the truth of that consideration admits of no denial. It is a Constitution which deals with the demarcation of powers, leaves to the courts of law the question of whether there has been any excess of power, and requires them to pronounce as void any act which is ultra vires. In the everyday work of this Court, we are accustomed to examining the validity of Acts of Parliament. Less often does the validity of an executive act come to be considered, but it stands upon the same footing. It is urged for that reason that we should refuse to adopt as applicable under our Constitution the view of the Court of Queen's Bench pronounced in 1840 and adopted as for the Colony of Victoria by the Privy Council in 1871, and that we should construe s 49 as not transferring to Australia that element in the law governing the privileges and powers of the House of Commons.

The answer, in our opinion, lies in the very plain words of s 49 itself. The words are incapable of a restricted meaning, unless that restricted meaning be imperatively demanded as something to be placed artificially upon them by the more general considerations which the Constitution supplies. Added to that simple reason are the facts of the history of this particular branch of the law. Students of English constitutional history are well aware of the controversy which attended the establishment of the powers, privileges and immunities of the House of Commons. Students of English constitutional law are made aware at a very early stage of their tuition of the judicial declarations terminating that controversy, and it may be said that there is no more conspicuous chapter in the constitutional law of Great Britain than the particular matter with which we are dealing. It is quite incredible that the framers of s 49 were not completely aware of the state of the law in Great Britain and, [166] when they adopted the language of s 49, were not quite conscious of the consequences which followed from it. We are therefore of opinion that the general structure of this Constitution, meaning by that the fact that it is an instrument creating a constitution of a kind commonly described as rigid in which an excess of power means invalidity does not provide a sufficient ground for placing upon the express words of s 49 an artificial limitation ...

Then it was argued that this is a constitution which adopts the theory of the separation of powers and places the judicial power exclusively in the judicature as established under the Constitution, the executive power in the executive, and restricts the legislature to legislative powers. It is said that the power exercised by resolving upon the imprisonment of two men and issuing a warrant to carry it into effect belonged to the judicial power and ought therefore not to be conceded under the words of s 49 to either House of the Parliament. It is correct that the Constitution is based in its structure upon the separation of powers. It is true that the judicial power of the Commonwealth is reposed exclusively in the courts contemplated by Chap III. It is further correct that it is a general principle of construction that the legislative powers should not be interpreted as allowing of the creation of judicial powers or authorities in any body except the courts which are described by Chap III of the Constitution. Accordingly, it is argued that a strong presumption exists against construing s 49 in a sense which would enable the particular power we have before us to be exercised by the Senate or the House of Representatives. It was pointed out that in the case of the Inter-State Commission s 101 had received a construction which made it impossible to invest the Inter-State Commission with the character of a court and confide to it judicial functions, because it was not a body which fell within Chap III. That was relied upon as an instance or example of the kind of construction or interpretation which we were urged to adopt in the case of s 49.

[167] The consideration we have already mentioned is of necessity an answer to this contention, namely, that in unequivocal terms the powers of the House of Commons have been bestowed upon the House of Representatives. It should be added to that very simple statement that throughout the course of English history there has been a tendency to regard those powers as not strictly judicial but as belonging to the legislature, rather as something essential or, at any rate, proper for its protection. This is not the occasion to discuss the historical grounds upon which these powers and privileges attached to the House of Commons. It is sufficient to say that they were regarded by many authorities as proper incidents of the legislative function, notwithstanding the fact that considered more theoretically – perhaps one might even say, scientifically – they belong to the judicial sphere. But our decision is based upon the ground that a general view of the Constitution and the separation of powers is not a sufficient reason for giving to these words, which appear to us to be so clear, a restrictive or secondary meaning which they do not properly bear.

The power contained in s 49 of the Constitution was finally exercised to enact the *Parliamentary Privileges Act 1987* (Cth). Section 3 defines "an offence against a House" to mean "a breach of the privileges or immunities, or a contempt, of a House or of the members or committees".

Parliamentary Privileges Act 1987 (Cth)

Essential element of offences

4 Conduct (including the use of words) does not constitute an offence against a House unless it amounts, or is intended or likely to amount, to an improper interference with the free exercise by a House or committee of its authority or functions, or with the free performance by a member of the member's duties as a member.

Powers, privileges and immunities

5 Except to the extent that this Act expressly provides otherwise, the powers, privileges and immunities of each House, and of the members and the committees of each House, as in force under section 49 of the Constitution immediately before the commencement of this Act, continue in force.

Contempts by defamation abolished

6 (1) Words or acts shall not be taken to be an offence against a House by reason only that those words or acts are defamatory or critical of the Parliament, a House, a committee or a member.

(2) Subsection (1) does not apply to words spoken or acts done in the presence of a House or a committee.

Penalties imposed by Houses

7 (1) A House may impose on a person a penalty of imprisonment for a period not exceeding 6 months for an offence against that House determined by that House to have been committed by that person.

(2) A penalty of imprisonment imposed in accordance with this section is not affected by a prorogation of the Parliament or the dissolution or expiration of a House.

(3) A House does not have power to order the imprisonment of a person for an offence against the House otherwise than in accordance with this section.

(4) A resolution of a House ordering the imprisonment of a person in accordance with this section may provide that the President of the Senate or the Speaker of the House of Representatives, as the case requires, is to have power, either generally or in specified circumstances, to order the discharge of the person from imprisonment and, where a resolution so provides, the President or the Speaker has, by force of this Act, power to discharge the person accordingly.

(5) A House may impose on a person a fine:

  (a) not exceeding $5,000, in the case of a natural person; or

  (b) not exceeding $25,000, in the case of a corporation,

for an offence against that House determined by that House to have been committed by that person.

(6) A fine imposed under subsection (5) is a debt due to the Commonwealth and may be recovered on behalf of the Commonwealth in a court of competent jurisdiction by any person appointed by a House for that purpose.

(7) A fine shall not be imposed on a person under subsection (5) for an offence for which a penalty of imprisonment is imposed on that person.

(8) A House may give such directions and authorise the issue of such warrants as are necessary or convenient for carrying this section into effect ...

Resolutions and warrants for committal

9 Where a House imposes on a person a penalty of imprisonment for an offence against that House, the resolution of the House imposing the penalty and the warrant committing the person to custody shall set out particulars of the matters determined by the House to constitute that offence ...

Parliamentary privilege in court proceedings

16 (1) For the avoidance of doubt, it is hereby declared and enacted that the provisions of article 9 of the Bill of Rights, 1688 apply in relation to the Parliament of the Commonwealth and, as so applying, are to be taken to have, in addition to any other operation, the effect of the subsequent provisions of this section.

(2) For the purposes of the provisions of article 9 of the Bill of Rights, 1688 as applying in relation to the Parliament, and for the purposes of this section, *proceedings in Parliament* means all words spoken and acts done in the course of, or for purposes of or incidental to, the transacting of the business of a House or of a committee, and, without limiting the generality of the foregoing, includes:

    (a) the giving of evidence before a House or a committee, and evidence so given;

    (b) the presentation or submission of a document to a House or a committee;

    (c) the preparation of a document for purposes of or incidental to the transacting of any such business; and

    (d) the formulation, making or publication of a document, including a report, by or pursuant to an order of a House or a committee and the document so formulated, made or published.

(3) In proceedings in any court or tribunal, it is not lawful for evidence to be tendered or received, questions asked or statements, submissions or comments made, concerning proceedings in Parliament, by way of, or for the purpose of:

    (a) questioning or relying on the truth, motive, intention or good faith of anything forming part of those proceedings in Parliament;

    (b) otherwise questioning or establishing the credibility, motive, intention or good faith of any person; or

    (c) drawing, or inviting the drawing of, inferences or conclusions wholly or partly from anything forming part of those proceedings in Parliament.

(5) In relation to proceedings in a court or tribunal so far as they relate to:

    (a) a question arising under section 57 of the Constitution; or

    (b) the interpretation of an Act;

neither this section nor the Bill of Rights, 1688 shall be taken to prevent or restrict the admission in evidence of a record of proceedings in Parliament published by or with the authority of a House or a committee or the making of statements, submissions or comments based on that record.

(7) Without prejudice to the effect that article 9 of the Bill of Rights, 1688 had, on its true construction, before the commencement of this Act, this section does not affect proceedings in a court or a tribunal that commenced before the commencement of this Act.

Section 9 of the *Parliamentary Privileges Act* removed the obstacle to judicial review that the High Court encountered in *R v Richards; Ex parte Fitzpatrick & Browne*. Since any warrant committing a person to custody must now give particulars of the alleged offence, it follows that any such allegation, and hence the validity of the warrant, will be subject to judicial review.

Section 16 builds upon the provision in the *Bill of Rights 1688* that the freedom of speech and proceedings in Parliament "ought not to be impeached ... in any court". (For a rare Australian example of an (unsuccessful) attempt to wind back this privilege, see the Parliamentary Privilege (Special Temporary Abrogation) Bill 2005 (SA), which sought to withhold the privilege from speakers revealing the names of police or public officials accused of paedophilia.) The purpose of s 16(3) is to counteract the limited interpretation given to Art 9 of the *Bill of Rights* in *R v Murphy* (1986) 5 NSWLR 18, where Hunt J had ruled that Art 9 did not prevent the cross-examination of witnesses, in criminal proceedings, in respect of their earlier statements to the Senate Committees investigating the allegations against Justice Lionel Murphy (see Chapter 13, §2(b)). In *Prebble v Television New Zealand Ltd* [1995] 1 AC 321 at 333, the Privy Council expressed the opinion that the ruling by Hunt J was wrong, and held that the practical effect of s 16(3) is merely to clarify what always was the effect of Art 9.

The effect of s 16(3) has provoked lively debate in State courts in relation to proceedings in federal Parliament. In 1994 Robert Katter, a Queensland member of the federal Parliament, made allegations in Parliament of sexual and other misconduct in connection with the granting of mining leases at Shoalwater Bay. His allegations reflected on the conduct of a Queensland company director, Peter Laurance. When Katter repeated his allegations on radio and television, he insisted that he was not "alleging anything except for the statements I have made inside Parliament"; but Laurance sued him for defamation. At the same time, he also sued the author of a written statement that Katter read out in Parliament. In a 1996 decision (reported as *Laurance v Katter* [2000] 1 Qd R 147), Katter's attempt to rely upon s 16(3) of the *Parliamentary Privileges Act* was rejected by the Queensland Court of Appeal. However, the two majority judges took very different approaches: Davies JA gave s 16(3) a limited operation, confined to protecting freedom of speech in Parliament, while Pincus JA held that it was wholly invalid, as infringing the implied constitutional freedom of political communication.

In *Rann v Olsen* (2000) 76 SASR 450, the Supreme Court of South Australia rejected both these approaches. In the context of ongoing accusations and counter-accusations in South Australian politics, the Leader of the State Opposition, Mike Rann, sued the then Premier, John Olsen, in respect of Olsen's statements to the press about evidence that Rann had given to a Commonwealth Parliamentary Committee. Rann had told the Committee that Olsen had leaked confidential information to the Opposition; Olsen had told journalists that this was a lie. The Court held that s 16(3) precluded any attempt by Olsen to question the truth of what Rann had told the Committee, and equally precluded any attempt by Rann to prove or rely on its truth. However, it did not prevent Olsen from relying on a defence of qualified privilege for the purpose of which he might prove the *fact* of Rann's statement to the Committee so long as he did not question its truth. While limiting the operation of s 16(3) to this extent, Doyle CJ was not prepared to accept the limited reading proposed by Davies JA in *Laurance v Katter*, since Parliament could not have intended its privileges to depend on "**[472]** a case by case judicial assessment of the impact ... of the relevant evidence" on Parliament's freedom of speech.

3. Representation

In the 41st Commonwealth Parliament elected on 9 October 2004, of the 150 members of the House of Representatives, 37 (24.7 per cent) were women – 17 in the Coalition government parties (as compared to 70 men), and 20 in the Labor Party opposition (as compared to 40 men). Of the 76 members of the Senate as at 1 July 2005, 27 (35.5 per cent) were female. While these figures reflect a gradual improvement of the ratio in recent decades, they still fall well short of gender equality. Bodies like the Women's Electoral Lobby have consistently argued that full equality of representation is needed to complete the original suffragist project of women's citizenship.

Deborah Cass and Kim Rubenstein, "Representation/s of Women in the Australian Constitutional System"
(1995) 17 *Adelaide Law Review* 3

[26] In order for the Australian constitutional system to reflect the principle of representative democracy in respect of women, women should feature as those who are *represented* (as voters); as those who are *representatives* (as members of parliament); and *in representations of* the constitutional system (in visual and textual descriptions) ...

[28] Representation in the Drafting of the Constitution
The first stage in the process of building a constitutional system based on representative democracy was the holding of a series of constitutional conventions in 1891, 1897 and 1898, at which the Constitution was drafted. Women were not merely *under represented* in this process, they were virtually not represented at all. At the 1891 Convention attended by all colonial legislatures and New Zealand, no women were present, and as none were eligible to vote in colonial elections none could contribute to the process by electing the delegates.

In 1894, South Australia had introduced universal franchise, and so South Australian women contributed to the 1897 Convention process by electing their representatives and, in the case of one particularly bold woman, even standing for office. But when Catherine Spence stood for election to the 1897 Convention as a South Australian delegate, she was the first woman to seek political office in Australia. Despite being named in the Liberal organisation's list of "10 Best Men", and polling a "creditable" 7383 votes, her bid was unsuccessful. Catherine Spence partly attributed her failure to comments by the South Australian Premier Charles Kingston, who cast doubt over her eligibility to stand as she was a woman, an attitude in keeping with prevailing legal doctrine in which married women had (along with lunatics and children) no civil legal capacity at common law … No women were present in 1897, nor were they in 1898.

Unless it is accepted, as was argued at the 1897 Convention, that women can be represented at the ballot box by "their relations and male friends", women were virtually excluded from this crucial constitution-making aspect of representative democracy …

[29] Representation in the Endorsement of the Constitution
The next phase in the making of Australia's most basic law was the holding in each State of a referendum to seek approval for the Constitution … [T]he popular mandate bestowed on our Constitution by the referendum process, is often touted as Australia's unique badge of democracy. The only problem with this argument is that the electorate which endorsed the Constitution comprised only half of the population in terms of gender …

Little wonder, then, the anger of many women in Victoria, Tasmania and New South Wales, who, having struggled since the 1860s for the right to vote, now saw the consequences of their exclusion from the franchise; they were effectively silenced in the constitution-making process. As one commented: "[i]t is manifestly unjust that this great national question of Federation should be decided by only half the adult population of New South Wales."

[30] This is a good example of how women of the time were caught in a classic cycle of discrimination. As they were not entitled to vote, they were not entitled to any say in the nature and content of the Constitution, the legal instrument which determined the very rights, such as voting, that they struggled to achieve. Some of the most basic rights of representation and citizenship (for example, determining what would be included in the basic law and voting for it) were denied them, because they were denied representation in the first place …

Representation as Voters
As women were excluded in the making or approving of the Constitution, so they were virtually excluded from voting for representatives in the new federal Parliament until 1902, when the vote was granted to all women except Aboriginal women in Queensland and Western Australia.

At the State level, the franchise had been extended over a period of some 25 years. South Australia was the first colony to grant women the right to vote in 1894 after the defeat of no less than six attempts in nine years. Western Australia granted women the franchise next in 1899, after three earlier attempts had been defeated. Then came the Commonwealth in June 1902, followed shortly thereafter by New South Wales in August 1902, and Tasmania in 1903. Queensland and Victoria held out against universal suffrage until 1905 and 1908 respectively, with Victoria having gone to the trouble of repealing the right it inadvertently granted to women ratepayers in 1863. Many of the early attempts to **[31]** extend the franchise were limited to women who owned property, or were married, and did not always extend to Aboriginal women …

[34] Representation as Members of the Parliament
Despite the opportunity for women to stand as representatives in the Parliament, the actual history of women's election to that role is not encouraging.

Apart from South Australia, where the right to stand was introduced in conjunction with the right to vote in 1894, the right to stand for election to Parliaments of the States was generally not introduced until around the period of the First World War. The right to stand for the Commonwealth Parliament was granted in 1903 along with the vote.

As to the actual election of women to Parliament in all States, apart from South Australia and Tasmania, women were elected fairly soon after the introduction of enabling legislation. In the Commonwealth, however, no women were elected to Parliament until 1943, when Enid Lyons won the seat in the House of Representatives and Dorothy Tangney entered the Senate.

The dearth of women representatives was not through any lack of willing candidates. Between 1902 and 1943, 39 women had unsuccessfully nominated for the lower house and five for the upper house.

Numerous reasons, many of which still resonate today, have been put forward for these dismal statistics. Haines attributes it to greater family responsibilities of women, the fact that women generally remained outside the party system, and, that when inside, they were given unwinnable seats. The idea of women representatives evoked fear on the part of male representatives: "The prospect of women occupying their hallowed parliamentary benches seemed to frighten most nineteenth-century Australian parliamentarians out of their wits."

Sensationalist, and contradictory comments were made to the effect that women representatives would be at once dangerous, and feminizing. "No Government would be safe against the persistent attacks of a feminine opposition"; "[d]o you want to bring them in here with their babies and their bottles".

The persistent failure of women to win seats continued well after the election of Enid Lyons and Dorothy [Tangney] In the twenty-five years between 1943 and 1969, women were successful on only five occasions, [35] and as Haines points out, as Enid Lyons was elected three times, only three different women represented the electorate during that period. At State level the figures are even worse. Of the 46 women who stood as State representatives, only seven were elected.

The most disturbing data however comes from the period of the 1960s and 70s, an era in which so-called second-wave feminism had advocated successfully for a range of initiatives. In this enlightened period, women responded enthusiastically to the idea of entering the public domain as representatives of the electorate. In an eight-year period between 1969 and 1977, no less than 161 women offered themselves as candidates for election to the House of Representatives. Only 44 of these were endorsed by either of the major parties, and only one, Joan Child, was elected. Equality of opportunity or not, clearly a system which produces such a run of statistics is open to question.

During the 1980s and the early 1990s, the figures have very gradually improved. At 8 November 1994, there were 136 women in Australian parliaments, out of 841 seats. This represents 16.17 per cent. It is clear from this evidence that merely providing the opportunity for women to become representatives is not sufficient to guarantee that the constitutional system is actually "representative". Since Federation, only 50 women out of a total of 1279 parliamentarians have been elected to federal Parliament. Despite the existence of equality in the formal sense, the reality has been that the representative nature of the Parliaments of Australia has been anything but equal in relation to women.

Even when women are elected, their representation in the media is often criticised as sexist and patronising. Julia Baird (*Media Tarts: How the Australian Press Frames Female Politicians* (Scribe Publications, 2004)) has argued that, although accusations of sexism are oversimple, her case studies of women whose promising political careers have ended in disappointment or even ignominy show that "[271] their policy work was obscured by a cult of personality over which they had very little control". Initially, they have had to contend with unrealistically high expectations, turning to excessively critical reactions of condemnation or disillusionment "[2] when they turn out to be human". "[7] [I]t is clear that a specific way of viewing women has frequently interfered with the way they are seen and the progress of their careers. The fact remains that the position of women is more tenuous and their grasp on power more slippery by virtue of their gender and the intense scrutiny – both sympathetic and hostile – of the media".

In India in 1996 an unsuccessful attempt was made to amend the Indian Constitution to require that one third of the seats in the lower Houses of the Union Parliament and of the State legislatures be reserved for women. The proposal built on an earlier amendment introducing a similar quota in village panchayats and other local government bodies. Since 1950, under Art 330 of the Constitution, India has had reserved parliamentary seats for members of the Scheduled Castes and Scheduled Tribes. Similarly, the New Zealand Parliament includes Maori members chosen by voters on the Maori Electoral Roll (*Electoral Act 1993* (NZ)).

In 1998, the Standing Committee on Social Issues of the New South Wales Legislative Council reported on proposals for dedicated Aboriginal seats in that Parliament (*Enhancing Aboriginal Political Representation: Inquiry into Dedicated Seats in the New South Wales Parliament* (1998)). It noted that Aboriginal people are under-represented at all levels of government and recommended measures to encourage their participation, particularly through the existing political parties. However, it concluded that the introduction of dedicated seats would be premature without further consultation with Aboriginal people, a community education campaign and an assessment of the level of support in political parties and the community (see also Queensland Legal, Constitutional and Administrative Review Committee, *Hands on Parliament: A Parliamentary Committee Inquiry Into Aboriginal and Torres Strait Islander Peoples' Participation in Queensland's Democratic Processes* (Report No 42, 2003)).

4. Voting and Elections

(a) "Directly chosen by the people"

Sections 7 and 24 of the Constitution require that the members of the Senate and the House of Representatives be "directly chosen by the people". Those words are the principal textual basis from which the High Court has drawn the implication that Australians possess a constitutionally protected freedom of political communication. Similarly, even though the Court held in *R v Pearson; Ex parte Sipka* (1983) 152 CLR 254 that s 41 does not confer an *express* right to vote (see Chapter 26, §2), it might be argued that ss 7 and 24 can support an *implied* right to vote. After all, these provisions require a "choice" by "the people", which, as s 7 makes clear, is to be made by electors "voting" at the ballot box.

In *McGinty v Western Australia* (1996) 186 CLR 140, Toohey J took the view that "[201] according to today's standards, a system which denied universal adult franchise would fall short of a basic requirement of representative democracy". Gaudron J stated: "[221] Notwithstanding the limited nature of the franchise in 1901, present circumstances would not, in my view, permit senators and [222] members of the House of Representatives to be described as 'chosen by the people' within the meaning of those words in ss 7 and 24 of the Constitution if the franchise were to be denied to women or to members of a racial minority or to be made subject to a property or educational qualification". Gummow J reached a similar conclusion at 287, as did McHugh J in *Langer v Commonwealth* (1996) 186 CLR 302 at 342.

Otherwise, the right to vote is governed by legislation.

Commonwealth Electoral Act 1918 (Cth)

93 (1) Subject to subsections (7) and (8) and to Part VIII, all persons:
   (a) who have attained 18 years of age; and
   (b) who are:
      (i) Australian citizens; or
      (ii) persons (other than Australian citizens) who would, if the relevant citizenship law had continued in force, be British subjects within the meaning of that relevant citizenship law and whose names were, immediately before 26 January 1984:
         (A) on the roll for a Division; or
         (B) on a roll kept for the purposes of the Australian Capital Territory Representation (House of Representatives) Act 1973 or the Northern Territory Representation Act 1922;
shall be entitled to enrolment.

(2) Subject to subsections (3), (4) and (5), an elector whose name is on the Roll for a Division is entitled to vote at elections of Members of the Senate for the State that includes that Division and at elections of Members of House of Representatives for that Division …

(7) A person who is:
   (a) within the meaning of the *Migration Act 1958*, the holder of a temporary visa; or
   (b) an unlawful non-citizen under that Act;
is not entitled to enrolment under Part VIII.

(8) A person who:
   (a) by reason of being of unsound mind, is incapable of understanding the nature and significance of enrolment and voting; or

(b) is serving a sentence of 3 years or longer for an offence against the law of the Commonwealth or of a State or Territory; or

(c) has been convicted of treason or treachery and has not been pardoned;

is not entitled to have his or her name placed on or retained on any Roll or to vote at any Senate
election or House of Representatives election.

Sections 94 and 94A exclude from enrolment Australian citizens living overseas who, when they
left, did not intend to resume residing in Australia within six years. It was only in 1962 that the
Act was amended to remove the exclusion of Aboriginal Australians from voting in federal
elections (see Chapter 5, §2).

Voting at federal elections has been compulsory since 1924. Section 245(1) of the *Commonwealth Electoral Act* states: "It shall be the duty of every elector to vote at each election". The
section establishes a penalty of $20 (or $50 if the matter is dealt with by a court) for electors who
fail to vote and cannot give a valid and sufficient reason for that failure. In *Judd v McKeon*
(1926) 38 CLR 380, only Higgins J was prepared to concede that a socialist who refused to vote
because all of the parties and candidates on offer were supporters of capitalism might legitimately
claim a "valid and sufficient reason" analogous to the allowance made for conscientious objection
on religious grounds in the case of military service.

In *Adelaide Company of Jehovah's Witnesses Inc v Commonwealth* (1943) 67 CLR 116,
Latham CJ said of s 116 of the Constitution: "**[123]** The prohibition in s 116 operates not only
to protect the freedom of religion, but also to protect the right of a man to have no religion".
It might similarly be argued that, if ss 7 and 24 of the Constitution confer a right to vote,
Parliament cannot compel electors to vote and that compulsory voting, as established by s 245 of
the *Commonwealth Electoral Act*, is constitutionally flawed. However, s 245 does not force a
person to make a choice. It requires attendance at the polling booth and the depositing of the
voting paper in the ballot box, but the voter need not mark the ballot paper.

Langer v Commonwealth suggests that compulsory voting is not inconsistent with ss 7 and
24 of the Constitution. Section 240 of the *Commonwealth Electoral Act 1918* (Cth) provided that
"[i]n a House of Representatives election a person shall mark his or her vote" by numbering every
square "1, 2, 3, 4 ..." until an exhaustive order of preference is stated. By s 268 any ballot paper
that fails to express an exhaustive preference is informal, provided that if one square is blank and
all others are numbered in sequence, the blank will be taken to express the voter's lowest
preference; and further that if there are only two candidates, a ballot paper will be formal if one is
marked "1", and the other is either left blank or given a number larger than 1. In addition, by
s 270(2), a ballot paper "shall not be informal" if it includes a sequence of consecutive numbers
beginning with "1", even if numbers are duplicated and even if one square is blank. Thus, a paper
numbered "1, 2, 3, 3 ..." will be counted as indicating a preference for candidates "1" and "2".
Under s 329A it was an offence, attracting up to six months' imprisonment, to "print, publish or
distribute ... any matter or thing with the intention of encouraging persons ... to fill in a ballot
paper otherwise than in accordance with" s 240.

At the 1993 federal election, Albert Langer urged electors to vote "1, 2, 3, 3 ...", with the
major parties being placed equal last. The Electoral Commission's counter-publicity emphasised
that a formal vote must number every square, using consecutive numbers. Langer sued in the
High Court for an injunction, arguing that the Commission's advertisements were "misleading
and intimidating", and would "have an effect ... [on] the Election such that it will no longer be
free or fair". His application for urgent relief was refused, but the question whether s 329A was
valid was reserved for the full Court's opinion. His written submissions maintained that s 329A
infringed the implied constitutional freedom of political communication. He also argued that
s 240 was invalid since its stipulations were inconsistent with the command in s 24 of the
Constitution that representatives be "directly chosen by the people", and the people, if choosing
freely, must be free not to choose by not numbering every square.

As a consequence of his submissions, Langer argued that there had not been a "free election"
in 1993, and hence that the Parliament then elected was invalid. This led him as a litigant in

person in argument before the High Court to assert (unsuccessfully) that both Gummow J and Brennan CJ should be disqualified from hearing the case, since Gummow's appointment as a judge, and Brennan's appointment as Chief Justice, had been made by the government formed from the Parliament elected in 1993. Langer conceded, however, that Brennan's appointment as a puisne Justice in 1981 had been valid, and accordingly that Brennan could at least continue to hear the case in that capacity.

In the result, all six judges held that s 240 was valid. By 5:1, Dawson J dissenting, it was then held that s 329A was valid, as a legitimate means of protecting the voting method validly prescribed by s 240.

Langer v Commonwealth
(1996) 186 CLR 302

Brennan CJ: [317] The legislative power over elections for the House of Representatives conferred by ss 31 and 51(xxxvi) is a plenary power and, as Isaacs J said in *Smith v Oldham* [(1912) 15 CLR 355 at 363] with reference to the power over federal elections: "The limits of plenary power end only with the subject matter in respect of which it may be exercised." Provided the prescribed method of voting permits a free choice among the candidates for election, it is within the legislative power of the Parliament. Section 24 of the Constitution does not limit the Parliament's selection of the method of voting by which a voter's choice is made known so long as the method allows a free choice. Section 240 permits a voter to make a discriminating choice among the candidates for election to the House of Representatives. An election in which members of the House of Representatives are elected pursuant to such a method of voting achieves what s 24 requires, namely, a House of Representatives composed of members directly chosen by the people.

It follows that the Parliament is empowered to prescribe a method of voting in an election for the House of Representatives that requires a voter to fill in a ballot paper in accordance with s 240, although that method requires a voter to choose by allocating preferences among candidates for whom the voter does not wish to vote. It is not to the point that, if a ballot paper were filled in otherwise than in accordance with s 240, the vote would better express the voter's political opinion.

Since s 240 can reasonably be regarded as prescribing a method of freely choosing members of the House of Representatives, a law which is appropriate and adapted to prevent the subversion of that method is within power. Section 329A is such a law. The saving provisions do not affect its validity. They are designed to minimise the exclusion of ballot papers from the scrutiny provided the voter's intention clearly appears from the voter's partial compliance with the method prescribed by s 240. But the saving provisions do not detract from the power to enact s 329A in order to protect what the Parliament intends to be the primary method of choosing members of the House of Representatives ...

The powers of the Parliament are impliedly limited so as to preserve that freedom of political discussion which is essential to the **[318]** maintenance of the Commonwealth system of representative government. But, as the judgments in the free speech cases have shown, the extent of the limitation depends on the particular circumstances, including especially the subject matter of the law which impairs the freedom. In *Australian Capital Television Pty Ltd v Commonwealth* [(1992) 177 CLR 106], *Theophanous v Herald & Weekly Times Ltd* [(1994) 182 CLR 104] and *Cunliffe v Commonwealth* [(1994) 182 CLR 272], I sought to explain the approach to be taken in determining the validity of a law impugned on the ground that it impairs the freedom of political discussion. In my view, if the impairment of the freedom is reasonably capable of being regarded as appropriate and adapted to the achieving of a legitimate legislative purpose and the impairment is merely incidental to the achievement of that purpose, the law is within power ...

Section 329A does not prohibit discussion about the operation or desirability of the method of voting prescribed by s 240 nor does it prohibit advocacy of its amendment or repeal. Section 329A operates in the context of the method of voting prescribed by s 240 and prohibits intentional encouragement of the filling in of ballot papers in a way which, if not within the saving provisions, will result in the exclusion of the ballot paper from the scrutiny and which, if within the saving provisions of s 270(2), will result in a diminished expression of the elector's preferences. The prohibition contained in s 329A is thus a means of protecting the method which Parliament has selected for the choosing of members of the House of Representatives. The restriction on freedom of speech imposed by s 329A is not imposed with a view to repressing freedom of political discussion; it is imposed as an incident to the protection of the s 240 method of voting.

If the Act had prescribed methods of voting alternative to those prescribed by s 240, there would be much to be said for the view that no law could preclude a person from encouraging voters to vote by an alternative method. The saving provisions do not prescribe an alternative method; they merely save from invalidity some ballot papers which are not filled in in accordance with the method which the [319] Act prescribes. Nor does s 329A prohibit a person from informing electors of the state of the law. It simply prohibits encouragement of voters to fill in their ballot papers otherwise than in accordance with the method of voting prescribed by the Act.

Toohey and Gaudron JJ similarly found that "[334] there is nothing in those cases to warrant a conclusion that the freedom operates to strike down laws which curtail freedom of communication, where that curtailment is reasonably capable of being viewed as appropriate and adapted to furthering or enhancing the democratic process". Only Dawson J dissented.

Dawson J: [323] The Constitution does not require the provision of any particular electoral system. Thus, the provision in s 240 for a preferential voting system is clearly within power notwithstanding that it requires a choice to be made in a specified manner and, standing alone, requires a [324] preference to be expressed in respect of each candidate. Whatever the system, the Constitution requires that a choice must be made and, as I pointed out in *Australian Capital Television Pty Ltd v Commonwealth* [(1992) 177 CLR 106 at 187], the choice involved must obviously be a genuine, or informed, choice which requires access on the part of the voter to the available alternatives in the making of the choice. Other members of the Court adopted a different approach and found in the concept of representative government or representative democracy an implied freedom of communication which was to be read into the Constitution. The freedom was said to embrace the discussion of government and political matters …

[325] Since, as I have said, the choice which is required by s 24 must be a genuine choice, those eligible to vote must have available to them the information necessary to exercise such a choice … [T]he power conferred by ss 31 and 51(xxxvi) may properly be regarded as a purposive power and it is therefore open to test the validity of a law enacted in the purported exercise of that power by asking whether the law is reasonably and appropriately adapted to the achievement of an end which lies within power. To my mind, s 329A (or, more accurately, the law inserting it in the Act) is not such a law. It is a law which is designed to keep from voters information which is required by them to enable them to exercise an informed choice. It can hardly be said that a choice is an informed choice if it is made in ignorance of a means of making the choice which is available and which a voter, if he or she knows of it, may wish to use in order to achieve a particular result.

If s 240 stood alone, s 329A would be supportable as a protection of the preferential system of voting provided by the Act. Upon any view, some limitations upon freedom of communication are necessary to ensure the proper working of any electoral system. However, the method of preferential voting which is established by the Act is that which may be discerned from ss 240, 268, 270 and 274 read together. Sections 268 and 270 qualify the method of voting prescribed by s 240 and s 270 makes available optional or selective preferential voting as opposed to full preferential voting. It is true that a voter cannot cast a formal vote by simply placing the number 1 in the square beside one candidate and leaving all the others blank. But the fact remains that the Act permits voters intentionally to record a preference for only one or some of the candidates standing for election by completing their ballot paper in the manner which I have described above. To prohibit communication of this fact (or at any rate communication in the form of encouragement) is to restrict the access of voters to information essential to the formation of the choice required by s 24 of the [326] Constitution. Thus, s 329A has the intended effect of keeping from voters an alternative method of casting a formal vote which they are entitled to choose under the Act.

It does not, to my mind, matter that the prohibition imposed by s 329A is confined to the conveying of information with the intention of encouraging persons voting at an election to fill in a ballot paper otherwise than in accordance with s 240. To impart information which can be used (and information about the availability of an optional or selective preferential vote is of that kind) is necessarily to encourage its use if the recipient of the information is so inclined. A person in making that information available to an eligible voter would, in the absence of active discouragement of its use, find it wellnigh impossible to prove that it was made available without any intention that those to whom it was made available should make use of it. To put the matter shortly, to make available useful information is ordinarily to encourage its use. This is particularly so in the context of an election. The effect of s 329A in any practical sense must, in my view, be to discourage, if not prevent, persons from imparting to eligible voters knowledge that the electoral system permits optional or selective preferential voting. It cannot, therefore, be a law which is reasonably and appropriately adapted to the achievement of an end which lies within the ambit of the relevant legislative power.

The High Court's decision was announced on 7 February 1996. The next day, at the instance of the Australian Electoral Commission, Beach J in the Supreme Court of Victoria granted an injunction (in force until the federal election due on 2 March) restraining Langer from "printing, publishing or distributing ... any matter or thing whatsoever with the intention of encouraging persons to vote" in a manner contrary to s 240. On 14 February, after Langer had continued to distribute leaflets contrary to that injunction, Beach J sentenced him to 10 weeks' imprisonment for contempt of court. On 23 February, Amnesty International described Langer in a press release as "the first prisoner of conscience in the country for over 20 years". Langer appealed to a Full Bench of the Federal Court of Australia. On 1 March 1996, the day before the federal election, his appeal against the injunction was dismissed (*Langer v Australian Electoral Commission (No 1)* (1996) 136 ALR 141); but on 7 March 1996, after the election was over, the Federal Court allowed his appeal against severity of sentence, and ordered his immediate release (*Langer v Australian Electoral Commission (No 2)* (1996) 59 FCR 463). He had been in prison a little over three weeks.

Although Langer was unsuccessful in his attack on ss 240 and 329A, he did have an impact at the polls. In 1996, approximately 46,000 people voted according to the method advocated by him, an increase of over 500 per cent on the 1993 election (C Field, "'Tweedledum and Tweedledee 1,2,3,3' – The Albert Langer Story" (Parliamentary Research Service, Commonwealth Parliament, Current Issues Brief No 14, 1995-96), 8). In its *Report of the Inquiry into all Aspects of the Conduct of the 1996 Federal Election and Matters Related Thereto* (Parliamentary Paper No 93 of 1997), the Joint Standing Committee on Electoral Matters recommended that ss 270(2) and 329A be repealed and that s 240 be amended to include the words "**[32]** consecutive numbers, without the repetition of any number". This recommendation was carried into effect by the *Electoral and Referendum Amendment Act 1998* (Cth). Section 240 now makes it clear that "1, 2, 3, 3 ..." no longer counts as a formal vote. At the time of the 2001 election, Langer continued to insist through a website campaign that the new s 240 is both unconstitutional and ineffective, since s 268 of the Act requires only that a formal vote should indicate "an" order of preference. However, by the time of the 2004 election, he had turned his attention and his website to a campaign against the war in Iraq.

(b)   Territory Senators

The addition of four senators representing the Territories was brought about by the *Senate (Representation of Territories) Act 1973* (Cth). Although the Act is dated 1973, it was actually passed in 1974 under the deadlock-breaking provisions of s 57 of the Constitution (see §6 below). The validity of the Act was narrowly upheld by the High Court in a 4:3 decision in *Western Australia v Commonwealth* (*First Territory Senators Case*) (1975) 134 CLR 201.

The issue was whether the Commonwealth Parliament had the legislative power to provide for the representation of Territories in the Senate. The Commonwealth argued that power was given by s 122 of the Constitution, which provides that the Commonwealth "may allow the representation of such territory in either House of the Parliament to the extent and on the terms which it thinks fit". On the other hand, the plaintiff States argued that ss 7-15 of the Constitution refer exclusively to senators representing the States. In particular, s 7 begins by stating that "The Senate shall be *composed of* senators for each State" (emphasis added).

The issue before the High Court is often portrayed as a striking example of indeterminacy in constitutional law. If one tries to work merely by legalistic analysis of the constitutional text, the apparent meaning of s 122 is in direct contradiction to the words in s 7. But, equally, if one tries to resolve the contradiction by appealing to more fundamental principles, the need for judicial choice still arises. The insistence throughout ss 7-15 on a concept of the Senate as a "States' House" reflects a belief in the federal principle, and hence in the idea that the States, through their representation in the Senate, should be able to maintain a countervailing voice against the lower House. On the other hand, there would seem to be a basic democratic assumption that all Australian citizens should be represented in both Houses of the federal Parliament regardless of whether they happen to live in a Territory or in a State. Thus, underlying the textual conflict between ss 7 and 122 is a fundamental conflict between the commitments to federalism and to democracy.

Four of the seven judges, McTiernan, Mason, Jacobs and Murphy JJ, effectively gave priority to democracy over federalism, though only Murphy J stated the issue explicitly in these terms. Barwick CJ, Gibbs and Stephen JJ dissented.

Western Australia v Commonwealth (*First Territory Senators Case*)
(1975) 134 CLR 201

Mason J: [270] The apparent opposition which arises from the reference to representation of the territories in s 122 and the absence of any such reference in ss 7 and 24 is irreconcilable only if it be assumed that Ch I in making provision for the composition of the Senate and the House is necessarily speaking for all time. To my mind this assumption is misconceived. Sections 7 and 24 should be regarded as making provision for the composition of each House which nevertheless, in the shape of s 122, takes account of the prospective possibility that Parliament might deem it expedient, having regard to the stage which a Territory might reach in the course of its future development, to give it representation in either House by allowing it to elect members of that House. To the framers of the Constitution in 1900 the existing condition of the Territories was not such as to suggest the immediate likelihood of their securing representation in either House, but the possibility of such a development occurring in the future was undeniable. The prospect of its occurrence was foreseen and in my view it found expression in s 122.

Understood in this light, ss 7 and 24 make exhaustive provision for the composition of each House until such time as Parliament might see fit to allow representation to a territory under s 122. This interpretation not only gives full scope to the language of that section but it supports and gives authority to the course of constitutional development by which in recent years Parliament might see fit to allow representation to a Territory ... in the House of Representatives, first by a member without voting rights, then by a member with qualified voting rights and finally by a member with unqualified voting rights, see the *Northern Territory Representation Act* 1922, the *Northern Territory* **[271]** *Representation Act* 1959, the *Northern Territory Representation Act* 1968.

The contrary view is that representation by membership can only be accorded to the people of a Territory on its admission as a State, a view which is assisted by the provision in s 7 that the senators shall be chosen by the people of the States, that is, new States as well as original States. However, it is a view which encounters difficulties when it is applied to the House of Representatives. If paramount effect is also to be given to the language of s 24 it is not easy to perceive why the citizens of the Northern Territory and the Australian Capital Territory are not presently to be numbered among "the people of the Commonwealth", although they would fall within that description in the event that the Territories were to be admitted as States. To my mind it is not a convincing answer to this difficulty to say that the House stands in a different position from the Senate, that the Territories may be accorded representation by membership in the House but not in the Senate, for s 122 contemplates no such distinction. The power which it confers on Parliament to allow representation of the Territories "on the terms it thinks fit" applies specifically "in either House of the Parliament".

Two matters remain to be mentioned. The first is the grim spectre conjured up by the plaintiffs of a Parliament swamping the Senate with senators from the Territories, thereby reducing the representation of the States disproportionately to that of an ineffective minority in the chamber. This exercise in imagination assumes the willing participation of the senators representing the States in such an enterprise, notwithstanding that it would hasten their journey into political oblivion. It disregards the assumption which the framers of the Constitution made, and which we should now make, that Parliament will act responsibly in the exercise of its powers.

Furthermore, such significance as the plaintiffs' argument may have is diminished when it is appreciated that the Constitution provides no safeguard against the pursuit by Parliament of a similar course at the expense of the original States in allowing for the representation of new States in the Senate. Although s 7 provides that equal representation of the original States shall be maintained in that chamber, neither the section nor the remaining provisions of Pt II of Ch I place any restriction on the number of senators which Parliament may accord to a new State as its representation in the Senate. Here, again, the assumption is that Parliament will act responsibly.

Murphy J: [283] The Constitution is designed for a democratic society. Except for the role of the Queen, which by convention has become largely formal, the Constitution is based on the concept of democracy. It was written against the background of the struggle, substantially fought out over the previous hundred and fifty years, for the representative form of popular democratic government. The framers of the Constitution had the benefit of the **[284]** American Declaration of Independence, the French Declaration of the Rights of Man and the Citizen, and work of writers such as Hamilton, Madison and Jay in the *Federalist Papers* and Mill in *Representative Government* (1861).

The American Declaration of Independence asserted that "governments are instituted among men, deriving their just powers from the consent of the governed" and its chief complaints against the King included:

"He has refused to pass other laws for the accommodation of large districts of people, unless those people would relinquish the *right of representation in the legislature; a right inestimable to them and formidable to tyrants only.*"

Hamilton, in the *Federalist Papers* (No 28) said:

"The whole power of the proposed government is to be in the hands of the representative people. This is the essential and, after all, only efficacious security for the rights and privileges of the people, which is attainable in a civil society."

Mill, in Ch 3 of *Representative Government*, said:

"The only government which can fully satisfy all the exigencies of the social state is one in which the whole people participate; ... the participation everywhere should be as great as the general degree of improvement of the community will allow; and that nothing less can be ultimately desirable than the admission of all to share in the sovereign power of the State. But as all cannot ... participate personally but some very minor proportions of the public business, it follows that the ideal type of perfect government must be representative."

and in Ch 7:

"In a really equal democracy every or any section will be represented, not disproportionately but proportionately. A majority of the electors would always have a majority of the representatives. But a minority of the electors would always have a minority of representatives. Man for man they would be as fully represented as the majority. Unless they are, there is no equal government but a government of inequality and privilege: one part of the people rule over the rest: there is a part whose fair and equal share of influence in the representation is withheld from them; contrary to all just government, but, above all, contrary to the principle of democracy, which professes equality as its very root and foundation."

Such sentiments pervaded the Constitution of the United States. This spirit of democracy was vigorously asserted in Australia, **[285]** and motivated the drive towards responsible government and independence from Imperial domination. The framers of our Constitution looked to the United States Constitution. Many of the provisions of our Constitution have obviously been borrowed from the United States model.

Victoria rightly contended that expressions such as "chosen ... by the people" in s 24 were directly borrowed from the United States Constitution. From this the argument ran that, as the United States Constitution only allows non-voting delegates to represent the territories in Congress, the same approach should be used in construing s 122.

Section 122 however, is a deliberate departure from the United States model. There is little doubt that s 122 was inserted to ensure that the privilege of membership in each House should not be denied forever to the people of the territories. This was accepted by authoritative textwriters from the earlier days.

After quoting John Quick and Robert Garran, *The Annotated Constitution of the Australian Commonwealth* (Angus & Robertson, 1901; repr Legal Books, 1995), 973 and W Harrison Moore, *The Constitution of the Commonwealth of Australia* (Murray, 1st ed 1902), 312, Murphy J noted that in 1910 the second edition of the latter work was "[286] more emphatic", asserting that s 122 "definitely includes ... a power to allot representation in either House of the Parliament to the extent and on the terms which Parliament thinks fit". He went on:

Murphy J: [286] If the contention of the plaintiffs is right, and the Parliament is not empowered by s 122 to allow representation to the territories by way of membership of the Senate, it would follow inevitably that Parliament could not under s 122 allow representation of territories by membership of the House of Representatives. The consequence would be that the *Australian Capital Territory Representation (House of Representatives) Acts* 1973 and the *Northern Territory Representation Act* 1922-1968 would both be invalid.

The Australian Capital Territory and the Northern Territory would have no membership in either House, and Parliament could not provide for membership of any territory in either House unless the Constitution was altered. This could only be done in the mode prescribed by s 128 of the Constitution. It could well be argued that such an alteration would not become law unless the majority of the electors voting in every State approved the proposed law (see the final paragraph of s 128).

The permanent deprivation of representation by membership in the Senate or the House of Representatives is a serious exclusion from the democratic process. These houses are our most important political institutions, the principal organs of our democracy; their decisions are vital to every Australian. Their importance to the people of the territories is not less than their importance to the people of the States. It is contrary to the democratic theme of the Constitution that Parliament should not be able to allow representation by membership in either House to territories at the time and on the terms which the Parliament considers appropriate.

[287] It has been argued in this case, as in a number of others, that the Constitution should not be construed in a way that gives Parliament powers it might abuse. In this case, the argument is that s 122 must be read down to exclude altogether the power of Parliament to allow any members in either House from any of the Territories, because if it is not read down, Parliament might abuse its power by allowing absurdly large numbers of senators from these two Territories or from the small island Territories or even the Antarctic Territory.

There is no such principle of construction. It is not in accordance with the respect that should characterize the relationship between Parliament, the Executive Government, and the Judiciary ... The framers of the Constitution did not distrust Parliament. In section after section, they left it to Parliament to provide for, or modify the provision for, important subjects. The expression, "until the Parliament otherwise provides", is to be found in numerous sections.

The minority view was put most firmly by Barwick CJ.

Barwick CJ: [227] The essentially federal nature of the new polity, the Commonwealth of Australia, is manifest throughout the Constitution. The power of alteration of the Constitution given by s 128 also emphasizes the federal structure of the Commonwealth. Each House of the Parliament may initiate a proposed law for the alteration of the Constitution. Only persons who are qualified to vote for the election of the House of Representatives may vote upon the proposed law and for its approval there must be a majority of such voters in a majority of the States as well as an [228] overall majority in the Commonwealth. To that federal nature, the maintenance of the relationship of the House of Representatives and the Senate and of the relationship of each respectively to the people of the Commonwealth and the States and of the Senate as the States' House is indispensable.

It is against this background that Ch VI must be read and construed. It is, in my opinion, quite inadmissible to conclude that this chapter was intended in any respect to alter, or qualify, the essential features of the federation or to permit of such a course or to create a power to do so: I cannot think that the founders of the Commonwealth intended that these essential features might be swept aside as it were by a bywind. Neither s 7 nor s 24 is prefaced with the words "subject to the Constitution": nor is s 122 prefaced with the words "notwithstanding any other provision of the Constitution". Some such qualification might well be expected if it had been intended that the provisions of s 7 or of s 24 could be displaced or qualified by a law made under s 122.

It is, in my opinion, clearly inadmissible to construe the Constitution as if the words "until the Parliament otherwise provides" prefaced both the whole of s 7 and of s 24. Where it is intended that the Parliament should have control of a Constitution provision, the Constitution expressly and unambiguously so provides. Indeed s 7 in each of its first three paragraphs is itself such an example. The limitation in the first paragraph of Parliamentary control to the nature of the electorate for voting purposes eloquently denies the possibility by construction of treating the whole of that first paragraph as subject to Parliamentary control and in particular as subject to an exercise of the power given by s 122.

Section 121 allows the admission of new States and empowers the Parliament when admitting a new State to determine the *extent* of its representation in either House of the Parliament. Being admitted as a State, the new State would be represented by senators in the Senate but there could be no question of any State new or original being represented as such in the House of Representatives. The members of the House do not *represent* States, they represent the people of the Commonwealth though elected in electoral divisions. Consequently, s 121 merely provides that included in the terms and conditions on which a new State may be admitted, there may be a term or condition as to the extent of representation in each House. The expression is not "representation of the new State in each House" because quite obviously ss 7 and 24 will operate with respect to the new State **[229]** when admitted and, as I have said, it is inappropriate to speak of representation of a State in the House of Representatives. But, not being an original State, the number of senators which the new State can elect to the Senate would need to be prescribed. To some extent s 24 will prescribe the representation of the residents of the new State who, because it is a State, become part of the people of the Commonwealth for the purpose of both sections. But there is scope for a limitation to be placed upon the number of members as well as upon the number of senators which the electors of the new State may elect: and such a limitation might be regarded as affecting the extent of the representation. Thus, by determining the "extent of representation", the numerical strength of the representation provided by the Constitution itself, may be determined by the Parliament at the point of, and as a term and condition of, the admission of the new State.

Section 122 is dealing with a totally different matter, namely, the acceptance of new Territories; that is to say, of new dependent Territories. It is quite clear that those who reside in any such Territory do not become people of the Commonwealth for the purposes of s 24: nor can the situation of a dependent Territory be in any sense approximated to that of a State. The Territories are governed by the new polity, the Commonwealth of Australia, and are not federally part of it. Thus, the matters upon which the Parliament may make laws to operate in such Territories are not federally circumscribed. A new State becomes part of that indissoluble union of which the Preamble to the *Constitution Act* speaks. In great contrast a Territory may be given independence and cease to be a Territory.

Consequently, s 122 is quite differently expressed to s 121. It speaks of allowing representation of the Territory in either House. Unlike the case of a new State, the Territory not being admitted to the federal structure, ss 7 and 24 do not provide for the representation of the Territory or of its residents.

In submitting that the expression "allow the representation of such Territory in either House" is apt to authorize a provision for representation by senators, the Commonwealth founds on the use of the word "representation" in s 121 … But the provision of a senator is not the form of representation which s 122 specifies. The word "representation" is not used with identical denotation in each section. There is no form of representation which the language of **[230]** s 122 compels. It could not be said that if representation is provided it must, in relation to the Senate, be by a senator with full rights and privileges of a senator for a State. Nor could it be said, in my opinion, that to make provision for a non-voting delegate would not be to allow representation. On the other hand, the federal nature of the Constitution and the sections to which I have referred, point against such a form of representation as would alter or affect such an essential part of the federation as to the relationship of the States to the Commonwealth and to one another provided by the establishment of the Senate as a "States House". It must be representation of a kind which does not qualify or impinge upon the unqualified specification of s 7 – "The Senate shall be *composed* of Senators for each State, directly chosen by the people of the State, voting, until the Parliament otherwise provides, as one electorate" ...

Further, the expression is "allow the representation of such territory in *either* House of the Parliament". To speak of the representation of a Territory in the House of Representatives is to my mind an indication against, rather than towards, the conclusion that representation by membership of the House of Representatives is contemplated. In that House the people of the Commonwealth are represented: States and Territories, in my opinion, cannot be ... Included in [the] other Territories, it must be remembered, are Norfolk Island, Christmas Island, and the Cocos Islands. The power contended for by the Commonwealth would include power to give each of these Territories senatorial representation, which might well be at least one senator per territory. The effect on the federation and on the Senate as the States House, of such a possibility needs no emphasis ...

[232] Some lesser connotation of the word "representation" must be found to make the Constitution, basically federal in nature, consistent throughout. To fit Pt VI into the Constitution as a whole, in my opinion, the expression "allow representation" must be construed so as to be consonant with and indeed to preserve and not to endanger or destroy an essential feature of federation, namely the maintenance of the Senate as the State House. In other words s 7 is relevantly a dominant provision and not subject to the exercise of the power given by s 122. The interpretation which, in my opinion, is the correct interpretation is that s 122 would at most permit the Parliament to allow the representation of a Territory in the Senate by a delegate who would not have the rights of a senator for a State, and who in any case, by whatever name designated, would not be entitled to be treated as a senator for a State or to vote on any questions before the Senate. Whether or not he was allowed to address the Senate on matters before it, in particular on matters which related exclusively to the affairs of the Territory, would be for the Parliament or perhaps, in default of Parliamentary prescription, for the Senate to decide.

The 4:3 decision in the *First Territory Senators Case* was not the end of the issue. McTiernan J, one of the four majority judges, retired in September 1976 at the age of 84 after a record 46 years on the Court. He had broken his hip while chasing a cricket and was absent from the Court for some months. According to David Marr, *Barwick* (Allen & Unwin, 1980), 290, McTiernan J then reluctantly retired after Barwick CJ refused to install a ramp so that he could return to the bench in a wheelchair. McTiernan J was replaced by Aickin J. Many observers predicted that Aickin J would have voted with the three dissenters on the *Territory Senators* issue, and hence that there might now be a 4:3 majority the other way. In these circumstances, Barwick CJ hinted strongly that the issue should be litigated again.

A-G (NSW); Ex rel McKellar v Commonwealth
(1977) 139 CLR 527

Barwick CJ: [532] [I]t should be noted that two States during the argument of these proceedings questioned the propriety of the Court's decision in *Western Australia v Commonwealth* [(1975) 134 CLR 201]. However, unfortunately as I think, neither State proffered any argument in support of this questioning. I say unfortunately because, if the decision is to be reconsidered, that reconsideration should take place before what, with due respect to the opinion of others, appears to me to be a serious departure from the federal nature of the Constitution, becomes entrenched in constitutional practice by the mere passage of time.

The Queensland government, led by Premier Joh Bjelke-Petersen, took the hint and initiated proceedings in *Queensland v Commonwealth (Second Territory Senators Case)* (1977) 139 CLR 585. As predicted, Aickin J voted with Barwick CJ. However, Gibbs and Stephen JJ, though still treating the earlier decision as wrong, insisted that it would not be right to overrule it merely because of a change in the composition of the bench. They therefore voted to affirm it, thus joining in a 5:2 majority supporting the legislation. (See the extracts in Chapter 13, §7, and note the qualification added by Gibbs J "**[601]** that if the Parliament were further to distort the federal balance by legislating to provide for the election of more senators for the Territories, that ... might be regarded as sufficient to justify a reconsideration of the question".)

(c)   One Vote One Value

The concept of representation was also considered in *A-G (Commonwealth); Ex rel McKinlay v Commonwealth* (1975) 135 CLR 1. It was argued that the election of 18 May 1974 had been held on the basis of a disproportionate electoral distribution and that there was reason to apprehend that the next election would be held on the same distribution of boundaries. The alleged maldistribution arose because, in terms of population, electorates for the House of Representatives were not of equal size. It was argued that this infringed the principle of "one vote, one value" and that provisions of the *Commonwealth Electoral Act 1918* (Cth) and the *Representation Act 1905* (Cth) were therefore invalid.

The question before the High Court was whether the Commonwealth Constitution requires adherence to the principle of "one vote, one value". The plaintiff relied on the words of s 24 of the Constitution, which require that the House of Representatives "shall be composed of members directly chosen by the people of the Commonwealth" and that, subject to other stipulations, "the number of members in the several States shall be in proportion to the respective numbers of their people". Only Murphy J accepted this argument.

A-G (Commonwealth); Ex rel McKinlay v Commonwealth
(1975) 135 CLR 1

Murphy J: [65] Great rights are often expressed in simple phrases ...

[The provisions of s 24] were clearly taken from Art I, s 2 of the Constitution of the United States of America which provides:

"1. The House of Representatives shall be composed of members chosen ... by the people of the several States ..."

"3. Representatives ... shall be apportioned among the several States which may be included within this Union, according to their respective numbers ..."

THE MEANING OF "BY THE PEOPLE" IN THE UNITED STATES CONSTITUTION

By a series of famous decisions, the United States Supreme Court has held that the words "chosen by the people" were themselves a guarantee of democracy ...

[66] These cases established that the words in Art 1, that representatives "shall be chosen by the people", contained a command of equal representation in the House of Representatives for equal numbers of people. In *Wesberry v Sanders* [376 US 1 at 7-9 (1964)] Warren CJ and Black, Douglas, Brennan, White and Goldberg JJ in the opinion of the Court, delivered by Black J stated:

"We hold that, construed in its historical context, the command of Art 1, s 2, that Representatives be chosen 'by the People of the several States' means that as nearly as is practicable one man's vote in a congressional election is to be worth as much as another's. This rule is followed automatically, of course, when Representatives are chosen as a group on a statewide basis, as was a widespread practice in the first fifty years of our Nation's history. It would be extraordinary to suggest that in such statewide elections the votes of inhabitants of some parts of a State, for example, Georgia's thinly populated Ninth District, could be weighted at two or three times the value of the votes of people living in more populous parts of the State, for example, the Fifth District around Atlanta ... We do not believe that the

Framers of the Constitution intended to permit the same vote-diluting discrimination to be accomplished through the device of districts containing widely varied numbers of inhabitants. To say that a vote is worth more in one district than in another would not only run counter to our fundamental ideas of democratic government, it would cast aside the principle of a House of Representatives elected 'by the People' a principle tenaciously fought for and established at the Constitutional Convention. The history of the Constitution, particularly that part of it relating to the adoption of Art 1, s 2, reveals that those who framed the Constitution meant that, no matter what the mechanics of an election, whether statewide or by districts, it was population which was to be the basis of the House of Representatives."

and later [376 US 1 at 17-8 (1964)]:

"No right is more precious in a free country than that of having a voice in the election of those who make the laws under which, as good citizens, we must live. Other rights, even the most basic, are illusory if the right to vote is undermined. Our Constitution leaves no room for classification of people in a way that unnecessarily abridges this right. In urging the people to adopt the Constitution, Madison said in No 57 of *The Federalist*: 'Who are to be the electors of the Federal Representatives? Not the rich more than the poor; [67] not the learned more than the ignorant; not the haughty heirs of distinguished names, more than the humble sons of obscure and unpropitious fortune. The electors are to be the great body of the people of the United States ...' Readers surely could have fairly taken this to mean, 'one person, one vote' ...

While it may not be possible to draw congressional districts with mathematical precision, that is no excuse for ignoring our Constitution's plain objective of making equal representation for equal numbers of people the fundamental goal for the House of Representatives. That is the high standard of justice and common sense which the Founders set for us."

The contention that variances were necessary in the drawing of congressional districts, to avoid the fragmentation of areas with distinct economic and social interests and the consequent dilution of effective representation of these interests in Congress was rejected as antithetical to the basic premise of the constitutional command to provide equal representation ...

[68] THE CONSTRUCTION OF SECTION 24.

In determining the meaning of s 24, certain principles of constitutional interpretation should be borne in mind.

"... it must always be remembered that we are interpreting a Constitution broad and general in its terms, intended to apply to the varying conditions which the development of our community must involve.

For that reason, where the question is whether the Constitution has used an expression in the wider or in the narrower sense, the Court should, in my opinion, always lean to the broader interpretation unless there is something in the context or in the rest of the Constitution to indicate that the narrower interpretation will best carry out its object and purpose." (*Jumbunna Coal Mine NL v Victorian Coal Miners' Association* [(1908) 6 CLR 309 at 367-8].)

"Constitutions made, not for a single occasion, but for the continued life and progress of the community may and, indeed, must be affected in their general meaning and effect by what Lord Watson in *Cooper v Stuart* [(1889) 14 App Cas 286 at 293] calls 'the silent operation of constitutional principles'." (*Commonwealth v Kreglinger* [(1926) 37 CLR 393 at 413], per Isaacs J.)

"We should avoid pedantic and narrow constructions in dealing with an instrument of government and I do not see why we should be fearful about making implications". (*Australian National Airways Pty Ltd v Commonwealth*, per Dixon J [(1945) 71 CLR 29 at 85].)

The House of Representatives. This name implies an organ of popular representative government.

Shall Be. The history of the United States Constitution shows that the use of the word "shall" throughout the Constitution was a deliberate departure from the exhortations or statements of philosophy in earlier instruments, such as the English Bill of Rights and the Virginia Declaration. It was a deliberate use of the language of command, an expression of imperative law (see Cahn, *The Great Rights* (1963), p 5).

Directly. This is clearly intended to ensure a direct popular election, allowing no intermediary, such as an electoral college.

Chosen by the People. The literal and commonsense construction of this important consti-tutional provision is a choosing by all **[69]** people capable of choosing, only excluding those incapable, such as minors and those of unsound mind.

It may have been accepted in 1900 that "chosen by the people" could exclude women and people without certain property. Women were then deprived of the vote in certain States and this was referred to obliquely in s 128 of the Constitution. Because of the silent operation of consti-tutional principles, this is no longer so. In 1975, any law of the Parliament which deprived persons of a right to representation or to vote on the ground of sex or lack of property would be incom-patible with the command that the House of Representatives be directly "chosen by the people". It would contravene s 24 and be thus unconstitutional ...

[70] DOES "CHOSEN BY THE PEOPLE" COMMAND EQUALITY?

In the present case, three main views have emerged on whether the phrase "chosen by the people" carries a command or a mandate of equal representation.

1. The phrase should be construed in the same way as it was by the United States Supreme Court but having as the standard of equality the alternatives of equal numbers of people and equal numbers of electors.

2. It contains a lesser requirement which, although related to equality, does not command that the number of people or electors be, as nearly as practicable equal (to the point of a good faith attempt at precise mathematical equality, or justification for departure from such a standard).

3. The words convey no mandate of any kind.

If the second view is accepted, it is not easy to see what standard would be used in determining when the members were "chosen by the people".

If the third view is accepted, it means simply that the Constitution does not require that the election for the House of Representatives be democratic. It would permit the most undemocratic deprivation or dilution of voting power, such as rotten boroughs, depriving women of a vote, and the imposing of property qualifications on voters. The State of New South Wales, intervening, adopted the stand that the Constitution would permit the mem-**[71]**-bers of the House of Representatives to be elected only by mayors and presidents of municipal and shire councils. It would mean also, as was argued, that a one member division could constitutionally contain twenty times the number of people or electors as another division in the same State and that one division could have twenty times the number of members as another division containing the same number of electors or people.

In my opinion, the first view is correct.

I am led to this conclusion by:

(a) The obvious importance placed on the phrase by its positioning in the opening sentence of that part of the Constitution devoted to the House of Representatives, and the fact that it is expressed in the language of command.

(b) The democratic theme of equal sharing of political power which pervades the Constitution. In 1902, the authority on the Constitution, Professor W Harrison Moore wrote:

> "The predominant feature of the Australian Constitution is the prevalence of the democratic principle, in its most modern guise." (*Constitution of the Commonwealth of Australia*, 1st ed (1902), p 327).

and

> "The great underlying principle is, that the rights of individuals are sufficiently secured by ensuring, as far as possible, to each a share, and *an equal share*, in political power." (My emphasis) (Ibid, p 329.)

(c) The reference is to the "people of the Commonwealth", which emphasizes the intention of sharing of political power.

(d) The absence of any other means of redress for those deprived of an equal share of represen-tation, even where it is grossly unequal. The argument was advanced that no guarantee of electoral equality should be read into the Constitution because it was left exclusively to the Parliament to do what was fair. If Parliament failed, the remedy was with the people. The hollowness of this argument has been made apparent by the history of maldistribution in the United States and in Australia. If the legislature fails to ensure fairness, and there is no constitutional right enforceable in the courts, where is the remedy? There is no provision for referendum or any other remedy which can be initiated by the people. Redistributions in Australia can be and have been delayed by the simple inaction of one House (see Paterson, "Federal Electorates and Proportionate Distribution", *Australian Law Journal*, vol 42 (1968), p 127). History here and elsewhere [72] reveals that with few exceptions, legislators who hold office because of an unbalanced electoral system will not act to change the system. The more unbalanced it becomes, the more severe are the consequences of correction and the more reluctant are the legislators to change it.

(e) The fact that the phrase was taken directly from the United States Constitution. The construction placed upon it by the United States Supreme Court that it commands electoral equality is compelling in its reasoning and applicable to our Constitution.

The framers of the Australian Constitution, in adopting the precise words of the United States Constitution were certainly aware of United States history. The struggles for independence, the declaration of independence, the revolutionary war, the framing of the United States Constitution, as well as the contributions to the liberty of man by the great figures of the United States, are part of the history of the English-speaking peoples. This history is part of our cultural heritage …

As we have seen, the Supreme Court in the United States held that the provision that the members shall be chosen "by the people" expresses the most basic right of the people and commands [73] that there shall be equal representation, an equal sharing of political power in the election in each State for the House of Representatives. It is a remarkable result if the same words carried into our Constitution and used for the same purpose of describing how the members shall be chosen are construed by our High Court as a vague philosophic statement requiring a direct choice but permitting the choosing to be by a few of the people only, with exclusions on grounds of sex or property, or other arbitrary criteria, and allowing the voting to be debased by unequal divisions or other devices.

As Jefferson said, *Writings*, Washington ed (1859), vol 4, p 506:

"Our peculiar security is the possession of a written Constitution. Let us not make it a blank paper by construction."

None of the other six judges accepted this approach.

Barwick CJ: [17] The problem which is thus presented to the Court is a matter of the legal construction of the Constitution of Australia, itself a legal document; an Act of the Imperial Parliament. The problem is not to be solved by resort to slogans or to political catch-cries or to vague and imprecise expressions of political philosophy. The question of the validity of an Act of the Parliament, namely, the *Electoral Act*, is to be decided by the meaning of the relevant text of the Constitution having regard to the historical setting in which the Constitution was created and the terms and operation of the Act in respect of the subject matter which, upon that construction, is committed by the Constitution to the Parliament. The only true guide and the only course which can produce stability in constitutional law is to read the language of the Constitution itself, no doubt generously and not pedantically, but as a whole: and to find its meaning by legal reasoning. I respectfully agree with Sir Owen Dixon's opinion that "there is no other safe guide to judicial decisions in great conflicts than a strict and complete legalism".

Barwick CJ rejected any analogy with the words "directly chosen by the people" in Art I of the United States Constitution, or with the Supreme Court's interpretation of those words.

Barwick CJ: [23] [I]t must always be borne in mind that the American colonies had not only made unilateral declarations of independence but had done so in revolt against British institutions and methods of government. The concepts of the sovereignty of Parliament and of ministerial responsibility were rejected in the formation of the American Constitution. Thus, not only does the American Constitution provide for a presidential system, but it provides for checks and balances based on the denial of complete confidence in any single arm of government.

In high contradistinction, the Australian Constitution was developed not in antagonism to British methods of government but **[24]** in co-operation with and, to a great extent, with the encouragement of the British Government. The Constitution itself is an Act of the Imperial Parliament which, except for a significant modification of the terms of s 74, is in the terms proposed by the Australian colonists and accepted by the British Government. Because that Constitution was federal in nature, there was necessarily a distribution of governmental powers as between the Commonwealth and the constituent States with consequential limitation on the sovereignty of the Parliament and of that of the legislatures of the States. All were subject to the Constitution. But otherwise there was no antipathy amongst the colonists to the notion of the sovereignty of Parliament in the scheme of government.

Also it is well known that the Constitution of the United States would not have been accepted except on the footing that it would be amended to include a Bill of Rights. It is very noticeable that no Bill of Rights is attached to the Constitution of Australia and that there are few guarantees. Not only are the powers given to the Parliament plenary but there is a large number of provisions in the Constitution which leave to the Parliament the power of altering the actual constitutional provisions. In other words, unlike the case of the American Constitution, the Australian Constitution is built upon confidence in a system of parliamentary Government with ministerial responsibility.

The contrast in constitutional approach is that, in the case of the American Constitution, restriction on legislative power is sought and readily implied whereas, where confidence in the parliament prevails, express words are regarded as necessary to warrant a limitation of otherwise plenary powers. Thus, discretions in parliament are more readily accepted in the construction of the Australian Constitution. The federating colonies committed themselves to what the Parliament, not what the House of Representatives, but the House of Representatives and the Senate, might do in relation to the franchise and the electoral distribution of the States, building in the safeguard of the equality of legislative power with one exception, in the two Houses.

In my opinion, in the construction of the Constitution of Australia, decisions of the Supreme Court upon the Constitution of the United States are frequently inapt, and none more so, in my opinion, than the decisions of the Supreme Court on Art 1.

In any event, Barwick CJ held that the criteria for electoral distributions set out in s 19 of the Electoral Act did ensure a reasonable approximation of equality. Gibbs J agreed in a separate judgment. The other four majority judges also agreed, but made some thoughtful concessions.

McTiernan and Jacobs JJ: [35] It is said that [equality of electoral divisions] is the meaning of the words "chosen by the people" in s 24. We do not think that any such exact content can by definition be given to these words. The words express a distinct concept or notion capable of application as a constitutional requirement but they are not words which can be re-written or paraphrased in such an exact manner ... Inequality of distribution of numbers between districts or divisions in respect of which members are chosen is one factor which may lead to a choice on the basis of such an unequal distribution being unable to be described as a choice by the people of the Commonwealth.

The people is the body of subjects of the Crown inhabiting the Commonwealth regarded collectively as a unity or whole, and the sum of those subjects regarded individually. To say that "people" means "electors" or "enfranchised subjects" is erroneous because it takes account only of the enfranchised subjects regarded indi-**[36]**-vidually but no account of the body of subjects regarded collectively as a unity. It is an accurate description only so long as the franchise is wide enough to satisfy the description "popular" but it would be nonsense to speak of a choice by a few who happened to be enfranchised (the foundation of an oligarchy) as a choice by the people (the foundation of a democracy).

Stephen J: [56] Three great principles, representative democracy (by which I mean that the legislators are chosen by the people), direct popular election, and the national character of the lower House, may each be discerned in the opening words of s 24. Nothing however is said as to the composition of electoral divisions. Only if some requirement as to their composition necessarily flows from one or other of these three principles can the plaintiffs' submissions be made good; and it can surely only be from the first, representative democracy in the sense in which I use that term, that some such requirement might be derived.

The principle of representative democracy does indeed predicate the enfranchisement of electors, the existence of an electoral system capable of giving effect to their selection of representatives and the bestowal of legislative functions upon the representatives thus selected. However the particular quality and character of the content of each one of these three ingredients of representative democracy, and there may well be others, is not fixed and precise. I take each in turn. The extent of the franchise; whether it extends to all residents or to all residents over a given age or is restricted, perhaps, to male British subjects over twenty-one, maybe with a superadded property qualification and whether more or less replete with disqualifications on grounds of incapacity or criminality or the like, it will none the less constitute an enfranchisement of electors. The electoral system, with its innumerable details including numbers and qualifications of representatives, single or multi-member electorates, voting methods and the various methods, including varieties of proportional representation, whereby the significance and outcome of the votes cast may be determined; in each there is scope for variety and no one formula can preempt the field as alone consistent with representative democracy. Again the [57] wide range of legislative functions which a legislature thus elected may possess is so clear in our federal polity, with its history of a variety of colonial legislatures, that it requires no elaboration.

It is, then, quite apparent that representative democracy is descriptive of a whole spectrum of political institutions, each differing in countless respects yet answering to that generic description. The spectrum has finite limits and in a particular instance there may be absent some quality which is regarded as so essential to representative democracy as to place that instance outside those limits altogether; but at no one point within the range of the spectrum does there exist any single requirement so essential as to be determinative of the existence of representative democracy.

To contend that the presence of what is described as "as near as practicable equality of numbers" within electoral divisions is essential to representative democracy, to a legislature "chosen by the people", is to deny proper meaning to language and to ignore long chapters in the evolution of democratic institutions both in this country and overseas, in which, representative democracy having been attained, its details have undergone frequent changes in response to community pressures but have failed to possess this feature of equality of numbers on which the plaintiffs now insist.

It is no doubt true that something approaching numerical equality of electors within electorates is an important factor, together with much else, in the attainment of what many will regard as representative democracy in its purest form, just as adult suffrage, free of discrimination on the grounds of race, sex, property or educational qualification will likewise aid in its attainment. But neither of these in absolute form is necessarily imported into the Constitution by the selection of representative democracy as the chosen mode of government for the nation.

This Court is not concerned to pass upon the relative merits of any particular democratic electoral system otherwise conforming to constitutional requirements nor to determine that any one of the very many features which go to make up such a system should conform to one particular model rather than to some other. The Constitution leaves this to legislatures to determine, in most instances, initially, to the legislature of the States – see ss 24, 29, 30, 31, 34(i) and (ii); or to the federal Parliament if it exercises its power to "otherwise provide". Having entrusted to these elected legislatures rather than to this Court these wide powers of shaping as they see fit the details of this nation's electoral system it is not for this Court to intervene so long as what is enacted is [58] consistent with the existence of representative democracy as the chosen mode of government and is within the power conferred by s 51(xxxvi).

At the time of federation the nature of the electoral system, as it would operate until such time as the federal Parliament might seek to intervene by "otherwise providing", was known to all since it was, in very large measure, already provided for by the existing colonial electoral laws. It was a system which contained such features as a franchise restricted to males in all but two of the States, with a property qualification applicable in one of the States, and a further restriction of the franchise to natural born or naturalized British subjects in all but one State. Section 25 of the Constitution recognized the disqualification of entire races which applied in Queensland and in what was then the Northern Territory of South Australia. The last sentence of s 25 and the terms of s 26 of the Constitution ensured that the proportionality of representatives to population should not operate initially so far as the representatives for Tasmania and Western Australia were concerned.

All these provisions are explicit indications that the Constitution in no way pretended to any perfect embodiment of some particular model of democratic principles; the federation of the colonies was an essentially practical and political affair, achieved after much negotiation and the outcome of extensive compromise.

In the light of all these considerations I regard it as quite unreal to seek to extract from the opening phrase of s 24 any requirement that boundaries of electoral divisions be determined either having regard to population numbers rather than numbers of electors or solely upon a footing of as near as practicable equality of numbers, whether of population or of electors.

Mason J: [61] All that the paragraph in s 24 requires is that there should be a direct choice of the members by the people – a prescription which does not cease to be satisfied because there is some, or even a marked, variation in the number of persons or electors in the electoral divisions within a State. The existence of such variations does not detract from the accuracy of the description of our existing electoral system as one in which the members of the House are directly chosen by the people of the Commonwealth.

It is perhaps conceivable that variations in the numbers of electors or people in single member electorates could become so grossly disproportionate as to raise a question whether an election held on boundaries so drawn would produce a House of Representatives composed of members directly chosen by the people of the Commonwealth, but this is a matter quite removed from the proposition that s 24 insists upon a practical equality of people or electors in single member electorates.

Despite these findings, the plaintiffs in *McKinlay's Case* were successful on two minor issues. According to sub-paras (i) and (ii) of s 24, "the number of members to be chosen in each State" is to be computed by reference to "the number of the people of the State, as shown by the latest statistics of the Commonwealth". According to the preamble to those two subparagraphs, this calculation is to be made "whenever necessary". However, ss 3-4 of the *Representation Act* provided that, in making this calculation, the Chief Electoral Officer was to rely on census figures. The first objection to this was that, in practice, it might mean that any redistribution might be based on population figures up to five years old. A further objection was that, since a redistribution was only to be made by reference to a census, and since the timing and frequency of the census is dependent on legislation, it might be possible to delay an electoral redistribution indefinitely. Barwick CJ, Gibbs, Stephen and Mason JJ held that these arrangements did not comply with the requirement that the calculation be made "whenever necessary" and accordingly that ss 3-4 of the *Representation Act* were invalid.

Further, s 12 of that Act provided that when an alteration had been made, and resulted in a change to the number of members to be elected in any State, "the alteration shall not affect – (a) any election held before the State had been redistributed into electoral divisions pursuant to the certificate ... , but shall affect any general election after such redistribution". Again, s 12(a) meant that it might be possible to postpone a redistribution indefinitely. For that reason, Barwick CJ, Gibbs, Stephen, Mason and Murphy JJ held s 12(a) to be invalid.

Sections 3-4 of the *Representation Act*, as successfully challenged in *McKinlay's Case*, had been the result of amendments made in 1938. This meant that all federal elections since 1938 had been conducted on the basis of unconstitutional statutory provisions, and possibly on the basis of electoral distributions that did not satisfy the constitutional requirements of s 24. Did this mean that all federal elections conducted since 1938 had been invalid, and hence that all Common-wealth Parliaments since 1938 had been invalidly constituted? If so, were all laws enacted by those Parliaments also invalid? The Court held that none of these consequences followed, but did not really explain why.

Barwick CJ: [34] The use of the then existing electoral divisions and of the then existing determination of the number of members of the House of Representatives chosen by the several States did not invalidate any election of members of the House of Representatives **[35]** which has already taken place; nor bring into doubt the validity of the membership of the Parliament.

Gibbs J, with whom Stephen and Mason JJ agreed on this point, attempted a fuller explanation.

Gibbs J: [53] Although it is obvious, it should be remarked that it does not follow from the fact that the *Representation Act* is in part invalid that the numbers chosen in the several States in the past have not been in their correct proportion. Even if it were established that the numbers were not or are not in their correct proportion (and there is no evidence to that effect), that would not mean that elections conducted in the past have been invalidly conducted, or that an election conducted in future on the basis of the existing determination as to the number of members to be chosen in the several States would be invalid. As I have already pointed out, there is an overriding constitutional duty to hold elections in certain circumstances. There is also a constitutional duty to ensure that each State is proportionately represented in the House of Representatives, but a failure to perform that duty does not invalidate an election held otherwise in compliance with the Constitution. Since, no doubt, the Parliament will act to give effect to the requirements of s 24 now that they have been pointed out, it is unnecessary to consider what remedies might be available if it did not.

McTiernan and Jacobs JJ did not need to address this puzzle. In their view, ss 3-4 of the *Representation Act* were valid and, although they agreed that s 12 was a problem, they stopped short of finding it invalid, holding only that it "**[41]** cannot validly operate in so far as by such an operation the number of members chosen in the several States would not be in proportion to the respective numbers of their people". Murphy J did not consider the past consequences that might flow from the invalidity of ss 3-4 and 12. However, he did point out that, on his view of the malapportionment issue, the coming election of 13 December 1975 would be unconstitutional since it "**[79]** will not be one in which the members will be 'chosen by the people' as the Constitution requires".

At the State level, the political issue of electoral malapportionment continued to be sensitive after *McKinlay's Case*. Most State Constitutions and Territory Self-Government Acts now mandate a limited tolerance of deviations from voter equality. For example, s 77 of the *Constitution Act 1934* (SA) requires that in an electoral redistribution for the South Australian Parliament the number of electors in any electorate should not deviate by more than 10 per cent from the electoral quota arrived at by dividing the number of electors by the number of electoral districts. Section 67D of the *Australian Capital Territory (Self-Government) Act 1988* (Cth) and s 28 of the *Constitution Act 1902* (NSW) also establish a 10 per cent margin, while s 13 of the *Northern Territory (Self-Government) Act 1978* (Cth) establishes a 20 per cent tolerance. However, both Queensland and Western Australia afford historical examples of skewed electoral boundaries devised by one political party that later came to benefit that party's opponents.

The skewed electoral boundaries in Western Australia, established by legislation including the *Acts Amendment (Electoral Reform) Act 1987* (WA), were challenged in *McGinty v Western Australia* (1996) 186 CLR 140. In *Australian Capital Television Pty Ltd v Commonwealth* (1992) 177 CLR 106 the High Court had held that the Constitution supports a judicially enforceable limitation on the power of the Commonwealth Parliament to interfere with the essential preconditions of the system of representative government, such as free discussion of political matters. In *Stephens v West Australian Newspapers Ltd* (1994) 182 CLR 211, a majority of the Court held that a counterpart limitation at the State level could be derived from the *Constitution Act 1889* (WA) (see Chapter 28, §4). While the focus in *Australian Capital Television* and *Stephens* was on freedom of political communication, it was argued in *McGinty* that, by parity of reasoning, both the Commonwealth and the Western Australian Constitutions could support an implication of equality in voting power.

At the 1993 Western Australian State election, the number of voters per electoral district differed markedly between districts, particularly as between metropolitan and rural electorates. For the Legislative Assembly, the largest of the metropolitan electorates, Wanneroo, had 26,580 enrolled voters, while the smallest of the rural electorates, Ashburton, had 9135 enrolled voters. In the Legislative Council, the disparity was even greater. The quota for the North Metropolitan Region was 34,161 votes, while the quota for the Mining and Pastoral Region was 9097 votes. James McGinty, the Labor Opposition Leader in Western Australia, challenged these electoral boundaries. He argued that a system of representative government was created by both the

Commonwealth and Western Australian Constitutions, each of which mandated equality of voting power in elections for the Western Australian Parliament. The High Court rejected that argument.

The majority consisted of Brennan CJ, Dawson, McHugh and Gummow JJ, with Toohey and Gaudron JJ dissenting. (Deane J, who might also have seemed likely to dissent, did not sit as he was about to take up his appointment as Governor-General.) The majority rejected the implication of voter equality and reaffirmed *McKinlay's Case*. They were also concerned to establish that any constitutional implication must be drawn from the text or structure of the relevant Constitution and not from an overarching concept of representative government.

McGinty v Western Australia
(1996) 186 CLR 140

Brennan CJ: [168] [I]t is ... impermissible to determine the validity of the 1987 Act by reference to its consistency with the requirements of a general principle of representative democracy. "Representative democracy" has been used as a shorthand description of the form of government prescribed by the Commonwealth Constitution in order to explain how the freedom to discuss governments and political matters is implied in the Constitution. As "the people" are to choose their elected representatives, it has been held that the people must be left free to discuss political and economic matters in order to perform their constitutional functions ...

Implications are not devised by the judiciary; they exist in the text and structure of the Constitution and are revealed or uncovered by judicial exegesis. No implication can be drawn from the Constitution which is not based on the actual terms of the Constitution, or on its structure ...

[170] The principle of "representative democracy" can be given the status of a constitutional imperative, but only in so far as the meaning and content of that principle are implied in the text and structure of the Constitution. The constitutional question for determination in this case cannot be stated as though it asks whether the distribution of electoral districts or of electoral regions is consistent with a general principle of representative democracy – especially if the content of "representative democracy" is derived from sources outside the Constitution. The constitutional question is whether there is inconsistency with the text and structure of the Constitution.

Unaffected by context, the phrase "chosen by the people" admits of different meanings. It might connote that candidates are chosen by popular direct election as distinct from election by an electoral college; or it might connote some requirement of equality or near equality of voting power among those who hold the franchise; or it might go further and import some requirement of a franchise that is held generally by all adults or all adult citizens unless there be substantial reasons for excluding them. Equally, these meanings might be attributed to the notion of "representative democracy" ...

[175] Assuming, without deciding, that the provisions of the Commonwealth Constitution impliedly preclude electoral distributions that would produce disparities of voting power – of whatever magnitude – among those who hold the Commonwealth franchise in a State, what do those provisions have to say with respect to the Constitutions and laws of the several States governing electoral distributions for State elections? In my opinion, the Commonwealth Constitution contains no implication affecting disparities of voting power among the holders of the franchise for the election of members of a State Parliament (hereafter "State disparities"). Far from containing an implication affecting State disparities, the text of Pts II and III of Ch I of the Commonwealth Constitution and the structure of the Constitution as a whole are inconsistent with such an implication. Sections 7, 8, 9 and 10 of the Constitution are expressed to relate only to elections for the Senate; ss 24, 25, 29 and 30 are expressed to relate only to elections for the House of Representatives; and s 41 is expressed to relate only to elections for either House of the Parliament of the Commonwealth. Not only are these sections expressly confined to elections for one or other House of the Commonwealth Parliament but they are all contained in Ch I of the Constitution which, being followed by Chs II and III, define the structure of the Commonwealth's three branches of government. Chapter V is the Chapter relating to the States and their Constitutions. The structure of the Constitution is opposed to the notion that the provisions of Ch I might affect the Constitutions of the States to which Ch V is directed.

Dawson J emphasised that, apart from specific provisions in the Constitution "**[182]** for the minimum requirements of representative government" and for "**[183]** certain other matters of machinery", "the form of representative government which we are to have is left to parliament".

Dawson J: [183] In particular, it is left to parliament to make laws determining the electoral divisions for which members of parliament may be chosen … In providing for those matters which are confided to it, parliament is required to determine questions of a political nature about which opinions may vary considerably. For example, the qualifications of electors are to be provided for by parliament under ss 8 and 30 and may amount to less than universal suffrage, however politically unacceptable that may be today. Thus, it may be seen that the form of representative government, including the type of electoral system, the adoption and size of electoral divisions, and the franchise are all left to parliament by the Constitution …

There are hundreds of electoral systems in existence today by which a form of representative government might be achieved. Their merits must be judged by a number of different criteria which are likely to be incompatible with one another … **[184]** There can be no implication that a particular electoral system, of the many available, is required by the Constitution. There is, of course, the express requirement that whatever system is employed it must result in a direct choice by the people. That must mean direct choice by the people through those eligible to vote at elections, but beyond that the matter of electoral systems, including the size of electoral divisions, and indeed whether to have divisional representation at all, is left to the parliament …

[185] Once it is recognised, as in my view it must be, that electorates of equal numerical size are not a necessary characteristic of representative government, the plaintiffs are driven in their argument to find in the system of representative government laid down by the Constitution a requirement that there be, as nearly as practicable, electorates of equal size. But that requirement is nowhere to be found in any express provision of the Constitution and this Court has denied in *McKinlay* [(1975) 135 CLR 1] that there is any basis for its implication. It is not to be found in the expression "directly chosen by the people" contained in ss 7 and 24. Indeed, ss 7 and 24 contain requirements which are to the contrary.

As Barwick CJ pointed out in *McKinlay* [135 CLR at 20] no Australian colony at the time of federation insisted upon practical equality in the size of electoral divisions and the view was then plainly open that problems of communication and access in geographically large electorates outside a metropolitan area justify different numerical sizes in electoral divisions. That is a view which obviously still prevails in Western Australia under the current legislation.

Clearly there is force in the contrary view which holds that the effect of unequal electoral divisions – malapportionment – is to weight the value of votes in the numerically smaller divisions. But the extra weight is only in the consequence that an elector in a smaller electorate is required to share his or her representative with a lesser number of electors than in the larger electorate. There are other ways, perhaps more significant, in which the value of a vote may be affected as, for example, where electoral divisions are defined in such a way as to allow one party in a two party system to return a majority of representatives with less than a majority of the total votes, which may occur whether or not malapportionment also exists. Disproportion of this kind may be intentionally caused by a gerrymander. Of course, the problems arising from malapportionment and disproportion would largely disappear if there were no electoral divisions within a State and a system of proportional representation were adopted – **[186]** something envisaged by s 29 of the Constitution. But such a system may be to the detriment of a two party system by encouraging the growth of splinter groups …

These considerations suggest that it would be unwise to freeze into a constitutional requirement a particular aspect of an electoral system the attraction of which might vary at different times, in different conditions and to different eyes. The wisdom of those who were responsible for framing our Constitution in recognising the political nature of such matters, and in leaving them to parliament, ought not to be overborne by drawing an implication which is neither apparent nor necessary …

In my **[189]** view the reasoning of the majority in [*McKinlay*] is compelling and I see no reason to depart from it.

It is true that in *McKinlay* McTiernan and Jacobs JJ suggested that the notion of equality is to some extent present in the words "chosen by the people" so that at some point electoral inequality might be inconsistent with a choice by the people. They rejected, however, any requirement of absolute equality or nearly as practicable equality. Similarly, Mason J said [135 CLR at 61]:

"It is perhaps conceivable that variations in the numbers of electors or people in single member electorates could become so grossly disproportionate as to raise a question whether an election held on boundaries so drawn would produce a House of Representatives composed of members directly chosen by the people of the Commonwealth, but this is a matter quite removed from the proposition that s 24 insists upon a practical equality of people or electors in single member electorates."

In my view, both McTiernan and Jacobs JJ and Mason J had in mind extreme situations markedly different from that which exists under the relevant Western Australian legislation.

As to the suggested implication of equality of voting power at the Commonwealth level, the judgments cannot be regarded as decisive, since Brennan CJ expressed no final opinion and Toohey and Gaudron JJ dissented. However, all six judges held that, even if there were such a requirement at Commonwealth level, it could not extend to State electoral systems. That left the alternative argument based on s 73(2) of the *Constitution Act 1889* (WA).

Section 73(2) was inserted in 1978. It entrenches Western Australian laws, including the Western Australian Constitution itself, against Bills of the several kinds specified in the provision. (As to the use of "entrenched" provisions in State Constitution Acts, see Chapter 11, §3.) The measures against which the "entrenchment" provisions are expressed to operate include, by s 73(2)(c), any Bill that "expressly or impliedly provides that the Legislative Council or the Legislative Assembly shall be composed of members other than members chosen directly by the people". In *McGinty*, it was argued that this provision supported a requirement of equality of voting power in Western Australian State elections. By 4:2, Toohey and Gaudron JJ dissenting, it was held that there was no such implication.

Brennan CJ: [178] From before Federation, the State has been so divided into electoral districts for the election of the Assembly and electoral provinces or regions for the election of the Council that there has been inequality in the voting power of electors in different parts of the State. Throughout this time, the holders of the franchise as it stood from time to time have directly chosen the members of the Council and the Assembly for their respective electoral districts and provinces. When s 73(2)(c) was inserted in the 1889 Act in 1978, it is impossible to suppose that the Parliament of Western Australia intended thereby to override the regime of electoral districts and provinces which were then, and had historically been, the electoral framework of the State. The language of s 73(2)(c) must be construed in the light of the constitutional history of the State and the circumstances existing when that provision was introduced. The purpose of that provision was not the creation of a new electoral regime; it was simply privative of the uncontrolled or partly-controlled power of constitutional amendment vested in the Parliament by s 73(1). The material purpose of the 1978 Act was expressed in its preamble as the making of further constitutional provision "to confirm the established constitutional provision aforesaid [relating to the Council, the Assembly and their powers] and to regulate the manner and form in which the powers of the Parliament of Western Australia may hereafter be exercised". Having regard to the history of the State's electoral laws and the context and operation of s 73(2)(c), it is impossible to find an implication other than the entrenchment of the system of electing members of the Council and the Assembly by direct popular vote. To find in s 73(2)(c) an implication that electoral power be equally distributed among the people of the State or among the people of the State possessing the franchise would be to find a legislative intention destructive of the means by which the enacting Parliament was elected.

Gaudron and Toohey JJ held that there was a relevant implication in the Commonwealth Constitution (in relation to federal elections), but joined in the unanimous view that any such implication at the federal level could not "flow on" to State elections. However, they also held (in dissent) that a similar implication could be discerned in s 73(2)(c).

Gaudron J: [222] [U]nless there is some relevantly different context, the words "chosen ... by the people" in s 73(2)(c) of the 1889 Act must be interpreted consistently with those same words in ss 7 and 24 of the Constitution. There is one difference: when s 73(2)(c) was inserted in the 1889 Act there was no constitutional provision which necessitated or, depending on population differences, might necessitate disparity in voting value, as is the case with ss 7 and 24 ... This means that there is no basis for any constitutional limitation in relation to voting equality of the kind necessary in relation to ss 7 and 24 of the Constitution. That aside, the words "chosen ... by the people" in s 73(2)(c) of the 1889 Act must, in my **[223]** view, be applied in the same way as they are in ss 7 and 24 of the Constitution. More particularly, they must be viewed as constituting a guarantee of democracy entrenched in the 1889 Act unless and until amended in accordance with s 73(2). And they must be applied in the light of contemporary circumstances, having regard to developments which have taken place in democratic standards.

In applying the words "chosen ... by the people", it is relevant to have regard to the fact that, in 1978, when those words were inserted in the 1889 Act, the 1947 Act allowed for significant disparity in voting value both for Legislative Council and Legislative Assembly elections. The extent of that disparity and the fact that it was countenanced until comparatively recent times militates, at least for the moment, against an approach to s 73(2)(c) which would require precisely the same standard as that now required by s 24 of the Constitution. Rather, that history provides a basis, at least for the moment, for a somewhat more generous margin of variation in voting value. But as with s 24 of the Constitution, the countenancing of voting inequality at one time does not, of itself, provide a basis for countenancing inequality at a later time. Ultimately, it is a question of what is required in the light of current democratic standards, including those which so recently applied in Western Australia.

In my view, the malapportionment which is detailed in the judgment of Toohey J is so great as to be distinctly at odds with democratic standards revealed in the electoral laws of the Commonwealth and the other Australian States referred to in his Honour's judgment. Moreover, the distinction between metropolitan and non-metropolitan areas is, as his Honour points out, arbitrary and inflexible and, that being so, it cannot be justified on the basis that it is reasonably capable of being seen as appropriate and adapted to the dispersed nature of the population in the remote regions of Western Australia or to any other matter or circumstance which might bear on effective parliamentary representation.

It was not argued that s 6 of the 1899 Act and ss 2A(2), (6) and (9) of the 1947 Act were invalid when enacted in 1987 or, indeed, at any particular time thereafter. Rather, the plaintiffs' case was that, at some unspecified time, the provisions became invalid and remain so, in the same way, presumably, as laws which are validly enacted under the defence power may cease to be laws with respect to defence and become void when hostilities have ceased. I am not convinced that that is the proper approach to be taken with respect to electoral **[224]** laws which are put into operation as and when elections have to be held.

The issue that arises with respect to s 6 of the 1899 Act and ss 2A(2), (6) and (9) of the 1947 Act is, in essence, whether they would have valid operation if elections were now held. Because that is the issue, the preferable course, in my view, is to answer the question in the case stated by saying, as earlier indicated, that if elections were now held, neither the members of the Legislative Council nor those of the Legislative Assembly would be "chosen ... by the people" within the meaning of those words in s 73(2)(c) of the 1889 Act. This is a minority view and it is, thus, unnecessary to consider what, if any, further relief is required by the answer I propose.

An attempted repeal of the *Electoral Distribution Act 1947* (WA), intended to clear the way for a new and more equal distribution, was struck down in *Attorney-General (WA) v Marquet* (2003) 217 CLR 545 (see Chapter 11, §3). The High Court held that the attempted repeal was blocked by s 13 of the 1947 Act, which effectively provided that "any Bill to amend this Act" must be passed by an absolute majority in both Houses of the State Parliament. After the election in February 2005, the re-elected government was finally successful in having Parliament change the system by enacting the *Electoral Amendment and Repeal Act 2005* (WA).

(d) A "level playing field"?

Much of the rhetoric of *McKinlay* and *McGinty* was repeated in 2004 when the Democratic Labor Party ("the DLP") sought to use the words "chosen by the people" as the basis for an attack on the validity of the party registration provisions in Pt XI of the *Commonwealth Electoral Act 1918* (Cth). The essential features of the registration scheme had been introduced by the *Commonwealth Electoral Legislation Amendment Act 1983* (Cth) as ancillary to a number of electoral changes made by that legislation. These included arrangements for the public funding of election campaigns by registered political parties; the inclusion on ballot papers of candidates' party identification; and the introduction of the simplified system of voting in Senate elections, which sets out lists of candidates in identified party groups and allows the elector to express a preference simply by giving a single vote to one party "above the line". In order for a political party to be registered for each of these purposes, it must either have current parliamentary representation (under para (a)(i) of the definition of "eligible political party" in s 123(1)), or be able to produce a list of at least 500 members (under para (a)(ii)).

A challenge to the validity of the Senate voting system was rejected by Gibbs CJ, sitting alone, in *McKenzie v Commonwealth* (1984) 57 ALR 747. The challenge depended in part on a claim that explicit reference to party identification infringed s 16 of the Constitution, which does not include party membership among the qualifications for senators. As to that, Gibbs CJ said that it did not follow "**[749]** that the Constitution forbids" the use of party identification and he saw "no reason to imply an inhibition on the use of a method of voting which recognizes political realities". It was also argued that the system "discriminate[s] against candidates who are not members of established parties or groups": this was said to infringe "general principles of justice", and also a requirement of "democratic methods" implied by the words "chosen by the people". Gibbs CJ was "prepared to assume" that such a requirement existed, but concluded (quoting what Stephen J had said in *McKinlay*): "[I]t cannot be said that any disadvantage … to candidates who are not members of parties or groups so offends democratic principles as to render the sections beyond the power of the Parliament to enact".

Before the 2001 federal election, the registration scheme was strengthened. By s 126(2A), introduced by the *Commonwealth Electoral Amendment Act (No 1)* 2000 (Cth), it was not permissible for a political party to claim as a member any person also claimed by another party (the "no overlap" rule); and by s 138A, inserted by the *Electoral and Referendum Amendment Act (No 1) 2001* (Cth), the Commission was given additional powers of reviewing the register with a view to deregistration.

After the 2001 election, the Commission sought to exercise its new powers by scrutinising the DLP's membership claims. In the 1960s and early 1970s the DLP had held the balance of power in the Senate, with four senators from 1967 to 1970, and five from 1970 to 1974. But its Senate representation was lost at the 1974 election and was never regained. Thus, under the registration system from 1984 onwards, the party had never been entitled to registration as "a Parliamentary party", but had been registered under the "500 member rule".

When the DLP refused to supply the names of its members, the Commission gave notice that it was considering the Party's deregistration. Thereupon John Mulholland, the Party's registered officer and its principal Senate candidate at the 2004 election, sought review of the Commission's decisions and conduct under the *Administrative Decisions (Judicial Review) Act 1977* (Cth). He also sought a writ of prohibition on the ground that the provisions purporting to authorise deregistration were invalid. Marshall J of the Federal Court dismissed these applications, as did a unanimous Full Bench of the Federal Court (*Mulholland v Australian Electoral Commission* (2003) 198 ALR 278) and a unanimous High Court (*Mulholland v Australian Electoral Commission* (2004) 220 CLR 181).

The constitutional challenge focused particularly on the requirement for a minimum of 500 members as a condition of registration, and on the exclusion by s 126(2A) of any attempt to count the same members by more than one political party. Gummow and Hayne JJ pointed out with some irony that the precise targets of the constitutional challenge had to be chosen with care. The party needed to strike out those provisions under which it might lose its registration, while leaving intact those provisions which gave it the benefits of registration: "**[231]** Were the appellant to succeed on the case put as to invalidity, a real question would arise as to whether that would be but a pyrrhic victory. It would be a substantial victory only if the application of the principles of severance left standing sufficient of Pt XI of the Act to preserve the registration of the DLP and the advantages it presently obtains by registration".

The result in the High Court was announced on 20 May 2004, but the reasons for judgment were not handed down until 8 September 2004, some 10 days after the federal election of 9 October 2004 had been announced. In those circumstances the Commission proceeded no further with any possible deregistration proceedings. However, at the ensuing election the DLP offered candidates for the Senate only in Victoria. It obtained 0.1356 of a quota, which was higher than the 0.1317 of a quota obtained by the Family First Party (though the latter, by exchanging preferences with other parties, obtained a Senate seat). The DLP also put forward candidates for the House of Representatives in the Victorian seats of Ballarat and McMillan (obtaining respectively 1.32 per cent and 0.35 per cent of the primary vote).

The constitutional challenge depended in part on the DLP's attempt to demonstrate a "burden" on its freedom of political communication. As to the failure of that attempt see Chapter 29, §3. The challenge also relied in part on return to the "discrimination" argument that had been considered by Gibbs CJ in *McKenzie v Commonwealth*, bolstered now by the reference made by Mason CJ in *Australian Capital Television* to the concept of a "level playing field". Finally, the challenge depended on implied limitations on the legislative power to regulate federal elections, supposedly to be derived from the words "chosen by the people". This aspect of the challenge was bolstered by reference to the Canadian case of *Figueroa v Canada (Attorney General)* [2003] 1 SCR 912, (2002) 227 DLR (4th) 1, where it was held that provisions in the *Canada Elections Act 1985* (Can) infringed the democratic rights implied by s 3 of the Canadian Charter of Rights and Freedoms 1982, by "**[946]** derogating from the capacity of marginal or regional parties to present their ideas and opinions to the general public" (227 DLR (4th) at 30). There, too, the impugned provisions established a system of party registration, carrying with it the right to list party identification on ballot papers. However, the Canadian requirement for registration was that "the party has officially nominated candidates in fifty electoral districts at the [next] general election". The Australian judges distinguished *Figueroa* on the ground that a requirement of 50 nominated *candidates* was far more onerous than a requirement of 500 *members*; and also because of the different constitutional principles involved. The suggested implication from the words "chosen by the people" was therefore rejected.

Mulholland v Australian Electoral Commission
(2004) 220 CLR 181

Gleeson CJ: [188] A notable feature of our system of representative and responsible government is how little of the detail of that system is to be found in the Constitution, and how much is left to be filled in by Parliament. In *Lange v Australian Broadcasting Corporation* [189 CLR 520 at 557], this Court said that ... the Constitution provides for "the fundamental features of representative government". In other cases, such as *Attorney-General (Cth); Ex rel McKinlay v Commonwealth* [(1975) 135 CLR 1], and *McGinty v Western Australia* [(1996) 186 CLR 140], it was pointed out that representative democracy takes many forms, and that the terms of the Constitution are silent on many matters that are important to the form taken by representative democracy in Australia, at a federal or State level, from time to time.

For example, while, in common with most democracies, Australia now has universal adult suffrage, this was not always so. At the time of the Constitution, most women in Australia did not have the right to vote. Aboriginal Australians have only comprehensively had the vote since 1962. Unlike most democracies, Australia now has a system of compulsory voting, but this did not exist at Federation. Members of the House of Representatives are now elected by a system of preferential voting. In the United Kingdom, as in the House of Representatives in the United States, and the

House of Commons in Canada, members of the House of Commons are elected on a first-past-the-post system. One of the most striking examples of the power given to Parliament to alter, by legislation, the form of our democracy concerns the composition of the Senate. There was a major change in the method of electing senators in 1948. For many years before then, the political party that dominated the House of Representatives usually controlled the Senate. With the introduction of proportional representation in 1948, there came to be a much larger non-government representation in the Senate. Furthermore, a legislative change in 1984, increasing the number of senators from ten per State to twelve per State, when combined with the system of proportional representation, produced the result that it is now unusual for a major party to control the Senate. This is of large political and practical significance. It was the result of legislative, not constitutional, change.

He quoted the contrast drawn by Barwick CJ in *McKinlay* between the Constitutions of the United States and Australia – the former drafted in a spirit of "**[23]** revolt against British institutions and methods of government", the latter "developed not in antagonism to British methods of government but **[24]** in co-operation with and, to a great extent, with the encouragement of the British Government".

Gleeson CJ: [189] That is a useful reminder of historical facts that explain not only what the Constitution says, but also what it does not say. The silence of the Constitution on many matters affecting our system of representative democracy and responsible government has some positive consequences. For example, if then current ideas as to the electoral franchise had been written into the Constitution in 1901, our system might now be at odds with our notions of democracy. The Constitution is, and was meant to be, difficult to amend. Leaving it to Parliament, subject to certain fundamental requirements, to alter the electoral system in response to changing community standards of democracy is a democratic solution to the problem of reconciling the need for basic values with the requirement of flexibility. As to responsible government, the deliberate lack of specificity on the part of the framers of the Constitution concerning the functioning of the executive was seen, in *Re Patterson; Ex parte Taylor* [(2001) 207 CLR 391 at 402-3], as an advantage. Constitutional arrangements on such matters need to be capable of development and adaptability.

Concepts such as representative democracy and responsible government no doubt have an irreducible minimum content, but community **[190]** standards as to their most appropriate forms of expression change over time, and vary from place to place. It is only necessary to consider the differences in the present electoral systems of New South Wales, Tasmania and New Zealand, all of which would be regarded as democratic, to see the point. The system in New South Wales is preferential voting of a kind that is orthodox in Australia. Tasmania has the Hare-Clark electoral system, which is unlike any other State system. New Zealand has changed from a first-past-the-post system to a system under which the Parliament has a number of members elected in single-seat constituencies, and a number elected by proportional representation from the lists of those parties obtaining a sufficient percentage of the national vote.

Federalism itself influenced the form of our government in ways that might be thought by some to depart from "pure democracy", if there is such a thing. Equal State representation in the Senate may be thought, and at the time of Federation was thought by some, to be inconsistent with a concept of voting equality throughout the Commonwealth. Voters in the smallest State ... elect the same number of senators as voters in the largest State. In this respect, the "value" of votes is unequal. That inequality is one aspect of Australian democracy which, exceptionally, is enshrined in the Constitution. Where the Constitution contains an express provision for one form of inequality in the value of votes, it dictates at least some caution in formulating a general implication of equality on that subject ...

[T]he overriding requirement that senators and members of the House of Representatives are to be "directly chosen by the people" ... imposes **[191]** a basic condition of democratic process, but leaves substantial room for parliamentary choice, and for change from time to time. The methods by which the present senators, and members of the House of Representatives, of the Australian Parliament are chosen are significantly different from the methods by which those in earlier Australian parliaments were chosen. Judicial opinion has been divided on the presently irrelevant question as to whether the Constitution guarantees universal suffrage. No one doubts, however, that Parliament had the power, as it did, to prescribe a minimum voting age, and, later, to reduce that age from 21 to 18. Whether Parliament would have the power to fix a maximum voting age is a question that has not yet arisen ...

[T]he respondent, and the Attorney-General of the Commonwealth intervening, accept that the choice required by the Constitution is a true choice with "an opportunity to gain an appreciation of the available alternatives" [*Lange*, 189 CLR at 560, quoting Dawson J in *Australian Capital Television* 177 CLR at 187]. In the course of argument, examples were given of forms of ballot paper prescribed for **[192]** use at elections which might not conform to that fundamental requirement. A ballot paper, for example, that had printed on it only one name, being that of the government candidate, requiring the name of any alternative candidate to be written in (a form not unknown in the past in some places), might so distort the process of choice as to fail to satisfy the test. Here, the rules in question preserve a full and free choice between the competing candidates for election. The electors are presented with a true choice. The available alternatives between candidates are set out on the ballot paper. The process of choice by electors is not impeded or impaired ...

[194] I accept ... that certain kinds or degrees of interference by the Australian Electoral Commission in the political process, including arrangements as to the form of the ballot paper, conceivably could be antithetical to the idea of representative democracy and direct choice. Even so, determining the electoral process in a representative democracy requires regulation of many matters, of major and minor significance, and the Constitution **[195]** gives Parliament a wide range of choice. In the context of a system of registration of political parties eligible to receive the privileges referred to earlier, the imposition of a requirement of some minimum level of support, the fixing of that level at 500 members, and the avoidance of abuse by the no overlap rule, are consistent with the constitutional concept of direct choice by the people and with representative government.

McHugh J: [206] [T]he Constitution prescribes only the irreducible minimum requirements for representative government, including the requirement that senators and members of the House of Representatives be "directly chosen by the people". The Constitution does not prescribe equality of individual voting power. Nor does it protect the secret ballot ...

[207] Hence, the Constitution does not mandate any particular electoral system, and, beyond the limited constitutional requirements outlined above, the form of representative government ... is left to the Parliament. This includes "the type of electoral system, the adoption and size of electoral divisions, and the franchise" [*McGinty*, 186 CLR at 183-4]. As a result, the Parliament may establish an electoral system that includes compulsory voting. It may specify a particular voting method – for example, preferential or proportional voting or first past the post voting [*McGinty* 186 CLR at 244]. It may provide for the election of an unopposed candidate and the election of a candidate on final preferences and may limit voters' ability to cast a formal vote and to vote against a candidate ...

The provisions of the Act that prescribe the "500 rule" and the "no-overlap rule" and confer power on the Commission to administer **[208]** those rules are laws "with respect to" elections. A law of the Parliament is made "with respect to" the subject matter of a power when it relates to or affects that subject matter and the connection is not "so insubstantial, tenuous or distant" that it cannot properly be described as a law with respect to that subject matter [*Re Dingjan; Ex parte Wagner* (1995) 183 CLR 323 at 369]. A law that regulates the method of voting in a federal election is a law with respect to elections, as is a law which protects the electoral or voting system that the Parliament selects. So too is a law that assists in the maintenance of the voting system and protects a particular method of voting ...

[210] The Parliament could reasonably take the view that some – maybe many – voters expect that parties identified on the ballot-paper are real political parties with some degree of public support, a genuine organisational structure and a leader. On that assumption, voters could be misled by a party that is a "front" party or a "decoy" party – that is, a party established only for the purpose of capturing preferences and channelling them to other candidates – or a party that has a very low level of public support. The "500 rule" therefore protects the electoral process by requiring that, before a party name can be placed on the ballot-paper, its sponsors demonstrate a minimum verifiable level of public support. As a result, the "500 rule" minimises voter confusion and prevents voters from being misled by parties with no Parliamentary representation and no substantial membership. Similarly, the object of the "no-overlap rule" is to prevent voters from being misled. It seeks to prevent Parliamentary parties or groups of 500 people from registering multiple parties, each with a "single issue" party name, calculated to catch the eye of voters and to channel preferences to another party (whose policies may be entirely unrelated to the name of the "single issue" party).

Without the challenged provisions, the electoral system is open to manipulation in the manner outlined above, particularly in the context of the Senate list system. The challenged provisions are therefore laws "with respect to" elections for the Senate and the House of Representatives because they have the legitimate objectives of preventing voter confusion or deception and assisting voters to make informed choices as to the person or party for whom they wish to vote ...

[211] Party endorsement on a ballot-paper is an important piece of information that many voters use when making a choice between candidates on their ballots. It is one of the "countless number of other circumstances and considerations" upon which the ability to cast a [212] fully informed vote depends. Because this is so, Mr Mulholland contends that the provisions that prescribe the "500 rule" and the "no-overlap rule" do not permit a "free and informed choice" or a "true choice" or a "fully informed" choice as required by ss 7 and 24. He contends that the restrictions deny voters important information by precluding the inclusion of the party name on the ballot-paper next to the name of a candidate endorsed by an unregistered party ... [T]he result of this denial of important information is that the choice made by voters ceases to be a "true choice", that is, a choice made with all the relevant information required for a meaningful exercise of the franchise in an informed manner. Moreover, because the Act provides for the ballot-paper to show the party endorsement of registered parties and prevents candidates of parties that do not meet the "500 rule" and the "no-overlap rule" from doing the same, Mr Mulholland contends that the Act permits voters to be misled ...

[213] At Federation, the inclusion on ballot-papers of political party endorsement of candidates for the Senate and the House of Representatives was not a requirement of the constitutionally prescribed system of representative government. Although, as long ago as the 18th century, politicians and commentators often referred to "party" in describing factions and adherents of particular policies, the modern political party is very much a 20th century development. It was not until 1983 that party endorsement was included on ballot-papers for federal elections. Nevertheless, the Constitution makes allowance for the "evolutionary nature of [214] representative government". It also recognises that "representative government is a dynamic rather than a static institution and one that has developed in the course of [the 20th] century" [*McGinty*, 186 CLR at 279-80]. It may be that the role of organised political parties and their influence on voters' choices within the Australian system of representative government have both developed to such an extent that that system requires that a candidate have the right to have his or her party endorsement noted on the ballot-paper.

However, even if the present conception of representative government requires recognition of the right of the candidates of genuine parties to have the party's name included on the ballot-paper alongside that of the candidate, it does not follow that every candidate of every "party" has that right.

Legislation enacted with the object of ensuring that voters are not misled by political parties is regulation of the electoral process that "is necessary in order that it may operate effectively" [*Levy v Victoria* (1997) 189 CLR 579 at 608]. The free choice of electors is not assisted by persons registering a single group of members multiple times with eye-catching "single issue" party names for the purpose of channelling preferences to other candidates. The Constitution accommodates the dynamic nature of the institution of representative government "by authorising the legislature to make appropriate provision from time to time" [*McGinty*, 186 CLR at 280-81]. This accords Parliament a broad scope to determine what is "appropriate" – within the boundaries of the constitutionally prescribed system of representative government. It is also open to the Parliament to hold the view that, important though party identification may be, the free choice of electors will be impaired and not improved by party identification of those parties which cannot or will not comply with the challenged provisions. Given previous decisions of the Court that the Constitution prescribes only the irreducible minimum requirements for representative government, the "500 rule" and the "no-overlap rule" fall within the scope of the legislative power of the Commonwealth with respect to elections. They do not infringe the true choice or fully informed choice requirements of the Constitution.

The Court was equally unanimous in rejecting the alternative argument that the provisions were invalid by reason of a "discriminatory" operation against the DLP.

Gleeson CJ: [192] Plainly, the reason for the 500 rule, in the wider context of a system of registered political parties for various purposes relating to the Act (a system which itself is not challenged by the appellant), is the view … that to qualify as a registered political party a group must have a certain minimum level of public support, and that an appropriate minimum level is established by a membership of 500. As to the first part of that, it is reasonably open to Parliament to consider that, bearing in mind the practical significance of political parties in the operation of the democratic process, it would deprive the concept of "party" of any real meaning if any two or more people, who happened to agree on even one issue, could demand recognition as a "party". It may be added, as was pointed out in argument, that in Australia there is a long history of electoral systems which discourage multiplicity of candidates by requiring candidates to deposit a sum of money which will be forfeited if they do not achieve a minimum number of votes. Similarly, there are long-standing requirements for nominations of candidates to be supported by a minimum number of people. Those are well-known forms of regulating candidature at elections which have never been regarded as infringing the electors' right of choice, or as involving unreasonable discrimination. A requirement that, to be eligible to be treated as a political party for the purposes of the Act, a group must have some minimum level of public support, is not materially different. As to the figure of 500, it is, no doubt, to an extent arbitrary, and there is no logical process by which it can be demonstrated that it should be more than, say, 100, or less than (as is the case in New South Wales) 750. Even so, the number 500 is not so large as to be outside the range of choice reasonably available to Parliament if a number is to be chosen at all.

Callinan J: [296] In my opinion the challenged provisions cannot be said to involve any *unreasonable* discrimination. The Constitution itself contemplates discrimination. Some might say that the election of an equal number of senators by each State discriminates against the more populous States. So too, a legislative entitlement to vote at age 18 years, may be thought by some to discriminate against people of 17 years. Lines must be drawn somewhere. The presence in the Constitution of ss 7, 8, 9, 24, 29, 30 and 34 provides a clear indication of the very broad power of the Parliament to make laws drawing those lines. Implicit in the challenged provisions are these propositions: political parties are comprised of people having a common political philosophy; political parties endorse and support candidates subscribing to that philosophy; endorsement by a political party may be a relevant matter **[297]** for electors to know; and, to be a real political party of relevance, entitling it to various privileges, it should have no fewer than 500 members who are not members of other parties. Provisions containing, or based upon those propositions do not discriminate in any unreasonable way against either a party or a candidate for election.

As I have pointed out, [in *Australian Capital Television*] only Mason CJ used the expression "level playing field" [177 CLR at 131]. The legislated rules apply to all in exactly the same way. Any discrimination that may occur, by denying candidates of unregistered parties of 2 to 499 members the same sort of notation on a ballot paper as a candidate endorsed by a registered party of, say 501 members, is to do no more than to draw the sort of line that the Constitution empowers the Parliament to draw, and that line has not been shown to have been unreasonably drawn here. Even if I were to accept that a political surface as true and level as a well-calibrated bowling green was required by the Constitution, I would hold that the Act here substantially provides for it.

5. Eligibility for Election

Section 163 of the *Commonwealth Electoral Act 1918* (Cth) specifies who is eligible to be elected to the federal Parliament.

Commonwealth Electoral Act 1918 (Cth)

163 (1) A person who:

(a) has reached the age of 18 years;

(b) is an Australian citizen; and

(c) is either:

(i)   an elector entitled to vote at a House of Representatives election; or

(ii) a person qualified to become such an elector;

is qualified to be elected as a Senator or a member of the House of Representatives.

The Constitution also places restrictions upon candidates for office. Section 43 provides that: "A member of either House of the Parliament shall be incapable of being chosen or of sitting as a member of the other House". Moreover, any person who falls within the disqualifying categories listed in s 44 of the Constitution "shall be incapable of being chosen or of sitting as a senator or a member of the House of Representatives". Many parliaments constructed on the Westminster model have disqualification provisions broadly similar to those in s 44. For the Commonwealth Parliament, s 44 remained dormant until 1975, when it was wakened in the controversial case of *Re Webster* (1975) 132 CLR 270.

Senator James Webster (Country Party, Victoria) was a shareholder in JJ Webster Pty Ltd, a small family company established by Webster's grandfather in 1920 to control the family's timber business. At the time of the 1974 election, Webster was also the managing director, secretary and manager of the company. At various times in 1973 and 1974 the company had submitted quotations and tenders, accepted offers, and entered into contracts for the supply of timber to Commonwealth departments. Insofar as contractual arrangements had resulted, the issue was whether the senator had "any direct or indirect pecuniary interest in any agreement with the Public Service of the Commonwealth" within the meaning of s 44(v).

Since its inception the High Court has been constituted as a Court of Disputed Returns to hear petitions disputing the validity of election results – initially under ss 192-193 of the *Commonwealth Electoral Act 1902* (Cth) (see *Chanter v Blackwood* (1904) 1 CLR 39) and now under ss 353-354 of the *Commonwealth Electoral Act 1918* (Cth). The legislation also provides (currently by s 376) that questions of qualification for election "may be referred by resolution to the Court of Disputed Returns by the House in which the question arises". The question of Senator Webster's position was referred in this way by the Senate.

A preliminary hearing took place before Barwick CJ, who initially proposed to refer the issue to the Full Court but then resolved to decide it himself by sitting as a single judge. In due course he held that Webster was not disqualified under s 44(v). Applying the rules of contract law relating to offer and acceptance, he held that each quotation submitted by the company was an offer, that acceptance occurred each time the government placed an order, that each such acceptance gave rise to a separate contract relating to that particular order, and that none of these separate contracts attracted the provisions of s 44(v).

Re Webster

(1975) 132 CLR 270

Barwick CJ: [279] The disqualification under s 44(v) as effected by s 45 of the Constitution, is automatic and does not depend upon a decision of the House or of the Court of Disputed Returns, though means are there provided of resolving the facts and their legal consequences. There being penal consequences of its breach, the paragraph should receive a strict construction.

Because of the evident purpose of the disqualification provision, it applies only to executory contracts, that is to say, to contracts under which at the relevant time something remains to be done by the contractor in performance of the contract … For the same reason, it has been said that "What are meant to be covered" (ie, by 22 Geo III c 45) "are contracts of a more permanent or continuing and lasting character, the holding and enjoying of which might improperly influence the action both of legislators and the Government": per Low J in *Tranton v Astor* [(1917) 33 TLR 383 at 386]. In somewhat the same vein, Montague Smith J in *Royse v Birley* [(1869) LR 5 CP 296 at 317] thought that what was contemplated was "a contract which would endure for some period of time" during which something remained to be done by the contractor. True it is that both **[280]** these judges were influenced to some extent by the presence in the statutes with which they were concerned of a disqualification which was "during the time" that the contractor held the contract. But, in my opinion, this requirement of something more than a "casual or transient" contract in order to found a disqualification, springs out of the purpose of the statute, in this case the Constitution, creating the disqualification.

It seems to me that, upon the proper construction of the paragraph, bearing in mind the purpose of its presence in the Constitution, the agreement to fall within the scope of s 44(v) must have a currency for a substantial period of time, and must be one under which the Crown could conceivably influence the contractor in relation to parliamentary affairs by the very existence of the agreement, or by something done or refrained from being done in relation to the contract or to its subject matter, whether or not that act or omission is within the terms of the contract. In the climate of the eighteenth century, the likelihood of such influence upon a government contractor could well be thought to be high. Accordingly, the mere existence of a supply contract justified the disqualification. But in modern business and departmental conditions the possibility of influence by the Crown is not so apparent: whilst it need not be certain, at least it must be conceivable, and in any case the possibility will arise from the continuing nature of the agreement. Further, it seems to me that the interest in the agreement of the person said to be disqualified must be pecuniary in the sense that through the possibility of financial gain by the existence or the performance of the agreement, that person could conceivably be influenced by the Crown in relation to Parliamentary affairs.

Whilst I am bound to say that I can point to no authoritative decision interpreting this section or its progenitors in this particular sense, I can say that, having carefully examined the decisions which have been given, I do not find any which would deny that interpretation. But, in my opinion, what I have said expresses the proper meaning and scope of s 44(v).

There would probably be little dissent from the general view of Barwick CJ that the purpose of s 44(v) has been superseded, that its wording is obscure and anachronistic and that its application should therefore be narrowly confined. Indeed, similar comments can be made about most of the disqualification provisions in s 44. Nonetheless, his decision not to refer *Webster's Case* to a larger bench attracted much criticism.

An immediate response to *Webster's Case* was the *Common Informers (Parliamentary Disqualifications) Act 1975* (Cth), which substituted far more modest penalties for those set out in s 46 of the Constitution. There was also immediate bipartisan agreement on the need for more substantive changes to s 44 itself. However, any further progress in this direction was overtaken by the political events of 1975 (see Chapter 12, §3). In 1981, the Senate Standing Committee on Constitutional and Legal Affairs produced a report, entitled *The Constitutional Qualifications of Members of Parliament* (Parliamentary Paper No 131 of 1981), which explored the ambiguities and anomalies of s 44 and recommended a package of reforms, including a proposal that some of its provisions, such as s 44(iii), be eliminated. No attempt has been made to implement this report.

In *Re Wood* (1988) 167 CLR 145, the High Court gave a clear warning. At the federal election of 11 July 1987, Robert Wood was elected as a senator for New South Wales. His election was challenged on the ground that he was a British citizen. The High Court, as the Court of Disputed Returns, held that Wood had not been validly elected, but that the election was not void as the problem could be solved by a further distribution of preferences. Wood's incapacity flowed simply from s 163(1)(b) of the *Commonwealth Electoral Act*, which requires that to be elected a person must be an Australian citizen. This statutory ground enabled the Court to avoid the problem of s 44(i) of the Constitution. The joint judgment added:

Re Wood
(1988) 167 CLR 145

The Court: [169] In answering these questions, it has not been necessary to determine whether Senator Wood was incapable of being chosen or of sitting as a senator by reason of the provisions of s 44(i) of the Constitution. The interpretation of s 44(i) and its applicability to an Australian citizen, who is also a citizen or who may, conceivably against his own wishes, be "entitled to the rights or privileges of … a citizen" of the United Kingdom or of countries other than Australia, are questions of great contemporary importance. As those questions were not fully argued, their resolution must be left for another day.

In *Sykes v Cleary* (1992) 176 CLR 77, that day arrived. At a federal by-election on 11 April 1992, Phil Cleary, an Independent, was elected to the seat of Wills, which had been held by former Prime Minister Bob Hawke. The Liberal Party candidate was John Delacretaz and the Labor Party candidate was Bill Kardamitsis.

Cleary had been a secondary school teacher employed by the Victorian Education Department under the *Teaching Service Act 1981* (Vic). Except for two days, he had been on leave without pay since 1 February 1990. He lodged his nomination for the seat of Wills on 20 March 1992. On the day of the election, 11 April 1992, he was still on leave without pay. The declaration of the poll, that is, the announcement of the winner of the poll, was held on 23 April 1992. However, earlier scrutineering left no doubt that Cleary had won. On 16 April 1992, he therefore resigned from the teaching service. Nevertheless, both on the day that he lodged his nomination and on election day, he was an "officer" under the *Teaching Service Act*. On this basis, the High Court unanimously held that Cleary held an "office of profit under the Crown" within the meaning of s 44(iv); and by 6:1, with Deane J dissenting, that he was incapable of being chosen or of sitting as a member of the House of Representatives.

Sykes v Cleary
(1992) 176 CLR 77

Mason CJ, Toohey and McHugh JJ: [95] The meaning of the expression "office of profit under the Crown" is obscure. Blackstone defined an "office" as "a right to exercise a public or private employment" and to take the "fees and emoluments thereunto belonging". Blackstone had in mind offices to which particular duties were attached and which entitled the holder to charge and retain fees for the performance of the services rendered by the office-holder.

It has been accepted in England that the disqualification of the holder of an "office of profit under the Crown" excludes permanent public servants, being officers of the departments of government, from membership of the House of Commons. Likewise, it has been accepted in Australia that a provision for disqualification expressed in the same terms excludes public servants, who are officers of the departments of government, from membership of the legislature. The exclusion of public servants from membership **[96]** of the House contributes to their exclusion from active and public participation in party politics. In this way, the disqualification played an important part in the development of the old tradition of a politically neutral public service.

The exclusion of permanent officers of the executive government from the House was a recognition of the incompatibility of a person at the one time holding such an office and being a member of the House. There are three factors that give rise to that incompatibility. First, performance by a public servant of his or her public service duties would impair his or her capacity to attend to the duties of a member of the House. Secondly, there is a very considerable risk that a public servant would share the political opinions of the Minister of his or her department and would not bring to bear as a member of the House a free and independent judgment. Thirdly, membership of the House would detract from the performance of the relevant public service duty.

The first respondent contends that the objects sought to be achieved by the disqualification of the holder of an "office of profit under the Crown" would sufficiently be served by confining the category of office-holders disqualified to that consisting of those who hold important or senior positions in government. History provides no support for this interpretation which would, in any event, fail to give effect to all the considerations or policies said to underlie the disqualification. In order to give effect to those considerations, the disqualification must be understood as embracing at least those persons who are permanently employed by government.

The first respondent seeks to find support for the interpretation for which he contends in judicial decisions relating to the word "office" in the context of revenue legislation. Thus, in *Grealy v Federal Commissioner of Taxation* [(1989) 24 FCR 405 at 411], the Full Court of the Federal Court said the word "usually connotes a position of defined authority in an organization, such as director of a company or tertiary educational body, president of a club or holder of a position with statutory powers". In other cases, it has been held that the word signifies a subsisting permanent substantive position which exists independently of the person who fills it from time to time. However, the meaning of "office" turns largely on the **[97]** context in which it is found and, in the light of the principal mischief which s 44(iv) and its predecessors were directed at eliminating or reducing, namely, Crown or executive influence over the House, such a restricted meaning cannot be given to "office" in s 44(iv).

Although a teacher is not an instance of the archetypical public servant at whom the disqualification was primarily aimed, a permanent public servant who is a teacher falls within the categories of public servants whose public service duties are incompatible, on the three grounds mentioned previously, with the duties of a member of the House of Representatives or of a senator. In this respect, the first respondent was a person who came within the statutory definition of "teachers", ie, "permanent officers employed in the [teaching] service". As such a permanent officer in the teaching service, he held an "office". So much may be deduced from the statutory definitions of "officer" and "employé", the latter connoting a temporary employee. Indeed, this was conceded in argument ...

Where an office in the teaching service is abolished, the holder of the office becomes an "unattached officer" and shall be deployed by the Chief General Manager to any other office which the Chief General Manager deems appropriate but, because "officer" is defined as meaning any person who holds an office, this does not mean that an "unattached" officer holds no office. And, even if the effect of the legislation is that an unattached officer ceases to hold an office within the meaning of the 1981 Act, the officer nonetheless remains a permanent employee of the Crown and is, for the purposes of s 44(iv), the holder of an office of profit under the Crown.

The taking of leave without pay by a person who holds an office of profit under the Crown does not alter the character of the office which he or she holds. The person remains the holder of an office, **[98]** notwithstanding that he or she is not in receipt of pay during the period of leave.

Application to office of profit under the Crown in right of a State
The reference in s 44(iv) to "*any* office of profit under the Crown" (emphasis added) is apt to include an office of profit under the Crown in right of a State. Not only are the words wide enough to achieve this result but also the last paragraph of the section proceeds on the footing that, but for that paragraph, a State Minister would hold an office of profit under the Crown in right of a State and be disqualified. If such an office of profit in a State stood outside s 44(iv), there would have been no need to exclude State Ministers from the disqualification. The Convention Debates reveal that the exclusion of State Ministers from the disqualification was put forward because it was believed that State Ministers otherwise would be disqualified because each of them was relevantly the holder of an office of profit under the Crown. The exclusion of State Ministers from the disqualification was designed to ensure their availability for election at the inception of the Commonwealth Parliament. The exclusion in the last paragraph of s 44 of those receiving certain payments as officers or members of the Queen's navy or army proceeded likewise on the footing that otherwise s 44(iv) would disqualify such persons. Both the text of s 44(iv) and the reason for the inclusion of the last paragraph in the section support the opinion of the commentators that the disqualification extends to State officers.

Moreover, the long-standing reasons for disqualifying Commonwealth public servants from membership of the Houses of Parliament have similar force in relation to State public servants. The risk of a conflict between their obligations to their State and their duties as members of the House to which they belong is a further incident of the incompatibility of being, at the same time, a State public servant and a member of the Parliament.

It follows that the first respondent, as the holder of an office of profit under the Crown, fell within s 44(iv) until he resigned that office on 16 April 1992.

The Commonwealth Solicitor-General, Gavan Griffith QC, argued that Cleary's position was saved by his resignation on 16 April 1992, as the question whether he was "incapable of being chosen" had to be answered at the point of time when he was "chosen". That time, it was argued, was the formal declaration of the poll. Since that occurred on 23 April 1992, one week after Cleary's resignation, he was not at that time the holder of an "office of profit under the Crown". It was on this basis that Deane J decided in Cleary's favour. However, the other six judges took a different view. They held that the expression "being chosen" in s 44 refers not to the declaration of the poll, nor even to the election day, but to the entire "**[100]** process of being chosen, of which nomination is an essential part". Thus, Cleary could only have avoided the operation of s 44(iv) by resigning before lodging his nomination on 20 March 1992.

It followed from the decision as to Cleary's position that the election for the seat of Wills was void and could not be cured by a recount. There had to be a fresh election. As both Kardamitsis and Delacretaz were again likely to be candidates, the Court considered their position as well. The facts as to these two candidates were summarised as follows:

Mason CJ, Toohey and McHugh JJ: [103] *Second respondent: facts*

The second respondent, Mr Delacretaz, was born in Switzerland on 15 December 1923 and, from the time of his birth, was a Swiss citizen. He migrated to Australia on 13 June 1951 and has lived in Australia since then. On 20 April 1960 he became naturalized as an Australian citizen pursuant to Div 3 of Pt III of the *Nationality and Citizenship Act* 1948 (Cth). In so doing, he renounced all allegiance to any sovereign or State of whom or of which he was a subject or citizen and took an oath of allegiance to Her Majesty the Queen, by which he swore to "be faithful and bear true allegiance to Her Majesty Queen Elizabeth the Second, her heirs and successors according to law" and "faithfully [to] observe the laws of Australia and fulfil [his] duties as an Australian Citizen".

However, he did not at any time make application to the Government of Switzerland to renounce or otherwise terminate his Swiss citizenship. He has held an Australian passport since 1960 and it is still current. He holds no other passport.

Under the law of Switzerland, a Swiss citizen will be released from his or her citizenship upon his or her demand if he or she has no residence in Switzerland and has acquired another nationality. The second respondent has made no such demand and is and was at all material times under the law of Switzerland a Swiss citizen and entitled to a Swiss passport to enter Switzerland without restriction and to reside in that country.

Third respondent: facts

The third respondent, Mr Kardamitsis, was born in Greece on 2 July 1952 and, from the time of his birth, was a Greek citizen. He came to Australia in 1969 as a migrant sponsored by his brother and has lived in Australia since then.

On 12 March 1975, he became an Australian citizen pursuant to Div 2 of Pt III of the *Australian Citizenship Act* 1948 (Cth). In so doing, he renounced all other allegiance and swore the oath of allegiance in a form similar to, but not identical with, that sworn by the second respondent. He did not at any time make application to the Government of Greece to discharge his Greek nationality.

When he became an Australian citizen, he surrendered a Greek passport which he then held. It had expired one or two years after he had migrated to Australia. Between 1969 and 1978, he did not **[104]** travel out of Australia. He was issued with an Australian passport on 24 April 1978, which was valid for five years, and a further Australian passport on 21 May 1987, which was valid for ten years and is still current. He entered Greece on his Australian passport for a holiday in 1978 and in 1987, and for the funeral of his mother in 1979 and of his father in 1990.

He has never received any social security or other like benefits from the Government of Greece. He has never stood for office in Greece or voted or been recorded as a voter in an election in Greece.

Since leaving Greece, he has not, to his knowledge, done any act, made any statement or acted in any manner which would place him under any acknowledgment of allegiance, obedience or adherence to Greece or any other foreign power. In becoming an Australian citizen, he took a conscious and serious step which he believed involved his breaking his bond of allegiance with Greece and his establishing a new bond of allegiance with Australia. He has habitually resided in Australia since leaving Greece. The centre of his interests is Australia, not Greece. His principal family ties are with Australia, not Greece. He has participated in public life in Australia and seeks further such participation. He has had no such participation in Greece and seeks none. He has a bond of attachment with Australia and not with Greece (except that Greece is part of his personal history), and he has inculcated the same bond in his children. Save that he has visited Greece on several occasions and that he has some family and friends in Greece, he has severed his links with Greece to the extent that any citizen of Greece can without applying to discharge his or her Greek citizenship.

Under the law of Greece, a Greek national will have his or her Greek nationality discharged if (a) he or she has acquired the nationality of another country with the permission of the appropriate Greek Minister; or (b) he or she has acquired the nationality of another country and later obtains the approval of the appropriate Greek Minister for the discharge of his or her Greek nationality. In the latter case, the discharge of Greek nationality becomes effective as from the date of the Greek Minister's approval … The third respondent has not sought to have his Greek nationality discharged and, accordingly, under the law of Greece, he is and was at all material times a Greek national.

Mason CJ, Toohey and McHugh JJ held, with Brennan and Dawson JJ agreeing, that since neither Kardamitsis nor Delacretaz had taken every possible step to divest themselves of foreign citizenship they remained "entitled to the rights or privileges of a subject or a citizen of a foreign power" within the meaning of s 44(i). They were therefore incapable of being chosen or of sitting as members of the House of Representatives. The joint judgment did not, however, leave the question of foreign citizenship to be determined entirely by the law of the foreign state concerned, as traditional international law would require.

Mason CJ, Toohey and McHugh JJ: [107] [T]here is no reason why s 44(i) should be read as if it were intended to give unqualified effect to that rule of international law. To do so might well result in the disqualification of Australian citizens on whom there was imposed involuntarily by operation of foreign law a continuing foreign nationality, notwithstanding that they had taken reasonable steps to renounce that foreign nationality. It would be wrong to interpret the constitutional provision in such a way as to disbar an Australian citizen who had taken all reasonable steps to divest himself or herself of any conflicting allegiance. It has been said that the provision was designed to ensure: "that members of Parliament did not have a split allegiance and were not, as far as possible, subject to any improper influence from foreign governments." What is more, s 44(i) finds its place in a Constitution which was enacted at a time, like the present, when a high proportion of Australians, though born overseas, had adopted this country as their home. In that setting, it could scarcely have been intended to disqualify an Australian citizen for election to Parliament on account of his or her continuing to possess a foreign nationality, notwithstanding that he or she had taken reasonable steps to renounce that nationality. In this respect it is significant that s 42 of the Constitution requires a member of Parliament to take **[108]** an oath or affirmation of allegiance in the form set out in the schedule to the Constitution.

What amounts to the taking of reasonable steps to renounce foreign nationality must depend upon the circumstances of the particular case. What is reasonable will turn on the situation of the individual, the requirements of the foreign law and the extent of the connexion between the individual and the foreign State of which he or she is alleged to be a subject or citizen. And it is relevant to bear in mind that a person who has participated in an Australian naturalization ceremony in which he or she has expressly renounced his or her foreign allegiance may well believe that, by becoming an Australian citizen, he or she has effectively renounced any foreign nationality.

Deane and Gaudron JJ dissented. Gaudron J argued that the matter should be considered solely within the framework of Australian law. Within that framework the two men had each been through a naturalisation ceremony "renouncing all other allegiance". Whether the law of Greece or Switzerland accepted the efficacy of that renunciation was, in her view, irrelevant.

In *Free v Kelly* (1996) 185 CLR 296 it was ultimately conceded that s 44(iv), as interpreted in *Sykes v Cleary*, must also result in the disqualification of Jackie Kelly, who had been elected in March 1996 as the Liberal member for Lindsay and at the time of her nomination had been an officer of the Royal Australian Air Force. That result led to two further inquiries (see Joint Standing Committee on Electoral Matters, *Report of the Inquiry into all Aspects of the Conduct of the 1996 Federal Election and Matters Related Thereto* (Parliamentary Paper No 93 of 1997), Ch 6; House of Representatives Standing Committee on Legal and Constitutional Affairs, *Aspects of Section 44 of the Australian Constitution* (Parliamentary Paper No 85 of 1997)). Both inquiries recommended substantial amendment of s 44.

At the October 1998 federal election, Heather Hill, standing on behalf of Pauline Hanson's One Nation Party, was elected as a senator for Queensland. Hill was born in the United Kingdom in 1960 (and thereby gained British citizenship) and migrated to Australia in 1971. In January 1998 she was granted Australian citizenship. The *Australian Citizenship Act 1948* (Cth) contained no requirement for the renunciation of foreign citizenship. She was only required to pledge her "loyalty to Australia and its people, whose democratic beliefs I share, whose rights and liberties I respect, and whose laws I will uphold and obey". It was not until November 1998 (after her election) that Hill became aware of steps that could be taken to renounce her British citizenship. She contacted the British High Commission, completed a declaration of renunciation, paid a fee of $135 and handed over her British passport.

Two petitioners challenged Hill's election on the basis that, at the time of her nomination, she did not satisfy the requirements of s 44(i) of the Constitution. The central issue was whether the United Kingdom was "a foreign power" under that section. Gleeson CJ, Gaudron, Gummow and Hayne JJ held that it was, and that Hill had not been duly elected (see the extract in Chapter 4, §8).

The reason why McHugh, Kirby and Callinan JJ reached no conclusion on the operation of s 44(i) was that they accepted a threshold challenge to the High Court's capacity to determine the question in proceedings instituted by petition. They held that the *Commonwealth Electoral Act 1918* (Cth) did not confer jurisdiction upon the Court, sitting as the Court of Disputed Returns, to determine such an issue. According to McHugh J, the question could be raised *only* "**[532]** on a referral by one of the Houses of Parliament" or "incidentally in determining whether an election should be set aside on the ground that the elected person has committed an 'illegal practice' by falsely declaring that he or she was" qualified to be elected.

This conclusion depended upon the interpretation of ss 353 and 354 of the *Commonwealth Electoral Act*. Section 353 provided that "[t]he validity of any election or return may be disputed by petition addressed to the Court of Disputed Returns and not otherwise". Section 354 constituted the High Court as "the Court of Disputed Returns"; conferred upon it jurisdiction to try the petitions referred to in s 353; and endowed it ("in respect of the petition") with "all the powers and functions of the Court of Disputed Returns". The question was whether these provisions could be read as including a grant of power to receive and determine petitions raising issues of disqualification under s 44 of the Constitution.

The Constitution provides its own mechanism for determining such issues by s 47, which provides that: "Until the Parliament otherwise provides, any question respecting the qualification of a senator or of a member of the House of Representatives ..., and any question of a disputed election to either House, shall be determined by the House in which the question arises". In respect of "any question of a disputed election" the Parliament has "otherwise provided" by ss 353 and 354 of the Electoral Act. In respect of "any question respecting ... qualification", it has "otherwise provided" by s 376.

Commonwealth Electoral Act 1918 (Cth)

376 Any question respecting the qualifications of a Senator or of a Member of the House of Representatives or respecting a vacancy in either House of the Parliament may be referred by resolution to the Court of Disputed Returns by the House in which the question arises and the Court of Disputed Returns shall thereupon have jurisdiction to hear and determine the question.

The immediate question in *Sue v Hill* was whether s 376 is intended to provide the *only* way of raising issues of disqualification in the High Court; or whether the words of ss 353 and 354 are wide enough to permit such a question to be raised by petition. Both mechanisms (that of ss 353-354 and s 376) are contained in Pt XXII of the Electoral Act, but the former mechanism is contained in Div 1 and the latter in Div 2. The argument which McHugh, Kirby and Callinan JJ accepted was that the two provisions were mutually exclusive.

Lurking behind that issue was another question, which the conflicting judgments do not directly resolve. As to "question[s] of a disputed election" it is clear that the mechanism now provided by ss 353-354 has excluded any continuing possibility of the Houses of Parliament resolving such issues for themselves under s 47 of the Constitution: s 353 provides that such issues may be dealt with by petition "and not otherwise". But as to "question[s] respecting ... qualification" the words "and not otherwise" do not appear in s 376, which says only that the issue "*may* be referred by resolution to the Court of Disputed Returns". Does that mean that, while s 376 gives each House the option of referring such issues to the High Court as a Court of Disputed Returns, each House also retains the option of determining such issues for itself, by reason of a continuing operation of s 47 of the Constitution?

This question arose in an acute form two weeks before the judgments in *Sue v Hill* were delivered, when the federal Opposition argued that Warren Entsch, parliamentary secretary to the Minister for Industry, was disqualified from continuing to sit in the House of Representatives. He held an interest in a private company, Cape York Concrete, which had won a $175,000 contract to supply concrete for an RAAF base. It was alleged that this amounted to a "pecuniary interest in any agreement with the Public Service of the Commonwealth" within the meaning of s 44(v) of the Constitution. The Opposition requested the Prime Minister to refer the matter to the High Court under s 376, but that request was refused. On 10 June 1999 the House of Representatives purported to determine the issue itself under s 47 of the Constitution by resolving (on the motion of Attorney-General Daryl Williams) that Entsch "does not have any direct or indirect pecuniary interest with the Public Service of the Commonwealth ... by reason of any contract entered into by Cape York Concrete" and was therefore "not incapable of sitting as a member of this House" (House of Representatives, *Parliamentary Debates* (*Hansard*), 10 June 1999, 6724). Whether the House in fact has power to pass such a resolution depends on whether s 376 of the *Electoral Act* has excluded its continuing power to do so, or has merely provided an alternative path that the House may use if it so chooses.

Whether the majority judgments in *Sue v Hill* have oblique implications for this question has been a matter for debate. What those judgments do determine (albeit only by a 4:3 majority) is that the "referral" mechanism in s 376 of the Act is not exclusive of the possibility that such issues may also be raised by petition under ss 353-354. As to the continuing effect of s 47 of the Constitution, the joint judgment of Gleeson CJ, Gummow and Hayne JJ offered only a cryptic reference to "**[480]** an argument in terrorem".

Sue v Hill
(1999) 199 CLR 462

Gleeson CJ, Gummow and Hayne JJ: [480] It was suggested that the situation might arise where, whilst there was pending a petition under Div 1 challenging an election by reason of constitutional ineligibility of the Senator or Member in question, that Senator or Member might take his or her seat and that, despite the pendency of the petition, the relevant chamber could proceed to determine the qualification itself without waiting for the determination of the petition and without making a reference under Div 2. However, questions respecting the exercise by the chambers of the Parliament of their constitutional authority bestowed by s 47 of the Constitution are not to be approached by reference to some distorting possibility.

At the least this seems to suggest that, if the relevant House of Parliament does still have power to answer such a question for itself under s 47 of the Constitution, the fact that it has already done so might not deter the High Court from giving a different answer in response to a petition under ss 353-354 of the Act.

Because the four majority judges held, as a matter of construction, that the petitions fell within the Court's jurisdiction under ss 353-354 of the Act, they had then to confront the further submission (as to which the three dissenting judges again expressed no opinion) that such a conferral of jurisdiction was itself unconstitutional. This involved a suggestion that particular functions of Courts of Disputed Returns are not of a "judicial" nature, and hence cannot validly be conferred upon a Ch III court. The main argument was that since *all* such functions are incidental or ancillary to the working of legislative institutions, they must be regarded as incidents of "legislative power" (and thus not of "judicial power"). The argument, resting on dicta in *Holmes v Angwin* (1906) 4 CLR 297, was rejected by the four majority judges. Gleeson CJ, Gummow and Hayne JJ concluded that: "**[484]** There is nothing in the nature of the resolution of disputed elections which places such controversies necessarily outside the exercise of the judicial power of the Commonwealth".

6. Resolving Deadlocks

Section 57 of the Constitution provides a means for resolving deadlocks between the House of Representatives and the Senate. It permits a double dissolution election and thereafter (if the deadlock persists) a joint sitting of both Houses, in effect as an alternative to the ordinary law-making process. A double dissolution election is called where the Prime Minister advises the Governor-General that, because of the Senate's failure to pass a Bill, both the House of Representatives and the whole of the Senate should be dissolved and a new election held (in contrast to the normal procedure under s 13 of the Constitution, whereby only half of the senators are elected at any particular time).

The procedure is designed to counterbalance the power of a hostile Senate to obstruct a government's legislative program. South Australia, Victoria and New South Wales have adopted broadly equivalent procedures, always with a similar purpose (see Chapter 11, §4). Normally, in the Westminster system the entitlement to govern is determined by voting strength in the lower House, and the Premier or Prime Minister is that person who is able to win a vote of confidence in that House. Consistently with the dominant role of the lower House in this respect, an upper House may usefully serve as a "House of review", that is, as a deliberative chamber subjecting legislative proposals to careful independent scrutiny. Beyond this, however, it is sometimes argued that a determined government should be able to implement its legislative program in spite of upper House opposition, and the s 57 machinery is perceived as intended to ensure that in practice (though not as a logical inevitability) this will be achieved.

Under s 57, there have been six double dissolutions of the Commonwealth Parliament – in 1914, 1951, 1974, 1975, 1983 and 1987. Only in 1974, however, was the double dissolution followed by a joint sitting of both Houses of Parliament. Both before and after the joint sitting in 1974, the Whitlam government's reliance on s 57 was tested in the High Court in a series of cases which, apart from particular issues of detail, raised the fundamental question of whether the provisions of s 57 are justiciable. Though the Court never reached unanimity on that issue, the majority view, reinforced by the practical effect of these decisions, was that compliance or non-compliance with the requirements of s 57 can be judicially determined, and that a finding of non-compliance will result in invalidity.

The 1974 double dissolution was granted by the Governor-General, Sir Paul Hasluck, on 11 April 1974. The ensuing election was held on 18 May 1974. The joint sitting was convened by the new Governor-General, Sir John Kerr, for 6 August 1974. On 1 August 1974, two Liberal Party senators sued in the High Court for declarations and injunctions to prevent the joint sitting from proceeding. The matter was argued before six judges of the High Court on 5 August 1974, with judgment being given orally late that afternoon.

Six Bills had been relied on as "triggers" for the 1974 double dissolution. Three, including the Senate (Representation of Territories) Bill 1973, related to electoral matters; two were Bills to establish the Medibank health scheme; and the sixth was the Petroleum and Minerals Authority Bill 1973 (the PMA Bill). Hasluck's proclamation dissolving the Parliament had recited that the conditions for a double dissolution "have been fulfilled" in respect of all of these Bills. Kerr's proclamation convening the joint sitting had included a similar recital, and had further proclaimed that at the joint sitting the members present "may deliberate" and "shall vote together" upon "each of" the six Bills. The plaintiffs argued that both proclamations were invalid, and hence that the joint sitting had not been validly convened. All six judges held that the High Court either would not or could not intervene at that stage to prevent the joint sitting. The joint sitting accordingly went ahead on 6-7 August 1974, and passed all six Bills.

One reason for the alleged invalidity of the proclamations was that each had specified six Bills as the basis for resort to s 57, whereas, it was argued, s 57 speaks throughout in the singular number of "any proposed law" or "the proposed law", and should therefore only be used in respect of one proposed law at a time. The Court rejected this argument.

Cormack v Cope
(1974) 131 CLR 432

Barwick CJ: [455] [I]t seems to me there is no need for any change in the language **[456]** of the section in order to justify a joint sitting discussing and voting upon more than one proposed law which has satisfied the prescription of the first paragraph of s 57. Because the proposed law must be identified with its earlier history, its earlier parliamentary history, it is of course necessary to use the singular. But there is nothing in the section, or in the evident reasons for its enactment which requires that only one proposed law should be so discussed and voted upon.

I have already indicated that the double dissolution is not granted in relation to or in respect of a particular law or, for that matter, particular laws. It is simply granted. The Houses are both dissolved. It is the second and third paragraphs of s 57 which control what is to happen after double dissolution in the law-making process, and it is the third paragraph which determines what shall be deliberated and voted upon at the joint sitting. Therefore, if this submission of the plaintiffs is to be made good one would need to find in the third paragraph of s 57 a limitation on the number of proposed laws which could be the subject of deliberation and voting at the joint sitting. I find no such limitation, and in particular I do not find it from the circumstance that the singular is used in describing what may be the subject of deliberation and voting. Indeed, it could not be otherwise because each proposed law as a unit in itself has to answer the prescription of the earlier part of s 57 and, in my opinion, could only be referred to as "the proposed law". The same can be said of each successive proposed law which is sought to be made the subject of deliberation and voting at the joint sitting.

I am quite conscious of the fact that such a view of s 57 leaves open the possibility that, as it were, a storehouse of proposed laws could be built up during the life of a Parliament so that after a double dissolution they might be presented at the one time to a joint sitting, thus making a considerable inroad upon the basic concept of the Constitution which provides for a bicameral system of Parliament. But whilst this is perhaps a possibility, it seems to me it is not to be prevented by what to my mind would not be merely a strained but an unwarranted construction of s 57. The control of such a possibility might lie in the formation and observance of parliamentary conventions designed to implement the spirit of parliamentary government as under the Constitution.

Menzies, Gibbs, Stephen and Mason JJ agreed.

The other main challenge to the two proclamations was that each of them had specifically relied on the PMA Bill. It was argued that the Bill had not satisfied the requirements of s 57 because when it was first considered by the Senate the Senate had not "failed to pass" it. What had happened was that on 13 December 1973 the Senate had adjourned the debate on the PMA Bill to be resumed when the Senate was to sit again in February 1974. As it happened, the Parliament was prorogued on 14 February 1974 and did not sit again until March 1974. On whether the adjournment on 13 December 1973 amounted to a "failure to pass", only Barwick CJ expressed a firm opinion. Gibbs and Mason JJ expressly refused to do so, while Stephen and Menzies JJ argued that the question was a matter for another day.

> **Menzies J: [463]** A particular point was taken in relation to the proposed law intituled Petroleum and Minerals Authority Act 1973. It was contended in respect of this proposed law that the conditions set out in the first paragraph of s 57 had not been complied with. If so, that proposed law should not have been taken into account by His Excellency the Governor-General, Sir Paul Hasluck, in granting a double dissolution and His Excellency the Governor-General, Sir John Kerr, was in error in proclaiming that the joint sitting may deliberate and shall vote upon it. Counsel for the State of New South Wales indicated that there may be other laws upon which the conditions provided by s 57 had not been complied with. However, as I have already indicated, that part of the proclamation naming the proposed laws to be deliberated and voted upon was surplusage and it cannot be regarded as any justification in law for the joint sitting deliberating and voting thereon. If such a proposed law is affirmed, and it is the case that the conditions set out in the first part of s 57 were not fulfilled with respect to it, the question of the validity of that law may become a question for this Court at a later time. If it does, the terms of the proclamation will not be relevant to the decision of that question. It will, in my opinion, be decided upon a determination of what happened in the Houses of Parliament – an inquiry which, upon a challenge to the validity of a law, this Court is competent to undertake ...
>
> **[464]** It should be added that it is not for the members of the Senate and the House of Representatives to decide whether or not a proposed law affirmed at a joint sitting has been enacted as a law. If and when the proposed law has been affirmed by the majority required by the section and has been assented to, it is open to challenge in the courts on the ground that it was not duly enacted because of non-compliance with the conditions which s 57 requires to be fulfilled. Non-compliance with constitutional requirements for the making of laws spells invalidity.

Barwick CJ was satisfied that the PMA Bill had not complied with the requirements of s 57. Moreover, he was not prepared to find that the reference to the Bill was mere "**[463]** surplusage", as Menzies J had done. Barwick CJ held that the reference to the PMA Bill rendered the Governor-General's proclamation void; that it followed that any proceedings at the joint sitting would also be void; and that in appropriate circumstances the Court would have both the power and the duty to so declare. However, even he thought it inappropriate to issue an injunction based upon these views in the context of the interlocutory hearing on 5 August 1974.

> **Barwick CJ: [456]** I turn now to the submission which has given me a great deal of difficulty. One part of the submission, however, is relatively clear. It **[457]** is said that in respect of the Petroleum and Minerals Authority Act 1973, the requisite interval of three months between the rejection by the Senate and the second passage of the bill by the House of Representatives did not elapse. In my opinion, the commencing point for the calculation of the interval of three months which the first paragraph of s 57 prescribes is the time when the Senate rejected the proposed law. No doubt there may be circumstances in which a decision of the precise date on which the Senate did so reject the proposed law would be difficult, but that is no reason for not adopting what is to my mind the proper construction of the section. It is clear enough that the event which begins the possibility of the use of the law-making process of s 57 is the Senate's rejection of the proposed law. I do not see any relevance to that law-making process of the date of the passage initially of a proposed law by the House of Representatives.
>
> Here the interlocutory nature of the proceedings obtrudes itself. If this were the hearing of a suit and the evidence stood as it stands now, I would have little difficulty in finding that in fact the proposed law consisting of the Petroleum and Minerals Authority Act 1973 did not qualify as a

proposed law which could be deliberated and voted upon in a joint sitting of the House under s 57. But this is not the final hearing and there was a claim made by the Attorney-General that issues of fact had yet to be examined ...

[459] I have given the question of the validity of the proclamation my **[460]** anxious consideration during the hearing of this matter and in the intervals of time for which it stood adjourned. I have no doubt the proclamation in terms goes beyond what s 57 empowers the Governor-General to do. The question ... is whether what I regard as an excess in the proclamation is so much part of its substance that the proclamation as a whole should be declared void. I have come to the conclusion it cannot be said now that it is unlikely that at a hearing the proclamation would be declared void. Indeed, the inclination in my mind at present is to think that there is a likelihood of a finding of invalidity.

Such a conclusion would provide ground on which to grant an interlocutory injunction if otherwise the circumstances were appropriate. However, it seems to me it is quite inappropriate to grant an injunction, either to restrain the holding of a joint sitting or to restrain the presentation to it of any particular item of business.

Barwick CJ had proceeded on the basis that the High Court had jurisdiction to intervene in the course of proceedings under s 57 by way of injunction, to pass judgment on the manner in which the Governor-General had exercised his powers under s 57 and, in an appropriate case, to declare that the Governor-General's acts were invalid.

Barwick CJ: [450] The dissolution by the Governor-General of both Houses of the Parliament is an act, an act of the Crown pursuant to the statutory power contained in s 57. The manner in which that act will be performed is not prescribed by s 57 though s 5 allows the dissolution of the House of Representatives or the prorogation of the Parliament to take place by proclamation "or otherwise". Thus, in the case of the dissolution of both Houses of the Parliament it is not so much a question of the conformity of the Governor-General's proclamation with any statutory provision, but rather of the lawfulness of the act of dissolution ...

[451] I should advert, at this point, to a submission made by the Attorney-General, of a very wide-ranging kind. It was submitted that the Governor-General, when performing his functions under s 57, was participating in the Parliamentary process of law-making so as to attract to all that he did what was referred to as the privileges of Parliament. Thus, according to the submission, this Court could **[452]** not inquire into the regularity of what the Governor-General had done or, indeed, into the regularity of any of the steps in the law-making process required by s 57.

The submission was founded on the fact that s 49 had brought to the Senate and the House of Representatives all the powers, privileges and immunities of the House of Commons in the United Kingdom as at the establishment of the Commonwealth. It was then recalled that the Commons from the time, at least, of the Bill of Rights in 1689, enjoyed certain privileges and immunities, one of which much emphasized by the Attorney-General was freedom of speech. The courts in the United Kingdom have traditionally refrained from any interference in the law-making activities of the Parliament. It was claimed that this restraint, if not indeed inability, on the part of the courts of the United Kingdom was part of the privileges and immunities of the Commons to which the House of Representatives and the Senate had succeeded by dint of s 49 of the Constitution.

But the submission, in my opinion, was basically misconceived. We are not here dealing with a Parliament whose laws and activities have the paramountcy of the Houses of Parliament in the United Kingdom. The law-making process of the Parliament in Australia is controlled by a written Constitution. This is particularly true of the special law-making process for which s 57 makes provision. It has been pointed out by the Privy Council in unequivocal language in the case of *Bribery Commissioner v Ranasinghe* [[1965] AC 172] that where the law-making process of a legislature is laid down by its constating instrument, the courts have a right and duty to ensure that that lawmaking process is observed ... **[453]** [That was a case] with respect to a Constitution which required a particular majority for the passage of an Act of a particular nature. The analogy in the case of s 57 is that the Constitution requires the various steps which I have outlined to be validly taken as a part of the law-making process. Speaking of the position of the Court in relation to such law-making processes, laid down by the constating instrument, Lord Pearce said in that case [[1965] AC at 194]: "The Court has a duty to see that the Constitution is not infringed and to preserve it inviolate," language which is singularly appropriate to the position of this Court in relation to the Australian Constitution.

Whilst it may be true the Court will not interfere in what I would call the intra-mural deliberative activities of the Parliament, it has both a right and a duty to interfere if the constitutionally required process of law-making is not properly carried out … What was said by the Chief Justice and Justices in *Osborne v* **[454]** *Commonwealth* [(1911) 12 CLR 321] can, in my opinion, be accepted if confined to the provisions of the Constitution with which the Court was then dealing. In my opinion, it is not acceptable as a statement of universal application, denying the Court jurisdiction to ensure observance of the conditions of the law-making process itself.

In *Osborne v Commonwealth* (1911) 12 CLR 321, most judges of the High Court expressed a tentative view that ss 53 and 54 of the Constitution are not justiciable. For example, Griffith CJ said that: "**[336]** Sections 53 and 54 deal with 'proposed laws', that is, Bills or projects of law still under consideration and not assented to – and they lay down rules to be observed with respect to proposed laws at that stage. Whatever obligations are imposed by these sections are directed to the Houses of Parliament *whose conduct of their internal affairs is not subject to review by a court of law*" (emphasis added). In *Cormack v Cope*, these italicised words were acceptable to Barwick CJ only if they were limited to ss 53 and 54. He preferred to rely upon the decision of the Privy Council in *Rediffusion (Hong Kong) Ltd v Att-Gen of Hong Kong* [1970] AC 1136. In that case, it was held that the Supreme Court of Hong Kong had jurisdiction to intervene in the legislative process to prevent the Legislative Council of Hong Kong from passing a proposed Bill that would have been repugnant to a law of the United Kingdom for the purposes of s 2 of the *Colonial Laws Validity Act*.

Barwick CJ: [454] Thus there are two distinct answers to the submission made by the Attorney-General. First of all, in my opinion, the Governor-General in convening a joint sitting or, for that matter, in dissolving both Houses, is not participating in the parliamentary process of lawmaking in any relevant sense. His act of dissolving both Houses and his direction for the convening of a joint sitting is in each instance an executive act. It is an act of the Crown in pursuance of a statute, the Constitution, and within the cognizance of this Court. The Crown's sole part in the parliamentary process of law-making does not begin until the proposed law has been passed by both Houses or affirmed in a joint sitting and is presented for the Royal assent.

Second, it is not the case in Australia, as it is in the United Kingdom, that the judiciary will restrain itself from interference in any part of the law-making process of the Parliament. Whilst the Court will not interfere in what I have called the intra-mural deliberative activities of the House, including what Isaacs J called "intermediate procedure" and the "order of events between the Houses" [12 CLR at 363], there is no parliamentary privilege which can stand in the way of this Court's right and duty to ensure that the constitutionally provided methods of law-making are observed.

Ordinarily, the Court's interference to ensure a due observance of the Constitution in connexion with the making of laws is effected by declaring void what purports to be an Act of Parliament, after it has been passed by the Parliament and received the Royal assent. In general, this is a sufficient means of ensuring that the processes of law-making which the Constitution requires are properly followed, and in practice so far the Court has confined itself to dealing with laws which have resulted from the parliamentary process. But nothing in that process has its precise analogy of or to that prescribed by s 57. In my opinion, the Court in point of jurisdiction is not limited to that method of ensuring the observance of the constitutional processes of law-making. It seems to me that in an appropriate, though no doubt unusual, case when moved by parties who have an interest in the regularity of the steps of the law-making process at the time intervention is sought, the Court is able, and indeed in a proper case bound, to interfere. The case of *Rediffusion (Hong Kong) Ltd v Attorney-General (Hong Kong)* [[1970] AC 1136] is illustra-**[455]**-tive of such a power … I would therefore reject entirely the Attorney-General's submission that this Court is powerless to decide upon the regularity of any of the steps in the law-making process under s 57, including the proclamation of the Governor-General purporting to convene a joint sitting.

Gibbs J agreed that the Court had jurisdiction to intervene; but unlike Barwick CJ, he felt no temptation to exercise it in the present case, preferring to adhere to "[467] the settled practice of this Court ... to refuse to grant relief in respect of proceedings within Parliament which may result in the enactment of an invalid law", since "the proper time for the Court to intervene is after the completion of the law-making process". Menzies J also appeared to put the point at least in terms of a settled practice, possibly even amounting to a denial of jurisdiction.

Menzies J: [464] It is a firmly established principle that this Court may declare or treat as invalid any law of the Parliament made without the authority of the Constitution. The exercise of this authority assumes the completion of the parliamentary process to turn a bill into an Act. It is no part of the authority of this Court, however, to restrain Parliament from making unconstitutional laws. It is of course convenient to speak of an unconstitutional law but the phrase means merely that **[465]** the purported law is not a law at all. This Court does not consider in advance whether if Parliament were to pass a particular bill it would result in a valid law. Another aspect of the same matter is that the introduction of a bill does not affect rights: it is the making of a law that does that. Then a person who has the requisite interest may challenge the validity of the law.

Closely associated with these principles is another principle of great constitutional importance, namely that the Court will not interfere with the proceedings of Parliament or the Houses of Parliament. The validity of the law that follows from what Parliament has done is one thing. The proceedings of Parliament that lead to a valid or an invalid law are another. It is not for this Court to prevent Parliament from doing what, in the opinion of this Court, will result in an invalid law. The Supreme Court of New South Wales in *Trethowan v Peden* [(1930) 31 SR (NSW) 183] did restrain the presentation for assent of a bill which it decided had not been passed as required by the Constitution of New South Wales. In *McDonald v Cain* [[1953] VLR 411] the Supreme Court of Victoria decided it had jurisdiction to declare that it was contrary to law to present a bill if it had not been passed by the majority required by the Victorian Constitution. But these cases are not authority for the proposition that a court can dictate to the members of the Houses of Parliament what they can or cannot deliberate and vote upon in a parliamentary proceeding. The correct general principle was clearly stated by this Court in *Osborne v Commonwealth* ...

[466] In my opinion the Court should not depart from the principles first established here in 1911. I would add but one reservation: it is that if by following some particular procedure in the making of a law it were possible to defeat the constitutional power of this Court to deal effectively with legislation when enacted that would give rise to a situation that has not yet been considered and which is unlikely to arise.

Mason J expressed no opinion on whether the Court could intervene in such cases. He held only that, even if such a jurisdiction exists, it ought not to be exercised on this occasion. Stephen J agreed with Menzies J that the High Court "[472] does not" intervene in the legislative process. However, he made it clear that "in my view this limitation of intervention by the Court depends not upon discretionary but jurisdictional grounds". McTiernan J held that none of the issues was justiciable.

The PMA Bill came before the High Court again in *Victoria v Commonwealth & Connor (PMA Case)* (1975) 134 CLR 81. This time, the Court held by 4:2, with McTiernan and Jacobs JJ dissenting, that the adjournment in the Senate on 13 December 1973 did not involve a "failure to pass", and accordingly that the Bill had not been validly enacted by the joint sitting.

Victoria v Commonwealth & Connor (PMA Case)
(1975) 134 CLR 81

Barwick CJ: [121] It is evident from the terms of the Constitution that the Senate was intended to represent the States, parts of the Commonwealth, as distinct from the House of Representatives which represents the electors throughout Australia. It is often said that **[122]** the Senate has, in this respect, failed of its purpose. This may be so, due partly to the party system and to the nature of the electoral system: but even if that assertion be true it does not detract from the constitutional position that it was in[t]ended that proposed laws could be considered by the Senate from a point of view different from that which the House of Representatives may take. The Senate is not a mere house of review: rather it is a house which may examine a proposed law from a stand-point different from that which the House of Representatives may have taken.

That a Bill needs consideration and debate is beyond question, though one cannot but observe that due to the dominance of the executive in the House of Representatives and perhaps, at times, in the Senate, opportunity for debate may be very attenuated. But, whatever the exigencies of party politics, the Constitution cannot be read as if laws ought to be passed by the Senate without debate, or as if the House of Representatives may in any respect command the Senate in relation to a Bill. Thus, in approaching the meaning of the word "fails" in s 57, it must be borne in mind that the Senate is both entitled and bound to consider a proposed law and to have a proper opportunity for debate and that its concurrence, apart from the provisions of s 57, is indispensable to a valid act of the Parliament.

It seems to me that the word "fails" in s 57 involves the notion that a time has arrived when, even allowing for the deliberative processes of the Senate, the Senate ought to answer whether or not it will pass the Bill or make amendments to it for the consideration of the House: that the time has arrived for the Senate to take a stand with respect to the Bill. If that time has arrived and the Senate rather than take a stand merely prevaricates, it can properly be said at that time to have failed to pass the Bill. In considering whether such a time has arrived, it may be that antecedent conduct of the Senate, particularly in relation to the proposed law, may be relevant. But it will be the conduct of the Senate itself and not the conduct or opinions or anticipatory statements of individual senators, whatever may be their party standing or party authority, which can have any relevance to the question whether, the situation having been reached where the Senate is called upon to give an answer on the Bill, it has failed to pass it ...

[123] In order to deny that the Senate has failed to pass the Bill, it may not be enough to say that all the processes available to the Senate in the consideration of a Bill have not been exhausted. It may be that even before those processes are exhausted the Senate may fail to pass within the meaning of s 57. In 1951 the reference of the Commonwealth Banking Bill to a select committee did not prevent the conclusion that the Senate had failed to pass, having regard to its entire conduct in regard to the Bill. It was said that the reference to the select committee in the particular circumstances was no more than prevarication. On other occasions and in different circumstances, the same conclusion perhaps may not be drawn from a reference of a Bill to a select committee.

However, I have no doubt that it cannot properly be said that when the Senate resolved on 13th December 1973 to adjourn the debate on the motion for a second reading until in effect the next sitting day, it had failed to pass the Bill. In my opinion, it could not be said that the time had arrived that day where the Senate was in any sense obliged to express itself definitively on the Bill. The concept of failure to pass must, it seems to me, mean more than "not pass". Failure in this sense imports, as I have said, the notion of the presence of an obligation as a House to take a definitive stand.

On this central issue, Gibbs, Stephen and Mason JJ agreed.

Stephen J: [168] The Senate, except as to money Bills, possesses legislative power in no way inferior to the House. It has full power of initiation, rejection and amendment of Bills coming from the House and even in the case of money Bills has the right freely to request amendments or to reject outright. These powers, unusual in a modern upper House, reflect the federal character of our polity. Having accorded to the smaller federating States Senate representation equal to that of the more populous States and having armed the Senate with far-reaching legislative powers the better to safeguard what were conceived to be State interests, there necessarily arose the spectre of legislative deadlock, which had been a familiar phenomenon in colonial bicameral legislatures.

A solution was called for, one which would satisfy the strong national aspirations for unity while not destroying the Senate's role as an effective guardian of States' rights. Section 57 was that solution. That a growing sense of nationhood, in combination with the discipline of the party system, would speedily diminish the Senate's active assertion of this role was, at the time of federation, foreseen by very few; that senators may seldom have assumed the role of guardians of the rights of their States cannot, however, [a]ffect the interpretation of the Constitution.

Few, if any, of the provisions of the Constitution occasioned so much debate as did s 57. It is clearly an extraordinary provision, a measure of last resort, introducing the unusual concepts of dissolution of an upper House and of temporary abandonment of the bicameral system, and this for the purpose of resolving disputes between the two plenipotent chambers. It would be a distortion of the history of the Constitutional Conventions to regard that solution which s 57 represents as involving no more than the simple and categorical remedy now suggested on behalf of the Commonwealth, that the will of the House should prevail and should do so without delay. It would indeed have been a simple task of draftsmanship so to provide, **[169]** but s 57 took no such form. Had it done so it would have destroyed that nice compromise between the rights of the States and those of the nascent Australian nation which was the aim of the federal compact and in the attainment of which the powers of the Senate were regarded as crucial. No less an authority than Barton J, with his unique understanding of what were the problems with which the various parts of the Constitution were intended to deal, has described the Constitution as designing the Senate "to be a House of greater power than any ordinary second chamber" and intended "to protect the States from aggression" (*Osborne v Commonwealth* [(1911) 12 CLR 321 at 353]) …

[170] Assume that in relation to any Bill coming before it the Senate may be seen to have engaged in those customary processes of debate, consideration and, in appropriate cases, inquiry by **[171]** select committee and the like which are the familiar practices of parliamentary democracy according to the Westminster model and which find local expression in Senate Standing Orders, those "orders with respect to … the order and conduct of its business and proceedings" which s 50 of the Constitution has empowered the Senate to make; assume also that examination does not reveal that in the particular instance there has been such an excessive indulgence in these processes, having regard to all the circumstances, including the importance, complexity and, perhaps, novelty of the measure in question, as will itself indicate that the law-making function has been abandoned in favour of mere dilatory evasion of that function. In such a case it cannot, in my view, be said that there has occurred any failure to pass the measure in question. The task of the Senate, in relation to Bills coming to it from the House, cannot be degraded to that of according to the legislative products of the House immediate and automatic indorsement, under threat of dissolution in the event of default.

A failure to pass will, then, not arise so long as the Senate is engaged in the normal processes of deliberation upon proposed laws; if advantage be taken of those same processes, designed for the proper consideration by legislators of the propriety and wisdom of measures, for ulterior purposes, for delaying, rather than considering and then passing or rejecting, a proposed law, the Senate will then, in terms of s 57, have failed to pass that proposed law. It is, I think, undesirable to resort to concepts of fault or of lack of bona fides in such a case, no doubt members of a legislature may employ every parliamentary device open to them in order to thwart the passage of legislation which they oppose and this without being in any way at fault or otherwise morally blameworthy. However, if by doing so the passage of legislation is delayed there will have arisen a failure to pass in terms of s 57 …

[172] Nothing in these facts suggests resort to delaying tactics. It was sought to supplement these facts with evidence of statements by the leaders of various political parties and by others, some in the Senate and some in the House, and by the use too of the fact that the Bill was ultimately defeated in the Senate, to give to the events of 13th December a colour which they otherwise lacked. I regard such a course as impermissible; it is with the actions of the Senate in its dealings with the Bill that the Court must be concerned; I would doubt whether any expressions of intention by a few individual members of Parliament, whatever may be the extent of party discipline and of unanimity of action and motives of various opposition parties, can ever assist in determining the quality of acts of a majority in a legislature.

On the basis of the above dicta, doubts have been raised as to the validity of the double dissolution granted in 1951 to Robert Menzies, as Prime Minister, by Sir William McKell, as Governor-General. The Banking Bill 1951 had been referred by the Senate to a Select Committee and Menzies had obtained a double dissolution by treating this as a "failure to pass". Yet the main proposition seeming to emerge from the *PMA Case* is that referral to a committee *may or may not* be a "failure to pass", depending on whether it is a legitimate part of the Senate's deliberative processes or an obstructionist or delaying tactic.

On the other hand, the *PMA Case* seems to exclude from judicial consideration most of the material by which the purpose or effect of the procedure adopted in the Senate might be characterised. The evidentiary material set out in the report of the *PMA Case* at 91-6 went well beyond what Stephen J called "[172] expressions of intention by a few individual members"; yet the Court declined to consider it. How, then, can the distinction between routine deliberative procedure and tactical "failure to pass" be drawn in any particular case? The dilemma may be partially eased by s 16(5) of the *Parliamentary Privileges Act 1987* (Cth), which provides that in questions arising under s 57, the limitations there imposed on the use of parliamentary material in court proceedings shall not "be taken to prevent or restrict the admission in evidence of a record of proceedings in Parliament … or the making of statements, submissions or comments based on that record".

Barwick CJ, Gibbs, Stephen and Mason JJ also considered and rejected the suggestion that the three-month period in s 57 should run from the time at which the House of Representatives first passed the Bill or, perhaps, from the time when that House had passed the Bill and it had been transmitted to the Senate. Barwick CJ and Stephen J had argued in *Cormack v Cope* that this construction was untenable. In the *PMA Case*, a four-judge majority held that the three-month period commences only when the Senate has "failed to pass" a Bill. Jacobs J dissented on this point. He held that the three-month period should run from the time at which the House had passed the Bill and transmitted it to the Senate, and that this approach was necessary in order to give a workable meaning to the concept of "failure to pass".

McTiernan J dissented on a more fundamental ground. As in *Cormack v Cope*, he held that the operation of s 57, and the various executive and legislative steps taken thereunder, were not justiciable. He quoted what Griffith CJ had said in *South Australia v Victoria* (*Boundaries Case*) (1911) 12 CLR 667: "[674] I assent to the argument that the jurisdiction of the High [675] Court, if any, is judicial and not political. So far, therefore, as a controversy requires for its settlement the application of political as distinguished from judicial considerations, I think that it is not justiciable under the Constitution".

McTiernan J: [135] In my opinion the question whether it is right to say that the Senate in truth rejected or failed to pass the Bill on 13th December 1973 is a political question. In my opinion it is not within the judicial power of the Commonwealth, vested by s 71 of the Constitution in the Court, to decide whether the recitals by the Governor-General in the proclamation dissolving both Houses were erroneous in fact or in law. "The crux of the matter," Frankfurter J said in *Baker v Carr* [369 US 186 at 287 (1962)], "is that courts are not fit instruments of decision where what is essentially at stake is the composition of those large contests of policy traditionally fought out in non-judicial forums, by which governments and the actions of governments are made and unmade". This inappropriateness of the issues of rejection of or failure to pass for judicial consideration may be designated "non-justiciability" … The Court would be going beyond its function if it entered upon an enquiry into the lawfulness and regularity of the course pursued at the joint sitting in respect of the proposed law before it was presented to the Governor-General for the Royal assent. **[136]** The traditional view is that courts do not undertake such an inquiry.

Although Jacobs J, in his dissenting judgment, had expressed a definite opinion on the substantive issues involved, he did not specifically hold that the issues were justiciable. Indeed, he used expressions which suggested that he was treating that as an open question. He outlined the practical difficulties which in his view would follow from the majority holding that the three-month period commences only when the Senate has "failed to pass" a Bill. One of these difficulties was that before the House of Representatives could pass a Bill for the second time, it would have to determine whether and when the Senate had "failed to pass" it.

Jacobs J: [196] [This] would be an invidious inquiry and determination and, what is more, if this litigation raises any justiciable issue at all, it would be an inquiry and determination on a factual situation in respect of which on the same or on additional facts propounded in evidence this Court, or indeed any other court of Australia which is invested with federal jurisdiction, might subsequently come to a contrary conclusion. That, it may be said, is a position in which persons in their private affairs are often placed ... But we are not dealing with private rights. We are dealing with public rights which lie at the heart of our constitutional democracy. The lives of the Government and of the national Parliament are in such a case at stake. In particular, the life of the elected Senate is at stake. If an error be made a Senate elected by the electorate for a certain period will be wrongly dissolved or on another view the dissolution itself may be void. It would indeed be an extraordinary result. It may be that this consideration is of even greater importance on the question whether the matter is justiciable before this Court at all, but it is by no means unimportant on the issue of construction if it be assumed that the issue is justiciable.

On the other hand, Barwick CJ, Gibbs, Stephen and Mason JJ held that the issues arising under s 57 were justiciable.

Barwick CJ: [117] It was, of course, conceded that the Court may declare invalid a law which does not fall within one of the topics assigned to the Parliament by the Constitution. But it was claimed that as long as an Act has received the Royal assent the Court cannot entertain the question whether it was passed in accordance with the constitutional requirements relating to the law-making processes. The argument had two distinct bases: first, that the question whether the constitutional law-making processes had been followed is not in any case a justiciable matter; second, that the decision of the Governor-General that the Bill was a proposed law within the operation of s 57, a decision to be implied from his assent to the Bill, was decisive and unex-**[118]**-aminable by the Court. There was another somewhat cognate submission, namely, that in any case the provisions of s 57 are directory only, so that failure to observe them will not produce invalidity.

The argument presented on behalf of the Commonwealth in the interlocutory proceedings in *Cormack v Cope* [(1974) 131 CLR 432] was of a different kind, though, as I have said, bent to the same conclusion as to the Court's competence. It was not repeated in terms in this case and in any case, for my part, it is sufficiently dealt with in that case. But the undeniable assertion there made that this Court is the guardian of the Constitution, and the authorities there cited, are fully relevant to the resolution of the submissions made in this case. Part of that Constitution provides for law-making processes. Section 57 is a notable example of that prescription. The Court, in my opinion, not only has the power but, when approached by a litigant with a proper interest so to do, has the duty to examine whether or not the law-making process prescribed by the Constitution has been followed and, if it has not, to declare that that which has emerged with the appearance of an Act, though having received the Royal assent, is not a valid law of the Commonwealth. Whether the Court should intervene before the Bill has received the Royal assent is a matter which does not now arise. I have already expressed my opinion that the Court has power to do so ...

[119] The defendants' further submission was that the "decision" of the Governor-General that the Bill was one which could be affirmed at the joint sitting and, thereafter, that it was proper for the receipt of the Royal assent, was not examinable by the Court and was decisive of the validity of the Act. In other words, it was submitted that the Governor-General had the power unexaminably to decide whether or not the conditions of s 57 had been satisfied. With that submission I express my complete disagreement. The powers given to the Governor-General by s 57 are statutory powers – the statute being an organic instrument – conditioned on the existence of facts. Any prerogatives in relation to the dissolution of Parliament which otherwise have been thought to exist would be conditioned and controlled by the express terms of the Constitution. They are not in any w[ay] conditioned on the Governor-General's opinion as to the facts. I can see no basis on which the Constitution can be read as giving the Governor-General a power to decide the facts on which the legality of his own actions or the validity of an Act may depend. Of course, the Governor-General must form a view for himself as to whether the circumstances of the proposed law satisfy the requirements of the first paragraph of s 57. But his power is contingent on the existence in fact of the conditions which that paragraph expresses: in my opinion, the power to decide the fact is reposed in this Court and in this Court alone. That is a facet of the undoubted position of the Court as the guardian of the Constitution.

The defendants made a related submission that the terms of s 57 are directory only. But there is no room, in my opinion, for the view that the terms of s 57 are merely directory so that failure to conform to its requirements will not affect the validity of what is done. What is laid down in s 57 is a process of lawmaking, and s 57 is a provision of the Constitution. It is quite inappropriate, in my opinion, to apply to such a section the distinctions between a directory and a mandatory statutory provision. The Court's decision in *Clayton v Heffron* [(1960) 105 CLR 214] does not **[120]** support a contrary conclusion: nor does the reasoning of the majority.

As to justiciability, Stephen J agreed with Barwick CJ, Gibbs and Mason JJ. However, he treated the question of whether s 57 is "mandatory" or merely "directory" (see Chapter 11, §4) as a separate question which, for the purposes of the *PMA Case*, did not need to be resolved.

One of the arguments relied on by the Commonwealth as suggesting that the requirements of s 57 are merely directory, and should thus not be regarded as justiciable, was that any finding of invalidity resulting from an incorrect use of s 57 would have unacceptable consequences. In the sequence of events in 1974, two vice-regal proclamations were in issue: the proclamation by Sir Paul Hasluck on 11 April 1974 dissolving both Houses of Parliament, and the proclamation by Sir John Kerr on 30 July 1974 convening the joint sitting. On the basis of the analysis that finally emerged from *Cormack v Cope* and the *PMA Case*, it did not matter that these proclamations relied in part on the PMA Bill, even though that Bill had failed to satisfy the requirements of s 57. Both proclamations were valid so long as there was at least one Bill which did satisfy those requirements.

Suppose, however, that the proclamations had relied on only one Bill, which had not satisfied the requirements of s 57. If the proclamation dissolving the Parliament were invalid, would that mean that the ensuing election would also be invalid, that the Parliament resulting from that election would be invalidly constituted and that all laws enacted by that Parliament would be invalidly passed? In *McKinlay's Case*, similar questions were brushed aside without really receiving a satisfactory answer. The four majority judges in the *PMA Case* did little better. They insisted that the drastic consequences envisaged above would not follow, but had difficulty in explaining why.

Barwick CJ: [120] Argument was presented to the Court as to what would be involved when the Governor-General dissolved the House without having the power so to do under the Constitution: that is to say, if he erroneously concluded that the conditions existed on which his power to dissolve depended. The dissolution itself is a fact which can neither be void nor be undone. If, without having power to do so, the Governor-General did dissolve both Houses, there would be no basis for setting aside the dissolution or for treating it as not having occurred. None the less, the double dissolution would not have been authorized, and therefore it would not satisfy the second paragraph of s 57 and provide a warrant for a joint sitting. The joint sitting, pursuant to the third paragraph of that section, which was dependent upon such a dissolution, which, though not void, was not lawful, would not have power to affirm any law. It is not necessary, in my opinion, to regard any part of s 57 as directory in order to conclude that, though the proclamation be unlawful, the sequential dissolution in fact occurred and was incapable of being disregarded, reversed or undone.

Stephen J: [178] In the case of s 57 no such consequences would, in my view, ensue; once the Governor-General has in fact dissolved both chambers, whether or not he is justified in doing so in terms of s 57, the existing Parliament will have been brought effectively to an end and the new Parliament which results from the issue of writs and the holding of an election following such dissolution will be quite unaffected by whatever may or may not have preceded that dissolution.

The third High Court action arising from the 1974 joint sitting was *Western Australia v Commonwealth* (*First Territory Senators Case*) (1975) 134 CLR 201. The main issue relating to the use of s 57 arose from the anxiety expressed by Barwick CJ in *Cormack v Cope* that a government might exploit or manipulate the possibility of a double dissolution by accumulating a "storehouse" or "stockpile" of double-dissolution "triggers", any one of which might be used at any time not to resolve the deadlock relating to that Bill but merely as a convenient "trigger" for a double dissolution at a time of the government's choosing. The focus of the *First Territory Senators Case* was on three enactments passed at the 1974 joint sitting: the *Commonwealth*

Electoral Act (No 2) 1973 (Cth), the *Senate (Representation of Territories) Act 1973* (Cth) and the *Representation Act 1973* (Cth). The first Act had been passed by the lower House on 4 April 1973, rejected by the Senate on 17 May 1973, passed again by the House on 23 August 1973 and rejected again by the Senate on 29 August 1973. The other two Bills were passed by the House on 30 May 1973, rejected by the Senate on 7 June 1973, passed again by the House on 27 September 1973 and rejected again by the Senate on 14 November 1973. Thus, by the time of the double dissolution on 11 April 1974, the Senate's second rejection of the Bill for the *Commonwealth Electoral Act (No 2)* was more than seven months old and the corresponding interval for the other two Bills was almost five months.

On 14 February 1974, after the three Bills had become available as double-dissolution "triggers", but before the proclamation of a double dissolution on 11 April 1974, the Parliament was prorogued until 28 February 1974. The intervention of a prorogation gave rise to two arguments. First, the normal effect of a prorogation is that all unfinished parliamentary business lapses, so that any bills still awaiting passage must be reintroduced at the next session. On this basis, it was argued that the availability of the three electoral Bills as double dissolution "triggers" had similarly lapsed. Second, it was said that when the Governor-General decided, on the Prime Minister's advice, to prorogue the Parliament he must be taken to have rejected, on the Prime Minister's advice, the alternative possibility of dissolving both Houses.

The Court had no difficulty in disposing of the arguments based upon the proroguing of Parliament. The Bills had not lapsed because at the time of the prorogation there were, within the Parliament, no unfinished processes remaining to be completed in respect of those Bills. By rejecting the Bills for a second time, the Senate had taken the final step in their parliamentary progress. The decision to prorogue did not affect the possibility of double dissolution because the two processes – one based on the executive's prerogative power, and the other on a specific grant of power in s 57 – were neither constitutionally comparable procedures nor politically alternative strategies. The Court also rejected the argument about "stockpiling" and "staleness", although considerable difficulty was felt by Barwick CJ.

Western Australia v Commonwealth (*First Territory Senators Case*)
(1975) 134 CLR 201

Barwick CJ: [221] In my opinion, to qualify as a proposed law which may be approved by a joint sitting convened pursuant to s 57, the bill must have twice not been passed by the Senate upon its presentation by the House of Representatives in conformity with the section and the second occasion on which the bill has not been passed must be so related in point of time to the date of the dissolution as to form part of the same current situation between the House and the Senate. The evident time sequence in s 57 progresses continuously towards the date of that proclamation. The action, if the House determines to re-present the bill, has a continuous currency which includes the act of dissolving the Houses. Whilst the implication of the word "thereupon" into the grant of the discretion, would appear to require too stringent an immediacy in the temporal relationship of the double dissolution to the second occasion of the non-passing of the bill by the Senate, there must in my opinion be such a temporal relationship as maintains the currency of the situation as a whole. Just as the implication of the word "thereupon" in relation to the discretion may involve too inflexible a relationship, so on the other hand, the implication of the words "at any time thereafter" would clearly destroy that currency of the situation which, to my mind the language and the structure of the section requires. This means, **[222]** in my opinion, that proposed laws which twice have not been passed by the Senate may not be stockpiled. They may not be laid aside against the possibility of a double dissolution founded on some event remote in time and unrelated to the situation in which the "stockpiled" or stale bill was twice rejected by the Senate: nor can they be laid aside until some later and relevantly remote time which may be considered more suitable for the making of a proclamation of double dissolution. On the other hand, time must be afforded to the Governor-General between the second time the bill has not been passed and the date of the proclamation, not merely to allow of consideration whether the discretion to dissolve ought to be exercised, but also to await the fate of other proposed laws which have been submitted or are in the course of being submitted to the process of s 57, assuming always that such other laws do form part of, or are substantially related to, the situation current at the time of the double dissolution. Bearing in mind the function of s 57 in providing the possibility of the electorate expressing its opinion on the matters in difference between the Houses of the Parliament, the language of s 57, in my opinion, sufficiently manifests the intention that action to enable that expression of opinion must be proximate to the time that difference emerged. It would be quite incongruous that at a considerable remove of time and after the business of the Parliament had been proceeding for very many months, it should be dissolved to enable the electorate to pass upon a question which would appear to have been shelved; to vote in relation to a bill or a difference between the Houses which had in truth become stale ...

I therefore conclude that, upon its proper construction, s 57 does require a temporal relationship between the time when the **[223]** Senate for a second time does not pass a proposed law and the date of the double dissolution. The situation as to the disagreement between the Houses of the Parliament as to the proposed law must be current at the time of the double dissolution. If the interval of time is so considerable as to warrant the conclusion that the proposed law is stale and that the situation which existed at the time of the second rejection is no longer current, it cannot, in my opinion, be brought forward to a joint sitting and there approved so as to become law. The continuity of the action under s 57, including as one of its progressing steps the double dissolution itself, must be substantially maintained.

I am not unaware of the difficulties involved in deciding whether in given circumstances this temporal relationship has been maintained. But, whether it has or not, is a matter of fact which ultimately this Court will be able to decide ...

[224] I have no difficulty in concluding that the Representation Bill was current at the date of the double dissolution. It related to the subject matter of the Senate (Representation of Territories) Bill which was secondly rejected on the same day. The period of four months less the duration of the Parliamentary recess is clearly not inordinate or indicative that the bill has become stale, laid aside, or that the Governor-General must have decided not to grant a double dissolution. In my opinion, both bills were proper to be approved by the joint sitting ...

After much consideration, I am not prepared to hold that the Electoral Bill failed to fulfil the temporal relationship which I have endeavoured to express as being required by s 57; that is to **[225]** say, the temporal relationship between the date of the Senate's second rejection of a bill and the date of the proclamation effecting a double dissolution. The time interval was indeed substantial, almost six months after allowing for the Parliamentary recess – particularly in relation to a Parliamentary term of three years or less. The possibility of the situation its rejection created, not being relevantly current at the date of the double dissolution, was indeed great and the fact that its subject matter was disparate from that of the proposed laws rejected much more proximately to the date of the double dissolution, though not definitive, is yet quite significant. The matter is on the borderline, but I am not of opinion that the Act resulting from the approval of the proposed law by the joint sitting should be held to be invalid.

For other judges, there was no such borderline issue. No time limit on the use of a Bill for a double dissolution could be read into s 57.

Stephen J: [251] It was contended that the Governor-General may only exercise his power under s 57 to dissolve both chambers simultaneously if he does so without undue delay after the Senate's second rejection of a bill twice passed by the House and that this limitation upon his power arises from the ordinary meaning of the words in s 57. Alternatively it was said that some such word as "thereupon" should be implied after the words "the Governor-General may" in the first paragraph of the section, thus leading to the same result; not to do so would involve, it was said, the unacknowledged insertion, in its stead, of words such as "at any time" and this would do violence to the whole sense of the section.

This interpretation has one obvious attraction, its acceptance would prevent the happening of what I have on an earlier occasion referred to as that wholesale impairment of the legislature's bicameral character which would occur were the House, by the repeated second passage of bills previously rejected by the Senate and which the Senate persisted in rejecting, to store up over a period a great number of measures which, following one double dissolution, might then be enacted at a joint sitting of both chambers.

However to accede to this submission would, I think, be to read into s 57 words which are not there and to do so without good reason. To read words into any statute is a strong thing and, in the absence of clear necessity, a wrong thing – *Thompson v Goold & Co* [[1900] AC 409 at 420]; a fortiori in the case of the Constitution. In *Bradley v Greenwich Board of Works* [(1878) 3 QBD 384 at 388], Cockburn CJ, speaking in a very different statutory context but where a not dissimilar contention had been urged, said, "we seek in vain for any limitation of the time within which the apportionment is to be completed. And as the legislature have fixed no limit it is impossible for us to introduce one". His Lordship's words apply aptly enough to the present case. Section 57 contains no ambiguity [252] which calls for resolution by the reading in of some such temporal limitation as is suggested; it presents no absurdity of operation if read as it stands, without any addition being made to its wording. None of the circumstances here exist which courts have regarded as justifying the reading into statutes of words other than those chosen by the legislators. Moreover where temporal limitations are intended to apply s 57 is careful to express them, it does so twice in its first paragraph; it must be all the less justifiable in such a case to seek to introduce a further such limitation where none is either expressed or called for as a matter of necessary intendment.

Mason and McTiernan JJ agreed.

Murphy J did not sit in the *PMA Case* because in *Cormack v Cope* he had appeared before the Court as Attorney-General and had argued the very issues which the *PMA Case* was to decide (see "High Court Practice as to Eligibility of Judges to Sit in a Case" (1975) 49 *Australian Law Journal* 110). In the *First Territory Senators Case* he agreed with the majority view set out above on the issue of "stockpiling" or "staleness". He also stressed the three explicit limitations of time contained in s 57. As to the first limitation, the three-month interval that must elapse before a second attempt to pass a Bill, he expressed his agreement with the dissenting view of Jacobs J in the *PMA Case*, and held that the three-month interval should run from the time when the House of Representatives first passed the Bill. He further argued:

> **Murphy J: [289]** These three limitations of time were not exceeded in respect of any of the three Acts, and there is no justification in the text of s 57 or the rest of the Constitution for implying any other limitation of time. The argument against doing so is strengthened by the consideration that if an issue whether a delay was unreasonable is justiciable, then the judiciary would be involved in attempting to resolve questions at the heart of the political process, far removed from the traditional exercise of judicial power.

In any event, Murphy J went on to agree with what McTiernan J had said in the *PMA Case*, namely, that issues relating to compliance with s 57 were not justiciable.

The formal questions stated for the Court's opinion in the *First Territory Senators Case* included specific questions as to whether the issues arising under s 57 were justiciable. In the formal order of the Court these questions were answered "Yes". Barwick CJ, Stephen and Mason JJ specifically so held. None of them gave elaborate reasons, since they had done so at length in the *PMA Case*. Gibbs J evidently assumed that the issue was settled by the *PMA Case*; indeed, he had said in the *PMA Case* that the issue had been settled by *Cormack v Cope*. Nevertheless, if an answer in favour of justiciability had appeared to be a clear majority view in the *PMA Case*, the majority now appeared narrower. McTiernan J did not repeat the arguments against justiciability which he had advanced in the *PMA Case*. Indeed, he did not refer to any of the issues arising under s 57, but confined his judgment to the question of legislative power under s 122. He also stated that "[233] I agree in the reasons of Mason J", but whether this agreement extended to the question of justiciability is doubtful. Conversely, Jacobs J, who in the *PMA Case* had avoided any direct expression of opinion as to justiciability, now firmly agreed with Murphy J that the issues were not justiciable.

> **Jacobs J: [275]** I did not find it necessary to determine but expressed some doubt in *Victoria v Commonwealth* (the *Petroleum and Minerals Authority Act Case*) [(1975) 134 CLR 81] whether there is any place for adjudication by this Court in questions of procedure which arise or may be

raised in relation to s 57 of the Constitution and the working out of the procedures there laid down. That doubt has crystallized. The reason may be simply expressed in one sentence. The procedure prescribed leads to the expression by the people of their preference in the choice of their elected representatives, a preference expressed with the knowledge that a joint [276] sitting of those representatives may need to take place, and no court in the absence of a clearly conferred power has the right to thwart or interfere with the people's expression of their choice. The people's expression cures any formal defects which may have previously existed. That is democratic government within the terms of the Constitution by which the people elected to be governed. The concern of this Court is with the respective limits of legislative power of the Commonwealth and the States and with the application to legislation, State or federal, of the provisions of the Constitution in order to test the substantial validity of that legislation. There is no indication that the Court was empowered to superintend the legislative procedures, above all a legislative procedure which involves as a consequence the election by the people of their representatives and as a sequel thereto a particular form of further legislative process.

Another issue re-canvassed in the *First Territory Senators Case* was the validity of the two proclamations issued as part of the events of 1974, that is, Sir Paul Hasluck's proclamation dissolving the Parliament and Sir John Kerr's proclamation convening the joint sitting. The *PMA Case* established that the PMA Bill had not complied with the requirements of s 57 and therefore that it should not have been included as a basis for the proclamations. Did its erroneous inclusion mean that the proclamations were invalid? In the *First Territory Senators Case*, the whole Court accepted the view that Menzies J had proposed in *Cormack v Cope*, namely that any erroneous recital in the proclamations was mere "surplusage" and could simply be ignored. As to this, even Barwick CJ was no longer prepared to dissent.

Barwick CJ: [225] I expressed a tentative view on this matter in my reasons for judgment in *Cormack v Cope* [(1974) 131 CLR 432]. A majority of the Justices participating in the decision of that case were of opinion that the Governor-General was not authorized to determine what could be discussed and approved at a joint sitting; but that so much of the Governor-General's proclamation as appeared to designate the bills to be the subject of the joint sitting was surplusage, not affecting the validity of the proclamation in so far as it convened the joint sitting. I doubted at that time that the statement in the proclamation that each of the specified proposed laws might be discussed and should be voted upon could be treated as surplusage. Statutory provisions allowing of a severance of part of a statutory instrument where that part is in excess of authority do not apply to the Governor-General's proclamation and it could scarce be denied that the inclusion in the proclamation of the reference to the proposed laws was intentional. However, I am not disposed to dissent on this point from the opinion of my brethren. I am [not] ready to do so because, having regard to the views expressed by them and by me, there is no likelihood that the error of doing more by such a proclamation than convene the joint sitting for a stated place and time will be repeated in the future.

Stephen J: [262] The power of the Governor-General to perform these two acts, of dissolution and of the convening of a joint sitting, is conferred for the purpose of the resolution of a legislative deadlock the existence of which has been attested by the happening of the events which I have described as the condition precedent. That power may only be employed, like other statutory powers, for the purpose for which it was conferred and where, as in the instances which I have given, it appears that it has been employed for quite other purposes its exercise will be unauthorized by s 57.

Just as the power may only be employed for the purpose authorized, so too the occasion created by the exercise of the power may only be employed for that purpose. Thus where a joint sitting is convened so that the members of both chambers may deliberate and vote together upon a particular proposed law they may not use the occasion for a different purpose and consider other proposed laws, whether or not the condition precedent has been satisfied in the case of those other laws …

[263] If, as in the present case, the proclamation refers to some measure which ought not to have been referred to this will amount to mere surplusage and the lawful agenda for the joint sitting will be the shorter. An erroneous intention will have been revealed but only as to that measure; the Governor-General will otherwise have intended that there should be submitted to a joint sitting measures the submission of which was in fact authorized; in relation to them the terms of s 57 will have been fully complied with. The position might have been otherwise if it had appeared from the proclamation that the joint sitting was convened so that it might deliberate upon all of the named measures or upon none at all. However there is nothing in the proclamation capable of conveying that unlikely intention and it is therefore unnecessary to consider what would, in those circumstances, have been the consequence.

In this passage Stephen J argued that the power of the Governor-General under s 57 is "**[262]** like other statutory powers" and "may only be employed ... for the purpose for which it was conferred". He was speaking of the power to convene a joint sitting. Is a similar principle also applicable to the power to dissolve both Houses? If the same principle does apply in both cases, what significance does it have for the events of 11 November 1975 (see Chapter 12, §3)? On that day, Sir John Kerr as Governor-General dismissed Gough Whitlam as Prime Minister and appointed Malcolm Fraser as caretaker Prime Minister in his place on condition that Fraser would immediately advise a double dissolution. Fraser duly tendered that advice on the basis of 21 Bills which had twice been rejected by the Senate and were therefore available to Whitlam as double-dissolution "triggers". However, the double dissolution granted to Fraser was not for the purpose of securing the passage of those 21 Bills. The available "triggers" were used as a convenient way of resolving quite a different kind of deadlock between the two Houses, one over supply, where the urgency of finding a resolution arose from the fear that funds would not be available for ordinary government services. Was this a case of the power conferred by s 57 being used for purposes other than those for which it was conferred? If so, does it follow that the ensuing double dissolution was not authorised by s 57?

In 2003, Prime Minister John Howard proposed that the power of the Senate to defeat government legislation be reduced. He favoured an amendment to s 57 to allow a government to call a joint sitting of both Houses of the federal Parliament after the Senate had rejected a Bill twice. A Bill passed at the joint sitting could then become law without the need for a double dissolution election. The Prime Minister released a discussion paper (*Resolving Deadlocks: A Discussion Paper on Section 57 of the Australian Constitution* (October 2003)) and appointed a Consultative Group on Constitutional Change to consult with Australians about the reform. Although the Group reported (*Resolving Deadlocks: The Public Response* (Parliamentary Paper No 235 of 2004)) that it was "**[8]** not convinced that the constitutional mechanism provided by section 57 is the best way of resolving legislative deadlocks", it also found that the Prime Minister's proposal "**[9]** received a rough passage in most of the Group's consultations. The clear prevailing body of opinion was that the option would increase executive governmental power at the expense of the Senate and render the Senate far less effective in performing its function of review. The Group concludes that the option would have virtually no chance of community acceptance either now or in the foreseeable future". In view of these findings, the Prime Minister announced in June 2004 that the proposal would not be put to a referendum.

7. Further References

Aroney, N, "Representative Democracy Eclipsed? The *Langer, Muldowney* and *McGinty* Decisions" (1996) 19 *University of Queensland Law Journal* 75.

Brooks, A, "A Paragon of Democratic Virtues? The Development of the Commonwealth Franchise" (1993) 12 *University of Tasmania Law Review* 208.

Campbell, E, *Parliamentary Privilege* (Federation Press, 2003).

Carne, G, "Representing Democracy or Reinforcing Equality?: Electoral Distribution and *McGinty v Western Australia*" (1997) 25 *Federal Law Review* 351.

Carney, G, *Members of Parliament: Law and Ethics* (Prospect, 2000).

Comans, CK, "Constitution, Section 57 – Further Questions" (1985) 15 *Federal Law Review* 243.

Evans, H, "*Fitzpatrick and Browne*: Imprisonment by a House of Parliament" in Lee, HP, and Winterton, G (eds), *Australian Constitutional Landmarks* (Cambridge University Press, 2003), 145.

Gleeson, M, "The Shape of Representative Democracy" (2001) 27 *Monash University Law Review* 1.

Harris, IC (ed), *House of Representatives Practice* (AGPS, 5th ed 2005).

Hinton, M, "Parliamentary Privilege and Police Powers in South Australia" (2005) 16 *Public Law Review* 99.

Holland, I, *Crime and Candidacy* (Parliamentary Research Service, Commonwealth Parliament, 2003), Current Issues Brief No 22 of 2002-03.

Katz, L, "The Simultaneous Dissolution of Both Houses of the Australian Federal Parliament, 1975" (1976) 54 *Canadian Bar Review* 392.

Kirk, J, "Constitutional Implications from Representative Democracy" (1995) 23 *Federal Law Review* 37.

Lindell, G, "Parliamentary Inquiries and Government Witnesses" (1995) 20 *Melbourne University Law Review* 383.

Lindell, G, and Bennett, R (eds), *Parliament: The Vision in Hindsight* (Federation Press, 2001).

Mason, A, "The Double Dissolution Cases" in Lee, HP, and Winterton, G (eds), *Australian Constitutional Landmarks* (Cambridge University Press, 2003), 213.

McKay, WR (ed), *Erskine May's Treatise on the Law, Privileges, Proceedings, and Usage of Parliament* (Butterworths, 23rd ed 2004).

Mercurio, B, and Williams, G, "The Australian Diaspora and the Right to Vote" (2004) 32 *University of Western Australia Law Review* 1.

Evans, H (ed), *Odgers' Australian Senate Practice* (AGPS, 11th ed 2004).

Orr, G, "Ballotless and Behind Bars: The Denial of the Franchise to Prisoners" (1998) 26 *Federal Law Review* 55.

Orr, G, and Williams, G, "Electoral Challenges: Judicial Review of Parliamentary Elections in Australia" (2001) 23 *Sydney Law Review* 53.

Pateman, C, "Feminism and Democracy" in Duncan, G (ed), *Democratic Theory and Practice* (Cambridge University Press, 1985).

Reid, GS, and Forrest, M, *Australia's Commonwealth Parliament 1901-1988* (Melbourne University Press, 1989).

Richardson, JE, "Federal Deadlocks: Origin and Operation of Section 57" (1962) 1 *University of Tasmania Law Review* 706.

Sawer, G, "Singulars, Plurals, and Section 57 of the Constitution" (1976) 8 *Federal Law Review* 45.

Twomey, A, "The Federal Constitutional Right to Vote in Australia" (2000) 28 *Federal Law Review* 125.

Twomey, A, "Free to Choose or Compelled to Lie? – The Rights of Voters after *Langer v The Commonwealth*" (1996) 24 *Federal Law Review* 201.

Walker, K, and Dunn, K, "Mr Langer is Not Entitled to be an Agitator: Albert Langer v Commonwealth" (1996) 20 *Melbourne University Law Review* 909.

Williams, G, *Human Rights under the Australian Constitution* (Oxford University Press, 1999), Ch 7.

Chapter 11

State Constitutions

1. Introduction

Initially as colonies of the British Empire, and nowadays as component units of the Australian federation, the Australian States have always been subject to external limitations on the legislative capacity of their Parliaments. The Imperial limits were expressed in the doctrines of repugnancy and extraterritoriality (see Chapter 4, §7). The federal limitations arise from the Commonwealth Constitution.

The various State Constitution Acts were originally enacted by the Imperial Parliament to provide each colony with its own institutions of representative government. However, as s 5 of the *Colonial Laws Validity Act 1865* (Imp) made clear (see Appendix), each local representative legislature had "full power to make laws respecting [its own] constitution, powers, and procedure". Accordingly, each State Parliament has from time to time re-enacted and amended its own Constitution Act.

The colonial constitutions in force on 1 January 1901 were expressly preserved in force by s 106 of the Constitution – to "continue as at the establishment of the Commonwealth ... until altered in accordance with the Constitution of the State". Section 107 made it clear that, except as to powers given exclusively to the Commonwealth or "withdrawn from the Parliament of the State", the existing legislative powers of the State Parliaments were to "continue". Similarly, s 108 ensured that, even in the areas of legislative power assigned to the Commonwealth, existing State legislation remained in force, along with the State's existing "powers of alteration and of repeal in respect of any such law". This last provision, however, was subject to the possibility of Commonwealth legislative override under s 109; and while s 106 preserved the State constitutions, it did so "subject to this Constitution", so that State legislative powers are subject to limitations arising from the Constitution itself.

These limitations are of three main kinds. First, areas of power *exclusively* vested in the Commonwealth Parliament are necessarily excised from the powers of the States. In practice the most important of these is the power in s 90 to levy duties of excise. In addition, some powers assigned to the Commonwealth by s 51 of the Constitution are effectively made exclusive by provisions in Ch V: for example, as to "Currency, coinage, and legal tender" (s 51(xii)) see s 115, and as to "naval and military defence" (s 51(vi)) see s 114.

Secondly, certain provisions of the Constitution *expressly* limit State legislative power (notably s 114, which provides that a State "shall not ... impose any tax on property of any kind belonging to the Commonwealth"). There are other express limitations whose effect on the States, although not spelled out explicitly, is clearly intended, and may indeed for practical purposes be their primary operation. These include s 117, the primary function of which is to prevent the

States from discriminating against residents of other States, and s 92, which commands that interstate "trade, commerce, and intercourse" shall be "absolutely free". Section 112 qualifies that command by permitting State "inspection laws", but adds that any such laws are subject to Commonwealth annulment.

Thirdly, since s 106 makes the State constitutions "subject to this Constitution", State legislative powers may be subject to limitations *implied* in the Constitution. The most obvious examples are those arising from federalism itself. Most other implications that may be discerned in the Commonwealth Constitution will operate primarily as limitations on *Commonwealth* legislative power; whether they also operate as limits on *State* legislative power is not always clear. If they do so operate, it is clear that they do so through the mechanism of the words "subject to this Constitution" in s 106. In *Theophanous v Herald & Weekly Times Ltd* (1994) 182 CLR 104, Deane J asserted that: "**[165]** The concurrent legislative powers of each State ... [are] derived from its constitution which ... is subjugated to the Constitution as a whole by s 106". However, this notion of "subjugation" seems unnecessarily strong. The better view appears to be that a limitation on Commonwealth legislative power will flow on through s 106 to limit State legislative power as well if, but only if, the limitation at State level is necessary to ensure the effectiveness of the limitation at Commonwealth level. As Dawson J observed in *McGinty v Western Australia* (1996) 186 CLR 140: "**[189]** The continuation by s 106 ... of the former colonial constitutions as State Constitutions is made 'subject to this Constitution', but this does not serve to apply to the States provisions of the Commonwealth Constitution which otherwise have no application to them".

In any event, these external limits on State legislative power, whether colonial or federal in origin, are relatively peripheral. The internal legislative power of the States, for most practical purposes, is plenary. The 19th-century Privy Council decisions referred to in Chapter 4, §3 established that, as their Lordships put it in *R v Burah* (1878) 3 App Cas 889, each colonial Parliament "**[904]** has, and was intended to have, plenary powers of legislation, as large, and of the same nature, as those of [the Imperial] Parliament itself". By contrast with the federal Parliament, with its circumscribed list of enumerated powers, the State Parliaments are invested with Australia's closest approximation to the British concept of "parliamentary sovereignty". That concept, however, contains its own limitation. According to its classic formulation by AV Dicey, the sovereignty of a "sovereign" Parliament is limited by the doctrine that it cannot bind its successors.

AV Dicey, *Introduction to the Study of the Law of the Constitution*
(Macmillan, 1st ed 1885, 10th ed 1959)

[64] Language has occasionally been used in Acts of Parliament which implies that one Parliament can make laws which cannot be touched by any subsequent Parliament, and that therefore the legislative authority of an existing Parliament may be limited by the enactments of its predecessors.

[65] That Parliaments have more than once intended and endeavoured to pass Acts which should tie the hands of their successors is certain, but the endeavour has always ended in failure. Of statutes intended to arrest the possible course of future legislation, the most noteworthy are the Acts which embody the treaties of Union with Scotland and Ireland. The legislators who passed these Acts assuredly intended to give to certain portions of them more than the ordinary effect of statutes. Yet the history of legislation in respect of these very Acts affords the strongest proof of the futility inherent in every attempt of one sovereign legislature to restrain the action of another equally sovereign body ...

[66] One Act, indeed, of the British Parliament might, looked at in the light of history, claim a peculiar sanctity. It is certainly an enactment of which the terms, we may safely predict, will never be repealed and the spirit will never be violated. This Act is the Taxation of Colonies Act, 1778 [providing that Parliament "will not impose any duty, tax, or assessment whatever, payable in any of his Majesty's colonies", with limited exceptions for the benefit of the colonies] ...

[67] The point calling for attention is that though policy and prudence condemn the repeal of the Taxation of Colonies Act, 1778, or the enactment of any law inconsistent with its spirit, there is

under our constitution no legal difficulty in the way of repealing or overriding this Act. If Parliament were tomorrow to impose a tax, say on New Zealand or on the Canadian Dominion, the statute imposing it would be a legally valid enactment. As stated in short by a very judicious writer [Alpheus Todd] – "It equally is certain that a Parliament cannot so bind its successors by the terms of any statute, as to limit the discretion of a future Parliament, and thereby disable the Legislature from entire freedom of action at any future **[68]** time when it might be needful to invoke the interposition of Parliament to legislate for the public welfare."

Whether this doctrine is sustainable has been among the most controversial aspects of Dicey's theory. Clearly, the doctrine is a paradoxical one: the inability to bind future parliaments, imposed as a limit on the "sovereignty" of the current parliament at any given time, is conceived of as necessary to ensure the unlimited "sovereignty" of future parliaments.

George Winterton ("The British Grundnorm: Parliamentary Supremacy Re-examined" (1976) 92 *Law Quarterly Review* 591) has identified three possible conceptions of "parliamentary sovereignty". In one conception, an illimitable continuing supremacy, Parliament cannot bind its successors in the sense that it might "**[593]** restrict the substantive power of future Parliaments", nor even in the sense that it might "impose procedural restrictions on them". (That is, it can neither prohibit laws on certain specified topics altogether, nor require that they be enacted according to a special procedure.) In another version, Parliament might "**[597]** change its procedure and the manner and form in which it legislates, but cannot impose limits on the content of legislation". In a third version, the institution of Parliament itself, including "the manner and form in which it exercises its power and the limitless ambit of its power", would be "the subject of a 'fundamental', unalterable rule".

Once we address our minds to the distinction between "substantive" and merely "procedural" limitations, it is possible to argue that restrictions of the latter kind are not inconsistent with parliamentary sovereignty. If restrictions of the latter kind are imposed it will still be true that legislative power is unlimited both as to the range of topics to which it can extend and as to the ways in which those topics may be regulated or dealt with. The restriction means only that, while this unlimited legislative power may be exercised on most issues in the normal manner, there are certain issues for which the power must be exercised in a special way.

For our purposes, the most significant features of the Australian State constitutions are, first, the extent to which their power approximates Dicey's conception of "parliamentary sovereignty"; and, second, the fact that, through constitutional "entrenchment" of restrictive legislative procedures, it has been found possible in certain respects for the State Parliaments to bind their successors.

2. State Legislative Power

(a)   Peace, Welfare and Good Government

The Constitution of each State, or in the case of Tasmania the *Australian Constitutions Act 1850* (Imp), confers a general legislative power on the Parliament of that State. For example, the *Constitution Act 1902* (NSW) states:

Constitution Act 1902 (NSW)

5 The Legislature shall, subject to the provisions of the Commonwealth of Australia Constitution Act, have power to make laws for the peace, welfare, and good government of New South Wales in all cases whatsoever.

The conferral of legislative power by some other State Constitutions differs slightly in wording, but is of the same effect in conferring a plenary legislative power. For example, s 2 of the *Constitution Act 1889* (WA) empowers the Parliament to "make laws for the peace, order, and good Government of the Colony of Western Australia", while s 16 of the *Constitution Act 1975* (Vic) states that the Victorian Parliament can make laws "in and for Victoria in all cases what-soever". However, for all States (including Victoria) the "peace, order and good government" formula is now imposed by s 2(1) of the *Australia Act 1986*.

It is sometimes suggested that the formula "peace, welfare [or order] and good government" in the grant of legislative power might be judicially construed as a limitation on parliamentary sovereignty. The courts would then have the power to ask themselves: Is this really a statute for the *peace* of New South Wales; for the *welfare* of New South Wales; or for the *good government* of New South Wales? If the answers to these questions were "No", the statute would be uncon-stitutional.

A suggestion that "peace, welfare and good government" are words of limitation was made by Street CJ in *Building Construction Employees and Builders' Labourers Federation of New South Wales v Minister for Industrial Relations* (*BLF Case*) (1986) 7 NSWLR 372. A challenge to the deregistration of the Building Construction Employees and Builders' Labourers Federation (BLF) had been dismissed by Lee J in the Supreme Court of New South Wales. The Union appealed, but before the appeal could be heard the New South Wales Parliament passed the *Builders Labourers Federation (Special Provisions) Act 1986* (NSW). That Act sought to remove doubts that had arisen in the hearing before Lee J. According to Kirby P: "**[395]** Its plain object was to remove any risk of an adverse determination of the appeal from Lee J. It amounts, in effect, although not in its terms, to a legislative judgment". It was argued before the New South Wales Court of Appeal that the Act was invalid because s 5 of the New South Wales Constitution did not empower the Parliament to abrogate certain fundamental rights. This argument failed.

Building Construction Employees and Builders' Labourers Federation of New South Wales v Minister for Industrial Relations (*BLF Case*)
(1986) 7 NSWLR 372

Street CJ: [383] It appears to be generally assumed that these words ["peace, welfare, and good government"] confer unlimited legislative power, comparable with that vested in the English Parliament itself. I can find no satisfactory basis for that assumption. The words, by their very terms, confine the powers conferred to "peace, welfare, and good government" of the body politic in respect of which the legislature is being established.

Assertions that these words convey plenary, or sovereign, power are to be found frequently in cases in which it has been felt necessary to reject any suggestion that the legislature in question is a mere delegate of the English Parliament and thus is not able to delegate further the law-making powers vested in it. Such suggestions have been uniformly rejected. But the rejection of such suggestions on the basis that the words confer plenary or sovereign power, does not necessarily import that the power is unlimited in scope.

Street CJ quoted the well-known passage from *R v Burah* (1878) 3 App Cas 889, declaring that a colonial legislature has "**[904]** plenary powers of legislation, as large, and of the same nature, as those of [the Imperial] Parliament itself"; but also that its powers "are expressly limited by the Act of the Imperial Parliament which created it, and it can, of course, do nothing beyond the limits which circumscribe these powers". As to this he said:

Street CJ: [384] This is a significant demonstration that a legislature may have "plenary powers of legislation, as large, and of the same nature, as those of Parliament itself" (ie the English Parliament) but may at the same time be subject to "limits which circumscribe these powers". This, in my view, is the position in which the New South Wales Parliament stands. It has plenary or sovereign powers. But they are circumscribed or limited by the requirement of "the peace, welfare, and good government of New South Wales". The limit may well be wide and extensive. Ultimately, however, it is a binding limit. Laws inimical to, or which do not serve, the peace, welfare, and good government of our parliamentary democracy, perceived in the sense I have previously indicated, will be struck down by the courts as unconstitutional ...

Dr Hogg in his *Constitutional Law of Canada* (1977) ... refers to the decision of the Privy Council in *Attorney-General for Saskatchewan v Canadian Pacific Railway Co* [1953] AC 594. Reference to the terms of the judgment in that case not only provide no support for Dr Hogg's proposition that the words "peace, order, and good government" confer plenary, unrestricted power; the judgment is in fact impliedly inconsistent with it. Their Lordships say of this phrase (at 613-614):

> "The words 'peace, order, and good government' are words of very wide import, and a legislature empowered to pass laws for such purposes had a very wide discretion."

In acknowledging the "very wide" import and discretion, the Privy Council has, it seems to me, impliedly accepted that the import and discretion is not unlimited ...

[385] As between the two Privy Council decisions I feel myself at liberty to express a clear preference for the existence of a limitation on the legislative power as impliedly recognised in *Attorney-General for Saskatchewan v Canadian Pacific Railway Co*. I agree with the view of Abel, as noted by Dr Hogg, that the critical phrase should not be treated as "a jingle" and that a court asks in relation to a statute "does this involve the peace of Canada? the order of Canada? the good government of Canada?" I see no warrant for glossing these apparently important words out of the *Constitution Act* and depriving them of their ordinary meaning and operation ...

There are to be found in the reports comments from great judges as far apart in the pages of history as Lord Coke and Sir Robin Cooke, the current President [in 1986] of the New Zealand Court of Appeal, asserting the power of the [386] courts to impose an ultimate test upon the constitutional validity of the enactments of a sovereign Parliament. In *Dr Bonham's Case* (1610) 8 Co Rep 107a at 118a; 77 ER 638 at 652, the Chief Justice said:

> "... And it appears in our books, that in many cases, the common law will controul Acts of Parliament, and sometimes adjudge them to be utterly void: for when an Act of Parliament is against common right and reason, or repugnant, or impossible to be performed, the common law will controul it and adjudge such Act to be void."

This brave assertion has not stood the test of time, and is regarded as having been denied by the *Bill of Rights* of 1688 and the *Act of Settlement* of 1700. But the ringing words of Lord Coke, one of the great civil libertarians of history, from whose lips the words due process of law issued repeatedly, may even yet provide encouragement for courts in putting down tyrannous legislation.

I shall not attempt to document the occasional assertions by English judges in the centuries that followed that reflected concern at the risk of the exercise of unbridled power by Parliament. They included *Day v Savadge* (1614) Hob 85 at 87; 80 ER 235 at 236-237 and *City of London v Wood* (1701) 12 Mod 669 at 687-688; 88 ER 1592 at 1601-1602 ...

Those assertions cannot be regarded as having commanded in themselves authoritative weight. They do, however, demonstrate apprehension on the part of judges of the risks inherent in the existence of absolute and unlimited power in the legislature.

Over 350 years after Lord Coke's judgment in *Dr Bonham's Case*, Sir Robin Cooke said in *New Zealand Drivers' Association v New Zealand Road Carriers* [1982] 1 NZLR 374 at 390:

> "... we have reservations as to the extent to which in New Zealand even an Act of Parliament can take away the rights of citizens to resort to the ordinary courts of law for the determination of their rights."

The conspicuous failure of the legislature to devise a wholly effective privative clause might, perhaps, be regarded as providing some support for these reservations.

Two years later Sir Robin Cooke in *Fraser v State Services Commission* [1984] 1 NZLR 116 at 121 said:

> "... This is perhaps a reminder that it is arguable that some common law rights may go so deep that even Parliament cannot be accepted by the Courts to have destroyed them."

The learned President renewed his assertion of ultimate judicial power in *Taylor v New Zealand Poultry Board* [1984] 1 NZLR 394 at 398:

> "... I do not think that literal compulsion, by torture for instance, would be within the lawful powers of Parliament. Some common law rights presumably lie so deep that even Parliament could not override them." ...

[387] I have a strong affinity for the judicial philosophy revived by Sir Robin Cooke in the 1980s. I am constrained, however, both by the absence of any decision commanding acceptance as

authoritative in which a doctrine of fundamental rights has actually been applied to invalidate a statute, and by Lord Reid's authoritative rejection of such a doctrine in *British Railways Board v Pickin* [1974] AC 765 at 782, to accept that there is no such doctrine standing alone. In any event the 1986 Act is not of such a character as to infringe any such doctrine. Parliament could have achieved its object in the same way as did the Commonwealth Parliament, that is to say without interference with the judicial process.

For my own part, I prefer to look to the constitutional constraints of "peace, welfare, and good government" as the source of power in the courts to exercise an ultimate authority to protect our parliamentary democracy, not only against tyrannous excesses on the part of a legislature that may have fallen under extremist control, but also in a general sense as limiting the power of Parliament. I repeat what I have said earlier – laws inimical to, or which do not serve, the peace, welfare, and good government of our parliamentary democracy, perceived in the sense I have previously indicated, will be struck down by the courts as unconstitutional. There is here a field of constitutional jurisprudence which has not yet been explored and developed. It may well become significant in the years ahead. Sir Robin Cooke's comments could be of relevance in this exploration and development. Standing alone, however, they do not, in my opinion, provide a safe independent basis for invalidating legislation that is otherwise within the constitutional authority of Parliament.

The dicta assembled by Street CJ, ranging from those of Sir Edward Coke (later Lord Coke) to those of Sir Robin Cooke (now Lord Cooke of Thorndon), suggested that, quite apart from any restrictive reading of the "peace, welfare and good government" formula, an independent line of authority beginning with *Dr Bonham's Case* in 1610 (see Chapter 3, §(2)(c)) could support a continuing judicial power to protect certain fundamental rights against legislative encroachment. That alternative line of authority, bolstered by numerous dicta of Murphy J in the High Court (see Chapter 28, §2), was considered most fully by Kirby P, though he ultimately rejected such an approach.

Kirby P: [404] Calling upon [a] long stream of authority, dating back to 1610, the BLF urge that there should be implied into the constitutional arrangements of New South Wales, a common law right "so deep" that the legislature could not invade it. This right assured the subject unimpeded pursuit of the entitlement to have a case before the Court determined according to law. In particular the right could not be destroyed by ad hominem legislation directed specifically and only at the termination of the right and, as well, at the termination of the entitlement to costs accrued in the normal way.

There are a number of answers to this stream of authority, at least so far as it is said to apply to the present case. The appeal to natural law and to a principle higher than parliamentary sovereignty is certainly out of line with the mainstream of current constitutional theory as applied in our courts. In *Liyanage* [*v The Queen* [1967] 1 AC 259] the attempt to argue that there are certain "fundamental principles" which inhibit legislative supremacy (the operations of the *Colonial Laws Validity Act* 1865 apart) was specifically rejected by the Privy Council ...: see also *Ibralebbe v The Queen* [1964] AC 900. Furthermore, Lord Reid in *British Railways Board v Pickin* [1974] AC 765 at 782 rejected the **[405]** notion of any such "right so deep", declaring it to be a notion incompatible with historical and constitutional facts:

> "... In earlier times many learned lawyers seem to have believed that an Act of Parliament could be disregarded in so far as it was contrary to the law of God or the law of nature or natural justice, but since the supremacy of Parliament was finally demonstrated by the Revolution of 1688 any such idea has become obsolete." ...

I agree with Lord Reid's conclusion. I do so in recognition of years of unbroken constitutional law and tradition in Australia and, beforehand, in the United Kingdom. That unbroken law and tradition has repeatedly reinforced and ultimately respected the democratic will of the people as expressed in Parliament. It has reflected political realities in our society and the distribution of power within it. I also do so in recognition of the dangers which may attend the development by judges (as distinct from the development by the people's representatives) of a doctrine of fundamental rights more potent than Parliamentary legislation. Such extra-constitutional notions must be viewed with reservation not only because they lack the legitimacy that attaches to the enactments ultimately sanctioned by the people. But also because, once allowed, there is no logical limit to their ambit. They may thereby undermine a rule of law and invite the only effective substitute, viz the rule of power. In the end, it is respect for long standing political realities and loyalty to the desirable notion of elected democracy that inhibits any lingering judicial temptation, even in a hard case, to deny loyal respect to the commands of Parliament by reference to suggested fundamental rights that run "so deep" that Parliament cannot disturb them.

This conclusion does not leave our citizens unprotected from an oppressive majority in Parliament. The chief protection lies in the democratic nature of our Parliamentary institutions. This much was emphasised in *Grace Bible Church v Reedman* (1984) 36 SASR 376 at 390; 54 ALR 571 at 585. It was the uniform approach to challenges such as the present in the authoritative decisions in Canada before the enactment of the Charter ...

A second protection lies in the power, referred to by Dicey, by which judges may construe legislation. In this sense, the sovereignty of Parliament is subject to the Rule of Law for, as Lord Diplock explained in *Black-Clawson International Ltd v Papierwerke Waldhof-Aschaffenburg AG* [1975] AC 591 at 638, under our Constitution, Parliament is sovereign only in respect of what it expresses by the words used in the legislation it has passed. I do not pause to examine the constitutional basis of this asserted power. Judges interpret the words. Often judges do surgery to legislation, in order to ensure **[406]** its consistency with basic constitutional assumptions. This, after all, is what Lord Wilberforce ultimately did in *Vestey [v Inland Revenue Commrs* [1980] AC 1148].

But if the legislation is clear, and though the judge considers it to be unjust or even oppressive, it is not for him to substitute his opinion for that of the elected representatives assembled in Parliament. In *Taylor v New Zealand Poultry Board* [[1984] 1 NZLR 394 at 398], Cooke J suggested that "I do not think that literal compulsion, by torture for instance, would be within the lawful powers of Parliament". Yet imprisonment, solitary confinement as a punishment and other severe physical and financial restraints have clearly been considered, even in recent times, to be within the power of Parliament. Substituting judicial opinion about entrenched rights for the lawful powers of Parliament, unless anchored in a Bill of Rights duly enacted, inevitably runs into the difficulties of defining what those "common law rights" are and of explaining how they are so basic that they cannot be disturbed. The developments in legislation on capital and corporal punishment illustrate the fact that perceptions of such "basic rights" are likely to vary in place and over time.

It is not necessary for me to consider in this case whether a power is reserved to the judiciary by the *Constitution Act* of 1902, s 5, to declare invalid a manifestly arbitrary and unjust law as repugnant to the Constitution on the grounds that it could not conceivably be, as the *Constitution Act* 1902, s 5, requires, a law "for the peace, welfare and good government of New South Wales". Those words have hitherto been seen as an ample grant of power "in all cases whatsoever". By their history, purpose and language these words may not be apt to provide a limitation on what the legislature may enact. In any case, if the legislature were to enact such a manifestly unacceptable statute as is postulated, it is unlikely to be restrained either by the Constitution Act, s 5, or the courts. Our protection against such predicaments remains, fundamentally, a political and democratic one. Whether there should be more significant legal protections is a matter of current debate in the Australian community. But that debate cannot influence the determination of the present summons. It must be resolved in accordance with the present law.

Glass JA reserved his opinion on this issue. Mahoney JA reached a similar result to Kirby P, while Priestley JA reached a similar conclusion to Street CJ.

Street CJ's suggestion that the words "peace, welfare and good government" do not convey plenary power was firmly squashed by the High Court in *Union Steamship Co of Australia Pty Ltd v King* (1988) 166 CLR 1. A similar suggestion as to Commonwealth power, based on the words "peace, order, and good government" in s 51, was rejected by the High Court in *Polyukhovich v Commonwealth* (*War Crimes Act Case*) (1991) 172 CLR 501.

In *Union Steamship*, it was argued that the words "peace, welfare, and good government of New South Wales" in s 5 of the *Constitution Act 1902* (NSW) did not merely confer power upon the New South Wales Parliament, but were also words of limitation. However, the Court accepted that the "peace, welfare and good government" formula has no special semantic significance, but is simply the conventional formula used by the Imperial Parliament when it wished to confer plenary power. The apparently interchangeable use of "peace, *welfare* and good government" and "peace, *order* and good government" provides support for this view. If "welfare" and "order" were taken seriously as legislative prescriptions, they would point in very different directions.

Union Steamship Co of Australia Pty Ltd v King
(1988) 166 CLR 1

The Court: [9] The power to make laws "for the peace, welfare, and good government" of a territory is indistinguishable from the power to make laws "for the peace, order and good government" of a territory. Such a power is a plenary power and it was so recognized, even in an era when emphasis was given to the character of colonial legislatures as subordinate law-making bodies. The plenary nature of the power was established in the series of historic Privy Council decisions at the close of the nineteenth century: *R v Burah* [(1878) 3 App Cas 889]; *Hodge v The Queen* [(1883) 9 App Cas 117]; *Powell v Apollo Candle Co* [(1885) 10 App Cas 282]; *Riel v The Queen* [(1885) 10 App Cas 675]. They decided that colonial legislatures were not mere agents or delegates of the Imperial Parliament.

Lord Selborne, speaking for the Judicial Committee in *Burah* [(1878) 3 App Cas at 904], said that the Indian Legislature "has, and was intended to have, plenary powers of legislation, as large, and of the same nature, as those of Parliament itself". Later, Sir Barnes Peacock in *Hodge* [(1883) 9 App Cas at 132], speaking for the Judicial Committee, stated that the legislature of Ontario enjoyed by virtue of the *British North America Act* 1867 (Imp): "authority as plenary and as ample within the limits prescribed by sect 92 as the Imperial Parliament in the plenitude of its power possessed and could bestow. Within these limits of subjects and area the local legislature is supreme, and has the same authority as the Imperial Parliament ..." In *Riel* Lord Halsbury LC, delivering the opinion of the Judicial Committee, rejected the contention that a statute was invalid if a court concluded that it was not calculated as a matter of fact and policy to secure the peace, order and good government of the territory. His Lordship went on **[10]** to say that such a power was "apt to authorize the utmost discretion of enactment for the attainment of the objects pointed to" [(1885) 10 App Cas at 678]. In *Chenard & Co v Joachim Arissol* [[1949] AC 127], Lord Reid, delivering the opinion of the Judicial Committee, cited *Riel* and the comments of Lord Halsbury LC with evident approval. More recently Viscount Radcliffe, speaking for the Judicial Committee, described a power to make laws for the peace, order and good government of a territory as "connot[ing], in British constitutional language, the widest law-making powers appropriate to a Sovereign": *Ibralebbe v The Queen* [[1964] AC 900 at 923].

These decisions and statements of high authority demonstrate that, within the limits of the grant, a power to make laws for the peace, order and good government of a territory is as ample and plenary as the power possessed by the Imperial Parliament itself. That is, the words "for the peace, order and good government" are not words of limitation. They did not confer on the courts of a colony, just as they do not confer on the courts of a State, jurisdiction to strike down legislation on the ground that, in the opinion of a court, the legislation does not promote or secure the peace, order and good government of the colony. Just as the courts of the United Kingdom cannot invalidate laws made by the Parliament of the United Kingdom on the ground that they do not secure the welfare and the public interest, so the exercise of its legislative power by the Parliament of New South Wales is not susceptible to judicial review on that score. Whether the exercise of that legislative power is subject to some restraints by reference to rights deeply rooted in our democratic system of government and the common law (see *Drivers v Road Carriers* [[1982] 1 NZLR 374 at 390]; *Fraser v State Services Commission* [[1984] 1 NZLR 116 at 121]; *Taylor v New Zealand Poultry Board* [[1984] 1 NZLR 394 at 398]), a view which Lord Reid firmly rejected in *Pickin v British Railways Board* [[1974] AC 765 at 782], is another question which we need not explore.

The unanimous judgment did concede that, insofar as State legislation still depends for its validity on some connection (however slight) with the territorial concerns of the State (see Chapter 4, §7(a)), that continuing requirement may nowadays depend on the "peace, welfare and good government" formula – presumably because the reference is to the "peace, welfare and good government" *of the State*. Apart from this residual concession, however, the attempt by Street CJ to derive a judicially enforceable limitation on legislative power from the words "peace, welfare and good government" was decisively rejected. Moreover, even that residual concession seems now to have been withdrawn, since the territorial limitation of State legislative power is apparently now to be derived not from the "peace, welfare and good government" formula but from the "text and structure" of the Commonwealth Constitution (see *BHP Billiton Ltd v Schultz* (2004) 211 ALR 523).

Note, however, that the final sentence from the judgment in *Union Steamship v King* leaves open the possibility that a limit on power might be found in "rights deeply rooted in our democratic system … and the common law". That possibility has been a topic of ongoing debate (see *Broken Hill Proprietary Co Ltd v Dagi* [1996] 2 VR 106; *Wake v Northern Territory* (1996) 109 NTR 1; *Kable v Director of Public Prosecutions (NSW)* (1996) 189 CLR 51; *Kruger v Commonwealth (Stolen Generations Case)* (1997) 190 CLR 1).

The issue arose again in *Durham Holdings Pty Ltd v New South Wales* (2001) 205 CLR 399. The *Coal Acquisition Act 1981* (NSW) vested coal in certain New South Wales land in the Crown in right of that State. The Act provided for payments to land owners, but from 1990 the amount was capped, thereby denying full compensation. If the acquisition had arisen under a Commonwealth statute, it would have breached the requirement in s 51(xxxi) of the Constitution that such acquisitions be made on "just terms". Durham Holdings Pty Ltd, a coal mining company, argued that the scheme was invalid because it exceeded the legislative powers of the New South Wales Parliament in providing for an acquisition of property without fair compensation. The Court of Appeal rejected this, and the High Court refused special leave to appeal because the argument "[437] would enjoy no prospects of success". After quoting the final two sentences of the extract from *Union Steamship* above, Gaudron, McHugh, Gummow and Hayne JJ continued:

Durham Holdings Pty Ltd v New South Wales
(2001) 205 CLR 399

Gaudron, McHugh, Gummow and Hayne JJ: [409] The question that the applicant posed for the Court of Appeal thus was whether or not the right to receive "just" or "properly adequate" compensation is such a "deeply rooted right" as to operate as a restraint upon the legislative power of the New South Wales Parliament. What the Court of Appeal said [*Durham Holdings Pty Ltd v State of New South Wales* (1999) 47 NSWLR 340 at 365] is true of the application to this Court, namely:

"The [applicant] was unable to point to any judicial pronouncements, let alone a decided case, which indicated, at any time, that any such principle existed in the common law of England, or of the **[410]** colonies of Australasia, or of Australia. It advocated the development of the common law, by the recognition of such a principle for the first time in this case."

The applicant sought to rely upon statements respecting the common law in decisions respecting the powers of several of the states of the United States before the inclusion in those written state constitutions of guarantees respecting the taking of property. However, what would be involved if the applicant's submission were accepted would not be the development of the common law of Australia. Rather, it would involve modification of the arrangements which comprise the constitutions of the states within the meaning of s 106 of the Constitution, and by which the state legislatures are erected and maintained, and exercise their powers.

The applicant must seek to introduce into the constitutional text, [and] in particular [into] s 2(2) of the Australia Act, a limitation not found there. Undoubtedly, having regard to the federal system and the text and structure of "[t]he Constitution of each State of the Commonwealth" (the phrase used in s 106 of the Constitution), there are limits to the exercise of the legislative powers conferred upon the parliament which are not spelled out in the constitutional text. However, the limitation for which the applicant contends is not, as a matter of logical or practical necessity, implicit in the federal structure within which state parliaments legislate. Further, whatever may be the scope of the inhibitions on legislative power involved in the question identified but not explored in *Union Steamship*, the requirement of compensation which answers the description "just" or "properly adequate" falls outside that field of discourse.

Callinan J found it unnecessary to address the issue and stated that he would "**[433]** reserve" his position on "the existence or otherwise, or the nature of, any unexpressed limits upon the legislative powers of the states". Kirby J reached the same conclusion as he had 15 years before in the *BLF Case* in rejecting limitations arising from the grant of State legislative power. However, he now suggested that limitations might arise from a different source.

> **Kirby J: [431]** In Australia, a state is not free-standing. Nor is it merely an historical colony given a different name. It is a state of the Commonwealth. It derives its constitutional status, as such, from the federal Constitution. It may be inferred, from that Constitution, that a State is a polity of a particular character. Thus s 107 of the Constitution provides, and requires, that each state should have a parliament. Such parliaments must be of a kind appropriate to a state of the Commonwealth and to a legislature that can fulfil functions envisaged for it by the Constitution. Ultimately, a "law of a State", made by such a parliament, could only be a "law" of a kind envisaged by the Constitution. Certain "extreme" laws might fall outside that constitutional presupposition.
>
> The significance of the contemporary realisation that the foundation of Australia's Constitution lies in the will of the Australian people has not yet been fully explored. It is not impossible that this conception would, in an extreme case, also reinforce the foregoing and affect judicial recognition of a purported "State law" that was not, in truth, a "law" at all. In Australia, considerations such as these, derived directly or indirectly from the Constitution, afford the likely future judicial response to any extreme affront masquerading as a State law. The answer lies in the implications derived from the Constitution, not in assertions by judges that the common law authorises them to **[432]** ignore an otherwise valid law of a state. Such an over-mighty assertion in relation to constitutional powers of lawmaking is as alien to our law as to our political realities. On the other hand, judicial derivation of implications from the federal Constitution is not alien but familiar.
>
> The present case, although apparently involving discrimination and arguably injustice to the applicant, falls far short of the extreme instance that would enliven any of the foregoing constitutional implications, assuming they had been invoked.

Jeffrey Goldsworthy has argued that courts do not possess the power to protect rights deeply rooted in the democratic system of government against abuse by parliament. He has rejected what he calls the "**[259]** The Argument From Extreme Cases" for such limits.

Jeffrey Goldsworthy, *The Sovereignty of Parliament: History and Philosophy*
(Clarendon Press, 1999)

[259] By far the most popular argument against the doctrine of parliamentary sovereignty is that no one could possibly be obligated to obey, and therefore **[260]** Parliament could not possibly have authority to enact, a statute that is blatantly and egregiously unjust or undemocratic. FA Mann, for example, invites us to imagine a statute depriving Jews of their nationality, prohibiting Christians from marrying non-Christians, dissolving marriages between blacks and whites, or confiscating the property of all red-haired women. 'Is it really suggested that English judges would have to apply and would in fact apply such a law? Do not evade the issue, do not avoid the legal test by asserting that, as we all hope and believe, no English parliament would ever pass such a statute.'

Allan also resorts to improbable, extreme examples. He insists that the courts could not possibly be justified in obeying a 'wicked' statute, which 'seriously contradicted the fundamental tenets of our political morality', such as one requiring all blue-eyed babies to be killed, depriving a large section of the population of the right to vote, or authorising officials to inflict punishment for whatever reason they should choose. Because it leads to the opposite conclusion, the doctrine of parliamentary sovereignty is an 'absurdity' that is 'bereft of any rational justification' ...

[261] The fatal flaw in this argument is that it treats moral and legal authority, and moral and legal obligation, as equivalents. It would be unreasonable to believe that a morally fallible legislature could have unlimited moral authority to enact laws, and that people would therefore have a moral obligation to obey whatever laws it might enact, no matter now undemocratic or unjust they might be. If legal authority to enact laws were the same as moral authority, then it would also be unreasonable to believe that such a legislature could have unlimited legal authority to enact laws. But there are good reasons for distinguishing between moral and legal authority, and between moral and legal obligation. They are reasons for thinking that a morally fallible legislature could have unlimited legal authority, despite having only limited moral authority, to enact laws. It follows that the doctrine of parliamentary sovereignty is not an absurdity, which legal officials cannot really accept.

It is not a logical or practical necessity that Parliament should have ultimate legal authority to decide what the law is. But it is a practical necessity that *some* institution have ultimate authority to decide any legal question that may arise, even if it is a different institution with respect to different types of questions. Otherwise the decisions of legal institutions would be no more than recommendations as to what the law is, and could not resolve disagreements between people with passionately opposed views. In the seventeenth century, this was often put in terms of obedience. 'Appeals must not be infinite', said one author [William Assheton], 'There must be some supreme power, in whose final determination (be it *right* or be it *wrong*) all inferiors must acquiesce and submit, otherwise, no controversies could be decided; nay, there could be no government, nothing but disorder and confusion in the world.' This goes too far. What is necessary is that on any legal question there must be an ultimate authority whose decisions are accepted as authoritatively stating the law, even if they are disobeyed because they are unjust.

If the judges rather than Parliament had this ultimate authority, we would be in the same predicament. Their decisions would have to be accepted as lawful even by people who, rightly or wrongly, believe them to be unjust. And because **[262]** judges, like legislators, are morally fallible, we would still face the danger of occasional, possibly egregious injustice. To adapt the words of Dudley Digges the younger, 'we cannot have any absolute security; in all governments it is necessary to trust somebody ... if you are weary of democracy you know the way to cast it off by placing judicial guardians over your Parliament, but have you any greater assurance than before? *Quis custodiet ipsos custodies*?' In other words, if it is useful to ask whether a statute requiring that blue-eyed babies be killed could possibly be valid, it is equally useful to ask whether a judicial decision that a blue-eyed baby be killed could possibly be valid. And if a negative answer to the former question justifies judges having authority to invalidate statutes, a negative answer to the latter question must justify officials other than judges having authority to invalidate judicial decisions. But who might they be, and to whom would we turn if *they* declared that blue-eyed babies must be killed? Such reasoning produces either a vicious circle, or an infinite regress, of authority to overrule egregiously unjust decisions. In practice, the chain of legal authority, and the availability of legal methods of overruling egregiously unjust decisions, must at some point come to an end. At that point, whichever institution has ultimate authority to decide a question must be trusted to exercise it responsibly. By itself, 'the possibility of the abuse of power, is no objection against that power ... for there can be no power at all, which is not accompanied with some trust; and there is no trust, but it possibly (morally speaking) may be broken'.

(b)   Constitutional Amendment

Each State Parliament has power to amend the constitution of its State, subject (as we shall see) to such binding "manner and form" requirements as the Parliament itself has been able to impose in the exercise of that power. The historical genesis both of the constituent power and of "manner and form" limitations lies in s 5 of the *Colonial Laws Validity Act 1865* (Imp) (see Appendix). That section gave to "every Colonial Legislature" full constituent power in respect of its own judicial system, and to "every Representative Legislature" full constituent power "to make Laws respecting the Constitution, Powers, and Procedure of such Legislature". Although the proviso at the end of s 5 ("provided that such Laws shall have been passed in such Manner and Form as may from Time to Time be required") restricted the power of the Australian States to amend their own constitutions, it is clear that the purpose of enacting the section was to establish that the colonies did have such a power. Each colonial Parliament was to have a continuing power to re-enact and re-write its own *Constitution Act*. In other words, these were flexible, not rigid, constitutions (see Chapter 1, §1).

At Federation on 1 January 1901, s 106 of the Australian Constitution ensured that, in each State, the *Constitution Act* of the former colony would "continue as at the establishment of the Commonwealth". Its continuance was "subject to this Constitution" and was also subject to alteration "in accordance with the Constitution of the State". In Queensland during World War I, the limits of what this might mean were tested in *Taylor v Attorney-General of Queensland* (1917) 23 CLR 457.

In 1908, after a protracted political deadlock between the two Houses of the Queensland Parliament, the *Parliamentary Bills Referendum Act 1908* (Qld) was enacted as a way of resolving such deadlocks in the future. The Act established an "alternative" legislative procedure: if a Bill was twice passed by the Legislative Assembly in two successive sessions, and twice rejected by the Legislative Council in two successive sessions, it might then be submitted to a referendum and, if approved, might then be presented for the Royal Assent.

In 1915, pursuant to this alternative procedure, A Bill to Amend the Constitution of Queensland by Abolishing the Legislative Council was passed by the Legislative Assembly but rejected by the Legislative Council. This was repeated in 1916. In 1917 the government proposed to put the Bill to a referendum. The Queensland Supreme Court granted an interlocutory injunction to prevent the referendum going ahead, but on appeal to the High Court the injunction was dissolved on condition that the Queensland government undertook to take no action on the referendum result until the constitutional issues had been determined by the High Court. The referendum went ahead, but produced a majority vote against the abolition proposal. Despite the referendum result, the High Court gave judgment on the issues of principle involved.

The first significant issue was whether the Queensland Parliament possessed the power to enact the *Parliamentary Bills Referendum Act*, that is, to create an alternative legislative procedure by-passing the Legislative Council. The High Court held that the Act was valid by relying upon s 5 of the *Colonial Laws Validity Act*. Adopting the language of s 5, Barton J said:

Taylor v Attorney-General of Queensland
(1917) 23 CLR 457

Barton J: [468] The Parliament of Queensland is a "representative legislature" and also a "colonial legislature" within the meaning of the Imperial Act. As such it is deemed always to have had, and it has had from 1865, "full power within its jurisdiction to establish Courts of judicature, and to abolish and reconstitute the same, and to alter the constitution thereof, and to make provision for the administration of justice therein." Also it is deemed always to have had, and it has had from 1865, "full power to make laws respecting the constitution, powers, and procedure of such legislature; provided that such laws shall have been passed in such manner and form as may from time to time be required by any Act of Parliament, letters patent, Order in Council, or colonial law for the time being in force" in Queensland. I take the constitution of a legislature, as the term is here used, to mean the composition, form or nature of the House of legislature where there is only one House, or of either House if the legislative body consists of two Houses. Probably the power does not extend to authorize the elimination of the representative character of the legislature within the meaning of the Act ...

The section is one of continuous vitality, and acts upon all laws as to the constitution and powers **[469]** of the legislature, so as to give them validity whether they were passed before or after 1865. It is true that the *Constitution Act of* 1867 provided for all laws passed thereunder to be enacted "by Her Majesty by and with the advice and consent of the Legislative Council and Legislative Assembly in Parliament assembled," and that the Constitution did not recognize the making of laws by any other authority. It is also true that in general the legislation of a body created by and acting under a written charter or constitution is valid only so far as it conforms to the authority conferred by that instrument of government, and that therefore attempted legislation, merely at variance with the charter or constitution, cannot be held an effective law on the ground that the authority conferred by that instrument includes a power to alter or repeal any part of it, if the legislation questioned has not been preceded by a good exercise of such power; that is, if the charter or constitution has not antecedently been so altered within the authority given by that document itself ... Normally, therefore, in the absence of such a provision as sec 5 of the Imperial Act, I should have been prepared to hold that the *Parliamentary Bills Referendum Act of* 1908, which, though it professed to be an amendment of the *Constitution Act of* 1867, was merely, in view of its provisions, an Act at variance with the Constitution, not preceded by a valid extension of the constitutional power, was therefore itself, as it stood, invalid. But in the present case the Imperial provision seems to me to take away the application of the principle I have stated to legislation of the kind which it authorizes. The *Parliamentary Bills Referendum Act* is a law "respecting the powers" of the Legislature in certain cases ... I feel bound to say that **[470]** in my opinion the words of the Imperial sec 5 cover such a case.

Isaacs J agreed. With the exception of any attempt to eliminate the Crown, which he thought could "**[474]** not [be] included in the ambit of such a power", he took a very broad view of the power.

Isaacs J: [474] I read the words "constitution of such legislature" as including the change from a unicameral to a bicameral system, or the reverse. Probably the "representative" character of the legislature is a basic condition of the power relied on, and is preserved by the word "such," but, that being maintained, I can see no reason for cutting down the plain natural meaning of the words in question so as to exclude the power of a self-governing community to say that for State purposes one House is sufficient as its organ of legislation. Some strong reason must be shown for cutting down the primary meaning of the words themselves applied to such a subject matter. I have shown why the grounds advanced for that purpose are insufficient ...

In my opinion, therefore, the full meaning of the words must be given to them, and, consequently, supposing there were no other authority to support the Queensland Referendum Act of 1908 than the *Colonial Laws Validity Act* 1865 – which is a standing general power of all representative legislatures outside and irrespective of their own separate Constitutions – the answer to the second question should be in the affirmative.

Once it was established that the *Parliamentary Bills Referendum Act* was valid, the question of whether its procedures could be used to abolish the Upper House received less attention. For one thing, the failure of the referendum meant that for the time being that question was moot. For another thing, the breadth of the power was so all-encompassing that it would necessarily extend to the abolition of the Upper House. Thus, Gavan Duffy and Rich JJ dealt with the particular issue of abolition as part of the general issue. After quoting s 5 of the *Colonial Laws Validity Act*, they went on:

Gavan Duffy and Rich JJ: [477] In our opinion the word "constitution" in this collocation means "nature," "composition," or "make up," and the enactment enables a representative legislature to alter its constitution as it chooses, to allot to the legislature such powers as it thinks fit, and to prescribe the method in which it shall conduct its proceedings. It may perhaps be that the legislature must always remain a representative legislature as defined by the Statute, but it is unnecessary in the present case to determine whether that is so or not. This seems to us the plain meaning of the words used, but it is urged that some less extended meaning should be given to them because of the earlier words of the section which run as follows: "Every colonial legislature shall have, and be deemed at all times to have had, full power within its jurisdiction to establish Courts of judicature, and to abolish and reconstitute the same, and to alter the constitution thereof, and to make provision for the administration of justice therein." It is said that the word "abolish" is used here where it is intended to give power to put an end to a Court, and that a similar word would have been used had it been intended to give power to destroy the Legislative Council, which is an integral part of the existing legislature. Had it been intended to give to a representative legislature power to enact that there should thereafter be no legislature, the word "abolish" might well **[478]** have been used, but the vice of the argument lies in a confusion between two distinct notions – the abolition of a legislature, and the abolition of a constituent part of such legislature. Mere alteration of the constitution of a legislature negatives the notion of the abolition of such legislature, but may entail the abolition of an integral part of it. The words of the section are properly chosen to express the powers sought to be conferred. It was intended that a colonial legislature should have power to constitute new Courts and to put an end to existing Courts, to determine whether specific Courts should continue to exist or should cease to exist, as well as to mould their form, prescribe their duties, and regulate their procedure, but it was not intended that a representative legislature should have power to produce anarchy by enacting that there should be no legislature; its powers are limited to determining what shall be the nature of the legislative body, what its powers of legislation, and what its methods of procedure. At the time the Legislature of Queensland passed the *Parliamentary Bills Referendum Act of* 1908, it was such a "representative legislature." It is said that the effect of that enactment was to provide that in certain cases laws should be made by the Legislative Assembly and the electors speaking by means of a referendum, instead of by the Legislative Assembly and the Legislative Council. We think its true effect was merely to limit the power of the Legislative Council by rendering its concurrence unnecessary in the making of laws in certain circumstances. But, however this may be, it is clear that it was a law within the competence of the then existing legislature, and that after its passage the Legislature of Queensland still remained a representative legislature within the meaning of the *Colonial Laws Validity Act*, and therefore competent to make laws with respect to its own constitution, powers, and procedure. It follows from what we have already said that a law to abolish the Legislative Council of Queensland would be such a law, for it would leave the Legislature of Queensland still a representative legislature within the meaning of the *Colonial Laws Validity Act*.

Taylor v Attorney-General of Queensland established that the Queensland Legislative Council could be abolished. This occurred in 1921 without a further referendum. Meanwhile, another landmark case had arisen in Queensland, this time from legislation affecting the constitution of the courts, and therefore falling within the first part of s 5 of the *Colonial Laws Validity Act*.

The *Industrial Arbitration Act 1916* (Qld) created a Court of Industrial Arbitration for the State of Queensland and envisaged that its President could also be appointed to the Supreme Court of Queensland. Appointment to the Court of Industrial Arbitration was to be for a renewable seven-year term. However, by s 6(6) of the Act, if the President was appointed to the Supreme Court, he or she "shall have in all respects and to all intents and purposes the rights, privileges, powers, and jurisdiction of a Judge of the Supreme Court in addition to the rights, privileges, powers, and jurisdiction conferred by this Act, and shall hold office as a Judge of the said Supreme Court during good behaviour, and be paid such salary and allowances as the Governor in Council may direct, which shall not be diminished or increased during his term of office as a Judge of the Supreme Court".

On the face of it, s 6(6) was an attempt to ensure that a Supreme Court appointment, where conferred on a person already holding the office of President, would carry with it all the normal guarantees of such an appointment, including a guarantee of tenure "during good behaviour" (that is, subject to misbehaviour) for life. However, throughout the litigation which followed, successive courts consistently held that s 6(6) was capable of authorising an appointment to the Supreme Court for a limited seven-year term. Moreover, they held that, as a matter of construction, it was not capable of authorising an appointment to the Supreme Court for life.

When Thomas McCawley was commissioned as the first President of the new Industrial Court, his commission purported to appoint him to the Supreme Court "during good behaviour". However, when he presented himself at the Supreme Court to take the judicial oath, members of the bar objected. It was argued that s 6(6) was unconstitutional if it was capable of authorising an appointment of a Supreme Court judge for a seven-year term. Section 15 of the *Constitution Act 1867* (Qld) declared that the commissions of all present and future Supreme Court judges "shall be, continue and remain in full force during their good behaviour".

In *McCawley v The King* [1920] AC 691, the Privy Council affirmed the power of the Queensland legislature to pass s 6(6), and thereby effectively to amend that State's Constitution.

Their Lordships held that this power could be exercised impliedly, that is, even in the absence of an express intention in s 6(6) to amend the *Constitution Act*.

McCawley v The King
[1920] AC 691

Lord Birkenhead (for their Lordships): **[703]** The first point which requires consideration depends upon the distinction between constitutions the terms of which may be modified or repealed with no other formality than is necessary in the case of other legislation, and constitutions which can only be altered with some special formality, and in some cases by a specially convened assembly.

The difference of view, which has been the subject of careful analysis by writers upon the subject of constitutional law, may be traced mainly to the spirit and genius of the nation in which a particular constitution has its birth. Some communities, and notably Great Britain, have not in the framing of constitutions felt it necessary, or thought it useful, to shackle the complete independence of their successors. They have shrunk from the assumption that a degree of wisdom and foresight has been conceded to their generation which will be, or may be, wanting to their successors, in spite of the fact that those successors will possess more experience of the circumstances and necessities amid which their lives are lived. Those constitution framers who have adopted the other view must be supposed to have believed that certainty and stability were in such a matter the supreme desiderata. Giving effect to this belief, they have created obstacles of varying difficulty in the path of those who would lay rash hands upon the ark of the constitution. It is not necessary, and indeed the inquiry would be a long one, to analyse the different methods which have been adopted in different countries by those who have framed constitutions under these safeguards. But it is important to realize with clearness the nature of the distinction. It is not a distinction which depends in the least upon the **[704]** differences between a unitary and a federal form of Government ...

Many different terms have been employed in the text-books to distinguish these two contrasted forms of constitution. Their special qualities may perhaps be exhibited as clearly by calling the one a controlled and the other an uncontrolled constitution as by any other nomenclature. Nor is a constitution debarred from being reckoned as an uncontrolled constitution because it is not, like the British constitution, constituted by historic development, but finds its genesis in an originating document which may contain some conditions which cannot be altered except by the power which gave it birth. It is of the greatest importance to notice that where the constitution is uncontrolled the consequences of its freedom admit of no qualification whatever. The doctrine is carried to every proper consequence with logical and inexorable precision. Thus when one of the learned judges in the Court below said that, according to the appellant, the constitution could be ignored as if it were a Dog Act, he was in effect merely expressing his opinion that the constitution was, in fact, controlled. If it were uncontrolled, it would be an elementary commonplace that in the eye of the law the legislative document or documents which defined it occupied precisely the same position as a Dog Act or any other Act, however humble its subject-matter.

The fundamental contention of the respondents in this appeal requires the conclusion that the constitution of Queensland is in the sense explained above a controlled constitution. The inquiry ought not to be, and in fact is not, a very difficult one; and it is proposed shortly to examine the principal points which arise; but it is important at the outset to notice **[705]** that the respondents do not find themselves in the position which they would occupy under any genuinely controlled constitution with which their Lordships are familiar. In such a case, confronted with the objections by which they are met in this appeal, they would have no difficulty in pointing to specific articles in the legislative instrument or instruments which created the constitution, prescribing with meticulous precision the methods by which, and by which alone, it could be altered. The respondents to this appeal are wholly unable to reinforce their argument by any such demonstration. And their inability has involved them in dialectical difficulties which are embarrassing and even ridiculous. They are, for instance, driven to contend – or at least they did in fact contend – that if it were desired to alter an article of the constitution it was in the first place necessary to pass a repealing Act; and in the second place by a separate and independent Act to make the desired change effective. Counsel for the respondents, in fact, though perhaps unnecessarily, went so far as to maintain that the attempted modification would not be effectively carried out by a single Act, even if such an Act incorporated the provisions of the two Acts which, in his view, required a separate existence.

Their Lordships prefer, however, to consider the matter in a manner more favourable to the respondents; and it would appear that their proposition may be more moderately stated in the following way. The constitution of Queensland is a controlled constitution. It cannot, therefore, be altered merely by enacting legislation inconsistent with its articles. It can only be altered by an Act which in plain and unmistakable language refers to it; asserts the intention of the Legislature to alter it; and consequentially gives effect to that intention by its operative provisions.

It must at once be observed that such a constitution as the respondents conceive of would be, so far as the Board is aware, unique in constitutional history. It is neither controlled nor is it uncontrolled. It is not controlled because posterity can by a merely formal Act correct it at pleasure. It is not uncontrolled because the framers have prescribed to their **[706]** successors a particular mode by which, and by which alone, they are allowed to effect constitutional changes.

Their Lordships are clearly of opinion that no warrant whatever exists for the views insisted upon by the respondents, and affirmed by a majority of the judges in the Courts below. It was not the policy of the Imperial Legislature, at any relevant period, to shackle or control in the manner suggested the legislative powers of the nascent Australian Legislatures. Consistently with the genius of the British people what was given was given completely, and unequivocally, in the belief fully justified by the event, that these young communities would successfully work out their own constitutional salvation.

3. Manner and Form Requirements

"Manner and form" requirements are restrictive procedures. They restrict the legislative powers of the Parliament by requiring that laws on certain topics may only be enacted by a special and more difficult procedure. The greatest challenge to Dicey's conception of parliamentary sovereignty presented by the Australian State constitutions lies not in any possible restriction of legislative power by phrases like "peace, order, and good government", but in judicial acceptance of the idea that, by introducing suitably worded "manner and form" requirements, a State Parliament can effectively limit the power of future Parliaments.

The idea that this might be possible has its origins in the proviso to s 5 of the *Colonial Laws Validity Act 1865* (Imp) ("provided that such Laws shall have been passed in such Manner and Form as may from Time to Time be required by any Act of [the Imperial] Parliament, Letters Patent, Order in Council, or Colonial Law for the Time being in force in the said Colony"). A similar proviso was re-enacted in s 6 of the *Australia Act 1986* (Cth), though now limited to "manner and form" requirements imposed by a law of the same Parliament. Moreover, the *Australia Act* version expresses the consequences of non-compliance ("shall be of no force or effect") in a way that seems designed to deny the effectiveness of infringing laws, without denying the power of a State Parliament to enact them. (By contrast, the effect of the proviso to s 5 of the *Colonial Laws Validity Act* was clearly to withhold legislative power.)

The decisive judicial test of the proviso in s 5 of the *Colonial Laws Validity Act* arose in New South Wales. Following the success of the Queensland Labor Party in abolishing the Queensland Upper House, the Labor Party in New South Wales attempted to follow suit. After an initial attempt in 1926 had failed, the conservative government of Premier Thomas Bavin sought in 1929 to forestall any future attempts by amending the *Constitution Act 1902* (NSW) to insert a new s 7A. As originally enacted in 1929, s 7A provided:

Constitution Act 1902 (NSW)

7A **(1)** The Legislative Council shall not be abolished nor, subject to the provisions of subsection six of this section, shall its constitution or powers be altered except in the manner provided in this section.

(2) A Bill for any purpose within subsection one of this section shall not be presented to the Governor for His Majesty's assent until the Bill has been approved by the electors in accordance with this section.

(3) On a day not sooner than two months after the passage of the Bill through both houses of the legislature, the Bill shall be submitted to the electors qualified to vote for the election of members of the Legislative Assembly. Such day shall be appointed by the legislature.

(4) When the Bill is submitted to the electors the vote shall be taken in such manner as the legislature prescribes.

(5) If a majority of the electors voting approve the Bill, it shall be presented to the Governor for His Majesty's assent.

(6) The provisions of this section shall extend to any Bill for the repeal or amendment of this section, but shall not apply to any Bill for the repeal or amendment of any of the following sections of this Act, namely, sections thirteen, fourteen, fifteen, eighteen, nineteen, twenty, twenty-one and twenty-two.

Section 7A meant that the Legislative Council could not be abolished without a referendum and also, by virtue of sub-s (6), that s 7A itself could not be amended or repealed without a referendum. Thus, if s 7A "entrenched" the constitutional status of the Legislative Council, sub-s (6) made this a "double entrenchment".

In 1930, a Labor government under Premier Jack Lang was returned to office with a large majority in the Legislative Assembly. Lang immediately announced his intention of abolishing the Legislative Council. The Legislative Council itself took the initiative and passed, without a referendum, a Bill purporting to repeal s 7A. The Legislative Assembly then passed the Bill. Two members of the Legislative Council sued in the New South Wales Supreme Court for an injunction to prevent the Bill from being presented to the Governor for the Royal Assent. The Lang government then introduced its own Bill purporting to abolish the Legislative Council without a referendum, and the plaintiffs sought an injunction in respect of that Bill too.

By 4:1, the New South Wales Supreme Court granted an interim injunction and declared that neither Bill could be presented for the Royal Assent without a referendum (*Trethowan v Peden* (1930) 31 SR (NSW) 183). The reasoning in *Trethowan v Peden* was as follows:

1. If s 7A had not been doubly entrenched, that is, if there had been no sub-s (6), the whole of s 7A could have been repealed.

2. On the same hypothesis, once s 7A was repealed, the Legislative Council could be abolished by an ordinary Act of Parliament.

3. Moreover, what could thus be done in two steps could also be done in a single step. There was no need first to repeal s 7A before abolishing the Legislative Council. Parliament could simply legislate to abolish the Legislative Council and, insofar as that legislation was inconsistent with s 7A, it would impliedly repeal that section.

4. However, the inclusion of sub-s (6) led to a different result. That sub-section could not be repealed by an ordinary Act of Parliament. It could only be repealed in the manner prescribed by s 7A itself, that is, by a referendum. Section 7A thus incorporated a "manner and form" requirement imposed by a law within the meaning of the proviso to s 5 of the *Colonial Laws Validity Act*.

The Lang government appealed to the High Court, which affirmed the Supreme Court's reasoning by 3:2, with Gavan Duffy CJ and McTiernan J dissenting. The High Court did not, however, affirm the decision to grant an interim injunction; that issue was carefully avoided.

Attorney-General (NSW) v Trethowan
(1931) 44 CLR 395

Rich J: [418] I regard it as clear that in so far as sec 5 [of the *Colonial Laws Validity Act*] enables the Legislature of New South Wales to fetter, restrain, or condition the exercise of its power of constitutional alteration, no prior statute of the Imperial Parliament can operate to enable it to ignore or set at nought any restraint, fetter, or condition it has seen fit to impose in the exercise of that power. On the other hand, in so far as sec 5 confers a power of constitutional alteration which it does not authorize the Legislature so to fetter, restrain, or condition, that power may be exercised in complete disregard of any fetter, restraint, or condition which may have been attempted. How far, then, does sec 5 permit of constitutional alterations which have the effect of controlling the future action of the Legislature? Two methods of controlling the operations of the Legislature appear to be allowed by the express terms of the section. The constitution of the legislative body may be altered; that is to say, the power of legislation may be reposed in an authority differently constituted. Again, laws may be passed imposing legal requirements as to manner and form in which constitutional amendments must be passed. In my opinion the efficacy of sec 7A depends upon the answer to the questions – does it fall within the proviso as to a requirement of manner and form? and does it introduce into the legislative body a new element? If the true answer to either of these questions is Yes, then the Legislative Council cannot be abolished without a referendum unless and until sec 7A is repealed, and sec 7A cannot be repealed except by a Bill approved at a referendum before it is presented for the royal assent. I think the whole matter is determined by the answer to these questions. They arise upon the text of the constating instrument, the *Colonial Laws Validity Act*. The Legislature of New South Wales is not sovereign, and no analogy can be drawn from the position of the British Parliament. The question is one of construction, and not of general reasoning as to the inherent right of a sovereign legislature to undo all that it has done. The first question is whether sub-sec 6, which is a colonial law for the time being in force, requires a manner and form in which a law repealing sec 7A must be passed. In my opinion it does ... The proviso [to sec 5] is not dealing with narrow questions of parliamentary **[419]** procedure ... In my opinion the proviso to sec 5 relates to the entire process of turning a proposed law into a legislative enactment, and was intended to enjoin fulfilment of every condition and compliance with every requirement which existing legislation imposed upon the process of law-making. This view is enough to dispose of the case; but if what is done under sub-sec 6 did not fall under the proviso, the question would still remain whether for the purpose of abolishing the Legislative Council and the purpose of repealing sec 7A a new element is not introduced into the legislative authority. It was conceded that under sec 5 it was competent to the legislature to establish a third Chamber whose assent would be required to complete any legislative act. It could not be denied that, if a third Chamber could be introduced, a body of persons of another character might also be created a constituent element of the legislature ... **[420]** An examination of sec 7A shows that a legislative body has been created for the purpose of passing or co-operating in passing a particular law. There is no reason why this authority need extend to all laws. It is enough to turn to the *Commonwealth of Australia Constitution Act* to find in sec 128 of the Constitution the prototype of sec 7A. The electors are called upon to approve or not of a certain class of Bill. In so doing they discharge a function of law-making ...

McCawley's Case [[1920] AC 691] reaffirms the full power of such a legislature as that of New South Wales, which passed sec 7A, to regulate its own constitution. Such a power naturally extends to the enactments of safeguards aimed at restraining improvident or hasty action. There is no reason why a Parliament representing the people should be powerless to determine whether the constitutional salvation of the State is to be reached by cautious and well considered steps rather than by rash and ill considered measures. *McCawley's Case* [[1920] AC at 703, 704] establishes that there is no difference in this respect between a **[421]** unitary and a federal system. Either may be rigid and controlled or flexible and uncontrolled. The only question is whether, on the construction of the constating instrument, the Imperial Parliament made a grant of power to the representative Legislature of New South Wales to prescribe to their successors a particular mode by which and by which alone constitutional changes may be effected. In my opinion, for the reasons given the constating instrument enabled that Legislature to introduce the referendum as such a mode because it constitutes a manner and form of legislation and includes the electorate as an element in the legislative authority in which the power of constitutional alteration resides.

I am, therefore of opinion that neither of the Bills in question may be lawfully presented to the Governor for the royal assent, and be validly assented to, until it is approved by a majority of the electors.

Dixon J: [425] This question must be answered upon a consideration of the true meaning and effect of the written instruments from which the Parliament of New South Wales derives its legislative power. It is not to be determined by the direct application of the doctrine of parliamentary sovereignty, which gives to the Imperial Parliament its supremacy over the law. It is the law, derived mediately or immediately from the Imperial Parliament, which gives to the Legislature of New South Wales its powers, and it is that law which determines the extent of those powers and the conditions which govern their exercise. The incapacity of the British Legislature to limit its own power otherwise than by transferring a portion or abdicating the whole of its sovereignty has been accounted for by **[426]** the history of the High Court of Parliament, and has been explained as a necessary consequence of a true conception of sovereignty. But in any case it depends upon considerations which have no application to the Legislature of New South Wales, which is not a sovereign body and has a purely statutory origin. Because of the supremacy of the Imperial Parliament over the law, the Courts merely apply its legislative enactments and do not examine their validity, but because the law over which the Imperial Parliament is supreme determines the powers of a legislature in a Dominion, the Courts must decide upon the validity as well as the application of the statutes of that legislature. It must not be supposed, however, that all difficulties would vanish if the full doctrine of parliamentary supremacy could be invoked. An Act of the British Parliament which contained a provision that no Bill repealing any part of the Act including the part so restraining its own repeal should be presented for the royal assent unless the Bill were first approved by the electors, would have the force of law until the Sovereign actually did assent to a Bill for its repeal. In strictness it would be an unlawful proceeding to present such a Bill for the royal assent before it had been approved by the electors. If, before the Bill received the assent of the Crown, it was found possible, as appears to have been done in this appeal, to raise for judicial decision the question whether it was lawful to present the Bill for that assent the Courts would be bound to pronounce it unlawful to do so. Moreover, if it happened that, notwithstanding the statutory inhibition, the Bill did receive the royal assent, although it was not submitted to the electors, the Courts might be called upon to consider whether the supreme legislative power in respect of the matter had in truth been exercised in the manner required for its authentic expression and by the elements in which it had come to reside.

This analysis of what a British court might do in such a case presupposes for the sake of argument that it could do something – or, as Dixon J put it, that the litigating parties could successfully raise the issue as one requiring judicial decision. Years later, Dixon CJ indicated that he had always doubted whether this was a possibility; that is, he doubted whether the Supreme Court had jurisdiction to intrude itself into the legislative process whether by injunction or otherwise. In *Hughes & Vale Pty Ltd v Gair* (1954) 90 CLR 203, he said: "**[204]** For myself I have long entertained a doubt as to the correctness of the decision of the Full Court of New South Wales in that case [*Trethowan's Case*] even on the terms of that Act". Subject to that procedural doubt, however, the above hypothetical formulation of an issue that might theoretically arise in the courts of the United Kingdom has a resonance – especially in the last three lines above – that has later come to assume an importance far transcending the immediate context of *Trethowan's Case*.

Having set up this elaborate hypothesis, Dixon J went on in *Trethowan's Case*:

Dixon J: [426] But the answer to this question, whether evident or obscure, would be deduced from the principle of parliamentary supremacy over the law. This principle, from its very nature, cannot determine the character or the operation of the constituent powers of the Legislature of New South Wales which are the result of statute. It is true that these constituent powers were meant to give to the constitution of New South Wales as much of the flexibility which in Great Britain arises **[427]** from the supremacy of Parliament as was thought compatible with the unity of the Empire, the authority of the Crown and the ultimate sovereignty of the Imperial Parliament. But this consideration, although generally of importance, affords small help in a question whether the constituent authority of a legislature in a Dominion suffices to enable it to impose a condition or a restraint upon the exercise of its power. The difficulty of the supreme Legislature lessening its own powers does not arise from the flexibility of the constitution. On the contrary, it may be said that it is precisely the point at which the flexibility of the British constitution ceases to be absolute. Because it rests upon the supremacy over the law, some changes which detract from that supremacy cannot be made by law effectively. The necessary limitations upon the flexibility of the constitution of New South Wales result from a consideration of exactly an opposite character. They arise directly or indirectly from the sovereignty of the Imperial Parliament. But in virtue of its sovereignty it was open to the Imperial Parliament itself to give, or to empower the Legislature of New South Wales to give, to the constitution of that State as much or as little rigidity as might be proper ...

[429] [Section 5 of the *Colonial Laws Validity Act*] both confers power and describes the conditions to be observed in its exercise. It authorizes a representative legislature to make laws respecting its own constitution, its own powers and its own procedure. This authority does not extend to the executive power in the constitution. But it is plenary save in so far as it may be qualified by a law which falls within the description of the proviso. The power to make laws respecting its own constitution enables the legislature to deal with its own nature and composition. The power to make laws respecting its own procedure enables it to prescribe rules which have the force of law [430] for its own conduct. Laws which relate to its own constitution and procedure must govern the legislature in the exercise of its powers, including the exercise of its power to repeal those very laws. The power to make laws respecting its own powers would naturally be understood to mean that it might deal with its own legislative authority. Under such a power a legislature, whose authority was limited in respect of subject matter or restrained by constitutional checks or safeguards, might enlarge the limits or diminish or remove the restraints. Conversely, the power might be expected to enable a legislature to impose constitutional restraints upon its own authority or to limit its power in respect of subject matter. But such restraints and limitations, if they are to be real and effective and achieve their end, must bind the legislature. If the legislature, nevertheless, continues to retain unaffected and unimpaired by its own laws the power given by this provision to legislate respecting its own powers, it is evident that it may always repeal the limitations and restraints which those laws purport to impose. Moreover, this means, as *McCawley's Case* establishes, that no formal repeal is necessary to resume the power and the legislature remains competent to make laws inconsistent with the restraints or limitations which its former statutes have sought to create. If and in so far, therefore, as sec 5 confers a superior and indestructible power to make laws with respect to the legislature's own powers, it cannot enable it to impose upon those powers any effective restraints or restrictions. How far is the power which it gives of this character? In other words, how far does sec 5 allow a constituent legislature to adopt a rigid constitution? There is no logical reason why the authority conferred over its own powers should not include a capacity to diminish or restrain that very authority. But, in giving every representative legislature the power to make laws respecting its own powers, sec 5 provides not only that the power shall subsist, but also [that it] shall be deemed at all times to have subsisted.

Considered apart from the proviso, the language in which this provision is expressed could not reasonably be understood to authorize any regulation, control or impairment of the power it describes. It does not say that the legislature may make laws [431] respecting its own powers including this power. But the proviso recognizes that the exercise of the power may to some extent be qualified or controlled by law. It describes the kinds of legislative instrument by which this may be done, and, with Acts of the Imperial Parliament, letters patent and orders in council, it includes a colonial law for the time being in force in the Colony. The expression "colonial law" is defined to include laws made for any Colony by the authority, other than the Imperial Parliament or His Majesty in Council, competent to make laws for the Colony (sec 1). The extent is limited to which such a law may qualify or control the power to make laws respecting the constitution, powers and procedure of the Legislature. It cannot do more than prescribe the mode in which laws respecting these matters must be made. To be valid, a law respecting the powers of the legislature must "have been passed in such manner and form as may from time to time be required by any ... colonial law" (*sc*, a law of that legislature) "for the time being in force." Its validity cannot otherwise be affected by a prior law of that legislature. In other words no degree of rigidity greater than this can be given by the legislature to the constitution.

The law proposed by the Bill to repeal sec 7A of the *Constitution Act* 1902 to 1929 answers the description "a law respecting the powers of the legislature" just as the provisions of sec 7A itself constitute a law with respect to those powers. But the proposal cannot be put into effect save by a law which "shall have been passed in such manner and form as may be required by any" prior law of the New South Wales Legislature. Unless it be void, sec 7A is undeniably a prior law of the New South Wales Legislature. It is no less a law of that Legislature because it requires the approval of the electors as a condition of its repeal. But it is not void unless this requirement is repugnant to sec 5 of the *Colonial Laws Validity Act*. No requirement is repugnant to that section if it is within the contemplation of its proviso, which concedes the efficacy of enactments requiring a manner or form in which laws shall be passed. If, therefore, a provision that a particular law respecting the powers of the Legislature may not be made unless it is approved by the electors, requires a manner or form in which such a law **[432]** shall be passed, then sec 7A is a valid law and cannot be repealed without the approval of the electorate.

Gavan Duffy CJ and McTiernan J dissented. McTiernan J, in his former capacity as Lang's Attorney-General, had played a leading role in the earlier attempt to abolish the New South Wales Legislative Council in 1926. He now argued that s 7A could not operate to impose a referendum requirement. He insisted that the Parliament could not cut down its own powers in a way that would bind future Parliaments and rejected the idea that a "manner and form" requirement could be imposed without any reduction in substantive legislative powers.

McTiernan J: [441] Sec 7A is a law respecting the powers of the Legislature (*Taylor v Attorney-General of Queensland* [(1917) 23 CLR 457]). The Legislature of New South Wales may, under sec 5 of the *Colonial Laws Validity Act*, restore any power to its fullest extent, which it has legislated to **[442]** diminish. If sub-sec 6 of sec 7A had not been enacted, no question would have arisen as to the power of the Parliament to enact a law to repeal sec 7A by the process or in the form in which laws are passed through the two Houses and assented to by the Governor in the name of His Majesty, or, if it would be necessary in the case, are reserved by the Governor for the assent of His Majesty and are assented to by His Majesty. Sub-sec 6 diminishes the power of the Legislature to repeal or amend sec 7A. The sub-section assumes to require that after the passage of a Bill to repeal or amend the section through both Houses the Legislature must take no further step in enacting the Bill into law for at least two months. If the persons designated by the section, who are outside Parliament, do not approve of the Bill, the Legislature is prevented from resuming the process of enacting the Bill into law and the Bill lapses. In my opinion, therefore, sub-sec 6 of sec 7A is not in substance a law dictating "manner": it is in substance a law depriving the Legislature of power. The words of the section measure the extent to which the power of the Legislature is cut down. It renders the King, the Legislative Council and the Legislative Assembly assembled in Parliament powerless to repeal the section unless an external body intervenes and approves of the repeal. In my opinion the Legislature, consisting of its three constituent elements in Parliament assembled, may, under sec 5 of the *Colonial Laws Validity Act*, resume the power to repeal sec 7A.

The High Court's decision was affirmed by the Privy Council in *Attorney-General for New South Wales v Trethowan* [1932] AC 526.

Several other States have also entrenched aspects of their Constitutions (see, for example, *Constitution Act 1867* (Qld), s 53; *Constitution Act 1934* (SA), ss 8, 10A and 88). The entrenchment mechanism need not take the form of a referendum. A less rigorous alternative may be used, such as an absolute majority in both Houses of Parliament (see *Constitution Act 1975* (Vic), s 18(2A)) or a two-thirds majority (see *Constitution Act 1934* (Tas), s 41A).

Trethowan's Case demonstrated that, if a "manner and form" provision is not "doubly entrenched", a parliament is free to legislate to remove the entrenchment and amend the protected provision. Despite this, there are examples of manner and form procedures that are not themselves entrenched (see, for example, *Constitution Act 1934* (Tas), s 41A). The case also established that, for measures affecting the constitution, powers and procedure of the State legislature, the requirement of submission to a referendum can be a "manner and form" requirement within the meaning of s 5 of the *Colonial Laws Validity Act*.

On the other hand, the High Court in *South-Eastern Drainage Board (SA) v Savings Bank of South Australia* (1939) 62 CLR 603 held that a mere requirement of a special declaratory form of words was not a "manner and form" requirement. Section 6 of the *Real Property Act 1886* (SA) stated that: "No law, so far as inconsistent with this Act, shall apply to land subject to the provisions of this Act, nor shall any future law, so far as inconsistent with this Act, so apply unless it shall be expressly enacted that it shall so apply 'notwithstanding the provisions of "*The Real Property Act* 1886"'." By the *South-Eastern Drainage Amendment Act 1900* (SA), land-owners were required to pay part of the costs of drainage construction. Under s 14, that liability was made a first charge on the land, enforceable as if the South-Eastern Drainage Board were a mortgagee. If this first charge prevailed over the rights of mortgagees under the *Real Property Act*, it detracted from the security of title given by that Act. However, it did not contain the "magic formula" which s 6 of that Act required.

The High Court held this did not matter: the normal rule applied that, to the extent of any inconsistency, the later Act prevailed and the earlier Act was to that extent impliedly repealed. The judges, with the exception of Evatt J, reached this conclusion by asking whether s 6 of the *Real Property Act* was a law "respecting the Constitution, Powers, and Procedure of such Legislature" within the meaning of s 5 of the *Colonial Laws Validity Act*. However, this was clearly the wrong question.

When an issue arises under s 5 of the *Colonial Laws Validity Act*, or nowadays under s 6 of the *Australia Act*, the first question to be asked is whether the law that is later in time is a law "respecting the Constitution, Powers, and Procedure of such Legislature". If and only if it is such a law, it then becomes necessary to ask whether the earlier law has prescribed any "manner and form" in which the later law must be passed. In the *South-Eastern Drainage Case* the Court should have asked whether the *South-Eastern Drainage Amendment Act*, and not the *Real Property Act*, was a law "respecting the Constitution, Powers, and Procedure of such Legislature". Since it clearly was not such a law, no question under s 5 of the *Colonial Laws Validity Act* should have arisen. Accordingly, it is sometimes suggested that the *South-Eastern Drainage Case* is flawed and is of no value as a precedent.

South-Eastern Drainage Board (SA) v Savings Bank of South Australia
(1939) 62 CLR 603

Latham CJ: [618] It was urged that sec 6 of the *Real Property Act* was a law which prescribed a manner and form for the passing of Acts of parliament and that therefore an Act passed not in such manner and form was not valid. But the proviso with respect to manner and form applies only to laws respecting the constitution of the legislature, the powers of the legislature, and the procedure of the legislature. Sec 6 is plainly not a provision affecting in any way the constitution of the legislature. Nor does it affect the powers of the legislature. It only purports to prescribe the contents of an Act which the legislature has power to pass. Nor does the section relate to any part of the procedure of the legislature in passing statutes. Accordingly, in my opinion, sec 6 of the *Real Property Act* cannot operate to deprive of effect any subsequent legislation of the South-Australian Parliament which, upon the natural construction of its terms, enacts a provision which is inconsistent with the *Real Property Act* 1886.

Evatt J: [633] [I]t is worth while to note what that section purports to do. It purports to control future parliaments of South Australia in any legislation affecting land under the *Real Property Act* by requiring that unless such legislation is couched in a certain literary form (ie, containing the words "notwithstanding the provisions of '*The Real Property Act* 1886'") it cannot affect land under the Act. For instance, it would not be sufficient if the Parliament used the phrase "*In spite of* the provisions of the *Real Property Act* 1886."

In my opinion the legislature of South Australia has plenary power to couch its enactments in such literary form as it may choose. It cannot be effectively commanded by a prior legislature to express its intention in a particular way. *Maugham* LJ has, I think, said something to this substantial effect in *Ellen Street Estates Ltd v Minister of Health* [[1934] 1 KB 590 at 597]. But this is an even clearer case. In my **[634]** opinion the decision in *Attorney-General for New South Wales v Trethowan* [[1932] AC 526] has nothing to do with the matter. Sec 6 is not a mere interpretation section, for it is not expressed to operate only so far as the contrary intention does not appear. It purports to lay down a rigid rule binding upon all future parliaments. It declares that, however clearly the intention of such parliaments may be expressed in an enactment, that intention shall not be given effect to unless it contains the magic formula. I think that the command in sec 6 was quite ineffective and inoperative.

Despite the confusion as to which Act was to be appraised to determine whether it touches "the Constitution, Powers, and Procedures of such Legislature", it is arguable that the *South-Eastern Drainage Case* makes a significant point. What most concerned Latham CJ was his apprehension that s 6 of the *Real Property Act* had purported "**[618]** to prescribe the contents" of future legislation. It is this that, consistently with the doctrine of parliamentary sovereignty, no Act of Parliament can be permitted to do. The effect of the *Colonial Laws Validity Act* in permitting "manner and form" requirements is thus acceptable only if, as to the desirable *content* of legislation, each new Parliament has a continuing freedom to judge what is desirable in response to the policy exigencies of its own time.

The assumption that the legislature cannot fetter its future freedom of action may extend in some contexts to the executive government as well. It is clear that when the Crown or one of its agencies enters into an ordinary commercial contract it is bound in the ordinary commercial way. However, attempts have been made to distinguish such commercial arrangements from those of a governmental character. In cases of the latter kind, it has been said that the Crown cannot bind itself, since to do so might fetter future policy judgments in a changed political context. Thus, in *Rederiaktiebolaget Amphitrite v The King* [1921] 3 KB 500 it was held that a Swedish ship entering British waters during World War I was lawfully detained by the British government despite a written undertaking that she would be allowed free passage.

Rederiaktiebolaget Amphitrite v The King (The Amphitrite)
[1921] 3 KB 500

Rowlatt J: [503] No doubt the Government can bind itself through its officers by a commercial contract, and if it does so it must perform it like anybody else … But this was not a commercial contract; it was an arrangement whereby the Government purported to give an assurance as to what its executive action would be in the future in relation to a particular ship in the event of her coming to this country with a particular kind of cargo. And that is, to my mind, not a contract for the breach of which damages can be sued for in a Court of law. It was merely an expression of intention to act in a particular way in a certain event. My main reason for so thinking is that it is not competent for the Government to fetter its future executive action, which must necessarily be determined by the needs of the community when the question arises. It cannot by contract hamper its freedom of action in matters which concern the welfare of the State.

The Supreme Court of South Australia arrived at a broadly similar view in *West Lakes Ltd v South Australia* (1980) 25 SASR 389. The plaintiff company entered into an agreement with the South Australian government for the planning and development of a residential suburb called West Lakes. The agreement followed earlier arrangements between the government and Development Finance Corporation Ltd. At each stage, these arrangements were embodied in "Indentures" which were ratified and given the force of law by State legislation.

The first three lines of Clause 1 of the Fourth Schedule to the 1969 Indenture, as ratified by the *West Lakes Development Act 1969* (SA), appeared to allow for the possibility that the regulations set out in the Fifth Schedule might be revoked or varied so long as this was done "explicitly", although the last four lines stipulated that this could not happen "without the prior written consent of the Corporation". Section 15(1) of the Act provided that the provisions of the Fourth Schedule "shall apply and have effect … as if … expressly enacted in this Act", while s 16(4) provided: "No regulation adding to, varying or revoking the regulations contained in the Fifth Schedule to the Indenture shall be published in the *Gazette* by the Minister or have effect before the final completion of the major works or before the Indenture ceases to have effect (whichever first occurs) except with the consent in writing of the Corporation".

In 1979, complaints by West Lakes residents about the floodlighting of a football oval in the area were referred to a Royal Commissioner, who recommended that the area should be floodlit. He further recommended that, for the purpose of making regulations to implement his recommendations, it should not be necessary to obtain the consent of West Lakes Ltd. Accordingly, the South Australian government prepared draft legislation to amend the *West Lakes Development Act* to provide that the consent of the company would not be required for any regulation giving effect to a recommendation of the Royal Commission. The company sought an injunction to prevent that Bill from being introduced into Parliament.

The action failed on two grounds. First, the Court held that a contractual obligation entered into by the executive government could not inhibit the power of Parliament to enact legislation or the right of Ministers of the Crown to propose such legislation.

West Lakes Ltd v South Australia
(1980) 25 SASR 389

King CJ: [390] Ministers of State cannot ... , by means of contractual obligations entered into on behalf of the State fetter their own freedom, or the freedom of their successors or the freedom of other members of parliament, to propose, consider and, if they think fit, vote for laws, even laws which are inconsistent with the contractual obligations. To enter into a contract containing a provision purporting to fetter members of parliament in their deliberations and to attempt to enforce any such contractual provision would, in my opinion, be the clearest breach of the privileges of the parliament and of the members thereof. The Ministers of State are members of parliament. As such they are free to propose, to consider, to discuss and to vote for any bill un-**[391]**-constrained by any contract entered into on behalf of the State. Indeed, I can find no indication in the indenture that it purports to fetter that freedom.

Secondly, it was held that in any event a requirement of written consent by a company was not a "manner and form" requirement within the meaning of s 5 of the *Colonial Laws Validity Act*.

King CJ: [396] I think, however, that it is quite clear that the bill under consideration is not a proposed law respecting any of the topics enumerated in s 5 of the *Colonial Laws Validity Act*. The question of whether the parliament can only exercise its powers to make laws respecting topics other than those enumerated in s 5 of the *Colonial Laws Validity Act* in the manner and form (if any) required by its own legislation or whether it may ignore any such requirement, is one of great constitutional importance. In view of the conclusions which I reached as to the other issues in the case, it is unnecessary for me to decide that question, and I think that it is undesirable therefore that I should express any view upon it. When it falls for decision, the question will involve a consideration of the way in which the constitutional principles discussed above are to be applied to a legislature which derives its authority from constitutional sources of the kind which are the foundation of the authority of the South Australian parliament. It will, moreover, involve a consideration of the true effect of the decision of the High Court in *South-Eastern Drainage Board (South Australia) v Savings Bank of South Australia* [(1939) 62 CLR 603].

A question might arise as to whether a particular statutory provision is truly a manner and form provision, which must be observed (at least as to legislation which falls within s 5 of the *Colonial Laws Validity Act*) as a condition of the validity of the Act, or whether it is a limitation or restraint of substance, which would not invalidate legislation inconsistent with the limitation or restraint. A requirement for a special majority in the parliament, such as the provision in the Ceylon constitution considered **[397]** in *Ranasinghe's* case [[1965] AC 172], might present special difficulty. The question whether the special majority provision related to manner and form did not arise in *Ranasinghe's* case. The *Colonial Laws Validity Act* did not apply and the case turned upon the provision being one of "the conditions of lawmaking that are imposed by the instrument which itself regulates the power to make law" [[1965] AC 172 at 197]. There must be a point at which a special majority provision would appear as an attempt to deprive the parliament of powers rather than as a measure to prescribe the manner or form of their exercise. This point might be reached more quickly where the legislative topic which is the subject of the requirement is not a fundamental constitutional provision. When one looks at extra-parliamentary requirements, the difficulty of treating them as relating to manner and form becomes greater. It is true that Dixon J in *Trethowan's* case [(1931) 44 CLR 394] gave "manner and form" a very wide meaning ... *Trethowan's* case, however, concerned a requirement that an important constitutional alteration be approved by the electors at a referendum. Such a requirement, although extra-parliamentary in character, is easily seen to be a manner and form provision because it is confined to obtaining the direct approval of the people whom the "representative legislature" represents. If, however, parliament purports to make the validity of legislation on a particular topic conditional upon the concurrence of an extra-parliamentary individual, group of individuals, organisation or corporation, a serious question must arise as to whether the provision is truly a law prescribing the manner or form of legislation, or whether it is not rather a law as to substance, being a renunciation of the power to legislate on that topic unless the condition exists ...

The Court was asked to construe the *West Lakes Development Act*, 1969, as meaning that the parliament may not legislate inconsistently with the provisions of the indenture without the consent of the plaintiff company. It was argued that the statute, so construed, prescribes a manner and form to be observed in legislation of that kind. Even if I could construe the statute according to the plaintiff's argument, I could not regard the pro-**[398]**-vision as prescribing the manner or form of future legislation. A provision requiring the consent to legislation of a certain kind, of an entity not forming part of the legislative structure (including in that structure the people whom the members of the legislature represent), does not, to my mind, prescribe a manner or form of lawmaking, but rather amounts to a renunciation *pro tanto* of the lawmaking power. Such a provision relates to the substance of the lawmaking power, not to the manner or form of its exercise. The point becomes clearer if one considers hypothetical (albeit extreme) examples such as provisions that legislation of a certain character might not be enacted without the consent of the governing body of a political party, or of an organization of employers or employees, or of an officer of the armed forces, or of any other individual, office holder, or body which does not form part of the representative legislative structure. It follows, in my view, that even if the statute bears the meaning attributed to it, it does not prescribe a manner or form of legislation and Parliament may legislate inconsistently with it. Parliament may therefore validly enact the bill which is under attack.

The principle stated by Rowlatt J in *The Amphitrite*, and by King CJ in *West Lakes*, is expressed as applying at the highest levels of legislative and executive power; but for individual Ministers, and for government officers and instrumentalities operating at subordinate levels, it is mirrored in the doctrine that they cannot "fetter their discretion" by binding themselves contractually to exercise their powers in a particular way (see, for example, *Watson's Bay and South Shore Ferry Co Ltd v Whitfield* (1919) 27 CLR 268). At all levels, the precise extent of the principle is open to debate. It is sometimes said that the contracts which can validly be made are those that affect "operational" matters as distinct from "policy" matters, or a government's "proprietary" interests as distinct from its "governmental" interests. There may also be overlap with the different principle that agreements with obvious implications for matters of government policy may sometimes be construed as not intended to create legal relations at all (see, for example, *Australian Woollen Mills Pty Ltd v Commonwealth* (1954) 92 CLR 424).

In *Ansett Transport Industries (Operations) Pty Ltd v Commonwealth* (1977) 139 CLR 54, Ansett complained that the grant of permits to rival companies, effectively enabling them to compete with Ansett in interstate air freight services, was in breach of an implied term in its agreements with the Commonwealth implementing the "two airlines" policy. The action failed because the High Court held by a 3:2 majority that no such term was implied. Barwick CJ and Aickin J dissented, and Gibbs J, though otherwise in the majority, agreed with them that such a term would not impermissibly have fettered discretion since the agreements "**[62]** have statutory approval". Murphy J disagreed. Mason J, who considered the point most fully, agreed that the *Amphitrite* principle was "**[74]** expressed too generally", but attempted to reconcile the need for "[p]ublic confidence in government dealings and contracts" with acknowledgment that "the public interest requires that neither the government nor a public authority can by a contract disable itself or its officer from performing a statutory duty or from exercising a discretionary power conferred by or under a statute by binding itself or its officer not to perform the duty or to exercise the discretion in a particular **[75]** way in the future".

In effect Mason J distinguished three types of case. First, where a public authority itself enters into a contract imposing "**[76]** an anticipatory fetter ... on [its] future exercise of [a] statutory power or discretion", the contract will simply be "invalid or ultra vires" because it is "incompatible" with the statute conferring the power.

Secondly, where the contract is made at a higher level of government, and the agency whose powers are affected is not itself a party to the contract, "it has been suggested" that although "the free and unfettered exercise of the discretion" must remain unimpaired, the contract will be enforceable in the limited sense that a breach of it will give rise to an action for damages, though not in the sense that it is amenable to injunction or specific performance. (This idea has been criticised on the ground that a public servant's awareness of a possible exposure to damages might effectively fetter his discretion just as much as a fully enforceable contract: see Dennis Rose, "The Government and Contract", in Paul Finn (ed), *Essays on Contract* (Law Book Co, 1987), 233.)

Finally, Mason J suggested that, when a contract of this latter kind is specifically approved by or enshrined in statute, the effect of the statute may sometimes be to "**[77]** impose on the repository of the discretion a duty to exercise it in conformity with [the contract]", so that in effect the discretion is "relevantly converted into a duty". In that event, he considered that the contract would be fully enforceable.

However, since this analysis depends on the operation of statute, even a statute of the kind suggested could presumably be repealed or amended. Accordingly, developers have frequently sought to ensure not only that their government contracts are incorporated into a statute, but that the statute is then "entrenched" by a "manner and form" provision (see KD MacDonald, "The Negotiation and Enforcement of Agreements with State Governments Relating to the Development of Mineral Ventures" (1977) 1 *Australian Mining and Petroleum Law Journal* 29, and comment thereon by Enid Campbell at 53-8). Yet *West Lakes* suggests that such attempted "entrenchment" is unlikely to be successful.

Nor is this an isolated case. In an earlier but similar case in Queensland, the Commonwealth Aluminium Corporation Pty Ltd ("Comalco") entered into an agreement with the State of Queensland in 1957 to enable it to undertake bauxite mining at Aurukun. The agreement was authorised by the *Commonwealth Aluminium Corporation Pty Ltd Agreement Act 1957* (Qld), which declared that the provisions of the agreement "shall have the force of law as though the Agreement were an enactment of this Act". The Act further provided (in s 4) that the agreement could be varied by agreement between the company and the responsible Minister, but that "no provision of the Agreement shall be varied nor the powers and rights of the company under the Agreement be derogated from except in such manner" and, further, that "[a]ny purported alteration of the Agreement not made and approved in such manner shall be void and of no legal effect whatsoever".

Under the *Mining Royalties Act 1974* (Qld), regulations were made which had the effect of increasing the royalties payable by the company under the agreement. The company protested that the 1957 Act had given the agreement the force of a "law"; that s 4 had prescribed a "manner and form" by which alone that "law" could be amended; and that the *Mining Royalties Act* was invalid because it purported to amend that "law" without satisfying the "manner and form" requirement. However, in *Commonwealth Aluminium Corporation Ltd v Attorney-General* [1976] Qd R 231, the Supreme Court of Queensland rejected these arguments by a 2:1 majority, holding that s 4 of the 1957 Act was *not* a "manner and form" provision, and accordingly that the Act might impliedly be repealed or amended by the normal operation of later legislation inconsistent with its provisions.

The broader political considerations that led King CJ to take a restrictive approach to the concept of "manner and form" in the *West Lakes* case may also affect other interpretive questions arising from the application of "manner and form" provisions. In *Attorney-General (WA) v*

Marquet (2003) 217 CLR 545, a majority of the High Court held that s 13 of the *Electoral Distribution Act 1947* (WA) was a "manner and form" provision. Section 13 required an absolute majority in both Houses of the State Parliament for "any Bill to amend this Act". It was held that s 13 was made effective by the continued operation, under s 6 of the *Australia Act 1986* (Cth), of the "manner and form" requirements formerly imposed by s 5 of the *Colonial Laws Validity Act*. Section 13 thus prevented the repeal of the 1947 Act by the Electoral Distribution Repeal Bill 2001 (WA), which would have cleared the way for a new electoral distribution based upon the idea of one vote one value (see Chapter 10, §4(c)).

To reach this conclusion, the Court had to answer two questions of construction. First, since the "manner and form" requirement was imposed by s 13 on "any Bill to amend this Act", it was necessary to determine whether a Bill to *repeal* the 1947 Act should be treated as a Bill to *amend* it. Secondly, it was necessary to decide whether legislation establishing a scheme for electoral distribution, and the bureaucratic machinery for its implementation, was "a law ... respecting the constitution, powers or procedure of the Parliament of the State" within the meaning of s 6 of the *Australia Act* (assumed for this purpose to have the same ambit as "laws respecting the constitution, powers and procedure" of representative legislatures in s 5 of the *Colonial Laws Validity Act*). The two issues were not unrelated, as Callinan J, who formed part of the majority, made clear. For one thing, it was debatable in relation to both issues whether the repeal Bill should be looked at in isolation, or whether there should be taken into account the cognate Electoral Amendment Bill 2001 (WA), by which it was proposed to introduce a new distribution once the 1947 Act was repealed.

Attorney-General (WA) v Marquet
(2003) 217 CLR 545

Callinan J: [628] In order to answer the questions raised by the applicants it is necessary to understand the nature and purpose of constitutions in this country and the history and conditions that have shaped their forms and provisions.

Western Australia is a vast State in a vast country. The population of both is unevenly distributed between metropolises and the country. In consequence, electorates vary in size, as do the demands of travel, communication, and servicing generally, upon those who represent their constituents. Equally it is obvious that there are many ways in which members of Parliaments may be elected, that is to say, democratically elected. Indeed, throughout the democratic world many different ways of electing representatives to Parliaments have been chosen. Similarly, Parliaments are not constituted according to any universal model. Even in Australia there is considerable variation. Queensland has a unicameral legislature. The terms of members of State upper houses vary considerably. Parliamentary representatives could be elected, as is the case with the Senate, on the basis of a single total State electorate, or, as with the House of Representatives, on the basis of one member for one electoral division, the boundaries of which are not immutable. The point is that Parliaments cannot be elected and operate without provision, indeed fairly elaborate provision, to enable them to do so. And it is against the background of these elementary propositions that the Constitution of Western Australia must be identified, and the legislation and the Bills to which reference has been made, must be examined.

The first of these to which I turn is the [*Electoral Distribution Act 1947* (WA)]. What work has it to do? The answer is, essential work, work of a kind that if not done, would not enable a legislature to be elected and to function. Section 3 reflects the choice ... of separate electoral divisions or districts for the election of members of the Parliament. Section 6 states the number of districts and distributes them (unevenly) between metropolitan areas as defined, effectively the capital Perth and its environs, and the rest of the State. Other provisions ... prescribe the times, persons, procedures, bases and other matters for the determination of the boundaries of, and numerical tolerances in, electoral divisions ...

[629] Without the [*Electoral Distribution Act*] or some like Act or replacement of it, elections for the Parliament of Western Australia could not be conducted ...

The problem in this area is obvious. What continuing vitality should a fetter imposed by a former Parliament have in relation to a later one? How heavily, definitely and finally, if at all, should the legislators of the past dictate the future? The answer must take into account that the whole intention of a constitution is to provide for the community that it is to govern a degree of genuine and effective, but not entirely inflexible, stability and certainty. The preference by and large of common law countries (apart from the United Kingdom) has been for Constitutions which are alterable in compliance only with a more strict, and, it may be accepted, less accessible process than the mere enactment of other, non-constitutional legislation. Section 128 of the Constitution of this country is itself an example of a provision requiring compliance with a strict process for its operation. By contrast, in some other countries there seems to have been a degree of instability which the presence of provisions such as s 13 ... and adherence to them help to avoid ...

[631] Opinion[s] as to the essentials ... of and for a constitution are not unanimous. In *McCulloch v Maryland* [17 US (4 Wheat) 315 at 406 (1819)] Marshall CJ delivering the opinion of the Court said this:

"A Constitution, to contain an accurate detail of all the subdivisions of which its great powers will admit, and of all the means by which they may be carried into execution, would partake of the prolixity of a legal code, and could scarcely be embraced by the human mind. It would, probably, never be understood by the public. Its nature, therefore, requires, that only its great outlines should be marked, its important objects designated, and the minor ingredients which compose those objects, be deduced from the nature of the objects themselves."

On the other hand, many constitutions contain quite elaborate detail with respect to matters which others eschew. Parts II and III of the Australian Constitution, for example, descend to the detail of the specification of the separate (State) electorates of Senators (s 7), the duration of their terms (ss 13 and 14), numbers of members of the House of Representatives (s 24), duration of the members' terms (s 28), and Part IV to the extent of the Parliament's powers with respect to the conduct of the business of Parliament.

It follows, in my opinion, that even though all draftspeople of Constitutions might not include the sort of detail as to the matters to which I have just referred, and those of a like kind in the [*Electoral Distribution Act*] ..., it cannot be said, that these are not at least fit matters for inclusion in, and forming part of a constitution, and, having been designated as such by a manner and form entrenchment provision, in this case s 13 of the [*Electoral Distribution Act*], should not be so regarded.

The matters to which I have referred, and the conclusion that I draw from them, that the [*Electoral Distribution Act*] forms part of the Constitution of the State, do not of themselves determine the meaning of and operation to be given to s 13 ..., but they heavily influence them. It immediately strikes the reader how anomalous it would be if "amend" when used in a constitution were to be read so narrowly as to exclude, or have no application to a repeal, so as to enable a legislature, without complying with the requirements of s 13, to obliterate or extinguish entirely part of the Constitution, but not to amend it even by the [632] addition or deletion of a mere word or phrase: that although the Parliament might not tinker with, it was entitled to annihilate a constitution or a substantial provision of it.

In my opinion therefore, "amend" in s 13 ... should be read to include and apply to a purported "repeal". The fact that other legislation, for example, s 44 of the *Interpretation Act* 1918 (WA) uses each of the words "altered, amended, or repealed" does not dictate any different conclusion. The context there is quite different. In any event, on occasions, the words may be used interchangeably, and on others either conjunctively or disjunctively, for further or greater assurance and completeness. The context here, of a constitution, requires an expansive reading. It is unnecessary for me to repeat the history of the [*Electoral Distribution Act*] and its precursors ... It is sufficient to say that the history is consistent with, and points to the conclusion which I have reached, that the purpose, and therefore the meaning to be given to s 13 of the [*Electoral Distribution Act*], was to immunise, consistently with the notion that constitutional change should be a matter of careful and detailed deliberation, the [*Electoral Distribution Act*] against change, whether partially or completely, except by stringent compliance with a manner and form provision.

Gleeson CJ, Gummow, Hayne and Heydon JJ: [565] The critical consideration is that defining electoral boundaries is legally essential to enable the election of the Parliament. Because that is so, "amend" cannot be understood as restricted to legislative changes that take the form of leaving the *Electoral Distribution Act* in operation albeit with altered legal effect. "Amend" must be understood as including changing the provisions which the *Electoral Distribution Act* makes, no matter what legislative steps are taken to achieve that end. In particular, it is not important whether the changes are made by one or more than one statute. The form in which the legislative steps to effect the change is framed is not determinative; the question is, what is their substance?

Because definition of electoral boundaries is legally essential to the election of the Parliament, repealing the *Electoral Distribution Act* must necessarily be a precursor to the enactment of other provisions on that subject of electoral boundaries. To read "any Bill to amend this Act" as confined to a Bill which will leave at least one provision of **[566]** the *Electoral Distribution Act* remaining in force, whether with the same or different legal operation, would defeat the evident purpose behind the introduction of the provision in 1904. That purpose was to ensure that no change could be made to electoral districts save by absolute majority of both Houses ...

Section 13 of the *Electoral Distribution Act* must be given the same meaning no matter whether the proposed legislation would advance or diminish the rights of particular electors. The construction question cannot be resolved by classifying the particular proposals that are made for new electoral boundaries as "desirable" or "undesirable", or as advancing human or other rights of electors in Western Australia. The content of the Bills which it is said have not validly been passed is irrelevant to whether either was a Bill to amend the *Electoral Distribution Act*. To assign a different meaning to s 13 according to the qualitative assessment that is made of the desirability of the proposed laws under consideration constitutes fundamental legal error ...

[572] The meaning to be given to the expression "constitution, powers or procedure of the Parliament" must be ascertained taking proper account of the history that lay behind the enactment of the *Australia Act*. In particular, it is necessary to give due weight to the learning that evolved about the operation of the *Colonial Laws Validity Act*, s 5 of which also spoke of "laws respecting the constitution, powers, and procedure" of the legislatures to which it applied.

In s 5 of the *Colonial Laws Validity Act* the expression "constitution, powers, and procedure" appeared in that part of the section which provided that a representative legislature "shall ... have, and be deemed at all times to have had, full power to make laws respecting" those subjects. The reference to manner and form requirements in the proviso to the section was treated as a condition upon which the full power referred to in s 5 was exercisable [*Attorney-General (NSW) v Trethowan* [1932] AC 526]. Section 6 of the *Australia Act* takes a different form. It provides directly for the requirement to observe manner and form. Nonetheless, the use of the expression "constitution, powers or procedure" in the *Australia Act* is evidently intended to build on the provisions of the *Colonial Laws Validity Act*. (The use of the conjunction "or" rather than "and" in the collocation is readily explained by the drafting change from grant of power to requirement to obey manner and form.)

On its face, the expression "constitution, powers or procedure" of a legislature describes a field which is larger than that identified as "the constitution" of a legislature. It is not necessary or appropriate to attempt to describe the boundaries of the areas within the field that the three separate integers of the expression "constitution, powers or procedure" cover, let alone attempt to define the boundaries of the entire field. In particular, it is not necessary or appropriate to explore what is encompassed by the reference in s 6 of the *Australia Act* to "powers or procedure" of a legislature, whether in relation to the ability of a legislature to entrench legislation about any subject or otherwise. It is enough to focus on the expression the "constitution" of the Parliament.

The "constitution" of a State Parliament includes (perhaps it is confined to) its own "nature and composition" [*Attorney-General (NSW) v Trethowan* (1931) 44 CLR 394 at 429]. The Attorneys-General for New South Wales and Queensland, intervening, both submitted that s 6 of the *Australia Act* should be read strictly and that, **[573]** accordingly, the "constitution" of a State Parliament should be understood as referring only to the general character of the legislature rather than the rules pursuant to which members are returned to a chamber.

For some purposes, the nature and composition of the Western Australian Parliament might be described sufficiently as "bicameral and representative". But the reference in s 6 of the *Australia*

Act to the "constitution" of a State Parliament should not be read as confined to those two descriptions ... That is, s 6 is not to be read as confined to laws which abolish a House, or altogether take away the "representative" character of a State Parliament or one of its Houses. At least to some extent the "constitution" of the Parliament extends to features which go to give it, and its Houses, a representative character. Thus, s 6 may be engaged in cases in which the legislation deals with matters that are encompassed by the general description "representative" and go to give that word its application in the particular case. So, for example, an upper House whose members are elected in a single State-wide electorate by proportional representation is differently constituted from an upper House whose members are separately elected in single member provinces by first past the post voting. Each may properly be described as a "representative" chamber, but the parliament would be differently constituted if one form of election to the upper House were to be adopted in place of the other.

Not every matter which touches the election of members of a Parliament is a matter affecting the Parliament's constitution. In *Clydesdale v Hughes* [(1934) 51 CLR 518 at 528], three members of the Court held that a law providing that the holding of a particular office did not disable or disqualify a person from sitting as a member of the Legislative Council of Western Australia was not a law which, for the purposes of s 73 of the 1889 Constitution, effected an alteration or change in the constitution of that House. Again, however, it is neither necessary nor appropriate to attempt to trace the metes and bounds of the relevant field.

The Repeal Bill and the Amendment Bill were respectively to do away with, and then provide an alternative structure for, the constitution of the two Houses of the Western Australian Parliament. The Repeal Bill did away with the scheme under which there were two Houses elected from 57 districts and six regions respectively, where the 57 districts were to be ascertained in accordance with the rules prescribed by s 6 of the *Electoral Distribution Act*. Those rules depended upon the division between the metropolitan and **[574]** other areas and the application of a tolerance of 15 per cent more or less. Upon the Repeal Bill coming into force the manner of effecting representation in the Parliament would have been at large. Considered separately, then, the Repeal Bill was for a law respecting the constitution of the Parliament of Western Australia.

The Amendment Bill, if it came into force, would have provided for 57 electoral districts and six electoral regions, but they would have been differently drawn from the way for which the *Electoral Distribution Act* provided. The criteria to be applied in drawing electoral boundaries under the Amendment Bill would have differed according to whether the electoral district had an area of less than 100,000 square kilometres. The tolerance in the smaller districts would have been reduced from 15 per cent to 10 per cent; in the larger districts the formula was more complicated, but again the tolerance was changed from 15 per cent. In addition, and no less significantly, under the Amendment Bill, the number of members of the Council would have been increased, from the 30 specified by s 5 of the *Constitution Acts Amendment Act* 1899, to 36. The Amendment Bill was for a law respecting the constitution of the Parliament of Western Australia.

Kirby J based his dissent primarily on his conclusion that the word "amend" in s 13 should be narrowly read so as not to extend to "repeal". He also held that the reference to laws respecting the "constitution" of a Parliament should be narrowly read so as not to extend to electoral arrangements. As to the word "amend", he noted that other Western Australian legislation had distinguished between "amendment" and wholesale "repeal", thus confirming the relevance of the usage suggesting that "amendment" stops short of "repeal". In addition, he thought that, in the context of electoral reform in Western Australia, the narrower meaning of "amend" was to be preferred on the basis of three "interpretive principles". The first was that any limitation on legislative power requires "**[596]** clear and unambiguous language". (He quoted the observation of Zelling J in *West Lakes Ltd v South Australia* (1980) 25 SASR 389, that "**[413]** given the general rule that the Acts of one Parliament do not bind its successors, it would require very clear words before a court would find that that was what had happened".) The second principle (as to which see Chapter 3, §4(c)) was that, in the absence of such language, the courts will ordinarily construe legislation so as to avoid the impairment of "fundamental rights" (in this case equality of voting rights): "**[601]** At the very least, where there is ambiguity or doubt in the applicable legislation, this Court ... should adopt the construction that advances fundamental rights in preference to one that attempts to 'entrench' against normal legislative repeal a provision giving effect to the last malapportionment of State electorates in the Commonwealth". The third principle (as to which see Chapter 19, §2(b)) was the settled practice "**[605]** that this Court will construe ambiguities in Australian legislation so as to avoid serious derogations from the international law of fundamental human rights" – in this case Art 25 of the International Covenant on Civil and Political Rights, which endorses the right to vote on a basis of "universal and equal suffrage".

4. Alternative Procedures

In 1932, the composition of the New South Wales Legislative Council was changed. Instead of its members being appointed by the Governor, they were to be elected by members of both Houses for a 12-year term. In 1978, the system was changed again and the current system of direct popular election was adopted. Following the change in 1932, s 5B was inserted into the *Constitution Act 1902* (NSW), and, incidentally to the change in 1978, s 5B was further amended. In its present form, s 5B provides:

Constitution Act 1902 (NSW)

Disagreements – referendum

5B (1) If the Legislative Assembly passes any Bill other than a Bill to which section 5A applies, and the Legislative Council rejects or fails to pass it or passes it with any amendment to which the Legislative Assembly does not agree, and if after an interval of three months the Legislative Assembly in the same Session or in the next Session again passes the Bill with or without any amendment which has been made or agreed to by the Legislative Council, and the Legislative Council rejects or fails to pass it or passes it with any amendment to which the Legislative Assembly does not agree, and if after a free conference between managers there is not agreement between the Legislative Council and the Legislative Assembly, the Governor may convene a joint sitting of the Members of the Legislative Council and the Members of the Legislative Assembly.

The Members present at the joint sitting may deliberate upon the Bill as last proposed by the Legislative Assembly and upon any amendments made by the Legislative Council with which the Legislative Assembly does not agree.

No vote shall be taken at the joint sitting.

(2) After the joint sitting and either after any further communication with the Legislative Council in order to bring about agreement, if possible, between the Legislative Council and the Legislative Assembly, or without any such communication the Legislative Assembly may by resolution direct that the Bill as last proposed by the Legislative Assembly and either with or without any amendment subsequently agreed to by the Legislative Council and the Legislative Assembly, shall, at any time during the life of the Parliament or at the next general election of Members of the Legislative Assembly, be submitted by way of referendum to the electors qualified to vote for the election of Members of the Legislative Assembly …

(3) If at the referendum a majority of the electors voting approve the Bill it shall be presented to the Governor for the signification of His Majesty's pleasure thereon and become an Act of the Legislature upon the Royal Assent being signified thereto, notwithstanding that the Legislative Council has not consented to the Bill.

(4) For the purposes of this section the Legislative Council shall be taken to have failed to pass a Bill if the Bill is not returned to the Legislative Assembly within two months after its transmission to the Legislative Council and the Session continues during such period.

(5) This section shall extend to any Bill whether it is a Bill to which section 7A applies or not. And in the application of this section to a Bill to which section 7A applies:

(a) the submission of the Bill to the electors by way of referendum in accordance with this section shall be a sufficient compliance with the provisions of section 7A which require the Bill to be submitted to the electors;

(b) the referendum under this section shall, notwithstanding anything contained in section 7A, be held upon a day which shall be appointed by the Governor; and

(c) the day so appointed shall, notwithstanding anything contained in subsection (2), be a day during the life of the Parliament and not sooner than two months after the Legislative Assembly has passed a resolution in accordance with that subsection for the purposes of such referendum.

The main purpose of s 5B is to provide an *alternative* legislative procedure – not only as an alternative to the normal legislative procedure in a Westminster parliament, that is, passage by both Houses plus the Royal Assent, but also as an alternative to the "restrictive" procedure established by s 7A of the *Constitution Act*. However, because s 5B affects the constitutional position of the Legislative Council and the operation of s 7A, the amendment inserting s 5B had itself to be passed by referendum in compliance with s 7A.

The difference between *alternative* and *restrictive* procedures is constitutionally of great significance: a "restrictive" procedure like that in s 7A of the New South Wales *Constitution Act* derogates from the usual principle of parliamentary sovereignty, by requiring that laws on certain topics cannot be passed by the ordinary parliamentary process at all. By contrast, on topics for which "alternative" procedures have been established, the normal parliamentary process remains fully available: the effect of the "alternative" procedure is simply to offer an additional option to a government which encounters difficulties in the normal process. Typically, such procedures are devised as a counter to the power of a hostile Upper House to obstruct a government's legislative program. The "double dissolution" procedure in s 57 of the Commonwealth Constitution (see Chapter 10, §6) is the most obvious Australian example.

The effect of s 5B was tested in 1959 and 1960, when a New South Wales Labor government, led by Premier Robert Heffron, again attempted to abolish the Legislative Council. This time it did so by attempting to proceed under s 5B rather than under s 7A. The Constitutional Amendment (Legislative Council Abolition) Bill 1959 (NSW) was passed by the Legislative Assembly on 2 December 1959. The Legislative Council rejected it the same evening. The Bill was again passed by the Legislative Assembly on 6 April 1960 and again rejected by the Legislative Council on the same day. What happened next is summarised below:

Clayton v Heffron
(1960) 105 CLR 214

Dixon CJ, McTiernan, Taylor and Windeyer JJ: [244] On 7th April 1960 the Legislative Assembly resolved on a message to the Council requesting, pursuant to the provisions of s 5B, a free conference with the Legislative Council with respect to the Bill. The message named ten managers whom the Assembly had appointed. The message was signed by the Speaker. On the message being reported to the Council, that Chamber adopted a resolution that this House does not consider that any situation has arisen whereby a free conference between managers of the Legislative Council and the Legislative Assembly is either necessary or proper and accordingly it refuses the request of the Legislative Assembly in its message dated 7th April 1960 … A message accordingly was sent to the Speaker. The Governor thereupon sent messages to the Houses convening a joint sitting of the members of the House to deliberate upon the Bill … The place named was the Legislative Council chamber and the date 20th April 1960: the members of the Council and of the Assembly were thereby required to give their attendance at the said time and place accordingly. Thereupon a resolution was passed in the Legislative Council to the effect that the House did not consider that a situation had arisen conferring constitutional power upon His Excellency the Governor to convene the joint sitting of members and the House resolved that for this constitutional reason the members of the House do not attend at or participate in such joint sitting.

In short, there was no "free conference between managers" of the kind envisaged by s 5B(1). The Legislative Council had declined to participate in such a conference and, although a joint sitting was held on 20 April 1960, it took place without the formal participation of the Legislative Council (even though 23 members of the Council did in fact attend).

On 12 May 1960, the Legislative Assembly resolved that the Constitutional Amendment (Legislative Council Abolition) Bill should be put to referendum. On the same day, five members of the Legislative Council instituted proceedings in the New South Wales Supreme Court, seeking an injunction to restrain any steps towards the holding of a referendum. An interim injunction was granted by McLelland CJ in Eq. The defendants demurred to the statement of claim and on 29 September 1960 a five-judge Full Court, presided over by Evatt CJ, upheld the demurrer by 4:1 (*Clayton v Heffron* (1960) 77 WN (NSW) 767). When the matter again came on for hearing before McLelland CJ in Eq, he dismissed the suit on the same grounds as had the Full Court. Thereupon the plaintiffs appealed to the High Court.

Whether the equitable remedy of injunction was an appropriate form of relief was debatable. However, at the hearing before the Full Supreme Court, that issue was disposed of by consent.

Clayton v Heffron
(1960) 77 WN (NSW) 767

Evatt CJ and Sugerman J: [774] It has been agreed between the parties that, for the purposes of these proceedings and in order to avoid the possibility that the Court might decide this application on grounds which left the main constitutional questions undecided, the defendants will concede that an injunction may be granted at the suit of those plaintiffs who are members of the Legislative Council against the defendants who are Ministers of the Crown and Members of the Executive Council restraining them from proceeding to take any steps towards the issue of a writ for the holding of a referendum if, in the events which have happened, it would be unconstitutional for the Bill to proceed to a referendum.

The leading judgment in the High Court was that of Dixon CJ, McTiernan, Taylor and Windeyer JJ. As to the above concession, they said:

Clayton v Heffron
(1960) 105 CLR 214

Dixon CJ, McTiernan, Taylor and Windeyer JJ: [233] How it is possible to support a claim for equitable relief of this nature it is difficult to understand. Indeed the constitution of the suit as a whole strikes one as an experiment against the success of which law equity and wisdom combine. As against the Ministers it is a claim that on the question in hand they be restrained from advising the Crown, executing the administrative functions which belong to them and permitting the expenditure of money which is available under supply or appropriation that has been or will be voted. As to the Electoral Commissioner, he is to be restrained from the performance of the functions which belong to him if and when the Governor issues his writ. This is to be done, moreover, at the suit of plaintiffs whose only interest is either as holders of offices of which the Bill if validly enacted might deprive them or as taxpayers, that is, members of the public, or in two cases members of other legislative bodies. All this is based upon the ground that properly interpreted and applied the law does not authorize the legislative measure proposed; and that is put on two grounds, namely, first, that the provision of the Constitution of New South Wales which purports to authorize such a proceeding is invalid, and second, that the provision contains requirements from which there have been fatal departures or at all events departures. The case in truth is one in which during the course of a legislative process which may or may not end in the adoption of the measure proposed, it is sought to obtain the interposition of a court of equity to enjoin those taken to be responsible for carrying forward the measure from further proceeding with it. It is evident enough that such a case has no analogy to *Attorney-General (NSW) v Trethowan* [[1932] AC 526]. The injunction was there granted by the majority **[234]** of the Supreme Court because a definite statutory prohibition made, so it was held, the step of presenting that Bill to the Governor for his assent unlawful: in the opinion of the Supreme Court, to enforce this distinct and imperative negative duty the remedy of injunction was available. Be that as it may (cf *Hughes and Vale Pty Ltd v Gair* [(1954) 90 CLR 203]) it can have nothing to do with an attempt to secure the intervention of a court of equity in a legislative process on the ground that the procedure is misconceived or alternatively has not been correctly pursued. It may be assumed that the suit would not have been entertained by the Supreme Court sitting in Equity, had it not been for a concession made by the defendants ... Upon the basis of this concession the Supreme Court entertained the suit ... Even so, (if the concession is given full effect) the Court in acting upon the concession must go beyond its function of deciding whether an Act of Parliament assented to by the Crown does not go beyond the legislative power of the Parliament so that it cannot form part of the law of the land and must enter upon an inquiry into the lawfulness and regularity of the course pursued within the Parliament [235] itself in the process of legislation and before its completion. It is an inquiry which according to the traditional view courts do not undertake. The process of law-making is one thing: the power to make the law as it has emerged from the process is another. It is the latter which the court must always have jurisdiction to examine and pronounce upon. Of course the framers of a constitution may make the validity of a law depend upon any fact, event or consideration they may choose, and if one is chosen which consists in a proceeding within Parliament the courts must take it under their cognizance in order to determine whether the supposed law is a valid law; but even then one might suppose only after the law in question has been enacted and when its validity as law is impugned by someone affected by its operation.

The joint judgment went on to hold that the Bill came within the terms of s 7A and *therefore* that it fell within s 7A as controlled or varied by s 5B(5). In other words, the device of setting up s 5B as an alternative to s 7A was successful. The joint judgment further held that the Bill's passage under s 5B would be valid and that the Legislative Council had twice "failed to pass" it within the meaning of s 5B(4).

There is a distinction between procedural requirements that are mandatory, that is, requirements which *must* be observed so that failure to do so results in invalidity, and those which are merely directory, that is, requirements which *should* be complied with but which do not necessarily invalidate an exercise of power for lack of strict compliance. In this instance the provisions for a free conference and a joint sitting were held to be merely directory.

Dixon CJ, McTiernan, Taylor and Windeyer JJ: [246] Would it be possible for the Court to investigate the legislative process and hold the enactment void because there had not been a conference of managers? There is no doubt that the words "after a free conference between managers" contain an implied direction that such a conference shall take place. In the same way the words relating to the joint sitting of members of the Houses import an intention that the Governor shall then exercise the authority to convene a joint sitting of members. But it is an entirely different thing to find in the direction an intention that a departure from the procedure shall spell invalidity in the statute when it is passed approved and assented to. In this case there are two matters with which we are dealing: the legislative power and the procedure for its exercise. The principles of the common law distinguished sharply between invalid attempts to exercise a legislative power and departures from the prescribed course for its exercise which may not or do not bring invalidity as a necessary consequence. In the end the distinction must be governed by the intention expressed by the legislature conferring the power and prescribing the steps to be taken in the course of its exercise. But commonly no express declaration is to be found in a statutory power as to the effect on validity of departures from the procedure laid down. The question is then determined by reference to the nature of the power conferred, the consequences which flow from its exercise, the character and purpose of the procedure prescribed. The power here is to enact a public general statute and the power to do this extends to a statute altering the constitution of the Legislature so that if the statute is to be void every future piece of legislation passed by the Legislature of the State so constituted will have no force or effect. The matter of procedure prescribed is a matter affecting the process in Parliament of legislating, a matter at once outside the ordinary scope of inquiry by the courts and also one not necessarily of public notoriety. The point of procedure concerns a step preliminary to the calling by the Governor of a joint sitting of the members of the two Houses. Such a meeting was convened in point of fact and a meeting of certain members of the two Houses took place at the time and place appointed. The point that in itself it could not amount to a joint meeting of members because the Council had resolved that its members should not attend is untenable. The preliminary step of appointing managers freely to confer rested on the co-operation of both Houses in a conflict. It would rest with either House to neglect the duty and so bring the **[247]** proceedings to nought. True it is that one contention is that a condition should be implied that the Council or the Assembly or for that matter neither of them may defeat the operation of s 5B by doing so. But once the conclusion is reached that a failure to perform the requirement of holding a free conference by managers spells invalidity of the ultimate statute, to make such an implication seems to amount to extracting from the interpretation which is first placed on the clause an implication to avoid a necessary consequence of that interpretation. On the other hand, before one reaches the conclusion that the failure to fulfil the requirement of holding a free conference will result in the invalidity of the law if adopted, it is natural to treat the fact that the Legislative Council may decline a conference of managers as a reason to be added to the other considerations for holding that it is not a matter going to validity. Lawyers speak of statutory provisions as imperative when any want of strict compliance with them means that the resulting act, be it a statute, a contract or what you will, is null and void. They speak of them as directory when they mean that although they are legal requirements which it is unlawful to disregard, yet failure to fulfil them does not mean that the resulting act is wholly ineffective, is null and void. It is almost unnecessary to say that the decided cases illustrating the distinction relate to much humbler matters than the validity or invalidity of the constitution of the Legislature of a State. But in them all the performance of a public duty or the fulfilment of a public function by a body of persons to whom the task is confided is regarded as something to be contrasted with the acquisition or exercise of private rights or privileges and the fact that to treat a deviation in the former case from the conditions or directions laid down as meaning complete invalidity would work inconvenience or worse on a section of the public is treated as a powerful consideration against doing so. Is it possible to imagine a stronger case of inconvenience than the invalidation perhaps at some future time of a constitutional provision possessing all the outward appearances of a valid law on the ground that when it was made managers of the Council had not met managers of the Assembly before the members of the two Houses were required by the Governor to meet? The argument for the plaintiffs suggested that the Governor's "power" to summon a joint meeting of members could not arise without a conference of managers. If that were all it would be enough to say that it is not a "power" in the ordinary sense and that in fact he did summon or convene the meeting without objection on the ground that he had interfered with the parliamentary process in a way which was **[248]** beyond the province of the Crown. But that is not the real point. The real point sought to be made is that a free conference is an essential condition of the ultimate validity of any statute enacted under s 5B. To that the answer is that according to the principles governing the invalidation of statutes for deviation from the legislative procedure laid down by law no such invalidity should be held to ensue as a consequence of the lack of a meeting of managers in a free conference.

Dixon CJ, McTiernan, Taylor and Windeyer JJ went on to hold that the validity of s 5B did not depend on its characterisation as a "manner and form" requirement under the proviso to s 5 of the *Colonial Laws Validity Act*. Section 5B was a valid exercise of the Parliament's plenary "peace welfare and good government" power in s 5 of the *Constitution Act*. Fullagar, Kitto and Menzies JJ agreed; but as to the operation of s 5B these three judges took different views. Fullagar J dissented from the conclusions in the joint judgment. He held that s 5B was mandatory and that since there had been no free conference, nor any joint sitting sufficiently complying with s 5B, its law-making procedure could not be used. Neither a subsequent referendum nor any subsequent Royal Assent could produce "**[265]** a valid Act of the legislature of New South Wales". Kitto and Menzies JJ also held that s 5B was mandatory. However, they held that it was subject to an implied condition that the Council must be willing to co-operate. Once the Council had refused to participate in a joint conference, the requirement that such a conference be held became inapplicable.

The end result was that the High Court held by 4:3 that the relevant provisions of s 5B were merely directory and not mandatory, and by 6:1 that, in the particular circumstances of *Clayton v Heffron*, the proposal to abolish the Legislative Council could properly be put to referendum even though there had neither been a free conference of managers nor a fully authorised joint sitting. On 29 April 1961 the Bill was duly submitted to a referendum, but failed.

Long before New South Wales adopted s 5B in 1932, both South Australia and Victoria had also introduced procedures for the resolution of deadlocks between the two Houses of their Parliaments. Indeed, the main South Australian version dates back to s 16 of the *Constitution Act Further Amendment Act 1881* (SA). As presently embodied in s 41 of the *Constitution Act 1934* (SA), it contemplates the situation where a Bill has been passed by the lower House in two successive Parliaments (with an election intervening); has been passed on the second occasion by an absolute majority in the lower House; and has failed on both occasions because it has been "rejected by the Legislative Council or failed to become law in consequence of ... amendments made therein by the Legislative Council". In that situation it shall be "lawful ... but not obligatory" for the Governor within six months to dissolve both Houses, *or* to issue writs for the election of two additional members for each Council district. Apart from the six months' limitation period (designed to prevent "stockpiling" or "staleness"), the mechanism remains substantially unchanged from that introduced in 1881. An alternative mechanism introduced in 1985, triggered by the Speaker's certification that a Bill is "of special importance", is now provided by s 28A.

The Victorian version embodied in ss 65A-65G of the *Constitution Act 1975* (Vic) was introduced in 2003. It replaced earlier procedures, first introduced as s 31 of the *Constitution Act 1903* (Vic), designed to resolve disputes between the Legislative Assembly and Legislative Council. The sections provide that a Bill becomes a "Disputed Bill" where it "has passed the Assembly and having been transmitted to and received by the Council not less than 2 months before the end of the session has not been passed by the Council within 2 months after the Bill is so transmitted, either without amendment or with such amendments only as may be agreed to by both the Assembly and the Council". A Dispute Resolution Committee, formed at the beginning of each Parliament and composed of members of both Houses, must then attempt to resolve the deadlock within 30 days of the Bill being referred to it by the Assembly. It may recommend that the Bill be passed as it stands, passed in an amended form or not passed at all. If the Committee cannot agree on a recommendation, or if its recommendation is not followed by either House, the Bill becomes a "Deadlocked Bill" in respect of which the Premier may advise the Governor to call an early election (but only for the Legislative Assembly). If after an election, whether or not it was called in respect of the Deadlocked Bill, the Bill again becomes a Disputed Bill, it may be put to a joint sitting of both Houses. If it receives the support of an absolute majority at that sitting, it is to be taken to have been passed by both Houses.

5. The *Ranasinghe* Principle

We now return to the mandatory conditions of valid legislation that are typified by the restrictive procedures in ss 7A and 7B of the *Constitution Act 1902* (NSW). The practical limitations on judicial enforcement of mandatory conditions of valid legislation such as ss 7A and 7B remain in considerable doubt. The doubt extends: (1) to when a Court can or should intervene (and, in particular, to whether it can or should intervene before the purported legislative process is complete); (2) to what remedies a Court can properly offer (and, in particular, whether an injunction to prevent the completion of the legislative process is an appropriate remedy); and (3) to how far, for the purpose of testing compliance with the procedural conditions, a Court can inquire into factual issues arising out of the "intra-mural" proceedings of the Houses of Parliament. However, subject to these doubts, it is clear in principle that so long as procedural requirements cannot be put aside as being merely "directory", they are judicially enforceable, and that a purported law which has not complied with the specified procedures for its enactment will be held to be invalid. Why is this so?

The answer given in *Attorney-General (NSW) v Trethowan* (1931) 44 CLR 395 depended on the proviso to s 5 of the *Colonial Laws Validity Act 1865* (Imp). In that case, the application of the proviso was treated as a matter of statutory interpretation. Yet as the British Empire evolved into a Commonwealth of Nations, whose members and former members continued to follow their own paths of constitutional development, the intriguing possibility emerged that, through exegesis of the proviso to s 5 of the *Colonial Laws Validity Act*, the High Court of Australia might have stumbled onto a more fundamental constitutional principle – not dependent on s 5 of the *Colonial Laws Validity Act*, but inherent in the very idea of law-making. This principle is that the process of making law is itself a process necessarily regulated by law; and accordingly that any purported exercise of law-making power will be valid only if it complies with the law-making procedures which the law for the time being requires. Where those procedures are prescribed by a written Constitution, they must be complied with because to do otherwise would constitute a failure to conform to the law-making process which the Constitution requires. Moreover, even where (as in the United Kingdom) there is no written Constitution, this principle might mean that if the Parliament at Westminster enacts statutory requirements as to how its sovereign law-making power is to be exercised in future cases, those requirements might be binding on future Parliaments in spite of the normal assumption that Parliament cannot bind its successors.

The first clear glimpse of such a principle can be seen in the judgment of Dixon J in *Trethowan's Case*, in the passage in which he speculates on what might have happened if a similar issue had arisen in the United Kingdom. If such a question did arise, he says that "**[426]** the Courts might be called upon to consider whether the supreme legislative power in respect of the matter had in truth been exercised in the manner required for its authentic expression and by the elements in which it had come to reside". The hypothesis is that in any case where a court is asked to enforce a purported law, or simply to determine whether it is a valid and therefore enforceable law, the questions that must be determined are whether "in truth" the relevant legislative power has been exercised (a) in the appropriate manner, and (b) by the appropriate elements, with the criteria for both (a) and (b) being themselves determined by law. Unless both (a) and (b) are satisfied, there is not "in truth" an "authentic expression" of the relevant legislative power and no law has been made.

The first significant indication that this kind of analysis did not depend merely on s 5 of the *Colonial Laws Validity Act* came in the South African case of *Harris v Minister of the Interior* [1952] 2 SALR 428. As the legal structure of apartheid was slowly erected in South Africa, especially from 1948 onwards, the Supreme Court of South Africa fought a rearguard action, using constitutional grounds to resist the racial division of the country. Eventually the Court was unsuccessful; but *Harris v Minister of the Interior* was a notable victory along the way.

The South African Constitution was contained in the *South Africa Act 1909* (UK). Within certain limits, the South African Parliament had power to amend its own Constitution.

South Africa Act 1909 (UK)

152 Parliament may by law repeal or alter any of the provisions of this Act: Provided that no provision thereof, for the operation of which a definite period of time is prescribed, shall during such period be repealed or altered: And provided further that no repeal or alteration of the provisions contained in this section, or in secs 33 and 34 (until the number of members of the House of Assembly has reached the limit therein prescribed, or until a period of ten years has elapsed after the establishment of the Union, whichever is the longer period) or in secs 35 and 137, shall be valid unless the Bill embodying such repeal or alteration shall be passed by both Houses of Parliament sitting together, and at the third reading be agreed to by not less than two-thirds of the total number of members of both Houses. A Bill so passed at such joint sitting shall be taken to have been duly passed by both Houses of Parliament.

Section 35 was amended by the *Representation of Natives Act 1936* (South Africa), which was passed at a joint sitting with the requisite two-thirds majority. As thus amended, s 35 provided:

35 (1) Parliament may by law prescribe the qualifications which shall be necessary to entitle persons to vote at the election of members of the House of Assembly, but no such law shall disqualify any person (other than a Native, as defined in sec 1 of the Representation of Natives Act, 1936) in the Province of the Cape of Good Hope who, under the laws existing in the Colony of the Cape of Good Hope at the establishment of the Union, is or may become capable of being registered as a voter from being so registered in the Province of the Cape of Good Hope by reason of his race or colour only or disqualify any Native, as so defined, who under the said Act would be or might become capable of being registered in the Cape Native voters' roll instituted under that Act from being so registered, or alter the number of the members of the House of Assembly who in terms of the said Act may be elected by the persons registered in the said roll, unless the Bill embodying such disqualification or alteration be passed by both Houses of Parliament sitting together, and at the third reading be agreed to by not less than two-thirds of the total number of members of both Houses. A Bill so passed at such joint sitting shall be taken to have been duly passed by both Houses of Parliament.

(2) No person (other than a Native as so defined) who at the passing of any such law is registered as a voter in any province shall be removed from the register by reason only of any disqualification based on race or colour.

The 1936 amendments had still left some non-European persons (that is, persons other than "natives") on the same electoral roll as those of European descent. However, the *Separate Representation of Voters Act 1951* (South Africa) introduced a system of rigorous segregation of Europeans and non-Europeans on separate electoral rolls. In *Harris v Minister for the Interior*, the validity of that enactment was challenged. The plaintiffs asserted that the Act was racially discriminatory as applied both to Europeans and to non-Europeans, and that, as to both categories, this discriminatory treatment amounted to "disqualification" within the meaning of s 35 of the *South Africa Act*. The Appellate Division of the Supreme Court accepted that argument. It was common ground that there had been no compliance with the requirements of a joint sitting or a two-thirds majority; the ordinary bicameral Parliament had simply passed the Act in the ordinary way. The question was whether any legal consequences followed from this.

The Appellate Division found that the power of the Parliament was limited by s 35. As the 1951 Act involved a "disqualification" of the kind referred to in s 35, it could only be enacted by the special procedure prescribed in that section. This finding involved the assertion of a binding "manner and form" requirement comparable to that in *Trethowan's Case*. However, in *Trethowan's Case* the binding operation of the requirement had been ascribed to s 5 of the *Colonial Laws Validity Act*. For the Union of South Africa, that ground of decision was no longer available, since the *Statute of Westminster 1931* (Imp) had excluded any further application of the *Colonial Laws Validity Act* to any law made by the Union. Instead, Centlivres CJ (with whom the other members of the Appellate Division agreed) identified a deeper ground.

Harris v Minister of the Interior
[1952] 2 SALR 428

Centlivres CJ: [463] Mr *Beyers* then contended that no country which, like the Union, emerged from a colony into a Dominion within the framework of the British Constitution can be a sovereign state unless it has a **[464]** sovereign Parliament functioning bicamerally in the same manner as the British Parliament and that if this is not so in the case of the Union, it cannot be a sovereign state unless it breaks completely with its past and abolishes the monarchy. I cannot agree with this contention. It seems to me to be based on the fallacy that a Dominion Parliament must necessarily be a replica of the British Parliament despite the fact that all Dominion Parliaments have constitutions which define the manner in which they must function as legislative bodies. There is nothing in the Statute of Westminster which in any way suggests that a Dominion Parliament should be regarded as if it were in the same position as the British Parliament. Indeed it would be surprising if the British Parliament in enacting the Statute of Westminster, which was agreed to by all Dominions, had gone out of its way to change the Constitution of a Dominion without a request

from that Dominion to do so. I have looked in vain at the official reports of the Imperial Conferences which led up to the passing of the Statute for any request by the Union to the British
Parliament for an alteration of its Constitution. On the contrary the authoritative voice of the
Union, as embodied in the joint resolution of the two Houses of Parliament, made it abundantly
clear that the Union did not desire any amendment of its Constitution and emphasised that the proposed Statute of Westminster should in no way derogate from the entrenched provisions of the
South Africa Act.

A State can be unquestionably sovereign although it has no legislature which is completely
sovereign. As Bryce points out in his *Studies in History and Jurisprudence* (1901 ed, Vol II, p 53)
legal sovereignty may be divided between two authorities. In the case of the Union, legal
sovereignty is or may be divided between Parliament as ordinarily constituted and Parliament as
constituted under sec 63 and the proviso to sec 152. Such a division of legislative powers is no
derogation from the sovereignty of the Union and the mere fact that that division was enacted in a
British Statute (viz the South Africa Act) which is still in force in the Union cannot affect the
question in issue.

I find it impossible to uphold the implications of Mr *Beyers'* contention, viz that after the
passing of the Statute of Westminster the Union found itself with a Constitution which had been
radically altered – a Constitution which enabled Parliament to sit either bicamerally or
unicamerally, no matter what the subject-matter of the legislation might be. The South Africa Act,
the terms and conditions of which were, as its preamble shows, agreed to by the respective Parliaments of the four original Colonies, created the Parliament of the Union. It is that Act and not the
Statute of Westminster which prescribes the manner in which the constituent elements of
Parliament must function for the purpose of passing legislation. While the Statute of Westminster
confers further powers on the Parliament of the Union, it in no way prescribes how that Parliament
must function in exercising those powers …

[468] [T]he Union is an autonomous state in no way subordinate to any other country in the
world. To say that the Union is not a sovereign state, simply because its Parliament functioning
bicamerally has not the power to amend certain sections of the South Africa Act, is to state a
manifest absurdity. Those sections can be amended by Parliament sitting unicamerally. The Union
is, therefore, through its Legislature able to pass any laws it pleases and it would be as false to say
that the Union is not a sovereign state as it would have been to say that the Republic of the Orange
Free State was not a sovereign state on the ground that it was provided in sec 26 of its Constitution
that no amendment could be made to it save by a three-fourths majority of the Volksraad in two
successive annual sessions. To go further afield, it would be surprising to a constitutional lawyer to
be told that that great and powerful country, the United States of America, is not a sovereign
independent country simply because its Congress cannot pass any legislation which it pleases.

The decision in *Harris v Minister of the Interior* was ineffectual as an attempt to halt the erection
of the apartheid system. The Parliament responded by enacting the *High Court of Parliament Act
1952* (South Africa), which set up members of Parliament as a High Court with the power to
reverse Supreme Court decisions, and this body proceeded to reverse the decision in *Harris v
Minister of the Interior*. However, the High Court of Parliament and its "decision" were in turn
declared invalid by the Supreme Court in *Minister of the Interior v Harris* [1952] 4 SALR 769.
At the 1953 election, the government increased its majority but still fell short of the numbers
required for a two-thirds majority at a joint sitting. Two joint sittings were held, but neither
produced a two-thirds majority. Then, in 1955, the government, by ordinary legislation, increased
the size of the Supreme Court's Appellate Division from six judges to 11 and required that in
constitutional matters all 11 judges should sit. At the same time, by the *Senate Act 1955* (South
Africa), the government increased the size of the Senate to enable it to secure the necessary two-
thirds vote in a joint sitting. At the end of 1955, the new Senate was elected and at the beginning
of 1956 a joint sitting, with a clear two-thirds majority, passed the *South Africa Act Amendment
Act 1956* (South Africa), which incorporated the provisions of the unsuccessful separate voting
legislation of 1951. In *Collins v Minister of the Interior* [1957] 1 SALR 552, the validity of the

Senate Act and of the *South Africa Act Amendment Act* was challenged in the Supreme Court, but the newly "stacked" Appellate Division held the legislation valid by 10 votes to one.

The possible implications of *Harris v Minister of the Interior* were explored by the Privy Council on appeal from Ceylon (now Sri Lanka) in *Bribery Commissioner v Ranasinghe* [1965] AC 172. The appellant Commissioner was a special prosecutor appointed under the *Bribery Act 1954* (Ceylon). His office had been created by the *Bribery Amendment Act 1958* (Ceylon), which had also created a new Bribery Tribunal before which persons prosecuted by the Commissioner were to be tried. In 1962, Pedrick Ranasinghe, who had been convicted by the Tribunal, successfully appealed to the Supreme Court of Ceylon on the ground that the Tribunal was unconstitutional (*Bribery Commissioner v Ranasinghe* (1962) 64 NLR 449). From that decision, the Commissioner appealed to the Privy Council.

The Constitution of Ceylon was conferred by the Ceylon (Constitution) Order in Council 1946, as amended in 1947. The *Ceylon Independence Act 1947* (Imp) made Ceylon independent of Imperial laws by provisions equivalent to those of the *Statute of Westminster*. By s 52, Supreme Court judges could not be removed except by the Governor-General on an address from both Houses of Parliament and by s 55 the "appointment, transfer, dismissal and disciplinary control" of other judicial officers was vested in a Judicial Service Commission. What Ranasinghe successfully argued was that members of the Bribery Tribunal were "judicial officers" whose appointment had not involved the Judicial Service Commission and hence did not comply with s 55 of the Constitution. The difficult question was whether this non-compliance made any difference. The answer depended on s 29 of the 1946 Constitution.

Ceylon (Constitution) Order in Council 1946

29 (1) Subject to the provisions of this Order, Parliament shall have power to make laws for the peace, order and good government of the Island …

(4) In the exercise of its powers under this section, Parliament may amend or repeal any of the provisions of this Order, or of any other Order of Her Majesty in Council in its application to the Island:

Provided that no Bill for the amendment or repeal of any of the provisions of this Order shall be presented for the Royal Assent unless it has endorsed on it a certificate under the hand of the Speaker that the number of votes cast in favour thereof in the House of Representatives amounted to not less than two-thirds of the whole number of Members of the House (including those not present).

Every certificate of the Speaker under this subsection shall be conclusive for all purposes and shall not be questioned in any court of law.

Section 29(4) was a "manner and form" requirement expressed to apply to any amendment or repeal of any "provisions of this Order". It did not require that constitutional amendments had to be passed in the lower House by a two-thirds majority, but only that there be a Speaker's certificate to that effect. Even if clear evidence were tendered that the Speaker's certificate had no factual basis, the final paragraph of sub-s (4) appears to mean that no court would be able to consider that evidence. The *Bribery Act* had been indorsed with a Speaker's certificate complying with s 29(4), but the *Bribery Amendment Act* carried no such certificate and presumably had not been passed by a two-thirds majority. The question was whether non-compliance with s 29(4) was fatal to validity. Their Lordships held that it was.

Bribery Commissioner v Ranasinghe
[1965] AC 172

Lord Pearce [194] The fact that the 1958 Bill did not have a certificate and was not passed by the necessary majority was not really disputed in the Supreme Court or before their Lordships' Board, but it has been argued that the court, when faced with an official copy of an Act of Parliament, cannot inquire into any procedural matter and cannot now properly consider whether a certificate was endorsed on the Bill. That argument seems to their Lordships unsubstantial, and it was rightly rejected by the Supreme Court. Once it is shown that an Act conflicts with a provision in the Constitution, the certificate is an essential part of the legislative process. The court has a duty to see that the Constitution is not infringed and to preserve it inviolate. Unless, therefore, there is some very cogent reason for doing so, the court must not decline to open its eyes to the truth. Their Lordships were informed by counsel that there were two duplicate original Bills and that after the Royal Assent was added one original was filed **[195]** in the Registry where it was available to the court. It was therefore easy for the court, without seeking to invade the mysteries of parliamentary practice, to ascertain that the Bill was not endorsed with the Speaker's certificate ...

[196] There remains the point which is the real substance of this appeal. When a sovereign Parliament has purported to enact a bill and it has received the Royal Assent, is it a valid Act in the course of whose passing there was a procedural defect, or is it an invalid Act which Parliament had no power to pass in that manner? ...

The appellant's argument placed much reliance on the opinion of this Board in *McCawley v The King* [[1920] AC 691]. Just as in that case the legislature of the then Colony of Queensland was held to have power by a mere majority vote to pass an Act that was inconsistent with the provisions of the existing Constitution of the Colony as to the tenure of judicial office, so, it was said, the legislature of Ceylon had no less a power to depart from the requirements of a section such as section 55 of the Order in Council, notwithstanding the wording of section 18 and section 29(4). Their Lordships are satisfied that the attempted analogy between the two cases is delusive and that *McCawley's* case, so far as it is material, is in fact opposed to the appellant's reasoning ...

[197] [T]he Board in *McCawley's* case took the view, which commends itself to the Board in the present case, that a legislature has no power to ignore the conditions of law-making that are imposed by the instrument which itself regulates its power to make law. This restriction exists independently of the question whether the legislature is sovereign, as is the legislature of Ceylon, or whether the Constitution is "uncontrolled," as the Board held the Constitution of **[198]** Queensland to be. Such a Constitution can, indeed, be altered or amended by the legislature, if the regulating instrument so provides and if the terms of those provisions are complied with: and the alteration or amendment may include the change or abolition of those very provisions. But the proposition which is not acceptable is that a legislature, once established, has some inherent power derived from the mere fact of its establishment to make a valid law by the resolution of a bare majority which its own constituent instrument has said shall not be a valid law unless made by a different type of majority or by a different legislative process. And this is the proposition which is in reality involved in the argument.

It is possible now to state summarily what is the essential difference between the *McCawley* case and this case. There the legislature, having full power to make laws by a majority, except upon one subject that was not in question, passed a law which conflicted with one of the existing terms of its Constitution Act. It was held that this was valid legislation, since it must be treated as pro tanto an alteration of the Constitution, which was neither fundamental in the sense of being beyond change nor so constructed as to require any special legislative process to pass upon the topic dealt with. In the present case, on the other hand, the legislature has purported to pass a law which, being in conflict with section 55 of the Order in Council, must be treated, if it is to be valid, as an implied alteration of the Constitutional provisions about the appointment of judicial officers. Since such alterations, even if express, can only be made by laws which comply with the special legislative procedure laid down in section 29(4), the Ceylon legislature has not got the general power to legislate so as to amend its Constitution by ordinary majority resolutions, such as the Queensland legislature was found to have under section 2 of its Constitution Act, but is rather in the position, for effecting such amendments, that that legislature was held to be in by virtue of its section 9, namely, compelled to operate a special procedure in order to achieve the desired result ...

[199] The legislative power of the Ceylon Parliament is derived from section 18 and section 29 of its Constitution. Section 18 expressly says "save as otherwise ordered in subsection (4) of section 29." Section 29(1) is expressed to be "subject to the provisions of this Order." And any power under section 29(4) is expressly subject to its proviso. Therefore in the case of **[200]** amendment and repeal of the Constitution the Speaker's certificate is a necessary part of the legislative process and any Bill which does not comply with the condition precedent of the proviso, is and remains, even though it receives the Royal Assent, invalid and ultra vires.

No question of sovereignty arises. A Parliament does not cease to be sovereign whenever its component members fail to produce among themselves a requisite majority, eg, when in the case of ordinary legislation the voting is evenly divided or when in the case of legislation to amend the Constitution there is only a bare majority if the Constitution requires something more. The minority are entitled under the Constitution of Ceylon to have no amendment of it which is not passed by a two-thirds majority. The limitation thus imposed on some lesser majority of members does not limit the sovereign powers of Parliament itself which can always, whenever it chooses, pass the amendment with the requisite majority ...

Their Lordships therefore are in accord with the view so clearly expressed by the Supreme Court "that the orders made against the respondent are null and inoperative on the grounds that the persons composing the Bribery Tribunal which tried him were not lawfully appointed to the Tribunal."

In *Victoria v Commonwealth & Connor* (*PMA Case*) (1975) 134 CLR 81, Gibbs J treated the *Ranasinghe* principle as applicable in every case "**[163]** where a legislature is established under or governed by an instrument which prescribes that laws of a certain kind may only be passed if the legislature is constituted or exercises its functions in a particular manner". He linked the *Harris* and *Ranasinghe* cases with *McCawley v The King* [1920] AC 691 and *McDonald v Cain* [1953] VLR 411, as deciding "that when the law requires a legislature to enact legislation in a particular manner, the courts may investigate whether the legislature has exercised its powers in the manner required". He stressed that the principle has nothing to do with "**[164]** whether or not a legislature is sovereign" or "forms part of a unitary or a federal system"; the only relevant distinction "is between legislatures which are, and those which are not, governed by an instrument which imposes conditions on the power to make laws". He appeared to suggest that, independently of the "manner and form" analysis derived from s 5 of the *Colonial Laws Validity Act* (and nowadays from s 6 of the *Australia Act*), the *Ranasinghe* principle might apply in Australia as a basis for judicial review.

This reasoning might enable the judicial enforcement of manner and form procedures enacted by the Commonwealth Parliament, which is not subject to s 6 of the *Australia Act*. For example, the *A New Tax System (Commonwealth-State Financial Arrangements) Act 1999* (Cth) provides in s 11(1) that "[t]he rate of the GST, and the GST base, are not to be changed unless each State agrees to the change", while the *Flags Act 1953* (Cth) establishes in s 3(2) that the Australian National Flag can be changed "if, and only if" the change is approved by a majority of Australians voting at a referendum. However, since these provisions are not themselves entrenched, they are legally ineffective: a future Parliament could amend or repeal them before changing the GST rate or adopting a new flag. Of course, the provisions may make it more difficult, as a matter of politics, to bring about change by ordinary legislation.

The absence of any attempt at double entrenchment may be due to uncertainty over whether it is possible to bind the Commonwealth Parliament with a manner and form provision. George Winterton (in "Can the Commonwealth Parliament Enact 'Manner and Form' Legislation?" (1980) 11 *Federal Law Review* 167) has argued that the federal Parliament can be bound by some such procedures, but that certain requirements could not be imposed. For example, an Act could not be entrenched by requiring for its amendment a special majority – say two thirds of either House of the Parliament – since ss 23 and 40 of the Constitution provide that questions arising in the Senate and the House of Representatives respectively are to be resolved by a simple majority. It would also not be possible to "**[192]** substitute a new legislature for the present Parliament, either by adding an additional element to the present legislative process (such as the consent of the electors or another body) or by creating a completely new body for the enactment of certain laws".

In 2003, the High Court rejected the possibility, at least as to State legislation, that enforcement of manner and form provisions might be possible on any basis other than s 6 of the *Australia Act 1986* (Cth). Kirby J, who was otherwise in dissent, endorsed this rejection.

Attorney-General (WA) v Marquet
(2003) 217 CLR 545

Gleeson CJ, Gummow, Hayne and Heydon JJ: [574] [T]he express provisions of s 6 [of the *Australia Act* 1986 (Cth)] can leave no room for the operation of some other principle, at the very least in the field in which s 6 operates, if such a principle can be derived from considerations of the kind which informed the Privy Council's decision in *Bribery Commissioner v Ranasinghe* [[1965] AC 172] and can then be applied in a federation.

Kirby J: [616] No common law principle of such a kind could stand against the clear grant of law-making power to a representative legislature of Australia, as provided in, and under, the Imperial legislation establishing that legislature and as confirmed in the colonial and State Acts that make up the State Constitutions as well as by the federal **[617]** Constitution itself. Unless the principle in *Ranasinghe* involves no more than an over-broad paraphrase of the provisions of s 5 of the [*Colonial Laws Validity Act*], it cannot, on its own, afford a higher source of law to impose a restraint upon the law-making power of the legislatures concerned. Where there is no higher source that underpins an inhibition on the law-making power of State Parliaments, the simple answer to the Privy Council's proposition in *Ranasinghe* is that the legislature enjoys full power to repeal the purported conditions or limitations on its law-making. Once it does so, it is not bound by those conditions or limitations. It is free to ignore them. They do not then control its "power to make laws".

Yet when Dixon J in *Trethowan's Case* contrasted the situation under a written constitution with that arising in England, and proceeded to formulate a justiciable question that might arise even under the English doctrine of "parliamentary sovereignty", he was not suggesting that such a question could arise *only* under that doctrine. His point, like that of Lord Pearce in *Ranasinghe*, was simply that the validity of a law-making procedure must itself depend on compliance with law. At a time when governments in many countries seem increasingly indifferent to legal constraints, it is a point rather to be reaffirmed than carelessly to be tossed aside.

6. Further References

Allan, TRS, "The Common Law as Constitution: Fundamental Rights and First Principles" in Saunders, C (ed), *Courts of Final Jurisdiction: The Mason Court in Australia* (Federation Press, 1996), 146.

Allan, TRS, "Legislative Supremacy and the Rule of Law: Democracy and Constitutionalism" (1985) 44 *Cambridge Law Journal* 111.

Allan, TRS, "The Limits of Parliamentary Sovereignty" [1985] *Public Law* 614.

Carney, G, "The Implied Freedom of Political Discussion – Its Impact on State Constitutions" (1995) 23 *Federal Law Review* 180.

Carney, G, "An Overview of Manner and Form in Australia" (1989) 5 *Queensland University of Technology Law Journal* 69.

Evans, J, "Mandatory and Directory Rules" (1981) 1 *Legal Studies* 227.

French, RS, "Manner and Form in Western Australia: An Historical Note" (1993) 23 *University of Western Australia Law Review* 335.

Goldsworthy, J, "Manner and Form in the Australian States" (1987) 16 *Melbourne University Law Review* 403.

Goldsworthy, J, "Manner and Form Revisited: Reflections on Marquet's Case" in Groves, M (ed), *Law and Government in Australia* (Federation Press, 2005), 18.

Goldsworthy, J, "The 'Principle in *Ranasinghe*': A Reply to HP Lee" (1992) 15 *University of New South Wales Law Journal* 540.

Johnston, P, "Method or Madness: Constitutional Perturbations and *Marquet's* Case" (2004) 7 *Constitutional Law and Policy Review* 25.

Killey, ID, "'Peace, Order and Good Government': A Limitation on Legislative Competence" (1989) 17 *Melbourne University Law Review* 24.

Lee, HP, "The Australia Act 1986: Some Legal Conundrums" (1988) 14 *Monash University Law Review* 298.

Lee, HP, "Manner and Form: An Imbroglio in Victoria" (1992) 15 *University of New South Wales Law Journal* 516.

Lumb, RD, *The Constitutions of the Australian States* (University of Queensland Press, 5th ed 1991).

Macintyre, C, and Williams, J (eds), *Peace, Order and Good Government: State Constitutional and Parliamentary Reform* (Wakefield Press and Australian Association of Constitutional Law, 2003).

O'Neill, N, "Blue-eyed Babies May be Murdered: Dicey's First Principle Upheld in the Court of Appeal" (1987) 12 *Legal Service Bulletin* 2.

Seddon, N, *Government Contracts: Federal, State and Local* (Federation Press, 3rd ed 2004).

Selway, B, *The Constitution of South Australia* (Federation Press, 1997).

Twomey, A, *The Constitution of New South Wales* (Federation Press, 2004).

Williams, G, "Entrenching the GST Rate" (1999) 1 *Constitutional Law and Policy Review* 61.

Winterton, G, "Constitutionally Entrenched Common Law Rights: Sacrificing Means to Ends?" in Sampford, C, and Preston, K (eds), *Interpreting Constitutions: Theories, Principles and Institutions* (Federation Press, 1996), 121.

Chapter 12

The Executive

1. The Executive

The federal executive includes the King or Queen, the Governor General, ministers (including the Prime Minister and Cabinet) and public servants employed by government departments. In this form, the executive is an adaptation of the Westminster system of government as it had evolved over centuries of constitutional development. At one time the monarchs of England ruled through autocratic means, making laws and dispensing justice through the courts in the exercise of the royal prerogative. Over time, they lost much of their personal power, especially in regard to legislation, which became the domain of Parliament. After the revolution of 1688, Parliament emerged as the dominant institution of government, with the power to make or unmake any law. The King or Queen remained formally responsible for the law's administration through public servants employed by and accountable to the Crown, but by constitutional convention it came to be recognised that, even in their higher executive functions, monarchs must act on the advice of their ministers, who must be members of Parliament and ultimately responsible to it.

Thus, when executive power is said to be exercised in the name of "the Crown", the ceremonial jewelled headpiece is used in a metonymous figure of speech as a depersonalised symbol of the monarch, who in turn is treated as a personalised symbol of what in other constitutional systems is usually referred to as "the State".

Town Investments Ltd v Department of the Environment
[1978] AC 359

Lord Simon of Glaisdale: [397] The crown as an object is a piece of jewelled headgear under guard at the Tower of London. But it symbolises the powers of government which were formerly wielded by the wearer of the crown; so that by the 13th century crimes were committed not only against the king's peace but also against "his crown and dignity": *Pollock and Maitland, History of English Law*, 2nd ed (1898), vol I, p 525. The term "the Crown" is therefore used in constitutional law to denote the collection of such of those powers as remain extant (the royal prerogative), together with such other powers as have been expressly conferred by statute on "the Crown".

So too "The Queen" indicates the person who by right of succession is entitled to wear the crown. But "Her Majesty" is evidently a symbolic phrase, betokening the power, the "mana", which is embodied in the person entitled to wear the crown ... "Her Majesty" in constitutional legal usage thus generally personifies the powers of "the Crown" – powers the nucleus of which legally and historically are those of The Queen, but which by constitutional convention (ie, in political reality) are exercised in the name **[398]** of The Queen by those who are nominally and legally her servants or agents.

Law Reform Commission of Canada,
The Legal Status of the Federal Administration
(Working Paper No 40, 1985)

[6] The survival of the Crown dates from a period in which all governmental functions flowed, in a more or less confused way, from the person of the Monarch. On the other hand, many institutions have evolved decisively towards a regime of separation of powers ... [The judiciary] is a truly separate and independent appendage of the State, although the appointment of judges and the administrative organization of the judiciary are the responsibility of the Executive ... Nevertheless, the courts are still [for Blackstone] "the King's Courts," mere extensions of royal justice ...

Historically, royal authority resulted in an integrated State. Legislative, judicial and executive functions proceeded directly from the individual person on the throne. Even today, the Queen sits in her Parliament, the courts are the Queen's courts, the Administration is a service of Her Majesty, the Monarch is the Head of State; she is defender of the Kingdom as Commander-in-Chief of the Armed Forces, and Defender of the Faith ... Many spiritual and temporal functions accordingly reside in an **[7]** institution which is absolute in every sense ...

Although British public law has undoubtedly evolved towards a system of separation of powers, this original integration of powers nonetheless inhibits modernization of this **[8]** area of the law. It presents two difficulties which are far from negligible.

On an essentially theoretical level, first, it must be observed that no activity of the State is really independent of the Crown ... [A]ll matters are transacted as if the Monarch were omni-present, the real embodiment of the State in all its parts. This fact is clearly reflected in current terminology, since we readily speak of Crown lands, a Crown prosecutor, a Minister of the Crown, the Speech from the Throne, Royal Assent, the Royal Mail, or simply the Crown, when we mean the Government. Not only does this constant reference to the Monarchy present problems in distinguishing all these entities from each other, but an effort is also necessary to overcome a close relational dependence with the Crown, which is reflected in filiations, privileges, immunities and exceptional powers ... Nevertheless, parliamentary and judicial functions have been clearly emancipated from Crown control (*Magna Carta, 1215*; *Case of Proclamations, 1611*; *Bill of Rights, 1689*; *Act of Settlement, 1701*). As such, they are not directly associated with the Crown, although they may be managed by it through the tabling of bills and the appointment of judges. In the case of the Government and the Administration, this differentiation has never been made, with the result that it is very difficult to conceive of executive action as an independent concept.

The second problem, directly connected to the first, results from the very impossibility of making a clear distinction between Crown and Government, Government and Administration, and Crown and Administration. In law, it is as if this trilogy were a single unit. In the first place, this is the result of history. By a series of transformations, the executive functions of the *Curia Regis* [the King's court] were transferred to the [King's] Council, then to the Privy Council, and finally ... to the Cabinet ... Under the leadership of Sir Robert Walpole, this Cabinet in fact became "the King's principal and trusted adviser." In this way by historical tradition and legal fiction, the Government and the Cabinet are associated directly with the Crown, and the latter personifies the Executive and the Administration ... **[9]** For de Smith, the civil service is defined with reference to the officers who make it up:

> [A] civil servant is a Crown servant appointed directly or indirectly by the Crown, and paid wholly out of funds provided by Parliament and employed in a Department of government.

These Departments or Offices usually have at their head a Minister of the Crown who is responsible to Parliament. The circle is thus complete. Civil servants, services, departments, Ministers and the Government are all merged in the Crown and benefit in various ways from some or all of its privileges.

The symbolism of the Crown is reflected in the Australian Constitution, which opens with the preamble "WHEREAS the people ... have agreed to unite in one indissoluble Federal Commonwealth under the Crown". Power is also conferred in a way that recognises the historic role of the monarch. Legislative power, for example, is granted by s 1 to the "Federal Parliament, which shall consist of the Queen, a Senate, and a House of Representatives" – though in practice, once a Bill has completed its passage through Parliament, the giving of the Royal Assent is nowadays a mere formality. It is not surprising then that governments are still referred to as "the Crown", though this would change if Australia became a republic (see Chapter 30, §3).

Since Federation, much of the power which at that time was still ascribed to the Queen has atrophied by unwritten convention (see, for example, s 59 of the Constitution). At the same time, the title of the monarch has changed. By the *Royal Titles Act 1953* (Imp), the Queen can take any title she thinks fit in territories outside the United Kingdom. In Australia, the *Royal Style and Titles Act 1973* (Cth) has approved her adoption of the title "Elizabeth the Second, by the Grace of God Queen of Australia and Her other Realms and Territories, Head of the Commonwealth".

2. Sources and Scope of Executive Power

Section 61 of the Constitution vests the executive power of the Commonwealth in the Queen; states that it is exercisable by the Governor-General as her representative; and provides that the power "extends to the execution and maintenance of this Constitution, and of the laws of the Commonwealth". The section is otherwise silent on the scope of the power (as compared, say, to the conferral of legislative power by s 51). The exercise of executive power has rarely been challenged on constitutional grounds in the High Court, leading Mason CJ, Deane and Gaudron JJ to state in *Davis v Commonwealth* (1988) 166 CLR 79 that the power "**[92]** has often been discussed but never defined". What is clear is that the executive may exercise the prerogative powers of the Crown (that is, the powers accorded to the Crown by the common law); the powers derived from Australia's status as a sovereign nation; and the powers conferred on the executive by statute.

(a)   Prerogative Power

The prerogative powers of the Crown in right of the Australian Commonwealth are nowadays regarded as incorporated in s 61. However, they may exist independently of and antecedently to it. For one thing, the Constitution is conceived of as coming into force "under the Crown", that is, as presupposing the antecedent existence of the Crown and its powers. For another thing, although the prerogatives were once thought to be "inherent" or "organic", they are probably now best understood as having their foundation in the special powers and privileges ascribed to the Crown by the common law.

Of course, some attributes of the Crown at common law arise simply from the fact that it is recognised as a legal person: for example, the executive can own property, enter into contracts and form companies (see *New South Wales v Bardolph* (1934) 52 CLR 455). Similarly, while the power to conduct a public inquiry by Royal Commission is usually understood as having its source in the royal prerogative (see, for example, Dixon J in *McGuinness v Attorney-General (Vic)* (1940) 63 CLR 73 at 93), Griffith CJ suggested in *Clough v Leahy* (1904) 2 CLR 139 that "**[156]** the power of inquiry" is not a prerogative right at all, but is simply an example of the power "of asking questions ... which every individual citizen possesses" (see also McHugh J in *North Ganalanja Aboriginal Corporation v Queensland* (1996) 185 CLR 595 at 634-5). However, to the extent that the Crown shares the capabilities of other legal persons, those capabilities cannot be regarded as having the quality of exclusive privilege that the idea of "prerogative" implies.

Adam Tomkins, *Public Law*
(Oxford University Press, 2003)

[81] In his *Commentaries* in the eighteenth century Blackstone offered a relatively narrow definition of prerogative power, when he wrote that the prerogative is 'in its nature singular and eccentrical [in] that it can only be applied to those rights and capacities which the king enjoys alone … and not to those which he enjoys in common with any of his subjects'. The important point of Blackstone's definition is that prerogative powers are unique to the Crown. For Blackstone, the prerogative is not a *carte blanche*, coming to the government's rescue whenever statutory authority runs out. Rather, the prerogative is a closed list of identifiable and discrete powers covering areas of government which are its especial province. Thus, individuals may not issue passports or ratify treaties (and neither for that matter may local authorities): these are tasks uniquely for the State, and are in English public law tasks that are the unique responsibility of the Crown and its Ministers, both being governed by the prerogative.

[82] Dicey, however, granted to the prerogative a far broader meaning. He wrote that the prerogative consists of the 'residue of discretionary or arbitrary authority which at any given time is legally left in the hands of the Crown'. It is this more expansive definition that has found judicial favour, Dicey's view having been expressly approved and followed in the leading House of Lords decision *Attorney-General v De Keyser's Royal Hotel* [[1920] AC 508]. Dicey's view of the prerogative is not only more expansive than Blackstone's: it is also considerably vaguer.

Dicey's view was echoed by Sir Frederick Pollock. In an editorial note in (1918) 34 *Law Quarterly Review* at 159, he wrote: "Prerogative is nothing more mysterious than the residue of the King's undefined powers after striking out those which have been taken away by legislation or fallen into desuetude". The trouble with attempts to reduce it to what Tomkins calls "**[81]** a closed list of identifiable and discrete powers" is that such lists have always been suspect. In mediaeval times it was thought that such a list could be found in the document known as *De Praerogativa Regis*, traditionally supposed to be a statute dating from the regnal year 17 Edward II (1323-24), and still included in compilations of English statutes as late as the 1880s as a statute "of uncertain date". In fact it had never been enacted as a statute (see H Fisher (ed), *The Collected Papers of Frederick William Maitland* (Cambridge University Press, 1911), 182-9). In *R v Prior of Lantonie* (1369) YB Trin 43 Edw III, fol 21, pl 12, its statutory authority was still unquestioned; but in *The Bishop of Ely's Case* (1475) YB Mich 15 Edw IV, fol 11, pl 17, a bench including Sir Thomas Littleton ruled that it was not a statute at all, but only "an affirmance of the common law", intended to clarify points that were doubtful. Littleton relied particularly on the fact that it was undated, but also on the fact that he recalled having seen Markham LCJ decide a case in a way that flatly disregarded its provisions (see also *In re Fawsley* (1382) Mich 6 Rich II in Chapter 3, §2(c)). In any event *De Praerogativa Regis* was a curious document, primarily concerned with the rights of the King in relation to the lands, the heirs, the wives and the widows of his tenants-in-chief under the feudal system. Perhaps the only provision of lasting significance was that "the King shall have Wreck of the Sea throughout the Realm, Whales and great Sturgeons taken in the Sea or elsewhere within the Realm, except in certain Places privileged by the King".

A more comprehensive compilation of common law pronouncements about the prerogative was undertaken by Sir John Comyns in 1736.

Sir John Comyns, *A Digest of the Laws of England*
(4th ed by Samuel Rose, A Strahan, 1800) vol 6, *sub voce* "Praerogative"

[28] (A) The King's Prerogative.
The king's prerogative comprehends all the liberties, privileges, powers and royalties allowed by the law to the crown of *England. Co L 90 b. St Praer 5. Vide Roy,* (A 1, 2).

For the king has not any prerogative, but such as the law allows. 12 *Co* 76. 2 *Inst* 496.63 …

[29] (B) Prerogative as to Foreign Nations ...

All the king's prerogatives relate to foreign states, or to his own subjects. The king and his progenitors have at all times been lords of the sea. 2 *Rol* 168 *l* 45. *Vide Navigation.*

And therefore the dominion of the whole sea which surrounds *England* belongs to the king ...

The king has authority to send ambassadors, envoys, &c to foreign states. *Vide Ambassador* (A) ...

To make leagues and alliances [with foreign states] belongs to the king only. 7 *Co* 25 *b* ...

All leagues ought to be upon record inrolled in *Chancery*, whereby every one may know who are in amity or enmity with the king, and who not. 4 *Inst* 152. 9 *Co* 31 *a* ...

[32] (C) Prerogatives in respect of the King's own Subjects; in Time of War ...

The king's prerogative in respect of his subjects, relates to war or the time of peace; for the king has the sole authority to declare war, or peace. 7 *Co* 25 *b*. *Vide ante*, (B 3) C *Parliament*, (H 24) ...

By the *st* 11 *H* 7.1 & 18 it is said, that every subject, by the duty of his allegiance, is bound to serve and assist his prince in his wars, &c.

But a man is not bound to serve the king out of the realm, except for wages. 1 *Roll* 166 *l* 10 *ad* 30.

Nor can he be sent by the king out of the realm to serve there. 2 *Inst* 47.

Though he be sent only to *Ireland. Ibid* ...

[33] The government and command of the *militia*, and all the forces by sea or by land, and of all forts belong only to the king.

And by the *st* 13 *Car* 2.6 it was declared, that the whole supreme government, command, and disposition of them, by the laws of *England*, ever was the undoubted right of the kings and queens of *England*; and that both or either of the houses of parliament ought not to pretend to the same ...

[34] (D) Prerogatives, which regard Time of Peace.

(D 1) Enacting of Laws

The king's prerogatives, which concern times of peace, relate, 1. To the enacting of laws. 2. Jurisdiction. 3. The nomination of officers. 4. Trade. 5. The revenue.

And therefore, no statute can be enacted without the royal assent. *Vide Parliament* ...

But the king ... cannot by his grant alter the law in any respect; as, he cannot give power to any to oust another of his land. 2 *Rol* 164 *l* ult.

(D 2) *Proclamations. When he may issue them.*] So, the king by his proclamation may enforce the execution of laws.

And therefore if the king by proclamation prohibits that which was before unlawful, the offence afterwards will be thereby aggravated. 12 *Co* 75.

So, the king by his proclamation may admonish his subjects, that they do not offend, under the penalty of the law. 12 *Co* 76 ...

By the *st* 31 *H* 8.8 the king, with the assent of the greater part of the privy council, might issue a proclamation, which should be obeyed as an act of parliament, and the offender to pay such forfeitures, and suffer such imprisonment as mentioned in the proclamation. But this is now repealed by the *st* 1 *Ed* 6.12.

(D 3) *When not.*] But the king cannot, by his proclamation, make a thing unlawful, which was before lawful; for the king cannot create an offence, by proclamation. 12 *Co* 75.

And therefore nothing will be punishable after a proclamation, which was not so before. *Ibid.*

So, he cannot by proclamation alter any part of the common law, statutes, or customs of the realm. *Ibid.*

And therefore a proclamation for the suspension of the execution of a statute, till the next parliament, is illegal and void. *Ibid* ...

[35] (D 4) *Dispensation. The nature and effect of it.*] A dispensation makes an act, otherwise prohibited, lawful to him to whom the dispensation is granted; for *dat jus. Vau* 333.

And this prerogative belongs to the king by the common law, in a case of necessity. *Hard* 446.448.

But dispensations are odious in law. 2 *Rol* (179) *l* 25 ...

(D 6) *In what cases the king may make a dispensation.*] If an act of parliament regards only the king's benefit, he, by his prerogative, may grant a dispensation of the statute. 2 *Rol* 179 *l* 47.

In which case the king, in respect of place, time or person, dispenses with a particular person, that he shall not incur the penalty of the statute. 7 *Co* 36 *b*.

As, if a statute prohibits a thing only *sub modo*, or under penalty. *Semb Hard* 110 ...

(D 7) *In what not.*] But the king cannot dispense with a thing, being *malum in se*. *Hard* 448 ...

[36] And therefore he cannot change or dispense with the common law, by his charter; as, if he grants that an alien shall inherit, it will be void. 2 *Rol* 115 ...

So, the king cannot dispense with *magna charta*, which is incorporated into the common law. *Ibid* ...

So, the king cannot dispense with an act of parliament, by which the subject has benefit. 2 *Rol* (179) *l* 50 ...

(D 8) *Pardon.*] So, the king may pardon all offences, of which a man is attainted, or convicted. *Vide Pardon* (A) ...

But the king cannot reverse a judgment against a criminal without legal process. 2 *Rol* 164 ...

[46] (D 28) *Erection of courts.*] The king, by his prerogative, may make what courts for the administration of the common law, and in what places, he pleases. *Vide Courts* (A).

But the king cannot erect a court of *Chancery*, or conscience; for the common law is the inheritance of the subject. 2 *Rol* 164 *l* 30 ...

[47] So, the erection of a new court, with a new jurisdiction, cannot be without an act of parliament. 4 *Inst* 200.

And if it be erected, the jurisdiction ought to be expressed; for nothing omitted shall be within such jurisdiction. *Ibid.*

So, the king cannot grant to a court, that it may proceed according to the civil law. 2 *Rush App* 77.

Nor can, by charter or commission, &c alter the common law. *Ibid* ...

(D 29) *Grant of commissions.*] The king may grant such commissions as are warranted, or allowed, by the common law, or by act of parliament. 4 *Inst* 163. 2 *Inst* 51. *Vide Justices*, (C 2) – (G 1, &c) ...

But the king cannot grant a commission not usual, nor allowed by act of parliament. 4 *Inst* 163 ...

So, the king cannot grant a commission for inquiry only, without power to hear and determine. *R* 12 *Co* 31. *Semb* 2 *Rol* 164 *l* 7.

In any event, as Evatt J noted in *Federal Commissioner of Taxation v Official Liquidator of EO Farley Ltd* (1940) 63 CLR 278, "**[320]** the royal prerogatives are so disparate in character and subject matter that it is difficult to assign them to fixed categories or subjects". Instead, he drew on his 1924 doctoral thesis (*The Royal Prerogative* (Law Book Co, 1987), 50) to propose a classification of prerogative powers into three main categories.

Republic Advisory Committee, *An Australian Republic: The Options*

(AGPS, The Report of the Republic Advisory Committee, 1993), vol 1

[145] One of the leading writers on the royal prerogative was Dr, later Justice, HV Evatt, who divided the prerogatives of the Crown into three categories as follows:

(i) 'executive prerogatives', under which the monarch had power to do various acts, eg execute treaties, declare war, make peace, coin money, incorporate bodies by royal charter, pardon offenders and confer honours;

(ii) 'immunities and preferences', such as the priority of Crown debts over those owed to other creditors, immunity from the ordinary process of the courts and freedom from distress for rent; and

(iii) 'property rights' such as the entitlement to royal metals, royal fish, treasure trove, and the ownership of the foreshore, the sea bed and its subsoil.

Commentators have disagreed as to whether the term 'prerogative' can be employed to refer to all of the non-statutory or common law powers of the Crown, or whether it should be confined to those powers which are unique to the Crown. It is clear, however, that, like other common law rights, the prerogatives are subject to legislation ...

All of the prerogatives of the Crown, except for those inapplicable to Australian conditions such as the ecclesiastical prerogatives, have been inherited by the Commonwealth or the States or both. The proprietary prerogatives passed to the Australian colonies and, except in so far as the Constitution transferred them to the Commonwealth, they remain with the States. Thus, in Australian law as in England, the Crown has 'original' or 'radical' title to all land; people hold land, theoretically, as tenants of the Crown, and (unless the land is in a Territory) that Crown is the Crown in right of the State. The preferences and immunities have been regarded as inherent in the concept of the Crown, so that each of the Australian polities inherited them at its inception; and the executive prerogatives have been divided between the Commonwealth and the States according to the division of legislative powers between them.

The executive prerogatives are incorporated in the 'executive power of the Commonwealth' which, by section 61 of the Constitution, is vested in the Queen **[146]** and exercisable on her behalf by the Governor-General (and which, by convention, is always exercised either on ministerial advice or by ministers and other officials authorised by the Governor-General to exercise particular powers). In the light of the Constitution's background in British constitutional history and the common law, section 61 has been treated as a shorthand prescription for incorporating the prerogative in the Crown in right of the Commonwealth; so that the full range of executive prerogatives relevant to Commonwealth legislative power is vested in the executive government of the Commonwealth, and the executive power of the Commonwealth, like the (common law) prerogatives, is subject to control by legislation.

The Crown in right of each State has also inherited those of the executive prerogatives which are relevant to the State's role in the federal system: the Crown in right of a State cannot, for example, make treaties or declare war, but it can pardon offenders and institute inquiries.

Because the prerogative powers depend on the common law, they are subject to modification by statute. This may happen in either of two ways. A statutory regime may *regulate* the exercise of a prerogative power, stripping it (for example) of discretionary elements and imposing criteria and procedures by which the exercise of the power is to be controlled, while still leaving the conceptual source of the power in the prerogative. Alternatively, a statutory regime may wholly supplant or *extinguish* the prerogative, so that what was formerly an inherent power of government now depends wholly on statute. The difference between regulation and extinguishment is often obscure: the history of appeals to the Privy Council, in Australia and elsewhere, is rich in examples. It was clear that the *Judicial Committee Acts 1833* and *1844* (Imp) had "regulated" the Queen's prerogative of granting special leave to appeal, and had done so without supplanting its essential prerogative nature; but other statutory provisions around the globe were held sometimes to "regulate" the prerogative, and sometimes to "extinguish" it (see *Attorney-General (Cth) v T & G Mutual Life Society Ltd* (1978) 144 CLR 161 at 176-80).

In *Attorney-General v De Keyser's Royal Hotel* [1920] AC 508, the United Kingdom government had requisitioned a hotel during World War I for use as the headquarters of the Royal Flying Corps. The requisition was made pursuant to regulations under the *Defence of the Realm Consolidation Act 1914* (UK), which provided for compensation; but when the hotel owners claimed compensation, the government asserted that it had acted in the exercise of a prerogative power to take property without compensation. As is often the case with prerogative claims, it was unclear whether such a prerogative had historically existed. In any event, the House of Lords held that the legislative scheme governed the matter, so that compensation was payable. However, as to the relation between the legislative power and the prerogative power, no two Law Lords took quite the same view.

Attorney-General v De Keyser's Royal Hotel Ltd
[1920] AC 508

Sir John Simon KC (in argument): [518] The prerogative … is the ultimate resource of the executive, and when there exists a statutory provision covering precisely the same ground there is no longer any room for the exercise of the Royal Prerogative. It has been taken away by necessary implication because the two rights cannot live together … **[519]** The prerogative is merged in the higher title derived by the Act of Parliament.

Lord Dunedin: [526] Now the view which I think prevailed in *In re A Petition of Right* [[1915] 3 KB 649] was that … the two systems could well stand side by side; and then, as there was no direct mention of the prerogative in the statutes, you were assisted by the general doctrine that the Crown is not bound by a statute unless specially mentioned … None the less, it is equally certain that if the whole ground of something which could be done by the prerogative is covered by the statute, it is the statute that rules. On this point I think the observation of the learned Master of the Rolls is unanswerable. He says [*In re De Keyser's Royal Hotel, Ld* [1919] 2 Ch 197 at 216]: "What use would there be in imposing limitations, if the Crown could at its pleasure disregard them and fall back on the prerogative?"

The prerogative is defined by a learned constitutional writer as "The residue of discretionary or arbitrary authority which at any given time is legally left in the hands of the Crown." Inasmuch as the Crown is a party to every Act of Parliament it is logical enough to consider that when the Act deals with something which before the Act could be effected by the prerogative, and specially empowers the Crown to do the same thing, but subject to conditions, the Crown assents to that, and by that Act, to the prerogative being curtailed.

Lord Atkinson: [539] It is quite obvious that it would be useless and meaningless for the Legislature to impose restrictions and limitations upon, and to attach conditions to, the exercise by the Crown of the powers conferred by a statute, if the Crown were free at its pleasure to disregard these provisions, and by virtue of its prerogative do the very thing the statutes empowered it to do. One cannot in the construction of a statute attribute to the Legislature (in the absence of compelling words) an intention so absurd. It was suggested that when a statute is passed empowering the Crown to do a certain thing which it might theretofore have done by virtue of its prerogative, the prerogative is merged in the statute. I confess I do not think the word "merged" is happily chosen. I should prefer to say that when such a statute, expressing the will and intention of the King and of the three estates of the realm, is passed, it abridges the Royal Prerogative while it is in force to this extent: that the Crown can only do the particular thing under and in accordance with the statutory provisions, **[540]** and that its prerogative power to do that thing is in abeyance. Whichever mode of expression be used, the result intended to be indicated is, I think, the same – namely, that after the statute has been passed, and while it is in force, the thing it empowers the Crown to do can thenceforth only be done by and under the statute, and subject to all the limitations, restrictions and conditions by it imposed, however unrestricted the Royal Prerogative may theretofore have been.

Lord Moulton: [554] What effect has this course of legislation upon the Royal Prerogative? I do not think that it can be said to have abrogated that prerogative in any way, but it has given to the Crown statutory powers which render the exercise of that prerogative unnecessary, because the statutory powers that have been conferred upon it are wider and more comprehensive than those of the prerogative itself. But it has done more than this. It has indicated unmistakably that it is the intention of the nation that the powers of the Crown in these respects should be exercised in the equitable manner set forth in the statute.

Lord Sumner: [561] I do not think that the precise extent of the prerogative need now be dealt with. The Legislature, by appropriate enactment, can deal with such a subject-matter as that now in question in such a way as to abate such portions of the prerogative as apply to it. It seems also to be obvious that enactments may have this effect, provided they directly deal with the subject-matter, even though they enact a modus operandi for securing the desired result, which is not the same as that of the prerogative. If a statute merely recorded existing inherent powers, nothing would be gained by the enactment, for nothing would be added to the existing law. There is no object in dealing by statute with the same subject-matter as is already dealt with by the prerogative, unless it be either to limit or at least to vary its exercise, or to provide an additional mode of attaining the same object. Even the restrictions (such as they were) imposed by the Defence Acts on any powers of requisitioning buildings in time of war were in no way inconsistent with an intention to abate the prerogative in this respect, if not absolutely, ... at least for so long as the statute operates. In truth, the introduction of Regulations so reasonable only strengthens the substance of the Royal authority by removing all semblance of arbitrary power ...

[562] My Lords, for these reasons I think that the Executive did not take possession under the prerogative, for the Defence Acts had superseded it.

Lord Parmoor: [568] The growth of constitutional liberties has largely consisted in the reduction of the discretionary power of the executive, and in the extension of Parliamentary protection in favour of the subject, under a series of statutory enactments. The result is that, whereas at one time the Royal Prerogative gave legal sanction to a large majority of the executive functions of the Government, it is now restricted within comparatively narrow limits. The Royal Prerogative has of necessity been curtailed, as a settled rule of law has taken the place of an uncertain and arbitrary administrative discretion ...

[575] The constitutional principle is that when the power of the Executive to interfere with the property or liberty of subjects has been placed under Parliamentary control, and directly regulated by statute, the Executive no longer derives its authority from the Royal Prerogative of the Crown but from Parliament, and that in exercising such authority the Executive is bound to observe the restrictions which Parliament has imposed in favour of the subject ... It would be an untenable proposition to suggest that Courts **[576]** of law could disregard the protective restrictions imposed by statute law where they are applicable. In this respect the sovereignty of Parliament is supreme.

The scope of the prerogative power in Australia, and the extent to which it has been displaced by statute, were central to the *Tampa* controversy in 2001. On 26 August 2001, 433 people, mainly Afghan, were rescued at sea in international waters from a sinking wooden fishing boat and were taken aboard the Norwegian commercial vessel the *MV Tampa*. Three days later the master of the *Tampa*, believing that some of the rescued people needed urgent medical treatment, asked for assistance from Australia. When this was not forthcoming, he took the *Tampa* into Australian territorial waters about four nautical miles off Christmas Island. The Howard government decided that the asylum seekers would not be permitted to land and 45 SAS troops boarded the ship. Proceedings were then initiated by the Victorian Council for Civil Liberties and by Eric Vadarlis, a Victorian solicitor, for a writ of habeas corpus (that is, an order for the release of the asylum seekers).

After a hastily convened hearing, North J of the Federal Court held on 11 September 2001 that the "rescuees" (as he called them) had been detained without lawful authority (*Victorian Council for Civil Liberties Inc v Minister for Immigration and Multicultural Affairs* (2001) 182 ALR 617). He ordered that they be released onto the mainland of Australia – after which they would again have been detained, but this time with the opportunity to make a visa application under the *Migration Act 1958* (Cth). The first step in his reasoning involved a finding that the handling of the rescuees aboard the *Tampa* had amounted to detention, since the government had shown itself "**[639]** committed to retaining control of the fate of the rescuees in all respects". North J held that a proposal to allow the rescuees to land at Nauru did not alter that finding: "Where complete control over people and their destiny is exercised by others it cannot be said that the opportunity offered by those others is a reasonable escape from the custody in which they are held". The second step in the reasoning involved a rejection of the government's argument that the expulsion of non-residents from Australian waters "**[644]** is a valid exercise of prerogative power". To this North J made two answers. The first was that it was doubtful whether the supposed prerogative had ever existed; the second was that, whatever the scope of the prerogative in this respect, it had now been wholly supplanted by the statutory scheme of the *Migration Act*. In *Robtelmes v Brenan* (1906) 4 CLR 395, Barton J, after noting the doubt as to whether such a prerogative existed, had concluded that in any event: "**[415]** The question today is one of statutory authority". And in *Mayer v Minister for Immigration and Ethnic Affairs* (1984) 55 ALR 587, Davies J had said: "**[591]** But whatever was, at one time, the common law prerogative power of the Crown in this matter, and that clearly was an arguable matter, at the present time the law with respect to the entry of persons to Australia and with respect to their expulsion is regulated by statute".

In the Full Court of the Federal Court on 18 September 2001, the decision of North J was reversed by 2:1, with Black CJ dissenting. French J, with whom Beaumont J agreed, held that the rescuees had not in fact been detained, and that the executive power of the Commonwealth extended to the expulsion of the rescuees and to their detention for that purpose.

Ruddock v Vadarlis (*Tampa Case*)
(2001) 183 ALR 1

French J: [48] The executive power can be abrogated, modified or regulated by laws of the Commonwealth. Its common law ancestor, the royal prerogative, was similarly subject to abrogation, modification or regulation by statute ...

The conceptual bases upon which it is said that statute law may abrogate or regulate the prerogative were variously proposed in *Attorney-General v De Keyser's Royal Hotel Ltd* [[1920] AC 508]. Implied **[49]** assent by the Crown, the futility of concurrent powers, one regulated and the other not, a presumption that the Crown resorts to statute rather than its unqualified power and simple parliamentary sovereignty encapsulate the approaches taken by the Law Lords in that case. In the end, however, there was nothing in their approaches which permitted avoidance of the need to construe the relevant statute to determine whether, by express words or necessary implication, it has any, and if so what, operation upon the prerogative power ...

The executive power of the Commonwealth under s 61 cannot be treated as a species of the royal prerogative, "The residue of discretionary or arbitrary authority which at any given time is legally left in the hands of the Crown": *De Keyser* [[1920] AC at 526]. While the executive power may derive some of its content by reference to the royal prerogative, it is a power conferred as part of a negotiated federal compact expressed in a written Constitution distributing powers between the three arms of government reflected in Chapters I, II and III of the Constitution and, as to legislative powers, between the polities that comprise the federation. The power is subject, not only to the limitations as to subject matter that flow directly from the Constitution but also to the laws of the Commonwealth made under it. There is no place then for any doctrine that a law made on a particular subject matter is presumed to displace or regulate the operation of the executive power in respect of that subject matter. The operation of the law upon the power is a matter of construction ...

[50] English courts have long recognised the general proposition of international law that:

> ... the supreme power of every state has a right to make laws for the exclusion or expulsion of a foreigner ... [*Re Adam* (1837) 1 Moo PC 460; 12 ER 889]

In that case the court recognised a power in the Governor in Council of the Colony of Mauritius "as the depositaries of the executive authority of the Crown, to remove at pleasure all aliens not protected by any special privilege" [at 470] ... The principle was explicitly recognised by the Privy Council in *Attorney-General (Can) v Cain* [[1906] AC 542 at 546]:

> One of the rights possessed by the supreme power in every State is the right to refuse to permit an alien to enter that State, to annex what conditions it pleases to the permission to enter it, and to expel or deport from the State, at pleasure, even a friendly alien, especially if it considers his presence in the State opposed to its peace, order, and good government, or to its social or material interests ...

[52] In my opinion, the executive power of the Commonwealth, absent statutory extinguishment or abridgement, would extend to a power to prevent the entry of non-citizens and to do such things as are necessary to effect such exclusion. This does not involve any conclusion about whether the executive would, in the absence of statutory authority, have a power to expel non-citizens other than as an incident of the power to exclude. The power to determine who may come into Australia is so central to its sovereignty that it is not to be supposed that the government of the nation would lack under the power conferred upon it directly by the Constitution, the ability to prevent people not part of the Australia community, from entering …

[53] It has been said that the common law of Australia knows no lettre de cachet or executive warrant pursuant to which either citizen or alien can be deprived of his freedom by mere administrative decision or action; *Re Bolton; Ex parte Beane* [(1987) 162 CLR 514 at 528] and *Chu Kheng Lim v Minister for Immigration, Local Government and Ethnic Affairs* [(1992) 176 CLR 1 at 19]. Those observations were made in the context of cases about the surrender of a resident of Australia to another country (*Re Bolton; Ex parte Beane*) and the validity of statutory provisions for the detention of unlawful non-citizens who arrived in Australia as boat people between November 1989 and December 1992 (*Chu Kheng Lim*).

Reliance was placed upon the observation by Davies J in *Mayer v Minister for Immigration and Ethnic Affairs* [(1984) 4 FCR 312 at 316] that whatever may have been the common law prerogative of the Crown "… at the present time the law with respect to the entry of persons to Australia and with respect to their expulsion is regulated by statute".

The reference[s] to the common law of Australia in *Beane* and *Lim* and to the common law prerogative of the Crown in *Mayer* do not deal with the question whether, absent statutory authorisation, s 61 of the Constitution confers upon the executive a power to exclude or prevent the entry of a non-citizen to Australia and powers incidental thereto. In my opinion, absent statutory authority, there is such a power at least to prevent entry to Australia. It is not necessary, for present purposes, to consider its full extent. It may be that, like the power to make laws with respect to defence, it will vary according to circumstances. Absent statutory abrogation it would be sufficient to authorise the barring of entry by preventing a vessel from docking at an Australian port and adopting the means necessary to achieve that result. Absent statutory authority, it would extend to a power to restrain a person or boat from proceeding into Australia or compelling it to leave …

[54] The question is whether the [*Migration Act 1958* (Cth)] operates to abrogate the executive power under s 61 to prevent aliens from entering into Australia. There are no express words to that effect. It is necessary then to look to whether by implication it has that effect …

In my opinion the Act, by its creation of facultative provisions, which may yield a like result to the exercise of executive power, in this particular application of it cannot be taken as intending to deprive the executive of the power necessary to do what it has done in this case. The Act confers power. It does not in the specific area evidence an intention to take it away. The term "intention" of course is a fiction. What must be asked is whether the Act operates in a way that is necessarily inconsistent with the subsistence of the executive power described. It is facultative. Its object is control of entry. Subject to certain specific provisions, such as those relating to the grant of protection visas, its object is not to confer rights upon non-citizens seeking to enter Australia. There are of course process rights at various stages of the visa [55] granting system including those arising under the provisions of Pt 8 relating to judicial review but they do not operate in the circumstances to which the executive power posited for the purposes of this case applies.

Black CJ dissented, holding that the power to expel people entering Australia illegally derives only from legislation, and not from power otherwise exercisable by the executive.

Black CJ: [6] It cannot be doubted that a nation-state has a sovereign power to exclude illegally entering aliens from its borders, and to legislate for this purpose … It is said that, in this case, the people rescued by the MV *Tampa* may be lawfully prevented from entering Australia in the exercise of this sovereign power, but not in exercise of power derived from legislation.

There is also no doubt that, as a general principle of law, there is no executive authority, apart from that conferred by statute, to subject anyone in Australia, citizen or non-citizen, to detention. In *Chu Kheng Lim* [176 CLR at 19], Brennan, Deane and Dawson JJ said:

> Since the common law knows neither lettre de cachet nor other executive warrant authorizing arbitrary arrest or detention, any officer of the Commonwealth Executive who purports to authorize or enforce the detention in custody of such an alien without judicial mandate will be acting lawfully only to the extent that his or her conduct is justified by valid statutory provision …

As a general principle, the executive cannot expel a person from Australia without statutory authority, although whether that principle applies to non-resident unlawful non-citizens is disputed here. But the Solicitor-General submitted that a **[7]** non-statutory executive power to prevent unlawful non-citizens from entering Australia carries with it necessary ancillary powers, which may include power to detain and expel an unlawful non-citizen for the purposes of protecting Australia's borders.

It may be accepted that ancillary powers of detention and expulsion must travel with a power to exclude. But on the view I take, the undoubted power of the executive to protect Australia's borders against the entry of unlawful non-citizens in times of peace derives only from statute ...

The Solicitor-General's principal argument was that the appellants acted in exercise of a prerogative power, which is embraced by s 61. It may be accepted that the power of the executive under s 61 includes powers accorded to the Crown at common law and the first question is, therefore, whether there is a prerogative power of the nature contended for by the Solicitor-General ...

[9] The doubts about the continued existence of [this] prerogative power ... raise the difficult question, on which opinion is divided, whether a particular prerogative power may revive after it has fallen into disuse. There is an argument that a long period of disuse extinguishes the prerogative, because it would be illusory to say that parliament has, in such circumstances, made a choice to leave the prerogative in the Crown's hands. Another view is that the prerogative may be revived in "propitious" circumstances, but not when it would be "grossly anomalous and anachronistic" (the phrase is taken from a dissenting judgment in *M'Kendrick v Sinclair* 1972 SC (HL) 25 at 60-61) ...

Some of these judicial and extra-judicial observations can be seen to support the proposition that prerogative powers can be extinguished, not merely **[10]** because legislation has been passed, but because the prerogative powers have become incompatible with modern constitutional jurisprudence. For example, considerations of this nature appear to emerge in the passage from the judgment of Holroyd J in [*Toy v Musgrove* (1888) 14 VLR 349 at 425] in which his Honour was "impressed" with the absence of any attempt to exercise the prerogative in three centuries. Lord Reid's speech in *Burma Oil Co (Burma Trading) Ltd v Lord Advocate* [[1965] AC 75 at 100] illustrates (in relation to a different prerogative power) the same approach:

> So ... we must try to see what the position was after it became clear that sovereignty resided in the King in Parliament. Any rights thereafter exercised by the King (or the executive) alone must be regarded as a part of sovereignty which Parliament chose to leave in his hands ...

Some of the historical reasons why the prerogative power to exclude aliens came to be viewed as at best doubtful are illuminated by the following passage where, having set out early authorities in support of its existence, Professor Holdsworth said:

> Nevertheless the influences which were making for a denial of this prerogative were beginning to be felt in the sixteenth century; and they gathered strength in the seventeenth, eighteenth, and early nineteenth centuries ... During the greater part of the eighteenth century, there appear to be very few instances in which the Crown used its prerogative to exclude or to expel aliens; and when, at the end of the century, it was thought desirable to exclude aliens, statutory powers were got ... These statutes were passed to exclude aliens who, it was though[t], might spread in England the ideas of the French Revolution. They were therefore opposed by the new Whigs who sympathized with these ideas. In 1816 Romilly, Mackintosh, and Denman denied that the Crown had the wide prerogative attributed to it by Eldon and Ellenborough; the same thesis was maintained in 1825 in a learned article in the *Edinburgh Review*; and in 1890 it was supported by Mr Craies.

In a footnote to this passage, Professor Holdsworth notes that the last occasion on which it appears that a prerogative power to expel or exclude non-citizens was in 1771, when the Crown directed that Jews "unable to pay the usual freight", should, unless they had a passport from an ambassador, be excluded from British territory ...

[11] The preponderance of opinion by the text writers supports the view that, by the end of the nineteenth century, in English jurisprudence, the power to exclude aliens in times of peace was not considered to be part of the prerogative ...

[12] This survey amply supports, in my view, the conclusion that it is, at best, doubtful that the asserted prerogative continues to exist at common law. The affirmative conclusion that the prerogative no longer exists may well be justified, but I do not find it necessary to express a concluded view on that matter. I proceed, however, to a discussion about the displacement of a prerogative power of this nature on the footing that its existence is entirely uncertain, and that there are no previous modern instances of its exercise ...

If it be accepted that the asserted executive power to exclude aliens in time of peace is at best doubtful at common law, the question arises whether s 61 of the Constitution provides some larger source of such a power. It would be a very strange circumstance if the at best doubtful and historically long-unused power to exclude or expel should emerge in a strong modern form from s 61 of the Constitution by virtue of general conceptions of "the national interest". This is all the more so when according to English constitutional theory new prerogative powers cannot be created: see ... *British Broadcasting Corp v Jones* [[1965] Ch 32 at 79] in which Diplock LJ said: "[I]t is 350 years and a civil war too late for the Queen's courts to broaden the prerogative".

The Australian cases in which the executive power has had an "interest of the nation" ingredient can be contrasted with those in which such a power has been asserted for coercive purposes. Thus, this executive power has been validly used to set up the Australian Bicentennial Authority and the CSIRO, but has been held not to be available to sustain deportation; detention or extradition of a fugitive; the arrest of a person believed to have committed a felony abroad; the arbitrary denial of mail and telephone services; or compulsion to attend to give evidence or to produce documents in an inquiry.

It is against this background that I now turn to consider the argument that if there is any prerogative or other non-statutory executive power, it has been **[13]** abrogated by the parliament through the enactment of the Migration Act 1958 (Cth) (the Act), as amended from time to time ...

[19] [R]eview of the [Migration Act] shows that it provides for a very comprehensive regime relating to – in the words of the long title – "the entry into, and presence in, Australia of aliens, and the departure or deportation from Australia of aliens." By virtue of the [*Border Protection Legislation Amendment Act 1999* (Cth)] that regime specifically extends to protection of Australia's sea borders. The regime is comprehensive in its coverage of powers of apprehension and detention. No doubt gaps can be found in the scheme, but the existence of these does not detract from the comprehensive character of the statutory regime. The conclusion to be drawn is that the parliament intended that in the field of exclusion, entry and expulsion of aliens the Act should operate to the exclusion of any executive power derived otherwise than from powers conferred by the parliament. This conclusion is all the more readily drawn having regard to what I have concluded about the nature and the uncertainty of the prerogative or executive power asserted on behalf of the Commonwealth.

The prospect of a successful High Court appeal was seemingly foreclosed by the *Border Protection (Validation and Enforcement Powers) Act 2001* (Cth), passed on 26 September 2001, which retrospectively authorised the detention of the rescuees and other acts done from 27 August to 27 September 2001. On 27 November 2001, the High Court refused an application by Vadarlis for special leave to appeal. By that time, the rescuees had been transferred to either Nauru or New Zealand. Accordingly, Gaudron, Gummow and Hayne JJ held that their original detention aboard the *Tampa* could no longer be challenged, and that the lawfulness of their detention in Nauru and New Zealand was a matter for the law of those countries. In refusing special leave, however, they stated that "the question of standing to seek ... relief under section 75(v) of the Constitution to compel observance of the law is an important constitutional question and might, in an appropriate case, attract the grant of special leave. The same is true of the question of executive and prerogative power examined in the Full Court, and also of the question of the validity of the *Border Protection (Validation and Enforcement Powers) Act*".

So far as the detention of the rescuees in Nauru was concerned, its validity under the *Immigration Act 1999* (Nauru) was upheld by the Supreme Court of Nauru in *Amiri v Director of Police* [2004] NRSC 1. In *Ruhani v Director of Police (No 2)* (2005) 219 ALR 270, that decision was upheld by the High Court of Australia in the exercise of its jurisdiction under the *Nauru (High Court Appeals) Act 1976* (Cth). Only Kirby J dissented.

The 2003 Iraq war, in which Australia participated as part of the "coalition of the willing", also raised questions about the prerogative. The Constitution does not state who can declare war for Australia or the circumstances in which Australia might go to war. The matter is governed by the prerogative. By contrast, Art 9 of the Japanese Constitution states that "the Japanese people forever renounce war as a sovereign right of the nation", while Art 1 of the United States Constitution vests the power "to declare war" in Congress and not the President. On 11 October 2002, Congress passed a *Joint Resolution to Authorize the Use of United States Armed Forces Against Iraq* (Public Law 107-243, 116 Stat 1498), which authorised the President "to use the Armed Forces of the United States as he determines to be necessary and appropriate in order to (1) defend the national security of the United States against the continuing threat posed by Iraq; and (2) enforce all relevant United Nations Security Council Resolutions regarding Iraq".

Geoffrey Lindell, "The Constitutional Authority to Deploy Australian Military Forces in the Coalition War against Iraq"
(2002) 5 *Constitutional Law and Policy Review* 46

[46] It is true that, unlike the constitutions of many other countries, the Commonwealth Constitution fails to refer explicitly to the powers of the executive to declare war and peace and also to deploy the armed forces. However, those powers are now taken to form part of the 'executive power of the Commonwealth' which is vested in the Governor-General as the Queen's representative under s 61 (and possibly also s 68) of the Constitution. The modern view is that the provisions of s 61 now include all the so-called 'prerogatives' of the Crown under the English common law ...

[47] The existence of these prerogatives has long been recognised. After indicating that the king's prerogatives included the power to make treaties with the governments of other countries, and also to receive and send ambassadors, Sir William Blackstone wrote during the 18th century: 'Upon the same principle the king has also the sole prerogative of making war and peace'.

These prerogatives were seen as 'the principal prerogatives of the king respecting the nation's intercourse with foreign nations'. The prerogatives in relation to war include the power to decide on the disposition and use that is made of the military forces even in the absence of a war.

The prerogative nature of the powers in question means that the powers may be exercised without parliamentary approval, subject only to the existence of any legislative provisions which regulate and control their exercise. The writer is not aware of any statutory provisions which regulate the power to declare war or limit the power to deploy military forces overseas.

A formal declaration of war was not thought to be necessary in this case [of Iraq], with the Commonwealth Government being content to rely on its interpretation of pre-existing resolutions passed by the UN Security Council. As a matter of international law, modern practice no longer seems to require a declaration of war to precede the commencement of hostilities. The announcement of Australia's participation in the war against Iraq was made by the Prime Minister at a press conference and in the House of Representatives later on the same day. A formal announcement involving the Governor-General was also thought to be unnecessary, despite the position occupied by the Governor-General as Commander in Chief, as provided in s 68 of the Constitution. The relevant decision was made by Cabinet and then passed on to the Chief of the Australian Defence Forces through the legal chain of command provided in ss 8, 9 and 9A of the *Defence Act 1903* (Cth).

Parliament was given the opportunity to debate the decision to use force in Iraq. The matter was brought before the House of Representatives on a motion by Prime Minister John Howard, who recognised that the "decision lies with the executive of government: the cabinet", but "[n]evertheless [thought it] appropriate that the parliament, at the first opportunity, have the chance to debate this motion. It is essential that the reason for that decision be made plain to the representatives of the people and that they have a full opportunity to debate them and to have their views recorded" (*Hansard*, House of Representatives, 18 March 2003, 12,506). The House passed the motion "endors[ing] the Government's decision to commit Australian Defence Force elements in the region to the international coalition of military forces prepared to enforce Iraq's compliance with its international obligations under successive resolutions of the United Nations Security Council, with a view to restoring international peace and security in the Middle East region" (*Hansard*, House of Representatives, 20 March 2003, 13,170). On the same day a motion passed in the Senate, where the government did not command a majority, called "for the Australian troops to be withdrawn and returned home" (*Hansard*, Senate, 20 March 2003, 9888).

It has been proposed that the prerogative power to go to war be changed by legislation. On 27 March 2003, the Defence Amendment (Parliamentary Approval for Australian Involvement in Overseas Conflicts) Bill 2003 was introduced by Senators Andrew Bartlett and Natasha Stott Despoja of the Australian Democrats. It would have amended the *Defence Act 1903* (Cth) to read:

Defence Amendment (Parliamentary Approval for Australian Involvement in Overseas Conflicts) Bill 2003

50C (1) Members of the Defence Force may be required to serve within the territorial limits of Australia.

(2) Subject to subsection (3), members of the Defence Force may not be required to serve beyond the territorial limits of Australia except in accordance with a resolution agreed to by each House of the Parliament authorising the service.

(3) The Governor-General may by proclamation declare that an emergency exists requiring the service beyond the territorial limits of Australia of members of the Defence Force, and such service may be required in accordance with such proclamation.

(4) If the Parliament is not in session when a proclamation under subsection (3) is made, it shall be summoned to meet within 2 days after the making of the proclamation ...

(7) For the purpose of this section, service beyond the territorial limits of Australia does not include service by members of the Defence Force:

(a) pursuant to their temporary attachment as provided by section 116B; or

(b) as part of an Australian diplomatic or consular mission; or

(c) on an Australian vessel or aircraft not engaged in hostilities or in operations during which hostilities are likely to occur; or

(d) for the purpose of their education or training; or

(e) for purposes related to the procurement of equipment or stores.

The Bill was debated in the Senate (*Hansard*, Senate, 10 February 2005, 106-34), but was not put to a vote.

(b)   Nationhood Power

In *Victoria v Commonwealth and Hayden* (*AAP Case*) (1975) 134 CLR 338, Mason J acknowledged that Commonwealth executive power "**[396]** is not unlimited". However, he asserted that, in addition to functions "ascertainable from the distribution of powers, more particularly the distribution of legislative powers, effected by the Constitution itself", the executive power must include responsibilities "**[397]** deduced from the existence and character of the Commonwealth as a national government". In context, this formulation was limited to executive power, since what was at issue in the *AAP Case* was a purely departmental initiative, with no statutory foundation at all (see Chapter 24, §1). In other contexts, it is now well settled that this aspect of the executive power can give rise to an ancillary legislative power by virtue of the express incidental power in s 51(xxxix), which enables Parliament to make laws with respect to "Matters incidental to the execution of any power vested by this Constitution ... in the Government of the Commonwealth".

Another aspect of this power is what Fullagar J spoke of in *Australian Communist Party v Commonwealth* (*Communist Party Case*) (1951) 83 CLR 1 as "the other power" (see Chapter 18, §6), that is, the "**[259]** inherent right of self-protection" that the Commonwealth as a nation must possess. Similarly, in *Burns v Ransley* (1949) 79 CLR 101 at 109-10, 116, and in *R v Sharkey* (1949) 79 CLR 121 at 148-9, the power was conceived of as enabling the Commonwealth to protect itself against subversion and sedition. In those cases, however, the power was spoken of as if it were an independent legislative power, directly implied in Ch II of the Constitution without reference to s 61. Thus, in the *Communist Party Case*, Fullagar J saw the power as "**[260]** depend[ing] really on an essential and inescapable implication which must be involved in the legal constitution of any polity", while Dixon J also ascribed it to a "**[188]** deeper or wider" source. In 1988, such expressions provoked a sharp retort from Wilson and Dawson JJ (with whom Toohey J agreed). They emphasised that what Dixon and Fullagar JJ had said in the *Communist Party Case* had been a minority view.

Davis v Commonwealth
(1988) 166 CLR 79

Wilson and Dawson JJ: [101] If the specifically enumerated powers are taken to include par (xxxix) of s 51, then we consider that in the ultimate analysis the Commonwealth Parliament does not possess any legislative power which could not be assigned to a particular provision or combination of provisions. Section 51(xxxix), it will be recalled, confers power to make laws with respect to matters incidental to the execution of any power vested by the Constitution in the Parliament or in either House thereof, or in the government of the Commonwealth, or in the federal judicature, or in any department or officer of the Commonwealth. The subject has been considered in the context of the suppression of seditious or subversive activities. In *Australian Communist Party v Commonwealth* ("the *Communist Party Case*") [(1951) 83 CLR 1 at 187-8], Dixon J did not doubt that particular laws upon those matters might be supported under powers obtained by combining the appropriate part of the text of s 51(xxxix) with the text of some other power, including the executive power under s 61. However, he found such an exercise **[102]** had an artificial aspect and preferred to find the source of the power to legislate against subversive conduct "in principle that is deeper or wider than a series of combinations of the words of s 51(xxxix) with those of other constitutional powers". The power was to be found, he said, in the very nature of the polity established by the Constitution and the capacity which it must of necessity have to protect its own existence.

But this view was a minority view. The majority of the members of the Court considered the validity of the impugned Act by reference to the question whether it was supported by s 51(xxxix) in association with either s 51(vi) or s 61 ...

We are unable to conceive of an implication of the kind described that would not be sufficiently and accurately described in the terms of s 61 supported by s 51(xxxix). Indeed, the execution and maintenance of the Constitution and of the laws of the Commonwealth are concepts which seem to us to comprehend all that is to be implied "from the existence and nature of the Constitution as the foundation of a body politic" ...

[103] [We] think it desirable to deprecate speaking of implied powers as distinct from the proper scope of the executive power conferred by s 61 lest the use of the term tend to suggest the existence of some new or independent source of power. The Commonwealth cannot be accorded a legislative power to cross the **[104]** boundaries between State and Commonwealth responsibility laid down by the Constitution. It is as axiomatic in constitutional law as it is elsewhere that the sum cannot be greater than its parts. Even if it be convenient in some circumstances to look at the totality rather than individual heads of power, the Commonwealth remains confined to that which is granted to it by the Constitution. Moreover, the range of activities which, not being expressly referred to elsewhere in the Constitution, are found on its proper construction to fall within s 61 will necessarily of their very nature lie outside the competence of the States for the reason that such powers will be exercisable only by the Commonwealth and for Commonwealth purposes. The truth is that the character and status of the Commonwealth as a national government are qualities which are themselves to be found within the confines of the Constitution.

In *Commonwealth v Tasmania* (*Tasmanian Dam Case*) (1983) 158 CLR 1, Wilson J had referred to the nationhood power as "**[203]** an inherent power to legislate". However, if the strictures in *Davis v Commonwealth* are accepted, such expressions should presumably be understood as an elliptical way of referring to the incidental power in s 51(xxxix), operating upon the executive power in s 61.

On that basis, it is now generally accepted that the "nationhood power" explains the validity of the various appropriations for cultural and other purposes listed by Latham CJ in *Attorney-*

General (Vic); Ex rel Dale v Commonwealth (Pharmaceutical Benefits Case) (1945) 71 CLR 237 at 254. Similarly, the effect of the *AAP Case* may be that the executive power in its "nationhood" aspect will support an appropriation of moneys from the Consolidated Revenue Fund under s 81 of the Constitution (see Chapter 24, §1).

In *New South Wales v Commonwealth (Seas and Submerged Lands Case)* (1975) 135 CLR 337, it was suggested that, quite apart from the Commonwealth's power over "external affairs" (s 51(xxix)), the nationhood power might enable the Commonwealth to legislate for the Australian territorial sea.

New South Wales v Commonwealth (Seas and Submerged Lands Case)
(1975) 135 CLR 337

Barwick CJ: [373] A consequence of creation of the Commonwealth under the Constitution and the grant of the power with respect to external affairs was, in my opinion, to vest in the Commonwealth any proprietary rights and legislative power which the colonies might have had in or in relation to the territorial sea, seabed and airspace and continental shelf and incline. Proprietary rights and legislative powers in these matters of international concern would then coalesce and unite in the nation. That, in my opinion, was the intendment of the Constitution. It is far easier to conclude that the Act of the Imperial Parliament setting up the federal Constitution intended to vest such matters of international consequence in the new Commonwealth, withdrawing them from the former colonies, than it was to decide that when an American State, already an independent nation in possession of international **[374]** rights, entered the Union, these rights became vested in the United States. Yet that is received doctrine in the United States expressed in decisions which have recently been affirmed: see *United States v California* [332 US 19 (1947)]; *United States v Texas* [339 US 707 (1950)]; *United States v Louisiana* [339 US 699 (1950)] and *United States v Maine* [420 US 515 (1975)] ...

This result conforms, in my opinion, to an essential feature of a federation, namely, that it is the nation and not the integers of the federation which must have the power to protect and control as a national function the area of the marginal seas, the seabed and airspace and the continental shelf and incline. This has been decided by the Supreme Courts of the United States and of Canada: see above citations and *Reference re Ownership of Offshore Mineral Rights* [[1967] SCR 792; 65 DLR (2d) 353] ... [The Canadian] Supreme Court's conclusion depends in no small degree upon the fact of Canada's independent nationhood and its recognition as such by the nations of the world. Appropriately, it is concluded that such international rights and obligations as derive from the Convention on the Territorial Sea devolve on Canada and not on any province of the federation. I can find no reason to differentiate in relevant respects the circumstances of this federation from those of the other great federations, except to say that the result of the cases to which I have referred more obviously flows in the case of our Constitution.

It is my opinion, therefore, that upon the enactment of the Constitution, any rights or powers which the former colonies might have had in the territorial sea, seabed and airspace or in **[375]** the continental shelf and incline became vested in the Commonwealth. The emergence of Australia as an independent nation state confirmed this situation.

A related manifestation of the nationhood power was relied on by the Commonwealth in *Commonwealth v Tasmania (Tasmanian Dam Case)* (1983) 158 CLR 1. The scheme of the *World Heritage Properties Conservation Act 1983* (Cth) was such that each of paras (a) to (d) of s 6(2) was designed to attract a different aspect of the external affairs power (see Chapter 19, §4(b)), whereas para (e) was designed to attract the nationhood power.

World Heritage Properties Conservation Act 1983 (Cth)

6 (2) A Proclamation may also be made under sub-section (3) in relation to identified property that is in a State and is property to which one or more of the following paragraphs applies or apply: ...
  (e) the property is part of the heritage distinctive of the Australian nation –

(i)   by reason of its aesthetic, historic, scientific or social significance; or

(ii) by reason of its international or national renown,

and, by reason of the lack or inadequacy of any other available means for its protection or conservation, it is peculiarly appropriate that measures for the protection or conservation of the property be taken by the Parliament and Government of the Commonwealth as the national parliament and government of Australia.

Once a proclamation had been made under s 6(2)(e), certain acts in respect of the property, such as the carrying out of excavation works or the cutting down of trees, became unlawful under s 9 unless the consent of the Minister had first been obtained.

Mason, Murphy and Brennan JJ, who held that para (b) was valid, had no need to consider para (e). Deane J also found that para (b) was valid, but went on to find that para (e) could not be supported by the nationhood power. Gibbs CJ, Wilson and Dawson JJ also held that para (e) was invalid. None of them denied that the nationhood power existed, but all denied that it was relevant in this instance.

Commonwealth v Tasmania (Tasmanian Dam Case)
(1983) 158 CLR 1

Wilson J: [203] The Commonwealth argues that, independently of any express legislative power conferred by the Constitution, the existence of the circumstances described in s 6(2)(e) of the Act brings into being an inherent power to legislate. The circumstances are the following: a heritage distinctive of the Australian nation, an absence or inadequacy of any other available means for its protection, and a conclusion that it is peculiarly appropriate that the Parliament and government of the Commonwealth should protect it. I am unable to accept the argument. I know of no occasion when a coercive law declaring certain conduct to be unlawful and imposing penalties has been enacted by the Parliament otherwise than pursuant to a given head of power. Such an approach to federal legislative power would **[204]** in my opinion be wholly subversive of the Constitution and cannot be permitted. I accept, so far as coercive laws are concerned, the emphatic statement of Latham CJ in the *Bank Case* [(1948) 76 CLR 1 at 184]:

> "The Constitution assigns only specific legislative powers to the Commonwealth Parliament. It is a Federal Constitution, not a unitary Constitution. This has been emphasised again and again in the judgments of this Court, and in no case more clearly than in the *Amalgamated Society of Engineers v Adelaide Steamship Co Ltd* [(1920) 28 CLR 129 at 150] where reference is made to the conclusion 'as to which this Court has never faltered, that the Commonwealth is a government of enumerated or selected legislative powers': see also at p 154: 'It is undoubted that those who maintain the authority of the Commonwealth Parliament to pass a certain law should be able to point to some enumerated power containing the requisite authority'."

It is unnecessary, for the purposes of this case, to consider the existence and scope of a non-coercive legislative power inherent in the fact of Australia's nationhood: cf *Victoria v Commonwealth and Hayden* [(1975) 134 CLR 338].

Deane J, the only majority judge to consider this issue, had a similar distinction in mind.

Deane J: [252] There are many statements in judgments in this Court which support the proposition that, in the context of s 51(xxxix) and s 61 of the Constitution, each of the Commonwealth Parliament and executive is vested with certain powers which are inherent in its existence or in the fact of Australian nationhood and international personality: see, generally, *Attorney-General (Vic) v Commonwealth* ("*Dale's Case*") [(1945) 71 CLR 237 at 269]; *Victoria v Commonwealth and Hayden* [134 CLR at 397, 412-23]. At the heart of such powers, there lies "the necessary power of the federal government to protect its own existence and the unhindered play of its legitimate activities": *Black's American Constitutional Law*, 2nd ed (1910), s 153, p 210, quoted by Dixon J in *Australian Communist Party v Commonwealth* [(1951) 83 CLR 1 at 188] and see, to the same effect, per Latham CJ in *Burns v Ransley* [(1949) 79 CLR 101 at 109-10]. The outer limits of such powers remain unexplored. They have been suggested, in the context of an appropriation of moneys from consolidated revenue, to include, eg, exploration itself in both physical and intellectual fields: see per Barwick CJ in *Victoria v Commonwealth and Hayden* [134 CLR at 362].

As one moves away from those matters which lie at the heart of the inherent powers of the Commonwealth, it becomes increasingly predictable that any such powers will be confined within areas in which there is no real competition with the States. There are, no doubt, areas within the plenitude of executive and legislative power shared between Commonwealth and States (see *Colonial Sugar Refining Co Ltd v Attorney-General (Cth)* [(1912) 15 CLR 182]; *Smith v Oldham* [(1912) 15 CLR 355]) which, while not included in any express grant of legislative power, are of real interest to the Commonwealth or national government alone. Even in fields which are under active State legislative and executive control, Commonwealth legislative or **[253]** executive action may involve no competition with State authority: an example is the mere appropriation and payment of money to assist what are truly national endeavours. It is unnecessary to pursue the subject here, however. It suffices, for present purposes, to say that I consider that the inherent powers of the Commonwealth could not, on any proper approach, be seen as including the power to enact a law imposing drastic restrictions of the type contained in s 9 of the Act in respect of "identified property" (as defined in s 3(2) of the Act) in relation to which the requirements of sub-ss (2)(e) and (3) of s 6 of the Act are satisfied. Those restrictions would involve the potential freezing of the "identified property" to which they were applied and would, to no small extent, override and displace the ordinary legislative and executive powers of the State, in which such property was situate, to authorize or regulate conduct thereon. The fact that particular physical property or artistic, intellectual, scientific or sporting achievement or endeavour is "part of the heritage distinctive of the Australian nation" may well be decisive of the question whether the protection, preservation or promotion of such property, achievement or endeavour may be made the object of an appropriation of money by the Commonwealth Parliament or of Commonwealth action to assist or complement actions of a State. In the absence of any relevant grant of power to the Commonwealth however, that fact cannot constitute the basis of some unexpressed power in the Commonwealth to arrogate to itself control of such property, achievement or endeavour or to oust or override the legislative and executive powers of the State in which such property is situate or such achievement or endeavour has been effected or is being pursued.

In *Davis v Commonwealth* (1988) 166 CLR 79, the Court considered the validity of the *Australian Bicentennial Authority Act 1980* (Cth). The plaintiff, Lou Davis, was an Aboriginal Australian who sought to market Bicentennial T-shirts bearing messages such as "200 YEARS OF SUPPRESSION AND DEPRESSION". He was unable to do so because ss 22 and 23 of the Act restricted the use of any symbol or logo associated with the Bicentenary as well as any use, in conjunction with "1788" or "1988", of words including "Bicentenary", "Bicentennial", "Sydney", "Melbourne", "First Settlement" or "200 years". Under the Act, Davis could not market his T-shirts without the Bicentennial Authority's consent, which was refused. The High Court unanimously held these provisions invalid, though the final order was limited to the words "200 years" as these were the only words directly in issue.

Davis v Commonwealth
(1988) 166 CLR 79

Mason CJ, Deane and Gaudron JJ: [92] The Commonwealth submits that its executive power under s 61 of the Constitution extends to the incorporation of a company in the Australian Capital Territory having as its object the commemoration of the Bicentenary throughout Australia ...

The scope of the executive power of the Commonwealth has often been discussed but never defined. By s 61 of the Constitution **[93]** it extends to the execution and maintenance of the Constitution. As Mason J observed in *Barton v Commonwealth* [(1975) 131 CLR 477 at 498], the power:

"extends to the execution and maintenance of the Constitution and of the laws of the Commonwealth. It enables the Crown to undertake all executive action which is appropriate to the position of the Commonwealth under the Constitution and to the spheres of responsibility vested in it by the Constitution."

These responsibilities [are] derived from the distribution of legislative powers effected by the Constitution itself and from the character and status of the Commonwealth as a national polity: *Victoria v Commonwealth and Hayden* ("the *AAP Case*") [(1975) 134 CLR 338 at 396-7]. So it is that the legislative powers of the Commonwealth extend beyond the specific powers conferred upon the Parliament by the Constitution and include such powers as may be deduced from the establishment and nature of the Commonwealth as a polity: see the discussion by Dixon J in *Australian Communist Party v Commonwealth* ("the *Communist Party Case*") [(1951) 83 CLR 1 at 187-8]. Dixon J expressed a like view of Parliament's power of appropriation when he said in *Attorney-General (Vic) v Commonwealth* ("the *Pharmaceutical Benefits Case*") [(1945) 71 CLR 237 at 271-2]:

"In deciding what appropriation laws may validly be enacted it would be necessary to remember what position a national government occupies and … to take no narrow view, but the basal consideration would be found in the distribution of powers and functions between the Commonwealth and the States."

The Constitution distributes the plenitude of executive and legislative powers between the Commonwealth and the States … On this footing, as Isaacs J pointed out in *Commonwealth v Colonial Combing, Spinning and Weaving Co Ltd* ("the *Wooltops Case*") [(1922) 31 CLR 421 at 437-9], s 61 confers on the Commonwealth all the prerogative powers of the Crown except those that are necessarily exercisable by the States under the allocation of responsibilities made by the Constitution and those denied by the Constitution itself. Thus the existence of **[94]** Commonwealth executive power in areas beyond the express grants of legislative power will ordinarily be clearest where Commonwealth executive or legislative action involves no real competition with State executive or legislative competence.

If we ask the question whether the commemoration of the Bicentenary is a matter falling within the peculiar province of the Commonwealth in its capacity as the national and federal government, the answer must be in the affirmative. That is not to say that the States have no interest or no part to play in the commemoration. Clearly they have such an interest and such a part to play, whether as part of an exercise in co-operative federalism or otherwise. But the interest of the States in the commemoration of the Bicentenary is of a more limited character. It cannot be allowed to obscure the plain fact that the commemoration of the Bicentenary is pre-eminently the business and the concern of the Commonwealth as the national government and as such falls fairly and squarely within the federal executive power.

Implicit in what we have just said is a rejection of any notion that the character and status of the Commonwealth as the government of the nation is relevant only in the ascertainment of the scope of the executive power in the area of Australia's external relations. In the legislative sphere the nature and status of the Commonwealth as a polity has sustained legislation against subversive or seditious conduct: *Burns v Ransley* [(1949) 79 CLR 101 at 116]; *R v Sharkey* [(1949) 79 CLR 121 at 148-9]; see the *Communist Party Case* [83 CLR at 187-8]. And there was no suggestion in the judgments in the *AAP Case* that the character and status of the Commonwealth as a national government was not relevant in ascertaining the scope of the executive power in its application domestically. Indeed, the judgments in that case contradict the suggestion, the Australian Assistance Plan being a domestic scheme.

From the conclusion that the commemoration of the Bicentenary falls squarely within Commonwealth executive power other consequences follow. The first is that the executive power extends to the incorporation of a company as a means for carrying out and implementing a plan or programme for the commemoration. There is no constitutional bar to the setting up of a corporate authority to achieve this object or purpose in preference to executive action through a Ministry of the Crown. Certainly there is no such bar to the incorporation of a company in the Australian Capital Territory, though we very much doubt that this procedure would enable the **[95]** Commonwealth to circumvent limitations or restrictions which would otherwise attach to the federal executive power in so far as it extends to the commemoration of the Bicentenary: cf *Johnson v Kent* [(1975) 132 CLR 164 at 169].

Section 51(xxxix) of the Constitution enables the Parliament to legislate in aid of an exercise of the executive power. So, once it is accepted that the executive power extends to the incorporation of the Authority with the object set out in cl 3 of its memorandum of association, s 51(xxxix) authorizes legislation regulating the administration and procedures of the Authority and conferring on it such powers and protection as may be appropriate to such an authority.

It may be possible to support this conclusion without recourse to s 51(xxxix). The requisite legislative power may be deduced from the nature and status of the Commonwealth as a national polity in just the same way as Dixon J in the *Communist Party Case* thought that legislation prohibiting specific acts of sedition could be upheld. However it is unnecessary for us to pursue this question.

Wilson and Dawson JJ in a joint judgment, and Toohey J in a separate judgment, substantially agreed. However, for the reasons already explained, they were anxious to make it clear that what was at stake was not an implied legislative power, but an aspect of the executive power under s 61, as acted upon by the incidental power in s 51(xxxix).

Brennan J maintained a wide view of the executive power. However, his view of the corresponding legislative power was more circumscribed. In a framework of s 51(xxxix) operating on s 61, he combined a wide view of s 61 with a narrow view of s 51(xxxix).

Brennan J: [107] The scope of the legislative power conferred by s 51(xxxix) in respect of matters incidental to the execution of the executive power of the Commonwealth depends, of course, on the scope of the executive power. The scope of s 61 has not been charted nor, for the reasons which [Mason J] stated [in the *AAP Case* (1975) 134 CLR 338 at 397-8], is its scope amenable to exhaustive definition. But it is not necessary to attempt an exhaustive definition in order to ascertain the operation of s 51(xxxix) in conjunction with s 61. The particular enterprise or activity in which the Executive Government engages or proposes to engage in execution of the executive power is the lynchpin of the legislative power, and it is necessary to determine only the existence of executive power to engage in that enterprise or activity ...

[109] Section 61 refers not only to the execution and maintenance of the laws of the Commonwealth (a function characteristically to be performed by execution of statutory powers); it refers also to "the **[110]** execution and maintenance of this Constitution" (a function to be performed by execution of powers which are not necessarily statutory). I respectfully agree with Jacobs J that the phrase "maintenance of this Constitution" imports the idea of Australia as a nation. I would briefly state my reasons for holding that the function which that phrase assigns to the Executive Government relates not only to the institutions of government but more generally to the protection and advancement of the Australian nation.

It is unnecessary to dwell upon the executive power to protect the nation, which Latham CJ in *Burns v Ransley* [(1949) 79 CLR 101 at 109-10], held to be the foundation for laws enacted under s 51(xxxix) for the protection and maintenance of the Government. Although Dixon J took the view that the power to legislate against subversive conduct came from a wider or deeper source (*Australian Communist Party v Commonwealth* [83 CLR at 187-8]), there can be no doubt that the Executive Government of the Commonwealth has an executive power to protect the nation.

This Court has not settled the questions whether and to what extent it is within the executive power of the Commonwealth for the Executive Government of the Commonwealth to exercise its prerogative powers or to engage in lawful activities or enterprises calculated to advance the national interest. Though the Constitution gives no express answer to these questions, the answer may be derived from what the Constitution was intended to do and has done. With great respect to those who hold an opposing view, the Constitution did not create a mere aggregation of colonies, redistributing powers between the government of the Commonwealth and the governments of the States. The Constitution summoned the Australian nation into existence, thereby conferring a new identity on the people who agreed to unite "in one indissoluble Federal Commonwealth", melding their history, embracing their cultures, synthesizing their aspirations and their destinies. The reality of the Australian nation is manifest, though the manifestations of its existence cannot be limited by definition. The end and purpose of the Constitution is to sustain the nation. If the executive power of the Commonwealth extends to the protection of the nation against forces which would weaken it, it extends to the advancement of the nation whereby its strength is fostered. There is no reason to restrict the executive power of the Commonwealth to matters within the heads of legislative power. So [111] cramped a construction of the power would deny to the Australian people many of the symbols of nationhood – a flag or anthem, eg – or the benefit of many national initiatives in science, literature and the arts. It does not follow that the Executive Government of the Commonwealth is the arbiter of its own power or that the executive power of the Commonwealth extends to whatever activity or enterprise the Executive Government deems to be in the national interest. But s 61 does confer on the Executive Government power "to engage in enterprises and activities peculiarly adapted to the government of a nation and which cannot otherwise be carried on for the benefit of the nation", to repeat what Mason J said in the *AAP Case* [134 CLR at 397]. In my respectful opinion, that is an appropriate formulation of a criterion to determine whether an enterprise or activity lies within the executive power of the Commonwealth. It invites consideration of the sufficiency of the powers of the States to engage effectively in the enterprise or activity in question and of the need for national action (whether unilateral or in co-operation with the States) to secure the contemplated benefit. The variety of enterprises or activities which might fall for consideration preclude[s] the a priori development of detailed criteria but, as cases are decided, perhaps more precise tests will be developed.

Despite these broad views of the underlying power, the whole Court held that the relevant provisions of the *Australian Bicentennial Authority Act* were invalid. Mason CJ, Deane and Gaudron JJ based this conclusion on a "proportionality" test. This was so even though these judges were prepared to envisage an "[99] implied legislative power" quite apart from the incidental power, and were also prepared to extend the power to "coercive laws".

Mason CJ, Deane and Gaudron JJ: [98] Apart from [one aspect] of s 22(6)(d)(i), the federal executive power authorizes the commemoration of the Bicentenary and what is incidental to it. Likewise, in the manner already discussed, federal legislative power extends to the same extent. In exercising that power the Parliament may protect the name of the Authority, authorize the prescription of appropriate official symbols for use by [99] the Authority and prohibit unauthorized use by others of the Authority's name or of those symbols, or likenesses of them, for the purpose of protecting their integrity. The implied legislative power, as well as the incidental power (s 51(xxxix)), enables Parliament to enact coercive laws: see *Burns v Ransley*. Consequently, if the provisions of ss 22 and 23 relating to the use of the Authority's name and prescribed symbols stood on their own we would uphold their validity.

If we look to s 22(1)(a) as it applies to prescribed expressions, the first six expressions prescribed by s 22(6)(d)(i) are expressions which may be used in conjunction with "1788", "1988" or "88", in connexion with a business, trade, profession or occupation, in a great variety of circumstances, without prejudicing in any way the commemoration of the Bicentenary or the attainment of the objects of the Authority. The expressions are commonly used by all sections of the community, particularly in this the Bicentennial year. There is every reason for thinking that a wide range of persons, companies and organizations have occasion to use them otherwise than for purposes of advertising and publicity, if only to record what they are doing in the Bicentennial year. And there is no reason for thinking that the protection of the integrity of the commemoration of the Bicentenary and the attainment by the Authority of its objects require the prohibition of such a use of the six prescribed expressions in the circumstances mentioned in s 22(1), subject only to the written consent of the Authority.

The difficulties do not stop at this point. Take the prescription of "Melbourne" and "Sydney" in par (d)(i). The use of "Family Law Conference Melbourne 1988", without the prior written consent of the Authority, in connexion with a conference of the legal profession in that city this year would infringe s 22(1)(a). Yet it is impossible to perceive how the prohibition of such a use contributes to the protection of the integrity of the commemoration of the Bicentenary or the attainment of the objects of the Authority. Many similar illustrations (eg, clothing or emblems displaying support for sporting teams) might be given of the use of a combination of "Melbourne" and "1988" or "Sydney" and "1988".

The illustrations given in the two preceding paragraphs indicate that the effect of the provisions is to give the Authority an extraordinary power to regulate the use of expressions in everyday use in this country, though the circumstances of that use in countless situations could not conceivably prejudice the commemoration of the Bicentenary or the attainment by the Authority of its [100] objects. In arming the Authority with this extraordinary power the Act provides for a regime of protection which is grossly disproportionate to the need to protect the commemoration and the Authority. It is therefore no answer to say that the Authority's power to refuse written consent is exercisable only for the purpose of ensuring such protection, assuming that to be a permissible construction of s 22(1).

Here the framework of regulation created by s 22(1)(a) with s 22(6)(d)(i) and (ii) reaches far beyond the legitimate objects sought to be achieved and impinges on freedom of expression by enabling the Authority to regulate the use of common expressions and by making unauthorized use a criminal offence. Although the statutory regime may be related to a constitutionally legitimate end, the provisions in question reach too far. This extraordinary intrusion into freedom of expression is not reasonably and appropriately adapted to achieve the ends that lie within the limits of constitutional power.

Wilson, Dawson and Toohey JJ substantially agreed. Brennan J reached the same result by carefully limiting the effect of the incidental power conferred by s 51(xxxix).

Brennan J: [111] The scope of the legislative power conferred by s 51(xxxix) in conjunction with s 61 depends on what the Executive Government has done or intends to do in execution of its power. Section 51(xxxix) confers a power to make a law not with respect to the subject-matter of an executive power of the Commonwealth, nor even with respect to a matter incidental to that subject-matter; it confers a power to make a law only with respect to a matter "incidental to the execution" of an executive power of the Commonwealth ...

[112] By reason of the confined scope of the power conferred by s 51(xxxix), the area within which a law enacted under that paragraph may create offences is necessarily confined. At least since the *Case of Proclamations* [(1611) 12 Co Rep 74; 77 ER 1352], the exercise of prerogative power has not been capable of creating a new offence. Nor can the exercise by the Executive Government of a non-statutory capacity create an offence. What offences can be created by a law with respect to a matter incidental to the execution of an executive power? In *R v Kidman* [(1915) 20 CLR 425 at 441] Isaacs J, noting that punishment is beyond the scope of the executive power, observed that "[p]unishment is an ordinary means employed by legislatures to guard and assist the executive power". This was the basis on which Latham CJ upheld the laws challenged in *Burns v Ransley*: see *Australian Communist Party v Commonwealth* [83 CLR at 211-12, 231]. However, the observation by Isaacs J does not emphasize that the offence-creating law must be in respect of a matter incidental to the *execution* of executive power, presumably because his Honour regarded punishment as something "quite unnecessary to the existence or exercise of the executive functions". With respect, this seems too extreme a view. Punishment may be necessary to protect the Executive Government's execution or attempted execution of its powers from being frustrated or impaired. But it is one thing to create offences in order to protect the efficacy of execution of executive power; it is another to create offences to supplement what the Executive Government has done or proposes to do. Where the Executive Government engages in activity in order to advance the [113] nation – an essentially facultative function – the execution of executive power is not the occasion for a wide impairment of individual freedom: cf the *Tasmanian Dam Case* [(1983) 158 CLR 1 at 203-4], per Wilson J. In my opinion, the legislative power with respect to matters incidental to the execution of the executive power does not extend to the creation of offences except in so far as is necessary to protect the efficacy of the execution by the Executive Government of its powers and capacities ...

[114] The first European settlement in Australia was an event of overwhelming significance in Australian history, albeit its significance for the Aboriginal inhabitants of 1788 was profoundly different from its significance for the European settlers of that time. The ensuing two centuries have changed but not eliminated differences in the significance of the event for different people; indeed, the significance of the event has taken on new aspects as the descendants of Aborigines and of Europeans and of both have appraised that significance for themselves in the light of their own experiences and as immigrants from all parts of the world have made their appraisement in the light of the history and culture of their places of origin. Whatever significance one chooses to assign to the event, it was a turning point in the history of those who now make up the Australian nation. In 1788, a system of law and government, religious and ethical beliefs, a money economy, the institution of private property, an urban and agrarian society, and forms of literacy and numeracy that were previously unknown in this country were introduced. Those innovations set the course of modern Australian development and, of course, radically and for ever changed the life, religion, culture, laws and institutions of Australian Aborigines. Although it is arguable that, since the first European settlement occurred in New South Wales, the commemoration should be regarded properly as a State affair, the first European settlement has undoubted significance for the whole of Australia. Giving to the executive power of the Commonwealth the scope which I have described, that power undoubtedly extends to the organizing of the commemoration of the Bicentenary and the stimulation of "an enduring consciousness of the historical basis and significance of that commemoration". The significance to be attributed to the first European settlement, as contemporary experience shows, is one of the abiding concerns of the Australian people. As the Bicentenary can properly be seen as a matter for commemoration by the Commonwealth, the executive power of the Commonwealth extends to the organization of the commemoration of the Bicentenary ... Section 51(xxxix) empowered the Parliament to make a law in aid of that activity. Putting aside ss 22 and 23 for the moment, the Act is supported by s 51(xxxix) of the Constitution ...

[116] The limits on the legislative power to enact penal laws under s 51(xxxix) [are] of especial importance when the relevant activity undertaken in execution of an executive power is the commemoration of an historical event. Such a commemoration may take many forms, according to the significance placed upon it. The form of national commemorations of historical events usually reflects the significance which the majority of people place upon the event. But there may well be minority views which place a different significance on the same event, as the present case illustrates. It is of the essence of a free and mature nation that minorities are entitled to equality in the enjoyment of human rights. Minorities are thus entitled to freedom in the peaceful expression of dissident views. In this case, the plaintiffs wish to raise a voice of protest against the celebratory commemoration of the Bicentenary, and the defendants contend that ss 22 and 23 are effective to muffle the intended protest. As a matter of construction, ss 22 and 23 do muffle the [117] intended protest. But it cannot be incidental to the organization of the commemoration of the Bicentenary to prohibit, under criminal sanctions, the peaceful expression of opinions about the significance of the events of 1788. By prohibiting the use of the symbols and expressions apt to express such opinions, ss 22 and 23 forfeit any support which s 51(xxxix) might otherwise afford.

In *Re Wakim; Ex parte McNally* (*Cross-vesting Case*) (1999) 198 CLR 511 (see Chapter 6, §3), Kirby J gave another possible example: he suggested that the cross-vesting scheme for the avoidance of jurisdictional conflicts between Australian courts might be rescued from invalidity by resort to the nationhood power.

Re Wakim; Ex parte McNally (*Cross-vesting Case*)
(1999) 198 CLR 511

Kirby J: [614] That power has been repeatedly recognised in decisions of this Court as deriving from Australia's very existence and character as a sovereign nation. It extends not only to Australia's external activities, but also internally. It is a source of power reflective of the unique position occupied by the Commonwealth within Australia's federal polity. In the past that power has been elaborated in connection with the Legislature and the Executive Government of the Commonwealth. But there is no reason of principle why it should not also apply in the case of the Judicature ...

[615] Federal legislation providing consent to the vesting of State jurisdiction in federal courts falls squarely within the purposes envisaged by the implied nationhood power as it relates to the Judicature. The legislation possesses an "Australian rather than a local flavour". It seeks to facilitate national co-operation and "co-ordination" in response to the "complexity ... of a modern national society" [*Victoria v Commonwealth and Hayden* (*AAP Case*) (1975) 134 CLR 338 at 412]. The Commonwealth, in its relationship with the States and Territories, is in a unique position to respond to the issues arising under the establishment of a national system of jurisdiction-sharing. It has done so for high national purposes.

Obviously, the implied nationhood power is strictly limited in its scope. It would be inconsistent with the distribution of powers provided by the Constitution were the nationhood power to be given an ambit that trespassed impermissibly upon the powers of the States. That would effect a disturbance of the federal balance. A characterisation of legislative purposes as "national" is not sufficient to attract the support of the nationhood power if those purposes fall within areas of law-making belonging to the States. But the cross-vesting legislation of the Commonwealth, in so far as it gives consent to the vesting of State jurisdiction in federal courts, cannot be characterised in that way. It is legislation which every Australian State and Territory supported in this Court. In no way does it encroach impermissibly upon the legislative domain of the States or [616] subvert the federal nature of the Constitution. On the contrary, it is clearly intended to support the legislative initiatives which the States have themselves taken. In the jurisprudence of this Court, the implied nationhood power is not limited to flags and symbols. It extends to co-operative national activities that are compatible with the Constitution and which reflect the modern needs of a dynamic and democratic federal polity.

In this passage Kirby J apparently envisaged an implied *legislative* power. Translating this into a postulate of legislative power under s 51(xxxix), as incidental to s 61, the relevant aspect of Commonwealth executive power would presumably lie in what Jacobs J identified in the *AAP Case* as the need for national initiatives of "[412] co-ordination and integration of ways and means of planning" for "the complexity and values of a modern national society". However, no argument of that kind had been advanced in *Re Wakim*, and Gummow and Hayne JJ emphatically argued that no such argument was possible.

Gummow and Hayne JJ: [581] No doubt the legislative and executive powers of the Commonwealth must be understood in light of the fact that the Commonwealth is established as the national polity. It may be, then, that there is power in the Commonwealth "to protect its own existence and the unhindered play of its legitimate activities". But whatever may be the content of any legislative power implied from the creation and existence of the Commonwealth as the national polity, that power does not authorise the Parliament to consent to the vesting of State jurisdiction in federal courts. Characterising a set of circumstances as having an Australian rather than a local flavour or as a desirable response to the complexity of a modern national society is to use [582] perceived convenience as a criterion of constitutional validity instead of legal analysis and the application of accepted constitutional doctrine.

A suggestion that the nationhood power might be used to supplement the statutory powers of expulsion arising from the immigration and aliens powers was flatly rejected in *Shaw v Minister for Immigration and Multicultural Affairs* (2003) 218 CLR 28. Kirby J said that: "[71] Where express powers are granted by the Constitution that are specifically relevant to the federal activity that is impugned [72] and where such powers are subject to well developed limitations upon their exercise directly derived from the constitutional language apt to that particular activity, no implied powers can cut a swathe through the Constitution to sustain an action otherwise beyond power". Callinan J added that, in any event: "[85] Constitutional implications may only be made in clear and unarguable cases of real necessity". Although these observations were apparently addressed to an argument couched in terms of an implied *legislative* power, the point made by Kirby J might equally apply to an attempted reliance on the incidental power in aid of a supposed executive power.

The suggestion made by Wilson J in the *Tasmanian Dam Case*, that the nationhood power cannot be invoked to support a "coercive" law, may need some refinement. The judgments in *Davis v Commonwealth* make it clear that if a regulatory provision is reasonably incidental, or proportionate, to the Commonwealth's legitimate national purpose, that provision can validly be enforced by a criminal sanction. (See also *Attorney-General (Vic); Ex rel Dale v Commonwealth* (*Pharmaceutical Benefits Case*) (1945) 71 CLR 237 in Chapter 24, §1.) Thus, the presence or absence of criminal sanctions seems not to be the issue: there is no problem about "coercive" laws in that penal sense. The problem lies rather in the extensive scope and intrusive nature of the regulatory provisions themselves.

The real point of *Davis v Commonwealth* seems best put by the judgments of Wilson and Deane JJ in the *Tasmanian Dam Case*. As Deane J put it, the "appropriation" power or the "nationhood" power, or some combination of them, can be used for a wide range of purposes relating to the "**[253]** protection, preservation or promotion" of some "particular physical property or artistic, intellectual, scientific or sporting achievement or endeavour". However, despite the wide ambit of the power, the scope for an ancillary resort to incidental legislative power is limited. It cannot be used to allow the Commonwealth "**[253]** to arrogate to itself control of such property, achievement or endeavour". Similarly, according to Brennan J in *Davis v Commonwealth* the power is "**[113]** essentially facultative".

(c) Power Conferred by Statute

Additional powers are often conferred upon the executive by statute. These may be new functions or may supplement the executive's existing powers. For example, in *Victoria v Commonwealth and Hayden* (*AAP Case*) (1975) 134 CLR 338, Jacobs J saw the "**[413]** executive power to formulate and co-ordinate plans and purposes" as extending to "**[412]** [i]nquiries on a national scale", including the power to establish inquiries such as a Royal Commission. However, because s 61 of the Constitution may not support the exercise of coercive powers by such inquiries, supplementary powers such as the ability to compel witnesses have been given by the *Royal Commissions Act 1902* (Cth).

Perhaps the most significant function conferred by statute is the capacity to make delegated legislation, that is, regulations, rules and other subordinate legislation (now collectively known under federal law as legislative instruments). Judicial scrutiny of such instruments to see whether they fall within the powers delegated by the statute is an important aspect of administrative law.

The scrutiny of delegated legislation is also, at least in principle, a central element in Parliament's control of the executive. Thus, in *Cobb & Co Ltd v Kropp* [1965] Qd R 285, broad regulatory powers delegated to the Queensland Commissioner for Transport were held to be valid because "**[290]** the Commissioner has at all times, as it were, a Parliamentary hand on his shoulder". In practice, however, the volume of delegated legislation is so vast that the effectiveness of parliamentary scrutiny has fluctuated considerably, and depends on a vigilant and efficient system of parliamentary committees, such as the Senate Standing Committee on Regulations and Ordinances. Under the Senate Standing Orders, that Committee has the task of reporting on "All regulations, ordinances and other instruments made under the authority of Acts of the Parliament, which are subject to disallowance or disapproval by the Senate".

The rules for disallowance by Parliament are set out in the *Legislative Instruments Act 2003* (Cth), a comprehensive regime for the making, registration, parliamentary scrutiny and periodic repeal of delegated legislation. Sections 24 and 25 require that all legislative instruments made after 1 January 2005 be registered "as soon as practicable", and s 38 requires that they be "laid before each House within 6 sitting days of that House" after registration. Any instrument not so tabled "ceases to have effect". Section 42 then allows 15 sitting days within which notice may be given of a motion to disallow the instrument. If such a motion is passed within that time, or if the notice has not been withdrawn and the motion has not been called on for a vote, the instrument "ceases to have effect".

In 1931 a protracted dispute about Senate disallowance of regulations made by the executive arose in respect of an earlier version of these provisions contained in the *Acts Interpretation Act 1901* (Cth). The resulting cases not only provided a wealth of doctrine relating to the effects of Senate scrutiny, but firmly established the constitutional validity in Australia of the British practice of delegating legislative powers to the executive government.

In the late 1920s, the Bruce-Page government set out to break the power of the Waterside Workers Federation (WWF). Section 3 of the *Transport Workers Act 1928* (Cth) provided that

"The Governor-General may make regulations, which, notwithstanding anything in any other Act ... , shall have the force of law" with respect to "the employment of transport workers, and in particular ... [their] engagement, service, and discharge ... , and the licensing of persons as transport workers, and for ... prohibiting the employment of unlicensed persons as transport workers". This power was unusual in that:

1. It authorised regulations which were to have the force of law *notwithstanding anything in any other Act*. That is, the Commonwealth executive was given the same power as the Parliament itself to override prior Acts of Parliament. Sometimes an Act contains a "Henry VIII clause", permitting that Act itself to be amended by regulation (see Legislative Assembly of Queensland, Scrutiny of Legislation Committee, *The Use of "Henry VIII Clauses" in Queensland Legislation* (January 1997)); but this Act permitted regulations to override *any* Act.

2. The power was to make regulations *with respect to* the employment of transport workers *for* a number of purposes, such as the regulation or prohibition of the employment of unlicensed persons as transport workers. This broad general power apparently authorised any regulations whatsoever "with respect to" the specified topics.

3. The Act did not set up a legal regime with respect to the employment of transport workers and then delegate to the executive the power to fill in the details. The *only* effect of the Act was to authorise the making of the regulations. Thus, so long as the regulations were "with respect to" the employment of transport workers, the Act set no limits and gave no guidance as to what the regulations should be.

The *Transport Workers Act* took effect on 24 September 1928. The next day, statutory rules were made under s 3 to establish a licensing system for waterside workers. The system was used to give licences only to workers who were not members of the WWF.

In October 1929, the Labor opposition led by James Scullin won a landslide election victory. However, the election was for the lower House only; in the Senate, Labor still held only seven of the 36 seats. On 15 May 1930, Scullin's first modest attempt to make regulations under the *Transport Workers Act* was disallowed by the Senate. He then undertook to repeal the Act, but instead, while he was out of Australia, his cabinet determined to use the Act to support the WWF. On 18 December 1930, Parliament rose for Christmas. On 19 December 1930, regulations were made under s 3 that provided that in waterfront employment "priority shall be given" to members of the WWF. There followed a long political and legal struggle, beginning when the regulations were upheld in *Huddart Parker Ltd v Commonwealth* (1931) 44 CLR 492 on the basis that they came within the trade and commerce power in s 51(i) of the Constitution.

The fact that the regulations were made the day after Parliament rose for Christmas had circumvented s 10 of the *Acts Interpretation Act*, which required that all regulations "be laid before each House of the Parliament" within 15 sitting days. Even when Parliament resumed in March 1931, the regulations were not tabled until the last possible moment. When finally tabled on 20 March 1931, they were promptly disallowed by the Senate; but the government responded on the same day by making new regulations in identical terms. Again the intention was to wait for 14 days before tabling; but this time the government was out-manoeuvred. On 26 March 1931, Sir George Pearce, the Senate opposition leader, produced the issue of the *Gazette* containing the regulations and quoted it in a speech. The Senate resolved that the document so quoted be tabled, and thereupon Pearce successfully moved for its disallowance.

This disallowance was upheld by the High Court in *Dignan v Australian Steamships Pty Ltd* (1931) 45 CLR 188. Judgment was given on 12 May 1931. On 15 and 22 May 1931, the government again made substantially the same regulations, which the Senate disallowed on 21 and 28 May 1931 respectively. The Senate then appealed to Sir Isaac Isaacs, as Governor-General, asking him to refuse his assent to any further reintroduction of the same regulations in defiance of the Senate. Isaacs refused to withhold his consent, stating that it was his duty to act on the advice of his ministers.

Hansard, Senate, 10 June 1931, vol 130

[2595] With deep respect, I have to inform you that I find it impossible, conformably with my duty, as I understand it, to comply with the request contained in the petition you have made the subject of your address ...

I do not understand from anything contained in the address that you question the legality of any regulation of the nature you have mentioned. At the same time I wish [2596] to assure you that I have, to the best of my ability, carefully re-examined the matter from this standpoint also, in order that no plain illegality should arise. My consideration of the relevant legislation and judicial decisions has led me to the belief that the advice of my legal adviser, the honorable the Attorney-General, is correct – that unless and until disallowed by either House of the Parliament such a regulation would be valid and have the force of law.

With respect to legality, therefore, it is obviously my duty to take the only course which would enable the proper tribunal for that purpose, the judiciary, to determine the question should it arise.

As to the constitutional propriety of my approval to such a regulation as is postulated by the address, it cannot be doubted that normally by constitutional practice ... I am bound to act upon the advice of my Ministers ...

My plain duty in such circumstances, as it appears to me, ... is simply to adhere to the normal principle of responsible government by following the advice of the Ministers who are constitutionally assigned to me for the time being as my advisers, and who must take the responsibility of that advice.

There were further exchanges of re-gazettal and Senate disallowance on 22 and 28 May, 8 and 11 June, 12 and 18 June, 18 and 26 June, 26 June and 29 July, 6 August and 16 October, 17 October and 12 November and 14 and 26 November. On 26 November 1931, the government had the last word by again re-making the regulations and then dissolving the Parliament.

On 17 July 1931, while the regulations of 26 June 1931 were in force, Victorian Stevedoring & General Contracting Co Pty Ltd, through its foreman Charles Meakes, gave preference to a non-member of the WWF, Aubrey Campbell. Cecil Dignan, a navigation inspector, laid charges against both the company and Meakes. Both were convicted by a magistrate. On appeal to the High Court it was argued that s 3 of the *Transport Workers Act* was invalid, but the High Court upheld its validity. The separation of powers doctrine (see Chapter 1, §4) was held to be no obstacle to the vesting of legislative power in the executive.

Dixon J offered an elaborate comparison of the Australian doctrine of "separation of powers" with the corresponding American doctrine as it had developed up to that time. He began by comparing the "vesting" provisions with which the first three Chapters of the Australian Constitution respectively begin (s 1 as to legislative power, s 61 as to executive power, s 71 as to judicial power) with the corresponding provisions at the beginning of each of the first three Articles of the United States Constitution. As to the latter he said:

Victorian Stevedoring & General Contracting Co Pty Ltd & Meakes v Dignan
(1931) 46 CLR 73

Dixon J: [89] In adopting this division of the functions of government, the members of the Convention of 1787 meant that the theory of the separation of powers should be embodied in the fundamental law which they were framing. They shared Gibbon's delight "in the frequent perusal of Montesquieu, whose energy of style and boldness of hypothesis were powerful to awaken and stimulate the genius of the age." To Madison he was "The oracle who is always consulted [90] and cited on this subject" (*The Federalist*, No 47). "No political truth," said Madison, "is certainly of greater intrinsic value, or is stamped with the authority of more enlightened patrons of liberty ... The accumulation of all powers, legislative, executive, and judiciary, in the same hands, whether of one, a few, or many, and whether hereditary, self-appointed or elective, may justly be pronounced the very definition of tyranny" (*ibid*).

The Constitution had been in operation hardly two years before the Judges took their stand upon this separation of powers and firmly declined to execute an act of Congress regulating claims to invalid pensions which, in their opinion, sought to give them duties outside judicial power. *Iredell* J, in his remonstrance to the President, submitted: "That the legislative, executive and judicial departments, are each formed in a separate and independent manner; and that the ultimate basis of each is the Constitution only, within the limits of which each department can alone justify any act of authority." *Jay* CJ, *Cushing, Wilson* and *Blair* JJ relied upon the same doctrine in their addresses to the President (*Hayburn's Case* [2 US (2 Dallas) 409 (1792)]. From this time the distribution of powers always received in the Supreme Court of the United States an interpretation which has ascribed to each department of government an incapacity to receive or to exert any power which according to its essential character was vested by the Constitution in another. "The different classes of power have been apportioned to different departments; and as all derive their authority from the same instrument, there is an implied exclusion of each department from exercising the functions conferred upon the others" (*Cooley's Constitutional Limitations*, 7th ed, ch v, p 126) ...

[91] But it is one thing to adopt and enunciate a basic rule involving a classification and distribution of powers of such an order, and it is another to face and overcome the logical difficulties of defining the power of each organ of government, and the practical and political consequences of an inflexible application of their delimitation. In the first place it was apparent that many things might be **[92]** done in the course of, or as ancillary to, the execution of one power which might also be done in virtue of another. For instance, the ascertainment of a state of facts upon testimony of witnesses may be incident to some executive action and is not confined to the judicial power ... Again, the power to make rules of procedure may be reposed in the Judiciary or exercised by the Legislature ... Further, although it may be true that the formulation of enforceable rules of conduct for the subject or the citizen, because they are considered expedient, is the very characteristic of law-making, yet it has always been found difficult or impossible to deny to the Executive, as a proper incident of its functions, authority to require the subject or the citizen to pursue a course of action which has been determined for him by the exercise of an administrative discretion. But in what does the distinction lie between a law of Congress requiring compliance with directions upon some specified subject which the administration thinks proper to give, and a law investing the administration with authority to legislate upon the same subject? The answer which the decisions of the Supreme Court of the United States supply to this question is formulated in the opinion of that Court delivered by *Taft* CJ in *Hampton & Co v United States* [276 US 394 at 406-7 (1928)]:– "It is a breach of the National fundamental law if Congress gives up its legislative power and transfers it to the President, or to the Judicial Branch, or if by law it attempts to invest itself or its members with either executive power or judicial power. This is not to say that the three branches are not co-ordinate parts of one government and that each in the field of duties may not invoke the action of the two other branches in so far as the action invoked shall not be an assumption of the constitutional field of action of another branch. In determining what it may do in seeking assistance from another branch, the extent and character of that assistance must be fixed according to common sense and the inherent necessities of the governmental co-ordination. The field of Congress involves all and many varieties of legislative action, and Congress has found it frequently **[93]** necessary to use officers of the Executive Branch, within defined limits, to secure the exact effect intended by its acts of legislation, by vesting discretion in such officers to make public regulations interpreting a statute and directing the details of its execution, even to the extent of providing for penalizing a breach of such regulations ... Congress may feel itself unable conveniently to determine exactly when its exercise of the legislative power should become effective, because dependent on future conditions, and it may leave the determination of such time to the decision of an Executive, or, as often happens in matters of State legislation, it may be left to a popular vote of the residents of a district to be affected by the legislation." He then quotes an often cited passage of another judgment [*Cincinnati, W & Z Railroad Co v Clinton County Commissioners*, 1 Ohio St 77 at 88 (1852)]:– "The true distinction, therefore, is, between the delegation of power to make the law, which necessarily involves a discretion as to what it shall be, and conferring an authority or discretion as to its execution, to be exercised under and in pursuance of the law. The first cannot be done; to the latter no valid objection can be made."

In *Mutual Film Corporation v Industrial Commission of Ohio* [236 US 230 at 245 (1915)] the vagueness of the principle is acknowledged, but its limits are restated thus:– "While administration and legislation are quite distinct powers, the line which separates ... their exercise is not easy to define in words. It is best recognized in illustrations. Undoubtedly the Legislature must declare the policy of the law and fix the legal principles which are to control in given cases: but an administrative body may be invested with the power to ascertain the facts and conditions to which the policy and principles apply. If this could not be done there would be infinite confusion in the laws, and in an effort to detail and to particularize, they would miss sufficiency both in provision and execution."

The latitude of application which such doctrines allow is evident. Indeed, one speculative writer has said: "The Courts have never had any criterion of validity except that of reasonableness, the common refuge of thought and expression in the face of undeveloped or unascertainable standards" ... And *Holmes* J, in a dissenting **[94]** opinion in *Springer v Government of the Phillipine Islands* [277 US 189 (1928)], has doubtless lent support to the notion that many of the consequences of the separation of powers are avoided in substance, although acknowledged in form ...

But in any case no decision of the Supreme Court of the United States, of which I am aware, allows Congress to empower the Executive to make regulations or ordinances which may overreach existing statutes.

Dixon J noted that the American doctrine had been complicated by the operation of the maxim *delegatus non potest delegare* ("a delegate may not itself delegate"), which "**[94]** has no application to the Australian Constitution". He then turned to the Australian position.

Dixon J: [96] When they adopted the distribution of powers which they found in the Constitution of the United States, the framers of the Constitution of the Commonwealth of Australia were, of course, by no means unaware of the significance given to the distribution and of the consequences flowing from it. But an independent consideration of the provisions of the Commonwealth Constitution unaided by any such knowledge cannot but suggest that it was intended to confine to each of the three departments of government the exercise of the power with which it is invested by the Constitution, the doing of that which can be done in virtue only of the possession of such a power. The arrangement of the Constitution and the emphatic words in which the three powers are vested by secs 1, 61 and 71 combine with the careful and elaborate provisions constituting or defining the repositories of the respective powers to provide evidence of the intention with which the powers were apportioned and the organs of government separated and described.

He considered the cases in which the High Court had insisted on a strict separation of judicial power: *New South Wales v Commonwealth* (*Wheat Case*) (1915) 20 CLR 54, *Waterside Workers' Federation of Australia v JW Alexander Ltd* (1918) 25 CLR 434, and *British Imperial Oil Co v Federal Commissioner of Taxation* (1925) 35 CLR 422 (see Chapter 14, §1).

Dixon J: [97] From these authorities it appears that, because of the distribution of the functions of government and of the manner in which the **[98]** Constitution describes the tribunals to be invested with the judicial power of the Commonwealth, and defines the judicial power to be invested in them, the Parliament is restrained both from reposing any power essentially judicial in any other organ or body, and from reposing any other than that judicial power in such tribunals. The same or analogous considerations apply to the provisions which vest the legislative power of the Commonwealth in the Parliament, describe the constitution of the Legislature and define the legislative power. Does it follow that in the exercise of that power the Parliament is restrained from reposing any power essentially legislative in another organ or body? In *Baxter v Ah Way* [(1909) 8 CLR 626] legislation of the Parliament was upheld conferring upon the Executive authority by proclamation to include goods in the category of prohibited imports. The maxim *Delegatus non potest delegare* was held to afford no ground of objection, and the plenary nature of the legislative power was emphasized. The separation of powers was not expressly mentioned ...

No further opportunity of dealing with the question seems to have occurred in this Court until a succession of cases arising out of regulations made under sec 4 of the *War Precautions Act* 1914-1916 were decided. But in none of them does the objection appear to have been raised that a legislative power had been given to the Executive which was not permitted because of the distribution of powers contained in the Constitution. Soon afterwards, however, a case was decided in which reliance was placed on the objection.

In *Roche v Kronheimer* [(1921) 29 CLR 329] the Court upheld the validity of sec 2 of the *Treaty of Peace Act* 1913, which empowered the Executive to make such regulations as appeared to it to be necessary for **[99]** carrying out or giving effect to the economic clauses of the Treaty of Versailles. In answer to an attack upon the regulation based upon the constitutional distribution of powers, the judgment of the Court, except *Higgins* J, said [29 CLR at 337]:– "It is enough to say that the validity of legislation in this form has been upheld in *Farey v Burvett* [(1916) 21 CLR 433]; *Pankhurst v Kiernan* [(1917) 24 CLR 120]; *Ferrano v Pearce* [(1918) 25 CLR 241]; and *Sickerdick v Ashton* [(1918) 25 CLR 506]." In none of these cases was the effect of the distribution of powers raised for consideration, although in three of them ... an argument raising it would have been relevant, and in two of these some difficulty might have been felt in treating the authority which had been exercised by the Executive as anything less than legislative. But the strength in time of war of the defence power, the exceptional nature of which had been much enlarged upon in *Farey v Burvett*, might conceivably have enabled the Court to confess and avoid an argument based upon the general doctrine of the separation of powers ...

The decision in *Kronheimer's Case* itself might also be reached without any denial of a constitutional rule confining to the Parliament any exercise of power which, apart from its subordinate character, would be essentially legislative. It might well be thought that no infringement of such a rule had been attempted by the enactment then in question, which left to the Executive the task of imposing upon the subject the legal duty of acting in conformity with an arrangement elaborately formulated in the Treaty. I think it certain that such a provision would be supported in America, and the passage in *Burah's Case* [(1878) 3 App Cas 889 at 906] appears to apply to it, in which **[100]** the Judicial Committee deny that in fact any delegation there took place. But sec 3 of the *Transport Workers Act* cannot, in my opinion, be regarded as doing less than authorizing the Executive to perform a function which, if not subordinate, would be essentially legislative. It gives the Governor-General in Council a complete, although, of course, a subordinate power, over a large and by no means unimportant subject, in the exercise of which he is free to determine from time to time the ends to be achieved and the policy to be pursued as well as the means to be adopted. Within the limits of the subject matter, his will is unregulated and his discretion unguided. Moreover, the power may be exercised in disregard of other existing statutes, the provisions of which concerning the same subject matter may be overridden.

When, at the beginning of this year, a regulation made under sec 3 of the *Transport Workers Act* came before us in *Huddart Parker Ltd v Commonwealth* [(1931) 44 CLR 492], the attack upon the validity of the section was based rather upon the scope of the commerce power, and but little reliance was placed upon the legislative character of the power conferred upon the Executive. But in the judgments of *Starke* J and of *Evatt* J and in my own judgment, with which *Rich* J expressed his agreement, the question was stated whether it was within the power of the Parliament to make a law which, in the language of *Starke* J [44 CLR at 506] "prescribes no rule in relation to such employment: it remits the whole matter to the regulation of the Governor in Council"; and the answer given by each of us was that *Roche v Kronheimer* decided that it is within the power of Parliament to do so. A reconsideration of the matter has confirmed my opinion that the judgment of the Court in that case does so mean to decide. It may be true that the nature of the case and the authorities cited as the ground of the decision are consistent with the explanation that it did no more than illustrate the potency of the defence power. But I think that the judgment really meant that the time had passed for assigning to the constitutional distribution of powers among the separate organs of government, an operation which confined the legislative power to the Parliament **[101]** so as to restrain it from reposing in the Executive an authority of an essentially legislative character. I, therefore, retain the opinion which I expressed in the earlier case that *Roche v Kronheimer* did decide that a statute conferring upon the Executive a power to legislate upon some matter contained within one of the subjects of the legislative power of the Parliament is a law with respect to that subject, and that the distribution of legislative, executive and judicial powers in the Constitution does not operate to restrain the power of the Parliament to make such a law. This does not mean that a law confiding authority to the Executive will be valid, however extensive or vague the subject matter may be, if it does not fall outside the boundaries of Federal power. There may be such a width or such an uncertainty of the subject matter to be handed over that the enactment attempting it is not a law with respect to any particular head or heads of legislative power. Nor does it mean that the distribution of powers can supply no considerations of weight affecting the validity of an Act creating a legislative authority … The interpretation by this Court of Chapter III of the Constitution and that of Chapters I and II which has now been adopted in view of *Roche v Kronheimer*, may appear to involve an inconsistency or, at least, an asymmetry, and there are not wanting those who think a course of judicial decision no sufficient warrant for anything so unsatisfactory. But the explanation should be sought not in a want of uniformity in the application to the different organs of government of the consequences of the division of powers among them, but in the ascertainment of the nature of the power which that division prevents the Legislature from handing over. It may be acknowledged that the manner in which the Constitution accomplished the separation of powers does logically or theoretically make the Parliament the exclusive repository of the legislative power of the Commonwealth. The existence in Parliament of power to authorize subordinate legislation may be ascribed to a conception of that legislative power which depends less upon juristic analysis **[102]** and perhaps more upon the history and usages of British legislation and the theories of English law. In English law much weight has been given to the dependence of subordinate legislation for its efficacy, not only on the enactment, but upon the continuing operation of the statute by which it is so authorised. The statute is conceived to be the source of obligation and the expression of the continuing will of the Legislature. Minor consequences of such a doctrine are found in the rule that offences against subordinate regulation are offences against the statute … and the rule that upon the repeal of the statute, the regulation fails … Major consequences are suggested by the emphasis laid in *Powell's Case* [(1885) 10 App Cas 282] and in *Hodge's Case* [(1883) 9 App Cas 117] upon the retention by the Legislature of the whole of its power of control and of its capacity to take the matter back into its own hands. After the long history of parliamentary delegation in Britain and the British colonies, it may be right to treat subordinate legislation which remains under parliamentary control as lacking the independent and unqualified authority which is an attribute of true legislative power, at any rate when there has been an attempt to confer any very general legislative capacity. But, whatever may be its rationale, we should now adhere to the interpretation which results from the decision of *Roche v Kronheimer*.

The decision that s 3 was valid cleared the way for an even more difficult puzzle concerning the effects of Senate disallowance. The chronology was as follows:

1. The *Waterside Employment Regulations*, which required the preferential hiring of trade union members, were made and gazetted on 26 June 1931.
2. The appellant company breached the regulations on 17 July 1931.
3. A summons was issued on 20 July 1931, with the case being heard by a magistrate on 24 July 1931 and the company being convicted.
4. On 29 July 1931, the regulations were disallowed by the Senate.

Under the *Acts Interpretation Act* as it then stood, any regulation thus disallowed "shall thereupon cease to have effect" (see now s 45 of the *Legislative Instruments Act*). However, as Dixon J analysed the chain of events, the regulations were validly in force from the time of their making on 26 June 1931 until the time of their disallowance on 29 July 1931. Therefore, on 24 July 1931, the company was duly convicted under a law then in force. Thus, at the time of the conviction, that conviction was valid and the High Court appeal had to be dismissed.

3. The Governor-General

In Australia, the Queen is represented in each State by its Governor and at the Commonwealth level by the Governor-General. Section 2 of the Constitution states that the Governor-General "shall have and may exercise in the Commonwealth during the Queen's pleasure, but subject to this Constitution, such powers and functions of the Queen as Her Majesty may be pleased to assign to him". These matters, including instructions issued by the monarch to the Governor-General, are dealt with in the *Letters Patent Relating to the Office of Governor-General of the*

Commonwealth of Australia, issued by the monarch under the prerogative power. The current Letters Patent were issued in 1984 (see Commonwealth *Gazette*, S 334, 24 August 1984).

Other than the statement in s 2 that "A Governor General appointed by the Queen shall be Her Majesty's representative in the Commonwealth", the Constitution says nothing about how the Governor-General is to be selected or the circumstances in which he or she can be dismissed. These matters are governed by unwritten constitutional convention (see Chapter 3, §4(d)). The current convention was settled in 1930, when an Imperial Conference resolved that, in appointing a Governor-General, the King "should act on the advice of His Majesty's ministers in the Dominion concerned". The resolution settled the public controversy that erupted after King George V initially refused to accept the Australian Prime Minister's advice that Sir Isaac Isaacs, then Chief Justice of the High Court, be appointed as Governor-General (see Zelman Cowen, *Isaacs Isaacs* (Oxford University Press, 1967), 191-207). It would follow from the convention regarding appointment that the monarch would be similarly bound to act on the advice of the Australian Prime Minister on any question relating to the dismissal of a Governor-General, though in fact no Governor-General of Australia has ever been dismissed.

The conventions came under fresh scrutiny amid the controversy that enveloped Dr Peter Hollingworth as Governor-General from 2001 to 2003. Allegations that he was unfit for the office were based in part on a finding by a Board of Inquiry that, before becoming Governor-General, he had as Archbishop of Brisbane allowed a priest to remain in the ministry after a confession of sexual abuse (*Report of the Board of Inquiry into Past Handling of Complaints of Sexual Abuse in the Anglican Church Diocese of Brisbane* (2003), tabled in the Queensland Parliament on 1 May 2003). Despite an apology and an admission that he had made a serious error of judgment, the view that he should resign was endorsed by a significant body of public opinion (76 per cent in one poll), as well as by the Leader of the Opposition, Simon Crean. Hollingworth resigned on 23 May 2003. The Letters Patent had first been amended (Commonwealth *Special Gazette*, S 151, 15 May 2003) to enable Sir Guy Green, the Governor of Tasmania, to act in the role until a new Governor-General was appointed.

George Winterton, "The Hollingworth Experiment"
(2003) 14 *Public Law Review* 139

[139] The appointment of Anglican Archbishop of Brisbane Peter Hollingworth as the 23rd Governor-General of Australia in June 2001 was unexpected, unconventional, and probably something of an experiment. When Hollingworth was effectively forced to resign after serving less than two years of his five-year term, the experiment was clearly seen to have failed. Yet the Hollingworth experiment sheds significant light on the office of Governor-General and the areas where it is deficient …

[140] The office of Governor-General has no prescribed "job description", nor is there universal agreement regarding its occupant's appropriate role. Many Australians, for example, consider Sir [141] William Deane an exemplary Governor-General, but there are also many who criticise him as unduly "activist" and consider the more restrained Sir Zelman Cowen (1977-1982) and Sir Ninian Stephen (1982-1989) as more appropriate exemplars. In earlier years, even after occupancy was confined to Australians following the appointment of Lord Casey (1965-1969), the office was rather remote; to the general public the Governor-General was a rather shadowy figure glimpsed at Anzac Day or Australia Day celebrations or the Melbourne Cup, but few understood the role. That changed after Sir John Kerr dismissed the Whitlam Government in November 1975, but after Kerr's departure in 1977 the office again subsided into semi-invisibility. That changed during the term of Sir William Deane (1996-2001) for several reasons. First, an unfortunate series of national disasters – Port Arthur, Black Hawk, the Interlaken canyoners and Childers – demonstrated the Governor-General's ability to represent the nation in a non-partisan manner, especially in an era of cynicism towards politicians. Secondly, Deane's focus on Aboriginal justice and reconciliation at a time when the Howard Government was de-emphasising these issues brought him unprecedented national attention. Thirdly, as part of [their] campaign against the republic,

monarchists exaggerated the significance of the office of Governor-General to bolster their claim that Australia already had an Australian Head of State – the Governor-General. (The monarch who appointed him was merely "The Sovereign".) These factors combined to emphasise the importance of the office and the necessity for its occupant to be morally unimpeachable, which worked to Hollingworth's detriment. The appointment of Major-General Michael Jeffery – a worthy but low profile appointee – as Hollingworth's successor could be interpreted as an attempt once again to alter expectations of the office …

[145] The principal lesson is that a Governor-General cannot survive in office without the confidence of the Australian people. Australians regard the Governor-General as their effective Head of State, partly due to the populist activism of Sir William Deane and monarchist arguments that the Governor-General is Australia's actual Head of State. The office is regarded as socially important and receives increasing media scrutiny, which helps to make it accountable to the people. Hollingworth's defenders claimed that he was the victim of a media "witch-hunt", but on this occasion the media reflected widespread community sentiment. There are two reasons why a Governor-General cannot survive in office against overwhelming public opposition. Probably the lesser reason is that a Governor-General cannot fulfil the office's role of national unifier and conscience without public support. The principal reason is that since the Governor-General's tenure lies in the Prime Minister's hands, public opposition to the Governor-General's continuation in office will eventually rebound on the Prime Minister, who will ultimately be forced to urge the Governor-General to resign.

The second lesson of the Hollingworth affair is that it is unsatisfactory that the *Constitution* is largely silent on the method of appointment and removal and the qualifications of the Governor-General. It merely provides that the Queen appoints the Governor-General who holds office "during [her] pleasure". It does not require Governors-General to be Australian, and until 1965 they were not, with the exception of two Labor appointments (Sir Isaac Isaacs (1931-1936) and Sir William McKell (1947-1953)).

While Governors-General fulfilled the dual role of effective local Head of State and British Ambassador (1901-1926), it was appropriate that they should be British and be appointed by the British Government (by the Colonial, later Dominions, Secretary through the monarch). Dominion Prime Ministers inherited the British Government's role in 1930. Hence the "genius" of our Constitution, much-vaunted by monarchists, whereby the Prime Minister and the Governor-General can each sack the other – a "High Noon" scenario where the outcome depends upon who draws first – is an accident of history, not a carefully constructed "check and balance".

Much of the day-to-day work of the Governor-General involves ceremony. As the Commander in Chief of Australia's military forces under s 68 of the Constitution, he or she attends military parades as well as national events such as Anzac Day. The Governor-General also receives visiting heads of state, opens sessions of the federal Parliament and receives the credentials of Ambassadors appointed to represent their nations in Australia. The Constitution also confers a number of non-ceremonial functions, including the powers to dissolve, prorogue and summon Parliament (s 5), exercise the executive power of the Commonwealth (s 61) and submit a proposed change to the Constitution to the people voting at a referendum (s 128).

Such powers are exercised by the Governor-General acting upon the advice of his or her ministers – sometimes because the Constitution confers the relevant power on the "Governor-General in Council" (meaning the Federal Executive Council referred to in ss 62 and 63 of the Constitution as providing such advice), but in other cases because of convention. However, the Governor-General is not limited to the passive acceptance of advice. As Wilson J stated in *FAI Insurances Ltd v Winneke* (1982) 151 CLR 342: "**[401]** He may be described as a rubber stamp, in the sense that his executive acts are based, and necessarily based, on the advice that he is given. But his responsibility is to administer the executive government, and to do so with integrity, discretion and a complete absence of political partiality. Bagehot's famous observation, that 'the sovereign has, under a constitutional monarchy such as ours, three rights – the right to be consulted, the right to encourage, the right to warn.' …, is still good law and good constitutional practice".

There are exceptions to the convention that the Governor-General should only act on advice. These are the "reserve powers", which the Governor-General can exercise in the absence of, or even contrary to, such advice. For example, in some circumstances the Governor-General may have an independent discretion to decide whom to appoint as Prime Minister – though in the normal situation where the government has lost an election, convention requires that the outgoing Prime Minister advise that the leader of the winning party be appointed as his successor, and in any genuinely doubtful case where a real discretion arises, the Governor-General should be guided as far as possible by the strengths of the rival parties in the popularly-elected House of Representatives. A clearer case of vice-regal discretion is the power to dismiss a Prime Minister who has lost a vote of confidence in that House but refuses to resign, though this situation too is generally governed by convention. There may also be a reserve power to dismiss the Prime Minister in other circumstances, but the grounds on which such a power might properly be exercised have remained controversial.

Republic Advisory Committee, *An Australian Republic: The Options*
(AGPS, The Report of the Republic Advisory Committee, 1993), vol 2

[256] The dismissal of a Prime Minister is the most dramatic and controversial of all exercises of reserve powers and is therefore regarded as 'a recourse of last resort, an ultimate weapon which is liable to destroy its user'. At least partly for that reason, there are very few precedents. No British Prime Minister has been dismissed by a monarch at least since 1834; and the development of representative democracy since then makes that precedent of very doubtful value. In a case decided in 1963 [*Adegbenro v Akintola* [1963] AC 614 at 631], the Privy Council noted that the dismissal of a British Prime Minister was 'not treated as being within the scope of practical politics'. Five Canadian Provincial governments were dismissed between 1878 and 1903; however, by the 1930s, 'the popular view, if not the [257] conventional wisdom, in Canada, was that the Governor-General's reserve powers had become little more than a constitutional Cheshire Cat: nothing remained but the smile'. In Australia the power to dismiss a government has been exercised twice. Both occasions generated such controversy that it is very doubtful whether they can be regarded as establishing the existence of any convention. They are discussed below.

There are two groups of situations in which, it seems to be accepted, the Governor-General may dismiss a Prime Minister:

- where the Prime Minister has been defeated in the lower House on a vote which is regarded as a vote of no confidence; and
- where the government is persisting in illegal or unconstitutional conduct.

There has been considerable debate in Australia as to whether the Governor-General may dismiss a Prime Minister who is unable to secure the passage of supply bills through the upper House.

No-confidence motion

Where the lower House passes a simple motion of no confidence in the Prime Minister, the convention is that he or she must either resign, thereby terminating the appointments of all other Ministers, or advise the Governor-General to dissolve Parliament (although the incumbent is probably entitled to a reasonable period to attempt to reverse the vote, particularly if the motion has been passed only because members of the incumbent's party or coalition were absent). If the incumbent does not take one or the other of these courses, the Governor-General is entitled to dismiss him or her. Even here, however, it has been stressed that dismissal should occur only if all attempts to induce the Prime Minister to do his or her duty have failed: it is only when others have clearly refused to adhere to convention that it becomes safe for the reserve power to be used to restore constitutional order ...

[258] *Illegality*

It appears to be accepted by commentators that there are circumstances in which a government can be dismissed because it is acting in breach of a fundamental constitutional principle. Professor Winterton argues that the power of dismissal may only be exercised where:

(a) it is clear that the government has 'persisted in breaching a fundamental constitutional provision';

(b) the government has ignored calls from the Governor-General to desist from this conduct; and

(c) the contravention is not 'justiciable' – that is, it cannot be brought before the courts …

[260] The issue of justiciability was raised by the only dismissal on grounds of illegality in Australian history. In the early part of 1932 New South Wales was in a dire financial position and the Labor Premier, Mr Lang, sought to cease making interest payments on the State's debts. The Federal Government took quite drastic steps to attempt to seize the State's revenue in order to discharge that interest liability (including ordering banks to pay to the Commonwealth amounts standing to the credit of the State). In an attempt to evade the Commonwealth scheme the State Government, among other measures, issued a circular ordering its officers to refrain from meeting expenditure by drawing cheques, to forward all moneys collected to the Treasury, and to insist on payments to the Government in cash or by bearer cheques. These orders were in direct conflict with a Commonwealth regulation which purported to order State officers to deal with money collected by them in the manner directed by the Federal Treasurer. On 12 May (a month after the offending orders were given) the Governor, Sir Philip Game, drew the Premier's attention to the conflict and asked that the circular be withdrawn on the basis that, otherwise, the Crown would be 'in the position of breaking the law of the land'. The next day, Friday 13th, the Premier refused to withdraw the circular and, upon being pressed to resign and refusing to do so, was dismissed. The Governor immediately commissioned the Leader of the Opposition, Mr Stevens, who then advised a dissolution of Parliament. In the ensuing election Mr Stevens was returned with a majority.

Although the dismissal took place in a complicated financial and political crisis, the only ground cited by the Governor for his action was the alleged illegality of the circular by reason of its conflict with the Commonwealth regulation. On this basis, the weight of opinion is that the Governor's decision was improper because the question of illegality could have been dealt with by the courts …

[261] *Prime Minister cannot obtain supply*

A refusal by the lower House to pass a supply bill would be regarded as an expression of no confidence in the Government, and would generally lead to resignation or dismissal on that basis. Different questions arise when supply is refused by the upper House (if, as is the case in Australia at the Commonwealth level and in most States, the upper House has power to refuse supply).

The second and best-known exercise of the reserve power of dismissal in Australia was the dismissal of Gough Whitlam's Labor Government by Governor-General Sir John Kerr in 1975 on the ground that it had not been able to obtain supply (the Senate having repeatedly deferred consideration of the Appropriation Bills) and was refusing to resign or advise a dissolution. Kerr appointed the Opposition Leader, Malcolm Fraser, as Prime Minister on the understanding that he could guarantee supply, would immediately advise a dissolution of both Houses and would lead a 'caretaker' government. The propriety of the Governor-General's action has been the subject of strong disagreement ever since, largely along party political lines but also among expert commentators without party affiliations, and in the absence of anything approaching agreement it cannot be said that the dismissal establishes as an accepted convention the power of a Governor-General to dismiss a government that cannot obtain supply. Fraser was, of course, returned with a large majority at the ensuing election. However, since people generally vote according to which government they prefer (which depends on a range of issues) rather than their view of the constitutional niceties, the result of an election which follows a dismissal does not prove anything about the constitutional propriety of the dismissal.

For Kerr it can be argued that government at the Federal level in Australia requires, as Sir Garfield Barwick put it, the 'confidence' of both Houses on supply in the sense that the Government must be able to secure the passage of supply bills through both Houses. The Government was therefore under an obligation to resign. On this view, action by the Governor-General was [262] necessary to resolve a deadlock which was threatening the economic fabric of the nation, and the Governor-General acted properly: he removed a government which was acting improperly and appointed one which would obtain funds for the administration of the country and would let the electorate resolve the deadlock between the Houses by advising a dissolution.

On another view it was wrong of Kerr to dismiss a government which continued to enjoy the confidence of the House of Representatives, the confidence of the Senate never having been regarded under principles of responsible government as a requirement for remaining in office. The Government's refusal to resign might have led to financial disaster, but that was a matter for the Government to explain to the Parliament and the electors, not a matter for the judgment of the Governor-General. Had the Government attempted to stay in office once supply had run out, and in doing so made payments from the Consolidated Revenue Fund without the authority of a parliamentary appropriation, that would have involved a breach of a fundamental constitutional principle (and the express words of section 83) and might well have justified dismissal; but that point had not been reached and, arguably, until that point was reached there was no sound basis for dismissing the Government. Kerr acted while there were still other conceivable options: a political solution to the crisis was still possible and obviously preferable to an exercise of the reserve power. Moreover, since the numbers in the Senate were equal, it was only through good luck that his actions resulted in supply being secured. Finally, he did not warn the Government of his intentions. (Had the Government known of the likelihood of dismissal its approach to events might have been different: it might have preferred to advise a dissolution and face the electors as an incumbent government rather than as a seemingly discredited opposition.) Even if the dismissal of Whitlam was justified in order to obtain an election it is arguable **[263]** that with the House of Representatives having expressed a want of confidence in Fraser, Whitlam should have been recommissioned for the caretaker period.

There is probably no satisfactory solution to the situation which arose in 1975.

What happened on 11 November 1975 was that the Governor-General, Sir John Kerr, dismissed the Whitlam Government in the purported exercise of a reserve power. The incoming caretaker Prime Minister, Malcolm Fraser, was then granted a double dissolution of Parliament under s 57 of the Constitution.

Ian Harris (ed), *House of Representatives Practice*
(AGPS, 5th ed 2005)

[462] The double dissolution of 11 November 1975 differed from earlier double dissolutions. Liberal Prime Minister Fraser who advised the Governor-General to grant a double dissolution had been Prime Minister only for a matter of hours and was not supported by a majority in the House. The bills which had satisfied the requirements of section 57 and which provided the technical grounds for the double dissolution had been introduced by the ALP Government, which had been dismissed from office earlier that day.

From July 1974, when the 29th Parliament commenced, to November 1975, 21 bills were regarded as fulfilling the requirements of section 57, having been twice rejected by the Senate. In addition there was Senate opposition to a considerable number of other government bills.

As with the 1974 double dissolution, the critical event leading up to the double dissolution concerned the passage of bills appropriating revenue for the ordinary annual services of the Government, namely, Appropriation Bills (Nos 1 and 2) 1975-76. It was on these bills that the Houses were in actual deadlock but they were not the bills in respect of which the double dissolution was granted. The deadlock in fact was broken when the Senate finally passed the appropriation bills on 11 November prior to the announcement of the proposed double dissolution ... These bills had been introduced into the House on 19 August 1975 and passed on 8 October. The bills were introduced into the Senate on 14 October. On 16 October the Senate agreed to the following amendment to the motion for the second reading in respect of each of the bills:

> **[463]** ... this Bill be not further proceeded with until the Government agrees to submit itself to the judgment of the people, the Senate being of the opinion that the Prime Minister and his Government no longer have the trust and confidence of the Australian people ...

A similar resolution had been agreed to by the Senate on the Loan Bill 1975 on the previous day. Meanwhile the House agreed to a motion which in part read:

Considering that the actions of the Senate and of the Leader of the Opposition will, if pursued, have the most serious consequences for Parliamentary democracy in Australia, will seriously damage the Government's efforts to counter the effect of world-wide inflation and unemployment, and will thereby cause great hardship for the Australian people:

(1) This House declares that it has full confidence in the Australian Labor Party Government;

(2) This House affirms that the Constitution and the conventions of the Constitution vest in this House the control of the supply of moneys to the elected Government and that the threatened action of the Senate constitutes a gross violation of the roles of the respective Houses of the Parliament in relation to the appropriation of moneys;

(3) This House asserts the basic principle that a Government that continues to have a majority in the House of Representatives has a right to expect that it will be able to govern;

(4) This House condemns the threatened action of the Leader of the Opposition and of the non-government parties in the Senate as being reprehensible and as constituting a grave threat to the principles of responsible government and of Parliamentary democracy in Australia, and

(5) This House calls upon the Senate to pass without delay the Loan Bill 1975, the Appropriation Bill (No 1) 1975-76 and the Appropriation Bill (No 2) 1975-76.

Following the passage of this resolution on 16 October 1975, and receipt of Senate messages communicating its resolutions on the appropriation and loans bills, a series of further messages concerning the bills were exchanged between the Houses:

- on 21 October the House asserted that the Senate's action on the appropriation bills was not contemplated within the terms of the Constitution and was contrary to established constitutional convention. On the same day in considering the Senate's resolution in relation to the loan bill the House resolved that the action of the Senate in delaying the passage of the bill for the reasons given in the Senate's resolution was contrary to the accepted means of financing a major portion of the defence budget and requested the Senate to pass the bill without delay;

- on 22 October the Senate asserted that its action in delaying the bills was a lawful and proper exercise within the terms of the Constitution and added several statements to support this view;

- on 28 October the House, in dealing with the Senate's message, denounced the Senate's action as a 'blatant attempt to violate section 28 of the Constitution for political purposes by itself endeavouring to force an early election for the House of Representatives' and resolved that it would uphold the established right of the Government with a majority in the House of Representatives to be the Government of the nation;

[464]• on 5 November the Senate rejected the House's claims and the House, when dealing with the Senate's reply, declared that the Constitution and its conventions vest in the House the control of the supply of moneys to the elected Government and that the action of the Senate constituted a gross violation of the roles of the respective Houses in relation to the appropriation of moneys. The House further declared its concern that the unprecedented and obstructive stand taken by the Senate in continuing to defer the passage of the bills was undermining public confidence in the parliamentary system of government; and

- a further resolution was agreed to by the Senate on the same day with respect to the Loan Bill 1975 [No 2] in the same terms as that agreed to on the first loan bill on 15 October but was not considered by the House.

Whilst these messages were being exchanged between the Houses, the House, on 22 October, introduced and passed appropriation bills similar to the first bills. Upon receipt of the bills, the Senate again resolved that the bills would not be further proceeded with until the Government agreed to submit itself to the judgment of the people. The Senate resolution on a third set of the bills was transmitted but was not considered by the House.

The Government was not only faced with the problem of continuing conflict with the Senate in respect of its legislative program. By early November, the moneys provided by the supply bills to maintain the public services of the country for the first five months of the financial year, pending the passage of the main appropriation bills, were becoming depleted and there were indications that there would be insufficient moneys to meet the necessary commitments of the Government at some time prior to 30 November.

A motion of want of confidence in the Government had been moved on 29 October and defeated and on 6 November, four sitting days later, Leader of the Opposition Fraser gave notice of a motion of censure of the Government based on the consequences of the appropriation bills failing to pass both Houses.

The next sitting day, 11 November, produced a sudden and dramatic climax of events. The Government allowed precedence to the motion of censure to which Prime Minister Whitlam moved an amendment censuring Leader of the Opposition Fraser.

During the lunch suspension Mr Whitlam went to Government House for a prearranged meeting with Governor-General Kerr. Mr Whitlam intended to advise His Excellency to approve an election for half the Senate, which was due in any case before 30 June 1976. During the course of the meeting the Governor-General terminated Mr Whitlam's commission as Prime Minister. The following is the text of the letter of dismissal:

[465] Government House
Canberra 2600
11 November 1975

Dear Mr Whitlam

In accordance with section 64 of the Constitution I hereby determine your appointment as my Chief Adviser and Head of the Government. It follows that I also hereby determine the appointments of all of the Ministers in your Government.

You have previously told me that you would never resign or advise an election of the House of Representatives or a double dissolution and that the only way in which such an election could be obtained would be by my dismissal of you and your ministerial colleagues. As it appeared likely that you would today persist in this attitude I decided that, if you did, I would determine your commission and state my reasons for doing so. You have persisted in your attitude and I have accordingly acted as indicated. I attach a statement of my reasons which I intend to publish immediately.

It is with a great deal of regret that I have taken this step both in respect of yourself and your colleagues.

I propose to send for the Leader of the Opposition and to commission him to form a new caretaker government until an election can be held.

Yours sincerely
(signed John R Kerr)

The Honourable E G Whitlam QC MP

At 2.34 that afternoon Mr Fraser announced to the House that the Governor-General had commissioned him to form a Government. The Governor-General informed the Speaker by letter that he had that day determined the appointment of Mr Whitlam and had commissioned and administered the oath of office to Mr Fraser as Prime Minister. In accepting the commission Prime Minister Fraser made the following undertakings in a letter to the Governor-General:

... I confirm that I have given you an assurance that I shall immediately seek to secure the passage of the Appropriation Bills which are at present before the Senate, thus ensuring Supply for the carrying on of the Public Service in all its branches. I further confirm that, upon the granting of Supply, I shall immediately recommend to Your Excellency the dissolution of both Houses of this Parliament.

My Government will act as a caretaker government and will make no appointments or dismissals or initiate new policies before a general election is held.

A few minutes before Mr Fraser made his announcement in the House, the Senate had passed the main appropriation bills. Following Mr Fraser's announcement, the House agreed to the following motion by Mr Whitlam:

That this House expresses its want of confidence in the Prime Minister and requests Mr Speaker forthwith to advise his Excellency the Governor-General to call the Honourable Member for Werriwa [Mr Whitlam] to form a Government.

In speaking to his motion Mr Whitlam stated:

There is no longer a deadlock on the Budget between the House of Representatives and the Senate. The Budget Bills have been passed. Accordingly, the Government which twice has been elected by the people is able to govern. Furthermore, as has been demonstrated this afternoon, the parties which the Prime Minister leads do not have a majority in the House of Representatives. The party I lead has a majority in the House of Representatives. It has never been defeated in the year and a half since the last election and in those circumstances it is appropriate, I believe, that you, Mr Speaker, should forthwith advise the Governor-General – waiting upon him forthwith to advise him – that the party I lead has the confidence of the House of Representatives, and you should apprise His **[466]** Excellency of the view of the House that I have the confidence of the House and should be called to form His Excellency's Government.

At 3.15pm the Speaker suspended the sitting and sought an appointment with the Governor-General to convey to him the terms of the House's resolution. An appointment was made for the Speaker to see the Governor-General at 4.45pm. At 4.30pm the Governor-General dissolved both Houses and at 4.45pm the double dissolution proclamation, in accordance with practice, was read by the Governor-General's Official Secretary on the steps of Parliament House. The sittings of the Houses did not resume. The double dissolution proclamation was signed before the Speaker was able to see the Governor-General and present the House's resolution to him …

On the following day Mr Scholes, as Speaker, wrote to the Queen expressing his serious concern that:

… the failure of the Governor-General to withdraw Mr Fraser's commission and his decision to delay seeing me as Speaker of the House of Representatives until after the dissolution of the Parliament had been proclaimed were acts contrary to the proper exercise of the Royal prerogative and constituted an act of contempt for the House of Representatives. It is improper that your representative should continue to impose a Prime Minister on Australia in whom the House of Representatives has expressed its lack of confidence and who has not on any substantial resolution been able to command a majority of votes on the floor of the House of Representatives.

It is my belief that to maintain in office a Prime Minister imposed on the nation by Royal prerogative rather than through parliamentary endorsement constitutes a danger to our parliamentary system and will damage the standing of your representatives in Australia and even yourself.

I would ask that you act in order to restore Mr Whitlam to office as Prime Minister in accordance with the expressed resolution of the House of Representatives …

On 17 November the Queen's Private Secretary, at the command of Her Majesty, replied that:

… the Australian Constitution firmly places the prerogative powers of the Crown in the hands of the Governor-General as the representative of The Queen of Australia. The only person competent to commission an Australian Prime Minister is the Governor-General and The Queen has no part in the decisions which the Governor-General must take in accordance with the Constitution. Her Majesty, as Queen of Australia, is watching events in Canberra with close interest and attention, but it would not be proper for her to intervene in person in matters which are so clearly placed within the jurisdiction of the Governor-General by the Constitution Act.

The election was held on 13 December 1975 and the Liberal-Country Party coalition gained a majority of seats in both Houses. None of the bills which formed the technical grounds for double dissolution was reintroduced by the new Government.

Earlier editions of the *House of Representatives Practice* included the full texts of the following documents:

Statement by the Governor-General, 11 November 1975
in JA Pettifer (ed), *House of Representatives Practice* (AGPS, 1981)

[58] I have given careful consideration to the constitutional crisis and have made some decisions which I wish to explain.

Summary

It has been necessary for me to find a democratic and constitutional solution to the current crisis which will permit the people of Australia to decide as soon as possible what should be the outcome of the deadlock which developed over supply between the two Houses of Parliament and between the Government and the Opposition parties. The only solution consistent with the Constitution and with my oath of office and my responsibilities, authority and duty as Governor-General is to terminate the commission as Prime Minister of Mr Whitlam and to arrange for a caretaker government able to secure supply and willing to let the issue go to the people.

I shall summarise the elements of the problem and the reasons for my decision which places the matter before the people of Australia for prompt determination.

Because of the federal nature of our Constitution and because of its provisions the Senate undoubtedly has constitutional power to refuse or defer supply to the Government. Because of the principles of responsible government a Prime Minister who cannot obtain supply, including money for carrying on the ordinary services of government, must either advise a general election or resign. If he refuses to do this I have the authority and indeed the duty under the Constitution to withdraw his Commission as Prime Minister. The position in Australia is quite different from the position in the United Kingdom. Here the confidence of both Houses on supply is necessary to ensure its provision. In the United Kingdom the confidence of the House of Commons alone is necessary. But both here and in the United Kingdom the duty of the Prime Minister is the same in a most important respect – if he cannot get supply he must resign or advise an election.

If a Prime Minister refuses to resign or to advise an election, and this is the case with Mr Whitlam, my constitutional authority and duty require me to do what I have now done – to withdraw his commission – and to invite the Leader of the Opposition to form a caretaker government – that is one that makes no appointments or dismissals and initiates no policies until a general election is held. It is most desirable that he should guarantee supply. Mr Fraser will be asked to give the necessary undertakings and advise whether he is prepared to recommend a double dissolution. He will also be asked to guarantee supply.

The decisions I have made were made after I was satisfied that Mr Whitlam could not obtain supply. No other decision open to me would enable the Australian people to decide for themselves what should be done.

Once I had made up my mind, for my own part, what I must do if Mr Whitlam persisted in his stated intentions I consulted the Chief Justice of Australia, Sir Garfield Barwick. I have his permission to say that I consulted him in this way.

The result is that there will be an early election for both Houses and the people can do what, in a democracy such as ours, is their responsibility and duty and theirs alone. It is for the people now to decide the issue which the two leaders have failed to settle.

Detailed Statements of Decisions

On 16 October the Senate deferred consideration of Appropriation Bills (Nos 1 & 2) 1975-76. In the time which elapsed since then events have made it clear that the Senate was determined to refuse to grant supply to the Government. In that time the Senate on no less than two occasions resolved to proceed no further with fresh Appropriation Bills, in identical terms, which had been passed by the House of Representatives. The determination of the Senate to maintain its refusal to grant supply was confirmed by the public statements made by the Leader of the Opposition, the Opposition having control of the Senate.

[59] By virtue of what has in fact happened there therefore came into existence a deadlock between the House of Representatives and the Senate on the central issue of supply without which all the ordinary services of the government cannot be maintained. I had the benefit of discussions with the Prime Minister and, with his approval, with the Leader of the Opposition and with the Treasurer and the Attorney-General. As a result of those discussions and having regard to the

public statements of the Prime Minister and the Leader of the Opposition I have come regretfully to the conclusion that there is no likelihood of a compromise between the House of Representatives and the Senate nor for that matter between the Government and the Opposition.

The deadlock which arose was one which, in the interests of the nation, had to be resolved as promptly as possible and by means which are appropriate in our democratic system. In all the circumstances which have occurred the appropriate means is a dissolution of the Parliament and an election for both Houses. No other course offers a sufficient assurance of resolving the deadlock and resolving it promptly.

Parliamentary control of appropriation and accordingly of expenditure is a fundamental feature of our system of responsible government. In consequence it has been generally accepted that a government which has been denied supply by the Parliament cannot govern. So much at least is clear in cases where a ministry is refused supply by a popularly elected Lower House. In other systems where an Upper House is denied the right to reject a money bill denial of supply can occur only at the instance of the Lower House. When, however, an Upper House possesses the power to reject a money bill including an appropriation bill, and exercises the power by denying supply, the principle that a government which has been denied supply by the Parliament should resign or go to an election must still apply – it is a necessary consequence of Parliamentary control of appropriation and expenditure and of the expectation that the ordinary and necessary services of government will continue to be provided.

The Constitution combines the two elements of responsible government and federalism. The Senate is, like the House, a popularly elected chamber. It was designed to provide representation by States, not by electorates, and was given by Sec 53 equal powers with the House with respect to proposed laws, except in the respects mentioned in the section. It was denied power to originate or amend appropriation bills but was left with power to reject them or defer consideration of them. The Senate accordingly has the power and has exercised the power to refuse to grant supply to the Government. The Government stands in the position that it has been denied supply by the Parliament with all the consequences which flow from that fact.

There have been public discussions about whether there is a convention deriving from the principles of responsible government that the Senate must never under any circumstances exercise the power to reject an appropriation bill. The Constitution must prevail over any convention because, in determining the question how far the conventions of responsible government have been grafted on to the federal compact, the Constitution itself must in the end control the situation.

Sec 57 of the Constitution provides a mean, perhaps the usual means, of resolving a disagreement between the Houses with respect to a proposed law. But the machinery which it provides necessarily entails a considerable time lag which is quite inappropriate to a speedy resolution of the fundamental problems posed by the refusal of supply. Its presence in the Constitution does not cut down the reserve powers of the Governor-General.

I should be surprised if the Law Officers expressed the view that there is no reserve power in the Governor-General to dismiss a Ministry which has been refused supply by the Parliament and to commission a Ministry, as a caretaker ministry which will secure supply and recommend a dissolution, including where appropriate a double dissolution. This is a matter on which my own mind is quite clear and I am acting in accordance with my own clear view of the principles laid down by the Constitution and of the nature, powers and responsibility of my office.

There is one other point. There has been discussion of the possibility that a half-Senate election might be held under circumstances in which the Government has not obtained **[60]** supply. If such advice were given to me I should feel constrained to reject it because a half-Senate election held whilst supply continues to be denied does not guarantee a prompt or sufficiently clear prospect of the deadlock being resolved in accordance with proper principles. When I refer to rejection of such advice I mean that, as I would find it necessary in the circumstances I have envisaged to determine Mr Whitlam's commission and, as things have turned out have done so, he would not be Prime Minister and not able to give or persist with such advice.

The announced proposals about financing public servants, suppliers, contractors and others do not amount to a satisfactory alternative to supply.

Sir Garfield Barwick, Letter of Advice to the Governor-General
in JA Pettifer (ed), *House of Representatives Practice* (AGPS, 1st ed 1981)

[60] Dear Sir John

In response to Your Excellency's invitation I attended this day at Admiralty House. In our conversation I indicated that I considered myself, as Chief Justice of Australia, free, on Your Excellency's request, to offer you legal advice as to Your Excellency's constitutional rights and duties in relation to an existing situation which, of its nature, was unlikely to come before the Court. We both clearly understood that I was not in any way concerned with matters of a purely political kind, or with any political consequences of the advice I might give.

In response to Your Excellency's request for my legal advice as to whether a course on which you had determined was consistent with your constitutional authority and duty, I respectfully offer the following.

The Constitution of Australia is a federal Constitution which embodies the principle of Ministerial responsibility. The Parliament consists of two houses, the House of Representatives and the Senate, each popularly elected, and each with the same legislative power, with the one exception that the Senate may not originate nor amend a money bill.

Two relevant constitutional consequences flow from this structure of the Parliament. First, the Senate has constitutional power to refuse to pass a money bill; it has power to refuse supply to the Government of the day. Secondly, a Prime Minister who cannot ensure supply to the Crown, including funds for carrying on the ordinary services of Government must either advise a general election (of a kind which the constitutional situation may then allow) or resign. If, being unable to secure supply, he refuses to take either course, Your Excellency has constitutional authority to withdraw his Commission as Prime Minister.

There is no analogy in respect of a Prime Minister's duty between the situation of the Parliament under the federal Constitution of Australia and the relationship between the House of Commons, a popularly elected body, and the House of Lords, a non-elected body in the unitary form of Government functioning in the United Kingdom. Under that system, a Government having the confidence of the House of Commons can secure supply, despite a recalcitrant House of Lords. But it is otherwise under our federal Constitution. A Government having the confidence of the House of Representatives but not that of the Senate, both elected Houses, cannot secure supply to the Crown.

But there is an analogy between the situation of a Prime Minister who has lost the confidence of the House of Commons and a Prime Minister who does not have the confidence of the Parliament, ie of the House of Representatives and of the Senate. The duty and responsibility of the Prime Minister to the Crown in each case is the same: if unable to secure supply to the Crown, to resign or to advise an election.

In the event that, conformably to this advice, the Prime Minister ceases to retain his Commission, Your Excellency's constitutional authority and duty would be to invite the Leader of the Opposition, if he can undertake to secure supply, to form a caretaker government (ie one which makes no appointments or initiates any policies) pending a general [61] election, whether of the House of Representatives, or of both Houses of the Parliament, as that Government may advise.

Accordingly, my opinion is that, if Your Excellency is satisfied in the current situation that the present Government is unable to secure supply, the course upon which Your Excellency has determined is consistent with your constitutional authority and duty.

Yours respectfully
(sgnd Garfield Barwick)

4. Control of the Executive

There are many mechanisms for keeping the executive in check. These include controls imposed by the executive upon itself, such as codes of conduct issued (and enforced) by a Prime Minister to regulate the behaviour of his or her ministers. Other forms of accountability include laws such as the *Freedom of Information Act 1982* (Cth), as well as the scrutiny provided by officers appointed under statute such as the Ombudsman (*Ombudsman Act 1976* (Cth)) and Auditor-General (*Auditor-General Act 1997* (Cth)), and by bodies like the Human Rights and Equal Opportunities Commission (*Human Rights And Equal Opportunity Commission Act 1986* (Cth)). Decision-making by ministers and their departments is also subject to review, whether it be by tribunal (particularly under the *Administrative Appeals Tribunal Act 1975* (Cth)) or by a court (particularly under the *Administrative Decisions (Judicial Review) Act 1977* (Cth), but also under the common law, as in the *Tampa* case above, or by the High Court through the "constitutional writs" guaranteed by s 75(v) of the Constitution). Parliament also has a key role in holding the executive to account under the conventions of responsible government.

(a) Responsible Government

The system of responsible government requires that, except in the exercise of their reserve powers, the Queen's representatives – the Governor in each State and the Governor-General – act on the advice of their ministers. In turn, the ministers must be members of parliament and therefore accountable to it (and ultimately to the people at the ballot box). Hence, s 64 of the Constitution states that "no Minister of State shall hold office for a longer period than three months unless he is or becomes a senator or a member of the House of Representatives".

Hugh Emy and Owen Hughes, *Australian Politics: Realities in Conflict*
(Macmillan, 2nd ed 1991)

[338] 'Responsible government' refers to a series of institutions and the political relations between them which interlock to provide both a system of government and a distinctive mode of organising and exercising the political power at the disposal of the state. The major components are as follows:

1. Executive authority, the power of final political decision, is vested in a ministry whose members in Australia must be members of Parliament – or must become so within three months of taking office – to whom they are individually and collectively responsible. The ministry is invariably divided into an inner ministry, or Cabinet, and an outer ministry. All ministers are responsible to Parliament for the affairs of their own departments (individual ministerial responsibility). All ministers are responsible to Parliament and the electorate for the overall conduct of government policy, irrespective of whether or not they sit in the Cabinet (collective ministerial responsibility).

2. Executive authority is also bifurcated between the ministry, which is responsible both to Parliament and electorate, and an appointed head of state, the Governor-General, who acts on the advice tendered to him by the Prime Minister on behalf of the ministry or government. The power of final political decision, ultimate (political) responsibility for policy, lies with the Cabinet, [339] whose deliberations are secret (or supposed to be), whose papers and proceedings are privileged, and whose meetings are chaired by the Prime Minister.

    The Governor-General acts as the final component in the legislative process, signing into law and thereby confirming the validity of laws duly passed by majorities in both Houses. The office of Governor-General is also supposed to possess a residual or reserve power to see that the government does not breach in some fundamental way the terms of the Constitution; and in particular, that it does not contravene the primary principles of legitimacy from which its authority to govern derives.

3. The executive may be dismissed, normally, in one of two ways: by losing an election or by losing a vote of confidence in the lower House. The latter is a device which signals it can no longer command majority support in the lower House. The actions and policies of the ministry are open to debate and scrutiny by members of both Houses.

4. The executive is supported and advised by a bureaucracy whose members form a career service – meaning, they are appointed and promoted on the basis of merit by independent selection procedures and not by political influence or patronage. They enjoy security of tenure and 'anonymity' – freedom from public praise or blame – on the understanding they

perform their functions objectively and to the best of their abilities; and that they do this no matter which party is in power; ie in carrying out their roles, they are meant to be neutral between parties. The final responsibility for the performance of, and policies enacted by, public servants, rests with ministers in Parliament.

5. What is central to responsible government is the concept of a direct chain of accountability running from officials to a minister and so to Cabinet; then from ministers and Cabinet to Parliament, and from Parliament and the Cabinet to the electorate.

These points outline the formal position. In practice matters are a good deal more complicated. One is dealing with the powers of, and the relations between, a number of separate institutions – Cabinet, Prime Minister, ministers, department, House of Representatives and Senate – and with a particular way of structuring the exercise of power between the executive and legislative arms of government. Since these powers and relations are continually evolving, there is always likely to be some gap between theory and practice.

A further problem with responsible government is [that] the key term *responsible* has different meanings which apply in different circumstances. One article identifies five different senses of responsibility. There has been a long-standing tension between the softer and the harder meanings of responsibility: one may speak of someone being 'responsible' in the broad sense of being *obliged* to answer for something, or being *in charge* of something or someone; or one may speak more definitively of someone being *accountable* or liable for something, which implies there are sanctions or penalties for poor performance. For example, it is a matter **[340]** of dispute whether 'ministerial responsibility' either does or should mean the minister's strict accountability to Parliament for departmental errors, entailing the real possibility of his or her resignation; or whether it means a more general responsibility to simply explain matters to Parliament when something goes wrong. Responsible government also embodies a normative conception of how government *ought* to be carried on, ie in an open and responsive, or tolerant and impartial manner. It can therefore signify 'acting responsibly', or exercising political power in a mature, objective and equitable way. So when someone is doubtful of the reality of responsible government, he or she may in fact be criticising just one or other particular senses of that elastic term 'responsibility'. One needs to remember, however, there may be other senses in which the term 'responsible government' still applies.

Nevertheless, there are four major problem areas with responsible government in Australia:

1. Problems with the chain of accountability: do ministers possess effective control over their departments? How much power do they have *vis-à-vis* their public servants? Do the latter behave and function as they are supposed to? This point merges with the next.

2. Problems with Parliament's control of ministers and the executive: can Parliament really 'call ministers to account', as the saying goes, or 'scrutinise the executive'? Does the apparent lack of ministerial resignations signal a weakness in the central doctrine of ministerial responsibility? Is it realistic these days to think that Parliament can dismiss the executive, or 'bring down' a government by an adverse vote? Do we have responsible *parliamentary* government or some more autocratic form of party government?

3. Problems created by the Senate's power to block supply under Section 53.

4. Problems created by the extent of discretion actually vested in the Governor-General by the Constitution, coupled with the point that a clear precedent now exists for the exercise of such discretion. It appears the Governor-General can intervene in the case of dispute between the two Houses over supply, and even dismiss a government with a majority in the lower House if it cannot, apparently, obtain supply.

In theory, a feature of responsible government is the capacity of parliament to scrutinise the actions of the executive. However, the dominance of the party system in Australia means that federal Parliament is usually controlled by the same party that forms the executive. Parliament may therefore be directed by, rather than acting as a check upon, the executive.

Ken Turner, "Parliament"

in Rodney Smith (ed), *Politics in Australia* (Allen and Unwin, 2nd ed 1993), 78

[82] The Ministry comes from within Parliament. The House of Representatives has apparent power to make and break governments, usually at the cost of its own dissolution. In 1975 the Senate also asserted its power to break governments. Yet in Australia the selection of the Government is normally by the voters, who determine clearly which party or coalition has a majority in the House of Representatives. Party discipline has long [83] been so strong that even criticism from within the majority party will be regarded as disloyalty.

By convention, the Government resigns if it no longer has the confidence of the lower house. A motion accepted as a want of confidence or censure motion takes precedence over all other business until disposed of. To 1980, 87 such motions or amendments had been moved. Despite their potential, increased use may have weakened their dramatic impact. Nineteen censure motions were moved in the period 1971-80 and their use has since increased further. Since Federation there have only been eight defeats on the floor leading a government to resign or to have Parliament dissolved; of these five were before 1910. The only cases since the early 1940s where the selection of government has been taken out of the hands of the voters have been Labor's assumption of office in 1941 without new elections, when the transfer of support of two Independents gave it a majority, and the Governor-General's appointment of a 'caretaker' government in 1975.

So Parliament does not normally make and unmake governments. Yet it does play an important role in the development of ministers. Coming from within Parliament, they have been trained in the expected roles, although Australian ministers have generally served much less lengthy apprenticeships than their British counterparts.

Similarly, Parliament has important apparent powers in checking public expenditure and supervising public administration, by asking questions, demanding answers, and holding ministers accountable. Yet the size, remoteness, and complexity of government are so great that backbenchers may not know what questions to ask. Parliament cannot be said to exercise control, yet it may contribute some supervision and redress of grievances, especially with the improvement of its committee system.

Clearly, 'parliamentary government' is not government by parliament or even government controlled by parliament. Parliament establishes expected roles including conventions of 'ministerial responsibility', and trains and influences ministers, whose actions it publicly attempts to scrutinise. Indeed most contemporary observers of its procedures are more likely to conclude that the Executive controls the Parliament, rather than the reverse ...

[84] With the support of its loyal majority, the Government has institutionalised advantages in the very procedures of Parliament. It controls the process of electing the Speaker and Chairman of Committees; usually determines times of sitting; appoints chairpersons of inquiries and decides their terms of reference and resources; amends Standing Orders (front benchers in the House dominating the membership of the Standing Orders Committee); curtails debate; timetables legislation and arranges the drafting of bills, effectively monopolising the initiation of legislation (not only of finance measures where its monopoly is constitutional). Within their departments, ministers will subsequently enjoy wide discretion in the detailed implementation of the statutes so created ...

Largely for the benefit of ministers, who thus have more time for their departments and less risk of awkward inquiries, the Australian Parliament is a 'part-time legislature' ... From 1901 to 1991, the House of Representatives averaged only 68 [85] sitting days per year ...

Australia's part-time legislature has had to cope with a greatly increased legislative load. From 1901 to 1910 the average number of Acts per year was 23, with an average of 25.1 hours afforded to each Act. In the period 1981-90, 172 Acts per year were passed, with an average of only 3.1 hours each.

In the 1990s, the legislative output of the federal Parliament continued to increase. For example, the published volumes of annual statutes rose from 5626 pages in 1995 to 8866 pages in 1999. Since then, the annual output (no longer consecutively paginated) has undergone a moderate decrease, though in 2001 the total pages of legislation, excluding title pages and tables of contents, came to 7821 (bolstered by the 1835 pages of the *Corporations Act 2001* (Cth) and the *Financial Services Reform Act 2001* (Cth)).

Where a parliament has an upper House in which the government does not have a majority (perhaps because it is elected by a different voting system, such as proportional representation), there may be greater opportunities for the scrutiny of government action. In the federal Parliament the Senate's powers have been enhanced by an expansion and entrenchment of the Senate committee system, initially at the instance of Lionel Murphy as Leader of the Opposition in the Senate in the 1960s. This has been aided by the fact that from 1981 until 2005 the Senate was controlled not by the government of the day but by a changing combination of the opposition, minor parties and independents.

The standing committees of the Senate (such as the Senate Legal and Constitutional Committee and the Senate Estimates Committee) conduct inquiries and report on matters referred to them by the Senate. Such matters include proposed legislation and major policy issues. Twice each year, the Senate also refers to these committees for examination and report the estimates of proposed annual expenditure of government departments and authorities. The estimates hearings enable Senators to question ministers and public officials about proposed expenditure and the operation of the programs for which they are responsible. The Senate also establishes select committees to investigate particular questions or particular instances of executive action. Examples include the Senate Select Committee on the Free Trade Agreement between Australia and the United States of America (Final Report tabled 5 August 2004) and the Select Committee for an Inquiry into a Certain Maritime Incident (Report tabled 23 October 2002), the latter on matters including the allegation by members of the executive that asylum seekers coming to Australia by boat had thrown their children overboard.

The federal election in October 2004 not only returned the Howard government but gave it control of the Senate. This took effect on 1 July 2005, when the membership of the Senate rotated as prescribed by s 13 of the Constitution. The control of the Senate by the government necessarily means that the opportunities for Senate scrutiny of the executive are lessened. While the Senate's scrutiny processes continue, they do so in an institutional setting where decisions to establish select committees or refer matters to the standing committees are effectively controlled by the executive through its majority in the Senate.

In the State Parliaments, upper Houses have also asserted a more active role in the scrutiny of government. In 1996, Michael Egan, the Treasurer in the Carr Labor Government, was the Leader of the Government in the Legislative Council, the upper House of the New South Wales Parliament. The Government lacked a majority of seats in that House. On 1 May 1996, the Legislative Council passed a resolution calling on Egan to table certain papers or deliver them to the Clerk. He failed to do so, since the Cabinet had earlier agreed that Ministers should decline to comply with such orders. On 2 May 1996, the Legislative Council passed a resolution, paras 2 and 3 of which adjudged Egan guilty of contempt (para 2), suspended him from the House for the remainder of the day (para 3(a)), and ordered him to attend the House on the next sitting day to explain his reasons for not complying with a number of orders of the House to table documents, including the order of 1 May 1996 (para 3(b)). When Egan refused to leave the House, the Usher of the Black Rod conducted him out of the chamber and the parliamentary precincts onto the footpath outside.

Egan brought an action seeking declarations that paras 2 and 3 of the resolution of 2 May 1996 were invalid and that his removal into the street was a trespass, since he had been removed beyond the parliamentary precincts. In *Egan v Willis* (1996) 40 NSWLR 650, the New South Wales Court of Appeal dismissed the claim that the resolutions were invalid, but held that a trespass had been committed. Egan appealed to the High Court. The issue before the High Court was limited to whether paras 2 and 3(a) of the resolution of 2 May 1996 were within the powers of the Legislative Council under the *Constitution Act 1902* (NSW).

An initial question was whether the issue was justiciable (see Chapter 13, §5(d)), that is, whether it could be determined by a court. While matters relating to the internal affairs of

Parliament have generally been regarded as non-justiciable, in this case a majority of the High Court was prepared to examine the powers of the Legislative Council because they were relevant to the claim that a trespass had been committed. According to Gaudron, Gummow and Hayne JJ: "**[438]** Questions respecting the existence of the powers and privileges of a legislative chamber may present justiciable issues when they are elements in a controversy arising in the courts under the **[439]** general law". The Court dismissed the appeal.

Egan v Willis
(1998) 195 CLR 424

Gaudron, Gummow and Hayne JJ: [451] It should not be assumed that the characteristics of a system of responsible government are fixed or that the principles of ministerial responsibility which developed in New South Wales after 1855 necessarily reflected closely those from time to time accepted at Westminster. Moreover, what are now federal and State co-operative legislative schemes involve the enactment of legislation by one Parliament which is administered and enforced by Ministers and officials at another level of government, not responsible to the enacting legislature.

A system of responsible government traditionally has been considered to encompass "the means by which Parliament brings the Executive to account" so that "the Executive's primary responsibility in its prosecution of government is owed to Parliament". The point was made by Mill, writing in 1861, who spoke of the task of the legislature "to watch and control the government: to throw the light of publicity on its acts". It has been said of the contemporary position in Australia that, whilst "the primary role of Parliament is to pass laws, it also has important functions to question and criticise government on behalf of the people" and that "to secure accountability of government activity is the very essence of responsible government". In *Lange v Australian Broadcasting Corporation* [(1997) 189 CLR 520 at 561], reference was made to those provisions of the Commonwealth Constitution which prescribe the system of responsible government as necessarily implying "a limitation on legislative and executive power to deny the electors and their representatives information concerning the conduct of the executive branch of **[452]** government throughout the life of a federal Parliament". The Court added:

> "Moreover, the conduct of the executive branch is not confined to Ministers and the public service. It includes the affairs of statutory authorities and public utilities which are obliged to report to the legislature or to a Minister who is responsible to the legislature."

In Australia, s 75(v) of the Constitution and judicial review of administrative action under federal and State law, together with freedom of information legislation, supplement the operation of responsible government in this respect.

In the United Kingdom, the responsibility or accountability of individual Ministers recently was identified in a publication by the Cabinet Office as a guide to Ministers as including:

> "Each Minister is responsible to Parliament for the conduct of his or her Department, and for the actions carried out by the Department in pursuit of Government policies or in the discharge of responsibilities laid upon him or her as a Minister. Ministers are accountable to Parliament, in the sense that they have a duty to explain in Parliament the exercise of their powers and duties and to give an account to Parliament of what is done by them in their capacity as Ministers or by their Departments."

On the other hand, the Court recently affirmed that the confidentiality of Cabinet deliberations reflects the principle of collective responsibility which "remains an important element in our system of government" [*Commonwealth v Northern Land Council* (1993) 176 CLR 604 at 615] ...

[453] One aspect of responsible government is that Ministers may be members of either House of a bicameral legislature and liable to the scrutiny of that chamber in respect of the conduct of the executive branch of government. Another aspect of responsible government, perhaps the best known, is that the ministry must command the support of the lower House of a bicameral legislature upon confidence motions. The circumstance that Ministers are not members of a chamber in which the fate of administration is determined in this way does not have the consequence that the first aspect of responsible government mentioned above does not apply to them. Nor is it a determinative consideration that the political party or parties, from members of which the administration has been formed, "controls" the lower but not the upper chamber. Rather, there may be much to be said for the view that it is such a state of affairs which assists the attainment of the object of responsible government of which Mill spoke in 1861 …

The arrangements made for New South Wales for the period following 1855 provided the elements of what now should be identified as a system of responsible government. There was an assumption of a measure of examination of the executive by the legislature as well as legislative control over taxation and appropriation of money. The consideration that the government of the day must retain the confidence of the lower House and that it is there that governments are made and unmade does not deny what follows from the assumption in 1856 by the Legislative Council of a measure of superintendence of the conduct of the executive government by the production to it of State papers …

The principle derived from the authorities and not challenged on this appeal is that the Legislative Council has such powers, privileges and immunities as are reasonably necessary for the proper exercise of its **[454]** functions. As Priestley JA emphasised in the Court of Appeal, to decide whether a particular power … is reasonably necessary for the Legislative Council to perform any constitutional function, it is necessary first to identify that function.

The primary function of the Legislative Council is indicated by s 5 of the *Constitution Act*. This is the exercise by the Legislative Council, as an element of the legislature, of its power, subject to the provisions of the Commonwealth Constitution, to make laws for the peace, welfare and good government of New South Wales in all cases whatsoever …

In addition, the long practice since 1856 with respect to the production to the Council of State papers, together with the provision in Standing Order 29 for the putting to Ministers of questions relating to public affairs and the convention and parliamentary practice with respect to the representation in the Legislative Council by a Minister in respect of portfolios held by members in the Legislative Assembly, are significant. What is "reasonably necessary" at any time for the "proper exercise" of the "functions" of the Legislative Council is to be understood by reference to what, at the time in question, have come to be conventional practices established and maintained by the Legislative Council …

[455] If a member will not produce documents sought by the House there may be some limits to the steps it may take in response. In *Barton v Taylor* [(1886) 11 App Cas 197 at 204-5] the Privy Council said:

> "[I]t may very well be, that the same doctrine of reasonable necessity would authorize a suspension until submission or apology by the offending member; which, if he were refractory, might cause it to be prolonged (not by the arbitrary discretion of the Assembly, but by his own wilful default) for some further time. The facts pleaded in this case do not raise the question whether that would be ultra vires or not. If these are the limits of the inherent or implied power, reasonably deducible from the principle of general necessity, they have the advantage of drawing a simple practical line between defensive and punitive action on the part of the Assembly. A power of unconditional suspension, for an indefinite time, or for a definite time depending only on the irresponsible discretion of the Assembly itself, is more than the necessity of self-defence seems to require, and is dangerously liable, in possible cases, to excess or abuse."

It is not necessary to say whether this is an accurate or exhaustive statement of the limits of the powers of the House. But one of the steps that the House may undoubtedly take is to resolve that the member be suspended for a limited time from the service of the House, and that is what happened here.

It was submitted that the House may not punish the member concerned but may coerce or induce compliance with its wish. To distinguish between punishing and merely inducing compliance may very well be difficult. Further, to state the distinction in these terms may distract attention from more important considerations of identifying … the power that has been exercised and whether, or to what extent, the courts may review [it] … But on no view of the authorities did the action taken in passing and implementing pars 2 and 3(a) of the resolution go beyond the boundary of what is permissible.

Kirby and Callinan JJ reached the same conclusion. McHugh J also held that, "**[458]** by reason of its being part of the Parliament of New South Wales", the Legislative Council had power to find Egan guilty of contempt and suspend him for his failure to produce the papers, so that Egan "**[480]** failed on the substantial issue". Nevertheless, McHugh J would formally have allowed the appeal because in his view the Court of Appeal lacked "**[466]** jurisdiction to determine the issue, an issue which after all concerns only the relationship between the House and **[467]** one of its members and the internal administration of the business of the House".

Egan v Willis was decided on 19 November 1998. In resolutions on 24 and 26 November 1998, the Legislative Council again required Egan to table certain documents or deliver them to the Clerk. Again Egan refused, this time claiming that the documents were protected by legal professional privilege or public interest immunity. In response, the Legislative Council again adjudged him guilty of contempt and he was suspended "for the remainder of the session or until he fully complies with this Order, whichever occurs first". Egan was again removed from the House by the Usher of the Black Rod. Again he sued on the basis that his removal from the House constituted an assault, arguing that he could not be required to table cabinet documents (which he said were protected by public interest immunity) and legal advice (which he said was protected by legal professional privilege).

Egan v Chadwick
(1999) 46 NSWLR 563

Spigelman CJ: [573] It is common ground that there has been no previous occasion on which a Minister has been suspended from a House of an Australian Parliament for failing to produce documents over which a claim of privilege has been made. Hitherto, in Australian parliamentary practice, a House has not sought to enforce demands to produce documents, when public interest immunity has been claimed.

This Court must decide what recognition should be given to a claim for public interest immunity in the context of determining the scope of a common law power to call for documents that satisfy the test of 'reasonably necessary for the performance' by the Legislative Council of its constitutional functions.

The determination of a claim of public interest immunity requires the balancing by the court of conflicting public interests. The immunity is not absolute. The plaintiff's submissions, put at their highest, in substance require the Court to accede to a "class claim" for Cabinet documents as a restriction on the power of the Legislative Council of a character which the courts have rejected in the case of litigation before courts. Alternatively, it is submitted, this Court should conduct a balancing exercise to similar effect …

[574] The high constitutional functions of the Legislative Council encompass both legislating and the enforcement of the accountability of the Executive. Performance of these functions may require access to information the disclosure of which may harm the public interest. Access to such information may, accordingly, be 'reasonably necessary for the performance of the functions of the Legislative Council'.

However, in my opinion, it is not reasonably necessary for the proper exercise of the functions of the Legislative Council to call for documents the production of which would conflict with the doctrine of ministerial responsibility, either in its individual or collective dimension. The power is itself, in significant degree, derived from that doctrine. The existence of an inconsistency or conflict constitutes a qualification on the power itself.

When the issue of access to Cabinet documents has arisen in the context of claims for public interest immunity in the course of litigation, the courts have recognised the significance of Cabinet confidentiality as an application of the princip[le] of collective responsibility. However, a distinction has been made between documents which disclose the actual deliberations within Cabinet and those which are described as "Cabinet documents", but which are in the nature of reports or submissions prepared for the assistance of Cabinet. With respect to the former the High Court has said:

"It has never been doubted that it is in the public interest that deliberations of Cabinet should remain confidential in order that the members of Cabinet may exchange differing views and at the same time maintain the principle of collective responsibility for any decision which may be made ... Despite the pressures which modern society places upon the principle of collective responsibility, it remains an important element in our system of government." [*Commonwealth v Northern Land Council* (1993) 176 CLR 604 at 615] ...

[576] [The] evidence indicates that the documents which the Legislative Council sought included documents which revealed the internal deliberations of the Cabinet. In my opinion, the Legislative Council does not have power to require the production of such documents.

In order to avoid inconsistency between the power to call for documents and one of the bases on which it has been determined that the power is reasonably necessary (namely executive accountability derived from responsible government), the power should, at least, be restricted to documents which do not, directly or indirectly, reveal the deliberations of Cabinet.

On the other hand, Spigelman CJ rejected the claim based on legal professional privilege.

Spigelman CJ: [578] I have not found it easy to reconcile the strength of the High Court's contemporary reasoning on the role of legal professional privilege (as exemplified most clearly in the result in *Carter* [*v Managing Partner, Northmore Hale Davy & Leake* (1995) 183 CLR 121], where access to information required for purposes of a criminal defence was denied) and the emphasis on the accountability function of the Legislative Council in *Egan v Willis*. I have concluded that the latter should prevail.

In performing its accountability function, the Legislative Council may require access to legal advice on the basis of which the Executive acted, or purported to act. In many situations, access to such advice will be relevant in order to make an informed assessment of the justification for the Executive decision. In my opinion, access to legal advice is reasonably necessary for the exercise by the Legislative Council of its functions.

What, if any, access should occur is a matter "of the occasion and of the manner" of the exercise of a power, not of its existence [*R v Richards; Ex parte Fitzpatrick and Browne* (1955) 92 CLR 157 at 162]. If the public interest is thereby harmed, the sanctions are political, not legal.

[579] My analysis, in the context of public interest immunity, of the scope of the power being limited in the case of inconsistency with the principles of collective or individual ministerial responsibility, may extend to documents covered by legal professional privilege at common law. That is not, however, because they are documents of that character. It is because their disclosure would have a consequence which gives rise to a conflict with the constitutional principle.

Meagher JA agreed with Spigelman CJ. Priestley JA generally agreed, but also went further. He drew an analogy with the courts' insistence (for example, in *Sankey v Whitlam* (1978) 142 CLR 1) that, when public interest immunity is claimed in court proceedings, the court will assess the validity of such a claim for itself. It was on this basis that he held that the Legislative Council could demand access to the Cabinet documents.

Priestley JA: [594] [I]n the adversary situations where public interest immunity may attach to documents to prevent their production, there is no doubt that the decision whether the doctrine attaches or not is, finally, not for the Executive to make, but for a court, after the court has had the documents produced to it. The court may not require to see the documents itself. It may be satisfied by evidence about the nature of the documents or other circumstances in the particular case that it should refuse production to the parties because of public interest immunity: but it undoubtedly has the power to compel production to itself even of cabinet documents, even though the power will in regard to certain cabinet documents be used with the highest degree of circumspection.

So, if in the adversary situations in which the case law has established public interest immunity may attach, a branch of government other than the Executive is trusted with the power to compel the production of documents for which the Executive claims such immunity, equally there should be no objection in the different situation that arises between the Executive and a House of Parliament, to the possession by another branch of government other than the Executive, of the same power; the more so when the power is necessary for the proper carrying out of the function of that branch of government.

The function and status of the Council in the system of government in New South Wales require and justify the same degree of trust being reposed in the Council as in the courts when dealing with documents in respect of which the Executive claims public interest immunity. In exercising its powers in respect of such documents the Council has the same duty to prevent publication beyond itself of documents the disclosure of which will, to adapt the words of Mason J in [*Commonwealth of Australia v John Fairfax & Sons Limited* (1980) 147 CLR 39 at 52], be inimical to the public interest because the security of the State, relations with other governments or the ordinary business of government will be prejudiced. When the Executive claims immunity on such grounds, the Council will have the duty, analogous to the duty of the court mentioned by Mason J ..., of balancing the conflicting public interest considerations. The carrying out of the duty will, in regard to certain cabinet documents, require the same very high degree of circumspection mandated for the courts by the High Court in the *Commonwealth v Northern Land Council* case ...

[595] One result of this view is that, notwithstanding the great respect that must be paid to such incidents of responsible government as cabinet confidentiality and collective responsibility, no *legal right* to *absolute* secrecy is given to any group of men and women in government, the possibility of accountability can never be kept out of mind, and this can only be to the benefit of the people of a truly representative democracy.

(b) Review by the High Court

The original jurisdiction that the High Court "shall have" is listed in s 75 of the Constitution. This includes the jurisdiction given by s 75(v) in "all matters ... [i]n which a writ of Mandamus or prohibition or an injunction is sought against an officer of the Commonwealth". This constitutionally secured power of controlling members of the executive ("officers of the Commonwealth") by issuing "constitutional writs" (see Chapter 13, §3(a)) has been tested in the immigration context as successive governments have sought to shield administrative decision-making from judicial scrutiny.

During the *Tampa* controversy of August–September 2001 (see §2(a) above), an early version of the Border Protection Bill 2001 (Cth) designed to validate actions of the kind taken by the Commonwealth against the *Tampa* contained several clauses (known as "privative clauses") restrictive of legal proceedings. While that version of the Bill was rejected by Parliament, s 7 of the version finally enacted, the *Border Protection (Validation and Enforcement Powers) Act 2001* (Cth), still provides that, in respect of the actions taken during the relevant period, "[p]roceedings, whether civil or criminal, may not be instituted or continued in any court ... [against] a Commonwealth officer", while s 6 provides that: "All action to which this Part applies is taken for all purposes to have been lawful when it occurred". However, the Act is narrowly tailored, applying only to specified actions during the specified period. In addition, in the enacted version a new s 9 provides that: "Nothing in this Part is intended to affect the jurisdiction of the High Court under section 75 of the Constitution".

The *Migration Reform Act 1992* (Cth) introduced a new Pt 8 into the *Migration Act 1958* (Cth), distinguishing between the migration decisions that are and are not judicially reviewable in the Federal Court, and limiting the grounds of review available even when review was not wholly excluded. The legislation was challenged in *Abebe v Commonwealth* (1999) 197 CLR 510 on the basis that it did not confer jurisdiction in the form of a "matter" as required by ss 75-77 of the Constitution (see the extract in Chapter 13, §5(b)). The challenge failed.

The plaintiff, Seniet Abebe, was an Ethiopian national whose claim to refugee status had been rejected by the Refugee Review Tribunal. She also brought a separate action in the High Court's original jurisdiction, as guaranteed by s 75(v) of the Constitution, in which she sought review of the Tribunal's decision on the grounds that had been excluded from the jurisdiction of the Federal Court. In these separate proceedings, her application for relief was unanimously rejected. Yet the fact that all members of the High Court elaborately considered her claim, and did so in the very same judgments that dealt with the constitutional issue, suggested a double signal. On the one hand, it pointedly reminded Parliament that, however far it may go in seeking to exclude the Federal Court from review of migration decisions, it cannot exclude the constitutionally guaranteed jurisdiction of the High Court. On the other hand, it demonstrated the additional workload that would accrue to the High Court if all challenges to decisions of the Refugee Review Tribunal were brought to that Court under s 75(v).

Nine months after *Abebe*, in dismissing an application under s 75(v) for certiorari to the Tribunal, McHugh J spelt out the effect of Pt 8 of the *Migration Act* on the High Court. In *Re Minister for Immigration and Multicultural Affairs; Ex parte Durairajasingham* (2000) 168 ALR 407, he stated that "[411] it difficult to see the rationale for the amendments to the Migration Act ... which now prevent this court from remitting to the Federal Court *all* issues arising under that Act which fall within this court's original jurisdiction". Further, "[t]he reforms brought about by the amendments are plainly in need of reform themselves if this court is to have adequate time for the research and reflection necessary to fulfil its role as 'the keystone of the federal arch' and the ultimate appellate court of the nation".

The workload problem for the High Court was created by s 485 of the *Migration Act*. Normally, under s 44 of the *Judiciary Act 1903* (Cth), the High Court may remit matters to lower courts for determination. Section 485(1) of the *Migration Act* reaffirmed this power, but sub-s (3) provided that, where a decision to which Pt 8 of the Act applied was remitted to the Federal Court, that Court "does not have any powers in relation to that matter other than the powers it would have had if the matter had been as a result of an application made under this Part". Hence, the High Court could not remit the whole of the "matter" before it, since the Federal Court had been denied the broader powers of review vested in the High Court by s 75(v) of the Constitution. The undue workload thus imposed on the High Court attracted considerable criticism (for example, Australian Law Reform Commission, *The Judicial Power of the Commonwealth: A Review of the Judiciary Act 1903 and Related Legislation* (Report No 2, October 2001), 117-20). However, in *Minister for Immigration and Multicultural Affairs v Yusuf* (2001) 206 CLR 323, the Court was able to relieve the pressure by interpreting the limited grounds of review available to the Federal Court in a manner sufficiently broad to enable that Court to hear many of the cases that could otherwise have been entertained only by the High Court under s 75(v).

Yusuf was followed by a legislative response. The *Migration Legislation Amendment (Judicial Review) Act 2001* (Cth), passed as part of a package of migration measures in the wake of the *Tampa* controversy, repealed Pt 8 and substituted a new regime that abolished judicial review of migration decisions made under the *Migration Act* as far as is constitutionally possible. The new s 474, entitled "Decisions under Act are final", stated:

Migration Act 1958 (Cth)

474 (1) A privative clause decision:

    (a) is final and conclusive; and

    (b) must not be challenged, appealed against, reviewed, quashed or called in question in any court; and

    (c) is not subject to prohibition, mandamus, injunction, declaration or certiorari in any court on any account.

(2) In this section:

privative clause decision means a decision of an administrative character made, proposed to be made, or required to be made, as the case may be, under this Act or under a regulation or other instrument made under this Act (whether in the exercise of a discretion or not), other than a decision referred to in subsection (4) or (5).

Section 484(1), as amended, provided: "The jurisdiction of the Federal Court and the Federal Magistrates Court in relation to privative clause decisions is exclusive of the jurisdiction of all other courts, other than the jurisdiction of the High Court under section 75 of the Constitution".

The passage of s 474 raised fundamental questions about the rule of law and the capacity of Parliament to shield administrative decision-making from judicial review. At the heart of these questions was the approach to privative clauses established in *R v Hickman; Ex parte Fox and Clinton* (1945) 70 CLR 598. In *Hickman*, a Local Reference Board constituted under the *National Security (Coal Mining Industry Employment) Regulations* (Cth) made an order on the basis of an erroneous finding that the matter was within the ambit of the coal mining industry. The High Court held that prohibition lay under s 75(v) of the Constitution. This decision was reached in spite of reg 17, which provided that the decision of a Local Reference Board "shall not be challenged, appealed against, quashed or called into question, or be subject to prohibition, mandamus or injunction, in any court on any account whatever". The conclusion of the High Court was consistent with a long line of authority holding that, where an Act purports to take away from the High Court jurisdiction to review the lawful ambit of power conferred on an officer of the Commonwealth, the Act is invalid to that extent. Dixon J, while joining with the majority as to the outcome, stated as a matter of general approach:

R v Hickman; Ex parte Fox and Clinton
(1945) 70 CLR 598

Dixon J: [614] The particular regulation is expressed in a manner that has grown familiar. Both under Commonwealth law, and in jurisdictions **[615]** where there is a unitary constitution, the interpretation of provisions of the general nature of reg 17 is well established. They are not interpreted as meaning to set at large the courts or other judicial bodies to whose decision they relate. Such a clause is interpreted as meaning that no decision which is in fact given by the body concerned shall be invalidated on the ground that it has not conformed to the requirements governing its proceedings or the exercise of its authority or has not confined its acts within the limits laid down by the instrument giving it authority, provided always that its decision is a bona fide attempt to exercise its power, that it relates to the subject matter of the legislation, and that it is reasonably capable of reference to the power given to the body.

Thus, the practical effect of "the *Hickman* principle" is that a decision protected by a privative clause has a limited immunity from review – but only from review on certain grounds, and even then only if the decision satisfies the qualifications noted in the final clauses of the passage above. These qualifications are often referred to as "the *Hickman* provisos".

According to Gaudron and Gummow JJ in *Darling Casino Ltd v New South Wales Casino Control Authority* (1997) 191 CLR 602 (quoting *R v Coldham; Ex parte Australian Workers' Union* (1983) 153 CLR 415 at 418), this cryptic statement by Dixon J was apparently designed to reconcile "[631] the prima facie inconsistency between one statutory provision which seems to limit the powers of the [decision-maker] and another provision, the privative clause, which seems to contemplate that the [decision] shall operate free from any restriction". The *Hickman* principle, though only obiter dicta, is frequently cited. Its application in respect of s 474 was considered by the High Court in *Plaintiff S157/2002 v Commonwealth* (2003) 211 CLR 476.

In 1997 the plaintiff applied for a protection visa. Under the *Migration Act* such a visa can be granted to a non-citizen to whom Australia has protection obligations under the 1951 United Nations Convention relating to the Status of Refugees, as amended by the 1967 Refugees Protocol. A delegate of the Minister for Immigration and Multicultural Affairs refused the application, and the plaintiff appealed to the Refugee Review Tribunal, which affirmed that refusal.

The plaintiff wished to seek judicial review of the decision of the Refugee Review Tribunal on the ground that it did not provide natural justice, primarily because it took into account material directly relevant and adverse to the plaintiff's claim without giving him notice of the material or an opportunity to address it. However, review of the Tribunal's decision was apparently precluded by s 474 of the *Migration Act*. The plaintiff then brought proceedings challenging the validity of that provision. He also challenged s 486A of the Act, which imposed a non-extendable time limit of 35 days on applications to the High Court for judicial review of privative clause decisions.

The High Court held ss 474 and 486A to be valid. It did so by interpreting them in a way that did not conflict with s 75(v). The result was that s 474 did not bar judicial review of decisions of the Refugee Review Tribunal in the High Court, at least on grounds of jurisdictional error. The order of the Court was: "[539] Section 474 would be invalid if, on its proper construction, it attempted to oust the jurisdiction conferred on the High Court by s 75(v) of the Constitution. However, on its proper construction, it does not attempt to do so. Section 474 is valid but does not apply to the proceedings the plaintiff would initiate".

Plaintiff S157/2002 v Commonwealth
(2003) 211 CLR 476

Gaudron, McHugh, Gummow, Kirby and Hayne JJ: [504] There are two basic rules of construction which apply to the interpretation of privative clauses. The first, which applies in the case of privative clauses in legislation enacted by the Parliament of the Commonwealth, is that "if there is an opposition between the Constitution and any such provision, it should be resolved by adopting [an] interpretation [consistent with the Constitution if] that is fairly open" [*R v Hickman; Ex parte Fox and Clinton* (1945) 70 CLR 598 at 616].

[505] The second basic rule, which applies to privative clauses generally, is that it is presumed that the Parliament does not intend to cut down the jurisdiction of the courts save to the extent that the legislation in question expressly so states or necessarily implies. Accordingly, privative clauses are strictly construed.

Quite apart from s 75(v), there are other constitutional requirements that are necessarily to be borne in mind in construing a provision such as s 474 of the Act. A privative clause cannot operate so as to oust the jurisdiction which other paragraphs of s 75 confer on this Court, including that conferred by s 75(iii) in matters "in which the Commonwealth, or a person suing or being sued on behalf of the Commonwealth, is a party". Further, a privative clause cannot operate so as to allow a non-judicial tribunal or other non-judicial decision-making authority to exercise the judicial power of the Commonwealth. Thus, it cannot confer on a non-judicial body the power to determine conclusively the limits of its own jurisdiction ...

[I]t was argued on behalf of the plaintiff that s 474(1)(c) of the Act is directly inconsistent with s 75(v) of the Constitution. However, s 474(1)(c) cannot be read in isolation from the definition of "privative clause decision" in s 474(2). That definition relevantly confines "privative clause decision[s]" to decisions "made, proposed to be made, or required to be made ... under this Act".

When regard is had to the phrase "under this Act" in s 474(2) of the Act, the words of that sub-section are not apt to refer either to [506] decisions purportedly made under the Act or, as some of the submissions made on behalf of the Commonwealth might suggest, to decisions of the kind that might be made under the Act. Moreover, if the words of the sub-section were to be construed in either of those ways, s 474(1)(c) would be in direct conflict with s 75(v) of the Constitution and, thus, invalid. Further, they would confer authority on a non-judicial decision-maker of the Commonwealth to determine conclusively the limits of its own jurisdiction and, thus, at least in some cases, infringe the mandate implicit in the text of Ch III of the Constitution that the judicial power of the Commonwealth be exercised only by the courts named and referred to in s 71.

Once it is accepted, as it must be, that s 474 is to be construed conformably with Ch III of the Constitution, specifically, s 75, the expression "decision[s] ... made under this Act" must be read so as to refer to decisions which involve neither a failure to exercise jurisdiction nor an excess of the jurisdiction conferred by the Act. Indeed so much is required as a matter of general principle. This Court has clearly held that an administrative decision which involves jurisdictional error is "regarded, in law, as no decision at all" [*Minister for Immigration and Multicultural Affairs v Bhardwaj* (2002) 209 CLR 597 at 614-15, 618, 646-7]. Thus, if there has been jurisdictional error because, for example, of a failure to discharge "imperative duties" or to observe "inviolable limitations or restraints", the decision in question cannot properly be described in the terms used in s 474(2) as "a decision ... made under this Act" and is, thus, not a "privative clause decision" as defined in ss 474(2) and (3) of the Act.

It followed from this conclusion that the time limit imposed by s 486A was also inapplicable, since that provision was also expressed to apply to "a privative clause decision". The joint judgment went on to determine the constitutional validity of s 474.

Gaudron, McHugh, Gummow, Kirby and Hayne JJ: [508] Because, as this court has held, the constitutional writs of prohibition and mandamus are available only for jurisdictional error and because s 474 of the Act does not protect decisions involving jurisdictional error, s 474 does not, in that regard conflict with s 75(v) of the Constitution and, thus, is valid in its application to the proceedings which the plaintiff would initiate. The plaintiff asserts jurisdictional error by reason of a denial to him of procedural fairness and thus s 474, whilst valid, does not upon its true construction protect the decision of which the plaintiff complains. A decision flawed for reasons of a failure to comply with the principles of natural justice is not a "privative clause decision" within s 474(2) of the Act.

The joint judgment's approach to s 474 resolved another problem as well. Its interpretation of s 474 (and also, as a result, of other provisions governing the remittal of matters) meant that the High Court could now remit matters back to the Federal Court, thereby reducing its workload.

In an earlier passage, the joint judgment had *rejected* the Commonwealth's reading of the *Hickman* principle as meaning that, so long as "the three *Hickman* provisos" were satisfied, the impugned decision would be protected even if it were otherwise vulnerable to attack. Instead, they said, the principle meant that, *unless* the provisos were satisfied, the decision would *not* be protected. The alternative reading of *Hickman* thus rejected had been used by the Commonwealth as a basis for suggestions of various legislative devices by which decision-making powers could be "read up" to the limits of constitutional validity. However, the joint judgment dismissed these suggestions.

Gaudron, McHugh, Gummow, Kirby and Hayne JJ: [511] It is important to emphasise that the difference in understanding what has been decided about privative clauses is real and substantive; it is not some verbal or logical quibble. It is real and substantive because it reflects two fundamental constitutional propositions, both of **[512]** which the Commonwealth accepts. First, the jurisdiction of this Court to grant relief under s 75(v) of the Constitution cannot be removed by or under a law made by the Parliament. Specifically, the jurisdiction to grant s 75(v) relief where there has been jurisdictional error by an officer of the Commonwealth cannot be removed. Secondly, the judicial power of the Commonwealth cannot be exercised otherwise than in accordance with Ch III. The Parliament cannot confer on a non-judicial body the power to conclusively determine the limits of its own jurisdiction.

To understand the three *Hickman* provisos as qualifying the powers of those who make privative clause decisions, rather than qualifying the protection which the privative clause affords, either assumes that the Act on its true construction provides no other jurisdictional limitation on the relevant decision making or other power or it assumes that the repository of the power can decide the limits of its own jurisdiction. For the reasons given earlier, the first assumption is wrong. The alternative assumption would contravene Ch III.

In submissions it was put by the Commonwealth that the reasoning in *Hickman* produced, as a matter of judicial interpretation of privative clauses, a result which might have been achieved by adoption of a legislative stipulation for the expansion of decision-making powers under the Act up to the boundaries of designated heads of power in s 51 of the Constitution. It has been explained earlier in these reasons that *Hickman* does not have such an operation. But something more should be said respecting the employment of a legislative device for the "reading up" of decision-making powers conferred upon the executive branch of government.

In argument, the Commonwealth suggested that the Parliament might validly delegate to the Minister "the power to exercise a totally open-ended discretion as to what aliens can and what aliens cannot come to and stay in Australia", subject only to this Court deciding any dispute as to the "constitutional fact" of alien status. Alternatively, it was put that the Act might validly be redrawn to say, in effect, "[h]ere are some non-binding guidelines which should be applied", with the "guidelines" being the balance of the statute. Other variations were canvassed.

The inclusion in the Act of such provisions to the effect that, notwithstanding anything contained in the specific provisions of that statute, the Minister was empowered to make any decision respecting visas, provided it was with respect to aliens, might well be ineffective. It is well settled that the structure of the Constitution does not preclude the Parliament from authorising in wide and general terms subordinate legislation under any of the heads of its legislative power. *Victorian Stevedoring and General Contracting Co Pty Ltd and Meakes v Dignan* [(1931) 46 CLR 73] may be cited for that proposition. But what may be [513] "delegated" is the power to make laws with respect to a particular head in s 51 of the Constitution. The provisions canvassed by the Commonwealth would appear to lack that hallmark of the exercise of legislative power identified by Latham CJ in *Commonwealth v Grunseit* [(1943) 67 CLR 58 at 82], namely, the determination of "the content of a law as a rule of conduct or a declaration as to power, right or duty". Moreover, there would be delineated by the Parliament no factual requirements to connect any given state of affairs with the constitutional head of power. Nor could it be for a court exercising the judicial power of the Commonwealth to supply this connection in deciding litigation said to arise under that law. That would involve the court in the rewriting of the statute, the function of the Parliament, not a Ch III court.

Finally, the issues decided in these proceedings are not merely issues of a technical kind involving the interpretation of the contested provisions of the Act. The Act must be read in the context of the operation of s 75 of the Constitution. That section, and specifically s 75(v), introduces into the Constitution of the Commonwealth an entrenched minimum provision of judicial review. There was no precise equivalent to s 75(v) in either of the Constitutions of the United States of America or Canada. The provision of the constitutional writs and the conferral upon this Court of an irremovable jurisdiction to issue them to an officer of the Commonwealth constitutes a textual reinforcement for what Dixon J said about the significance of the rule of law for the Constitution in *Australian Communist Party v Commonwealth* [(1951) 83 CLR 1 at 193]. In that case, his Honour stated that the Constitution:

> "is an instrument framed in accordance with many traditional conceptions, to some of which it gives effect, as, for example, in separating the judicial power from other functions of government, others of which are simply assumed. Among these I think that it may fairly be said that the rule of law forms an assumption."

The reservation to this Court by the Constitution of the jurisdiction in all matters in which the named constitutional writs or an injunction are sought against an officer of the Commonwealth is a means of [514] assuring to all people affected that officers of the Commonwealth obey the law and neither exceed nor neglect any jurisdiction which the law confers on them. The centrality, and protective purpose, of the jurisdiction of this Court in that regard places significant barriers in the way of legislative attempts (by privative clauses or otherwise) to impair judicial review of administrative action. Such jurisdiction exists to maintain the federal compact by ensuring that propounded laws are constitutionally valid and ministerial or other official action lawful and within jurisdiction. In any written constitution, where there are disputes over such matters, there must be an authoritative decision-maker. Under the Constitution of the Commonwealth the ultimate decision-maker in all matters where there is a contest, is this Court. The Court must be obedient to its constitutional function. In the end, pursuant to s 75 of the Constitution, this limits the powers of the Parliament or of the executive to avoid, or confine, judicial review.

For Gleeson CJ, too, the question was primarily one of statutory interpretation. However, he adopted a broader, more contextual approach to the factors to be considered in such a process.

Gleeson CJ: [490] In the present context, there is a question whether a purported [491] decision of the tribunal made in breach of the assumed requirements of natural justice, as alleged, is excluded from judicial review by s 474. The issue is whether such an act on the part of the tribunal is within the scope of the protection afforded by s 474. Consistent with authority in this country, this is a matter to be decided as an exercise in statutory construction, the determinative consideration being whether, on the true construction of the Act as a whole, including s 474, the requirement of a fair hearing is a limitation upon the decision-making authority of the tribunal of such a nature that it is inviolable. The line of reasoning developed by Dixon J in *Hickman* and later cases identifies the nature of the task involved, and the question to be asked. By identifying the task as one of statutory construction, all relevant principles of statutory construction are engaged. It cannot be suggested that Dixon J was formulating a principle of construction which excluded all others. On the contrary, by treating the exercise as a matter of construction he was opening the way for the application of other principles as well. Those principles have been stated by this Court on many occasions, and are as well known to Parliament as *Hickman* itself …

[492] Decisions as to whether a person is someone to whom Australia owes protection obligations often turn upon questions of law; sometimes complex and difficult questions of law. Although it is the provisions of the Act concerning protection visas that are directly relevant in the present case, they are only part of a wider, and more detailed, pattern of legislation which, in a variety of respects, affects fundamental human rights and involves Australia's international obligations.

In such a context, the following established principles are relevant to the resolution of the question of statutory construction.

First, where legislation has been enacted pursuant to, or in contemplation of, the assumption of international obligations under a treaty or international convention, in cases of ambiguity a court should favour a construction which accords with Australia's obligations.

Secondly, courts do not impute to the legislature an intention to abrogate or curtail fundamental rights or freedoms unless such an intention is clearly manifested by unmistakable and unambiguous language. General words will rarely be sufficient for that purpose. What courts will look for is a clear indication that the legislature has directed its attention to the rights or freedoms in question, and has consciously decided upon abrogation or curtailment. As Lord Hoffmann recently pointed out in the United Kingdom [*R v Home Secretary; Ex parte Simms* [2000] 2 AC 115 at 131], for Parliament squarely to confront such an issue may involve a political cost, but in the absence of express language or necessary implication, even the most general words are taken to be "subject to the basic rights of the individual".

Thirdly, the Australian Constitution is framed upon the assumption of the rule of law. [In *Church of Scientology v Woodward* (1982) 154 CLR 25 at 70] Brennan J said:

> "Judicial review is neither more nor less than the enforcement of the rule of law over executive action; it is the means by which executive action is prevented from exceeding the powers and functions assigned to the executive by law and the interests of the individual are protected accordingly."

Fourthly, and as a specific application of the second and third **[493]** principles, privative clauses are construed "by reference to a presumption that the legislature does not intend to deprive the citizen of access to the courts, other than to the extent expressly stated or necessarily to be implied" [*Public Service Association (SA) v Federated Clerks' Union* (1991) 173 CLR 132 at 160].

Fifthly, a principle of relevance to *Hickman* is that what is required is a consideration of the whole Act, and an attempt to achieve a reconciliation between the privative provision and the rest of the legislation. In the case of the Act presently under consideration, that is a formidable task. There may not be a single answer to the question. But the task is not to be performed by reading the rest of the Act as subject to s 474, or by making s 474 the central and controlling provision of the Act.

The Commonwealth's argument as to the effect of s 474, in its application to the proceedings contemplated by the plaintiff, is inconsistent with the above principles. In essence, the argument is that the amendment of the Act which introduced s 474 brought about a radical transformation of the pre-existing provisions. From that time, there were no "imperative duties", and no "inviolable limitations" on the powers and jurisdiction of decision-makers under the Act. When s 474 says that constitutional writs do not lie, it means that, subject to "the *Hickman* conditions", breaches of the Act do not involve jurisdictional error. The "*Hickman* conditions" are that a decision is a bona fide attempt to exercise power, that it relates to the subject matter of the legislation, and that is reasonably capable of reference to the power. Applying that to a decision to refuse a protection visa under s 65 of the Act, it will always necessarily relate to the subject matter of the legislation, it will always be reasonably capable of reference to power given to the decision-maker, and so long as it is a bona fide attempt to exercise the power conferred by s 65, all the conditions necessary for legally valid decision-making will have been satisfied. Australia's international protection obligations will be fulfilled by the executive government's bona fide attempt to fulfil them.

The theory behind this argument appears to be that, in whatever statutory context it is found, a privative provision controls the meaning of the remainder of the statute, and, in the case of a conferral of jurisdiction upon a decision-maker, expands that jurisdiction in such a way that excess of jurisdiction will only occur in the event of a breach of one of the "conditions" mentioned. That is difficult to reconcile with the actual decision in *Hickman*. And, in the context of the Act, and decisions as to protection visas, it is impossible to reconcile with the principles of statutory construction stated above.

As French J observed in *NAAV v Minister for Immigration and Multicultural and Indigenous Affairs* [(2002) 193 ALR 449 at 542], the Act is "replete with **[494]** official powers and discretions, tightly controlled under the Act itself and under the regulations by conditions and criteria to be satisfied before those powers and discretions can be exercised". In that case, and a number of related cases heard at the same time, the Full Court of the Federal Court dealt with several different kinds of challenge to decisions under the Act, and the operation of s 474 in relation to each of them. Here we are concerned with only one kind of challenge, involving a claim of denial of natural justice. A rejection of the Commonwealth's global approach to the operation of s 474 does not mean that the opposite conclusion follows in relation to every possible kind of challenge to a decision.

The principles of statutory construction stated above lead to the conclusion that Parliament has not evinced an intention that a decision by the Tribunal to confirm a refusal of a protection visa, made unfairly, and in contravention of the requirements of natural justice, shall stand so long as it was a bona fide attempt to decide whether or not such a visa should be granted. Decision-makers, judicial or administrative, may be found to have acted unfairly even though their good faith is not in question. People whose fundamental rights are at stake are ordinarily entitled to expect more than good faith. They are ordinarily entitled to expect fairness. If Parliament intends to provide that decisions of the Tribunal, although reached by an unfair procedure, are valid and binding, and that the law does not require fairness on the part of the Tribunal in order for its decisions to be effective under the Act, then s 474 does not suffice to manifest such an intention.

It follows that, in my view, if the Tribunal's decision in relation to the plaintiff was taken in breach of the rules of natural justice, as is alleged, then it is not within the scope of protection afforded by s 474. It is not, relevantly, a decision to which s 474 applies.

Since *Plaintiff S157* was decided, the immigration matters to reach the High Court by way of s 75(v) have included *Dranichnikov v Minister for Immigration and Multicultural Affairs* (2003) 197 ALR 389 and *Re Minister for Immigration and Multicultural Affairs; Ex parte Applicant S20/2002* (2003) 198 ALR 59. In the former case the applicant succeeded: orders for prohibition, certiorari and mandamus were made absolute. In the latter case the applicant failed; but Kirby J (who dissented) took the opportunity to emphasise again that "**[95]** what is afforded by [s 75(v) of] the Constitution is a beneficial remedy of the greatest importance and utility". McHugh and Gummow JJ, in the leading majority judgment, also emphasised that the "**[65]** minimum measure of judicial review" that s 75(v) "entrenches" could no longer be ignored: "The decisions upon s 75(v), which extend across the whole period of the court's existence, may have been overlooked or discounted by administrative lawyers as being largely of immediate concern for industrial law. That, as this litigation illustrates, can no longer be so".

5. Further References

Barwick, G, *A Radical Tory* (Federation Press, 1995), Ch 24.

Basten, J, "Constitutional Elements of Judicial Review" (2004) 15 *Public Law Review* 187.

Beaton-Wells, C, "Judicial Review of Migration Decisions: Life After *S175*" (2005) 33 *Federal Law Review* 141.

Campbell, E, and Groves, M, "Privative Clauses and the Australian Constitution" (2004) 4 *Oxford University Commonwealth Law Journal* 51.

Cooray, LJM, *Conventions, the Australian Constitution and the Future* (Legal Books, 1979).

Evans, G (ed), *Labor and the Constitution 1972-1975* (Heinemann Educational, 1977).

Evans, S, "The Rule of Law, Constitutionalism and the MV Tampa" (2002) 13 *Public Law Review* 94.

Evans, S, 'Continuity and Flexibility: Executive Power in Australia" in Craig, P, and Tomkins, A (eds), *Power and Accountability in Comparative Perspective* (Oxford University Press, 2005), 89.

Evatt, HV, *The King and His Dominion Governors* (Legal Books, 2nd ed 1990).

Evatt, HV, *The Royal Prerogative* (Law Book Co, 1987).

Jackson, D, "Development of Judicial Review in Australia over the last 10 Years: The Growth of Constitutional Writs" (2004) 12 *Australian Journal of Administrative Law* 22.

Kelly, P, *November 1975: The Inside Story of Australia's Greatest Political Crisis* (Allen & Unwin, 1995).

Kerr, D, and Williams, G, "Review of Executive Action and the Rule of Law under the Australian Constitution" (2003) 14 *Public Law Review* 219.

Lindell, G, "Responsible Government" in Finn, PD (ed), *Essays on Law and Government: Principles and Values* (Law Book Co, 1995) vol 1, 75.

Lindell, G, *Responsible Government and the Australian Constitution: Conventions Transformed into Law?* (Law and Policy Paper 24, Federation Press and Centre for International and Public Law, 2004).

McHugh, MH, "Tensions between the Executive and the Judiciary" (2003) 6 *Judicial Review* 111.

Meyerson, D, "Rethinking the Constitutionality of Delegated Legislation" (2003) 11 *Australian Journal of Administrative Law* 45.

Meyerson, D, "State and Federal Privative Clauses: Not So Different After All" (2005) 16 *Public Law Review* 39.

Pearce, DC, and Argument, S, *Delegated Legislation in Australia* (LexisNexis Butterworths, 3rd ed 2005).

Renfree, HE, *The Executive Power of the Commonwealth of Australia* (Legal Books, 1984).

Richardson, JE, "The Executive Power of the Commonwealth" in Zines, L (ed), *Commentaries on the Australian Constitution* (Butterworths, 1977), 50.

Robertson, H, "Truth, Justice and the Australian Way: *Plaintiff S157 of 2002 v Commonwealth*" (2003) 31 *Federal Law Review* 373.

Saunders, C, "The National Implied Power and Implied Restrictions on Commonwealth Power" (1984) 14 *Federal Law Review* 267.

Sawer G, *Federation under Strain* (Melbourne University Press, 1977).

Seddon, N, "The Crown" (2000) 28 *Federal Law Review* 245.

Selway, B, "All at Sea: Constitutional Assumptions and 'the Executive Power of the Commonwealth'" (2003) 31 *Federal Law Review* 495.

Selway, B, "Mr Egan, the Legislative Council and Responsible Government" in Stone, A, and Williams, G (eds), *The High Court at the Crossroads: Essays in Constitutional Law* (Federation Press, 2000), 35.

Selway, B, "The Constitutional Role of the Queen in Australia" (2003) 32 *Common Law World Review* 248.

Smith, D, *Head of State: the Governor General, the Monarchy and the Dismissal* (Macleay Press, 2005).

Spigelman, JJ, "Integrity and Privative Clauses" in Pearce, D (ed), *AIAL National Lecture Series on Administrative Law No 2* (Australian Institute of Administrative Law, 2004), 43.

Stephen, N, "The Governor-General as Commander-in-Chief" (1984) 14 *Melbourne University Law Review* 563.

"Symposium on Executive Power" (2005) 16 *Public Law Review* 276.

Twomey, A, *The Constitution of New South Wales* (Federation Press, 2004), Ch 12.

Whitlam, G, *The Truth of the Matter* (Melbourne University Press, 3rd ed 2005).

Williams, G, "The Power to Go to War: Australia in Iraq" (2004) 15 *Public Law Review* 5.

Winterton, G, "1975: The Dismissal of the Whitlam Government" in Lee, HP, and Winterton, G (eds), *Australian Constitutional Landmarks* (Cambridge University Press, 2003), 229.

Winterton, G, "The Evolution of a Separate Australian Crown" (1993) 19 *Monash University Law Review* 1.

Winterton, G, "The Evolving Role of the Australian Governor-General" in Groves, M (ed), *Law and Government in Australia* (Federation Press, 2005), 44.

Winterton, G, "The Limits and Use of Executive Power by Government" (2003) 31 *Federal Law Review* 421.

Winterton, G, *Parliament, the Executive and the Governor-General* (Melbourne University Press, 1983).

Zines, L, *The High Court and the Constitution* (Butterworths, 4th ed 1997), Chs 9 and 12.

Chapter 13

The High Court
and Constitutional Litigation

1. The Platonic High Court

The first two barristers to argue a case before the High Court were named Wise and Sly. The argument was heard in Sydney on 6 November 1903 (after earlier ceremonial sittings in October at Melbourne, Sydney and Brisbane). Wise appeared for the Commonwealth and Sly represented the plaintiff in a case that the Supreme Court of New South Wales had decided on 20 August 1903 (*Hannah v Dalgarno* (1903) 3 SR (NSW) 495).

A telephone wire that was being repaired in Elizabeth Street, Sydney, had broken, falling across an electric trolley-wire and electrocuting the horse that drew Robert Hannah's hansom cab. In an action brought under the *Claims against the Commonwealth Act 1902* (Cth) against James Dalgarno as a nominal defendant representing the Commonwealth, Hannah recovered damages of £200. A majority in the full Supreme Court affirmed that verdict. At the Sydney sitting on 15 October the High Court had granted Dalgarno leave to appeal; but the plaintiff successfully argued that leave to appeal should be rescinded. How, argued Sly, could a Supreme Court decision on 20 August be the subject of an appeal to a High Court which at that date did not yet exist? Even as a statutory matter, the existence of the Court as an avenue of appeal could not predate the *Judiciary Act 1903* (Cth), which constituted the Court ("shall consist of the Chief Justice and two other Justices"), and regulated its jurisdiction and procedure. That Act was assented to on 25 August, five days *after* the Supreme Court decision in *Hannah v Dalgarno*. By s 35 of that Act the High Court's appellate jurisdiction "shall extend to" several enumerated categories of judgments, including those "given or made before the commencement of this Act";

but none of the categories thus made retrospective extended to *Hannah v Dalgarno*. Wise replied on behalf of the defendant that none of this mattered:

Hannah v Dalgarno
(1903) 1 CLR 1

Wise KC (in argument): **[4]** [T]he defendant, apart from the *Judiciary Act* has a constitutional right to appeal by virtue of sec 73 of the Constitution. By sec 71 of the same Act, the judicial power of the Commonwealth is vested not only in federal Courts but also in such Courts of the States as the Parliament invests with federal jurisdiction. The *Claims against the Commonwealth Act* (No 21 of 1902, sec 6) gave the Supreme Court of New South Wales jurisdiction to try this case in the first instance. The papers are entitled "In the Supreme Court of New South Wales, Federal jurisdiction". There was, therefore, a right of appeal to this Court, but there was no Court to appeal to.

Griffith CJ: You say the High Court was potentially in existence all the time.

Wise KC: That is so. The *Judiciary Act* does not constitute the Court, it only determines the number of judges. The Court existed potentially from the date of the establishment of the Constitution. Therefore, sec 35 of the *Judiciary Act* does not affect the position.

This argument depended on two provisions of the Constitution: s 71, which provides that Commonwealth judicial power *"shall be vested* in a Federal Supreme Court, to be called the High Court of Australia"; and s 73, which provides that the High Court *"shall have jurisdiction*, with such exceptions ... as the Parliament prescribes, to hear and determine appeals from all judgments ... [of any] court exercising federal jurisdiction" (emphases added). The argument was that these provisions immediately became operative on 1 January 1901.

Although the Court thought it prudent, as a matter of discretion, to rescind the defendant's leave to appeal, this did *not* involve a rejection of Wise's argument.

Griffith CJ (for the Court): **[10]** It is important to remember that the powers of the Parliament [under s 73 of the Constitution], so far as regards the appellate jurisdiction of the Court, are limited to prescribing "exceptions" from the otherwise unrestricted jurisdiction conferred by the Constitution ... But it has no authority to create any additional appellate jurisdiction. The authority, therefore, if any, of this Court to hear the case now before us is to be sought not in the *Judiciary Act* but in the Constitution itself, and sec 35 of that Act is to be regarded, not as a provision for creating rights of appeal, but as a provision making exceptions from the jurisdiction conferred by the Con-**[11]**-stitution and prescribing regulations as to its exercise. Had then the High Court jurisdiction to entertain appeals from judgments pronounced before the passing of the *Judiciary Act*? The Court, as the embodiment of the judicial power inherent in every Sovereign State, is an essential part of the structure of the Commonwealth. Sec 73 of the Constitution has been in force from the establishment of the Commonwealth, although the power of the High Court could not, of course, be exercised until the Court was actually constituted by the Parliament. With regard to judgments pronounced by the Supreme Court, in the exercise of their State jurisdiction before the passing of the *Judiciary Act*, the right of appeal to the High Court was to be subject to the same conditions and restrictions as appeals to His Majesty in Council until those conditions and restrictions were altered by the Parliament. In the meantime, if ... the prescribed time had elapsed before the actual establishment of the High Court, without an assertion by the unsuccessful party of his right to appeal to His Majesty, his right was gone. But as to appeals from federal Courts or Courts exercising federal jurisdiction other considerations arise. There is much force in the contention that the jurisdiction of those Courts was, from the first, intended to be subject to the right of appeal to the High Court, and that that right, being a right conferred by the Constitution itself upon suitors, could not be lost or taken away by mere inaction of the Parliament, or in any other way except by actual legislation prescribing exceptions. The temporary inability to exercise a statutory right by reason of a delay which, from the nature of the case, was inevitable, in the passing of an Act to determine the number of Judges of the High Court, could not, in this view, operate as a destruction or diminution of the right itself.

[12] On the other hand it may be said that the words of sections 71 and 73 of the Constitution are words of futurity, that a right of appeal to a non-existent Court is illusory, and that a right of appeal involves an incidental right to take proceedings for giving effect to it, which cannot be taken until the Court of appeal itself exists ... The question is one of difficulty and importance. It is, however, a matter for our discretion to say whether so important a question should be decided in the present case. And considering the nature of the case, which is, we think, on the border line ... , we think that our discretion would be most fitly exercised by refusing leave to appeal.

This judgment just stopped short of holding that, despite the Parliament's initial delay in bringing it into existence, the High Court had been an essential part of the Australian constitutional universe even before it existed. On that view, under the Australian Constitution, the High Court is like Heidegger's God: it *is*, even when it does not *exist*.

2. Appointment and Removal of Judges

As originally adopted, s 72 of the Constitution provided:

Constitution of the Commonwealth of Australia

72. The Justices of the High Court and of the other courts created by the Parliament –
  (i.)   Shall be appointed by the Governor-General in Council:
  (ii.) Shall not be removed except by the Governor-General in Council, on an address from both Houses of the Parliament in the same session, praying for such removal on the ground of proved misbehaviour or incapacity:
  (iii.) Shall receive such remuneration as the Parliament may fix; but the remuneration shall not be diminished during their continuance in office.

In *New South Wales v Commonwealth* (*Wheat Case*) (1915) 20 CLR 54, the limited provision in para (ii) for removal from office – apparently the only way in which a judge can cease to hold office except voluntarily – was treated as meaning that High Court judges had guaranteed tenure for life. That remained the position until 1977, and resulted in some very long tenures. In 1950 Rich and Starke JJ resigned at the ages of 87 and 79 respectively; in 1975 McTiernan J resigned at the age of 84, after a record 46 years on the Court.

By referendum in 1977, another seven paragraphs were added to s 72, essentially for the purpose of establishing a compulsory retirement age. For the High Court this is fixed at 70; for other federal courts the *maximum* is 70, with power for the Parliament to prescribe a lower age. Those judges already appointed before 1977 remained entitled to tenure for life. However, Sir Harry Gibbs (first appointed to the Court on 4 August 1970) was appointed as Chief Justice on 12 February 1981; and Sir Anthony Mason (first appointed on 21 September 1972) was appointed as Chief Justice on 6 February 1987. Although in each of these cases the initial appointment was for life, the new final paragraph of s 72 was interpreted as meaning (first) that appointment as Chief Justice was an "appointment" to which the new compulsory retirement age of 70 was attached; and (second) that acceptance of the appointment implied an abandonment of any continuing entitlement to serve as a puisne justice for life.

(a)   Appointment

There have been 45 appointments to the High Court, including the current seven judges (see Appendix and Francesca Dominello and Eddy Neumann, "Background of Justices" in Tony Blackshield, Michael Coper and George Williams (eds), *The Oxford Companion to the High Court of Australia* (Oxford University Press, 2001), 48). Most judges have been over 50 when appointed, with an average of around 53 years. The last person appointed before the age of 50 was Mary Gaudron, who joined the Court at age 43 in 1987. Owen Dixon was appointed at the same age in 1929. Only two judges have been appointed younger: Herbert Vere Evatt was 36 and

Edward McTiernan was 38 when the two were appointed in December 1930. On the other hand, William Owen, aged 62, is the oldest person to have joined the Court.

The Justices have come from a relatively narrow section of Australian society. In almost every case, a person has been appointed directly from being a barrister or judge. Unlike judges on final courts in other nations, none has been appointed from a full-time academic position (although Dyson Heydon, appointed in 2003 after more than two decades as a barrister and judge, had been a Professor and Dean of the University of Sydney Law Faculty in the 1970s and early 1980s). Every one of the 45 judges has been of an Anglo-Celtic background, with only one, Michael Kirby, being openly gay and only two, Gaudron and Susan Crennan, being female.

The appointments have often been "political". The first Commonwealth Prime Minister, Sir Edmund Barton, appointed himself to the High Court; his brother judges, Sir Samuel Griffith and Richard O'Connor, were also seasoned veterans of colonial and federating politics. Sir Samuel Griffith had been both Premier and Chief Justice of Queensland. Sir Isaac Isaacs, Sir John Latham, Sir Garfield Barwick and Lionel Murphy had all been Commonwealth Attorneys-General before appointment to the High Court. While some appointments have been controversial, the decision of whom to appoint and the criteria for their selection remain questions for the federal executive alone.

Rachel Davis and George Williams, "Reform of the Judicial Appointments Process: Gender and the Bench of the High Court of Australia"
(2003) 27 *Melbourne University Law Review* 819

[823] The only provision in the *Australian Constitution* relating to the process of appointment to the High Court is s 72(i), which states that Justices of the Court '[s]hall be appointed by the Governor-General in Council'. In practice, this means that the Governor-General makes the appointment acting on the advice of the government of the day. Other than prohibiting the appointment of judges who have reached the retirement age of 70 years, the *Constitution* makes no mention of qualifications or background, and contains no other procedural requirements. It does not even require that an appointee be qualified as a lawyer.

The *High Court of Australia Act 1979* (Cth) is slightly more prescriptive. Section 7 requires that an appointee be a judge of a federal or state court, or have been enrolled as a legal practitioner in Australia for not less than five years. Section 6 states that, before making an appointment, the 'Attorney-General shall ... consult with the Attorneys-General of the States' (no mention is made of the Attorneys-General of the territories). However, the extent and form of consultation is not specified and it is unclear whether this process has any real effect on the appointment ...

According to former federal Attorney-General Daryl Williams, appointees to the High Court are chosen on 'the essential criterion' of merit, a basic policy that has been confirmed by ... Attorney-General, Philip Ruddock. As for more specific criteria: 'It is enough to say that outstanding professional skills and personal qualities, such as integrity and industry, are required, together with a proper appreciation of the role of the Court.' Currently, the Attorney-General consults with both the state and territory Attorneys-General prior to an appointment being made to the High Court. With respect to federal appointments generally, the Attorney-General also holds confidential consultations, or 'informal discussions', with various individuals, including 'the Chief Justice (or equivalent) of the relevant court', 'legal professional bodies such as the Law Council and the Bar Association or Law Society' of the relevant state or territory, 'serving and former judges, the Attorney-General's ministerial and parliamentary colleagues, [and] appropriate community groups' ...

[824] It does not appear that those 'consulted' are requested to assess candidates against specific criteria, but are instead simply asked for their personal opinion or 'impression'. According to Sir Harry Gibbs, the extent to which the views of those consulted are actually taken into account varies, as does the extent of consultations. As former federal Attorney-General Michael Lavarch has said: 'If equity could be said to vary depending on the size of the Chancellor's foot, then the selection process, for Commonwealth judges at least, can alter with each Attorney-General'.

After 'consulting', the Attorney-General informs Cabinet of his or her recommendation – or recommendations, in the case of more than one vacancy. At the time of the … appointment [of Dyson Heydon] made to the High Court in February 2003, the Attorney-General also conducted private interviews with candidates but did not indicate what questions were put to candidates, or how this information was used in the selection process.

Cabinet then considers the Attorney-General's recommendation and may accept it or may decide on an entirely different person. It is unclear what information, other than the candidate's name, Cabinet has before it when it makes its decision. However, the limited evidence available of instances where an Attorney-General's preferred candidate has not been accepted by Cabinet demonstrates that the choice has been influenced by considerations as diverse as the potential appointee's 'politics, state of origin, friendships, and the views of sitting Justices'.

[825] The Attorney-General, after securing the agreement of the nominee chosen by Cabinet, 'formally recommends' the appointment to the Governor-General. In practice, then, the Governor-General in Council has no active involvement in the process and the decision is entirely in the hands of a small group in the executive. The lack of established criteria (beyond the vague notion of 'merit'), and of an entrenched process of public consultation, means that appointments to the High Court have been accurately described as being 'the gift' of the executive government.

In 1993, Commonwealth Attorney-General Michael Lavarch released a discussion paper (*Judicial Appointments – Procedure and Criteria*) that explored ways of making the appointment process more open to public scrutiny, and the resulting spread of appointments more representative. Since then, many proposals have been put forward for reform, including the adoption of criteria (rather than merely the idea of "merit") to guide the process and the establishment of a judicial appointments commission to advise on the making of appointments.

(b)   Removal

The 1977 referendum rebutted the implication of tenure for life that the High Court had drawn from s 72(ii) of the Constitution. However, the text of s 72(ii) remains unchanged. It provides that federal judges, including the Justices of the High Court, can *only* be removed by "the Governor-General in Council on an address from both Houses of Parliament in the same session praying for such removal on the ground of proved misbehaviour or incapacity".

Presumably, in any clear or obvious case of misbehaviour, the misbehaviour would readily be regarded as "proved" and both Houses of Parliament would act accordingly in a non-partisan manner. However, in any controversial or ambiguous case, it is difficult to see how the machinery envisaged by s 72(ii) could be made to work objectively. The only sustained attempts to establish a case for removal from the High Court related to Murphy J – initially through the criminal prosecution brought against him and other former ministers of the Whitlam government in *Sankey v Whitlam* (1978) 142 CLR 1; and then, when that prosecution collapsed, through a series of allegations centred on the so-called "*Age* tapes" (alleged transcripts of intercepted phone conversations, as published by the Melbourne *Age* on 2 February 1984).

The first attempts to establish whether or not there were grounds for removal of Murphy J under s 72(ii) involved two Senate Committees, reporting respectively on 24 August 1984 and 31 October 1984 (Parliamentary Papers Nos 168/1984 and 271/1984). The first committee cleared Murphy J of all allegations arising from the "*Age* tapes", but gave rise to a fresh allegation by Clarrie Briese CSM. As to that allegation, and also as to a further allegation by Judge Paul Flannery, the second committee yielded five different views, in some instances apparently partisan and in others heavily qualified. The overall effect was inconclusive. At that stage Ian Temby QC, as Commonwealth Director of Public Prosecutions, laid criminal charges against Murphy J. On 5 July 1985 a jury acquitted Murphy J of the Flannery charge but convicted him of the Briese charge. That conviction was overturned on appeal (*R v Murphy* (1985) 4 NSWLR 42), and on 28 April 1986 a second jury acquitted Murphy J of the Briese charge. However, before he could return to the Court a new Parliamentary Commission of Inquiry, constituted by three retired State and federal judges, was established to review all aspects of his private and public life. At the time of Murphy J's death in 1986 that Commission had assembled 42 allegations; had determined that 28 of them were lacking in substance; and had set aside the remaining 14 to be explored in more detail. The Commission's work was never completed. In spite of two-and-a-half years of travail, the entire saga offered little hope of a manageable fact-finding procedure by which the two Houses of Parliament might arrive at, or for that matter reject, a finding of "proved misbehaviour or incapacity". Nor did it shed much meaningful light on what that expression might mean.

AR Blackshield, "The 'Murphy Affair'"

in Jocelynne Scutt (ed), *Lionel Murphy: A Radical Judge* (McCulloch Publishing, 1987), 230

[253] In 1901, when the Constitution first came into force, the *Annotated Constitution of the Australian Commonwealth* prepared by John Quick and Robert Garran had expounded the meaning of 'proved misbehaviour' for purposes of section 72 by quoting a passage from an earlier classic, Alpheus Todd's *Parliamentary Government in England*. Todd had written:

> Misbehaviour includes, firstly, the improper exercise of judicial functions; secondly, wilful neglect of duty, or non-attendance; and thirdly, a conviction for any infamous offence, by which, although it be not connected with the duties of his office, the offender is rendered unfit to exercise any office or public franchise.

Clearly, if Todd's enumeration is an exhaustive statement of the kinds of 'misbehaviour' that call for removal under section 72, the only basis on which Justice Murphy's judicial position could ever have been under threat would have been a criminal conviction on a sufficiently serious charge.

[254] Before the first Senate Committee, Murphy's lawyers had argued that 'misbehaviour' should indeed be restricted along the lines suggested by Todd; and as early as 24 February 1984, an opinion from the Commonwealth Solicitor-General, Gavan Griffith QC, had taken a similar view. But a later opinion given to the Committee by CW Pincus QC on 14 May 1984 had argued for a wider view:

> I think it is for Parliament to decide whether any conduct alleged against a judge constitutes misbehaviour sufficient to justify removal from office. There is no 'technical' relevant meaning of misbehaviour and in particular it is not necessary, in order for the jurisdiction under s 72 to be enlivened, that an offence be proved.

The only significant pronouncement of the Parliamentary Commission of Inquiry established in May 1986 also took a wider view. In a ruling on the meaning of 'misbehaviour' on 5 August 1986 (tabled in Parliament on 21 August 1986), all three members of the Commission seemed inclined to accept a submission that Todd's enumeration never had been an accurate reflection of the traditional British position. But in any event, all three of them convincingly held that the Australian provision should *not* be regarded as perpetuating the British position, but as a distinctive fresh start.

As between the wider and narrower views of what section 72 requires, the wider view seems clearly correct. Its only deficiency, in the version expounded by Pincus QC and by the three Parliamentary Commissioners, is a logical paradox. The essential point, as Pincus observes, is that there is no relevant 'technical' meaning of misbehaviour; but what this really means is that Parliament's power of removal cannot *legally* be defined at all. Yet inevitably, as Mr Pincus and the Commissioners set out their views, they were in the position of legal authorities expounding a legal opinion. They were simultaneously informing us of the section's legal meaning, and asserting that it has no legal meaning.

In the Pincus opinion, this self-negation was at most only latent. The three Commissioners, however, met the paradox head on, making it clear that, as they understood it, their wide definition of 'misbehaviour' involved legal propositions to be arrived at by a process of legal construction. Andrew Wells QC spoke of section 72 as 'a code', and sought to emulate 'the approach that a Court should adopt' to 'construing' such a code. Commissioner Blackburn also spoke of 'solving this problem of construction'. All three of them sought to avoid the paradox of self-invalidation by insisting that, though the concept of 'misbehaviour' was a wide one, it was not an unlimited one; and that the limits which they sought to articulate were legal limits.

This, however, is precisely the problem. Assume that the crucial words 'proved misbehaviour' do have a legal meaning. Then, if Parliament did present an address by both Houses to the Governor-General, and if in response to that address the Governor-General did in fact remove a judge from office, the judge would be entitled to appeal to the High Court of Australia, arguing that the Parliament (and the Governor-General) had not correctly understood or applied their legally circumscribed powers. Commissioner Lush tentatively suggested that, in 'the present state of Australian jurisprudence', such an issue would indeed be justiciable. By contrast, in the practical world of institutional possibility, any adjudication on such an issue would seem to me quite unthinkable.

Section 72 has a double purpose: to ensure that no one but Parliament can [255] remove a judge from office, but also to ensure that Parliament *can*. The power of removal is the ultimate and the only check on judicial authority: it would simply be unworkable to subject this power to an appeal to that very authority. (The *reductio ad absurdum* would be to imagine that all seven judges might be removed on addresses from both Houses of Parliament, and that all seven judges thus removed might then appeal to themselves.)

It is just for this reason that I would contend that the meaning of 'proved misbehaviour' must rest solely on the Parliament's judgment in any given case, and that its *potential* meaning thus has no legal limits at all. No doubt this proposition is itself a legal proposition, and the High Court could be asked to say whether this proposition is correct. But, if it did so decide, it could then have nothing further to say. The central point of section 72 is that removal is a matter for Parliament; and the *only* relevant function of the High Court would be to ensure that Parliament's power was not eroded by the interference of any other body, including itself.

Commissioner Wells had a different suggestion: that if a judge were removed the High Court might be able to review the Parliament's 'verdict' in the same way as a court of appeal can review a jury's verdict: namely, by asking 'whether there was evidence upon which the jury ... could fairly have arrived at the verdict from which the appeal was brought'. It is, perhaps, just conceivable that if a judge were to be removed on the basis of clearly inadequate evidence, the High Court might be able to intervene in this way. But in the world of practical politics, even this degree of control by the Court on the Parliament's control of the Court seems difficult to imagine. Besides, Wells' analogy with a jury verdict re-emphasised the central problem. The issue he postulated was whether the jury, 'subject to a proper direction in law', could fairly have arrived at its verdict. But who, in the case of the Parliament's 'verdict', is to give this direction in law? The only acceptable answer is that the Parliament itself must do so.

This does not mean that there are no limits on the Parliament's scope for removal of judges. But it means that the limits are essentially political, not legal, in nature. If Parliament were to impute 'misbehaviour' to a judge who picked his nose on the bench, I would be among the first to protest. But in doing so I would be advancing a political, not a legal, argument. I would be contending that Parliament *ought not* to remove a judge on such a ground. Equally, I would for the most part accept the good sense of the various suggestions and cautions advanced by the three Commissioners as to what might or might not be sufficiently serious to warrant removal. I would stress, however, that their comments were valid as *political advice* which each individual member of Parliament was free to accept or reject, not as *legal instruction* by which the Parliament or its members were in any way bound. The removal is vested exclusively and entirely in the Australian Commonwealth Parliament; and whether or not the grounds exist for its exercise is also a question exclusively for Parliament.

3. Jurisdiction and Procedure

(a)   Jurisdiction

Unlike the Supreme Court of the United States, the High Court combines its distinctive federal functions with those of an ordinary court of appeal for the States in matters of general law. The Court's appellate jurisdiction is outlined by s 73 of the Constitution. It embraces (i) appeals from within the High Court itself (typically from a single Justice to a larger bench) in matters arising within the Court's original jurisdiction; (ii) appeals from any "federal court, or court exercising federal jurisdiction", *and also* (regardless of any federal element) appeals from the State Supreme Courts or any other State courts from which it was formerly possible to appeal to the Privy Council; and (iii) appeals, on questions of law, from the Inter-State Commission envisaged by ss 101-103 of the Constitution. This last possibility has been a dead letter for most of the High Court's history (see Chapter 14, §1 and Chapter 27, §1(a)).

The three classes of appellate jurisdiction enumerated in s 73 are often said to be "exclusive and exhaustive". However, in this respect as in others the extent to which Ch III of the Constitution is or is not applicable to the courts of the Territories has been problematic (see the cases discussed in Chapter 6, §5). In *Porter v The King; Ex parte Chin Man Yee* (1926) 37 CLR 432, it was held that the High Court's appellate jurisdiction does extend to those courts; and that decision has consistently been reaffirmed even though a Territory court is not regarded as falling within s 73(ii) of the Constitution since it is neither a "federal court" nor a "court exercising federal jurisdiction". The explanation accepted in the *Boilermakers' Case* (*R v Kirby; Ex parte Boilermakers' Society of Australia* (1956) 94 CLR 254) was that s 73, and indeed Ch III as a whole, "**[290]** has reference only to the federal system of which the Territories do not form a part". But any assumption that Territory courts lie wholly outside the universe of Ch III can no longer be accepted, and appeals from the Territories to the High Court have increasingly been perceived as anomalous (see, for example, Gaudron J in *Re Governor, Goulburn Correctional Centre; Ex parte Eastman* (1999) 200 CLR 322 at 337).

In *Ruhani v Director of Police* (2005) 219 ALR 199, the High Court held that jurisdiction could be conferred upon the High Court to determine appeals from the Supreme Court of Nauru. Kirby J concluded, partly on the basis of the Territories example, that the categories of appellate jurisdiction enumerated in Ch III are *not* "exclusive and exhaustive". He therefore felt able to hold that the *Nauru (High Court Appeals) Act 1976* (Cth) was valid as a conferral on the High Court of additional appellate jurisdiction. However, no other judge held that the jurisdiction had been conferred on this basis. In particular, Callinan and Heydon JJ reaffirmed that s 73 defines the Court's appellate jurisdiction "**[265]** in a clearly exclusive way". They found it "**[264]** unthinkable that the founders would have considered it necessary, or desirable, to make provision for the bringing of appeals to the High Court from another dominion or colony of the Empire, let alone from a foreign country".

The other members of the Court in *Ruhani* were less emphatic. McHugh J approached the issue by weighing up competing indicia of whether or not the jurisdiction could be characterised as "appellate", though one factor he adduced as telling against that characterisation was that "**[212]** the jurisdiction to hear an 'appeal' under the Nauru Appeals Act is not jurisdiction falling within s 73 of the Constitution". Gleeson CJ noted that the argument for a valid conferral of appellate jurisdiction "**[200]** would face the formidable obstacle of a long line of authority" reaffirming the *Boilermakers* view of Ch III as "an exhaustive statement of the manner in which the judicial power of the Commonwealth is or may be vested"; but he found it "**[201]** unnecessary to examine [the argument] in greater detail". Similarly, Gummow and Hayne JJ noted that the "**[228]** exhaustive and exclusive nature of the provisions of Ch III" had been confirmed in *Re Wakim; Ex parte McNally* (*Cross-Vesting Case*) (1999) 198 CLR 511; but they also noted that Territory appeals "are not readily reconciled with that view" and concluded: "**[228]** This is not an appropriate occasion to consider further the present state of authority in this area. It is sufficient to say that … there appear no grounds of textual necessity or constitutional expediency which would warrant any distortion of Ch III beyond what may presently be required by the case law concerning s 122".

All of the appellate jurisdiction conferred by s 73 is subject to such "exceptions" and "regulations" as the Parliament may prescribe. However, as to appeals from State Supreme Courts, the legislative power to prescribe exceptions or regulations is limited. As to any matter in which, in 1901, an appeal lay from a State Supreme Court to the Privy Council, no statutory enactment can prevent the High Court from hearing and determining an appeal. In such matters, of course, the

High Court itself may decline to hear an appeal; and the Parliament may provide (as it has done since 1984 by s 35 of the *Judiciary Act 1903* (Cth)) that appeals from any State court require the special leave of the High Court itself. The validity of this requirement was affirmed in *Smith Kline & French Laboratories (Aust) Ltd v Commonwealth* (1991) 173 CLR 194.

As to appeals in federal jurisdiction, the Parliament's power to prescribe "exceptions" or "regulations" has no such limits (see *Watson v Commissioner of Taxation* (1953) 87 CLR 353; *Cockle v Isaksen* (1957) 99 CLR 155). Thus, Commonwealth statutes may contain particular provisions excluding or limiting the possibility of appeal to the High Court, or allowing it only on specified conditions (see, for example, *Family Law Act 1975* (Cth), s 95).

The original jurisdiction of the High Court – that is, the range of matters in which action may be initiated in the Court – is outlined in the Constitution by ss 75 and 76. Section 75 lists matters in which the Court "shall have original jurisdiction"; s 76 lists additional matters in which original High Court jurisdiction may be conferred by the Parliament. Oddly, these areas of jurisdiction left to Parliament's discretion include matters "arising under this Constitution, or involving its interpretation". In those matters the Court's original jurisdiction is conferred by s 30(a) of the *Judiciary Act*. Section 76 also allows the High Court to be given original jurisdiction in any matters arising "under any laws made by the Parliament"; in Admiralty and maritime matters; and in matters where "the same subject-matter [is] claimed under the laws of different States". Before the creation of the Federal Court of Australia in 1976, the original jurisdiction conferred on the High Court was extensive; but since then it has been cut back so that today, apart from constitutional cases, the only other area of jurisdiction still assigned to the High Court by s 30 of the *Judiciary Act* relates to "(c) trials of indictable offences against the laws of the Commonwealth" (though the last example was *R v Brewer* (1942) 66 CLR 535).

Apart from the *Judiciary Act*, the effect of s 76(ii) is that other "laws made by the Parliament" may add to the original jurisdiction of the Court from time to time. Thus, in *Ruhani v Director of Police* (2005) 219 ALR 199, the provision for appeals from Nauru, though couched in the language of "appellate" jurisdiction, was treated as a grant of "original" jurisdiction – in the sense that the appeal to the High Court "**[212]** engages the judicial power of the Commonwealth for the first time", or "**[225]** represents the first engagement in Australia of any judicial power". Moreover, although the issues raised on appeal were to be determined solely by the law of Nauru, they gave rise to a matter "arising under" a law made by the Parliament because such a law "**[202]** may pick up the law of Nauru as the law to be applied in determining rights and liabilities in issue in an exercise of federal jurisdiction". As McHugh J put it, the Commonwealth law "**[215]** identifies Nauruan law as the *factum* by reference to which the Act operates and Nauruan law as the law to be applied in the resolution of proceedings brought under the Act ... **[218]** [It] adopts the substantive law of Nauru as the substantive law by reference to which the rights and duties of the parties are to be ascertained". Gummow and Hayne JJ took a similar view: "**[226]** A law made by the Parliament ... **[227]** may answer the relevant constitutional description even though it defines rights and obligations by adoption of, or by reference to, the laws of another polity", since "without that federal law there would be no subject-matter for determination by this Court". Both they and McHugh J invoked the example of *Hooper v Hooper* (1955) 91 CLR 529, where the post-war *Matrimonial Causes Act 1945* (Cth) had picked up, for the purposes of a limited federal jurisdiction, the matrimonial laws of the State or Territory in which the petitioner was domiciled. In that case the Court had held that the State or Territory laws thus picked up became "**[536]** part of the law of the Commonwealth" and that, equally, the Parliament might have chosen to define the rights of the parties "**[537]** by reference to the law of England or the law of New Zealand". In addition, McHugh J relied on *Western Australia v Commonwealth* (*Native Title Act Case*) (1995) 183 CLR 373, where the joint judgment, though rejecting the possibility that a federal statute could pick up the common law in this way, had conceded that: "**[484]** There can be no objection to the Commonwealth making a law by adopting as a law of the Commonwealth a text which emanates from a source other than the Parliament. In such a case the text **[485]** becomes, by adoption, a law of the Commonwealth and operates as such".

It was on this basis that Gleeson CJ, McHugh, Gummow and Hayne JJ were able to hold that the avenue of appeal had been validly created. Kirby J, though also holding the legislation valid, declined to accept this solution because, in his view, what was patently intended as "appellate jurisdiction" could only be described as "original jurisdiction" by "**[240]** extended mental gymnastics": "**[236]** Whilst the chosen language cannot determine conclusively the character of the jurisdiction, it would require an unreasonable alteration of the character of the jurisdiction … to turn the language of *appeals* into the substance of *original* jurisdiction. Prudent conjuring with words is the stuff of constitutional interpretation. Magic belongs elsewhere". He added, however, that if he had felt able to accept the use of the word "original" he would have agreed with the reasoning outlined above: "**[249]** The Australian federal law simply picks up the Nauruan law. It treats it as a *factum* upon which the exercise of this Court's jurisdiction is performed".

Callinan and Heydon JJ made no such concession. They held that the legislation was wholly invalid, and dismissed the majority's use of the term "original jurisdiction" as "**[263]** inapt and wrong". They did so in part because the view it implied of the earlier Nauruan proceedings "would be an affront to all elementary principles of comity … **[264]** In some unexpressed way, this Court is now, it is urged, bound to proceed as if … a decision has not been made and no trial has taken place. To proceed in that way would be to proceed in the teeth of the most clearly expressed language possible".

The original jurisdiction that the High Court "shall have" is limited to the rather anomalous collection of matters listed in s 75 of the Constitution. Most of them involve some aspect of inter-governmental relationships with other countries; or with the Commonwealth as a government; or between States or residents of different States. The unifying principle detected by Isaacs J in *Australasian Temperance and General Mutual Life Assurance Society Ltd v Howe* (1922) 31 CLR 290 was that "**[306]** [i]n every one of them the principle of *political identification or differentiation is present*" (the italics are his). Perhaps the most anomalous item in this collocation is the jurisdiction in matters arising "under any treaty" conferred by s 75(i), and invoked (apparently for the first time) in *Re East; Ex parte Nguyen* (1998) 196 CLR 354. The result of that case left it in doubt whether s 75(i) has any significant content at all. The applicant complained that the failure to provide him with an interpreter in County Court proceedings infringed the *Racial Discrimination Act 1975* (Cth); and that this was a matter arising "under any treaty" because the Act gives effect to the 1966 International Convention on the Elimination of all Forms of Racial Discrimination. However, the remedies sought by the applicant were not envisaged by the Act, and the remedies and procedures that it did envisage had not been pursued. For these reasons among others, the Court dismissed the application on the ground that there was no "matter"– thus leaving unresolved the question whether, if there had been a "matter", it would have been a matter arising "under any treaty".

One possible answer was that no such judicially cognisable matter can ever arise. The analysis would be that until a treaty is implemented by Australian legislation, it cannot give rise to a matter in Australian law (see Chapter 19, §2(b)); but that once a treaty has been implemented by legislation, any relevant matter arises under the legislation, not under the treaty. In a separate judgment Kirby J argued against "**[133]** ascribing ignorant stupidity to the founders" by adopting such an analysis; but the point remains unresolved. The solution favoured by Kirby J was that a matter should be regarded as "arising under" a treaty "if, directly or indirectly, the right claimed or the duty asserted owes its existence to the treaty, depends upon the treaty for its enforcement or directly or indirectly draws upon the treaty as the source of the right or duty in controversy". When Kirby J applied this test in *Ruhani v Director of Police* (2005) 219 CLR 199 he held that it was not satisfied. The legislation investing the High Court with jurisdiction to entertain appeals from Nauru had been enacted pursuant to an Agreement made in 1976 between the Common-wealth of Australia and the Republic of Nauru and annexed to the legislation. However, Kirby J held that the substantive issues raised by the instant appeal (and presumably by any appeal) did not "**[248]** depend on the construction or effect of … the 1976 Agreement", but only on "the interpretation of various laws of Nauru". Similarly, Callinan and Heydon JJ held that the matter

"**[268]** [s]elf-evidently … does not arise under a treaty. It arises under Nauruan law exclusively". Gleeson CJ did not refer to this question, while McHugh, Gummow and Hayne JJ found it unnecessary to consider the issue.

In general the only jurisdiction of practical significance secured to the Court by s 75 is that conferred by s 75(v) in respect of "all matters … [i]n which a writ of Mandamus or prohibition or an injunction is sought against an officer of the Commonwealth". For example, most of the many cases concerning the powers of the Industrial Relations Commission and its predecessors under s 51(xxxv) of the Constitution have arisen by way of orders nisi for mandamus or prohibition under s 75(v). There is no reference in s 75(v) to writs of certiorari, but the power to issue writs of mandamus and prohibition has been held to imply an ancillary jurisdiction to grant certiorari (see *Pitfield v Franki* (1970) 123 CLR 448; *R v Cook; Ex parte Twigg* (1980) 147 CLR 15; *Re Coldham; Ex parte Brideson* (1989) 166 CLR 338). Because the expressions "jurisdiction" and "prohibition" are used in s 75 with constitutional force, and because the Crown is not an element of the judicature established by Ch III of the Constitution, Gaudron and Gummow JJ in *Re Refugee Tribunal; Ex parte Aala* (2000) 204 CLR 82 at 92-3 acceded to the view of Kirby J (at 133-4) that in this context the writs should be referred to as "constitutional writs" rather than "prerogative writs". The High Court's power to issue writs is further spelled out by s 33 of the *Judiciary Act*; but it seems clear that no such statutory provision could *limit* the jurisdiction that s 75(v) declares that the Court "shall have".

The fact that the High Court's jurisdiction under s 75(v) is constitutionally unassailable (except by referendum) appears to set a significant limit to legislative attempts to shield executive decision-making from judicial scrutiny. Restrictions on the jurisdiction of the Federal Court in such matters were held valid in *Abebe v Commonwealth* (1999) 197 CLR 510 (see §5(b) below); and from time to time as further restrictions on judicial review have been proposed, especially in regard to immigration decisions, it has been suggested that the Parliament might seek to exclude the jurisdiction even of the High Court. However, it does not appear that any legislative restrictions could have that effect. In *Plaintiff S157/2002 v Commonwealth* (2003) 211 CLR 476, the restrictions inserted in 2001 into the *Migration Act 1958* (Cth) were interpreted so as not to impinge on s 75(v); but the joint judgment in that case also insisted that "**[512]** the jurisdiction of this Court to grant relief under s 75(v) of the Constitution cannot be removed by or under a law made by the Parliament"; that "the jurisdiction to grant s 75(v) relief where there has been jurisdictional error by an officer of the Commonwealth cannot be removed"; and that s 75(v) provides "**[513]** an entrenched minimum provision of judicial review" which "constitutes a textual reinforcement" of the rule of law (see Chapter 12, §4(b)).

By s 77(ii) of the Constitution the Parliament may make laws "defining the extent to which the jurisdiction of any federal court shall be exclusive" of State court jurisdiction. It may also define the jurisdiction of federal courts other than the High Court (s 77(i)); and may make laws "investing any court of a State with federal jurisdiction" (s 77(iii) – see Chapter 6, §3). So far as the High Court is concerned, the power to make its jurisdiction exclusive has been exercised by s 38 of the *Judiciary Act* – in relation to matters arising "directly" under any treaty; suits brought by one State against another, or by the Commonwealth against a State or vice versa; and "matters in which a writ of mandamus or prohibition is sought against an officer of the Commonwealth or a federal court".

(b)　Initiating a Constitutional Case

Constitutional matters may be appealed to the High Court from the decisions of lower courts. The *Judiciary Act* also makes elaborate provision for removal into the High Court from any other State or federal court of "[a]ny cause or part of a cause arising under the Constitution or involving its interpretation" (s 40(1)); and (where all parties consent and the High Court "is satisfied that it is appropriate … having regard to … the public interest") of any other cause or part of a cause involving federal jurisdiction (s 40(2) and (4)). By s 42 any matter thus removed into the

High Court *may* be remitted to the court of origin, and *shall* be so remitted if the High Court finds that it lacks original jurisdiction to deal with it.

Matters commenced directly in the High Court may initially be heard by a single judge, but are often referred to a full bench by way of case stated or questions reserved. Section 18 of the *Judiciary Act* provides that a judge of the Court "may state any case or reserve any question for the consideration of a Full Court, or may direct any case or question to be argued before a Full Court, and a Full Court shall thereupon have power to hear and determine the case or question". These alternative procedures are explained below by Frank Jones, Registrar of the High Court from 1980 to 1995.

FWD Jones, "High Court Procedure under the Judiciary Act"
(1994) 68 *Australian Law Journal* 442

[442] *Case Stated*

The terms "case stated" and "questions reserved" by a justice are often used interchangeably …

A case stated is the procedure adopted when the parties can agree to the "constitutional facts" which they believe the court should have before it in order to properly consider the constitutional validity of the legislation which has been impugned.

There was a reluctance in the past, to allow the parties to determine the **[443]** "constitutional facts", the court being the custodian of the Constitution and equally the surveillant of constitutional facts.

Times have changed – in the past it was the practice of the court to have a justice find the facts and then formally state a case for the consideration of the Full Court. The workload of the court through the 1980s, and today, is such that a justice has not the time to conduct lengthy fact-finding hearings. The preferred course is for the parties to agree to the facts; the alternative is remitter of the fact-finding exercise to either the Federal Court or a Supreme Court of a State or Territory.

The usual procedure is for the parties to exchange drafts of the facts which they think are relevant until they agree. This process can take some considerable time when the facts are complex, and it is necessary that they be carefully particularised because of the need to have an accurate factual basis on which to found a constitutional argument. When the parties have agreed to the facts and the form of questions for consideration of the Full Court, a directions hearing is arranged by the registrar. The hearing is usually before the Chief Justice although other justices may state a case or reserve questions. On the occasions that the parties are not in complete agreement, the Chief Justice will use some judicial persuasion to bring the parties together and he may, if necessary, reformulate the questions …

The Chief Justice having formally indicated that he will state the case, the party having the carriage of the matter prepares an engrossed copy of the case stated for the signature of the Chief Justice. A case-stated book is then prepared in consultation with the registrar or deputy registrars. The case-stated book may contain only the stated case, however, there may be annexures such as the pleadings in the matter or, as was recently the case, the second reading speech of the Parliament …

[444] *Questions Reserved*

A justice most commonly reserves questions for the consideration of the Full Court in those cases where there are "pure" questions of law which can be referred without any agreed facts, or, where the facts as found by a lower court, such as on a s 40 of the *Judiciary Act* 1903 removal can be used as the factual background.

The "question reserved" procedure has recently been used in *Capital Duplicators Pty Ltd v Australian Capital Territory* [(1992) 177 CLR 248; directions hearing 18 December 1991], a case where the defendants demurred to the whole of the statement of claim pleading that no cause of action arose because the licence fee in question was not a duty of excise within the meaning of s 90 of the Constitution. Alternatively, if the licence fee was a duty of excise, it was not invalidly exacted by the defendants.

The court ordered that the second of the above issues be heard first, the question as ultimately framed by the court was:

"Does Ch IV of the Commonwealth Constitution operate so as to preclude the Legislative Assembly of the Australian Capital Territory from exercising the power to impose duties of excise within the meaning of s 90 of the Constitution?"

The subsequent answer of the court to the question was "Yes".

The above question involved only the parties, and the Commonwealth and Northern Territory as intervenors. If the additional questions raised by the demurrer, namely, whether the licence fee was an excise, or, whether the provisions of the Act were invalid as being a law with respect to a "classification of materials for the purpose of censorship" were heard together, there would have been interventions by Solicitors-General on behalf of all the States. If the basic constitutional question had been answered in the negative, their arguments on whether or not the licence fee was an excise would have been superfluous. By splitting the case and hearing the preliminary question first there was a considerable saving in hearing time and, most importantly, of the costs and time of the intervenors.

An alternative form of stated case is the parties' agreement on a "special case", as provided for in the *High Court Rules 2004* (Cth). The chief advantage is that, under r 27.08.5, "The Court may draw from the facts stated and documents identified in the special case any inference, whether of fact or law, which might have been drawn from them if proved at a trial".

In another version of the same article, Jones explains the procedure, at one time in frequent High Court use, for bringing a question of law before the Court by way of demurrer (see *High Court Rules*, r 27.07). In the old English system of written pleadings, retained in New South Wales until 1970, a "demurrer" was a written pleading by which to challenge the legal sufficiency of the opponent's pleadings. It asserted that even if all the opponent's averments of fact could be proven, those facts were not legally capable of producing the effect contended for. For purposes of deciding the pure question of law thus presented, it was *assumed* on the hearing of argument on the demurrer that all the factual averments were true.

FWD Jones, "The Story Behind the Headlines: Constitutional Procedures"
(1994) 12 *Australian Bar Review* 148

[149] The High Court Rules have retained the demurrer as a form of pleading when all other Australian courts, except the Supreme Court of Queensland, have discarded it as a form of pleading. What is a demurrer? What does it achieve? Sir Owen Dixon described the effect of a demurrer in the following terms [*South Australia v Commonwealth* (1961) 108 CLR 130 at 141-2]:

All that such a demurrer does is to deny the legal sufficiency of the facts alleged in the pleading, that is the sufficiency to entitle the plaintiff to a legal remedy.

[150] The virtue of proceedings by demurrer is that in an appropriate case it enables a quick decision to be given on a question of law when that will dispose of the whole action. Sometimes, however, particularly when the pleadings are defective, the demurrer will not lead to any final decision but will result only in delay of the proceeding and an increase in costs.

There are difficulties with the practical workings of demurrers where, for instance, the defendant has difficulty in accepting the allegations made by the plaintiff in the statement of claim. This is because it is basic to a demurrer that it admits for the purpose of its disposal all allegations of fact made in the statement of claim. The only facts which can be taken as admitted for this purpose are those which are expressly or impliedly averred in the statement of claim itself. The court cannot take as admitted a fact which is not averred but which is an inference from facts which are averred in the pleadings. This limitation on the use of facts and inferences has led to the decline in the use of the demurrer as a procedure for bringing constitutional cases before the High Court.

The Commonwealth is becoming increasingly reluctant to demur in constitutional cases whereas it was the common practice in the immediate post war period. It will only demur in those cases where there are few facts and where the question involved is one of the constitutional construction of legislation.

Both the procedure by way of demurrer and the formulation of "questions reserved" provide an efficient means of enabling constitutional questions to be raised before the High Court. They assist in defining the scope of the constitutional questions to be answered as well as the (often limited) factual basis upon which such questions are to be determined.

(c) Interveners and Amici Curiae

According to the traditional model of litigation, the task of a court "[533] is to determine disputes that are brought before it by parties who appear before it … [536] The general principle is that the parties are entitled to carry on their litigation free from the interference of persons who are strangers to the litigation" (*United States Tobacco Co v Minister for Consumer Affairs* (1988) 20 FCR 520). Despite this, the States and the Commonwealth have readily been given leave to intervene in constitutional matters – initially as a matter of judicial discretion, and since 1976 pursuant to ss 78A and 78B of the *Judiciary Act*.

Section 78A(1) provides for an automatic right of intervention by the Attorneys-General of the Commonwealth and the States in any "matter arising under the Constitution or involving its interpretation" that comes before an Australian court. In addition, s 78B requires that, whenever such a matter arises, a notice "specifying the nature of the matter" must be given to the Attorneys-General of the Commonwealth and the States. (For the purposes of both these provisions, "the States" include the Australian Capital Territory and the Northern Territory.) The purpose is to give the Attorneys-General an opportunity to intervene in the proceedings, or to seek their removal into the High Court under s 40. Until the notice has been given, and a reasonable time has elapsed to enable the Attorneys-General to consider their response, "it is the duty of the court not to proceed in the cause".

A survey by Enid Campbell ("Intervention in Constitutional Cases" (1998) 9 *Public Law Review* 225) of the 33 constitutional decisions handed down by the High Court between 1994 and 1997 found that at least one Attorney-General intervened in 29 of those cases, with a total of 95 interventions by Attorneys-General, or on average nearly three intervening Attorneys-General per case. In the four cases in which no Attorney-General had intervened, the Commonwealth, or a party sued on behalf of the Commonwealth, was in any event the defendant.

No statutory right of intervention in constitutional cases is granted to private persons or to non-government bodies, such as public interest organisations. The Court has generally been reluctant to permit non-governmental interests to appear as interveners or to assist the Court by offering submissions as *amici curiae*. An intervener becomes a party to proceedings, albeit in relation to a particular issue or issues (and as a party, is subject to a costs order); an *amicus curiae* (literally a "friend of the court") is a non-party who assists the Court.

The limits of the *amicus curiae* role were stressed by Gummow J in *APLA Ltd v Legal Services Commissioner (NSW)* (2005) 219 ALR 403, where New South Wales regulations restricting publicity relating to personal injury litigation were unsuccessfully challenged. The plaintiffs were an association of lawyers engaged in such litigation, along with a firm and an individual practitioner so engaged; the *amici* were the Redfern Legal Centre and the Combined Community Legal Centres Group NSW Inc. Between the advertisements issued by the plaintiffs and the publicity issued by the *amici* there might conceivably have been a material difference. The plaintiffs' advertisements, unlike those of the *amici*, were "commercial", and hence less likely to fall within the implied constitutional freedom of political communication and more likely, for purposes of s 92, to be characterised as "trade and commerce" rather than "intercourse". Thus, one possible outcome would have been that the impugned regulations could validly apply to the plaintiffs' advertisements but not to the publicity issued by the *amici*. Because these possibilities had been fully argued without objection, Gummow J considered them. However, he pointed out that, while evidence about the publicity used by the *amici* might have been sufficient to warrant their admission as interveners, their limited role as *amici* did not strictly permit them to tender such evidence (though "[438] counsel for the *amici* skilfully sought to draw [it] … into the general consideration of the issues"). Nor would the *amici* have been entitled to "[447] any declaratory relief".

Apart from the *Judiciary Act* provisions that came into force in 1976, neither interveners nor *amici curiae* are entitled to appear except by leave of the Court. The steamship companies and marine engineers who appeared in *In re Judiciary and Navigation Acts* (1921) 29 CLR 257 were apparently there by reason of orders made under ss 91 and 92 of the *Judiciary Act 1903* (Cth), as part of the special reference procedure that was utilised (but held to be invalid) in that case. Even then, the Institute of Marine Engineers confined themselves to adopting the arguments made on behalf of Victoria. In *Australian Railways Union v Victorian Railways Commissioners* (*ARU Case*) (1930) 44 CLR 319, even States were refused leave to intervene. The approach that the Court had taken in *Victoria v Commonwealth* (*Federal Roads Case*) (1926) 38 CLR 399 would have allowed all States to intervene to oppose the Commonwealth's view of the extent of its powers; but in the *ARU Case* they sought to *support* the Commonwealth argument that State Railways Commissioners, as employers, were subject to the arbitral powers of the Commonwealth Court of Conciliation and Arbitration. Only Isaacs CJ would have given the States leave to do so.

Australian Railways Union v Victorian Railways Commissioners
(1930) 44 CLR 319

Starke J: [330] I agree that leave should be refused. The only question in this case is whether the Commonwealth has constitutional power under the arbitration provisions to affect an organ of the State, namely, the railway service. The States do not wish to **[331]** argue that power does not subsist in the Commonwealth. Therefore there is no necessity for them to appear, and no need for us to hear them. There are sufficient representatives here to put that view, and to oppose it. An appearance by the States would be utterly useless.

Dixon J: [331] I agree that leave to intervene should be refused. I think we should be careful to allow arguments only in support of some right, authority or other legal title set up by the party intervening. Normally parties, and parties alone, appear in litigation. But, by a very special practice, the intervention of the States and the Commonwealth as persons interested has been permitted by the discretion of the Court in matters which arise under the Constitution. The discretion to permit appearances by counsel is a very wide one; but I think we would be wise to exercise it by allowing only those to be heard who wish to maintain some particular right, power or immunity in which they are concerned, and not merely to intervene to contend for what they consider to be a desirable state of the general law under the Constitution without regard to the diminution or enlargement of the powers which as States or as Commonwealth they may exercise.

The view expressed by Dixon J was decisive until recent times, leaving very little scope for intervention by non-government interests.

In *Brandy v Human Rights and Equal Opportunity Commission* (1995) 183 CLR 245 and *Kruger v Commonwealth* (*Stolen Generations Case*) (1997) 190 CLR 1, the Public Interest Advocacy Centre and the International Commission of Jurists, respectively, were refused leave to intervene, apparently for the traditional reasons. But at the hearing of oral argument in *Superclinics Australia Pty Ltd v CES* (11-12 September 1996, unreported and ultimately settled), a different view narrowly prevailed. The respondent plaintiff in that case alleged that her doctor had been negligent in failing to detect her pregnancy, thus depriving her of the opportunity for an abortion. The trial judge had held that this claim disclosed no enforceable cause of action because, in the circumstances, an abortion would have been unlawful. As to whether that was an accurate statement of the law of abortion in New South Wales, the Court of Appeal (in *CES v Superclinics (Australia) Pty Ltd* (1995) 38 NSWLR 47) had expressed three different views.

When the case reached the High Court John McCarthy QC, on behalf of the Australian Catholic Health Care Association and the Australian Catholic Bishops' Conference, sought leave for those organisations to be heard as *amici curiae* for the purpose of arguing that the current understanding of the lawfulness of abortions in New South Wales was wrong. This was accepted by a "statutory majority" (that is, in a Court of six, by three judges including the Chief Justice), and the organisations were given leave to appear as *amici curiae*. This "**[137]** radically transformed the case from one of medical negligence to *the* test case on abortion" (Jo Wainer, "Abortion Before the High Court" (1997) 8 *Australian Feminist Law Journal* 133) and when the case resumed the next day, an application for leave to intervene as *amici curiae* was made by the Abortion Providers Federation of Australasia and its President. Leave was again granted. At the end of the day, without having reached the issues raised by the interventions, the hearing was adjourned to a later date to be fixed. The parties ultimately settled the matter and it never returned to the High Court.

It was against this background that the cases of *Levy v Victoria* (1997) 189 CLR 579 and *Lange v Australian Broadcasting Corporation* (1997) 189 CLR 520 were argued in the High Court. They were heard together because notice had been given that *Levy* would raise the issue, ultimately determined in *Lange*, whether *Theophanous v Herald & Weekly Times Ltd* (1994) 182 CLR 104 and *Stephens v West Australian Newspapers Ltd* (1994) 182 CLR 211 should be overruled. Those cases had recognised a "constitutional defence" to actions against media organisations for defamation of political figures. Several media proprietors, the journalists' association (the Media, Entertainment and Arts Alliance) and the Australian Press Council sought leave to appear as interveners or *amici* to argue that *Theophanous* should *not* be overruled – an argument which would not necessarily be put by any of the governmental interveners in the case. Leave was granted to the media proprietors to intervene in the proceedings and to the journalists' association and the Australian Press Council to act as *amici*.

Levy v Victoria
(1997) 189 CLR 579

Brennan CJ: [601] [A] non-party whose interests would be affected directly by a decision in the proceeding – that is, one who would be bound by the decision albeit not a party – must be entitled to intervene to protect the interest liable to be affected. This, indeed, is the explanation of many of the cases in which intervention has been allowed in probate and admiralty cases and in other cases where an intervener and a party are privies in estate or interest.

But the legal interests of a person may be affected in more indirect ways than by being bound by a decision. They may be affected by operation of precedent – especially a precedent of this Court – or by the doctrine of stare decisis. Apart from the obsolete exception contained in s 74 of the Constitution, an exercise of the jurisdiction conferred on this Court is not subject to appeal nor to review by any **[602]** other Court. As this Court's appellate jurisdiction extends to appeals, whether directly or indirectly, from all Australian courts, a decision by this Court in any case determines the law to be applied by those courts in cases that are not distinguishable. A declaration of a legal principle or rule by this Court will govern proceedings that are pending or threatened in any other Australian court to which an applicant to intervene is or may become a party. Even more indirectly, such a declaration may affect the interests of an applicant either by its extra-curial operation or in future litigation. Ordinarily, such an indirect and contingent affection of legal interests would not support an application for leave to intervene. But where a substantial affection of a person's legal interests is demonstrable (as in the case of a party to pending litigation) or likely, a precondition for the grant of leave to intervene is satisfied. Nothing short of such an affection of legal interests will suffice. This accords with the view of Dixon J in *Australian Railways Union v Victorian Railways Commissioners* [(1930) 44 CLR 319 at 331] ...

[603] Jurisdiction to grant leave to intervene to persons whose legal interests are likely to be substantially affected by a judgment exists in order to avoid a judicial affection of such a person's legal interests without that person being given an opportunity to be heard.

Nevertheless, an indirect affection of legal interests enlivens no absolute right to intervene. The assumption is that the Court will determine the law correctly, so that the indirect affection of an applicant's legal interest is simply the inevitable consequence of the exercise by this Court of its jurisdiction as the final Court in the Australian hierarchy. On that assumption, no undue prejudice is suffered by a person whose interests will be affected by the decision. The exercise of this Court's jurisdiction to determine controversies between parties is not, and could not be, conditioned on allowing intervention by all those whose interests are susceptible to affection by the Court's judgments. Such a condition would virtually paralyse the exercise of that jurisdiction. The principles of natural justice which control the exercise of curial power must take account of the nature of the jurisdiction to be exercised.

However, where a person having the necessary legal interest to apply for leave to intervene can show that the parties to the particular proceeding may not present fully the submissions on a particular issue, being submissions which the Court should have to assist it to reach a correct determination, the Court may exercise its jurisdiction by granting leave to intervene. The grant may be limited, if appropriate, to particular issues and subject to such conditions, as to costs or otherwise, as will do justice as between all parties. In that situation, intervention may prevent an error that would affect the interests of the intervener. Of course, if the intervener's submission is merely **[604]** repetitive of the submission of one or other of the parties, efficiency would require that intervention be denied ...

The hearing of an amicus curiae is entirely in the Court's discretion. That discretion is exercised on a different basis from that which governs the allowance of intervention. The footing on which an amicus curiae is heard is that that person is willing to offer the Court a submission on law or relevant fact which will assist the Court in a way in which the Court would not otherwise have been assisted. In *Kruger v Commonwealth* [transcript of 12 February 1996 at 12], speaking for the court, I said in refusing counsel's application to appear for a person as amicus curiae:

> "As to his application to be heard as amicus curiae, he fails to show that the parties whose cause he would support are unable or unwilling adequately to protect their own interests or to assist the Court in arriving at the correct determination of the case. The Court must be cautious in considering applications to be heard by persons who would be amicus curiae lest the efficient operation of the Court be prejudiced. Where the Court has parties before it who are willing and able to provide adequate assistance to the Court it is inappropriate to grant the application."

It is not possible to identify in advance the situations in which the Court will be assisted by submissions that will not or may not be presented by one of the parties nor to identify the requisite capacities of an amicus who is willing to offer assistance. All that can be said is that an amicus will be heard when the Court is of the opinion that it **[605]** will be significantly assisted thereby, provided that any cost to the parties or any delay consequent on agreeing to hear the amicus is not disproportionate to the assistance that is expected.

Kirby J: [650] [T]his court should maintain a tight rein on interventions. Where they are allowed, the Court should impose terms which protect the parties from the costs and other burdens which interventions may occasion. However, some of the rigidities of earlier procedural restrictions are not now appropriate. This is especially so because of this Court's function of finally declaring the law of **[651]** Australia in a *particular* case for application to *all* such cases. The acknowledgment of the fact that courts, especially this Court, have unavoidable choices to make in finding and declaring the law, makes it appropriate, in some cases at least, to hear from a broader range of interveners and amici curiae than would have appeared proper when the declaratory theory of the judicial function was unquestioningly accepted. The opinion of Dixon J, a committed proponent of that theory, was stated in *Australian Railways Union v Victoria Railways Commissioners*. It is cited by Brennan CJ in this case. However, since those words were written, this Court has become the final court of appeal for Australia. There has also developed a growing appreciation that finding the law in a particular case is far from a mechanical task. It often involves the elucidation of complex questions of legal principle and legal policy as well as of decided authority. This appreciation has inevitable consequences for the methodology of the court. Those consequences remain to be fully worked out.

In the United States of America and Canada, the practice of hearing submissions from interveners and amici curiae is well established. Such practice is particularly common where matters of general public interest are being heard in the higher appellate courts. In recent years, some Australian courts have also favoured a more liberal approach to permitting interveners and amici. So far, that course has not recommended itself to this Court.

There is no need for undue concern about adopting a broader approach. The Court itself retains full control over its procedures. It will always protect and respect the primacy of the parties. Costs and other inhibitions and risks will, almost always, discourage officious busybodies. Those who persist can usually be recognised and easily rebuffed. The submissions of interveners and amici curiae will typically be conveyed, for the most part, in writing. But sometimes oral argument by them will be useful to the Court. Such interests may occasionally have perspectives which help the court to see a problem in a context larger than that which the parties are willing, or able, to offer. That wider context is particularly appropriate to an ultimate national appellate court. It is especially relevant to a constitutional case.

Nothing in the Australian Constitution prevents such a procedural course. Conforming to the Constitution, this Court should adapt its procedures, particularly in constitutional cases or where large issues of legal principle and legal policy are at stake, to ensure that its eventual **[652]** opinions on contested legal questions are informed by relevant submissions and enlivened by appropriate materials.

In the present matter, I would have allowed the Council for Civil Liberties and other relevant bodies, had they applied, to make brief submissions on the constitutional controversy ... subject to the same strict conditions as applied to other interveners and amici. If necessary, the relevant bodies could have been restricted to written submissions. But I would have allowed them a voice.

The more liberal approaches of Brennan CJ and Kirby J in *Levy* (and of Kirby J in subsequent cases such as *Attorney-General (Cth) v Breckler* (1999) 197 CLR 83 and *Commissioner of Taxation v Scully* (2000) 201 CLR 148) have not led to a significant increase in intervention in constitutional cases by non-government interests. Intervention in constitutional cases remains dominated by government interests.

(d)   Deciding Constitutional Cases

In matters "affecting the constitutional powers of the Commonwealth", s 23(1) of the *Judiciary Act* prevents the High Court from reaching any decision "unless at least three Justices concur". The effect of this provision is illustrated by what happened in *Field Peas Marketing Board (Tas) v Clements & Marshall Pty Ltd* (1948) 76 CLR 414. An appeal from Williams J at first instance was initially heard by the five other Justices available, but Rich J (aged 85) then withdrew due to illness, leaving the other four Justices equally divided.

Field Peas Marketing Board (Tas) v Clements & Marshall Pty Ltd
(1948) 76 CLR 414

Latham CJ: [416] The Court is equally divided in opinion. In a case which did not involve any question affecting the constitutional powers of the Commonwealth the result would be that the decision of *Williams* J would be affirmed, and the appeal would be dismissed ... It may be suggested, however, that the present case is governed by s 23(1) ... This case involves a question of the interpretation of s 92 of the Commonwealth Constitution. The Commonwealth is not a party to the action, but the decision with respect to this question may inferentially affect the constitutional powers of the Commonwealth ... **[417]** Section 92 binds both the Commonwealth and the States and in some cases a decision upon the interpretation of s 92 may therefore be a decision upon a question affecting the constitutional powers of the Commonwealth. Three Justices do not concur in a decision upon this question and therefore it appears to me that a proper course is to abstain from giving a decision upon it, with the result that the judgment of *Williams* J should remain and the appeal should be dismissed. My brother *Starke* is of opinion that the case should be remitted to *Williams* J. All the other members of the Court agree in the result that the appeal should be dismissed.

The more usual result of an equal division of opinion is governed by s 23(2) of the *Judiciary Act*. Generally speaking, where a matter is before a full bench of the High Court on appeal (including appeals from a single Justice of the Court), the decision below is affirmed: that is, the presumption is that that decision will stand unless a majority of the High Court decides otherwise. In other cases (generally speaking, when there is no previous decision to attract the benefit of such a presumption), "the opinion of the Chief Justice … shall prevail". In 1981 Murphy J suggested that these provisions were unconstitutional.

Federal Commissioner of Taxation v St Helens Farm (ACT) Pty Ltd
(1981) 146 CLR 336

Murphy J: [387] Those directions are of questionable validity. If Parliament can direct that on an even division a certain judgment follows, for example that in certain cases, the opinion of the Chief Justice or if he is absent, the opinion of the Senior Justice present, shall prevail, presumably it can direct that in those or other cases the opinion of the junior or some other Justice shall prevail, and of course it can change the directions from time to time. If Parliament can direct that a Full Court consisting of less than all the Justices shall not give a decision on a question affecting the constitutional powers of the Commonwealth, unless at least three Justices concur in the decision, (see s 23(1)), presumably it can direct that the decision shall not be given unless it is unanimous. If Parliament can give such directions, why can it not direct that no decision shall be given which invalidates an Act (or on a question affecting the validity of an Act) or which challenges the validity of any governmental action, or which is adverse to the Government, unless the decision is unanimous. Section 79 of the Constitution states that "The federal jurisdiction of any court may be exercised by such number of judges as the Parliament prescribes". Assuming this is intended to apply to the High Court, it does not authorize directions on how the individual opinions or votes of justices should be transformed into judgments of the Court, which seems to be well within the sphere of the judicial branch. The validity of these provisions has not been raised, perhaps because the main provision that an appeal fails if it does not attract a majority conforms to a widespread convention … The provision about equal division in the original jurisdiction does not. It is very disturbing that an Act or State Act **[388]** should be held invalid on an even division of this Court.

4. Appeals to the Privy Council

At the time of federation, the retention of Privy Council appeals, especially in relation to constitutional cases, had been a contentious issue (see JA La Nauze, *The Making of the Australian Constitution* (Melbourne University Press, 1972), 248-69). The Australian draft had proposed to make the High Court of Australia the final arbiter of constitutional questions. The British government, apparently with some connivance behind the scenes by influential Australian judges, including Sir Samuel Griffith, insisted that appeals to the Privy Council be retained. The eventual compromise, embodied in s 74 of the Constitution, was that in certain specified cases no appeal to the Privy Council should lie unless the High Court gave a certificate "that the question is one which ought to be determined by Her Majesty in Council". In other cases, the normal avenues of appeal to the Privy Council remained.

The specified cases requiring a certificate were those "upon any question, howsoever arising, as to the limits inter se of the Constitutional powers of the Commonwealth and those of any State or States, or as to the limits inter se of the Constitutional powers of any two or more States". As it turned out, only one such certificate was ever granted (in *Attorney-General (Commonwealth) v Colonial Sugar Refining Co Ltd* [1914] AC 237).

Not every constitutional case involved an inter se question. In *James v Cowan* [1932] AC 542, the Privy Council held (at 560) that s 92 did not do so; and in *O'Sullivan v Noarlunga Meat Ltd* [1957] AC 1, their Lordships confirmed the assumption that a finding of inconsistency under s 109 of the Constitution did not involve such a question either. In that case the High Court had refused an inter se certificate on the basis that there was no inter se matter (*O'Sullivan v Noarlunga Meat Ltd (No 2)* (1956) 94 CLR 367), since the application of s 109 "**[374]** has always been regarded as a question, not between powers, but between laws made under powers". The Privy Council adopted the same distinction.

The requirement of an inter se certificate ensured that the High Court could control the extent to which questions affecting the federal distribution of powers might go to the Privy Council. But this control had two qualifications. First, as the above cases illustrate, it was assumed that the Privy Council had power to determine any issues on which its own jurisdiction depended, and hence to determine whether or not a particular type of question did involve an inter se question. Second, the control exerted by the High Court extended only to appeals from the High Court. So long as it remained possible to appeal to the Privy Council direct from a State Supreme Court, whether by leave of that Court or by leave of the Privy Council, it was possible for an inter se matter to by-pass the High Court altogether.

The provision in s 40 of the *Judiciary Act 1903* for "removal" into the High Court was originally an attempt to block this loophole in s 74. Another strategy to the same end was embodied in s 39. Section 39(1) deprived State courts of any *State* jurisdiction they might other-wise have had in matters of federal law, including constitutional law; and sub-s (2) then invested them with *federal* jurisdiction in respect of the very same matters, but subject to conditions. Originally the conditions were designed to ensure that, apart from the possibility of an appeal to the High Court, the State Court's decision would be "final and conclusive". Those words were understood (apparently on the basis of *Cushing v Dupuy* (1880) 5 App Cas 409) as blocking all appeals except those depending solely on the royal prerogative: that is, appeals by special leave of the Privy Council itself. Since 1968 the condition in sub-s (2) has blocked *all* appeals, "whether by special leave or otherwise".

As perceived by those State judges bent on retaining Privy Council appeals, s 39 was unconstitutional. That issue was central to the struggle surrounding the discovery in *D'Emden v Pedder* (1904) 1 CLR 91 of an "implied immunity of instrumentalities" doctrine, and the use of that doctrine in *Deakin v Webb* (1904) 1 CLR 585, to make the salaries of Commonwealth officers, including cabinet ministers, immune from State income taxation (see Chapter 7, §2).

When *Deakin v Webb* was initially before the Supreme Court of Victoria (*In re the Income Tax Acts (No 4)* (1904) 29 VLR 748), that Court had "distinguished" *D'Emden v Pedder*. The High Court decision in *Deakin v Webb*, rejecting such a distinction, was handed down on 28 October 1904. On 3 November, Isaac Isaacs applied to the High Court on behalf of Victoria for an "inter se certificate" (see (1904) 1 CLR at 619-31). That application was refused.

By this time the issue of State taxation of Commonwealth salaries was pending in several other cases, including that of the Deputy Postmaster-General for Victoria, Colonel Frank Outtrim. The Supreme Court of Victoria heard that case on 10 February 1905. Isaacs, again repre-senting Victoria, told the Court that the proceedings "had been instituted in order that an appeal might be taken to the Privy Council against the decision of the Court". Counsel for both sides admitted that the case was governed by the High Court decision in *Deakin v Webb*; "and the Full Court, stating that it was bound by that decision, intimated that it would give judgment for Colonel Outtrim, with costs" (see *The Argus*, 11 February 1905, 15, col 3).

From that decision Hodges J, in the Supreme Court of Victoria, granted leave to appeal direct to the Privy Council, bypassing the High Court (*In re the Income Tax Acts* [1905] VLR 463). In granting leave to appeal, he held that s 39 of the *Judiciary Act* was invalid. In deciding the appeal (*Webb v Outrim* [sic] [1907] AC 81), the Privy Council also so held. However, its decision was flawed by an elementary misconception of the Australian Constitution and the role it assigns to the courts. It affirmed that, by contrast with the United States, which **[88]** has erected a tribunal which possesses jurisdiction to annul a statute upon the ground that it is unconstitutional", the position in Australia was that, apart from the possibility of repugnancy to paramount Imperial laws, State legislation was immune to constitutional challenge: "[N]o authority exists by which its validity can be questioned or impeached".

The High Court was furious. In *Baxter v Commissioners of Taxation (NSW)* (1907) 4 CLR 1087, the Court had little difficulty in deciding that the substantive holding in *Webb v Outtrim* need not be followed, since it had usurped the Court's own exclusive function of determining inter se questions. However, the holding as to s 39 posed a greater difficulty. It was not until

Commonwealth v Limerick Steamship Co Ltd and Kidman (1924) 35 CLR 69 that a majority of the Court (Isaacs, Rich and Starke JJ) held that s 39(2)(a) was valid. Even then, they did so by distinguishing *Webb v Outtrim*, so as not to repudiate it directly (see AR Blackshield, *The Abolition of Privy Council Appeals* (Adelaide Law Review Research Papers No 1, 1978), 8-10). Recurring tensions between the two courts were apparent until appeals to the Privy Council were finally abolished altogether (see AR Blackshield, "The Last of England: Farewell to their Lordships Forever" (1982) 56 *Law Institute Journal* 779).

Part of the compromise embodied in s 74 of the Constitution was that, apart from inter se matters, "this Constitution shall not impair" the possibility that special leave to appeal from the High Court to the Privy Council might be granted by the Privy Council itself as a matter of royal prerogative. However, although s 74 insisted that "this Constitution" did not itself work such an impairment, it went on to say that "[t]he Parliament may make laws limiting the matters in which such leave may be asked". In 1968 this power to "limit" appeals from the High Court was exercised by the Gorton government's *Privy Council (Limitation of Appeals) Act 1968* (Cth): thereafter special leave to appeal from the High Court could be sought only where the High Court itself had heard an appeal from a State Supreme Court on a matter of purely State law. At the same time s 39 of the *Judiciary Act* was amended to its present form. The power to "limit" was further exercised by the Whitlam government's *Privy Council (Appeals from the High Court) Act 1975* (Cth), which provided that special leave could not be asked for "unless the decision of the High Court was given in a proceeding that was commenced in a court before the date of commencement of this Act". In short, the 1968 Act had exercised the power to "limit" by abolishing *some* appeals; and the 1975 Act had further exercised the power to "limit" by abolishing any remaining appeals apart from cases already in the pipeline. The 1968 Act was held valid (by the Privy Council) in *Kitano v Commonwealth* [1976] AC 99. The 1975 Act was held valid (by the High Court) in *Attorney-General (Cth) v T & G Mutual Life Society Ltd* (1978) 144 CLR 161. The cumulative effect of the two Acts was to prevent applications for "special leave to appeal" – that is, for "prerogative appeals". All other appeals from the High Court had been blocked since 1901, by virtue of the provision in s 73 of the Constitution that the High Court's judgment shall be "final and conclusive".

The effect of the Acts on the doctrine of precedent was considered by the High Court in *Viro v R* (1978) 141 CLR 88, where the Court held that it was no longer bound by any Privy Council decision. The hierarchy of precedent follows the hierarchy of appeal; and so long as it was possible to appeal from High Court to Privy Council, their Lordships' decisions had bound the High Court. With the ending of the hierarchical relation that was no longer the case. The Privy Council had hitherto been, and as to appeals from the States still was, an Australian "apex" court. However, the High Court was now also an "apex" court, coequal with the Privy Council. It followed that the Court should treat Privy Council decisions as if they were its own, with the same degree of precedent force, but no more.

The greater judicial "activism" that seemed to be manifest in the High Court in the 1980s and early 1990s was the cumulative product of many social and individual forces. It had started to become apparent in the 1960s, in cases like *Mutual Life & Citizens' Assurance Co Ltd v Evatt* (1968) 122 CLR 556, where Barwick CJ accepted the High Court's responsibility for developing the law "**[563]** as appropriate to current times in Australia"; or *Uren v John Fairfax & Sons Ltd* (1966) 117 CLR 118, where the Court successfully asserted that developments of the common law in Australia and England might diverge. But the Court's declaration in *Viro* of its emancipation from binding Privy Council authority seemed like a coming of age.

Yet what was liberating for the High Court was a source of problems for State Supreme Courts, since the possibility of appeal from those courts direct to the Privy Council survived. What if, on the very same issue, one litigant appealed to the Privy Council and another to the High Court? If the two coequal "apex" courts gave conflicting decisions, which one ought the State courts to follow? The hierarchical model suggests that both would be equally binding; but that leads to an intolerable contradiction. In *Viro v R* most judges suggested that in such a case the

State courts should invariably follow the High Court; but they gave no convincing explanation of why this should be the case. In *National Employers' Mutual General Association Ltd v Waind (No 2)* [1978] 1 NSWLR 466, a special five-judge Bench of the New South Wales Court of Appeal announced that, for its part, it would never again grant leave to appeal to the Privy Council. To do so it had to be affirmatively satisfied that the matter "ought" to be determined by the Privy Council rather than by the High Court; and now that High Court and Privy Council ranked equally, that could never be said. In *Australian Government Workers' Association v Armstrong* (1980) 25 SASR 441, the Supreme Court of South Australia took a similar view. In *Southern Centre of Theosophy Inc v South Australia* (1979) 145 CLR 246, it was argued that the cumulative effect of the 1968 and 1975 Acts had extinguished *any* surviving prerogative basis for appeals to the Privy Council, including appeals from the States; but the High Court rejected this argument.

All these problems were finally resolved by the *Australia Act 1986* (see Chapter 4, §8 and Appendix). By abolishing the last remaining possibilities of appeal from the States, that Act confirmed the High Court's position as the only "apex" court with power to shape the development of Australian law, and thereby finally gave the Court (in 1986!) a foundation for independence in doing so.

Appeals to the Privy Council have now been abolished in most other British Commonwealth countries. In New Zealand, the appeal was abolished by the *Supreme Court Act 2003* (NZ), which substituted an appeal within New Zealand to a newly constituted Supreme Court. However, when Jamaica attempted in 2004 to abolish Privy Council appeals and to substitute an appeal to a regional court, the Caribbean Court of Justice, the Privy Council held in *Independent Jamaica Council for Human Rights (1998) Ltd v Marshall-Burnett and Attorney-General (Jamaica)* [2005] 2 AC 356 that the legislation was invalid. The appellate jurisdiction could not be vested in the Caribbean Court of Justice because its independence from legislative and executive interference was insufficiently guaranteed; and Parliament would not have intended to abolish the Privy Council appeal if nothing was put in its place.

5. The Limits of Power

(a)   Judicial Parsimony

One way of practising "judicial self-restraint" is an adherence to doctrines, procedures or canons of judicial wisdom which ensure that constitutional questions will only be decided when it becomes judicially necessary to do so. If the rationale for judicial review depends upon the Court's *duty* to police and enforce the Constitution, then the rationale might only be available when the duty is inescapable.

The United States Supreme Court has developed a rich repertoire of avoidance devices, most of which have parallels in Australian High Court practice, though sometimes only in a rudimentary form. Henry J Abraham, *The Judicial Process* (Oxford University Press, 7th ed 1998, 386-410), has distilled the American practice into "sixteen great maxims of judicial self-restraint". Among them is the so-called precept of "judicial parsimony":

Henry J Abraham, *The Judicial Process*
(Oxford University Press, 7th ed 1998)

[403] [I]f a case or controversy can be decided on any other than constitutional grounds – such as by statutory construction ... – the Court will be eager to do so. For normally it will not decide questions of a constitutional nature unless absolutely necessary to the decision of the case, and even then it will draw such a decision as narrowly as possible, [404] being ever loath to formulate a rule of constitutional law broader than is clearly required by the precise facts to which it is to be applied. Nor will it anticipate a question of constitutional law in advance of the necessity of deciding it.

In Australia, the refusal to "anticipate" issues has frequently been voiced in cases involving the "corporations" power, s 51(xx) of the Constitution. Thus, in *Strickland v Rocla Concrete Pipes Ltd* (*Concrete Pipes Case*) (1971) 124 CLR 468, Barwick CJ declined "**[490]** to set as it were the outer limits of the reach of the power", and explained his refusal by reference to the traditional case method, followed by the High Court in constitutional and common law matters alike. Similarly, in *Actors and Announcers Equity Association v Fontana Films Ltd* (1982) 150 CLR 169, Brennan J invoked "**[218]** the practice of this Court in interpreting the Constitution case by case, deciding only so much as is necessary to decide the case in hand ... Hewing close to the issues raised by each case, the Court avoids the possibility of having its judgment applied to issues that were not envisaged in the arguments before it and which may have implications emerging only in the future". More recently, when four members of the Court in *Re Patterson; Ex parte Taylor* (2001) 207 CLR 391 made a constitutional ruling which was not necessary to the decision, Gummow J (who dissented) later remarked, in *Re Minister for Immigration and Multicultural Affairs; Ex parte Meng Kok Te* (2002) 212 CLR 162, that the unsatisfactory outcome "**[200]** may demonstrate the wisdom in the practice of the Court determining a case on the basis of constitutional invalidity only when it cannot found the order it makes on other grounds". Eventually, that aspect of *Re Patterson* was overruled.

Abraham's account of the practice in the United States Supreme Court places special emphasis on its reluctance to reach issues of constitutional principle if the case at hand can be decided by interpreting the relevant statute. For example, he quotes Felix Frankfurter's response when counsel told the Supreme Court in *Peters v Hobby*, 349 US 331 (1955), that he did not wish to win on a narrow ground of statutory construction. Justice Frankfurter answered: "The question is not whether you want to win the case on that ground or not. The Court reaches constitutional issues last, not first". The High Court has similarly tended to insist on a process of statutory construction before proceeding to the consideration of constitutional issues. However, this has not necessarily been for reasons of "parsimony" or "judicial restraint". Instead, it has often reflected the distinctive Australian approach to the characterisation of impugned legislation for the purpose of determining whether it falls within legislative power. Thus, it was in the context of expounding his own approach to characterisation that Latham CJ, in *Bank of NSW v Commonwealth* (*Bank Nationalisation Case*) (1948) 76 CLR 1, quoted what the Privy Council had said in *Great West Saddlery Co Ltd v The King* [1921] 2 AC 91: "**[117]** The only principle that can be laid down ... is that legislation the validity of which has to be tested must be scrutinized in its entirety in order to determine its true character". It was in that sense that Latham CJ went on to say: "**[186]** In determining the validity of a law it is in the first place obviously necessary to construe the law and to determine its operation and effect (that is, to decide what the Act actually does), and in the second place to determine the relation of that which the Act does to a subject matter in respect of which it is contended that the relevant Parliament has power to make laws".

More recently, however, the repeated insistence in the Gleeson Court on an initial process of statutory construction has seemed less concerned with characterisation, and more with the parsimonious avoidance of constitutional issues. Thus, in *Re Minister for Immigration and Multicultural and Indigenous Affairs; Ex parte Ame* (2005) 218 ALR 483, Kirby J ascribed this approach expressly to the need "**[500]** to avoid unnecessary invalidation of legislation, where a dispute can be resolved without recourse to such a drastic constitutional remedy". A striking example is *Plaintiff S157/2002 v Commonwealth* (2003) 211 CLR 476 (see Chapter 12, §4(b)), where the Court concluded that ss 474 and 486A of the *Migration Act 1958* (Cth) were valid, since it was able to interpret them in a way that did not conflict with s 75(v) of the Constitution. Another example is *Coleman v Power* (2004) 220 CLR 1, where three of the four majority judges (Gummow, Kirby and Hayne JJ) were able to quash a conviction for "insulting words" under s 7(1)(d) of the *Vagrants, Gaming and Other Offences Act 1931* (Qld) on the basis that, as they construed the provision, it had no application to the appellant. Accordingly, those three judges had no need to decide the constitutional issue of whether the provision was valid.

In that case, all seven judges considered the construction of s 7(1)(d) before turning to consider its validity, though not all of them explained why this was appropriate. Gleeson CJ stated simply that "**[21]** [t]he first step is to construe the statutory language", while Gummow and Hayne JJ said: "**[68]** Little direct attention was given to first construing the relevant provisions. Yet that is where the inquiry must begin". Kirby J gave a fuller explanation.

Coleman v Power
(2004) 220 CLR 1

Kirby J: [84] I agree with the approach of the other members of this Court. The first step is to construe the law itself.

This is so, whether the law in question is a federal, State or Territory law. It is so, whether the constitutional rule is one expressly stated or implied from the language and structure of the Constitution. Adopting this approach conforms to the longstanding instruction of this Court in cases of suggested constitutional invalidity. It is an approach regularly taken where there is any possibility of doubt concerning the meaning and operation of the impugned law. In *R v Hughes* [(2000) 202 CLR 535 at 565-6] I explained why this approach is taken:

"In considering the validity or otherwise of the legislation ... said to be invalid, it is necessary, at the threshold, to elucidate the meaning and operation of the provisions in question. This is an elementary point. However it is important in the present case. If particular provisions claimed to be unconstitutional have no operation in the circumstances of the matter before the Court, it is irrelevant, and therefore unnecessary, to determine their validity. Constitutionality is not normally decided on a hypothesis inapplicable to the resolution of a particular dispute. If, upon a true construction of the legislation, it operates in a way that does no offence to the language and structure of the Constitution, it is irrelevant that, had it been construed in a different way, it might **[85]** have done so. This Court will not answer constitutional questions on the basis of assumptions that have no practical or legal consequence for the case in hand."

The foregoing observations apply, word for word, to the present case. However, in saying this I do not embrace a naïve belief that interpretation of a contested provision can be wholly disjoined in a case such as this from constitutional questions that have been raised. Or that statutory interpretation is a simple matter of taking out a dictionary and using it to find the meaning of the contested words, read in isolation. History, context, legislative purposes, considerations of human rights law and basic common law assumptions – as well as constitutional principle – can all play a part ...

The need to interpret a statute before its validity is considered was restated by Kirby J in *APLA Ltd v Legal Services Commissioner (NSW)* (2005) 219 ALR 403 – though he also recognised again that it will often be "**[471]** impossible, or unhelpful, to consider the meaning of a law disjoined from its constitutional context". In that case, the preliminary construction of the impugned legislation was "of no assistance", but Kirby J invoked as a "counterpart" the "rule of prudence" and common practice that confines the consideration of constitutional issues "to those that need to be decided in order to ... dispose of the proceedings". This meant that "immaterial consideration of constitutional issues is avoided" and the "solemn responsibility ... of deciding arguments of constitutional invalidity" is "confined to those cases where such questions must be decided ... to reach dispositive orders". Accordingly, though the regulations in that case had been challenged on five main constitutional grounds, Kirby J dealt with only two of them.

In *Coleman v Power*, the need to give prior consideration to issues of interpretation was also emphasised by Heydon J.

Heydon J: [115] I agree that the other members of the Court correctly approach the appeal on the basis that the first question in the present case ought to be whether the conduct of the appellant fell within the meaning of the expression "insulting words" in s 7(1)(d)... That is the correct approach because if that first question is answered "No", the next question, whether s 7(1)(d) effectively burdens the freedom of communication on government and political matters, does not arise; but if that first question is answered "Yes", the construction of **[116]** s 7(1)(d) as a whole, independently of as well as in its particular application to the appellant, must be embarked on in order to determine whether s 7(1)(d) burdens the freedom of communication and other questions.

Heydon J emphasised that this was so although the parties "**[116]** did not in fact rigorously approach the appeal that way". Yet he also complained that this had left the proceedings before the High Court in an unsatisfactory state:

Heydon J: [118] [N]othing in the careful reasons for judgment of the learned magistrate suggests that the appellant contended that s 7(1)(d) was limited to conduct intended or reasonably likely to provoke unlawful physical retaliation ... Nor do the notice of appeal to the District Court, the District Court's reasons for judgment, or the notice of application for leave to appeal to the Court of Appeal. The Court of Appeal necessarily assumed that the appellant had contravened s 7(1)(d), since it only granted leave to appeal in relation to constitutional questions. The same assumption was made in the appellant's amended notice of appeal to this Court, the notices issued under s 78B of the *Judiciary Act 1903* (Cth) and the appellant's written and oral argument in this Court: indeed the latter made it explicit. **[119]** The respondents were given no opportunity by the appellant's submissions to address a construction of s 7(1)(d) under which an intention to provoke, or reasonable likelihood of provoking, unlawful physical retaliation is a necessary element. It is true that questions were raised in argument which, if answered one way, would support that construction, that the Attorney-General of Queensland and the other respondents were given leave to file notes concerning the history and meaning of s 7(1)(d) and that the appellant was given leave to respond to them. However, in their notes the respondents did not deal with, and in his response the appellant did not advance, the proposition that s 7(1)(d) was limited to conduct which was intended or reasonably likely to provoke unlawful physical retaliation. Indeed, ... the appellant appears to have had a conscious preference for a wide construction of s 7(1)(d), because the wider its construction, the more likely it was to fall foul of all the requirements of the constitutional test. The appellant eschewed a submission that s 7(1)(d) was, on its true construction, so narrow that he had not contravened it.

In short, the respondents, though they had ample occasion to advance their submissions on the true construction of s 7(1)(d), have not had an opportunity in any of the four courts which have dealt with these proceedings to controvert the specific elements of any formulation by the appellant of the competing construction. This is but one of the aspects in which this Court's approach to the issues raised by the appeal is hampered by the want of a satisfactory procedural background.

Heydon J linked this problem with another issue, on which the claims of judicial parsimony came into conflict with those of constitutional fidelity. According to the twofold test laid down in *Lange v Australian Broadcasting Corporation* (1997) 189 CLR 520, the appellant in *Coleman v Power* needed to establish: (1) that the impugned legislation imposed a "burden" on the freedom of political communication; and (2) that the burden thus imposed was not "reasonably appropriate and adapted" to a legitimate end in a manner compatible with responsible and representative government (see Chapter 28, §5). Yet on appeal to the High Court the respondents had *conceded* the existence of a sufficient "burden" to satisfy the first of these tests, leaving only the second issue to be argued.

Heydon J: [120] It would be necessary to examine this concession if the outcome of the appeal turned on its correctness. However, it does not. The concession may be assumed to be correct for the purposes of the next question, but that assumption implies no decision as to its actual correctness.

It is, however, unsatisfactory that the case is to be decided on an assumption that s 7(1)(d) fails the test enunciated in the question. To some extent that is because analysis of the present problem should address the problem in its entirety, rather than examining only part of it. It is also because, in dealing with the next question whether s 7(1)(d) is reasonably appropriate and adapted to serve a legitimate end, it is necessary to assess whether the burden it places on freedom of communication is heavy or light. The task which consideration of the first limb would require to be carried out, though superficially obviated by the concession, in this case returns in another guise in considering the second limb.

McHugh J took the view that in these circumstances the Court *could not* express an opinion on whether or not a "burden" existed: since there was no issue between the parties, there was nothing to be judicially decided.

> **McHugh J: [44]** In my view – in constitutional and public law cases as well as private law cases – parties can concede issues even though the issue is a legal issue. The only power with which this Court is invested is judicial power together with such power as is necessary or incidental to the exercise of judicial power in a particular case. The essence of judicial power is the determination of disputes between parties. If parties do not wish to dispute a particular issue, that is their business. This Court has no business in determining issues upon which the parties agree. It is no answer to that proposition to say that this Court has a duty to lay down the law for Australia. Cases are only authorities for what they decide. If a point is not in dispute in a case, the decision lays down no legal rule concerning that issue. If the conceded issue is a necessary element of the decision, it creates an issue estoppel that forever binds the parties. But that is all. The case can have no wider *ratio decidendi* than what was in issue in the case. Its precedent effect **[45]** is limited to the issues.

As it happened, McHugh J was of the view that the concessions made by the respondents were in fact properly made. Kirby J also took that view. However, he disagreed with the suggestion that such a concession, whether rightly or wrongly made, could fetter judicial decision-making:

> **Kirby J: [89]** I do not agree with McHugh J that parties can control this Court's application of the Constitution and foreclose constitutional decision-making merely by their private arrangements or assertions in court. In my opinion, this is completely inconsistent with this Court's duty to the Constitution when a matter is before the Court for decision. In effect, McHugh J's views on this issue would allow parties to control the exercise of a portion of the judicial power. Such a possibility has only to be stated to be seen as incompatible with constitutional principle.

However, in *Combet v Commonwealth* (2005) 221 ALR 621, Kirby J joined with McHugh J in deploring the fact that the joint majority judgment in that case had disposed of the issue by adopting a statutory construction which had not been advanced by either party, and had not been adequately argued in court.

(b)   "Matters"

The High Court has steadfastly refused to give advisory opinions and, when the Parliament attempted to legislate to enable it to do so, the attempt was held to be unconstitutional. The attempt was made by Pt XII of the *Judiciary Act 1903* (Cth), as inserted in 1910 under the heading: "Reference of Constitutional Questions". By s 88: "Whenever the Governor-General refers to the High Court for hearing and determination any question of law as to the validity of any Act or enactment of the Parliament the High Court shall have jurisdiction to hear and determine the matter". By s 89, on any such reference, "the matter shall be heard and determined by a Full Court consisting of all [available] Justices". By s 93: "The determination of the Court upon the matter shall be final and conclusive and not subject to any appeal".

This reference procedure was first invoked in relation to amendments in 1920 to the *Navigation Act 1912* (Cth). The amendments were to come into force on a date to be proclaimed; the question of their validity was referred to the Court before any proclamation was made. Parties represented included the Attorneys-General of the Commonwealth, Victoria and Western Australia; the shipowners; and the Institute of Marine Engineers. Owen Dixon for the Victorian Attorney-General took a preliminary objection to Pt XII of the *Judiciary Act*. It must have been enacted in reliance on s 76 of the Constitution ("any matter (i) arising under this Constitution, or involving its interpretation"): "**[258]** But the word 'matter' there means a claim of right in litigation between parties, and an abstract question of law is not a 'matter'." By 5:1, the Court accepted this argument. Higgins J dissented; Isaacs J was absent overseas.

In re Judiciary and Navigation Acts
(1921) 29 CLR 257

Knox CJ, Gavan Duffy, Powers, Rich and Starke JJ: [264] Mr *Leverrier*, for the Commonwealth, contended that a determination of the Court pronounced under this Part of the Act was, on the true construction of those sections, merely advisory and not judicial. In our opinion this is untenable. After carefully considering the provisions of Part XII, we have come to the conclusion that Parliament desired to obtain from this Court not merely an opinion but an authoritative declaration of the law. To make such a declaration clearly is a judicial function, and such a function is not competent to this Court unless its exercise is an exercise of part of the judicial power of the Commonwealth. If this be so, it is not within our province in this case to inquire whether Parliament can impose on this Court or on its members any, and if so what, duties other than judicial duties, and we refrain from expressing any opinion on that question … **[265]** The question then is narrowed to this: Is authority to be found under sec 76 of the Constitution for the enactment of Part XII of the *Judiciary Act*? Sec 51(XXXIX) does not extend the power to confer original jurisdiction on the High Court contained in sec 76. It enables Parliament to provide for the effective exercise by the Legislature, the Executive and the Judiciary, of the power conferred by the Constitution on those bodies respectively, but does not enable it to extend the ambit of any such power. It is said that here is a matter arising under the Constitution or involving its interpretation, and that Parliament by sec 30 of the *Judiciary Act* has conferred on this Court original jurisdiction in all matters arising under the Constitution or involving its interpretation. It is true that the answer to the question submitted for our determination does involve the interpretation of the Constitution, but is there a matter within the meaning of sec 76? We think not. It was suggested in argument that "matter" meant no more than legal proceeding, and that Parliament might at its discretion create or invent a legal proceeding in which this Court might be called on to interpret the Constitution by a declaration at large. We do not accept this contention; we do not think that the word "matter" in sec 76 means a legal proceeding, but rather the subject matter for determination in a legal proceeding. In our opinion there can be no matter within the meaning of the section unless there is some immediate right, duty or liability to be established by the determination of the Court. **[266]** If the matter exists, the Legislature may no doubt prescribe the means by which the determination of the Court is to be obtained, and for that purpose may, we think, adopt any existing method of legal procedure or invent a new one. But it cannot authorize this Court to make a declaration of the law divorced from any attempt to administer that law. The word "matter" is used several times in Chapter III of the Constitution (secs 73, 74, 75, 76, 77), and always, we think, with the same meaning. The meaning of the expression "in all matters between States" in sec 75 was considered by this Court in *South Australia v Victoria* [(1911) 12 CLR 667]. *Griffith* CJ said that it must be a controversy of such a nature that it could be determined upon principles of law, and in this *Barton* J agreed. *O'Connor* J said that the matter in dispute must be such that it can be determined upon some recognized principle of law. *Isaacs* J said that the expression "matters" used with reference to the Judicature, and applying equally to individuals and States, includes and is confined to claims resting upon an alleged violation of some positive law to which the parties are alike subject, and which therefore governs their relations, and constitutes the measure of their rights and duties. *Higgins* J appeared to think that the expression involved the necessity of the existence of some cause of action in the party applying to the Court for a declaration … All these opinions indicate that a matter under the judicature provisions of the Constitution must involve some right or privilege or protection given by law, or the prevention, redress or punishment of some act inhibited by law. The adjudication of the Courts may be sought in proceedings *inter partes* or *ex parte*, or, if Courts had the requisite jurisdiction, even in those administrative **[267]** proceedings with reference to the custody, residence and management of the affairs of infants or lunatics. But we can find nothing in Chapter III of the Constitution to lend colour to the view that Parliament can confer power or jurisdiction upon the High Court to determine abstract questions of law without the right or duty of any body or person being involved.

Note that the same restrictive meaning of the word "matter" or "matters" is said to govern *all* the usages of the term in ss 73 to 77 inclusive. Thus the jurisdiction that may be conferred on other federal courts under s 77, as well as that which may be given to the High Court under s 76, is confined to concrete "matters" in the above sense. For example, in *Collins v Charles Marshall Pty Ltd* (1955) 92 CLR 529, s 31(1) of the *Conciliation and Arbitration Act 1904* (Cth), purporting to make appeals to the Commonwealth Court of Conciliation and Arbitration exclusive, was held to be invalid. It had sought to confer on the Arbitration Court appellate jurisdiction in a variety of proceedings, including "proceedings arising under this Act" and "proceedings arising under an order or award or involving the interpretation of an order or award". Such proceedings, said a unanimous High Court, did not constitute a "matter".

In such cases the claim to validity depends on the finding of a "matter". But occasionally it may happen that a claim to legislative validity depends upon showing that *no* jurisdiction involving a "matter" has been conferred. In 1973 the Whitlam government proposed to abolish all remaining appeals to the Privy Council (see now the *Privy Council (Appeals from the High Court) Act 1975* (Cth)). To pre-empt or circumvent that proposal, the Queensland Parliament under Premier Johannes Bjelke-Petersen enacted the *Appeals and Special Reference Act 1973* (Qld), which provided for a reference to the Privy Council by the Queen or by the Attorney-General ("for hearing and consideration and advice thereon") of any "questions or matters which, whether as part of any cause or otherwise, ... arise under or concern any law in force in Queensland". The language used was closely modelled on that of the *Judicial Committee Act 1833* (Imp). In *Commonwealth v Queensland* (*Queen of Queensland Case*) (1975) 134 CLR 298, the High Court held that the Queensland legislation was unconstitutional – in part because, although by convention Privy Council judgments are couched in the form of humble advice to Her Majesty, the Judicial Committee is "**[309]** in substance and reality ... 'an independent court of law' " (see *Ibralebbe v The Queen* [1964] AC 900 at 919). It followed that the Queensland Act was invalid – both as an attempt to confer jurisdiction inconsistently with Ch III of the Constitution, and as an attempt to circumvent the controlled regime of Privy Council appeals embodied in Ch III or evolved through the subsequent accretions to and implementation of its provisions. The State of Queensland had tried to avoid these conclusions by arguing that no jurisdictional "matters" were involved. The attempt was not successful.

Commonwealth v Queensland (*Queen of Queensland Case*)
(1975) 134 CLR 298

Jacobs J: [325] The argument on behalf of the defendants depends upon the submission that a reference of the proposed questions to the Judicial Committee, although it is a reference of a "matter" under s 4 of the 1833 Act, is not a reference of a "matter" under either s 75 or s 76 of the Constitution in that the questions proposed to be asked in the reference are hypothetical questions.

It was held in *In re Judiciary Act* 1903-1920 and *In re Navigation Act* 1912-1920 [(1921) 29 CLR 257] that the determination of questions of law on a reference to the High Court was clearly a judicial function and could only be made, if at all, on an exercise of part of the judicial power of the Commonwealth. It was of course held that the determination of such questions, when they do not arise in a legal proceeding where there is some immediate right, duty or liability to be established by the determination of the Court, does not fall within the judicial power which may be exercised under Ch III ... But it was also held ... that Ch III was an exhaustive statement of the judicial power which may be conferred under the chapter ...

In re Judiciary Act 1903-1920 and *In re Navigation Act* 1912-1920 was not decided as a case where it was sought to impose a non-judicial function upon the High Court. If it had been, the law as then understood might not have caused this to be an invalidating characteristic. It was decided on the grounds which I have stated and has never been overruled.

[326] It should be remarked that the contrary view, that an "advisory" decision involves no exercise of judicial power, would mean that on any subject of our constitutional or Commonwealth law a Supreme Court of a State could be invested with this power and could exercise it with no possibility of appeal to this Court ... but with an appeal to the Judicial Committee ... It is unreal to regard this as of no consequence because the declarations of law are merely "opinions". No community could appreciate the significance of a distinction in such a context between judicial and non-judicial power. Much reliance was placed upon the statement of Lord Loreburn LC in *Attorney-General (Ontario) v Attorney-General (Canada)* [[1912] AC 571 at 589] that the answers to referred questions "are only advisory and will have no more effect than the opinions of the law officers". But though this is so in the sense that no parties are immediately bound by the determination as a res judicata, the decision is, "an authoritative declaration of the law" [29 CLR at 264] ...

[327] In my opinion the judicial power delineated in Ch III is exhaustive of the manner in and the extent to which judicial power may be conferred on or exercised by any court in respect of the subject matters set forth in ss 75 and 76, "matters" in those sections meaning "subject matters". This is so not only in respect of federal courts but also in respect of State courts whether or not they are exercising federal jurisdiction conferred on them under s 77(iii). In respect of the subject matters set out in ss 75 and 76 judicial power may only be exercised within the limits of the kind of judicial power envisaged in Ch III and if in respect of those matters an investing with federal jurisdiction of a State court does not enable it to perform the particular judicial function, then in respect of those matters the State court cannot under any law exercise that judicial function. Therefore, if in respect of those matters a State court exercising federal jurisdiction cannot give "advisory opinions" it cannot in respect of the same matters give such opinions in exercise of some State jurisdiction ...

[328] What is true of a court within the territorial boundaries of a State is equally true of the Judicial Committee. Once it is recognized that the Judicial Committee is a judicial body and that it exercises judicial power and once it is recognized that Ch III of the Constitution is an exhaustive statement of the kind of judicial power which may be conferred or exercised in respect of the subject matters set out in ss 75 and 76 it is of no consequence in the present context that the Judicial Committee may consider and determine "matters" under s 4 of the 1833 Act which are not "matters" under s 75 and 76. The subject matters under those sections of the Constitution may only be considered and determined in exercise of the kind of judicial power envisaged under Ch III of the Constitution ... The effect of the *Commonwealth of Australia Constitution Act* 1900 is to limit the prerogative to refer any matter to the Judicial Committee for the exercise of its judicial power in relation thereto (including its power to give an advisory opinion upon a question of law) by extinguishing the same at least in respect of subject matters of judicial power which fall within Ch III of the Constitution.

When a question of law arises in the course of a criminal trial, most States have a mechanism for referring it to an appellate court for determination. The *Criminal Code* (Qld) provides for such a referral in s 669A. In a case where the accused has been acquitted, s 669A(5) stipulates that the result of the reference shall not affect the acquittal; but in other cases this stipulation would not preclude the possibility of a fresh indictment. In *Mellifont v Attorney-General (Queensland)* (1991) 173 CLR 289, the trial judge had ruled in favour of the accused on a point of law. The prosecution then entered a nolle prosequi (indicating that they were unwilling to proceed), and the accused was discharged. The issue was referred under s 669A to the Court of Criminal Appeal, which ruled in favour of the prosecution. The accused, who had been warned to expect a fresh indictment in the event of such a ruling, then sought to appeal against the ruling to the High Court. That Court's appellate jurisdiction, conferred by s 73 of the Constitution, extends to "all judgments, decrees, orders, and sentences" of State and federal courts. The question therefore was whether this formula included a ruling on a reference under s 669A. By 6:1, with Brennan J dissenting, the High Court held that it did.

Mellifont v Attorney-General (Queensland)
(1991) 173 CLR 289

Mason CJ, Deane, Dawson, Gaudron and McHugh JJ: [303] In *In re Judiciary and Navigation Acts* [(1921) 29 CLR 257 at 266-7] ... [t]he Court, with the sole dissent of Higgins J, ... stated that the legislature:

"cannot authorize this Court to make a declaration of the law divorced from any attempt to administer that law ... we can find nothing in Chapter III of the Constitution to lend colour to the view that Parliament can confer power or jurisdiction upon the High Court to determine abstract questions of law without the right or duty of any body or person being involved."

The passage contains two critical concepts. One is the notion of an abstract question of law not involving the right or duty of any body or person; the second is the making of a declaration of law divorced or dissociated from any attempt to administer it.

In *O'Toole* [*v Charles David Pty Ltd* (1990) 171 CLR 232], it was explicitly recognized that answers given by the full court of a court to questions reserved for its consideration in the course of proceedings in a "matter" pending in that court do not constitute an advisory opinion or abstract declaration of the kind dealt with in *In re Judiciary and Navigation Acts* whether or not those answers, of themselves, determine the rights of the parties. Such answers are not given in circumstances divorced from an attempt to administer the law as stated by the answers; they are given as an integral part of the process of determining the rights and obligations of the parties which are at stake in the proceedings in which the questions are reserved. Once this is accepted, as indeed it must be, it follows inevitably that the giving of the answers is an exercise of judicial power because the seeking and the giving of the answers constitutes an important and influential, if not decisive, step in the judicial determination of the rights and liabilities in issue in the litigation ...

[304] The consequence is that the answers fall within the description "judgments, decrees, orders" in s 73 of the Constitution. The difficulties and inconveniences which would flow from a contrary conclusion were identified in *O'Toole* and there is no occasion to repeat them here. It follows that *Fisher v Fisher* [(1986) 161 CLR 438] and *Swiss Aluminium* [*Australia Ltd v Federal Commissioner of Taxation* (1987) 163 CLR 421] were incorrect to the extent that they decided that no appeal lies to this Court from answers given to a special or stated case where those answers do not determine the parties' rights. In that respect they should not be followed.

However, this conclusion does not dispose of the objection to jurisdiction in the present case. The Attorney-General's power under the Code to refer a point of law to the Court of Criminal Appeal for its consideration arises only if the accused has been acquitted of the charge in the indictment or if the accused has been discharged in respect of that charge after counsel for the Crown, as a result of a ruling by the trial judge on that point of law, has informed the court that the Crown will not proceed further upon the indictment in respect of that charge. In other words, in the case of discharge, the exercise of the power to refer and the exercise of jurisdiction by the Court pursuant to the reference both proceed on the footing that no further proceedings on the indictment in respect of the relevant charge will be taken. Consequently, the ruling on the point of law pursuant to the reference will not play any part in the subsequent determination of the charge on the indictment. Likewise, in the case of acquittal, the ruling on the reference has no impact on the acquittal. In this respect, the decision on the point of law referred stands in a different position from answers given by a full court to questions reserved in a stated case in the situation previously discussed.

Although the indictment itself cannot serve as a vehicle for the further determination of the charge in consequence of the statement by counsel for the Crown and the subsequent filing of the nolle prosequi, the reference and the decision on the reference *arise out of* the proceedings on the indictment and are a statutory extension of those proceedings ... **[305]** The Crown sought the reference in order to establish that the trial judge's ruling was wrong in various respects. In this situation, the decision on the reference was made with respect to a "matter" which was the subject-matter of the legal proceedings at first instance and was not divorced from the ordinary administration of the law. The decision is therefore to be distinguished from the abstract declaration sought by the Executive Government in *In re Judiciary and Navigation Acts*. That opinion was academic, in response to an abstract question, and hypothetical in the sense that it was unrelated to any actual controversy between parties.

True it is that the purpose of seeking and obtaining a review of the trial judge's ruling was to secure a correct statement of the law so that it would be applied correctly in future cases. However, in our view, in the context of the criminal law, that does not stamp the procedure for which s 669A(2) provides as something which is academic or hypothetical so as to deny that it is an exercise of judicial power ... The fundamental point, as it seems to us, is that s 669A(2) enables the

Court of Criminal Appeal to correct an error of law at the trial. It is that characteristic of the proceedings that stamps them as an exercise of judicial power and the decision as a judgment or order within the meaning of s 73 ...

It follows that, in our opinion, *Saffron v The Queen* [(1953) 88 CLR 523] ... **[306]** was wrongly decided and should not be followed. It also follows that the objection to jurisdiction must be overruled. In reaching that conclusion we should state that we do not rely on the fact that it was foreshadowed to the applicant that a fresh indictment would be presented against him in the event of a "successful" reference and that, at any subsequent trial, the decision of the Court of Criminal Appeal ... would have been applied. In our view the decision of the Court of Criminal Appeal would have grounded an appeal to this Court, subject to the grant of special leave, even if the Crown did not propose to issue a fresh indictment.

The question of this Court's jurisdiction cannot turn on whether or not the Crown decides to present a fresh indictment against the applicant.

The applicant in *Mellifont* faced the imminent threat of a fresh prosecution. The joint majority judgment treated that as irrelevant, though Toohey J regarded it as "**[326]** a consideration". In *Croome v Tasmania* (1997) 191 CLR 119 there was no such imminent threat. In Tasmania, "carnal knowledge of any person against the order of nature" and "indecent practice between male persons" were criminal offences under ss 122 and 123 of the *Criminal Code* (Tas) respectively. In 1994, the Human Rights Committee established by Art 28 of the International Covenant on Civil and Political Rights 1966 found that these provisions were an "arbitrary interference with privacy" within the meaning of Art 17 of the Covenant (Human Rights Committee, Communication No 488/1992, UN Doc CCPR/C/50/D/488/1992 (8 April 1994)). In response, the *Human Rights (Sexual Conduct) Act 1994* (Cth) enacted into Australian law the relevant language of Art 17, insofar as it applied to "sexual conduct involving only consenting adults acting in private". In *Croome v Tasmania*, Rodney Croome and Nicholas Toonen sought to establish that the *Criminal Code* was inconsistent with that enactment, thus attracting the operation of s 109 of the Constitution.

Had either of the plaintiffs been prosecuted under the *Criminal Code*, that contention would necessarily have arisen for decision; but the Tasmanian authorities declined to prosecute. Despite this, the plaintiffs initiated an action in the High Court seeking a declaration that the Commonwealth Act had effectively triggered the operation of s 109. Tasmania sought to have the writ set aside on the ground that there was no "matter" in which the High Court could assert jurisdiction, and also on the ground that the plaintiffs lacked standing to raise the issue (see §5(c) below). The Tasmanian objection failed. At the hearing the argument based on "standing" was abandoned and the High Court unanimously held that there was a relevant "matter".

Croome v Tasmania
(1997) 191 CLR 119

Brennan CJ, Dawson and Toohey JJ: [124] A "matter" must be distinguished from the action or judicial proceeding which is commenced in order to obtain a determination of **[125]** a controversy between the parties. The "matter" is not the proceeding but the subject of the controversy which is amenable to judicial determination in the proceeding. Such a controversy has particular characteristics. In *In re Judiciary and Navigation Acts* [(1921) 29 CLR 257 at 265-6], the majority of the Court said:

> "In our opinion there can be no matter within the meaning of [s 76] unless there is some immediate right, duty or liability to be established by the determination of the Court ... But [the Legislature] cannot authorize this Court to make a declaration of the law divorced from any attempt to administer that law."

Speaking of this passage, the majority in *Mellifont v Attorney-General (Q)* [(1991) 173 CLR 289 at 303] said it contained "two critical concepts":

"One is the notion of an abstract question of law not involving the right or duty of any body or person; the second is the making of a declaration of law divorced or dissociated from any attempt to administer it."

The Solicitor-General for Tasmania submits that the plaintiffs' action does not seek to establish any immediate right, duty or liability nor is the Court called upon to administer the relevant law. However, the question of law that the plaintiffs seek to raise is not whether they or either of them has engaged in conduct proscribed by s 122(a) or (c) or by s 123 of the Code; nor whether the plaintiffs should be prosecuted, convicted or punished for their conduct. The question is whether those provisions operate and, since the enactment of s 4 of the *Human Rights (Sexual Conduct) Act*, have operated in Tasmania. The Solicitor-General's submission that no prosecution under the Code is pending or threatened does not touch that question.

It is a long-standing doctrine that a "matter" may consist of a controversy between a person who has a sufficient interest in the subject and who asserts that a purported law is invalid and the polity whose law it purports to be. In *Toowoomba Foundry Pty Ltd v Commonwealth* [(1945) 71 CLR 545 at 570], Latham CJ said:

"The plaintiff has relied upon the practice of the Court in allowing the constitutional validity of statutes and regulations and orders made thereunder to be challenged by interested persons in actions claiming only declarations of invalidity: See, eg, *Attorney-*[126]*General for NSW v Brewery Employés Union of NSW* [(1908) 6 CLR 469]; *Colonial Sugar Refining Co Ltd v Attorney-General (Cth)* [(1912) 15 CLR 182]. More recently, see *Victorian Chamber of Manufactures v Commonwealth (Prices Regulations)* [(1943) 67 CLR 335] and *Victorian Chamber of Manufactures v Commonwealth (Women's Employment Regulations)* [(1943) 67 CLR 347]. It is now, I think, too late to contend that a person who is, or in the immediate future probably will be, affected in his person or property by Commonwealth legislation alleged to be unconstitutional has not a cause of action in this Court for a declaration that the legislation is invalid."

It is a misconception of the principle in *In re Judiciary and Navigation Acts* to suggest that, in proceedings for a declaration of invalidity of an impugned law, no law is administered unless the executive government has acted to enforce the impugned law. The law that is being administered in such proceedings is not the impugned law but the constitutional or administrative law which determines the validity or invalidity of the impugned law. Thus Gavan Duffy, Rich and Starke JJ in *James v South Australia* [(1927) 40 CLR 1 at 40] identified a "right, title, privilege or immunity" claimed under the Constitution as the criterion of a matter arising under the Constitution or involving its interpretation. A declaration of validity or invalidity of an impugned law administers the law governing the controversy about the impugned law. If it were otherwise, there would be no jurisdiction in this Court to determine an action by the Attorney-General of a State for a declaration that a challenged Commonwealth law is invalid. Yet an action of that kind is the classical vehicle for exercising this Court's constitutional jurisdiction.

Gaudron, McHugh and Gummow JJ also referred to the passage from *In re Judiciary and Navigation Acts* set out above, and to the exegesis of it in *Mellifont*. They went on:

Gaudron, McHugh and Gummow JJ: [136] There is nothing in the references in *In re Judiciary and Navigation Acts* to the administration of the law which provides any foundation for the submissions of the State in this case. The administration referred to is that of the courts in dispensing justice. The concern of the Court in *In re Judiciary and Navigation Acts* was to establish that Ch III is an exhaustive statement of that judicial power which may be conferred for the exercise of federal jurisdiction. A determination of questions of law on a reference by the Executive Government to the High Court could only be made, if at all, in exercise of the judicial power of the Commonwealth. A determination of such questions, if they do not arise in a legal proceeding where there is some immediate right, duty or liability to be established by the determination of the Court, does not fall within that judicial power which may be exercised under Ch III. This accords with the analysis given by Jacobs J in *Commonwealth v Queensland* [134 CLR at 325] ...

Their Honours in *In re Judiciary and Navigation Acts* are not to be taken as lending support to the notion that, where the law of a State imposes a duty upon the citizen attended by liability to prosecution and punishment under the criminal law, and the citizen asserts that, by operation of s 109 of the Constitution, the law of the State is invalid, there can be no immediate right, duty or liability to be established by determination of this Court, in an action for declaratory relief by the citizen against the State, unless the Executive Government of the State has, at least, invoked legal process against the particular citizen to enforce the criminal law.

They, too, pointed out that in constitutional challenges to Commonwealth legislation, a declaration of invalidity is often the only relief granted or sought; and they, too, quoted the list of examples given by Latham CJ in *Toowoomba Foundry Pty Ltd v Commonwealth*.

Gaudron, McHugh and Gummow JJ: [137] The Solicitor-General sought to distinguish the authorities referred to by Latham CJ as applicable only to proceedings in which the attack was on the validity of laws of the Commonwealth. There is no reason in logic for such a confinement of those authorities to exclude a proceeding in which declaratory relief is sought as to the invalidity of the law of a State. Particularly is this so where the plaintiff is a citizen seeking to establish that s 109 of the Constitution has operated relevantly to remove the requirement of observance of the State criminal law. In the present case, the provisions of the Code affect the plaintiffs in their person by imposing duties which require the observance of particular norms of conduct and attach liability to prosecution and subsequent punishment for disobedience.

Observations by Dixon J in *Federal Council of the British Medical Association v Commonwealth* [(1949) 79 CLR 201 at 257] are in point. The issue there was whether s 7A of the *Pharmaceutical Benefits Act* 1947 (Cth) was invalid as imposing a form of civil conscription within the meaning of s 51(xxiiiA) of the Constitution. Section 7A provided that a medical practitioner was not to write prescriptions otherwise than on a prescription form supplied by the Commonwealth. A penalty for non-compliance was imposed. The first plaintiff was a body corporate, the Federal Council of the British Medical Association in Australia, one of the objects of which was to advance the general interests of the medical profession. Dixon J doubted if a corporate body had a title to maintain the suit, it lacking a sufficient material interest which would be prejudiced by the operation of the statute. However, his Honour continued:

> "But the point is of no importance, because there are six other plaintiffs all of whom practise medicine or surgery. The interest which they have is enough to enable them to complain, if the **[138]** legislation is invalid as a whole or if severable provisions are invalid which would directly affect the practice of medicine or surgery."

There was no suggestion that it was necessary for the plaintiffs to show that there already had been set in motion against them the punitive provisions of the legislation. It was significant enough that the plaintiffs "faced possible criminal prosecution".

The definition of federal jurisdiction by reference to specified classes of "matters" has given rise to much recondite learning. For example, in *R v Bevan; Ex parte Elias and Gordon* (1942) 66 CLR 452, Starke J said that when a matter arises under s 76(i) of the Constitution, the High Court is "**[465]** clothed with full authority essential for the complete adjudication of the matter and not merely the interpretation of the Constitution". In cases like *Philip Morris Inc v Adam P Brown Male Fashions Pty Ltd* (1981) 148 CLR 457, similar reasoning led the High Court to say that, once the Federal Court takes jurisdiction in the federal aspects of a "matter", its jurisdiction extends to "**[531]** the whole of such matter". This concept of the "whole" of a matter, as implicitly differentiated from "parts" of a matter, was considered in *Abebe v Commonwealth* (1999) 197 CLR 510.

The *Migration Reform Act 1992* (Cth) had introduced into the *Migration Act 1958* (Cth) a new Pt 8, distinguishing between those migration decisions that are and are not judicially reviewable in the Federal Court. Section 475, when read with s 486, provided that the Federal Court's jurisdiction to review decisions of the Refugee Review Tribunal was "exclusive of the jurisdiction of all other courts other than the jurisdiction of the High Court under s 75 of the Constitution". However, s 476 then limited the grounds of review by excluding grounds such as denial of natural justice, or an exercise of power being "so unreasonable that no reasonable person could have so exercised the power" (that is, "*Wednesbury* unreasonableness" in the sense explained by *Associated Picture Houses Ltd v Wednesbury Corporation* [1948] 1 KB 223). In *Abebe v Commonwealth* the validity of these restrictions was unsuccessfully challenged.

The fact that the legislation operated by first conferring on the Federal Court an apparently unlimited power to review the Tribunal's decisions, and then withdrawing part of that power, was presumably not a promising basis for constitutional attack. Even if the grant and withdrawal were conceived of sequentially, "[226] it is the general conception of English law that what Parliament enacts it may repeal". Moreover, as held in *Georgiadis v Australian and Overseas Tele-communications Corporation* (1994) 179 CLR 297, "[306] a right which has no existence apart from statute is one that, of its nature, is susceptible of modification or extinguishment". Instead, the argument focused on the fact that in ss 75-77 of the Constitution all of the references to the jurisdiction which may be conferred upon federal courts are expressed in terms of "matters". It was said that when Parliament chooses to confer jurisdiction, it must do so with respect to a "matter", and must give jurisdiction over the whole of that "matter". To give jurisdiction to review a Tribunal decision, but to limit the jurisdiction so that it could only be exercised on some of the grounds which would normally be available, would involve an attempt to confer juris-diction over only part of a "matter". This, it was argued, is not permitted by the Constitution. At the very least, it was said, this must be so when the same Tribunal decision remains reviewable with no restriction on the available grounds by the High Court in the exercise of its constitu-tionally guaranteed jurisdiction under s 75(v) of the Constitution. Gleeson CJ, McHugh, Kirby and Callinan JJ rejected this argument and upheld the legislation; Gaudron, Gummow and Hayne JJ dissented.

Abebe v Commonwealth
(1999) 197 CLR 510

Gleeson CJ and McHugh J: [525] Nothing in the terms of s 77 or Ch III of the Constitution requires the Parliament to give a federal court authority to decide every legal right, duty, liability or obligation inherent in a controversy between subjects or between a subject and the Crown merely because it has jurisdiction over some aspect of the controversy. Nor does anything in s 77 or Ch III of the Constitution require a federal court dealing with a legal controversy to have authority to deal with every legal ground that a party wishes to put forward. It is true that a "matter" is concerned with the rights, duties and liabilities of particular parties in concrete situations and that, when a "matter" exists, it cannot be identified without reference to some law or state of affairs described in s 75 or s 76, and which exists independently of the jurisdiction of a court or its procedures. But that does not mean that, if the Parliament wishes to confer jurisdiction on a federal court in respect of "matters" arising under a particular law or state of affairs, it can only define the jurisdiction of that court by reference to the totality of the rights, privileges, powers and duties that arise under that law or state of affairs ...

As long as the law defining or investing jurisdiction is one "with respect to" any of the "matters", as so understood, it will be a law **[526]** authorised by s 77. The conferring of a power to make laws "with respect to" a subject "is as wide a legislative power as can be created", as Latham CJ pointed out in *Bank of NSW v Commonwealth* [(1948) 76 CLR 1 at 186]. A law which changes, regulates or abolishes rights, duties, powers and privileges relating to a subject is made "with respect to" that subject. That being so, a law defines the jurisdiction of a federal court with respect to any of the "matters" mentioned in ss 75 and 76 when it defines the authority of that court to decide what are the rights of parties in a proceeding that may be brought in that court with respect to any of those "matters". Thus, a law authorised by s 77 may confer or invest jurisdiction in a federal or State court over the whole range of rights, powers, privileges and liabilities arising from the operation of a law or the existence of a state of affairs answering any of the descriptions in ss 75 and 76 of the Constitution. On the other hand, a s 77 law may validly confer or invest jurisdiction in respect of some only of those rights, powers, privileges and liabilities and may even limit the remedies which are available to a person affected by a breach of those rights ...

[528] The existence of a "matter" … cannot be separated from the existence of a remedy to enforce the substantive right, duty or liability. That does not mean that there can be no "matter" unless the existence of a right, duty or liability is established. It is sufficient that the moving party claims that he or she has a legal remedy in the court where the proceedings have been commenced to enforce the right, duty or liability in question. It does mean, however, that there must be a remedy enforceable in a court of justice, that it must be enforceable in the court in which the proceedings are commenced and that the person claiming the remedy must have sufficient interest in enforcing the right, duty or liability to make the controversy justiciable. Questions of standing cannot be divorced from the notion of a "matter" …

[529] Once it is accepted that a "matter" cannot be identified without regard to the remedies available in the court where it is litigated, it necessarily follows that the same legal controversy can give rise to separate matters because different courts may provide different remedies. Until the "fusion" of law and equity, for example, a person might obtain an injunction to restrain a continuing breach of contract in the Court of Chancery and damages for the breach in action at law. That position continued in New South Wales until the "fusion" of law and equity occurred in 1970. Similarly, an employee may be able to **[530]** obtain an order from an industrial court that a term of the employment contract is void because it is harsh or unconscionable and at the same time have a right to obtain an order from a court of general jurisdiction that the term is unjust or unfair under legislation such as the *Trade Practices Act* or the *Contracts Review Act* 1980 (NSW). In both cases, the "matter" determined in one court is separate and independent from the "matter" determined in the other court even though each "matter" arises out of the same factual substratum …

[531] In construing provisions such as s 77(i), it is necessary to keep in mind that the Constitution is an instrument of government, not easily or readily amended, and intended to endure indefinitely. To hold that the Parliament cannot confer federal jurisdiction in respect of the matters mentioned in ss 75 and 76 unless the Parliament gives the relevant court jurisdiction to dispose of the whole controversy between the parties would create immense practical problems for the administration of federal law which the makers of the Constitution can hardly have intended. Such a holding would seem to deny the Parliament the right to have specialist federal courts or courts whose jurisdiction was limited by reference to remedies, geographical areas or monetary limits. It would also seem to deny the Parliament the power to prevent federal courts from dealing with certain subject matters such as title to land or actions in contract or from granting certain remedies such as injunctions or prerogative relief. Historically, governments have found it useful to create courts of limited jurisdiction, and it was, and is, usual for the jurisdiction of magistrates' courts to be limited in such a fashion …

[532] The plaintiff contends that, once Parliament has laid down a regime of legal rights or duties and conferred jurisdiction on a court to deal with a controversy as to whether one of those rights or duties has been breached, it can not prevent that court from dealing with the whole controversy. On these hypotheses, the Parliament has only three options. They are (i) not creating the right or duty at all; (ii) creating the right or duty and preventing all courts (other than this Court) or some courts (such as courts of inferior jurisdiction) from dealing with any part of the controversy and (iii) creating the right or duty and investing every court, irrespective of its status, with every remedy needed to settle the whole controversy. These options are so rigid and impractical that only the clearest constitutional language could compel them. In so far as the exercise of appellate jurisdiction or administrative review, in particular, is concerned, the interpretation of s 77(i) for which the plaintiff contends would seem to deny the Parliament any choice as to the form that the appeal or review would take. Nothing in the language of Ch III forces such limited and rigid choices on the Parliament …

[534] Thus, the subject matter for decision by a federal court may embrace the whole controversy between the parties or part of it. The law defining the jurisdiction of the court may provide limited remedies for the successful party or every remedy that is necessary to do justice between the parties and which is appropriate to the exercise of judicial power by a federal court. The choice is one for the Parliament.

In the present case, the Parliament has chosen to restrict severely the jurisdiction of the Federal Court to review the legality of decisions of the Refugee Review Tribunal. That restriction may have significant consequences for this Court because it must inevitably force or at all events invite applicants for refugee status to invoke the constitutionally entrenched s 75(v) jurisdiction of this Court. The effect on the business of this Court is certain to be serious. Nevertheless, we can see nothing in ss 75, 76 and 77 of the Constitution which prevents the Parliament from enacting ss 476, 485 and 486 of the Act.

Gaudron, Gummow and Hayne JJ dissented. Gaudron J held that the functions given to the Federal Court by Pt 8 of the Act did not involve an exercise of judicial power, understood as "**[555]** the power to make final and binding determinations as to some immediate right, duty or obligation put in issue by the parties". The "right" at issue here, she said, was not the plaintiff's right to have the Tribunal's decision set aside, but the Minister's right "to act upon or give effect to" that decision. Since that right of the Minister could be challenged in the High Court on grounds not available to the Federal Court, the Federal Court could not finally determine it. Hence it was unable to exercise judicial power. It followed also that Pt 8 did not give rise to a "matter". Gummow and Hayne JJ reached the same conclusion.

Gummow and Hayne JJ: [569] The Commonwealth contended that the provisions are valid **[570]** because, although there can be no "matter" and no exercise of judicial power without there being an adjudication of rights or duties, here the rights the subject of adjudication are those conferred by Pt 8 – the right to have the decision set aside on any of the stated grounds. The fact that other rights might be adjudicated in an application under s 75 of the Constitution was, so it was contended, irrelevant. The applicant contended, on the other hand, that there is no "matter" and there is no exercise of judicial power because the controversy between the parties is whether the Tribunal acted in accordance with law. That controversy is wider than a controversy about the grounds specified in Pt 8 and is not quelled by the decision of the Federal Court ...

[571] The fact that Pt 8 entitles a person dissatisfied with a decision of the Refugee Review Tribunal to commence a proceeding in the Federal Court does not mean that the proceeding relates to a matter. Much of the argument advanced in favour of the validity of Pt 8 proceeded from the unstated premise that the existence of a matter can be demonstrated by showing that a litigant may commence a proceeding.

But the majority of the Court in *In re Judiciary and Navigation Acts* [(1921) 29 CLR 257] rejected the contention that "matter" means no more than legal proceeding. It was held there that "matter" in s 76 means the subject matter for determination in a legal proceeding rather than the proceeding itself. Thus, to say that a party may bring a proceeding under Pt 8 does not mean that the subject of the proceeding is a "matter". The answer put forward on behalf of the Commonwealth was, in effect, that the "matter" was not the right to bring a proceeding but the right to have the Tribunal's decision set aside if one or more of the grounds specified in Pt 8 was established. That invites attention to what are the rights or duties that are to be judicially established.

No doubt a lay observer may say that the grievance of a person like the present applicant is that she was not granted refugee status. But no person who claims to be a refugee has any right recognised in law to have the merits of the executive's decision about refugee status reconsidered and decided in the exercise of the judicial power of the Commonwealth. By contrast, however, and as indicated earlier in these reasons, an applicant for refugee status does have a right to have the executive make its decision about an application for a protection visa in accordance with law. And that right may be vindicated by seeking the exercise of the judicial power of the Commonwealth. Thus, to cast the issue in terms of rights and duties, what is significant for immediate purposes is that the Tribunal has a duty to reach its decision according to law and an applicant to that Tribunal has a right enforceable in the exercise of federal judicial power to have it do so. That right does not find its origin in Pt 8 of the Act ...

[572] What Pt 8 of the Act seeks to do is to say that some, but not all, allegations of breach of that duty may be raised in and decided by the Federal Court. The inevitable consequence of limiting the kinds of allegation that may be made is that the Federal Court can never conclude that the decision challenged was made according to law. It may decide only that the particular grounds of challenge that were raised in the proceeding were not made out. The statute forbids it from embarking on some aspects of the more general inquiry whether the decision was made according to law ...

[574] Consideration of what orders the Federal Court may make is important because it reveals a more fundamental difficulty than a narrow point about the remedies that may be granted or a point about severance. What the difficulties about the possible forms of order that may be made under Pt 8 illustrate is that the rights and duties of the parties are not adjudicated in a proceeding under that Part. Only *some* of the considerations affecting their rights and duties may be agitated and decided and the controversy between them is not quelled by any decision in the proceeding. There is, therefore, no conferring on the Federal Court of jurisdiction over a "matter" arising under a law made by the Parliament, within the meaning of s 77(i) and s 76(ii) of the Constitution.

In *Attorney-General (Vic); ex rel Black v Commonwealth* (*DOGS Case*) (1981) 146 CLR 559 (see the extract in §5(c) below), the persons initiating the action had obtained the fiat of the Attorney-General for Victoria, and were therefore able to sue in his name. In *Re McBain; Ex parte Australian Catholic Bishops Conference* (2002) 209 CLR 372 there was a more unusual resort to this procedure. In *McBain v Victoria* (2000) 177 ALR 320, Sundberg J had held in the Federal Court that s 8 of the *Infertility Treatment Act 1995* (Vic), which required women undergoing reproductive treatment to be married or in a de facto relationship, was inoperative by reason of inconsistency with the *Sex Discrimination Act 1984* (Cth). Dr John McBain had applied to the Federal Court for a declaration to that effect, joining as respondents the State of Victoria; its Minister for Health; its Infertility Treatment Authority; and an individual patient to whom McBain proposed to provide the treatment. None of these four respondents chose to appeal against the decision. However, Sundberg J had given leave to counsel representing the Australian Catholic Bishops Conference and the Australian Episcopal Conference of the Roman Catholic Church to appear as *amici curiae* to oppose McBain's application. In the absence of an appeal, the Australian Catholic Bishops Conference applied to Callinan J of the High Court for an order nisi for certiorari addressed to Sundberg J with a view to quashing his decision. Callinan J issued an order nisi returnable before the Full Court.

The constitution of these proceedings gave rise to conceptual difficulties. It was not clear that the Catholic Bishops had standing in the matter; nor was it clear that there was a "matter" to which they were parties. If there was a "matter", its boundaries and its substratum of relevant facts were also unclear. Moreover, while it had been established that under s 75(v) of the Constitution the High Court may issue certiorari to a judge of the Federal Court (*R v Gray; Ex parte Marsh* (1985) 157 CLR 351), there was no precedent for the use of certiorari proposed in this case. In order to cure these difficulties, the Catholic Bishops applied to the Commonwealth Attorney-General for a fiat. This was granted in August 2001, shortly before the case was due to be argued, and gave rise to a separate proceeding (*Re McBain; Ex parte Attorney-General (Cth)*) which was argued together with the Catholic Bishops' application. However, it was not clear that the fiat had cured all the difficulties: indeed, it gave rise to a further anomaly. The Commonwealth was already appearing in the principal proceedings to *support* the Bishops' claim that there was no inconsistency between the two laws, but to *oppose* their argument that the *Sex Discrimination Act* was unconstitutional. The Attorney-General's fiat was granted only in respect of the former issue. The extent of these difficulties became vividly apparent when the case was argued before the High Court (see *Re McBain; Ex parte Australian Catholic Bishops Conference*, transcript of argument, 4-6 September 2001).

In the end the decisive issues were, first, whether there was a "matter" and, secondly, since certiorari is a discretionary remedy, whether (on the assumption that there was a "matter") the writ should be issued in this case. On the first issue the Court divided 4:3. Gleeson CJ, Gaudron, Gummow and Hayne JJ held that neither application gave rise to a "matter" of which the Court could take cognisance. McHugh and Callinan JJ, dissenting on this point, held that there was a "matter", while Kirby J agreed with them at least as to the Attorney-General's relator action. As to the discretionary issue, Gleeson CJ expressed no final view. The other six judges all held that, on discretionary grounds, certiorari should be refused.

The majority view that the Court had no "matter" before it was put most fully by Gaudron and Gummow JJ. They referred to a number of judicial formulations, all harking back to the ruling in *Re Judiciary and Navigation Acts* that "matter" means "[265] the subject matter for determination in a legal proceeding", and hence that "there can be no matter ... unless there is some immediate right, duty or liability to be established by the determination of the Court".

Re McBain; Ex parte Australian Catholic Bishops Conference
(2002) 209 CLR 372

Gaudron and Gummow JJ: [405] These statements suggest that the task of identification of the "matter" said to be the subject of the present litigation is to be approached as a tripartite inquiry: first, the identification of the subject-matter for determination in each of [the two proceedings] C22 and C6; secondly, the identification of the right, duty or liability to be established in each **[406]** proceeding; thirdly, the identification of the controversy between the parties to C22 and C6 for the quelling of which the judicial power of the Commonwealth is invoked. Whilst each of these inquiries may be pursued separately, all are related aspects of the basal question, "is there a 'matter' in the sense required by Ch III of the Constitution?" In our view, there is no such "matter", and this is so whether the moving party here is seen either as the Attorney-General or [as] the ecclesiastical authorities.

There is no controversy apparent between the applicants and the respondents, Sundberg J and Dr McBain. The latter has the protections against action against him by the State of Victoria of the declaration made in his favour, in particular par 3 thereof. But no relief by way of prohibition is sought against him. The learned judge has no interest in the matter; he has discharged the duty to exercise the judicial power of the Commonwealth in the proceeding which came before him and the orders have been entered. His Honour has acted within the jurisdiction conferred by para (b) of s 39B(1A) of the *Judiciary Act* and there has been no enlivening of the appellate processes of the Federal Court.

The subject-matter for determination in each proceeding is whether there is an error of law on the face of the record of the Federal Court, represented by the outcome of the proceeding before Sundberg J, and the purging of that record by administration of a remedy in the nature of certiorari. None of the applicants presents a claim for declaratory relief ... Rather, the whole of the relief the applicants seek is directed to the outcome of the particular proceeding which was disposed of in the Federal Court ...

In [*Truth About Motorways Pty Ltd v Macquarie Infrastructure Investment Management Ltd* [(2000) 200 CLR 591 at 612], Gaudron J said:

> "Absent the availability of relief related to the wrong which the plaintiff alleges, no immediate right, duty or liability is established by the Court's determination. Similarly, if there is no available **[407]** remedy, there is no administration of the relevant law. Thus, as Gleeson CJ and McHugh J pointed out in *Abebe v Commonwealth* [(1999) 197 CLR 510 at 527], '[i]f there is no legal remedy for a "wrong", there can be no "matter".'"

However, it would be to invert the reasoning in *Truth about Motorways* to say that, if there is no "wrong", nevertheless there is a "matter" so long as there is an available remedy.

Though conceding that the requirement of "some immediate right, duty or liability to be established by the determination of the Court" did not imply that the parties must have correlative interests therein, Gaudron and Gummow JJ saw that requirement as decisive in the present case.

Gaudron and Gummow JJ: [408] The Bishops and the Episcopal Conference may have a sharp difference in opinion with those such as the interveners who favour the provision of treatment to persons in the position of Ms Meldrum and who advocate the removal of the restrictions imposed by s 8 of the State Act. The concern of the Bishops and the Episcopal Conference is that the decision of Sundberg J provides a precedent which would influence the outcome of future litigation in which they or others seek relief upholding the validity of s 8 and allied provisions ... Hence the subject-matter of this litigation is the purging, by order of this Court, of the record of the Federal Court.

However, those concerns and objectives of the ecclesiastical authorities do not represent a claim by them in this present litigation of a right, title, privilege or immunity under the

Constitution; nor do they present, necessarily and directly rather than incidentally, an issue upon the interpretation of the Constitution. In short, the controversy between these parties and the respondents to these applications is not one which comprises a "matter" described in s 76(i) of the Constitution.

Reference has been made earlier in these reasons to authority in this Court that the Attorneys-General stand in a somewhat special position respecting matters which arise under the Constitution. The State of Victoria was a party to the proceeding in the Federal Court in which the Commonwealth Attorney might, by statute, have intervened or whose removal into this Court might have been obtained, again by statute. Where (on relation or otherwise) an Attorney initiates an action respecting validity, it usually has been against the Commonwealth or a State or States, as the case may be. The result will be a declaration binding the other polity or polities and an effective exercise of judicial power. That is not the result where, as here, relief is sought, not against the State whose law is in question, but [against] a federal judicial officer.

If the Attorney had intervened in the Federal Court proceeding or caused its removal into this Court, the Attorney may have been maintaining a "particular right, power, or immunity in which [he was] **[409]** concerned" [*Australian Railways Union v Victorian Railways Commissioners* (1930) 44 CLR 319 at 331]. The decision in *Mellifont v Attorney-General (Qld)* [(1991) 173 CLR 289] provides an analogy. There, the Attorney-General appealed from answers to questions of law referred to the Queensland Court of Appeal by way of a procedure designed to secure a reversal of a ruling at trial and thereby secure a correct statement of the law ... The decision of the Court of Criminal Appeal was held to involve the exercise of judicial power by that Court because the procedure was directed to correcting errors in a criminal trial. Thus, the decision fell within the words "judgments, decrees, orders" in s 73 of the Constitution and this Court had jurisdiction to entertain an appeal from it.

It also may be said that the Attorney would have been maintaining a particular right, power or immunity in which he was concerned if he had instituted a proceeding in which declaratory relief had been sought respecting the operation of s 109 of the Constitution upon the State Act. But even then it is not easy to see how this would be so where the relief sought by the Commonwealth Attorney would affirm the operation of a State law in the face of s 109. Normally it would be for the State Attorney-General to represent the interest of the public of that State in vindicating the laws of that State ...

However, in any event, the "very special practice" respecting Attorneys-General which Dixon J described in *Australian Railways Union v Victorian Railways Commissioners* [44 CLR at 331] does not extend to the advancement of what the Executive Government considers to be the desirable interaction between particular State and federal laws, by the Attorney-General pursuing the course he has in this litigation. Here the Attorney (both as an intervener and on the relation of the Episcopal Conference) seeks to re-open closed litigation between other parties and to purge the record of the Federal Court of an order which is at odds with an allegedly desirable state of constitutional affairs. The point may be expressed as a reflection of the limits of the judicial **[410]** power of the Commonwealth or of the absence of any claim by the Attorney-General to a right, title, privilege or immunity under the Constitution which is necessary to give rise to a "matter" under s 76(i). Whether acting on relation or otherwise, the Attorney-General, consistently with Ch III, cannot have a roving commission to initiate litigation to disrupt settled outcomes in earlier cases, so as to rid the law reports of what are considered unsatisfactory decisions respecting constitutional law.

McHugh, Kirby and Callinan JJ dissented in part since they held that there *was* a "matter" of which the Court could take cognizance.

McHugh J: [412] When a person claims that the writ of certiorari should issue to quash an order or decision of a lower court, tribunal or public **[413]** authority, the claim gives rise to a "matter" within the meaning of Ch III of the Constitution. The claim asserts that the *record* of the court, embodying the order, is defective and that the order is of no force and effect. It gives rise to a controversy – concerning "some immediate right, duty or liability to be established by the determination of the Court" [*Re Judiciary and Navigation Acts* (1921) 29 CLR 257 at 265] – with the maker of, and any party supporting, the order or decision. If the order or decision is that of a court, it is irrelevant that it may have settled a controversy between parties who are strangers to the applicant for certiorari ... A claim for certiorari gives rise to a new and different controversy from that involved in the proceedings that gave rise to the order. It gives rise to a separate "matter". The contrary view could only be maintained if the dissenting view in *Abebe v Commonwealth* [(1999) 197 CLR 510] had prevailed ...

A stranger to the proceedings that gives rise to the relevant *record* may apply for certiorari to quash an order or judgment contained in the record. The judgment of Blackburn J in *R v Justices of Surrey* [(1870) LR 5 QB 466] is frequently cited for this proposition, although earlier cases had also recognised the right of a stranger to obtain certiorari. The rule that a stranger to the proceedings can apply for certiorari to quash an order, made without jurisdiction, has the same historical basis as the rule that a stranger can apply for prohibition to quash such an order. Permitting strangers to apply for certiorari helps to ensure that "the prescribed order of the administration of justice" is not disobeyed. In *Worthington v Jeffries* [(1875) LR 10 CP 379 at 382] ... Brett J said:

> **[414]** [T]he ground of decision, in considering whether prohibition is or is not to be granted, is not whether the individual suitor has or has not suffered damage, but is, whether the royal prerogative has been encroached upon by reason of the prescribed order of administration of justice having been disobeyed. If this were not so, it seems difficult to understand why a stranger may interfere at all.

Perhaps a better reason – particularly in a federal system where cases deal with questions of constitutional validity – is that, if the losing party does not appeal, a judgment or order made without jurisdiction will become a precedent. Hence, the public interest may be enhanced by allowing a stranger to apply for certiorari to quash such a judgment or order. As Barwick CJ pointed out in *R v Federal Court of Australia; Ex parte WA National Football League* [(1979) 143 CLR 190 at 204], such considerations "apply with equal, if not greater, force with respect to matters where jurisdiction depends on constitutional competence". In similar vein, Professor Wade has written [(1967) 83 *Law Quarterly Review* 499 at 503] that certiorari "is designed to keep the machinery of justice in proper working order by preventing inferior tribunals and public authorities from abusing their powers". These statements of Barwick CJ and Professor Wade apply with equal force to *records* of curial proceedings, made within jurisdiction, but which on their face demonstrate an error of law.

Given that a stranger may apply for certiorari, it is not surprising that the Attorney-General, when representing the Crown in cases within the Attorney's jurisdiction, always has standing to apply for the issue of certiorari even though he or she was not a party to the proceedings in the lower court or tribunal. That is because the Crown, as guardian of the public interest, has an interest in seeing that tribunals stay within their jurisdiction and that they do justice according to law ...

Accordingly, in my opinion, both applications for certiorari give rise to a matter in the original jurisdiction of this Court. In both proceedings, the applicants contend that the record of the Federal Court should be quashed because it shows an error of law on its face. The controversy between the applicants and the respondents is whether the order of the Federal Court does show an error of law on its face and whether the applicants are entitled to have certiorari issue to quash the order. Other controversies between the parties – such as standing **[415]** – are incidental to those issues. In some cases, the existence of a matter may depend on the plaintiff or applicant having standing. But "neither the concept of 'judicial power' nor the constitutional meaning of 'matter' dictates that a person who institutes proceedings must have a direct or special interest in the subject matter of those proceedings" [*Truth About Motorways Pty Ltd v Macquarie Infrastructure Investment Management Ltd* (2000) 200 CLR 591 at 611]. True it is that no matter exists for constitutional purposes unless "there is a remedy available at the suit of the person instituting the proceedings in question" [200 CLR at 612]. Here there is a remedy available to the applicants. Subject to the exercise of the Court's discretion, even a stranger may obtain certiorari even though he or she is not a person aggrieved by the order made in the proceedings.

The fact that the applicants were not parties to the proceedings in the Federal Court is irrelevant, as is the fact that the Federal Court order settled a controversy between the respondents. A stranger has the right to assert that the record of a court is defective for want of jurisdiction or for error of law on the face of the record. That claim of right gives rise to a justiciable controversy against the maker of the record and those who were parties to its making.

Finally ..., the controversy between the parties arises under the Constitution and is therefore a "matter" within the meaning of the Constitution.

Callinan J broadly agreed with McHugh J. Indeed, he suggested that the decision in *Mellifont v Attorney-General (Qld)* may nowadays "**[476]** provide a basis for a broad view of what is a 'matter' and ... perhaps, the absence of an 'immediate' right, duty, privilege or liability may not of itself always be decisive". Kirby J, too, was prepared to hold that the Court was seised of a "matter", at least in the relator action authorised by the Attorney-General's fiat.

However, even these three judges who held that there was a relevant "matter" agreed that the applications should be dismissed on discretionary grounds. Moreover, Gaudron, Gummow and Hayne JJ said that, even if they had discerned a relevant "matter", they too would have declined on discretionary grounds to issue certiorari. Various factors were adduced as pointing to this denial of discretionary relief. For example, it was said that an unknown number of doctors (including McBain), acting in good faith upon the decision of Sundberg J, might have carried out IVF treatments for which, if the decision were now overturned, they might find themselves liable to prosecution under the Victorian Act. Some of those treatments might already have been completed; others might have to be abandoned prematurely. Again, it was said that the Episcopal Conference, having been permitted to make submissions to Sundberg J as an *amicus*, had abandoned its application to be joined as a party to the Federal Court proceedings. Had it persisted and been joined as a party, it would have had a right to appeal, and for that reason it would not have been permitted to proceed by way of certiorari. As McHugh J put it, "**[425]** the Conference's failure to seek to become a party cannot put it in a better position than it would be in if it had been a party". Similarly, the belated entry into the proceedings by the Commonwealth Attorney-General was judged against his earlier failure to intervene in the Federal Court proceedings, or to seek their removal into the High Court, in response to notification under s 78B of the *Judiciary Act*. In addition, Kirby J noted that "**[456]** all of the actual parties to the proceedings before Sundberg J were content with the outcome of those proceedings"; and McHugh J noted that, in particular, the Victorian government, which might have had an interest in contesting the decision, was evidently content to accept it. It had not appealed, nor had it made any attempt to repeal or amend the legislation. Its attitude made it doubtful "**[425]** whether it would enforce its legislation even if there was no declaration of invalidity ... **[426]** One must assume that the Victorian government thinks that it is in the public interest of that State to accept the correctness of the order made by Sundberg J".

(c)   Standing

The requirement that a plaintiff must have *locus standi*, and the restrictive criteria by which that requirement must be satisfied, have their origins in a version of the public/private distinction going back to mediaeval times. Traditionally, if as between individual neighbouring occupiers of land, the amenity of one was impaired by the land use of the other, the afflicted individual had a personal remedy for "private nuisance". However, if a whole neighbourhood was affected so that the grievance affected the local community generally, no individual plaintiff had a private right of action. "Public nuisance" was a public concern, and required a public remedy. This meant either that the author of the nuisance was prosecuted for a criminal misdemeanour, or that the Attorney-General, as the chief law officer of the Crown in its capacity as *parens patriae*, could institute proceedings in the public interest for an injunction to abate the nuisance. As time went on this remedy was modified in two ways.

First, it came to be accepted that proceedings for "public nuisance" could be initiated by a private individual in the Attorney-General's name. The Attorney-General's consent was required, but was usually given (by the granting of a "fiat"). The action is thus brought by the Attorney-General "on the relation of" ("*ex rel*") the real plaintiff; but the latter (the "relator") has the control and conduct of the proceedings, and pays the costs. The "relator" may be someone directly affected by the nuisance, but need not be. In modern times municipal councils have frequently brought "relator" actions.

Secondly, it was held in *Sowthall v Dagger* (1535) YB Mich 27 Henry VIII, fol 27, pl 10, that a private individual could sue for damages in respect of a "public nuisance" if he had suffered "greater hurt or inconvenience than everyman had" – that is, if he could demonstrate some "particular" or "special" damage, over and above the annoyance to the general public. In a wide range of "public interest" cases, including those raising issues of constitutional validity, these two developments – the relator action, and the possibility that a sufficient degree of "special" interest might give an individual plaintiff standing to sue – are the main ways that private citizens may use the courts to ventilate issues of public importance.

In *Re McBain; Ex parte Australian Catholic Bishops Conference* (2002) 209 CLR 372 (see the extract in §5(b) above), the Commonwealth Attorney-General was already on the record (in part to defend the validity of Commonwealth legislation), but then granted his fiat to the prosecutors for other aspects of their case, thus giving rise to separate relator proceedings. Hayne J insisted that the Attorney-General could not then be permitted to intervene in the relator proceedings, since he could not appear on both sides of the record: once the Attorney-General grants his fiat, he "**[473]** has complete charge of the litigation at all times … **[474]** Although it is said that by the fiat the Attorney-General 'lends standing' to the relator, such metaphors must not obscure the fact that it is and remains the Attorney's proceeding". Gaudron and Gummow JJ appeared to agree with Hayne J on this issue: identifying it as one of several issues arising from the "**[402]** procedural imbroglio" before them, they suggested that it might be governed by the dictum of Lord Cottenham LC in *Attorney-General v Ironmongers' Co* (1841) Cr & Ph 208 at 218, 41 ER 469 at 474 – namely, that once the Attorney-General granted his fiat, he "**[218]** was the party prosecuting the cause, and … the only party whom the Court could recognise in that character; and, therefore, that [the Court] could not hear the Attorney-General against the relator, or the relator against the Attorney-General". By contrast, Kirby J saw no problem with this aspect of the case.

A good example of a relator action is *Attorney-General (Vic) (ex rel Black) v Commonwealth* (*DOGS Case*) (1981) 146 CLR 559. The relators, members of the DOGS organisation ("Defence of Government Schools"), sued through the Victorian Attorney-General in an effort to establish that State aid to church schools violated the mandate in s 116 of the Constitution that "[t]he Commonwealth shall not make any law for establishing any religion". They also sought to establish that they had standing to raise the issue in their own right on the basis that the alleged depletion of resources available to State schools had a special impact on those relators who were parents of children attending State schools; or those who were teachers in State schools; or simply those who as taxpayers had an interest in the allocation of Commonwealth revenue. Because the action failed on the merits, the issue of whether any of the plaintiffs had sufficient individual standing to sue was never clearly resolved. Stephen and Wilson JJ expressly refused to consider the issue. Murphy J was prepared to take an extremely broad view of standing, while Gibbs J reaffirmed the traditional view.

Attorney-General (Vic); ex rel Black v Commonwealth (*DOGS Case*)
(1981) 146 CLR 559

Murphy J: [634] It is a traditional duty of the Attorney-General of Australia to defend the validity of Acts. It would be incongruous and unrealistic to hold that only the Attorney-General could challenge the validity of an Act. To require a person who is not and will not be affected by the coercive operation of an Act to obtain the fiat of the Attorney-General of Australia or of a State would put enforcement of constitutional guarantees at the mercy of political pressures exercisable through parliaments, although the purpose of the constitutional guarantees was to provide certain protection, even against parliaments. A citizen's right to invoke the judicial power to vindicate constitutional guarantees should not, and, in my opinion, does not, depend upon obtaining an Attorney-General's consent. Any one of the people of the Commonwealth has the standing to proceed in the courts to secure the observance of constitutional guarantees. Objections to wide standing have no merit. Experience in other countries, especially the United States, has shown that the "floodgates" argument is baseless, and that procedures are available to deal with frivolous challenges.

The United States Supreme Court in *Baker v Carr* [369 US 186 at 204 (1962)] said:

"Have the appellants alleged such a personal stake in the outcome of the controversy as to assure that concrete adverseness which sharpens the presentation of issues upon which the court so largely depends for illumination of difficult constitutional questions? This is the gist of the question of standing."

The conduct of the [present] case by the plaintiffs and their presentation of factual and legal material has taken the question beyond assurance to actual demonstration of that "concrete adverseness which sharpens the presentation of the issues" referred to in *Baker v Carr*.

Gibbs J: [588] At the outset there arises the question whether the plaintiffs or any of them have standing to bring this action. In my opinion it is clear that the Attorney-General for Victoria has a locus standi to sue for declarations of the invalidity of the Acts in question in so far as they apply to schools in Victoria. Indeed in *Victoria v Commonwealth* (the *Roads Case*) [(1926) 38 CLR 399] proceedings were brought by two States and their Attorneys-General to challenge the validity of an Act on the ground that it was not a proper exercise of the power conferred by s 96, and the Court said [38 CLR at 407], that the action was properly constituted. In *Attorney-General (Vic) v Commonwealth* (the *Clothing Factory Case*) [(1935) 52 CLR 533 at 556], Gavan Duffy CJ, Evatt and McTiernan JJ said:

"In our opinion, it must now be taken as established that the Attorney-General of a State of the Commonwealth has a sufficient title to invoke the provision of the Constitution for the purpose of challenging the validity of Commonwealth legislation which extends to, and operates within, the State whose interests he represents."

In *Attorney-General (Vic) v Commonwealth* (the *Pharmaceutical Benefits Case*) [(1945) 71 CLR 237 at 272], Dixon J said that this statement expressed the settled doctrine of the Court, and himself restated the principle by saying that the Attorney-General of a State has "a locus standi to sue for a declaration wherever his public is or may be affected by what he says is an ultra vires act on the part of the Commonwealth or of another State". Those statements of principle would I think be applicable in the present case, where **[589]** the Acts operate on the State of Victoria itself, and on schools within the State. It does not seem to me material that the State of Victoria has accepted the grants of financial assistance made under the Acts. The State is perfectly entitled to say that it will accept the financial assistance if the Acts are valid and the conditions are binding, but that it nevertheless wishes to challenge the validity of the Acts and the conditions. The Commonwealth however says that the *Appropriation Acts* under which moneys are paid for the assistance of schools in the Territories ... have no operation in Victoria, and that the Attorney-General for Victoria has no standing to challenge their validity. With all respect I cannot agree. I remain of the opinion which I expressed in *Victoria v Commonwealth and Hayden* (the *AAP Case*) [(1975) 134 CLR 338 at 381], which was the case of a challenge to an *Appropriation Act*, that "it is involved in the very nature of the Constitution that either the Commonwealth or a State should have standing to institute legal proceedings when the other has exceeded its constitutional authority." Mason J expressed a similar view in the same case, but Stephen J disagreed and Murphy J was inclined to agree with him, although he said that if it were claimed that the appropriation or expenditure were in breach of any constitutional prohibition then the position might be different. In my opinion even where no question arises as to the limits inter se of the powers of the Commonwealth and the State, the Attorney-General of a State may sue to compel the Commonwealth to observe the fundamental law of the Constitution, which the citizens of any State [have] an interest to maintain, although it may not be such a special interest as would enable them as individuals to bring the suit. On the other hand, as at present advised, I gravely doubt whether the other plaintiffs have standing to sue; I hardly think that the fact that they are taxpayers, and in some cases parents of children at government schools, gives them a special interest in the subject matter of the action within the principles stated in the cases collected in *Australian Conservation Foundation Inc v Commonwealth* [(1980) 146 CLR 493]. However in Canada an exception to the general principle appears to have been recognized in constitutional cases (*Thorson v Attorney-General (Canada) (No 2)* [[1975]

1 SCR 138; (1974) 43 DLR (3d) 1] and since, for reasons which will appear, it is unnecessary to decide whether **[590]** these individual plaintiffs have standing, I would express no concluded opinion on the question.

In *Australian Conservation Foundation Inc v Commonwealth* (1980) 146 CLR 493 – to which Gibbs J referred in the *DOGS Case* – Gibbs, Stephen and Mason JJ, with only Murphy J dissenting, affirmed the decision of Aickin J that the Australian Conservation Foundation did *not* have standing to challenge approvals, under the *Environment Protection (Impact of Proposals) Act 1974* (Cth), for a tourist resort in central Queensland. That, however, was not a constitutional case; and even for non-constitutional cases, the traditional requirements there reaffirmed may no longer be strictly enforced. In *Onus v Alcoa of Australia Ltd* (1981) 149 CLR 27, the High Court held that the tribal guardians of the Gournditch-jmara Aboriginal people had a "special interest" in the preservation of their tribal relics, sufficient to give them standing to invoke the provisions of the *Archaeological and Aboriginal Relics Preservation Act 1972* (Vic). The *Conservation Foundation Case* was distinguished, but arguably on unsatisfactory grounds that concealed a real shift of emphasis (see AR Blackshield, "Alcoa Decision on Standing: How Liberal?" (1981) 6 *Legal Service Bulletin* 28). Later cases in the Federal Court and elsewhere have appeared to take a much more liberal view of "standing" in environmental cases than the High Court had done before *Onus v Alcoa* (see, for example, *Australian Conservation Foundation v Minister for Resources* (1989) 19 ALD 70).

For constitutional cases, it would seem that this more liberal approach to "standing" has now been confirmed. In *APLA Ltd v Legal Services Commissioner (NSW)* (2005) 219 ALR 403, lawyers wishing to publish advertisements relating to personal injury litigation were held to have standing to challenge the validity of a regulation restricting such advertisements, even though (as Gummow J put it) there was no suggestion "**[436]** that any of the plaintiffs (or their employees) face prosecution under the Regulation for any conduct in which they have previously, or are currently, engaged". Nor did the plaintiffs need to demonstrate any prospect of disciplinary proceedings under the *Legal Profession Act 1987* (NSW); "it is sufficient that they wish to engage in conduct as part of their ordinary business practices for which they *may* encounter prosecution" (emphasis added). Kirby J agreed: "**[469]** It is enough that each of them wishes to engage … in conduct that would be impermissible under the Regulation". He noted, however, the Court's discretion to refuse relief "if the effect on the individual plaintiffs were too remote, theoretical or *de minimis*".

In *Combet v Commonwealth* (2005) 221 ALR 621, the five majority judges had no need to consider the issue of standing, since they held that the plaintiffs' claim was unsuccessful in any event. However, McHugh and Kirby JJ, who dissented on the substantive issue, both went on to hold that the requirement of standing was satisfied. The claim was that expenditure on government advertising to promote proposals for new industrial relations legislation was invalid for want of a relevant parliamentary appropriation. The plaintiffs were Greg Combet as secretary of the Australian Council of Trade Unions (which along with its members was directly affected by the proposed legislative changes, and had mounted its own advertising campaign against them) and Nicola Roxon as shadow Attorney-General.

Both McHugh and Kirby JJ held that Roxon had standing, simply because she was a member of the House of Representatives with "**[651]** a special interest in ensuring that public moneys are not expended inconsistently with the terms of [the Appropriation Act] passed by the Parliament of which she is a member". McHugh J appeared to assume that her role as shadow Attorney-General was also a sufficient basis for standing; Kirby J expressly refused to decide whether that was the case. Neither judge found it necessary to decide whether Combet had standing; but Kirby J was inclined to an affirmative answer in his instance also.

Combet v Commonwealth
(2005) 221 ALR 621

McHugh J: [650] In *British Medical Association v Commonwealth* [(1949) 79 CLR 201 at 257], Dixon J doubted that the Federal Council of the British Medical Association in Australia, one of whose objects was to advance the general interests of the medical profession in Australia, had standing to challenge federal legislation that imposed a form of civil conscription within the meaning of s 51(xxiiiA) of the Constitution. His Honour said that it "may be doubted whether this body has, as a corporation, a sufficient material interest, which would be prejudiced by the operation of the Act, to give it a title to maintain the suit". Similarly, in *Real Estate Institute of NSW v Blair* [(1946) 73 CLR 213], Latham CJ, Starke J and Dixon J were of the opinion that the Real Estate Institute of NSW had no standing to challenge legislation that made provision for the housing of members and ex-members of the armed forces. Their Honours thought that the Institute, in contrast to its members, had no material interest in the operation of the legislation. By parity of reasoning, the ACTU has no material interest in the operation of Act No 1. The Secretary of the ACTU is even further removed from the operation of the Act. It may be that the [above] decisions and *dicta* ... require reconsideration in the light of subsequent developments in the law of "standing" in relation to general law matters. It is not necessary, however, to determine whether the first plaintiff has standing.

Kirby J: [706] I am not convinced that the first plaintiff, Mr Combet, lacked standing of his own to initiate the proceedings. Assimilating him (as the defendants accepted) to the ACTU, his interest in challenging the advertising campaign, funded from the public purse, was clearly related to the role that the ACTU was playing in the political and industrial debate concerning the proposed amendments to federal workplace relations laws ...

The first plaintiff, and the organisation he represents, have a real and substantial interest to curtail a purported reliance on an appropriation of public money for the Executive Government's advertising campaign. He, and the ACTU, have a direct interest to attempt to prevent the drawing of such money from the Treasury without ... a parliamentary appropriation for that purpose. Such an interest, whilst raising public law considerations, probably involves in this case the kind of mercantile and economic "special interests" often given weight in decisions on standing in private litigation ...

British Medical Association v Commonwealth and *Real Estate Institute of NSW v Blair* ... were decided more than **[707]** fifty years ago, before this Court elaborated its views on the requirements of standing in public interest litigation. The cited decisions have been overtaken by subsequent developments of legal doctrine ... [B]ased on the current law (as stated in *Onus* and similar cases), it is likely that the ACTU, as represented by the first plaintiff, has standing in this matter.

Earlier, in *Croome v Tasmania* (1997) 191 CLR 119, the shift to a more liberal view of standing was suggested only indirectly: the Tasmanian argument that the plaintiffs lacked "standing" was *abandoned* at the hearing, and the actual decision allowing the action to proceed was only on the ground that there was a "matter" amenable to the Court's jurisdiction. However, Gaudron, McHugh and Gummow JJ emphasised that it was impossible to disaggregate the two issues.

Croome v Tasmania
(1997) 191 CLR 119

Gaudron, McHugh and Gummow JJ: [132] The State no longer seeks a stay on the ground that the plaintiffs lack a special interest in the subject-matter of the action which is sufficient to support their standing to sue for a declaration. It appears that the State took this step to amend the summons on the footing that it regarded the issue of standing as one distinct from the alleged absence of a "matter" within the meaning of s 76 of the Constitution. The Solicitor-General for the State expressed the distinction he sought to make by submitting that "firstly, you have got to have a matter and then once you have a matter ... the issue of standing to contest the matter arises".

During the course of argument it became apparent that the attempted severance in this case between questions going to [standing] … and those directed to the constitutional requirement of the exercise of federal jurisdiction with respect to a "matter" was conceptually awkward, if not impossible …

Where the issue is whether federal jurisdiction has been invoked **[133]** with respect to a "matter", questions of "standing" are subsumed within that issue. The submission made in the present case, to the effect that a proceeding in which a citizen seeks a declaration of invalidity of a law of a State, by reason of the operation of the Constitution, is liable to be struck out unless there is attempted enforcement of the State law against the citizen, indicates the interdependence of the notions of "standing" and of "matter".

That view accords with the doctrine of the Supreme Court of the United States with respect to the identification in Art III of the Constitution of the United States of judicial power with "cases" and "controversies". *In Philip Morris Inc v Adam P Brown Male Fashions Pty Ltd* [(1981) 148 CLR 457 at 508], Mason J described the formulation of "matter" in *In re Judiciary and Navigation Acts* as not departing from the American concept of "cases" and "controversies".

In *FW/PBS, Inc v Dallas* [493 US 215 at 231 (1990)], standing was said to be perhaps the most important of the jurisdictional doctrines affecting the scope of the judicial power of the United States. Subsequently, in delivering the Opinion of the Court in *Lujan v Defenders of Wildlife* [504 US 555 at 560 (1992)], Scalia J spoke of the "core component of standing" as "an essential and unchanging part of the case-or-controversy requirement of Article III".

Accordingly, in the course of [these] reasons, it will be necessary to advert to issues perhaps better sub-classified as going to standing, when dealing with those heads of the summons which the State still presses.

In that spirit, they concluded their judgment by saying:

Gaudron, McHugh and Gummow JJ: [138] The conduct by the plaintiffs of their personal lives in significant respects is overshadowed by the presence of ss 122 and 123 of the Code. The policy of the law which animates the operation of the Australian legal system includes the encouragement, and indeed the requirement, of observance of the law. That particularly is so of the norms of conduct required or forbidden by the criminal law. Breach thereof is attended by risk of prosecution and punishment and also may have consequences for the broader civil legal order as it applies to the individual. Thus, doctrines turning upon illegality play a significant part in the operation of the law of tort and contract. The covenant in the lease taken by the second plaintiff is an example, no doubt repeated in the daily lives of many citizens. [The plaintiff, as the tenant of residential premises, had covenanted not to use the premises for any illegal purpose.]

The Constitution may deny to the law in question, wholly or in part, validity as an operative part of the legal order. Section 109 may achieve that result in respect of the law of a State. Where it is established, in the exercise of the judicial power of the Commonwealth, that s 109 does so operate, there is met by the Constitution a call of great importance to the ordinary citizen. Such a person is, to continue with terms used by Gibbs CJ [*University of Wollongong v Metwally* (1984) 158 CLR 447 at 457-8], "entitled to know" whether there continues a requirement to observe that State law.

In the circumstances of this case, the claim to declaratory relief is not to be denied at the threshold on the ground that relief is sought prematurely and to establish the legal character of a state of affairs not yet come to pass. If s 109 operates here, as the plaintiffs seek to establish at the trial or other final disposition of their action, it presently operates upon the provisions of the Code and has done so since the commencement of the Act.

Moreover, as we have sought to indicate, the plaintiffs have a "real interest" and do not seek to raise a question which is abstract or hypothetical. The State, by the Director of Public Prosecutions, **[139]** has not prosecuted but, even if it were open for it to do so, it has not disabled itself from prosecuting hereafter. The DPP does not take the position that no offences have been committed nor that the offences do not continue.

The other three judges were less explicit about the overlap between the two issues. However, they too treated the plaintiffs' "sufficient interest" as a necessary element in their finding of a "matter". Moreover, they opined that the concession as to standing was "rightly made".

Brennan CJ, Dawson and Toohey JJ: [126] However, … a justiciable controversy does not arise unless the person who seeks to challenge the validity of the law has a sufficient interest to do so. In *British Medical Association v Commonwealth* [(1949) 79 CLR 201 at 257], Dixon J doubted whether the plaintiff Association had "a sufficient material interest, which would be prejudiced by the operation of the [impugned] Act" – parts of the *Pharmaceutical Benefits Act* 1947 (Cth) and the Pharmaceutical Benefits Regulations – "to give it a title to maintain the suit" for a declaration of invalidity. But his Honour held that the other plaintiffs in the action, who were practitioners of medicine or surgery, possessed the necessary interest. The "sufficient material interest" which, being **[127]** prejudicially affected by a law, founds a cause of action to seek a declaration of invalidity of a law, is not confined to professional or trading interests. In *Pharmaceutical Society of Great Britain v Dickson* [[1970] AC 403 at 433] Lord Upjohn said:

> "This principle is not confined to trade. A person whose freedom of action is challenged can always come to the court to have his rights and position clarified, subject always, of course, to the right of the court in exercise of its judicial discretion to refuse relief in the circumstances of the case."

A person with a sufficient interest to raise a justiciable controversy as to the validity of a law is regarded as having or claiming a right to a declaration and that right satisfies the requirement of some "right, duty or liability to be established by the determination of the Court".

No distinction in principle can be drawn between a controversy as to the validity of a law on the ground that it exceeds legislative power and a controversy as to the operation of a State law which is said to be inconsistent with a law of the Commonwealth and, to that extent, "invalid" by reason of s 109 of the Constitution. In both cases, invalidity releases a plaintiff from a liability or obligation which the impugned law purports to impose.

We do not wish now to assent to the broad proposition that any person who desires or intends to act in contravention of a law has, by reason merely of that desire or intention, a cause of action to seek a declaration of invalidity of the law. It may be that the curial discretion to refuse relief warrants acceptance of that broad proposition but, in the present case, it is not necessary to decide the question.

It is conceded that the plaintiffs have standing to bring the action seeking declarations of invalidity of the impugned provisions of the Code. That concession, if rightly made, establishes that they have a sufficient interest to support an action for a declaration that the impugned provisions of the Code are "invalid" by reason of s 109 of the Constitution. In our opinion, the concession of standing was rightly made not by reason of their intention to engage in conduct of the kind pleaded in par 7 (though that intention may be relevant to the exercise of a discretion to grant or refuse a declaration) but by reason of their having engaged in such conduct.

The plaintiffs plead that they have engaged in conduct which, if the impugned provisions of the Code were and are operative, renders them liable to prosecution, conviction and punishment. The fact that the Director of Public Prosecutions does not propose to prosecute does not remove that liability. Liability to prosecution under the impugned provisions of the Code will be established if the Court were to **[128]** determine the action against the plaintiffs even if liability to conviction and punishment under those provisions cannot be determined by civil process. Controversy as to the operative effect of the impugned provisions of the Code will be settled and binding on the parties. The plaintiffs have a sufficient interest to support an action for a declaration of s 109 invalidity.

Consistently with the blurring in *Croome v Tasmania* of the separate requirements that the plaintiff have "standing" and that there be a "matter", Gleeson CJ and McHugh JJ suggested in *Abebe v Commonwealth* (1999) 197 CLR 510 that the existence of a "matter" requires that "**[528]** the person claiming the remedy must have sufficient interest in enforcing the right, duty or liability to make the controversy justiciable". However, this statement requires qualification in the light of *Truth About Motorways Pty Limited v Macquarie Infrastructure Investment Management Ltd* (2000) 200 CLR 591. Macquarie Infrastructure Investment Management Ltd managed two unit trusts, one of the assets of which was the "Eastern Distributor" toll road in Sydney. Macquarie issued a prospectus in 1996 inviting members of the public to purchase units in the trusts. A "social action group" formed a company, Truth About Motorways Pty Ltd, which brought proceedings contending that the prospectus was misleading and deceptive in overstating traffic volumes, and that Macquarie was therefore in breach of s 52 of the *Trade Practices Act 1974* (Cth). Truth About Motorways had not suffered any loss or damage, had no assets other than a subscribed capital of $3 and had no business other than the prosecution of the proceedings. It was able to bring the action because s 80 of the *Trade Practices Act* enabled the Federal Court to grant injunctive relief on the application of "any ... person", while s 163A provided that "a person" could institute proceedings. Macquarie challenged the validity of ss 80 and 163A, arguing that as Truth About Motorways had no interest in the proceedings there was no justiciable controversy and therefore no "matter", so that jurisdiction could not be conferred upon the Federal Court. The High Court rejected this argument. Kirby J, for example, found "**[648]** nothing in the word 'matter' ... which demands a particular requirement as to standing". However, the result was subject to some careful qualifications.

Truth About Motorways Pty Ltd v Macquarie Infrastructure Investment Management Ltd
(2000) 200 CLR 591

Gaudron J: [611] The classes of matter in respect of which the judicial power of the Commonwealth is engaged are specified in ss 75 and 76 of the Constitution and include matters "in which a writ of Mandamus or prohibition or an injunction is sought against an officer of the Commonwealth". It is well established that prohibition may issue to a person who has neither a direct nor special interest in the subject matter of the proceedings constituted by an application to obtain that relief. That being so, there is no basis for concluding that either the concept of "judicial power" or the constitutional meaning of "matter" dictates that a person who institutes proceedings must have a direct or special interest in the subject matter of those proceedings. Indeed that proposition is denied by the very rule that the Attorney-General as the representative of the public interest – not as a person having a direct or special interest – may bring proceedings with respect to a public wrong.

Once it is accepted that neither the concept of "judicial power" nor the constitutional meaning of "matter" dictates that a person who institutes proceedings must have a direct or special interest in the subject matter of those proceedings, it follows as was pointed out in *Bateman's Bay Local Aboriginal Land Council v Aboriginal Community Benefit Fund Pty Ltd* [(1998) 194 CLR 247 at 262] that, for the purposes of Ch III of the Constitution, "questions of 'standing', when they arise, are subsumed within the constitutional requirement of a 'matter'." This does not mean that, for the purposes of Ch III, questions of standing are wholly irrelevant.

There may be cases where, absent standing, there is no justiciable controversy. That may be because the court is not able to make a final and binding adjudication. To take a simple example, a court could not make a final and binding adjudication with respect to private rights other than at the suit of a person who claimed that his or her right was **[612]** infringed. Or there may be no justiciable controversy because there is no relief that the court can give to enforce the right, duty or obligation in question.

The relationship between "standing" and available relief was adverted to by Aickin J in *Australian Conservation Foundation v Commonwealth* [146 CLR at 511]. In that case his Honour observed:

> "it is an essential requirement for locus standi that it must be related to the relief claimed. The 'interest' of a plaintiff in the subject matter of an action must be such as to warrant the grant of the relief claimed. I do not mean that, where the relief is discretionary, locus standi depends on showing that the discretion must be exercised favourably. What is required is that the plaintiff's interest should be one related to the relief claimed".

That passage not only poses the test to be applied when there is a question of standing but, in my view, discloses the significance of standing to the existence of a matter for the purposes of Ch III of the Constitution.

There is no matter within the constitutional meaning of that term unless there is a remedy available at the suit of the person instituting the proceedings in question. That follows from the essential features of "matter" identified in *In re Judiciary and Navigation Acts* [(1921) 29 CLR 257 at 265-6]. It was said in that case:

> "there can be no matter ... unless there is some immediate right, duty or liability to be established by the determination of the Court ... [And the legislature] cannot authorize [the] Court to make a declaration of the law divorced from any attempt to administer that law."

Absent the availability of relief related to the wrong which the plaintiff alleges, no immediate right, duty or liability is established by the Court's determination. Similarly, if there is no available remedy, there is no administration of the relevant law. Thus, as Gleeson CJ and McHugh J pointed out in *Abebe v Commonwealth* [(1999) 197 CLR 510 at 526-7], "[i]f there is no legal remedy for a 'wrong', there can be no 'matter'."

Provided there is a remedy which is appropriately related to the wrong in question, whether the remedy derives from the general law or is created by statute, nothing in Ch III of the Constitution prevents Parliament from modifying the general rule that only the Attorney-General may bring proceedings with respect to a public wrong and permitting any person to institute proceedings of that kind. If it does **[613]** so, and if there is a remedy appropriate to the asserted wrong, there is, in my view, a matter for the purposes of Ch III of the Constitution ...

The present matter was argued solely on the basis that, for proceedings with respect to a public wrong to constitute a matter for the purposes of Ch III of the Constitution, a private individual must have some special interest in the subject matter of those proceedings. It is therefore not appropriate to express a concluded view whether, in the circumstances of this case, an appropriate remedy is available. The view has been taken in the Federal Court that, notwithstanding the terms of s 80A(1) of the Act, s 80 permits of an order requiring corrective advertising at the request of a person other than the Minister or the Commission. If so, the relief sought pursuant to s 80 of the Act appears appropriate to the wrong complained of ...

There may be cases where a bare declaration that some legal requirement has been contravened will serve to redress some or all of the harm brought about by that contravention. *Ainsworth v Criminal Justice Commission* [(1992) 175 CLR 564] was such a case. But a declaration cannot be made if it "will produce no foreseeable consequences for the parties" [*Gardner v Dairy Industry Authority (NSW)* (1977) 18 ALR 55 at 69]. That is not simply a matter of discretion. Rather, a declaration that produces no foreseeable consequences is so divorced from the administration of the law as not to involve a matter for the purposes of Ch III of the Constitution. And as it is not a matter for those purposes, it cannot engage the judicial power of the Commonwealth.

(d)   Justiciability

The American doctrine that "political questions" are not justiciable (see *Baker v Carr*, 369 US 186 (1962)) has not played any similarly prominent role in High Court jurisprudence, though distant echoes of it may sometimes be detected.

Commonwealth v Tasmania (*Tasmanian Dam Case*)
(1983) 158 CLR 1

Mason J: [125] [T]he Court would undertake an invidious task if it were to decide whether the subject-matter of a convention is of international character or concern. On a question of this kind the Court cannot substitute its judgment for that of the executive government and Parliament ... Whether the subject-matter as dealt with by the convention is of international concern, whether it will yield, or is capable of yielding, a benefit to Australia, whether non-observance by Australia is likely to lead to adverse international action or reaction, are not questions on which the Court can readily arrive at an informed opinion. Essentially they are issues involving nice questions of sensitive judgment which should be left to the executive government for determination. The Court should accept and act upon the decision of the executive **[126]** government.

Castlemaine Tooheys Ltd v South Australia
(1990) 169 CLR 436

Mason CJ, Brennan, Deane, Dawson and Toohey JJ: [473] [I]t would place the Court in an invidious position if the Court were to hold that only such regulation of interstate trade as is in fact necessary for the protection of the community [is valid] ... The question whether a particular legislative enactment is a necessary or even a desirable solution to a particular problem is in large measure a political question best left for resolution to the political process. The resolution of that problem by the Court would require it to sit in judgment on the legislative decision, without having access to all the political considerations that played a part in the making of that decision, thereby giving a new and unacceptable dimension to the relationship between the Court and the legislature of the State.

More typically, however, and arguably even in the above examples, denials of "justiciability" have reflected the traditional separation of powers (see Chapter 1, §4) or, rather, the traditional British conventions of inter-institutional comity and mutual deference between the principal organs of government. In particular, matters relating to the internal affairs of Parliament have generally been regarded as non-justiciable (see Chapter 10, §6 and Chapter 23, §1). In addition, the Court has traditionally not regarded as "justiciable" those exercises of executive power derived from the royal prerogative (see Chapter 12, §2(a)), though this limitation appears to be weakening as prerogative power itself is reconceptualised in more functional terms. In *R v Toohey; Ex parte Northern Land Council* (1981) 151 CLR 170, planning regulations made by the Administrator of the Northern Territory under the *Planning Act 1979* (NT) expanded the area of the "town" of Darwin from 142 sq km to 4350 sq km, thereby excluding the latter area from the operation of the *Aboriginal Land Rights (Northern Territory) Act 1976* (Cth). Toohey J, as Aboriginal Land Commissioner, had held that he could not entertain a claim relating to land within the area thus enlarged – on the basis that since the Administrator represented the Crown, no regulation made by him could be challenged by an imputation of bad faith or ulterior motive. Whether the Administrator should in fact be regarded as representing the Crown was the subject of conflicting dicta in the High Court; but all six majority judges held that, even if that were the case, the regulation was open to challenge. In *FAI Insurances Ltd v Winneke* (1982) 151 CLR 342, the appellant company had been an approved insurer under the *Workers Compensation Act 1958* (Vic) for 20 years until 1981, when its approval was not renewed. The power to grant or refuse renewals was vested in the Governor in Council and exercised, after a decision at cabinet level, by a formal Order in Council; but the High Court held that this did not shield the decision from judicial scrutiny or from the rules of natural justice. In both cases Murphy J dissented on separation-of-powers grounds.

It was in relation to executive power that Gummow J, when on the Federal Court, had to consider the justiciability of allegations that the Commonwealth government, in making arrangements for extradition, had both exceeded its powers, and abused those powers by misleading and deceptive conduct. Although he held that in this instance the allegations were not made out, he also held that such allegations were justiciable.

Re Ditfort; Ex parte Deputy Commissioner of Taxation
(1988) 83 ALR 265

Gummow J: [284] The expression "non-justiciable", when used in relation to international relations conducted by Australia, identifies several distinct legal rules or principles. First, "non-justiciability" has special application with regard to the law of evidence. While the courts are entitled to take judicial notice of the course of open and notorious international events of a public nature, in some cases of doubt they accept as conclusive statements provided to the courts by the executive government … The statements so received have dealt with such questions as the extent of foreign territory, the existence of a state of war, belligerency or neutrality, the existence of foreign States and the **[285]** identity of persons constituting the governments of recognised States. The statements provided by the executive certify that the Australian Government "recognises" a particular state of affairs: see the terms of the certificate in *Corporate Affairs Commission v Bradley* [[1973] 1 NSWLR 382] (at 390). The terms of such certificates are subject to interpretation by the courts but, once so construed, the certificates are "conclusive". The expression "conclusive" is used not only in the sense that evidence is not admissible to contradict the certificates (*Carl Zeiss Stiftung v Rayner & Keeler Ltd (No 2)* [1967] 1 AC 853 at 901) but also, it seems, in the sense that the certificates cannot be questioned in proceedings for judicial review under s 75(v) of the Constitution or s 39B of the Judiciary Act …

In the present case, the respondent does not rely on "non-justiciability" in this sense. However, I should at this stage emphasise that British decisions upon "non-justiciability" or the "unreviewability" of decisions made by the British Government are to be viewed with some care before what there is said is treated as applicable in this country. In *Attorney-General v Nissan* [1970] AC 179 at 237, and in *CCSU v Minister for Civil Service* [1985] 1 AC 374 at 418, Lords Pearson and Roskill respectively spoke of the exercise of various prerogative powers of the Crown in right of the United Kingdom (including the treaty making power) as of such a nature and subject matter as not to be amenable to the judicial process. However, even in Britain, the threshold question of whether an act in question was done under the prerogative power will be for the court to decide, the point being that if it was, the court may then decide it will not inquire further into the propriety of that act … To decide whether a question is "non-justiciable" is not to decide the alleged non-justiciable question itself.

In Australia, with questions arising in federal jurisdiction, one looks not to the content of the prerogative in Britain, but rather to s 61 of the Constitution, by which the executive power of the Commonwealth was vested in the Crown. That power extends to the execution and maintenance of the Constitution and of the laws of the Commonwealth and enables the Crown to undertake all executive action appropriate to the spheres of responsibility vested in the Commonwealth. One such sphere is the conduct of relations with other countries, including the acquisition of international rights and obligations, and in this sphere the executive power of the Commonwealth is exclusive of that of the States …

The result is that a question as to the character and extent of the powers of the executive government in relation to the conduct of relations with other countries may give rise to a matter which arises under or involves the interpretation of s 61 of the Constitution and will so affect the interests of **[286]** a plaintiff as to give the necessary standing. These circumstances will provide a subject matter for the exercise of federal jurisdiction pursuant to Ch III of the Constitution. In such a case no question of "non-justiciability" ordinarily will arise. In Britain, putting to one side any questions that may arise consequent upon membership of the European Economic Community, there will be no directly comparable situations.

The position in Australia is illustrated by the litigation in *Barton v Commonwealth* (1974) 131 CLR 477 … There, the High Court entertained proceedings instituted by prospective deportees from Brazil in which they sought a declaration that a request to that country for their detention there pending a request for their extradition to Australia was "*ultra vires* and beyond the executive government of Australia". It may be observed that the plaintiffs plainly had an immediate concern in the outcome, so there was no question of lack of standing.

This judgment was quoted with approval by Kirby J, sitting alone, in *Thorpe v Commonwealth (No 3)* (1997) 144 ALR 677. In that case Kirby J struck out a statement of claim by an Aboriginal Australian who had sought a declaratory order in effect requiring the Commonwealth, through its representatives in the United Nations General Assembly, to move a resolution that the General Assembly should exercise its power under Art 96 of the United Nations Charter to "request the International Court of Justice to give an advisory opinion" as to whether Australia's treatment of its Indigenous peoples was in breach of a fiduciary duty owed to them by the Commonwealth government. Specifically, the plaintiff sought three declarations: (1) a declaration as to the existence of a fiduciary duty; (2) a declaratory order directing the Commonwealth to initiate the General Assembly resolution; and (3) a declaratory order directing the Commonwealth to negotiate with the plaintiff about the terms of the resolution and about his right to be heard for the purpose of giving evidence and making submissions in any ensuing proceedings in the International Court of Justice.

Although Kirby J struck out all three claims on the basis that no "matter" was involved, his treatment of that issue in relation to the second and third of the proposed declarations showed that it could not be disaggregated from the question of "justiciability". At the hearing before Kirby J the plaintiff Robert Thorpe was assisted by a legal practitioner, Len Lindon, whose own statement of claim relating to the treatment of Aboriginal peoples (filed under the *nom de théâtre* "Limbo") had previously been struck out (see *Re Citizen Limbo* (1989) 92 ALR 81). Kirby J relied in part on the reasoning of Brennan J in that earlier case.

Thorpe v Commonwealth (No 3)
(1997) 144 ALR 677

Kirby J: [689] During argument, it was submitted that the Court would, at least, allow the pleading to stand with respect to the first declaration. If necessary, it would sever that declaration from the remainder and permit, in effect, the issue presented by Toohey J's opinion in *Mabo (No 2)* [(1992) 175 CLR 1 at 203-5] to go forward for judicial determination in this case. I cannot agree. A declaration limited to that sought in para 1 of Mr Thorpe's writ would, on its own, be entirely theoretical. This Court from its earliest days has indicated that it will not act in that way. At some future time the detail of this jurisprudence may warrant reconsideration by the Court. However, it is inconceivable that such reconsideration would arise on a vehicle presented by Mr Thorpe's writ confined to the first declaration.

For these reasons, the first declaration cannot stand alone. It either survives or falls, depending upon the fate of the two succeeding declarations ...

[690] What Mr Thorpe is, in effect, seeking, by the second and third declarations, is that this Court should set out to control the way in which the Commonwealth conducts Australia's international relations ... I assume for present purposes that, were such declarations to be made, the Commonwealth would seek to conform to their terms in order to comply with the Court's declaration of its legal duty. However, in no case that could be cited, nor any that I have discovered in my own researches, has this Court purported to intrude in such a way in the conduct of Australia's international activities. The reason why no such case could be found is plain enough although the explanation may be advanced in various ways. It might be said that the subject matters of the declarations are not the kind of "immediate right, duty or liability" grounded in a legal norm which would present a "matter" to enliven the jurisdiction of this Court under the Constitution ... But it might also be said that the issues presented by the declarations lacked "judicially discoverable and manageable standards for resolving" a justiciable issue. Traditionally in this country, as under like constitutional provisions in the United States, the courts have been extremely reluctant to pass upon the conduct of international relations. As a matter of history, this reluctance is probably inherited, in Australia at least, from the traditional approach of the courts of England in reviewing the exercise of the prerogatives of the Sovereign, including in the conduct of relations with other States. Gummow J pointed out, when a Judge of the Federal Court of Australia [*Re Ditfort; Ex parte Deputy Commissioner of Taxation* (1988) 83 ALR 265 at 285], that care must be exercised in the use of English authority on this point because the source of power in Australia to conduct relations with other States (and with international organisations) resides in the Constitution of which this Court is the guardian, not (at least normally) in the residue of the prerogatives of the Crown.

The Commonwealth argued that this Court would never make declarations 2 and 3 as sought, or anything like them. To do so would involve a wholly impermissible invasion of the constitutional prerogatives of the Executive Government of the Commonwealth. By s 61 of the Australian Constitution, the executive power of the Commonwealth is vested in the Queen. That power **[691]** extends to all executive action appropriate to the spheres of responsibility vested in the Commonwealth .... Different views may exist as to the scope of justiciability and the delineation of questions marked off as "not justiciable". In *Re Ditfort*, Gummow J was disinclined to surrender entirely the reviewability of executive conduct against the touchstone of the Australian Constitution, even in matters of international relations. It may be that, in an extreme case, difficult to imagine, a court might hold that particular executive conduct went beyond the constitutional warrant although the Commonwealth supported it by reference to the conduct of external affairs. However that may be, the essential point to which most judicial authority on this question returns is one grounded in the separation of powers which the Constitution mandates.

Brennan J explained this in *Re Limbo* [(1989) 92 ALR 81] where "Citizen Limbo" (Mr Lindon) had sought declarations that certain acts of, and omissions by, the Commonwealth were contrary to international law (including the Genocide Convention). Brennan J said [92 ALR at 82-3]:

> [W]hen one comes to a court of law it is necessary always to ensure that lofty aspirations are not mistaken for the rules of law which courts are capable and fitted to enforce. It is essential that there be no mistake between the functions that are performed by the respective branches of government. It is essential to understand that courts perform one function and the political branches of government perform another. One can readily understand that there may be disappointment in the performance by one branch or another of government of the functions which are allocated to it under our division of powers. But it would be a mistake for one branch of government to assume the functions of another in the hope that thereby what is perceived to be an injustice can be corrected. Unless one observes the separation of powers and unless the courts are restricted to the application of the domestic law of this country, there would be a state of confusion and chaos which would be antipathetic not only to the aspirations of peace but to the aspirations of the enforcement of any human rights.

Later his Honour went on [92 ALR at 85]:

> The proposed plaintiffs seem to have mistaken the branch of government to which their plea must be directed. However disappointing it may be to have their pleas directed to the political branches of government but rejected, their pleas are political pleas … This Court cannot assume a function of determining the truth of political issues unless those issues are critical to the existence of some power. The statement of claim provides no foundation for expecting that such a foundation is alleged or would be made out.

[692] Those words apply to the present case. It is true, as Mr Lindon said for Mr Thorpe, that the mere involvement of a political or controversial question does not mean that a court lacks jurisdiction, that a controversy is not a "matter" for the purpose of the Constitution, that a cause of action lacks viability or that the issue tendered is non-justiciable. In *Melbourne Corporation v Commonwealth* [(1947) 74 CLR 31 at 82] Dixon J pointed out:

> The Constitution is a political instrument. It deals with government and governmental powers. The statement is, therefore, easy to make though it has a specious plausibility. But it is really meaningless. It is not a question whether the considerations are political, for nearly every consideration arising from the Constitution can be so described, but whether they are compelling.

This is not the case in which to explore the question of justiciability and the relevance of the "political questions" doctrine developed around a similar constitutional language and structure in the United States. In *Baker v Carr* [369 US 186 at 211 (1962)], Brennan J of the Supreme Court of the United States, delivering the judgment of that Court, acknowledged that many questions touching foreign relations would fall within that doctrine … However, the Court went on there to suggest that it was an "error to suppose that every case or controversy which touches foreign relations lies beyond judicial cognizance" [369 US at 211]. This conclusion reflects that to which Gummow J came in *Re Ditfort*. It takes the judge, hearing a contested argument about justiciability, to the foundation of that principle. That foundation lies in the separation of powers required by the Constitution. Is the question tendered, of its nature, such as is apt to a court performing court-like functions? If it is not, it matters little in practical terms whether the court, facing an objection, rules that it lacks jurisdiction for want of a "matter" engaging its powers, or [whether] it says that any such "matter" would be non-justiciable. In either event, the court's duty is plain. It should stop the proceedings forthwith …

[693] The Court has no knowledge of the many considerations which would have to be taken into account in deciding whether Australia should seek such a resolution from the General

Assembly. It has no means of knowing how any such application would affect Australia's international relations generally or its relations with particular countries or its other activities within the United Nations and its agencies. These are all matters which the Australian Constitution reserves to the executive government of the Commonwealth. They defy judicial application. They turn on a multitude of considerations unknown to this Court. They are matters upon which the Australian Government speaks to the international community with a single voice. That voice is the voice of the executive government chosen from the Parliament elected by the people of Australia. It is not the voice of this Court.

As for the intra-mural proceedings of Parliament, denials of their justiciability can usually be traced, in Australia, to the distinction drawn in *Osborne v Commonwealth* (1911) 12 CLR 321 between ss 53 and 54 of the Constitution, and s 55. Section 53 limits the powers of the Senate with respect to Money Bills, and especially Appropriation Bills. Section 54 requires that Appropriation Bills "deal only with such appropriation" (see Chapter 24, §1); that is, that the limited powers of the Senate with respect to such Bills will not be unfairly exploited. The two paragraphs of s 55 require (first) that laws imposing taxation "shall deal only with the imposition of taxation", and (second) that such laws "shall deal with one subject of taxation only" (with some latitude for customs and excise tariffs) (see Chapter 23, §1). What *Osborne v Commonwealth* suggested was that s 55 is justiciable, but that ss 53 and 54 are not.

In that case the *Land Tax Assessment Act 1910* (Cth) had been challenged on the basis of both paragraphs of s 55. The challenge failed on both counts. Since s 55 was not infringed, the question whether there would have been a justiciable issue if it had been infringed did not arise for decision. All discussion of that question was obiter. The suggested distinction, tentatively accepted by all but Higgins J, rested on two main arguments. One was that the first paragraph of s 55 states a clear legal consequence that is to follow if that paragraph is infringed: those parts of the impugned law which go beyond the imposition of taxation "shall be of no effect". This suggests that the Court must determine whether or not that consequence has ensued: that is, that the issue is justiciable. The second paragraph of s 55 specifies no such clear consequence, but it would be anomalous if the first paragraph were justiciable and the second not.

The second argument was that ss 53 and 54 refer throughout to "proposed laws" (or "any proposed law" or "the proposed law"). They should therefore be read as referring to Bills that are still in the course of passage through Parliament; and issues arising at that stage must be "intra-mural" issues to be policed by the Parliament itself. By contrast, both paragraphs of s 55 refer to "laws" – that is, to enactments which have completed their passage through the Parliament, and may be presented to the Court for a pronouncement upon their legal validity.

One difficulty with this argument is that s 57, like ss 53 and 54, speaks throughout of "any proposed law" or "the proposed law". Yet it is now clear that issues of compliance with s 57 are justiciable (see Chapter 10, §6). If issues arising under s 53 had been similarly justiciable, the constitutional crisis of 1975 (see Chapter 12, §3) might have taken a very different course. Perhaps for this reason, the distinction drawn in *Osborne v Commonwealth* has regularly been reaffirmed (see *Northern Suburbs Cemetery Reserve Trust v Commonwealth* (1993) 176 CLR 555 at 578; *Western Australia v Commonwealth* (*Native Title Act Case*) (1995) 183 CLR 373 at 482).

While the Court has maintained its insistence on the non-justiciability of s 53 of the Constitution, it may now be more willing to intervene in "intra-mural" issues of parliamentary privilege and procedure: see *Egan v Willis* (1998) 195 CLR 424 in Chapter 12, §4(a).

6. Remedies

(a) Invalidity

Many constitutions offer a range of remedies, including damages, for a breach of their terms, and in particular for contraventions of protected rights or freedoms. Among the fundamental rights guaranteed by Pt III of the Constitution of India, Art 32(1) declares that "the right to move the

Supreme Court by appropriate proceedings for the enforcement of the rights conferred by this Part" is itself guaranteed; and Art 32(2) goes on to specify that the rights may be enforced by "directions or orders or writs, including writs in the nature of *habeas corpus, mandamus*, prohibition, *quo warranto* and *certiorari*, whichever may be appropriate". Other examples include s 24(1) of the Canadian Charter of Rights and Freedoms ("Anyone whose rights or freedoms, as guaranteed by this Charter, have been infringed or denied may apply to a court of competent jurisdiction to obtain such remedy as the court considers appropriate and just in the circumstances") and s 38 of the 1996 South African Constitution ("Anyone listed in this section has the right to approach a competent court, alleging that a right in the Bill of Rights has been infringed or threatened, and the court may grant appropriate relief").

Even in the absence of an express provision, the United States Constitution has been held to confer a right to damages. In *Bivens v Six Unknown Named Agents of the Federal Bureau of Narcotics* 403 US 388 (1971), a search of Webster Bivens' home and person had violated the guarantee in the Fourth Amendment to the United States Constitution against "unreasonable searches and seizures". The United States Supreme Court held by 6:3 that, regardless of any action in tort that might be available to him under State law, Bivens was entitled to a federal cause of action, with a remedy in damages based directly on the violation of his constitutional rights. Later cases have held that the *Bivens* cause of action is limited in scope. It may not arise where there are legislative indications to the contrary, or adequate alternative remedies (see, for example, *Bush v Lucas*, 462 US 367 (1983); *Schweiker v Chilicky*, 487 US 412 (1988)); the liability accrues only to the individual agents or officers whose action directly infringed the plaintiff's constitutional rights, not to the government or the instrumentality for which they purported to act (see *Federal Deposit Insurance Corporation v Meyer*, 510 US 471 (1994)); and the individual officer will be protected by a qualified immunity from suit if it would not have been clear to a reasonable officer that he or she was acting unlawfully (as was held to be the case in *Saucier v Katz*, 533 US 194 (2001), but not in *Groh v Ramirez*, 540 US 551 (2004)).

By contrast, the Australian Constitution makes no mention of what is to occur where it is infringed, and has been interpreted by the High Court to offer little in the way of remedies. In cases where one government or its representative challenges the validity of the legislative or executive action of another government, a bare declaration of invalidity is usually a sufficient outcome. Indeed, where the challenge has been referred to a full bench by way of case stated (as in *Amalgamated Society of Engineers v Adelaide Steamship Co Ltd* (*Engineers' Case*) (1920) 28 CLR 129 and *Australian Communist Party v Commonwealth* (*Communist Party Case*) (1951) 83 CLR 1), or by way of questions reserved (as in *Commonwealth v Tasmania* (*Tasmanian Dam Case*) (1983) 158 CLR 1), the substantive outcome will usually consist simply of the Court's answers to the questions posed. For example, the answers given in the *Tasmanian Dam Case* established that certain provisions of the *World Heritage Properties Conservation Act 1983* (Cth) and regulations made thereunder were valid, and accordingly that the development envisaged by the *Gordon River Hydro-Electric Power Development Act 1982* (Tas) could not proceed without Commonwealth consent. But the Court declined to answer a further question whether the Premier of Tasmania must direct the Hydro-Electric Commission to abandon the project; and when counsel proposed an injunction to that effect, Gibbs CJ is said to have protested indignantly: "*Of course* the Tasmanian government will comply with the law as this Court has declared it to be!"

Even in such cases, however, injunctive relief may sometimes be granted. In *Combet v Commonwealth* [2005] HCA 61, the majority of the Court rejected an argument that certain expenditures out of consolidated revenue had not been authorised by a relevant parliamentary appropriation; but Gummow, Hayne, Callinan and Heydon JJ added that, had the argument succeeded, the plaintiffs would still have had to surmount "**[168]** the very considerable difficulty" explored in *Victoria v Commonwealth and Hayden* (*AAP Case*) (1975) 134 CLR 338, where Jacobs J observed "**[412]** that any relief granted by the court against an illegitimate expenditure would need carefully and precisely and exhaustively to delineate those expenditures in respect of which relief is granted. The practical impossibility of so doing may well prevent the granting of relief by way of quia timet injunction or even by way of declaration". On the other hand McHugh and Kirby JJ, who dissented in *Combet v Commonwealth*, were not only prepared to make a declaration that the impugned expenditures had *not* been authorised, but took pains to fashion a form of injunction sufficiently precise to avoid the problem to which Jacobs J had referred.

Both the difficulty of framing injunctive relief, and the importance of doing so, may seem particularly acute in cases where the issue of constitutional validity is the primary issue. In constitutional cases where the moving party is a private individual directly affected by the legislation whose validity is challenged, the success of the challenge will normally entitle the individual only to a finding that the law is invalid (and thus void *ab initio*), and to the benefit of whatever legal consequences may flow from this. The Court has not recognised any further entitlement to compensation. The effect is that the Constitution arms the citizen, it is sometimes said, with a "shield" but not with a "sword", its function being to protect the citizen against unlawful governmental action.

In 1939, after 10 years of victories in the courts founded on s 92, which guarantees that interstate trade, commerce and intercourse shall be "absolutely free", the South Australian dried fruits grower Frederick James brought an action in the High Court seeking damages for the Commonwealth's repeated invasions of his premises and seizures of his property. In *James v Commonwealth* (1939) 62 CLR 339, Dixon J, sitting alone, held that James was entitled to damages in tort for four specific seizures of dried fruits. As to each of those seizures the Commonwealth's officers might normally have claimed a defence of lawful authority; but the finding that the relevant statutory provisions were invalid negated that defence. It was only in that sense that the operation of s 92 assisted James' claim to damages.

James v Commonwealth
(1939) 62 CLR 339

Dixon J: [361] In his judgment in *James v Cowan* [(1930) 43 CLR 386 at 418], a judgment which Lord *Atkin* described as "convincing", *Isaacs* J ... described the right protected by sec 92 as a personal right attaching to the individual **[362]** and not attaching to the goods. He spoke of the right as the possession of the individual Australian protected from State interference by sec 92. But it does not appear that his Honour was considering the question whether sec 92 conferred upon the individual a private right, breach of which involves an action for damages. Standing in the Constitution as it does, the provision should not, I think, be construed as dealing with the private rights of individuals under the civil law. Although, in point of grammar, it is expressed in the affirmative, it amounts to a negative in universal terms denying power, authority and competence, denying them to governments. I do not think that sec 92 affords the plaintiff a cause of action sounding in damages. It would be ridiculous to apply to the provisions of a Constitution any of the considerations disclosed by the authorities [on whether the statutory creation of a public duty gives rise to a correlative private right to damages for breach of that duty] ... Prima facie a constitution is concerned with the powers and functions of government and the restraints upon their exercise. There is, in my opinion, no sufficient reason to regard sec 92 as including among its purposes the creation of private rights sounding in damages. It gives to all an immunity from the exercise of governmental power. But to find whether a governmental act be wrongful the general law must be applied. Sec 92 will do no more than nullify an alleged justification. The plaintiff cannot, therefore, recover damages under sec 92 independently of any tort by the Commonwealth.

The assumption that this analysis applies to all constitutional limitations on legislative and executive power was affirmed in *Lange v Australian Broadcasting Corporation* (1997) 189 CLR 520. It was reaffirmed in *Kruger v Commonwealth* (*Stolen Generations Case*) (1997) 190 CLR 1, where Brennan CJ, Toohey and Gaudron JJ, substantially supported by Gummow J, held that, even if the provisions authorising the forced removal of Aboriginal children from their families were unconstitutional, any resulting entitlement to damages would depend on the ordinary principles of tort law. No remedy was available against the Commonwealth or its officers for a breach of constitutional rights.

Kruger v Commonwealth (*Stolen Generations Case*)
(1997) 190 CLR 1

Brennan CJ: [46] The Constitution reveals no intention to create a private right of action for damages for an attempt to exceed the powers it confers or to ignore the restraints it imposes. The causes of action enforceable by awards of damages are created by the common law (including for this purpose the doctrines of equity) supplemented by statutes which reveal an intention to create such a cause of action for breach of its provisions. If a government does or omits to do anything which, under the general law, would expose it or its servants or agents to a liability in damages, an attempt to deny or to escape that liability fails when justification for the act done or omission made depends on a statute or an action that is invalid for want of constitutional support. In such a case, liability is not incurred for breach of a constitutional right but by operation of the general law. But if a government does or omits to do something the doing or omission of which attracts no liability under the general law, no liability in damages for doing or omitting to do that thing is imposed on the government by the Constitution.

It follows that no right of action distinct from a right of action in tort or for breach of contract arises by reason of any breach of the protections claimed by the plaintiffs in the paragraphs of the respective **[47]** amended statements of claim.

Gaudron J considered the issue only in relation to the plaintiffs' claims based on s 116 and on an implied constitutional freedom of movement and association.

Gaudron J: [124] It is convenient to turn first to s 116. By its terms, s 116 does no more than effect a restriction or limitation on the legislative power of the Commonwealth. It is not, "in form, a constitutional guarantee of **[125]** the rights of individuals" [*Attorney-General (Vic); Ex rel Black v Commonwealth* (1981) 146 CLR 559 at 605]. It does not bind the States: they are completely free to enact laws imposing religious observances, prohibiting the free exercise of religion or otherwise intruding into the area which s 116 denies to the Commonwealth. It makes no sense to speak of a constitutional right to religious freedom in a context in which the Constitution clearly postulates that the States may enact laws in derogation of that right. It follows, in my view, that s 116 must be construed as no more than a limitation on Commonwealth legislative power. More precisely, it cannot be construed as impliedly conferring an independent or free-standing right which, if breached, sounds in damages at the suit of the individual whose interests are thereby affected.

Freedom of movement and of political communication stand in a somewhat different position … They are freedoms which, of their nature are universal, in the sense that they necessarily operate without restriction as to time or place. That being so, they necessarily restrict State legislative power and thus, may be described as giving rise to general, although … not absolute freedoms. Even so, it does not follow that the Constitution gives an independent or free standing right to move in society and to associate with one's fellow citizens which, if breached, sounds in damages.

The right to move in society and to associate with one's fellow citizens is an aspect of personal liberty which is jealously guarded by the common law and which is abridged only to the extent that it is inconsistent with positive rights, including property rights, or to the extent that statute law validly provides to the contrary. Personal liberty is protected by the Constitution to the extent that freedom of movement and association are impliedly mandated by it. However, there is no basis, in my view, for construing the Constitution as conferring an additional right over and above those provided by the common law. Moreover, the relevant rights provided by the common law are properly vindicated by actions for trespass to the person and for false imprisonment, actions which sound in damages, including, in **[126]** appropriate cases, exemplary damages. There is, thus, no necessity to invent a new cause of action.

Gummow J: [146] *Bivens* [*v Six Unknown Named Agents of the Federal Bureau of Narcotics* 403 US 388 (1971)] has received **[147]** some favourable attention in New Zealand. However, current authority in this Court suggests there is no such doctrine in Australia in respect of executive action in excess of constitutional authority or in contravention of a constitutional prohibition beyond liability under the common law for tortious or other wrongful acts …

The reasoning in the Australian authorities has not proceeded on the footing that, because a constitutional guarantee operates to impose a restraint upon legislative power (as does s 51(xxxi)) or to confer an immunity upon the individual in respect of certain activity (as does s 117), it follows that the guarantee confers a "right" which must have a remedy in the form of substantive relief upon a personal cause of action. Such a conclusion does not necessarily follow from the premise.

Moreover, *Bivens* has attracted much unfavourable comment in the United States, including the statement that the *Bivens* doctrine is "so devoid of constitutional legitimacy ... and so harmful in its consequences" that the Supreme Court itself should consider overruling *Bivens*. The decision is only to be understood against the limited waiver of the tort immunity of the United States by the *Federal Torts Claims Act* 1946, and by the limitation of the *Civil Rights Act* 1871 to deprivation of federal rights by State or local **[148]** officials acting under colour of State law ...

The treatment by the *Judiciary Act* of the tort liability of the Commonwealth has been quite different to that of the United States. So also is the relationship between the common law and the federal Constitution.

(b)   Reading Down and Severance

Even when a particular statutory provision, or a particular application of such a provision, is held to be unconstitutional, that does not necessarily mean that the entire statute will fail. In cases where the High Court holds that a particular application of a provision would be invalid, it is often able to preserve the validity of the provision in its other applications by reading it down so as not to apply where it cannot validly do so, while still having a meaningful operation in other cases that are within power. Where this is not possible, a court may still "sever", that is, cut away, the offending parts of an Act, leaving the remainder with a valid operation. These techniques enable a court to "save" parts of an Act instead of striking down all of it.

These techniques were developed judicially by analogy with American precedents (as to severance see particularly the *Bootmakers' Case (No 2)* (1910) 11 CLR 1). Their purpose is to give effect so far as possible to Parliament's intention. However, that means that the outcome depends on judicial assessment of whether the operation remaining to the Act after "reading down" or "severance" is one that Parliament would have intended if the challenged provisions were to fail. For that reason, many Australian parliaments have enacted general statutory directives to "reading down" or "severance", as an indication of their intention. The main directive of this kind at the Commonwealth level is s 15A of the *Acts Interpretation Act 1901* (Cth). (There are similar State provisions, such as the *Acts Interpretation Act 1954* (Qld), s 9.)

Acts Interpretation Act 1901 (Cth)

15A Every Act shall be read and construed subject to the Constitution, and so as not to exceed the legislative power of the Commonwealth, to the intent that where any enactment thereof would, but for this section, have been construed as being in excess of that power, it shall nevertheless be a valid enactment to the extent to which it is not in excess of that power.

A good example of reading down is *Wilson v Minister for Aboriginal and Torres Strait Islander Affairs* (1996) 189 CLR 1. Having held that the functions to be conferred on a "person" under s 10 of the *Aboriginal and Torres Strait Islander Heritage Protection Act 1984* (Cth) could not validly be performed by a judge, the Court then saved the validity of the Act by reading down the word "person" so as not to include a judge! Another example, which in the 1970s and 1980s had far-reaching consequences, was *Russell v Russell* (1976) 134 CLR 495, the first major challenge to the *Family Law Act 1975* (Cth). In a deeply divided Court the substantial validity of the Act was preserved by a reading down solution devised by Mason J (with whom Stephen J agreed on this point); but thereafter the scope to which the permissible jurisdiction of the Family Court had thus been read down was initially treated by both Court and Parliament as if it had set the outer limits of constitutional power. Both Mason and Stephen JJ were driven to protest that this was a misunderstanding. As Stephen J put it in *Dowal v Murray* (1978) 143 CLR 410: "**[424]** It would be a coincidence indeed were particular legislation ever to contain a standard or test available for purposes of 'reading down' which happened also precisely to correspond with the extent of the particular constitutional power found to be capable of supporting that legislation as so read down".

There are limits to the effectiveness of legislative devices intended to ensure severability. The difficulty in *Strickland v Rocla Concrete Pipes Ltd* (*Concrete Pipes Case*) (1971) 124 CLR 468 was the complexity of the challenged legislation, the *Trade Practices Act 1965* (Cth). The operative provisions in s 35 (as to restrictive agreements) and s 36 (as to restrictive practices) were expressed in quite general terms, not tied to any specific head of Commonwealth power and not limited to Commonwealth power. Then s 7(1)(a) sought to give those sections a valid sphere of operation under s 51(i) of the Constitution; s 7(1)(b) sought to give them another area of operation under the incidental power attached to s 51(i); s 7(1)(c) another again, incidental to Commonwealth executive power; s 7(1)(d) another under s 122 of the Constitution, and s 7(1)(e) as "incidental" to s 122. Then s 7(2) sought to give s 35 a sphere of operation based on s 51(xx) of the Constitution and s 7(3) did the same for s 36. The intention in separating out these spheres was that if any of these operations of ss 35 and 36 was invalid, those sections could still operate validly in the other spheres. The High Court majority held, however, that the resulting jigsaw-puzzle arrangement – requiring the Court to draw out from s 35 (for example) one law aided by s 7(1)(a) (applying to all persons and corporations, but only in interstate trade), and a different law aided by s 7(2) (applying to both interstate and intrastate trade, but only to "s 51(xx) corporations") – went beyond any legitimate technique of severance or reading down under s 15A of the *Acts Interpretation Act* or otherwise. As Menzies J stated: "**[506]** Parliament cannot direct courts to reconstruct out of the ruins of one invalid law of general application a number of valid laws of particular application".

In 1993 the federal parliamentary drafting office experimented with a more ambitious form of severability provision, inserted, for example, as a new s 7A in the *Industrial Relations Act 1988* (Cth), now renamed the *Workplace Relations Act 1996* (Cth).

Workplace Relations Act 1996 (Cth)

7A **(1)** Unless the contrary intention appears, if a provision of this Act:
- (a) would, apart from this section, have an invalid application; but
- (b) also has at least one valid application;

it is the Parliament's intention that the provision is not to have the invalid application, but is to have every valid application.

(2) Despite subsection (1), the provision is not to have a particular valid application if:
- (a) apart from this section, it is clear, taking into account the provision's context and the purpose or object underlying this Act, that the provision was intended to have that valid application only if every invalid application, or a particular invalid application, of the provision had also been within the Commonwealth's legislative power; or
- (b) the provision's operation in relation to that valid application would be different in a substantial respect from what would have been its operation in relation to that valid application if every invalid application of the provision had been within the Commonwealth's legislative power.

(3) Subsection (2) does not limit the cases where a contrary intention may be taken to appear for the purposes of subsection (1).

(4) This section applies to a provision of this Act, whether enacted before, at or after the commencement of this section.

(5) In this section:

application means an application in relation to:
- (a) one or more particular persons, things, matters, places, circumstances or cases; or
- (b) one or more classes (however defined or determined) of persons, things, matters, places, circumstances or cases;

invalid application, in relation to a provision, means an application because of which the provision exceeds the Commonwealth's legislative power;

valid application, in relation to a provision, means an application that, if it were the provision's only application, would be within the Commonwealth's legislative power.

The same clause was used as s 208 of the *Native Title Act 1993* (Cth); and amending legislation was drafted to insert it as an all-purpose provision into the *Acts Interpretation Act 1901* (Cth) as a new s 15AAA. However, in 1995 that proposed amendment was abandoned. The new s 7A had come into force on 30 March 1994, after *Re Dingjan; Ex parte Wagner* (1995) 183 CLR 323 had been argued before the High Court. But on 14 February 1995 the Commonwealth submitted further argument in *Dingjan's Case* to the effect that the provisions of the *Industrial Relations Act* there in question could be saved by s 7A. In the end the Court held only that s 7A could not be applied retrospectively; but the sharp exchanges during oral argument gave such strong indications that the provision was not judicially acceptable that the proposed amendment to the *Acts Interpretation Act* was withdrawn.

On the other hand, s 7A remains in the *Workplace Relations Act* even after its further amendment by the *Workplace Relations Amendment (Work Choices) Act 2005* (Cth). Indeed, it is given a supplement. The existing Sch 1B (entitled "Registration and Accountability of Organisations", and applying to associations of both employers and employees, as well as to a new category of "enterprise associations") is recast so that it now depends primarily on the corporations power (s 51(xx)) rather than the conciliation and arbitration power (s 51(xxxv)). For example, under ss 18A and 18B of the Schedule, an association is registrable if the majority of its members are "federal system employers" or "federal system employees". For employers, this means that a majority of members must be "constitutional corporations", or engaged in businesses that bring them within some other head of power (such as interstate trade or banking). For "federal system employees" there are similar classes or categories. For both employer and employee associations a new s 18D then provides that if, when majority membership is assessed to determine registrability, the inclusion of a particular class would mean that Parliament "would not have sufficient legislative power" to provide for registration, the definition of "federal system employers" or "federal system employees" is to be applied "as if it did not include a reference to that class".

7. Precedent and Overruling

The doctrine of precedent, or *stare decisis*, imports an expectation that the High Court will normally follow its own prior decisions. However, the High Court is an "apex" court, the highest court in the national appellate hierarchy. While this means that all other Australian State and federal courts are bound by the law as enounced by the High Court, it entails no necessary logical conclusion as to whether, or when, the High Court should regard itself as bound by its own decisions. Generally, most "apex" courts have concluded, on the basis of their supervisory responsibility for sound development of the law, that they should *not* be bound by their own decisions. Until 1966 the notable exception was the House of Lords in its capacity as the "apex" court for the legal systems of the United Kingdom. The idea that the House was absolutely bound by its own decisions, first suggested in *Beamish v Beamish* (1861) 9 HL Cas 273; 11 ER 735, had itself been endowed with the binding authority of a House of Lords decision in *London Tramways Co v London County Council* [1898] AC 375. This self-referential precedent gave rise to a paradox: the rule that the House was bound by its own decisions could only be abolished by overruling the *London Tramways Case*, but the rule made such an overruling impossible. When the rule was eventually changed, this paradox was circumvented by a Practice Statement [1966] 1 WLR 1234 – incidentally giving strong support to the view that the rules of precedent are not rules of law, but only rules of practice, and can therefore be changed simply by the adoption of a different practice.

In any event, the House of Lords' experiment with irreversible auto-limitation was always an anomaly. It was attributed sometimes to the idea that the House of Lords, when it functions as an appellate court, is really a committee of the House of Lords as the upper chamber of the Westminster Parliament, and that its decisions have therefore a kind of legislative status. The Judicial Committee of the Privy Council, though frequently constituted by the same personnel as the (judicial) House of Lords, had never adopted a similar practice of being bound by its own decisions. From the beginning the High Court of Australia made it clear that in this respect it would follow the practice of the Privy Council.

Australian Agricultural Co v Federated Engine-Drivers & Firemen's Association (*Engine-Drivers' Case*)
(1913) 17 CLR 261

Isaacs J: [275] In *Read v Bishop of Lincoln* [[1892] AC 644 at 655], after full consideration of the subject, Lord *Halsbury* LC, as to previous decisions of the Judicial Committee, laid down ... the rule to be followed in these terms:– "Whilst fully sensible of the weight to be attached to such decisions, their Lordships are at the same time bound to examine the reasons upon which the decisions rest, and to give effect to their own view of the law."

There we have laid down for us, by the tribunal by which we are in most respects controlled, that it is the primary duty of even that august tribunal, to consider for itself at the instance of every suitor before it, what is the law by which he is bound. A prior decision does not constitute the law, but is only a judicial declaration as to what the law is. The declaration, unless that of a superior tribunal, may be wrong, in the opinion of those whose present function is to interpret and enforce the law; and if the reasons given appear when examined to be unsound, then, say the Judicial Committee, they are bound "to give effect to their own view of the law"; other-**[276]**-wise Judges arrogate to themselves the position of legislators. The Privy Council has in fact reconsidered its own decisions on various subjects for various reasons, and has overruled them ...

Nothing could be more decisive than the general rule quoted from *Read* v *Bishop of Lincoln*; and further, nothing could more strongly emphasize the fact that the doctrine of the House of Lords is anomalous and rests upon its anomalous position in the constitutional and juristic history of England, than the circumstance that it was the same learned Judge, Lord *Halsbury*, who delivered the widely differing pronouncements in the House of Lords and the Privy Council respectively [that is, in the *London Tramways Case* [1898] AC 375 and in *Read v Bishop of Lincoln*].

As late as 1907 Sir *Frederick Pollock*, in a note to *Bright v Hutton* [(1852) 3 HLC 341, as annotated in 88 Revised Reports 126 at 127], observes in contradistinction to the House of Lords, that "the Judicial Committee does not hold itself bound to follow its own previous rulings, neither do American Courts of last resort." And I may add, that neither of those illustrious tribunals, fortified as they both are by long experience ... , trembles at the spectre of instability. That is a danger which the good sense of those tribunals, and every other, always where necessary sufficiently guards against.

Unless, therefore, this Court is to be regarded as possessing a **[277]** nearer approach to infallibility than the Privy Council – and I am unable to press such a claim – no reason presents itself to my mind for refusing to follow the guidance of that august tribunal whose determinations are final in a higher and more decisive sense than any we are empowered to give ...

[278] The oath of a Justice of this Court is "to do right to all manner of people *according to law.*" Our sworn loyalty is to the law itself, and to the organic law of the Constitution first of all. If, then, we find the law to be plainly in conflict with what we or any of our predecessors erroneously thought it to be, we have, as I conceive, no right to choose between giving effect to the law, and maintaining an incorrect interpretation. It is not, in my opinion, better that the Court should be persistently wrong than that it should be ultimately right.

Whatever else may be said with respect to the reconsideration of former decisions ... so much at least emerges as is undoubtedly beyond challenge, that where a former decision is clearly wrong, and there are no circumstances **[279]** countervailing the primary duty of giving effect to the law as the Court finds it, the real opinion of the Court should be expressed.

In my opinion, where the prior decision is manifestly wrong, then, irrespective of consequences, it is the paramount and sworn duty of this Court to declare the law truly.

In the House of Lords, the willingness to "depart from" previous decisions, as announced in the 1966 Practice Statement, led paradoxically to a greater degree of formalism in the handling of precedent. Before 1966 their Lordships had developed a rich repertoire of techniques for "departing from" their own prior decisions without a formal overruling. In the years after 1966, the overt acknowledgment of the power to "depart" led to anxious, and often contradictory, attempts to identify the criteria for the exercise of this power. In Australia, these developments coincided with a period when the High Court – which had never been formally bound by House of Lords decisions but until the 1960s had invariably followed them for the sake of comity and Imperial or Commonwealth uniformity – was striking out on its own independent path. Yet a further paradox was that the formalism with which the House of Lords infused the problem of self-overruling began to be emulated in the High Court for the first time. In *Attorney-General (NSW) v Perpetual Trustee Co (Ltd)* (1952) 85 CLR 237, Dixon J had remarked comfortably that: "**[243]** This Court has adopted no very definite **[244]** rule as to the circumstances in which it will reconsider an earlier decision". The High Court's more recent approach to the issue has been far less relaxed.

The question of overruling is now approached by the High Court in two stages. At neither level is it sufficient to show that the impugned decision is "wrong". The arguments in favour of adherence to precedent thus get two bites at the cherry. The first question is whether the question of overruling will be entertained at all. In *Evda Nominees Pty Ltd v Victoria* (1984) 154 CLR 311, the Court adopted a rule of practice that a party may not challenge the correctness of a prior decision unless leave is given to do so. Since then that rule has consistently been applied. Deane J dissented in *Evda Nominees*, protesting that, in his opinion, "**[316]** counsel representing a party does not require the permission of the Court to present or to continue to present argument that is relevant to the decision in the case, including argument seeking to show that a previous decision of the Court is wrong and should not be followed". In later cases he continued to doubt the correctness of the rule. More recently, similar doubts have been expressed by Kirby J; for example, in *Re Colina; Ex parte Torney* (1999) 200 CLR 386 he stated: "**[407]** Once a matter is before the Court, it is my view that the Constitution requires the Court to dispose of the controversy which it presents in accordance with law. No rule of practice can shackle or limit the judicial obligation in that regard". (See also *Brownlee v The Queen* (2001) 207 CLR 278 at 312-15.)

Assuming that leave has been given to argue that an earlier decision should be reopened, the question of whether it should actually be overturned will still receive anxious consideration, often with no unanimous answer. For attempted checklists of the factors to which the Court may sometimes give weight in deciding whether to overrule a prior decision of its own, see Lyndel V Prott, "When Will a Superior Court Overrule Its Own Decision?" (1978) 52 *Australian Law Journal* 304 and Bryan Horrigan, "Towards a Jurisprudence of High Court Overruling" (1992) 66 *Australian Law Journal* 199. One should of course be aware of the danger that such checklists may artificially complicate the issue by giving to the factors identified an unwarranted degree of precision and argumentative weight.

In a constitutional context the factors thought to justify overruling were formulated by Gibbs CJ in *Commonwealth v Hospital Contribution Fund* (1982) 150 CLR 49 at 56-8. That formulation was applied in a non-constitutional context when the Court overruled its notorious decision in *Curran v Federal Commissioner of Taxation* (1974) 131 CLR 409.

John v Federal Commissioner of Taxation
(1989) 166 CLR 417

Mason CJ, Wilson, Dawson, Toohey and Gaudron JJ: [438] [I]n *Commonwealth v Hospital Contribution Fund* [(1982) 150 CLR 49 at 56-8], Gibbs CJ, with whom Stephen J and Aickin J agreed, specified four matters which in that case justified departure from earlier decisions. The first was that the earlier decisions did not rest upon a principle carefully worked out in a significant succession of cases. The second was a difference between the reasons of the justices constituting the majority in one of the earlier decisions. The third was that the earlier decisions had achieved no useful result but on the contrary had led to considerable inconvenience. The fourth was that the earlier decisions had not been independently acted on **[439]** in a manner which militated against reconsideration, as had been the case in *Queensland v Commonwealth* [(1977) 139 CLR 585].

See also *Esso Australia Resources Ltd v Federal Commissioner of Taxation* (1999) 201 CLR 49 at 71 (overruling the decision in *Grant v Downs* (1976) 135 CLR 674).

The joint judgment in *John's Case* went on to note the argument that, in cases of statutory interpretation, the Court should not allow adherence to precedent to divert it from what it now regards as "**[440]** the true intent of the statute". This point is sometimes advanced even more strongly in relation to decisions involving the interpretation of the Constitution.

Leslie Zines, *The High Court and the Constitution*
(Butterworths, 4th ed 1997)

[433] The High Court has never regarded itself as bound by its own decisions and in the area of constitutional law the principle of *stare decisis* is regarded as having somewhat less force than in other areas of the law, for the obvious reason that parliament cannot rectify the consequences of a decision of the High Court on the Constitution …

Barwick CJ and Murphy J have been the chief exponents of the view that no judicially devised formula can replace the text. Judicial reasoning "may not be used as a substitute for the Constitution. Always the Constitution remains the text": *Damjanovic and Sons Pty Ltd v Commonwealth* (1968) 117 CLR 390 at 396; *Victoria v Commonwealth* (1971) 122 CLR 353 at 378 per Barwick CJ. "The task is to apply the Constitution, not the judicial decisions": *Buck v Bavone* (1976) 135 CLR 110 at 137 … per Murphy J. Other judges, while accepting the duty of a judge to interpret the Constitution, have expressed concern about the instability that may result from each judge construing the Constitution individually without sufficient regard for past decisions and rules, principles and doctrines created and developed by those decisions. One might add that the authority of the court as an institution may also be at stake. On the other hand, it seems highly inappropriate, in the case of a constitution intended to endure for a very long time and to serve the needs of succeeding generations, that past decisions should not be departed from when new social problems arise or later experience shows those decisions to be inadequate or socially damaging. "Fresh interpretations of grants of legislative power and of constitutional guarantees may be needed to adapt them to new or changed conditions": *Hughes and Vale Pty Ltd v New South Wales (No 1)* (1953) 87 CLR 49 at 76 per McTiernan J.

There have been some striking examples of refusal by members of the High Court to defer to precedent when this conflicts with their own perceptions of what the Constitution requires. In *Breavington v Godleman* (1988) 169 CLR 41, Deane, Wilson and Gaudron JJ argued that when action was brought in any Australian jurisdiction for a tort committed in any other Australian jurisdiction, the outcome must be governed by the *lex loci delicti* (the law of the place of the tort), thus giving to that law the "full faith and credit" which s 118 of the Constitution demands. In *McKain v RW Miller & Co (SA) Pty Ltd* (1991) 174 CLR 1, that approach failed to win majority acceptance, though again supported by Deane and Gaudron JJ. When the issue arose again 15 months later, Deane and Gaudron JJ yet again adhered to their earlier view.

Stevens v Head
(1993) 176 CLR 433

Deane J: [461] I have given careful consideration to the question whether I should abandon the views which I expressed in my judgments in *Breavington v Godleman* [(1988) 169 CLR 41] and

McKain [(1991) 174 CLR 1. The perception that this country is a single nation with a unitary system of law, in the sense that I explained in *Breavington v Godleman*, lies at the heart of my understanding of the structure and working of the Constitution. Any denial of that perception seems to me to be flawed by an unjustifiable underestimation of the extent of the compact between the Australian people and a mistaken denial of the fundamental imperative embodied in s 118 of that compact. I am fully conscious of the weight of the considerations which support the view that a decision of the Court which still enjoys majority support should be treated by an individual member of the Court as being as binding upon him or her as it is on the members of every other Australian court. There are, however, weighty statements of authority which support the proposition that, in matters of fundamental constitutional importance, the members of this Court are obliged to adhere to what they see as the requirements of the **[462]** Constitution of which the Court is both a creature and the custodian. Ultimately, I have come to the conclusion that I should adhere to the views which I expressed in *Breavington v Godleman* and *McKain*.

Gaudron J: [464] There are constitutional provisions which permit of different views as to their meaning or, more often, as to their effect in a particular case. But in the context of covering cl 3 of the Constitution whereby the people of Australia were united in a Federal Commonwealth ..., s 118 of the Constitution is not one of them. Either its requirement that "[f]ull faith and credit ... be given ... to the laws ... of every State" means that the laws of the State which govern an act as it happens also govern the legal consequences of that act or it means nothing of any constitutional significance at all. And, if s 118 does not have constitutional significance of the kind I have indicated, we are not a united Federal Commonwealth but an alliance which can at any stage be revealed as an alliance of "separate countries in private international law". It follows that I not only differ from the contrary view of the majority in *McKain*, I also consider that that view is wrong and fundamentally so. In my view and because the Constitution prevails over the pronouncements of **[465]** this Court upon it, the decision in that case, so far as it concerns s 118 of the Constitution, should not be followed.

Eventually, in *John Pfeiffer Pty Ltd v Rogerson* (2000) 203 CLR 503, Gaudron J was able to participate in a joint judgment with Gleeson CJ, McHugh, Gummow and Hayne JJ, effectively overruling *McKain v Miller* and *Stevens v Head* on the basis of a concept of the federal system derived in part from s 118, and noting that: "**[533]** Reconsideration ... is not precluded by the fact that *McKain* and *Stevens* have not stood for very long".

Again, in *Re Tracey; Ex parte Ryan* (1989) 166 CLR 518, Deane and Gaudron JJ spelled out from their understanding of Ch III of the Constitution rigorous limits on the extent to which criminal offences, other than genuine "service offences", could be tried by courts martial or other military tribunals. In *Re Nolan; Ex parte Young* (1991) 172 CLR 460 they were joined by McHugh J. However, in neither case did their approaches attract majority support. When the issue arose again in *Re Tyler; Ex parte Foley* (1994) 181 CLR 18, McHugh J yielded to the force of precedent; but Deane and Gaudron JJ again adhered to their previous views. McHugh J observed pointedly that, since this was now the third occasion on which a majority of the Court had affirmed the validity in such cases of trials by service tribunals, "**[39]** [b]oth the **[40]** Parliament and those responsible for the administration of service discipline could be fairly excused for thinking that the constitutional question had been settled". Yet in *Re Colonel Aird; Ex parte Alpert* (2004) 220 CLR 308, Kirby J was able to point out that the Court remained as "**[331]** sharply divided" as ever, and expressed himself to be "**[337]** [n]ot for the first time ... in agreement with the approach of Deane J" (see Chapter 18, §5).

In *Coleman v Power* (2004) 220 CLR 1, Callinan J quoted what Deane J had said in *Stevens v Head* in support of his view that the absence of any challenge to *Lange v Australian Broadcasting Corporation* (1997) 189 CLR 520 "**[109]** may not relieve me of the necessity, if I am conscientiously of the view that it, as a decision of this Court, no matter that it be recent and unanimous, is incompatible with the Constitution, of deciding whether I am bound not to follow it, rather than obliged to apply it". He also quoted what Barwick CJ had said in *Queensland v Commonwealth (Second Territory Senators Case)* (1977) 139 CLR 585. In that case, Barwick CJ held that the Court's earlier decision in *Western Australia v Commonwealth* (*First Territory Senators Case*) (1975) 134 CLR 201 should be overruled.

Queensland v Commonwealth (*Second Territory Senators Case*)
(1977) 139 CLR 585

Barwick CJ: [593] As to the first of these submissions, it is fundamental to the work of this Court and to its function of determining, so far as it rests on judicial decision, the law of Australia appropriate to the times, that it should not be bound in point of precedent but only in point of conviction by its prior decisions. In the case of the Constitution, it is the duty, in my opinion, of each Justice, paying due regard to the opinions of other Justices past and present, to decide what in truth the Constitution provides. The area of constitutional law is pre-eminently an area where the paramount consideration is the maintenance of the Constitution itself. Of course, the fact that a particular construction has long been accepted is a potent factor for consideration: but it has not hitherto been accepted as effective to prevent the members of the Court from departing from an earlier interpretation if convinced that it does not truly represent the Constitution. There is no need to refer to the instances in which the Court has departed from earlier decisions upon the Constitution, some of long standing. The Constitution may be rigid but that does not imply or require rigidity on the part of the Court in adherence to prior decisions. No doubt to depart from them is a grave matter and a heavy responsibility. But convinced of their error, the duty to express what is the proper construction is paramount. It is worthwhile, I think, to recall what Sir Isaac Isaacs said in *Australian Agricultural Co v Federated Engine-Drivers and Firemen's Association of Australasia* [(*Engine-Drivers' Case*) (1913) 17 CLR 261 at 278] ...

What I have written relates to longstanding decisions. Reluctance to depart from them when thought to be wrong springs from the length of time they have stood and apparently been accepted. But that reluctance can have no place, in my opinion, in relation to a recent decision. To refuse to decide in a constitutional case what one is convinced is right because there is **[594]** a recent decision of the Court is, to my mind, to deny the claims of the Constitution itself and to substitute for it a decision of the Court. If both old and new decisions construing the Constitution, of whose error the Court is convinced, must none the less be followed, then, to use Sir Isaac Isaacs' expression, perpetuation of error rather than the maintenance of the Constitution becomes the paramount duty. I find no validity in the submission that the recency of the Court's former decision gives it a quality which precludes critical examination of it or, indeed, departure from it.

However, the *First Territory Senators Case* was upheld because Gibbs and Stephen JJ declined to depart from it, even though they had dissented from it at the time and still thought it was wrongly decided.

Gibbs J: [597] I have considered again, with care, the judgments in *Western Australia v Commonwealth* [(1975) 134 CLR 201], but with all respect to those who take a different view I remain of the opinion that the decision in that case was erroneous ...

[598] It then becomes necessary for me to decide whether I ought to follow the decision of the majority in *Western Australia v Commonwealth*, notwithstanding that I believe it to be wrong. There is of course no doubt that this Court is not bound by its own decisions. Further, it has been said, and with some **[599]** justification, that "the doctrine of stare decisis should not be so rigidly applied to the constitutional as to other laws" (see the passage cited by Isaacs J in *Australian Agricultural Co v Federated Engine-Drivers and Firemen's Association of Australasia* [(1913) 17 CLR 261 at 278]) because in such cases the Parliament cannot legislate to correct the errors of the courts. It has been said, too, that since this Court has the duty of maintaining the constitution, it has a duty to overrule an earlier decision if convinced that it is plainly wrong. In the case already cited, Isaacs J went on to say [(1913) 17 CLR 261 at 278]:

"Our sworn loyalty is to the law itself, and to the organic law of the Constitution first of all. If, then, we find the law to be plainly in conflict with what we or any of our predecessors erroneously thought it to be, we have, as I conceive, no right to choose between giving effect to the law, and maintaining an incorrect interpretation. It is not, in my opinion, better that the Court should be persistently wrong than that it should be ultimately right."

But like most generalizations, this statement can be misleading. No Justice is entitled to ignore the decisions and reasoning of his predecessors, and to arrive at his own judgment as though the pages of the law reports were blank, or as though the authority of a decision did not survive beyond the rising of the Court. A Justice, unlike a legislator, cannot introduce a programme of reform which sets at nought decisions formerly made and principles formerly established. It is only after the most careful and respectful consideration of the earlier decision, and after giving due weight to all the circumstances, that a Justice may give effect to his own opinions in preference to an earlier decision of the Court.

It would be futile to attempt to state any succinct general principle by which the Court should be guided in deciding whether to overrule an earlier decision of its own. Some cases may be clear enough. On the one hand the Court would be slow to disturb a decision which applied a principle that had been carefully worked out in a succession of cases, and had been more than once reaffirmed. On the other hand, a judgment which had been given per incuriam, and was in conflict with some other decision of the Court, or with some well-established principle, might be readily reviewed. However the present case does not lie at either of these extremes, and I have had much difficulty in deciding what course my duty requires. As the plaintiffs have urged, the decision in *Western Australia v Commonwealth* was recently given, and by a narrow majority. It has not **[600]** been followed in any other case. It involves a question of grave constitutional importance. But when it is asked what has occurred to justify the reconsideration of a judgment given not two years ago, the only possible answer is that one member of the Court has retired, and another has succeeded him. It cannot be suggested that the majority in *Western Australia v Commonwealth* failed to advert to any relevant consideration, or overlooked any apposite decision or principle. The arguments presented in the present case were in their essence the same as those presented in the earlier case. No later decision has been given that conflicts with *Western Australia v Commonwealth*. Moreover, the decision has been acted on; senators for the Territories have been elected under the legislation there held valid. To reverse the decision now would be to defeat the expectations of the people of the Territories that they would be represented, as many of them believed that they ought to be represented, by senators entitled to vote – expectations and beliefs that were no less understandable because in my view they were constitutionally erroneous, and that were encouraged by the decision of this Court.

When, in *The Tramways Case (No 1)* [(1914) 18 CLR 54 at 69], Barton J said that "Changes in the number of appointed Justices can ... never of themselves furnish a reason for review" of a previous decision, it may be that not all who had become his brethren agreed with him, but his statement in my respectful opinion ought to be regarded as, in general, correct, having regard to "the need for continuity and consistency in judicial decision" to which he there referred. Still less should the replacement of one Justice by another in itself justify the review of an earlier decision. Having considered all the circumstances that I have mentioned I have reached the conclusion that it is my duty to follow *Western Australia v Commonwealth*, although in my view it was wrongly decided.

He did, however, add the qualification "**[601]** that if the Parliament were further to distort the federal balance by legislating to provide for the election of more senators for the Territories, that would be a circumstance that might be regarded as sufficient to justify a reconsideration of the question whether *Western Australia v Commonwealth* should continue to be followed".

Stephen J, too, declined to depart from the earlier decision in spite of his earlier dissent. He suggested that the issue "**[603]** was very much one upon which different minds might reach different conclusions, no one view being inherently entitled to any pre-eminence as conforming better than others to principle or to precedent. In such a context phrases such as 'plainly wrong' and 'manifest error', which have gained currency in this field, are merely pejorative".

This result strongly reinforced the tradition that departure from precedent cannot be justified merely by a change in the composition of the bench. As Barton J had put it much earlier, in *R v Commonwealth Court of Conciliation and Arbitration; Ex parte Brisbane Tramways Co Ltd*

(No 1) (1914) 18 CLR 54: "**[69]** Changes in the number of appointed Justices can ... never of themselves furnish a reason for review".

However, such precepts are not always observed. In *Re Patterson; Ex parte Taylor* (2001) 207 CLR 391, McHugh, Kirby and Callinan JJ joined Gaudron J – who had dissented alone in *Nolan v Minister for Immigration and Ethnic Affairs* (1988) 165 CLR 178 – in overruling *Nolan*; but in February 2003 Gaudron J resigned from the bench and was replaced by Heydon J. Thereupon, in *Shaw v Minister for Immigration and Multicultural Affairs* (2003) 218 CLR 28, Heydon J joined Gleeson CJ, Gummow and Hayne JJ in overruling *Patterson* and reinstating *Nolan*, leaving McHugh, Kirby and Callinan JJ in dissent. Kirby J protested that "**[50]** this Court should not use chance happenings affecting its composition to change its recent statements of the governing law", and added:

Shaw v Minister for Immigration and Multicultural Affairs
(2003) 218 CLR 28

Kirby J: [55] I recognise that, in respect of the meaning of the Constitution, the duty of each Justice is to the **[56]** fundamental law of the nation. In the history of this Court the rule of obedience to a majority holding of the Court on a point of law has not been uniformly treated as applying in the same way to a constitutional ruling. Nevertheless, whilst adhering to (and often expressing) individual views concerning the meaning of the Constitution, it is normal for Justices of this Court to give effect to majority rulings on the Constitution, if only to avoid the spectacle of deliberate persistence in attempts to overrule recent constitutional decisions on identical questions on the basis of nothing more intellectually persuasive than the retirement of a member of a past majority and the replacement of that Justice by a new appointee who may hold a different view.

Those who recognise the stabilising element of the doctrine of precedent in our legal system (even to the extent of suggesting the need for leave of this Court to re-argue a matter determined by past authority) will ordinarily accept a determination of a rule, especially where that determination is recent and concerns exactly the same legal issue. Otherwise, every important constitutional decision will be resubmitted for redetermination following new appointments until the dissenter gets his or her way ... [The view] endorsed in *Nolan* [(1988) 165 CLR 178] but overruled in *Re Patterson* [(2001) 207 CLR 391] should not continue to revisit this Court awaiting the hoped for arrival of a majority to give effect to an opinion about the Constitution dismissed in the past in an authoritative decision on the point ...

[72] The success of the Minister's persistent submission in the conclusion of the new majority gathered in this case, following a change of membership of the Court, is a sharp reminder of the opinionative character of constitutional doctrine. Some citizens and some judges may wish that it were otherwise, but ultimately a case such as the present obliges us to face the facts ... [W]hat matters in the end is the conclusion of a majority of this Court. Indeed, there could not be a clearer illustration of that truth. Reason, history, principle, words, adverse risks and legal precedent, all bend in the wind of transient majorities. One day ... it may be hoped that a new majority in this Court will gather around the view of the Constitution favoured by the majority in *Re Patterson* and that that view will be restored.

Gleeson CJ, Gummow and Hayne JJ retorted, in a joint judgment, that the ruling of the four judges in *Re Patterson* had *not* been "authoritative", since the four judges had given different emphases to the factual elements on which the application of their ruling depended. Earlier, in *Re Minister for Immigration and Multicultural Affairs; Ex parte Meng Kok Te* (2002) 212 CLR 162, Gummow J had suggested that "**[200]** the divergent reasoning [in *Patterson*] ... dooms an attempt to discern a ... ratio decidendi for [that aspect of] the decision. If the Court is to depart from previous decisions, particularly those involving the interpretation and application of the provisions of the Constitution, then it should be taken as having done so only in circumstances where what was decided in the earlier case, or (as here) cases, has been overthrown and replaced by fresh doctrine, the content of which is readily discernible". Picking up on that theme, the joint judgment in *Shaw* observed:

Gleeson CJ, Gummow and Hayne JJ: [44] Any consideration of the significance to be attached to *Patterson* must involve the determination whether *Patterson* was effective to take the first step of overruling the earlier decision in *Nolan v Minister for Immigration and Ethnic Affairs*. In our view, the Court should be taken as having departed from a previous decision, particularly one involving the interpretation of the Constitution, only where that which purportedly has been overthrown has been replaced by some fresh doctrine, the elements of which may readily be discerned by the other courts in the Australian hierarchy. On that approach to the matter ... *Patterson* plainly fails to pass muster ...

[45] The decision in *Patterson* does not rest upon a principle carefully worked out in a significant succession of decisions; the contrary ... is the case. Secondly, the treatment of [the constitutional issue] in *Patterson* was not necessary for the decision, because there was a clear alternative basis for the decision. Thirdly, the inconvenience flowing from the existence of *Patterson* is indicated by reference to *Long* [*v Minister for Immigration and Multicultural and Indigenous Affairs* [2002] FCA 1422 (unreported, 19 November 2002)]. Finally, the Minister has moved as quickly as may be in this Court to obtain a reconsideration of *Patterson*.

In this paragraph the joint judgment was applying the criteria for overruling laid down in *John v Federal Commissioner of Taxation* (1989) 166 CLR 417.

The protest of Kirby J in *Shaw* echoed similar pleas in the United States Supreme Court. In *Mitchell v WT Grant Co*, 416 US 600 (1974), for example, Justice Stewart protested: "**[636]** A basic change in the law upon a ground no firmer than a change in our membership invites the popular misconception that this institution is itself little different from the two political branches of Government. No misconception could do more lasting injury to this Court and to the system of law which it is our abiding mission to serve". Despite this, the changing membership of that Court has resulted in the frequent overruling of decisions on constitutional issues, since that Court too has accepted that justices should be more willing to overrule if they conclude that to do so is to achieve a better interpretation of what the Constitution requires.

Indeed, the explicit recognition in that Court that overruling *changes* the law, in a way that is incompatible with "the declaratory theory of law", has led to acceptance of the practice of *prospective* overruling, by which the Court not only makes new law but, like a legislative institution, asserts the power to specify the precise point of time at which the new law is to displace the old. However, despite some initial flirtations with the possibility that such a practice might be adopted in the High Court, it now appears to have been decisively rejected. In *Oceanic Sun Line Special Shipping Company Inc v Fay* (1988) 165 CLR 197, a case in which a High Court majority refused to change the law, Deane J observed that, if there were to be a change, it "**[257]** should be prospective only"; and in *Bropho v Western Australia* (1990) 171 CLR 1, the Court laid down one interpretive approach for statutes "**[23]** enacted before the publication of the decision in the present case" and a different approach for statutes "enacted subsequent to this decision". However, in that case Brennan J dissociated himself from any suggestion of prospective overruling; and in *Ha v New South Wales* (1997) 189 CLR 465, the Court declined to entertain any such strategy. Brennan CJ, McHugh, Gummow and Kirby JJ, with the support of Dawson, Toohey and Gaudron JJ, stated that "**[503]** [t]his Court has no power to overrule cases prospectively", since such a course would be "**[504]** inconsistent with judicial power".

8. Further References

Bennett, JM, *Keystone of the Federal Arch* (AGPS, 1980).

Blackshield, AR, "'Practical Reason' and 'Conventional Wisdom': The House of Lords and Precedent" in Goldstein, L (ed), *Precedent in Law* (Clarendon Press, 1987), 107.

Blackshield, AR, Coper, M, and Williams, G (eds), *The Oxford Companion to the High Court of Australia* (Oxford University Press, 2001).

Boeddu, G, and Haigh, R, "Terms of Convenience: Examining Constitutional Overrulings by the High Court" (2003) 31 *Federal Law Review* 167.

Brennan, G, "The Privy Council and the Constitution" in Lee, HP, and Winterton, G (eds), *Australian Constitutional Landmarks* (Cambridge University Press, 2003), 312.

Burmester, H, "Locus Standi" in Lee, HP, and Winterton, G (eds), *Australian Constitutional Perspectives* (Law Book Co, 1992), 148.

Campbell, E, "Unconstitutionality and its Consequences" in Lindell, G (ed), *Future Directions in Australian Constitutional Law* (Federation Press, 1994), 90.

Campbell, E, and Lee, HP, *The Australian Judiciary* (Cambridge University Press, 2001).

Cane, P (ed), *Centenary Essays for the High Court of Australia* (LexisNexis Butterworths Australia, 2004).

Coper, M, *Encounters with the Australian Constitution* (CCH, 1988), Ch 3.

Evans, G, "The Most Dangerous Branch? The High Court and the Constitution in a Changing Society" in Hambly, D, and Goldring, J (eds), *Australian Lawyers and Social Change* (Law Book Co, 1976), 13.

Evans, S, and Donaghue, S, "Standing to Raise Constitutional Issues in Australia" in Moens, GA, and Biffot, R (eds), *The Convergence of Legal Systems in the 21st Century* (CopyRight Publishing, 2002), 53.

Galligan, B, *Politics of the High Court* (University of Queensland Press, 1987).

Goldring, J, *The Privy Council and the Australian Constitution* (Unitas Law Press, 1996).

Irving, H, "Advisory Opinions, the Rule of Law, and the Separation of Powers" (2004) 4 *Macquarie Law Journal* 105.

Jackson, DF, "Practice in the High Court of Australia" (1997) 15 *Australian Bar Review* 187.

Kenny, S, "Constitutional Fact Ascertainment" (1990) 1 *Public Law Review* 134.

Kenny, S, "Intervenors and Amici Curiae in the High Court" (1998) 20 *Adelaide Law Review* 159.

Keyzer, P, "When is an Issue of 'Vital Constitutional Importance'? Principles Which Guide the Reconsideration of Constitutional Decisions in the High Court of Australia" (1999) 2 *Constitutional Law and Policy Review* 13.

Lindell, G, "The Justiciability of Political Questions: Recent Developments" in Lee, HP, and Winterton, G (eds), *Australian Constitutional Perspectives* (Law Book Co, 1992), 180.

Lindell, G, "The Murphy Affair in Retrospect" in Lee, HP, and Winterton, G (eds), *Australian Constitutional Landmarks* (Cambridge University Press, 2003), 280.

Lynch, A, "Dissent: The Rewards and Risks of Judicial Disagreement in the High Court of Australia" (2003) 27 *Melbourne University Law Review* 724.

Lynch, A, "The Gleeson Court on Constitutional Law: An Empirical Analysis of its First Five Years" (2003) 26 *University of New South Wales Law Journal* 32.

Mason, A, "The Regulation of Appeals to the High Court of Australia: The Jurisdiction to Grant Special Leave to Appeal" (1996) 15 *University of Tasmania Law Review* 1.

Mason, A, "The Use and Abuse of Precedent" (1988) 4 *Australian Bar Review* 93.

Mason, K, "Prospective Overruling" (1989) 63 *Australian Law Journal* 526.

Opeskin, B, and Wheeler, F (eds), *The Australian Federal Judicial System* (Melbourne University Press, 2000).

Palmer, A, and Sampford, C, "Judicial Retrospectivity in Australia" (1995) 4 *Griffith Law Review* 170.

Patapan, H, *Judging Democracy: The New Politics of the High Court of Australia* (Cambridge University Press, 2000).

Stephen, N, "Judicial Independence – A Fragile Bastion" (1982) 13 *Melbourne University Law Review* 334.

Thomson, JA, "Appointing Australian High Court Justices: Some Constitutional Conundrums" in Lee, HP, and Winterton, G (eds), *Australian Constitutional Perspectives* (Law Book Co, 1992), 251.

Williams, J, "Re-thinking Advisory Opinions" (1996) 7 *Public Law Review* 205.

Williams, G, "The Amicus Curiae and Intervener in the High Court of Australia: A Comparative Analysis" (2000) 28 *Federal Law Review* 365

Winterton, G, "Appointment of Federal Judges in Australia" (1987) 16 *Melbourne University Law Review* 185.

Zines, L, *Cowen and Zines's Federal Jurisdiction in Australia* (Federation Press, 3rd ed 2002).

Chapter 14

The Separation of Judicial Power

1. The Separation of Federal Judicial Power

The differentiation between the three main functions of government – legislative, judicial and executive – and the separation of powers between them, is dealt with in Chapter 1, §4. As early as *New South Wales v Commonwealth (Wheat Case)* (1915) 20 CLR 54, the High Court decided that the strict insulation of judicial power was a fundamental principle of the Constitution. Under s 101 of the Constitution, "the execution and maintenance ... of the provisions of this Constitution relating to trade and commerce, and of all laws made thereunder", is entrusted to an Inter-State Commission ("There shall be an Inter-State Commission ..."). But in fact the Commission did not come into being until the passage of the *Inter-State Commission Act 1912* (Cth). Three years later in the *Wheat Case* the High Court held by 4:2 (with Barton and Gavan Duffy JJ dissenting) that the Act was invalid because it purported to invest the Commission with "judicial power". This was so even though s 101 of the Constitution proclaims that the Commission is to have "such *powers of adjudication* and administration as the Parliament deems necessary" (emphasis added).

New South Wales v Commonwealth (Wheat Case)
(1915) 20 CLR 54

Isaacs J: [88] By the first Chapter the legislative power of the Commonwealth is vested in a Parliament, consisting of the Sovereign and two Houses, and for this purpose the Governor-General is the Royal representative. By Chapter II, headed "The Executive Govern-[89]-ment," the executive power of the Commonwealth is vested in the Sovereign simply, the Governor-General again being the representative. There might be some ambiguity as to what is meant by executive power, arising from the fact that sometimes in relation to the British Constitution the Judiciary are classed among the executive officers of the Crown ... And in one sense Judges do execute laws. They execute laws relating to the Judiciary, by performing their judicial functions. But, in the contrasted sense, executive powers are distinct from judicial powers.

And in order to avoid misapprehension as to what is meant by the executive power of the Commonwealth, to be vested in the Sovereign as "the Executive Government" it is specifically defined as the one which "extends to the execution and maintenance of this Constitution, and of the laws of the Commonwealth." The phraseology is important to remember.

This language accords with *Blackstone*, vol I, p 270, who observes that "though the making of laws is entirely the work of a distinct part, the legislative branch, of the sovereign power, yet the manner, time, and circumstances of putting those laws in execution must frequently be left to the discretion of the executive magistrate."

Chapter II, taken alone, left, as a matter of law, the means and method of executing and maintaining the laws entirely to the Sovereign's discretion, and tacitly subjected the exercise of the power only to the conventions of responsible government.

Chapter III is headed "the Judicature," and vests the judicial power of the Commonwealth not in the Sovereign simply, or as he may in Parliament direct, but in specific organs, namely, Courts strictly so called. They are the High Court, such other federal Courts as Parliament creates, and such other Courts as it invests with federal jurisdiction. There is a mandate to create a High Court; there is a discretionary power to create other federal Courts; and there is a discretionary power to invest with federal jurisdiction such Courts as Parliament finds already in existence, that is, State Courts. But that exhausts the judicature. And as to federal Courts, the Justices are to have a specific tenure. And the distinct [90] command of the Constitution is that whatever judicial power – that is, in the contrasted sense – is to be exerted in the name of the Commonwealth, must be exercised by these strictly so called judicial tribunals ...

[T]he mandate is to create an Inter-State Commission. That *primâ facie* is not language implying a Court of Justice, but rather implying an executive body. Of course, a Parliament of [91] plenary power may do as it pleases, but this section is a direction to the Parliament, and intended to bind the Parliament to follow that direction. The *raison d'être* of the Commission is manifestly "the execution and maintenance, within the Commonwealth, of the provisions of this Constitution relating to trade and commerce, and of all laws made thereunder." Those words are practically a repetition of the phraseology of sec 61, the introductory executive section. The Commission, in short, is to be a department under the Crown to assist in executing and maintaining trade and commercial law in Australia.

The mandate arises as a necessity from the provisions of sec 102. It is common knowledge that, at the time the Constitution was framed, railway rates in some adjacent colonies were of a fiercely competitive nature, "cut-throat rates" was what they were termed, and were not only productive of loss, and artificial diversion of trade and commerce, but also of irritation.

Sec 102 enabled Parliament to correct this, but between the parliamentary majority for the moment and the State railway systems, there was interposed by the final clause of the section the opinion of a body free from political control, and having the function of "adjudging" whether any given preference or discrimination was undue and unreasonable or unjust to any State complaining of it ... The adjudication contemplated by sec 102 is not that of a Court. It is rather discretion or judgment in sense of the well-considered statesmanlike opinion, and is not measurable by any legal standard. It resembles an authoritative report, which the Constitution makes a condition precedent to parliamentary action.

But when making the adjudication of the Commission a *sine quâ non* of rate correction, a mandate to create the Commission was essential and was given. Obviously I should say the Commission so far was not a Court, but a great, perhaps a unique government Expert Department, dealing with Inter-State trade and commerce in railways ...

[92] This would make it in no respect different in inherent character from the American Inter-State Commission, which is recognized even with its most recent extended powers as an administrative body only ...

Thus the Constitution provided for the possible establishment of a novel administrative and consultative organ with incidental quasi-judicial functions, very much as a Commissioner of Patents has to exercise quasi-judicial functions before exercising the executive act of issuing a patent, or a Collector of Customs has sometimes in a quasi-judicial way to examine and come to a conclusion on the dutiability of goods, and the conclusion is sometimes made a binding one. The usefulness of the Commission was not necessarily to stop at sec 102. It might be seen that the commerce provisions of the Constitution or the Commonwealth laws would be greatly aided if the same body were to have its authority extended, and the ordinary administrative departments might be materially assisted by such an extension.

That, in my opinion, is the true import of the power given to Parliament in sec 101. The extension would in no respect alter the character of the Commission, or convert it from an executive to a judicial branch. The dominant words in section 101 are "the [93] execution and maintenance of the provisions of the Constitution relating to trade and commerce, and of all laws made thereunder." Those words denote the purpose and nature of the power to be conferred, and mark their limit. Courts do not execute or maintain laws relating to trade and commerce. Those words imply a duty to actively watch the observance of those laws, to insist on obedience to their mandates, and to take steps to vindicate them if need be. But a Court has no such active duty: its essential feature as an impartial tribunal would be gone, and the manifest aim and object of the constitutional separation of powers would be frustrated. A result so violently opposed to the fundamental structure and scheme of the Constitution requires, as I have before observed, extremely plain and unequivocal language.

Reading the section as I have read it, does no violence to any part of the instrument; on the contrary it harmonizes it. It gives the same effect to the words "execute and maintain the laws" in the three places where they, or like words, are found, viz, sec 51(VI), sec 61 and sec 101.

It also avoids serious consequences, hardly supposable as intended. For instance, the Commonwealth's argument either assumes the Commission to be a federal Court created by the Parliament within the meaning of sec 71, in which case the tenure of the members departs from sec 72, or it assumes it to be an additional Court, exercising true judicial power, though sec 71 is exhaustive in its terms.

Further, if it be the first class of Court, it may be authorized under the assumedly unlimited words of sec 101, combined with sec 77, to try criminal cases, and even ... to entertain appeals from all State Courts or any other federal Court except the High Court in relation to commerce litigation. Indeed, in reply to a question by the Court, learned counsel for the Commonwealth claimed that the Inter-State Commission could now validly try such a case as the *Vend Case* [(1911) 14 CLR 387], or Customs prosecutions. It would be rather remarkable to permit two laymen to overrule a lawyer in a criminal case ...

[94] On the other hand, if it be an excrescent Court of Justice, quite outside the Judicature Chapter of the Constitution, sec 80 would be inapplicable to it. This would lead to a most astounding result. Parliament by virtue of its alleged unlimited power under sec 101 could confer both criminal and civil jurisdiction on a body presumably in the main consisting of non-lawyers, and could enable it to try offences even on indictment without the security of sec 80 in relation to a jury. Not only so, even Parliament could not enable this Court to re-examine the facts in case of error, or the sentence, however severe, unless absolutely illegal.

On the whole I reject the notion of the Commission as a Court of Justice, and regard its quasi-judicial powers, where given, as incidental and assistant to its main and paramount purpose, as in the making of some executive order ...

The immediate result of the *Wheat Case* was that the Inter-State Commission was rendered powerless. The first Commissioners had been appointed in 1913. After their original seven-year terms expired in 1920 no fresh appointments were made, and in 1950 the *Inter-State Commission Act 1912* (Cth) was repealed. A new Act re-establishing the Commission was passed by the Whitlam government in 1975, but that government was dismissed before the Act could be proclaimed. The legislation was revived and amended by the Hawke government in 1983 and a new Inter-State Commission was appointed in 1984. However, in 1989, even though the tenure of its members is guaranteed by s 103 of the Constitution, the Inter-State Commission was again abolished (see Michael Coper, "The Second Coming of the Fourth Arm: The Role and Functions of the Inter-State Commission" (1989) 63 *Australian Law Journal* 731).

The reasoning in the *Wheat Case* was taken further in *Waterside Workers' Federation of Australia v JW Alexander Ltd* (1918) 25 CLR 434. The original conception of the Commonwealth Court of Conciliation and Arbitration established under s 51(xxxv) of the Constitution was that it should consist of only one judge, a "President", who should also double as a High Court judge. Accordingly, the *Commonwealth Conciliation and Arbitration Act 1904* (Cth) provided in s 11 that the Commonwealth Court of Conciliation and Arbitration "shall be a Court of Record, and shall consist of a President", while s 12(1) provided:

Commonwealth Conciliation and Arbitration Act 1904 (Cth)

12 (1) The President shall be appointed by the Governor-General from among the Justices of the High Court. He shall be entitled to hold office during good behaviour for seven years, and shall be eligible for re-appointment, and shall not be liable to removal except on addresses to the Governor-General from both Houses of the Parliament during one session ... praying for his removal on the ground of proved misbehaviour or incapacity.

The "removal" provisions in s 12(1) paralleled those in s 72 of the Constitution, but with a difference. The "removal" contemplated by s 12(1) of the Act was from a renewable seven-year term. As s 72 of the Constitution stood in 1917, it said nothing about any limited term of office. "Removal" was the *only* way in which a judge's term of office might come to an end except at the judge's initiative.

The first President appointed "from among the Justices of the High Court" was O'Connor J. In 1906 Higgins J was selected to replace him, but first requested a year in which to get established on the High Court. He began his first seven-year term as President in 1907 and a second term in 1914.

In 1918 the Waterside Workers' Federation alleged that an employer, JW Alexander Ltd, was in breach of an award. The employer responded by arguing that the Arbitration Court was invalidly constituted because the President's seven-year term was incompatible with s 72 of the Constitution. By 5:2, with Higgins and Gavan Duffy JJ dissenting, the High Court construed s 72, as it then stood, as impliedly requiring life tenure for federal judges. That aspect of *Alexander's Case* was later challenged in *Shell Co of Australia v Federal Commissioner of Taxation* [1931] AC 275, but the Privy Council did not decide the issue. Thereafter, the requirement of life tenure stood unchallenged until 1977, when s 72 was amended by referendum to provide for compulsory retirement at 70 years of age.

In *Alexander's Case*, the consequential issue was whether Higgins J, appointed to the Arbitration Court merely for a renewable seven-year term, could validly discharge: (1) its arbitral functions, including the making of awards; and (2) its judicial functions, including the enforcement of awards. By differently-constituted majorities, it was held that the arbitral functions were validly conferred, but that the judicial functions were not. This meant that in *Alexander's Case* itself the relevant award had validly been made by Higgins J as an arbitrator but could not validly be enforced by him as a judge. The decisive distinction between judicial and arbitral functions was drawn by Isaacs and Rich JJ.

Waterside Workers' Federation of Australia v JW Alexander Ltd
(1918) 25 CLR 434

Isaacs and Rich JJ: [462] Industrial disputes extending beyond the limits of any one State embrace so many possible divergencies ... that direct legislation in advance is incapable of being applied to them. No one can foresee for any appreciable period the legislative requirements of industrial peace in any one industry, much less in all industries of the Commonwealth which are common to more than one State ... Nevertheless, it was thought necessary that such disputes should not go uncontrolled but that the control **[463]** should be exercised only by means of conciliation and arbitration. That is essentially different from the judicial power. Both of them rest for their ultimate validity and efficacy on the legislative power. Both presuppose a dispute, and a hearing or investigation, and a decision. But the essential difference is that the judicial power is concerned with the ascertainment, declaration and enforcement of the rights and liabilities of the parties as they exist, or are deemed to exist, at the moment the proceedings are instituted; whereas the function of the arbitral power in relation to industrial disputes is to ascertain and declare, but not enforce, what in the opinion of the arbitrator ought to be the respective rights and liabilities of the parties in relation to each other ...

[464] [The arbitrator's award] stands precisely in the same position as a valid Act enacting the identical mutual rights and liabilities. They exist, and are expected to be observed. Their creation is not the ordinary work of a Court of law. In the New South Wales Report of the Commission on Strikes 1891 (p 34, par 28) it is said:– "It should be remembered that a Court of arbitration is not like an ordinary Court of law. There is no fixed code of law which it interprets, and its decision is only a declaratory statement as to what it thinks just and expedient." It will be noticed in that extract that a "Court of arbitration" as distinct from "Court of law" is spoken of as a well known tribunal ...

A Court of law has no power to give effect to any but rights recognized by law. In *Blackburn v Vigors* [(1887) 12 App Cas 531 at 543] Lord *Macnaghten* observed: "I apprehend that it is not the function of a Court of justice to enforce or give effect to moral obligations which do not carry with them legal or equitable rights." In the *Ruabon Steamship Co v London Assurance* [[1900] AC 6 at 9-10] Lord *Halsbury* LC said: "It seems to me a very formidable proposition indeed to say that any Court has a right to enforce what may seem to them to be just, apart from common law or Statute." So per Lord *Loreburn* LC in *Dewar v Goodman* [[1909] AC 72 at 76].

The two functions therefore are quite distinct. The arbitral function is ancillary to the legislative function, and provides the *factum* upon which the law operates to create the right or duty. The judicial function is an entirely separate branch, and first ascertains whether the alleged right or duty exists in law, and, if it binds it, then proceeds if necessary to enforce the law. Not only are they different powers, but they spring from different sources in the **[465]** Constitution. The arbitral power arises under sec 51(xxxv); the judicial power under sec 71. The latter section contains, in the words "such other Federal Courts as the Parliament creates," the implied grant of power to create Courts other than the High Court. There is no other grant of that power in the Constitution – except as to territories (sec 122). The two powers being distinct and separate in nature and origin, it follows that, when an award is once made, the dispute is settled and the arbitral function is at an end ... Enforcement by a Court is an entirely separate matter. It arises on breach or threatened breach. But that is the case with every right. A right of property or a contractual right may exist, and, if violated, the law provides for its enforcement. But breach is not presumed. It follows that enforcement is in its nature an entirely separate process from the creation of the right.

But it happens that in the Act both processes are provided for. And it is urged (1) that Parliament has made it a *sine quâ non* that the organ to arbitrate and to enforce shall be a Court of law; (2) that a Court of law can only be created provided the Justice has a life tenure under sec 72; (3) that Parliament by sec 12 of the Act openly violated sec 72 of the Constitution, and so enforcement is unlawful; (4) that Parliament has bound up arbitration and enforcement inseparably, and therefore the whole Act is futile. The mere statement of the chain of reasoning compels the admission that, on the basis contended for, Parliament must have deliberately set to work to destroy the fabric it professed to create. We are unable so to read the legislation.

It is a cardinal rule of construction that all documents are to be construed *ut res valeat magis quam pereat* ... More cogent is that rule when we are considering whether the work of Parliament representing the will of the whole people shall be undone. And still **[466]** more cogent is the rule when that work has been so acted on ... that many thousands of men and women are today pursuing their occupations on the faith of it, and industries all over the Commonwealth, whose progress was threatened, are carrying on in reliance on the awards of the Court the operations necessary for the service, the comfort and even the existence of the nation. So far from finding any ground for annihilating the Statute and everything that has been done under it, we think it plainly good as to the arbitral portion of it.

Powers J agreed. As to the validity of the arbitral procedure, only Barton J dissented. Higgins and Gavan Duffy JJ, who held that s 72 did not require life tenure, thought the Act was wholly valid. Griffith CJ did require life tenure and did not feel able to distinguish between judicial and arbitral functions, but pointed out that Higgins J did have life tenure in his capacity as a High Court judge, and could validly be "assigned" to additional duties for a shorter term.

Griffith CJ: [447] The language of sec 12 … demands careful examination. It says nothing in express terms about the tenure, *eo nomine*, of the President's office, but it provides that he shall be appointed "from among the Justices of the High Court," that is, that he shall be a person who already as a Justice of the High Court holds judicial office during good behaviour. Again, it is not expressed that he is to be appointed for any definite term, but that he shall "be entitled to hold office" for a period of seven years. The word "appoint," which in modern times is often used to designate an executive act by which an office, old or new, is conferred upon a person, is not in law confined to that meaning …

The word does not of itself import any particular duration or tenure of office. Whenever used, its meaning may, and indeed must, be controlled by the subject matter and the context. If the subject matter is an office in the ordinary service of the State the duration connoted is during pleasure. If it is a Federal judicial office the tenure connoted is during the life of the officer, subject **[448]** again to the context. Thus, in sec 72 of the Constitution the power to appoint is a power to appoint for life. In sec 103 the power to appoint is a power to appoint for seven years. In sec 12 of the Arbitration Act the word is used in a new and unusual context. The person to be appointed has already a life tenure of the qualifying office of Justice. No additional remuneration is conferred upon him, and there is nothing in the words used to suggest that any new or additional personal right or advantage is to be given him. On the contrary, the suggested words of limitation are words of additional privilege, and he is not bound, but "entitled," at his own will to discharge the duties of President for seven years …

I am therefore of opinion that the word "appointed" must in its actual context be read as meaning "assigned," and the provision must, in accordance with what I conceive to be the manifest intention of the Parliament, be construed as the imposition of a new judicial duty, although of imperfect obligation, upon a person who already holds a permanent judicial office under the Constitution …

I do not think that this Court can, consistently with its previous decisions or with common sense, dissect the Arbitration Act, and hold, contrary to the plain intention of Parliament, that the President, a single person, is validly appointed for some of its purposes and not appointed for the others. In my opinion, his appointment **[449]** if bad in part is bad altogether. To hold otherwise is to make, not to declare, the law, and to declare a very different law from that enacted by the Parliament.

Yet this was precisely what happened. The conferral of *arbitral* functions on the Arbitration Court was held valid by 6:1; the conferral of its *judicial* functions was held invalid by 4:3. Griffith CJ voted with Higgins and Gavan Duffy JJ to hold, in dissent, that the vesting of judicial power was valid; Isaacs, Rich and Powers JJ voted with Barton J to hold it invalid.

The immediate response to *Alexander's Case* was a legislative amendment transferring the enforcement of awards to Courts of Petty Sessions. However, in 1926 the Bruce-Page government embarked on a major reconstruction of the Conciliation and Arbitration Court. Its enforcement powers were restored, and, to overcome the problem of *Alexander's Case*, the reliance on seven-year terms was abandoned. The Court was reconstituted as staffed by "Judges" holding office for life, with a "Chief Judge" instead of a "President".

Of course, if the joint judgment of Isaacs and Rich JJ in *Alexander's Case* meant that arbitral and judicial functions must be kept strictly separate, the 1926 amendments did not solve the problem at all, but merely perpetuated (indeed reintroduced) the very problem that those judges had complained of. However, this continuing problem was overlooked for 30 years, until it finally became the basis for the decision in the *Boilermakers' Case* – reported in the High Court as *R v Kirby; Ex parte Boilermakers' Society of Australia* (1956) 94 CLR 254, and in the Privy Council as *Attorney-General (Commonwealth) v The Queen* [1957] AC 288.

In *Victorian Stevedoring & General Contracting Co Pty Ltd & Meakes v Dignan* (1931) 46 CLR 73 (see the extract in Chapter 12, §2(c)), Dixon J had suggested that, by virtue of the separation of powers, Parliament is restrained "**[98]** *both* from reposing any power essentially judicial in any other organ or body, *and* from reposing any other than that judicial power in such tribunals" (emphasis added). That dictum embodies two propositions:

1. That the judicial power of the Commonwealth cannot be vested in any tribunal other than a Ch III court (that is, one established or authorised by Ch III of the Constitution); and

2. That a Ch III court cannot be invested with anything other than judicial power (except for those ancillary powers that are strictly incidental to its functioning as a court).

The combined effect of these propositions is that judicial and non-judicial power cannot be mixed up in the same tribunal. This is what the *Boilermakers' Case* held. The possibility of such an argument had already been hinted at: for example, in *R v Foster; Ex parte Commonwealth Life (Amalgamated) Assurances Ltd* (1952) 85 CLR 138, Dixon, Fullagar and Kitto JJ had remarked: "[155] Whether and how far judicial and arbitral functions may be mixed up is another question, one which fortunately the Court has never been called upon to determine".

In the *Boilermakers' Case*, the Metal Trades Employers' Association sought to enforce a no-strike clause in an award. The Arbitration Court had made an order requiring the union to comply with the award, and a further order fining the union for contempt of court by reason of disobedience to the earlier order. In the High Court, the union obtained an order nisi from McTiernan J calling upon the judges of the Arbitration Court to show cause why a writ of prohibition should not issue, on the ground that the vesting of judicial power in a body also exercising non-judicial power was unconstitutional. By 4:3, with Williams, Webb and Taylor JJ dissenting, the order nisi was made absolute.

R v Kirby; Ex parte Boilermakers' Society of Australia (*Boilermakers' Case*)
(1956) 94 CLR 254

Dixon CJ, McTiernan, Fullagar and Kitto JJ: [267] In a federal form of government a part is necessarily assigned to the judicature which places it in a position unknown in a unitary system or under a flexible constitution where Parliament is supreme. A federal constitution must be rigid. The government it establishes must be one of defined powers; within those powers it must be paramount, but it must be incompetent to go beyond them. The conception of independent governments existing in the one area and exercising powers in different fields of action carefully defined [268] by law could not be carried into practical effect unless the ultimate responsibility of deciding upon the limits of the respective powers of the governments were placed in the federal judicature. The demarcation of the powers of the judicature, the constitution of the courts of which it consists and the maintenance of its distinct functions become therefore a consideration of equal importance to the States and the Commonwealth. While the constitutional sphere of the judicature of the States must be secured from encroachment, it cannot be left to the judicial power of the States to determine either the ambit of federal power or the extent of the residuary power of the States. The powers of the federal judicature must therefore be at once paramount and limited. The organs to which federal judicial power may be entrusted must be defined, the manner in which they may be constituted must be prescribed and the content of their jurisdiction ascertained. These very general considerations explain the provisions of Chap III of the Constitution which is entitled "The Judicature" and consists of ten sections. It begins with s 71 which says that the judicial power of the Commonwealth shall be vested in a Federal Supreme Court to be called the High Court of Australia and in such other courts as the Parliament creates or it invests with federal jurisdiction. There is not in s 51, as there is in the enumeration of legislative powers in Art I, s 8, of the American Constitution, an express power to constitute tribunals inferior to the Federal Supreme Court. No doubt it was thought unnecessary by the framers of the Australian Constitution who adopted so definitely the general pattern of Art III but in their variations and departures from its detailed provisions evidenced a discriminating appreciation of American experience. On the other hand, the autochthonous expedient of conferring federal jurisdiction on State courts required a specific legislative power and that is conferred by s 77(iii). What constitutes judicial power is not stated. But the subject matter of its exercise is defined with some particularity ...

[269] Had there been no Chap III in the Constitution it may be supposed that some at least of the legislative powers would have been construed as extending to the creation of courts with jurisdictions appropriate to the subject matter of the power. This could hardly have been otherwise

with the powers in respect of bankruptcy and insolvency (s 51(xvii)) and with respect to divorce and matrimonial causes (s 51(xxii)). The legislature would then have been under no limitations as to the tribunals to be set up or the tenure of the judicial officers by whom they might be constituted. But the existence in the Constitution of Chap III and the nature of the provisions it contains make it clear that no resort can be made to judicial power except under or in conformity with ss 71-80. An exercise of a legislative power may be such that "matters" fit for the judicial process may arise under the law that is made. In virtue of that character, that is to say because they are matters arising under a law of the Commonwealth, they belong to federal judicial power. But they can be dealt with in federal jurisdiction only as the result of a law made in the exercise of the power conferred on the Parliament by s 76(ii) or that provision considered with s 71 and s 77. Section 51(xxxix) extends to furnishing [270] courts with authorities incidental to the performance of the functions derived under or from Chap III and no doubt to dealing in other ways with matters incidental to the execution of the powers given by the Constitution to the federal judicature. But, except for this, when an exercise of legislative powers is directed to the judicial power of the Commonwealth it must operate through or in conformity with Chap III. For that reason it is beyond the competence of the Parliament to invest with any part of the judicial power any body or person except a court created pursuant to s 71 and constituted in accordance with s 72 or a court brought into existence by a State. It is a proposition which has been repeatedly affirmed and acted upon by this Court ... Indeed to study Chap III is to see at once that it is an exhaustive statement of the manner in which the judicial power of the Commonwealth is or may be vested. It is true that it is expressed in the affirmative but its very nature puts out of question the possibility that the legislature may be at liberty to turn away from Chap III to any other source of power when it makes a law giving judicial power exercisable within the Federal Commonwealth of Australia. No part of the judicial power can be conferred in virtue of any other authority or otherwise than in accordance with the provisions of Chap III ...

[271] There is, of course, a wide difference – and probably it is more than one of degree – between a denial on the one hand of the possibility of attaching judicial powers accompanied by the necessary curial and judicial character to a body whose principal purpose is non-judicial in order that it may better accomplish or effect that non-judicial purpose and, on the other hand, a denial of the possibility of adding to the judicial powers of a court set up as part of the national judicature some non-judicial powers that are not ancillary but are directed to a non-judicial purpose. But if the latter cannot be done clearly the former must be then completely out of the question.

A number of considerations exist which point very definitely to the conclusion that the Constitution does not allow the use of courts established by or under Chap III for the discharge of functions which are not in themselves part of the judicial power and are not [272] auxiliary or incidental thereto. First among them stands the very text of the Constitution. If attention is confined to Chap III it would be difficult to believe that the careful provisions for the creation of a federal judicature as the institution of government to exercise judicial power and the precise specification of the content or subject matter of that power were compatible with the exercise by that institution of other powers. The absurdity is manifest of supposing that the legislative powers conferred by s 51 or elsewhere enabled the Parliament to confer original jurisdiction not covered by ss 75 and 76 ... To one instructed only by a reading of Chap III and an understanding of the reasons inspiring the careful limitations which exist upon the judicial authority exercisable in the Federal Commonwealth of Australia by the federal judicature brought into existence for the purpose, it must seem entirely incongruous if nevertheless there may be conferred or imposed upon the same judicature authorities or responsibilities of a description wholly unconnected with judicial power. It would seem a matter of course to treat the affirmative provisions stating the character and judicial powers of the federal judicature as exhaustive. What reason could there be in treating it as an exhaustive statement, not of the powers, but only of the judicial power that may be exercised by the judicature? It hardly seems a reasonable hypothesis that in respect of the very kind of power that the judicature was designed to exercise its functions were carefully limited but as to the exercise of functions foreign to the character and purpose of the judicature it was meant to leave the matter at large. Unfortunately, as perhaps it has turned out to be, the joint judgment delivered in *In re Judiciary and Navigation Acts* [(1921) 29 CLR 257], by the majority of the Court, distinguished between the two conclusions ...

[274] With reference to the federal judicature, the true contrast in federal powers is not between judicial power lying within Chap III and judicial power lying outside Chap III. That is tenuous and unreal. It is between judicial power within Chap III and **[275]** other powers. To turn to the provisions of the Constitution dealing with those other powers surely must be to find confirmation for the view that no functions but judicial may be reposed in the judicature. If you knew nothing of the history of the separation of powers, if you made no comparison of the American instrument of government with ours, if you were unaware of the interpretation it had received before our Constitution was framed according to the same plan, you would still feel the strength of the logical inferences from Chaps I, II and III and the form and contents of ss 1, 61 and 71. It would be difficult to treat it as a mere draftsman's arrangement. Section 1 positively vests the legislative power of the Commonwealth in the Parliament of the Commonwealth. Then s 61, in exactly the same form, vests the executive power of the Commonwealth in the Crown. They are the counterparts of s 71 which in the same way vests the judicial power of the Commonwealth in this Court, the federal courts the Parliament may create and the State courts it may invest with federal jurisdiction. This cannot all be treated as meaningless and of no legal consequence.

Probably the most striking achievement of the framers of the Australian instrument of government was the successful combination of the British system of parliamentary government containing an executive responsible to the legislature with American federalism. This meant that the distinction was perceived between the essential federal conception of a legal distribution of governmental powers among the parts of the system and what was accidental to federalism, though essential to British political conceptions of our time, namely the structure or composition of the legislative and executive arms of government and their mutual relations. The fact that responsible government is the central feature of the Australian constitutional system makes it correct enough to say that we have not adopted the American theory of the separation of powers. For the American theory involves the Presidential and Congressional system in which the executive is independent of Congress and office in the former is inconsistent with membership of the latter. But that is a matter of the relation between the two organs of government and the political operation of the institution. It does not affect legal powers. It was open no doubt to the framers of the Commonwealth Constitution to decide that a distribution of powers between the executive and legislature could safely be dispensed with, once they rejected the system of the independence of the executive. But it is only too evident from the text of the Constitution that that was not their decision. In any case the separation of the **[276]** judicial powers from other powers is affected by different considerations. The position and constitution of the judicature could not be considered accidental to the institution of federalism: for upon the judicature rested the ultimate responsibility for the maintenance and enforcement of the boundaries within which governmental power might be exercised and upon that the whole system was constructed. This would be enough in itself, were there no other reasons, to account for the fact that the Australian Constitution was framed so as closely to correspond with its American model in the classical division of powers between the three organs of government, the legislature, the executive and the judicature. But, whether it was necessary or not, it could hardly be clearer on the face of the Constitution that it was done. The fundamental principle upon which federalism proceeds is the allocation of the powers of government. In the United States no doubts seem to have existed that the principle should be applied not only between the federal Government and the States but also among the organs of the national Government itself ...

[278] The judicial power, like all other constitutional powers, extends to every authority or capacity which is necessary or proper to render it effective. The judicial power of which s 71 speaks is not to be defined or limited in any narrow or pedantic manner. With respect to the matters comprised within ss 76, 77, 78 and 79, it rests with the Parliament to make laws affecting its content or exercise. Legislative powers too are involved in some of the provisions of ss 71, 72, 73 and 74. And it must not be forgotten that s 51(xxxix) expressly empowers the Parliament to make laws with respect to matters incidental to the execution of any power vested by the Constitution in the federal judicature. What belongs to the judicial power or is incidental or ancillary to it cannot be determined except by ascertaining if it has a sufficient relation to the principal or judicial function or purpose to which it may be thought to be accessory. On more than one occasion of late attempts have been made in judgments in this Court to make it clear that a function which, considered independently, might seem of its own nature to belong to another division of power, yet, in the place it takes in connection with the judicature, falls within the judicial power or what is incidental to it … There are not a few subjects which may be dealt with administratively or submitted to the judicial power without offending against any constitutional precept arising from Chap III. It may be too that the manner in which they have been traditionally treated or in which the legislature deals with them in the particular case will be decisive: see *Davison's Case* [(1954) 90 CLR 353] …

[289] Independently, therefore, of certain considerations which it will be necessary to discuss, it is difficult to see what escape there can be from the conclusion that the Arbitration Court, though under s 51(xxxv) of the Constitution there is legislative power to give it the description and many of the characteristics of a court, is established as an arbitral tribunal which cannot constitutionally combine with its dominant purpose and essential functions the exercise of any part of the strictly judicial power of the Commonwealth. The basal reason why such a combination is constitutionally inadmissible is that Chap III does not allow powers which are foreign to the judicial power to be attached to the courts created by or under that chapter for the exercise of the judicial power of the Commonwealth.

On appeal, the Privy Council affirmed the High Court decision.

Attorney-General (Commonwealth) v The Queen
[1957] AC 288

Lord Simonds (for their Lordships): [311] The problem can now be stated. Is it permissible under the Constitution of the Commonwealth of Australia for the Parliament to enact that upon one body of persons, call it tribunal or court, arbitral functions and judicial functions shall be together conferred? The problem can be solved only by an examination of the Constitution itself. The expression "arbitral functions" is here used to describe compendiously the functions exercisable by the Court other than its judicial functions …

That the Constitution is based upon a separation of the functions of government is clearly to be seen in its structure, which closely follows the model of the American Constitution. **[312]** By section 1, which is contained in Chapter I, "The Parliament," it is provided that the legislative power of the Commonwealth shall be vested in a Federal Parliament, and the following 59 sections deal broadly with its composition and powers … By section 61, which is the first section of Chapter II, "The Executive Government," it is provided that the executive power of the Commonwealth is vested in the Queen and is exercisable by the Governor-General as the Queen's representative and extends to the execution and maintenance of the Constitution and of the laws of the Commonwealth. The following nine sections of Chapter II deal with the exercise of executive power. By section 71, which is the first section of Chapter III, "The Judicature," it is provided that the judicial power of the Commonwealth shall be vested in a Federal Supreme Court to be called the High Court of Australia and in such other Federal Courts as the Parliament creates and in such other courts as it invests with federal jurisdiction. The following nine sections of Chapter III deal with the appointment of judges, their tenure of office and remuneration, the appellate jurisdiction of the High Court, appeals to the Queen in Council, the original and additional jurisdiction of the High Court, the power of the Parliament to define jurisdiction and certain other matters.

Such is the bare structure of the Constitution and it will be necessary to look more closely into some of its provisions. But enough has been said to suggest that in the absence of any contrary provision the principle of the separation of powers is embodied in the Constitution. Section 1, which vests legislative power in a Federal Parliament, at the same time negatives such power being vested in any other body. In the same way section 71 and the succeeding sections, while affirmatively prescribing in what courts the judicial power of the Commonwealth may be vested and the limits of their jurisdiction, negative[ ] the possibility of vesting such power in other courts or extending their jurisdiction beyond these limits. It is to Chapter III alone that the Parliament must have recourse if it wishes to legislate in regard to the judicial power. That Chapter is in its terms detailed and exhaustive, and their Lordships dissent from the contention **[313]** sometimes explicitly, sometimes implicitly, advanced that, inasmuch as there is no express prohibition of other legislation in this field, it is open to the Parliament to turn from Chapter III to some other source of power.

Yet this general proposition is subject to a qualification, and it is a qualification which powerfully supports the proposition. For in section 51, the final matters in respect of which the Parliament is empowered to make laws are found in placitum (xxxix) ... This placitum looks forward to the vesting of power in the Federal Judicature which is found in Chapter III: it assumes such vesting and empowers the Parliament to make laws in respect of matters incidental to the execution of such power. The conferment of such a limited power of legislation in section 51 makes it very clear that it is in Chapter III alone that a larger power is contained. There could not well be a clearer case for the application of the maxim "Expressio unius exclusio alterius."

The argument so far appears to lead irresistibly to the conclusion that it is only in Chapter III that legislative authority is to be found to vest the judicial power of the Commonwealth. If so, it is to the provisions of that Chapter that one must look to find authority for the vesting in a court powers and functions which are not judicial or to vest in a body of persons exercising non-judicial functions part of the judicial power of the Commonwealth. The problem is advisedly stated in this alternative form, because it appears to their Lordships (to use words familiar in connexion with another much debated section) that it would make a mockery of the Constitution to establish a body of persons for the exercise of non-judicial functions, to call that body a court and upon the footing that it is a court vest in it judicial power ... [314] The question, in whatever form it is stated, is whether and how far judicial and non-judicial power can be united in the same body. Their Lordships do not doubt that the decision of the High Court is right and that there is nothing in Chapter III, to which alone recourse can be had, which justifies such a union.

The judgment in the Privy Council was given on 19 March 1957, but amendments to the *Conciliation and Arbitration Act* (assented to on 30 June 1956) had already divided the former Court of Conciliation and Arbitration into a Conciliation and Arbitration *Commission*, and a Commonwealth Industrial *Court*. In subsequent restructuring, the strict demarcation between a judicial Court and a non-judicial Commission has been steadfastly maintained.

The effect of the *Boilermakers' Case* was that the Court of Conciliation and Arbitration had been invalidly constituted ever since its restructuring in 1926, 30 years earlier. Part III of the 1956 amending Act purported to preserve the validity of awards and orders during those 30 years. Presumably, on the analogy of *Alexander's Case*, the making of industrial awards had been valid, since under the 1926 legislation the Court was validly invested with its non-judicial arbitral powers. As to the Court's judicial orders for the period 1926-36, by s 49(2) of the 1956 Act they were "deemed to be orders of the [newly created] Commonwealth Industrial Court". The validity of these saving provisions has never been challenged.

In 1956 the *Boilermakers' Case* was a 4:3 decision, and in later decades the necessity for its rigid quarantining of judicial from non-judicial powers remained controversial. In 1974 the High Court seemed almost to be inviting an argument that the case should be overruled.

R v Joske; Ex parte Australian Building Construction Employees & Builders' Labourers' Federation
(1974) 130 CLR 87

Barwick CJ: [90] The principal conclusion of the *Boilermakers' Case* was unnecessary, in my opinion, for the effective working of the Australian Constitution or for the maintenance of the separation of the judicial power of the Commonwealth or for the protection of the independence of courts exercising that power. The decision leads to excessive subtlety and technicality in the operation of the Constitution without, in my opinion, any compensating benefit. But none the less and notwithstanding the unprofitable inconveniences it entails it may be proper that it should continue to be followed. On the other hand, it may be thought so unsuited to the working of the Constitution in the circumstances of the nation that there should now be a departure from some or all of its conclusions.

Mason J: [102] I agree also that a serious question arises as to the course which this Court should adopt in relation to the princip[al] conclusion reached in *R v Kirby; Ex parte Boilermakers' Society of Australia*. However, it is not a question which needs to be considered in order to resolve this case.

Two years later, in *R v Joske; Ex parte Shop Distributive & Allied Employees Association* (1976) 135 CLR 194, it looked as if the time for an overruling had arrived. In a challenge to the supervisory powers of the Commonwealth Industrial Court over the internal affairs of trade unions, it was argued that statutory provisions had sought to confer non-judicial power on the Industrial Court in contravention of the *Boilermakers' Case*. In reply the respondents argued that *Boilermakers* was wrongly decided. The case was originally argued before a Court of five judges. Once the *Boilermakers* issue emerged, it was adjourned to be re-argued before a Court of seven. However, the case was ultimately disposed of on the ground that the relevant sections did not, after all, confer non-judicial power. The *Boilermakers* issue did not need to be resolved.

A further challenge is now unlikely because, since the 1970s, the underlying rationale of the *Boilermakers* doctrine has shifted. In *Boilermakers*, an essential rationale was the need to insulate from political interference the special judicial responsibility for "the maintenance of the Constitution". Leslie Zines has suggested that this rationale applies peculiarly to the High Court, so that the position of other federal courts could be distinguished (*The High Court and the Constitution* (Butterworths, 4th ed 1997), 212-13). Zines concedes, however, that while such a distinction might be drawn on policy grounds, the textual and structural arguments that were relied on in the *Boilermakers' Case* admit no such distinction. And, in any event, there has been a shift in recent years towards a different rationale: one that treats the courts as the bulwarks or bastions of individual liberty, and thereby implies that their role in policing constitutional limits on government has as much to do with the protection of individual freedom as with the federal distribution of powers. Nowadays it is on this basis, rather than that of federalism, that the *Boilermakers* doctrine is most frequently upheld.

This wider rationale is reflected, for instance, in the assertion by Deane J in *Street v Queensland Bar Association* (1989) 168 CLR 461 that the Constitution "**[521]** contains a significant number of express or implied guarantees of rights and immunities", and that "[t]he most important of them is the guarantee that the citizen can be subjected to the exercise of Commonwealth judicial power only by the 'courts' designated by Ch III". The shift in emphasis was signalled by Jacobs J in *R v Quinn; Ex parte Consolidated Foods Corporation* (1977) 138 CLR 1, when the Court held that the power of the Registrar of Trade Marks to order the removal of a trade mark from the register did not involve judicial power.

R v Quinn; Ex parte Consolidated Foods Corporation
(1977) 138 CLR 1

Jacobs J: [11] The historical approach to the question whether a power is exclusively a judicial power is based upon the recognition that we have inherited and were intended by our Constitution to live under a system of law and government which has traditionally protected the rights of persons by ensuring that those rights are determined by a judiciary independent of the parliament and the executive. But the rights referred to in such an enunciation are the basic rights which traditionally, and therefore historically, are judged by that independent judiciary which is the bulwark of freedom. The governance of a trial for the determination of criminal guilt is the classic example ...

[12] The right to have a trade mark remain upon a register is not such a right as I have described.

2. The Separation of State Judicial Power

While there is a strong textual and structural basis for the separation of powers in the Commonwealth Constitution, the same is not true of the State constitutions. In both *Clyne v East* (1967) 68 SR(NSW) 385 and *Building Construction Employees and Builders' Labourers Federation of New South Wales v Minister for Industrial Relations* (1986) 7 NSWLR 372, it was held that the separation of powers is not constitutionally entrenched in the *Constitution Act 1902* (NSW). In the latter case, Kirby P stated that "[401] far from providing a constitutional protection, separation and entrenchment of the judiciary ..., the *Constitution Statute* and the *Constitution Act* both specifically contemplated that, in respect of New South Wales, power would be held by the legislature not just to impinge upon courts and the judicial function but even to abolish, alter or vary such courts".

The first edition of this book suggested (at 902) that in New South Wales a different result might now be possible as a result of the *Constitution (Entrenchment) Amendment Act 1992* (NSW), which was carried in a referendum held on 25 March 1995 and assented to on 2 May 1995. That Act amended s 7B of the *Constitution Act* to add to the provisions thereby "entrenched" (see Chapter 11, §3) the provisions for judicial independence and security of tenure contained in Pt 9 of the *Constitution Act* (as inserted by the *Constitution (Amendment) Act 1992* (NSW)). However, in *Kable v Director of Public Prosecutions (NSW)* (1996) 189 CLR 51, an argument to that effect failed. It failed in part on the technical ground that all of the material events in *Kable* had taken place before 2 May 1995 (when the new entrenchment provisions came into force). But it also failed on the more substantial ground that the protections of judicial independence now entrenched in the New South Wales Constitution were insufficient to furnish either the textual indicia of a strict constitutional insulation of judicial independence, or the long-established historical tradition of such insulation, which were found for the Commonwealth of Australia in the *Boilermakers' Case* and for Ceylon in *Liyanage v The Queen* [1967] 1 AC 259 (see §7 below).

Kable v Director of Public Prosecutions (NSW)
(1996) 189 CLR 51

Dawson J: [77] The appellant contended that the *Constitution Act* 1902 embodies a separation of powers whereby the judicial power of the State is separated from its legislative and executive powers ... However, there is nothing in the structure of the *Constitution Act* 1902 to support this contention ...

Whilst Pt 9 of that Act is headed "The Judiciary" nowhere does it provide that the judicial power of the State is vested in the judiciary. Section 53, which is contained in Pt 9, provides that no holder of judicial office may be removed from office save on an address of both Houses of Parliament seeking removal on the ground of proved misbehaviour or incapacity. There are additional provisions relating to the suspension of judicial office and the fixing or changing of retirement age. Section 56 provides that Pt 9 does not prevent abolition by legislation of a judicial office whether that be done directly or indirectly by the abolition of a court or part of a court.

While these provisions are concerned with the preservation of judicial independence, they cannot be seen as reposing the exercise of judicial power exclusively in the holders of judicial office. Nor can they be seen as precluding the exercise of non-judicial power by persons in their capacity as holders of judicial office. They clearly do not constitute an exhaustive statement of the manner in which the judicial power of the State is or may be vested. Had Pt 9 attempted such an exercise it would have cut across a long history of [78] the exercise of non-judicial power by the courts and the exercise of judicial power by bodies exercising non-judicial functions.

The *Constitution Act* 1902 may be contrasted with the provisions of the Commonwealth Constitution, in particular ss 1, 61 and 71. Those sections respectively vest the legislative power of the Commonwealth in the Parliament, the executive power in the Executive and the judicial power in the Judicature. Section 1 appears at the commencement of Ch I, which is headed "The Parliament". Section 61 appears at the commencement of Ch II which is headed "The Executive Government". Section 71 appears at the commencement of Ch III which is headed "The Judicature". In *R v Kirby; Ex parte Boilermakers' Society of Australia* [(1956) 94 CLR 254 at 275] this Court held that this pattern could not be treated as a "mere draftsman's arrangement" or as "meaningless and of no legal consequence". It is because the judicial power of the Commonwealth is vested by Ch III in those courts which it identifies and is dealt with nowhere else (save for s 51 (xxxix)) that this Court was compelled to conclude that no functions other than judicial functions may be reposed in the federal judicature and that no powers which are foreign to the judicial power may be attached to courts created by or under that chapter. Not only that, but it was recognised that the position and constitution of the federal judicature was bound up in the federal structure established by the Constitution, "for upon the judicature rested the ultimate responsibility for the maintenance and enforcement of the boundaries within which governmental power might be exercised" [94 CLR at 276].

The latter consideration has no application to the judicature of a State and the failure of the New South Wales Constitution to vest judicial power exclusively in the judicature must be fatal to any contention that the separation of that power from the other powers of government is a constitutional requirement. Even if it could be said that it was required, it might, in contrast to the requirement imposed by the Commonwealth Constitution, be disregarded by an Act of Parliament, for in that respect the New South Wales Constitution is "uncontrolled" [*McCawley v The King* [1920] AC 691 at 704]. It remains true, therefore, as was said by the New South Wales Court of Appeal in *Clyne v East* [(1967) 68 SR(NSW) 385], that the structure and provisions of the *Constitution Act* 1902 provide no ground for importing into it a principle of separation of powers.

[79] The appellant placed reliance upon the Privy Council decision of *Liyanage v R* [[1967] 1 AC 259] in which it was held that the Constitution of Ceylon contained a separation of powers notwithstanding that it was silent as to the vesting of judicial power. But the judicature in Ceylon was in existence before the Constitution and was operating under the Courts Ordinance which contained the jurisdiction and procedure of the courts established under the Charter of Justice in 1833. The Charter provided that "the entire administration of justice, civil and criminal therein, shall be vested exclusively in the courts erected and constituted by this Our Charter". There was, for this reason, so the Privy Council found, no need to make specific reference in the Constitution to the vesting of judicial power, but the organisation of that instrument was otherwise such as to manifest "an intention to secure in the judiciary a freedom from political, legislative and executive control". The Constitution's silence as to the vesting of judicial power was, the Privy Council said, "consistent with its remaining, where it had lain for more than a century, in the hands of the judicature". It was, it said [[1976] 1 AC at 287-8], "not consistent with any intention that henceforth it should pass to or be shared by, the executive or the legislature".

There is no such background to the New South Wales Constitution which inherited the United Kingdom model under which the extent to which a separation of powers was observed was conventional rather than compelled by any constitutional mandate. The New South Wales Court of Appeal was clearly correct in concluding in *Clyne v East* that, notwithstanding that the Supreme Court of New South Wales also owes its origin to a Charter of Justice, no basis could be found in the provisions of the *Constitution Act* 1902 for isolating judicial power from the other powers of government.

Brennan CJ, Toohey and McHugh JJ reached the same conclusion. However, since Toohey and McHugh JJ joined Gaudron and Gummow JJ in holding that the relevant legislation was invalid on a different ground, this rejection of the "separation of powers" point might be regarded, strictly speaking, as not necessary to the decision – especially since the argument also failed on the narrower ground that any effect of the entrenchment provisions was not retrospective. Nevertheless, there was a clear majority view that, despite the entrenchment of Pt 9, the *Constitution Act 1902* (NSW) does not effect a separation of powers.

3. Defining Judicial Power

One reason for the absence of direct challenges to the *Boilermakers* decision is that, in practice, it has frequently been circumvented. The definitions of what does and does not constitute "judicial power" are sufficiently imprecise to allow a significant measure of pragmatic flexibility. The classic definition of judicial power was given by Griffith CJ.

Huddart, Parker & Co Pty Ltd v Moorehead
(1909) 8 CLR 330

Griffith CJ: [357] I am of the opinion that the words "judicial power" as used in sec 71 of the Constitution mean the power which every sovereign authority must of necessity have to decide controversies between its subjects, or between itself and its subjects, whether the rights relate to life, liberty or property. The exercise of this power does not begin until some tribunal which has power to give a binding and authoritative decision (whether subject to appeal or not) is called upon to take action.

The imprecise nature of this definition, and indeed of other definitions, has meant that tribunals whose functions might seem to overlap with "judicial power" have nevertheless sometimes been regarded as validly constituted if the particular grant of power is appropriately tailored to the legislative purpose. A good example is the decision in 1970 that the functions of the Trade Practices Tribunal, as defined by the *Trade Practices Act 1965* (Cth), did not involve judicial power and were thus validly conferred. Part IV of the Act conferred upon the Tribunal powers to hear proceedings instituted by the Commissioner of Trade Practices and to make determinations and orders in respect of those proceedings. It was held, with Menzies J dissenting, that the Tribunal did not exercise judicial power.

R v Trade Practices Tribunal; Ex parte Tasmanian Breweries Pty Ltd
(1970) 123 CLR 361

Kitto J: [373] The question is whether the powers which Pt VI thus purports to confer are within the concept of the judicial power of the Commonwealth. Questions of this general description are often difficult to decide, for it has not been found possible to frame an exhaustive definition of judicial power. But this is not to say that the expression is meaningless. The uncertainties that are met with arise, generally if not always, from the fact that there is a "borderland in which judicial and administrative functions overlap" (*Labour Relations Board of Saskatchewan v John East Iron Works Ltd* [[1949] AC 134 at 148], so that for reasons depending upon general reasoning, analogy or history, some powers which may appropriately be treated as administrative when conferred on an administrative functionary may just as appropriately be seen in a judicial aspect and be validly conferred upon a federal court. The judgments in *R v Davison* [(1954) 90 CLR 353] provide illustrations of this.

But I do not think that any such difficulty confronts us here. There are no traditional concepts to be applied as there were in *R v Davison*, and two considerations, one negative and the other positive, appear to me ... to require the conclusion that the powers entrusted to the Tribunal are essentially non-judicial. The powers must, of course, be performed in a judicial manner, that is to say with judicial fairness and detachment, but the same is true of many administrative powers. Close examination of the relevant provisions of the Act shows, I think, that on the one hand no exercise of any of the Tribunal's powers is an adjudication (in the proper sense of the word), and that on **[374]** the other hand the result achieved by an exercise of any of the powers is a result foreign to the nature of judicial power.

In *Labour Relations Board of Saskatchewan v John East Iron Works Ltd* [[1949] AC at 149], Lord Simonds for the Privy Council said:

"It is a truism that the conception of the judicial function is inseparably bound up with the idea of a suit between parties, whether between Crown and subject or between subject and subject."

This is not to say that some powers may not be held to be judicial though no adjudication in a lis inter partes is involved, for there may be sufficient justification for such a conclusion in an analogy with an admittedly judicial function, or in the fact that the power is ancillary to a judicial function, or in some such consideration: see *R v Davison*. But in general the notion is there, even if in the background, of arbitrament upon a question as to whether a right or obligation in law exists ... Thus a judicial power involves, as a general rule, a decision settling for the future, as between defined persons or classes of persons, a question as to the existence of a right or obligation, so that an exercise of the power creates a new charter by reference to which that question is in future to be decided as between those persons or classes of persons. In other words, the process to be followed must generally be an inquiry concerning the law as it is and the facts as they are, followed by an application of the law as determined to the facts as determined; and the end to be reached must be an act which, so long as it stands, entitles and obliges the persons between whom it intervenes, to observance of the rights and obligations that the application of law to facts has shown to exist. It is right, I think, to conclude from the cases on the subject that a power which does not involve such a process **[375]** and lead to such an end needs to possess some special compelling feature if its inclusion in the category of judicial power is to be justified.

The characteristics and content of "judicial power" have not proved susceptible to precise definition. In *Tasmanian Breweries*, Windeyer J observed that "**[394]** the concept seems ... to defy, perhaps it were better to say transcend, purely abstract conceptual analysis". In *Chu Kheng Lim v Minister for Immigration, Local Government and Ethnic Affairs* (1992) 176 CLR 1, McHugh J noted that "**[67]** [t]he line between judicial power and executive power in particular is very blurred", and that classification of a power "frequently depends upon a value judgment ..., having regard to the circumstances which call for its exercise ... The application of analytical tests and descriptions does not always determine the correct classification. Historical practice plays an important, sometimes decisive, part". And in *R v Quinn; Ex parte Consolidated Foods Corporation* (1977) 138 CLR 1, Aickin J concluded that "**[15]** in substance all that the courts have been able to say towards a definition has been the formulation of negative propositions by which it has been said that no one of a list of factors is itself conclusive and perhaps the presence of all is not conclusive".

In short, while "judicial power" may have a number of indicia (for example, that it is exercised with judicial fairness and detachment), none of these indicia is by itself decisive. Whether a power can be said to be "judicial" depends upon the indicia found in the power being "weighed up" against those which are absent, or against other indicia to the contrary.

AR Blackshield, "The Law"
in *Power in Australia: Directions of Change*
(Centre for Continuing Education, Australian National University, 1981), 171

[185] "Judicial power" is *controlled* power, in the sense that its exercise must be based on authoritative legal materials; the rules, principles, conceptions and standards applied must be drawn from existing law. But this clear central conception becomes elusive and unhelpful as it shades over into either one of two opposite types of case.

On the one hand, it is sometimes argued that the application of ... "standards" – "equity and good conscience"; "good cause"; "oppressive, unreasonable or unjust"; "just and equitable"; "proper", "just and equitable", "necessary ... to do justice", "as the court thinks just" – lies beyond the scope of judicial power because, in applying such standards, the individual persons who compose the tribunal cannot proceed mechanically or even "objectively", but must necessarily bring into play their own subjective evaluations. Overwhelmingly, such arguments have failed. Yet in *R v Spicer; Ex parte Australian Builders' Labourers' Federation* [(1957) 100 CLR 277], standards such as "tyrannical", "oppressive", "unreasonable conditions", were rejected as "vague and general", giving "more the impression of an attempt to afford some guidance in the exercise of what one may call an industrial discretion than to provide a legal standard governing a judicial decision". More compatibly with the general course of decision, the *Tasmanian Breweries* case [(1970) 123 CLR 361] held that "contrary to the public interest" was also not a sufficiently justiciable standard. Windeyer J explained [at 399-400] that the phrase

> seems to me to embody considerations much further removed from traditional judicial concepts than those which the words "just and equitable" express when applied in a controversy between parties. The public interest is a concept which attracts indefinite considerations of policy that are more appropriate to law-making than to adjudication according to existing law. The Act directs the Tribunal as to matters it is to "take into account" ... The generality of

these matters prevents their providing objectively determinable criteria. In the result the jurisdiction of the Tribunal to make determinations and orders depending upon its view of where the public interest lies ... seems to be an exercise of a legislative or administrative function of government rather than of the judicial power.

On the other hand, it is sometimes argued that the formulation of legislative guidelines so tightly defined, or so automatic in their prescription of consequences, as to leave the court *no leeway for choice at all* in its application of the predetermined law, is also incompatible with the idea of "judicial power". In *Palling v Cornfield* [(1971) 123 CLR 52], for example, it was argued that Parliament could not validly reduce a court to a *mere* rubber stamp, by enabling a prosecutor to request a sentencing procedure which, on proof of certain elementary facts, must mandatorily be followed. This kind of **[186]** argument, too, has failed.

Nevertheless, both these extreme kinds of case clearly challenge the central conception of "judicial power" ... What appears to be meant by the insistence on the need to apply "existing law" is that the application of the authoritative legal materials must leave the judges *some* room for independent interpretive judgment, *but not too much*. The crucial question, "How much?", is not really approached ... [The insistence on "existing law" is] like *Hamlet* without the prince ... [It] sets the stage for the play of judicial power – provides the flats, backdrops and props – but tells us nothing about the drama which is played out on the stage. To choose a more workmanlike metaphor, the emphasis on "existing law" tells us something about the judge's indispensable tools of trade, but not about what he does with them.

The missing ingredient thus elided from the heart of "judicial power" is perhaps supplied, in two very different ways, by two judgments from other jurisdictions often quoted in the Australian decisions. The first is from Oliver Wendell Holmes:

A judicial inquiry investigates, declares and enforces liabilities as they stand on present or past facts and under laws *supposed* already to exist ... The nature of the final act determines the nature of the previous inquiry. As the judge is bound to declare the law he must know or discover the facts *that establish* the law [*Prentis v Atlantic Coast Line Co*, 211 US 210 at 226-7 (1908) (emphases added)].

What matters is not whether or not the ultimate decision is *in fact* a predetermined inference from existing rules of law, but whether the judge *believes*, and *acts as if*, the principles he applies are derived from the existing legal materials. If this seems a hazardously subjective criterion on which to base an explication of "judicial power", it is worth recalling how faithfully it parallels Max Weber's insistence on "subjective interpretation" – on the explication of "social action" in terms of the "subjective meaning" attached to it *by the actor himself* – as the key to sociological "understanding" ...

The other famous quotation is from Palles CB in *R v Local Government Board* [(1902) 2 IR 349 at 373 (emphases added)]:

I have always thought that to erect a tribunal into a "Court" or "jurisdiction", so as to make its determinations judicial, the essential element is that it should have power, *by its determination* within jurisdiction, to impose liability or affect rights. By this I mean that the liability is imposed, or the right affected *by the determination only*, and not by the fact determined, and so that the liability will exist, or the right will be affected, although the determination be wrong in law or in fact.

[187] The key to "judicial power" is neither in law nor in facts, but in the "determination" *by the judge* which is interposed between these. He went on to reiterate even more clearly what for him was the real significance of "judicial power": that a judge's decision within jurisdiction (and hence validly exercising "judicial power") will have binding force and effect for the parties *even if the underlying interpretation of the law or the facts is wrong*.

In the end all that can be said is that, in order to be "judicial", power must *somehow* be circumscribed and controlled, whether by the law or the facts (or by both). We cannot even think of this as an "objective" circumscription or control; what matters is that the judge is *subjectively* constrained by his intellectual duty to keep faith with the integrity of the law and the facts as he sees them. Even then, as judges become more self-conscious in their sensitivity to the indeterminacy of the authoritative legal materials, it is interesting to see the emphasis shifting from control by "the law", to control by the facts, as the key to judicial power. "Judicial power" is involved, however indeterminate the standards to be applied, because [per Walsh J in *Cominos v Cominos* (1972) 127 CLR 588 at 593-4]

> The court is not at liberty ... to act upon broad policy considerations, unrelated to the facts of the particular case ... It must decide what are the circumstances of the case. It must consider the question, what settlement, if any, for the benefit of all or any of the parties to the marriage and the children of the marriage, would be in those circumstances just and equitable ... In my opinion, the court when so acting is clearly engaged in the exercise of judicial power ...

Two other themes running through the cases should be noted in closing. One is that a court has a "duty" to act: whatever other discretions it may have, it typically lacks discretion both in the sense that it cannot embark on action of its own initiative but must wait until a claim is filed or an application is made, and in the sense that it *must* then determine the issues raised by that claim or application. The other is that judicial power must be exercised "with judicial fairness and detachment" [123 CLR at 373]; and this has several aspects.

One aspect, stressed by Jacobs J in *R v Quinn; Ex parte Consolidated Food Corporation* [138 CLR 1 at 11], is judicial independence ... A second aspect, already emerging from the preceding discussion, is that **[188]** the circumscribing "control" of attention to the facts and the law sets limits on the considerations which a court may take into account: "Irrelevant matters ... which have no rational connexion with the policy of the [legal materials] but would be expressive only of the personal predilections of the Court, cannot be allowed by it to play any part in its decision" [*Talga v MBC International Ltd* (1976) 133 CLR 622 at 634]. A third aspect is the nice distinction made in 1979 by Brennan J: even when personal predilections *do* enter into judgment, what sways each judge is not his view of the judgment *he* should deliver, but his view of the judgment *the court* should deliver. No doubt this is still his view: but it is a view in which professional and institutional values, and understanding of the authoritative legal materials, are both intertwined with and among the objects of personal evaluation.

4. Judicial Power and Non-Judicial Tribunals

One consequence of the *Boilermakers' Case* is that federal judicial power cannot be vested in a non-judicial body. The issue arises where a power conferred on an administrative, or quasi-judicial, tribunal appears to have attributes of both judicial and non-judicial power. Long before the *Boilermakers' Case*, in *British Imperial Oil Co v Federal Commissioner of Taxation* (1925) 35 CLR 422, Owen Dixon KC (with him Robert Menzies) had convinced the High Court that a Board of Appeal established under the *Income Tax Assessment Act 1922* (Cth) could not have a taxpayer's "case" referred to it, since this would involve judicial power. However, a year later the Court accepted the validity of amendments that replaced the "Board of Appeal" by a "Board of Review", and avoided some of the language that had caused difficulty in the earlier case.

Federal Commissioner of Taxation v Munro
(1926) 38 CLR 153

Isaacs J: [175] The difference in point of status and nature of function between the new Board of Review and the original Board of Appeal is the difference between daylight and dark. When Parliament has shown so unmistakably its resolve to steer clear of the judicial rocks plainly charted in the earlier case, it would be a serious matter to impute an intention which would wreck the legislation and confuse the finances. In the former legislation the Board of Appeal was linked up in character with the High Court and the Supreme Court of the State, and an appeal on law points was given to this Court in its appellate jurisdiction. That was an unmistakable and an inseparable indication that the Board of Appeal was intended by Parliament to exercise "judicial power." ... But there are many functions which are either inconsistent with strict judicial action, as the arbitral functions in *Alexander's Case* [(1918) 25 CLR 434], or are consistent with either strict judicial or executive action. If inconsistent with judicial action the question is at once answered. If consistent with either strictly judicial or executive action, the matter must be examined further. In a sense the function may [176] involve so-called judicial conduct in a wider sense than the dispensing of the King's justice as understood in the law. It may be merely the incidental or ancillary determination of circumstances as a *factum* for the operation of the legislative will. The dispensing of royal justice by means of the King's judicial power is in itself a primary function; the ascertainment or determination in a judicial manner of facts, whether controverted or not, for the purpose of carrying out executive functions in a just way is a secondary or incidental function attached to and taking its dominant character from the main purpose. The very same process may thus, in some instances, be either judicial or executive ... The whole relevant legislation must, in such a case, be looked to in order to pronounce upon the question as to which category the particular function belongs to. If, for instance, the Legislature could validly go on to give the tribunal jurisdiction to enforce the decision by execution, the function would be judicial, since the concept of judicial power includes enforcement. If, however, the Legislature could not validly add that jurisdiction, then, in the absence of other controlling expressions – as in the *British Imperial Oil Co's Case* [(1925) 35 CLR 422] – one would say the function assigned was not judicial ... [177] The character of the function often takes its colour largely from the primary character of the functionary, and depends also on how the decision is made binding and how enforced. Government could not be carried on without some administrative power of finally determining disputed facts ...

[178] The decisions of the Board of Review may very appropriately be designated, in Lord *Haldane's* words, "administrative awards", but they are by no means of the character of decisions of the Judicature of the Commonwealth ... I would say, speaking with considerable experience in each of the three departments of government, that, if a legislative provision of the present nature be forbidden, then a very vast and at present growing page of necessary constitutional means by which Parliament may in its discretion meet, and is at present accustomed to meet, the requirements of a progressive people, must, in my opinion, be considered as substantially obliterated ... The Constitution, it is true, has broadly and, to a certain extent, imperatively separated the three great branches of government, and has assigned to each, by its own authority, the appropriate organ. But the Constitution is for the advancement of representative government, and contains no word to alter the fundamental features of that institution ...

[180] It is always a serious and responsible duty to declare invalid, regardless of consequences, what the national Parliament, representing the whole people of Australia, has considered necessary or desirable for the public welfare. The Court charged with the guardianship of the fundamental law of the Constitution may find that duty inescapable. Approaching the challenged legislation with a mind judicially clear of any doubt as to its propriety or expediency – as we must, in order that we may not ourselves transgress the Constitution or obscure the issue before us – the question is: Has Parliament, on the true construction of the enactment, misunderstood and gone beyond its constitutional powers? It is a received canon of judicial construction to apply in cases of this kind with more than ordinary anxiety the maxim *Ut res magis valeat quam pereat*. Nullification of enactments and confusion of public business are not lightly to be introduced. Unless, therefore, it becomes clear beyond reasonable doubt that the legislation in question transgresses the limits laid down by the organic law of the Constitution, it must be allowed to stand as the true expression of the national will.

On appeal the Privy Council upheld this decision, specifically adopting the reasoning of Isaacs J (*Shell Co of Australia Ltd v Federal Commissioner of Taxation* [1931] AC 275).

Nonetheless, there are limits to the extent to which "overlap" of administrative and judicial functions will be tolerated. A sharp reminder of those limits was given in *Brandy v Human Rights and Equal Opportunity Commission* (1995) 183 CLR 245, where amendments in 1992 and 1993 to the *Racial Discrimination Act 1975* (Cth) were unanimously held to be invalid.

Before the 1992 amendments the Human Rights and Equal Opportunity Commission was empowered to make "determinations" in response to complaints of racial discrimination, and the respondents to such determinations might voluntarily choose to comply. However, in the absence of voluntary compliance a successful complainant had no direct means of *enforcing* the Commission's determination. Instead, a complainant had to make a fresh application to the Federal Court, which, after a complete rehearing, could make such orders as it thought fit. In *Maynard v Neilson* [1988] EOC ¶92-226, Wilcox J criticised that procedure as a costly and unnecessary duplication. The 1992 amendments were drafted in response to that criticism. As introduced primarily by the *Sex Discrimination and other Legislation Amendment Act 1992* (Cth) (and further modified by the *Law and Justice Legislation Amendment Act 1993* (Cth)), a new s 25ZAA required, with certain exceptions, that determinations by the Commission be registered in the Federal Court. Thereupon, by s 25ZAB, a determination was to have effect "as if it were an order made by the Federal Court" unless the respondent applied to that Court for review. In such a case, by s 25ZAC, the Court "may review all issues of fact and law" and "make such orders as it thinks fit", but "new evidence" could not be adduced except by leave of the Court. No change was made to s 25Z(2), which provided that a determination made by the Commission "is not binding or conclusive between any of the parties".

Both of the joint judgments in *Brandy's Case* made it clear that before the 1992 amendments, although the Commission's "determinations" had many of the hallmarks of judicial power, the fact that the determinations were not directly enforceable had been a saving factor. The power to make an *unenforceable* determination was not "judicial" and could thus be validly entrusted to an administrative body. However, both judgments also held that, by providing machinery for direct enforcement of the determinations, the 1992 amendments had removed the one factor which had rendered the determinations non-judicial.

Brandy v Human Rights and Equal Opportunity Commission
(1995) 183 CLR 245

Deane, Dawson, Gaudron and McHugh JJ: [267] Difficulty arises in attempting to formulate a comprehensive definition of judicial power not so much because it consists of a number of factors as because the combination is not always the same. It is hard to point to any essential or constant characteristic. Moreover, there are functions which, when performed by a court, constitute the exercise of judicial power but, when performed by some other body, do not. These difficulties were recognised by the Court in *Precision Data Holdings Ltd v Wills* [(1991) 173 CLR 167 at 188-9]:

> "The acknowledged difficulty, if not impossibility, of framing a definition of judicial power that is at once exclusive and exhaustive arises from the circumstance that many positive features which are essential to the exercise of the power are not by themselves conclusive of it. Thus, although the finding of facts and the making of value judgments, even the formation of an opinion as to the legal rights and obligations of parties, are common ingredients in the exercise of judicial power, they may also be elements in the exercise of administrative and legislative power."

One is tempted to say that, in the end, judicial power is the power exercised by courts and can only be defined by reference to what courts do and the way in which they do it, rather than by recourse to any other classification of functions. But that would be to place reliance upon the elements of history and policy which, whilst they are legitimate considerations, cannot be conclusive.

It is traditional to start with the definition advanced by Griffith CJ in *Huddart, Parker and Co Pty Ltd v Moorehead* [(1909) 8 CLR 330 at 357] in which he spoke of **[268]** the concept of judicial power in terms of the binding and authoritative decision of controversies between subjects or between subjects and the Crown made by a tribunal which is called upon to take action. However, it is not every binding and authoritative decision made in the determination of a dispute which constitutes the exercise of judicial power. A legislative or administrative decision may answer that description. Another important element which distinguishes a judicial decision is that it determines existing rights and duties and does so according to law. That is to say, it does so by the application of a pre-existing standard rather than by the formulation of policy or the exercise of an adminis-trative discretion. Thus Kitto J in *R v Gallagher; Ex parte Aberdare Collieries Pty Ltd* [(1963) 37 ALJR 40 at 43] said that judicial power consists of the "giving of decisions in the nature of adjudications upon disputes as to rights or obligations arising from the operation of the law upon past events or conduct". But again, as was pointed out in *Re Cram; Ex parte Newcastle Wallsend Coal Co Pty Ltd* [(1987) 163 CLR 140 at 149], the exercise of non-judicial functions, for example, arbitral powers, may also involve the determination of existing rights and obligations if only as the basis for prescribing future rights and obligations.

However, there is one aspect of judicial power which may serve to characterise a function as judicial when it is otherwise equivocal. That is the enforceability of decisions given in the exercise of judicial power. In *Waterside Workers' Federation of Australia v JW Alexander Ltd* [(1918) 25 CLR 434 at 451] Barton J said:

"It is important to observe that the judicial power includes with the decision and the pronouncement of judgment the power to carry that judgment into effect between the contending parties. Whether the power of enforcement is essential to be conferred or not, when it is conferred as part of the whole the judicial power is undeniably complete."

And in *Federal Commissioner of Taxation v Munro* [(1926) 38 CLR 153 at 176] Isaacs J pointed out that the concept of judicial power includes enforcement: the capacity to give a decision enforceable by execution. It was this characteristic of judicial power which was emphasised by Latham CJ in *Rola Co (Australia) Pty Ltd v Commonwealth* [(1944) 69 CLR 185 at 198-9]. He pointed to the fact that in *Huddart, Parker & Co Pty Ltd v Moorehead* Griffith CJ referred not only to the giving of a binding and authoritative decision as being indicative of the exercise of judicial power, but also spoke of such a decision being given by a tribunal "called upon to take action". Thus, Latham CJ pointed out [69 CLR at 199], where a **[269]** tribunal is able to give a binding and authoritative decision and is able to take action so as to enforce that decision, "all the attributes of judicial power are plainly present".

However, notwithstanding the reference by Griffith CJ to a tribunal "called upon to take action", it is not essential to the exercise of judicial power that the tribunal should be called upon to execute its own decision. As Dixon CJ and McTiernan J observed in *R v Davison* [90 CLR at 368], an order of a court of petty sessions for the payment of money is made in the exercise of judicial power, but the execution of such an order is by means of a warrant granted by a justice of the peace as an independent administrative act.

Turning to the present case, it is apparent that the Commission's functions point in many respects to the exercise of judicial power. It decides controversies between parties and does so by the determination of rights and duties based upon existing facts and the law as set out in Pt II of the *Racial Discrimination Act*. Indeed, the relevant function of the Commission is essentially to determine whether the provisions of ss 9 and 15, which prohibit certain kinds of racial discrimination, have been contravened. That is clearly indicative of the exercise of judicial power, for, as Starke J said in *Victorian Chamber of Manufactures v Commonwealth (Industrial Lighting Regulations)* [(1943) 67 CLR 413 at 422]:

"The Constitution remits to the judicial power of the Commonwealth the jurisdiction and authority to determine whether a subject has or has not contravened a law or regulation of the Commonwealth."

Moreover, the remedies which the Commission may award include damages as well as declaratory or injunctive relief and, according to whether they may be viewed as punitive or otherwise, make its functions closely analogous to those of a court in deciding criminal or civil cases. And as Isaacs J remarked in *Federal Commissioner of Taxation v Munro* [38 CLR at 175] the punishment of crime or the trial of actions for breach of contract or for civil wrongs is "appropriate *exclusively* to judicial action".

However, if it were not for the provisions providing for the registration and enforcement of the Commission's determinations, it would be plain that the Commission does not exercise judicial power. That is because, under s 25Z(2), its determination would not be binding or conclusive between any of the parties and would be unenforceable. That situation is, we think, reversed by the registration provisions.

[270] Under s 25ZAA registration of a determination is compulsory and under s 25ZAB the automatic effect of registration is, subject to review, to make the determination binding upon the parties and enforceable as an order of the Federal Court. Nothing that the Federal Court does gives a determination the effect of an order. That is done by the legislation operating upon registration. The result is that a determination of the Commission is enforceable by execution under s 53 of the *Federal Court Act*. It is the determination of the Commission which is enforceable and it is not significant that the mechanism for enforcement is provided by the Federal Court. The situation stands in contrast to the situation which was superseded by the 1992 amendments to the *Racial Discrimination Act*. Under the earlier provisions, the Federal Court had to be satisfied of a breach of the Act before making an order for itself.

The Commonwealth, intervening, submitted that by virtue of the review procedure provided by s 25ZAC the registration of a determination is the commencement of proceedings in the Federal Court so that if a determination becomes enforceable it is by reason of the adjudication of the Federal Court, that being a court constituted in accordance with Ch III of the Constitution and capable of exercising judicial power.

The plain answer to that submission is that a registered determination may not be subjected to review but has effect as an order of the Court from the moment of registration. True it is that it cannot be enforced pending the institution or completion of a review, but it remains an order of the Court. The right to review is exercisable only by a respondent to a determination. If he or she fails to apply for review within twenty-eight days, the determination becomes enforceable forthwith. The Commonwealth sought to counter this answer by submitting that the procedure is analogous to the entry of judgment by default, but the analogy cannot be sustained.

A judgment entered by default is nonetheless a judgment of the court whose rules provide for such a course. The circumstances in which judgment may be entered are prescribed by the court itself and the process is one which is commenced and brought to a conclusion in accordance with those rules. The circumstances in which a determination may be made by the Commission are prescribed by the Act and, except upon a review, the Federal Court is precluded from any consideration of those circumstances either upon the registration of a determination or in relation to its enforcement. The determination remains the determination of the Commission and in no sense becomes the determination of the Federal Court.

If the registration of a determination of the Commission cannot be seen as the commencement of proceedings in the original jurisdiction of the Federal Court, then the existence of the review procedure does **[271]** not bear upon the question whether the determination was made in the exercise of judicial power. That is obvious in the case of a determination for which no review is sought, but it is equally the case where a review is sought. The existence or exercise of a right of appeal from a decision made in the exercise of judicial power does not convert that decision into one of an administrative kind.

The way in which the Commonwealth sought to use the review procedure was to say that its comprehensive nature was such as to indicate that the jurisdiction of the Federal Court was original and not by way of appeal. Because a determination might be registered and enforced without recourse to review, that argument cannot succeed in any event, but the review procedure, despite its name, does not indicate a proceeding in the original jurisdiction of the Federal Court. The court "may" review all issues of law and fact but is not required to do so. It would be unlikely to do so in the absence of some specified ground for disturbing the Commission's determination. Moreover, upon a review a party cannot adduce new evidence without the leave of the Court. Whether "new evidence" is the same as fresh evidence is not clear, but its exclusion points to a proceeding by way of appeal – an appeal by rehearing and not de novo – rather than a proceeding in the original jurisdiction of the Court. Thus the review procedure provided does not support the suggestion that the registration of a determination of the Commission is the commencement of a fresh proceeding in the Federal Court.

Mason CJ, Brennan and Toohey JJ reached the same result, holding that "**[264]** so much of the Act as provides for the registration and enforcement of a determination is invalid".

Brandy limited the capacity of the federal Parliament to establish non-judicial tribunals with effective powers of dispute resolution. The decision stopped the proliferation of non-judicial bodies and was a factor in the creation of a Federal Magistrates Court. This effect of *Brandy* is arguably at odds with the economic and social imperative for the informal, speedy and cost-effective resolution of some disputes. On the other hand, to allow the functions of a court to be vested in tribunals may undermine a person's right to a fair hearing by a properly constituted judicial body.

Brandy also cast doubt on the validity of other existing tribunals. In *Fourmile v Selpam Pty Ltd* (1998) 152 ALR 294 and *Wilkinson v Clerical Administrative and Related Employees*

Superannuation Pty Ltd (1998) 152 ALR 332, the Federal Court struck down the enforcement powers of the National Native Title Tribunal and the Superannuation Complaints Tribunal, respectively. In the High Court, however, the latter decision was unanimously reversed.

The Superannuation Complaints Tribunal was established by the *Superannuation (Resolution of Complaints) Act 1993* (Cth) to review decisions made by superannuation fund trustees. Section 14 allowed complaints to the Tribunal on the basis that a decision was "unfair or unreasonable", while s 37 provided that the Tribunal had "all the powers, obligations and discretions that are conferred on the trustee" and could vary a trustee's decision or substitute a new decision. The Tribunal's decisions were enforced by complementary legislation. Section 31(1) of the *Super-annuation Industry (Supervision) Act 1993* (Cth) stated that standards might be prescribed by regulation; and under s 34 trustees were required to ensure compliance with such standards or be guilty of an offence. By virtue of reg 13.17B of the *Superannuation Industry (Supervision) Regulations* (Cth), a standard applicable to the operation of a regulated superannuation fund was that "the trustee … must not fail, without lawful excuse, to comply with an order, direction or determination of the Superannuation Complaints Tribunal". A superannuation fund became a regulated superannuation fund, and thereby gained taxation and other benefits, if its trustee elected that the *Superannuation Industry (Supervision) Act* should apply in relation to the fund.

Attorney-General (Cth) v Breckler
(1999) 197 CLR 83

Gleeson CJ, Gaudron, McHugh, Gummow, Hayne and Callinan JJ: [110] [T]he question is whether the Complaints Act, in particular the provisions for the determination by the Tribunal of complaints against trustees of regulated superannuation funds, brings about a conclusive determination as to the existing rights and entitlements of members, either inter se or against the trustee or both, and as to the existing duties and responsibilities of the trustee. Does a determination by the Tribunal of a complaint offend Ch III because it creates, to adapt what was said by Kitto J in *R v Trade Practices Tribunal; Ex parte Tasmanian Breweries Pty Ltd* [(1970) 123 CLR 361 at 374], in a passage frequently applied in this Court, a new charter by reference to which the existence of the rights or obligations of the parties to the complaint are to be decided between those persons or classes of persons? Is the existence of the determination something which "entitles and obliges" the parties to observance of the deemed decision of the trustee?

In *Brandy v Human Rights and Equal Opportunity Commission* [(1995) 183 CLR 245], the mere registration in the Federal Court of the determination by the Commission gave it the effect of an order of that Court. Registration, an administrative act, converted a non-binding administrative determination into a determination of the character identified by Kitto J, namely a binding, authoritative and curially enforceable determination. It followed that the legislation which so provided contravened Ch III.

The present case does not fall under that proscription for several reasons. The first is founded in the terms of the trust deed constituting the Plan. The evident purpose as well as the effect of the variations of the trust deed … were to change the terms themselves of the charter by reference to which the rights and obligations of the trustees and the members of the Plan were, as a matter of private law, to be determined and decided. The trustees became expressly obliged by cl 1.2 to observe the requirements which have their source in the Supervision Act and the Supervision Regulations. These included obligations to observe determinations by the Tribunal under the Complaints Act (reg 13.17B). Thus, the **[111]** determination by the Tribunal involved not the exercise of the sovereign power referred to by Griffith CJ in *Huddart, Parker & Co Pty Ltd v Moorehead* [(1909) 8 CLR 330] but the arbitration of a dispute using procedures and criteria adopted by the constituent trust instrument, the existing charter, for the resolution of certain disputes arising thereunder.

Secondly, even without a provision in the trust deed such as cl 1.2, the situation would bear a similar character. The application of the provisions of the Complaints Act was possible only because the Plan had the status of a regulated superannuation fund. The attainment of that status was the product of the exercise of an election provided to the trustees by the Supervision Act. Given the importance of attracting the operation of Pt IX of the Income Tax Act, cases may readily be imagined where it would be a breach of trust not to exercise the election so as to obtain the revenue benefits which follow, albeit at the concomitant price of attracting the regulatory regime of which the Tribunal is a component. The availability of an election of this nature may be, and in the context of the present legislative scheme is, a decisive pointer in favour of validity.

Thirdly, the Complaints Act and the Supervision Act take the existence of a determination by the Tribunal as a criterion by reference to which legal norms are imposed and remedies provided for their enforcement ... A determination which "constitutes the factum by reference to which" [*Tasmanian Breweries* 123 CLR at 378] legislation operates to confer curially enforceable rights and liabilities does not necessarily involve the exercise of judicial power. The provisions we have discussed would involve what Mason CJ, Brennan and Toohey JJ identified in *Brandy v Human Rights and Equal Opportunity Commission* [183 CLR at 261] as "an independent exercise of judicial power" to give effect in this way to a determination by the Tribunal.

Reference also should be made to a consideration which, although not necessarily decisive, strengthens the case for validity which is otherwise made out. It is that the Complaints Act does not purport to give determinations of the Tribunal that conclusive character which **[112]** would prevent collateral challenge in proceedings to compel observance of those determinations. Section 37(3) of the Complaints Act obliges the Tribunal to make a determination in writing which affirms the decision of the trustee in question, remits it, varies it, or sets it aside by substituting the decision of the Tribunal for that of the trustee. Upon such variations or substitutions, s 41(3)(a) operates by specifying that the decision of the Tribunal is "for all purposes" to be taken to be a decision of the trustee. That proposition is qualified by the phrase "other than the making of a complaint about the decision" so as to avoid a situation whereby the machinery beginning with the operation of s 14 is again set in motion, this time in respect of the Tribunal's deemed decision. Conferral upon the determination of the Tribunal of the status of a decision of the trustee does not bring with it a preclusive effect which immunises the determination, and thus its status, from attack in properly constituted curial proceedings ...

The present situation may be contrasted to that in *R v Trade Practices Tribunal; Ex parte Tasmanian Breweries Pty Ltd.* Section 51 of the *Trade Practices Act* (Cth) considered in that case stipulated that the effect of a determination by the Trade Practices Tribunal that a restriction in an agreement was contrary to the public interest was that the agreement thereafter became "unenforceable" as regards the observance of the restriction. The validity of the determination was, s 102(1) provided, not to be "challenged, reviewed or called in question in any proceedings". However, s 102(2) provided that this did not limit the exercise of any jurisdiction of this Court to issue a writ of prohibition, mandamus or certiorari or an injunction. The validity of the legislation was upheld. In the present case, the avenues for collateral challenge are broader than in *Tasmanian Breweries*.

In *Luton v Lessels* (2002) 210 CLR 333, the High Court held by 6:0 that the functions of the Child Support Registrar (a position created by the *Child Support (Registration and Collection) Act 1988* (Cth)) did not involve judicial power. The registration of liability for child support under that Act did not do so because it was "**[357]** an entirely administrative act which requires the Registrar to decide whether the statutory criteria for registration are met". More importantly, the Registrar's power under the *Child Support (Assessment) Act 1989* (Cth) to assess the rate of child support payable by a particular parent (or to reduce or remit the assessment by a so-called "departure determination" where the existing determination would be "unjust and inequitable") did not involve judicial power because it did not "determine a question about the existence of any right or obligation", but merely provided "the **[358]** factum on which other provisions of the Assessment Act and the Registration and Collection Act operate, thereby creating new rights and new obligations which are to govern the future".

Luton v Lessels
(2002) 210 CLR 333

Gaudron and Hayne JJ: [360] Several points emerge from an examination of ... the Assessment Act. First, as mentioned at the outset, the Registrar's assessment, whether as an administrative assessment or as a departure determination, is the factum by reference to which the statute *creates* rights for the future which then are to be enforced by resort to the courts; the assessment does not adjudge existing rights. Secondly, the Registrar's assessment, again whether as an administrative assessment or as a departure determination, is not final. It is open to the processes of objection and then "appeal" to a court. Thirdly, so far as administrative assessments are concerned, the statutory processes are wholly administrative. So far as departure determinations are concerned, the Registrar may make such a determination, but need not if the issues are "too complex". If the Registrar does make a departure determination, the party dissatisfied can object and if still dissatisfied go to a court; if the Registrar does not make such a determination, again the party dissatisfied can object and then go to court. In either event the Court will decide the question afresh, without regard to what the Registrar has done.

Callinan J: [387] It is common ground that it is not always possible to define a power or function as being exclusively administrative or judicial. Powers may overlap, and some functions or powers may be conferred on either a court or an administrative body. It has also been said (in the context of a consideration of the power of a Registrar of Trademarks) that some functions "may, chameleon like, take their colour from their legislative surroundings or their recipient" [*R v Quinn; Ex parte Consolidated Foods Corporation* (1977) 138 CLR 1 at 18]. And as both *Harris* [*v Caladine* (1991) 172 CLR 84] and *Brandy v Human Rights and Equal Opportunity* **[388]** *Commission* [(1995) 183 CLR 245] decide, the availability and nature of a review by a court are relevant considerations.

I would prefer to state a test by reference to several questions, not all of which will be of equal importance in every case. First, is the exercise to be undertaken under the relevant scheme, one which calls for independence and tenure of a kind traditionally enjoyed by judges? Secondly, does the scheme require the making of findings on disputed facts, or as to the law to be applied? Thirdly, is the relevant decision made by reference to a formula or a fairly standard set of criteria? Fourthly, is the decision appealable? Fifthly, if it is, what is the nature of the appeal? Sixthly, is the decision likely, as a legal or as a practical matter to serve as a precedent for decisions in future similar instances? Seventhly, has the legislature expressed a view about the nature of the process involved? Eighthly, is the process to be followed of a kind that has traditionally been undertaken by courts? Ninthly, does the decision relate to pre-existing rights and obligations, or does it create new ones? Tenthly, is the decision enforceable by the maker of it or by the institution of which he or she is a member? And, last, is there any other feature of the process which is historically of an administrative or a non-judicial kind?

5. Exceptions to the *Boilermakers' Case*

The *Boilermakers' Case* firmly rejected any notion that the grants of power in s 51 – for example, para (xvii) as to bankruptcy, or para (xxii) as to divorce and matrimonial causes – could be construed as "**[269]** extending to the creation of courts with jurisdictions appropriate to the subject matter of the power". Nevertheless some anomalous sources of judicial power outside the framework of Ch III have been acknowledged. Thus, appeals to the High Court from Territory courts are commonly assumed to depend on an exercise of legislative power under s 122. (Territory courts are regarded neither as "federal courts" nor as exercising "federal jurisdiction".) The difficulty of reconciling such appeals with the *Boilermakers* assumption that Ch III is exhaustive and exclusive has attracted increasing comment in recent years, but without judicial resolution (see the cases in Chapter 6, §5).

Again, in *R v Richards; Ex parte Fitzpatrick and Browne* (1955) 92 CLR 157, the Commonwealth Parliament was treated as having an independent judicial power to punish for contempt of Parliament; and in *R v Bevan; Ex parte Elias and Gordon* (1942) 66 CLR 453, it was held that courts martial and other military tribunals were validly established under the defence power in s 51(vi). In *R v Cox; Ex parte Smith* (1945) 71 CLR 1, Dixon J explained that this was only "**[23]** an apparent exception" to the general rule, since such tribunals "do not form part of the judicial system administering the law of the land", and to give them jurisdiction even over civilians "would involve no infringement upon the judicial power of the Commonwealth". However, the position of military tribunals has since become increasingly controversial (see Chapter 18, §5). In *Re Woolley; Ex parte Applicants M276/2003 (by their next friend GS)* (2004) 210 ALR 369, McHugh J took the view that while the power of Parliament to punish for contempt "**[382]** is an exception that is more apparent than real", the judicial power of military tribunals is "a true exception that can be explained only on historical grounds".

Two other exceptions to the *Boilermakers* principle have assumed general importance. These are the assignment of judicial functions to administrative officers (by delegation under continuing judicial supervision) and the assignment of non-judicial functions to judges (as *personae designatae*, that is, in their personal capacity). In recent years this latter exception has in turn given rise to a further doctrine – an exception to the exception – forbidding the assignment to any judges exercising federal judicial power of functions "incompatible" with the exercise of federal judicial power. This "incompatibility" doctrine has now emerged as a separate limitation on the functions that may validly be assigned to judges, supplementing and perhaps even supplanting in some respects the "separation of powers" doctrine itself.

(a)   Delegation of Judicial Power

For many years, particularly in the bankruptcy and matrimonial jurisdictions, a vexed issue was whether "the judicial power of the Commonwealth" could be exercised by court registrars, masters or other senior administrative officers of the court. In *R v Davison* (1954) 90 CLR 353, it was held that the making of a sequestration order involved "judicial power" that could not validly be entrusted to a registrar or deputy registrar under the *Bankruptcy Act 1924* (Cth). In *Kotsis v Kotsis* (1970) 122 CLR 69, it was held that the federal jurisdiction conferred on the Supreme Court of New South Wales by the *Matrimonial Causes Act 1959* (Cth) could only be exercised by "the Court", so that a Deputy Registrar had no power to make an order for costs. The parallel case of *Knight v Knight* (1971) 122 CLR 114 took a similar view for a Master in the Supreme Court of South Australia. However, in *Commonwealth v Hospital Contribution Fund of Australia* (*HCF Case*) (1982) 150 CLR 49, those latter decisions were overruled. It was held that a Master of the Supreme Court of New South Wales could properly be seen as "**[59]** part of the organization through which the powers and jurisdiction of the court were exercised", in both federal and State jurisdiction. Consistently with that view, in 2005 the Masters of the Supreme Court of New South Wales were reconstituted as "Associate Judges".

The focus in all these cases was on State Supreme Courts in which federal jurisdiction is vested; but in the *HCF Case* Mason J suggested that a similar tolerance might be extended to masters or registrars in federal courts as well, "**[64]** provided that the exercise [of jurisdiction] is subject to review or appeal". Similarly, Murphy J said that, for federal courts as well, "**[66]** Parliament may authorize the exercise of its jurisdiction by officers or others who are not justices provided that these are under the real supervision and control of the justices of the court".

These suggestions as to the position in a federal court were taken up and developed in *Harris v Caladine* (1991) 172 CLR 84, where the High Court was asked to determine the validity of rules made under the *Family Law Act 1975* (Cth) that had delegated to Registrars of the Family Court of Australia the power to make certain orders. Mason CJ, Deane, Dawson, Gaudron and McHugh JJ held that the delegation was valid. Brennan and Toohey JJ dissented.

Mason CJ and Deane J analysed the reasoning in *Kotsis v Kotsis* as depending on the premise that a "court" is constituted solely by its judges, so that when the judicial power of the Commonwealth is vested in the "courts" referred to in s 71 of the Constitution, it is vested only in their judges. They added, however, that "**[91]** the ways in which a court may be organized or structured for the purpose of exercising its jurisdiction … admit of considerable variation". As Windeyer J had noted in *Kotsis v Kotsis*, the courts of record at common law had originally sat *en banc*, with the idea of a court being constituted by a single judge developing later. Against that background, said Mason CJ and Deane J, legislation in the Australian States providing "**[91]** that the Supreme Court shall consist not only of judges but also of masters" was "a further stage in the process of evolutionary development in the constitution of courts". The *HCF Case* had recognised that development as affecting the use of the word "court" in s 77(iii) of the Constitution, and a similar view should now be taken of its use in s 71.

Harris v Caladine
(1991) 172 CLR 84

Mason CJ and Deane J: [93] Now that it has been established by the *HCF Case* [(1982) 150 CLR 49] that some part of the federal jurisdiction of a State court may be exercised by a master or registrar in conformity with State legislation, it becomes difficult, if not impossible, to assert that s 71 vests the exercise of judicial power in the judges of the courts specified in the section. It makes little sense either as a matter of logic or policy to require that the power be exercised solely by federal judges to the exclusion of officers of a court when, in the case of invested federal jurisdiction, the power may be exercised by officers of State courts. More importantly, as a matter of construction, it is not permissible to read s 71 as speaking differently in its application to federal and State courts.

The difficulties which have invariably attended attempts to define judicial power in a comprehensive fashion and to identify those functions which constitute an exercise of the power and those that do not provide yet another reason for refusing to imply in s 71 a restriction limiting the exercise of all federal jurisdiction to judges. It was pointed out in *Queen Victoria Memorial Hospital v Thornton* [(1953) 87 CLR 144 at 151], that "[m]any functions perhaps may be committed to a court which are not themselves exclusively judicial, that is to say which considered independently might belong to an administrator." Subsequently, in *Davison* [(1954) 90 CLR 353 at 368], it came to be acknowledged that the exercise of judicial power included a range of functions which might be given to courts or administrators. If a particular function can be entrusted to an administrator, there is nothing inherent in the function itself which requires that it must be discharged by a judge when it is entrusted to a court ...

[94] The legislative power of Parliament to authorize the exercise by officers of the Family Court of part of its jurisdiction, powers and functions is subject to some limitation, as is the power of the Court to delegate some part of its jurisdiction, powers and functions, whether in the exercise of its rule-making power under s 123 of the *Family Law Act* 1975 (Cth) ("the Act") or in the exercise of its inherent jurisdiction. The limitation is that the legislative power and the power of delegation cannot be exercised in a manner that is inconsistent with the continued existence of the Family Court as a federal court constituted under Ch III. In other words, both the legislative power and the power of delegation must be exercised in conformity with the requirement that the Court's federal jurisdiction, powers and functions are to be exercised by a court whose members are judges appointed pursuant to s 72 of the Constitution. Because a federal court, in common with other courts, may be organized or structured in a variety of ways for the purpose of the exercise of its jurisdiction, it does not follow that all the jurisdiction, powers and functions of the Family Court must be exercised by a judge or judges of that Court. But the requirement does mean that the judges of the Court do effectively control and supervise the exercise of its jurisdiction, powers and functions by participating in the hearing and determination of cases and otherwise by having the capacity to review the decisions of officers of the Court and other persons to whom jurisdiction, powers and functions may be delegated ...

[95] It seems to us that, so long as two conditions are observed, the delegation of some part of the jurisdiction, powers and functions of the Family Court as a federal court to its officers is permissible ... The first condition is that the delegation must not be to an extent where it can no longer properly be said that, as a practical as well as a theoretical matter, the judges constitute the court. This means that the judges must continue to bear the major responsibility for the exercise of judicial power at least in relation to the more important aspects of contested matters. The second condition is that the delegation must not be inconsistent with the obligation of a court to act judicially and that the decisions of the officers of the court in the exercise of their delegated jurisdiction, powers and functions must be subject to review or appeal by a judge or judges of the court. For present purposes it is sufficient for us to say that, if the exercise of delegated jurisdiction, powers and functions by a court officer is subject to review or appeal by a judge or judges of the court on questions of both fact and law, we consider that the delegation will be valid. Certainly, if the review is by way of hearing de novo, the delegation will be valid. The importance of insisting on the existence of review by a judge or an appeal to a judge is that this procedure guarantees that a litigant may have recourse to a hearing and a determination by a judge.

McHugh J agreed, though in his view the essential condition was not merely that there be "review by a judge or an appeal to a judge", but that it be "**[164]** a hearing de novo ... [t]hat is to say, ... a complete rehearing of the facts and the law as they exist when the Justice or judge reviews the order made by the officer".

(b)   Persona Designata Rule

Building on earlier cases such as *Medical Board of Victoria v Meyer* (1937) 58 CLR 62, it has been held that although it is impermissible to supplement the judicial functions of a federal judge by adding non-judicial functions, a person who happens to be a federal judge may validly be appointed or assigned to perform non-judicial functions provided that the appointment or assignment is addressed to the individual person. Such functions may be conferred even if federal judicial tenure is the criterion by which that person was selected. The argument is well illustrated by the holding in the Federal Court that Davies J, of that Court, was validly appointed also as a Deputy President of the Administrative Appeals Tribunal.

Drake v Minister for Immigration & Ethnic Affairs
(1979) 46 FLR 409

Bowen CJ and Deane J: [413] The general argument that it was constitutionally impermissible for Davies J to be appointed a Deputy President of the Tribunal confuses the appointment of a person, who has the qualification of being a judge of a court created by the Parliament, to perform an administrative function with the purported investing of a court created under Ch III of the Constitution with functions which are properly administrative in their nature. Davies J's appointment as a presidential member was a personal appointment. Before he could be validly appointed as a presidential member, it was necessary that he hold one of a number of designated qualifications. It so happened that the qualification which he held was that he was a judge of this Court. The appointment was of him to the office of Deputy President of the Tribunal and not a conferring of functions or duties on the court of which he was already a member.

There is nothing in the Constitution which precludes a justice of the High Court or a judge of this or any other court created by the Parliament under Ch III of the Constitution from, in his personal capacity, being appointed to an office involving the performance of administrative or executive functions including functions which are quasi-judicial in their nature. Such an appointment does not involve any impermissible attempt to confer upon a Ch III court functions which are antithetical to the exercise of judicial power. Indeed, it does not involve the conferring of any functions at all on such a court. The attack on the validity of the appointment of Davies J ... must be rejected.

The first significant application of this doctrine in the High Court was the 3:2 decision in *Hilton v Wells* (1985) 157 CLR 57. The case arose from a Federal Police investigation into allegations of bribery and corruption in procuring the early release of prisoners from New South Wales prisons. The evidence of the alleged conspiracy was in part obtained by telephone tapping pursuant to warrants issued by judges of the Federal Court under s 20 of the *Telecommunications (Interception) Act 1979* (Cth), which authorised the issue of such warrants by "a Judge". By s 18, the word "Judge" was defined to mean "a Judge of the Federal Court of Australia" or of the Australian Capital Territory Supreme Court or (subject to arrangements) of the Supreme Court of a State or the Northern Territory. In a challenge to the admissibility of the phone-tapping evidence, it was argued that s 20 of the Act was unconstitutional. The challenge failed.

Hilton v Wells
(1985) 157 CLR 57

Gibbs CJ, Wilson and Dawson JJ: [67] The power conferred by s 20 is not ancillary or incidental to any judicial function. If s 20 confers power on the courts of which the judges to which it refers are members, it will therefore be invalid in so far as the court on which it confers the power is the Federal Court of Australia. It will be equally invalid in so far as it invests the Supreme Courts of the States with non-judicial power since s 77(iii) of the Constitution, which enables the Parliament to make laws investing any court of a State with federal jurisdiction, does not enable the Parliament to require the State courts to exercise non-judicial power: *Queen Victoria Memorial Hospital v Thornton* [(1953) 87 CLR 144] ...

[69] The question ... then is whether s 20 confers powers on (inter alia) the Federal Court, or on the judges individually as designated persons. It is a question which involves fine distinctions, which some may regard as unsatisfactory. Most of the authorities in which the question is discussed ... concern the question whether the decision of a judge who was a member of the Supreme Court of a State but who was exercising particular statutory functions was the decision of the Supreme Court within s 73 of the Constitution, so that an appeal lay to this Court. In the first case in which the question arose, *Holmes v Angwin* [(1906) 4 CLR 297], a statute of Western Australia provided that disputed elections were to be heard and determined by the "Supreme Court" to be constituted by a single judge. It was held that no appeal lay to the High Court from the decision of this tribunal, because it was not a decision of the Supreme Court within s 73 of the Constitution. Griffith CJ said [4 CLR at 306-7], that "the real tribunal is a new tribunal consisting of a Judge of the Supreme Court as a persona designata ...". ... [The Court was] influenced by the **[70]** nature of the power conferred, which was regarded [at 305] as "different from the kind of matters which the Supreme Courts of this and the other States were primarily constituted to deal with", and by the provisions of the statute which indicated that the applicable procedure, and the manner of enforcement of the decision, differed from those ordinarily applicable to the Supreme Court and which precluded an appeal to the Full Court of the Supreme Court. A similar conclusion was reached in *CA MacDonald Ltd v South Australian Railways Commissioner* [(1911) 12 CLR 221]. In that case a South Australian Act of 1847 provided that compensation for land compulsorily acquired was to be assessed by a jury presided over by a judge, commissioner or sheriff, but a later statute, of 1881, provided that either party might apply for an order for a trial of the question "in the Supreme Court", and that when a judge ordered a question of compensation to be tried "before the Court", the question should be stated in the form of an issue, that the verdict and judgment should be "under and subject to the control and jurisdiction of the Supreme Court as in ordinary actions therein" and that the rights of the parties should be the same as in the case of an ordinary action tried under the *Supreme Court Act* 1878 (SA). However, a judgment was not enforceable as a judgment of the Supreme Court and this circumstance was relied on by the members of this Court in reaching the conclusion that the jurisdiction was conferred upon the judge of the Supreme Court as a persona designata, and that his judgment was not a judgment of the Supreme Court ...

[72] It clearly appears from these authorities that where a power, judicial or non-judicial, is conferred by statute upon a court or a judge, it is not necessarily conferred on the court or the judge as such – the question is one of construction. Where the power is conferred on a court, there will ordinarily be a strong presumption that the court as such is intended. Where the power is conferred on a judge, rather than on a court, it will be a question whether the distinction was deliberate, and whether the reference to "judge" rather than to "court" indicates that the power was intended to be invested in the judge as an individual who, because he is a judge, possesses the necessary qualifications to exercise it. Even if it were to be assumed that the fact that the power conferred by s 20 is conferred on "a Judge" gives rise to a prima facie presumption that it is conferred on the judge as such, and that he will determine it as a **[73]** member of the court to which he belongs, we consider that there are sufficient indications in the statute to rebut that presumption. In the first place it is clear that if the judge is a member of the Supreme Court of a State, or of the Supreme Court of the Northern Territory, the power is not conferred on the Supreme Court of the State or Territory, but upon the judge as a designated person. Unless the Governor-General has made arrangements with the Governor of the State or the Administrator of the Northern Territory, no

677

judge of the Supreme Court of the State or Territory will be invested with power by s 20, and if those arrangements are made they will not necessarily be applicable to all of the judges of the Supreme Court of the State, and cannot be applicable to all the judges of the Supreme Court of the Northern Territory. Since when s 20 refers to "a Judge" it in some cases refers to a judge as a designated person, it is unlikely that the Parliament intended in other cases to refer to the judge as such and to confer power on the court. Secondly, the nature of the power conferred is of importance in deciding whether the judge on whom it is conferred is intended to exercise it in his capacity as a judge or as a designated person. If the power is judicial, it is likely that it is intended to be exercisable by the judge by virtue of that character; if it is purely administrative, and not incidental to the exercise of judicial power, it is likely that it is intended to be exercised by the judge as a designated person. Thirdly, none of the provisions of the *Federal Court of Australia Act 1976* (Cth), as amended, or of the rules thereunder is rendered applicable to the exercise of power under s 20. By s 19(1) of that Act the Federal Court has such original jurisdiction as is vested in it by laws made by the Parliament and s 20 of the *Telecommunications (Interception) Act* does not express an intention to invest the court with jurisdiction. Under s 20 the judge makes no order and nothing that he does is enforced under the *Federal Court of Australia Act*. He grants a warrant, the effect of which depends entirely upon the *Telecommunications (Interception) Act*.

For these reasons we conclude that s 20 confers no power on the Federal Court and does not infringe the rule laid down in the *Boilermakers' Case* [(1956) 94 CLR 254]. It was submitted by Mr Ellicott that the separation of judicial and administrative power is not merely a matter of verbal formulae and that is, of course, correct. If the nature or extent of the functions cast upon judges were such as to prejudice their independence or to conflict with the proper perform-**[74]**-ance of their judicial functions, the principle underlying the *Boilermakers' Case* would doubtless render the legislation invalid. But the exercise of the functions conferred by s 20 would not have that result. The section designates the judges as individuals particularly well qualified to fulfil the sensitive role that the section envisages, and confers on them a function which is not incompatible with their status and independence or inconsistent with the exercise of their judicial powers.

For these reasons we hold that s 20 of the *Telecommunications (Interception) Act* is a valid enactment of the Commonwealth Parliament.

Mason and Deane JJ effectively dissented.

Mason and Deane JJ: [78] The question which we have to determine as a matter of statutory construction is whether the functions entrusted to a Federal Court judge by s 20 are entrusted to him personally as someone who is detached from the court or in his capacity as a judge of the court of which he is a member in which event they become functions of the court ...

[81] In the present case, the function of issuing warrants is conferred upon all the judges of the Federal Court indiscriminately. It is exercisable by a judge of that Court in circumstances in which he is not appointed to a separately constituted tribunal. If the function is exercisable by him otherwise than in his character as a judge it must be because he is intended to discharge the function personally, detached from his judicial office as a member of the Federal Court. In saying this we reject the notion that functions may be entrusted to a person as a judge, but not as a member of the court to which he belongs. The metaphysical notion of a judge acting in his character or capacity as a judge, at large, so to speak, detached from the court of which he is a member, cannot be supported as a matter of legal theory.

There are compelling reasons why the Court should strictly maintain and apply established principle by insisting upon a clear expression of legislative intention before holding that functions entrusted to a judge of a federal court are exercisable by him personally. The ability of Parliament to confer non-judicial power on a judge of a Ch III court, as distinct from the court to which he belongs, has the potential, if it is not kept within precise limits, to undermine the doctrine in the *Boilermakers' Case*. One may ask: what is the point of our insisting, in conformity with the dictates of the *Boilermakers' Case*, that non-judicial functions shall not be given to a Ch III court, if it is legitimate for Parliament to adopt the **[82]** expedient of entrusting these functions to judges personally in lieu of pursuing the proscribed alternative of giving the functions to the court to which the judges belong? The answer is that the independence of the federal judiciary which is protected by the *Boilermakers' Case* will be preserved in a substantial way if, in accordance with the principle expressed by Dixon J in *Meyer* [(1937) 58 CLR 62 at 97], we continue to acknowledge that Parliament may confer non-judicial functions on a federal judge only where there is a clear expression of legislative intention that the functions are to be exercised by him in his personal capacity, detached from the court of which he is a member.

Nor is the point which we have just made necessarily dependent on the authority of the *Boilermakers' Case*. Even without that decision, there is much to be said for the view that the underlying concept of the separation of powers which the Constitution prescribes as "a safeguard of individual liberty" (see *R v Davison* [(1954) 90 CLR 353 at 380-2]) would itself support adherence to the principle which we have discussed. Cardozo CJ, speaking of the separation of powers under the Constitution of the State of New York in *In re Richardson* [160 NE 655 at 657 (1928)], observed:

> "From the beginnings of our history, the principle has been enforced that there is no inherent power in Executive or Legislature to charge the judiciary with administrative functions except when reasonably incidental to the fulfilment of judicial duties ... The exigencies of government have made it necessary to relax a merely doctrinaire adherence to a principle so flexible and practical, so largely a matter of sensible approximation, as that of the separation of powers. Elasticity has not meant that what is of the essence of the judicial function may be destroyed ...".

And see, generally, *R v Trade Practices Tribunal; Ex parte Tasmanian Breweries Pty Ltd* [(1970) 123 CLR 361] and the discussion by Hamilton in *The Federalist*, No 78 (1788). Indeed, it may be arguable that, conformably with the underlying concept of the separation of powers, it is beyond the power of the Parliament to attach to the holding of judicial office as a member of a Ch III court an unavoidable obligation to perform as a designated person, detached from the relevant court, administrative functions which are unrelated to the exercise of the jurisdiction of that court. However, these are questions which have not been argued in the present case and it is unnecessary for us to deal with them.

[83] In the United States, as in Australia, it has been recognized that non-judicial functions may be entrusted to judges personally and not in their capacity as judicial officers, but, it seems, on the footing that a duty of acceptance cannot be imposed: *In re Richardson* [160 NE at 659]. This recognition is no doubt subject to the general qualification that what is entrusted to a judge in his individual capacity is not inconsistent with the essence of the judicial function and the proper performance by the judiciary of its responsibilities for the exercise of judicial power. In *United States v Ferreira* [54 US (13 Howard) 40 (1851)], the Supreme Court considered that certain statutes of Congress could not validly confer on the judges of the Territorial Court of Florida and later a district judge of the United States in their judicial capacity the duty of adjudging claims for loss by Spanish officers and inhabitants arising out of the operations of the American army in Florida and reporting to the Secretary of the Treasury who, on being satisfied that the decisions were just and equitable, was bound to pay. The Supreme Court went on to decide, in the words of Taney CJ [54 US at 47]:

> "The authority conferred on the respective judges was nothing more than that of a commissioner to adjust certain claims against the United States; and the office of judges, and their respective jurisdictions, are referred to in the law, merely as a designation of the persons to whom the authority is confided, and the territorial limits to which it extends."

In concluding that the judges were appointed as commissioners, the court was influenced by the circumstance that the statutes were designed to give effect to the United States' obligations under a treaty with Spain by which the United States bound itself to establish a tribunal to adjust the claims. Upon analysis, the case is analogous to *Drake's Case* [(1979) 46 FLR 409] in that ... the tribunal established for the purposes of the treaty was a special tribunal consisting of the judges as commissioners rather than as members of a court ... Accordingly, the decision cannot be regarded as authority for the proposition that the courts will generally lean in favour of preserving the validity of legislation entrusting non-judicial functions to judges by concluding that they are to be exercised personally.

Another reason for adhering to a strict application of settled principle is that when a function is entrusted to a judge by reference to his judicial office the legislators and the community are entitled to [84] expect that he will perform the function in that capacity. To the intelligent observer, unversed in what Dixon J accurately described – and emphatically rejected – as "distinctions without differences" (*Meyer* [58 CLR at 97]), it would come as a surprise to learn that a judge, who is appointed to carry out a function by reference to his judicial office and who carries it out in his court with the assistance of its staff, services and facilities, is not acting as a judge at all, but as a private individual. Such an observer might well think, with some degree of justification, that it is all an elaborate charade ...

[86] We therefore conclude that the function of issuing warrants was imposed upon the judges of the Federal Court not as designated individuals but as a function to be performed by them as judges of that Court in their capacity as such. That being so, we are unable to participate in the negative answer which the majority of the Court has given to the first question removed into this Court ... For our part we refrain from giving a definite answer to this question in the absence of argument on the Commonwealth Solicitor-General's proposed submission that the Court should reconsider the *Boilermakers' Case*. In view of the majority's conclusion that s 20 is valid in any event, there is no point in embarking on a consideration of that submission.

Hilton v Wells was a 3:2 decision in a five-judge Court, but, in *Jones v Commonwealth* (1987) 71 ALR 497, when a seven-judge Court was asked to reconsider *Hilton v Wells*, a 6:1 majority refused to do so. The sole dissenter was Gaudron J.

Following *Hilton v Wells*, the *Telecommunications (Interception) Act 1979* (Cth) was amended in 1987 to make it clear that a judge who authorised a telephone tap was doing so as a *persona designata*. The use of the term "a Judge" and its troublesome definition in s 18 were abandoned. Instead, the relevant powers were conferred on an "eligible judge".

Telecommunications (Interception) Act 1979 (Cth)

6D (1) In this Act, unless the contrary intention appears:
"**eligible Judge**" means a Judge in relation to whom a consent under subsection (2) and a declaration under subsection (3) are in force;
"**Judge**" means a person who is a Judge of a court created by the Parliament.
(2) A Judge may by writing consent to be nominated by the Minister under subsection (3).
(3) The Minister may by writing declare Judges in relation to whom consents are in force under subsection (2) to be eligible Judges for the purposes of this Act.
(4) An eligible Judge has, in relation to the performance or exercise of a function or power conferred on an eligible Judge by this Act, the same protection and immunity as a Justice of the High Court has in relation to proceedings in the High Court.

The validity of these new provisions was considered by the High Court in *Grollo v Palmer* (1995) 184 CLR 348. In the absence of Gaudron J, the case was decided by a Court of six judges. All six acknowledged that the 1987 amendments had made it clear that the function was entrusted to judges as *personae designatae* and not as members of a Court; but what was now considered more anxiously was whether the performance of such a role in the criminal investigation process was compatible with judicial office even for a *persona designata*.

Grollo v Palmer
(1995) 184 CLR 348

Brennan CJ, Deane, Dawson and Toohey JJ: [362] The applicant submits that the important principle of separation of powers expounded in *Boilermakers* should not be undermined by acceptance of the power of the legislative or the executive branches of government to repose non-judicial power in individual judges when that power cannot be reposed in the courts they constitute. The distinction which the conception of persona designata draws between judges and the courts to which they are appointed is said to be too fine and specious to be supported. The distinction (so the **[363]** argument runs) is formal not substantial and it is apt to convert the principle of separation of powers into a mockery. In practice, the system of "eligible Judges" has resulted in the conferring of power to issue warrants on thirty of the thirty-five judges of the Federal Court; the warrants are signed by the judge [so] as to indicate the judge's judicial status and the judges have, in respect of that function, a statutory immunity which is "the same protection and immunity as a Justice of the High Court ... in relation to proceedings in the High Court". The conception of persona designata is said to serve as a charade concealing the reality that a non-judicial power has been conferred on the judges of a Ch III court. It is submitted that the conception of persona designata should be abolished to maintain the integrity of the *Boilermakers* principle. In Canada, Laskin CJ expressed agreement with the proposition that "the whole persona designata conception could be scrapped without the slightest inconvenience or the least distortion of legal principles" [*Herman v Deputy Attorney-General of Canada* [[1979] 1 SCR 729 at 732; (1978) 91 DLR(3d) 3 at 4-5].

The submission that this Court should follow that lead must be rejected. The conception of persona designata has been invoked when the vesting of a non-judicial power, which could not be vested in a court consistently with Ch III of the Constitution, has been supported as a vesting of the power in individual judges detached from the courts they constitute. But the conception of "persona designata" is not always invoked in the same sense. Sometimes it is invoked as an aid to, or a descriptive expression in, statutory interpretation, connoting an individual judge detached from the court to which the judge is appointed. It is in this sense that the term is used when the question is whether the legislature has intended to vest the power in the court or in individual judges detached from the court. It was in that sense that the term was relevant ... in *Hilton v Wells* [(1985) 157 CLR 57] and it was in that sense that the usefulness of the term was disparaged by Laskin CJ. Sometimes the term is invoked as a shorthand expression of a limitation on the principle of *Boilermakers*, acknowledging that there is no necessary inconsistency with the separation of powers mandated by Ch III of the Constitution if non-judicial power is vested in individual judges detached from the court they constitute. It is in the latter sense that the term falls for **[364]** consideration in this case.

Summarising the qualifications expressed in *Hilton v Wells* – particularly by Mason and Deane JJ, but also by Gibbs CJ, Wilson and Dawson JJ – the joint judgment said:

Brennan CJ, Deane, Dawson and Toohey JJ: [364] The conditions thus expressed on the power to confer non-judicial functions on judges as designated persons are twofold: first, no non-**[365]**-judicial function that is not incidental to a judicial function can be conferred without the judge's consent; and, second, no function can be conferred that is incompatible either with the judge's performance of his or her judicial functions or with the proper discharge by the judiciary of its responsibilities as an institution exercising judicial power ("the incompatibility condition"). These conditions accord with the view of the Supreme Court of the United States in *Mistretta v United States* [488 US 361 at 404 (1989)] where the court said:

> "This is not to suggest, of course, that every kind of extrajudicial service under every circum-stance necessarily accords with the Constitution. That the Constitution does not absolutely prohibit a federal judge from assuming extrajudicial duties does not mean that every extra-judicial service would be compatible with, or appropriate to, continuing service on the bench; nor does it mean that Congress may require a federal judge to assume extrajudicial duties as long as the judge is assigned those duties in an individual, not judicial, capacity. The ultimate inquiry remains whether a particular extrajudicial assignment undermines the integrity of the Judicial Branch."

The incompatibility condition may arise in a number of different ways. Incompatibility might consist in so permanent and complete a commitment to the performance of non-judicial functions by a judge that the further performance of substantial judicial functions by that judge is not practi-cable. It might consist in the performance of non-judicial functions of such a nature that the capacity of the judge to perform his or her judicial functions with integrity is compromised or impaired. Or it might consist in the performance of non-judicial functions of such a nature that public confidence in the integrity of the judiciary as an institution or in the capacity of the indivi-dual judge to perform his or her judicial functions with integrity is diminished. Judges appointed to exercise the judicial power of the Commonwealth cannot be authorised to engage in the performance of non-judicial functions so as to prejudice the capacity either of the individual judge or of the judiciary as an institution to discharge effectively the responsibilities of exercising the judicial power of the Commonwealth. So much is implied from the separation of powers mandated by Chs I, II and III of the Constitution and from the conditions necessary for the valid and effective exercise of judicial power.

The applicant submits that judicial integrity is compromised and public confidence in the exercise of the jurisdiction of the Federal Court is prejudiced by the conferral of power on judges of the Federal Court to issue interception warrants. First, it is said that an obligation **[366]** – either statutory or common law – not to disclose the information on which the judge may have decided to issue an interception warrant compromises the judge's duty to exercise the jurisdiction of the Court. If a judge cannot reveal the information which was given to him or her on an application for the issue of an interception warrant and the judge is subsequently asked to exercise jurisdiction in a matter arising from the issue of the warrant or relating to the information given extra-curially, no disclosure can be made to the parties of the judge's prior involvement in, or knowledge of, the matter. Bias might be apprehended in any case in which the validity of an interception warrant is in issue by reason of the large proportion of Federal Court judges who are eligible judges and who, if not involved in the issue of the warrant in the particular case, would have formed a view about the manner in which the power to issue an interception warrant should be exercised. These arguments are "troubling" but, as with the courts in the United States, the argument can be met by the adoption of an appropriate practice. A judge who has issued a warrant in a particular matter can ensure that he or she does not sit on any case to which the warrant relates. That is the practice followed when a judge has received information extra-curially which might prove embarrassing to the impartial hearing and determination of a case. Of course, the risk of such a situation arising and, in particular, of a judge discovering late in the day that he or she had issued a warrant on the basis of which evidence is to be tendered, is increased when there are but few judges appointed to a court. In the Australian Capital Territory, for example, it would be prudent for a resident judge of the Supreme Court of the Australian Capital Territory not to accept an appointment. But that is a matter for individual judges. However, as in *Mistretta* [488 US at 407]:

"We are somewhat more troubled by [the] argument that the Judiciary's entanglement in the political work of the Commission undermines public confidence in the disinterestedness of the Judicial Branch ... The legitimacy of the Judicial Branch ultimately depends on its reputation for impartiality and nonpartisanship. That reputation may not be borrowed by the political Branches to cloak their work in the neutral colors of judicial action."

If the issuing of interception warrants were reasonably to be **[367]** regarded as a judicial participation in criminal investigation, it would be a function which could not be conferred on a judge without compromising the judiciary's essential separation from the executive government. The judicial method of deciding questions in controversy has no application in exercising the power to issue an interception warrant. Not only is the application for an interception warrant made ex parte; the very issue of a warrant and the identity of the judge who issued it are not disclosed. Unlike a warrant to enter, search and seize, its execution may go undetected by the person against whom or against whose interests the warrant is executed. Unlike a warrant to enter, search and seize, there is no return made on the execution of the warrant which permits a determination of its lawfulness, a review of its due execution and a disposition of the fruit of the execution. Because of the secrecy necessarily involved in applying for and obtaining the issue of an interception warrant, no records are kept which would permit judicial review of a judge's decision to issue a warrant. Nor are reasons given for such a decision. The decision to issue a warrant is, for all practical purposes, an unreviewable in camera exercise of executive power to authorise a future clandestine gathering of information. Understandably a view might be taken that this is no business for a judge to be involved in, much less the large majority of the judges of the Federal Court.

Yet it is precisely because of the intrusive and clandestine nature of interception warrants and the necessity to use them in today's continuing battle against serious crime that some impartial authority, accustomed to the dispassionate assessment of evidence and sensitive to the common law's protection of privacy and property (both real and personal), be authorised to control the official interception of communications. In other words, the professional experience and cast of mind of a judge is a desirable guarantee that the appropriate balance will be kept between the law enforcement agencies on the one hand and criminal suspects or suspected sources of information about crime on the other. It is an eligible judge's function of deciding independently of the applicant agency whether an interception warrant should issue that separates the eligible judge from the executive function of law enforcement. It is the recognition of that independent role that preserves public confidence in the judiciary as an institution ...

[368] Clearly views may differ as to the desirability of judges being involved in the issue of interception warrants. But the issue before the Court is one of the validity of legislation. Relevantly, the legislation is not invalid unless what we have referred to as the incompatibility condition precludes the vesting of the power to issue interception **[369]** warrants. For the reasons given earlier, that is not the case.

Only McHugh J held that to assign to "eligible Judges" the function of issuing warrants for telephone tapping was incompatible with their judicial office.

McHugh J: [377] The persona designata exception to the *Boilermakers'* principle must ... give way when the exercise of non-judicial functions impairs a federal judge's ability to perform judicial functions or when it would give rise to a reasonable doubt as to the independence or impartiality of a federal judge. In either case, Parliament cannot constitutionally invest executive power in a federal judge as persona designata. As the Supreme Court of the United States pointed out in *Mistretta v United States* [488 US 361 at 407 (1989)]:

> "The legitimacy of the Judicial Branch ultimately depends upon its reputation for impartiality and nonpartisanship. That reputation may not be borrowed by the political Branches to cloak their work in the neutral colors of judicial action."

If, therefore, reasonable people, not trained to discover "distinctions without differences", might reasonably apprehend that the functions undertaken by a judge as persona designata impaired his or her ability to carry out judicial functions or conflicted with the judge's independence or impartiality, those non-judicial functions cannot constitutionally be invested in a person who is a member of a federal court. Furthermore, since the Constitution requires that the exercise of judicial power be separated from the exercise of executive power, **[378]** those who assert the compatibility of the non-judicial and judicial functions of a person who holds office as a federal judge have the burden of proving that those functions are compatible ...

The question ... therefore is whether investing persons who are judges of the Federal Court with the power to authorise the issue of warrants is incompatible with the exercise of the judicial functions of judges of that court. In my opinion, the functions undertaken by Federal Court judges acting as persona designata in accordance with the Act are of such a nature and are exercised in such a manner that public confidence in the ability of the judges to perform their judicial functions in an independent and impartial manner is likely to be jeopardised. That being so, the power to authorise the issue of interception warrants is incompatible with the exercise of the functions of a judge of a federal court ...

[379] Open justice is the hallmark of the common law system of justice and is an essential characteristic of the exercise of federal judicial power. Participation in secret, ex parte administrative procedures that approve the acts of federal law enforcement officers by those who hold federal judicial office contravenes the spirit of the requirement that **[380]** justice in the federal courts should be open; it weakens the perception that the federal courts are independent of the federal government and its agencies. Much of the litigation in the Federal Court is between the ordinary citizen and the federal government and its agencies. The maintenance of public confidence in the independence and impartiality of the Federal Court judges in hearing disputes between the citizen and the government and its agencies is contingent upon the public perception that the judges of the federal courts are impartial and entirely independent of the executive arm of government. That public perception must be diminished when the judges of the Federal Court are involved in secret, ex parte administrative procedures, forming part of the criminal investigative process, that are carried out as a routine part of their daily work.

But even more importantly, the hearing of applications for warrants by eligible judges is likely to give rise to direct conflicts with their judicial functions. Proceedings may come before the Court, as they have in this case, directly or indirectly involving the subjects of the telephone interception warrants authorised by a judge of the Federal Court. Highly prejudicial information in relation to a person may have been secretly provided to the judge, information upon which the judge may have relied in authorising the issue of the warrant. Because the applications and the identity of judges are secret, the parties to proceedings are not aware that the judge is in possession of information that is prejudicial to one of them; the affected party is unable to ask the judge to disqualify him or herself on the grounds of apprehended bias. What is worse is that arguably the judge [381] cannot reveal the information to them without breaching a statutory obligation of secrecy that was imposed on him or her when, as persona designata, the judge approved the issue of the warrant …

[382] Not only are the nature and mode of performance of the functions of issuing warrants likely to impact upon public confidence in the independence and impartiality of judges of the Federal Court, but the terms of the Act reinforce that impression. Although the Act gives power to the judges of a federal court as persona designata, it seeks to clothe the function of authorising warrants with as much judicial status as possible. The references in the Act are to an "eligible Judge" or simply to a "Judge". It appears that the legislative intention is to associate the judicial status of the judge as closely as possible with the process of issuing interception warrants without actually conferring the power on the judge as a judge. Even sophisticated readers of the Act will readily, perhaps inevitably, fail to see the distinction which the Act draws between a federal judge and the person who holds that office. It is this combination of inconsistent aims that led Mason and Deane JJ in *Hilton v Wells* [(1985) 157 CLR 57 at 84] to characterise the formal [383] investiture of warrant-issuing powers in the judges as individuals rather than as judges as an "elaborate charade". This close association of judicial and non-judicial functions makes it likely that the general public will conclude that the federal judiciary is involved in secretly approving police investigative and invasive procedures …

[384] Telephone interception with its attendant invasion of the privacy of the citizen is regrettably an essential tool of law enforcement officers if they are to combat the evil of organised crime. Because telephone interceptions necessarily involve infringements of the right to privacy, the national Parliament has regarded it as essential that the interceptions only take place with the approval of some person or tribunal independent of the criminal investigative agencies that are authorised to intercept telephone conversations. Persons who hold office as judges of the federal courts are unquestionably well suited to carry out such a role under the Act. The sense of public duty that is characteristic of those judges has resulted in over 85 per cent of the judges of the Federal Court becoming "eligible Judges" to perform the non-judicial work that the national Parliament has inferentially asked them to perform. But many other persons and tribunals, the law officers of the Commonwealth and retired judges among them, are also well fitted to carry out the functions that the Act purports to vest in eligible judges. Under the Constitution, it is to those persons and tribunals and not to the federal judges that the Parliament must turn if independent approval is to remain a condition of telephone interception permitted by the Act. Authorisation by federal judges is incompatible with the separation of executive and judicial power mandated by our Constitution.

Gummow J agreed with the majority. He expressed some sympathy with the views of McHugh J (and of Gaudron J in *Jones v Commonwealth*), but in the end felt able to hold that the legislation was valid because he was satisfied that its prohibitions on disclosure could be interpreted so as not to apply in any case where they might conflict with a judicial duty of disclosure.

6. The Incompatibility Doctrine

Thus far the conceptual structure was clear, though sometimes criticised as artificial. In the *Boilermakers' Case* the High Court of Australia and the Privy Council had affirmed a rigid constitutional principle prohibiting any combination of non-judicial power with "the judicial power of the Commonwealth", as vested by and exercised under Ch III of the Constitution. In *Hilton v Wells*, the High Court had affirmed by a 3:2 majority an exception to the *Boilermakers* principle: a person who exercises federal judicial power may validly be appointed or assigned to perform a non-judicial function in his or her personal capacity, if the person is appointed or assigned as an individual *persona designata*. In *Grollo v Palmer*, the Court had recognised (but by majority had failed to apply) an exception to the exception: the *persona designata* doctrine does *not* avail to support the performance by a federal judge of a non-judicial function if that function is "incompatible" with the holding of judicial office.

In 1996 the "incompatibility" doctrine was extended considerably further. In *Wilson v Minister for Aboriginal and Torres Strait Islander Affairs* (1996) 189 CLR 1, it was applied, by a 6:1 majority, to invalidate the appointment of Justice Jane Mathews, a judge of the Federal Court, to prepare a report under s 10 of the *Aboriginal and Torres Strait Islander Heritage Protection Act 1984* (Cth) in relation to the Hindmarsh Island bridge development (see Chapter 21, §4). Under ss 9-10 of the Act, the Minister has power to make declarations for "the protection and preservation ... from injury or desecration" of areas "of particular significance to Aboriginals in accordance with Aboriginal tradition". The power to make such a declaration arises where certain preconditions are satisfied, including a requirement under s 10(1)(c) that the Minister has received and considered a report "from a person nominated by him". That person is required by s 10(3) to publish a notice "inviting interested persons to furnish representations in connection with the report"; to "give due consideration to any representations so furnished"; and to "attach them to the report". The matters to be dealt with in the report, as specified by s 10(4), include "the particular significance of the area to Aboriginals" and "the extent of the area that *should* be protected" (emphasis added).

A majority of the High Court, with Kirby J dissenting, held that the formation of opinions and the giving of advice involved in the making of the report were incompatible with the constitutional independence of the judiciary from the executive government. The precise way in which the "incompatibility" doctrine was held to operate was explained with care, through a contrast with the common law doctrine of "incompatibility". Under the latter, if a person is appointed to two incompatible offices, one office is automatically vacated; and at least in the older version of the doctrine, the office to be vacated was the one first held. The constitutional doctrine, however, does not vacate either appointment. Certainly it could not vacate the judicial appointment: "**[16]** No common law doctrine can alter the security of the tenure ... created [by s 72 of the Constitution]". Instead, the doctrine operates "to sterilise the power to interfere with the protection which the Constitution gives to the independence of Ch III judges".

Accordingly, the doctrine did not operate directly to invalidate Justice Mathews' appointment, to vacate her office or to render her report a nullity. The doctrine operates primarily as a limit on federal legislative power. Thus, in a case where a federal statute specifically authorised the appointment of a judge to undertake functions "incompatible" with judicial office, the statutory provision authorising such an appointment would be invalid. The invalidity of any purported appointment would be merely consequential on the invalidity of the empowering statute. In this instance, however, the statute made no such specific provision: by s 10(1)(c) the reporter was identified merely as "a person nominated by [the Minister]". In its natural reading the word "person" would include a judge; but since the nomination of a judge would be unconstitutional, the word "person" must be read down so as *not* to include a judge. Thus construed, the Act had never authorised the appointment of Justice Mathews.

Wilson v Minister for Aboriginal and Torres Strait Islander Affairs
(1996) 189 CLR 1

Brennan CJ, Dawson, Toohey, McHugh and Gummow JJ: [16] In the present case, the category of incompatibility that arises for consideration is "the performance of non-judicial functions of such a nature that public confidence in the integrity of the judiciary as an institution or in the capacity of the individual judge to perform his or her judicial functions with integrity is diminished" [*Grollo v Palmer* (1995) 184 CLR 348 at 365].

Bearing in mind that public confidence in the independence of the judiciary is achieved by a separation of the judges from the persons exercising the political functions of government, no functions can be conferred on a Ch III judge that would breach that separation. The separation that is relevant here is separation in the performing of the particular non-judicial function; the principle does not touch personal relationships or relationships outside the area of governmental activity between judges and those who perform legislative or executive functions. Those relationships are matters for judicial sensitivity but not of constitutional significance. Constitutional incompatibility has the effect of limiting legislative and executive power. Where it has that effect, it is discovered on the face of the statute, or on the face of those measures taken pursuant to a statute, that purports or purport to confer a non-judicial function on a Ch III judge. That is not to say that constitutional incompatibility is a matter of mere form. The operation of the statute or of the measures taken pursuant to it is ascertained by looking to the circumstances in which the purported function might be performed. Where a non-judicial power is purportedly conferred, **[17]** constitutional incompatibility is ascertained by reference to the function that has to be performed to exercise the power.

The statute or the measures taken pursuant to the statute must be examined in order to determine, first, whether the function is an integral part of, or is closely connected with, the functions of the Legislature or the Executive Government. If the function is not closely connected with the Legislature or the Executive Government, no constitutional incompatibility appears. Next, an answer must be given to the question whether the function is required to be performed independently of any instruction, advice or wish of the Legislature or the Executive Government, other than a law or an instrument made under a law (hereafter "any non-judicial instruction, advice or wish"). If an affirmative answer does not appear, it is clear that the separation has been breached. The breach is not capable of repair by the Ch III judge on whom the function is purportedly conferred, for the breach invalidates the conferral of the function. If the function is one which must be performed independently of any non-judicial instruction, advice or wish, a further question arises: Is any discretion purportedly possessed by the Ch III judge to be exercised on political grounds – that is, on grounds that are not confined by factors expressly or impliedly prescribed by law? In considering these questions, it will often be relevant to note whether the function to be performed must be performed judicially, that is, without bias and by a procedure that gives each interested person an opportunity to be heard and to deal with any case presented by those with opposing interests. An obligation to observe the requirements of procedural fairness is not necessarily indicative of compatibility with the holding of judicial office under Ch III, for many persons at various levels in the executive branch of government are obliged to observe those requirements. But, conversely, if a judicial manner of performance is not required, it is unlikely that the performance of the function will be performed free of political influence or without the prospect of exercising a political discretion.

A judge who conducts a Royal Commission may have a close working connection with the Executive Government yet will be required to act judicially in finding facts and applying the law and will deliver a report according to the judge's own conscience without regard to the wishes or advice of the Executive Government except where those wishes or advice are given by way of submission for the judge's independent evaluation. The terms of reference of the particular Royal Commission and of any enabling legislation will be significant. Similarly, where a judge is appointed as a presidential member of the Administrative Appeals Tribunal, the function of **[18]** deciding applications must be performed independently of any instruction, advice or wish of the Executive Government. The tribunal must give what it considers to be the correct or preferable decision. And that is so even in those cases where government policy is a relevant factor for consideration and the powers of the tribunal are limited to the affirming of, or recommending the reconsideration of, the decisions of a Minister … Independence from the Legislature and the Executive Government in the sense thus explained is essential to the constitutional compatibility of performing a non-judicial function with the holding of office as a Ch III judge.

The only power conferred by s 10 of the Act is the power conferred on the Minister to make a declaration. A report is no more than a condition precedent to the exercise of the Minister's power to make a declaration. The function of a reporter under s 10 is not performed by way of an independent review of an exercise of the Minister's power. It is performed as an integral part of the process of the Minister's exercise of power. The performance of such a function by a judge places the judge firmly in the echelons of administration, liable to **[19]** removal by the Minister before the report is made and shorn of the usual judicial protections, in a position equivalent to that of a ministerial adviser.

The reporter is not expressly required to hold a hearing, but may nevertheless be obliged to observe requirements of procedural fairness. That obligation is not significant. Significantly, the competing interests of Aboriginal applicants and of others whose proprietary or pecuniary interests are liable to be affected by the making of a declaration have to be determined. Such a determination is essentially a political function. A reporter may choose to act independently of the Minister in determining the interests to be preferred, but the Act does not require the reporter to disregard ministerial instruction, advice or wish in preparing the report. The report may be prepared so as to accord with ministerial policy. If the Minister has no policy instruction or intimation to give to the reporter, the reporter himself or herself must make political decisions: "the extent of the area that *should be* protected", "the prohibitions and restrictions *to be made*" and "the duration of any declaration". These decisions are not necessarily made by finding the nature and extent of an Aboriginal connection with the land or by an assessment of the extent to which Aboriginal beliefs or lifestyles are under threat. The decisions to be made by a reporter are political in character. In addition, the reporter is required by s 10(4)(g) to furnish advice to the Minister upon a question of law, namely, the extent to which the area in question is or may be protected by or under a law of a State or Territory. Yet the giving to the executive of advisory opinions on [20] questions of law is quite alien to the exercise of the judicial power of the Commonwealth. The separation of the Ch III judge acting as reporter from the Minister has been breached. The function of reporting is therefore incompatible with the holding of office as a Ch III judge.

It seems that the criteria of incompatibility above expressed have not always been observed in practice. However, disconformity of practice with constitutional requirement is no inhibition against truly expounding the text and implications of the Constitution. Indeed, any practice of departure from the constitutional requirement makes the necessity to declare the requirement more imperative. It cannot be avoided by a judge choosing to adopt a procedure designed to erect a *cordon sanitaire* between the judge and the Legislature or the Executive Government. The Constitution is concerned not with the conduct of a judge who exercises his or her discretion to maintain independence from the Legislature or the Executive Government but with the limits on legislative and executive power that might be exercised to confer a function bridging the separation of the Judiciary from the Legislature and the Executive Government.

In the present case, no doubt Justice Mathews would have followed a judicial or quasi-judicial procedure and her Honour's report might well evidence an independence of view as to the course which she regards as a desirable one for a Minister to follow. Nevertheless, if the Act be read down as it must, it follows that the function was one which the Minister could not properly nominate her to perform, nor one which her Honour was capable of accepting.

Kirby J: [47] When the stated principles are applied to the undisputed facts of the present case there is no constitutional invalidity either in the Act pursuant to which Justice Mathews was nominated as reporter or in the conduct of the Minister in so nominating her.

The separation of powers dividing the judiciary from the other branches of government remains intact. There is a clear divorce, in law and in appearance, between Justice Mathews's appointment as a judge of the Federal Court (on the one hand) and her other appointments to non-judicial duties under legislation enacted by the Parliament, including that of reporter here in question (on the other). The duties of reporter were not imposed on a federal court. Although it is true that Justice Mathews is described as a "Justice" in the documentation of her inquiry, this is but a normal courtesy, commonly observed in [48] Australia. At no time did Justice Mathews concurrently perform duties as a federal judge and duties as a reporter. The Minister did not appoint her as reporter until her consent was first signified.

The actual duties of a reporter are considerably closer to those of the holder of a judicial office than, say, the duties of an "eligible judge" in providing a warrant for telephone interception which the authority of this Court has upheld. Justice Mathews is in no way involved in functions incompatible with those of a judge as, for example, involvement in criminal investigation and prosecutorial duties arguably is. On the contrary, the very reason for her appointment to provide a report in the instant case is clearly to utilise the particular qualities which are normal to a judge in Australia: accuracy in the application of the law; independence and disinterestedness in evaluating evidence and submissions; neutrality and detachment; and efficiency and skill in the provision of a conclusion ... I am unpersuaded that the appointment ... is inconsistent with the Constitution.

There was no suggestion of any incompatibility in the performance of the limited function of reporting with Justice Mathews's primary commission as a judge in the Federal Court ... Far from the provision of a report damaging the federal judiciary, or Justice Mathews personally, I consider that the Australian community, in such an inquiry, would feel much more comfortable that the task of reporting was being performed by a judge, with nothing to gain or fear by the discharge of the accepted duty. Far from sapping and undermining the separation of powers, the provision of such a report of potential importance to Australians – Aboriginal and non-Aboriginal alike – would be in complete harmony with a century of unbroken experience during which numerous reports on troublesome and controversial subjects have been provided to the Executive Government by appointed judges, federal and state.

Whilst it is true that most of the functions of the reporter in this case would be carried out in private, the same is often true of Royal Commissions and other inquiries. It is always so in the case of "eligible judges" authorising warrants under the *Telecommunications (Interception) Act* 1979. Unlike such "eligible judges", Justice Mathews's nomination was publicly announced. Some of her proceedings were conducted in public. And she was subject to the rules of procedural fairness which could be enforced in the Federal Court.

Opinions may differ as to the desirability or seemliness of a federal **[49]** judge accepting such a nomination. Doubtless, in accepting nomination, Justice Mathews would have considered the sensitivity of the matters upon which she was required to report, the need, in that task, to respect both the interests of justice and the interests of Aboriginal tradition and the advantage of calling upon her judicial experience to suggest procedures which could be followed by later reporters who do not have the long and wide experience in state and federal courts which her Honour has enjoyed. This, it will be remembered, is the precise way, 20 years ago, that the Administrative Appeals Tribunal began under its first presidential members all of whom, initially, were federal judges. Guidance of great value was given for those, of differing background and qualifications, whose appointments followed. Novel functions (including, in that case, the review of Ministerial decisions on matters of policy and the provision of recommendations to Ministers) were performed by persons who, although tribunal members performing non-judicial duties, were also federal judges. The advantages were clear and wholly beneficial. A rigid rule would not only have been contrary to Australia's legal history. It would have deprived the Commonwealth of judicial experience and wisdom where the novelty of the functions and the sensitivity of their proper performance suggested the special utility of utilising federal judges. Far from eroding public confidence in the integrity of the federal judiciary as an institution and the independence of its members, the use of federal judges ensured the impartiality of the Tribunal, its compliance with the law and its high reputation amongst members of the community.

It is no less useful or beneficial in the performance of the function of reporter under the Act in this instance. Just as in the case of the Administrative Appeals Tribunal there are some ... who are unsympathetic to the functions [and] unwilling themselves to perform them ..., the same is doubtless true of a reporter under the Act. But no constitutional principle requires that the width of the legislative language ("any person") should be narrowed or that the discretion of the Executive Government to choose a "person" who happens to be a Federal Court judge to provide the report, should be circumscribed.

In my view and with great respect to those of a different opinion, the contrary conclusion represents a significant narrowing of the application of the accepted authority of this Court in *Hilton* and *Grollo*, if not of the authority itself. If the suggested test is impermissible closeness to the Legislature or the Executive Government and their respective functions, the activities of a federal judge, **[50]** secretly and anonymously authorising telephonic intercepts, [are] clearly much closer to the functions of the other branches than are those of a statutory reporter, publicly identified, evaluating evidence and submissions, judicially reviewable and presenting a report which reality suggests would inevitably find its way into the public domain, save for any specially confidential parts. Yet by the authority of this Court, *Hilton* and *Grollo* permit the former and that authority was not challenged. This case will prohibit the latter. It is said that "historically" judges have been vested with functions such as authorising the issue of warrants. So they have. But they have also, in our history, been called upon to report to the Executive upon difficult and sensitive questions. History does not stand still.

In my respectful opinion, the decision in this case involves a departure from long-standing practice in Australia ...; a rejection of the principles found to be appropriate in the more rigid constitutional context considered by the Supreme Court of the United States; an undue constriction of the Parliament's decision to authorise utilisation of "any person" as a reporter; and a serious limitation on the privilege of the Executive Government to choose a person, who happens to be a judge, where the sensitivity and importance of the particular case is considered by it to warrant that course.

In this decision, the "incompatibility" doctrine was treated merely as an exception to the permissible use of the *persona designata* device. However, in *Kable v Director of Public Prosecutions (NSW)* (1996) 189 CLR 51 the reach of the "incompatibility" doctrine was extended considerably further. The effect of that decision is considered in Chapter 15, §2.

7. Legislative Usurpation

(a)   Interference with the Judicial Process

The contemporary rationale for a strict separation of judicial power tends to emphasise independence from the executive government. However, it is equally applicable to cases where the legislature attempts to interfere with the workings of the courts, or itself seeks to exercise or "usurp" judicial power, for example by determining the result of an individual case in a way that amounts to "legislative judgment". "Usurpation" occurs when, by retrospective legislation or otherwise, a legislature purports to predetermine the outcome in an individual case. "Interference" entails an attempt to change the direction or outcome of pending judicial proceedings.

The notions of "usurpation of judicial power" or of "legislative judgment" entered into contemporary currency through a Privy Council decision in 1965, reported as *Liyanage v The Queen* [1967] 1 AC 259. In that case 11 persons had been tried by the Supreme Court of Ceylon (now Sri Lanka) on charges arising from an attempted *coup d'état* on 27 January 1962. Special legislation was passed redefining the relevant offences and penalties, modifying the laws of evidence, providing for trial by three judges without a jury and retrospectively validating the defendants' arrest without warrant and pre-trial detention. The legislation was "deemed ... to have come into operation on January 1, 1962" and was "limited in its application to any offence against the State alleged to have been committed on or about January 27, 1962".

The Constitution of Ceylon had been conferred by the Ceylon (Constitution) Order in Council 1946, as amended in 1947. Although it contained no specific provision "vesting" judicial power, the Privy Council found in it sufficient indications of a concern for judicial independence to warrant a conclusion that the Constitution was intended to embody a separation of powers. On that basis, their Lordships held the legislation to be unconstitutional.

Liyanage v The Queen
[1967] 1 AC 259

Lord Pearce (for their Lordships): [289] [I]n their Lordships' view ... there exists a separate power in the judicature which under the Constitution as it stands cannot be usurped or infringed by the executive or the legislature ...

But do the Acts of 1962 ... usurp or infringe that power? It goes without saying that the legislature may legislate, for the generality of its subjects, by the creation of crimes and penalties or by enacting rules relating to evidence. But the Acts of 1962 had no such general intention. They were clearly aimed at particular known individuals who had been named in a White Paper and were in prison awaiting their fate. The fact that the learned judges declined to convict some of the prisoners is not to the point. That the alterations in the law were not intended for the generality of the citizens or designed as any improvement of the general law is shown by the fact that the effect of those alterations was to be limited to the participants in the January coup and that, after these had been dealt with by the judges, the law should revert to its normal state.

But such a lack of generality in criminal legislation need not, of itself, involve the judicial function, and their Lordships are not prepared to hold that every enactment in this field which can be described as ad hominem and ex post facto must inevitably usurp or infringe the judicial power.

Nor do they find it necessary to attempt the almost impossible task of tracing where the line **[290]** is to be drawn between what will and what will not constitute such an interference. Each case must be decided in the light of its own facts and circumstances, including the true purpose of the legislation, the situation to which it was directed, the existence (where several enactments are impugned) of a common design, and the extent to which the legislation affects, by way of direction or restriction, the discretion or judgment of the judiciary in specific proceedings. It is therefore necessary to consider more closely the nature of the legislation challenged in this appeal.

Mr Gratiaen succinctly summarises his attack on the Acts in question as follows. The first Act was wholly bad in that it was a special direction to the judiciary as to the trial of particular prisoners who were identifiable (in view of the White Paper) and charged with particular offences on a particular occasion. The pith and substance of both Acts was a legislative plan ex post facto to secure the conviction and enhance the punishment of those particular individuals. It legalised their imprisonment while they were awaiting trial. It made admissible their statements inadmissibly obtained during that period. It altered the fundamental law of evidence so as to facilitate their conviction. And finally it altered ex post facto the punishment to be imposed on them.

In their Lordships' view that cogent summary fairly describes the effect of the Acts. As has been indicated already, legislation ad hominem which is thus directed to the course of particular proceedings may not always amount to an interference with the functions of the judiciary. But in the present case their Lordships have no doubt that there was such interference; that it was not only the likely but the intended effect of the impugned enactments; and that it is fatal to their validity. The true nature and purpose of these enactments are revealed by their conjoint impact on the specific proceedings in respect of which they were designed, and they take their colour, in particular, from the alterations they purported to make as to their ultimate objective, the punishment of those convicted. These alterations constituted a grave and deliberate incursion into the judicial sphere. Quite bluntly, their aim was to ensure that the judges in dealing with these particular persons on these particular charges were deprived of their normal discretion as respects appropriate sentences. They were compelled to sentence each offender on conviction to not less than ten years' imprisonment, and compelled to order con-**[291]**-fiscation of his possessions, even though his part in the conspiracy might have been trivial ...

If such Acts as these were valid the judicial power could be wholly absorbed by the legislature and taken out of the hands of the judges. It is appreciated that the legislature had no such general intention. It was beset by a grave situation and it took grave measures to deal with it, thinking, one must presume, that it had power to do so and was acting rightly. But that consideration is irrelevant, and gives no validity to acts which infringe the Constitution. What is done once, if it be allowed, may be done again and in a lesser crisis and less serious circumstances. And thus judicial power may be eroded ... **[292]** In their Lordships' view the Acts were ultra vires and invalid.

An argument alleging interference with the federal judicial process had limited success in *Chu Kheng Lim v Minister for Immigration, Local Government and Ethnic Affairs* (1992) 176 CLR 1. However, a more ambitious argument alleging usurpation of judicial power was rejected. At issue was the validity of the *Migration Amendment Act 1992* (Cth), assented to on 6 May 1992, which had added to the *Migration Act 1958* (Cth) a new Div 4B entitled "Custody of certain non-citizens". The amendments had been rushed through Parliament in extraordinary circumstances to prevent the hearing of applications for release pending in the Federal Court.

The "designated persons" to whom Div 4B applied were identified in s 54K as having "been on a boat in the territorial sea of Australia after 19 November 1989 and before 1 December 1992". Of the two groups of Cambodian "boat people" who were plaintiffs in the High Court proceedings, one group of 22 plaintiffs had arrived in Australian territorial waters on 27 November 1989, and the other group of 13 plaintiffs had arrived on 31 March 1990. The amendments were expressed to take effect from the date of assent, 6 May 1992, and provided that, after that commencement, "a designated person must be kept in custody" until he or she were either to leave Australia, or be given an entry permit. Specifically, s 54R provided: "A court is not to order the release from custody of a designated person". Moreover, s 54N(1) provided that: "a designated person ... not in custody immediately after commencement" was liable to be detained without warrant. Section 54N(2) added that this applied even to "a designated person … whose release was ordered by a court".

The joint judgment of Brennan, Deane and Dawson JJ held, first, that up to the time of the 1992 amendments the plaintiffs' detention had been unlawful and, second, that if similar provisions were enacted in relation to Australian citizens, they would violate the separation of powers. As to the second point they said:

Chu Kheng Lim v Minister for Immigration, Local Government and Ethnic Affairs
(1992) 176 CLR 1

Brennan, Deane and Dawson JJ: [26] The Constitution is structured upon, and incorporates, the doctrine of the separation of judicial from executive and legislative powers. Chapter III gives effect to that doctrine in so far as the vesting of judicial power is concerned. Its provisions constitute "an exhaustive statement of the manner in which the judicial power of the Commonwealth is or may be vested … No part of the judicial power can be conferred in virtue of any other authority or otherwise than in accordance with the provisions of Chap III" [*R v Kirby; Ex parte Boilermakers' Society of Australia* (1956) 94 CLR 254 at 270]. Thus, it is **[27]** well settled that the grants of legislative power contained in s 51 of the Constitution, which are expressly "subject to" the provisions of the Constitution as a whole, do not permit the conferral upon any organ of the Executive Government of any part of the judicial power of the Commonwealth. Nor do those grants of legislative power extend to the making of a law which requires or authorizes the courts in which the judicial power of the Commonwealth is exclusively vested to exercise judicial power in a manner which is inconsistent with the essential character of a court or with the nature of judicial power.

There are some functions which, by reason of their nature or because of historical considerations, have become established as essentially and exclusively judicial in character. The most important of them is the adjudgment and punishment of criminal guilt under a law of the Commonwealth. That function appertains exclusively to and "could not be excluded from" the judicial power of the Commonwealth [*R v Davison* (1954) 90 CLR 353 at 368]. That being so, Ch III of the Constitution precludes the enactment, in purported pursuance of any of the sub-sections of s 51 of the Constitution, of any law purporting to vest any part of that function in the Commonwealth Executive …

If the first element – ie "non-citizen" – of the definition of "designated person" for the purposes of Div 4B had been omitted with the consequence that those provisions purported to apply to Australian citizens, Div 4B would be plainly beyond the legislative competence of the Parliament and invalid. The reason for that would not only be the absence of any relevant head of Commonwealth legislative power to found the application to citizens of this country of laws of the kind contained in Div 4B. It would also be that Div 4B, if not confined to non-citizens, would purport both to authorize involuntary imprisonment of citizens by executive designation and to deprive the courts of jurisdiction to order that a citizen, who had been so designated by the Executive, be released from custody if his or her detention in custody was found to be unlawful. Such a conferral upon the Executive of an essentially unexaminable power to imprison a citizen would, for the reasons given above, be inconsistent with the Constitution's doctrine of the separation of judicial from executive and legislative power and its exclusive vesting of judicial power in the courts. Ultimately, the critical question in the present case is whether the effect of the confinement of the application of the provisions of Div 4B to non-citizens or aliens is to avoid such conflict between the provisions of Div 4B and Ch III of the Constitution.

Insofar as Div 4B authorised "**[29]** involuntary imprisonment … by executive assignation", they held it to be valid because, in the case of aliens, "**[32]** the conferral upon the Executive of authority to detain … an alien in custody for the purposes of expulsion or deportation … is neither punitive in nature nor part of the judicial power of the Commonwealth" (see the extract in Chapter 15, §1). As to the alleged "usurpation" of judicial power they said:

Brennan, Deane and Dawson JJ: [34] It should be mentioned that it was argued on behalf of the plaintiffs that the provisions of Div 4B, including ss 54L and 54N, were invalid as "a usurpation" of the judicial power of the Commonwealth for the reason that they apply only to a class which is "so limited by definition as to amount in substance to a specification of individuals" and "were enacted in order to affect the outcome of known or prospective legal proceedings by those individuals". In support of that argument, particular reliance was placed upon the words "whose release was ordered by a court" in s 54N(2), the provision of s 54R, the judgment of the Privy Council in *Liyanage v The Queen*, the judgment of Street CJ in *BLF v Minister for Industrial Relations* and comments in the judgments of some members of this Court in *Polyukhovich v The Queen* [(1991) 172 CLR 501]. The conclusion that the powers to detain in custody conferred by Div 4B are an incident of the executive powers of exclusion, admission and deportation and, being non-punitive in character, are not part of the judicial power of the Commonwealth, effectively disposes of that argument except in so far as it relates to **[35]** the severable provisions of ss 54R and (arguably) 54U, as to which see below. The fact that proceedings seeking an order for release of the plaintiffs were pending in the Federal Court did not have the effect that the conferral by Div 4B, or the subsequent exercise, of a new executive power of detention constituted a usurpation of, or an impermissible interference with, the exercise of the judicial power of the Commonwealth. In that regard, we would note that the words "whose release was ordered by a court" in s 54N(2) must, in our view, be construed as a reference to an order made by a court before the commencement of Div 4B and as not purporting to authorize an executive overriding of an order made by a court after the commencement of that Division.

The only aspect of the plaintiffs' case not defeated by these arguments was the attack on s 54R ("A court is not to order the release from custody of a designated person").

Brennan, Deane and Dawson JJ: [35] Section 54R provides that a court "is not to order the release from custody of a designated person" … [The section] does not purport to exclude a person to whom the Department has purportedly given "a designation" from challenging his or her status as a "designated person". The section must, however, be read with s 54U which provides that a statement by a Departmental officer that the Department has given a person "a designation described in paragraph (e) of the definition [of designated person]" is "conclusive evidence" of that fact. Subject to the effect of that section, s 54R is inapplicable to a person who does not satisfy all of the six elements of the definition of a "designated person". On the other hand, if a person does satisfy all those elements and is a "designated person" for the purposes of the Division, s 54R purports to direct the courts, including this Court, not to order his or her release from custody regardless of the circumstances.

If it were apparent that there was no possibility that a "designated person" might be unlawfully held in custody under Div 4B, it would be arguable that s 54R did no more than spell out what would be the duty of a court of competent jurisdiction in any event. If that were so, s 54R would be devoid of significant content. In fact, of course, it is manifest that circumstances could exist in which a "designated person" was unlawfully held in custody by a person purportedly acting in pursuance of Div 4B. The reason why that is so is that the status of a person as a "designated person" does not automatically cease when detention in custody is no longer authorized by Div 4B … **[36]** Once it appears that a designated person may be unlawfully held in custody in purported pursuance of Div 4B, it necessarily follows that the provision of s 54R is invalid.

Ours is a Constitution "which deals with the demarcation of powers, leaves to the courts of law the question of whether there has been any excess of power, and requires them to pronounce as void any act which is ultra vires" [*R v Richards; Ex parte Fitzpatrick and Browne* (1955) 92 CLR 157 at 165]. All the powers conferred upon the Parliament by s 51 of the Constitution are, as has been said, subject to Ch III's vesting of that judicial power in the courts which it designates, including this Court. That judicial power includes the jurisdiction which the Constitution directly vests in this Court in all matters in which the Commonwealth or a person being sued on behalf of the Commonwealth is a party or in which mandamus, prohibition or an injunction is sought against an officer of the Commonwealth (s 75(v)). A law of the Parliament which purports to direct, in unqualified terms, that no court, including this Court, shall order the release from custody of a person whom the Executive of the Commonwealth has imprisoned purports to derogate from that direct vesting of judicial power and to remove ultra vires acts of the Executive from the control of this Court. Such a law manifestly exceeds the legislative powers of the Commonwealth and is invalid. Moreover, even to the extent that s 54R is concerned with the exercise of jurisdiction other than this Court's directly vested constitutional jurisdiction, it is inconsistent with Ch III. In terms, s 54R is a direction by the Parliament to the courts as to the manner in which they are to exercise their jurisdiction. It is one thing for the Parliament, within the limits of the legislative power conferred upon it by the Constitution, to grant **[37]** or withhold jurisdiction. It is a quite different thing for the Parliament to purport to direct the courts as to the manner and outcome of the exercise of their jurisdiction. The former falls within the legislative power which the Constitution, including Ch III itself, entrusts to the Parliament. The latter constitutes an impermissible intrusion into the judicial power which Ch III vests exclusively in the courts which it designates.

We have given consideration to whether s 54R can legitimately be read down to bring it within legislative power. In our view, it cannot. Any effective reading down would involve the introduction of some qualification to exclude any interference with the directly vested constitutional jurisdiction of this Court. In so far as this Court is concerned, such a reading down would largely deprive the section of its effective content. More important, in so far as the residual jurisdiction of this Court and the jurisdiction of other courts are concerned, any effective reading down would necessarily involve a complete and impermissible reformulation of the terms of s 54R so as to transform an impermissible directive about the manner in which jurisdiction is to be exercised into a provision withdrawing jurisdiction. On the other hand, s 54R is clearly severable from the other provisions of Div 4B. Its invalidity does not give rise to consequential invalidity of any other provision.

Gaudron J agreed with these conclusions, though as to ss 54L and 54N she emphasised more forcefully that they were valid only insofar as they stayed strictly within the constitutional meaning of "aliens". Mason CJ, Toohey and McHugh JJ held that even s 54R was valid, but only because they felt able to "read it down" in the way that the final paragraph above declined to do.

Mason CJ: [12] [I]t would be quite extraordinary to ascribe to Parliament an intention to require a court not to release a person held in unlawful custody. Unless a clear and unambiguous intention to do so appears from a statute, it should not be construed so as to infringe the liberty of the subject. Furthermore, such a clear and unambiguous intention is not sufficiently manifested by the use of general words ...

The only argument against the interpretation of s 54R which I find compelling is that the section, so interpreted, may achieve nothing. The section achieves nothing if it does no more than instruct the courts to act in conformity with the substantive provisions of Div 4B, that being something which the courts would be bound to do in any event. To construe the section in this way, it is suggested, would be to ignore the presumption that words are not used in a statute without a meaning and are not superfluous ... **[13]** However, this presumption or rule of construction is of limited application ...

In this case, s 54R presents a ... choice between one construction which involves superfluity and another which infringes the liberty of the individual and purports to require the courts not to release a person held in unlawful custody, thereby setting at naught the fundamental principle that no person shall be imprisoned except pursuant to lawful authority. Plainly enough, the presumption or rule of construction is not strong enough to enable the second construction to prevail.

(b)   The Trial Process

The contemporary approach to the strict separation of judicial power as reflecting the role of the courts as a bulwark of individual liberties was foreshadowed very early in the history of the Constitution, by one of the most influential commentators of the time.

W Harrison Moore, *The Constitution of the Commonwealth of Australia*
(Maxwell, 2nd ed 1910, repr Legal Books, 1997)

[321] It would be dangerous to attempt an exhaustive statement of the cases in which judicial functions may be exercised under the Constitution by authorities other than the Courts established or invested with jurisdiction under sec 71. But ... it may be accepted as a general rule that the separation of powers in the Constitution imports within the range of Commonwealth action that the legality of any governmental action, or the existence of any right, or the liability to any penalty, cannot be determined elsewhere than in the Courts: that determination is a part of the judicial power of the Commonwealth. This limitation upon administrative action is well illustrated by the case of Executive inquiries. The Commissioner or officer questioning a witness and requiring him to answer, could not be empowered to fine or imprison the recalcitrant witness. **[322]** Nor could such authority by any determination of its own, create, by the mere force of that determination, a duty to answer the questions. The question whether the witness is bound to answer the questions can only be determined by the Court which is invoked to impose the penalties, and which then has to determine for itself whether there was a duty or whether it was broken.

The rule which assigns the judicial power of the Commonwealth to Courts is thus a safeguard against arbitrary power more important than at first appears and importing restrictions upon the power of Parliament more extensive than is at first realized. It is not merely that the Legislature may not constitute itself or any other body unauthorized by the Constitution, a Court of justice with functions which might be validly performed by a Court regularly constituted, *ie* the determination, after hearing, of rights according to law. If this were all that is imported by the separation of powers, it would be of small importance legally, for a power of this nature is very rarely usurped by a Legislature. The temptation to which Legislatures are liable, to which American Legislatures have succumbed, and which American Courts have met by the allegation of an invasion of judicial power, is to apply a new rule to past acts or events, or to deal with a specific matter of injury or wrong independently of all rule. However mischievous and dangerous may be *ex post facto* laws and *privilegia*, their very mischief lies in the fact that they are something other than judicial acts; that what should have been done in a judicial way and according to law has been done by the assumption of arbitrary power. The grant of judicial power **[323]** to a special organ means that if the matter be one which from its nature is proper for judicial determination alone, the Legislature cannot deal with it otherwise, or authorize anyone, even a Court properly constituted, to deal with it except in the way of adjudication. Thus, as already seen, the question whether a witness has incurred a penalty for refusing to answer questions in an Executive inquiry is essentially one for judicial determination. It would be unconstitutional for the Legislature to constitute itself, or one of its committees, or the Executive body pursuing the inquiry, a tribunal for determining the question upon a regular investigation of the facts and a consideration of the law. But it would be none the less unconstitutional for the Legislature to enact without regard to either law or facts that the penalties had been incurred and should be suffered by the witness. In one sense the act is not "judicial," for no Court could properly have acted in such a way. But it is an excess of legislative power and an invasion of the judicial power because it affects to deal with an essentially judicial matter in a non-judicial way. On the same grounds, the power to adjudicate possessed by a Court imports the observance of principles of legal administration essential to the judicial office. The full extent of these principles cannot be easily determined; but whatever they are, they may not be interfered with by the Legislature. The Constitution empowers the Legislature to regulate the *incidents* of judicature – this power is expressly conferred in sec 51(xxxix) – but any interference with the essentials of judicial administration is a deprivation of judicial power and an attempt to require the Court to act in a non-judicial way ... **[324]** The Legislature may declare generally who shall be competent witnesses, what shall be admissible as evidence, and how proof may be made. It may even declare that certain things shall be *primâ facie* evidence of the matter in dispute, and thus affect the burden of proof. This, however, is subject to the qualification that the matter proved must have a reasonable relation to the matter in issue and a real tendency to establish it – the inference must not be "purely arbitrary, unreasonable, unnatural or extraordinary." To go further and pre-determine the probative force of evidence so as absolutely to exclude a party from rebutting it would be an interference with the judicial office and void.

The limits of legislative interference with evidentiary burdens of proof were tested in *Actors & Announcers Equity Association v Fontana Films Pty Ltd* (1982) 150 CLR 169. In that case the High Court upheld, as a law with respect to "trading ... corporations" under s 51(xx) of the Constitution, the controversial "secondary boycott" provision – s 45D – added in 1977 to the

Trade Practices Act 1974 (Cth). Broadly, s 45D prohibited trade union activities, pursuant to a dispute with an employer, which affected the trading activities of other corporations in their dealings with the employer. As to the decision that this prohibition was valid, see Chapter 17, §3. Our present concern is with s 45D(5), which provided that where two or more officers of a union engaged in concerted conduct, the union itself was *deemed* to engage in that conduct, unless it could show "that it took all reasonable steps" to prevent it. By 5:2 this provision was held to be invalid. It failed because it had, as Mason J put it, "**[211]** a very remote connexion with corporations, a connexion so remote that the provision cannot be characterized as a law with respect to corporations". Only Murphy J gave any full explanation of why this was so.

Actors & Announcers Equity Association v Fontana Films Pty Ltd
(1982) 150 CLR 169

Murphy J: [213] Presumptions are a useful and common device for facilitating proof. Judges have recognized, that is adopted, a myriad of presumptions. These make the legal system operable. Statutory presumptions are a way of correcting the recent tendency to abandon the common law method of adapting the law (including evidence and proof) to the changing society. The justification for all presumptions is human experience of the association between the known and the presumed facts or circumstances.

It is within the general incidental power (s 51(xxxix)) or the specific powers in ss 51 or 52 of the Constitution to provide that one fact or circumstance shall be presumed from the existence of another, provided there is a rational basis for the presumption. Where there is no rational basis for the presumption, then in my opinion Parliament has no power to require a court to act upon the presumption. To do so would be to undermine the judicial **[214]** power. Clearer still, a law that proof of one fact is deemed to be proof of another fact, so that the party against whom the second fact is alleged is prevented from attempting to disprove it, undermines the judicial power. This does not apply where the second fact is merely another description of, or an inevitable consequence of, the first fact. Sometimes deemed may only mean presumed. Also "deeming" may be used merely as a shorthand method of legislating, so that when the provisions as a whole are considered the vice is only in the form, not the substance. But here the deeming provision in s 45D(5) and the reference to it in s 45D(6) create a statutory fiction (see Griffith CJ in *Muller v Dalgety & Co Ltd* [(1909) 9 CLR 693 at 694]), so that the conclusion is to be made even if it is contrary to the fact. In the light of experience of Australian industrial relations, it cannot rationally even be presumed that the conduct in concert of two or more members of an organization of employees is the conduct of the organization. The conduct is often unsupported by or occasionally opposed by the organization ... The effect of s 45D(5) and (6) is that if two or more members or officers of an organization of employees engaged in prohibited conduct in concert this would be deemed to be the conduct of the organization (unless it could establish that it took all reasonable steps to prevent the participants from engaging in that conduct) exposing it to severe consequences. Such a law is not authorized by the corporations' power or the general incidental power in s 51(xxxix). The legislative powers in s 51 are subject to the Constitution, including Ch III, The Judicature. It is not consistent with the exercise of judicial power that the courts be required to make findings contrary to fact or to adjudge persons guilty or civilly liable upon proof of facts from which a rational conclusion of guilt or liability does not follow but on the basis of a legislative conclusion which is unexaminable judicially. A similar attempt to penalize persons on the basis of legislative or executive opinions unexaminable in the courts was rejected in *Australian Communist Party v Commonwealth* [(1951) 83 CLR 1].

Unlike a presumption, the purpose and effect of a deeming provision is to prevent any attempt, by either party, to prove the truth. Legislative provision for suppression of the truth in judicial proceedings is inconsistent with the exercise of judicial power and **[215]** unconstitutional.

One feature of the law held invalid in *Liyanage v The Queen* was its retrospective operation. It is generally thought important that laws defining the elements of criminal guilt should operate only for the future, so that guilt or innocence are determined by judicial application of rules or criteria already publicly spelled out at the time of the alleged offences. Accordingly, the traditional approach has been that, where possible, the courts will construe a law imposing criminal penalties so as not to operate retrospectively. However, the corollary of that approach is that an Act will operate retrospectively if Parliament has made that intention unmistakably clear.

The standard Australian example of this approach is *R v Kidman* (1915) 20 CLR 425. The defendants were charged with conspiracy to defraud the Commonwealth by profiteering on supplies to the armed forces in World War I. The offence of "conspiracy to defraud the Commonwealth" had been added to the Commonwealth *Crimes Act 1914* (Cth) by amendment in 1915. The amendment was assented to on 7 May 1915, but required that it "be deemed to have been in force" from 29 October 1914. The High Court upheld these provisions. Most of the judgments specifically held that the Commonwealth did have power to enact a retrospective criminal law. However, Griffith CJ held only that the legislation was not in the relevant sense "retrospective", since it merely gave statutory declarative form to an offence already existing at common law. At one stage the judgment of Isaacs J appeared to reflect a similar assumption.

The issue arose again in *Polyukhovich v Commonwealth* (*War Crimes Act Case*) (1991) 172 CLR 501. Section 9(1) of the *War Crimes Act 1945* (Cth), as inserted by the *War Crimes Amendment Act 1988* (Cth), provided that an Australian citizen or resident was guilty of an indictable offence if he or she "committed a war crime" in Europe between 1 September 1939 and 8 May 1945. The problem was whether the *War Crimes Amendment Act* amounted to a retrospective criminal law, and whether in that or other ways it deviated so fundamentally from normal judicial processes as to violate an implied guarantee arising from Ch III of the Constitution. In part, this involved the question whether *Kidman* should be overruled.

Ivan Polyukhovich did not originally raise these issues. The Commonwealth maintained that the law was valid either under the defence power (s 51(vi)) or under the external affairs power (s 51(xxix)), and both sides initially argued the case in terms of those heads of power. It was Deane J who raised in the course of argument the possibility that the law might infringe a constitutional implication to be found in Ch III of the Constitution; and the case was reargued on that basis.

A 6:1 majority upheld the Act as a law with respect to "external affairs", but for those judges who considered the issue it was not a law with respect to "defence". Only Brennan J held that it was not within either power. Significantly, his conclusion was heavily influenced by the element of retrospectivity. Thus, he might have accepted the argument under the "external affairs" power were it not for the Act's "disconformity" to international law, and particularly to its condemnation of retrospective criminal law. Again, the argument that the Act might legitimately relate to "defence", by helping to set standards of conduct applicable in future wars, was rejected by him because of the Act's retrospectivity and selective application (see the extract in Chapter 18, §1).

Both Deane and Gaudron JJ held that the Act was "within power" as a law with respect to external affairs. Nevertheless, both of them ended up agreeing with Brennan J that the Act was invalid. They did so on the ground that it was incompatible with Ch III of the Constitution.

Polyukhovich v The Queen (*War Crimes Act Case*)
(1991) 172 CLR 501

Deane J: [606] The main objective of the sometimes inconvenient separation of judicial from executive and legislative powers had long been recognized at the time of the federation. It is to ensure that "the life, liberty, and property of the subject [is not] in the hands of arbitrary judges, whose decisions [are] then regulated only by their own opinions, and not by any fundamental principles of law" (Blackstone, *Commentaries*, 17th ed (1830), vol I, p 269; and see, **[607]** to like effect, Story, *Commentaries on the Constitution of the United States* (1833), §1568). That objective will, of course, be achieved only by the Constitution's requirement that judicial power be vested exclusively in the courts which it designates if the judicial power so vested is exercised by those courts in accordance with the essential attributes of the curial process (cf *Re Tracey; Ex parte Ryan* [(1989) 166 CLR 518 at 580]). Indeed, to construe Ch III of the Constitution as being concerned only with labels and as requiring no more than that the repository of judicial power be called a court would be to convert it into a mockery, rather than a reflection, of the doctrine of separation of powers. Common sense and the provisions of Ch III, based as they are on the assumption of traditional judicial procedures, remedies and methodology ... , compel the conclusion that, in insisting that the judicial power of the Commonwealth be vested only in the courts designated by Ch III, the Constitution's intent and meaning were that that judicial power would be exercised by those courts acting as courts with all that that notion essentially requires. Accordingly, the Parliament cannot, consistently with Ch III of the Constitution, usurp the judicial power of the Commonwealth by itself purporting to exercise judicial power in the form of legislation. Nor can it infringe the vesting of that judicial power in the judicature by requiring that it be exercised in a manner which is inconsistent with the essential requirements of a court or with the nature of judicial power ...

[608] Prima facie, the relevant substantive law for determining rights and liabilities is the law which operated at the time of the circumstances from which those rights and liabilities are alleged to arise. Thus, it is a rule of construction that it is to be presumed that it was not the legislative intent that a statutory provision which affects rights or liabilities should operate retrospectively. Nonetheless, the focus of civil litigation is upon the determination of rights and liabilities under the law as it exists at the time of the proceedings. Civil legislation which operates retrospectively in the sense that it extinguishes or alters pre-existing rights or liabilities or deems rights and liabilities which it creates to have existed at an earlier time may, depending on the circumstances, be susceptible of legitimate criticism as unfair or unjustified. Such legislation will not, however, contravene the doctrine of separation of powers merely because it retrospectively creates, extinguishes or alters civil rights and liabilities or because it requires the courts to recognize and enforce, in subsequent civil litigation, the retrospective operation of its provisions ... Putting to one side cases of impermissible interference with the proper discharge of judicial power by the courts, it will do so only if it is properly to be seen as involving a purported legislative exercise of the judicial function. Except in quite extreme cases (eg a statute providing that there be a verdict for the plaintiff in the amount of $500,000 in pending defamation proceedings in a court), the boundary between what is permissible as falling within the limits of legislative power and what is forbidden as a usurpation of judicial power is likely to be blurred in civil matters. The reason is that both the legislature and the judicature may, within the limits of their respective functions under the doctrine of separation of powers, each settle questions of rights and liabilities under the civil law. The position is different, however, in the case of a law which operates to make criminal an act which was not a crime when done. I turn to explain why that is so. For convenience of discussion, I shall refer to such a law as an "ex post facto criminal law".

There are some functions which, by reason of their nature or because of historical considerations, have become established as incontrovertibly and exclusively judicial in their character. One – and the most important – of such functions is the adjudgment of guilt of a person accused of a criminal offence. As such, that function is a matter "appertaining exclusively to [judicial] power" [609] (per Griffith CJ, *Waterside Workers' Federation of Australia v JW Alexander Ltd* [(1918) 25 CLR 434 at 444]) which "could not be excluded from the judicial power": see, eg, *R v Davison* [(1954) 90 CLR 353 at 368-9, 383]. It follows that, subject only to limited qualifications ... , the Parliament is incapable of vesting jurisdiction to try a person accused of an offence against a law of the Commonwealth otherwise than in one of the "courts" contemplated by Ch III or of directing that part of such jurisdiction be exercised in a manner inconsistent with the requirements of that Chapter. More important for present purposes, the Parliament is incapable of substituting a legislative enactment of criminal guilt of an offence against a law of the Commonwealth for a trial by a Ch III court ...

The basic tenet of our penal jurisprudence is that every citizen is "ruled by the law, and by the law alone". The citizen "may with us be punished for a breach of law, but he can be punished for nothing else" (Dicey, *Introduction to the Study of the Law of the Constitution*, 10th ed (1959), p 202). Thus, more than two hundred years ago, Blackstone taught (see *Commentaries* (1830), vol I, pp 45-46) that it is of the nature of law that it be "a rule *prescribed*" and that ... an enactment which proscribes otherwise lawful conduct as criminal will not be such a rule unless it applies only to future conduct ...

[I]t is basic to our penal jurisprudence that a person who has disobeyed no relevant law is not guilty of a crime. Of its nature, a crime "is an act committed, or omitted, in violation of a public law, either forbidding or commanding it" (Blackstone, *Commentaries* (1830), vol IV, p 5). It necessarily involves a **[610]** contravention of a prohibition contained in an existing applicable valid law ... Accordingly, the whole focus of a criminal trial is the ascertainment of whether it is established that the accused in fact committed a past act which constituted a criminal contravention of the requirements of a valid law which was applicable to the act at the time the act was done. It is the determination of that question which lies at the heart of the exclusively judicial function of the adjudgment of criminal guilt ...

[612] A statutory provision, such as s 9 of the Act, that a "person who" in the past "committed" a specified act "is guilty of" a punishable crime prescribes no rule of conduct. It prohibits nothing. It trespasses upon the exclusively judicial field of determining whether past conduct was a crime, that is to say, whether it was in fact an act or omission which the law "prohibited with penal consequences". Within that field, it negates the ordinary curial process by enacting, and requiring a finding of, criminal guilt regardless of whether there was in fact any contravention of any relevant law. If the specified act was not prohibited by such a law when done, such a statutory provision is a retroactive legislative declaration of past criminal guilt when in fact there was none. If it nominates, either individually or by reference to an identifiable group, the person or persons who have committed the specified act, it constitutes a Bill of Attainder or a Bill of Pains and Penalties, depending upon the punishment. In such a case, the statutory provision constitutes a legislative declaration of guilt without any trial at all. Plainly, it involves a usurpation of judicial power ...

The position is less obvious where such a statutory provision does not nominate a particular person or group of persons but identifies **[613]** the persons whom it makes punishable for past "crime" by reference only to their having committed some past act which was not criminal when done. In such a case, there will be a need for a trial to determine whether a particular accused falls within the class of those whose past conduct is retroactively made criminal. Nonetheless, such a statutory provision declaring past conduct to have been a criminal offence constitutes a usurpation of judicial power in that, once it is established that the accused has committed the past act, the question whether that act constituted a criminal contravention of the law is made simply irrelevant. To that extent, curial determination of criminal guilt is ousted by legislative decree. The point can be illustrated by dividing the legislation in such a case into its essential components. One component ... is the requirement that there be a "trial" in the courts, in which judicial process must be observed, to determine whether it is established beyond reasonable doubt that a particular person knowingly engaged in the designated conduct. The second component is the enactment that, if it be established that the particular person did in fact engage in that past conduct which was not criminal when done, he is guilty of a punishable crime. That second component of the legislation invades the heart of the exclusively judicial function of determining criminal guilt, that is to say, of determining whether past conduct constituted a criminal contravention of the law. It pre-empts and negates what would otherwise be an inevitable judicial determination that, since the act of the particular person did not constitute a criminal contravention of any Commonwealth law which was applicable at the time when it was done, that person committed no crime under our law. In the place of that inevitable judicial determination, it imposes a legislative enactment of past guilt which it requires the courts, in violation of the basic tenet of our criminal jurisprudence and the doctrine of separation of judicial from legislative and executive powers, to apply and enforce. It is simply not to the point that the first component of the legislation camouflages the usurpation of judicial power involved in the second by requiring a display of the full panoply of judicial process for the purpose of determining whether it is established beyond reasonable doubt that the accused person knowingly did a specified act which was not criminal when done.

It follows ... that Ch III's exclusive vesting of the judicial power of the Commonwealth in courts acting as such does not, at least prima facie, permit the conviction of a person by a court under a statute which declares that a person is guilty of a punishable crime if he has done a past **[614]** act which was not criminal when done. There are two closely related reasons why the process leading up to such a conviction would prima facie contravene the doctrine of separation of powers embodied in Ch III. It is convenient to restate them in summary form. First, the legislature's interference in that process would go beyond the limits of the legislative function under a constitution structured upon the separation of judicial and legislative powers in that it would involve a usurpation and partial exercise of what lies at the heart of the exclusively judicial function in criminal matters, namely, the determination of whether the accused person has in fact done an act which constituted a criminal contravention of the then applicable law. Second, a court's participation in that process would also be inconsistent with the doctrine of the separation of powers in that it would represent an abdication of the judicial function of determining in a criminal trial whether past conduct had contravened the law in favour of the legislature's decree that a past non-criminal act is to be punished as a crime.

Deane J went on to consider whether there were other features of the Constitution that might weigh against this conclusion; but in fact those he found reinforced it. Chapter III implies "[614] an assumption of traditional judicial procedures, remedies and methodology"; it confers "juris-diction", and gives it to "courts"; and it does so by reference to "matters", as defined by Isaacs J in *South Australia v Victoria* (*Boundaries Case*) (1911) 12 CLR 667 as "[715] confined to claims resting upon an alleged violation of some positive law". Then there was the existence of s 80, which, said Deane J, "[615] assumes, what would in any event be implicit in the requirement of trial by jury, that the question of guilt or innocence will be determined by reference to criminality or otherwise as at the time of the alleged offence".

The United States Constitution provides (in Art I, §9, cl 3): "No Bill of Attainder or ex post facto law shall be passed". Clearly the drafters of the Australian Constitution, working from the American model, chose not to include such a clause. On that ground it was argued that the Court could not now imply one. However, Deane J rebutted that argument by invoking the well-established view of the United States Supreme Court (initially in *Calder v Bull*, 3 US (3 Dallas) 387 (1798), but reaffirmed, for example, in *United States v Brown*, 381 US 437 (1965)) that the prohibition in Art I, §9, cl 3 is merely an explicit reaffirmation of what is in any event implicit in the separation of powers. As to *R v Kidman*, Deane J said:

> **Deane J: [622]** The basis of Griffith CJ's conclusion in *Kidman* [(1915) 20 CLR 425]... was that the law was not really an ex post facto criminal law at all. In his Honour's view, conduct which constituted conspiracy to defraud the Commonwealth had already been a crime at common law before the enactment of the 1915 Act. On that view [20 CLR at 436-7], all that the 1915 Act did was to enact "in the form of a Statute the unwritten law of the Commonwealth". Griffith CJ's view that the legislation in *Kidman* was not an ex post facto criminal law in the narrow sense in which I have been using that phrase, was apparently shared by Isaacs J. The judgments of a majority of the Court proceeded, however, on the assumption that the 1915 Act was a truly ex post facto criminal law. That being so, *Kidman* is properly to be seen as providing technical authority for a denial of the proposition that Ch III of the Constitution precludes the enactment by the Parliament of such a law. However, in circumstances where the effect of Ch III and the question of the validity of that proposition were neither raised in argument nor considered in any of the judgments and where the case was decided before the implications of the adoption by Ch III (and by the Constitution as a whole) of the doctrine of the separation of judicial from administrative and legislative power had been critically examined in this Court, the authority of *Kidman* in that regard is weak indeed. This Court is the creation and the servant of the Constitution. It would be quite wrong for it to treat an implicit decision of its own in an earlier case on a point which was neither raised in argument nor considered in the judgments as of itself providing a justification for refusing to acknowledge the implications of Ch III's fundamental guarantee of judicial process.

Gaudron J took a similar view, but analysed more sharply the sense in which a retrospective criminal law is a "legislative usurpation" of judicial power.

> **Gaudron J: [703]** An essential feature of judicial power is that it be exercised in accordance with the judicial process. I attempted to identify the features of that process in *Harris v Caladine* [(1991) 172 CLR 84 at 150-2], and in *Re Nolan; Ex parte Young* [(1991) 172 CLR 460 at 496]. To adopt the words of Kitto J in *R v Trade Practices Tribunal; Ex parte Tasmanian Breweries Pty* **[704]** *Ltd*

[(1970) 123 CLR 361 at 374], the essential features of that process include the determination of legal rights, obligations or consequences by the ascertainment of the facts as they are and as they bear on the matter for determination, and the identification of the applicable law, followed by an application of that law to those facts. Those features may be more or less obvious, depending on the issues involved and the nature of the law to be applied. At one extreme, the law to be applied may require the assigning of future rights and obligations attaching to or in consequence of a legal relationship in the exercise of a judicial discretion in which no particular matter is decisive. At the other extreme, the law may assign distinct legal consequences by reason that a person has committed a particular proscribed act. Criminal laws are laws of the latter kind. But whatever the issues and whatever the nature of the law being applied, the power vested in a court can be exercised only on the basis of the discovered facts and by application of the law which determines the legal consequences attaching to those facts.

A power to be exercised by the application of law to facts invented by Parliament or invented according to some statutory formula or prescription would not be a power to be exercised in accordance with the judicial process and would not be judicial power. That is not to say that statutory fictions may not be employed in the course of and for the purpose of formulating the legal rights, obligations or consequences attaching to a relationship or to conduct. And, of course, they may be applied by the courts when those rights, obligations or consequences are in issue. However, the relationship or the conduct which is the basis of those rights, obligations or consequences must be real and not fictitious. A law assigning legal consequences on the basis of fictitious or invented facts may sometimes, on that account, be characterized as other than a law on a subject matter within legislative power: see *Actors and Announcers Equity Association v Fontana Films Pty Ltd* [(1982) 150 CLR 169]. Quite apart from that consideration, a law conferring power on a court to determine legal consequences on the basis that a person is who he is not or on the basis that he did what he did not would be invalid for offending Ch III. It would be invalid because the power in question would involve a travesty of the judicial process and would, thus, be a power which, by virtue of s 71, could not validly be conferred on a court.

Equally, it would be a travesty of the judicial process if, in proceedings to determine whether a person had committed an act proscribed by and punishable by law, the law proscribing and **[705]** providing for punishment of that act were a law invented to fit the facts after they had become known. In that situation, the proceedings would not be directed to ascertaining guilt or innocence (which is the function of criminal proceedings and the exclusive function of the courts), but to ascertaining whether the Parliament had perfected its intention of declaring the act in question an act against the criminal law. That is what is involved if a criminal law is allowed to take effect from some time prior to its enactment. Of course, the position is different if the law re-enacts an earlier law which applied when the acts were committed ... [However], in my view, a law would not be a law reenacting an earlier law if it purported to apply cumulatively upon it. And the position is different again in the case of a law which acts retrospectively upon civil rights, obligations or liabilities. The function of a court in civil proceedings is the determination of present rights, obligations or liabilities. In that context, a retrospective civil law is very much like a statutory fiction in that it is a convenient way of formulating laws which, by their application to the facts in issue, determine the nature and extent of those present rights, obligations or liabilities ...

As Deane J points out in this case, the significance of Ch III was neither raised nor considered in *Kidman*. Accordingly, in my **[706]** view, *Kidman* is authority only for what it actually decided, namely, that it is within the legislative power of the Parliament to create a statutory offence taking effect prior to its enactment if it merely gives statutory form to an earlier common law offence. However, if *Kidman* is authority for some wider proposition, then in my view, for the reasons given by Deane J, it should be re-examined. In particular, it does not rest upon a principle that has been carefully worked out in a succession of cases and, it is not a decision which, outside the present case, appears to have been acted upon: see *Commonwealth v Hospital Contribution Fund* [(1982) 150 CLR 49 at 56-7].

The true nature of what is commonly called an "ex post facto law" or a "retroactive law" is revealed in the judgment of Powers J in *Kidman* [20 CLR at 457] where his Honour described a law of that kind as "a law by which, after an act has been committed which was not punishable ... at the time it was committed, the person who committed it is declared to have been guilty of a crime and to be held liable to punishment". As is there made clear, it is the statute or the Act of the Parliament, and not the determination of a court, by which a person is declared to have been guilty. That is the usurpation (see *Liyanage v The Queen* [[1967] 1 AC 259 at 289]) of power which is exclusively judicial ...

The usurpation of judicial power by a law which declares a person guilty of an offence produces the consequence that the application of that law by a court would involve it in an exercise repugnant to the judicial process. It is repugnant to the judicial process because the determination of guilt or innocence is foreclosed by the law. The only issue is whether the person concerned was a person declared guilty by the law. And all that involves is the determination, as a matter of fact, whether some person is the person, or answers the description (whatever form it takes) of the persons, declared guilty by the Act. It does not involve, and indeed negates, that which is the essence of judicial power in a criminal proceeding, namely, the determination of guilt or innocence by the application of the law to the facts as found. Accordingly, such a law **[707]** is invalid as infringing s 71 because it involves the exercise by Parliament of a power which can be exercised only by the courts named or indicated in s 71 and because its application by a court would involve it in exercising a power repugnant to the judicial process. If *Kidman* holds otherwise, it should no longer be followed.

Brennan J had no need to consider this issue; he had reached the same conclusion by more traditional means. However, Mason CJ, Dawson and McHugh JJ rejected the argument almost entirely. In their view, *Kidman* was still good law, and the war crimes legislation was valid.

Mason CJ: [532] According to the widely-accepted statement of Griffith CJ in *Huddart, Parker & Co Pty Ltd v Moorehead* [(1909) 8 CLR 330 at 357], judicial power in s 71 means "the power which every sovereign authority must of necessity have to decide controversies between its subjects, or between itself and its subjects whether the rights relate to life, liberty or property".

A more comprehensive statement of the content of judicial power is contained in the judgment of Kitto J in *R v Trade Practices Tribunal; Ex parte Tasmanian Breweries Pty Ltd* [123 CLR at 374-5] ... This statement contemplates as one element in the exercise of judicial power the application to the facts of a pre-existing or antecedent legal principle or standard, though it does not require that the rule or standard should have been ascertained or precisely defined before the determination is made in the exercise of judicial power. The need for an inquiry into what the law is presupposes that there may be uncertainty as to the nature, scope or content of the principle or standard to be applied. Indeed, it is widely **[533]** recognized that courts, in exercising their judicial power, make and alter law in the sense of formulating new or altered legal principles.

There is nothing in the statements which I have quoted to suggest that an exercise of judicial power necessarily involves the application to the facts of a legal principle or standard formulated in advance of the events to which it is sought to be applied. Indeed, there is powerful authority in this Court which supports the proposition that the application to the facts of a retrospective law which operates on past conduct so as to create rights and liabilities is an instance of the exercise of judicial power. In *Nelungaloo Pty Ltd v Commonwealth* [(1947) 75 CLR 495], the validity of the *Wheat Industry Stabilization Act (No 2) 1946* (Cth) was upheld, even though it validated an order for the acquisition of wheat, the validity of which was in issue in proceedings pending when the statute was enacted. The statute affected rights in issue in the litigation ...

More recently, in *Australian Building Construction Employees' and Builders Labourers' Federation v Commonwealth* [(1986) 161 CLR 88], this **[534]** Court rejected the contention that the *Builders Labourers' Federation (Cancellation of Registration) Act 1986* (Cth) was invalid because it was an exercise of judicial power or because it involved an interference with judicial power. The contention was that the impugned statute, which cancelled the registration of the plaintiff union as a registered organization, abrogated the function of this Court in pending proceedings concerning the cancellation of that registration. The Court drew a distinction between legislation affecting substantive rights in issue in litigation and legislative interference with the judicial process itself. *Liyanage v The Queen* [[1967] 1 AC 259], where the statutes were directed to the trial of particular persons charged with particular offences on a particular occasion, was a case which fell into the second of the two categories.

It is contended that the power of the Parliament to enact a retrospective or retroactive law dealing with substantive rights or liabilities does not extend to a law which makes past conduct a criminal offence. Such a law, it is said, stands in a very different position. It is suggested that support is to be found in Blackstone's *Commentaries* ...

[535] But nowhere does Blackstone assert that it is beyond the power of Parliament to enact such a law, and still less that such a law would constitute an interference with the exercise of judicial power. He held strongly to the view that Parliament had power to enact that which was unreasonable and was vehemently opposed to the pretension that the courts had power to reject a statute on the ground that it was unreasonable "for that were to set the judicial power above that of the legislature, which would be subversive of all government": *Commentaries* (1830), vol I, p 91.

Article I, s 9, cl 3 and Art I, s 10, cl 1 of the United States Constitution prohibit any State as well as Congress from passing a bill of attainder or an ex post facto law. A bill of attainder is a legislative enactment which inflicts punishment without a judicial trial; initially a bill of attainder provided for punishment by death but in the context of the constitutional prohibition such a bill is now regarded as including what was formerly a bill of pains and penalties: *Cummings v Missouri* [71 US (4 Wallace) 277 (1867)]. An ex post facto law, of which a bill of attainder was, or might be, an instance, is a retrospective law which makes past conduct a criminal offence ...

The distinctive characteristic of a bill of attainder, marking it out from other ex post facto laws, is that it is a legislative enactment adjudging a specific person or specific persons guilty of an offence constituted by past conduct and imposing punishment in respect of that offence. Other ex post facto laws speak generally, leaving it to the courts to try and punish specific individuals.

The constitutional prohibition against bills of attainder and ex post facto laws was not an expression of the antecedent common law of England. So much was acknowledged by Chase J in *Calder v Bull* [3 US (3 Dallas) 386 at 389 (1798)] when he said:

> "The prohibition against [State legislatures] making any ex post facto laws was introduced for greater caution, and very probably arose from the knowledge, that the parliament of Great Britain claimed and exercised a power to pass such laws, under the denomination of bills of attainder, or bills of pains and penalties; the first inflicting capital, and the other less, [536] punishment. These acts were legislative judgments; and an exercise of judicial power."

The absence of any similar prohibition in our Constitution against bills of attainder and ex post facto laws is fatal to the plaintiff's argument except in so far as the separation of powers effected by our Constitution, in particular the vesting of judicial power in Ch III courts, imports a restraint on Parliament's power to enact such laws. In this respect the prohibition against bills of attainder has been seen "as an implementation of the separation of powers, a general safeguard against legislative exercise of the judicial function, or more simply – trial by legislature": *United States v Brown* [381 US 437 at 442 (1965)]. This doctrine applies to bills of attainder but not to the generality of other ex post facto laws. That is because it is of the essence of the prohibition of a bill of attainder "that it proscribes legislative punishment of specified persons – not of whichever persons might be judicially determined to fit within properly general proscriptions duly enacted in advance": Tribe, *American Constitutional Law*, 2nd ed (1988), p 643. The application of the doctrine depends upon the legislature adjudging the guilt of a specific individual or specific individuals or imposing punishment upon them. If, for some reason, an ex post facto law did not amount to a bill of attainder, yet adjudged persons guilty of a crime or imposed punishment upon them, it could amount to trial by legislature and a usurpation of judicial power. But if the law, though retrospective in operation, leaves it to the courts to determine whether the person charged has engaged in the conduct complained of and whether that conduct is an infringement of the rule prescribed, there is no interference with the exercise of judicial power ...

[539] In the light of what I have said earlier about the plaintiff's argument, the decision in *Kidman* was plainly correct. It has frequently been cited in subsequent decisions of the Court without any hint of disapproval ... The only qualification relevant to the plaintiff's argument that needs to be made is that the separation of powers effected by our Constitution would invalidate a bill of attainder on the ground that it involves a usurpation of judicial power. To the extent that Higgins J seems to suggest that such a bill, if enacted by the Parliament, would be valid, I am unable to agree.

[540] True it is that the judgments in *Kidman* to which I have referred do not make any mention of the separation of powers. That is readily understandable. The challenge to the validity of the

1915 Act was, and could only be, that it was an ex post facto law, for it was not a bill of attainder. Before the present case it had never occurred to anyone to suggest that an ex post facto law of the kind under consideration here, not being a bill of attainder, could amount to a usurpation of judicial power because such an ex post facto law simply does not amount to a trial by legislature. It leaves for determination by the court the issues which would arise for determination under a prospective law.

This rejection of the approach suggested by Deane J was emphatic. But notice the crucial concession that a Bill of Attainder would be "**[539]** a usurpation of judicial power" and would thus lie beyond the powers of the Commonwealth Parliament. At least to this limited extent, Mason CJ must, after all, be seen as accepting the view that some limits on legislative power are implied in Ch III of the Constitution. Moreover, McHugh J also agreed "**[721]** that the enactment of a Bill of Attainder or a Bill of Pains and Penalties would infringe the provisions"; and Dawson J, though not fully committing himself, was willing to make the same assumption. Thus Mason CJ, Deane, Gaudron and McHugh JJ all supported the view that a Bill of Attainder would be invalid, with Dawson J at least inclining strongly in that direction as well.

The margin in *Polyukhovich* becomes even narrower when the judgment of Toohey J is taken into account. How far he would agree with Deane and Gaudron JJ he did not finally need to decide, since he took the view that this case did not involve "retroactivity" in the relevant sense. However, he clearly accepted the broad thrust of their arguments.

Toohey J: [689] It is not the case that a law (even a criminal law) that operates retroactively thereby offends Ch III of the Constitution. It is only if a law purports to operate in such a way as to require a court to act contrary to accepted notions of judicial power that a contravention of Ch III may be involved. It is conceivable that a law, which purports to make criminal conduct which attracted no criminal sanction at the time it was done, may offend Ch III, especially if the law excludes the ordinary indicia of judicial process. Such a law may strike at the heart of judicial power: see *Liyanage v The Queen*. But it is unnecessary to pursue this topic further **[690]** because, as will appear, I do not consider that the Act, in its application to the information laid against the plaintiff, is retroactive in any offensive way. Likewise, I find it unnecessary to consider whether the decision in *R v Kidman* is consistent with the operation of Ch III as described in this judgment, though it is apparent that I do not share dicta which may be thought to suggest that an ex post facto law can never offend Ch III … The Court was not invited to overrule *Kidman* and, in the absence of full argument on the point, it is preferable to say no more on this aspect.

Toohey J's actual holding was extremely narrow: in its application to *this* information against *this* accused, the Act was not "retroactive in any offensive way".

To sum up, Deane and Gaudron JJ held the Act invalid on the basis of an inconsistency with Ch III of the Constitution. Brennan J agreed with them in the result, though he treated the retrospectivity of the law as a reason for denying a sufficient connection with the relevant heads of power, rather than an infringement of an overriding limitation on power. Mason CJ, Dawson and McHugh JJ held that the Act was valid. This latter result prevailed because of the view expressed by Toohey J, but only on the very narrow ground adopted by him. The legislation thus survived constitutional challenge by 4:3. At the same time, Toohey J evinced strong sympathy for the reasoning of Deane and Gaudron JJ, though neither his position nor that of Brennan J can be added to that of Deane and Gaudron JJ to produce a majority. Apart from the actual result of the case – and, of course, apart from the 6:1 holding as to the external affairs power – the only clear majority holding is the view adopted by at least four judges that a "Bill of Attainder" would be inconsistent with the provision for judicial power in Ch III.

In *Polyukhovich*, Deane J held that federal courts cannot be required to exercise power in a manner "**[607]** inconsistent with the essential requirements of a court or with the nature of judicial power". Brennan, Deane and Dawson JJ took a similar view in *Chu Kheng Lim* (at 27), while *Kable v Director of Public Prosecutions (NSW)* (1996) 189 CLR 51 (see Chapter 15, §2) extends the same proposition to State courts as well, at least if they are capable of exercising federal judicial power. Accordingly, the refusal in *Sorby v Commonwealth* (1983) 152 CLR 281 to treat the privilege against self-incrimination as constitutionally entrenched may need to be reassessed. In that case, Gibbs CJ stated that "**[298]** Parliament can, in relation to a trial by jury, alter the rules of evidence, or the rules relating to the onus of proof".

Dicta in *Chu Kheng Lim* and *Polyukhovich* suggest that the "essential requirements of a court" might include the idea that a court must hold a "fair trial" (or, conversely, is incapable of holding an "unfair trial"). If this is correct, the core components of the criminal trial, such as the presumption of innocence or even certain rules of evidence, may be constitutionally prescribed. According to Gaudron J in *Re Nolan; Ex parte Young* (1991) 172 CLR 460, the entrenched component might include an "**[496]** open and public enquiry (subject to limited exceptions), the application of the rules of natural justice, the ascertainment of the facts as they are and as they bear on the right or liability in issue and the identification of the applicable law, followed by an application of that law to those facts".

In *Dietrich v The Queen* (1992) 177 CLR 292, a majority of the High Court held that the power of a court to order a stay where an unfair trial would otherwise result may be exercised where an accused is charged with a serious offence and, through no fault of his or her own, is unable to obtain legal representation. This conclusion was framed as an extension of the common law rule governing the right to fair trial, rather than a constitutional imperative. However, in obiter dicta, Deane and Gaudron JJ suggested that the common law rights thus protected were, as Deane J put it, "**[326]** entrenched by the Constitution's requirement of the observance of judicial process and fairness". Whether, if need be, the Court would be prepared to "constitutionalise" the common law reasoning in *Dietrich* has been the subject of debate.

However, since the focus of *Dietrich* was on the *discretionary* nature of the power to order a stay of proceedings, that debate must now take account of *Nicholas v The Queen* (1998) 193 CLR 173. The earlier decision in *Ridgeway v The Queen* (1995) 184 CLR 19 concerned heroin imported into Australia, in breach of the *Customs Act 1901* (Cth), by law enforcement officers who sold it to John Ridgeway in an attempt to entrap him. A majority of the High Court held that evidence of the importation of heroin should not have been admitted because, at common law, a judge has the discretion "**[33]** to exclude, on public policy grounds, all evidence of an offence or an element of an offence procured by unlawful conduct on the part of law enforcement officers". In 1996, in response to *Ridgeway*, the federal Parliament inserted a new Pt 1AB into the *Crimes Act 1914* (Cth). It applied to "controlled operations" in which law enforcement officers engaged in otherwise illegal conduct to obtain evidence for prosecutions concerning narcotic goods under s 233B of the *Customs Act*. The Part also had a retrospective operation, s 15X providing that in defined circumstances:

Crimes Act 1914 (Cth)

15X In determining, for the purposes of a prosecution for an offence against section 233B of the *Customs Act 1901* or an associated offence, whether evidence that narcotic goods were imported into Australia in contravention of the *Customs Act 1901* should be admitted, the fact that a law enforcement officer committed an offence in importing the narcotic goods, or in aiding, abetting, counselling, procuring, or being in any way knowingly concerned in, their importation is to be disregarded.

It was argued in *Nicholas* that s 15X was invalid because it directed a court to exercise a discretionary power in a manner inconsistent with the essential character of a court or the nature of judicial power. A majority, with McHugh and Kirby JJ dissenting, held that s 15X was valid.

Brennan CJ noted that "**[188]** [s]ome characteristics of a court ..., including the duty to act and to be seen to be acting impartially", can be seen to flow from the fact that the process of judgment, being "**[187]** founded on the antecedent rights and liabilities of the parties", requires the court to "find the facts and apply the law which, at the relevant time, prescribe those antecedent rights and liabilities". However, it was not inconsistent with this that the fact-finding process should to some extent be regulated by statute.

Nicholas v The Queen
(1998) 193 CLR 173

Brennan CJ: [188] A law that purports to direct the manner in which judicial power should be exercised is constitutionally invalid. However, a law which merely prescribes a court's practice or procedure does not direct the exercise of the judicial power in finding facts, applying law or exercising an available discretion … Section 15X does not impede or otherwise affect the finding of facts by a jury. Indeed, it removes the barrier which *Ridgeway* [(1995) 184 CLR 19] placed against tendering to the jury evidence of an illegal importation of narcotic goods where such an importation had in fact occurred. Far from being inconsistent with the nature of the judicial power to adjudicate and punish criminal guilt, s 15X facilitates the admission of evidence of material facts in aid of correct fact finding …

The judicial power of a court is defined by the matters in which jurisdiction has been conferred upon it. The conferral of jurisdiction prima facie carries the power to do whatever is necessary or convenient to effect its exercise. The practice and procedure of a court may be prescribed by the court in exercise of its implied power to do **[189]** what is necessary for the exercise of its jurisdiction but subject to overriding legislative provision governing that practice or procedure. The rules of evidence have traditionally been recognised as being an appropriate subject of statutory prescription. A law prescribing a rule of evidence does not impair the curial function of finding facts, applying the law or exercising any available discretion …

[191] If s 15X had simply declared that evidence of an illegal importation should be admitted, denying any discretion in the trial judge to exclude the evidence, the provision would simply have enlarged the evidentiary material available to a jury to assist it to find the facts truly. It would have been a mere procedural law assisting in the court's finding of material facts. No exception could be taken to such a law … But s 15X leaves the trial judge with a discretion to reject evidence of importation of narcotic goods in an authorised controlled operation, requiring only that in exercising the discretion, the illegal conduct of law enforcement officers should be disregarded. The existence of the judicial discretion does not alter the classification of the law as a law governing the admission of evidence and therefore a law governing procedure. The procedure for determining the admission of evidence of illegal importation is affected, but the judicial function of fact finding is unchanged and the judicial power to be exercised in determining guilt remains unaffected.

Gaudron J reached the same conclusion. In doing so, she carefully laid out what she saw as the essential requirements of a court.

Gaudron J: [208] In my view, consistency with the essential character of a court and with the nature of judicial power necessitates that a court not be required or authorised to proceed in a manner that does not ensure equality before the law, impartiality and the appearance of impartiality, the right of a party to meet the case made against him or her, the independent determination of the matter in controversy by application of the law to facts determined in accordance with rules and procedures which truly permit the facts to be ascertained and, in the case of criminal proceedings, the determination of guilt or innocence by **[209]** means of a fair trial according to law. It means, moreover, that a court cannot be required or authorised to proceed in any manner which involves an abuse of process, which would render its proceedings inefficacious, or which brings or tends to bring the administration of justice into disrepute.

In *Ridgeway*, she had been prepared to hold that reliance on evidence unlawfully obtained by law enforcement officers is always an abuse of process. However, she now deferred to the more cautious view of the majority in that case.

Gaudron J: [210] Although Mason CJ, Deane and Dawson JJ anchored the public policy considerations which underpin the *Ridgeway* discretion in "the integrity of the administration of criminal justice" [184 CLR at 39], they stopped short of the view which I took, namely that the prosecution of an offence, which is the culmination of illegal action on the part of law enforcement authorities, is an abuse of process because its "inevitable consequence … is to weaken public confidence in the administration of justice" [184 CLR at 78]. Accordingly, it follows from what was said by Mason CJ, Deane and Dawson JJ in *Ridgeway* and, also, from the fact that *Ridgeway* identified a discretion rather than a rule of general application that it cannot be said that every prosecution for an offence induced by the illegal action of law enforcement officers weakens confidence in the judicial process ...

Properly construed, s 15X does no more than exclude the bare fact of illegality on the part of law enforcement officers from consideration **[211]** when determining whether the *Ridgeway* discretion should be exercised in favour of an accused person. So construed, it is clear that it does not prevent independent determination of the question whether that evidence should be excluded or, more to the point, independent determination of guilt or innocence. And so construed, it is also clear that it neither authorizes nor requires a court to proceed in circumstances which bring or tend to bring the administration of justice into disrepute. And although it is perhaps not quite so clear, it does not offend against the requirements of equal justice ...

[Section] 15X does not negate the *Ridgeway* discretion. It leaves the discretion to be exercised in any case in which it is invoked and, in that respect, the applicant's situation is no different from that which obtained in *Ridgeway*. And the principle of equality before the law is not infringed simply because, in the exercise of a discretion of the kind identified in *Ridgeway*, evidence is or may be excluded in one case and not in another. Indeed, it is the very essence of a discretion of that kind that the result of its exercise may vary according to the circumstances of the case.

By contrast, McHugh and Kirby JJ took the view that s 15X was invalid.

McHugh J: [224] Section 15X operates on the hypothesis that law enforcement officers have committed an offence against s 233B and that it is their criminal conduct that has brought into existence an essential element of the charge against the accused. Yet the section then directs courts exercising the judicial power of the Commonwealth to disregard the critical fact that the offence by the accused exists as a result of the criminal conduct of a law enforcement officer. That is to say, s 15X directs those courts to shut their eyes to a fact that, according to *Ridgeway*, is crucial in determining whether the integrity of the processes of federal courts are being demeaned. Expressly and by implication, the Parliament is saying to courts exercising federal jurisdiction in respect of importations occurring before s 15X was enacted: "Although the evidence may convincingly demonstrate to you that a law enforcement officer has committed a crime in order to establish an essential element of the crime for which he or she has prosecuted the accused, you must disregard the fact that that officer has committed that crime. You must disregard that fact even though the High Court of Australia in *Ridgeway* [184 CLR at 41] regarded that fact as crucial in holding that 'the public interest in maintaining the integrity of the courts and of ensuring the observance of the law and minimum standards of propriety by those entrusted with powers of law enforcement' outweighed the public interest in convicting the guilty." I cannot accept the claim that such a direction does not infringe the judicial power of the Commonwealth.

Section 15X in my opinion is not comparable with those enactments, commonly found in the statutes of the Parliament and the legislatures of the States, that regulate judicial discretions by requiring this or that matter to be taken into account ... It is a direction to a court exercising federal jurisdiction that it cannot have regard to a **[225]** fact that is relevant and often critical in determining whether the court's processes are being demeaned. It is true that under *Ridgeway* the ultimate issue is whether evidence establishing an element of a criminal charge should be rejected. But if that evidence is rejected, it is partly, perhaps wholly, because the processes of the court would be demeaned if the evidence was admitted. What s 15X does is to prevent a court exercising federal jurisdiction from considering a fact which is a relevant step in determining whether its process is being demeaned ...

[Section] 15X is no mere evidentiary rule or rule of practice. It strikes at the capacity of a court, exercising federal jurisdiction, to **[226]** protect its processes. True it is that the section does not take that power away from such a court. But it does direct that court to disregard a fact that in *Ridgeway* was, and in other cases might be, critical to the exercise of the power ...

Consistently with maintaining the independence of the federal judiciary which Ch III of the Constitution guarantees to the nation, the federal courts cannot transfer to the Parliament of the Commonwealth the power or responsibility for defining what is an abuse of their process. Parliament, for example, cannot prevent a litigant from invoking the jurisdiction of this Court by declaring conduct to be an abuse of process when it is not. Similarly, Parliament cannot prevent this Court from protecting its process by declaring conduct not to be an abuse of process when it is an abuse of process. It is a necessary corollary of the last proposition that Parliament cannot hamper this Court or other federal courts in determining whether conduct is an abuse of process or has a tendency to undermine public confidence in their administration of justice.

In any event, the majority view in *Nicholas* is narrowly focused, and depends on the view that the discretion exercised in *Ridgeway* is theoretically unimpaired. In *Loveridge v Commissioner of Police (SA)* (2004) 89 SASR 72, White J, of the Supreme Court of South Australia, in declining to execute a 24-year-old warrant for extradition to Western Australia which he saw as an abuse of process, suggested that if s 18 of the *Service and Execution of Process Act 1992* (Cth) were construed as excluding the inherent power to stay or dismiss proceedings for abuse of process, it might be invalid. In making that suggestion he relied on what had been said in *Nicholas* both by Gaudron J (in the majority, at 208-9) and by McHugh J (in dissent, at 226).

8. Equal Justice

The positions of Deane, Toohey and Gaudron JJ in *Polyukhovich* were further developed in *Leeth v Commonwealth* (1992) 174 CLR 455, where Deane and Toohey JJ discerned in the Constitution a broad underlying value of "equality", or at least "equal treatment". Gaudron J found that wider question "[501] unnecessary to decide", but enounced a more precise concept of "[502] equal justice ... [as] fundamental to the judicial process". While later cases have rejected the far-reaching implication proposed by Deane and Toohey JJ, they have given support to the narrower version suggested by Gaudron J.

The issue arose in *Leeth* in the relatively narrow context of the terms upon which Commonwealth prisoners are confined in State jails. Pursuant to the co-operative arrangement envisaged by s 120 of the Constitution, the standard practice has been for Commonwealth prisoners to be housed in State jails. Until 1989 this practice was regulated by the *Commonwealth Prisoners Act 1967* (Cth). Section 4 of that Act required that, after a "federal offender" was sentenced, the sentencing judge should follow the practices and criteria of the relevant State in fixing a minimum non-parole period. This meant that, within the one prison, State and Commonwealth prisoners alike would have comparable parole expectations; but that, as amongst Commonwealth prisoners incarcerated in different States, non-parole periods varied widely. Richard Leeth, convicted under the *Customs Act 1901* (Cth) for importing cannabis in commercial quantities, complained that this inequality of treatment was unconstitutional.

Leeth was convicted and sentenced in August 1989. In July 1990 the *Crimes Legislation (Amendment) Act 1989* (Cth) came into force. That Act repealed the *Commonwealth Prisoners Act*, and introduced into the *Crimes Act 1914* (Cth) a new Pt IB dealing with the "Sentencing, Imprisonment and Release of Federal Offenders". The relevant procedures were thus elaborately regulated by Commonwealth law. However, the new provisions picked up and applied to Commonwealth prisoners held in a State or Territory prison any "law of [that] State or Territory that provides for the remission or reduction of State or Territory sentences" (s 19AA) and required that those laws be taken into account in calculating a non-parole period (ss 19AF and 19AG). A transitional provision in the amending legislation (s 30(1)) also required that any non-parole period imposed under the old 1967 Act be treated "as if it were a non-parole period that had been duly fixed" under the new Pt IB. Accordingly, Leeth's main argument was that s 4 of the 1967 Act had been invalid. Deane, Toohey and Gaudron JJ accepted this argument.

Leeth v Commonwealth
(1992) 174 CLR 455

Deane and Toohey JJ: [483] The grants of Commonwealth legislative power contained in s 51 of the Constitution are expressly made "subject to" the Constitution. They are confined by a variety of overriding express guarantees and prohibitions. Their prima facie content is also confined by a general principle of construction that they should not be interpreted as authorizing the infringement of a number of implications to be drawn either from the Constitution as a whole or from some one or more of its particular provisions. Thus, it is now well settled that there is to be deduced from the nature of the federal system which the Constitution establishes, including the assumption of the continued existence of the States as viable political entities, an implied confinement or restriction of the grants of Commonwealth legislative power contained in s 51 which, except to the extent that the nature of a specific power otherwise indicates, precludes the enactment by the Parliament of laws which discriminate against the States by subjecting them or their **[484]** instrumentalities to special burdens or disabilities. That implied confinement or restriction operates to preclude discriminatory treatment either of the States or their instrumentalities generally or of a particular State or State instrumentality.

The States themselves are, of course, artificial entities. The parties to the compact which is the Constitution were the people of the federating Colonies. It is the people who, in a basic sense, now constitute the individual States just as, in the aggregate and with the people of the Territories, they constitute the Commonwealth. The implied confinement or restriction of Commonwealth legislative powers to preclude the singling out of the States and their instrumentalities for discriminatory treatment has, however, been uniformly defined in terms which protect only the artificial entities or organs of government rather than the constituent people. Any constitutional protection of the people themselves from arbitrary or discriminatory treatment must be found, if at all, in other express or implied doctrines or provisions. Nonetheless, the implication which protects the States and their instrumentalities is relevant for present purposes for two reasons. First, it would be somewhat surprising if the Constitution, which is concerned with matters of substance, embodied a general principle which protected the States and their instrumentalities from being singled out by Commonwealth laws for discriminatory treatment but provided no similar protection of the people who constitute the Commonwealth and the States. Secondly, the Constitution's adoption, by implication rather than express statement, of the general principle protecting the States and their instrumentalities from discriminatory treatment illustrates the general approach of the framers of the Constitution to the underlying doctrines or principles upon which it is structured. That approach was to incorporate underlying doctrines or principles by implication drawn both from the nature of the Federation and from any particular express provisions of the Constitution which reflect or implement those doctrines or principles. In the context of that approach, specific provisions of the Constitution which reflect or implement some underlying doctrine or principle are properly to be seen as a manifestation of it and not as a basis for denying its **[485]** existence by invoking the inappropriate rule of expressio unius. Thus, the specific provisions of the Constitution preserving and protecting the Constitutions (Constitution, s 106), powers (s 107), laws (s 108) and territory (s 123) of the States do not preclude the implication of a more general principle protecting their continued existence and political viability. Again, the Constitution contains no detailed statement of the content or implications of the doctrine of the separation of judicial power from executive and legislative powers which it implements by expressly vesting the judicial power of the Commonwealth in Ch III courts (s 71), the legislative power of the Commonwealth in the Parliament (s 51) and the executive power of the Commonwealth in the Crown (s 61). The adoption of that doctrine of the common law as part of the very structure of the Constitution is, however, apparent …

In *Commonwealth v Kreglinger & Fernau Ltd and Bardsley* [(1926) 37 CLR 393 at 411-12], Isaacs J pointed out "that it is the duty of this court, as the chief judicial organ of the Commonwealth, to take judicial notice, in interpreting the Australian Constitution, of every fundamental constitutional doctrine existing and fully recognized at the time the Constitution was passed". The doctrine of legal equality is in the forefront of those doctrines. It has two distinct but related aspects. The first is the subjection of all persons to the law: "every man, whatever be his rank or condition, is subject to the ordinary law … and amenable to the jurisdiction of the ordinary tribunals" [AV Dicey, *Introduction to the Study of the Law of the Constitution* (10th ed 1959), 193]. The second involves the underlying or inherent theoretical equality of all persons under the law and before the courts. The common law may discriminate between individuals **[486]** by reference to relevant differences and distinctions, such as infancy or incapacity, or by reason of conduct which it proscribes, punishes or penalizes. It may have failed adequately to acknowledge or address the fact that, in some circumstances, theoretical equality under the law sustains rather than alleviates the practical reality of social and economic inequality. Nonetheless, and putting to one side the position of the Crown and some past anomalies, notably, discriminatory treatment of women, the essential or underlying theoretical equality of all persons under the law and before the courts is and has been a fundamental and generally beneficial doctrine of the common law and a basic prescript of the administration of justice under our system of government. Conformably with its ordinary approach to fundamental principles, the Constitution does not spell out that general doctrine of legal equality in express words. The question arises whether it adopts it as a matter of necessary implication. In our view, several considerations combine to dictate an affirmative answer to that question.

For one thing, there is the conceptual basis of the Constitution. As the preamble and s 3 of the *Commonwealth of Australia Constitution Act* 1900 (Imp) make plain, that conceptual basis was the free agreement of "the people" – all the people – of the federating colonies to unite in the Commonwealth under the Constitution. Implicit in that free agreement was the notion of the inherent equality of the people as the parties to the compact. Indeed, covering cl 5 (s 5) expressly enacted the first aspect of the common law doctrine of legal equality, namely, that "[t]his Act" – which included the actual terms of the Constitution (s 9) – "and all laws made by the Parliament of the Commonwealth under the Constitution, shall be binding on the courts, judges, and people ... of every part of the Commonwealth".

For another thing, the doctrine of legal equality is, to a significant extent, implicit in the Constitution's separation of judicial power from legislative and executive powers and the vesting of judicial power in designated "courts" ... Those provisions not only identify the possible repositories of Commonwealth judicial power. They also dictate and control the manner of **[487]** its exercise. They are not concerned with mere labels or superficialities. They are concerned with matters of substance. Thus, in Ch III's exclusive vesting of the judicial power of the Commonwealth in the "courts" which it designates, there is implicit a requirement that those "courts" exhibit the essential attributes of a court and observe, in the exercise of that judicial power, the essential requirements of the curial process ... At the heart of that obligation is the duty of a court to extend to the parties before it equal justice, that is to say, to treat them fairly and impartially as equals before the law ...

Finally, once it is appreciated that it is the ordinary approach of the Constitution not to spell out the fundamental common law principles upon which it is structured, the existence of a number of specific provisions which reflect the doctrine of legal equality serves to make manifest rather than undermine the status of that doctrine as an underlying principle of the Constitution as a whole. Among those specific provisions are: the guarantee against discrimination between persons in different parts of the country in relation to customs and excise duties (Constitution, ss 86, 88, 90), other Commonwealth taxes (s 51(ii)) and bounties (ss 51(iii), 86, 90); the guarantee that the Commonwealth shall not, by any law or regulation of trade, commerce or revenue, give preference to one State or any part thereof over another State or part thereof (s 99); the guarantee of freedom of interstate trade, commerce and intercourse (s 92); the guarantee of direct suffrage and equality of voting rights among those qualified to vote (ss 24, 25); the guarantee that no religious test shall be required as a qualification for any office or public trust under the Commonwealth (s 116) ...

[488] The doctrine of legal equality is not infringed by a law which discriminates between people on grounds which are reasonably capable of being seen as providing a rational and relevant basis for the discriminatory treatment. In one sense, almost all laws **[489]** discriminate against some people since almost all laws operate to punish, penalize or advantage some, but not all, persons by reference to whether their commands are breached or observed. While such laws discriminate against those whom they punish or penalize or do not advantage, they do not infringe the doctrine of the equality of all persons under the law and before the courts. To the contrary, they assume that underlying legal equality in that they discriminate by reference to relevant differences. Again, laws which distinguish between the different needs or responsibilities of different people or different localities may necessarily be directed to some, but not all, of the people of the Commonwealth. Provided that the differentiation of and between those to whom they are addressed does not involve discrimination of a kind that infringes their inherent equality as people of the Commonwealth, such laws will not infringe the doctrine of equality under the law and before the courts.

Even where a law does infringe the doctrine of legal equality, the nature of the particular grant of legislative power may be such as to rebut the assumption that such discrimination was unauthorized by the relevant provision of the Constitution. Thus, for example, a law which deprives a particular person of his or her property, albeit on just terms, for a purpose in respect of which the Parliament has power to make laws, may discriminate against the person who is deprived of his or her property but will nonetheless be clearly within the intended ambit of the legislative power conferred by s 51(xxxi). Similarly, a legislative power to make special laws with respect to a particular class of persons, such as aliens (Constitution, s 51(xix)) or persons of a particular race (s 51(xxvi)), necessarily authorizes discriminatory treatment of members of that class to the extent which is reasonably capable of being seen as appropriate and adapted to the circumstance of that membership. Again, the nature of a Commonwealth legislative power may be such as to authorize laws which discriminate between persons in different geographical areas: defence (s 51(vi)), quarantine (s 51(ix)) and medical services such as immunization (s 51(xxiiiA)) may provide examples. In contrast, a law which discriminates against the members of such a class or the persons in such a geographical area in a way or to an extent which goes beyond the discrimination which the relevant **[490]** legislative power appears, from its nature, to be intended to authorize will exceed the limits of that legislative power.

Quite apart from the nature of a particular grant of legislative power, the Constitution's doctrine of the legal equality of the people of the Commonwealth must be adjusted to the extent necessary to accommodate discriminatory treatment which other provisions of the Constitution clearly contemplate. Thus, the Constitution, in providing for the exercise of the judicial power of the Commonwealth by both State and federal courts, implicitly contemplates the application, in the course of that exercise, of the different procedural laws, rules and practices of the courts concerned. Those different procedural laws, rules and practices may, in some circumstances, be of critical importance to the outcome of litigation, including criminal proceedings. Nonetheless, the doctrine of the legal equality of the people of the Commonwealth must be adjusted to accommodate them at least to the extent that the application of the procedural laws, rules and practices of a particular court is a necessary concomitant of the vesting by the Parliament of part of the judicial power of the Commonwealth in that court. Again, s 120 of the Constitution requires each State to make provision for the detention in its prisons of persons accused or convicted of offences against the laws of the Commonwealth, and for the punishment of persons convicted of such offences. The conditions of imprisonment may vary from State to State and, to that extent, a person imprisoned in one State for an offence against a law of the Commonwealth may be more harshly treated than a person imprisoned for the same offence in another State. If the Constitution's doctrine of legal equality would otherwise preclude such different treatment, it must be modified to permit it at least to the extent that it is a necessary concomitant of the use of State prisons to punish Commonwealth offenders. Neither of those adjustments of the doctrine of legal equality suffices, however, to save s 4(1) of the Act from invalidity.

They conceded that s 4(1) would have been valid if it had authorised the sentencing judge to have regard to the non-parole periods applicable in the State where the sentence would be *served*; the problem lay in the reference to the State in which the sentence was *imposed*. The former criterion would have "**[491]** enabled account to be taken of actual differences in the conditions of imprisonment in different States and Territories", whereas s 4(1) "operated arbitrarily to require a court to treat the State or Territory in which a federal offender was convicted as *the* relevant consideration for determining which of a number of greatly varying legislative schemes should govern the fixing of a non-parole period".

Deane and Toohey JJ: [492] The Commonwealth is one country and the criminal laws of the Commonwealth are part of one system of law to which all within the Commonwealth are equally subject. The view is simply not open that the place within the Commonwealth in which a person happens to be convicted of an offence against a law of the Commonwealth is so critical to the determination of the appropriate non-parole period that it could provide a rational basis for a law which expressly required that a person convicted in Sydney serve more than twice the minimum term of imprisonment of a person convicted in Perth. It is true that s 4(1) did not in terms impose that grossly discriminatory treatment of a person convicted in Sydney vis-a-vis a person convicted of an identical offence in Perth. All that s 4(1) did was to endorse whatever happened to result from the application of whatever non-parole system was operating in the States and internal Territories at any particular time. The fact that the extent of the actual discriminatory treatment of persons in relevantly equal or comparable circumstances was left to be determined in that way tends, however, to emphasize rather than to mitigate the lack of any rational basis for it.

Gaudron J: [501] On the view that I take of s 30(1) of the Crimes Amendment Act, it is unnecessary to decide whether, as argued on behalf of the plaintiff, the legislative power of the Commonwealth under s 51 of the Constitution is subject to an implied general limitation forbidding laws which discriminate (in the sense used in argument) on the basis of the State or Territory in which some event took place. In my view this case raises the much narrower issue of whether the Parliament may require a court named or indicated in s 71 of the Constitution to exercise a power by reference to a criterion or to criteria which will necessarily result in discrimination of the kind discussed ...

It has often been said that judicial power has not proved susceptible of exhaustive or exclusive definition. A definition of judicial power must take account of its varying character: in some cases, the content of the power will stamp it as one which can only be exercised by courts; in others, the content will indicate that it is a power with a "double aspect", in the sense that Parliament may choose whether to confer it on a court ... or on some other body. Another feature which renders "judicial power" difficult to define is **[502]** that it cannot be defined only in terms of its content. It is necessary to have regard to the manner in and the processes by which the power is or is to be exercised.

It is an essential feature of judicial power that it should be exercised in accordance with the judicial process. A legislative direction which would require a power vested in a court to be exercised other than in accordance with that process is necessarily invalid. Its effect would be to take the power outside the concept of "judicial power" ... [and thus to] infringe the prohibition deriving from s 71 which limits the powers which may be conferred on a court to those which are judicial or ancillary or incidental to judicial power. Of course, it might be that, in some cases, a direction of that kind would be severable, so that the power, when shorn of the direction, is validly conferred.

All are equal before the law. And the concept of equal justice – a concept which requires the like treatment of like persons in like circumstances, but also requires that genuine differences be treated as such – is fundamental to the judicial process. Questions of constitutional prohibition aside, if the substantive law assigns significance to some matter that in reality it does not have, it thereby becomes a matter to be taken into account in the way that the law requires. And in that way, the law may treat things which are relevantly different as though they are not, or even treat things that are not different as though they are. But that is not the same as the conferral of a power of the kind purportedly conferred by s 4(1) of the repealed Act. In the former case, a legal distinction is created or denied and the law is stated by reference to the existence or absence of that distinction. In the latter case, there is a directive to exercise a general power in different ways according to a factual matter, namely, the State or Territory in which the accused person stood trial.

The power purportedly conferred by s 4(1) of the repealed Act varied in nature and in content, not according to the nature of the offence or the circumstances of its commission, but according to the place of conviction. As such, and in the ordinary course of events, the exercise of that power would involve a failure to treat like offences against the laws of the Commonwealth in a like manner and also a failure to give proper account to genuine **[503]** differences. That is only another way of saying that s 4(1) was discriminatory. But, stated in these terms, it is clear that a power of that kind is one that treats people unequally. As such its exercise is inconsistent with the judicial process.

Mason CJ, Dawson and McHugh JJ rejected these arguments.

Mason CJ, Dawson and McHugh JJ: [467] There is no general requirement contained in the Constitution that Commonwealth laws should have a uniform operation throughout the Commonwealth. There is, of course, the implication drawn from the federal structure erected by the Constitution that prevents the Commonwealth from legislating in a way which discriminates against the States by imposing special burdens or disabilities upon them or in a way which curtails their capacity to exercise for themselves their constitutional functions. There are also specific provisions prohibiting discrimination or preference of one kind or another, but these are confined in their operation ...

[469] It is at least theoretically possible that, in legislating for the treatment of offenders in a particular manner, the Parliament may discriminate against particular offenders or classes of offenders in such a way that the legislation travels beyond matters which are incidental to the main power. The legislation might for that reason be invalid, but that would not be because it offended any implied prohibition against the exercise of legislative power in a discriminatory manner. In the present case, the non-parole period to be served by federal offenders was a matter which was clearly incidental to the main legislative power and the contrary was not suggested ...

In *R v Kirby; Ex parte Boilermakers' Society of Australia* it was held that Ch III of the Constitution, of which s 71 is the first section, imposes a separation of judicial power from the other powers of government ... But to speak of judicial power in this context is to speak of the function of a court rather than the law which a court is to apply in the exercise of its function. Of course, legislation **[470]** may amount to a usurpation of judicial power, particularly in a criminal case, if it prejudges an issue with respect to a particular individual and requires a court to exercise its function accordingly. It is upon this principle that bills of attainder may offend against the separation of judicial power. But a law of general application which seeks in some respect to govern the exercise of a jurisdiction which it confers does not trespass upon the judicial function. It may well be that any attempt on the part of the legislature to cause a court to act in a manner contrary to natural justice would impose a non-judicial requirement inconsistent with the exercise of judicial power, but the rules of natural justice are essentially functional or procedural and, as the Privy Council observed in the *Boilermakers' Case* [[1957] AC 288 at 317], a fundamental principle which lies behind the concept of natural justice is not remote from the principle which inspires the theory of separation of powers.

In this case, however, the legislation in question did not require a court invested with federal jurisdiction to perform a function which could be described as non-judicial. The sentencing of offenders, including in modern times the fixing of a minimum term of imprisonment, is as clear an example of the exercise of judicial power as is possible ...

Even if it is accepted for the purpose of argument that any fundamental departure by the legislature from the principle that like offenders should be treated in a like manner may involve the **[471]** imposition upon a court of a non-judicial function, it is in our view apparent that to require a court, in the case of a federal offender, to have regard to the sentencing practices of the State in which he is convicted involves no such departure. To require a court to do so does not convert the sentencing process into some process of a non-judicial kind but merely reflects the manner in which the Commonwealth, within the means made available to it by the Constitution, has chosen in the administration of its criminal law to operate through the existing State systems.

To say as much is, of course, to take the matter further than we need do. There is no requirement that the actual sentence of a federal offender be fixed having regard to local circumstances. The sentencing judge may, as in this case, have regard to the sentences imposed in other States in order to achieve as far as possible a measure of consistency. The restrictions of which the plaintiff complains relate merely to the fixing of the minimum term which, whilst it is undoubtedly part of the punishment imposed, is also closely linked to the parole system to be applied to the offender and has a bearing upon the administration of the prison in which he must serve his sentence. We can see no departure from the judicial function if a court within our federal system is required, in fixing the minimum term of imprisonment of a federal offender, to have regard to those matters to which it would have regard if the law of the State in which the offender was convicted were applicable.

The decisive vote was that of Brennan J. He agreed with Mason CJ, Dawson and McHugh JJ that the legislation in this case was valid, but he also partly agreed with Deane and Toohey JJ. For him, the crucial distinction was between a Commonwealth *offender* (that is, a person convicted of an offence against Commonwealth law), and a Commonwealth *prisoner* (that is, an offender who has been sentenced to a term of imprisonment). Issues of sentencing relate to the treatment of Commonwealth *offenders*, and in this context there is indeed a requirement that all offenders be treated as equals. Questions of parole relate to the treatment of Commonwealth *prisoners*, and under the existing imprisonment system the relevant category must be, for example, "prisoners in New South Wales gaols".

Brennan J: [475] If the plaintiff's arguments were directed against a law prescribing different maximum penalties for the same offence, there would be much force in them. The maximum penalties prescribed for offences determine the extent of the judicial power to send an offender to prison and the corresponding liability of an offender to be sent to prison. It would be offensive to the constitutional unity of the Australian people "in one indissoluble Federal Commonwealth", recited in the first preamble to the *Commonwealth of Australia Constitution Act* 1900, to expose offenders against the same law of the Commonwealth to different maximum penalties dependent on the locality of the court by which the offender is convicted and sentenced. It follows that the maximum penalty prescribed for a breach of the law must be the same irrespective of the locality of the court before which the offender is tried and sentenced. On the other hand, where an offence against a law of the Commonwealth is defined to contain an element of locality within Australia, an offence against that law will attract a penalty for conduct that may not attract a penalty, or may not attract so severe a penalty, if committed outside the locality. Such a law, which discriminates between conduct in one part of Australia and like conduct in another part must find support in the power under which the law is **[476]** purportedly enacted ...

Section 4 of the *Commonwealth Prisoners Act*, however, does not relate to the exercise of the judicial power to send an offender to prison; nor does it relate to the reduction or remission of sentences. It relates to the exercise of the executive power to release Commonwealth prisoners from the prisons to which they are respectively sent, which is quite a different thing ...

[478] Section 4 of the *Commonwealth Prisoners Act* does not discriminate among offenders against laws of the Commonwealth in respect of the maximum penalties to which they are exposed; it **[479]** discriminates among Commonwealth prisoners in respect of the determination of the condition limiting the executive power to release them on parole ... [Although it] discriminates among Commonwealth prisoners serving sentences for the same kind of offence, the practical ground of distinction is their incarceration in prisons shared with State and Territory prisoners. That is not only a rational ground of discrimination; it is a necessary ground. To aggregate as a class all Commonwealth prisoners who have been convicted of the same kind of offence by courts in different parts of Australia and, by reference to that overall classification, to find an impermissible discrimination among them is to mistake the classification relevant to the operation of s 4 of the *Commonwealth Prisoners Act*. Given the desirability of maintaining the same regime for fixing minimum terms to be served by all prisoners in a State or Territory prison before becoming eligible for parole, the relevant classification is Commonwealth prisoners who are serving their custodial sentences in the prisons of the respective States and Territories. As among the members of those respective classes of Commonwealth prisoners, s 4 ... works no discrimination. Each of them acquires eligibility for parole under the same laws. If it were otherwise, the system contemplated by s 120 of the Constitution would be impracticable ...

Once it is appreciated that ss 4 and 5 relate to the regime for releasing on parole Commonwealth prisoners who will serve their sentences in the prisons of the State and Territory in which the court is sitting ..., the differences in the State and Territory laws to be **[480]** applied to Commonwealth prisoners are seen as no more than the inevitable consequence of the constitutionally sanctioned expedient of incarcerating in the same prisons offenders against laws made under federal powers and offenders against State laws.

The distinction between the approach of Deane and Toohey JJ and that of Gaudron J was brought into sharp relief by the latter's judgment in *Kruger v Commonwealth* (*Stolen Generations Case*) (1997) 190 CLR 1, where she reaffirmed her own analysis in *Leeth* but repudiated the broader "equality" doctrine envisaged by Deane and Toohey JJ. The issue was whether the *Aboriginals Ordinance 1918* (NT) was valid insofar as it authorised the forced removal of Aboriginal children from their families and their communities. The Ordinance was challenged in part on the ground that this discriminatory and unequal treatment of Aboriginal children offended a general "doctrine of legal equality" derived from *Leeth*. Gaudron J held that, on her own more limited view of the "equality" doctrine, that aspect of the plaintiffs' challenge must fail.

Kruger v Commonwealth (*Stolen Generations Case*)
(1997) 190 CLR 1

Gaudron J: [112] The plaintiffs rest their argument in support of an implied guarantee of legal equality on what was said by Deane and Toohey JJ in *Leeth v Commonwealth* [(1992) 174 CLR 455 at 489]. In that case, their Honours expressed the view … that, as a matter of necessary implication and subject to certain exceptions, the Constitution provides a guarantee of legal equality …

In *Leeth*, I expressed the view, to which I still adhere, that Ch III operates to preclude the conferral on courts of discretionary powers which are conditioned in such a way that they must be exercised in a discriminatory manner. If that view is correct, there is a limited constitutional guarantee of equality before the courts, not an immunity from discriminatory laws which, in essence, is what is involved in the argument that there is an implied constitutional guarantee of equality.

Several provisions of the Constitution are expressly concerned to prevent discrimination: the power to legislate with respect to taxation is subject to the requirement that laws on that topic "not … discriminate between States or parts of States" [s 51(ii)]; the power to legislate with respect to bounties is subject to the requirement that they **[113]** "be uniform throughout the Commonwealth" [s 51(iii)]; customs duties are to be uniform [s 88]; trade, commerce and intercourse among the States are to be absolutely free [s 92], by which is meant free from "discriminatory burdens of a protectionist kind" [*Cole v Whitfield* (1988) 165 CLR 360 at 394]. And by s 117, "[a] subject of the Queen, resident in any State, shall not be subject in any other State to any disability or discrimination which would not be equally applicable to him if he were a subject of the Queen resident in such other State."

There is a dual aspect to s 117: it operates to prevent discrimination; it also sanctions discrimination so far as concerns persons who are not subjects of the Queen. It is not the only provision of the Constitution which sanctions different treatment for different people. Thus, as Deane and Toohey JJ acknowledged in *Leeth*, the power to make laws with respect to aliens and persons of a particular race necessarily allows for different treatment for different classes of people. And their Honours also acknowledged that "the nature of a Commonwealth legislative power may be such as to authorise laws which discriminate between persons in different geographical areas", giving defence, quarantine and medical services as possible examples [174 CLR at 489].

Section 25 of the Constitution also sanctions discriminatory laws and allows that, for the purposes of determining the number of members of the House of Representatives to be chosen in each State, "if by the law of any State all persons of any race are disqualified from voting at elections for the more numerous House of the Parliament of the State, then, in reckoning the number of the people of the State or of the Commonwealth, persons of that race resident in that State shall not be counted". Moreover, until 1967, the Constitution, itself, was blatantly discriminatory. Until repealed in that year, s 127 provided, in terms completely contrary to any notion of equality, that "[i]n reckoning the numbers of the people of the Commonwealth, or of a State or other part of the Commonwealth, Aboriginal natives [should] not be counted". That latter provision precludes any implication of equality benefiting Aboriginal Australians in respect of events which occurred before its repeal in 1967 …

[T]he constitutional provisions which sanction and those which operate to prevent discriminatory laws so combine, in my view, that there is no room for any implication of a constitutional right of equality beyond that deriving from Ch III. That deriving from Ch III has no bearing on **[114]** the validity of the Ordinance. It follows that the Ordinance was not invalid by reason that it was contrary to an implied constitutional right to or guarantee of equality.

Dawson J, with whom McHugh J agreed, expressed some support for the view of Gaudron J (at least as to a requirement of *procedural* "due process" derived from Ch III). While Gummow J appeared to express no opinion on that more limited issue, both he and Dawson JJ emphatically rejected the broader approach of Deane and Toohey JJ in *Leeth*.

Dawson J: [63] The separation of judicial power from the other powers of government precludes the legislature from investing a court created by or under Ch III of the Constitution with non-judicial powers that are not ancillary but are directed to some non-judicial purpose. A Ch III court cannot be made to perform a function which is of a non-judicial nature or is required to be performed in a non-judicial manner. Chapter III may, perhaps, be regarded in this way as affording a measure of due process, but it is due process of a procedural rather than substantive nature. As was pointed out in *Leeth v Commonwealth* [174 CLR at 469], "to speak of judicial power in this context is to speak of the function of a court rather than the law which a court is to apply". However, for the reasons which I have already given, the plaintiffs are unable to resort to the separation of powers so far as the territories are concerned and in any event their argument goes much further than the requirements of Ch III in asserting a guarantee of equality before and under the law ...

It is true that [in *Leeth*] Deane and Toohey JJ found a doctrine of legal equality in the Constitution, but the reasoning which led to that conclusion did not commend itself to other members of the Court nor, with the greatest of respect, does it now commend itself to me. An analogy for the doctrine of equality was, it was said, to be discerned in the implied prohibition against Commonwealth legislation which discriminates against the States or subjects them or their instrumentalities to special burdens or disabilities. It would be surprising, it was suggested, if the Constitution "embodied a general principle which protected the States and their instrumentalities from being singled out by Commonwealth laws for discriminatory treatment but provided no similar protection of the people who constitute the [64] Commonwealth and the States" [174 CLR at 484]. With respect, I do not find that situation surprising at all. The limitation upon the powers of the Commonwealth Parliament which prevent[s] it from discriminating against the States is derived from different considerations entirely ... Moreover the Constitution is in many respects inconsistent with a doctrine of legal equality.

Section 51 (xxvi), as Deane J recognised in the *Tasmanian Dam Case* [(1983) 158 CLR 1 at 273], "remains a general power to pass laws discriminating against or benefiting the people of any race". Similarly, s 51(xix) enables the Commonwealth Parliament to make laws which discriminate in favour of or against aliens. Discrimination in relation to the qualification to vote in federal elections is clearly envisaged by the Constitution and equality of voting power is not guaranteed. And until 1967 (which is after the last alleged act of detention ended), ss 51(xxvi) and 127 excluded Aboriginals for specified purposes. It is unnecessary to provide an exhaustive list of those respects in which the Constitution does not support the suggested doctrine of equality, for Deane and Toohey JJ recognised in *Leeth* that "the nature of the particular grant of legislative power may be such as to rebut the assumption that such discrimination was unauthorised by the relevant provision of the Constitution" or may need to be "adjusted to the extent necessary to accommodate discriminatory treatment which other provisions of the Constitution clearly contemplate" [174 CLR at 489-90]. To recognise as much is surely to undermine any basis for asserting that the Constitution assumes a doctrine of equality.

Not only that, but where the Constitution requires equality it does not leave it to implication. It makes provision for it by prohibiting discrimination, preference or lack of uniformity in specific instances. For example, the power of the Commonwealth Parliament to make laws with respect to taxation conferred by s 51(ii) must not be exercised so as to discriminate between States or parts of States. [65] Section 88 provides for uniform customs duties and s 51(iii) provides for uniform bounties. Section 92, in requiring trade, commerce and intercourse among the States to be absolutely free, prohibits discrimination of a protectionist kind. Section 99 forbids the Parliament to give preference to one State or any part thereof over another State or any part thereof by any law or regulation of trade, commerce or revenue. And s 117 provides that a subject of the Queen, resident in any State, shall not be subject in any other State to any disability or discrimination which would not be equally applicable to him if he were a subject of the Queen resident in such other State. In *Leeth*, Deane and Toohey JJ said that the existence of these specific provisions "which reflect the doctrine of legal equality serves to make manifest rather than undermine the status of that doctrine as an underlying principle of the Constitution as a whole" [174 CLR at 487]. That statement not only denies the accepted canon of construction expressed in the maxim expressio unius, exclusio alterius; it turns it on its head. And as one commentator [Leslie Zines] has observed:

"If various provisions aimed at preventing discrimination, preference and lack of uniformity are merely reflections of a general principle of equality, it can be similarly reasoned that the specific powers given to the Commonwealth Parliament are merely examples of a general principle, mentioned from time to time by delegates, that the Commonwealth Parliament was to be given power over all subjects which could not be as effectively dealt with by the States."

The inappropriateness of the expressio unius maxim arose, in their Honours' view, from what was said to be the "ordinary approach of the Constitution not to spell out the fundamental common law principles upon which it is structured" [174 CLR at 487] because "the general approach of the framers of the Constitution ... was to incorporate underlying doctrines or principles by implication" [174 CLR at 484]. With respect, that is not the case. Guarantees of equality before the law and due process were specifically rejected, not because they were already implicit and therefore unnecessary, but because they were not wanted. Indeed, if there was a need to make specific provision for equality where that was intended, it would suggest that there is no principle of equality underlying the Constitution and that were such a doctrine intended, specific provision would have been made for it. But to be fair to Deane and Toohey JJ, they did not, I think, base a doctrine of **[66]** equality principally upon the existence of these specific provisions. They referred to considerations of a more fundamental kind.

The ultimate source of the doctrine was said to lie in the common law ... However, whilst the rule of law requires the law to be applied to all without reference to rank or status, the plain matter of fact is that the common law has never required as a necessary outcome the equal, or non-discriminatory, operation of laws. It is not possible, in my view, to dismiss the discriminatory treatment of women at common law or such matters as the attainder of felons as "past anomalies". To do so is to treat the doctrines of the common law with selectivity. Moreover, the supremacy of parliament, which is itself a principle of the common law, necessarily leaves the common law subject to alteration without reference to notions of equality. The common law thus provides no foundation for a doctrine of equality, at all events substantive equality as opposed to the kind of procedural equality envisaged by the rule of law.

But even if a doctrine of substantive equality were discernible in the common law, it would not appear that it was ... adopted in the drafting of the Constitution. Apart from anything else, it is clear that the Commonwealth Parliament was intended to have the capacity, in the exercise of its legislative powers, to alter the common law ... Nevertheless, in **[67]** *Leeth* Deane and Toohey JJ expressed the view that such a doctrine had been adopted in the Constitution by necessary implication by reason of its conceptual basis and because it is "implicit in the Constitution's separation of judicial power from legislative and executive powers and the vesting of judicial power in designated 'courts'" [174 CLR at 486].

In referring to the conceptual basis of the Constitution, Deane and Toohey JJ had in mind the preamble and covering cl 3 of the *Commonwealth of Australia Constitution Act* which refer to the agreement of the people of the various colonies to unite in a Federal Commonwealth. Their Honours took the view [174 CLR at 486] that "[i]mplicit in that free agreement was the notion of the inherent equality of the people as the parties to the compact". It may be observed that a degree of equality was lacking in the free agreement of which their Honours spoke, in that the referendum expressing that agreement excluded most women and many Aboriginals. But the important thing is that the Constitution to which the people agreed plainly envisages inequality in the operation of laws made under it. Moreover, those who framed the Constitution deliberately chose not to include a provision guaranteeing due process or the equal protection of the laws and it was with those omissions that the people agreed to the Constitution. It is not possible, in my view, to read into the fact of agreement any implications which do not appear from the document upon which agreement was reached. Not only does a doctrine of equality ... not appear from the Constitution, but the very basis upon which it was drafted was that matters such as that were better left to parliament and the democratic process ...

[68] [I]t is possible to regard the separation of judicial power from the other powers of government as affording a measure of due process but it is due process of an essentially procedural rather than a substantive kind. What is clear is that Ch III says nothing, either expressly or by implication, requiring equality in the operation of laws which courts created by or under that Chapter must administer. Those courts have an obligation to administer justice according to law. No doubt that duty is to do justice according to valid law, but Ch III contains no warrant for regarding a law as invalid because the substantive rights which it confers or the substantive obligations which it imposes are conferred or imposed in an unequal fashion ...

For these reasons, I would respectfully reject the conclusion reached by Deane and Toohey JJ that there is a doctrine of equality to be found by implication in the Constitution. For the same reasons I would reject the plaintiffs' claim based upon that doctrine. I would affirm the proposition contained in the judgment of Mason CJ, McHugh J and myself in *Leeth* [174 CLR at 467] that there is no general requirement contained in the Constitution that Commonwealth laws should have a uniform operation throughout the Commonwealth.

Brennan CJ, while he too held that no generalised requirement of "**[45]** substantive equality" could assist the Aboriginal plaintiffs in *Kruger*, expressed no opinion as to the existence or scope of such a requirement. His rejection of the plaintiffs' argument depended mainly on the conclusion that no such requirement could "restrict the power conferred by s 122" over Australian Territories. He added also that "**[44]** [e]ven in the federal provisions of the Constitution, some legislative inequality is contemplated by s 51(xix) and (xxvi)", that is, the "aliens" power and the "races power". However, he made the point in carefully limited terms, noting only that these provisions "destroy the **[45]** argument that all laws of the Commonwealth must accord substantive equality to all people irrespective of race". Beyond that, he neither reaffirmed nor retracted the position he had taken in *Leeth*.

Only Toohey J was willing to defend the position that he and Deane J had taken in *Leeth*. Quoting passages from the judgments of Brennan and Gaudron JJ in *Leeth*, he protested that "**[95]** a view of *Leeth* which confines any doctrine of equality to the joint judgment of Deane J and myself does less than justice to the reasons of Brennan J and Gaudron J". However, even he felt unable to hold on the pleadings that the *Aboriginals Ordinance* was invalid by reason of the substantive inequality of treatment which it embodied, though he did perceive a possible issue which would need to be determined if the litigation proceeded to trial.

Despite Toohey J's unrepentant adherence to *Leeth* and Brennan CJ's apparent reservations, the cumulative effect of the positions taken in *Kruger* by Dawson, Gaudron, McHugh and Gummow JJ appears to mean that the "doctrine of legal equality" suggested by Deane and Toohey JJ in *Leeth* has now been decisively rejected. On the other hand, the more limited doctrine proposed by Gaudron J, and at least partially endorsed in *Kruger* by Dawson and McHugh JJ, appears still to be maintainable.

9. Further References

Boas, G, "*Dietrich*, the High Court and Unfair Trials Legislation: A Constitutional Guarantee?" (1993) 19 *Monash Law Review* 256.

Brown, AJ, "The Wig or the Sword? Separation of Powers and the Plight of the Australian Judge" (1992) 21 *Federal Law Review* 48.

Campbell, E, "Rules of Evidence and the Constitution" (2000) 26 *Monash University Law Review* 312.

De Meyrick, J, "Whatever Happened to Boilermakers?" (1995) 69 *Australian Law Journal* 106 (Part I), 189 (Part II).

Gerangelos, P, "The Separation of Powers and Legislative Interference with Judicial Functions in Pending Cases" (2002) 30 *Federal Law Review* 1.

Gerangelos, P, "The Decisional Independence of Chapter III Courts and Constitutional Limitations on Legislative Power: Notes from the United States" (2005) 33 *Federal Law Review* 391.

Hope, J, "A Constitutional Right to a Fair Trial? Implications for the Reform of the Australian Criminal Justice System" (1996) 24 *Federal Law Review* 173.

Jackson, DF, "The Australian Judicial System: Judicial Power of the Commonwealth" (2001) 24 *University of New South Wales Law Journal* 737.

Kirk, J, "Constitutional Implications (II): Doctrines of Equality and Democracy" (2001) 25 *Melbourne University Law Review* 24.

Kirk, L, "Chapter III and Legislative Interference with the Judicial Process: *Abebe v Commonwealth* and *Nicholas v The Queen*" in Stone, A, and Williams, G (eds), *The High Court at the Crossroads*: *Essays in Constitutional Law* (Federation Press, 2000), 119.

Lacey, W, "Inherent Jurisdiction, Judicial Power and Implied Guarantees under Chapter III of the Constitution" (2003) 31 *Federal Law Review* 57.

Malcolm, D, "The State Judicial Power" (1991) 21 *University of Western Australia Law Review* 7.

McHugh, MH, "Does Chapter III of the Constitution Protect Substantive as Well as Procedural Rights?" (2001) 21 *Australian Bar Review* 235.

Meyerson, D, "Extra-Judicial Service on the Part of Judges: Constitutional Impediments in Australia and South America" (2003) 3 *Oxford University Commonwealth Law Journal* 181.

Murphy, MD, "Judicial Registrars of Federal Courts: Widening the Supervised Exercise of Delegated Judicial Power" (1997) 6 *Journal of Judicial Administration* 226.

Opeskin, B, and Wheeler, F (eds), *The Australian Federal Judicial System* (Melbourne University Press, 2000).

Perry, MA, "Chapter III and the Powers of Non-Judicial Tribunals: *Breckler* and Beyond" in Stone, A, and Williams, G (eds), *The High Court at the Crossroads*: *Essays in Constitutional Law* (Federation Press, 2000), 148.

Roberts, H, "Retrospective Criminal Laws and the Separation of Judicial Power" (1997) 8 *Public Law Review* 170.

Saunders, C, "Concepts of Equality in the Australian Constitution" in Lindell, G (ed), *Future Directions in Australian Constitutional Law* (Federation Press, 1994), 209.

Schoff, P, "The Electoral Jurisdiction of the High Court as the Court of Disputed Returns: Non-judicial Power and Incompatible Function?" (1997) 25 *Federal Law Review* 317.

Twomey, A, *The Constitution of New South Wales* (Federation Press, 2004), Ch 13.

Twomey, A, "Reconciling Parliament's Contempt Powers with the Constitutional Separation of Powers" (1997) 8 *Public Law Review* 88.

Walker, K, "Disputed Returns and Parliamentary Qualifications: Is the High Court's Jurisdiction Constitutional" (1997) 20 *University of New South Wales Law Journal* 257.

Walker, K, "Persona Designata, Incompatibility and the Separation of Powers" (1997) 8 *Public Law Review* 153.

Wheeler, F, "Due Process, Judicial Power and Chapter III in the New High Court" (2004) 32 *Federal Law Review* 205.

Wheeler, F, "Original Intent and the Doctrine of the Separation of Powers in Australia" (1996) 7 *Public Law Review* 96.

Wheeler, F, "The *Boilermakers* Case" in Lee, HP, and Winterton, G (eds), *Australian Constitutional Landmarks* (Cambridge University Press, 2003), 160.

Wheeler, F, "The Rise and Rise of Judicial Power under Chapter III of the Constitution: A Decade in Overview" (2001) 20 *Australian Bar Review* 283.

Williams, G, *Human Rights under the Australian Constitution* (Oxford University Press, 1999), Ch 8.

Winterton, G, "The Separation of Judicial Power as an Implied Bill of Rights" in Lindell, G (ed), *Future Directions in Australian Constitutional Law* (Federation Press, 1994), 185.

Zines, L, *The High Court and the Constitution* (Butterworths, 4th ed 1997), Chs 9, 10.

Chapter 15

Judicial and Non-Judicial Detention

1. Introduction

In *Chu Kheng Lim v Minister for Immigration, Local Government and Ethnic Affairs* (1992) 176 CLR 1, the High Court substantially upheld the validity of amendments to the *Migration Act 1958* (Cth) providing for the detention in custody of two groups of asylum seekers specifically targeted by the amendments. In explaining why the provisions would have been invalid if applicable to Australian citizens, Brennan, Deane and Dawson JJ formulated a broad constitutional principle that (subject to certain well established exceptions) the involuntary detention of a citizen in custody may only be ordered by a court, and in consequence of a judicial finding of criminal responsibility. However, the precise scope of that principle, and indeed whether such a principle exists at all, has remained controversial.

The formulation in *Chu Kheng Lim* was applicable only to cases of detention under a law of the Commonwealth, since it was proposed as a consequence of the exclusive provision made by Ch III of the Constitution for the judicial power of the Commonwealth. However, in *Kable v Director of Public Prosecutions (NSW)* (1996) 189 CLR 51 a related principle was enounced for the States on the basis that a State court whose functions include the exercise of Commonwealth judicial power may not be given functions "incompatible" with the exercise of that power. Again, the precise extent of the *Kable* principle has remained uncertain.

The principle suggested in *Chu Kheng Lim* was formulated as follows.

Chu Kheng Lim v Minister for Immigration, Local Government and Ethnic Affairs
(1992) 176 CLR 1

Brennan, Deane and Dawson JJ: [27] In exclusively entrusting to the courts designated by Ch III the function of the adjudgment and punishment of criminal guilt under a law of the Commonwealth, the Constitution's concern is with substance and not mere form. It would, for example, be beyond the legislative power of the Parliament to invest the Executive with an arbitrary power to detain citizens in custody notwithstanding that the power was conferred in terms which sought to divorce such detention in custody from both punishment and criminal guilt. The reason why that is so is that, putting to one side the exceptional cases to which reference is made below, the involuntary detention of a citizen in custody by the State is penal or punitive in character and, under our system of government, exists only as an incident of the exclusively judicial function of adjudging and punishing criminal guilt. Every citizen is "ruled by the law, and by the law alone" and "may with us be punished for a breach of law, but he can be **[28]** punished for nothing else" [AV Dicey, *Introduction to the Study of the Law of the Constitution*, Macmillan, 10th ed 1959, at 202]. As Blackstone wrote, relying on the authority of Coke:

"The confinement of the person, in any wise, is an imprisonment. So that the keeping [of] a man against his will ... is an imprisonment ... To make imprisonment lawful, it must either be by process from the courts of judicature, or by warrant from some legal officer having authority to commit to prison; which warrant must be in writing, under the hand and seal of the magistrate, and express the causes of the commitment, in order to be examined into (if necessary) upon a habeas corpus."

There are some qualifications which must be made to the general proposition that the power to order that a citizen be involuntarily confined in custody is ... entrusted exclusively to Ch III courts. The most important is that which Blackstone himself identified in the above passage, namely, the arrest and detention in custody, pursuant to executive warrant, of a person accused of crime to ensure that he or she is available to be dealt with by the courts. Such committal to custody awaiting trial is not seen by the law as punitive or as appertaining exclusively to judicial power. Even where exercisable by the Executive, however, the power to detain a person in custody pending trial is ordinarily subject to the supervisory jurisdiction of the courts, including the "ancient common law" jurisdiction, "before and since the conquest", to order that a person committed to prison while awaiting trial be admitted to bail. Involuntary detention in cases of mental illness or infectious disease can also legitimately be seen as non-punitive in character and as not necessarily involving the exercise of judicial power. Otherwise, and putting to one side the traditional powers of the Parliament to punish for contempt and of military tribunals to punish for breach of military discipline, the citizens of this country enjoy, at least in times of peace, a constitutional immunity from being imprisoned by Commonwealth [29] authority except pursuant to an order by a court in the exercise of the judicial power of the Commonwealth.

Explaining why this immunity did not assist the plaintiffs in *Chu Kheng Lim*, these judges said:

Brennan, Deane and Dawson JJ: [29] While an alien who is actually within this country enjoys the protection of our law, his or her status, rights and immunities under that law differ from the status, rights and immunities of an Australian citizen in a variety of important respects. For present purposes, the most important difference ... lies in the vulnerability of the alien to exclusion or deportation. That vulnerability flows from both the common law and the provisions of the Constitution ... [I]ts effect is significantly to diminish the protection which Ch III of the Constitution provides, in the case of a citizen, against imprisonment otherwise than pursuant to judicial process ...

[30] In this Court, it has been consistently recognized that the power of the Parliament to make laws with respect to aliens includes not only the power to make laws providing for the expulsion or deportation of aliens by the Executive but extends to authorizing the [31] Executive to restrain an alien in custody to the extent necessary to make the deportation effective. The clearest example is *Koon Wing Lau v Calwell* [(1949) 80 CLR 533] ...

[32] It can therefore be said that the legislative power conferred by s 51(xix) of the Constitution encompasses the conferral upon the Executive of authority to detain (or to direct the detention of) an alien in custody for the purposes of expulsion or deportation. Such authority to detain an alien in custody, when conferred upon the Executive in the context and for the purposes of an executive power of deportation or expulsion, constitutes an incident of that executive power. By analogy, authority to detain an alien in custody, when conferred in the context of and for the purposes of executive powers to receive, investigate and determine an application by that alien for an entry permit and (after determination) to admit or deport, constitutes an incident of those executive powers. Such limited authority to detain an alien in custody can be conferred on the Executive without infringement of Ch III's exclusive vesting of the judicial power of the Commonwealth in the courts which it designates. The reason why that is so is that, to that limited extent, authority to detain in custody is neither punitive in nature nor part of the judicial power of the Commonwealth. When conferred upon the Executive, it takes its character from the executive powers to exclude, admit and deport of which it is an incident.

In later cases arising under the *Migration Act*, the validity of provisions for the detention of asylum seekers in custody has consistently been reaffirmed.

2. The Incompatibility Doctrine

The evolution of the "incompatibility" doctrine is traced in Chapter 14, §6. In the *Boilermakers' Case* the High Court of Australia (*R v Kirby; Ex parte Boilermakers' Society of Australia* (1956) 94 CLR 254) and the Privy Council (*Attorney-General (Commonwealth) v The Queen* [1957] AC 288) treated Ch III of the Constitution as excluding any combination of non-judicial power with the judicial power of the Commonwealth. In *Hilton v Wells* (1985) 157 CLR 57, the majority accepted an exception to the *Boilermakers* principle: a federal judge can be appointed to perform non-judicial functions provided that those functions can be construed as assigned to the individual as a *persona designata* and not in a judicial capacity. In *Grollo v Palmer* (1995) 184 CLR 348, the Court recognised an exception to the exception: the *persona designata* doctrine does *not* apply if the functions to be performed are "incompatible" with the holding of judicial office. And in *Wilson v Minister for Aboriginal and Torres Strait Islander Affairs* (1996) 189 CLR 1, this principle was applied to invalidate the appointment of Justice Jane Mathews as a reporter under s 10 of the *Aboriginal and Torres Strait Islander Heritage Protection Act 1984* (Cth).

In *Wilson*, the "incompatibility" doctrine was treated merely as an exception to the permissible use of the *persona designata* device. However, in *Kable v Director of Public Prosecutions (NSW)* (1996) 189 CLR 51 (decided six days later on 12 September 1996) the reach of the "incompatibility" doctrine was greatly extended in a case where no suggestion of appointment as *personae designatae* was involved.

The *Community Protection Act 1994* (NSW) empowered the Supreme Court of New South Wales to make "preventive detention orders".

Community Protection Act 1994 (NSW)

5(1) On an application made in accordance with this Act, the Court may order that a specified person be detained in prison for a specified period if it is satisfied, on reasonable grounds:

(a) that the person is more likely than not to commit a serious act of violence; and

(b) that it is appropriate, for the protection of a particular person or persons or the community generally, that the person be held in custody.

(2) The maximum period to be specified in an order under this section is 6 months.

(3) An order under this section may be made against a person:

(a) whether or not the person is in lawful custody, as a detainee or otherwise; and

(b) whether or not there are grounds on which the person may be held in lawful custody otherwise than as a detainee.

(4) More than one application under this section may be made in relation to the same person.

Under s 15, an order could only be made against a person pursuant to s 5(1) if the Court was satisfied that the case against that person had been made out "on the balance of probabilities". Section 14 provided that proceedings under the Act "are civil proceedings", and as such were to be conducted according to the rules of evidence applicable to such proceedings. Despite the general applicability of s 5(1), the operation of the Act was limited by s 3 as follows:

3 (1) The object of this Act is to protect the community by providing for the preventive detention (by order of the Supreme Court made on the application of the Director of Public Prosecutions) of Gregory Wayne Kable.

(2) In the construction of this Act, the need to protect the community is to be given paramount consideration.

(3) This Act authorises the making of a detention order against Gregory Wayne Kable and does not authorise the making of a detention order against any other person.

(4) For the purposes of this section, Gregory Wayne Kable is the person of that name who was convicted in New South Wales on 1 August 1990 of the manslaughter of his wife, Hilary Kable.

The Act was passed because Kable, while in gaol for the manslaughter of his wife, had written letters apparently threatening the safety of his children and his deceased wife's sister, with whom the children were now living. The structure of the Act, as Toohey J pointed out, was anomalous: while most of its provisions were framed in language of general application, the effect of s 3 was to confine its operation to Kable as a named individual. Toohey J ascribed the anomaly to "[89] amendments made while the Bill was in progress through Parliament, without sufficient attention being paid to their impact on other provisions of the Act".

One argument against the Act was that its singling out of an individual person for detention, and its use of *preventive* detention in the absence of any actual additional crime, amounted to a "legislative judgment" or a "legislative usurpation of judicial power" within the meaning of *Liyanage v The Queen* [1967] 1 AC 259. That argument, however, depended upon a strict constitutional "separation of powers", whereas in cases such as *Clyne v East* (1967) 68 SR(NSW) 385 it had been held that the *Constitution Act 1902* (NSW) embodies no such separation. A possible answer to that objection was that amendments to the *Constitution Act* in 1995 had entrenched judicial independence to such an extent that, as thus amended, the *Constitution Act* now *might* embody a separation of powers. But that argument was rejected in *Kable* (see the extract in Chapter 14, §2). Accordingly, in the absence of any "separation of powers" at the State level, an attack on the *Community Protection Act* based on the concept of "legislative judgment" necessarily failed.

Instead, a majority of the High Court invoked the "incompatibility" doctrine, holding that the function conferred on the Supreme Court by the *Community Protection Act* was "incompatible" with its exercise of federal judicial power. Thus, the point was not that the Act was an inappropriate exercise of (State) *legislative* power, but that the function assigned to the Supreme Court was incompatible with the exercise by that Court of (federal) *judicial* power. The case was decided by a 4:2 majority, with Brennan CJ and Dawson J dissenting. Toohey J began by making a point that most of the other judges appeared *not* to regard as necessary to the decision: namely, that "federal jurisdiction" was involved *in this very case*.

Kable v Director of Public Prosecutions (NSW)
(1996) 189 CLR 51

Toohey J: [94] The respondent accepted that in the present case the Supreme Court was exercising federal jurisdiction vested in it by s 39 of the Judiciary Act. The reason for the concession was that the appellant was relying upon what the Solicitor-General for New South Wales described as "federal constitutional points", not only before this Court but at first instance and on appeal to the Court of Appeal. The reference to "federal constitutional points" was a reference to submissions made on behalf of the appellant that an implication is to be drawn from the Commonwealth Constitution that legislation, whether federal or State, that is directed against or discriminates against an individual is invalid. In addition the appellant relied upon s 80 of the Constitution to argue [95] that a charge of the offence created by the Act must be tried by a judge and jury ... Thus, it was said, federal jurisdiction was attracted in the present case ...

The appellant's senior counsel was at pains to eschew any notion that his submission involved challenging the well-established doctrine [96] that, in investing judicial power in the States, the Parliament must take the State courts as it finds them. For instance, the appellant accepted that State courts may be vested with non-judicial powers and functions. His argument was that a State court exercising federal jurisdiction, in the sense discussed earlier, could not be the recipient of powers and functions which were incompatible with the very nature of judicial power. In other words, the issue as presented by the appellant was not one of judicial versus legislative or executive power but of incompatibility with the essence of judicial power. Hence, no question of taking the courts as the Parliament finds them truly arose. It follows that passages in the judgments of this Court which emphasise that the courts of a State are the judicial organs of the State and not of the Commonwealth do not resolve the questions now facing this Court. By reason of the issues raised in the case, the Supreme Court exercised federal jurisdiction. It is not the investing of the Supreme Court with federal jurisdiction that is in issue; it is the exercise of federal jurisdiction by the Supreme Court in the circumstances arising under the Act that is challenged.

In *Grollo v Palmer* [(1995) 184 CLR 348] the Court held that the vesting in designated judges of the Federal Court of the power to issue interception warrants was not incompatible either with the judge's performance of his or her judicial functions or with the proper discharge by the judiciary of its responsibilities as an institution exercising judicial power. Nevertheless the Court emphasised [184 CLR at 365] that "no function can be conferred that is incompatible ... with the proper discharge by the judiciary of its responsibilities as an institution exercising judicial power". It is true that the proposition was enunciated in the context of the power to confer non-judicial functions on judges as designated persons but in my view it holds good whenever Ch III of the Constitution is operative. And *Mistretta v United States* [488 US 361 (1989)], to which the majority judgment refers with approval, is couched in terms of constitutional doctrine ... [and] "the integrity of the Judicial Branch".

The appellant's argument of incompatibility of function rests on several foundations. But fundamentally it relies upon the nature of the Act whereby the Supreme Court may order the imprisonment of a person although that person has not been adjudged guilty of any criminal offence. The Supreme Court is thereby required to participate **[97]** in a process designed to bring about the detention of a person by reason of the Court's assessment of what that person might do, not what the person has done.

The Act speaks of likelihood "to commit a serious act of violence". If the power to detain were the consequence of the actual commission of a serious act of violence, it might be little different from the power to impose an indeterminate sentence to be found in various statutes. In those cases, however, some prior conduct in the form of the commission of an offence of a prescribed nature is the basis upon which an indeterminate sentence may be ordered. The appellant's complaint is that, while prior conduct may bring him to the attention of the authorities, no such conduct is identified as the basis for the making of an order under s 5. No doubt prior conduct has an evidentiary part to play; without it there could hardly be a conclusion that the appellant was more likely than not to commit a serious act of violence. In that respect it was a relevant consideration that the appellant had been charged with the murder of his wife and that subsequently he pleaded guilty of manslaughter, a plea which was accepted by the Crown by reason of his diminished responsibility. But the order for his detention was not made by reason of his commission of that offence. Likewise, it may have been a relevant consideration, in terms of the Act, that the appellant was facing 17 charges alleging contravention of s 85s of the *Crimes Act* 1914 (Cth) in making improper use of postal services by sending threatening letters to various persons including his children. But the Act required no determination of his guilt for any of those offences as a condition of the order made against him ...

[98] Preventive detention under the Act is an end in itself. And the person so detained "is taken to be a prisoner within the meaning of the Prisons Act 1952". It is not an incident of the exclusively judicial function of adjudging and punishing criminal guilt. It is not part of a system of preventive detention with appropriate safeguards, consequent upon or ancillary to the adjudication of guilt ... In the present case the Act requires the Supreme Court to exercise the judicial power of the Commonwealth in a manner which is inconsistent with traditional judicial process.

The extraordinary character of the legislation and of the functions it requires the Supreme Court to perform is highlighted by the operation of the statute upon one named person only. In this respect the Act is virtually unique. It does not define "a specified person" by reference to any class or category and it carries no consequences for any person, other than the appellant, to whom its language might otherwise be applicable.

The Act answers that aspect of incompatibility which was identified in *Grollo v Palmer* as "the performance of non-judicial functions of such a nature that public confidence in the integrity of the judiciary as an institution ... is diminished" [184 CLR at 365]. The function exercised by the Supreme Court under the Act offends Ch III which, as I said in *Harris v Caladine* [(1991) 172 CLR 84 at 135], reflects an aspect of the doctrine of separation of powers, serving to protect not only the role of the independent judiciary but also the personal interests of litigants in having those interests determined by judges independent of the legislature and the executive. The function offends that aspect because it requires the Supreme Court to participate in the making of a preventive detention order where no breach of the criminal law is alleged and where there has been no determination of guilt. On that ground I would hold the Act invalid. It is not possible to sever s 5 from the rest of the Act which exists only to give effect to that section ...

[99] If the Act operated on a category of persons and a defence to an application for a preventive detention order was confined to a challenge that the criteria in s 5(1) had not been met, different questions might arise. In that situation the judicial power of the Commonwealth might not be involved ... But here the judicial power of the Commonwealth is involved, in circumstances where the Act is expressed to operate in relation to one person only, the appellant, and has led to his detention without a determination of his guilt for any offence.

Gaudron J quoted what Isaacs J had said in *R v Murray and Cormie; Ex parte Commonwealth* (1916) 22 CLR 437: "**[452]** The Constitution, by Ch III, draws the clearest distinction between federal Courts and State Courts, and ... recognises in the most pronounced and unequivocal way that they remain 'State Courts'." However, she demonstrated by close technical analysis that most of the provisions of Ch III draw no such distinction. For example, s 79 refers to "[t]he federal jurisdiction of *any court*" (emphasis added); s 71 deals even-handedly with such "federal courts as the Parliament creates" and such "other courts as it invests with federal jurisdiction"; and s 73, in conferring the High Court's appellate jurisdiction, is similarly even-handed as between State and federal courts. Against that background Gaudron J went on:

Gaudron J: [101] [If s 72 and s 77] are put to one side, the provisions of Ch III clearly postulate an integrated Australian court system for the exercise of the judicial power of the Commonwealth, with this Court at its apex as a constitutional court and as a court exercising appellate jurisdiction for the whole of Australia, and with no distinction, so far as concerns the judicial power of the Commonwealth, between State courts and federal courts created by the Parliament ...

Again, s 77 does not distinguish between State courts and federal courts created by the Parliament as repositories of the judicial power of the Commonwealth. It does, however, recognise that the other courts which may be invested with federal jurisdiction are State courts. When s 77 is considered in conjunction with s 72 which, as earlier indicated, provides as to the appointment, tenure and remuneration of the members of this Court and federal courts created by the Parliament, it is correct to say, by reference to those provisions, that **[102]** Ch III recognises that this Court and other federal courts are creatures of the Commonwealth and that State courts are the creatures of the States ...

[I]t follows that it is for the States and for the States alone to determine the appointment, tenure and remuneration of State judges and the structure, organisation and jurisdictional limits of State courts. In that sense, it is correct to say, as it often is [said], that the Commonwealth must take State courts as it finds them. However, it should be remembered that that dictum originates in the judgment of Griffith CJ in *Federated Sawmill, Timberyard and General Woodworkers' Employees' Association (Adelaide Branch) v Alexander* [(1912) 15 CLR 308], a case involving the question whether jurisdictional limits imposed by State law on a State court applied in matters of invested federal jurisdiction. It was in that context that his Honour said [15 CLR at 313] that "when the Federal Parliament confers a new jurisdiction upon an existing State Court it takes the Court as it finds it, with all its limitations as to jurisdiction, unless otherwise expressly declared" – a vastly different statement from the unqualified proposition that the Commonwealth must take a State court as it finds it.

Neither the recognition in Ch III that State courts are the creatures of the States nor its consequence that, in the respects indicated, the Commonwealth must take State courts as it finds them detracts from ... one of the clearest features of our Constitution, namely, that it provides for an integrated Australian judicial system for the exercise of the judicial power of the Commonwealth. Moreover, neither that recognition nor that consequence directs the conclusion that State Parliaments may enact whatever laws they choose with respect to State courts. If Ch III requires that State courts not exercise particular powers, the Parliaments of the States cannot confer those powers upon them. That follows from covering cl 5, which provides that the Constitution is "binding on the courts, judges, and people of every State and of every part of the Commonwealth, notwithstanding anything in the laws of any State", and from s 106, by which the Constitution of each State is made subject to the Australian Constitution. And so much was recognised in

Commonwealth v Queensland [(1975) 134 CLR 298 at 315] where it was said that State legislation in violation of "the principles that underlie Ch III" is invalid.

The question whether the Constitution requires that State courts not have particular powers conferred upon them depends, in my view, on a proper understanding of the integrated judicial system for which Ch III **[103]** provides – the "autochthonous expedient", as it has been called [*Boilermakers' Case* (1956) 94 CLR 254 at 268]. One thing which clearly emerges is that, although it is for the States to determine the organisation and structure of their court systems, they must each maintain courts, or, at least, a court for the exercise of the judicial power of the Commonwealth. Were they free to abolish their courts, the autochthonous expedient, more precisely, the provisions of Ch III which postulate an integrated judicial system would be frustrated in their entirety. To this extent, at least, the States are not free to legislate as they please.

Two other matters of significance emerge from a consideration of the provisions of Ch III. The first is that State courts are neither less worthy recipients of federal jurisdiction than federal courts nor "substitute tribunals", as they have sometimes been called [*Commonwealth v Limerick Steamship Co Ltd and Kidman* (1924) 35 CLR 69 at 116]. To put the matter plainly, there is nothing anywhere in the Constitution to suggest that it permits of different grades or qualities of justice, depending on whether judicial power is exercised by State courts or federal courts created by the Parliament.

The second and, perhaps, the more significant matter which emerges from a consideration of the provisions of Ch III is, as I pointed out in *Leeth v Commonwealth* [(1992) 174 CLR 455 at 498-9], that State courts, when exercising federal jurisdiction "are part of the Australian judicial system created by Ch III of the Constitution and, in that sense and on that account, they have a role and existence which transcends their status as courts of the States". Once the notion that the Constitution permits of different grades or qualities of justice is rejected, the consideration that State courts have a role and existence transcending their status as State courts directs the conclusion that Ch III requires that the Parliaments of the States not legislate to confer powers on State courts which are repugnant to or incompatible with their exercise of the judicial power of the Commonwealth.

The prohibition on State legislative power which derives from Ch III is not at all comparable with the limitation on the legislative power of the Commonwealth enunciated in *R v Kirby; Ex parte Boilermakers' Society of Australia*. The *Boilermakers'* doctrine, as it is sometimes called, prevents the Parliament of the Commonwealth from conferring judicial power on bodies other than courts and prevents it from conferring any power that is not judicial power or a power incidental thereto on the courts specified in s 71 of the Constitution. It also prevents the Parliament from conferring functions on judges in their individual capacity if the functions are inconsistent with the exercise of judicial power in the sense explained in *Grollo v* **[104]** *Palmer*. The limitation on State legislative power is more closely confined and relates to powers or functions imposed on a State court, rather than its judges in their capacity as individuals, and is concerned with powers or functions that are repugnant to or incompatible with the exercise of the judicial power of the Commonwealth.

Although the limitation is one relating to the conferral of powers on courts, rather than on judges in their capacity as individuals, it is, nevertheless, one that is closely related to the limitation on Commonwealth power to confer functions on judges of this and other federal courts in their capacity as individuals. In both cases the limitation derives from the necessity to ensure the integrity of the judicial process and the integrity of the courts specified in s 71 of the Constitution.

It remains to be considered whether the power purportedly conferred on the Supreme Court by s 5(1) of the Act is repugnant to or incompatible with the exercise of the judicial power of the Commonwealth ...

[106] The proceedings which the Act contemplates are not proceedings otherwise known to the law. And except to the extent that the Act attempts to dress them up as legal proceedings (for example, by referring to the applicant as "the defendant", by specifying that the proceedings are civil proceedings and by suggesting that the rules of evidence apply), they do not in any way partake of the nature of legal proceedings. They do not involve the resolution of a dispute between contesting parties as to their respective legal rights and obligations. And as already indicated, the applicant is not to be put on trial for any offence against the criminal law. Instead, the proceedings are directed to the making of a guess – perhaps an educated guess, but a guess nonetheless – whether, on the balance of probabilities, the appellant will commit an offence of the kind specified in the definition of "serious act of violence". And, at least in some circumstances, the Act directs that that guess be made having regard to material which would not be admissible as evidence in legal proceedings.

It is well settled that some functions take their character from the way in which they are to be exercised and, thus, from the body on which they are conferred. Accordingly, some functions which are not essentially judicial in character are, nonetheless, properly characterised as judicial if conferred on a court. Chapter III permits the conferral of such functions on courts. And, of course, there is nothing to prevent the Parliaments of the States from conferring powers on their courts which are wholly non-judicial, so long as they are not repugnant to or inconsistent with the exercise by those courts of the judicial power of the Commonwealth.

The power purportedly conferred by s 5(1) of the Act requires the making of an order, if the conditions specified in s 5(1) are satisfied, depriving an individual of his liberty, not because he has breached any law, whether civil or criminal, but because an opinion is formed, on the basis of material which does not necessarily constitute evidence admissible in legal proceedings, that he "is more likely than not" to breach a law by committing a serious act of violence as defined in s 4 of the Act. That is the antithesis of the judicial process, **[107]** one of the central purposes of which is, as I said in *Re Nolan; Ex parte Young* [(1991) 172 CLR 460 at 497], to protect "the individual from arbitrary punishment and the arbitrary abrogation of rights by ensuring that punishment is not inflicted and rights are not interfered with other than in consequence of the fair and impartial application of the relevant law to facts which have been properly ascertained". It is not a power that is properly characterised as a judicial function, notwithstanding that it is purportedly conferred on a court and its exercise is conditioned in terms usually associated with the judicial process.

Moreover, when regard is had to the precise nature of the function purportedly conferred by s 5(1), the matters to be taken into account in its exercise and its contrariety to what is ordinarily involved in the judicial process, the effect of s 5(1) is, in my view, to compromise the integrity of the Supreme Court of New South Wales and, because that court is not simply a State court but a court which also exists to exercise the judicial power of the Commonwealth, it also has the effect of compromising the integrity of the judicial system brought into existence by Ch III of the Constitution.

The integrity of the courts depends on their acting in accordance with the judicial process and, in no small measure, on the maintenance of public confidence in that process. Particularly is that so in relation to criminal proceedings which involve the most important of all judicial functions, namely, the determination of the guilt or innocence of persons accused of criminal offences. Public confidence cannot be maintained in the courts and their criminal processes if, as postulated by s 5(1), the courts are required to deprive persons of their liberty, not on the basis that they have breached any law, but on the basis that an opinion is formed, by reference to material which may or may not be admissible in legal proceedings, that on the balance of probabilities, they may do so.

Mention should be made of one other aspect of the function purportedly conferred on the Supreme Court by s 5(1) of the Act. Public confidence in the courts requires that they act consistently and that their proceedings be conducted according to rules of general application. That is an essential feature of the judicial process. It is that feature which serves to distinguish between palm tree justice and equal justice. Public confidence cannot be maintained in a judicial system which is not predicated on equal justice.

The Act, in several of its provisions, suggests that an application under s 5(1) is to be determined in accordance with rules generally applicable in legal proceedings. In this respect, I have already referred to the description of the appellant as "the defendant", the description **[108]** of the proceedings as "civil proceedings" and the suggestion that the rules of evidence apply when, in significant respects, they do not. Mention has also been made of s 16 which provides for proceedings under s 5(1) to be "commenced by summons in accordance with rules of court". In truth, the proceedings contemplated by s 5(1) are unique with unique procedures and with rules which apply only to the appellant. They are proceedings which the Act attempts to dress up as proceedings involving the judicial process. In so doing, the Act makes a mockery of that process and, inevitably, weakens public confidence in it. And because the judicial process is a defining feature of the judicial power of the Commonwealth, the Act weakens confidence in the institutions which comprise the judicial system brought into existence by Ch III of the Constitution.

McHugh J: [111] *State courts are part of an Australian judicial system*

At federation each Colony had courts. Each Colony had a Supreme Court from which an appeal could be taken to the Privy Council. **[112]** The right of appeal from the State Supreme Courts to the Privy Council continued after federation. In addition, s 74 of the Constitution preserved the prerogative right of Her Majesty in Council to grant leave to appeal from decisions of the High Court ... However, s 74 also gave the Parliament power to "make laws limiting the matters" in which special leave to appeal from the High Court to the Privy Council could be asked. That power extended to abolishing all matters in respect of which leave could be sought. Nevertheless, until that power was exercised, the Constitution intended that, subject to the grant of a certificate by the High Court in respect of an inter se matter, Australia should have an integrated system of State and federal courts administering a single body of common law under the supervision of the Judicial Committee of the Privy Council which stood at the apex of the system.

Unlike the United States of America where there is a common law of each State, Australia has a unified common law which applies in each State but is not itself the creature of any State. Perhaps the validity of that proposition is not as readily apparent to a State judge bound by the authority of his or her own Full Court or Court of Appeal as it is to a judge of a federal court who must apply the common law. In an extra-judicial paper published in 1957, Sir Owen Dixon pointed out that, if there is no statutory law in the case, an Australian judge sitting in the original jurisdiction of the High Court "proceeds to administer the common law as an entire system. He ascertains its content as best he may. Among the judicial decisions to which he may turn those of the State whose law he finds that he must apply will have no higher authority than the decisions of any other State and the authority of the decisions will be persuasive only and not imperative" ...

[114] An essential part of the machinery for implementing that supervision of the Australian legal system and maintaining the unity of the common law is the system of State courts under a Supreme Court with an appeal to the High Court under s 73 of the Constitution ... Without the continued existence of a right of appeal from the Supreme Court of each State to the High Court, it would be difficult, indeed probably impossible, to have the unified system of common law that the Constitution intended should govern the people of Australia ...

It follows that State courts exercising State judicial power cannot be regarded as institutions that are independent of the administration of the law by this court or the federal courts created by the Parliament of the Commonwealth. In exercising federal jurisdiction, a court of a State administers the same law as the Federal Court of Australia when it exercises the identical federal jurisdiction. In exercising federal jurisdiction, a State court must deduce any relevant common law principle from the decisions of all the courts of the nation and not merely from the decisions of the higher courts of its State. A judge exercising the federal jurisdiction invested in a State court must see the common law in exactly the same way that a judge of a federal court created under s 71 of the Constitution sees it.

Furthermore, a State court when it exercises federal jurisdiction invested under s 77(iii) is not a court different from the court that exercises the judicial power of the State. The judges of a State court who exercise the judicial power of the State are the same judges who exercise the judicial power of the Commonwealth invested in their courts pursuant to s 77(iii) of the Constitution. Indeed, it is not uncommon for a judge of a State court to administer State legislation in the course of the exercise of federal jurisdiction. It is common ground, for example, that in this very case Levine J made his order in the exercise of federal jurisdiction because he became seized of federal jurisdiction when the appellant contended that the Act was in breach of the Constitution.

Under the Constitution, therefore, the State courts have a status and a role that extends beyond their status and role as part of the State judicial systems. They are part of an integrated system of State and federal courts and organs for the exercise of federal judicial power as **[115]** well as State judicial power. Moreover, the Constitution contemplates no distinction between the status of State courts invested with federal jurisdiction and those created as federal courts. There are not two grades of federal judicial power ...

Legislatures cannot alter or undermine the constitutional scheme set up by Ch III

It is axiomatic that neither the Commonwealth nor a State can legislate in a way that might alter or undermine the constitutional scheme set up by Ch III of the Constitution. The Parliament of the Commonwealth, for example, has no power under s 77(iii) of the Constitution to invest State courts with non-judicial functions except as an incident in the grant of judicial power. Similarly, a State cannot legislate for issues arising under Ch III to be referred to the Judicial Committee of the Privy Council or some other body for determination or advice in a manner that conflicts with the principles of Ch III. In *Commonwealth v Queensland* [134 CLR at 314-15], in a judgment with which Barwick CJ, Stephen and Mason JJ agreed, Gibbs J held that it is implicit in Ch III that a State cannot legislate in a way that has the effect of violating "the principles that underlie Ch III".

[116] Because the State courts are an integral and equal part of the judicial system set up by Ch III, it also follows that no State or federal parliament can legislate in a way that might undermine the role of those courts as repositories of federal judicial power. Thus, neither the Parliament of New South Wales nor the Parliament of the Commonwealth can invest functions in the Supreme Court of New South Wales that are incompatible with the exercise of federal judicial power ... [T]he Act does not seek to interfere with the invested federal jurisdiction of the Supreme Court. On its face it is directed to the exercise of State, not federal, jurisdiction. But for present purposes that is irrelevant. The compatibility of State legislation with federal judicial power does not depend on intention. It depends on effect. If, as Gibbs J pointed out in *Commonwealth v Queensland*, State legislation has the effect of violating the principles that underlie Ch III, it will be invalid.

Courts exercising federal jurisdiction must be perceived to be free from legislative or executive interference

One of the basic principles which underlie Ch III and to which it gives effect is that the judges of the federal courts must be, and must be perceived to be, independent of the legislature and the executive government. Given the central role and the status that Ch III gives to State courts invested with federal jurisdiction, it necessarily follows that those courts must also be, and be perceived to be, independent of the legislature and executive government in the exercise of federal jurisdiction. Public confidence in the impartial exercise of federal judicial power would soon be lost if federal or State courts exercising federal jurisdiction were not, or were not perceived to be, independent of the legislature or the executive government.

In the case of State courts, this means they must be independent and appear to be independent of their own State's legislature and executive government as well as the federal legislature and government. Cases concerning the States, the extent of the legislative powers of the States and the actions of the executive governments of the States frequently attract the exercise of invested federal jurisdiction. The Commonwealth Government and the residents and governments of other States are among those who litigate issues in the courts of a State. Quite **[117]** often the government of the State concerned is the opposing party in actions brought by these litigants. Public confidence in the exercise of federal jurisdiction by the courts of a State could not be retained if litigants in those courts believed that the judges of those courts were sympathetic to the interests of their State or its executive government.

While nothing in Ch III prevents a State from conferring non-judicial functions on a State Supreme Court in respect of non-federal matters, those non-judicial functions cannot be of a nature that might lead an ordinary reasonable member of the public to conclude that the court was not independent of the executive government of the State. A State law which gave the Supreme Court powers to determine issues of a purely governmental nature – for example, how much of the State Budget should be spent on child welfare or what policies should be pursued by a particular government department – would be invalid. It would have the effect of so closely identifying the Supreme Court with the government of the State that it would give the appearance that the Supreme Court was part of the executive government of the State. The law would fail not because it breached any entrenched doctrine of separation [of] powers in the State Constitution but because it gave the appearance that a court invested with federal jurisdiction was not independent of its State government.

In addition, in the case of the Supreme Court, although non-judicial functions may be vested in that court, they cannot be so extensive or of such a nature that the Supreme Court would lose its identity as a court. Thus, a State can invest its Supreme Court with a jurisdiction similar to that ... presently exercised in the federal sphere by the Administrative Appeals Tribunal. The Supreme Court would not lose its identity as the Supreme Court of the State merely because it was given a jurisdiction similar to that of that Tribunal. Nor could such a jurisdiction lead any reasonable person to conclude that the Supreme Court was part of the executive government of the State. However, a State could not legislate to abolish all other jurisdictions of the Supreme Court and invest it with no more than a jurisdiction similar to that Tribunal. To do so would make a mockery of the principles contained in Ch III of the Constitution.

Furthermore, although nothing in Ch III prevents a State from conferring executive government functions on a State court judge as persona designata, if the appointment of a judge as persona designata gave the appearance that the court as an institution was not independent of the executive government of the State, it would be invalid. No doubt there are few appointments of a judge as persona [118] designata in the State sphere that could give rise to the conclusion that the court of which the judge was a member was not independent of the executive government. Many Chief Justices, for example, act as Lieutenant-Governors and Acting Governors. But, given the long history of such appointments, it is impossible to conclude that such appointments compromise the independence of the Supreme Courts or suggest that they are not impartial. Similarly, a law that provided for a judge of a State court to be appointed as a member of an Electoral Commission fixing the electoral boundaries of the State would not appear to suggest that the court was not impartial. However, a State law which purported to appoint the Chief Justice of the Supreme Court to be a member of the Cabinet might well be invalid because the appointment would undermine confidence in the impartiality of the Supreme Court as an institution independent of the executive government of the State.

It follows therefore that, although New South Wales has no entrenched doctrine of the separation of powers and although the Commonwealth doctrine of separation of powers cannot apply to the State, in some situations the effect of Ch III of the Constitution may lead to the same result as if the State had an enforceable doctrine of separation of powers ...

[119] *The Act has the tendency to undermine public confidence in the impartiality of the Supreme Court of New South Wales ...*

[121] The Parliament of New South Wales has the constitutional power to pass legislation providing for the imprisonment of a particular individual. And that is so whether the machinery for the imprisonment be the legislation itself or the order of a Minister, public servant or tribunal. Moreover, there is no reason to doubt the authority of the State to make general laws for preventive detention when those laws operate in accordance with the ordinary judicial processes of the State courts. However, whatever else the Parliament of New South Wales may be able to do in respect of the preventive detention of individuals who are perceived to be dangerous, it cannot, consistently with Ch III of the Constitution, invoke the authority of the Supreme Court to make the orders against the appellant by the methods which the Act authorises. This is because the Act and its procedures compromise the institutional impartiality of the Supreme Court ...

[124] At the time of its enactment, ordinary reasonable members of the public might reasonably have seen the Act as making the Supreme Court a party to and responsible for implementing the political decision of the executive government that the appellant should be imprisoned without the benefit of the ordinary processes of law. Any person who reached that conclusion could justifiably draw the inference that the Supreme Court was an instrument of executive government policy. That being so, public confidence in the impartial administration of the judicial functions of the Supreme Court must inevitably be impaired. The Act therefore infringed Ch III of the Constitution and was and is invalid.

Dawson J: [82] The suggestion that the Constitution does not permit of two grades of judiciary exercising the judicial power of the Commonwealth, or that Ch III does not draw the clear distinction between State and federal courts which it has hitherto been thought to, simply ignores the fact that the Constitution ensures security of tenure and of remuneration in respect of judges of courts created by or under Ch III but does not do so in respect of judges of State courts invested with federal jurisdiction. It equally ignores the fact that the Constitution does not require that State courts only exercise judicial power. The suggestion that the Act is invalid because it compromises the institutional impartiality of the Supreme Court of New South Wales ignores the fact that the mechanisms for ensuring judicial impartiality and independence – security of tenure and remuneration, and separation from the other arms of government – are not constitutionally prescribed for State courts notwithstanding that they are prescribed for courts created by or under Ch III. It is difficult to conceive of a clearer distinction …

And yet the appellant's argument, as I understand it, is that the Commonwealth Constitution, and Ch III in particular, precludes a State court, as the potential or actual repository of federal jurisdiction, from having functions conferred upon it by the State legislature which are incompatible with Ch III. Either that or, so the appellant's argument goes, a law, such as s 39(2) of the *Judiciary Act* 1903 (Cth), **[83]** which invests a State court with federal jurisdiction, is inconsistent with a State law conferring a function upon that court which is incompatible with Ch III and must, for that reason, prevail over the State law under s 109 of the Constitution.

It may be said at the outset that such an argument simply denies the proposition, hitherto accepted without question, that Ch III, and s 77(iii) in particular, treats State courts as existing institutions. The result is that, so long as they are in fact courts, Ch III is unconcerned with whether they comply with the requirements of Ch III for courts created by or under that chapter. State courts are not created by or under Ch III and, provided they are courts within the meaning of s 77(iii), it matters not for the purposes of Ch III what functions they perform in exercising the jurisdiction vested in them by State legislation. That is for the State legislature to determine …

Whether State courts invested with federal jurisdiction are part of the federal judicature or not is a question of little practical significance, save perhaps in considering the application of the incidental power conferred by s 51(xxxix). They remain State courts even though, when exercising federal jurisdiction, they may be **[84]** regarded as a component of the federal judicature. There is no one court system in Australia. Each of the States has its own hierarchy which is governed by State legislation. The federal courts created under s 71 of the Constitution constitute a different system. Of course, the whole can be regarded as an entirety … But our legal system, though integrated, is not a unitary system. The States are distinct jurisdictions … The system is a federal system and, while the framers of the Constitution might have established a judicial system which was neither State nor federal but simply Australian, they did not do so. It is therefore dangerous to attempt to draw conclusions from the fact that the Australian legal system may be regarded as a whole. It may be, but as a matter of legal analysis that is to stop short of an appreciation of its different parts …

[85] Once it is recognised that there is no requirement in the New South Wales Constitution that courts in that State perform solely judicial functions and that, notwithstanding that characteristic, they are nevertheless courts which may be invested with federal jurisdiction under s 77(iii) of the Commonwealth Constitution, any question of incompatibility with Ch III upon the ground that the State court is required to perform executive or legislative functions must disappear. Certainly those functions may not be performed by a federal court created by or under Ch III. That is because the federal court is precluded by the separation of judicial power from performing them. But as far as State courts are concerned there is no incompatibility with Ch III because that chapter accepts those courts as existing institutions which may be invested with federal jurisdiction notwithstanding that they are not subject to any doctrine of separation of powers.

It may be that, in referring to incompatibility, the appellant used the word in the sense in which it was used by the majority in *Grollo v Palmer* where it was said that the ability of parliament to confer a non-judicial function on a judge of a Ch III court as a designated person rather than as a judge is subject to the limitation that the non-judicial function must not be incompatible either with the judge's performance of his or her judicial functions or with the proper discharge by the judiciary of its responsibilities as an institution exercising judicial power. So much, it was said in that case [184 CLR at 365], was to be "implied from the separation of powers mandated by Chs I, II and III of the Constitution and from the conditions necessary for the valid and effective exercise of judicial power".

But the judicial power of which the majority were there speaking was the judicial power exercised by a federal court created by or under Ch III – a Ch III court. The nature of that judicial power is, as was acknowledged in *Grollo*, very much determined by the separation of powers which the Constitution requires to be observed in relation to such a court … What is incompatible with the exercise of the judicial power of the Commonwealth by a Ch III court may not be incompatible with the exercise of the judicial power of the **[86]** Commonwealth by a court which is not restricted by any separation of powers. As *Grollo* makes clear, the concept of incompatibility is derived from the separation of powers and does not have a life of its own independent of that doctrine. Five members of the Court recognised that very point in *Wilson v Minister for Aboriginal and Torres Strait Islander Affairs* [(1996) 189 CLR 1 at 15] where they said that *"Grollo* was concerned with constitutional incompatibility, *derived from* the constitutional separation of the functions of the Judiciary from the functions of the Parliament and the Executive". (Emphasis added.)

In any event, no question of incompatibility in the sense in which the concept was used in *Grollo* arises in this case. In that case, the persona designata doctrine was held to justify the giving of an executive function to a judge of a Ch III court. Incompatibility was raised only to demonstrate that the persona designata doctrine has its limits. In this case, where the New South Wales court is not affected by any separation of powers, there is no call for the invocation of the persona designata doctrine and no question of incompatibility arises from the vesting in the court of an executive function. Nor can it be said in these circumstances that a particular type of executive function is incompatible with the exercise of judicial power any more than it can be said that a particular type of judicial function is inconsistent with the exercise of executive or legislative power. The reasons, which are readily apparent, for the adoption of a separation of powers in a federal structure do not have the same force in a unitary state. Be that as it may, New South Wales has not adopted that doctrine so that there can be no incompatibility between the exercise of judicial power and the exercise of executive or legislative power by a court of that State. And there can be no incompatibility with Ch III arising from that situation because it was within the contemplation of those who framed that chapter that federal jurisdiction might be vested in State courts exercising executive or legislative functions as well as judicial powers.

Among the questions arising from the majority judgments are the following.

1. At all stages of the proceedings Kable had sought to challenge the validity of the *Community Protection Act* by arguments based on the Commonwealth Constitution. (One such argument, not pursued before the High Court, was that the Act infringed an implied constitutional guarantee of equality of the kind discussed in *Leeth v Commonwealth* (1992) 174 CLR 455.) It was therefore possible to say that, at every stage of the proceedings in the Supreme Court of New South Wales, the Court was exercising "the judicial power of the Commonwealth". This element in the *Kable* litigation was emphasised particularly by Toohey J, and also perhaps by Gummow J. However, the other majority judgments appear to be predicated simply on the fact that the New South Wales Supreme Court *sometimes* exercises the judicial power of the Commonwealth, with no suggestion that its having done so *in this very case* was a necessary basis for the decision. In later cases, that more restrictive suggestion has not been renewed (see §5 below).

2. The earlier discussions of the "incompatibility" doctrine treated it merely as an exception to the *persona designata* doctrine. In *Kable* there is no question of *personae designatae*, and the "incompatibility" doctrine is treated as a wider concomitant of *any* exercise of "the judicial power of the Commonwealth". Does this mean that the "incompatibility" doctrine has become a "free-standing principle" of the kind deplored by McHugh J in *McGinty v Western Australia* (1996) 186 CLR 140 at 231-2 (see the extract in Chapter 28, §5)?

3. In *Breavington v Godleman* (1988) 169 CLR 41, Deane J developed a broad conception of "a unitary national system of law" within which the courts and judicial proceedings of every part of the Commonwealth should be seen as integral parts of one consistent and coherent whole (see the extract in Chapter 6, §6). Later cases such as *John Pfeiffer Pty Ltd v Rogerson* (2000) 203 CLR 503 have confirmed that conception. A similar view is expounded at length in *Kable* – especially by McHugh and Gummow JJ – along with an emphasis on the High Court's role as the "apex" of this unitary system. How exactly do these conceptions and emphases give inferential support to the application of the "incompatibility" doctrine? Note especially the rejection of any such inference by Dawson J.

3. Protective Detention

In *Chu Kheng Lim v Minister for Immigration*, though Brennan, Deane and Dawson JJ saw "**[27]** involuntary detention of a citizen in custody by the State [as] penal or punitive in character", arising "only as an incident of the exclusively judicial function of adjudging and punishing criminal guilt", they noted a number of exceptions, including involuntary detention in cases of mental illness or infectious disease. These traditional categories of involuntary detention, *not* requiring judicial "due process", were further explored in *Kable*, where the uniquely targeted provisions of the *Community Protection Act* were contrasted with what might have been acceptable as "**[608]** a system of preventive detention with appropriate safeguards, consequent upon or ancillary to the adjudication of guilt".

Apart from these accepted exceptional categories, the combined effect of *Chu Kheng Lim* and *Kable* suggests that the detention of a person against their will may be constitutionally permissible only when determined by a court, and only when the determination conforms to the traditional procedures and safeguards of the judicial process. This suggestion was one focus of argument in *Kruger v Commonwealth* (*Stolen Generations Case*) (1997) 190 CLR 1. The argument focused specifically on ss 16 and 67 of the *Aboriginals Ordinance 1918* (NT).

Aboriginals Ordinance 1918 (NT)

16 (1) The Chief Protector may cause any aboriginal or half-caste to be kept within the boundaries of any reserve or aboriginal institution or to be removed to and kept within the boundaries of any reserve or aboriginal institution, or to be removed from one reserve or aboriginal institution to another reserve or aboriginal institution, and to be kept therein.

(2) Any aboriginal or half-caste who refuses to be removed or kept within the boundaries of any reserve or aboriginal institution when ordered by the Chief Protector, or resists removal, or who refuses to remain within or attempts to depart from any reserve or aboriginal institution to which he has been so removed, or within which he is being kept, shall be guilty of an offence against this Ordinance.

(3) Sub-section (1) of this section shall not apply to any aboriginal or half-caste –
   (a) who is lawfully employed by any person; or
   (b) who is the holder of a permit to be absent from the reserve or aboriginal institution in question; or
   (c) who is a female lawfully married to and residing with a husband who is substantially of European origin or descent; or
   (d) for whom, in the opinion of the Chief Protector, satisfactory provision is otherwise made.

Section 67 authorised the making of regulations for the effectual carrying out of the Ordinance, in particular by "providing for the control, care and education of aboriginals or half-castes in aboriginal institutions and for the supervision of such institutions" and by "prescribing the conditions on which aboriginal and half-caste children may be apprenticed to or placed in the service of suitable people".

The Human Rights and Equal Opportunity Commission, appraising the effect of this and similar laws throughout Australia in its report *Bringing Them Home: Report of the National Inquiry into the Separation of Aboriginal and Torres Strait Islander Children from their Families* (Sterling Press, 1997), felt able to "**[37]** conclude with confidence that between one in three and one in ten Indigenous children were forcibly removed from their families and communities in the period from approximately 1910 until 1970". Five of the plaintiffs in *Kruger* were Aboriginal Australians who, as children in the Northern Territory, had been forcibly removed from their families pursuant to the *Aboriginals Ordinance*. The sixth plaintiff was an Aboriginal mother whose child had been taken from her. It was argued that the removals had involved "involuntary detention" of a kind that, according to *Chu Kheng Lim* and *Kable*, could only be ordered by a court, and hence that they had entailed an exercise of Commonwealth judicial power otherwise than by a Ch III court (or alternatively that, even if such an exercise of power was permissible in the Territories because Ch III of the Constitution had no application, what was done had infringed a more general doctrine of separation of powers).

For Brennan CJ these arguments failed because of "**[44]** the accepted doctrine" that Ch III has no application in the Territories. Gaudron J rejected that doctrine, while Toohey and Gummow JJ were also strongly inclined to doubt it. However, all three of these judges rejected the plaintiffs' argument on a different ground. This was that, in the context of a facial challenge to the Northern Territory Ordinance (that is, a challenge limited to grounds of invalidity apparent on the face of the Ordinance), the ostensible concern of the Ordinance with Aboriginal welfare precluded any finding that the forced removal and institutional confinement of Aboriginals was "punitive", and hence any finding that it fell within the constitutionally sensitive category of "involuntary detention" which requires the decision of a court. Indeed, having regard to the breadth of the exceptions acknowledged in *Chu Kheng Lim* and in *Kable*, Gaudron J now doubted whether any constitutional requirement that involuntary detention be subject to judicial "due process" was maintainable at all. Dawson J, with whom McHugh J agreed, adopted similar reasoning. But he also agreed with Brennan CJ that even if the decisions that were taken did involve the exercise of judicial power, the argument would still fail because Ch III has no application in the Territories.

Kruger v Commonwealth (Stolen Generations Case)
(1997) 190 CLR 1

Toohey J: [84] In general terms, the power to order involuntary detention is an incident of judicial power. In *Chu Kheng Lim v Minister for Immigration* [(1992) 176 CLR 1 at 28] Brennan, Deane and Dawson JJ spoke of

> "the general proposition that the power to order that a citizen be involuntarily confined in custody is, under the doctrine of the separation of ... powers enshrined in our Constitution, part of the judicial power of the Commonwealth entrusted exclusively to Ch III courts."

That proposition was affirmed by a majority of the Court in *Kable v Director of Public Prosecutions (NSW)* [(1996) 189 CLR 51].

However, both decisions recognise that there are qualifications to the general proposition that involuntary detention is necessarily an incident of the judicial function of adjudging and punishing criminal guilt. The qualifications to which Brennan, Deane and Dawson JJ referred include detention in cases of mental illness or infectious disease and committal to custody awaiting trial. Their Honours left open "whether the defence power in times of war will support an executive power to make detention orders" [176 CLR at 28 n 66]. And in *Lim* itself the Court upheld a law conferring upon the executive authority to detain an alien in custody for the purposes of expulsion or deportation. The point is that there are qualifications to the general proposition so that it cannot be said in absolute terms that the power to detain in custody is necessarily an incident of judicial power.

Judged by current standards, the involuntary detention of an Aboriginal pursuant to such a provision as s 16 of the Ordinance could hardly be brought within any of the recognised exceptions to the general proposition. Conscious of this, the Commonwealth submitted that the welfare and protection object of the legislation must be judged by the values and standards prevailing at the time. The plaintiffs' reply was that, even by the standards prevailing in 1918, the Ordinance was one which expressly contemplated permanent institutionalisation and carried an unqualified power of indefinite detention, unlimited by the objects or circumstances of necessity said to justify that power.

[85] A welfare purpose is evident in the legislation, emphasised by the legislative history to which reference has been made. The Chief Protector (and later the Director) was the legal guardian of Aboriginals. His duties, identified in s 5(1), included the distribution of forms of "relief or assistance to the Aboriginals", the supply of food and shelter, medicine, provision for custody, maintenance and education and

> "(f) to exercise a general supervision and care over all matters affecting the welfare of the Aboriginals, and to protect them against immorality, injustice, imposition and fraud".

Section 6(1) empowered the Chief Protector

"to undertake the care, custody, or control of any Aboriginal or half-caste, if, in his opinion it is necessary or desirable in the interests of the Aboriginal or half-caste for him to do so".

The responsibility for welfare cast upon the Chief Protector is at odds with the notion that the powers conferred by the Ordinance are of themselves punitive and necessarily involve the exercise of judicial power ... While this does not necessarily provide an answer to other bases of the plaintiffs' claim, the argument based on judicial power cannot succeed.

Gaudron J: [109] The plaintiffs rely for their argument with respect to Ch III on statements in *Chu Kheng Lim v Minister for Immigration* which point in favour of a broad immunity from detention in custody save by order of a court in consequence of a determination of criminal guilt. Thus, it was said in the joint judgment of Brennan, Deane and Dawson JJ [176 CLR at 28-9] ... that "the citizens of this country enjoy, at least in times of peace, a constitutional immunity from being imprisoned by Commonwealth authority except pursuant to an order by a court in the exercise of the judicial power of the Commonwealth". Their Honours explained [176 CLR at 27] the immunity on the basis that "the involuntary detention of a citizen in custody by the State is penal or punitive in character and, under our system of government, exists only as an incident of the exclusively judicial function of adjudging and punishing criminal guilt".

Arrest and custody pursuant to warrant pending trial, detention by reason of mental illness or infectious disease, and punishment for contempt of Parliament and for breach of military discipline were recognised by Brennan, Deane and Dawson JJ in *Lim* as exceptions to **[110]** the immunity which their Honours would there acknowledge. And of course, it was held in *Lim* that aliens might lawfully be detained in custody for the purposes of expulsion and deportation and, also, for the purposes of the receipt, investigation and determination of applications for admission to this country.

At one level, the existence of so many acknowledged exceptions to the immunity for which the plaintiffs contend and the fact that those exceptions serve so many different purposes tell against the implication of a constitutional rule that involuntary detention can only result from a court order. And that is so even if the supposed rule is one that is subject to exceptions. Of greater significance, however, is the consideration that it cannot be said that the power to authorise detention in custody is exclusively judicial except for clear exceptions. I say clear exceptions because it is difficult to assert exclusivity except within a defined area and, if the area is to be defined by reference to exceptions, the exceptions should be clear or should fall within precise and confined categories.

The exceptions recognised in *Lim* are neither clear nor within precise and confined categories. For example, the exceptions with respect to mental illness and infectious disease point in favour of broader exceptions relating, respectively, to the detention of people in custody for their own welfare and for the safety or welfare of the community. Similarly, it would seem that, if there is an exception in war time, it, too, is an exception which relates to the safety or welfare of the community.

Once exceptions are expressed in terms involving the welfare of the individual or that of the community, it is not possible to say that they are clear or fall within precise and confined categories. More to the point, it is not possible to say that, subject to clear exceptions, the power to authorise detention in custody is necessarily and exclusively judicial power. Accordingly, I adhere to the view that I tentatively expressed in *Lim*, namely, that a law authorising detention in custody is not, of itself, offensive to Ch III.

Moreover, the acknowledgment by Brennan, Deane and Dawson JJ in *Lim* that the immunity there enunciated does or may not operate in war time is, in my view, inconsistent with the notion of a general immunity from involuntary detention deriving from Ch III of the Constitution. The defence power, as with the power to legislate with respect to the other matters specified in s 51, is "subject to [the] Constitution". It is, thus, equally subject to the limitations deriving from Ch III as is the power to legislate with respect to those other matters.

I do not doubt that there is a broad immunity similar to, but not **[111]** precisely identical with that enunciated by Brennan, Deane and Dawson JJ in *Lim*. In my view, however, it does not derive from Ch III. Rather, I am of the view that the true constitutional position is that, subject to certain exceptions, a law authorising detention in custody, divorced from any breach of the law, is not a law on a topic with respect to which s 51 confers legislative power. The defence power may be an exception to that proposition. And the proposition does not extend to laws with respect to quarantine or laws with respect to aliens and the influx of criminals. It may be that an exception should also be acknowledged with respect to the race power. It is however arguable that that power only authorises laws for the benefit of "the people of [a] race for whom it is deemed necessary to make special laws".

If, as I think, the legislative power conferred by s 51 of the Constitution does not extend to authorise laws conferring a power of detention divorced from criminal guilt, unless they are laws with respect to the topics or, perhaps, some of the topics to which reference has been made, that is another reason for concluding that there is no similar immunity deriving from Ch III. On that basis, there is no necessity for any such implication. At least that is so with respect to the powers conferred by s 51. However and no matter the position with respect to s 51, it can only be said that s 122 does not authorise laws for the detention of persons in custody, divorced from a breach of the law, if that provision is subject to some express or implied limitation in that regard. Because, in my view, the power to authorise detention in custody is not exclusively judicial in character, Ch III is not the source of any such limitation. It follows that the Ordinance was not invalid by reason that it purportedly conferred judicial power contrary to Ch III of the Constitution.

Gummow J: [161] A power of detention which is punitive in character and not consequent upon **[162]** adjudgment of criminal guilt by a court cannot be conferred upon the Executive by a law of the Commonwealth.

The question whether a power to detain persons or to take them into custody is to be characterised as punitive in nature, so as to attract the operation of Ch III, depends upon whether those activities are reasonably capable of being seen as necessary for a legitimate non-punitive objective. The categories of non-punitive, involuntary detention are not closed.

The powers of the Chief Protector to take persons into custody and care under the 1918 Ordinance were, whilst that law was in force, and are now, reasonably capable of being seen as necessary for a legitimate non-punitive purpose (namely the welfare and protection of those persons) rather than the attainment of any punitive objective.

This is apparent from various matters. There is the creation of legal guardianship in the Chief Protector by s 7, the specification in s 5(1) of the duties of the Chief Protector, the conditioning of the power under s 6 by an opinion as to exercise of the power being necessary or desirable in the interests of the persons in question for the Chief Protector to take them into care and custody, the exclusion from the operation of s 16 of those persons for whom, in the opinion of the Chief Protector, "satisfactory provision is otherwise made", and the existence before 1918 of long-established statutory regimes in the colonies and States which were directed to the welfare and protection of other indigenous persons.

4. Immigration Detention

Ahmed Al-Kateb arrived in Australia by boat in December 2000 without a passport or visa. He was taken into detention under the *Migration Act 1958* (Cth). Section 189 states that, if an officer knows or reasonably suspects that a person in the migration zone is an unlawful non-citizen, the officer must detain the person. Section 196 further provides:

Migration Act 1958 (Cth)

196 (1) An unlawful non-citizen detained under section 189 must be kept in immigration detention until he or she is:

    (a)   removed from Australia under section 198 or 199; or

    (b)   deported under section 200; or

    (c)   granted a visa.

    (2) To avoid doubt, subsection (1) does not prevent the release from immigration detention of a citizen or a lawful non-citizen.

(3) To avoid doubt, subsection (1) prevents the release, even by a court, of an unlawful non-citizen from detention (otherwise than for removal or deportation) unless the non-citizen has been granted a visa.

In January 2001, Al-Kateb lodged an application for a protection visa under the *Migration Act* on the basis that he was a non-citizen to whom Australia has protection obligations under the 1951 Convention relating to the Status of Refugees. His application was refused and subsequent appeals failed. In these circumstances, s 198(6) of the *Migration Act* required "[a]n officer [to] remove as soon as reasonably practicable an unlawful non-citizen". In June 2002, Al-Kateb himself indicated that he wanted to leave Australia for "Kuwait, and if you cannot please send me to Gaza". In August he also stated "I wish voluntarily to depart Australia, and ask the Minister to remove me from Australia as soon as reasonably practicable".

However, Al-Kateb was born in Kuwait in 1976 of Palestinian parents. His birth in Kuwait did not confer Kuwaiti citizenship, and the absence of a Palestinian state left him as a "stateless person", a term defined by the 1954 Convention relating to the Status of Stateless Persons as a person "who is not considered as a national by any State under the operation of its law". The Commonwealth sought unsuccessfully to remove him to Egypt, Jordan, Kuwait and Syria as well as to Palestinian territories (which required the co-operation of Israel).

Al-Kateb applied to the Federal Court for a declaration that he was being "unlawfully detained" and an order that he be released. That Court dismissed his application: von Doussa J found that all reasonable steps had been taken to remove him, but that "removal from Australia is not reasonably practicable at the present time as there is no real likelihood or prospect of removal in the reasonably foreseeable future". However, other proceedings which raised the same issue produced a different result. In *Minister for Immigration and Multicultural and Indigenous Affairs v Al Masri* (2003) 197 ALR 241, the Full Court of the Federal Court held that a person in a like position was entitled to be released from immigration detention if and when the purpose of removal becomes incapable of fulfilment.

In April 2003, pending the determination of his High Court appeal, Al-Kateb was released from immigration detention by Federal Court order made with the consent of the parties. By a majority of 4:3, the High Court then dismissed the appeal. Each judge gave detailed reasons except for Heydon J, who agreed with Hayne J. The majority, McHugh, Hayne, Callinan and Heydon JJ, addressed two issues. First, they held that, as a matter of statutory construction, the *Migration Act* authorises detention even if a detainee has no prospect of being removed from Australia in the reasonably foreseeable future. Second, they held that the Act was within Commonwealth legislative power. On the first issue, Hayne J found the statute "[643] intractable":

Al-Kateb v Godwin
(2004) 219 CLR 562

Hayne J: [639] It may be accepted that "as soon as reasonably practicable" [in s 198 of the *Migration Act*] assumes that the event concerned can happen, and that, if there is any uncertainty, it is about *when* the event will happen, not *whether* it will ...

In the case of a stateless person, there may be many countries which could properly be approached and asked to receive the person. Whether one of those countries agrees to take the person will ordinarily depend upon matters beyond the power of Australia. Indeed, whether the country of nationality of a non-citizen who is not stateless will receive that person, if expelled from Australia, will ordinarily depend upon matters beyond this country's power to control, perhaps even influence.

What follows is that the most that could ever be said in a particular case where it is not now, and has not been, reasonably practicable to effect removal, is that there is *now* no country which will receive a particular non-citizen whom Australia seeks to remove, and it cannot *now* be predicted when that will happen. Nor is it to say that the time for performing the duty imposed by s 198 has come. The duty remains unperformed: it has not yet been practicable to effect removal. That is not to say that it will *never* happen.

This appellant's case stands as an example of why it cannot be said that removal will never happen. His prospects of being removed to what is now the territory in Gaza under the administration of the Palestinian Authority are, and will continue to be, much affected by political events in several countries in the Middle East. It is not possible to predict how those events will develop. The most that can be decided with any degree of certainty is whether removal can be effected *now* or can be effected in the future pursuant to arrangements **[640]** that *now* exist. Of course, it must be accepted in the present appeal that, as the primary judge found, "there is no real likelihood or prospect of [the appellant's] removal in the reasonably foreseeable future", but that does not mean it will *never* occur. Whether and when it occurs depends largely, if not entirely, upon not only the course of events in the Middle East (his preferred destination being Gaza) but also upon the willingness of other countries to receive stateless Palestinians.

Because there can be no certainty about whether or when the non-citizen will be removed, it cannot be said that the Act proceeds from a premise (that removal will be possible) which can be demonstrated to be false in any particular case. And unless it has been practicable to remove the non-citizen it cannot be said that the time for performance of the duty imposed by s 198 has arrived. All this being so, it cannot be said that the purpose of detention (the purpose of removal) is shown to be spent by showing that efforts made to achieve removal have not so far been successful. And even if, as in this case, it is found that "there is no real likelihood or prospect of [the non-citizen's] removal in the reasonably foreseeable future", that does not mean that continued detention is not for the purpose of subsequent removal.

As so interpreted, the Act was held not to infringe Ch III of the Constitution:

Hayne J: [647] The line which was drawn in the joint reasons [in *Chu Kheng Lim v Minister for Immigration* (1992) 176 CLR 1 at 33] was a line between detention "reasonably capable of being seen as necessary for the purposes of deportation or necessary to enable an application for an entry permit to be made and considered" and detention not so limited. The former was said not to contravene Ch III; the latter was said to be punitive and contrary to Ch III. Three points may be made about this division.

First, to ask whether the law is limited to what is reasonably capable of being seen as necessary for particular purposes may be thought to be a test more apposite to the identification of whether the law is a law with respect to aliens or with respect to immigration. No doubt account must be taken of the fact that the provisions now in question impose the obligation to detain upon the Executive. If the relevant power is identified (as their Honours appear to have identified it) as the *executive* power to deport or exclude, it may readily be accepted that the legislative conferral of authority to detain in custody for the purposes of an executive power identified in that way would be an incident of that power.

It is important to notice, however, that the sections now in question (like the provisions under consideration in *Chu Kheng Lim*) require, rather than authorise, detention. True it is that the requirement is made of the Executive: an "officer" must detain. But the provision is mandatory; the legislature requires that persons of the identified class be detained and kept in detention. No discretion must, or even can, be exercised. No judgment is called for. The only disputable question is whether the person is an unlawful non-citizen. And the courts can readily adjudicate any dispute about that. There is, therefore, nothing about the decision-making that must precede detention which bespeaks an exercise of the judicial power. Nor is there any legislative judgment made against a person otherwise entitled to be at liberty in the Australian community. The premise for the debate is that the non-citizen does not have permission to be at liberty in the community.

[648] Secondly, for my part, I would not identify the relevant power in quite so confined a manner as is implicit in the joint reasons in *Chu Kheng Lim*. The relevant heads of power are "aliens" and "immigration". The power with respect to both heads extends to preventing aliens entering or remaining in Australia except by executive permission. But if the heads of power extend so far, they extend to permitting exclusion from the Australian community – by prevention of entry, by removal from Australia, *and* by segregation from the community by detention in the meantime.

That is why I do not consider that the Ch III question which is said now to arise can be answered by asking whether the law in question is "appropriate and adapted" or "reasonably necessary" or "reasonably capable of being seen as necessary" to the purpose of processing and removal of an unlawful non-citizen. Those are questions which it is useful to ask in considering a law's connection with a particular head of power. For the reasons given earlier, the sections now in question are laws with respect to aliens and with respect to immigration. In part that is because a law to exclude a non-citizen from joining the Australian community is a law with respect to those two heads of power.

Thirdly, the line which their Honours drew in the joint reasons in *Chu Kheng Lim* depended upon first concluding [176 CLR at 27] that, with certain exceptions, "the involuntary detention of a citizen in custody by the State is penal or punitive in character and, under our system of government, exists only as an incident of the exclusively judicial function of adjudging and punishing criminal guilt". Their Honours described this as "a constitutional immunity from being imprisoned by Commonwealth authority except pursuant to an order by a court in the exercise of the judicial power of the Commonwealth" [176 CLR at 28-9].

As Gaudron J demonstrated in *Kruger* [*v Commonwealth* (1997) 190 CLR 1 at 109-10], the line which their Honours drew in *Chu Kheng Lim* is a line which is difficult to identify with any certainty. It is a line which appears to assume that there is only a limited class of cases in which executive detention can be justified. And that assumption is at least open to doubt. But doubtful or not, it is an assumption which turns upon the connection between such detention and the relevant head of power, not upon the identification of detention as a step that can *never* be taken except in exercise of judicial power. That is why it is important to recognise that once the step is taken, as it was in *Chu Kheng Lim*, of deciding that mandatory detention of unlawful non-citizens can validly be provided without contravention of Ch III, it is plain that unlawful non-citizens **[649]** have no general immunity from detention otherwise than by judicial process.

At least in many cases it will be right to say that a law authorising detention divorced from any breach of the law is not a law with respect to a head of power and for that reason is invalid. As Gaudron J pointed out in *Kruger* [190 CLR at 111], the powers with respect to defence, quarantine and the influx of criminals may stand as exceptions to that observation. But so too do the aliens and immigration powers in so far as they empower the making of laws with respect to the exclusion of persons from Australia and the Australian community.

In that, exclusionary, operation the laws do not infringe the limitations on power which follow from the separation of judicial power from the executive and legislative powers. If the line to be drawn is, as suggested in the joint reasons in *Chu Kheng Lim*, a line that depends upon connection with the relevant heads of power, these laws in their exclusionary operation have that connection.

If the line to be drawn attaches importance to the characterisation of the consequences as punitive, it must be recognised that the consequences which befall an unlawful non-citizen whom the Executive cannot quickly remove from Australia are not inflicted on that person as punishment for any actual or assumed wrongdoing. They are consequences which come about as the result of a combination of circumstances. They flow, in part, from the non-citizen entering or remaining in Australia without permission, in part from the unwillingness of the Executive to give the non-citizen that permission, and in part from the unwillingness of other nations to receive the person into their community or their unwillingness to permit that person to travel across their territory. The first of those considerations may be laid at the feet of the unlawful non-citizen concerned. Indeed, there may be other features of individual cases in which the unwillingness of others to receive the unlawful non-citizen can be seen to flow from the non-citizen's own conduct. These would include not only cases where the non-citizen impedes removal (by destroying identity documents or refusing to co-operate in the obtaining of new documents) but also cases of deportation on "character" grounds in which receiving countries are unwilling to accept persons who have committed criminal offences, or criminal offences of particular kinds, while living in Australia.

It is no less important to recognise that the consequences befalling an unlawful non-citizen whom the Executive cannot quickly remove from Australia fall on that person because otherwise he or she will gain the entry to the Australian community which the Executive has decided should not be granted.

But at its root, the answer made to the contention that the laws now **[650]** in question contravene Ch III is that they are *not* punitive. It is necessary to explain why that is so.

The explanation depended on a passage from HLA Hart, *Punishment and Responsibility* (Clarendon Press, 1968) in which, for the jurisprudential purpose of giving a "**[1]** morally tolerable account" of "the institution of criminal punishment", Hart had effectively proposed a stipulative definition of "punishment" as retribution "**[5]** for an offence against legal rules ... imposed and administered by an authority constituted by a legal system against which the offence is committed". Hayne J argued that because confinement in an Immigration Centre did not fall within the terms of this definition, it could not be regarded as "punishment":

Hayne J: [650] Two features of the immigration detention for which the *Migration Act* now provides ... are then important. First, immigration detention is not detention for an offence. There is now no offence of entering or being found within Australia as a prohibited immigrant. Yet the law permitting detention otherwise than for an offence is a law with respect to a head of power. Secondly, where a non-citizen has entered or attempted to enter Australia without a visa, detention of that person excludes that person from the community which he or she sought to enter. Only in the most general sense would it be said that *preventing* a non-citizen making landfall in Australia is punitive. Segregating those who make landfall, without permission to do so, is not readily seen as bearing a substantially different character. Yet the argument alleging invalidity would suggest that deprivation of freedom will *after a time* or in some circumstances *become* punitive.

Only if it is said that there is an immunity from detention does it become right to equate detention with punishment that can validly be exacted only in exercise of the judicial power. Once it is accepted, as it was by all members of the Court in *Chu Kheng Lim*, that there can be **[651]** detention of unlawful non-citizens for some purposes, the argument from the existence of an immunity must accept that the immunity is not unqualified. The argument must then turn to the identification of those qualifications. That must be done by reference to the purpose of the detention. Neither the bare fact of detention nor the effluxion of some predetermined period of time in detention is said to suffice to engage Ch III. And because the purposes must be gleaned from the content of the heads of power which support the law, it is critical to recognise that those heads of power would support a law directed to excluding a non-citizen from the Australian community, by preventing entry to Australia or, after entry, by segregating that person from the community.

It is essential to confront the contention that, because the time at which detention will end cannot be predicted, its indefinite duration (even, so it is said, for the life of the detainee) is or will become punitive. The answer to that is simple but must be made. If that is the result, it comes about because the non-citizen came to or remained in this country without permission. The removal of an unlawful non-citizen from Australia then depends upon the willingness of some other country to receive that person. If the unlawful non-citizen is stateless, as is Mr Al-Kateb, there is no nation state which Australia may ask to receive its citizen. And if Australia is unwilling to extend refuge to those who have no country of nationality to which they may look both for protection and a home, the continued exclusion of such persons from the Australian community in accordance with the regime established by the *Migration Act* does not impinge upon the separation of powers required by the Constitution.

As Judge Learned Hand said in his dissenting opinion in *United States v Shaughnessy* [195 F 2d 964 at 971 (2nd Cir 1952)]:

"An alien, who comes to our shores and the ship which bears him, take the chance that he may not be allowed to land. If that chance turns against them, both know, or, if they do not, they are charged with knowledge, that, since the alien cannot land, he must find an asylum elsewhere; or, like the Flying Dutchman, forever sail the seas. When at his urgence we do let him go ashore – *pendente lite* so to say – we may give him whatever harborage we choose, until he finds shelter elsewhere if he can."

(The decision of the Second Circuit Court of Appeals, from which Judge Hand dissented, was reversed by the Supreme Court of the United States [*Shaughnessy v Mezei* 345 US 206 (1953)].) To adopt and adapt what Hand J said in that case [195 F 2d at 971]:

[652] "Think what one may of a statute ... when passed by a society which professes to put its faith in [freedom], a court has no warrant for refusing to enforce it. If that society chooses to flinch when its principles are put to the test, courts are not set up to give it derring-do."

McHugh J: [584] Nor does the continued detention of a person who cannot be deported immediately infringe Ch III of the Constitution. Chapter III is always infringed where the detention of a person other than by a curial order – whatever the purpose of the detention – is authorised by a law of the Commonwealth *and* imposes punishment. However, a law authorising detention will not be characterised as imposing punishment if its object is purely protective. *Ex hypothesi*, a law whose object is purely protective will not have a punitive purpose. That does not mean, however, that a law authorising detention in the absence of a curial order, but whose object is purely protective, cannot infringe Ch III of the Constitution. Even a law whose object is purely protective will infringe Ch III if it prevents the Ch III courts from determining some matter that is a condition precedent to authorising detention.

A law requiring the detention of the alien takes its character from the purpose of the detention. As long as the purpose of the detention is to make the alien available for deportation or to prevent the alien from entering Australia or the Australian community, the detention is non-punitive. The Parliament of the Commonwealth is entitled, in accordance with the power conferred by s 51(xix) and without infringing Ch III of the Constitution, to take such steps as are likely to ensure that unlawful non-citizens do not enter Australia or become part of the Australian community and that they are available for deportation when that becomes practicable. As Latham CJ pointed out in *O'Keefe v Calwell* [(1949) 77 CLR 261 at 278]:

> "Deportation is not necessarily punishment for an offence. The Government of a country may prevent aliens entering, or may deport aliens ... Exclusion in such a case is not a punishment for any offence. Neither is deportation ... The deportation of an unwanted immigrant (who could have been excluded altogether without any infringement of right) is an act of the same character: it is a *measure of protection of the community* from undesired infiltration and *is not punishment for any offence*." (emphasis added)

It is open to the Parliament, therefore, to enact legislation that requires unlawful non-citizens to be detained so as to ensure that they do not enter Australia or the Australian community and can be deported when, and if, it is practicable to do so. To hold that Parliament cannot do so would mean that any person who unlawfully entered Australia and could not be deported to another country could thwart the operation of the *Migration Act*. It would mean that such **[585]** persons, by their illegal and unwanted entry, could become de facto Australian citizens unless the Parliament made it a criminal offence with a mandatory sentence for a person to be in Australia as a prohibited immigrant ...

Nothing in ss 189, 196 or 198 purports to prevent courts, exercising federal jurisdiction, from examining any condition precedent to the detention of unlawful non-citizens. Nor is it possible to hold that detention of unlawful non-citizens – even where their deportation is not achievable – cannot be reasonably regarded as effectuating the purpose of preventing them from entering Australia or entering or remaining in the Australian community. Indeed, detention is the surest way of achieving that object. If the Parliament of the Commonwealth enacts laws that direct the executive government to detain unlawful **[586]** non-citizens in circumstances that prevent them from having contact with members of or removing them from the Australian community, nothing in the Constitution – including Ch III – prevents the Parliament doing so. For such laws, the Parliament and those who introduce them must answer to the electors, to the international bodies who supervise human rights treaties to which Australia is a party and to history. Whatever criticism some – maybe a great many – Australians make of such laws, their constitutionality is not open to doubt.

In dissent, Gleeson CJ, Gummow and Kirby JJ held that the appeal should be allowed on the basis of their construction of the statute.

Gleeson CJ: [575] The Act does not in terms provide for a person to be kept in administrative detention permanently, or indefinitely. A scheme of mandatory detention, operating regardless of the personal characteristics of the detainee, when the detention is for a limited purpose, and of finite duration, is one thing. It may take on a different aspect when the detention is indefinite, and possibly for life. In its application to the appellant, the Act says that he is to be kept in administrative detention until he is removed, and that he is to be removed as soon as reasonably practicable. That could mean that the appellant is to be kept in administrative detention for as long as it takes to remove him, and that, if it never becomes practicable to remove him, he must spend the rest of his life in detention …

[577] Where what is involved is the interpretation of legislation said to confer upon the Executive a power of administrative detention that is indefinite in duration, and that may be permanent, there comes into play a principle of legality, which governs both Parliament and the courts. In exercising their judicial function, courts seek to give effect to the will of Parliament by declaring the meaning of what Parliament has enacted. Courts do not impute to the legislature an intention to abrogate or curtail certain human rights or freedoms (of which personal liberty is the most basic) unless such an intention is clearly manifested by unambiguous language, which indicates that the legislature has directed its attention to the rights or freedoms in question, and has consciously decided upon abrogation or curtailment. That principle has been re-affirmed by this Court in recent cases. It is not new … [In *Potter v Minahan* (1908) 7 CLR 277 at 304], O'Connor J referred to a passage from the fourth edition of *Maxwell on Statutes* which stated that "[i]t is in the last degree improbable that the legislature would overthrow fundamental principles, infringe rights, or depart from the general system of law, without expressing its intention with irresistible clearness" …

It is submitted for the respondents that the terms of the statute are general, but tolerably clear, and that if there is a silence on the particular problem raised by the case of the appellant, that is only because it is sufficiently covered by the general words. I am unable to accept that submission. The Act provides that the appellant must be kept in detention until he is removed from Australia under s 198, and s 198 provides that he must be removed as soon as reasonably practicable. The Act does not say what is to happen if, through no fault of his own or of the authorities, he cannot be removed. It does not, in its terms, deal with that possibility. The possibility that a person, regardless of personal circumstances, regardless of whether he or she is a danger to the community, and regardless of whether he or she might abscond, can be subjected to indefinite, and perhaps [578] permanent, administrative detention is not one to be dealt with by implication.

In s 196, the period of detention of the appellant is defined by reference to the fulfilment of the purpose of removal under s 198. If that purpose cannot be fulfilled, the choice lies between treating the detention as suspended, or as indefinite. In making that choice I am influenced by the general principle of interpretation stated above. I am also influenced by the consideration that the detention in question is mandatory, not discretionary. In a case of uncertainty, I would find it easier to discern a legislative intention to confer a power of indefinite administrative detention if the power were coupled with a discretion enabling its operation to be related to the circumstances of individual cases, including, in particular, danger to the community and likelihood of absconding. The absence of any reference to such considerations, to my mind, reinforces the assumption that the purpose reflected in s 196 (removal) is capable of fulfilment, and supports a conclusion that the mandated detention is tied to the validity of that assumption.

Gummow J also addressed the constitutional issue, "[609] [l]est silence be taken as any assent".

Gummow J: [609] A majority of the Court in *Lim* accepted the proposition that the power of the Parliament to authorise, and that of the Executive to implement, the detention of aliens is limited by reference to the purpose of that detention. In their joint judgment, Brennan, Deane and Dawson JJ held that laws authorising the administrative detention of aliens will only be valid [176 CLR 1 at 33]:

> "if the detention which they require and authorize is limited to what is reasonably capable of being seen as necessary for the purposes of deportation or necessary to enable an application for an entry permit to be made and considered".

Their Honours went on to explain that, were laws authorising immigration detention not so limited, the authority of the Executive to detain could not properly be characterised as being an incident of the power to exclude, admit and deport. In these circumstances, the detention would properly be characterised as punitive and would [610] thereby offend against the principle that the judicial power of the Commonwealth can only be vested in Ch III courts.

In a separate judgment in *Lim*, McHugh J expressed a similar view, and one which likewise focused on the purpose of detention as the criterion upon which the constitutional validity of the detention was to be assessed. His Honour said [176 CLR 1 at 65-6]:

"If a law authorizing the detention of an alien went beyond what was reasonably necessary to effect the deportation of that person, the law might be invalid because it infringed the provisions of Ch III of the Constitution. Similarly, if a law, authorizing the detention of an alien while that person's application for entry was being considered, went beyond what was necessary to effect that purpose, it might be invalid because it infringed Ch III."

McHugh J later added [176 CLR 1 at 71]:

"Although detention under a law of the Parliament is ordinarily characterized as punitive in character, it cannot be so characterized if the purpose of the imprisonment is to achieve some legitimate non-punitive object ... But if imprisonment goes beyond what is reasonably necessary to achieve the non-punitive object, it will be regarded as punitive in character."

Gaudron J analysed the issue not in terms of the limitations on legislative power imposed by Ch III, but rather as an issue of characterisation and the scope of that legislative power. In her Honour's view, which was further developed in *Kruger*, a law that was not appropriate and adapted to regulating the entry of aliens or facilitating their departure could not be characterised as a valid law with respect to naturalisation and aliens under s 51(xix).

Although it proceeds on a different basis, the result of Gaudron J's analysis is consistent with the view expressed by Brennan, Deane, Dawson and McHugh JJ that the power of the Parliament to authorise the administrative detention of aliens is not at large and that the power does not extend to authorise detention for any purpose selected by the Parliament.

There may be situations in which a law authorising the detention of aliens is "so insubstantial, tenuous or distant" in its connection with aliens that "it ought not to be regarded as enacted with respect to the specified matter falling within the Commonwealth power" [Dixon J in *Melbourne Corporation v Commonwealth* (1947) 74 CLR 31 at 79]. However, between the reasons dictating invalidity in *Lim*, those **[611]** advanced by Brennan, Deane, Dawson and McHugh JJ are to be preferred.

Consistently with McHugh J's analysis in *Lim*, it could not seriously be doubted that a law providing for the administrative detention of bankrupts in order to protect the community would be a law with respect to bankruptcy and insolvency (s 51(xvii)), or that a law providing for the involuntary detention of all persons within their homes on census night would be a law with respect to census and statistics (s 51(xi)). If such laws lack validity, it is not by reason of any limitation in the text of paras (xvii) and (xi) but by the limitation in the opening words of s 51, "subject to this Constitution", which attract any limitation required by Ch III.

In considering any limitation required by Ch III, it is not to the point that if no such limitation applies persons may be deprived of their liberty and detained without commission of and conviction for any offence, so that to require of the Parliament that it attain its objective of detention by means of the criminal law is to allow form to triumph over substance. That which the Constitution may require is an expression of supreme authority in the Australian system of government.

The nature of the Ch III limitation

The respective submissions in the present case fixed upon the question whether the detention authorised by the Act was punitive or non-punitive in character. This reflects the general discussion in *Lim* and *Kruger* of the Commonwealth's power to impose administrative detention. However, there is often no clear line between purely punitive and purely non-punitive detention ...

[612] [The] coincidence of punitive and non-punitive purposes is not uncommon. In *Veen v The Queen (No 2)* [(1988) 164 CLR 465 at 476], this Court recognised that among the purposes which inform a criminal sentence are not only the punitive purposes of deterrence, retribution and reform, but also what may be seen as the non-punitive purpose of protection of society. Once it is accepted that many forms of detention involve some non-punitive purpose, it follows that a punitive/ non-punitive distinction cannot be the basis upon which the Ch III limitations respecting administrative detention are enlivened.

Accordingly, the focusing of attention on whether detention is "penal or punitive in character" is apt to mislead. As Blackstone noted, in a passage quoted by Brennan, Deane and Dawson JJ in *Lim* [176 CLR at 28], "[t]he confinement of the person, in any wise, is an imprisonment" and one which, subject to certain exceptions, is usually only permissible if consequent upon some form of judicial process. It is primarily with the deprivation of liberty that the law is concerned, not with whether that deprivation is for a punitive purpose. The point is encapsulated in the statement in *Hamdi v Rumsfeld* [542 US 507 at 554-5 (2004)] by Scalia J (with the concurrence of Stevens J), made with reference to Blackstone and Alexander Hamilton [*The Federalist*, No 84], that:

> "The very core of liberty secured by our Anglo-Saxon system of separated powers has been freedom from indefinite imprisonment at the will of the Executive."

In *Witham v Holloway* [(1995) 183 CLR 525 at 534], Brennan, Deane, Toohey and Gaudron JJ observed:

> "[N]othing is achieved by describing some proceedings as 'punitive' and others as 'remedial or coercive'. Punishment is punishment, whether it is imposed in vindication or for remedial or coercive purposes. And there can be no doubt that imprisonment **[613]** and the imposition of fines, the usual sanctions for contempt, constitute punishment."

It is convenient here to return to the joint judgment in *Lim*. Having established that the involuntary detention of a citizen can generally only exist as an incident of the exclusively judicial power of adjudging and punishing criminal guilt, Brennan, Deane and Dawson JJ noted that the protection afforded by Ch III to aliens was not so far reaching. The principal reason for this is that, absent some authority conferred by statute, aliens have no right to enter or reside in Australia. The aliens power (s 51(xix)) and the immigration power (s 51(xxvii)) empower the Parliament to establish the conditions upon which aliens enter, reside in and leave Australia. It has long been recognised that this includes the power to deport aliens on such terms as the legislature thinks fit. As a consequence of this, the Parliament has the power to authorise the Executive to detain aliens for the purposes of "deportation or expulsion", and as an incident to the executive powers to "receive, investigate and determine an application by that alien for an entry permit" [176 CLR at 32].

However, the purposes are not at large. The continued viability of the purpose of deportation or expulsion cannot be treated by the legislature as a matter purely for the opinion of the executive government. The reason is that it cannot be for the executive government to determine the placing from time to time of that boundary line which marks off a category of deprivation of liberty from the reach of Ch III. The location of that boundary line itself is a question arising under the Constitution or involving its interpretation, hence the present significance of the *Communist Party Case* [(1951) 83 CLR 1]. Nor can there be sustained laws for the segregation by incarceration of aliens without their commission of any offence requiring adjudication, and for a purpose unconnected with the entry, investigation, admission or deportation of aliens. To that latter proposition there should be **[614]** entered the caveat expressed by Brennan, Deane and Dawson JJ in *Lim* as follows [176 CLR at 28 fn 66]:

> "It is unnecessary to consider whether the defence power in times of war will support an executive power to make detention orders such as that considered in *Little v Commonwealth* [(1947) 75 CLR 94]."

The reasoning of the three dissenting judges was invoked by Kirby J, by analogy, in *Ruhani v Director of Police (No 2)* (2005) 219 ALR 270, to support the conclusion that, as a matter of Nauruan law, the provisions of the *Immigration Act 1999* (Nauru) could have no application to the asylum seekers brought to Nauru against their will pursuant to arrangements with the Australian government after the *Tampa* incident in 2001 (see Chapter 12, §2(a)). He saw the *Al-Kateb* dissents as illustrating the principle that a statute "**[288]** apparently drawn in general language" may be "inapplicable ... in a given case because the hypothesis upon which the statute is expressed does not apply". He distinguished the majority decision in *Al-Kateb* by pointing out that the Nauruan legislation, unlike that in Australia, had to be construed in the context of express constitutional guarantees of individual liberty. However, Kirby J was in sole dissent: Gleeson CJ, Gummow, Hayne and Heydon JJ held in a joint judgment that the detention in Nauru was valid.

The judgments in *Al-Kateb* raised a host of other interpretive and historical issues, as well as the relevance of decisions in Hong Kong (*Tan Te Lam v Superintendent of Tai A Chau Detention Centre* [1997] AC 97), the United Kingdom (*R v Governor of Durham Prison; Ex parte Singh* [1984] 1 All ER 983) and the United States (*Zadvydas v Davis*, 533 US 678 (2001)) that led to the release of detainees. Disagreement was expressed most sharply by McHugh and Kirby JJ, who continued their exchanges on the High Court's role in interpreting the Constitution (see Chapter 8, §3) and on the use of international law in that process (see Chapter 19, §2(c)).

McHugh J: [588] It is not true, as Kirby J asserts, that "indefinite detention at the will of the Executive, and according to its opinions, actions and judgments, is alien to Australia's constitutional arrangements". During the First and Second World Wars, the National Security Regulations authorised the detention of persons who, in the opinion of the Executive government, were disloyal or a threat to the security of the country. Many persons born in Germany were detained under these Regulations in both wars, while many persons born in Italy were detained under the relevant regulation during the Second World War. However, detention was not confined to those born in the countries with which Australia was at war. As the detention of members of the Australia First Movement demonstrates, foreign birth was not a necessary condition of detention. PR Stephensen, one of the leaders of that Movement, was detained for almost 3½ years.

During the First World War, reg 55(1) of the War Precautions Regulations 1915 (Cth) provided that where the Minister for Defence

"has reason to believe that any naturalized person is disaffected or disloyal, he may, by warrant under his hand, order him to be detained in military custody in such place as he thinks fit during the continuance of the present state of war".

The validity of that regulation was upheld by this Court in *Lloyd v Wallach* [(1915) 20 CLR 299]. The Court unanimously held that the regulation was validly made under the *War Precautions Act* 1914 (Cth) which was enacted under the defence power. No member of the Court suggested that the regulation infringed Ch III of the Constitution.

During the Second World War, reg 26 of the National Security (General) Regulations 1939 (Cth) provided:

"The Minister may if satisfied with respect to any particular person that with a view to prevent that person acting in any manner prejudicial to the public safety or the defence of the Commonwealth it is necessary to do so make an order ... directing that he be **[589]** detained in such place and under such conditions as the Minister from time to time determines ..."

This Court unanimously upheld the validity of the regulation in *Ex parte Walsh* [[1942] ALR 359] ...

During the greater part of the period when reg 26 was in force, the relevant Minister was Dr HV Evatt, who had been a Justice of this Court and was later to become President of the United Nations General Assembly. According to a speech he gave in Parliament on 19 July 1944, 6,174 persons were detained under this regulation at the time when he became the Minister and 1,180 persons were still detained under the regulation in July 1944. He does not appear to have thought that, in making orders under reg 26, he was acting in breach of Ch III of the Constitution.

Nor am I aware of anybody else suggesting that detention under these Regulations infringed Ch III of the Constitution. The purpose of the detention was not punitive but protective. I see no reason to think that this Court would strike down similar regulations if Australia was again at war in circumstances similar to those of 1914-1918 and 1939-1945.

McHugh J conceded that Al-Kateb's situation was "**[581]** tragic". He also noted that "**[594]** [e]minent lawyers who have studied the question firmly believe that the Australian Constitution should contain a Bill of Rights". However, he concluded that "**[595]** the justice or wisdom of the course taken by the Parliament is not examinable in this or any other domestic court" since "[i]t is not for courts ... to determine whether the course taken by Parliament is unjust or contrary to basic human rights". Kirby J responded tartly:

Kirby J: [616] "Tragic" outcomes are best repaired before they become a settled rule of the Constitution. As McHugh J observed in recent extracurial remarks ["The Strengths of the Weakest Arm", paper delivered at the Australian Bar Association Conference, Florence, 2 July 2004]:

"[I]t is difficult to believe that Australia would have been as politically free a country as it is today if the High Court had upheld the validity of the legislation challenged in the *Communist Party Case*. If that legislation had survived, its legacy must have influenced the way that we give effect to political rights and freedoms."

We should be no less vigilant than our predecessors were. As they did in the *Communist Party Case*, we also should reject Executive assertions of self-defining and self-fulfilling powers. We should deny such interpretations to federal law, including the Act ...

[617] *Response to the criticism*: I cannot agree with much of what McHugh J has written in his reasons, including that part responding to the foregoing reasons of my own. There will be other occasions where I will have written a more substantial exposition of the contested issues than in this case and where it will therefore be more appropriate to enter debate over such matters. However, it is necessary to respond to McHugh J's specific criticisms. Otherwise, it might be thought that they are unanswerable; and that is far from the case.

Detention under the Constitution: The express subjection of the legislative power to the judicial power in the Australian Constitution is not a mere formality. The existence and predominance of the judicial power necessarily implies constitutional limitations on the use of the heads of legislative power in Ch I (or the powers of the executive under Ch II) of the Constitution in providing for unlimited detention without the authority of the judiciary. This is because such a power of detention can turn into punishment in a comparatively short time. And punishment, under the Constitution, is the responsibility of the judiciary; not of the other branches of government.

In another extracurial paper, with which I respectfully agree, **[618]** McHugh J has pointed to the implications that may exist in Ch III in order that the judiciary, as there provided, should be effective. Many of these implications remain to be elaborated. His Honour suggested that there would be a "[g]radual acceptance that Ch III protects due process rights" ["Does Chapter III of the Constitution Protect Substantive as Well as Procedural Rights?" (2001) 21 *Australian Bar Review* 235 at 238]. In my opinion, impeccable and persuasive views such as this should be given effect within the Court in legal and constitutional exposition. They should not be confined to papers for the academy and the profession. If the opinion is sound, it applies to judicial decisions, unless binding authority coerces a judge to a different conclusion …

[620] *Wartime cases and actions*: In his reasons, McHugh J cites Australian cases and official conduct during the two World Wars to establish the proposition that arbitrary and unrestricted detention by the Executive or under legislation is possible, even usual, in Australia in time of war.

I accept that cases exist that lend support to the conclusion that such detention has occurred and that such powers have been upheld by this Court. However, these cases are the Australian equivalent to the decision of the Supreme Court of the United States in *Korematsu v United States* [323 US 214 (1944)]. There the Supreme Court, by majority, upheld the detention of an American-born citizen of Japanese ancestry (and hence many of a like background). Such cases are now viewed with embarrassment in the United States and generally regarded as incorrect. We should be no less embarrassed by the local **[621]** equivalents. Certainly, the necessities of war require adaptation of the Constitution and specifically of the power to make laws with regard to defence. However, such necessities cannot support the elimination of constitutional requirements, including those appearing in Ch III. This is because, by the opening words of s 51, the legislative power with respect to defence is subjected to the Constitution, including Ch III.

This point was well made by Barak P for the Supreme Court of Israel, sitting as the High Court of Justice in *Beit Sourik Village Council v Government of Israel* [HCJ 2056/04 at [86]]. That case concerned a challenge by Palestinian villagers to the "security fence" or wall being constructed on their land. In the course of reasons that upheld some of the petitions, Barak P cited an earlier decision of the Court in *The Public Committee against Torture in Israel v The Government of Israel* [HCJ 5100/94 at 845] in which, after referring to the implications of the decision for national security, he had said:

> "This is the destiny of a democracy – she does not see all means as acceptable, and the ways of her enemies are not always open before her. A democracy must sometimes fight with one arm tied behind her back. Even so, a democracy has the upper hand. The rule of law and individual liberties constitute an important aspect of her security stance. At the end of the day, they strengthen her spirit and this strength allows her to overcome her difficulties."

I do not doubt that if Australia were faced with challenges of war today, this Court, strengthened by the post-War decision in the *Communist Party Case* and other cases since, would approach the matter differently than it did in the decisions which McHugh J has cited with apparent approval. Respectfully, I regard them as of doubtful authority in the light of legal developments that occurred after they were written.

The actions of Attorney-General Evatt, referred to by McHugh J, have been described by a biographer as a "cancer" which greatly damaged his reputation. According to the biographer, the initial arrests of wartime detainees were authorised by the Minister of the Army, on a military submission, not by Dr Evatt, who sought to have most of the detainees freed. However that may be, the instances hardly amount to a proud moment in Australian **[622]** law. Nor are they ones that should be propounded as a precedent and statement of contemporary legal authority.

The decision meant that Al-Kateb was required to re-enter immigration detention pending his removal from Australia, which depended upon a state of Palestine being created or some other nation being willing to receive him.

The reasoning in *Al-Kateb* was applied in another case handed down the same day, *Minister for Immigration and Multicultural and Indigenous Affairs v Al Khafaji* (2004) 219 CLR 664. The Court held that Abbas Al Khafaji, an Iraqi national whom the Australian government had been unable to remove and who it was found had no real prospect of successful removal in the foreseeable future, must also continue to be detained.

Another decision handed down that day, *Behrooz v Secretary of the Department of Immigration and Multicultural and Indigenous Affairs* (2004) 219 CLR 486, arose out of an "escape" by six people, including Mahran Behrooz, from the Woomera Immigration Reception and Processing Centre in the far north of South Australia. Charges were laid under s 197A of the *Migration Act*, which provides: "A detainee must not escape from immigration detention. Penalty: Imprisonment for 5 years". In his defence, Behrooz sought to argue that "**[502]** if the conditions of detention were so obviously harsh as to render them punitive, then the detention went beyond that which was authorised by the Act". The defence failed in the High Court, with Kirby J dissenting. It was held that, while inhumane conditions may attract the criminal law and entitle a person to remedies in tort, for instance for breach of a duty of care, they do not affect the legality of the immigration detention. As Gleeson CJ stated:

Behrooz v Secretary of the Department of Immigration and Multicultural and Indigenous Affairs
(2004) 219 CLR 486

Gleeson CJ: [499] [T]here is no warrant for concluding that, if the conditions of detention are sufficiently harsh, there will come a point where the detention itself can be regarded as punitive, and an invalid exercise of judicial power. Whatever the conditions of detention, the detention itself involves involuntary deprivation of liberty. For a citizen, that alone would ordinarily constitute punishment. But for an alien, the detention is an incident of the exclusion and deportation to which an alien is vulnerable. Harsh conditions of detention may violate the civil rights of an alien. An alien does not stand outside the protection of the civil and criminal law. If an officer in a detention centre assaults a detainee, the officer will be liable to prosecution, or damages. If those who manage a detention centre fail to comply with their duty of care, they may be liable in tort. But the assault, or the negligence, does not alter the nature of the detention. It remains detention for the statutory purpose identified above. The detention is not for a punitive purpose. The detainee is deprived of his or her liberty, but not as a form of punishment. And the detainee does not cease to be in immigration detention within the meaning of the Act.

In response to these decisions, a number of political leaders called for an Australian Bill of Rights (see Chapter 30, §4). They included the Federal President of the Australian Labor Party, Dr Carmen Lawrence; the leader of the Australian Democrats, Senator Andrew Bartlett; and Greens MHR Michael Organ. For her part, Immigration Minister Amanda Vanstone reviewed the cases of 24 people who claimed to be stateless, and decided to grant bridging visas to Al-Kateb, Al Khafaji and seven others so that they were released from detention.

Two months later, the High Court rejected another attack on mandatory immigration detention, this time from a different angle. The applicants in *Re Woolley; Ex parte Applicants M276/2003 (by their next friend GS)* (2004) 210 ALR 369 were four children of Afghani nationality, aged 15, 13, 11 and seven, whose parents had brought them to Australia in 2001. Their applications for a visa had been refused and review proceedings had not yet concluded. Detained in the Baxter Immigration Detention Centre, they sought release through orders for habeas corpus, prohibition and injunction, directed to the Minister for Immigration and to Kit Woolley, the centre manager. The applicants did not dispute that they were "unlawful non-citizens" under the *Migration Act*, but argued that the regime of mandatory detention set out in the Act did not apply to children. This was unanimously rejected by the Court on the basis that the Act was expressed in clear terms, with no exceptions made for children ("non-citizen", for example, was defined by s 5 as "a person who is not an Australian citizen"). According to Gleeson CJ: "[371] It is hardly likely that Parliament overlooked the fact that some of the persons covered by those definitions would be children. Human reproduction, and the existence of families, cannot have escaped notice".

The second argument was that the Act was invalid to the extent that it applied a regime of mandatory detention to children. This, too, was unanimously rejected. The applicants did not seek to have *Chu Kheng Lim* re-opened (though the indications were that if they had it would have been reaffirmed), and that decision was applied to defeat their argument. It was held that the mandatory detention of unlawful non-citizen children could validly be enacted under the "aliens" power (s 51(xix)), and that this was not incompatible with any freedom from involuntary detention that might be derived from Ch III of the Constitution. The decision also suggested that, after *Al-Kateb*, any such freedom might now need to be reformulated.

Re Woolley; Ex parte Applicants M276/2003 (by their next friend GS)
(2004) 210 ALR 369

McHugh J: [383] [In *Chu Kheng Lim v Minister for Immigration* (1992) 176 CLR 1, Brennan, Deane and Dawson JJ] said that it would be beyond the legislative power of the Parliament to invest the Executive with an arbitrary power to detain citizens in custody notwithstanding that the power was conferred in terms which sought to divorce such detention in custody from both punishment and criminal guilt. Their Honours justified this premise on the basis that [176 CLR at 27]:

> "[P]utting to one side the exceptional cases ..., the involuntary detention of a citizen in custody by the State is penal or punitive in character and, under our system of government, exists only as an incident of the exclusively judicial function of adjudging and punishing criminal guilt."

From this premise, their Honours drew the conclusion that, apart from some exceptional cases, there exists, for citizens, "at least in times of peace, a [384] *constitutional immunity* from being imprisoned by Commonwealth authority except pursuant to an order by a court in the exercise of the judicial power of the Commonwealth" [176 CLR at 28-9].

With great respect, the reason given by their Honours does not support their premise. If no more appears, a law which authorises the Executive to detain a person should be classified as "penal or punitive in character" and a breach of the separation of powers doctrine. But it is too far to say that, subject to specified exceptions, detention by the Executive *is always* penal or punitive and can only be achieved as the result of the exercise of judicial power. Accordingly, their Honours' conclusion that in times of peace, citizens enjoy a constitutional immunity from being imprisoned by Commonwealth authority except under an order by a court in the exercise of the judicial power of the Commonwealth cannot stand.

Whether detention is penal or punitive must depend on all the circumstances of the case. Logically, the fact that courts punish persons by making orders for detention by the Executive cannot lead to the conclusion – subject to exceptions or otherwise – that detention by the Executive is necessarily penal or punitive. In *Lim*, Brennan, Deane and Dawson JJ identified as exceptions to the "constitutional immunity" detention in custody without bail pending the determination of a criminal charge and detention because of infectious disease or mental illness. Detention imposed in these cases has never been and could not be characterised as punitive or penal. Their Honours also recognised cases of contempt of Parliament and imprisonment by military tribunals as exceptions to the rule that only courts could order detention by the Executive. And their Honours expressly held that detention pending the investigation and determination of an application for a visa is not an exercise of the "judicial power of the Commonwealth". Although their Honours found it unnecessary to consider the issue, where the nation is at war even a citizen may be detained by the Executive, acting under Parliamentary authority, if, in the opinion of the Executive, the citizen is disloyal or acts in any manner prejudicial to the safety or defence of the Commonwealth. Moreover, from time to time, even courts make orders for the detention of persons by the Executive that cannot possibly be characterised as penal or punitive. An order committing a person to an institution after acquittal of a criminal charge on the ground of insanity or mental illness is a notable example. Another example is an order committing a person to be detained without bail pending trial. At different times, courts have also been given power to order the detention of persons who were adjudged mentally ill or who were debtors.

In *Lim* [176 CLR at 55], Gaudron J said that she was:

[385] "not presently persuaded that legislation authorizing detention in circumstances involving no breach of the criminal law and travelling beyond presently accepted categories is necessarily and inevitably offensive to Ch III."

Her Honour expressed herself even more strongly in *Kruger v Commonwealth* [190 CLR at 110]. She said that "it is not possible to say that, subject to clear exceptions, the power to authorise detention in custody is necessarily and exclusively judicial power." In *Al-Kateb v Godwin* [208 ALR at 188-91, 200], Hayne J, with whose judgment Heydon J agreed on this point, referred to the judgment of Gaudron J in *Kruger* and was clearly of the same opinion as her Honour. In my opinion, the statement of her Honour in *Kruger* was correct and the *dictum* of Brennan, Deane and Dawson JJ in *Lim* to the contrary should not be followed.

That persons are ordinarily detained by the Executive only as the result of an order made in judicial proceedings is by itself an indication that a law that authorises detention without a judicial order is, as a matter of substance, punitive in nature. However, the object for which the law authorises or requires the detention of a person is an even stronger indication of whether the detention is penal or punitive in nature. If no more appears than that the law authorises or requires detention, the correct inference to be drawn from its enactment is likely to be that, for some unidentified reason, the legislature wishes to punish or penalise those liable to detention without the safeguards of a judicial hearing. It would nevertheless be a rare case where nothing more appears to throw light on whether the law is punitive or penal in nature. The terms of the law, the surrounding circumstances, the mischief at which the law is aimed and sometimes the parliamentary debates preceding its enactment will indicate the purpose or purposes of the law. As Callinan J made plain in *Al-Kateb* [208 ALR at 198], it is the purpose of the law that authorises detention that is the "yardstick" for determining whether the law is punitive in nature. Hence, the issue of whether the law is punitive or non-punitive in nature must ultimately be determined by the law's purpose, not an *a priori* proposition that detention by the Executive other than by judicial order is, subject to recognised or clear exceptions, always punitive or penal in nature. Indeed, leaving aside the cases of punishment for contempt of Parliament or breach of military law, the so-called exceptions to the "constitutional immunity" rule can be explained only by the fact that the *purpose* of the detention in those "exceptional" cases is not punitive or penal in nature.

The most obvious example of a non-punitive law that authorises detention is one enacted solely for a protective purpose. Thus, detention may be necessary to protect the detainee (as in the case of mental illness), to protect others (as in the case of infectious disease) or to protect the community (as in the case of those suspected of being disloyal during wartime). A power will not be regarded as purely protective, however, if one of its principal objects or purposes is punitive. The dividing line between a law whose purpose is protective and one whose purpose is punitive is often difficult to draw. This is particularly so where a protective law has acknowledged consequences that, standing alone, would make the law punitive in nature. Protective laws, for example, may also have some deterrent aspect which the legislature intended. However, the law will not be [386] characterised as punitive in nature unless deterrence is one of the principal objects of the law and the detention can be regarded as punishment to deter others. Deterrence that is an intended consequence of an otherwise protective law will not make the law punitive in nature unless the deterrent aspect itself is intended to be punitive.

Accordingly, it cannot be said that detention by the Executive in circumstances involving no breach of the criminal law is necessarily penal or punitive in nature, and therefore involves an exercise of judicial power. Nor does it follow that at least in times of peace, citizens enjoy a constitutional immunity from being imprisoned by Commonwealth authority except under an order made by a court in the exercise of the judicial power of the Commonwealth. Rather, it is necessary to characterise the law that authorises or requires detention and to consider all the circumstances of the case. In particular, the purpose of a law that authorises or requires the detention of a person by the Executive is determinative. If the purpose of such a law is purely protective, detention by the Executive under that law will not be regarded as penal or punitive in nature.

However, this did not mean that the Constitution imposed no restraint on the power of the Commonwealth Parliament to authorise detention by the executive government. For one thing, McHugh J adopted the suggestion made by Gaudron J in *Kruger v Commonwealth*: namely, that "**[111]** a law authorising detention in custody, divorced from any breach of the law" will normally not be referable to any head of Commonwealth power.

McHugh J: [386] The foregoing discussion has assumed that, but for Ch III of the Constitution, a federal law that authorises the Executive to detain a person without a judicial order would be a valid law. In many – probably most – cases of federal laws that authorise Executive detention without a judicial order, however, a Ch III question does not arise. That is because most heads of federal legislative power do not authorise the making of such laws. The Federal Parliament has no general power to make laws with respect to imprisonment or detention. Furthermore, with the exception of the powers relating to naturalisation and aliens, race, marriage, divorce, bankruptcy and the influx of criminals, the subject matters with respect to which the Parliament may make laws do not intrinsically refer to human beings. Consequently, in most cases, a federal law that authorises or requires detention without a judicial order can be supported only if the detention is incidental to the subject matter of the grant of federal legislative power. Given the doctrines of the separation of powers and the rule of law and the decisions in *Australian Communist Party v Commonwealth* [(1951) 83 CLR 1] and *Nationwide News Pty Ltd v Wills* [(1992) 177 CLR 1], justifying such laws as being incidental to a s 51 grant of power will prove difficult. The defence and quarantine powers are probably exceptions. As a result, most heads of federal legislative power do not seem expansive enough to justify a law that authorises or requires detention divorced from a breach of law. In *Kruger* [190 CLR at 111], Gaudron J said, correctly in my opinion, that the immunity from involuntary detention does not derive from Ch III, but rather that:

> "subject to certain exceptions, a law authorising detention in custody, divorced from any breach of the law, is not a law on a topic with respect to which s 51 confers legislative power. The defence power may be an exception to that proposition. And the proposition does not extend to laws with respect to quarantine or laws with respect to aliens and the influx of criminals. It may be that an exception should also be acknowledged with respect to the race power." (footnotes omitted)

In this passage McHugh J unequivocally endorses what Gaudron J said in *Kruger*, as asserting "**[386]** correctly" that any restraint on the power to authorise detention "does not" derive from Ch III. Yet he does not envisage such a clear dichotomy as she did between issues arising from Ch III, and issues of characterisation. He began this part of his judgment by posing the question "**[381]** whether, though textually laws with respect to aliens, ss 189 and 196 of the Act are not laws 'with respect to' the power conferred by s 51(xix) *because* they infringe the requirements of Ch III of the Constitution" (emphasis added): that is, he envisages that a law might not be referable to a head of power *because of* a constraint on legislative power arising from Ch III. He recognises that constraints drawn from Ch III "**[392]** are constitutional limitations on legislative power", but assumes that they can be relevant (and even decisive) at the stage of characterisation. (Compare in Chapter 25, §2(b) the blurring in *Re State Public Services Federation; Ex parte Attorney-General (WA)* (1993) 178 CLR 249 of the traditional sequential approach which turns to limitations on power only after a law is held to be otherwise "within power".) It follows, on McHugh J's analysis, that the relevant tests of validity – and apparently the *only* relevant tests – are those appropriate under Ch III.

> **McHugh J: [388]** What, then, is the appropriate test or principle for determining whether a law of the Parliament infringes Ch III of the Constitution when it authorises the Executive to detain an alien – or for that matter a citizen – without an order made in the exercise of judicial power? The applicants contend that the test for assessing the validity of a law that authorises the Executive to detain an alien requires a two-stage process:
> (1) identify a legitimate non-punitive objective to which the law is directed; and
> (2) if such an objective can be identified, determine whether the law that authorises detention is "reasonably necessary" or "reasonably capable of being seen as necessary" or "appropriate and adapted" to achieve that purpose or objective.
> They argue that this test involves considerations of proportionality.

All three of the formulae listed in the second stage above had been used in *Chu Kheng Lim* – "reasonably capable of being seen as necessary" by Brennan, Deane and Dawson JJ; "appropriate and adapted" by Gaudron J; and "reasonably necessary" by McHugh J himself (see 176 CLR at 33, 57 and 71 respectively). However, McHugh J now rejected all three.

> **McHugh J: [389]** Until the decision of the Court in *Al-Kateb*, the weight of judicial *dicta* … favoured the "reasonably capable of being seen as necessary" test. In *Al-Kateb*, the Court had to determine whether ss 189 and 196 of the Act infringed Ch III of the Constitution by requiring the continued detention of an alien who could not be deported in the reasonably foreseeable future. A majority of Justices held that, although the sections required the detention of Al-Kateb until he could be deported, they were valid because they had the non-punitive purposes of facilitating his deportation and segregating him from the Australian community. None of the Justices in the majority in that case applied the "reasonably capable of being seen as necessary" test as the determinative test for ascertaining whether the purpose of the detention was punitive …
> **[390]** [Callinan J,] like Hayne J and Heydon J and myself, … saw the validity of the detention … as depending simply on whether its purpose was to impose punishment on the detainee.
> **[391]** The reasoning in *Al-Kateb* is therefore inconsistent with the applicants' argument that the issue of punitive purpose must be determined by reference to whether the law itself is "reasonably necessary" for or "reasonably capable of being seen as necessary" for the achievement of a non-punitive purpose. A law that authorises detention will not offend the separation of powers doctrine as long as its *purpose* is non-punitive. As I indicated in *Lim* [176 CLR at 71]:
> > "[T]he lawful imprisonment of an alien while that person's application for entry is being determined is not punitive in character because the purpose of the imprisonment is to prevent the alien from entering into the community until the determination is made. But if imprisonment goes beyond what is reasonably necessary to achieve the non-punitive object, it will be regarded as punitive in character."
> Thus, if a law that authorises the imprisonment of an asylum seeker also has the purpose of keeping the detainee in solitary confinement without justification or otherwise has a purpose of subjecting the detainee to cruel and unusual punishment, it would go beyond what was necessary to achieve its non-punitive object. It would have a punitive purpose. It would go beyond what is necessary to prevent the detainee from entering the Australian community while his or her application for a visa is being determined. As questions of proportionality do not arise in the Ch III context, tests such as whether the impugned law is "reasonably necessary" for or "reasonably capable of being seen as necessary" for the achievement of a non-punitive purpose have no application when assessing whether the law infringes Ch III.

Notice in this passage how McHugh J explains his earlier use of the expression "reasonably necessary" by asserting that, if a law with a legitimate non-punitive purpose is shown also to have an additional punitive purpose, it will be invalid because *in that sense* it "go[es] beyond" what is necessary for its legitimate purpose. However, his analysis ignores the accepted use of "proportionality" tests in cases where the characterisation of a law depends on its purpose (see

Chapter 16, §8), despite his insistence on the *purpose* of an authorised detention as the key to its validity. Instead, he turns to the use of "proportionality" as "**[391]** an appropriate concept where there is a constitutional limitation on legislative power".

> **McHugh J: [392]** In such cases, the question for resolution is whether a law that directly or in effect conflicts with the constitutional limitation is nevertheless valid because its operation is proportionate to some legitimate end compatible with the limitation. The separation of judicial power and the prohibition on the legislature conferring judicial power on any body other than a Ch III court are constitutional limitations on legislative power. But questions of proportionality cannot arise in the context of Ch III. A law that confers judicial power on a person or body that is not authorised by or otherwise infringes Ch III cannot be saved by asserting that its operation is proportionate to an object that is compatible with Ch III. The judicial power of the Commonwealth can be exercised only by courts that conform with the requirements of Ch III. It cannot be invested in non-judicial tribunals even if such investiture would be a reasonable and appropriate or proportionate means of achieving an end that is compatible with Ch III.

However, he proceeded to spell out more fully the idea that, although the detention provision was "**[381]** textually" within power because of its legitimate non-punitive purpose, it might nevertheless infringe Ch III if it were shown also to have an additional punitive purpose.

> **McHugh J: [392]** The respondents contend that the detention regime authorised by ss 189 and 196 serves several legitimate non-punitive purposes ...
>
> **[393]** The Act certainly has these purposes or objects. However, that is not conclusive. If ss 189 and 196 have or either of them has a punitive purpose as well as a non-punitive purpose, those sections or that section will almost certainly infringe Ch III. A law may infringe that Chapter even if the punitive or penal sanction is not imposed for breach of the law or the existence of the fact or reason for the punishment is not transparent. If the purpose of the law is to *punish* or *penalise* the detainee without identifying the fact, reason or thing which gives rise to the punishment or penalty, then, as a matter of substance it gives rise to the strong inference that it is a disguised exercise of judicial power. Chapter III looks to the substance of the matter and cannot be evaded by formal cloaks. If an Act has a punitive purpose but the reason for the punishment cannot be identified, it should ordinarily be regarded as an exercise of judicial power. It should be seen as imposing a punishment or penalty because of who the person punished or penalised is or what that person has done. On that hypothesis, it is an exercise of judicial power in the classical sense of the term. Nevertheless, it is important to recognise the distinction for Ch III purposes between purpose and effect. This distinction is a matter of substance, not form. It is not enough that the effect of the law is no different from the infliction of punishment. If the effect of the law is not readily distinguishable from the effect of inflicting punishment, a rebuttable inference will arise that the purpose of the law is to inflict punishment. But, in determining whether a law authorises or requires punishment to be inflicted in breach of Ch III of the Constitution, it is the purpose of the law that is decisive.

Drawing on an analysis by Kristie Dunn and Jessica Howard, "Reaching behind Iron Bars: Challenges to the Detention of Asylum Seekers" (2003) 4 *The Drawing Board: An Australian Review of Public Affairs* 45, the applicants had identified a number of features of the detention provisions which, they submitted, did have the effect of rendering the detention punitive. Those most fully considered were, first, that the detention was for an indefinite period, and, secondly, that the provisions applied to children in the same way as to adults. On both points, the applicants' arguments were unanimously dismissed.

In particular, the argument based on the absence of any maximum time limit was treated as effectively disposed of by *Al-Kateb v Godwin*. As Hayne J expressed it: "**[428]** Once it is accepted, as I do, that the aliens and immigration powers support a law directed to excluding a non-citizen from the Australian community (by segregating that person from the community) the effluxion of time, whether judged alone or in the light of the vulnerability of those who are detained, will not itself demonstrate that the purpose of detention has passed from exclusion by segregation to punishment". In this respect, however, McHugh J added a qualification:

McHugh J: [394] In *Lim*, Brennan, Deane and Dawson JJ regarded the prescribed maximum time limit on detention for which the Act then provided as one element that rendered the Executive's powers of detention under the Act reasonably capable of being seen as necessary for the purpose of making and considering entry applications. However, in light of the surrounding circumstances, the Court did not regard this element as determinative. Indeed, I thought that the length of detention in light of the administrative burden on the Department to investigate and determine entry applications was relevant. I said [176 CLR at 71-2] that, while the detention might be "inordinately long" in that case, this did not make it punitive. No doubt cases may also arise where the connection between the alleged purpose of detention and the length of detention becomes so tenuous that it is not possible to find that the purpose of the detention is to enable visa applications to be processed pending the grant of a visa. If the law in question has such a tenuous connection, the proper inference will ordinarily be that its purpose is punitive. The fact that the law may also have a non-punitive purpose will not save it from invalidity.

The Human Rights and Equal Opportunity Commission was given leave to intervene in the case and put to the Court a number of articles and reports dealing with the mental health effects of long-term immigration detention on children. The Court found this material to be of little use. Gummow J noted that "**[403]** the bulk of this material is anecdotal in nature, has not been tested and is not specific to the situation of the individual applicants". The Commission's own report, *A Last Resort? National Inquiry into Children in Immigration Detention* (Parliamentary Paper No 134 of 2004) was delivered in April 2004. The major findings included that "**[5]** Australia's immigration detention laws, as administered by the Commonwealth, and applied to unauthorised arrival children, create a detention system that is fundamentally inconsistent with the *Convention on the Rights of the Child*" and that "**[6]** [c]hildren in immigration detention for long periods of time are at high risk of serious mental harm".

The Court also had before it detailed submissions showing that the Australian regime of mandatory detention for asylum seekers was in breach of international conventions and customary international law, including the adverse ruling of the United Nations Human Rights Committee in *Bakhtiyari v Australia* (UNHCR Communication No 1069/2002, 29 October 2003). The submissions also contrasted the Australian regime unfavourably with those in force in Canada, the United States, the United Kingdom and New Zealand. McHugh J, in particular, reviewed all this material at length (at 399-402). Nevertheless, he concluded:

McHugh J: [402] However, the issue in this Court is not whether the detention of the present applicants is arbitrary according to international jurisprudence, whether it **[403]** constitutes a breach of various Conventions to which Australia is a party or whether it is contrary to the practice of other states. It is whether Parliament has the *purpose* of punishing children who are detainees so that, for the purpose of the Constitution, the Parliament has exercised or authorised the Executive to exercise the judicial power of the Commonwealth. On that very different issue, the international jurisprudence and the practice of other states do not assist. That is because the purpose of ss 189 and 196 is a protective purpose – to prevent unlawful non-citizens, including children, from entering the Australian community until one of the conditions in s 196(1) is satisfied. If that is the purpose of the provisions, as I think it is, the Parliament has not exercised, nor authorised the Executive to exercise, the judicial power of the Commonwealth. Whether or not Australia may be in breach of its international obligations cannot affect that constitutional question.

Kirby J also found this material to be of no assistance:

Kirby J: [416] Under the Constitution, all valid laws made by the Australian Parliament are binding "on the courts, judges, and people of every State and of every part of the Commonwealth". For an Australian court, a refusal to apply, and to give effect to, provisions of a valid federal act is not an available option. Fundamental to the Australian Constitution is respect for the rule of law. If the law is clear and constitutionally valid, it is the duty of Australian courts to apply its terms. This is so whatever judges or others may think about the content and effect of the law. Under our constitutional arrangements, changes to the content of such laws normally depend upon the political process ...

[419] In *Minister for Immigration and Multicultural and Indigenous Affairs v B* [(2004) 206 ALR 130 at 170-3], I traced the series of parliamentary and other official reports by which, over the past decade, the Australian Parliament has been made aware of official concerns about the requirements of mandatory detention of unlawful arrivals in general, and the detention of vulnerable people, such as children and unaccompanied minors, in particular. Notwithstanding these reports, and several recommendations for alteration of the system of mandatory detention, including in the case of children, the system has been maintained unchanged. The Act has not been amended in any relevant respect. On the contrary, the procedures have been continued despite an intervening change of federal government and **[420]** considerable public debate on the subject. It cannot be said that the policy, including as it relates to the detention of children, is the result of oversight, ignorance, inattention or mistake. It is the product of a deliberate decision of successive governments and the Australian Parliament, enacted and maintained in force under the broad scope of the "aliens" power granted by the Constitution ...

[422] In the light of this history and on the face of the public record of the Parliament, the suggestion that there has been some oversight, mistake or a failure to consider the immigration detention of children in Australia is fanciful. Detention is the deliberate policy of the Australian Parliament, repeatedly affirmed. In default of a constitutional basis for invalidating it, it is the duty of this Court to give effect to the Act, whatever views might be urged about the wisdom, humanity and justice of that policy ...

[423] [A]ssuming that there is a breach of international law established by the failure of the Act, and the administration of the Act, to comply with the treaties binding Australia, such a breach does not, as such, affect the validity of the provisions of the Act or the duty of this Court to give effect to those provisions as part of a valid law of this nation. In construing any ambiguities in such law, it is legitimate for a court to interpret the law, so far as its language permits, to avoid departures from Australia's international obligations. However, where, as here, the law is relevantly clear and valid (and is the result of a deliberately devised and deliberately maintained policy of the Parliament) a national court, such as this, is bound to give it effect according to its terms. It has no authority to do otherwise.

5. Preventive Detention

Both *Baker v The Queen* (2004) 210 ALR 1 and *Fardon v Attorney-General (Queensland)* (2004) 210 ALR 50 involved unsuccessful attempts to use *Kable* to invalidate State legislation. At issue in *Baker* was a 1997 amendment to s 13A of the *Sentencing Act 1989* (NSW).

In November 1973, Virginia Morse was abducted from her home near Collarenebri, in northwestern New South Wales. She was taken, gagged and blindfolded, across the State border to Queensland, where she was tortured, raped and eventually shot. Convicted of this atrocity, Allan Baker and Kevin Crump were sentenced in 1974 to life imprisonment. The trial judge told them: "I believe you should spend the rest of your lives in jail and there you should die. If ever there was a case where life imprisonment means what it says ... this is it".

Under s 13A of the *Sentencing Act*, a person who had completed at least eight years of a sentence of life imprisonment could apply to the Supreme Court for a determination of sentence (effectively involving the fixing of a minimum sentence, after which parole might be possible). On 24 April 1997, an application made by Crump was successful: his minimum non-parole sentence was set to expire in 2003. However, in 2001, a new s 154A inserted into the *Crimes (Administration of Sentences) Act 1999* (NSW) imposed extraordinarily rigorous criteria for the parole of "a serious offender the subject of a non-release recommendation", including a need for the Parole Board to be satisfied that the offender "is in imminent danger of dying, or is incapacitated to the extent that he or she no longer has the physical ability to do harm to any person".

A more immediate result of the 1997 determination in Crump's case was that s 13A of the *Sentencing Act* was amended so that "a person who is the subject of a non-release recommendation" was required to complete 20 years' imprisonment (rather than eight years) before making an application. Subsection (1) defined a "non-release recommendation" as "a recommendation or observation, or an expression of opinion, by the original sentencing court that (or to the effect that) the person should never be released from imprisonment". In addition, a new sub-s (3A) declared that such a person "is not eligible" for a fresh determination "unless the Supreme Court … is satisfied that special reasons exist that justify making the determination". When Baker applied for a determination under this new regime, the judge found that there were no "special reasons" and the application was refused.

Baker invoked the *Kable* principle on two main grounds. First, the fact that the amendments related only to those "the subject of a non-release recommendation" was said to be excessively selective. Secondly, it was said that since the requirement of "special reasons" could have no possible content or meaning, its effect was to involve the Supreme Court in a "charade", masking the reality of a legislative judgment that those affected were never to be released.

The selectivity argument rested partly on the fact that the practice of sentencing judges in making or not making non-release recommendations had varied widely (so that the absence of such a recommendation was not necessarily an indication of a less shocking offence); partly on the fact that the persons subject to such recommendations in New South Wales in 1997 were a limited and identifiable class; and partly on the fact that the persons affected had been identified by name, in the course of the parliamentary debate on the 1997 amendment, in a way that appeared to suggest that the amendment was specifically intended for them:

New South Wales, *Parliamentary Debates*
Legislative Assembly, 8 May 1997

Mr Paul Whelan (Ashfield, Minister for Police): [8337] Allan Baker, Kevin Crump, Michael Murphy, Leslie Murphy, Gary Murphy, John Travers, Michael Murdoch, Stephen Jamieson, Matthew Elliot, Bronson Blessington – these animals represent pure evil. These animals deserve never to see the exit sign at the prison gate. These animals are reviled and shunned by anyone who has ever heard of their heinous crimes. There is not a person in our community who does not need protection from these animals and the security of knowing they will never again be free.

The decision of the Supreme Court in redetermining Kevin Garry Crump's life sentence has caused grave concern in the community. Crump and Baker committed one of the most revolting crimes this nation has ever seen. Put simply, they deserve to die in gaol …

The Kable experience has shown this Parliament the invalidity of individual-specific legislation. For this Parliament to introduce and consider Crump-specific legislation, in light of the Kable case, would not only be irresponsible but cruel and unusual punishment for the victims of his crimes. It would be a bill which would be likely to be struck down by the High Court. It would be a bill which would unfairly and unrealistically raise the expectation of the public and victims like Brian Morse. This Government will not inflict more pain, more heartache nor will it raise false hopes …

Proposing legislation that is constitutionally sound is the Government's primary objective so as not to give Crump and these nine other animals any hope for the future. The public expects nothing less. It expects real change not insane responses that will not work. In relation to this class of offenders the Government has responded by introducing this bill. This bill is effectively the toughest sentencing legislation ever introduced into this Parliament. It will provide the bleakest possible futures for these men – amongst the most dangerous in custody in this State …

[8338] [T]he bill tells judges that we, the Parliament and the community, do not expect these most serious offenders ever to be released.

Baker's constitutional challenge was unsuccessful. Kirby J was the only dissenter.

Baker v The Queen
(2004) 210 ALR 1

Gleeson CJ: [5] When the 1997 amendments to s 13A … were made, there was a limited number of prisoners serving life sentences who had been the subject of non-release recommendations. Their identities, and the circumstances of their crimes, were widely known. The New South Wales Parliament decided that, in the scheme of s 13A, they should be treated as exceptional cases. It made special, and different, provision for them. As a matter of legislative power, the Parliament was entitled to do so. Senior counsel for the appellant acknowledged ... that, if Parliament had simply named the persons in question and excluded them from the operation of s 13A, then his *Kable* argument would not have arisen. It might be argued, as a matter of legislative policy, that it was unreasonable of Parliament to single out for special, and disadvantageous, treatment those prisoners who had been sentenced by judges who were willing to make non-release recommendations when others who had also committed heinous crimes might have escaped such recommendations because of the inclinations of a particular sentencing judge. As a matter of policy, I see the force of that argument, but its significance in terms of legislative power is another matter. Parliament may have taken the view that at least those people in the position of the appellant should be subject to a special regime, and if others whose crimes were just as serious were given the benefit of more favourable treatment then that would have to be accepted. It is evident from the parliamentary material referred to in argument that the view was taken that public opinion demanded some form of legislative recognition of the fact that, included amongst prisoners serving life sentences, there were people whose crimes were so extreme that sentencing judges had been moved to recommend that they should never be released. As a matter of legislative power, it was open to the New South Wales Parliament to enact legislation reflecting such opinion. The distinction drawn by the legislature was not arbitrary. If, for any reason, one wanted to identify prisoners who had committed the most heinous crimes, searching for those who had been the subject of a non-release recommendation would be at least a good start. In the view of **[6]** some people, it would be unreasonable to stop there, and unfair to discriminate solely on that ground. Choices of that kind, however, are generally within legislative competence.

Persons who were the subject of a non-release recommendation had one thing in common: the legislature knew that the judges who sentenced them thought that their crimes were so serious that, in their cases, imprisonment for life should mean exactly that. There may have been other cases where sentencing judges held the same opinion, but did not express it. Even so, the fact that a particular judge expressed such an opinion is, as a matter of fact, indicative of the gravity of the conduct of an offender. It was within the power of the Parliament to select such an expression of opinion as an indication that the offending was of the most serious kind. The Parliament was entitled to create a special regime for the most serious offenders, and to select as the criterion for distinguishing the most serious offenders the making of a non-release recommendation. The selection was not arbitrary, and the criterion was not irrelevant. If it was unfair, its unfairness could have been thought to lie in the consequence that some other offenders of a most serious kind received more favourable treatment.

There is a further consideration that Parliament is entitled to take into account when legislating about crime and punishment. Parliament is not functioning in a hermetically sealed environment. The public are aware that there are some prisoners whose crimes have attracted judicial condemnation of the utmost severity, and that such condemnation, at least in the past, has sometimes taken the form of an expression of opinion that a particular prisoner should remain in custody for life. The complex legal and political issues that surrounded the 1989 "truth-in-sentencing" legislation in New South Wales resulted from a notorious difference between the appearance and the reality of some sentences. When Parliament decided to permit prisoners who had been sentenced for "life" to apply for determinate sentences, which to the public would almost certainly appear to be lower than their original sentences, it was foreseeable that it would want to address, and perhaps reserve for special treatment, the most extreme cases, however those cases were to be identified.

The joint judgment of McHugh, Gummow, Hayne and Heydon JJ also rejected the argument. Insofar as the argument rested simply on the limited number and known identity of the persons affected, they held that it was defeated by earlier dicta, initially in *Leeth v Commonwealth* (1992) 174 CLR 455 and then in *Nicholas v The Queen* (1998) 193 CLR 173, by which the decision in *Liyanage v The Queen* [1967] 1 AC 259 had been distinguished. The impugned legislation in *Liyanage* had been characterised as "**[290]** a special direction to the judiciary as to the trial of particular prisoners who were identifiable ... [as part of] a legislative plan ex post facto to secure the conviction and enhance the punishment of those particular individuals". In *Leeth*, however, Mason CJ, Dawson and McHugh JJ had distinguished *Liyanage* by drawing a contrast between, on the one hand, legislation which "**[470]** prejudges an issue with respect to a particular individual … [and on the other hand] a law of general application which seeks in some respect to govern the exercise of a jurisdiction which it confers".

In *Nicholas*, s 15X of the *Crimes Act 1914* (Cth) was held to fall into the latter class. Section 15X was introduced in 1996 to overcome the effect of the decision in *Ridgeway v The Queen* (1995) 184 CLR 19 (see the extract in Chapter 14, §7(b)). It provided that when a court is determining the admissibility of evidence in a prosecution for drug importation, the fact that the evidence was obtained unlawfully "is to be disregarded". At the time when s 15X came into force, the enforcement tactics concerned had been used in a finite number of cases, and the identity of those against whom charges had been laid was known. (The High Court was told that there were "**[191]** half a dozen [cases] in New South Wales and Victoria".)

Despite this, the fact that s 15X applied not only to the pending prosecutions, but also to any future prosecutions in similar circumstances, was sufficient to save it. As Toohey J put it in *Nicholas*: "**[203]** There is nothing in the relevant provisions which singles out an individual, as in *Kable v Director of Public Prosecutions (NSW)*, or which singles out a particular category of persons. It is simply the fact that by applying to controlled operations commenced before [a specified date], s 15X necessarily operates only by reference to accused persons to whom those operations related. In the same way, it might be said that the *War Crimes Act* 1945 (Cth) [considered in *Polyukhovich v Commonwealth* (*War Crimes Act Case*) (1991) 172 CLR 501] necessarily applied only to the conduct of a limited number of persons. But that did not lead to any declaration of invalidity".

In *Baker*, the joint judgment took a similar view. Since "**[16]** it could not be said that the appellant was the sole and direct 'target' of the 1997 Act", their Honours thought it "unnecessary to determine what would have been the consequences of such a conclusion". Insofar as the argument rested on a notion of "discrimination", the joint judgment pointed out that while such a notion is relevant in cases under s 92 or s 117 of the Constitution, this was not such a case; and any attempt to invoke some wider constitutional implication of equality "**[15]** would have to overcome" the majority reasoning in *Leeth*. Insofar as it rested on an assumption that the making of a non-release recommendation was not itself an exercise of judicial power, they answered that while it is true that, in the process of "trial and conviction on indictment", the exercise of judicial power is "**[16]** ordinarily … exhausted by a finding of guilt or acceptance of a plea of guilty followed by sentence", nevertheless the making of judicial recommendations for or against clemency had been sufficiently common in the history of criminal trials that they should be accepted "as one of the historical instances [of judicial power] identified in *R v Davison* [(1954) 90 CLR 353 at 369]".

The other main issue in *Baker* turned on the supposed vacuity of "special reasons" as a criterion which judges were required to apply.

Gleeson CJ: [6] The weight of the appellant's *Kable* argument was put upon the requirement of "special reasons" in s 13A(3A) … [T]hat requirement was said to be devoid of content, and illusory. On that premise, in its application to people the subject of non-release recommendations, s 13A involved the Supreme Court in a charade. The legislature was using the forms of judicial procedure to mask the reality of the legislative decree, which was that these people were never to be released. On that premise, as a matter of principle, the case would be very close to *Kable*. It is the premise that is in contest …

[7] There is nothing unusual about legislation that requires courts to find "special reasons" or "special circumstances" as a condition of the exercise of a power. This is a verbal formula that is commonly used where it is intended that judicial discretion should not be confined by precise definition, or where the circumstances of potential relevance are so various as to defy precise definition. That which makes reasons or circumstances special in a particular case might flow from their weight as well as their quality, and from a combination of factors.

It is the duty of a court to give meaning to the requirement of "special reasons" in sub-s (3A) unless that is impossible. That elementary principle of statutory interpretation cannot be ignored. Section 31 of the *Interpretation Act* 1987 (NSW) provides that an Act shall be construed so as not to exceed legislative power ... As Bowen LJ said in *Curtis v Stovin* [(1889) 22 QBD 513 at 517], "if it is possible, the words of a statute must be construed so as to give a sensible meaning to them".

Once sub-s (3A) was approached in that spirit, it followed that what Whelan had said in the Legislative Assembly debate ought not to be regarded as relevant.

Gleeson CJ: [7] It is inappropriate and impermissible to use speeches made in Parliament to seek to evade the statutory command in s 31 of the *Interpretation Act*, or fundamental principles of statutory interpretation. The use that can be made of such extrinsic material is governed by s 34 of the *Interpretation Act*. Where a dispute about the meaning of a statutory provision ... arises the Court is not entitled to treat what was said by a member of Parliament in the course of political debate as some kind of evidence of legislative bad faith. The duty of the Court, reinforced by the *Interpretation Act* ..., is to give meaning to the whole of s 13A unless it is impossible to do so.

The only issue of statutory interpretation ... is whether the expression "special reasons" is devoid of content, so that it is impossible for any case to satisfy the requirement. It is not to be overlooked that, now that the appellant is left only with his *Kable* argument, it suits his purposes to contend that he can never make out a case of "special reasons". That was not his primary argument in the Supreme Court, where his counsel was strongly contending that the requirements of sub-s (3A) could be, and were, satisfied ...

[8] The structure of s 13A is to distinguish between ordinary cases for the application of the section and a special class of case, being the cases referred to in sub-ss (3)(b) and (3A). In the special cases, it is necessary for there to be "special reasons" to justify the making of a determination ... In the ordinary case, the Supreme Court is directed by sub-s (9) to have regard to all relevant matters. Its attention is also directed specifically to certain matters. It would be absurd to construe "special reasons" in sub-s (3A) as excluding from consideration any matter covered by sub-s (9), because sub-s (9) covers all relevant matters. That would leave for consideration only irrelevant matters. The legislation does not require such a construction, and the principles of statutory interpretation referred to earlier argue strongly against it. Questions of weight and degree may arise. To take one specific example, sub-s (9) directs attention to the age of an offender at the time of the commission of the offence as a relevant matter in the ordinary case. In a particular case, the offender may have been a juvenile at the time of the offence. (This example, it should be added, is not purely hypothetical. One of the persons the subject of a non-release recommendation was 14 at the time of the offence.) It would be open to a judge to treat that as a special reason for the purposes of sub-s (3A). By reason of sub-s (9), age is always relevant, although in some cases its significance may be small. In a particular case, it may have a special significance. It would not necessarily be conclusive, but it would be open for consideration. To take another example, mentioned in the Court of Criminal Appeal, assistance given to the authorities in the detection of crime, sometimes involving extreme danger, could be a relevant matter in the ordinary case. There may also be particular circumstances in which, either [alone] or in combination with other factors, it could amount to a special reason in one of the special cases.

Examples of this kind cannot be dismissed as fanciful. We are not dealing with an argument that it is difficult to satisfy the requirements of sub-s (3A). We are dealing with an argument that it is impossible to satisfy the requirements because the statutory phrase "special reasons" is, in this context, devoid of content. We are dealing with a legal argument aimed at demonstrating invalidity, not a political argument aimed at demonstrating the desirability of legislative amendment.

The appellant's submission, that it will always be impossible to establish "special reasons" under sub-s (3A), was not simply a rhetorical overstatement of a complaint about unfairness. It was the basis for the contention that, in its application to persons the subject of non-release recommendations, the **[9]** legislative scheme was a charade, and the Supreme Court's judicial process was being used merely to implement a legislative intention that such persons would never be released. In order to make that argument good, it is not sufficient to show that it is difficult to establish special reasons, or that successful applications are likely to be rare. It is necessary to show that it is impossible to establish special reasons, and that no application could succeed. That has not been shown.

What followed from these conclusions was that the exercise of judicial power had not been impaired. Even if the challenged provisions had been found in Commonwealth legislation, no infringement of Ch III would be involved. It followed that there was no possibility of invalidity at the State level and that the question of *Kable* incompatibility simply did not arise.

In the earlier case of *HA Bachrach Pty Ltd v Queensland* (1998) 195 CLR 547, certain land at Morayfield, north of Brisbane, had been rezoned for a shopping centre. The plaintiff had unsuccessfully appealed to the Planning and Environment Court against the rezoning. A further appeal was pending in the Queensland Court of Appeal when the *Local Government (Morayfield Shopping Centre Zoning) Act 1996* (Qld) was passed, giving legislative approval to the rezoning. In a joint unanimous judgment, a five-judge High Court (Gleeson CJ, Gaudron, Gummow, Kirby and Hayne JJ) held that no interference with the judicial process was involved. The enactment of planning legislation does not preclude the subsequent enactment of exceptions for particular cases; and the functions of a court under such legislation are not the kind of functions that "[562] appertain exclusively to the judicial power". The Court noted that: "[561] *Kable* took as a starting point the principles applicable to courts created by the Parliament under s 71 and to the exercise by [562] them of the judicial power of the Commonwealth under Ch III. If the law in question here had been a law of the Commonwealth and it would not have offended those principles, then an occasion for the application of *Kable* does not arise". That aspect of *Bachrach* was followed in *Silbert v Director of Public Prosecutions (WA)* (2004) 217 CLR 181, in relation to the *Crimes (Confiscation of Profits) Act 1988* (WA). It was followed again in *Baker*. The joint judgment quoted the relevant passage from *Bachrach* with approval, as indicating "[9] the appropriate approach in the present appeal":

> **McHugh, Gummow, Hayne and Heydon JJ: [9]** If the provisions of the 1997 Act under challenge had been laws of the Commonwealth, they would have complied with the principles found in Ch III of the Constitution for the exercise of federal jurisdiction by federal courts ... **[10]** That being so, the appellant's attack on validity cannot succeed ...
>
> **[16]** The doctrine in *Kable* is expressed to be protective of the institutional integrity of the State courts as recipients and potential recipients of federal jurisdiction. If the State law in question confers jurisdiction of a nature which would meet the more stringent requirements for the exercise by the Supreme Court of judicial power under investment by federal law, there is no occasion to enter upon the question of whether the less stringent requirements of *Kable* are met. Counsel for the Attorney-General of the Commonwealth encapsulated the point in his submissions that, if a law satisfied the stricter tests required with respect to the judicial power of the Commonwealth, then the Court did not have to go on to ask whether it satisfied the lesser hurdle presented by the reasoning in *Kable*.

Notice that, while this passage denies the relevance of *Kable* in any case where the functions conferred on State courts would be acceptable for a federal court, it also envisages that, in any case where the *Kable* principle is relevant, it is sufficient that the State court involved is *potentially* a recipient of federal jurisdiction. A similar approach was taken in *North Australian Aboriginal Legal Aid Service Inc v Bradley* (2004) 218 CLR 146, where, contrary to what might have been thought (see Chapter 6, §5), it was held that the Territories are also subject to the *Kable* principle. The joint judgment accepted Gaudron J's statement in *Ebner v Official Trustee in Bankruptcy* (2000) 205 CLR 337 that, "[363] as courts created pursuant to s 122 of the Constitution may also be invested with the judicial power of the Commonwealth, it should now be recognised, consistently with the decision in *Kable*, that the Constitution also requires that those courts be constituted by persons who are impartial and who appear to be impartial".

In *Baker*, in sole dissent, Kirby J insisted that what had been said by Whelan and others in the Legislative Assembly "[19] leaves no doubt that the purpose of the Bill ... was to ensure that, in its application to the appellant and the other named prisoners, there would be no repetition of the possibility opened up by the order made in the case of Mr Crump". Whelan's statement made it

"**[26]** quite clear that the purpose of the impugned provisions was to tell 'judges that we, the Parliament and the community, do not expect these most serious offenders ever to be released' ... **[27]** Reading these passages should create a heightened vigilance on the part of a court such as this, whose duty is to protect the integrity of the judicial power and, relevantly, to repel attempts to 'dress up' as a judicial function the making of orders which, in truth, are designed to implement the clearly stated parliamentary objective that the named 'animals', including the appellant, never 'see the exit sign at the prison gate'." The enactment "was an attempt to involve the judiciary in the performance of punitive decisions effectively already determined by Parliament itself".

He also held that "the legislation is *ad hominem* in nature" since its operation "is clearly confined to the nominated prisoners". On this point he thought that *Nicholas* was distinguishable: although, at the time of its enactment, the legislation in that case was applicable only to five identified persons, the class of cases to which it applied "was stated in terms of general application", so that more instances might occur in the future. By contrast, in the *Baker* case, "there could never be any addition to the class of prisoners serving existing life sentences against whom there was a judicial 'non-release recommendation' made at the time they were originally sentenced". The class was closed.

Kirby J accepted the argument that it was "**[31]** seriously arbitrary and discriminatory" to delimit the class by reference to the making of a "non-release recommendation", given that the judicial practice with respect to such declarations had varied so widely according to judicial "**[32]** differences of personality, temperament and emotion". In *Ryan v The Queen* (2001) 206 CLR 267, he and Hayne J had warned that judicial emotions should be kept in check in such cases. In *Jamieson, Elliott and Blessington* (1992) 60 A Crim R 68 – the Janine Balding case, involving three of the 10 men now affected by s 13A(3A) – a New South Wales Court of Criminal Appeal presided over by Gleeson CJ had expressly disapproved of the practice of making such recommendations, saying in part that "**[80]** especially where the offender is a young person, and there are so many different possibilities as to what might happen in the future, it is normally not appropriate for a sentencing judge to seek to anticipate decisions that might fall to be made by other persons, and in other proceedings, or under other legislation, over the ensuing decades". In any event, said Kirby J, such recommendations had no legal effect. "**[32]** For Parliament to select non-normative, non-binding and possibly emotional remarks in one judge's reasons for sentence as the ground, decades later, to control the judicial orders of contemporary judges is to impose on the latter obligations of arbitrary conduct by reference to a discriminatory criterion". It was discriminatory because the result in such cases was effectively to exclude any possibility of a redetermination of sentence, whereas in cases where no such recommendation was made such redeterminations "*have* been made ... in crimes of comparable gravity (including crimes by triple murderers)".

Kirby J acknowledged that the exercise of a discretion conditioned on "special reasons" may sometimes be "**[34]** a permissible, even orthodox, exercise of judicial power". However, he insisted that the phrase "special reasons" must be read in context. The relevant context was supplied in part by the history of the legislation (including the parliamentary debates), and in part by the implicit contrast between "**[35]** special" and "ordinary" reasons, which suggested that the "ordinary" reasons for a redetermination would not be sufficient. This was borne out by the fact that in Baker's case itself, very strong supportive evidence of rehabilitation, "**[21]** exemplary" behaviour, and "very low" risk of recidivism, had not been considered sufficient to meet the need for "special reasons". The examples of what might constitute "special reasons" referred to in the judgment of Gleeson CJ were dismissed by Kirby J as "**[36]** fantastic possibilities of heroic prison rescues or intramural community service", in any event dependent on "chance possibilities ordinarily outside the prisoner's own control", and thus confirming that the "exception" for "special reasons" was "included to permit the conscription of judges of the New South Wales Supreme Court into a charade pretending to the availability of discretion ... when in truth it was intended to ensure that the judges could never, in law or fact, order the eligibility for release of any of the named offenders".

Kirby J also held that the impugned legislation was effectively retroactive, since it "[27] undoubtedly has the effect [28] of altering the punishment which the appellant and other affected prisoners were to suffer under the judicial sentence imposed upon them at the time of their initial convictions". As is now usual in constitutional cases, Kirby J appealed to international law, contending that a retroactive increase in punishment was in breach of the 1966 International Covenant on Civil and Political Rights. Moreover, he noted that one of the persons named in Parliament, Bronson Blessington, had been 14 years old at the time of his offence – so that, in its application to him, the substantive effect of the legislation was clearly in breach of the prohibition, in Art 37 of the 1989 Convention on the Rights of the Child, of "life imprisonment without possibility of release" as a punishment for "offences committed by persons below eighteen years of age".

Despite this comment by Kirby J, and the more oblique reference by Gleeson CJ to the special factors involved, the Blessington case has remained controversial. In *R v Blessington* (2005) 190 FLR 47, Dunford J held that the amendments introduced on 8 May 1997 in response to Crump's case did not apply retrospectively – so that Blessington's application, originally lodged in November 1996, was not affected by those amendments. Subsequently, the *Sentencing Legislation Further Amendment Act 1997* (NSW), apparently intended only for Blessington, had attempted to make the provisions retrospective; but Dunford J held that, while this was effective for the requirement of "special reasons", it did not subject Blessington's application to a waiting period (since the application had already been made). Nor did a 1999 amendment increasing the waiting period to 30 years affect his existing application. Moreover, Dunford J added that, since all these various amendments had clothed the original non-release recommendation in "legal effect and authority", the recommendation might now be appealable.

The New South Wales Parliament promptly responded by enacting the *Crimes (Sentencing Procedure) Amendment (Existing Life Sentences) Act 2005* (NSW). It applies the various statutory restrictions to all non-release recommendations made "before, on, or after" the latest date of assent, and provides that all such cases must be dealt with judicially on the limited basis (excluding any reduction of an existing life sentence) now embodied in Sch 1 to the *Crimes (Sentencing Procedure) Act 1999* (NSW), "and not otherwise".

More generally, Kirby J protested in *Baker* against "[17] an unduly narrow appreciation of the doctrine, in effect treating *Kable* as a constitutional guard-dog that would bark but once". He insisted that constitutional issues call for an approach to legislation "from the standpoint of substance, not mere form ...; [18] not a narrow approach befitting consideration of the validity of regulations made under a *Dog Act*". He was wary of the rule-of-thumb derived from *Bachrach* and *Silbert* that, if a law would be compatible with Ch III of the Constitution if enacted at federal level, it must necessarily be valid under *Kable*. He conceded that the testing of State legislation against the standards of Ch III "[25] may sometimes be a useful step"; but he warned that because it "involves an hypothesis prone to artificiality ..., care must be taken to avoid unnecessary dependence on such fictions. The safer course is to measure the State legislation by reference to the *Kable* standard, and not to become unduly diverted by considering what would have been the case if the State law were something it was not".

He discounted the references made in *Kable* to loss of public confidence in the courts: "[23] A court is not well placed to estimate with precision the impact, if any, of particular legislation upon public opinion. At most, the reference to this consideration constitutes a legal fiction, constructed by judges in an attempt to explain and objectify their conclusions". The importance of *Kable* is "[25] not for the protection of the judiciary, as such, but for the protection of all people in the Commonwealth". On the other hand, in a sideswipe at the decision in *Austin v Commonwealth* (2003) 215 CLR 185 (see Chapter 25, §2(c)), he asserted: "Upholding the constitutional implication expressed in *Kable* is at least as important for the defence of the independence and integrity of the judiciary in this country as giving effect to a hitherto undis-covered constitutional implication limiting the imposition of federal taxes on some State judicial pension rights".

Finally, in the parliamentary debate of May 1997 Kirby J saw a chilling example of "**[20]** the bidding contest in extreme punishments in which the members of Parliament had become involved", and warned that: "Subject to the Constitution, only the courts of this country stand as guardians of proportionality and the avoidance of serious excesses and departures from … human rights". The laws at issue in *Baker* and *Fardon* were in his view "**[39]** extreme examples of invasions of the real functions secured to the State judiciary by the Australian Constitution as stated … in *Kable*", and the failure of the majority to strike them down "shows that that decision is a dead letter. At least it is so until a future time perceives its importance for the protection of fundamental rights in this country".

The principle emerging from *Bachrach*, *Silbert* and *Baker* – that *Kable* can have no application to a law which would not offend Ch III if enacted at federal level – was not sufficient to resolve the issue in *Fardon v Attorney-General (Queensland)*, since there was no consensus on whether the challenged law would be valid if enacted at Commonwealth level. The law in question was the *Dangerous Prisoners (Sexual Offenders) Act 2003* (Qld), which authorised "interim detention orders" (under s 8), and "supervision orders" or "continuing detention orders" (under s 13), to be made by the Supreme Court of Queensland in relation to a "prisoner". The word "prisoner" was defined for this purpose by s 5(6) as meaning "a prisoner detained in custody who is serving a period of imprisonment for a serious sexual offence, or serving a period of imprisonment that includes a term of imprisonment for a serious sexual offence, whether the person was sentenced to the term or period of imprisonment before or after the commencement of this section". The appellant, Robert Fardon, fell within this definition because, on 30 June 1989, he was sentenced to 14 years' imprisonment for rape, sodomy and assault. That sentence was due to expire on 30 June 2003; but the *Dangerous Offenders (Sexual Offenders) Act* came into force on 6 June, and an interim detention order was made against Fardon on 27 June. After further interim protection orders on 31 July and 2 October, a "continuing detention order" was made on 6 November 2003, authorising detention in custody "for an indefinite term for control, care and treatment". Under s 40 of the *Judiciary Act 1903* (Cth) an appeal to the Queensland Court of Appeal was removed into the High Court, where an appeal against the first interim detention order was already pending.

Gummow J was inclined to think that a similar scheme enacted at Commonwealth level would *not* have been constitutional.

Fardon v Attorney-General (Queensland)
(2004) 210 ALR 50

Gummow J: [73] Upon the hypothesis propounded by the Commonwealth, the significant result of the foregoing is that a person may be held in detention in a corrective facility, to use the modern euphemism, by order of a court exercising federal jurisdiction and by reason of a finding of criminal propensity rather than an adjudication of criminal guilt. That invites attention to two related propositions.

The first is that expressed as follows by Gaudron J in *Re Nolan; Ex parte Young* [(1991) 172 CLR 460 at 497]:

"[I]t is beyond dispute that the power to determine whether a person has engaged in conduct which is forbidden by law and, if so, to make a binding and enforceable declaration as to the consequences which the law imposes by reason of that conduct lies at the heart of exclusive judicial power."

The making by the Supreme Court of a continuing detention order under s 13 is conditioned upon a finding, not that the person has engaged in conduct which is forbidden by law, but that there is an unacceptable risk that the person will commit a serious sexual offence.

That directs attention to the second proposition and to what was said by Brennan, Deane and Dawson JJ in *Chu Kheng Lim v Minister for Immigration, Local Government and Ethnic Affairs* [(1992) 176 CLR 1 at 27-8]. That litigation directly concerned the detention of aliens with no title to enter or remain in Australia, not the situation of citizens such as the appellant. However, their

Honours earlier in their judgment [176 CLR at 27] had said that, putting aside the cases of detention on grounds of mental illness, infectious disease and ... other "exceptional cases", there was a constitutional principle derived from Ch III that:

"the involuntary detention of a citizen in custody by the State is penal or punitive in character and, under our system of government, exists only as an incident of the exclusively judicial function of adjudging and punishing criminal guilt".

That passage was applied as a step in the reasoning in *Kable* [(1996) 189 CLR 51] of Toohey J and Gummow J, and is reflected in that of Gaudron J and McHugh J.

It must be said that the expression of a constitutional principle in this form has certain indeterminacies. The first is the identification of the beneficiary of the principle as "a citizen". That may readily be understood given the context in *Lim* of the detention of aliens with no title to enter or remain in Australia and their liability to deportation processes. But in other respects aliens are not outlaws; many will have a statutory right or title to remain in Australia for a determinate or indeterminate period and at least for that period they have the protection afforded by the Constitution and the laws of Australia. There is no reason why the **[74]** constitutional principle stated above should not apply to them outside the particular area of immigration detention with which *Lim* was concerned. Subsequent references in these reasons to "a citizen" should be read in this extended sense.

Another indeterminacy concerns the phrase "criminal guilt". In *Chief Executive Officer of Customs v Labrador Liquor Wholesale Pty Ltd* [(2003) 216 CLR 161 at 198], Hayne J, after referring to the unstable nature of a dichotomy between civil and criminal proceedings, went on:

"It seeks to divide the litigious world into only two parts when, in truth, that world is more complex and varied than such a classification acknowledges. There are proceedings with both civil and criminal characteristics: for example, proceedings for a civil penalty under companies and trade practices legislation. The purposes of those proceedings include purposes of deterrence, and the consequences can be large and punishing."

However, what is involved here is the loss of liberty of the individual by reason of adjudication of a breach of the law. In such a situation, as Kirby J remarked in *Labrador* [216 CLR at 179], that loss of liberty is "ordinarily one of the hallmarks reserved to criminal proceedings conducted in the courts, with the protections and assurances that criminal proceedings provide".

I would prefer a formulation of the principle derived from Ch III in terms that, the "exceptional cases" aside, the involuntary detention of a citizen in custody by the State is permissible only as a consequential step in the adjudication of criminal guilt of that citizen for past acts. That central conception is consistent with the holding in *Polyukhovich v Commonwealth* [(1991) 172 CLR 501] that the conduct may not have been forbidden by law when it was engaged in; the detention under federal legislation such as that upheld in *Polyukhovich* still follows from a trial for past, not anticipated, conduct.

That formulation also eschews the phrase "is penal or punitive in character". In doing so, the formulation emphasises that the concern is with the deprivation of liberty without adjudication of guilt rather than with the further question whether the deprivation is for a punitive purpose.

Further, "punishment" and cognate terms have an indeterminate reference, and are "heavily charged with subjective emotional and intellectual overtones". The indeterminacy of the term "punishment" is illustrated by the division of opinion in the United States Supreme Court in *Kansas v Hendricks* [521 US 346 (1997)]. The Kansas law under challenge in that case established procedures for the commitment of those who by reason of a "mental abnormality" or a "personality disorder" were likely to engage in "predatory acts of sexual violence". The issues **[75]** (resolved in favour of validity) ... were treated by the Supreme Court as turning on the classification of commitment under the law as "punishment". The majority contrasted detention for the purpose of protecting the community from harm and "the two primary objectives of criminal punishment: retribution and deterrence" [521 US at 361-2]. This Court has looked at the objectives of the sentencing process rather more broadly ...

Preventative detention regimes attached by legislation to the curial sentencing process upon conviction have a long history in common law countries. The *Habitual Criminals Act* 1905 (NSW) and Pt II of the *Prevention of Crime Act* 1908 (UK) are examples of such legislation. It may be accepted that the list of exceptions to which reference was made in *Lim* [176 CLR at 28] is not closed. But it is not suggested that regimes imposing upon the courts functions detached from the sentencing process form a new exceptional class, nor that the detention of the mentally ill for treatment is of the same character as the incarceration of those "likely to" commit certain classes of offence.

Another of the well-understood exceptions to which the Court referred in *Lim*, with a citation from Blackstone, was committal to custody, pursuant to executive warrant of accused persons to ensure availability to be dealt with by exercise of the judicial power. But detention by reason of apprehended conduct, even by judicial determination on a *quia timet* basis, is of a different character and is at odds with the central constitutional conception of detention as a consequence of judicial determination of engagement in past conduct.

It is not to the present point ... that federal legislation ... [might] provide for detention without adjudication of criminal guilt but by a judicial process of some refinement. The vice ... would be in the nature of the outcome, not the means by which it was obtained.

Hayne J: [103] Subject to one exception, I agree in the reasons of Gummow J. The exception is that I would reserve my opinion about whether federal legislation along the lines of the Act would be invalid. As Gummow J points out, no sharp line can be drawn between criminal and civil proceedings or between detention that is punitive and detention that is not. And once it is accepted, as it has been in Australia, that protection of the community from the consequences of an offender's re-offending is a legitimate purpose of sentencing, the line between preventative detention of those who have committed crimes in the past (for fear of what they may do in the future) and punishment of those persons for what they have done becomes increasingly difficult to discern. So too, when the propensity **[104]** to commit crimes (past or future) is explained by reference to constructs like "anti-social personality disorder" and it is suggested that the disorder, or the offender's behaviour, can be treated, the line between commitment for psychiatric illness and preventative detention is difficult to discern. Indeed, the premise for the decisions of the Supreme Court of the United States upholding State civil commitment statutes is that the statutes do not differ in substance or effect from a legislative regime providing for the confinement of some who suffer psychiatric illness.

I acknowledge the evident force in the proposition that to confine a person for what he or she might do, rather than what he or she has done, is at odds with identifying the central constitutional conception of detention as a consequence of judicial determination of engagement in past conduct. Nonetheless, I would reserve for further consideration, in a case where it necessarily falls for decision, whether legislation requiring a federal court to determine whether a person previously found guilty of an offence should be detained beyond the expiration of the sentence imposed, on the ground that the prisoner will or may offend again, would purport to confer a non-judicial function on that court.

Kirby J, who was otherwise in dissent, agreed with Gummow J on this issue. Gleeson CJ found the issue "**[56]** unnecessary ... to decide", and the other majority judges were silent. They did, however, emphasise the difference between the rigorous requirements under Ch III for the exercise of federal judicial power, and the weaker requirements arising under *Kable* at the State level. Thus, while *Bachrach* and *Baker* hold that enactments that would be valid at federal level must necessarily be valid at State level, *Fardon* insists that a law that would be invalid if enacted at federal level may nevertheless be valid at State level.

Callinan and Heydon JJ: [110] This Court did not in *Kable* hold ... that in all respects, a Supreme Court of a State was the same, and subject to the same constraints, as a federal court established under Ch III of the Constitution. Federal judicial power is not identical with State judicial power. Although the test, whether, if the State enactment were a federal enactment, it would infringe Ch III of the Constitution, is a useful one, it is not the exclusive test of validity. It is possible that a State legislative conferral of power which, if it were federal legislation, would infringe Ch III of the Constitution, may nonetheless be valid. Not everything by way of decision-making denied to a federal judge is denied to a judge of a State. So long as the State court, in applying legislation, is not called upon to act and decide, effectively as the alter ego of the legislature or the executive, so long as it is to undertake a genuine adjudicative process and so long as its integrity and independence as a court are not compromised, then the legislation in question will not infringe Ch III of the Constitution.

In this instance, the six majority judges had no doubt that the detention procedures established by the *Dangerous Prisoners (Sexual Offenders) Act* were valid.

Gleeson CJ: [52] The constitutional objection to the legislative scheme is not based, or at least is not directly based, upon a suggested infringement of the appellant's human rights. The objection is based upon the involvement of the Supreme Court of Queensland in the process. It is the effect of the legislation upon the institutional integrity of the Supreme Court, rather than its effect upon the personal liberty of the appellant, that is said to conflict with the requirements of the Constitution. There is a paradox in this. As Charles JA pointed out in *R v Moffatt* [[1998] 2 VR 229 at 260] (a case in which there was an unsuccessful challenge, on similar grounds, to Victorian legislation providing for the imposition of indefinite sentences on dangerous persons convicted of certain serious offences), it might be thought surprising that there would be an objection to having detention decided upon by a court, whose proceedings are in public, and whose decisions are subject to appeal, rather than by executive decision. Furthermore, as Williams JA pointed out in this case, there is other Queensland legislation [s 163 of the *Penalties and Sentences Act 1992* (Qld)] under which indefinite detention may be imposed at the time of sentencing violent sexual offenders who are regarded as a serious danger to the community. If it is lawful and appropriate for a judge to make an assessment of danger to the community at the time of sentencing, perhaps many years before an offender is due to be released into the community, it may be thought curious that it is inappropriate for a judge to make such an assessment at or near the time of imminent release, when the danger might be assessed more accurately.

There are important issues that could be raised about the legislative policy of continuing detention of offenders who have served their terms of imprisonment, and who are regarded as a danger to the community when released. Substantial questions of civil liberty arise. This case, however, is not **[53]** concerned with those wider issues. The outcome turns upon a relatively narrow point, concerning the nature of the function which the Act confers upon the Supreme Court. If it is concluded that the function is not repugnant to the institutional integrity of that Court, the argument for invalidity fails.

Gleeson CJ went on to recall the tragic history of the *Veen* case: a life sentence reduced to a term of 12 years by a compassionate High Court in *Veen v The Queen (No 1)* (1979) 143 CLR 458, only to see a new life sentence, imposed after further killing, upheld by the High Court in *Veen v The Queen (No 2)* (1988) 164 CLR 465. He noted the wish expressed by Deane J in *Veen (No 2)* for a statutory system which could "**[495]** avoid the disadvantages of indeterminate prison sentences by being based on periodic orders for continuing detention in an institution other than a gaol and provide a guarantee of regular and thorough review by psychiatric and other experts". He also quoted at length from the observations of Chief Judge Clement Haynsworth (United States Court of Appeals, Fourth Circuit), in *United States v Chandler*, 393 F 2d 920 (1968), emphasising that ultimately: "**[929]** The law must proceed upon the assumption that man, generally, has a qualified freedom of will, and that any individual who has a substantial capacity for choice should be subject to its sanctions". (Compare Lon L Fuller, *The Morality of Law* (Yale University Press, 1964), 162-7.) Gleeson CJ summed up these reflections by saying:

Gleeson CJ: [55] The way in which the criminal justice system should respond to the case of the prisoner who represents a serious danger to the community upon release is an almost intractable problem. No doubt, predictions of future danger may be unreliable, but, as the case of *Veen* shows, they may also be right. Common law sentencing principles, and some legislative regimes, permit or require such predictions at the time of sentencing, which will often be many years before possible release. If, as a matter of policy, the unreliability of such predictions is a significant factor, it is not necessarily surprising to find a legislature attempting to postpone the time for prediction until closer to the point of release.

Turning to the *Kable* issue, he said:

Gleeson CJ: [56] The decision in *Kable* established the principle that, since the Constitution established an integrated Australian court system, and contemplates the exercise of federal jurisdiction by State Supreme Courts, State legislation which purports to confer upon such a court a function which substantially impairs its institutional integrity, and which is therefore incompatible with its role as a repository of federal jurisdiction, is invalid.

The New South Wales legislation in question in that case provided for the preventive detention of only one person, Mr Kable. As was pointed out by Dawson J, the final form of the legislation had a number of curious features, because of its parliamentary history. It was originally framed as a law of general application, but an amendment confined its application to the appellant. The object of the statute in its final form was said to be to protect the community by providing for the preventive detention of Gregory Wayne Kable. Toohey J said that the extraordinary character of the legislation and of the functions it required the Supreme Court to perform was highlighted by the operation of the statute upon one named person only. In that respect, he said, the statute was virtually unique. Senior counsel for the appellant in the case argued that the legislation was not a carefully calculated legislative response to a general social problem; it was legislation *ad hominem*. That argument was accepted. The members of the Court in the majority considered that the appearance of institutional impartiality of the Supreme Court was seriously damaged by a statute which drew it into what was, in substance, a political exercise.

The minor premise of the successful argument in *Kable* was specific to the legislation there in question. It is the major premise – the general principle – that is to be applied in the present case ...

[T]he suggested ground of invalidity is that identified in the decision in *Kable*; a ground based upon the involvement of the Supreme Court in the decision-making process as to detention. Indeed, in the course of argument, senior counsel for the appellant acknowledged that his challenge to the validity of the Act would disappear if the power to make the relevant decision were to be vested in a panel of psychiatrists (or, presumably, retired judges).

[57] The Act is a general law authorising the preventive detention of a prisoner in the interests of community protection. It authorises and empowers the Supreme Court to act in a manner which is consistent with its judicial character. It does not confer functions which are incompatible with the proper discharge of judicial responsibilities or with the exercise of judicial power. It confers a substantial discretion as to whether an order should be made, and if so, the type of order. If an order is made, it might involve either detention or release under supervision. The onus of proof is on the Attorney-General. The rules of evidence apply. The discretion is to be exercised by reference to the criterion of serious danger to the community. The Court is obliged, by s 13(4) of the Act, to have regard to a list of matters that are all relevant to that criterion. There is a right of appeal. Hearings are conducted in public, and in accordance with the ordinary judicial process. There is nothing to suggest that the Supreme Court is to act as a mere instrument of government policy. The outcome of each case is to be determined on its merits.

It might be thought that, by conferring the powers in question on the Supreme Court of Queensland, the Queensland Parliament was attempting to ensure that the powers would be exercised independently, impartially, and judicially. Unless it can be said that there is something inherent in the making of an order for preventive, as distinct from punitive, detention that compromises the institutional integrity of a court, then it is hard to see the foundation for the appellant's argument ...

It cannot be a serious objection to the validity of the Act that the law which the Supreme Court of Queensland is required to administer relates to a subject that is, or may be, politically divisive or sensitive. Many laws enacted by parliaments and administered by courts are the outcome of political controversy, and reflect controversial political opinions. The political process is the mechanism by which representative democracy functions. It does not compromise the integrity of courts to give effect to valid legislation. That is their duty. Courts do not operate in a politically sterile environment. They administer the law, and much law is the outcome of political action.

It was argued that the test, posed by s 13(2), of "an unacceptable risk that the prisoner will commit a serious sexual offence" is devoid of practical content. On the contrary, the standard of "unacceptable risk" was referred to by this Court **[58]** in *M v M* [(1988) 166 CLR 69] in the context of the magnitude of a risk that will justify a court in denying a parent access to a child. The Court warned against "striving for a greater degree of definition than the subject is capable of yielding" [166 CLR at 78]. The phrase is used in the *Bail Act* 1980 (Q), which provides that courts may deny bail where there is an unacceptable risk that an offender will fail to appear (s 16). It is not devoid of content, and its use does not warrant a conclusion that the decision-making process is a meaningless charade.

In some of the reasons in *Kable*, references were made to the capacity of the legislation there in question to diminish public confidence in the judiciary. Those references were in the context of a statute that was held to impair the institutional integrity of a court and involve it in an *ad hominem* exercise. Nothing that was said in *Kable* meant that a court's opinion of its own standing is a criterion of validity of law. Furthermore, nothing would be more likely to damage public confidence in the integrity and impartiality of courts than judicial refusal to implement the provisions of a statute upon the ground of an objection to legislative policy. If courts were to set out to defeat the intention of Parliament because of disagreement with the wisdom of a law, then the judiciary's collective reputation for impartiality would quickly disappear. This case involves no question of the interpretation of an ambiguous statute, or of the application of the common law. It concerns a specific challenge to the validity of a State law on the ground that it involves an impermissible attempt to resolve a certain kind of problem through the State's judicial process.

McHugh J: [60] [T]he legislation that the Court declared invalid in *Kable* was extraordinary. Section 3(1) of that Act declared that the object of the Act was "to protect the community by providing for the preventive detention … of Gregory Wayne Kable." Section 3(3) declared that it "authorises the making of a detention order against Gregory Wayne Kable and does not authorise the making of a detention order against any other person." It was thus *ad hominem* legislation that, although dressed up as a Supreme Court legal proceeding, had been enacted for the purpose of ensuring that Kable remained in prison when his sentence expired …

The differences between the legislation considered in *Kable* and the Act are substantial. First, the latter Act is not directed at a particular person but at all persons who are serving a period of imprisonment for "a serious **[61]** sexual offence" [ss 2, 5, 13]. Second, when determining an application under the Act, the Supreme Court is exercising judicial power. It has to determine whether, on application by the Attorney-General, the Court is satisfied that "there is an unacceptable risk that the prisoner will commit a serious sexual offence" if the prisoner is released from custody [s 13(2)]. That issue must be determined in accordance with the rules of evidence [s 13(3)]. It is true that in form the Act does not require the Court to determine "an actual or potential controversy as to existing rights or obligations" [*R v Trade Practices Tribunal; Ex parte Tasmanian Breweries Pty Ltd* (1970) 123 CLR 361 at 375]. But that does not mean that the Court is not exercising judicial power. The exercise of judicial power often involves the making of orders upon determining that a particular fact or status exists. It does so, for example, in the cases of matrimonial causes, bankruptcy, probate and the winding up of companies. The powers exercised and orders made by the Court under this Act are of the same jurisprudential character as in those cases. The Court must first determine whether there is "an unacceptable risk that the prisoner will commit a serious sexual offence". That is a standard sufficiently precise to engage the exercise of State judicial power. Indeed, it would seem sufficiently precise to constitute a "matter" that could be conferred on or invested in a court exercising federal jurisdiction. Third, if the Court finds that the Attorney-General has satisfied that standard, the Court has a discretion as to whether it should make an order under the Act and, if so, what kind of order [s 13(5)]. The Court is not required or expected to make an order for continued detention in custody. The Court has three discretionary choices open to it if it finds that the Attorney-General has satisfied the "unacceptable risk" standard. It may make a "continuing detention order", a "supervision order" or no order [s 13(5)]. Fourth, the Court must be satisfied of the "unacceptable risk" standard "to a high degree of probability" [s 13(3(b)]. The Attorney-General bears the onus of proof. Fifth, the Act is not designed to punish the prisoner. It is designed to protect the community against certain classes of convicted sexual offenders who have not been rehabilitated during their period of imprisonment. The objects of the Act expressed in s 3 are:

> "(a) to provide for the continued detention in custody or supervised release of a particular class of prisoner to ensure adequate protection of the community; and
>
> (b) to provide continuing control, care or treatment of a particular class of prisoner to facilitate their rehabilitation."

Sixth, nothing in the Act or the surrounding circumstances suggests that the jurisdiction conferred is a disguised substitute for an ordinary legislative or **[62]** executive function. Nor is there anything in the Act or those circumstances that might lead to the perception that the Supreme Court, in exercising its jurisdiction under the Act, is acting in conjunction with, and not independently of, the Queensland legislature or executive government.

Does the Act compromise the institutional integrity of the Supreme Court of Queensland?

With great respect to those who hold the contrary view, nothing in the Act or the surrounding circumstances gives any ground for supposing that the jurisdiction conferred by the Act compromises the institutional integrity of the Supreme Court of Queensland. Nothing in the Act gives any ground for concluding that it impairs the institutional capacity of the Supreme Court to exercise federal jurisdiction that the Federal Parliament has invested or may invest in that Court. Nothing in the Act might lead a reasonable person to conclude that the Supreme Court of Queensland, when exercising federal jurisdiction, might not be an impartial tribunal free of governmental or legislative influence or might not be capable of administering invested federal jurisdiction according to law ...

[65] In my opinion, ... *Kable* is a decision of very limited application. That is not surprising. One would not expect the States to legislate, whether by accident or design, in a manner that would compromise the institutional integrity of their courts. *Kable* was the result of legislation that was almost unique in the history of Australia. More importantly, however, the background to and provisions of the *Community Protection Act* pointed to a legislative scheme enacted solely for the purpose of ensuring that Mr Kable, alone of all people in New South Wales, would be kept in prison after his term of imprisonment had expired. The terms, background and parliamentary history of the legislation gave rise to the perception that the Supreme Court of that State might be acting in conjunction with the New South Wales Parliament and the executive government to keep Mr Kable in prison. The combination of circumstances which gave rise to the perception in *Kable* is unlikely to be repeated. The *Kable* principle, if required to be applied in future, is more likely to be applied in respect of the terms, conditions and manner of appointment of State judges or in circumstances where State judges are used to carry out non-judicial functions, ... than in the context of *Kable*-type legislation.

In this case, it is impossible to conclude that the Queensland Parliament or the executive government of that State might be working in conjunction with the Supreme Court to continue the imprisonment of the appellant. Nor is it possible to conclude that the Act gives rise to a perception that the Supreme Court of Queensland might not render invested federal jurisdiction impartially in accordance with federal law. The Act is not directed to a particular person but to a class of persons that the Parliament might reasonably think is a danger to the community. Far from the Act giving rise to a perception that the Supreme Court of Queensland is acting in conjunction with the Queensland Parliament or the executive government, it shows the opposite. It requires the Court to adjudicate on the claim by the Executive that a prisoner is "a serious danger to the community" in accordance with the rules of evidence and "to a high degree of probability". Even if the Court is satisfied that there is an unacceptable risk that the prisoner will commit a serious sexual offence if released from custody, the Court is not required to order the prisoner's continued detention or supervised release. Furthermore, the Court must give detailed reasons for its order, reasons that are inevitably subject to public scrutiny. It is impossible to hold, therefore, **[66]** that the Queensland Parliament and the executive government intend that the appellant's imprisonment should continue and that they have simply used the Act "to cloak their work in the neutral colors of judicial action" [*Mistretta v United States*, 488 US 361 at 407 (1989)]. On the contrary, the irresistible conclusion is that the Queensland Parliament has invested the Supreme Court of Queensland with this jurisdiction because that Court, rather than the Parliament, the executive government or a tribunal such as a parole board or a panel of psychiatrists, is the institution best fitted to exercise the jurisdiction.

Again in sole dissent, Kirby J expanded on the themes he had raised in *Baker*.

Kirby J: [82] The appellant points out that the sentences of imprisonment imposed on him in 1989 have been served in their entirety. Nevertheless, pursuant to orders made under the Act, the appellant has remained a prisoner, incarcerated in the Townsville Correctional Centre after the date of the expiry of his sentences. This has occurred without allegation, still less proof, of any further offence by **[83]** him, or breach of the law. He complains that, effectively, his judicial punishment has been extended ...

> "[b]ecause opinions have been formed, probably on material which would not be admissible in a legal proceeding and on a standard other than beyond reasonable doubt, that [he] will commit a serious sexual offence as defined if released from custody, or at least unsupervised custody, after completing [his] sentenced terms of imprisonment" [*Attorney-General (Q) v Fardon* [2003] QCA 416 at [91]].

Experts in law, psychology and criminology have long recognised the unreliability of predictions of criminal dangerousness. In a recent comment, Professor Kate Warner remarked:

> "[A]n obstacle to preventive detention is the difficulty of prediction. Psychiatrists notoriously overpredict. Predictions of dangerousness have been shown to have only a one-third to 50% success rate. While actuarial predictions have been shown to be better than clinical predictions – an interesting point as psychiatric or clinical predictions are central to continuing detention orders – neither are accurate."

Judges of this Court have referred to such unreliability. Even with the procedures and criteria adopted, the Act ultimately deprives people such as the appellant of personal liberty, a most fundamental human right, on a prediction of dangerousness, based largely on the opinions of psychiatrists which can only be, at best, an educated or informed "guess". The Act does so in circumstances, and with consequences, that represent a departure from past and present notions of the judicial function in Australia.

As the Act's provisions show, it targets people who "will almost inevitably be unpopular with the community and the media who can be expected to take considerable interest in orders of the type sought under the Act" [[2003] QCA 416 at [91]]. As framed, the Act is invalid. It sets a very bad example, which, unless stopped in its tracks, will expand to endanger freedoms protected by the Constitution. In this country, judges do not impose punishment on people for their beliefs, however foolish or undesirable they may be regarded, nor for future crimes that people fear but which those concerned have not committed. In strictly limited circumstances, the judiciary permits "executive interference with the liberty of the individual" where "the purpose of the imprisonment is to achieve some **[84]** legitimate non-punitive object" [*Lim* 176 CLR at 71]. Despite some attempts to give the Act that appearance, that is not the true meaning and effect of its terms. The appellant's continued imprisonment is unlawful. Having served his lawful sentences, he should be released forthwith ...

[85] I do not pretend that the ultimate issue raised by these proceedings is cut and dried. The validity of similar enactments has repeatedly divided the Supreme Court of the United States ... In this country, the *Kable* principle has so far proved a weak protection against State legislation said to have intruded impermissibly into the judicial function. In only one case has the principle been upheld and applied by this Court, namely in *Kable* itself. What was seen at first to be an important assurance that the State judiciary in Australia (certainly the named Supreme Courts) enjoyed many of the constitutional protections of the federal judiciary, has repeatedly been revealed as a chimera.

[86] I disagree with this approach .... In my opinion, *Kable* is especially important when the rights of unpopular minorities are committed to the courts. That is when legislatures may be tempted to exceed their constitutional powers, involving the independent judiciary in incompatible activities so as to cloak serious injustices with the semblance of judicial propriety. Against such risks, Ch III of the Constitution stands guard. This Court should be vigilant to uphold such protection. That is what the principle in *Kable* requires ...

Too much has been made of the differing ways in which the majority in *Kable* expressed their respective reasons for upholding the constitutional objection to the *Community Protection Act* 1994 (NSW), challenged in that case. The essential idea was relatively clear and simple. Because State courts (and unavoidably State Supreme Courts named in the Constitution) may be vested with federal jurisdiction which they are then bound to exercise, they must exhibit certain basic qualities as "courts" fit for that function.

In short, State courts must remain at all times curial receptacles proper to the exercise of federal jurisdiction. Although they are not, as such, federal courts, subject to the express strictures of Ch III, their inclusion in the integrated judicature of the Commonwealth, the provisions for appeals from them to federal courts and the facility for the vesting of federal jurisdiction all imply that they cannot be required by State law to perform functions inconsistent with ("repugnant to") Ch III.

In particular instances of challenge, it falls to the courts themselves (ultimately this Court), to explain the contents of the *Kable* principle. The principle must be given meaning in a context that respects the different constitutional origins and histories of State courts; but which also upholds the implications necessary to their undoubted place within the judicature envisaged by the federal Constitution. Just as the States of Australia are not, constitutionally speaking, merely the colonies renamed, so State courts, after Federation (and specifically State Supreme Courts named in the Constitution) derive particular functions and characteristics from the federal Constitution itself. These requirements are not identical to those imposed explicitly on federal courts. However, they cannot be so different from such requirements as to undermine the integrated scheme for the national judicature which the Constitution creates.

Self-evidently, a conclusion that legislation infringes the Constitution and is for that reason invalid is a serious one. The only justification for such a conclusion can be the Constitution itself. It cannot depend on the whim of judges to set aside an unliked law that has been made by the vote of a majority of the representatives of the people, elected to Parliament. However, just as the **[87]** legislators have their functions under the Constitution, so do the courts. If any branch of government neglects, or exceeds, its functions, the harmony envisaged by the Constitution is disturbed.

Within the system of representative government created by the Constitution, legislators sometimes respond to waves of community fear and emotion, occasionally promoted by sections of the media. As this Court demonstrated in *Australian Communist Party v Commonwealth* ("the *Communist Party Case*") [(1951) 83 CLR 1], its function, derived from the Constitution, responds to a time frame that is much longer than that of the other branches of government. Inevitably, it affords a constitutional corrective to transient passions and, sometimes, to ill-considered laws repugnant to the timeless constitutional design.

This is what I take *Kable* to require. It forbids attempts of State Parliaments to impose on courts, notably Supreme Courts, functions that would oblige them to act in relation to a person "in a manner which is inconsistent with traditional judicial process" [189 CLR at 98]. It prevents attempts to impose on such courts "proceedings [not] otherwise known to the law", that is, those not partaking "of the nature of legal proceedings" [189 CLR at 106]. It proscribes parliamentary endeavours to "compromise the institutional impartiality" of a State Supreme Court [189 CLR at 121]. It forbids the conferral upon State courts of functions "repugnant to judicial process" [189 CLR at 134].

Recent, and not so recent, experience teaches that governments and parliaments can, from time to time, endeavour to attract electoral support by attempting to spend the reputational currency of the independent courts in the pursuit of objectives which legislators deem to be popular. Normally, this will be constitutionally permissible and legally unchallengeable. However, as *Kable* demonstrates, a point will be reached when it is not, however popular the law in question may at first be. The criteria for the decision are stated in *Kable* in general terms. Yet such is often the case in constitutional adjudication. Evaluation and judgment are required of judicial decision-makers responding, as they must, to enduring values, not to immediate acclaim.

Protection of the legal and constitutional rights of minorities in a representative democracy such as the Australian Commonwealth is sometimes unpopular. This is so whether it involves religious minorities, communists, illegal drug importers, applicants for refugee status, or persons accused of **[88]** offences against anti-terrorist laws. Least of all is it popular in the case of prisoners convicted of violent sexual offences or offences against children. Yet it is in cases of such a kind that the rule of law is tested. As Latham CJ pointed out long ago, in claims for legal protection, normally, "the majority of the people can look after itself": constitutional protections only really become important in the case of "minorities, and, in particular, of unpopular minorities" [*Adelaide Company of Jehovah's Witnesses Inc v Commonwealth* (1943) 67 CLR 116 at 124]. It is in such cases that the adherence of this Court to established constitutional principle is truly tested, as it is in this case.

[90] There are five features in the Act which, combined, indicate an attempted imposition upon the judges of the Supreme Court of Queensland functions repugnant to Ch III of the federal Constitution as explained in *Kable*. These features severally authorise the Supreme Court … to order:

(1)   The civil commitment of a person to a prison established for the reception of prisoners, properly so-called;

(2)   The detention of that person in prison, in the absence of a new crime, trial and conviction and on the basis of the assessment of future re-offending, not past offences;

(3)   The imprisonment of the person in circumstances that do not conform to established principles relating to civil judicial commitment for the protection of the public, as on a ground of mental illness;

(4)   The imposition of additional judicial punishment on a class of prisoners selected by the legislature in a manner inconsistent with the character of a court and with the judicial power exercised by it; and

(5)   The infliction of double punishment on a prisoner who has completed a sentence judicially imposed by reference, amongst other things, to the criterion of that person's past criminal conduct which is already the subject of final judicial orders that are (or shortly will be) spent at the time the second punishment begins.

As to the last feature, Kirby J again held (as he had done in *Baker*) that the imposition of continuing detention involved an additional retroactive punishment; and also (or alternatively) that it infringed the rule against double jeopardy. As to his first point, he said:

Kirby J: [90] Generally speaking, in Australia, the involuntary detention of a person in custody by any agency of the state is viewed as penal or punitive in character. In Australian law, personal liberty has always been regarded as the most fundamental of rights. Self-evidently, liberty is not an absolute right. However, to deprive a person of liberty … is a grave step. If it is to extend for more than a very **[91]** short interval …, it requires the authority of a judicial order.

These rules explain a fundamental principle that lies deep in our law. Ordinarily, it requires officers of the Executive Government, who deprive a person of liberty, to bring that person promptly before the judicial branch, for orders that authorise, or terminate, the continued detention. The social purpose behind these legal obligations is to divorce, as far as society can, the hand that would deprive the individual of liberty from the hand that authorises continued detention. The former, which normally lies in the Executive branch, is taken to be committed to the deprivation of liberty for some purpose. The latter is taken to be independent and committed only to the application in the particular case of valid laws. The operation of the writ of *habeas corpus* is another assurance, afforded to the judiciary, requiring the prompt legal justification of any contested deprivation of liberty. So precious does our legal system regard every moment of personal freedom …

The necessary involvement of the judiciary in adjudging and punishing criminal guilt is a fixed feature of the courts participating in the integrated judicature of the Commonwealth, provided for in the Constitution. Precisely because liberty is regarded as so precious, legal provisions derogating from liberty (and especially those that would permit the Executive Government to deprive a person of liberty) are viewed by courts with heightened vigilance. Normally, a law providing for the deprivation of the liberty of an individual will be classified as punitive. As a safeguard against expansion of forms of administrative detention without court orders, our legal system has been at pains to insist that detention in custody must ordinarily be treated as penal or punitive, precisely because only the judiciary is authorised to adjudge and punish criminal **[92]** guilt. Were it other-wise, it would be a simple matter to provide by law for various forms of administrative detention, to call such detention something other than "punishment", and thereby to avoid the constitutional protection of independent judicial assessment before such deprivation is rendered lawful.

It is true that a limited number of exceptions to this constitutional scheme have been acknow-ledged by this Court. They include immigration detention of "unlawful non-citizens" for the purposes of deportation or to enable an application for an entry permit to be made and determined; quarantine detention for reasons of public health; detention of the mentally ill and the legally insane for the protection of the community; and analogous non-punitive, protective orders permitted by valid legislation. This Court has assumed, or suggested, that the imposition by federal and State courts of sentences that involve indefinite periods of imprisonment is compatible with Ch III. Such provisions have a long history. In intermediate courts, they have been held compatible with *Kable*.

This Court has also made it clear that the list of permissible burdens upon liberty, classified as "non-punitive," is not closed.

Nonetheless, where, as in the case of the Act, a new, different and so far special attempt is made by State legislation to press the judiciary into a function not previously performed by it, it is necessary to evaluate the new role by reference to fundamental principles. The categories of exception to deprivations of liberty treated as non-punitive may not be closed; but they remain exceptions. They are, and should continue to be, few, fully justifiable for reasons of history or reasons of principle developed by analogy with the historical derogations from the norm. Deprivation of liberty should continue to be seen for what it is ...

In the case of the Act, the drafter has not even attempted a change of nomenclature to disguise the reality of the order assigned to the judiciary ... The person the subject of the order is a "prisoner", convicted of a previous crime. He or she is already detained in prison and must be so at the time of the application and order. If the order under the Act is made, he or she is nominally detained as a "serious danger to the community". However, such continued detention is served in a prison and the detainee, **[93]** although having completed the service of imprisonment, remains a "prisoner". The detention continues under the "continuing detention order". From the point of view of the person so detained, the imprisonment "continues" exactly as it was.

Where a court is concerned with the constitutional character of an Act, its attention is addressed to actuality, not appearances. Were it otherwise, by the mere choice of legislative language and the stroke of a pen, the requirements of the Constitution could be circumvented ...

The same point was made in *Chu Kheng Lim v Minister for Immigration* [176 CLR at 27]:
"In exclusively entrusting to the courts designated by Ch III the function of the adjudgment and punishment of criminal guilt under a law of the Commonwealth, the Constitution's concern is with substance and not mere form."

The same rule must apply to the evaluation of a State law said to be incompatible with Ch III ... Invalidity does not depend on verbal formulae or the proponent's intent. It depends upon the character of the law. Effectively, the Act does not provide for civil commitment of a person who has completed a criminal sentence. Had it done so, one would have expected commitment of that person to a different (non-prison) institution, with different incidents, different facilities, different availability of treatment and support designed to restore the person as quickly as possible to liberty ...

Occasionally, for a very short interval and in exceptional circumstances, civil commitment to prison may occur. But that is not the character of the Act. It contemplates lengthy commitment, generally with assessment and reassessments at annual intervals. In Australia, we formerly boasted that even an hour of liberty was precious to the common law. Have we debased liberty so far that deprivation of liberty, for yearly intervals, confined in a prison cell, is now regarded as immaterial or insignificant? Under the Act, just as in the law invalidated in *Kable*, the prisoner could theoretically be detained for the rest of **[94]** the prisoner's life. This could ensue not because of any *past* crime committed, but because of a prediction of *future* criminal conduct ...

On its face, the Act hardly makes any effort to pretend to a new form of "civil commitment". To the extent that it does, it fails to disguise its true character, namely punishment. And, by Australian constitutional law, punishment as such is reserved to the judiciary for breaches of the law. An order of imprisonment as punishment can therefore only be made by a court following proof of the commission of a criminal offence, established beyond reasonable doubt where the charge is contested, in a fair trial at which the accused is found guilty by an independent court of the offence charged. Here there has been no offence; no charge; no trial ... Instead, because of a prisoner's antecedents and criminal history, provision is made for a new form of additional punishment utilising the courts and the corrective services system in a way that stands outside the judicial process hitherto observed in Australia.

He concluded:

[101] This Court should not resolve the arguments of the parties in the present proceedings unaware of what has gone before. History evidences many patterns of unacceptable intrusions by other sources of power into the independence of the judiciary. These should not be dismissed as irrelevant to Australia. They have occurred in "highly civilised" countries, with strong legal and judicial traditions …

One pattern of intrusion into judicial functions may be observed in what occurred in Germany in the early 1930s. It was provided for in the acts of an elected government. Laws with retroactive effect were duly promulgated. Such laws adopted a phenomenological approach. Punishment was addressed to the estimated character of the criminal instead of the proved facts of a crime. Rather [102] than sanctioning specified criminal conduct, the phenomenological school of criminal liability procured the enactment of laws prescribing punishment for identified "criminal arche-types". These were the *Volksschädlinge* (those who harmed the nation). The attention of the courts was diverted from the *corpus delicti* of a crime to a preoccupation with the "pictorial impression" of the accused. Provision was made for punishment, or additional punishment, not for specific acts of proved conduct but for "an inclination towards criminality so deep-rooted that it precluded [the offender's] ever becoming a useful member of the … community".

This shift of focus in the criminal law led to a practice of not releasing prisoners at the expiry of their sentences. By 1936, in Germany, a police practice of intensive surveillance of discharged criminals was replaced by increased utilisation of laws permitting "protective custody". The German courts were not instructed, advised or otherwise influenced in individual cases. They did not need to be … Offenders for whom such punishments were prescribed were transferred from civil prisons to other institutions, such as lunatic asylums, following the termination of their criminal sentence. Political prisoners and "undesirables" became increasingly subject to indeterminate detention.

In the *Communist Party Case* [83 CLR at 187-8], Dixon J taught the need for this Court to keep its eye on history, including recent history, so far as it illustrated the over-reach of governmental power. He and his generation of Australian judges were aware of the challenge to the capacity of the judiciary to defend the rule of law. This Court should not allow the passage of fifty years since this insight to dull its memory or its appreciation of the distortions of the judicial power that are now being attempted. The principle in *Kable* was a wise and prudent one, defensive of judicial independence in Australia … I dissent from the willingness of this Court, having stated the principle, now repeatedly to lend its authority to [its] confinement … This has been done virtually to the point where the principle itself has disappeared at the very time when the need for it has greatly increased, as this case shows.

6. Further References

Allan, J, "'Do the Rights Thing' Judging? The High Court of Australia in Al-Kateb" (2005) 24 *University of Queensland Law Journal* 1.

Carne, G, "Detaining Questions or Compromising Constitutionality?: The *ASIO Legislation Amendment (Terrorism) Act 2003* (Cth)" (2004) 27 *University of New South Wales Law Journal* 524.

Carney, G, "*Wilson & Kable*: The Doctrine of Incompatibility – An Alternative to Separation of Powers?" (1997) 13 *Queensland University of Technology Law Journal* 175.

Handsley, E, "Do Hard Laws Make Bad Cases? – The High Court's Decision in *Kable v Director of Public Prosecutions (NSW)*" (1997) 25 *Federal Law Review* 171.

Hardcastle, R, "A Chapter III Implication for State Courts: *Kable v Director of Public Prosecutions*" (1998) 3 *Newcastle Law Review* 13.

Johnston, P, and Hardcastle, R, "State Courts: The Limits of *Kable*" (1998) 20 *Sydney Law Review* 216.

Meagher, D, "The Status of the Kable Principle in Australian Constitutional Law" (2005) 16 *Public Law Review* 182.

Wood, D, "A One Man Dangerous Offenders Statute – The Community Protection Act 1990 (Vic)" (1990) 17 *Melbourne University Law Review* 497.

Chapter 16

Characterisation
and the Trade and Commerce Power

1. Introduction

Sections 51 and 52 of the Constitution assign broad legislative powers relating to a range of subjects and purposes to the Commonwealth Parliament. In constitutional discourse the term "characterisation" refers to the process of determining whether a law falls within one of these heads of power by ascertaining the *subject-matter* or the *purpose* of the law. While this chapter is intended as a general overview of the process of characterisation of laws by reference to those subjects and purposes, illustrations are drawn in particular from the first of the powers listed in s 51, the "trade and commerce" power.

2. Characterisation

The simplest view of "characterisation", and, indeed, of the whole process of judicial review of legislation, is encapsulated in a famous American statement by Justice Roberts in *United States v Butler*, 297 US 1 (1936).

United States v Butler
297 US 1 (1936)

Roberts J: [62] When an act of Congress is appropriately challenged in the courts as not conforming to the constitutional mandate the judicial branch of the Government has only one duty – to lay the article of the Constitution which is invoked beside the statute which is challenged and to decide whether the latter squares with the former.

This approach reflects the "legalism" of the decision in *Amalgamated Society of Engineers v Adelaide Steamship Co Ltd* (*Engineers' Case*) (1920) 28 CLR 129. It assumes that the question is simply whether the subject-matter on which the federal Parliament has legislated "squares with" one of the designated subject-matters on which it has the power to legislate. If it does, the legislation is valid; and so long as there is no other express or implied restriction, no further question arises. However, the process of "characterisation" is neither as simple nor as simple-minded as this quotation suggests.

The misleadingly intuitive appeal of such an approach may be strongest in those cases where legislative power is defined by reference to a specified subject-matter. In conventional High

Court doctrine most of the powers granted by s 51 are assumed to be of this kind. In those cases, the passage from *United States v Butler* may at least be analytically helpful in suggesting that an intellectual inquiry at two different levels is involved. The constitutional text identifies a particular definitional area and the question is whether the subject of the impugned legislation falls within that area. If it does, the law will be valid. Logically, therefore, the first task would be to define the limits of the subject-matter area, while the second task would be to determine whether the challenged law lies within those limits. It is this second task that is referred to as *characterisation*. The first task is one of *constitutional interpretation*.

If both these levels of inquiry involved either the factual identification of objectively given "subject-matters", or the precise definitional elucidation of conceptual "essences", the approach of *United States v Butler* might be plausible. Usually, however, the questions to be answered lend themselves neither to self-evident objectivity nor to definitional certitude. The difficulties arise at both levels: although it is convenient to talk of the first task as one of "interpreting" the head of power, and the second task as "characterising" the law, this second task is also an interpretive one, as we shall see.

Moreover, as the High Court has often acknowledged, an approach to these tasks in any particular context must be limited by that context. Accordingly, the Court has usually chosen to concentrate on the second task (of characterising the *law*), approaching the first task (of defining the *power*) only to the limited extent that is necessary to resolve the immediate characterisation issue.

A judicial approach to characterisation at one time much in vogue depended on ascertaining the "pith and substance" of the relevant law. The phrase had originated in the Privy Council in the context of Canadian appeals relating to the distribution of powers under the *British North America Act 1867* (Imp) (see, for example, *Union Colliery Company of British Columbia v Bryden* [1899] AC 580: "**[587]** the whole pith and substance of the enactments"). That Act specified one list of legislative powers assigned to the Dominion of Canada (s 91) and another list assigned to the Provinces (s 92). The typical situation was that each list contained a head of power to which the impugned legislation might plausibly be assigned. The problem was therefore one of determining which of two competing characterisations of the law was the more appropriate. In that context, it was understandable that the question was approached by attempting, as the Privy Council did in *Russell v The Queen* (1882) 7 App Cas 829, to identify "**[839]** [t]he *true nature and character* of the legislation … **[840]** in order to ascertain the class of subject to which it *really* belongs" (emphasis added).

In other cases where the expression "pith and substance" or similar expressions were used, the problem was also one of choosing between *competing* characterisations, one of which would be clearly forbidden to the enacting legislature (see, for example, for Northern Ireland *Gallagher v Lynn* [1937] AC 863). The early doctrine of "reserved State powers" (see Chapter 7, §3) in effect postulated a similar choice for Australia. Yet this model of *competing* characterisations (and hence of a search for "pith and substance") was clearly less appropriate for the Australian Constitution, which follows the United States model by having only one list of enumerated powers (for the federal or central legislature). The question in an Australian case is not whether the topic of legislation should be characterised as falling within a specified Commonwealth power or a specified State power, but only whether it can be characterised in a way that brings it within Commonwealth power.

The frequent use of the phrase "pith and substance" as a key to characterisation led to other uses of the phrase in other constitutional contexts: for instance, in determining whether the effect of a law was to interfere with freedom of interstate trade under s 92. Especially in those other contexts, however, the phrase went out of fashion after the Privy Council decision in *Commonwealth v Bank of New South Wales* (*Bank Nationalisation Case*) [1950] AC 235. In that case, the *Banking Act 1947* (Cth) was held invalid because it infringed s 92. The Act would have nationalised Australian banking by progressively prohibiting "the carrying on of banking business by private banks". In the present context, what is important is that the *Banking Act* was *not* held invalid by reason of any want of legislative power, since its subject-matter and operation did fall within the Commonwealth's banking power in s 51(xiii) of the Constitution. The Privy Council did not deal with that issue at all, since it was an "inter se question", in relation to which the Privy Council had no jurisdiction (see Chapter 13, §4). In the High Court, the argument that the law should not be characterised as a law with respect to banking was accepted only in the dissenting judgment of Rich and Williams JJ, who adopted a "pith and substance" approach. Latham CJ rejected the *words* "pith and substance", but not necessarily the underlying idea. Although parts of his judgment remain influential, it was Dixon J who spelled out the broader view of characterisation that nowadays prevails.

Bank of NSW v Commonwealth (*Bank Nationalisation Case*)
(1948) 76 CLR 1

Latham CJ: [182] It was argued for the defendants that the 1947 Act was valid because it related to and affected banks and banking and therefore "touched and concerned" banking and was "relevant" to the subject matter of banking. The plaintiffs, on the other hand, argued that the constitutional validity of legislation should be determined by enquiring what was the "pith and substance" of the law; whether the legislation had what was called "substantial impact" upon an authorized subject matter ...

[183] There are in my opinion grave difficulties in the way of accepting the proposition that a law which "touches and concerns" an authorized subject matter is valid unless it contravenes some express prohibition to be found in the Constitution ...

[184] [T]he Constitution must be read as a whole, and each power conferred upon the Federal Parliament must be read in the context of the words prescribing the other legislative powers of the Parliament.

The Constitution assigns only specific legislative powers to the Commonwealth Parliament. It is a Federal Constitution, not a unitary Constitution. This has been emphasised again and again in the judgments of this Court, and in no case more clearly than in the *Amalgamated Society of Engineers v Adelaide Steamship Co Ltd* [(1920) 28 CLR 129 at 150] where reference is made to the conclusion "as to which this court has never faltered, that the Commonwealth is a government of enumerated or selected legislative powers" ... Accordingly, no single power should be construed in such a way as to give to the Commonwealth Parliament a universal power of legislation which would render absurd the assignment of [185] particular carefully defined powers to that Parliament. Each provision of the Constitution should be regarded, not as operating independently, but as intended to be construed and applied in the light of other provisions of the Constitution. Thus an endeavour should be made to "reconcile the respective powers ... and give effect to all": *Citizens Insurance Co of Canada v Parsons* [(1881) 7 App Cas 96 at 109] ... If the fact that a statute "touched and concerned" a matter within the power of the Commonwealth Parliament were held to be sufficient to establish its validity, there would be no distribution of powers between Commonwealth and States – the Commonwealth would have complete power of controlling by law all persons and things in Australia, subject only to such prohibitions as the Constitution contains ...

Nor, on the other hand, am I of opinion that the phrase "pith and substance," in spite of its frequent use by high authorities, solves any difficulties. It lends itself to emphatic asseveration, but it provides but little illumination. It is a metaphorical phrase possibly derived from "pith and marrow" in patent law. *Wills* J in *Incandescent Gas Light Co v De Mare Incandescent Gas Light System Ltd* [(1896) 13 RPC 301 at 332], said of the latter phrase:– "'Pith' is a great deal less than the substance of the vegetable structure of which it is part, and 'marrow' a great deal less than the substance of the animal structure of which it is part. Metaphors are very apt to mislead, as they are seldom close enough to the things to which they are applied." The difference, if any, between "pith" and "substance" is not explained.

The distinction marked by the phrase is a distinction between "pith and substance" as representing "primary object and effect" and incidental application to other matter: *Attorney-General for Canada v Attorney-General for Quebec* [[1947] AC 33 at 44]. The case of *Prafulla Kumar Mukherjee v Bank of Commerce* [(1947) LR 74 Ind App 23 at 43] shows that there is no difference between asking: "What is the pith and substance of a statute?" and asking: "What is its true nature and character?" In *Great West Saddlery Co Ltd v The King* [[1921] 2 AC 91 at 117] it was said with respect to the construction of statutes for the purpose of **[186]** determining constitutional validity: "The only principle that can be laid down for such cases is that legislation the validity of which has to be tested must be scrutinized in its entirety in order to determine its true character." But there is no rule which will settle all cases. A question of *ultra vires* "must be determined in each case as it arises, for no general test applicable to all cases can safely be laid down": *Attorney-General for Alberta v Attorney-General for Canada* [[1939] AC 117 at 129].

A power to make laws "with respect to" a specific subject is as wide a legislative power as can be created. No form of words has been suggested which would give a wider power. The power conferred upon a Parliament by such words in an Imperial statute is plenary – as wide as that of the Imperial Parliament itself: *R v Burah* [(1878) 3 App Cas 889]; *Hodge v The Queen* [(1883) 9 App Cas 117]. But the power is plenary only with respect to the specified subject. In determining the validity of a law it is in the first place obviously necessary to construe the law and to determine its operation and effect (that is, to decide what the Act actually does), and in the second place to determine the relation of that which the Act does to a subject matter in respect of which it is contended that the relevant Parliament has power to make laws. A power to make laws with respect to a subject matter is a power to make laws which in reality and substance are laws upon the subject matter. It is not enough that a law should refer to the subject matter or apply to the subject matter: for example, income tax laws apply to clergymen and to hotel-keepers as members of the public; but no-one would describe an income tax law as being, for that reason, a law with respect to clergymen or hotel-keepers. Building regulations apply to buildings erected for or by banks; but such regulations could not properly be described as laws with respect to banks or to banking.

It has often been decided that the motives of Parliament, and, as a general rule, the objects which a Parliament seeks to achieve, are not relevant to questions of constitutional validity: see cases cited in *South Australia v Commonwealth* (*Uniform Tax Case*) [(1942) 65 CLR 373 at 424-5]. The operation and effect of a customs duty on certain goods is to make the importation of those goods subject to the duty imposed. That is what the law does. The motive of Parliament may have been to assist a particular industry or business. When validity is in question, that fact is irrelevant. An indirect consequence of the law may be to ruin some other industry or business. That fact also is irrelevant.

[187] Thus when a question arises as to the validity of legislation it is the duty of the Court to determine what is the actual operation of the law in question in creating, changing, regulating or abolishing rights, duties, powers or privileges, and then to consider whether that which the enactment does falls in substance within the relevant authorized subject matter, or whether it touches it only incidentally, or whether it is really an endeavour, by purporting to use one power, to make a law upon a subject which is beyond power.

Dixon J: [332] To my mind the argument is answered by the principles of constitutional interpretation which this Court adopted early in its history and from which, I believe, it has never intentionally departed.

They are well expressed in a passage from the judgment of *O'Connor* J in the *Jumbunna Coal Mine, No Liability v Victorian Coal Miners' Association* [(1908) 6 CLR 309 at 367] which I shall quote:– "Where it becomes a question of construing words used in conferring a power of that kind on the Commonwealth Parliament, it must always be remembered that we are interpreting a Constitution broad and general in its terms, intended to apply to the varying conditions which the development of our community must involve. For that reason, where the question is whether the Constitution has used an expression in the wider or in the narrower sense, the Court should, in my opinion, always lean to the broader interpretation unless there is something in the context or in the rest of the Constitution to indicate that the narrower interpretation will best carry out its object and purpose."

The foundation of these principles is expressed by *Higgins* J in *Attorney-General for New South Wales v Brewery Employés Union of New South Wales* [(*Union Label Case*) (1908) 6 CLR 469 at 611] where he says, "although we are to interpret the words of the Constitution on the same principles of interpretation as we apply to any ordinary law, these very principles of interpretation compel us to take into account the nature and scope of the Act that we are interpreting – to remember that it is a Constitution, a mechanism under which laws are to be made, and not a mere Act which declares what the law is to be." His Honour proceeds to quote from *Story, Commentaries*, 2nd ed, s 455: **[333]** "While, then, we may well resort to the meaning of single words to assist our inquiries, we should never forget, that it is an instrument of government that we are to construe" [6 CLR at 612].

The purpose of the enumeration of powers in s 51 is not to define or delimit the description of law that the Parliament may make upon any of the subjects assigned to it. Speaking generally, the legislative power so given is plenary in its quality. The purpose of the enumeration is to name a subject for the purpose of assigning it to that power. The names or descriptions employed are usually of the briefest kind. It is true that certain powers do involve a description amounting almost to a formal definition; examples are pars (iii), (xxiv) and (xxv), (xxxv), (xxxvii), (xxxviii) and (xxxix). But more often they are the most general names of general topics.

To borrow the words of *Gray* J delivering the opinion of the Supreme Court in *Juilliard v Greenman* [110 US 421 at 439 (1884)]: "the Constitution ... by apt words of designation or general description, marks the outlines of the powers granted to the National Legislature; but it does not undertake, with the precision and detail of a code of laws, to enumerate the subdivisions of those powers, or to specify all the means by which they may be carried into execution."

The power with respect to banking seems to me a plain example of the designation of a broad subject without any indication of the means by which it is to be dealt with or of the existence of limits upon the description of laws to be made with respect thereto. To say that it is not a question of what limits there may be upon the description of legislation but of the definition of the subject to which they may be addressed, and that continuance is an attribute of the subject, is not, I think, a satisfactory answer. For the question is whether there should be extracted from the word "banking" and its content an intention that, among other things, it should continue, that it should remain consensual, or that it should be a matter between subject and subject. Such an intention narrows the definition of the subject in a way which reduces the area, not of relevance, but rather of legislative discretion or policy. Of course "banking" describes an activity which is carried on and in that sense continues. But no-one would feel that it was anything but an ordinary use of the word to say that a statute declaring that banking should no longer be carried on was a law about banking. It is as easy to explain the addition of the words "also ... the incorporation of banks and the issue of paper money" as made **[334]** to remove any doubt and to insure that those subjects were included as to infer an actual intention that "banking" should have a restrictive or narrow construction.

For the reasons I have indicated, I am unable to accept the view that the word "banking" should have ascribed to it anything but the wide meaning and flexible application of a general expression designating, as a subject of legislative power, a matter forming part of the commercial economic and social organization of the community. I see no sufficient reason for importing into it any of the three limitations suggested, viz, (1) confining the power to laws for the governance of a continuing activity, to something that does not go beyond regulation, (2) the limitation of the conception of banking to transactions entirely consensual, and (3) to transactions between subject and subject.

When the *Bank Nationalisation Case* reached the Privy Council (*Commonwealth v Bank of New South* Wales [1950] AC 235), their Lordships endorsed Latham CJ's "**[312]** just criticism" of phrases like "pith and substance", observing memorably that such phrases "**[313]** but illustrate the way in which the human mind tries, and vainly tries, to give to a particular subject-matter a higher degree of definition than it will admit".

Despite his rejection of "pith and substance", Latham CJ seems finally to fall back on the question whether laws "**[186]** in *reality and substance* are laws *upon* the subject matter" (emphasis added). Yet his emphasis on the phrase "with respect to" suggests that this cannot really be the question. This is another reason why the simple model of characterisation in *United States v Butler* is inadequate. That model would be plausible only if the question were whether or not a law could be characterised as being "on" the permitted subject. But the question posed by the opening words of s 51 is whether the law is one "with respect to" the specified topic – a broader and looser question. Moreover, in answering this question, the Court does not demand to be satisfied that the challenged law *is* a law "with respect to" the relevant topic, but only that it can *fairly be described* in that way. Or, as the Court nowadays often puts the question: is there a *sufficient connection* between the law and a head of power?

3. Sufficient Connection

The contemporary acceptance that what is required for a law to be validly enacted under the Constitution is *no more than* a sufficient connection with a head of power is the end result of a series of cases in the 1970s and 1980s concerning the validity of successive amendments to the *Family Law Act 1975* (Cth). The combined effect of *Lansell v Lansell* (1964) 110 CLR 353 and of *Russell v Russell* (1976) 134 CLR 495 was that most of those amendments were dependent for validity not on s 51(xxii) ("Divorce and matrimonial causes ...") but on s 51(xxi) ("Marriage"). The question was therefore whether they could be characterised as laws with respect to marriage. In response to this question Gibbs J, in particular, insisted that the connection with marriage must be "close". For example, in *R v Lambert; Ex parte Plummer* (1980) 146 CLR 447 he observed that in some cases "**[457]** the connexion between the operation of the law and the relationship of marriage may be so tenuous that such a law cannot be said to be a law with respect to marriage", and that everything depends "on the closeness of the connexion between the law and the marriage relationship".

In *Gazzo v Comptroller of Stamps (Vic)* (1981) 149 CLR 227, Stephen and Aickin JJ joined Gibbs CJ in holding that s 90 of the *Family Law Act* lacked a sufficiently close connection with "marriage". That section provided that maintenance agreements, and transfers of property pursuant to such agreements or to orders of the Family Court, should be exempt from "any duty or charge under any law of a State or Territory". Mason and Murphy JJ, in dissent, would have held that the provision was valid. In particular, Murphy J protested that, through the requirement of a "close" connection, "**[255]** [t]he once-discredited doctrine of reserved powers of the States, is having a triumphant, if unacknowledged, resurgence".

Several of the cases involved legislative attempts to extend the jurisdiction of the Family Court in custody matters by deeming the expression "a child of a marriage" to extend to a child (for example, an ex-nuptial child of one spouse, or a grandchild of one spouse) who was "treated by the husband and wife as a child of their family, if, at the relevant time, the child was ordinarily a member of the household of the husband and wife". The cumulative effect of *In Marriage of Cormick* (1984) 156 CLR 170, *R v Cook; Ex parte C* (1985) 156 CLR 249 and *Re F; Ex parte F* (1986) 161 CLR 376 was that none of the children concerned could claim a sufficiently close connection with the relevant marriage. However, Deane J dissented in *R v Cook*; and in *Re F; Ex parte F* Mason J joined him in admitting to second thoughts about the requisite connection with "marriage". They suggested that the need for close scrutiny of the "connection" between particular children and particular marriages should never have arisen because, on the conventional broad approach to problems of characterisation, the regulation of rights and obligations towards different classes of children might always have lain "**[389]** within the central area of the grant of legislative power". In a passage now endorsed as authoritative, they said:

Re F; Ex parte F
(1986) 161 CLR 376

Mason and Deane JJ: [387] There are two important and related general principles which must be borne in mind in determining the ambit of the legislative power conferred by the various paragraphs of s 51 of the Constitution ... The first is that the different grants of legislative power contained in the paragraphs of s 51 are not mutually exclusive and are not to be read down by reference to some presumption that they are ...

The second ... is that a single law can possess more than one character in the sense that it can properly be characterized as a law with respect to more than one subject-matter. It suffices for constitutional validity if any one or more of those characters is within a head of Commonwealth legislative power. In determining validity, it is not necessary to single out the paramount character. It is enough that the law "fairly answers the description of a law 'with respect to' one given subject-matter appearing in s 51" **[388]** regardless of whether it is, at the same time, more obviously or equally a law with respect to some other subject-matter: see *Actors and Announcers Equity Association v Fontana Films Pty Ltd* [(1982) 150 CLR 169 at 192-4]. In a case where a law fairly answers the description of being a law with respect to two subject-matters, one of which is and the other of which is not a subject-matter appearing in s 51, it will be valid notwithstanding that there is no independent connexion between the two subject-matters. Thus, if the operation of a particular law is such that the law fairly answers the description of being "with respect to ... Marriage", it will be within the legislative power conferred by s 51(xxi) notwithstanding that it more obviously or equally answers the description of being a law with respect to some other subject-matter, such as a particular class of children, and regardless of the absence of any independent connexion between marriage and that other subject-matter ...

[389] [A] law which directly and on its face operates upon or affects the subject of "marriage" – eg, a law which operates to confer rights or impose obligations upon the parties to a marriage or third persons by reference to or arising out of marriage – comes within the central area of the grant of legislative power contained in s 51(xxi) and must ... be characterized as a law with respect to marriage. Such a law cannot properly be denied that characterization by reason of the fact that the members of this Court disapprove of its content or consider that it operates to make marriage the source of rights and duties ... which go beyond what is desirable or appropriate ... Put differently, it would be contrary to basic constitutional principle to confine the reach of the legislative power conferred by s 51(xxi) by reference to preconceived notions of the matters with which a law with respect to marriage should or should not deal or to adopt the approach that a law should be denied characterization as a law with respect to marriage if, regardless of its operation, matters with which it dealt were thought by members of this Court to lack some requisite independent connexion with the institution or relationship of marriage.

Where a law does not on its face directly operate upon or affect marriage, validity under s 51(xxi) will depend upon the nature and strength of any connexion between what the law does and marriage: **[390]** "for on the one hand the subject-matter may itself involve or include a penumbra of things that are incidental, consequential and ancillary and a law as to some aspects of these things would not be ultra vires, and on the other hand the operation of a law upon any subject may not be apparent on its face but yet be clear when the actual practical working of cause and effect is perceived": per Dixon CJ in the *Marriage Act Case* [(1962) 107 CLR 529 at 543]. Even in such a case, it is to the operation of the law that regard must be had for the purposes of characterization and that operation of itself can create or exhibit the relationship with marriage necessary to justify characterization as a law pursuant to s 51(xxi) of the Constitution notwithstanding that the law directly and more obviously operates upon some other subject-matter which would lack any obvious independent connexion with marriage. All that is necessary is that any connexion between what the law does and "Marriage" is sufficient to enable the law to be fairly characterized not only as a law with respect to that other subject-matter but also as a law with respect to marriage. If the sufficient and necessary connexion does not exist and the particular laws cannot fairly be so characterized, however, that does not mean that every law with respect to the subject-matter with which that law deals is necessarily denied characterization as being also a law with respect to marriage for the purposes of s 51(xxi). The fact that one law dealing with a subject-matter that is not within a specific grant of legislative power cannot properly be characterized as a law with respect to marriage simply does not mean that a different law dealing with that same subject-matter must also be denied such characterization.

In *Fisher v Fisher* (1986) 161 CLR 438 this approach finally prevailed, this time in relation to s 79(8) of the *Family Law Act*, which permitted continuance of property proceedings after one of the parties to a marriage had died. Mason and Deane JJ again affirmed that such a law is "**[453]** within the central area of the marriage power, without there being any occasion to engage in discussion about the need for a connexion with the subject-matter of the power, whether close or otherwise". In any event they added that discussion of a "connexion" "is more appropriately undertaken when the operation of the law is not on the subject-matter of the power, but on something which is incidental to it". They added also that "[e]ven in such a case it is a mistake to insist on the existence of a 'close' connexion"; and that "while the actual decision in *Gazzo v Comptroller of Stamps (Vic)* must be respected unless and until it is overruled, ... the authority of that case should be confined to its particular facts" since "the reasoning underlying the decision [was] fundamentally unsound".

Initially, the phrase "sufficient connection" had been introduced by way of contrast with those cases where the challenged law is said to be "on" the relevant topic: that is, where the entities or activities regulated by the challenged provision are themselves examples of the very category delineated by the words of the constitutional grant. These latter cases are nowadays said to lie within the "core" of the power, perhaps in homage to the distinction drawn by HLA Hart, "Positivism and the Separation of Law and Morals" (1958) 71 *Harvard Law Review* 593 between "**[607]** a core of settled meaning" and "a penumbra of debatable cases". By contrast, a "sufficient connection" was sought where the law was not "on" the very topic, but could only be brought within power by the words "with respect to" (or perhaps by the incidental powers considered in §6 below). However, the phrase "sufficient connection" is wide enough to cover both types of case, and is increasingly used in that way. For example, in *Re Dingjan; Ex parte Wagner* (1995) 183 CLR 323, McHugh J summarised the contemporary view as follows.

Re Dingjan; Ex parte Wagner
(1995) 183 CLR 323

McHugh J: **[368]** In determining whether a law is 'with respect to' a head of power **[369]** in s 51 of the Constitution, two steps must be taken. First, the character of the law must be determined. That is done by reference to the rights, powers, liabilities, duties and privileges which it creates. Secondly, a judgment must be made as to whether the law as so characterised so operates that it can be said to be connected to a head of power conferred by s 51. In determining whether the connection exists, the practical, as well as the legal, operation of the law must be examined. If a connection exists between the law and a s 51 head of power, the law will be 'with respect to' that head of power unless the connection is, in the words of Dixon J [*Melbourne Corporation v Commonwealth* (1947) 74 CLR 31 at 79], 'so insubstantial, tenuous or distant' that it cannot sensibly be described as a law 'with respect to' the head of power.

The permissiveness of this approach to characterisation, and its avoidance of rigid definitional boundaries, reflect the broad approach to constitutional interpretation derived (in the United States) from *McCulloch v Maryland*, 17 US (4 Wheat) 316 (1819) and (in Australia) from *Jumbunna Coal Mine NL v Victorian Coal Miners' Association* (1908) 6 CLR 309 (see Chapter 7, §6). That broad approach was again reaffirmed when the basic principles of characterisation were summarised by six members of the High Court (with whom Kirby J separately agreed) in *Grain Pool of Western Australia v Commonwealth* (2000) 202 CLR 479. The case involved an unsuccessful challenge to the *Plant Variety Rights Act 1987* (Cth) and *Plant Breeder's Rights Act 1994* (Cth), which provided for the grant of "plant variety rights", a novel form of intellectual property. The central issue was whether, in creating such rights, the Acts possessed a sufficient connection with the power over "Copyrights, patents of inventions and designs, and trade marks" in s 51(xviii) of the Constitution.

In *Attorney-General (NSW) v Brewery Employés Union of NSW* (*Union Label Case*) (1908) 6 CLR 469, the words of s 51(xviii) – specifically in that case "trade marks" – had been treated as technical legal terms which must therefore be held strictly to the legal meaning that they had in 1900 (see Chapter 8, §5). That approach, however, was heavily influenced by the now-discredited doctrine of "reserved State powers"; and, in giving emphatic endorsement to a broader approach, the joint judgment in the *Grain Pool* case quoted extensively from the dissenting judgment of Higgins J in *Union Label*.

Grain Pool of Western Australia v Commonwealth
(2000) 202 CLR 479

Gleeson CJ, Gaudron, McHugh, Gummow, Hayne and Callinan JJ: [491] The plaintiff contends that the operation of s 51(xviii) with respect to patents of inventions is limited by what it identifies as certain traditional principles of patent law. In particular, it submits that there are certain fixed minimum requirements for the "intellectual effort" required of inventors respecting novelty and inventive step, that there is a crucial distinction between process and product claims, and that the term "patents" imports a constitutional requirement of the scope of the monopoly rights which must be granted and limits the permissible statutory qualifications to those rights. The statutes here in question are said to fail to satisfy these criteria ...

[492] The general principles which are to be applied to determine whether a law is with respect to a head of legislative power such as s 51(xviii) are well settled. They include the following. First, the constitutional text is to be construed "with all the generality which the words used admit" [*R v Public Vehicles Licensing Appeal Tribunal (Tas); Ex parte Australian National Airways Pty Ltd* (1964) 113 CLR 207 at 225-6]. Here the words used are "patents of inventions". This, by 1900, was "a recognised category of legislation (as taxation, bankruptcy)", and when the validity of such legislation is in question the task is to consider whether it "answers the description, and to disregard purpose or object" [*Stenhouse v Coleman* (1944) 69 CLR 457 at 471]. Secondly, the character of the law in question must be determined by reference to the rights, powers, liabilities, duties and privileges which it creates. Thirdly, the practical as well as the legal operation of the law must be examined to determine if there is a sufficient connection between the law and the head of power. Fourthly, as Mason and Deane JJ explained in *Re F; Ex parte F* [(1986) 161 CLR 376 at 388]:

> "In a case where a law fairly answers the description of being a law with respect to two subject matters, one of which is and the other of which is not a subject matter appearing in s 51, it will be valid notwithstanding that there is no independent connection between the two subject matters."

Finally, if a sufficient connection with the head of power does exist, the justice and wisdom of the law, and the degree to which the means it adopts are necessary or desirable, are matters of legislative choice.

In a passage in the joint judgment of the Court in *Nintendo Co Ltd v* [493] *Centronics Systems Pty Ltd* [(1994) 181 CLR 134 at 160] upholding the validity of the *Circuit Layouts Act* 1989 (Cth), the Court attended to the first of these matters, the construction of the terms of s 51(xviii) with the generality admitted by the words used. Their Honours said:

> "The grant of Commonwealth legislative power which sustains the [*Circuit Layouts Act*] is that contained in s 51(xviii) of the Constitution with respect to 'Copyrights, patents of inventions and designs, and trade marks'. It is of the essence of that grant of legislative power that it authorises the making of laws which create, confer, and provide for the enforcement of, intellectual property rights in original compositions, inventions, designs, trade marks and other products of intellectual effort."

In the present case, the plaintiff contends that the final phrase in this passage should not be read so as to treat as sufficient to attract this head of power *any* product of intellectual effort. Those supporting validity contend that the legislation here is valid without such a wide reading of the power. That which constitutes the invention for the Varieties Act is "the origination" of the "new plant variety" (s 5(a)) and for the Breeder's Rights Act it is "the breeding" of the plant variety (s 10(b)). It will be necessary to return to these submissions.

What is of immediate significance for present purposes is the reference in *Nintendo* by their Honours to *R v Brislan; Ex parte Williams* [(1935) 54 CLR 262] and *Jones v Commonwealth (No 2)* [(1965) 112 CLR 206]. Those authorities dealt with the inherent scope for expansion of the application of the power with respect to postal, telegraphic, telephonic "and other like services" in s 51(v) of the Constitution. This serves to emphasise a point of significance in the present case. Later developments in scientific methods for the provision of telegraphic and telephonic services were contemplated by s 51(v). Likewise, it would be expected that what might answer the description of an invention for the purpose of s 51(xviii) would change to reflect developments in technology.

Consistently with the general principles which we have identified above, an appropriate approach to the interpretation of s 51(xviii) is that appearing in what was then the dissenting judgment of Higgins J in *Attorney-General (NSW) v Brewery Employés Union of NSW* (the *Union Label Case*) [(1908) 6 CLR 469]. Higgins J observed that trade marks were "artificial products of society" [6 CLR at 611]. Further, whilst "we are to ascertain the meaning of 'trade marks' as in 1900", trade marks usage in 1900 "gives us the central type; it does not give us the circumference of the power" [6 CLR at 610] with respect to trade marks provided **[494]** for by s 51(xviii). The centre of the thing named – trade marks – was to be taken with the meaning as in 1900 to find the circumference of the power. However, it would be "a mistake to treat the centre as the radius".

Higgins J continued [6 CLR at 611-12]:

"Power to make laws as to any class of rights involves a power to alter those rights, to define those rights, to limit those rights, to extend those rights, and to extend the class of those who may enjoy those rights. In the same clause of s 51, power is given to make laws with respect to 'copyrights' (rights of multiplying copies of books, &c); with respect to 'patents' (rights to make or sell inventions); and with respect to 'trade marks' (rights to use marks for the purposes of trade). The power to make laws 'with respect to' these rights, involves a power to declare what shall be the subject of such rights. In the second place, although we are to interpret the words of the Constitution on the same principles of interpretation as we apply to any ordinary law, these very principles of interpretation compel us to take into account the nature and scope of the Act that we are interpreting – to remember that *it is a Constitution, a mechanism under which laws are to be made, and not a mere Act which declares what the law is to be.*" (Original emphasis.)

His Honour went on to deal, as an instance of the application of these principles, with the decision of the United States Supreme Court in *Re Klein* [42 US (1 Howard) 277 (1843)]. Higgins J said of that case [6 CLR at 610]:

"At the making of the United States Constitution, the word 'bankruptcy' had the original English meaning of an adverse proceeding by a creditor against a fraudulent debtor. This was the meaning from the beginning (34 & 35 Hen VIII c 4), and at the time of the American Constitution. Yet it was held that Congress, under its power 'to establish uniform laws on the subject of bankruptcies throughout the United States', had power to make a law for the voluntary sequestration of their estates by debtors – power to allow a voluntary bankruptcy at the instance and for the benefit of the debtor. It was also held that the Act was valid, although the word 'bankruptcy' was properly applicable only to traders. In short, Congress had the same power to widen the scope of bankruptcy law **[495]** as the English Parliament possessed, and as it in fact exercised after the American Revolution."

Similar reasoning, with respect to the bankruptcy power (s 51(xvii)) is found in the judgment of Gibbs CJ in *Storey v Lane* [(1981) 147 CLR 549 at 557-8]. Gibbs CJ said:

"It may be accepted that in 1901, both in England and Australia, an insolvent debtor might still have been imprisoned under an order of a punitive kind, ie an order made as a punishment rather than as a means of execution, and that there was no power in courts of bankruptcy to grant relief in such a case. But the provisions of laws made under s 51(xvii) were not intended to be stereotyped so as to confine the power of the Parliament to the legislative provisions existing in 1901 as to bankruptcy and insolvency. If the powers of the courts of bankruptcy to relieve debtors against imprisonment imposed as a consequence of the failure to pay their debts was inadequate in 1901, the Parliament had power to extend them. A law which empowers a court of bankruptcy to order the release from prison of a debtor against whom a bankruptcy petition has been presented, and who is imprisoned because of his failure to pay a provable debt or a penalty payable in consequence of the non-payment of a provable debt, or because of his non-compliance with an order to pay a provable debt, is a law with respect to bankruptcy."

The judgment of the Court in *Nintendo* and those of Higgins J and Gibbs CJ, delivered across the lifespan of the Court, exemplify the first of the general principles of constitutional interpretation to which reference has been made. They reflect what the foundation members of the Court had intended by their adoption in *Baxter v Commissioners of Taxation (NSW)* [(1907) 4 CLR 1087 at 1105] of a passage of the judgment of Story J delivering the opinion of the Court in *Martin v*

Hunter's Lessee [14 US (1 Wheat) 304 (1816) at 326]. In that well-known statement with respect to the interpretation of the United States Constitution, Story J had stressed that the legislative powers of the Congress were expressed "in general terms", so as "to provide [not] merely for the exigencies of a few years, but ... to endure through a long lapse of ages, the events of which were locked up in the inscrutable purposes of Providence".

These words do not suggest ... any notion that the boundaries of the power conferred by s 51(xviii) are to be ascertained solely by identifying what in 1900 would have been treated as a copyright, patent, design or **[496]** trade mark. No doubt some submissions by the plaintiff would fail even upon the application of so limited a criterion. However, other submissions ... fail because they give insufficient allowance for the dynamism which, even in 1900, was inherent in any understanding of the terms used in s 51(xviii).

The statement of "**[492]** general principles" in *Grain Pool* has repeatedly been relied on as authoritative in recent judgments. For example, in *Re Maritime Union of Australia; Ex parte CSL Pacific Inc* (2003) 214 CLR 397 in the context of s 51(i), the trade and commerce power, *Grain Pool* was treated as authority for its second principle (the decisive importance of identifying "the rights, powers, liabilities, duties and privileges" that the challenged legislation creates) and also for the principle "**[414]** that, where a connection exists between the law in question and the head of power which is not insubstantial, tenuous or distant, that connection is not displaced by the lack of some further or additional connection".

These cases demonstrate that, of the differing approaches to characterisation in the *Bank Nationalisation Case*, the one which has remained most influential is that of Dixon J. What he said in that case had two distinct aspects. First, he insisted that "banking" as a subject-matter of legislative power must be understood in a broad and general way, avoiding artificial definitional limitations. (Note that he, too, quoted approvingly from the judgment of Higgins J in *Union Label*.) Secondly, he insisted that within the area of subject-matter thus broadly defined, the kind of law that the Commonwealth can make is not restricted at all; within each granted area of subject-matter, legislative power is plenary.

However, this second proposition requires some qualification. In some instances, the words of one power may fetter the scope of another power. The normal result flowing from the *Engineers' Case* is that this kind of cross-reference between powers does *not* occur: each head of power must be construed independently, so that one grant of power cannot be used to "read down" another. Thus, a broad reading of the Commonwealth's "external affairs" power in s 51(xxix) of the Constitution is not refuted by the fact that such a reading entirely swallows up other grants of power, such as s 51(xxx), so as to render them otiose (see *New South Wales v Commonwealth (Seas and Submerged Lands Case)* (1975) 135 CLR 337 at 471, 497). Again, in *Pidoto v Victoria* (1943) 68 CLR 87, the High Court held that the limited ambit of s 51(xxxv) (which gives power to provide for the regulation of industrial relations, but only through "conciliation and arbitration") could not be used to inhibit attempts to regulate industrial relations on the basis of some other power (in that case the defence power, s 51(vi)). The *Pidoto* case arose when the Commonwealth used its wartime defence power to restrict the rights of workers, and expand the powers of the Commonwealth Court of Conciliation and Arbitration, by means of a series of *National Security (Industrial Peace) Regulations* (Cth).

Pidoto v Victoria
(1943) 68 CLR 87

Latham CJ: [101] The first objection to the Regulations submitted by the State of Victoria is based upon s 51(xxxv) of the Constitution, which confers upon the Commonwealth Parliament power to make laws with respect to "conciliation and arbitration for the prevention and settlement of industrial disputes extending beyond the limits of any one State." It is contended that this provision implies a negative – that it means, not only that the Commonwealth Parliament shall have power to legislate in relation to the industrial disputes there defined and in the manner there prescribed, but also that the Commonwealth Parliament shall not have power to deal with any other industrial matter or with any industrial dispute in any other manner. In my opinion this argument cannot be supported. Section 51(xxxv) is a positive provision conferring a specific power. The particular terms in which this power is conferred are not, in my opinion, so expressed as to be capable of being so construed as to impose a limitation upon other powers positively conferred. Further, if s 51(xxxv) were construed so as to prevent the Parliament from dealing with industrial matters except under that specific provision, similar reasoning would lead to the conclusion that the Commonwealth Parliament could not (under *any* legislative power) provide for the use of conciliation and arbitration in relation to any other matter than inter-State industrial disputes. It must, I think, be conceded, for example, that the Commonwealth Parliament can, in legislating with respect to the public service of the Commonwealth (Constitution, s 52(ii)), provide for conciliation and arbitration in relation to matters such as wages, conditions and hours, whether or not any dispute about those matters is industrial, and whether or not it extends beyond the limits of any one State. In my opinion the objection to the *Industrial Peace Regulations* based upon s 51(xxxv) of the Constitution must be rejected, because it finds no support in the words of this provision for the implied prohibition suggested.

However, this principle – that one grant of power cannot be used to "read down" another – may not apply "**[24]** where the wording of a particular power expressly extracts from or restricts what otherwise might be included within it" (Leslie Zines, *The High Court and the Constitution* (Butterworths, 4th ed 1997)). In short, we have a primary rule that each head of power should be construed independently according to its natural meaning, so that one head of power cannot be used to limit the scope of another; but we also have a secondary rule that sometimes, by way of exception to the primary rule, the restrictions expressed in one head of power may operate to restrict the scope of other heads of power as well.

An example is s 51(xiii), which authorises legislation with respect to "Banking, other than State banking". In *Bourke v State Bank of New South Wales* (1990) 170 CLR 276 it was held that the words "other than State banking" are a limit not only on the "banking" power, but also on other heads of power such as the "corporations" power, s 51(xx). This meant that if a law is enacted in reliance on some head of power other than s 51(xiii), it can validly operate on State banking so long as it cannot be characterised as "**[288]** a law with respect to banking"; but once it *can* be characterised as a law with respect to banking, it must observe the limits which s 51(xiii) imposes on such a law: that is, it must not "touch or concern State banking, except to the extent that any interference with State banking is so incidental as not to affect the character of the law as **[289]** one with respect to banking other than State banking".

The test suggested by Leslie Zines may not always be easy to apply. On that test the limitation in s 51(xiii) can restrict the use of other heads of power because it is expressed as an exception: the words "other than" have the effect of carving the topic of "State banking" out of what would otherwise be a general power with respect to banking. The refusal in *Pidoto v Victoria* to restrict other grants of power by reference to the words of s 51(xxxv) would be appropriate because those words are not expressed by way of exception, but by way of definitional circumscription of an affirmative grant. Yet the difference between these two modes of expression may be more apparent than real. For example, the words of s 51(i) express an affirmative grant of power, with respect to "[t]rade and commerce with other countries, and among the States"; yet perhaps the major inference judicially drawn from those words has been an implied exclusion of any power with respect to intrastate trade.

Another example that initially evoked differing judicial reactions is s 51(xxii), giving power with respect to "[d]ivorce and matrimonial causes; and *in relation thereto*, parental rights, and the custody and guardianship of infants" (emphasis added). The exclusion of any other issues relating to custody and parental rights is merely inferential from the words of the affirmative grant, yet in *Russell v Russell* (1976) 134 CLR 495 Barwick CJ and Gibbs J held that, because such issues were excluded from the scope of s 51(xxii), they must also be excluded from the scope of s 51(xxi), which confers power to make laws with respect to "marriage". Stephen, Mason and Jacobs JJ took the contrary view, which is now regarded as correct. As Mason J stated: "**[465]** In the interpretation of the Constitution it is a mistake to assume too readily that the presence of a particular head of power reflects an assumption on the part of the framers that the subject matter was not included in another head of power. A competing hypothesis of at least equal strength is that the former head of power was expressed as it was because doubts were entertained as to the scope of the latter".

4. Subject-Matter and Purpose

The approach to characterisation that is nowadays generally accepted is said to be based on the ascertainment of a *sufficient connection* between the law and a head of power. This suggests that the legislative purpose of the law is no business of the court. As Latham CJ put it in the *Bank Nationalisation Case*, "[186] the motives of Parliament, and, as a general rule, the objects which a Parliament seeks to achieve, are not relevant to questions of constitutional validity". When the principles laid down in *R v Burah* (1878) 3 App Cas 889 were applied to the grants of legislative power in s 51 of the Constitution, the result, according to the *Engineers' Case* (1920) 28 CLR 129, was to rule out any possibility of implied limitations on Commonwealth law-making power – in part because it was "[151] inappropriate" for the courts "to determine political necessities": any "extravagant" use of power was "a matter to be guarded against by the constituencies and not by the Courts". Consistently with that theme, the Court has repeatedly insisted that the process of characterisation does not involve political judgments or subjective evaluations, but can be performed objectively on strict legalistic principles.

Australian National Airways Pty Ltd v Commonwealth (*ANA Case*)
(1945) 71 CLR 29

Rich J: [70] Some of the arguments addressed to the Court in the cases now before us lead me to preface my reasons by observations which I should otherwise have thought so trite as to be superfluous ... Now, it cannot be too clearly understood that this Court is not in the smallest degree concerned to consider whether such a project is politically, economically, or socially desirable or undesirable. It is concerned only with the questions whether it is within the constitutional powers of the Commonwealth Parliament to pass an Act, or for the regulation-making authority to make a regulation, of the type which has been called in question, and if so whether the Act or regulation is, in whole or part, a valid exercise of power ... [O]ur task is purely legal. It is to examine those provisions of the Constitution which confer legislative power upon the Commonwealth Parliament and to see whether the legislation which has been challenged is wholly, or if not wholly to some extent, within one or more of the powers which the framers of the Constitution thought fit to confer upon it.

Such statements have been repeated many times. They would seem to leave little foothold for the latter-day suggestion (considered in §8 below) that the validity of a statute might depend upon its passing a test of "proportionality": that is, that the statute must be seen to be "appropriate" or "adapted" to its legislative purpose. The question of what is "appropriate" or "[well] adapted" would be a question which no court could appropriately entertain.

However, even if that view be accepted, the relevance of "purpose" to characterisation cannot be excluded altogether. For one thing, it is clearly relevant in the process of statutory construction whereby the legal scope and operation of a law is determined as a precursor to the process of characterisation. There is a long tradition of statutory interpretation, going back to *Heydon's Case* (1584) 3 Co Rep 7a, 76 ER 637, that suggests that the purpose of a statute is an essential guide to its interpretation. Similarly, s 15AA(1) of the *Acts Interpretation Act 1901* (Cth) provides: "In the interpretation of a provision of an Act, a construction that would promote the purpose or object underlying the Act (whether that purpose or object is expressly stated in the Act or not) shall be preferred to a construction that would not promote that purpose or object".

Moreover, there are other complications. The exclusion of any reference to legislative "purpose" is most persuasive in those cases where the challenged law is said to lie at the "core" of the constitutional grant of power. So long as the subject-matter of a law is itself clearly located within the ambit of the constitutional grant of power, the way that Parliament deals with that subject-matter, and its purpose in doing so, are judicially irrelevant. In terms of subject-matter, the proffered law "squares with" the grant of power and no other question arises. Indeed, what judges find attractive about the "subject-matter" approach may be that the questions involved in identifying a "subject-matter", and then determining whether an enactment relates to that "subject-matter", appear to be questions that can be answered impartially and objectively without entering into the political value-judgments that questions of legislative "purpose", and "appropriateness" to that "purpose", apparently entail.

However, in cases where a law is not "on" the very subject-matter of the constitutional grant, so that its validity must depend on finding a "sufficient connection", that connection will frequently be established by reference to the *purpose* of the law. Moreover, while most heads of power in s 51 can plausibly be conceived of as delineating a "subject-matter", there are some that the Court has understood as involving a legislative "purpose". Such purposive powers include the "defence" power (s 51(vi)); and also the "external affairs" power (s 51(xxix)) insofar as it enables the Commonwealth to implement international treaties and conventions. For these "purposive" powers, it is nowadays generally acknowledged that a different approach to the task of characterisation is required, depending on what is commonly described as a test of "proportionality" (see §8 below). The contrast between these "purposive" powers and "subject matter" powers rests primarily on the passage from the judgment of Dixon J in *Stenhouse v Coleman* (1944) 69 CLR 457 to which the joint judgment in *Grain Pool* referred.

Stenhouse v Coleman
(1944) 69 CLR 457

Dixon J: [471] [U]nlike most other powers conferred by s 51 of the Constitution, [the defence power] involves the notion of purpose or object. In most of the paragraphs of s 51 the subject of the power is described either by reference to a class of legal, commercial, economic or social transaction or activity (as trade and commerce, banking, marriage), or by specifying some class of public service (as postal installations, lighthouses), or undertaking or operation (as railway construction with the consent of a State), or by naming a recognized category of legislation (as taxation, bankruptcy). In such cases it is usual, when the validity of legislation is in question, to consider whether the legislation operates upon or affects the subject matter, or in the last case answers the description, and to disregard purpose or object. An example will be found in *Victorian Stevedoring and General Contracting Co Pty Ltd v Dignan* [(1931) 46 CLR 73 at 103]. But "a law with respect to the defence of the Commonwealth" is an expression which seems rather to treat defence or war as the purpose to which the legislation must be addressed. This peculiarity in the power has caused no departure from the practice that excludes from investigation the actual extrinsic motives and intentions of legislative authorities. But, however it may be expressed, whether by the words – "scope", "object", "pith", "substance", "effect" or "operation", the connection of the regulation with defence can scarcely be other than purposive, if it is within the power. No doubt it is possible that the "purpose" here may be another example of what Lord *Sumner* described as "one of those so-called intentions which the law imputes; it is the legal construction put on something done in fact" (*Blott's Case* [[1921] 2 AC 171 at 218]). For apparently the purpose must be collected from the instrument in question, the facts to which it applies and the circumstances which called it forth.

The examples given of "subject matter" powers were those described "**[471]** by reference to a class of legal, commercial, economic or social transaction or activity (as trade and commerce, banking, marriage), or by specifying some class of public service (as postal installations, lighthouses), or undertaking or operation (as railway construction with the consent of a State), or by naming a recognized category of legislation (as taxation, bankruptcy)". Yet none of these is objectively given in a way that can meaningfully be defined or identified independently of purposive human activity. On the contrary, each of them refers to a socially constructed institution that can only be understood by reference to the human purposes involved.

When Higgins J observed in the *Union Label Case* (1908) 6 CLR 469 that trade marks were "**[611]** artificial products of society", he contrasted this with the fixed denotation of a word like "cattle": "Cattle are concrete, physical objects, and the boundaries of the class are fixed by external nature". His point was that a class like "cattle" was closed, whereas a class composed of "artificial products of society" might be extended. (Of course, developments in the science of genetic modification have made the contrast in this respect between "cattle" and "trade marks" less clear than Higgins J supposed.) In any event, what for our purposes is important about "artificial products of society" – including all of the matters listed by Dixon J in *Stenhouse v Coleman* – is not merely that the content of a conception like "trade marks" or "bankruptcy" may change, but that the enterprise or institution referred to can only be understood in purposive terms. The "purposes" involved are those of the individual persons who avail themselves of the relevant institutional forms, or perhaps the "purposes" of a human society in developing such institutional forms. What is different about a "purposive power" such as "defence" is only that the purpose is coextensive with the power itself; that is, what the Commonwealth is authorised to do is to pursue the specified purpose, and its legislation will be valid if it can reasonably be considered conducive to that purpose.

In short, the distinction between "purposive" powers and "subject matter" powers is blurred. For example, with the development of new electronic and telecommunications technologies, the old-fashioned lighthouse has become increasingly obsolete, as its function of directing shipping is taken over by new navigational aids. The new technology has the same purpose as a lighthouse, but in no way resembles a lighthouse. Would the regulation of such technologies fall within s 51(vii) of the Constitution ("Lighthouses, lightships, beacons and buoys")? Or would it not?

5. Dual Characterisation

Attempts at characterisation sometimes tend to assume that each statute must possess only one subject-matter (its "pith and substance"). For example, because the law in *R v Barger* (1908) 6 CLR 41 was a law to regulate the manufacture of agricultural implements, it was said to follow that it could not also be a law with respect to taxation (see the extract in Chapter 7, §3). There are signs of this approach in the judgment of Latham CJ in *Melbourne Corporation v Commonwealth* (1947) 74 CLR 31 and in that of Barwick CJ in *Victoria v Commonwealth* (*Payroll Tax Case*) (1971) 122 CLR 353 (see the extracts in Chapter 25, §2(a)). However, this rigid either/or approach has now been discredited.

The issue in *Fairfax v Federal Commissioner of Taxation* (1965) 114 CLR 1 was whether s 11 of the *Income Tax and Social Services Contribution Assessment Act 1961* (Cth) was validly enacted under the Commonwealth's taxation power in s 51(ii) of the Constitution. Section 11 inserted a new Div 9B into Pt III of the *Income Tax and Social Services Contribution Assessment Act 1936* (Cth). Division 9B provided for the assessment of income taxation and could be used to induce superannuation funds to invest in Commonwealth bonds by exempting them from income tax if they did so and by subjecting them to a special rate of tax if they did not. The Court held that s 11 was valid under s 51(ii). The argument that the provisions could be characterised as a law with respect to "taxation" was presented by Anthony Mason QC as Solicitor-General for the Commonwealth.

Fairfax v Federal Commissioner of Taxation
(1965) 114 CLR 1

Mason QC (in argument): [3] *R v Barger* [(1908) 6 CLR 41] does not establish any limitation upon the taxation power. The question always is whether the law in question is a law with respect to taxation. To determine this question it is necessary to characterize the law by having regard to its terms, not by going behind the terms to seek the motive of the legislature or by having regard to indirect consequences of the law. Regard is had to the terms of the law to ascertain its direct legal operation. If a law is characterized as one with respect to a head of Commonwealth power, in the instant case taxation, it does not matter that it also affects a matter not included in the heads of Commonwealth power. The earlier characterization is decisive of the question. The only operation which Act No 17 of 1961 has upon the rights of any person is in the matter of taxation. That the law is properly characterized as one in respect of taxation is seen not only upon an examination of the rights and liabilities which it directly affects, but also upon an examination of the character of the law into which it is introduced ... The provisions of Act No 17 of 1961 operate not directly as a regulation of investment by trustees of superannuation funds, but operate directly in relation to taxation rights and liabilities producing a result in relation to investment by trustees of such funds. It may be that the statute operates to encourage trustees to a course of conduct which will enable them to take advantage of the exemption, but it does so by reason of encouragement, not of command or prohibition. To hold that the statute was not a law with respect to taxation one would have to find some positive command to or a prohibition not to invest in a certain way. The present law cannot be characterized as one imposing a penalty, and not as one dealing with taxation.

There were two main strands to this argument. The first was that, so long as a law can fairly be characterised as being a law "with respect to" a subject-matter that is within Commonwealth power, it does not matter that it might also be characterised as bearing upon some other subject-matter that is not within power. Only the first characterisation is relevant. The second strand adopted what Latham CJ said in the *Bank Nationalisation Case*: namely, that in characterising a law the focus should be on its direct legal operation, as ascertained from its text and from the legal rights and liabilities affected thereby. This second strand, nowadays regularly and ritualistically invoked in High Court judgments, was also much in vogue in the 1950s and 1960s – especially in the judgments of Kitto J, who delivered the leading judgment in *Fairfax*.

Kitto J: [6] The argument for invalidity not unnaturally began with the proposition that the question to be decided is a question of substance and not of mere form; but the danger quickly became evident that the proposition may be misunderstood as inviting a speculative inquiry as to which of the topics touched by the **[7]** legislation seems most likely to have been the main preoccupation of those who enacted it. Such an inquiry has nothing to do with the question of constitutional validity under s 51 of the Constitution. Under that section the question is always one of subject matter, to be determined by reference solely to the operation which the enactment has if it be valid, that is to say by reference to the nature of the rights, duties, powers and privileges which it changes, regulates or abolishes; it is a question as to the true nature and character of the legislation: is it in its real substance a law upon, "with respect to", one or more of the enumerated subjects, or is there no more in it in relation to any of those subjects than an interference so incidental as not in truth to affect its character? ...

The need to distinguish between form and substance appears from what has just been said. The possibility has to be recognized, as it was in the United States as long ago as *McCulloch v Maryland* [17 US (4 Wheat) 316 at 423 (1819)], that under the guise of exercising one or more of the powers of the Parliament legislation may in truth endeavour only to accomplish objects beyond those powers ... Accordingly the task of characterizing laws according to subject matter must be performed with care lest mere words mislead. The Court, as Higgins J said in *R v Barger* [6 CLR at 118] "is not to be bound by the name which Parliament has chosen to give the Act" – one may add, or has chosen to give anything else – "but is to consider what the Act is in substance – what it does, what it commands or prescribes". The appellant's argument in its final form accepted this as its real starting point and proceeded to say that s 11, though it is couched in terms of taxation and wears the badge of a tax law prominently upon it, really operates to expose trustees of superannuation funds to a liability which it miscalls a tax, a liability which in truth is a penalty or sanction for a failure to pursue a prescribed course of conduct by such trustees with respect to the investment of moneys. For this reason, it was said, s 11 is in substance not a law upon taxation but only a law upon the subject of the investment of such moneys. Thus the argument endeavours to lift **[8]** the section out of its formal surroundings in an Income Tax Assessment Act, to treat the use it makes of the terminology and machinery of taxation legislation as a veil to be removed, and to exhibit it as in truth but an attempt to regulate, with sanctions, the investment of superannuation fund moneys ...

[10] In Australia ... the distribution of powers has greatly influenced decision, particularly in the majority judgment in *R v Barger*, upon which the appellants' argument in the present case is largely founded. While affirming that in deciding whether a law is supported by the taxation power it is irrelevant [11] to inquire into the ultimate indirect consequences of the operation of the law – for no conclusion can be built upon them save as to the motives of the legislators – the majority of the Court accepted the view that it is legitimate to draw an inference from what appears on the face of the law as to whether the substantial purpose is, on the one hand, to raise revenue or, on the other hand, to regulate the conduct of persons by providing for a sanction in the form of a pecuniary impost to be incurred by departure from a specified course. Griffith CJ and Barton and O'Connor JJ treated the task of choosing the correct inference as one to be performed against a background provided by the doctrine, to which they were adherents, that the Constitution was to be interpreted as intending to reserve to the States all such powers as were not expressly conferred upon the Commonwealth. From this doctrine they took as the background of their thinking in *Barger's Case* the proposition that "taxation" in s 51(ii) of the Constitution has a special meaning, that it refers only to taxation not imposed as a means of regulating the domestic affairs of the States. Confronted by an Act which purported to provide for a duty of excise to be paid upon manufactured goods if certain conditions of employment in the course of manufacture were not observed, their Honours saw on the face of it an intention to use the taxation power as a mere means of regulating conditions of employment, a matter "reserved", as they considered, to the States; and they concluded that the end aimed at was the substance, the taxing means employed was mere form, and that the law was therefore outside the true limits of the power.

In so far as the judgment insisted upon testing the validity of the law by reference to its substantial operation, it has been approved by the Privy Council in *WR Moran Pty Ltd v Deputy Commissioner of Taxation* [[1940] AC 838 at 849] and neither the dissenting members of the Court in *Barger's Case* nor any Judge since has wished to disagree. But it is by no means a settled doctrine that a law which purports to provide for a tax upon behaviour is in substance not a law with respect to taxation if it exhibits on its face a purpose of suppressing or discouraging the behaviour and is to be explained more convincingly as a means to that end than as a means to provide the Government with revenue. Indeed, to espouse such a doctrine would be to fall into the error already mentioned, of confusing the distinction between form and substance with the distinction between the major and the minor [12] importance which a reading of the Act suggests that those who passed it may have attributed to the various aspects of its operation. In my opinion the judgment of the majority in *Barger's Case* provides no satisfactory guide in the case before us, partly because the doctrine of the reserved powers of the States, in the wide form in which it was held by their Honours, has long since been exploded (see *Amalgamated Society of Engineers v Adelaide Steamship Co* [(1920) 28 CLR 129 at 154]), but, more fundamentally, because we ought to maintain the principle which may be stated in words taken from the judgment of Clark J in *United States v Sanchez* [340 US 42 at 44 (1950)]: "It is beyond serious question that a tax does not cease to be valid merely because it regulates, discourages, or even definitely deters the activities taxed ... The principle applies even though the revenue obtained is obviously negligible, *Sonzinsky v United States* [300 US 506 at 513-14 (1937)] or the revenue purpose of the tax may be secondary, *J W Hampton & Co v United States* [276 US 394 (1928)]. Nor does a tax statute necessarily fall because it touches on activities which Congress might not otherwise regulate" ...

[13] In the result I think that this case should be decided against the appellants upon the broad principle which Sir Owen Dixon stated in *Melbourne Corporation v Commonwealth* [(1947) 74 CLR 31 at 79]: "Speaking generally, once it appears that a federal law has an actual and immediate operation within a field assigned to the Commonwealth as a subject of legislative power, that is enough. It will be held to fall within the power unless some further reason appears for excluding it. That it discloses another purpose and that the purpose lies outside the area of federal power are considerations which will not in such a case suffice to invalidate the law". The operation of s 11 is to replace a total exemption from all income tax with a conditional special liability to income tax on "investment income". The legislative policy is obvious and may be freely acknowledged: it is to

provide trustees of superannuation funds with strong inducement to invest sufficiently in Commonwealth and other public securities. The raising of revenue may be of secondary concern. But the enactment does not prescribe or forbid conduct. Its character is neither fully nor fairly described by saying that it makes trustees of superannuation funds liable to pay for failing to do what the legislature wishes. To adapt the language of Higgins J in *R v Barger*, the substance of the enactment is the obligation which it imposes, and the only obligation imposed is to pay income tax. In substance as in form, therefore, the section is a law with respect to taxation.

Menzies J: [17] Whether or not a law is one with respect to taxation cannot be determined by looking at its economic consequences, however apparent they must have been at the time of its enactment; nor is an enquiry into the motives of the legislature permissible. There may be laws ostensibly imposing tax which, nevertheless, are not laws with respect to taxation. For example, a special prohibitive tax upon the income derived from the sale of heroin or from the growing or treatment of poppies for the production of heroin may not be a law with respect to taxation but rather a law made **[18]** for the suppression of the trade in that drug by imposing penalties described as taxes for participation in it. The reason for denying to such a law the character of a law with respect to taxation would not be either its economic consequences or the motive behind its enactment. It would simply be that its true character is not a law with respect to taxation. The problem is, therefore, to ascertain from the terms of the law impugned its true nature and character.

In this case, there is no reason – apart from the likely consequences upon the investing of the assets of the superannuation fund and the motives imputed to the legislature – for denying to s 11, which relates to exemption from income tax, the character of a law with respect to taxation. The consequences and imputed motives, for the reason which I have given, do not deprive the law of its character as such a law.

In *State Chamber of Commerce and Industry v Commonwealth* (*Second Fringe Benefits Tax Case*) (1987) 163 CLR 329 at 353-4, Mason CJ, Wilson, Dawson, Toohey and Gaudron JJ disapproved of the dictum of Menzies J as to the "**[18]** true character" of a law directed to the suppression of heroin. They pointed out that it was inconsistent with the dual characterisation approach developed in other cases, and indeed with that developed by Kitto J in *Fairfax*.

Fairfax was followed in *Herald & Weekly Times Ltd v Commonwealth* (1966) 115 CLR 418. The relevant grant of legislative power was s 51(v) of the Constitution, as extended to radio by *R v Brislan; Ex parte Williams* (1935) 54 CLR 262 and to television by *Jones v Commonwealth (No 2)* (1965) 112 CLR 206 (see Chapter 8, §5).

Grants of television licences on conditions were authorised by s 81 of the *Broadcasting and Television Act 1942* (Cth). In 1965, the Act was amended to set limits on the ownership or control of commercial television stations. By s 92E, a television licence could not be granted to a company if the grant would result in a contravention of ss 92 or 92C. By s 92, no person could have a "prescribed interest", that is, more than a 5 per cent shareholding, in more than two television licences, or in more than one in any capital city. By s 92C, no person could be a director of two or more companies together controlling three or more licences. Attached to each commercial television licence was a condition that these prohibitions not be infringed. It was argued that both the subject-matter of the conditions attaching to the licences and the prohibitions on "prescribed interests" were beyond the scope of s 51(v).

The case was argued in two stages. On behalf of the media proprietors, Keith Aickin QC initially challenged the validity of the *conditions* attached to the television licences. He argued that the subject-matter of the conditions was not within power. Anthony Mason QC, again appearing as Solicitor-General for the Commonwealth, rebutted that argument.

Herald & Weekly Times Ltd v Commonwealth
(1966) 115 CLR 418

Mason QC (in argument): [430] It was established by *R v Brislan; Ex parte Williams* [(1935) 54 CLR 262] and *Jones v Commonwealth (No 2)* [(1965) 112 CLR 206] that Parliament can legislate on the subject of the selection of the operator of a television station. That proposition is based on the fact that the selection of the operator is part of the subject with respect to which the power is conferred. It follows that Parliament can legislate so as to prescribe characteristics for the selection of the operator. There is no relevant limit on the characteristics which Parliament may prescribe. The contrary argument must proceed on the footing that unless the criteria are shown to be part of or have a relevant connexion with the subject-matter the law ceases to be a law on the subject-matter because of the character of the criterion. We contend that if the selection of the operator is part of the subject-matter and a law on the selection of the operator is within power a law does not cease to be within power because criteria are selected which are unrelated to the subject-matter.

The claim made by Mason QC is not quite unlimited: "**[430]** There is no *relevant* limit on the characteristics which Parliament may prescribe" (emphasis added). The implication seems to be that there may be some limits to the conditions that Parliament can impose on a licensing scheme, but that none was relevant to the facts of this case.

Faced with this attack on the argument made by Aickin QC, Hibbert Newton QC switched his argument for the plaintiffs to a different issue. He argued that the *prohibitions* on "prescribed interests", insofar as they directly regulated or prohibited conduct, were not within power. The Court rejected both arguments. Again, the leading judgment was that of Kitto J.

Kitto J: [433] The provisions now in question are superimposed upon this licensing system. At one stage of the plaintiffs' argument it was contended, in regard to such of the provisions now under attack as subject a licence to conditions, or as prescribe criteria for the eligibility of a company to receive a licence, that the question whether they are valid as having the character of laws with respect to television services depends wholly upon the nature of the conditions or criteria. To uphold this contention would be to overlook the fact that any provision which operates to create or delimit a power in given circumstances to relax in favour of a television station the general prohibition upon television transmission has, of necessity, by reason of the very fact that it has that operation, the character of a law with respect to television services. It is not necessary, in order that a provision so operating shall be within the constitutional power, that the persons, things, situations or events referred to in it shall themselves possess characteristics which supply a further link with the subject of television services …

[434] The main attack, however, is directed against so much of Div 3 as, if valid, creates offences consisting of certain kinds of conduct on the part of persons who are not the holders of television licences. Plainly enough, the attack must succeed unless the conduct which is thus made unlawful is so relevant to the subject of television services that a law forbidding it is a law with respect to that subject …

[436] It is unnecessary here to describe the challenged provisions in greater detail. One need only read them to agree with the plaintiffs that they cast a net so wide as to cover many a concrete case that may be imagined, where it is most unlikely that the person concerned would find himself in a position to exercise any form or degree of control, or even of influence, in relation to any television licence or television station. But it does not follow that for this reason they are beyond power, unless the assumption be accepted which the plaintiffs' argument in truth made, that a law cannot be with respect to television services unless there can be seen, in every kind of case that it covers, some likelihood of there being an opportunity of influence or control in respect of a television service. The assumption, in my opinion, unduly limits the notion of substantial connexion upon which the Constitution insists when it uses the expression "with respect to". Undoubtedly it is right to scrutinize minutely the effect of a challenged law in all the variety of cases to which it applies according to its terms; but when that has been done the broader inquiry remains: what, then, is the law really doing by the operation which the scrutiny reveals that it has? For it is the answer to that question that shows whether the law is really one "with respect to" the relevant subject matter of power. The answer to it here surely is that the offence provisions are setting up a barrier against, not indeed the probability, but the possibility that a person who may be able by reason of any of a number of legal or business relationships, to influence the exercise of the rights conferred by one television licence may be able, by reason of such a relationship, to influence the exercise of the rights conferred by another television licence. If it were correct to say of any of the relationships that in no case could it carry with it a special opportunity to exert such an influence, the relevant provision would no doubt lack the necessary connexion with the subject matter of power. But this cannot be said of any of the relationships which the division describes. Each gives rise to a situation which according to ordinary experience **[437]** may, in some cases at least, support an endeavour to affect the control or management of a television station or its operation under its licence. And, as everyone knows, even the faintest of voices may sometimes carry the day.

Thus the provisions in question operate as part of a legislative plan to insulate the control and management of activities connected with the exercise of a television licence against the possibility of influence by a person who may occupy any of the specified positions of potential influence over like activities in relation to another such licence. It necessarily follows that the provisions are laws upon the subject of television licences and therefore upon the subject of television services.

The plaintiffs contend, in effect, that the situations by reference to which the provisions are made to apply are so arbitrarily selected, and the possibility that any capacity for influence will actually arise or exist by reason of some of them at least is so remote, that the provisions cannot be regarded as in their entirety characterized by a purpose of preserving licences from influences tainted by associations with other licences. It may be conceded that in some of the cases to which they apply, the described situations will often, or even generally, afford no foothold at all for an exertion of influence. Yet it is impossible, in my opinion, to avoid the conclusion, even upon consideration of the most extreme illustrations of the working of the provisions, that together they form a means, and are enacted as a means, for effectuating a desired end which is within power, namely that of ensuring freedom of competition between television services. How far they should go was a question of degree for the Parliament to decide, and the fact that the Parliament has chosen to go to great lengths – even the fact, if it be so, that for many persons difficulties are created which are out of all proportion to the advantage gained – affords no ground of constitutional attack.

In the first paragraph above, Kitto J rejected the argument that *conditions* attached to a television licence might be invalid because the subject-matter of the conditions was not within power. The answer to that argument was simply that a law for the licensing of television services was necessarily a law "with respect to" those services, and the nature of the conditions attached to the licence did not affect that conclusion. Kitto J then turned to the separate argument attacking the provisions that *prohibited* the holding of "prescribed interests". Initially, he conceded the main thrust of this argument: the prohibited conduct must itself be "**[434]** *so relevant to* the subject of television services that a law forbidding it is a law *with respect to* that subject" (emphasis added). However, he went on to argue that this test had been satisfied. At this stage the focus of his reasoning shifted from a question of subject-matter to one of purpose – namely, "**[437]** that of ensuring freedom of competition between television services". That purpose was within power because it relates to the subject-matter of television services. The remaining question was how far the constitutional power extended to the particular means of pursuing that purpose. In his final paragraph, Kitto J seems to be saying that, so long as the *end* or *purpose* is within power, the choice of *means* to that end is entirely a matter for Parliament.

Together, *Fairfax* and *Herald & Weekly Times* established that, in characterising a law, the High Court is not overtly concerned with the policy that the law embodies, but only with whether it can fairly be described as a law "with respect to" a specified subject-matter. So long as a law can be so described, it does not matter that it might also be described by some other characterisation that might cast doubt upon its validity.

That approach was reinforced and applied in *Murphyores Incorporated Pty Ltd v Commonwealth* (1976) 136 CLR 1, this time in the context of s 51(i). The *Customs Act 1901* (Cth) gave power under s 112 to make regulations prohibiting exports. The *Customs (Prohibited Exports) Regulations* (Cth) (made under s 112, and applying in part to substances gained by the processing or treatment of minerals) provided in reg 9(3): "The exportation from Australia of goods to which this regulation applies is prohibited unless an approval in writing ... issued by the Minister of State for Minerals and Energy ... is produced to the Collector".

The plaintiff companies were engaged in sand mining on Fraser Island in Queensland. Their operations produced zircon and rutile concentrates, for which they sought export approval under reg 9(3). The plaintiffs were informed that no decision on their application would be made until an inquiry had been undertaken under s 11 of the *Environment Protection (Impact of Proposals) Act 1974* (Cth). Under that section, the Minister for the Environment could direct an inquiry into the environmental aspects of any matter referred to in s 5, which declared that the purpose of the Act was to ensure that environmental issues "are fully examined and taken into account" in "the making of, or the participation in the making of, decisions and recommendations" by the Australian Government or on its behalf. The plaintiffs challenged the validity of the Commonwealth enactments. Both reg 9(3) and the *Environment Protection (Impact of Proposals) Act* were held to be valid.

Murphyores Incorporated Pty Ltd v Commonwealth
(1976) 136 CLR 1

Mason J: **[18]** The power conferred by s 51 (i) enables the Parliament to prohibit, regulate and control the importation and exportation of **[19]** goods, matters which lie at the heart of trade and commerce with other countries ...

The power to legislate with respect to trade and commerce with other countries, including as it does power to prohibit and regulate the exportation of goods from Australia, necessarily comprehends the power to select and identify the persons who engage in, and the goods which may become the subject of, that activity ... It is then for Parliament in its wisdom or for the person to whom Parliament delegates the power to decide who may export and what goods may be exported. The means and the criteria by which this choice is to be made are for Parliament to decide. There is nothing in the subject matter of the constitutional power which justifies the implication of any limitation on Parliament's power of selection. It does not follow, for example, that because the subject of the power is trade and commerce, selection of the exporter or of the goods to be exported must be made by reference to considerations of trading policy.

It is enough that the law operates on the topic of trade and commerce with other countries. A law which absolutely or conditionally prohibits exportation of goods is a law that operates on that topic. It is not a law which ceases to deal with that topic because it confers a discretion, unlimited in scope, to permit exportation of particular goods. In this respect it differs from a law whose connexion with the subject matter of power is more remote, when the limits of a statutory discretion may become important in characterizing the law ...

The point here is that by imposing a conditional prohibition on exportation, a prohibition which may be relaxed according to the **[20]** exercise of a discretion, the law is dealing with exportation of goods, a matter at the heart of trade and commerce with other countries. It is not to the point that the selection may be made by reference to criteria having little or no apparent relevance to trade and commerce; it is enough that the law deals with the permitted topic and it does not cease to deal with that topic because factors extraneous to the topic may be taken into account in the relaxation of the prohibition imposed by the law. It is now far too late in the day to say that a law should be characterized by reference to the motives which inspire it or the consequences which flow from it ...

[22] It is one thing to say that the trade and commerce power does not enable the Commonwealth to regulate and control directly matters standing outside the subject matter of power, such as the environmental aspects of mining in Queensland. It is quite another thing to say that the Commonwealth cannot in the exercise of that power make laws which have a consequential and indirect effect on matters standing outside the power, even by means of prohibiting conditionally engagement in trade and commerce with other countries. It is no objection to the validity of a law otherwise within power that it touches or affects a topic on which the Commonwealth has no power to legislate.

These principles have been applied more recently outside the field of trade and commerce, the most notable example being in *Herald and Weekly Times Ltd v Commonwealth* [(1966) 115 CLR 418] ...

[23] [That case] makes it clear that if an unqualified prohibition against participation in an activity is within constitutional power, a qualified or conditional prohibition is necessarily within power.

R v Barger [(1908) 6 CLR 41], which might have been thought to assist the plaintiffs, can no longer be regarded as having authority. It depended on the now discredited doctrine of reserved powers. The minority who rejected this doctrine had no difficulty in holding the legislation to be valid. The decision of this Court in *Fairfax v Federal Commissioner of Taxation* [(1965) 114 CLR 1], it should now be acknowledged, swept away the last vestigial remnants of *Barger's Case*.

Stephen J: [11] The federal Parliament, having power to legislate with respect to overseas trade and commerce, is legislating concerning a matter at the very heart of that subject matter when it prohibits the exportation of specified classes of goods, and none the less so when its legislation takes the form of a power to make regulations prohibiting all export of particular classes of goods coupled with a dispensing power. Such a regulation remains one within the four corners of the trade and commerce power since its subject matter is the exportation of goods.

In those instances in which the legislative power of the Commonwealth is granted in purposive terms, as in s 51(vi), it is necessary, in determining constitutional validity, to have regard to purpose and this applies no less to administrative acts than to legislation; hence reference, in such cases as *Shrimpton v Commonwealth* [(1945) 69 CLR 613 at 630], to the need to ensure that the stream does not rise above its source. But where the source of power is found in non-purposive subject-matter, as in s 51(i) the same problem does not present itself. Thus once legislation addresses itself to the subject matter of the prohibition of exports, central to the trade and commerce power, a regulation implementing that prohibition will inherently be within subject matter; so also will **[12]** be an administrative decision relaxing, or failing to relax, that prohibition in a particular case; so long as that is the nature of the decision it will be within power and there is no question of the stream rising above its source. The source is trade and commerce with other countries and the stream, of legislation, regulation and administrative decision, flows from it and concerns one and the same subject matter, all within constitutional power.

The administrative decision whether or not to relax a prohibition against the export of goods will necessarily be made in the light of considerations affecting the mind of the administrator; but whatever their nature the consequence will necessarily be expressed in terms of trade and commerce, consisting of the approval or rejection of an application to relax the prohibition on exports. It will therefore fall within constitutional power. The considerations in the light of which the decision is made may not themselves relate to matters of trade and commerce but that will not deprive the decision which they induce of its inherent constitutionality for the decision will be directly on the subject matter of exportation and the considerations actuating that decision will not detract from the character which its subject matter confers upon it.

The principle of dual characterisation developed in *Fairfax, Herald & Weekly Times* and *Murphyores* was further developed by Stephen J in *Actors and Announcers Equity Association v Fontana Films Pty Ltd* (1982) 150 CLR 169 (see the extract in Chapter 17, §3). Indeed, he made it clear that the problem is one of multiple characterisations, since "**[192]** a law may possess a number of quite disparate characters". Among these it is an error to search for one uniquely "true" character of the law. Moreover, it is equally an error to search for its "predominant" character. "**[194]** It will be enough if the law fairly answers the description of a law 'with respect to' one given subject matter appearing in s 51, regardless of whether it may equally be described as a law with respect to other subject matters", and regardless of whether those other descriptions would be within power or not. This approach is now frequently applied by the High Court, and significantly broadens the scope of federal legislative power (see, for example, *Northern Suburbs General Cemetery Reserve Trust v Commonwealth* (1993) 176 CLR 555 in Chapter 23, §1(a)).

6. The Trade and Commerce Power

Even apart from the latitude afforded by the principle of "dual characterisation", the potential reach of s 51(i) ("Trade and commerce with other countries, and among the States") is obviously very broad. The words "trade" and "commerce" also occur in s 92 of the Constitution, which speaks of "trade, commerce, and intercourse". There too the words have been broadly construed.

W & A McArthur Ltd v Queensland
(1920) 28 CLR 530

Knox CJ, Isaacs and Starke JJ: [546] The terms "trade, commerce and intercourse" are not terms of art. They are expressions of fact, they are terms of common knowledge, as well known to laymen as to lawyers, and better understood in detail by traders and commercial men than by Judges. But as Judges we are taken to know and do in fact in this instance know the general import of the words. The particular instances that may fall within the ambit of the expression depend upon the varying phases and development of trade, commerce and intercourse itself ... "Trade and commerce" between different countries – we leave out for the present the word "intercourse" – has never been confined to the mere act of transportation [547] of merchandise over the frontier. That the words include that act is, of course, a truism. But that they go far beyond it is a fact quite as undoubted. All the commercial arrangements of which transportation is the direct and necessary result form part of "trade and commerce." The mutual communings, the negotiations, verbal and by correspondence, the bargain, the transport and the delivery are all, but not exclusively, parts of that class of relations between mankind which the world calls "trade and commerce."

Section 51(i) enables the Commonwealth both to regulate and to participate in trade and commerce with other countries and among the States. The *Australian National Airlines Act 1945* (Cth) established the Australian National Airlines Commission, later privatised and now absorbed by Qantas, which was authorised to operate an airline service interstate (and also to operate to and from or within any Territory). In *Australian National Airways Pty Ltd v Commonwealth* (*ANA Case*) (1945) 71 CLR 29, the High Court held that the creation and operation of the airline service were valid: the power to legislate with respect to interstate trade and commerce could be used by the Commonwealth to establish its own government-owned instrumentality to engage in such trade and commerce. In *Australian Coastal Shipping Commission v O'Reilly* (1962) 107 CLR 46, the Court took a similar view in relation to the Australian Coastal Shipping Commission. However, in the *ANA Case* other sections of the Act, which attempted to confer a monopoly upon the airline, were held invalid under s 92.

Australian National Airways Pty Ltd v Commonwealth (ANA Case)
(1945) 71 CLR 29

Dixon J: [80] It is convenient ... to consider first whether, putting on one side the effect of s 92, the leading provisions of the *Airlines Act* can be regarded as an exercise of the commerce power. It is objected that they cannot be supported under that power because it contemplates the legislative regulation of overseas and inter-State trade and commerce and not the entry of the Government itself into that field of activity ...

[81] I am of opinion that this argument ought not to be accepted. It plainly ignores the fact that it is a Constitution we are interpreting, an instrument of government meant to endure and conferring powers expressed in general propositions wide enough to be capable of flexible application to changing circumstances. It confuses the unexpressed assumptions upon which the framers of the instrument supposedly proceeded with the expressed meaning of the power. A law authorizing the government to conduct a transport service for inter-State trade, whether as a monopoly or not, appears to me to answer the description, a law with respect to trade and commerce amongst the States. It is only by importing a limitation into the descriptive words of the power that such a law can be excluded.

As to the provision of air services to a Territory, Dixon J said in relation to the Commonwealth's Territories power in s 122 of the Constitution (see Chapter 6, §5):

Dixon J: [85] We should avoid pedantic and narrow constructions in dealing with an instrument of government and I do not see why we should be fearful about making implications. It is absurd to contemplate a central government with authority over a territory and yet without power to make laws, wherever its jurisdiction may run, for the establishment, maintenance and control of communications with the territory governed. The form or language of s 122 may not be particularly felicitous but, when it is read with the entire document, the conclusion that the legislative power is extensive enough to cover such a matter seems inevitable.

Nevertheless, the judicial interpretation of s 51(i) has been inhibited by at least three factors:

1. The reference in s 51(i) is to two areas of power: "trade and commerce with other countries" and "trade and commerce ... among the States". What is omitted is any mention of trade and commerce within a State. As a result, most judges have felt obliged to construe s 51(i) in such a way as not to allow the Commonwealth to encroach too far upon the area of power so pointedly not granted to it. As Gibbs J remarked in *Attorney-General (WA) v Australian National Airlines Commission* (1976) 138 CLR 492, the dichotomy between interstate and intrastate trade suggested by s 51(i) "**[502]** must be maintained however much inter-dependence may now exist between those two divisions of trade and however artificial the distinction may be thought to be".

2. The words of s 51(i) are adapted from those of the "Commerce Clause" in the United States Constitution (Art I, § 8, cl 3), which empowers the United States Congress "[t]o regulate Commerce with foreign Nations, and among the several States". The American version adds a third category, "[commerce] with the Indian Tribes", reflecting the recognition of native American peoples as distinct political units. Despite the close verbal parallels, the Australian version has been far less widely used by the Parliament than its American equivalent, and far less widely construed by the courts. One reason for this is that the list of Commonwealth legislative powers in the Australian s 51 comprises 39 items (or 40 including para (xxiiiA)), whereas the corresponding list in the American Art I, § 8 comprises only 18. Many of the Australian items (such as s 51(xiii) as to "banking") spell out explicitly areas of power which in the United States emerged only through judicial exposition of what was implied in the "Commerce Clause". To that extent, the Australian framers drew on American experience. The more limited list of powers in Article I, § 8 of the United States Constitution has meant that virtually all of the controversial expansions of United States congressional power have had to take place under the aegis of the "Commerce Clause", whereas similar developments in Australia have drawn on a much wider range of powers, for example the "corporations" power, s 51(xx), or the "external affairs" power, s 51(xxix). Thus, the more dramatic expansions of the American "Commerce Clause" have not been perceived as either necessary or appropriate in Australia. The American expansion has depended in part on the "commingling" doctrine; that is, the idea that interstate and intrastate trade are so commercially interdependent that congressional power to regulate the former must necessarily extend into the latter. By contrast, the High Court of Australia has consistently refused to espouse any such doctrine.

3. A particular problem in Australia is the need to harmonise s 51(i) with s 92. The Common-wealth is authorised by s 51(i) to make laws with respect to "trade and commerce ... among the States", with no apparent limit on the kinds of laws that can be made so long as they are "with respect to" that topic. At the same time, however, s 92 places trade and commerce among the States beyond the reach of some kinds of laws, since "trade, commerce, and inter-course among the States ... shall be absolutely free". Thus, an interpretation that expands the scope of interstate trade and commerce for purposes of s 51(i), and thereby enlarges Commonwealth power, might also entail a parallel expansion in the scope of interstate trade and commerce for the purposes of s 92, and thereby restrict Commonwealth power. In the *ANA Case*, for example, the Commonwealth was able to establish a government-owned

interstate airline because to do so was to make a law with respect to interstate trade and commerce. However, it was unable to give the airline a monopoly because that would have infringed s 92.

The High Court's resistance to Commonwealth encroachment on areas of purely intrastate trade has overtones of "reserved State powers": the Commonwealth power is narrowly construed to ensure that it does not encroach on matters properly of concern to the States. The early cases applying the "reserved State powers" doctrine all involved heads of power other than s 51(i), but in each of them the supposed need to maintain a sharp distinction between interstate and intrastate trade for the purposes of s 51(i) was used as an argument for a narrow reading of the other heads of power (see, for example, the extract from *R v Barger* (1908) 6 CLR 41 in Chapter 7, §3). Those cases thus depended on the idea, now generally discredited, that the limitations on one grant of power can be used to impose corresponding limitations on other grants of power. However, the abolition of this larger doctrine of "reserved State powers" did not necessarily abolish a narrower version, operating solely within the ambit of s 51(i) and supposedly based on its explicit distinction between interstate and intrastate trade.

Even this narrower version needs to be stated with caution. It is not that s 51(i) reserves the power of regulating intrastate trade to the States. It is simply that it does not grant that power to the Commonwealth. As Barwick CJ said in *Strickland v Rocla Concrete Pipes Ltd* (*Concrete Pipes Case*) (1971) 124 CLR 468: "[488] Section 51(i) contains no explicit or implicit prohibition and does not reserve the subject of intrastate trade to the States".

The need for a strict observance of the boundary between overseas and interstate trade (which the Commonwealth may regulate) and intrastate trade (which it may not) was spelled out clearly in *R v Burgess; Ex parte Henry* (1936) 55 CLR 608, along with the High Court's consequent resistance to any analogy with the United States "commingling" doctrine. *R v Burgess* involved the validity of s 4 of the *Air Navigation Act 1920* (Cth), which authorised the making of regulations "for the control of air navigation in the Commonwealth and the territories". This broad language had been used because, in 1920, it was agreed that the States would legislate to "refer" to the Commonwealth, under s 51(xxxvii), legislative power over the whole topic of air navigation. However, only the Tasmanian referral legislation ever came into force. The Commonwealth was thus faced with the need to defend, by invoking specific grants of power in s 51, legislation which had not been drafted with those grants of power in mind.

To this end Sir Edward Mitchell KC and his junior Alan Taylor relied both on s 51(xxix), the external affairs power, and on s 51(i), the trade and commerce power. As to the first, see Chapter 19, §4(a). As to the second, Mitchell argued that "[622] [t]here is a plenary power over inter-State trade and commerce, and a limited power over intra-State trade and commerce. In order to have effective control over inter-State traffic, there must be control over intra-State traffic … [623] The Commonwealth has power under the trade and commerce power to make regulations in relation to aircraft engaged in inter-State trade and commerce, and, to ensure the safety of inter-State commerce the Commonwealth can make its air-navigation regulations applicable also to aircraft flying intra-State". The argument failed. The Court held that, although air navigation "in the Territories" could be regulated under s 122 of the Constitution, air navigation "in the Commonwealth" was a general subject-matter that the Commonwealth could regulate only in limited aspects. Section 51(i) was held to imply a clear distinction between interstate and intrastate trade and commerce, to which a general provision for "air navigation in the Commonwealth" could not conform.

R v Burgess; Ex parte Henry
(1936) 55 CLR 608

Latham CJ: [627] Uniform rules designed to secure the airworthiness of aircraft and the competency of pilots, and uniform flying rules as to flight, the passing of aircraft in flight, and in particular ascent from and descent to aerodromes, are clearly **[628]** desirable in the interests of all who use the air for flying. If the rules, eg, for landing upon an aerodrome, are not uniform, so that one pilot lands in a clockwise direction while another pilot, in the same place, obeying another set of rules, lands in an anti-clockwise direction, there is very grave risk of serious accident. Upon these and similar considerations the argument is based that in order to deal effectively with the subject of aircraft flying between the States or between Australia and other countries the Commonwealth Parliament must also have the power to deal with aircraft flying only within the limits of one State which use, as a matter of absolute necessity, the same air, and as a matter of practical necessity, the same aerodromes.

The illustrations which have been given indicate the difficulties of any double control of aviation and might well be used to support the contention that it is wise or expedient that there should be a single control of this subject matter. Considerations of wisdom or expediency cannot, however, control the natural construction of statutory language. The Constitution gives to the Commonwealth Parliament power over inter-State and foreign trade and commerce and does not give to it power over intra-State trade and commerce, although these subjects are obviously in many respects very difficult to separate from each other. On several occasions the argument has been pressed upon this court that, where inter-State or foreign and intra-State maritime trade and commerce are so intermingled that it is practically essential to control all of them as one subject matter, the Commonwealth Parliament has power under sec 51(i) and sec 98 of the Constitution to deal with intra-State navigation and shipping. A similar argument could be applied to railways the property of any State with respect to which the Commonwealth has power to legislate under the trade and commerce power (See Constitution, sec 98). This argument, however, has always been rejected by the court. Although foreign and inter-State trade and commerce may be closely associated with intra-State trade and commerce, the court has uniformly held that the distinction drawn by the Constitution must be fully recognized, and that the power to deal with the former subject does not involve an incidental **[629]** power to deal with the latter subject ... It is true that in the United States of America a similar contention has been approved by the Supreme Court in such cases as *Southern Railway Co v United States* [222 US 20 at 26 (1911)], where the court found that there was such a close or direct relation or connection between the inter-State and intra-State traffic when moving over the same railroad "as to make it certain that the safety of the inter-State traffic and of those who are employed in its movement will be promoted in a real or substantial sense by applying the requirements of these (Federal) acts (which required the installation of certain safety appliances) to vehicles used in moving the traffic which is intra-State as well as to those used in moving that which is inter-State". The decisions of this court, however, have definitely declined to adopt such a principle, and have therefore left the problem which is indicated by the illustrations above ... to be solved by some form of co-operation between the Commonwealth and the States. A new problem would be raised if in any given case it were established by evidence in respect of a particular subject matter that the intermingling of foreign and inter-State trade and commerce with intra-State trade and commerce was such that it was impossible for the Commonwealth Parliament to regulate the former without also directly regulating the latter. No such evidence, however, has been presented in this case, and it will be necessary to deal with such a question only when it is directly raised.

Applying the decisions of this court to which I have referred, and in the absence of any evidence of the character which I have just mentioned, I find myself compelled to reject the contention that if the Commonwealth Parliament has power to legislate with respect to inter-State and foreign aviation, it must therefore also have power to regulate intra-State aviation.

Dixon J: [670] The concluding words of sec 4 purport to enable the Governor-General to make regulations for the purpose of providing for the control of air navigation in the Commonwealth. This part of the section is not expressed as in any way relating to trade and commerce with other countries and among the States. It refers to air navigation as an entire subject; it contains no indication of any intention on the part of the legislature to deal with transportation by air as trade and commerce with other countries and among the States. It makes no distinction between air carriage of goods and passengers and all the matters preparatory to flying by air, incidental thereto or consequent thereon, which are comprehended under the expression "air navigation." It makes no distinction between flying across and flying within the boundaries of a State.

In reference to air navigation, as to broadcasting, the suggestion has **[671]** been made that its control does not admit of the distinction between what is inter-State and what is confined to one State; that to regulate inter-State flying effectively air navigation must be controlled as a whole. The inconvenience and difficulty of maintaining the distinction needs no demonstration. But the legislative power is to make laws with respect to inter-State commerce, and, under the power, the domestic commerce of a State can be affected only to the extent necessary to make effectual its exercise in relation to commerce among the States ...

[672] The express limitation of the subject matter of the power to commerce with other countries and among the States compels a distinction however artificial it may appear and whatever inter-dependence may be discovered between the branches into which the Constitution divides trade and commerce. This express limitation must be maintained no less steadily in determining what is incidental to the power than in defining its main purpose. But, in any case, the second limb of sec 4 of the *Air Navigation Act* 1920 does not appear to me to be based at all on the commerce power. "Air navigation" is an indefinite expression and might be used to describe transport by air. But its association in the Act with the convention for the regulation of aerial navigation shows that it is intended to cover a much wider field. The legislature has not addressed itself to the use of aircraft as instruments of inter-State commerce and then, in order to ensure the effectiveness of the regulations adopted for that purpose, gone on to take or authorize consequential measures in relation to aircraft not so used. The second limb of the section might have been capable of support if it had been expressly confined to inter-State air navigation.

Evatt and McTiernan JJ: [677] It is impossible to accept the theory of the Commonwealth that its power to legislate with respect to inter-State trade necessarily extends to all aircraft engaged solely in intra-State trade, by reason of the possible "commingling," in air routes and air ports, of the aircraft proceeding intra-State with the aircraft proceeding inter-State. No doubt, by virtue of sec 109 of the Constitution, State laws or regulations of transport may be invalidated by valid Commonwealth laws or regulations dealing with the subject matter of transport. Moreover, the rejection of the "commingling" theory does not deny that there may be occasions when parts of intra-State aviation will be seen to occupy so direct and proximate a relationship to inter-State aviation that the agents and instruments of the former will be drawn within the ambit of the Federal power, for otherwise the particular Commonwealth regulation of inter-State commerce would be entirely frustrated and nullified. But this does not mean that the Commonwealth Parliament is legislating with respect to intra-State trade but only that legislation with respect to inter-State trade may operate in respect of or against persons, matters and things which, though not themselves directly involved in inter-State trade, are brought into a sufficiently proximate relationship with such trade.

These conclusions were reaffirmed in the 1960s, again in relation to air navigation, though with some development of the final concession by Evatt and McTiernan JJ that *some* aspects of intrastate trade might have "**[677]** a sufficiently proximate relationship" with interstate trade. In *Airlines of NSW Pty Ltd v New South Wales* (*First Airlines Case*) (1965) 113 CLR 1, the High Court had held that a New South Wales licensing system for aircraft operating solely within the State was not inconsistent with Commonwealth regulations made under the *Air Navigation Act 1920* (Cth). In part, this was because the Commonwealth regulations (by reg 6) were expressed to have no application to purely intrastate flights. Following that decision, both governments amended their legislation, and returned to the High Court in *Airlines of NSW Pty Ltd v New South Wales (No 2)* (*Second Airlines Case*) (1965) 113 CLR 54. Again, the Court found no inconsistency. It did, however, hold that the Commonwealth regulations were valid (with the exception of a new reg 200B – see Chapter 9, §4).

Regulation 6(1) had been amended by a new para (f), which extended the regulations to "all air navigation within Australian territory of a kind not specified", that is, to purely intrastate aviation. By reg 198: "An aircraft shall not be used in regular public transport operations except under the authority of and in accordance with a [Commonwealth] licence". By reg 199(3), a Commonwealth licence for "other than an interstate service" may be issued "upon such conditions, in addition to compliance with these Regulations, as the Director-General considers necessary". By a new reg 199(4), in deciding whether to issue a licence for purely intrastate aviation, the Director-General shall "have regard to matters concerned with the safety, regularity and efficiency of air navigation and to no other matters". As to the validity of regs 198-199, Kitto and Windeyer JJ relied solely on s 51(i); McTiernan J relied solely on the Commonwealth's "external affairs" power in s 51(xxix); Menzies and Owen JJ relied on both heads of power; and Barwick CJ thought that both were applicable but preferred s 51(i). Taylor J dissented. In his view the new Commonwealth regulations were wholly invalid.

Airlines of NSW Pty Ltd v New South Wales (No 2) (*Second Airlines Case*)
(1965) 113 CLR 54

Kitto J: [113] [T]he licensing system in its application to wholly intra-State air services is limited so as to serve only the purpose of aiding and protecting the safety, regularity and efficiency of air navigation generally. It is at this point that the crucial question arises. In so far as regs 198 and 199 aid and protect the safety, regularity and efficiency of intra-State air navigation, have they the character of a law with respect to any subject or subjects of federal legislative power?

I pause to make the point that that and nothing else is the question. In *R v Burgess; Ex parte Henry* [(1936) 55 CLR 608] both *Latham* CJ and *Dixon* J took their stand against the introduction into Australian constitutional law of some of the vague standards which at times have been accepted in relation to the reach of the commerce power under the Constitution of the United States and have resulted in a greatly diminished importance in that country of the distinction between inter-State and intra-State commerce. The course of American decision since 1936 has been away from some of the indefinite tests of validity (under the commerce power) to which *Dixon* J referred in his quotations from American cases. The distinction is no longer held to be that which *Hughes* CJ expressed in *Schechter Poultry Corporation v United States* [295 US 495 at 546 (1935)], namely between direct and indirect effects of intra-State transactions upon inter-State commerce. But the principle remains that of the *Shreveport Rate Cases* [234 US 342 (1914)] namely that federal intervention is constitutionally authorized because of "matters having such a close and substantial relation to interstate traffic that the control is essential or appropriate to the security of that traffic, to the efficiency of the interstate service, and to the maintenance of conditions under which interstate commerce may be conducted upon fair terms and without molestation or hindrance" [234 US at 351]. Thus it is held, upon consideration of economic effects, that the reach of the commerce power extends to "those intra-State activities which in a substantial way interfere with or obstruct the exercise of the granted power": *United States v* **[114]** *Wrightwood Dairy Co* [315 US 110 at 119 (1942)]; *Wickard v Filburn* [317 US 111 at 120-5 (1942)]. The doctrine rests on the premise that "in certain fact situations the federal government may find that regulation of purely local or intra-State commerce is 'necessary or proper' to prevent injury to inter-State commerce": *Polish National Alliance v National Labour Relations Board* [322 US at 653]. In applying this doctrine the Supreme Court has "required clear findings" and has insisted upon "suitable regard to the principle that whenever the federal power is exerted within what would otherwise be the domain of state power, the justification of the exercise of the federal power must clearly appear": [322 US 643 at 653 (1944)] … But this is doubtless because the Court has been alive to the width of the doctrine and the danger of its getting out of hand. As the Court itself said in *Mandeville Island Farms v American Crystal Sugar Co* [334 US 219 at 233 (1948)] the *Shreveport* decision "substituted judgment as to practical impeding effects upon inter-State commerce for rubrics concerning its boundaries as the basic criterion of effective congressional action".

The establishment of these criteria in the United States has evoked in that country itself criticisms of which we would do well to take notice. It was *Frankfurter* J who described them as "less than unwavering bright lines": *Baker v Carr* [369 US 186 at 283 (1962)]. One other quotation will be enough. I take it from the writings of Dr *Bernard Schwartz*, Professor of Law at New York University: "Decisions like those just discussed illustrate the extent to which the Supreme Court has departed from the concept of dual federalism which had previously governed its approach to cases involving the relationship of federal and State authority. For the older view that the federal power over commerce could not be exercised over local transactions, which were within the exclusive area of State authority, has been substituted the notion of a plenary power of the national

Government over commerce. If wheat production intended by the farmer solely for his domestic consumption can be regulated by Congress because of its possible effect upon interstate commerce, however indirect it may be, there are, in practice, no restrictions upon federal regulation of even so-called purely local commerce. **[115]** And, if this is true, the American system is clearly no longer one of dual federalism". *American Constitutional Law* (1955) p 170.

The Australian union is one of dual federalism, and until the Parliament and the people see fit to change it, a true federation it must remain. This Court is entrusted with the preservation of constitutional distinctions, and it both fails in its task and exceeds its authority if it discards them, however out of touch with practical conceptions or with modern conditions they may appear to be in some or all of their applications. To import the doctrine of the American cases into the law of the Australian Constitution would in my opinion be an error. The Constitution supplies its own criteria of legislative power. To ask, as we are bound to do, whether a given federal law having an operation upon intra-State commerce is, in that operation, a law "with respect to" commerce with other countries or among the States (or is within some other head of federal power) is of course to ask a question which is not so precise that different answers may not appeal to different minds. But at least it is a legal question, a question of ascertaining the true character of the law by a consideration of what it does "in the way of changing or creating or destroying duties or rights or powers": *South Australia v Commonwealth* [(1942) 65 CLR 373 at 424]. It is the question the Constitution in terms presents.

It must, of course, be considered in the light of the nature of the particular form of commerce to which the law relates. It is, I think, a question as to whether, when the factual situation in which the law operates is understood, the law by its operation upon the intra-State section of the relevant form of commerce is seen to operate also upon the actual conduct of an activity or collection of activities in respect of which federal power exists, eg, the actual carrying on of activities forming part of the overseas and inter-State sections of that form of commerce. Where the intra-State activities, if the law were not to extend to them, would or might have a prejudicial effect upon matters merely consequential upon the conduct of an activity within federal power, eg where the profit or loss likely to result from inter-State commercial air navigation would or might be affected, that mere fact would not suffice, in my judgment, to make the law a law "with respect to" that activity itself. But, by contrast, where the law, by what it does in relation to intra-State activities, protects against danger of physical interference the very activity itself which is within federal power, the conclusion does seem to me to be correct that in that application the law is a law within the grant of federal power.

[116] We must therefore answer the question before us in the light of the nature of air navigation as it exists as a phenomenon of life in Australia and its Territories at the present time. In respects which hardly need to be emphasized it is *sui generis* among methods of transport, and indeed among all forms of trade and commerce. The speed at which modern aircraft move through the skies; their constant liability to sudden and wide deviation in flight by reason of mechanical or human deficiencies, the vagaries of the weather, the behaviour of other aircraft and other causes; the multiplicity of flights required to satisfy the demands of modern life; the multiplicity and inter-relation of the routes to be served; all these matters and more combine to make air navigation in this country a complex of activities of such a kind that what happens at any given time and place in the course of an air operation may substantially, even dramatically, affect other air operations close or distant in time or space. The significance of distances, of geographical relationships, is necessarily different for a problem concerning air navigation than for a problem concerning any other form of transport. Moreover it must be kept in mind that while many examples of air navigation are within federal legislative power because they are themselves a form of commerce with other countries or among the States or because they are carried on within or into or out of Territories of the Commonwealth, or because they use as aerodromes places acquired by the Commonwealth for public purposes, many other examples of air navigation may be within federal legislative power because the purposes with which they are carried on are purposes incidental to matters over which such power extends. Purposes incidental to defence, or to postal services, or to the conduct of the public business of the Commonwealth (eg, the conveyance of the Governor-General or of Ministers in the discharge of their official functions) provide obvious illustrations. It is probably true that there is no head of federal power to which the flying of aircraft may not be incidental, eg, the use of aircraft by the Commonwealth Banking Corporation may no doubt be made a subject of federal legislation under s 51(xiii) of the Constitution. With all this in mind, it is impossible to assume in advance that any impairment of the safety, regularity or efficiency of intra-State air navigation will leave unimpaired the safety, regularity and efficiency of the other departments into which air navigation may be divided for constitutional purposes. It follows from these considerations, in my opinion, that a federal law which provides a method of controlling regular public transport services by air with regard only to the safety, regularity and efficiency of air navigation **[117]** is a law which operates to protect against real possibilities of physical interference the actual carrying on of air navigation, and therefore is, in every application that it has, a law "with respect to" such air navigation as is within federal power, and none the less so because it is also legislation with respect to that intra-State air navigation which is not within the power.

In my opinion regs 198 and 199 are for these reasons valid laws of the Commonwealth, even in their application to regular public transport operations conducted wholly within the borders of a single State.

Compare the above with *R v Burgess*. In the *Second Airlines Case*, the focus was on a precisely drafted set of regulations. In *R v Burgess*, the focus was on the empowering words in an Act which authorised the making of regulations "for the control of air navigation in the Commonwealth". The differing focus might be a factor in explaining the different decisions.

7. Incidental Powers

Extensions to the concept of interstate trade and commerce have often depended on the Commonwealth's "incidental" powers. The "express incidental power" is provided by s 51(xxxix) of the Constitution, which gives power to legislate with respect to "[m]atters incidental to the execution of any power vested by this Constitution in the Parliament ... , or in the Government of the Commonwealth, or in the Federal Judicature, or in any department or officer of the Commonwealth". In addition, the Court has consistently held that each head of power in s 51 contains an "implied incidental power".

The difference between the "express" and "implied" incidental powers is obscure. Indeed, it may be that there is no difference: as PH Lane has suggested (*The Australian Federal System* (Law Book Co, 2nd ed 1979), the inclusion of the express incidental power, so far as it applies to legislative powers, may be "**[347]** pleonastic" (that is, redundant). On the other hand, what is clearly distinctive about the express incidental power is that it operates not only in respect of the legislative powers granted by the Constitution, but also in respect of the executive and judicial powers so granted. That is, s 51(xxxix) permits what Lane calls "**[347]** a legislative crossover: the legislature, the controlling and active arm of government, can deal with matters incidental to powers vested in the other arms of government". For example, this operation of s 51(xxxix) upon the executive power conferred by s 61 is frequently adduced as a textual basis for the so-called "nationhood power" (see Chapter 12, §2(b)). Be that as it may, the extension of every head of power by an implied incidental power has been affirmed since the High Court's earliest days.

D'Emden v Pedder
(1904) 1 CLR 91

Griffith CJ (for the Court): [109] It is only necessary to mention the maxim, *quando lex aluquid concedit, concedere videtur et illud sine quo res ipsa valere non potest*. In other **[110]** words, where any power or control is expressly granted, there is included in the grant, to the full extent of the capacity of the grantor, and without special mention, every power and every control the denial of which would render the grant itself ineffective. This is, in truth, not a doctrine of any special system of law, but a statement of a necessary rule of construction of all grants of power, whether by unwritten constitution, formal written instrument, or other delegation of authority, and applies from the necessity of the case, to all to whom is committed the exercise of powers of government.

Grannall v Marrickville Margarine Pty Ltd
(1955) 93 CLR 55

Dixon CJ, McTiernan, Webb and Kitto JJ: **[77]** Nothing which has been said above implies that under the power conferred by s 51(i) of the Constitution to make laws with respect to trade and commerce with other countries and among the States legislation of the Commonwealth Parliament can never reach or touch production. In the first place, the power is to legislate *with respect to* trade and commerce. The words "with respect to" ought never to be neglected in considering the extent of a legislative power conferred by s 51 or s 52. For what they require is a relevance to or connection with the subject assigned to the Commonwealth Parliament ... In the next place, every legislative power carries with it authority to legislate in relation to acts, matters and things the control of which is found necessary to effectuate its main purpose, and thus carries with it power to make laws governing or affecting many matters that are incidental or ancillary to the subject-matter.

In this passage, the power conferred by s 51(i) is said to be extended *both* by the presence of the words "with respect to" *and* by the implied "incidental" power to regulate matters "**[77]** the control of which is found necessary to effectuate its main purpose". Although these are presented as separate reasons for treating the grant of power expansively, it seems doubtful whether there is any example of a law being characterised as valid on the basis supplied by one of these rationales, which could not equally have been upheld on the other basis. At the least, there is a broad overlap not only between the express and implied incidental powers, but between both of them and the extended reach of power supplied by the words "with respect to". Both in satisfying the test supplied by those words and in findings of "incidental power", we have seen that what the High Court requires is a *sufficient connection* of the matter sought to be regulated with the main grant of power.

The extended reach of legislative power under s 51(i) has usually been conceived of as depending on "incidental" power. Generally, it will be the "implied" incidental power that is in issue; or, rather, such cases will fall within the area in which it makes no difference whether the "express" or "implied" incidental power is invoked. What does make a difference is whether the use of the incidental power is restricted, in the context of s 51(i), by the Court's acute sensitivity to Commonwealth "encroachment" into the domain of purely intrastate trade. The comments of Dixon CJ in *Wragg v NSW* (1953) 88 CLR 353 have been influential.

Wragg v NSW
(1953) 88 CLR 353

Dixon CJ: [385] The distinction which is drawn between inter-State **[386]** trade and the domestic trade of a State for the purpose of the power conferred upon the Parliament by s 51(i) to make laws with respect to trade and commerce with other countries and among the States may well be considered artificial and unsuitable to modern times. But it is a distinction adopted by the Constitution and it must be observed however much inter-dependence may now exist between the two divisions of trade and commerce which the Constitution thus distinguishes. A legislative power, however, with respect to any subject matter contains within itself authority over whatever is incidental to the subject matter of the power and enables the legislature to include within laws made in pursuance of the power provisions which can only be justified as ancillary or incidental. But even in the application of this principle to the grant of legislative power made by s 51(i) the distinction which the Constitution makes between the two branches of trade and commerce must be maintained. Its existence makes impossible any operation of the incidental power which would obliterate the distinction.

Dixon CJ was referring to trade and commerce both with other countries *and* among the States. However, it is arguable that laws relating to trade and commerce with other countries are less likely to impinge upon intrastate trade, and thus that the scope for the incidental power to operate may be correspondingly greater. *O'Sullivan v Noarlunga Meat Ltd* (1954) 92 CLR 565 is a classic example. That case involved the effect of a licence under the *Commerce (Meat Export) Regulations* (Cth), which were made under the *Customs Act 1901* (Cth). Regulation 5 provided that all premises used for the slaughter, treatment and storage of meat, meat products or edible offal, for export were to be registered. Regulation 4B laid down elaborate health requirements with which registered premises had to comply.

The immediate issue was whether, under s 109 of the Constitution, these regulations were inconsistent with similar South Australian legislation (so that the holder of a Commonwealth licence would have no need for a State licence as well). Dixon CJ, Fullagar and Kitto JJ found an inconsistency. McTiernan, Webb and Taylor JJ found none. In this 3:3 division of opinion, the Chief Justice's view prevailed pursuant to s 23(2) of the *Judiciary Act 1903* (Cth).

Webb and Taylor JJ, finding no inconsistency, expressed no view on the validity of the regulations under s 51(i). For them the issue did not strictly arise. The other four judges held the regulations to be valid. For McTiernan J it was sufficient that "[580] the standards required for registered establishments have a real causative relation to the fitness of the meat and other products to enter the stream of trade and commerce with other countries". The leading judgment, with which Dixon CJ and Kitto J agreed, was that of Fullagar J.

O'Sullivan v Noarlunga Meat Ltd
(1954) 92 CLR 565

Fullagar J: [595] The Commonwealth is legislating to ensure that only meat of a certain grade and quality shall be exported, and the law [reg 4B] is clearly a law with respect to trade and commerce with other countries. The power given by s 51 (i) extends to authorizing the total prohibition of the **[596]** export of any commodity, and *a fortiori* it includes a power to prohibit the export of any commodity except upon compliance with prescribed conditions.

But the regulations go further than this … Regulation 5 prohibits the use of any premises for the slaughter of meat for export unless those premises are registered, and a penalty is imposed by reg 99 on any use of premises which is in breach of reg 5 … The question which emerges is whether the Commonwealth power with respect to trade and commerce with other countries extends to authorizing legislation regulating and controlling the slaughter of meat for export. In my opinion it does so extend.

The question obviously tends to open up a wide field of speculation as to the extent of the power in question. But it will be wise, I think, to avoid that field, and to concentrate attention on the particular case before us and the particular commodity with which that case is concerned. It will be wise also, I think, to begin by obtaining as clear a conception as possible of what is meant by the expression "slaughter for export". It would perhaps have been better if we had had some evidence before us as to Australia's export trade in meat, and as to the processes involved in the killing and preparation of meat for export and for home consumption respectively. But it seems to be safe to say that Sir *Garfield Barwick* was entirely right when he said that the expression "slaughter for export" is used in the relevant legislation as a composite expression which would be understood objectively in the trade. Whether "slaughter for export" is taking place is not, from the point of view of the legislator, a question which depends entirely on some intention in the mind of the owner or slaughterer of a beast – an intention which may change from time to time as operations proceed. The whole process from killing to packing **[597]** will be conditioned in certain respects by the predetermined destination of the meat, and "slaughter for export" is, in the mind of the legislator, a definite objective conception distinct from slaughter for home consumption. It does not, of course, follow that any corresponding position exists with regard to any commodity other than meat. It may very well be, for example, that such an expression as "mining metals for export" or "sowing wheat for export" is meaningless except by reference to some subjective element.

Probably fifty years ago in the United States such legislation as that contained in the *Commerce (Meat Export) Regulations* would have been held to lie outside the federal commerce power. A sharp distinction seems to have been drawn between manufacture or production on the one hand

and commerce, conceived essentially as the movement of goods, on the other hand ... Today, however, it seems most probable that such legislation would be held within the power to regulate commerce with foreign nations. It is possible indeed that the killing and treatment of stock for export might be regarded as themselves part of the course of commerce with foreign nations, but in any case I think they would be held to be matters within the commerce power ... It was argued that the regulations in question here are a direct regulation of the very subject matter of the power, that they control steps taken in the actual course of trade and commerce with other countries. But, even if counsel for the State of South Australia be right in saying that the course of commerce with other countries does not begin until a later stage, I am of opinion that the regulations must be held valid on the broad general principle of constitutional interpretation adopted in the earliest days of this Court. In *D'Emden v Pedder* [(1904) 1 CLR 91 at 110], the Court accepted the famous enunciation of the principle by *Marshall* CJ in *M'Culloch v Maryland* [17 US (4 Wheat) 159 at 206 (1819)], as "a most welcome aid and assistance" and said: "Where any power or control is expressly granted, there is included in the grant, to the full extent of the capacity of the grantor and without special mention, every power and every **[598]** control the denial of which would render the grant itself ineffective".

It is true that the Commonwealth possesses no specific power with respect to slaughter-houses. But it is undeniable that the power with respect to trade and commerce with other countries includes a power to make provision for the condition and quality of meat or of any other commodity to be exported. Nor can the power, in my opinion, be held to stop there. By virtue of that power all matters which may affect beneficially or adversely the export trade of Australia in any commodity produced or manufactured in Australia must be the legitimate concern of the Commonwealth. Such matters include not only grade and quality of goods but packing, get-up, description, labelling, handling, and anything at all that may reasonably be considered likely to affect an export market by developing it or impairing it. It seems clear enough that the objectives for which the power is conferred may be impossible of achievement by means of a mere prescription of standards for export and the institution of a system of inspection at the point of export. It may very reasonably be thought necessary to go further back, and even to enter the factory or the field or the mine. How far back the Commonwealth may constitutionally go is a question which need not now be considered, and which must in any case depend on the particular circumstances attending the production or manufacture of particular commodities. But I would think it safe to say that the power of the Commonwealth extended to the supervision and control of all acts or processes which can be identified as being done or carried out for export. The "slaughter for export" of stock is such an act or process, and, in my opinion, the *Commerce (Meat Export) Regulations* are within the legislative power conferred upon the Commonwealth by s 51(i).

Note that Fullagar J did not exclude the possibility that the regulations might be valid as "**[597]** a direct regulation of the very subject matter of the power". He found it unnecessary to determine that issue because, in any event, the regulations came within the implied incidental power. On that basis he sought to extend the reach of the "trade and commerce power" back *before* the commencement of the transactions constituting trade with other countries to "**[598]** the factory or the field or the mine". Extension to *later* activities may also be possible. On one interpretation of *Crowe v Commonwealth* (1935) 54 CLR 69 – which permitted enforcement of the *Dried Fruits Export Control Act 1924* (Cth) by Australian agencies in the United Kingdom and Canada – the decision entailed an extension of the power to activities *after* the transactions constituting "trade and commerce ... with other countries", though in that case too there was ambiguity as to whether *all* of the transactions to be regulated might not simply be part of "trade and commerce with other countries", and hence within the core of the power.

On either basis, such results are in striking contrast with the Dixon Court's reluctance in the 1950s to adopt a similar extended view of the scope of "trade and commerce ... among the States" for the purposes of s 92. This may have been because an "implied" incidental power attaches to s 51(i) but not to s 92; or because of the idea that grants of power should be broadly construed, while restrictions on power should be strictly construed. Or it may have been simply because in *Noarlunga* and *Crowe* the focus was on overseas as distinct from interstate trade.

In *Attorney-General (WA) v Australian National Airlines Commission* (1976) 138 CLR 492, the comparison was between s 51(i) and the Territories power in s 122. Section 19(2) of the *Australian National Airlines Act 1945* (Cth) empowered the Australian National Airlines Commission to transport passengers and goods by air between a place in a State and a place in another State and between a place in a Territory and a place in Australia outside that Territory. Since 1945, that power had been exercised under the business name Trans-Australia Airlines (TAA), competing with the privately owned Ansett Airlines pursuant to the Commonwealth's "two airlines" policy. By a new s 19B(1) inserted in 1973: "The Commission may, to the extent provided by sub-s (2), transport passengers or goods for reward by air or by land, or partly by air and partly by land, between places in the one State". Under s 19B(2), such powers "may be exercised for the purposes of the efficient, competitive and profitable conduct of the business of the Commission".

Under the 1973 amendments, TAA proposed that its Perth-Darwin service would stop at Port Hedland in Western Australia, thus including an intrastate service between Perth and Port Hedland. Without the stop at Port Hedland, the Perth-Darwin route was said to be uneconomic. Ansett Airlines brought a relator action through the West Australian Attorney-General for a declaration that s 19B was invalid. The result was complex. By 3:2, Barwick CJ and Gibbs J dissenting, s 19B was held to be valid insofar as it relied upon the Territories power. However, Barwick CJ, Gibbs and Stephen JJ held that s 19B was invalid insofar as it relied on s 51(i). Murphy J dissented, arguing for a broader view of s 51(i). Mason J held that since s 19B was valid under the Territories power, its validity under s 51(i) "**[521]** need not be decided".

A separate issue was raised as to whether the valid operation of s 19B could be saved from its invalid operation under s 15A of the *Acts Interpretation Act 1901* (Cth) by being "read down" to exclude its invalid operation. Stephen and Mason JJ held that the valid operation of s 19B, that is, the operation depending upon s 122 rather than s 51(i), could be saved. This issue did not arise for Barwick CJ and Gibbs J, who found the legislation invalid on both counts, nor for Murphy J, who found the legislation valid on both counts. The pivotal judgment – accepting the use of s 122 but rejecting the use of s 51(i) – was that of Stephen J.

Attorney-General (WA) v Australian National Airlines Commission
(1976) 138 CLR 492

Stephen J: [508] Does, then, s 51(i), by its grant of legislative power over interstate trade and commerce, incidentally include a grant of power to legislate for intrastate trade and commerce when its only relationship to interstate trade and commerce lies in the fact that the purpose of engagement in such intrastate activity is to conduce to the efficiency, competitiveness and profitability of the interstate activity?

The authorities in this Court on the scope of that implied incidental power which attaches to each specific grant of power as to subject matter provide, in my view, a clear negative answer to the question posed. It is primarily to decisions upon s 51(i) that attention must be directed since, as Dixon CJ pointed out in *Victoria v Commonwealth* [(1957) 99 CLR 575 at 614] the nature and subject of the **[509]** particular head of power in question will be critical in determining what is incidental to that particular power …

It is notable that in considering the extent of the incidental power in the case of s 51(i) particular emphasis has always been placed upon the distinction drawn by the Constitution between those aspects of trade and commerce assigned to Commonwealth legislative competence and that which is left to the States …

The effect of this constitutional division of power over trade and commerce between the Commonwealth and the States has led to a quite narrowly confined ambit being given to the incidental power in the case of s 51(i), at least where what is in question is possible intrusion into the field of intrastate trade and commerce …

[510] In *Airlines of New South Wales Pty Ltd v New South Wales (No 2)* [(1965) 113 CLR 54 at 78] Barwick CJ, having affirmed earlier rejection of the notion that any commingling of the two divisions of trade and commerce could enlarge the subject matter of Commonwealth legislative power, said that nevertheless Commonwealth power might include within its sweep intrastate trade and commerce if that were necessary for the Commonwealth law to be "effective" as to interstate trade. The Chief Justice went on to say that the fact that international or interstate carriage by air may profit by, or to a significant degree depend upon, the level of intrastate carriage by air did not warrant the conclusion that the Commonwealth might stimulate and encourage the latter so as to foster the former. Kitto J drew a distinction between a law protecting from the danger of physical interference an activity within power and one which prevents prejudice to matters merely consequential to such an activity, as for instance the profitability of interstate commercial air navigation. Only the former, he said, would be within power. Taylor J adopted as a test of extent of power whether its exercise was necessary to the safety and efficiency of interstate air navigation. Menzies J did likewise; he spoke of power to control intrastate air navigation if "necessary for the effectual control" of interstate air navigation; was it, he asked, "necessary to make effectual" the latter? Windeyer J would have required some imperilling of the safety of interstate air navigation before intrastate air navigation could come within Commonwealth competence.

In the light of the foregoing it is apparent that the permitted exercise of the power conferred by s 19B, and which is described in [511] sub-s (2) as "incidental", extends beyond the ambit of that incidental power which s 51(i) carries with it. It follows that the validity of s 19B cannot gain any support by reliance upon s 51(i); nor can the resultant deficiency of power be wholly made good by recourse to s 122, those deficiencies do not lie only in areas related to Commonwealth Territories, where alone s 122 can be called in aid.

I accordingly conclude that s 19B is ultra vires the legislative power of the Commonwealth. However it does not therefore wholly fail; s 15A of the *Acts Interpretation Act* may come to its aid affording it validity over a restricted range of application. Section 19B of the *Australian National Airlines Act* is well suited to the application to it of the provisions of s 15A of the *Acts Interpretation Act* and if those provisions be applied, the section being read down to the extent necessary to bring it within power, it will retain a substantial sphere of operation and will, in my view, apply in its full vigour in relation to territory air services and to air services between a Territory and other parts of Australia.

By contrast, in holding that the Territories power could support landing rights at Port Hedland, Stephen J did not necessarily rely on "implied incidental power" at all. He inclined to think that it might be sufficient to say that the power to legislate for the Territories under s 122 is "plenary". In *Lamshed v Lake* (1958) 99 CLR 132 at 143, Dixon CJ had taken a different view, and the point remains undetermined. In any event, on either basis, Stephen J held that s 19B was valid under s 122, although not under s 51(i).

Stephen J: [514] In considering the permissible scope of laws enacted under s 122 there is, I think, no reason for the exclusion of laws whose connexion with "the government of a territory" is confined to the production of desirable qualities in functions of government; thus a law which has as its object the reduction in cost of or the improvement in the efficiency of some governmental activity related to a Territory is, I think, a law with respect to the government of that Territory. In this respect the position is in marked contrast to that governing the scope of incidental powers to be implied in s 51(i) and which I have already noticed. I may say that it is not clear to me that any question of implied incidental legislative power can arise in the case of s 122, which itself confers a plenary legislative power, leaving little room for any implication of incidental power. Rather than speak of an implied incidental power in connexion with s 122 it [515] may be preferable to regard the express words of grant as including within the power the entirety of power necessary to legislate for the government of a Territory. However if, as has sometimes been suggested in the authorities, there be implied incidental powers in the case of s 122, neither authority nor general principle calls for their restriction to that which is "necessary" or "essential" to the effective exercise of the express power to legislate for the government of a Territory; and if not so restricted it should, in my view, extend to the authorization of that which will render a function of territorial government more efficient, competitive and profitable.

The Parliament, charged with the general government of Territories, has created a corporation to conduct, in competition with whatever services private enterprise may care to furnish, airline services providing, inter alia, communications with those Territories. In the preamble to the legislation by which it has effected this it has recited its intention of ensuring that, among other things, "the development of the Territories is promoted with the utmost expedition". The taking of steps to promote the efficiency of those airline services is, I think, very much a part of the subject matter described as "the government of a Territory". Because the airline service in question is one funded by government that government must also necessarily be concerned with its profitability. Its competitiveness with any rival service is but a reflex of efficiency and profitability.

As to s 51(i), Murphy J dissented. He argued for a wide interpretation of the power, uninhibited by any distinction between intrastate and interstate trade.

Murphy J [528] The Constitution did not create a partnership between the Commonwealth and the six States for the government of the nation, nor does it express in detail the various powers of the national government. It indicates the broad areas of the powers within the scope of the legislative branch, many of which were not used in the early days of the Federation. The extent to which the national legislative powers could become interwoven was probably not realized then but now they form a matrix enabling Parliament to authorize the carrying out of the functions of a modern national government …

[529] *The Commerce Power.* This is perhaps the greatest legislative power and is at the heart of the federal system. It is the first legislative power in the Constitution and is necessary for the national government of our federation.

"Trade and commerce … among the States" is a comprehensive phrase and should not be construed narrowly. Although usually abbreviated to "interstate trade and commerce", it means trade and commerce which concerns more than one State.

The legislative power was adopted from the United States Constitution. The scope of the Australian power to make laws "with respect to" trade and commerce among the States is at least as wide as, if not wider than, the United States power "to regulate" commerce among the States. The commerce power under our Constitution is not exclusive to the national legislature as it is under the doctrine developed in the United States. There is thus less reason for construing the power narrowly here than there. Yet it has been construed narrowly. One reason for this is to avoid the destructive effects of what I consider to be a misreading of s 92 of the Constitution … Another reason is the persistence of the doctrine that the national legislative powers are to be limited so that the reserved power of the States is not invaded. In this case, the reserved power is that over intrastate trade and commerce.

The scope of the legislative power with respect to trade and commerce among the States should not be ascertained by assuming a division between interstate and intrastate commerce. Sections 51(i) and 92 of the Constitution make a [530] distinction between trade and commerce among the States and that which is not, but do not make trade and commerce among the States and intrastate trade and commerce mutually exclusive. The Constitution does not mention intrastate trade and commerce and contains nothing which suggests a rigid separation between the two. Almost any act of trade and commerce among the States can be regarded as a series or combination of acts which from another point of view are intrastate commerce. "Commerce among the States must of necessity be commerce with the States …" [*Gibbons v Ogden*, 22 US (9 Wheat) 1 at 196 (1824)].

Even if there were such a division and mutual exclusion, legislative power with respect to trade and commerce among the States and legislative power with respect to intrastate trade and commerce would not be mutually exclusive. The States were not given exclusive power over intrastate trade and commerce. The Commonwealth may override the suggested dividing line, for the words "with respect to" in s 51 and the incidental aspect which is attached to each head of power authorize laws dealing not only with trade and commerce among the States but with intrastate trade and commerce and with acts or transactions which are not trade and commerce, as long as these are with respect to, that is relevant to, trade and commerce among the States. The maintenance of the supposed division and the further insistence … that even the use of the incidental power in s 51(xxxix) cannot obliterate the division, keeps the pre-*Engineers* ghosts walking. This approach minimizes the trade and commerce power and inhibits its use …

The sections in question authorize intrastate transport for the purposes of efficient competitive and profitable conduct of the interstate transport of the Commission. These criteria adopted by Parliament are well within the scope of the commerce power. It is permissible for Parliament to take account of commercial effects in legislating under the commerce power. It would be as illogical to exclude commercial considerations [531] from the construction of the commerce power as it would be to exclude defence considerations from the defence power (s 51(vi)) or industrial considerations from the industrial power (s 51(xxxv)). I find no basis in the Constitution for the distinction that Kitto J drew between physical and economic effects upon "interstate commercial air navigation" in *Airlines of New South Wales v New South Wales (No 2)* [(1965) 113 CLR 54 at 115].

The cautious use of "incidental power" to extend the scope of s 51(i) where the focus is on "trade and commerce … among the States" is in contrast not only with the result arrived at under the Territories power, but also with the result in those cases under s 51(i) where the focus is on "trade and commerce with other countries". A final example of that type of case is *Burton v Honan* (1952) 86 CLR 169. Under s 229 of the *Customs Act 1901* (Cth), imported goods involved in customs offences were forfeited to the Crown. By s 262, a conviction for a relevant offence "shall have effect as a condemnation of the goods". It was held that these provisions were valid as being incidental to "trade and commerce with other countries". As in *Noarlunga* and *Crowe v Commonwealth*, it appeared to be ambiguous whether the forfeiture provisions were treated as arising "directly" within the core of the power, or as incidental to it.

Burton v Honan
(1952) 86 CLR 169

Dixon CJ: [177] The authority of the Commonwealth Government to impose forfeitures may be said to arise directly … as a matter fairly within the scope of the substantive power to deal with, on the one hand, Customs duties, and, on the other, importation under the commerce power. But another view of the matter is to treat the power to impose a forfeiture in the case of offences as something which is incidental to the main power. There has in this Court been some discussion as to the use of par (xxxix) of s 51 in cases where the extent of the subject matter of a substantive power of the Commonwealth is involved, and the question is whether a provision in a statute may be supported as directed to carrying out the main power by providing for a matter incidental to the subject matter. The view which I personally have expressed is that everything which is incidental to the main purpose of a power is contained within the power itself so that it extends to matters which are necessary for the reasonable fulfilment of the legislative power over the subject matter in accordance with the maxim *quando lex aliquid alicui concedit, concedere et illud videtur sine quo res ipsa valere non potest* … [I]t has appeared to me that par (xxxix) of s 51 is related not so much [178] to matters incidental to the subjects placed under the legislative power of the Commonwealth but rather to matters which arise in the execution of the various powers reposed in the Legislature, the Judiciary and the Executive. But the distinction is for present purposes immaterial because it produces the same result, namely, that the Parliament may in the exercise of any of the substantive powers given by s 51 make all laws which are directed to the end of those powers and which are reasonably incidental to their complete fulfilment.

In this passage the availability of the "incidental" powers, whether express or implied, is said to involve an indeterminate criterion of "reasonableness" – that is, what is "[178] reasonably incidental" or "[177] necessary for the reasonable fulfilment of the legislative power". This standard might appear to invite value judgments as to whether the legislative strategy adopted is an "appropriate" or "proportionate" way of achieving its purpose. In *Burton v Honan* it was on just this ground that Honan sought, without success, to impugn the forfeiture provisions.

Dixon CJ: [178] It is said that goods … are exposed to forfeiture notwithstanding that they go into home consumption and are released from the control of the Customs for that purpose, and that they may be found in the hands of persons who have dealt with them quite honestly and have acquired apparent title to them as the last of a line of successive people all dealing in perfect bona fides and for value.

As to s 262, it is said that a forfeiture may result ... of goods which are in the hands of a person who has obtained them innocently after they have gone into home consumption, and that by the conviction of the offender who imported them unlawfully into the country the innocent purchaser is left with no right to contest the legality of the forfeiture but has lost his goods in consequence of a proceeding to which he is not a party.

The preliminary question with which we are concerned is whether those two features of the operation of the provisions drive it beyond the application of the incidental power. On that subject, which is one of degree, we have had the advantage of a discussion on both sides, which has drawn our attention to the material considerations. On one side it is pointed out that injustice may occur to individuals who are innocent, and that they may be involved in the loss of property for which they can only have a recompense by recourse to the person who has sold it, who may, of course, not be able to restore the purchase money. On the other side it is pointed out that in the history of English and Australian Customs legislation forfeiture provisions are common, drastic and far-reaching ... [179] These matters of incidental powers are largely questions of degree, but in considering them we must not lose sight of the fact that once the subject matter is fairly within the province of the Federal legislature the justice and wisdom of the provisions which it makes in the exercise of its powers over the subject matter are matters entirely for the Legislature and not for the Judiciary.

In the administration of the judicial power in relation to the Constitution there are points at which matters of degree seem sometimes to bring forth arguments in relation to justice, fairness, morality and propriety, but those are not matters for the judiciary to decide upon. The reason why this appears to be so is simply because a reasonable connection between the law which is challenged and the subject of the power under which the legislature purported to enact it must be shown before the law can be sustained under the incidental power.

8. Proportionality

In *Burton v Honan* Dixon CJ conceded that, when the validity of an enactment depends on "the incidental power", the sufficiency of its connection with the main head of power may be a matter of degree. An enactment might thus be invalid because it stretches the connection with legislative power so far that the link becomes tenuous, or breaks: the legislation "goes too far". The judgment that a provision "goes too far" may seem to suggest that the law is being evaluated in terms of "[179] justice, fairness, morality and propriety". However, Dixon CJ was concerned to deny that any such evaluation is involved. In part, this was simply a way of insisting that, in *Burton v Honan* itself, the forfeiture provision was not to be rejected as unconstitutional simply because it had operated harshly and unjustly in relation to Burton (an innocent purchaser who had lost his car). However, it also reaffirmed a broader insistence that, on issues of constitutional validity, the Court will limit itself to a value-free assessment of whether the impugned law is "within power".

Compare this with the equivocal effect of the famous passage from *McCulloch v Maryland*, 17 US (4 Wheat) 316 (1819), at 421, employed by the High Court in *Jumbunna Coal Mine NL v Victorian Coal Miners' Association* (1908) 6 CLR 309 (see the extracts in Chapter 7, §6). On the one hand, the passage from *McCulloch v Maryland* insists on a broad interpretation of constitutional powers, with generous allowance for legislative judgment; on the other hand, this approach is extended only to enactments that are "appropriate" or "plainly adapted" to a legitimate end. In recent years, initially in decisions concerning the "external affairs" power, the requirement that laws be "appropriate" or "adapted" or "proportionate" to their purpose has developed into an important test of constitutional validity.

In *Nationwide News Pty Ltd v Wills* (1992) 177 CLR 1, an innovative judgment by Mason CJ carried this approach significantly further. That case concerned s 299(1)(d)(ii) of the *Industrial Relations Act 1988* (Cth), which gave sweeping protection to the Industrial Relations Commission against written or verbal criticism. Four judges held that the provision was invalid because it infringed an implied constitutional commitment to freedom of political discussion. The other three judges, led by Mason CJ, reached the same result by holding that the law was not "within power". For Mason CJ, the "purposive" criteria ("appropriate", "proportionate" and "adapted") could legitimately be used in any case where the purpose of a challenged law was relevant to its characterisation. This was so in regard to external affairs because, where a law is designed to fulfil Australia's obligations under an international treaty, it is that purpose of the law which gives it a sufficient connection with "external affairs". Another example could be found in cases concerning the "defence" power, where the characterisation of a law will usually depend not on whether it relates to the subject-matter of "defence", but on whether it is conducive to the purpose of "defence". What Mason CJ added in *Nationwide News* was that, in any case where the validity of a law depends upon bringing it within "the incidental power", it will usually be the purpose of the law that must be relied on to establish a sufficient connection with the constitutional power. Accordingly, he said, in these cases too, the Court must inquire not merely into the purpose of the law, but also into whether the means adopted are an "appropriate" and "proportionate" way of achieving that purpose.

Nationwide News Pty Ltd v Wills
(1992) 177 CLR 1

Mason CJ: [27] To sustain the validity of s 299(1)(d)(ii) on the footing that it comes within the scope of the incidental reach of the power, it must appear that there is a relevant and sufficient connexion with the subject-matter of the power. In determining whether such a connexion exists, it is material to have **[28]** regard to the purpose of the provision and to the reasonableness of the connexion between that law and the subject-matter of the power. It has been said that the "end or purpose of the provision ... will give the key" [*Bank Nationalisation Case* (1948) 76 CLR 1 at 354] and there is authority to support the proposition that, if the purpose of the provision is within power, it is valid, notwithstanding that the difficulties created for many persons are out of all proportion to the advantage gained.

   Herald and Weekly Times Ltd v Commonwealth [(1967) 115 CLR 418] was such a case. In furtherance of a policy of ensuring freedom of competition between television services, which was within power, the statute established a regulatory regime covering many concrete situations where it was most unlikely that the person concerned would be able to exercise any degree of control or even influence. In some situations, there was no foothold for the exercise of influence. Nevertheless, the statute was held to be valid. Kitto J ... said [115 CLR at 437]:

   > "How far they should go was a question of degree for the Parliament to decide, and the fact that the Parliament has chosen to go to great lengths – even the fact, if it be so, that for many persons difficulties are created which are out of all proportion to the advantage gained – affords no ground of constitutional attack."

   That statement seems to suggest that, if the purpose of the impugned law is within power, that is enough, no matter that the connexion between the law and the subject-matter is remote and that the difficulties created for many persons affected are out of all proportion to the advantage gained. Taken in isolation, the statement may also appear to suggest that matters of degree are for Parliament and not for the Court.

   Nevertheless, it has long been accepted that it is for the Court to determine whether there is a reasonable connexion between the law and the subject-matter of the power and that this is very often **[29]** largely a question of degree. In other words, the question of degree is not merely a matter for Parliament; although the Court will give weight to the view of Parliament, it is a matter for the Court in determining whether a reasonable connexion exists.

   Despite the observations of Kitto J quoted above, this Court has held that, in characterizing a law as one with respect to a permitted head of power, a reasonable proportionality must exist between the designated object or purpose and the means selected by the law for achieving that object or purpose. The concept of reasonable proportionality is now an accepted test of validity on the issue of ultra vires. It is a test which governs the validity of statutes as well as that of regulations. So, in *Castlemaine Tooheys Ltd v South Australia* [(1990) 169 CLR 436 at 473-4], in deciding whether a law was appropriate and adapted to the protection of the environment, in which event the law would have been valid, it was necessary to consider whether the adverse or extraordinary consequences of the law were disproportionate to the achievement of the relevant protection.

As an illustration he cited *Davis v Commonwealth* (1988) 166 CLR 79 (see Chapter 12, §2(b)):

Mason CJ: [30] *Davis* [(1988) 166 CLR 79] establishes two propositions. First, that, even if the purpose of a law is to achieve an end within power, it will not fall within the scope of what is incidental to the substantive power unless it is reasonably and appropriately adapted to the pursuit of an end within power, ie, unless it is capable of being considered to be reasonably proportionate to the pursuit of that end. Secondly, in determining whether that requirement of reasonable proportionality is satisfied, it is material to ascertain whether, and to what extent, **[31]** the law goes beyond what is reasonably necessary or conceivably desirable for the achievement of the legitimate object sought to be attained and, in so doing, causes adverse consequences unrelated to the achievement of that object. In particular, it is material to ascertain whether those adverse consequences result in any infringement of fundamental values traditionally protected by the common law, such as freedom of expression.

The purpose of s 299(1)(d)(ii) is, without any doubt, to protect the Commission, and its members, with a view to preserving its reputation and public confidence in its determinations. Subject to the requirement of reasonable proportionality, the attainment of these objects would enhance the prevention and settlement of interstate industrial disputes by means of conciliation and arbitration and thus fall within the purview of s 51(xxxv) ... The problem is that the means chosen is far more restrictive than the protection conferred by the law of contempt upon the courts and the administration of justice and that the means chosen, if valid, makes it an offence to criticize the Commission or any of its members, even if the criticism is based on facts which are true and consists of comments which are fair ...

[33] In considering whether the protection sought to be given to the Commission is so disproportionate as to lead to the conclusion that the protection stands outside the incidental scope of the substantive power, two points are, in my view, of paramount importance. First, as the courts have come to the conclusion that only the degree of protection accorded to the courts and the administration of justice by the law of contempt can reasonably be justified in the public interest, how can this Court now decide, consistently with that view, that a much larger degree of protection of the Commission and its members is capable of being considered to be justified in the public interest? ... [N]o one could deny that, in the highly charged, contentious world of industrial relations, the reputation of the Commission for integrity, objectivity and fairness is vitally important. Public acceptance of the Commission's determinations is essential to the stability of industrial peace and harmony. But no less important is the interest of the public in ensuring that the Commission and its activities should be open to public scrutiny and criticism. That interest, it seems to me, is just as fundamental in the case of the Commission as it is in the case of the courts and the administration of justice. Viewing the question from the perspective of the need to protect the Commission, there may be a case for saying that the Commission's need is greater than that of the courts. Because the Commission is **[34]** not a court, its decision-making processes differ from curial processes and it deals with industrial disputes, it can be said that it does not have the standing and status in the public mind which the court system enjoys. On this argument, its reputation needs a greater degree of protection. I am prepared to assume, without deciding, that there is force in this argument. However, it is in any event outweighed by the strength of the public interest in public scrutiny and freedom to criticize.

This conclusion leads me into the second point of relevance to the issue of proportionality. In deciding an issue of proportionality in the context of the incidental scope of a substantive legislative power, the Court must take account of and scrutinize with great anxiety the adverse impact, if any, of the impugned law on such a fundamental freedom as freedom of expression, particularly when that impact impairs freedom of expression in relation to public affairs and freedom to criticize public institutions. Recognition of the paramount importance of freedom of expression and of criticism of public institutions has strongly influenced the formulation of the principles of the law of contempt. It is inevitable that recognition of that importance must govern the Court's present decision on whether s 299(1)(d)(ii) has a relevant connexion with the subject-matter of the legislative power.

It is fascinating to compare this judgment, written by Mason CJ in 1992, with his arguments as Solicitor-General in 1965 in *Fairfax* and in *Herald & Weekly Times*. The judgment in *Nationwide News* uses much of the same thematic material, but deploys it to produce an almost opposite result. The end result of *Fairfax* was that, provided the purpose of a law is sufficient to establish its connection with a subject-matter of legislative power, the fact that the legislative means adopted "[437] are out of all proportion ... affords no ground of constitutional attack". On the other hand, in *Nationwide News*, the lack of proportion in such a case became a ground for constitutional attack.

McHugh J took a similar view to that of Mason CJ, but with greater deference to the traditional approach to characterisation. Dawson J also reached the same result, but rejected Mason CJ's reliance upon the "proportionality" test. He approached the issue solely in terms of whether there was "a sufficient connection" with the head of power. Quoting what Dixon CJ had said in *Burton v Honan*, he added:

> **Dawson J: [87]** [I]t is for this reason that, in an exercise of the kind which [88] must be undertaken in this case, limited assistance is to be derived from the concept of reasonable proportionality. No doubt a law which is inappropriate or ill-adapted for the purpose of achieving a legitimate end may fail for want of a power. But it fails not because the Court considers the law to be inappropriate or ill adapted but because the very fact that the law is inappropriate or ill adapted prevents there being a sufficient connexion between the law and a relevant head of power. The question is essentially one of connexion, not appropriateness or proportionality, and where a sufficient connexion is established it is not for the Court to judge whether the law is inappropriate or disproportionate ...
>
> **[89]** Reasonable proportionality may provide a test of validity where a purposive power is concerned. Then the question is what the legislation operates *for*, not what it operates *upon*. That is to say, purpose rather than connexion with any particular subject-matter must then be the test. When a power is not purposive (and most of the powers in s 51 are not) the ultimate question is not whether the law is reasonably adapted to the achievement of a purpose, but whether it has a sufficient operation upon – a sufficient connexion with – something forming part of the subject-matter of the power. For that reason, the concept of reasonable proportionality is of limited assistance where purposive powers are not involved and the danger in employing it is that it invites the Court to act upon its view of the desirability of the impugned legislation rather than upon the connexion of the legislation with the subject-matter of the legislative power.

The extent to which Mason CJ had tried to introduce "proportionality" into the process of characterisation was obviously controversial. However, the plaintiffs in *Cunliffe v Commonwealth* (1994) 182 CLR 272 tried to stretch it even further. They argued that purposive criteria could be invoked in all problems of characterisation. This extension was rejected, with the Court continuing to draw the line where Mason CJ had drawn it in *Nationwide News*; that is, "proportionality" may be relevant in cases where characterisation depends on purpose, including cases that depend on the incidental power.

Cunliffe involved a challenge to Pt 2A of the *Migration Act 1958* (Cth). Part 2A regulated the giving of "immigration assistance" and the making of "immigration representations" by requiring persons (including legal practitioners) providing such services on a professional or organisational basis to be registered under the Act. At issue was whether Pt 2A was a valid enactment under the Commonwealth's "aliens" power (s 51(xix) of the Constitution). Since Pt 2A did not operate directly on "aliens", but on persons wishing to provide advice and assistance to "aliens", it was argued that if it was to be characterised as a law with respect to "aliens" this must be by virtue of the incidental power. It was further submitted that reliance on the incidental power must depend on the "purpose" of the law and hence on whether it was appropriate and proportionate to that purpose.

The whole Court rejected this argument on the ground that Pt 2A could be characterised directly as a law with respect to "aliens" without resort to the incidental power. Brennan, Toohey and McHugh JJ all quoted what Stephen J had said in *Actors and Announcers Equity Association v Fontana Films Pty Ltd* (1982) 150 CLR 169: "**[195]** A law forbidding certain acts of third parties for the reason that they were both intended, and also likely, to harm aliens would surely be as central to the grant of power with respect to aliens as a law which required aliens to do or refrain from particular conduct". On this basis, the need for resort to arguments about incidental power (and hence about "proportionality") did not strictly arise. Nevertheless, Mason CJ in particular maintained his view that where the validity of a law depends upon the "incidental power", it may be relevant to determine whether the law satisfies the test of reasonable proportionality.

The use of "proportionality" was again invoked in *Leask v Commonwealth* (1996) 187 CLR 579. As in *Cunliffe*, the argument failed. In seven separate judgments the Court discussed the proper role of "proportionality" in relation to characterisation at length. However, the effect of what was said has been variously understood. On one view, in *Leask* as in *Cunliffe*, the effect is to draw the line where Mason drew it in *Nationwide News* – accepting the relevance of "proportionality" where validity depends on the *purpose* of the law in question, and accepting that this may *sometimes* be the case where the argument for validity depends on the incidental power, with the area of disagreement confined to whether or not it can be said that arguments about incidental power are *usually or typically* dependent on arguments about legislative purpose. On another view, the various judgments in *Leask* represent a significant move away from reliance on "proportionality" as an aid to characterisation.

The *Financial Transaction Reports Act 1988* (Cth) was aimed at hindering the unlawful cash economy, including tax evasion and money laundering. Section 7 required "cash dealers" to report transactions that involved the transfer of $10,000 or more. Under s 31(1), it was an offence to seek to avoid s 7 by splitting transactions into multiple amounts of less than $10,000. More precisely, the parties to such a transaction were guilty of an offence "if … it would be reasonable to conclude" that their purpose was to avoid the reporting requirements. Whether it was reasonable so to conclude was to be determined on the basis of factual criteria, including "any explanation made by the person as to the manner or form in which the transactions were conducted". There was room for debate (which the High Court judgments did not resolve) as to whether or not these last quoted words made adequate provision for the element of *mens rea* that the common law has traditionally regarded as an essential element in criminal liability. To the extent that s 31(1) did *not* adequately provide for *mens rea*, its effect was to create a strict liability offence. It was this that the plaintiffs relied upon as "disproportionate" to the purpose of the Act.

The Commonwealth argued that s 31(1) was valid *either* under s 51(xii) of the Constitution (as a law with respect to "Currency, coinage, and legal tender"), *or* under s 51(ii) (as a law with respect to "Taxation …"). The whole Court held that the provision was valid. Brennan CJ, Dawson, McHugh and Gummow JJ held that it was a law with respect to "currency" (and reached no final view as to "taxation"). Kirby J held that it was valid as a law with respect to "taxation" (and reached no final view as to "currency"). Toohey and Gaudron JJ held that it was valid under both heads of power. However, the significant feature of the judgments was not the choice between "currency" and "taxation", but the discussion of the principles to be applied, under either head of power, in determining whether the law fell within the implied incidental power – and, in particular, the extent to which, in determining such a question, notions of "purpose" and "proportionality" might be relevant.

Although the various judicial statements in *Leask* can be read as a reaffirmation of the limits asserted in *Cunliffe*, it seems clear that within those limits all members of the Court affirmed a more cautious view of the extent to which questions of "purpose" and "proportionality" may be relevant to characterisation. In particular, there was a shared emphasis that a finding of incidental power depends simply on a "sufficient connection" with the main head of power, and that while such a connection may sometimes be established by the purpose of the challenged law, it may also frequently be established simply by the factual subject-matter or practical operation of the law.

Leask v Commonwealth
(1996) 187 CLR 579

Dawson J: [599] Even if s 31(1) did create an offence of absolute or strict liability, I do not think that the argument which the plaintiff seeks to put would be available to him. To say that a law is not reasonably capable of being seen as appropriate and adapted to achieving an object or purpose within power or is not reasonably proportionate to some object or purpose within power is to posit a proposition or propositions which do not assist in determining the validity of the law. The expressions are borrowed from other jurisdictions and their usefulness is limited; indeed, it may be thought that they confuse rather than clarify the processes by which the validity of a law under our Constitution must be determined.

The words "appropriate" and "adapted" appear to have their origin in the judgment of the United States Supreme Court delivered by Marshall CJ in *McCulloch v Maryland* [17 US (4 Wheat) 159 at 206 (1819)], where the following passage appears:

"Let the end be legitimate, let it be within the scope of the constitution, and all means which are appropriate, which are plainly adapted to that end, which are not prohibited, but consist with the letter and spirit of the constitution, are constitutional."

But the context in which those words were uttered makes it plain beyond argument that they did not envisage a restriction upon the powers of Congress. On the contrary, they were spoken in rejection of an argument that Congress was restricted in the exercise of the powers otherwise vested in it by the constitution by the addition to its enumerated powers of the power to make "all laws which shall be necessary and proper, for carrying into execution the foregoing powers, and all other powers vested by this constitution, in the government of the United States, or in any department thereof" [17 US at 202] ...

[600] Notwithstanding that Marshall CJ intended the words "appropriate" and "adapted" to signify anything but a requirement that the means adopted by the legislature to achieve a constitutionally valid end must be proportionate to that end, they have been taken up and used, in conjunction with a so-called principle of proportionality, to suggest just such a requirement ...

The concept of reasonable proportionality has its origin in Europe, where it was developed as an instrument for the review of legislative and administrative acts. In the jurisprudence of the European Court of Justice the principle of proportionality emerged from the legal systems of member states of the European Community as a general principle of European Community law. The principle was written into the Treaty establishing the European Economic Community (the Treaty of Rome) by the Treaty on European Union (the Maastricht Treaty) ... in the following terms:

"Any action by the Community shall not go beyond what is necessary to achieve the objectives of this Treaty."

The inappropriateness of such a concept in Australian constitutional law where legislative power is with few exceptions conferred by reference to subject matter rather than aims or objectives is immediately apparent. It is even more apparent when regard is had to the manner in which the principle is applied. For example, in a case involving a challenge to a prohibition ... **[601]** upon the use in agriculture of a certain substance, it was submitted that the prohibition infringed the principle of proportionality. The European Court of Justice stated the principle as follows [*R v Minister for Agriculture, Fisheries and Food; Ex parte FEDESA* [1990] 5 ECR I-4023 at I-4063]:

"[T]he lawfulness of the prohibition of an economic activity is subject to the condition that the prohibitory measures are appropriate and necessary in order to achieve the objectives legitimately pursued by the legislation in question; when there is a choice between several appropriate measures recourse must be had to the least onerous, and the disadvantages caused must not be disproportionate to the aims pursued."

In deciding whether the measure in question satisfied that test ..., the Court considered the practicability of the measure, the possibility that it might lead to a black market, the relative merits of prohibition and the dissemination of information and advice, and the appropriateness of causing financial hardship to certain traders. When considering whether a law is with respect to a particular head of power in our Constitution, such matters are not relevant. They are essentially political rather than judicial considerations.

The fact that the legislative powers conferred upon the Commonwealth Parliament by s 51 of the Constitution are expressed to be with respect to subject matters means that a law is within power if the acts, facts, matters or things upon which it operates fall within the description of one or more heads of power ...

[602] Establishing the requisite connection is often a matter of degree, but once it is established, it does not matter that the legislature has chosen a means of achieving its aim which goes further than is necessary or desirable. That is a matter for the legislature. As Dixon CJ said in *Burton v Honan* [(1952) 86 CLR 169 at 179]:

"[O]nce the subject matter [of the law] is fairly within the province of the Federal legislature the justice and wisdom of the provisions which it makes in the exercise of its powers over the subject matter are matters entirely for the Legislature and not for the Judiciary."

Or as Kitto J said in *Herald and Weekly Times Ltd v Commonwealth* [(1966) 115 CLR 418 at 437]:

"[T]he fact that the Parliament has chosen to go to great lengths – even the fact, if it be so, that for many persons difficulties are created which are out of all proportion to the advantage gained – affords no ground of constitutional attack."

To introduce the concept of proportionality, whether it be via the notion that a law must be reasonably appropriate and adapted to some end in view or by any other route, is to introduce a concept which is alien to the principles which this Court has hitherto applied in determining the validity of laws passed by the Commonwealth Parliament. Putting purposive powers to one side, so far as I am able to discern the attempt to do so has been made only in relation to the incidental power which is to be implied as an aspect of each of the substantive heads of power in s 51, that is to say, the power to legislate with respect to all those things which are reasonably incidental to the complete fulfilment of the power. In this context it is important to appreciate that, whilst it is correct to speak of implied incidental powers, each head of power is but one grant of power. As Brennan J said in *Cunliffe* [182 CLR at 318]: "the core and incidental aspects of a power are not separated; the power is an entirety." No doubt as one moves closer to the outer limits of a power, the purpose of a law which lies at "the circumference of the subject [matter of the power] or can at best be only incidental to it" [*Bank Nationalisation Case* (1948) 76 CLR 1 at 354] becomes important, because "by divining the purpose of a law from its effect and [603] operation, its connection with the subject of the power may appear more clearly" [182 CLR at 319]. "Purpose" in that connection is merely an aspect of what the law does in fact and the test remains one of sufficient connection. If that connection is established, it matters not how ill-adapted, inappropriate or disproportionate a law is or may be thought to be.

The purpose of a law passed pursuant to a head of power is a different thing from the purpose of the head of power. In *Cunliffe* [182 CLR at 296] Mason CJ, whilst recognising that most of the heads of power in s 51 are not of a purposive nature, thought that:

"that does not mean that faithful pursuit of purpose is a relevant or critical element only in those cases in which one is concerned with the reach of an implied incidental power in conjunction with a specific power which is truly purposive."

However, to speak of the purpose of a non-purposive power is merely to speak of its subject matter. To take this case, the purpose of the power to make laws with respect to currency can be nothing more than the authorisation of legislation upon the subject of currency. Nevertheless, Mason CJ continued [182 CLR at 296-7]:

"Faithful pursuit of purpose is necessarily a relevant consideration when the validity of a law is sought to be sustained on the ground that it is designed to achieve an end within power, even though it operates on a subject matter beyond power. In cases of this kind, in considering whether there is a substantial or sufficient connection between the impugned provision and the relevant law, it may be material to inquire whether the provision is capable of being reasonably considered to be appropriate and adapted to the end in view. The requirement that there be an affirmative answer to that inquiry implies that 'a reasonable proportionality must exist between the designated object or purpose and the means selected by the law for achieving that object or purpose'."

I must confess that I have some difficulty with that passage. I assume that in speaking of "a substantial or sufficient connection between the impugned provision and the relevant law", his Honour was speaking of a substantial or sufficient connection between the impugned provision and the relevant head of power. And if that is so, "the end in view" must mean the end or purpose of the head of power. But as I **[604]** have said, most heads of power do not have an end or purpose other than the authorisation of legislation upon their subject matter and whether a law is upon a subject-matter depends upon its connection with that subject matter. If, on the other hand, "the end in view" to which his Honour refers is the end of the legislation, this is only a relevant consideration if it assists in determining whether the requisite connection between the law and the subject matter of a head of power is established. If it is established, the proportionality or appropriateness of the means selected by the Parliament to achieve the end in view are matters for it alone ...

[605] For these reasons, it is my view that the relevant test of the validity of a law made under one of the substantive heads of power in s 51 of the Constitution is that of sufficiency of connection with its subject matter. That is so whether or not in characterising the law it is necessary to invoke the implied incidental power. As I said in *Cunliffe*, the disproportion of a law to an end asserted to be within power may suggest that the law is actually a means of achieving another end which is beyond power. And no doubt there is a question of judgment involved in deciding whether a law exhibits a sufficient connection with the subject matter of a head of power. But that does not involve a judgment as to the desirability of legislation, and the danger with expressing the test in terms of proportionality is that it suggests that the court is concerned with the desirability of legis-lation. The Court does not for the purpose of determining validity under s 51 inquire into whether a law either is necessary to achieve an end or infringes fundamental values in a manner not justified by the pursuit of that end. That is not, of course, to deny that, before construing a law as interfering with basic common law freedoms, the Court requires the clearest expression of intent. Whatever the position may be in other legal systems, the terms "appropriate and adapted" and "reasonable proportionality" are best avoided when enunciating a test to determine whether a law exceeds a non-purposive head of power under s 51 of our Constitution.

The situation may be different where the purpose of a law is a crucial determinant of validity, as it is where a power is conferred in purposive terms. Taking the defence power for example, a court must **[606]** ask whether a law is for the purpose of defence. There is no subject matter as there is with other powers – lighthouses or external affairs, for example – and it is therefore not possible to delineate the boundaries of the power by reference to subject matter: the acts, facts, matters or things upon which a law with respect to defence may operate are, at least in war-time, virtually without limits. To determine the validity of a law said to be supported by a purposive power, a court must ask whether it is a law for the specified purpose, and the court may have to inquire into whether the law goes further than is necessary to achieve that purpose. That is an exercise in proportionality.

The situation is also different where a law is said to fall foul of a constitutional limitation on legislative power. As Brennan CJ points out in this case, and as I accepted in *Australian Capital Television Pty Ltd v Commonwealth* [(1992) 177 CLR 106 at 195], it may be within power to legislate in a way that affects an immunity conferred by a limitation on power where to do so is merely incidental to the achievement of a legitimate end. In such a situation one is concerned with the resolution of a tension between two principles and notions of proportionality may be relevant.

Note that while Dawson J rejects the use of proportionality as an aid to characterisation in relation to subject-matter powers, even when the incidental aspect of such powers comes into play, he concedes that it may be a legitimate aid to characterisation in relation to purposive powers such as the defence power. He also concedes that proportionality may be relevant in determining whether a law infringes a constitutional limitation. He thus acknowledges the widespread use of such tests in deciding whether a law that pursues a legitimate purpose or object, and does so within a clear grant of power, may nevertheless be invalid by reason of limitations on how the power can be exercised (whether the limitations are express, as with ss 92 and 117, or implied, as with the freedom of political communication).

Brennan CJ and Gummow J agreed with Dawson J, as did McHugh J, who stated: "**[616]** Where, however, the dominant subject matter of an impugned law is not itself a head of federal power, but that law has ostensibly been passed to achieve some purpose falling within a subject of Commonwealth power, the sub-test of proportionality may sometimes prove helpful in determining whether the subject matter of the impugned law is sufficiently connected to the subject of federal power". He argued that this should be seen as part of the general question of whether a law has a "sufficient connection" with a head of power. Toohey J, as he had done in *Cunliffe*, sought to reserve the use of the word "proportionality" *only* for cases where the problem is that an otherwise valid law impinges on the values protected by some express or implied limitation on the way in which legislative power is exercised. Gaudron J rejected that attempt at a definitional limit. She continued to insist that "proportionality" "[616] is one of several considerations that may be taken into account in determining purpose, whenever that is in issue and for whatever reason, and, also, in determining whether a law is relevantly connected with a particular subject or with a head of constitutional power". Kirby J did not resolve the issue, but located his discussion of proportionality within a review of the characterisation process.

> **Kirby J: [634]** In considering the sufficiency of the suggested connection between the law, so characterised, and the constitutional head of power relied on, some recent observations in this Court have remarked that it may be useful to apply a test of "proportionality" to the impugned provision. This test has not enjoyed universal favour. Behind the expressed doubts lies more than resistance to a legal concept with an origin outside the common law. The risk that assessments of proportionality may take a court into evaluation of policy and judgment on the desirability of the means employed by the law **[635]** occasions the hesitation to embrace the notion of proportionality as a universal criterion for constitutional validity. Distinctions have been drawn (repeated in this case) between the value of the concept in cases where the constitutional power is conferred in purposive terms, cases where the power is expressed as restricted by a limitation and other cases. Such distinctions find no reflection in the concept of proportionality in the legal systems from which that concept was originally derived. They were not mentioned in the authorities by which the concept originally found its way into the jurisprudence of this Court. They are difficult to reconcile with the essential idea of proportionality. They are not universally accepted by the opinions expressed within the Court. It is difficult, in principle, to embrace the proposition that proportionality might be an appropriate criterion for some paragraphs of s 51 of the Constitution yet impermissible in respect of others. The same basic question is in issue in every case: namely where the boundary of federal constitutional power lies. Whilst there is no settled doctrine on the use of the concept of proportionality in resolving constitutional disputes, recent cases suggest a growing acceptance of the notion as a useful test of general application. It may provide a means to help the mind of the decision-maker to answer the question whether the impugned law is "in truth" one with respect to a designated grant of power, as mandated by Kitto J in *Fairfax v Federal Commissioner of Taxation* [(1965) 114 CLR 1 at 7]. That question is not readily answered by repeating, as a mantra, the puzzle: "Does the law have sufficient connection with the constitutional head of power?" In the words "sufficient" and "connection" lie much room for differences of opinion. Such well-worn phrases merely state what the judicial task is. They do not really elucidate how it is to be performed. That is why the attempt has been made by some members of the Court to find a subsidiary or additional test which, because of its functional nature, may be useful in the task of characterisation. Proportionality is certainly a concept of growing influence on our law more generally. I consider that it may sometimes be helpful in the context of constitutional characterisation …
>
> Consistent with the function of this Court, neither the task of characterisation nor the application of the concept of proportionality **[636]** affords any authority for judging the desirability of the law or the means employed by the lawmaker. Provided the law is within power, the means adopted will not ordinarily be a matter for the court.

The issues of whether, and in what conceptual setting, the incidental aspect of a power may be subject to a requirement of proportionality did not strictly arise in *Leask*, since the whole Court agreed that proportionality had no role to play in *this* case. Indeed, not even Mason CJ would have suggested that it did. His argument in *Nationwide News* and *Cunliffe* was only that the doctrine has a role to play in ascertaining validity under the incidental aspect of a power, not where a law falls squarely under the central aspect of a non-purposive power. Section 31(1) of the *Financial Transaction Reports Act* was a law within the central area of a head of power, whether that head of power was thought to be "currency" or "taxation". Accordingly, as stated by Gummow J: "**[624]** No recourse to ancillary or incidental legislative power is necessary to sustain [its] validity".

9. Further References

Fitzgerald, BF, "Proportionality and Australian Constitutionalism" (1993) 12 *University of Tasmania Law Review* 263.

Lee, HP, "Proportionality in Australian Constitutional Adjudication" in Lindell, G (ed), *Future Directions in Australian Constitutional Law* (Federation Press, 1994), 126.

Kirk, J, "Constitutional Guarantees, Characterisation and the Concept of Proportionality" (1997) 21 *Melbourne University Law Review* 1.

McCann, D, "First Head Revisited: A Single Industrial Relations System under the Trade and Commerce Power" (2004) 26 *Sydney Law Review* 75.

Phillips, PD, "The Trade and Commerce Power" in Else-Mitchell, R (ed), *Essays on the Australian Constitution* (Law Book Co, 2nd ed 1961), 129.

Selway, B, "The Rise and Rise of the Reasonable Proportionality Test in Public Law" (1996) 7 *Public Law Review* 212.

Zines, L, "Characterisation of Commonwealth Laws" in Lee, HP, and Winterton, G, (eds), *Australian Constitutional Perspectives* (Law Book Co, 1992), 33.

Zines, L, "Engineers and the 'Federal Balance'" in Coper, M, and Williams, G (eds), *How Many Cheers for Engineers?* (Federation Press, 1997), 81.

Zines, L, *The High Court and the Constitution* (Butterworths, 4th ed 1997), Chs 2-4, 17.

Chapter 17

The Corporations Power

1. *Huddart Parker* Overthrown

For over half a century, the "corporations" power conferred by s 51(xx) of the Constitution was largely ignored as a basis for Commonwealth legislation because of the decision in *Huddart, Parker & Co Pty Ltd v Moorehead* (1909) 8 CLR 330. That decision held that the power could not support the *Australian Industries Preservation Act 1906* (Cth) (an early version of "anti-trust" or "trade practices" legislation). It was not until *Huddart Parker* was overruled in *Strickland v Rocla Concrete Pipes Ltd* (*Concrete Pipes Case*) (1971) 124 CLR 468 that the modern development of the power began.

The *Australian Industries Preservation Act* applied to "foreign corporations, and trading or financial corporations formed within the limits of the Commonwealth". Sections 5(1) and 8(1) prohibited such corporations from engaging in certain restrictive trade practices, such as "unfair competition" or "monopolisation". Isaacs J, in dissent, read s 51(xx) broadly enough to accommodate these provisions. The other judges, including Higgins J, did not. They agreed that the power should be construed narrowly, but were not able to agree on an appropriate interpretation. Their approach reflected the perceived need to protect "the reserved powers of the States", an idea abandoned in 1920 in *Amalgamated Society of Engineers v Adelaide Steamship Co Ltd* (*Engineers' Case*) (1920) 28 CLR 129. A related factor was the fear that a broader interpretation might prove uncontrollable. This gave rise to Higgins' list of "horribles" (PH Lane, *The Australian Federal System* (Law Book Co, 2nd ed 1979), 160).

Huddart, Parker & Co Pty Ltd v Moorehead
(1909) 8 CLR 330

Higgins J: [409] If the argument for the Crown is right, the results are certainly extraordinary, big with confusion. If it is right, the Federal Parliament is in a position to frame a new system of libel laws applicable to newspapers owned by corporations, while the State law of libel would have to remain applicable to newspapers owned by individuals. If it is right, the Federal Parliament is competent to enact licensing Acts, creating a new scheme of administration and of offences applicable only to hotels belonging to corporations. If it is right, the Federal Parliament may enact that no foreign or trading or financial corporation shall pay its **[410]** employés less than 10s per day, or charge more than 6 per cent interest, whereas other corporations and persons would be free from such restrictions. If it is right, the Federal Parliament can enact that no officer of a corporation shall be an Atheist or a Baptist, or that all must be teetotallers. If it is right, the Federal Parliament can repeal the *Statute of Frauds* for contracts of a corporation, or may make some new *Statute of Limitations* applicable only to corporations. Taking the analogous power to make laws with regard to lighthouses, if the respondent's argument is right, the Federal Parliament can license a lighthouse for the sale of beer and spirits, or may establish schools in lighthouses with distinctive doctrinal teaching, although the licensing laws and the education laws are, for ordinary purposes, left to the State legislatures.

In his dissenting judgment, Isaacs J attempted to set limits to the power.

Isaacs J: [393] What, then, on ordinary principles of construction, is the extent of the power to make laws in respect of "foreign corporations, and trading or financial corporations formed within the limits of the Commonwealth?" … In the first place, it is a separate and independent power complete in itself, and additional to the commerce power. The commerce power is exercisable wherever that subject exists, whether individuals or corporations are engaged in it. The power over corporations is exercisable wherever these specific *objects* are found, irrespective of whether they are engaged in foreign or Inter-State commerce, or commerce confined to a single State. Next, it is clear that the power is to operate only on corporations of a certain kind, namely, foreign, trading, and financial corporations. For instance, a purely manufacturing company is not a trading corporation; and it is always a preliminary question whether a given company is a trading or financial corporation or a foreign corporation. This leaves entirely outside the range of federal power, as being in themselves objects of the power, all those domestic corporations, for instance, which are constituted for municipal, mining, manufacturing, religious, scholastic, charitable, scientific, and literary purposes, and possibly others more nearly approximating a character of trading; a strong circumstance to show how and to what extent the autonomy of the States was intended to be safeguarded. The federal power was sufficiently limited by specific enumeration, and there is no need to place further limits on the words of the legislature. Another thing is clear, that corporations to come within the legislative reach of the Commonwealth must be corporations already existing. It is not a power to create corporations. When such a power was intended to be given it was expressly mentioned as in paragraph (xiii), and federal incorporation necessarily includes a granting of all capacities and the enactment of all ancillary provisions for internal procedure, even though these matters would otherwise be **[394]** exclusively within State jurisdiction … Foreign corporations are *ex vi termini* already existing, and the Australian trading and financial corporations subject to the power are those "*formed* within the limits of the Commonwealth". The words quoted would be meaningless if the power of creation, either in the first instance, or by way of adding capacities were included …

[395] I take the power to legislate "for the peace, order, and good government of the Commonwealth with respect to foreign corporations, and trading and financial corporations formed within the limits of the Commonwealth" to be a power to act upon certain beings, which are found and remain in actual existence, possessing a fixed identity, a defined ambit of potentiality, having certain capacities and faculties unalterable by the Commonwealth, beings ready to act within their sphere of capabilities in relation to the people of the Commonwealth. Necessarily you cannot legislate for such corporations except with respect to some extraneous circumstances or events, whether trade, or finance, or contracts, &c, and there is nothing in the Constitution which says anything about the object, primary or secondary. I adhere to my view regarding purpose, motive, and objects expressed in *Barger's Case* [(1908) 6 CLR 41]. The power does not look behind the charter, or concern itself with purely internal management, or mere personal preparation to act; it views the beings upon which it is to operate in their relations to outsiders, or, in other words, in the actual exercise of their corporate powers, and entrusts to *the Commonwealth Parliament the regulation of the conduct of the corporations in their transactions with or as affecting the public*. Many of the matters that in one aspect are internal – such as balance sheets, registers of members, payment of calls, &c – may in another aspect and in certain circumstances be important elements in connection with outward transactions, and have a direct relation to them, and so fall incidentally within the ambit of federal power. The same may be said of legal proceedings, remedies, and so on, including winding up proceedings so far as necessary to satisfy creditors, but **[396]** not so far as extinction. But whether any given provision is part of the federal power or not must, as I view it, depend on whether it includes or is necessarily incidental to *the control of the conduct of the corporations in relation to outside persons*.

By overruling the majority judgments in *Huddart Parker*, the *Concrete Pipes Case* raised the question of whether the dissenting view of Isaacs J had been correct. In some respects, this remains unresolved. Note that in the above passage Isaacs J discusses two separate questions:

1. *Which corporations* come within Commonwealth power under s 51(xx)? When is a corporation "a s 51(xx) corporation"?
2. *What aspects or activities* of a corporation can be regulated under s 51(xx)?

The answer to question 1 is given by s 51(xx) itself: "foreign corporations", and "trading or financial corporations formed within the limits of the Commonwealth". The problem is how to construe these words. Insofar as Isaacs J gave them a narrow construction (excluding, for example, corporations "[393] constituted for municipal, mining, manufacturing, religious, scholastic, charitable, scientific, and literary purposes") it now seems clear that he was wrong. Addressing question 2 is more difficult. Two views, a narrow and a wide view, border the range of possible answers:

1. The clue is in the categories of corporations specified as being within power: "foreign corporations", and Australian-based "trading" or "financial" corporations. Thus the aspects or activities that the Commonwealth can regulate must have something to do with the characteristic that brings corporations within Commonwealth power. This would mean, for example, that only the trading activities of trading corporations could be regulated.
2. There are no limits at all. Provided a corporation has the characteristics that bring it within s 51(xx), any aspect or activity of that corporation can be regulated by the Commonwealth. It is this possibility that evokes the fears expressed by Higgins J.

From one point of view, both of the above questions relate to the *interpretation of the power* delineated in s 51(xx), rather than to the appropriate *characterisation of a law* (for example, the *Australian Industries Preservation Act*). For Isaacs J this was natural enough since his *Huddart Parker* judgment was for him a first attempt to chart the limits of the legislative power. However, in the cases surveyed below from the 1970s and 1980s, the continued focus on these two questions may have been misleading in not focusing sufficiently on the characterisation of the particular law under challenge, as later cases such as *Re Dingjan; Ex parte Wagner* (1995) 183 CLR 323 have increasingly tended to do.

The *Concrete Pipes Case* was a challenge to aspects of the *Trade Practices Act 1965* (Cth). Under s 35, agreements between competitors restricting competition were made "examinable". The examinable restrictions were defined to include those in agreements made by s 51(xx) corporations. In the result the 1965 Act was held *not* to be valid, since its intricate way of invoking and combining *different* sources of legislative power was not acceptable to the Court (see Chapter 13, §6(b)). Nevertheless, the Court also held that s 51(xx) was available to support a law of this kind. (It did not, however, attempt to answer the questions raised by Isaacs J in *Huddart Parker*.) The leading judgment was delivered by Barwick CJ, who as Attorney-General in the Menzies Government in 1962 had initiated the drive for trade practices reform that culminated in the 1965 Act.

Strickland v Rocla Concrete Pipes Ltd (*Concrete Pipes Case*)
(1971) 124 CLR 468

Barwick CJ: [484] I address myself to the first question namely – should this Court now accept its decision in *Huddart, Parker & Co Pty Ltd v Moorehead* [(1909) 8 CLR 330] as a correct construction of s 51(xx) of the Constitution. I am clearly of opinion that it should not. However, out of respect for those Justices who formed the majority in deciding that case and having regard to the time which has elapsed since the decision was given, I should offer some analysis of the decision and state my reasons as concisely as possible for thinking that it was erroneous …

[485] The case was decided in the year 1909 at a time when the current doctrine of this Court was that the construction of the words of the Constitution by which legislative power is granted to the Parliament should be approached on the footing that there were certain legislative areas reserved by the Constitution to the States and that the Constitution should not be read as authorizing the Parliament to invade those areas unless as a necessary incident to the exercise of some granted power. This was the so-called reserved powers doctrine which was exploded and unambiguously rejected by this Court in the year 1920 in the decision of the *Amalgamated Society of Engineers v Adelaide Steamship Co Ltd* ("the *Engineers' Case*") [(1920) 28 CLR 129] …

[488] It is plain enough from a reading of the reasons given by the majority in *Huddart, Parker & Co Pty Ltd v Moorehead* that the influence of the then current reserved powers doctrine was so strong that the Court was driven to emasculate the legislative power given by s 51(xx) and to confine it in substance to the statutory recognition of corporations falling within the terms of the paragraph and the fixing of the conditions upon which they might enter trade in Australia: for the rest, their trading activities in intra-State trade [were] a matter for the State legislation exclusively …

[489] I therefore conclude that the reasoning of this Court in *Huddart, Parker & Co Pty Ltd v Moorehead* was in error and that it ought not be accepted now by this Court. The question then remains whether the Court's decision that s 5(1) and s 8(1) were invalid ought to be overruled …

[Those sections] were clearly laws regulating and controlling amongst other things the trading activities of foreign corporations and trading and financial corporations formed within the limits of the Commonwealth. In my opinion such laws were laws with respect to such corporations. They dealt with the very heart of the purpose for which the corporation was formed, for whether a trading or financial corporation, by assumption, its purpose is to trade, trade for constitutional purposes not being limited to dealings in goods. cf *Bank of New South Wales v Commonwealth* (*Bank Nationalization Case*) [(1948) 76 CLR 1]. If the corporation is exercising its powers it will be carrying out trading operations and in that pursuit making agreements with others in matters of trade. Agreements to restrict trade or endeavouring to monopolize it are activities in trade with which the law has been familiar for centuries. Sections 5(1) and 8(1) in controlling such activities are in my opinion clearly laws with respect to the topic of s 51(xx). I would conclude therefore that s 5(1) and s 8(1) were valid and that the Court's decision to the contrary in *Huddart, Parker & Co Pty Ltd v Moorehead* should be overruled.

However, having regard to Sir Samuel Griffith's remark in *Huddart, Parker & Co Pty Ltd v Moorehead* [8 CLR at 345] and what was said in argument in these appeals I ought to observe that it does not follow either as a logical proposition, or, if in this instance there be a difference, as a legal proposition, from the validity of those sections, that any law which in the range of its command or prohibition includes foreign corporations or trading or financial corporations formed within the limits of the Commonwealth is **[490]** necessarily a law with respect to the subject matter of s 51(xx). Nor does it follow that any law which is addressed specifically to such corporations or some of them is such a law. Sections 5(1) and 8(1), in my opinion, were valid because they were regulating and controlling the trading activities of trading corporations and thus within the scope of s 51(xx). But the decision as to the validity of particular laws yet to be enacted must remain for the Court when called upon to pass upon them. No doubt, laws which may be validly made under s 51(xx) will cover a wide range of the activities of foreign corporations and trading and financial corporations: perhaps in the case of foreign corporations even a wider range than in the case of other corporations: but in any case, not necessarily limited to trading activities. I must not be taken as suggesting that the question whether a particular law is a law within the scope of this power should be approached in any narrow or pedantic manner.

We were invited in the argument of these appeals to set as it were the outer limits of the reach of the power under this paragraph of s 51. This for my part I am not prepared to do: and indeed I do not regard the Court as justified in doing so. The method of constitutional interpretation is the same as that with which we have long been familiar in the common law. The law develops case by case, the Court in each case deciding so much as is necessary to dispose of the case before it …

[491] [This] answers the second of the questions which earlier I thought were raised by these appeals. A law requiring the registration of trading agreements restrictive of trade to which a foreign corporation or a trading or financial corporation formed within the limits of the Commonwealth is a party, and requiring the corporation to give particulars of such an agreement under penalty of a fine for failing to do so, appears to me clearly to be a law with respect to corporations of the kind described. As I have said, the making of such an agreement in the course of trade is truly a trading activity. Such a law is a law regulating and controlling the trading activities of such corporations.

Menzies J: [507] For the most part, subject matter [in s 51] is expressed impersonally; indeed, it is only in pars (xix), (xx) and (xxvi) that the subject matter is persons. Each of these paragraphs presents its own problems. For instance, can Parliament, by legislation under par (xix), provide widowers' pensions for aliens notwithstanding that par (xxiiiA) does not authorize the provision[ ] of widowers' pensions? … [C]ould Parliament, by a law under par (xxvi), make, if it thought necessary, laws governing all the trading activities of people of particular races? … **[508]** [T]he very generality of a subject matter defined by reference to persons of a particular description provokes the question whether it is intended that the Parliament should have the power to make any laws outside constitutional prohibitions with regard to persons of these descriptions. Is any law commencing "Every alien shall …" a valid law? I do not think it is necessary here to determine whether the Attorney-General's affirmative submission is correct because all we are here concerned with is a law relating to the trading of trading corporations formed within Australia. Prima facie such a law is within power …

[511] I am not prepared to attempt to define the limits of the power conferred by s 51(xx). I content myself with saying that a law such as s 5 of the *Australian Industries Preservation Act* governing the conduct of its business by a trading corporation formed within the limits of the Commonwealth is within the power of the Parliament by virtue of s 51(xx).

The *Concrete Pipes Case* gave a clear indication that the Commonwealth could enact trade practices legislation by relying chiefly upon s 51(xx). The Commonwealth promptly responded by enacting the *Restrictive Trade Practices Act 1971* (Cth), which was superseded by the *Trade Practices Act 1974* (Cth). The course of High Court decision-making on s 51(xx) since the *Concrete Pipes Case* has mostly been confined to particular issues, proceeding on the case-by-case basis foreshadowed by Barwick CJ. The first issue to be addressed was the meaning of "trading or financial corporations".

2. Which Corporations?

In *New South Wales v Commonwealth* (*Incorporation Case*) (1990) 169 CLR 482, a majority of the Court stated: "**[498]** To fall within the [foreign corporations] limb, a corporation must be … formed outside the limits of the Commonwealth". Otherwise, the focus of attention and debate has been on the characteristics of "trading" and "financial" corporations.

The crucial issue in *R v Trade Practices Tribunal; Ex parte St George County Council* (1974) 130 CLR 533 was whether the attempt to bring the St George County Council within the *Trade Practices Act* as a "trading corporation" was to be assessed by reference to the *original purposes* for which the Council was incorporated, or by reference to its *current activities*. On either basis the character of the County Council was ambiguous. Under the *Local Government Act 1919* (NSW), it could have been given a wide range of local government functions. However, the only functions which it had been given related to the supply of electricity and electrical appliances. Barwick CJ and Stephen J preferred the "activities" test. They therefore held that the County Council was a "trading corporation" because of its substantial trading. Gibbs and Menzies JJ preferred the "purposes" test. They consequently held that the County Council was not a "trading corporation" because it had been "**[564]** constituted for the purposes of local government to provide an essential service to the inhabitants". McTiernan J agreed with the latter result, but for slightly different reasons.

If *St George County Council* had seemed to favour the "purposes" test, *R v Federal Court of Australia; Ex parte WA National Football League* (*Adamson's Case*) (1979) 143 CLR 190 went the opposite way. Under the rules of the National Football League, a club could not field a player registered with another club unless the player had been given a clearance by the appropriate State football league. Brian Adamson, "**[194]** a young man, twenty-five years of age, who has developed skill as a player of Australian Rules football," was registered with the West Perth football club and applied for a clearance from the Western Australian National Football League to play for a club in South Australia. His request was refused. He brought an action under s 45(2) of the *Trade Practices Act 1974* (Cth) claiming restraint of trade. The Act was applicable only if the football clubs and leagues were "trading corporations" within the meaning of s 51(xx) of the Constitution, as transcribed by s 4 of the Act.

Barwick CJ, Mason, Murphy and Jacobs JJ all applied an "activities" test – although Murphy J asserted that a corporation will fall within s 51(xx) if either test applies. These four judges held that corporations engaged in league football were "trading corporations" because of their substantial trading activities. Gibbs J applied a "purposes" test. He held that the league corporations were not "trading corporations" because of their original purposes. Stephen J, with whom Aickin J agreed, used an amalgam of the purposes and activities tests (without distinguishing between them) to reach the same result as Gibbs J.

While *Adamson's Case* established the activities test, it raised another question. Do the trading activities of a corporation need to be its *predominant* activities for it to be a trading corporation, or need they only be a *substantial part* of its business? *Adamson's Case* did not settle this point. Barwick CJ and Murphy J applied an activities test based on the latter approach: indeed, Murphy J stated that such activities need only be "[239] not insubstantial". Mason J, with whom Jacobs J agreed, gave obiter support to the latter approach, but based his decision on a finding that the corporation's "[235] principal activity" was trading.

R v Federal Court of Australia; Ex parte WA National Football League (*Adamson's Case*)
(1979) 143 CLR 190

Mason J: **[233]** "Trading corporation" is not and never has been a term of art or one having a special legal meaning. Nor … was there a generally accepted definition of the expression in the nineteenth century. Essentially it is a description or label given to a corporation when its trading activities form a sufficiently significant proportion of its overall activities as to merit its description as a trading corporation …

[234] Not every corporation which is engaged in trading activity is a trading corporation. The trading activity of a corporation may be so slight and so incidental to some other principal activity, viz religion or education in the case of a church or school, that it could not be described as a trading corporation. Whether the trading activities of a particular corporation are sufficient to warrant its being characterized as a trading corporation is very much a question of fact and degree. It is to this question, as it arises in relation to the facts of this case, that I now turn.

The trading activities [of the football leagues] … are so extensive as to leave no doubt in my mind that they are trading corporations. The WA League and the SA League are engaged in trading activities on a very substantial scale. The WA League has as its principal object the promotion, control, management and encouragement of Australian Rules football matches and competitions. It controls and manages the competition between the Perth clubs, adjudicating on disputes between clubs and on complaints against officials and players, imposing penalties where they are considered appropriate. The clubs are members of the League and pay a small subscription to it. The proceeds of each League competition match are received by the League. Under its constitution the WA League retains 20 per cent of these proceeds or such greater percentage as it may require, and the balance is equally divided among the member clubs. In the last three years the amounts distributed among the member clubs have been (1975) $525,921, (1976) $594,722 and (1977) $754,133. Total gate receipts derived in the last two years have been (1976) $1,102,150 and (1977) $1,310,587. Total revenue received by the League in those years has been (1976) $1,290,196 and (1977) $1,630,314. Apart from gate receipts from competition matches the League has a variety of other sources of income. They include: (a) receipts from interstate and other matches which it promotes or arranges; (b) receipts from broadcasting and television rights granted in respect of games which it promotes or arranges; (c) income from promotion, sponsorship and advertising; (d) rent for use of part of its premises; (e) catering rights at Subiaco Oval in Perth which it holds on lease; (f) income from the sale of, and advertising revenue from, its weekly **[235]** programme. The income from sales in the last three years was as follows: (1975) $58,066, (1976) $58,427 and (1977) $84,876.

The SA League has a principal object which is similar to that of its sister League in WA. It engages in, and derives income from, similar activities to those engaged in by the WA League. It is entitled to gate receipts from matches which it arranges, matches in which a team representing the SA League participates, and matches in which its clubs participate. The SA League owns Football Park which is the principal venue for football in Adelaide. The constitution of the League requires that a certain proportion of its income be credited to a fund for the development and maintenance of Football Park. The constitution contains other provisions authorizing a distribution of portion of the League's revenue amongst the member clubs. The amounts distributed to clubs in the past two years have been (1976) $470,000 and (1977) $515,000. In the same period gate receipts from grounds other than Football Park amounted to (1976) $702,174 and (1977) $821,180. In the same period the income derived at Football Park was (1976) $560,635 and (1977) $706,892. Other sources of revenue are – (a) members' subscriptions at Football Park, sale of season, presale and other tickets; (b) hire of Football Park; (c) catering fees; (d) advertising rights and sponsorships; (e) car park receipts; (f) interstate matches; (g) television and broadcasting fees.

The prosecutors' case is that the trading activities of the two Leagues are incidental to their main objects which are the promotion and encouragement of the sport as a recreation. This to my mind is an inversion of the true position. To me it seems that the sport is promoted and encouraged as a means of ensuring the receipt of the large financial returns which are associated with it. The financial revenue of the Leagues is so great and the commercial means by which it is achieved so varied that I have no hesitation in concluding that trading constitutes their principal activity. In saying this I treat all their activities which I have listed and which produce revenue as trading activities. I do not limit the concept of trading to buying and selling at a profit; it extends to business activities carried on with a view to earning revenue.

Likewise, in my opinion West Perth is a trading corporation, though it stands in a somewhat different category. Its principal objects are to foster Australian Rules football, to provide facilities for playing it and to provide recreational and sporting facilities for its members. According to its constitution, the income and property of the club are to be applied solely towards **[236]** the promotion of the objects of the club. It is expressly provided that no part of the income and property shall be paid or transferred, directly or indirectly, to the members. The fact that no part of the club's revenue or profit can be distributed to the members is a circumstance to be taken into account in deciding whether it is a trading corporation, though in my judgment it is outweighed by other considerations which point to the conclusion that West Perth is a trading corporation.

West Perth derives income from two main sources: first, from the operations of its football team in the competition run by the WA League; secondly, from various trading activities which it conducts. The first source of income includes the distribution received by it as a member club of the WA League and membership fees for admission to matches in which its teams participate. The second source of income is from bar trading and catering. Its gross income from bar trading was (1976) $116,277 and (1977) $139,644. Its net profit on trading in those years was (1976) $41,087 and (1977) $49,925. A third and minor source of income is revenue from the sale of club ties, objects and souvenirs.

The fact that West Perth is a club and that therefore its sales of liquor and food are largely made to members does not in my view affect its character as a trading corporation. There is no reason why an incorporated club which is heavily engaged in trading activities should not be held to be such a corporation, despite the fact that its trading activities are related to its character as a club and that it provides social functions, amenities and services for its members.

The principal activity of the Club is its participation as a member club of the WA League in the competitions which it runs. Indeed, that is West Perth's major source of income. The comment which Fletcher Moulton LJ made of the Crystal Palace Club in *Walker v Crystal Palace Football Club Ltd* [[1910] 1 KB 87] applies with equal force to West Perth. His Lordship said: "Here is a company that carries on the game of football as a trade, getting up and taking part in football matches." The only qualification to be made is that West Perth does not arrange or manage the competition matches.

The evidence gives some indication of the promotion and encouragement of country and junior football by the club. This activity may well enhance its prospects of recruiting players and strengthen its competitive position as a member club of the WA League. But even if it proceeds from loftier motives, it is [237] consistent with the club having the character of a trading corporation. The trader is sometimes inspired by altruism. Consequently, it is my opinion that West Perth, like the two Leagues, is a trading corporation.

Stephen J: [217] [I] have the misfortune of disagreeing with other members of the Court. I will state quite shortly my reasons for doing so.

There is, I think, no doubt but that the three bodies here in question are corporations: it is their character as "trading" corporations that I do not accept …

[218] These income-producing activities are no doubt in the nature of trade and in one sense it can be of little significance that the spectacles which the [West Perth] Club promotes involve teams of footballers. The staging of sporting spectacles may quite well provide that activity from which a trading corporation derives its income. However the fact that it is Australia's most popular spectator sport, football, which is in question is, in another sense, of great importance. It explains why it is that the Club has thousands of fee-paying members who yet derive no profits from the Club, why its unpaid committee members devote their time as its officers, why the whole complex of ardently supported clubs, of State leagues and of national associations exist and thrive, those responsible for their promotion being content to find their reward in the satisfaction of their enthusiasm for football. It is this enthusiasm that accounts for the phenomenon of corporations which are not trading corporations yet through whose tills large revenues pass …

[219] It does what it does to promote football, the income that comes its way being no doubt eagerly gathered in, but only as a means of better promoting its predominant purpose, the fostering of football …

[220] So much for the Club. Much of what I have said of it applies also to the Western Australian League. Its stated principal objects are to promote, control, manage and encourage the game of football, arranging matches and competitions. The evidence of what in fact are its activities shows them to be just that, no more and no less. Like the Club it takes advantage of the opportunities open to it to derive profits, but only those opportunities which arise incidentally in the carrying out of those very activities which it engages in in the furtherance of its principal objects. In doing this it of course trades: it charges for television, broadcasting and catering rights at the matches it organizes and for the sale of its programmes and advertising space in those programmes, it gets money for promotion, sponsorship and advertising, it collects, and retains for itself a proportion of, gate takings at matches. But, as all who participated in the *St George County Council Case* agreed, to engage in trade is not in itself to be a trading corporation …

The purpose for which the League was formed was not that of engaging in trade, nor have its activities deviated from the effecting of the purposes of its formation; its intended functions have proved to be its actual functions and these do not consist of the engaging in trade. Such trading as it undertakes is incidental to and a by-product of its principal activities and is undertaken the better to perform those activities. Accordingly I do not regard it as a trading corporation …

I have laid considerable stress upon the incidental character of the trading activities of these corporations and have done so because I think that there may well be a distinction between trading which is incidental to, and is undertaken in the course of [221] carrying out, some other principal non-trading activity and trading which is engaged in as a distinct and unconnected activity. Were the Club or the League, assuming power to do so and so as to meet a need for additional funds, to become a retail trader, say in groceries, very different questions might then arise and it might be no answer that the purpose of entering into that trade was to apply the resultant profits to the fostering of football.

Although *Adamson's Case* concerned leagues and clubs in Western Australia and South Australia, the Australian Rules football code had first been developed in Melbourne, and continues to occupy a special place in that city's urban culture. However, it was no doubt a mere coincidence that in *Adamson's Case* all four of the majority judges came from Sydney, while two of the three dissenting judges came from Melbourne.

In *Re Ku-ring-gai Co-operative Building Society (No 12) Ltd* (1978) 22 ALR 621 a Full Court of the Federal Court held that co-operative building societies providing finance for their members were "financial corporations" within the meaning of s 51(xx).

Re Ku-ring-gai Co-operative Building Society (No 12) Ltd
(1978) 22 ALR 621

Deane J: [642] ["Financial corporation"] does not refer to solvency. An obvious reference point is to the activity of commercial dealing in finance. Another possible reference point is the provision of management or advisory services in relation to financial matters. I use the words "dealing in finance", for want of a better expression, to refer to transactions in which the subject of the transaction is finance (such as borrowing or lending money) as distinct from transactions (such as the purchase or sale of particular goods for a monetary consideration) in which finance, although involved in the payment of the price, cannot properly be seen as constituting the subject of the transaction. A common but not invariable characteristic of the relevant type of transaction is that the obligation on each side is to pay money. The borrowing and lending which the applicants were formed to engage in and in which they in fact engage are dealings in finance in this sense.

In *State Superannuation Board of Victoria v Trade Practices Commission* (1982) 150 CLR 282, Mason, Murphy and Deane JJ approached "financial corporations" in the same way as *Adamson's Case* approached "trading corporations": that is, a corporation is a "financial" corporation if it engages in financial activities. The State Superannuation Board of Victoria managed and administered a superannuation fund providing pensions for public servants. The Board was required to furnish information and produce documents to the Trade Practices Commission relating to loans made by the Board. The Commission alleged that the loans may have amounted to exclusive dealing under s 47(1) of the *Trade Practices Act*.

  State Superannuation Board is significant because the majority held that, in order for a corporation to be a "financial corporation", its financial activities need not be its predominant activities, but need only form a substantial proportion of its total activities. Gibbs CJ and Wilson J dissented on this point, arguing that a financial corporation is characterised by its predominant financial activities. They did not regard that test as satisfied where, as here, the "**[298]** business of dealing in finance" was merely "ancillary or incidental to the ... primary activity of administering the [superannuation] scheme".

State Superannuation Board of Victoria v Trade Practices Commission
(1982) 150 CLR 282

Mason, Murphy and Deane JJ: [303] It is our view that the Court's approach to the ascertainment of what constitutes a "financial corporation" should be the same as its approach to what constitutes a "trading corporation", subject to making due allowance for the difference between "trading" and "financial". After all, the two adjectives form part of the general category "and trading or financial corporations formed within the limits of the Commonwealth". The two classes are not mutually exclusive – a corporation may be a financial as well as a trading corporation ...

  [304] [T]here is nothing in *Adamson* [(1979) 143 CLR 190] which lends support for the view that the fact that a corporation carries on independent trading activities on a significant scale will not result in its being properly categorized as a trading corporation if other more extensive non-trading activities properly warrant its being also categorized as a corporation of some other type.

  If there be any difference in the comments made by the majority in *Adamson* it is one of emphasis only. And it is important to note that they were all directed to the issue as it arose for decision, an issue relating to a sporting club and the league with which it was affiliated; they were not aimed at the corporation which has not begun, or has barely begun, to carry on business. It might well be **[305]** necessary to look to the purpose for which such a corporation was formed in order to ascertain whether it is a corporation of the kind described.

  Like the expression "trading corporation", the words "financial corporation" are not a term of art; nor do they have a special or settled legal meaning. They do no more than describe a corporation which engages in financial activities or perhaps is intended so to do. The nature and the extent or volume of a corporation's financial activities needed to justify its description as a financial corporation do not call for much discussion in the present case. A finance company is an obvious example of a financial corporation because it deals in finance for commercial purposes, whether by way of making loans, entering into hire purchase agreements or providing credit in other forms, and this activity is not undertaken for the purpose of carrying on some other business. However, just as a corporation may be a trading corporation, notwithstanding that its trading activities are entered into in the course of carrying on some primary or dominant undertaking, so also with a corporation which engages in financial activities in the course of carrying on its primary or dominant undertaking. Thus a corporation which is formed by an employer to provide superannuation benefits for its employees and those of associated employers may nevertheless be a financial corporation if it engages in financial activities in order to provide or augment the superannuation benefits ...

[306] The facts as we have recited them demonstrate beyond any question that the appellant engages in financial activities on a very substantial scale. Even if we confine our attention to such aspects of the appellant's investment activities as involve the making of commercial and housing loans, its business in this respect is very substantial and forms a significant part of its overall activities. No doubt these activities are all entered into for the end purpose of providing superannuation benefits to contributors, but, as we have seen, this circumstance constitutes no obstacle to the conclusion that the appellant is a financial corporation.

Mason, Murphy and Deane JJ did not entirely exclude the "purposes" test. They spoke of "[305] a corporation which engages in financial activities or perhaps is intended so to do", and envisaged that for "[304[a corporation which has not begun, or has barely begun, to carry on business" the "purposes" test might be decisive. Similarly, Gibbs CJ and Wilson J did not abandon the "purposes" test in their dissent. They conceded that *Adamson's Case* required them to "[295] give greater weight to the current activities test than we would otherwise have thought appropriate"; but they still thought it "[297] not irrelevant ... [but] appropriate and indeed necessary to start with the proposition that here is a statutory body which is formed to carry out a governmental function".

In *Fencott v Muller* (1983) 152 CLR 570, Oakland Nominees Pty Ltd had no current activities. It was a shelf company formed to facilitate a conveyancing transaction. Mason, Murphy, Brennan and Deane JJ, who had hitherto favoured the "activities" test, now held that it was a "trading or financial corporation" by applying the "purposes" test. They argued that, in the absence of any current activities, the character of the corporation should be determined by the purposes for which it was created. Gibbs CJ, Wilson and Dawson JJ dissented, holding that the corporation was not a s 51(xx) corporation under either the activities test or the purposes test.

Fencott v Muller
(1983) 152 CLR 570

Mason, Murphy, Brennan and Deane JJ: [601] Oakland has not engaged in trading activities. Nor has it engaged in any financial activity, for it has not hitherto engaged in any financial transactions. And so the question arises whether a corporation with objects and powers appropriate for a trading or financial corporation can bear that character before it engages in any trading or financial activity. That question did not arise for consideration in *Adamson's Case* [(1979) 143 CLR 190]. The majority judgments in that case which held that the established activities of the football [602] league concluded its character as a trading corporation did not suggest that trading activities are the sole criterion of character. Absent those activities, the character of a corporation must be found in other indicia. While its constitution will never be completely irrelevant, it is in a case such as the present where a corporation has not begun, or has barely begun, to carry on business that its constitution, including its objects, assumes particular significance as a guide (see *State Superannuation Board (Vic) v Trade Practices Commission* [(1982) 150 CLR 282 at 304]). Oakland's memorandum and articles of association reveal that the objects for which it was established include engaging in financial activities and carrying on a large variety of businesses, though it lay dormant – "on the shelf" – after its incorporation. In the circumstances of the present case, there is no better guide to its character than its constitution and its constitution establishes its character as a trading or financial corporation. It is immaterial whether it is a trading corporation or a financial corporation or which of those characters its future activities may give it.

Gibbs CJ: [589] I have said that the purposes for which a corporation is formed may be relevant in determining its character. That will be particularly so when the corporation has not yet begun, or has only just commenced, the activities which it was intended to carry on. However, in deciding what are the purposes for which a corporation is formed, the objects clause of its memorandum of association is an inadequate and may be a misleading guide. For many years it has been the practice of those drawing memoranda of association to give to companies powers to engage in multifarious activities, many of which bear no relation to the actual or intended affairs of the company. Over sixty years ago Lord Wrenbury referred to this practice when in *Cotman v Brougham* [[1918] AC 514 at 522] he said that this "pernicious practice" which was in active operation when he was a **[590]** junior at the bar "has arrived now at a point at which the fact is that the function of the memorandum is taken to be, not to specify, not to disclose, but to bury beneath a mass of words the real object or objects of the company with the intent that every conceivable form of activity shall be found included somewhere within its terms" ... [T]o accept that the intended as well as the actual functions of the corporation are relevant for the purpose of determining its character, does not mean that it is permissible to look at the memorandum of association alone for that purpose. The whole of the evidence as to the intended operations of the corporation is relevant and is likely to show, as it shows in the present case, that many of the objects in the memorandum were inserted out of an abundance of caution, with no intention of describing the activities in which the company is actually engaged or is likely to engage.

In the present case the evidence shows that at no time during its existence has Oakland been intended to engage, and at no time has it engaged, in trading or financial activities. It is not a corporation of the kind to which par 51(xx) refers.

The determination of whether a company with no activities (such as a shelf company) is a trading or financial corporation has now been made more difficult. The practice referred to by Gibbs CJ of drafting the constitution of a company so "that every conceivable form of activity shall be found included somewhere within its terms" has been the subject of reform. Since 1998, a company need not have a constitution and can instead adopt the "replaceable rules" in the *Corporations Act 2001* (Cth). The High Court has not addressed how it would characterise a company that has adopted these generic rules instead of developing its own constitution.

Commonwealth v Tasmania (*Tasmanian Dam Case*) (1983) 158 CLR 1 led to further development on the question "What corporations?". The Hydro-Electric Commission was a government-controlled corporation created by the *Hydro-Electric Commission Act 1944* (Tas)) that planned to build a dam on the Franklin river system in Tasmania. The aim was to generate electricity that would be sold to consumers. Mason, Murphy, Brennan and Deane JJ held that it was a "trading corporation", with Gibbs CJ in dissent. While Wilson and Dawson JJ saw no need to decide, the latter added that if need be he would agree with Gibbs CJ.

Commonwealth v Tasmania (*Tasmanian Dam Case*)
(1983) 158 CLR 1

Mason J: [155] This question must be answered in the affirmative for reasons which may be shortly stated in this way:

1. The decision in *R v Trade Practices Tribunal; Ex parte St George County Council* [(1974) 130 CLR 533] is no longer to be regarded as correct. A majority of the Court in *R v Federal Court of Australia; Ex parte WA National Football League* [(1979) 143 CLR 190] considered it to have been wrongly decided: see also *State Superannuation Board v Trade Practices Commission* [(1982) 150 CLR 282 at 304].

2. As Barwick CJ observed in his dissenting judgment in *St George County Council*, the connexion of the corporation with the government of a State will not take it outside s 51(xx). In making this statement, his Honour referred to certain features of the County Council in that case and stated that they did not take the council outside the category of "trading corporations". The features were (1) that it was incorporated under the *Local Government Act* 1919 (NSW); (2) that it had power to levy a loan rate; (3) that there was a limitation on profit-making to

ensure that the council performed a public service for the county district; and (4) that in reticulating electricity to the district it was performing a public service.

3. The Commission's connexion with the government of Tasmania is certainly closer than the connexion of St George County Council with the government of New South Wales. And the Commission's position in the structure of government is certainly more important than that of the County Council. The Commission is the State authority responsible for generating and distributing electrical power in the State. It constructs and manages the relevant dams, generating plants and other works and makes the policy decisions and recommendations to the Minister in connexion with its functions. But in *Launceston Corporation v Hydro-Electric Commission* [(1959) 100 CLR 654] it was decided that the Commission was an **[156]** independent statutory corporation and it was not a servant or agent of the Crown. Since then the Commission's Act has been amended, notably by the inclusion of ss 15A and 15B. Section 15A enables the Minister to notify the Commission of the policy objectives of the government with respect to any matter relating to generation, distribution, etc of electrical energy. Section 15B enables the Minister to give a direction to the Commission with respect to the performance of its functions, subject to certain limitations and qualifications. The Commission may object to the direction. If the Minister does not withdraw the direction or qualify it in a manner acceptable to the Commission, the matter is then submitted to the Governor for decision (s 15B(4) and (5)). The Commission is bound to comply with the direction, subject to any withdrawal or modification and subject to a decision of the Governor. However, it is specifically provided that the Minister's power to give a direction does not make the Commission a servant or agent of the Crown or confer on the Commission any status, privilege or immunity of the Crown (s 15B(9)). Accordingly, it is not suggested that the decision in *Launceston Corporation* has been eroded by legislative developments.

4. The trading activities of the Commission therefore form a much less prominent feature of its overall activities than was the case with *St George County Council*. The Commission has an important policy-making role. It is the generator of electrical power for Tasmania for distribution to the public and for this purpose it engages on a large scale in the construction of dams and generating plants. In this respect its operations are largely conducted in the public interest.

5. However, *WA National Football League* demonstrates that these considerations do not exclude the Commission from the category of "trading corporations". The majority judgment in *State Superannuation Board* pointed out that the case decided that a trading corporation whose trading activities take place so that it may carry on some other primary or dominant undertaking (which is not trading) may nevertheless be a trading corporation.

6. The agreed facts show that the Commission sells electrical power in bulk and by retail on a very large scale. This activity in itself designates the Commission as a trading corporation.

7. The final question, one raised on behalf of the Commission, is whether it is possible to treat for the purposes of s 51(xx) a corporation as a trading corporation in relation to its trading activities and as a non-trading corporation in relation to its non-**[157]**-trading activities. My earlier conclusion that the legislative power is not confined to the trading activities of trading corporations is in one sense an answer to this submission. The other answer is that s 51(xx) designates as the subject of the power the corporate persona itself, ie the artificial person created by incorporation. There is no suggestion in the paragraph that it is looking to some hypothetical or notional incorporation which covers only the trading activities of a trading corporation.

Gibbs CJ: [116] To say that the Commission is a "trading corporation" is to rob those words of all distinctive meaning. Of course the Commission is a corporation and it trades. But the words "trading corporations" in s 51(xx) describe corporations of a particular character. It must follow that in deciding whether a corporation answers the description, it is necessary to determine its true character. In *R v Trade* **[117]** *Practices Tribunal; Ex parte St George County Council*, I thought that the purpose for which a corporation was formed provided the discrimen by which its character should be determined. Subsequent cases have shown that in determining the character of the corporation the Court must consider all the circumstances relating to the corporation – its activities as well as the purposes of its formation ... I have so recently discussed this question, in *Fencott v Muller* [(1983) 152 CLR 570 at 588-9], that I need do no more than repeat what I then said:

"... a corporation cannot take its character from activities which are uncharacteristic, even if those activities are not infrequently carried on. It may indeed be wrong to insist on finding activities that are 'primary' or 'predominant', but it is equally wrong to be satisfied with activities that are 'substantial', if the latter activities do not, in all the circumstances, show that the corporation has a character which the Constitution requires."

The Commission is not a trading corporation. It is a corporation sui generis. Its activities include trading – in that it supplies electricity for profit – and trading on a substantial scale, but they include also the construction on a large scale of generating plants and works for the distribution of electricity to enable it to keep Tasmania supplied with electricity; in that respect it discharges a public function of vital importance to the State. It performs other governmental functions of less importance (under Pts X and XI). It is in some respects subject to ministerial power, and is accorded special powers and privileges similar to some which the Crown enjoys, although it is not the servant of the Crown: *Launceston Corporation v Hydro-Electric Commission*. It is "a public authority with public purposes, as distinct from a private undertaking engaged upon a merely commercial enterprise, and ... its powers are to be exercised for the good of the State": *Launceston Corporation v Hydro-Electric Commission* [100 CLR at 661]. Its trading activities, although significant, do not indicate its true character.

3. What Aspects or Activities?

In most of the above cases, the question "What aspects or activities of a corporation can be regulated under s 51(xx)?" was not directly addressed. Some incidental points were clarified in *R v Australian Industrial Court; Ex parte CLM Holdings Pty Ltd* (1977) 136 CLR 235. That case established that, where the activities of a s 51(xx) corporation were validly regulated, the conduct of individual persons taking part in those activities, such as company directors, could incidentally be regulated as well.

In *Actors and Announcers Equity Association v Fontana Films Pty Ltd* (1982) 150 CLR 169, the Court still did not deal directly with the regulation of a corporation's activities. The issue was whether s 45D of the *Trade Practices Act* was valid. Section 45D protected a corporation against a "secondary boycott", that is, against action, such as trade union action, which prevents a supplier of a corporation from maintaining supplies to it. The whole Court upheld this as a valid law with respect to s 51(xx) corporations, although certain ancillary provisions were held invalid on other grounds. The legislative purpose thus upheld was protection of corporations rather than regulation of them. The case also provided an opportunity for extensive discussion of how far the "corporations" power might extend.

Actors and Announcers Equity Association v Fontana Films Pty Ltd
(1982) 150 CLR 169

Gibbs CJ: [182] The words of par (xx) suggest that the nature of the corporation to which the laws relate must be significant as an element in the nature or character of the laws, if they are to be valid ... In other words, in the case of trading and financial corporations, laws which relate to their trading and financial activities will be within the power. This does not mean that a law under s 51(xx) may apply only to the foreign activities of a foreign **[183]** corporation, for ex hypothesi the law will be one for the peace, order and good government of the Commonwealth. It means that the fact that the corporation is a foreign corporation should be significant in the way in which the law relates to it. For present purposes, however, it is enough that it is established by *Strickland v Rocla Concrete Pipes Ltd* [(1971) 124 CLR 468] that a law which governs the trading activities of trading corporations formed within the limits of the Commonwealth is within the scope of s 51(xx) ... Of course, the law in the present case does not regulate or govern the activities of trading corporations; it regulates the conduct of others. But the conduct to which the law is directed is conduct designed to cause, and likely to cause, substantial loss or damage to the business of a trading corporation formed within the limits of the Commonwealth. I can see no reason in principle why such a law should necessarily fall outside the scope of s 51(xx). A law may be one with respect to a trading corporation, although it casts obligations upon a person other than a trading corporation.

As between the narrow view of s 51(xx) (requiring some connection with the trading activities of a trading corporation) and the broad view (requiring no such connection), Stephen J made no attempt to choose. Instead, he turned directly to the characterisation of s 45D(1)(b)(i), and undertook a major restatement of the approach to characterisation.

Stephen J: [190] The law contained in s 45D(1)(b)(i) is composed of three elements: the existence of conduct by persons in concert which impedes a dealing in goods or services; the fact that that dealing is a dealing to which those persons are not themselves parties, and the presence of resultant and intended actual or likely detriment to one of the parties to the dealing, it being a corporation. It would no doubt be possible to describe the law by reference to any one of these elements, the conduct, the dealing or the detriment suffered by a corporation, [ignoring] in each instance the two other elements. The law could thus be described as one about concerted action affecting dealings, about dealings in goods or services or about detriment to corporations. But each such description would suffer from excessive width since it is only certain forms of concerted action, only dealings between those not parties to such actions and only detriment of a particular kind, suffered by a corporation, that the law affects. Its true character can only be conveyed by a description which picks up each of the elements, as does the description of it as a law prohibiting concerted action directed against a corporation's dealings in goods and services. Any attempt further to refine the description, while it may succeed in confining the subject matter of the law to one only of its elements, will necessarily lead to a departure from accuracy.

What I have said touches upon one of the major difficulties involved in the process of characterization. An accurate description of any at all complex law will necessarily be relatively detailed if it is to encompass the several elements which together go to make up the impugned law. However, constitutional grants of power such as those in s 51 are customarily expressed quite differently – succinctly and in terms of wide generality. Thus, when an accurate, and hence relatively detailed, description of a law is sought to be matched against one or other of the tersely expressed grants of **[191]** legislative power contained in s 51 of the Constitution, it will not infrequently be found that different parts of the description of the law fall within different paragraphs of s 51; still other parts may be found to fall within none of those enumerated grants of power, because they concern elements of the law which are the subject only of State legislative power ...

[192] To recognize that a law may possess a number of quite disparate characters is, then, to accept reality. Few laws will involve only one element. Even the simplest form of law will commonly contain two elements when it forbids, regulates or mandates particular conduct on the part of a particular class of person. The conduct and the class will form distinct elements and if each happens to bear a relationship to different grants of legislative power the law may often be equally appropriately described by reference to either. If a law also includes reference to another class of persons, those affected by the conduct in question, a third element will thereby be introduced. Many laws will, because of the relatively complex concepts to which they give effect, involve still further elements. These elements may, of course, all bear one and the same character. However, where they do not, any search for a single character by which to describe the law is likely to prove fruitless.

Were constitutional dogma to require such a search to be pursued, the difficulty in choosing between competing elements might readily lead different minds, perhaps influenced by quite subjective considerations, to varying conclusions as to the dominant character of a law. But to accept as constitutionally permissible the fact that a law may bear several characters, each as valid as the other because each is reasonably capable of fairly describing the law as a whole, disposes of the need to rely upon what may prove to be quite subjective reasons for selecting one particular description only. With the disappearance of subjective criteria, the process of characterization then becomes less uncertain and more a matter of logic than of idiosyncratic assertion.

Once it is recognized that a law may possess several distinct characters, it follows that the fact that only some elements in the description of a law fall within one or more of the grants of power in s 51 or elsewhere in the Constitution will be in no way fatal to its validity. So long as the remaining elements, which do not fall within any such grant of power, are not of such significance that the law cannot fairly be described as one with respect to one or more of such grants of power then, however else it may also be described, the law will be valid. If a law enacted by the federal legislature can be fairly described both as a law with respect to a grant of power to it and as a law with respect to a matter or matters left to the States, that will suffice to support its validity as a law of the Commonwealth ...

[194] It follows that in testing validity the task is not to single out one predominant character of a law which, because it can be said to prevail over all others, leads to the attaching to the law of one description only as truly apt. It will be enough if the law fairly answers the description of a law "with respect to" one given subject matter appearing in s 51, regardless of whether it may equally be described as a law with respect to other subject matters. This will be so whether or not those other subject matters appear in the enumeration of heads of legislative power in s 51.

If the task of characterization be approached in this fashion, s 45D(1)(b)(i) may be seen clearly enough to possess the character of a law with respect to trading corporations, whatever other characters it may also possess. What it does is to forbid conduct which has for its purpose, and which in addition would have or be likely to have the effect, of causing substantial loss or damage to a corporation. To that may be added the fact that the forbidden conduct is described, in the opening words of s 45D(1), in terms directly relating it to the trading activities of corporations. Whatever other descriptions might also be assigned to it, to fail to include as one characterization of it that of a law about corporations would seem to me to be to ignore the obvious. To describe it as a law with respect to trading corporations seems entirely apt; it does no more than recognize what is the manifest purpose and direct effect of the law. The connexion with corporations forms a crucial component of the law, making wholly inappropriate any description of that connexion as being merely "so incidental as not in truth to affect its **[195]** character" – per Kitto J in *Fairfax v Federal Commissioner of Taxation* [(1965) 114 CLR 1 at 7].

The centrality of that connexion is emphasized, rather than diminished, by the fact that the prohibition which the law imposes is not addressed to corporations but rather to those who act with a purpose of harming them. That the law takes this form is dictated by its aim of protecting corporations from a particular harm; in such a prohibitory law the focus will necessarily be upon the acts of those who intend harm. A law forbidding certain acts of third parties for the reason that they were both intended, and also likely, to harm aliens would surely be as central to the grant of power with respect to aliens as a law which required aliens to do or refrain from particular conduct: the intended object of another's conduct is no less central, no less significant, in bestowing a character upon a law than is the actor to whom that law directly speaks ...

It was also contended that because s 45D(1)(b)(i) refers to substantial loss or damage to "the business" of a corporation this introduced invalidity because a corporation's "business" is capable of extending so as to include far more than its trading activities. This argument is founded upon the assumption that s 51(xx) is confined to the trading activities of trading corporations. Even were such an assumption well-founded, the present contention would nevertheless fail because, in this sub-paragraph, "business" must clearly be given a meaning consistent with context and that requires that its meaning should be confined to a corporation's trading activities.

Mason J stressed that the prohibition on secondary boycotts "**[200]** necessarily has an effect on corporations in their trading activities":

Mason J: [204] The judgments in *Strickland*, in *R v Trade Practices Tribunal; Ex parte St George County Council* [(1974) 130 CLR 533 esp at 542-3], and more recently in *R v Federal Court of Australia; Ex parte WA National Football League* [(1979) 143 CLR 190], do not attempt to define the limits of the corporations power. They proceed upon the footing that the power **[205]** extends to the regulation of the trading activities of foreign corporations and trading and financial corporations formed within the limits of the Commonwealth, without deciding whether it travels further ...

The appellants seek to draw a distinction between a law which regulates the trading activities of a trading corporation and a law which protects such activities. When we speak of a law which regulates the trading activities of a trading corporation we mean a law which controls the subject matter by prohibiting the corporation from engaging in certain trading activities or permitting it so to do either absolutely or subject to condition. Such a law is within power because it necessarily operates directly on the subject of the power – it is a law about trading corporations. But when we speak of a law which protects the trading activities of a trading corporation our statement is not so specific. It may be understood as signifying a law which operates directly on the subject of the power. So understood the law is within power and valid. But it may be understood in a different sense so as to denote a law which, though it protects the trading activities of trading corporations, does so by a legal operation outside the subject matter of the power. A law which prohibits the levying of taxes and duties on trading activities **[206]** generally may be said to protect or promote the trading activities of corporations, but it is neither a law with respect to corporations nor a law with respect to trading corporations. It protects the trading activities of non-corporations as well as protecting the trading activities of corporations and the protection which it gives to non-corporations is not merely incidental to the protection given to corporations. The law does not operate directly upon corporations and it cannot be characterized as a law about them.

The Solicitor-General for the Commonwealth submits that if there is a power to prohibit the activities or the trading activities of trading corporations, it necessarily follows that there is a legislative power to protect these activities. He refers to the observations of Starke J in *Bank of NSW v Commonwealth* [(1948) 76 CLR 1 at 304], where his Honour expressed the view that the power enabled the Parliament to prohibit activities of corporations. However, his Honour said nothing about a law which protects corporations or their trading activities. The Solicitor-General's submission is correct so long as it is understood that by a law which protects the trading activities of trading corporations he means a law which has a direct legal operation on the subject of the power. Such a law is within power and valid.

Despite this focus on the "trading activities" of trading corporations, Mason J went out of his way to argue that s 51(xx) is not limited to such activities.

Mason J: [207] I should not wish it to be thought from what I have said that the corporations power is confined in its application to trading corporations to laws that deal with their trading activities. The subject of the power is corporations – of the kind described; the power is not expressed as one with respect to the activities of corporations, let alone activities of a particular kind or kinds. A constitutional grant of legislative power should be construed liberally and not in any narrow or pedantic fashion. This, the correct approach to the interpretation of legislative powers conferred by the Constitution, was expressed by this Court in its unanimous judgment in *R v Public Vehicles Licensing Appeal Tribunal (Tas); Ex parte Australian National Airways Pty Ltd* [(1964) 113 CLR 207 at 225-6], in these words:

> "The simplest approach, however, to the problem is simply to read the paragraph and to apply it without making implications or imposing limitations which are not found in the express words. We must remember that it is part of the Constitution and go back to the general counsel to remember that it is a constitution we are construing and it should be construed with all the generality which the words used admit. See per O'Connor J in the *Jumbunna Case* [(1908) 6 CLR 309 at 367, 368]."

See also *New South Wales v Commonwealth* [(1975) 135 CLR 337 at 470-1].

Nowhere in the Constitution is there to be found a secure footing for an implication that the power is to be read down so that it relates to "the trading activities of trading corporations" and, I would suppose, correspondingly to the financial activities of financial corporations and perhaps to the foreign aspects of foreign corporations. Even if it be thought that it was concern as to the trading activities of trading corporations and financial activities of financial corporations that led to the singling out in s 51(xx) of these domestic corporations from other domestic corporations it would be mere speculation to say that it was intended to confine the legislative power so given to these activities. The competing hypothesis, which conforms to the accepted approach to the construction of a legislative power in the Constitution is that it was intended to confer comprehensive power with respect to the subject matter so as to ensure that all conceivable matters of national concern would be **[208]** comprehended. The power should, therefore, in accordance with that approach, be construed as a plenary power with respect to the subjects mentioned free from the unexpressed qualifications which have been suggested.

Murphy J took an even broader approach.

Murphy J: [212] The power is, of course, plenary; it enables Parliament to make comprehensive laws covering all internal and external relations of foreign trading and financial corporations. It extends to authorize a "Companies Act" providing for the formation, operation and dissolution of trading and financial corporations. Except in a very artificial sense, the power is not available to deal with the formation of foreign corporations, but no doubt authorizes laws dealing with their operation and dissolution. The power obviously authorizes laws dealing with the trading (or financial) operations of such corporations; for example, Parliament can legislate for the standards of products manufactured or sold by foreign and trading corporations and has done so (see ss 62 and 63 of the Act). However, the power is not confined to laws dealing with the trading or financial operations of trading or financial corporations (nor to foreign operations of foreign corporations). It extends to laws dealing with industrial relations so that in relation to such corporations Parliament, uninhibited by limitations expressed in s 51(xx[x]v), may legislate directly about the wages and conditions of employees and other industrial matters. [In] *R v Federal Court of Australia; Ex parte WA National Football League* I stated that "The corporations power may be used not only to protect persons who trade with trading corporations, but also to protect trading corporations in regard to those who deal with them". This aspect of the power is not confined to trading corporations nor to protecting them only from those who deal with them. It enables Parliament to protect trading, financial and foreign corporations from others and to protect others from such corporations. Parliament could, if it wished, enact a comprehensive criminal and civil code dealing with the protection of foreign trading and financial corporations, their property and affairs, and also the protection of others in relation to such corporations.

The view of Murphy J that the power could be used to regulate industrial relations, "[212] uninhibited by limitations expressed in" s 51(xxxv), was effectively conceded (though not decided) in *Victoria v Commonwealth (Industrial Relations Act Case)* (1996) 187 CLR 416 (see §3 below) and was taken up by the Howard government in the *Workplace Relations Amendment (Work Choices) Act 2005* (Cth) as the basis for "a simplified national system" of industrial relations in which conciliation and arbitration under s 51(xxxv) are reduced to a peripheral role.

In *Actors Equity* Aickin J agreed with Mason J. Effectively, therefore, Mason, Murphy and Aickin JJ committed themselves to a view of the power that was not confined to any nexus with "trading activities". By contrast, Gibbs CJ and Wilson J retained such a nexus. Stephen J, as we have seen, avoided any comment on the more general scope of s 51(xx).

Brennan J also refused to commit himself on the issue. However, his approach seemed consonant with a broader view of the power. This was that a law authorised by s 51(xx) is one that *discriminates* between corporations and other legal persons, in the sense that corporate involvement is the *discrimen* by which the sphere of operation of the law is identified.

Brennan J: [216] When a law confers a right or imposes a duty upon particular persons or upon a class of persons or affects their rights or liabilities, and thereby discriminates between them and the public at large, the discrimination is an essential element of the right or duty and is therefore material to the character of the law in question. That is not to say that the character of the law is to be determined for all purposes by reference merely to the persons or class of persons whose rights or duties are augmented or altered by its provisions. Every element of the rights or duties which it creates or alters is material to its character.

A problem arises when the relevant head of power is expressed as a power to make laws with respect to persons ... If a law augments or alters the rights and duties of one or more of the classes of corporations mentioned in par (xx) and thereby discriminates between those corporations and the public at large, is that sufficient to bring the law within the head of power? Or is it necessary that the rights and duties which the law augments or alters should be rights or duties affecting particular activities or relationships? And, if so, what are those particular activities or relationships? ...

[218] The command of s 45D of the *Trade Practices Act* 1974 (Cth) ... is addressed indifferently to all persons ... The section is concerned with the rights of corporations, not with their duties, and such discrimination as the law effects flows from the conferring of protection upon them in the carrying on of their businesses. In a sense, this case presents the obverse of the problem faced in the *Rocla Pipes Case*. If a law discriminates between one or more of the classes of corporations mentioned in par (xx) and the public at large by imposing upon corporations of such a class a duty as to the manner in which they conduct their trading activities and the law falls accordingly within the ambit of the power conferred by that paragraph, is a law which discriminates by protecting the trading activities of those corporations within the ambit of the power?

If corporations are the special beneficiaries of the protection which the law affords, it is not to the point to say that the law is not expressed to bind them. The relevant question is whether a law which gives the businesses of corporations the protection specified in s 45D is within the ambit of the power. Before examining the terms of the section, two observations should be made.

First, the practice of this Court in interpreting the Constitution case by case, deciding only so much as is necessary to decide the case in hand is of particular importance when the head of power has not hitherto been the subject of extensive judicial exegesis. Hewing close to the issues raised by each case, the Court avoids the possibility of having its judgment applied to issues which were not envisaged in the arguments before it and which may have implications emerging only in the future. The development of principle from the concrete issues of particular cases may be slow, but it gives assurance that the principle will not be unsuited to the solution of practical problems. It follows that it is undesirable to answer a question left open in an earlier case unless an answer is evoked by the issues in the case in hand. In the present case, it is not necessary to determine whether any law which discriminates between corporations mentioned in par (xx) and the public at large is a law falling within the ambit of the corporations power; but it is **[219]** necessary to determine whether a law which affords a discriminatory protection to the businesses of trading corporations formed within the limits of Australia is valid.

Second, to determine the validity of s 45D it is desirable to commence with what has been judicially established as falling within the ambit of the power ... Clearly enough, neither *Rocla Pipes* nor any of the cases which followed it [has] held that the conferring of a right upon corporations mentioned in par (xx), as distinct from the imposition of duties upon them, gives to a law the character of a law with respect to those corporations. But what is the difference in point of constitutional principle between two laws each of which discriminates between corporations mentioned in par (xx) and the public at large, one of which imposes a duty upon those corporations affecting the conduct of their trading activities, the other of which confers a protection upon those corporations in the conduct of the same activities? There is none, for a law which affects those corporations in the conduct of their trading activities exhibits the same nexus with those corporations whether it regulates or whether it protects their trading activities ...

[220] The subject matter which the provision selects as the object of its protection is "the business" of the corporation. That was the subject matter to which Menzies J referred ... in *Rocla Pipes*. His reference to "business" may be compared with the references to "trading activity" in other judgments in *Rocla* **[221]** *Pipes*. In *R v Trade Practices Tribunal; Ex parte St George County Council* and in *R v Federal Court of Australia; Ex parte WA National Football League*, trading activity rather than the carrying on of business was regarded as material to the character of a corporation falling within the description of trading corporation. At all events, the concepts of business and trade are not coextensive (cf *Hornsby Shire Council v Salmar Holdings Pty Ltd* [(1972) 126 CLR 52 at 54, 56, 60]), and there may be some business of a trading corporation which is not trading activity ...

[222] Where the subject matter affected by a law is trading activity, the law affects the heart of the purpose for which trading corporations are formed or a significant activity in which they are engaged. That circumstance gives a clear pointer to the character of the law. But if the law affects also more peripheral matters, it does not necessarily lose its character as a law with respect to trading corporations; indeed the additional subject matter may confirm the character which would otherwise be attributed to the law ...

[Section 45D] discriminates between trading corporations and the public at large, protects the trading activities of those corporations together with any non-trading businesses carried on by them, and confers upon them rights of action to enforce the protection which the provision accords. It is a law with respect to trading corporations within the power conferred upon the Parliament by par (xx).

In *Commonwealth v Tasmania* (*Tasmanian Dam Case*) (1983) 158 CLR 1, the Commonwealth sought to rely upon the "corporations" power to support ss 7 and 10 of the *World Heritage Properties Conservation Act 1983* (Cth).

World Heritage Properties Conservation Act 1983 (Cth)

7 Where the Governor-General is satisfied that any identified property is being or is likely to be damaged or destroyed, he may, by Proclamation, declare that property to be property to which section 10 applies.

10 (1) In this section –
"foreign corporation" means a foreign corporation within the meaning of paragraph 51(xx) of the Constitution;
   "trading corporation" means a trading corporation within the meaning of paragraph 51(xx) of the Constitution.
   (2) Except with the consent in writing of the Minister, it is unlawful for a body corporate that –
   (a)   is a foreign corporation;
   (b)   is incorporated in a Territory; or
   (c)   not being incorporated in a Territory, is a trading corporation formed within the limits of the Commonwealth,
whether itself or by its servant or agent –
   (d)   to carry out any excavation works on any property to which this section applies;
   (e)   to carry out operations for, or exploratory drilling in connection with, the recovery of minerals on any property to which this section applies;
   (f)   to erect a building or other substantial structure on any property to which this section applies or to do any act in the course of, or for the purpose of, the erection of a building or other substantial structure on any property to which this section applies;
   (g)   to damage or destroy a building or other substantial structure on any property to which this section applies;
   (h)   to kill, cut down or damage any tree on any property to which this section applies;
   (j)   to construct or establish any road or vehicular track on any property to which this section applies;
   (k)   to use explosives on any property to which this section applies; or
   (m)   if an act is prescribed for the purposes of this paragraph in relation to particular property to which this section applies, to do that act in relation to that property.
   (3) Except with the consent in writing of the Minister, it is unlawful for a body corporate of a kind referred to in sub-section (2), whether itself or by its servant or agent, to do any act, not being an act the doing of which is unlawful by virtue of that sub-section, that damages or destroys any property to which this section applies.
   (4) Without prejudice to the effect of sub-sections (2) and (3), except with the consent in writing of the Minister, it is unlawful for a body corporate of the kind referred to in paragraph (2)(c), whether itself or by its servant or agent, to do, for the purposes of its trading activities, an act referred to in any of paragraphs (2) (d) to (m) (inclusive) or an act referred to in sub-section (3).

Note the difference in s 10 between sub-ss (2) and (3) (on the one hand) and sub-s (4) (on the other). Subsections (2) and (3) prohibit a wide range of activities if done by any corporation falling within paras (a) to (c) of sub-s (2). Subsection (4) prohibits the same activities if done by a trading corporation "for the purposes of its trading activities".

   The Hydro-Electric Commission planned to build a dam to generate electricity, and the purpose of generating electricity was to sell it. Thus, if the Commission was a "trading corporation", the building of the dam was an activity for the purposes of its trading activities.

   Overall, five judges, Gibbs CJ, Mason, Murphy, Brennan and Deane JJ, held that s 10(4) was valid. Mason, Murphy and Deane JJ held that all the provisions in s 10 were valid: that is, that all the prohibitions could validly be imposed on a corporation under s 51(xx), including those in s 10(2) and (3). Brennan J, as in *Actors Equity*, was loath to decide the larger issue, that is, whether the permissible regulation of trading corporations is limited by the need for a nexus with their "trading activities". All that was necessary in this case was to decide that s 10(4) was valid. Accordingly, his judgment stopped there. Gibbs CJ agreed with this narrower proposition: he too held that s 10(4) was valid, albeit in his view inapplicable because he did not accept that the Commission was a "trading corporation". As on other issues in the *Tasmanian Dam Case*, Wilson and Dawson JJ dissented.

Commonwealth v Tasmania (Tasmanian Dam Case)
(1983) 158 CLR 1

Mason J: [148] [I]t has been affirmatively established that the power extends to the regulation and the protection of the trading activities of trading corporations … Whether the power goes further remains to be decided. Barwick CJ, Murphy, Brennan JJ and I have indicated that it does … It would be unduly restrictive to confine the power to the regulation and protection of the trading activities of trading corporations. After all, the subject-matter of the power is persons, not activities. The suggested restriction might possibly deny to Parliament power to regulate borrowing by trading corporations, notwithstanding that there is much to be said for the view that one of the objects of s 51(xx) was to enable Parliament to regulate transactions between the categories of corporation mentioned and the public, indeed to enable Parliament to protect the public, should the need arise, in relation to the operations of such corporations.

There is, certainly, no sound reason for denying that the power should extend to the regulation of acts undertaken by trading corporations for the purpose of engaging in their trading activities. I do not understand Mr Merralls to deny that in some instances at least the power extends that far.

There is more to be said for the view that the scope of the power is to be ascertained by reference to those matters, whatever they may be, [that] are relevant to the trading character of a trading corporation. Thus, it might be said that the power extends to, but does not travel beyond, such aspects of a trading corporation's structure, business and affairs, as have relevance to its character as a trading corporation. This view of the power would, if accepted, enable Parliament to enact legislation regulating (and prohibiting) acts and activities engaged in by a trading corporation for the purpose of engaging in its trading activities.

However, it seems to me that there are three powerful objections to the adoption of this limited construction. The first is that this **[149]** approach to the scope of the power in its application to the classes of corporations mentioned, though it has some plausibility in the case of trading corporations, has none at all in the case of financial and foreign corporations. It can scarcely have been intended that the scope of the power was to be limited by reference to the foreign aspects of foreign corporations and the financial aspects of financial corporations. And it would be irrational to conclude that the power is plenary in the case of those corporations, but limited in the case of trading corporations.

The second objection is that the interpretation fails to give effect to the principle that a legislative power conferred by the Constitution should be liberally construed. And the final objection is that a power to make laws with respect to corporations (of designated categories), as in the case of a power with respect to natural persons, would seem naturally to extend to their acts and activities. In *Koowarta* [(1982) 153 CLR 168 at 209] Stephen J, when referring to the power conferred by s 51(xxvi) with respect to the people of any race, said that "The content of the laws which may be made under it are left very much at large" and that "they may be directed to any aspect of human activity".

There is nothing in the context of s 51(xx) which compels the conclusion that the language in which the power is expressed should be given a restricted interpretation … [W]e should recognize that the power confers a plenary power with respect to the categories of corporation mentioned …

[152] [T]he Commission submits that s 7 is invalid because it selects damage to or destruction of property as the basis of the power to make a proclamation and not an act or prohibited act of a foreign or trading corporation. An event having no necessary connexion with trading or foreign corporations is made the occasion for prohibiting them from damaging property. This demonstrates something that is evident from other provisions of the Act, namely that the object of s 10 is to protect the Western Tasmania Wilderness Area. The Parliament has exercised the corporations power to achieve this end, not for some overriding purpose having a connexion with trading and foreign corporations. But the point is **[153]** that the legislative power with respect to trading and foreign corporations is not, on the view which I have expressed, in any sense purposive. It is enough that the law has a real relationship with the subjects of the power; it matters not, when the power is not purposive, that the object of the exercise is to attain some goal in a field that lies outside the scope of the Commonwealth power. A law which prohibits trading and foreign corporations from doing an act is a law about trading and foreign corporations, notwithstanding that it is also a law about the act which is prohibited. It is a law which imposes obligations on such corporations enforceable by injunctions. Consequently, it is simply impossible to say that the law has no substantial connexion with trading and foreign corporations.

Gibbs CJ: [119] Apart from s 10(4), the connexion between ss 7 and 10 and the topic of trading corporations is not direct and substantial – it is exiguous and unreal. It is apparent that the relationship between trading corporations and the operative provisions of s 10 is merely incidental – the section is applied to trading corporations only in an attempt to use s 51(xx) as a source of power which would not otherwise exist. The true character of the section is not that of a law with respect to trading corporations.

However, s 10(4) applies only where the forbidden acts are done by a body corporate of the kind described in the section "for the purposes of its trading activity". Notwithstanding some doubts as to whether the connexion made by s 10(4) with trading corporations by the use of those words is merely contrived, I consider that the sub-section does have a sufficient connexion with the topic of power granted by s 51(xx). I would therefore hold s 10(4) to be valid.

On the question, "What aspects or activities of a corporation can be regulated under s 51(xx)?", the *Tasmanian Dam Case* and *Actors Equity* were inconclusive. It had earlier been accepted that s 51(xx) at least empowers the Commonwealth to regulate the trading activities of trading corporations. The holding in the *Tasmanian Dam Case* as to s 10(4) pressed this further, extending the power to laws that regulate a trading corporation *with regard to activities undertaken for the purpose of its trading activities*. Whether the power extended further again, all the way to Higgins' list of "horribles", remained undecided, although three judges in the *Tasmanian Dam Case* expressed the view that it did.

However, that question may ultimately be destined to remain undecided. *Re Dingjan; Ex parte Wagner* (1995) 183 CLR 323 was potentially another opportunity to determine whether the "wide view" of s 51(xx) was correct. Since the *Tasmanian Dam Case*, three new judges had been appointed to the Court (Toohey, Gaudron and McHugh JJ), replacing one judge who took a wide view of the power (Murphy J) and two who had taken a narrow view (Gibbs CJ and Wilson J). But the answers now given by the Court as thus reconstituted suggested that the question "What aspects or activities ... ?", as a question about the scope of Commonwealth power, may simply have been the wrong question. As Stephen J had perceived most clearly in *Actors Equity*, the Court is not ultimately concerned with the characterisation *of corporations or their activities* but with the characterisation *of laws*.

A 1992 amendment to the *Industrial Relations Act 1988* (Cth) gave the Industrial Relations Commission the power to examine unfair contracts imposed on independent contractors. Such contracts could be set aside wholly or in part or varied under s 127B. By s 127A(1)(a)(ii), the power extended only to contracts for services relating "to the performance of work by the independent contractor, other than work for the private and domestic purposes of the other party to the contract". By s 127C(1), the power extended only to cases where the contract fell within Commonwealth legislative power. Included on this basis were cases: "(a) in relation to a contract to which a constitutional corporation is a party; (b) in relation to a contract relating to the business of a constitutional corporation; (c) in relation to a contract entered into by a constitutional corporation for the purposes of the business of the corporation". By s 127C(2), "constitutional corporation" was defined by reference to s 51(xx) of the Constitution.

The relevant corporation, Tasmanian Pulp and Forest Holdings Ltd, was not itself a party to the relevant contract. Timber for the company's woodchip mill was harvested and transported to the mill by independent contractors, including Mr and Mrs Wagner. They, in turn, had entered into sub-contracts with Mr and Mrs Dingjan and Mr and Mrs Ryan. The sub-contractors, supported by the Transport Workers Union, sought review and variation of their contract under s 127A. Since the company was not a party to the contract, s 127C(1)(a) and (c) were not applicable. The only basis on which the Act could apply was s 127C(1)(b).

By 4:3, the Court found that s 127C(1)(b) could not be supported under s 51(xx) and that the provision could not be read down to a valid operation by applying s 15A of the *Acts Interpretation Act 1901* (Cth). The main dissenting judgment was that of Gaudron J, with whom Mason CJ and Deane J agreed. In holding that s 127C(1)(b) was valid, these three judges took a wider view of the constitutional power than the four judges who found it invalid; and indeed Mason CJ stressed again that in his view the power is "plenary". Yet among the four majority judges Toohey and McHugh JJ also stressed that the power is "plenary". To that extent, it is arguable that the wider view of s 51(xx) prevailed.

Yet in all the judgments the focus was not on a wider or narrower answer to the question "What aspects or activities … ?", but on whether there was the sufficient connection with "trading or financial corporations" that general principles of characterisation require. The narrowest view of this question was that of Dawson J, who said: "**[346]** For a law to be a valid law with respect to a trading or financial corporation, the fact that it is a trading or financial corporation should be significant in the way in which the law relates to it". In using this language he was simply adhering to his own dissenting view in the *Tasmanian Dam Case*, as adapted in turn from that of Gibbs CJ in *Actors Equity* and ultimately from Walsh J in the *Concrete Pipes Case*.

McHugh J, like Toohey J, stressed the "plenary" scope of s 51(xx); yet for him, as for Dawson J, the necessary standard of relevance for purposes of characterisation was that of "significance". A law enacted under s 51(xx) must be significant "**[369]** for the activities, functions, relationships or business of the corporation". A law which "merely refers to or operates upon" those aspects or elements of corporate identity will not be sufficient.

Re Dingjan; Ex parte Wagner
(1995) 183 CLR 323

McHugh J: [368] The corporations power, like all s 51 powers, is a plenary grant of power. It is to be construed with all the generality that its words will admit. Unlike most of the powers conferred by s 51, however, the corporations power is directed to persons and not subject matters such as trade, commerce, taxation or quarantine. Although laws that regulate the activities, functions, relationships or business of corporations are clearly laws with respect to corporations, the power conferred by s 51(xx) also extends to any subject that affects the corporation. As long as the law in question can be characterised as a law with respect to trading, financial or foreign corporations, the Parliament of the Commonwealth may regulate many subject matters that are otherwise outside the scope of Commonwealth legislative power. Laws that protect s 51(xx) corporations from the conduct of non-corporations, for example, are laws with respect to s 51(xx) corporations. Thus a law that penalises persons who impose secondary boycotts that are designed to and likely to cause substantial damage to the business of corporations is a law with respect to those corporations, notwithstanding that its principal purpose is to outlaw secondary boycotts.

It does not follow, however, that s 51(xx) authorises any law that operates on conduct that relates to the activities, functions, relationships or business of trading, financial or foreign corporations. The law must be a law "with respect to" a corporation of the kind described by s 51(xx). That means that the law must have "a relevance to or connection with" [*Grannall v Marrickville Margarine Pty Ltd* (1955) 93 CLR 55 at 77] a s 51(xx) corporation. It is not enough, however, that the law "should refer to the subject matter or apply to the subject matter" [76 CLR at 186].

In determining whether a law is "with respect to" a head of power **[369]** in s 51 of the Constitution, two steps must be taken. First, the character of the law must be determined. That is done by reference to the rights, powers, liabilities, duties and privileges which it creates. Secondly, a judgment must be made as to whether the law as so characterised so operates that it can be said to be connected to a head of power conferred by s 51. In determining whether the connection exists, the practical, as well as the legal, operation of the law must be examined. If a connection exists between the law and a s 51 head of power, the law will be "with respect to" that head of power unless the connection is, in the words of Dixon J [*Melbourne Corporation v Commonwealth* (1947) 74 CLR 31 at 79], "so insubstantial, tenuous or distant" that it cannot sensibly be described as a law "with respect to" the head of power.

Where a law purports to be "with respect to" a s 51(xx) corporation, it is difficult to see how it can have any connection with such a corporation unless, in its legal or practical operation, it has significance for the corporation. That means that it must have some significance for the activities, functions, relationships or business of the corporation. If a law regulates the activities, functions, relationships or business of a s 51(xx) corporation, no more is needed to bring the law within s 51(xx). That is because the law, by regulating the activities, etc, is regulating the conduct of the corporation or those who deal with it. Further, if, by reference to the activities or functions of s 51(xx) corporations, a law regulates the conduct of those who control, work for, or hold shares or office in those corporations, it is unlikely that any further fact will be needed to bring the law within the reach of s 51(xx).

It is not enough, however, to attract the operation of s 51(xx) that the law merely refers to or operates upon the existence of a corporate function or relationship or a category of corporate behaviour. The activities, functions, relationships and business of s 51(xx) corporations are not the constitutional switches that throw open the stream of power conferred by s 51(xx). In *Actors and Announcers Equity Association v Fontana Films Pty Ltd* [(1982) 150 CLR 169 at 222], Brennan J said:

> "It is of the nature of the power that it is a power to make laws with respect to corporate persons, not with respect to functions, activities or relationships."

[370] So, where a law seeks to regulate the conduct of persons other than s 51(xx) corporations or the employees, officers or shareholders of those corporations, the law will generally not be authorised by s 51(xx) unless it does more than operate by reference to the activities, functions, relationships or business of such corporations. A law operating on the conduct of outsiders will not be within the power conferred by s 51(xx) unless that conduct has significance for trading, financial or foreign corporations. In most cases, that will mean that the conduct must have some beneficial or detrimental effect on trading, financial or foreign corporations or their officers, employees or shareholders. Thus, laws that regulate conduct that promotes or protects the functions, activities, relationships or business of such corporations or laws that regulate conduct conferring benefits on those corporations are laws with respect to s 51(xx) corporations even though they are also laws with respect to that conduct.

But a law that does no more than make some activity of a s 51(xx) corporation the condition for regulating the conduct of an outsider will ordinarily not be a law with respect to those corporations. If a law regulates conduct that has no significance for s 51(xx) corporations, it is not a law with respect to those corporations even if that conduct is connected to or even based on what a corporation does. Thus, a law that sought to regulate the remuneration of employment contracts made by financial analysts would not be a law with respect to s 51(xx) corporations even if the work of the analysts was entirely based upon the business activities of corporations. Laws that seek to regulate such contracts are laws with respect to employment contracts, but they are not laws with respect to corporations.

Sections 127A, 127B, 127C(1)(b) combined to give the Industrial Relations Commission jurisdiction to set aside or vary a contract that was unfair, harsh or against the public interest if the contract was one "relating to the business of" a s 51(xx) corporation. The term "relating to" is extremely wide. But it predicates the existence of a relationship between a contract and the business of a s 51(xx) corporation. In some statutes, the context of the term "relating to" requires that the relationship be substantial or direct. Nothing in s 127C or in the rest of the Act, however, requires that the relationship required by s 127C(1)(b) should be narrowly construed. In its natural and ordinary meaning, the provision requires no more than a relationship, whether direct or indirect, between a contract and the business of a s 51(xx) corporation ...

[371] The validity of s 127C(1)(b) does not depend upon the directness or indirectness of the relationship between the contract and the business of a s 51(xx) corporation ... [but] upon whether a contract referred to in s 127A has significance for such a corporation. A contract would have significance if it conferred some benefit or imposed some detriment on a s 51(xx) corporation or if it affected the activities, functions, relationships or business of such a corporation. But the jurisdiction conferred by s 127C(1)(b) is not dependent upon the contract having any effect on, or any other significance for, the corporation. The Commission is given jurisdiction to intervene and set aside a contract on the bare condition that the contract relates to the business of a s 51(xx) corporation. Whether the unfairness, harshness or contrariety to the public interest of the contract has any consequences or significance for the corporation is of no relevance whatever. Jurisdiction to make orders arises once a relationship between the contract and the business of a s 51(xx) corporation exists. That is not enough in my opinion to make ss 127A, 127B and 127C(1)(b) a law with respect to a s 51(xx) corporation. It follows that s 127C(1)(b), as enacted, was not authorised by s 51(xx) of the Constitution.

Brennan J adhered to his own earlier test of "discriminatory operation": that is, a law is valid under s 51(xx) if it selects the involvement of trading or financial corporations as the *discrimen* that determines its ambit of operation. Yet he also assimilated this test to that of "significance".

Brennan J: [337] [In *Actors Equity Association v Fontana Films Pty Ltd* 150 CLR at 183] Gibbs CJ postulated as a test of validity that the constitutional character of a corporation "should be significant in the way in which the law relates to it". That test was accepted by Dawson J in the *Tasmanian Dam Case* [(1983) 158 CLR 1 at 316]. Though I see no error in this approach, it leaves much to judicial impression from case to case. If the constitutional character be "significant" to the relationship with the law, it must be because the character of the corporation is the factor which attracts the operation of the law. If that be so, I perceive no distinction between that test and a test of discriminatory operation. I prefer to state the test as one of discrimination, for that test admits of an objective ascertainment of the rights, duties, powers or privileges which the law creates or affects ...

[339] The legislative power conferred by s 51(xx) is not a power to make laws with respect to *things relating to* corporations or *things relating to the businesses of* corporations. A law of that kind bears the character of a law with respect to constitutional corporations only if the relationship governed by the law affects constitutional corporations in a discriminatory manner. If this be the test by which the character of a law is determined, constitutional corporations must be affected in some respect sufficiently material to give significance to their discriminatory treatment.

The minority held that s 127C(1)(b) was valid. Where it might have an application beyond power, they held that it could be read down under s 15A of the *Acts Interpretation Act*. In so holding, Gaudron J focused as McHugh J had done on "**[364]** the business functions, activities or relationships of constitutional corporations"; but unlike him she thought it sufficient that a law be "expressed to operate on or by reference to" those modes of corporate presence. For her there was no superadded requirement of "significant" or "substantial" connection.

Gaudron J: [364] When s 51(xx) is approached on the basis that it is to be construed according to its terms and not by reference to unnecessary implications and limitations, it is clear that, at the very least, a law which is expressed to operate on or by reference to the business functions, activities or relationships of constitutional corporations is a law with respect to those corporations. In this regard, it is sufficient to note that, **[365]** although the business activities of trading and financial corporations may be more extensive than their trading or financial activities, those corporations, nonetheless, take their character from their business activities. As was pointed out by Gibbs CJ in *Actors and Announcers Equity Association of Australia v Fontana Films Pty Ltd* [150 CLR at 185], "[i]t is the business of a trading corporation to trade, and its business is its trading". So too, it is the business of a financial corporation to engage in financial transactions and its business consists of the transactions in which it engages. And a foreign corporation is simply a corporation formed outside Australia that carries on business in Australia.

As their business activities signify whether or not corporations are trading or financial corporations and the main purpose of the power to legislate with respect to foreign corporations must be directed to their business activities in Australia, it follows that the power conferred by s 51(xx) extends, at the very least, to the business functions and activities of constitutional corporations and to their business relationships ...

[366] It is possible that, as a matter of construction, ss 127A and 127B extend to the review and variation of some aspect of a contract that has no connection with the business activities of a constitutional corporation and which, thus, is separate and distinct from the business functions and activities which an individual performs for the corporation or the business relationship which he or she has with it. If they do, a question arises whether s 51(xx) extends to authorise laws binding on individuals with respect to matters which travel beyond the corporate functions and activities in which they participate or the relationships which they have with a constitutional corporation. The same question arises if ss 127A and 127B allow a contract to be varied so that it has an operation unrelated to the business of a constitutional corporation.

The question whether ss 127A and 127B operate pursuant to s 127C(1)(b) in some respect that is unrelated to the business activities of a constitutional corporation can be put to one side. It does not arise on the facts of this case. So too, the question whether s 51(xx) authorizes that operation need not be pursued. Clearly, s 127C(1)(b) can be read down pursuant to s 15A of the *Acts Interpretation Act* 1901 (Cth), if necessary, to apply to contracts only to the extent that they relate to the business of a constitutional corporation ...

[367] As already indicated, even if ss 127A and 127B are construed to operate with respect to matters which travel beyond the business functions and activities which an individual performs for a constitutional corporation or the business relationship he or she has with it, no question of constitutional validity arises in this case. This case is concerned solely with the rights and obligations of persons, namely, the prosecutors, who entered into a contractual relationship with a trading corporation, the Company, for the performance of work by or in consequence of which it, the company, carries out its business activities. And it is concerned only with that work and the rights and obligations arising out of or in connection with that work. When applied to the facts and circumstances with which this case is concerned, ss 127A and 127B operate no differently from a law providing that a person who contracts with a constitutional corporation to procure the performance of work by or in consequence of which it, the corporation, carries out its business activities shall not procure that work on terms that are unfair, harsh or against the public interest. As already explained, that operation, being an operation on persons who are in a business relationship with a constitutional corporation in respect of matters the subject of their particular relationship, is within the power conferred by s 51(xx).

By stipulating repeatedly that s 51(xx) extends "at the very least" to laws of the kind thus described, Gaudron J intimated that behind her approach to the question of characterisation lay a broader view of constitutional power. Moreover, while her approach to characterisation required a connection with corporate "business", hers was the most permissive version of what that connection might be.

Mason CJ joined her in dissent, expressed his agreement with her reasoning and reiterated his own earlier view that s 51(xx) "[333] must be construed as a plenary [334] power ... not limited to the regulation of the functions, activities and relationships of constitutional corporations ... which can be described as business functions, activities and relationships". He also insisted that "the characterisation of a law is [not] to be determined [merely] by reference to its direct legal operation". Yet in formulating the requisite degree of connection with corporate identity and activity, his dissenting judgment picked up all the competing epithets from the majority judgments: "significant", "sufficient" and "substantial". In his view, a law should be characterised in a way that secures its validity whenever it "exhibits in its practical operation a substantial or sufficient connection with the relevant head of power". In this case it was enough that "[335] the contract 'relates to' the business operations of the corporation in a substantial and significant practical sense".

To the question "*What aspects or activities* of a corporation can be regulated under s 51(xx)?" *Dingjan's Case* gives no precise answer. Nor does it determine whether the Commonwealth can enact laws providing that "A corporation shall ..." or "A corporation shall not ...". Instead, both the majority and the dissenting judgments signal that these abstract questions as to the potential scope of the power may no longer be the relevant questions. In *Dingjan's Case* all seven judges accepted that the critical question must be *what degree of relevance or connection* to "constitutional corporations" is necessary for characterisation as a law "with respect to" those corporations,

Whether the requisite relevance or connection must be "significant", "substantial" or "sufficient" still leaves room for judicial disagreement. One might also ask in which direction the requisite connection should run. Is it that a focus on corporate identity or activity must have been a sufficient conceptual influence in the fashioning of the law? Or is it that the operation of the law must have a sufficient practical effect upon corporate identity and activity? Either way, the clear shift of focus in *Dingjan's Case* to the question of characterisation means that abstract questions of the outer limits of power are bypassed. If ever Higgins' list of "horribles" assumes legislative reality, the ensuing judicial determination will not depend on whether or not the scope of s 51(xx) in principle extends so far, but on whether the effect of the law upon "constitutional corporations" is sufficiently substantial or significant to enable it to be characterised as a law "with respect to" those corporations.

It is partly for this reason that the judgment of Brennan CJ, Toohey, Gaudron, McHugh and Gummow JJ in *Victoria v Commonwealth* (*Industrial Relations Act Case*) (1996) 187 CLR 416 adds little to the explication of legislative power under s 51(xx). In a long, intricate judgment that worked sequentially through some 50 separate issues relating to sections of the Act, the tendency in *Dingjan* to focus on the characterisation of specific provisions rather than on the outer limits of power was reinforced. The Court upheld extensive changes to the *Industrial Relations Act*, introduced by the *Industrial Relations Reform Act 1993* (Cth) and the *Industrial Relations Amendment Act (No 2) 1994* (Cth). The enactment of the new provisions was founded in part on the external affairs power, and in part on the corporations power.

Although three States had instituted proceedings to challenge the legislation, only Western Australia challenged the provisions that primarily relied on s 51(xx); and at the hearing that challenge was abandoned. "[188] Subject to one possible exception, it was conceded in argument by Western Australia ... that the Parliament has power to legislate as to the industrial rights and obligations of constitutional corporations ... and their employees". Accordingly, the validity of such legislation was "[189] not in issue". The *Workplace Relations Amendment (Work Choices) Act 2005* (Cth) is enacted on the assumption that Western Australia's concession was correct.

The only significant context in which the Court found it necessary in the *Industrial Relations Act Case* to enter upon a detailed discussion of s 51(xx) was that of "secondary boycotts". The original provisions upheld in *Actors Equity* had substantially been re-enacted as Div 7 of Pt VI of the *Industrial Relations Act*, but with additional protections for trade unions. In holding both the "boycott" provisions and the ancillary protections for trade unions valid, the Court simply applied *Actors Equity*. In holding that the impact of the provisions upon third parties was valid, the Court simply distinguished *Dingjan*.

4. Incorporation

Throughout the case-by-case development of the "corporations" power since the *Concrete Pipes Case*, other difficult questions remained unresolved. In particular, there was speculation from *Concrete Pipes* onwards as to whether the Commonwealth could enact its own corporations law that would regulate all aspects of companies, including their incorporation.

In 1990 the issue was finally resolved in a way that dramatically reasserted limits on Commonwealth power under s 51(xx). In *New South Wales v Commonwealth* (*Incorporation Case*) (1990) 169 CLR 482 the Court held, with Deane J dissenting, that s 51(xx) does *not* enable the Commonwealth to regulate the process of incorporation. This was because the power is delineated by reference to "trading and financial corporations formed within the limits of the Commonwealth", that is, to corporations which have already been formed.

The *Incorporation Case* concerned the major legislative package by which the Commonwealth first sought to establish its national regime of corporations and securities law. The *Corporations Act 1989* (Cth) was based upon the assumption that s 51(xx) empowered the Commonwealth to legislate for the incorporation of a company if the subscribers to the memorandum of association intended that its activities would substantially be trading or financial activities.

New South Wales v Commonwealth (*Incorporation Case*)
(1990) 169 CLR 482

Mason CJ, Brennan, Dawson, Toohey, Gaudron and McHugh JJ: [497] The power conferred by s 51(xx) is not expressed as a power with respect to a function of government, a field of activity or a class of relationships but as a power with respect to persons, namely, corporations of the classes therein specified: *Actors and Announcers Equity Association v Fontana Films Pty Ltd* [(1982) 150 CLR 169 at 182, 216] and *Commonwealth v Tasmania* (the *Tasmanian Dam Case*) [(1983) 158 CLR 1 at 157, 202, 240, 269, 314]. The Commonwealth contention is that the words "formed within the limits of the Commonwealth" serve merely to distinguish local trading or financial corporations from foreign corporations. No doubt the words do serve that function but their plain meaning goes beyond the mere drawing of that distinction. The expressions "trading or financial" and "formed within the limits of the Commonwealth" serve to restrict the classes of domestic corporation which can be the subject of Commonwealth power. To fall **[498]** within one limb of the power, a corporation must satisfy two conditions: it must be formed within the limits of the Commonwealth and it must be a trading or financial corporation. To fall within the other limb, a corporation must be a foreign corporation, that is, a corporation formed outside the limits of the Commonwealth. The distinction based on the place of formation is obvious, but the basis of the distinction is formation. The word "formed" is a past participle used adjectivally, and the participial phrase "formed within the limits of the Commonwealth" is used to describe corporations which have been or shall have been created in Australia. (Clearly enough, the phrase is used to describe corporations formed after as well as those formed before federation.) The subject of a valid law is restricted by that phrase to corporations which have undergone or shall have undergone the process of formation in the past, present or future. That is to say, the power is one with respect to "formed corporations". That being so, the words "formed within the limits of the Commonwealth" exclude the process of incorporation itself. Such corporations are distinguished from corporations which have been or shall have been created outside the limits of Australia.

No doubt, as the Commonwealth submitted, the words "with respect to" in s 51 of the Constitution are words of wide import and par (xx), being a grant of legislative power, "should be construed with all the generality which the words used admit": *R v Public Vehicles Licensing Appeal Tribunal (Tas); Ex parte Australian National Airways Pty Ltd* [(1964) 113 CLR 201 at 225]. But the generality imported by the words "with respect to" cannot expand a power over existing ("formed") corporations into a power to form corporations. The power conferred by s 51(xx) to make laws with respect to artificial legal persons is not a power to bring into existence the artificial legal persons upon which laws made under the power can operate ...

[501] Moreover, the history of s 51(xx) confirms that the language of the paragraph was not directed towards the subject of incorporation. That the Convention Debates may be used to establish the subject to which the paragraph was directed is made clear by *Cole v Whitfield* [(1988) 165 CLR 360 at 385]; see also *Port MacDonnell Professional Fishermen's Association Inc v South Australia* [(1989) 168 CLR 340 at 375-7]. And the draft bills prepared by the Conventions of 1891, 1897 and 1898 have long been considered a legitimate aid in the interpretation of the provisions of the Constitution: see *Tasmania v Commonwealth and Victoria* [(1904) 1 CLR 329 at 333, 350].

The successive drafts of s 51(xx) before it reached the form in which it appears in the Constitution confirm that that paragraph is concerned with existing corporations and was not intended to confer power to legislate for their creation. The origin of s 51(xx) is to be found in s 15(i) of the

Federal Council of Australasia Act 1885 (Imp). The draft Bill presented to the National Australasian Convention held in Sydney in 1891 contained in cl 52 a power to **[502]** legislate with respect to "The status in the commonwealth of foreign corporations, and of corporations formed in any state or part of the commonwealth". It is apparent that this provision gave no power to make laws with respect to the incorporation of companies. The power was confined to the status of corporations. The word "formed", therefore, meant "which have been formed". Indeed, at that Convention the question was raised whether the delegates should amend cl 52(19) to deal with the incorporation of companies. Sir Samuel Griffith replied "I do not think we should. There are a great number of different corporations. For instance, there are municipal, trading and charitable corporations, and these are all incorporated in different ways according to the law obtaining in the different states ... What is important, however, is that there should be a uniform law for the recognition of corporations ... I think the states may be trusted to stipulate how they will incorporate companies, although we ought to have some general law in regard to their recognition": *Convention Debates* (Sydney 1891) vol I, p 686. The clause was adopted without amendment: *Convention Debates* (Sydney 1891) vol I, p 952.

Clause 50 of the draft Bill presented to the Adelaide Convention in 1897 conferred legislative power with respect to "XXII Foreign corporations, and trading corporations formed in any State or part of the Commonwealth". The clause was no longer limited to laws with respect to the status of corporations and Commonwealth power over local corporations was restricted to trading corporations. But there is no reason to suppose that, by deleting the words "the status in the commonwealth of" and inserting the word "trading", those who drafted the provision intended to alter the meaning of the words "formed in". The clause was adopted with the addition of the words "or financial" after the word "trading": *Convention Debates* (Adelaide 1897) vol III, p 1230. The clause in its final form appeared as s 51(xx) in the draft Bill presented to the Convention held in Melbourne in 1898, the words "within the limits of the Commonwealth" having been substituted for the words "in any State or part of the Commonwealth". It was adopted in that form ...

There is thus no ground for thinking that s 51(xx) was framed with the intention of conferring upon the Commonwealth the power to provide for the incorporation of companies. Indeed, the history of the paragraph plainly indicates that the draftsmen of the provision did not contemplate that it should confer any power otherwise than in respect of corporations already formed. Contemporary opinion, which was reflected in the decision in *Huddart Parker* [(1909) 8 CLR 330], is to be seen in the following passage from Quick and Garran, *Annotated Constitution of the Australian Commonwealth* **[503]** (1901), where the authors say, at p 607:

"It would therefore seem that this provision refers to companies created under State laws. Such bodies, once launched, will come within the control of Federal legislation. Under this power it would probably be competent for Parliament to convert a corporation created by State authority into a Federal corporation; to enlarge the scope of its operations and business; to confer on a local corporation certain powers which would be beyond the jurisdiction of the States Governments to grant."

The scheme of the *Corporations Act* is based upon an apparent acceptance of the view that the character of a company as a trading or financial corporation is to be determined by the nature of its activities, either actual or intended. It is unnecessary in this case to embark upon an examination of the authorities dealing with this topic – see, eg, *State Superannuation Board v Trade Practices Commission* [(1982) 150 CLR 282]; *Fencott v Muller* [(1983) 152 CLR 570] – but it may be observed that the limitation imposed upon the reach of s 51(xx) by the requirement that, in the case of domestic corporations, they be of a trading or financial character, would create undeniable difficulties if that paragraph were to be construed as extending to the incorporation of companies. The fact that the character of a corporation may vary, so that it may be at one time a trading or financial corporation and not at another, makes it less likely at least that s 51(xx) was intended to confer power upon the Commonwealth to incorporate companies over which its power of regulation might fluctuate, possibly without knowledge upon either side. The complexity of the Act in attempting to cope with that difficulty demonstrates the problem which stems from construing s 51(xx) so as to include a power to legislate for the creation of corporations within the confines otherwise imposed by that paragraph. But it is sufficient for our purposes to observe that such a construction is supported by neither the language of the provision, nor its history nor authority.

Deane J: [504] It was contended in argument that par (xx)'s grant of legislative power with respect to foreign corporations could not extend to the making of a law governing the incorporation of foreign corporations. I do not accept that contention. Incorporation means **[505]** the acquisition or conferral of corporate personality under the law. A plenary legislative power "with respect to" particular kinds of corporation extends, as a matter of mere language, to laws dealing with both the incorporation and the liquidation of such corporations just as a plenary legislative power with respect to "copyrights", "patents", "designs" or "trade marks" extends to laws dealing with the creation and extinguishment of those particular kinds of industrial property. It is true that it has often been said that comity among nations requires some local recognition of foreign corporations. Nonetheless, the circumstances in which, the extent to which and the procedures by which corporate personality is to be accorded under our system of law to foreign corporations are patently matters for our local law ... That being so, it appears to me to be plain that par (xx)'s grant of legislative power with respect to foreign corporations cannot properly be confined to exclude the power to make laws defining the circumstances and establishing the procedures under and by which artificial entities invested with corporate personality under other systems of law may acquire or enjoy such personality under the law of this country. At least in that sense, a law providing for the local incorporation of "foreign corporations" is a law within the grant of power with respect to such corporations.

The argument that par (xx)'s grant of legislative power "with respect to ... trading or financial corporations formed within the limits of the Commonwealth" should be construed as not extending to laws with respect to the incorporation of such corporations focussed upon the word "formed". The legislative power could not, so it was said, extend to authorize laws governing the formation of such corporations since, until they are formed, they do not exist as the subject-matter of the power. Any superficial appeal of that argument does not, in my view, survive close examination. One objection to it is that it fails to distinguish between the abstract subject-matter of the legislative power and concrete instances of that subject-matter. One might as well say that a legislative power with respect to locally manufactured motor vehicles would not extend to laws governing the local manufacture of motor vehicles or that the legislative power with respect to lighthouses does not **[506]** extend to laws governing the erection of lighthouses since, until it is manufactured locally or erected, neither the locally manufactured motor vehicle nor the lighthouse exists as such. Another objection is that the argument fails to accord proper scope to the words "with respect to" in s 51 or to the settled principle which requires that par (xx), which is a constitutional grant of plenary legislative power, be liberally, and not narrowly or technically, construed: "it should be construed with all the generality which the words used admit" (per Dixon CJ, Kitto, Taylor, Menzies, Windeyer and Owen JJ, *R v Public Vehicles Licensing Appeal Tribunal (Tas); Ex parte Australian National Airways Pty Ltd*) [113 CLR at 225]. In that regard, it is important to note that the basis of the argument is a reading of the word "formed" as meaning "which have already been formed at the time of application of the relevant law". That constrictive interpretation of the word seems to me to be quite unjustified. In the context of the use of the phrase "formed within the limits of the Commonwealth" in contradistinction to "foreign", the word "formed" is properly to be understood as representing a use of the past participle as part of an adjectival phrase which is without temporal significance. As Stephen J pointed out in *Mikasa (NSW) Pty Ltd v Festival Stores* [(1972) 127 CLR 617 at 660-1], such a merely descriptive use of the past participle is "common enough", it "is not the past tense ... , it is neutral in temporal meaning and applies equally to the future as to the past" (see, also, per Murphy J, *Kathleen Investments (Aust) Ltd v Australian Atomic Energy Commission* [(1977) 139 CLR 117 at 159]). When the word "formed" is so understood, it affords no basis for excluding the formation or incorporation within the limits of the Commonwealth of trading and financial corporations from the scope of the legislative power granted by the second limb of par (xx). To the contrary, it tends to focus attention upon that aspect of the grant of power ...

[511] Reference should be made to two subsidiary arguments advanced in favour of the view that laws dealing with incorporation were beyond the ambit of par (xx). The first can be shortly disposed of. It was to the effect that that view is supported by what was said in the course of the Convention Debates and by contemporary commentators (see, in particular, Quick and Garran, *Annotated Constitution of the Australian Commonwealth*, (1901), p 607 §198; but cf Sir Robert Garran, "Memoranda on Constitutional Questions", in Commonwealth Parliamentary Papers

(1934-1937) vol II, p 73). The first answer to that argument is that the few brief references in the Convention Debates are far from compelling (see, eg, *Convention Debates* (Adelaide 1897) vol III, p 439) and one can point to contrary statements in early authority (see W Harrison Moore, *Constitution of the Commonwealth of Australia* (1902), p 148). The second answer is a more fundamental one … It is that it is not permissible to constrict the effect of the words which were adopted by the people as the compact of a nation by reference to the intentions or understanding of those who participated in or observed the Convention Debates (see *Breavington v Godleman* [(1989) 169 CLR 41 at 131-3]).

The second subsidiary argument was, as I followed it, essentially an appeal to convenience. It was said that the words "trading or financial" in par (xx) significantly restrict the corporations to which the grant of legislative power extended. That being so, it would be productive of difficulty and inconvenience to construe par (xx) as conferring a legislative power with respect to the incorporation of those corporations only. One answer to this argument is that it assumes an unduly restrictive connotation of the phrase "trading or financial corporations" in par (xx) … **[512]** In any event, there is a more complete answer to the argument of inconvenience based on the consideration that the grant of legislative power with respect to local trading or financial corporations does not extend to all corporations. It is that, while that consideration might well be seen by the Parliament as calling for restraint in the exercise of the legislative power, it does not provide any legal justification for denying the generality of a plenary grant of legislative power with respect to the designated class of corporation. If even further answer to an argument based upon the alleged inconvenience of uniform companies legislation in relation to trading and financial corporations be needed, it is plain enough. It is that the advantages of such national companies legislation with respect to such corporations seem to me overwhelmingly to outweigh the alleged inconvenience.

It follows from what has been said above that I am of the view that the legislative power which the second limb of par (xx) confers upon the Parliament with respect to local trading or financial corporations extends to authorize the making of laws governing the formation or incorporation of such corporations. That is the effect of the words of the Constitution when they are construed in accordance with the principles applicable to the construction of a plenary grant of legislative power.

Despite this strong dissent by Deane J, the *Incorporation Case* meant that any Commonwealth power to legislate for a corporations law was denied. Instead, the Commonwealth was driven to rely on the co-operative arrangements with the States explained in Chapter 6, §3.

5. Further References

Corcoran, S, "Corporate Law and the Australian Constitution: A History of Section 51(xx) of the Australian Constitution" (1994) 15 *Journal of Legal History* 131.

Crawford, J, "The High Court and the Corporations Power: Incorporation 'Reserved' to the States" [1990] *Australian Corporation Law Bulletin* 32.

Kennett, G, "Constitutional Interpretation in the *Corporations Case*" (1990) 19 *Federal Law Review* 223.

Lindell, G, "The Corporations and Races Powers" (1984) 14 *Federal Law Review* 219.

Lloyd, BL, "The Constitutional Validity of the Trade Practices Act and Regulation of the Conduct of Holding Companies" (1993) 21 *Federal Law Review* 279.

McQueen, R, "Why High Court Judges Make Poor Historians: The Corporations Act Case and Early Attempts to Establish a National System of Company Regulation in Australia" (1990) 19 *Federal Law Review* 245.

Ramsay, IM, "Company Law and the Economics of Federalism" (1990) 19 *Federal Law Review* 169.

Stewart, A, "Federal Labour Law and New Uses for the Corporations Power" (2001) 14 *Australian Journal of Labour Law* 145.

Zines, L, *The High Court and the Constitution* (Butterworths, 4th ed 1997), Ch 5.

Chapter 18

The Defence Power

1. The Nature of the Power

The central High Court doctrine in this area can be summed up in one sentence: the defence power waxes and wanes. That is, at the height of a global war the measures that Parliament can enact may extend into virtually every aspect of Australian life, and may involve far greater control and co-ordination of the national economy than is normally possible. In times of peace, the scope of the defence power will be much more limited; but although the power is "elastic", it does not immediately snap back at the end of a period of international conflict to its limited peacetime scope. The transition back into peacetime conditions may justify a continuation of some wartime measures, and new measures may be needed to cope with that transition.

Behind the particular issues lie deeper problems of doctrine and judicial method, which were given their classic formulation by Dixon J in a series of judgments during World War II. Among the cases involved was *Andrews v Howell* (1941) 65 CLR 255, where the Court (Rich ACJ, Dixon and McTiernan JJ, with Starke J dissenting) upheld the validity of the *National Security (Apple and Pear Acquisition) Regulations* (Cth). (Their object was "to minimize the disorganization in the marketing of apples and pears likely to result from the impracticability of exporting sufficient quantities … because of the effects upon shipping of the present war".)

Andrews v Howell
(1941) 65 CLR 255

Dixon J: [278] In dealing with that constitutional power, it must be remembered that, though its meaning does not change, yet unlike some other powers its application depends upon facts, and as those facts change so may its actual operation as a power enabling the legislature to make a particular law. In the same way the operation of wide general powers conferred upon the Executive by the Parliament in the exercise of the power conferred by sec 51(vi) is affected by changing facts. The existence and character of hostilities, or a threat of hostilities, against the Commonwealth are facts which will determine the extent of the operation of the power. Whether it will suffice to authorize a given measure will depend upon the nature and dimensions of the conflict that calls it forth, upon the actual and apprehended dangers, exigencies and course of the war, and upon the matters that are incident thereto.

In *Stenhouse v Coleman* (1944) 69 CLR 457, the Court upheld regulations conferring on the Minister a wide discretionary power to make orders controlling the sale or distribution of "essential articles", provided that his actual orders had a sufficient connection with defence.

Stenhouse v Coleman
(1944) 69 CLR 457

Dixon J: [469] When the question is whether a measure is incidental or conducive to the prosecution of a war that is being fought, the solution of the question is bound to depend much less upon the abstract formulation of the general test or criterion to be applied than upon a correct ascertainment of the true nature and operation of the provisions impugned and of their bearing upon the prosecution of the war.

The bearing of any particular legislative or executive act upon the prosecution of this or any other war is necessarily the product of factors or conditions the operation of which is likely to be intricate.

If the actual and possible factors could be openly and exhaustively examined and laid bare before it, a court would probably find little difficulty in deciding whether a given measure was, or was not, incidental or conducive to the prosecution of the war. But in many cases this cannot be done. Apart from other reasons, information and considerations which may have guided the authors of a statutory instrument under attack may be of such a nature that they cannot be publicly canvassed without prejudicing the conduct of the war or imperilling the national interest. In any case, there are limitations upon the material which a court can receive or take into account for the purpose of considering the validity of a general law. If the form of the power makes the existence of some special or particular state of fact a condition of its exercise, then, no doubt, the existence of that state of fact may be proved or disproved by evidence like any other matter of fact. But ordinarily the court does not go beyond matters of which it may take judicial notice. This means that for its facts the court must depend upon matters of general public knowledge. It may be that in this respect the field open to the court is wider than has been commonly supposed … But, however that may be, common experience shows that much of the difficulty and of the uncertainty that attends the discussion of the validity of a purported exercise of legislative power, **[470]** defined like the defence power by reference to the end to which it is directed, arises from the inferential, not to say speculative, character of the grounds connecting the provision with the prosecution of the war. It is for that reason no doubt that those supporting the validity of a measure so often place reliance upon the presumption in favour of validity. The question is one of law and not of fact, and in such a case a presumption seldom provides a solution; at best it supplies a step in legal reasoning. But where the validity of a legislative instrument is affected by what is planned or is going forward in relation to the prosecution of the war, the presumption is, so to speak, reinforced by the respect which the court pays to the opinion or judgment of the other organs of government with whom the responsibility for carrying on the war rests. When, for example, it appears that a challenged regulation is a means adopted to secure some end relating to the prosecution of the war, the court does not substitute for that of the Executive its own opinion of the appropriateness or sufficiency of the means to promote the desired end. But great as must be the weight given to these considerations, it is finally the court which must form and act upon a judgment upon the question whether the legislation, be it direct or be it subordinate, is a true exercise of the legislative power with respect to defence …

[471] Some of the difficulties which have been felt in the application of that power seem to me to be due to the circumstance that, unlike most other powers conferred by s 51 of the Constitution, it involves the notion of purpose or object … [T]he purpose must be collected from the instrument in question, the facts to which it applies and the circumstances which called it forth. It is evident that among these circumstances the character of the war, its notorious incidents, and its far-reaching consequences must take first place. In some cases they must form controlling considerations, because from them will appear the cause and the justification for the challenged measure. They are considerations arising from matters about which, in case of doubt, courts can inform themselves by looking at materials that are the subject of judicial notice.

The course of the war has taught us that, in grave emergencies, it may be necessary, in exercise of the defence power, to assume control of the greater part of the human and material resources of the nation. The character of a war and the state of emergency at a **[472]** given time may justify measures which at another time would be unwarranted. One difficulty to which this elastic application of the defence power gives rise is that regulations, the necessity or justification for which would be conceded during the emergency which called them forth, may continue unrevoked when the emergency may have passed and conditions may have assumed a normal appearance.

The following themes emerge from these passages:

1. The defence power is "elastic": it "waxes and wanes", "ebbs and flows". It is "a fixed concept with a changing content". Its scope depends on Australia's defence needs at any given time, and as these needs fluctuate so does the scope of the power.

2. The defence power is a "purpose" power; it authorises the Commonwealth to legislate not on a specified subject-matter, but for a specified purpose. A law is justified not because it is on the topic of defence, but because it is, or reasonably may be, conducive to a defence purpose or object. Although this analysis is widely accepted, it has not been unanimous. Starke J was unyielding in his insistence that "defence" was a subject-matter for legislation, to be approached much like other heads of power. Accordingly, during World War II High Court majorities commonly upheld regulations because they were for the *purpose* of defence, while Starke J dissented because they were not on the *topic* of defence (see, for example, *Australian Woollen Mills Ltd v Commonwealth* (1944) 69 CLR 476).

3. The conditions that determine the scope of the power as it "waxes and wanes" are factual conditions – for example, whether Australia is currently at war or facing a real or perceived threat of invasion, and the immediate military and economic needs of Australia at such a time. The most obvious facts are external to Australia, but internal conditions are also important. Most of these are political, international, economic and social in nature and are likely to be notorious as matters of common knowledge. They are thus the kind of facts of which courts take "judicial notice", that is, facts that judges can draw from their personal knowledge without requiring evidentiary proof.

4. Where "judicial notice" is insufficient to show that a measure is for the purpose of defence, there are difficulties of inference and proof that *Stenhouse v Coleman* does not solve. The success of military and other policies is rarely certain; and a demonstration that a particular measure will contribute to victory, or will enhance defence preparedness, cannot reasonably be expected. What is required is that a measure can reasonably be regarded as one that might achieve a defence objective. Even when there are "facts" that will satisfy that limited test, the High Court may be ill equipped to find them (see Susan Kenny, "Constitutional Fact Ascertainment" (1990) 1 *Public Law Review* 134). Indeed, such "facts" may not even be open to evidentiary proof. For one thing, they may depend on information that, especially in wartime, governments may not be able to make public. Moreover, these "facts" are likely to be matters of opinion or judgment in areas where the separation of powers requires that such judgments be made by the executive and not by the courts. For these reasons, courts are likely to accord substantial deference to legislative and executive judgment, thereby giving very wide latitude to government policies that might be conducive to defence. The extent of this latitude may "wax and wane" along with the scope of the defence power itself, becoming very broad indeed in times of total war.

5. Despite this deference, the question of whether a particular law is authorised by s 51(vi) is a question of constitutional law that must be determined by a court. The separation of powers means that neither the legislature nor the executive can pre-empt the judicial function by purporting to determine the constitutional question in advance. Evidence of the beliefs and intentions of the legislature or executive may help to answer the constitutional question, but it must ultimately be answered by the High Court as the only authoritative interpreter of the Constitution. The Parliament cannot be the judge of its own constitutional power.

Because defence is a "purpose" rather than a "subject-matter" power, the relevant question of characterisation is one of proportionality, rather than whether the law is sufficiently connected to the subject-matter. This requires the High Court to determine whether the challenged law can be seen to be reasonably appropriate and adapted to achieving a defence purpose. That approach, implicit in many of the cases decided during World War II, was made explicit in *Polyukhovich v Commonwealth* (*War Crimes Act Case*) (1991) 172 CLR 501.

Ivan Polyukhovich was the first person to be tried in Australia (but eventually acquitted) under the *War Crimes Amendment Act 1988* (Cth). The Act almost completely rewrote the original *War Crimes Act 1945* (Cth) to permit the prosecution and trial in Australia of Australian residents alleged to have committed war crimes in Europe during World War II. The High Court, with Brennan J in dissent, held that the Act was within Commonwealth legislative power with respect to "external affairs". Deane and Gaudron JJ held that it was nonetheless invalid because it violated a fundamental "implied guarantee" against retrospective criminal laws (see Chapter 14, §7(b)). Brennan J reached the same result as Deane and Gaudron JJ, but without resort to an "implied guarantee".

Having held that the law could not be upheld as one with respect to "external affairs", Brennan J turned to s 51(vi). Presumably, the original *War Crimes Act* was valid as part of the transitional process arising from the fact that Australia had been involved in World War II; but that justification could hardly be relied on in 1988. Instead, it was argued that the 1988 Act might be conducive to *future* defence needs: by vigorously pursuing allegations of past war crimes now, Australia might help to establish strong international standards against wartime atrocities which might protect Australian men and women fighting in future wars. Brennan J rejected this argument and held that the legislation could not be supported by s 51(vi). He had earlier hinted at a similar view in *R v Bolton; Ex parte Beane* (1987) 162 CLR 514.

Polyukhovich v Commonwealth (*War Crimes Act Case*)
(1991) 172 CLR 501

Brennan J: [592] Although the Act is capable of having a relevant deterrent effect and may, on that account, be said to be "appropriate and adapted" to serve defence purposes (as the original *War Crimes Act* was thought to do), the validity under s 51(vi) of a law enacted in a time of peace depends upon whether the Parliament might have reasonably considered the means which the law embodies for achieving or procuring the relevant defence purpose to be appropriate and adapted to that end, a question of reasonable proportionality: see per Deane J in the *Tasmanian Dam Case* [(1983) 158 CLR 1 at 260]; *Richardson* [*v Forestry Commission* (1988) 164 CLR 261 at 291, 311- 12, 336, 345-6]. In times of war, laws abridging the freedoms which **[593]** the law assures to the Australian people are supported in order to ensure the survival of those freedoms in times of peace. In times of peace, an abridging of those freedoms – in this case, freedom from a retrospective criminal law – cannot be supported unless the Court can perceive that the abridging of the freedom in question is proportionate to the defence interest to be served. What is necessary and appropriate for the defence of the Commonwealth in times of war is different from what is necessary or appro- priate in times of peace: *Richardson* [164 CLR at 326], per Dawson J. "That is because the question of appropriateness and adaptation falls for determination by reference to the circumstances which engage the power": per Gaudron J in *Re Tracey; Ex parte Ryan* [(1989) 166 CLR 518 at 597]. The formation of the critical judgment as to whether the means adopted by a law are appropriate and adapted to serve defence purposes is entrusted to the Court: *Stenhouse v Coleman* [(1944) 69 CLR 457 at 470].

The means which the Act adopts to secure future adherence to the laws and customs of war not only trample upon a principle which is of the highest importance in a free society, namely, that criminal laws should not operate retrospectively, but also select a specific group of persons from a time long past out of all those who have committed, or are suspected of having committed, war crimes in other armed conflicts. Respect for the laws and customs of war cannot be secured by a law having such an oppressive and discriminatory operation.

The other six judges did not need to consider the "defence" power because they held that the Act could be supported by the "external affairs" power. Despite this, Toohey and Gaudron JJ briefly did so and agreed with Brennan J.

2. War

Like most of the cases heard during World War II, *Andrews v Howell* and *Stenhouse v Coleman* involved challenges to the validity of regulations made under the *National Security Act 1939* (Cth). The power of delegated legislation given by that Act was extremely broad, and the regulations themselves often gave wide discretionary powers to the Governor-General to be exercised on the basis of his opinion that it was necessary or expedient to do so. Where regulations were held to be invalid, it was either because the making of such regulations was not authorised by the Act, or because, if the Act did authorise such regulations, the Act itself was to that extent not a valid exercise of legislative power under s 51(vi).

In *Farey v Burvett* (1916) 21 CLR 433, Isaacs J appeared to envisage a separate executive power to respond to wartime emergencies, independent of s 51(vi). He suggested that the provisions of s 61 of the Constitution (vesting executive power in the Governor-General) "[452] carry with them the royal war prerogative, and all that the common law of England includes in that prerogative". He then treated the express incidental power (s 51(xxxix)) as operating on s 61 to ensure "[452] in the most ample and absolute terms ... the full power and duty of taking every measure of defence which the circumstances may require". Although these suggestions have a certain resonance in later decisions on the "nationhood power" (see Chapter 12, §2(b)), they have never been tested. In any event, the *National Security Regulations* (Cth) made during World War II, like the *War Precautions Regulations* (Cth) made during World War I, were made by the executive government with statutory authority, and were therefore open to constitutional scrutiny under s 51(vi).

According to Isaacs J in *Farey v Burvett*, the scope of the defence power is virtually unlimited during a time of total war when the existence of Australia is threatened. It becomes a "[454] paramount" source of power – overriding all constitutional restraints on the exercise of power, such as s 92; displacing the normal distribution of power between Commonwealth and States; and compelling judicial deference to legislative and executive judgment to the point of total acquiescence. Isaacs J argued that the limits of the defence power are "[453] bounded only by the requirements of self-preservation" and that "[455] [i]f the measure questioned may conceivably in such circumstances even incidentally aid the effectuation of the power of defence, the Court must hold its hand and leave the rest to the judgment and wisdom and discretion of the Parliament and the Executive it controls – for they alone have the information, the knowledge and the experience and also, by the [456] Constitution, the authority to judge of the situation and lead the nation to the desired end".

The dicta of Isaacs J were clearly too sweeping and have not met later judicial acceptance. Subsequent decisions have held that laws passed under s 51(vi) are subject to constitutional guarantees such as s 51(xxxi) (*Minister for the Army v Dalziel* (1944) 68 CLR 261) and s 92 (*Gratwick v Johnson* (1945) 70 CLR 1). However, much of what Isaacs J said is *almost* acceptable. Even when the necessary qualifications are added, the scope of s 51(vi) in a time of total war is extremely wide. During World War II, judicial deference to government claims for a massive expansion in the scope of the defence power was almost complete.

Brian Galligan, *Politics of the High Court*
(University of Queensland Press, 1987)

[120] Japan's entry into the war, although not unexpected, was dramatic and its advances were astonishing. Pearl Harbour was attacked on 7 December 1941, Singapore fell on 15 February 1942, Darwin was bombed on 19 February 1942 and the American forces in the Philippines surrendered on 6 May 1942. The shock of Pearl Harbour was in many respects an immense relief for Australia since it brought the United States directly into the war with Japan. The fall of Singapore was a more traumatic experience because it exploded the popular myth that Australia was secure behind the protective umbrella of British naval power. As Curtin predicted: "The fall of Singapore opens

the Battle of Australia." Soon Australian troops were fighting grimly in Southern Papua, part of Australia's trust territories, and a Japanese landing on Australia's own shores seemed imminent ...

[121] Under Labor administration ... there was ruthless direction of industry and considerable expansion of government works by the Allied Works Council. A myriad of national security regulations controlled virtually every aspect of Australian life; there were labour controls, price controls, profit controls and rationing. In his pleas to the American people for increased help in March 1942, Curtin could vouch for the maximum commitment of his own country's resources. Australia was "a nation stripped for war", he said; business interests were subject to "iron control and drastic elimination of profits"; and the sacred rights and privileges of trade unions had been suspended. This was possible only because the High Court allowed enormous expansion of the section 51(vi) defence power during this period of grave national emergency ...

[126] It has long been recognized that a federal system is predisposed towards weak national government. Whereas strong government requires a concentration of political power and the ability to act forcefully and quickly, the Australian federal system, following the American model, divides basic government powers between two levels of government, each sovereign in its own sphere. It further weakens the national level of government by fragmenting power among its three branches, legislative, executive and judicial, and by dividing the legislature into two separate houses, each constituted on a different principle of representation. During the national crisis of World War II this complicated system of fragmented powers was effectively suspended. Under the defence power, Australia had, for all practical **[127]** purposes, a unitary government. The national legislature was unified: in the first instance because the opposition-controlled Senate dared not oppose the Curtin government, as it had the Scullin government in the 1930s, because of far greater pressures for national solidarity in time of war; and after 1943 because the Senate was also controlled by Labor. Furthermore, parliament delegated virtually the whole area of defence to the executive. Under the National Security Act of 1939 the executive was given sweeping powers "for securing the public safety and the defence of the Commonwealth ... and for prescribing all matters which ... are necessary or convenient ... for the more effectual prosecution of the present war".

Presiding over and sanctioning this transformation of the Australian constitution was the High Court. Rich said in one of the defence cases that a country with a federal form of government that becomes involved in a war which necessitated the direction of its whole resources to defence, "cannot hope to survive unless it submits itself for the time being to what is in effect a dictatorship with power to do anything which can contribute to its defence" [*Dawson v Commonwealth* (1946) 73 CLR 157 at 177] ...

In the spirit of *Farey v Burvett* (1916) [21 CLR 433] the Court first upheld the National Security Act that allowed the executive to govern by national security regulation. It subsequently allowed regulations controlling prices, the workforce and the production and distribution of goods. These regulations were typically drawn in the broadest terms and gave the appropriate minister absolute discretion. For example, regulation 59 of the National Security (General) Regulations allowed a minister to make orders providing for "regulating, restricting or prohibiting the production, ... movement, ... distribution, sale, purchase ... of essential articles", while "essential articles" were defined as articles "appearing to a Minister to be essential for the defence of the Commonwealth or the efficient prosecution of the war, or to be essential to the life of the community". The constitutional validity of this open-ended regulation was upheld by the Court. More specifically, in the commercial field the Court allowed regulations controlling landlord and tenant relations and rents, fixing maximum and minimum prices of shares, prohibiting advertising for special occasions such as Christmas, and adjusting contracts to take account of war conditions [*Silk Bros Pty Ltd v State Electricity Commission of Victoria* (1943) 67 CLR 1; *Miller v Commonwealth* (1946) 73 CLR 187; *Ferguson v Commonwealth* (1943) 66 CLR 432; *Peacock v Newtown Marrickville and General Co-operative Building Society No 4 Ltd* (1943) 67 CLR 25].

Many of the regulations that the Court allowed as valid exercises of the defence **[128]** power were only very indirectly linked to defence. For instance, the Court upheld a national marketing scheme for apples and pears on the basis that the export part of the crop was now subject to war restraint on shipping. Starke, a fairly regular and quite sarcastic dissenter in many of the defence cases concerning economic regulation, claimed that the apple and pear marketing regulations had no relation whatever to the "economic front", but merely propped up one sector of the economy that had been affected by war. Starke accused the Court of accepting arguments that led to the conclusion that "in time of war the Commonwealth had complete power to legislate in respect of the social and economic conditions of Australia". He reminded his fellow judges that "after all, the government of Australia is a dual system based upon a separation of powers" [*Andrews v Howell* (1941) 65 CLR 225 at 273]. The Court even went as far as declaring constitutional the restriction of drinking hours in the name of national defence. Starke again disagreed and called this regulation "one of those irritating orders and restrictions upon freedom of action which is arbitrary and capricious, serves no useful purpose, and has no connection whatever with defence" [*de Mestre v Chisholm* (1944) 69 CLR 51 at 63] …

[129] The defence power, however, was not completely without limits. The Court disallowed the federal government's attempt to regulate the working conditions of state public servants engaged in routine administrative work that had nothing to do with the war effort [*R v Commonwealth Court of Conciliation and Arbitration; Ex parte Victoria* (1942) 66 CLR 488]. It also overruled a mixed bag of federal attempts to regulate admission to universities, to control the making of insect sprays, and to set general standards for artificial lighting in factories [*R v University of Sydney; Ex parte Drummond* (1943) 67 CLR 95; *Wertheim v Commonwealth* (1945) 69 CLR 601; *Victorian Chamber of Manufactures v Commonwealth* (*Industrial Lighting Regulations*) (1943) 67 CLR 413].

The defence cases demonstrate the broad discretion that judges have for greatly expanding one part of the constitution when they are convinced that circumstances warrant such expansion. If the judges had been concerned only with technical evaluation of the cases before them, they might have sided with Starke in disallowing many of the Labor administration's industrial and economic regulations that were only indirectly related to defence. But the judges themselves were acutely aware of the seriousness of the national crisis. Latham and Dixon had been directly involved in diplomatic work in Tokyo and Washington in the early years of the war and were privy to the great efforts that the Australian nation had to make in order to survive until the tide of battle turned in the Allies' favour. In such a crisis the Court was prepared to allow virtually every regulation of individual and economic freedom. Approving the overall thrust of the Labor administration's war effort, the Court rarely quibbled over detailed regulations.

This pattern is illustrated by a series of cases concerning the employment of women in industry during World War II, and attempts to ensure that they had reasonable working conditions and fair wages. "Fairness" was understood to require that female wages must be at least 60 per cent of comparable wages for men. It was clear that certain "vital industries", such as the manufacture of munitions, were directly "defence-related", and hence that the deployment of women in these industries was within s 51(vi). There were other industries closer to normal civilian life in which a nexus with wartime conditions could also be claimed – for example, the many areas where women filled specific gaps left by men departing for war; or the industries which, though not "defence-related", were still "vital" to maintaining the continuity of the Australian community and economy under wartime conditions.

Lynn Beaton, "The Importance of Women's Paid Labour: Women at Work in World War II"

in Margaret Bevege, Margaret James and Carmel Shute (eds),
Worth Her Salt: Women at Work in Australia (Hale & Iremonger, 1982), 84

[85] The outbreak of World War II created a critical need for vast increases in the number of women in the paid workforce. This necessitated a temporary reversal of the relative promotion of women's two functions, a reversal which highlighted the usually imperceptible participation of women in the paid workforce. The ideological promotion of the working woman gave her a social significance and visibility that enabled her to fight against the exploitation of low wages and poor conditions. The promotional change is shown clearly by Andrée Wright, who has recorded changes in the image of femininity as portrayed in the *Australian Women's Weekly* through the war years. The working woman not only became 'visible' but attained primacy over her housewife

counterpart: 'During the early war years, up to 1942, homemaking and motherhood remained the most important job.' As the need for increased supplies of female labour became paramount, the *Australian Women's Weekly* began to change the image of its heroine: 'As long as women were needed in the workforce, magazine propaganda painted an attractive image of the working woman.' But as soon as the war was over, the 'working woman' ceased to exist for the *Women's Weekly*, being replaced by 'the bride' ...

[86] At first there was a general reluctance to allow women into new fields of employment at all. But as the war proceeded it became evident that, if the country was to make the most of its resources, women would have to [87] take over men's jobs to release men for combatant duty. This realisation brought strong opposition from both sides of the industrial fence. Male labour would not tolerate the intrusion of cheap labour into their fields of employment; and employers, although willing to employ women in any capacity, were totally opposed to paying them higher wages ...

[88] In March 1942, to facilitate the necessary entry of women into the required areas of employment, the Labor Government instituted the Women's Employment Board (WEB) to rule on cases pertaining to the wages and conditions of women entering jobs for which no previous female rates had been designated. The WEB met with dogged opposition throughout its short life. The interests of capital opposed its existence, threatened its validity in every way conceivable, and when all else failed they simply refused to pay women the rates awarded by the WEB, on the grounds that the Board was constitutionally invalid ...

The WEB's first challenge came at its inception. It was to consist of two employer representatives, two representatives of labour and an independent judge. The government, as one of the largest employers of women in men's jobs, appointed one of the employer representatives and invited the Associated Chamber of Manufactures to nominate the other. They refused to do so ... This delay prevented the Board [89] from functioning until May 1942. In September the Senate disallowed by one vote the National Security Regulations under which the Board was constituted, and on the same day the Victorian Chamber of Manufactures and Hecla Electric appealed to the High Court to test the Board's legal validity. The WEB had just made its first comprehensive ruling covering the wages of female metal workers in nineteen firms. It [90] awarded them 90 per cent of the male rate after a one-month probation period on 60 per cent.

The Labor Government responded by introducing the Women's Employment Bill, which bypassed the need for the National Security Regulations and showed its determination to defend the WEB. The Prime Minister saw the Board as an essential part of the country's war mobilisation, vital at this stage due to the imminent threat of the Japanese advances in the Pacific. Curtin stated that unless the Board was maintained 'Australia's war effort will be gravely impeded. In addition the organisation of the labour resources of this country and the diversion on a large scale of women to employment in war production and essential industries will be rendered practically impossible.'

Arthur Calwell, a member of the Labor Government, threatened a double dissolution if the Senate rejected the bill, saying 'as a matter of fact the best thing that could happen to this Parliament now that it is becoming unworkable because of the intransigence of the Opposition in the Senate would be to have a double dissolution so that the people might decide the issue'. The bill was allowed to pass through the Senate, but the challenges to the Board's existence continued.

The powers of the Women's Employment Board depended initially on regulations made under the *National Security Act 1942* (Cth). So long as those regulations remained in force, the Board's determinations were validly made. However, the Senate's disallowance of those regulations meant not only that the Board could make no further determinations, but that its prior determinations could no longer operate. Thus one purpose of the *Women's Employment Act 1942* (Cth) was to restore those determinations to continuing effect. The Board's power to make further determinations was restored by enshrining the regulations in a schedule to the Act. However, by further regulations made pursuant to the Act in December 1942, parts of the scheduled regulations were repealed and replaced by new provisions. Those new provisions were disallowed by the Senate in March 1943, but that disallowance did not alter the fact that the repeal of the scheduled regulations had already taken effect. The resulting tangles were sorted out in *Victorian Chamber of Manufactures v Commonwealth* (*Women's Employment Case*) (1943) 67 CLR 347 at

358-74. The main issue was whether the *Women's Employment Act* was valid: that is, whether it had a sufficient connection to the defence power.

Victorian Chamber of Manufactures v Commonwealth
(*Women's Employment Case*)
(1943) 67 CLR 347

Latham CJ: [356] The first question which arises concerns the validity of the *Women's Employment Act*. This Act is entitled: "An Act to encourage and regulate the employment of women for the purpose of aiding the prosecution of the present war." It is argued for the plaintiffs that the general subject of the encouragement and regulation of the employment of women is not and cannot be so connected with the prosecution of the war as to authorize the Parliament to legislate upon that subject under the defence power. It is further argued that even if there is any authority under the defence power of the Commonwealth Parliament to deal with the employment of women, there is no authority to deal with such employment in the manner in which the relevant legislation has dealt with it, because that legislation is not limited by any reference to women engaged in work which is directly associated with the war, but extends to all kinds of work which may be done by women if that work had not formerly been done by women either at all, or usually, or in a particular establishment.

The war has withdrawn, and necessarily withdrawn, large numbers of men from their normal work into the fighting and other war services. In order to supply the needs of the fighting services, and to maintain the activities of the civil population which are necessary both for the purpose of supplying such services and for the continued existence of the community, replacement of the men who have given **[357]** up their customary work has become an important matter. As men are no longer available in sufficient numbers, it has become necessary to resort to the services of women. The Act and the Regulations, as is apparent from their terms, are designed to deal with these new circumstances ...

The legislation does not (as it might have done) compel women to work; it provides means for determining their wages and conditions of employment in the hope that the offer of such wages and conditions will encourage them to work.

In my opinion the legislation, that is, the Act and the Regulations, deals with a problem which has arisen from the war, and with which it may reasonably be considered to be necessary to deal in order to promote the successful prosecution of the war. The legislation is directed towards the efficient supply of goods and services, both for the army and for the civil community, by organizing the labour power of the community, in so far as it may depend upon the work of women, who in large numbers have been brought into such employment by reason of war exigencies. Legislation to deal with such a war-created problem (whether considered in relation to the general community or to the fighting services) is, in my opinion, within the power to legislate with respect to the naval and military defence of the Commonwealth conferred upon the Parliament by s 51(vi) **[358]** of the Constitution. The method of dealing with the problem and the extent to which it should be dealt with are matters for the consideration of the legislature and not of the courts ... I am of opinion that legislation with respect to the encouragement and regulation of the employment of women has a real and substantial relation to the prosecution of the war and is calculated in an appreciable degree to advance it.

McTiernan and Rich JJ agreed that the legislation was valid. Williams J also agreed, but considered that the Act should have made it clearer that the employment of women in industry was only a temporary measure limited to the duration of the war. He seized on counsel's use of the expression "new women", meaning those women brought in to replace men in traditional male occupations because of the wartime emergency.

Williams J: [398] It is unfortunate that the *Women's Employment Act* does not contain an express provision, similar to that contained in the *National Security Act*, s 19, that the operation of the Act is limited to the present war; but, having regard to the date upon which the preceding regulations made under the *National Security Act* were first enacted, to the preamble to the *Women's*

Employment Act, to the fact that s 5 could only operate while the *National Security Act* remained in force, to the provisions of s 6(*a*), to the reference in reg 5A to the "emergency created by the present war," and to the nature of the work to be done by females described in reg 6; it can be inferred that the operation of the Act is intended to be **[399]** limited in this way, and that the females to whom it applies are females substituted in work for men who have enlisted in the armed forces or who have changed from their usual employment to other work on account of the war ...

[402] In order to determine whether legislation is within the defence power it is necessary to examine the substance and purpose of the legislation in order to ascertain what it is that the legislature is really doing. But if the real substance and purpose is such that the legislation is capable even incidentally of aiding the effectuation of the power then it is in my opinion within the ambit of the power ... [I]t is important to bear in mind that a state of war creates a situation that is abnormal and temporary, so that, since legislation of the Commonwealth Parliament, including legislation under the defence power, can only be valid if **[403]** and in so far as it falls within the ambit of an enumerated power, laws which can only be justified by the enlarged operation of the defence power which occurs in an emergency must not extend beyond what is reasonably required to cope with such abnormal and temporary conditions (*Adelaide Company of Jehovah's Witnesses Inc v Commonwealth* [(1943) 67 CLR 116 at 161-3]).

It is conceivable to my mind that the regulation by Commonwealth legislation of the terms and conditions of employment of these "new women," as they were called during the argument, can aid in the prosecution of the war. The industries in which they may in some instances become employed may be industries which are not associated with the prosecution of the war, but it is employment in industry which in the case of the first two classes has become vacant because of the war and in the third class has been created by the war. The only express power to control industry conferred upon the Commonwealth Parliament by the Constitution is that contained in s 51, placitum xxxv, to make laws with respect to conciliation and arbitration for the prevention and settlement of industrial disputes extending beyond the limits of any one State. As *Isaacs* and *Rich* JJ pointed out in their joint judgment in *Waterside Workers' Federation of Australia v JW Alexander Ltd* [(1918) 25 CLR 434], this power is limited to legislation with respect to a particular method of dealing with such disputes; that is to say, it presupposes a dispute, a hearing or investigation and a decision ... A power which can only be exercised in this way and which is confined to industrial disputes extending beyond the limits of any one State would not give the Commonwealth Parliament sufficient control over industry in time of war. The operation of the ambit of the defence power in time of war must therefore be enlarged to enable the Parliament to exercise more control over industry than it is able to exercise in time of peace. It is unnecessary in the present case to decide the difficult problem whether this operation should be enlarged to control all industry, because the *Women's Employment Act* seeks only to control a particular aspect of industry. A sudden transfer of males due to the war from certain industries and the substitution **[404]** of females in their place can obviously create new industrial conditions which ought to be controlled by legislation. These conditions would exist throughout the whole of the Commonwealth and could only be effectively and expeditiously dealt with by the Commonwealth Parliament. As the Act has the character of a law with respect to defence, it is a matter for the Commonwealth Parliament to decide the nature of the legislation by which these conditions shall be controlled, including the question as to what work in the three defined cases is suitable for the employment of the "new women".

Starke J, in sole dissent, insisted on seeing the issue as one of "subject matter".

Starke J: [380] The war, no doubt, has raised many social, industrial and economic problems for Australia. But, extensive as is the defence power, I cannot agree that it enables the Commonwealth to seize control of the whole social, industrial and economic conditions of Australia and legislate for them as it thinks proper ...

[381] The Regulations are not limited, as we have seen, to employment of women in industry for war purposes, but for any purpose. Indeed, the Regulations make a special provision for employment of females for war purposes ... The determination of the question whether the legislation in question is with respect to defence or with respect to taxation involves the same method of approach. It does not differ because one power relates to defence and the other to taxation. The fundamental question in both cases is the same, namely: To what subject matter in substance does the law or the regulation relate? As the question is one of degree, differences of opinion must arise. But in the present case the *Women's Employment Regulations* are not regulations with respect to defence either in substance or in form but regulations for the purpose of regulating and controlling the employment of all women in certain categories regardless of the question whether the work to be performed relates or **[382]** does not relate to defence. The Federal Parliament is not authorized to make any such law, and the Act and Regulations as they exist or as amended are consequently invalid. The contrary opinion must lead to results that cannot now be foreseen, but I apprehend that the regulation of conditions relating to employment in industry in Australia will pass to the Commonwealth in time of war. The determinations and awards of wages boards and arbitration courts can all be overridden and the Parliament itself will have authority to regulate wages and conditions in relation to employment in industry. This may or may not be advantageous to Australia, but it is inconsistent, I think, with the Federal system of government adopted by the Constitution.

In *R v Commonwealth Court of Conciliation and Arbitration; Ex parte Victoria* (1944) 68 CLR 485, the balance shifted. Rich and Williams JJ voted with Starke J to prohibit an application of the *Women's Employment Act* to female assessors in the taxation branch of the Victorian Treasury. The original *Women's Employment Regulations* (Cth) had been limited to "women employed in industry". Now that limit had been repealed. For Williams J this made a crucial difference and, like Rich and Starke JJ, he found that the new regulations could not be supported by the defence power. Latham CJ and McTiernan J dissented.

Australian Woollen Mills Ltd v Commonwealth* (1944) 69 CLR 476 involved a separate initiative under the *National Security (Female Minimum Rates) Regulations* (Cth), which empowered the Commonwealth Court of Conciliation and Arbitration to increase the minimum rates of pay for women in "vital industries". There was no suggestion that this initiative was confined to "new women". Indeed, reg 8(b) provided that, in fixing appropriate wage levels, the Court "shall not have regard to any submission that it is necessary to offer a differential monetary inducement or attraction to promote the recruitment of female labour for vital industries". In these circumstances, Starke J concluded that the regulations "**[494]** do not fall within the category of laws with respect to naval or military defence, but within the category of laws for the improvement and betterment of the social and industrial conditions of females engaged in certain specified industries, which is a subject matter within the constitutional power of the States". This, however, reflected his insistence on "subject matter" rather than "purpose". The other judges found that the regulations were valid.

Australian Textiles Pty Ltd v Commonwealth* (1945) 71 CLR 161 also concerned the *National Security (Female Minimum Rates) Regulations*. New amendments after the Japanese had agreed to surrender, and only three days before they formally did so, had increased the protection for women in "vital industries" by requiring that the wages for adult women should not be less than 75% of "the corresponding minimum male rate". The High Court held that the amendments were valid, with only Starke J dissenting: "**[171]** We have lived so long in an atmosphere of make-believe ... that it is hard to return to realities".

3. Post-War

The last gasp of the *Women's Employment Regulations* came in *R v Foster* (1949) 79 CLR 43. Throughout the period of post-war reconstruction the government had repeatedly extended the operation of wartime controls – initially until the end of 1946 by the *National Security Act 1946* (Cth); then until the end of 1947 by the *Defence (Transitional Provisions) Act 1946* (Cth); and thereafter by similarly titled enactments from year to year. As late as March 1949 the High Court had acquiesced (*Hume v Higgins* (1949) 78 CLR 116). However, in April 1949 the Court heard challenges to the continued operation of three different sets of regulations: wage-fixing under the *Women's Employment Regulations*; petrol rationing under the *National Security (Liquid Fuel) Regulations* (Cth); and court-enforced preferential housing for ex-service personnel under the

National Security (War Service Moratorium) Regulations (Cth). In June 1949, six judges (Starke J was on leave) gave a unanimous judgment that put an end to all three regulations, and laid down what amounted to a policy statement for all such issues thereafter.

R v Foster
(1949) 79 CLR 43

The Court: [81] The fighting in the recent war ceased in September 1945, over three years ago ...

When actual hostilities have ceased the scope of application of the defence power necessarily diminishes, but the cessation of hostilities leaves behind various matters which can legitimately be made the subject of Commonwealth legislation as being incidental to the execution of the defence power in the past. This Court has already held that after hostilities have ceased laws may be sustained **[82]** under the defence power as valid because they deal with conditions which have been brought about by the exercise of the defence power itself (*Dawson v Commonwealth* [(1946) 73 CLR 157]; *Miller v Commonwealth* [(1946) 73 CLR 187]; *Real Estate Institute of New South Wales v Blair* [(1946) 73 CLR 213]; *Sloan v Pollard* [(1947) 75 CLR 445]; *Hume v Higgins* [(1949) 78 CLR 116]; *Jenkins v Commonwealth* [(1947) 74 CLR 400]). Thus Federal regulation of matters which are brought within Federal power only by reason of the defence power need not necessarily cease with the actual fighting ...

The substantial argument in support of the regulations, the validity of the continuance of which is now challenged, is that the defence power authorizes, beyond the period of obvious war emergencies, laws which are directed to dealing with the consequences of war. The Constitution does not confer upon the Commonwealth Parliament any power in express terms to deal with the consequences of war, but there are some consequences which undeniably fall within the scope of the legislative power with respect to defence. Repatriation and rehabilitation of soldiers is an obvious case. Rebuilding of a city which had been destroyed **[83]** or damaged by bombing would be another case. Laws relating to such matters would, however, be valid not merely because they dealt with consequences of a war, but because such laws can fairly be regarded as involved incidentally in a full exercise of a power to make laws with respect to defence.

The effects of the past war will continue for centuries. The war has produced or contributed to changes in nearly every circumstance which affects the lives of civilized people. If it were held that the defence power would justify any legislation at any time which dealt with any matter the character of which had been changed by the war, or with any problem which had been created or aggravated by the war, then the result would be that the Commonwealth Parliament would have a general power of making laws for the peace, order and good government of Australia with respect to almost every subject. Nearly all the limitations imposed upon Commonwealth power by the carefully framed Constitution would disappear and a unitary system of government, under which general powers of law-making would belong to the Commonwealth Parliament, would be brought into existence notwithstanding the deliberate acceptance by the people of a Federal system of government upon the basis of the division of powers set forth in the Constitution. We proceed to state reasons why the Court should not ascribe an operation so far-reaching and, indeed, revolutionary, to the defence power.

On the other hand, this Court, in discharging the duties imposed upon it by the Constitution, should be careful now and in the future (as it has been in the past in the many decisions with respect to the defence power) not to take a narrow view of the problems with which the Commonwealth Government has to deal when it is entrusted with the supreme responsibility of the defence of the country.

The solution of the difficulties thus presented cannot be achieved by the application of any mechanical hard and fast rule. It is not possible to do more than lay down general principles and to apply them to the circumstances, varying in time and place, which are to be found in a modern community. In stating and in applying the principles we do not forget that in contemplation of law a state of war still exists, although armed conflict has long since been at an end. But this Court has never subscribed to the view that the continued existence of a formal state of war is enough in itself, after the enemy has surrendered, to bring or retain within the legislative power over defence the same wide field of civil regulation and control as fell within it while the country was engaged in a **[84]** conflict with powerful enemies. The Court has not, of course, put out of consideration the fact that a state of peace has not yet been brought about by treaty or otherwise or the fact that enemy territory is still in Allied occupation. But we have treated these as but circumstances to be considered, that is, as factors in a total situation governing the practical application of the legislative power with respect to defence. They are, however, factors which can have little bearing upon the question whether any of the three regulations now challenged still remain in valid operation. It is a question which must depend upon that aspect of the defence power which authorizes legislation on matters incidental to the termination of hostilities, to the disestablishment and disposal of arrangements set up in the course of prosecuting the war and to the restoration of the country to conditions of peace. In winding up the arrangements made for war and restoring a community organized for war to a state in which it can resume peaceful courses the legislature may continue for a space this or that war-time control. For it may be incidental to defence to continue the control and regulation of a particular subject matter for a time after the cessation of hostilities and also to maintain such control while legislative provision is being made for the necessary re-adjustment. The sudden removal of all controls is not demanded by the collapse of enemy resistance. Given regulations or controls may no longer find a justification in the considerations which the active prosecution of the war supplied. Yet the very fact that the controls or regulations have been established may create a situation which must be maintained for a reasonable time while some other legislative provision is made. But the Court must see with reasonable clearness how it is incidental to the defence power to prolong the operation of a war measure dealing with a subject otherwise falling within the exclusive province of the States and unless it can do so it is the duty of the Court to pronounce the enactment beyond the legislative power.

No one doubts that the defence power will justify some legislation directed to the transition period between war and peace and some legislation which operates even after the full establishment of peace. But it does not place within Federal legislative authority every social, economic or other condition that might not have arisen except for the war. Where a state of facts exists which though outside the chief or central purpose of the power, namely, the armed defence of the country, is from a practical point of view entirely due to war, legislation to deal with it may fall within the defence power. For in that event such legislation may well be incidental **[85]** to the exercise of the power. Examples have already been given as in the case of the returned soldier (whether wounded or ill or not) and the destroyed city. But there are many matters which result from a plurality of causes of which the war is one. To point to the war as a contributory cause can hardly be enough. The recent war has produced some changes in almost every part of our lives. This fact does not mean that the whole life of man is to be regarded as a war consequence. It is obvious that to determine whether any given attempt to continue laws or regulations in force for an extended period after the end of hostilities is valid, it is necessary to consider in detail the nature and application of the particular measure.

In *Illawarra District Council v Wickham* (1959) 101 CLR 467, one question was whether, by an amendment assented to on 4 November 1955, the operation of the *Re-establishment and Employment Act 1945* (Cth), which provided for preferential hiring of ex-service personnel, could validly be extended until 2 September 1958. A separate question was whether, by an amendment assented to on 1 October 1958, the scheme could validly be further extended until 30 June 1960. Both questions were answered in the negative.

4. Peace

Even in times of peace, the defence power enables the Commonwealth to maintain "defence preparedness", and therefore to deal with "**[254]** such matters as the enlistment (compulsory or voluntary) and training and equipment of men and women in navy, army and air force, the provision of ships and munitions, the manufacture of weapons and the erection of fortifications" (*Australian Communist Party v Commonwealth* (*Communist Party Case*) (1951) 83 CLR 1).

Moreover, the conduct and organisation of enterprises primarily linked to "defence" may also involve ancillary or corollary activities less clearly related to defence.

In *Commonwealth v Australian Commonwealth Shipping Board* (1926) 39 CLR 1, the High Court held that s 51(vi) did not extend to a statutory provision empowering the Australian Commonwealth Shipping Board to enter into an agreement for the supply, delivery and erection of six steam turbo-alternators. The Board was incorporated under the *Commonwealth Shipping Act 1923* (Cth).

Commonwealth v Australian Commonwealth Shipping Board
(1926) 39 CLR 1

Knox CJ, Gavan Duffy, Rich and Starke JJ: [9] The Parliament only has such power as is expressly or by necessary implication vested in it by the Constitution. There is no power which enables the Parliament or the Executive Government to set up manufacturing or engineering businesses for general commercial purposes ... The naval and defence power coupled with the incidental power conferred by sec 51(XXXIX) was also relied upon. Extensive as is that power, still it does not authorize the establishment of businesses for the purpose of trade and wholly unconnected with any purpose of naval or military defence. It was suggested, however, that the dockyard and workshops on Cockatoo Island were required for the purposes of the naval defence of the Commonwealth, and that it was impracticable to maintain them efficiently for that purpose unless the managing body – the Shipping Board – was authorized to enter upon general manufacturing and engineering activities, because the cost of maintenance of the works would be excessive and the working staff would be unable to obtain proper experience. Despite the practical difficulties facing the Commonwealth in the maintenance of its dockyard and works, the power of naval and military defence does not warrant these activities in the ordinary conditions of peace, whatever be the position in time of war or in conditions arising out of or connected **[10]** with war.

Isaacs and Higgins JJ held, as a matter of statutory construction, that s 14(4) of the *Commonwealth Shipping Act* did not give the Board the power to enter into the agreement. They therefore did not need to reach the constitutional issue, but Isaacs J added: "**[12]** I am unable to find such a meaning in sub-sec 4 of sec 14, and if I could, I should be unable to find its justification in the Constitution".

The *Shipping Board Case* is difficult to reconcile with *Attorney-General (Vic) v Commonwealth* (*Clothing Factory Case*) (1935) 52 CLR 533, which held that the Commonwealth could, under s 51(vi), establish a clothing factory to manufacture uniforms not only for the defence forces but for other bodies such as Commonwealth and State government departments and the Boy Scouts Association.

Attorney-General (Vic) v Commonwealth (Clothing Factory Case)
(1935) 52 CLR 533

Gavan Duffy CJ, Evatt and McTiernan JJ: [558] This brings us to the question whether the legislative power in respect of defence is a sufficient warrant for the legislation so construed and so applied to the facts. It is obvious that the maintenance of a factory to make naval and military equipment is within the field of legislative power. The method of its internal organisation in time of peace is largely a matter for determination by those to whom is entrusted the sole responsibility for the conduct of naval and military defence. In particular, the retention of all members of a specially trained and specially efficient staff might well be considered necessary, and it might well be thought that the policy involved in such retention could not be effectively carried out unless that staff was fully engaged. Consequently, the sales of clothing to bodies outside the regular naval and military forces are not to be regarded as the main or essential purpose of this part of the business, but as incidents in the maintenance for war purposes of an essential part of the munitions branch of the defence arm. In such a matter, much must be left to the discretion of the Governor-General and the responsible Ministers.

In these circumstances, we hold that the objections of the plaintiff, as far as they are based upon the Constitution, should fail. The plaintiff relied upon the case of *Commonwealth v Australian Commonwealth Shipping Board* [(1926) 39 CLR 1], where this Court held that an agreement made between the Australian Commonwealth Shipping Board and the Municipal Council of Sydney was beyond the powers of the former body ...

[559] The decision does not contain a complete definition of the limits of the defence power, and the statement of the majority of the Court in relation to the defence power that "extensive as is that power, still it does not authorize the establishment of businesses for the purpose of trade and wholly unconnected with any purpose of naval and military defence", does not assist the present plaintiff, because the purpose of naval and military defence has been impressed upon the operations of the clothing factory from the very commencement.

Rich J agreed; but Starke J dissented, applying the *Shipping Board Case*. In the *Communist Party Case*, Fullagar J described the *Clothing Factory Case* as "**[254]** perhaps border-line".

5. Military Justice

The defence power enables the Commonwealth to maintain a system of military discipline in the armed forces. *Re Tracey; Ex parte Ryan* (1989) 166 CLR 518 raised the question of what types of offences might be proscribed under s 51(vi) by the *Defence Force Discipline Act 1982* (Cth). Most of the offences in Pt III of the Act relate to service discipline; but Divs 5 and 7 of Pt III overlap with the ordinary criminal law (as Div 5A now does as well). Moreover, s 61 provides that any act or omission which would be a criminal offence if committed in the Australian Capital Territory is triable as a service offence if committed by a service member anywhere. The question is the extent to which a military jurisdiction should thus be permitted to encroach on that of the ordinary civilian courts. In *O'Callahan v Parker*, 395 US 258 (1969), the United States Supreme Court had initially answered a similar question by limiting the military jurisdiction to charges with a "service connexion"; but in *Solorio v United States*, 483 US 435 (1987), that decision was overruled as unworkable.

In *Re Tracey*, the seven members of the Australian High Court took four different views. Mason CJ, Wilson and Dawson JJ accepted the view expressed in *Solorio*; that is, they held that any offence committed by a service member may be treated as a service offence and may therefore be proscribed under s 51(vi).

Re Tracey; Ex parte Ryan
(1989) 166 CLR 518

Mason CJ, Wilson and Dawson JJ: [543] [B]oth as a matter of history and of contemporary practice, it has commonly been considered appropriate for the proper discipline of a defence force to subject its members to penalties under service law for the commission of offences punishable under civil law even where the only connexion between the offences and the defence force is the service membership of the offender. Such legislation is based upon the premise that, as a matter of discipline, the proper administration of a defence force requires the observance by its members of the standards of behaviour demanded of ordinary citizens and the enforcement of those standards by military tribunals. To act in contravention of those standards is not only to break the law, but also to act to the prejudice of good order and military discipline. It is appropriate that such conduct should be punished in the interests **[544]** not only of the community but of the defence force as well. There can be little doubt that in war-time or upon overseas service such considerations warrant the treatment of civil offences as service offences and it is open to the legislature to regard the position in peace-time as warranting similar treatment. Good order and military discipline, upon which the proper functioning of any defence force must rest, are required no less at home in peace-time than upon overseas service or in war-time ...

[545] It follows that, if offences against military law can extend no further than is thought necessary for the regularity and discipline of the defence forces (see *Groves v Commonwealth* [(1982) 150 CLR 113 at 125]), this limitation would not preclude Parliament from making it an offence against military law for a defence member to engage in conduct which amounts to a civil offence. It is open to Parliament to provide that any conduct which constitutes a civil offence shall constitute a service offence, if committed by a defence member.

The strongest opposing view was that of Deane J.

Deane J: [585] It suffices for present purposes to say that the disciplinary powers of military tribunals excluded from the reach of Ch III of the Constitution are, in their application to members of armed forces within the jurisdiction of the ordinary courts in time of peace and general civil order, confined in the two fundamental respects already mentioned, namely, (i) they are essentially disciplinary in their nature in the sense of being concerned either with exclusively disciplinary offences or with the disciplinary aspects of other service-related offences ... and (ii) they are supplementary in their character in that they do not supplant the jurisdiction or function of the ordinary courts in **[586]** relation to the general community aspects of conduct which also constitutes an offence under the ordinary criminal law ...

It follows from what has been said above that a Commonwealth legislative scheme which purports to confer upon military tribunals, which are not Ch III courts, jurisdiction to administer a comprehensive system of criminal law and which, in cases where that jurisdiction is exercised, supplants the jurisdiction of the ordinary courts to deal with the general community aspects of conduct which also constitutes an offence under ordinary law necessarily trespasses upon the judicial power which Ch III vests exclusively in the courts which it designates and is, at least to the extent of the trespass, invalid.

For Gaudron J, the test of validity was whether the challenged law was "**[597]** reasonably capable of being regarded as appropriate and adapted" to the purposes of s 51(vi). In her view, s 51(vi) had two relevant purposes: "defence" and "control of the armed forces". She did not believe that the latter purpose justified any overlap whatever with the range of offences covered by "ordinary criminal justice". For Brennan and Toohey JJ, what mattered was not the nature of the charge but the function of the proceedings. An enactment under s 51(vi) would be valid if the hearing of proceedings by a service tribunal could reasonably be regarded as conducive to service discipline.

In *McWaters v Day* (1989) 168 CLR 289 it seemed that the Court was able to extract a consensus from *Re Tracey*. The joint unanimous judgment purported to find in *Re Tracey* a principle to which all judges, save perhaps Gaudron J, had supposedly subscribed: namely, "**[297]** that the Discipline Act was to be interpreted so as to ensure that the military disciplinary code it enacted was cumulative upon and not exclusive of the ordinary criminal law". On that basis the *Defence Force Discipline Act* was construed, for purposes of s 109 of the Constitution, so as not to exclude the application of the *Traffic Act 1949* (Qld) to a soldier charged with driving under the influence in the grounds of an army barracks. However, the apparent consensus soon vanished.

In *Re Nolan; Ex parte Young* (1991) 172 CLR 460, a case involving the falsification of an army pay list, Mason CJ and Dawson J adhered to the position they had shared with Wilson J in *Re Tracey*; McHugh J, who had replaced Wilson J, agreed with Deane J; and the other members of the Court repeated their previously stated views. In short, for Mason CJ and Dawson J, the disciplinary proceedings were valid because Sergeant Young was a "service member". For Brennan and Toohey JJ, they were valid because the proceedings, which involved a charge of falsifying service documents, were conducive to "service discipline". McHugh J added his dissenting voice to those of Deane and Gaudron JJ, producing a 4:3 result; but beneath the result, deep and unresolved disagreements remained. Three years later *Re Tyler; Ex parte Foley* (1994) 181 CLR 18 again left the issue unresolved, although once again the view of Mason CJ and Dawson J combined with that of Brennan and Toohey JJ to produce a majority result. McHugh J now accepted that result, on the basis that *Re Tracey* and *Re Nolan* should be treated as binding. Deane and Gaudron JJ again adhered to their previous views (see Chapter 13, §7).

Almost a decade elapsed without further challenge to the uneasy majority arrived at, both in *Re Nolan* and in *Re Tyler*, by combining two different approaches (those of Mason CJ and Brennan J, as supported respectively by Dawson and Toohey JJ). In 2003, Richard Tracey QC, who as a Defence Force Magistrate had been the respondent in *Re Tracey*, told a conference audience that, in practice, service tribunals in Australia had adopted the more restrictive test of military jurisdiction favoured by Brennan and Toohey JJ (the "service connection" test) rather than the potentially more inclusive test initially favoured by Mason CJ, Wilson and Dawson JJ (the "service status" test) ("The Constitution and Military Justice" (Paper presented at The Australian Constitution in Troubled Times: The Annual Public Law Weekend, Centre for International and Public Law, Australian National University, 8 November 2003), 175). He noted that in applying this test the military authorities "[13] have adopted a conservative approach ... Where doubt exists, cases are referred to the appropriate Director of Public Prosecutions. Protocols have been developed under which consultation regularly occurs between military lawyers and DPP solicitors before any decisions are made about whether charges, which have civilian counterparts, should be dealt with in service tribunals or civil courts".

When the issue reached the High Court again in *Re Colonel Aird; Ex parte Alpert* (2004) 220 CLR 308, most judges were also content to adopt the "service connection" test. To that extent, the view of Brennan and Toohey JJ has now prevailed. As to the appropriate result, however, the Court was as deeply divided as ever. Gleeson CJ, Gummow and Hayne JJ joined McHugh J in holding that the alleged offence had enough of a "service connection" to be tried by court martial. Kirby, Callinan and Heydon JJ dissented.

In two respects, the facts were very different from those of the earlier trilogy of cases. First, each of the earlier cases had involved some form of petty fraud or falsification of papers, whereas Private Stewart Alpert was charged with raping an 18-year-old British backpacker on a Thai beach. Secondly, the offence was said to have been committed while Alpert was serving overseas, whereas all of the previous Australian cases had involved offences allegedly committed in Australia. Because of this, McHugh J pointed out during argument that the relevant legislation might be justified under the "external affairs" power. However, the Commonwealth defended its enactments solely on the basis of the defence power.

Section 9 of the *Defence Force Discipline Act 1982* (Cth) provided that the arrangements made in the Act for the trial of service offences (including those defined by picking up the provisions of the *Crimes Act 1900* (ACT)) applied "both in and outside Australia but do not apply in relation to any person outside Australia unless that person is a defence member or a defence civilian". Counsel for Alpert conceded that the Act might validly have applied to a charge arising while he was on active duty in Malaysia, but contended that it could not validly apply to a charge arising while he was on leave in Thailand, effectively as a tourist.

Re Colonel Aird; Ex parte Alpert
(2004) 220 CLR 308

McHugh J: [321] As I explained [in *Re Tyler* (1994) 181 CLR 18 at 37] ... the "divergent reasoning of the majority judges in *Re Tracey* [(1989) 166 CLR 518] and *Re Nolan* [(1991) 172 CLR 460] means that neither of those cases has a ratio decidendi" ... *Re Tyler* also failed to obtain a majority of Justices in favour of any particular construction of the defence power in relation to offences by service personnel.

The difference between the views of Mason CJ, Wilson and Dawson JJ and on the other hand Brennan and Toohey JJ in these cases is the difference between the "service status" view of the jurisdiction and the "service connection" view of that jurisdiction. The "service status" view – which is now applied in the United States – gives a service tribunal jurisdiction over a person solely on the basis of the accused's status as a member of the armed forces. The "service connection" view of the jurisdiction requires a connection between the service and the offence. It was the view formerly accepted in the United States ...

[322] The argument of the parties in the present case accepted, sometimes expressly but more often by assumption, that the general words of s 51(vi) of the Constitution must be read down to comply with Ch III of the Constitution, as interpreted in the trilogy of *Tracey*, *Nolan* and *Tyler*. Since those cases, it seems to have been generally accepted – indeed it was accepted by the Judge Advocate in the present case – that the proper test is the "service connection" test and not the "service status" test ...

The prosecutor contends that, while he was in Thailand, he had no connection with the Army. He points out that, when the offence allegedly occurred, he was on leave in Thailand ... He was wearing civilian attire at all material times. He did not enter Thailand under any military arrangement or for any military purposes and his visit to Thailand was for recreational purposes only ... [H]e paid for his own accommodation, meals and incidental expenses. The prosecutor concedes, however, that, if he had committed the alleged offence while he was in Malaysia, his offence would be within the jurisdiction of the service tribunal because his presence would be connected to his military service. But he contends his presence in Thailand was unconnected with his Army service ...

[323] In determining whether the standards of conduct imposed on Defence Force personnel by reference to the legislation of the Australian Capital Territory have the potential to maintain and enhance the discipline of the Defence Force, an important factor is that, when overseas, they are likely to be perceived by the government of the foreign country and members of the local population as representatives of the Australian government. In this respect, they are different from ordinary Australians who visit a foreign country as tourists. It is not to the point that, so far as dress and other matters are concerned, they cannot be distinguished from an ordinary Australian tourist. If a soldier on recreation leave is involved in conduct that is prohibited by the *Crimes Act* of the Australian Capital Territory, it is likely that that conduct will also be unlawful under the laws of the foreign country or at all events regarded as undesirable conduct. And it is not unlikely that the local citizenry will soon become aware that the person involved ... was a member of the Australian Defence Force. It is a likely consequence of such conduct, therefore, that the local citizenry will be critical of its occurrence and may even become hostile to Australian Defence Force members.

Moreover, even if the local citizens do not become aware of the soldier's connection with the Australian Defence Force, it is likely that the government of the country will be aware of the identity of the soldier. If such conduct occurred regularly, it might have the consequence that the government of the foreign country would deny entry to Australian Defence Force members in so far as they seek to visit areas for rest and recreation. If that happened, it would have a direct impact on the morale and discipline of the Defence Force. It is possible that in extreme cases the unruly behaviour of personnel would cause a foreign country to refuse entry to Australian Defence Force members for Defence Force purposes such as training exercises. It may be that some conduct that is an offence under the law of the Australian Capital Territory in its relation to the Jervis Bay Territory has no relation to the defence power. If so, the operation of s 61 of the [*Defence Force Discipline Act 1982* (Cth)] would have to be read down to exclude such conduct.

However, even if some of the standards of conduct required by the *Crimes Act* of the Australian Capital Territory go beyond the defence power – go beyond what is required for maintaining the discipline and morale of the Defence Force – the prohibition against rape goes to the heart of maintaining discipline and morale in the Defence Force. Rape and other kinds of sexual assault are acts of violence. It is central to a disciplined defence force that its members are not persons who engage in uncontrolled violence. And it need hardly be said that other members of the Defence Force will be reluctant to serve with personnel who are guilty of conduct that ... amounts to rape or sexual assault. This may be out of fear for personal safety or rejection **[324]** of such conduct or both. Such reluctance can only have a detrimental effect on the discipline and morale of the armed services.

Accordingly, the standard of conduct imposed by the legislation of the Australian Capital Territory in respect of the offence of sexual intercourse without consent "can reasonably be regarded as substantially serving the purpose of maintaining or enforcing service discipline" [*Re Tracey*, 166 CLR at 570].

Gleeson CJ, Gummow and Hayne JJ reached the same conclusion. Callinan and Heydon JJ agreed with McHugh J that the relevant test was one of "service connection", but dissented as to how that test should be applied.

Callinan and Heydon JJ: [359] If the test of service connection is to be applied on the basis that it will be satisfied if the acts alleged constitute an undisciplined application of force, or conduct that would be regarded as abhorrent by other soldiers, then it is difficult to see how any serious crime committed anywhere, including in Australia, under any circumstances would not be susceptible to the military jurisdiction exclusively. The further consequence would be the denial to the soldier and the prosecuting authority of trial by jury. It is sometimes overlooked that the prosecuting authority and the community which it represents have as great and as real an interest in trial by jury as the person on trial.

We do not, with respect, therefore subscribe to the view that to ask the question whether the discipline of the military service will be enhanced by a certain measure or course, is to ask the same question as "Is there a service connexion?" Any measure for the proscription of any form of misconduct has as its end, discipline. If enhancement of discipline is to be effectively the only test, there will be very few offences of any kind, committed anywhere, in any countries, which will escape the all-enveloping net of "service connexion" ...

[360] The difference between a soldier on leave in a foreign country in which he is neither on active duty, serving nor based, and a civilian tourist is not to be overstated. Nor are we persuaded that criminal misconduct, unrelated to the performance of a soldier's military duties is likely to provoke greater protest or reluctance on the part of another country to admit and harbour Australians, including, relevantly Australian military units, than criminal misconduct by Australian tourists. Equally it might be asserted that misbehaviour by other Australian groups of visitors to foreign countries, whether organized formally or informally or not, such as sporting teams and their followers, would be likely to provoke protest and resistance to the reception of Australians generally, including members of its defence forces. Strictly these are factual matters and no fact material to them appears in the case stated or otherwise. But this is clear, misbehaviour, criminal and otherwise, whether committed by soldiers or civilians reflects badly on a nation and is capable of adversely affecting its interests. It would be a form of chauvinism to regard another nation and its people as being incapable of drawing a distinction between the behaviour of a soldier on leave from a base in a third country in an entirely civilian setting, and the behaviour of a soldier there actually under military orders or carrying out military duties. It would be equally chauvinistic to regard the country in which the criminal conduct has occurred as being incapable of detecting it and trying and punishing an offender for it ...

The majority also stress the importance of discipline and morale in the defence forces and McHugh J makes factual assertions about the reluctance of both male and female military personnel to serve with rapists. Again, these are factual issues which neither the case stated nor any evidence touches on. But it may be assumed that the importance of morale in a defence force is no doubt very great. It is **[361]** likely to be put at serious risk however if charges against soldiers in respect of criminal misconduct committed on leave in a foreign country in circumstances totally unrelated to their military activities and duties, are to be heard and determined by court martial in Australia without a jury. Indeed, the knowledge that the military authorities have the right to intrude into the private life of soldiers, and to discipline them in military proceedings for conduct far removed from their military service, and that in such proceedings there is no right to a committal and a jury, is likely to prove a disincentive to enlistment itself, let alone to morale.

Kirby J: [331] In its earlier decisions, this Court was sharply divided. So it is in this case. Only one member of the Court, McHugh J, who participated in two of the earlier decisions, remains. In one of those cases, he expressed the opinion that "unless a service tribunal is established under Ch III of the Constitution, it has jurisdiction to deal with an 'offence' by a member of the armed services *only* if such an 'offence' is exclusively disciplinary in character or is concerned with the disciplinary aspect of conduct which constitutes an offence against the general law" [*Re Nolan*, 172 CLR at 499]. In a later case [*Re Tyler*, 181 CLR at 39], his Honour said that he "remain[ed] convinced that the reasoning of the majority Justices in *Re Nolan* and *Re Tracey* is erroneous". Now, this "erroneous" view of the Constitution is not only applied but even extended by a divided decision of this Court …

This case illustrates the way in which, when wrong turnings are made in constitutional interpretation, they are often pushed further by their beneficiaries. Because I would not permit this to happen, I would answer the question in the stated case: "Yes".

Kirby J noted recurrent criticisms of the military justice system, including those of the Commonwealth Parliament's Joint Standing Committee on Foreign Affairs, Defence and Trade (*Military Justice in the Australian Defence Force*, Parliamentary Paper No 125 of 1999) and of earlier inquiries (there reproduced as appendices) conducted by Brigadier AR Abadee in 1997 and by the Commonwealth Ombudsman in 1998. He concluded:

Kirby J: [352] The very fact that there have been three major investigations into "military justice" or the "military judicial system" in Australia in quick succession speaks volumes about the seriousness of the problems that tend to be endemic in such a system. The culture of the military is not one in which independent and impartial resolution of charges comes naturally. These considerations reinforce the need for great caution in expanding the reach of the system of service tribunals, particularly in time of peace …

[353] The services have sometimes endeavoured to cut themselves off from ordinary law. [354] In special and limited circumstances, where it is proportional and appropriate for national defence, it must be so, at least for a short time, as during actual conflict. But under the Australian Constitution, the armed services are not divorced from civil law. Indeed, they exist to uphold it. It is the duty of this Court to maintain the strong civilian principle of the Constitution. It is one of the most important of Australia's legacies from British constitutional law.

It is particularly important to adhere to this time-honoured approach at a time when increased demands are being made for greater executive and legislative power. At such a time, as in the past, we should maintain the function of the courts to ensure that military power is only deployed in accordance with the Constitution. This is not an occasion to enhance the operation of military tribunals. The directions in which the expansion of military law can sometimes lead may be seen in other countries. They afford a warning that this Court should heed …

[355] Applying the approach expressed in the successive reasons of Brennan and Toohey JJ in this court, I would therefore reject the validity of the proceedings against the prosecutor. Civilian jurisdiction [356] in Thailand in could conveniently and appropriately have been invoked in this case. It is the jurisdiction that should have been exercised. The jurisdiction of the service tribunal was only available under the Constitution for the limited purpose of maintaining or enforcing service discipline, properly so called. In the context of the exceptional character of service tribunals, standing outside Ch III, the crime of rape allegedly committed by the prosecutor, whilst a tourist off duty, in the circumstances described in the special case, was not one to which service discipline applied.

The present is not a time to expand, beyond this Court's established authority, the jurisdiction and powers of military tribunals in Australia – any more than the power of indefinite punishment or detention at the will of the Parliament and Executive Government. It is at times like the present that this Court – as it has done in the past – must adhere steadfastly to the protection of basic civil rights in Australia's constitutional arrangements. Other final courts are doing so. We should be no less vigilant.

In June 2005, the Senate Foreign Affairs, Defence and Trade References Committee (*The Effectiveness of Australia's Military Justice System*, Parliamentary Paper No 134 of 2005) delivered a scathing assessment of the military justice system in Australia. The bipartisan report found that "[xxvii] substantive injustices" had occurred but that "[xxv] High Court challenges to the military justice system in Australia [have] achieved little success in terms of fundamentally changing the system". The Committee's major recommendations were that "[54] all suspected criminal activity in Australia be referred to the appropriate State/Territory civilian police for investigation and prosecution before the civilian courts" and that "[55] the investigation of all suspected criminal activity committed outside Australia be conducted by the Australian Federal Police".

6. Cold War: The *Communist Party Case*

Although it is common to expound the scope of s 51(vi) in terms of different wartime or peace-time "phases", the "elastic" nature of the power means that such "phases" cannot be exhaustively defined. For example, the "phases" approach may not adequately explain the scope of the defence power during wars – such as the Gulf War of 1991, the Iraq War of 2003 or the so-called "War on Terror" – that may involve Australian troops but not directly the defence of territorial Australia. Indeed, the words "naval and military defence" in s 51(vi) have been given such little weight that a real or perceived escalation of terrorist activity within Australia might expand the defence power even in the absence of a formally declared "war".

The major decisions of the decade after World War II were *Australian Communist Party v Commonwealth* (*Communist Party Case*) (1951) 83 CLR 1 and *Marcus Clark & Co Ltd v Commonwealth* (*Capital Issues Case*) (1952) 87 CLR 177. In one sense, both were "peacetime" cases. However, the period was also one of "Cold War" and included a war in Korea in which Australian troops were involved. Indeed, the *Communist Party Dissolution Act 1950* (Cth), by which the newly elected Menzies government sought to ban the Australian Communist Party, was introduced into Parliament on the very day that the first Australian forces landed in Korea. Among the more remarkable features of the Act were the nine recitals that prefaced the legislation.

Communist Party Dissolution Act 1950 (Cth)

AND WHEREAS the Australian Communist Party, in accordance with the basic theory of communism, as expounded by Marx and Lenin, engages in activities or operations designed to assist or accelerate the coming of a revolutionary situation, in which the Australian Communist Party, acting as a revolutionary minority, would be able to seize power and establish a dictatorship of the proletariat:

AND WHEREAS the Australian Communist Party also engages in activities or operations designed to bring about the overthrow or dislocation of the established system of government of Australia and the attainment of economic, industrial or political ends by force, violence intimidation or fraudulent practices ...

AND WHEREAS it is necessary, for the security and defence of Australia and for the execution and maintenance of the Constitution and of the laws of the Commonwealth, that the Australian Communist Party, and bodies of persons affiliated with that Party, should be dissolved and their property forfeited to the Commonwealth, and that members and officers of that party or of any of those bodies and other persons who are communists should be disqualified from employment by the Commonwealth and from holding office in an industrial organization a substantial number of whose members are engaged in a vital industry:

The intended effect of these recitals was to bring the legislation within s 51(vi) ("the security and defence of Australia") and also within the legislative power incidental to s 61 ("the execution and maintenance of the Constitution and of the laws of the Commonwealth").

Section 4 of the Act declared the Communist Party to be an unlawful association, provided for its dissolution and enabled the appointment of a receiver to manage its property. Section 7(1) provided that a person was liable to five years' imprisonment if he or she knowingly committed acts that included continuing to operate as a member or officer of the Party or carrying or displaying anything indicating that he or she was in any way associated with the Party.

Section 5 provided the machinery for declarations by the Governor-General that other organisations were unlawful. The provision targeted bodies that supported or advocated communism, were affiliated with the Party or whose policies were substantially shaped by members of the Party or "Communists". Once unlawful, an association would be dissolved under s 6 and a receiver appointed under s 8. An organisation could be declared unlawful under s 5(2) where the "Governor-General is satisfied that a body of persons is a body of persons to which this section applies and that the continued existence of that body of persons would be prejudicial to the security and defence of the Commonwealth or to the execution or maintenance of the Constitution or of the laws of the Commonwealth".

Under s 9(2), the Governor-General could declare any person to be a "Communist" or member of the Party by exercising a similar discretion to that laid out in s 5(2). "Communist" was defined by s 3 to mean "a person who supports or advocates the objectives, policies, teachings, principles or practices of communism, as expounded by Marx and Lenin". Once declared, a person could not hold office in the Commonwealth public service or in industries declared by the Governor-General to be vital to the security and defence of Australia (s 10). Should a person wish to contest a declaration by the Governor-General, he or she could do so under s 9(4), although s 9(5) provided that "the burden shall be upon him to prove that he is not a person to whom this section applies".

An important issue in the *Communist Party Case* was whether the alleged factual basis on which the Parliament sought to rely could be given further weight or made conclusive by the recitals in the preamble to the Act. Whether the Parliament could by its own legislative recitals in effect pre-empt the High Court's judgment as to the adequacy of the connection with "defence" was answered succinctly by McTiernan J in the opening paragraphs of his judgment. All judges, except Latham CJ, reached the same conclusion.

Australian Communist Party v Commonwealth (*Communist Party Case*)
(1951) 83 CLR 1

McTiernan J: [205] This stated case raises the question whether the *Communist Party Dissolution Act* 1950 is valid or invalid and also a preliminary question which relates to the recitals forming the part of the preamble of the Act beginning with the fourth recital. This preliminary question is whether the decision of the main question depends on the judicial determination or ascertainment of the facts stated in those recitals. Neither of these judicial processes is a prerequisite to the Court's noticing the recitals. The Court gives to recitals the effect which they have as such and no judicial inquiry into the facts stated in them is necessary to determine that matter, the effect of the recitals. Their effect is that they contain Parliament's reasons for passing the Act; express the opinions which Parliament held; they conclusively show Parliament held those opinions and believed, presumably, that what is recited is true. The recitals are in no way decisive of the question whether the Act is valid or invalid, for that is a judicial question which only the judicature has the power to decide finally and conclusively. If any fact stated in a recital is material to the question whether the Act is valid or invalid, the fact would need to be judicially determined or ascertained. The recitals are not judicial findings and do not bind the judicature on any question within its own exclusive province. The judicature, of course, treats the recitals with respect and regards the views which they express as possible but cannot concede that they are probative of any matter of fact which is material to the question whether the Parliament had or had not the power to pass this Act. The Constitution does not **[206]** allow the judicature to concede the principle that the Parliament can conclusively "recite itself" into power.

There were two alternative grounds on which the Commonwealth maintained that the Act was valid: either the defence power, or what both Dixon and Fullagar JJ called "the other power". "The other power", now found in a more expansive and benevolent guise as "the nationhood power" (see Chapter 12, §2(b)), was viewed as a power to defend the existing system of government. It was conceived of either as an attribute of "the executive government of the Commonwealth" under s 61 of the Constitution, so that the relevant legislative power would then arise from the operation of s 51(xxxix) upon s 61, or as simply inherent in the existence of the Commonwealth as a national government.

What particularly troubled Dixon J was that ss 5(2) and 9(2) of the Act gave the executive an unreviewable discretion to proscribe organisations and persons that it viewed as prejudicial to Australia's defence. (Note, however, that Dixon J's view that "**[179]** [t]he counsels of the Crown" were unreviewable would no longer be accepted: see *R v Toohey; Ex parte Northern Land Council* (1981) 151 CLR 170 and *FAI Insurances Ltd v Winneke* (1982) 151 CLR 342.)

Dixon J: [178] [Section 5(2)] leaves to the opinion of the Governor-General in Council every element involved in the application of the proposition. Thus it would be for the Governor-General in Council to judge of the reach and application of the ideas expressed by the phrases "security and defence of the Commonwealth", "execution of the Constitution", "maintenance of the Constitution", "execution of the laws of the Commonwealth", "maintenance of the laws of the Commonwealth" and "prejudicial to". In the second place the expression by the Governor-General in Council of the result in a properly framed declaration is conclusive. In the case of the Governor-General in Council it is not possible to go behind such **[179]** an executive act done in due form of law and impugn its validity upon the ground that the decision upon which it is founded has been reached improperly, whether because extraneous considerations were taken into account or because there was some misconception of the meaning or application, as a court would view it, of the statutory description of the matters of which the Governor-General in Council should be satisfied or because of some other supposed miscarriage. The prerogative writs do not lie to the Governor-General. The good faith of any of his acts as representative of the Crown cannot be questioned in a court of law (*Duncan v Theodore* [(1917) 23 CLR 510 at 544]). An order, proclamation or declaration of the Governor-General in Council is the formal legal act which gives effect to the advice tendered to the Crown by the Ministers of the Crown. The counsels of the Crown are secret and an inquiry into the grounds upon which the advice tendered proceeds may not be made for the purpose of invalidating the act formally done in the name of the Crown by the Governor-General ...

[185] The matters of which the Governor-General is to be satisfied are described most indefinitely – activities prejudicial to security and defence, activities prejudicial to the execution or maintenance of the Constitution or of the laws of the Commonwealth. The source in s 61 of the Constitution of much of the language of the second expression and the frequent use in relation to the prosecution of two actual and existing wars in statutory instruments of expressions like the first do not make it less true that as they are used here they express no specific connection with the subject matter of the defence power and no specific connection with any definite course of subversive conduct or design. The sub-sections commit to the Governor-General in Council complete authority over the application of these vague expressions; and how they are applied is left to depend upon the conceptions of the Executive Government.

With reference to "the other power", Dixon J said:

Dixon J: [193] I think that it would be impossible to say of a law of the character described, which depends for its supposed connection with the power upon the conclusion of the legislature concerning the doings and the designs of the bodies or person to be affected and affords no objective test of the applicability of the power, that it is a law upon a matter incidental to the execution and maintenance of the Constitution and the laws of the Commonwealth. Indeed, upon the very matters upon which the question whether the bodies or persons have brought themselves within a possible exercise of the power depends, it may be said that the Act would have the effect of making the conclusion of the legislature final and so the measure of the operation of its own power.

Turning to the defence power, he said:

Dixon J: [196] At the date of the royal assent Australian forces were involved in the hostilities in Korea, but the country was not of course upon a war footing, and, though the hostilities were treated as involving the country in a contribution of force, the situation bore little relation to one in which the application of the defence power expands because the Executive Government has become responsible for the conduct of a war. I think that the matter must be considered substantially upon the same basis as if a state of peace ostensibly existed. Is it possible, however, to sustain the Act on the ground that under the influence of events the practical reach and operation of the defence power had grown to such a degree as to cover legislation providing no objective standard of liability relevant to the subject of the power but proceeding directly first by the pronouncement of a judgment by means of recitals and then in pursuance of the recitals acting directly against a body named, and bodies and persons described, in derogation of civil and proprietary rights? ...

[197] It ought not, I think, to be denied that the events of the time, some of which I have briefly enumerated, bring within the practical application of the defence power measures which would not have been considered competent – for example, in the state of affairs prevailing when this Court held its first sittings. But hitherto it has been supposed that only the supreme emergency of war **[198]** itself would extend the operation of the power so far as to support a legislative provision which on a subject not by its own nature within the defence power affects the status, property and civil rights of persons *nominatim* or by other identification without any external test of liability upon which the connection of the provisions with power will depend ...

[199] When s 4 names a voluntary association, declares it unlawful and by force **[200]** of the Act dissolves it, and when ss 8 and 15(1) attach the consequence of deprivation of property and s 7 attaches the consequence of a restriction of the civil rights of the members, it provides for matters which, considered as specific subjects, are not of their own nature within any of the enumerated powers of the Commonwealth Parliament and prima facie lie only within the province of the States. If the operation of the law upon the right of association, the common property and the civil rights of the members were made by the statute to depend upon the actual existence or occurrence of any act, matter or thing having a specific relation to the purposes of the power with respect to defence, then, notwithstanding that the immediate subject of the provision did not of its own nature form part of the subject matter of the power, the provision would be brought within it as ancillary to the main purpose of the power. Again, prima facie no opinion of the Parliament as to the actual existence or occurrence of some matter or event which would provide a specific relation of the subject of a law with power can suffice to give the law that relation. It would, for example, be impossible for the Parliament by reciting that a society for research in radio physics planned or carried on experiments causing or likely to cause an interference with wireless transmission to bring within s 51(v) (postal, telegraphic, &c services) an enactment naming the society and dissolving it *brevi manu*. It would be impossible to bring under s 51(xviii) (patents) a direct grant of a monopoly for a specified manufacturing process by reciting that it was an invention. The pronouncements by Parliament which the recitals in the Act contain, combined with the declaration of unlawfulness and decree of dissolution made by s 5 and the forfeiture imposed by s 15(1), were said by the plaintiffs to amount together to an invasion or usurpation of judicial power. In the case of s 15(1) it was also said that, except by a lawful exercise of judicial power, such a forfeiture could not be imposed by reason of s 51(xxxi) of the Constitution. As I am deciding the case on the ground of want of affirmative legislative power, I shall not deal with these arguments, but I mention them because they illustrate the substantial effect and nature of the provisions in question. There should be no confusion about the essential nature of the connection with the defence power which the recitals seek to supply. Essentially it consists in the past acts, the tenets and opinions and the present propensities or tendencies of persons and associations of persons.

Where legislation, subordinate or principal, purporting to exercise the defence power has stated the purpose for which it was enacted **[201]** or adopted, this expression of purpose has received effect. In relation to a power largely directed to purpose its importance is evident. It is true that the expression of the nature and existence of the purpose has left open the question whether nevertheless the legislation failed as an exercise of the defence power, because of the nature of the provisions, the prevailing situation, the facts, the remoteness of the means adopted from the avowed object, or some other consideration. But here, so far as the preambles express the existence and the nature of the purpose animating the legislation, that may be conceded. It is, however, but a small step. What is in question is so much of the recitals as concern not the opinions and purposes of the legislature, but the opinions and purposes of the persons against whom the provisions are directed and their past actions. Again, the case is not one where a course of conduct is required or forbidden but only a knowledge of facts outside judicial notice would enable the Court to see how the pursuit of that course of conduct would promote or prejudice, as the case may be, an object within the defence power. It is enough to mention *Sloan v Pollard* [(1947) 75 CLR 445] and *Jenkins v Commonwealth* [(1947) 74 CLR 400], the facts of which provide sufficient illustrations. In such a case the result which the rule laid down produces or is calculated to produce is within the defence power and all that is lacking is an understanding of the process of causation between the conduct prescribed or prohibited and the result. That can be proved. There is no need to stop to inquire precisely how much effect a recital by the legislature of facts of such a nature should receive; for it is not this case. But, to my mind, recitals of such a character, stating how a law will operate, or for that matter recitals stating the purpose for which an enactment is made, stand on an altogether different footing from what is the essential matter here. The essential matter here is a statement to the effect that persons or bodies of persons have been guilty of acts which might have been penalized in advance under the defence power and have a propensity to commit like acts, this being recited as affording a supposed connection between the defence power and the operative provisions enacted, provisions dealing with the persons or bodies directly by name or description.

At the risk of repetition it is perhaps desirable to add that the case is not one where the legislation is dealing with a subject matter undeniably within power. If the legislature directly dissolved a marriage between named parties, it would at all events be dealing with divorce, whatever other objections might be found [202] to the Act. If it directly enacted that a named alien should be deemed naturalized or that a person or persons named or described should be denied the use of the postal, telegraphic and telephonic services, it would likewise be upon the very subject of power. Whatever recitals it thought fit to make would have such effect as it was taken to intend, and whatever conditions it imposed would be valid, subject always, of course, to the relevance of positive restrictions that might be found elsewhere in the Constitution.

It must be evident that nothing but an extreme and exceptional extension of the operation or application of the defence power will support provisions upon a matter of its own nature prima facie outside Federal power, containing nothing in themselves disclosing a connection with Federal power and depending upon a recital of facts and opinions concerning the actions, aims and propensities of bodies and persons to be affected in order to make it ancillary to defence.

It may be conceded that such an extreme and exceptional extension may result from the necessities of war and, perhaps it may be right to add, of the imminence of war. But the reasons for this are to be found chiefly in the very nature of war and of the responsibility borne by the government charged with the prosecution of a war.

Fullagar J contrasted laws with the "direct and immediate object" of defence with what he called "the secondary aspect" of s 51(vi).

Fullagar J: [253] [P]erhaps partly because of its "purposive" character, the power given by s 51(vi) has two aspects. The tendency of the decisions of this Court, given in the course of two great wars and during the aftermath of each, has been to hold up the two aspects in sharp contrast one to another, and the dividing line between them has hitherto been regarded as sharp and clear – perhaps as sharper and clearer than it will ultimately be found to be. In its first aspect, s 51(vi) authorizes the making of laws which have, as their direct and immediate object, the naval and military defence of the Commonwealth and of the several States. This power is clearly not confined to time of war: see, eg, *Farey v Burvett* [(1916) 21 CLR 433 at 453], per *Isaacs* J; *Adelaide Company of Jehovah's Witnesses Inc v Commonwealth* [(1943) 67 CLR 116 at 132, 133], per *Latham* **[254]** CJ; *Hume v Higgins* [(1949) 78 CLR 116 at 133, 134], per *Dixon* J; and cf the reference by *Williams* J in *Koon Wing Lau v Calwell* [(1949) 80 CLR 533 at 584] to matters "which could reasonably be considered to be a threat to the safety of Australia in the event of some future war". It is obvious that such matters as the enlistment (compulsory or voluntary) and training and equipment of men and women in navy, army and air force, the provision of ships and munitions, the manufacture of weapons and the erection of fortifications, fall within this primary aspect of the defence power. These things can be undertaken by the Commonwealth as well in peace as in war, because they are *ex facie* connected with "naval and military defence". From any legitimate point of view of a court their only possible purpose or object is naval and military defence ...

What I have called the secondary aspect of the defence power has so far only been invoked and expounded in connection with an actual state of war in which Australia has been involved. It has hitherto, I think, been treated in the cases as coming into existence upon the commencement or immediate apprehension of war and continuing during war and the period necessary for post-war readjustment. In a world of uncertain and rapidly changing international situations it may well be held to arise in some degree upon circumstances which fall short of an immediate apprehension of war. In its secondary aspect the power extends to an infinite variety of matters which could not be regarded in the normal conditions of national life as having any connection with defence. Examples now familiar are the prices of goods and the rationing of goods, rents and the eviction of tenants, the transfer of interests [255] in land, and the conditions of employment in industry generally. It may be that, on its true analysis, this secondary aspect of the defence power depends wholly on s 51(xxxix) of the Constitution. On this view, the effect of a national emergency is that the matters which I have mentioned, and very many others, become "matters incidental to the execution" of the power of the Executive to deal with the emergency. Having in mind this secondary or extended aspect of the power, *Dixon* J, in *Andrews v Howell* [(1941) 65 CLR 255 at 278], said of the power given by s 51(vi):– "Though its meaning does not change, yet, unlike some other powers, its application depends upon facts, and, as those facts change, so may its actual operation as a power enabling the legislature to make a particular law ... The existence and character of hostilities, or a threat of hostilities, against the Commonwealth are facts which will determine the extent of the operation of the power." Other passages to a similar effect could be cited. In such passages the "facts" referred to are the basic facts which give rise to the extension of the power. Such facts have always hitherto been matters of public general knowledge, and matters, therefore, of which a court can and will take judicial notice. But, given the basic fact of (say) war, the question will still arise, whenever the validity of a particular law is in question, whether that law can be related to the extended power, or whether it is a law with respect to a matter incidental to the power of the Executive to wage war. The matter is, in effect, taken in two stages. At the first stage, the existence of war or national emergency is recognized as bringing into play the secondary or extended aspect of the defence power. This is done simply as a matter of judicial notice, and it provides the justification for a presumption of validity which might not otherwise exist in the case of an enactment which on its face bore no relation to any constitutional power. At the second stage the enactment in question is examined with regard to its character as a step to assist in dealing with the emergency ... The question which arises at this second stage may itself turn on **[256]** particular facts as distinct from the overriding general fact of war or national emergency. Such facts may relate to the operation of the law in question or to a state of affairs which calls for its enactment. Whether any and what evidence of such facts is admissible must depend on the circumstances of each particular case ...

[258] That under the defence power a law may, at least in time of war, be made to operate upon the opinion of a designated person, and that that opinion may supply the only link between the defence power and the legal effect of the opinion is well established. It is sufficient to refer to *Lloyd v Wallach* [(1915) 20 CLR 299] (cf *Liversidge v Anderson* [[1942] AC 206]; *Ex parte Walsh* [[1942] ALR 359]; *Little v Commonwealth* [(1947) 75 CLR 94]; and *Reid v Sinderberry* [(1944) 68 CLR 504]). It may be thought that herein lies an exception to an elementary rule of constitutional law which has been expressed metaphorically by saying that a stream cannot rise higher than its source. It was stated in *Shrimpton v Commonwealth* [(1945) 69 CLR 613 at 629, 630] in these terms:– "Finality, in the sense of complete freedom from legal control, is a quality which cannot be given under our Constitution to a discretion, if ... it is capable of being exercised for purposes, or given an operation, which would or might go outside the power from which the law or regulation conferring the discretion derives its force." Cf *Dawson v Commonwealth* [(1946) 73 CLR 157 at 181, 182]. The "discretion" may, of course, be the discretion of the legislature itself, exercised by the very fact of the enactment of a law. Or it may be the discretion of the Governor-General or a Minister, intended to be legally effective by the operation of an enacted law upon it. The validity of a law or of an administrative act done under a law cannot be made to depend on the opinion of the law-maker, or the person who is to do the act, that the law or the consequence of the act is within the constitutional power upon which the law in question itself depends for its validity. A power to make laws with respect to lighthouses does not authorize the making of a law with respect to anything which is, in the opinion of the law-maker, a lighthouse. A power to make a proclamation carrying legal consequences with respect to a lighthouse is one thing: a power to make a similar proclamation with respect to anything which in the opinion of the Governor-General is a lighthouse is another thing.

As to "the other power", Fullagar J said: "**[261]** I think that it is so far of a different nature from the defence power that a law cannot be made under it imposing legal consequences on a legislative or executive opinion which itself supplies the only link between the power and the legal consequences of the opinion". Fullagar J concluded that the validity of the Act must turn on the fact that it was directed to a particular voluntary association.

Fullagar J: [261] I come now to the Act itself. The most conspicuous feature of the Act is s 4, and the most conspicuous feature of s 4 is that it does not purport to impose duties or confer rights or prohibit acts or omissions, but purports simply to declare a particular unincorporated voluntary association unlawful and to dissolve it. It is, one supposes, to be classed as a public enactment as distinct from a private enactment, but it is, or at least is extremely like, what the Romans would have called a *privilegium*. Such a law (for I would not deny to it the character of a law) may well be within the competence of the Commonwealth legislative power, which is, within its constitutional limits, plenary (cf *Abitibi Power & Paper Co Ltd v Montreal Trust Co* [[1943] AC 536 at 548]). It would be impossible, I should think, to challenge s 4 if the Parliament had power to make laws with respect to voluntary associations or with respect to communists. It would be a law "with respect to" each of those "matters". So an Act of the Parliament dissolving the marriage of A with B would be a law with respect to divorce. It would be a *privilegium*, but what the Act actually did would be a thing which fell within a class of subject matter on which the Parliament was authorized to legislate. The Parliament has power to make laws with respect to divorce, and the Act is a law which effects a divorce. It is a *privilegium*, but it is a good law. But, if the Parliament enacts a *privilegium* which on its face bears no relation to any head of legislative power, it is likely to be extremely difficult to justify it under any head of power. In such a case (and s 4 is an example of such a case) there can, in my opinion, be no presumption of validity, and the Act, if it is to be upheld at all, can only be upheld on the basis of special and particular facts relating to the person or class who or which is the subject of the *privilegium* ...

[262] It should be observed at this stage that nothing depends on the justice or injustice of the law in question. If the language of an Act of Parliament is clear, its merits and demerits are alike beside the point. It is the law, and that is all. Such a law as the *Communist Party Dissolution Act* could clearly be passed by the Parliament of the United Kingdom or of any of the Australian States. It is only because the legislative power of the Commonwealth Parliament is limited by an instrument emanating from a superior authority that it arises in the case of the Commonwealth Parliament. If the great case of *Marbury v Madison* [5 US (1 Cranch) 137 (1803)] had pronounced a different view, it might perhaps not arise even in the case of the Commonwealth Parliament; and there are those, even today, who disapprove of the doctrine of *Marbury v Madison*, and who do not see why the courts, rather than the legislature itself, should have the function of finally deciding whether an Act of a legislature in a Federal system is or is not within power. But in our system the principle of *Marbury v Madison* is accepted as axiomatic, modified in varying degree in various cases (but **[263]** never excluded) by the respect which the judicial organ must accord to opinions of the legislative and executive organs ...

[266] This Act can, in my opinion, only be supported, if it can be supported at all, as an exercise of the defence power in what I have called its extended or secondary aspect. I do not think it can be supported under the other power invoked, whether that power be regarded as based on the joint operation of s 61 and s 51(xxxix) of the Constitution or on an implication from the existence and nature of the Constitution as the foundation of a body politic. The reason for this is that the provisions of the Act operate on opinions, and those opinions include an opinion as to matters on which the validity of those provisions depends. There is, as I have pointed out, a notable difference between the first group of provisions (headed by s 4) on the one hand and the second and third groups of provisions (headed by ss 5 and 9) on the other hand. But, in the last analysis, they stand on the same footing, and their validity depends on the same considerations. Section 4 is a directly enacted *privilegium* based on announced opinions of the Parliament, which involve an opinion as to matters on which power depends. Sections 5 and 9 operate on opinions of the Governor-General, which involve an opinion as to matters on which power depends. The decisions of this Court establish that such enactments may (not that they always will) be valid in cases where the secondary aspect of the defence power comes into existence by virtue of a judicially noticed emergency. No decision establishes that such enactments may be valid as exercises of the other power invoked by the Parliament in this case, and I have already expressed my opinion that there is no secondary aspect of this other power corresponding to the secondary aspect of the defence power.

[267] The question whether the Act can be supported as an exercise of the defence power in its secondary aspect must, in my opinion, depend entirely on judicial notice. The coming into existence of this secondary aspect has never been treated as depending on anything else. Nor could it, in my opinion, be treated as depending on anything else. It is only when the existence of the secondary aspect has been established by judicial notice of an emergency that evidence has ever been admitted to connect the enactment in question with power ...

[The] ultimate problem lies, I think, in the question whether judicial notice can be taken of matters sufficient to bring into operation that extended aspect of the defence power which was the basis of the decisions in *Lloyd v Wallach*; *Ex parte Walsh*, and *Little v Commonwealth*. On the whole I do not think that it can.

[268] Four things are to be remembered throughout. The first, which may or may not by itself be of vital importance, is that the date as at which the matter must be considered is 20th October 1950. The second is that the Parliament had, and has, undoubted powers to deal with such a situation as is envisaged by the preamble. The only question is whether it has power to deal with it by the particular means adopted. The third is that the particular means adopted is a means which has hitherto been recognized as valid only in time of, and by virtue of, a clear and great national danger. It is a means, moreover, which may – from a practical, though not perhaps from a technical and analytical, point of view – be thought to involve a degree of relaxation of a fundamental constitutional rule. Finally, it must not be forgotten that the defence power is, as I have said, a power concerned with protection against external enemies. If, therefore, a situation is to be found which will justify the Act in question as an exercise of an extended defence power, it must be an international situation. It is necessary to be on guard against letting in considerations appropriate only to the other power on which reliance is placed and which I have felt must be rejected.

On the one hand, I am not prepared to hold that nothing short of war or an immediate threat of war can bring into play a fully extended defence power. Each situation which arises must be examined as and when it arises. On the other hand, I think that the Court would be justified in taking judicial notice of a good many of the matters suggested by Mr *Barwick* as proper matters for judicial notice. But I have come to the conclusion that, if one keeps steadily in mind the important factors which I have enumerated, one cannot judicially notice in this case a state of affairs which would justify holding a measure having the peculiar features of the *Communist Party Dissolution Act* valid as an exercise of an extended defence power.

Both Dixon and Fullagar JJ rejected any possible relevance of "the other power" to the *Communist Party Case* because, as Fullagar J stated, that power can never extend to a law "**[261]** imposing legal consequences on a legislative or executive opinion which itself supplies the only link between the power and the legal consequences of the opinion". By contrast, Fullagar J held that the "secondary" or "extended" aspect of the defence power might extend this far. In other words, the defence power might confer an uncontrolled discretion to determine the facts on which the exercise of the discretion depends, but only at the fullest extent of its "secondary" aspect. Thus, the question was whether, not on the basis of legislative recitals, but on the basis of facts of which the Court could take judicial notice, there was a sufficiently serious national or international emergency to extend the power that far. All judges other than Latham CJ found that there was not, and therefore that the Act was invalid.

Before his appointment to the High Court as Chief Justice in 1935, Latham had served in the federal Parliament as Attorney-General and Opposition Leader and had established a reputation as a committed anti-communist. In the *Communist Party Case* he was in sole dissent.

Latham CJ: [141] I propose to refer to some general considerations affecting the nature of the defence power and of the power to make laws to protect the existence of constitutional government.

These powers are ... essentially different in character from most, if not all, of the other legislative powers of the Commonwealth Parliament. The exercise of these powers can be intelligent only when they are used in relation to some national objective which is concerned with protecting the country against what is regarded as a danger. The most important question which arises in these cases is whether legislation for such a purpose approved by Parliament cannot be valid unless it is also approved by a court after hearing evidence as to the existence of national danger.

These powers are perhaps the most important powers intrusted to the Parliament of the Commonwealth. The continued existence of the community under the Constitution is a condition of the exercise of all the other powers contained in the Constitution, whether executive, legislative or judicial. The preservation of the existence of the Commonwealth and of the Constitution of the Commonwealth takes precedence over all other matters with which the Commonwealth is concerned. As Cromwell said, "Being comes before well-being". The Parliament of the Commonwealth and the other constitutional organs of the Commonwealth cannot **[142]** perform their functions unless the people of the Commonwealth are preserved in safety and security.

Any Government which acts or asks Parliament to act against treason or sedition has to meet the criticism that it is seeking not to protect government, but to protect *the Government*, and to keep itself in power. Whether such a criticism is justified or not is, in our system of government, a matter upon which, in my opinion, Parliament and the people, and not the courts, should pass judgment ...

The exercise of these powers to protect the community and to preserve the government of the country under the Constitution is a matter of the greatest moment. Their exercise from time to time must necessarily depend upon the circumstances of the time as viewed by some authority. The question is – "By what authority – by Parliament or by a court?"

Latham CJ then set out, listed as (a) to (f), the matters that "**[142]** are, or normally may be, taken into account in ascertaining whether dangers exist against which laws passed under the defence power may be directed". They included "**[144]** extensive examination of the international situation, the views upon which may determine whether action should be taken against an external power ... [and whether] another country is a friend or not – whether a change in its government or in the policy of its government is likely". He saw these as "matters of judgment, not of fact in the ordinary sense. It can only be a question of opinion and not a question of fact upon which a court can make a decision as to whether the international situation is 'set fair' or 'stormy' and in what quarter a storm is likely to arise". He concluded:

Latham CJ: [145] The Government and Parliament are responsible to the electorate for the policy of "fight" or "not fight" which they adopt after such consideration as is thought proper has been given to all the above matters.

The matters mentioned under the above headings (a) to (f) are mainly matters purely of policy and of opinion. They are not actual or objective facts which can be "found" by a court. Such matters of "fact" as are involved have no significance except in relation to some policy. Many of the relevant matters, as already stated, could never be made public. The plaintiffs contend that the view of the Government and Parliament, based upon the considerations mentioned, is irrelevant when the validity of legislation is to be determined. If a court agrees with Parliament that certain legislative action is really for the defence of Australia the Court will hold an Act to be valid. If the Court disagrees with **[146]** the view of Parliament, then it must, it is argued, hold the Act to be invalid ...

[149] In my opinion the arguments for the plaintiffs show no adequate appreciation of the functions of the executive and of Parliament in a system of government under a Federal constitution. The governing questions in relation to defence and to the protection of constitutional government are questions of policy with which a court has nothing to do. It is not the case that all the questions which arise in government are "questions of fact" or "questions of law" – the former possibly for a jury and the latter for a court. When those responsible for the safety of the country determine to go to war they may be moved by all kinds of considerations and circumstances, many of which could never be stated in the form of categorical propositions which would be capable of proof by legally admissible evidence. Entry into a war may be determined from one point of view readily and easily as a matter of self-preservation. But where some people take this view others may take a contrary view. It is notorious that in 1939 and 1940, though Parliament and the Government considered that the defence of Australia made it necessary to fight Germany, there were those in Australia and elsewhere who contended that the war was merely an "imperialist adventure" that had nothing whatever to do with the defence of Australia ...

[154] [I]t is not for a court (either at the present stage of these cases, or at any later stage) to ask or to answer the question whether or not it agrees with the view of Parliament that the Australian Communist Party and organizations and persons associated with it are enemies of the country. It is for the Government and Parliament to determine that question, and they have already determined it. Whether they are right or wrong is a political matter upon which the electors, and not any court, can pass judgment. The only question for a court, therefore, is whether the provisions of the Act have a real connection with the activities and possibilities which Parliament has said in its opinion do exist and do create a danger to Australia.

Latham CJ held that such a connection existed and thus that the Act was valid.

Latham CJ: [155] Actual fighting in the Second World War ended in 1945, but only few peace treaties have been made. The Court may, I think, allow itself to be sufficiently informed of affairs to be aware that any peace which now exists is uneasy and is considered by many informed people to be very precarious, and that many of the nations of the world (whether rightly or wrongly) are highly apprehensive. To say that the present condition of the world is one of "peace" **[156]** may not unfairly be described as an unreal application of what has become an outmoded category. The phrases now used are "incidents", "affairs", "police action", "cold war". The Government and Parliament do not regard the present position as one of perfect peace and settled security, and they know more about it than the courts can possibly know as the result of considering legally admissible evidence. I have already referred to the authorities which show that neither the technical existence of war nor actual fighting is a condition of the exercise of the defence power. At the present time the Government of Australia is entitled, in my opinion, under the defence power to make preparations against the risk of war and to prepare the community for war by suppressing, in accordance with a law made by Parliament, bodies believed by Parliament to exist for the purpose (*inter alia*) of prejudicing the defence of the community and imperilling its safety. It is immaterial whether the courts agree with Parliament or not.

The maxim referred to by Fullagar J that "**[258]** a stream cannot rise higher than its source" is relevant in two ways. First, the Commonwealth Parliament cannot control the limits of its own power. Its "source" of power is the Constitution. Whether an enactment falls within an area of power granted to the Parliament by the Constitution must ultimately be determined not by the Parliament but by the High Court. This explains the reservations expressed by Gaudron J in *Nolan v Minister for Immigration & Ethnic Affairs* (1988) 165 CLR 178 at 192 as to how far the Parliament could use its power in respect of "aliens" (s 51(xix)) to determine the legal definition of "aliens". It may also explain the decision in *New South Wales v Commonwealth* (*Incorporation Case*) (1990) 169 CLR 482 that the Parliament cannot use its power in respect of "corporations" (s 51(xx)) to prescribe the process by which "corporations" are formed. The Supreme Court of the United States has taken a similar view. In *Employment Division, Department of Human Resources of Oregon v Smith*, 494 US 872 (1990), the Court departed from its earlier decision in *Sherbert v Verner*, 374 US 398 (1963), abandoning the stringent criteria there applied to laws affecting the First Amendment right to free exercise of religion (as extended to the States by the Fourteenth Amendment). The United States Congress sought to reverse that result, reinstating *Sherbert v Verner* by enacting the *Religious Freedom Restoration Act 1993*. But in *City of Boerne v Flores*, 521 US 507 (1997), the Supreme Court held that the 1993 Act was itself unconstitutional. Even though the United States Congress is explicitly empowered to *enforce* the Fourteenth Amendment, it has no power to determine its legal interpretation: "**[644]** If Congress could define its own powers by altering the Fourteenth Amendment's meaning, no longer would the Constitution be 'superior paramount law, unchangeable by ordinary means'."

Secondly, an administrative decision-maker cannot, on the basis of unexaminable opinion, be permitted to control the limits of his or her administrative power. Nor can an administrative discretion be so broad that it enables the decision-maker to make decisions on matters lying wholly outside the grant of power. The point is illustrated by Fullagar J's reference to *Shrimpton v Commonwealth* (1945) 69 CLR 613, where the parties, Mary Shrimpton and Florence Thornton, were respectively purchaser and vendor in a Melbourne conveyancing transaction. Under the *Economic Organization Regulations* (Cth) made under the *National Security Act 1939* (Cth), such transactions required the Treasurer's approval. By reg 9(2) "the Treasurer may, in his absolute discretion, grant the consent, either unconditionally or subject to such conditions as he thinks fit, or refuse to grant the consent". In *Shrimpton v Commonwealth* the Treasurer imposed two conditions: that the purchase price be paid in cash, and that the purchaser deposit Commonwealth bonds worth £350 in her bank. The High Court held that this latter condition could not validly be imposed. Either reg 9(2) must be read down to limit the conditions that could be imposed to those of relevance to the particular transaction, or it must be struck down as wholly invalid.

None of this means that administrative discretions may not be extremely broad. According to Leslie Zines, *The High Court and the Constitution* (Butterworths, 4th ed 1997), the exclusion of discretions conditioned wholly on the decision-maker's opinion "**[221]** does not mean that a discretion cannot be given to, say, an administrator when the matter would lie clearly within the subject matter however the discretion was exercised. If the legislation is concerned with a subject which is undoubtedly within Commonwealth power and gives a discretion to an officer which affects or creates rights and liabilities within that subject, it is a law with respect to that subject". The distinction is illustrated by *Ex parte Walsh and Johnson; In re Yates* (1925) 37 CLR 36 (see Chapter 20, §2. So long as the discretion conferred by s 8AA of the *Immigration Act 1901* (Cth) was limited to "immigrants", both the grant and the exercise of the discretion were valid; but once an attempt was made to base the grant of discretion on the "trade and commerce" power (s 51(i)), it could not be made to depend on the Minister's "satisfaction" that trade and commerce were affected.

The decision in the *Communist Party Case* was handed down on 9 March 1951. A week later, Menzies called an early election at which communism was the main issue. (The Liberal Party's campaign slogan in Tasmania was "Menzies or Moscow".) Menzies won the election held on 28 April 1951 and immediately set out to gain the power to ban the Australian Communist Party by way of a referendum under s 128 of the Constitution. There is evidence to suggest that Menzies received support in drafting the proposed amendments from an unlikely (and inappropriate) source: Chief Justice Latham. Clem Lloyd ("Not Peace But a Sword! – The High Court under JG Latham" (1987) 11 *Adelaide Law Review* 175 at 202) has uncovered correspondence in which Latham remarks that he has had "an informal talk with the Prime Minister" regarding constitutional amendments and that he had "made some suggestions to him".

The referendum proposal put to the people on 22 September 1951 sought to add to the Constitution a new s 51A, including in sub-s (1): "The Parliament shall have power to make such laws for the peace, order and good government of the Commonwealth with respect to communists or communism as the Parliament considers to be necessary or expedient for the defence or security of the Commonwealth or for the execution or maintenance of this Constitution or of the laws of the Commonwealth". Note the absence of the qualifying words "subject to this Constitution", which govern the existing grants of power in ss 51 and 52. The amendment would also have conferred an express power to re-enact the *Communist Party Dissolution Act*. The referendum failed by a narrow margin (2,317,927 "yes" votes to 2,370,009 "no" votes).

The *Capital Issues Case* was decided 18 months after the *Communist Party Case*. In the meantime, the Korean War had escalated as a result of the entry of China into the conflict on 22 April 1951. Even before that, Menzies spoke publicly of an impending "World War III" (see, for example, *Sydney Morning Herald*, 3 March 1951). It seemed that Australia was faced with an emergency requiring extensive defence preparation. The case concerned the *Defence Preparations Act 1951* (Cth). Like the *Communist Party Dissolution Act*, it was prefaced with a series of recitals – for example, that "a state of international emergency" existed "in which it is essential that preparations for defence should be immediately made". Section 4 authorised the Governor-General to "make regulations for or in relation to defence preparations".

The *Defence Preparations (Capital Issues) Regulations* (Cth) were made pursuant to s 4. These prohibited the borrowing of money upon security and the issue of share capital over a certain limit unless accompanied by the consent of the Treasurer. Marcus Clark & Co Ltd sought to borrow £100,000, partly for renovations to their retail outlets and partly for a new bedding factory. The Treasurer refused his consent and the company sought a declaration from the High Court that the regulations were invalid. However, unlike the *Communist Party Dissolution Act*, the *Capital Issues Regulations* had made elaborate provision for judicial review of the Treasurer's decision, including a requirement in reg 17 that a person "taking proceedings in a court for relief ... may apply to the court for an order directing the Treasurer to state in writing the facts and matters by reason of which … the refusal of consent … was for purposes of or in relation to defence preparations". In response to an order made under this regulation by McTiernan J, the Treasurer filed a detailed statement (reported in (1952) 87 CLR at 182-96). On that basis the Court held by 4:2, with Williams and Kitto JJ dissenting, that the Act and the regulations were valid. The *Communist Party Case* was distinguished.

Marcus Clark & Co Ltd v Commonwealth (Capital Issues Case)
(1952) 87 CLR 177

Dixon CJ: [215] [U]nlike the law held invalid in *Australian Communist Party v Commonwealth* [(1951) 83 CLR 1], this **[216]** case does afford objective tests by which its connection, or want of connection, with the defence power may be seen or ascertained; its provisions do specify a course to be pursued and considerations and purposes to be effectuated the operation and practical consequences of which will show whether the measure does tend or might reasonably be considered to conduce to or to promote or to advance the defence of the Commonwealth. On its face it is directed against the raising of money in a way which the Treasurer judges to be prejudicial to purposes that are described as purposes for or in relation to defence preparations, the scope and meaning of the term "defence preparations" being made sufficiently clear. The judicial remedies available to ensure that the judgment or discretion of the Treasurer does not go beyond what is the true scope and meaning of "defence preparations" may or may not prove adequate to the purpose but at all events it is the intention of the regulations that his determination of that question should not be conclusive.

Fullagar J: [252] I would observe at the outset that there is, in my opinion, nothing in any of the judgments of any of the majority in the *Australian* **[253]** *Communist Party v Commonwealth* which affords the slightest assistance to the plaintiff in the present case. That case, as I understand it, turned wholly on the nature of the law in question, and not at all upon the subject matter of that law. I should have thought it indisputable that the matters mentioned in the preamble to the *Communist Party Dissolution Act* 1950 were matters upon which the Parliament could legislate under the defence power in peace or in war. But the provisions of the law actually enacted were of an altogether exceptional and peculiar character. The statute did not merely prescribe rules of conduct or create duties or impose prohibitions. In the first place it imposed, of its own mere force and without the possibility of judicial intervention, what were really penalties upon a particular specified organisation. And, in the second place, it attached, of its own mere force, what were really penal consequences to the formation of an opinion of the Executive, not judicially examinable, that a person or a body of persons was engaged, or likely to become engaged, in activities prejudicial to defence. Laws having such a character had been held valid under the defence power in *Lloyd v Wallach* [(1915) 20 CLR 299]; *Ex parte Walsh* [[1942] ALR 359] and *Little v Commonwealth* [(1947) 75 CLR 94], but only when the actual engagement of the Commonwealth in a great war could be said to have expanded the scope of the defence power to an extent approaching its maximum. In the *Communist Party Case* I was prepared to take judicial notice of a disturbed international situation affecting Australia and of certain matters which were forcibly put by Mr *Barwick*, but those matters did not appear to me to justify a decision that laws of so exceptional a character fell in October 1950 within the defence power. I do not think that the view taken by four of the five other justices who formed the majority differed substantially from mine. The Act and the regulations which are in question in the present case do not possess the exceptional character which belonged to ss 4, 5 and 9 of the *Communist Party Dissolution Act*.

I think that the only relevance of the *Communist Party Case* in the present case lies in the fact that it is recognised in all of the judgments delivered in that case that a situation falling short of actual war may so expand the scope of the defence power as to enable the Parliament to legislate with respect to subject matters which have *ex facie* no relation to naval and military defence. This was, indeed, I think, implicit in most of the general statements of the nature of the defence power, although before the *Communist* **[254]** *Party Case* what I called the secondary aspect of the defence power had never been invoked except in time of war. It is clearly implicit in the well-known passage in the judgment of *Dixon* J in *Andrews v Howell* [(1941) 65 CLR 255 at 278]. But it is expressly stated and emphasised in the *Communist Party Case* ...

[255] I have not been able to see any sound reason for saying that s 4(2) is invalid. I would not be prepared to regard the fact that the words "defence preparations" occur in every paragraph as conclusive – as I think we were, in effect, invited to do by counsel for the defendants. And I express no opinion as to the validity of such provisions in what *Isaacs* J once called a period of "profound peace". No one would regard the present state of peace as very "profound". The view taken of the situation by the Parliament and the Government is expressed in the second recital in the preamble, and facts which may be judicially noticed go a considerable distance towards supporting that view. It is impossible for a court to say that it is not justified. And it seems to me equally impossible to say that the execution of a substantial defence programme is not quite likely to bring about economic strains and dislocations of such a nature that, unless they can be controlled by the authority constitutionally responsible for defence, the defence programme itself may be imperilled or impeded ...

[255] I am of opinion ... that the Capital Issues Regulations are a valid exercise of powers conferred by s 4(2) of the Act. It may be said that the provisions of reg 17(1) and (2) are conclusive on the question, for they prohibit a refusal of consent or the imposition of a condition upon consent "except for purposes of or in relation to defence preparations", and, although the words "defence preparations" must be given a wide meaning in the light of the preamble and s 4(2) of the Act, the opinion has already [256] been expressed that s 4(2) is valid. But some such limitation or restriction upon the discretion to refuse consent or impose a condition would have to be implied: cf *Shrimpton v Commonwealth* [(1945) 69 CLR 613]. And the question arises whether a measure imposing a prohibition of certain borrowings and capital issues is a measure of the character authorised by s 4(2). It appears to me that the view may reasonably be entertained that the "expansion of the capacity of Australia to produce or manufacture goods or to provide services" for one purpose will be aided by measures tending to limit or restrict the production or manufacture of goods or the provision of services for other purposes. It appears to me also that such measures may also be thought quite reasonably to conduce to the diversion of resources from other purposes to the purposes contemplated by s 4(2). If these conclusions are reached, the regulations must be held valid. They are, in my opinion, valid.

One obvious difference between the *Communist Party Case* and the *Capital Issues Case* was that, in the latter, the regulations made careful provision for judicial review, including a procedure whereby the Treasurer gave a justification for his decision, the persuasiveness of which could be assessed by the Court. Another difference was that the *Capital Issues Case* concerned economic rights, whereas the *Communist Party Case*, although it too affected property rights, primarily concerned civil and political rights. Although the judgments did not dwell on this theme, the *Communist Party Case* is widely regarded as an outstanding example of the High Court's potential role in protecting civil liberties and the rule of law.

7. Further References

"Australian Military Law", Thematic Issue (2005) 28 *University of New South Wales Law Journal*.

Brown, RA, "Military Justice in Australia: W(h)ither Away? The Effects of *Re Tracey; Ex parte Ryan*" (1989) 13 *Criminal Law Journal* 263.

Cain, F, and Farrell, F, "Menzies' War on the Communist Party, 1949-1951" in Curthoys, A, and Merritt, J (eds), *Australia's First Cold War, 1945-1953* (Allen & Unwin, 1984), vol 1, 109.

"Counter-Terrorism Laws", Thematic Issue (2004) 27 *University of New South Wales Law Journal*.

Douglas, R, "A Smallish Blow for Liberty? The Significance of the Communist Party Case" (2001) 27 *Monash University Law Review* 253.

Derham, DP, "The Defence Power" in Else-Mitchell, R (ed), *Essays on the Australian Constitution* (Law Book Co, 2nd ed 1961), 157.

Gilbert, CD, "'There Will be Wars and Rumours of Wars': A Comparison of the Treatment of Defence and Emergency Powers in the Federal Constitutions of Australia and Canada" (1980) 18 *Osgoode Hall Law Journal* 307.

Head, M, "The Military Call-Out Legislation – Some Legal and Constitutional Questions" (2001) 29 *Federal Law Review* 273.

Kirby, M, "HV Evatt, the Anti-Communist Referendum and Liberty in Australia" (1990) 7 *Australian Bar Review* 93.

Lee, HP, *Emergency Powers* (Law Book Co, 1984).

Mitchell, M, and Voon, T, "Defence of the Indefensible? Reassessing the Constitutional Validity of Military Service Tribunals in Australia" (1999) 27 *Federal Law Review* 499.

Sawer, G, "Defence Power of the Commonwealth in Time of Peace" (1952-1954) 6 *Res Judicata* 214.

Sawer, G, "The Defence Power of the Commonwealth in Time of War" (1946) 20 *Australian Law Journal* 295.

Sugerman, B, and Dignam, W, "The Defence Power and Total War" (1943) 17 *Australian Law Journal* 207.

Symposium, "The Constitution and Military Justice" (1990) 20 *University of Western Australia Law Review* 4.

Williams, G, "Reading the Judicial Mind: Appellate Argument in the *Communist Party Case*" (1993) 15 *Sydney Law Review* 3.

Williams, G, "The Suppression of Communism by Force of Law: Australia in the Early 1950s" (1996) 42 *Australian Journal of Politics and History* 220.

Winterton, G, "The *Communist Party* Case" in Lee, HP, and Winterton, G (eds), *Australian Constitutional Landmarks* (Cambridge University Press, 2003), 108.

Zines, L, *The High Court and the Constitution* (Butterworths, 4th ed 1997), Ch 11.

Chapter 19

International Law
and the External Affairs Power

1. Introduction

Australia's status as an independent sovereign member of the community of nations developed only gradually after Federation, particularly as a result of the two world wars (see Chapter 4, §§5-8). Many aspects of the Commonwealth's power to pass laws with respect to "external affairs" under s 51(xxix) of the Constitution have therefore not yet been fully explored.

In recent years, most attention has focused on the use of the power to pass legislation giving effect within Australia to international obligations that Australia has incurred under international treaties and conventions. In some cases, as with human rights guarantees or environmental protection, the topics or activities regulated by such legislation have been located solely within Australia, or even solely within a particular State. Persons who object to the use of s 51(xxix) as a basis for such legislation are wont to ask in such cases: "What's international about it?" Our concern in this Chapter is to trace the High Court's answers to this question and to explore other aspects of the power.

2. International Law and the Constitution

(a)   The Power to Enter into Treaties

Australia is a signatory to a multitude of international instruments such as treaties and conventions. In recent years, the nation has acceded to agreements ranging from multilateral instruments like the Rome Statute of the International Criminal Court to bilateral instruments like the Australia-US Free Trade Agreement. By December 2005, Australia had entered into 2544 international instruments (according to the *Australian Treaties Library* <www.austlii.edu.au/au/other/dfat/>). Some of these merely amend treaties that have already been entered into, and some treaties have been terminated or replaced. Hence, in 1995, by which time the *Australian Treaties Library* listed 2273 instruments, the Department of Foreign Affairs and Trade came up with a lower figure in finding that Australia was a party to approximately 920 substantive and operating treaties (Senate Legal and Constitutional References Committee, *Trick or Treaty: Commonwealth Power to Make and Implement Treaties*, Parliamentary Paper No 474 of 1995, [2.4]-[2.6]).

The power to commit Australia to international agreements lies with the federal executive as an aspect of its prerogative power (see Chapter 12, §2(a)). It alone has the power to decide which treaties Australia does and does not accede to. However, recent reforms have meant that Parliament does play a part in the deliberative process.

Hilary Charlesworth, Madelaine Chiam, Devika Hovell and George Williams, "Deep Anxieties: Australia and the International Legal Order"
(2003) 25 *Sydney Law Review* 423

[439] In 1961, Prime Minister Menzies had announced a commitment to table in both Houses of Parliament the text of treaties Australia had signed but not yet ratified or to which Australia contemplated accession. Except for urgent cases, treaties were to be tabled at least 12 sitting days before proposed ratification or accession. The aim of this measure was to keep Parliament informed about treaty matters. The executive maintained this practice until the late 1970s, when treaties began to be tabled in bulk after periods of about six months. Bulk tabling meant that many of the tabled treaties had already been ratified and that Australia had assumed new, and sometimes significant, international obligations without any parliamentary scrutiny ...

Increasing dissatisfaction with Parliament's desultory role in the treaty-making process, in particular the perception that reduced Parliamentary involvement produced a 'democratic deficit', led to a 1995 Senate inquiry into the treaty-making power and the external affairs power. Many of the recommendations from the inquiry were implemented by the new Coalition government in its 1996 reforms to the treaty-making process. The Senate inquiry had recommended that the reforms be introduced by legislation, but they were ultimately introduced by resolution.

The reforms had five aspects:

- The tabling in Parliament of all treaty actions proposed by the Government in Parliament for at least 15 sitting days before binding action is taken. Treaty actions which the Minister for Foreign Affairs certifies to be particularly urgent or sensitive, involving significant commercial, strategic or foreign policy interests, are exempted from this requirement;
- The preparation of a National Interest Analysis (*NIA*) for each treaty, outlining [440] information including the obligations contained in the treaty and the benefits for Australia of entering into the treaty;
- The establishment of the parliamentary Joint Standing Committee on Treaties (*JSCOT*);
- The establishment of the Treaties Council comprising the Prime Minister, Premiers and Chief Ministers; and
- The establishment on the internet of the Australian Treaties Library.

In August 2002, the Minister for Foreign Affairs announced refinements to the tabling process. Treaties of major political, economic or social significance are now tabled for 20 sitting days, while other treaties continue to be tabled for 15 sitting days ...

[441] JSCOT has been the most influential of all of the 1996 reforms ... [It] is empowered to inquire into and report upon:

1. matters arising from treaties and related National Interest Analyses and proposed treaty actions presented or deemed to be presented to Parliament;
2. any question relating to a treaty or other international instrument, whether or not negotiated to completion, referred to the committee by:
   (a) either House of the Parliament; or
   (b) a Minister; and
   (c) such other matters as may be referred to the committee by the Minister for Foreign Affairs and on such conditions as the Minister may prescribe.

The JSCOT process works in tandem with the tabling of treaties in Parliament. JSCOT must review treaties within the defined 15 or 20 day sitting day period for the treaties, although extensions are possible in exceptional circumstances. The review process generally involves an examination of the accompanying NIA, public submissions and a public hearing on the treaty. Those called on to address the Committee at public hearings usually include representatives from relevant government departments, relevant non-government and other private organisations and any other individuals whom the Committee deems appropriate. At the end of the process, JSCOT issues a report containing its recommendations as to whether and in what circumstances the treaty should be ratified.

JSCOT had issued 53 reports as at 1 September 2003. The usual practice is for a single report to include reviews of a number of treaties, normally all the treaties tabled at a particular time. In line with its powers, however, JSCOT has also produced a number of single issue reports. These reports have concerned matters **[442]** of particular economic, social, cultural or political significance and include reports on the Statute of the International Criminal Court, the Multilateral Agreement on Investment (*MAI*), the World Trade Organisation, Australia's extradition policy and the Kyoto Protocol to the Climate Change Convention.

In general, JSCOT has recommended the taking of binding treaty action by the executive. Its practice of preferring consensus outcomes to majority/dissenting reports means it would be unusual for the Committee to make a strong finding against the government. It also makes displays of political partisanship within the Committee extremely rare. The Committee seems to take a politic approach to its reports and is more likely to make recommendations that will be adopted by government than take a strong stance that may be ignored.

It is clear, however, that the Committee does not consider itself simply to be a rubber stamp for executive action. The tenor of JSCOT reports suggests a committee confident of its position and influence within government and one unafraid of criticising government where appropriate. The Committee found fault, for example, with the 'inadequate' consultation that Treasury conducted in relation to the MAI. The Committee criticised Treasury's role with respect to the MAI, 'not to accuse it of wrong doing but to draw attention to how excessive zeal for a cause in which it believes can sometimes blind an organisation' ...

[443] The Coalition government's attitude towards JSCOT has been generally enthusiastic, although it is slow to respond to JSCOT recommendations. It is not unusual for responses to JSCOT reports to be issued up to a year after the recommendations were made. The government is also aware of the potential implications of ignoring JSCOT recommendations. The Minister for Foreign Affairs has stated that 'any government would need to think very carefully of the political consequences before it ignored a unanimous JSCOT recommendation'. It is difficult to assess the accuracy of this statement, however, as the recommendations of JSCOT and the intentions of the executive have so far appeared to coincide ...

One analysis of the JSCOT process, in relation to Australia's multilateral economic diplomacy, agreed that it adds an important layer to the management of international law within Australia. It also concluded, however, that:

> For all the committee's activism, and for all its unusual non-partisanship, the JSCOT initiative has been unable to alter substantially the way in which Australia's foreign economic policy has been made .... [W]e conclude that the **[444]** main role of JSCOT in the realm of trade diplomacy has been as a tool of political management, a means by which the executive can channel protest, deflect opposition, and in essence legitimize its own policy preferences.

The JSCOT process may have thus become a mechanism through which public anxieties about Australia's relationship with international law are reduced ... Despite the enhanced transparency of the treaty-making process under JSCOT ... it seems that the executive has retained its dominant role in Australia's relationship with international law.

(b)   International Law and the Legal System

Historically, it was often assumed that rules of international law were automatically incorporated into the English common law. In *Triquet v Bath* (1764) 3 Burr 1478, 97 ER 936, Lord Mansfield remembered earlier judges as saying "**[1481]** [t]hat the law of nations, in its full extent was part of the law of England". However, that was at a time when both common law and international law were still evolving and relatively fluid, and when international norms depended not on treaty-making but almost entirely on "customary international law" – that is, a distillation of the accepted practice of nation states. Its underlying rationale thus fitted easily into that of the unwritten common law. In modern times, in both England and Australia, this "incorporation" theory has largely been supplanted by a "transformation" theory – that is, that the international legal order and that of the nation state are separate legal systems, so that developments in international law have no direct effect for domestic purposes unless a deliberate law-making act by the proper law-making authority has "transformed" the international rule into a rule of domestic law.

Of course, in the common law tradition, judges as well as legislators have authority to determine the law; and in *Nulyarimma v Thompson* (1999) 165 ALR 621 Merkel J, while accepting the "transformation" theory, held that an authoritative decision to adopt a norm of international law as part of Australian law could be made by courts as well as by parliaments. That, however, was a dissenting view. As international legal obligations have increasingly depended on treaties, Australian courts have consistently denied that they can have any effect for domestic legal purposes until they are given that effect through legislation. Already in *Brown v Lizars* (1905) 2 CLR 837, the High Court held that neither the courts nor the Crown could give effect to an extradition treaty in the absence of legislation. In *Chow Hung Ching v The King* (1948) 77 CLR 449, Dixon J emphasised that the executive action of ratifying a treaty, thus committing Australia to it internationally, is effective only externally, with "**[478]** no legal effect upon the rights and duties of the subjects of the Crown". Later judges, including Mason CJ and McHugh J in *Dietrich v The Queen* (1992) 177 CLR 292, have repeatedly reaffirmed the point. As Gibbs CJ stated in *Kioa v West* (1985) 159 CLR 550, "**[570]** treaties do not have the force of law unless they are given that effect by statute".

Even if the common law still has a capacity to "incorporate" norms of international law, it would seem that this could now extend only to customary international law. Moreover, any norms thus "incorporated" would attain only common law status and thus could be overridden by statute. In *Polites v Commonwealth* (1945) 70 CLR 60, where the plaintiff argued that under international law his Greek nationality precluded liability to military service in Australia, the High Court held that, even if that were so, the clear provisions of the *National Security Act 1939* (Cth) would prevail.

All this might suggest that, in the absence of legislation, international law can have little influence on Australian law. In recent years, however, this has come under challenge. Discussing the effect of the 1966 International Convention on the Elimination of All Forms of Racial Discrimination in *Gerhardy v Brown* (1985) 159 CLR 70, Brennan J made a powerful statement of the effect of international human rights norms upon "**[125]** sovereign powers".

Gerhardy v Brown
(1985) 159 CLR 70

Brennan J: [125] The recognition and observance of human rights and fundamental freedoms by a State involves a restraint on the untrammelled exercise of its sovereign powers in order to ensure that the dignity of human beings within each State is respected and that equality among human beings prevails. Clearly enough, human rights and fundamental freedoms are not to be understood as the rights and freedoms which a person has under a particular legal system; they **[126]** are rights and freedoms which every legal system ought to recognize and observe. They are inalienable rights and freedoms that a human being possesses simply in virtue of his humanity, independently of any society to which he belongs, independently of the legal regime which governs it, and independently of any right or freedom that he might acquire by entering into a special relationship with another. The term connotes the rights and freedoms which must be recognized and observed, and which a person must be able to enjoy and exercise, if he is to live as he was born – "free and equal in dignity and rights".

However, when the possibility of "a restraint on ... sovereign powers" was tested in *Kruger v Commonwealth (Stolen Generations Case)* (1997) 190 CLR 1, it was met with a more orthodox response. The plaintiffs claimed that the *Aboriginals Ordinance 1918* (NT), which authorised the forced removal of Aboriginal children from their families and traditional culture, was uncon-stitutional. In part, this claim depended on an argument that the practices thus authorised had amounted to "cultural genocide" within the meaning of the Convention on the Prevention and Punishment of the Crime of Genocide, which entered into force on 12 January 1951. The practices complained of by the plaintiffs had continued well after that date; but the Ordinance upon which the High Court litigation was focused had been made in 1918, over 30 years before the Convention entered into force. To overcome that problem, the plaintiffs argued, as Gaudron J put it, that the Convention had merely given "**[104]** expression to an enduring peremptory norm of [customary] international law". As thus effectively narrowed to a question of whether the 1918 Ordinance fell within the definition of "genocide" in the 1951 Convention, the plaintiffs' claim failed. According to the Convention, the acts there referred to, including the forcible transfer of children, constitute "genocide" when committed "with intent to destroy" an ethnic, racial or religious group. However, the ostensible purpose of the 1918 Ordinance was one of paternalistic protection. The whole Court held that this made it impossible to find the genocidal "intent" required by the Convention.

Kruger v Commonwealth (*Stolen Generations Case*)
(1997) 190 CLR 1

Dawson J: [70] The Genocide Convention was ratified by Australia on 8 July 1949 and entered into force on 12 January 1951. The 1918 Ordinance therefore pre-dates it by more than three decades. The *Genocide Convention Act* 1949 (Cth) gave parliamentary approval to the ratification by Australia of the Genocide Convention, but there is no legislation implementing the Genocide Convention in this country.

The definition of "genocide" in the Genocide Convention is as follows:

"In the present Convention, genocide means any of the following acts committed with intent to destroy, in whole or in part, a national, ethnical, racial or religious group, as such:

(a) Killing members of the group;

(b) Causing serious bodily or mental harm to members of the group;

(c) Deliberately inflicting on the group conditions of life calculated to bring about its physical destruction in whole or in part;

(d) Imposing measures intended to prevent births within the group;

(e) Forcibly transferring children of the group to another group."

The first thing that may be said is there is nothing in the 1918 Ordinance, even if the acts authorised by it otherwise fell within the definition of genocide, which authorises acts committed with intent to destroy in whole or in part any Aboriginal group. On the contrary ... the powers conferred by the 1918 Ordinance were required to be exercised in the best interests of the Abori-ginals concerned or of the Aboriginal population generally. The acts authorised do not, therefore, fall within the definition of genocide contained in the Genocide Convention.

In any event, the Convention has not at any time formed part of Australian domestic law. As was recently pointed out in *Minister for* **[71]** *Immigration and Ethnic Affairs v Teoh* [(1995) 183 CLR 273], it is well established that the provisions of an international treaty to which Australia is a party do not form part of Australian law unless those provisions have been validly incorporated into our municipal law by statute. Where such provisions have not been incorporated they cannot operate as a direct source of individual rights and obligations.

In short, international law is not a "higher law" like the Constitution with which statutes must comply. Decisions like *Polites v Commonwealth* demonstrate that parliaments can legislate incon-sistently with international norms (see also *Horta v Commonwealth* (1994) 181 CLR 183 in §3(b) below).

This does not, however, prevent international law being applied in more indirect ways; and it is as an interpretive influence that it has had an increasingly important impact on Australian law. Its use as an aid to interpretation where a statute has been enacted to give domestic effect to a treaty or convention is authorised by s 15AB(2) of the *Acts Interpretation Act 1901* (Cth).

Members of the High Court have gone further – accepting, as Brennan, Deane and Dawson JJ put it in *Chu Kheng Lim v Minister for Immigration* (1992) 176 CLR 1, that courts "**[38]** should, in a case of ambiguity, favour a construction of a Commonwealth statute which accords with the obligations of Australia under an international treaty".

International law is also used in the development of the common law. In recognising "traditional native title" in *Mabo v Queensland (No 2)* (1992) 175 CLR 1, Brennan J stated: "**[42]** The common law does not necessarily conform with international law, but international law is a legitimate and important influence on the development of the common law, especially when international law declares the existence of universal human rights".

More controversially, the High Court has had recourse to international norms in the scrutiny of federal administrative decision-making. It held in *Minister for Immigration and Ethnic Affairs v Teoh* (1995) 183 CLR 273 that Commonwealth decision-makers may need to take account of international treaties ratified by Australia (in that case the 1989 Convention on the Rights of the Child), since such a treaty can give rise to a "legitimate expectation" that government decisions will conform with the treaty.

Minister for Immigration and Ethnic Affairs v Teoh
(1995) 183 CLR 273

Mason CJ and Deane J: [286] It is well established that the provisions of an international treaty to which Australia is a party do not form part of Australian law unless **[287]** those provisions have been validly incorporated into our municipal law by statute. This principle has its foundation in the proposition that in our constitutional system the making and ratification of treaties fall within the province of the Executive in the exercise of its prerogative power whereas the making and the alteration of the law fall within the province of Parliament, not the Executive. So, a treaty which has not been incorporated into our municipal law cannot operate as a direct source of individual rights and obligations under that law. In this case, it is common ground that the provisions of the Convention have not been incorporated in this way ...

But the fact that the Convention has not been incorporated into Australian law does not mean that its ratification holds no significance for Australian law. Where a statute or subordinate legislation is ambiguous, the courts should favour that construction which accords with Australia's obligations under a treaty or international convention to which Australia is a party, at least in those cases in which the legislation is enacted after, or in contemplation of, entry into, or ratification of, the relevant international instrument. That is because Parliament, prima facie, intends to give effect to Australia's obligations under international law ...

[288] Apart from influencing the construction of a statute or subordinate legislation, an international convention may play a part in the development by the courts of the common law. The provisions of an international convention to which Australia is a party, especially one which declares universal fundamental rights, may be used by the courts as a legitimate guide in developing the common law. But the courts should act in this fashion with due circumspection when the Parliament itself has not seen fit to incorporate the provisions of a convention into our domestic law. Judicial development of the common law must not be seen as a backdoor means of importing an unincorporated convention into Australian law ... Much will depend upon the nature of the relevant provision, the extent to which it has been accepted by the international community, the purpose which it is intended to serve and its relationship to the existing principles of our domestic law.

In the present case, however, we are not concerned with the resolution of an ambiguity in a statute. Nor are we concerned with the development of some existing principle of the common law. The critical questions to be resolved are whether the provisions of the Convention are relevant to the exercise of the statutory discretion and, if so, whether Australia's ratification of the Convention can give rise to a legitimate expectation that the decision-maker will exercise that discretion in conformity with the terms of the Convention ...

[291] [R]atification of a convention is a positive statement by the executive government of this country to the world and to the Australian people that the executive government and its agencies will act in accordance with the Convention. That positive statement is an adequate foundation for a legitimate expectation, absent statutory or executive indications to the contrary, that administrative decision-makers will act in conformity with the Convention ... It is not necessary that a person seeking to set up such a legitimate expectation should be aware of the Convention or should personally entertain the expectation; it is enough that the expectation is reasonable in the sense that there are adequate materials to support it ...

The existence of a legitimate expectation that a decision-maker will act in a particular way does not necessarily compel him or her to act in that way. That is the difference between a legitimate expectation and a binding rule of law. To regard a legitimate expectation as requiring the decision-maker to act in a particular way is tantamount to treating it as a rule of law. It incorporates the provisions of the unincorporated convention into our municipal law by the back door ...

But, if a decision-maker proposes to make a decision inconsistent with a legitimate expectation, procedural fairness requires that the persons affected should be given notice and an adequate opportunity of **[292]** presenting a case against the taking of such a course.

The *Teoh* principle was expressed to operate in the absence of "**[291]** statutory or executive indications to the contrary". Its impact appeared to be blunted by a Joint Statement by the Minister for Foreign Affairs, Senator Gareth Evans, and the Attorney-General, Michael Lavarch, on 10 May 1995, which provided an executive indication, and foreshadowed a legislative indication, that treaties should not give rise to a "legitimate expectation". The Administrative Decisions (Effect of International Instruments) Bill was then introduced into the federal Parliament in 1995, but was not passed by the time of the March 1996 election. A further executive statement (reproduced at (1997) 8 *Public Law Review* 120), issued by the Attorney-General, Daryl Williams, and the Minister for Foreign Affairs, Alexander Downer, was provided by the Howard government on 25 February 1997. Further legislative indications have also been attempted. However, the Administrative Decisions (Effect of International Instruments) Bills of 1997 and 1999 lapsed with the 1998 and 2001 elections, respectively.

In *Re Minister for Immigration and Multicultural Affairs; Ex parte Lam* (2003) 214 CLR 1, an applicant for review of a deportation decision sought unsuccessfully to rely on *Teoh*. A five-judge Court held unanimously that *Teoh* did not apply. As Gleeson CJ put it: "**[14]** The applicant lost no opportunity to advance his case. He did not rely to his disadvantage on the statement of intention. It has not been shown that there was procedural unfairness ... [or] a failure properly to take into account the interests of the applicant's children". The joint judgment of McHugh and Gummow JJ went further, seizing the opportunity for a sustained critique both of the concept of "legitimate expectation", and of its use in *Teoh* in relation to unincorporated treaties. McHugh J had dissented in *Teoh*, while Gummow J, when *Lam* was argued before the Court on 24 June 2002, had protested in relation to the phrase "legitimate expectation": "I cannot go on writing judgments about things I do not understand".

McHugh and Gummow JJ saw English decisions such as *R v North and East Devon Health Authority; Ex parte Coughlan* [2001] QB 213 as representing "**[24]** an attempted assimilation ... of doctrines derived from European civilian systems". They rejected this as inappropriate for Australia because "a written federal constitution, with separation of the judicial power, necessarily presents a frame of reference which differs from both the English and other European systems referred to above". Their own more limited approach, "**[25]** stop[ping] short of giving the doctrine of legitimate expectation a substantive operation", was supported by decisions in New Zealand (notably *Thames Valley Electric Power Board v NZFP Pulp & Paper Ltd* [1994] 2 NZLR 641) and in Canada (notably *Baker v Canada* [1999] 2 SCR 817, (1999) 174 DLR (4th) 193, and *Mount Sinai Hospital Center v Quebec (Minister of Health and Social Services)* [2001] 2 SCR 281, (2001) 200 DLR (4th) 193). Consistently with those decisions, they maintained that the doctrine of "legitimate expectation" should not be extended beyond the limited basis acknowledged by McHugh J in his dissenting judgment in *Teoh*, and earlier by Brennan J in *Attorney-General (NSW) v Quin* (1990) 170 CLR 1.

Re Minister for Immigration and Multicultural Affairs; Ex parte Lam
(2003) 214 CLR 1

McHugh and Gummow JJ: [27] In his dissenting judgment in *Teoh* [(1995) 183 CLR 273 at 311-12], McHugh J questioned whether, given the development in Australian case law of the requirements of procedural fairness, the doctrine of legitimate expectations was left with any distinct role. His Honour said:

"I think that the rational development of this branch of the law requires acceptance of the view that the rules of procedural fairness are presumptively applicable to administrative and similar decisions made by public tribunals and officials. In the absence of a clear contrary legislative intention, those rules require a decision-maker 'to bring to a person's attention the critical issue or factor on which the administrative decision is likely to turn so that he may have an opportunity of dealing with it' [*Kioa v West* (1985) 159 CLR 550 at 587]. If that approach is adopted, there is no need for any doctrine of legitimate expectations. The question becomes, what does fairness require in all the circumstances of the case?"

Earlier, in *Quin* [(1990) 170 CLR 1 at 39], Brennan J had said:

"So long as the notion of legitimate expectation is seen merely as indicating 'the factors and kinds of factors which are relevant to any consideration of what are the things which must be done or afforded' to accord procedural fairness to an applicant for the exercise of an administrative power [*Macrae v Attorney-General (NSW)* (1987) 9 NSWLR 268 at 285], the notion can, with one important proviso, be useful. If, but only if, the power is so created that the according of natural justice conditions its exercise, the **[28]** notion of legitimate expectation may usefully focus attention on the content of natural justice in a particular case; that is, on what must be done to give procedural fairness to a person whose interests might be affected by an exercise of the power. But if the according of natural justice does not condition the exercise of the power, the notion of legitimate expectation can have no role to play. If it were otherwise, the notion would become a stalking horse for excesses of judicial power."

These statements by McHugh J and Brennan J should be accepted as representing the law in Australia. The decision in *Teoh* does not require any contrary or other understanding of the law.

McHugh and Gummow JJ pointed out that, in cases before *Teoh*, the "legitimate expectations" asserted had a definite subject-matter with a factual basis in general public knowledge. For example, *FAI Insurances Ltd v Winneke* (1982) 151 CLR 342 had involved the periodic renewal of an approval previously granted for the conduct of insurance business, while *Heatley v Tasmanian Racing and Gaming Commission* (1977) 137 CLR 487 had involved the expectation that members of the public be admitted to sporting venues. Aickin J had stated what was involved in that case as "**[509]** an expectation on the part of members of the public that they will continue to receive the customary permission to go on to racecourses upon the payment of a stated fee". The situation in *Teoh*, McHugh and Gummow JJ suggested, was not comparable with any of these.

McHugh and Gummow JJ: [31] It is one thing for a court in an application for judicial review to form a view as to the expectations of Australians presenting themselves at the gates of football grounds and racecourses. It is quite another to take **[32]** ratification of any convention as a "positive statement" made "to the Australian people" that the executive government will act in accordance with the convention and to treat the question of the extent to which such matters impinge upon the popular consciousness as beside the point ...

If *Teoh* is to have continued significance at a general level for the principles which inform the relationship between international obligations and the domestic constitutional structure, then further attention will be required to the basis upon which *Teoh* rests. The case involved ratification by the Executive of a treaty which had not been followed by any relevant exercise of legislative power to make laws with respect to external affairs. It was remarked in the *Industrial Relations Act Case* [(1996) 187 CLR 416 at 486] that there may be some treaties with a subject-matter identified in terms of aspiration which cannot enliven the power conferred by s 51(xxix) of the Constitution. But that does not necessarily mean that the executive act of ratification is to be dismissed as platitudinous; an international responsibility to the contracting state parties or other international institutions has been created.

In any event, it was not suggested that *Teoh* concerned a treaty of this limited nature. However, in general, ratification, as an executive act, did not in the domestic constitutional structure thereby confer [33] rights upon citizens or impose liabilities upon them. In that sense the ratified treaty was not "self-executing" and lacked "direct application" in that domestic system.

Nevertheless, in various respects, an unincorporated treaty, left in that state, may be invoked in various ways in the conduct of domestic affairs. For example, a peace treaty will, without legislation, change the status of enemy aliens in Australian courts [*Porter v Freudenberg* [1915] 1 KB 857]. Further, the taking of a step by the executive government in the conduct of external affairs, whilst of itself neither creating rights nor imposing liabilities, may supply a step in a broader process of resolution of justiciable disputes. The so-called "disguised extradition" cases are an example. The treatment of public policy objections in the conflict of laws may be another. More frequently encountered are the rules of statutory interpretation which favour construction which is in conformity and not in conflict with Australia's international obligations ...

However, in the case law a line has been drawn which limits the normative effect of what are unenacted international obligations upon discretionary decision-making under powers conferred by statute and without specification of those obligations. The judgments in *Teoh* accepted the established doctrine that such obligations are not mandatory relevant considerations attracting judicial review for jurisdictional error. The curiosity is that, nevertheless, such matters are to be treated, if *Teoh* be taken as establishing any general proposition in this area, as mandatory relevant considerations for that species of judicial review concerned with procedural fairness.

The reasoning which as a matter of principle would sustain such an [34] erratic application of "invocation" doctrine remains for analysis and decision. Basic questions of the interaction between the three branches of government are involved. One consideration is that, under the Constitution (s 61), the task of the Executive is to execute and maintain statute law which confers discretionary powers upon the Executive. It is not for the judicial branch to add to or vary the content of those powers by taking a particular view of the conduct by the Executive of external affairs. Rather, it is for the judicial branch to declare and enforce the limits of the power conferred by statute upon administrative decision-makers, but not, by reference to the conduct of external affairs, to supplement the criteria for the exercise of that power.

Clearly this final paragraph suggests that, by attaching requirements of procedural fairness to the expectation that Australia would abide by its treaty obligations, the majority judgments in *Teoh* exceeded the appropriate limits of judicial power. Yet the point that, under Australia's constitutional arrangements, the ratification of a treaty by the executive government does not of itself give rise to any "mandatory relevant considerations" in Australian domestic law was recognised by *Teoh* itself; while the possibility that a ratified treaty may nevertheless *indirectly* affect domestic legal processes was acknowledged above by McHugh and Gummow JJ.

(c)   International Law and Constitutional Interpretation

Despite the use of international law in statutory interpretation and in developing the common law, the High Court has been reluctant to use such norms in interpreting the Constitution. Kirby J is the only current Justice to do so. He first articulated his "interpretive principle" in *Newcrest Mining (WA) Ltd v Commonwealth* (1997) 190 CLR 513, in relation to the guarantee of just terms for the acquisition of property in s 51(xxxi). He then elaborated upon his approach in *Kartinyeri v Commonwealth* (*Hindmarsh Island Bridge Case*) (1998) 195 CLR 337, where he held (in dissent) that the "races power" in s 51(xxvi) does not extend to "[411] laws detrimental to, or discriminatory against, the people of any race (including the Aboriginal race) by reference to their race".

Kartinyeri v Commonwealth (*Hindmarsh Island Bridge Case*)
(1998) 195 CLR 337

Kirby J: [417] Where the Constitution is ambiguous, this Court should adopt that meaning which conforms to the principles of universal and fundamental rights rather than an interpretation which would involve a departure from such rights. Such an approach has, in recent years, found favour in New Zealand – where Cooke P (as Lord Cooke of Thorndon then was) has referred to the "duty of the judiciary to interpret and apply national constitutions … in the light of the universality of human rights" [*Tavita v Minister of Immigration* [1994] 2 NZLR 257 at 266]. Likewise, in interpreting the Canadian Charter of Rights and Freedoms, that country's Supreme Court has frequently had regard to international instruments. To do so does not involve the spectre, portrayed by some submissions in these proceedings, of mechanically applying international treaties, made by the Executive Government of the Commonwealth, and perhaps unincorporated, to distort the meaning of the Constitution. It does not authorise the **[418]** creation of ambiguities by reference to international law where none exist. It is not a means for remaking the Constitution without the "irksome" involvement of the people required by s 128. There is no doubt that, if the constitutional provision is clear and if a law is clearly within power, no rule of international law, and no treaty (including one to which Australia is a party) may override the Constitution or any law validly made under it. But that is not the question here … Where there is ambiguity, there is a strong presumption that the Constitution, adopted and accepted by the people of Australia for their government, is not intended to violate fundamental human rights and human dignity. Such violations are ordinarily forbidden by the common law and every other statute of this land is read, in the case of ambiguity, to avoid so far as possible such a result. In the contemporary context it is appropriate to measure the prohibition by having regard to international law as it expresses universal and basic rights. Where there is ambiguity in the common law or a statute, it is legitimate to have regard to international law. Likewise, the Australian Constitution, which is a special statute, does not operate in a vacuum. It speaks to the people of Australia. But it also speaks to the international community as the basic law of the Australian nation which is a member of that community.

Kirby J's "interpretive principle" has not been accepted by other members of the Court. For example, in *AMS v AIF* (1999) 199 CLR 160, Gleeson CJ, McHugh and Gummow JJ observed that "**[180]** reliance … upon several international instruments to which this country is a party did not advance [the] arguments … As to the Constitution, its provisions are not to be construed as subject to an implication said to be derived from international law". In *Kartinyeri*, Gummow and Hayne JJ stressed that, even in the interpretation of statutes, disconformity to international law is irrelevant when the language of the statute is "**[386]** unambiguous". Beyond that, they said, the argument that "a rule for the construction of legislation passed in the exercise of the legislative power" could be used "to limit the content of the legislative power itself" had "failed in *Polites* and in *Horta* and it should fail here".

Despite such reactions, Kirby J has remained unrepentant in his use of international law: see, for example, *Attorney-General (WA) v Marquet* (2003) 217 CLR 545 at 603-7; *Coleman v Power* (2004) 220 CLR 1 at 91-6 (compare Gleeson CJ at 27-30); *Baker v The Queen* (2004) 210 ALR 1 at 36-8; and *Re Minister for Immigration and Multicultural and Indigenous Affairs; Ex parte Ame* (2005) 218 ALR 483 at 517-19, where he draws support from the controversial opinion of the United States Supreme Court in *Roper v Simmons*, 543 US 551 (2005). Even where the international materials have proved to be of no assistance, or to offer no support for his conclusions, Kirby J has scrupulously considered their possible relevance. An example is *Re Colonel Aird; Ex parte Alpert* (2004) 220 CLR 308 (see Chapter 18, §5), where he said in part:

Re Colonel Aird; Ex parte Alpert
(2004) 220 CLR 308

Kirby J: [344] Some members of this Court have objected to this notion, believing it to be inconsistent with the history and function of the Constitution as a charter for national government. My own view is that the Constitution, like all other law in Australia, now operates in a context profoundly affected **[345]** by international law. Context is always a vital consideration in deriving legal rules.

In the twenty-first century, national final courts must accommodate the global context in which municipal law, including constitutional law, has its operation. The proliferation of international law, especially in the last three decades, demands of this Court recognition that "[w]e cannot have trade and commerce in world markets and international waters exclusively on our terms, governed by our laws, and resolved in our courts" [*The Bremen v Zapata Off-Shore Co*, 407 US 1 at 9 (1971)]. In giving meaning to the Australian Constitution, this Court is therefore inevitably influenced by conceptions of the world in which the Constitution operates and the application of the constitutions and laws of other nation states that impinge upon it.

Ignoring international law will sometimes result not only in chaos and futility. It will reduce the enlargement of the international rule of law, to which municipal, regional and international law together contribute. In particular, to be unconcerned about any relevant universal principle of international law, when giving meaning to an uncertain or ambiguous provision of a national constitution, is to "act on [a] blinkered view [and] to wield power divorced from responsibility" [*Semanza v Prosecutor, International Criminal Tribunal for Rwanda*, ICTR-97-20-A (Decision of 31 May 2000), Separate Opinion of Judge Shahabuddeen, para 25].

The decisions of national courts, in so far as they affect the operation of universal principles of international law, contribute to the content of public international law, as the Statute of the International Court of Justice recognises. In making such decisions …, municipal courts exercise a form of international jurisdiction. They should do so alert to any applicable rules of international law and so as to avoid, as far as they lawfully can, conflict with such rules. It makes little sense to acknowledge such obligations in connection with other municipal laws but to deny them when it comes to the national constitution. **[346]** Even the Supreme Court of the United States, long resistant to the use of international law in its constitutional decisions, has lately taken that law into account in constitutional elaboration [*Atkins v Virginia*, 536 US 304 at 316 (2002); *Lawrence v Texas*, 539 US 558 at 572-3 (2003)]. This Court should do likewise.

In 2004, the 4:3 division of the Court in *Al-Kateb v Godwin* (2004) 219 CLR 562 (see Chapter 15, §4) provoked a particularly sharp exchange between Kirby and McHugh JJ. The focus was on Kirby J's reliance on "the legal instruments that have declared the human rights and fundamental freedoms of humanity" since World War II.

Al-Kateb v Godwin
(2004) 219 CLR 562

McHugh J: [589] [C]ontrary to the view of Kirby J, courts cannot read the Constitution by reference to the provisions of international law that have become accepted since the Constitution was enacted in 1900. Rules of international law at that date might in some cases throw some light on the meaning of a constitutional provision. Interpretation of the term "aliens" by reference to the *jus soli* or *jus sanguinis* is an example. But rules of international law that have come into existence since 1900 are in a different category.

The claim that the Constitution should be read consistently with the rules of international law has been decisively rejected by members of this Court on several occasions. As a matter of constitutional doctrine, it must be regarded as heretical. In *Polites v The Commonwealth* [(1945) 70 CLR 60], the Court accepted that, so far as the language of a statute permits, it should be interpreted and applied in conformity with the established rules of international law. That is a rule of construction of long standing. The rationale for the rule is that the legislature is taken not to have intended to legislate in violation of the rules of international law **[590]** *existing* when the legislation was enacted. Accordingly, the law is construed as containing an implication to that effect. But, as *Polites* decided, the implication must give way where the words of the statute are inconsistent with the implication. No doubt the rule of construction had some validity when the rules of international law were few and well-known. Under modern conditions, however, this rule of construction is based on a fiction. Gone are the days when the rules of international law were to be found in the writings of a few well-known jurists.

Under Art 38 of the Statute of the International Court of Justice, international law includes: (1) international conventions establishing rules recognised by contesting states, (2) international custom, as evidence of a general practice accepted as law and (3) the general principles of law recognised by civilised nations. International custom may be based on:

"diplomatic correspondence, policy statements, press releases, the opinions of official legal advisers, official manuals on legal questions ... executive decisions and practices, orders to naval forces etc, comments by governments on drafts produced by the International Law Commission, state legislation, international and national judicial decisions, recitals in treaties and other international instruments, a pattern of treaties in the same form, the practice of international organs, and resolutions relating to legal questions in the United Nations General Assembly" [Ian Brownlie, *Principles of Public International Law* (Oxford University Press, 6 ed 2003), p 6].

Given the widespread nature of the sources of international law under modern conditions, it is impossible to believe that, when the Parliament now legislates, it has in mind or is even aware of all the rules of international law. Legislators intend their enactments to be given effect according to their natural and ordinary meaning. Most of them would be surprised to find that an enactment had a meaning inconsistent with the meaning they thought it had because of a rule of international law which they did not know and could not find without the assistance of a lawyer specialising in international law or, in the case of a treaty, by reference to the proceedings of the Joint Standing Committee on Treaties. In *Minister for Immigration and Ethnic Affairs v Teoh* [(1995) 183 CLR 273 at 316 (emphasis added)], counsel for the Minister told this Court that Australia was "a party to *about* 900 treaties". When one adds to the rules contained in those treaties, the general principles of law recognised by civilised nations and the rules derived from international custom, it becomes obvious that the rationale for the rule that a statute contains an **[591]** implication that it should be construed to conform with international law bears no relationship to the reality of the modern legislative process. Be that as it may, the rule of construction recognised in *Polites* ... is too well established to be repealed now by judicial decision.

However, this Court has never accepted that the Constitution contains an implication to the effect that it should be construed to conform with the rules of international law. The rationale for the rule and its operation is inapplicable to a Constitution – which is a source of, not an exercise of, legislative power. The rule, where applicable, operates as a statutory implication. But the legislature is not bound by the implication. It may legislate in disregard of it. If the rule *were* applicable to a Constitution, it would operate as a restraint on the grants of power conferred. The Parliament would not be able to legislate in disregard of the implication ...

[592] Most of the rules now recognised as rules of international law are of recent origin. If Australian courts interpreted the Constitution by reference to the rules of international law now in force, they would be *amending* the Constitution in disregard of the direction in s 128 of the Constitution. Section 128 declares that the Constitution is to be amended only by legislation that is approved by a majority of the States and "a majority of all the electors voting". Attempts to suggest that a rule of international law is merely a factor that can be taken into account in interpreting the Constitution cannot hide the fact that, if that is done, the meaning of the Constitution is changed whenever that rule changes what would otherwise be the result of the case. The point is so obvious that it hardly needs demonstration. But a simple example will suffice to show the true character of what is done if courts take a post-1900 rule of international law into account. Immediately before the rule was recognised, our Constitution had meanings that did not depend on that rule. Either the rule of international law has effect on one or more of those meanings or it has no effect. If it has an effect, its invocation has altered the meaning of the Constitution overnight. As a result, a court that took the rule into account has amended the Constitution without the authority of the people acting under s 128 of the Constitution. It has inserted a new rule into the Constitution ...

Many constitutional lawyers – probably the great majority of them – now accept that developments inside and outside Australia since 1900 may result in insights concerning the meaning of the Constitution that were not present to earlier generations. Because of those insights, **[593]** the Constitution may have different meanings from those perceived in earlier times ...

Failure to see the difference between taking into account political, social and economic developments since 1900 and taking into account the *rules* of international law is the error in the approach of those who assert that the Constitution must be read in conformity with or in so far as it can be read conformably with the rules of international law. Rules are specific. If they are taken into account as *rules*, they amend the Constitution. That conclusion cannot be avoided by asserting that they are simply "context" or elucidating factors. Rules are too specific to do no more than provide insights into the meanings of the constitutional provisions. Either the rule is already inherent in the meaning of the provision or taking it into account alters the meaning of the provision. No doubt from time to time the making or existence **[594]** of (say) a Convention or its consequences may constitute a general political, social or economic development that helps to elucidate the meaning of a constitutional head of power. But that is different from using the *rules* in that Convention to control the meaning of a constitutional head of power. Suppose the imposition of tariffs is banned under a World Trade Agreement. If that ban were taken into account – whether as context or otherwise – in interpreting the trade and commerce power, it would add a new rule to the Constitution. It would require reading the power to make laws with respect to trade and commerce as subject to the rule that it did not extend to laws that imposed tariffs. Such an approach, in the words of Dixon J, cannot be "countenanced" [70 CLR at 78] …

Eminent lawyers who have studied the question firmly believe that the Australian Constitution should contain a Bill of Rights which substantially adopts the rules found in the most important of the international human rights instruments. It is an enduring – and many would say a just – criticism of Australia that it is now one of the few countries in the Western world that does not have a Bill of Rights. But, desirable as a Bill of Rights may be, it is not to be inserted into our Constitution by judicial decisions drawing on international instruments that are not even part of the law of this country. It would be absurd to suggest that the meaning of a grant of power in s 51 of the Constitution can be elucidated by the enactments of the Parliament. Yet those who propose that the Constitution should **[595]** be read so as to conform with the rules of international law are forced to argue that rules contained in treaties made by the executive government are relevant in interpreting the Constitution. It is hard to accept, for example, that the meaning of the trade and commerce power can be affected by the Australian government entering into multilateral trade agreements. It is even more difficult to accept that the Constitution's meaning is affected by rules created by the agreements and practices of other countries. If that were the case, judges would have to have a "loose-leaf" copy of the Constitution. If Australia is to have a Bill of Rights, it must be done in the constitutional way – hard though its achievement may be – by persuading the people to amend the Constitution by inserting such a Bill.

Kirby J: [622] A majority of this Court may not yet have accepted the interpretive principle that I favour. However, in 1904, a majority did not accept the principle later upheld in *Amalgamated Society of Engineers v Adelaide Steamship Co Ltd* [(1920) 28 CLR 129] as a fundamental interpretive principle of the Constitution. It has been applied ever since. In 1921, a majority of this Court did not accept the interpretation of the structure of the Constitution (and of the requirements of Ch III) adopted in 1956 in *R v Kirby; Ex parte Boilermakers' Society of Australia* [(1956) 94 CLR 254]. In *Gould v Brown* [(1998) 193 CLR 346] a majority could not be found to strike down part of the State cross-vesting legislation. Following changes to the membership of the Court, **[623]** a majority was assembled little more than one year later in *Re Wakim; Ex parte McNally* [(1999) 198 CLR 511]. There are many similar cases.

The understanding of the Constitution in this Court is constantly evolving. The interpretive principle that I have expressed is but another step in the process of evolution.

With great respect to the opinion of Dixon J in *Polites v Commonwealth* (and to those who have later embraced that view) his Honour's notion of the influence of international law on the interpretation of the Australian Constitution can scarcely be treated as the last word. In 1945, when *Polites* was decided, the Australian Constitution was commonly regarded as little more than a statute of the United Kingdom Parliament, binding in Australia for that reason. In most cases – including many constitutional cases – the decisions of this Court were subject to appeal to the Privy Council. Notions of national independence and distinctive legal thinking in Australia were tamed by these realities. Because of entirely new realities today our thinking is necessarily different.

In 1945, the international community was quite different. The Crown of the United Kingdom was still sovereign over a fifth of humanity. Many colonial empires survived. Government by representative democracy and the rule of law were the exception. The global economy was primitive when compared with today. Integrating technology was quite limited. The United Nations had not yet been formed when the decision in *Polites* was handed down in April 1945. The institutions of the world community had not yet been created. The legal instruments that have declared the human rights and fundamental freedoms of humanity had not yet been adopted. In these circumstances, to have expected even so great a judge as Dixon J to foresee the legal expressions of human rights and fundamental freedoms, founded in the notions of human dignity and the principle of justice recognised in the Charter of the United Nations and to appreciate their impact on our Constitution, is to expect too much. He, and our other predecessors, are excused for not foreseeing these developments. Contemporary judges are not excused for ignoring them.

McHugh J objects to the use of the "rules" of international law to inform the interpretive principle that I favour. "Rules" is a word I have not used, preferring as I do "principles" or "basic principles". McHugh J accepts that phenomena other than international law can **[624]** "result in insights concerning the meaning of the Constitution that were not present to earlier generations". Once this concession is made, the difference between McHugh J and myself is narrowed. International law, including as it declares universal human rights and fundamental freedoms, exists in the form of "rules" and discourse. This is the tangible manifestation. "[P]olitical, social or economic developments", which McHugh J accepts *can* throw light on the meaning of the Constitution, generally appear in other forms. But if they can have their influence in the form in which they exist, so can the "rules" of international law in the form in which they manifest themselves. They do not *bind* as other "rules" do. But the principles they express can *influence* legal understanding …

Whatever may have been possible in the world of 1945, the complete isolation of constitutional law from the dynamic impact of international law is neither possible nor desirable today. That is why national courts, and especially national constitutional courts such as this, have a duty, so far as possible, to interpret their constitutional texts in a way that is generally harmonious with the basic principles of international law, including as that law states human rights and fundamental freedoms.

In practice, this development presents no significant difficulty for a legal system such as Australia's. In part, this is because of the profound influence on the most basic statements of international law (and specifically of the law of human rights and fundamental freedoms) of Anglo-American lawyers and the concepts that they derived from the common law. In part, it is because such rights and freedoms express the common rights of all humanity. They pre-existed their formal expression.

[625] *Consistency with s 128 of the Constitution*: Nor, contrary to the opinion of McHugh J, is the interpretive principle that I favour inconsistent with the provisions of s 128 of the Constitution governing its formal amendment. If this argument were valid, it would apply equally to other decisions of this Court in which the Court has given new meaning to the constitutional text and expounded new rights and duties.

The Constitution provides [for both] formal amendment and judicial reinterpretation. From the earliest days of federation both means of adjustment and change have been followed, to the advantage of the Commonwealth and its people. It is idle to suggest otherwise. This Court has played its role in adapting the Constitution to changing times where that was proper and compatible with the constitutional text and legal principle. The developments of international law since 1945 represent no more than another change requiring adaptation.

Courts declaring new rights: It is true that, consistently with the Constitution, it is not part of the judicial function to insert a comprehensive Bill of Rights into the Constitution. Nor may the judiciary "by the back door" incorporate an international treaty (even one ratified by Australia) as part of Australian law where the Parliament has not done so by legislation. Whether a Bill of Rights should be adopted in Australia by legislation, constitutional amendment or at all, is a political question. The limits inherent in the interpretive principle favouring consistency with the principles of international law, specifically the international law of human rights and fundamental freedoms, must be observed by the courts. Where the Constitution or a valid national law are clear, the duty of a court, which derives its power and authority from the Constitution, is to give effect to the law's requirements. As such, international law is not part of, nor superior to, our constitutional or statute law. Unless incorporated, it is not part of our municipal law.

Nevertheless it is incorrect, with respect, to say that Australian courts, including this Court, have no function in finding "rights" in the text of the Constitution. Some of this Court's decisions, declaring what are in effect "rights", would have been regarded by the founders as astonishing. In deriving a number of them, McHugh J has played a notable part [Kirby J referred in a footnote to *Kable v Director of Public Prosecutions (NSW)* (1996) 189 CLR 51, *Lange v Australian Broadcasting Corporation* (1997) 189 CLR 520, and *Austin v Commonwealth* (2003) 215 CLR 185. He added that "A non-constitutional case of the same character is *Mabo v Queensland (No 2)* (1992) 175 CLR 1 at 15-16."]. Thus, the courts in Australia are also law-makers; **[626]** but in a confined and restricted way acting in accordance with the Constitution and established legal principle.

I do not agree with McHugh J that the content of the trade and commerce power, expressed in the Constitution, is unaffected by the great changes that have occurred in global trade since 1901; nor influenced by multilateral, regional and bilateral agreements in which Australia has participated. With respect, to suggest that, were it otherwise, judges would need a "loose-leaf" copy of the Constitution trivialises a serious question.

If the defence power expands and contracts, as it does, by reference to the needs of war and a state of profound peace, so it is with the trade and commerce power and every other federal head of power in the Australian constitutional list. In the case of most powers, the differences may not always be so noticeable or profound as in cases concerning the defence power. However, in terms of constitutional principle, the concept must be the same.

In any event, constitutional lawyers do indeed have "loose-leaf" copies of the Constitution in which the text is elaborated by the decisions of this and other courts, and which refer to contextual, historical and other materials essential to the evolving understanding of what the Constitution means and how it operates. I have simply indicated the need, in the present age, to add a reference to one of the most important legal developments that is occurring and to which national constitutions must adapt, namely the growing role of international law, including the law relating to human rights and fundamental freedoms.

The approach of other countries: The constitutional courts of many other countries now adopt the interpretive approach that I favour. They reject the approach that McHugh J supports in this case. It is true that in some cases, the new process of reasoning has been stimulated by express constitutional provisions requiring that regard be had to the **[627]** provisions of international law. This is so, for example, under the new Constitution of the Republic of South Africa. However, the Constitutional Court of South Africa has said that, even if such an express provision did not exist in the text, international law would necessarily have been considered where it was relevant.

It is also true that in some cases, the references to the developing jurisprudence of international and regional courts and other bodies have been stimulated by the existence of human rights provisions in the national constitution expressed in terms similar to the international and regional statements of human rights and fundamental freedoms. This is not a significant consideration in the Australian context. However, the willingness of national constitutional courts to look outside their own domestic legal traditions to the elaboration of international, regional and other bodies represents a paradigm shift that has happened in municipal law in recent years. There are many illustrations in the decisions of the courts of, for example, Canada, Germany, India, New Zealand, the United Kingdom and the United States ...

[629] Therefore, with every respect to those of a contrary view, opinions that seek to cut off contemporary Australian law (including constitutional law) from the persuasive force of international law are doomed to fail. They will be seen in the future much as the reasoning of Taney CJ in *Dred Scott v Sandford* [60 US 393 (1857)], Black J in *Korematsu* [*v United States* 323 US 214 (1944)] and Starke J in *Ex parte Walsh* [[1942] ALR 359 at 360] are now viewed: with a mixture of curiosity and embarrassment. The dissents of McLean J and Curtis J in *Dred Scott* strongly invoked international law to support the proposition that the appellant was not a slave but a free man. Had the interpretive principle prevailed at that time, the United States Supreme Court might have been saved a serious error of constitutional reasoning; and much injustice, indifference to human indignity and later suffering might have been avoided. The fact is that it is often helpful for national judges to check their own constitutional thinking against principles expressing the rules of a "wider civilization".

My conclusion is no more a judicial attempt to "amend[ ] the Constitution under the guise of interpretation" than were the many decisions of this Court, in which McHugh J participated, where the process of interpretation produced a significant change to earlier **[630]** understandings of that document. If one new interpretation is forbidden, so are others. We should not declare interpretations impermissible just because we do not agree with them. As McHugh J has written elsewhere [*News Ltd v South Sydney District Rugby League Football Club Ltd* (2003) 215 CLR 563 at 580]:

> "Questions of construction are notorious for generating opposing answers, none of which can be said to be either clearly right or clearly wrong."

These words apply equally to constitutional construction.

3. External Affairs

(a)   Relations with Other Countries

Although in *Australian Communist Party v Commonwealth* (*Communist Party Case*) (1951) 83 CLR 1 the High Court refused to allow the Commonwealth to abolish the Australian Communist Party (see Chapter 18, §6), there were earlier cases after World War II in which the Court upheld prosecutions of communists for sedition. One such case was *Burns v Ransley* (1949) 79 CLR 101; another was *R v Sharkey* (1949) 79 CLR 121. Section 24A of the *Crimes Act 1914* (Cth) defined "seditious intention" to include an intention "to excite disaffection against the Government or Constitution of any of the King's Dominions". In *R v Sharkey*, the High Court held that this was valid as a law with respect to "external affairs".

R v Sharkey
(1949) 79 CLR 121

Latham CJ: [136] The Commonwealth of Australia is a political organization which is associated with other Dominions by political conventions which are recognized both by the King's Dominions and internationally. The relations of the Commonwealth with all countries outside Australia, including other Dominions of the Crown, are matters which fall directly within the subject of external affairs ... The preservation of friendly **[137]** relations with other Dominions is an important part of the management of the external affairs of the Commonwealth. The prevention and punishment of the excitement of disaffection within the Commonwealth against the Government or Constitution of any other Dominion may reasonably be thought by Parliament to constitute an element in the preservation of friendly relations with other Dominions.

The emphasis in *R v Sharkey* on relations with other British Dominions reflects a common judicial hypothesis advanced, for example, by Evatt and McTiernan JJ in *R v Burgess; Ex parte Henry* (1936) 55 CLR 608 at 684-5; Barwick CJ in *New South Wales v Commonwealth* (*Seas and Submerged Lands Case*) (1975) 135 CLR 337 at 360; and the joint judgment in *Victoria v Commonwealth* (*Industrial Relations Act Case*) (1996) 187 CLR 416 at 482. This is that the term "external affairs", rather than "foreign affairs", was chosen to make it clear that the power was meant to extend to relations with the United Kingdom and other parts of the British Empire. The United Kingdom and its possessions were not, in 1901, conceived of as "foreign" to Australia. "Foreign relations" were conducted by the British government on behalf of the whole British Empire. From that Imperial point of view, internal relations within the Empire were domestic, not "foreign", affairs. Australia's intra-Imperial relations were, however, "external" to Australia. Thus, relationships with Britain were "external affairs" even though they would not then have been regarded as "foreign affairs" (compare today *Sue v Hill* (1999) 199 CLR 462 in Chapter 4, §8).

What Latham CJ said in *R v Sharkey* was not confined to the "**[136]** preservation of friendly **[137]** relations with other Dominions", but extended to relations with "**[136]** all countries outside Australia". Brennan J in *Koowarta v Bjelke-Petersen* (1982) 153 CLR 168 extended this to relations with other "international persons", including the whole contemporary range of international organisations, and especially the United Nations and its various agencies.

The judges in the *Seas and Submerged Lands Case* differed as to whether the "external affairs" power entitled the Commonwealth to assert its sovereignty over Australia's territorial sea, though a majority held that it did. They differed also in the extent to which they relied on the 1958 Geneva Conventions on the law of the sea in resolving this issue. Only McTiernan J based his judgment solely on the Geneva Conventions, while only Jacobs J refused to rely on them at all. However, all seven judges agreed that assertion of sovereignty over Australia's continental shelf was valid. The underlying reason for this was that the whole idea of the "continental shelf", and of national rights in respect thereof, had emerged since World War II distinctly as a product of international relations and international law. Australia's rights to that part of the submarine land mass therefore necessarily arose in the context of "external affairs".

New South Wales v Commonwealth (Seas and Submerged Lands Case)
(1975) 135 CLR 337

Stephen J: [449] It is international intercourse between nation states which is the substance of a nation's external affairs. Treaties and conventions to which a nation may become a part form, no doubt, **[450]** an important part of those affairs, but "external affairs" will also include matters which are not consensual in character; conduct on the part of a nation, or of its nationals, which affects other nations and its relations with them are external affairs of that nation, for instance, conduct in "violation of international comity", *R v Burgess; Ex parte Henry* [(1936) 55 CLR 608 at 669], per Dixon J; thus s 51(xxix) has been held to justify a law making it an offence to excite disaffection within Australia against the government or constitution of any of the King's Dominions: *R v Sharkey* [(1947) 79 CLR 121]. I would not think that it is essential to validity that such a law be restricted to the protection of good relations within the King's Dominions.

(b)   Matters External to Australia

According to Barwick CJ in the *Seas and Submerged Lands Case*, the external affairs power extends to anything "**[360]** which in its nature is external to ... Australia", or according to Mason J "**[471]** to matters or things geographically situated outside Australia". These suggestions were reinforced in later cases, and finally assumed decisive importance in *Polyukhovich v Commonwealth* (*War Crimes Act Case*) (1991) 172 CLR 501. The issue was whether, in 1988, the Commonwealth Parliament could legislate to identify as "war crimes" certain crimes committed in Europe during World War II, and to provide for the trial, in present-day Australia, of persons now Australian citizens or residents who might have committed such crimes. All judges other than Brennan J held that s 51(xxix) contained a sufficient grant of power to support such a law. Mason CJ, Deane, Dawson and McHugh JJ held that this conclusion could be based on the bare fact that the geographical location in which the relevant acts were alleged to have been done was physically external to Australia.

Polyukhovich v Commonwealth (War Crimes Act Case)
(1991) 172 CLR 501

Deane J: [602] Whatever may have been the position before the emergence of Australia as a fully independent sovereign State, it should now be accepted that any law which can properly be characterized as a law with respect to any matter, thing or person occurring or situate outside Australia is a law with respect to "External affairs" for the purposes of s 51(xxix) ... [That conclusion is] supported by the consideration that Commonwealth laws with respect to matters, things or persons outside Australia are likely to operate in areas where there will commonly be no competing State interests with the result that, in the absence of Commonwealth legislative power, there would be a lacuna in the plenitude of combined legislative powers of the various Parliaments of the Australian federation. It has long been **[603]** recognized in this Court that, subject to express and implied constitutional limitations and guarantees, no such lacuna exists in legislative authority in relation to internal matters: see, eg, *Colonial Sugar Refining Co Ltd v Attorney-General (Cth)* [(1912) 15 CLR 182 at 214-15]; *Smith v Oldham* [(1912) 15 CLR 355 at 360-1, 365]; *R v Duncan;*

Ex parte Australian Iron and Steel Pty Ltd [(1983) 158 CLR 535 at 590-1]. With the emergence of Australia as a fully sovereign and independent nation, there remains no acceptable basis for maintaining any such lacuna in the combined powers of the Parliaments of the federation to legislate for this country with respect to extraterritorial matters beyond that resulting from the limitations which the Constitution itself expressly or impliedly imposes ...

To the extent that they provide for the trial and punishment of Australian citizens and residents for acts committed outside Australia and having a specified relationship with the 1939-1945 war or armed conflict which occurred in Europe, the provisions of the Act are clearly a law or laws with respect to matters or things which occurred or were done outside Australia. It follows from what has been said above that, at least to that extent, the Act is a law with respect to "External affairs" within the meaning of that phrase as used in s 51(xxix).

Brennan J rejected this approach. When legislation implementing a treaty has its operation wholly inside Australia, critics are wont to ask: "What's international about it?" Confronted in *Polyukhovich* with legislation attaching legal consequences to events and actions that had taken place wholly outside Australia, Brennan J posed a neat inversion of the question. He asked: "What's Australian about it?"

Brennan J: [550] [I]t is argued that, although there must be some connexion between the extraterritorial operation of a State law and the extraterritorial persons, things or events on which a State law operates (*Port MacDonnell Professional Fishermen's Association Inc v South Australia* [(1989) 168 CLR 340 at 372]), no such connexion is required in the case of a Commonwealth law. If such a connexion were required, so the argument runs, there would be a lacuna in the plenitude of legislative powers which the Australian legislatures, Commonwealth and State, together possess ...: see per Jacobs J in the *Seas and Submerged Lands Case* [(1975) 135 CLR 337 at 497]. But the powers conferred by the Constitution are not to be expanded beyond their true scope merely to supply what is thought, from the public viewpoint, to be a desirable or convenient power. Limits on power are the measure of private immunity from legislative action by the State. The legislative powers of the Parliament are limited by the terms of the Constitution, and the connotation of the phrase "external affairs" must be ascertained from its context and purpose. Accepting fully that s 51(xxix) is not to be narrowly construed (*Commonwealth v Tasmania* (the *Tasmanian Dam Case*) [158 CLR at 220-1]), nevertheless the power thereby conferred is limited ... I do not understand the phrase "external affairs" to sweep into Commonwealth power every person who exists or every relationship, set of circumstances or field of activity which exists or occurs outside Australian territory. The "affairs" which are the subject matter of the power are, in my view, **[551]** the external affairs of Australia; not affairs which have nothing to do with Australia. Although affairs which exist or occur outside Australia may be described as "external" in a geographical sense, I would not hold that the Constitution confers power to enact laws affecting affairs which, though geographically external, have nothing to do with Australia. There must be some nexus, not necessarily substantial, between Australia and the "external affairs" which a law purports to affect before the law is supported by s 51(xxix) ...

[552] It is, of course, for the Parliament to determine in the first instance whether there is any connexion between Australia and a relationship, set of circumstances or field of activity which exists or occurs outside Australia and which a proposed law would purportedly affect, but, if the legislative judgment cannot reasonably be supported, the law will be held to be outside the power conferred by s 51(xxix): see *Richardson* [*v Forestry Commission* (1988) 164 CLR 261 at 296]; *Gerhardy v Brown* [(1985) 159 CLR 70 at 139]. It leaves no great lacuna in the plenitude of Australian legislative power to deny the character of a law with respect to external affairs to a law which does no more than affect something or somebody unconnected with Australia occurring or existing outside Australia. To take an extreme example: would a law be properly characterized as a law with respect to external affairs if it imposed a criminal penalty on a person who, being a citizen and resident of France, had dropped litter in a Parisian street forty years ago? The limits of the power conferred by s 51(xxix) are, in a real sense, a guarantee of the immunity from harassment by Australian law of persons who, having no connexion with Australia, engage in conduct elsewhere which does not affect Australian interests or concerns.

Brennan J did not accept as a sufficient "Australian connexion" the fact that the legislation was limited to prosecution of persons who were now Australian residents or citizens. However, Toohey J, while agreeing with Brennan J on the need for some "Australian connexion" if events in Europe were to qualify as an "external affair", found a sufficient connexion in the mere fact of Australia's involvement as a belligerent in World War II. Gaudron J agreed with Brennan J that externally located "external affairs" must have an element of Australian interest or concern, but she also agreed with Mason CJ that Parliament's decision to legislate showed conclusively that this element was present. Mason CJ had explicitly rejected any suggestion that the Court should satisfy itself of Australia's interest or concern in the issue: "[530] It is enough that Parliament's judgment is that Australia has an interest or concern. It is inconceivable that the Court could overrule Parliament's decision [531] on that question".

In *Polyukhovich*, Mason CJ, Deane, Dawson and McHugh JJ all seemed to indicate that mere externality, with no "Australian connexion", is sufficient to enliven the external affairs power. However, *Horta v Commonwealth* (1994) 181 CLR 183 was strangely inconclusive on the point. On the one hand, the reason for the decision was once again that a valid exercise of the external affairs power was sufficiently demonstrated by the mere fact of geographical "externality". On the other hand, the joint judgment seemed at pains to leave open the question of whether some additional element, beyond mere "externality", is needed.

Horta involved a challenge to legislation passed pursuant to a 1989 bilateral treaty between Australia and Indonesia for the joint exploitation of petroleum resources in the Timor Gap. The Timor Gap was an area claimed by both nations as part of the continental shelf but not within the territorial waters of either. Ultimately, the plaintiffs hoped to challenge the validity, under international law, of Indonesia's assertion of sovereignty over East Timor. On that basis, it was argued that the 1989 treaty was void in international law, and so could not validly be implemented under s 51(xxix). Clearly, the High Court was anxious to avoid these difficult and politically sensitive questions, and in particular to avoid a situation in which a municipal court (that is, one operating within a national legal system) might be called upon to judge the legality of treaty activity under international law. The holding that the relevant areas of the seabed were geographically "external" to Australia, and that this was enough to support the validity of the legislation, enabled the Court to dispose of the litigation in short order.

Horta v Commonwealth
(1994) 181 CLR 183

The Court: [194] Regardless of whether the mere fact that a matter or thing is territorially outside Australia is of itself sufficient to bring a matter or thing within the phrase "External affairs" for the purposes of s 51(xxix) or whether one or other of those additional factors is necessary, it is clear that the area of the Timor Gap and the exploration for, and the exploitation of, petroleum resources within that area all fall within that phrase. Each of those matters is geographically external to Australia. There is an obvious and substantial nexus between each of them and Australia. As the enactment of the Act demonstrates, they are all matters which the Parliament recognizes as affecting or touching Australia. That being so, the enactment of a law with respect to one or all of those matters is prima facie within the legislative power conferred by s 51(xxix) …

There can be circumstances in which a law which is prima facie within the legislative power conferred by s 51(xxix) is nonetheless outside the legislative powers of the Parliament by reason of some [195] other provision of the Constitution, express or implied, to which the legislative power conferred by s 51(xxix) is subject. However, no such circumstances exist in the present case. It was submitted on behalf of the plaintiffs that the enactment of the two Acts would be beyond the legislative power conferred by s 51(xxix) if the Treaty were void under international law either on the ground that it was contrary to international law or on the ground that Australia's entry into or performance of it would be in breach of Australia's obligations under international law. There is, however, a short answer to that submission. That answer is that even if the Treaty were void or unlawful under international law or if Australia's entry into or performance of the Treaty involved a breach of Australia's obligations under international law, the Act and the Consequential Act would not thereby be deprived of their character as laws with respect to "External affairs" for the purposes of s 51(xxix). Neither s 51(xxix) itself nor any other provision of the Constitution confines the legislative power with respect to "External affairs" to the enactment of laws which are consistent with, or which relate to treaties or matters which are consistent with, the requirements of international law. In particular, there is simply no basis either in s 51(xxix) or in any other provision of the Constitution for the plaintiffs' submission that the legislative power conferred by s 51(xxix) must be confined within the limits of "Australia's legislative competence as recognized by international law".

The actual holding in *Horta* would tend to support the view that mere externality is enough. That view was reaffirmed by the joint judgment of Brennan CJ, Toohey, Gaudron, McHugh and Gummow JJ in *Victoria v Commonwealth* (*Industrial Relations Act Case*) (1996) 187 CLR 416. They quoted what Dawson J had said in *Polyukhovich*, and added citations to "**[485]** [s]imilar statements" in *Polyukhovich* by Mason CJ, Deane, Gaudron and McHugh JJ before concluding that these statements "must now be taken as representing the view of the court". The issue therefore appears to be settled. However, Kirby J warned in *Re Patterson; Ex parte Taylor* (2001) 207 CLR 391 that geographical externality cannot be used as a basis for "**[497]** [s]elf-fulfilling prophesies": one could not, for example, determine an issue of whether the expulsion of aliens fell within s 51(xxix) by expelling them to a foreign destination and then arguing that the power applied because the destination was foreign.

(c)   International Law

Polyukhovich also shed light on the ways in which international law, through the operation of treaties and otherwise, can attract the "external affairs" power. Apart from the "externality" ground, the Commonwealth's argument in *Polyukhovich* had sought to bring the *War Crimes Amendment Act* within the "external affairs" power on several other grounds.

Since only Brennan J had rejected the "externality" ground, he was the only judge for whom it was necessary to consider the Commonwealth's alternative arguments, although Toohey J also did so. Central to the reasoning of Brennan J in rejecting these other arguments was his view that the intricate statutory definition of "war crimes" did not faithfully adhere to the definition of "war crimes" under international law, and certainly not under international law as it was at the time of the alleged offences during World War II.

Brennan J reviewed a number of arguments – for example, that s 51(xxix) applied because the prosecution of war crimes was "**[558]** a matter for serious international concern", or because the legislation was a response to "**[591]** resolutions and recommendations of the United Nations General Assembly" and other international bodies, or because international law recognises a "universal jurisdiction" to prosecute the perpetrators of international crime. This last proposition was illustrated by the old concept of "piracy *iure gentium*", that is, the idea that a pirate can be tried and convicted by any nation because the act of piracy is contrary to the law of nations. The "universal jurisdiction" to prosecute war criminals is the modern equivalent of this. The point is not that nations are obliged to exercise this "universal jurisdiction", nor even that the international community is concerned that it be exercised, but simply that every nation is entitled, or at liberty, to do so and that, by asserting this jurisdiction, Australia was simply availing itself of a "right" or facility extended to it by international law.

Polyukhovich v Commonwealth (*War Crimes Act Case*)
(1991) 172 CLR 501

Brennan J: [562] Although the terminology which equates universal jurisdiction with a right might be open to question, I would hold that a law which vested in an Australian court a jurisdiction recognized by [563] international law as a universal jurisdiction is a law with respect to Australia's external affairs. Australia's international personality would be incomplete if it were unable to exercise a jurisdiction to try and to punish offenders against the law of nations whose crimes are such that their subjection to universal jurisdiction is conducive to international peace and order. As the material drawn from international agreements and UNGA [United Nations General Assembly] resolutions acknowledges, international law recognises a State to have universal jurisdiction to try suspected war criminals whether or not that State is under an obligation to do so and whether or not there is any international concern that the State should do so.

However, the claim to be exercising "universal jurisdiction" could only be valid if the prosecution was for an international crime as defined by international law. For Brennan J, the "[589] disconformity" of the legislation to international law was fatal to the Commonwealth's arguments, whether based on "universal jurisdiction" or otherwise.

Toohey J generally agreed with Brennan J on these issues. However, as to the exercise of "universal jurisdiction", he held that, despite the artificiality and difficulty of the legislation, it did sufficiently evince an intention to conform to international law. For him, therefore, the Act came within s 51(xxix) on this ground, as well as on the ground of "externality".

4. Implementing Treaties

(a)   First Approaches

By far the most controversial question concerning s 51(xxix) has been the extent to which Commonwealth power is triggered by the existence of international treaties or conventions to which Australia is a party. The focus is on the extent to which obligations imposed on Australia as a party to such treaties can be carried out under s 51(xxix) by legislation implementing the treaty provisions within Australia.

The view that s 51(xxix) authorises laws within Australia to implement the provisions of an international treaty has been expressed since the earliest years of federation. In *Victoria v Commonwealth* (*Industrial Relations Act Case*) (1996) 187 CLR 416, the joint judgment quoted statements to that effect by Barton J in *McKelvey v Meagher* (1906) 4 CLR 265 at 286 and by Alfred Deakin as Attorney-General in 1902. However, the first clear judicial use of that view as a basis for decision was by Higgins J in *Roche v Kronheimer* (1921) 29 CLR 329. In that case the Court upheld the validity of the *Treaty of Peace Act 1919* (Cth), which implemented within Australia the provisions of the Treaty of Peace signed at Versailles after World War I. Most members of the Court relied on the "defence" power, but Higgins J reached the same conclusion based upon the "external affairs" power.

The decisive step was taken in *R v Burgess; Ex parte Henry* (1936) 55 CLR 608. The High Court held that the *Air Navigation Act 1920* (Cth) was not supported by the trade and commerce power (s 51(i) – see Chapter 16, §6), but was valid insofar as it authorised the making of regulations "for the purpose of carrying out and giving effect to" the International Convention for the Regulation of Aerial Navigation signed at Paris in 1919. The actual regulations were held invalid because they did not adhere sufficiently to the Convention.

Latham CJ, Evatt and McTiernan JJ all spoke of the legislative implementation of treaties as valid under s 51(xxix) in quite unqualified terms. Evatt and McTiernan JJ went further than Latham CJ in arguing that, even in the absence of a binding obligation, the power would extend to implementation within Australia of recommendations of the International Labour Organization. Despite some peripheral comments on that question in the *Industrial Relations Act Case*, the precise effect of "recommendations" must still be regarded as open.

R v Burgess; Ex parte Henry
(1936) 55 CLR 608

Evatt and McTiernan JJ: [679] The main argument advanced in denial of the competence of the Commonwealth Parliament to authorize the making of regulations to secure the execution of the Aerial Navigation Convention, was that a perusal of the convention shows that there is nothing "outside" Australia, but only matters, things and persons "within" Australia, which are to be regulated by the Governor-General, and that the inevitable result is to invade the domestic jurisdiction of the States ...

At a much earlier point of time Professor *Harrison Moore* argued that the existence of an international convention did not, of itself, bring the subject matter of the convention within the Commonwealth's legislative jurisdiction over "external affairs." He said:– "The power to give effect to international arrangements must, it would seem, be limited to matters which *in se* concern external relations; a matter in itself purely domestic, and therefore within the exclusive power of the States, cannot be drawn within the range of Federal power merely because some arrangement has been made for uniform national action. Thus, there is at the present time an international movement for the amelioration of labour conditions, and the International Union has arrived at some agreements for uniformity of legislation. It is submitted that the Commonwealth could not by adhering to an international agreement for the regulation of factories and workshops, proceed to legislate upon that subject in supersession of the laws of the States" (*Harrison Moore*: *Commonwealth of Australia*, 2nd ed (1910), pp 461, 462).

[680] It will be noticed that *Harrison Moore's* comment was made at a time when it was not fully appreciated that the Commonwealth's powers under secs 51 and 52 of the Constitution must first be recognized and interpreted *before* it is possible to determine the extent of "the exclusive power of the States." In this respect the Commonwealth Constitution differs essentially from that of Canada (*Huddart Parker Ltd v Commonwealth* [(1931) 44 CLR 492 at 526-8]). That this is the proper method of approach to the construction of the Constitution was recognized in portion of the judgment in the much discussed *Engineers' Case* [(1920) 28 CLR 129]. Accordingly it is wrong to prejudice the examination of the content of the subject "external affairs" by assuming or asserting in advance that there are certain matters such as conditions and terms of employment which are necessarily excluded from Commonwealth legislation in exercise of the power ...

[681] In relation to the Commonwealth Constitution very much the same argument as was presented by *Harrison Moore* in 1910 in relation to the "external affairs" power is repeated by those who contend that under art 405 of the Treaty of Versailles, Australia is "a federal State, the power of which to enter into conventions on labour matters is subject to limitations." It is true that such subject matters as air navigation, the manufacture of munitions, the suppression of the drug traffic and standard hours of work in industry are not made express or separate subject matters of Commonwealth legislative power. But there is, in our view, an undoubted capacity in His Majesty to enter into international conventions dealing with any of these subject matters and necessarily binding upon and in respect of the Commonwealth. In truth, the King's power to enter into international conventions cannot be limited in advance of the international situations which may from time to time arise. And in our view the fact of an international convention having been duly made about a subject brings that subject within the field of international relations so far as such subject is dealt with by the agreement. Accordingly (to pursue the illustration) Australia is not **[682]** "a federal State the power of which to enter into conventions on labour matters is subject to limitations." ...

[687] It would seem clear, therefore, that the legislative power of the Commonwealth over "external affairs" certainly includes the power to execute within the Commonwealth treaties and conventions entered into with foreign powers. The legislative power in sec 51 is granted "subject to this Constitution" so that such treaties and conventions could not be used to enable the Parliament to set at nought constitutional guarantees elsewhere contained, such, for instance, as secs 6, 28, 41, 80, 92, 99, 100, 116, or 117. But it is not to be assumed that the legislative power over "external affairs" is limited to the execution of treaties or conventions; and, to pursue the illustration previously referred to, the Parliament may well be deemed competent to legislate for the carrying out of "recommendations" as well as the "draft international conventions" resolved upon by the

International Labour Organization or of other international recommendations or requests upon other subject matters of concern to Australia as a member of the family of nations. The power is a great and important one. Having regard to the statement of the Privy Council in *British Coal Corporation v The King* [[1935] AC 500 at 518], recently repeated in *James' Case* [[1936] AC 578], it would not be in accordance with established canons of construction to attempt to assign precise limits to its content ... No suggestion has been made that the entry into the convention was merely a device to procure for the Commonwealth an additional domestic jurisdiction and that suggestion could easily be refuted by referring to the setting up under chapter VIII of the Convention of the Permanent International Commission for Air Navigation.

Starke and Dixon JJ both speculated as to possible limitations on the power.

Starke J: [658] The Commonwealth cannot do what the Constitution forbids. But otherwise the power is comprehensive in terms and must be commensurate with the obligations that the Commonwealth may properly assume in its relations with other Powers or States. It is impossible, I think, to define more accurately, at the present time, the precise limits of the power. It may be, as *Willoughby* suggests in connection with the treaty-making power in the Constitution of the United States, that the laws will be within power only if the matter is "of sufficient international significance to make it a legitimate subject for international co-operation and agreement" (*Willoughby on The Constitutional Law of the United States*, 2nd ed (1929), p 519).

Dixon J: [669] If a treaty were made which bound the Commonwealth in reference to some matter indisputably international in character, a law might be made to secure observance of its obligations if they were of a nature affecting the conduct of Australian citizens. On the other hand, it seems an extreme view that merely because the Executive Government undertakes with some other country that the conduct of persons in Australia shall be regulated in a particular way, the legislature thereby obtains a power to enact that regulation although it relates to a matter of internal concern which, apart from the obligation undertaken by the Executive, could not be considered as a matter of external affairs. The limits of the power can only be ascertained authoritatively by a course of decision in which the application of general statements is illustrated by example.

R v Burgess established that the implementation within Australia of some international treaties was valid. The possible limitation suggested by Starke J (to matters "**[658]** of sufficient international significance" to be "a legitimate subject for international co-operation and agreement") did not need to be resolved since, even if this test applied, the subject of international air navigation clearly satisfied it. The same applied to the possible limitation suggested by Dixon J (to matters "**[669]** indisputably international in character"). Equally, insofar as the reasoning of Latham CJ, Evatt and McTiernan JJ extended beyond these limits, it was wider than was necessary for the actual decision.

Despite the scope given to the power, the regulations made under the *Air Navigation Act* were held invalid as they were not sufficiently tailored to the provisions of the Convention. The idea was that, since Commonwealth power arises from the purpose of implementing a convention, the resulting legislation must be confined to that purpose in order to be valid.

Evatt and McTiernan JJ: [687] [I]t is a necessary corollary of our analysis of the constitutional power of Parliament to secure the performance of an international **[688]** convention that the particular laws or regulations which are passed by the Commonwealth should be in conformity with the convention which they profess to be executing. In other words, it must be possible to assert of any law which is, *ex hypothesi*, passed solely in pursuance of this head of the "external affairs" power, that it represents the fulfilment, so far as that is possible in the case of laws operating locally, of all the obligations assumed under the convention. Any departure from such a requirement would be completely destructive of the general scheme of the Commonwealth Constitution, for, as we are assuming for the moment, it is only because, and precisely so far as, the Commonwealth statute or regulations represent the carrying into local operation of the relevant portion of the international convention, that the Commonwealth Parliament or Executive can deal at all with the subject matters of the convention. Doubtless this requirement does not necessarily preclude the exercise of wide powers and discretions by the Parliament or the Executive of the Commonwealth, for the international convention may itself contemplate that such powers and discretions should be exercisable by the appropriate authority of each party to the convention. Everything must depend upon the terms of the convention, and upon the rights and duties it confers and imposes. But the general requirement must be fulfilled or the Commonwealth will be exceeding its lawful domain.

Starke J dissented on whether the regulations were valid. He reaffirmed the legitimacy of a broad choice of legislative means.

Starke J: [659] The power is wide in terms, but its limits cannot be transcended. All means which **[660]** are appropriate, and are adopted to the enforcement of the convention and are not prohibited, or are not repugnant to or inconsistent with it, are within the power. The power must be construed liberally, and much must necessarily be left to the discretion of the contracting States in framing legislation, or otherwise giving effect to the convention. For instance, general safety and other regulations may be necessary for supplementing the convention, and probably exemptions are legitimate where it appears unnecessary or undesirable that the provisions of the convention should apply … A construction of the power that enables a ready application of the convention to various circumstances and conditions is preferable to one that insists upon an inflexible and rigid adherence to the stipulations of the convention. After all, we should remember that the power is conferred for the purpose of carrying out an international and not a mere local agreement.

After *R v Burgess*, new regulations were made under the *Air Navigation Act*. They laid down rules for the use of "aerodynes", that is, aerodynamic aircraft. By r 51(1): "An aerodyne shall not, except when departing or landing, fly over an aerodrome at a lower height than 2,300 feet". This was based on r 39(a) in Annex D to the 1919 International Convention for the Regulation of Aerial Navigation, which stated: "Flight over a landing area at a lower height than 700 metres is prohibited for aerodynes, save in the case of a departure or landing".

Henry Goya Henry used a light aircraft to take members of the public for joyrides along the perimeter of Mascot aerodrome in Sydney. In *R v Burgess* he had been prosecuted for flying without a licence; that prosecution failed when the regulations were held to be invalid. Under the new regulations he was prosecuted again. He was charged with breaching r 51(1). This raised the issue of whether the rule was a valid implementation of r 39(a) of the Convention. It was assumed throughout that 2300 feet was a near enough approximation of 700 metres (a precise equivalent would be 2296 ft 7 inches). However, by r 38 of the Convention "a neutral zone, situated along the perimeter of the landing area and at the approaches to the hangars, may be set apart for aerodynes manoeuvring on the ground". Goya Henry's flights were in the "neutral zone" and, since the Convention prohibited low flying only in the "landing area", he was not in breach of the Convention. He was in breach of the Australian rule because it extended to the whole "aerodrome": that is, it covered not only the "landing area" but also the "neutral zone".

In *R v Poole; Ex parte Henry (No 2)* (1939) 61 CLR 634, Rich, Starke, Evatt and McTiernan JJ held that r 51(1) was valid. Rich J stated that the wider Australian prohibition was "**[644]** a not improper method" of ensuring strict obedience to the Convention rule. Evatt found that "**[656]** the added area is necessarily ancillary to the landing area proper, so that the prohibition imposed may fairly be regarded as incidental" to that stated in the Convention. Hence, according to Evatt J, it was possible to regard r 51(1) as "sufficiently stamped with the purpose" of implementing the Convention. McTiernan J saw no discrepancy; the Convention rule could not be interpreted as strictly confined to the "landing area". Latham CJ dissented. Dixon J did not decide the issue.

A new set of *Air Navigation Regulations* (Cth), this time based on the 1944 Chicago Convention on International Civil Aviation, was considered in *Airlines of NSW Pty Ltd v New South Wales (No 2)* (*Second Airlines Case*) (1965) 113 CLR 54. As in *R v Burgess*, the Commonwealth sought to support the validity of the regulations by relying on both s 51(i) and s 51(xxix), this time with confusing results. The whole Court held that reg 200B was invalid because it would have authorised the holder of a Commonwealth licence to conduct air operations, including purely intrastate operations (see Chapter 9, §4). The other significant regulations were held to be valid – under s 51(i) by five judges (see Chapter 16, §6) and under s 51(xxix) by four judges. In particular, Barwick CJ held that, although the Convention imposed no obligation to set up a licensing system, it said "[91] nothing … inconsistent with the inception and maintenance of such a system", which was therefore acceptable as "an appropriate means of securing the observance of those regulations which are properly made in carrying out the Convention". However, Barwick CJ added that he would "prefer" to rely upon s 51(i), since this would "fully support" the regulations on "a wider basis". If Barwick CJ's observations on s 51(xxix) are set aside as obiter dicta, the Court was evenly divided on the use of s 51(xxix). In any event, insofar as the case can be regarded as deciding by a narrow majority that the use of s 51(xxix) in the circumstances was valid, it is still inconclusive on the issue of whether a treaty need be on a matter of inherent international significance, since any requirement of that kind was clearly satisfied by the topic of air navigation.

(b)   The Expanding Power

Uncertainty about the scope of the power was resolved by two landmark cases: *Koowarta v Bjelke-Petersen* (1982) 153 CLR 168 and *Commonwealth v Tasmania* (*Tasmanian Dam Case*) (1983) 158 CLR 1. In *Koowarta*, the High Court considered whether the *Racial Discrimination Act 1975* (Cth) was validly enacted under either the races power (s 51(xxvi) – see Chapter 21, §2) or the external affairs power. The *Racial Discrimination Act* was enacted to implement Australia's obligations under the 1966 International Convention on the Elimination of All Forms of Racial Discrimination. On whether the power of treaty implementation is subject to a limitation of the kind suggested by Starke and Dixon JJ in *R v Burgess*, *Koowarta* was still equivocal. Mason, Murphy and Brennan JJ saw no such limitation. Gibbs CJ, Aickin and Wilson JJ adopted the limitation proposed by Dixon J: that a treaty can be implemented within Australia only if its subject-matter is "[669] indisputably international in character". Stephen J thought there must be some limitation, but that this formulation was too narrow. He held that what was really required was that the treaty be on a matter of "[217] international concern", apparently a version of the test proposed by Starke J. He agreed with Mason, Murphy and Brennan JJ that the *Racial Discrimination Act* was valid on the ground that it is nowadays "[218] undoubted" that the suppression of racial discrimination is of international concern.

Koowarta v Bjelke-Petersen
(1982) 153 CLR 168

Gibbs CJ: [192] The crucial question … is whether under the power given by s 51(xxix) the Parliament can enact laws for the execution of any treaty to which it is a party, whatever its subject-matter, and in particular for the execution of a treaty which deals with matters that are purely domestic and in themselves involve no relationship with other countries or their inhabitants. In the most important of the cases … in which it has been held that laws to give effect to treaties can validly be made under the external affairs power, the treaties in question had, in themselves, an international element; they affected the relations between Australia and other countries in some direct way … **[193]** In no case has it been decided whether or not the Parliament has power to give effect to a treaty which deals with a matter that is entirely domestic, and affects only Australians within Australia, and their relations to each other, and does not involve any relationship between Australia or Australians and other countries or their citizens. The question which now falls for decision is therefore an open one …

[198] There are strong arguments which support the conclusion that s 51(xxix) does not empower the Parliament to give effect in Australia to every international agreement, whatever its character, to which Australia is a party. If the Parliament is empowered to make laws to carry into effect within Australia any treaty which the Governor-General may make, the result will be that the executive can, by its own act, determine the scope of Commonwealth power. Moreover, the power might be attracted not only by a formal agreement, such as a treaty, but also by an informal agreement: see *R v Burgess; Ex parte Henry* [(1936) 55 CLR 608 at 687]. If the view of Evatt and McTiernan JJ is correct, the executive could, by making an agreement, formal or informal, with another country, arrogate to the Parliament power to make laws on any subject whatsoever. It could, for example, by making an appropriate treaty, obtain for the Parliament powers to control education, to regulate the use of land, to fix the conditions of trading and employment, to censor the press, or to determine the basis of criminal responsibility – it is impossible to envisage any area of power which could not become the subject of Commonwealth legislation if the Commonwealth became a party to an appropriate international agreement. In other words, if s 51(xxix) empowers the Parliament to legislate to give effect to every international agreement which the executive may choose to make, the Commonwealth would be able to acquire unlimited legislative power. The distribution of powers made by the Constitution could in time be completely obliterated; there would be no field of power which the Commonwealth could not invade, and the federal balance achieved by the Constitution could be entirely destroyed.

Of course it has been established, since the *Engineers' Case* [(1920) 28 CLR 129 at 154], that it is an error to read s 107 of the Constitution, which continues the powers of the Parliaments of the States, "as reserving any power from the Commonwealth that falls fairly within the explicit terms of **[199]** an express grant in sec 51, as that grant is reasonably construed, unless that reservation is as explicitly stated". However, in determining the meaning and scope of a power conferred by s 51 it is necessary to have regard to the federal nature of the Constitution. "Accordingly, no single power should be construed in such a way as to give to the Commonwealth Parliament a universal power of legislation which would render absurd the assignment of particular carefully defined powers to that Parliament": *Bank of NSW v Commonwealth* [(1948) 76 CLR 1 at 184-5], per Latham CJ ...

[200] No effective safeguard against the destruction of the federal character of the Constitution would be provided by accepting the suggestion of Evatt and McTiernan JJ in *R v Burgess; Ex parte Henry* [55 CLR at 687], that the power given by s 51(xxix) might not be attracted if "the entry into the convention was merely a device to procure for the Commonwealth an additional domestic jurisdiction". It would be unlikely that an international agreement would be entered into as a mere device. It would not be enough to establish bad faith to show that the executive, when it made a treaty, was fully aware that the Parliament had no legislative power to deal with the subject-matter of the treaty except that which would arise under s 51(xxix) once the treaty was concluded. Suppose, for example, that the executive genuinely believed that working hours should be reduced (or increased), that Australia ought to [join] in an international agreement to that effect, and that it would be beneficial if, by entering into an agreement, the Parliament acquired a legislative competence it otherwise lacked. The entry into the agreement in those circumstances could hardly be described as a mere device, or as done in bad faith. The doctrine of bona fides would at best be a frail shield, and available in rare cases.

If the "extreme view" is adopted, and the broadest possible interpretation is given to the words of s 51(xxix), that paragraph would mean that the power of the Commonwealth Parliament could be expanded by simple executive action, and expanded in such a way as to render meaningless that "limitation and division of sovereign legislative authority" which is "of the essence of federalism": *Spratt v Hermes* [(1965) 114 CLR 226 at 274]. It is apparent that a narrower interpretation of par (xxix) would at once be more consistent with the federal principle upon which the Constitution is based, and more calculated to carry out the true object and purpose of the power which, after all, is expressed to relate, not to internal or domestic affairs, but to external affairs. I conclude, therefore, that the view of Evatt and McTiernan JJ must be rejected, and that a law which gives effect within Australia to an international **[201]** agreement will only be a valid law under s 51(xxix) if the agreement is with respect to a matter which itself can be described as an external affair. I consider that a law which carries into effect the provisions of an international agreement will only have the character of a law with respect to external affairs if the provisions to which it gives effect answer that description ...

What I have said is not intended to suggest that there is a limited class of matters which, by their nature, constitute external affairs, and that only such matters are subject to the power conferred by s 51(xxix). Any subject-matter may constitute an external af[f]air, provided that the manner in which it is treated in some way involves a relationship with other countries or with persons or things outside Australia. A law which regulates transactions between Australia and other countries, or between residents of Australia and residents of other countries, would be a law with respect to external affairs, **[202]** whatever its subject-matter. However, ... I consider that a matter does not become an external affair simply because Australia has entered into an agreement with other nations with regard to it ...

In support of the argument that the Act is within the power conferred by s 51(xxix), the learned Solicitor-General for the Commonwealth naturally placed considerable reliance on the circumstance that the protection of human rights against racial discrimination had, by the time that the Act was passed, become a topic which was the subject of much international debate. There is no doubt that many countries of the world have, or profess, a deep concern that human rights and fundamental freedoms should be observed, and that racial discrimination should be eliminated, throughout the world. There is no need for me to refer to the international conventions and declarations in which that concern has been expressed. The fact that many nations are concerned that other nations should eliminate racial discrimination within their own boundaries does not mean that the domestic or internal affairs of any one country thereby become converted into international affairs. There may be legitimate international concern as to the domestic affairs of a nation. An Australian law which is designed to forbid racial discrimination by Australians against Australians within the territory of Australia does not become international in character, or a law with respect to external affairs, simply because other nations are interested in Australia's policies and practices with regard to racial discrimination.

Murphy J: [241] [I]t is no valid objection that the *Racial Discrimination Act* 1975 deals, as it does, with internal affairs. Preservation of the world's endangered species, maintenance of universal standards of human rights, control of traffic in drugs of dependence, elimination of infectious diseases, and many others, are for Australia as well as other nations, internal as well as external affairs. The States' contentions are a hardly disguised representation of the State reserved powers doctrine rejected in *Amalgamated Society of Engineers v Adelaide Steamship Co Ltd* ("the *Engineers' Case*"), but now having a new lease (see *Gazzo v Comptroller of Stamps (Vic)* [(1981) 149 CLR 227]). The argument is that the external affairs power [is] insufficient to implement certain treaties into which the Executive Government can enter (of which the Convention is an example), and that implementation can be secured only by the co-operation of State Parliaments. Victoria contended that certain provisions of the *Narcotic Drugs Act* 1967 (Cth) (implementing the Single Convention on Narcotic Drugs) were invalid as beyond the competence of the Parliament; and that a law (pursuant to a treaty obligation) to prevent the emergence of slavery in any part of Australia would also be invalid. No satisfactory test was advanced for deciding which treaties Parliament could implement and which would require action by the States. If these contentions are correct, then as I said in *New South Wales v Commonwealth* ("the *Seas and Submerged Lands Case*") [(1975) 135 CLR 337 at 503] "Australia would be an international cripple unable to participate fully in the emerging world order." The Constitution envisages no division of external affairs power between the Parliament and the State Parliaments. The Parliament, in exercising the external affairs power (as well as its other powers), is entitled to make laws for the peace order and good government of the Commonwealth, that is, of the people as a whole, notwithstanding the opposition of any State Government or Parliament. The exercise of that power is not an intrusion upon the people of the States. The people of the States are entitled as well as obliged to have the legislative and executive conduct of those affairs which are part of Australia's external affairs carried out by the Parliament and Executive Government of Australia.

The crucial judgment of Stephen J said:

Stephen J: [216] [Two limitations] recur in some judgments in this Court: that to fall within power, treaties must be bona fide agreements between states and not instances of a foreign government lending itself as an accommodation party so as to bring a particular subject-matter within the other party's treaty power; and that to fall within power a treaty must deal with a matter of international rather than merely domestic concern.

Limitations such as these accord better with the terms of our Constitution than with that of the United States, where the power is with respect not to "external affairs" but to treaties. For courts to deny legitimacy, under a power to make foreign treaties, to what is in form a treaty and no sham presents very real difficulties. But where the grant of power is with respect to "external affairs" an examination of subject-matter, circumstance and parties will be relevant whenever a purported exercise of such power is challenged. It will not be enough that the challenged law gives effect to treaty obligations. A treaty with another country, whether or not the result of a collusive arrangement, which is on a topic neither of especial concern to the relationship between Australia and that other **[217]** country nor of general international concern will not be likely to survive that scrutiny ...

[A]reas of what are of purely domestic concern are steadily contracting and those of international concern are ever expanding. Nevertheless the quality of being of international concern remains, no less than ever, a valid criterion of whether a particular subject-matter forms part of a nation's "external affairs". A subject-matter of international concern necessarily possesses the capacity to affect a country's relations with other nations and this quality is itself enough to make a subject-matter a part of a nation's "external affairs". And this being so, any attack upon validity, either in what must be the very exceptional circumstances which could found an allegation of lack of bona fides or where there is said to be an absence of international subject-matter, will still afford an appropriate safeguard against improper exercise of the "External affairs" power.

It is there that an analogy may be drawn between the defence power and the external affairs power. In cases on the defence power this Court has determined the validity of legislative measures by reference to their capacity to assist the purpose of defence ... It will be open to the Court, in the case of a challenged exercise of the external affairs power, to adopt an analogous approach, testing the validity of the challenged law by reference to its connexion with international subject-matter and with the external affairs of the nation ...

[218] That prohibition of racial discrimination, the subject-matter of the *Racial Discrimination Act*, now falls squarely within the concept I regard as undoubted. That a consequence would seem to be an intrusion by the Commonwealth into areas previously the exclusive concern of the States does not mean that there has been some alteration of the original federal pattern of distribution of legislative powers. What has occurred is, rather, a growth in the content of "External affairs". This growth reflects the new global concern for human rights and the international acknowledgment of the need for universally recognized norms of conduct, particularly in relation to the suppression of racial discrimination ...

[220] Even were Australia not a party to the Convention, this would not necessarily exclude the topic as a part of its external affairs. It was contended on behalf of the Commonwealth that, quite apart from the Convention, Australia has an international obligation to suppress all forms of racial discrimination because respect for human dignity and fundamental rights, and thus the norm of non-discrimination on the grounds of race, is now part of customary international law, as both created and evidenced by state practice and as expounded by jurists and eminent publicists. There is, in my view, much to be said for this submission and for the conclusion that, the Convention apart, the subject of racial discrimination should be regarded as an important aspect of Australia's external affairs, so that legislation much in the present form of the *Racial Discrimination Act* would be supported by power conferred by s 51(xxix). As with slavery and genocide, the failure of a nation to take steps to suppress racial discrimination has become of immediate relevance to its relations with the international community. In *New South Wales v Commonwealth* [135 CLR at 450] I said that included in external affairs were "matters which are not consensual in character; **[221]** conduct on the part of a nation, or of its nationals, which affects other nations and its relations with them". I then cited particular passages from the judgments in *R v Sharkey* [(1949) 79 CLR 121] which provide instances of such non-consensual matters forming a part of Australia's external affairs.

In the present cases it is not necessary to rely upon this aspect of the external affairs power since there exists a quite precise treaty obligation, on a subject of major importance in international relationships, which calls for domestic implementation within Australia. This in itself, without more, suffices to bring the *Racial Discrimination Act* within the terms of s 51(xxix).

Stephen J's judgment supports two lines of argument on s 51(xxix). One is that the power can be used to implement an international treaty at least when the treaty deals with an issue of "international concern". The other is that, even in the absence of a treaty, an "international concern", to which Australia in its international relations might consider it necessary or prudent to respond by appropriate legislation within Australia, might be enough to bring that legislation within the scope of s 51(xxix).

The ratio decidendi of *Koowarta* – the "lowest common denominator" of the four majority judgments – might be formulated thus: the implementation of a treaty is a valid use of power under s 51(xxix) *at least* when the subject-matter is of "international concern". However, even though the test of "international concern" may be the "lowest common denominator" of *Koowarta*, it should be remembered that it was relied on only by Stephen J, and thus that *Koowarta* may stand for nothing more than its result.

The legal issue in the *Tasmanian Dam Case* turned largely on the problem of what had been decided in *Koowarta*. The dissenting judges in the *Tasmanian Dam Case* would clearly have preferred that any use of s 51(xxix) to implement international treaties be subject to the limitation proposed by Dixon J in *R v Burgess*. Two of them, Gibbs CJ and Wilson J, had also dissented in *Koowarta*, and Dawson J, as Solicitor-General for Victoria, which along with Western Australia had intervened in *Koowarta*, had argued a similar view. But all three of these judges now settled for the "lowest common denominator" of *Koowarta*, that is, the test proposed by Stephen J, as the best that could now be salvaged. They held that the building of a dam in south-west Tasmania was not of "international concern".

Commonwealth v Tasmania (*Tasmanian Dam Case*)
(1983) 158 CLR 1

Gibbs CJ: [101] Whether a matter is of international concern depends on the extent to which it is regarded by the nations of the world as a proper subject for international action, and on the extent to which it will affect Australia's relations with other countries. For myself, I should have preferred a more precise test. However, the result is that unlike some other powers, but like the defence power, the application of the external affairs power "depends upon facts, and as those facts change so may its actual operation as a power enabling the legislature to make a particular law": *Andrews v Howell* [(1941) 65 CLR 255 at 278].

The Convention, and the recommendation, in their relevant aspects, and as applicable to Australia, deal with matters entirely domestic – matters which contemplate action within Australia, which involve no reciprocity of relationship with other nations (as a convention regarding the protection of historic memorials from bombardment might do) and which do not directly affect the interests of other nations, eg, by protecting them from actual or potential risks (as a convention relating to the eradication of diseases or the prohibition of the illegal export of cultural property might do). The protection of the environment and the cultural heritage has **[102]** been of increasing interest in recent times, but it cannot be said to have become such a burning international issue that a failure by one nation to take protective measures is likely adversely to affect its relations with other nations, unless of course damage or pollution extends beyond the borders. If one nation allows its own natural heritage (and no other) to be damaged, it is not in the least probable that other nations will act similarly in reprisal, or that the peace and security of the world will be disturbed – in this respect, damage to the heritage stands in clear contrast to such practices as racial discrimination ... The question whether the subject-matter of the Convention is one of international concern within the test propounded by Stephen J is one of some difficulty, because, since the external affairs power, like the defence power, "applies to authorize measures only to meet facts" (cf *Australian Textiles Pty Ltd v Commonwealth* [(1945) 71 CLR 161 at 181]), the Court must form its own impression of the facts, in part on the basis of judicial notice. In the present case I regard as decisive the fact that the Convention does not impose any obligation on the Commonwealth to enact legislation for the protection of any part of the national heritage within Australia; and of course the recommendation does not purport to do so. I also take into account my opinion that relations with other countries are not likely to be significantly affected by whatever action Australia takes in relation to the protection of the Parks. These considerations, and the nature of the matters with which the Convention and the recommendation deal, lead me to the conclusion that the external affairs power has not been attracted in the present case.

For the four majority judges in the *Tasmanian Dam Case*, Mason, Murphy, Brennan and Deane JJ, the problem of binding precedent was less acute. On the "lowest common denominator" view, *Koowarta* had established the validity of treaty implementation at least when "international concern" was present. However, that was no obstacle to asserting a wider principle. Mason J rejected the test of "international concern" as too "[123] elusive" and as yielding no "[125] acceptable criteria or guidelines".

Mason J: [124] It is submitted that the suggested requirement that the subject-matter must be "of international concern" means that it must be international in character in the sense that there is a mutuality of interest or benefit in the observance of the provisions of the convention. Thus, we are invited to say that a convention by which the contracting parties agree to enact domestic laws requiring **[125]** persons in motor vehicles to wear seat belts does not deal with a matter of international concern because no nation can derive a benefit from the wearing of seat belts in another country. This is by no means self-evident. Drivers and passengers cross international boundaries. They are likely to observe in other countries the practices which they observe at home. International co-operation resulting in a convention insisting on compliance with uniform safety standards may well benefit all countries. The illustration is instructive because it demonstrates how difficult it is to say with accuracy of any treaty or convention that observance of its provisions will not benefit a contracting party.

The point is that if a topic becomes the subject of international co-operation or an international convention it is necessarily international in character – the existence of co-operation and the making of a convention establish that the subject-matter is an appropriate vehicle for the creation of international relationships or, in the case of a bilateral treaty, a relationship between the parties to it. And participation in a convention indicates a judgment on the part of participating nations that they will derive a benefit from it. All this indicates an absence of any acceptable criteria or guidelines by which the Court can determine the "international character" of the subject-matter of a treaty or convention. The existence of international character or international concern is established by entry by Australia into the convention or treaty.

In any event, as I observed in *Koowarta* [(1982) 153 CLR 168 at 229], the Court would undertake an invidious task if it were to decide whether the subject-matter of a convention is of international character or concern. On a question of this kind the Court cannot substitute its judgment for that of the executive government and Parliament. The fact of entry into, and of ratification of, an international convention, evidences the judgment of the executive and of Parliament that the subject-matter of the convention is of international character and concern and that its implementation will be a benefit to Australia. Whether the subject-matter as dealt with by the convention is of international concern, whether it will yield, or is capable of yielding, a benefit to Australia, whether non-observance by Australia is likely to lead to adverse international action or reaction, are not questions on which the Court can readily arrive at an informed opinion. Essentially they are issues involving nice questions of sensitive judgment which should be left to the executive government for determination. The Court should accept and act upon the decision of the executive **[126]** government and upon the expression of the will of Parliament in giving legislative ratification to the treaty or convention.

Murphy J did not reject the test of "international concern" but treated it as only one of several different criteria, any one of which was sufficient to attract power under s 51(xxix).

Murphy J: [171] It is preferable that the circumstances in which a law is authorized by the external affairs power be stated in terms of what is sufficient, even if the categories overlap, rather than in exhaustive terms. To be a law with respect to external affairs it is sufficient that it: (a) implements any international law, or (b) implements any treaty or convention whether general (multilateral) or particular, or (c) implements any recommendation or request of the United Nations organization or subsidiary organizations such as the World Health Organization, the United Nations Education, Scientific and **[172]** Cultural Organization, the Food and Agriculture Organization or the International Labour Organization, or (d) fosters (or inhibits) relations between Australia or political entities, bodies or persons within Australia and other nation States, entities, groups or persons external to Australia, or (e) deals with circumstances or things outside Australia, or (f) deals with circumstances or things inside Australia of international concern.

The fact that a subject becomes part of external affairs does not mean that the subject becomes, as it were, a separate, plenary head of legislative power. If the only basis upon which a subject becomes part of external affairs is a treaty, then the legislative power is confined to what may reasonably be regarded as appropriate for implementation of provisions of the treaty. This does not mean that either all of the provisions must be implemented or else none can be implemented. It does not mean that there must be any rigid adherence to the terms of the treaty. Again, if the subject of external affairs is some other circumstance, the legislative power will extend to laws which could reasonably be regarded as appropriate for dealing with that circumstance.

The world's cultural and natural heritage is, of its own nature, part of Australia's external affairs. It is the heritage of Australians, as part of humanity, as well as the heritage of those where the various items happen to be. As soon as it is accepted that the Tasmanian wilderness area is part of world heritage, it follows that its preservation as well as being an internal affair, is part of Australia's external affairs.

Brennan J sympathised with the wish to set limits on treaty implementation under s 51(xxix), but adhered to his own view in *Koowarta* that this could be done by insisting on the strictly controlled implementation of a treaty obligation. Deane J, on the other hand, argued that the whole issue had already been settled by *R v Burgess*. He read the judgment of Latham CJ along with that of Evatt and McTiernan JJ as yielding a binding majority view.

All this covered only a small part of the spectrum of "external affairs" as it might have been explored in the *Tasmanian Dam Case*. The case arose because, in 1983, the newly elected Hawke Labor Government had taken action under the *World Heritage Properties Conservation Act 1983* (Cth) to stop the damming of the Franklin river system in Tasmania. The foundations for the purported exercise of power under s 51(xxix) were laid in s 6 of the Act. Section 6 was linked to and formed the basis of the operative provisions in s 9 of the Act.

World Heritage Properties Conservation Act 1983 (Cth)

6 (1) A Proclamation may be made under sub-section (3) in relation to identified property that is not in any State.

(2) A Proclamation may also be made under sub-section (3) in relation to identified property that is in a State and is property to which one or more of the following paragraphs applies or apply:

    (a) the Commonwealth has, pursuant to a request by the State, submitted to the World Heritage Committee under Article 11 of the Convention that the property is suitable for inclusion in the World Heritage List provided for in paragraph 2 of that Article, whether the request by the State was made before or after the commencement of this Act and whether or not the property was identified property at the time when the request was made;

    (b) the protection or conservation of the property by Australia is a matter of international obligation, whether by reason of the Convention or otherwise;

    (c) the protection or conservation of the property by Australia is necessary or desirable for the purpose of giving effect to a treaty (including the Convention) or for the purpose of obtaining for Australia any advantage or benefit under a treaty (including the Convention);

    (d) the protection or conservation of the property by Australia is a matter of international concern (whether or not it is also a matter of domestic concern), whether by reason that a failure by Australia to take proper measures for the protection or conservation of the property would, or would be likely to, prejudice Australia's relations with other countries or for any other reason …

(3) Where the Governor-General is satisfied that any property in respect of which a Proclamation may be made under this sub-section is being or is likely to be damaged or destroyed, he may, by Proclamation, declare that property to be property to which section 9 applies ...

9 (1) Except with the consent in writing of the Minister, it is unlawful for a person, whether himself or by his servant or agent –

    (a)   to carry out any excavation works on any property to which this section applies;

    (b)   to carry out operations for, or exploratory drilling in connection with, the recovery of minerals on any property to which this section applies;

    (c)   to erect a building or other substantial structure on any property to which this section applies or to do any act in the course of, or for the purpose of, the erection of a building or other substantial structure on any property to which this section applies:

    (d)   to damage or destroy a building or other substantial structure on any property to which this section applies;

    (e)   to kill, cut down or damage any tree on any property to which this section applies;

    (f)   to construct or establish any road or vehicular track on any property to which this section applies;

    (g)   to use explosives on any property to which this section applies; or

    (h)   if an act is prescribed for the purposes of this paragraph in relation to particular property to which this section applies, to do that act in relation to that property.

(2) Except with the consent in writing of the Minister, it is unlawful for a person, whether himself or by his servant or agent, to do any act, not being an act the doing of which is unlawful by virtue of sub-section (1), that damages or destroys any property to which this section applies.

(3) If an application of sub-sections (1) and (2) of this section in relation to particular property, being property that is relevant property by virtue of a particular paragraph or particular paragraphs of sub-section 6 (2), would be within the powers of the Parliament if the property were relevant property by virtue only of that paragraph or those paragraphs, it is intended that sub-sections (1) and (2) of this section should have that application in relation to the property whether or not the property is also relevant property by virtue of another paragraph or paragraphs of sub-section 6 (2).

(4) In sub-section (3), "relevant property" means property in respect of which a Proclamation may, by virtue of sub-section 6 (2), be made under sub-section 6 (3).

Each of the paragraphs of s 6(2) was designed to invoke a different aspect of "external affairs", usually on the basis of dicta from the judgments in *Koowarta*. Thus, para (a) impliedly asserted that the power in respect of "external affairs" was applicable simply because the Tasmanian wilderness area had been the subject of a submission by Australia to the World Heritage Committee (an international organisation). Paragraph (b) implied the sufficiency of an international obligation whether or not there was any treaty. Paragraph (c) raised the converse issue of an international treaty whether or not it imposed any obligation. Paragraph (d) implied the sufficiency of "international concern".

Of the four majority judges in the *Tasmanian Dam Case*, only Murphy J held that all four of the relevant paragraphs of s 6(2) were valid. The other majority judges, Mason, Brennan and Deane JJ, decided only that s 6(2)(b) was valid, thus accepting the mere existence of an international obligation as enough to attract s 51(xxix). This did not mean the other paragraphs were invalid, only that these three judges did not decide their validity.

The three dissenting judges, Gibbs CJ, Wilson and Dawson JJ, held that s 6(2)(b) was invalid. Extracting from *Koowarta* a test of "international concern", they held that the Act did not pass the test. In any event, they also held that the Convention for the Protection of the World Cultural and Natural Heritage 1972 did not impose any "obligation". On this latter question the reasoning of both the majority and the dissenting judges was circular. The Convention was drafted so that, in its application to a federal country, it imposed an obligation if the central government had the constitutional power to discharge it, but not otherwise.

Convention for the Protection of the World Cultural and Natural Heritage
Opened for signature 16 November 1972; *entered into force* 17 December 1975;
(1972) 11 *International Legal Materials* 1358

Article 34

The following provisions shall apply to those States Parties to this Convention which have a federal or non-unitary constitutional system:

(a) with regard to the provisions of this Convention, the implementation of which comes under the legal jurisdiction of the federal or central legislative power, the obligations of the federal or central government shall be the same as for those States Parties which are not federal States;

(b) with regard to the provisions of this Convention, the implementation of which comes under the legal jurisdiction of individual constituent States, countries, provinces or cantons that are not obliged by the constitutional system of the federation to take legislative measures, the federal government shall inform the competent authorities of such States, countries, provinces or cantons of the said provisions, with its recommendation for their adoption.

If we start with an assumption that implementation of the Convention falls within Commonwealth power under s 51(xxix), then para (a) applies. Hence the Commonwealth has an *obligation* to implement the Convention; hence legislation discharging that obligation falls within s 51(xxix). Conversely, if we assume that there is *no* constitutional basis for legislation under s 51(xxix), then para (b) applies. Hence the Commonwealth has no obligation to implement the Convention, but only to make appropriate recommendations to the States. Hence there is no basis for legislation under s 51(xxix). Either way, the initial assumption is confirmed.

The four majority judges held that the Commonwealth had an international obligation to protect "world heritage" items and that legislation within Australia to carry out that obligation would be valid under s 51(xxix). However, it did not follow that the legislation in fact enacted was valid. Both Brennan and Deane JJ had difficulties with the operative provisions in s 9.

In *R v Burgess*, Evatt and McTiernan JJ had asserted the power of the Commonwealth to carry out its obligations under *any* international treaty, but had also insisted that such legislation must strictly conform to the treaty. Starke J had taken a more permissive view of the latitude available to the Commonwealth in its choice of means to fulfil its obligations. Barwick CJ held in the *Second Airlines Case* that the Commonwealth, in making regulations to carry out the Convention, was free to devise its own "appropriate" means, in that case a licensing system, for securing the observance of the regulations. For Brennan and Deane JJ in the *Tasmanian Dam Case*, this word "appropriate" was of crucial importance and gave rise to what has since been commonly referred to as a test of "proportionality" (see Chapter 16, §8).

Commonwealth v Tasmania (Tasmanian Dam Case)
(1983) 158 CLR 1

Deane J: [259] [A] law would not properly be characterized as a law with respect to external affairs if it failed to carry into effect or to comply with the particular provisions of a treaty which it was said to execute … or if the treaty which the law was said to carry into effect was demonstrated to be no more than a device to attract domestic legislative power: *Burgess' Case* [(1936) 55 CLR 608 at 687, 642, 669]; *Koowarta* [(1982) 153 CLR 168 at 231, 260]. More importantly, while the question of what is the appropriate method of achieving a desired result is a matter for the Parliament and not for the Court (see *Poole (No 2)* [(1939) 61 CLR 634 at 644, 647-8, 655]; *Airlines of NSW (No 2)* [(1965) 113 CLR 54 at 136]), the law must be capable of being reasonably considered to be appropriate and adapted to achieving what is said to impress it with the character of a law with respect to external affairs; cf per Starke J, speaking of the scope of the regulation-making power, in *Burgess' Case* [55 CLR at 659-60] and in *Poole (No 2)* [(1939) 61 CLR 634 at 647], and per Barwick CJ in **[260]** *Airlines of NSW (No 2)* [113 CLR at 86]. In that regard, the purpose which a law operating upon a domestic subject-matter is intended to achieve (eg, the carrying into effect of a treaty, the performance of an international obligation or the obtaining of an international benefit) is likely to assume an importance in deciding questions of characterization in relation to s 51(xxix) which is comparable to its importance in characterization in relation to the defence power (s 51(vi)) since it will commonly be that purpose which, in the factual context, is called in aid to provide the character of a law with respect to external affairs. As Dixon J observed in *Burgess' Case* [55 CLR at 674]:

"It is apparent that the nature of this power necessitates a faithful pursuit of the purpose, namely, a carrying out of the external obligation, before it can support the imposition upon citizens of duties and disabilities which otherwise would be outside the power of the Commonwealth. No doubt the power includes the doing of anything reasonably incidental to the execution of the purpose. But wide departure from the purpose is not permissible, because under colour of carrying out an external obligation the Commonwealth cannot undertake the general regulation of the subject-matter to which it relates."

Implicit in the requirement that a law be capable of being reasonably considered to be appropriate and adapted to achieving what is said to provide it with the character of a law with respect to external affairs is a need for there to be a reasonable proportionality between the designated purpose or object and the means which the law embodies for achieving or procuring it. Thus, to take an extravagant example, a law requiring that all sheep in Australia be slaughtered would not be sustainable as a law with respect to external affairs merely because Australia was a party to some international convention which required the taking of steps to safeguard against the spread of some obscure sheep disease which had been detected in sheep in a foreign country and which had not reached these shores. The absence of any reasonable proportionality between the law and the purpose of discharging the obligation under the convention would preclude characterization as a law with respect to external affairs notwithstanding that Tweedledee might, "contrariwise", perceive logic in the proposition that the most effective way of preventing the spread of any disease among sheep would be the elimination of all sheep. The law must be seen, with "reasonable clearness", upon consideration of its operation, to be "really, and not fancifully, colourably, or ostensibly, referable" to and explicable by the purpose or object which is said to provide its character: cf, as **[261]** regards the defence power, *R v Foster* [(1949) 79 CLR 43 at 84]; *Shrimpton v Commonwealth* [(1945) 69 CLR 613 at 623-4]; *Marcus Clark and Co Ltd v Commonwealth* [(1952) 87 CLR 177 at 215-16, 256]. In that regard, the "peculiar" or "drastic" nature of what the law provides or the fact that it pursues "an extreme course" is relevant to characterization: cf *R v Foster* [79 CLR at 96-7] …

[266] The overall effect of s 3(2), s 6(2) and (3), s 9(1) and s 13(1) is that all of the prohibitions contained in paragraphs (a) to (g) (inclusive) of s 9(1) are automatically imposed in respect of any property which is proclaimed by the Governor-General pursuant to s 6(3) regardless of their appropriateness for the purpose of **[267]** protecting or conserving the property and regardless of whether any relationship at all exists between all or any of the prohibited acts and the nature and source of likely damage to the property. In these circumstances, there is a lack of any reasonable proportionality between the provisions of s 9(1)(a) to (g) and the purpose of protecting and conserving the relevant property. Those paragraphs are not capable of being reasonably considered to be appropriate and adapted to achieving that purpose. Since it is the purpose of protecting and conserving the property and thereby complying with the obligations under the Convention (or achieving one of the other international objectives referred to in s 6(2)(a), (b), (c) and (d)) that is said to warrant characterization as a law with respect to external affairs, it follows that, in the absence of the necessary relationship with that purpose, pars (a) to (g) (inclusive) of s 9(1) of the Act cannot be sustained by s 51(xxix). They are invalid.

Section 9(1)(h) and s 9(2) are in a different category. Paragraph (h) of s 9(1) prohibits the doing, without the consent of the Minister, of an act which is prescribed for the purposes of the paragraph in relation to particular property to which s 9 applies. The power to prescribe such acts is vested in the Governor-General by s 21. It is not an arbitrary power and must be construed in its context. It is exercisable only in respect of property which has been prescribed by the Governor-General pursuant to s 6(3) upon his being satisfied that the property is being or is likely to be damaged or destroyed. In that context and in the context of s 6(2), the power to prescribe an act for the purposes of par (h) is limited by the purpose for which it exists, namely, the purpose of preventing or avoiding damage or further damage to or destruction of the particular property, and is exercisable only in relation to an act which could reasonably be considered to be a possible cause of, or a contributing factor to, such damage or further damage or destruction: see *R v Toohey; Ex parte Northern Land Council* [(1981) 151 CLR 170]. Section 9(2) provides that, except with the consent in writing of the Minister, it is unlawful for a person to do any act, not being an act the doing of which is unlawful by virtue of sub-s (1), that damages or destroys any property to which the section applies.

Section 9(1)(h) and s 9(2) are, by reason of the provisions of s 15A of the *Acts Interpretation Act* 1901, severable from the invalid provisions of paragraphs (a) to (g) (inclusive) of s 9(1). Both s 9(2) and s 9(1)(h) are capable of being considered as appropriate and adapted to the purpose of discharging the international obligation under the Convention to protect or conserve the relevant property. That being so and subject to any general constitutional limitations, including whether "just terms" were required or **[268]** provided, they are within the legislative competence of the Parliament pursuant to s 51(xxix) of the Constitution.

It was submitted, by Tasmania, that the relevant provisions of the Act are not within s 51(xxix) because, to the extent that they represent implementation of the Convention, that implementation is partial only. It should be apparent from what has been said that I do not accept the proposition that a law under s 51(xxix) for the carrying into effect of a treaty or for the discharge of treaty obligations must, as a condition of validity, carry into effect the whole treaty or completely discharge all the obligations. It is competent for the Parliament, in a law under s 51(xxix), partly to carry a treaty into effect or partly to discharge treaty obligations leaving it to the States or to other Commonwealth legislative or executive action to carry into effect or discharge the outstanding provisions or obligations or leaving the outstanding provisions or obligations unimplemented or unperformed. On the other hand, if the relevant law "partially" implements the treaty in the sense that it contains provisions which are consistent with the terms of the treaty and also contains significant provisions which are inconsistent with those terms, it would be extremely unlikely that the law could properly be characterized as a law with respect to external affairs on the basis that it was capable of being reasonably considered to be appropriate and adapted to giving effect to the treaty.

Brennan J reasoned in a like manner. Both he and Deane J held that most of s 9(1) was invalid, and for Brennan J s 9(2) was invalid as well. Deane J also held that the provisions were invalid insofar as they effected an "acquisition of property" in breach of s 51(xxxi) (see Chapter 27, §2(c)). Mason J rejected these arguments; he and Murphy J held that both s 9(1) and (2) were valid.

(c)   Successors to the Tasmanian Dam Case

The *Tasmanian Dam Case* was followed in *Richardson v Forestry Commission* (1988) 164 CLR 261. Though Wilson and Dawson JJ had dissented in the *Tasmanian Dam Case*, each now accepted it as binding. The *Lemonthyme and Southern Forests (Commission of Inquiry) Act 1987* (Cth) established a Commission to investigate whether the Lemonthyme and Southern Forests areas in Tasmania could qualify to be nominated as a world heritage area under the 1972 Convention for the Protection of the World Cultural and Natural Heritage. During the period of investigation, s 16(1) of the Act prohibited certain works from occurring within the areas, including forestry operations and the construction of roads. Wilson and Dawson JJ joined Mason CJ, Brennan and Toohey JJ in holding the Act to be valid.

Richardson v Forestry Commission
(1988) 164 CLR 261

Dawson J: [320] In *Commonwealth v Tasmania* ("the *Tasmanian Dam Case*") [(1983) 158 CLR 1], the majority took the view that legislation implementing the Convention for the Protection of the World Cultural and Natural Heritage was a valid exercise of the external affairs power contained in s 51(xxix) of the Constitution. That view was taken, as I read the judgments, upon the basis that subject to **[321]** express constitutional prohibitions, any matters covered by a bona fide international treaty are, by their very inclusion in the treaty, brought within the ambit of the external affairs power. As will be apparent from my reasons for judgment in the *Tasmanian Dam Case*, I am unable to accept that view. No doubt the activities involved in concluding an international agreement fall within the description of external affairs, but that does not to my mind bring the subject-matter of the agreement, if it is otherwise entirely domestic, within that description. In my view it is quite wrong to conclude that, because the scope of matters which are the subject of treaties has in modern times greatly expanded, the scope of the external affairs power has undergone the same expansion. The fact that an agreement is international in character does not necessarily mean that the matters with which it deals cease to be of a domestic nature and become part of the country's external affairs. Just as, in another context, the Constitution requires us to distinguish between interstate and intrastate trade, so we must distinguish between affairs which are external and those which are not. And just as the fact that a contract is made over State boundaries will not determine whether the subject-matter of the contract is interstate or intrastate trade, so the fact that an agreement is made internationally will not determine whether its subject-matter is external or domestic in character. Since there is no practical limit to those matters which may form the subject of international agreement, the result of taking the opposite view is that there is no practical limit to the scope of the external affairs power. That is to say, the result is that par (xxix) has the potential to obliterate the division of legislative power otherwise effected by s 51. Simply as a matter of construction, I cannot believe that such a result was ever intended.

However, I do not refer to these considerations merely to reiterate a view which did not find favour in the *Tasmanian Dam Case*. I mention them to indicate that my difference with the majority is upon a matter of fundamental importance. The course which I should adopt in these circumstances is not altogether clear. Plainly enough, if, as is the case, I do not think that the Constitution admits of any other interpretation, it is the words of the Constitution rather than authority which should govern any decision I might make. If I were asked to do so, I should find the greatest difficulty, notwithstanding the course taken in *Queensland v Commonwealth* [(1977) 139 CLR 585], in deciding that the Constitution said something which I thought it did not. This Court has never held itself to be bound by its own decisions and ultimately it is the Constitution itself, and not **[322]** authority, which must dictate the answers which we give: see *Australian Agricultural Co v Federated Engine-Drivers and Firemen's Association of Australasia* [(1913) 17 CLR 261 at 275-9], per Isaacs J; the *Tramways Case (No 1)* [(1914) 18 CLR 54 at 70], per Isaacs J.

Precedent must, however, have a part to play, even in the interpretation of a constitution. Considerations of practicality make it necessary that the law should, as far as possible, take a consistent course. The constant re-examination of concluded questions is incompatible with that aim. That is why this Court has adopted the practice of requiring leave to be granted before it will allow a previous decision to be re-argued: *Evda Nominees Pty Ltd v Victoria* [(1984) 154 CLR 311]. The parties in the present case did not seek to question the decision in the *Tasmanian Dam Case*. In these circumstances, and having made my own view clear, it is, I think, proper to proceed upon the same basis as did the argument in this case and to assume the authority of that decision.

The *Tasmanian Dam Case* does, I think, provide an answer in the present case because whatever else it decided, it did decide that the legislative implementation of an international treaty concluded in good faith is within the ambit of the external affairs power. True it is that the *Tasmanian Dam Case* appears to have decided more than this. As I read the judgments of the majority, it is enough to attract legislative power if, even though there is no treaty, a subject-matter is of sufficient international concern ... Although the majority did not necessarily place any reliance upon the judgment of Stephen J in *Koowarta v Bjelke-Petersen* [(1982) 153 CLR 168], that conclusion flows logically from the view which he expressed that the implementation of a treaty is not automatically an exercise of the external affairs power; the subject-matter of the treaty must also be a matter of international concern. Stephen J saw the requirement of international concern as a restriction upon the power and I was prepared to view it in that way in the *Tasmanian Dam Case*. But in reality, as the decision in the latter case shows, the fact that a matter is the subject of a bona fide treaty makes it difficult to say that it is not a matter of international concern and, if international concern is the touchstone, why is a treaty necessary at all? Why is **[323]** international concern over a matter not sufficient of itself to bring it within the external affairs power?

If the scope of the matters which may be the subject of treaties has greatly expanded in recent years, the scope of those matters which may be the subject of international concern is even wider. It is not, therefore, surprising to find a search for some limit to the breadth which, upon this expansive view, the external affairs power apparently possesses.

Deane and Gaudron JJ (in dissent on this point) held that most of the interim protection measures prescribed by s 16(1) were invalid. They insisted on confining validity to the precise, "proportionate" implementation of treaty obligations. Gaudron J stated: "**[347]** Because s 16 must be viewed as affording general environmental protection rather than protection of the qualities and features which may be of outstanding universal value, it is not on the material before the Court reasonably capable of being viewed as appropriate **[348]** or adapted to the circumstance that the areas may be or contain areas constituting part of the world heritage".

The *Tasmanian Dam Case* was also followed in *Queensland v Commonwealth* (*Tropical Rainforests Case*) (1989) 167 CLR 232. On 15 December 1988, by a proclamation under s 6(3) of the *World Heritage Properties Conservation Act 1983* (Cth), certain areas in north-east Queensland were declared to be property to which the protective provisions in s 9 of that Act applied. Queensland challenged the validity of the proclamation, asserting that the relevant areas had not been demonstrated to qualify as "world cultural heritage" or "world natural heritage". Australia had submitted the areas to the World Heritage Committee for inclusion on the World Heritage List under the 1972 Convention for the Protection of the World Cultural and Natural Heritage. After evaluation, the Bureau of the Committee had accepted the "inscription of the Property to the World Heritage List".

In a joint judgment, Mason CJ, Brennan, Deane, Toohey, Gaudron and McHugh JJ rejected outright the idea that a court "**[242]** can decide for itself as an issue of fact whether the Wet Tropical Rainforests ... [are] part of the natural heritage". They held that: "As the inclusion of the property in the List is conclusive of its status in the eyes of the international community, it is conclusive of Australia's international duty to protect and conserve it. Its inclusion is therefore conclusive of the constitutional support for the proclamation of 15 December 1988". For Dawson J, what was conclusive was the mere fact that Australia itself had identified the area as part of its natural heritage, since that was enough to give rise to "**[248]** an international obligation to protect it ... regardless of any further assessment".

The principles established in the *Tasmanian Dam Case* were again reaffirmed in *Victoria v Commonwealth* (*Industrial Relations Act Case*) (1996) 187 CLR 416. The *Industrial Relations Reform Act 1993* (Cth) was introduced by the Keating government. It amended the *Industrial Relations Act 1988* (Cth) by adding what were then a new Pt VIA and a new Pt VIB. Part VIA enshrined a range of workers' rights in respect of such matters as minimum wages, equal pay, unfair dismissal and parental leave. Its claim to validity depended primarily on the "external affairs" power, since the new protections extended to workers were said to implement the requirements of various Conventions and Recommendations adopted by the General Conference of the International Labour Organization in its annual meetings at Geneva. Part VIB provided for the enforcement of new forms of "certified agreements" and "enterprise flexibility agreements". Its claim to validity depended primarily on the "corporations" power in s 51(xx) of the Constitution (see Chapter 17, §3). The claims to validity based on s 51(xxix) were largely upheld, primarily in a joint judgment by Brennan CJ, Toohey, Gaudron, McHugh and Gummow JJ. In a separate judgment Dawson J concurred in the result. The joint judgment took the opportunity for a strong reaffirmation of the *Tasmanian Dam Case*, stressing (as Latham CJ had done in *R v Burgess*) that there had been "**[478]** a continual expansion in the range of the subject matter of treaties", and stressing also that this expansion had been well under way and widely recognised by the beginning of the 20th century.

Victoria v Commonwealth (*Industrial Relations Act Case*)
(1996) 187 CLR 416

Brennan CJ, Toohey, Gaudron, McHugh and Gummow JJ: [479] The "oldest international organization in the world", the International Telecommunication Union, was established in 1865 as the International Telegraph Union. By the turn of the century about 30 states were members. The Universal Postal Union was inaugurated in 1874. India and Canada obtained separate votes in the Universal Postal Union and, in 1885, the Australian colonies collectively obtained one vote ... The International Convention for the Protection of Industrial Property was signed at Paris in 1883 and it provided for the establishment at Berne of the office of the International Union for the Protection of Industrial Property. The result was to provide international recognition for the rights of inventors. The rights of authors of literary and artistic works were given similar recognition by the Berne Convention of 1886.

Before 1900, modern international arbitration had developed, beginning with the Alabama Award of 1872; bilateral treaties greatly extended state submission of future disputes. This process was further advanced with the Hague Convention for the Pacific Settlement of International Disputes 1899, which established the Permanent Court of International Arbitration.

There was activity also in the fields of what now would be called international human rights, world health and environmental protection. The Geneva Convention 1864 laid the foundations of the International Red Cross. The General Act for dealing with the Suppression of Slavery in Africa, signed at Brussels in 1890, provided for the **[480]** maintenance of a bureau to collect all information on measures connected with matters dealt with under the General Act. Abuses against inhabitants of the Pacific Islands were a major concern of the Imperial Government. This had been reflected in the *Pacific Islanders Protection Acts* of 1872 and 1875 (UK) and the establishment of the High Commissioner for the Pacific.

Conventions were negotiated affecting health and the environment. The Convention of London, signed by the African colonial powers in 1900, sought to preserve the native fauna of that continent; a convention signed at Berne in 1878 sought to prevent recurrence of the damage done to the wine industry by the phylloxera epidemics of the preceding decade; and several conventions dealt with the threat to public health by the spread of cholera and the plague ...

[482] The phrase "External affairs" was adopted in s 51(xxix) of the Constitution in preference to "foreign affairs" so as to make it clear that the power comprehended both the relationship between the Commonwealth of Australia and other parts of the then British Empire and the relationship with foreign countries ... [T]he Commonwealth of Australia was established at a time of evolving law and practice in the external relations between sovereign powers and between the self-governing units of the Empire. It would be a serious error to construe par (xxix) as though the subject matter of those relations to which it applied in 1900 were not continually expanding. Rather, the external relations of the Australian colonies were in a condition of continuing evolution and, at that time, were regarded as such. Accordingly, it is difficult to see any justification for treating the content of the phrase "external affairs" as crystallised at the commencement of federation, or as denying it a particular application on the ground that the application was not foreseen or could not have been foreseen a century ago.

From the foundation of the Commonwealth ..., informed observers took the view that the power to legislate with respect to external affairs included power to legislate with respect to treaties, in so far as they affected Australia, which had been concluded by the Imperial Government. Thus, in *McKelvey v Meagher* [(1906) 4 CLR 265 at 286], Barton J said that it was probable that the external affairs power "includes power to legislate as to the observance of treaties between Great Britain and foreign nations". Writing as **[483]** Attorney-General in 1902, Deakin dealt as follows with the omission of the words "and treaties" from s 51(xxix):

> "The omission, as appears from the debates, was solely to prevent any assumption arising that the Commonwealth claimed an independent power of making treaties. Legislation with respect to the enforcement of treaty obligations is clearly within the scope of 'external affairs'."

The legislative power was designed to authorise the implementation of treaty obligations which bound Australia. At the time of federation the source of such obligations was action taken by the

Imperial authorities. However, given the scope of the legislative power, it was at least implicit that it would authorise the implementation of treaty obligations accepted independently by the Commonwealth of Australia, if and when the Executive Branch of government attained the competence to do so.

There was some suggestion in the submissions of the plaintiff States in the present case that what has come to pass with the legislation they seek to impugn is something beyond contemplation at the time of the adoption of the Constitution. Any such proposition is, as we have endeavoured shortly to illustrate, too widely stated. The treaties which were part of the subject matter of foreign relations in 1900, and the treaties that have since been made, embrace an ever-expanding range of topics.

The joint judgment resisted any attempt to limit the ratio decidendi of the *Tasmanian Dam Case*. Counsel had submitted that, if we assume that protection of World Heritage properties is a matter of "international concern", then the actual *result* in the *Dam Case* could have been reached on the basis suggested by Stephen J in *Koowarta* – so that, although all four majority judges had asserted a wider view of the power, those wider assertions (being not necessary to the decision) were only obiter dicta. However, that analysis was decisively rejected.

Brennan CJ, Toohey, Gaudron, McHugh and Gummow JJ: [484] [T]he Solicitor-General for Victoria contended for a criterion of validity which resembled that adopted by Stephen J or alternatively that of the minority judges in *Koowarta*. He submitted that, even upon this limited footing, the result in the *Tasmanian Dam Case* [(1983) 158 CLR 1] would have been the same. Therefore, the submission proceeded, there was no occasion to seek leave to reopen the correctness of the *Tasmanian Dam Case*.

The difficulty in the path of these submissions is that subsequently the majority in the *Tasmanian Dam Case* adopted the broader view. It is not to the point that the same result might have been achieved by application of the view previously taken by Stephen J. It is to seek to distort the principles of stare decisis and of ratio decidendi to contend that a decision lacks authority because it might have been reached upon a different path of legal reasoning to that which was actually followed. That would be to replace what was decided by that **[485]** which might have been decided. According to basic constitutional principle, and with qualifications not presently relevant, the intrusion of Commonwealth law into a field that has hitherto been the preserve of State law is not a reason to deny validity to the Commonwealth law provided it is, in truth, a law with respect to external affairs.

However, the joint judgment also emphasised the *limits* of the *Tasmanian Dam Case*. The treaty must embody precise obligations rather than mere vague aspirations, and the legislation must be "appropriate and adapted" to the implementation of those obligations.

Brennan CJ, Toohey, Gaudron, McHugh and Gummow JJ: [486] There may be some treaties which do not enliven the legislative power conferred by s 51(xxix) even though their subject matter is of international concern. For example, Professor Zines has suggested that a treaty expressed in terms of aspiration (for example "to promote full employment") cannot support a law which adopts one of a variety of possibly contradictory ways that might be selected to fulfil the aspiration ...

When a treaty is relied on under s 51(xxix) to support a law, it is not sufficient that the law prescribes one of a variety of means that might be thought appropriate and adapted to the achievement of an ideal. The law must prescribe a regime that the treaty has itself defined with sufficient specificity to direct the general course to be taken by the signatory states ...

Where the legislative power is said to be enlivened by a treaty binding on the Commonwealth of Australia, and the law prescribes a regime affecting a domestic subject matter, a question arises as to the **[487]** connection which must exist between the law and the treaty. To be a law with respect to "external affairs", the law must be reasonably capable of being considered appropriate and adapted to implementing the treaty. Thus, it is for the legislature to choose the means by which it carries into or gives effect to the treaty provided that the means chosen are reasonably capable of being considered appropriate and adapted to that end. But that is not to say that an obligation imposed by treaty provides the outer limits of a law enacted to implement it. The term "purpose" has been used to identify the object for the advancement or attainment of which a law was enacted. Hence, the statement by Brennan J in *Cunliffe v Commonwealth* [(1994) 182 CLR 272 at 322] that the external affairs power has "a purposive aspect". As this phrase indicates, care is required in relevant analysis. Where a treaty relating to a domestic subject matter is relied on to enliven the legislative power conferred by s 51(xxix) the validity of the law depends on whether its purpose or object is to implement the treaty ... In this context, purpose is not something found in the head of power. Rather, it is a test for determining whether the law in question is reasonably capable of being considered as giving effect to the treaty and therefore as being a law upon a subject which is an aspect of external affairs.

It has been said that a law will not be capable of being seen as appropriate and adapted in the necessary sense unless it appears that there is "reasonable proportionality" between that purpose or object **[488]** and the means adapted by the law to pursue it. The notion of "reasonable proportionality" will not always be particularly helpful. The notion of proportion suggests a comparative relation of one thing to another as respects magnitude, quantity or degree; to ask of the legislation whether it may reasonably be seen as bearing a relationship of reasonable proportionality to the provisions of the treaty in question appears to restate the basic question. This is whether the law selects means which are reasonably capable of being considered appropriate and adapted to achieving the purpose or object of giving effect to the treaty, so that the law is one upon a subject which is an aspect of external affairs.

Pursuant to this test the Court in fact held that, at least on the evidence available, certain elements in the legislation could *not* be supported as "appropriate and adapted" to the purpose of implementing the relevant Conventions. In the first place, termination of employment without "valid reason" was prohibited by s 170DE(1); and s 170DE(2) then added that "[a] reason is not valid if, having regard to ... the employee's capacity and conduct ... , the termination is harsh, unjust or unreasonable". The joint judgment held that this latter provision, though severable, was invalid as going beyond what was required by the ILO Convention Concerning Termination of Employment at the Initiative of the Employer (adopted 22 June 1982).

Brennan CJ, Toohey, Gaudron, McHugh and Gummow JJ: [517] Section 170DE(2) goes beyond the terms of the Convention because Art 4 of the Convention only requires the employer to comply with the equivalent of s 170DE(1). The question, therefore, is whether the selection of the criteria of harsh, unjust or unreasonable termination is an expression of the manner of the implementation of the Convention which, as we have indicated, is a matter for the Parliament, or whether s 170DE(2) is not reasonably capable of being considered appropriate and adapted to implementing the Convention obligations.

Article 4 of the Convention requires that employment not be terminated without a valid reason. Article 5 provides that a number of grounds "inter alia, shall not constitute valid reasons for termination". Those grounds, even if they would otherwise have constituted valid reasons for termination, are deemed not to be valid reasons. The use of the words "inter alia" recognises that the list in Art 5 is not an exhaustive one. There obviously will be other reasons for termination which, having regard to the capacity and conduct of the employee and the operational requirements of the employer, are not valid. However, the Convention does not specify in detail what those reasons are. It leaves the general word "valid" as the cornerstone of Art 4.

Section 170EDA(1) provides for a shifting onus of proof. Where an application alleges that a termination was not for a valid reason, the onus lies on the employer to prove that there was a valid reason (para (a) of s 170EDA(1)) but, even if the employer does so, the employee may still prove that the termination was harsh, unjust or unreasonable: para (b) of s 170EDA(1). Paragraph (a) is clearly supported by Art 9(2) of the Convention which provides that the methods of implementation of the Convention in relation to "the burden of proving the existence of a valid reason for the termination as defined in Article 4 of this Convention shall rest on the employer" or an alternative method detailed in the Article. There is no indication in the Convention that the onus might be a shifting one, requiring the employer to prove valid reasons for termination in some cases and the employee to prove that the reasons were not valid in other cases.

It is this shifting onus in s 170EDA(1) which indicates that the inclusion of the "harsh, unjust or unreasonable" test is an additional ground of unlawful termination that goes beyond the requirement for the reason for termination to be valid. The terms "harsh, unjust or unreasonable" are not merely a synonym for "valid". Had the Parliament recognised the terms as being synonyms, or even the harsh, unjust or unreasonable test as being a subset of grounds that were not **[518]** "valid", then there would be no reason for changing the onus from employer to employee between paras (a) and (b) of s 170EDA(1).

The changing onus in s 170EDA(1) indicates that the harsh, unjust or unreasonable criterion is broader than what otherwise would be the test for validity. This is reinforced by the nature of s 170DE(2) which, in contrast to s 170DE(1) and Art 4 of the Convention, goes not to the reason for termination but to the overall effects of the termination. It recognises that, whilst a reason for termination might be a valid one, the overall effect of the termination in the circumstances might be harsh, unjust or unreasonable. This supports the conclusion that the inclusion of the "harsh, unjust or unreasonable" criterion does not implement the terms of the Convention but goes beyond its requirements and adds an alternative ground for making terminations unlawful. For these reasons, ss 170DE(2) and 170EDA(1) are, at least in part, invalid.

In the second place, termination of employment for certain specified unacceptable reasons was prohibited by s 170DF(1). These included, by para (f) of that subsection, "race, colour, sex, sexual preference, age, physical or mental disability, marital status, family responsibilities, pregnancy, religion, political opinion, national extraction or social origin". Some items on this list were expressly specified by Art 1(a) of the ILO Convention Concerning Discrimination in Respect of Employment and Occupation (adopted 4 June 1958); others (including "age", "physical disability" and "sexual preference") had been determined "after consultation with representative employer's and worker's organisations" in the manner prescribed by Art 1(b). But the inclusion of "mental disability" was neither required by Art 1(a), nor apparently the subject of consultation pursuant to Art 1(b). However, "**[532]** as the material relating to consultation was not fully canvassed at the hearing" it was held that, rather than make an order of invalidity, "the better course is to give no answer in respect of that ground".

In the third place, the provisions contained in Pt VIB, Div 4, recognising a limited right of workers to strike, were generally accepted as giving (partial) effect to the "right to strike" proclaimed by Art 8 of the International Covenant on Economic, Social and Cultural Rights, and hence as valid under s 51(xxix). Within the limits of the "right to strike" as thus recognised, s 170PG(2) protected striking employees against the possibility of common law action. This, too, was held to be valid. But s 170PG(3) conferred similar protection against possible actions for breach of contract upon employers engaging in a lockout of employees; and although this was ultimately held to be valid under s 51(xxxv), it was not accepted as a valid use of power under s 51(xxix).

That the main "right to strike" provisions were held to be valid, although they stopped short of the full extent of the "right to strike" recognised by Art 8 of the International Covenant, was also significant. More generally, the joint judgment clearly held that partial implementation of a treaty is sufficient. The original view of Evatt and McTiernan JJ that, in order to claim validity under s 51(xxix), an enactment must implement the relevant treaty in its entirety, was rejected. However, this was so with a significant qualification. After quoting from the judgment of Deane J in the *Tasmanian Dam Case* at 268, Brennan CJ, Toohey, Gaudron, McHugh and Gummow JJ stated: "**[459]** Deficiency in implementation of a supporting Convention is not necessarily fatal to the validity of a law; but a law will be held invalid *if the deficiency is so substantial as to deny the law the character of a measure implementing the Convention* or it is a deficiency which, when coupled with other provisions of the law, make it substantially inconsistent with the Convention" (emphasis added).

In this instance, the Court expressly held that the new Pt VIA, Div 5 was valid as an implementation of the ILO Convention Concerning Equal Opportunities and Equal Treatment for Men and Women Workers: Workers with Family Responsibilities (adopted 23 June 1981): "**[524]**

[T]he circumstance that only part of the broad obligations imposed on Australia by the Family Responsibilities Convention is implemented in the Division ... is no objection to its validity". Similarly, as already noted, the "right to strike" provisions were held to be valid even though they "[546] can only represent a partial implementation of the right referred to in the Covenant ... because of the limited circumstances in which they are applicable".

At several points in the 1993 legislation the Parliament purported to rely not only on ILO Conventions, but also on the "Recommendations" by which the broad provisions of the Conventions had been fleshed out. The *Industrial Relations Act Case* was thus a potential opportunity for authoritative pronouncement on the suggestion by Evatt and McTiernan JJ in *R v Burgess* that mere "Recommendations" of the International Labour Organization might also be the occasion for legislation under s 51(xxix). In fact, however, the joint judgment was inconclusive on this point. At most, the Recommendations relied upon were relevant as signifying that the particular measures thereby recommended would be an "appropriate and adapted" means of satisfying the Convention. Thus, the reference to "parental leave" in the Recommendation Concerning Equal Opportunities and Equal Treatment for Men and Women Workers: Workers with Family Responsibilities (Recommendation No 165, adopted 23 June 1981) was referred to as giving additional support to the conclusion that the "parental leave" provisions in the new Pt VIA, Div 5, were "appropriate and adapted" as a means of giving effect to the similarly titled Convention of the same date.

The issue evoked a more general, but still equivocal, comment in relation to s 170BC(3)(b) of the Act, which required the Industrial Relations Commission to make orders requiring "equal remuneration for work of equal value" only if such an order "can reasonably be regarded as appropriate and adapted to giving effect to" (i) one or more of the relevant Conventions, or (ii) the Recommendation Concerning Equal Remuneration for Men and Women Workers for Work of Equal Value (Recommendation No 90, adopted 29 June 1951) or the Recommendation Concerning Discrimination in Respect of Employment and Occupation (Recommendation No 111, adopted 25 June 1958). As to this the joint judgment said:

> **Brennan CJ, Toohey, Gaudron, McHugh and Gummow JJ: [509]** The section refers separately to a measure being reasonably regarded as appropriate and adapted for giving effect to Recommendation No 90 or Recommendation No 111. That provision can be supported under s 51(xxix) if, but only if, the terms of these Recommendations themselves can reasonably be regarded as appropriate and adapted to giving effect to the terms of the Conventions to which they relate. In our view, they can be so regarded. Hence measures that fall within the terms of s 170BC(1) and implement the terms of the Recommendations will fall within the terms of s 170BC(3)(b)(i). On this line of reasoning, the words "can reasonably be regarded as appropriate and adapted to" in s 170BC(3)(b) may be superfluous in relation to the Recommendations but are obviously designed to cover the situation where the Recommendations are relied upon of themselves to support an exercise of the external affairs power. This is a point which, at this stage, it is not necessary to decide.

Compare the second sentence of this paragraph ("if, but only if") with the final sentence ("not necessary to decide").

(d)   Undermining the "federal balance"?

Four months after the *Tasmanian Dam Case*, Dawson J delivered the Southey Memorial Lecture at Melbourne University Law School. He painted a picture of sweeping changes being made to the Constitution "[354] upon the initiative of the Commonwealth supported by the interpretation given to the Constitution by the High Court", which if put to referendum would have been rejected, and which cumulatively result in almost unlimited Commonwealth power.

Sir Daryl Dawson, "The Constitution – Major Overhaul or Simple Tune-up?"

(1984) 14 *Melbourne University Law Review* 353

[358] I suppose that I must start with the *Dams Case* [(1983) 158 CLR 1] although I do so with some apology. The case has been so overlaid with the environmental theme, which has little relevance to the decision and none to my observations tonight, that it seems almost futile and even tedious to attempt to confine the case to what it really decides. On any view of that decision, it must now be said that the potential scope of Commonwealth legislative power is coextensive with the potential scope of international agreement. Since there is no theoretical limit to what may be the subject-matter of international agreement, the external affairs power may, as a matter of constitutional theory, be regarded as open-ended. Of course, there are practical limits. International obligations are not assumed lightly. It is unlikely that an international obligation would be undertaken merely for the sake of acquiring domestic legislative power and, if it were, the exercise would run the risk of being held to lack good faith and hence ineffective to achieve its purpose.

But the point remains that even with existing treaties to which Australia is a party, the Commonwealth presently has the capacity to cut a swathe through the areas hitherto thought to be within the residual powers of the States.

The number of treaties or international agreements, bilateral or multilateral, to which Australia is a party, runs into the hundreds. But ... the most significant so far as Commonwealth legislative power is concerned must surely be the Human Rights Covenants. To take some examples from the International Covenant on Economic, Social and Cultural Rights: Article 1 provides that all peoples have the right of self-determination. By virtue of that right they freely determine their political status and freely pursue their economic, social and cultural development. Article 4 recognizes that, in the enjoyment of those rights provided by the state in conformity with the Covenant, the state may subject such rights only to such limitations as are determined by law only in so far as this may be compatible with the nature of these rights and solely for the purpose of promoting the general welfare in a democratic society. Article 7 recognizes the right of everyone to the enjoyment of just and favourable conditions of work. Article 10 recognizes that the widest possible protection should be accorded to the family and that special measures of protection and assistance should be taken on behalf of all children and young persons without any discrimination for reasons of parentage or other conditions. Article 11 recognizes the right of everyone to an adequate standard of living for [359] himself and his family, including adequate food, clothing and housing, and to the continuous improvement of living conditions. And so on. No one could deny the desirability of the standards laid down by the articles of the covenant but no one, at the same time, could deny that they provide a broad base for legislative activity ...

To be sure, a Commonwealth law purporting to implement an international treaty must be able to be seen to be doing so. But with treaties written in language more appropriate to the political slogan than the precise regulation of human behaviour, the scope offered to the legislator remains wide. It has been said that it is not possible for the Commonwealth, once Australia enters into a treaty, to legislate with respect to the subject-matter of the treaty as if that subject-matter were a new and independent head of Commonwealth legislative power. But once it is accepted, as appears to be necessary, that it is not possible to implement a treaty by simply reproducing its terms in a domestic form, then any restraint suggested by that view is illusory. Clearly the Court will exercise its powers to ensure that Commonwealth legislation keeps to the treaty, but having regard to the views expressed in the *Dams Case*, the confines will not be narrowly drawn. In any event, it is patent that the construction of the external affairs power which has now found favour offers to the Commonwealth new and independent heads of power on a potentially limitless range of subjects, whatever restrictions are imposed or latitude allowed in the implementation of a particular treaty.

Against the background of these strongly held views, the judicial approach adopted by Dawson J in *Richardson v Forestry Commission* and the *Tropical Rainforests Case* involved an intriguing combination of strategies. In both cases, he deferred to the majority view and accepted the *Tasmanian Dam Case* as binding precedent while nevertheless continuing strongly to assert his own contrary view. He also pushed the decision in the *Tasmanian Dam Case* to its logical extremes, while keeping open the possible limits that might be derived from the idea of "international concern". In his last major judicial utterance on the topic, he again adhered to this strategy.

Victoria v Commonwealth (*Industrial Relations Act Case*)
(1996) 187 CLR 416

Dawson J: [564] In seeking to support the validity of those provisions of the *Industrial Relations Act* 1988 (Cth) which are challenged in these cases, the Commonwealth placed reliance upon its power to legislate under s 51(xxix) of the Constitution with respect to "External affairs". Those provisions, as the name of the Act would suggest, deal with industrial relations but in important respects travel beyond the **[565]** limits which the Constitution imposes upon the power of the Commonwealth to legislate with respect to that subject matter. Those limits confine Common-wealth power to the making of laws with respect to "Conciliation and arbitration for the prevention and settlement of industrial disputes extending beyond the limits of any one State". It is evident that the intention which lay behind the imposition of those limits was that the States should remain responsible for industrial relations within their borders except where, because of the interstate nature of a dispute, its prevention or settlement might be beyond the capacity of any one State. It was then, and only then, that the Commonwealth was to have power to prevent or settle the dispute, and then only by means of conciliation or arbitration.

For a long time the Commonwealth has found these restrictions on its power irksome. Com-mencing in 1910 it has sought amendments to the Constitution to remove them. None of these amendments have received the majority of votes required by s 128 for the amendment of the Constitution. The Commonwealth made its last unsuccessful attempt at amendment in 1946, this time by the insertion of the following paragraph in s 51 of the Constitution:

"(xxxivA) Terms and conditions of employment in industry, but not so as to authorise any form of industrial conscription".

It is ironical, to say the least, that the Commonwealth should seek and, upon the view adopted by the majority in these cases, find in the external affairs power a way to disregard the restrictions imposed upon it by s 51(xxxv) and to legislate in a manner denied to it by the continued refusal of the electors to amend the Constitution.

Not only is it ironical, but the result is such as to call into question the construction which produces it. It is one thing to say that the enumerated legislative powers given to the Common-wealth by s 51 may overlap. It is quite another thing to say that the carefully drawn limits upon one power may be disregarded in the construction of another. Where those limits are in the form of an exception to a power otherwise given – for example, the exception of State banking from the banking power – they must surely be given effect whatever paragraph of s 51 is under consi-deration. And even where the **[566]** limits are to be found in the definition of the subject matter of the power – as is the case with s 51(xxxv) – they must surely be taken into account in the construction of s 51 as a whole.

This is not to deny the plenary nature of the powers conferred by s 51, but before a power can be given full effect, its proper scope must be determined. For example, the power to legislate with respect to corporations under s 51(xx) is undoubtedly a plenary power, but that did not relieve the Court of the task of construing its terms to ascertain its meaning. And if the injunction that the Court should lean towards a broader rather than a narrower interpretation of the Constitution means that it should abandon the basic principle of construction that an instrument should be construed as a whole, then I respectfully dissent from its application in the present context.

What then is the construction of the external affairs power which supports legislation with respect to industrial matters which are confined to Australia and which are otherwise regarded by the Constitution as being of a domestic nature and does so in a manner which disregards the limits imposed by s 51(xxxv) upon Commonwealth power with respect to such matters? It is a construction which adopts the view that the legislative implementation of an international treaty made in good faith is within the ambit of the external affairs power. I have elsewhere expressed my disagreement with that view ...

[567] To say that any matter covered by a bona fide international treaty is, by its very inclusion in the treaty, brought within the ambit of the external affairs power is to say that the matters upon which there might be valid Commonwealth legislation are limited only by the capacity of the executive to conclude a treaty upon them. Effectively, it means that it is for the executive and not the Court to determine the scope of the external affairs power, for upon that view no distinction can be drawn in terms of subject matter between what might be described as external affairs and what might not. Yet that is a distinction which s 51(xxix) itself requires to be drawn by the use of the term "External affairs".

To adopt the view that a matter must exhibit some characteristic other than its inclusion in a treaty to fall within the external affairs power is not to adopt a restrictive interpretation of that power, nor is it to rely upon implications drawn from the federal nature of the Constitution. It is simply to recognise and apply the distinction which is necessarily made by s 51(xxix) between those matters which are [568] external affairs and those which are not. True it is that such a distinction is also required because otherwise s 51(xxix) would have the capacity to obliterate the division of power which is a necessary feature of any federal system and of our federal system in particular. But it is a distinction which is expressly made by the language used in s 51(xxix) and is not dependent upon implication ...

Australia is a federation and a "fragmentation" of the decision-making process is part and parcel of a federal system. Indeed, it is one of the reasons for choosing that system of government and may be seen as a virtue rather than as a vice ... [569] Accepting, as we must, that the system of government chosen by the people for this country is a federal system, it is difficult to see why "such a fragmentation of the decision-making process" – which is nothing more than a division of power – should be "altogether too disturbing to contemplate" ...

[T]he Commonwealth Parliament ... has specific power to make laws with respect to external affairs and matters incidental thereto, in addition to its other enumerated powers which may also be employed to implement treaties. The external affairs power is a broad power but for a law to fall within its terms, it must, in my view, operate upon something which is external to Australia. That is to give the power no narrow construction. A glance at the many treaties entered into by Australia in recent years shows that laws implementing the vast majority of them would deal with matters having an external aspect sufficient to satisfy such a test. But a law which has an entirely domestic operation cannot, in my view, be a law with respect to external affairs merely because it implements a treaty or is upon a subject matter which is of international concern ...

[572] Notwithstanding that I find nothing in the reasons of the majority in these cases which causes me to doubt the views which I have expressed above and in previous cases, I nevertheless think that I should adhere to the course which I adopted in *Richardson* [(1988) 164 CLR 261] ... [573] The parties in this case, as in *Richardson*, did not seek to contest the authority of the *Tasmanian Dam Case* and, proceeding upon the basis of that decision, I agree with the orders proposed by the majority.

The decision in the *Tasmanian Dam Case* remains controversial. A typical criticism is that of LJM Cooray and S Ratnapala ("The High Court and the Constitution – Literalism and Beyond" in Gregory Craven (ed), *The Convention Debates: Commentaries, Indices and Guide* (Legal Books, 1986), 203). They take up in more emphatic terms the concerns expressed by Dawson J in his Southey Memorial Lecture. As they put it, since 1901 the Constitution "[203] has undergone a transformation which has resulted in the translocation of substantial powers from the States to the central government", and has been "judicially executed ... without the approval of the people" by "an extraordinary legal subterfuge". They are especially critical of what they call "[225] the Murphy-Mason principle of broad interpretation". Clearly, what underlies such criticisms is the apparent expansion of Commonwealth legislative power involved.

5. Further References

Blackshield, AR, "Damadam to Infinities! The Tourneyold of the Wattarfalls" in Sornarajah, M (ed), *The South West Dam Dispute: The Legal and Political Issues* (University of Tasmania, 1983), 37.

Cass, D, "Traversing the Divide: International Law and Australian Constitutional Law" (1998) 20 *Adelaide Law Review* 73.

Charlesworth, H, "Dangerous Liaisons: Globalisation and Australian Public Law" (1998) 20 *Adelaide Law Review* 57.

Charlesworth, H, Chiam, M, Hovell, D, and Williams, G (eds), *The Fluid State: International Law and National Legal Systems* (Federation Press, 2005).

Coper, M, *Encounters with the Australian Constitution* (CCH, 1988), Ch 1.

Coper, M, *The Franklin Dam Case* (Butterworths, 1983).

Coper, M, "The Role of the Courts in the Preservation of Federalism" (1989) 63 *Australian Law Journal* 463.

Cranwell, G, "The Treaty Making Process in Australia: A Report Card on Recent Reforms" (2001) *Australian International Law Journal* 177.

Hovell, D, and Williams, G, "A Tale of Two Systems: The Use of International Law in Constitutional Interpretation in Australia and South Africa" (2005) 29 *Melbourne University Law Review* 95.

Kirby, M, "The Australian Use of International Human Rights Norms: From Bangalore to Balliol – A View from the Antipodes" (1993) 16 *University of New South Wales Law Journal* 363.

Lacey, W, "Judicial Discretion and Human Rights: Expanding the Role of International Law in the Domestic Sphere" (2004) 5 *Melbourne Journal of International Law* 108.

Lacey, W, "A Prelude to the Demise of Teoh: The High Court Decision in *Re Minister for Immigration and Multicultural Affairs; Ex parte Lam*" (2004) 26 *Sydney Law Review* 131.

Lacey, W, "In the Wake of *Teoh*: Finding an Appropriate Government Response" (2001) 29 *Federal Law Review* 219.

Lee, HP, "The High Court and the External Affairs Power" in Lee, HP, and Winterton, G (eds), *Australian Constitutional Perspectives* (Law Book Co, 1992).

McDermott, PM, "External Affairs and Treaties: The Founding Fathers' Perspective" (1990) 16 *University of Queensland Law Journal* 123.

Opeskin, B, and Rothwell, D (eds), *International Law and Australian Federalism* (Melbourne University Press, 1997).

Sampford, C, and Round, T, *Beyond the Republic: Meeting the Global Challenges to Constitutionalism* (Federation Press, 2001).

Saunders, C, "Articles of Faith or Lucky Breaks? The Constitutional Law of International Agreements in Australia" (1995) 17 *Sydney Law Review* 150.

Simpson, A, and Williams, G, "International Law and Constitutional Interpretation" (2000) 11 *Public Law Review* 205.

Thomson, JA, "Is it a Mess? The High Court and the *War Crimes* Case: External Affairs, Defence, Judicial Power and the Australian Constitution" (1992) 22 *University of Western Australia Law Review* 197.

Walker, K, "International Law as a Tool of Constitutional Interpretation" (2002) 28 *Monash University Law Review* 85.

Walker, K, "Treaties and the Internationalisation of Australian Law" in Saunders, C (ed), *Courts of Final Jurisdiction: The Mason Court in Australia* (Federation Press, 1996), 204.

Williams, D, "Treaties and the Parliamentary Process" (1996) 7 *Public Law Review* 199.

Zines, L, *The High Court and the Constitution* (Butterworths, 4th ed 1997), Ch 13.

Zines, L, "The *Tasmanian Dam* Case" in Lee, HP, and Winterton, G (eds), *Australian Constitutional Landmarks* (Cambridge University Press, 2003), 262.

Chapter 20

The Immigration and Aliens Powers

1. The White Australia Policy

This chapter concerns the Commonwealth's legislative powers with respect to "Immigration and emigration" (s 51(xxvii)) and "Naturalization and aliens" (s 51(xix)). Whether, independently of legislation, the exclusion or expulsion of aliens falls within the grant of Commonwealth executive power in s 61, as it was said to do during the *Tampa* controversy of 2001, is considered in Chapter 12, §2(a). That chapter also examines (in §4(b)) the extent to which the federal Parliament can exclude immigration decisions made by the executive from judicial review. A related issue, the scope for the mandatory detention of asylum seekers, even for an indefinite time, is considered in Chapter 15, §4.

Until the 1960s the political focus in this area was mainly on the "White Australia" policy – at first staunchly maintained by most Australians, but increasingly found unacceptable as the 20th century went on. Among its most vigorous defenders was Sir Isaac Isaacs. Throughout the "White Australia" period, the relevant Commonwealth legislation (usually involving amendments to the *Immigration Act 1901* (Cth)) relied mainly on the immigration power. The early case of *Potter v Minahan* (1908) 7 CLR 277 is typical of cases from this period in two important respects. One relates to the definition of "immigrant", the other to the "dictation test".

James Minahan was born in Victoria on 4 October 1876. His mother's name was Winifred Minahan. As Griffith CJ noted, she bore "**[286]** a British name" and "may be assumed to have been of British race". The reputed father was a Chinese named Teung Ming, with whom James' mother lived as his wife; but Griffith CJ held that "**[286]** [h]aving regard to conditions in Victoria in 1876, and to the relations between Chinese [men] and European women at that time", no presumption of marriage arose. On that assumption James acquired his mother's nationality (British) and his mother's domicil (Victoria).

When James was five years old his father returned to China, taking James with him. Winifred saw them off at the ship. The father still received money from his partnership in a country store in Victoria, to which he meant at first to return. But some 12 years later, when James was 18 or so, the father died, still in China. Before he died he gave James a copy of his birth certificate, "**[287]** apparently as a document establishing his right to return to Victoria". According to James, he planned to do so, but first sought to obtain the Chinese equivalent of a Bachelor of Arts degree (with the idea "**[313]** of better teaching Chinese to Australian boys of Chinese origin", said Isaacs J sceptically). He took examinations at three-year intervals in 1899, 1902 and 1905, but failed each time. He then decided to return to Australia.

The "prohibited immigrants" under s 3 of the *Immigration Restriction Act 1901* (Cth) included "any person who fails to pass the dictation test: that is to say, who, when an officer dictates to him not less than fifty words in any prescribed language, fails to write them out in that language". On arriving in Australia Minahan was met by a Customs officer, who testified: "**[279]** I told him I was going to read out … a passage of not less than fifty words in English, and I required him to write them in English. I said:– 'Here is paper and pencil … If you write them you will be allowed to land, and if you fail to write them you will not be allowed to land. I will read the passage slowly, and if you say you can write it I will read it out slowly again.' … [After reading the passage] I then asked him if he could write it, and he said he could not". Thereupon Minahan was charged, by Police Constable LF Potter, with being a prohibited immigrant. A magistrate dismissed the information on the ground that Minahan was not an "immigrant". Potter's appeal to the High Court was dismissed. One reason was that since the Customs officer had never actually dictated a passage, there had been no dictation test within the meaning of the Act. For Isaacs and Higgins JJ this was the sole reason, and for O'Connor J the primary reason. On this point Barton J was inclined to agree and Griffith CJ to dissent.

In other cases, the "dictation test" was a successful technique for excluding unwanted immigrants. On the other hand, strict judicial scrutiny of the "dictation test" became one way in which courts were sometimes able to mitigate the operation of government policy. The best-known example concerned the left-wing Czech novelist Egon Kisch. In 1934 Kisch was one of many celebrities invited to speak at a left-wing anti-war conference organised by the "United Front". Pursuant to a government campaign against communism, Commonwealth Attorney-General Robert Menzies sought to prevent the entry to Australia of several of the proposed speakers, including Kisch. The advance publicity was such that, when Kisch first arrived at Circular Quay aboard the SS *Straithaird*, the captain of the ship refused him permission to land, believing Kisch to be a prohibited immigrant. Kisch applied to the High Court for a writ of habeas corpus, which was granted by Evatt J sitting alone (*R v Carter; Ex parte Kisch* (1934) 52 CLR 221). Meanwhile, Kisch had broken his leg while attempting to jump off the ship. After winning the habeas corpus proceedings, he was carried ashore in a chair and taken to a police station where he was subjected to a "dictation test" in Scottish Gaelic. However, the High Court held, with Starke J dissenting, that this did not amount to a dictation test "in any European language" as was then required by the *Immigration Restriction Act*.

R v Wilson; Ex parte Kisch
(1934) 52 CLR 234

Dixon J: [244] I am disposed to think that [the expression "any European language"] means here to convey that a test is provided for immigrants depending upon a proper familiarity with some form of speech which in some politically organized European community is regarded as the common means of communication for all purposes, either throughout the whole body or throughout a complete society, if the political organization is composed of more than one community **[245]** of people. The provision means to supply that test as one which might properly be laid down by the Legislature for intending immigrants, however afterwards it might be applied in administration.

Adopting such a test, it appears to me that the Gaelic language has been shown to be at the present time an ancient form of speech spoken by a remnant of people inhabiting the remoter portion of the British Isles. Scottish Gaelic has also been shown to be quite a distinct form of speech from Irish Gaelic and other Celtic forms, and to have a separate identity which would make it not proper to treat it as merely a dialectical form of a general speech which is spoken on both sides of the Irish Sea. The remnant of people who speak this language is fast diminishing. If it were relevant to ascertain what the Legislature would have thought about Scotch Gaelic, if, in 1901, it had adverted to the question we have to decide, it might be right to look at the figures of the census of 1901 showing how many spoke it. But I do not think the date of 1901 is the period to be looked to for the purpose of inquiring whether Scotch Gaelic is now a language which properly answers the meaning we have assigned to the expression "an European language" in the *Immigration Restriction Act*. What are the attributes which the expression connotes, depends upon the general meaning which, of course, it possessed in 1901. But whether a particular form of speech possesses those attributes depends upon the facts and circumstances now affecting that form of speech. The figures show that, whilst it may be true that the areas of the country in which it is spoken have not been diminished so that it cannot be said that English, as an invader of the territory, has driven it back into narrower confines, yet within those areas there are very few people indeed who use that speech as their sole means of communication with their fellows. The inference appears to me to be very strong that in a modern community it has not been found a practicable medium for carrying on the affairs of daily life. People, who might otherwise have been able to preserve it, are called upon to mix in a society which either will not or cannot use it as a common means of communication. It is a speech which probably contains a vocabulary ill-fitted to deal with modern conditions. It is spoken by a people who appear to lead somewhat special lives, and do not move about and mix in the general life of **[246]** the whole community in Great Britain. In the Law Courts it is not a recognized form of speech, nor is it for any official purposes, though, of course, its existence is officially acknowledged as a fact. All these circumstances lead me to think that we cannot treat the matter philologically, and, because so treated it is a language, hold that the dictation test may be administered in it. The matter must be treated practically. Although it is quite untrue philologically to say that it is a dialect of some other standard speech, yet it is correct that in the British community it takes the same place and serves the same practical purpose as one of the more highly differentiated and persistent dialects spoken in the various English counties might take. It appears to me, therefore, that this speech spoken by so few people can be described as a European language only philologically, and that in the ordinary course of discussion of such a matter as educational tests for immigration it would not be understood as answering the meaning of the expression "an European language."

Four months later this decision led to one of the more outspoken public criticisms of the High Court. An editorial in the Sydney *Sun* on 13 April 1935 spoke of the Court's "**[4]** keen, microscopic vision for splits in hairs", and added: "When the amendments are made we should invite him to jump ashore again to see whether the new Act pleases the High Court any better than the old, or whether the ingenuity of five bewigged heads cannot discover another flaw ... Well may the Caseys and the Kellys cry, like the historic British monarch, for some gallant champion to rid them of this pestilent Court. Perhaps there is a better way. If the High Court were given some real work to do the Bench would not have time to argue for days on the exact length of the split in the hair, and the precise difference between Tweedledum and Tweedledee".

In *R v Dunbabin; Ex parte Williams* (1935) 53 CLR 434, the High Court was called upon to decide whether the newspaper company and the editor responsible for these comments should be punished for contempt of court. (The applicant was the same Dulcie Williams who was responsible for *R v Brislan; Ex parte Williams* (1935) 54 CLR 262 (see Chapter 8, §5). Albert Piddington KC (as to whom see Chapter 27, §1) appeared for her in both cases, and also appeared for Egon Kisch in all of the latter's High Court applications.) The result was that both the company and the editor were found guilty of contempt of court. The company was fined £200 and the editor £50. In earlier contempt proceedings against the *Sydney Morning Herald*, Evatt J, sitting alone, had declined to make any punitive order (*R v Fletcher; Ex parte Kisch* (1935) 52 CLR 248). However, in *Dunbabin* only Starke J dissented. In his typical gruff way he held that the editorial was obviously in contempt of court, but that, just as obviously, the Court would be foolish to take any notice of it. It seems likely that the approach of Starke J would nowadays be preferred.

2. "Once an immigrant always an immigrant"

Now return to *Potter v Minahan*, this time for the primary issue of whether Minahan was an "immigrant". On this issue a majority of three judges ruled in Minahan's favour, holding that he was not an "immigrant" – Griffith CJ by construing that word as used in the Constitution; O'Connor J by construing it as used in the Act; and Barton J "**[299]** whether measured by the Constitution or the Statute law". On this issue Isaacs and Higgins JJ dissented. For them the decision in Minahan's favour rested only on the failure to administer a "dictation test".

Despite the confused and overlapping majorities by which Minahan finally succeeded, the decision can now be regarded as establishing two significant principles: that the entry into Australia of a person who is not an "immigrant" cannot be regarded as coming within the "immigration" power (s 51(xxvii)); and that a person is not an "immigrant" if, at the time of entry into Australia, he or she is already a member of the Australian community who is merely "coming home" (though the various majority and minority judgments offered widely differing theories of what might constitute "membership" of the Australian "community").

Potter v Minahan
(1908) 7 CLR 277

Griffith CJ: [288] I do not think that the present case can be determined by the mere application of the rules either of nationality or of domicil. There is no doubt that a British subject coming to the **[289]** Commonwealth from another part of the British Dominions may be an immigrant within the meaning of the Constitution.

But anterior, both in order of thought and in order of time, to the concepts of nationality and domicil is another, upon which both are founded, and which is, I think, an elementary part of the concept of human society, namely, the division of human beings into communities. From this it follows that every person becomes at birth a member of the community into which he is born, and is entitled to remain in it until excluded by some competent authority. It follows also that every human being (unless outlawed) is a member of some community, and is entitled to regard the part of the earth occupied by that community as a place to which he may resort when he thinks fit. In the case of *Musgrove v Chun Teeong Toy* [[1891] AC 272] it was held that an alien (though an alien friend) has no legal right to enter a country of which he is not a national. Yet, unless he is outlawed from human society, he must be entitled to enter some community. So, by process of exclusion, we ascertain at least one part of the world to which every human being, not an outlaw, can claim the right of entry when he thinks fit.

At birth he is, in general, entitled to remain in the place where he is born. (There may be some exceptions based upon artificial rules of territoriality.) If his parents are then domiciled in some other place, he perhaps acquires a right to go to and remain in that place. But, until the right to remain in or return to his place of birth is lost, it must continue, and he is entitled to regard himself as a member of the community which occupies that place. These principles are self-evident, and do not need the support of authority …

The return of such a person to his native land after temporary **[290]** absence has never, so far as I have any acquaintance with the English language, been described as "immigration." That word is not a technical term of art, and when used in sec 51(xxvii) of the Constitution must receive its ordinary signification unless the context requires some other meaning to be adopted …

The respondent … was entitled by the circumstances of his birth to regard Victoria as his home. Upon the facts as found by the magistrate he has not himself, nor has anyone by whose acts he is bound, done anything to deprive him of that right, or to confer on him a right to enter or remain in any other part of the world, except so far as his British nationality may confer any such right.

It follows, in my judgment, that, although entry into another part of the British Dominions might and probably would have been immigration, his return to the Commonwealth was not immigration within the meaning of sec 51(xxvii) of the Constitution.

O'Connor J: [304] [I]t is always necessary, in cases such as this where a Statute affects civil rights, to keep in view the principle of construction stated in *Maxwell on Statutes*, 4th ed, p 121:– "There are certain objects which the legislature is presumed not to intend; and a construction which would lead to any of them is therefore to be avoided." …

Mr *Duffy* relied strongly on this principle, and urged that there was one right which it would not be assumed the legislature intended to take away except by express words or necessary implication. That is the right of every British subject born in Australia, and whose home is in Australia, to remain in, depart from, or re-enter Australia as and when he thought fit, unless there was in force in Australia a positive law to the contrary. The existence of that right is, to my mind, beyond serious controversy. It follows as a matter of reason from one of the fundamental principles of international law. Speaking generally, every person born within the British Dominions is a British sub-**[305]**-ject and owes allegiance to the British Empire and obedience to its laws. Correlatively he is entitled to the benefit and protection of those laws, and is entitled, among other things, to entry and residence in any part of the King's Dominions except in so far as that right has been modified or abolished by positive law. But the British Empire is subdivided into many communities, some of them endowed by Imperial Statute with wide powers of self government, including the power to make laws which, when duly passed and assented to by the Crown, will operate to exclude from their territories British subjects of other communities of the Empire. To this extent the British subject's right to enter freely into any part of the King's Dominions may be modified by Statute law. The right is founded on the obligations of national allegiance. International law recognizes for purposes of allegiance only sovereign nationalities – not sub-divisions of a nation – and in questions between the British Empire and other nations Australian nationality cannot be recognized. But in questions between the Australian community and its members it would seem to follow that the principle which regulates rights as between the British Empire and its subjects must be applied in determining the relations of the Australian community to its members. A person born in Australia, and by reason of that fact a British subject owing allegiance to the Empire, becomes by reason of the same fact a member of the Australian community under obligation to obey its laws, and correlatively entitled to all the rights and benefits which membership of the community involves, amongst which is a right to depart from and re-enter Australia as he pleases without let or hindrance unless some law of the Australian community has in that respect decreed the contrary. It cannot be denied that, subject to the Constitution, the Commonwealth may make such laws as it may deem necessary affecting the going and coming of members of the Australian community. But in the interpretation of those laws it must, I think, be assumed that the legislature did not intend to deprive any Australian-born member of the Australian community of the right after absence to re-enter Australia unless it has so enacted by express terms or necessary implication.

Higgins J: [320] It is urged that there is an Australian species of British nationality; that a man born in Australia is an **[321]** "appendage to the soil"; that when a man goes back to the land of his birth he is not "immigrating," &c. I cannot find any foundation for these contentions. Throughout the British Empire there is one King, one allegiance, one citizenship. I use this last word, not in the Roman or in the American sense, but only because there is no suitable abstract noun corresponding to the word "subject" … Even when England and Scotland were distinct kingdoms under one King, from 1603 to 1707, there was no distinction recognized between English and Scottish citizenship. There was not one local allegiance for the subjects of England, and another local allegiance for the subjects of Scotland. All the King's subjects are members of one great society, bound by the one tie of allegiance to the one Sovereign, even as children hanging on to the ropes of a New Zealand swing. The top of the pole is the point of union: *Calvin's Case* [(1608) 2 St Tr 559]. The fact of birth on British soil made the respondent a British subject, owing allegiance and entitled to protection; but that is all. I know of no principle of British law to the effect that a man has some peculiar right to resort to one particular part of the Empire as distinguished from other parts. He is free to move at will throughout the Empire, unless some law forbid him; and this right he has by virtue of his natural liberty: *libertas naturalis est facultas ejus quod cuique facere libet nisi quod jure prohibetur (Bracton)*. It is a fundamental characteristic of British law that British subjects are free to act except so far as they are forbidden … If the argument of the respondent's counsel were urged against the exclusion of any British subjects from Australia, I could understand it. It might be urged that Parliament cannot be supposed to have meant to interfere with the right of all British subjects to go and come within the Empire. But the Court has already decided that the Act does apply so as to exclude even British subjects: *Attorney-General for the Commonwealth v Ah Sheung* [(1906) 4 CLR 949] … If the respondent's theory is to be deduced from the nature of **[322]** human society, there would be equally strong ground for deducing also a right to subsistence, and a right to share in the land of the country; but such rights are unknown to British law.

If the central holding in *Potter v Minahan* was that persons "coming home" are not within the reach of the immigration power, the corollary was that any person entering Australia who is not "coming home" *is* within the reach of that power – and can therefore be prevented from entering

THE IMMIGRATION AND ALIENS POWERS

the country (or having entered, can be deported). That this extends to mere "visitors" – and even to British subjects – was made clear in *R v Macfarlane; Ex parte O'Flanagan and O'Kelly* (*Irish Envoys' Case*) (1923) 32 CLR 518. Father Michael O'Flanagan and John O'Kelly had come to Australia, under the auspices of Archbishop Daniel Mannix, to campaign against the agreement for an "Irish Free State" excluding Northern Ireland. The public furore that followed can be gauged by the following item from the *Sydney Morning Herald*.

The Sydney Morning Herald
21 March 1923

[13] IRISH DELEGATES
REPUBLICAN ENVOYS.
PROTESTS IN MELBOURNE.

MELBOURNE, Tuesday.

The visit to Melbourne of two members of the Irish Oversea Mission is already causing trouble, not merely on account of the strong feeling which is apparent in Protestant circles, but principally among a certain section of Roman Catholics. The latter have emphatically protested against utterances made on Saturday and Sunday by the visitors, whose object it has been stated is to speak to Irish sympathisers in Australia and to enlighten them on the position in Ireland, thus giving them an opportunity of "hearing the other side". The delegates, the Rev Father O'Flannagan and Mr JJ Kelly, will consult with leaders of Irish opinion in Australia in de Valera's name, to try and find a way to lasting and honourable peace in Ireland.

Letters, signed by Roman Catholics, are appearing in the Press, and clearly show that strong exception is being taken to the object of the mission. One writer states: "What we Irish out here want to know is: If the Irish hierarchy to a man backed by 98 per cent of the Irish people, support the Free State Government, why should the Rev Father O'Flannagan be out here to try and upset that Government? Why is he not at home in his little country parish attending to the wants of his people, instead of working against his own bishops?"

In a letter to the "Argus", a correspondent, who signs himself "Australian Catholic," states: "Is there no end to the humiliation continually being heaped upon Victorian Catholics by certain Irish-born ecclesiastics, who, apparently, fail to realise that, after all, their country supplies only a very small moiety of the 272,860,000 adherents to the Church throughout the world? We Australian Catholics resent strongly the efforts of these clergymen to associate our Church with the treason and sedition of their countrymen in Ireland."

At a meeting of the King William Royal Orange Lodge, a motion was agreed to "That this Orange Lodge, consisting of 500 members, strongly and emphatically protests against the disloyal speeches which were delivered at the Exhibition Building and St Patrick's Hall, on Saturday and Sunday last, involving the honour of the Empire. We strongly object to the mission of the two Republican delegates and respectfully call on the Prime Minister to protect the Commonwealth from the dissemination of such treasonable and seditious sentiments."

Throughout April 1923 the controversy continued. Finally, at the end of the month, the two men were arrested on charges of sedition. In May, while the criminal charges were pending, they were summoned to appear before a Board established under s 8A of the *Immigration Act* to show cause why they should not be deported. (A recommendation by the Board was a basis for deportation.) The High Court unanimously refused to intervene in the hearing before the Board. Four of the five judges based their decision on a holding that the use of s 8A in such a case was constitutionally valid. The only dissenter was Higgins J, but he also held that High Court intervention at this stage was premature, since, if the proceedings were to result in an unlawful deportation order, the two men would then be able to apply for habeas corpus.

The first constitutional issue was whether the *Immigration Act* could apply to British subjects: even Higgins J somewhat ambiguously held that it could, though in *Potter v Minahan* he had spoken of all British subjects throughout the Empire as belonging to "[321] one great society" with "one tie of allegiance to the one Sovereign". It may be that some lingering wish on his part to maintain the freedom of British subjects "to move at will throughout the Empire" contributed to his dissent on the other two constitutional issues involved. First, he held that the "immigration" power did not extend to a person entering Australia merely as a temporary "visitor", with no intention of permanent settlement. Secondly, he held that the power was applicable only to "[574] the act of immigrating" – that is, that it could only be exercised at the point of entry into Australia, so that once having been allowed to enter the country, the "Irish envoys" had passed beyond the reach of the "immigration" power. On both these points the other four judges took a wider view of the power, spelled out most emphatically by Isaacs J.

R v Macfarlane; Ex parte O'Flanagan and O'Kelly (*Irish Envoys' Case*)
(1923) 32 CLR 518

Isaacs J: [552] The second objection suggests that the Constitution was looking, not to the nature of the persons who might immigrate and how they if admitted might affect the community, but to the mere mode or time of their arrival. Obviously, if the "act" of immigrating were the sole subject matter of legislation, nothing happening before or after that "act" could be dealt with by Parliament. An attempt to enter upon false credentials, if unsuccessful, could not be legislated for, since there would be no actual "immigration." And on that hypothesis also, no legislative condition imposed, even before arrival [553] and to operate afterwards by force of the Act, could be insisted on … If, however, it be once admitted that the law independently could impose subsequently arising obligations, then the method of creating them is entirely within the discretion of the Legislature, and its choice of means cannot be questioned unless contrary to some provision in the Constitution. The dictionary was appealed to for the meaning of the word "immigration." Like many other words in our language, it is more or less flexible. But what I regard as a very valuable as well as authoritative declaration as to the interpretation of statutes, is contained in a judgment of the Privy Council in the case of *The Lion* [(1869) LR 2 PC 525 at 530]. There Lord *Romilly* said: "The meaning of particular words in an Act of Parliament, to use the words of *Abbott* CJ in *R v Hall* [(1882) 1 B & C 123 at 136; 107 ER 47 at 51], 'is to be found not so much in a strict etymological propriety of language, nor even in popular use, as in the subject or occasion, on which they are used.'" That statement is extremely apposite here. The word "immigration" was not inserted in reliance on some lexicographer's opinion of what that word conveyed in the various collocations in which it might be found. It was adopted on the occasion when (*inter alia*) governmental powers which experience had shown were not exercisable with full advantage to the whole of Australia were transferred either exclusively or supremely to the Commonwealth. It had come to be seen that the piecemeal and not wholly identical treatment of the subject of "immigration," as it came to be called, by the separate Colonies was far from satisfactory or effective; either from an Australian or an Imperial standpoint. It was an urgent question awaiting early treatment by the single hand of a united people by the light of experience. The history of that experience is enlightening, but, it will be seen, is confirmatory only of the meaning properly and normally attachable to the words as they stand in a national grant of legislative power. "Immigration and emigration" is the simple but unqualified subject of power, and no words could be wider to enable a Parliament to deal territorially with all that is comprised within the operations connoted [554] by the words. Immigration, for instance, connotes the persons who immigrate and their movements, including departures, travel, arrival, entry, and presence after arrival. Legislation with reference to immigration means legislation to control the matter; and it includes legislation, if Parliament so desires, for the encouragement as well as the restriction of immigration. It could hardly be contended that the Federal Parliament, if it were minded to encourage a particular form of immigration, could not lawfully include in its scheme a method of settling the immigrants after they arrived and providing for their wants … But if the argument of the "instant of entry," and that alone, be fallacious when applied to the encouragement of immigration, how can it be correct when applied to restriction? It is perforce conceded that there is power of absolute exclusion, as well as of absolute admission. But the suggestion is that there is no *via media*. The Commonwealth has, it is conceded, unlimited power over immigration, but – so runs the argument – it has not power to admit immigrants conditionally … I am at a loss to understand how any solid foundation can exist for the contention.

Where there is power to prohibit absolutely, there must be power to relax that prohibition without entirely surrendering it ... Look at the matter practically. Parliament, let us suppose, is willing and anxious that eligible immigrants shall be admitted, but determined that dangerous persons shall be excluded ... **[555]** Say, for instance, insane persons or tuberculous persons are prohibited. A man arrives and, to all appearance and so far as examination can discover, he is neither insane nor tuberculous. Nevertheless, after admission he may manifest symptoms which show that he had at the instant of arrival one or other of those afflictions latent in his system and on the point of manifestation. What is the Commonwealth to do? Is it definitely to refuse what may be a valuable citizen, or definitely and irrevocably to receive what may be a dangerous element into its midst? Why, within the ample scope of the immigration power, can it not say:– "We will admit you conditionally; if within three months or three years you manifest insanity or tuberculosis, then we shall regard you as having been a lurking danger when you entered, and you must leave. If, however, that time passes, and you appear still free from insanity or tubercle, then we definitely receive you as an inhabitant of Australia"? I cannot understand why a Legislature, having the extensive power as formulated in *R v Burah* [(1878) 3 App Cas 889 at 904], cannot, in the absence of limiting words at least, take the middle course as I have indicated it. It must not by any means be taken that I am suggesting that as the limit of the power. Far from it. Except in the case of a person Australian born, who having abandoned this country as his home is readmitted and so restored to his original status, an "immigrant" – that is, a person whose original home was elsewhere and who comes to this country for any purpose – remains an "immigrant" as long as he is in Australia. As to him, while in Australia, the rule holds "Once an immigrant always an immigrant," and the Parliamentary power is never abandoned and cannot be abandoned. It seems to me a needless and improper restriction of language to alter the word "immigration," normally denoting the broad social movement of persons from abroad and passing into this country, to the microscopic verbal expression "immigration" denoting merely the momentary and isolated act of entering the country.

As to the supposed exclusion of "visitors" from the reach of the power, Isaacs J went on:

Isaacs J: [555] The third objection is scarcely consistent with the second. It is that "visitors," – however criminal, immoral, or diseased, or **[556]** degraded, or of whatsoever race or colour – are entirely outside the true notion of "immigration," and beyond the power of the Commonwealth Parliament to exclude. Let me give some striking examples of what this means. "Prohibited immigrants," as defined, include (among others) the following: idiots, persons suffering from a serious transmissible disease, or pulmonary tuberculosis, or any loathsome or dangerous communicable disease, or any defect liable to render them a charge on a public or charitable institution, persons convicted of crime and imprisoned within five years, prostitutes, and persons living on prostitution, and persons who advocate the overthrow by force or violence of the established government of the Commonwealth or of any State. The argument unadorned is simply that such persons if they come as "visitors" – no limit being suggested to the period of time or the object of their visit – are free to enter the Commonwealth, bring their dangers with them and mingle with the general population, with such results as may be expected to follow. Is our Constitution so grotesque as is represented? ... It is contended that there is no power but as to "immigration" or possibly "aliens." But the power as to "aliens" leaves a huge gap, sufficient in itself to paralyse the Commonwealth unless "immigration" covers it. Why are "visitors" not within the immigration power? It is said that "immigration" connotes "settlement," or at least "some continuance" in the country. "Settlement" probably means a permanent adoption as a home. But, short of that, where can any line be drawn? And when is it to be drawn? If the first objection is good, then the intention to "settle" or "to have some continuance" of stay must exist and must be capable of being predicated at the moment of the "act" of entering – or otherwise the second objection is unfounded. But in that event, if a person arrives and genuinely has formed no intention as to his future stay or departure, leaving that to be determined after inquiry so that he may leave in a week or remain for life, then, according to the extraordinary suggestion, he is a "visitor," and so he cannot be excluded ... **[557]** [O]nce admitted, he is admitted, it is said, with all his imperfections and cannot be removed, though the next week he determines to remain a component part of the Australian people. It is a most fantastic result of the vaunted power of a great people to control its own destiny, that it cannot even preserve its immunity from all the evils that afflict humanity, physical, moral or anarchistic, provided only they come to us in the embodiment of a "visitor." A power to legislate "with respect to" immigration, even assuming that word has the limitation of meaning suggested, necessarily includes the power of preventing it by any means and to any extent desired, and therefore of excluding any specified class of persons irrespective of their present intention. But, in truth, such a fantastic result as would ensue from the contention referred to has never, as might well be supposed, been the accepted thesis of the people of Australia, or indeed of any part of the Empire. The history of this country and its development has been, and must inevitably be, largely the story of its policy with respect to population from abroad. That naturally involves the perfect control of the subject of immigration, both as to encouragement and restriction with all their incidents. This control, I hold, the Commonwealth Parliament possesses in amplitude.

Before Federation the governmental power of controlling immigration had been very extensively exercised by the various Colonies for many years. At the time the Constitution was framed it was obviously one of immense importance to the present and future well-being of the continent. From various aspects it was essential to place it on a proper footing … [U]nless the recited power is sufficiently broad to meet, not only possible, but very probable, movements of population from other parts of the world towards Australia, we have but a crippled Constitution wherewith to meet the necessities of the future. That it is ample, in relation to this power, to protect the people of Australia physically, racially, industrially and socially, is, to my mind, perfectly clear, not only from the inherent meaning of its terms as already construed, but also when we consider how the word "immigration" **[558]** was understood in Australia in 1900 … Immigration had been dealt with in several forms before Federation. Assisted immigration had been the legislative policy of all the Colonies in one way or another for many years. At last it prejudicially affected the remuneration and other conditions of labour, and was gradually … abolished. Among the methods that had been adopted in part of Australia was the introduction of colored labour, and the subject eventually excited keen opposition and did much to arouse a sentiment that is of paramount national significance, a determination to preserve a White Australia. How that sentiment is possible of effectuation, consistently with the notion that colored "visitors" (if not aliens) have an unchallengeable right of entry into Australia, passes my comprehension. If coolies or others (not being aliens) can enter Australia without challenge as "visitors," and can afterwards at will become "inhabitants" irremovable by the Commonwealth, what guarantee do all the industrial laws and arbitration awards afford in the face of such a mass of unskilled labour as would be thrown on the market – to say nothing of the social consequences? But, besides the encouragement of immigration, the subject, even before Federation, took on another phase, that of restriction … The Chinese, for some ten years, had immigrated in considerable number to Australia, and a shipping strike had occurred by reason of the employment of Chinese on steamers. An Intercolonial Conference in 1880 had considered the advisability of concerted action of all the Colonies both in representation to the Imperial Government and in local legislation. Disputes between Colonies took place on the subject of introducing Chinese labour, and representations were made to the Home Authorities by New Zealand and all the Australian Colonies except Western Australia … **[559]** Legislation was enacted, but Australia was then under separate Governments, and some Chinese entered in the Northern Territory and found their way to other parts of the continent. In March 1888 a ship called the *Afghan* arrived in Melbourne with Chinese passengers for various parts … [A] severe political crisis ensued, and the Courts were called upon to determine the rights of the Chinese to land. The legal proceedings can be read in the cases of *Ex parte Leong Kum* [(1888) 9 NSWLR (L) 250], *Ex parte Woo Tin* [(1888) 9 NSWLR (L) 493], *Ex parte Lo Pak* [(1888) 9 NSWLR (L) 221] and *Ex parte Lau You Fat* [(1888) 9 NSWLR (L) 269]. [Another] Intercolonial Conference was held, and is thus recited in the Queensland Act of 1888:– "Whereas at a meeting of representatives of Australasian Governments, held at Sydney in the month of June one thousand eight hundred and eighty-eight, it was amongst other things resolved that it is desirable that uniform Australasian legislation should be adopted for the restriction of Chinese *immigration*: And whereas the provisions of this Act were approved of by such representatives as the basis of such uniform legislation," &c. The Act (which in more or less similar terms became common in Australia) begins the later type of "Immigration Restriction Acts." Its essential features were:– (1) Exception from its operation of (a) persons accredited by a Government; (b) persons born in the Colony; (c) exempted persons. (2) It affects every person described as affected irrespective of his intention to remain in the Colony for any definite or indefinite time or purpose. (3) Entry into the Colony by any Chinese passenger by water was forbidden, except in accordance with the Act, under pecuniary penalty and liability to imprisonment. (4) Entry by a Chinese by land, which was of course through another Colony, without a permit rendered him liable to like penalties and also deportation to the Colony whence he came ...

[561] Another phase or type of legislation soon appeared. In 1891 ... South Australia passed an Act called the *Immigration Limitation Act*. It provided that on arrival of any ship an officer was to go on board and, if he found among the "passengers" *any person* who (1) was convicted of felony elsewhere or (2) was indigent as well as lunatic, idiot, deaf, dumb, blind, &c, and likely to become a public charge, a bond should be required for five years to pay any expenses of maintenance; and, by sec 3, if during the five years the passenger should be convicted of felony or misdemeanour or should be publicly maintained, his cost of maintenance should be recouped to the State or institution incurring it. Again there is no limitation to persons intending to settle permanently or for any continuance of time. In 1896 the question of coloured immigration became somewhat acute. South Australia ... passed an Act extending the Immigration Restriction Acts to coloured immigrants. Assent was reserved, but never given. There were political difficulties in the way of an Imperial or international character that were fully recognized by the Colonies. In 1897 the Federal Convention met, and resulted in entrusting this great national power to Australia as a whole. It is demonstrably plain that the Australian Colonies were, under the name of "immigration restriction," endeavouring to deal with the arrival of persons from abroad who, if they came into Australia at all, might, from their personal attributes or characteristics, in some way, according to national standards, operate against the welfare of the people of Australia. No limitation or test in point of purpose or time was thought of: it was *the presence* here of the immigrants described that was deemed undesirable – except on the terms and conditions expressed. And unauthorized arrival in some cases was met by deportation from one Colony to another. It was not the "act" of crossing that was thought detrimental to the Colony: it was the class of "persons" [562] who were objectionable. It was the simple and solid fact of transference of such persons into Australia – styled "immigration" – that was provided against ... Who could imagine that, when "immigration" was entrusted to the Commonwealth Parliament, Chinese visitors were to be henceforth free from interference? Such a contention puts back the clock of Australian history a quarter of a century.

Note how Isaacs J introduces the aphorism "[555] Once an immigrant always an immigrant". Although he purports to be quoting a common saying, it is generally assumed that the phrase was his own, and in later cases it was inseparably linked with his name. He uses the phrase to suggest that any person who, at the time of original entry to Australia, is not "coming home", is forever after subject to the reach of the "immigration" power. The alternative view is that, at some indeterminate time after entry into Australia, a migrant becomes so completely "absorbed" into the Australian community as to be beyond any continued reach of the power. Once "absorbed", such a person is as much "at home" as the Australian-born part-Chinese in *Potter v Minahan*. This notion of "absorption" is imprecise, since it postulates a gradual process that cannot be pinpointed as occurring at any precisely identifiable time. It may also reflect an underlying policy of "assimilation" at odds with later policies of multiculturalism.

Nevertheless, the "absorption" view is now regarded as correct, although there has never been a definitive High Court judgment to that effect. As late as the 1960s it was thought to be still in doubt which view of the "immigration" power should be applied – the "absorption" view or "Once an immigrant always an immigrant". An article by PH Lane, "Immigration Power" (1966) 39 *Australian Law Journal* 302, advocating the "absorption" view, had some influence in inducing the modern consensus. In retrospect, the decisive turning point had been the majority decision in *Ex parte Walsh and Johnson; In re Yates* (1925) 37 CLR 36.

The case arose from the seamen's strike of 1925, the climax to a militant campaign by the leaders of the Australian Seamen's Union, Tom Walsh and Jacob Johnson. A new s 8AA was added to the *Immigration Act*, specifically for the purpose of deporting the two men.

Immigration Act 1901 (Cth)

8AA (1) If at any time the Governor-General is of opinion that there exists in Australia a serious industrial disturbance prejudicing or threatening the peace, order or good government of the Commonwealth, he may make a Proclamation to that effect ...

(2) When any such Proclamation is in force, the Minister, if he is satisfied that any person not born in Australia has been concerned ... in acts directed towards hindering or obstructing ... the transport of goods or the conveyance of passengers in relation to trade or commerce with other countries or among the States, *or* the provision of services by any department or public authority of the Commonwealth, *and* that the presence of that person in Australia will be injurious to the peace, order or good government of the Commonwealth in relation to matters with respect to which the Parliament has power to make laws, may ... summon the person to appear before a Board ... to show cause why he should not be deported from the Commonwealth [emphasis added].

The purpose of this amendment was spelled out (in *Hansard*, House of Representatives, 8 July 1925) by Dr Earle Page, who spoke of "**[778]** certain persons who have come to this country from abroad ... these imported leaders of labour ... undesirables from abroad who try to set at nought the laws and traditions of this country". However, Walsh (born in Ireland in 1871) had migrated to New South Wales in 1893, while Johnson (born in Holland in 1885) had migrated to New South Wales in 1910 and was naturalised in 1913.

The Court held by 5:0 that the "immigration" power could not validly apply to Walsh, since he was already a member of the Australian community before the Commonwealth came into existence – that is, one limit on the "immigration" power is that it can only apply to persons entering Australia after 1 January 1901. While this conclusion in itself no longer has practical significance, it suggests the important principle that, although Parliament can exercise its powers retrospectively, no retrospective law can be made to alter the legal situation at an earlier time unless the enacting parliament would have had power to effect such an alteration *at that earlier time*. Higgins J gave effect to this view by holding that the new s 8AA was invalid. The other judges "read it down" so as to operate only in respect of arrivals after federation. On that basis the section was validly enacted, but could not apply to Walsh.

A majority consisting of Knox CJ, Higgins and Starke JJ reached similar views as to Johnson. The "immigration" power could not extend to anyone who had become part of the Aust-ralian community. For Higgins J, s 8AA was invalid, and for the other two judges it was to be "read down" so as not to apply to Johnson.

Ex parte Walsh and Johnson; In re Yates
(1925) 37 CLR 36

Knox CJ: [62] The power undoubtedly extends to every person who is, at the relevant time, an immigrant, that is to say, a person coming into Australia who is not at the time of entry a member of the Australian community. If the question be whether he is entitled to enter Australia, the question for decision is whether at that time he is not a member of the Australian community and is therefore subject to the immigration power. If the question be whether he is entitled to remain in Australia, or, stated otherwise, whether he may be lawfully expelled from Australia under a law made under the authority of this power, and of this power only, the question for decision is whether he is, at the time when it is sought to expel him, a person who is not a member of the Australian community and who is therefore subject to the immigration power. On any given day any person either is or is not a member of the Australian community. If on a given day a person seeking to enter Australia be exempt from the operation of a law made under this power purporting to prohibit his admission, he cannot, in my opinion, be on that day subject to the operation of a law made under the same power purporting to authorize his expulsion. The liability of any person to inclusion **[63]** within the ambit of this power ... must, in my opinion, be determined on the same considerations whether the law made under the power be directed to restricting his right to enter the Commonwealth or to destroying his right to remain there. The decision in *Potter v Minahan*

[(1908) 7 CLR 277] clearly establishes ... that a person whose permanent home is in Australia and who therefore is a member of the Australian community is not, on arriving in Australia from abroad, an immigrant ... It is true that in that case the person in question was born in Australia and lived in Victoria for a few years before the institution of the Commonwealth in 1901, but none of the Justices who took part in the decision treated these facts as of themselves decisive ... There is nothing in the reasons given by any member of the Court which suggests that the decision would have been the other way if the respondent in that case had, by birth or residence in Australia, acquired a home there after the institution of the Commonwealth instead of before that event ... **[64]** It seems to me to follow from the opinions expressed in that case, that a person who has originally entered Australia as an immigrant may, in course of time and by force of circumstances, cease to be an immigrant and become[ ] a member of the Australian community. He may, so to speak, grow out of the condition of being an immigrant and thus become exempt from the operation of the immigration power. The power to make laws with respect to immigration would, no doubt, extend to enable Parliament either to prohibit absolutely or to regulate as it might think fit immigration into Australia, but, in my opinion, it does not extend to enable Parliament to prohibit or regulate anything which is not immigration, and the decision in *Potter v Minahan* shows that, when the person seeking to enter the Commonwealth is a member of the Australian community, his entry is not within the **[65]** power to make laws with respect to immigration. I agree with the opinion expressed by my brother *Starke* in *R v Macfarlane* [(1923) 32 CLR 518 at 581] that Parliament has authority under this power to expel or deport from the Commonwealth any person who does not belong to the people of Australia, but I can find no reason for extending that authority so as to include within the scope of this power persons who have become members of the Australian community.

Isaacs and Rich JJ agreed as to Walsh (that is, as to persons already within the Commonwealth in 1901), but dissented as to Johnson.

Isaacs J: [81] I have expressed my own view emphatically in the *O'Flanagan Case* [(1923) 32 CLR 518], that once a person immigrates into Australia he is always subject to the power of the Parliament under construction. I endeavoured to crystallize my view into the maxim "Once an immigrant always an immigrant." A person arriving as an immigrant into the Commonwealth comes *subject to all the constitutional powers of the Parliament of Australia*. Its permission to him to enter may be either conditional or **[82]** unconditional. He has no right to enter Australia against the will of its people. He can enter only in pursuance of their will, and subject to their constitutional right to qualify or withdraw that permission at any time or under any circumstances they think proper. No Parliament – for Parliament is only the legislative instrument of the people – can either by action or inaction surrender or weaken or forfeit that national power. Immigration, as I have explained in the *O'Flanagan Case*, is not obliterated for ever by the mere passage across the frontier, nor by the momentary leap over a barrier which magically and instantaneously transforms a Hindoo or a Kanaka, for example, into an Australian. If such were its meaning, the cherished national policy of Australia would indeed be in peril. And it would only nominally lessen the peril if the Hindoo or the Kanaka by immediately adopting Australia as his "home," as it is said, could, so to speak, dig himself into this Commonwealth, so as to be irrevocably, so far as the Commonwealth power is concerned, a member of the people of the Commonwealth – a true Australian – and thereby escape the immigration power for ever. He could afterwards, as it is said, irrespective of nationality, of sentiment, of customs, of everything except his resolve to stay in Australia indefinitely as his "home," remain here or travel back and forwards, leave when he pleased, enter as he chose, and claim all the rights of a native-born Australian who had never abandoned his country. For this Court to so hold would, in my opinion, be a tragedy. The immigration power would practically be a dead letter once the frontier was passed, whatever shred of theory remained ...

[84] Dr *Evatt* urged ... that, once an immigrant becomes *in fact* incorporated into the mass of the community, he escapes from the reach of the constitutional power. Before analyzing that contention I may premise that such incorporation could hardly be asserted if in violation of a law existing at the time it occurred. For instance, if a surreptitious entry were made, and concealed until actual settlement took place, it would probably be conceded to be ineffectual. But if entry were permitted on stated terms and before settlement was completed, which might not occur for years, suppose a law was passed extending the term of probation, would the settlement *in fact*, contrary to the extending law, be effective to annul the constitutional power as to that individual? I am not sure what the contention would be in that case. I answer the question decidedly in the negative. But supposing the settlement takes place before the alteration of the law, the contention then is that never afterwards can the constitutional power of the Australian people apply even retrospectively to the individual in question. And now let me analyze the contention. It is and must be simply this: Until an immigrant, *whenever he arrives* in Australia, has settled down so as in fact to have his "home" in Australia as a home which he finally adopts without intention of ever leaving Australia, he is still an immigrant, whose "movement" of immigration is uncompleted. That is to say, his "immigration" is still a presently existing fact on which the Commonwealth power can operate. Let me at once point out one most startling and serious, but unavoidable, consequence of this curious doctrine … **[85]** [I]f continued "movement" is the test of continuing immigration, and if the indefinite word "home" is the test whether the immigration is still in progress, then *many persons who immigrated into Australia before the establishment of the Commonwealth were, even after its establishment and for many years, and may be still, in "movement" and so within the immigration power of the Commonwealth Parliament.* It would as to them be always a fighting question of fact whether they have even now definitely adopted Australia as their "home" and escaped the immigration power. To me that is wholly inconsistent with the clear-cut view of the Constitution that I have adopted, namely, that where there was entry by any person into the Commonwealth prior to the birth of the Commonwealth, then, if that person still remains here, he is entirely outside the immigration power of the Commonwealth.

But in truth there lurks in the contention … a basic fallacy which, if not eliminated, leads to disastrous results. It ignores the fundamental principle that it is the original entry, the "immigration," that attracts the power; that all that takes place afterwards takes place by virtue of and flowing from the original permission, and must be based on that permission; that that permission was originally and always remains a matter of law, that *the law is an essential element in determining whether or not a man is originally or has become and remains an Australian, having a right to be here* (the very argument assumes it), and, lastly, that the law may be altered retrospectively so as to remove from the relevant circumstances that essential element of legal right to be present on Australian territory. Let me give a concrete illustration. For example, an Italian (to take a member of a great foreign European country) or a Hindoo (in order to include British subjects as well as aliens) arrives at the Port of Sydney in 1925, and desires to enter the Commonwealth. He is, of course, subject there and then to the immigration power. There may be no immigration law made under that power, or the law may say nothing as to him. He enters. He settles and perhaps marries, and so acts that he becomes domiciled within a year, and is so satisfied with his surroundings that he abandons all intention of leaving Australia. If of foreign nationality **[86]** he becomes naturalized so as to enjoy certain advantages which an alien cannot have. Australia is his "home" as far as *he* can make it so. It is said he is incorporated into the Australian community. Then he begins activities designed to establish anarchical and terroristic or treasonable societies. Parliament retrospectively enacts that all persons immigrating as from 1924 shall be deportable as prohibited immigrants, if they are found engaging in such practices. Is it the law of the Constitution that he is immune? Cannot Parliament, acting for the people of the Commonwealth, alter or even revoke the permission which was given tacitly to immigrate into Australia? Or, phrasing it differently, cannot Parliament, by virtue of the legislative authority, said to be as wide for local purposes as that of the Imperial Parliament, regulate *ab initio* its permission to him to enter and reside in Australia? Can he say in opposition to such an enactment: "I have made my home here in fact, and that fact which has taken place and has legal force only by permission of the Parliament has obliterated the fact that I immigrated; that my immigration is annulled for all legal purposes, and now it is beyond the power of the Commonwealth to remove me"? By what authority and on what principle, I would ask, can this Court refuse to acknowledge the binding force of a Commonwealth Act retrospectively declaring the law as to the original immigration of the man into Australia – a subject it could have controlled at its inception? I believe this is the first time in the history of British jurisprudence that such a doctrine has ever been pressed upon a Court … It would be a ruling which would write a new chapter on constitutional law, entirely foreign to the whole theory and practice of the British constitution (see *The Ironsides* [(1862) 31 LJ PM & A 129 at 131]), quite contrary to the law laid down by Lord *Selborne* in *R v Burah* [(1878) 3 App Cas 889 at 904], and contrary to the view of Lord *Macnaghten* in *Colonial Sugar Refining Co v Irving* [[1905] AC 369], contrary to the decision of this Court in *R v Kidman* [(1915) 20 CLR 425], and not supported by any restriction or limitation **[87]** found in our written Constitution. I repeat as to the immigration supposed: "Once an immigrant always an immigrant." Suppose further, while enjoying the full permission to remain in Australia, after making his home here he leaves for Italy or India on a visit merely. So long as the *statute law* remains unaltered, he is, in law, on his return not immigrating, and he may enter unchallenged. But if in his absence the law is altered, so as to declare him a prohibited immigrant by a retrospective alteration, express or implied, of the former permissive law, as at the date of his original entry, has he the right to force his way in? Again I apply "Once an immigrant always an immigrant." We must, of course, carefully discriminate between the constitutional power and the statute. *I apply the aphorism only to the power, not to the statute.* He may not be always an immigrant, taking the statute as the test; or rather he may not always, according to that test, be a prohibited immigrant. But, for the purposes of the *power*, the aphorism holds without exception … Whatever the Federal Parliament can do or permit, it can undo or recall.

Despite this unyielding stand on the constitutional issue, Isaacs and Rich JJ agreed that the deportation proceedings must fail, but only on a procedural point under the terms of s 8AA. The summons issued to Walsh and Johnson had recited the Minister's satisfaction of *all* the matters mentioned in sub-s (2), adding no specific details but simply transcribing the statutory language exactly. Isaacs and Rich JJ held that this was inadequate because it gave no indication to Walsh and Johnson (nor even to the Board) of the charges they had to answer; and no proof that the Minister was ever "satisfied" of any relevant acts.

The language of sub-s (2) was important for another reason as well. The reference to "trade and commerce" supported an argument that the legislation might be valid under s 51(i); the reference to services by any Commonwealth "department or public authority" supported a similar argument based on s 52(ii); and the reference to "matters with respect to which the Parliament has power to make laws" supported an argument based on *all* the heads of power in s 51. In addition, the Commonwealth relied on s 51(xxxix), the express incidental power, as read in conjunction with *any* of the provisions in s 51, or alternatively in conjunction with the executive power of "execution and maintenance … of the laws of the Commonwealth" given by s 61. Isaacs and Rich JJ, in dissent, accepted validity on most of these grounds. The three majority judges rejected them. Higgins J did so on the idiosyncratic ground (expressly rejected by Starke J, and clearly incompatible with the now-settled approach to heads of Commonwealth power) that because the Commonwealth had purported to rely primarily on the "immigration" power, it *could not* now support the legislation by invoking alternative heads of power. But Higgins J also agreed with the main point on which Knox CJ and Starke J relied.

Ex parte Walsh and Johnson; In re Yates
(1925) 37 CLR 36

Knox CJ: [69] The only connection between this law and the trade and commerce power is … that the law may come into operation if the Minister is satisfied that the person sought to be affected by it has at some time been concerned in acts directed towards hindering or obstructing transactions which are part of inter-State or foreign trade or commerce. But, although participation in such acts may be the matter as to which the Minister is satisfied in accordance with the earlier provisions of the sub-section, the person concerned in those acts is liable to deportation, if the Minister is satisfied that his presence in Australia will be injurious to the peace, order or good government of the Commonwealth in relation to (for example) divorce and matrimonial causes or invalid and old-age pensions. The reference to acts directed towards hindering trade or commerce is introduced into the enactment, not for the purpose of prohibiting such acts, or of enabling persons committing or attempting to commit them to be punished for, or prevented from, doing so, but merely for the purpose of furnishing a condition precedent to the exercise by the Minister of the power of deportation. So far as foreign or inter-State trade or commerce is concerned, the enactment prohibits no act, enjoins no duty, creates no offence, imposes no sanction for disobedience to any command, prescribes no standard or rule of conduct. It purports to do no more than arm the Minister with power to prevent an injury, the nature of which is not defined, to the peace, order or good government of the Commonwealth in relation to any matter in respect of which the Parliament has power to make laws. And that power may be exercised although the person dealt with has never been concerned in any transaction of inter-State or foreign commerce, or in hindering or attempting to hinder any such transaction, if the Minister is satisfied of the existence of an alternative condition precedent. The enactment does not purport in any respect to authorize, prohibit, regulate, or affect any transaction which is included in the subject matter described as "trade and commerce with other countries, and among [70] the States," or to prescribe any rule of conduct for any person engaged in such trade and commerce. The real aim and object of the enactment is to authorize the Minister to deport from the Commonwealth any person whose presence in Australia will, in his opinion, be injurious to the peace, order or good government of the Commonwealth in relation to any matter with respect to which the Parliament has power to make laws. An Act with this as its only real aim and object, having no connection with foreign or inter-State trade or commerce beyond that which I have indicated, cannot, in my opinion, consistently with the use of words in their ordinary meaning, be described as an Act with respect to trade and commerce with other countries and among the States.

The idea here developed picked up a submission made on behalf of Walsh and Johnson by Dr HV Evatt (at 50-1). It emerged more fully in *Australian Communist Party v Commonwealth* (*Communist Party Case*) (1951) 83 CLR 1 as the doctrine that, in the words of Fullagar J, "[258] a stream cannot rise higher than its source" (see Chapter 18, §6).

In the *Irish Envoys' Case* Isaacs J had argued that a Commonwealth Parliament wishing to *encourage* immigration must surely be able to establish "[554] a method of settling the immigrants after they arrived and providing for their wants". Although he then swung back into his cry of "Once an immigrant always an immigrant", it is possible to discern here the seeds of an alternative approach. This is that the "immigration" power is exhausted once a person has been "absorbed" into the Australian community – but that the process (and therefore the power) of "immigration" *includes the process of absorption*. Hence, for persons who make a new home in Australia, the process of "immigration" comprises not only the initial entry into the country but also the more gradual process of settling into a "home". Even before the "absorption" theory had gained full acceptance, this two-stage analysis of the steps to which the "immigration" power extends was elaborated in *O'Keefe v Calwell* (1949) 77 CLR 261.

In that case only Latham CJ and Dixon J found it necessary to consider the constitutional issue. Once again, the majority were able to rule against deportation on non-constitutional grounds. Annie O'Keefe, formerly Annie Maas, was a native of Celebes (Sulawesi). When the Japanese invaded Borneo in 1942, she and her husband Samuel Jacob, with their eight children, escaped. At that time the island was a Dutch possession and the whole family were Dutch subjects. They were evacuated by an Australian warship, which brought them to Australia, where they had another child. Annie Maas had not voluntarily chosen to enter Australia, and initially had no intention of permanent settlement. But after her husband, while working for the Dutch intelligence service, was killed in a plane crash in 1944, she and her children stayed on in Melbourne. In 1947 she married John O'Keefe and thus became a British subject.

Meanwhile, on 16 January 1947, she had obtained a "certificate of exemption" under s 4 of the *Immigration Act*, acting on advice from the Immigration Department in response to an inquiry about how to regularise her position. Under s 4 such a certificate could be granted to "any person who … is liable to be prohibited under this Act from entering or remaining in the Commonwealth". But s 4 also provided that a person whose "certificate of exemption" had *expired* was liable on that ground to be declared a prohibited immigrant. After several extensions, O'Keefe's certificate expired on 31 December 1948. In February 1949 the Minister for Immigration, Arthur Calwell, declared her to be a prohibited immigrant, and she was served with a notice requiring her to leave Australia.

The whole procedure was lawful only if, on 16 January 1947, the "certificate of exemption" was validly granted – that is, only if *on that day* she was a person "liable" to be prohibited from remaining in the Commonwealth. In one sense she *was* so liable. At any time within five years after her entry into Australia (that is, at any time up to September 1947) she might have been required to submit to a dictation test under s 5 of the Act; and on failing such a test she would have been liable to be declared a prohibited immigrant. However, looking at her position on 16 January 1947, Rich, McTiernan, Williams and Webb JJ held that this kind of contingent liability was not what was meant by the word "liable" in s 4 of the Act. Hence her "certificate of exemption" was not validly granted under s 4, and all subsequent proceedings based upon it were also invalid. On this issue of construction, Latham CJ and Dixon J dissented. Accordingly they, and only they, had to consider whether s 4 could validly apply to such a case. They held that it could (that is, that O'Keefe could validly be deported).

O'Keefe v Calwell
(1949) 77 CLR 261

Latham CJ: [276] It is … argued that the plaintiff has now made her home in Australia and has become a member of the Australian community, so that the *Immigration Act* can no longer be applied to her – *Potter v Minahan* [(1908) 7 CLR 277]. In January 1947, when she applied for and was granted a certificate of exemption, she was an alien awaiting return to her own country when conditions permitted. Laws with respect to immigration may properly control, not only the act of entry into Australia, but also the conditions upon which persons not already members of the Australian community may be permitted to remain in Australia. The basis of s 4 of the Act is that persons may be permitted to remain in Australia for limited periods, which may be extended from time to time, so that … they are not remaining in Australia in contravention of the Act. The exemption may be for any period – days, months or years. There is no time limit prescribed in the Act. But such persons … cannot, during that period, become members of the Australian community so as to become entitled to remain here permanently. It is true that the plaintiff has married an Australian husband, has an Australian home, has children who are going to school here, has joined her husband's church, and has her whole life here. But a person cannot become a member of the Australian community by his own act when he has been admitted and has been allowed to remain in Australia only under a temporary permit authorized by statute. Section 4 expressly provides that such a person, who originally could have been excluded altogether, may be deported in accordance with the provisions of the section.

There is in my opinion no ground for holding that such provisions cannot be enacted under a power to make laws with respect to immigration. Such a power is a power to make laws with respect to the whole subject of immigration – with respect to each and every element in immigration. "Immigrants" include persons who are intending settlers in a country other than their own and seek to enter (or do enter) that country and to remain in it for the purpose of making a permanent home there, or who, having entered another country without any original intention to settle there, do in fact endeavour to remain in that country as members of the community. Control of immigration involves control of the admission of such persons and determination whether such admission is to be allowed **[277]** to be permanent or only temporary. Such control is the means of determining the composition of the population of a country in respect of the admission of external elements. Admission of any person not already a member of the community may, under a power to make laws with respect to immigration, be allowed or prevented either completely or partially and subject to conditions as Parliament thinks proper. There could be no effective control of the subject of immigration if it were not possible to limit the entry and stay of persons who claimed that they were only making a short visit, or if it were not possible to deport persons who were allowed into the country only for a specified period and who then changed their minds and wished to remain permanently. Immigration into a country, if completed, involves two elements, (*a*) entry into the country, and (*b*) absorption into the community of the country. Both of these elements can be controlled under a power to make laws with respect to immigration. It is unnecessary and somewhat unconvincing to seek to justify legislation as immigration legislation upon the basis of a contention that *any* entry into a country is "immigration" … Such legislation is justified as legislation upon the subject of immigration because without control of the entry of all persons not already members of the community there cannot be control of the second element – possible absorption into the community. Thus laws with respect to immigration may impose conditions of entry upon such persons and may provide for the limitation of the period during which they are to be permitted to remain in Australia, and may lawfully provide for their deportation upon the expiry of that period.

Dixon J: [287] Without the guidance of decided cases I should have regarded the legislative power with respect to immigration contained in s 51 (xxvii) of the Constitution as ample justification for s 4 in its application to such a case as that of the plaintiff. Its valid operation upon her does not appear to me to depend upon the question whether the manner of her entry and the reasons for her continued presence here warrant the application to her of the word immigrant. The purpose of s 4 is to provide a means of ensuring that persons who come here ostensibly or actually for a temporary stay do not make Australia their permanent home. Whether or not a person who comes here for a temporary purpose may be said to have done anything which comes within some allowable meaning of the word "immigration" itself, it must, as I think, be within the power with respect to immigration to take measures to see that he does not remain here. It is a constitutional power carrying with it everything necessary or proper for the fulfilment of its purpose and it must be incidental to the power to provide for the admission of strangers on terms that they leave after a specified period and do not so to speak turn themselves into settlers. In the same way similar terms may be imposed on those whose entry has been allowed designedly or inadvertently but who have not any title to stay …

[288] Once the plaintiff came under s 4 and received an exemption certificate no attempt on her part to make Australia her permanent home could prevent the operation of the provision. The legislation adopts the machinery of an exemption certificate to prevent persons entering or remaining except by consent and then so long only as the consent continues. If that is within the legislative power with respect to immigration, as I think it is, it is difficult to understand how a person holding an exemption could by nevertheless resolving to make Australia her permanent home and by identifying herself with this country pass from the operation the Constitution allows to the provision. Had she become by lapse of time and long continued acceptance a member of the community before receiving her exemption it might have been otherwise. However, those are not the facts. But a construction has been given to the constitutional power with respect to immigration by a series of cases. After what was said … by *Cussen* J in *Ah Sheung v Lindberg* [[1906] VLR 323] and by this Court in *Chia Gee v Martin* [(1905) 3 CLR 649], *Potter v Minahan* and *R v Macfarlane; Ex parte O'Flanagan and O'Kelly* [(1923) 32 CLR 518], it seems impossible to do other than treat the power over immigration as relating to all movement of strangers into the Commonwealth independently of the intention of the persons who enter. So long as the new arrival is a stranger and not one of the people of Australia the legislature may deal with the question whether he enters and on what terms he enters or remains. See particularly per *Starke* J in *R v Macfarlane* [32 CLR at 580]. The Act is construed accordingly. See per *McMillan* J in *Mann v Ah On* [(1905) 7 WALR 182]. The chief point of distinction relied upon for the plaintiff was that when the plaintiff reached Australia she came involuntarily. She exercised no choice but was brought by a naval vessel as an evacuee from a scene of Japanese invasion. It is no doubt a distinction in fact. But I cannot see how it takes the case outside the principle. If the principle is that the intention of the person entering is irrelevant, it cannot matter that the plaintiff had no intention except to do what she was told and to escape from the Japanese. If the principle is that it is incidental to the immigration power to control the entry and presence in Australia of all strangers lest they settle here, then the circumstances of the entry and the intention or want of intention of the visitor are equally irrelevant.

The principle enunciated by Latham CJ is that immigration involves "[277] two elements", entry and absorption, *both* of which can be regulated under the immigration power. That principle is now generally accepted (see *R v Forbes; Ex parte Kwok Kwan Lee* (1971) 124 CLR 168). It received a somewhat unsatisfactory application in *R v Director-General of Social Welfare; Ex parte Henry* (1975) 133 CLR 369 – a decision on the validity of the *Immigration (Guardianship of Children) Act 1946* (Cth). Under that Act "every immigrant child" was placed under Ministerial guardianship "until the child reaches the age of twenty-one years or leaves Australia permanently, or until the provisions of this Act cease to apply to and in relation to the child, whichever first happens". A majority of the Court held that this provision must be "read down" so as not to apply to a child who had been "absorbed" into the Australian community, but that as so read down it was valid. Whether "absorption" would be completed only upon the child turning 21, or by some earlier and more gradual process, was not entirely resolved, though most judges seemed to favour the latter view, and Murphy J insisted that the child's 18th birthday must nowadays be an upper limit. Only Jacobs J saw a lingering "half truth" in the old maxim "Once an immigrant always an immigrant".

R v Director-General of Social Welfare; Ex parte Henry
(1975) 133 CLR 369

Jacobs J: [384] It must however be borne in mind that in [the earlier] cases the extent of the immigration power was being explored in the particular aspect of deportation. Useful as they are in determining the meaning of the word "immigration" and the general nature of the power it is important not to transpose concepts apposite to the aspect of deportation into other aspects of the power ... It does not follow that because a person has entered Australia and been permitted to remain here and to become a member of the Australian community, therefore no law ... whose validity depends upon the immigration power can validly apply to such a person. It is within the immigration power not only to control entry and absorption into the Australian community of persons not born in Australia but also, as an incident of the power, to make laws which so relate to the special needs or special characteristics of immigrants that the subject matter of a law dealing particularly with immigrants may be valid as a law with respect to immigration even where the subject matter generally is not one upon which the Commonwealth has power to leg-**[385]**-islate. There is truth in the aphorism that the power is in respect of immigration and not immigrants. But there is truth also in the aphorism "Once an immigrant, always an immigrant". Like most aphorisms in the law they are both no more than half-truths and they solve nothing. In relation to deportation a day comes, it has been held, when an immigrant is absorbed into the Australian community so that he cannot thereafter be deported under the immigration power. But the concept of absorption into the Australian community, though it is a useful consideration in all aspects of the power, has a different content in the context of deportation from that which it has in other contexts of the immigration power. So long as an immigrant has a special need or so long as Australia has a special need from him then so long may the Commonwealth legislate in respect of that special need of the immigrant or the country; and this may be so even if he has become a member of the Australian community in that he can no longer be deported. Of course it could be said that so long as an immigrant has a special need or Australia has a special need from him then he has not been absorbed into the Australian community. But it can only be correct provided that it is then kept clear that the words "absorption into the Australian community" are used in this context with different content and application from those in the context of deportation. Therefore, State laws discriminating against immigrants politically economically or socially could be avoided by a Commonwealth law prohibiting such discrimination. Likewise forms of discrimination by individuals could be prohibited in respect of all, or any particular class of, immigrants; and the law would be valid even though the particular immigrant had been so far absorbed into the community that he could no longer be deported.

3. Naturalisation and Aliens

Progressively, since *Ex parte Henry*, the focus of legislative and bureaucratic activity, and hence of constitutional exegesis, has tended to shift away from s 51(xxvii) to s 51(xix). In the earlier cases it was often suggested that the "aliens" power might in some ways be broader than the "immigration" power – primarily because alienage, being a legal status, is displaced by a formal legal grant of naturalisation or citizenship, not by a gradual process of "absorption". In *Potter v*

Minahan Higgins J had fastidiously avoided using the word "citizenship" "**[321]** in the Roman or in the American sense"; but more recently, the contrast between "aliens" and "citizens" has been used as a legal and conceptual device to define the membership of the Australian community.

(a)   Citizenship

The Constitution does not mention citizenship (except in s 44(i), which provides that a "citizen of a foreign power" cannot be a member of the federal Parliament). Certainly, it contains nothing like the 14th Amendment to the United States Constitution, which states: "All persons born or naturalized in the United States and subject to the jurisdiction thereof, are citizens of the United States and of the State wherein they reside". In speaking of the political community that constitutes the Commonwealth, the Australian Constitution instead refers to "the people", for instance when s 24 identifies the electorate for the House of Representatives as "the people of the Commonwealth", or when s 53 excludes any Senate amendment that would increase any "charge or burden on the people".

The development of the law of Australian citizenship was thus left to Parliament. The first Act on the subject was the *Nationality and Citizenship Act 1948* (Cth), which in 1973 was retitled the *Australian Citizenship Act 1948* (Cth). In *Hwang v Commonwealth* (2005) 222 ALR 83, McHugh J, sitting alone, rejected a challenge to the validity of the Act. He did so on the basis that the power to make laws with respect to citizenship "**[86]** arises simply from the emergence of Australia as an independent nation, it is because of *the fact* that it is an independent sovereign nation and that other nations recognise it as such". He also held that such power arises "from the express and implied powers of the Parliament of the Commonwealth to declare who are the persons who are members of the Australian community. It arises partly by implication out **[87]** of the Parliament's status as the national Parliament and its entitlement to define who are 'the people' who make up the Australian community. And it arises partly out of its express power to make laws with respect to immigration, naturalisation and aliens". He noted in this context that the "frequent reference to 'the people' of the Commonwealth" in the Constitution "is a synonym for citizenship of the Commonwealth".

An amendment to the *Australian Citizenship Act* in 1993 introduced a new preamble, reciting the legislative assumptions on which "citizenship" nowadays depends.

Australian Citizenship Act 1948 (Cth)

Australian citizenship represents formal membership of the community of the Commonwealth of Australia; and Australian citizenship is a common bond, involving reciprocal rights and obligations, uniting all Australians, while respecting their diversity; and

Persons granted Australian citizenship enjoy these rights and undertake to accept these obligations
   by pledging loyalty to Australia and its people, and
   by sharing their democratic beliefs, and
   by respecting their rights and liberties, and
   by upholding and obeying the laws of Australia

Under s 13, a person granted citizenship is expected to have "an adequate knowledge of the responsibilities and privileges of Australian citizenship". The 1993 amendments replaced the former requirement of an "oath of allegiance" with a "pledge of commitment", in which the prospective citizen must repeat the undertakings set out in the second recital above. To that extent, a "normative" conception of citizenship is superimposed on its legal significance.

Kim Rubenstein, "Citizenship and the Centenary – Inclusion and Exclusion in 20th Century Australia"

(2000) 24 *Melbourne University Law Review* 576

[578] [The] legal formal notion [of citizenship] is primarily concerned with the legal status of individuals within a community. For instance, in Australia citizens are contrasted with permanent residents, temporary residents and unlawful non-citizens ...

The normative notion of citizenship is not as concerned with these legal questions; rather, it sees membership as becoming 'increasingly universalistic and open-ended'. Citizenship is discussed in non-legal, normative frameworks in a variety of ways, primarily in terms that look to the material circumstances of life within the polity, and notably to questions of social membership and substantive equality. In this way the normative notion is much broader than the legal notion. It is a progressive project which is not just concerned with legal citizens, but with persons and the way persons should act and be treated as members of a community. In fact, there is a disjuncture between the legal notion, which is an exclusive one, and the normative notion, which seeks to be inclusive and universal ...

[579] The *Australian Constitution* ... is the formal legal starting point for understanding citizenship. However, 'citizenship' is largely omitted from its terms, a situation influenced by various factors. As colonies of the United Kingdom, Australians were obviously legally British subjects at the beginning of the 20th century. It might be imagined that Australian citizenship was not of concern to those drafting the *Constitution* because citizenship was missing from our legal lexicon. However, that is far [580] from the case. Citizenship concerned the drafters acutely and they made a conscious effort to exclude the term from Australia's foundational legal document.

John Quick, a delegate to the Constitutional Conventions and later commentator with Robert Garran on the *Constitution*, sought to include a definition of Australian citizenship when he argued that the Commonwealth should have the power, under what is now s 51 of the *Constitution*, over Commonwealth citizenship. Discussion of citizenship had also occurred when debating what is now s 117 of the *Constitution*, which is concerned with discrimination between residents of the various States. However, the drafters of the *Constitution* resolved to leave the legal concept of the Australian citizen vague and undefined, as they feared that all attempts to define citizenship would land them in 'innumerable difficulties'. The debate over Quick's proposal largely concerned the problem of categorisation: how to deal with people of other races, particularly Chinese and Indian residents, who had originated in other British colonies? If 'citizens' were defined as subjects of the Queen, then not only would Chinese people from Hong Kong be treated differently from those from other parts of China, but they would also be able to claim citizenship of the Commonwealth ...

The historical and social evolution of membership of Australia from the late 1850s lays the foundations of the theme running through this article – exclusion and inclusion – and is still relevant to notions of citizenship today. From the 1850s onwards, all the colonies were in agreement about restricting Asian, particularly Chinese, immigration. Anti-Chinese sentiment developed during the gold rush era, when many Chinese men arrived on contracts formed through agents in China to replace the labour lost to the goldfields. By 1859 there were 42 000 Chinese people in Victoria, which amounted to a ratio of about one in 12 to 14 Europeans. The Victorian Legislative Council established a Select Committee on [581] Chinese Immigration in 1857 to frame a Bill to control the flood of Chinese immigration, resulting in 'An Act to Regulate the Residence of Chinese Population in Victoria'. Twenty-three years later these concerns were voiced at the Australasian Inter-Colonial Conference of December 1880 – January 1881. A report to the British government at the conclusion of the conference stated: 'In all the six Colonies a strong feeling prevails in opposition to the unrestricted introduction of Chinese, this opposition arising principally from a desire to preserve and perpetuate the British type in the various populations.' ...

[582] Issues regarding membership were definitely a national issue, of concern to the whole Commonwealth, not just to the individual colonies. In fact, one piece of legislation introduced into the first Commonwealth Parliament was the Immigration Restriction Bill 1901 (Cth). The debate over the Bill resembles the debates over the question of citizenship in the Convention Debates. Alfred Deakin was at pains to point out that the Bill involved touching 'the profoundest instinct of individual or nation – the instinct of self-preservation – for it is nothing less than the national

manhood, the national character, and the national future that are at stake.' Moreover, he referred to the **[583]** *Constitution* as 'contain[ing] within itself the amplest powers to deal with this difficulty [immigration] in all its aspects.' This fear and antagonism towards aliens, such as Chinese immigrants, contributed to a particularly 'Australian' sense of nationhood ...

In the first part of the 20th century, there was active discussion about Australian citizenship, even though it was not yet a formal legal term. As Irving argues, citizenship was a term of popular usage 'in speeches, in the press, in the rules and charters of organisations, and in debates about political entitlements'. This notion of citizenship 'entailed commitment, belonging, and contribution'. This reflects the normative, universal notion of citizenship then in use. However, in law the major distinction of membership in Australia for the first 50 years of the Commonwealth was between British subjects and aliens. At common law, a person's formal legal status was determined by their allegiance to the monarch, whether by birth or through naturalisation. Even so, David Dutton has explained that a

> *de facto* administrative Australian citizenship operated during the period which arose from the necessity of distinguishing between those British subjects who were permanent residents and belonged to the Commonwealth (in the sense that they could not be deported), and those British subjects who were merely visitors or who were yet to reside in Australia long enough to be regarded as belonging.

Thus there were three forms of membership – those who were British subjects permanently residing in Australia, those who were British subjects and temporarily in Australia, and those who were not British subjects and were aliens. This **[584]** broader distinction between aliens and British subjects, which framed Australian citizenship in the first 50 years of the 20th century, has continued to this day with the current distinction between citizen and non-citizen. The preference for British subjects has disappeared relatively recently ...

[587] Australia has only recently commemorated the 50th anniversary of the *Australian Citizenship Act 1948* (Cth). Notwithstanding this short history, it would be fair to assume that once Parliament decided to define Australian citizenship in a legislative framework, a clear meaning would evolve. However, this has not been **[588]** the case. The *Australian Citizenship Act 1948* (Cth) offers a definition of citizenship stripped bare. While the Act tells us who is a citizen and who can lose their citizenship, it tells us nothing about the legal consequences of citizenship. Yet, the definition of citizenship in itself, and some of the matters dealt with in the Act, reflect some more fundamental aspects of membership of the community. As Karen Slawner reminds us, the '[l]egal definitions of citizenship always incorporate what is considered to be desirable activity.'

Although the definition of an Australian citizen has changed since the inception of the Act in 1948, the present formulation is reasonably clear. A person can become an Australian citizen:

1 by birth, if at the time of the person's birth in Australia, at least one parent is an Australian citizen or an Australian permanent resident;
2 by adoption, if adopted by an Australian citizen;
3 by descent, if a parent is an Australian citizen and registers the child's name at an Australian consulate within 18 years of the birth; or
4 by grant of citizenship.

While transparent, two significant issues of exclusion arise from the definition as it presently stands. The previous nationality by birthplace rule was changed on 20 August 1986. The nationality by birthplace, or *jus soli*, principle was abandoned for a specific reason. The new rule limited citizenship to those born in Australia to a parent who was an Australian citizen or permanent resident ...

[589] This is a transparent use of citizenship as a device of exclusion. It is not about including everyone born in Australia as a member of the community, but rather determining first and foremost whom we want and whom we do not want to be part of the Australian community.

Another transparent area of the Act which asserts whom we want as a member of the Australian community is the section relating to the grant of Australian citizenship. This is within the Minister's discretion and is based upon a variety of factors that the Minister must take into account. These matters incorporate 'desirable activity' into the definition of citizenship. For instance, the applicant must be a permanent resident, over 18, and able to understand the nature of the application. This reflects the importance placed upon a conscious acceptance or consent to becoming a member of the community. In addition, the person has to have lived in Australia for a period of two years in the five years preceding the application, and this includes a period of 12 months in the two years before the application. This emphasises the value of residence in a community as an expression of membership. Also, the person has to be of good character, have a basic knowledge of English and an adequate knowledge of the responsibilities and privileges of Australian citizenship. This reflects further characteristics of whom we want to include as fellow members – people whom we trust and respect, people with whom we can communicate, and people who will understand what we expect of them as fellow members. Moreover, the applicant must be likely to reside or continue to reside in Australia, or maintain a close and continuing association with Australia. Each of these factors tells us something about citizenship as a legal status representing a form of membership of the **[590]** community.

Despite the persistence of exclusionary legal conceptions of citizenship, both in Australia and elsewhere, what Rubenstein calls "**[578]** the normative notion of citizenship" has expanded in most communities towards more inclusive egalitarianism. The privileges, obligations and status of citizenship are conceived of (with limited exceptions, notably for minor children) as extending to all members of the community as a matter of right.

Barry Hindess, "Multiculturalism and Citizenship"
in Chandran Kukathas (ed), *Multicultural Citizens: The Philosophy and Politics of Identity*
(Centre for Independent Studies, 1993), 33

[34] In the tradition of Western political thought, citizenship has normally been identified with the status of an independent member of a community that is self-governing in two rather different respects. First, in relation to outsiders, the community is free to determine its own laws and its own government. In particular, then, its identity as a political unit is not determined primarily by the fact of its subordination to some particular ruler – as was the case, for example, for most of the important political units of feudal Europe and for many imperial possessions throughout history. Second, with regard to its own membership, the community is a republic, in which any governing minority should be seen as answerable to the community as a whole. To say that members of such a community are independent is to say that they are not dependent on others for their legal standing as **[35]** members of the community: they are not, for example, chattels, indentured servants or minors.

Only a minority of the world's population have ever been citizens in this sense. Most have not belonged to communities of the relevant kind, or they have belonged to such communities, but not as independent members …

Rights and Obligations
First, there are questions to do with the rights and obligations involved in the status of citizenship, and with the attributes required of persons if they are to be the subjects of those rights and obligations. The most important issues here concern the role of citizens in the government of the community and the status of rights in relation to government. In its strongest form, the republican tradition of political thought maintains that the community should be governed and defended by the collective activity of its citizens. From this point of view each citizen is an officer of the community, and the personal attributes and qualities of individual citizens may therefore be regarded as matters of legitimate concern for the community as a whole. Machiavelli's *Commentaries*, for example, suggest that the liberty of individual citizens is crucially dependent on the liberty of their community, and also that the latter in turn requires the maintenance of appropriate virtues amongst the citizenry. The possession of courage, integrity, moral sensitivity and practical intelligence is an obligation of citizenship.

Where the commitment to active citizen participation in government is relaxed, we also find some relaxation of the insistence on citizen virtue. Republicanism in the strong participatory sense just noted has normally been associated with the small city states of ancient Greece and of early modern Europe. Larger communities have usually been thought to require governments of other kinds, depending for the most part on the consent of citizens rather than on their active involvement

– except perhaps on an intermittent basis. The *Federal-*[36]*-ist Papers*, for example, argue that government in the modern world should be representative or indirect for two reasons. The one that concerns us at this point is a matter of size: a nation small enough to be governed directly by its citizens would not be large enough to defend itself against powerful states. A republic able to defend its independence must therefore also be one in which the great majority of citizens can play little direct part in government. Since, on this view, citizens would not normally be officers of the community the virtues that could reasonably be required of them must be correspondingly less demanding. In effect, the problem of ensuring that citizens are virtuous is reconceptualised as a matter of institutions rather than a matter of persons.

However, even where citizens are not called upon to play an active part in the government of their community they are generally expected to participate at some level in a common culture. The community of citizens is also thought to be a moral community in which a minimum of shared values helps sustain, and is in turn sustained by, the life of what is often called civil society – a sphere of social interaction, not directly controlled by government, in which citizens engage with others and discuss matters of general concern.

On the matter of rights, the requirement that citizens play their part in the life of the community would seem to imply a corresponding responsibility on the part of the community to ensure that its citizens are not prevented from so doing. This is a matter of political and civil liberties, at least in the first instance: the freedom to air one's views in public discussion and to initiate legal proceedings. But it has sometimes also been thought to involve economic support. It is in such terms, for example, that the Athenians justified payment of citizens from the poorer classes for the performance of public services …

Even if they play no active part in government, citizens are still expected to participate in the life of civil society – and influential traditions of social-policy analysis have argued that government has an obligation to ensure that citizens have the wherewithal to do so. On [37] the one hand, …, this is now regarded as a matter of the social rights of citizenship. On the other hand, community action to prevent the emergence of a disaffected underclass is often regarded as a matter of elementary prudence.

Finally, the rights of citizens (and others) have often been understood in a rather different sense as securing their standing as independent persons. If their independence is to have any real force then such rights cannot be subordinated to the will of the community as it might be expressed at any particular point in time. The Roman doctrine of the rule of laws (rather than of men) and the early modern doctrine of natural rights both carry this implication. Such views of the rights of citizens imply a correspondingly relaxed understanding of the requirements of virtue: citizens have rights irrespective of whether their fellow citizens see them as virtuous. This point brings us to the second, and more important, argument of the *Federalist Papers* in favour of representative government. Such a form of government would be democratic (in the sense that the people rule) but it would also provide the benefits of constitutionalism. In effect, the tensions between competing governmental powers would defend the rights of citizens against any capricious will of the majority.

Exclusiveness

The second perspective from which the understanding of citizenship can be approached concerns its exclusive character. The qualities required of persons if they are to be regarded as bearers of the rights and obligations considered above are hardly sufficient to distinguish the citizens of any given community from non-citizens, some of whom might also possess the requisite qualities. Likewise, an important part of the common culture of the citizens and many of their shared values will also be shared by at least some outsiders; and much of what they do not share could be acquired by them without too much difficulty. The qualities required of Athenian citizens, for example, were often thought to be present in members of other Greek communities, and sometimes even among non-Greeks.

Following the Enlightenment, the qualities required of citizens have frequently been understood in universalistic terms – that is, they have been regarded as qualities that are possessed or may be acquired by any normal human individual. However, since communities of citizens invariably inhabit a world of numerous autonomous political units, to be a citizen is always to be a member of one community [38] amongst others. The community to which a citizen belongs will be a community of citizens (and others), but it will also be identified as a community in other ways. Athenian citizens, for example, had to be sons of Athenian citizens (and of Athenian mothers from the middle of the fifth century) ... Notions of descent (and the apparently more respectable surrogate notion of a distinctive national culture that cannot readily be acquired by persons who are not born into it) have always played an important part in the way citizenship has been understood within particular communities. In the modern period, such notions have generally coexisted in uneasy relationship with other principles of inclusion and exclusion. Germany, Israel and Japan are examples of Western democracies in which citizenship is restricted primarily in terms of descent. Elsewhere the legal requirements of citizenship are usually less restrictive ...

Egalitarianism

Perhaps the feature that most distinguishes the understandings of citizenship that have developed in the modern West from those that are best known from classical antiquity and the early modern period is their radical egalitarianism ... [In] three striking respects ... the egalitarianism of contemporary accounts of citizenship distinguishes them from their earlier counterparts. Citizenship in Athens and in Rome was a matter of a limited set of statuses within a larger and highly differentiated network of statuses. First, citizens were divided (largely according to wealth, at least in the first instance) into legally defined classes with distinct rights and obligations. Second, most members of the community could not be citizens, if only because they were not legally regarded as independent persons. Third, even if we leave to one side inhabitants of subject territories, numerous independent persons were subject to the laws of the community but did not possess the political rights of citizens. Metics in Athens, for example, were personally free non-citizens who were nevertheless subject to taxation and liable for military service.

[39] With some qualifications, the most influential of contemporary Western understandings of citizenship have been egalitarian in all three respects. First, citizens are not divided into legally defined classes or estates. Indeed, since the Enlightenment it has been difficult to mount an intellectually respectable case for any such division between citizens – although sterling efforts were once made to defend property qualifications for the franchise. If we are to believe the authors of the *Federalist Papers*, representative government offers all the benefits of constitutionalism without the need for competition between estates. Second, almost all members of the community are legally regarded as independent persons, and therefore as citizens (children now being the only significant exceptions). The third issue is more problematic. Although there are significant alien minorities in all societies, the predominant Western view seems to be that all permanent residents should normally have the status of citizen. Even those who would restrict citizenship on grounds of descent tend to be egalitarian in this respect. The assumption is that non-citizens may be present in the community but only on a temporary basis. They would normally be expected to move on, or else, if they were eligible, to become citizens.

Despite the expectation that permanent residents will take up "citizenship" through a legal process of naturalisation, it appears that such a legal process can always be reversed. In that sense, the saying "Once an alien always an alien" may have more validity than the famous aphorism relating to immigrants. The Australian legislation relating to naturalisation has always provided for its reversal; see now s 21 of the *Australian Citizenship Act 1948* (Cth). In *Meyer v Poynton* (1920) 27 CLR 436, Starke J had no doubt that the similar provision in s 11 of the *Naturalization Act 1903* (Cth) was valid. In *Nolan v Minister for Immigration and Ethnic Affairs* (1988) 165 CLR 178, Gaudron J was content to assume that "**[192]** [t]he power to legislate with respect to naturalization and aliens seems necessarily to carry with it a power to revoke the grant of naturalization"; and in *Re Minister for Immigration and Multicultural Affairs; Ex parte Meng Kok Te* (2002) 212 CLR 162 Gleeson CJ cited *Meyer v Poynton* as authority for the unqualified proposition that: "**[171]** The power conferred by s 51(xix) includes a power to determine legal status".

It is also clear that, even after "absorption" into the community, a non-naturalised alien remains within s 51(xix) and thus liable to deportation (see, for example, *Kenny v Minister for Immigration and Ethnic Affairs* (1993) 115 ALR 75). Previous editions of this book asserted that any doubt on this point had been settled in *Pochi v Macphee* (1982) 151 CLR 101. Some doubt resurfaced in 2002 when it was suggested in *Meng Kok Te* that *Pochi v Macphee* had been undermined by the reasoning of four judges in *Re Patterson; Ex parte Taylor* (2001) 207 CLR 391 (see §3(b) below). However, the doubt proved to be shortlived. *Pochi v Macphee* was reaffirmed and instead it was the authoritative status of *Re Patterson* that was cast into doubt.

(b)   Persons Born in Britain

In the early cases, one reason for emphasis on the "immigration" power was that, at least from the *Irish Envoys' Case* (1923) 32 CLR 518 onwards, that power would extend to the deportation of British subjects travelling on British passports – whereas, in the days of a British Empire bound, in the words of Higgins J in *Potter v Minahan* (1908) 7 CLR 277, by "[321] one tie of allegiance to the one Sovereign", it was assumed that a British subject could not be an "alien". In that respect, as Isaacs J noted in the *Irish Envoys' Case*, the "aliens" power left "[556] a huge gap". Today, however, changes in the citizenship laws of both Australia and the United Kingdom have removed the basis for that assumption. The effect of the relevant statutory changes was first examined judicially in 1988.

Therrance Nolan (a citizen of the United Kingdom and, as such, a subject of the Queen) had come to Australia in 1967 at the age of nine, and by 1985 had lived in Australia for 18 years – more than half of which he had spent in prison. An order for his deportation was made under s 12 of the *Migration Act 1958* (Cth) – which at the time of *Pochi v Macphee* had applied to "an alien" convicted of certain offences, but which now, as amended in 1984, applied to "a person who is a non-citizen". The High Court, with Gaudron J dissenting, held that Nolan's deportation was valid under the "aliens" power, and hence that there was no need to consider its possible validity under the "immigration" power.

Nolan v Minister for Immigration and Ethnic Affairs
(1988) 165 CLR 178

Mason CJ, Wilson, Brennan, Deane, Dawson and Toohey JJ: [183] As a matter of etymology, "alien", from the Latin *alienus* through old French, means belonging to another person or place. Used as a descriptive word to describe a person's lack of relationship with a country, the word means, as a matter of ordinary language, "nothing more than a citizen or subject of a foreign state": *Milne v Huber* [17 Fed Cas (US) 403 (1843)]. Thus, an "alien" has been said to be, for the purposes of United States law, "one born out of the United States, who has not since been naturalized under the constitution and laws" [17 Fed Cas at 406]. That definition should be expanded to include a person who has ceased to be a citizen by an act or process of denaturalization and restricted to exclude a person who, while born abroad, is a citizen by reason of parentage. Otherwise, it constitutes an acceptable general definition of the word "alien" when that word is used with respect to an independent country with its own distinct citizenship. The word could not, however, properly have been used in 1900 to identify the status of a British subject vis-à-vis one of the Australian or other colonies of the British Empire for the reason that those colonies were not, at that time, independent nations with a distinct citizenship of their own. At that time, no subject of the British Crown was an alien within any part of the British Empire. Even after federation, Australia did not immediately enjoy the international status of an independent nation. The terms "British subject" and "subject of the Queen" were essentially synonymous. The British Empire continued to consist of one sovereign State and its colonial **[184]** and other dependencies with the result that there was no need to modify either the perception of an indivisible Imperial Crown or the doctrine that, under the common law, no subject of the Queen was an alien in any part of Her Majesty's dominions …

The transition from Empire to Commonwealth and the emergence of Australia and other Dominions as independent sovereign nations … inevitably changed the nature of the relationship between the United Kingdom and its former colonies and rendered obsolete notions of an indivisible Crown. A separate Australian citizenship was established by the *Nationality and Citizenship Act* 1948 (Cth), now known as the *Australian Citizenship Act* 1948. That Act and statutes of other

Commonwealth countries, particularly the *British Nationality Act* 1948 (UK), reflected and formalized the diminished importance of the notion of "British subject". It became accepted as a "truism" that, although "there is only one person who is the Sovereign ... , ... in matters of law and government the Queen of the United Kingdom ... is entirely independent and distinct from" the Queen of (eg) Canada or Australia: per May LJ, *R v Foreign Secretary; Ex parte Indian Association* [[1982] QB 892 at 928]. The fact that a person who was born neither in Australia nor of Australian parents and who had not become a citizen of this country was a British subject or a subject of the Queen by reason of his birth in another country could no longer be seen as having the effect, so far as this country is concerned, of precluding his classification as an "alien". It is not that the meaning of the word "alien" had altered. That word is and always has been appropriate to describe the status, vis-à-vis a former colony which has emerged as an independent nation with its own citizenship, of a non-citizen who is a British subject by reason of his citizenship of a different sovereign State. But the word is not and never has been appropriate to describe within any part of the territory (whether colonial or otherwise) of a single sovereign State the status of a person who is one of the subjects of that particular State.

So much was recognized by this Court in 1982 in *Pochi v Macphee* [(1982) 151 CLR 101]. In that case, an attack was made on the validity of the then s 12 of the Act. For present purposes, the important differences between the provisions of the Act in the form under consideration in *Pochi* and the provisions under consideration in this case are that the section then applied to an "alien" as distinct from a "non-citizen" and that the *Migration Act* contained (at the time of **[185]** the decision in *Pochi*) a definition of "alien" which excluded, among others, persons who had the status of "a British subject". Persons having "the status of a British subject" were, however, defined ... in a way which produced the result that the word "alien" included, for the purposes of the then s 12, citizens of some countries (particularly the Solomon Islands) who were British subjects (and also subjects of the Queen). It was argued that such persons could not be "aliens" for the purposes of the legislative power conferred by s 51(xix) ... That argument was rejected by the Court in plain and unambiguous words. The leading judgment was that of Gibbs CJ. His Honour, having traced the alteration in the concept of "British subject" and the development of Australian citizenship, concluded that the plaintiff's argument was "based on a false assumption and must fail" for the reason that, pursuant to the legislative power granted by s 51(xix) with respect to "aliens", "the Parliament can ... treat as an alien *any person* who was born outside Australia, whose parents were not Australians, and who has not been naturalized as an Australian" [151 CLR at 109-10] (emphasis added). Two of the other three members of the Court in *Pochi*, Mason and Wilson JJ, concurred in the judgment of Gibbs CJ. It follows that the basis of the decision in *Pochi* is inconsistent with the plaintiff's argument in the present case.

Nolan had attempted to resist these arguments by relying on the reference to "the Crown of the United Kingdom" in the preamble to the *Commonwealth of Australia Constitution Act 1900* (Imp), as repeated and expanded in s 2 of that Act ("covering clause 2"). He had also relied on the use of the expression "subject of the Queen" in ss 34(ii) and 117 of the Constitution. The joint judgment found it "**[185]** unnecessary to pursue that point beyond saying that those references cannot alter, or avoid the consequences of, the emergence of Australia as an independent nation, the acceptance of the **[186]** divisibility of the Crown which was implicit in the development of the Commonwealth as an association of independent nations and the creation of a distinct Australian citizenship". These developments meant that, although the word "alien" still had the same "abstract meaning", its "practical designation" had changed. As to s 117, they suggested – as Toohey J had effectively done in *Street v Queensland Bar Association* (1989) 168 CLR 461 at 553-4 (see Chapter 26, §5) – that in that context "subject of the Queen" now means "a subject of the Queen in right of Australia".

The dissenting judgment of Gaudron J took a different view of Nolan's position.

Gaudron J: [189] [In] the early common law of England alien status was identified as absence of allegiance to the Crown: see, eg, *Calvin's Case* [(1609) 7 Co Rep 1a; 77 ER 377]; *Blackstone's Commentaries*, 8th ed, vol 1, p 366. Allegiance to the Crown became synonymous with being a British subject. The status of British subject served as a useful point of identification during the days of the Empire when the status in English law of persons resident in the colonies was in question: see *In re Johnson; Roberts v Attorney-General* [[1903] 1 Ch 821]; *Gavin Gibson & Co Ltd v Gibson* [[1913] 3 KB 379]. Whether it would have served with equal utility to identify, after federation, the status in Australian law of persons resident in some other part of the Empire must be open to doubt. However, there can be no doubt that the status of British subject no longer serves as the point of distinction between aliens and non-aliens in Australian law, for, as was pointed out by Gibbs CJ in *Pochi v Macphee* [151 CLR at 109], with the coming into force of the *British Nationality Act* 1981 (UK) the status of British subject is restricted to a narrow group, and if that status serves to distinguish between aliens and non-aliens in Australian law "almost all Australian citizens, born in Australia, would … be aliens".

An alien (from the Latin *alienus* – belonging to another) is, in essence, a person who is not a member of the community which constitutes the body politic of the nation state from whose perspective the question of alien status is to be determined. For most purposes it is convenient to identify an alien by reference to the want or absence of the criterion which determines membership of that community. Thus, where membership of a community depends on citizenship, alien status corresponds with non-citizenship; in the case of a community whose membership is conditional upon allegiance to a monarch, the status of alien corresponds with the absence of that allegiance. At least this is so where the criterion for membership of the community remains constant.

There is no specific criterion identified for membership of the community constituting the Australian body politic. By various steps, largely coinciding with the transformation of the Empire into **[190]** the British Commonwealth of Nations constituted by sovereign and independent nation states, the statutory description of members of the Australian community has been changed from "British subjects" to "Australian citizens". Until the concept of citizenship was introduced by the *Nationality and Citizenship Act* 1948 (Cth), later known as the *Australian Citizenship Act* 1948 (Cth) ("the Citizenship Act"), membership of the community of the body politic of Australia coincided with possession of the status of British subject at least if the person concerned was resident in Australia. That situation continued after the coming into force of the Citizenship Act, for, although the Act introduced the concept of Australian citizenship and prescribed the method of its acquisition (including by naturalization) by s 7(1), an Australian citizen was also a British subject. Following amendments in 1969, an Australian citizen was described as having the status of a British subject. After the Citizenship Act was proclaimed, Australian citizens acquired their status as British subjects by virtue of their Australian citizenship. However, the Act continued to accord a special position … to British subjects who were not Australian citizens. By amendment in 1984 (taking effect from 1 May 1987) all reference to the "status of British subject" and to the special position of British subjects was removed from the Act, and Australian citizenship became the sole statutory description of membership of the Australian nation.

Neither the Citizenship Act nor the *Migration Act*, in terms, makes Australian citizenship the exclusive criterion for admission to membership of the community constituting the body politic of Australia. However, given that no other criterion is supplied, either by the general law or by statute, and that (as from its amendment in 1984) s 12 of the *Migration Act* posits the deportation only of persons who are non-citizens, it must be accepted that the intendment of s 12 of the *Migration Act*, when viewed in the context of the amendments made to the Citizenship Act, was that Australian citizenship should be (or perhaps, should become) the criterion for admission to membership of the community constituting the body politic of Australia.

There can be no doubt as to the power of the Parliament to enact laws prescribing the conditions currently prescribed by the Citizenship Act for the acquisition of citizenship and treating non-citizens thereafter entering Australia as aliens, at least if then entering Australia for the first time. But s 12 of the *Migration Act* goes further. It deals with non-citizens who entered Australia at any time, provided that they have not been permanently resident for ten years or ten years when periods of imprisonment are disregarded. Because **[191]** of its scope s 12 can only be supported as a valid exercise of legislative power with respect to aliens if all persons who fall within its ambit were at all times aliens within the meaning of that expression in s 51(xix) of the Constitution, or, if not having been aliens, it is within legislative power to transform their status from non-alien to alien by reason of their not having become Australian citizens.

When the plaintiff entered Australia in 1967 a British subject was excluded from the definition of an "alien" appearing in s 5 of the Citizenship Act. That exclusion continued until 1 May 1987, when the 1984 amendments to the Citizenship Act came into force. Of course, the statutory definition of "alien" cannot control the constitutional meaning of "alien" as a person not a member of the community constituting the body politic of Australia. Nevertheless, the statutory definition does illustrate the historical and legal fact that until the 1984 amendments to the Citizenship Act, a British subject occupied a special position in the Australian community. That "special position" survived the introduction of citizenship consequent upon the enactment of the Citizenship Act in 1948, and is further illustrated by reference to the *Commonwealth Electoral Act* 1918 (Cth) which, by s 39(1) (until its amendment in 1984) accorded the right to vote to British subjects who had been permanently resident in Australia for six months. It is hard to conceive that persons who were excluded from the statutory definition of alien by virtue of their being British subjects, and who were entitled (subject to a six month residence qualification) to participate in the election of the government of the day, were aliens in the sense of not being members of the community constituting the body politic of Australia. However, it seems to me that that is not the critical consideration.

As at 1967 (and at least for some time thereafter) persons resident in Australia were, as a matter of law, members of the community constituting the body politic of Australia by virtue of their allegiance to the Crown ie by virtue of their being British subjects. At that stage no legislative distinction was made by reference to the several and distinct capacities of the Queen as Head of State of several and distinct sovereign nations: allegiance to the Crown was allegiance to the Crown and not simply to the Crown in right of Australia. It may be that since amendment in 1973 that distinction is to be found in the Oath of Allegiance contained in Sched 3 of the Citizenship Act. However, even if the distinction was then made, that distinction did not effect any immediate change to the special position statutorily accorded to British subjects.

It is unnecessary to identify precisely when the criterion for **[192]** admission to membership of the community constituting the body politic of Australia changed from allegiance to the Crown to citizenship involving allegiance to the Crown in right of Australia. Certainly it did not occur prior to 1973. Because the plaintiff, as a British subject, came to and took up residence in Australia prior to 1973, he was, in my view, not then an alien. It remains to be considered whether it is within legislative power to transform a non-alien person into an alien by reason of that person not having acquired citizenship.

The power to legislate with respect to naturalization and aliens seems necessarily to carry with it a power to revoke the grant of naturalization and a power to define the circumstances in which a non-alien may become an alien. However, those powers are not at large. In *Pochi* Gibbs CJ, with whom Mason and Wilson JJ agreed, observed [151 CLR at 109] that "the Parliament cannot, simply by giving its own definition of 'alien', expand the power under s 51(xix) to include persons who could not possibly answer the description of 'aliens' in the ordinary understanding of the word". Nor, in my view, can the Parliament expand the power by constituting a non-alien an alien if there has not been some relevant change in the relationship between that person and the community constituting the body politic of Australia, including, eg, the abandonment of membership of the community, or the acquisition of membership of some other nation community. It seems to me that such was the condition which the common law attached to the transformation from non-alien to alien status: see *Thomas v Acklam* [(1824) 2 B & C 779; 107 ER 572]; *Auchmuty v Mulcaster* [(1826) 5 B & C 770; 108 ER 287]. However, the condition did not necessarily involve any positive act on the part of the person concerned. In *In re Stepney Election Petition; Isaacson v Durant* [(1886) 17 QBD 54], eg, the status of Hanoverians resident in England was altered by operation of different laws of succession (rather than by choice of the individuals concerned) when, after the death of William IV, different monarchs succeeded to the thrones of England and Hanover …

[193] As the transformation from non-alien to alien requires some relevant change in the relationship between the individual and the community, it is not, in my view, open to the Parliament to effect that transformation by simply redefining the criterion for admission to membership of the community constituting the body politic of Australia. Nor, in my view, does a mere failure on the part of a non-alien to acquire citizenship involve any fundamental alteration of his or her relationship with that community. Of course, it might be otherwise if citizenship were offered and refused in circumstances such that refusal could properly be seen as a revival of an earlier allegiance to some other nation or as an abandonment of allegiance to Australia. But mere inactivity in the face of legislative change (perhaps not understood by, or not known to, the person concerned) cannot, in my view, transform a non-alien into an alien. It follows that s 12 of the *Migration Act* cannot be upheld as a valid exercise of the power to legislate with respect to aliens in so far as it operates with respect to persons who were non-aliens prior to its coming into operation.

The view which I have expressed is to some extent at variance with the statement by Gibbs CJ in *Pochi* [151 CLR at 109-10] that "the Parliament can … treat as an alien any person who was born outside Australia, whose parents were not Australians, and who has not been naturalized as an Australian". However, it may be questioned whether that statement was intended to encompass persons who … had acquired non-alien status before Parliament so acted. Moreover, that statement needs to be read in the context of his Honour's earlier acknowledgment that the extent of Parliament's power to define an alien had not been fully explored in argument.

Note the insistence by Gaudron J that Parliament's "[192] power to define the circumstances" in which a person may become an alien cannot be simply "at large" – including her use of the comment by Gibbs CJ in *Pochi v Macphee* (1982) 151 CLR 101 that "[109] the Parliament cannot, simply by giving its own definition of 'alien', expand the power under s 51(xix)". There are overtones here of the doctrine in *Australian Communist Party v Commonwealth* (*Communist Party Case*) (1951) 83 CLR 1 that "[258] a stream cannot rise higher than its source" (see Chapter 18, §6) – that is, that Parliament cannot be allowed to regulate the limits of its own constitutional power. Yet if "alienage" is a legal status must not *some* power to define its legal conditions and attributes be a part of what s 51(xix) comprehends?

The dissenting judgment of Gaudron J in *Nolan* was apparently vindicated in *Re Patterson; Ex parte Taylor* (2001) 207 CLR 391. Graham Taylor, a British subject, migrated to Australia as a young child with his parents in 1966. He never took out Australian citizenship but came to hold a visa that enabled him to stay in Australia. In 1996, he pleaded guilty to offences involving sexual assaults upon children. Upon his release from prison, he was arrested and detained after his visa was cancelled under s 501(3) of the *Migration Act*. Taylor (the prosecutor) sought relief on three grounds. First, that the decision to cancel his visa had been made, not by "the Minister" as required by s 501(3), but by Senator Kay Patterson (the respondent), who was Parliamentary Secretary to the Minister. Second, that s 501(3) could not apply to Taylor because he was not an "alien" within the meaning of s 51(xix). Third, that Patterson had exercised her discretion under s 501(3) on the erroneous basis that Taylor would thereafter have had an opportunity to make representations to her.

Six judges dismissed Taylor's first argument, thus vindicating the extensive practice of assigning ministerial duties to assistant ministers and parliamentary secretaries. Only McHugh J found it unnecessary to decide that point. Five judges accepted Taylor's third argument. Gleeson CJ, Gaudron, Gummow and Hayne JJ took that as the basis for their decision. McHugh J indicated that he agreed on that issue with Gummow and Hayne JJ, and had initially agreed on that basis that Patterson's decision must be quashed. However, in response to the division of opinion in the rest of the Court, he addressed his judgment primarily to the second, constitutional point. Although the consideration of this issue was not strictly necessary, since Taylor had succeeded on his third ground, each judge went on to examine it. In the end, four judges (Gaudron, McHugh, Kirby and Callinan JJ) held that *Nolan* should be overruled. By contrast, Gummow and Hayne JJ, with whom Gleeson CJ agreed, affirmed *Nolan* and held that Taylor was an "alien" within the meaning of s 51(xix).

Re Patterson; Ex parte Taylor
(2001) 207 CLR 391

Gummow and Hayne JJ: [468] [P]ersons may acquire the status or character of alienage by reason of supervening constitutional and political events not involving any positive act or assent on the part of the person concerned. A British subject could be rendered an alien **[469]** by reason of loss of territory of the British Crown. This might come about, as in the case of the recognition by Britain of the independence of the United States, by statute recognising a new sovereignty over the territory in question ...

The relationship between Australia and New Guinea provides a striking instance of the loss of citizenship by reason of constitutional changes. The *Papua New Guinea Independence Act 1975* (Cth) provided that Australia ceased to have any sovereignty, sovereign rights or rights of administration in respect of or appertaining to the whole or any part of Papua New Guinea. In exercise of the regulation-making power conferred by s 6, reg 4 of the Papua New Guinea Independence (Australian Citizenship) Regulations provided that a person who immediately before independence day on 16 September 1975 was an Australian citizen and who, on independence, became a citizen of Papua New Guinea, ceased on that day to be an Australian citizen.

Plainly, Gibbs CJ was correct when, in *Pochi v Macphee* [(1982) 151 CLR 101 at 109], he **[470]** said that "the Parliament cannot, simply by giving its own definition of 'alien', expand the power under s 51(xix) to include persons who could not possibly answer the description of 'aliens' in the ordinary understanding of the word". However, the situation that arose with the establishment of the independent state of Papua New Guinea and the supporting Australian legislation considered above may suggest that Gibbs CJ expressed the power too narrowly, or that he did not mean to state it exhaustively, when he said in the same passage in *Pochi v Macphee* [at 109-10]:

> "[T]he Parliament can in my opinion treat as an alien any person who was born outside Australia, whose parents were not Australians, and who has not been naturalized as an Australian".

The prosecutor, on the other hand, contends that the formulation by Gibbs CJ is too wide. This is said to be because there has to be a qualification or exception to the reach of the legislative power to put beyond its exercise those who were not aliens when they arrived in Australia and who had been absorbed into the Australian community before the constitutional and political developments in relations between the United Kingdom and Australia which otherwise would bring them within the scope of the power.

That submission, for several reasons, should not be accepted. First, there is a real likelihood that persons born in the United Kingdom after the commencement in 1949 of the [*Australian Citizenship Act 1948* (Cth)] were objects for the exercise of the aliens power in s 51(xix) of the Constitution. The status of British subject conferred or recognised in Australia by force of imperial legislation no longer existed at the time of the birth of the prosecutor. Part I of the [*British Nationality and Status of Aliens Act 1914* (Imp)], which had defined those who were natural born British subjects, had been repealed by the [*British Nationality Act 1948* (UK)]; the [*Nationality Act 1920* (Cth)] which had adopted Pt I in Australia had been repealed by the Citizenship Act. Thereafter, there remained no imperial legislation applying in Australia by paramount force or adopted in Australia which defined those who were British subjects or who had the status of British subjects by reference to allegiance owed to the Imperial Crown. After 1949, in determining those who were British subjects or who had that status for the purposes of Australian law, one turned only to the Citizenship Act ...

The matter may be looked at somewhat differently by asking whether, at the time of the purported application to him of s 501(3) of the *Migration Act* by the decision of the respondent, the prosecutor was a citizen or subject of a foreign state and had not become an Australian citizen. That was the interpretation given to "alien" in the joint judgment of six members of the court in *Nolan v Minister for* **[471]** *Immigration and Ethnic Affairs* [(1988) 165 CLR 178] ...

The prosecutor seeks to escape the consequences of this reasoning by emphasising (i) that he did not enter Australia as an alien in the constitutional sense; and (ii) that supervening political and constitutional developments and events over which he has had no control cannot be effective to render him an alien in the constitutional sense. We have indicated above the serious doubts as to whether proposition (i) can be accepted. In any event, proposition (ii) should be rejected. The prosecutor had not taken the steps which the Citizenship Act afforded for the acquisition of Australian citizenship. His past enjoyment of the statutory status, under Australian law, of a British subject gave him, under that law, certain advantages other aliens did not possess. But the prosecutor had enjoyed those advantages as an alien, not because he was placed in some intermediate position where, although a British citizen for the purposes of the law of the United Kingdom, and not a citizen for the purposes of Australian law, in Australia he was not to be considered an alien ...

[472] The prosecutor seeks to redefine alienage for the purposes of s 51(xix) of the Constitution as one who at the time the issue arises is not a member of the Australian community. He denies the competence of the Parliament to transform that relationship between the individual and the community by legislative redefinition of the criterion for admission and continued membership of it. The prosecutor submits that he had become a member of the Australian community in the necessary sense and that legislation which would lead to his classification as an "unlawful non-citizen" was ineffective to change that relationship by rendering him an alien.

The notion of an Australian community and of the absorption into it of persons not born in Australia appears first to have been developed ... in *Potter v Minahan* [(1908) 7 CLR 277] ...

There is no reason to conflate the criteria by which there is gauged the scope of the powers of the Parliament on the one hand with respect to naturalisation and aliens, and on the other with respect to [473] immigration and emigration. The distinct considerations which led to the inclusion of the two heads of power in s 51 suggest otherwise. Further, the notion of absorption into the Australian community is one which, the decisions of the court with respect to the immigration power show, is not easy of application and turns into constitutional facts many details of the lives of individuals.

Gaudron J, reaffirming her dissenting view in *Nolan*, held that Taylor was not an "alien" within s 51(xix). However, although the parties had accepted as common ground that because he had been absorbed into the Australian community he could not be treated as an "immigrant" within s 51(xxvii), Gaudron J held that he was not beyond the reach of the immigration power, since that power does extend to "[413] the conferral of visas on persons who have migrated to Australia", and hence to the cancellation of such visas. She therefore finished up agreeing with Gleeson CJ, Gummow and Hayne JJ that Taylor's visa could validly be cancelled. On the other hand, McHugh, Kirby and Callinan JJ agreed with Gaudron J that *Nolan* should be overruled; and for them this meant that the power to cancel a visa conferred by s 501(3) had no valid application.

McHugh J: [432] A striking example of the changing nature of [Australia's relationship with the United Kingdom] is found in *Sue v Hill* [(1999) 199 CLR 462 at 490] where a majority of this court held that, "since at least the commencement of the *Australia Act 1986* (Cth)", the United Kingdom was a "foreign power" within the meaning of s 44(i) of the Constitution although it had not been a "foreign power" in 1901 and for long after. But it is one thing to say that a person born in England is the subject of a foreign power and another thing to say that such a person is an alien for the purpose of the Constitution.

Until the relationship between the United Kingdom and Australia evolved to the stage that the United Kingdom became a foreign power, it was impossible to maintain that a person born in the United Kingdom and a subject of the Queen was an alien within the meaning of s 51(xix) ...

[U]pon the completion of the evolutionary process, the subjects of the Queen born and living in Australia became subjects of the Queen of Australia. Henceforth, by a mystical process, they owed their allegiance to the Queen of Australia, not the Queen of the United Kingdom ...

But upon what legal or logical basis can this Court distinguish between subjects of the Queen of the United Kingdom born in Australia and those subjects of the Queen born outside, but living in, Australia when the evolutionary process was complete? I can see none. Birth within the sovereign's territories was the criterion by which the common law distinguished the subject of the sovereign from the alien. But that fact provides no ground for a court distinguishing between the subjects of the evolutionary process. It is also true that subjects of the [433] Queen born in the United Kingdom continued to owe allegiance to the Queen in right of the United Kingdom. But that was not incompatible with them also owing allegiance to the Queen of Australia *as subjects of that Queen* while they continued to live in Australia. Whether or not they were aliens, they were under the protection of and owed allegiance to the Queen of Australia as long as they lived here. If they were subjects of the Queen living here immediately before the end of the evolutionary process, there is no constitutional reason why they could not become subjects of the Queen of Australia as well as subjects of the United Kingdom. *Sue v Hill* holds that this dual allegiance prevents them from being members of the federal Parliament. But nothing in the Constitution indicates that allegiance to the Queen in two capacities makes a person born in the United Kingdom an alien for the purpose of the Constitution. Indeed s 117 of the Constitution strongly supports the opposite conclusion ...

In 1901, "subject of the Queen" in s 117 meant subject of the Queen of the United Kingdom of Great Britain and Ireland. In *Nolan* [165 CLR at 186], six Justices of this Court, answering the argument that the terms of s 117 were inconsistent with a British subject being an alien, referred to the changes in the relationship between the United Kingdom and Australia and said:

> "Those developments necessarily produced different reference points for the application of the word 'alien'. Inevitably, the practical designation of the word altered so that, while its abstract meaning remained constant, it encompassed persons who were not citizens of this country even though they might be British subjects or subjects of the Queen by reason of their citizenship of some other nation. We would add that, to the extent that there would otherwise be inconsistency in the use of the words 'subject of the Queen' in the Constitution, it should be resolved by treating those words as referring, in a modern context, to a subject of the Queen in right of Australia: cf *Royal Style and Titles Act* 1973 (Cth)."

The proposition in the first and second sentences in this passage can **[434]** be readily accepted if it is confined to British subjects of the Queen who arrived in Australia after the completion of the evolutionary process that made Australians subjects of the Queen of Australia. It is simply an application of the principle that, although the meaning of a constitutional term remains constant, its denotation – the matters, persons or things to which it applies – may change. The proposition in the third sentence may also be accepted for present purposes although it ranks as one of the most radical propositions in the constitutional jurisprudence of the court. It is *that* radical because it relies on external events to change the *meaning* or connotation of a constitutional term and not merely its application or denotation. It changes the meaning of "subject of the Queen" in s 117 and other sections of the Constitution from subject of the Queen of the United Kingdom to subject of the Queen of Australia. It repudiates the declaration in Covering Clause 2 of the Constitution that "[t]he provisions of this Act referring to the Queen shall extend to Her Majesty's heirs and successors in the sovereignty of the United Kingdom." Moreover, it changes the meaning of "subject of the Queen" to accommodate the expanded denotation of "aliens" in s 51(xix) although the grant of that power is conferred "subject to this Constitution", a process of reasoning that reverses the ordinary rule of statutory and constitutional construction.

Whatever may be said of the process of legal reasoning that led to the proposition in the third sentence of the above passage in *Nolan*, however, it makes the language of a number of constitutional provisions consistent with the realities that have accompanied Australia's emergence as an independent nation. I would not seek to overturn the proposition in the third sentence although it may have been more consistent with the 1901 meaning to read "subject of the Queen" in the Constitution "as referring to the subjects of the Queen in any of those rights, including as Queen of Australia." What the above passage from *Nolan* does not deal with, however, is the effect that the change of meaning of "subject of the Queen" had on the rights that s 117 gave to subjects of the Queen before the completion of the evolutionary process.

Immediately prior to the completion of that process, a subject of the Queen, resident in a State, had the right to ignore any law that subjected that person to any disability or discrimination in another State that "would not be equally applicable to him if he were a subject of the Queen" resident in that other State. Moreover, the subject of the Queen had the right to seek the protection of the courts from any **[435]** executive action taken under a law that infringed s 117. I cannot accept that the constitutional rights of some subjects of the Queen granted by s 117 of the Constitution simply disappeared at some unidentified and unidentifiable time by reason of the change in the relationship between the executive governments of the United Kingdom and Australia. No bell rang or could have been rung to tell British-born subjects of the Queen, resident in an Australian State, that from that moment they no longer had the rights that s 117 of the Constitution conferred on them. No bell rang or could have been rung to inform them that henceforth they could be subjected to disabilities and discriminations that could not be imposed on Australian-born subjects of the Queen of the United Kingdom. Ironically, before the decision in *Nolan*, the concern was not that overseas-born subjects of the Queen would lose their s 117 rights but that Australian-born subjects would do or had done so.

I accept, as *Nolan* holds, that "subject of the Queen" in s 117 has evolved to mean subject of the Queen of Australia. By parity of reasoning, however, subjects of the Queen, resident in Australia at the end of the evolutionary process, became subjects of the Queen of Australia, irrespective of their place of birth. That meant that the rights conferred on them by s 117 were protected.

Once it is accepted that a person is the subject of the Queen for the purpose of the Constitution, that person cannot be an alien for the purpose of the Constitution. It is not a matter of Australian citizenship – a term that the Constitution does not use – but of the distinction that the Constitution draws between a subject of the Queen and one who is not, that is to say, an alien. That distinction was not altered because of the enactment of the *British Nationality Act* 1948 (UK) … That Act and the cognate legislation of the Commonwealth countries "envisaged two national statuses – citizenship of a Commonwealth country as well as the common status of a British subject or Commonwealth citizen." Nor was the distinction altered by the enactment of the *British Nationality Act* 1981 (UK). Nor can the distinction that the Constitution draws be altered by the Parliament defining aliens to include some persons who are subjects of the Queen of Australia. In *Pochi v Macphee* [151 CLR at 109], Gibbs CJ pointed out that "the Parliament cannot, simply by giving its **[436]** own definition of 'alien', expand the power under s 51(xix) to include persons who could not possibly answer the description of 'aliens' in the ordinary understanding of the word."

Prior to the completion of the evolutionary process that made the United Kingdom a foreign power, the Parliament could not have asserted that British subjects, living in Australia, were aliens. In 1925, in *Ex parte Walsh and Johnson; Re Yates* [(1925) 37 CLR 36] this court held that the Federal Government had no power to deport two union officials although they were born overseas and fell within the scope of the relevant legislation. Both officials were British subjects … Although Sir Robert Garran, Solicitor-General of the Commonwealth, relied on many heads of federal power to support the application of the legislation to the two men, he made no attempt to rely on the aliens power. It would be a curious result if seventy-six years later the Federal Government now had the power to deport them.

Gleeson CJ, Gaudron, Gummow and Hayne JJ held that in its application to Taylor s 501(3) was valid, and his visa could be cancelled. Gaudron, McHugh, Kirby and Callinan JJ held that *Nolan* was wrongly decided. The only judge common to both majorities was Gaudron J.

For most practical purposes it is sufficient to assume that every human being in Australia is either an alien or a citizen, so that the two terms can effectively be used to define each other. On that assumption a citizen is a "non-alien", and an alien (as the statutory usage since 1984 has awkwardly assumed) is a "non-citizen". However, the result in *Patterson* implied that this dichotomy cannot be maintained for all purposes. According to the majority view in *Patterson*, Taylor had never become a citizen, but he had never become an alien either.

In *Re Minister for Immigration and Multicultural Affairs; Ex parte Meng Kok Te* (2002) 212 CLR 162, two men holding permanent resident visas contended that they too were neither citizens nor aliens. Meng Kok Te was born in Cambodia, Dung Chi Dang in Vietnam. Both had sought refuge in Australia in the early 1980s. Despite repeated criminal convictions for which they now faced deportation, both men claimed to have been absorbed into the Australian community. That absorption would place them beyond the reach of the "immigration" power, and (on their interpretation of *Patterson*) beyond the reach of the "aliens" power as well. However, their argument was rejected by a unanimous Court.

Re Minister for Immigration and Multicultural Affairs; Ex parte Meng Kok Te
(2002) 212 CLR 162

Gleeson CJ: [169] At the time of his arrival here, the prosecutor was an alien … He was never a British subject. He has never become an Australian citizen. In 1983, the Migration Act was amended to include a definition of non-citizen. The prosecutor is a non-citizen. So long as he held a visa, he was a "lawful non-citizen". Without such a visa, he is liable to removal. …

The prosecutor acknowledges that he is a non-citizen; but denies that he is an alien. In *Pochi* [151 CLR at 109-10] Gibbs CJ said that, for the purposes of s 51(xix), Parliament can treat as an alien "any person who was born outside Australia, whose parents were not Australians, and who has not been naturalised as an Australian". The prosecutor is such a person. In *Nolan* [(1988) 165 CLR 178], six Justices of this Court approved that statement, and treated as an acceptable definition of the term "alien", as adapted to Australia, a statement by a United States court [*Milne v Huber*, 17 Fed Cas 403 at 406 (1843)] that, in the United States, an alien is "one born out of the United States, who has not since been naturalised under the constitution and laws".

It is contended that although the prosecutor was born out of Australia, and his parents were not Australian, and he has not taken up Australian citizenship and thus become naturalised as an Australian, he is, nevertheless, not an alien. That contention involves two steps. First, it is said, four members of this Court in *Patterson* [(2001) 207 CLR 391] recognised the existence of a class of persons in Australia who, although not citizens, are not aliens. Secondly, it is said, the prosecutor is a member of that class. The second step, of course, depends upon the definition of the class referred to in the first step; but on that point there are differences in the reasons given by the four Justices who, on this issue, were in a majority in *Patterson* ...

[170] The prosecutor contends that, at the date of the cancellation of his visa, he had ceased to be an alien by reason that (a) he owed allegiance to the Queen of Australia, and to no other power; and/or (b) he was a member of the community constituting the body politic of Australia; and/or (c) he had been absorbed into the Australian community.

If the reasoning in *Pochi* and *Nolan* is correct, each of those three propositions is beside the point. As a person who was born outside Australia, whose parents were not Australian, and who has never become an Australian citizen, the prosecutor would be someone whom Parliament was entitled to treat as an alien.

There is no majority in *Patterson* for the view that any one of the propositions referred to in (a), (b), or (c) above, if established, would sustain the prosecutor's case. Each proposition can be traced to aspects of the reasoning of one or more of the four Justices who comprised the majority, but there was no majority view that either (a), or (b), or (c), if made good, would require a conclusion that the prosecutor is not an alien. On the other hand, six Justices in *Nolan* jointly expressed a view which, if correct, would mean that neither all, nor any, of the propositions, if established, would entitle the prosecutor to succeed. That is the current, inconclusive, state of authority ...

In *Robtelmes v Brenan* [(1906) 4 CLR 395], in 1906, this Court, following the opinion of international jurists, and decisions of courts of the highest authority in England and the United States, held that it is an attribute of sovereignty that every State is entitled to decide what aliens shall or shall not become members of its community. Griffith CJ [4 CLR at 400] quoted the statement of the Privy Council [*Attorney-General (Canada) v Cain and Gilhula* [1906] AC 542 at 546] that "[o]ne of the rights possessed by the supreme power in every State is the right to refuse to permit an alien to enter that State, to annex what conditions it pleases to the permission to enter it, and to expel or deport from the State, at pleasure, even a friendly alien, especially if it considers his presence in the State opposed to its peace, order, and good government, or to its social or material interests" ...

[171] The legislative powers conferred upon the Parliament by pars (xix) and (xxvii) of s 51 of the Constitution are intended to enable the exercise of that power and responsibility. It is a large responsibility, vital to the welfare, security and integrity of the nation. From the beginning, the power to make laws with respect to aliens has been understood as a wide power, equipping the Parliament with the capacity to decide, on behalf of the Australian community, who will be admitted to formal membership of that community. Alienage is a legal status. Naturalisation is the act in the law by which a person who was formerly an alien ceases to be one. The power conferred by s 51(xix) includes a power to determine legal status. When an alien is permitted to enter Australia, as in the case of the prosecutor, ordinarily such permission is, by virtue of the legislative scheme pursuant to which it is granted, conditional. An alien retains the status of alienage until that status is removed by the process of naturalisation. It is for Parliament to decide, from time to time, what that process will involve.

Mason CJ said in *Cunliffe v Commonwealth* [(1994) 182 CLR 272 at 295] that the aliens power provides a more expansive source of power than the immigration power. Immigration and emigration are activities. Immigration is "an activity which ex vi termini is one day to be completed and looks forward (usually, at any rate) to that day". That does not mean that only a person who intends to settle in Australia is an immigrant for the purposes of the power ... [or that the power] is in all respects limited in time to the duration of that activity. But a law which purports to expel, or authorise the expulsion of, a person who has become absorbed into the Australian community, so that the **[172]** activity of immigration has ceased, will not bear the character of a law with respect to immigration. If, however, the person in question entered as an alien, and that status has not altered, then such a law may be supported by the power to make laws with respect to aliens. As Mason CJ said, in *Cunliffe* [182 CLR at 295], "an alien who has been absorbed into the Australian community ceases to be an immigrant, though remaining an alien".

The concept of absorption into the Australian community, vague as it may be, has been developed as a method of indicating that the activity of immigration in which a person has engaged has come to an end. But it does not mean that the person has lost the status of an alien. Many immigrants become resident aliens. One of the aspects of the power given by par (xix) is a power in the Parliament to determine, by legislation, how an alien may alter that status. It includes, for example, a power to provide by legislation that a person who is an alien does not cease to be an alien otherwise than by going through a formal procedure which includes acknowledgment of the obligations and responsibilities of Australian citizenship. And, as I indicated in *Patterson* [207 CLR at 400], whilst I accept that Parliament cannot, by some artificial process of definition, ascribe the status of alienage to whomsoever it pleases, par (xix) empowers the Parliament to decide who will be granted Australian citizenship, who will be treated as aliens, and by what process and upon what conditions persons may lose their status of alienage. The Australian community, through Parliament, decides who will be admitted to what the *Australian Citizenship Act* now describes as the formal membership of the community represented by citizenship, "a common bond, involving reciprocal rights and obligations", and the terms and conditions on which such admission will take place.

It was the historical relationship between Australia and the British Empire, and the status of British subjects, that gave rise to the issue in *Patterson*. If the prosecutor in this case had been born in Hong Kong, or Canada, or Gibraltar, that relationship may have been relevant here. But putting to one side the position of British subjects, there are many people who entered Australia as aliens, who have lived here for long periods and have become absorbed into the community, whose activity of immigration has long since ceased, but who have never sought formal membership of the community. There may be various reasons why they have not done so. In some cases, such a step might require the renunciation of other rights and privileges, or the severance of ties they wish to maintain. Whether by design, or simply as the result of neglect, they remain aliens ...

[173] Finally, as I indicated in *Patterson*, under pars (xix) and (xxvii) of s 51, subject to one qualification, Parliament has the power to determine the legal basis by reference to which Australia deals with matters of nationality and immigration, to create and define the concept of Australian citizenship, to prescribe the conditions on which such citizenship may be acquired and lost, and to link citizenship with the right of abode. The qualification is that, as Gibbs CJ said in *Pochi* [151 CLR at 109], Parliament cannot, simply by giving its own definition of "alien", expand the power under s 51 (xix) to include persons who could not possibly answer the description of "aliens" in the ordinary understanding of the word. However, within the class of those who could answer that description, Parliament can determine to whom it will be applied.

Gleeson CJ did not accept any of the three propositions that had been relied on to show that the status of alienage had ceased to apply. As to the two men's "allegiance to the Queen", he (and indeed the whole Court) saw no more than the "local allegiance" traditionally ascribed to resident aliens, and consistent with their alienage. As to the other two propositions he said:

Gleeson CJ: [175] The prosecutor's second proposition, that he is a member of the community constituting the body politic of Australia, appears on examination to involve no more than a restatement of the issue for decision and a bare assertion that the issue should be decided in favour of the prosecutor. I find it difficult to understand what this contention adds to the first and third propositions on which the prosecutor relies. If neither the first nor the third proposition takes the prosecutor outside the constitutional category of a person whom Parliament is entitled to treat as an alien, then it does not advance the matter to construct an antonym for "alien" and assert that it covers the prosecutor.

The power conferred upon Parliament by s 51(xix) includes a power to decide who will be entitled to membership of the Australian body politic. That power, as has been noted, is not unqualified; but there is no reason to doubt that it extends to denying such membership to a person who arrived in this country as an alien, and has never taken up Australian citizenship ...

The third proposition is that the prosecutor has become absorbed into the Australian community. The major premise is that the status of alienage can be lost by absorption into the community. The minor premise is that such absorption has occurred in the case of the prosecutor.

As to the minor premise, the case of the prosecutor provides an example of the vagueness of the concept of absorption, which is accepted as relevant to the immigration power. In *Patterson* [207 CLR at 434-5], McHugh J, referring to the practical difficulties involved in treating British subjects resident in Australia as having their legal status affected by the process of evolution in Australia's relations with the [176] United Kingdom, said that "no bell rang" to inform them when the changes in their status occurred. That is fair comment. It would have been equally fair comment in that case to say that no bell rang to inform Mr Taylor when he became absorbed into the Australian community. Yet all members of the Court accepted that at that time, whenever it was, he ceased to be subject to the immigration power. As is exemplified by the concept of absorption into the community, the silence of bells does not deny the legal significance of gradual change. However, the present case does not turn upon the particular circumstances of the prosecutor, or upon questions as to how the process of absorption into the community is affected by matters of criminal and custodial history. This is because the major premise is to be rejected.

It is true that, in *Patterson*, Kirby J, with whom Callinan J agreed on this point, explicitly referred to the absorption into the Australian community of a class of persons (British subjects) as a reason for treating them as beyond the aliens power as well as beyond the immigration power. There was no majority in *Patterson* for that view. And, in any event, the prosecutor does not belong to that class. Treating absorption into the community as relevant to the status of alienage is inconsistent with earlier judicial views as to the width of par (xix) compared with par (xxvii), to which I have referred above. In my opinion, it is wrong in principle. For reasons already discussed, while absorption reflects the fact that an activity of immigration has come to an end, it may co-exist, and commonly co-exists, with a legal status of alienage. Resident aliens may be absorbed into the community, but they are still aliens.

Gummow J added that, even if there had been a relevant doctrine of "absorption", it could only be a common law doctrine, and hence liable to "[195] displacement by statute". As to the supposed acquisition of an Australian "allegiance", he said:

Gummow J: [195] [The prosecutor] relied upon the statement by McHugh J in *Re Patterson; Ex parte Taylor* [207 CLR at 428-9], made with reference to Holdsworth, that the common law rules concerning subjects and aliens "centre around" the duty of allegiance owed by the subject to the Crown. Holdsworth was speaking of the appearance in England in the course of the thirteenth century of the beginnings of "the modern rules of the common law, which define the persons who are to be accounted as British subjects". He went on to say that the doctrine of allegiance had its roots in the feudal idea of personal fealty and, significantly, that "it [196] is the duty of allegiance ... which differentiates the subject from the alien".

That latter proposition, if it was designed by Holdsworth to apply to the state of the common law in England when he wrote between the World Wars, was erroneous. The principles respecting allegiance provided no sufficient discrimen between subjects and aliens. It may be that Holdsworth's subsequent treatment of the restatement of the common law in *Calvin's Case* [(1608) 7 Co Rep 1a; 77 ER 377] ... and the differentiation between alien friends and alien enemies indicates that his proposition respecting allegiance as the discrimen between subjects and aliens was intended to refer only to the position in the Middle Ages. In any event, it supplies no such discrimen in modern times ...

[198] An individual may be under concurrent obligations of allegiance to more than one state ... [In 1947] Sir Hersch Lauterpacht said that the English law respecting the obligations of

allegiance owed by resident aliens was fully in conformity with existing international practice. He added:

> "The alien resident in a foreign country continues to owe allegiance to the sovereign of his own State. That allegiance expresses itself in [199] his continued subjection to the laws of his own country – though, more often than not, the home State considers it convenient to limit its claims to jurisdiction with regard to the acts of its nationals when abroad. But, while continuing to be bound by allegiance to his own State, the alien becomes subject to another allegiance – that concomitant with the protection of the law which shelters him ..."

The four judges who had been in the majority in *Re Patterson* were equally emphatic in holding that what that case decided had no application to the present case.

Gaudron J: [178] Although there was some difference in the reasons of those who constituted the majority in *Re Patterson*, that case clearly held that provisions of the Act permitting the detention and removal of non-citizens were invalid in their application to a person who had been born in the United Kingdom, had entered Australia before the coming into effect, in 1987, of the *Australian Citizenship Amendment Act* 1984 (Cth) (the 1984 Act) and had been absorbed into the Australian community but had not taken out Australian citizenship. Because the prosecutor in that case had been absorbed into the Australian community, the provisions of the Act ... could not be supported in their application to him as an exercise of the power to legislate with respect to "immigration and emigration". Thus, the question was whether the prosecutor was an alien for the purposes of s 51(xix) of the Constitution.

By reason that the prosecutor in *Re Patterson* was a British subject by birth, it was held in that case that he had not been an alien when he entered Australia. And it was further held that he had not been transformed into an alien either by reason of the emergence of the separate capacity of the Queen as Queen of Australia or by reason of [179] the amendments to the *Australian Citizenship Act* ...

Because the prosecutor in *Re Patterson* had not entered Australia as an alien, that case is the obverse of the present. That being so, *Re Patterson* does not assist the prosecutor's argument which is predicated on the proposition that, notwithstanding the Citizenship Act, an alien may become a non-alien other than by the conferral of Australian citizenship.

Before turning to the argument advanced on behalf of the prosecutor, it is necessary to say something of Australian citizenship. Citizenship is a statutory, not a constitutional concept. The relevant constitutional concepts with which this case are concerned are "alien", the singular form of the word used in s 51(xix) of the Constitution, and, by way of constitutional distinction, "non-alien". Thus, the fact that the prosecutor is not an Australian citizen is irrelevant if he is not an alien.

It may at once be accepted that the power conferred by s 51(xix) of the Constitution to legislate with respect to "naturalization and aliens" is a power that is confined by the concept of "alien" – a concept which is not at large. Thus, the power to legislate with respect to naturalisation and aliens is not a power to declare that a person who is a non-alien, as was the prosecutor in *Re Patterson*, is an alien in the absence of some change in the relationship of that person with the Australian body politic. So, too, it may be accepted that the notion of "alien" is and always has been linked with a person's place of birth. Thus, s 51(xix) of the Constitution does not permit the Parliament to legislate so as to provide that a person born in Australia to an Australian citizen is an alien.

To say that the Parliament's power to legislate so as to deprive a person who is, by birth, or who has become a member of the body politic of his or her status as a non-alien is limited is not to say that there is any limitation on the power of the Parliament to legislate as to the circumstances in which and the procedures by which an alien born person may be admitted to membership of the Australian body politic and, thus, cease to be an alien. Nor is it to say that a person may cease to be an alien other than in the circumstances and by the procedures designated by Parliament.

The process whereby an alien born individual attains the status and entitlements that attach to a non-alien is called "naturalization". The argument for the prosecutor is predicated on the proposition that the common law permits and the Constitution recognises that that process can occur other than in the circumstances and by the procedures designated by Parliament. That proposition is without foundation.

[180] In *Pochi v Macphee*, Gibbs CJ observed [151 CLR at 111] that "[i]t was well settled at common law that naturalisation could only be achieved by Act of Parliament – even action by the Crown under the prerogative could not give an alien the status of a British subject". Holdsworth states that that was recognised "as early as, and probably before, the beginning of the fifteenth century … and … was accepted as a settled rule of law in *Calvin's Case*". In *Calvin's Case* [77 ER at 385] it was said that "the King by his letters patent may make a denizen, but cannot naturalise him to all purposes, as an Act of Parliament may do". And Quick and Garran, writing in 1901, noted that "[f]ormerly the only mode of obtaining naturalization was by a special Act of Parliament passed for each individual seeking to be naturalized; but by the Act 7 and 8 Vict c 66, the British Parliament provided a general procedure by which approved aliens could acquire the status of natural-born subjects of the Queen".

Once it is accepted … that the common law does not permit and, for many centuries, has not permitted an alien born person to acquire the status and entitlements that attach to a person who acquires membership of the Australian body politic by birth except in accordance with statute, it follows that the Constitution recognises neither of the processes which the prosecutor calls in aid in this case and that neither process can or does limit the power of Parliament to define or limit the circumstances in which an alien born person may acquire membership of the Australian body politic and, thereby, cease to be an alien. And when Parliament so legislates, it legislates exhaustively on the topic.

At least since 1948, the Citizenship Act has exhaustively provided with respect to the circumstances in which persons who are alien born – a class which, as was held in *Re Patterson*, does not include persons who entered Australia as British subjects in the same circumstances as did the prosecutor in that case – may become members of the Australian body politic by the acquisition of Australian citizenship. It cannot be disputed that the prosecutor was alien born and has not obtained Australian citizenship in accordance **[181]** with the Citizenship Act. He is, therefore, an alien.

What Kirby and Callinan JJ had suggested in *Patterson* was not that, in the case of a person who came to Australia as an alien, the status of alienage can be dissolved by absorption into the community, but only that, in the case of a person who was *not* an alien, absorption into the community may be a reason for denial that the status of alienage can subsequently be imposed upon him or her by external events. *Meng Kok Te* affirms a different proposition: that although the process of "absorption" liberates an "immigrant" from the grip of the immigration power, no similar process can liberate an "alien" from the grip of the aliens power. On that point there was no significant dissent from Gleeson CJ's insistence that, even when aliens have been absorbed into the community, "**[176]** they are still aliens". For example, Gaudron J held that alienage cannot be extinguished "**[180]** except in accordance with statute", and that no process of absorption can "limit the power of Parliament to define or limit the circumstances in which an alien born person may acquire membership of the Australian body politic and, thereby, cease to be an alien". Similarly, McHugh J held that: "**[188]** Those who enter a common law country as aliens can only acquire citizenship and the status of non-aliens by legislation".

Both Kirby and Callinan J left open the possibility that (as Kirby J put it) there might be "**[217]** extreme cases" in which "non-citizens … might exceptionally be regarded as outside the aliens power" (for example, "a ninety-year-old non-citizen … [who] had lived peacefully in Australia virtually all her life"). As to those cases Kirby J said only that "**[218]** [t]he facts of the applicants' cases fall so far short of such instances that it is unnecessary to canvass them further". Callinan J found a "**[228]** conclusive" answer to the applicants' claims in "the fact that their criminal activities are incompatible with absorption within the community" – "even if I were to assume", he said hypothetically, "that a non-citizen may come to be beyond the reach of the aliens power after absorption". Accordingly, he was able to say: "**[229]** For the reasons given by Gaudron J I would seriously doubt whether 'absorption' can put persons such as the applicants beyond the reach of the aliens power. I do not need however to decide this appeal on that basis, and refrain from doing so, sharing as I do, some of the concerns expressed by Kirby J with respect to very long term residents of Australia". In short, all four of the judges who had been in the majority in *Patterson* on the constitutional issue had reaffirmed the correctness of that decision in *Meng Kok Te*. But in February 2003 Gaudron J resigned from the bench and was replaced by Heydon J; and when the issue next arose for decision, *Patterson* was overruled and *Nolan* was restored.

Jason Shaw was born in the United Kingdom and brought to Australia by his parents in 1974 when he was 18 months old. He grew up in Australia, and never travelled abroad, but never applied for citizenship either. On the grounds of a "substantial criminal record" from the age of 14 onwards, his visa was cancelled in 2001 under s 501 of the *Migration Act*. The question was whether, in its application to Shaw, s 501 was a valid exercise of the power with respect to "aliens". Gleeson CJ, Gummow, Hayne and Heydon JJ held that it was, and that *Patterson* should be overruled. McHugh, Kirby and Callinan JJ dissented.

Shaw v Minister for Immigration and Multicultural Affairs
(2003) 218 CLR 28

Gleeson CJ, Gummow and Hayne JJ: [36] Much of the applicant's argument proceeded from the premise that, because the expression "British subject" could be applied to him, he was not an alien. That premise is flawed. First, "British subject" is not a constitutional expression; it is a statutory expression. Secondly, and more fundamentally, if "British subject" was being used as a synonym for "subject of the Queen", an expression which is found in the Constitution, that usage would assume that there was at the time of federation, and there remains today, a constitutional and political unity between the UK and Australia which 100 years of history denies.

[37] The status of subjects of the Crown derived from the mediaeval common law in England. The term "British subject" seems first to have appeared at the time of the Union with Scotland. Article IV of the Articles of Union ensured trade and navigation rights to "all the subjects of the United Kingdom of Great Britain". Thereafter, the *British Nationality and Status of Aliens Act* 1914 (UK) (the 1914 UK Act) deemed to be "natural-born British subjects" those "born within His Majesty's dominions and allegiance": s 1(1). Hence the statement that the 1914 UK Act "was based on the conception of a common British nationality of all subjects of the Crown throughout the Commonwealth and Empire, which had grown out of, and perpetuated, the common law doctrine of allegiance to the King" [*Halsbury's Laws of England*, 3rd ed, vol 1, par 1023].

In their commentary on the covering clauses of the Constitution, Quick and Garran rightly pointed out that:

> "[t]he relation of the Commonwealth to the Empire, and the relation of the Federal and State Governments of the Commonwealth to one another, can hardly be appreciated apart from a sound study of the principle of sovereignty."

They distinguished between "legal sovereignty" (as, for example, the sovereignty of the British Parliament), "political sovereignty" (the sovereignty of the people), and "titular sovereignty" (the sovereignty of the Queen). As HWR Wade was later to point out, in 1955, there comes a point in debate about "sovereignty" and related concepts where the legal and the political intersect. As long ago as 1935, in *British Coal Corporation v The King* [[1935] AC 500 at 520], Viscount Sankey LC said of the possibility that the British Parliament might repeal the Statute of Westminster ... that it was "theory" and had "no relation to realities". The "realities" to which Lord Sankey referred were the political realities of the separation of the dominions from the UK which had occurred and which found reflection in the Statute of Westminster. These political realities informed the relevant body of law and are reflected in the later observation by Sir Robert Menzies that constitutional law combines elements of history, statutory interpretation and political philosophy ...

[38] The constitutional term "subject of the Queen" must be understood in the light of the development and evolution of the relationship between Australia and the UK and between the UK and those other countries which recognise the monarch of the UK as their monarch. In particular, the expression "subject of the Queen" can be given meaning and operation only when it is recognised that the reference to "the Queen" is not to the person but to the office. That recognition necessarily entails recognition of the reality of the independence of Australia from the UK.

At the time of his birth, the applicant was, by force of the UK statute then in force, the *British Nationality Act* 1948 (UK) (the 1948 UK Act) (s 1(1)), a "citizen of the [UK] and Colonies" and "by virtue of" that citizenship he had "the status of a British subject". This status was the creation of and derivative from UK statute law, because its existence was dependent upon the possession of UK citizenship, itself a statutory concept.

In Australia, by virtue of s 7 of the Citizenship Act, the applicant, "by virtue of" his citizenship of the UK, was classified as a "British subject". This Australian legislative status conferred on such persons certain advantages under other Australian statutes, such as those dealing with the franchise and the issue of passports.

The passage of the Citizenship Act and the 1948 UK Act and legislation in other Commonwealth countries followed negotiations between the governments concerned. The new arrangements reflected significant changes in the Imperial system which had taken place since federation ...

[39] It may be that there never was a single nationality law throughout the British Empire. In 1901, the Home Office in the UK established an inter-departmental committee to consider the state of the law of naturalisation in the British Empire. That committee pointed to a number of difficulties that followed from disparate and local laws governing naturalisation throughout the British Empire. These matters were taken up at Imperial conferences in 1902, 1907 and 1911, and in 1914 the UK Parliament enacted the 1914 UK Act to deal with some of the problems that were seen to have emerged. Even under that Act, however, the naturalising power was to be exercisable by the self-governing dominions without reference to the UK. So much, of course, was entirely consistent with the provision of s 51(xix) of the Constitution by which the Parliament of the Commonwealth had power with respect to naturalisation and aliens. [40] The 1914 UK Act and the 1948 UK Act both assumed that questions of naturalisation were within the powers of the dominion legislatures. The understanding of the expression "subject of the Queen", and the light which that understanding casts on the ambit of the aliens power cannot, then, attribute significance to the adoption of the expression "British subject" in UK legislation. Rather, "subject of the Queen", with its implicit reference to notions of sovereignty, must recognise that at least by 1948 the subjects of the Queen to which reference was made were subjects of the monarch in right of Australia, not subjects of the monarch in right of the UK.

The Citizenship Act, then styled the *Nationality and Citizenship Act* 1948 (Cth), came into force on 26 January 1949. Undoubtedly, to a significant degree, that statute depended upon the aliens power. Under UK law, Irish citizens ceased to be British subjects on 1 January 1949. Special provision, of a favourable nature, was made in s 8 of the Citizenship Act with respect to Irish citizens. In addition, Irish citizens might acquire Australian citizenship by following the procedures and conditions of s 12 which were less rigorous than those stipulated by s 15 for other aliens. Further, the statute created its own class of aliens which was narrower than the class of what might be called "constitutional aliens". This is apparent from the terms of the definition in s 5(1) of "alien" as meaning "a person who is not a British subject, *an Irish citizen* or a protected person" (emphasis added). It also should be noted that the "protected persons" spoken of included those in British protectorates who were aliens in the ordinary sense of the term but were taken out of that category for the purposes of the legislation.

The classification by s 7 of the Citizenship Act of the citizens of the UK, Canada, New Zealand, the Union of South Africa, Newfoundland, India, Pakistan, Southern Rhodesia and Ceylon, as British subjects in Australian law by virtue of that citizenship, also was an exercise of the legislative power with respect to aliens. The new statutory status rendered those persons a class of aliens with special advantages in Australian law, as mentioned above. It can hardly be said that, as the relevant political facts and circumstances stood in 1948, those citizens could not possibly answer the description of aliens in the ordinary understanding of that word.

The Constitution was, to use Isaacs J's expression, made not "for a single occasion", but for "the continued life and progress of the community" [*Commonwealth v Kreglinger & Fernau Ltd and Bardsley (Skin Wool Case)* (1926) 37 CLR 393 at 413]. The Constitution took effect at a time when "the Crown" was said to be "indivisible" and when the common law notion of allegiance to that "Crown" informed the statutory use of the [41] term "British subject". But, as was explained in *Sue v Hill* [(1999) 199 CLR 462 at 497-503], in 1900 the term "the Crown" was used in constitutional theory in several distinct senses. In particular, the expression "the Crown in right of ..." was used to distinguish between the newly created governmental units within the Empire. Harrison

Moore made the point that, in the statutes establishing the Canadian and Australian federations, the Imperial Parliament had "unquestionably treated these entities as distinct persons" ...

The development of the "autonomous Communities" recognised by the Imperial Conference of 1926 proceeded by steps and over periods which had different consequences for the reading of various provisions of the Constitution. To ask when Australia actually achieved complete constitutional independence or other questions phrased in similar terms is to assume a simple answer to a complex issue, rather than to attend to the particular matter arising under the Constitution or involving its interpretation which has arisen for decision. In that regard, Gaudron J said in *Sue v Hill* [199 CLR at 526]:

> "To acknowledge that, in some constitutional provisions, some words and phrases are capable of applying to different persons or things at different times is not to change the meaning of those provisions. It is simply to give them their proper meaning and effect." ...

At times when elements of the UK government still participated or had the power to participate in Australian legislative, executive and judicial affairs, in particular until 1986 in the affairs of the States, it was difficult to classify the UK as a "foreign **[42]** power" within the meaning of s 44(i) of the Constitution. The decision in *Sue v Hill* proceeded on that footing.

On the other hand, s 34 of the Constitution acknowledges the possibility of change in the relationship between the UK on the one hand and Australia on the other. It does so by providing that the Parliament may alter the qualifications for elections so as to eliminate any requirement that candidates "be a subject of the Queen, either natural-born or for at least five years naturalised under a law of the United Kingdom" ...

Once it be decided that the text of the Constitution contemplates changes in the political and constitutional relationship between the United Kingdom and Australia, it is impossible to read the legislative power with respect to "aliens" as subject to some implicit restriction protective from its reach those who are not Australian citizens but who entered Australia as citizens of the UK and colonies under the 1948 UK Act. It was unnecessary to reach that conclusion in *Re Patterson; Ex parte Taylor* [(2001) 207 CLR 391], but it should now be reached.

References in argument to the statutory status of a "British subject" are apt to obscure the undoubted truth that, by 1948, the Imperial Crown, indivisible in nature, with an undivided allegiance, was no longer apparent, whether in this country or the UK. Such references also obscure the realisation that, in the pre-1948 law, the status of a natural-born British subject was statute based, particularly in the 1914 UK Act. There never was a common law notion of "British subject" rendered into an immutable element of "the law of the Constitution". This is so, whether that term be as understood to Diceyans in the UK or to lawyers in this country ...

[43] It remains to refer to s 117 of the Constitution. This operates in favour of "[a] subject of the Queen, resident in any State". The Citizenship Act no longer provides for any status of "British subject". Nor has the law of the UK, since 1 January 1983, used the term as a status enjoyed in relation to citizenship. Does this mean that, like the expression in the Schedule to the Constitution, "the United Kingdom of Great Britain and Ireland", s 117 is to be read as it would have been read in 1901? The answer must be "no", lest the section be deprived of any useful operation. The reading of the text should accommodate the evident purpose of s 117 in present conditions. That purpose is the protection of citizens (but not aliens) resident in one State against the relevant disability or discrimination in another State.

The conclusion reached is that the applicant entered Australia as an alien in the constitutional sense. *Re Minister for Immigration and Multicultural Affairs; Ex parte Meng Kok Te* establishes that, this being so, he did not lose that status by reason of his subsequent personal history in this country. Upon the cancellation of his visa, he became an "unlawful non-citizen" within the meaning of the Act.

This case should be taken as determining that the aliens power has reached all those persons who entered this country after the commencement of the Citizenship Act on 26 January 1949 and who were born out of Australia of parents who were not Australian citizens and who had not been naturalised. The scope of any earlier operation of the power does not fall for consideration.

In a brief concurring judgment, Heydon J went further. He found it "**[87]** unsatisfactory" that the case had been conducted on the assumption that "in 1901 British subjects were not aliens", so that the discussion "concentrated on the question of when and how the change occurred". He thought the question should be left open of whether, from an Australian viewpoint, British subjects (or at least some of them) had already been "aliens" as from 1 January 1901.

The three remaining members of the majority in *Patterson* – McHugh, Kirby and Callinan JJ – all continued to affirm its correctness, but this time in dissent.

McHugh J: [46] There are only two heads of federal constitutional power that could arguably extend the operation of s 501 to a person such as the applicant who is a British citizen and who arrived in Australia in 1974. The first is the immigration power; the second is the aliens power. A long line of authority establishes that the immigration power does not authorise the Parliament to make laws with respect to persons who have immigrated to Australia, made their permanent homes here and become members of the Australian community. Accordingly, the immigration power did not authorise the enactment of s 501 in so far as it purports to apply to the applicant.

The aliens power, however, gives the Parliament greater power over immigrants than the immigration power. In *Nolan v Minister for* **[47]** *Immigration and Ethnic Affairs* [(1988) 165 CLR 178], this Court held that any immigrant who has not taken out Australian citizenship is an alien for the purpose of s 51(xix) of the Constitution. On that view of the aliens power, the Parliament can legislate for the deportation of persons who are British citizens and have been permanent residents of Australia for many years. In *Nolan*, the Court upheld an order of the Minister deporting Nolan, a citizen of the United Kingdom who had lived permanently in Australia since 1967 but who had not taken out Australian citizenship.

In *Re Patterson; Ex parte Taylor* [(2001) 207 CLR 391], however, a majority of this Court held that *Nolan* should be overruled in so far as it held that all British citizens living in Australia who had not taken out Australian citizenship were aliens for the purpose of the Constitution. Taylor was a British citizen who had arrived in Australia in 1966 and had since lived here permanently. However, he had not taken out Australian citizenship. A majority of the Court held that s 501 of the Act could not constitutionally authorise the deportation of Taylor.

As I pointed out in *Re Minister for Immigration and Multicultural Affairs; Ex parte [Meng Kok] Te* [212 CLR at 187], *Re Patterson* has no ratio decidendi. The four majority Justices were Gaudron, Kirby and Callinan JJ and myself. Gaudron J held that Taylor was a member of the body politic that constituted the Australian community and that British citizens who were members of that body politic and had been in Australia before 1987, were not aliens within the meaning of the Constitution. Kirby J held that Taylor was not an alien when he arrived in Australia, that he "had been absorbed into the people of the Commonwealth" [207 CLR at 492] and that the Parliament could not retrospectively declare him to be an alien. I held that British immigrants who settled in Australia before 1973 were subjects of the Queen of Australia and could not be "aliens" for the purpose of the Constitution. I selected 1973 as the earliest date on which the constitutional power to legislate with respect to aliens could apply to British immigrants. I did so because 1973 was the year in which the Parliament enacted the *Royal Style and Titles Act* 1973 (Cth). But I expressed the view that the relevant date "maybe later" [207 CLR at 436]. Callinan J agreed with the reasoning of both Kirby J and myself.

Although *Re Patterson* has no ratio decidendi, "it still has precedential authority in respect of circumstances that 'are not reasonably distinguishable from those which gave rise to the **[48]** decision'" [212 CLR at 187]. It is not possible, however, to say that the present case is not reasonably distinguishable from *Re Patterson*. The only material fact in *Re Patterson* that was common to all majority judgments was that Taylor had arrived in Australia in 1966. *Re Patterson* is therefore only an authority for the proposition that a British citizen is not an alien if that person arrived in Australia in or before 1966 and has lived here permanently since that time. Even if the relevant year be extended to 1973, it does not assist the applicant in this case: he did not migrate to Australia until 1974. Accordingly, the applicant cannot rely on *Re Patterson* as an authority that supports his claim that the Act cannot constitutionally authorise the Minister to revoke his visa and render him liable to deportation.

Despite *Re Patterson* having no precedential value for the purpose of *this* case, I remain convinced that *Re Patterson* was correctly decided. Having read the reasons of Callinan J, I am also convinced that his Honour is correct in holding [218 CLR at 85] that the evolutionary process by which the term "subject of the Queen" in s 117 of the Constitution became "subject of the Queen of Australia" was not completed until 3 March 1986. Until that date, therefore, Australians, born or naturalised, and British citizens permanently residing in Australia owed their allegiance to the "Crown of the United Kingdom of Great Britain and Ireland". Until that date, they were subjects of the Queen of the United Kingdom of Great Britain and Ireland for the purpose of s 117 of the Constitution, and were entitled to the protection of that section. When the evolutionary process ended, British citizens then permanently residing in Australia became subjects of the Queen of Australia by the same evolutionary process that had transformed the Queen of the United Kingdom of Great Britain and Ireland into the Queen of Australia. For the reasons that I gave in *Re Patterson*, subjects of the Queen of Australia are not aliens for the purpose of the Constitution.

It follows that the applicant, who arrived in Australia in 1974 and was permanently living in Australia on 3 March 1986, is a subject of the Queen of Australia. He is not an alien.

Kirby J, also, now agreed with Callinan J that the critical date was 3 March 1986, when the *Australia Acts* came into force (see Chapter 4, §8); and both of them continued to speak of earlier British arrivals like Shaw as having been absorbed into the Australian community. Thus, Kirby J pleaded for greater "[64] understanding of the peculiar transitional Australian position of the significant number of British assisted immigrants who came to Australia as part of our community and enjoyed a special status in the nation because, at the time, they were regarded as sharing a common allegiance and a common membership of our community".

In *Meng Kok Te*, both Kirby and Callinan JJ had suggested that the two men involved in that case had *not* in fact been absorbed into the community. As Kirby J there put it: "[218] Far from showing allegiance or being absorbed into the Australian body politic, the repeated conduct of the applicants constitutes a public renunciation of the norms of the community … [since] each of the applicants has repeatedly broken this country's laws". Indeed, as we have seen, Callinan J was able to take "[228] the fact that their criminal activities are incompatible with absorption within the community" as the basis of his actual decision. Both judges, however, now declined to take a similar view of Shaw's criminal record. Callinan J chose to "[79] adhere to the view, that persistent serious criminal activity *from soon after the inception of residence here* is likely to be regarded as antipathetic to absorption into the general community" (emphasis added), but declined to apply that view to Shaw, since "[86] in this case the applicant had been living in Australia for more than twelve years before his first conviction, and that occurred when he was still a child. In my view the applicant had [already] been absorbed into the Australian community by the time that he came to the notice of the criminal courts. And, in any event, I would not regard that first conviction, occurring as it did when he was so young, as putting him beyond the community of ordinary Australians".

(c)   Persons Born in Australia

Scattered through the series of cases dealing with the status of former "British subjects" were frequent references to place of birth as the decisive criterion distinguishing aliens from non-aliens. For example, in *Patterson* McHugh J noted that at common law "[432] [b]irth within the sovereign's territories was the criterion by which the common law distinguished the subject of the sovereign from the alien", while in *Meng Kok Te* Gaudron J thought "[179] it may be accepted that the notion of 'alien' is and always has been linked with a person's place of birth". Hayne J, for his part, thought in *Meng Kok Te* that: "[220] Alienage is a status fixed by reference to descent and place of birth". However, when the criterion of "place of birth" was invoked in 2004 by a plaintiff born in Australia, but excluded from Australian citizenship by s 10(2) of the *Australian Citizenship Act 1948* (Cth), Gummow, Hayne and Heydon JJ explained that birth was not, after all, the decisive criterion, while Gleeson CJ and Kirby J held that there was no constitutional restriction on the Parliament's power to define the limits of "citizenship" in a way that excluded the plaintiff, and thereby to render her an alien.

The disputed provisions of s 10(2) had been introduced into the Act by amendment in 1986 in response to a series of cases occurring during the previous year. Alvin Au Yeung was born at Bourke, New South Wales, in December 1983. By virtue of s 10 of the *Australian Citizenship Act*, as it then stood, he became an Australian citizen by birth. His parents had come to Australia on tourist visas in 1982. They had worked at the RSL Club in Bourke, and had hoped to buy a restaurant in the Riverina; but, having overstayed their visas, they were forced to leave in September 1984, taking Alvin with them. Because Alvin was an Australian citizen, his parents complained on his behalf to the Human Rights Commission, which reported to Parliament on 28 March 1985. The Commission found that, as compared with other Australian children, Alvin had suffered discrimination contrary to Art 24 of the 1966 International Covenant on Civil and Political Rights: "**[4]** Treating him as a mere appendage of his parents is to ignore his independent rights". On the other hand, his rights "**[5]** should not be looked at in isolation from the position of his immediate family". It followed that his parents "should have been permitted to stay with him in Australia", and that the discretionary power to deport conferred by s 18 of the *Migration Act 1958* (Cth) had been wrongly exercised.

Human Rights Commission Report No 10, *The Human Rights of Australian-Born Children: A Report on the Complaint of Mr and Mrs RC Au Yeung*
(Parliamentary Paper No 80 of 1985)

[10] [T]he Commission *recommends* that Mr and Mrs Au Yeung be permitted to return to Australia as permanent residents and that in other cases involving the human rights of the Australian born children of parents who are not citizens of Australia recognition is given to the paramountcy of the human rights of these children in the making of immigration decisions concerning their parents. The Commission further *recommends* that consideration be given to the question whether Australia's international obligations in the field of human rights require it automatically to grant citizenship to the children of non-citizens born in Australia. Whilst the human rights of Australian citizens must invariably be observed, is it necessary for the children of prohibited non-citizens to become Australian citizens merely because they are born in Australia? It would seem that the current practice, in cases like this, is to treat them as if they were not citizens with the result that their human rights are denied. This is an unjust result, and it may be fairer in the long run to change the rule that birth in Australia automatically results in Australian citizenship, provided that otherwise stateless children born in Australia are granted Australian citizenship. The Commission observes, further, that more effective supervision of temporary entrants would remove or substantially reduce the kind of problem presented in this case.

A similar issue involving Taygan Yilmaz (born in Melbourne in 1982) and his brother Alkan Yilmaz (born in Sydney in 1984) arose in 1985 (see Human Rights Commission Report No 15, *The Human Rights of Australian-Born Children: A Report on the Complaint of Mr and Mrs M Yilmaz* (Parliamentary Paper No 310 of 1985)). The Commission repeated its earlier recommendations, but added that Art 24(3) of the International Covenant – requiring that every child have the right "to acquire a nationality" – could be satisfied in various ways, of which citizenship by birth was only one. (It could equally be satisfied, for instance, if a child were given citizenship, or a right to acquire it, by "**[6]** the country of which the parents are nationals".) Again, however, the Commission warned that any legislative change "should be such as to ensure that the child, if it would otherwise be stateless, has Australian nationality".

Four months after this second report, a similar issue was considered by the High Court in *Kioa v West* (1985) 159 CLR 550. The Court held, with only Brennan J dissenting, that Australia's international obligations in such cases were not legally relevant. However, Elvina Kioa and her parents were allowed to remain in Australia since the High Court also held (with Gibbs CJ dissenting) that the decision to deport them had involved a denial of natural justice.

In 1986, the Hawke government responded to the Human Rights Commission reports by amending s 10 of the *Australian Citizenship Act* to limit the circumstances in which citizenship is automatically acquired by birth. As further amended in 1989, s 10 now provides as follows:

Australian Citizenship Act 1948 (Cth)

10 (1) Subject to this section, a person born in Australia after the commencement of this Act shall be an Australian citizen.

(2) Subject to subsection (3), a person born in Australia after the commencement of the *Australian Citizenship Amendment Act 1986* shall be an Australian citizen by virtue of that birth if and only if:

    (a) a parent of the person was, at the time of the person's birth, an Australian citizen or a permanent resident; or

    (b) the person has, throughout the period of 10 years commencing on the day on which the person was born, been ordinarily resident in Australia.

(3) Subject to subsection (5), a person shall not be an Australian citizen by virtue of this section if, at the time of the person's birth, a parent of the person was an enemy alien and the birth occurred in a place then under occupation by the enemy.

(5) Subsection (3) does not apply in relation to a person if, at the time of the person's birth, a parent of the person:

    (a) was an Australian citizen or a permanent resident; and

    (b) was not an enemy alien.

(6) A reference in this section to a permanent resident does not include a reference to a person who is, for the purposes of the *Migration Act 1958*, an exempt non-citizen.

The Commission's enjoinder that no child should be rendered a stateless person was satisfied by an amendment to s 23D of the Act, which provides a process by which a person can gain Australian citizenship if born in Australia with no other citizenship and no entitlement to acquire such other citizenship.

The effect of the 1986 amendment was considered by the High Court in 2004. Tania Singh (the plaintiff) was born in Mildura, Victoria, in February 1998 and remained in Australia from the time of her birth. Both of her parents were Indian citizens and accordingly she too was, by descent, a citizen of India. However, because neither of her parents was an Australian citizen or a permanent resident, she was not an Australian citizen under the amended version of s 10 of the *Australian Citizenship Act*.

Section 198 of the *Migration Act* provided for the removal from Australia of non-citizens who do not hold a visa (referred to in the Act as "unlawful non-citizens"). The plaintiff argued that the application of this provision in her case was not supported by the "aliens" power. She maintained that, because she was born in Australia, she could not for constitutional purposes be regarded as an alien. The High Court rejected her argument by 5:2, with McHugh and Callinan JJ dissenting. Her contention that the word "aliens" in s 51(xix) was limited to the fixed legal meaning which it bore in 1900 provoked extensive reflections on "originalism", founders' intention, and the use of the Convention Debates.

Singh v Commonwealth
(2004) 209 ALR 355

Gummow, Hayne and Heydon JJ: [400] The plaintiff submitted that, at the time of federation, "aliens" had an accepted and fixed legal meaning which, subject to two immaterial exceptions, excluded from its embrace any person born in Australia. (The two exceptions concerned children of foreign diplomats and children of occupying armies.) This, the plaintiff submitted, was the meaning which the common law of England had attributed to the word "alien" since as long ago as *Calvin's Case* [(1608) 7 Co Rep 1a; 77 ER 377] and it was not within the powers of the federal Parliament to give any new or different content to that term. That is, the plaintiff contended … that the word "aliens" had a meaning which was fixed by the common law as expressed in *Calvin's Case* and that that "common law meaning" fixed the outer limits to the power given to the Parliament by s 51(xix) …

[401] The defendants … submitted that the power to make laws with respect to naturalization and aliens confers on the Parliament power to make laws determining to whom is attributed the status of alien. That power was said not to be unqualified. It was said that "while this Court may determine the 'outer boundaries' of the word 'aliens' in accordance with the Constitution, the Parliament may enact laws to define 'aliens' within the penumbra of the 'ordinary understanding' of the word". The reference to the "ordinary understanding of the word" was an allusion to what Gibbs CJ said in *Pochi v Macphee* [(1982) 151 CLR 101 at 109]:

"Clearly the Parliament cannot, simply by giving its own definition of 'alien', expand the power under s 51(xix) to include persons who could not possibly answer the description of 'aliens' in the ordinary understanding of the word." …

[402] It is … important to emphasise the point made by Fullagar J in *Australian Communist Party v Commonwealth* ("the *Communist Party Case*") [(1951) 83 CLR 1 at 258] by reference to the metaphor that a stream cannot rise higher than its source. As his Honour said:

"A power to make laws with respect to lighthouses does not authorize the making of a law with respect to anything which is, in the opinion of the law-maker, a lighthouse."

To adapt that dictum to the present case, a power to make laws with respect to aliens does not authorise the making of a law with respect to any person who, in the opinion of the Parliament, is an alien. That Parliament has made a law which a party or intervener asserts to be a law with respect to aliens presents the constitutional question for resolution; it does not provide an answer.

These reasons seek to demonstrate that a central characteristic of the status of "alien" is, and always has been, owing obligations to a sovereign power other than the sovereign power in question. The plaintiff has that characteristic. The problem to which Gibbs CJ adverted in *Pochi* and Fullagar J adverted in the *Communist Party Case* does not arise …

[403] The plaintiff's contention that "aliens" had a fixed legal meaning at federation assumed not only that this meaning was to be ascertained by reference to the common law but also that the meaning, once ascertained, defined the outer limits of the power of the Parliament. These reasons will seek to demonstrate that, at federation, "aliens" did not have a fixed legal meaning ascertained by reference to the common law. What had been the common law at the time of *Calvin's Case* had been overtaken by statute and by subsequent developments of legal thought in England and in Europe. It is as well, however, to go on to say something further about … [the assumption] that a meaning ascertained in the way for which the plaintiff contended defined the outer limits of the constitutional power.

To say of a constitutional expression, like "aliens", that its content is "immutable" invites controversy which may be more remarkable for its heat than for the light shed on the underlying issue. The relevant question is not whether the meaning of "aliens" is immutable, it is whether, as a matter of construction, the law now in question (here s 198 of the *Migration Act*) can be supported in its operation with respect to the plaintiff as a law with respect to naturalization and aliens.

In undertaking that question of construction, to identify the meaning conveyed, at the time of federation, by the words used in the Constitution is more than a matter of historical interest. It is an essential step in the task of construction. That is not to say, however, that seeking an understanding of the meaning of a constitutional expression like "aliens", when used at the time of federation, permits or requires searching for the subjective intention of the framers. It does not. Metaphorical references to "the founders' intention" are as apt to mislead in the constitutional context as are references to the intentions of the legislature when construing a statute or references to the intentions of the parties to a contract when considering its construction. Rather, the question is one of construing the relevant constitutional provisions. That task of construction cannot be undertaken without knowing what particular constitutional expressions meant, and how words were used, at the time of federation. But the task does not end with the results of that inquiry. Always, the Constitution is to be construed bearing steadily in mind that it is an instrument of government intended to endure.

[404] Numerous cases decided by this Court reveal that constitutional expressions may have a different operation 50 or 100 years after federation from the operation they would have had in

1901. *Sue v Hill* [(1999) 199 CLR 462], and its consideration of whether Great Britain is now to be regarded as a foreign power, and *Grain Pool of Western Australia v Commonwealth* [(2000) 202 CLR 479], with its discussion of whether legislation concerning the grant of plant variety rights was a law with respect to copyrights, patents of invention and designs and trademarks, are but two recent examples.

It may be that tools like the distinction between connotation and denotation or the distinction between concepts and conceptions are thought to be useful in understanding or explaining decisions like *Sue v Hill*. There is at least a risk, however, that using such tools directs attention to their content and to their utility rather than to the analytical task they are being used to undertake.

For present purposes, all that need be noted are two related points. First, to require the identification of the historical meaning of constitutional terms does not confine the operation of the Constitution to the applications which those who wrote it may have had in mind. To confine it in that way would be to fall into the error of seeking the subjective intention of the founders. Secondly, the identification of the historical meaning of a constitutional term like "aliens" is not complete if all that is done is to give a list of the particular circumstances to which the word was applied at federation.

After tracing the statutory modifications of the common law concept of "alienage", they said:

Gummow, Hayne and Heydon JJ: [411] The word "aliens" may have had a fixed legal meaning in the 17th century. (Even then the legislature had altered the rules about alienage in some respects.) By the end of the 19th century the word did not bear the meaning it did at the time of *Calvin's Case*. There had been numerous legislative [412] interventions in the subject. But there was one feature about the use of the word that was constant: it was that the alien "belonged to another". Often that was expressed by reference to the concept of allegiance and often it was expressed in terms that, by their definitions, assumed that the world could be divided into two groups. Either one was a British subject or one was an "alien". And those groups were defined by reference to the nature of the allegiance they owed. During the 19th century, large numbers of persons emigrated from the British Isles to America and from Europe to the British Isles and America. During the latter half of that century legal thought in Britain and Europe grappled with the consequences of these movements. What may once have been the common law understanding of alienage yielded to these new circumstances. "Aliens", even if it had once had a fixed legal meaning, did not bear such a meaning by the end of the 19th century. But what did remain unaltered was that "aliens" included those who owed allegiance to another sovereign power, or who, having no nationality, owed no allegiance to any sovereign power.

On this basis, they held against the plaintiff.

Gummow, Hayne and Heydon JJ: [414] The plaintiff alleges that because a person in her circumstances would have fallen outside the class identified by British law in 1901 as "aliens" the federal Parliament has no power, under the naturalization and aliens power, to make a law, the application of which to the plaintiff depends … upon her parents not being natural-born or naturalized citizens of Australia. Identification of membership of the class described as "aliens" in 1901 depended in Britain not only upon common law rules, but also upon the application of particular statutory modifications of those rules. To say, then, as the plaintiff does, that "aliens" is a word that had an accepted and fixed legal meaning in 1901 would be accurate only if it were to be understood as saying no more than that resort to the then applicable law in Britain would have revealed whether or not an individual fell within the reach of that term.

To understand the constitutional reference to "aliens" as confined to those who, in 1901, by then existing British law, would have been treated by a British court as an alien would be to confine the meaning of the word too narrowly. It would be to give meaning to the word by listing those to whom it could then have been applied rather than by identifying the characteristics of the legal status to which the word refers. The central characteristic of that status is, and always has been, owing obligations ("allegiance") to a sovereign power other than the sovereign power in question (here Australia). That definition of the status of alienage focuses on what it is that gives a person the status: owing obligations to another sovereign power. It does not seek to define the status, as the plaintiff sought to submit, by pointing to what is said to take a person *outside* its reach …

[415] The previous decisions of the Court do not require the conclusion that those born within Australia who, having foreign nationality by descent, owe obligations to a sovereign power other than Australia are beyond the reach of the naturalization and aliens power. Observations in *Potter v Minahan* [(1908) 7 CLR 277], a case ultimately about the meaning of "immigrant" in a statute, concerning the consequences of birth in Australia were not directed to the present problem, and took no account of the question whether the defendant owed allegiance to any foreign power. In *Pochi* [(1982) 151 CLR 101 at 109-10], Gibbs CJ said that Parliament could "treat as an alien any person who was born outside Australia, whose parents were not Australians, and who has not been naturalized as an Australian". Mr Pochi met all three of these conditions. It would be wrong, however, to take what was said **[416]** by Gibbs CJ as necessarily treating a person born in Australia as beyond the reach of the aliens power. That question did not arise and was not decided in *Pochi* ...

Rather, the meaning of "aliens" was conveniently described in the joint reasons of six members of the Court in *Nolan v Minister for Immigration and Ethnic Affairs* [(1988) 165 CLR 178 at 183] where it was said that "alien" "[u]sed as a descriptive word to describe a person's lack of relationship with a country ... means, as a matter of ordinary language, 'nothing more than a citizen or subject of a foreign state'." It was common ground that the plaintiff is a citizen of India. She is, therefore, a citizen of a foreign state. She is a person within the naturalization and aliens power.

Gleeson CJ and Kirby J agreed that the plaintiff had failed to establish a fixed constitutional meaning of "alien" as at 1900; but they did not attempt to supply an alternative essentialist "definition" of alienage (or its "central characteristic") as Gummow, Hayne and Heydon JJ had done. Instead, they considered it sufficient to hold that there was nothing in the Constitution to prevent the Parliament making legislative excisions from the category of "citizenship".

Gleeson CJ: [357] [S]ubject to a qualification, Parliament, under pars (xix) and (xxvii) of s 51, has the power to determine the legal basis by reference to which Australia deals with matters of nationality and immigration, to create and define the concept of Australian citizenship, to prescribe the conditions on which such citizenship may be acquired and lost, and to link citizenship with the right of abode. In that regard, Brennan, Deane and Dawson JJ said in *Chu Kheng Lim v Minister for Immigration* [(1992) 176 CLR 1 at 25], that the effect of Australia's emergence as a fully independent sovereign nation with its own distinct citizenship was that alien in s 51(xix) of the Constitution had become synonymous with non-citizen. The qualification is that Parliament cannot, simply by giving its own definition of "alien", expand the power under s 51(xix) to include persons who could not possibly answer the description of "aliens" in the Constitution. Within the class of persons who could answer that description, Parliament can determine to whom it will be applied, and with what consequences. Alienage is a status, and, subject to the qualification just mentioned, Parliament can decide who will be treated as having that status for the purposes of Australian law and, subject to any other relevant constitutional constraints, what that status will entail.

Everyone agrees that the term "aliens" does not mean whatever Parliament wants it to mean. Equally clearly, it does not mean whatever a court, or a judge, wants it to mean. When a judicial decision is made in the course of judicial review of legislative action, for the purpose of determining constitutional validity, it is made by reference to a standard other than current public opinion. In a representative democracy, the will of Parliament is the most authentic and legitimate expression of public opinion. It may be imperfect, but it is through the political process, culminating in legislative action, that public policy is formed and imposed. It is not the role of the judiciary to give effect to an understanding of public opinion in opposition to the will of Parliament. When a law enacted by Parliament, which represents, or purports to represent, current community values, is declared unconstitutional and invalid, the judicial arm of government is imposing a restraint upon the power of a democratically elected legislature by reference to a written instrument, the Constitution. The source of the restraint is the legal effect of the instrument; not the will of the judiciary. The legal effect of the instrument is determined by the meaning of the text.

It is in the nature of law that rules laid down in the past, whether the past be recent or distant, bind conduct in the future. It is in the nature of a written, federal Constitution that a division of governmental power, necessarily involving limitations upon such power, agreed upon in the past, binds future governments. **[358]** That the terms of the agreement were to have that future operation is a matter relevant to an understanding of their meaning, but the role of a court is to understand

and apply the meaning of the terms, not to alter the agreement. Respect for the constitutional settlement is the primary obligation of a constitutional court. The source of this Court's power is the Constitution itself. There is no other. The role of the Court stems from the meaning and effect of the terms of that instrument. The stream of judicial review cannot rise above its source.

The power of judicial review, which is inherent in the structure of a federal union, was treated as axiomatic by the framers of the Australian Constitution. The decision in *Marbury v Madison* [5 US (1 Cranch) 137 (1803)] was 100 years old when this Court was established. Furthermore, as Alfred Deakin reminded Parliament when the Bill for an Act to establish this Court was being debated, the legislatures in the Australian colonies were all of limited power, and colonial courts were accustomed to declaring those limits. The historical context is critical to the existence of a power of judicial review. The legitimacy of judicial review depends upon adhering to a technique of deciding the meaning, and therefore the legal effect, of the Constitution that is consistent with the nature of the power being exercised. Judicial review of the validity of legislative action by reference to the Constitution is conducted upon the hypothesis that the terms, express and implied, of a written instrument, brought into existence more than a century ago, bind present and future parliaments, and courts. That instrument cannot be amended by Parliament, or by a simple majority of Australian voters, or by a court. Its meaning controls the exercise of governmental power. In some respects that meaning is clear. In some respects it is contestable. What the Constitution does not say may be as significant as what it says. On any view, it is a legal instrument written in the past that controls the exercise of power in the present, and (subject to the possibility of amendment in accordance with its own terms) in the future ...

[359] The Australian Constitution contains many terms that have a legal meaning, and that are naturally understood and applied by courts with reference to their legal meaning. To confine attention to s 51, they include bounties, insurance, bills of exchange, promissory notes, bankruptcy, insolvency, copyrights, patents of inventions and designs, trade marks, naturalization, aliens, corporations, trading corporations, marriage, divorce, matrimonial causes, custody and guardianship of infants, service and execution of process, and conciliation and arbitration. The concepts which those terms signify, in the context of the Constitution, can only be identified by reference to legal usage and understanding. Thus, when a dispute arose as to whether an incorporated local government authority that sold electrical appliances was a "trading corporation" within the meaning of s 51(xx), the question was not resolved by consulting a dictionary, and looking up the meaning of the noun "corporation", and the verb "to trade". This Court held that, although the authority in question was a corporation, and although it traded, it was not a trading corporation [*R v Trade Practices Tribunal; Ex parte St George County Council* (1974) 130 CLR 533]. In reaching that conclusion, the Court looked to the history of the development of corporations law, and noted that, at and around the time of Federation, legal authorities treated trading corporations and municipal corporations as entities of a different kind. The relevance of contemporary legal usage was that it formed part of the context in which the expression "trading corporations" was adopted, and an understanding of the context was necessary to a conclusion about the constitutional meaning of the expression. Furthermore, as Gaudron and Gummow JJ said in *Re Refugee Tribunal; Ex parte Aala* [(2000) 204 CLR 82 at 93], some expressions used in the Constitution, such as "a writ ... of prohibition", or "patents of inventions", have no meaning other than as technical legal expressions. A knowledge of the law, including legal history, is indispensable to an appreciation of their essential characteristics ...

[360] Meaning is always influenced, and sometimes controlled, by context. The context might include time, place, and any other circumstance that could rationally assist understanding of meaning. I referred above to the meaning of "aliens" in s 51(xix). That is a brief description of the immediate context in which "aliens" appears, but the context is much wider than that. It includes the whole of the instrument, its nature and purpose, the time when it was written and came into legal effect, other facts and circumstances, including the state of the law, within the knowledge or contemplation of the framers and legislators who prepared the Constitution or secured its enactment, and developments, over time, in the national and international context in which the instrument is to be applied ...

[361] One consideration of special importance to the meaning of a constitutional instrument is its general nature and purpose: an instrument of government, expressed in broad and general terms,

designed to speak to a future that, as the founders well understood, was in many respects beyond their capacity to foresee. In his speech on the Judiciary Bill, Alfred Deakin said [Commonwealth of Australia, *Parliamentary Debates*, House of Representatives, 18 March 1902]:

"[The] Constitution was drawn, and inevitably so, on large and simple lines, and its provisions were embodied in general language, because it was felt to be an instrument not to be lightly altered, and indeed incapable of being readily altered; and, at the same time, was designed to remain in force for more years than any of us can foretell, and to apply under circumstances probably differing most widely from the expectations now cherished by any of us. Consequently, drawn as it of necessity was on simple and large lines, it opens an immense field for exact definition and interpretation."

He also said:

"… our written Constitution, large and elastic as it is, is necessarily limited by the ideas and circumstances which obtained in the year 1900. It was necessarily precise in parts, as well as vague in other parts. That Constitution remains verbally unalterable except by the process of amendment … But the nation lives, grows, and expands. Its circumstances change, its needs alter, and its problems present themselves with new faces. The organ of the national life which preserving the union is yet able from time to time to transfuse into it the fresh blood of the living present, is the Judiciary[,] the High Court of Australia or Supreme Court in the United States. It is as one of the organs of Government which enables the Constitution to grow and to be adapted to the changeful necessities and circumstances of generation after generation that the High Court operates. Amendments achieve direct and sweeping changes, but the court moves by gradual, often indirect, cautious, well considered steps, that enable the past to join the future, without undue collision and strife in the present."

[362] There is no inconsistency between Alfred Deakin's statement that the written Constitution is necessarily limited by the ideas and circumstances which obtained in the year 1900, and his statement that it is capable of responding to changing circumstances and necessities. He distinguished between interpretation and amendment. The ideas and circumstances of 1900 influenced what the Constitution says, and what it does not say. They form part of the context in which the meaning of the written words is to be understood. Changing times, and new problems, may require the Court to explore the potential inherent in the meaning of the words, applying established techniques of legal interpretation …

Gleeson CJ also considered the use to be made of the Convention Debates.

Gleeson CJ: [363] The public record of the Convention Debates is evidence of what some people, involved in the framing of the Constitution, said about various drafts of the instrument. It is a partial record of the drafting history of most of the provisions of the Constitution. It reveals what some people understood, knew, believed, thought, or intended about the proposed instrument, and the circumstances surrounding some of the events involved in its preparation. For the reasons already given, what the record shows about the subjective beliefs or intentions of some people may be interesting but, of itself, is not a relevant fact. Many people, in Australia and the United Kingdom, were involved, directly or indirectly, in decisions about the form of the Constitution. Not all of them participated in the Convention Debates. Furthermore, as at all gatherings of lawyers or politicians, those who had the most to say were not necessarily the best informed or the most influential. A search for the collective, subjective intention of the framers of the Constitution would be impossible, and the individual subjective intention of any one of them, if it could be established, would not be relevant, because it would not advance any legitimate process of reasoning to a conclusion about the meaning of the text. Nevertheless, the drafting history of the Constitution, including the record of the Convention Debates, may be capable of throwing light on the meaning of a provision. Whether this will be so depends upon the nature of the problem of interpretation **[364]** that arises, the nature of the information that is gained from the drafting history, and the relevance of that information to the solution of the problem. Whether information is capable of assisting in the rational solution, by a legitimate process of reasoning, of a problem about the meaning of the text, depends upon the nature of the problem, and the nature of the information.

An example is given in *Cheng v The Queen* [(2000) 203 CLR 248 at 269]. In the course of a debate, on 4 March 1898, there was an exchange between Mr Barton and Mr Isaacs concerning the drafting of what is now s 80, relating to trial by jury. The exchange was helpful in the resolution of the question considered in *Cheng*, not because it revealed what Mr Isaacs and Mr Barton believed the clause meant, (their belief was a legally irrelevant fact), but because it threw light on the purpose and object of the provision, a matter of importance to the process of legal interpretation. What was involved was a commonplace exercise in purposive construction. The record of what occurred was regarded, as long ago as 1901, as capable of assisting the ascertainment of the meaning of s 80. [He referred to J Quick and R Garran, *The Annotated Constitution of the Australian Commonwealth* (Angus & Robertson, 1901; repr Legal Books, 1995), 808.] Earlier inhibitions about taking advantage of that assistance have now been abandoned. Reference to the record may be made, not for the purpose of seeking the subjective intention of people involved in the drafting, "but for the purpose of identifying the contemporary meaning of language used, the subject to which that language was directed and the nature and objectives of the movement towards federation" [*Cole v Whitfield* (1988) 165 CLR 360 at 385]. The reference, in *Cole v Whitfield*, to "identifying the contemporary meaning of language used", that is, its meaning at the time of the Convention Debates, directs attention to the historical context in which language, the subject of a problem of interpretation, was used. For the reasons already given, an understanding of that context is often a valuable, and sometimes necessary, aid to deciding meaning. To deny the relevance of the contemporary meaning of the language used in 1900 would not only be contrary to what was said in *Cole v Whitfield*, it would be contrary to one of the most elementary principles of legal interpretation, which is that a text must be understood in its context.

Applying this approach, he decided against the plaintiff.

Gleeson CJ: [366] In 1900, the major legal systems of the Western world adopted different approaches to the concept of alienage, and to correlative concepts of citizenship or allegiance. Broadly, the two leading theories were one which attached controlling importance to descent, and one which attached controlling importance to place of birth. The common law of England adhered to the second theory, but by 1900 the United Kingdom Parliament had intervened to modify the common law in significant respects. The questions of nationality, allegiance and alienage were matters on which there were changing and developing policies, and which were seen as appropriate for parliamentary resolution. The complex racial circumstances that resulted from Imperial expansion complicated the issues even further. The reasons of Gummow, Hayne and Heydon JJ demonstrate that, in the case of someone such as the plaintiff, an Indian citizen, born in Australia of Indian citizens, there was in 1900 no established legal requirement that she be excluded from the class of aliens. At the least, it was a matter appropriate to be dealt with by legislation. In *Grain Pool of Western Australia v Commonwealth* [202 CLR at 501] the joint judgment, referring to "cross-currents and uncertainties" in the law relating to patents and registered designs at the time of Federation, said "it plainly **[367]** is within the head of power in s 51(xviii) to resolve them". It seems to me that, given the legal context in which the Constitution was written, it is equally plain that it was within the head of power given by s 51(xix) for Parliament to decide whether a person such as the plaintiff should be treated as an alien.

The different view of the meaning of "aliens" taken by McHugh and Callinan JJ depended, in part, on their understanding of the role of historical materials in constitutional interpretation.

McHugh J: [368] Section 51(xix) of the Constitution empowers the Parliament of the Commonwealth to make laws with respect to "aliens". By necessary implication or assumption, that grant of power recognises that an alien is a person who can be identified by reference to some criterion or criteria that exists or exist independently of any law of the Parliament or indeed of the Constitution itself. It is a corollary of that implication or assumption that the Parliament of the Commonwealth cannot itself define who is an alien. Thus, s 51(xix) implies or assumes that an alien can be defined – but not by the Parliament.

It must follow, then, that that paragraph also implies or assumes that, when the Constitution was enacted in 1900, the term had a meaning that would be understood objectively by the Australian people. The persons who fall within or outside that meaning may change over the years. Australia's evolving independence from the United Kingdom, its steps towards becoming a sovereign nation, the acceptance of the divisibility of the Crown and the evolution of the Crown from an Imperial to a national office have led to changes in the denotation of the term "aliens". Hence, a person born in the United Kingdom who is resident in Australia may now be regarded as an alien in Australia for constitutional purposes even though such a person would not have been regarded as an alien in 1900. It may even be that experience of political or social developments has given or may give insights that lead later generations of Australians to define the constitutional term "aliens" itself in a way that does not fully accord with its perceived meaning in 1900. But if the persons who fall within the denotation of the term change or the connotation of the term changes, it will be because of events that occur independently of laws made by the Parliament. To deny that proposition is to deny the binding effect – indeed the legitimacy – of the Constitution itself.

[369] In the Australian colonies in 1900, the essential meaning – the connotation – of the term "alien" was a person who did not owe permanent allegiance to the Crown. And, subject to three exceptions, in 1900 *and now*, birth in Australia, irrespective of parentage, gave and still gives rise to an obligation of permanent allegiance to the sovereign of Australia. Even if it is permissible in 2004 to give the constitutional term "aliens" a *meaning* different from that which it had in 1900 – itself a contestable proposition – the Commonwealth has referred to no circumstance external to the Constitution which demonstrates that the essential meaning of the term in 1900 no longer applies. Indeed, even under a "progressivist" theory of constitutional interpretation, it is hard to conceive of the essential meaning of a constitutional term being entirely displaced and another meaning substituted for it.

Under the law of India at the time of her birth, Ms Singh acquired Indian citizenship at birth because her parents are Indian citizens. However, it is of no relevance in determining the meaning of the constitutional term "aliens" that, under the law of another country, a person, born in this country, may be a citizen of, and owe obligations of allegiance to the sovereign of, the foreign country. Equally irrelevant to determining the meaning of "aliens" in s 51(xix) are concepts of nationality and citizenship. Discussion of those concepts in this constitutional context merely invites error. What was, and is now, central to the meaning of the constitutional term "aliens" is the existence of an obligation of permanent allegiance to *our* sovereign – once the Queen of the United Kingdom but now, according to the doctrine of this Court, the Queen of Australia. Because the Commonwealth contends that Ms Singh is an alien – and therefore within the operation of s 51(xix) – it must show that upon her birth, she came under no obligation of permanent allegiance to the Queen of Australia. Not only has the Commonwealth failed to show that that is the case, it has not attempted to, nor could it, do so.

The unanswerable logic of Ms Singh's claim that she is not an alien can be seen in the following polysyllogism:

An alien is a person who does not owe permanent allegiance to the Queen of Australia.

A person ... born in Australia owes an obligation of permanent allegiance to the Queen of Australia.

Therefore, a person born in Australia is not an alien.

Ms Singh was born in Australia.

Therefore, Ms Singh is not an alien ...

[372] What, then, is the meaning of the term "aliens" in s 51(xix) and how is it to be ascertained? ...

There is no consensus as to any single approach to the interpretation of the Constitution. Commentators on the constitutional jurisprudence of this Court claim that all the methodologies that it has used are subject to criticism. Current High Court jurisprudence on constitutional interpretation favours some form of textualism. The basic premise of a textualist approach is that the text has ultimate primacy, although history and extrinsic materials may be relevant to explain the meaning of the text.

Because the Constitution is contained in a statute of the Imperial Parliament and the people of the Commonwealth have agreed to be governed under the Constitution, it seems obvious that the best guides to its interpretation are the general rules of statutory interpretation. The fundamental rule of statutory interpretation is that the meaning of an enactment is the meaning that its makers intended. Intention in the context of statutory interpretation is "an obvious fiction". But it is "a useful judicial construct because the judge is required to make the choices that best express the statutory text's meaning" [WD Popkin, *Statutes in Court: The History and Theory of Statutory*

Interpretation (Duke University Press, 1999), 211]. In **[373]** the case of the Constitution, the intention is that of those who framed it. Their intention is determined objectively. Their subjective beliefs and assumptions as to its meaning are irrelevant.

In applying the rules of statutory construction to the Constitution, Justices of this Court have always taken into account that it is no ordinary statute. They have recognised that it is an instrument difficult to amend, designed for the ages and intended as the blueprint for governing a federation consisting of a central and six regional governments as well as a number of territories. The makers of the Constitution and the people of the Australian colonies who approved the Constitution laid down a blueprint for the government of the nation for the indefinite future, subject to the power of the people to consent to its amendment under s 128 of the Constitution. The Constitution must be interpreted with that fundamental premise in mind. Because that is so, its provisions must not be interpreted pedantically or narrowly. They must be interpreted flexibly and purposively and, subject to the text and structure, in the manner best fitted to the contemporary needs of a federal system. Many provisions of the Constitution are framed in terms wide enough to allow this to be done. Dixon J recognised this in *Australian National Airways Pty Ltd v Common-wealth* [(1945) 71 CLR 29 at 81] when he said that:

> "[I]t is a Constitution we are interpreting, an instrument of government meant to endure and conferring powers expressed in general propositions wide enough to be capable of flexible application to changing circumstances." ...

[374] In interpreting the Constitution, historical and other materials often throw light on its meaning. They can be considered, for example, in order to identify the mischief to which the words of the Constitution were directed, to identify the purpose of the relevant constitutional concept or to determine the specialised meaning of constitutional terms. Latham CJ once pointed out that the Commonwealth was not born into a vacuum. Behind its making was a body of constitutional conventions and common law rules and principles that governed the relationship of the Crown and the people of the Australian colonies and gave content to the Constitution's language. In addition, many constitutional words and phrases are legal terms of art with a rich pre-federation history of which the framers would have been aware. Further, as I pointed out in *Theophanous v Herald & Weekly Times Ltd* [(1994) 182 CLR 104 at 196]:

> "The true meaning of a legal text almost always depends on a background of concepts, principles, practices, facts, rights and duties which the authors of the text took for granted or understood, without conscious advertence, by reason of their common language or culture."

A most striking example of background throwing light on the meaning of a constitutional provision is the decision in *Cole v Whitfield*. In *Cole*, the Court used history to read down the words in s 92 of the Constitution that "trade ... among the States ... shall be absolutely free" to cover cases only where interstate trade was burdened by laws that were discriminatory in a protectionist sense. In a line of cases dealing with "trial ... by jury" in s 80 of the Constitution, the Court used history to look for the "essential" characteristics of a jury as they were understood at common law in 1900. The Court identified these essential features by considering the historical evolution of juries in the United Kingdom and Australia before and around 1900 and the purpose of the relevant section of the Constitution. The Court then considered these "essential" aspects in their historical context.

When those who framed the Constitution included the term "aliens", they did so against a background of British and colonial history that, for at least six centuries, had regarded an alien as a person who did not owe permanent **[375]** allegiance to the Crown. The makers of our Constitution enacted s 51(xix) knowing that the principle that a person who did not owe permanent allegiance to the Crown was an alien was an entrenched rule of the common law, a rule as central to the unwritten constitution of the United Kingdom and its colonies as could be found. They also knew that, upon birth in any part of the Crown's dominions, the new born child immediately owed permanent allegiance to the Crown and was entitled to claim a reciprocal duty of protection on the part of the Crown, unless the child fell into one of three categories to which I shall later refer. In 1900, no-one in Australia who knew anything about the subject would think for a moment that a person, born in any part of the Crown's dominions, was an alien unless the child fell into one of the three categories.

The three exceptions, who were aliens despite their birth within the Crown's dominions, were (1) any person "[386] whose father was an enemy alien and who was born within a part of the British dominions that at the time of the person's birth was in hostile occupation"; (2) any person "born within British dominions whose father was an alien and, at the time of the person's birth, was an ambassador or other diplomatic agent accredited to the Crown by the sovereign of a foreign state"; and (3) "a child of a foreign sovereign born within British dominions".

McHugh J: [375] It is a mistake to think that in 1900 an alien was simply a person who was not a British subject. In the then structure of the Empire, a person who was not a British subject was an alien. Nevertheless, "non-British subject" was not the "essential meaning" of the term "alien" in 1900. If it were, the term would have that meaning until amended under s 128 of the Constitution. Most Australians would now be aliens. It is more accurate to say that in 1900 an alien was a person who was not a "subject of the Queen". The essence of the term "alien" was the lack of permanent allegiance to the Crown. While the Crown remained indivisible, a British subject was outside the denotation of the term "alien". However, when the Crown divided, so to speak, the denotation of the term "subject of the Queen" changed. As a result, British subjects no longer owed permanent allegiance to the Queen of Australia and became "aliens" in Australia.

Against this background, the inevitable conclusion is that in s 51(xix) of the Constitution the term "aliens" means persons who do not owe permanent allegiance to the Queen of Australia. It is only a half-truth to say that an alien is a person who owes permanent or even temporary allegiance to another country. Indeed, in the case of a stateless person, it is not even a half-truth. The meaning of "aliens" in the Constitution does not turn on whether under the law of another country the person in question owes a duty of allegiance to that country. It turns on whether that person owes a duty of permanent allegiance to the Queen of Australia.

McHugh J then turned to the historical materials to demonstrate this. He concluded:

McHugh J: [396] In 1900, then, it was inconceivable in the Anglo-Australian world that a person, born in Australia, could be an alien unless that person came within one of the three exceptions to the rule. In *Potter* [*v Minahan*], this Court accepted that every person born within Australia was a subject of the King and owed permanent allegiance to the King. As a corollary, that person was also entitled to the benefit and protection of the King. Further, as the joint judgment of the Court in *Nolan* accepted, the meaning of the constitutional term "aliens" has not changed since federation, although persons who were once outside its application are now within it. This change in the application of the term is the result of a number of significant developments since federation. They include:

(a) the gradual emergence of Australia as an independent, sovereign nation (which arguably culminated with the passage of the *Australia Acts* 1986 (Cth) and (UK));

[397] (b) the acceptance of the divisibility of the Crown (implicit in the development of the Commonwealth as an association of independent nations);

(c) the creation of a distinct Australian citizenship commencing in 1948 with the passage of the *Nationality and Citizenship Act* and the *British Nationality Act* 1948 (UK); and

(d) the acceptance by this Court that the phrase "subject of the Queen" in the Constitution no longer means "subject of the Queen of the United Kingdom" but "subject of the Queen of Australia".

Ms Kim Rubenstein has correctly characterised these changes in the application of the term "aliens" as changes in its denotation. Hence, while the meaning (or connotation) of "aliens" has remained constant, the classes of persons falling within that meaning have changed. As Windeyer J noted in *Ex parte Professional Engineers' Association* [(1959) 107 CLR 208 at 267]: "Law is to be accommodated to changing facts. It is not to be changed as language changes."

Rightly or wrongly, this Court took the bold step in *Nolan* of holding that, in light of the developments described above, a natural born British subject (that is, a person born in the United Kingdom) may be regarded as an alien in Australia for constitutional purposes. However, cases such as *Nolan*, *Re Patterson* and *Shaw* concerned persons born in the United Kingdom who had not become naturalised as Australian citizens. Once it is accepted that after 1948 such persons were the subjects of a foreign power *and not* subjects of the Queen of Australia, those decisions are not open to criticism. But they do not address the position of persons born in Australia of alien parents. Such persons are subjects of the Queen of Australia. They are qualified to stand for the House of Representatives unless they fall within the terms of s 44(i) of the Constitution. By force of s 117 of the Constitution, while resident in any State, they cannot be subjected "in any other State to any disability or discrimination which would not be equally applicable to [them] if [they] were a subject of the Queen resident in such other State." Upon birth, like the children of native born Australian parents, they come under an obligation of permanent allegiance to the Queen of Australia and a duty to obey the law, including the law of treason. Moreover, because they are "subjects of the Queen", they are members of the Australian community and among "the people of the Commonwealth". The "essential meaning" of the term "aliens" in 1900 and now does not include a person born in Australia who owes permanent allegiance to the Queen of Australia. For that reason, Ms Singh is not an alien.

The common law tradition on which the plaintiff relied was exemplified, for example, in the comment of WS Holdsworth, *A History of English Law*, vol 9 (Methuen: Sweet & Maxwell, 3rd ed 1944) that: "**[75]** [A]ll persons born on English soil, no matter what their parentage, owed allegiance to, and were therefore subjects of the king". The refusal of the majority justices to accept this tradition as definitive for the 21st century seemed in part to reflect a resistance to what Kirby J called "**[421]** the feudal history lying at the heart of this birthright idea". The plaintiff had attempted to demonstrate the continued relevance of the common law doctrine by pointing to the continued centrality of the Crown in Australia's constitutional system; but this may not have been tactically prudent.

> **Kirby J: [430]** In response to the suggestion that the role of the Crown in the Constitution necessarily endorsed a type of feudal notion of allegiance, subservience and duty implicit in the approach of birthright to nationality, there are many answers.
>
> From the start, the relationship with the Crown in Australia has been a comparatively light burden, if burden at all. It was freely adopted and retained in the Constitution. It has adapted in its Antipodean environment to the needs of this country. The adaptation of the Constitution to the practical and statutory change in the position of the Queen as Queen of Australia has been recognised in many cases. These cases, in turn, demonstrate the capacity of the Constitution to move with international and national realities.
>
> Constitutional notions of membership of the Australian community, and of who constitute the "people of the Commonwealth", have kept pace with these changes. It is unrealistic, indeed highly artificial, to conceive of such membership today in feudal terms. The constitutional text does not require it. Legal principle and historical independence deny it. By parity of reasoning, the word "aliens" adapts as the counterpart to modern notions of Australian nationality. These changes permit enlargement of the federal power to make laws with respect to "aliens" beyond that which would generally have been accepted at the time the Constitution came into force.

Similarly, in insisting that the "birthright idea" had been ousted by a conception of alienage as "**[414]** owing obligations ('allegiance') to a sovereign power other than the sovereign power in question", the joint judgment of Gummow, Hayne and Heydon JJ may have reflected an underlying shift in High Court jurisprudence from a depersonalised conception of "the Crown" to a transpersonal conception of "sovereignty".

The dissenting judgment of McHugh J relied partly on the historical tradition of *Calvin's Case* (1609) 7 Co Rep 1a, 77 ER 377, and partly on the assertion by AV Dicey (*A Digest of the Laws of England with Reference to the Conflict of Laws* (Stevens, 1896)) that: "**[176]** The child of aliens, if born within any country subject to the Crown, is a natural-born British subject". But he also relied on the High Court decision in *Potter v Minahan* (1908) 7 CLR 277, with which this chapter began. Quoting from all five judgments in that case, he pointed out that Griffith CJ had insisted that "**[289]** every person becomes at birth a member of the community into which he is born, and is entitled to remain in it until excluded by some competent authority"; that this principle was subject only to "exceptions based upon artificial rules of territoriality"; and that these ideas were "self-evident, and do not need the support of authority", since they constituted "an elementary part of the concept of human society". Barton J had described James Minahan as "**[293]** a natural-born British subject by virtue of his birth within the British Dominions", while O'Connor J had stated as a general principle of law: "**[304]** [E]very person born within the British Dominions is a British sub-**[305]**-ject and owes allegiance to the British Empire and obedience to its laws. Correlatively he is entitled to the benefit and protection of those laws". Indeed, O'Connor J had added: "A person born in Australia … becomes by reason of [that] fact a member of the Australian community under obligation to obey its laws, and correlatively entitled to all the rights and benefits which membership of the community involves". Even the dissenting judges, Isaacs and Higgins JJ, had conceded (as Higgins J put it) that: "**[321]** The fact of birth on British soil made the respondent a British subject, owing allegiance and entitled to protection".

Gummow, Hayne and Heydon JJ brushed *Potter v Minahan* aside by pointing out that the actual decision related to the meaning of the word "immigrant" in a statute – though in fact, of the three majority judges, only O'Connor J had addressed the issue exclusively at that level. They also maintained that dicta like those just quoted "**[415]** were not directed to the present problem, and took no account of … whether the defendant owed allegiance to any foreign power". Kirby J referred to *Potter v Minahan* only as showing that, even at that time, the birthright principle was "**[421]** subject to well-settled exceptions recognised in the common law at the time of the Constitution's making".

Both in *Potter v Minahan* and in *Singh v Commonwealth*, the person in question had been born in Victoria. In *Re Minister for Immigration and Multicultural and Indigenous Affairs; Ex parte Ame* (2005) 218 ALR 483, a similar question arose with respect to birth in Papua before 1975 – that is, before the emergence of Papua New Guinea as an independent nation. However, the Court was unanimous in dismissing any continuing claim to Australian citizenship.

Amos Ame was born in Papua in 1967, in the highland district where all four of his grandparents had also been born. At that time s 10 of the *Australian Citizenship Act 1948* (Cth) still operated to confer Australian citizenship on any person born in "Australia", defined for this purpose as including Papua. However, in 1975 the new Constitution of Papua New Guinea conferred "automatic citizenship" on any "person born in the country … who has two grand-parents born in the country". At the same time Australian regulations, made under s 6 of the *Papua New Guinea Independence Act 1975* (Cth), provided that any Australian citizen thus acquiring citizenship of the newly independent Papua New Guinea "ceases … to be an Australian citizen". A unanimous High Court, with Kirby J agreeing in a separate judgment, held that this provision was valid both under s 122 of the Australian Constitution (the Territories power) and under s 51(xix) (naturalisation and aliens).

The "citizenship" conferred on natives of Papua by the 1975 Act had always been less than "real" citizenship, since it had not been accompanied by any automatic right to enter or remain in mainland Australia; and the transfer of citizenship was seen as a natural and appropriate concomitant of the transfer of sovereignty. (In particular, as Kirby J emphasised, it was fully consistent with customary international law and state practice in such cases.) These factors would probably have been sufficient to defeat an attack on the Australian regulations, quite apart from the decisions in *Shaw* and *Singh*. However, the joint judgment of six members of the Court invoked those decisions as negating any relevant limitation on the legislative power in s 51(xix). In particular, those decisions were treated as confirming that "**[495]** the legal status of alienage has as its defining characteristic the owing of allegiance to a foreign sovereign power", and that "changes in the national and international context in which s 51(xix) is to be applied may have an important bearing upon its practical operation".

For his part, Kirby J continued to protest that the decision in *Shaw* "**[514]** exposes to expulsion and seriously unfair treatment subjects of the Queen who have lived in mainland Australia for years", and to hope that *Shaw* might some day "be reversed as its offensiveness to constitutional concepts of nationality and allegiance becomes obvious, and before more wrongs are done under it". Despite this, he "accepted that the constitutional doctrine in *Nolan* has, for the time being, been restored"; and on that basis he agreed that the Australian regulation depriving native Papuans of Australian citizenship was a valid exercise of power under s 51(xix) as well as under s 122. He stressed, however, that the decision under s 122 was limited to *external* Territories, and that the decision under s 51(xix) "**[516]** affords no precedent for any deprivation of constitutional nationality of other Australian citizens whose claim on such nationality is stronger in law and in fact than that of the applicant".

4. Further References

Coper, M, "The Reach of the Commonwealth's Immigration Power: Judicial Exegesis Unbridled" (1976) 50 *Australian Law Journal* 351.

Chesterman, J, and Galligan, B (eds), *Defining Australian Citizenship: Selected Documents* (Melbourne University Press, 1999).

Christodoulidis, EA (ed), *Communitarianism and Citizenship* (Ashgate, 1998).

Crock, M, *Immigration and Refugee Law in Australia* (Federation Press, 1998).

Crock, B, and Saul, B, *Future Seekers: Refugees and the Law in Australia* (Federation Press, 2002).

Dauvergne, C, "Citizenship, Migration Laws and Women: Gendering Permanent Residency Statistics" (2000) 24 *Melbourne University Law Review* 280.

Finlay, HA, "The Immigration Power Applied" (1966) 40 *Australian Law Journal* 120.

Migrants and the Law: An Annotated Bibliography (AGPS, 1995).

Palfreeman, AC, *The Administration of the White Australia Policy* (Melbourne University Press, 1967).

Rubenstein, K, *Australian Citizenship Law in Context* (Lawbook Co, 2002).

Ryan, KW, "Immigration, Aliens and Naturalization in Australian Law" in O'Connell, DP (ed), *International Law in Australia* (Law Book Co for Australian Institute of International Affairs, 1965), 465.

Shafir, G (ed), *The Citizenship Debates: A Reader* (University of Minnesota Press, 1998).

Sornarajah, M, "Deportation of Aliens and Immigrants from Australia" (1985) 34 *International and Comparative Law Quarterly* 498.

Taylor, G, "Citizenship Rights and the Australian Constitution" (2001) 12 *Public Law Review* 205.

Taylor, S (ed), *Nationality, Refugee Status and State Protection: Explorations of the Gap between Man and Citizen* (Special Edition of *Law in Context*, vol 22(2), Federation Press, 2005).

Wells, B, "Aliens: The Outsiders in the Constitution" (1996) 19 *University of Queensland Law Journal* 45.

Wood, D, "Deportation, the Immigration Power, and Absorption into the Australian Community" (1986) 16 *Federal Law Review* 288.

Chapter 21

The Races Power

1. Introduction

As initially drafted, s 51(xxvi) was a power to make laws with respect to: "The people of any race, *other than the aboriginal race in any State,* for whom it is deemed necessary to make special laws". In 1967, the Australian people voting at a referendum deleted the words in italics.

The intended purpose of s 51(xxvi) was expressed at the 1898 Convention in Melbourne by Sir Edmund Barton, later Australia's first Prime Minister and one of the first judges of the High Court. He argued that s 51(xxvi) was necessary to enable the Commonwealth to "[228] regulate the affairs of the [229] people of coloured or inferior races who are in the Commonwealth" (*Official Record of the Debates of the Australasian Federal Convention* (1891-98, repr Legal Books 1986), vol 4, Melbourne 1898). Summarising the effect of s 51(xxvi), John Quick and Robert Garran, *The Annotated Constitution of the Australian Commonwealth* (Angus & Robertson, 1901; repr Legal Books, 1995), said: "[622] It enables the Parliament to deal with the people of any alien race after they have entered the Commonwealth; to localise them within defined areas, to restrict their migration, to confine them to certain occupations, or to give them special protection and secure their return after a certain period to the country whence they came".

Some delegates spoke strongly against such a use of legislative power. Josiah Symon QC, a former Attorney-General of South Australia, argued: "[250] It is monstrous to put a brand on these people when you admit them. It is degrading to us and our citizenship to do such a thing. If we say they are fit to be admitted amongst us, we ought not to degrade them by putting on them a brand of inferiority" (*Official Record of the Debates of the Australasian Federal Convention* (1891-98, repr Legal Books 1986), vol 4, Melbourne 1898). However, lest it be thought that s 51(xxvi) might confer any protection from racial discrimination, Quick and Garran continued: "[623] On the contrary, it would seem that by sub-sec xxvi the Federal Parliament will have power to pass special and discriminating laws relating to 'the people of any race,' and that such laws could not be challenged on the ground of unconstitutionality".

2. "Special laws"

The scope of s 51(xxvi), as amended in 1967, was first considered in *Koowarta v Bjelke-Petersen* (1982) 153 CLR 168. In that case, the High Court held that the *Racial Discrimination Act 1975* (Cth) was valid as a law with respect to "external affairs" under s 51(xxix) of the Constitution. The Commonwealth had also argued that the Act was valid under s 51(xxvi). Five judges, with Murphy J dissenting and Mason J not deciding, rejected this argument. They held that the *Racial Discrimination Act* protected all races and not any one particular race, and thus was not a "special law" for "the people of any race".

Koowarta v Bjelke-Petersen
(1982) 153 CLR 168

Gibbs CJ: [186] It would be a mistake to suppose that s 51(xxvi) was included in the Constitution only for the purpose of enabling the Parliament to make laws for the special protection of people of particular races. Quick and Garran, in their *Annotated Constitution of the Australian Commonwealth* (1901), correctly observed, at p 623, that by "sub-sec xxvi the Federal Parliament will have power to pass special and discriminating laws relating to 'the people of any race'." Such laws might validly discriminate against, as well as in favour of, the people of a particular race. As Professor Sawer has pointed out in an article, "The Australian Constitution and the Australian Aborigine", published in the *Federal Law Review*, vol 2 (1966) 17, at p 20 – "... (xxvi) was intended to enable the Commonwealth to pass the sort of laws which before 1900 had been passed by many States concerning 'the Indian, Afghan and Syrian hawkers; the Chinese miners, laundrymen, market gardeners, and furniture manufacturers; the Japanese settlers and Kanaka plantation labourers of Queensland, and the various coloured races employed in the pearl fisheries of Queensland and Western Australia'. Such laws were designed 'to localize them within defined areas, to restrict their migration, to confine them to certain occupations, or to give them special protection and secure their return after a certain period to the country whence they came'." However, it is clear that under s 51(xxvi), in its present form, the Parliament has power to make laws prohibiting discrimination against people of the Aboriginal race by reason of their race.

However ss 9 and 12 are not directed to the protection of people of the Aboriginal race. They prohibit discrimination generally on the ground of race; that is, they protect the persons of any race from discriminatory action by reason of their race. On behalf of the Commonwealth it was submitted that the Act is a special law within par (xxvi) because it selects as its subject the people of any race against whom discrimination on racial grounds is, or may be, practised. This argument cannot be accepted, for it gives insufficient weight to the words "for whom it is deemed necessary to make special laws". It is true that in some contexts the word "any" can be **[187]** understood as having the effect of "all", but it would be self-contradictory to say that a law which applies to the people of all races is a special law. It is not possible to construe par (xxvi) as if it read simply "The people of all races". In the context provided by par (xxvi), the word "any" is used in the sense of "no matter which". The Parliament may deem it necessary to make special laws for the people of a particular race, no matter what the race. If the Parliament does deem that necessary, but not otherwise, it can make laws with respect to the people of that race. The opinion of Parliament that it is necessary to make a special law need not be evidenced by an express declaration to that effect; it may appear from the law itself. However, a law which applies equally to the people of all races is not a special law for the people of any one race.

Wilson J: [244] The learned Solicitor-General for the Commonwealth argues that there is no necessary singularity attaching to the phrase "the people of any race". He observes that if the Act were to contain a section which specifically applied its provisions to discrimination against the people of a particular race there could be no doubt that the law was **[245]** within the power. If then there followed a series of provisions applying the Act in turn to the people of every race in Australia then in his submission the same result would follow. What can be done severally can be done in a global way ...

This ingenious submission cannot be accepted. If the Act can apply with respect to the people of any race at all who may happen to be the victims of discrimination on account of their race, then it is not a special law. It is a general law directed to the elimination of all racial discrimination in the community. The power contained in s 51(xxvi) is activated when the Parliament discerns circumstances which in its view give rise to a necessity to make a special law. That necessity can arise only from circumstances considered to be compelling in relation to a section of the community, namely, the people of a particular race or races. As the Chief Justice has observed, the power is apt to enable the Parliament, if it considered it necessary to do so, to prohibit racial discrimination against the people of the Aboriginal race.

Stephen, Aickin and Brennan JJ also held that the Act could not be upheld as a "special law" for "the people of any race".

For Gibbs CJ, Aickin and Wilson JJ it was necessary to decide this issue since in their view the Act was not valid under the "external affairs" power. For the judges who decided, by a 4:3 majority, that the Act was valid as a law with respect to "external affairs", it was not strictly necessary to discuss the argument under s 51(xxvi). For that reason, Mason J abstained from any examination of the issue. Murphy J also held that since the "external affairs" power provided a sufficient basis for validity, it was "**[242]** unnecessary" to deal with the argument based on s 51(xxvi). However, Murphy J added that in his opinion the Act was valid under s 51(xxvi). In an "Appendix", he listed "Numerous books, articles and government reports [that] starkly outline the discrimination suffered by Australian Aborigines". In a further obiter dictum he said: "**[242]** In par (xxvi) 'for' means 'for the benefit of'. It does not mean 'with respect to', so as to enable laws intended to affect adversely the people of any race. If 'with respect to' or some similar expression were intended, it would have been used, as it is in other parts of s 51 (see the opening words and pars (xxxi) and (xxxvi))".

Commonwealth v Tasmania (*Tasmanian Dam Case*) (1983) 158 CLR 1 concerned the validity of the *World Heritage Properties Conservation Act 1983* (Cth). For ss 6 and 9 of the Act, the Commonwealth claimed legislative power under the "external affairs" and "nationhood" powers; for ss 7 and 10, under s 51(xx), the "corporations" power; and for ss 8 and 11, under s 51(xxvi). The pattern was that s 8 laid a foundation upon which s 11 then imposed substantive prohibitions.

World Heritage Properties Conservation Act 1983 (Cth)

8 (1) It is hereby declared that it is necessary to enact this section, section 11 and sub-sections 13(7) and 14(5) as special laws for the people of the Aboriginal race.

(2) A reference in this section to an Aboriginal site is a reference to a site –

(a) that is, or is situated within, identified property; and

(b) the protection or conservation of which is, whether by reason of the presence on the site of artefacts or relics or otherwise, of particular significance to the people of the Aboriginal race.

(3) Where the Governor-General is satisfied that an Aboriginal site is being or is likely to be damaged or destroyed or that any artefacts or relics situated on an Aboriginal site are being or are likely to be damaged or destroyed, he may, by Proclamation, declare that site to be a site to which section 11 applies …

11 (1) Except with the consent in writing of the Minister, it is unlawful for a person, whether himself or by his servant or agent –

(a) to carry out any excavation works on any site to which this section applies;

(b) to carry out operations for, or exploratory drilling in connection with, the recovery of minerals on any site to which this section applies;

(c) to erect a building or other substantial structure on any site to which this section applies or to do any act in the course of, or for the purpose of, the erection of a building or other substantial structure on any site to which this section applies;

(d) to damage or destroy any artefacts or relics situated on any site to which this section applies;

(e) to remove any artefacts or relics from any site to which this section applies;

(f) to kill, cut down or damage any tree on any site to which this section applies;

(g) to construct or establish any road or vehicular track on any site to which this section applies;

(h) to use explosives on any site to which this section applies; or

(j) if an act is prescribed for the purposes of this paragraph in relation to a particular site to which this section applies, to do that act in relation to that site.

(2) Except with the consent in writing of the Minister, it is unlawful for a person, whether himself or by his servant or agent, to do any act, not being an act the doing of which is unlawful by virtue of sub-section (1) –

(a) that damages or destroys; or

(b) that is likely to result in damage to or the destruction of,

any site to which this section applies or any artefacts or relics on any site to which this section applies.

(3) Except with the consent in writing of the Minister, it is unlawful for a person, whether himself or by his servant or agent, to do any act preparatory to the doing of an act that is unlawful by virtue of sub-section (2).

The Commonwealth's justification for these provisions was summarised as follows:

Commonwealth v Tasmania (Tasmanian Dam Case)
(1983) 158 CLR 1

Gibbs CJ: [65] The subject area is said to be part of the cultural heritage because it contains significant Aboriginal archaeological sites. It is not clear that there are significant sites within the subject area, although there are certainly significant sites within the Parks. Two caves, Kutikina Cave (formerly known as Fraser Cave) and Deena Reena Cave, which are situated within the area of 780 hectares which is to vest in the Commission in 1990, are alleged to be "two of the seven archaeologically richest limestone cave sites in the Western Pacific region". It is alleged that the former cave is an immensely rich archaeological site and that recent radiocarbon dating of deposit at basal levels of the site indicated human occupation dated to beyond 20,000 years ago. Older material is at present being radiocarbon dated. Carbon samples from hearths in Deena Reena Cave have been dated to about 19,000 years ago. There are other caves in the lower Franklin River valley whose contents have not yet been investigated. It is alleged that investigations suggest that archaeological deposits contained in the limestone caves along the lower Franklin River valley are likely to transform archaeological knowledge, of the stone tool technology of Ice Age man in Tasmania. Those cave sites, it is said, contain evidence of the economic and cultural systems of their inhabitants, who, in prehistoric times, were the most southerly dwelling human beings on earth. It is further alleged that archaeological sites along the river terraces of the Denison and Franklin Rivers, together with the archaeological cave sites, make it highly probable that the subject area is capable of providing archaeologists and scholars generally with a comprehensive picture of settlement of a whole river system by early man and his more recent Aboriginal descendants. A site upon Flat Island, recently radiocarbon dated to 15,000 years ago, is said to be the only known open archaeological site of such antiquity in Tasmania. The Commonwealth asserts that the proposed inundation would result in the loss and destruction of irreplaceable evidence concerning the occupation and settlement of an entire river system by Ice Age man and his more recent Aboriginal descendants, and that the flooding of the archaeological cave sites of the lower Franklin River valley would destroy their outstanding universal cultural and historical value.

Mason, Murphy, Brennan and Deane JJ held that this use of s 51(xxvi) was valid. Gibbs CJ, Wilson and Dawson JJ dissented. However, Deane J also held that s 11 amounted to an "acquisition of property" without just terms contrary to s 51(xxxi). He therefore joined Gibbs CJ, Wilson and Dawson JJ in holding ss 8 and 11 invalid.

Brennan J: [242] Section 51(xxvi) of the Constitution was amended in 1967 by deleting the words "other than the aboriginal race in any State" from the original text which granted power to make laws with respect to "[t]he people of any race, other than the aboriginal race in any State, for whom it is deemed necessary to make special laws". No doubt par (xxvi) in its original form was thought to authorize the making of laws discriminating adversely against particular racial groups: see Quick and Garran, *Annotated Constitution of the Australian Commonwealth* (1901), p 623. The approval of the proposed law for the amendment of par (xxvi) by deleting the words "other than the aboriginal race" was an affirmation of the will of the Australian people that the odious policies of oppression and neglect of Aboriginal citizens were to be at an end, and that the primary object of the power is beneficial. The passing of the *Racial Discrimination Act* manifested the Parliament's intention that the power will hereafter be used only for the purpose of discriminatorily conferring benefits upon the people of a race for whom it is deemed necessary to make special laws.

Where Parliament seeks to confer a discriminatory benefit on the people of the Aboriginal race, par (xxvi) does not place a limitation upon the nature of the benefits which a valid law may confer, and none should be implied. It was submitted that, as ss 8 and 11 do not confer legal rights, powers or privileges upon Aboriginal people in addition to the legal rights, powers or privileges conferred upon the public generally, those provisions are not supported by par (xxvi). Is it sufficient that the discriminatory benefit is found in the special importance or significance which the people of a race attach to the rights, powers or privileges generally conferred? In *Koowarta* [(1982) 153 CLR at 211] **[243]** Stephen J noted that the "necessary special quality might perhaps be sufficiently attracted by facts dehors the legislation". The concept of "race" suggests the answer.

"Race" is not a term of art; it is not a precise concept: see *Ealing London Borough Council v Race Relations Board* [[1972] AC 342 at 362], per Lord Simon of Glaisdale. There is, of course, a biological element in the concept. The UNESCO studies on race and racial discrimination reveal some difficulty in giving a precise definition even to this element. Senor Hernan Santa Cruz, the Special Rapporteur on Racial Discrimination, in his report to the United Nations ("Special Study on Racial Discrimination in the Political, Economic, Social and Cultural Spheres" (1971, UN Document No E/CN4/Sub 2/307/Rev 1, pp 12-13)) traces some of the findings of experts:

"A conference of experts assembled in Moscow by UNESCO in August 1964 to give their views on the biological aspects of the race question, adopted a set of proposals on this subject. They stated inter alia that all men living today belong to a single species and are derived from a common stock (article I); that pure races in the sense of genetically homogeneous populations do not exist in the human species (article III); and that there is no national, religious, geographic, linguistic or cultural group which constitutes a race ipso facto (article XII). The proposals concluded:

'The biological data given above stand in open contradiction to the tenets of racism. Racist theories can in no way pretend to have any scientific foundation.' ...

Popular notions of 'race', however, have frequently disregarded the scientific evidence. Prejudice and discrimination on the ground of race, colour or ethnic origin occur in a number of societies, where physical appearance – notably skin colour – and ethnic origin are accorded prime importance."

A need to identify the biological element of the concept followed the enactment of a Race Relations Act in New Zealand and in England. In New Zealand the question arose in *King-Ansell v Police* [[1979] 2 NZLR 531]. Richardson J said [[1979] 2 NZLR at 542]:

"... all four expressions 'race', 'colour', 'national origins' and 'ethnic origins' are concerned with antecedent rather than acquired characteristics.

It does not follow that the identifying characteristics must be genetically determined at birth. The ultimate genetic ancestry of any New Zealander is not susceptible to legal proof. Race is clearly used in its popular meaning."

[244] His Honour discounted the importance of, if not the necessity for, scientific proof of the biological element:

"The real test is whether the individuals or the group regard themselves and are regarded by others in the community as having a particular historical identity in terms of their colour or their racial, national or ethnic origins."

In England in *Mandla v Dowell Lee* [[1983] QB 1 at 19], Kerr LJ in reference to the words "race or ethnic or national origins" said: "they clearly refer to human characteristics with which a person is born and which he or she cannot change, any more than the leopard can change his spots." Membership of a race imports a biological history or origin which is common to other members of the race, but Richardson J is surely right in denying the possibility of proving ultimate genetic ancestry. However, in my respectful opinion, I do not think his Honour was propounding his "real test" of common regard as being conclusive or exhaustive. Actual proof of descent from ancestors who were acknowledged members of the race or actual proof of descent from ancestors none of whom were members of the race is admissible to prove or to contradict, as the case may be, an assertion of membership of the race. Though the biological element is, as Kerr LJ pointed out, an essential element of membership of a race, it does not ordinarily exhaust the characteristics of a racial group. Physical similarities, and a common history, a common religion or spiritual beliefs and a common culture are factors that tend to create a sense of identity among members of a race and to which others have regard in identifying people as members of a race. As the people of a group identify themselves and are identified by others as a race by reference to their common history, religion, spiritual beliefs or culture as well as by reference to their biological origins and physical similarities, an indication is given of the scope and purpose of the power granted by par (xxvi). The kinds of benefits that laws might properly confer upon people as members of a race are benefits which tend to protect or foster their common intangible heritage or their common sense of identity. Their genetic inheritance is fixed at birth; the historic, religious, spiritual and cultural heritage are acquired and are susceptible to influences for which a law may provide. The advancement of the people of any race in any of these aspects of their group life falls within the power.

A law which, on its face, does not discriminate in favour of the people of a race, may nevertheless be valid if it discriminates in favour of those people by its operation upon the subject-matter to [245] which it relates. That involves no departure from the ordinary processes of constitutional interpretation. The characterization of a law requires that the operation of the law be ascertained by reference to its terms and their application to the circumstances in which the law operates ...

I would not construe par (xxvi) as requiring the law to be "special" in its terms; it suffices that it is special in its operation. Section 8 ensures that s 11 is special in its operation. It was argued that such a construction was impliedly rejected in *Koowarta*, for the proscribing of racial discrimination must surely have been a matter of special significance for the people of the Aboriginal race. If racial discrimination were peculiarly a practice affecting Aborigines, there would be much force in the argument. But victims of racial discrimination may sadly be found in many races: the people of many races may say with Shylock (*The Merchant of Venice*, Act III, Scene I):

"If you prick us, do we not bleed? if you tickle us, do we not laugh? if you poison us, do we not die? and if you wrong us, shall we not revenge?"

Deane J: [272] As Professor Sawer comments ("The Australian Constitution and the Australian Aborigine", *Federal Law Review*, vol 2 (1966), p 17), the architects of the Constitution paid no attention at all to the position of the Aboriginal people of Australia. Their express exclusion from the provisions of s 51(xxvi) could not be attacked as adversely discriminatory since that grant of power was primarily seen as a power to permit adverse discrimination against the people of a particular race rather than as a power to pass a law for the benefit or protection of such people ... As it became increasingly clear that Australia, as a nation, [273] must be diminished until acceptable laws be enacted to mitigate the effects of past barbarism, the exclusion of the people of the Aboriginal race from the provisions of s 51(xxvi) came to be seen as a fetter upon the legislative competence of the Commonwealth Parliament to pass necessary special laws for their benefit. The referendum of 27th May, 1967 ... was carried by an overwhelming majority of the voters in every State of the Commonwealth. The power conferred by s 51(xxvi) remains a general power to pass laws discriminating against or benefiting the people of any race. Since 1967, that power has included a power to make laws benefiting the people of the Aboriginal race.

Look carefully at the last two sentences. In the first of them Deane J appears to reaffirm the majority view in *Koowarta* that the power in s 51(xxvi) may be exercised *for or against* the interests of a particular race. The second sentence might be read as consistent with that view – but might also be read as asserting that, contained within the general power to legislate for the benefit or detriment of particular races, there is now, since the 1967 referendum, a power relating to Aboriginals which can only be used for their benefit. Deane J went on:

Deane J: [273] It is unnecessary, for the purposes of the present case, to consider the meaning to be given to the phrase "people of any race" in s 51(xxvi). Plainly, the words have a wide and non-technical [274] meaning: see, eg, *King-Ansell v Police*; *Mandla v Dowell Lee*. The phrase is, in my view, apposite to refer to all Australian Aboriginals collectively. Any doubt[ ] which might otherwise exist in that regard[ ] is removed by reference to the wording of par (xxvi) in its original form. The phrase is also apposite to refer to any identifiable racial sub-group among Australian Aboriginals. By "Australian Aboriginal" I mean, in accordance with what I understand to be the conventional meaning of that term, a person of Aboriginal descent, albeit mixed, who identifies himself as such and who is recognized by the Aboriginal community as an Aboriginal ...

The relationship between the Aboriginal people and the lands [275] which they occupy lies at the heart of traditional Aboriginal culture and traditional Aboriginal life. Past violations of Aboriginal culture and of Aboriginal life, both traditional and otherwise, have not obliterated the fundamental importance to the Aboriginal people of Australia of their ancient sites. To the contrary, one effect of the years since 1788 and of the emergence of Australia as a nation has been that Aboriginal sites which would once have been of particular significance only to the members of a particular tribe are now regarded, by those Australian Aboriginals who have moved, or been born, away from ancient tribal grounds, as part of a general heritage of their race. The dual requirement that a declaration can only be made in respect of a site if it is both "of outstanding universal value" and "of particular significance to the people of the Aboriginal race" means that only those Aboriginal sites which are of extraordinary significance qualify for protection and conservation under ss 8 and 11. A law protecting such sites is, in one sense, a law for all Australians. It appears to me, however, on any approach to language, that a law whose operation is to protect and preserve sites of universal value which are of particular importance to the Aboriginal people is also a special law for those people ...

[276] Viewed as a matter of substance, a special law which protects the persons or the property or the activities of Aboriginal people is not only a law with respect to the prohibited actions against such persons, property or activities. It is also a law with respect to people of the Aboriginal race ... In my view, a law which protects those – and only those – endangered Aboriginal sites included in the "cultural heritage" which satisfy the requirement that they are of particular significance to people of the Aboriginal race is not only a law with respect to Aboriginal sites. It is a law ... which comes within the primary scope of the grant of legislative power to make laws with respect to the people of any race for whom it is deemed necessary to make special laws. The reference to "people of any race" includes all that goes to make up the personality and identity of the people of a race: spirit, belief, knowledge, tradition and cultural and spiritual heritage. A power to legislate "with respect to" the people of a race includes the power to make laws protecting the cultural and spiritual heritage of those people by protecting property which is of particular significance to that spiritual and cultural heritage.

By contrast, for Gibbs CJ, Wilson and Dawson JJ, a law for the preservation of archaeological relics "of significance to all mankind" was not a "special law" for the people of any one race.

Gibbs CJ: [109] The nature of the power conferred by s 51(xxvi), to make laws with respect to "the people of any race for whom it is deemed necessary to make special laws" was recently considered in *Koowarta* [(1982) 153 CLR 168]. To come within s 51(xxvi) a law must be a law with respect to the people of a particular race, and it must be a special [110] law. A law will be special if it has some special connexion with the people of a race; it will not answer that description if it applies equally to people of all races. History strongly supports the view that "for" in par (xxvi) means "with reference to" rather than "for the benefit of" – it expresses purpose rather than advantage – but that is not particularly relevant in the present case ...

Although the protection or conservation of a site to which s 11 applies must be of particular significance to the people of the Aboriginal race, the site itself must be of outstanding universal value, since otherwise it cannot form part of the cultural heritage or natural heritage. A site which may be of very great significance to the people of the Aboriginal race will not be within the section if it is not of outstanding universal value. The prohibitions in s 11 are directed to the protection of the site generally, and not to the preservation of any particular feature of the site which may give it significance to members of the Aboriginal race. What is more important, members of the Aboriginal race have no special rights or privileges, and no special obligations, in relation to a site to which s 11 applies. They have no greater right of access to the site than anyone else, and they are affected by the prohibitions contained in s 11 in the same way as other people. If the Minister consented to the removal of the artefacts and relics from a site, eg, to enable them to be the subject of scientific study or to be kept safe, he could allow them to be taken to a place to which people other than those of the Aboriginal race had access and members of the Aboriginal race did not. True it is that in such a case a member of the Aboriginal race might apply to review the decision of the Minister to give his consent (see s 13(7)) but so also could other persons and [111] organizations (see s 13(5)). In short, ss 8 and 11 confer no rights and impose no duties on members of the

Aboriginal race as such, or on other persons in relation to their dealings with members of the Aboriginal race. The sections are not a law with respect to people of the Aboriginal race.

If this view were wrong, the validity of the law would depend on the question whether any of the sites the subject of either of the two proclamations is of particular significance to the people of the Aboriginal race. That would be a question of mixed law and fact. In my opinion the law would not be a special law for the people of the Aboriginal race only because the site contained artefacts and relics dating from prehistoric times, even though those artefacts and relics were left by the race which originally inhabited Tasmania. Artefacts and relics of such antiquity are of significance to all mankind; a law for their protection is not a special law for the people of any one race.

Subsequent research confirming the significance of the artefacts and relics in the caves is summarised by Josephine Flood, *Archaeology of the Dreamtime: The Story of Prehistoric Australia and its People* (Angus & Robertson, revised ed 1999), 118-38. The artefacts and animal remains found in Kutikina Cave (pronounced to rhyme with "miner") have been dated back to about 20,000 BP (that is, before the present, with "the present" conventionally understood to mean about 1950 AD). Other sites are even older: Warreen Cave, discovered in 1986 to the east of Kutikina, contains evidence of human occupation going back as far as 35,000 BP, and becoming intense around 24,000 BP. In both these caves the artefacts include not only stone scrapers, but knives made of Darwin glass (that is, the glass formed by the melting of rocks when a meteorite hits the earth).

Ironically, the archaeological and cultural significance of the area became apparent only because the Tasmanian Hydro-Electric Commission, in the environmental impact statement that accompanied the proposal to dam the area, had claimed that it contained nothing of archaeological interest and no evidence of Aboriginal use. In 1999 the story was told to an interviewer from Flinders University.

Rhys Jones in conversation with Vincent Megaw, "Confessions of a Wild Colonial Boy"
(2000) 50 *Australian Archaeology* 12

[21] [I]n 1981 the Tasmanian Hydro-Electric Commission was going to make this huge dam on the Gordon, Franklin and other rivers of south west Tasmania. They had done a large environmental impact statement ... stating that in this country there was nothing archaeological and no evidence of Aboriginal use. Certainly, ethnographically there wasn't. One of the things that I had written, in 1974 was an Appendix to Tindale's, *The Tribes of Australia*, a monumental tribal atlas of Australia. In the piece on Tasmanian tribes I had this big area marked 'Unoccupied' in the south-west of the island and the Hydro-Electric Commission took that map of mine and said that this area had always been unoccupied and therefore they didn't need to carry out an archaeological survey.

Yet we then said, 'Look, go into the valleys', and we did. Some limestone caves had just been found by the Sydney Speleological Society a year or so earlier ... We went to one of these caves which was then called 'Fraser Cave' which had been named by Kevin Kiernan, one of the speleologists, after the then Federal Prime Minister, Malcolm Fraser ... I was taken into Fraser Cave, Kutikina Cave as it is now called, by Kevin Kiernan and his team. There we were, at night, we had travelled up the Franklin against the flow all day. It was cold and raining and we got into this dark empty space with no rain and I thought that we were in a grove until Kevin turned on the light and then, bang, there was this huge deposit! It took about two or three seconds, you could see that the deposit was full of artefacts with *Monomilch* or soft calcite deposit on top. Really major discoveries are made instantly; I don't mean the actual discovery of the artefacts, but the realisation of the implications ... Clearly the top of this deposit was from the end of the last Ice Age. There was a rubble of limestone, which is last Ice Age, periglacial conditions, it was full of artefacts, thousands of artefacts, and smashed and broken wallaby bones. This is the southernmost part of the world that humans got to during the height of the last Ice Age. Humans never got that far south in South [22] America, and South Africa is on a more northerly latitude. To me there was this global thing, these were people and here before me was the great span of humankind associated with the great ice sheets, in both north and southern Hemispheres.

Ironically, too, in view of the importance for constitutional purposes of the tension between the special significance of the sites for Tasmanian Aboriginals, and their broader significance for what Jones called "[22] the great span of humankind", more recent exploration of the sites has at times been delayed by tension between their archaeological significance as evidence of human prehistory and their spiritual significance for Tasmanian Aboriginals. The latter perspective was especially sensitive because the period of archaeological discovery from the 1970s onwards coincided with the period in which Indigenous Tasmanians were contesting the myth that their peoples had become "extinct". In such a context, gestures of co-operative goodwill could some-times misfire. The suggestion that "Fraser Cave" be given an Aboriginal name was made in 1981 by the Tasmanian Archaeological Society; but the Nomenclature Board established under s 20A of the *Survey Co-ordination Act 1944* (Tas) then drew up a list of possible names without consulting any Aboriginal representative body, and continued to resist the name "Kutikina" even after it was proposed by the Tasmanian Aboriginal Centre. (The name is that of a spirit presence, conceived of as protecting the cave and its chambers against intruders.) Increasingly, the archaeological enterprise was itself perceived as suspect, since its emphasis on the importance of the caves as part of the common heritage of mankind was perceived as undermining their unique sensitivity as Aboriginal sacred sites.

By 1995 these tensions had culminated in Federal Court litigation, instituted by the Tasmanian Aboriginal Land Council against archaeologists from La Trobe University to demand the return of six assemblages (five of them from the southern forests area) originally taken under permit with Land Council co-operation between 1987 and 1992. The archaeologists sought more time for analysis; the Land Council insisted that the original permits had expired. Olney J granted an interim injunction on 5 July 1995, and extended it on 28 July until "serious matters of fact and law" could be tried (*Sainty v Allen*, unreported, No VG 643/1995). The litigation was terminated when Tasmania's Minister for Environment and Land Management, John Cleary, ordered the return of the artefacts to the Tasmanian government.

On 14 November 1995 the *Aboriginal Lands Act 1995* (Tas) received the Royal assent. The Tasmanian Aboriginal Land Council was reconstituted by s 5 of the Act, and by s 27 13 Tasmanian sites including Kutikina Cave, Ballawinne Cave, and Wargata Mina Cave, were "vested in the Council in trust for Aboriginal persons in perpetuity". In 1999 John Mulvaney and Johan Kamminga, *Prehistory of Australia* (Allen & Unwin, 1999) lamented that because of "[356] the rupture" between archaeologists and the Land Council, "archaeological fieldwork is largely sus-pended in Tasmania … [It is] paradoxical and disappointing that archaeologists are seen as the 'enemy'. At present both sides are losers. We can only hope that archaeological fieldwork and analysis can recommence in co-operative partnership, devoid of mutual acrimony and confron-tation".

In the same year as these words were written, the *Tasmanian Wilderness World Heritage Area Management Plan 1999* was adopted. In contrast to an earlier management plan adopted in 1992, it made elaborate provision for Aboriginal management, prescribing for instance that "[98] surveys pertaining to Aboriginal values are to be done in partnership with the Tasmanian Aboriginal community". Happily, under the auspices of the 1999 plan, it appears that such partnerships are now being re-established, so that archaeological work based on findings at Kutikina and elsewhere can resume.

3. Native Title

In *Western Australia v Commonwealth* (*Native Title Act Case*) (1995) 183 CLR 373, the validity of the *Native Title Act 1993* (Cth) was upheld under s 51(xxvi). In response to *Mabo v Queensland (No 2)* (1992) 175 CLR 1, the Act provided for the determination of future claims to native title, and also for the validation of extinguishments of native title occurring after the *Racial Discrimination Act* came into force in 1975.

Western Australia v Commonwealth (*Native Title Act Case*)
(1995) 183 CLR 373

Mason CJ, Brennan, Deane, Toohey, Gaudron and McHugh JJ: [459] The constitutional character of the *Native Title Act* may now be examined. The Act removes the common law defeasibility of native title, and secures the Aboriginal people and Torres Strait Islanders in the enjoyment of their native title subject to the prescribed exceptions which provide for native title to be extinguished or impaired ... The Act confers its protection upon native title holders who, ex hypothesi, are members of a particular race. As "[t]he relationship between the Aboriginal people and the lands which they occupy lies at the heart of traditional Aboriginal culture and traditional Aboriginal life" [*Tasmanian Dam Case* (1983) 158 CLR 1 at 274-5], the significance of security in the enjoyment of native title by the Aboriginal people of Western Australia who hold native title is undoubted ...

[460] The races power, unlike the aliens power or the corporations power, is not expressed to be a power to make laws simply with respect to persons of a designated character. It must be "deemed necessary" that "special laws" be made for "the people of any race". As the phrases quoted prescribe the conditions of legislative power, it is said that this Court must determine for itself whether an impugned enactment satisfies those conditions. Western Australia submits that, while it is concededly for the Parliament to deem a law to be necessary, it is the duty of the Court to determine whether the law answers the constitutional description. So much can be accepted ...

If ... the requirement that a law enacted under s 51(xxvi) be special were held to evoke a judicial evaluation of the needs of the people of a race or of the threats or problems that confronted them in order to determine whether the law was, or could be deemed to be, "necessary", the Court would be required to form a political value judgment. Yet it is clear that that judgment is for the Parliament, not for the Court. If the Court retains some supervisory jurisdiction to examine the question of necessity against the possibility of a manifest abuse of the races power, this case is not the occasion for an examination of that jurisdiction. The removal of the common law general defeasibility of native title by the *Native Title Act* is sufficient to demonstrate that the Parliament could properly have deemed that Act to be "necessary".

"Special" qualifies "law"; it does not relate to necessity. Therefore the special quality of a law must be ascertained by reference **[461]** to its differential operation upon the people of a particular race, not by reference to the circumstances which led the Parliament to deem it necessary to enact the law. A special quality appears when the law confers a right or benefit or imposes an obligation or disadvantage especially on the people of a particular race. The law may be special even when it confers a benefit generally, provided the benefit is of special significance or importance to the people of a particular race. That was the view of the majority in the *Tasmanian Dam* case, where the protection of objects of significance to Aboriginal cultural heritage was held to be supported by the races power albeit the same objects were items of cultural heritage under an international treaty the protection of which was supported by the external affairs power ...

[462] [On that basis] the *Native Title Act* is "special" in that it confers uniquely on the Aboriginal and Torres Strait Islander holders of native title (the "people of any race") a benefit protective of their native title. Perhaps the Act confers a benefit on all the people of those races. The special quality of the law thus appears. Whether it was "necessary" to enact that law was a matter for the Parliament to decide and, in the light of *Mabo (No 2)*, there are no grounds on which this Court could review the Parliament's decision, assuming it had power to do so.

The *Native Title Act* being thus valid under s 51(xxvi), there was no need to consider the Commonwealth's alternative claim to validity based on the "external affairs" power in s 51(xxix). This argument, too, involved characterisation of the Act as a "special law". Specifically, the argument was that the *Native Title Act* was a "special measure" authorised by s 8(1) of the *Racial Discrimination Act 1975* (Cth), and thus ultimately by Art 1(4) of the International Convention on the Elimination of All Forms of Racial Discrimination 1966 (which permits "[s]pecial measures ... for the sole purpose of securing adequate advancement of certain racial or ethnic groups ... in order to ensure such groups ... equal enjoyment or exercise of human rights and fundamental freedoms"). In *Gerhardy v Brown* (1985) 159 CLR 70, the *Pitjantjatjara Land Rights Act 1981* (SA) had been upheld as a "special measure". As State legislation, that Act did not need support from the "external affairs" power, but it did need to be reconciled with the *Racial Discrimination Act* in order that the latter Act would not override it by virtue of s 109 of the Constitution.

The *Native Title Act* itself had laid the foundation for an argument based on s 51(xxix) by the last two recitals in its Preamble.

Native Title Act 1993 (Cth)

The Parliament of Australia intends that the following law will take effect according to its terms and be a special law for the descendants of the original inhabitants of Australia.

The law, together with initiatives announced at the time of its introduction and others agreed on by the Parliament from time to time, is intended, for the purposes of paragraph 4 of Article 1 of the International Convention on the Elimination of All Forms of Racial Discrimination and the *Racial Discrimination Act 1975*, to be a special measure for the advancement and protection of Aboriginal peoples and Torres Strait Islanders, and is intended to further advance the process of reconciliation among all Australians.

Moreover, to allay apprehensions that the validation of past extinguishments would involve a "suspension" or "rolling back" or even "implied repeal" of the *Racial Discrimination Act*, the *Native Title Act* as originally enacted included another provision, arguably self-contradictory:

7 **(1)** Nothing in this Act affects the operation of the *Racial Discrimination Act 1975*.

(2) Subsection (1) does not affect the validation of past acts by or in accordance with this Act.

The argument based on the "external affairs" power was not expressly considered in the *Native Title Act Case*. However, the joint judgment did comment on the relationship between the *Native Title Act* and the *Racial Discrimination Act*, pointing out that while, on the one hand, the *Native Title Act* "**[462]** validates or permits the validation of past acts" whose operation to extinguish native title might otherwise have been inhibited by the *Racial Discrimination Act*, on the other hand it also extended to holders of native title a new form of statutory protection, parallel to that of the *Racial Discrimination Act* but "more specific and more complex ... **[463]** [T]he *Racial Discrimination Act* protects native title holders against *discriminatory* extinction or impairment of native title. The *Native Title Act*, on the other hand, protects native title holders against *any* extinction or impairment of native title subject to the specific and detailed exceptions which that Act prescribes or permits".

The question of whether s 51(xxvi), as applied to Australia's Indigenous peoples, extends only to legislation *for their benefit*, was not explored in the *Native Title Act Case*. Nor was the question of whether the *Native Title Act* qualified as a "special measure" under s 8(1) of the *Racial Discrimination Act*. The latter question would have raised an issue analogous to the constitutional issue (though not identical with it), since a "special measure" must be for the *sole* purpose of benefiting the relevant racial group (see Brennan J in *Gerhardy v Brown* at 135-7). However, although Western Australia argued that the *Native Title Act* was inconsistent with the *Racial Discrimination Act* (and in view of s 7(1) must therefore be "inoperative"), the point of the argument was *not* that the *Native Title Act* discriminated *against* Aborigines and Torres Strait Islanders (by making their land titles subject to extinguishment, and retrospectively permitting the validation of past extinguishment). Had that argument been put, it might well have raised the constitutional question. Instead, however, the argument was that the *Native Title Act* discriminated *in favour of* Aborigines, and must hence be rendered inoperative by s 7(1). In dismissing *that* argument, the joint judgment found it "**[483]** difficult to identify the legal purpose which [s 7] is intended to serve".

In any event, the 1998 amendments to the *Native Title Act* restated its relationship to the *Racial Discrimination Act*. The amended version of s 7 reads as follows:

7 (1) This Act is intended to be read and construed subject to the provisions of the *Racial Discrimination Act 1975*.

(2) Subsection (1) means only that:

(a) the provisions of the *Racial Discrimination Act 1975* apply to the performance of functions and the exercise of powers conferred by or authorised by this Act; and

(b) to construe this Act, and thereby to determine its operation, ambiguous terms should be construed consistently with the *Racial Discrimination Act 1975* if that construction would remove the ambiguity.

(3) Subsections (1) and (2) do not affect the validation of past acts or intermediate period acts in accordance with this Act.

In *Western Australia v Ward* (*Miriuwung-Gajjerong Case*) (2002) 213 CLR 1, Gleeson CJ, Gaudron, Gummow and Hayne JJ said of this amended version: "**[97]** One effect of this section is that, contrary to what otherwise might follow from the fact that the [*Native Title Act*] is a later Act of the federal Parliament, the [*Native Title Act*] is not to be taken as repealing the [*Racial Discrimination Act*] to any extent. The significance of s 7(3) is to make it clear that, notwithstanding the continued paramountcy of the [*Racial Discrimination Act*] stated in the earlier sub-sections, the effect of the validation achieved by the [*Native Title Act*] is to displace the invalidity which otherwise flowed from the operation of the [*Racial Discrimination Act*]. It is unnecessary to consider whether s 7 may have other operations".

4. For the Benefit of a Race?

Whether a law relating to Indigenous peoples enacted under s 51(xxvi) must be a law *for their benefit* remains a point of contention. The comments of Brennan and Deane JJ in the *Tasmanian Dam Case* have sometimes been read as supporting the view of Murphy J in *Koowarta* that the 1967 referendum, in bringing Aboriginals within the reach of the "races" power, did so in such a way that the power can only be used for their benefit. In *Chu Kheng Lim v Minister for Immigration* (1992) 176 CLR 1, Gaudron J remarked that Murphy J's approach "**[56]** has much to commend it".

In *Kruger v Commonwealth* (*Stolen Generations Case*) (1997) 190 CLR 1, she again found it "**[111]** arguable that that power only authorises laws for the benefit of 'the people of [a] race for whom it is deemed necessary to make special laws'." Brennan CJ and Gummow J expressed no opinion on the issue. They did point out that the mere existence of s 51(xxvi) permits some kind of differential treatment of "the people of any race", as does s 51(xix) for "aliens", so that these provisions are inconsistent with any general constitutional implication of "equality" (see Chapter 14, §8). However, Brennan CJ stressed that he was speaking "**[44]** [w]ithout attempting to ascertain the operation of these subparagraphs", while Gummow J observed that s 51(xxvi) had permitted detrimental as well as beneficial legislation "**[155]** at least in its original form".

The issue arose again in *Kartinyeri v Commonwealth* (*Hindmarsh Island Bridge Case*) (1998) 195 CLR 337. But again it remained unresolved. The case had a tortuous history (see Margaret Simons, *The Meeting of the Waters: The Hindmarsh Island Affair* (Hodder, 2003)). Hindmarsh Island ("Kumarangk"), situated in the Murray River delta in South Australia, had traditionally been connected to the mainland only by a cable-drawn vehicular ferry. During the 1980s there was a steady development on the island foreshores of marina berths and supporting commercial services (including a chandlery and a licensed tavern); and in 1989, as a condition of planning approval for a further marina development, it was proposed that the island be linked to the mainland by a bridge, which was to be constructed by a private company but vested in the local council. The development was opposed on environmental grounds, and also on Aboriginal heritage grounds, since the island, and the Goolwa Channel area in which it was located, were part of the traditional home of the Ngarrindjeri people.

It was on the latter basis that the Commonwealth Minister for Aboriginal and Torres Strait Islander Affairs, Robert Tickner, was asked to exercise his powers under the *Aboriginal and Torres Strait Islander Heritage Protection Act 1984* (Cth), which empowers the responsible Minister to make emergency and other declarations "for and in relation to the protection and preservation" of "significant Aboriginal area[s]". In the course of successive approaches to the Minister, the full extent of the claim only gradually emerged; but by April 1994 he was receiving representations about "secret/sacred information … concerning the creation and renewal of life", and by May 1994 he had received a further representation from a group of Ngarrindjeri women, claiming to be the custodians of secret "women's business" for which the island had traditionally been used, and which could not be disclosed to Ngarrindjeri men, nor to other men. On that basis the Minister made an interim declaration under s 9 of the Act on 12 May 1994, and, on 23 May 1994, appointed Professor Cheryl Saunders to report to him under s 10 of the Act "to enable me to consider whether under s 10(1) I may make a declaration".

In the course of her inquiry Saunders was given extensive evidence of the alleged "women's business", which she collected and presented in sealed envelopes. Other witnesses, including other Ngarrindjeri women, gave evidence that the alleged "women's business" was a fabrication put forward by the Ngarrindjeri opponents of the bridge as a strategic device. Despite that evidence, Saunders' report accepted the authenticity of the "women's business"; and on 9 July 1994 the Minister made a declaration under s 10 of the Act, based on Saunders' report which he had received the previous day. In deference to the Ngarrindjeri women's claim that details of the alleged "women's business" could be disclosed only to women, Tickner did not himself examine the detailed evidence in the sealed envelopes.

On 15 February 1995, both the declaration and the report were quashed in the Federal Court by O'Loughlin J (*Chapman v Minister for Aboriginal and Torres Strait Islander Affairs* (1995) 133 ALR 74); and on 7 December 1995 that decision was affirmed by a Full Court of the Federal Court (*Norvill v Chapman* (1995) 133 ALR 226). It was held that Saunders' advertisement inviting submissions had not adequately identified the affected area or the issues for the purposes of s 10(3); and that the Minister had not adequately discharged his statutory obligation to give the matter his own consideration (including his own assessment of the sealed evidence relating to "women's business").

Meanwhile, the South Australian government had appointed its own Royal Commission to investigate the competing claims. On 21 December 1995, two weeks after the decision in *Norvill v Chapman*, the Royal Commissioner, Iris Stevens, made a finding that the alleged "women's business" had been fabricated by the Ngarrindjeri women in order to halt the construction of the bridge (*Report of the Hindmarsh Island Bridge Royal Commission*, 1995).

On 16 January 1996, Tickner, nominated Justice Jane Mathews of the Federal Court to prepare a second report. To overcome the problem identified in *Norvill v Chapman*, he announced that, when the time came for ministerial action on Mathews' report, he would delegate his functions to a female colleague, Senator Rosemary Crowley.

On 25 March 1996, after a change of government, the new Minister for Aboriginal and Torres Strait Islander Affairs, Senator John Herron, announced that he had asked Mathews to complete her report for the benefit of the incoming government. However, the validity of her nomination was then challenged in further litigation. In *Wilson v Minister for Aboriginal and Torres Strait Islander Affairs* (1996) 189 CLR 1, the High Court held that Mathews' nomination was not authorised by the Act: since the statutory function of reporting to the Minister was incompatible with judicial office, the word "person" in s 10(1)(c) must be construed so as not to include a holder of federal judicial office (see Chapter 14, §6).

On 17 September 1996, 11 days after the High Court decision, the Mathews Report was tabled in the Senate. It turned out that, quite apart from the invalidity of her nomination, Mathews had encountered another difficulty. The Ngarrindjeri claimants had given their evidence to Mathews on the understanding that the new Minister, Senator Herron, would delegate ministerial consideration of the report to a female colleague, just as his predecessor had undertaken to do.

But, subsequently, Senator Herron had announced that he would consider the matter himself. Thereupon the Ngarrindjeri women had withdrawn much of the detailed evidence they had given to Mathews. In the end, therefore, Mathews' report was to the effect that, on the evidence now available to her, she was unable to find that the women's claim had been substantiated.

In the wake of this second miscarriage of procedures under the 1984 Act, the *Hindmarsh Island Bridge Act 1997* (Cth) was enacted to preclude any possibility of further proceedings under that Act, even though the original 1994 application on behalf of the Ngarrindjeri women was still pending. The only substantive provision of the new legislation was s 4.

Hindmarsh Island Bridge Act 1997 (Cth)

4 Provisions facilitating construction etc of the bridge

(1) The Heritage Protection Act does not authorise the making of a declaration in relation to the preservation or protection of an area or object from any of the following activities:

    (a) the construction of a bridge, and associated works (including approaches to the bridge), in the Hindmarsh Island bridge area;

    (b) work or other activities in that area preparatory to, or associated with, that construction;

    (c) maintenance on, or repairs to, the bridge and associated works;

    (d) use of the bridge and associated works;

    (e) the removal of materials from, or dumping of materials in, the pit area in connection with any of the activities mentioned in paragraphs (a), (b) and (c).

(2) The Heritage Protection Act does not authorise the Minister to take any action after the commencement of this Act in relation to an application (whether made before or after the commencement of this Act) that relates (wholly or partly) to activity covered by paragraph (1)(a), (b), (c), (d) or (e).

The removal of "the Hindmarsh Island bridge area" from the scope of the 1984 Act was intended to preclude any further possible claim that the area had "secret/sacred" significance for Ngarrindjeri women. Whether or not such a claim was well founded, the preclusion of any further inquiry seemed adverse to the interests of the Ngarrindjeri women concerned.

Moreover, whether the 1997 Act was conceived of as an independent enactment or as an amendment to the 1984 Act, the power to enact it could only be derived from s 51(xxvi). In that context, it was foreshadowed that unresolved issues as to the scope of s 51(xxvi) might finally arise for decision (see Commonwealth of Australia, *Parliamentary Debates,* House of Representatives, 26 March 1997, 3277-8). Accordingly, the question before the High Court was whether the *Hindmarsh Island Bridge Act* was validly enacted under s 51(xxvi).

The Commonwealth argued that there are no limits to the power so long as the law affixes a consequence based upon race. In other words, it was not for the High Court to examine the positive or negative impact of the law. On the first day of the hearing, the Commonwealth Solicitor-General, Gavan Griffith QC, suggested that the races power "is infected, the power is infused with a power of adverse operation". He also acknowledged its "direct racist content", in the sense of "a capacity for adverse operation". The following exchange then occurred:

Kartinyeri v Commonwealth (*Hindmarsh Island Bridge Case*)
(Transcript of Argument, High Court of Australia, 5 February 1998)

Kirby J: Can I just get clear in my mind, is the Commonwealth's submission that it is entirely and exclusively for the Parliament to determine the matter upon which special laws are deemed necessary or whatever the words say or is there a point at which there is a justiciable question for the Court? I mean, it seems unthinkable that a law such as the Nazi race laws could be enacted under the race power and that this Court could do nothing about it.

Griffith QC: Your Honour, if there was a reason why the Court could do something about it, a Nazi law, it would, in our submission, be for a reason external to the races power. It would be for some wider over-arching reason.

The case was decided by only six judges, Callinan J having disqualified himself from deciding the matter (see Sydney Tilmouth and George Williams, "The High Court and the Disqualification of One of its Own" (1999) 73 *Australian Law Journal* 72). The challenge failed by 5:1, with Kirby J dissenting, because, in the words of Brennan CJ and McHugh J: "**[356]** Once the true scope of the legislative powers conferred by s 51 [is] perceived, it is clear that the power which supports a valid Act supports an Act repealing it". It was common ground that the 1984 Act was valid; hence it necessarily followed that a later modification of its operation must also be valid. Accordingly, Brennan CJ and McHugh J did not need to address the scope of s 51(xxvi). Indeed, they thought it "**[358]** not only unnecessary but misleading" to do so, since the issue could only arise if one of "two false assumptions" was made: either that the power to make a law does not extend to its repeal, or that a repealing Act "may not possess the same character as the law repealed". They thought that no statement of opinion could have judicial authority "in a case where such a statement can be made only on an assumption that is false".

The other four judges did address the scope of the races power. The plaintiffs had argued that the words "the people of any race" require legislation for *all* the people of the relevant race, so that the power could not be used to single out some Aboriginal people from others. Gaudron, Gummow, Hayne and Kirby JJ rejected that argument, holding that s 51(xxvi) can support a law with respect to a sub-group of a particular race. Secondly, the plaintiffs had argued that the power is confined to laws for the *benefit* of the people of the relevant race (or, alternatively, that its operation with respect to people of the Aboriginal race is so confined). The Court failed to settle this issue. Gummow and Hayne JJ held that the power could be used to withdraw a statutory benefit granted to Aboriginal people (and at least in that sense to impose a disadvantage). Kirby J accepted the plaintiffs' argument. Gaudron J, while developing her own approach, conceded that in practice it might yield the same result as that of Kirby J.

Gaudron J's position was distinctive. Despite her tentative comments in the *Stolen Generations Case* she found it impossible to assign to s 51(xxvi) a differential operation for Aboriginal peoples, as compared with its operation for peoples of other races. However, she focused on the requirement that a racially discriminatory law enacted under s 51(xxvi) must be "deemed necessary" by Parliament, and held that, although the Court could not pre-empt this judgment of necessity, it could determine whether such a judgment was "reasonable". The justiciable question which she thus identified was whether the discriminatory enactment is "appropriate and adapted to a relevant difference".

Kartinyeri v Commonwealth (*Hindmarsh Island Bridge Case*)
(1998) 195 CLR 337

Gaudron J: [361] The 1967 amendment was one that might fairly be described in today's terms as a "minimalist amendment". As a matter of language and syntax, it did no more than remove the then existing exception or limitation on Commonwealth power with respect to the people of the Aboriginal race. And unless something other than language and syntax is to be taken into account, it operated to place them in precisely the same constitutional position as the people of other races.

The "Yes" case for the 1967 referendum identified two **[362]** purposes attending the proposed law, which upon its approval in accordance with s 128 of the Constitution, deleted the words "other than the aboriginal race in any State" … The first was to "remove any ground for the belief that, as at present worded, the Constitution discriminates in some ways against people of the aboriginal race". The other was "to make it possible for the Commonwealth Parliament to make special laws for the people of the Aboriginal race, wherever they may live". Given the limited nature of the purposes thus disclosed and given, also, that as a matter of language and syntax, the amendment was apt to achieve those purposes, and only those purposes, it is not possible, in my view, to treat s 51(xxvi) as limited to laws which benefit Aboriginal Australians if it is not similarly limited with respect to the people of other races.

If, prior to 1967, s 51(xxvi) extended to authorise laws which were not for the benefit of the people of a particular race, it is difficult to see that the 1967 amendment ... could have altered that position. However, two matters were advanced in support of the proposition that it did. The first was that, by 1967, international standards and community values were such that racial discrimination was not to be tolerated. The second was that it was intended by the electors that the amendment would enable the Parliament to legislate [363] for the benefit of Aboriginal people and only for their benefit. Given the terms of the "Yes" case to which reference has already been made, it is doubtful whether the intention of the electorate was as stated. However, that issue may be put to one side.

Whatever the international standards and community values in 1967 and whatever the intention of those voting in the 1967 referendum, the bare deletion of an exception or limitation on power is not, in my view, capable of effecting a curtailment of power. On the contrary, the consequence of an amendment of that kind is to augment power. Accordingly, if, prior to 1967, s 51(xxvi) authorised special laws which were not for the benefit of the people of a particular race, the referendum did not, in my view, alter that position.

There are two matters with respect to s 51(xxvi) which are beyond controversy. The first is that the debates of the Constitutional Conventions ... reveal an understanding that it would authorise laws which discriminated against people of "coloured races" and "alien races". The second is that s 51(xxvi) does not simply confer power to legislate with respect to "the people of any race". It confers power to legislate with respect to "the people of any race for whom it is deemed necessary to make special laws".

Were s 51(xxvi) simply a power to legislate with respect to "the people of any race", there would, in my view, be no doubt that Parliament might legislate in any way it chose so long as the law in question differentiated in some way with respect to the people of a particular race or dealt with some matter of "special significance or importance to the[m]" [*Western Australia v Commonwealth* (*Native Title Act Case*) (1995) 183 CLR 373 at 461]. However, the words "for whom it is [364] deemed necessary to make special laws" must be given some operation. And they can only operate to impose some limit on what would otherwise be the scope of s 51(xxvi) ...

[A]lthough I expressed the view in *Chu Kheng Lim v Minister for Immigration* [(1992) 176 CLR 1 at 56] that there was much to commend the view that, in s 51(xxvi), "for" means "for the benefit of", that view cannot be maintained in the face of the constitutional debates earlier referred to. Even so, the words "for whom it is deemed necessary to make special laws" must be given some operation and, as already indicated, they can only operate as a limit to the power conferred by s 51(xxvi) ...

[365] The criterion for the exercise of power under s 51(xxvi) is that it be deemed *necessary* – not expedient or appropriate – to make a law which provides differently for the people of a particular race or, if it is a law of general application, one which deals with something of "special significance or importance to the people of [that] particular race". Clearly, it is for the Parliament to deem it necessary to make a law of that kind. To form a view as to that necessity, however, there must be some difference pertaining to the people of the race involved or their circumstances or, at least, some material upon which the Parliament might reasonably form a political judgment that there is a difference of that kind. Were it otherwise, the words "for whom it is deemed necessary to make special laws" would have no operation and s 51(xxvi) would simply be a power to make laws for the people of any race.

Once it is accepted that the power conferred by s 51(xxvi) may only be exercised if there is some material upon which the Parliament might reasonably form a judgment that there is a difference necessitating some special legislative measure, two things follow. The first is that [366] s 51(xxvi) does not authorise special laws affecting rights and obligations in areas in which there is no relevant difference between the people of the race to whom the law is directed and the people of other races. A simple example will suffice. Rights deriving from citizenship inhere in the individual by reason of his or her membership of the Australian body politic and not by reason of any other consideration, including race. To put the matter in terms which reflect the jurisprudence that has developed with respect to anti-discrimination law, race is simply irrelevant to the existence or exercise of rights associated with citizenship. So, too, it is irrelevant to the question of continued membership of the Australian body politic. Consequently, s 51(xxvi) will not support a law depriving people of a particular racial group of their citizenship or their rights as citizens. And race is equally irrelevant to the enjoyment of those rights which are generally described as human rights and which are taken to inhere in each and every person by reason of his or her membership of the human race.

The second matter which flows from the requirement that there be some matter or circumstance upon which the Parliament might reasonably form the judgment that there is some difference pertaining to the people of a particular race which necessitates some special law is that the law must be reasonably capable of being viewed as appropriate and adapted to the difference asserted. A similar view was expressed by Deane and Toohey JJ in *Leeth v Commonwealth* [(1992) 174 CLR 455 at 489], it being said by their Honours that s 51(xxvi) authorises "discriminatory treatment of members of [a particular race] to the extent which is reasonably capable of being seen as appropriate and adapted to the circumstance of that membership". Although they did not explain why that was so, the requirement flows, in my view, from the need for there to be some material or circumstance from which it might reasonably be concluded by the Parliament that there is some difference necessitating a special law. Unless the law in question is reasonably capable of being viewed as appropriate and adapted to the difference which is claimed, it could not be concluded that the Parliament formed the view that there was such a difference.

I have attempted to explain the need for a law to be reasonably capable of being viewed as appropriate and adapted to some difference which the Parliament might reasonably judge to exist by reference to the language of s 51(xxvi). However, the matter may also be expressed in terms used in the *Native Title Act Case*. A law which deals differently with the people of a particular race and which is not reasonably capable of being viewed as appropriate and adapted to a difference of the kind indicated has no rational basis and is, thus, a **[367]** "manifest abuse of the races power" [183 CLR at 460]. So, too, it would be irrational and, thus, a manifest abuse of the races power if Parliament were to enact a law requiring or providing for the different treatment of the people of a particular race if it could not reasonably form the view that there was some difference requiring their different treatment.

Because the power conferred by s 51(xxvi) of the Constitution is premised on there being some matter or circumstance pertaining to the people of a particular race upon which the Parliament might reasonably conclude that there is a real and relevant difference necessitating the making of a special law, its scope necessarily varies according to circumstances as they exist from time to time. In this respect the power conferred by par (xxvi) is not unlike the power conferred by s 51(vi) to legislate with respect to defence. And as with the defence power, a law that is authorised by reference to circumstances existing at one time may lose its constitutional support if circumstances change.

Although the power conferred by s 51(xxvi) is, in terms, wide enough to authorise laws which operate either to the advantage or disadvantage of the people of a particular race, it is difficult to conceive of circumstances in which a law presently operating to the disadvantage of a racial minority would be valid. It is even more difficult to conceive of a present circumstance pertaining to Aboriginal Australians which could support a law operating to their disadvantage. To put the matter another way, prima facie, at least, the circumstances which presently pertain to Aboriginal Australians are circumstances of serious disadvantage, which disadvantages include their material circumstances and the vulnerability of their culture. And prima facie, at least, only laws directed to remedying their disadvantage could reasonably be viewed as appropriate and adapted to their different circumstances.

Notwithstanding that it is difficult to envisage circumstances in **[368]** which a law which operated to the disadvantage of the people of a racial minority might validly be enacted under s 51(xxvi) of the Constitution, the test of constitutional validity is not whether it is a beneficial law. Rather, the test is whether the law in question is reasonably capable of being viewed as appropriate and adapted to a real and relevant difference which the Parliament might reasonably judge to exist. It is the application of that test to today's circumstances, so far as they are known, that leads to the conclusion that prima facie, at least, s 51(xxvi) presently only authorises laws which operate to the benefit of Aboriginal Australians ...

The mere fact that the power conferred by s 51(xxvi) of the Constitution is limited in the manner indicated does not provide an answer ... [A] plenary power to legislate on some topic or with respect to some subject matter carries with it the **[369]** power to repeal or amend existing laws on that topic or with respect to that subject matter ... [However], in the case of the amendment or partial repeal of a law enacted under s 51, a question may arise whether the law, as it stands after its alteration, retains its character as a law with respect to a matter within Commonwealth legislative power.

The plaintiffs contend that, as the Bridge Act does not, in terms, purport to repeal or amend any existing Commonwealth law, its validity is to be determined on the basis that it stands separate and apart from any such law, including the Heritage Protection Act. Were the Bridge Act a separate enactment which, for example, purported to forbid a State Minister from making a declaration under State law having the same or similar effect as a declaration under the Heritage Protection Act, it would be difficult, if not impossible, to conceive of a present difference which the Parliament might reasonably judge to exist between the Ngarrindjeri people and people of other races so as to necessitate that particular law. But the Bridge Act does not affect a State law. It affects a Commonwealth law, namely, the Heritage Protection Act and it affects it by limiting its field of operation. Because it limits the field in which the Heritage Protection Act operates, it operates, to that extent, to repeal that Act.

[370] The validity of the Heritage Protection Act is not in question. And in the view that I take, there is no reason to doubt that, at all relevant times, it has been, and continues to be a valid law under s 51(xxvi) of the Constitution. And subject to the qualifications previously mentioned, s 51(xxvi) not only authorises the Heritage Protection Act but, also, authorises its partial repeal.

Gummow and Hayne JJ reached the same conclusion as Gaudron J as to the 1967 referendum, but not as to the scope of s 51(xxvi). In what may have been intended as a significant distinction, they emphasised at the outset that the rights withdrawn from the Ngarrindjeri women were statutory rights, as distinct from rights subsisting in the common law.

Gummow and Hayne JJ: [376] The Bridge Act curtails the operation of another law of the Commonwealth, not the enjoyment of any substantive common law rights. It demonstrates the general proposition ... that what the Parliament may enact it may repeal. First, the Bridge Act limits in a particular respect the declaration-making authority of the Minister under the Heritage Protection Act. Further, the Bridge Act removes any privilege conferred by the **[377]** Heritage Protection Act upon Aboriginals or Aboriginal groups who applied or might apply seeking such declaration in respect of areas or objects in the Hindmarsh Island bridge area or the pit area, as defined in the Bridge Act ...

[378] It is true that "unlike the aliens power or the corporations power", s 51(xxvi) "is not expressed to be a power to make laws simply with respect to persons of a designated character". A law will only answer the constitutional description in s 51(xxvi) if it (i) is "deemed necessary" (ii) that "special laws" (iii) be made for "the people of any race".

The term "deem" may mean "to judge or reach a conclusion about something". Here, the judgment as to what is "deemed necessary" is that of the Parliament. Nevertheless, it may be that the character of a law purportedly based upon s 51(xxvi) will be denied to a law enacted in "manifest abuse" of that power of judgment. Even if such a restraint (in addition to those stated or implied elsewhere in the Constitution, such as in s 51(xxxi)) exists there is no occasion for its application to the Bridge Act. The scope of **[379]** the Heritage Protection Act was such that, if the various conditions required by that law were satisfied, the Minister might ... have made declarations under ss 10 and 12 with respect to the Hindmarsh Island bridge area and the pit area. Such a declaration would have been subject to disallowance by either legislative chamber, as s 15 contemplated. There is no "manifest abuse" of its power of legislative judgment for the Parliament to accelerate matters by determining that, in respect of particular areas, the Ministerial power of declaration was withdrawn. It was for the Parliament to make its assessment of the circumstances which led it to deem it necessary to enact the Bridge Act.

The requirement that the Bridge Act be "special" does not relate to the matter of necessity. The presence of the special quality of the Bridge Act is to be ascertained "by reference to its differential operation upon the people of a particular race". Here, "the people of a particular race" are those spoken of in s 4 of the Heritage Protection Act. They are those Aboriginals and particular communities or groups of Aboriginals for whom areas or objects to which the Heritage Protection Act applied were of particular significance in accordance with Aboriginal tradition. In respect of areas and objects within the Hindmarsh Island bridge area …, the Bridge Act withdrew the potentiality of that special protection which would flow from declarations by the Minister and would continue for the life of such declarations.

As just indicated, "differential operation" is that which gives to any law based upon s 51(xxvi) its character as a "special" law. Once it is accepted, as it has been, that a law may make provision for some only of a particular race, it follows that a valid law may operate differentially between members of that race. That is the situation with the Bridge Act. Moreover, as was said in the joint judgment in the *Native Title Act Case* [183 CLR at 461]:

> "A special quality appears when the law confers a right or benefit or imposes an obligation or disadvantage especially on the people of a particular race."

Here, the Bridge Act imposes a disadvantage, of the nature identified above, with respect to areas and objects within the Hindmarsh Island bridge area and the pit area. The disadvantage is in the contraction of the field of operation of the Heritage Protection Act, itself a law which is to be taken as supported by s 51(xxvi).

Although they disclaimed any such submission, the position **[380]** assumed by the plaintiffs in denying the validity of the Bridge Act would deny to the Parliament the competence to limit the scope of a special law by a subsequent legislative determination that something less than the original measure was necessary. The Parliament might make that judgment for various reasons, including changes in the circumstances which had led it to enact that original special law.

It is true, but not to the point, that the differential treatment of those upon whom the law operates by conferral of a right or benefit may also impose an obligation or disadvantage upon others. In various provisions of the Constitution, notably ss 51(ii), 102 and 117, the terms "discriminate" and "discrimination" appear … The judicial exegesis in this Court upon "discrimination" in constitutional law largely has been concerned with its meaning as a restriction … upon legislative power. Section 51(xxvi) stands in a different position. The requirement of differential operation, spelled out from the use of the phrase "special laws", is a criterion of validity not a cause of invalidity. It is "of the essence of" a law supported by s 51(xxvi) "that it discriminates between the people of the race for whom the special laws are made and other people" [153 CLR at 261].

The differential operation of the one law may, upon its obverse and reverse, withdraw or create benefits. That which is to the advantage of some members of a race may be to the disadvantage of other members of that race or of another race. Extreme examples, given particularly the lessons of history (including that of this country), may be imagined. But such apprehensions cannot, in accordance with received doctrine, control what otherwise is the meaning to be given today to heads of federal legislative power.

Thus, in the *Territorial Senators Case* [*Western Australia v Commonwealth* (1975) 134 CLR 201 at 271], Mason J spoke of "the grim spectre conjured up by the plaintiffs of a Parliament swamping the Senate with senators from the Territories, thereby reducing the representation of the States disproportionately to that of an ineffective minority in the chamber". This was to disregard the assumption "which we should now make, that Parliament will act responsibly in the exercise of its powers". In the same case, Jacobs J spoke against **[381]** the construction of the words of the Constitution "by some distorting possibility" [134 CLR at 275].

However, three further points may briefly be made. First, as a matter of construction, a legislative intention to interfere with fundamental common law rights, freedoms and immunities must be "clearly manifested by unmistakable and unambiguous language" [*Coco v The Queen* (1994) 179 CLR 427 at 437]. Secondly, the doctrine of *Marbury v Madison* [5 US (1 Cranch) 137 (1803)] ensures that courts exercising the judicial power of the Commonwealth determine whether the legislature and the executive act within their constitutional powers. Thirdly, the occasion has yet to arise for consideration of all that may follow from Dixon J's statement that the Constitution [*Australian Communist Party v Commonwealth* (1951) 83 CLR 1 at 193]: "is an instrument framed in accordance with many traditional conceptions, to some of which it gives effect, as, for example, in separating the judicial power from other functions of government, others of which are simply assumed. Among these I think that it may fairly be said that the rule of law forms an assumption."

Kirby J: [411] I have concluded that the race power in par (xxvi) of s 51 of the Constitution does not extend to the enactment of laws detrimental to, or discriminatory against, the people of any race (including the Aboriginal race) by reference to their race ...

Textual and contextual indications of non-discrimination

No authority of this Court requires the rejection of the plaintiffs' submission about the meaning of par (xxvi). It is therefore necessary to start the elucidation of its requirements with the text, viewed in its context. First, the power is not simply to make laws with respect to "[t]he people of any race". In this regard par (xxvi) is to be contrasted with par (xix) which affords such a plenary power, relevantly, with respect to "aliens". In par (xxvi), words have been added which must have work to do. They are intended to send signals of meaning to the reader of the paragraph. The requirement that laws made under par (xxvi) by reference to race should be "deemed necessary" and should be "special" cannot be dismissed as mere surplusage. In a constitutional text noted for its brevity, the additional words must clearly have the purpose of putting a limitation on what would otherwise be an unbridled race power.

It may be assumed that the drafters of par (xxvi) would have been aware of the sharply divided opinions which were evident in the Conventions: some of the delegates viewing detrimental or adversely discriminatory laws by the new Parliament as "disgraceful". On the face of things, therefore, the stated preconditions to the use of the race power were intended to indicate a brake on legislation with respect to "the people of any race". All people in the Commonwealth were people of a "race". Most of the settlers would probably, in 1901, have regarded themselves as people of the British race or, perhaps, Caucasians. Clearly, a race power for "special" laws was not intended to have application to them.

Secondly, the words of qualification in par (xxvi) must be read as a composite idea. The parts combine to impose a control on the laws which may be made under the paragraph. As a matter of language, the words are consistent with an operation that is non-detrimental and has no adverse discrimination about it. This is particularly so if the structure, purpose and other features of the Constitution support that meaning. The word "for" is ambiguous. It could mean "for the **[412]** benefit of". Or it could mean "in respect of". The history of the power in its original form tends to favour the latter meaning. However, a textual argument against that meaning is that, where the framers of the Constitution intended that idea, it was so expressed. Thus it was done in pars (xxxi), (xxxvi) ("in respect of"); in par (xxii) ("in relation thereto"); and in par (xxxii) ("with respect to"). The test of necessity in par (xxvi) is a strong one. It is to be distinguished from advisability, expedience or advantage. Its presence in par (xxvi) indicates that a particular *need* might enliven the *necessity* to make a special law. It has been held by this Court, and was conceded by the Commonwealth, that ultimately and in "extreme cases" the existence of such necessity was justiciable. Various formulae were urged to emphasise the severe limits of the jurisdiction to review the posited necessity. But in my view, the legislation contested here is subject to judicial review. There appears nothing in the agreed facts about the Ngarrindjeri, or the section of them constituted by the plaintiffs, which calls forth the power in par (xxvi) on the ground of necessity by reference to the race of such people. The only necessity evident in the facts (and stated in the long title to the Bridge Act) is the necessity "to facilitate the construction of the [bridge]". The fact that any law made under the race power must be deemed "necessary" and must answer to the description of "special" marks such a law out from all other laws that may be made by the Parliament. It tenders to the Parliament, and ultimately to this Court, criteria of limitation which must be given meaning according to the understanding of the Constitution read today.

Other paragraphs of s 51 contain concepts, the content of which has varied during the history of the Commonwealth because they are read with different eyes at different times in the light of different necessities. The clearest example is par (vi) which relates to the defence of the Commonwealth ... It is therefore unsurprising that we, who look at par (xxvi) in 1998, read the adjectival clause which qualifies the power ... to make laws with respect to "the people of any race" informed by the experience of a century of federal government. In that century the concept of what it is, in the nature of law, that may be deemed "necessary" and in a "special" form for the people of a race, by reference to race, cannot, and should not, be understood as it might **[413]** have been in 1901. Such a static notion of constitutional interpretation completely misunderstands the function which is being performed.

Thirdly, a crucial element in the history of the constitutional text is the amendment of par (xxvi) in 1967. Because there have been so few amendments to the Australian Constitution, it has not hitherto been necessary to develop a theory of the approach to be taken to the meaning of the text where a provision is altered. In deriving the meaning of the altered provision, conventional rules of statutory construction permit a court to take into account the legislative change. But this is much more important in elucidating a constitutional text. This is especially so in Australia because of the necessity, exceptionally, to involve the electors of the Commonwealth in the law-making process. That step requires that this Court, to understand the amendment, should appreciate, and give weight to, the purpose of the change. The stated purpose here was to remove two provisions in the Constitution which, it had ultimately been concluded, discriminated against Australian Aboriginals. Whatever the initial object of the original exception to par (xxvi), by the time that the words were removed, the amendment did not simply lump the Aboriginal people of Australia in with other races as potential targets for detrimental or adversely discriminatory laws. It was the will of the Australian Parliament and people that the race power should be significantly altered. If the Constitution were not to be changed to provide the power to make laws with respect to the advancement of Aboriginal people and to forbid discrimination on racial grounds (as Mr Wentworth had proposed), it was to be altered, at least, to remove their exclusion from the Parliament's law-making power in order that the Parliament might have the power to make special laws with respect to them. To construe the resulting power in par (xxvi) as authorising the making of laws detrimental to, and discriminatory against, people on the ground of race, and specifically Aboriginal race, would be a complete denial of the clear and unanimous object of the Parliament in proposing the amendment to par (xxvi). It would amount to a refusal to acknowledge the unprecedented support for the change, evident in the vote of the electors of Australia. This Court should take notice of the history of the amendment and the circumstances surrounding it in giving meaning to the amended paragraph.

Fourthly, although the source and application of the protection from adverse discrimination on the ground of race differs in the United States of America, it is helpful to consider the approach of that country's Supreme Court to such laws. There, legislation that enacts detrimental discrimination on such grounds is considered **[414]** "constitutionally suspect" [*Bolling v Sharpe*, 347 US 497 at 499 (1954)]. Such enactments will therefore be subject to the "most rigid scrutiny" [*Korematsu v United States*, 323 US 214 at 216 (1944)], and held to be "justifiable only by the weightiest of considerations" [*Washington v Davis*, 426 US 229 at 242 (1976)]. The Court will not simply rely on the view of the relevant legislature as to the purpose or effect of the challenged law. Arguments of inconvenience and potential political embarrassment for the Court fall on deaf judicial ears in that country. It is no different in Australia although the constitutional foundations are different. This Court ... often finds itself required to make difficult decisions which have large economic, social and political consequences.

Unworkability of the "manifest abuse" test

In order to explain why the Australian Parliament could not, under the Constitution, enact racist laws such as those made in Germany during the Third Reich and in South Africa during apartheid – a result by inference accepted as totally alien to the character and meaning of our Constitution – counsel for the Commonwealth argued that it was enough that this Court retained a supervisory jurisdiction although one limited to invalidity of laws in cases where the Parliament's reliance upon par (xxvi) was a "manifest abuse" of that power. Such a test has found favour with some of the Justices in this case. As I understand the test of "manifest abuse", it is to be confined to legislation which the Court considers to be "extreme", "outrageous" or "completely unacceptable". In evaluating whether such a test is a legally viable, and therefore an acceptable, one, it is instructive to examine how, in practice, a law that has an adverse discriminatory effect may not at first appear, on its face, to constitute a "manifest abuse" or an "outrageous" exercise of the enabling power.

Take first the former laws of South Africa, which illustrate this point most clearly. The principal legislative manifestation of apartheid was the *Group Areas Act*. It categorised the population according **[415]** to racial "groups". It provided for the proclamation of "controlled areas" in *relation* to a particular group. It forbade members of other groups owning or occupying land within them. However, the legislation did not, on its face, actually differentiate between particular groups. All three groups were prohibited from acquiring land in certain areas. Yet, in effect, whilst the legislation obliged major relocation of "Bantus" and "coloureds", it had very few consequences for "whites". How could such a law, or one having similarities to it, be said to be, on its face, a "manifest abuse"? Doubtless it did have, and its equivalent would have, persuasive defenders arguing that it was open to the Parliament to deem such a special law to be necessary.

A similar conclusion could be reached in relation to other legislation enacted by the South African Parliament under apartheid. The *Prohibition of Mixed Marriages Act* (which banned marriages between "Europeans" and "non-Europeans") and the *Immorality Act* (which prohibited sexual contact between "whites" and "coloureds") applied equally to all racial groups.

Likewise, it is difficult to be sure that some of the early legislation enacted by the Third Reich would be struck down under the "manifest abuse" test. For example, the first anti-Semitic law enacted by the regime, the *Law for the Restoration of the Professional Civil Service* 1933 (Ger), provided that civil servants of "non-Aryan" descent were to be retired. Arguably, on its face, this would be insufficient to amount to a "manifest abuse". Australian **[416]** employment laws have frequently contained provisions requiring certain public servants to be Australian citizens or British subjects – most of those being of the Caucasian race. Yet in Germany this power was immediately used to dismiss thousands of Germans of the Jewish race from their posts. Such statutes, beginning with apparently innocuous provisions, laid the ground for worse to follow. They formed the precursors for more abhorrent legislation during the subsequent decade.

Laws such as those set out above would, now, be expressly forbidden by the constitutions of both Germany and South Africa. Yet, in Australia, if s 51(xxvi) of the Constitution permits all discriminatory legislation on the grounds of race excepting that which amounts to a "manifest abuse", many of the provisions which would be universally condemned as intolerably racist in character would be perfectly valid under the Commonwealth's propositions. The criterion of "manifest abuse" is inherently unstable. The experience of racist laws in Germany under the Third Reich and South Africa under apartheid was that of gradually escalating discrimination. Such has also been the experience of other places where adverse racial discrimination has been achieved with the help of the law. By the time a stage of "manifest abuse" and "outrage" is reached, courts have generally lost the capacity to influence or check such laws …

The laws of Germany and South Africa to which I have referred **[417]** provide part of the context in which par (xxvi) is now understood by Australians and should be construed by this Court. I do not accept that in late twentieth century Australia that paragraph supports detrimental and adversely discriminatory laws when the provision is read against the history of racism during this century and the 1967 referendum in Australia intended to address that history. When they voted in that referendum, the electors of this country were generally aware of that history. They knew the defects in past Australian laws and policies. And they would have known that the offensive legal regimes in Germany during the Third Reich and South Africa under apartheid were not the laws of uncivilised countries. Both in Germany and in South Africa the special laws enacted would probably have been regarded as unthinkable but a decade before they were made. They stand as a warning to us in the elaboration of our Constitution.

The purpose of the race power in the Australian Constitution, as I read it, is therefore quite different from that urged for the Commonwealth. It permits special laws for people on the grounds of their race. But not so as adversely and detrimentally to discriminate against such people on that ground.

Kirby J also relied on the "interpretive principle" which he had expounded in *Newcrest Mining (WA) Ltd v Commonwealth* (1997) 190 CLR 513: namely, that in cases of ambiguity the Constitution, like statutory enactments, should be construed in accordance with international law, and particularly with international norms declaratory of human rights (see Chapter 19, §2(c)).

The Hindmarsh Island Bridge was officially opened on 4 March 2001; but the litigious saga was not yet over. Following the Saunders Report, the developers had sued a range of defendants, including both Saunders and Tickner, for damages in respect of the delay that Tickner's 1994 declaration had caused to the bridge and marina development. They relied on various causes of action including breach of a common law duty of care; breach of statutory duty under the *Heritage Protection Act*; misfeasance in public office; and misleading or deceptive conduct within the meaning of the *Trade Practices Act 1974* (Cth). In *Chapman v Luminis Pty Ltd (No 4)* (2001) 123 FCR 62, von Doussa J held that none of these claims was sustainable. His findings also cast serious doubt on the credibility of the plaintiffs and their Ngarrindjeri supporters as witnesses. Conversely, he rejected the plaintiffs' attack on the credibility of Doreen Kartinyeri, the principal representative of the claimant group.

In reaching these conclusions, von Doussa J found it necessary to consider the plaintiffs' allegation that the Ngarrindjeri women's account of secret "women's business" was a fabrication with no authentic foundation. He conceded that debate on this issue was likely to "[177] continue amongst the anthropologists, Ngarrindjeri people and in other sections of the community, and will continue to be influenced by entrenched positions, political considerations and self interest" – to such an extent "that any further attempt by forensic process to establish the existence or non-existence of the knowledge as part of genuine Aboriginal tradition will be fraught with difficulty". He found, however, that "[181] on the evidence before this Court" he could not be satisfied that the plaintiffs "have established on the balance of probabilities that restricted women's knowledge as revealed to Dr Fergie and Professor Saunders was not part of genuine Aboriginal tradition".

Von Doussa J emphasised that the evidence before him was different from that before the South Australian Royal Commission. In order to assess the factual issues, he had ordered that evidence relating to the alleged "women's business" "[153] be received in a court closed to the [154] public and to all men, save for the Judge whose role and presence was an inevitable part of the exercise of judicial power under Chapter III of the Constitution" (see *Chapman v Luminis Pty Ltd (No 2)* (2000) 100 FCR 229). For this purpose male lawyers were excluded, and each party was represented by two female lawyers only. As a basis for the examination of Tickner – also in closed session – von Doussa J made confidential findings about the contents of the sealed envelopes, and circulated them in draft form to the parties' female counsel for the purpose of submissions thereon. His final judgment in 2001 was "[155] necessarily imprecise as to the content of the restricted women's knowledge to preserve its confidentiality", but noted that his detailed findings of fact about the contents of the sealed envelopes had been conveyed "to the female lawyers who participated in the receipt of the evidence", and "will be available to any court of appeal that considers the matter". They had "been sealed up and will be held secured in the records of the Court but will not otherwise be recorded or published".

In the *Hindmarsh Island Bridge Case*, Kirby J concluded that laws made under s 51(xxvi) with respect to "[411] the people of any race (including the Aboriginal race)" can only be for their benefit. The more subtle approach of Gaudron J might for practical purposes yield the same result, at least where Aborigines are concerned. Gummow and Hayne JJ took the opposite view, at least for cases involving the withdrawal of statutory benefits (as distinct from common law rights). Brennan CJ and McHugh J declined to consider the scope of the power at all. With the Court thus divided 2:2:2, the issue remains unresolved.

In October 2003 the Senate's Legal and Constitutional References Committee, in its report *Reconciliation: Off Track* (Parliamentary Paper No 207 of 2003), recommended that s 51(xxvi) be amended to authorise the Commonwealth Parliament "to make special laws only for the benefit of any particular race". Any amendment of that kind, however, would require a further referendum.

5. Further References

De Plevitz, L, and Croft, L, "Aboriginality under the Microscope: The Biological Descent Test in Australian Law" (2003) 3 *Queensland University of Technology Law and Justice Journal* 104.

Dubler, R, "Race and the Constitution" (2002) 76 *Australian Law Journal* 456.

French, R, "The Race Power: A Constitutional Chimera" in Lee, HP, and Winterton, G (eds), *Australian Constitutional Landmarks* (Cambridge University Press, 2003), 180.

Lindell, G, "The Corporations and Races Powers" (1984) 14 *Federal Law Review* 219.

Malbon, J, "Avoiding the *Hindmarsh Island Bridge* Disaster: Interpreting the Race Power" (2002) 6 *Flinders Journal of Law Reform* 44.

Malbon, J, "The Race Power under the Australian Constitution: Altered Meanings" (1999) 21 *Sydney Law Review* 80.

McCorquodale, J, "The Legal Classification of Race in Australia" (1986) 10 *Aboriginal History* 7.

Reilly, A, "Reading the Race Power: A Hermeneutic Analysis" (1999) 23 *Melbourne University Law Review* 476.

Williams, G, "Race and the Australian Constitution: From Federation to Reconciliation" (2000) 38 *Osgoode Hall Law Journal* 643.

Williams, G, Gageler, S, and Lindell, G, "October Symposium: The Races Power" (1998) 9 *Public Law Review* 265.

Williams, J, and Bradsen, J, "The Perils of Inclusion: The Constitution and the Race Power" (1997) 19 *Adelaide Law Review* 95.

Chapter 22

The Industrial Relations Power

1. Introduction

Section 51(xxxv) of the Constitution gives the Commonwealth a limited power to regulate industrial relations. The power extends only to the techniques ("conciliation and arbitration") and only to the industrial disputes ("extending beyond the limits of any one State") to which the grant of power refers. These restrictions have meant that both Labor and Coalition governments have also turned to other powers in s 51 to regulate industrial relations. Indeed, the century-old scheme based upon s 51(xxxv) has now largely been displaced by the *Workplace Relations Amendment (Work Choices) Act 2005* (Cth). That Act, which relies primarily on the Commonwealth's corporations power (s 51(xx)), brings about a single national system of workplace relations law that includes an Australian Fair Pay Commission and the prescription of minimum working conditions by legislation.

Another important source of power is s 51(xxxvii), which gives the Commonwealth power in respect of matters referred to the Commonwealth by the Parliament of any State. Under the *Commonwealth Powers (Industrial Relations) Act 1996* (Vic), the Victorian Parliament conferred on the Commonwealth wide-ranging powers over industrial relations within Victoria. This Act makes the need for the Commonwealth to rely upon s 51(xxxv), or indeed upon any other s 51 power, within that State otiose.

The centrepiece of Commonwealth legislation under s 51(xxxv) had been the creation of bodies to undertake the task of "conciliation and arbitration". The Commonwealth Court of Conciliation and Arbitration was established by the *Commonwealth Conciliation and Arbitration Act 1904* (Cth). Originally, the Court had only one judge – a "President". The Act provided that this was to be a justice of the High Court, initially O'Connor J. Higgins J became President in September 1907, and it was under his aegis that the Court assumed its distinctive role in Australian industrial relations. The pattern was set by his famous "Harvester judgment" (*Ex parte HV McKay* (1907) 2 CAR 1), in which he introduced the concept of the "**[4]** minimum wage". The nexus with the High Court was broken in 1926, when a Chief Judge was appointed in place of the President and two additional judges were created. Thereafter, the powers conferred on the Court were frequently amended. In 1928, for example, the Nationalist government led by Stanley Bruce made major extensions to the Court's "penal" powers; and in 1929 it tried unsuccessfully to abolish the Court altogether.

In 1956 the High Court decided by 4:3 in *R v Kirby; Ex parte Boilermakers' Society of Australia* (*Boilermakers' Case*) (1956) 94 CLR 254 that the Court of Conciliation and Arbitration was invalidly constituted, on the ground that judicial and non-judicial power were impermissibly combined in the same tribunal. The Privy Council affirmed the decision in *Attorney-General (Cth) v The Queen* [1957] AC 288 (see Chapter 14, §1). In response, the Menzies government amended the *Conciliation and Arbitration Act* to effect a severance of judicial and non-judicial functions. The powers of conciliation and arbitration were vested in a Conciliation and Arbitration *Commission* (with its "presidential members" still entitled to judicial status, title and security of tenure), while the judicial powers were vested in a new Commonwealth Industrial *Court*.

In 1977 the Industrial Court was absorbed into the newly created Federal Court of Australia. In 1985 the Hancock Report (*Report of the Committee of Review into Australian Industrial Relations Law and Systems* (1985)) recommended the reestablishment of a separate Australian Labour Court. The Court was not to be reintegrated with the Commission, but their judges were to have joint commissions. A first attempt to implement the Hancock Report (the Industrial Relations Bill 1987 (Cth)) was withdrawn before the 1987 election, while the modified version finally enacted (the *Industrial Relations Act 1988* (Cth)) omitted the new Labour Court. However, under the *Industrial Relations Reform Act 1993* (Cth) a new Industrial Relations Court of Australia was created to replace the Industrial Division of the Federal Court. Meanwhile, the 1988 Act had abolished the old Conciliation and Arbitration Commission, and substituted a new Industrial Relations Commission. With one exception, Justice JF Staples, all members of the old Commission were automatically appointed to the new one. The new title given to the Commission reflected the new title of the Act, and both reflected a shift away from the earlier focus on "conciliation and arbitration".

In 1996, the federal Parliament substantially amended the *Industrial Relations Act*, and the Act was re-titled, this time as the *Workplace Relations Act 1996* (Cth). The work of the Industrial Relations Court was returned to the Federal Court, where it had resided before 1993. By further amendments in 2005, an extensive jurisdiction was vested also in the Federal Magistrates Court.

2. The Industrial Relationship

In the early years, especially when Higgins J was President of the Commonwealth Court of Conciliation and Arbitration, constitutional issues often arose in the form of questions stated by him for the opinion of the High Court. (In *Federated Saw Mill &c Employes of Australasia v James Moore & Son Proprietary Ltd* (*Woodworkers' Case*) (1909) 8 CLR 465 at 485, Griffith CJ's response was an acerbic complaint that the questions ought not to have been submitted to the High Court at all!) In modern times such issues have reached the High Court more usually by application for a writ of prohibition under s 75(v) of the Constitution. The argument is that the Commission has exceeded its jurisdiction, or is proposing to do so.

Not all such applications raise constitutional issues. The party seeking prohibition may wish to claim that the Commission is exceeding its *statutory* powers. The constitutional cases are those where it is argued that particular proceedings in the Commission, or particular provisions in the Act, exceed the Commonwealth's *constitutional* powers.

Constitutional power under s 51(xxxv) is confined to the prevention and settlement of *industrial* disputes. The argument that a dispute is not "industrial" can arise in two different ways. It may be argued that the relationship between the parties is not an industrial *relationship*, or that the subject of the dispute is not an industrial *matter*. These arguments may overlap. From 1929 onwards the High Court insisted that to have an industrial relationship the disputant employers and employees must be engaged in an "industry". Initially, this requirement had been construed broadly. From 1920 onwards it was construed increasingly narrowly; but in 1983 the initial broad approach was restored to favour.

The initial broad approach to the meaning of "industrial disputes" was proclaimed in *Jumbunna Coal Mine NL v Victorian Coal Miners' Association* (1908) 6 CLR 309. It was prompted by an argument that the phrase "industrial disputes" as used in the Constitution should be confined to disputes relating to the production or manufacture of goods, and hence that the definition of the word "industry" in the *Conciliation and Arbitration Act* was too wide – since it would extend, for example, to cooks, stewards, waiters and hairdressers. In finding that the words used in s 51(xxxv) "**[367]** are large enough to cover all of them", O'Connor J stated: "It was to remedy the evils of industrial disturbances extending beyond the territorial limits of any one State that the power in question was conferred. It must have been well known to the framers of the Constitution that such disturbances are not confined to industries connected directly or indirectly with manufacture or production".

Most of the early cases on "implied immunities" of government instrumentalities, as well as the overthrow of that doctrine in *Amalgamated Society of Engineers v Adelaide Steamship Co Ltd* (*Engineers' Case*) (1920) 28 CLR 129, were reflections of an ongoing struggle over the powers of the Commonwealth Court of Conciliation and Arbitration. In *Federated Amalgamated Government Railway and Tramway Service Association v New South Wales Railway Traffic Employes Association* (*Railway Servants' Case*) (1906) 4 CLR 488, the "immunities" doctrine had been used to insulate State government agencies, in their capacity as employers, from the operation of the Commonwealth arbitration system. This was the aspect of the "immunities" doctrine which Higgins and Isaacs JJ, from 1906 onwards, were most determined to oppose. Even before the *Engineers' Case*, their efforts had steadily extended the access of State employees to federal arbitration. If the early cases such as *Railway Servants* reflected the tendency of judges like Griffith CJ to limit the effective powers and functions of the Commonwealth arbitration system, the later cases (and above all *Engineers*) reflected the tendency of judges like Isaacs J to extend those powers. Indeed, it is sometimes said that the overthrow of the "immunities" doctrine arose from the determination of Isaacs J to maximise the impact of the Commonwealth arbitration system. (The same can be said of the doctrinal developments relating to s 109 of the Constitution, and especially the "cover the field" test.)

A somewhat different reading of the history was suggested by the unanimous judgment in *R v Coldham; Ex parte Australian Social Welfare Union* (*CYSS Case*) (1983) 153 CLR 297. The Court suggested that the extension of the Commonwealth system to State government employees had indeed been a serious problem. The "immunities" doctrine had provided a mechanism through which the problem could be managed; but once that doctrine was abolished, a different solution was needed, and the gradual narrowing thereafter of the judicial concept of "industry" was a direct response to this need. Indeed, the *CYSS* judgment suggested that this narrower approach to "industry" had already begun to appear in *Federated Municipal and Shire Council Employees' Union of Australia v Melbourne Corporation* (*Municipalities Case*) (1919) 26 CLR 508. In that case, the employers, the municipal corporations, had argued that the Arbitration Court had no jurisdiction because "the making, maintenance, control and lighting of public streets" did not constitute part of an "industry". The two dissenting judges, Barton and Gavan Duffy JJ, accepted that argument. Higgins and Powers JJ rejected it, as did the joint judgment of Isaacs and Rich JJ. Isaacs and Rich JJ denied that "industrial disputes" could be limited to operations carried on for profit or involving manual labour.

Federated Municipal and Shire Council Employees' Union of Australia v Melbourne Corporation (*Municipalities Case*)
(1919) 26 CLR 508

Isaacs and Rich JJ: [554] Industrial disputes occur when, in relation to operations in which capital and labour are contributed in co-operation for the satisfaction of human wants or desires, those engaged in co-operation dispute as to the basis to be observed, by the parties engaged, respecting either a share of the product or any other terms and conditions of their co-operation. This formula excludes the two extreme contentions of the claimant and the respondents respectively. It excludes, for instance, the legal and the medical professions, because they are not carried on in any intelligible sense by the co-operation of capital and labour and do **[555]** not come within the sphere of industrialism. It includes, where the necessary co-operation exists, disputes between employers and employees, employees and employees, and employers and employers. It implies that "industry," to lead to an industrial dispute, is not, as the claimant contends, merely industry in the abstract sense, as if it alone effected the result, but it must be acting and be considered in association with its co-operator "capital" in some form so that the result is, in a sense, the outcome of their combined efforts. It also implies that "an industry," in the relevant sense, is not confined to a single enterprise, but means a class of operations in which all persons, employers and employees, are engaged on the same field of industry – not necessarily of commerce – provided by the society in which they exist.

This paragraph was clearly intended to offer a broad, expansive approach to the concept of "industry", and hence to that of "industrial disputes". However, the *CYSS Case* suggests that in fact this approach turned out to lay the foundation for a narrower view of these concepts.

In *Australian Insurance Staffs' Federation v Accident Underwriters' Association* (*Insurance Staffs' Case*) (1923) 33 CLR 517 it was held that claims by employees of banks and insurance companies gave rise to "industrial disputes". Knox CJ and Gavan Duffy J, in dissent, treated "industry" as limited to "[523] undertakings carried on for the purpose of gain and wholly or mainly by means of manual labour". The rest of the Court rejected these limits, again clearly intending to lay down a broad view of "industrial disputes". Isaacs and Rich JJ repeated their formula from the *Municipalities Case*, and proceeded to elaborate upon it.

Australian Insurance Staffs' Federation v Accident Underwriters' Association (*Insurance Staffs' Case*)
(1923) 33 CLR 517

Isaacs and Rich JJ: [527] The second contention involves the essential nature of the business of banks and insurance companies in relation to industrial operations. There can, no doubt, be found in accredited works on finance and politics, references both to banking and insurance as departments of industry. These references are certainly of some force as indicating that the expression "industrial disputes" applied to those cases is not so inapt as the respondents' argument would suggest. But we rest upon the inherent fact of the nature of the part that banking and insurance both play in the scheme of national industrial activity. They are indispensable portions of the general industrial mechanism. Without the aid of the capital and credit furnished by bankers the present system of industrial organization would collapse. They directly furnish an essential instrument of production. Insurance companies increase the productivity of capital actually employed in industry by diminishing the uncertainty of its continuance. Unexpected losses are replaced, the risk of these being transferred to the accumulated fund that the insurance business provides. Banks and insurance companies alike, though in varying circumstances, provide for industry one essential commodity – capital; and without them modern industrial operations would be impossible. They perform their services to industry in many ways, adapting their assistance to the protean needs of society. We are utterly unable to sever legally what the hard facts of life have so closely united, and, therefore, conclude that the disputes now referred to us answer the description of "industrial disputes" within the meaning of the Constitution.

In later years, when a narrower view of "industry" became established, this passage made it possible to explain the *Insurance Staffs' Case* on the basis that the businesses of banking and insurance, though not themselves part of "industry", were within the scope of s 51(xxxv) as ancillary or incidental to industry.

The decisive turning point was *Federated State School Teachers' Association of Australia v Victoria* (*School Teachers' Case*) (1929) 41 CLR 569, where Knox CJ, Gavan Duffy and Starke JJ held that teachers in State government schools were not engaged in an "industry" and hence could not be parties to an "industrial dispute". Rich J concurred, applying his earlier joint judgments with Isaacs J to conclude that "[591] the relation of the State to its teachers does not include the important element ... [of] capital and labour co-operating to produce a result which is the outcome of their combined efforts". Only Isaacs J dissented.

Federated State School Teachers' Association of Australia v Victoria
(*School Teachers' Case*)
(1929) 41 CLR 569

Knox CJ, Gavan Duffy and Starke JJ: [573] Economists, notably Mr *JA Hobson* (*The Industrial System*), say that a scientific interpretation requires us to include in the word "industry" processes which are concerned with services **[574]** such as the administrative services of public officials and the skilled professional advice of doctors and lawyers. But the Constitution is not a thesis upon economics. It is an instrument of Government, dealing, in sec 51 pl XXXV, with a subject matter – industrial disputes – in the ordinary and popular acceptation of that term ...

The economic view has never been accepted by this Court: it is too wide. That confining the description of the ph[r]ases to operations carried on by manual labourers is rejected as too narrow (*Insurance Staffs' Case* [(1923) 33 CLR 517]). And the view that the sphere of industrialism is to be found in operations in which the relation of employer and employee subsists is also, in our opinion, too wide: it approaches the economic view, and would bring within the range of the industrial power of the Commonwealth services of all kinds whatever. It cannot, we think, be supported, for it ignores the use of the words "industrial" in the composite expression "industrial dispute" in the Constitution.

[575] Testing this case, therefore, by the other suggested criteria or badges of industrialism, can it be said that the educational activities of the States constitute an industry? So far as the matter is one of fact, we would say that they cannot. They bear no resemblance whatever to an ordinary trade, business or industry. They are not connected directly with, or attendant upon, the production or distribution of wealth; and there is no co-operation of capital and labour, in any relevant sense, for a great public scheme of education is forced upon the communities of the States by law. It was said that if the activities were carried on by a private person, such as a schoolmaster, then the operations would be described as a business, a trade, or an industry. Shortly, that argument is met by the fact that a private person could no more carry on this system of public education than he could carry on His Majesty's Treasury or any of the other executive departments of Government; and if he were authorized to do so, which is almost inconceivable, then he would no more carry on an industry than the State does now.

Isaacs J: [577] The contention sounds like an echo from the dark ages of industry and political economy. It not merely ignores the constant currents of life around us, which is the real danger in deciding questions of this nature, but it also forgets the memorable industrial organization of the nations, not for the production or distribution of material wealth, but for service, national service, as the service of organized industry must always be. Examination of this contention will not only completely dissipate it, but will also serve to throw material light on the question in hand generally. The contention is radically unsound for two great reasons. It erroneously conceives the object of national industrial organization and thereby unduly limits the meaning of the terms "production" and "wealth" when used in that connection. But it further neglects the fundamental character of "industrial disputes" as a distinct and insistent phenomenon of modern society. Such disputes are not simply a claim to share the material wealth jointly produced and capable of registration in statistics. At heart they are a struggle, constantly becoming more intense on the part of the employed group engaged in co-operation **[578]** with the employing group in rendering services to the community essential for a higher general human welfare, to share in that welfare in a greater degree. (See, for instance, Lord *Askwith's* work on *Industrial Problems and Disputes*, at p 25.) All industrial enterprises contribute more or less to the general welfare of the community, and this is a most material consideration when we come to determine the present question apart from the particular contention raised at the Bar.

That contention, if acceded to, would be revolutionary. Some of the industries up to the present recognized as legitimately within the ambit of the Constitution, would have to be regarded as outside its limits; for instance, musicians and actors and tramway employees, pilots of ships, street lighters and cinema operators. How could it reasonably be said that a comic song or a jazz performance, or the representation of a comedy, or a ride in a tramcar or motor-bus, piloting a ship, lighting a lamp or showing a moving picture is more "material" as wealth than instruction, either cultural or vocational? Indeed, to take one instance, a workman who travels in a tramcar a mile from his home to his factory is no more efficient for his daily task than if he walked ten yards, whereas his technical training has a direct effect in increasing output. If music or acting or personal transportation is admitted to be "industrial" because each is productive of wealth to the employer as his business undertaking, then an educational establishment stands on the same footing. But if education is excluded for the reason advanced, how are we to admit barbers, hairdressers, taxi-cab drivers, furniture removers, and other occupations that readily suggest themselves? And yet the doctrine would admit manufacturers of intoxicants and producers of degrading literature and pictures, because these are considered to be "wealth." The doctrine would concede, for instance, that establishments for the training of performing dogs, or of monkeys simulating human behaviour, would be "industrial," because one would have increased material wealth, that is, a more valuable dog or monkey, in the sense that one could exchange it for more money. If parrots are taught to say "Pretty Polly" and to dance on their perch, that is, by concession, industrial, because it is the production of wealth. But if Australian youths are trained to read and write **[579]** their language correctly and in other necessary elements of culture and vocation making them more efficient citizens, fitting them with more or less directness to take their place in the general industrial ranks of the nation and to render the services required by the community, that training is said not to be wealth and the work done by teachers employed is said not to be industrial. The consequence, it is said, is that employment in the service rendered to the community by education is not one which can give rise to Commonwealth arbitration. That is certainly not my view and is legally, economically and historically opposed to a vast and formidable array of recorded opinion.

In *R v Commonwealth Court of Conciliation and Arbitration; Ex parte Victoria* (*Public Service Case*) (1942) 66 CLR 488, it was held that Victorian State public servants were not engaged in an "industry". The case involved manual workers as well as clerical and professional employees in government departments. The case arose under the *National Security (Industrial Peace) Regulations* (Cth), but the terms used in the Regulations were expressed to have the same meaning as in the *Conciliation and Arbitration Act*. Latham CJ at 502 quoted the dissent of Isaacs J in the *School Teachers' Case*: even in dissent, Isaacs J had conceded that "**[584]** Crown officials engaged in administering true, essential governmental authority" would not come within s 51(xxxv). McTiernan J at 520 quoted what Griffith CJ had said in *Jumbunna Coal* ("**[333]** the term 'industry' should be construed as including all forms of employment"); but explained that, of course, Griffith CJ had only meant industrial forms of employment. In *R v Commonwealth Court of Conciliation and Arbitration; Ex parte Victoria* (1944) 68 CLR 485, the restrictive view of the word "industry" in the *Public Service Case* was applied to the use of the word in the *Women's Employment Regulations* (Cth) (see Chapter 18, §2).

In 1959 a somewhat wider view was taken in *R v President of Commonwealth Conciliation and Arbitration Commission; Ex parte Professional Engineers Association* (1959) 107 CLR 208, where it was held that the employment of engineers was not excluded from the scope of "industrial disputes" by the fact that the employer was a State department or agency. The attempt to exclude State governmental functions from the ambit of "industrial disputes" altogether was seen as a revival of notions rejected in the *Engineers' Case*.

R v President of the Commonwealth Conciliation and Arbitration Commission; Ex parte Professional Engineers' Association
(1959) 107 CLR 208

Windeyer J: [272] Counsel for the States started with the proposition that disputes are either industrial or not industrial. That is logically incontestable; and, as was said by counsel in *Repton v Hodgson* [(1850) 3 HLC 72 at 79-80; 10 ER 28 at 31] in a sentence which *Jordan* CJ brought to light in an essay, "Like Sinclair's well-known division of sleeping into two sorts, namely, sleeping with or sleeping without a nightcap, it would seem to exhaust the subject". But the presence or absence of the quality "industrial" in a dispute is not as indisputably apparent as the presence or absence of a nightcap on a sleeper. And to collect a miscellany of diverse elements referred to in different judgments as characteristics of industrialism, and treat them all as either collectively or individually significant, so that the presence or absence of one may be decisive is, in my view, fallacious. It can lead to a sophistic sorites. It was, however, contended that these difficulties were surmounted by treating the occupation of the employer as the cardinal factor. Then it was said that, as government is not industry, a complete antithesis exists between activities which are governmental and those which are industrial. Our task it was then suggested was, in counsel's words, to see in each case "whether the particular activity can truly be said to be governmental or industrial". Thus, instead of being asked to say whether a particular project, enterprise or undertaking in which engineers were employed was by reason of its nature one in which an industrial dispute could occur, we were asked to consider whether it was or was not a governmental project, enterprise or undertaking. What for the purposes of this argument was meant by "governmental" was stated only in broad generalities such as "government organization for solving a communal problem", and whether as a way of dealing with "a communal need" it was "akin to the ordinary departments of state". It was also said that whether any activity was industrial or governmental was to be determined by seeing whether it was "more akin to the type-specimen government or the type-specimen industry". This last phraseology was apparently derived from remarks of *Latham* CJ in his judgment in the *Victorian Public Servants' Case* [(1942) 66 CLR 488 at 501]. It may, no doubt, sometimes be helpful, to adopt for the social sciences this method of classification, familiar in natural history; but it can only be satisfactory if the type-specimens with which comparisons are to be made are postulated, and their relevant attributes so ascertained that in making [273] comparisons *propria* can be distinguished from *accidentia*. If not, the result is a mere logomachy. But the dialectical difficulties of following the path suggested can, I think, be disregarded, for the simple reason that it seems to me that here it is the wrong path. The question is not to be solved by asking is a particular activity governmental; because, for the matter in hand, the assumed complete antithesis between industrial and governmental activities does not exist … The States' argument drove them to contend that workers in, at all events some, nationalized industries – electricity supply was given as an illustration – were incapable of being disputants in an industrial dispute. Yet they had to concede that immediately before the particular undertaking was taken over by the State, the same workers had been engaged in industry. If at the actual time of the take-over a dispute was in progress at the works it would [274] apparently have begun as an industrial dispute but become translated. This and other extravagant illustrations only expose the fundamental fallacy. A nationalized industry is clearly a government undertaking, but it is still an industry …

[276] We heard some muffled echoes of old arguments. But we cannot open our ears to them. Doctrines discarded by the decision in the *Engineers' Case* [(1920) 28 CLR 129] cannot be revived to defeat the claim of these latter-day engineers. The effect of the *Engineers' Case* in relation to some of these matters has been stated by *Dixon* J, as he then was, in *West v Commissioner of Taxation (NSW)* [(1937) 56 CLR 657 at 681] and in the *Essendon Corporation Case* [(1947) 74 CLR 1 at 19-22]. There is nothing in these cases or in the *Victorian Public Servants' Case* which, as I read the judgments, curtails in any way the rule that the power under par (xxxv) applies to industrial disputes to which a State is a party.

However, any relaxation was short-lived. In *Pitfield v Franki* (1970) 123 CLR 448 the Court held by 4:1, with Walsh J dissenting, that fire fighting was not an "industry". Perhaps this was a catalyst, for from that point onwards members of the Court began increasingly to question such decisions. In 1975 in *R v Marshall; Ex parte Federated Clerks Union of Australia* (1975) 132 CLR 595 the Court held by 4:1, McTiernan J dissenting, that credit unions were an "industry", and thus that their employees were eligible for membership of a registered union. Mason J went further, saying: "[608] My own inclination would be to adopt a somewhat wider view, more akin to the opinions expressed by Griffith CJ and O'Connor J in the *Jumbunna Coal Mine Case* [(1908) 6 CLR 309], as appropriate to the nature and scope of the power [609] and the underlying purpose which it was designed to achieve, although I acknowledge that a more restricted view has thus far prevailed".

Despite such encouraging dicta, when the Association of Australian University Staff sought registration under the *Conciliation and Arbitration Act*, they did so not by a direct challenge to the *School Teachers' Case*, but by arguing that they came within the exception established by the

AUSTRALIAN CONSTITUTIONAL LAW AND THEORY

Insurance Staffs' Case: that is, that the work of universities was "ancillary or incidental to industry". In *R v McMahon; Ex parte Darvall* (1982) 151 CLR 57, the Court indignantly rejected that suggestion as giving (in the words of Gibbs CJ) "**[62]** a completely distorted picture of the functions of the universities", although Gibbs CJ also stated: "**[63]** In *R v Holmes; Ex parte Public Service Association (NSW)* [(1977) 140 CLR 63 at 74], I said that the reasons given by O'Connor J in *Jumbunna Coal Mine NL v Victorian Coal Miners' Association* [(1908) 6 CLR 309] appeared to me convincing. Since no attempt was made in the present case to argue that the views of Griffith CJ and O'Connor J in that case should be treated as correct, notwithstanding their rejection in later cases, it is unnecessary to consider whether, if their reasons had been adopted, a different result would have been reached in the present case".

In the *CYSS Case*, a unanimous seven-judge Court announced a return to the *Jumbunna* approach. The Community Youth Support Scheme (CYSS) had been established by the Fraser government in 1976 to provide "appropriate activities to help unemployed young people maintain their morale and orientation towards work". It was not a job-creation scheme, but a program of support and job-skills development for unemployed young people, operating in each State through State, Electorate and Local Committees. The Local Committees employed "project officers" to carry out the scheme's objects. The Australian Social Welfare Union served a log of claims on the Local Committees relating to the pay and conditions of "project officers". The Full Bench of the Conciliation and Arbitration Commission held, by majority, that there was no "industrial dispute" because CYSS was not an "industry". The Social Welfare Union brought an action in the High Court to quash this finding. In a single joint judgment the Court concluded that the claims by the "project officers" did give rise to an "industrial dispute".

R v Coldham; Ex parte Australian Social Welfare Union (*CYSS Case*)
(1983) 153 CLR 297

The Court: [304] As the decision in *Federated Amalgamated Government Railway and Tramway Service Association v New South Wales Railway Traffic Employés Association* ("the *Railway Servants' Case*") [(1906) 4 CLR 488] indicated, and as subsequent developments would demonstrate, the early interpretation of s 51(xxxv) was dominated by a continuing political and legal controversy arising from federal-State conflicts. A, if not the, focal point of that controversy was the question whether the power conferred by s 51(xxxv) enabled the Commonwealth to confer jurisdiction on the Commonwealth Court of Conciliation and Arbitration ("the Arbitration Court") to settle disputes between State instrumentalities or statutory authorities and their employees. The *Railway Servants' Case* answered that question in the negative, applying the doctrine of intergovernmental immunities to State railway authorities. The effect of the doctrine before *Amalgamated Society of Engineers v Adelaide Steamship Co Ltd* ("the *Engineers' Case*") [(1920) 28 CLR 129] made it inevitable in cases affecting State instrumentalities and authorities that the meaning of the expression "industrial dispute" … was of secondary importance … The Court was more concerned with the nature and extent of the restrictions **[305]** imposed by the doctrine than with the scope of the legislative power …

[306] There was no major obstacle to the acceptance of an interpretation of the arbitration power in accordance with that favoured by Griffith CJ or O'Connor J in *Jumbunna* [(1908) 6 CLR 309], so long as the Court held firmly to the doctrine of intergovernmental immunities. If, however, the Court were to abandon that doctrine, as it did in the *Engineers' Case*, then a broad interpretation of the power would expose once again the problem posed by the possible exercise of jurisdiction by the Arbitration Court over State instrumentalities or authorities and their employees.

Federated Municipal and Shire Council Employees' Union of Australia v Melbourne Corporation ("the *Municipalities' Case*") [(1919) 26 CLR 508] **[307]** was a harbinger of things to come. The importance of the immunities doctrine to the interpretation of the arbitration power was recognized by the division of the hearing into two stages. By majority (Isaacs, Higgins, Gavan Duffy, Powers and Rich JJ, with Griffith CJ and Barton J dissenting) the Court held that municipalities established under State laws were not State government instrumentalities in relation to the making, maintenance, control or lighting of public streets. The judgments of the majority contain strong indications that the doctrine might have no application in Australia at all, but that question remained to be decided by the *Engineers' Case* ...

The joint judgment of Isaacs and Rich JJ, which involved a retreat on the part of Isaacs J from the position which he occupied in *Jumbunna*, was to influence the future course of decisions. According to their Honours industrial disputes can only occur in an industry in which capital and labour co-operate to provide goods or services for the community ...

[308] Thus, notwithstanding Isaacs J's comment in *Jumbunna*, the approach of Isaacs and Rich JJ necessarily involved a search for a dispute in an industry ...

The doctrine of intergovernmental immunities was overthrown in the *Engineers' Case* where it was decided that a dispute between an organization of employees and a Minister of the Crown for a State acting under the authority of a State statute as an employer in the conduct of a trading enterprise was an "industrial dispute" within s 51(xxxv). The *Railway Servants' Case* was overruled. The new development opened the way to the exercise by the Arbitration Court of jurisdiction over disputes between State instrumentalities and their servants ...

[309] The limits of the power, according to the interpretations which began to find favour in the *Municipalities' Case*, were revealed in *Federated State School Teachers' Association of Australia v Victoria* ("the *Schoolteachers' Case*") [(1929) 41 CLR 569]. The majority of the Court decided that State schoolteachers were not engaged in industry. Isaacs J alone dissented, though adhering to the joint judgments in which he had participated in the *Municipalities' Case* and the *Insurance Staffs' Case*.

The main judgment in the *Schoolteachers' Case* was that of Knox CJ, Gavan Duffy and Starke JJ. Rich J, who was also in the majority, delivered a separate judgment. The decision in the case was the first to involve a clear rejection of the wide views which had been expressed by members of the Court in *Jumbunna*. There is no indication in the majority judgment in the *Schoolteachers' Case* of any chain of reasoning which leads to that rejection. The closest approximation to a reason for rejecting the view that, in accordance with the ordinary meaning of the phrase, "industrial disputes" in s 51(xxxv) "includes, at all events, a dispute between employer and employee as to their reciprocal [*sic*] rights and duties" (the *Municipalities' Case*, per Higgins J [26 CLR at 575]) is the statement in the joint judgment of Knox CJ, Gavan Duffy and Starke JJ [41 CLR at 574] that "the view that the sphere of industrialism is to be found in operations in which the relation of employer and employee subsists ... cannot ... be supported, for it ignores the use of the word 'industrial' in the composite expression 'industrial dispute' in the Constitution".

[310] That statement is plainly per incuriam in that the view which their Honours were rejecting, far from ignoring the word "industrial", relied upon the word to define the composite expression "industrial disputes" in the sphere of relations between employers and employees.

It is evident from the judgments in the *Professional Engineers' Case*, particularly those of Dixon CJ and Taylor J [(1959) 107 CLR 208 at 235-7, 258-61], that their Honours regarded the judgments in the *Schoolteachers' Case* with rather less than complete satisfaction. And in more recent decisions members of this Court have indicated a willingness to reconsider a return to a broader interpretation of the constitutional power, more in line with that favoured by Griffith CJ and O'Connor J in *Jumbunna* ...

The absence of a disclosed chain of reasoning leading to a rejection of the broader view is but one of several powerful reasons why we should now embark upon that reconsideration. Another is that the course of judicial exposition of s 51(xxxv) has not resulted in a settled interpretation of the power. True it is that the judgments in the *Professional Engineers' Case*, proceeding from an acceptance of the correctness of the decision in the *Schoolteachers' Case*, reflected a view of s 51(xxxv) which was uniform, or substantially so ... In the *Professional Engineers' Case* the Court was not asked to reconsider the *Schoolteachers' Case* or to discard it in favour of the *Jumbunna* interpretation. Indeed, the correctness of the *Schoolteachers' Case* was common ground between the parties, each side seeking to use the decision to its advantage. In the result the Court was able to distinguish the professional engineers from the school-[311]-teachers. As has so often been the case, the judgments were directed to the resolution of a particular facet of an old problem – a dispute between a State and its engineers. It has, of course, been explicitly or implicitly acknowledged from time to time that the *Schoolteachers' Case* is not consistent with the *Jumbunna* interpretation in all its generality (*R v Commonwealth Court of Conciliation and Arbitration; Ex parte Victoria* ("the *State Public Servants' Case*") [(1942) 66 CLR 488]; *Pitfield v Franki* [(1970) 123 CLR 448 at 455]; *Holmes* [(1977) 140 CLR 63 at 74)]. For the most part these cases, like the *Schoolteachers' Case* and the *Professional Engineers' Case*, related to a dispute between a State or State authority and its servants with the attendant difficulties which disputes of this kind bring in their train. In that area the *Schoolteachers' Case* has occupied a central place in the reasoning in a number of cases since it was decided. However, in our opinion that is not a sound reason for refusing to re-examine the basic interpretation of the constitutional power.

We have already noted that before the *Engineers' Case* the scope and extent of the power was a secondary question, subsidiary in importance to the doctrine of intergovernmental immunity. Since the *Engineers' Case* the interpretation of s 51(xxxv) has been dominated by the continuing problems which have arisen in association with disputes between States and State authorities and their employees. The rejection of the doctrine of intergovernmental immunity did not result in the acceptance of the broad interpretation which had previously prevailed in *Jumbunna*. Instead, it resulted in an apparent contraction of the power as members of the Court based their exclusion of disputes involving certain categories of State employees on different interpretations of the term "industrial disputes". The interaction between the abandonment of the doctrine and the contraction of the power is best seen in the *Municipalities' Case* and Isaacs J's change of heart between *Jumbunna* and the *Municipalities' Case*.

The final factor, yet to be elaborated, which calls for reconsideration is the superior attraction, both in point of legal reasoning and in consequence, of the broad interpretation of the provision over the later versions, especially that of Isaacs and Rich JJ in the *Municipalities' Case* and the *Insurance Staffs' Case*. In this respect, a remarkable feature of the judgments in the two last mentioned cases – as in the *Schoolteachers' Case* – is the absence of discussion of the *Jumbunna* interpretation and of the reasons for departing from **[312]** it …

The correct approach to the construction of the expression "industrial disputes" in s 51(xxxv) was, we think, expressed by Higgins J in the *Municipalities' Case* [26 CLR at 572-5] and the *Insurance Staffs' Case* [33 CLR at 528-30], reflecting the view earlier expressed by O'Connor J in *Jumbunna* shorn of its association with the doctrine of intergovernmental immunities. The words are not a technical or legal expression. They have to be given their popular meaning – what they convey to the man in the street. And that is essentially a question of fact. That the expression is "industrial disputes", not "disputes in an industry", as Higgins J noted, makes quite inexplicable the emphasis given in the later cases to limitations on the power derived from the meaning of the word "industry". Perhaps this development is to be explained, though not justified, by the amendment made to the Act in 1911 which defined the word "industry" in terms of the undertaking of the employer and the calling, service, employment or industrial occupation of the employee. It may be that the framework of the Act played some part in shaping the interpretation of the constitutional power, although as early as *Jumbunna* Isaacs J, who with Rich J was to base his later interpretation on the concepts of "industry" and "industrialism", had been quick to perceive that the Act might possibly contemplate a narrower notion of "industrial disputes" than that envisaged by s 51(xxxv). An alternative explanation is that it was apprehended that, unless some such limitation based on "industry" was introduced, the category of "industrial disputes" might be unlimited. If there was such an apprehension, it was a misapprehension. The content of the popular understanding of the composite expression sets the limits on the category.

It is, we think, beyond question that the popular meaning of "industrial disputes" includes disputes between employees and employers about the terms of employment and the conditions of work. Experience shows that disputes of this kind may lead to industrial action involving disruption or reduction in the supply of goods or services to the community. We reject any notion that the adjective "industrial" imports some restriction which confines the constitutional conception of "industrial disputes" to disputes in productive industry and organized business carried on for the purpose of making profits. The popular meaning of the expression no doubt extends more widely to embrace disputes between parties **[313]** other than employer and employee, such as demarcation disputes, but just how widely it may extend is not a matter of present concern.

It is also unnecessary to consider whether or not disputes between a State or a State authority and employees engaged in the administrative services of the State are capable of falling within the constitutional conception. It has been generally accepted, notwithstanding the *Engineers' Case*, that the power conferred by s 51(xxxv) is inapplicable to the administrative services of the States (see the *Professional Engineers' Case* [107 CLR at 233]). If the reasons hitherto given for reaching that conclusion are no longer fully acceptable, it may be that the conclusion itself finds support in the prefatory words of s 51 where the power is made "subject to this Constitution" (cf *Holmes* 140 CLR at 90]). The implications which are necessarily drawn from the federal structure of the Constitution itself impose certain limitations on the legislative power of the Commonwealth to enact laws which affect the States (and vice versa). The nature of those limitations was discussed in *Melbourne Corporation v Commonwealth* [(1947) 74 CLR 31], *Victoria v Commonwealth* ("the *Pay-roll Tax Case*") [(1971) 122 CLR 353], and the other cases there cited. If at least some of the views expressed in those cases are accepted, a Commonwealth law which permitted an instrumentality of the Commonwealth to control the pay, hours of work and conditions of employment of all State public servants could not be sustained as valid, but as Walsh J pointed out in the *Pay-roll Tax Case* [122 CLR at 410], the limitations have not been completely and precisely formulated and for present purposes the question need not be further examined.

One effect of this decision was to reawaken the underlying issue in the *Railway Servants' Case* and the *Engineers' Case* as to the extent to which State governments, as employers, are amenable to Commonwealth conciliation and arbitration proceedings. The inconclusive comments in the *CYSS Case* as to whether the principle in *Melbourne Corporation v Commonwealth* (1947) 74 CLR 31 might set limits to State exposure were revisited, still inconclusively, in a series of dicta throughout the 1980s. As examined in Chapter 25, §2(b), the issue was finally resolved in *Re Australian Education Union; Ex parte Victoria* (1995) 184 CLR 188.

3. Industrial Matters

The relaxation achieved by the *CYSS Case* related primarily to the expectation that an "industrial dispute" is one which can be seen as arising out of an industrial *relationship*. Traditionally, there has been a further requirement that an "industrial dispute" must be one which relates to an industrial *matter*. Here, too, a less rigorous conception of "industry" would result in a widening of the constitutional power. However, the actual powers of the Industrial Relations Commission have never been co-extensive with the scope of constitutional power, since the constitutional power was mediated through a *statutory* definition of "industrial dispute", for instance in s 4(1) of the *Workplace Relations Act 1996* (Cth). That definition required, inter alia, that an "industrial dispute" be "about matters pertaining to the relationship between employers and employees". To the extent that s 4(1) reflected an older view of "industrial matters", the full potential flow-on effect of the *CYSS Case* was not realised.

For "industrial matters", the history is one of an initially broad approach (as typified by *Australian Tramway Employee's Association v Prahran & Malvern Tramways Trust* (*Union Badge Case*) (1913) 17 CLR 680) which gradually came to be narrowed. In between lies *R v Kelly; Ex parte Victoria* (1950) 81 CLR 64. The aspect of that decision which is relevant here is the holding that a federal award could not regulate the trading hours of butchers' shops because this was not an "industrial matter".

R v Kelly; Ex parte Victoria
(1950) 81 CLR 64

The Court: [84] The term "industrial matters" is defined by s 4 as meaning "all matters pertaining to the relations of employers and employees". The definition goes on to provide that the term includes a number of specified matters, but the subject matter of clause 16A [of the award] cannot be brought within any of these, unless perhaps it be "(*a*) matters or things affecting or relating to work done or to be done." We do not think that the subject matter (the closing of shops as distinct from the work of employees in shops) is a "matter pertaining to the relations of employers and employees." The words "pertaining to" mean "belonging to" or "within the sphere of," and the expression "the relations of employers and employees" must refer to the relation of an employer as employer with an employee as employee. The time at which a shopkeeper (who may or may not employ anybody) may open and close his shop is not a "matter" which belongs to or is within the sphere of the relation of that shopkeeper as employer with any person as employee. Nor is it, in our opinion, a matter affecting work done or to be done within the meaning of par (*a*) of the definition. Trading hours of an employer are not the same subject as working hours of an employee, and a prescription of trading hours as distinct from working hours does not "affect or relate to work done or to be done." Provisions with respect to trading hours may affect the turnover of shopkeepers who employ persons and so indirectly affect their ability to pay award rates, and this state of affairs may in turn affect the relations of those shopkeepers and their employees. But this is the most that can be said, and it is obviously not enough. It shows only the possibility of an indirect, consequential and remote effect upon the relations of the last-mentioned persons. All kinds of matters, eg supply and prices of raw material, the state of the money market, may affect the capacity of employers to pay wages at a certain standard. But these are not industrial matters within the definition contained in s 4 of the Act. What *O'Connor* J said in *Clancy v Butchers' Shop Employees Union* [(1904) 1 CLR 181 at 207] is as true of the Commonwealth Act here in question as it was of the New South Wales Act there under consideration. His Honour said: "If once we begin to introduce and include in its scope" (ie the scope of the Act) "matters indirectly affecting work in the industry, it becomes very difficult to draw any line so as to prevent the power of the Arbitration Court from being extended to the regulation and control of businesses and industries in every part." **[85]** In the case of Commonwealth legislation with respect to the same subject matter any such extension would seem inevitably to involve an excess of the power conferred by s 51 (xxxv) of the Constitution.

A significant feature of this passage is the way in which the argument as to the statutory definition of "industrial matters" shifts to a constitutional argument. Significant also is the reference to *Clancy v Butchers' Shop Employés Union* (1904) 1 CLR 181 at 207. O'Connor J was dealing in that case with the *Industrial Arbitration Act 1901* (NSW), but his comment has often been used to justify a limited view of "industrial disputes" in s 51(xxxv). It is said that unless the Commission's powers are strictly confined in this way, it might turn out to have a general power to regulate all aspects of the economy.

In the wake of the *CYSS Case*, it was widely assumed that the Court would take a broader view of "industrial matters" along with its return to a broader view of "industrial disputes". Although there were hints to this effect in the *CYSS Case* itself, the real shift came in *Federated Clerks' Union (Aust) v Victorian Employers' Federation* (1984) 154 CLR 472. That case concerned the powers of a State Industrial Relations Commission under s 34(1) of the *Industrial Relations Act 1979* (Vic). The State Commission had made an award requiring that any phasing in of technological change be preceded by full consultation. The Court held that this was an "industrial matter". Gibbs CJ dissented in part; he agreed as to the actual implementation of new technology, but not as to any preliminary attempt "**[485]** to give the union and the employees an opportunity to influence … what is purely a management decision".

Federated Clerks' Union (Aust) v Victorian Employers' Federation
(1984) 154 CLR 472

Mason J: [488] From the decided cases the following propositions may be extracted: (1) a matter does not become an "industrial matter" or the subject of an "industrial dispute" simply because it is a matter with respect to which persons who are employers and employees are disputing …; (2) in order to constitute an "industrial matter" and become the subject of an "industrial dispute" what is demanded must have a relevant connexion with the relationship of employer and employee … or, as it has been put more narrowly, "the relationship of employer and employee must be directly involved in the demand" …, a connexion resting on an indirect effect or consequence being insufficient for this purpose …; (3) a demand by employees for something of a management or managerial nature has no relevant connexion with the relationship of employer and employee and is not an "industrial matter" ...; and (4) likewise, a demand for something of a political or social nature is for the same reason not an "industrial matter" ...

Of these propositions, the first two plainly reflect the statutory definitions of "industrial dispute" and "industrial matters" contained in s 4 of the *Conciliation and Arbitration Act* ... The same comment may be made of ...[cases involving] the statutory definitions of *The Industrial Conciliation and Arbitration Acts* 1932 *to* 1955 (Q) ... These decisions, together with those sustaining the first two propositions, far from reflecting a common or general understanding of what the two expressions mean, give effect to the statutory definitions and to the particular relationship which exists between them, reinforced by arguments arising from the perceived purpose of the relevant Act and the role of the tribunal. The reasoning on which they are based is to be contrasted with that in *R v Coldham; Ex parte Australian Social Welfare Union* [(1983) 153 CLR 297 at 312-13] where the Court, unimpeded by statutory definition, gave effect to the popular meaning of the expression "industrial disputes" by observing "the expression no doubt extends more widely to embrace disputes between parties other than employer and employee, such as demarcation disputes" ...

[490] The third proposition which I have extracted from the decided cases is in one respect the product of the second proposition and in another the product of other considerations. When the Court in *Kelly* [81 CLR at 84] rejected the claim that a dispute between an organization of employees and an organization of employers as to the trading hours of shopkeepers was an industrial dispute, it did so on the ground that it was not enough to show that what was demanded might possibly have "an indirect, consequential and remote effect upon" the relations of employers and employees, ... [and] went on to quote the remarks of O'Connor J in *Clancy v Butchers' Shop Employés Union* [(1904) 1 CLR 181 at 207] ...

Kelly did not distinguish between employers' decisions which are management decisions or managerial in character and those which are not. That distinction was made by Barwick CJ in [*R v Commonwealth Conciliation and Arbitration Commission; Ex parte*] *Melbourne and Metropolitan Tramways Board* [(1966) 115 CLR 443 at 451-2] where, after acknowledging that industrial disputes and awards may consequentially have an impact on the management of an enterprise and upon otherwise unfettered managerial discretions, [he] observed that "the management of the enterprise is not itself a subject matter of industrial dispute". A demand that no two-man tram or bus service shall be converted to a one-man operation was, according to his Honour, a demand which directly concerned only the management of the transport system. The distinction echoes in a more precise way the comment of O'Connor J in *Clancy* and other early statements that industrial tribunals were not empowered to adjudicate about the manner in which an employer should conduct his business ...

The problem with the concept of management or managerial [491] decisions standing outside the area of industrial disputes and industrial matters is that it does not provide a clear distinction. There are many decisions made by management which are capable of giving rise to an industrial matter and becoming the subject of an industrial dispute ... Whether the concept of management or managerial decisions can be sustained as an absolute and independent criterion of jurisdiction, even in the context of the *Conciliation and Arbitration Act*, is an important question that may require future consideration. In saying this I do not underrate the importance of the comment made by O'Connor J in *Clancy*. The prospect of industrial tribunals regularly reviewing business policy decisions made by employers, and thereby controlling the economy to a substantial extent, is indeed a daunting one. On the other hand, the popular understanding of an industrial dispute extends to any dispute between employees and employers that may result in the dislocation of industrial relations, eg, by the withdrawal of labour or the introduction of work or other bans. What is more, reflection on the serious impact on the community of industrial dislocation suggests that the scope and purpose of statutes regulating conciliation and arbitration and industrial relations extend to the conferment of jurisdiction on industrial tribunals in relation to industrial disputes in their broadest conception.

The exclusion of "managerial discretions" from "industrial matters" was finally repudiated in *Re Cram; Ex parte NSW Colliery Proprietors' Association Ltd* (1987) 163 CLR 117. At issue was the definition of "industrial matters" in complementary legislation establishing the Coal Industry Tribunal – the *Coal Industry Act 1946* (Cth) and the *Coal Industry Act 1946* (NSW).

Re Cram; Ex parte NSW Colliery Proprietors' Association Ltd
(1987) 163 CLR 117

The Court: [135] [W]e return to the statement already quoted by O'Connor J in *Clancy* [(1904) 1 CLR 181 at 207]. That statement probably echoes in some respects what was received doctrine at an earlier time – that it was the prerogative of management to decide how a business enterprise should operate and whom it should employ, without the workforce having any stake in the making of such decisions. In that climate of opinion, disputes about the making of such decisions, despite their impact on working conditions and work to be done, might not necessarily be regarded as industrial matters susceptible of resolution by industrial arbitration. Over the years that climate of opinion has changed quite radically, perhaps partly as a result of the extended definition of "industrial matters" in s 4 of the *Conciliation and Arbitration Act* and partly a result of a change in community attitudes to the relationship between employer and employee. The judgment of Isaacs and Rich JJ in *Tramways Employes* [(1913) 17 CLR 680 at 693-4] reflects the first of these factors. No doubt our traditional system of industrial conciliation and arbitration has itself contributed to a growing recognition that management and labour have a mutual interest in many aspects of the operation of a business enterprise. Many management decisions, once viewed as the sole preroga- tive of management, are now correctly seen as directly affecting the relationship of employer and employee and constituting an "industrial matter".

A dispute about the level of manning is a good example. It has a direct impact on the work to be done by employees; it affects the volume of work to be performed by each employee and the conditions in which he performs his work. So also with the mode of recruitment of the workforce. The competence and reliability of the workforce has a direct impact on the conditions of work, notably as they relate to occupational health and observance of safety standards. Employees, as well as management, have a legitimate interest in both these matters.

Why then is not the proposed employment of non-union labour or the refusal to abide by a system of recruitment which gives preference to union labour a matter directly affecting the relations of employer and employee? The decision in *R v Gaudron; Ex parte Uniroyal Pty Ltd* [(1978) 141 CLR 204] shows that it is. There the Court held **[136]** that a dispute about preference in employment for a particular class of members of a union was a dispute as to an "industrial matter" as defined by s 4 of the *Conciliation and Arbitration Act* …

In reaching this conclusion we reject the suggestion, based on the remarks of Barwick CJ in *Melbourne & Metropolitan Tramways Board* [(1966) 115 CLR 443 at 451-2], that managerial decisions stand wholly outside the area of industrial disputes and industrial matters. There is no basis for making such an implication. It is an implication which is so imprecise as to be incapable of yielding any satisfactory criterion of jurisdiction: see *Federated Clerks Union* [(1984) 154 CLR 472 at 490-1]. Indeed, the difficulty of making such an implication is accentuated by the fact that the extended definition of "industrial matters" proceeds on the footing that many management decisions are capable of generating an industrial dispute.

These considerations indicate that the objection voiced by O'Connor J in *Clancy* to the regulation and control of business enterprises by industrial tribunals is not a matter that goes to the jurisdiction of the tribunals. Rather it is an argument why an industrial tribunal should exercise caution before it makes an award **[137]** in settlement of a dispute where that award amounts to a substantial interference with the autonomy of management to decide how the business enterprise shall be efficiently conducted. The evident importance of arming such tribunals with power to settle industrial disputes capable of disrupting industry is a powerful reason for refusing to read down the wide and general definition of "industrial matters" in the Commonwealth and State Acts by reference to any notion of managerial prerogatives as such.

Neither the *Federated Clerks' Case* nor *Re Cram* dealt with the definition of "industrial disputes" in the *Conciliation and Arbitration Act*; and neither the *Industrial Relations Act 1988* (Cth) nor the *Workplace Relations Act 1996* (Cth) materially changed that definition. Instead, those Acts appeared to proceed on a legislative assumption that the Court's new expansive view had now been so thoroughly entrenched by the *Federated Clerks' Case* and by *Re Cram* that there was no longer any need to work with extended statutory definitions of "industrial matters" at all. But this legislative assumption was ill-founded. In 1994, a unanimous seven-judge Court affirmed the wider view of "industrial disputes" now ascribed to s 51(xxxv) *of the Constitution*, yet refused to depart from the narrower view of "industrial matters" formerly established as the Court's interpretation of the definition contained *in the Act*. Specifically, the Court reaffirmed the correctness of *R v Portus; Ex parte ANZ Banking Group Ltd* (1972) 127 CLR 353, which had held that a union demand for "union dues" to be deducted by employers from employees' wages did not involve an "industrial matter" within the meaning of the *Industrial Relations Act*. In earlier times, "industrial matters" had been found in *Australian Tramway Employes Association v Prahran and Malvern Tramway Trust* (*Union Badge Case*) (1913) 17 CLR 680 (a demand that tram conductors be allowed to wear a union membership badge on their watch-chains) and *Federated Clothing Trades of the Commonwealth of Australia v Archer* (*Archer's Case*) (1919) 27 CLR 207 (a demand, in the context of a dispute about the use of outworkers, that all garments "**[209]** shall bear the name of the actual manufacturer on a label ... to be sewn on a prominent part of the garment"); but the Court declined to build on these precedents.

Re Alcan Australia Ltd; Ex parte Federation of Industrial, Manufacturing and Engineering Employees
(1994) 181 CLR 96

The Court: [105] Neither the broader approach to s 51(xxxv) of the Constitution nor the definition of "industrial dispute" in s 4(1) of the Act provides any basis, in our view, for a reconsideration of *R v Portus*. The question is not one involving s 51(xxxv); it is simply a question of the meaning of the definition of "industrial dispute" in s 4(1). And although there are some minor differences between that definition and the relevant definitions previously found in the *Conciliation and Arbitration Act*, the requisite nature of the subject matter of a dispute remains precisely the same, namely, that it pertain to the employment relationship involving employers, as such, and employees, as such.

Nor is the Federation's argument advanced by the *Union Badge Case* or by *Archer's Case*. As was said in *R v Kelly* [81 CLR at 85], "[w]hether an employer should permit his employee to wear a particular badge when on duty seems plainly a matter pertaining to the relations between an employer as employer and an employee as employee". *Archer's Case* is, perhaps, not so plain ... However, when the claim is viewed as one directed to distinguishing between garments made by the manufacturers' employees and those made by sub-contractors or out-workers, it is, in our view, one that is directly related to the work performed or to be performed by employees. And that is well within the employer-employee relationship.

The claim in *Archer's Case* was directed to strengthening the position of employees, presumably trade unionists, vis-à-vis the position of independent contractors who, presumably, were not members of a union. On that basis, there are clear similarities between that claim, the claim in the *Union Badge Case* and the **[106]** claim in this case. All three have an aspect directed to strengthening the position of trade unions or of employees who are members of a union. That aspect, when viewed in isolation, concerns employees as members of a union, not as employees. And although there are remarks in the *Union Badge Case* that provide clear support for the view that the words "industrial disputes" in s 51(xxxv) of the Constitution should be given their popular meaning, a view which was later adopted in the *CYSS Case* ..., there is nothing in that case or in *Archer's Case* to suggest that a claim directed to strengthening the position of a union or union members is, without more, a matter pertaining to the employment relationship involving employers, as such, and employees, as such.

There are, in our view, three matters which tell persuasively against reconsideration of *R v Portus*. The first is that the principle on which it proceeds, namely, that for a matter to "pertain to the relations of employers and employees" it must affect them in their capacity as such, has been accepted as correct in a number of subsequent cases ... The second is that Parliament re-enacted, in s 4(1) of the Act, words which are almost identical with those considered in *R v Portus*. There is abundant authority for the proposition that where the Parliament repeats words which have been judicially construed, it is taken to have intended the words to bear the meaning already "judicially attributed to [them]" [*Barras v Aberdeen Steam Trawling & Fishing Co* [1933] AC 402 at 446], although the validity of that proposition has been questioned. But the presumption is considerably strengthened in the present case by the legislative history of the Act. **[107]** The Committee of Review into the Australian Industrial Relations Law and Systems, whose report preceded the enactment of the Act, recommended that the jurisdiction of the tribunal be extended to the limits of the constitutional power under s 51(xxxv). Yet Parliament adopted, in almost identical terms, the language of the former Act into the Act, and the Minister acknowledged in his Second Reading Speech that the jurisdiction was to be limited by "the requirement that disputes relate to matters concerning employers and employees". These considerations reinforce the presumption that Parliament did not intend to overturn *R v Portus*.

The third matter that tells against a reconsideration of *R v Portus* is that, academic criticism notwithstanding, there is no reason to think it is in any way affected by error. The considerations which lead to the conclusion that a dispute as to deduction of union dues (at least, where authorized by individual employees) is an industrial dispute within s 51(xxxv) of the Constitution, tend in favour of the conclusion that the subject matter does not pertain to the relationships of employers and employees in their capacity as such. Those considerations, which depend on the nature and role of trade unions in Australia, show that although the subject matter pertains to a relationship between employers and employees, it is a relationship involving employees as union members and not at all as employees.

Since its amendment in 2005 the *Workplace Relations Act* no longer depends for its operation upon the expressions "industrial disputes" and "industrial matters"; and when it continues to use those expressions in describing the operation of State legislation, it stipulates that "the ordinary meaning of those expressions" shall apply.

4. "Conciliation and arbitration"

Apart from the requirement that an exercise of power under s 51(xxxv) must relate to "*industrial disputes*", the constitutional power is also restricted in other ways. It is limited to "industrial *disputes*"; they must be "disputes *extending beyond the limits of any one State*"; the purpose is "the *prevention and settlement*" of such disputes; and Parliament is limited in its choice of means of pursuing that purpose since the power is only to make laws with respect to "*Conciliation and arbitration* for the prevention and settlement of industrial disputes".

The starting points for judicial exegesis of these criteria are found in the series of *Whybrow* cases beginning with *Australian Boot Trade Employés Federation v Whybrow & Co (No 1)* (1910) 10 CLR 266, which built upon *Federated Saw Mill &c Employes of Australasia v James Moore & Son Pty Ltd* (*Woodworkers' Case*) (1909) 8 CLR 465. In the *Woodworkers' Case* and in *Whybrow (No 1)*, the majority (Griffith CJ and O'Connor J in *Woodworkers*, joined by Barton J in *Whybrow*) held that a federal award could not override a determination by a Victorian Wages Board. Ordinarily, State awards could be so overridden, but the Wages Boards in Victoria had a special statutory basis which legally bound a federal arbitrator. This holding reflected the concept of "reserved State powers" (see Chapter 7, §3), but it also depended on the fact that the Commonwealth power was limited to "conciliation and arbitration".

In the *Woodworkers' Case* and in *Whybrow (No 1)* the words "conciliation and arbitration" in s 51(xxxv) led to two distinct points. First, since the function of "conciliation and arbitration" is not a legislative function, it must follow that a conciliator or arbitrator cannot change the law – and hence must obey the law. Secondly, although all judges recognised that governmental initiatives in industrial arbitration were different from the older forms of "private" arbitration, it was said that the process of "arbitration" must still retain the essential characteristics of its "private" form. These include a conception of the arbitrator as a delegate of the disputant parties: the arbitrator can do anything that the parties themselves could do, but only what the parties themselves could do. Hence the arbitrator is bound by the law. These points never extended so far as to put

State industrial arbitration awards beyond the reach of federal power: clearly a (federal) arbitral award could vary a previous (State) award which would otherwise bind the parties, just as it could vary their contractual obligations. The argument was only that State determinations *with statutory force* lay beyond arbitral reach.

Federated Saw Mill &c Employes of Australasia v James Moore & Son Pty Ltd (*Woodworkers' Case*)
(1909) 8 CLR 465

Griffith CJ: [492] [T]he power is not a general power to make laws for the settlement of industrial disputes. A power conferred in such terms would *primâ facie* authorize an invasion of the whole field of the conditions of employment so far as might be necessary for their settlement. The power is limited to making laws for their settlement by arbitration. The term "arbitration" connotes a judicial tribunal, by whatever name it is called and however constituted, and, although the functions of the tribunal differ from those of ordinary tribunals in that they are not limited to determining existing causes of action, but extend to **[493]** prescribing conditions to be observed in future contracts of employment, the tribunal is no less a tribunal. To my mind the obligation to decide in accordance with the law is implied in the notion of the creation of a tribunal. Otherwise the members of the tribunal would not be judicial persons at all, but dictators exercising the power of legislation, not of adjudication.

It is gravely maintained, however, that the tribunal which the Parliament may establish for the settlement of industrial disputes is not bound by any State laws relating to domestic trade, and that, although the Parliament itself could not make a law inconsistent with the State law, it can under the language of pl xxxv authorize its creature, the tribunal of arbitration, to disregard the State law, to free persons from any obligation to obey it, and even impose penalties upon persons who do obey it, because such power is necessary for the effective settlement of industrial disputes …

I find it difficult to treat such an argument with due gravity. It may be necessary, in order to allay political agitation, for the legislature to repeal or alter an existing law, but it cannot be said to be necessary that a tribunal appointed to settle disputes by arbitration should have a dispensing power authorizing it to supersede or abrogate a law or excuse obedience to it, unless, indeed, it is assumed that a dispute cannot be settled unless one (and of course only one) of the parties to the dispute gets all that **[494]** he asks. This would be an entirely novel meaning of the word, and would put the tribunal above the law. *Sic volo, sic jubeo, mea sit pro lege voluntas.*

Australian Boot Trade Employés Federation v Whybrow & Co (No 1)
(1910) 10 CLR 266

Barton J: [293] "Arbitration" is a term which, taken by itself, connotes a process for the settlement of disputes by submitting them to the decision of a tribunal selected by the parties or accepted by them, **[294]** and an agreement by both to be bound by the decision, which is commonly called the award. The submission may include questions of pure law, of mixed law and fact, or of fact alone, according to the terms in which the dispute is submitted or referred to arbitration; and beyond all question the award is a judicial determination. That at least has never been the subject of doubt … The tribunal, then, being judicial, its office is to decide questions of fact, and in respect of such conclusions to declare or apply existing laws, save so far as either party may voluntarily and lawfully renounce the benefit of them. It is resorted to simply and solely because the parties cannot come to an agreement on the questions submitted, and therefore desire that the tribunal should make an agreement for them, by which they mutually consent beforehand to be bound. The range, then, of an arbitrator's authority, if the submission is wide enough, is co-extensive with the powers of the parties to settle their dispute without him. Whatever they can lawfully agree to, he may lawfully award. If, however, they desire him to make for them an agreement in breach of the mandate of positive law, he is powerless to do so. As they can each surrender strict legal rights by agreement, so he can bind them to such surrenders by award, if they give him power to do so. But it is one thing for a party to waive a legal right, and another thing for the tribunal to impair the obligation of a law or to attempt to make a new one. That is out of the question, because it is not a conceivable function of a judicial tribunal in a civilized country. There may be legislatures which prefer to set up tribunals with despotic powers to wave aside legislation which does not please them, but the Imperial Parliament is not such a legislature, nor is the Parliament of the Commonwealth. The office of an arbitrator is like that of a Judge to the extent that it is for him to declare the law and not to make it.

Does the function then lose its judicial character when the arbitration is for the settlement of industrial disputes? Clearly the nature of the subject matter cannot destroy that character, and therefore the tribunal is as clearly bound to obey the legislature in an industrial arbitration as in one of the primary kind. The parties may be large organizations of employés on one side, **[295]** they may be individual employers or organizations of employers on the other. That does not affect the essential character of the tribunal. Nor is it affected by the fact that the matters for settlement include the future as well as the existing contractual relations of the parties. In this case, again, the tribunal is invoked because the parties cannot agree – are still in dispute; and here, too, the arbitrator can do for the parties that which they might lawfully do for themselves if they could agree; but he can do no more. If either or both of them wish him to decide in contravention of positive law, he remembers that the law binds both him and them, and the appeal is in vain.

In *R v Commonwealth Court of Conciliation and Arbitration; Ex parte Whybrow & Co* (1910) 11 CLR 1 (the second of the *Whybrow* cases), such observations led to an argument that the *Conciliation and Arbitration Act* was fundamentally flawed because what it provided for was not "arbitration". The argument focused on s 30 of the Act (which paralleled s 109 of the Constitution by providing that federal awards should prevail over inconsistent State laws); and also on s 38(f), which gave power "to declare by any award or order that any practice, regulation, rule, custom, term of agreement, condition of employment or dealing whatsoever determined by an award in relation to any industrial matter shall be a common rule of any industry in connection with which the dispute arises". No final decision was given as to either s 30 or s 38(f). It was said that even if they did exceed legislative power, they were severable. On the broader issue, the challenge failed. The whole Court accepted the analysis of Isaacs J.

R v Commonwealth Court of Conciliation and Arbitration; Ex parte Whybrow & Co
(1910) 11 CLR 1

Isaacs J: [49] The next question in logical order is the validity of the *Conciliation and Arbitration Act*. That is challenged on two grounds. It is said in the first place that it is radically unconstitutional and illegal, because the tribunal is altogether compulsory, leaving no possible choice of arbitrator or arbitrators to the parties. It is urged that the word "arbitration" connotes such a possible choice. I do not agree with that ... Arbitration is I conceive correctly defined by Lord *Trayner* in *McMillan & Son Ltd v Rowan & Co* [(1903) 40 Sc LR 265 at 267] in these words:– "An agreement to submit to arbitration simply means that the parties have agreed to have their differences determined otherwise than by a Court of law, but does not even suggest whether the Court they have chosen for themselves shall consist of one member or many or how many members."

The essence of the matter ... is that *the differences are to be decided otherwise than by a Court of law.*

So long as that essential feature is preserved, Parliament is free to provide the constitution of the tribunal, and to say whether or not the parties ... may or may not have a voice in its selection. This appears really incontrovertible when it is remembered that the chief object of the constitutional power was to maintain industrial peace for the benefit of the community at large, and [it] was, therefore, not introduced for the sole purpose of determining or averting a private quarrel concerning only the immediate parties. The trouble or possible trouble being public, and probably urgent, Parliament acting for the public is entrusted with the power to appoint a tribunal, and at once, which it thinks will act fairly between all parties concerned. It is, however, contended that this view is barred by what is called the every-day conception of the term arbitration. But where is there found any definite every-day import other than that I have indicated?

[50] Doubtless, every reference to arbitration at common law out of Court was by agreement as to the matters to be referred, as to the persons to whom they were to be referred, and as to the powers of those persons to decide. No agreement to submit to arbitration was complete at common law ... until an arbitrator was appointed. The result at common law was that, among other things, a person wholly or partially incapable of entering into a contract was to that extent incapable of submitting a dispute to arbitration. Infants and married women (see, for instance, *Strachan v Dougall* [(1851) 7 Moo PC 365; 13 ER 920]) were instances of total or restricted capacity to submit to arbitration. The whole position, therefore, necessarily rested on agreement.

If, therefore, I thought the test of arbitration were the capacity or power to agree, I would at once accede to the present argument. But to apply that test appears to me to mistake surrounding and temporary circumstances for inherent permanent attributes. Learned counsel have not asserted that because an infant possesses only a limited capacity to contract the *Arbitration Act* is therefore inapplicable to affect him except so far as his contractual power extends. And if the suggested test fails there, it fails in my opinion altogether. It is impossible, in the face of the numerous Acts passed by the British Parliament on the subject of arbitration, to maintain that arbitration ceases to be arbitration unless it retains its voluntary character.

The issue as to s 38(f) – the "common rule" provision – was finally settled in the third of the *Whybrow* cases. The whole Court held that the making of a "common rule" for a whole industry was not an exercise of the power of conciliation and arbitration.

Australian Boot Trade Employés Federation v Whybrow & Co (No 2)
(1910) 11 CLR 311

Barton J: [323] The common rule provisions contained in sec 38 of the *Commonwealth Conciliation and Arbitration Act* 1904-1910 are similar to those [in the *Industrial Arbitration Act* 1901 (NSW)] ... But the Parliament of Australia has not the plenary power which the legislature of New South Wales exercised when it made these provisions. To be valid, they must be at least incidental to the attainment of the object of arbitration for the settlement of industrial disputes as that term is used in sub-sec xxxv. I do not think they are so. To empower the Court to declare that any condition of employment, or the like, prescribed by its award shall be a common rule binding the whole industry and all engaged in it, is plainly to extend the authority of the Court beyond the ambit of the dispute and to bind persons other than the disputants by the decisions of the Court. This can by no means be considered as in its nature incidental to the settlement of a dispute which only the disputants brought or could bring before the Court. The award itself is the means prescribed for the settlement of the dispute as between the actual parties. If the award did more it would be an excess of jurisdiction to that extent, even if expressly confined in its operation to the immediate parties and their industrial affairs. If it not only included more than the subject matter of the dispute but involved others than the parties the case would be worse. How then can it be bettered, if the attempt is made to produce any such effect either as to parties or subject matter by nominally separating the operations and giving the name of a common rule to the excess? The process cannot possibly be merely incidental to that which depends for its validity upon the limitation of the adjudication to the subject matter of the dispute and the parties thereto. And the mere citing of persons not parties to the dispute, even by serving [324] process on them instead of calling upon them, generally and not even by name, in an advertisement, would not make that lawful which previously lacked constitutional warrant.

I am of opinion, therefore, that the common rule provisions are not within the power given to Parliament to make laws in respect of arbitration for the settlement of the class of industrial disputes specified in sub-sec xxxv.

But it is contended that the power is one to legislate as to arbitration for the prevention as well as for the settlement of such disputes.

In the first place I own myself unable to understand how there can be an arbitration to prevent a dispute. There must be something to arbitrate upon. There must be parties and a subject matter before a resort can be had to arbitration. If people are agreed and at peace, a request from one to the other that they should arbitrate would be, to put it mildly, an amiable eccentricity. There would be no subject matter, nor would there be parties, for there would be no cause of division between employers and employés to make them take sides, and without it how could they arbitrate? But even if there could be arbitration for the prevention of a dispute, giving that name to any vague discontent with an indefinable cause, how can it be supposed that, with an eye to such preventive arbitration, the Constitution has authorized laws for citing, and for making regulations to bind, all the persons engaged in an industry, including those who have never even heard of the mere murmur that is made to pass for the subject matter of an arbitration. If I spoke more plainly of such a suggestion I could not speak of it respectfully. It is enough to express one's inability to follow it.

But it may be said ... that the thing intended by clause xxxv is arbitration for the prevention, not of disputes as they arise, but of disputes in general, by citing all those engaged in an industry, and dealing with them in the first instance by way of common rule. The provision the validity of which is challenged is of a different character. It presupposes an award *inter partes* in the first instance, and a common rule as an extension of it or of part of it. There is the additional difficulty, that such a proceeding would not be in **[325]** substance an arbitration, as that term is known either at common law or in any Statute passed before July 1900. It cannot therefore be taken to have been within the contemplation of those who framed the Constitution.

In part, Barton J was responding to an argument that a "common rule" might *prevent* disputes, so that making such a rule in the course of arbitration might constitute "arbitration for the prevention ... of industrial disputes". His answer is in effect that conciliation might be a means of "prevention and settlement" of industrial disputes, but that arbitration, by its nature, can only be a means of "settlement". Griffith CJ was inclined to a different solution. He read s 51(xxxv) distributively, so that "conciliation" can only be used for the prevention of industrial disputes and "arbitration" only for their settlement. O'Connor, Isaacs and Higgins JJ rejected both these suggestions. Despite this, the holding that "arbitration" requires specific parties, engaged in a dispute which needs to be "settled", has tended in practice to shift the emphasis to "settlement" rather than "prevention".

From time to time individual judges complain that this has unduly narrowed the power by overlooking the constitutionally authorised goal of "prevention ... of industrial disputes". Perhaps the most significant reminder of this neglected aspect of the power came in *Re Federated Storemen and Packers Union of Australia; Ex parte Wooldumpers (Vic) Ltd* (*Wooldumpers Case*) (1989) 166 CLR 311, where the High Court held that the Conciliation and Arbitration Commission had no jurisdiction to entertain an "impending dispute" arising from a worker's dismissal, essentially because it did not fall within the ambit of an existing dispute. Hence its resolution would not be conducive to the "settlement" of that dispute. Although the "prevention" aspect of the power was not directly raised, Mason CJ, Deane and Gaudron JJ noted its potential scope. For example, Mason CJ suggested that, although the definition of "industrial dispute" in s 4(1) of the *Conciliation and Arbitration Act* included "a threatened, impending or probable dispute", this formula did not exhaust the power conferred by s 51(xxxv) – so that other disputes, "**[320]** fall[ing] short of being threatened, impending or probable", might be within legislative competence. The boldest comment came from Deane J.

Re Federated Storemen and Packers Union of Australia; Ex parte Wooldumpers (Vic) Ltd (Wooldumpers Case)
(1989) 166 CLR 311

Deane J: [327] Conciliation and arbitration have as important roles to play in preserving interstate industrial peace in areas where it exists as in restoring it in areas where differing interests or aspirations, or local differences or disputes have degenerated to a stage where interstate industrial dispute and disruption have occurred or are pending. The grant of legislative power contained in s 51(xxxv) of the Constitution plainly recognizes that that is so. Its emphasis is as much upon conciliation and arbitration for the "prevention" of interstate "industrial disputes" in the abstract as it is upon conciliation and arbitration for the "settlement" of particular identified interstate "industrial disputes" which have actually broken out. Obviously, the most effective way in which the process of conciliation and arbitration can prevent the occurrence of interstate industrial disputes is by the conciliation of differences before the actual threshold of dispute is reached or, if actual dispute has broken out, by resolving it by conciliation or arbitration before it assumes an interstate character. Yet the *Conciliation and Arbitration Act* 1904 (Cth), presumably reflecting a constricted view of the scope of the legislative power conferred by s 51(xxxv) particularly in relation to conciliation, firmly bases the jurisdiction of the Australian Conciliation and Arbitration Commission upon the identification of some specific **[328]** interstate industrial dispute which has at least progressed to the stage of being "threatened", "impending", "probable" or "likely" and in respect of which a determination can be made of both "the matters in dispute" and "the parties". This gives rise to the paradox that access to the national tribunal entrusted with conciliation and arbitration for the prevention of interstate industrial disputes is barred unless the potential disputants become qualified to invoke jurisdiction by exacerbating their differences to the stage where there is an actual, threatened, impending, probable or likely specific identified dispute of interstate proportions.

Despite these dicta, the "prevention" aspect of the power remains underdeveloped. Moreover, the narrow conception of arbitration laid down in the *Whybrow* cases was not challenged in the *Wooldumpers Case;* and the view that s 51(xxxv) does not extend to the making of a common rule has continued to prevail (see §5 below).

If the arbitral tribunal cannot "legislate" under s 51(xxxv), since its power is confined to arbitration, the Parliament itself cannot "legislate" directly with respect to industrial relations under that power either, except in ways which establish or are incidental to a system of conciliation and arbitration. The limits of Parliament's power were tested in *Waterside Workers' Federation v Commonwealth Steamship Owners' Association* (1920) 28 CLR 209, in a challenge to what was then s 28(2) of the *Conciliation and Arbitration Act*. That section provided that, after an initial term fixed by the arbitral tribunal and until it is altered otherwise, "the award shall … continue in force until a new award has been made". Although this provision was held to be valid, Isaacs, Rich and Powers JJ dissented. They reasoned that, because the industrial settlement as thus continued in force reflected the result of a legislative process, it no longer reflected the result of a process of arbitration, and thus was not the kind of settlement which alone is authorised by s 51(xxxv).

The majority (Knox CJ, Higgins, Gavan Duffy and Starke JJ) rejected this characterisation of the effect of s 28(2). They held that it was merely incidental to the arbitration system, or perhaps incidental to Parliament's function in establishing and regulating such a system.

Waterside Workers' Federation of Australia v Commonwealth Steamship Owners' Association
(1920) 28 CLR 209

Knox CJ: [218] It is clear that this power does not authorize the Commonwealth Parliament to regulate conditions of employment by direct legislation, *eg*, to prescribe by Act of Parliament the minimum rate of wage to be paid or the maximum number of hours to be worked. It is, I think, equally clear that the power in question does authorize the Commonwealth Parliament to set up a tribunal with plenary and unrestricted power to prevent or settle two-State industrial disputes by conciliation and arbitration. It follows, in my opinion, that the Commonwealth Parliament has power to prescribe by legislation the manner in which, and the conditions on which, the tribunal so constituted shall carry out its functions and exercise the jurisdiction conferred upon it. The Commonwealth Parliament cannot settle a dispute or make an award by legislative enactment, but it has power, in my opinion, to enact that the tribunal which is set up for the purpose of settling industrial disputes shall, if it makes an award, comply with conditions prescribed by Parliament. This power to constitute a tribunal with plenary power to act according to its unfettered discretion, in my opinion, carries with it power to constitute a tribunal for the same purpose with circum-scribed or limited powers … **[219]** It cannot be successfully contended that it was beyond the power of Parliament to enact both a minimum and a maximum period for the continuance in force of any award that might be made under the Act, and in my opinion it is clear that the two sub-sections of sec 28 in effect do no more than this, though a power is reserved to the Court of Arbitration to put an end to an award at any time after the expiration of the "specified period" referred to in sub-sec 1. Under this provision the continuance in force of an award beyond the specified period is placed absolutely under the control of the tribunal constituted by the Act, and I cannot find in the provisions of this section any attempt on the part of Parliament to prescribe conditions of employment by legislative enactment.

Isaacs and Rich JJ: [228] Parliament may give what powers it pleases **[229]** to the arbitrator; it may limit his powers as it pleases; it may make the exercise of these powers conditional, and may make any determination of the arbitrator law. But it cannot, consistently with the terms of its legislative power in relation to industrial disputes, impose any obligations or alter rights by any provision which dispenses with arbitration; it cannot go beyond the actual decision of the arbitrator, or alter his decision, or make any provision for settlement of the dispute binding that does not involve his own decision, or that extends beyond his own decision or adoption. The settlement, the complete settlement, of industrial disputes is limited to "arbitration", which consists in judicial examination into the circumstances of each particular case as to how, and for how long, ordinary rights should be varied in the interests of industrial peace. And all the ancillary provisions of the law that we find in the Act so far as they are valid must be incidental only to the arbitrator's own decision. But if Parliament can, irrespective of the merits of the particular case, make a general enactment, operating mechanically and setting aside ordinary legal rights of employers and employees beyond anything awarded, the words and the spirit of the constitutional provision are alike broken. And, if Parliament can do it in this case, we can see no limit to its power. If it has such complete power that it can lengthen the arbitrator's period, it can shorten it. If [the arbitrator] thinks a certain wage should last for five years, Parliament may, notwithstanding his decision, alter the period to one year. And if the parties have expressly agreed under sec 24 to a fixed term and ended their dispute on that definite basis, then, as that is, when certified, "deemed to be an award," and consequently within sec 28(2), Parliament, if the view we are contesting be right, can validly alter the deliberate agreement of the parties – fixed (say) for one year – so as to make it binding on them for twenty years …

[232] The result is that in enacting sec 28(2) Parliament is departing from arbitration and enacting, as if it were a plenary Legislature, what new and independent obligations outside the arbitrator's award shall subsist between individuals as an industrial law. We consider that incompetent … Parliament can always give the arbitrator affirmative power to extend an award if he, on a review of the circumstances, thinks it just. But, not having done so, its own direct assumption of the power appears to us unwarranted, and we are obliged so to declare.

These arguments were recycled 80 years later in *Re Pacific Coal Pty Ltd; Ex parte Construction, Forestry, Mining and Energy Union* (*CFMEU Case*) (2000) 203 CLR 346, and again the High Court divided 4:3 in favour of legislative validity. But this time, instead of seeking to extend the operation of award provisions, the Parliament had established a mechanism for their dismemberment.

The *Workplace Relations and Other Legislation Amendment Act 1996* (Cth) (the WROLA Act) marked a further stage in the progressive shift away from compulsory arbitration as a means of regulating industrial relations. Pursuant to a policy of "award simplification", the issues that could be submitted to arbitration were restricted to a list of 20 "allowable award matters", catalogued in a new s 89A(2) of the *Workplace Relations Act* and including such matters as "rates of pay generally", "parental leave, including maternity and adoption leave" and "superannuation". Other matters, such as disciplinary measures, study leave and occupational health and safety, could no longer be the subject of awards.

The WROLA Act imposed similar restrictions on existing awards. Item 50(1) of the "transitional provisions" set out in Sch 5, Pt 2, provided that, at the end of an 18-month interim period, "each award ceases to have effect to the extent that it provides for matters other than allowable award matters". During the interim period, the Industrial Relations Commission was empowered to vary awards so as to deal only with "allowable award matters"; and "as soon as practicable after the end of the interim period", item 51(2) required the Commission to vary awards "to remove provisions that ceased to have effect".

Pursuant to that provision the Coal Mining Industry (Production and Engineering) Consolidated Award, made in 1997, was varied in July 1998 by the deletion of non-allowable matters. The variation was challenged on the ground that s 3 of the WROLA Act, which gave legal effect to the transitional provisions in items 50 and 51 of the Schedule, was invalid.

It was common ground that the new legislative restrictions on future awards were valid. As Gleeson CJ explained, s 51(xxxv) "[354] confers [355] the power to establish and maintain, and, where it is considered appropriate, alter, the system. The Parliament, in the exercise of the power, legislates to institute, vary, modify, or abrogate, the system". Accordingly, the challenge in the *CFMEU Case* was directed only to the mandatory provisions for variation of existing awards. However, although these provisions were characterised by Pt 2 of Sch 5 as "transitional", their impact was of great practical significance because existing awards with very extensive coverage were preserved in force by s 148 of the Act.

A majority of the Court, Gleeson CJ, Gummow, Hayne and Callinan JJ, held that the provisions were valid. Gaudron, McHugh and Kirby JJ dissented. The majority view depended in part on ascribing a narrow meaning to the declaration in Item 50(1) that, except as to allowable matters, "each award ceases to have effect".

Re Pacific Coal Pty Ltd; Ex parte Construction, Forestry, Mining and Energy Union (*CFMEU Case*)
(2000) 203 CLR 346

Gummow and Hayne JJ: [405] [W]hile the Commonwealth Parliament has power to make laws with respect to conciliation and arbitration, the fact that it has exercised that power in ways that have had profound effects on the ordering of relations between employers and employees does not mean that the Parliament cannot choose to dismantle the structure it has erected. The power to make a law includes a power of repeal … [T]he focus upon awards and their enforcement does not mean that the individual contract of employment between employer and employee cannot be the primary source of the conditions of employment of a particular employee. An objective of the legislation under consideration here is that wages and conditions of employment be determined as far as possible by the agreement of employers and employees …

[413] Having regard to the various provisions of the WROLA Act and the *Workplace Relations Act* that we have mentioned, we do not consider [414] that item 50 should be read as intending to do more than remove any support (that is, any "effect") which the *Workplace Relations Act* may otherwise have given to those provisions of awards which were not allowable award matters. To understand why that is so, it is necessary to consider what is meant by giving "effect" to an award. First (and obviously) the effect in question is legal effect. That is, when it is said that effect is given to an award, it means that the provisions of the award are of legal significance; legally enforceable rights, duties, powers and privileges are created.

Secondly, it is necessary to recall that an award is the arbitrated or conciliated outcome of a process that takes place, usually, between employers, or groups of employers, and one or more registered organisations representing the interests of employees. As is apparent from what we have said about the Coal Award, an award will often contain provisions that would find no place in an individual contract of employment … The award is therefore cast in terms of generality rather than in terms of the stipulations which together make up a particular contract of employment between an employer and an employee.

Thus, when "effect" is given to an award, it is given legal consequences which attach to individuals, groups or organisations because of the particular status which the award is given by the legislation pursuant to which it was made. When that legislation gives rights to, or imposes obligations on, individuals that are rights or obligations referable to the award, they are rights and obligations conferred by the legislation …

To read item 50 as intended to deny any and all legal effect to the award provisions with which it dealt, no matter whether that effect was legislative or contractual, would attribute to it an intention to regulate the terms and conditions of employment of individual employees [415] which would be entirely antithetical to the stated object of the *Workplace Relations Act* as being to ensure that primary responsibility for such matters "rests … at the workplace or enterprise level". In addition, if reading it in that way would lead to invalidity, that would be a further, perhaps even conclusive, reason not to do so if there were some other available construction consistent with validity. But we need not, and do not, base our construction of s 3 and item 50 on those last-mentioned considerations. Rather, we consider that the "effect" with which item 50 was concerned was the legal effect given to awards by the Commonwealth conciliation and arbitration legislation, and not any wider legal effect that would be attributable to the incorporation of particular awards or provisions of awards in individual contracts of employment …

[417] Once the nature of the rights, duties, powers and privileges which the legislation changes, regulates or abolishes [is] properly identified, it is apparent that s 3 of the WROLA Act (in so far as it gives effect to items 50 and 51(1), (2) and (3)) is a law with respect to conciliation and arbitration within s 51(xxxv). It is a law the subject matter of which is the extent to which legislatively pre-scribed consequences are to attach to the outcome of conciliation and arbitration processes carried out by persons and bodies established and regulated by legislation enacted within power. That is, it is a law taking away part of what the legislature had validly given, namely, legal effect to awards resulting from processes of conciliation and arbitration that had been legislatively prescribed and regulated within power …

[420] Those who challenged validity contended that because item 50 sought to terminate the effect of some, but not all, provisions of the Coal Award, the award as varied … would be signifi-cantly different from the award as it was originally made. It was contended that the variation could not be characterised as having any relevant connection with the original interstate industrial dispute that gave rise to the award and that, for that reason, the variation fell outside the ambit of s 51(xxxv) …

[421] It was submitted that the remaining, effective provisions of the award could not be said to be the product of a process of conciliation and arbitration for the prevention and settlement of interstate industrial disputes. It was said that those provisions were not the product of that process because that process had produced an altogether different award from the award to which the Act would give effect after the interim period. Thus, so it was argued, the provisions now in question were not laws with respect to conciliation and arbitration because they produced a "result" different from the result of conciliation and arbitration …

This way of putting the argument can be seen to be no more than a restatement … of arguments with which we have dealt above. Speaking of the "result" of conciliation and arbitration distracts attention from the relevant inquiry: to identify the rights, duties, powers and privileges that have been changed, regulated or abolished. The relevant "result", then, is not just what has previously been published as an arbitrator's award or as a conciliated consent award; the relevant "result" is the rights, duties, powers and privileges to which that process gave rise. And the question that must be asked about the legislation that now is in question is what rights, duties, powers and privileges that legislation changes. The argument about difference in result when examined, can be seen to be one which, directly or indirectly, seeks to attribute relevant legal significance to particular provi-sions of awards other than the significance that was given to those provisions by the legislation. For the reasons we have given earlier, we do not accept that s 3 and the relevant items of Sch 5 deal with more than that legislative effect.

Gaudron J: [372] [I]n their unmodified form, ss 148(1) and 149(1) of the principal Act which, respectively, give effect to awards and extend the operation of awards, are valid. They are valid because they give effect to or continue the effect of the outcome of conciliation and arbitration until set aside or a new award is made. However, if Parliament legislates to give effect to some only of the terms of an award, or, more precisely, to deny effect to some terms whilst continuing the effect of others, it is not legislating with respect to the outcome of the processes of conciliation and arbitration. It is creating a new outcome from the combined processes of legislation and arbitration or, perhaps, the combined processes of conciliation, arbitration and legislation. In substance, the position is the same as if Parliament were to legislate directly to supplement the terms of an award.

It follows that s 3 of the WROLA Act, to the extent in issue in these proceedings, cannot be supported on the same constitutional basis as ss 148(1) and 149(1) of the principal Act.

As will later appear, Parliament could have amended s 148(1) of the principal Act to withdraw all legislative support from awards containing non-allowable award matters. And it could also have legislated to require the Commission to review awards containing non-allowable award matters to determine whether it was desirable that they should continue to make provision with respect to those matters and directing it, if it found their continued operation undesirable, to vary the awards by deleting those provisions. Of course, the award as varied would be a valid exercise of the conciliation and arbitration power only if it retained a requisite connection with the dispute in respect of which it was made. But Parliament has taken neither course.

In substance, Parliament has attempted, itself, to review the awards of the Commission and to vary them in the exercise of legislative power. It has substituted its decision for that of the arbitrator. A law which substitutes an outcome that is different from the outcome of the processes of conciliation and arbitration is not a law with respect to conciliation and arbitration.

McHugh J: [387] Section 51(xxxv), like s 51(xxxi) of the Constitution, is what Dixon J has referred to as a "compound conception" [*Grace Brothers Pty Ltd v Commonwealth* (1946) 72 CLR 269 at 290]. It initially describes a power to legislate with respect to two processes – "conciliation and arbitration", which are disjunctive in the sense that the process can be either conciliation or arbitration. But the width of legislative power that would otherwise flow from a power to legislate with respect to these processes is confined by the conjunctive requirement that the process be directed to achieving an objective. The existence of the objective is indicated by the word "for", and the specified objective is "the prevention and settlement of industrial disputes extending beyond the limits of any one State" ...

[388] [I]t is a mistake to isolate the elements of s 51(xxxv) of the Constitution, interpret them, and then ask whether the legislation in question is legislation with respect to the sum of those individual interpretations. It must be always kept in mind that the power in s 51(xxxv) is a power to legislate with respect to a process that is designed to achieve a particular objective ...

The "process limb" of the compound conception in s 51(xxxv) has given rise to several requirements which this Court has considered are necessary concomitants of the words used to describe the process. The relevant process in this case is "arbitration" ... There can be no arbitration for constitutional purposes unless there is a **[389]** genuine dispute in existence between two parties which is determined by the tribunal acting judicially and applying the principles of natural justice. Since, by hypothesis, the parties have been unable to agree, the tribunal must make an agreement for them ...

[I]t would be pointless to compel parties to submit to an arbitrator if the arbitrator's subsequent decision could be completely ignored by the parties without legal sanction. In the case of parties voluntarily submitting to arbitration, the parties themselves agree to be "bound by the decision". But at least in the case of compulsory arbitration, legislative provisions are needed to make the outcome of the arbitration binding on the parties ...

[390] If a statute set up a sophisticated process of non-voluntary *arbitration* but contained a provision that the arbitrator's award would have no legal effect, it is not easy to accept that it would be an arbitration for the purpose of s 51(xxxv) of the Constitution. Depending on all the circumstances, it might be upheld as a law with respect to conciliation but it is hard to accept that the law provided for arbitration for the settlement of an industrial dispute. If the parties can ignore the "arbitrated" result, the process does not bind them and the arbitration has not settled the dispute. At best, it suspends the continuance of the dispute for as long as the parties agree to act in accordance with the "arbitrated" award ...

Because the compound conception ... in s 51(xxxv) involves some notion of the enforceability of the outcome, I cannot accept the argument of the respondents that the legislation is valid because the impugned provisions do not affect the settlement of the dispute but only its enforceability. That argument seeks to divorce the notion of an arbitrated settlement from its enforceability ...

The decided cases in this Court on the conciliation and arbitration power show that, if legislation affecting the enforceability of an award retains the integrity of the award as an outcome of conciliation or arbitration, that legislation will generally be a law with respect to s 51(xxxv).

That this result flows from the authorities is not surprising. It is a result dictated by a principled application of the text of the Constitution. The compound conception in s 51(xxxv) includes a **[391]** process and an objective. Assuming that the process meets its constitutional description, then a law with respect to the outcome simpliciter of that process will generally be a law with respect to the compound conception because the outcome is the embodiment of the constitutionally dictated objective.

However, a law which operates upon the outcome in such a way so as to not deal with it as an outcome simpliciter will not necessarily be a law with respect to the compound conception. If the law deals with only part of the outcome, the outcome will not necessarily retain its status as the end of the constitutionally dictated objective of the process …

[397] In my opinion, items 50 and 51 do operate to deprive the award of its status as the achievement of the constitutionally dictated objective of the process. They are not laws with respect to the outcome of the constitutional process directed at settling the original dispute. The process of reaching an arbitrated settlement necessarily involves trade-**[398]**-offs being made between the competing claims of the parties. The arbitrator may consider that it is just to impose an obligation on a party (obligation A) in return for granting that party a compensating right (right B). In constructing the award, the arbitrator would have been working on the assumption that the term of the award giving effect to right B would have the same legal status and enforceability as the term of the award giving effect to obligation A, and that no single term of the arbitrated outcome would in the future achieve a preferred legal status over any other term. If it were otherwise, the arbitrator could not confidently impose obligation A as the quid pro quo for the granting of right B. The arbitrator would be forced to guess which terms might be unenforceable in the future. In striking of the appropriate balance, the arbitrator would be forced to apply some "discounting factor" to those terms because in the future they may be of no utility to a party – no more substantial in reality than "buildings on a movie set – structures with the appearance of reality but having no substance behind them" [*Yanner v Eaton* (1999) 201 CLR 351 at 376].

Callinan J: [450] There may very well be, as McHugh J points out, elements of compromise in the affected award some of which may not readily be able to be isolated. But it might equally be said that an award such as this one may contain elements repugnant to parties bound by it. It may even be anathematical in whole to some parties, but the industrial regime in this country has nonetheless for a very long time operated to impose awards upon such parties. It does not therefore seem to me to be anomalous that the challenged provisions might in some way affect the balance of compromises (if any) contained in it. However, in any event item 51(3) provides that the Commission when varying an award may also vary it, so that in relation to an allowable award matter, the award is expressed in a way that reasonably represents the entitlements of employees in respect of that matter as provided in the award in force immediately before the interim period. In short, it might confidently be expected that any concern about the prospective loss of a benefit achieved by a compromise would usually be the subject of debate and argument in the Commission.

All of the mechanisms of "award simplification" employed in the WROLA Act were taken further by the *Workplace Relations Amendment (Work Choices) Act 2005* (Cth). However, since that Act no longer depends primarily on s 51(xxxv), the arguments of the dissenting judges in the *CFMEU Case* would appear to be no longer relevant.

In later proceedings concerning Item 25 of Pt 1 of Sch 5 to the WROLA Act, which inserted s 111AAA into the principal Act, the Court unanimously held that the amendment must be given its full effect. Section 111AAA(1) provided: "If the Commission is satisfied that a State award or State employment agreement governs the wages and conditions of employment of particular employees …, the Commission must cease dealing with the industrial dispute in relation to those employees, unless the Commission is satisfied that ceasing would not be in the public interest". The Federal Court had held that this provision did not apply to proceedings already constituted before s 111AAA came into force (*Re McIntyre v Transport Workers' Union of Australia; Ex parte Attorney-General (Queensland)* (2000) 105 FCR 584); but in *Attorney-General (Queensland) v Australian Industrial Relations Commission* (2002) 213 CLR 485 the High Court reversed that decision, holding that s 111AAA applied to all proceedings in the Commission, regardless of when they were commenced. In undertaking this further assessment of the impact of the WROLA Act on the industrial arbitration regime, the joint judgment of Gaudron, McHugh, Gummow and Hayne JJ noted that "**[499]** many of the features of that regime still exist", but found it "convenient to describe the relevant provisions in the past tense".

5. Paper Disputes

Many of the potential problems arising from the early cases were overcome by the central role in the Commonwealth arbitration system assigned to "registered organisations", both of employees and of employers. This allowed the High Court's refusal to countenance a "common rule" to be largely overcome. If the parties to a dispute in an industry are "registered organisations", then an arbitral award made binding on the employees' union and on the employers' organisation is effectively binding on the whole industry. The watershed here was *Burwood Cinema Ltd v Australian Theatrical and Amusement Employees' Association* (1925) 35 CLR 528.

In that case the Australian Theatrical and Amusement Employees' Association had served a log of claims on theatre owners throughout Australia, thereby generating a "paper dispute". The Burwood Cinema objected that it could not be a party to any dispute since its employees were all satisfied with their working conditions. (On similar facts in *R v Commonwealth Court of Conciliation and Arbitration; Ex parte William Holyman & Sons Ltd* (1914) 18 CLR 273 the High Court had granted prohibition.) The firm of Lillyman & White also objected that it could not be a party to the dispute because it employed no union members. By 4:2, Knox CJ and Gavan Duffy J dissenting, the Court held that both employers were parties as to whom a binding award could be made. Insofar as *Holyman's Case* decided otherwise, it was overruled.

Burwood Cinema Ltd v Australian Theatrical and Amusement Employees' Association
(1925) 35 CLR 528

Isaacs J: [539] Approaching ... the matter by the light of the three leading principles – namely, those of (1) the *Engineers' Case* [(1920) 28 CLR 129], (2) *Brunton's Case* [[1913] AC 747] and (3) the cases establishing the broad construction of pl xxxv – it is clear that that placitum embraces whatever at a given moment answers the essential conception of an "industrial dispute" in 1900. Industry itself is constantly changing: scientific, social and other causes bring about great transformations. Disputes will necessarily vary accordingly. Causes, forms of manifestation and subjects of difference will change; organization may become more or less complete, or may become more or less detailed; but, so long as the fundamental concept of "industrial dispute" is present, none of these evolutionary modifications prevent[s] the matter from being within the ambit of power. Indeed, it is of the essence of a Constitution that it is intended by its generality to adapt itself to the growth of the nation. "Industrial disputes" certainly include conflicts of greater or less intensity among those **[540]** co-operating in a given industry with reference to the conditions of their co-operation. "Co-operation" in the industry is not from the standpoint of the Constitution restricted to actual contractual relations. Every employer that enters the competitive field of the industry is co-operating to carry it on, in the broader sense in which the people of the Commonwealth are interested. That sense is national service and supply, the interruption of which is the evil dealt with in pl xxxv. So also is every employee a co-operator in the same sense, for his labour is not to be looked on as a mere commodity, as if he were a machine, animate like the horse or inanimate like a steam-engine. The nexus of all the co-operators is the industry itself, irrespective of how its ownership or its operative arrangements are subdivided. If we confine our attention for the moment to disputes between employers and employed, we have to visualize the disputants respectively as portions of groups representing capital and labour. "Employer" and "employee" are terms which denote, not individuals contracting with each other whose industrial relations arise out of and are limited by their specific contracts, but membership of a group with which the individual has identified himself in relation to a given industry. The concept has grown out of the necessity for collective bargaining and collective action, involving organization more or less formal and more or less complete. Long before 1900 the identification of the individual with the group was thoroughly established. In 1892 in Dr Garran's Report on New South Wales it was stated, that "the federation of labour and the counter-federation of employers is the characteristic feature of the labour question in the present epoch." Without such identification there never can be effective action to meet the difficulties of modern industrial life … I may at once quote one paragraph from the unanimous interim report, dated 8th March 1917, of the Reconstruction Committee on Joint Standing Industrial Councils presented to Mr Lloyd George when Prime Minister (Cd 8606) … Par 23 is as follows:– "It may be desirable to state here our considered opinion that an essential condition of **[541]** securing a permanent improvement in the relations between employers and employed is that there should be adequate organization on the part of both employers and work-people. The proposals outlined for joint co-operation throughout the several industries depend for their ultimate success upon there being such organization on both sides; and such organization is necessary also to provide means whereby the arrangements and agreements made for the industry may be effectively carried out." Why is "organisation" an "essential condition"? Plainly, because an "industry or some selected branch of it" is for the purpose regarded as one entity … Every competitor acts and interacts, and more or less affects the rest of those on the same field. If, then, sec 51(xxxv) of the Australian Constitution is to be faithfully applied in the broad sense already adopted, so as to be effective to cope with the destructive evil of industrial warfare – an evil which, if unchecked, would threaten all national welfare – it must necessarily be competent to provide by conciliation and arbitration for the "essential condition" referred to. That is to say, while the "common rule" as one extreme is excluded, so a limitation to individual contract as the other extreme is also excluded. Employers who voluntarily enter and compete on the same field of industry and thereby affect the industrial relations of all others on that field – unionist and non-unionist – cannot escape the result of their voluntary action by merely excluding union labour.

Starke J: [548] Industrial disputes are, as a rule, collective disputes. They may arise between two sets of workmen, as in the case of demarcation or discipline disputes. Or, as is more common, between employers or a class of employers on the one side and a large aggregation of workmen on the other. In the latter case the dispute often relates to the terms on which future employment shall be given, not only to men then employed, but to all men who may subsequently be engaged in the trade or calling in which the dispute has arisen. Thus the dispute may be whether preference shall be given by those employing a certain class of labour to the members, present and future, of some association of employees, or whether all members of that association, present and future, shall, if employed, have the benefit of better terms and conditions, and so forth. It is clear, therefore, that the existence of an industrial dispute does not depend upon the actual relation of employer and employee or of master and servant, between the participators in the dispute. It is equally clear that absolute definiteness of the individuals engaged in the dispute cannot be essential, for in industrial disputes, claims and demands are usually made for the benefit of "the ever changing body of workmen that constitute the trade" (see *Hudson's Case* [(1923) 32 CLR 413 at 454]). An industrial dispute is constituted, both historically and in point of fact, where a difference exists between workmen themselves, or perhaps between employers themselves, or between employers or classes of employers, and workmen engaged in some common industry or calling, concerning industrial conditions affecting a class so engaged and not merely affecting **[549]** individual and definite members thereof. An industrial relationship, and not a contractual relationship, is all that is necessary to constitute an industrial dispute. The nexus is to be found in the industry or in the calling or avocation in which the participators are engaged. This description does not, perhaps, exhaust the constitutional power of the Commonwealth in relation to industrial disputes … , but it covers most of the field and is a sufficient guide for the determination of the main questions stated in this case. Associations of large bodies of men are, however, defective in legal personality, and it is expedient, at least for the purposes of legal representation, and probably also for the purpose of "collective bargaining," that they should be organized in some form.

All this was recognized, in my opinion, by this Court in the *Jumbunna Coal Mine, No Liability, v Victorian Coal Miners' Association* [(1908) 6 CLR 309], which upheld the provisions of the Arbitration Act relating to the incorporation of associations of workmen, and also of employers, or organizations, as they are termed in the Act. Such organizations, to my mind, "represent and stand in the place of their members" and must, to be effective, have "right and authority to act on their account" (see Encyclopaedia Britannica, 11th ed, sub "Representation").

But this Court has not yet, I think, adopted so broad a view. A series of cases suggests that this principle of representation does not enable an organization itself to raise an industrial dispute. The acts of the individuals constituting the organization were, in each case, examined in detail for the purpose of determining whether the workmen themselves ... made common cause, common demands, and took concerted action in support of their demands ... And in *Holyman's Case* [(1914) 18 CLR 273] ... **[550]** [this Court] prohibited the making of an award against employers whose employees had signed a statement that they had no dispute with their employers and were satisfied with their conditions of labour ... **[551]** Now, however, three members of the Court, who took part in *Holyman's Case* or applied its principle in other cases, have reached the conclusion that *Holyman's Case* cannot be supported, and my brother *Higgins*, sitting alone, has also, I think, departed from the principle of that case.

Under these circumstances, I feel free, and, indeed, bound, to give effect to my own view. *Holyman's Case* was, in my opinion, wrongly decided. An organization registered under the Arbitration Act is not a mere agent of its members: it stands in their place, and acts on their account and is a representative of the class associated together in the organization. It is, as my brother *Higgins* said, "a party principal," and "not a mere agent or figurehead." The acts and conduct of its members are relevant, no doubt, upon the question whether the dispute submitted to the Court by the organization or referred to it by other means is real or illusory, but otherwise their acts and conduct are immaterial.

The decision in the *Burwood Cinema Case* was further developed in *Metal Trades Employers Association v Amalgamated Engineering Union* (1935) 54 CLR 387. In 10 disputes in the metal trades industry Beeby J, in the Commonwealth Court of Conciliation and Arbitration, proposed an award which would bind the employers as to all employees. When employers in South Australia objected, Beeby J stated a case for the High Court on whether the Arbitration Court could make an award which would bind employers in respect of all employees, whether members of a union or not. Latham CJ, Rich, Evatt and McTiernan JJ, with Dixon J dissenting, held that a union demand in respect of "all persons employed" gave rise to an industrial dispute under s 51(xxxv); and that, in order to settle that dispute between the union and the employers, an arbitral award could bind the employers in respect of all employees, including non-unionists.

Metal Trades Employers Association v Amalgamated Engineering Union
(1935) 54 CLR 387

Latham CJ: [402] The first question which arises in this matter is whether there may be an industrial dispute between employees (A) and employers (B) as to terms of employment of other employees (C) in the same industry in which employees (A) are engaged in cases where none of the employees (A) are themselves employed by some or even by any of the employers (B).

A dispute exists only between the disputants. Generally and naturally it relates to their mutual industrial relations. But there is no reason why it should not relate to the industrial relations between one set of the disputants and third persons. In actual experience preference to unionists is an industrial matter which is a common source of industrial disputes between unionists and their employers. In such disputes the contention of the disputants essentially relates to the employment or non-employment by one set of disputants of third persons who are not parties to the dispute. Such a matter is of great industrial importance alike to unionists and non-unionists (as well as to employers), but only unionists ... are parties to the dispute on the side of the employees. There does not appear to be any reason in principle for denying that the terms upon which non-unionists may be employed may be as much the subject matter of an industrial dispute as the question whether non-unionists shall be employed at all.

[403] Unionists may be concerned and apprehensive with respect to any matters which may affect the terms upon which their employers can afford to employ them. If other employers are at liberty to employ non-unionists at lower rates of wages, the competitive efficiency of employers employing unionists may be seriously prejudiced, and the continued employment of the unionists may be jeopardized. Employers of unionists may take the same view. It is to be expected that the opinions of those engaged in industry will vary upon this subject. Some will regard it as a matter of principle, others as a matter of interest. Divergence of views is well illustrated in this very case. Four unions have definitely claimed that employers should give to non-unionists the same conditions as to unionists, while two unions have appeared before the Court to oppose that claim. Employers in New South Wales, Victoria and Tasmania argued in the same way as the four unions mentioned, while employers in South Australia supported the arguments of the two opposing unions. The question of the terms upon which non-unionists may be employed can hardly be denied to be industrial in character, and it is obvious that it may become the subject of a dispute – between employers and employees, or between employers and employers, or between employees and employees.

The question which arises cannot however be decided merely by determining that the subject matter of the claim made may be the subject of an industrial dispute. The Act authorizes the settlement of industrial disputes only by conciliation or by arbitration. Conciliation may bring about an agreement: arbitration may result in an award. An agreement between two persons may produce an effect upon third persons, but it can impose duties or confer rights only upon those who make the agreement. Similarly an award may produce an effect upon third persons, but it can directly affect the legal relations only of those who were parties to the arbitration proceedings of which it is the result. In industrial arbitration the conception of "parties" is extended by a doctrine of representation which is in itself associated with the idea of "industrial disputes." Industrial disputes are essentially group contests – there is always an industrial group on at least one side. [404] A claim of an individual employee against his employer is not in itself an industrial dispute. If it professes to be based upon an existing right (as, for example, a contract of employment, or an award …) such a claim may give rise to litigation in the civil Courts – but it is not an industrial dispute. If a claim is made by an individual employee for some improvement in his pay or conditions of employment the refusal of the claim by his employer may result in a personal dispute, but this in itself would not be an industrial dispute. One necessary element of an industrial dispute, as distinguished from other disputes, is the circumstance that a demand is made by or upon a group of employers or employees. Thus an industrial organization is engaged in such a dispute when it makes what may be called an industrial demand on behalf of its members, present and future. In a forensic sense the organization is the party to the dispute, though it asks for nothing for itself as an organization. In another sense, the existing members of the organization are the parties to the dispute. The object of the dispute is to obtain rights for them or to cause them to become subject to obligations. The future members of the organization, though not in existence as such, are also regarded as represented in the dispute by the organization (*Burwood Cinema Ltd v Australian Theatrical and Amusement Employees' Association* [(1925) 35 CLR 528]).

The conception of industrial arbitration is closely similar in these respects to that of an industrial dispute. The parties to the proceedings always include some group which makes or resists a demand for an award which will impose duties or confer rights upon or in relation to the members of the group. This conception underlies the provision in sec 29 of the Act that members of an organization shall be bound by an award, though they have not individually taken any part in the arbitration proceedings. Any statement that an industrial award binds only disputants who are parties to the arbitration proceedings must be understood in [this] extended sense …

[405] These considerations do not affect the principle that the Commonwealth Court of Conciliation and Arbitration cannot impose duties or confer rights upon persons who are neither parties to, nor represented in any manner in, the dispute or the arbitration proceedings.

It does not, however, follow that an industrial award, by imposing duties upon such parties (which are owed only to other such parties), cannot affect the possible employment of third persons who are not such parties in any sense. It is true that the procedural provisions of the Act limit the legal effect of an award to persons who either directly are, or by reason of representation are regarded as being, such parties. But the terms of an award may prevent the creation of specified legal relations between a party and third persons. An obvious example is found in the admitted proposition that an award may grant preference to unionists. So far as the award creates legal relations between persons, it affects only the parties to the dispute and to the proceedings. But it prevents the lawful employment of non-unionists and therefore prohibits the creation of a contract of employment between employers and non-unionists, even though the latter were not parties to or heard in the arbitration proceedings ...

[408] It has been argued before us that the question which arises is concluded by the decision [as to a common rule] in *Australian Boot Trade Employees' Federation v Whybrow & Co* [(1910) 11 CLR 311] ... The ground of that decision, however, is to be found in the principle that an award, whether made for the purpose of preventing or for the purpose of settling an industrial dispute, could not bind others than the disputants. Accordingly it was determined that an award could not extend beyond the area of the dispute so as to regulate the whole of an industry irrespective [409] of the extent of the dispute. But it was not denied that the award could deal with the whole subject matter of the industrial dispute. That subject matter may include a controversy as to the industrial relations of disputants with strangers to the dispute. If so, there is nothing in the principles upon which *Whybrow's Case* was decided which prevents the making of an award dealing with that controversy (cf *George Hudson Ltd v Australian Timber Workers' Union* [(1923) 32 CLR 413 at 439]). These considerations provide a reply to the objection that the proposed award would be legislative rather than arbitral in character.

It has been urged, as an *argumentum ab inconvenienti* in support of the contention that the Act does not contemplate an award being made which deals with the relations of disputants to persons who are not disputants, that great confusion will arise if such awards are made. Unionists doing identical work may, it is pointed out, in some cases belong to either of two or possibly more unions, but as long as awards deal with the relation of employers to unionists and not with the relation of employers to non-unionists, it is possible to ascertain which award applies in any given case. It is urged that, if awards in general are framed upon the model of the proposed award in this case, it will sometimes be impossible for an employer to know to which award he should refer in order to ascertain the terms upon which he could lawfully employ a non-unionist. The difficulty is a real one, but its existence or possible existence cannot be decisive of the legal questions raised. The risk of such confusion arising and the desirability, indeed the necessity, of preventing it, will doubtless be present to the mind of the Arbitration Court. The matter is in the hands of the Court, which will doubtless take pains to prevent more than one award being so expressed as to be applicable in any given case.

Dixon J: [428] In *The Builders' Labourers' Case* [(1914) 18 CLR 224] this Court relinquished the endeavour to find in the circumstance that a dispute has been raised by an organization for the purpose of obtaining an award a reason sufficient in itself for denying that the dispute is genuine. It also decided that a formal demand for improved conditions of pay and work, if refused, affords prima facie evidence of a dispute. From that time the formulation of claims by registered organizations of employers became a procedure recognized as sufficient to found the Court's jurisdiction to make an award unless some particular reason appeared for saying that there could not be, or was not, a dispute. The validity of the provisions in the Act dealing with the formation, registration and incorporation, of associations or organizations of employees and employers had been sustained in *Jumbunna Coal Mine, No Liability v Victorian Coal Miners' Association* [(1908) 6 CLR 309] upon the ground that they are incidental to the power of preventing and settling industrial disputes by conciliation and arbitration. They were considered so incidental because the power could not be effectively exercised if individual employees only could be dealt with and if no continuing representatives of the employees existed who could arrive at a permanent settlement of the dispute by collective bargaining and be the means of securing obedience to an award when the Court settled it; see per *O'Connor* J in the *Jumbunna Coal Mine Case* [6 CLR at 359], whose judgment appears to be the source of many of the conceptions developed in the later decisions. The curious consequence has ensued that organizations, existing under a law upheld on the ground that their formation and registration conduced to the easier and more permanent settlement by conciliation and arbitration of disputes independently arising, have come to be the instruments for propounding the claims by which industrial disputes are created so that the Court of Conciliation and Arbitration may regulate wages and conditions of employment.

Despite the impact of these decisions on the practice of industrial relations in Australia, the main point of *Whybrow (No 2)* has always remained unshaken: the power of "conciliation and arbitration" does not extend to the making of a "common rule" for an entire industry. However much the *Burwood Cinema Case* and the *Metal Trades Case* may have weakened or circumvented the practical effect of this restriction, the conceptual restriction remains.

Of course, since the exclusion of a "common rule" depends on the Court's interpretation of s 51(xxxv), the Parliament has been able in recent years to authorise the making of a "common rule" under other heads of power, for example in relation to the Territories, the Commonwealth public service, and Victoria under its referral of powers (see the *Workplace Relations Act 1996* (Cth), Part VI, Div 5 – repealed in 2005 but so that any "common rules" already established remain in force on a transitional basis). More generally, under the expanded "defence" power during World War II, the *National Security (Industrial Peace) Regulations* (Cth) specifically conferred a power to declare "that any term of an order or award shall be a common rule of any industry in connexion with which the dispute arose". However, when the Chifley government attempted in 1947 to re-enact that provision on a permanent basis as a new s 41(1) of the *Conciliation and Arbitration Act*, the High Court unanimously declared it invalid, reaffirming the traditional doctrine.

R v Kelly; Ex parte Victoria
(1950) 81 CLR 64

The Court: [79] [N]o distinction can be drawn between the present case and *Whybrow's Case* [(1910) 11 CLR 311] on the basis of any difference between the language of the old s 38(*f*) and the new s 41(1). The reasoning of all the judgments in *Whybrow's Case* makes it quite plain that it is by reason of its inherent nature that the common rule is held to be outside the constitutional power. That which is actually **[80]** authorized by s 41(1) is exactly the same thing as that which was authorized by s 38(*f*), and it was held that that very thing could not be constitutionally authorized. This was because the constitutional power is limited to conciliation and arbitration between disputing parties, and to make a common rule is to go outside the scope of conciliation and arbitration and to assume a function of general industrial legislation ...

If, then, the common rule is to be upheld in this case, it is necessary that *Whybrow's Case* should be overruled, and we were invited to overrule it. *Whybrow's Case* ought not, in our opinion, to be overruled. The decision has stood for forty years, the reasoning of the judgments commends itself to us as unanswerable, and the main argument presented to us, while it has commanded consideration, does not seem to us to cast any doubt upon that reasoning ...

[81] The most substantial argument for the common rule, however, rested on a series of cases which begins with *Burwood Cinema Ltd v Australian Theatrical & Amusement Employees' Association* [(1925) 35 CLR 528] and may be said to end with *Metal Trades Employers' Association v Amalgamated Engineering Union* [(1935) 54 CLR 387] ... **[82]** In the first of these cases, the *Burwood Cinema Case*, the reasons for judgment give no support to the proposition that power to make a common rule can validly be given to the court or to a conciliation commissioner. *Isaacs* J expressly says that "the common rule as one extreme is excluded" [35 CLR at 541]. The principle upon which the doctrine of the *Metal Trades Case* rests is "that the interest which an organization of employees possesses in the establishment or maintenance of industrial conditions for its members gives a foundation for an attempt on its part to prevent employers employing anyone on less favourable terms. As a result an industrial dispute may be raised by it with employers employing none of its members, and an award may be made binding such employers and regulating the terms and conditions upon which they may employ unionists or non-unionists" (per *Dixon* J in *R v Commonwealth Court of Conciliation and Arbitration; Ex parte Kirsch* [(1938) 60 CLR 507 at 537-38]). But in such a case there is *ex hypothesi* a dispute between the organization and the employers whom it is sought to affect by the award. The award does not affect any non-disputant. It does not create (as the common rule would create) actual rights and duties as between persons who are non-disputants. According to the theory of the *Metal Trades Case* it does nothing that is "foreign to arbitration" (per *Isaacs* J in *Arnall's Case* [(1929) 43 CLR 29 at 44]). This is made plain by *Latham* CJ in the *Metal Trades Case* [54 CLR at 408]. A common rule *does* effect a result which is "foreign to arbitration." The distinction may seem technical, and the practical result of observing it may be, as Mr *Ashburner* said, merely to compel the joining of many additional parties as respondents before the court or commissioner – but any parties so joined would not be bound by an award made in relation to the dispute unless they were parties, not only to the proceedings, but also to the dispute. The distinction has been observed and emphasised throughout the whole series of cases, it is a clear and logical distinction, and, in our opinion, it ought to be observed and the power to make a common rule denied.

From time to time it was thought that the High Court might be chipping away at the *Burwood Cinema Case*. In *Re Finance Sector Union of Australia; Ex parte Financial Clinic (Vic) Pty Ltd* (1993) 178 CLR 352, it was held by a 4:3 majority that an arbitrable "industrial dispute" could arise from a union demand that employers' contributions to superannuation for employees who were union members must be paid into a single specified superannuation scheme, but not from the extension of such a demand to contributions in respect of employees who were not members of the union.

The dissenting judgment of Brennan, Dawson and McHugh JJ traced the developments by which superannuation had emerged as an industrial issue: initially through the High Court decision in *Re Manufacturing Grocers' Employees Federation of Australia; Ex parte Australian Chamber of Manufactures* (1986) 160 CLR 341, and thereafter through the 1986 *National Wage Case* (1986) 301 CAR 611 and the *Occupational Superannuation Standards Act 1987* (Cth). Against that background they argued that, as between the union and the employers, a demand that all superannuation premiums be paid into a single fund, including those in respect of employees who were *not* union members, was a matter of legitimate concern. However, the majority rejected that view. The joint judgment of Mason CJ, Deane, Toohey and Gaudron JJ explained that any union claim in respect of non-members "**[363]** must relate to the employer-employee relationship of the employers and employees who are, or are treated as, the parties to the dispute". The *Metal Trades Case* had remained within this limit because the decision in respect of non-members was confined to their wages and working conditions. "**[361]** If a claim does travel beyond wages and conditions as they apply to individual employees, it is necessary to inquire whether it pertains 'to the relationship between employers and employees' as required by s 4(1) of the Act". An affirmative answer could be given for a union claim that all employees, including non-members, "**[364]** receive superannuation contributions in the same amount or at the same level", but not for a claim that such contributions should all be paid to a single fund – at least not if the claim was driven by "nothing more than a desire to bring about a situation in which there is a single industry superannuation scheme".

This decision must be read in the light of an earlier decision in 1993, in which it was clear that the Court was holding fast to its traditional doctrines. The prosecutors, applicants for prohibition, had argued that, now that the *CYSS Case* had shifted the emphasis to "industrial disputes", and thus away from "disputes in an industry", the fact that all the parties involved were engaged in a single "industry" could no longer be used as the nexus or unifying factor sufficing to knit their grievances into a single "dispute". The Court rejected this argument.

Re Australasian Meat Industry Employees' Union; Ex parte Aberdeen Beef Co Pty Ltd
(1993) 176 CLR 154

Mason CJ, Brennan, Deane, Dawson, Toohey and Gaudron JJ: [159] It is true that in *R v Coldham; Ex parte Australian Social Welfare Union* [(1983) 153 CLR 297 at 312] the Court pointed out that the phrase used in s 51(xxxv) of the Constitution is "industrial disputes" and not "disputes in an industry" …

However, recognizing that the expression "industrial disputes" in the Constitution is used in its popular and not in any narrow sense, does not prevent the existence of an identifiable industry from providing the nexus or unifying factor which combines in a single industrial dispute a number of demands made on behalf of a number of employees to a number of employers … [I]t remains possible to identify specific industries and in most cases it is still true to say, as Isaacs J did in *Jumbunna Coal Mine NL v Victorian Coal Miners' Association* [(1908) 6 CLR 309 at 373] and *R v Commonwealth Court of Conciliation and Arbitration; Ex parte Jones; Ex parte W Cooper & Sons* ("the *Builders' Labourers' Case*") [(1914) 18 CLR 224 at 242], that "the *nexus* of an industrial dispute is 'the industry' itself". It may now be the case, given the wider meaning attributed to "industrial dispute", that it is no longer invariably necessary to discern a particular industry before it is possible to find the existence of an industrial dispute. Other factors may provide the nexus. But the words of Starke J in *Burwood Cinema Ltd v Australian Theatrical and Amusement Employees' Association* [(1925) 35 CLR 528 at 548-9] still provide a general guide:

> "An industrial dispute is constituted, both historically and in point of fact, where a difference exists between workmen **[160]** themselves, or perhaps between employers themselves, or between employers or classes of employers, and workmen engaged in some common industry or calling, concerning industrial conditions affecting a class so engaged and not merely affecting individual and definite members thereof. An industrial relationship, and not a contractual relationship, is all that is necessary to constitute an industrial dispute. The nexus is to be found in the industry or in the calling or avocation in which the participators are engaged."

It is not of great significance that there was no exact coincidence between the activities carried on in the respective States in respect of which demands were made. It is of greater significance that those upon whom or in respect of whom the demands were made had a community of interest. That factor may exist because of the employers' or employees' participation in a single industry and is present here. A dispute involving parties having a community of interest is likely to be a single industrial dispute despite differences between the activities of those parties. In this case a single industry can be identified in which there is a history of common industrial regulation by a single award containing the same classifications as were adopted by the log of claims.

However, at the political level, the more recent terminological preference for the label "workplace relations" rather than "industrial relations" has reflected the legislative objective of locating the "nexus" in the individual "workplace", rather than in the entire "industry".

6. "Beyond the limits of any one State"

The *Burwood Cinema Case* permitted the making of awards effectively binding throughout a particular industry, thus achieving in practice much of the impact of a "common rule". It also greatly reduced the significance of the need for industrial disputes "extending beyond the limits of any one State". Since "registered organisations" of employers and employees are themselves constituted on a federal basis, the service of a log of claims by a union on an employer organisation will usually suffice to bring into existence an interstate dispute. However, when a dispute arises from actual industrial dislocation there may still be difficulty in showing that it extends "beyond the limits of any one State". The most striking example was the climax to a long history of unrest in the Hunter Valley coalfields in New South Wales.

Under the *War Precautions Act 1914* (Cth), the Commonwealth government increased the output, prices and wages at mines in the Hunter Valley. The Act was repealed in 1920, but regulations relating to coal were extended to 1921. From 1920 on, the colliery owners insisted that under post-war conditions output, prices and wages must be reduced. The Miners' Federation filed a log of claims in 1920 that led to a further wage increase, while the owners filed a log in 1922 for wage reductions, which were refused. A further wage increase was granted in 1925, but was largely negated by intermittent closure by the owners. After 1927 the new conservative government in New South Wales under Premier Thomas Bavin took up the owners' demands. Conferences called by Bavin in 1928 proposed a price reduction of four shillings per ton, which was based, in part, on miners' wages being cut by one shilling per ton. In February 1929 the miners rejected the Bavin plan. Thereupon the owners gave the miners 14 days' notice that all the Hunter Valley mines would close down, to reopen only when the miners accepted the wage cut. The result was a stoppage that put 10,000 men out of work for 16 months.

Throughout 1929 efforts to get the mines reopened broke down. Eventually the New South Wales government gave an ultimatum that if the miners did not accept the Bavin plan it would take over the mines at Cessnock, Pelton and Rothbury and reopen them on reduced wages. The threat of compulsory reopening led to unrest in Victoria and Queensland. The miners in those States feared that reduction of wages in New South Wales would flow on to them. On 16 December 1929 the New South Wales government reopened the Rothbury mine, and the Commonwealth Court of Conciliation and Arbitration intervened for the first time. Beeby J called a compulsory conference on 17-18 December 1929. When it failed, he found that "an industrial dispute of which the Court can take cognizance exists or is threatened and impending". On 19 December 1929 he made an interim award fixing wages at pre-lockout rates. Despite an impassioned dissent by Isaacs J, the High Court granted prohibition on the ground that the dispute was confined to New South Wales.

Caledonian Collieries Ltd v Australasian Coal and Shale Employees' Federation (No 1)
(1930) 42 CLR 527

Gavan Duffy, Rich, Starke and Dixon JJ: **[552]** [It is] well established that to constitute an industrial dispute there must be disagreement between people or groups of people who stand in some industrial relation upon some matter which affects or arises out of the relationship. Such a disagreement may cause a strike, a lock-out, and disturbance and dislocation of industry; but these are the consequences of the industrial dispute, and not the industrial dispute itself, which lies in the disagreement. It is only because this meaning of the words "industrial dispute" **[553]** was adopted that the Court of Conciliation and Arbitration has been able to exercise the function of prescribing rates of wages and conditions of employment at the instance of organizations which have done little more than formulate and deliver logs of demands with which employers have not complied. But upon this conception of an industrial dispute, it cannot extend beyond the limits of any one State unless in each of two or more States, at one time, the disagreement exists between people or groups who stand in some industrial relation ...

[554] From these facts let it be assumed that the miners in Queensland and Victoria were strongly opposed to any reduction of wages in New South Wales, not only upon principle, but because their own wages would be endangered by such a reduction, and that they were prepared to stop the production of coal in order to aid the general resistance to the attempt in New South Wales to lower wages. But how does all this make the lowering of wages a matter of dispute between miners and mine-owners **[555]** in Queensland or Victoria? The closing of the mines in the northern district of New South Wales greatly increased the selling price of coal, and unless and until these mines resumed production at lower costs no one contemplated a reduction in Victoria or Queensland. It is said that the action of the miners in these States and their leaders there and in New South Wales manifested or imported a demand on all mine-owners jointly throughout the three States that existing wages and conditions should remain unaltered, and that nothing but uniform acceptance by each and all of these owners could prevent a disagreement with all of them which would amount to a dispute, and therefore that the continuance of the mine-owners' demands in New South Wales for a reduction resulted in a dispute. This artificial view of the matter was supported by the contention that if a demand was made upon a number of employers that each and all should give concessions, the refusal of these concessions by one of them created a disagreement or dispute with all, notwithstanding that the rest complied with the demand. Another view relied upon was that the Victorian and Queensland miners impliedly required from their employers an assurance that come what might in New South Wales their wages would not be affected. This view imputes to the miners a demand for an immediate promise or contract that wages should in no event be reduced in future, although events in New South Wales might put the Victorian and Queensland proprietors in the dilemma of reducing wages or closing the mines. But the truth is that the conduct of the men and of their leaders imported no request or demand upon their employers in either of these two States. Their employers would not understand that anything was asked of them, nor would they be understood as either requiring anything of, or refusing anything to, the men. Mr *Browne*, for the

Australian Coal and Shale Employees' Federation, in an endeavour to avoid the consequences of this view, boldly argued that an inter-State dispute existed whenever men in two States combined for the common interest in resisting the demands made in one State. The contention cannot be sustained in view of *Holyman's Case* [(1914) 18 CLR 273]. This dispute in New South Wales did not extend to Victoria or **[556]** Queensland. Was its extension threatened, impending or probable? No desire or attempt to reduce wages and no question about wages would arise between men and owners in Queensland or Victoria out of the present situation, unless and until the mines resumed in New South Wales at a reduced cost of production. But this would mean the settlement of the dispute in New South Wales. It would not extend to Queensland or Victoria although its settlement might so affect the trade in coal in those States that new similar disputes might there arise. A limit imposed alike by the Act and by the Constitution upon the jurisdiction of the Court of Conciliation and Arbitration is that it must be exercised by award so as to settle the dispute. (See per *Isaacs* J and *Rich* J in *Archer's Case* [(1919) 27 CLR 207 at 212].) On 19th December there was no dispute in relation to wages, whether existing, threatened, impending or probable, which could be so settled, between the men and the proprietors in Victoria or Queensland. For these reasons Judge *Beeby* had no jurisdiction to make his interim award of that date, which is accordingly invalid.

Isaacs J: [538] On 16th December 1929 the Government of New South Wales reopened the Rothbury coal mine in the northern district of that State. That was the culmination of a series of events that profoundly affected not merely the State of New South Wales but practically all Australia. There had been months of inactivity on that mine field, months of struggle and endurance on both sides, severe privations on one side and great losses on the other, months of vain negotiation between the northern proprietors and their former employees, in which the then Prime Minister and the Premier of New South Wales had taken part. Disorder arose, and life was lost. There can be no question as to the fact that at that time an industrial dispute of a very bitter character existed between the proprietors of the northern collieries and the miners formerly employed by them, in which the respective disputants were maintaining at great sacrifices to themselves what they asserted to be their just rights. But it is also a painful truth that their strife was causing untold injury to the general community, and in every reasonable sense it was of an Australian character. On the day the Rothbury mine opened and the disturbance occurred, the news of what had happened was rapidly known by radio in Victoria and Queensland. It became alarmingly evident that a great industrial conflagration was imminent. No one can possibly doubt that on 16th, 17th and 18th December the emergency, be its legal designation what you will, had assumed proportions in area and general effect entirely beyond the power of any one State to control. At that juncture the machinery of the Federal Arbitration Court was set in motion. It is the only tribunal in Australia armed with the authority of the whole people to preserve or restore industrial peace where a conflict of national extent is imminent or in progress. By direction of Chief Judge *Dethridge*, a compulsory conference was summoned by Judge *Beeby*, and held before him on 17th and 18th December. It was ineffectual to secure agreement. His Honor then … [took] judicial notice of events that every rational adult in Australia was aware of, and arrived at the conclusion that "an industrial dispute of which the **[539]** Court can take cognizance exists or is threatened and impending," and he referred the dispute into Court for hearing and determination.

That finding has been criticized as vague and fatally indistinct, so as to render all subsequent proceedings void. The objection is, to me, incomprehensible. The law, when it prescribes a duty, does not demand impossibilities. At the stage reached by Judge *Beeby* on 18th December, with the evidence then available to him, it would have been as easy to delimit the precise locality and incidents of an advancing thunderstorm as to mark out with the suggested definiteness the boundaries as to parties and the items of subject matter included or to be included in the dispute. Obviously, the inter-State dispute he found to exist consisted of the uncontroverted dispute in New South Wales and the stoppages of coal-miners in Victoria and Queensland. That is clear from his reference to the affidavits of Davies and Lowden in his order of 19th December. There was manifest urgency to restore working conditions as soon as possible without prejudicing any party. He then made an interim award for New South Wales, temporarily restoring the previously existing rates and wages, and so removing the local cause of disorder in that region of the dispute … He distinctly stated that the interim award was "without prejudice to the parties on the full hearing of the dispute." The beneficent effect of the interim award was immediately apparent. The effect on the Wonthaggi miners is definitely shown by Mr McVicar's evidence. He says as to meetings of the miners before the opening of Rothbury:– "The general sentiment and expressions of opinion by members were that if a reduction did take place at any particular colliery in New South Wales, *it would reflect itself on members in Victoria.* Their reason for expressing that opinion was that the awards under which they are working at the present time are practically awards made by various tribunals, and what affected one State affected the whole of the States. They naturally thought that *if New South Wales went to work under a reduction in wages, it would automatically apply to Victoria.*" Acting on this belief, the Wonthaggi miners **[540]** stopped work. But as soon as Judge *Beeby* made his interim award and announced his intention to examine the position further, they were at once instructed to return to work, and they were thoroughly satisfied to do so. At two mines in Queensland work was resumed where the danger of the reduction being operative had also been apprehended … No one can reasonably doubt that had Judge *Beeby's* temporary award not been challenged but acted upon, the subsequent deplorable disorder and disorganization that have occurred would have been averted. But his intervention has on many grounds been attacked as unlawful. The present applications are in substance for a decision of this Court nullifying what he has done, forbidding him to proceed further with the work of pacification, and casting the controversy once again into the furnace of open industrial conflict. If that is the inexorable requirement of the law, then the Court must do it regardless of consequences, and leave the reproach with the law: for reproach it would be if the law so demanded.

Viewing the matter for myself, however, from the strictest legal standpoint, the only aspect from which I allow myself to regard it for this purpose, I hold most firmly, and I hope to make it clear why I so hold, that the Court's duty is to refuse to take the course suggested. In my opinion, the circumstances not only justified, but loudly demanded, the intervention of the Arbitration Court. That intervention was the interposition of the national law to save the community from the loss and suffering of a national calamity, and it has been rightfully and properly exercised.

The *Caledonian Collieries Case (No 1)* involved the problem of "interstateness" when a dispute arises from actual industrial dislocation within a single State. A different problem arises when similar industrial dislocations erupt more or less simultaneously in different States. Do the cumulative incidents evince a dispute "extending beyond the limits of any one State"? Or is each of them "a single-State dispute" with parallels or echoes of other "single-State disputes"? In *R v Commonwealth Conciliation and Arbitration Commission; Ex parte Australian Workers' Union* (*Pinkenba Case*) (1957) 99 CLR 505, the Waterside Workers Federation was involved in demarcation disputes in three States, but the High Court held that each was a separate "single-State dispute". The Court found that the disputes "**[511]** from their very nature must involve separate and unconnected industrial questions".

In *R v Turbet; Ex parte Australian Building Construction Employees and Building Labourers' Federation* (1980) 144 CLR 335 the result went the other way. In 1976 the Builders Labourers' Federation launched a campaign for exclusive representation of labourers on all building sites in Australia. This led to a series of demarcation disputes with other unions – notably the Federated Ironworkers' Association. At the Loy Yang power station construction site in the Latrobe Valley in Victoria, a private company, Electric Power Transmission Pty Ltd, contracted to supply and erect steel structures to support the boilers. To this end, it was to produce 33,000 tonnes of structural steel in Sydney and transport it to the site. The company wished to employ four labourers at the site to unload and sort the steel, but each union insisted that its members be employed. The result was a series of bans and stoppages and an accumulation of 2000 tonnes of unsorted steel. The High Court held by 4:1, with Aickin J dissenting, that (as Mason J put it) "**[350]** we have here, not a series of isolated and disconnected intrastate disputes, but a continuing dispute between two nation-wide unions which extends to major construction sites throughout Australia and, as it unfolds, catches up employers in various States and Territories". At any one time the dispute "may affect construction sites in one State only, but this is only to say that … there is an immediate manifestation in one State only of a continuing underlying industrial dispute which is nation-wide in extent".

When the issue of whether the States, as employers, could be subject to the federal arbitration system was finally resolved in *Re Australian Education Union; Ex parte Victoria* (1995) 184 CLR 188 (see Chapter 25, §2(b)), the majority of the Court also took a relaxed view of "interstateness". The immediate issues related to public service employment in only one State, Victoria. The Victorian government argued that, as its dispute with its public sector employees must necessarily be confined within the boundaries of that State, it could not be an "interstate dispute". The Court, with Dawson J in sole dissent, rejected this argument.

Re Australian Education Union; Ex parte Victoria
(1995) 184 CLR 188

Mason CJ, Brennan, Deane, Toohey, Gaudron and McHugh JJ: [235] The matters on which the prosecutor relied were the limitation of a State's jurisdiction and activities within its own boundaries, the lack of a common interest as between States in the business of "State government", and the traditional autonomy that State governments and their colonial predecessors have enjoyed with respect to the engagement and termination of the services of public servants. Inevitably the argument rests rather heavily on the difference between private and public service employment. When all these matters are taken into account, it is suggested that two conclusions should be drawn: (1) that disputes of the kind in question necessarily remain at the level of intrastate disputes between a State and its public servants and do not merge into or become part of a wider interstate dispute; and (2) that disputes do not have an interstate quality as that requirement must be understood in the context of s 51(xxxv). The second suggested conclusion rests on the notion that it could not have been contemplated when the Constitution was adopted and enacted that s 51(xxxv) would apply to disputes between States and their employees.

The prosecutor's submission is inconsistent with the course of decisions in this Court. Ever since the decision in the *Engineers' Case* [(1920) 28 CLR 129] it has been consistently recognised that a dispute between an **[236]** organisation of employees and a Minister of the Crown for a State acting under the authority of a statute of that State as an employer can amount to an interstate industrial dispute within the meaning of s 51(xxxv) … In the *Professional Engineers' Case* [(1959) 107 CLR 208], to which we have previously referred, the Court held that there was an interstate industrial dispute between the State of New South Wales and various Government departments on the one hand and employed engineers on the other hand. Subsequently, in the *Social Welfare Union Case* [(1983) 153 CLR 297], where the narrow conception of "industrial dispute" was rejected and the popular meaning of the term adopted, the correctness of the decisions in the *Engineers' Case* and in the *Professional Engineers' Case* was accepted. And, in *Re Lee; Ex parte Harper* [(1986) 160 CLR 430], the Court held that the power conferred by s 51(xxxv) would extend to an interstate dispute to which an organisation representative of State school teachers was a party.

In the cases referred to in the preceding paragraph, the primary question for consideration by the Court was not whether a relevant dispute had, or would have, the requisite interstate quality but, in the *Engineers' Case*, whether the doctrine of implied intergovernmental immunity was to be accepted so as to impose limits on the power conferred by s 51(xxxv) and, in the other cases, whether the dispute was, or a relevant dispute would be, "industrial". However, in each of the cases, the Court proceeded on the footing that a dispute between a State (or its agency) and its employees could give rise to an interstate industrial dispute. The acceptance by a unanimous Court in the *Social Welfare Union Case* of the popular meaning of the expression "industrial dispute" in s 51(xxxv) and the rejection of the narrow meaning based on the concept of a dispute in an industry does not affect the conclusion on "interstateness" reached in the cases. The reasoning to that conclusion is unaffected by that change.

The notion that interstate employers must have a common business or operate in a particular industry as a pre-condition of the existence of interstate industrial dispute has never been accepted. Although statements have been made which assert that the nexus or unifying factor which combines in a single industrial dispute a number of demands made on behalf of a number of employees is "the industry" itself [*Jumbunna Coal Mine NL v Victorian Coal Miners' Association* (1908) 6 CLR 309 at 373], the nexus may also be found in the calling or vocation in **[237]** which the participants are engaged ... And, in the final analysis, the adoption of the popular meaning of "industrial dispute" and the rejection of the view that there must be a dispute in an industry, is fatal to the contention that the necessary nexus or unifying factor must be found in the industry.

In *Aberdeen* [(1993) 176 CLR 154 at 160], the joint judgment stated:

"It is not of great significance that there was no exact coincidence between the activities carried on in the respective States in respect of which demands were made. It is of greater significance that those upon whom or in respect of whom the demands were made had a community of interest. That factor may exist because of the employers' or employees' participation in a single industry and is present here. A dispute involving parties having a community of interest is likely to be a single industrial dispute despite differences between the activities of those parties."

Whether such a community of interest exists in a particular case may depend upon a combination of industrial, economic and financial considerations.

True it is that the functions and operations of the States and their agencies are confined very substantially, if not wholly, within the boundaries of the particular State ... As against that consideration is to be set the common interest which the State employees have in seeking and obtaining uniform terms and conditions **[238]** across State boundaries as well as the common interest which the employers as public sector employers have in resisting the demands.

In *Merchant Service Guild of Australasia v Commonwealth Steamship Owners' Association (No 3)* (1920) 28 CLR 495, it was held that "disputes extending beyond the limits of any one State" must relate to "**[503]** the terms and conditions of industrial operations in Australia only". The overruling of that decision in *R v Foster; Ex parte Eastern and Australian Steamship Co Ltd* (1959) 103 CLR 256 reflected Australia's evolving status as a Dominion, freed from fetters of "extraterritorial incompetence" (see Chapter 4, §5), as well as a recognition that terms of employment on ships outside Australia could be an "industrial matter" affecting Australian industrial relations. It also reflected the broad acceptance of "paper disputes" initiated by "registered organisations" that had come to prevail since the *Burwood Cinema Case*.

7. Logs of Claims

A second issue as to s 51(xxxv) was raised by the industrial dispute in the Hunter Valley coalfields. As a consequence of the *Caledonian Collieries Case (No 1)*, which overturned the award of 19 December 1929, the miners' union, the Coal and Shale Employees' Federation, sought to bring the matter within federal power by way of a log of claims served on mine owners. The log of claims was largely based on one served in 1927 with a view to proceedings in a special tribunal under the *Industrial Peace Act 1920* (Cth), but never pursued because the chairman of the tribunal was ill. In respect of an interim award made by Beeby J on 23 January 1930, one day after the High Court's decision in the *Caledonian Collieries Case (No 1)*, the Court again granted prohibition. It held, again with Isaacs J as the only dissentient, that the log of claims was not "genuine", but only a device to overcome the High Court's first decision.

Caledonian Collieries Ltd v Australasian Coal and Shale Employees' Federation (No 2)
(1930) 42 CLR 558

Gavan Duffy, Rich, Starke and Dixon JJ: [577] In *R v Hibble; Ex parte Broken Hill Pty Co* [(1921) 29 CLR 290 at 299], *Knox* CJ, *Gavan Duffy* J, *Powers* J, *Rich* J and *Starke* J said in their joint judgment:– "It is settled law under the Arbitration Act that a dispute must be real and genuine (*Tramways Case (No 2)* [(1914) 19 CLR 43]). Whether it be real and genuine is always a question of fact, and upon proceedings **[578]** in prohibition the fact must be determined by this Court on its own independent view of the evidence." Nothing in the *Burwood Cinema Case* [(1925) 35 CLR 528] ... conflicts in any way with this proposition, which is, indeed, only a restatement of the view long held and frequently acted upon by this Court that "in all cases the Court is bound to be satisfied of the existence and reality of the dispute" (per *Isaacs* J in the *Builders' Labourers' Case* [(1914) 18 CLR 224 at 246]). In this case there was and is a very real and grave dispute between the parties to these proceedings, but, as we have held in our previous judgment, it was, on and up to 19th December, the date of Judge *Beeby's* first award, confined to New South Wales. The matter of the dispute was whether wages should be reduced on the northern coalfields. It was generally believed that if, as a result of such a reduction of wages, the price of coal upon that field fell, wages must be reduced upon all other fields. The question we have to decide is, in substance, whether the formulation, five days later, of a paper demand for increased wages, shorter hours and more advantageous conditions and its refusal could and did operate … to bring into being a real and genuine dispute, or a real and genuine extension of the existing dispute. We think that it is quite clear that the Council revived and remodelled the demands of 1927 for the purpose of attempting to confer upon Judge *Beeby* authority to deal with the existing dispute upon the northern coalfields of New South Wales. The rejection by the men at the meetings between 4th and 10th December of the terms which their leaders had put before them, and, as the President of the Federation said, "recommended as the best possible terms which could be secured from the proprietors for a resumption of work," the opening of Rothbury by the New South Wales Government with non-union labour, and the excitement and violence displayed on the fields on 16th December, had combined to make the intervention of the Federal Court welcome. The resolution of 13th December to extend and intensify the dispute beyond the limit of this State shows that this intervention was **[579]** already contemplated. The telegram on 16th December to Wonthaggi calling for a stoppage there, and asking for an urgent wire reporting it, leaves no doubt of its purpose and of the plan followed. When next day members of the Council who were not at Court turned to the consideration of a log of demands, can it be doubted that they were animated by the same purpose? The service of a log would be the natural way in which an attempt to give jurisdiction would be made. Indeed, in ordinary circumstances where the remaining materials were at hand for the manufacture of a real inter-State dispute, it might be enough to create one. But in this case particular difficulties were inherent in the situation. A determined struggle had been long in progress in New South Wales for the reduction of wages. The closing of the northern mines had made it possible for other mines to work profitably, but while this in some districts prompted thoughts of increased wages, it was clear to all concerned that ultimately wages on the northern field would determine wages elsewhere. At the same time while the northern mines remained closed there was no question of reduction elsewhere. This made it impossible to extend the real issue in the north beyond the boundaries of the State. Its extension could come about only by the opening of the northern mines under conditions enabling the sale of coal at lower prices, which meant, of course, the settlement of the question there. Accordingly, if an industrial dispute extending beyond New South Wales was to be promoted upon the subject of wages, no course was open but to demand that wages should be raised. But is it credible that at this juncture the Council of the Federation sincerely propounded to the proprietors of the northern collieries for immediate answer a bona fide demand upon which they were resolved to insist that the proprietors should raise wages, shorten hours and afford further advantages? We think that the truth is that all parties regarded the formulation of these demands as nothing but a step towards enabling the Arbitration Court to deal with the trouble in New South Wales.

Isaacs J: [567] This controversy has certainly reached an amazing position. For the second time, in the name of the law of the Commonwealth, the coal-miners and the proprietors have been compulsorily brought into the Arbitration Court to compose by impartial methods a serious national industrial quarrel that has caused, and is still causing, widespread injury in the community; and for the second time, in the name of the same law, they are summarily ejected from that tribunal, with the conflict still active and its consequences unaverted. I am unable to agree that on the facts before us this is the true result of the relevant Australian law, imperfect as it undoubtedly is …

[568] Now, in approaching the question "Was there on 23rd January 1930 an existing or probable inter-State industrial dispute within the meaning of the Constitution and the Act?" it is of the highest importance to bear in mind the essential nature of those enactments. It is, if I may venture to say so, the main essential vice of the contentions put forward against the "reality" or "genuineness" of the dispute, that the matter is regarded as if such a dispute concerned the immediate disputants only. That narrows improperly the conception of what will suffice to constitute a

real dispute. I have so often expressed my own view that the public welfare is the governing consideration, and made allusion to skilled authorities, legal and economic, that I shall merely, as to my
own expressions, refer to what I said on that subject in the *Tramways Case (No 2)* [19 CLR at 85] ...

[569] Here the argument for the applicants eliminates the public aspect, looks at the matter as
concerning merely the relations of the contestants, and treats it in the narrowest possible way by
urging, for instance, that for two years prior to December 1929 there had been no demand made on
the proprietors. What does that matter to the public so long as the demand when made in December
was intended to be persisted in to the point of insistence in the Arbitration Court, which the law has
made the only lawful duelling ground? The reality of an "industrial dispute" in the sense required
by the Constitution is satisfied whatever the motives or objects of the demand and whatever its
reasonableness or unreasonableness, **[570]** whether it is of long standing or a creation of yesterday,
whether there was prior dissatisfaction or not, and whether the defendants expect their claims to be
yielded or granted in full or not, so long only as the demandants now insist on their claims and in
some way seek to enforce them, even if that way be through the legitimate avenue of the Arbitration Court, which is the constitutional substitute for force. All those and similar considerations
are non-essentials, for, whether they are present or absent, the public loss in case of stoppage is just
the same. In my opinion we should abandon any attempt to confine industrial disputes by applying
technical limitations in order to test reality. Such disputes are hard facts of life, they are not rigid in
character, they are of constantly changing form and methods of origin to meet advancing
circumstances, and they are easily recognizable as facts – too often by their effects – whenever and
however they arise. Judge-made limitations of reality are just as effective to control the existence
and extent of industrial disputes as was King Canute's command to stay the waves of the ocean. If
only the simple principle, so clearly enunciated [in *Melbourne Tramway and Omnibus Co v
Tramway Board* [1919] AC 667 at 674] by the Privy Council, be applied to the present case – the
touchstone of public welfare – and the relevant legislation interpreted with that as a guide, we
should at once escape from this labyrinth of confusion. There is, in this connection, a matter which
appears to permeate the argument for the applicants and to give it a false colour. It is the artificial
doctrine of the "reality" of an industrial dispute. That a dispute must be "real" or "genuine" is in
one sense undoubted. We know there are sham-fights, mere simulacra of battles, where everything
is in show, and no one intends to strike a blow or fire a bullet. It is possible that industrial demands
may be made and refusals given merely for parade, everyone aware that nothing serious is intended
and that all is a pretence and a form and never to be pursued. But the "reality" or "genuineness" of
that dispute, like that of any other legal relation between citizens, must be determined by the
reasonable effect upon each that is to be attributed by what is actually said and done by the other in
the given circumstances. According to accepted methods in British Courts, it is not to be attained
by a system of thought-reading to the disregard of actual acts and words, **[571]** and more especially
to the disregard of direct reputable testimony. And when it is seen that the claims are in earnest and
are persisted in to the fighting point, notwithstanding firm refusals, we are not to wait for casualties
to convince us that the combat is real.

The emphasis on "paper disputes" has led to additional problems. A log of claims is regarded as
setting the "ambit" of a dispute (often by what is popularly called an "ambit claim"), and all
subsequent awards or deliberations must stay within that "ambit". The original idea emerged from
the second of the *Whybrow* cases. The wage for apprentices awarded by Higgins J in the Arbitration Court was calculated on a basis which in some instances yielded higher wages than the
union had claimed. It was held in effect that since this part of the award had exceeded the ambit
of the dispute, it could not be regarded as arbitration for the settlement of the dispute.

R v Commonwealth Court of Conciliation and Arbitration; Ex parte Whybrow & Co
(1910) 11 CLR 1

Isaacs J: [61] I cannot escape the judicial conclusion that as to some apprentices more has been
awarded than was asked for and refused, and therefore more than was in dispute. And in my

opinion the Court had no greater jurisdiction to award a higher wage than was asked, than it had to reduce wages below what were actually in dispute. It is the *dispute* that has to be regarded and adjudicated upon … There is nothing in the world to prevent employers or employés from making their respective demands as wide as they please; but when they choose to select one particular limited demand as the subject or point of dispute, and refer that to the Court, then that is what the Court has to decide. It may give anything between the maximum and the minimum limits of the dispute, but it can pass neither further forward than the maximum, nor further back than the minimum. As unfortunately the maximum has **[62]** been passed, the award is in respect of that branch invalid.

In order to give rise to a "dispute", and in order to set its "ambit", a log of claims must make reasonably intelligible and reasonably specific demands. It is the rejection of these demands that constitutes a "dispute". If the claims are too imprecise, there is no "industrial dispute" under s 51(xxxv). This idea can be traced to a judgment by Barton ACJ in 1913.

Merchant Service Guild of Australasia v Newcastle & Hunter River Steamship Co Ltd (No 1)
(1913) 16 CLR 591

Barton ACJ: [616] It is common ground that there must be parties and a subject matter before resort can be had to arbitration. Arbitration is in itself a judicial proceeding for adjusting a difference between two or more parties as to something. It is argued that parties may differ about something without being in dispute. The parties and the difference, it is said, may co-exist, and yet the thing or subject matter be so little defined that the stage of actual dispute has not been reached. But, if the thing is undefined, it is nebulous. I must leave to quicker-witted people the duty of defining an arbitration upon the nebulous. If A complains that his wages are too low, and his employer, B, denies it, how can C arbitrate between them without first finding out what A's wage is, what A claims that it ought to be, and whether B refuses to pay it? The same thing occurs when A says his hours are too long. If A says that B's manager is tyrannical and B denies it, how can C arbitrate between them without finding out what are the alleged instances of tyranny, and whether B admits them? The object of the arbitration in such a case is not merely to procure a general reproof of the manager, but to prevent a continuance or recurrence of specific conduct. To my mind it is impossible to arbitrate unless the subject matter is definite.

In context, this was the old argument that s 51(xxxv) cannot extend to "arbitration for the prevention" of industrial disputes. "Prevention" would take place *ex hypothesi* before a dispute had crystallised into sufficiently definite form, and hence before there was anything to arbitrate. In later years, such arguments have sometimes been used to deny the validity or adequacy of a log of claims. Usually, however, the High Court has refused to endorse such denials. So long as there is an "intelligible" dispute, that is enough.

The classic attack on a log of claims as "**[157]** ambiguous and indefinite, uncertain and contradictory" was in *R v Association of Professional Engineers of Australia; Ex parte Victoria* (1957) 100 CLR 155. The log of claims had sought to establish minimum salary levels of £1650 per annum for a qualified engineer and £2200 per annum for a chartered engineer, but made no specific salary claims above those levels. Instead, it envisaged that beyond those levels employers should negotiate individual salaries with employees. A five-judge High Court held unanimously that the claim was sufficiently definite to be the basis of a "dispute".

R v Association of Professional Engineers of Australia; Ex parte Victoria
(1957) 100 CLR 155

The Court: [161] It would serve no useful purpose to go over all the criticisms that have been made of this log as indefinite. It may at once be conceded that at, so to speak, the edges of the application of the definition of engineering duties there may be uncertainty as to this or that given case. It may be conceded that qualifications coming from a large number of academical sources may satisfy the definition of professional engineer. It may be conceded too that uncertainty may be found in saying whether this or that individual falls within the definition of qualified or of chartered engineer although that uncertainty will less frequently occur. But we think the substance or general scope and reach of these definitions cannot be attended by much doubt. The demand for minimum salaries is perfectly clear. It is not, we think, open to any real doubt that, subject to the minimum salaries, the general **[162]** demand is that salaries shall be fixed on an individual basis with the help of the intervention on behalf of the engineer of representatives of the association. It is, we think, impossible to suppose that the officers of the Governments who received this log are unaware of its central intendment … No doubt demands which are not intelligible or convey nothing clearly to the mind of the person to whom they are addressed may fail in giving rise to an industrial dispute. The doctrine by which this Court has allowed paper demands to form evidence, sufficient evidence, of a real dispute has not hitherto been qualified by any principle which requires paper demands to be in any specific form or to be incapable of misreading or misconstruction. It surely must be sufficient that the party to whom they are addressed ought fairly to understand what he is requested to do on the specific matters which form the subject of the alleged grievance. Every case of this description must stand on its own basis. But it is sufficient to say in the present case that this log is very far from exhibiting such a vagueness or uncertainty as to make it incapable of giving rise to an industrial dispute with which a conciliation commissioner may deal.

In *R v Portus; Ex parte McNeil* (1961) 105 CLR 537, there was no log of claims. The Australian Federation of Air Pilots, after initial demands on the airlines, broke off negotiations and refused to submit to conciliation or arbitration. A conciliation commissioner found that a dispute existed between the airlines and individual pilots, which he proposed to conciliate. The Federation sought prohibition to prevent him from doing so.

R v Portus; Ex parte McNeil
(1961) 105 CLR 537

Dixon CJ, Kitto, Taylor and Windeyer JJ: [544] [I]t is said that … there was no industrial matter in contest. Proposals for discussion and negotiation were put forward and different views were adopted but there was not, it was said, a distinct issue or disagreement; there was, so to speak, no *litis contestatio*. The answer to this lies in the facts: there was a very distinct disagreement about a whole subject matter backed by a preliminary resort to or threat of industrial dislocation. An industrial dispute may exist without a formulation of a definite and clear cut demand followed by an equally definite and clear cut refusal. Familiarity with paper disputes consisting of carefully drawn logs of demand and general refusals has perhaps led to a somewhat artificial conception of what amounts to an industrial dispute. But an attempt to gain higher rewards by means first of negotiation and then of pressure and threatened dislocation is no less an industrial dispute because the exact stand taken by the respective parties may be less definite and precise than a paper log would be apt to make it.

In *Re State Public Services Federation; Ex parte Attorney-General (WA)* (1993) 178 CLR 249, it had been anticipated that the Court would resolve the issue of when, after the *CYSS Case*, Commonwealth awards might be applied to State governments as employers. As it turned out, the Court found it unnecessary to resolve that issue. Instead, it held that the Industrial Relations Commission had erred in finding that the log of claims gave rise to an "industrial dispute". The log had claimed, for all employees to be covered by the proposed award, a flat weekly wage of $5000 together with a flat weekly allowance of $2500. The Court held that a claim for entitlements of $7500 a week, regardless of qualifications or duties, was so unreal that it was not capable of giving rise to a dispute – not even as an "ambit claim".

The main judgment was that of Toohey J. The other six judges all agreed that the bald demand for remuneration of $7500 a week presented an insuperable problem, but they differed from Toohey J in their diagnosis of precisely what the problem was. They were all at pains to insist that they were not undermining the established doctrines of "ambit claims" and "paper disputes". The problem as they saw it was rather that, since the demand for $7500 a week could not be taken seriously at face value, it failed to establish any "ambit" at all. If such a demand were to be construed so as to give it some workable meaning, it must be understood as an open-ended invitation to the Industrial Relations Commission to assess what it considered to be appropriate scales of remuneration, unrestricted by any outer limit or "ambit". However, this kind of open-ended power could not validly be conferred on the Commission.

Re State Public Services Federation; Ex parte Attorney-General (WA)
(1993) 178 CLR 249

Toohey J: [289] It has been said that the expression "genuine dispute" is tautologous. And so it is in the sense that "either there is a dispute as defined in s 4(1) of the Act or there is not" [*Re Printing and Kindred Industries Union; Ex Parte Vista Paper Products Pty Ltd* (1993) 113 ALR 421 at 429]. The use of the qualifier "genuine" has crept into the language of industrial law, no doubt so as to put a brake on the service of demands which are not in truth sought by the members of the union in question and which seek merely to attract the jurisdiction of the Commission ...

[290] While the expression "genuine dispute" may be tautologous, the term "genuine demand" is not necessarily so. It does serve the purpose of focusing attention on the reality of the demand made and the motive with which it is made. If the demand is not genuine, in the sense described, failure to accede to it does not give rise to an industrial dispute. As the Court said in *R v Ludeke; Ex parte Queensland Electricity Commission* [(1985) 159 CLR 178 at 181]: "[T]he demands must be bona fide in the sense that they are being genuinely advanced."

It is no answer to the contention that an industrial dispute exists merely to show that the demands made in a log of claims have little prospect of success and that they do no more than set the ambit **[291]** within which conditions of employment may be negotiated and, if negotiations are unsuccessful, determined by the Commission. But a log may be so far-fetched, so lacking in industrial reality that it cannot possibly be treated seriously. It may be asked: where then do you draw the line? The answer is that while it is not always possible to draw a line, it may be possible nevertheless to say whether something, in this case a particular log, falls on one or other side of it.

The minimum weekly wage of $5,000 and the minimum weekly allowance of $2,500 contained in the log lack all industrial reality. They have no relationship with any prevailing wage rates or allowances paid under existing awards and cannot be within the contemplation of those whom the log seeks to embrace. There is no attempt to distinguish between categories of employees, even allowing for the fact that a "minimum" is sought. That factor alone highlights the unreality of the claim. In argument, counsel for the respondents attempted to defend the minimum wage by pointing to rates of inflation and to the inability of predicting the value of money in years to come. But again, that only points up the unreality of the demand. Clause 4 of the proposed award contains a provision to cater for cost of living adjustments; therefore, the figures of $5,000 and $2,500 can only be seen as current rates for which demand is made. But the figures were apparently not seen by the Commission as obstacles to the finding of an industrial dispute. Rather, the Commission saw them as difficulties in the way of making an award if SPSF fails "in due course to particularize with greater exactitude the conditions of employment sought to be implemented in the context of any existing arrangements".

It is true that the purpose of the doctrine of ambit serves "not to determine the validity of a claim or log of claims, but to ensure that there exists an appropriate relationship between the dispute, especially a paper dispute, and the award which settles that dispute" [*R v Holmes; Ex parte Victorian Employers' Federation* (1980) 145 CLR 68 at 76] ... **[292]** But the doctrine of ambit does not of itself provide an answer to a challenge that the demand made in a log of claims is not genuine.

In *Ludeke* [159 CLR at 181] the Court said:

"Because disagreement rather than disturbance or dislocation of industrial relations is the essential characteristic of an industrial dispute, a 'paper dispute' evidenced by delivery and non-acceptance of a log of claims is sufficient to create such a dispute."

But the Court, immediately thereafter, spoke of the need for the dispute to be "real and genuine". There is nothing in the judgment which stands in the way of rejecting as not genuine a demand which is not genuinely advanced. Evatt J correctly identified the issue when he asked whether the demand is genuine or a pretended demand [*Australian Tramway and Motor Omnibus Employees' Association v Commissioner for Road Transport and Tramways (NSW)* (1938) 58 CLR 436 at 442]. Where the demand is not genuine there can be no disagreement for there is in truth nothing to disagree about ...

[294] In my view the considerations relied upon by the Commission do not lead to a conclusion that service of the log of claims on the Western Australian and Queensland employers gave rise to an industrial dispute; the log does not evidence a demand genuinely made.

Mason CJ, Deane and Gaudron JJ: [267] It is sometimes said that a "paper dispute" must be a "genuine dispute". That means no more than that written demands must be genuine demands. If not – if, for example, they are part of a hoax or if they are intended to dress up a purely intrastate dispute – their rejection will not involve any disagreement and, thus, will not result in a dispute at all.

To ascertain whether demands are "genuine demands", it is sometimes asked whether the demands are seriously advanced **[268]** or, in the case of demands by or on behalf of employees, whether they are advanced with a view to "obtaining improved terms and conditions ... within the framework of the claims made" [159 CLR at 183]. This last formulation is one that takes account of the doctrine of ambit and allows that a demand may be genuine notwithstanding that neither the union making it nor its members are "intent on obtaining forthwith every item which is mentioned in the log of claims or the particular terms and conditions of employment in the form and in the amounts in which they are expressed in the log" [159 CLR at 182-3].

Given the doctrine of ambit and given that there is nothing inherently artificial about written demands, or "paper disputes", it will not often be the case that a written demand with respect to the wages or conditions of employees will be other than a genuine demand. Generally speaking, and whether the question falls for decision in this Court or in the Commission, a demand, as to the wages or conditions of employees made by an organization of employees and authorised by its rules and in accordance with its procedures, will be treated as a genuine demand unless it is plainly fanciful or unless it appears that the demand was made merely to dress up some other claim which, on its own, would not constitute a dispute as defined in s 4(1) of the *Industrial Relations Act* 1988 (Cth) ("the Act").

The question whether a claim is properly described as fanciful is one that can only be answered in the light of general industrial **[269]** standards and general patterns of industrial regulation. These are matters peculiarly within the experience and expertise of the Commission and, thus, this Court accords considerable weight to its findings with respect to the genuineness of demands and the existence or otherwise of a dispute arising out of those demands.

Notwithstanding that the Commission found there was a dispute arising out of the log of claims involved in the SPSF matters, there are features which indicate that its demand, if read according to its terms, is, in truth, fanciful. The notion of weekly earnings of $7,500 for all employees, regardless of skill, qualification, or the nature of the work performed, is one that is at odds with established wage fixing principles. And, unless one subscribes to some extravagant, post-modern notion of equal pay involving the same rate of pay regardless of the work or the worker concerned, it is one that is at odds with those general theories and concepts that fashion those principles. Nor is the claim explicable as an ambit claim in which there is some in-built allowance for inflation for the claim contains an express stipulation that wages and allowances should be adjusted for cost of living increases. These matters persuade us that the demand, if read strictly according to its terms, must be treated as fanciful and, hence, not a genuine demand.

Given that the matter has been pursued this far, presumably at considerable expense, it is reasonable to assume that SPSF is pursuing some more realistic claim than the one that emerges from a strict reading of its demand. In our view, it is reasonable to assume that SPSF's claim is for increased wages and allowances as determined by the Commission. It is also reasonable to assume that it would have been so understood by those bodies on whom it was served. On that basis, it is necessary to consider whether a bare claim for increased wages and conditions as determined by the Commission gives rise to an industrial dispute as defined in s 4(1) of the Act.

There are two interrelated matters that serve to indicate [that it does not] ... The first is that the Commission is not a general regulatory body. It is a tribunal established for the conciliation and arbitration of [270] disputes ... Its regulatory powers are activated only in consequence of a dispute and only with respect to the matters in dispute. A bare claim that employees should be paid increased wages and allowances as determined by the Commission is, in effect, a claim that the Commission should have general regulatory powers with respect to the wages and allowances of those employees.

The Commission has only those powers that the Act confers upon it. It is well settled that a claim that it should have other or additional powers is not a claim that is "about matters pertaining to the relationship between employers and employees" as required by the definition of "industrial dispute" in s 4(1) of the Act, no matter that the powers in question, if exercised, might affect matters pertaining to that relationship. Thus a claim that the Commission should have or should exercise general regulatory power, whether made in terms which predicate an improvement, a reduction or, even, maintenance of existing wages and conditions, is not a claim that gives rise to an industrial dispute as defined in s 4(1) of the Act. That is not to deny that there may be circumstances involving a bare claim of that kind amounting to an industrial dispute as defined in s 4(1) of the Act – particularly, if regard is had to that part of the definition that speaks of "a situation that is likely to give rise to an industrial dispute". But in that event, it will be the overall circumstances that constitute or give rise to the dispute, not merely the rejection of a claim for wages or conditions as determined by the Commission.

The second matter that indicates that a bare claim for increased wages and allowances as determined by the Commission does not give rise to an industrial dispute is that the assent or dissent of employers is entirely irrelevant to what is demanded. Indeed, the [271] claim proceeds on that very basis. And assuming jurisdiction were thus attracted, increases awarded by the Commission would take effect by virtue of the Act and quite independently of the assent of the employers concerned. The irrelevance of the assent or dissent of employers flows from the assumption which is embedded in the claim, namely, that the Commission has or may acquire general regulatory power as the result of a claim of the kind under consideration. The validity of that assumption is denied by the decisions of this Court in which it has been held that a demand as to a matter on which assent or dissent is irrelevant may give rise to "a contrariety of opinion" [*R v Graziers' Association of NSW; Ex parte Australian Workers' Union* (1956) 96 CLR 317 at 323], but does not give rise to a dispute.

We would read the log of claims as involving a claim for increased wages and allowances as determined by the Commission. However, and as already indicated, a claim of that kind does not give rise to an industrial dispute as defined in s 4(1) of the Act.

It seems that the refusal to find a "dispute" in this case should be treated as an isolated response to a singular "fanciful" claim, and not as opening up to general reconsideration the body of traditional doctrines and practices erected on the foundation of the *Burwood Cinema Case*. This was made clear in *Attorney-General (Qld) v Riordan* (1997) 192 CLR 1, where again it was argued that certain logs of claims did not give rise to an "industrial dispute" because they lacked "reality" and "genuineness". In finding that the claims did give rise to an "industrial dispute", the Court made it clear that *Re State Public Services Federation; Ex parte Attorney-General (WA)* should not be taken to have undermined the idea of "paper disputes".

Attorney-General (Qld) v Riordan
(1997) 192 CLR 1

Kirby J: [39] Australia's industrial law and practice cannot be understood in a vacuum. Each has derived from the historical evolution of the understanding of the conciliation and arbitration power in the Constitution. So-called "paper disputes" represent a procedural device to overcome limitations thought to be inherent in the process of arbitration and apparent obstacles presented by the requirement of "interstateness". The latter, clearly expressed in the constitutional grant of power, would, if narrowly construed, have prevented the growth of the jurisdiction of the federal tribunal.

In the early years of this century that growth was conceived to be linked to the desirable development of a national economy. The early Justices of this Court, who accepted and thereby facilitated the log of claims procedure, did so conscious of the fact that, although upon one view it was an artificial device, it would provide a simple means of creating an interstate industrial dispute by "concerted action against ... employers in [different] States for the making and enforcing of the same demands" [*Jumbunna Coal Mine NL v Victorian Coal Miners' Association* (1908) 6 CLR 309 at 352]. The same Justices who upheld the device were also clearly affected by the memory of the dislocation caused by the industrial strikes which had paralysed Australia in the 1890s. Isaacs J said as much, explaining how the convulsion which had then occurred had "greatly influenced the introduction of the power in the Constitution" [*Builders' Labourers' Case* (1914) 18 CLR 224 at 241]. To avoid the repetition of the damaging interstate industrial disputation of the 1890s, a simple procedure to attract jurisdiction to the new Commonwealth Court of Conciliation and Arbitration was seen as doubly attractive. It would further the new body's national influence. It would also avoid the necessity to rely upon strikes and lock-outs as "real" evidence of an interstate industrial dispute. The procedure was also seen as more appropriate and seemly to a federal tribunal then constituted as a court. To require that the court's jurisdiction should depend upon the creation of a strike, which was illegal, was less attractive than the adoption of a formal initiating process, such as a demand with log of claims. In this way the Commonwealth Court of Conciliation and Arbitration, supported by this Court, came to enlarge the popular notion which the words "industrial disputes" might otherwise have conveyed. So-called "paper disputes" were permitted. Once permitted, they soon became the standard means of invoking federal jurisdiction. Of course, **[40]** the words "industrial disputes" in the Constitution and the statute remained to be given meaning ...

More recently, the apparent extravagance of some union claims has attracted fresh criticism on the basis that such practices might tend to divert attention from "the actual industrial situation" [*Re Printing and Kindred Industries Union; Ex parte Vista Paper Products* (1993) 113 ALR 421 at 433]. The procedures imposed on the Commission by constitutional decisions have sometimes been criticised as "primitive, time-wasting and often expensive" [*R v Alley; Ex parte NSW Plumbers & Gasfitters Employees' Union* (1981) 153 CLR 376 at 396]. However, there remains considerable scope for flexibility, particularly where the prevention of disputes is concerned. The constitutional power in that regard is still largely undeveloped, despite the fact that it has been called to attention by this Court in several decisions. Notwithstanding the critics, the **[41]** demand and log of claims procedure has many advantages. It is a relatively simple way of invoking the Commission's jurisdiction. If the necessary steps are properly carried out, its legal effectiveness is undoubted. It has enhanced the position of unions and employer organisations. It has contributed to the equalisation of costs of labour throughout Australia and hence to the growth of a national economy. Disputes in other fields of the law are regularly created, and defined, by the exchange of correspondence. Although, as they have developed in the industrial relations context, "paper disputes" have artificial, formalistic features, they are now so deeply entrenched in the long-standing authority of this Court and in Australia's industrial practice that they should not be disturbed. No party to the present proceedings directly challenged the log of claims procedure as such. It is an established means of creating and defining "industrial disputes" in this country. It should remain so.

8. Further References

Buchanan, RJ, and Neil, IM, "Industrial Law and the Constitution in the New Century: An Historical Review of the Industrial Power" (2001) 20 *Australian Bar Review* 256.

Creighton, B, and Stewart, A, *Labour Law* (Federation Press, 4th ed 2005).

"Development in Australian Workplace Laws", Special Feature (2005) 10 *Deakin Law Review*.

Ford, WJ, "The Constitution and the Reform of Australian Industrial Relations" (1994) 7 *Australian Journal of Labour Law* 105.

Ford, WJ, "Reconstructing Australian Labour Law: A Constitutional Perspective" (1997) 10 *Australian Journal of Labour Law* 1.

Frazer, A, "Parliament and the Industrial Power" in Lindell, G, and Bennett, R (eds), *Parliament: The Vision in Hindsight* (Federation Press, 2001), 93.

Higgins, HB, *A New Province for Law and Order* (Constable, 1922; Dawsons of Pall Mall, 1968 reprint).

Kirby, MD, "Industrial Conciliation and Arbitration in Australia – A Centenary Reflection" (2004) 17 *Australian Journal of Labour Law*, 229.

Macken, JJ, *Australian Industrial Laws: The Constitutional Basis* (Law Book Co, 2nd ed 1980).

Pittard, M, and Naughton, R, *Australian Labour Law: Cases and Materials* (Butterworths, 4th ed 2003).

Williams, G, *Labour Law and the Constitution* (Federation Press, 1998).

Williams, N, and Gotting, A, "The Interrelationship between the Industrial Power and Other Heads of Power in Australian Industrial Law" (2001) 20 *Australian Bar Review* 264.

Chapter 23

Taxation and Excise

1. The Taxation Power

The Commonwealth's taxation power, s 51(ii) of the Constitution, has been crucial to the evolution of Australia's federal structure. Its importance has been cemented by the High Court's interpretation of s 96, which has enabled the Commonwealth to wrest the field of income taxation away from the States (see Chapter 24, §2(b)). The taxation power has also assumed greater importance through the Court's interpretation of s 90, which makes the levying of certain taxes, notably duties of excise, exclusive to the federal Parliament.

Section 51(ii) gives the Commonwealth the power to legislate with respect to "taxation". It uses this power to raise the greater part of its revenue, most obviously by income taxation and taxes on goods and services. The power of taxation is expressly limited by the requirement that it not be used to "discriminate between States or parts of States" (see Chapter 6, §4). On the other hand, the power to distribute the resulting revenues (for example, under s 96) is not so limited.

Other provisions of the Constitution relevant to the Commonwealth's taxation power are ss 53 and 55. Section 53 provides that "[p]roposed laws ... imposing taxation, shall not originate in the Senate", and restricts the Senate's power to amend such laws (though not its power to reject them). Because it refers only to "proposed laws", and therefore to the internal workings of the federal Parliament, the High Court has held that s 53 is not justiciable – that is, it is not appropriate for adjudication by a court (*Osborne v Commonwealth* (1911) 12 CLR 321 – see Chapter 13, §5(d)). Despite occasional doubts, that view has repeatedly been confirmed, for example by a passage in *Western Australia v Commonwealth* (*Native Title Act Case*) (1995) 183 CLR 373 (at 482) which has since been repeated by the majority judgment in *Permanent Trustee Australia Ltd v Commissioner of State Revenue* (2004) 220 CLR 388 at 409.

Osborne v Commonwealth took the opposite view in relation to the first paragraph of s 55, which requires that laws imposing taxation shall deal only with the imposition of taxation, and that any provision dealing with other matters "shall be of no effect". This provision was said to be justiciable because the reference is to "laws" rather than "proposed laws", and because the words "shall be of no effect" prescribe a precise legal consequence of breach.

Despite the absence of these indicia, a similar conclusion has been extended to the second paragraph of s 55, which requires that laws imposing taxation "shall deal with one subject of taxation only" (see *State Chamber of Commerce and Industry v Commonwealth* (1987) 163 CLR 329). However, challenges to legislation on this ground have regularly failed, since the concept of a "subject of taxation" has been very loosely applied. As Dixon J explained in *Resch v Federal Commissioner of Taxation* (1942) 66 CLR 198, the purpose of s 55 is political, rather than legal; and accordingly the expression "subject of taxation" "[223] must be taken as contemplating broad distinctions between possible subjects of taxation based on common understanding and general conceptions, rather than on any analytical or logical classification". The "main or substantial subject of the tax" is to be "gathered from a general consideration" of the impugned legislation, bearing in mind "that it is for the legislature to choose its own subject and that its choice is fettered neither by existing nomenclature nor by categories that have been adopted for other purposes". Once the main subject has been ascertained, the question whether ancillary provisions have introduced a different subject must be answered "by considering their natural connection with or relevance to the main subject".

Infringements or potential infringements of the first paragraph of s 55 have also been extremely rare, in part because of the practice of splitting tax legislation into two enactments – one to "deal only with the imposition of taxation", and one to provide the machinery for assessing and collecting the tax (see, for example, the *Income Tax Act 1986* (Cth) and the *Income Tax Assessment Act 1997* (Cth)). In *Moore v Commonwealth* (1951) 82 CLR 547, Dixon J referred to this as "[569] a tried and venerated procedure for escaping the hitherto ineffectual menaces of s 55". How far that procedure was strictly necessary was debated inconclusively in *Re Dymond* (1959) 101 CLR 11. The uncertainty has now been resolved by the joint majority judgment in *Permanent Trustee Australia Ltd v Commissioner of State Revenue* (2004) 220 CLR 388, which endorses the view of Higgins J in *Osborne v Commonwealth* that the words used in *both* paragraphs of s 55 – "shall deal only with the imposition of taxation", and "shall deal with one subject of taxation only" – are broad enough "[373] to allow the insertion of any provision which is fairly relevant or incidental to the imposition of a tax on one subject of taxation". It also endorses the view of Starke J in *Federal Commissioner of Taxation v Munro* (1926) 38 CLR 153 that because the words are not "shall only impose taxation", but "shall deal only with the imposition of taxation", it follows that "[215] it is not unlawful to include in a taxing Act provisions incidental and auxiliary to the assessment and collection of the tax". Starke J added that this "would include provisions for administration, returns, assessments, reviews of [216] assessments and so forth"; and that neither the Assessment Acts nor the Tax Acts "deal with any matter other than the imposition of taxation".

There was no dissent in *Permanent Trustee* from the Court's acceptance of these views, though Kirby J expressed "[469] much more hesitation" about the matter and McHugh J expressed no opinion. The joint judgment means that the traditional "[419] practice or convention of splitting Bills between a taxing Act and an assessment Act" has been unnecessary, at least so far as s 55 is concerned. Nevertheless, the joint judgment suggested that the practice should be continued in order to ensure that an Assessment Act "will not be a [420] law imposing taxation with respect to which s 53 will restrict the powers of the Senate".

(a) What is a Tax?

The central question arising in relation to s 51(ii) is: "What is a tax?" If an exaction is a tax, then the law that imposes it can be characterised as a law with respect to the subject-matter of s 51(ii). In *Matthews v Chicory Marketing Board* (Vic) (1938) 60 CLR 263, the question was whether a Victorian levy upon producers of chicory was an excise duty, in which event it infringed s 90 of the Constitution; and since excise is a form of taxation (loosely, a tax on goods), it was necessary first to determine whether the levy was a "tax". In answering this question, Latham CJ laid down what has become the classic definition of a "tax". Citing *Lower Mainland Dairy Products Sales Adjustment Committee v Crystal Dairy Ltd* [1933] AC 168 at 175, he held that a tax "[276] is a compulsory exaction of money by a public authority for public purposes, enforceable by law, and is not a payment for services rendered".

A series of recent cases beginning with *Air Caledonie International v Commonwealth* (1988) 165 CLR 462 has made it clear that Latham CJ's definition was not complete or exhaustive. Section 7 of the *Migration Amendment Act 1987* (Cth) sought, as from 1 January 1988, to impose a "fee for immigration clearance" upon international airline passengers entering Australia. It did this by inserting s 34A into the *Migration Act 1958* (Cth). The "fee" was set by regulation at $5. The plaintiffs argued that the "fee" was a "tax" for the purposes of s 55 of the Constitution and thus that s 55 prevented the insertion of s 34A into the *Migration Act*, which dealt with matters other than the "imposition of taxation".

Air Caledonie International v Commonwealth
(1988) 165 CLR 462

The Court: [466] In *Lower Mainland Dairy Products Sales Adjustment Committee v Crystal Dairy Ltd* [[1933] AC 168 at 175], the Privy Council identified three features which sufficed to impart to the levies involved in that case the character of a "tax". Those features were that the levies: were compulsory; were for public purposes; and were enforceable by law. In *Matthews v Chicory Marketing Board (Vic)* [(1938) 60 CLR 263 at 276], Latham CJ adopted those three features as the basis of what has subsequently been recognized in this Court as an acceptable general statement of positive and negative attributes which, if they all be present, will **[467]** suffice to stamp an exaction of money with the character of a tax … More recently this Court has drawn attention to other criteria, namely, that a tax is not by way of penalty and that it is not arbitrary (see *MacCormick v Federal Commissioner of Taxation* [(1984) 158 CLR 622 at 639]; *Deputy Federal Commissioner of Taxation v Truhold Benefit Pty Ltd* [(1985) 158 CLR 678 at 684]).

There are three comments which should be made in relation to the above general statement of Latham CJ. The first is that it should not be seen as providing an exhaustive definition of a tax. Thus, there is no reason in principle why a tax should not take a form other than the exaction of money or why the compulsory exaction of money under statutory powers could not be properly seen as taxation notwithstanding that it was by a non-public authority or for purposes which could not properly be described as public. The second is that, in *Logan Downs Pty Ltd v Queensland* [(1977) 137 CLR 59 at 63], Gibbs J made explicit what was implicit in the reference by Latham CJ to "a payment for services rendered", namely, that the services be "rendered to" – or (we would add) at the direction or request of – "the person required" to make the payment. The third is that the negative attribute – "not a payment for services rendered" – should be seen as intended to be but an example of various special types of exaction which may not be taxes even though the positive attributes mentioned by Latham CJ are all present. Thus, a charge for the acquisition or use of property, a fee for a privilege and a fine or penalty imposed for criminal conduct or breach of statutory obligation are other examples of special types of exactions of money which are unlikely to be properly characterized as a tax notwithstanding that they exhibit those positive attributes. On the other hand, a compulsory and enforceable exaction of money by a public authority for public purposes will not necessarily be precluded from being properly seen as a tax merely because it is described as a "fee for services". If the person required to pay the exaction is given no choice about whether or not he acquires the services and the amount of the exaction has no discernible relationship with the value of what is acquired, the circumstances may be such that the exaction is, at least to the extent that it exceeds that value, properly to be seen as a tax.

The Court held that the "fee for immigration clearance" was a tax, and hence that its introduction into the *Migration Act* infringed s 55. However, the Court did not follow through on the literal effect of s 55, which provides that "any provision therein dealing with any other matter shall be of no effect". That would have meant that the whole of the *Migration Act* would be rendered ineffective *except* for the provision imposing the immigration clearance fee. Instead, the Court held that the law to be denied any legal effect was the one which would produce the unconstitutional consequence: "**[472]** It follows that the effect of the conclusion that s 34A was a law imposing taxation is that s 7 of the *Migration Amendment Act* 1987 was ineffective to amend the *Migration Act* by adding s 34A to its provisions".

The scope of the term "tax" was further widened by the decision in *Australian Tape Manufacturers Association Ltd v Commonwealth* (1993) 176 CLR 480. That case concerned Part VC of the *Copyright Act 1968* (Cth), which had been inserted by the *Copyright Amendment Act 1989* (Cth). The 1989 Act was passed to deal with the widespread practice of taping of sound recordings in breach of copyright. Part VC provided for the payment of a "royalty" to copyright owners and in return permitted the copying of sound recordings for private and domestic use. Under s 135ZZP(1), the "royalty" was payable by the vendor of each blank tape when first sold, let or hired or otherwise distributed in Australia. The "royalty" was payable to a "collecting society", a company whose members were copyright owners. By 4:3, with Dawson, Toohey and McHugh JJ dissenting, it was held that s 135ZZP(1) imposed a tax and that the 1989 Act was therefore invalid as infringing s 55 of the Constitution.

Australian Tape Manufacturers Association Ltd v Commonwealth
(1993) 176 CLR 480

Mason, Brennan, Deane and Gaudron JJ: [500] The argument that the levy is not a tax rests on the broad propositions that it is not exacted by a public authority, nor is it exacted for public purposes. The two propositions are based on the influential statement by Latham CJ in *Matthews v Chicory Marketing Board (Vic)* [(1938) 60 CLR 263 at 276] that a tax "is a compulsory exaction of money by a public authority for public purposes, enforceable by law, and is not a payment for services rendered". Although the elements in this statement have been recognized as the positive and negative attributes of a tax, this Court has held that the statement is not an exhaustive definition of what is a tax and has attached important qualifications to the statement.

One such qualification relates to the propositions on which the Commonwealth relies to support its contention that the levy is not a tax. In *Air Caledonie International v Commonwealth*, the Court said [(1988) 165 CLR 462 at 467]:

[501] "(T)here is no reason in principle ... why the compulsory exaction of money under statutory powers could not be properly seen as taxation notwithstanding that it was by a non-public authority or for purposes which could not properly be described as public".

That approach was implicit in the reasons given by Dixon J in *Vacuum Oil Co Pty Ltd v Queensland* [(1934) 51 CLR 108] for rejecting the contention that the obligation imposed upon sellers of petrol to purchase and pay for a specified quantity of power alcohol at a specified price was a tax. His Honour said with reference to the compulsory payment [(1934) 51 CLR 108 at 125]:

"It is not a liability to the State, or to any public authority, or *to any definite body or person authorized by law to demand or receive it.*" (Emphasis added.)

It would seem to be a remarkable consequence if a pecuniary levy imposed for public purposes by a non-public authority acting pursuant to a statutory authority falls outside the concept of a tax simply because the authority which imposes the levy is not a public authority, when the amount of the levy is to be expended on public purposes, more particularly, if those purposes are Commonwealth purposes. It is scarcely to be contemplated that the character of the impost as a tax depends upon whether the authority is a public authority, unless it be a case in which the character of the authority will be relevant and influential in deciding whether the purposes on which the moneys raised are to be expended are themselves public. Of course, it is a misnomer to describe an authority as non-public when one of its functions is to levy, demand or receive exactions to be expended on public purposes. To that extent, at least, the authority should be regarded as a public authority. But the better view is that it is not essential to the concept of a tax that the exaction should be by a public authority.

The next question is whether it is necessary that the exaction should be for public purposes if the exaction is to be characterized as a tax ...

[503] In Australia, the fact that a levy is directed to be paid into the Consolidated Revenue Fund has been regarded as a conclusive indication that the levy is exacted for public purposes. But neither principle nor Australian authority provides any support for the converse proposition that an exaction is not a tax if it is not to be paid into the Consolidated Revenue Fund. The requirement imposed by s 81 of the Constitution that all revenue or moneys raised or received by the Executive

Government form one Consolidated Revenue Fund is not, and cannot constitute, a criterion for what is a tax. The purpose of s 81, like that of its Imperial ancestor 27 Geo III c 13 (1787), was to ensure that the revenues of the Crown, including taxes, were brought together in one Consolidated Revenue Fund under the control of Parliament. To hold that revenues or moneys that are not treated in **[504]** accordance with the requirements of s 81 cannot be taxes to which s 81 applies is circuitous reasoning and deprives s 81 of any effective content.

In the present case, it was not contended that, if an exaction does not form part of the Consolidated Revenue Fund, it cannot be said that it was raised for public purposes and therefore is not a tax. But it is necessary to deal with the argument. The essence of the argument is that the expression "public purposes" is to be equated to "governmental purposes". It is sought by the use of the adjective "governmental" to convey the notion that the critical purposes are such that they can be effectuated only with the expenditure of moneys standing to the credit of the Consolidated Revenue Fund. If that proposition be correct, then an exaction not raised or received by the Executive Government, for example, an exaction raised and received by an independent statutory authority pursuant to a power conferred by statute, could not constitute a tax. As Parliament has power to authorize a statutory authority to levy and receive a tax, that general proposition must be rejected ...

The only possible reason, apart from those already rejected, for holding that the provision in question in this case is not a law imposing taxation is that an expropriation from one group for the benefit of another as an incident of legislative regulation of interests on a subject-matter within power, with a view to bringing about what is conceived to be an equitable outcome, is not an exaction for public purposes and is therefore not a tax. In one sense it may be said that the purpose is private in that it concerns the interests of the two groups only. But, in truth, the legislative solution to the problem proceeds on the footing that it is imposed in the public **[505]** interest. Indeed, the purpose of directing the payment of the levy to the collecting society for ultimate distribution of the net proceeds to the relevant copyright owners as a solution to a complex problem of public importance is of necessity a public purpose ...

[507] In the result, we are of the opinion that the levy is a tax. It does not fall within any of the well-recognized descriptions of fees or charges which stand outside the concept of a tax. It is not a fee for a licence or privilege or for a service rendered; it is not a charge for the acquisition or use of property; and it is certainly not a fine or penalty. Moreover, it has the characteristics of an excise; it is imposed upon the vendors of blank tapes in respect of the sale of the tapes and it is a charge which the vendor will, in the ordinary course of business, pass on to the purchaser.

In his dissenting judgment McHugh J said:

McHugh J: [529] A compulsory exaction of money by a public authority for public purposes which is enforceable by legal process will be classified as a tax unless the exaction is a reasonable payment for services rendered to or on behalf of the payee or unless the exaction is a penalty for a breach of the law. However, in *Air Caledonie International v Commonwealth* [165 CLR at 467], this Court said, by way of dicta, that "there is no reason in principle ... why the compulsory exaction of money under statutory powers could not be properly seen as taxation notwithstanding that it was by a non-public authority or for purposes which could not properly be described as public".

I am unable to accept the proposition that a compulsory exaction of money under a statutory power may be a tax although it is not raised for public purposes. A compulsory exaction of money under statutory authority is not by itself sufficient to constitute a payment of tax. If it was, any compulsory transfer of money from one person to another, pursuant to a statutory scheme, would constitute taxation. Moreover, so far as I am aware, no case has yet decided that a compulsory exaction could be a tax even though it was not raised for public purposes. In *Air Caledonie*, the amount of the fee imposed on travellers, although collected by the airlines, was a debt due to the Commonwealth by the airlines whether or not the fee had been or could be collected from the traveller. In *United States v Butler* [297 US 1 at 61 (1936)], the Supreme Court of the United States said:

> "A tax, in the general understanding of the term, and as used in the Constitution, signifies an exaction for the support of the Government. The word has never been thought to connote the expropriation of money from one group for the benefit of another."

This passage emphasises that the chief feature of a tax is that it is raised to finance government expenditure. It is raised "for the benefit of the Consolidated Revenue" [*R v Barger* (1908) 6 CLR 41 at 82] ...

[530] Before a compulsory exaction of money under statutory authority can constitute a tax, it must, in my opinion, be raised for some public, that is, governmental, purpose. In the setting of the Constitution, it must be raised for the purposes of the Commonwealth to "be applied to the payment of the expenditure of the Commonwealth" [Constitution, s 82].

In the context of Pt VC of the *Copyright Act*, the levy imposed by s 135ZZP does not constitute a tax. It is not paid into Consolidated Revenue, and it is not imposed for the purposes of government or of any public or statutory authority. Neither the Commonwealth nor its agents nor any public authority is involved in the exaction of the payments or, for that matter, the distribution of the funds raised by those payments. The levy is collected by, and is the property of, a private collecting society which is administered and controlled by the copyright owners. It is imposed as part of a scheme which makes lawful the domestic copying of copyright works by the use of blank tapes and provides for the compensation of the copyright owners by means of a fund, financed by imposing a levy on the vendors of blank tapes.

A point noted in *Air Caledonie* is that a tax is not a penalty. This distinction was important in *Northern Suburbs General Cemetery Reserve Trust v Commonwealth* (1993) 176 CLR 555, a case that is also significant in demonstrating how laws enacted under s 51(ii) can be used to achieve purposes unrelated to taxation. In reaching that conclusion, the Court applied the accepted approach to characterisation expressed in decisions such as *Fairfax v Federal Commissioner of Taxation* (1965) 114 CLR 1 (see the extract in Chapter 16, §5).

The *Training Guarantee (Administration) Act 1990* (Cth) set out a minimum level of expenditure (calculated as a percentage of an employer's annual national payroll) that employers should spend on employment-related training. The Act provided that an employer's "training guarantee shortfall" in any year equalled the amount that an employer was required by the Act to spend on employment-related training, less the amount actually spent. Under the *Training Guarantee Act 1990* (Cth), the employer was liable to pay the amount of the "training guarantee shortfall" to the Commonwealth. Such amounts were to be paid into a Training Guarantee Fund. The Court held that the Acts were valid under s 51(ii). The exaction imposed by the *Training Guarantee Act* was characterised as a tax rather than a penalty.

Northern Suburbs General Cemetery Reserve Trust v Commonwealth
(1993) 176 CLR 555

Mason CJ, Deane, Toohey and Gaudron JJ: [566] It is beyond question that the Act imposes a compulsory levy, exacted by the Commonwealth itself and enforceable by law. And s 34 of the Administration Act provides that the moneys so **[567]** collected are to be applied for certain enumerated public purposes. In *Air Caledonie International v Commonwealth* [(1988) 165 CLR 462 at 466-7], this Court affirmed that it "suffice(s) to stamp an exaction of money with the character of a tax" if those positive attributes are present in combination with the negative attribute identified by Latham CJ in *Matthews v Chicory Marketing Board (Vic)* [(1938) 60 CLR 263 at 276], namely, that the levy is "not a payment for services rendered". But, as the Court emphasized in *Air Caledonie*, this proposition is not to be applied as an exhaustive definition of a tax. In particular, the negative attribute "not a payment for services rendered" should be seen "as intended to be but an example of various special types of exaction which may not be taxes even though the positive attributes ... are all present" [165 CLR at 467] for the reason that the presence of other characteristics may indicate that the exaction is not in its true character a tax ...

[569] [T]he fact that the revenue-raising burden is merely secondary to the attainment of some other object or objects is not a reason for treating the charge otherwise than as a tax. One might as well suggest that a protective customs duty is not a tax because its primary object is the protection of a particular local manufacturing industry from overseas competition.

If a law, on its face, is one with respect to taxation, the law does not cease to have that character simply because Parliament seeks to achieve, by its enactment, a purpose not within Commonwealth legislative power. In *Osborne v Commonwealth* [(1911) 12 CLR 321], the Court rejected a challenge to the validity of the *Land Tax Act* 1910 (Cth) and the *Land Tax Assessment Act* 1910 (Cth) which was based on the ground that their object was to prevent residents owning large areas of land or to prevent landholders from residing out of Australia or to prevent absentees from holding land in Australia. Subsequently, in *Radio Corporation Pty Ltd v Commonwealth* [(1938) 59 CLR 170 at 179-80], Latham CJ (with whom Rich, Starke and McTiernan JJ agreed) said:

> "After *Osborne v Commonwealth*, it is difficult to contend that an Act relating to taxation is invalid because it is designed for the purpose of carrying out a policy of the Commonwealth **[570]** Parliament which affects matters which are themselves not directly within the legislative power of the Parliament."

Fairfax v Federal Commissioner of Taxation [(1965) 114 CLR 1] likewise demonstrated that, in the characterization of a law with respect to taxation, the legislative purpose has limited relevance. That case concerned the validity of statutory provisions which denied to trustees of superannuation trusts the general exemption from liability to income tax on the investment income of the trust, unless the investments … contained a specified proportion of Commonwealth and other public securities …

[571] The characterization of the charge is complicated by the circumstance that the legislature has not stated whether the charge is a tax or a penalty when it could easily have done so. But, in the ultimate analysis, the considerations pointing to a tax rather than a penalty are decisive. Neither the Act nor the Administration Act mandates or proscribes conduct of any kind. The legislative provisions do not make it an offence to fail to spend the minimum training requirement; nor do they provide for the recovery of civil penalties for such a failure. Consequently, the charge is not a penalty because the liability to pay does not arise from any failure to discharge antecedent obligations on the part of the person on whom the exaction falls. The fact that the legislature has singled out those who do not spend the minimum training requirement as the class to bear the burden of the charge and to quantify the amount of the liability by reference to the shortfall does not deprive the charge of the character of a tax.

[572] The law "'fairly answers the description of a law "with respect to" one given subject-matter appearing in s 51' regardless of whether it is, at the same time, more obviously or equally a law with respect to some other subject-matter" [*Re F; Ex parte F* (1986) 161 CLR 376 at 387-8]. Accordingly, the conclusion that the Act and the Administration Act are laws with respect to taxation is unaffected by the omission of the purpose of raising revenue from the statement of legislative objects.

The joint judgment in *Australian Tape Manufacturers* noted that, in cases where a levy was paid into Consolidated Revenue, this had been seen as "**[503]** a conclusive indication that the levy is … for public purposes". But that presumption, too, is rebuttable. The *Child Support (Registration and Collection) Act 1988* (Cth) and the *Child Support (Assessment) Act 1989* (Cth) provided that a person caring for a child (typically one parent), and entitled to payments of child support (typically from the other parent), can choose to register the payments under those Acts. Thereupon the liability to make the payments becomes a debt owing to the Commonwealth. The payments are collected by the Commonwealth and paid into Consolidated Revenue and amounts equivalent to those collected are paid out of Consolidated Revenue to the person caring for the child. Despite this use of Consolidated Revenue, it was unanimously held in *Luton v Lessels* (2002) 210 CLR 333 that the liabilities thus created did not involve a "tax".

Luton v Lessels
(2002) 210 CLR 333

Gaudron and Hayne JJ: [352] It is clear that the Registration and Collection Act provides for the compulsory exaction of money which is to be paid to the Commonwealth. It is equally clear that it is inappropriate to speak of the exaction being in payment for any services rendered by the

Commonwealth. Further, it may readily be assumed that the scheme for which the Registration and Collection Act provides is a scheme which is seen as being of public benefit, even though its principal focus can also be seen as being on the performance of each individual's obligation to provide child support for his or her child or children, and the satisfaction of the need, and the right, of that child or those children to that support. It by no means follows, however, that the Registration and Collection Act as a whole, or particular provisions of it, are properly described as a law imposing taxation.

All of the features which Latham CJ identified in *Matthews v Chicory Marketing Board (Vict)* [(1938) 60 CLR 263] as typical of a tax – compulsory exaction, by a public authority, for public purposes, enforceable by law, and not being payment for services rendered – are important. The presence or absence of none of them, however, is determinative of the character of the legislation said to impose a tax. It is necessary, in every case, to consider all the features of the legislation ...

[354] Sections 81, 82 and 83, taken together, give effect to the proposition described by [Arthur] Durell in his work on Parliamentary Grants:

"The prohibition of raising taxes without parliamentary authority would be nugatory if the proceeds, even of legal taxes, could be expended at the will of the sovereign. The right, therefore, of appropriation was a logical consequence of the right of levying supplies." ...

It follows that every *tax* that is raised must be paid into the **[355]** Consolidated Revenue Fund. But the converse is not universally true. Not *every* sum that statute requires to be paid to the Commonwealth, and which is paid into the Consolidated Revenue Fund, is a tax ...

What marks the present exactions apart from other exactions that have been held to be taxes is that in every case the sum exacted ... [is] the amount which otherwise would be due and payable by the payer in satisfaction of an existing obligation owed by that payer to the carer of a child ...

There is, therefore, under the Registration and Collection Act, more than the mere earmarking of a compulsory exaction for a particular application. Imposing a financial burden on one group in society for the benefit of another group in society will often constitute a tax. Pointing to some identifiable relationship between the group of payers and the group of recipients or even to some relationship between a particular payer and a particular recipient will not usually require some different conclusion. Under the Registration and Collection Act, however, the obligation to make a payment to the carer of the child is replaced by the obligation to pay the same amount to the Commonwealth. That obligation is coupled with the creation of a new right in the carer to have the Commonwealth pay the carer whatever the payer thereafter gives up – whether by making a payment to the Commonwealth or by suffering a compulsory deduction from salary or wages. The combination of these features – the substitution of a new obligation to the Commonwealth equal to an existing obligation which is terminated, coupled with the substitution of new rights in the carer against the Commonwealth equal to the extent to which the payer performs his or her obligation to the Commonwealth – takes this compulsory exaction outside the description of "taxation".

Callinan J: [383] [T]hese observations can fairly be made about the scheme established by the two Acts. Their purpose is not to raise revenue for the Commonwealth. The scheme does not contemplate any net benefit to the Commonwealth. The scheme does not confer any direct benefit upon the general community. It does not seek to exact money from the community. It may apply to, and require deductions from a social security pension or benefit payable by the Government (s 72AA of the Collection Act), features which hardly give the scheme the appearance of one for the exaction of a tax. The beneficiaries of the scheme are of a limited class: children whose parent or parents would seek to **[384]** avoid their moral and legal obligations owed to them. The Collection Act extinguishes the debt payable pursuant to the Assessment Act by a liable parent to an eligible carer: it creates a debt payable by a liable parent to the Commonwealth. And, it is important to note, s 76 of the Collection Act confers rights to payment upon an eligible carer of an equivalent amount by the Commonwealth. The result that the Collection Act is intended to achieve, and the means by which it is achieved, have some similarity to what happens when a creditor assigns a debt to another ...

These aspects of the scheme would be immediately sufficient to put beyond doubt any question that it is not one for the exaction of a tax but for the recent decision of this Court in *Australian Tape Manufacturers Association Ltd v Commonwealth* [(1993) 176 CLR 480] ... The Court was narrowly divided as to the characterisation of the legislative scheme there. It was held … that the royalty was imposed for a "public purpose", namely the compensation of relevant copyright holders. If a purpose of compensating copyright holders is a public purpose, it is not immediately apparent why a purpose of ensuring that child carers receive maintenance for children, should not also be so regarded. The majority … regarded the relevant enactment as one for the exaction of money from one group for redistribution for the benefit of another group, with a view to bringing about what was seen to be an equitable outcome. There was no necessary correspondence between a copyright holder and the purchaser of a blank tape, who might not even use the tape to copy copyright material. By contrast, the amounts payable under this scheme are paid to the Commonwealth by a particular debtor in relation to a particular child or children, and an equivalent amount is paid to the particular person entitled to that amount of child support. It is this feature which makes *Australian Tape Manufacturers Association* distinguishable and it is unnecessary to consider the Commonwealth's submission that it should be permitted to reopen that case …

[385] [T]his scheme does not involve an exaction by a public authority for a public purpose of the kind discussed in [*Air Caledonie International v Commonwealth* (1988) 165 CLR 462]. A person assessed under this scheme may have no ultimate choice but to pay the assessment to the Commonwealth, but the compulsion to pay only arises, if, and only if, the payer has not otherwise discharged the obligation that a parent owes to his or her child or children. It is parenthood that is, and continues to be the source of the obligation.

(b)   Fees for Services

Matthews v Chicory Marketing Board confirmed what the wording of s 53 implies: namely, that a "fee for services" is not a tax, even if it is compulsory. Three elements commonly need to be established to show that an exaction is a fee for services:

1.   there is a specific identifiable service;
2.   the fee is payable by the person who receives the service; and
3.   the fee is proportionate to the cost of the service.

An example of a fee for services that is therefore not a tax was given in *Harper v Victoria* (1966) 114 CLR 361. The *Marketing of Primary Products Act 1958* (Vic) required that all eggs sold by retail in Victoria be graded and tested by the Egg and Egg Pulp Marketing Board and be stamped to indicate grade and quality. Section 41C(5) required that "[e]very person presenting eggs" for this purpose "shall pay to the Board for the grading testing marking and stamping of such eggs such fee or fees as may be fixed by the Board to defray the expenses incurred therefor". Under s 48(1)(ba), all such fees collected by the Board were to be included in the funds of the Board, from whose surplus payments were made to producers. This meant that any under-estimation of the cost of grading, testing, marking and stamping of eggs would be recouped before the surplus payable to producers was determined and any over-estimation would increase the amount of that surplus.

It was argued that the fee imposed by s 41C(5) was beyond State power as a duty of excise. As a first step, it was necessary to show that the fee was a tax. Instead, it was held to be a fee for services rendered. McTiernan J stressed that the purpose of the fee "[377] is to defray the cost of those services", and that the accounting plan in s 48(1)(ba) "shows pretty clearly that the fees are not devoted to building up consolidated revenue". Owen J stressed that the amount of the fee "[382] is determined by the cost to the Board or the cost, as estimated by the Board, of rendering those services". Taylor and Menzies JJ agreed.

Earlier, in *Parton v Milk Board (Vic)* (1949) 80 CLR 229, it was held that legislation requiring "every dairyman" and "every owner of a milk depot" to contribute to a fund run by a government agency imposed a tax. The money was to be used for governmental purposes, such as measures under other legislation aimed at improving the quality of milk in Victoria. The fund was also to finance the activities of the Victorian Milk Board, including the promotion of milk consumption. In characterising the exaction as a tax and not as a fee for services, Dixon J pointed out that "[258] the Board performs no particular service for the dairyman or the owner of a milk depot for which his contribution may be considered as a fee or recompense".

In *Air Caledonie* the Commonwealth argued that the fee imposed by s 34A of the *Migration Act* could not be a tax because it was a fee for services. The Court rejected this argument.

Air Caledonie International v Commonwealth
(1988) 165 CLR 462

The Court: [468] It is clear that the "fee" purportedly exacted by s 34A possessed all of the positive attributes which have been accepted in this Court as prima facie sufficient to stamp an exaction of money with the character of a tax: it was compulsory; it was exacted by a public authority (the Commonwealth itself) for public purposes (consolidated revenue: see Constitution, s 81); it (or its "amount") was enforceable by law. It is therefore necessary to consider whether there was something special about the fee (eg a "fee for services") or the circumstances in which it was purportedly exacted (eg as a penalty for an offence) which, notwithstanding the presence of those positive attributes, might preclude its characterization as "taxation".

If the fee had been exacted only in those cases where the arriving [469] passenger was not an Australian citizen, it would have been arguable that, regardless of whether it was a "fee for services", it was not a tax. In that event, and notwithstanding the countervailing analogy of a customs duty which is clearly a tax, there might have been some force in an argument to the effect that it was to be seen as a charge imposed upon the passenger for the privilege of entering Australia or as a licence fee and that the requirement that the airline operator collect the fee (and pay the amount of it to the Commonwealth if not collected from the passenger) could not convert it into a tax. However, as has been seen, the fee was payable by, and in respect of, both citizens and non-citizens arriving on an international airline flight. The only exemption was of those whom the Executive might see fit to prescribe by regulation. The right of the Australian citizen to enter the country is not qualified by any law imposing a need to obtain a licence or "clearance" from the Executive. In the case of such a returning citizen, the impost could not be regarded as a charge for the privilege of entry. It has not been, and it could not sensibly be, suggested that the provisions of s 34A could be transformed, by any acceptable process of severance or reading down, from provisions imposing clearance "fees" upon, or with respect to, arriving airline passengers generally into provisions discriminating against visiting non-citizens or non-nationals by imposing a form of entry fee only in relation to them. Accordingly, the question whether the provisions of s 34A are properly to be characterized as a law "imposing taxation" must be answered on the basis that they applied indifferently with respect to returning citizens and visiting non-citizens. That being so, s 34A was a law "imposing taxation" if the fee which it purported to exact from, or with respect to, returning citizens was, for relevant purposes, properly to be characterized as a tax. The only basis upon which it has been suggested that the fee which the section purported to impose for "the clearance of" a returning citizen was not taxation was that it represented a fee "for services".

In one sense, all taxes exacted by a national government and paid into national revenue can be described as "fees for services". They are the fees which the resident or visitor is required to pay as the quid pro quo for the totality of benefits and services which he receives from governmental sources. It is, however, clear that the phrase "fees for services" in s 53 of the Constitution cannot be read in that general impersonal sense. Read in context, the reference to "fees for services" in s 53 should, like the reference to "payment for services rendered" in ... the judgment of [470] Latham CJ in *Matthews v Chicory Marketing Board* [(1938) 60 CLR 263 at 276], be read as referring to a fee or charge exacted for particular identified services provided or rendered individually to, or at the request or direction of, the particular person required to make the payment.

At least in a case of the ordinary Australian citizen returning by air from overseas, the description of the purported impost (see s 34A(1)) as a "fee for immigration clearance of that passenger" did not suffice to make the impost a "fee for services" in any relevant sense. As has been said, such a citizen had, under the law, the right to re-enter the country, without need of any Executive fiat or "clearance", for so long as he retained his citizenship. The subjection of such a citizen to administrative procedures at the point of entry (see Migration Regulations, reg 4) may be necessary, in the public interest, to enable the entry of non-citizens to be prevented or controlled and to enable proper administrative records and procedures to be kept or followed in relation to the arrival and departure of citizens and non-citizens alike. A requirement that a returning citizen submit, in the public interest, to the inconvenience of such administrative procedures at the end of a journey cannot, however, properly be seen as the provision or rendering of "services" to, or at the request or direction of, the citizen concerned. Nor is it possible to find in s 34A (or in any other provision of the Act) any identification of particular services provided or rendered to the individual passenger for which the impost could relevantly be regarded as a fee or quid pro quo. As has been seen, the section neither fixed the amount of the fee nor indicated the considerations to which the Executive was required to pay regard in prescribing it. In these respects, the impost which s 34A purported to exact is to be contrasted with the nominated statutory fee of ten dollars (no other having been prescribed) for the processing of a particular individual's application to become an approved pathologist which was held not to be a tax in *General Practitioners Society v Commonwealth* [(1980) 145 CLR 532]. Indeed, one need do no more than refer to the second reading speech of the responsible Minister, to which both sides referred the Court, to confirm that the moneys intended to be raised by the purported impost were not related to particular services to be supplied to particular passengers but were intended to provide, when paid into consolidated revenue, a general off-setting of the administrative costs of certain areas of the relevant Commonwealth Department, including, for example, the administrative costs involved in maintaining facilities for the issue of visas in overseas countries and "general administrative overheads". Therefore, the fee **[471]** which s 34A purported to exact was, at least in so far as it related to passengers who were Australian citizens, a tax and the provisions of the section were, for relevant purposes, a law "imposing taxation".

The later case of *Airservices Australia v Canadian Airlines International Ltd* (1999) 202 CLR 133 has important implications for "user pays" systems of access to federal government services. Section 66 of the *Civil Aviation Act 1988* (Cth) empowered the Civil Aviation Authority (CAA) to impose charges upon aircraft operators to recoup the cost of providing certain services. The charges were based on the maximum take-off weight of aircraft, and were set at a level that would defray the costs of CAA across its Australian "network" and include a further rate of return of 7.5 per cent on the assets of CAA. Section 67 provided that the amount of the charge "shall be reasonably related to the expenses incurred" by CAA and "shall not be such as to amount to taxation". This was presumably inserted to prevent the rest of the Act being rendered invalid by s 55 of the Constitution in the event that s 66 was held to impose a tax.

Charges were levied against Compass Airlines for air traffic, rescue and fire fighting and meteorological services. In order to secure payment after Compass went into liquidation, CAA imposed a statutory lien under the Act on aircraft used by Compass. The aircraft were leased by Compass, and the owners of the aircraft brought proceedings arguing that the charges infringed s 67. The charges were said to be taxes, and not fees for services, because they did not accurately reflect the actual cost to CAA of providing the services to Compass. Compass, it was argued, was indirectly subsidising other aircraft operators because it would have been assessed for lower charges if factors such as the routes actually flown by Compass had been included in the calculation. This argument succeeded before Branson J in the Federal Court and on appeal to the Full Court of the Federal Court. It was, however, rejected by the High Court, which held, with Callinan J not deciding, that the charges were not taxes.

Airservices Australia v Canadian Airlines International Ltd
(1999) 202 CLR 133

Gleeson CJ and Kirby J: [176] [T]he judges in the Federal Court regarded it as fatal to the ability of the CAA to demonstrate that the charges were not such as to amount to taxation that they were not related to the value to Compass of the particular services and facilities provided to Compass or to the cost to the CAA of providing those particular services and facilities. The corollary appears to be that, if an instrumentality of government provides services or facilities on a user-pays basis, but does not seek to **[177]** relate its charges to the value of the services, or the cost of providing them, to particular users, then although its total revenues from that activity do not exceed its total expenses, (or total expenses plus a reasonable rate of return on capital), what is involved is taxation …

The Constitution, in s 53, contrasts proposed laws imposing taxation with proposed laws for the payment of fees for licences, or fees for services. However, there is no strict dichotomy. The problem is one of characterisation …

What is it that would give a charge the character of one which was such as to amount to taxation? The most likely possibility would be that the charge was "devoted to building up consolidated revenue" [*Harper v Victoria* (1966) 114 CLR 361 at 377]. Compliance with the first limb of s 67 would go a long way towards negating that possibility. In the present case, the charges were not set so as to provide the Commonwealth with a source of additional revenue, and it was accepted that, if they were, they would be likely to fall foul of both limbs of s 67. The critical matter is said to be the lack of relationship between the manner in which the charges were calculated and the value to Compass of, or the cost to the CAA of providing to Compass, the particular services and facilities which it used. The question is not whether this makes the charges unfair; the question is whether it makes them taxes. The answer to the question has wide implications for instrumentalities of government operating in an environment in which the users of services and facilities are expected to bear the cost of providing them, even where such users have no practical choice but to use the services and facilities, and where some of the "services" are in the nature of public regulation and control. Do charges bear the legal character of taxation because some individual users or consumers pay more than the cost of the particular services which they use? In Australia, postal services, transportation services, educational services, and health services, amongst others, and many facilities, are provided by governments, or **[178]** government instrumentalities, in circumstances where charges are imposed which take account of such factors as price sensitivity or capacity to pay, or which seek to equalise costs between, for example, rural and urban consumers, or which in some other way exhibit characteristics similar to those of the charges presently in question. It is not to the point that such pricing of services may have an economic effect, equivalent, or similar, to taxation. What is presently in issue is whether what is involved is taxation within the meaning of s 67 of the Act which, in turn, is to be understood in a wider constitutional context.

If it is necessary to concentrate upon the position of the individual user of a particular service, it is difficult to understand why one would prefer either of two different tests: the value of the service to the user, or the cost to the provider, in deciding whether there was taxation …

Not all taxation has as its primary purpose the raising of revenue; and some forms of taxation are notoriously inefficient means to that end. An objective of raising revenue is not, therefore, a universal determinant. Even so, the presence or absence of such an objective will often be significant.

In this case: the charges were not imposed to raise revenue; the charges were undoubtedly charges for the provision of services and facilities; the charges were imposed to recover the cost of providing such services and facilities across the entire range of users; the charges for categories of services were reasonably related to the expenses incurred in relation to the matters to which the charges related; the services and facilities were, of their nature, part of an activity which must be highly integrated in order to be effective; there was a rational basis for such discrimination between users as existed.

[179] In those circumstances, there is no warrant for concluding that the charges amounted to taxation on the ground that they exceeded the value to particular users of particular services or the cost of providing particular services to particular users.

Gaudron J, with whom Hayne J agreed, reached the same conclusion.

Gaudron J: [192] In a commercial context of the kind described, it seems to me that, notwithstanding that charges apply differently to different users and reflect neither the cost nor the value of the particular service rendered, they are properly characterised as fees for service if three conditions are met. The first is that they are levied only against persons who use the services. The second is that they are levied against all such users. The third is that there is a commercial justification for discriminating between different users.

It is not in issue that only those who used or availed themselves of the services and facilities provided by the Authority were liable to pay the charges now in question and that all such users were liable to a charge for their use. Moreover, where services are provided by a public sector monopoly on a commercial basis, there is a sound reason for fixing prices according to price sensitivity or demand elasticity. Put at its simplest, if those who are price sensitive are forced out of the market, the cost to others will necessarily increase. That being so, the landing and en route charges are, in my view, properly to be characterised as fees for services and do not involve any element of taxation.

McHugh J also focused on the relationship between the charge and the actual services provided, and in doing so sought to clarify how "fees for services" should be understood in light of contemporary government "user pays" practices.

McHugh J: [237] If it were correct that there must be a relationship between the particular charge levied and the particular service received, statutory authorities would be constrained to relating charges to the marginal cost of providing the service in order that the charges not amount to taxation. Where the statutory authority has high fixed costs and low variable costs, this constraint would mean that it would not be able to fully recover its costs. In that case, the statutory purpose, such as that underlying the Act, could not be achieved. The issue then, is whether such a consideration can be legitimately taken into account in determining whether a charge is taxation or a fee for services …

[238] [I]n my opinion, in characterising a charge as a fee for services or taxation, it is legitimate to take account of the changing circumstances of government which are exemplified by the devolving of functions from government departments to statutory authorities or other corporate bodies which, under the terms of their enabling statutes, have a monopoly on the provision of a certain service and are directed by the legislature to provide those services on a "user pays" basis. Charges by such authorities and bodies should be seen as essentially cost driven, imposed on users for the purpose of reimbursing the cost of services provided. They should not be **[239]** approached as if they were imposed simply to raise revenue for the general government of the country …

[240] [T]he following elements of the statutory context and the circumstances of this case indicate that the charges are properly characterised as fees for services: the services were provided by a statutory authority which had as one of its statutory functions the provision of those services or services of that general type; the position of the statutory authority in providing the services approximated that of a natural monopolist; the statutory authority was (at least impliedly) directed under statute to recover the costs of providing those services from the users of those services; the statutory authority exhibited a large degree of financial independence from the executive government and was intended to operate on a commercial basis; and the pricing structure which gave rise to the lack of a discernible relationship between the value of the services provided on a particular occasion and the charge levied for those services … was a reasonably and appropriately adapted means of achieving a legitimate public purpose (other than revenue raising) which was related to the functions, powers or duties of the statutory authority.

These matters support the inference that the lack of a discernible relationship arises from factors, commercial in nature, related to implementing the "user pays" principle of public policy by a body which is financially separate from government. They therefore negate the inference that the particular pricing structure arises from a revenue-raising purpose. Where the total charges recovered for providing the services exceed[ ] the total cost of providing the services, however, a rebuttable presumption naturally arises that the pricing structure is employed for a revenue-making purpose.

Here the evidence disclosed that the rates of the charges were calculated by making an estimate of the total outgoings of the Authority for the 1991-92 year, adding to this figure 7.5 per cent of the value of the Authority's assets (representing the rate of return on assets) and subtracting the interest charges. There is no suggestion that the figure of 7.5 per cent is an unreasonable rate of return on the assets in question. But can that 7.5 per cent rate of return be properly included in the "costs" of the Authority?

[241] The degree of financial autonomy of the Authority from the executive government indicates that a reasonable rate of return on assets from the Authority to the Commonwealth may be legitimately considered to be the cost to the Authority of utilising capital provided by the Commonwealth to provide the services in question …

The rate of return required by the Commonwealth arose as an incident of the Commonwealth utilising the Authority to provide the services in question. The Commonwealth required that its assets provide a reasonable rate of return so that there was no opportunity cost to the Commonwealth of allowing a semi-autonomous statutory authority to tie up what would be Commonwealth assets if the functions of providing the services in question had not been devolved to the Authority. But the overarching purpose of the requirement, as discerned from the operation of the Act, was to allow the Authority to provide the services in question while minimising the opportunity cost to the Commonwealth. It was not to "replenish the Treasury" ...

It follows that in the statutory context of this case the lack of a discernible relationship between the charge levied for, and the value of, a particular service provided on a particular occasion, does not destroy the prima facie character of the charges as fees for services. All the charges in question are therefore properly regarded as fees for services and do not amount to taxation.

(c)   A Tax Cannot be Arbitrary

MacCormick v Federal Commissioner of Taxation (1984) 158 CLR 622 suggests that a fee is not a tax if it is arbitrary (that is, based on other than ascertainable criteria – see also *Giris Pty Ltd v Federal Commissioner of Taxation* (1969) 119 CLR 365). The *Taxation (Unpaid Company Tax – Vendors) Act 1982* (Cth) and the *Taxation (Unpaid Company Tax – Promoters) Act 1982* (Cth) were drafted to recoup revenue lost to the government through tax avoidance schemes that "asset-stripped" companies, leaving them without the assets to pay the taxes for which they were liable. The legislation sought to impose tax liability upon the vendors and promoters of "asset-stripped" companies. The legislation was held to be valid.

MacCormick v Federal Commissioner of Taxation
(1984) 158 CLR 622

Gibbs CJ, Wilson, Deane and Dawson JJ: [639] The exactions in question answer the usual description of a tax. They are compulsory. They are to raise money for governmental purposes. They do not constitute payment for services rendered ... They are not penalties since the liability to pay the exactions does not arise from any failure to discharge antecedent obligations on the part of the persons upon whom the exactions fall ... They are not arbitrary. Liability is imposed by reference to criteria which are sufficiently general in their application and which mark out the objects and subject matter of the tax ...

A further submission was made by the plaintiffs that recoupment tax under the relevant legislation is an incontestable tax and for this reason is beyond the power of the Parliament. Recognition is to be found in the cases of the doctrine that the incontestability of a tax may go to its validity. The principle which lies behind the doctrine is a more general one of elementary constitutional law. It is simply that the legislature cannot determine conclusively for itself its power to enact legislation by putting beyond examination compliance with the constitutional limits upon that power. As was pointed out in *Deputy Commissioner of Taxation v Hankin* [(1959) 100 CLR 566 at 576-7], the point is "that which was so much discussed in *Australian Communist Party v* **[640]** *Commonwealth* [(1951) 83 CLR 1], and which is sometimes expressed by saying that 'a stream cannot rise higher than its source'." In the latter case, Fullagar J put the matter clearly when he said [83 CLR at 258]:

> "The validity of a law or of an administrative act done under a law cannot be made to depend on the opinion of the law-maker, or the person who is to do the act, that the law or the consequence of the act is within the constitutional power upon which the law in question itself depends for its validity. A power to make laws with respect to lighthouses does not authorize the making of a law with respect to anything which is, in the opinion of the law-maker, a lighthouse. A power to make a proclamation carrying legal consequences with respect to a lighthouse is one thing: a power to make a similar proclamation with respect to anything which in the opinion of the Governor General is a lighthouse is another thing."

In other words, where, as is ordinarily the case under the Commonwealth Constitution, the validity of the law depends upon its characterization as a law with respect to a particular subject matter by reference to the criteria which the law itself fixes for its operation, the law cannot be so characterized if, in effect, it goes on to provide that it will have that operation regardless of whether those criteria are, in truth, satisfied.

The particular doctrine in relation to taxation was expressed by Dixon CJ in *Deputy Federal Commissioner of Taxation v Brown* [(1958) 100 CLR 32 at 40], in these terms:

"Although there is no judicial decision to that effect, it has, I think, been generally assumed that under the Constitution liability for tax cannot be imposed upon the subject without leaving open to him some judicial process by which he may show that in truth he was not taxable or not taxable in the sum assessed, that is to say that an administrative assessment could not be made absolutely conclusive upon him if no recourse to the judicial power were allowed."

See also per Williams J at p 52.

For an impost to satisfy the description of a tax it must be possible to differentiate it from an arbitrary exaction and this can only be done by reference to the criteria by which liability to pay the tax is imposed. Not only must it be possible to point to the criteria themselves, but it must be possible to show that the way in which they are applied does not involve the imposition of liability in an arbitrary or capricious manner. In *Giris Pty Ltd v Federal Commissioner of Taxation* [(1969) 119 CLR 365 at 378-9], Kitto J pointed out that the expression "incontestable tax" in the sense in which it is used in **[641]** *Hankin* and *Brown* "refers to a tax provided for by a law which, while making the taxpayer's liability depend upon specified criteria, purports to deny him all right to resist an assessment by proving in the courts that the criteria of liability were not satisfied in his case". The purported tax is thereby converted to an impost which is made payable regardless of whether the circumstances of the case satisfy the criteria relied upon for characterization of the impost as a tax … Such an incontestable impost is not a tax in the constitutional sense and a law imposing such an impost is not a law with respect to taxation within s 51(ii). It is in this sense that an incontestable tax is invalid.

However, the liability which the legislation imposes to pay recoupment tax is not incontestable in this sense. One of the criteria of liability for recoupment tax is a pre-existing, unpaid liability on the part of a target company to pay company tax. The fact that a person not liable to pay company tax but liable to pay a different tax in the form of recoupment tax has a limited right or no right at all to contest the liability of the relevant target company for company tax is not to the point. It is the existence of the overdue company tax which is one of the criteria of liability for recoupment tax and that existence is established once an assessment of company tax is made and any objection has been finalized or the period for objecting has expired and the tax remains unpaid at the relevant time. Liability to pay recoupment tax does not arise until these events have occurred and it arises only upon the assessment of those persons to whom the legislation applies. The assessment of those persons is open to the ordinary processes of review and appeal. This is because the 1982 Assessment Act incorporates the relevant parts of the *Income Tax Assessment Act* relating to the assessment and collection of tax, including review and appeal.

The issues in *MacCormick* were raised again in *Deputy Federal Commissioner of Taxation v Truhold Benefit Pty Ltd* (1985) 158 CLR 678, in a further challenge to the recoupment provisions of the *Taxation (Unpaid Company Tax) Assessment Act 1982* (Cth). Section 6(2) of the Act was a complex provision that enabled the Commissioner of Taxation to assess for taxation a person entitled to participate in the capital distribution of a company that had been "asset-stripped". It was argued that s 6(2) was invalid because it imposed taxation in an arbitrary manner since the personal liability to pay tax in s 6(2) arose where the Commissioner formed an opinion that it would be unreasonable for the company to be liable to pay the tax. This was supported by an argument that the person actually assessed for the tax under s 6(2) need not have a connection with the transaction that stripped the company of its assets. These arguments were unanimously rejected and s 6(2) was held to be valid.

Deputy Federal Commissioner of Taxation v Truhold Benefit Pty Ltd
(1985) 158 CLR 678

Gibbs CJ, Mason, Wilson, Deane and Dawson JJ: [684] In *MacCormick v Commissioner of Taxation* [(1984) 158 CLR 622] it was held that the recoupment tax, for which the Act provides, answers the usual description of a tax. Amongst the characteristics which were said by the majority to bring it within that description was the fact that the tax is not arbitrary. This was, as the relevant passage shows, a reference to the fact that liability can only be imposed by reference to ascertainable criteria with a sufficiently general application and that the tax cannot lawfully be imposed as a result of some administrative decision based upon individual preference unrelated to any test laid down by the legislation. To say that a tax may not be arbitrary in that sense does not, of course, preclude the pejorative description of a tax as arbitrary in the sense that the criteria which are laid down for its application give it a harsh or unreasonable incidence with regard to either its subject-matter or objects. To describe a tax as arbitrary in the latter sense is to do so in a manner which does not go to its validity …

[687] What may be unreasonable having regard only to the situation of the relevant company or its shareholders may not be unreasonable when considered in the context within which the Commissioner is required to form his opinion. That context is provided by s 6, in which sub-ss (1), (2) and (3) should be read together. When so read, each is clearly part of an overall design to ensure that recoupment tax, when it has become payable, will be paid by some person or persons falling within the description provided by the legislation. If recovery from a company otherwise liable to pay is not possible because it has ceased to exist, or because it is insolvent, or if it is unreasonable by reason of a sale of its shares into different hands, then liability may be passed further along the chain which commences with the transaction which resulted in the stripping of the target company. The Commissioner is to be guided and controlled by the policy and purpose of the enactment and, whatever the width of his discretion, it is not unexaminable should he exceed the limits which may be discerned from its provisions: *Giris Pty Ltd v* **[688]** *Federal Commissioner of Taxation* [(1969) 119 CLR 365]. The legislation does not contemplate the formation of an opinion by the Commissioner in an arbitrary manner and any attack upon it on that ground cannot, in our view, succeed.

In *Austin v Commonwealth* (2003) 215 CLR 185 the challenge was to a federal tax, described as a "superannuation contributions surcharge", levied on State judicial officers by the *Superannuation Contributions Tax (Members of Constitutionally Protected Superannuation Funds) Assessment and Collection Act 1997* (Cth) and the *Superannuation Contributions Tax (Members of Constitutionally Protected Superannuation Funds) Imposition Act 1997* (Cth). Although the Court struck down the laws as infringing the immunity of the States from certain Commonwealth laws (see Chapter 25, §2(c)), it rejected an argument that the laws were also invalid because they imposed a liability by reference to criteria so incapable of ascertainment or lacking in general application as to deny them the description of "laws … with respect to … Taxation" under s 51(ii). While Kirby J was moved to deplore "**[286]** the unpleasant complexity of federal superannuation law", the legislative criteria were held to be sufficiently certain to withstand challenge on such grounds.

Austin v Commonwealth
(2003) 215 CLR 185

Gaudron, Gummow and Hayne JJ: [269] It may well be said of the federal laws respecting superannuation enacted over the last twenty years that collectively and individually they fall well short of the Benthamite ideal referred to in *Byrnes v The Queen* [(1999) 199 CLR 1 at 13]. This advocates the drafting of laws which mark out the line of the citizen's conduct by visible directions rather than turn the citizen loose "into the wilds of perpetual conjecture". Further, the plaintiffs gave colour to their submissions by emphasising what they saw as the harsh or unreasonable incidence of the tax imposed upon them by reference both to its subject matter and its objects. But, as the plaintiffs recognised, with reference to [*Deputy Federal Commissioner of Taxation v Truhold Benefit Pty Ltd* (1985) 158 CLR 678], such matters do not go to validity.

However, in *MacCormick* [(1984) 158 CLR 622 at 639], one of the characteristics which were said by the majority to bring the impost there in question within the description of a tax for the purposes of s 51(ii) of the Constitution was that it was "not arbitrary" ...

[270] The plaintiffs complain that different actuaries ... can reasonably differ in working out the amount of their surchargeable contributions ... That is because the "eligible actuary" identified in s 9(5) will be making assumptions and judgments on such variables as mortality rates, retirement age, marital status, age differences between spouses and the like ...

The submissions by the plaintiffs are foreclosed by what was said by Kitto J in *Giris* [(1969) 119 CLR 365 at 379]:

"There is no need to cite authority for the general proposition that the operation of a law with respect to taxation may validly be made to depend upon the formation of an administrative opinion or satisfaction upon a question, eg, as to the existence of a fact or circumstance, or as to the quality (eg, the reasonableness) of a person's conduct, or even as to the likelihood of a consequence of **[271]** the operation of the law in an individual case, as in s 265 [of the *Income Tax Assessment Act 1936* (Cth)] where the question is whether the exaction of an amount of tax will entail hardship."

In such situations there has been no "abdication" of legislative authority. This objection to validity fails.

2. Excise Duties

Section 90 of the Constitution makes *exclusive* so much of the Commonwealth's taxation power under s 51(ii) as relates to "duties of customs and of excise", and also makes exclusive the granting of "bounties on the production or export of goods". Section 90 is prefaced by the words: "On the imposition of uniform duties of customs ..." Uniform duties of customs were imposed by the Federal Parliament on 8 October 1901.

The apparent absence in economic discourse of any settled meaning for the expression "duties of excise" is reflected in the difficulty encountered by the High Court in developing a legal operation for the term. What is clear is that a duty of excise is a tax on goods (rather than on services). "Customs duties" are also taxes on goods; but that term is traditionally used for duties on imported goods imposed at the point of import. In 1901 this led John Quick and Robert Garran to say, by contrast, that: "**[837]** The fundamental conception of the term [excise] is that of a tax on articles produced or manufactured in a country" (*The Annotated Constitution of the Australian Commonwealth* (Angus & Robertson, 1901; repr Legal Books, 1995)).

A narrow interpretation of s 90, like that of Quick and Garran, might be suggested by the context of the provision, particularly ss 88 and 93. This, and the pre-Federation debates over trade policy (see *Cole v Whitfield* (1988) 165 CLR 360 in Chapter 27, §1(b)), suggest that the exclusive power given to the Commonwealth by s 90 might have been intended as applicable only to tariff policy – in other words, "**[297]** that the taxes forbidden to the States by that section were **[298]** taxes which, because of their application to imported or locally produced goods, would interfere with the Commonwealth's tariff policies: that is, taxes which in their application discriminated between imported and local produced goods" (Peter Hanks, *Constitutional Law in Australia* (Butterworths, 2nd ed 1996)).

On the other hand, the movement of High Court decisions to a wider view of "excise" has been justified on the basis that the purpose of s 90 is to safeguard the centralised control of the national economy. As Dixon J suggested in an oft-quoted statement in *Parton v Milk Board (Vic)* (1949) 80 CLR 229: "**[260]** In making the power of the Parliament of the Commonwealth to impose duties of customs and of excise exclusive it may be assumed that it was intended to give the Parliament a real control of the taxation of commodities and to ensure that the execution of whatever policy is adopted should not be hampered or defeated by State action".

(a)   First Approaches

In 1904 the first use of the "reserved State powers" doctrine (see Chapter 7, §3) related not to the grants of concurrent power in s 51 of the Constitution, but to the exclusive Commonwealth power to levy excise duties under s 90. In *Peterswald v Bartley* (1904) 1 CLR 497, the Court gave a relatively narrow meaning to the expression "duties of excise", partly with a view to leaving undisturbed the pre-1900 New South Wales system of brewers' licensing fees. The overtones of "reserved State powers" in that case were made unacceptable by *Amalgamated Society of Engineers v Adelaide Steamship Co Ltd* (*Engineers' Case*) (1920) 28 CLR 129. However, a concern to preserve adequate fiscal powers, or revenue capabilities, for the States is still sometimes expressed as a reason for preferring a narrower meaning of "excise", since to bring a tax within the definition of "excise" is to say that no State can impose such a tax.

The brewer's licence fee considered in *Peterswald v Bartley* was held not to be an excise on the ground that, although it was related to the production or manufacture of goods, it was not a tax on goods. The fee was fixed at a nominal flat rate regardless of the quantity of beer produced and was an adjunct of a genuine licensing system. It was not a case where the licensing system was a device for collecting a tax.

Peterswald v Bartley
(1904) 1 CLR 497

Griffith CJ (for the Court): [509] With respect to the Australian use of the term [duties of excise], we are entitled to take notice of the sense in which it had been understood and used in the legislation of the various States. We know that in some of them there were in existence for many years "duties of excise", properly so called, imposed on beer, spirits and tobacco. There were other charges which were never spoken of as excise duties, such as fees for publicans' licences, and for various other businesses, such as slaughtermen's, auctioneers', and so forth, but these were not commonly understood in Australia as included under the head of excise duties. Bearing in mind that the Constitution was framed in Australia by Australians, and for the use of the Australian people, and that the word "excise" had a distinct meaning in the popular mind, and that there were in the States many laws in force dealing with the subject, and that when used in the Constitution it is used in connection with the words "on goods produced or manufactured in the States", the conclusion is almost inevitable that, whenever it is used, it is intended to mean a duty analogous to a customs duty imposed upon goods either in relation to quantity or value when produced or manufactured, and not in the sense of a direct tax or personal tax. Reading the Constitution alone, that seems to be the proper construction to be put on that term …

[510] [I]f a particular industry is one which exists only by the permission of the State, the forbidding of the carrying on of that industry in that State is within the power of its legislature, and they may impose upon it any condition or restriction they think fit. Therefore, such a tax is not, *primâ facie*, a tax upon particular goods, but a condition imposed by Statute upon persons who are engaged in producing them … **[511]** [T]he subject matter is one which the legislature of New South Wales has power to regulate, – that is to say the carrying on of any business – in the exercise of the police power of the State. It is not disputed that it can regulate the manufacture of an article, though it has no power to impose a tax upon the thing itself. From that point of view we look at the Statute in question to see whether it was passed for the purpose of regulating or controlling the manufacture of this particular article, beer. The Act provides in substance that a person who proposes to carry on the business of manufacturing beer must give the name and place where he intends to carry it on, and pay a licence fee. Whether there is also a federal excise duty upon the manufactured beer is quite immaterial. Further, the licence not only empowers the licensee to manufacture beer, but entails the liability to have the premises entered by an inspector for the purpose of taking samples of the beer made there, in order to ascertain whether there is any adulteration or not. The provision, therefore, is one of several conditions imposed upon the manufacturer for regulating the trade, which is one of the primary functions of a State legislature.

Note especially the two key elements of a duty of excise set out by Griffith CJ; that is, it is a tax imposed upon goods (1) "either in relation to quantity or value" and (2) at the point of time when the goods are "produced or manufactured".

The reasoning, although not necessarily the result, in *Peterswald v Bartley* was flawed in two ways. The first problem was the influence of the "reserved State powers" doctrine. The second problem was unnecessary deference to the Privy Council, which had dealt with a superficially similar problem in constitutional appeals from Canada.

Section 122 of the Canadian Constitution (the *British North America Act 1867* (Imp)) provided: "The Customs and Excise Laws of each Province shall, subject to the Provisions of this Act, continue in force until altered by the Parliament of Canada". But, by s 92, each Province retained exclusive power in relation to "Direct Taxation within the Province in order to [*sic*] the raising of a Revenue for Provincial Purposes". This implies that the raising of revenue by "direct taxation" is not an excise. The Canadian distribution of powers, and the language in which it is expressed, are so different from those in Australia as to seem of little help; but despite this, *Peterswald v Bartley* began a tradition of deference to Privy Council decisions on Canada's s 92. In practice, this meant deference to John Stuart Mill, since the relevant Privy Council judgments, beginning with *Bank of Toronto v Lambe* (1887) 12 App Cas 575, had been dominated by a passage from his *Principles of Political Economy* (1848).

John Stuart Mill, *Principles of Political Economy*
(1848; Longmans Green & Co, 1936) Book V, Ch 3

[371] §I. TAXES are either direct or indirect. A direct tax is one which is demanded from the very persons who, it is intended or desired, should pay it. Indirect taxes are those which are demanded from one person in the expectation or intention that he shall indemnify himself at the expense of another: such as the excise or customs. The producer or importer of a commodity is called upon to pay a tax on it, not with the intention to levy a peculiar contribution upon him, but to tax through him the consumers of the commodity, from whom it is supposed that he will recover the amount by means of an advance in price.

The acceptance of this passage in *Peterswald v Bartley* was a final reason for the decision: the Court could see nothing to distinguish the fee from "**[512]** a direct tax upon the manufacturer".

Yet acceptance of the distinction between direct and indirect taxes confused the notion of "a tax on goods". On the one hand, *Peterswald v Bartley* had held that excise duties were limited to taxes imposed upon goods at the point of manufacture. On the other hand, if the essence of an "excise" is that it is indirect, that is, that the burden of the tax is not borne by the person who pays the tax but is passed on to the ultimate consumer, then it does not matter whether the tax is imposed at the manufacturing stage or not. The idea of "a tax on goods" thus came to mean that the tax is attached to the goods at some stage (not necessarily that of manufacture), and travels with them, as a component of their price or value, through all subsequent dealings until final consumption.

(b)   Widening Views of "excise"

The gradual widening of the High Court's definition of "excise" involved a movement away from the *Peterswald v Bartley* notion of a tax on the "quantity or value" of goods "when produced or manufactured". The crucial steps in this shift were *Matthews v Chicory Marketing Board (Vic)* (1938) 60 CLR 263, in relation to "quantity or value", and *Parton v Milk Board (Vic)* (1949) 80 CLR 229, in relation to "when produced or manufactured". In each of these cases, the leading judgment was that of Dixon J, supported in *Matthews* by Rich and Starke JJ and in *Parton* by Rich and Williams JJ. In each case, Latham CJ and McTiernan JJ dissented.

In *Matthews v Chicory Marketing Board*, the Victorian Chicory Marketing Board proclaimed a levy, under the *Marketing of Primary Products Act 1935* (Vic), to be paid by all producers of chicory "at the rate of £1 for every half acre, or part thereof, of the area planted by such producer with chicory during the year ending 30th June, 1937". By 3:2, it was held that the levy was an excise and therefore invalid.

Matthews v Chicory Marketing Board (Vic)
(1938) 60 CLR 263

Dixon J: [299] The history of the word "excise" does not disclose any very solid ground for saying that, according to any established English meaning, an essential part of its connotation is, or at any time was, that the duty called by that name should be confined to goods of domestic manufacture or production. The application of the word by economists and others to duties so confined is scarcely logical proof that the word is inapplicable to inland duties levied on commodities independently of the place of manufacture. But, of course, it is a factor to be weighed …

[302] The chief purpose of the foregoing discussion of the considerations governing the connotation of the word "excise" is to show that, although, as it is used in the Commonwealth Constitution, it describes a tax on or connected with commodities, there is no ground for restricting the application of the word to duties calculated directly [303] on the quantity or value of the goods. A definition which makes quantity and value the only basis of taxation which would satisfy the notion of "excise" has no foundation either in history, economic or fiscal principle, nor in any accepted specialization. The basal conception of an excise in the primary sense which the framers of the Constitution are regarded as having adopted is a tax directly affecting commodities.

The levy made by the Chicory Marketing Board is not ascertained by direct reference to the quantity or value of the chicory produced. It is imposed upon a producer, and presumably under the definition of that word he must actually obtain some chicory from the crop he has sown before he satisfies that description. But the basis of his assessment is not what he garners but what he plants. By calculating the levy upon the number of half acres which the producer plants with chicory the board makes it at least theoretically possible that owing to a failure of his crop the levy upon him has little or no relation to his actual production of chicory. But the basis adopted for the levy has a natural, although not a necessary, relation to the quantity of the commodity produced. Although many other factors go to the determination of the actual quantity of chicory produced, the area planted is, if not the chief, at all events a controlling element. By adopting area planted as the criterion of the amount of the levy upon each producer the board has taxed the production of the commodity as effectually as if it had selected, for instance, the weight of the chicory gathered in its raw state, the quantity treated or the gross returns. For it has placed upon an essential step in production, namely, planting, an impost computed quantitatively. There is no distinction of substance and scarcely any even of form between levying a tax upon the area planted and levying a tax upon the act of planting the area. The levy is directed to the normal case of a man reaping even as he sows. The fact that the tax would also fall upon a chicory farmer whose expectations are disappointed through some of the mischances of agriculture does not seem to me to make the levy any less a tax upon production. The natural or practical relations between manufacture or production and activities or conditions chosen as the tests or standards of liability to taxation depend, not upon logical definitions, but upon the actual course of industrial organization and technique and of the productive arts.

[304] If the word "excise" received a meaning which confined its application to taxes the relation of which to the commodity concerned was of some narrow and strictly defined nature, as, for instance, by an arithmetical relation to quantity, it would not only miss the principle contained in the use of the word "excise," but it would expose the constitutional provision made by sec 90 to evasion by easy subterfuges and the adoption of unreal distinctions. To be an excise the tax must be levied "upon goods," but those apparently simple words permit of much flexibility in application. The tax must bear a close relation to the production or manufacture, the sale or the consumption of the goods and must be of such a nature as to affect them as the subjects of manufacture or production or as articles of commerce. But if the substantial effect is to impose a levy in respect of the commodity the fact that the basis of assessment is not strictly that of quantity or value will not prevent the tax falling within the description, duties of excise.

In *Parton v Milk Board*, the *Milk Board Act 1933* (Vic) established a Milk Board to regulate the supply of milk in Melbourne. Under s 30(1)(a), the Board was to be financed by a levy upon "every dairyman ... who sells or distributes milk in the metropolis" and "every owner of a milk depot who sells or distributes milk to any person in the metropolis". The levy was to be determined by the Board at an amount not exceeding "one-quarter of a penny per gallon for every gallon of milk so sold or distributed". A majority of the Court, Rich, Dixon and Williams JJ, found that the levy was an excise. Latham CJ and McTiernan J again dissented.

Parton v Milk Board (Vic)
(1949) 80 CLR 229

Dixon J: [258] In my opinion the levy of the contribution does amount to the imposition of a duty of excise. In stating as briefly as I can my reasons for this conclusion I shall begin by mentioning the characteristics of the contribution in virtue of which I think it is a duty of excise. In the first place I think that it is clearly a tax. It is a compulsory exaction. It is an exaction for the purposes of expenditure out of a Treasury fund. The expenditure is by a government agency and the objects are governmental. It is not a charge for services ... **[259]** The contribution is a compulsory levy by a public authority for public purposes and that is enough to show that it is a tax ...

In the next place it is a tax upon goods. It is a levy of an eighth or a tenth of a penny upon every gallon of milk sold or distributed in the metropolis by a dairyman or a milk depot. That means a tax upon the milk sold or distributed for consumption in Melbourne. It is not a licence fee payable as a condition of a right to carry on a business. On the other hand it is a trading tax. "Customs and excise duties are, in their essence, trading taxes, and may be said to be more concerned with the commodity in respect of which the taxation is imposed than with the particular person from whom the tax is exacted": *Attorney-General for British Columbia v Kingcome Navigation Co* [[1934] AC 45 at 59]. Again the exaction is not a tax imposed upon the dairyman and owner of a milk depot because they are selected as the parties to the trading who should bear a particular contribution but on the contrary it is imposed on them as the persons to pay, it being a matter of indifference which of the parties ultimately bears the burden and the tax having from its nature a tendency to enter into the price obtained for the milk. The tax is therefore indirect [[1934] AC at 57] ... "The leading characteristic of an indirect tax is that it is susceptible of being passed on and customs and excise duties ordinarily exhibit this characteristic" (*Matthews v Chicory Marketing Board* [(1938) 60 CLR 263 at 285], per *Starke* J). It is a sales tax and as I understand it that is generally regarded as an excise.

Finally it falls within the definition of "excise" given by the *Encyclopaedia Britannica*, 11th ed, vol 10, and adopted by the *Oxford English Dictionary sv* viz: "a term now well known in public finance, signifying a duty charged on home goods, either in the process of their manufacture or before their sale to the home consumers."

Only if the conception of what is an excise is limited by the condition that the tax must be levied on the manufacturer, that is to **[260]** say upon the goods while they are still in his hands, can I see any escape from the conclusion that the levy of the contribution is an excise.

I cannot adopt the view that this is an essential feature of the conception. What probably is essential is that it should be a tax upon goods before they reach the consumer. Though in *Commonwealth & Commonwealth Oil Refineries v South Australia* [(1926) 38 CLR 408 at 435] *Higgins* J said: "Excise means a duty on the manufacture, production &c in the country itself; and it matters not whether the duty is a duty imposed at the moment of actual sale or not, or sale and delivery, or consumption." In making the power of the Parliament of the Commonwealth to impose duties of customs and of excise exclusive it may be assumed that it was intended to give the Parliament a real control of the taxation of commodities and to ensure that the execution of whatever policy is adopted should not be hampered or defeated by State action. A tax upon a commodity at any point in the course of distribution before it reaches the consumer produces the same effect as a tax upon its manufacture or production. If the exclusive power of the Commonwealth with respect to excise did not go past manufacture and production it would with respect to many commodities have only a formal significance ...

[261] In *Matthews v Chicory Marketing Board (Vic)* I examined the history of the word "excise" and its meaning and I shall not go over the same ground again. It is probably a safe inference from *Atlantic Smoke Shops, Ltd v Conlon* [[1943] AC 550], which has since been decided, that a tax on consumers or upon consumption cannot be an excise.

(c)   The Tangled Web of Dennis Hotels

In *Parton v Milk Board*, Dixon J suggested that he would not regard as an excise "**[263]** something like the licence fee of a licensed victualler calculated on the amount expended by him in the previous year in purchasing liquor". This very situation arose in *Dennis Hotels Pty Ltd v Victoria* (1960) 104 CLR 529. Despite his dictum in *Parton v Milk Board*, Dixon CJ held that the licence fee was an excise.

If *Dennis Hotels* began with a change of mind, it ended in a tangle from which the High Court has never managed entirely to escape. *Dennis Hotels* saw the Court almost evenly divided. The way in which the division was resolved established a precedent that satisfied no one, yet which the Court repeatedly felt unable to overrule or reconsider.

A company held a "victualler's licence" for its hotel under the *Licensing Act 1928* (Vic). It had also held a series of "temporary licences" for booths and bars at sporting fixtures and at agricultural shows. The company challenged the validity of the fees for both licences. Under s 19(1)(a) of the *Licensing Act*, the fee for the victualler's licence was 6 per cent of the cost of all liquor purchased for the premises during the 12 months ending on 30 June preceding the application for grant or renewal of the licence. By s 19(1)(b), the fee for a temporary licence was £1 per day, plus 6 per cent of the cost of all liquor purchased for sale under that licence.

For Dixon CJ, McTiernan and Windeyer JJ, both licence fees were "excise duties". For Fullagar, Kitto and Taylor JJ, neither fee was an excise. Only Menzies J distinguished between the two types of licence. He held that the fee for a "temporary licence" was an excise duty but that the fee for a "victualler's licence" was not.

Dennis Hotels Pty Ltd v Victoria
(1960) 104 CLR 529

Dixon CJ: [538] In *Parton v Milk Board (Vic)* [(1949) 80 CLR 229 at 263] I had occasion to state why in my opinion the character of the levy dealt with in *Hartley v Walsh* [(1937) 57 CLR 372] showed that it could not be a duty of excise. I said: "Not only was the imposition upon the proprietor of the packing shed and one measured, at least as to the maximum, by the fruit handled, but the fruit was the fruit of the previous year. This appears to me to place the imposition more in the category of **[539]** a licence fee in respect of a business calculated on past business done." Had I stopped there, I would have had nothing to repent. But I did not stop there; I went on with an illustration: "something like the licence fee of a licensed victualler calculated on the amount expended by him in the previous year in purchasing liquor, which I should not regard as an excise." No doubt I had the system obtaining in Victoria in mind. But an examination of the system has convinced me that the illustration was entirely wrong ...

It is, I believe, an undeniable proposition that, subject to ... unimportant exceptions ..., because of the provisions of the *Licensing Act* no liquor can be bought by retail in Victoria unless in respect of it someone has paid, has become liable to pay or will be placed in a situation which will from the necessity of the case involve him in paying to the Victorian Treasury an amount equal to six per cent of the wholesale selling price of the liquor.

That proposition means to me that the provisions impose an excise duty within the meaning of s 90. It is a tax. It is a tax **[540]** "upon" the goods. It is the kind of tax which tends to be recovered by the person paying it in the price he charges for the goods which bear the imposition ...

[546] The provisions deal with the distribution of liquor in Victoria as a continuous operation and impose the tax accordingly. That is one reason why it appears to me to be quite immaterial that the payment of the tax made in, say, January of a given year is calculated on the liquor purchased during the twelve months ending on the last day of the previous June for sale on the premises or as the **[547]** case may be. It is also a reason why it has seemed unnecessary to go into the question of the obtaining of a new licence and the assessment of tax for the commencing year ...

The fact that the licensing of a licensed victualler and for that matter the registration of a club forms part of the method of controlling the sale of liquor, the conduct of hotels and so on appears to me quite immaterial, as does the question whether the licence in the hands of the licensee is a valuable privilege for which the payment of the tax may be regarded as part of the consideration. Section 90 is quite unconcerned with the position of the individual. It is concerned wholly with the demarcation of authority between Commonwealth and State to tax commodities. Duties of excise and of customs are denied to the States simply because of their effect on commodities. Whether a tax is a duty of excise must be considered by reference to its relation to the commodity as an article of commerce. The six per cent upon the wholesale selling price of liquor appears to me simply to be a tax upon liquor, a tax imposed on liquor on its way to the consumer by whatever **[548]** channel it may proceed: it is in other words an addition to the excises the Commonwealth Parliament has chosen to impose on liquor.

McTiernan and Windeyer JJ agreed. By contrast, Fullagar, Kitto and Taylor JJ held, for different reasons, that the licence fees were not "excise duties". Fullagar J attempted to purge the case law of its distortions and return to *Peterswald v Bartley*, though not to its use of Canadian precedents or to the "reserved State powers" doctrine.

Fullagar J: [553] When it has been decided that the particular exaction in question is a tax, the question is then sometimes asked whether it is a "direct" tax or an "indirect" tax. As to this, I would say that, with the greatest respect, I think it a pity that this distinction was ever raised or mentioned in relation to s 90. I do not think it is capable of throwing any light on s 90. Attention to it may be thought to have been invited by the concluding words of the "definition" of *Griffith* CJ in *Peterswald v Bartley* [(1904) 1 CLR 497 at 509]. His Honour's words were "and not in the sense of a direct tax or personal tax". But I understand his Honour to have intended by those words not to add anything by way of definition to what he had already said, but merely to give an example, by way of contradistinction, of something which would not be a duty of excise. I gather from a recent article *Judicial Review under Section 90 of the Constitution – An Economist's View – Pt* 1 by Professor *HW Arndt* that the distinction between "direct" and "indirect" taxes is now discredited among economists. But in any case I do think that the whole subject of s 90 and duties of excise has been clouded by reference to a number of decisions of the Privy Council, which have interpreted and clarified s 92(II) of the Canadian Constitution but have no real bearing on s 90 of our own ...
[554] There can be no such justification for "the use of Mill's analysis", or for the use of Canadian precedents, when we come to interpret our own s 90, which was adopted in a quite different setting and employs much more specific terminology.

When we have found that an exaction which is in question is a tax, and when we have put aside the Canadian Constitution and the decisions on it as irrelevant, we come to the critical questions. These may be stated as being three in number – (1) Must it be a tax "upon goods"? – (2) Must it be imposed upon the production or manufacture of goods? – (3) Must it be imposed by reference to quantity or value of the goods? The questions so stated raise for consideration, though not in the same order, the three elements regarded by the Court in *Peterswald v Bartley* as essential.

Probably no one would dissent from the broad proposition that it is an essential element in the character of a duty of excise that it should be a tax "upon goods". But the whole weight of that expression is carried by, and ambiguity lurks in, the humble preposition, for which is sometimes substituted a prepositional phrase such as "in respect of", or "in relation to". Taxes may be charged upon property, real or personal, in the sense that there is a direct remedy against the property for recovery of the tax. But nothing of that kind is meant when we speak, in the present universe of discourse, of a tax "upon goods". Goods as such cannot pay taxes: there must be a person to pay them. And what is meant by saying that a tax is a tax upon goods is that the person by whom the tax is payable is charged by reason of, and by reference to, some specific relation subsisting between him and particular goods. A tax will be rightly regarded as a tax upon goods if the person upon whom it is imposed is charged by reason of and by reference to the fact that he is the owner, importer, exporter, manufacturer, producer, processor, seller, purchaser, hirer or consumer of particular goods. This list may not be exhaustive.

Duties of customs and duties of excise are particular classes of taxes "upon goods". The relation of taxpayer to goods which characterizes a duty of customs is found in the importation or exportation of goods. The taxpayer is taxed by reason of, and by reference to, his importation or exportation of goods. The relation is implicit in the term itself, which has acquired an established meaning, so that difficulty is seldom felt as to whether a particular [555] exaction is or is not a duty of customs. It has often been observed that the meaning of the term "duty of excise" is not so well established, and the crucial question in the present case, as I see it, is: What is the relation of taxpayer to goods which characterizes a "duty of excise" as that term is used in the Constitution and particularly in s 90?

The answer to this question given by the Court in *Peterswald v Bartley* was that the necessary relation is to be found in the manufacture or production of goods – that what characterizes a duty of excise is that the taxpayer is taxed by reason of, and by reference to, his production or manufacture of goods. The relation is treated as implicit in the term itself ... After full consideration, and necessarily with the greatest respect for the contrary view, I am of opinion that the answer given in *Peterswald v Bartley* was right and should be applied in the present case.

Kitto and Taylor JJ agreed with Fullagar J that the various licence fees were not "excise duties", but for different reasons. Kitto J adopted the notion of "direct" and "indirect" taxes. He married this to an emphasis on the "criterion of liability" adopted in the taxing statute, that is, the fact or element which the legislature had specified as attracting the incidence of the tax.

Kitto J: [559] [A] tax is not a duty of excise unless the criterion of liability is the taking of a step in a process of bringing goods into existence or to a consumable state, or passing them down the line which reaches from the earliest stage in production to the point of receipt by the consumer. Indeed, the fact which in general justifies the description of an excise duty as an indirect tax, in the sense of John Stuart Mill's dichotomy, is that when, in the ordinary case, excise duty [560] becomes payable, it amounts to a statutory addition to the cost of a particular act or operation in the process of producing or distributing goods, so that in the costing of the goods in relation to which the act or operation is done, for the purpose of arriving at a selling price to be charged to the next recipient in the chain that leads to the ultimate consumer, the duty paid in respect of those goods may enter – and therefore, according to the natural course of business affairs, will enter – as a charge relating to those goods specifically ... As *Matthews v Chicory Marketing Board (Vic)* [(1938) 60 CLR 263 shows, it is not essential that in every case that may arise the act or process which attracts the tax shall succeed in its purpose: through some mischance it may happen that no goods issue from the activity to be passed down the line to the consumer, and therefore there may be no opportunity to pass the tax on. But the impost is nevertheless a duty of excise if it operates as a tax upon the taking of a step in a process of producing or distributing goods.

To say so much is to exclude a tax which has no closer connexion with production or distribution than that it is exacted for the privilege of engaging in the process at all. The cases decided in this Court have been marked by much diversity of opinion on some points, but I think it may be taken as settled that a tax is not a duty of excise unless the criterion of liability is such as I have mentioned.

The decisive judgment was that of Menzies J, who held that the fee for the "temporary licence" was an excise duty but that the fee for a "victualler's licence" was not.

Menzies J: [589] [T]he position has now been reached that although an excise duty is a tax on the [590] production or manufacture of goods, a tax upon the sale or purchase of goods manufactured in Australia at any point before sale for consumption is to be regarded as a tax on production or manufacture; and furthermore, that a tax may be an excise notwithstanding that quantity or value of goods is not the basis of the duty. This position I feel bound to accept notwithstanding the reservations I would otherwise have about the glosses upon the main proposition ... It is also to be observed that in the cases, there are many statements to the effect that an excise duty is an indirect tax, but there is a good deal to be said for the view expressed by *Starke* J on more than one occasion that this particular classification is one of convenience rather than logic and the fact that a duty is "indirect" is no more than one factor in favour of the conclusion that it is an excise. This is the view taken by the Court in *Browns Transport Pty Ltd v Kropp* [(1958) 100 CLR 117 at 129], but it is said: "It would perhaps be going too far to say that it is an essential element of a duty of excise that it should be an 'indirect' tax. But a duty of excise will generally be an indirect tax, and, if a tax appears on its face to possess that character, it will generally be because it is a tax upon goods rather than a tax upon persons" …

[591] Coming back now to the victualler's licence fee, I am disposed to regard it as an indirect tax in that not only are consumers likely to pay more for liquor than would be the case if licence fees were not charged, but, further, notwithstanding s 19(3), licensed victuallers probably endeavour to pass on to consumers the full amount of what they pay as licence fees; it is not, however, a sales or a purchase tax because, as I have already stated, a dealing with the goods does not expose the licensed victualler to liability for tax; the tax is upon the person seeking a licence to sell liquor upon particular premises in the future, not upon the liquor already purchased for sale at those premises although it is calculated upon such purchases; it is a tax upon persons, like that considered in *Browns Transport Pty Ltd v Kropp*, namely, a tax upon a licensed victualler as the price for his franchise to carry on a business, the most important element of which is to sell liquor from the licensed premises independently of whether the liquor is produced in Australia or abroad, or partly in Australia and partly abroad. It is not in truth a tax on the production or manufacture of liquor, and none of the decided cases require that it should be treated as such a tax. For these reasons, I have come to the conclusion that the licensed victualler's fee is not a duty of excise …

I find greater difficulty about the character of the fee for a temporary licence. It seems to me that once a temporary licence is granted, every purchase of liquor for sale under that licence, whether it be of local or overseas production, does attract tax at the rate of six per cent of the purchase price. In these circumstances I feel constrained by *Parton v Milk Board (Vic)* to treat such fees to the extent that they are upon purchases of liquor produced in Australia, as duties of excise.

Evidently, Menzies J saw *Parton v Milk Board* as binding, but had no wish to extend it. He therefore felt able to hold that the victualler's licence fee was not an "excise" because, even though the fee was calculated on the basis of the plaintiff's purchases of liquor, these were past purchases. Hence, the new licence could have no operation in relation to *that* liquor. By contrast, the temporary licence fee was calculated on the basis of the very liquor to be sold under that licence. He felt bound by *Parton v Milk Board* to hold that a fee thus computed was a tax on that liquor, that is, an excise. No other judge accepted this distinction: in particular, Windeyer J objected that "[595] the two imposts are similar in their general economic consequences", and that the supposed distinction involved "considerations so nice as to be artificial". Besides, he said, it "overlooks the way in which a publican's business is conducted".

In the result, the view of Menzies J added to those of Dixon CJ, McTiernan and Windeyer JJ meant that the temporary licence fee was an excise, while the view of Menzies J added to those of Fullagar, Kitto and Taylor JJ meant that the victualler's licence fee was not an excise. On one view of the doctrine of precedent, only the decision is binding. On a more orthodox view, what is binding is the ratio decidendi, the reason for the decision; yet the only reason for the result is the distinction drawn by Menzies J. Thus, the proposition for which *Dennis Hotels* appears to be authority is a proposition which only one of the seven judges accepted.

In *Bolton v Madsen* (1963) 110 CLR 264, the High Court unanimously applied the "criterion of liability" test propounded by Kitto J in *Dennis Hotels*. However, in *Anderson's Pty Ltd v Victoria* (1964) 111 CLR 353, Barwick CJ rejected the suggestion that this was the only applicable test. In his view its focus on verbal criteria and on the "direct legal effect" of the tax was too formalistic. The one brief moment of unanimity in *Bolton v Madsen* was shattered.

(d)   Alcohol, Tobacco and Petrol

In *Western Australia v Hamersley Iron Pty Ltd (No 1)* (1969) 120 CLR 42 and *Western Australia v Chamberlain Industries Pty Ltd* (1970) 121 CLR 1 the High Court considered provisions of the *Stamp Act 1921* (WA) imposing stamp duty on receipts. Insofar as the receipts were given to acknowledge payment for the sale of goods, the majority in a narrowly divided Court held that the duty was effectively a tax on the goods and hence invalid as an "excise". This provoked an angry State reaction. The States embarked on a search for other forms of revenue to replace the lost duties on sale-of-goods receipts, and among the more successful results was the *Tobacco Act 1972* (Tas), substantially held valid in *Dickenson's Arcade Pty Ltd v Tasmania* (1974) 130 CLR 177.

Part III of the Act prohibited the retail sale of tobacco without a licence. The licence fee was modelled on *Dennis Hotels*, and computed by reference to the average monthly stock value over a 12-month period ending six months before the commencement of the licence. A flat fee of $2 was payable if the average monthly stock value was under $500, with a sliding scale of up to 30 per cent of that average for greater amounts. By 5:1, with McTiernan J dissenting, this fee was held not to be an excise because of its adherence to the formula in *Dennis Hotels*.

Dickenson's Arcade Pty Ltd v Tasmania
(1974) 130 CLR 177

Barwick CJ: [188] There being no reason for decision common to the majority of the Justices, the Court's decision in *Dennis Hotels Pty Ltd v Victoria* [(1960) 104 CLR 529], in my opinion, is authority only in relation to the statutory and factual situation it resolved and in relation to a case which has, if not precisely, at least substantially and indistinguishably the same statutory and factual situation. Cf Lord Haldane in *Great Western Railway Co v Owners of ss "Mostyn"* [[1928] AC 57 at 71-2]. I do not consider myself bound by any of the several reasons given by the individual Justices for the conclusion to which they came: and, in particular, I do not regard myself as bound to use any of those reasons as a base on which to construct some further or other conclusion. If to decide this case it were necessary to choose that view expressed in that case which most commends itself to me, my present inclination would be to prefer the views expressed by Sir Owen Dixon, my brother McTiernan and Sir Victor Windeyer.

[189] However, after due consideration, I have come to the conclusion that I do not have to make any such choice. I have been troubled by the question whether the statutory and factual situation in the present case is so substantially similar to that with which the Court dealt in *Dennis Hotels Pty Ltd v Victoria* that I should regard the decision in the case quite apart from any of the reasoning of any of the Justices as compelling a decision in this so far as the licensing provisions of the Act are concerned. Clearly enough, the draftsman, in using his evident ingenuity in constructing the Act, built upon the decision in that case in expressing the mode of calculating the licence fee payable under Pt III of the Act. By using an ambiguous expression in s 11(3)(a), namely "the average value ... of the tobacco handled in a month" and by choosing that average for the period during six months before the commencement of the period of the licence, the draftsman thought to remove the specification of the fee one step further from a clear case of an excise as found by the Court in *Dennis Hotels Pty Ltd v Victoria*, in the instance of the temporary victualler's fee. However, after consideration, I have come to think that the statutory and factual situation in this case is so substantially similar to and not distinguishable from the statutory and factual situation in *Dennis Hotels Pty Ltd v Victoria*, the temporary victualler's and the temporary packet licences apart, that though, if the matter were fully open for decision, I would not be prepared, as at present advised, to so decide, I have come to think that I ought to apply the decision in *Dennis Hotels Pty Ltd v Victoria* to this case and to regard that decision as decisive of the validity of the licensing provisions in this Act. I cannot confess to any great satisfaction in taking that course but, in the circumstances, I am prepared on the authority of the precise decision in that case, but as I have indicated not because of any of its reasoning, to hold that the provisions with respect to the fee payable for a tobacco vendor's licence do not impose a duty of excise.

Gibbs J: [226] *Dennis Hotels Pty Ltd v Victoria* is authority for the proposition that legislation which provides for the grant of a licence to sell goods, on payment of a licence fee, the quantum of which is based on the value of the goods purchased for the premises in a previous year, does not impose a tax directly related to the goods ... The case is authority for what was decided, namely, that a licence fee quantified by reference to the amount paid or payable for goods purchased during a period preceding that in respect of which the licence was granted was not a duty of excise. The same result would clearly follow if the quantification were by reference to the amount obtained from the sale of goods during a preceding period. No doubt these questions, if undecided, would be very arguable but that is no ground for re-opening the decision. The close division of opinion in that case was not on any question of constitutional principle but on the application of the principles to a particular form of licence fee. The decision having been pronounced by a majority of a Full Bench of the Court, after full consideration, should be regarded as settling the question. In any case the later authorities cast no doubt upon its correctness.

Mason J adopted a narrow view of *Dennis Hotels*, but nevertheless held that the retail tobacconist's licence fee was not an excise.

Mason J: [240] *Dennis Hotels* [(1960) 104 CLR 529] is not authority for the universal proposition that, in order to constitute an excise, a licence fee must be calculated by reference to the quantity of goods sold under the licence, thereby enabling the duty to be passed on to a purchaser and that it is not enough that the licence fee is calculated by reference to the quantity of goods sold by the licensee or on the premises before the licence commenced to operate. The decision related to fees prescribed for a licence to sell liquor by retail; it has no necessary application to fees prescribed for a licence to manufacture or process goods to which in my opinion different considerations apply.

Although I doubt whether I should have been inclined, even in the context of the *Licensing Act* 1958 (Vic) to draw a distinction between licence fees prescribed by reference to the quantity of goods sold under the licence and those prescribed by reference to goods sold in an antecedent period, this circumstance does not warrant my declining to follow the authority of *Dennis Hotels* in its application to licence fees of a like kind. The decision has been accepted as authoritative in later cases. The narrowness of the majority and the manner in which it was composed are not enough to warrant a reconsideration of the decision.

The decision on the retail tobacconist's licence fee was clearly a concession to the States. However, it was narrowly limited and grudgingly made. It did not herald any judicial cutback to a narrower definition of excise. In *MG Kailis (1962) Pty Ltd v Western Australia* (1974) 130 CLR 245, decided on the same day as *Dickenson's Arcade*, Mason J applied the above distinction (limiting *Dennis Hotels* to licences for retail businesses as opposed to manufacturing or processing businesses) to hold that a Western Australian fish processing licence fee was an excise. McTiernan and Menzies JJ joined Mason J in a 3:2 result, though they did so on different grounds.

Part II of the *Tobacco Act* considered in *Dickenson's Arcade* imposed a "consumption tax": that is, the persons assessed for tax were those who actually smoked or chewed the tobacco. The tax was fixed at 7.5 per cent of the value of the tobacco consumed, but was payable at the time of consumption only if it had not already been paid. The Act itself made no provision for any such earlier payment; but as a "convenient method for the collection of the tax" the regulations authorised retail tobacconists to collect the tax at the point of retail sale pursuant to "arrangements" with the Commissioner of Taxes. The Commissioner was required to make such "arrangements" with every applicant for a tobacconist's licence. Purchasers were not required to pay the tax at the point of sale, but could lodge a return and pay the tax to the Commissioner after consumption if they so chose. Menzies, Gibbs and Stephen JJ, with Mason J agreeing in principle, held that this was not an excise and was valid.

Gibbs J: [221] Since *Parton v Milk Board (Vic)* [(1949) 80 CLR 229] no member of the Court has dissented from, and almost every member who has had occasion to discuss the matter has expressly affirmed, the proposition that a tax imposed on consumption is not a duty of excise … It might be said that these expressions of opinion are not binding because it was not necessary to decide in any of these cases whether a tax imposed on consumption was an excise, but the very greatest weight should be given to the fact that on this issue unanimity has been reached after a fluctuation of judicial opinion … **[222]** Once it is accepted, as it must be, that "duties of excise" for the purposes of s 90 cannot include all the miscellaneous taxes that have been regarded in England, and in some cases arising under the Constitution of the United States, to be excises, it seems to me that established usage (notwithstanding some divagations) favours the conclusion that a tax on the consumption of goods is not a duty of excise within the meaning of that expression as used in s 90 of the Constitution. To say that the control by the Commonwealth Parliament of the taxation of goods will not be complete, or that its fiscal policy may be hampered, if the States can impose a tax at the point of consumption, is in my opinion not decisive against this view. The question cannot be answered by having regard to the position of the Commonwealth alone. The Constitution is a federal constitution, and s 90 is intended to effect a distribution of the power to impose taxation between the Commonwealth and the States. Of course, the section confers no power on the Commonwealth, which derives its power to impose taxation from s 51(ii), but it denies power to the States. The extent of the denial must be found in the words of the section themselves rather than in economic, social or political theory. Section 90 does not refer to taxes on goods but to duties of customs and of excise. Upon its proper construction s 90 stops short of denying power to the States to impose taxes on consumption.

In reaching this conclusion I have not derived any assistance from the theory that a duty of excise would generally be an indirect tax … **[223]** I share the regret, expressed by Fullagar J in *Dennis Hotels Pty Ltd v Victoria* [104 CLR at 553-4], that a discussion of the difference between direct and indirect taxation, which in relation to Canada is rendered necessary by the words of s 92(2) of the *British North America Act*, should ever have been thought to be relevant or useful in relation to s 90 …

In *Bolton v Madsen* [110 CLR at 271], the Court said: "It is now established that for constitutional purposes duties of excise are taxes directly related to goods imposed at some step in their production or distribution before they reach the hands of consumers." The Court went on to make it clear that in its opinion it is the criterion of liability that determines whether or not a tax is a duty of excise. It is not enough that the imposition produces a similar, or even the same, economic or practical effect as that which a duty of excise would have produced. The tax will only be an excise if the person taxed is … rendered liable because he has taken a step in the production or distribution of goods … In my opinion the statement in *Bolton v Madsen* should be accepted as an authoritative expression of principle. In deciding whether a tax is a duty of excise the Court must identify the criterion of liability under the statute which imposes the tax …

[224] It is now possible to consider the validity of the tax imposed by Pt II of the Act. The label given to it – "Tax on the consumption of tobacco" – is not of importance. However, in my opinion Pt II on its proper construction does impose a tax which is correctly described by that label, that is, a tax on consumption. It is true … that for practical reasons a purchaser is likely to pay the tax to the retailer or his agent at the time when he buys his tobacco. However, the purchaser is not bound to make payment until he has in fact consumed the tobacco and the retailer is not liable for any tax which he does not collect. It is, in my opinion, impossible to say that Pt II, when properly construed, imposes a tax on the last retail sale of tobacco. It is immaterial, if in fact it is true, that the tax has substantially the same practical effect as a tax imposed on the last retail sale. The criterion of liability is consumption. The tax is not an excise.

McTiernan J dissented because he held that a tax on consumption was an excise; Barwick CJ dissented because he held that what Pt II imposed was not a consumption tax at all.

Barwick CJ: [190] Tobacco is not smoked or chewed in the precise amount which is purchased, unless the purchase be of a single cigarette or cigar. No doubt the latter is common enough amongst those given to the delights of cigar smoking but rarely, I should think, even in penurious circumstances, is a single cigarette purchased. Generally speaking, the tobacco is purchased in packets of cigarettes or in **[191]** bulk quantities, ready rubbed, flaked or in block. The purchased quantity is smoked by the purchaser at intervals, their frequency depending on individual habit, inclination and opportunity. It is a casual habit in the sense that no current record is kept or likely to be kept or even a mental impression made or retained of the occasion on which something is smoked. Indeed, the habitual smoker may not be conscious of the fact as distinct from the experience of smoking. The smoker in general will not be conscious in particular of the time or occasion of the separate acts of "consumption" or be capable of recollection of them after the event. Nor is any identification made of the thing smoked with the time and circumstances of its acquisition, whether by purchase or by gift. Perhaps a part or, at times, the whole of what is purchased is given away, either on one occasion or over a period of time …

The donee of tobacco, eg a cigarette, may but does not necessarily identify its brand and, perhaps, in many situations, does not care. Whether or not the donor, or for that matter his donor, has paid an appropriate amount of tax in respect of the cigarette can scarcely be known. All this may equally be true of the friend or acquaintance who is given a "fill" of his pipe. Thus, a person who has been given tobacco may not have the means of knowing the value for the purposes of the Act of what he smokes. Bearing in mind the habits of mankind in offering cigarettes and tobacco not merely to friends but to the merest acquaintance on social occasions, the idea that the agreeable recipient of the convivial cigarette or pipe fill should come under an obligation to make a return or give a notification of having smoked the gift and within seven days of that event – no doubt rarely remembered at the end of an evening of stimulating social intercourse – to pay a tax of seven and a half per cent of the value of that cigarette or pipe fill upon pain of a criminal prosecution, is so ludicrous that it is to my mind inconceivable that a legislature should so intend. Examples of a like kind crowd in upon the mind. It could scarcely be conceived that the elderly gentleman, resting after a life-time of labour, **[192]** eking out his days in the sunshine on park bench or wall, quietly cutting a pipeful from a block of tobacco provided by friend or charity, and after rubbing it to a suitable tilth, smoking it in contentment, was intended to be required to notify his self-indulgence and pay within seven days, if he could but remember the occasion, a tax of seven and a half per cent of the value of the pipeful or perhaps of only so much of the pipeful as he smoked before dropping off to sleep in the sun. Of course, if he could but ascertain it, he might find, not by direct evidence but by inference, that someone had paid the tax at the point of purchase so that he was after all not liable to tax on his smoking in the sun. I cannot believe, however, that any such operation of the Act is intended. My incredulity of such a fanciful operation being intended by a legislature leads me to conclude in the absence of clear and unambiguous words that it was not intended to tax the consumption of tobacco in all circumstances, including the case of tobacco given to the smoker or chewer. That means, in my opinion, that it was intended only to tax the consumption of tobacco by or at the instance of a purchaser of tobacco purchased by or for him. I find nothing in the language of the Act to compel a contrary conclusion …

[193] Thus I conclude that, upon its proper construction, the Act imposes a tax not upon consumption of tobacco in any and all circumstances by any person, but only upon the consumption by or at the instance of a purchaser of tobacco purchased by retail. It intends that the tax will be paid by the purchaser and that payment will be made in anticipation of consumption at the time of purchase and as part of the purchase transaction. It is, in my opinion, a tax upon the movement of the tobacco into consumption …

[194] The intended operation of the Act is that the tax is payable only by the purchaser of the tobacco and it is intended to be collected at the point of purchase. Such a tax is not, in my opinion, a tax upon consumption in the sense of the decisions of this Court. It is not a tax, as I construe the Act, unconnected with the purchase of tobacco; indeed, it is essentially connected with such purchase. In my opinion, it constitutes a tax upon a step in the movement of the tobacco into consumption. In the relevant sense it is a tax upon the tobacco. It is a duty of excise.

Mason J, though upholding the "consumption tax" as set out in the Act, held that, when it was read in conjunction with the collection arrangements in the regulations, it was an excise. Thus, while accepting Pt II of the Act as valid, he joined Barwick CJ and McTiernan J in holding the regulations invalid; and on that point, in a 3:3 division, the Chief Justice's view prevailed.

Mason J: [243] It is evident then that the regulations require that arrangements be made between the Commissioner and every proprietor of a retail tobacco business or the occupier of the premises in which that business is carried on, for the appointment of a tax collector in respect of the premises whose duty it is to receive payments of tax made at the time when tobacco is sold by retail to buyers. Consequently, the tax which is imposed by the Act is levied at the time of the last retail sale at the place at which the tobacco is sold. It is levied before or at the time of delivery to the purchaser, who will in many circumstances be a person other than the ultimate consumer. The tax is therefore levied in respect of the goods before they pass into the hands of the consumer and it is calculated by reference to their value according to the retail sale price. The amount of the tax is paid directly by the purchaser.

Once the provisions of the regulations are taken into account, the effect of the tax, so it seems to me, is that it is an excise. It is a levy on the sale of goods calculated by reference to their value and imposed before they pass into the hands of the consumer in circumstances where the amount of the tax is paid by the ultimate purchaser.

In *HC Sleigh Ltd v South Australia* (1977) 136 CLR 475, the Court considered a petrol tax imposed by the *Business Franchise (Petroleum) Act 1974* (SA) in the form required by *Dennis Hotels*: a licence fee based upon a percentage of the value of petroleum products sold during the year ending on the preceding 30 June. Barwick CJ, Gibbs, Stephen, and Mason JJ applied *Dennis Hotels* to hold that it was not an excise, while Murphy J agreed in the result. Jacobs J, who dissented, read *Dickenson's Arcade* as standing for the following proposition:

HC Sleigh Ltd v South Australia
(1977) 136 CLR 475

Jacobs J: [522] Where the fee is for a licence to conduct on particular premises the business of selling by retail to the public in unrestricted quantities a product containing a drug and where the fee for the licence in respect of a following period is calculated upon the turnover of the product at the licensed premises during a preceding period, the fee is not a duty of customs or excise within the meaning of s 90.

Thus understood, he thought that *Dickenson's Arcade* could be fitted into "**[522]** a coherent pattern of decision" in the excise cases which should be followed. However, he went on to say:

Jacobs J: [523] [A]lthough the pattern of decision is still coherent it is showing signs of strain or distortion. On the one side there is the pressure of the decisions which have invalidated levies even where the legislature's expressed purpose was the creation of a fund devoted to the **[524]** rationalization and improvement of the industry on whose production the levy has been sought to be imposed. On the other side there is a "bulge" whereby taxes in some circumstances at least can lawfully be raised by licence fees calculated by reference to the value or quantity of turnover in a commercial activity even though the purpose of the tax is unrelated to any purpose of rationalization or improvement of the industry reflected in that commercial activity. This, I think, is a danger signal …

Where on an examination of the legislation as a whole it appears that the purpose of the licensing is the facilitation of the collection of the tax and not the control of commercial operations in respect of the product in its course from production to consumption, then at least the tax will be a duty of excise within the meaning of s 90. Whether or not any particular piece of legislation should be so regarded cannot be deduced from a formula. The answer will depend on a consideration of the operation of the legislative provisions in the conditions of our society with which the Court is familiar and of which, if it be thought necessary in a particular case, the Court can be more particularly informed.

Having examined the subject legislation I am not left in any doubt whatsoever that the licensing of the businesses is no more than a convenient mechanism for collecting the so-called licence fees …

[525] It has been submitted that the effect of this conclusion would be to overturn the course of past authority: *Dennis Hotels Pty Ltd v Victoria* [(1960) 104 CLR 529]; *Dickenson's Arcade Pty Ltd v Tasmania* [(1974) 130 CLR 177] … upon which the financial relationship between the States and the Commonwealth has come to depend. In my opinion the first of the above cases did not establish that a licence fee where the fee is calculated on trading in a prior period is in every case not a duty of excise …What has happened is that decisions that a licence fee is not necessarily a duty of excise where the amount of the fee is calculated on the basis of dealings in a commodity for a preceding period [have] been taken by the legislature to be a decision that a licence fee cannot be a duty of excise provided that the fee is so calculated. This has been treated as a so-called "logical" consequence and the State has chosen to pass legislation accordingly. So-called "logical" extensions of a past decision are seldom a sufficient ground for forecasting a future decision, because a regard only to the so-called logic fails to take account of the further factors which make the later case not merely an application but an extension of the earlier decision. Moreover, the financial relationship between the **[526]** States and the Commonwealth has not come to depend on the course of decision of this Court in this respect. The attempted effectuation of the idea that by setting up a licensing system in respect of dealing in any commodity at all, the States can overcome the s 90 embargo on imposition of excise duties is of comparatively recent origin. It must be curbed now before the Court is faced either with the virtual supersession of s 90 or a need at some later time to cry halt. In my opinion the time is now.

I am prepared to distinguish *Dennis Hotels Pty Ltd v Victoria* and *Dickenson's Arcade v Tasmania* upon the ground that in both of them there was present in the impugned legislation a concatenation of factors – the nature of the product and the licensing of premises for the sale of the product – sufficient to enable it to be held that the calculation of the licence fee by reference to the value or quantity of the product dealt with in a preceding period was no more than a method of quantification of that licence fee and not a tax upon the product dealt with in the preceding period. I find it quite impossible to say that of legislation where the licence is no more than a mechanism for collection of a tax.

On the other hand, Stephen J rejected any attempt to limit *Dennis Hotels* or *Dickenson's Arcade* by having regard to the nature of the product being taxed.

> **Stephen J: [496]** I find no valid ground for distinction in the fact that in *Dickenson's Case* and in its predecessor, *Dennis Hotels Pty Ltd v Victoria,* the licence in question related to the licensing of premises for the sale of consumables, liquor and tobacco, which some may see as falling within a particular class broadly described as drugs. To introduce into this already difficult area of the law a ground of distinction dependent upon the character of the goods in question and which involves the notion of a class of goods of uncertain scope is neither called for by prior authority nor is it, in my view, likely to contribute either to greater certainty of result or to what might be thought to be desirable policy ends.

In *Gosford Meats Pty Ltd v New South Wales* (1983) 151 CLR 599, Mason and Deane JJ applied the distinction between licences for retail and licences for production or manufacture to hold that (despite its use of a *Dennis Hotels* formula) an annual licensing fee for the operation of an abattoir or slaughterhouse was an excise. They were joined in that conclusion, on different grounds, by Brennan and Murphy JJ, while Gibbs, Wilson and Dawson JJ dissented. In *HC Sleigh* Murphy J had called for a radical return to a narrower concept of "excise": in order for a State tax to be struck down as an excise duty, it "**[527]** must be one on production or manufacture within the State … and must discriminate against such local production or manufacture". That approach might have seemed to leave s 90 with a very limited scope indeed, since it would not be likely that a State legislature would "discriminate" against its own local industries. It turned out, however, in *Gosford Meats* that what Murphy J meant by a "discriminatory" tax on local production or manufacture was a measure singling out the very process of production or manufacture as attracting the incidence of the tax.

Similarly, in *Hematite Petroleum Pty Ltd v Victoria* (1983) 151 CLR 599, Murphy J joined Mason, Brennan and Deane JJ in holding that an annual pipeline operation fee imposed by the *Pipelines Act 1967* (Vic) was an excise. The plaintiffs owned two pipelines that conveyed hydrocarbons from one plant to another. Until 1981, the pipelines had been subject to an annual pipeline operation fee of $35 per kilometre, giving a maximum payment of $7080. In 1981, the Act was amended to impose a fee in respect of the pipelines of $10 million each. Gibbs CJ and Wilson J dissented, while Dawson J did not sit because, as Solicitor-General for Victoria, he had advised the Victorian government that the pipeline fee was valid.

Hematite Petroleum Pty Ltd v Victoria
(1983) 151 CLR 599

Gibbs CJ: [617] On any possible view of its effect, s 90 itself confers on the Parliament only a very limited power to control the economy. There are many taxes which have a tendency to enter into the price of commodities but which are not excises, and which are accordingly within the power of the States to impose. Payroll tax is an obvious example. There are many other legislative measures which a State can take either to discourage or to encourage production and manufacture. On the one hand it can fix quotas on production or manufacture, or indeed forbid production or manufacture altogether; on the other hand it can, for example, favour producers and manufacturers by reducing their taxes and the charges made to them for power and freight, and by building ports and railways for their use and providing them with other assistance. Thus s 90 does not go very far towards giving the Commonwealth exclusive control of or influence over the production or manufacture of goods. Moreover, s 109 of the Constitution, which invalidates State laws to the extent to which they are inconsistent with laws of the Commonwealth, plays a major part in preventing any State law from frustrating Commonwealth legislative policy. The presence of s 109 may well have rendered it unnecessary to include in s 90 a reference to duties of excise for the purpose of invalidating a State excise duty which counteracted the effect of a Commonwealth tariff.

The power conferred on the Commonwealth by s 51(ii) to make laws with respect to taxation is unaffected by s 90. The Parliament may impose a tax whether it is an excise or not. On the other hand, s 90 seriously restricts the taxing power of the States; it narrows, artificially, the field of taxation open to them. The inability of the States to impose duties of excise has created greater difficulties for the States since the uniform tax arrangements have virtually prevented them from imposing income taxes. One view of experts in the field of public finance is that the wide extension made by this Court to the definition of "excise" is "one of the greatest impediments preventing the achievement of a rational and lasting division of financial powers in the Australian federal system": Mathews and Jay, *Federal Finance* (1972), p 318. One result must surely tend to be that the States will impose some forms of taxation which, although constitutionally permissible, are less economically desirable than taxes now categorized as duties of excise ...

[622] Clearly the payment of the fee is a condition of the right to use the pipeline. The amount of the fee does not depend on the extent to which the pipeline is used ... [F]or the purposes of the *Pipelines Act*, it is immaterial whether the pipelines carry any particular quantity of, or indeed any, hydrocarbons. If the Minister, acting under s 37, limited the pressure at which the pipeline might be operated, or prohibited the use of the pipeline or part of it for a time, no rebate would be allowed in respect of any fee already paid. If it were known that in a forthcoming year the use of the pipeline would be prohibited for a time, the fee payable would not be affected. If, perhaps as the result of some disaster, no oil could be produced from Bass Strait, and the use of the pipeline stopped entirely, no part of the fee would be repayable. No doubt in those circumstances, as a matter of practicality, the plaintiffs might not wish to seek a renewal of the licence, but they could not recover the fee if already paid. If it appeared that in a particular year the plaintiffs would carry a greater (or lesser) amount of liquid hydrocarbons than in the previous licence period, that would be quite irrelevant to the amount of fee payable.

The conclusion appears to me inescapable that the fee is not imposed because the hydrocarbons are carried; it is imposed as a condition of the right to carry them.

Moreover, there is neither a natural nor a necessary relationship between the fee fixed and the quantity or value of the hydrocarbons conveyed ...

The very size of the impost, the fact that it is exacted in respect of pipelines carrying the products of the Bass Strait oil wells and the comparison with the pipeline operation fee charged in respect of other pipelines naturally give rise to the suspicion that the fees charged for the licences for the trunk pipelines are designed to avoid the limitation which s 90 imposes on the taxing power of the States. However, a tax is not an excise simply because it is large and discriminatory and aimed at companies which carry on a business thought to be lucrative enough to enable them to pay it ... **[624]** The pipeline operation fee is in my opinion not a tax upon or directly affecting goods; it is what it purports to be, a fee for a licence to use the pipeline. It is not a duty of excise.

Mason J: [630] [I]t has been generally accepted that the grant of exclusive power to impose duties of excise in conjunction with a like power to impose customs duties ... "was intended to give the Parliament a real control of the taxation of commodities and to ensure that the execution of whatever policy it adopted should not be hampered or defeated by State action" (*Parton v Milk Board (Vic)* [(1949) 80 CLR 229 at 260], per Dixon J ...). Excise duties, like customs duties, are significant instruments for raising revenue. What is more important is that Parliament, possessing exclusive power to impose both forms of duties, can protect and stimulate home production by fixing appropriate levels of customs and excise duties. And it can lower the level of domestic prices by lowering customs and excise duties. By lowering customs duties alone it can put pressure on Australian producers and manufacturers to become more competitive.

If the States had power to impose excise duties then the Commonwealth Parliament's power to protect and stimulate home production and influence domestic price levels might be compromised. It is possible that by an exercise of the taxation power the Commonwealth could effectively prevent the States from imposing excise duties. A law enacted under s 51(ii) providing that no excise duties should be payable on designated goods would, by virtue of s 109, prevail over any inconsistent State law. This is not a reason for denying that the object of granting exclusive power to the Commonwealth was as I have expressed it to be. The Commonwealth's control is stronger if it possesses exclusive power; then there is no potential for conflict between Commonwealth and State legislation. The possibility of the imposition of taxes on goods by the States in the period prior to the enactment of inconsistent legislation by the Commonwealth undermines the Commonwealth's real control of the taxation of commodities and provides a further reason for rejecting the existence of s 109 as a basis for narrowing the ambit of **[632]** the Commonwealth's exclusive power under s 90. In any case, to make the power exclusive is to free its exercise from some of the political controversies and constraints which would inevitably surround any attempt by the Commonwealth Parliament to pass inconsistent legislation designed solely to override a State law ...

That the object of the power was to secure a real control over the taxation of commodities provides strong support for a broad view of what is an excise, one which embraces all taxes upon or in respect of a step in the production, manufacture, sale or distribution of goods, for any such tax places a burden on production. A tax on goods sold, like a tax on goods produced, is a burden on production, though less immediate and direct in its impact. It is a burden on production because it enters into the price of the goods – the person who is liable to pay it naturally seeks to recoup it from the next purchaser. As the tax increases the price of the goods to the ultimate consumer, and thereby diminishes or tends to diminish demand for the goods, it is a burden on production.

To justify the conclusion that the tax is upon or in respect of the goods it is enough that the tax is such that it enters into the cost of the goods and is therefore reflected in the prices at which the goods are subsequently sold. It is not necessary that there should be an arithmetical relationship between the tax and the quantity or value of the goods produced or sold (*Matthews v Chicory Marketing Board (Vic)* [(1938) 60 CLR 263 at 304]), still less that such a relationship should exist in a specific period during which the tax is imposed ...

[634] Here the significant features of the pipeline operation fee are: (1) that it is levied only upon a trunk pipeline, ie, the gas and fuel Corporation pipeline, the Gas Liquids pipeline and the crude oil pipeline, through which flow the entirety of the hydrocarbons recovered from the Bass Strait fields; (2) that it is a fee payable for permission to operate a pipeline ... which the plaintiffs otherwise hold a permit to own and use; (3) that the fee is a special fee which is extraordinarily large in amount, having no relationship at all to the amount of the fees payable for other pipeline operation licences – the fee payable for a trunk pipeline is $10,000,000 whereas the fee payable for any other pipeline is $40 per kilometre; and (4) that the fee is payable before an essential step in the production of refined spirit can take place – the transportation of the hydrocarbons from Longford to Long Island Point where the refinery is situated.

The coexistence of these features indicates that the pipeline operation fee payable by the plaintiffs is not a mere fee for the privilege of carrying on an activity; it is a tax imposed on a step in the production of refined petroleum products which is so large that it will inevitably increase the price of the products in the course of distribution to the consumer. The fee is not an exaction imposed in respect of the plaintiffs' business generally; it is an exaction of such magnitude imposed in respect of a step in production in such circumstances that it is explicable only on the footing that it is imposed in virtue of the quantity and value of the hydrocarbons produced from the Bass Strait fields. To levy a tax on the operation **[635]** of the pipelines is a convenient means of taxing what they convey for they are the only practicable method of conveying the hydrocarbons to the next processing point.

(e)   The Grip of Precedent

As a result of *Dennis Hotels*, *Dickenson's Arcade* and *HC Sleigh*, the States were able to levy prior-period licensing fees on alcohol, tobacco and petrol. In subsequent years, these taxes came to form an increasingly large percentage of State revenue, and the States' financial dependency on them was increasingly seen as a reason not to overrule the decisions. In *Evda Nominees Pty Ltd v Victoria* (1984) 154 CLR 311, a challenge to the *Business Franchise (Tobacco) Act 1974* (Vic), the High Court refused to hear argument on whether *Dennis Hotels* and *Dickenson's Arcade* should be reconsidered. Only Deane J would have allowed the argument to be presented (see Chapter 13, §7).

In *Philip Morris Ltd v Commissioner of Business Franchises (Vic)* (1989) 167 CLR 399, the *Business Franchise (Tobacco) Act* was challenged again. It provided for a wholesale licence fee using a *Dennis Hotels* formula: a flat fee of $50, plus an ad valorem fee of 25 per cent of the value of the tobacco sold in relation to the last preceding month but one. As in *Evda Nominees*, leave was sought to challenge the correctness of the decisions in *Dennis Hotels*, *Dickenson's Arcade* and *HC Sleigh* (now collectively referred to as "the franchise cases"). However, Mason CJ announced at the hearing that the Court had once again decided, with Deane J again dissenting, that the franchise cases would not be reconsidered. The hearing continued on the basis that the plaintiff would attempt to distinguish the cases. When judgments were handed down, the attack on the licence fee had failed by 5:2, with Brennan and McHugh JJ dissenting. The majority judges gave three different sets of reasons for this result.

Philip Morris Ltd v Commissioner of Business Franchises (Vic)
(1989) 167 CLR 399

Mason CJ and Deane J: [438] [T]he fact that *Dennis Hotels* [(1960) 104 CLR 529] stands as authority for a result, rather than for any strand of reasoning common to a majority of Justices, has on two occasions led to its being followed due to the close similarity between the facts of the respective cases. In this way the supposed principle has arisen that a fee for a licence to conduct a business calculated by reference to sales made by the business in a past period is not to be viewed as an excise. But, as we have sought to demonstrate, no such principle in truth exists. The reasoning underlying such a principle is inconsistent with the broad approach of the authorities in cases not involving licence fees, which insist on a range of criteria being taken into account. As we have said, there is no basis for claiming a rigid dichotomy between licence fees and excise duties.

However, on the authority of *Dennis Hotels*, *Dickenson's Arcade* [(1974) 130 CLR 177 and *HC Sleigh* [(1977) 136 CLR 475], the States have enacted laws imposing licence fees calculated upon trading in an antecedent period in businesses of liquor and tobacco retailing and sale of petroleum products. In *Evda Nominees* [(1984) 154 CLR 311] and again in argument in this case the Court decided not to reopen the three earlier cases. There are powerful considerations against overruling the actual decisions in those cases. Financial arrangements which are of great importance to the governments of the States and perhaps to the economy of the nation have been made for a long time past on the faith of these decisions. The power of this Court to overrule its previous decisions would not be properly exercised to disturb those arrangements unless, in the light of later insights into the true meaning of the Constitution, obedience to its terms or the interests of certainty in those arrangements clearly demanded that those decisions be reconsidered. That cannot presently be said of at least the first two of the trilogy of cases. *Dennis Hotels* and *Dickenson's Arcade* can be rationalized by reference to traditional considerations relating to the licensing of dealings in alcohol and tobacco and to the particular characteristics of those items of personal consumption ...

[439] The basis upon which the decision in *Dennis Hotels* can be accepted is, we think, to be found in the circumstance that the impost took the form of a fee for a licence to sell liquor and that legislation providing for the issue of liquor licences has traditionally been of a regulatory character arising from the various public interest considerations relating to the sale and consumption of alcohol. The regulatory character of the legislation was a factor in the majority decision that the victualler's licence fee under s19(1)(a) was not an excise ... *Dennis Hotels* may be regarded as an example of a licensing fee which does not amount to an excise because the imposition of the licensing fee is an element in regulatory legislation controlling the sale and distribution of a parti-cular commodity, which is designed to protect the public interest in the light of the characteristics of that commodity ...

[440] The Court has refused to retreat from its decision in *Dennis Hotels* because of the need to ensure certainty in the area of State business franchise fees relating to alcohol. Similar policy arguments dictate that the same view be taken of *Dickenson's Arcade*. It would be possible to achieve this result by confining the two decisions strictly to their facts and going no further, in accordance with the approach indicated by Barwick CJ in *Dickenson's Arcade*. Attractive though that course may be to those who, like ourselves, disagree with the decisions in those cases to the extent that they held that the licence fees were not duties of excise, we have come to the conclusion that we should not follow it. It appears to us that the effect of that course would be merely to force the States to impose artificiality and inefficiency in business and taxing procedures in order to ensure that taxing laws in the special fields of alcohol and tobacco enjoyed the protection of those decisions. The preferable approach is to accept *Dennis Hotels* and *Dickenson's Arcade* as authority for the proposition that, in the special fields of licences to sell alcohol and tobacco, a licence fee which would otherwise be regarded as a duty of excise will not be so regarded if it can properly be characterized as a fee for carrying on business and if it is calculated by reference to sales made during a period other than the period of the licence.

Liquor licensing has a unique history and it is not easy to imagine a range of commodities whose characteristics and history would lead to a similar outcome. However, in our opinion, a similar view may be taken of tobacco, though it lacks the long history of legislative regulation that has been a feature of the merchandising of liquor. Tobacco and tobacco products have like characteristics which invite regulatory control and that control is appropriate to sale and distri-bution of the commodities. In the case of neither is a tax imposed in relation to sale or distribution likely to be passed on as a significant component of the cost of different and dissimilar manu-factured goods. It is on this footing that we would uphold the decision in *Dickenson's Arcade*.

For the purpose of deciding the present case it is unnecessary to **[441]** reconsider *HC Sleigh*. Whether it stands conveniently with *Dennis Hotels* and *Dickenson's Arcade* is not a matter that we need to determine, though it may well be that petroleum products are not to be treated in the same way as alcohol and tobacco.

Dawson J invoked the Federal Convention Debates of the 1890s, which the Court had used in *Cole v Whitfield* (1988) 165 CLR 360 and was later to use in *New South Wales v Commonwealth* (*Incorporation Case*) (1990) 169 CLR 482. He argued that historically, and especially in the context of s 93, the concept of "excise duty" should be confined "**[466]** to a tax upon goods produced or manufactured in a State". He expressed strong sympathy for the approach of *Peterswald v Bartley* and of Fullagar J in *Dennis Hotels*. But, given the repeated lack of majority support for those approaches, he settled for the "criterion of liability" approach adopted in *Bolton v Madsen*.

In *Commonwealth & Commonwealth Oil Refineries Ltd v South Australia* (1926) 38 CLR 408, Isaacs J had contrasted a tax "**[426]** so connected with the production of the article sold ... as in effect to be a method of taxing the production of the article" with a tax "unconnected with production and imposed merely with respect to the sale of the goods as existing articles of trade and commerce". The latter was said not to be an excise. Without quoting Isaacs J, Toohey and Gaudron JJ drew a similar contrast. Accordingly they found that the licence fee was not an excise since it "**[485]** affects tobacco products in their character as articles of commerce rather than in their character as goods manufactured in Australia".

In dissent, Brennan and McHugh JJ pointed to "[461] several substantial features" of the tax imposed by s 10(1) that distinguished it from the taxes upheld in the franchise cases.

Brennan J: [463] [T]he proximity of the relevant period to the licence period, the shortness of the licence period, the imposition of an ad valorem tax calculated at rates reaching 30 per cent on the value of tobacco sold which is to be borne only once in the course of distribution and the revenue raising and non-regulatory purpose of the scheme all tend to show that the tax is not merely a fee for a licence to carry on a business of selling tobacco but is in substance a tax upon the tobacco sold in the relevant period or to be sold in the licence period.

Coastace Pty Ltd v New South Wales (1989) 167 CLR 503 raised similar issues in relation to the *Business Franchise Licences (Tobacco) Act 1975* (NSW). It was argued together with *Philip Morris* and produced a similar result.

The extent of the judicial disarray revealed in *Philip Morris* and *Coastace* in relation to "the franchise cases" led to speculation that the time might have come for the Court to reconsider all the cases on s 90 with a view to a "fresh start". However, whereas in *Cole v Whitfield* the Court was able to agree unanimously on a "fresh start" in the interpretation of s 92 of the Constitution, no such unanimity could be expected in relation to excise duties, where the underlying policy divisions remained as sharp as ever. Thus, there was a perception that any attempt to reopen the underlying issues might only result in yet another unsatisfactory and narrowly divided decision. Moreover, the outcome would be unpredictable: any litigants who succeeded in persuading the Court to reconsider "the franchise cases" might find themselves worse off than before.

The Australian Capital Territory Legislative Assembly, in the exercise of its powers under the *Australian Capital Territory (Self-Government) Act 1988* (Cth), legislated for a system of licensing fees for the wholesale or retail sale of X-rated videos. Based upon the *Dennis Hotels* formula, the licences were issued monthly on the payment of a "franchise fee" equal to 40 per cent of the wholesale value of videos supplied in the month occurring two months before the licence period, except that the initial payment for the first two months (the "advance fee") was based on an estimate of the value of videos to be supplied during that period. Two companies, a wholesaler and a retailer, argued that the fees infringed s 90.

The opening round in the litigation was *Capital Duplicators Pty Ltd v Australian Capital Territory (No 1)* (1992) 177 CLR 248. By 4:3, the High Court held that s 90 makes Commonwealth power exclusive as against the Territories as well as the States (see Chapter 6, §5). That decision cleared the way for *Capital Duplicators Pty Ltd v Australian Capital Territory (No 2)* (1993) 178 CLR 561. The Commonwealth and all six States intervened, but for those who had hoped that this might be the occasion to "do a *Cole v Whitfield*" the result was an anti-climax. The Australian Capital Territory argued for a return to the original narrow reading in *Peterswald v Bartley*, and was broadly supported by South Australia. No other State adopted a similar strategy. The main concern of the other five States was that the Court should not overrule *Dennis Hotels* and *Dickenson's Arcade*.

The States, apart from South Australia, having chosen to argue for the status quo, got exactly that. Brennan and McHugh JJ, who dissented in *Philip Morris*, now threw in their lot with Mason CJ and Deane J. The result was a 4:3 decision rejecting any departure from the line of development since *Parton v Milk Board* and, within that framework, refusing again to reconsider *Dennis Hotels* or *Dickenson's Arcade*. The majority also held that the "licensing fees" for X-rated videos were invalid as an excise duty, for reasons cobbled together from those relied on in *Philip Morris* by Mason CJ and Deane J, by Brennan J, and by McHugh J.

Capital Duplicators Pty Ltd v Australian Capital Territory (No 2)
(1993) 178 CLR 561

Mason CJ, Brennan, Deane and McHugh JJ: [596] [T]he legislation cannot be described merely as a regulatory scheme in which the licensing fees are simply an element in an overall regime of controlling the distribution of "X" videos to the public. The principal elements of the legislation are directed to the raising of revenue rather than to the creation of a regulatory scheme designed to protect the public.

There is no restriction whatsoever in the Act on the class of videos which can be sold; any video, no matter how violent or pornographic, may be sold. Nor is there any restriction on the class of purchasers; the Act does not preclude the sale of any video to children. Likewise, there is no restriction on advertising or display. And the conditions to be satisfied by an applicant for a licence under s 5 relate more obviously to the capacity of the applicant to pay the fees than to the protection of the public in connection with the distribution of violent and pornographic videos. Accordingly, the Act falls outside the category of regulatory schemes affecting liquor and tobacco which Mason CJ and Deane J held in *Philip Morris* [(1989) 167 CLR 399] could support the exaction of a licence fee on the footing that it is not an excise.

Furthermore, the size of the fee (40 per cent) is larger than the fee exacted in the other franchise cases and clearly exceeds the cost of implementing the scheme. No endeavour was made to justify the size of the fee on that score. Indeed, the true nature of the exaction is to be discerned from s 21 which refers to the fee being "payable in relation to the supply or offer for retail sale" of the videos. **[597]** Hence, the purpose of exacting the licensing fees is not simply regulatory but has a very substantial revenue purpose.

In the view of Brennan J in *Philip Morris*, the fact that the legislative scheme is not regulatory and the substantial size of the fee are factors which are relevant in the characterisation of the licence fee as an excise. In addition, the advance fee, being calculated by reference to sales made under the licence, plainly is an exaction made as a step in the process of distribution under the licence. And, though the franchise fee is calculated by reference to sales made in a past period, that period is no more than two months earlier than the licence period, each being for one month only. The proximity of the prior period to the period of the licence is a factor pointing in the direction of an excise because the transactions in the past period may well provide a reliable forecast of the transactions which will occur during the currency of the licence. Thus, the exaction is imposed not merely on the taxpayer's past dealings with the goods but in circumstances in which the magnitude of the past dealings with the goods is a likely indicator of the measure of the taxpayer's dealings with the goods during the term of the licence. With the exception of the non-regulatory character of the licensing scheme, the same factors would, on the view of McHugh J in *Philip Morris*, lead to the view that the exactions in the present case are excise duties.

In the result, in the light of the reasoning of the members of the Court in *Philip Morris*, the conclusion is inevitable that certain licence fees imposed by the Act are an excise.

In dissent, Dawson, Toohey and Gaudron JJ reaffirmed what they had said in *Philip Morris*.

(f)   *The States Lose $5 Billion*

The course of decisions on s 90 since *Parton v Milk Board* in 1949 had progressively narrowed the scope for the States to levy taxes on goods, and *Capital Duplicators (No 1)* subjected the Territories to the same limitation. The franchise cases gave the States some leeway to raise taxation by imposing prior-period licence fees, but by 1997 the revenue-raising potential of this exception was being pushed to its limits. New South Wales alone raised an estimated $852 million from tobacco licence fees in the 1995-96 financial year.

The *Business Franchise Licences (Tobacco) Act 1987* (NSW) prohibited the sale of tobacco, by wholesale or retail, unless the seller held a licence under the Act. Under s 41(1) of the Act, the cost of a retailer's licence was calculated as being $10 plus an amount equal to a specified percentage of the value of tobacco sold by the applicant during the month beginning two months before the beginning of the month in which the licence expired, disregarding any such tobacco purchased from a licensee. Until 28 August 1989 the specified percentage was 30 per cent, but a series of increases meant that from 28 June 1995 the specified percentage was 100 per cent.

The plaintiffs in *Ha v New South Wales* (1997) 189 CLR 465 operated a duty free store in Sydney, where they sold tobacco by retail without holding a licence under the *Business Franchise Licences (Tobacco) Act*. Their argument that the New South Wales licence fee in respect of tobacco infringed s 90 was heard together with a similar argument by another plaintiff company, Walter Hammond & Associates, which sold tobacco for resale in New South Wales. In response, New South Wales, supported by all other States, the Australian Capital Territory and the Northern Territory, argued that the High Court should reconsider its interpretation of s 90 and reverse the trend of decisions beginning with *Parton v Milk Board*. In essence, the States sought to have the Court choose between the approach in *Peterswald* and that in *Parton v Milk Board*. In doing so, they put at risk the exception provided by the franchise cases. Despite that risk, they calculated that this was the time to press for a new interpretation of s 90. Mason CJ and Deane J had left the Court and their replacements, Gummow and Kirby JJ, had yet to be tested.

As it turned out, Gummow and Kirby JJ joined Brennan CJ and McHugh J in holding the New South Wales tobacco licence fee to be invalid, leaving Dawson, Toohey and Gaudron JJ dissenting as before. Moreover, though the majority just stopped short of overruling *Dennis Hotels* and *Dickenson's Arcade*, it was clear that their reasoning imposed stringent limits on any future resort to those cases, and hence on the possibility that the States and Territories might continue to raise significant revenue from franchise fees.

Ha v New South Wales
(1997) 189 CLR 465

Brennan CJ, McHugh, Gummow and Kirby JJ: [490] As Brennan J said in *Philip Morris Ltd v Commissioner of Business Franchises (Vict)* [(1989) 167 CLR 399 at 445]:

"If there be any rock in the sea of uncertain principle, it is that a tax on a step in the production or distribution of goods to the point of receipt by the consumer is a duty of excise." ...

[491] To support the overturning of such a long and consistent line of authority, the defendant's submissions needed to show a clear departure from the text of the Constitution. They submitted that *Parton* [(1949) 80 CLR 229] had departed without warrant from what they identified as the narrow view of "duties of excise" expressed by Griffith CJ, speaking for the court in *Peterswald v Bartley* [(1904) 1 CLR 497] ...

[497] So long as a State taxing statute taxes the sale or distribution of imported goods and goods of local production or manufacture indifferently and equally, the statute, it is said, cannot be characterised as a law imposing duties of excise. This submission proceeds on the footing that a criterion of liability must be local production or manufacture and that a statute which imposes a tax indifferently on goods irrespective of their origin does not impose a duty of excise. If this submission were accepted, the State power of taxation would extend in effect to the taxation of any commodity provided the taxing statute is not expressed to tax solely goods of local production or manufacture. The importation of an insignificant quantity of the **[498]** commodity would permit State taxation of the commodity provided it applied indifferently to the imported quantity and the quantity that is locally produced. In the present case, for example, even if the substantive effect of the tax were found to burden Australian production or manufacture of tobacco, the importation of a small percentage of the tobacco sold in Australia would permit the imposition of the tax under a State law. If accepted, the submission would frustrate whatever purpose might be attributed to s 90. That approach to the characterisation of laws impugned for contravention of s 90 was rejected as far back as *Peterswald v Bartley* [1 CLR at 511] itself:

"In considering the validity of laws of this kind we must look at the substance and not the form."

In the *Commonwealth Oil Refineries Case* [(1926) 38 CLR 408 at 423] Isaacs J said:

"The prohibitions of ss 90 and 92 of the Constitution may be transgressed not merely by a direct and avowed contravention. They are transgressed also by a statute – whatever its ultimate purpose may be, and however its provisions are disguised by verbiage or characterisation, or by numerous and varied operations lengthening the connective chain, or by otherwise paying titular homage to the supreme law of the Constitution – if it operates in the end by its own force so as to do substantially the same thing as a direct contravention would do, either in attaining a forbidden result or in using forbidden means. The relevant constitutional prohibitions include both means and results. It is no justification for using forbidden means that permissible results are sought, nor for securing forbidden results that lawful means are employed."

When a constitutional limitation or restriction on power is relied on to invalidate a law, the effect of the law in and upon the facts and circumstances to which it relates – its practical operation – must be examined as well as its terms in order to ensure that the limitation or restriction is not circumvented by mere drafting devices. In recent cases, this court has insisted on an examination of the practical operation (or substance) of a law impugned for contravention of a constitutional limitation or restriction on power. On that approach, even if the narrower view of "duties of excise" were accepted, the question whether the imposts on the sellers of tobacco under the Act burden Australian-produced tobacco products would **[499]** have to be answered. However, for reasons stated above, the question is whether the imposts are an inland tax on a step in the distribution of tobacco products.

If it were not for the factors to which reference will be made in considering what have been known as the franchise cases, the defendants' submissions could and would have been dismissed by reference simply to the line of authority following *Parton* and culminating in the *Capital Duplicators Case (No 2)* [(1993) 178 CLR 561]. No further analysis of the arguments supporting those submissions would have been called for. The repetition on this occasion does nothing to enhance their cogency, despite the care and vigour with which they were presented. *Evda Nominees Pty Ltd v Victoria* [(1984) 154 CLR 311] and the *Capital Duplicators Case (No 2)* show that mere repetition of arguments does not require the court to reopen settled authority to reconsider the arguments, at least where "the States have organized their financial affairs in reliance on them" [154 CLR at 316]. In the present case, however, the States, fully appreciating that the attack on the doctrine based on *Parton*, if successful, would destroy the reasoning in the franchise cases and conscious of the factors on which the plaintiffs rely to limit the protection which the franchise cases give to the States' tax base, chose to invite the court to re-examine the *Parton* doctrine which has been accepted for nearly half a century.

Perhaps the States and Territories were conscious of the risk that the taxes in question in this case might be held to fall outside the protection offered by the franchise cases. However that might be, as the present case requires a declaration of the limits of the protection offered by the franchise cases so as to accord with the *Parton* doctrine, it seems right to accede to the defendants' application to reopen the *Parton* line of cases. But the correctness of the doctrine they establish must now be affirmed. Therefore we reaffirm that duties of excise are taxes on the production, manufacture, sale or distribution of goods, whether of foreign or domestic origin. Duties of excise are inland taxes in contradistinction from duties of customs which are taxes on the importation of goods. Both are taxes on goods, that is to say, they are taxes on some step taken in dealing with goods. In this case, as in the *Capital Duplicators Case (No 2)*, it is unnecessary to consider whether a tax on the consumption of goods would be classified as a **[500]** duty of excise.

Note that the majority left open whether a consumption tax is an excise. Accordingly, there must now be doubt as to the correctness of that aspect of the decision in *Dickenson's Arcade*. In *Ha*, the majority went on to consider whether the tobacco licence fee was merely a licence to carry on a business and therefore not an excise.

Brennan CJ, McHugh, Gummow and Kirby JJ: [500] This is substantially the same question as that which arose in *Coastace Pty Ltd v New South Wales* [(1989) 167 CLR 503] in which imposts under the legislation as it stood between 28 January and 27 July 1987 were held to be valid. Since 1987, as we have seen, the variable component of licence fees calculated under s 41 of the Act [has] been increased by increasing the specified rate from 30 per cent of the value of tobacco sold in a relevant period to 100 per cent.

The imposts in *Coastace* were held to be valid by a majority whose opinions were markedly dissimilar. In particular, Mason CJ and Deane J upheld the imposts for reasons which their Honours had stated more extensively in their judgment in *Philip Morris*. In that case, their Honours expressed the view that liquor and tobacco were commodities that invite regulatory control and, that being so, they were prepared to accept the correctness of *Dennis Hotels* [(1960) 104 CLR 529] and *Dickenson's Arcade* on a special basis ...

[501] We are respectfully unable to accept the basis on which Mason CJ and Deane J accepted *Dennis Hotels* and *Dickenson's Arcade*. Were it not for that basis, Mason CJ and Deane J would have joined Brennan and McHugh JJ in holding the imposts in *Philip Morris* and *Coastace* to be duties of excise and, on that account, invalid. The concordance in their Honours' views was manifested in their joint judgment in the *Capital Duplicators Case (No 2)*.

It is therefore unnecessary to canvass again the question whether the decisions in the franchise cases can be reconciled with the doctrine based on *Parton*. That exercise was undertaken by Brennan J in *Philip Morris* and we agree with the analysis and conclusions in his Honour's judgment. In *Philip Morris*, McHugh J was also in dissent. His Honour rejected the authority of the earlier franchise cases as support for any proposition save the validity of the imposts upheld in those cases. We do not apprehend that, in the result, there is any dissimilarity in the approach taken by the two Justices in dissent. Both Brennan J and McHugh J pointed to the proximity of the relevant period to the licence period, the shortness of the licence period, the size of the tax imposed ad valorem and the fact that it is to be borne only once in the course of distribution as indicia that were inconsistent with the tax being merely a licence fee having – to use the test stated by Kitto J in *Dennis Hotels* [104 CLR at 560] – "no closer connection with production or distribution than that it is exacted for the privilege of engaging in the process at all". Brennan J added a reference [167 CLR at 463] to "the revenue raising and non-regulatory purpose of the scheme".

Those factors are present and relevant ... **[502]** in this case. Moreover, an amount equal to 75 or 100 per cent of the value of tobacco sold during a relevant period is levied by the Act. That amount could not conceivably be regarded as a mere fee for a licence required as an element in a scheme for regulatory control of businesses selling tobacco. The Act contains minimal provisions controlling businesses selling tobacco, chiefly those contained in s 36(2) which authorises the refusal of a licence to a person who has been convicted of an offence under s 59 of the *Public Health Act* 1991 (NSW) or, pursuant to s 36(2AA), if the Chief Commissioner is satisfied that "the issue of a licence would be contrary to the public interest". Subject to these provisions, renewal of a licence requires merely the due payment of the fees exacted. The licence fee is manifestly a revenue-raising tax imposed on the sale of tobacco during the relevant period. The licensing system is but "an adjunct to a revenue statute" [104 CLR at 576 per Taylor J] ...

[503] We are conscious that this judgment has the most serious implications for the revenues of the States and Territories. But, in the light of the significantly increasing tax rates imposed by State and Territory laws under the insubstantial cloak of the *Dennis Hotels* formula, the Court is faced with stark alternatives: either to uphold the validity of a State tax on the sale of goods provided it is imposed in the form of licence fees or to hold invalid any such tax which, in operation and effect, is not merely a fee for the privilege of selling the goods. Section 90 of the Constitution, by prescribing the exclusivity of the Commonwealth's power to impose duties of excise, resolves the question. So long as a State tax, albeit calculated on the value or quantity of goods sold, was properly to be characterised as a mere licence fee this Court upheld the legislative power of the States to impose it. But once a State tax imposed on the seller of goods and calculated on the value or quantity of goods sold cannot be characterised as a mere licence fee, the application of s 90 must result in a declaration of its invalidity.

The majority judgment considered whether it would be possible to limit the overruling of *Dennis Hotels* and *Dickenson's Arcade* to prospective effect, but concluded that this "**[504]** would be a perversion of judicial power".

Brennan CJ, McHugh, Gummow and Kirby JJ: [504] In any event, the decision of this Court is not to overrule *Dennis Hotels* or *Dickenson's Arcade*. They may stand as authorities for the validity of the imposts therein considered. Properly understood, the test of "no closer connection" as stated by Kitto J in *Dennis Hotels* and explained by Brennan J in *Philip Morris* is maintained. It is not necessary now to reconsider *H C Sleigh*, though the reservation expressed as to that case in the *Capital Duplicators Case (No 2)* will not have passed unnoticed. However, the consequence of rejecting the view that alcohol and tobacco are commodities that are in a special category for s 90 purposes means that *Philip Morris* and *Coastace* were wrongly decided.

In dissent, Dawson, Toohey and Gaudron JJ again argued for a return to *Peterswald v Bartley*.

Dawson, Toohey and Gaudron JJ: [508] [I]t is plainly incorrect to assert that a tax upon a commodity at any point in the course of distribution before it reaches the consumer has the same effect as a tax upon its manufacture or production. Not only is it an incorrect assertion but it fails to comprehend that the purpose of making the power to impose excise duties exclusive to the Commonwealth was to prevent impairment by the States of the common external tariff. A tax upon the manufacture or production of goods increases the cost of those goods without effecting a corresponding increase in the cost of imported goods of the same kind. Any protection afforded by customs duties imposed upon the imported goods is thereby reduced. But a tax imposed upon a step **[509]** in the distribution of goods which falls indiscriminately upon locally produced and imported goods does not have that effect.

No doubt in saying that a tax imposed on production or manufacture and a tax imposed upon a step in the distribution of goods had the same effect, Dixon J had in mind the early classification of duties of excise as indirect taxes. An indirect tax was said to be one that has a tendency to be passed on in the price of goods whereas a direct tax was said to be one that tends to be borne by the person upon whom it is imposed. The distinction between indirect and direct taxes is now recognised as being economically unsound because market forces determine whether a tax will be passed on or not and there is nothing inherent in a particular tax which enables it to be classified as direct or indirect. Thus all taxes, even income tax, will be passed on to a greater or lesser extent depending upon market forces and the dichotomy between direct and indirect taxes is no longer seen as a satisfactory means of distinguishing between excise duties and other taxes. … [Moreover], just as it is not possible to draw any practical distinction between direct and indirect taxes, so it is not possible to discern any direct or necessary connection between the ultimate price of goods and their cost of production or manufacture. Again, market forces will determine the effect of price upon demand and hence upon production or manufacture. For that reason it is not possible to say that a tax upon a step in the distribution of goods is in effect a tax upon their production or manufacture. And, of course, a tax which falls upon a step in the distribution of imported and locally produced goods alike can hardly be regarded as a tax upon the production of the imported goods.

Once the reasons given in *Parton* for extending the meaning of duties of excise are recognised as unsound, the extension is without any justification in economic or constitutional terms. In particular, it disregards the correlation between duties of customs and duties of excise which reveals the true purpose of s 90 and which identifies the limits placed by the Constitution upon the term "duties of excise" …

[512] A State tax which fell selectively upon imported goods would, of course, be a customs duty and be prohibited by s 90. A State tax which fell selectively upon goods manufactured or produced in that State would be an excise duty and be prohibited by s 90. A State tax which discriminated against interstate goods in a protectionist way would offend s 92 and be invalid. But those three instances do not exhaust the categories of taxes upon goods and do not support, as a legal conclusion, the proposition that the Commonwealth was intended to have an exclusive power to tax commodities … [C]learly a State tax – a tax upon sale, for example – which does not fall selectively upon imported goods or locally produced or manufactured goods and does not discriminate against interstate goods, offends against none of the prohibitions imposed by the Constitution. In particular, such a tax would not affect freedom of interstate trade because all goods would compete in the State on the same footing: there would be no discrimination of a protectionist kind …

[514] Whether a tax which falls upon locally produced goods discriminates against those goods in favour of imported goods is a question of substance, not form. It is the answer to that question which, upon the correct view of duties of excise, determines whether the tax is an excise duty. The clearest case is, of course, where a customs duty exists so as to afford a measure of protection to the home product and a selective tax upon a product of that kind extinguishes or substantially diminishes the protection. But there would be discrimination with a selective tax even where there was no relevant customs duty. The tariff policy in that case must be that imported goods of the relevant kind compete with locally produced goods upon an equal footing in the home market and a tax imposed selectively upon the local production of those goods would burden them in relation to imported goods and so impair the policy …

[517] In the present cases, the licence fees, regarded as taxes upon goods, fall indiscriminately upon tobacco products regardless of whether they are locally manufactured or produced or are imported. In 1994, approximately 60 per cent of Australian tobacco was grown in Queensland, 37 per cent in Victoria and 3 per cent in New South Wales. There were three domestic manufacturers of tobacco products, two of which had their factories in New South Wales and one of which had its factory in Victoria. It was not suggested, and could not be suggested, that free trade among the States was affected by the fees imposed under the Act. The imposition of those fees operated in a manner which did not discriminate against interstate tobacco products, nor did it protect New South Wales tobacco products.

The total value of domestic consumption in terms of retail sales of tobacco products in 1994 was $5,389 million, of which imported tobacco products represented in retail value about 4 per cent. Thus imported tobacco products represented only a very small percentage of the tobacco market. It was suggested in argument that this was a reason for concluding that form would triumph over substance if the licence fees were held not to constitute duties of excise.

It would seem that the argument proceeded on the footing that, had New South Wales chosen to impose a tax on the production or manufacture of tobacco or tobacco products, it would have raised almost the same amount of revenue from practically the same sources as it did by the imposition of the licence fees. To approach the matter in that way is, however, to mistake the purpose of s 90. The purpose of that section was not to restrict the revenue raising capacity of the States. Equally, its purpose was not to secure to the Commonwealth a revenue base: that is the function of s 51(ii). Rather, the purpose of s 90 was to preclude State imposts on goods which would undermine the common external tariff regardless of the revenue which the States would be compelled to forgo by reason of the prohibition. Thus, in [518] these cases it is the nature of the impost and not the revenue involved which is important and it is the fact that the impost falls upon domestic and imported goods alike which is the substance of the matter. It is not to the point that only a small amount of tobacco products sold in New South Wales, or in Australia generally, is imported. Whatever the proportion, the level of protection, if any, which the Commonwealth has chosen to give tobacco products produced or manufactured in Australia remains unaffected.

The majority in *Ha* hinted strongly that the petrol exception in *HC Sleigh* could no longer stand; and although they upheld the actual results in *Dennis Hotels* (for alcohol) and *Dickenson's Arcade* (for tobacco), it was clear that this was limited to the specific taxes (at relatively modest levels) actually imposed in those cases. The generic exception for alcohol and tobacco suggested by Mason CJ and Deane J in *Philip Morris* did not find favour.

The immediate result for the States was catastrophic. Not only was the collection of franchise fees brought to an end, but billions of dollars in franchise revenue that had been collected unlawfully was liable to be repaid. The loss in State revenue was estimated to be some $5 billion a year. The Commonwealth intervened with an urgent rescue package increasing Commonwealth customs and excise duties on tobacco and petrol and sales taxes on alcohol, with the proceeds (other than administrative costs) to be paid to the States as "revenue replacement grants" under s 96. Moreover, the Commonwealth imposed a "franchise fees windfall tax" of 100 per cent on any amount that a State might be liable to repay to a taxpayer as having been invalidly collected: see the *Franchise Fees Windfall Tax (Imposition) Act 1997* (Cth) and the *Franchise Fees Windfall Tax (Collection) Act 1997* (Cth) (see also *Roxborough v Rothmans of Pall Mall Australia Ltd* (2001) 208 CLR 516 and *British American Tobacco Australia Ltd v Western Australia* (2003) 217 CLR 30). Pursuant to the Intergovernmental Agreement on the Reform of Commonwealth-State Financial Relations entered into in June 1999, these temporary measures have now been subsumed into the arrangements for a broadly based goods and services tax (GST), collected by the Commonwealth with the whole of the revenues distributed to the States (see Chapter 24, §2(c)).

With most "taxes on goods" now included in the Commonwealth GST regime, it may be that the kinds of State revenue measures that have given rise to such persistent problems under s 90 will no longer arise. In that event, the deep judicial divisions still manifest in the 4:3 decision in *Ha* may be destined to remain unresolved.

3. Further References

Arndt, HW, "Judicial Review under Section 90 of the Constitution: An Economist's View" (1952) 25 *Australian Law Journal* 667.

Caleo, C, "Section 90 and Excise Duties: A Crisis of Interpretation" (1987) 16 *Melbourne University Law Review* 296.

Cass, DZ, "Lionel Murphy and Section 90 of the Australian Constitution" in Coper, M, and Williams, G (eds), *Justice Lionel Murphy – Influential or Merely Prescient?* (Federation Press, 1997), 19.

Coper, M, "The High Court and Section 90 of the Constitution" (1976) 7 *Federal Law Review* 1.

Coper, M, *Encounters with the Australian Constitution* (CCH, 1988), Ch 5.

Cremean, DJ, "Consumption Taxes, Licence Fees and Excise Duties" (1974) 9 *Melbourne University Law Review* 735.

Dixon, N, "Section 90 – Ninety Years On" (1993) 21 *Federal Law Review* 228.

Galligan, B, *Politics of the High Court* (University of Queensland Press, 1987), Ch 4.

Gibbs, H, "'A Hateful Tax'? Section 90 of the Constitution" in *Upholding the Australian Constitution* (The Samuel Griffith Society, Proceedings of the Fifth Conference of The Samuel Griffith Society, 1995), 121.

Hanks, P, "Section 90 of the Commonwealth Constitution: Fiscal Federalism or Economic Unity?" (1986) 10 *Adelaide Law Review* 365.

Hannan, AJ, "Finance and Taxation" in Else-Mitchell, R (ed), *Essays on the Australian Constitution* (Law Book Co, 2nd ed 1961), 247.

Johnston, P, "A Taxing Time: The High Court and the Tax Provisions of the Constitution" (1993) 23 *University of Western Australia Law Review* 362.

McLeod, N, "State Taxation: Unrequited Revenue and the Shadow of Section 90" (1994) 22 *Federal Law Review* 476.

Moore, JD, "Tax Reform and State Taxation: A Perspective" in Mathews, RL (ed), *Tax Reform and the States* (Centre for Research on Federal Financial Relations, Australian National University, 1985).

Opeskin, B, "Section 90 of the Constitution and the Problem of Precedent" (1986) 16 *Federal Law Review* 170.

Pearson, G, and Lehmann, G, "Are State Payroll Taxes Unconstitutional?" (1990) 24 *Taxation in Australia* 864.

Sampathy, P, "Section 90 of the Constitution and Victorian Stamp Duty on Dealings in Goods" (2002) 4 *Journal of Australian Taxation* 133.

Shapiro, P, and Petchey, J, "'Shall become Exclusive': An Economic Analysis of Section 90" (1994) 70 *Economic Record* 171.

Sharp, PG, "The First Paragraph of Section 55" (2005) 33 *Federal Law Review* 569.

Williams, J, "'Come in Spinner': Section 90 of the Constitution and the Future of State Government Finances" (1999) 21 *Sydney Law Review* 627.

Chapter 24

The Spending Powers

1. The Appropriation Power

Section 81 of the Constitution enables Parliament to appropriate money out of the Consolidated Revenue Fund (that is, to authorise its expenditure) "for the purposes of the Commonwealth". Under s 83, an appropriation must be made by law – that is, by a law of the federal Parliament. Under s 54, a "proposed law" that appropriates money must deal only with such appropriation. Like s 53, s 54 is thought to be non-justiciable (see Chapter 23, §1).

The effect of ss 81 and 83 is that government expenditure requires a parliamentary appropriation of moneys. Historically, this has been one of the most basic ways in which Parliament has controlled the executive; the requirement dates back to the Petition of Right acceded to by Charles I in 1628 (see Chapter 3, §2(d)). Whether it is open to a further measure of judicial control has given rise to difficult theoretical and practical questions.

A central issue concerning s 81 is – in what circumstances may the Parliament appropriate money under s 81? That is, what are "the purposes of the Commonwealth"? The High Court's first exposure to arguments based on s 81 of the Constitution was in *Attorney-General (Vic); Ex rel Dale v Commonwealth* (*Pharmaceutical Benefits Case*) (1945) 71 CLR 237. That decision concerned the *Pharmaceutical Benefits Act 1944* (Cth), which established a scheme of free medicine, obtainable (under s 8) from approved chemists upon prescription by a doctor using a Commonwealth form. Under the Act, the scheme was funded by appropriations made under s 81 from the Consolidated Revenue Fund. The Medical Society of Victoria sought a declaration that the Act was invalid, and an injunction against any expenditure under its provisions or for its purposes.

The detailed regulatory scheme in the Act did not depend primarily on penal sanctions for its enforcement, but rather on an elaborate system of "approvals", powers of inspection and indirect sanctions or inducements. The penal provisions in the Act related mainly to offences of fraud, impersonation and the like. The only direct penal sanction for medical practitioners was in s 22, which made it an offence for a medical practitioner to write a prescription on a Commonwealth form unless satisfied by personal examination that the prescription was necessary for the treatment of the patient.

Attorney-General (Vic); Ex rel Dale v Commonwealth (*Pharmaceutical Benefits Case*)
(1945) 71 CLR 237

Latham CJ: [251] At one stage of the argument it was suggested on behalf of the plaintiff that the appropriation power is limited to purposes for which the Commonwealth Parliament has power to make laws for the reason that, with the exception of s 96 (which provides for financial grants by the Commonwealth to States), the only power to appropriate moneys to be found in the Constitution is that contained in s 51(xxxix). It was said that the power to spend money is incidental to the execution of the Commonwealth powers to make laws with respect to the other subject matters mentioned in s 51, and it was suggested that, apart from placitum (xxxix), there might not have been power to expend money in connection with the various matters mentioned in placita (i) to (xxxviii).

In my opinion this argument cannot be accepted. Each power to make laws with respect to a particular subject matter includes a power to make a law providing for the expenditure of money in relation to that subject matter. For example, the power contained in s 51(vii) to make laws with respect to lighthouses, lightships, beacons and buoys in itself includes a power to provide for the expenditure of money in relation to lighthouses, &c. The position is the same with respect to the other subjects mentioned in s 51 …

Appropriation may be, and normally is, made by a Commonwealth statute, but there are many provisions in the Constitution itself which either appropriate or authorize the appropriation of moneys. I refer to s 3 – salary of the Governor-General; s 48 – allowances to Members of Parliament; s 66 – salaries of Ministers; s 72 – salaries of judges; s 84 – payments to transferred State officers; s 85 – payments for State property taken over by the Commonwealth. Sections 87, 89, 93 and 94 all relate to payments to be made by the Commonwealth to the States. Section 96 expressly authorizes the Parliament to grant financial assistance to any State; ss 105 and 105A provide for the application of Commonwealth money towards payment of interest and principal of the debts of the States. Under s 122 the Commonwealth Parliament may spend Federal moneys as it thinks fit in the Territories of the Commonwealth.

It is plain, therefore, that appropriations are made, or may be made, by law otherwise than under the powers contained in s 51(xxxix) of the Constitution.

[252] It was argued for the plaintiff that the phrase "the purposes of the Commonwealth" in s 81 refers to legislative purposes of the Commonwealth, that is, purposes for which the Commonwealth Parliament has power to make laws. It is plain that the Commonwealth has executive and judicial purposes as well as legislative purposes. The very existence of the Commonwealth, apart from any legislation, creates some purposes of the Commonwealth: See *Commonwealth v Colonial Combing, Spinning and Weaving Co Ltd* [(1922) 31 CLR 421 at 441]. But as laws may be made with respect to executive and judicial purposes, legislative purposes could be held to include the other purposes mentioned. The principal argument for the plaintiff was that a Commonwealth purpose (for which alone appropriation of money is said to be legitimate) must be found in powers conferred upon the Parliament by some other provision than s 81; that s 81 conferred no legislative power whatever, but was based upon the assumption that the purposes of the Commonwealth were defined or limited by other provisions of the Constitution; so that "the purposes of the Commonwealth" must be construed as meaning "purposes for which the Commonwealth Parliament has power to make laws." …

[253] What are purposes of the Commonwealth within the meaning of the section?

I approach the consideration of this question with the prima facie opinion that the words "purposes of the Commonwealth" (which plainly *include* purposes "in respect of which the Parliament has power to make laws") are not identical in meaning with the latter words. I have already stated my opinion that each such power includes a power to authorize the expenditure of money. A meaning is given to the words "to be appropriated for the purposes of the Commonwealth" if they are read as intended to show positively that there may be other Commonwealth purposes than those in respect of which power to make laws is given elsewhere in the Constitution. Otherwise the words have no legal effect whatever.

[254] What then is the authority which can determine what purposes are purposes of the Commonwealth? As the appropriation is to be made by law (s 83), the natural answer is – the authority which makes Commonwealth laws, that is, the Commonwealth Parliament, not the executive authority which administers laws when made nor the judicial authority which interprets and applies the laws. Thus, in my opinion, the Commonwealth Parliament has a general, and not a limited, power of appropriation of public moneys. It is general in the sense that it is for the Parliament to determine whether or not a particular purpose shall be adopted as a purpose of the

Commonwealth. I take as illustrations some past appropriations for purposes in relation to which the Parliament has approved the expenditure of moneys but where, when the purposes are considered in themselves, there is no power to legislate with respect to the matters to which the expenditure relates. In some cases there is only an appropriation of money for the purpose stated, in other cases there are statutes containing detailed provisions for the establishment of organizations for the purpose of spending the money. I mention appropriations for Antarctic exploration, medical research, literary grants and pensions, subscriptions to international organizations, such as the Agricultural Institute at Rome, public health, assistance to distressed Australians abroad … The application of Commonwealth moneys to these objects, so far as it merely involves the expenditure of money, is, in my opinion, authorized by the Constitution. Such expenditures do not interfere with the rights of the States or of any persons, and if the Commonwealth Parliament approves the expenditure there is, in my opinion, full legal justification for the expenditure …

[256] [T]he determination whether a particular purpose should be regarded and adopted as a Commonwealth purpose is a political matter. If the proposed limitation to "legislative purposes" in the sense stated is rejected, no test has been suggested which would enable a court to undertake a judicial review upon any legal basis of the multifarious expenditure which a Parliament may consider it necessary or desirable to undertake.

The words "purposes of the Commonwealth" should not, in my opinion, be construed as meaning for the governmental purposes of the political organism called the Commonwealth. In the introductory provision of s 51 (that laws are to be made for the peace, order and good government of the Commonwealth) the word "Commonwealth" is used to describe the people of the Commonwealth in the area which is the Commonwealth in the geographical sense. The laws of the Commonwealth operate directly upon the people of Australia, and it is the good government of those people with which the Constitution is concerned, not the government of the Government itself. In s 81 in the phrase "the purposes of the Commonwealth" the word "Commonwealth" should, in my opinion, be interpreted in the same sense. The word "Commonwealth" there plainly does not mean the geographical area known as the Commonwealth. Neither, in my opinion, does it mean the Commonwealth as a political organism. I see no reason for limiting the words "the purposes of the Commonwealth" to governmental purposes in the sense of the discharge of legislative, judicial or executive functions. The word "Commonwealth" in this section refers to the people who, by covering clause 3 of the Constitution, are "united in a Federal Commonwealth under the name of the Commonwealth of Australia."

For these reasons, in my opinion, the provisions of s 81 can fairly be read as intended to mean that it is the Commonwealth Parliament, and not any court, which is entrusted with the power, duty and responsibility of determining what purposes shall be Commonwealth purposes, as well as of providing for the expenditure of money for such purposes.

This conclusion, however, relates only to laws providing for the expenditure of money. It does not follow that the Commonwealth Parliament, because it can, as it were, subscribe towards the support of what it considers to be worthy objects, can take legislative control of matters relating to any such objects in respect of which there is no other grant of legislative power. A company may have power to **[257]** subscribe to a hospital or a football club without having power to conduct a hospital or to organize and control a football club.

I illustrate the position as I understand it by taking public health legislation as an example. Under s 51(ix) the Commonwealth Parliament has power to make laws with respect to quarantine. Quarantine legislation may be regarded in most, if not all, of its aspects as a particular form of public health legislation. In relation to quarantine the Commonwealth Parliament has full powers of legislation. It can not only provide that money shall be spent upon quarantine, but it can devise and put into operation a whole compulsory system of quarantine under which duties can be imposed upon persons and penalties inflicted for breach of the law. But in relation to other aspects of public health the Commonwealth (once again leaving out of account the Territories) has no such power of legislation. The Commonwealth can, in my view, authorize the expenditure of public money on inquiries, investigations, research and advocacy in relation to matters affecting public health. But the Parliament could not pass a law requiring citizens of the States to keep their premises clean or to submit to vaccination or immunization. The power to appropriate and expend money, however wide that power may be, does not enable the Commonwealth to extend its legislative powers beyond those marked out and defined by the Constitution, although (in my opinion) those powers include a general appropriation power.

Although Latham CJ refused to impose any limit on the expression "the purposes of the Commonwealth", it did not follow that s 81 enabled the Parliament to enact any legislation whatever. Parliament could appropriate money to any policy area, and the money thus appropriated could then be expended, but s 81 could not support Commonwealth implementation of policies by ordinary legislation. It could not "**[257]** put into operation a whole compulsory system ... under which duties can be imposed upon persons and penalties inflicted for breach of the law". It was on this basis that the challenge to the *Pharmaceutical Benefits Act* succeeded.

Latham CJ: [258] The question therefore is whether the *Pharmaceutical Benefits Act* falls within the sphere of Commonwealth legislative power. If it is an Act for the appropriation of money, s 51(xxxix) of the Constitution would authorize the inclusion in the Act of provisions to prevent the use of the money for purposes other than those declared by Parliament. But the power to make laws for the appropriation of money can go no further than this. If the Act can properly be described as an Act for the appropriation of money with safeguards against wrongful expenditure of the money, it is in my opinion valid. If, on the other hand, it is an Act which, though it appropriates money, is really an Act for the control of doctors, chemists, sale of drugs and the conduct of persons who deal with doctors and chemists, then in my opinion it is invalid, for the reason that the Act is an Act with respect to subjects which are not committed to the Federal Parliament ...

[263] The Act is far more than an appropriation Act; it is just the kind of statute which might well be passed by a parliament which had full power to make such laws as it thought proper with respect to public health, doctors, chemists, hospitals, drugs, medicines and medical and surgical appliances. The Commonwealth Parliament has no such power. The result of a contrary view would be that, by the simple device of providing for the expenditure of a sum of money with respect to a particular subject matter, the Commonwealth could introduce a scheme which in practice would completely regulate and control that subject matter. The Commonwealth Parliament would thus have almost unlimited legislative power. The careful delimitation of Commonwealth powers made by the Constitution prevents the adoption of such an opinion.

On the meaning of "the purposes of the Commonwealth", the *Pharmaceutical Benefits Case* yielded no majority view. McTiernan J took the same broad view as Latham CJ, holding that "**[273]** [t]he purposes of the Commonwealth are, I think, such purposes as the Parliament determines", but held that the Act was valid. Dixon J, with whom Rich J agreed, leant towards a narrower view, but held that the Act was invalid "**[268]** even with the widest conceivable construction of the power of appropriation". They accordingly had no need to reach any conclusion on what "the purposes of the Commonwealth" might mean. Starke and Williams JJ held that the Act was invalid by construing "purposes" narrowly. As Williams J put it: "**[282]** These purposes must all be found within the four corners of the Constitution".

Starke J: [266] The purposes of the Commonwealth are those of an organized political body, with legislative, executive and judicial functions, whatever is incidental thereto, and the status of the Commonwealth as a Federal Government. And where else but from the Constitution and other Acts conferring authority upon the Commonwealth can its purposes or functions be discovered? Those purposes include matters in respect of which it can make laws by virtue of the Constitution or any other Act, and they also include the exercise of executive and judicial functions vested in the Commonwealth by the Constitution or by any other Act. Among other purposes of the Commonwealth must also be included, I think, matter arising from the existence of the Commonwealth and its status as a Federal Government. Thus, I should think that moneys appropriated for payment &c of members of Parliament, exploration and so forth, would be within the authority of the Commonwealth.

But the *Pharmaceutical Benefits Act* 1944 is beyond any purpose of the Commonwealth. No legislative, executive or judicial function or purpose of the Commonwealth can be found which supports it, and it cannot be justified because of the existence of the Commonwealth or its status as a Federal Government.

The decision in *Victoria v Commonwealth and Hayden* (*AAP Case*) (1975) 134 CLR 338 left the meaning of "purposes of the Commonwealth" similarly unresolved. In that case there was no question, as there was in the *Pharmaceutical Benefits Case*, of "[257] a whole compulsory system … under which duties can be imposed upon persons and penalties inflicted for breach of the law". What was before the High Court was a two-line item in an Appropriation Act relating to the Australian Assistance Plan. The Plan envisaged the establishment and financing of Regional Councils for Social Development throughout Australia. The appropriation was to be spent, through the Regional Councils, on social welfare activities such as family day care programs, counselling services for families and Community Health and Welfare Centres. The *Appropriations Act (No 1) 1974* (Cth) authorised expenditure from the Consolidated Revenue Fund of $4,667,794,000 to be applied for the purposes set out in the Schedule. The Schedule allocated $141,637,000 to the Department of Social Security, including, in Div 530:

Appropriations Act (No 1) 1974 (Cth)

4. Australian Assistance Plan

01. Grants to Regional Councils for Social Development	$5,620,000
02. Development and Evaluation	$350,000
Total	**$5,970,000**

Victoria brought an action seeking a declaration that the appropriation of $5,970,000 was beyond power, and an injunction against any expenditure thereof. By 4:3 (McTiernan, Stephen, Jacobs and Murphy JJ, with Barwick CJ, Gibbs and Mason JJ dissenting), the High Court rejected the challenge. McTiernan, Mason and Murphy JJ affirmed the broad view of Commonwealth "purposes". Barwick CJ and Gibbs J took a narrow view, while Jacobs J assumed for purposes of argument that such a view was correct. Stephen J expressed no opinion: he held that the plaintiffs' challenge failed because they lacked standing to raise the issue (see Chapter 13, §5(c)).

Barwick CJ appealed to the original intention of the framers of the Constitution that the surplus revenues of the Commonwealth should be returned to the States. In particular, he relied on ss 87 and 94 of the Constitution. Section 87 had provided that, for a transitional 10-year period, the Commonwealth's annual expenditure should be limited to one quarter of its revenue, and that the balance "shall, in accordance with this Constitution, be paid to the several States" or applied towards interest on State debts. Section 94 had empowered the Parliament, after a transitional five-year period, to "provide, on such basis as it deems fair, for the monthly payment to the several States of all surplus revenue of the Commonwealth". That provision had been rendered ineffectual by the decision in *New South Wales v Commonwealth* (*Surplus Revenue Case*) (1908) 7 CLR 179, which permitted the Commonwealth to pay unused money into trust accounts for use in future years, thus effectively leaving no "surplus" for disbursement to the States. However, Barwick CJ found it possible to discern in these provisions a continuing principle entitling the States to receive the Commonwealth's "surplus revenue", that principle being reflected in more recent times in the need for State reimbursement grants under the uniform tax scheme (see §2(b) below). Thus, the underlying plan was one in which the federal allocation of fiscal capacities would parallel the federal allocation of legislative powers: a *limited* allocation of power to the Commonwealth, with the residue secured to the States. On that basis, he held that a limited scope for appropriations under s 81 was part of the fundamental federal plan.

Victoria v Commonwealth and Hayden (*AAP Case*)
(1975) 134 CLR 338

Barwick CJ: [356] The fact, if that be the right conclusion, that the payment of the surplus revenue was left in the control of the Parliament does not detract, in my opinion, from the basic concept of limiting the power of the Commonwealth, itself a legislative power, to appropriate and spend the

Consolidated Revenue Fund as part of the distribution of legislative power by which the federation was effected. The failure to agree upon a permanent formula for distributing the revenue does not deny the essentially federal nature of the financial provisions of the Constitution. In my opinion, the words of s 81 do involve a restraint of the Commonwealth's power of appropriation and expenditure of the Consolidated Revenue Fund and ss 81 and 83 were part of what I may call the distribution of the available governmental revenue of the federation as between Commonwealth and States ...

[358] In line with the limitation on Commonwealth expenditure out of the revenues of customs and excise, with the power to make grants to States under s 96 and with the provision for surplus revenue to be paid to the States, the power of appropriation and of expenditure of the Consolidated Revenue Fund in my opinion is limited to appropriation and expenditure for Commonwealth purposes. Although appropriated but unspent money was denied the quality of surplus revenue for the constitutional purpose (see *New South Wales v Commonwealth* [(1908) 7 CLR 179]) and although the undoubted demands on the Consolidated Revenue Fund including the amount of grants under s 96 may reduce in present times the extent of surplus revenue, the right of the State to the distribution of such surplus revenue remains. Whilst s 94 is expressed in facultative rather than mandatory terms, if there is at any time surplus revenue which the Commonwealth may not appropriate and expend, the practical effect must be that that surplus can only be and will be made available to the States, though the Parliament may determine the basis of its distribution ... [T]he sense of the Court's decision in *New South* [359] *Wales v Commonwealth* is, in my opinion, that if there be a surplus, the Commonwealth is required to make it available to the States on a basis fixed by the Parliament ...

[360] In my opinion, the words "for the purpose[s] of the Commonwealth" were intended to and do limit the legislative power of the Commonwealth to appropriate and authorize the expenditure of the Consolidated Revenue Fund. They must be construed and applied in the light of the circumstances and constitutional provisions to which I have referred. It follows inevitably, in my opinion, that they cannot be writ out of the Constitution by deciding that any purpose which the Parliament considers to be a Commonwealth purpose is an authorized purpose. That is but an example of "words meaning what I says they mean", a notion more likely to be found in fantasy than in constitutional law.

There can be no doubt, in my opinion, that those who framed the Constitution realized that there were purposes for which money could be spent which were purposes of the Commonwealth and purposes which were not. Hence there exist words of limitation. Sections 81 and 83 in combination require that there shall be an appropriation by law and an authority to expend the Consolidated Revenue Fund for a Commonwealth purpose. That means, in my opinion, that such a purpose must be seen in the law, either expressly or referentially by description. It must be possible to decide that the law containing the appropriation and authority to expend is valid within the constitutional limitation.

That limitation may be fully satisfied by the express terms of the appropriation, eg in the Second Schedule of the Act, Div 101 Senate 1 Salaries and Payments in Nature of Salaries; or those terms may need to be supplemented by further material describing the activities of the body mentioned in the appropriation, eg as in the present case where the notation "Australian Assistance Plan" needs to be supplemented by description of the activities embraced in the Plan. There may be Acts other than the Appropriation Acts, some of a long-standing nature and others of an annual nature, which control the nature and level of the expenditure of the appropriated sums, eg appropriations for the departments of State, where public service legislation and staffing arrangements pursuant to it, provide the necessary statutory authority. Further, as an incident of an Act on some topic assigned [361] by the Constitution to the Parliament, an appropriation may be made by a section of that Act, thus providing money to service its other provisions.

But, however evidenced or demonstrated, the purpose of the appropriation, ie the purpose on or for which the appropriated money may be spent, must, in my opinion, both appear and satisfy the limitation present in the words of s 81, "for the purposes of the Commonwealth" ...

When the Court decides that the required purpose of an appropriation is lacking, it does not amend the Appropriation Act. It declares that the authority to expend money out of the Consolidated Revenue Fund upon the item in question is beyond the power of the Parliament; that there is no law to satisfy s 83; that money may not lawfully be drawn from the Treasury in pursuance of that purported authority.

What then are purposes of the Commonwealth within s 81? The Commonwealth is a polity of limited powers, its legislative power principally found in the topics granted by ss 51 and 52: its executive power is described as extending to the execution and maintenance of the Constitution and of the laws of the Commonwealth. **[362]** No doubt some powers, legislative and executive, may come from the very formation of the Commonwealth as a polity and its emergence as an international state. Thus it may be granted that in considering what are Commonwealth purposes, attention will not be confined to ss 51 and 52. The extent of powers which are inherent in the fact of nationhood and of international personality has not been fully explored. Some of them may readily be recognized: and in furtherance of such powers money may properly be spent. One such power, for example, is the power to explore, whether it be of foreign lands or seas or in areas of scientific knowledge or technology. Again, there is power to create departments of State, for the servicing of which, as distinct from the activities in which the departments seek to engage, money may be withdrawn from the Consolidated Revenue Fund.

But, to anticipate a submission with which I must later deal, to say that a matter or situation is of national interest or concern does not, in my opinion, attract any power to the Commonwealth. Indeed, any student of the Constitution must be acutely aware of the many topics which are now of considerable concern to Australia as a whole which have not been assigned to the Commonwealth. Perhaps the most notable instance is in relation to the national economy itself. There is but one economy of the country, not six: it could not be denied that the economy of the nation is of national concern. But no specific power over the economy is given to the Commonwealth. Such control as it exercises on that behalf must be effected by indirection through taxation, including customs and excise, banking, including the activities of the Reserve Bank and the budget, whether it be in surplus or in deficit. The national nature of the subject matter, the national economy, cannot bring it as a subject matter within Commonwealth power.

However, to whatever source it be referred, any act or activity of the Commonwealth must fall within the confines of some power, legislative or executive, derived from or through the Constitution. In this connexion, I have not included any reference to the judicial power because, in my view, such a reference would be irrelevant to the matter in hand. In the long run, whether the attempt is made to refer the appropriation and expenditure to legislative or to executive power, it will be the capacity of the Parliament to make a law to govern the activities for which the money is to be spent, which will determine whether or not the appropriation is valid. With exceptions that are not relevant to this matter and which need not be stated, the executive may only do that which has been or could be the subject of valid legislation. Consequently, **[363]** to describe a Commonwealth purpose as a purpose for or in relation to which the Parliament may make a valid law, is both sufficient and accurate. In my opinion, the expression in s 51(xxxi) of the Constitution "for any purpose in respect of which the Parliament has power to make laws;" is a reasonable synonym for the expression "the purposes of the Commonwealth" in s 81 …

Is the Australian Assistance Plan … a purpose of the Commonwealth? Is it something the Commonwealth may lawfully implement? I have no doubt it is not. There is no granted power which either alone, or in combination with other powers, could support a scheme for the rearrangement of the Australian community into regions for deriving financial support directly from the Commonwealth or for integration of social welfare schemes or welfare planning as such. Nor is there power to grant money to or through the Regional Councils. An Act of the Parliament which sought to authorize the carrying out of the Plan, including its financial provisions, would, in my opinion, be beyond the power of the Parliament.

The statement of defence suggests that the Plan is supportable by reference to a number of powers granted by s 51. Because, for example, old age pensioners or migrants might be the object of some scheme or co-ordination by a Regional Council, it is said that the Plan may properly be regarded as a provision with respect to old age pensions or immigration. But such a claim is clearly insupportable. See, for example, Sir John Latham's discussion of legislative subject matter in *Bank of New South Wales v Commonwealth* [(1948) 76 CLR 1 at 182-7]. A statute authorizing the Plan could not, in my opinion, be regarded as a law with respect to old age pensions or immigration or any of the other subject matters to which reference was made in argument.

It was then suggested that, because social welfare itself and, in particular, the co-ordination of the efforts of a large number of **[364]** diverse agencies was a national problem, there was power in the national Parliament to deal with it, by appropriation of funds as well as by particular legislation. But, as I have already pointed out, to describe a problem as national, does not attract power. Though some power of a special and limited kind may be attracted to the Commonwealth by the very setting up and existence of the Commonwealth as a polity, no power to deal with matters because they may conveniently and best be dealt with on a national basis is similarly derived. However desirable the exercise by the Commonwealth of power in affairs truly national in nature, the federal distribution of power for which the Constitution provides must be maintained.

In my opinion, no power resides in the Commonwealth to implement and carry out a social welfare plan such as the Australian Assistance Plan. It follows, in my opinion, that that Plan is not a purpose of the Commonwealth within the meaning of the language of s 81.

Mason J rejected the argument for a textual limit on "the purposes of the Commonwealth".

Mason J: [393] The case for confining the expression "for the purposes of the Commonwealth" to activities which fall within the exercise of powers legislative, executive and judicial, committed to the Commonwealth under the Constitution has its attractions, based largely as it is, on important considerations stemming from the distribution of powers and the consequential division of functions between the Commonwealth and the States. The existence of an unlimited power of appropriation would, it was said, be quite inappropriate to, and inconsistent with, the distribution of powers so carefully contrived by the Constitution. A limited power of appropriation would play a powerful part in keeping the Commonwealth within the bounds assigned to it by that instrument.

Likewise, the existence of s 94 of the Constitution, which provides for the distribution to the States of the surplus revenue of the Commonwealth, was urged as an additional reason for restricting Commonwealth appropriations to purposes falling within the area of responsibility assigned to the Commonwealth under the Constitution. The application of the section was curtailed when this Court decided in *New South Wales v Commonwealth* [(1908) 7 CLR 179] that it gives the States no interest in moneys appropriated but not expended. So construed the section allows the Parliament to give priority to appropriations for Commonwealth purposes, even by means of permanent or standing appropriations to trust accounts into which moneys are paid from Consolidated Revenue pursuant to the authority conferred by the appropriation. As the section merely assumes, without stipulating, that there will be a surplus, the entitlement which it gives to the States to participate in the distribution of surplus revenue leaves them very much at the mercy of the Commonwealth.

In this situation the more limited is the Commonwealth's power of appropriation the greater is the prospect that the States have of securing by a distribution of surplus revenue a financial provision which is more commensurate with their needs. Conversely, if the power of appropriation is unlimited, the smaller will be the amount of a surplus available for distribution to the States. This observation is subject to the important qualification that even if **[394]** the power of appropriation be unrestricted, its exercise is necessarily influenced by the limited scope of the Commonwealth's legislative, executive and judicial powers, a matter to be discussed later.

However, the support which these considerations give to the plaintiffs' case [is], I think, out-weighed by other factors which point to an opposite conclusion.

The annual appropriations are a central feature of the financial arrangements made for the government of the country. It is not lightly to be supposed that the framers of the Constitution intended to circumscribe the process of parliamentary appropriation by the constraints of constitutional power and thereby to expose the items in an Appropriation Act to judicial scrutiny and declarations of invalidity. Consequences more detrimental and prejudicial to the process of Parliament would be difficult to conceive. Any item in the Act would be subject to a declaration of invalidity after the Act is passed, even after the moneys in question are withdrawn from Consolidated Revenue and perhaps even after the moneys are expended, for an appropriation, if it be unlawful and subject to a declaration of invalidity, does not cease to have that character because acts have taken place on the faith of it.

The adverse consequences of a narrow view of s 81 do not stop at this point. It has been the practice, born of practical necessity, in this country and in the United Kingdom, to give but a short description of the particular items dealt with in an Appropriation Act. No other course is feasible because in many respects the items of expenditure have not been thought through and elaborated in detail. How is the short description of an item contained in the schedule to the Act to serve as the fulcrum of constitutionality? If it fails to throw sufficient illumination on the area of doubt, is the Court to have regard to supplementary material, as it has been invited to do in this case, and if so, to what material will it have recourse? These questions, which to my mind admit of no satisfactory solution, illustrate the problems inherent in the narrow construction offered by the plaintiffs and the hazards attending the processes of Parliament if that construction is accepted.

Another consequence of the plaintiffs' view of s 81 is that it would deprive the Commonwealth of the power to make grants for purposes thought to be deserving of financial support by government, yet standing outside the area of Commonwealth power, and not involving any exercise of the Commonwealth's executive power. Over the years there have been many instances of appropriations made by the Parliament to persons and bodies and for purposes **[395]** which appear to have little, if any, connexion with the functions and powers of the Commonwealth under the Constitution. On the plaintiffs' argument these appropriations are invalid. The consequence would be that public money has been illegally withdrawn from the Treasury and paid away. And for the future the Commonwealth, subject to the authority which s 122 provides, could make such grants only through the agency of the States under s 96.

Although some have discovered in s 96 of the Constitution a power to make grants to the States which would not otherwise exist, the section should in my view be seen as a provision which puts beyond question the power of Parliament to attach conditions to grants made to the States, as to which doubts would certainly have existed had explicit provision not been made. But it could scarcely be doubted that in the absence of s 96 the Parliament would have enjoyed the power to make unconditional grants to the States. So much at least would be implied from the relationship subsisting between the Commonwealth and the States as constituent elements in the federation and the possession by the Commonwealth of its taxation and other financial powers. The presence of s 96 is therefore not a reason for confining s 81 as the plaintiffs would suggest ...

[396] It follows, then, that I would give to the words "for the purposes of the Commonwealth" in s 81 the meaning ascribed to them by Latham CJ in the *Pharmaceutical Benefits Case* [(1945) 71 CLR 237 at 256], that is, for such purposes as Parliament may determine.

On this basis, Mason J agreed with McTiernan and Murphy JJ that "the purposes of the Commonwealth" extended to any purposes that the Parliament might choose to pursue. However, he also agreed with Barwick CJ and Gibbs J that the Australian Assistance Plan was invalid in its expenditure of the appropriated money.

Mason J: [396] But this is not to say that the Commonwealth has an unlimited executive power or that a statutory appropriation provides lawful authority for the engagement by the Commonwealth in particular activities. An appropriation, as I have explained, has a limited effect. It may provide the necessary parliamentary sanction for the withdrawal of money from Consolidated Revenue and the payment or subscription of money to a particular recipient or for a particular purpose but it does not supply legal authority for the Commonwealth's engagement in the activities in connexion with which the moneys are to be spent. Whether the Commonwealth can engage in any specific activities depends upon the extent of the Commonwealth's legislative, executive and judicial powers.

Here, no legislation having been enacted to give effect to the Australian Assistance Plan, we must look to the executive power. In the words of s 61, the executive power of the Commonwealth "extends to the execution and maintenance of this Constitution, and of the laws of the Commonwealth". Although the ambit of the power is not otherwise defined by Ch II it is evident that in scope it is not unlimited and that its content does not reach beyond the area of responsibilities allocated to the Commonwealth by the Constitution, responsibilities which are ascertainable from the distribution of powers, more particularly the distribution of legislative powers, effected by the Constitution itself and the character and status of the Commonwealth as a national government. The provisions of s 61 taken in conjunction with the federal **[397]** character of the Constitution and the distribution of powers between the Commonwealth and the States make any other conclusion unacceptable. Moreover, it is a view of the executive power which is confirmed by the past decisions of this Court (see *Commonwealth v Colonial Combing, Spinning and Weaving Co Ltd* ("the *Wooltops Case*") [(1922) 31 CLR 421 at 432]; *Commonwealth v Australian Commonwealth Shipping Board* [(1926) 39 CLR 1 at 10]).

However, in ascertaining the potential scope of the power there are several important considerations which need to be kept steadily in mind. First, the incidental power contained in s 51(xxxix) taken in conjunction with other powers, notably s 61 itself, adds a further dimension to what may be achieved by the Commonwealth in the exercise of other specific powers. So in *Burns v Ransley* [(1949) 79 CLR 101] and *R v Sharkey* [(1949) 79 CLR 121], ss 24A, 24B and 24D of the *Crimes Act* 1914-1946 (Cth) were held to be supported by the combination of ss 51(xxxix) and 61. Secondly, the Commonwealth enjoys, apart from its specific and enumerated powers, certain implied powers which stem from its existence and its character as a polity (*Australian Communist Party v Commonwealth* [(1951) 83 CLR 1 at 187-8]). So far it has not been suggested that the implied powers extend beyond the area of internal security and protection of the State against disaffection and subversion. But in my opinion there is to be deduced from the existence and character of the Commonwealth as a national government and from the presence of ss 51(xxxix) and 61 a capacity to engage in enterprises and activities peculiarly adapted to the government of a nation and which cannot otherwise be carried on for the benefit of the nation.

It is in the exercise of this capacity that the Commonwealth has established the Commonwealth Scientific and Industrial Research Organization to undertake scientific research on behalf of the nation. The *Science and Research Act* 1951, as amended, is an exercise of the power conferred by s 51(xxxi) and s 61 or perhaps of implied power. So also the Commonwealth may expend money on inquiries, investigation and advocacy in relation to matters affecting public health, notwithstanding the absence of a specific legislative power other than quarantine – see the *Pharmaceutical Benefits Case* [71 CLR at 257]. No doubt there are other enterprises and activities appropriate to a national government which may be undertaken by the Commonwealth on behalf of the nation. The functions appropriate and adapted to a national government will vary from time to time. As time unfolds, as circumstances and **[398]** conditions alter, it will transpire that particular enterprises and activities will be undertaken if they are to be undertaken at all, by the national government.

However, the executive power to engage in activities appropriate to a national government, arising as it does from an implication drawn from the Constitution and having no counterpart, apart from the incidental power, in the expressed heads of legislative power, is limited in scope. It would be inconsistent with the broad division of responsibilities between the Commonwealth and the States achieved by the distribution of legislative powers to concede to this aspect of the executive power a wide operation effecting a radical transformation in what has hitherto been thought to be the Commonwealth's area of responsibility under the Constitution, thereby enabling the Commonwealth to carry out within Australia programmes standing outside the acknowledged heads of legislative power merely because these programmes can be conveniently formulated and administered by the national government …

[399] It would be an unrewarding exercise to recapitulate the principal elements in the Plan as they emerge from the documents. It is sufficient to say that it is not confined, as the defence might suggest, to the co-ordination on a national basis of welfare services otherwise provided and to be provided. It makes provision for the establishment and financing of Regional Councils for social development throughout Australia. The pilot programme records that in the first full year twenty-nine bodies received administrative grants only and a further six Councils received capitation grants for expenditure on social welfare services covering a wide range of social welfare activities including such activities as family day care programmes, parent education programmes, family counselling services, home help and housekeeper services, provision of community and other centres. The function of the Regional Councils is to stimulate interest in activity in the broad field of social development …

[400] The elements of the Plan have not yet been enshrined in legislation. At this time it exists as an administrative scheme only. However, the pilot programme contemplates that enabling legislation will be introduced into the Parliament. Plainly enough the legislation contemplated is not an exercise of the power conferred by s 96. Nowhere in the documents is it suggested that the scheme is to be administered by or through the States. Likewise, despite the Solicitor-General's vigorous asseverations to the contrary, it seems clear that the programme is not an experimental programme conducted with a view to determining or formulating a policy according to which s 96 grants might be made to the States.

The documents indicate that the elements of the scheme are to be a direct responsibility of the Commonwealth, acting not through the States and their agencies, but independently of them. They also show that, although the pilot programme is experimental in the sense that alterations to the programme will be made in the light of experience gained, the Plan as such has been put forward and adopted as a continuing social welfare scheme. So it is that the establishment of regional councils has not been undertaken as an experiment but as a deliberate step in a social welfare scheme which calls for the setting up of regional councils throughout Australia, operating not under the aegis of the States, but independently of and perhaps in competition with them and their institutions.

In the light of what I have already said as to the extent of the appropriation power, the *Appropriation Act*, in so far as it relates to item 530.4, the item in question, is a valid exercise of that power conferred by s 81. However, in my view the activities which call for the expenditure of this money, the elements which comprise the scheme known as the Australian Assistance Plan, stand largely, if not wholly, outside the boundaries of the executive power of the Commonwealth. I acknowledge that some part of the moneys appropriated could find their way into the hands of citizens in the form of pensions within the meaning of s 51(xxiii) and (xxiiiA), but this is consequential upon the establishment and operation of the regional councils which, as I understand [401] it, is central to the creation of the bureaucratic organization envisaged by the Australian Assistance Plan. The carrying into execution of that Plan is in my view outside the realm of the executive power of the Commonwealth and should be restrained by injunction.

Jacobs J apparently assumed the correctness of the narrow view that any exercise of Commonwealth power under s 81 must be for a "purpose of the Commonwealth" having a foothold within the framework of the constitutional text. However, one such foothold was the Commonwealth's prerogative power, which is an important implicit aspect of the executive power under s 61. For him, this was an answer to the question raised by Mason J about the executive government's capacity to spend the appropriated moneys. It also opened up a wide range of legislative powers – supported, if need be, by the "incidental" power in s 51(xxxix).

Jacobs J: [404] Nor is it correct that Parliament may only appropriate moneys in respect of a purpose which is already the subject of legislation of the Australian Parliament. The Constitution does not say so and there is no place for such an implication. The argument overlooks the wide area in which moneys may be expended by the Executive Government, that is to say, by the Queen exercising her prerogative through the Governor-General on the advice of the Executive Council. When moneys are voted to the Queen by Parliament for the purposes declared by the Parliament, it falls [405] within the prerogative to determine whether or not those moneys will be expended for that purpose and how, within the expression of the purpose to which the moneys have been appropriated, the expenditure will be made. Legislation is only needed when Parliament chooses to replace or affect the prerogative powers by legislation which either extends or limits or simply reproduces in the form of executive or other authority the powers previously comprehended within the prerogative. The exercise of the prerogative of expending moneys voted by Parliament does not depend on the existence of legislation on the subject by the Australian Parliament other than the appropriation itself. This exercise of the prerogative is in no different case from other exercises of the prerogative which fall within the powers of the Executive Government of the Commonwealth under s 61 of the Constitution. If legislation were a prerequisite it would follow that the Queen would never be able to exercise the prerogative through the Governor-General acting on the advice of the Executive Council; she would always exercise executive power by authority of the Parliament. This cannot be suggested. It would, if correct, result in an inability of Australia to declare war, make treaties, appoint officers of State and members of the public service of the Commonwealth and do all the multitude of things which still fall within the prerogative, unless there was a general or special sanction of an Act of Parliament.

The Constitution envisages the exercise of the prerogative through the Governor-General in those matters appertaining to the Government of the Commonwealth in its provision by s 61 that the executive power of the Commonwealth extends to the execution and maintenance of the Constitution. Except so far as the Constitution makes particular provision in respect of matters otherwise within the prerogative, the prerogative remains unaffected. It was always intended that, subject to the Constitution and its expression of the subject matters of Commonwealth power, to a large extent the prerogative would be exercised on all matters of Australian concern by the Crown on the advice of Australian Ministers rather than on the advice of United Kingdom Ministers. The extent of its exercise on such advice has throughout the years of federation been a growing extent. The area of its exercise on the advice of Australian Ministers is limited by the terms of the Constitution. Primarily its exercise is limited to those areas which are expressly made the subject matters of Commonwealth legislative power. But it cannot be strictly limited to those subject matters. The prerogative is now exercisable by the Queen through the Governor-General acting on the advice of the Executive **[406]** Council on all matters which are the concern of Australia as a nation. Within the words "maintenance of this Constitution" appearing in s 61 lies the idea of Australia as a nation within itself and in its relationship with the external world, a nation governed by a system of law in which the powers of government are divided between a government representative of all the people of Australia and a number of governments each representative of the people of the various States.

It does not follow that any subject matter of the exercise of the prerogative which is properly exercisable through the Governor-General on the advice of the Executive Council cannot be the subject of legislation which may deny or limit or replace the prerogative by legislative provision. The same is true of any executive power expressly conferred by the Constitution, though of course the exercise of either executive or legislative power is subject to the provisions of the Constitution. The power to legislate in respect of matters falling within the prerogative arises under s 51(xxxix) in so far as it does not arise under any other particular head of power. Alternatively the [source] of power is the inherent sovereignty of the Australian Parliament in all subject matters which lie within the province of the Government of the Commonwealth of Australia. The Parliament is sovereign over the Executive and whatever is within the competence of the Executive under s 61, including or as well as the exercise of the prerogative within the area of the prerogative attached to the Government of Australia, may be the subject of legislation of the Australian Parliament. However, although the Parliament may legislate in respect of any subject matter which is within the prerogative so far as it is exercisable through the Governor-General on the advice of the Executive Council, it does not follow that legislation is necessary before a prerogative power is exercised.

After summarising the departmental documents that outlined the Plan, Jacobs J went on:

Jacobs J: [409] With this material before the Court, the argument proceeded to a further stage. Part of the expenditure by the Government pursuant to the appropriation would under the Australian Assist-**[410]**-ance Plan in this pilot phase, as it has been called, be by way of capitation grants to the Regional Councils. These Councils could spend the grants so made on any or all of the capital or maintenance costs of the services outlined in Ch 4 of the Discussion Paper and many of those services would in the case of persons who did not otherwise fall within a class comprehended in a subject matter of Commonwealth power be outside any particular head of Commonwealth power. Part of the expenditure might, and probably would, thus be on matters which, viewed in isolation, did not fall directly within a subject of general Commonwealth power. In this situation, it is submitted, the whole appropriation is bad and an injunction may be granted by the Court restraining expenditure generally. The basis of the submission is an analogy between the appropriation and the expenditure pursuant thereto and the principles which govern the construction of legislation of the Australian Parliament which imposes duties and obligations. Such legislation is not valid if it may in its execution transcend the limits of power or if part thereof is within power and an inseverable part is beyond power. It is submitted that, just as legislation will be invalid if it may inseverably operate on a matter or in a matter beyond power as well as on matters or in matters within power, so an appropriation will be wholly beyond power if some part thereof, not severable in the appropriation from the remainder, may be expended in respect of matters which do not fall within the power of the Commonwealth to legislate generally. This is a very far-reaching submission and would invalidate a very large number of items in any Appropriation Act.

But it is in my opinion a submission which cannot be sustained. It does not give weight to the nature of the relief which may be granted by the Court. The submission must depend on the invalidity of the actual appropriation of moneys. It can have no weight if it is the threatened expenditure alone which can be impugned. In my opinion the appropriation by the Commonwealth Parliament of moneys of the Commonwealth to the purposes stated in the *Appropriation Act* cannot by itself be the subject of legal challenge. The appropriation is a matter internal to the Government of the Commonwealth. It may not make valid anything which cannot be validated. That depends on the breadth of the Commonwealth power of appropriation and expenditure expressed in s 81 and on the meaning of the words therein "for the purposes of the Commonwealth". However, even when those words are given a limited meaning it does not follow that the *Appropriation Act* or any part thereof can be declared invalid. **[411]** The appropriation is no more than an earmarking of the money, which remains the property of the Commonwealth. All it does is to disclose that the Parliament assents to the expenditure of the moneys appropriated for the purposes stated in the appropriation. The Crown may then within the law governing appropriation of its money expend those moneys …

There must be an appropriation by Parliament. Section 81 requires that revenue or moneys be appropriated in the manner imposed by the Constitution and under s 83 the appropriation must be made by law. This is the expression in our Constitution of the requirement established in English constitutional law that the revenues raised by authority of Parliament must be voted to the Crown by Parliament. Section 83 is not in itself a limitation on the power of the Parliament to appropriate moneys and should not be read as meaning "by a law on a subject matter in respect of which the power is otherwise conferred on the Parliament to legislate". The section does not say that and there is no need for such an implication. The limitation, if any, is to be found in the words "purposes of the Commonwealth" in s 81.

Although the appropriation made on the message from the Governor-General is clearly evidence of an intention to expend the moneys for the purposes stated in the appropriation, relief can only be given in respect of so much of the expenditure pursuant to the appropriation as lies outside the purposes for which an appropriation can be made. The appropriation cannot make lawful that which is unlawful but it does nothing which can attract to its operation the principles which have been developed in respect of Commonwealth legislation creating rights, obligations and duties. It is for a plaintiff to identify any expenditure which is impugned and to frame a prayer for relief in terms which will enjoin that expenditure and that only.

There is no analogy between the validity of legislation and the validity of expenditure. In the former case it is the intention of the Parliament which is the subject of scrutiny and if the Parliament discloses an intention that its legislation shall apply or be capable of applying inseverably to matters and things within power and to matters and things outside power then the whole legislation is inseverably invalid. On the other hand, if the Executive Government expends or proposes to expend money the only relevant act or intention is that of expending or proposing to expend particular **[412]** sums. No question of any "overall" intention can arise. There is in law no "scheme" of expenditure as there can be a scheme of legislation. It follows that any relief granted by the court against an illegitimate expenditure would need carefully and precisely and exhaustively to delineate those expenditures in respect of which relief is granted. The practical impossibility of so doing may well prevent the granting of relief by way of quia timet injunction or even by way of declaration. The complex interrelation between the heads of power within the competence of the Commonwealth would make it very difficult to frame relief except in general and therefore impermissible terms. Clearly much of the proposed expenditure of $5,970,000 would fall within Commonwealth power in respect of social welfare generally or in respect of the social welfare of particular groups or classes of persons. No form of relief appropriate only to so much of the sum of $5,970,000 as may be claimed to be proposed expenditure beyond Commonwealth power has been, or apparently could be, formulated. No argument was presented to the Court which would require such a formulation.

For these reasons alone the plaintiffs have made out no case for relief even on the assumption that some part of the proposed expenditure may be beyond Commonwealth power. That assumption, however, does not appear to me to be correct. Moneys may be appropriated and therefore expended pursuant to that appropriation "for the purposes of the Commonwealth". It appears to me that the view of the majority of the Court in *Attorney-General (Vic) v Commonwealth* was that the power of appropriation was limited by the nature and purposes of the Government of the Commonwealth but that, on the other hand, the purposes of the Commonwealth may not only fall within a subject matter of general or particular power prescribed in the Constitution but may also be other purposes which now adhere fully to Australia as a nation externally and internally sovereign: cf per Starke J [71 CLR at 266]. The growth of national identity results in a corresponding growth in the area of activities which have an Australian rather than a local flavour. Thus, the complexity and values of a modern national society result in a need for co-ordination and integration of ways and means of planning for that complexity and reflecting those values. Inquiries on a national scale are necessary and likewise planning on a national scale must be carried out. Moreover, the complexity of society, with its various interrelated needs, requires co-ordination of services designed to **[413]** meet those needs. Research and exploration likewise have a national, rather than a local, flavour.

In two ways the Australian Assistance Plan is in substance within the powers of the Commonwealth. First, it is an expenditure of money in the exercise by the Commonwealth of its executive power to formulate and co-ordinate plans and purposes which require national rather than local planning and of its legislative power to appropriate its funds accordingly. Secondly, in so far as the proposed expenditure does not fall directly within a specific power of the Commonwealth it is an expenditure of money which is incidental to the execution by the Commonwealth of its wide powers respecting social welfare. A considerable part of the proposed expenditure falls or may fall directly within Commonwealth power either in respect of specific subject matter or in respect of particular classes of persons but in so far as some expenditure may be outside Commonwealth powers in respect of specific subject matters or in respect of particular classes of persons it seems to me that the expenditure falls within the incidental power in s 51(xxxix). The purposes of the Commonwealth certainly include all the purposes comprehended within the subject matters of s 51 in respect of which the Commonwealth may legislate, including the subject matter comprised in s 51(xxxix). The purposes of the Commonwealth include purposes comprehended within the Commonwealth power in respect of matters incidental to the execution of the legislative power to appropriate and the executive power to expend moneys for the purposes of the Commonwealth. Moneys may therefore be appropriated and expended for that purpose as well as for purposes wholly comprehended within the other subject matters of Commonwealth power. Appropriation and expenditure of moneys for the purposes of the Commonwealth may therefore be made for purposes comprehended within the power of the Commonwealth in respect of matters incidental to the execution of the legislative power to appropriate and the executive power to expend moneys for purposes comprehended within other subject matters of power. In every case it is necessary to determine whether the expenditure, if it is not for the purposes of the Commonwealth in what may compendiously in the light of this analysis be described as a primary sense, is nevertheless incidental to the execution of the power to expend moneys for the purposes of the Commonwealth in that primary sense.

In speaking here of matters "incidental" to the execution of the legislative power of appropriation or the executive power of spending, Jacobs J had in mind a difficult distinction between *incidents of* the primary topic or enterprise and matters merely *incidental to* it. This, for him, was the key to the difference between "express" and "implied" incidental powers in s 51. He saw the implied incidental power read into each grant of power in s 51 as extending only to matters which are truly "incidents of" the primary subject-matter. He argued that the express incidental power in s 51(xxxix) casts a wider net – not only extending to all of the Commonwealth's legislative, executive and judicial powers, but enabling the Parliament to legislate on matters which are neither part of the primary subject-matter nor even "incidents" of it, but which it is appropriate to deal with incidentally to such subject-matter. He concluded:

Jacobs J: [415] The proposed 1974-1975 expenditure of the Commonwealth, classified in the 1974-1975 Budget papers as expenditures upon welfare, health and social security, but not including education, are the largest expenditures by classification which it makes. The total for the relevant year is $4,673,000,000 out of a total budgeted expenditure of $16,274,000,000. See *Hansard*, House of Representatives, First Session – First Period, p 1295. The Executive Government has taken the view that these expenditures are unco-ordinated among themselves and are unco-ordinated with social welfare expenditures made independently by and in the various States. It has also determined that it is desirable to involve people at community level in the devising and planning of welfare services. The claim that planning for co-ordination and rationalization of welfare services and expenditure thereon is beyond power has hardly been pressed. Where it is claimed that the Commonwealth has transgressed the limits of power is in including within the funds made available at community level amounts by way of the so-called "capitation grants" which may be expended on aspects of social welfare other than aspects within the limits of express powers conferred in s 51. It has not been established that payment of these "capitation grants" is not incidental to the execution of the power to appropriate and expend moneys for the purposes comprehended within the Commonwealth powers contained in s 51(xxiii) and (xxiiiA) as well as the powers possessed by the Commonwealth in respect of particular groups and classes of persons in the community for whose social welfare the Commonwealth may generally provide. In my opinion no cause of action is disclosed by the pleadings and I would dismiss the action.

McTiernan, Murphy and Jacobs JJ held that the Australian Assistance Plan was valid. Barwick CJ, Gibbs and Mason JJ held that it was not. The judgment of Stephen J was therefore crucial. He rejected the challenge to the Plan by holding that Victoria had no standing to mount it.

Stephen J: [386] When an item in an Appropriation Act is attacked as ultra vires it is not in any real sense the Commonwealth Parliament's legislative power that is attacked but rather the taking of the first step in the expenditure of moneys on a particular purpose. As was said by Isaacs and Rich JJ in *Commonwealth v Colonial Ammunition Co Ltd* [34 CLR at 224] when speaking of the parliamentary appropriation of moneys:

> "The object of Parliament in such a case is financial, not regulative. In doing that, it is not concerned with general legislation, and is acting wholly alio intuitu …"

This peculiar character of Appropriation Acts was, until 1963, made the more apparent by the then standing orders governing parliamentary procedure on money bills. Under that procedure, borrowed from what is still the British practice, the passage of an Appropriation Bill in the lower house was a mere formality, all significant proceedings being conducted in committee of the whole … Lord Palmerston described an Appropriation Bill passed under that procedure as no more than "a form that is required by the Constitution, and not a Bill to give rise to any discussion" (Todd, *Parliamentary Government in England* (1867), vol 1, p 529).

It is, then, with this special type of Act of Parliament that the present proceedings are concerned. It is an Act which, while a necessary precondition to lawful disbursement of money by the Treasury, is not in any way directed to the citizens of the Commonwealth; **[387]** it does not speak in the language of regulation, it neither confers rights or privileges nor imposes duties or obligations. It only permits of moneys held in the Treasury being paid out, upon the Governor-General's warrant, to departments of the Government. Its importance is essentially confined to the polity in question, here the federal polity; the control which, by its means, is exercised by the legislature over proposed government expenditure is of significance within the framework of that polity but has no direct effect upon the powers or interests of the other component parts of the federation, the States.

How then can the present plaintiffs, the State of Victoria and its Attorney-General, have any standing to complain of this legislative authorization of proposed federal expenditure? The answer is, in my view, that they cannot. The State itself has no concern with the mode of expenditure of federal revenue unless it be associated with some claim to surplus revenue of the Commonwealth under s 94 of the Constitution, but the present proceedings are no more appropriate to raise any such claim than were those in *Attorney-General (Vic); Ex rel Dale v Commonwealth* ("the *Pharmaceutical Benefits Case*"); I would adopt what Latham CJ there said. The plaintiffs did not seek to support standing by reference to surplus revenue, no doubt both because of the Commonwealth's use of trust funds, sanctioned in *New South Wales v Commonwealth* and exemplified, in refined form, in s 7 of the present Appropriation Act and because, in any event, the very large deficit budgeted for effectively eliminates it from consideration ...

[390] In the light of the foregoing I conclude that where the federal legislation which is impugned is no more than an Appropriation Act, whose provisions not only do not extend to and operate within any State and do not affect, still less interfere with, public rights but have no ordinary law making function at all, not purporting to govern the conduct of the citizens of any State or of the Commonwealth and having no injurious effect upon their trading activities or other rights, the Attorney-General of a State has no standing to sue. There is here nothing which can operate so as to "hamper the freedom of citizens of the State" (per O'Connor J, in the *Union Label Case* [(1908) 6 CLR 469 at 553]) because what is complained of is not truly an instance of law making but rather an example of the exercise of fiscal control over the executive by the legislature.

[391] To express this conclusion is to acknowledge that, whatever might be the outcome of appropriate proceedings brought by an individual federal taxpayer or by the Commonwealth Attorney-General, the allegedly ultra vires expenditure by the Commonwealth of its own funds which this Appropriation Act is said to authorize may not be attacked in a declaratory action instituted by the Attorney-General of another political entity, the State of Victoria. So expressed, the proposition accords well enough with concepts of inter-governmental relationships within a federation and does, I think, no violence to, but rather conforms with, the previous work of this Court, referred to by Dixon J in the *Pharmaceutical Benefits Case* [71 CLR at 272], of applying to our federal system a doctrine developed in the English unitary system.

For Barwick CJ, Gibbs and Mason JJ, the State's standing arose from its interest in ensuring that the Commonwealth did not exceed its powers. Barwick CJ suggested that the State might also have standing because of its interest, under s 94, in the Commonwealth's surplus revenue.

The effect of the *AAP Case* has been summarised as follows:

Davis v Commonwealth
(1988) 166 CLR 79

Mason CJ, Deane and Gaudron JJ: [95] An appropriation for a valid exercise of the executive power of the Commonwealth is necessarily an appropriation for a purpose of the Commonwealth within the meaning of s 81 of the Constitution, even if one adopts a narrow view of the expression "purposes of the Commonwealth" in that section. In one sense this is by the way. There has been a long-standing controversy about the meaning of "purposes of the Commonwealth" in s 81. In the *Pharmaceutical Benefits Case* [(1945) 71 CLR 237] Latham CJ and McTiernan J considered that the expression meant in effect such purposes as the Parliament may adopt as purposes of the Commonwealth, whereas Rich, Starke, Dixon and Williams JJ thought that it meant purposes otherwise within the province of the Commonwealth ... Subsequently in the *AAP Case* [(1975) 134 CLR 338] McTiernan, Mason and Murphy JJ concluded that s 81 enabled the Parliament to appropriate for such purposes as it may determine. Jacobs J considered that the validity of an appropri-[96]-ation is not justiciable and is therefore not susceptible to legal challenge. The case therefore stands as an authority for the proposition that the validity of an appropriation act is not ordinarily susceptible to effective legal challenge. It is unnecessary to consider whether there are extraordinary circumstances in which an appropriation of money by the Parliament may be susceptible to such challenge. It suffices to say that, if there be such cases, the present is not one of them.

However unsatisfactory this summation may be as a ratio decidendi, it appears to be accurate as a prediction. Indeed, in *Combet v Commonwealth* (2005) 221 ALR 621, it was not even argued that the appropriation in question was invalid. Instead, it was argued that the Howard government's expenditure on an advertising campaign to promote its proposals for change to Australia's industrial relations system was invalid because it had not been authorised by the *Appropriation Act (No 1) 2005* (Cth). Accordingly, the issue was one of statutory construction.

The Schedule to the Act appropriated funds for expenditure by the Department of Employment and Workplace Relations. The essential features of the appropriation were as follows:

	Departmental Outputs	Administered Expenses	Total
Outcome 1 – Efficient and effective Labour market assistance	$1,235,216,000	$1,970,400,000	$3,205,616,000
Outcome 2 – Higher productivity, Higher pay workplaces	$140,131,000	$90,559,000	$230,690,000
Outcome 3 – Increased workforce Participation	$72,205,000	$560,642,000	$632,847,000
Total	**$1,447,552,000**	**$2,621,601,000**	**$4,069,153,000**

According to a definition in s 3 of the Act, the *total* amount entered at the foot of the column headed "Departmental Outputs" was to be treated as a single "departmental item".

When the case was argued before the High Court, the issue mainly debated was whether the advertising campaign could reasonably be seen as sufficiently conducive to the objectives of "higher productivity" and "higher pay workplaces" to justify the expenditure being made from the moneys appropriated to "Outcome 2" above. However, the joint judgment of Gummow, Hayne, Callinan and Heydon JJ held that this question did not even arise. They conceded that the sums allocated to "Administered Expenses" were governed by s 8(2) of the Act, which provided that expenditure "for an administered item for an outcome of an entity" (in this case the Department) "may only be applied for expenditure for the purpose of carrying out activities for the purpose of contributing to achieving that outcome". By contrast, they held that the sums allocated to "departmental outputs" were governed by s 7(2) of the Act, which required that expenditure "for a departmental item … may only be applied for the departmental expenditure of the entity". Accordingly, though the specification of "outcomes" served to limit the purposes for which moneys appropriated for "administered expenses" could be used, there was no such limit on the use of moneys appropriated for "departmental outputs". Since the advertising expenditure could be regarded as a "departmental output", it did not matter whether it was conducive to the stated objectives or not.

In the table above the appropriations in the column for "departmental outputs", as well as those in the column for "administered expenses", are allocated among the three objectives or "outcomes" listed at the left hand side. In declining to attach significance to this allocation in the case of "departmental outputs", the joint judgment relied on an explanatory note attached to s 3 of the Act, stipulating that "the amounts set out opposite outcomes, under the heading 'Departmental outputs', are 'notional'. They are not part of the item, and do not in any way restrict the scope of the expenditure authorised by the item".

Gleeson CJ reached the same result, but did not accept the above reasoning. He insisted that every appropriation must be for a stated purpose, and that every expenditure must be sufficiently related to a purpose so stated. However, he accepted the Commonwealth's argument that the expenditure *was* sufficiently related to "Outcome 2", since "**[630]** promotion of public acceptance of workplace relations policy and legislative change", like departmental advice on the policy, "**[629]** could rationally be regarded as contributing to [that] outcome". He accepted the plaintiffs' submission that the outcomes were stated "at a very high level of abstraction", but added: "Provided such statements are not so general, or abstract, as to be without meaning, they represent Parliament's lawful choice as to the manner in which it identifies the purpose of an appropriation … If Parliament formulates the purposes of appropriation in broad, general terms, then those terms must be applied with the breadth and generality they bear". He quoted (at 623) what Jacobs J had said in the *AAP Case*: "**[404]** Provided that purposes are stated it is a matter for the

Parliament how minute and particular shall be the expression of purposes in any particular case". He also quoted what Murphy J had said in that case: "**[422]** The purpose of any appropriation may be indicated generally. 'One-line' appropriations are valid".

McHugh and Kirby JJ dissented. They held that advertisements of the kind in question could not be justified as conducive to any of the specified "outcomes", and that this was decisive since those "outcomes" controlled expenditures on "departmental outputs" as well as on "administered expenses". They vehemently rejected the construction placed on the Act by the joint majority judgment as contrary to the regime presupposed by the Portfolio Budget Statements that accompanied the introduction of the Appropriation Bill into Parliament; by the *Financial Management and Accountability Act 1997* (Cth); and by other documents explaining the accounting methods and principles of financial management on which the annual Budget was based. In the light of that regime they held that the specification of "outcomes" was intended as a limitation on *all* expenditures, since without such a limitation none of the elaborate mechanisms for control of government expenditure through independent audit, annual departmental reports, and scrutiny by parliamentary committees would have any meaningful criteria. As McHugh J put it, if the "outcomes" did not supply such criteria, they "**[646]** would be but pious aspirations which departments could disregard if and when they pleased".

The note attached to s 3 of the Act was explained by McHugh and Kirby JJ as attaching the epithet "notional" only to the *amounts* that were specified for "Departmental Outputs", not to the specified "outcomes". It was these *amounts* that were said "not … [to] restrict the scope of the expenditure" on the relevant departmental item. On that reading, the whole of the total amount of $1,447,552,000 was available for departmental expenditure on any one of the three specified "outcomes"; the amount expended on Outcome 2 might be more, or less, than $140,131,000. But any expenditure must be related to one or another of the stated "outcomes".

Both McHugh and Kirby JJ stressed that the construction adopted by the joint majority judgment had not been adequately explored in argument. As Kirby J put it: "**[701]** That point was only dealt with in passing, and then in response to isolated questions from the Court … To dispose of these proceedings, as the joint reasons do, on an unconvincing interpretation of the Appropriation Act, alien to the Constitution and to Australian parliamentary practice, advanced by no party, hypothesised from the Bench and answered on the run, is an unreasonable way of concluding such an important controversy". McHugh J emphasised not only that such a construction had *not* been relied on in argument by the Commonwealth Solicitor-General, but that his answers to questions had consistently assumed the opposing construction. For example, the Solicitor-General had spoken of "**[645]** a very simple situation in which the three administered items set out against each outcome are items that can only be spent in relation to that outcome, *whereas the departmental item, which is the 1.4 billion, can be spent on any or all of the three outcomes*" (emphasis by McHugh J). When McHugh J asked him whether this meant "that the Outcomes were not controlling in respect of Departmental Outputs", he answered: "Yes … Except to the extent that one must be within one of them". Later, he repeated "that the Act has defined the expenditure in terms of Outcomes. A certain sum of money is limited to Outcome 2 and a certain sum of money can be applied, at departmental discretion, to Outcomes 1, 2 or 3".

Both McHugh and Kirby JJ invoked the dictum of Latham CJ in the *Pharmaceutical Benefits Case*, that, consistently with the requirement of "purposes" in s 81 of the Constitution, "**[253]** there cannot be appropriations in blank, appropriations for no designated purpose, merely authorizing expenditure with no reference to purpose. An Act which merely provided that a minister or some other person could spend a sum of money, no purpose of the expenditure being stated, would not be a valid appropriation Act". As McHugh J put it: "**[648]** The construction favoured by the joint judgment contravenes this principle, for it appears to authorise an agency to spend money on whatever outputs it pleases … A statute of the Federal Parliament should not be construed in a way that gives rise to questions of its constitutional invalidity unless the words of the statute make it clear that such a construction was intended". For his part Kirby J invoked *Brown v West* (1990) 169 CLR 195 as a precedent that should have been followed. In that case the dictum of Latham CJ about "appropriations in blank" had been linked with the Privy Council's insistence, in *Auckland Harbour Board v The King* [1924] AC 318, that "**[326]** no money can be taken out of the consolidated Fund ... excepting under a distinct authorization from Parliament itself". At issue in *Brown v West* was an increase in postal allowances for members of Parliament, which was held not to comply with the statutory regime by which such allowances were to be determined. An attempt to save the increased allowances by arguing that they were covered by a parliamentary appropriation was rejected by a unanimous Court. For Kirby J in *Combet v Commonwealth*, this insistence on the need for "a distinct authorization" reflected "**[686]** centuries of constitutional history ... This Court should not retreat from the clear rule expressed in that case".

2. The Grants Power

Section 96 states: "During a period of ten years after the establishment of the Commonwealth and thereafter until the Parliament otherwise provides, the Parliament may grant financial assistance to any State on such terms and conditions as the Parliament thinks fit". The section did not appear in the draft constitution approved by the Australasian Federal Convention in March 1898. It was added at a Premiers' Conference following the failure of the New South Wales referendum in June that year. Moreover, it was intended to be only a transitional provision, as its opening words indicate. Despite this, it has proved to be a significant vehicle for the Commonwealth's arrogation to itself of additional regulatory powers. It has also proved to be even more intractable to judicial control than the provision for appropriations in s 81.

(a)   The Early Cases

Victoria v Commonwealth (*Federal Roads Case*) (1926) 38 CLR 399 is one of the shortest, yet one of the most significant, judgments handed down by the High Court. The *Federal Aid Roads Act 1926* (Cth) authorised the Commonwealth Parliament to make agreements with the States for the making and remaking of roads with Commonwealth financial support in the form of s 96 grants. To finance work on the roads, it was envisaged that grants of £20 million over 10 years would be made to the States, with the money being allocated according to a State's population and area. Two States sought a declaration from the High Court that the Act was invalid. The Court's decision in full was:

Victoria v Commonwealth (*Federal Roads Case*)
(1926) 38 CLR 399

The Court: [406] The Court is of the opinion that the *Federal Aid Roads Act* No 46 of 1926 is a valid enactment.

It is plainly warranted by the provisions of sec 96 of the Constitution, and not affected by those of sec 99 or any other provisions of the Constitution, so that exposition is unnecessary.

The action is dismissed.

In *Deputy Federal Commissioner of Taxation (NSW) v WR Moran Pty Ltd* (1939) 61 CLR 735, Latham CJ treated s 96 both as virtually unreviewable by a court and as enabling the Common-wealth, with no real restriction, to make such grants and to impose such conditions as "**[763]** it thinks proper". The *Wheat Industry Assistance Act 1938* (Cth) was part of an exercise in "co-operative federalism" for the benefit of Australian wheat growers. A Commonwealth excise tax on flour was collected from flour millers, and the proceeds were granted to the States under s 96 of the Constitution on condition that the money be distributed to growers in proportion to the quantities of wheat they produced, thereby effectively maintaining a price of 5s 2d per bushel. If the price of wheat rose above that figure, the growers would be taxed and the proceeds would be used to recompense the millers. Tasmania was a special problem because virtually no wheat was grown there. Accordingly, the total revenue from Tasmanian millers was granted to the State government and, by virtue of Tasmanian legislation (the *Flour Tax Relief Act 1938* (Tas)), it was used to reimburse the millers. In 1997 a similar use of s 96 was proposed as a way of resolving the financial crisis arising from the decision in *Ha v New South Wales* (1997) 189 CLR 465 (see Chapter 23, §2(f)).

In *Moran's Case* it was argued that the Commonwealth legislation infringed s 51(ii) and (iii) of the Constitution, which require respectively that taxation laws shall not "discriminate between States or parts of States", and that "[b]ounties on the production or export of goods … shall be uniform throughout the Commonwealth". The High Court, with Evatt J dissenting, rejected these arguments and held that the Commonwealth legislation was valid.

Deputy Federal Commissioner of Taxation (NSW) v WR Moran Pty Ltd
(1939) 61 CLR 735

Latham CJ: [763] Section 96 is a means provided by the Constitution which enables the Commonwealth Parliament, when it thinks proper, to adjust inequalities between States which may arise from the application of uniform non-discriminating Federal laws to States which vary in **[764]** development and wealth. Discrimination is prohibited in laws with respect to taxation (sec 51(ii)). Bounties must be uniform (sec 51(iii)). Laws or regulations of trade, commerce or revenue must not give preference to one State or part thereof over another State or part thereof (sec 99). But these "equal" laws may produce very unequal results in different parts of Australia. A uniform law may confer benefits upon some States, but it may so operate as to amount to what is called "a Federal disability" in other States. Sec 96 provides means for adjusting such inequalities in accordance with the judgment of Parliament. That section is not limited by any prohibition of discrimination. There is no general prohibition in the Constitution of some vague thing called "discrimination". There are the specific prohibitions or restrictions to which I have referred. The word "discrimination" is sometimes so used as to imply an element of injustice. But discrimination may be just or unjust. A wise differentiation based upon relevant circumstances is a necessary element in national policy. The remedy for any abuse of the power conferred by sec 96 is political and not legal in character.

Even this passage might be read as confining grants under s 96 to a limited purpose, such as the redress of "**[754]** a Federal disability" arising from the unequal operation of an equally applicable law. In any event, when the High Court decision was affirmed by the Privy Council, their Lordships deliberately spoke in "**[858]** the language of caution".

WR Moran Pty Ltd v Deputy Commissioner of Taxation for New South Wales
[1940] AC 838

Viscount Maugham (for their Lordships): [857] There are no restrictions whatever in this section, and it is clear that while the section remains in operation, the Parliament – apart from the restrictions contained in s 51, which must be considered in a moment – may in the matter of financial assistance discriminate between States as much as it thinks fit.

Their Lordships have accordingly to bear in mind, first, that s 51(ii) prohibits discrimination between States or parts of States, but is not concerned to deal with the matter of equality of burden; and secondly, that s 96 does not prohibit discrimination. It is difficult to see any ground for an attack on the scheme, or on the various Acts which carry it into effect, in so far as that attack is really based on the exercise by the Commonwealth Parliament of its powers under s 96. Those powers are plainly being used for the purpose of preventing an unfairness or injustice to the State of Tasmania, or, indirectly, to some or all of its population. Such discrimination as may result between millers or their customers in Tasmania and in the other States is a by-product, **[858]** so to speak, of the endeavour to equalize the burden of the legislation by diminishing the special burden on Tasmania; and it is of first importance to note that this is brought about by an exercise of power under s 96, which does not itself prohibit discrimination. Great reliance was placed by the appellants on the scheme; but, in the view of their Lordships, the scheme adds nothing to the argument; for there is nothing in s 51 to prevent the Commonwealth Parliament from passing measures in concert with any State or States with a view to a fair distribution of the burden of the taxation imposed, provided always that the Act imposing taxes does not itself discriminate in any way between States or parts of States, and that the Act granting pecuniary assistance to a particular State is in its purpose and substance unobjectionable. In other words, it seems to their Lordships, as it seemed to the High Court, that the various Commonwealth and State Acts, if considered together as part of an organic whole, contain nothing which is prohibited in the Constitution.

In coming to this conclusion their Lordships wish to make it clear that, as at present advised, they do not take the view that the Commonwealth Parliament can exercise its powers under s 96 with a complete disregard of the prohibition contained in s 51(ii), or so as altogether to nullify that constitutional safeguard. The prohibition is of considerable importance; and the Constitution should be construed bearing in mind that it is the result of an agreement between six high-contracting parties with, in some respects, very different needs and interests. Cases may be imagined in which a purported exercise of the power to grant financial assistance under s 96 would be merely colourable. Under the guise or pretence of assisting a State with money, the real substance and purpose of the Act might simply be to effect discrimination in regard to taxation. Such an Act might well be ultra vires the Commonwealth Parliament. Their Lordships are using the language of caution because such a case may never arise, and also because it is their usual practice in a case dealing with constitutional matters to decide no more than their duty requires. They will add only that, in the view they take of the matter, some of the legislative **[859]** expedients – objected to as ultra vires by Evatt J in his forcible dissenting judgment – may well be colourable, and such Acts are not receiving the approval of their Lordships.

The first paragraph of this passage appears to support an unqualified view of the Commonwealth's power to make grants to the States "on such terms and conditions as the Parliament thinks fit". However, the second paragraph makes it clear that their Lordships were addressing themselves only to the limited question of whether s 14 of the *Wheat Industry Assistance Act*, which provided for a special grant to Tasmania, was "discriminatory" in an unacceptable sense. That is, they were endorsing this use of s 96 but not necessarily all possible uses. The final paragraph makes this limited scope of their Lordships' decision quite explicit. They saw no need to explore the possible limits of s 96 "**[859]** in the present case", but did concede that a "**[859]** merely colourable" use of s 96 might be invalid.

Despite these qualifications, the authority of *Moran's Case* has been added to that of the *Federal Roads Case* as supporting the proposition that resort to s 96 has no judicially enforceable limits. In 1942 this proposition became the basis for a major restructuring of Australian federalism.

(b)   *The* Uniform Tax Cases

In most federations, income tax is collected by both the central and the regional governments. This was the pattern in Australia until World War II. State taxation departments collected the Commonwealth's income tax on its behalf, so that even under the system of double taxation each taxpayer paid only one lot of tax. However, since 1942 the central feature of Australian "fiscal federalism" has been a reversal of this arrangement. Income tax has been levied only by the Commonwealth, with a proportion of the proceeds, calculated to represent each State's "share", then being distributed to the States in the form of Commonwealth grants under s 96.

The validity of these arrangements was upheld in *South Australia v Commonwealth* (*First Uniform Tax Case*) (1942) 65 CLR 373 and reaffirmed in *Victoria v Commonwealth* (*Second Uniform Tax Case*) (1957) 99 CLR 575. The *Uniform Tax Cases* bore out the prophecy of Alfred Deakin, one of Australia's first Prime Ministers, that the States would find themselves "**[97]** legally free, but financially bound to the chariot wheels of the Central Government" (A Deakin, *Federated Australia: Selections from Letters to the* Morning Post *1900-1910* (JA La Nauze (ed), Melbourne University Press, 1968)).

The *First Uniform Tax Case* arose out of four Commonwealth enactments that together established the Commonwealth's monopoly over income tax:

1. The *Income Tax Act 1942* (Cth) fixed Commonwealth income tax at very high rates – up to 18 shillings in the pound.

2. The *States Grants (Income Tax Reimbursement) Act 1942* (Cth) provided in s 4 that: "In every financial year during which this Act is in operation in respect of which the Treasurer is satisfied that a State has not imposed a tax upon incomes, there shall be payable by way of financial assistance to that State the amount set forth in the Schedule to this Act against the name of that State, less an amount equal to any arrears of tax collected by or on behalf of that State during that financial year".

3. The *Income Tax (War-time Arrangements) Act 1942* (Cth) provided for the transfer to the Commonwealth of State public servants engaged in assessment or collection of income tax, along with the property of State taxation departments, such as equipment and office space.

4. The *Income Tax Assessment Act 1942* (Cth) provided in s 221 that, in order to ensure Commonwealth revenue for the "efficient prosecution of the present war", no taxpayer should pay any State income tax until after he or she had paid Commonwealth income tax for the relevant year.

Four States challenged this regime. The case was heard by only five judges, since Dixon J was in Washington as Australian war-time Ambassador. The High Court rejected the challenge. Starke J dissented as to the validity of the *States Grants (Income Tax Reimbursement) Act* and the *War-time Arrangements Act*, and Latham CJ dissented as to the validity of the latter Act.

It is sometimes said that the *First Uniform Tax Case* was decided in wartime on the basis of the "defence power" and that the *Second Uniform Tax Case* then reaffirmed it in peacetime on the basis of the doctrine of precedent. However, this oversimplifies the position. The 1942 scheme depended on four separate enactments, each of which was independently held valid. Only the transfer of officers and facilities from the States' taxation departments to the Commonwealth was specifically upheld by reference to the Commonwealth's defence power. McTiernan J also relied on the defence power to support s 221 of the *Income Tax Assessment Act*; but the finding that s 221 was valid was the only aspect of the *First Uniform Tax Case* overruled in the *Second Uniform Tax Case*.

The decisive step in the *First Uniform Tax Case* was not the holding that any one of the four pieces of legislation was valid. Rather, it was the Court's insistence that if each of the four Acts was valid, the scheme as a whole was valid. Accordingly, the Court assessed the validity of each of the four Acts separately, and refused to entertain any argument based on their cumulative effect as a scheme.

South Australia v Commonwealth (First Uniform Tax Case)
(1942) 65 CLR 373

Latham CJ: [409] [T]he controversy before the Court is a legal controversy, not a political controversy. It is not for this or any court to prescribe policy or to seek to give effect to any views or opinions upon policy. We have nothing to do with the wisdom or expediency of legislation. Such questions are for Parliaments and the people. It has been argued that the Acts now in question discriminate, in breach of sec 51(ii) of the Constitution, between States. The Court must consider and deal with such a legal contention. But the Court is not authorized to consider whether the Acts are fair and just as between States – whether some States are being forced, by a political combination against them, to pay an undue share of Commonwealth expenditure or to provide money which other States ought fairly to provide. These are arguments to be used in Parliament and before the people. They raise questions of policy which it is not for the Court to determine or even to consider ...

[411] *The Acts as a Scheme.* – In the first place it is contended by the plaintiffs that the Acts together constitute a "scheme" directed towards an unlawful object, namely, the exclusion of State

Parliaments from the sphere of legislation upon income tax … The contention that an Act which does not refer to or incorporate any other Act, and which when considered by itself is not invalid, may be held to be invalid by reason of the enactment of other Acts, whether valid or invalid, meets many difficulties. Parliament, when it passes an Act, either has power to pass that Act or has not power to pass that Act. In the former case it is plain that the enactment of other valid legislation cannot affect the validity of the first-mentioned Act if that Act is left unchanged. The enactment of other legislation which is shown to be invalid equally cannot have any effect upon the first-mentioned valid Act, because the other legislative action is completely nugatory and the valid Act simply remains valid.

Latham CJ held that the *Income Tax Act* was valid, since "[412] it is not possible for the Court to impose limitations upon the Parliament as to the rate of tax which it proposes to impose upon the people. There is no legal principle according to which a tax of 10s in the pound should be held to be valid, but a tax of 11s or 15s or 18s or 20s should be held to be invalid". As to the *States Grants (Income Tax Reimbursement) Act*, he said:

Latham CJ: [415] *The Grants Act.* – It is now necessary to deal with the far-reaching and fundamental general objection which is made to the *Tax Act* considered in association with the other Acts, but which is particularly directed against the *Grants Act*.

This objection is based upon the following principle which, it is argued, applies to all Commonwealth legislative powers, namely – the Commonwealth cannot direct its legislative powers towards destroying or weakening the constitutional functions or capacities of a State. (A corresponding rule should, it is said, be applied in favour of the Commonwealth as against the States.) In another form the principle is said to be that the Commonwealth cannot use its legislative powers to destroy either "the essential governmental functions" or "the normal activities" of a State …

[416] Upon [s 4 of the *Grants Act*] the following preliminary comments may be made: –

(*a*) The Act does not purport to repeal State income-tax legislation. The Commonwealth Parliament cannot do this. It cannot repeal an Act which it has no power to enact … Plainly the Commonwealth Parliament could not enact separate income-tax Acts for separate States. Nor can it repeal such Acts enacted by the States.

(*b*) The *Grants Act* does not require, in order that a State should qualify for a grant, that the State – or rather the State Parliament – should abdicate, or purport to abdicate, its power to impose taxes upon incomes. A State Parliament could not bind itself or its successors not to legislate upon a particular subject matter, not even, I should think, by referring a matter to the Commonwealth Parliament under sec 51(xxxvii) of the Constitution – but no decision upon that provision is called for in the present case. The grant becomes payable if the Treasurer is satisfied that a State has not in fact imposed a tax upon incomes in any particular year during the operation of the Acts.

(*c*) The Act does not purport to deprive the State Parliament of the power to impose an income tax. The Commonwealth Parliament cannot deprive any State of that power: see Constitution, secs 106, 107. Notwithstanding the *Grants Act* a State Parliament could at any time impose an income tax. The State would then not benefit by a grant under the Act, but there is nothing in the *Grants Act* which could make the State income-tax legislation invalid.

[417] (*d*) The *Grants Act* offers an inducement to the State Parliaments not to exercise a power the continued existence of which is recognized – the power to impose income tax. The States may or may not yield to this inducement, but there is no legal compulsion to yield.

The Commonwealth may properly induce a State to exercise its powers (eg the power to make roads: See *Victoria v Commonwealth* [(1926) 38 CLR 399]) by offering a money grant. So also the Commonwealth may properly induce a State by the same means to abstain from exercising its powers. For example, the Commonwealth might wish to exercise the powers given by the Constitution, sec 51(xiii) and (xiv) to legislate with respect to banking, other than State banking, and insurance, other than State insurance. The Commonwealth might wish to set up some Federal system of banking or insurance without any State competition. If the States were deriving revenue from State banking or State insurance, they might be prepared to retire from such activities upon receiving what they regarded as adequate compensation. The Commonwealth could properly, under Commonwealth legislation, make grants to the States upon condition of them so retiring. The States could not abdicate their powers by binding themselves not to re-enter the vacated field, but if the

Commonwealth, aware of this possibility, was prepared to pay money to a State which in fact gave up its system of State banking or insurance, there could be no objection on this ground to the validity of the Commonwealth law which authorized the payment.

But the position is radically different, it is urged, if the so-called inducement practically amounts to coercion. Admittedly the Commonwealth Parliament could not pass a law compelling a State to surrender the power to tax incomes or prohibiting the exercise of that power by a State. Equally, it is said, the Commonwealth cannot lawfully make an offer of money to a State which, under the conditions which actually exist, the State cannot, on political or economic grounds, really refuse.

This identification of a very attractive inducement with legal compulsion is not convincing. Action may be brought about by temptation – by offering a reward – or by compulsion. But temptation is not compulsion. A person whose hand is physically propelled by another person against his will so that it strikes a blow is not guilty of assault. But it would be no defence to allege that he really could not help striking the blow because he was offered £1,000 for doing it.

The argument referred to in this passage, that the Commonwealth "[415] cannot direct its legislative powers towards destroying or weakening the constitutional functions or capacities of a State", was a variant of the argument that Garfield Barwick KC was later to put successfully in *Melbourne Corporation v Commonwealth* (1947) 74 CLR 31 (see Chapter 25, §2(a)). The answer given by Latham CJ was that, so long as the legislation could be characterised as being "with respect to" a head of Commonwealth power, it was necessarily valid.

Latham CJ: [423] There is no universal or even general opinion as to what are the essential functions, capacities, powers, or activities of a State. Some would limit them to the administration of justice and police and necessary associated activities. There are those who object to State action in relation to health, education, and the development of natural resources. On the other hand, many would regard the provision of social services as an essential function of government. When Lord *Watson* said in *Coomber v Justices of Berks* [(1883) 9 App Cas 61 at 74] that "the administration of justice, the maintenance of order, and the repression of crime are among the primary and inalienable functions of a constitutional government," he was not purporting to give an exhaustive definition of the functions of government. In a fully self-governing country where a parliament determines legislative policy and an executive government carries it out, any activity may become a function of government if parliament so determines. It is not for a court to impose upon any parliament any political doctrine as to what are and what are not functions of government, or to attempt the impossible task of distinguishing, within functions of government, between essential and non-essential or between normal or abnormal. There is no sure basis for such a distinction. Only the firm establishment of some political doctrine as an obligatory dogma could bring about certainty in such a sphere, and Australia has not come to that.

Thus the principle for which the plaintiffs contend must be applied, if at all, in protection of all that a State chooses to do, and it must mean that Commonwealth legislation cannot be directed to weaken or destroy any State function or activity whatsoever.

But it cannot be denied that Commonwealth legislation may be valid though it does in fact weaken or destroy, and even is intended **[424]** to weaken or destroy, some State activity. Sec 109 shows that this must be so in many cases. Commonwealth laws have in fact put an end to the existence of State Courts of Bankruptcy and State Patent, Trade Mark and Copyright Departments. The Commonwealth laws are not invalid on that account. They have produced the results stated just because they are valid.

It is true that the Commonwealth Parliament has no power to make laws with respect to the capacity and functions of a State Parliament. It has already been stated that the Commonwealth Parliament could not pass a law to prohibit a State Parliament from legislating in general or from legislating upon some particular subject matter. But this limit upon the power of the Commonwealth Parliament does not arise from any prohibition or limitation to be implied from the Constitution. It is simply the result of the absence of power in the Commonwealth Parliament to pass laws with respect to the functions or powers of State Parliaments. The Commonwealth Parliament cannot legislate with respect to any subject whatever unless a power to do so is conferred on it by the Constitution. No power such as that mentioned is given by the Constitution to the Parliament.

But the Acts in question are not laws with respect to State functions. They do not command or prohibit any action by the State or by the State Parliament.

Indirect Effects of Laws. – A law may produce an effect in relation to a subject matter without being a law with respect to that subject matter. Questions of motive and object are irrelevant to the question of the true nature of a law. The nature (or "substance" if that word is preferred) of a law is to be determined by what it does, not by the effect in relation to other matters of what the law does. A prohibition of import or a very high duty in a customs tariff may bring about the closing of business enterprises in a State. But the tariff is not a law with respect to those enterprises. Similarly a State law may prohibit the carrying on of occupations with the result that they are necessarily abandoned, with perhaps great consequential loss to the Commonwealth in customs duties or income-tax receipts. But the State law does not for this reason become a law with respect to customs duties or income tax. The true nature of a law is to be ascertained by examining its terms and, speaking generally, ascertaining what it does in relation to duties, rights or powers which it creates, abolishes or regulates. The question may be put in these terms: "What does the law do in the way of changing or creating or destroying duties or rights or powers?" The consequential effects are irrelevant for this purpose. Even though an indirect **[425]** consequence of an Act, which consequence could not be directly achieved by the legislature, is contemplated and desired by Parliament, that fact is not relevant to the validity of the Act …

[426] The problem, as explained in the *Engineers' Case* [(1920) 28 CLR 129], is the different, though not always easy, problem of deciding whether a particular Commonwealth law falls within a head of Commonwealth power: if it does, it is immaterial that the States may also have power to legislate on the matter. If the law falls within the Commonwealth power, the law is valid and fully operative, notwithstanding any State law. *Barger's Case* [(1908) 6 CLR 41] is an illustration of the difficulty of deciding whether a particular law really does fall within a granted power, but … *Barger's Case* in all of the judgments rejects considerations of indirect consequences as being irrelevant material.

[427] Thus, although the Commonwealth Parliament cannot validly pass laws limiting the functions of State Parliaments – and *vice versa* – the *Tax Act* and the *Grants Act* are not invalid on that ground. They do not give any command or impose any prohibition with respect to the exercise of any State power, legislative or other. The *Tax Act* simply imposes Commonwealth taxation, and is authorized by sec 51(ii) of the Constitution. The *Grants Act* authorizes payments to States which choose to abstain from imposing income tax, and is valid by reason of sec 96 of the Constitution, unless it is bad as involving some prohibited discrimination or preference …

[429] *Conclusion as to Tax Act and Grants Act.* – Thus the objections to the *Tax Act* and the *Grants Act* fail, whether those Acts are considered separately or as part of a scheme to bring about the abandonment by the States of the raising of revenue by taxation of incomes.

It is perhaps not out of place to point out that the scheme which the Commonwealth has applied to income tax of imposing rates so high as practically to exclude State taxation could be applied to other taxes so as to make the States almost completely dependent, financially and therefore generally, upon the Commonwealth. If the Commonwealth Parliament, in a grants Act, simply provided for the payment of moneys to States, without attaching any conditions whatever, none of the legislation could be challenged by any of the arguments submitted to the Court in these cases. The amount of the grants could be determined in fact by the satisfaction of the Commonwealth with the policies, legislative or other, of the respective States, no reference being made to such matters in any Commonwealth statute. Thus, if the Commonwealth Parliament were prepared to pass such legislation, all State powers would be controlled by the Commonwealth – a result which would mean the end of the political independence of the States. Such a result cannot be prevented by any legal decision. The determination of the propriety of any such policy must rest with the Commonwealth Parliament and ultimately with the people. The remedy for alleged abuse of power or for the use of power to promote what are thought to be improper objects is to be found in the political arena and not in the Courts.

It was on this point that Starke J dissented.

Starke J: [442] The government of Australia is a dual system based upon a separation of organs and of powers. The maintenance of the States and their powers is as much the object of the Constitution as the maintenance of the Commonwealth and its powers. Therefore it is beyond the power of either to abolish or destroy the other. The limited grant of powers to the Commonwealth cannot be exercised for ends inconsistent with the separate existence and self-government of the States, nor for ends inconsistent with its limited grants ...

It cannot be doubted that the Commonwealth cannot expressly prohibit the States from exercising their powers of taxation, and that those powers cannot, subject to the provisions of the Constitution, sec 51(xxxviii), be appropriated by the Commonwealth nor abdicated by the States. The question in this case comes back to this: What is the object and operation of the *States Grants Act*? It purports in sec 4 to grant financial assistance to the States, but is it linked up with an object that is beyond the powers of the Commonwealth, namely, to control the exercise by the States of their powers to impose taxes upon income? ...

[443] In my opinion, the object of the Act is not merely to grant financial assistance to the States, but there is linked up in it an object and an end that is inconsistent with the limited grant of power given by sec 96 to the Commonwealth, namely, making the Commonwealth the sole effective taxing authority in respect of incomes and compensating the States for the resulting loss in income tax. The argument that the *States Grants Act* leaves a free choice to the States, offers them an inducement but deprives them of and interferes with no constitutional power, is specious but unreal. And it does not meet the substance of the States' position that the condition of the Act relates to a matter in respect of which the Commonwealth has no constitutional power whatever, and yet by force of the condition and not as a consequence of the exercise of any power conferred upon the Commonwealth, the grant of assistance to the States is withdrawn unless they comply with its terms. The real object of the condition is that already stated, and it is in my judgment neither contemplated by nor sanctioned by the Constitution, and in particular by sec 96 thereof. As I have said, all State legislation and functions might ultimately be so controlled and supervised. The possibility of the abuse of a power is not, however, an argument against the existence of a power. But if the extent of the power claimed by the Commonwealth leads to "results which it is impossible to believe ... the statute contemplated ... there is good reason for believing that the construction which leads to such results cannot be the true construction of the statute" (*R v Clarence* [(1888) 22 QBD 23 at 65]). A legitimate use of the powers contained in sec 96 may be found in the *Road Grants Case* (*Victoria v Commonwealth* [(1926) 38 CLR 399]), where the Commonwealth and the State of Victoria entered into an agreement, the object of which was to aid the State in the construction and reconstruction of certain roads. Incidentally the making of roads would be an aid to trade and commerce, and possibly also to defence: See *Federal Aid Roads Act* 1926 (No 46 of 1926). No doubt means can be found to give the States financial assistance without crippling them in the exercise of their powers of self-government if the Commonwealth taxation creates economic difficulties for them. But I cannot agree that the provisions of sec 96 enable the Commonwealth to condition that assistance upon the States abdicating their powers of taxation or, **[444]** which in substance is the same thing, not imposing taxes upon income. In my opinion, it follows that the *States Grants (Income Tax Reimbursement) Act* 1942 is not within the power or authority of the Commonwealth Parliament.

After World War II, the *States Grants (Income Tax Reimbursement) Act* was repealed but its broad scheme repeated on a permanent basis by the *States Grants (Tax Reimbursement) Act 1946* (Cth). The priority for the collection of Commonwealth income tax under s 221 of the *Income Tax Assessment Act* had been expressed to expire one financial year after World War II. In 1946, this time limit was repealed and the stated purpose of the priority altered from "for the efficient prosecution of the present war" to "for the purposes of the Commonwealth".

In 1957 this revised scheme was challenged in the *Second Uniform Tax Case*. Dixon CJ, McTiernan, Kitto and Taylor JJ held that the priority given to Commonwealth income tax over any State income tax in s 221 was invalid. Williams, Webb and Fullagar JJ dissented on this point. The main issue was the use of Commonwealth grants under s 96 to compensate the States for their lost income tax revenues. The whole Court held that this use of s 96 was valid.

Victoria v Commonwealth (Second Uniform Tax Case)
(1957) 99 CLR 575

Dixon CJ: [601] The whole plan of uniform taxation has thus become very much a recognised part of the Australian fiscal system. How far it really rests on the validity of the condition which forms an integral part of the *Tax Reimbursement Acts* and of s 221(1)(*a*) of the *Income Tax and Social Services Contribution Assessment Act* is, I think, open to question. But on the footing that it does so, the Court is now invited to depart from the decision in *South Australia v Commonwealth* [(1942) 65 CLR 373], either by treating it as wrongly decided or by distinguishing it as a decision resting in an essential degree on the scope of the defence power in time of war. Having regard to the lapse of time in which no State has taken proceedings seeking judicial relief against the statutes, to overrule the decision or even so to distinguish it must involve a grave judicial responsibility.

In the present proceedings the argument for the States took a course which differed from that adopted in the earlier case. It was more restricted. Then all four enactments assented to on 7th June 1942 were impugned as together forming a legislative scheme or plan of an unconstitutional character. The *"Arrangements" Act* has of course done its work and is spent. Of the three remaining statutory elements necessary to the "plan" or "scheme" upon which the argument in the earlier case based the attack, it was recognised that the validity of the *Taxing Act* must be conceded. There are two such Acts at present, the *Income Tax and Social Services Contribution Acts* 1956 (Nos 28 and 102). On its face such a measure is simply a taxing Act every word of which is within the power to make laws with respect to taxation. All that could be said is that the rates of tax are doubtless higher than they would have been if there were no "tax reimbursement" to the States. Each of the two provisions left, that is to say, s 221 of the *Assessment Act* and the *Tax Reimbursement Act*, is made the subject of a separate attack, on the ground that it lies outside the legislative power to which it has been referred and moreover attempts an unconstitutional interference with the States. The constitutional power to which s 221 is referred is of course that given by s 51(ii) of the Constitution with perhaps s 51(xxxix) operating in aid, and that to which the *Tax Reimbursement* provisions are referred is the power contained in s 96 of the Constitution.

[602] But while the ground for impugning validity in the case of each enactment is confined to a separate argument of *ultra vires* and is not based on the disclosure of an unconstitutional plan or scheme by the enactments considered in combination, reliance is placed on the planned inter-connexion of the provisions as giving each a purpose which may be material in considering whether it is a true exercise of the legislative power upon which its validity depends.

The question whether s 96 suffices to support the enactment of the *States Grants (Tax Reimbursement) Act* 1946-1948 is the first matter to decide. It is affected more by decided cases than is the validity of s 221 which, as it seems to me, has the support of no judicial decision except *South Australia v Commonwealth* …

[605] [I]t is apparent that the power to grant financial assistance to any State upon such terms and conditions as the Parliament thinks fit is susceptible of a very wide construction in which few if any restrictions can be implied. For the restrictions could only be implied from some conception of the purpose for which the particular power was conferred upon the Parliament or from some general constitutional limitations upon the powers of the Parliament which otherwise an exercise of the power given by s 96 might transcend. In the case of what may briefly be described as coercive powers it may not be difficult to perceive that limitations of such a kind must be intended. But in s 96 there is nothing coercive. It is but a power to make grants of money and to impose conditions on the grant, there being no power of course to compel acceptance of the grant and with it the accompanying term or condition.

Dixon CJ then discussed the *Federal Roads Case* and *Moran's Case*, referring to them as "**[605]** what amounts to a course of decisions upon s 96 all amplifying the power and tending to a denial of any restriction upon the purpose of the appropriation or the character of the condition". As to the statutory provisions held valid in *Moran's Case*, he said:

Dixon CJ: [606] Now it might have been thought **[607]** that these provisions were outside s 96 because they gave no assistance to the State as a body politic but used it only as a conduit or an agency by which the moneys would be distributed among the wheat growers of the State … In fact, however, the provision was considered to amount to financial assistance to the State notwithstanding that the State was bound to distribute the money it received to the wheat grower.

The decision, which was affirmed in the Privy Council [[1940] AC 838], without express reference to this use of s 96, must mean that s 96 is satisfied if the money is placed in the hands of the State notwithstanding that in the exercise of the power to impose terms and conditions the State is required to pay over the money to a class of persons in or connected with the State in order to fulfil some purpose pursued by the Commonwealth and one outside its power to effect directly. I should myself find it difficult to accept this doctrine in full and carry it into logical effect, but the decision shows that the Court placed no limitation upon the terms or conditions it was competent to the Commonwealth to impose under s 96 and regarded the conception of assistance to a State as going beyond and outside subventions to or the actual supplementing of the financial resources of the Treasury of a State ...

[609] In the present attack upon the validity of the *Tax Reimbursement Act* 1946-1948 the two States that are plaintiffs naturally rest heavily upon the argument that the Act is a law for the restriction or control of the States in the exercise of their taxing powers, that on its face the purpose appears of compelling the States to abstain from imposing taxes upon income. If s 96 came before us for the first time for interpretation, the contention might be supported on the ground that the true scope and purpose of the power which s 96 confers upon the Parliament of granting money and imposing terms and conditions did not admit of any attempt to influence the direction of the exercise by the State of its legislative or executive powers. It may well be that s 96 was conceived by the framers as (1) a transitional power, (2) confined to supplementing the resources of the Treasury of a State by particular subventions when some special or particular need or occasion arose, and (3) imposing terms or conditions relevant to the situation which called for special relief of assistance from the Commonwealth. It seems a not improbable supposition that the framers had some such conception of the purpose of the power. But the course of judicial decision has put any such limited interpretation of s 96 out of consideration. In any case it must be borne in mind that the power conferred by s 96 is confined to granting money and moreover to granting money to governments. It is not a power to make laws with respect to a general subject matter, which for reasons such as I gave in *Melbourne Corporation v Commonwealth* [(1947) 74 CLR 31], may be taken to fall short of authorising a special attempt to control the exercise of the constitutional powers of the States where there is a connexion with some part of the subject matter of the federal [610] power. The very matter with which the power conferred by s 96 is concerned relates to State finance. Further there is nothing which would enable the making of a coercive law. By coercive law is meant one that demands obedience. As is illustrated by *Melbourne Corporation v Commonwealth*, the duty may be imposed, not on the State or its servants, but on others and yet its intended operation may interfere unconstitutionally with the governmental functions of the State in such a way as to take the law outside federal power. But nothing of this sort could be done by a law which in other respects might amount to an exercise of the power conferred by s 96. For the essence of an exercise of that power must be a grant of money or its equivalent and beyond that the legislature can go no further than attaching conditions to the grant. Once it is certain that a law which is either valid under s 96 or not at all does contain a grant of financial assistance to the States, the further inquiry into its validity could not go beyond the admissibility of the terms and conditions that the law may have sought to impose. The grant of money may supply the inducement to comply with the term or condition. But beyond that no law passed under s 96 can go.

Once the interpretation is accepted in full which the decisions in *Victoria v Commonwealth* [(1926) 38 CLR 399], and in *Moran's Case* [(1939) 61 CLR 735; [1940] AC 838] combine to place upon the section it becomes difficult indeed to find safe ground for saying that the condition of the grant of financial assistance may not be that a particular form of tax shall not be imposed by the State. The interpretation flowing from these two decisions is not consistent with the view that there must be a need for relief or a reason for giving assistance which is not itself created by the Commonwealth legislation connected with the grant. It is inconsistent with the view that the terms or conditions cannot require the exercise of governmental powers of the State and require the State to conform with the desires of the Commonwealth in the exercise of such powers. It seems a short step from this to saying that the condition may stipulate for the exercise or non-exercise of the State's general legislative power in some particular or specific respect. Once this step is taken it becomes easier to ask than to answer the question – "Why then does this not apply to the legislative power of imposing this or that form of taxation?"

In short the result of my consideration of the two prior decisions upon s 96 has been to convince me that the decision of the majority **[611]** of the Court with respect to the *Tax Reimbursement Act* in *South Australia v Commonwealth* was but an extension of the interpretation already placed upon s 96 of the Constitution. The three decisions certainly harmonise and they combine to give to s 96 a consistent and coherent interpretation and they each involve the entire exclusion of the limited operation which might have been assigned to the power as an alternative.

Before the meaning of s 96 and the scope of the power it gives had been the subject of judicial decision no one seems to have been prepared to speak with any confidence as to its place in the constitutional plan and its intended operation. It may be said perhaps that while others asked where the limits of what could be done in virtue of the power the section conferred were to be drawn, the Court has said that none are drawn; that any enactment is valid if it can be brought within the literal meaning of the words of the section and as to the words "financial assistance" even that is unnecessary. For it may be said that a very extended meaning has been given to the words "grant financial assistance to any State" and that they have received an application beyond that suggested by a literal interpretation.

But even if the meaning of s 96 had seemed more certain, it would, in my opinion, be impossible to disregard the cumulative authority of the three cases I have discussed and conclude that ss 5 and 11 of the *Tax Reimbursement Act* are invalid. I therefore think that the validity of that Act must be upheld.

Dixon CJ treated the cumulative effect of the *Federal Roads Case*, *Moran's Case* and the *First Uniform Tax Case* as decisively establishing that the Commonwealth may attach any conditions it wishes to a s 96 grant. Simultaneously, however, he outlined the narrower view he might have taken "**[609]** if s 96 came before us for the first time". Note the limitations that he felt able to impose without controverting these decisions. The power is confined "to granting money and moreover to granting money to governments". It is not "a power to make laws with respect to a general subject matter", though this is double-edged: in *Melbourne Corporation*, he had held that a "general" power of that kind might be subject to an implied limitation so as not to extend to interference with the States' constitutional functions, but the passage in the *Second Uniform Tax Case* seems to say that because the grants power necessarily "**[610]** relates to State finance", it is subject to no such limitation.

In addition, Dixon CJ suggested that s 96 cannot be used to "enable the making of a coercive law" (that is, "one that demands obedience"). This, too, may be equivocal. In ruling out "coercive" laws, he may have meant only that, in laying down policies which it wishes the States to follow, the Commonwealth can use a carrot but not a stick. The "coercive" laws that he excludes would then be only those which exert "coercion" on the States. This would rule out certain kinds of legislative sanctions, rather than any legislative policies.

On the other hand, his insistence that s 96 is only a "spending" power suggests that under s 96 the Commonwealth is confined to those policies that essentially involve the distribution of money. It can confer financial benefits on the States, or on others through the "conduit" of the States, but it cannot impose a regulatory scheme designed to order the behaviour of citizens as most "ordinary" legislation does. Such "ordinary" legislation could only be justified by reference to a specific head of legislative power, not as a mere by-product of "spending".

The *First Uniform Tax Case* is sometimes regarded as "**[325]** the high-water mark of the doctrine from the *Engineers' Case*" (PJ Hanks, *Constitutional Law in Australia* (Butterworths, 2nd ed 1996)). This is partly because the refusal to consider the implications of the legislative "scheme" exemplified the literal approach to statutory construction laid down in the *Engineers' Case*, and partly because of the outright rejection (except by Starke J) of the kind of argument which was later to succeed in *Melbourne Corporation*.

A feature of the "new federalism" announced by the Fraser government in 1976 was an undertaking to allow the States to re-impose personal income tax. The framework for such a re-entry was provided by the *Income Tax (Arrangements with the States) Act 1978* (Cth). No State took advantage of this legislation and it was repealed in 1989.

(c)   Fiscal Imbalance

State reimbursement under the uniform tax scheme has been in the form of "general revenue grants", supplemented where necessary by "special assistance grants". In addition, the States have received "specific purpose grants" tied through s 96 conditions to expenditure for a specific purpose. The implementation of Commonwealth policies in fields such as tertiary education, where the Constitution gives the Commonwealth no legislative power, was initially dependent entirely on such grants, though it seems that in relation to the funding of universities the Commonwealth's reliance on s 96 has now been abandoned (see *Higher Education Funding Amendment Act (No 2) 1992* (Cth) and subsequent legislation).

While "special assistance grants" have been one solution to the problem of "horizontal fiscal imbalance", "specific purpose grants" have been a major source of the problem of "vertical fiscal imbalance". These terms are explained below:

Russell Mathews, *Revenue Sharing in Federal Systems*
(Centre for Research on Federal Financial Relations, Australian National University, Research Monograph No 31, 1980)

[10] *Vertical Fiscal Imbalance*

The growth of the public sector and the shift to responsibility sharing among governments have made it difficult for most federations to maintain vertical fiscal balance, defined as a situation in which governments at each level can command the financial resources necessary for them to carry out their expenditure responsibilities and be held accountable for both spending and taxing decisions. Because expenditure needs change over time, vertical balance implies the existence of a flexible source of taxation revenue for each unit of government.

The factors contributing to vertical fiscal imbalance have been, first, the concentration of financial power and flexible revenue sources, in particular income taxes with their progressive rate structures and built-in revenue elasticity, in the hands of federal governments; and, second, the rapid growth in the costs of providing education, health, transport, urban and other services for which the states (and in some countries, local governments) continue to have the main responsibility. Federal taxation revenues have thus tended to grow at a faster rate than gross domestic product, while demographic, social and structural changes affecting the economy have tended to encourage state expenditures to increase more rapidly than gross domestic product.

[11] The resulting budgetary imbalances have led to political pressures from state and local governments for the transfer of revenue sources from federal governments or, alternatively, for intergovernmental grants in the form of general revenue-sharing payments. Where these vertical fiscal adjustments have taken the form of the opening up of tax room for lower-level governments by a reduction in federal tax rates, or of co-ordinated decisions based on mutual agreement about levels of taxes and how they are to be shared, there has been no conflict between revenue sharing and fiscal responsibility. Where, however, grants or other revenue-sharing arrangements have depended on unilateral decisions by federal governments which have broken the link between spending and taxing decisions for both granting and recipient governments, there has been a loss of accountability and a weakening of democratic controls over all the governments concerned. The situation is not improved where state governments are able to mobilise political power to offset the superior financial power of federal governments; although bargaining strength may be more equal under these circumstances, there is no reason to believe that any revenue-sharing arrangements which result from the bargaining will achieve vertical fiscal balance.

Horizontal Fiscal Imbalance

The need for state and local governments to extend the range and increase the scale of public goods and services has also accentuated the problem of horizontal fiscal imbalance, even in countries where federal governments have responsibility for making social welfare payments to individuals. Horizontal fiscal balance may be defined as a situation in which each unit within a particular level of government (eg each state in a federal system) has the capacity to provide services at a standard comparable to that of other units provided that it imposes taxes and charges at a comparable standard. Horizontal **[12]** fiscal balance does not imply uniformity of service provision or uniformity of revenue-raising arrangements as between units of government within the same level. It is the capacity of governments to provide comparable services, provided they impose comparable taxes and charges, which needs to be equal in a state of horizontal fiscal balance. Two governments with equal fiscal capacity may decide on different levels of service provision and revenue raising, and on different patterns of expenditure and taxation, without causing a departure from horizontal fiscal balance.

However, because the different units of government within a particular level cannot be expected to have equal fiscal capacity (involving both equality of revenue-raising capacity and equality in costs of providing comparable services) except by chance, horizontal fiscal balance in a federal system implies the existence of some sort of revenue-sharing arrangements or equalisation grants to remove the inequalities.

It is possible to conceive of a system of responsibility sharing without revenue sharing, and the achievement of vertical fiscal balance is not necessarily dependent on some form of revenue sharing or intergovernmental grants arrangements. But intergovernmental fiscal equalisation arrangements in one form or another are a necessary condition for horizontal fiscal balance.

Indeed, it may reasonably be claimed that an effective system of fiscal equalisation is one of the principal requirements for an efficient, equitable and responsive federal system. It is the means of reconciling equality and diversity, of giving all citizens in the federation access to public goods and services on a comparable basis while simultaneously permitting greater freedom of choice in relation to the scale, pattern and financing of those services.

The goods and services tax (GST) introduced by the Howard government during its second term of office ushered in a new approach to these problems. The GST came into effect from 1 July 2000, levied at a flat rate of 10 per cent on a wide range of goods and services. In return for an agreement by the States to remove or review certain State taxes, the Commonwealth guaranteed that the proceeds of the GST would be wholly transferred to the States. Some have seen this arrangement as an innovative and effective solution to the endemic problems of Australian fiscal federalism; others have argued that it undermines the autonomy of the States even further by making them more dependent on funding controlled by the Commonwealth.

Cheryl Saunders, "Federal Fiscal Reform and the GST"
(2000) 11 *Public Law Review* 99

[101] The main features of the new federal fiscal arrangements are set out in the Intergovernmental Agreement on the Reform of Commonwealth-State Financial Relations. The Agreement, in turn, implements the principles agreed by governments at the Special Premiers' Conference on 13 November 1998 … The Agreement is expressed to come into effect on 1 July 1999 and is scheduled to the *A New Tax System (Commonwealth-State Financial Arrangements) Act* 1999 (Cth) (the Act).

A key undertaking in the Agreement concerns the distribution of all GST revenue to the States and Territories. Additional grants or interest-free loans will continue to be made by the Commonwealth to the States for the first few years … After the first two years, the Agreement requires GST revenues to be distributed [among] the States and Territories in accordance with fiscal equalisation principles … A carefully worded clause undertakes that there will be no reduction in specific purpose payments as part of the tax reform process.

A second key undertaking prescribes the unanimous agreement of all State and Territory governments, the "endorsement" of the Commonwealth government, and passage of legislation by the Commonwealth Parliament, as prerequisites for variation of the rate of the GST …

A third series of provisions in the Agreement concerns the efficiency and integrity of the taxation system in general. Both the Commonwealth and the States undertake to "cease to apply" certain taxes, immediately or at a future agreed time. The [102] revenue thus foregone by the States will be taken into account for the purpose of calculating their entitlement to additional payments during the transitional period ....

[103] The Act provides for the payment to the States of the revenue raised by the GST in the form of GST Revenue Grants. A formula prescribes the manner in which each State's grant is to be determined annually. The formula depends in part on each State's "relativities factor". This is to be determined by the Treasurer each year and, before doing so, the Treasurer "must consult each of the States". The Act does not refer to the Commonwealth Grants Commission, whose reports have always provided the basis for calculation of relativities, nor to the Ministerial Council, charged with the responsibility of "discussion of [Commonwealth Grants Commission] recommendations regarding relativities" under cl 42(iv) of the Agreement. The States are described as "entitled" to the GST grants and the moneys are "appropriated accordingly". However, the grants are to be paid in amounts and at times determined by the Treasurer. All determinations by the Treasurer under the Act are "conclusively presumed to be correct" ...

[104] In some respects, the changes in federal financial arrangements that accompany the introduction of the GST are an improvement on current arrangements. Some unsatisfactory State taxes are abolished and replaced by the more efficient GST. Revenue redistribution is placed on a more principled and less arbitrary footing, providing the States with access to a revenue source that can be expected to grow. There is potential for revenue redistribution to be removed from the annual intergovernmental political agenda altogether or, at least, from the meetings of Heads of Government, giving them the opportunity to focus on other things.

The scheme has problems as well, however, from the standpoint of fiscal federalism and it is not yet clear where the balance of advantage will lie.

Most obviously, the immediate effect of the scheme is to increase the vertical fiscal imbalance and to make the States more dependent on revenue redistribution from the Commonwealth. This might matter less if the State entitlement to GST revenues were secure. In this regard, both the fact and the manner of incorporation of the arrangements in legislation, by reference to State "entitlements" are significant. Legislation can be changed, however. Interestingly enough, this particular change is not expressed to be subject to prior State consent.

Issues of the accountability of governments to their Parliaments are also largely ignored ... An arrangement that suggests that changes in the rate or base of taxation imposed by one sphere of government [are] dependent on agreement by another presents obvious difficulties for accountability, as generally conceived. The complication that the requirement for the agreement by the other governments is unenforceable in law arguably detracts from accountability further, by confusing the issue.

This difficulty might have been overcome, at least in part, by a clear recognition that the old link between tax and spending no longer applies in the same form and by making the replacement procedures as transparent as possible. In other words, the Act might have acknowledged that in Australia, for reasons of public convenience, most taxation is raised by one sphere of government on behalf of the others, as well as itself. It does not do so, however. There is nothing in the Act to suggest that the GST is anything other than a Commonwealth tax, redistributed by the Commonwealth to the States as "grants". Apart from the requirement for State consent to changes to the rate and base, which is motivated by the desire to be perceived to cap the GST rather than to share decision-making with the States, there is little reflection of the intergovernmental nature of the scheme in the Act. There is no mention, for example, of the Ministerial [105] Council through which the consultation with the States on a range of matters is supposed to occur.

From the standpoint of accountability at the State level, the situation is worse. The States also have parliamentary systems, which assume that State governments are accountable to State Parliaments for decisions about taxing and spending. This principle is displaced to a degree when State governments receive substantial sums by way of grants, which they have not themselves raised by taxation. The GST arrangements present the further difficulty that State governments are ostensibly involved in decisions about increasing taxes, the proceeds of which will flow to them as grants, but again without authority from State Parliaments.

At the same time, through the Agreement, State governments have foresworn the imposition of certain State taxes as long as the Agreement is in force. These undertakings are not enforceable in law either. Unless a State complies, however, it might find that its GST grant is cut. Australian experience with the uniform income tax shows that this is a powerful means of deterring the States from reimposing taxes that they have abandoned but which still lie within their constitutional power. This feature of the GST legislation suggests the sobering possibility that Australian federal history may be about to repeat itself.

According to the New South Wales Treasury (*2005-06 Budget Papers* (Budget Paper No 2), Ch 8), that State expected to receive $16,796 million in the form of Commonwealth grants over the 2005-06 financial year. This was made up of $10,675 million in General Purpose Payments (composed of a $10,410 million GST Revenue Grant and a $265 million National Competition Policy Payment) and $6121 million in Specific Purpose Payments.

New South Wales Treasury, *2005-06 Budget Papers*
(Budget Paper No 2), Ch 8

[14] Vertical Fiscal Imbalance ...
The introduction of the GST worsened this imbalance because States abolished a number of their own taxes. The Commonwealth collects over 80 percent of the taxation revenue (including the GST), but is responsible for around 54 percent of own-purpose outlays. The States collect around 16 percent of taxation revenue and account for around 39 percent of own-purpose outlays. Commonwealth grants now account for around 40 percent of New South Wales' revenues, compared with slightly over one-third before the introduction of the GST.

Horizontal Fiscal Equalisation
GST revenue grants are allocated among the States according to the principle of horizontal fiscal equalisation which states:
- State governments should receive funding from the pool of goods and services tax revenue and health care grants such that, if each made the same effort to raise revenue from its own sources and operated at the same level of efficiency, each would have the capacity to provide services at the same standard ...

[15] Comparison with Equal Per Capita Funding
In 2005-06, New South Wales will receive $10,410 million of the total GST pool of $37,287 million. But New South Wales receives significantly less in GST revenue grants than if funding were based solely on population shares.
- New South Wales' GST revenue grants in 2005-06 will be $1,526 per capita or 16 percent less than the average of all the States;
- The average GST revenue grant in 2005-06 for New South Wales and Victoria (the donor States) will be $1,537 per capita, compared with an average of $2,211 per capita for the recipient States ...

In 2005-06, New South Wales and Victoria will subsidise the recipient States by $3,363 million, compared with an equal per capita distribution. New South Wales alone will transfer $2,010 million, or $295 per capita, to the recipient States ...

[16] Comparison with GST Generated by States
An alternative method of measuring the level of transfers from donor to recipient States is to compare GST revenue grants with the amount of GST generated by activity in each State.

On this basis, activity in New South Wales is estimated to generate around $13.2 billion in GST revenue in 2005-06, while receiving GST revenue grants of around $10.4 billion. This is a cross-subsidy to other States of around $2.8 billion, or $407 per capita. New South Wales receives around 79 cents for every $1 in GST generated in this State.

(d)   Limits?

Clause 5(v) of the 1999 Intergovernmental Agreement on the Reform of Commonwealth-State Financial Relations provides: "The Commonwealth will continue to provide Specific Purpose Payments (SPPs) to the States and Territories and has no intention of cutting aggregate SPPs as part of the reform process set out in this Agreement". Thus, apart from the use of s 96 as the mechanism by which the proceeds of the GST will be portioned out to the States, the section will continue to be used for the implementation of Commonwealth policy through "specific purpose grants".

It seems clear that the tailoring of GST Revenue Grants to "relativities factors" as between States is unlikely to raise constitutional problems. One effect of the High Court decision in *Moran's Case* was that s 96 is not subject to the prohibitions on discrimination and preference contained in ss 51(ii) and 99 of the Constitution.

In other respects, too, "specific purpose grants" may be used not only to overcome an *absence* of Commonwealth legislative power, but to circumvent specific *restrictions* on Commonwealth legislative power. For example, one express limitation is the requirement in s 51(xxxi) that any acquisition of property for Commonwealth purposes be "on just terms"; but in *Pye v Renshaw* (1951) 84 CLR 58, the Court allowed the use of s 96 to circumvent the need for "just terms" by holding that, because a grant made under s 96 is not itself an "acquisition of property" by the Commonwealth, it is not subject to s 51(xxxi).

On the other hand, it has been established that s 96 is subject to s 116 of the Constitution, which provides in part: "The Commonwealth shall not make any law for establishing any religion". When the use of s 96 as a channel for Commonwealth funds to Church schools was challenged in *Attorney-General (Vic); Ex rel Black v Commonwealth* (*DOGS Case*) (1981) 146 CLR 559, the plaintiffs argued that s 96 is constrained by s 116. The question did not strictly arise for decision, since the Court held by 6:1 (with Murphy J dissenting) that the aid to Church schools did not involve "establishing any religion". Nevertheless, the Court took the view that laws made under s 96 are subject to s 116.

Attorney-General (Vic); Ex rel Black v Commonwealth (*DOGS Case*)
(1981) 146 CLR 559

Gibbs J: [592] The question is whether if the conditions of a grant of financial assistance require the State to which the grant is made to establish a religion within the meaning of that section, the Act by which the grant is authorized is invalid as contrary to s 116. It is plain, as *Deputy Federal Commissioner of Taxation (NSW) v WR Moran Pty Ltd* [(1939) 61 CLR 735] shows, that a condition may be imposed under s 96 for the purpose of persuading a State to do something which the Commonwealth itself could not do. *Pye v Renshaw* [(1951) 84 CLR 58] provides another example. The cases show that the Parliament has wide power to fix the terms and conditions of a grant made under s 96. In *Victoria v Commonwealth* (the *Roads Case*) [(1926) 38 CLR 406], it was said that the *Federal Aid Roads Act* 1926 was "plainly warranted by the provisions of s 96 of the Constitution, and not affected by those of s 99 or any other provision of the Constitution", and the statement that grants made under s 96 are not affected by any other provision of the Constitution was repeated in *Deputy Federal Commissioner of Taxation (NSW) v WR Moran Pty Ltd*. On the other hand, in *Adelaide Company of Jehovah's Witnesses Inc v Commonwealth* [(1943) 67 CLR 116 at 123], Latham CJ said that s 116 "prevails over **[593]** and limits all provisions" [of the Constitution] "which give power to make laws", and McTiernan J [67 CLR at 156] said that the section "imposes a restriction on all the legislative powers of Parliament". I consider that the ordinary rules of statutory construction should be applied, and that ss 96 and 116 should be read together, the result being that the Commonwealth has power to grant financial assistance to any State on such terms and conditions as the Parliament thinks fit, provided that a law passed for that purpose does not contravene s 116. It is one thing to say that the Parliament, by a condition imposed under 96, could achieve a result which it lacks power to bring about by direct legislation, but quite another to say that the Parliament can frame a condition for the purpose of evading an express prohibition contained in the Constitution. As the Judicial Committee pointed out in *WR Moran Pty Ltd v Deputy Federal Commissioner of Taxation (NSW)* [[1940] AC 838 at 855], the powers given by s 51 of the Constitution are expressly made "subject to this Constitution" which includes s 96. On the other hand, s 116 is not expressed to be subject to the Constitution. Of course the same is true of s 99, but that section speaks of "any law or regulation of trade, commerce or revenue" and a law under s 96 cannot properly be regarded as such a law: see *Deputy Federal Commissioner of Taxation (NSW) v WR Moran Pty Ltd* [61 CLR at 775]. However, whether or not the provisions of s 51 can be "completely disregarded" in deciding upon the validity of a law made under s 96 (as to which see *WR Moran Pty Ltd v Deputy Federal Commissioner of Taxation (NSW))* [[1940] AC at 858-9], I consider that the Parliament, acting under s 96, cannot pass a law which conflicts with s 116. To take an unlikely example, an Act which granted money to a State on condition that the State would prohibit entirely the exercise of a particular religion would, in my opinion, be a law for prohibiting the free exercise of that religion, and would be invalid.

Wilson J: [657] I have already expressed the opinion that a law which finds its authority in s 96 is nevertheless subject to s 116. For the purpose of examining the validity of the States Grants legislation by reference to the latter section I have assumed that the laws were otherwise authorized by the former section. I turn now to consider the plaintiffs' attack based on s 96 ... The plaintiffs submit that the essential feature of the scheme is that it is the Commonwealth, either Parliament or the Minister or his delegate, that makes every relevant decision in connection with a grant. The State may elect whether or not to accept the grant, and that is all. The only function of the State is to pay money, in amounts fixed by the Commonwealth, to a school or school system nominated by the Commonwealth, to make an agreement with the school authority in terms which are determined by the Commonwealth, to receive repayment from a school authority of such amounts as the Commonwealth determines ought to be re-paid by a school authority in the event of a breach of the agreement with the State, and then to repay that amount to the Commonwealth. In many cases, capital grants paid to a school enable the erection of buildings owned by the religion sponsoring the school. The conditions attached to the grant require the school authority of the school or school system as the case may be to relate directly to the Commonwealth, for example, in accounting for moneys spent, and in the provisions of statistical information.

In these circumstances, the plaintiffs submit that the grants cannot be described as grants of financial assistance to the **[658]** States within the meaning of s 96. They give no assistance to a State as a body politic but use it merely as a conduit or an agency by which moneys are distributed to schools and school systems upon conditions fixed by the Commonwealth ...

[659] The plaintiffs distinguish *Moran*, notwithstanding an apparent similarity to the present case, as basically different. They observe that the legislation in that case, the *Wheat Industry Assistance Act* was promoted by the States, that the Commonwealth was a partner in the scheme and made the grants at the instigation of the States as bodies politic, albeit that they were eventually to be paid to a class of persons. The machinery of State government was necessarily involved in the administration of the scheme, and it was wrong therefore to describe the States as mere agents of the Commonwealth, with no discretionary responsibility.

I must confess that I have great sympathy with the plaintiffs' argument. The legislation provides a striking contrast in the discretion that is accorded to the States in the administration of the grants for government schools and the virtually total disregard of the States, save only for the barest acknowledgment of the formalities required by s 96, in the administration of the grants for non-government schools. The contrast is all the more remarkable in the context of a constitution which in the distribution of power within the federation does not confer on the Commonwealth Parliament a specific legislative power with respect to education.

But unfortunately for the success of their argument, the plaintiffs mistake policy for law. The Court is not concerned with the wisdom or the expediency of the former, and the features of the scheme of which the plaintiffs complain are of this character. In the present state of the authorities, the legislation satisfies the requirements of s 96 for a valid law. It is a non-coercive law which in terms grants money to each of the States **[660]** "by way of financial assistance to the State". The freedom of each State to decide whether to accept or reject the grant, however restricted it may be in a political sense, is legally fundamental to the validity of the scheme, and its existence as a matter of law cannot be denied. The conditions attaching to the grant are those to be determined by the Commonwealth, but this has always been so. It is not necessary that the grant should benefit the State Treasury directly, or that the purpose of the grant should be within the express legislative power of the Commonwealth, or that the State should be the instigator or even a party to the initiation of the scheme.

In addition to the significance of the State's decision to accept the grant, the necessity for it then to enter into an agreement with the eventual recipient of a grant is also significant. The State enters into that agreement, not as an agent for the Commonwealth, but as a principal.

Wilson J finally decided that, "[659] [i]n the present state of the authorities", the use of s 96 as an instrument of Commonwealth policy was valid. The earlier precedents, especially *Moran's Case*, were not challenged in the *DOGS Case*. If such a challenge had been attempted, Wilson J suggested that he would have had "[659] great sympathy" with such an argument. Note that since *Viro v R* (1978) 141 CLR 88 the High Court has not regarded itself as bound by Privy Council decisions: that is, it would now be possible for the High Court to reject *Moran's Case*, whereas no such rejection was possible in either of the *Uniform Tax Cases*.

What Wilson J took up in the *DOGS Case* from the judgment of Dixon CJ in the *Second Uniform Tax Case* was not the idea that s 96 cannot be used for "coercive" laws; he held explicitly that State aid to Church schools is not in that sense "coercive". What he adopted were the "misgivings" expressed by Dixon CJ about the use of State governments, through conditional grants under s 96, "[658] only as a conduit or an agency" for the implementation of Common-wealth policy.

Such "misgivings" have several grounds. One is that to use a State government as a mere "conduit" reduces it to a mechanical instrumentality of Commonwealth policy, leaving the State with no governmental policy-making function of its own (there may be overtones here of *Melbourne Corporation v Commonwealth* (1947) 74 CLR 31 – see Chapter 25, §2(a)). A second reason for concern is that expressed by Latham CJ in *Bank of NSW v Commonwealth* (*Bank Nationalisation Case*) (1948) 76 CLR 1: that "[184] no single power should be construed in such a way as to render absurd the assignment of [185] particular carefully defined powers to that Parliament". If this is true of the specific enumerated heads of power in s 51, one would equally expect it to be true of s 96. Indeed, the main criticism of the use of "specific purpose grants" since the 1950s has been of the way they have enabled the Commonwealth to dominate policy-making in areas where the Constitution assigns it no power at all.

In one sense, the grants power has provided a solution to the problem of "vertical fiscal imbalance". For expensive public responsibilities such as roads, schools and hospitals, one aspect of "imbalance" is that the States have the necessary legislative power, while the Commonwealth has the necessary revenue. The use of s 96 has eased this problem by allowing the transfer of resources to the seats of relevant power, and since July 2000 the flow of "GST Revenue Grants" has increasingly provided the States with a secure revenue base (though perhaps still not an adequate base).

However, this enhanced revenue base still involves dependency on resources raised and dis-tributed through Commonwealth laws and policies. Moreover, the States' critical lack of revenue had partly come about because of the uniform tax scheme, and hence because of the use of s 96. Thus, in another sense it was the use of s 96 that had escalated the traditional problem of "vertical fiscal imbalance". Recall that one of Mathews' major concerns over "vertical fiscal imbalance" was the breaking of "[11] the link between spending and taxing decisions". The judgments made in raising revenue, and the judgments made in expending it, were in his view most responsibly made if both are made by the same power-wielders, who are sensitive to their interdependence. His main concern was not so much with responsibility in a budgetary or accountancy sense, as with fundamental political principles of democratic responsibility and accountability to the electorate. Saunders' suggestion that we might rethink these fundamental principles on the basis of "[104] a clear recognition that the old link between tax and spending no longer applies" remains to be fully developed.

Finally, Commonwealth policy may have been distorted because its implementation through "specific purpose grants" has *not* in fact given the Commonwealth unlimited policy-making control. If the Commonwealth's entry into a field is ultimately through a "spending" power, its political objectives will be determined accordingly. In some of the major areas of Commonwealth intervention over the past four decades, the original impetus seems to have come from a political need to find a new and electorally attractive form of public largesse. Later modifications have come from the need to reduce the amount of largesse. Either way, the policy-making focus is on the distribution of money. The result is that whole areas of policy, on topics ranging from universities to nursing homes, have been determined, not by constructive assessment of the functional needs of such institutions and their clientele, but on the basis of the goals set by successive governments for their system of money-distribution. Obviously, all responsible policy-making gives some weight to such factors. However, the argument is that, in areas covered by "specific purpose grants" under s 96, the money-distribution tail has wagged the policy dog.

3. Further References

Coper, M, *Encounters with the Australian Constitution* (CCH, 1988), Ch 5.

Galligan, B, *Politics of the High Court* (University of Queensland Press, 1987), Ch 4, 148-57.

Gerard, G, "A Reply to the AAP Case" (1977) 2 *University of New South Wales Law Journal* 105.

Mathews, RL, and Grewal, B, *The Public Sector in Jeopardy: Australian Fiscal Federalism from Whitlam to Keating* (Centre for Strategic Economic Studies, Victoria University, 1997).

Saunders, C, "The Development of the Commonwealth Spending Power" (1978) 11 *Melbourne University Law Review* 369.

Saunders, C, "The Uniform Income Tax Cases" in Lee, HP, and Winterton, G (eds), *Australian Constitutional Landmarks* (Cambridge University Press, 2003), 62.

Saunders, C, "Towards a Theory for Section 96" (1987-88) 16 *Melbourne University Law Review* 1 (Pt I), 699 (Pt II).

Chapter 25

Intergovernmental Immunities

1. Intergovernmental Immunities

Australian federalism has been shaped both by the express prohibitions of discrimination and preference in ss 51(ii) and 99 of the Constitution, and by "intergovernmental immunities" – that is, by the idea that the Commonwealth and the States might (impliedly) be wholly or partly immune from each other's laws. However, the express provisions have been interpreted in a way that has rendered them largely ineffective (see Chapter 6, §4). Instead, it has been left to intergovernmental immunities to maintain the autonomy and integrity of the two tiers of government.

According to the reciprocal doctrine of "implied immunity of instrumentalities" spelled out in *D'Emden v Pedder* (1904) 1 CLR 91 and *Federated Amalgamated Government Railway and Tramway Service Association v New South Wales Railway Traffic Employes Association* (*Railway Servants' Case*) (1906) 4 CLR 488, the two levels of government established by the Constitution were wholly immune from each other's laws. At least in their "governmental" functions, neither State nor Commonwealth governments could be touched in any way by the operation of legislation emanating from the other level of government. Any such impact was thought to be inconsistent with its "sovereignty" as a political entity. These immunities were swept aside by *Amalgamated Society of Engineers v Adelaide Steamship Co Ltd* (*Engineers' Case*) (1920) 28 CLR 129.

In the decades after the *Engineers' Case*, and particularly after Sir Isaac Isaacs left the bench, the High Court cautiously returned to the idea that there must be some things that the Commonwealth could not do to the States, and also some things which the States could not do to the Commonwealth. However, unlike the earlier doctrine, the later doctrines of State immunity from Commonwealth laws and Commonwealth immunity from State laws have not been neatly reciprocal.

In both respects, the cautious and qualified return to the idea of some implied limitations on legislative power was due mainly to the influence of Sir Owen Dixon. In *Australian Railways Union v Victorian Railways Commissioners* (*ARU Case*) (1930) 44 CLR 319, a series of interventions from the bench by Dixon J redirected the argument (as initially presented by HV Evatt KC and Robert Menzies KC) until in the end the Court was being invited to reconsider whether the *Railway Servants' Case* had in fact been overruled by the *Engineers' Case*. It obviously had been, and the end result was to reaffirm that position. However, the case gave Dixon J an opening to state his understanding of "**[390]** the rule adopted ... in the *Engineers' Case*".

Australian Railways Union v Victorian Railways Commissioners (*ARU Case*)
(1930) 44 CLR 319

Dixon J: [390] This rule I understand to be that, unless, and save in so far as, the contrary appears from some other provision of the Constitution or from the nature or the subject matter of the power or from the terms in which it is conferred, every grant of legislative power to the Commonwealth should be interpreted as authorizing the Parliament to make laws affecting the operations of the States and their agencies, at any rate if the State is not acting in the exercise of the Crown's prerogative and if the Parliament confines itself to laws which do not discriminate against the States or their agencies.

In formulating this passage Dixon J was drawing together possible exceptions or qualifications which he found secreted in passages of the *Engineers' Case* itself.

Amalgamated Society of Engineers v Adelaide Steamship Co Ltd (*Engineers' Case*)
(1920) 28 CLR 129

Knox CJ, Isaacs, Rich and Starke JJ: [143] It is proper, at the outset, to observe that this case does not involve any prerogative "in the sense of the word," to use the phrase employed by the Privy Council in *Theodore v Duncan* [[1919] AC 696 at 706] "in which it signifies the power of the Crown apart from statutory authority." Though much of the argument addressed to us on behalf of the States rested on the prerogative, this distinction was not observed, but it exists, and, so far as concerns prerogative in the sense indicated, it is unnecessary to consider it. In several recent cases the Judicial Committee has had the broader question under consideration, as in … *Bonanza Creek Gold Mining Co v The King* [[1916] AC 566], but in none of these was it found necessary to determine it. It is manifest that when such a question is involved in a decision, the nature of the prerogative, its relation to the Government concerned, and its connection with the power under which it is sought to be affected, may all have to be considered … If in any future cases concerning the prerogative in the broader sense, or arising under some other Commonwealth power – for instance, taxation, – the extent of that power should come under consideration so as to involve the effect of the principle stated in **[144]** … the *Bonanza Creek Case*, and its application to the prerogative or to the legislative or executive power of the States in relation to the specific Commonwealth power concerned, the special nature of the power may have to be taken into account …

[156] *Deakin v Webb* [(1904) 1 CLR 585] and *Lyne v Webb* [(1904) 1 CLR 585] were cases in which it was held that the State *Income Tax Act* of Victoria did not validly extend to tax moneys which had been received as Commonwealth salary. The decision was rested on two grounds … The first ground is that taxation of a person who is a Federal officer necessarily, *per se*, so far as it reaches money he received as salary, and although it so reaches that money by reason of provisions which apply generally to the whole community without discrimination, is an interference with the means employed by the Commonwealth for the performance of its constitutional functions … **[157]** Having regard to the principles we have stated, the first ground is erroneous. An act of the State Legislature discriminating against Commonwealth officers might well be held to have the necessary effect of conflicting with the provision made by the Commonwealth law for its officers relatively to the rest of the community.

From the *ARU Case* onwards, allusions to possible problems with taxation laws, "discriminatory" laws, or laws interfering with prerogative powers became a recurring theme in the judgments of Dixon and Evatt JJ. However, the suggestion by Dixon J in the *ARU Case* that the *Engineers* approach to Commonwealth powers might not apply as against a State government "**[390]** acting in the exercise of the Crown's prerogative" has subsequently received little support. In *Victoria v Australian Building Construction Employees' and Builders Labourers' Federation* (1982) 152 CLR 25 at 92-3, Mason J pointed out that, in later cases, Dixon J himself had readily upheld the validity of Commonwealth laws affecting or overriding the prerogative rights of the States. Mason J concluded that an implication shielding State prerogative rights and powers from Commonwealth legislation has "**[93]** no secure foundation ... and the weight of judicial opinion, based on the thrust of the reasoning in the *Engineers' Case*, is against it".

In *West v Commissioner of Taxation (NSW)* (1937) 56 CLR 657 and *Federal Commissioner of Taxation v Official Liquidator of EO Farley Ltd* (1940) 63 CLR 278, both Dixon and Evatt JJ explored these issues at length. A striking feature of the judgments of Dixon J was the way he built upon his own paraphrases of the *Engineers' Case* from one judgment to the next.

West v Commissioner of Taxation (NSW)
(1937) 56 CLR 657

Dixon J: [681] Surely it is implicit in the power given to the Executive Government of the Commonwealth that the incidents and consequences of its exercise shall not be made the subject of special liabilities or burdens under State law. The principles which have been adopted for determining for the purposes of sec 109 whether a State law is consistent with a Federal statute are no less applicable when the question is whether the State law is consistent with the Federal Constitution. Since the *Engineers' Case* [(1920) 28 CLR 129] a notion seems to have gained currency that in interpreting the Constitution no implications can be made. Such a method of construction would defeat the intention of any instrument, but of all instruments a written constitution seems the last to which it could be applied. **[682]** I do not think that the judgment of the majority of the court in the *Engineers' Case* meant to propound such a doctrine. It is inconsistent with many of the reasons afterwards advanced by *Isaacs* J himself for his dissent in *Pirrie v McFarlane* [(1925) 36 CLR 170 at 191]. Indeed, he there refers to "the natural and fundamental principle that, where by the one Constitution separate and exclusive governmental powers have been allotted to two distinct organisms, neither is intended, in the absence of distinct provision to the contrary, to destroy or weaken the *capacity* or *functions* expressly conferred on the other." He adds: "Such attempted destruction or weakening is prima facie outside the respective grants of power." There is little justification for seeking to find in the *Engineers' Case* authority for more than was decided. The importance alike of the principle there applied and of the application given to it is sufficiently great and far reaching. It is a principle adopted for the interpretation of the legislative powers of the Parliament. The principle is that whenever the Constitution confers a power to make laws in respect of a specific subject matter, prima facie it is to be understood as enabling the Parliament to make laws affecting the operations of the States and their agencies. The prima facie meaning may be displaced by considerations based on the nature or the subject matter of the power or the language in which it is conferred or on some other provision in the Constitution. But, unless the contrary thus appears, then, subject to two reservations, the power must be construed as extending to the States. The first reservation is that in the *Engineers' Case* the question was left open whether the principle would warrant legislation affecting the exercise of a prerogative of the Crown in right of the States. The second is that the decision does not appear to deal with or affect the question whether the Parliament is authorized to enact legislation discriminating against the States or their agencies ...

[683] In so describing the effect of the decision, I have done little but repeat what I said on a former occasion (*Australian Railways Union v Victorian Railways Commissioners* [(1930) 44 CLR 319]). But, in spite of its compendiousness, I believe it to be an accurate enough statement of the law laid down by which we are to be guided. It is, perhaps, desirable to add that, in applying the general principle to a legislative power of the Commonwealth, the words at the head of secs 51 and 52, "Subject to this Constitution," must not be overlooked and that these words together with sec 106 and perhaps sec 107 may be of great importance in a question how far a law of the Commonwealth may affect the States.

Notice the words "capacity" and "functions", italicised (by Isaacs J) in the passage which Dixon J quotes from *Pirrie v McFarlane* (1925) 36 CLR 170. We shall see that in more recent judgments these words, sometimes combined and sometimes contrasted, have been used in an attempt to give precision to the scope of intergovernmental immunities.

2. Commonwealth Laws and the States

(a)   *The* Melbourne Corporation *Principle*

The *Engineers' Case* had said: "**[155]** The principle we apply to the Commonwealth we apply also to the States". So too, the above judgments moved even-handedly from what the Commonwealth could do to the States, to what a State could do to the Commonwealth. In *Melbourne Corporation v Commonwealth* (1947) 74 CLR 31, however, these vague notions coalesced into a doctrine that set limits only on what the Commonwealth could do to the States.

During World War II the Commonwealth Bank was given power to oversee the private banks and to control the supply of money and credit. The *Banking Act 1945* (Cth) sought to make these arrangements permanent. By applying the Act, Prime Minister and Treasurer Ben Chifley proposed to compel the States and their authorities, including local government authorities, to bank with the Commonwealth Bank. Section 48 of the Act provided that: "Except with the consent in writing of the Treasurer, a bank shall not conduct any banking business for a State or for any authority of a State, including a local governing authority". The Melbourne City Council was notified that it was to be specified as an authority to which s 48 applied. The Council sought to have s 48 declared invalid.

Melbourne Corporation v Commonwealth
(1947) 74 CLR 31

Dixon J: [78] The prima-facie rule is that a power to legislate with respect to a given subject enables the Parliament to make laws which, upon that subject, affect the operations of the States and their agencies. That, as I have pointed out more than once, is the effect of the *Engineers' Case* [(1920) 28 CLR 129] stripped of embellishment and reduced to the form of a legal proposition. It is subject, however, to certain reservations and this also I have repeatedly said. Two reservations, that relating to the prerogative and that relating to the taxation power, do not enter into the determination of this case and nothing need be said about them. It is, however, upon the third that, in my opinion, this case turns. The reservation relates to the use of **[79]** federal legislative power to make, not a general law which governs all alike who come within the area of its operation whether they are subjects of the Crown or the agents of the Crown in right of a State, but a law which discriminates against States, or a law which places a particular disability or burden upon an operation or activity of a State, and more especially upon the execution of its constitutional powers. In support of such a use of power the *Engineers' Case* has nothing to say. Legislation of that nature discloses an immediate object of controlling the State in the course which otherwise the Executive Government of the State might adopt, if that Government were left free to exercise its authority. The control may be attempted in connection with a matter falling within the enumerated subjects of federal legislative power. But it does not follow that the connection with the matter brings a law aimed at controlling in some particular the State's exercise of its executive power within the true ambit of the Commonwealth legislative power. Such a law wears two aspects. In one aspect the matter with respect to which it is enacted is the restriction of State action, the prescribing of the course which the Executive Government of the State must take or the limiting of the courses available to it. As the operation of such a law is to place a particular burden or disability upon the State in that aspect it may correctly be described as a law for the restriction of State action in the field chosen. That is a direct operation of the law.

In the other aspect, the law is connected with a subject of Commonwealth power. Conceivably that connection may be made so insubstantial, tenuous or distant by the character of the control or restriction the law seeks to impose upon State action that it ought not to be regarded as enacted with respect to the specified matter falling within the Commonwealth power. If so, the law fails simply because it cannot be described as made with respect to the requisite subject matter. But, if in its second aspect the law operates directly upon a matter forming an actual part of a subject enumerated among the federal legislative powers, its validity could hardly be denied on the simple ground of irrelevance to a head of power. Speaking generally, once it appears that a federal law has an actual and immediate operation within a field assigned to the Commonwealth as a subject of legislative power, that is enough. It will be held to fall within the power unless some further reason appears for excluding it. That it discloses another purpose and that the purpose lies outside the area of federal power are considerations which will not in such a case suffice to invalidate the law ...

[80] In the case of most legislative powers assigned to the Commonwealth some ingenuity would be needed to base a law squarely upon the subject matter of the power and at the same time effect by it a restriction or control of the State in respect of some exercise of its executive authority or for that matter in respect of the working of the judiciary or of the legislature of a State. The difficulty of using most federal powers in that way arises from the character of the subjects of the powers. It is, for instance, difficult to see how any law based on the power with respect to light-houses, astronomical observations, fisheries, weights and measures, bills of exchange or marriage could be aimed at controlling States in the execution of their functions. But to attempt to burden the exercise of State functions by means of the power to tax needs no ingenuity, and that, no doubt, is why that power occupies such a conspicuous place in the long history both in the United States and here of the question how far federal power may be used to interfere with the States in the exercise of their powers ...

[81] What is important is the firm adherence to the principle that the federal power of taxation will not support a law which places a special burden upon the States. They cannot be singled out and taxed as States in respect of some exercise of their functions. Such a tax is aimed at the States and is an attempt to use federal power to burden or, may be, to control State action. The objection to the use of federal power to single out States and place upon them special burdens or disabilities does not spring from the nature of the power of taxation. The character of the power lends point to the objection but it does not give rise to it. The federal system itself is the foundation of the restraint upon the use of the power to control the States. The same constitutional objection applies to other powers, if under them the States are made the objects of special burdens or disabilities. Not of course all powers, for some of them are concerned with the States specially or contemplate some measure in particular relation to a State. Examples can be seen in pars (xxxi), (xxxii), (xxxiii), and (xxxiv) of s 51. The meaning and nature of the power cannot be left out of account. Of this the defence power is a conspicuous example. But plainly the greater number of powers contemplate legislation of general application.

I do not think that either under the Constitution of the United States or *The British North America Act* or the Commonwealth Constitution has countenance been given to the notion that the legislative powers of one government in the system can be used in order directly to deprive another government of powers or authority committed to it or restrict that government in their exercise, notwithstanding the complete overthrow of the general doctrine of reciprocal immunity of government agencies and the discrediting of the reasoning used in its justification. For that reason the distinction has been constantly drawn between a law of general application and a provision singling out governments and placing special burdens **[82]** upon the exercise of powers or the fulfilment of functions constitutionally belonging to them. It is but a consequence of the conception upon which the Constitution is framed. The foundation of the Constitution is the conception of a central government and a number of State governments separately organized. The Constitution predicates their continued existence as independent entities. Among them it distributes powers of governing the country. The framers of the Constitution do not appear to have considered that power itself forms part of the conception of a government. They appear rather to have conceived the States as bodies politic whose existence and nature are independent of the powers allocated to them. The Constitution on this footing proceeds to distribute the power between State and Commonwealth and to provide for their inter-relation, tasks performed with reference to the legislative powers chiefly by ss 51, 52, 107, 108 and 109.

In the many years of debate over the restraints to be implied against any exercise of power by Commonwealth against State and State against Commonwealth calculated to destroy or detract from the independent exercise of the functions of the one or the other, it has often been said that political rather than legal considerations provide the ground of which the restraint is the consequence. The Constitution is a political instrument. It deals with government and governmental powers. The statement is, therefore, easy to make though it has a specious plausibility. But it is really meaningless. It is not a question whether the considerations are political, for nearly every consideration arising from the Constitution can be so described, but whether they are compelling.

A truism that has been invoked is that the possibility that a power may be abused is no reason for restricting the power by construction. Doubtless it formed a proper objection to the view now completely discredited that an agency of one government was not in that character amenable in any degree to a power of the other lest some exercise of the power might interfere with the due performance of the functions of the agency. But as an objection it is not in point where the question is whether an actual attempt to restrict or control the State in the exercise of a function forming part of its executive power is or is not permitted by the Constitution.

The considerations I have just mentioned have been used in relation to the question what the federal Government may do with reference to the States and the question of what a State may do with reference to the federal Government. But these are two quite different questions and they are affected by considerations that are not the same. The position of the federal government is necessarily **[83]** stronger than that of the States. The Commonwealth is a government to which enumerated powers have been affirmatively granted. The grant carries all that is proper for its full effectuation. Then supremacy is given to the legislative powers of the Commonwealth.

These two considerations add great strength to the implication protecting the Commonwealth from the operation of State laws affecting the exercise of federal power. But they also amplify the field protected. Further, they limit the claim of the States to protection from the exercise of Commonwealth power. For the attempt to read s 107 as the equivalent of a specific grant or reservation of power lacked a foundation in logic. Accordingly the considerations upon which the States' title to protection from Commonwealth control depends arise not from the character of the powers retained by the States but from their position as separate governments in the system exercising independent functions. But, to my mind, the efficacy of the system logically demands that, unless a given legislative power appears from its content, context or subject matter so to intend, it should not be understood as authorizing the Commonwealth to make a law aimed at the restriction or control of a State in the exercise of its executive authority. In whatever way it may be expressed an intention of this sort is, in my opinion, to be plainly seen in the very frame of the Constitution.

It should not be assumed that the judgment of Dixon J can be taken as sufficiently or comprehensively explaining the principle for which *Melbourne Corporation* is authority. While five judges, with McTiernan J dissenting, accepted the argument of Garfield Barwick KC that s 48 was invalid, they each had a different emphasis.

Starke J: [70] The federal character of the Australian Constitution carries implications of its own. As I have said before, "the government of Australia is a dual system based upon a separation of organs and of powers. The maintenance of the States and their powers is as much the object of the Constitution as the maintenance of the Commonwealth and its powers. Therefore it is beyond the power of either to abolish or destroy the other" (*South Australia v Commonwealth* [(1942) 65 CLR 373 at 442]; *R v Commonwealth Court of Conciliation and Arbitration; Ex parte Victoria* [(1942) 66 CLR 488 at 515]). The same principle was applied to the dual system of government under the Constitution of the United States of America. "Neither Government may destroy the other nor curtail in any substantial manner the exercise of its powers" (*Metcalf v Mitchell* [269 US 514 at 523 (1926)]) …

[74] I cannot **[75]** agree that the presence or absence of discrimination affords a decisive test or legal criterion of constitutional power. As was pointed out in *New York v United States* [326 US 572 at 587 (1946)] by *Stone* CJ, *Reed, Murphy* and *Burton* JJ, a tax which is not discriminatory "may nevertheless so affect the State, merely because it is a State that is being taxed, as to interfere unduly with the State's performance of its sovereign functions of government." It is a practical question, whether legislation or executive action thereunder on the part of a Commonwealth or of a State destroys, curtails or interferes with the operations of the other, depending upon the character and operation of the legislation and executive action thereunder. No doubt the nature and extent of the activity affected must be considered and also whether the interference is or is not discriminatory but in the end the question must be whether the legislation or the executive action curtails or interferes in a substantial manner with the exercise of constitutional power by the other.

Latham CJ adopted a different approach, but he too was uncomfortable with the idea of "discrimination", and found the idea of "undue interference" **[61]** rather vague". For him, as for Williams J, the essential point was one of "characterisation". However, this approach depended on the now discredited technique of "either/or" characterisation (as reflected in decisions such as *R v Barger* (1908) 6 CLR 41 – see Chapter 7, §3). For Dixon J, in the passage set out above, a characterisation as restricting the powers of the States might possibly mean that a Commonwealth law dependent on incidental power would fail (for want of a sufficient connection); but where the law fell within a core area of Commonwealth legislative power "**[78]** its validity could hardly be denied" on such a ground. By contrast, for Latham CJ and Williams J, the mere fact that a law was characterised as restricting the power of the States was sufficient to preclude its characterisation as a valid Commonwealth law.

> **Latham CJ: [60]** I have some difficulty in understanding how "discrimination" in a precise sense can be shown in a law applying only to one person or class of persons in respect of a particular subject matter. Discrimination appears to me to involve differences in the treatment of two or more persons or subjects. Legislation with respect only to one **[61]** or more persons or with respect only to one or more subjects is not, I suggest with respect, properly described as discriminating against other persons or other subjects simply because it leaves them alone … In *New York v United States* [326 US 572 (1946)] and the other cases to which I have referred in which it has been held that a law may be invalid on the ground of "discrimination," the word "discrimination" is, I think, really used in the sense explained … in *New York v United States* – that is, singling out another government and specifically legislating about it.
>
> But why should legislation "discriminating" in this – or any other sense – against States or Commonwealth (as the case may be) be held to be invalid? It is true that taxation laws made by the Commonwealth Parliament must not discriminate between States or parts of States – Constitution, s 51(ii). But this specific provision against discrimination in the case of this class of laws emphasises the absence from the Constitution of any provision prohibiting Federal legislation "discriminating" against the States or prohibiting State legislation "discriminating" against the Commonwealth.
>
> In my opinion the reason why such legislation is invalid is that what is called "discrimination" shows that the legislation is really legislation by the Commonwealth with respect to a State or State functions as such and not with respect to the subject in respect of which it is sought to bind the State – or, in the case of a State law specifically dealing with and seeking to control Commonwealth functions, that the State Parliament is really endeavouring to make laws with respect to the Commonwealth or Commonwealth functions as such. The Commonwealth Parliament has no power to make laws with respect to State governmental functions as such, and the State Parliaments have no power to make laws with respect to Commonwealth governmental functions as such. It is upon this ground, in my opinion, that what is called "discriminatory" legislation may properly be held to be invalid. I refer to what I said upon this subject in *West v Commissioner of Taxation* [(1937) 56 CLR 657 at 668, 669].
>
> Similarly, federal legislation which, though referring to a subject of federal power, is really legislation about what is clearly a State governmental function, may be said to "interfere unduly" with that function and therefore to be invalid. "Undue" interference is a rather vague conception, and an attempt to apply it as a standard **[62]** for determining the validity of legislation would invite and would certainly produce differences of opinion which would often be due to other than objective considerations. In my opinion the invalidity of a federal law which seeks to control a State governmental function is brought about by the fact that it is in substance a law with respect to a subject as to which the Commonwealth Parliament has no power to make laws. Though there will sometimes be difficulties in applying such a criterion, this is a more satisfactory ground of decision than an opinion that a particular federal "interference" with a State function reaches a degree which is "undue".

Rich J, like Starke J, approached the issue from the viewpoint of an implied immunity rather than by "characterisation". He held that the problem might arise in "**[66]** two classes of case":

Rich J: [66] The view once prevailed that any legislative or executive act of the Commonwealth which would, if valid, interfere with the free exercise by a State or its instrumentalities of their legislative or executive powers was *pro tanto* invalid. At a very early stage, however, there were decisions inconsistent with this view, and it was finally exploded by the *Engineers' Case*. There is no general implication in the framework of the Commonwealth Constitution that the Commonwealth is restricted from exercising its defined constitutional powers to their fullest extent by a supposed reservation to the States of an undefined field of reserved powers beyond the scope of Commonwealth interference. But this is always subject to the provisions of the Commonwealth Constitution itself. That Constitution expressly provides for the continued existence of the States. Any action on the part of the Commonwealth, in purported exercise of its constitutional powers, which would prevent a State from continuing to exist and function as such is necessarily invalid because inconsistent with the express provisions of the Constitution, and it is to be noted that all the powers conferred by s 51 are conferred "subject to this Constitution". Such action on the part of the Commonwealth may be invalid in two classes of case, one, where the Commonwealth singles out the States or agencies to which they have delegated some of the normal and essential functions of government, and imposes on them restrictions which prevent them from performing those functions or impede them in doing so; another, where, although the States or their essential agencies are not singled out, they are subjected to some provision of general application, which, in its application to them, would so prevent or impede them. Action of the former type would be invalid because there is nothing in the Commonwealth Constitution to authorize such action by the Commonwealth. A general income tax Act which purported to include within its scope the general revenues of the States derived from State taxation would be an instance of the latter.

These differing approaches left in doubt the precise criteria on which Commonwealth "interference" with State functions might be invalid, as well as the extent to which *Melbourne Corporation* might be seen as the culmination of a gradual shift away from the *Engineers' Case*.

A major reappraisal of both the *Engineers' Case* and *Melbourne Corporation* came in *Victoria v Commonwealth* (*Payroll Tax Case*) (1971) 122 CLR 353. The *Payroll Tax Act 1941* (Cth) imposed a 2.5 per cent tax on all wages paid by an employer. Section 3 of the related *Payroll Tax Assessment Act 1941* (Cth) defined "employer" to include "(a) the Crown in right of a State; (b) a municipal corporation or other local governing body or a public authority constituted under any State Act". However, although all seven judges reaffirmed the principle of *Melbourne Corporation*, none of them was willing to apply it to invalidate the payroll tax. The levying of the tax on the States by the Commonwealth was therefore held to be valid. The judgment of Barwick CJ echoed his argument as counsel in *Melbourne Corporation*, as adopted in that case by Latham CJ: he treated the problem simply as one of "characterisation".

Victoria v Commonwealth (Payroll Tax Case)
(1971) 122 CLR 353

Barwick CJ: [372] [I]t is to my mind clear that the Constitution in providing for the States did not give the Commonwealth legislative power over them, or their powers and functions of government, as subject matters of legislation. That the Government cannot "aim" its legislation against a State, its powers or functions of government is both true and fundamental to our constitutional arrangements. But, in my opinion, this does not derive from any implied limitation upon any legislative power granted to the Commonwealth. It is true simply because the topics of legislation allotted to the Commonwealth by the Constitution do not include the States themselves nor their governmental powers or functions as a subject matter of legislative power. As will appear from my understanding of the judgments in *Melbourne Corporation v Commonwealth* [(1947) 74 CLR 31], a law of the Commonwealth which in substance takes a State or its powers or functions of government as its subject matter is invalid because it cannot be supported upon any granted legislative power. If the subject matter of the law is in substance the States or their powers or functions of government, there is no room, in my opinion, for holding it to be at the same time and in the same respects a law upon one of the enumerated topics in s 51 ... Of course, a law may be at the same time thought to be a law with respect to either of two of the topics enumerated in s 51 and it may be satisfactory in such a case not to trouble to say with respect to which of the two subject matters the law should preferably be referred. But when a law may possibly be regarded as having either of two **[373]** subjects as its substance, one of which is within Commonwealth power and the other is not, a decision must be made as to that which is in truth the subject matter of the law. Although usually not an appropriate course in determining whether a law is a law on an enumerated topic, in such a case, the decision of what is the subject matter of the law may be approached somewhat in the manner the validity of a law claimed to be within one of the two mutually exclusive lists in the Canadian Constitution is determined. The law must be upon one or other of the subjects. It cannot be on both. Thus, in my opinion, to decide that the law in question is a law having the States or their powers or functions of government for its subject matter, is to decide that it cannot be a law "justified by the power to make laws with respect to" one of the topics enumerated in s 51. In other words, it seems to me to follow necessarily from the decision of the Court in the *Engineers' Case* [(1920) 28 CLR 129], and from the reasons given for that decision, that the validity of a Commonwealth law will be determined by its relation to a granted subject matter of legislative power construed as a provision of an act of the Imperial Parliament, "read naturally in the light of the circumstances in which it was made". By that direct approach no warrant will, in my opinion, be found in the Constitution for a law of which the powers or functions of a State is or are in truth the subject matter. It is for lack of an appropriate subject matter rather than the presence of an implied limitation upon some granted power that such a law, in my opinion, would fail. That, in my opinion, is the real ground of and, in any case, the only acceptable ground for, the decision in *Melbourne Corporation v Commonwealth*.

The reflections of Windeyer J on the *Engineers' Case* are set out in Chapter 7, §4. His insistence on the full scope of Commonwealth power matched that of Barwick CJ. However, he rejected the latter's reliance on "either/or" characterisation.

Windeyer J: [399] I do not think that much is to be gained by either elaboration or paraphrase of the phrase "with respect to". "Characterization" is the now common jargon... **[400]** The question under s 51 is always whether a particular enactment is within Commonwealth power. It is never whether it invades a State's domain. The question is one of subsumption under a particular description. It is not one of classification into categories mutually exclusive; for a law may be quite properly described as with respect to more than one subject ...

[401] [I]n my view of the matter, implications have a place in the interpretation of the Constitution: and I consider it is the sense that Dixon J intended when in *Australian National Airways Pty Ltd v Commonwealth* [(1945) 71 CLR 29 at 85] he said: "We should avoid pedantic and narrow constructions in dealing with an instrument of government and I do not see why we should be fearful about making implications." His Honour, when Chief Justice, repeated this observation in *Lamshed v Lake* [(1958) 99 CLR 132 at 144]. I said, in *Spratt v Hermes* [(1965) 114 CLR 226 at 272], that it is well to remember it. I still think so. The only emendation **[402]** that I would venture is that I would prefer not to say "making implications", because our avowed task is simply the revealing or uncovering of implications that are already there ...

[403] The position that I take is this: The several subject matters with respect to which the Commonwealth is empowered by the Constitution to make laws for the peace, order and good government of the Commonwealth are not to be narrowed or limited by implications. Their scope and amplitude depend simply on the words by which they are expressed. But implications arising from the existence of the States as parts of the Commonwealth and as constituents of the federation may restrict the manner in which the Parliament can lawfully exercise its power to make laws with respect to a particular subject matter. These implications, or perhaps it were better to say underlying assumptions of the Constitution, relate to the use of a power not to the inherent nature of the subject matter of the law. Of course whether or not a law promotes peace, order and good government is for the Parliament, not for a court, to decide. But a law, although it be with respect to a designated subject matter, cannot be for the peace, order and good government of the Commonwealth if it be directed to the States to prevent their carrying out their functions as parts of the Commonwealth.

Owen J agreed with Barwick CJ, while McTiernan J gave a judgment to the same effect. Menzies, Walsh and Gibbs JJ each wrote separate judgments broadly endorsing the approach of Dixon, Rich and Starke JJ in *Melbourne Corporation*, but none of them actually applied *Melbourne Corporation* to invalidate the legislation.

Gibbs J: [421] The reasons given for the decision in *Melbourne Corporation v Commonwealth* do not reveal one ground common to all of the judgments upon which the decision of the majority rested. In my opinion, however, it is not right to regard the case simply **[422]** as a decision that s 48 of the *Banking Act*, properly understood, was not a law for the peace, order and good government of the Commonwealth with respect to banking. In my opinion the decision is authority for the view that although s 48 was such a law it was invalid because it infringed an implied restriction on the power of the Commonwealth …

[423] [I]t seems to me that the federal nature of the Constitution, and its scheme and purpose, do not give rise to any implication that no general law imposing taxation may validly be extended to the States. Such an implication goes beyond what is required to preserve and protect the position of the States as independent members of the federation, and would, on the other hand, lead to complexities and difficulties in many cases. I hold that there should not be implied in the Constitution a limitation upon the legislative powers of the Commonwealth that would render invalid **[424]** any law to the extent to which it purports to impose a tax upon the States. No doubt, however, laws imposing taxation upon the States will be more likely than many other laws to offend against the limitations that apply generally to Commonwealth powers.

It then becomes necessary to determine whether the legislation in the present case is rendered invalid by any such general limitation on Commonwealth power. It is unnecessary to discuss fully the subject of the implied limitations on the power of the Commonwealth to make laws binding on the States. Such matters as the extent of the Commonwealth power to affect the prerogative, or whether the Commonwealth can compel the States to make appropriations of money in satisfaction of liabilities imposed on them, or can impair or affect the Constitution of a State, do not fall for consideration. Still less is it necessary to discuss the implications that may be made as to the immunity of the Commonwealth from action by the States. In my respectful opinion, the view of Sir Owen Dixon, that a Commonwealth law is bad if it discriminates against States, in the sense that it imposes some special burden or disability upon them, so that it may be described as a law aimed at their restriction or control, should be accepted. With all respect, however, I am not disposed to agree that a law which is not discriminatory in this sense is necessarily valid if made within one of the enumerated powers of the Commonwealth. A general law of the Commonwealth which would prevent a State from continuing to exist and function as such would in my opinion be invalid. It is true that in many cases a law which offended in this way would prove to be discriminatory, and I am conscious of the imprecision of the test so far as it applies to general and nondiscriminatory laws. The further formulations of the test by Rich and Starke JJ in the *Melbourne Corporation Case* are not free from difficulty. To say that what the Constitution impliedly forbids is a law which would prevent the States from performing the normal and essential functions of government or impede them in doing so is to draw a distinction between essential and inessential functions of government which is inappropriate to modern conditions and has probably never been valid (cf per Windeyer J in *Ex parte Professional Engineers' Association* [(1959) 107 CLR 208 at 274-6]). To inquire whether a law curtails or interferes in a substantial manner with the exercise of constitutional power by the States leads only to the further question what is the constitutional power of the States that is protected. For the purposes of the present case it is, however, unnecessary to attempt to resolve these difficulties because the pay-roll tax in its present form would not be invalid on any **[425]** view of the question. Although in some cases it may be possible to show that the nature of a tax on a particular activity, such as the employment of servants, renders the continuance of that activity practically impossible, it has not been shown that the tax in the present case prevents the States from employing civil servants or operates as a substantial impediment to their employment. The tax has now been imposed upon and paid by the States for nearly thirty years, and it has not been shown to have prevented the States from discharging their functions or to have impeded them in so doing. They may have less money available for public purposes because they have to pay the tax, but that could be said in every case in which a tax is imposed on the States, and in itself it cannot amount to an impediment against State activity sufficient to invalidate the tax.

The question that remains is whether the legislation discriminates against the States. Section 15 of the *Assessment Act* provides that the provisions of Pt III (which deals generally with the liability to the tax) shall not apply to wages paid by certain employers. These exemptions are not so extensive that it can be said that the tax is aimed at the States, but one particular exemption, granted by par (bb) of s 15 ... exempts from the tax the wages paid to the employees of most private schools in Australia but it does not exempt wages paid by the States to teachers whom they employ. The wages paid to teachers in State schools amount in total to a large sum and their inclusion for the purpose of the assessment of pay-roll tax is far from being insignificant. It might, therefore, be said that the State is under a substantial burden which is not placed generally on other persons who employ school teachers. Although I do not regard this as altogether an easy question, I have reached the conclusion that it is not right to look at the matter in that way. It was understandable that the legislature should have wished to assist the advancement of education by exempting the wages paid by schools which were not conducted for profit or gain. Most taxing statutes contain provision for exemptions and exceptions, **[426]** and it is of the nature of such statutes that not all taxpayers are treated with absolute equality. The fact that certain private employers are given an exemption which is denied to the States does not necessarily mean that the statute discriminates against the States in the sense defined by Sir Owen Dixon. The question is, to some extent, one of degree. The most that can be said is that in respect of one field of employment the State is taxed although certain private employers escape. If the position of the States is compared with that of private employers generally, it is not possible to say that the States are under such a special burden or disability that the legislation is aimed at the restriction or control of the States.

(b)   Restatement: Two Principles

In *Commonwealth v Tasmania* (*Tasmanian Dam Case*) (1983) 158 CLR 1, *Melbourne Corporation* was again discussed but not applied. Commonwealth legislation halted the construction of the Franklin Dam in Tasmania by the Tasmanian Hydro-Electric Commission. It was argued that this was a direct interference with the State's hydro-electric program and that it affected so much of its land mass as to warrant limitation on the use of Commonwealth power for the sake of the "federal balance". The argument got short shrift.

Commonwealth v Tasmania (*Tasmanian Dam Case*)
(1983) 158 CLR 1

Mason J: [128] The only relevant implication that can be gleaned from the Constitution ... is that the Commonwealth cannot, in the exercise of its legislative powers, enact a law which discriminates against or "singles out" a State or imposes some special burden or disability upon a State or inhibits or impairs the continued existence of a State or its capacity to function. This implied prohibition – for it is in truth an implied prohibition despite the endeavour of Barwick CJ in *Victoria v Commonwealth* ("the *Pay-roll Tax Case*" [(1971) 122 CLR 353 at 372-3]), to deal with it as a matter of characterization – has been recognized and discussed in many cases ... **[129]** The precise limits of the prohibition have not been formulated ... and there is no need here to essay a more precise formulation ... What is important for present purposes is that the implied prohibition reflects in point of expressed principle as much as can legitimately be extracted from the miscellany of considerations on which Tasmania relies. So much and no more can be distilled from the federal nature of the Constitution and ritual invocations of "the federal balance" ...

[139] Mr Ellicott, submits, in my view correctly, that in order to come within the prohibition it is not necessary to show that the law discriminates against a State, though discrimination in itself will attract the principle. It is enough that the Commonwealth law inhibits or impairs the continued existence of a State or its capacity to function. It is then suggested that the prohibition strikes down a Commonwealth law which inhibits, impairs or curtails any governmental function of a State in a material way. But this is to rewrite the principle. What it does is to prohibit impairment of the capacity of the State to function as a government, rather than to prohibit interference with or impairment of any function which a State government undertakes ...

To fall foul of the prohibition ... it is not enough that Commonwealth law adversely affects the State in the exercise of some governmental function as, for instance, by affecting the State in the exercise of a prerogative. Instead, it must emerge that there is a substantial interference with the State's capacity to govern, an interference which will threaten or endanger the continued functioning of the State as an essential constituent element in the federal system.

Deane J: [280] A broad submission was developed on behalf of Tasmania to the effect that ... the relevant provisions ... "are invalid because they interfere with, inhibit, curtail or impair the legislative and executive functions of the State of Tasmania and the prerogative of the Crown in right of Tasmania in relation to the lands". Mr Ellicott, for Tasmania, **[281]** emphasized that this submission did not involve any attempt to reassemble the pieces of the "exploded" doctrine of the reserve powers of the States ...

The fact that the Wilderness National Parks comprise more than 11 per cent of the land area of Tasmania provided a setting in which this submission was advanced with an effectiveness that, in my view, does not survive closer scrutiny. The declaration, in Reg 2 of the Regulations under the Act, of the Wilderness National Parks as part of the natural heritage, which is the only provision which relates to the whole of the Wilderness National Parks, did not involve any operative interference at all with the legislative or executive powers of Tasmania in respect of that land. Nor, in my view, can the actual prohibitions and restrictions which the Act, Regulations and proclamations impose in respect of more limited areas properly be seen as in any way inconsistent with the continued existence of Tasmania or its capacity to function.

The mere fact that land is Crown land or waste land provides, under the Constitution, no immunity against the paramount legislative powers of the Commonwealth. This is underlined by the express grant of power in s 51(xxxi) of the Constitution to make laws with respect to the acquisition of property on just terms from any State. The relevant provisions ... do restrict the legislative and executive powers of Tasmania in that they operate to invalidate any inconsistent Tasmanian law. That is, however, the case with every valid law of the Commonwealth. To that extent, they no doubt "interfere with, inhibit, curtail or impair the legislative and executive functions of the State of Tasmania". They do not, however, in any relevant sense, involve "a discriminatory attack" upon the exercise by Tasmania of its executive authority.

Brennan J: [214] This is not a case of a Commonwealth law purporting to restrict the use by the central departments of government or by Parliament or by the Supreme Court of the buildings appointed for their use in performing their respective functions. The Commonwealth measures impose restrictions on the use of part of the Parks and expose the whole of the Parks to the possibility of restriction if the conditions specified in the Act were satisfied ... To affect that land in that way is not to impair the functioning of the executive government of the State, though the measures limit the areas within which the executive government may make its will effective. The Commonwealth measures diminish the powers of the [Tasmanian] executive government but they do not impede the processes by which its powers are exercised ... **[215]** A restriction upon the doing of specified acts in the exercise of an executive power to use and to control the use of waste lands is no invalid intrusion upon the exercise of that power.

Note the "two limbs" of the *Melbourne Corporation* principle identified by Mason J: that is, (1) a Commonwealth law may not discriminate against a State and (2) such a law may not inhibit or impair its continued existence or capacity to function. That the first limb could operate independently, as itself a sufficient ground for invalidity, appeared to be confirmed by *Queensland Electricity Commission v Commonwealth* (1985) 159 CLR 192, where a Commonwealth law was struck down as "discriminating" against the State of Queensland.

On 19 April 1985, over 30 trade unions had imposed a 24-hour land, sea and air blockade on Queensland in protest against Queensland legislation curtailing trade union rights and banning strikes by electricity workers. By the *Conciliation and Arbitration (Electricity Industry) Act 1985* (Cth), the Commonwealth sought to establish a special procedure for expedited settlement of the dispute in the Commonwealth Conciliation and Arbitration Commission. Section 6(1) of the Act applied to "the industrial dispute between the Electrical Trades Union ... and certain authorities that was found to exist ... on 18 April 1985". The Queensland Electricity Commission was a party to that dispute.

Queensland Electricity Commission v Commonwealth
(1985) 159 CLR 192

Mason J: [217] This review of the authorities shows that the principle is now well established and that it consists of two elements: (1) the prohibition against discrimination which involves the placing on the States of special burdens or disabilities; and (2) the prohibition against laws of general application which operate to destroy or curtail the continued existence of the States or their capacity to function as governments ... The second element of the prohibition is necessarily less precise than the first; it protects the States against laws which, complying with the first element because they have a general application, may nevertheless produce the effect which it is the object of the principle to prevent.

Three comments should be made in relation to the prohibition as it has been expressed. First, the principle prohibits discrimination against a particular State as well as against the States generally. Discrimination against a particular State, at least so long as it involves the imposition of a special burden or disability on that State, by isolating it from the general law applicable to others, including other States, falls squarely within the principle. Secondly, notwithstanding ... the emphasis given [in] its application to the exercise of executive power by the States, the principle, as Stephen J indicated in *Koowarta* [(1982) 153 CLR 168 at 216], protects legislatures as well as executive governments. Thirdly, it does not follow that every law which deprives a State of a right, privilege or benefit which it enjoys will amount to discrimination in the sense already discussed. A law which deprives a State of a right, privilege or benefit not enjoyed by others, so as to place the State on an equal footing with others, is not a law which isolates the State from the general law. So, in *Federal Commissioner of Taxation v Official Liquidator of EO Farley Ltd* [(1940) 63 CLR 278 at 313-14] Dixon J suggested that a Commonwealth law enacted under s 51(xvii) might regulate the Crown's priority in **[218]** payment of debts in bankruptcy and insolvency, both in respect of the Commonwealth and the States ... And this leads to the more general proposition that the Commonwealth Parliament may by an exercise of its legislative powers abrogate a prerogative of the States without necessarily offending the prohibition against discrimination.

The prohibition against discrimination operates to strike down laws which apply to agencies of a State as well as to a State itself: see, eg, *Melbourne Corporation* [(1947) 74 CLR 31 at 78-9]. Although there has been no examination of what is meant by "agencies of a State" in this context, there is no reason for thinking that the expression is confined to authorities which represent the Crown in the sense that they are entitled to the shield of the Crown ... The object of the implied prohibition is to protect the State in the exercise of its functions from the operation of discriminatory laws whether the functions are discharged by the executive government or by an authority brought into existence by the State to carry out public functions even if the authority acts independently and is not subject to government direction and even if its assets and income are not property of the State. And it is significant that s 48 of the *Banking Act*, held to be invalid in *Melbourne Corporation*, was directed not only to a State but also to an "authority of a State, including a local governing authority". Accordingly, it is of no moment whether the plaintiffs in the first action, other than the Queensland Electricity Commission, represent the Crown in right of the State of Queensland. It is enough that they are agencies of the State, brought into existence for a public purpose ...

[219] There can be no objection to an exercise of the conciliation and arbitration power which establishes a particular tribunal or a particular procedure for the settlement of disputes in one industry, say the electricity industry. In relation to that industry Parliament might, if it saw fit, require that, in the interests of expedition, the jurisdiction of the Commission be exercised by a Full Bench. It might even provide that disputes in that industry be not referred to a State industrial authority but be determined by the Commission itself. Such a law would apply to all without differentiation. But when the Parliament singles out disputes in the electricity industry to which agencies of the State of Queensland are parties and subjects them to special procedures which differ from those applying under the principal Act to the prevention and settlement of industrial disputes generally, and of industrial disputes in the electricity industry in particular, it discriminates against the agencies of the State by subjecting them to a special disability in isolating them from the general law contained in the principal Act ...

[220] In some situations it will transpire that a provision, which on its face appears to discriminate against a particular State, ceases to have that character, when attention is given to the nature of the law and the purpose and effect which it has. The deprivation of a right, privilege or benefit, not enjoyed by others, is one illustration. And it may be that action on the part of a State or its agencies may be of such a kind as to call for a special exercise of a particular federal power in circumstances where that exercise involves no real discrimination against the State. Here, however, the provisions are so extreme in their operation that they could not be sustained on this footing.

Deane J suggested that, even when the principle is infringed by the impact on one or more States of "a law of general application", that may still be because the case can be seen, in the circumstances, as one of discrimination.

Deane J: [248] The fact that a general law imposes a particularly onerous burden upon the States (or upon a particular State) does not necessarily mean that the law relevantly discriminates against them (or it). To be caught by the reservation, the law must, as has been indicated above, discriminate in the sense that its operation involves a singling out of the States to make them "the objects of special burdens or disabilities" ... That is not to say that a law cannot discriminate against the States in the relevant sense if it is cast in general terms and is of apparently general application. Quite apart from the case where such a general law applies to the States in a way which would prevent them from performing their essential functions or which would impede them in so doing ... , a general law may operate in the context of particular **[249]** circumstances to single out the States for discriminatory treatment. The character of a law as a law of general application is ordinarily a factor, and sometimes a conclusive factor, militating against the conclusion that it discriminates against the States or a State in the relevant sense. The question whether a law does so discriminate against the States or a particular State is however, for the purposes of the law of the Constitution, a question of substance which is not susceptible of being resolved by the mere inquiry whether, as a matter of form, the law is a general or a special one. The point may be conveniently illustrated by reference to the *Pay-roll Tax Case* [(1971) 122 CLR 353]. The decision in that case was that Commonwealth legislation imposing a general pay-roll tax to be paid by employers on wages paid to their employees validly applied to the States and their agencies. The fact that the States' pay-rolls were particularly large no doubt meant that the effect of the legislation was particularly onerous in its application to them in the sense that they paid more tax than all or most other employers. That did not, however, mean that the legislation was discriminatory against the States in the sense that it singled them out to be made objects of special burdens or disabilities. On the other hand, if the legislation had been confined to the imposition upon all employers other than the Crown in right of the Commonwealth of liability to pay-roll tax upon wages paid to "public servants", it might still properly have been seen, as a matter of form, as a law of general application. Such confined legislation would, nonetheless, have discriminated against the States in the relevant sense for the reason that, as a matter of substance, its operation would have been, in circumstances where the States and State instrumentalities were the only non-Commonwealth employers of "public servants", to single out the States for the imposition of a special burden.

Nor is the question whether an impugned law relevantly discriminates against the States or a particular State susceptible of resolution merely by reference to whether the formal criterion of its operation satisfies the requirements of some formularized test. The fact that the formal operation of a law is to impose a burden or disability upon the States or State instrumentalities by reference to their character as such will ordinarily suffice to establish that, as a matter of substance, the law relevantly discriminates against the States. The failure of a law to operate by reference to such a formal criterion of liability will not, however, preclude a conclusion that, as a matter of substance, the law relevantly so discriminates. That question of substance must ultimately be resolved by reference to the actual operation of the law in the circumstances. If, as a matter of substance, the actual operation of the law is to discriminate against **[250]** the States or a particular State in the relevant sense, it will be within the scope of the reservation regardless of how disguised the substance may be by ingenious expression or outward form.

Gibbs CJ, Mason, Wilson and Dawson JJ found the *Conciliation and Arbitration (Electricity) Act* wholly invalid. Deane and Brennan JJ found the Act invalid only in certain respects.

In *Australian Capital Television Pty Ltd v Commonwealth* (1992) 177 CLR 106, the *Political Broadcasts and Political Disclosures Act 1991* (Cth) had introduced into the *Broadcasting Act 1942* (Cth) a new Pt IIID, headed "Political Broadcasts", intended to limit and control political broadcasts at election times. The scheme affected the States in two ways:

1. The same regulatory scheme was applied to Commonwealth elections by s 95B, to Territory elections by s 95C and to State elections by s 95D.

2. In each of those three sections, there were separate subsections (ss 95B(3), 95C(4) and 95D(3)) prohibiting political advertising "for or on behalf of the government, or a government authority", of the Commonwealth, of the Territories and of the States.

The majority held Pt IIID invalid because it infringed the implied freedom of political communication. Brennan and Dawson JJ, who dissented on that issue, were the only judges who needed to consider an alternative challenge based on *Melbourne Corporation*. Dawson J held that the challenge on this ground also failed. Brennan J held that sub-ss (3) and (4) of s 95D, which dealt specifically with State elections, were invalid; but that the restrictions on State government advertising in ss 95B(3) and 95C(4) were valid, since they did not "**[164]** affect the functioning of the States", nor did they "single out the States: rather they ensure that the position of the States is the same as the position of all other governments and persons". McHugh J had no need to consider this issue, since he held that Pt IIID was invalid on the ground of the implied freedom. However, he agreed with Brennan J that the *Melbourne Corporation* principle was infringed by sub-ss (3) and (4) of s 95D.

Australian Capital Television Pty Ltd v Commonwealth
(1992) 177 CLR 106

McHugh J: [241] In my opinion, the provisions of s 95D(3) and (4) are invalid in so far as they operate to prohibit the advertising of political matter in an election to a State Parliament or to a local government authority of a State. They are invalid because their immediate object is to control the States and their people in the exercise of their constitutional functions.

At federation, each of the colonies had its own legislature and executive, governed and controlled by a Constitution, based on the **[242]** institutions of representative government and responsible government. The terms of ss 106 and 107 of the Constitution necessarily give rise to the inference that, subject to the alteration of the Constitution under s 128, the States are to continue as independent bodies politic with their own Constitutions and representative legislatures ...

To be consistent with the constitutional premise of the States continuing as independent bodies politic with their own Constitutions and representative legislatures, a power conferred by s 51 of the Constitution should not be construed as authorising the Commonwealth to make a law whose immediate object is to interfere with the electoral processes authorised by those Constitutions unless the contrary intention is plainly evident in the section. The powers conferred by s 51 are conferred "subject to this Constitution". The inference to be drawn from the continuance of the States as independent bodies politic with their own Constitutions and representative legislatures is that, subject to a plain intention to the contrary, the powers of the Commonwealth do not extend to interfering in the constitutional and electoral processes of the States. It is for the people of the State, and not for the people of the Commonwealth, to determine what modifications, if any, should be made to the Constitution of the State and to the electoral processes which determine what government the State is to have. The use of a Commonwealth power to make a law which "discloses an immediate object of controlling" the processes by which the people of the States elect their governments in accordance with their Constitutions should be seen as not "within the true ambit of the Commonwealth legislative power" [*Melbourne Corporation v Commonwealth* (1947) 74 CLR 31 at 79] …

[244] Section 95D(4) is invalid, therefore, in so far as it applies to elections for the Parliaments of the State. Section 95D(3) is also invalid. In so far as it applies to the State holding the election in question, it is "a law aimed at the restriction or control of a State in the exercise of its executive authority" [74 CLR at 83]. It constitutes an interference with the functions of the State as an independent body politic. Moreover, since local government authorities are authorities of the States to which the States have delegated the authority to govern in respect of particular areas of the States, s 95D cannot validly apply to their elections. It follows that s 95D(3), in so far as it applies to the State holding an election, and s 95D(4) are invalid and not authorised by s 51(v) of the Constitution.

In *R v Coldham; Ex parte Australian Social Welfare Union* (*CYSS Case*) (1983) 153 CLR 297, an important issue relating to the possible application of *Melbourne Corporation* was left open. That case dramatically widened the definition of "industry" for the purposes of s 51(xxxv) of the Constitution, thereby exposing State governments, as employers, to Commonwealth conciliation and arbitration proceedings (see Chapter 22, §2). This raised the question of whether *Melbourne Corporation* might be invoked to set limits on this exposure.

The question was examined without resolution in *Re Lee; Ex parte Harper* (1986) 160 CLR 430 and again in *Re State Public Services Federation; Ex parte Attorney-General (WA)* (1993) 178 CLR 249. An incautious obiter dictum in the first of these cases was corrected in the second, although arguably in an equally unorthodox way.

Re Lee; Ex parte Harper
(1986) 160 CLR 430

Mason, Brennan and Deane JJ: [453] Although the purpose of the implied limitations is to impose some limit on the exercise of Commonwealth power in the interest of preserving the existence of the States …, the implied limitations must be read subject to the express provisions of the Constitution. Where a head of Commonwealth power, on its true construction, authorizes legislation the effect of which is to interfere with the exercise by the States of their powers to regulate a particular subject-matter, there can be no room for the application of the implied limitations.

Re State Public Services Federation; Ex parte Attorney-General (WA)
(1993) 178 CLR 249

Mason CJ, Deane and Gaudron JJ: [271] [W]e should point out that the statement made in *Re Lee; Ex parte Harper* [(1986) 160 CLR 430 at 453], that the implied limitations must be read subject to the express provisions of the Constitution, should not be understood as excluding consideration of implications derived from the Constitution until the scope of s 51(xxxv) is ascertained by reference to its terms alone. Rather, the scope of that provision must be ascertained by reference not only to its text but also to its **[272]** subject matter and the entire context of the Constitution, including any implications to be derived from its general structure.

Brennan J: [274] The passage [in *Re Lee; Ex parte Harper*] should not be read as suggesting that the scope of a State immunity implied by the general provisions of the Constitution can be ascertained by considering the overriding effect of a valid Commonwealth law on an inconsistent exercise of State power. The tentative view was expressed in that case that the implied limitations "do not protect the States from the consequences of the exercise by the Commonwealth of the powers granted to it by the Constitution which contemplate their application to the States". So much must be accepted. But the critical question is the scope of the relevant Commonwealth power. The **[275]** true construction of s 51(xxxv) would have to be ascertained before the effect of that provision on any countervailing implication could be determined.

It is clear that implications derived from the general structure of the Constitution may qualify express provisions conferring legislative power. Thus in *Queensland Electricity Commission v Commonwealth* [(1985) 159 CLR 192], it was held that a law enacted under the power conferred by s 51(xxxv) was invalid for conflict with an implied limitation. The proposition that "implied limitations must be read subject to the express provisions of the Constitution" does not in terms acknowledge that the construction of a head of legislative power is itself ascertained by reference to the entire context of the Constitution and that its scope may be limited by implication ... The construction of s 51(xxxv) or, for that matter, the construction of any other legislative power in s 51, calls for a consideration of the text of the power, its subject matter and the general constitutional context. None of these factors can be considered in isolation, nor is there a sequence to be followed in considering one factor before another.

These passages from the *State Public Service Case* were approved in *Re Australian Education Union; Ex parte Victoria* (1995) 184 CLR 188. However, all the above passages should be compared with the approach of Dixon J in *Melbourne Corporation*. Dixon J envisaged that one *first* determines whether a challenged law is "within power" (the characterisation question); and, if the law passes that test, one *then* proceeds to ask whether the law is nevertheless invalid as offending some express or implied limitation on the Commonwealth's use of its powers. The passage in *Re Lee; Ex parte Harper* would preserve this priority, but in such a way that a favourable answer to the characterisation question might preclude any meaningful inquiry into implied limitations. The passages in the *State Public Service Case* reject any sequential priority: in this model, all constitutional arguments bearing on the extent or the use of power must be weighed up together as aspects of one undifferentiated whole.

It was *Re Australian Education Union* that finally dealt with the substantive issue of what protection (if any) *Melbourne Corporation* might give to State governments as respondent employers under the federal system of industrial arbitration. The underlying dispute concerned redundancy packages offered to Victorian public school teachers and public sector health workers. Unions representing the school teachers and health workers had sought to have the redundancy issue covered by federal awards. With some qualifications the Court held by 6:1, with Dawson J dissenting, that the Commonwealth industrial relations system, including Commonwealth industrial awards, could apply to persons employed in the administrative services of the State: that is, that the so-called "administrative services exception" to the operation of s 51(xxxv) could no longer be sustained. However, it was held that the decision of the Victorian government to dismiss public servants on grounds of redundancy could not be overridden by federal awards.

Re Australian Education Union; Ex parte Victoria
(1995) 184 CLR 188

Mason CJ, Brennan, Deane, Toohey, Gaudron and McHugh JJ: [228] The prosecutor submitted that the statements in the *Tasmanian Dam Case* [(1983) 158 CLR 1], when they refer to impairment of a State's capacity "to function as a government", extend to any impairment of capacity to exercise government functions. The prosecutor's submission is not in accordance with the natural meaning of the words used. Nor does it accord with the substance of the views expressed in a number of judgments in which the implied limitation has been discussed ...

[229] In our view, the prosecutor's submission on this point is against the weight of modern authority and draws a distinction which is unsatisfactory. To say that the limitation protects the existence of the States and their capacity to function as a government is to give effect more accurately to the constitutional foundation for the implied limitation identified by Dixon J in the passages earlier quoted from *Australian Railways Union* [(1930) 44 CLR 319 at 391-2], including s 106 of the Constitution. To press the limitation as far as the prosecutor seeks to take it would travel beyond the language of s 106 and would confer protection on **[230]** the exercise of powers by the States to an extent which is inconsistent with the subordination of those powers to the powers of the Commonwealth through the operation of s 109 of the Constitution. And the argument, if successful, would protect a substantial part of a State's workforce from the impact of federal awards, notwithstanding that the operation of those awards in relation to school teachers, health workers and other categories of employees would not destroy or curtail the existence of the State or its capacity to function as a government.

The fact is that the existence of the States and their Constitutions and their capacity to function as governments would not be impaired by the operation of federal awards made in respect of the vast majority of the employees sought to be covered by the logs of claims, at any rate if the award provisions were confined to minimum wages and working conditions which take appropriate account of any special functions or responsibilities which attach to them. The freedom of State governments to determine terms and conditions of employment of employees would be restricted but that is a consequence of the application of the arbitration power to States. Whether the making of a comprehensive award would result in a relevant impairment is another question which we leave for later discussion.

We are unable to accept the distinction which the prosecutor drew between "governmental functions" and trading functions. The argument was that States function as a government when carrying out public functions for a public purpose. On this view, health, education and police functions are governmental functions, Indeed, it is difficult to see why, on this view, trading functions are not governmental, if they are undertaken by government in the public interest. The distinction is unsatisfactory for that reason ...

A long-standing problem with the administrative services exception is that it has always been difficult to define or describe what is meant by the expression "the administrative services of a State" and it cannot mean all employees of the State who do some administrative work. The Solicitor-General for New South Wales, who argued that the exception was supported by the implied limitation, suggested that some guidance as to the meaning of the expression may be provided by the distinction between "policy" and "operational" decisions sometimes discussed in the law of torts in the context of government liability. The guidance, if it can be so called, is obscure. The Solicitor-General was on stronger ground in contending that the exercise of legislative, administrative and judicial power is, and has always been, regarded as governmental. But the correlation between the exercise of these powers and the exception is by no means [231] apparent. What is more, the exception is not related in any way to the implied limitation or to the purpose which it serves. That purpose protects the State and its capacity to function as a government. The exception consists of a category of employees and is not directed to functions of government and even less to capacity to function as a government ...

The Solicitor-General for South Australia contended that the implied limitation protects the integrity or autonomy of a State. In this respect he drew a distinction between external services (not protected) and internal services (protected). Internal services were said to include policy formulation, reporting to Parliament, the collection and administration of government revenue and the provision of services to Parliament and the judiciary. It was claimed that the protection would embrace, among others, the Treasury, the Attorney-General's Department, court staff and the police. It was conceded that the content of an award was a relevant consideration. Thus the Commission could regulate remuneration and disputes about remuneration and other payments to employees but it could not prescribe employment qualifications, eligibility and termination procedures. The latter, so the argument runs, would impair the integrity or autonomy of the State. It will be convenient to deal a little later with this argument which, in our view, has some force ...

Our rejection of the particular submissions made by the prosecutor and supporting interveners other than that advanced by South Australia as to the scope and content of the implied limitation leads us, subject to consideration of one gloss put forward by the prosecutor, to express the scope and content of the limitation in this way. The limitation consists of two elements: (1) the prohibition against discrimination which involves the placing on the States of special burdens or disabilities ("the limitation against discrimination") and (2) the prohibition against laws of general application which operate to destroy or curtail the continued existence of the States or their capacity to function as governments ...

[232] At this point it is convenient to consider South Australia's argument based on impairment of a State's "integrity" or "autonomy". Although these concepts as applied to a State are by no means precise, they direct attention to aspects of a State's functions which are critical to its

capacity to function as a government. It seems to us that critical to that capacity of a State is the government's right to determine the number and identity of the persons whom it wishes to employ, the term of appointment of such persons and, as well, the number and identity of the persons whom it wishes to dismiss with or without notice from its employment on redundancy grounds. An impairment of a State's rights in these respects would, in our view, constitute an infringement of the implied limitation. On this view, the prescription by a federal award of minimum wages and working conditions would not infringe the implied limitation, at least if it takes appropriate account of any special functions or responsibilities which attach to the employees in question. There may be a question, in some areas of **[233]** employment, whether an award regulating promotion and transfer would amount to an infringement. That is a question which need not be considered. As with other provisions in a comprehensive award, the answer would turn on matters of degree, including the character and responsibilities of the employee.

In our view, also critical to a State's capacity to function as a government is its ability, not only to determine the number and identity of those whom it wishes to engage at the higher levels of government, but also to determine the terms and conditions on which those persons shall be engaged. Hence, Ministers, ministerial assistants and advisers, heads of departments and high level statutory office holders, parliamentary officers and judges would clearly fall within this group. The implied limitation would protect the States from the exercise by the Commission of power to fix minimum wages and working conditions in respect of such persons and possibly others as well. And, in any event, Ministers and judges are not employees of a State ...

However, the rejection of the arguments put forward by the prosecutor and the intervening States – arguments which would have given the implied limitation a wide-ranging operation – means that the Commission has power to make awards binding the States and their agencies in relation to minimum wages and working conditions which take account of the special functions and responsibilities, if any, of a broad range of public servants and employees ... **[234]** On the other hand, as we have indicated, the operation of the implied limitation would preclude the Commission from making an award binding the States in relation to qualifications and eligibility for employment, term of appointment and termination of employment, at least on the ground of redundancy. It would also preclude the Commission from making an award binding the States in relation to the terms and conditions of employment or engagement of persons such as Ministers, ministerial assistants and advisers, heads of department and senior office holders – as well as parliamentary officers and judges. What impact the implied limitation would have on the power of the Commission to make an award prescribing particular minimum terms and conditions of employment for particular classes of employees, eg, term of appointment, procedures and criteria for promotion and transfer, and termination on grounds other than redundancy, was a question which was not explored in detail in the arguments presented to this Court.

Dawson J rejected the distinctions drawn by the majority.

Dawson J: [249] Difficulty is inevitably encountered in attempting to identify the point at which a law, particularly a law of general application, may prevent a State from functioning effectually as an independent unit. The difficulty may be less in the case of a discriminatory law. In the light of the *Engineers' Case* [(1920) 28 CLR 129], it is necessary to start with the proposition that a law under s 51(xxxv) may bind a State and its instrumentalities, but having regard to the nature and scope of State employment, there is no readily discernible line between those aspects of the relationship between a State and its employees which may be externally regulated without interference with the capacity of the State to function independently and those which may not. If the determination of the number and identity of persons to be employed is critical to the functioning of a State, then so too will be the wages and conditions of employment, for the former cannot be determined in isolation from the latter, if only because of the budgetary considerations which constrain any government. It is obvious that if, for example, a State is required to pay a substantial increase in wages to its teachers (who are employed in significantly large numbers), it may have as much impact on the State's budget and the implementation of **[250]** its policies as an award prohibiting redundancies in that workforce. It is similarly artificial to draw a line between those employed at the higher levels of government and those employed at the lower levels. To do so is merely to revive the distinction between industrial and non-industrial functions which is of little relevance in the context of industrial disputes as they are now viewed. A State can function only through those whom it employs, whatever the level of employment, and the external regulation of the terms and conditions of employment of those employed at the lower levels may, if for no other reason than their numbers, be as destructive of the capacity of a State to function as an independent unit as the regulation of the terms and conditions of those employed at the higher levels.

There was also an argument put to the Court based upon the "discrimination" limb of the implied immunity, that is, the limb applied in the *Queensland Electricity Case*. This argument was rejected. Section 111(1)(g) of the *Industrial Relations Act 1988* (Cth) empowered the Commission to dismiss a matter or refrain from further hearing a matter "if it appears ... that further proceedings are not necessary or desirable in the public interest"; but in 1992, s 111(1A) was inserted into the Act. That section provided that the Commission could not exercise the discretion conferred by s 111(1)(g), but must proceed to a hearing, in matters involving "an order, award, decision or determination of a State industrial authority" that "cannot be dealt with by a State arbitrator by compulsory arbitration". Section 111(1A) was introduced after new Victorian legislation had replaced the previous State system of compulsory arbitration with a system of individual employment agreements, and the purpose of the new Commonwealth provision was to ensure that employees had access to the federal system in such cases. The majority judgment, with which Dawson J agreed on this point, held that s 111(1A) did not breach the "discrimination" limb of the implied immunity.

Mason CJ, Brennan, Deane, Toohey, Gaudron and McHugh JJ: [239] The prosecutor submitted that s 111(1A) discriminates against Victoria and employers and employees in that State by denying them recourse to s 111(1)(g). The new provision is said to discriminate against Victoria and any other State that enacts similar legislation; alternatively, it is said that the legislation is aimed at Victoria.

No doubt the events which had recently taken place in Victoria, particularly the enactment of the Victorian legislation, were the occasion for the introduction of s 111(1A) but that is not enough to justify characterization of the provision as one which is aimed at Victoria. The provision is framed in general terms and is capable of applying to any State which introduces a system similar to the Victorian system. The fact that Victoria is the only State presently affected by s 111(1A) is not a compelling consideration, though it could conceivably be so in the absence of a rational and relevant connection between the basis on which that provision denies access, the application of s 111(1)(g) and the exercise of the powers conferred by the last-mentioned provision.

Whether s 111(1A) discriminates against Victoria, its employers and employees in the sense of being aimed at them is not a question to be **[240]** determined by reference to the subjective motives of the legislators; rather, it is a question of determining what was the purpose of the enactment, a matter which is to be ascertained by reference to the substance and actual operation of the law in the circumstances to which it applies. That was the approach which the Court adopted in *Queensland Electricity Commission* where the members of the Court, as we understand the judgments, examined the substance and operation of the statutory provisions in reaching their conclusions with respect to the validity of the impugned provisions.

The prosecutor contended that there is no logical connection between refusing to make an award in the public interest pursuant to s 111(1)(g) and the absence of a system of compulsory arbitration in a State. That argument cannot be accepted. If the view be taken, as it has been taken by the Commonwealth Parliament that, in the public interest, industrial disputes should be resolved by means of compulsory arbitration, it is logical for the Parliament to conclude that a power given to the Commission to refrain from proceeding where it is in the public interest to do so should only be exercisable when an alternative system of compulsory arbitration is available. Further, the introduction of s 111(1A) can be supported on the ground that it eliminated or alleviated problems that would arise once State compulsory arbitration was no longer available. Applications under s 111(1)(g) would involve delay, even if the Commission decided to proceed due to the absence of compulsory arbitration. And, if the Commission were to decline to proceed and leave the dispute to voluntary arbitration, interstate industrial disputes might not be resolved satisfactorily.

In the result, *Australian Education Union* was something of a Pyrrhic victory both for the trade unions and for the State. The Court held that the Commonwealth arbitration system *could* extend to industrial relations within the State public service to the extent that awards could validly be made on matters such as minimum wages and working conditions; but could *not* extend into areas of policy judgment which a State might wish to make in relation to its public service employment structure, since this would obtrude upon the "integrity" or "autonomy" of the State. Thus the Commonwealth system could *not* extend to the wages and working conditions of State "**[233]** Ministers, ministerial assistants and advisers, heads of departments and high level statutory office holders, parliamentary officers and judges". Similarly, decisions by the Victorian government to dismiss public servants on grounds of redundancy were within its governmental prerogatives, and could *not* be overridden by federal awards. Despite the vagueness of "integrity" and "autonomy" as criteria of immunity, and despite the Court's rejection of the analogy suggested by the New South Wales Solicitor-General with "**[230]** the distinction between 'policy' and 'operational' decisions … in the law of torts", *Australian Education Union* in fact subjects State governments to federal law at an operational level, while according them an immunity for policy decisions and for employment conditions "**[233]** at the higher levels of government".

The two specific examples thus provided of State immunity from Commonwealth interference have proved to be more restrictive than the above account might suggest. In *Australian Education Union* these had appeared to be *only* examples, illustrative of a broad principle protecting the "integrity" and "autonomy" of a State. However, when this decision came to be applied in *Victoria v Commonwealth* (*Industrial Relations Act Case*) (1996) 187 CLR 416, there was no talk of "integrity" or "autonomy". The specific examples above were treated as rigid factual categories into which the principles of *Australian Education Union* had now been distilled. If the legislative provisions there in question (amendments to the *Industrial Relations Act* introduced by the *Industrial Relations Reform Act 1993* (Cth)) affected holders of "high level" State public office, or State dismissals on the ground of redundancy, then either the provisions thus offending were invalid, or (as in fact happened) they must be "read down" under s 15A of the *Acts Interpretation Act 1901* (Cth) to avoid that invalid operation. If not, there appeared to be no other basis on which *Melbourne Corporation* or *Australian Education Union* might be invoked.

The issue was considered most fully in relation to the "minimum wage" provisions introduced into the *Industrial Relations Act* as Div 1 of a new Pt VIA, and intended primarily as a "safety net" for workers in States with no industrial arbitration system of their own. The joint judgment first dealt with an argument that this "discriminated" against those States.

Victoria v Commonwealth (*Industrial Relations Act Case*)
(1996) 187 CLR 416

Brennan CJ, Toohey, Gaudron, McHugh and Gummow JJ: [500] The provisions of Div 1 of Pt VIA are of general application and do not distinguish between employees of a State and other employees. And there is no suggestion that, in their practical operation, they operate upon States and their employees differently from other employers and employees. Rather, the argument that the provisions are discriminatory was put on the basis that "if a particular State does not maintain a compulsory arbitration system for its employees, the State and its employees are subjected to the power of the Commission to impose a common rule which fixes minimum wages for those employees" while other States are not. That argument mistakes the nature and effect of the provisions in question.

The provisions of Div 1 of Pt VIA are directed to ensuring that persons whose wages are not protected by an award (whether State or federal) or by an agreement which prevails over awards may obtain the benefit of a minimum wages order under s 170AE. The class of persons in respect of whom an order may be made is selected, not by reference to employment by or in a State, but by reference to practical criteria which take account of the general pattern of industrial regulation and of the way in which the rights of wage earners are generally protected in Australia …

The question whether a provision is discriminatory is to be determined from the purpose of the enactment ascertained "by reference to the substance and actual operation of the law in the circumstances to which it applies" [*Re Australian Education Union; Ex parte Victoria* (1995) 184 CLR 188 at 240]. Given that, first, the criteria selected to determine those for whom an order may be made under s 170AE bear a real and rational relationship with the general system of wage fixation as it has developed in this country and, secondly, that it cannot be said that the provisions of Div 1 of Pt VIA necessarily operate with different impact on or in Western Australia, there is no basis for holding that the provisions in question discriminate against that State or, indeed, any other State which elects not to maintain an industrial system involving compulsory arbitration.

As to the argument that the Commonwealth could not validly extend such legislation to the holders of "high level" State public office, the joint judgment accepted the argument but dealt with it by a "reading down" solution.

Brennan CJ, Toohey, Gaudron, McHugh and Gummow JJ: [501] [Section] 6 specifies that the Act binds the Crown in various capacities, including "in right of … each of the States". That provision governs the application of the substantive provisions of the Act. In so far as the substantive provisions are expressed in general terms or in terms wide enough to apply to or permit of orders regulating the terms and conditions of those employed at the higher levels of government, the question is not whether, on that account, those provisions are invalid in their application to the States, but whether s 6 is invalid in its specification that the Act and, thus, those provisions bind the States.

Section 6 of the Act is not, in terms, subject to any limitation or prohibition. More particularly, it is not, in terms, made subject to those matters pertaining to State employees which were identified in *Re Australian Education Union* as falling within the scope and content of the implied limitation recognised in the *Melbourne Corporation* Case [(1947) 74 CLR 31]. The question thus arises whether, pursuant to s 7A(1) of the Act or s 15A of the *Acts Interpretation Act* 1901 (Cth) (the Interpretation Act), s 6 can be read as not binding the States with respect to those matters, particularly as not binding them with respect to the terms and conditions of those employed at the higher levels of government …

[503] In the present case, s 6 purports to subject the States to a regime which specifies certain terms and conditions with respect to employment generally and which, in relation to other matters, permits the Commission to regulate the terms and conditions on which persons are employed. That is an area in which the legislative power of the Parliament is limited in the manner explained in *Re Australian Education Union*. The nature and subject matter of the Act suggest the limitation by which s 6 may be read down within constitutional power if its provisions would otherwise infringe that limitation. In other words, s 6 can be read as binding the States to the extent that the provisions of the Act do not prevent them from determining the number of persons they wish to employ, the term of their appointment, the number and identity of those they wish to dismiss on redundancy grounds and the terms and conditions of those employed at the higher levels of government.

As to the "discrimination" limb of *Melbourne Corporation*, the Court took a similar view in relation to the provision for "certified agreements" in Div 2 of the new Pt VIB: because the provisions "**[541]** are of general application and do not distinguish between the States, as employers, and other employers" their operation was not discriminatory.

Elsewhere in Pt VIA of the Act the reading down of s 6 was similarly relied on to limit the operation (but thereby preserve the validity) of the equal pay provisions in Div 2; the unfair dismissal and anti-discrimination provisions in Div 3; the parental leave provisions in Div 5; and the conferral of civil immunity on a limited "right to strike" in Div 4 of Pt VIB.

(c)　　Restatement: One Principle

In 1983 it was still possible to argue that the *Melbourne Corporation* principle did *not* apply to invalidate federal legislation simply because it "discriminated" against one or more States (in the sense that it singled out a State or its agencies as the subject of special legislation not applicable to other legal subjects). The following is an example.

AR Blackshield, "Damadam to Infinities! The Tourneyold of the Wattarfalls"

in M Sornarajah (ed), *The South West Dam Dispute: The Legal and Political Issues*
(University of Tasmania, 1983), 37

[57] This leaves … the idea that a Commonwealth law cannot "discriminate" against the States (or against any one of them) in the sense that it "singles out" one or all States as the target of "some special burden or disability", and that any law thus "aimed at" the States will on that ground alone be invalid. In [the *Tasmanian Dam Case* (1983) 158 CLR 1 at 128], as in [*Victoria v Australian Building Construction Employees' and Builders Labourers' Federation* (1982) 152 CLR 25 at 93], Mason J in particular still treats this as a valid independent limb of the *Melbourne Corporation* [(1947) 74 CLR 31] principle: a law will be invalid *either* if it "discriminates" in the above sense, *or* if it "impairs the continued existence of a State or its capacity to function". Later in his judgment [158 CLR at 139] he repeats that "discrimination in itself will attract the principle" — though only as an aside to the observation that proof of discrimination "is not necessary", since "it is enough that the Commonwealth law inhibits or impairs the continued existence of a State or its capacity to function". Yet, surely the essential point of *Melbourne Corporation* itself was that "discrimination" was neither necessary nor sufficient.

Admittedly, the judgment of Dixon J repeatedly spoke of "discrimination" as a self-sufficient and self-executing test: "to isolate the State from the general system" so as to "place it under a particular disability" was for him a sufficient sin. But even in his judgment, the crucial conjunctions tended to shift. His initial rejection of "a law which discriminates against States" *or* burdens a State ("especially … [in] its constitutional powers") became a rejection of laws "singling out governments *and* placing special burdens" on the powers "constitutionally belonging to them". And he stressed that the prohibition, "in whatever way it may be expressed", must in the end be derived from "the very frame of the Constitution" [74 CLR at 84, 79, 81-3].

The judgments which treated the problem simply as one of characterisation also spoke of "discrimination", but much more equivocally. Latham CJ, for instance, held that s 48 of the Banking Act was invalid because it "singles out States and State agencies and creates a rule for them and for no others"; it was thus "in substance legislation about States and State authorities" [74 CLR at 62]. But this was a conscious attempt to make sense of the use of "discrimination" as a "disqualifying category". He complained that the concept of "discrimination" is anomalous in such a context: discrimination "between States or parts of States" may be hard enough to measure in practice, but at least it satisfies our logical and grammatical expectation that discrimination will involve a selection *between* one object and another. (Discrimination, like conspiracy, takes two.) To avoid this problem his Honour proceeded to redefine "discrimination" (for the purpose in hand) as "singling out another government and specifically legislating about it"; but this still left him puzzled as to why "discrimination" (in this "or any other sense") was invalid. His attempt to resolve this puzzle led him into "characterisation"; but his explanation, limiting the "disqualifying category" to laws "with respect to State governmental functions as such" [74 CLR at 61], was indistinguishable from the principle adopted by the other concurring judges … Williams J also used the language of "discrimination" and "characterisation"; but for him, more clearly than for Latham CJ, a law was only invalid if it gave "directions to the States as to the manner in which they shall exercise their executive, legislative or judicial governmental functions" in a way that intruded into "the constitutional affairs of the States" … [58] He expressly declined to hold that a law was "necessarily invalid" simply because of discrimination "against a State or States" [74 CLR at 99-100].

Starke J also expressly rejected the view "that the presence or absence of discrimination affords a decisive test or legal criterion of constitutional power" [74 CLR at 75] … Rich J [74 CLR at 66] spoke of "two classes of case", one "discriminatory" and one not. But both of them illustrated his general theme that a law was unacceptable only if it would "prevent a State from continuing to exist and function as such". His first class (where a law "singles out the States" *and* imposes restrictions on the "essential functions of government") showed that a discriminatory law was invalid only if it also infringed his more fundamental test; his second class showed that a law was invalid if it infringed that test in the absence of any discrimination at all. In the second class "discrimination" is not necessary; in the first it is not sufficient.

In 1985, adherence to this kind of argument appeared to be precluded by the *Queensland Electricity Case* – both by the actual result in that case and by the dictum of Mason J that the *Melbourne Corporation* principle "**[217]** consists of two elements", one of which is a self-sufficient "prohibition against discrimination which involves the placing on the States of special burdens or disabilities". Now, however, in *Austin v Commonwealth* (2003) 215 CLR 185, the joint judgment of Gaudron, Gummow and Hayne JJ (joined on this issue by Kirby J) has rejected the dictum of Mason J, and proposed a fundamental conceptual return to the earlier under-standing. Perhaps this conceptual shift is intended to facilitate the rationalising project of Dawson, Toohey and Gaudron JJ in *Re Residential Tenancies Tribunal (NSW); Ex parte Defence Housing Authority* (*Henderson's Case*) (1997) 190 CLR 410 (see §3 below): namely, to assimilate State immunity under *Melbourne Corporation* to Commonwealth immunity under *Commonwealth v Cigamatic Pty Ltd (In Liquidation)* (1962) 108 CLR 372.

In *Austin v Commonwealth*, Robert Austin (a judge of the Supreme Court of New South Wales) and Kathryn Kings (a Master of the Supreme Court of Victoria) sought to test their liabi-lity to a federal tax, the "superannuation contributions surcharge". The legislative scheme was collateral to a wider scheme for taxing superannuation benefits in the hands of employers (in their capacity as "superannuation providers") – usually with the practical result that the burden of the tax would be passed on to the members of the superannuation scheme by reduction of their benefit payments. In most Australian States, however, judicial pensions do not depend on a contributory superannuation scheme, but are paid out of consolidated revenue (with no contri-butions and no separate fund).

To ensure that the incidence of the "superannuation contributions surcharge" fell equally on all "high income earners", the Commonwealth enacted the *Superannuation Contributions Tax (Members of Constitutionally Protected Superannuation Funds) Assessment and Collection Act 1997* (Cth). According to the usual practice, adopted (perhaps unnecessarily – see Chapter 23, §1) in order to ensure compliance with s 55 of the Constitution, the actual imposition of the surcharge was effected by a short separate statute, the *Superannuation Contributions Tax (Members of Constitutionally Protected Superannuation Funds) Imposition Act 1997* (Cth). That Act was expressed to apply to a range of "constitutionally protected funds" established by State legis-lation, as originally identified by reg 14 of the *Income Tax Regulations* (Cth). Among the State enactments there referred to were the *Judges' Pensions Act 1953* (NSW) and the *Supreme Court Act 1986* (Vic), upon which the pension entitlements of the plaintiffs respectively depended.

The *Assessment and Collection Act* constructed a notional scheme whereby every person entitled to a pension under the legislative provisions referred to was deemed to have made "surchargeable contributions" which by s 9(4) of the Act were equivalent, in any financial year, to "the actuarial value of the benefits that accrued to [that person]", together with "the value of the administration expenses and risk benefits provided in respect of [that person]". The actuarial calculations required to establish these notional values were to be carried out according to formulae found partly in s 9 of the Act and partly in Regulations. The fictitious "surchargeable contributions" thus imputed to a taxpayer were then taxed in the hands of the taxpayer, since the Commonwealth assumed that any attempt to impose the tax directly upon a State government would be precluded by s 114 of the Constitution.

The burden thus imposed on State Supreme Court judges was substantial, and would escalate dramatically for those who remained on the bench beyond their earliest pensionable retirement date. In Austin's case, if he retired as soon as he became eligible for a pension (at age 62), his accumulated "superannuation contributions surcharge" would be over $300,000; if he stayed on the bench until age 72, it would be over $550,000. To ease this burden, in 1998 New South Wales amended its *Judges' Pensions Act* to allow judges to commute their pension entitlements to a sufficient extent to enable them to pay the surcharge.

By s 7, the Commonwealth Act did not apply to a person whose "membership" of a notional superannuation scheme arose "because he or she is a judge of a court of a State at the commencement of this Act" (that is, as at 7 December 1997). This exemption did not apply to

Austin because he was not appointed until August 1998. The Commonwealth maintained that the exemption did not apply to Kings either, on the ground that she was not a "judge"; but the High Court held unanimously that under the Victorian legislation she was relevantly a "judge", and was therefore not subject to the surcharge.

The Court was comprised of six justices, since Callinan J did not sit. By 5:1, Kirby J dissenting, the Court held that, in its application to State judicial officers, the legislation infringed the *Melbourne Corporation* principle. Gaudron, Gummow and Hayne JJ were concerned to insist that "discrimination" alone would *not* suffice to attract invalidity.

Austin v Commonwealth
(2003) 215 CLR 185

Gaudron, Gummow and Hayne JJ: [246] It is important … to examine what is involved in the notion of "discrimination" said to be drawn from *Melbourne Corporation* and succeeding decisions respecting intergovernmental immunities. The notion of "immunity" here is concerned with freedom from legislative affectation. In *Re State Public Services Federation; Ex parte Attorney-General (WA)* [(1993) 178 CLR 249 at 296], Toohey J identified a debate underlying *Queensland Electricity Commission v Commonwealth* [(1985) 159 CLR 192]: "as to whether discrimination against a State is but an illustration of a law impairing **[247]** the capacity of a State to govern or whether it has a standing of its own".

It is necessary also to distinguish the specific reference in s 51(ii) to discrimination. A law with respect to taxation, in general, does not discriminate in the sense spoken of in s 51(ii) if its operation is general throughout the Commonwealth even though, by reason of circumstances existing in one or more of the states, it may not operate uniformly …

The phrase in s 51(ii) is "discriminate between". Likewise, in other provisions of the Constitution where "discrimination" is used expressly, notably ss 102 and 117, and in judicial interpretation of the Constitution, notably that of s 92, the primary sense is of "discrimination between". The essence of the notion of discrimination is said to lie in the unequal treatment of equals or the equal treatment of those who are not equals, where the differential treatment and unequal outcome is not the product of a distinction which is appropriate and adapted to the attainment of a proper objective.

The submission in the present litigation respecting *Melbourne Corporation* is that, at least in their application to the first plaintiff, the laws in question are beyond the taxation power because they discriminate against New South Wales by singling it out to place upon it special burdens or disabilities, the attainment of a constitutionally improper objective. But, even if that be so, where is the first step, the unequal treatment of equals or equal treatment of the unequal?

They went on to quote several passages querying the concept of "discrimination". One was from the judgment of Latham CJ in *Melbourne Corporation*. Another was from the joint judgment in *Re Australian Education Union; Ex parte Victoria* (1995) 184 CLR 188, noting that, although in *Melbourne Corporation* Dixon J spoke primarily of discrimination, he "**[227]** clearly had in mind" that Commonwealth power "cannot be exercised to destroy or curtail the existence of the States or their continuing to function as such". A third was the paradox spelled out by Laurence Tribe, *American Constitutional Law* (Foundation Press, 3rd ed 2000): "**[1233]** [T]he very concept of an *immunity* (as reflected in the intergovernmental immunity doctrine) is more than a claim to *equal treatment*; indeed, it is a claim to *special* treatment beyond that to which otherwise similarly situated parties are entitled".

Gaudron, Gummow and Hayne JJ: [248] At some stages in the argument in the present case it was suggested to be sufficient to render the legislation invalid in its application to the first plaintiff and other State judicial officers that the legislation treated **[249]** them differently to beneficiaries under … unfunded private sector schemes … by imposing the taxation liability upon them rather than the provider of the benefits. This differential treatment was said, without more, to attract the *Melbourne Corporation* doctrine … That would appear to give "discrimination" a standing on its own which in this field of discourse it does not have.

There is, in our view, but one limitation, though the apparent expression of it varies with the form of the legislation under consideration. The question presented by the doctrine in any given case requires assessment of the impact of particular laws by such criteria as "special burden" and "curtailment" of "capacity" of the States "to function as governments". These criteria are to be applied by consideration not only of the form but also "the substance and actual operation" of the federal law. Further, this inquiry inevitably turns upon matters of evaluation and degree and of "constitutional facts" which are not readily established by objective methods in curial proceedings ...

[257] To fix separately upon laws addressed to one or more of the States and upon laws of so-called "general application", and to present the inquiry as differing in nature dependent upon the form taken by laws enacted under the one head of power, tends to favour form over [258] substance ... It is to attend insufficiently to what in this realm of discourse is the essential question in all cases. This is whether the law restricts or burdens one or more of the States in the exercise of their constitutional powers. The form taken by a particular law may, as Dawson J explained in ... *Queensland Electricity* [159 CLR at 260] ..., assist more readily in answering that question, but in all cases the question must be addressed.

In *Queensland Electricity*, Mason J may have taken a contrary view. His Honour said [159 CLR at 217] that the principle applied in *Melbourne Corporation* ... consists of two elements ... However, that is to be read with an earlier passage in that judgment [159 CLR at 216]. Mason J, with reference to what had been said by Dixon J in the *Banking Case* concerning laws of general application, there said:

> "Plainly, his Honour was speaking of a law which, though referable to a head of legislative power, is, by reason of its impact on the States and their functions, inconsistent with the fundamental constitutional conception which underlies the prohibition against discrimination."

That "fundamental constitutional conception" has proved insusceptible of precise formulation. Nevertheless, an understanding of it is essential lest propositions such as those expressed by Mason J in *Queensland Electricity* take on, by further judicial ex[e]gesis, a life of [259] their own which is removed from the constitutional fundamentals which must sustain them.

Gaudron, Gummow and Hayne JJ went on to draw attention to passages in the *Tasmanian Dam Case* and *Western Australia v Commonwealth* (*Native Title Act Case*) (1995) 183 CLR 373 placing emphasis on the *capacity* of the State and its organs to function. From *Melbourne Corporation* itself, and from *Re Australian Education Union*, they quoted passages extending the protection to judicial functions and organs. As to that extension they said:

Gaudron, Gummow and Hayne JJ: [261] As a general proposition, it is for the State of New South Wales, as for the other States, to determine the terms and conditions upon which it appoints and remunerates the judges of its courts. The concept of remuneration includes provision of retirement and like benefits to judges, spouses and other dependants. There is, as the Supreme Court of Canada pointed out in *R v Beauregard* [[1986] 2 SCR 56 at 83; (1986) 30 DLR (4th) 481 at 501], "a close relationship between salaries and pensions", both being "remunerative benefits". The State of New South Wales chose to discharge its responsibilities for the establishment and maintenance of its judicial branch by providing the unfunded and non-contributory scheme in the NSW Pensions Act ...

[262] In respect of that State legislative choice, the federal laws in contention impose no fiscal burden directly upon the State. It is the first plaintiff, not the State, who is the taxpayer. Does the absence of that immediate fiscal burden upon the State compel the conclusion that there has been but a "speculative and uncertain" impairment by the federal law of the exercise by the State of its freedom to discharge as it decides its constitutional functions respecting the remuneration of the judicial branch? Does the federal law merely affect the ease of the working of the judicial branch?

The provision of secure judicial remuneration at significant levels serves to advantage and protect the interest of the body politic in several ways. Secure judicial remuneration at significant levels assists, as the United States Supreme Court has emphasised [*United States v Hatter*, 532 US 557 at 568 (2001)], to encourage persons learned in the law, in the words of Chancellor Kent written in 1826, "to quit the lucrative pursuits of private business, for the duties of that important station".

It also, as the Victorian Attorney-General indicated when introducing legislation to provide some relief against the effects of the surcharge legislation, assists the attraction to office of persons without independent wealth and those who have practised in less well paid areas. Further, the Supreme Court of the United States has stressed that such provision helps "to secure an independence of mind and spirit necessary if judges are 'to maintain that nice adjustment between individual rights and governmental powers which constitutes political liberty'" [532 US at 568]. The Supreme Court went on to refer to the statement by Chief Justice John Marshall [at the Virginia State Convention in 1829] that an **[263]** ignorant or dependent judiciary would be the "greatest scourge ... ever inflicted".

Views may vary from time to time as to the relevant importance of these considerations and the measures to give effect to them. But in the constitutional framework in this country these are matters, respecting State judges, for determination by State legislatures. That constitutional framework also constrains those legislatures, in particular, by requiring them to take as they find federal laws of "general application" as part of the system enjoyed by the whole community. Hence the statement by Frankfurter J in *O'Malley v Woodrough* [307 US 277 (1939) at 282]:

> "To subject them to a general tax is merely to recognize that judges are also citizens, and that their particular function in government does not generate an immunity from sharing with their fellow citizens the material burden of the government whose Constitution and laws they are charged with administering."

However, that is not the present case. Section 5 of the Protected Funds Assessment Act speaks of "high-income members of constitutionally protected superannuation funds". They are taxed in a fashion which differs from that required by the Surcharge Imposition Act and the Surcharge Assessment Act. A law taxing them is not in the sense of the authorities a law of "general application" ... Those persons whose surchargeable contributions ... are worked out by reference to the notional surchargeable contributions factor ... are a particular group of State employees and officers. Their selection for attention by the federal legislature as "high-income members" of the non-contributory unfunded schemes in question suggests that, for the purposes of the *Melbourne Corporation* doctrine, they are those employees and officers "at the higher levels of government" spoken of in *Australian Education Union* [184 CLR at 233]. At all events, there is no doubt that the first plaintiff is such an individual.

The case stated had asked whether the legislation was invalid because it discriminated against New South Wales, or imposed a particular disability or burden upon its activities. Gaudron, Gummow and Hayne JJ preferred a narrower question: namely, whether the imposition of the "surcharge" was placed beyond Commonwealth power "**[264]** by a sufficiently significant impairment of the exercise by the State of its freedom to select the manner and method for discharge of its constitutional functions respecting the remuneration of the judges of the courts of the State". They answered that the impairment was indeed sufficiently significant.

However, they emphasised again that the invalidity of the law did *not* depend merely on the discriminatory treatment of State judicial officers as compared with other taxpayers. Nor did it depend on the proposition – suggested by recent "**[268]** narrowly divided decisions of the United States Supreme Court", such as *New York v United States*, 505 US 144 (1992), *Printz v United States*, 521 US 898 (1997), and *Reno v Condon*, 528 US 141 (2000) – "**[269]** that consistently with, and perhaps in development of, the reasoning in *Australian Education Union*, it is critical to the constitutional integrity of the States that they alone have the capacity to give directions to their officials and determine what duties they perform. That is a large proposition [which is] best left for another day".

Gleeson CJ was content to express the relevant principle in terms of "discrimination", while McHugh J noted the repeated judicial analyses of the *Melbourne Corporation* principle as having "two elements".

McHugh J [281]: Given this long line of judicial exposition of the principle, I am unable to agree with that part of the reasons of the joint judgment [which asserts] that the *Melbourne Corporation* principle involves only "one limitation, though the apparent expression of it varies with the form of the legislation under consideration". With respect, since *Queensland Electricity Commission* it has been settled doctrine that there are two rules arising from the necessary constitutional implication. It is true that the joint judgment of six members of this Court, including myself, **[282]** in *Re Australian Education Union; Ex parte Victoria* said that it was unnecessary in that case to decide whether "there are two implied limitations, two elements or branches of one limitation, or simply one limitation" [184 CLR at 227]. But that statement provides no basis for rejecting the statement of Mason J in *Queensland Electricity Commission* [159 CLR at 217] that "the principle is now well established and that it consists of two elements". Nor does it provide any basis for rejecting the statement of Gibbs CJ in the same case [159 CLR at 206] that "it is clear, however, that there are two distinct rules, each based on the same principle, but dealing separately with general and discriminatory laws".

Perhaps nothing of substance turns on the difference between holding that there are two rules and holding that there is one limitation that must be applied by reference to "such criteria as 'special burden' and 'curtailment' of 'capacity' of the States 'to function as governments'". If there is a difference in content or application, it may lead to unforeseen problems in an area that is vague and difficult to apply. If there are no differences, no advantage is to be gained by jettisoning the formulation of Mason J in *Queensland Electricity Commission*.

As the present case is concerned with ... burdens on State judicial officers, the federal legislation is not directed at the States themselves. But that fact does not prevent the application of the *Melbourne Corporation* principle. In *Melbourne Corporation* itself, the legislation was directed at the private banks. But it was invalid because it restricted the banking choices open to State governments and their authorities. It prevented them – because it prevented the private banks – from entering into relationships concerning the use and placement of State government funds and borrowings ...

[283] Nothing in the Constitution or in the principle of *Melbourne Corporation* prevents the federal Parliament from subjecting State judicial officers to general taxation, provided that it does not discriminate against them as State judicial officers. But the matter is constitutionally different when federal legislation taxes State judicial officers in a way that differs from other income earners. Such a law will be invalid unless the discrimination is such that it has no practical impact on the relationship between the State and the judicial officer. The matter may be one of degree. Drawing the line between a law that treats State judicial officers differently from other income earners and is valid and a law that disadvantages them in a real sense and is invalid may not always be easy. But it must be drawn if the States are to be free from federal laws that impose special burdens or disabilities on their constitutional arrangements relating to the administration of justice.

Here the federal law discriminates against State judicial officers in a way that interferes in a significant respect with the States' relationships with their judges. It interferes with the financial arrangements that govern the terms of their offices, not as an incidence of a general tax applicable to all but as a special measure designed to single them out and place a financial burden on them that no one else in the community incurs. The Commonwealth does not dispute that the relevant federal legislation treats the first plaintiff and other State judicial officers differently from the way federal laws concerned with the superannuation contributions surcharge deal with other "high income earners". Private "high income earners" do not have the surcharge imposed on them. In their case, the surcharge is imposed on **[284]** their superannuation provider. The federal legislation assumes – no doubt with good reason – that the surcharge will be passed on to the high income earner in his or her capacity as a member of the superannuation scheme in the form of reduced benefits. But in so far as the federal legislation deals with these private "high income earners", it does not impose any surcharge on them personally. It does not make them liable to pay a debt of hundreds of thousands of dollars, as these federal laws make State judicial officers liable to pay ...

[285] So serious was the likely effect on the relationship between State judicial officers and the State of New South Wales that the State felt compelled to enact the *Judges' Pensions Amendment Act* 1998 (NSW). That Act amended the *Judges' Pensions Act* 1953 (NSW) to provide for the commutation of pensions to enable the payment of the superannuation contributions surcharge. As the New South Wales Attorney-General pointed out in his Second Reading Speech in the Legislative Council, the amendments were "essential to provide judges and other persons entitled to a pension or reversionary pension under the Act with a mechanism to pay the superannuation contributions surcharge from the benefit they are entitled to receive". Thus, the result of the present federal legislation concerning superannuation contributions surcharges is that the State of New South Wales and other States have been forced for practical reasons to enact legislation to pay a lump sum to their judges who retire so that they can if they wish commute part of their benefits to pay the surcharge debt. Thus, the practical effect of the federal legislation is to require the States to pay a sum of money to a retiring State judge to be paid to the Commonwealth, a payment that the Commonwealth accepts or assumes it could not directly require the States to pay.

Kirby J dissented. He agreed, "**[295]** with some hesitation", that for this purpose Kings was a "judge" (to whom, since she was appointed in 1993, the surcharge did not apply), but did not agree that its application to Austin infringed the *Melbourne Corporation* principle. This was so even though he agreed "**[299]** with much of the analysis" in the joint judgment.

Kirby J: [301] In so far as a difference has emerged in this case between the joint reasons and the reasons of McHugh J, I agree with the former that the two aspects of the implied limitation upon federal legislative power, noted in past decisions, are essentially manifestations of the one constitutional implication. Both are referable to the underlying conception concerning the nature of the Australian federation. I share the view that each identified defect is to be determined by reference to the effect of the impugned legislation on the continuing existence of the States, and whether there is an impermissible degree of impairment of the State's constitutional functions. The presence of discrimination against a State may be an indication of an attempted impairment of its functions as the Constitution envisaged them. But any discrimination against States must be measured against that underlying criterion. It affords the touchstone of the implied limitation explained in the Court's decision in *Melbourne Corporation*. It has been described as the "firm ground" upon which the reasoning in that case stands [*Payroll Tax Case* (1971) 122 CLR 353 at 402] ...

[304] I contest the proposition that imposition of [the surcharge] has a significant and detrimental effect on the power of a State to determine the terms and conditions affecting the remuneration of its judges. This Court has repeatedly upheld the broad power of the Federal Parliament to make laws with respect to taxation in the most ample terms. A wide power is essential for the effective discharge by the Commonwealth of all of its national responsibilities, as envisaged by the Constitution. Self-evidently, taxation laws of general application have long had important consequences for the States, their instrumentalities, employees and officers, including those holding high positions in the government of the States such as judges. Yet this Court has repeatedly resisted attempts by the States to narrow the federal taxation power, or to secure immunity from federal taxes, by reference to implied limitations on the Commonwealth's law-making capacity to affect the States. It did so most recently in the challenges to the federal payroll tax and to the fringe benefits tax. As a matter of constitutional principle, no different approach should be adopted with respect to the laws here in question.

Nor does the evidence support the argument of the first plaintiff that "not many Judges should be prepared to continue to serve after the first opportunity for retirement". A review, conducted by the New South Wales Government Actuary's Office on the judges' pension scheme of that State ..., noted that "[j]udges who retire at older ages have always received a lower value of benefit since payments will on average be paid for shorter periods". Whilst commenting, fairly, that "[t]he effect of the surcharge is that in future [judges] will also receive lower amounts of pension payments, which is a perverse outcome for longer service", the data produced **[305]** suggests that, despite financial disincentives, many judges in the past have continued to serve until the statutory retiring age ... The evidence before this Court does not establish the proposition – nor is it open to reasonable inference – that the established pattern of judicial service would alter significantly following the introduction of the surcharge. There is every reason to believe that it would not.

Despite financial disadvantages, appropriate appointees will continue to be attracted to, and elect to remain within, judicial office, federal and State. They will do so because of the nonfinancial features of judicial office. The submission that the new federal surcharge would alter this, in ways seriously damaging to the government of the States, is speculative, hypothetical and unproved. It should be rejected. Whatever arguments exist for improving the general level of judicial remuneration in Australia, having regard to its relative decline in recent decades, they have no bearing upon the constitutional validity of the federal law challenged in this case.

I would infer that *some* potential appointees, suitable for appointment as State judges, might now reject the offer of judicial appointment because of the comparative decline of the financial rewards in consequence of the surcharge. Yet given the general applicability of the surcharge in some form upon high income earners, most potential appointees would be likely to face a decline in post-retirement income even if they were to remain in their alternative employment. *Some*, who are appointed, might now elect to leave office earlier than they otherwise would have done. But there have always been injustices and anomalies in laws imposing taxation, as in the judicial pension scheme itself. The surcharge has now been in operation for five years whilst this case was being conceived, argued and decided. I would reject any suggestion that, in that time, there has been a fall off in the number and quality of judicial appointments, State or federal, in this country … The inducements typically lie elsewhere – in the interest and responsibility of the work; the status and public respect for the judicial office; the opportunity for a change of direction involving broader public service; and the respite from the intense pressures of other legal employment. Such inducements remain unchanged …

[306] The first plaintiff argued that the mechanism by which the surcharge was imposed, upon the superannuation member rather than the provider, constituted an impermissible discrimination against State judges, rendering the legislation invalid. However, mere discrimination does not amount to impermissible interference by the Federal Parliament in the basic constitutional functions of a State. As the joint reasons point out, discrimination does not have an independent operation in this context. It is only if the discrimination has the effect of impairing the constitutional functions of the State that the federal prohibition implied from the Constitution is enlivened …

[307] In my view, the effect of the federal legislation impugned in these proceedings does not even come close to jeopardising the selection and retention of State Supreme Court judges. It falls far short of impairing, in a substantial degree, the State's capacity to function as an independent constitutional entity. The decision of this Court to the contrary pushes the implied constitutional prohibition to a new and radical application that has no foundation in the Constitution. Since the impugned federal laws were enacted, the New South Wales Parliament has demonstrated the capacity of that State to adapt the pension arrangements for its judges … to the new federal legislation, in order to ameliorate any hardships to retired judges or other beneficiaries under the judicial pension scheme … Such measures contradict the suggestion of a relevant constitutional impairment.

The surcharge, applying as it does directly to judges in the position of the first plaintiff, imposes a financial burden upon them. That is true. But it is a burden that is imposed by a valid federal taxation law, [308] and, as such, has to be borne by those subject to it. Compared with some other lawyers and certain other income earners, judicial officers in Australia may not be particularly well remunerated. Yet, compared to the great mass of the population – including many of those subject to the superannuation contributions surcharge, they are very well remunerated indeed. It is unconvincing to suggest that the burden exacted by the impugned law could affect the proper discharge of the judicial role of persons such as the first plaintiff, their determination of matters coming before them in their judicial capacity or their integrity in carrying out their respective functions. In these circumstances I am unconvinced by the argument that the State judicial institution is damaged or weakened in a way that substantially impairs the capacity of the States to function as the Constitution envisaged.

3. State Laws and the Commonwealth

Melbourne Corporation raised the question: Are there certain things that Commonwealth legislation cannot do to the States? We turn now to the converse question: Are there certain things that State legislation cannot do to the Commonwealth? Our initial focus is on two groups of cases that seem to suggest contrary answers. At the least, they reflect divergent strains in the development of Australian federalism since the *Engineers' Case*.

The basic assumption underlying the doctrine of "implied immunity of instrumentalities" was that, as the Commonwealth and State political and legal orders coexist in the same geographical territory, each must normally be immune from the other's laws. Once that doctrine was rejected by the *Engineers' Case*, one might have expected the opposite assumption: that when Commonwealth and State coexist in the same geographical territory each of them must normally be subject to the other's laws. The actual results in *Pirrie v McFarlane* (1925) 36 CLR 170 and *West v Commissioner of Taxation* (1937) 56 CLR 657 are consistent with such an assumption. When, in *Pirrie v McFarlane*, the Commonwealth, in the form of Air-Craftsman Thomas McFarlane, entered into the legal regime of the State of Victoria, he became subject to the State's road traffic and drivers' licence laws. When, in *West's Case*, the Commonwealth, in the form of Edward West's pension cheque, entered into the legal regime of the State of New South Wales, it became subject to the State's income tax laws.

Pirrie v McFarlane arose out of proceedings brought in Victoria against a member of the Royal Australian Air Force. McFarlane, who did not have a driver's licence, had been ordered to drive an Air Force car to pick up a flight-lieutenant. During this journey, McFarlane was stopped by Constable William Pirrie, a member of the Victorian Police force, and charged under s 6 of the *Motor Car Act 1915* (Vic) with driving a motor vehicle on a public highway without a licence. The question was whether the *Motor Car Act* could apply to a member of the Commonwealth Defence Force. Knox CJ, Higgins and Starke JJ held that it could. As Higgins J put it: **[219]** The result of this case … will be to make it clear that a soldier is also a citizen and must obey the laws of the State in which he is, as well as the Federal laws".

Pirrie v McFarlane
(1925) 36 CLR 170

Starke J: [226] The Commonwealth power of defence cannot exempt soldiers from the obligation of all State law, nor can the power of the States to regulate the use of motor-cars within their territories be used so as to abrogate or derogate from the Commonwealth power of defence … [T]he *Motor Car Act* regulates the use of motor-cars in Victoria, and is designed to preserve the public safety and security. That is a subject matter wholly within the domain of the States and prima facie one in which they have plenary power to make laws for the peace, order and good government of the States and to bind all persons within their respective territories. The argument denying the power of the States to affect Commonwealth officers based upon some prohibition expressed or implied **[227]** in the Constitution can no longer be sustained (*Engineers' Case* [(1920) 28 CLR 129] …). So the immunity claimed in this case must rest upon [inconsistency with] some law enacted by the Parliament … How, then, is the *Motor Car Act* 1915, and particularly sec 6 thereof, inconsistent with any law of the Commonwealth?

A soldier or a member of the Air Force does not cease to be a citizen: if he commits an offence against the ordinary criminal law, he can be tried and punished as if he were a civilian … **[228]** An Air Force is organized under the Defence and Air Force Acts with all necessary arms and equipment for training in peace and service in war. And its government, discipline and military duty are provided for on much the same lines as in Great Britain. These Acts restrict to some extent the civil rights and duties of soldiers, but nowhere do they do they exempt them from obedience to civil law … The *Motor Car Act*, it is said, will paralyze the Defence Forces of the Commonwealth and impair the efficiency of their service: they cannot, in Victoria, be trained in peace nor used in war without the sanction of the State. Extravagant arguments such as this may well be considered when the State passes legislation calculated to lead to such dangerous consequences … All the State has done in this case is to regulate **[229]** the use of motor-cars and to require all citizens to observe provisions for the preservation of public safety and security. The Act is directed to acts of a purely local character, and its object is peculiarly within the authority of the State. It is not aimed particularly at the Defence Forces of the Commonwealth, nor is it in opposition to any express provision of the laws of the Commonwealth. A civil duty is, no doubt, established for all citizens using the public highways of Victoria, reasonable in itself and in no wise interfering with or infringing the military duties and obligations of the Defence Forces of the Commonwealth ... [T]he Commonwealth has ample legislative power to maintain its Forces free from any inconvenient legislation of the States.

Isaacs and Rich JJ dissented. In part they relied on the Commonwealth's exclusive power with respect to defence. Thus, Isaacs J argued that where "[191] a power – such as defence or [192] customs – is *expressly*, by secs 106 and 107, eliminated from State Constitutions, because made *exclusive* by sec 52, and transferred *eo nomine* to the Commonwealth, its control is necessarily by force of the very words of the Constitution placed outside the ambit of the State Constitutions and beyond any power of the State to affect it. No State Act can operate on that extraneous field" (the italics are his). In part, they relied on s 109 of the Constitution, arguing in effect that regulations under the *Defence Act 1903* (Cth) and the *Air Force Act 1923* (Cth) had "covered the field". In part, however, both Isaacs and Rich JJ relied on an implied immunity.

> **Isaacs J: [204]** [A] Judge, a Minister of the Crown, a member of Parliament ... have each a special status which for the due performance of their public functions carries with it special duties, rights and immunities that are outside the scope of ordinary citizenship. It would be illegal to do anything to weaken their obligation or their power to render the necessary public service ... But, taking the case of a Federal Judge or a Commonwealth member of Parliament, can it be seriously contended that in relation to the actual performance of their official duties they are – simply because they are also citizens – bound to conform to State statutory directions? I hold without reservation that not even prima facie have they any obligation to observe State law *in the performance of their Commonwealth duties*. And I hold that, even supposing there is not a syllable in any Commonwealth Act which directly or indirectly relieves them of that obligation. Once the assumption is made that their act is one of actual performance of Commonwealth official duty required by the Commonwealth law, then any State law which **[205]** intervenes and prescribes any limitation or qualification or condition on the performance of that duty is necessarily inconsistent with the Constitution or some Commonwealth law made under it. If a State law prescribed that no person should write notes in a book unless it had red covers, then, though there is not a word to the contrary in any Federal law, a Federal Judge could, when acting as such, disregard it. But, if Judges and members of Parliament are by the very nature of their duties to be left to their free exercise, unfettered by State legislation, how can that be denied to the Commonwealth Army and Navy created to preserve the existence of the country?

> **Rich J: [220]** The Police Magistrate [held] ... that on its construction the statute did not apply to the defendant when acting in his character of soldier ... [This] point does not depend on any doubt as to verbiage. It depends entirely on constitutional law. That constitutional law goes back at last to a question whether the State Parliament can validly regulate the official duties of Commonwealth officials ...
>
> **[221]** [E]ven apart from any special provision of Commonwealth law, I am unable to see how a State law can validly dictate to the Commonwealth in what manner or under what conditions it is to perform the executive functions expressly and exclusively committed to it by the Constitution.

The question whether, in the winding-up of a company, a State law could regulate the payment of creditors by overriding the priority otherwise given to debts owed to the Crown in right of the Commonwealth, first arose in *Federal Commissioner of Taxation v Official Liquidator of EO Farley Ltd* (1940) 63 CLR 278, where Dixon and Evatt JJ explored issues similar to those they had raised in *West's Case*. Could State legislation defer or destroy the priority of Crown debts in a winding-up? Could Commonwealth legislation assert a priority for debts to the Commonwealth Crown? The discussion was hypothetical, since the issue did not arise directly. The winding-up was under the *Companies Act 1899* (NSW), which made no special provision affecting the priority of debts to the Crown, and in any event did not bind the Crown.

In re *Foreman & Sons Pty Ltd; Uther v Federal Commissioner of Taxation* (*Uther's Case*) (1947) 74 CLR 508 raised the issue again, but this time the statutory context had changed. The winding-up was not under the "old" provisions of the *Companies Act 1899* (NSW), but under the "new" provisions of the *Companies Act 1936* (NSW). These "new" provisions, ss 282 and 297, bound the Crown and ruled out any priority for debts to the Crown in right of the Common-wealth. Latham CJ, Rich, Starke and Williams JJ held that when the Commonwealth, in the form of a creditor making a claim in the winding-up of a company, entered into the legal regime of the State of New South Wales, it became subject to the State's winding-up laws.

In re Foreman & Sons Pty Ltd; Uther v Federal Commissioner of Taxation (*Uther's Case*)
(1947) 74 CLR 508

Latham CJ: [520] The principle enunciated and applied [in *Melbourne Corporation* (1947) 74 CLR 31] ... cannot, in my opinion, be applied in favour of the Commonwealth in the same way as it may properly be applied in favour of a State. A State has no means of protecting itself against Commonwealth legislation if that legislation is valid. The position in the case of the Common-wealth, however, is very different. The Commonwealth Constitution, s 109, provides that when a law of a State is inconsistent with a law of the Commonwealth the latter shall prevail and the former shall, to the extent of the inconsistency, be invalid. This provision, as has often been pointed out, relates only to State laws which, apart from s 109, would be valid. A valid Commonwealth law prevails over an otherwise valid State law where the latter is inconsistent with the former. Accordingly, the Commonwealth Parliament is in a position to protect the Commonwealth against State legislation which, in the opinion of the Parliament, impairs or interferes with the performance of Commonwealth functions or the exercise of Commonwealth rights ...

[521] Accordingly, there is no need to invoke any principle of non-interference with governmental functions for the purpose of protecting the prerogative right of the Commonwealth to priority in payment of debts due to the Commonwealth. The Commonwealth Parliament has the means of protection in its own hands, and by suitable legislation can prevent the application of inconsistent State legislation. I do not suggest, however, that, because the Commonwealth has an extensive power of protecting itself in relation to its governmental functions against State legislation, the result is that any State legislation with respect to the Commonwealth should be held to be valid unless the Commonwealth Parliament produces counter-legislation. There are some subjects which are completely beyond State legislative power; for example, the functions of the Governor-General in relation to the summoning and the dissolution of the Commonwealth Parliament are matters with respect to which State legislatures have no power whatever. The Parlia-ment of New South Wales has power to make laws "for the peace, welfare and good government of New South Wales in all cases whatsoever" – *Constitution Act* 1902 (NSW), s 5. Laws upon the subjects mentioned would not be laws for the peace, &c, of New South Wales. Any State legislation relating to such matters would be invalid and the Commonwealth Parliament would not be put to the necessity of passing a statute inconsistent with a State statute which attempted to regulate such matters.

Thus some matters of Commonwealth concern are entirely beyond State legislative power. Is the Commonwealth prerogative right of priority in respect of debts owed to the Commonwealth one of these matters?

The Commonwealth of Australia was not born into a vacuum. It came into existence within a system of law already established. To much of that law the Commonwealth is necessarily subject; for example, the Commonwealth has no general power to legislate with respect to the law of property, the law of contract, the law of tort. In relation to those subjects, speaking generally, it lives and moves and has its being within a system of law which consists of the common law (in the widest sense) and the statute law of the various States. The question of the application of general law to the Commonwealth came before this Court in *Pirrie v McFarlane* [(1925) 36 CLR 170]. It was there held **[522]** that general provisions in a Traffic Act relating to motor cars applied to the Commonwealth when there was no Commonwealth law with which the State law was inconsistent ... Provision for the ranking of debts *inter se* in the liquidation of companies in the forum of a State is a common feature of ordinary company law. It is as much a part of the general law of the community as a traffic law. It usually involves distinction between classes of creditors. It is a general law which can be applied to the Commonwealth where the Commonwealth is a creditor in the same way as to other creditors. If the State legislation abolishes or reduces the priority in payment to which the Commonwealth is entitled at common law the Commonwealth may, by Commonwealth legislation, prevent that State law from operating. But, in my opinion, until the Commonwealth Parliament passes such legislation, the State law is applicable according to its terms.

Dixon and McTiernan JJ dissented. McTiernan J thought that the new configuration of State and Commonwealth legislation gave rise to an "inconsistency" under s 109 of the Constitution, thereby rendering the State legislation inoperative. Dixon J took a larger ground.

Dixon J: [528] We are here concerned with nothing but the relation between the Crown in right of the Commonwealth as a creditor for public moneys and the subjects of the Crown as creditors for private moneys. There are no conflicting claims between State and Commonwealth. The conflict is between the Commonwealth and its own subjects. What title can the State have to legislate as to the rights which the Commonwealth shall have as against its own subjects?

The fact that the priority claimed by the Commonwealth springs from one of the prerogatives of the Crown is an added reason, a reason perhaps conclusive in itself, for saying that it is a matter lying completely outside State power. But there is the antecedent consideration that to define or regulate the rights or privileges, duties or disabilities, of the Commonwealth in relation to the subjects of the Crown is not a matter for the States. General laws made by a State may affix legal consequences to given descriptions of transaction and the Commonwealth, if it enters into such a transaction, may be bound by the rule laid down. For instance, if the Commonwealth contracts with a company the form of the contract will be governed by s 348 of the *Companies Act*. Further, State law is made applicable to matters in which the Commonwealth is a party by s 79 of the *Judiciary Act*. But these applications of State law, though they may perhaps be a source of confusion, stand altogether apart from the regulation of the legal situation which the Commonwealth, as a Government, shall occupy with reference to private rights. Take two examples. At common law the King in virtue of his prerogative might effectually assign, or take an assignment of, a legal chose in action, at all events if it were for a debt or thing certain. No law of the State could deprive the Crown in right of the Commonwealth of this special capacity or impose, for instance, the necessity of **[529]** notice in writing. Again, in the interval before the *Claims against the Commonwealth Act* 1902 made the Commonwealth liable for tort no State law could have done so …

A federal system is necessarily a dual system. In a dual political system you do not expect to find either government legislating for the other. But supremacy, where it exists, belongs to the Commonwealth, not to the States. The affirmative grant of legislative power to the Parliament over the subjects of bankruptcy and insolvency may authorize the enactment of laws excluding or reducing the priority of the Crown in right of the States in bankruptcy and it has been held that the taxation power extends to giving the Commonwealth a right to be paid taxes before the States are paid (*South Australia v Commonwealth* [(1942) 65 CLR 373]). But these are the results of express grants of specific powers, plenary within their ambit, to the Federal legislature, whose laws, if within power, are made paramount. Because of their content or nature, the **[530]** express powers in question are considered to extend to defining the priority of debts owing to the States or postponing State claims to taxes. The legislative power of the States is in every material respect of an opposite description. It is not paramount but, in case of a conflict with a valid Federal law, subordinate. It is not granted by the Constitution. It is not specific, but consists in the undefined residue of legislative power which remains after full effect is given to the provisions of the Constitution establishing the Commonwealth and arming it with the authority of a central government of enumerated powers. That means, after giving full effect not only to the grants of specific legislative powers but to all other provisions of the Constitution and the necessary consequences which flow from them.

It is a fundamental constitutional error to regard the question of the efficacy of s 282 of the *Companies Act* 1936 of New South Wales as if it were an exercise of an express grant, contained in the Constitution, to the States of a power to make laws with respect to the specific subject of the winding up of insolvent companies. It is a provision enacted in intended pursuance of a general legislative power to make laws for the peace, welfare, and good government of New South Wales in all cases whatsoever. The content and strength of this power are diminished and controlled by the Commonwealth Constitution. It is of course a fallacy, in considering what a State may or may not do under this undefined residuary power, to reason from some general conception of the subjects which fall within it as if they were granted or reserved to the States as specific heads of power. But no fallacy in constitutional reasoning is so persistent or recurs in so many and such varied applications. In the present case the fallacious process of reasoning could not begin from s 107 as the error has so commonly done in the past. For it is not a question whether the power of the Parliament of a Colony becoming a State continues as at the establishment of the Commonwealth. The Colony of New South Wales could not be said at the establishment of the Commonwealth to have any power at all with reference to the Commonwealth. Like the goddess of wisdom the Commonwealth *uno ictu* sprang from the brain of its begetters armed and of full stature. At the same instant the Colonies became States; but whence did the States obtain the power to regulate the legal relations of this new polity with its subjects? It formed no part of the old colonial power. The Federal constitution does not give it. Surely it is for the peace, order and good government of the Commonwealth, not for the peace, welfare and good government of New South Wales, **[531]** to say what shall be the relative situation of private rights and of the public rights of the Crown representing the Commonwealth, where they come into conflict. It is a question of the fiscal and governmental rights of the Commonwealth and, as such, is one over which the State has no power ...

How far s 109 of the Constitution may protect from the operation of State laws the consequences which are affixed by law **[532]** to what Federal legislation enacts is perhaps a question; but I suppose that, if it sufficiently appears that the purpose of the Federal law is to bring about the consequences, a State law which defeats them must be regarded as inconsistent. However, as I am of opinion that the State law cannot affect the prerogative rights of the Crown ... , it is unnecessary to pursue the question.

Dixon J's arguments did not succeed in *Uther's Case*, but 15 years later *Commonwealth v Cigamatic Pty Ltd (In Liquidation)* (1962) 108 CLR 372 raised the issue again. Again the case turned on ss 282 and 297 of the *Companies Act*, and again the Commonwealth claimed the priority over other creditors to which it would be entitled apart from those provisions. By this time Sir Owen Dixon had been Chief Justice for 10 years, and this time his view prevailed.

Commonwealth v Cigamatic Pty Ltd (In Liquidation)
(1962) 108 CLR 372

Dixon CJ: [376] In the first instance the Commonwealth rests its claim on the right at common law of the Crown to priority of payment when in any administration of assets debts of equal degree due to the Crown and due to subjects of the Crown come into competition. This right arose from the sovereignty of the Crown and was **[377]** accordingly expressed in terms of prerogative but it is today one of the fiscal rights of government and of course it clearly attaches to the Commonwealth. The claim of the Commonwealth in the present case resting on this right is, however, denied on the ground that by force of the State *Companies Act* it is excluded. This conclusion is doubtless supported, if not completely at all events to no inconsiderable degree, by the judgments of the majority in *Uther v Federal Commissioner of Taxation* [(1947) 74 CLR 508], but it seems to me now as it seemed to me then to imply a fundamental proposition about the power of legislatures of the States which ought not to be entertained. The proposition that is implied is that an exercise of State legislative power may directly derogate from the rights of the Commonwealth with respects to its people. It is a proposition which must go deep in the nature and operation of the federal system. There can be no doubt as to the nature or the source of the right of the Commonwealth in an administration of assets to be paid in preference to subjects of the Crown if there is a competition among debts of equal degree. It springs from the nature of the Commonwealth as a government of the Queen. Therefore to treat those rights as subject to destruction or modification or qualification by the legislature of a State must mean that under the Constitution there resides in a State or States a legislative power to control legal rights and duties between the Commonwealth and its people. Indeed in *Uther's Case* [74 CLR at 523] *Rich* J actually says: "In so far as the right of the Crown in the right of the Commonwealth to rank as a preferential creditor is based merely on the prerogative of the Crown as such, I see no reason why the State legislature cannot validly abridge or abolish it just as it could any other Crown prerogative of this sort". Except by adopting such a doctrine I cannot see how it could be thought that State legislative power could directly deprive the Commonwealth of the priority to which it is entitled under the law derived from the prerogative. Believing, as I do, that the doctrine thus involved is a fundamental error in a constitutional principle that spreads far beyond the mere preference of debts owing to the Commonwealth, I do not think we should treat *Uther's Case* as a decisive authority upon that question which we should regard as binding. It is not a question, as it appears to me, of interpreting some positive power of the State over a given subject matter. It is not a question of making some implication in favour of the Commonwealth restraining some acknowledged legislative power of the State. If you express the priority belonging to the **[378]** Commonwealth as a prerogative of the Crown in right of the Commonwealth, the question is whether the legislative powers of the States could extend over one of the prerogatives of the Crown in right of the Commonwealth. If, as in modern times I think it is more correct to do, you describe it as a fiscal right belonging to the Commonwealth as a government and affecting its Treasury, it is a question of State legislative power affecting to control or abolish a federal fiscal right. It is not a question of the authority of the power of a State to make some general law governing the rights and duties of those who enter into some description of transaction, such as the sale of goods, and of the Commonwealth in its executive arm choosing to enter into a transaction of that description. It is not a question of the exercise of some specific grant of power which according to the very meaning of the terms in which it is defined embraces the subject matter itself: for it is not the plan of the Constitution to grant specific powers to the States over defined subjects. It is, I think, a question which cannot be regarded as simply governed by the applicability of the principles upon which *Melbourne Corporation v Commonwealth* [(1947) 74 CLR 31] depended. In truth it imports a principle which if true would apply generally with respect to the legal rights of the Commonwealth in relation to its subjects. I do not speak of legal rights which are the immediate product of federal statute and so protected by s 109 of the Constitution. But because it imports such a principle I think we ought not to give effect to the view taken in *Uther's Case* that s 297 of the *Companies Act*, 1936 of New South Wales operated directly to nullify the priority to which the Commonwealth might have been entitled. I shall not recapitulate the reasons against this conclusion which I gave in *Uther's Case*.

Windeyer J agreed with Dixon CJ. Menzies J delivered a separate judgment, with which Owen J concurred, adopting what Dixon J had said in *Uther's Case*. Kitto J agreed with both Dixon CJ and Menzies J. McTiernan and Taylor JJ dissented, adhering to *Uther's Case*.

Note the following points in respect of *Uther's Case* and *Cigamatic*:

1. In *Uther's Case*, Latham CJ treated the winding-up provisions as "**[522]** a general law" that could apply to the Commonwealth "in the same way as to other creditors". That, of course, would be consistent with *Pirrie v McFarlane* and *West's Case*. On the other hand, Dixon J argued that where the effect of a law is "**[528]** to define or regulate" the rights of the Commonwealth, it is not "a general law" but a special law, which a State has no power to make.

2. Why would such a law be a "special law"? It may be because the subject-matter of the law is a royal prerogative. In *Uther's Case* Dixon J sees this as "**[528]** an added reason, ... perhaps conclusive in itself" for denying State legislative power. However, in *Cigamatic* he prefers to analyse the fiscal claims of governments in a more functional way that does not expressly invoke the "prerogative" at all.

3. It may be a "special law", and therefore beyond State power, because it interferes in the relations between the Commonwealth as a body politic and its subjects. The implication would be that these relationships must be regulated only by Commonwealth legislation and not by State legislation.

4. The assumption that the States and the Commonwealth will normally be subject to each other's laws was expressly rejected by Dixon J in *Uther's Case*. He stated that: "**[529]** In a dual political system you do not expect to find either government legislating for the other".

5. Part of the background to Dixon J's approach is the basic assumption of Australian federalism that, when issues of "supremacy" arise, it is the Commonwealth that must be

"supreme". This assumption is reflected not only in s 109, but in covering clause 5 of the *Commonwealth of Australia Constitution Act 1900* (Imp).

6.   The effect of the *Engineers' Case* is that grants of power must be read according to their natural meaning, with no artificial restrictions imposed by constitutional "implications". That means that the grants of Commonwealth power in s 51 of the Constitution will often have the effect of authorising the Commonwealth to pass laws that affect the States. However, this reasoning does not work in reverse, since the Constitution contains no similar grants of specific State powers. The State legislative powers granted by the various State Constitutions, and recognised or preserved by ss 106-108 of the federal Constitution, are only in general terms. The specific pegs or footholds that enable the Commonwealth to legislate in a way that affects the States have no counterpart at the State level.

Some of the above points might allow us to "explain" *Cigamatic* as establishing a limited exception to the general principle illustrated by *Pirrie v McFarlane*. Some of them would not. It seems clear, both in *Uther's Case* and in *Cigamatic*, that Sir Owen Dixon saw himself as establishing "[377] a constitutional principle" that "must go deep in the nature and operation of the federal system". If we accept the validity of such a principle, then perhaps it is *Pirrie v McFarlane* that needs to be explained as an "exception". Alternatively, we may have to conclude that *Pirrie v McFarlane* is itself an example of the "fundamental error" that in *Cigamatic* Dixon CJ was seeking to root out.

It is evident that the principle that Dixon CJ had in mind was linked with his earlier dicta in *Essendon Corporation v Criterion Theatres Ltd* (1947) 74 CLR 1, and with those of Fullagar J in *Commonwealth v Bogle* (1953) 89 CLR 229. In *Essendon Corporation* the High Court held that the Commonwealth was not liable to municipal rates in respect of premises at Essendon in Victoria which, from September 1942 to September 1944, had been taken over and occupied by Commonwealth military forces for wartime purposes. The decision rested primarily on the ground that a statutory provision imposing liability on "any person who occupies" property should not be construed as applicable to the Crown in right of the Commonwealth.

Essendon Corporation v Criterion Theatres Ltd
(1947) 74 CLR 1

Dixon J: [18] [T]he aspect in which the occupation of the land by the Commonwealth should be regarded is not that of passive ownership but of the actual carrying on of measures of defence. At all events I so regard the matter and prefer to base my decision upon the ground that the Constitution does not permit the State to tax that kind of action of the Commonwealth ... Clearly enough the Commonwealth took and retained possession of the land in executing a function of government. Let it be added, should there still be those who think it matters, one of "the primary and inalienable functions of a constitutional government" (*Coomber v Justices of Berks* [(1883) 9 App Cas 61 at 74]). The imposition of the tax that is attempted is directly upon the Commonwealth itself and to make it **[19]** worse the occasion of the imposition is the act of the Commonwealth in so taking and retaining possession of the land. I believe that I am on sound ground in saying that the constitution does not allow this ...

[22] To my mind the incapacity of the States directly to tax the Commonwealth in respect of something done in the exercise of its powers or functions is a necessary consequence of the system of government established by the Constitution. It is hardly necessary at this stage of our constitutional development to go over the considerations which make it impossible to suppose that the Constitution intended that the States should levy taxes upon the Commonwealth – the nature of the Federal Government, its supremacy, the exclusiveness or paramountcy of its legislative powers, the independence of its fiscal system and the elaborate provisions of the Constitution governing the financial relations of the central government to the constituent States. To describe the establishment of the Commonwealth as the birth of a nation has been a commonplace. It was anything but the birth of a taxpayer.

The idea that a tax liability might be directly imposed upon the Commonwealth by State law would not, I think, have been entertained, if it had not been for misapprehensions which obtain concerning the effect of the *Engineers' Case* [(1920) 28 CLR 129]. One such misapprehension is that the decision meant that the Constitution implies nothing; that it means nothing that it does not say in express words.

The issue in *Commonwealth v Bogle* was whether an increase in accommodation charges at a Commonwealth migrant hostel violated the *Prices Regulation Act 1948* (Vic). The Court held that it did, and that the Act was applicable because the corporatised entity managing the hostel did not represent "the Crown". Dixon CJ and Kitto J agreed (and Webb J "**[255]** substantially" agreed) with the judgment of Fullagar J.

Commonwealth v Bogle
(1953) 89 CLR 229

Fullagar J: [259] In the view which I have ultimately taken of this case it is not necessary to decide whether the Commonwealth is bound by the *Prices Regulation Act* (Vic). I think I should say, however, that, in my opinion, the Commonwealth is not bound by that Act, and, if I had thought that the Commonwealth, as the party with whom the defendant contracted, was the proper plaintiff in this action, I should have held that the defence to which I have referred failed. To say that a State can enact legislation which is binding upon the Commonwealth in the same sense in which it is binding upon a subject of the State appears to me to give effect to a fundamental mis-conception. The question whether a particular State Act binds the Crown in right of a State is a pure question of construction. The Crown in right of the State has assented to the statute, and no constitutional question arises. If we ask whether the same statute binds the Crown in right of the Commonwealth, a question of construction may arise on the threshold. In considering that question we are, or should be, assisted by a presumption that references to the Crown are references to the Crown in right of the State only. If the answer to the question of construction be that the statute in question does purport to bind the Crown in right of the Commonwealth, then a constitutional question arises. The Crown in right of the State has assented to the statute, but the Crown in right of the Commonwealth has not, and the constitutional question, to my mind, is susceptible of only one answer, and that is that the State Parliament has no power over the Commonwealth. The Commonwealth – or the Crown in right of the Commonwealth, or whatever you choose to call it – is, to all intents and purposes, a juristic person, but it is not a juristic person which is subjected either by any State Constitution or by the Commonwealth Constitution to the legislative power of any State Parliament. If, for instance, the Commonwealth Parliament had never enacted **[260]** s 56 of the *Judiciary Act* 1903-1950, it is surely unthinkable that the Victorian Parliament could have made a law rendering the Commonwealth liable for torts committed in Victoria. The Common-wealth may, of course, become affected by State laws. If, for example, it makes a contract in Victoria, the terms and effect of that contract may have to be sought in the *Goods Act* 1928 (Vic) (see *Federal Commissioner of Taxation v Official Liquidator of EO Farley Ltd (In Liquidation)* [(1940) 63 CLR 278 at 308] and *In re Richard Foreman & Sons Pty Ltd; Uther v Federal Commis-sioner of Taxation* [(1947) 74 CLR 508 at 528]). But I should think it impossible to hold that the Parliament of Victoria could lawfully prescribe the uses which might be made by the Common-wealth of its own property, the terms upon which that property might be let to tenants, or the terms upon which the Commonwealth might provide accommodation for immigrants introduced into Australia.

These judgments in *Essendon Corporation* and *Commonwealth v Bogle* went beyond the issues which the Court actually had to decide. Nevertheless, the two judgments were clearly intended as major statements of principle that appear to complement the reasoning of Sir Owen Dixon in *Uther's Case* and *Cigamatic*.

In *Commonwealth v Bogle*, Fullagar J conceded that the Commonwealth "**[260]** may, of course, become affected by State laws". He gave the example that, when the Commonwealth makes a contract in Victoria, it may be governed by the *Goods Act 1928* (Vic). In *Federal*

Commissioner of Taxation v Official Liquidator of EO Farley Ltd (1940) 63 CLR 278, Dixon J had said: "**[308]** In many respects the executive government of the Commonwealth is affected by the condition of the general law". He, too, gave the example of contracts. In *Uther's Case*, Dixon J again acknowledged these "**[528]** applications of State law". But he thought they "stand altogether apart from the regulation of the legal situation which the Commonwealth, as a government, shall occupy with reference to private rights".

This distinction may be one way of reconciling *Cigamatic* with *Pirrie v McFarlane*. Yet the limits of the "affected by" doctrine, as it is sometimes called, are hazy. The conception may be broad enough to include *Pirrie v McFarlane*: by directing McFarlane's car along St Kilda Road, the Commonwealth was availing itself of a State facility, and ought thus to submit itself to the regulatory regime controlling the use of that facility. But why is it not also broad enough to extend to the situation in *Farley's Case*, *Uther's Case* and *Cigamatic*, where the Commonwealth was seeking to participate in a State winding-up in a State Supreme Court under a State company law?

The tension between *Pirrie v McFarlane* and *Cigamatic* has run deep in Australian constitutional theory. Generally, those commentators who saw *Pirrie v McFarlane* as fundamental have had trouble in accepting (or even understanding) *Cigamatic*, while those who saw *Cigamatic* as fundamental have had trouble with *Pirrie v McFarlane*.

RP Meagher and WMC Gummow, "Sir Owen Dixon's Heresy"
(1980) 54 *Australian Law Journal* 25

[27] [I]n 1962 a new doctrine entered the realm of constitutional law in this country. It was laid down by the majority of the High Court in *Commonwealth v Cigamatic Pty Ltd* [(1962) 108 CLR 372], a decision which overruled *Uther's* case [(1947) 74 CLR 508] and placed in the Australian constitutional pantheon the dissenting judgment of Dixon J (as he then was) in *Uther's* case …

[28] We believe there are some eleven propositions to be teased out from the judgments … and that taken both collectively and individually they offer no logical basis for any such doctrine as that which they have been said to support. We now turn to these eleven heads and set out our views upon each of them.

(a) Much is said of the significant place of s 109 in the scheme of the Constitution; but in truth, the terms of that section support no general principle (i) of Commonwealth superior *power* or (ii) immunity of the Commonwealth from the exercise of the State legislative power; rather they assume a concurrence of *power* which produces a conflict in *legislation*.

(b) It is no reason to deny validity to a State law otherwise within legislative competence, that it has an impact upon a prerogative enjoyed by the Crown in another right; if it is for the peace, welfare and good government of New South Wales to legislate that, in respect of the winding up of a New South Wales incorporated company, Crown debts of New South Wales and other States and Dominions, and the United Kingdom, are to be limited to special statutory priority, why should the law be taken beyond power when it attemp[t]s to reach the Crown in the right of the Commonwealth?

(c) To say that before 1901 the Colonies could not legislate in respect of the Commonwealth and nothing since then has given the States such power, is to misstate the position because: (i) it assumes the States can only legislate in respect of subject-matter in existence when the respective colonies attained responsible government in the nineteenth century, which would confine their present legislative reach to persons of extraordinary longevity and to corporations of respectable antiquity, and (ii) it denies the undoubted propositions that the States have plenary power to legislate in respect of any subject-matter from time to time within that power, and that that power flowed in the first instance from the Imperial legislation establishing their present organs of responsible government and was confirmed by a later Imperial Act, namely the Australian Constitution [s 107] …

(d) To say that a State law of the kind in question cannot be for the peace, welfare and good government of the State because it touches the Commonwealth does not resolve the issue because:

(i) it falsely assumes that each law permits only of one characterisation, whereas the High Court itself has made it clear that this is not so; (ii) it overlooks the assumption in the **[29]** Constitution that in various fields both State and Commonwealth may validly and concurrently legislate pursuant to concurrent legislative powers ... ; (iii) it assumes that laws for the peace, order and good government of the Commonwealth and the peace, welfare and good government of the States are mutually exclusive classes whereas this is not the case; and (iv) it does not heed the consideration that had the States not otherwise been competent to touch the Commonwealth, there would have been no need to express s 52 of the Constitution as conferring exclusive powers or to enact s 114 of the Constitution.

(e) To speak of the relations of the Commonwealth and "its people" overlooks the residence of each of those persons in their respective States and obscures the true issue, namely one of the adjustment of concurrent claims made over those persons by the Commonwealth and the States.

(f) The reference to s 79 of the *Judiciary Act* 1903 (Cth) is inapposite; all that section does is to select a law for application in a Federal Court, as is provided for by Ch III of the Constitution.

(g) The Commonwealth was not born by parthenogenesis, nor in the manner of Athena; it was called into existence by an Imperial Statute, it is not to be seen in isolation from the constitutional matrix of Imperial legislation over a long period which contains the Commonwealth together with the Imperial and State Crowns, and the question is not whether the Commonwealth has "submitted itself" to State legislative power but whether on the true construction of all the Imperial laws involved it is preserved thereby from State legislation.

(h) References to the Commonwealth "waiving" its immunity by, for example, entering into contracts for the sale of goods are logically incoherent; either the State law is valid when enacted or not at all, and no reason can be advanced for assessing such validity from time to time in the light of current Commonwealth executive action.

(i) The express disavowal of reliance on the *Melbourne Corporation* doctrine removes from the new dogma any foundation in necessity for preservation of Commonwealth governmental functions; thus it could not be suggested that the prerogative right at stake in both *Uther's* case and in *Cigamatic* was essential to government in the sense of that term as expounded in the *Melbourne Corporation* case.

(j) There is nothing inherent in the nature of any prerogative right which places it in any special class so as to suggest it is given special immunisation from infection by any State legislation; the "prerogative" is no more than a general term used to identify a wide range of executive powers. As Sir Frederick Pollock explained long ago, "prerogative is nothing more mysterious than the residue of the King's undefined powers after striking out those which have been taken away by legislation or fallen into desuetude" ...

(k) In truth, the *Cigamatic* doctrine, in its various formulations, is but a revival in fresh garb of one aspect of the immunity of instrumentalities doctrine, which in both of its operations was discarded in the *Engineers' Case* [(1920) 28 CLR 129]. So much is apparent from the comments of Jacobs J in *Maguire v Simpson* [(1977) 139 CLR 362 at 404], wherein he spoke of the "question whether the reasoning in *Cigamatic* involves revival of the doctrine of implied immunity of instrumentalities and whether it is essentially consistent with the *Engineers' Case*". It is to be hoped that the High Court will at the earliest opportunity be invited to reconsider, and [will] reconsider, the correctness of the decision in *Cigamatic*.

It is generally accepted that the Commonwealth can submit itself and its instrumentalities to State law by its own legislation (see *Taxation Debts (Abolition of Crown Priority) Act 1980* (Cth) and *Crown Debts (Priority) Act 1981* (Cth), which reverse the practical effect of the *Cigamatic* decision). Indeed, it may be that the "affected by" doctrine can be explained as depending on a submission by conduct. An early example of submission by legislation was the *Commonwealth Salaries Act 1907* (Cth), in which the long dispute over State taxation of federal salaries was resolved in favour of the States by the Commonwealth Parliament itself. That act of submission was held to be valid in *Chaplin v Commissioner of Taxes for South Australia* (1911) 12 CLR 375.

A current example, the full significance of which is still debated, is s 64 of the *Judiciary Act 1903* (Cth), which provides: "In any suit to which the Commonwealth or a State is a party, the rights of parties shall as nearly as possible be the same, and judgment may be given and costs awarded on either side, as in a suit between subject and subject". Once a suit has commenced, s 64 has the effect of submitting the Commonwealth and its instrumentalities to State laws (see also *Judiciary Act*, ss 79 and 80). In *Maguire v Simpson* (1977) 139 CLR 362, for example, it was held that an action filed in the Supreme Court of New South Wales by the Commonwealth Trading Bank, a Commonwealth instrumentality, had attracted the *Limitation Act 1969* (NSW), which barred the action as out of time.

Commonwealth v Evans Deakin Industries Ltd (1986) 161 CLR 254 also concerned s 64. The principal contractor engaged by the Commonwealth for construction work at Eagle Farm airport in Brisbane had gone into liquidation, leaving the sub-contractor (Evans Deakin) unpaid. The sub-contractor then sued the Commonwealth, seeking to enforce a charge on the moneys owed by the Commonwealth to the contractor, pursuant to the *Subcontractors' Charges Act 1947* (Qld). The Court, with Brennan J dissenting, held that s 64 rendered the 1947 Act applicable. By contrast, in *Deputy Commissioner of Taxation v Moorebank Pty Ltd* (1988) 165 CLR 55, the High Court held that s 64 does not apply where its effect is precluded by other Commonwealth legislation: "**[64]** In particular, where a Commonwealth legislative scheme is complete upon its face, s 64 will not operate to insert into it some provision of State law for whose operation the Commonwealth provisions can, when properly understood, be seen to have left no room".

In *Allders International Pty Ltd v Commissioner of State Revenue (Vic)* (1996) 186 CLR 630, it was held that Victorian stamp duty could not be levied on the lease of a duty free store at Tullamarine airport, since the airport was a place "acquired by the Commonwealth for public purposes" within the meaning of s 52(i) of the Constitution (and hence subject to the Commonwealth's exclusive legislative power). In so deciding the Court followed *Worthing v Rowell and Muston Pty Ltd* (1970) 123 CLR 89, which had decided that no State law could operate within any "Commonwealth place". The effect of that decision had been overcome by the *Commonwealth Places (Application of Laws) Act 1970* (Cth), but that legislation contained an exception for State laws imposing taxes. When *Allders* was argued before the High Court, the respondent had unsuccessfully sought leave to argue that *Worthing v Rowell and Muston* should be overruled, in part on the ground of alleged inconsistency with *Pirrie v McFarlane*. Accordingly, the decision for the appellant in *Allders* immediately gave rise to suggestions that *Pirrie v McFarlane* had impliedly been overturned. The matter came to a head in *Re Residential Tenancies Tribunal (NSW); Ex parte Defence Housing Authority* (*Henderson's Case*) (1997) 190 CLR 410, when leave was given to argue that *Cigamatic* should be overruled.

In 1992, the Defence Housing Authority (DHA), a Commonwealth body established by the *Defence Housing Authority Act 1987* (Cth), took a 10-year lease of a home unit at Epping in Sydney on terms that DHA would then sublet the unit to defence personnel. The unit was then sold (subject to the lease) to Dr Arvin Henderson, who thus became the head lessor. Relying upon s 24 of the *Residential Tenancies Act 1987* (NSW), he and his wife sought to enter and inspect the premises. DHA refused their request. The Hendersons then sought orders from the Residential Tenancies Tribunal of New South Wales that DHA was bound by the *Residential Tenancies Act* and that they be allowed to enter and inspect the premises and to have a copy of the key. DHA disputed the Tribunal's jurisdiction by obtaining an order nisi for prohibition in the High Court.

DHA relied upon four grounds in seeking to prohibit further proceedings in the Tribunal. First, it argued that, in purporting to confer jurisdiction upon the Tribunal over DHA, the *Residential Tenancies Act* was inconsistent with the *Defence Housing Authority Act* and was therefore invalid under s 109 of the Constitution. The Court, with Kirby J dissenting, rejected this submission. Second, DHA submitted that the *Residential Tenancies Act* was invalid in so far as it purported to apply to DHA because it dealt with a matter within the exclusive power of the Commonwealth under s 52(ii) of the Constitution. The Court, with Kirby J again dissenting, rejected this argument, interpreting s 52(ii) as a mere transitional provision, intended only to exclude any continuing operation of State law upon "**[506]** the persons or property of a department of the State public service" transferred to the Commonwealth after its establishment under s 69 of the Constitution. While s 52(ii) had operated thus to perfect the initial transfer to the

Commonwealth of State defence departments, it could have no wider operation in relation to the Department of Defence as now constituted. Third, DHA argued that the *Residential Tenancies Act* did not extend to DHA given the immunity of the Commonwealth from State laws as expounded in *Cigamatic*. This argument was unanimously rejected. Fourth, it was said that s 64 of the *Judiciary Act 1903* (Cth) had no application to the proceedings before the tribunal. Although the answers given to the previous submissions meant that it was strictly unnecessary for this argument to be addressed, there were indications by members of the Court that s 64 did not apply because the proceedings in the tribunal were not judicial proceedings amounting to a "suit" under s 64. (Similarly, in *Commonwealth v Western Australia* (*Mining Act Case*) (1999) 196 CLR 392, it was held that applications to mining wardens in Western Australia for exploration leases did not give rise to a "suit" attracting the operation of s 64.)

On the issue of the scope and operation of the *Cigamatic* doctrine, the Court in *Henderson's Case*, with Kirby J dissenting, reaffirmed the correctness of *Cigamatic*. However, in doing so, the majority made it clear that the doctrine does not amount to a general immunity of the Commonwealth and its agencies from State laws, but stands for a more limited proposition. This conclusion rested upon a series of difficult distinctions.

Re Residential Tenancies Tribunal (NSW); Ex parte Defence Housing Authority (Henderson's Case)
(1997) 190 CLR 410

Dawson, Toohey and Gaudron JJ: [438] It was submitted by the DHA and by the Attorney-General for the Commonwealth intervening that State laws cannot by their own force bind the Crown in right of the Commonwealth. That submission was said to be supported by the decision of this Court in *Commonwealth v Cigamatic Pty Ltd (in liq)* [(1962) 108 CLR 372], but in truth it represents a basic misconception of what was decided in that case.

In the present context, the Crown in right of the Commonwealth means the government of the Commonwealth exercising the executive power vested in it by s 61 of the Constitution. That power includes the prerogatives of the Crown because the setting in which the Crown is invested with executive power is that of the common law and the prerogatives of the Crown are those rights, powers, privileges and immunities which it possesses at common law. Of course, those prerogatives are not immutable but, being derived from the common law, are susceptible to statutory alteration or abolition where the necessary legislative power exists. Under s 61 the executive power vested in the Crown is exercisable by the Governor-General as the Crown's representative. The activities of the Commonwealth government are conducted formally on behalf of the Crown through the Governor-General acting on the advice of the Federal Executive Council. The Federal Executive Council consists of the Crown's Ministers of State drawn, subject to a minor qualification, from the House of Representatives and the Senate. In reality, the Crown acts in its day to day activities through the agency of its public service and through other institutions or instrumentalities created for the purpose. The Crown's functions nowadays extend beyond the traditional, or clearly regal, functions of government to activities of an entrepreneurial or commercial kind which, in general, were previously engaged in only by subjects of the Crown.

It is necessary at the outset to observe a distinction between the capacities of the Crown on the one hand, by which we mean its rights, powers, privileges and immunities, and the exercise of those capacities on the other. In referring to the capacities of the Crown so defined, we **[439]** are speaking of the same thing of which Dixon J spoke when he used the words "capacity or functions" in *West v Commissioner of Taxation (NSW)* [(1937) 56 CLR 657 at 682] in quoting from the dissenting judgment of Isaacs J in *Pirrie v McFarlane* [(1925) 36 CLR 170 at 191]. Elsewhere he used other expressions to convey essentially the same meaning, such as the "governmental rights and powers belonging to the Federal executive as such" [*Federal Commissioner of Taxation v Official Liquidator of EO Farley Ltd* (1940) 63 CLR 278 at 308] or "the rights or privileges, duties or disabilities, of the Commonwealth in relation to the subjects of the Crown" [*In re Foreman & Sons Pty Ltd; Uther v Federal Commissioner of Taxation* (1947) 74 CLR 508 at 528]. In *Cigamatic*

[108 CLR at 378], Dixon CJ also spoke of the "legal rights of the Commonwealth in relation to its subjects" and that expression is, as shall appear, of some use in applying the principle which he expounded.

The purpose in drawing a distinction between the capacities of the Crown and the exercise of them is to draw a further distinction between legislation which purports to modify the nature of the executive power vested in the Crown – its capacities – and legislation which assumes those capacities and merely seeks to regulate activities in which the Crown may choose to engage in the exercise of those capacities.

In *Cigamatic* it was held that a State legislature had no power to impair the capacities of the Commonwealth executive, but at the same time it was recognised that the Commonwealth might be regulated by State laws of general application in those activities which it carried on in common with other citizens. Dixon J had earlier drawn the same distinction in *Federal Commissioner of Taxation v Official Liquidator of EO Farley Ltd* [63 CLR at 308] where he said:

"In many respects the executive government of the Commonwealth is affected by the condition of the general law. For instance, the general law of contract may regulate the formation, performance and discharge of the contracts which the Commonwealth finds it necessary to make in the course of the ordinary administration of government. Where there is no Federal statute affecting the matter, an exercise of the legislative power of the State over the general law of contract might incidentally apply in the case of the Commonwealth alike with the citizen ... There is, however, a clear distinction between the general law, the content or condition of which, though a matter for the legislatures of the States, may **[440]** incidentally affect Commonwealth administrative action, and, on the other hand, governmental rights and powers belonging to the Federal executive as such."

The fundamental principle which lies behind those observations is that which was recognised in *Melbourne Corporation v Commonwealth* [(1947) 74 CLR 31], namely, that the Constitution is predicated upon the continued separate existence of the Commonwealth and the States, not only in name, but as bodies politic to which the Constitution proceeds to distribute powers of government. In the application of the principle, however, it is necessary to differentiate between the Commonwealth on the one hand and the States on the other.

For the Commonwealth is given enumerated legislative powers which by reason of their content, context or subject matter may authorise it to affect the executive capacities of a State. Where that is so, the basic principle does not afford the State any protection from an exercise of Commonwealth legislative power having that effect. In the exercise of its legislative powers the Commonwealth is supreme and its laws prevail over State laws under s 109 of the Constitution. However, Commonwealth legislative powers are impliedly restricted so as to preclude their exercise by the making of laws singling out a State or the States so as to impose a special burden on them or inhibiting or impairing the continued existence of the States or their capacity to function. In that way, the States are preserved in "their position as separate governments in the system exercising independent functions" [74 CLR at 83] subject to any Commonwealth legislative power which, on its true construction, may be exercised to affect the State.

The States, on the other hand, do not have specific legislative powers which might be construed as authorising them to restrict or modify the executive capacities of the Commonwealth. The legislative power of the States is an undefined residue which, containing no such authorisation, cannot be construed as extending to the executive capacities of the Commonwealth. No implication limiting an otherwise given power is needed; the character of the Commonwealth as a body politic, armed with executive capacities by the Constitution, by its very nature places those capacities outside the legislative power of another body politic, namely a State, without specific powers in that respect. Having regard to the fundamental principle recognised in *Melbourne Corporation v Commonwealth*, only an express provision in the Constitution could authorise a State to affect the capacities of the Commonwealth executive and there is no such authorisation.

As we have said, the specific heads of power granted to the **[441]** Commonwealth Parliament may as a matter of construction extend to the alteration of the capacities of the Crown in right of the States. Of course, those powers may extend to altering the capacities of the Crown in right of the Commonwealth, at all events where those capacities derive their existence from the common law and are not defined by the Constitution. Indeed, it is of the very nature of executive power in a system of responsible government that it is susceptible to control by the exercise of legislative power by Parliament. The power conferred on the Commonwealth Parliament by s 78 of the Constitution is a clear example of a power pursuant to which the capacities of the Crown in right of the State could be altered. In particular, that section, with its explicit mention of "laws conferring rights to proceed against … a State", would support Commonwealth legislation conferring a right to proceed against the Crown in right of a State within the ambit of federal judicial power. Its terms also expressly authorise legislation of a similar kind in relation to the Crown in right of the Commonwealth. Dixon J in *Uther* suggested that the bankruptcy and insolvency power granted to the Commonwealth Parliament by s 51(xvii) might extend as a matter of construction to laws excluding or reducing the priority of the Crown in right of a State in the payment of debts due to it. Obviously, that power could be relied upon to exclude or reduce the priority of the Crown in right of the Commonwealth in the payment of debts due to it. But the fundamental point made in *Cigamatic* is that in the absence of a like power being conferred upon the States, the priority of the Crown in right of the Commonwealth in the payment of debts is not something over which the States have legislative power.

In *Cigamatic* this Court adopted the view which Dixon J had expressed in dissent in *Uther*. Both cases were concerned with the power of a State legislature to restrict or abolish a particular capacity enjoyed by the Crown in right of the Commonwealth – its prerogative right to the payment of all debts due to it in priority to all other debts of equal degree. The view which was adopted treats that prerogative as part of the definition of Commonwealth executive power going, as it does, to the rights or privileges of the Crown in right of the Commonwealth. The fact that it was a prerogative power that was involved made it plain that the capacities of the Commonwealth executive were involved. Identifying and defining prerogatives and ascertaining which of them subsist in the Crown in right of the Commonwealth may not be an exercise which can be carried out with precision. But the important consideration is whether a suggested capacity is enjoyed by the Commonwealth executive, not its character **[442]** as a prerogative or otherwise. The principle that a State law cannot affect the capacities of the Commonwealth executive clearly extends beyond those rights, powers, privileges or immunities which might be described as having their origin in the prerogative.

Both in *Uther* and *Cigamatic* a distinction is drawn between State laws affecting Commonwealth executive capacities and State laws of general application regulating activities carried on by the Crown in the exercise of those capacities in the same manner as its subjects …

In that passage [108 CLR at 378] Dixon CJ spoke of the legal rights of the Commonwealth in relation to its subjects. Sometimes that relationship **[443]** will be one of equality: for example, the capacity of the Crown to enter into contracts is no more or less than that of its subjects. Sometimes the relationship will be one of privilege or immunity on the part of the Crown alone: for example, the right to the payment of debts in priority to others. Where the relationship is one of privilege or immunity it is immediately apparent that any diminution of the privilege or immunity will alter the relationship of the Crown with its subjects. But it is equally so when the relationship is one of equality and the Crown is singled out and treated differently, for the relationship then ceases to be one of equality.

When Dixon CJ spoke of general laws he meant laws of general application which bind the Crown and its subjects alike. Such laws are laws which do not have an impact upon any relationship of equality. But a State law which discriminates against the Commonwealth government and imposes a disability upon it will have an impact upon such a relationship and will constitute an interference with its executive capacities. In the same way, a Commonwealth law which discriminates against a State and imposes a disability upon it will constitute an interference with State executive capacities. Thus in *Queensland Electricity Commission v Commonwealth* [(1985) 159 CLR 192] a Commonwealth law which discriminated against the State of Queensland restricting the remedies available to the State in relation to the settlement of industrial disputes was, by implication, held to be beyond the power of the Commonwealth parliament under s 51(xxxv) of the Constitution. Similarly, in *Melbourne Corporation v Commonwealth* a Commonwealth law which placed a special disability upon States by, in effect, preventing them from banking with a private bank, was held to interfere with their governmental functions and to be invalid. On the other hand, as Dixon J pointed out, if the Commonwealth lawfully established a monopoly in banking the States would have to put up with it.

There is nothing in the principles recognised in *Melbourne Corporation v Commonwealth* or in any extrapolation of those principles to be found in the judgment of Dixon J in *Uther* or in the reasons of the majority in *Cigamatic* which would suggest that the Crown or its agents enjoy any special immunity from the operation of laws of general application, State or federal. Indeed, the contrary is **[444]** affirmed. The rule of law requires such a result ...

[445] [I]n *Commonwealth v Bogle* [(1953) 89 CLR 229] Fullagar J, with whom Dixon CJ and Webb and Kitto JJ agreed, denied that a State statute might bind the Commonwealth. He was speaking generally, and not of a State statute purporting to interfere with the executive capacities of the Commonwealth. Indeed, in direct contrast with observations made in the authorities discussed above, he said [89 CLR at 259]:

> "To say that a State can enact legislation which is binding upon the Commonwealth in the same sense in which it is binding upon a subject of the State appears to me to give effect to a fundamental misconception."

Those words are obiter and are, in any event, contrary to the later decision of this Court in *Cigamatic*. They form no part of the reasoning leading to the actual conclusion in *Bogle* and in the light of *Cigamatic* it can hardly be said that Dixon CJ and Kitto J, in agreeing to the reasoning and conclusion of Fullagar J in *Bogle*, were assenting to that proposition.

In any event, and with the greatest of respect, the proposition is **[446]** insupportable. Of course, as a matter of construction ... , a court may conclude that a statute was not intended to bind the Crown, but that is not to say that a State parliament lacks the power to bind the Crown in right of the Commonwealth and its agencies. It cannot do so where the result would affect the executive capacities of the Commonwealth for the reasons already given. But the Commonwealth executive is not above the law and where a State statute is applicable it forms part of the law ...

[447] In an effort to recognise practical realities in a situation in which the Commonwealth executive increasingly engages in transactions upon the same basis as ordinary citizens in a State, Fullagar J acknowledged that the Commonwealth may be "affected by State laws" [89 CLR at 260] in, for example, entering into a contract in a State. But it is impossible to say what is meant by "affected by State laws" if it does not mean that the Crown in right of the Commonwealth is bound by them. As we have said, it is not a matter of choice for the Commonwealth executive whether or not it is bound by the law of the land. If in regulating activities engaged in by the Crown and its subjects alike a State statute extends as a matter of construction to the Crown in right of the Commonwealth, then that Crown is bound by the statute in the same way as the subject is bound, subject always to any inconsistency with a valid Commonwealth law.

Nothing has emerged in this case to indicate any purported alteration or denial of the executive capacity of the Crown in right of the Commonwealth by the provisions of the Residential Tenancies Act. The DHA is the creature of the *Defence Housing Authority Act* and that Act is predicated upon the existence of a legal system of which the *Residential Tenancies Act* forms a part. The latter Act does nothing to alter or deny the function of the DHA, notwithstanding that it regulates activities carried out in the exercise of that function in the same way as it regulates the same activities on the part of others. If, and to the extent that, the DHA in carrying out its functions is acting in the exercise of the executive capacity of the Commonwealth, the *Residential Tenancies Act* neither alters nor denies that capacity notwithstanding that it regulates its exercise.

Brennan CJ also distinguished the capacities and functions of the Crown in right of the Commonwealth (which are protected by an immunity) from particular transactions in which it may choose to engage in exercise of its capacities and functions (which are not). He concluded that "**[428]** absent Commonwealth statutory authority, the Crown in right of the Commonwealth cannot authorise its servants or agents to perform their functions in contravention of the criminal laws of a State and cannot confer immunity upon them if, in performing those functions, they contravene those laws. For that reason, *Pirrie v McFarlane* was, in my respectful opinion, rightly decided".

McHugh and Gummow JJ also held that DHA was not entitled to the benefit of the *Cigamatic* doctrine and thus was subject to the *Residential Tenancies Act*. However, in reaching this conclusion, they rejected the distinction drawn by Brennan CJ, Dawson, Toohey and

Gaudron JJ. McHugh J, who had advocated a strong conception of *Cigamatic* immunity as a member of the New South Wales Court of Appeal in *Australian Postal Commission v Dao* (1985) 3 NSWLR 565, now appeared to adhere to that conception.

McHugh J: [454] It follows from *Cigamatic* that, once the executive power of the Commonwealth arising from s 61 of the Constitution has authorised a relationship creating rights and duties, a State has no power to alter that relationship even by a law that operates generally within the State. I do not think that the validity of this proposition turns on any distinction between the capacities of the Commonwealth and the exercise of them. It is not a distinction which I find illuminating in this constitutional context. Nor can I see anything in the judgment of Dixon CJ in *Cigamatic* which supports such a distinction.

The executive capacity of the Commonwealth can only mean its legal right or power to do or refrain from doing something. I cannot see any constitutional rationale for a doctrine that would hold, for example, that the States cannot prevent the Commonwealth from entering into a specific class of contract but can alter the legal rights and obligations of the Commonwealth and the subject once they have **[455]** entered into a contract of that class. Moreover, the distinction between a capacity of the Commonwealth and its exercise is not easily drawn. If a State law prevents the Commonwealth from using its contractual right to forfeit a lease or terminate an employment, is the State law fettering a Commonwealth capacity or only the exercise of it?

In most cases, State law including the common law will govern the creation of a relationship between the Commonwealth and a subject even when the creation of the relationship arises from the Constitution's grant of executive power. If the Commonwealth chooses to enter into the relationship without negating the consequences of relevant State law, it necessarily submits to the State law governing the incidents of the relationship. But, for the reasons given by Dixon CJ in *Cigamatic*, once the Commonwealth has entered into such a relationship and created legal rights and duties in accordance with that State law, it is not open to the State to change their nature or effect. If the Commonwealth enters into a contract relying on the grant of executive power conferred by s 61 of the Constitution, a State has no power to change the consequences of that contract even by a law of general application ...

[457] Whether or not a general law of the State validly applies to a Commonwealth servant or agent acting in the course of his or her duties depends on a number of considerations, the chief of which are the nature of the Commonwealth activity upon which the servant or agent is engaged and the act or omission which the State law purports to regulate. In my opinion, however, the answer to the question whether a servant or agent of the Commonwealth Crown must obey a State law does not depend on any general proposition that the Commonwealth cannot authorise its servants or agents to perform their duties contrary to the penal laws of a State.

In determining whether a Commonwealth authorisation of executive activity is outside the law of a State, one naturally begins with the proposition that the Constitution is superimposed on a background of common law rules and principles. Except where those rules and principles are inconsistent with the grant of executive power under the Constitution or a federal statute made pursuant to the Constitution, the carrying out of Commonwealth executive activity must conform with those rules. By the Bill of Rights 1688 and probably by the common law, the Crown had no power to authorise its servants to ignore the law. But in a federation that does not mean that the Executive Government of one polity of the federation is bound to obey the law of another polity in that federation. The rule that the Crown cannot give its agents any dispensation to ignore a statute was formulated for a unitary system of government. Just as the common law rule of the supremacy of Parliament had to be modified to accord with the Constitution, so must the rule that the Crown cannot authorise a breach of a law be modified to accord with the division of legal power between the Commonwealth and the States. In a federation, an anterior question must be answered before that rule has any operation. That question is, is there a law that the servants and agents of the relevant Sovereign must obey? It follows therefore that, in determining whether the Commonwealth Crown has power to authorise its servants or agents to disobey a State law, the first question is, is the State law binding on the Commonwealth Crown? Only when that question is answered can one determine whether the Commonwealth Crown can authorise its servants to ignore the law of a State.

If a State law attempted to discriminate against the exercise of an executive activity arising from the operation of s 61 of the Constitution, it would be plainly invalid for the reasons given by **[458]** Dixon J in *West v Commissioner of Taxation (NSW)*. On the other hand, a general law that merely regulates the manner or mode of performing an activity which a servant or agent of the Commonwealth carries out in the course of executing functions and duties arising from the operation of s 61 of the Constitution is unlikely to constitute an infringement of those extraordinary capacities or powers of the Commonwealth to which I have referred. Such laws are to be contrasted with State laws that purport to bind the Commonwealth itself in exercising the capacities and powers conferred by s 61 of the Constitution alone or in conjunction with other powers of the Commonwealth. State laws purporting to have that effect can only operate as interpretation clauses. They show that the State law is intended to apply to the Commonwealth. However, they can do so only to the extent that the Commonwealth submits to the law by express words or conduct or by inference from its silence. But that is all.

Like McHugh J, Gummow J rejected "**[472]** any distinction between the capacities of the Commonwealth and their exercise", but for different reasons. He restated the Dixon-Fullagar "affected by" doctrine as accepting that the "**[473]** Commonwealth lives and moves within the Australian common law", which "may be qualified or replaced by State legislation with a general operation in respect of certain kinds of transaction or business activity". For him the relevant distinction was that drawn by Dixon J in *Farley's Case* – *accepting* the operation of "this general body of law as it affected dealings by the Executive Government of the Commonwealth in the course of the orderly administration of government", but *denying* the validity of "State laws which would detract from or adversely affect the very governmental rights of the Commonwealth". The law considered in *Uther* and *Cigamatic* was of the latter kind because it involved "the destruction, modification or qualification by New South Wales law of a fiscal right of pre-eminence otherwise enjoyed by the Commonwealth Treasury". On the other hand, Gummow J's careful restatement of this as the *relevant* distinction stopped short of any express acceptance or endorsement of its *correctness*. His actual decision was only that the Parliament, in creating the DHA, had not "**[472]** imparted to it the preferences, immunities and exceptions, including that zone of immunity conferred by the *Cigamatic* doctrine, which are enjoyed by the Executive Government".

Only Kirby J argued (in dissent) that *Cigamatic* should now "**[509]** be reverently laid to rest". As to the argument that the States could have had no power before 1901 to regulate a then non-existent Commonwealth, he pointed out "**[504]** that the States are themselves creations of the Constitution", as parts of an entirely new regime in which the Commonwealth and the States "are intended ... to operate together, and in relation to each other". In this "**[507]** integrated federal polity ... [i]t is not a diminution of the sovereignty of the Commonwealth to accept that laws made by Australian citizens through their State parliaments may, in defined circumstances, bind the Commonwealth. This is no more than the fulfilment of the integrated federal system of government established by the Constitution. It is also the assurance of the rule of law by which all those present in a State (or otherwise affected) are bound by valid legislation". He found the "accepted by" doctrine "**[504]** so uncertain of meaning and operation as to cast doubt on **[505]** the integrity of the immunity principle itself", which was in any event "unacceptably unstable and uncertain". He suggested that any "**[507]** coherent implied immunity of the Commonwealth" must depend on reciprocal application of the *Melbourne Corporation* principle, so that a "State parliament could not legislate in a way that would impair the **[508]** integrity or autonomy of the Government of the Commonwealth".

The joint judgment of Dawson, Toohey and Gaudron JJ may itself be read as an attempt to restate the *Cigamatic* immunity as a reciprocal counterpart to *Melbourne Corporation* (see Francesca Dominello, "Intergovernmental Immunities and Judicial Reasoning" in Tony Blackshield, Michael Coper, and George Williams (eds), *The Oxford Companion to the High Court of Australia* (Oxford University Press, 2001), 344 at 346). In the first place, the distinction between the Commonwealth's "capacities" (which the States cannot regulate) and the "exercise" of those capacities (which they may) seems intended to mirror the insistence of Mason J in the *Tasmanian*

Dam Case that what *Melbourne Corporation* protects is a State's "**[129]** capacity to function ... rather than ... any function which a State government undertakes". Second, the joint judgment asserts that *Cigamatic* and *Melbourne Corporation* reflect the same "**[440]** fundamental principle", with differences arising only "[i]n the application of the principle". The detailed exposition of these differences then parallels Dixon J's account in *Uther's Case*. (Yet, far from asserting divergent unfoldings of a shared fundamental principle, Dixon J had asserted in *Uther* that the starting points in State and Commonwealth power are "**[530]** in every material respect of an opposite description".) Finally, the joint judgment restates *Cigamatic* in the language of equality and discrimination, apparently to demonstrate consonance with the so-called "discrimination" limb of *Melbourne Corporation* (but see now *Austin v Commonwealth* in §2(c) above).

Whether the restatement in *Henderson's Case* will be accepted as authoritative remains unclear. In *Commonwealth v Western Australia* (*Mining Act Case*) (1999) 196 CLR 392, Hayne J outlined the relevant principles in terms of the judgment delivered by Dawson, Toohey and Gaudron JJ, though conceding that: "**[471]** The content and application of these principles has been controversial and it may well be that there is still room for doubt about them". McHugh J noted that his own views in *Henderson's Case* "**[421]** do not fully accord with" what Hayne J had said, adding: "No doubt it will some day be necessary to determine whether the views expressed by Dawson, Toohey and Gaudron JJ ... have finally settled the question of the States' capacity to bind the Commonwealth. But it is not necessary to do so for the purposes of this case".

4. Further References

Coper, M, *Encounters with the Australian Constitution* (CCH, 1987), Ch 4.

Coper, M, and Williams, G (eds), *The Cauldron of Constitutional Change* (Centre for International and Public Law, ANU, 1997).

Dixon, N, "Limiting the Doctrine of Intergovernmental Immunity" (1993) 9 *Queensland University of Technology Law Journal* 1.

Douglas, N, "'Federal' Implications in the Construction of Commonwealth Legislative Power: A Legal Analysis of Their Use" (1985) 16 *University of Western Australia Law Review* 105.

Doyle, JJ, "1947 Revisited: The Immunity of the Commonwealth from State Law" in Lindell, G (ed), *Future Directions in Australian Constitutional Law* (Federation Press, 1994), 47.

Evans, G, "Rethinking Commonwealth Immunity" (1971) 8 *Melbourne University Law Review* 521.

Howard, C, "Some Problems of Commonwealth Immunity and Exclusive Legislative Powers" (1972) 5 *Federal Law Review* 31.

Kneebone, S, "Claims against the Commonwealth and States and Their Instrumentalities in Federal Jurisdiction: Section 64 of the Judiciary Act" (1996) 24 *Federal Law Review* 93.

Lee, HP, "Commonwealth Liability to State Law – The Enigmatic Case of *Pirrie v McFarlane*" (1987) 17 *Federal Law Review* 132.

Ong, DSK, "The Federal Balance: The Australian Constitution and its Implied Power, Implied Prohibition and Incidental Powers" (1984) 14 *Melbourne University Law Review* 660.

Penhallurick, C, "Commonwealth Immunity as a Constitutional Implication" (2001) 29 *Federal Law Review* 151.

Rose, D, "The Commonwealth Places (Application of Laws) Act 1970" (1971) 4 *Federal Law Review* 263.

Sackville, R, "The Doctrine of Immunity of Instrumentalities in the United States and Australia: A Comparative Analysis" (1969) 7 *Melbourne University Law Review* 15.

Simpson, A, "The Australian Education Union Case: A Quiet Revolution?" (1998) 7 *Griffith Law Review* 30.

Simpson, A, "State Immunity from Commonwealth Laws: *Austin v Commonwealth* and Dilemmas of Doctrinal Design" (2004) 32 *University of Western Australia Law Review* 44.

Sawer, G, "State Statutes and the Commonwealth" (1961) 1 *University of Tasmania Law Review* 580.

Twomey, A, "Federal Limitations on the Legislative Power of the States and the Commonwealth to Bind One Another" (2003) 31 *Federal Law Review* 507.

Zines, L, "The Binding Effect of State Law on the Commonwealth" in Groves, M (ed), *Law and Government in Australia* (Federation Press, 2005), 1.

Zines, L, *The High Court and the Constitution* (Butterworths, 4th ed 1997), Ch 14.

Zines, L, "Sir Owen Dixon's Theory of Federalism" (1965) 1 *Federal Law Review* 221.

Chapter 26

Civil and Political Freedoms

1. Human Rights

Perceptions of human rights can be affected by social, economic and cultural background. Thus, human rights may be viewed differently by men and women, as well as by Australians above and below the poverty line. Context is important. As Brennan J suggested in *Gerhardy v Brown* (1985) 159 CLR 70, "**[126]** an attempt to define human rights and fundamental freedoms exhaustively is bound to fail, for the respective religious, cultural and political systems of the world would attribute differing contents to the notions of freedom and dignity and would perceive at least some differences in the rights and freedoms that are conducive to their attainment". Despite this, certain rights are widely accepted as being "universal", that is, as belonging to every human being irrespective of legal status or cultural, economic or other circumstances.

Louis Henkin, *The Age of Rights*
(Columbia University Press, 1990)

[2] Human rights are rights of individuals in society. Every human being has, or is entitled to have, "rights" – legitimate, valid, justified claims – upon his or her society; claims to various "goods" and benefits. Human rights are not some abstract, inchoate "good"; they are defined, particular claims listed in international instruments such as the Universal Declaration of Human Rights and the major covenants and conventions. They are those benefits deemed essential for individual well-being, dignity, and fulfillment, and that reflect a common sense of justice, fairness, and decency. In the constitutional jurisprudence of the United States … individual rights have long been thought of as consisting only of "immunities," as limitations on what government might do *to* the individual. Human rights, on the other hand, include not only these negative "immunity claims" but also positive "resource claims," claims to what society is deemed required to do *for* the individual. They include liberties – freedom *from* (for example, detention, torture), and freedom *to* (speak, assemble); they include also the right to food, housing, and other basic human needs.

Human rights are universal: they belong to every human being in every human society. They do not differ with geography or history, culture or ideology, political or economic system, or stage of societal development. To call them "human" implies that all human beings have them, equally and in equal measure, by virtue of their humanity – regardless of sex, race, age; regardless of high or low "birth," social class, national origin, ethnic or tribal affiliation; regardless of **[3]** wealth or poverty, occupation, talent, merit, religion, ideology, or other commitment. Implied in one's humanity, human rights are inalienable and imprescriptible: they cannot be transferred, forfeited, or waived; they cannot be lost by having been usurped, or by one's failure to exercise or assert them.

Human rights are *rights*; they are not merely aspirations, or assertions of the good. To call them rights is not to assert, merely, that the benefits indicated are desirable or necessary; or, merely, that it is "right" that the individual shall enjoy these goods; or even, merely, that it is the duty of society to respect the immunity or provide the benefits. To call them "rights" implies that they are claims "as of right," not by appeal to grace, or charity, or brotherhood, or love; they need not be earned or deserved. The idea of rights implies entitlement on the part of the holder in some order under some applicable norm; the idea of human rights implies entitlement in a moral order under a moral law, to be translated into and confirmed as legal entitlement in the legal order of a political society. When a society recognises that a person has a right, it affirms, legitimates, and justifies that entitlement, and incorporates and establishes it in the society's system of values, giving it important weight in competition with other societal values.

Human rights imply the obligation of society to satisfy those claims. The state must develop institutions and procedures, must plan, must mobilize resources as necessary to meet those claims. Political and civil rights require laws, institutions, procedures, and other safeguards against tyranny, against corrupt, immoral, and inefficient agencies or officials. Economic and social rights in modern society require taxation and spending and a network of agencies for social welfare. The idea of human rights implies also that society must provide some system of remedies to which individuals may resort to obtain the benefits to which they are entitled or be compensated for their loss ...

Human rights are claims upon society. These claims may derive from moral principles governing relations between persons, but it is society that bears the obligation to satisfy the claims. Of course, the official representatives of society must themselves respect individual freedoms and immunities; political society must also act to protect the individual's rights against private invasion. As regards claims to economic and social benefits, society must act as insurer to provide them if individuals cannot provide them for themselves. Thus, government must protect me from assault by my neighbor, or from wolves, and must ensure that I have bread or hospitalization; in human rights terms my rights are **[4]** against the state, not against the neighbor or the wolves, the baker, or the hospital. The state may arrange to satisfy my claims by maintaining domestic laws and institutions that give me, say, rights and remedies in tort against my neighbor, or administrative remedies against a corrupt, misguided, or inefficient bureaucrat, or access to public schools or health services. Those legal rights and remedies against individuals or agencies within society give effect to my human rights claims upon society.

The idea of human rights has implications for the relation of the individual's rights to other public goods. It is commonly said that human rights are "fundamental." That means that they are important, that life, dignity, and other important human values depend on them; it does not mean that they are "absolute," that they may never be abridged for any purpose in any circumstances. Human rights enjoy a prima facie, presumptive inviolability, and will often "trump" other public goods. Government may not do some things, and must do others, even though the authorities are persuaded that it is in the society's interest (and perhaps even in the individual's own interest) to do otherwise; individual human rights cannot be lightly sacrificed even for the good of the greater number, even for the general good of all. But if human rights do not bow lightly to public concerns, they may be sacrificed if countervailing societal interests are important enough, in particular circumstances, for limited times and purposes, to the extent strictly necessary ...

The idea of rights accepts that some limitations on rights are permissible but the limitations are themselves strictly limited. Public emergency, national security, public order are weighty terms, bespeaking important societal interests, but they are not to be lightly or loosely invoked, and the conception of national security or public order cannot be so large as to swallow the right. Derogations are permitted only in time of a public emergency that threatens the life of the nation, not as a response to fears (warranted or paranoid) for other values, or for the security of a particular regime. Even in an authentic emergency, a society may derogate from rights only to the extent strictly required by the exigencies of the situation, and even such necessary derogations must not involve invidious inequalities, and may not derogate from basic rights: they must not invade the right to life, or involve torture or cruel, inhuman punishment, slavery or servitude, conviction of crime under ex post facto laws, denial of rights as a person before the law, or violate freedom of thought, conscience, or religion. Moreover, considerations of public emergency permitting derogations, or of national security or public order permitting limitations on certain rights, refer to a universal standard, monitored by external scrutiny and judgment ...

[5] I have referred to rights as claims *upon* society, not *against* society. In the ideology of rights, human rights are not "against society," against the interest of society; on the contrary, the good society is one in which individual rights flourish, and the promotion and protection of every individual's rights are a public good. There is an aura of conflict between individual and society only in that individual rights are asserted against government, against those who represent society officially, and because the human rights idea often requires that an individual's right be preferred to some other public good. But this apparent conflict between individual and society is specious; in the longer, deeper view, the society is better if the individual's rights are respected.

The process of determining universal human rights in the international sphere began after World War II with the creation of the United Nations in 1945 and the adoption by its General Assembly, on 10 December 1948, of the Universal Declaration of Human Rights. After recognising the "inherent dignity and ... the equal and inalienable rights of all members of the human family", the Declaration sets out a list of basic rights as "a common standard of achievement for all peoples and all nations". These rights include:

Universal Declaration of Human Rights 1948

3 Everyone has the right to life, liberty and security of person.

4 No one shall be held in slavery or servitude; slavery and the slave trade shall be prohibited in all their forms.

5 No one shall be subjected to torture or to cruel, inhuman or degrading treatment or punishment.

16 (1) Men and women of full age, without any limitation due to race, nationality or religion, have the right to marry and to found a family. They are entitled to equal rights as to marriage, during marriage and at its dissolution.

(2) Marriage shall be entered into only with the free and full consent of the intending spouses.

(3) The family is the natural and fundamental group unit of society and is entitled to protection by society and the State.

17 (1) Everyone has the right to own property alone as well as in association with others.

(2) No one shall be arbitrarily deprived of his property.

18 Everyone has the right to freedom of thought, conscience and religion; this right includes freedom to change his religion or belief, and freedom, either alone or in community with others and in public or private, to manifest his religion or belief in teaching, practice, worship and observance.

19 Everyone has the right to freedom of opinion and expression; this right includes freedom to hold opinions without interference and to seek, receive and impart information and ideas through any media and regardless of frontiers.

20 (1) Everyone has the right to freedom of peaceful assembly and association.

(2) No one may be compelled to belong to an association.

26 (1) Everyone has the right to education. Education shall be free, at least in the elementary and fundamental stages. Elementary education shall be compulsory. Technical and professional education shall be made generally available and higher education shall be equally accessible to all on the basis of merit.

(2) Education shall be directed to the full development of the human personality and to the strengthening of respect for human rights and fundamental freedoms. It shall promote understanding, tolerance and friendship among all nations, racial or religious groups, and shall further the activities of the United Nations for the maintenance of peace.

(3) Parents have a prior right to choose the kind of education that shall be given to their children.

Like *Magna Carta*, this instrument has had an influence that far exceeds its legal effect. While the Universal Declaration now forms part of customary international law and is thus seen as binding on all nations, it cannot be enforced in Australian courts. This does not, however, detract from its cultural, political and symbolic importance. The Declaration is invoked throughout the world – the website <http://www.unhchr.ch/udhr/index. htm> of the United Nations has over 300 translations – and can be a rallying point for those who claim they have been denied their universal rights.

The Universal Declaration was bolstered by the International Covenant on Civil and Political Rights and the International Covenant on Economic, Social and Cultural Rights, both of which were adopted by the General Assembly on 16 December 1966. The Covenants, having attained the requisite number of ratifications, entered into force internationally in 1976 and were ratified by Australia in 1980 and 1976, respectively.

These Covenants establish different regimes for civil and political rights on the one hand, and economic, social, and cultural rights on the other. This division, as contrasted to the single list of universal rights in the Universal Declaration, has proved to be controversial, and the differences between the two categories of rights are often hard to establish. According to Peter Bailey (*Human Rights: Australia in an International Context* (Butterworths, 1990)): "**[12]** If civil and political rights can be described as the rights which enable individuals to operate freely within the political system and to be protected from arbitrary action in the administration of the law, including particularly the criminal law, then economic, social and cultural rights can be described as allowing people to own property, to work in fair conditions and to be guaranteed an adequate standard of living and facilities for education and the enjoyment of life and of the culture in which they live or have been brought up". Accordingly, the International Covenant on Civil and Political Rights recognises rights such as "freedom of expression" (Art 19) and "equal protection of the law" (Art 26), while the International Covenant on Economic, Social and Cultural Rights provides that the State will "recognize the right of every-one to social security" (Art 9) and "to an adequate standard of living" (Art 11). The Covenants also differ in the obligations they impose on states. (The emphases below have been added).

International Covenant on Civil and Political Rights
Adopted 16 December 1966; *entered into force* 23 March 1976;
999 UN Treaty Series 171

2 (2) Where not already provided for by existing legislative or other measures, each State Party to the present Covenant undertakes *to take the necessary steps*, in accordance with its constitutional processes and with the provisions of the present Covenant, *to adopt such legislative or other measures as may be necessary* to give effect to the rights recognized in the present Covenant.

(3) Each State Party to the present Covenant undertakes:

(*a*) To ensure that any person whose rights or freedoms as herein recognized are violated shall have an effective remedy, notwithstanding that the violation has been committed by persons acting in an official capacity;

(*b*) To ensure that any person claiming such a remedy shall have his right thereto determined by competent judicial, administrative or legislative authorities, or by any other competent authority provided by the legal system of the State, *and to develop the possibilities of judicial remedy*;

(*c*) To ensure that the competent authorities shall enforce such remedies when granted.

International Covenant on Economic, Social and Cultural Rights
Adopted 16 December 1966; *entered into force* 3 January 1976;
993 UN Treaty Series 3

2 (1) Each State Party to the present Covenant undertakes *to take steps*, individually and through international assistance and co-operation, especially economic and technical, *to the maximum of its available resources*, with a view to *achieving progressively* the full realization of the rights recognized in the present Covenant by all appropriate means, including particularly the adoption of *legislative measures*.

The weaker obligation imposed by the latter Covenant is in part a reflection of the need for compromise in securing international acceptance for such an instrument; but it also reflects the functional recognition that what Henkin calls "resource claims" may not be amenable to the same degree of legal enforcement as is usually demanded for civil and political rights.

Although Australia has ratified both Covenants and thereby agreed to assume the obligations they set out, the Covenants are not enforceable under Australian law unless they have been incorporated by legislation (see Chapter 19, §2(b)). Some of the rights in the Covenants and in other like international instruments have been incorporated in an ad hoc fashion, for instance by the *Racial Discrimination Act 1975* (Cth) and the *Sex Discrimination Act 1984* (Cth). However, there is no comprehensive national law or Bill of Rights that does so. The first example of such a law at the State and Territory level is the *Human Rights Act 2004* (ACT), which incorporates many of the rights in the International Covenant on Civil and Political Rights (see Chapter 30, §4).

In 1991, Australia also acceded to the (first) Optional Protocol to the International Covenant on Civil and Political Rights. Under Art 2, "individuals who claim that any of their rights enumerated in the Covenant have been violated and who have exhausted all available domestic remedies" may submit a written complaint (a "communication") to the Human Rights Committee of the United Nations. What follows from a complaint is cautiously structured. If, after considering the response of the national government concerned, the Human Rights Committee is satisfied that the complaint is made out, Art 5(4) provides that "[t]he Committee shall forward its views to the State Party concerned and to the individual". It is then left to the national government to indicate whether or how it will respond to those views. Although the pressure exerted for a positive response depends on moral and political persuasion rather than legal sanction, it may (for example) induce the federal Parliament to legislate to bring domestic law into line with the Covenant. An example is the *Human Rights (Sexual Conduct) Act 1994* (Cth) (see *Croome v Tasmania* (1997) 191 CLR 119 in Chapter 13, §5(b) and (c)), which was enacted in response to the Human Rights Committee's view of the first Australian complaint submitted to it. The Committee found that the Tasmanian *Criminal Code Act 1924*, which made sexual activity between consenting adult males a crime, was inconsistent with the right of privacy set out in Art 17 of the Covenant on Civil and Political Rights. On the other hand, despite eight further adverse findings against Australia (including four in 2003), the law has not since been changed to be brought into conformity with the Covenant.

Henkin's distinction between "immunities" ("**[2]** limitations on what government might do *to* the individual") and "resource claims" ("claims to what society is deemed required to do *for* the individual") broadly corresponds to the distinction drawn by the International Covenants between "civil and political rights" (to be protected by effective remedies, especially judicial remedies), and "economic, social and cultural rights" (to be realised through progressive implementation, particularly legislation). Henkin understands human rights as importing not merely "**[3]** entitlement in a moral order under a moral law", but also a demand that this moral entitlement be "translated into and confirmed as legal entitlement in the legal order of a political society". Yet, as the above distinctions make clear, the legal mechanisms by which this translation is effected, and the degree of force that it carries, may vary considerably.

In Wesley Hohfeld's famous attempt to clarify the use of entitlement language in the law (see Chapter 8, §5), he reserved the word *right* (in its legal sense) for situations where an individual claim is correlated with an enforceable legal *duty* to respect that claim. A *privilege* or *liberty* in Hohfeld's sense is something less than a "right"; its correlative is not an enforceable "duty" to allow the activity in question, but merely the absence of any enforceable legal "right" to obstruct that activity. The traditional common law usage referring merely to "civil liberties" rather than "civil rights" is thus highly significant. In Hohfeld's analysis, "immunities" are different from both "rights" and "liberties": the correlative of an *immunity* is a *disability*, that is, an absence of legal *power* to affect the individual's legal position in the relevant respect. Although there are difficulties in applying Hohfeld's analysis to public law, it seems clear that Henkin is correct in treating constitutional "immunities" as synonymous with "limitations on what government might do *to* the individual": that is, the "immunity" would appear to be necessarily correlative with a limitation on government power.

In Australian constitutional discourse there are frequent references to "freedoms" or liberties; to "immunities"; and to "limitations on legislative and executive power" – but rarely to positive rights. For example, in *Lange v Australian Broadcasting Corporation* (1997) 189 CLR 520, a unanimous High Court stated that ss 7 and 24 of the Constitution, which give rise to an implied freedom of political communication, "**[560]** do not confer personal rights on individuals. Rather they preclude the curtailment of the protected freedom by the exercise of legislative or executive power". Similarly, the express provisions in the Constitution that might protect individuals are usually expressed as limitations on power rather than as positive rights. For example, s 116, dealing with freedom of religion, begins: "The Commonwealth shall not make any law ...". The only apparent exception to this usage is s 117, which focuses on the position of the individual and forbids the imposition of "any disability or discrimination" based on out-of-State residence. We shall see that some judges have understood this as conferring a unique kind of *individual* "immunity", and have contrasted this with the more usual model of limitations on power. Even then, this "immunity" is understood as analytically distinct from a "right".

These terminological distinctions affect the remedies available when a constitutional freedom is infringed. They mean that, except in the case of proceedings under s 117, a person will be entitled to a declaration that the law is invalid but not to any further relief such as damages for any injury caused by the breach (see Chapter 13, §6(a)). Conversely, when s 117 is invoked, the "individual immunity" view will mean that plaintiffs are entitled to a declaration that the impugned provision does not apply to them, but *not* to a declaration that the provision is invalid.

2. Right to Vote

The express guarantees of rights or freedoms in the Australian Constitution are not only con-strictively worded, but in any event are strikingly limited in number and scope. One possible example is s 41, which might be viewed as guaranteeing a right to vote in federal elections for anyone entitled to vote for the lower house of a State Parliament. As early as 1901, however, John Quick and Robert Garran had suggested that the section is merely a transitional provision, designed to preserve the voting rights of South Australian women until the new Commonwealth Parliament could enact a uniform federal franchise (*The Annotated Constitution of the Australian Commonwealth* (Angus & Robertson, 1901; repr Legal Books, 1995), 483-7). On this view, once the *Commonwealth Franchise Act 1902* (Cth) had been passed, s 41 had no continuing operation in relation to people who acquired an entitlement to vote in State elections at any time after 1902.

In *King v Jones* (1972) 128 CLR 221, the High Court was asked to apply s 41 to resolve a political controversy over the lowering of the voting age to 18 years. In New South Wales and Western Australia this had happened in 1970 and in South Australia in 1971. The Whitlam government made a similar change at the federal level in 1973, and the remaining States then followed suit. However, in 1972, the McMahon federal government was still resisting any change. Susan King, the 18-year-old daughter of the South Australian Attorney-General, argued that she was an "adult person" by virtue of both social and legal acceptance, relying as to the latter on the *Age of Majority (Reduction) Act 1970* (SA). As an "adult person", she argued that she was entitled by s 41 to exercise voting rights in federal elections equivalent to those she had acquired in South Australia. The following exchange took place during argument:

King v Jones
(1972) 128 CLR 221

LK Murphy (in argument): [224] I propose to call as a witness a professor of sociology who is an expert on the subject of the development of persons to maturity and who is able to give direct evidence and expert opinion evidence upon matters of fact material to the submission that persons of eighteen years of age and upwards in Australia are mature persons.

Barwick CJ: The Court will not receive evidence at this point. It will first decide the construction of the Constitution. When argument is finished we will reserve our view on that and whether we resume the hearing.

That is, the Court would consider the reception of sociological evidence only if the word "adult" in s 41 was open to a shift in meaning. In the end, the whole Court held that it was not. The constitutional use of the word was held to be fixed with the meaning it had in 1901.

Stephen J: [268] The section may be viewed from two aspects, as a restraint upon Commonwealth legislative power or as a Constitutional guarantee; I prefer the latter view, regarding it as ensuring that those State electors to whom it refers will not be excluded from any federal franchise which the federal Parliament may enact. It guarantees an entitlement to the federal franchise for those State-enfranchised electors who fall within its terms. So regarded there can be no place, in its interpretation, for the well-established doctrine that the import or meaning of a Constitutional grant of legislative power or of an immunity from legislative interference, when "expressed in general propositions wide enough to be capable of flexible application to changing circumstances" – per Dixon J in *Australian National Airways Pty Ltd v Commonwealth* [(1945) 71 CLR 29 at 81] – may "only be appreciated when considered, as the years go on, in relation to the vicissitudes of fact which from time to time emerge": *James v Commonwealth* [(1936) 55 CLR 1 at 43]. On the contrary its function would suggest that it will have a constant operation so far as concerns the character of the class in whose favour it guarantees a right to the federal franchise ...

[271] [I]f "adult" in s 41 is to be given some meaning other than that of having attained the age of twenty-one years, it is likely to be a meaning which, used in a Constitution to secure important political rights to the citizens of federating colonies, was both certain and uniform throughout the Commonwealth. It may be objected that other phrases employed in the Constitution have proved difficult to describe as possessing certainty of meaning but "adult person" is not concerned with any definition of fields of legislative power, it deals with no broad concepts of freedom; there is no reason why it should involve any obscurity of language such as is perhaps inherent in other parts of the Constitution. On the contrary it is in subject matter such as s 41 that certainty of expression may be anticipated, as may Commonwealth-wide uniformity of meaning ... A meaning of "adult" which would enable a particular State, by appropriate State legislation, to enfranchise large numbers of persons under the age of twenty-one and, by the operation of 41, confer upon them the federal franchise ... is one not lightly to be attributed to the framers of the Constitution.

On the limited "transitional" reading of s 41 suggested by Quick and Garran, the issue discussed in *King v Jones* could never have arisen – because, although King had "acquire[d] a right to vote at elections for ... the Parliament of [her] State", she had done so 70 years too late. *King v Jones* was not, however, decided on that basis. Barwick CJ approached the case "**[229]** on the assumption that a franchise derived from a State law made subsequent to the enactment of the Constitution is within s 41 – a matter of construction which it is unnecessary presently to resolve". Walsh and Stephen JJ made similar assumptions. Gibbs J remarked: "**[259]** The view of Quick and Garran ... is far from clearly correct, but I find it unnecessary to express a final opinion upon it". Menzies J was more definite.

Menzies J: [246] The character of s 41 is that of a permanent constitutional provision. It is not a provision to make temporary arrangements for the period between the establishment of the Constitution and the making of Commonwealth laws. It applies to a person, who, in 1901, had or who, in the future, acquires particular voting rights by the laws of a State.

Despite the dicta in *King v Jones*, the Court in *R v Pearson; Ex parte Sipka* (1983) 152 CLR 254 accepted the "transitional" view of s 41 by a 6:1 majority, with Murphy J dissenting. Section 45 of the *Commonwealth Electoral Act 1918* (Cth) provided that: "Claims for enrolment ... which are received by the Registrar after six o'clock in the afternoon of the day of the issue of the writ for an election shall not be registered until after the close of the polling at the election". On 3 February 1983, the Governor-General granted Prime Minister Malcolm Fraser a double disso-lution of both Houses of the federal Parliament under s 57 of the Constitution. The date for the issue of the writs was fixed as the following day, 4 February 1983, and the election for 5 March 1983. In the High Court on 16 February 1983, four persons entitled to vote in a New South Wales election, but effectively excluded from the federal election by s 45 of the Act, asserted a right to vote on the basis of s 41. The majority view that s 41 had not been infringed was stated in two joint judgments, one by Gibbs CJ, Mason and Wilson JJ and the other by Brennan, Deane and Dawson JJ.

R v Pearson; Ex parte Sipka
(1983) 152 CLR 254

Brennan, Deane and Dawson JJ: [276] The primary question which arises in all four applications is whether the right to vote which is protected or guaranteed by s 41 extends beyond a right possessed by a person under a law of the State when a federal franchise was enacted by a law of the Commonwealth. If the answer is no, then none of the prosecutors can succeed because, apart from any other consideration, none of them is of sufficient age to have enjoyed such a right. Put **[277]** differently, the primary question is whether s 41 of the Constitution preserved to each State, after the Commonwealth Parliament enacted laws prescribing the Commonwealth franchise, a power to extend that franchise in that State. If the argument for the prosecutors be correct, a State can, by extending the franchise for its own "more numerous House of the Parliament", extend the Commonwealth franchise ...

The meaning and purpose of s 41 may be gleaned from its terms and context and by reference to the circumstances in which the section was to operate immediately after Federation. At Federation the qualifications of electors of the more numerous Houses of the Parliaments of the respective States were not uniform. In particular, South Australia and Western Australia were the only States in the Commonwealth which ha[d] extended the franchise to women of the age of twenty-one and over. The right to vote in each State was nevertheless taken as the qualification of electors of members of the House of Representatives and of the Senate "[u]ntil the Parliament **[278]** otherwise provides" (ss 30, 8). The constitutional franchise thus conferred upon the people of the Commonwealth to elect the Parliament was defined by the laws of the respective States. That definition of the constitutional franchise was to yield to a statutory franchise when the Parliament, thereunto empowered by s 51(xxxvi), defined the qualification of electors throughout the Commonwealth. It was anticipated that, at some time after Federation, the Parliament would enact a uniform qualification of electors of members of the Parliament. Section 128 made particular provision for halving the votes cast in referenda in any State in which adult suffrage prevailed "until the qualification of electors of members of the House of Representatives becomes uniform throughout the Commonwealth" ...

Though it is right to see s 41 as a constitutional guarantee of the right to vote, the means by which that guarantee is secured is itself definitive of the extent of the guarantee. Voting, that is, the exercise of an existing right to vote, at elections of the Commonwealth Parliament cannot "be prevented by any law of the Commonwealth". But s 41 does not in terms confer a right to vote. If a right to vote is claimed by an elector in reliance upon the statutory franchise now prescribed by the laws of the Commonwealth, those laws are definitive of the right and s 41 has no work to do. But if **[279]** and so long as a right to vote was claimed by an elector in reliance upon the constitutional franchise – whether existing at the establishment of the Commonwealth or the result of a later modification before the prescription of a statutory franchise by the Commonwealth Parliament – s 41 precluded any law of the Commonwealth from preventing the exercise of that voting right. In other words, those who, by State laws, were able to acquire a right to vote at elections of the more numerous House of the State and who, by reason of ss 30 and 8, thereby acquired the right to vote at elections of the Parliament of the Commonwealth, were entitled to continue voting at the latter elections so long as they continued to be entitled to vote at elections of the more numerous House of the State Parliament. They could not be prevented by any law of the Commonwealth from doing so.

The applicants seek to extend the operation of s 41 beyond this point by converting the prohibition against preventing a person from voting at a federal election into a source of a right to vote at such an election. If s 41 were given this operation, the power conferred upon the Parliament to legislate for a uniform franchise would be destroyed. A Parliament of a State would be empowered to give the federal franchise to those whom the Commonwealth Parliament has excluded or disqualified, for example, property owners who do not live in the State, aliens, prohibited immigrants or convicts under sentence for more serious offences.

If that operation were accorded to s 41, the Parliament of a State would be empowered to increase the number of its electors for the purposes of s 128 beyond the number entitled under the uniform franchise. Such an operation of s 41, though surprising and unsatisfactory, might be warranted if the text of the Constitution demanded it. But that operation is wholly unsupported by the terms of s 41. It is impermissible to construe a provision relating to the prevention of the exercise of a right to vote as the source of the right itself. The right to vote to which s 41 relates is the constitutional franchise conferred ["until the Parliament otherwise provides"] by ss 30 and 8. The purpose of s 41 is clear from its constitutional context: it was to ensure that those who enjoyed the constitutional franchise should not lose it when the statutory franchise was enacted. The statute was to govern the subsequent acquisition of the right to vote at federal elections. The persons to whom s 41 applies are the persons who acquired the right to vote pursuant to ss 30 and 8. After the Parliament enacted the *Commonwealth Franchise Act* 1902, which was entitled "An act to provide for an Uniform Federal Franchise", no person could acquire the right to vote at federal elections save in accordance with its terms …

[280] It follows, of course, that the practical effect of s 41 is spent. Most of the electors who acquired a right to vote at federal elections under ss 30 and 8 of the Constitution would have died. Since 12 June 1902, when the *Commonwealth Franchise Act* came into force, no person has acquired a right to vote the exercise of which is protected by s 41. None of the present applicants is a person to whom s 41 applies.

Murphy J: [268] An interpretation which requires that "adult person", must in 1983 be read as referring to centenarians, cannot be correct …

Section 41 is one of the few guarantees of the rights of persons in the Australian Constitution. It should be given the purposive interpretation which accords with its plain words, with its context of other provisions of unlimited duration, and its contrast with transitional provisions. Constitutions are to read broadly and not pedantically. Guarantees of personal rights should not be read narrowly. A right to vote is so precious that it should not read out of the Constitution by implication. Rather every reasonable presumption and interpretation should be adopted which favours the right of people to participate in the elections of those who represent them.

Plain meaning. The purpose conveyed by its plain words is a constitutional guarantee that every adult person who has a right to vote at State elections shall not be prevented by any Commonwealth law from voting at federal elections. The only sensible meaning is that the persons described are entitled to vote in federal elections. The respondents contend that s 41 does not confer any right to vote at federal elections; it merely says that no Commonwealth laws shall prevent the persons described from voting in federal elections and that the right to vote must be found elsewhere. This ridicules the constitutional guarantee. Such a pedantic interpretation should not be adopted to nullify this important personal right. Further, like other constitutional statutory provisions s 41 is presumed to be prospective, ambulatory and constantly speaking. Its words are not transitional …

[271] Quick and Garran favoured a restricted interpretation of s 41 based on their account of the Convention Debates and this was followed by other early scholars (see Harrison Moore (*The Constitution of the Commonwealth* (1902)) and Solicitor-General Garran (*Opinions of the Attorneys-General of the Commonwealth of Australia* (1981), p 695[)]). However, Quick and Garran's account of the Debates in this respect [is] not entirely satisfactory. At the [272] Constitutional Convention on 3 March 1898 the precursor to s 41 was debated. It was in these terms:

> "No elector who has at the establishment of the Commonwealth, or who afterwards acquires, a right to vote at elections for the more numerous House of the Parliament of a state, shall, whilst the qualification continues, be prevented by any law of the Commonwealth from exercising such right at elections for either House of Parliament." …

Mr Barton recognized that the clause would have a continuing operation notwithstanding the introduction of any Commonwealth franchise and expressed fears of the extent to which the State franchise and consequently the Commonwealth franchise in that State might be extended. He said "any state might alter from time to time its suffrage for its House of Assembly, and, having altered it, notwithstanding the existence of the Commonwealth the person who acquired under that alteration a right to vote for the House of Assembly in that particular state might vote – although the extension of the suffrage gave it not only to women, but, perhaps, to such a class as the young persons of sixteen years of age who are now agitating in some places for a vote – notwithstanding the different suffrages of other states, at elections for either House of the Commonwealth … as they were given that right under the law of the state, they, by the operation of this clause, would be entitled to the benefit of every successive alteration of the law, no matter to what length or depth it went, and in such a way that they would be entitled to influence, and very strongly influence the composition of both Houses of the Parliament" (p 1841).

To meet the objection that as the clause stood there will be "an indefinite power in the hands of the States to constantly enlarge the franchise", Mr Isaacs proposed that it be altered to read "Any elector who has, at the establishment of the Commonwealth, or who afterwards, and before the Parliament prescribes the qualification of electors for the Houses of Parliament, acquired a right to vote etc." (see p 1851) That proposal was never adopted. Section 41 omits the very restrictions which Mr Isaacs proposed. Unfortunately Quick and Garran in *The Annotated Constitution of the Australia Commonwealth* do not disclose fully these references to the continuing operation of the clause and although suggesting that there were several possible interpretations of s 41 preferred that which in fact reflects the unadopted proposal of Mr Isaacs. The respondents now contend likewise. The argument is unacceptable.

Murphy J also argued that the need for s 41 as a genuine and continuing guarantee was illustrated by its role in securing the federal franchise to Aborigines before 1962. In fact his history was wrong. Because of the narrow interpretation favoured by Quick and Garran, s 41 had no such impact (see Chapter 5, §2).

In 1988, a referendum proposal to delete s 41 and substitute a new provision unambiguously guaranteeing a right to vote was defeated in every State. In 1992, the High Court held in *Australian Capital Television Pty Ltd v Commonwealth* (1992) 177 CLR 106 that, because ss 7 and 24 of the Constitution establish a system of representative government based on democratic elections, they impliedly protect the individual rights upon which such a system depends, such as freedom of political communication (see Chapter 28, §3). Although this implication has been held not to require *equality* of voting rights (see *McGinty v Western Australia* (1996) 186 CLR 140 in Chapter 10, §3(c)), the bare *existence* of a right to vote may be more fundamental. Thus, even if the reasoning in *R v Pearson* as to s 41 is maintained, the result might now be reversed on the basis that there is an implied constitutional right to vote.

3. Trial by Jury

At first glance, s 80 appears to guarantee the right to trial by jury for offences arising under Commonwealth laws. At second glance, it is clear that the guarantee operates only where there is a "trial on indictment". The High Court has repeatedly held that the application of these words lies wholly within the discretion of the Commonwealth Parliament. It is Parliament that, in creating an offence and providing for its trial and punishment, determines whether the trial shall be summary or on indictment, and thereby determines whether or not there shall be trial by jury. Section 80 might thus be translated: "There shall be trial by jury in those cases where the law provides that there shall be trial by jury". The result is tautological and offers no guarantee at all.

The origins of this view lie in *R v Bernasconi* (1915) 19 CLR 629, where Isaacs J said: "**[637]** If a given offence is not made triable on indictment at all, then sec 80 does not apply", and in *R v Archdall & Roskruge; Ex parte Carrigan and Brown* (1928) 41 CLR 128, where Higgins J quoted s 80 and said: "**[139]** that is to say, if there be an indictment, there must be a jury; but **[140]** there is nothing to compel procedure by indictment".

In a famous joint dissent in *R v Federal Court of Bankruptcy; Ex parte Lowenstein* (1938) 59 CLR 556, Dixon and Evatt JJ argued for a wider interpretation of s 80. The case arose out of s 217 of the *Bankruptcy Act 1924* (Cth), which provided that, when charged with an offence under the Act, a bankrupt could be tried summarily and, if convicted, imprisoned for up to six months. Dixon and Evatt JJ would have held that s 217 infringed s 80 of the Constitution.

R v Federal Court of Bankruptcy; Ex parte Lowenstein
(1938) 59 CLR 556

Dixon and Evatt JJ: [580] The Commonwealth Constitution contains no guarantee against deprivation of life, liberty or property without due process of law, like the fifth and fourteenth amendments of the United States Constitution. To establish personal liberty by constitutional restrictions upon the exercise of governmental power was not a guiding purpose in framing the Australian instrument, which in this respect departs widely from its American model. It is true that checks against legislative encroachment on individual freedom are not completely absent from the Australian Constitution. There are two or three; and one of them, that contained in sec 80 relating to trial by jury, cannot be dismissed from consideration ...

[581] Having before them the provisions contained in art III(2) of the American Constitution and in the fifth, sixth and seventh amendments upon the subject of trial by jury, the framers of our Constitution thought fit for some reason to include in the instrument an adaptation from the original article, although their faith in the palladium of justice was not strong enough to induce them to complete its shrine by transcribing the provisions of the amendments. The third paragraph of art III(2) of the United States Constitution contains the words: "The trial of all crimes, except in cases of impeachment, shall be by jury." The definition of the words "all crimes" in this sweeping declaration had proved no easy matter ... Whether for this or some more subtle reason, when the provision was written into the Commonwealth Constitution, where it stands as sec 80, the corresponding declaration was given the form following, viz, "The trial on indictment of any offence against any law of the Commonwealth shall be by jury." In this formula the difficulty lies not in the words "any offence" but in the words "trial on indictment." In *R v Archdall* [(1928) 41 CLR 128 at 139, 140] *Higgins* J paraphrases the words as meaning – "if there be an indictment, there must be a jury; but there is nothing to compel procedure by indictment." It is a queer intention to ascribe to a constitution; for it supposes that the concern of the framers of the **[582]** provision was not to ensure that no one should be held guilty of a serious offence against the laws of the Commonwealth except by the verdict of a jury, but to prevent a procedural solecism, namely, the use of an indictment in cases where the legislature might think fit to authorize the court itself to pass upon the guilt or innocence of the prisoner. There is high authority for the proposition that "the Constitution is not to be mocked." A cynic might, perhaps, suggest the possibility that sec 80 was drafted in mockery; that its language was carefully chosen so that the guarantee it appeared on the surface to give should be in truth illusory. No court could countenance such a suggestion, and, if this explanation is rejected and an intention to produce some real operative effect is conceded to the section, then to say that its application can always be avoided by authorizing the substitution of some other form of charge for an indictment seems but to mock at the provision. But, even if this means of avoidance be allowable, what is meant by an indictment? In English law it is a bill of accusation preferred before a grand jury and found true by the oaths of at least twelve men whereupon it is to be prosecuted at the suit of the King. But in Australia the word has inevitably been used in a wider sense. Since 9 Geo IV c 83, the means of putting a prisoner upon his trial before a petit jury has been by an accusation under the hand of a law officer or prosecutor for the King. Grand juries have been little used. The accusation at different times and in different States has been variously called an information, an indictment and a presentment.

[583] What then is the essence of a "trial upon indictment" which sec 80 insists shall be by jury? For ourselves we should have thought that to find an answer it was necessary to look for the substantial elements common to the recognized forms of procedure so called and going to make up the conception of prosecution upon indictment. We think that the first of them would be seen to be that some authority constituted under the law to represent the public interest for the purpose took the responsibility of the step which put the accused on his trial; the grand jury, the coroner's jury or the coroner, the law officer or the court. A second element, we think, would be found in the liability of the offender to a term of imprisonment or to some graver form of punishment. We should not have taken the view that sec 80 was intended to impose no real restriction upon the legislative power to provide what kind of tribunal shall decide the guilt or innocence on a criminal charge ...

[584] We admit the difficulties which the form of sec 80 creates, but to treat such a constitutional provision as producing no substantial effect seems rather to defeat than to ascertain its intention.

On the other hand, Latham CJ and McTiernan J held, apparently on the basis of *R v Archdall*, that s 80 had no effective meaning. Rich and Starke JJ expressed no opinion either way. Accordingly, neither of the opposing views had majority support.

Nevertheless, in subsequent cases, the narrow reading of s 80 has repeatedly been treated as "settled". In *Zarb v Kennedy* (1968) 121 CLR 283, that reading was unanimously asserted by a full seven-judge Court for the first time, but the point had been argued very briefly and was dealt with equally briefly. In *Li Chia Hsing v Rankin* (1978) 141 CLR 182, the narrow view of s 80 was again affirmed. However, in this case Murphy J made his fullest statement of a view he had first advanced in *Beckwith v The Queen* (1976) 135 CLR 569: namely, that Dixon and Evatt JJ were right in *Lowenstein's Case* and that s 80 should be read as "[198] a guarantee of a fundamental right to trial by jury in criminal cases (at least in serious ones)".

In *Kingswell v The Queen* (1985) 159 CLR 264, Murphy J's argument was taken up and developed in a powerful dissent by Deane J. Brennan J also dissented, but stopped short of questioning the earlier cases. The joint judgment of Gibbs CJ, Wilson and Dawson JJ, with whom Mason J agreed on this point, once again affirmed the narrow interpretation of s 80.

The *Customs Act 1901* (Cth) imposed forfeitures and penalties for customs offences. Section 233B set out offences of "attempting" to import or "aiding and abetting" importation of narcotic drugs. Under s 235, the penalties for such an offence depended upon a finding by a judge, rather than a jury, as to whether or not a "commercial quantity" of narcotic goods was involved, with the maximum sentence varying accordingly (up to life imprisonment).

Kingswell v The Queen
(1985) 159 CLR 264

Gibbs CJ, Wilson and Dawson JJ: [276] Section 80 requires that if there is a trial on indictment of any offence against any law of the Commonwealth it shall be by jury. The sections now in question do not provide to the contrary. If there is a trial by jury the ordinary incidents of such a trial will apply; the judge will continue to exercise his traditional functions, and, for the purpose of imposing a sentence within the limits fixed by the law, will form his own view of the facts, provided that that view is not in conflict with the verdict of the jury. Section 80 says nothing as to the manner in which an offence is to be defined. Since an offence against the law of the Commonwealth is a creature of that law, it is the law alone which defines the elements of the offence. The fact that s 80 has been given an interpretation which deprives it of much substantial effect provides a reason for refusing to import into the section restrictions on the legislative power which it does not express. It has been held that s 80 does not mean that [277] the trial of all serious offences shall be by jury; the section applies if there is a trial on indictment, but leaves it to the Parliament to determine whether any particular offence shall be tried on indictment or summarily. This result has been criticized, but the Court has consistently refused to reopen the question and the construction of the section should be regarded as settled.

Deane J: [298] The guarantee of s 80 of the Constitution was not the mere expression of some casual preference for one form of criminal trial. It reflected a deep-seated conviction of free men and women about the way in which justice should be administered in criminal cases. That conviction finds a solid basis in an understanding of the history and functioning of the common law as a bulwark against the tyranny of arbitrary punishment. In the history of this country, the **[299]** transition from military panel to civilian jury for the determination of criminal guilt represented the most important step in the progress from military control to civilian self-government.

In *Spratt v Hermes* [(1965) 114 CLR 226 at 244] however, Barwick CJ expressed the view that the inclusion of the words "on indictment" in the relevant provision of s 80 had the result that "[w]hat might have been thought to be a great constitutional guarantee has been discovered to be a mere procedural provision" ... If that view be correct and the ostensible guarantee of the section be, in any event, no more than "a mere procedural provision" whose operation can be avoided at whim by the Parliament, there can be little objection in principle to an insular and narrow construction of its terms. If, on the other hand, the section is properly to be seen as embodying a fundamental and substantive constitutional guarantee of trial by jury, the settled principles of legal interpretation applicable to such a guarantee require that it be broadly interpreted and applied ...

Regardless of whether one traces the common law institution of trial by jury to Roman, Saxon, Frankish or Norman origins, the underlying notion of judgment by one's equals under the law was traditionally seen as established in English criminal law, for those who had the power to be heard, at least by 1215 when the Charter of that year provided, among other things, that no man should be arrested, imprisoned, banished or deprived of life otherwise than by the lawful judgment of his equals ("per legale judicium parium suorum") or by the law of the land. Modern scholarship would indicate that much of the traditional identification of trial by jury with Magna Carta was erroneous. It is, however, clear enough that the right to trial by jury in criminal matters was, by the fourteenth **[300]** century, seen in England as an "ancient" right. In the centuries that followed, there was consistent reiteration ... of the fundamental importance of trial by jury to the liberty of the subject under the rule of law ... When British settlements were established in other parts of the world, trial by jury in criminal matters was claimed as a "birthright and inheritance" under the common law and as an institution to be established and safeguarded to the extent that local circumstances would permit ...

In *R v Snow* [(1915) 20 CLR 315 at 323], Griffith CJ described the constitutional guarantee which s 80 contains as "a fundamental law of the Commonwealth". The rationale and the essential function of that guarantee are the protection of the citizen against those who customarily exercise the authority of government: legislators who might seek by their laws to abolish or undermine "the institution of 'trial by jury' with all that was connoted by that phrase in constitutional law and in the common law of England" (per Griffith CJ); administrators who might seek to subvert the due process of law or be, or be thought to be, corrupt or over-zealous in its enforcement; judges who might be, or be thought to be, over-remote from ordinary life, over-censorious or over-responsive to authority ...

[301] Trial by jury also brings important practical benefits to the administration of criminal justice. A system of criminal law cannot be attuned to the needs of the people whom it exists to serve unless its administration, proceedings and judgments are comprehensible by both the accused and the general public and have the appearance, as well as the substance, of being impartial and just. In a legal system where the question of criminal guilt is determined by a jury of ordinary citizens, the participating lawyers are constrained to present the evidence and issues in a manner that can be understood by laymen. The result is that the accused and the public can follow and understand the proceedings. Equally important, the presence and function of a jury in a criminal trial and the well-known tendency of jurors to identify and side with a fellow-citizen who is, in their view, being denied a "fair go" tend to ensure observance of the consideration and respect to which ordinary notions of fair play entitle an accused or a witness. Few lawyers with practical experience in criminal matters would deny the importance of the institution of the jury to the maintenance of the appearance, as well as the substance, of impartial justice in criminal cases ...

The institution of trial by jury also serves the function of protecting both the administration of justice and the accused from the rash judgment and prejudices of the community itself. The nature of the jury as a body of ordinary citizens called from the community to try the particular case offers some assurance that the community as a whole will be more likely to accept a jury's verdict than it would be to accept the judgment of a judge or magistrate who might be, or be portrayed as being, over-responsive to authority or remote from the affairs and concerns of ordinary people ...

[302] That is not, of course, to close one's eyes to reality and assert that the traditional criminal trial by jury is without any identifiable weaknesses ... The safeguards surrounding trial by jury have never represented a guarantee that juries, unlike other human agencies of the community, will never get it wrong. Unavoidably, there will be the rare case in which a properly instructed jury's verdict of guilty can be demonstrated to constitute a miscarriage of justice warranting the interference of an appellate court. Perhaps more importantly, contemporary circumstances have raised new questions about, and placed additional strains upon, the institution of the criminal trial by jury. There is, eg, obvious force in the argument that a jury of ordinary men and **[303]** women selected at random from the community lacks the knowledge and experience necessary to sit in responsible judgment upon the type of scientific dispute between specialists that may arise in the course of a criminal trial or upon the detailed technical questions which may be involved in the trial of white collar and computer crime. Indeed, under the existing practice whereby a jury is deprived even of the transcript of expert evidence, it would seem inevitable that the members of a jury will sometimes be faced with an effective choice between determining complicated technical questions by reference to the unlikely touchstone of the surface plausibility of disputing experts or opposing counsel and abrogating their own function in favour of any views which they might attribute to the trial judge. In that regard, there is much to be said in favour of the introduction of a system of "court witnesses" or expert "assessors" to advise or guide a lay jury in such areas. Again, the pervasiveness of the influence of organs of the media and their concern, for whatever motive, to stimulate and satisfy the public interest in the news which they purvey has inevitably led to problems involving the extent to which freedom of public discussion should or effectively can be restricted to protect and preserve the impartiality and public anonymity of the members of criminal juries and the confidentiality of their deliberative processes. Notwithstanding such actual or potential weaknesses, however, the institution of trial by jury remains as important a safeguard of the liberties of free men and women as it ever was and, if it be effective, the constitutional guarantee of jury trial will remain as much a fundamental law of the Constitution as it was at the time when the Constitution was adopted by the people of the Australian colonies.

After a review of the changing historical uses and modes of the "indictment" procedure in England and in the Australian colonies, Deane J said:

Deane J: [310] In my respectful view, Dixon and Evatt JJ were correct in their conclusion [in *R v Federal Court of Bankruptcy; Ex parte Lowenstein* (1938) 59 CLR 556 at 582] that there lies at the heart of the concept of "trial on indictment" in s 80 the notion of the trial of a "serious offence". I am, however, unable to accept their Honours' view that the criterion of what constitutes, for relevant purposes, a serious offence is that it be punishable by any term of imprisonment at all. In the light of the foregoing, it appears to me that the correct criterion of what constitutes a serious offence is that it not be one which can appropriately be dealt with summarily by justices or magistrates ...

[318] The conclusion to which I have finally come is that, notwithstanding the contrary trend in subsequent judgments in this Court, the views expressed by Dixon and Evatt JJ in *Lowenstein*, as qualified in the manner which I have mentioned, should be accepted **[319]** as a correct statement of the effect of the reference to "trial on indictment" in s 80 of the Constitution. On that construction, the guarantee of the section is applicable in respect of any trial of an accused charged with an offence against a law of the Commonwealth in circumstances where the charge is brought by the State or an agency of the State and the accused will, if found guilty, stand convicted of a "serious offence" ... [A] particular alleged offence will ... be a "serious offence" if it is not one which could appropriately be dealt with summarily by justices or magistrates in that conviction will expose the accused to grave punishment. It is unnecessary, for the purposes of the present case, to seek to identify more precisely the boundary between offences which are not and offences which are capable of being properly so dealt with. I have, however, indicated the tentative view that that boundary will ordinarily be identified by reference to whether the offence is punishable, when prosecuted in the manner in which it is being prosecuted, by a maximum term of imprisonment of more than one year.

Both Brennan and Deane JJ dissented in *Kingswell* on the ground that, by establishing a different sentencing regime for offences involving a "commercial quantity" of narcotic substances, the Parliament had in effect created a distinct and separate offence that attracted its own separate operation of the guarantee in s 80. Deane J based this on his conclusion that s 80 must be read as "**[319]** an effective restraint upon Commonwealth legislative power" – a conclusion, he said, which "necessitates the approach that the words of the fundamental law which it embodies must ... be given their full force and effect". Brennan J, without addressing that wider question, treated the matter simply as one of construction of the word "offence".

When the issue was revisited in *Cheng v The Queen* (2000) 203 CLR 248, the discussion focused primarily on the judgment of Brennan J in *Kingswell*; but again his analysis was adopted only in dissent (by Gaudron and Kirby JJ). The majority evinced some sympathy for Brennan J's approach in principle, but held that the "commercial quantity" provisions in the *Customs Act* did not in fact create a distinct offence. As for the judgment of Deane J in *Kingswell*, it continued to attract little support. Gleeson CJ, Gummow and Hayne JJ refused to reopen *Kingswell* (partly because the defendants in *Cheng* had pleaded guilty), but were generally supportive of the current interpretation of s 80. McHugh and Callinan JJ went further, explicitly reaffirming the majority view in *Kingswell*.

Cheng v The Queen
(2000) 203 CLR 248

McHugh J: [292] What ... is the mischief at which s 80 is aimed? When the section is read in the light of its United States counterpart, its drafts and the discussion at the Constitutional Conventions, it is plain that it took the form that it did to avoid the mischief that would result if Parliament could not determine which offences against the laws of the Commonwealth were to be tried by juries. The words of s 80 were deliberately and carefully chosen to give the Parliament the capacity to avoid trial by jury when it wished to do so ...

[295] Whether one looks at text, history or purpose, the answer is the same: the approach to the construction of s 80 accepted by the majority in *Kingswell* and by this Court in earlier cases is correct. Section 80 is not a great guarantee of trial by jury for serious matters. It guarantees trial by jury only when the trial is on indictment. Whether the offence is tried or triable on indictment depends in the first instance on Parliament's classification of the offence. Such a conclusion is unlikely to be acceptable to many civil libertarians or those who believe that serious criminal offences should be tried by juries. But it is what our Constitution mandates. A contrary result can only be reached, in my respectful opinion, by disregarding the plain meaning of s 80, its drafting history and its purpose.

Even if one came to the conclusion that s 80 had, or may have had, a purpose other than that which its plain words suggest, a real question would arise as to what meaning could be placed on the section to give effect to that purpose. Those Justices who have rejected the accepted interpretation of s 80 ... have not been able to agree, however, as to the meaning that should be given to the phrase "trial on indictment" in s 80 ...

[296] Not only are each of [their] formulations [of "trial on indictment"] significantly different from each other, but each uses a category of indeterminate reference – "grave form of punishment", "serious matter", "grave punishment", "serious criminal offences", "serious offence", "appropriately be dealt with summarily". Each of them would provoke as much, probably more, uncertainty of application as the "not self-determining" term "all Crimes" in the corresponding provision in the Constitution of the United States. They would leave every Justice free to decide each case according to the opinion of the Justice as to whether the offence or the punishment was sufficiently serious or grave to require a jury trial. There would be no objective criteria to which the Justice could turn to determine the question. Contrary to what Deane J may have thought in *Kingswell*, history would give present-day Justices little assistance in determining whether the trial of an offence could "appropriately be dealt with summarily". At all events, history would authorise summary trials in many cases that would seem to modern eyes to require a jury trial if s 80 is to be regarded as a real guarantee of trial by jury ...

[298] Undoubtedly there are many offences where courts would have no doubt that they were serious offences requiring trial by jury. Treason, murder and rape are examples. But in the regulatory State, there are many offences where judges and justices would probably often disagree as to whether they met the criteria laid down by Dixon, Evatt, Murphy or Deane JJ. History is unlikely to offer much of a guide. In the United States, the indeterminacy of the "cruel and unusual punishments" clause of that country's Constitution has provoked much debate and corresponding uncertainty concerning its application. It seems likely that the suggestions of the above Justices as to the meaning of s 80 would create similar uncertainty as to the reach of the section. Would charges of indecent assault, indecent exposure, larceny, embezzlement, falsification of accounts, fraudulent misappropriation, false pretences, corruption, receiving, malicious injury or forgery require a trial by jury? They are merely some of the serious offences that are, or have been, able to be tried summarily in State courts, sometimes only with the consent of the accused and sometimes without his or her consent. Are these offences serious matters which would require trial by jury if enacted by the Commonwealth? Would it make a difference if the maximum sentence in respect of such offences is (say) two years? Is two or three years for corporate fraud such a serious matter involving such grave punishment that it would require a jury trial in the case of a federal offence? Would it be relevant that the facts of the case suggest a sentence of no more than one year? Would the length of sentences that could be imposed in State jurisdictions for summary offences be relevant in determining the application of s 80?

These questions suggest that to adopt the views of Dixon and Evatt JJ or Murphy J or Deane J would provoke much uncertainty as to the application of s 80 and create a new and fertile field of constitutional jurisprudence. Unsatisfactory consequences cannot alter constitutional meanings but they should make us hesitate before adopting the meaning of a constitutional provision which is contrary to its text, history and purpose ...

[299] Even if I thought that the current interpretation ... accepted by the majority in *Kingswell* was incorrect, the difficulties of judicially formulating a workable principle would make me hesitate before rejecting the authority of the cases that give effect to the current interpretation. My hesitation would be increased by the knowledge that in 1988 a substantial majority of the Australian people refused to approve an amendment to s 80. That amendment would have required a jury trial where the person was being tried "for an offence, where the accused is liable to imprisonment for more than two years or any form of corporal punishment". The proposed amendment made exceptions for a trial for contempt of court and certain cases tried before a court-martial. It is true that the amendment was defeated as part of a package of four amendments and that a majority of the people may have favoured it. But at least this much can be said: the people did not feel so strongly in favour of trial by jury that they were prepared to accept the remaining amendments so that they could have trial by jury "for an offence, where the accused is liable to imprisonment for more than two years or any form of corporal punishment".

Gaudron and Kirby JJ took a more robust view of s 80, on the basis that, as Gaudron J put it, "**[278]** constitutional guarantees are to be construed liberally and not pedantically confined".

Kirby J: [306] Section 80 of the Australian Constitution ... has led to some of the sharpest divisions of opinion in the history of this Court. The present proceedings are no exception.

In the early days of the Court, the opinion prevailed that the section was no more than a procedural requirement, a position seemingly incompatible with its inclusion within the enduring provisions of Ch III of the Constitution. Yet, even in those dark days, there were occasional glimmers of light. Thus, in 1915, Griffith CJ suggested that s 80 was a "fundamental law of the Commonwealth" [*R v Snow* (1915) 20 CLR 315 at 323]. In 1936, Evatt J, extracurially, derided the prevailing view as tautological because it rendered illusory the protections of the Constitution and put them "at the will of the very Parliament whose action it was intended to restrict by safeguarding the rights of the citizen". In 1938, Dixon and Evatt JJ wrote a strong dissent castigating the opinion of their colleagues as one which attributed a "queer intention" to the **[307]** Constitution and allowed it to be "mocked" [*R v Federal Court of Bankruptcy; Ex parte Lowenstein* (1938) 59 CLR 556 at 581-2]. Although individual Justices were from time to time persuaded to the minority view, the majority opinion remained that s 80 was not a constitutional guarantee but a mere procedural provision. That view was expressed as late as 1985 in the decision that comes under re-examination in these proceedings [*Kingswell*] …

Then, it seemed, a change came over the Court's exposition of the requirements of s 80. In 1986, in *Brown v The Queen* [(1986) 160 CLR 171 at 201], Deane J declared that the section was a "constitutional guarantee … for the benefit of the community as a whole". Other members of the Court on that occasion acknowledged that s 80 afforded a meaningful guarantee protective of substantive rights. In 1993, in *Cheatle v The Queen* [(1993) 177 CLR 541], a unanimous Court declared that s 80 protected the essential features of criminal trial by jury …

Then the earlier formalism returned. The most recent decisions on s 80, whilst sometimes containing a passing nod to the view of the section as a fundamental guarantee of the Constitution, have confined its operation to an ineffective hortation. The old view, it seems, is, for a time, to prevail again. The logic and necessity of giving a constitutional effect to s 80 is to be rejected. Whereas other provisions of Ch III are strictly invoked to strike down beneficial national legislation [*Re Wakim; Ex parte McNally* (1999) 198 CLR 511] or to invalidate longstanding national practice [*Wilson v Minister for Aboriginal and Torres Strait Islander Affairs* (1996) 189 CLR 1], s 80 of the Constitution is, it would appear, to be viewed as a withered "guarantee" of no substantive use to those facing trial for federal offences in Australian courts. It might just as well not have been included in the Constitution.

Because … I cannot accept this view of the meaning of s 80 and because I reject a turning back to such a sterile opinion about **[308]** its requirements, I must explain my point of difference …

[321] [The argument that s 233B established separate offences] would necessitate the drawing of lines and the classification of particular considerations … Similar problems must be faced by construing the words on "indictment" as constitutionally equivalent to the specification of offences that are "serious". But the alternative to drawing such lines is the adoption of a construction of s 80 of the Constitution that deprives the section of any ultimate constitutional efficacy. In a choice between adjusting to a difficulty and surrender to the Parliament of untrammelled power, which the constitutional text, if it has a purpose, was designed to deny, the former will ordinarily be the correct path of constitutional construction. It is the path that the Court should take here …

[T]he Attorney-General laid much emphasis upon the intention of the framers of the Constitution. Once again, this Court was taken through the debates at the Constitutional Conventions to show how many of the framers (some of whom later as Justices of the Court gave effect to their opinions) regarded the notion that s 80 of the Constitution was a guarantee of individual rights as "clap-trap". It was on this footing that the submission was advanced that it was perfectly possible, indeed affirmatively expected, that s 80 could be rendered nugatory by "mere drafting devices". Such an approach, deeply offensive to a principled construction of the Constitution, needs to be answered. It is my opinion that the framers of the Constitution did not intend, nor did they enjoy the power to require, that their subjective expectations, wishes or hopes should control all succeeding generations of Australians who live under the protection of the Constitution. The history of s 80 and debates or **[322]** writings about its expected operation may certainly be read for illumination and guidance. But the consideration that governs the meaning of the constitutional text is the ascertainment, with the eyes of the present generation, of the essential characteristics of the text read as a constitutional charter of government. We are not chained to the expectations of 1900.

For purposes of the immediate issue in *Cheng*, Gaudron and Kirby JJ based their dissents on the approach of Brennan J in *Kingswell*. However, in the earlier decision of *Re Colina; Ex parte Torney* (1999) 200 CLR 386, Kirby J had held that "**[422]** the proper construction of s 80 of the Constitution is that favoured by Deane J in *Kingswell*". In that case it was held that the inherent power of federal judges to punish for contempt of court did not attract s 80 – for McHugh and Callinan JJ because such proceedings are not tried "on indictment"; for Gleeson CJ, Gummow and Hayne JJ because the inherent power flows directly from Ch III of the Constitution, and hence not from "any law of the Commonwealth" within the meaning of s 80 at all. Kirby J dissented from these conclusions; Gaudron J did not sit.

In *Cheng*, the decisions in *Brown v The Queen* (1986) 160 CLR 171 and *Cheatle v The Queen* (1993) 177 CLR 541 were treated by Kirby J as apparent harbingers of change that were then superseded by a return to "**[307]** the earlier formalism". In fact, the focus of *Brown* and

Cheatle is different. *Kingswell*, as reaffirmed in *Cheng*, is concerned to delimit the range of offences to which s 80 applies; *Brown* and *Cheatle* are concerned with the consequences of s 80 for those offences to which it applies (that is, those that under Commonwealth law are triable "on indictment"). If, in the light of *Cheng*, it appears that *Brown* and *Cheatle* did not foreshadow acceptance of the view of Deane J in *Kingswell*, it would equally be a mistake to infer that *Cheng* has weakened or undermined the decisions in *Brown* and *Cheatle*.

In *Brown*, the Court considered s 7 of the *Juries Act 1927* (SA), which permits an accused to waive his or her right to a jury trial. It was held that the provision was not applicable to a person charged with a Commonwealth offence, "**[200]** for such an application would give s 7 an operation inconsistent with s 80 of the Constitution". Normally, when a trial on indictment for a Commonwealth offence is held in a State court, the relevant State procedural laws are adopted by s 68 of the *Judiciary Act 1903* (Cth); but since s 7 was inapplicable the Court held that it was not picked up by s 68. Brennan and Dawson JJ agreed with Deane J that the right to a jury trial *could not* be waived because it is a "**[201]** constitutional guarantee ... for the benefit of the community as a whole", not just for the individual. Gibbs CJ and Wilson J held (in dissent) that the right *could* be waived since it was primarily an individual right, "**[190]** wholly directed to effectively securing to an accused person presented for trial on indictment the right to ... the verdict of a jury". Both views treated s 80 as a meaningful guarantee protecting significant rights. It was on this ground that, until the decision in *Cheng*, *Brown* was seen by some as a step towards majority acceptance of Deane J's judgment in *Kingswell*.

In *Cheatle*, the issue was whether a trial judge in South Australia, in a trial under s 86A of the *Crimes Act 1914* (Cth), was entitled to accept a majority verdict, that is, 10 out of 12 jurors, as was permitted by s 57 of the *Juries Act*. The High Court held in a joint unanimous judgment that jury unanimity is an essential element of the "trial by jury" guaranteed by s 80. Accordingly, s 57 of the *Juries Act* was "read down" so as not to have any application to a Commonwealth "trial on indictment".

Cheatle v The Queen
(1993) 177 CLR 541

The Court: [550] THE REQUIREMENT OF UNANIMITY: HISTORY
As a matter of history, the common law's insistence that the verdict of the petty jury on a criminal trial be by agreement of all the jurors can be traced back at least to the judgment of the Common Bench, delivered by Thorpe CJ, in an *Anonymous Case* [(1367) YB 41 Lib Ass 11] in 1367 when "it was finally settled ... that (the) verdict must be unanimous". The origin of that requirement of unanimity would seem to lie not in any reasoned development of principle but in a requirement of the concurrence of twelve jurors in the verdict in the early days when jurors performed the function of local witnesses in trial by compurgation. Be that as it may, the common law has, since the fourteenth century, consistently and unequivocally insisted upon the requirement of unanimity. The requirement was, at one stage, subjected to some distinguished criticism, mainly for the reason that it constituted the **[551]** foundation and explanation of the practice in earlier times of carrying the jurors around "in a wagon" with the assize – "without meat or drinke, fire or candle" – until they were starved or frozen into agreement. In more recent times, however, the requirement has commonly been seen as constituting "an essential and inseparable part" [*Newell v The King* (1936) 55 CLR 707 at 713] of the right to trial by jury and an important "protection" of the citizen against wrongful conviction ...

It suffices to say that, by 1900, trial by jury was firmly established by legislation in each of the federating Colonies as the universal method of trial of serious crime. In the legislation of each Colony, some of the traditional characteristics of the common law institution of criminal trial by jury were assumed rather than specifically prescribed. That was certainly the case as regards the requirement of unanimity. Notwithstanding the absence of any specific legislative provision in that regard, it was recognized, as a basic principle of the administration of criminal justice in each of the Colonies, that the verdict of a criminal jury could be returned only by the agreement of all the jurors ...

[552] It follows from what has been said above that the history of criminal trial by jury in England and in this country up until the time of Federation establishes that, in 1900, it was an essential feature of the institution that an accused person could not be convicted otherwise than by the agreement or consensus of all the jurors. It is well settled that the interpretation of a constitution such as ours is necessarily influenced by the fact that its provisions are framed in the language of the English common law, and are to be read in the light of the common law's history. In the context of the history of criminal trial by jury, one would assume that s 80's directive that the trial to which it refers must be by jury was intended to encompass that requirement of unanimity.

THE REQUIREMENT OF UNANIMITY: PRINCIPLE

Considerations of principle also support the conclusion that the requirement of unanimity is an essential feature of the trial by jury guaranteed by s 80. Regardless of the origins of the requirement that the verdict of a criminal jury be unanimous, the common law's unwavering insistence upon the requirement since the fourteenth century has endowed it with the authority of settled doctrine. Indeed, the requirement constitutes one of the hallmarks of the common law institution of criminal trial by jury in that there is a significant difference in nature between a deliberative process in which a verdict can be returned only if consensus or agreement is reached by all jurors and a process in which a specified number of jurors can override any dissent and return a majority verdict. The requirement of a unanimous verdict ensures that the representative **[553]** character and the collective nature of the jury are carried forward into any ultimate verdict. A majority verdict, on the other hand, is analogous to an electoral process in that jurors cast their votes relying on their individual convictions. The necessity of a consensus of all jurors, which flows from the requirement of unanimity, promotes deliberation and provides some insurance that the opinions of each of the jurors will be heard and discussed. Thereby, it reduces the danger of "hasty and unjust verdicts". In contrast, and though a minimum time might be required to have elapsed before a majority verdict may be returned, such a verdict dispenses with consensus and involves the overriding of the views of the dissenting minority.

Moreover, the common law's insistence upon unanimity reflects a fundamental thesis of our criminal law, namely, that a person accused of a crime should be given the benefit of any reasonable doubt. It is true that there is no logical inconsistency involved in the co-existence in the law of the criminal onus of proof and majority verdicts of guilt. Nonetheless, assuming that all jurors are acting reasonably, a verdict returned by a majority of the jurors, over the dissent of others, objectively suggests the existence of reasonable doubt and carries a greater risk of conviction of the innocent than does a unanimous verdict …

[560] SOME ARGUMENTS AGAINST UNANIMITY

Several distinct arguments were advanced against the conclusion that the requirement of unanimity is implicit in s 80's guarantee of trial by jury. In our view, none of them is persuasive. It suffices to make specific reference to three of them.

(i) *There were some undesirable characteristics of trial by jury in 1900*

Considerable reliance was placed by the Crown and some of the intervening Attorneys-General on the fact that some aspects of trial by jury, as it existed in the Australian Colonies at the time of Federation, are inconsistent with both the contemporary institution, and generally accepted standards of a modern democratic society. In particular, criminal juries in 1900 were constituted exclusively by males who satisfied some minimum property qualification. There is, it was argued, no more justification for the perception that s 80 incorporates the requirement of unanimity than there would be for the approach that the section requires the preservation of those undesirable aspects of trial by jury in 1900. The answer to that argument is, however, clear enough. It is that to abrogate the requirement of unanimity involves an abandonment of an essential feature of the institution of trial by jury. In contrast, a liberalization of the qualifications of jurors involves no more than an adjustment of the institution to conform with contemporary standards and to bring about a situation in which it is more truly representative of the community.

Neither the exclusion of females nor the existence of some property qualification was an essential feature of the institution of trial by jury in 1900. The relevant essential feature or requirement of the institution was, and is, that the jury be a body of persons representative of the

wider community. It may be that there are certain unchanging elements of that feature or requirement such as, for example, that the panel of jurors be randomly or impartially selected rather than
chosen by the prosecution or the State. The restrictions and qualifications of jurors which either
advance or are consistent with it may, however, vary with contemporary standards and perceptions.
The exclusion of women and unpropertied persons was, presumably, seen as justified in earlier
days by a then current perception that the only true representatives of the wider community were
men of property. It would, however, be absurd to **[561]** suggest that a requirement that the jury be
truly representative requires a continuation of any such exclusion in the more enlightened climate
of 1993. To the contrary, in contemporary Australia, the exclusion of females and unpropertied
persons would itself be inconsistent with such a requirement.

(ii) Unanimity was not necessary in the case of civil juries in some Colonies

At common law, unanimity was required in the case of both criminal and civil juries. By the
time of Federation, however, the legislation of some of the Australian Colonies provided for the
return of a majority verdict by a civil jury. The legislative provisions to that effect mean, so it was
argued, that the requirement of unanimity could not have been seen as an essential feature of the
institution of trial by jury in 1900. Again, the answer to the argument is clear enough. It is that it is
a mistake to see those legislative modifications in relation to civil juries as undermining the status
of the requirement of unanimity as an essential feature of the institution of criminal trial by jury
adopted by s 80 ...

(iii) Argument of convenience

The third argument to which specific reference should be made was to the effect that there are
powerful practical considerations favouring the acceptance of majority verdicts in criminal trials in
contemporary Australia. There are two answers to that argument. First, the abandonment, for
reasons of contemporary convenience **[562]** or practical utility, of an essential feature of the
criminal trial by jury which is guaranteed by s 80 of the Constitution is not a matter for this Court.
It is a matter for the people of Australia for whose protection the guarantee, including the requirement of unanimity, was adopted. Secondly, it is not, in any event, apparent that considerations of
contemporary convenience or practical utility favour an abandonment of the requirement of
unanimity in the case of a criminal jury. To the contrary, one can point to strong support for the
view that the requirement of unanimity of a criminal jury is, on balance, in the public interest in
this country. In particular, it is far from evident that the reduction in the number of cases in which a
criminal jury is unable to return a verdict, which could be expected to result from an abandonment
of the requirement of unanimity, would be of sufficient significance to outweigh the disadvantages
which would result from such a course.

Since *Cheatle*, the High Court has been asked in a number of cases to determine whether adaptations of the jury process are consistent with s 80. In each case, the Court has held that the
provision has not been infringed. The decisions demonstrate that, although there are essential
characteristics of a "trial by jury" under s 80 such as unanimity and perhaps that "**[560]** jurors be
randomly or impartially selected" (as to which see *Katsuno v The Queen* (1999) 199 CLR 40),
innovation remains possible as to other aspects of the jury process. Within this framework, it is
possible for legislation to modify the traditional jury process – for example, in response to the
increasing length and complexity of trials.

In *Brownlee v The Queen* (2001) 207 CLR 278 it was argued that s 22(a)(i) of the *Jury Act
1977* (NSW) must be read down so as not to apply to a Commonwealth "trial on indictment". It
provided that, if members of a jury have been discharged, the remaining members "shall be
considered as remaining" a properly constituted jury, provided that in a criminal case the number
of jurors is not reduced below 10. It was also argued that a s 80 jury cannot, by a court order
under s 54(b) of the *Jury Act*, be permitted to separate after they retire to consider their verdict.
Although the Court rejected both arguments, Gaudron, Gummow and Hayne JJ conceded as to
the first that "**[318]** questions of degree" may be involved, so that "there is much force in the
contention that no reduction below 10 is permissible".

In *Cheung v The Queen* (2001) 209 CLR 1, it was argued that a "trial by jury" under s 80 carries with it the requirement that "**[39]** all important factual **[40]** questions determinative of criminal punishment … be isolated and decided by the jury, not by the judge". This was rejected by the whole Court, which found that the determination of facts as part of the sentencing process could properly be left to the trial judge alone. In further decisions in *Fittock v The Queen* (2003) 217 CLR 508 and *Ng v The Queen* (2003) 217 CLR 521, the Court held that the practice of empanelling "reserve" or "additional" jurors (in case, for example, a juror dies or is discharged) is also consistent with the concept of a "trial by jury" under s 80.

Both *Brown* and *Cheatle* were perceived at the time as making the unresolved disagreement in *Kingswell* seem more anomalous. However, it is clear that, logically, they did not bear on that disagreement. Questions about what s 80 requires *in those cases in which it applies* do not determine *when it applies*. *Cheatle* remains the strongest example of a forceful application of s 80 in those cases to which it applies. But there was no doubt that the Cheatles were to be tried "on indictment" and, if there had been any doubt as to whether that procedure was appropriate, nothing in the High Court's reasoning would have resolved such a doubt. Accordingly, neither *Brown* nor *Cheatle* did anything to strengthen or weaken the argument of Deane J in *Kingswell*. Equally, the decision in *Cheng* does nothing to detract from the force of the decisions in *Brown* and *Cheatle*.

4. Freedom of Religion

Section 116 contains four separate guarantees: the Commonwealth shall not make any law "for establishing any religion", "for imposing any religious observance" or "for prohibiting the free exercise of any religion", and "no religious test shall be required as a qualification for any office or public trust under the Commonwealth". Most of the case law on s 116 has concerned the "free exercise" clause. The first indication of a narrow judicial approach came in *Krygger v Williams* (1912) 15 CLR 366. The *Defence Act 1903* (Cth) had introduced a system of compulsory peace-time military training. By s 135, "every person who in any year, without lawful excuse, evades or fails to render the personal service required by this Part shall be guilty of an offence". By s 143(3), "all persons liable to be trained … who are forbidden by the doctrines of their religion to bear arms shall so far as possible be allotted to non-combatant duties". Edgar Krygger was charged with failure to render service under s 135. He told the magistrate: "**[367]** I decline to render military service because it is opposed to the will of God … Attendance at drill is against my conscience and the will of God … To me it is as much a sin in the sight of God as gambling, racing, or any other sin … If I went to military training I would be **[368]** prohibited from the free exercise of my religion". His appeal was heard by Griffith CJ and Barton J, both of whom impatiently dismissed the suggestion that s 116 was infringed.

Krygger v Williams
(1912) 15 CLR 366

Griffith CJ: [369] Sec 116 of the Constitution provides that "the Commonwealth shall not make any law for … prohibiting the free exercise of any religion" – that is, prohibiting the practice of religion – the doing of acts which are done in the practi[c]e of religion. To require a man to do a thing which has nothing at all to do with religion is not prohibiting him from a free exercise of religion. It may be that a law requiring a man to do an act which his religion forbids would be objectionable on moral grounds, but it does not come within the prohibition of sec 116 …

[370] Careful provision has been made by the legislature for the case of those who really have conscientious objections to war … [E]verybody knows that in warfare not all the duties are of a combatant nature. I will only take as an illustration the ambulance corps, the duty of which is not to take life but to save it …

The real objection taken by the appellant is not to being trained so as to become efficient for taking life, but to being trained so that in time of war he may be competent to assist in saving life, and that is called a conscientious objection. For my own part, I do not think that such an objection is any excuse for a refusal to obey a positive law. All our laws, I think, where there is any ground for thinking that real conscientious objection **[371]** may exist, make careful provision for the protection of people's consciences, as does this Act. But to base a refusal to be trained in non-combatant duties upon conscientious grounds is absurd.

Barton J: [372] [T]he *Defence Act* is not a law prohibiting the free exercise of the appellant's religion, nor is there any attempt to show anything so absurd as that the appellant could not exercise his religion freely if he did the **[373]** necessary drill. I think this objection is as thin as anything of the kind that has come before us.

Adelaide Company of Jehovah's Witnesses Inc v Commonwealth (*Jehovah's Witnesses Case*) (1943) 67 CLR 116 is generally regarded as reinforcing the grudging approach in *Krygger*. The case involved a wartime challenge to the *National Security (Subversive Associations) Regulations* (Cth). Regulation 3 provided: "Any body corporate or unincorporate, the existence of which the Governor-General … declares to be in his opinion, prejudicial to the defence of the Common-wealth or the efficient prosecution of the war, is hereby declared to be unlawful". Once declared unlawful, an association was dissolved under the Regulations and its property could be occupied and forfeited. On 17 January 1941, the Governor-General made a declaration in relation to the Adelaide Company of Jehovah's Witnesses Inc. On the same day, a Commonwealth officer attempted to occupy the Jehovah's Witnesses' Kingdom Hall in Adelaide and to exclude them from meeting there.

The Regulations were described by Starke J as "**[154]** arbitrary, capricious and oppressive"; and the crucial provisions were held invalid as exceeding the scope of the Commonwealth's defence power under s 51(vi) of the Constitution. On the other hand, the Court held by 5:0 that the Regulations did not infringe s 116. It was said that freedom is meaningful only in an ordered framework and that, consistently with s 116, the Commonwealth could take steps to secure that framework. According to Rich J, the protection offered by s 116 is "**[149]** not absolute. It is subject to powers and restrictions of government essential to the preservation of the community. Freedom of religion may not be invoked to cloak and dissemble subversive opinions or practices and operations **[150]** dangerous to the common weal".

It is sometimes said that in the *Jehovah's Witnesses Case* the High Court devalued or discounted religious rights, but upheld property rights. At most this seems accurate only in relation to Latham CJ and McTiernan J, whose strongest disapprobation was reserved for the Commonwealth seizure and closure of Kingdom Hall. While Latham CJ took a narrow view of "freedom of religion", he balanced this to some extent with a wide view of "religion". Indeed, it was in part because Latham CJ took such a broad view of "religion", and of the range of activities that might be involved in its exercise, that he then felt able to argue that the freedom of religion could not be absolute and that it must be "**[132]** possible to reconcile religious freedom with ordered government".

Adelaide Company of Jehovah's Witnesses Inc v Commonwealth (*Jehovah's Witnesses Case*)
(1943) 67 CLR 116

Latham CJ: [123] 3. Section 116 applies in express terms to "any religion," "any religious observance," the free exercise of "any religion" and any "religious test." Thus the section applies in relation to all religions, and not merely in relation to some one particular religion.

It would be difficult, if not impossible, to devise a definition of religion which would satisfy the adherents of all the many and various religions which exist, or have existed, in the world. There are those who regard religion as consisting principally in a system of beliefs or statement of doctrine. So viewed religion may be either true or false. Others are more inclined to regard religion as prescribing a code of conduct. So viewed a religion may be good or bad. There are others who pay greater attention to religion as involving some prescribed form of ritual or religious observance. Many religious conflicts have been concerned with matters of ritual and observance. Section 116 must be regarded as operating in relation to all these aspects of religion, irrespective of varying opinions in the community as to the truth of particular religious doctrines, as to the goodness of conduct prescribed by a particular religion, or as to the propriety of any particular religious observance. What is religion to one is superstition to another. Some religions are regarded as morally evil by adherents of other creeds. At all times there are many who agree with the reflective comment of the Roman poet – *"Tantum religio potuit suadere malorum."*

The prohibition in s 116 operates not only to protect the freedom of religion, but also to protect the right of a man to have no religion. No Federal law can impose any religious observance. Defaults in the performance of religious duties are not to be corrected by Federal law – *Deorum injuriae Diis curae.* Section 116 proclaims not only the principle of toleration of all religions, but also the principle of toleration of absence of religion.

[124] 4. It was suggested in argument that no system of beliefs or code of conduct or form of ritual could be protected under the section unless the general opinion of the present day regarded the belief or conduct or ritual as being really religious. It is true that in determining what is religious and what is not religious the current application of the word "religion" must necessarily be taken into account, but it should not be forgotten that such a provision as s 116 is not required for the protection of the religion of a majority. The religion of the majority of the people can look after itself. Section 116 is required to protect the religion (or absence of religion) of minorities, and, in particular, of unpopular minorities …

[125] At all periods of human history there have been religions which have involved practices which have been regarded by large numbers of people as essentially evil and wicked. Many religions involve the idea of sacrifice, and the practice of sacrifice has assumed the form of human sacrifice or animal sacrifice as appears in the Old Testament, and in many other sacred writings and traditions. So also religions have differed in their treatment of polygamy. Polygamy was not reproved in the Old Testament; it has been part of the Mormon religion; it is still an element in the religion of millions of Mohammedans, Hindus, and other races in Asia. The criminal religions in India are well known. The Thugs of India regarded it as a religious duty to rob and to kill. The practice of suttee, involving the immolation of the widow upon the funeral pyre of her husband, was for centuries a part of the Hindu religion.

These examples are sufficient to show that religious belief and practice cannot be absolutely separated either from politics or from [126] ethics. An inconsistency between religious and political duty has often appeared in history. The early Christians refused to take part in the worship of the Emperor as divine, just as Christian converts in Korea refuse to take part in Shinto ceremonial. In each case the State view is that the ceremony which has been made obligatory is merely political in character – a form of "saluting the flag" – but the other view of the question is that it is something which requires a true believer to abjure part of his cherished faith.

Section 116, however, is based upon the principle that religion should, for political purposes, be regarded as irrelevant. It assumes that citizens of all religions can be good citizens, and that accordingly there is no justification in the interests of the community for prohibiting the free exercise of any religion.

7. The examples which have been given illustrate the difficulty of the problem with which a court is confronted when it is asked to determine whether or not a particular law infringes the constitutional provision by prohibiting "the free exercise of … religion." Can any person, by describing (and honestly describing) his beliefs as practices as religious exempt himself from obedience to the law? Does s 116 protect any religious belief or religious practice, irrespective of the political or social effect of that belief or practice?

It has already been shown that beliefs entertained by a religious body as religious beliefs may be inconsistent with the maintenance of civil government. The complete protection of all religious beliefs might result in the disappearance of organized society, because some religious beliefs, as already indicated, regard the existence of organized society as essentially evil …

The word "free" is used in many senses, and the meaning of the word varies almost indefinitely with the context. A man may be said to be free when he is not a slave, but he is also said to be free when he is not imprisoned, and is not subject to any other form of physical restraint. In another sense a man is only truly free when he has the freedom of thought and expression, as well as of physical movement. But in all these cases an obligation to obey laws which apply **[127]** generally to the community is not regarded as inconsistent with freedom ...

[130] [I]n 1900 it had been thoroughly established in the United States that the provision **[131]** preventing the making of any law prohibiting the free exercise of religion was not understood to mean that the criminal law dealing with the conduct of citizens generally was to be subject to exceptions in favour of persons who believed and practised a religion which was inconsistent with the provisions of the law. The result of this approach to the problem has been the development of the principle which has been applied in the later cases ... according to which it is left to the court to determine whether the freedom of religion has been *unduly* infringed by some legislative provision. This view makes it possible to accord a real measure of practical protection to religion without involving the community in anarchy.

10. There is, therefore, full legal justification for adopting in Australia an interpretation of s 116 which had, before the enactment of the Commonwealth Constitution, already been given to similar words in the United States. This interpretation leaves it to the court to determine whether a particular law is an undue infringement of religious freedom.

A similarly broad view of "religion" was taken by the High Court in *Church of The New Faith v Commissioner of Pay-Roll Tax (Vic)* (1983) 154 CLR 120, which concerned a provision that religious institutions were exempt from pay-roll tax. Under the First Amendment to the United States Constitution, it had been decided that support for religious institutions through tax exemptions was *not* unconstitutional as an "establishment of religion" (*Walz v Tax Commission of the City of New York*, 397 US 664 (1970)). In Australia, under s 116, the constitutional issue was not even raised. Instead, the issue was whether the Church of The New Faith, which promoted "Scientology", could claim to be a "religious institution" entitled to the exemption. The Court held that it could, and in doing so spelt out criteria that might be used to determine what is "religion" for the purposes of s 116.

Church of The New Faith v Commissioner of Pay-Roll Tax (Vic)
(1983) 154 CLR 120

Mason ACJ and Brennan J: [135] [T]he area of legal immunity marked out by the concept of religion cannot extend to all conduct in which a person may engage in giving effect to his faith in the supernatural. The freedom to act **[136]** in accordance with one's religious beliefs is not as inviolate as the freedom to believe, for general laws to preserve and protect society are not defeated by a plea of religious obligation to breach them ... Religious conviction is not a solvent of legal obligation. Thus, in *Jehovah's Witnesses Inc* [(1943) 67 CLR 116] a prohibition against subversion of the war effort was not circumvented by the pacifist ideals of the Jehovah's Witnesses ... , even though s 116 protects both freedom of religious opinion and the free exercise of religion. In the United States, where similar constitutional guarantees are to be found in the First Amendment, the free exercise clause was held not to exempt the Mormons from the law forbidding polygamy ... In *Reynolds v United States* [98 US 145 at 167 (1979)], the Supreme Court held that to excuse polygamy on religious grounds would "make the professed doctrines of religious belief superior to the law of the land, and in effect ... permit every citizen to become a law unto himself. Government could exist only in name under such circumstances." Conduct in which a person engages in giving effect to his faith in the supernatural is religious, but it is excluded from the area of legal immunity marked out by the concept of religion if it offends against the ordinary laws, ie if it offends against laws which do not discriminate against religion generally or against particular religions or against conduct of a kind which is characteristic only of a religion.

We would therefore hold that, for the purposes of the law, the criteria of religion are twofold: first, belief in a supernatural Being, Thing or Principle; and second, the acceptance of canons of conduct in order to give effect to that belief, though canons of conduct which offend against the ordinary laws are outside the area of any immunity, privilege or right conferred on the grounds of religion. Those criteria may vary in their comparative importance, and there may be a different intensity of belief or of acceptance of canons of conduct among religions or among the adherents to a religion. The tenets of a religion may give primacy to one particular belief or to one particular canon of conduct. Variations in emphasis may distinguish one religion from other religions, but they are irrelevant to the determination of an individual's or a group's freedom to profess and exercise the religion of his, or their, choice.

Wilson and Deane JJ: [173] In *Adelaide Company of Jehovah's Witnesses Inc v Commonwealth* [67 CLR at 124] Latham CJ referred to the difficulty, if not the impossibility, of framing an acceptable definition of religion for the purposes of s 116 of the Constitution and commented that it "is not for a court, upon some a priori basis, to disqualify certain beliefs as incapable of being religious in character". Notwithstanding that there may be grounds for attributing a wider meaning to the word "religion" in the context of a constitutional guarantee against the establishment of a religion than in the context of a statutory exemption from a pay-roll tax, we are of the view that the above comment of Latham CJ, with which we respectfully agree, is in point in answering the question whether Scientology is a religion for the purposes of the present case. There is no single characteristic which can be laid down as constituting a formularized legal criterion, whether of inclusion or exclusion, of whether a particular system of ideas and practices constitutes a religion within a particular State of the Commonwealth. The most that can be done is to formulate the more important of the indicia or guidelines by reference to which that question falls to be answered. Those indicia must, in the view we take, be derived by empirical observation of accepted religions. They are liable to vary with changing social conditions and the relative importance of any particular one of them will vary from case to case. We briefly outline hereunder what we consider to be the more important of them. In so doing, we are conscious of the fact that we are, of necessity, venturing into a field which is more the domain of the student of comparative religion than that of the lawyer.

[174] One of the more important indicia of "a religion" is that the particular collection of ideas and/or practices involves belief in the supernatural, that is to say, belief that reality extends beyond that which is capable of perception by the senses. If that be absent, it is unlikely that one has "a religion". Another is that the ideas relate to man's nature and place in the universe and his relation to things supernatural. A third is that the ideas are accepted by adherents as requiring or encouraging them to observe particular standards or codes of conduct or to participate in specific practices having supernatural significance. A fourth is that, however loosely knit and varying in beliefs and practices adherents may be, they constitute an identifiable group or identifiable groups. A fifth, and perhaps more controversial, indicium … is that the adherents themselves see the collection of ideas and/or practices as constituting a religion.

Murphy J declined to attempt even this degree of definition. In a judgment backed by a bibliography of 133 items on social, psychological and other aspects of religion, he argued that *any* attempt "[150] to determine what religion is … poses a threat to religious freedom". He had taken a similar stand in *Attorney-General (NSW) v Grant* (1976) 135 CLR 587. In that case the formation of the Uniting Church was opposed by some Presbyterians, who saw it as involving fundamental changes in religious doctrine. They argued that their General Assembly had no power to make such changes; that the union was invalid; and that property formerly held on trust for the Presbyterian Church was still so held. Although the *Presbyterian Church of Australia Act 1971* (NSW) clearly governed the matter, Murphy J refused to consider the issues at all, since for courts to decide "[612] questions of doctrine, practice or procedure in ecclesiastical government" would "exceed the judicial sphere and interfere with religious freedom".

In *Kruger v Commonwealth (Stolen Generations Case)* (1997) 190 CLR 1, an attempt was made to invoke s 116 as protecting the tribal culture of Aboriginal families and communities in the Northern Territory. That raised the vexed preliminary issue of whether s 116 applies in the Territories. Gaudron J held that it is so applicable (though she added that "[123] s 116 is directed to laws made by the Commonwealth, not laws enacted by the legislature of a self-governing Territory"), and Toohey and Gummow JJ were strongly inclined to agree. On that basis, the plaintiffs' substantive argument was that the *Aboriginals Ordinance 1918* (NT), insofar as it had authorised the forced removal of Aboriginal children from their tribal culture, was invalid as a law "for prohibiting the free exercise of any religion".

In principle, Gaudron J accepted that argument, though noting that it depended on issues of fact which could only be determined at trial. She also rejected any notion that, while grants of power should be broadly construed, limitations on power should be strictly construed. Toohey J also evinced some degree of sympathy with the argument, but found it impossible on the basis of the limited material before the Court to conclude that the Ordinance had been made with the constitutionally forbidden purpose (that is, that it was a law "*for* prohibiting the free exercise of any religion"). Brennan CJ held flatly that "**[40]** [t]o attract invalidity under s 116, a law must have the purpose of achieving an object which s 116 forbids" and that "[n]one of the impugned laws has such a purpose". Gummow J appeared to take a very narrow view of the constitutional protection afforded to the "free exercise of ... religion", harking back to *Krygger*. In his view, the Ordinance was valid because "**[161]** [n]o conduct of a religious nature was proscribed or sought to be regulated in any way". He did, however, add that the Ordinance might be given a different construction on the basis of "extrinsic materials, the relevance and admissibility of which would be an issue at trial". Dawson J, with whom McHugh J agreed, disposed of the issue on the ground that s 116 has no application in the Territories. But he added that "**[60]** if I am wrong in that conclusion, I would agree with Gummow J, for the reasons given by him, that the 1918 Ordinance contains nothing which **[61]** would enable it to be said that it is a law for prohibiting the free exercise of any religion".

Kruger v Commonwealth (*Stolen Generations Case*)
(1997) 190 CLR 1

Gaudron J: **[124]** There are two issues involved ..., namely, whether the Ordinance was a law "prohibiting the free exercise of any religion" and, if so, whether it was a law "*for* prohibiting" it (emphasis added) ...

[130] The expression "prohibiting the free exercise of any religion" suggests that, in that respect, s 116 is concerned only with laws which, in terms, ban religious practices or otherwise forbid the free exercise of religion. Some support for that view is to be found in the statement of Griffith CJ in *Krygger v Williams* [(1912) 15 CLR 366 at 369] that "a law requiring a man to do an act which his religion forbids [might] be objectionable on **[131]** moral grounds, but it does not come within the prohibition of s 116". Moreover, as Barwick CJ pointed out in *Attorney-General (Vict); Ex rel Black v Commonwealth* [(1981) 146 CLR 559 at 580-1], s 116 is directed to "the *making* of law", not "the administration of a law".

There are two matters, one textual, the other contextual, which in my view, tell against construing s 116 as applying only to laws which, in terms, ban religious practices or otherwise prohibit the free exercise of religion. First, s 116 speaks of the exercise of religion, and it follows, as Latham CJ pointed out in *Adelaide Company of Jehovah's Witnesses Inc* [(1943) 67 CLR 116 at 124], that "it is intended to protect from the operation of any Commonwealth laws acts which are done in the exercise of religion." The contextual consideration is that, putting s 122 to one side, the Commonwealth has no power to legislate with respect to religion, and, thus, a law which, in terms, prohibits religious practice would, ordinarily, not be a law on a subject matter with respect to which the Commonwealth has any power to legislate. These considerations provide powerful support for the view that s 116 was intended to extend to laws which operate to prevent the free exercise of religion, not merely those which, in terms, ban it.

Another matter which points in favour of construing s 116 as extending to laws which prevent the free exercise of religion, not merely those which, in terms, effect a prohibition in that regard, is the need to construe constitutional guarantees liberally, even limited guarantees of the kind effected by s 116. In this respect, it is inconsistent with established principles of constitutional construction to construe constitutional guarantees as concerned with form rather than substance. So too, it is inconsistent with established principle to interpret constitutional guarantees "pedantically" [*Bank of*

NSW v Commonwealth (1948) 76 CLR 1 at 349 per Dixon J] so that they may be circumvented by legislative provisions which purport to do indirectly what cannot be done directly.

[132] The matters to which reference has been made compel the conclusion that s 116 extends to laws which prevent the free exercise of religion. And the need to construe guarantees so that they are not circumvented by allowing to be done indirectly what cannot be done directly has the consequence that s 116 extends to provisions which authorise acts which prevent the free exercise of religion, not merely provisions which operate of their own force to prevent that exercise.

Again, the question whether the Ordinance authorised acts which prevented the free exercise of religion involves factual issues which cannot presently be determined. However, if Aboriginal people had practices and beliefs which are properly characterised as a religion for the purposes of s 116, and if, as would seem likely, those practices were carried out in association with other members of the Aboriginal community to which they belonged or at sacred sites or other places on their traditional lands, removal from their communities and their traditional lands would, necessarily, have prevented the free exercise of their religion. Whether or not that was the case remains to be decided. But on the assumption that it was, the question arises whether the Ordinance was a law "for prohibiting the free exercise of any religion".

In *Adelaide Company of Jehovah's Witnesses Inc* [67 CLR at 132], Latham CJ observed in relation to s 116 that "[t]he word 'for' shows that the purpose of the legislation in question may properly be taken into account in determining whether or not it is a law of the prohibited character." In my view, that is not entirely accurate. The use of the word "for" indicates that purpose is the criterion and the sole criterion selected by s 116 for invalidity. Thus, purpose must be taken into account. Further, it is the only matter to be taken into account in determining whether a law infringes s 116.

In emphasising that purpose is the criterion selected by s 116, I do not overlook observations to the effect, for example, that s 116 is not infringed by laws which "prevent persons or bodies from disseminating subversive principles or doctrines or those prejudicial to the defence of the Commonwealth or the efficient prosecution of the war" [67 CLR at 149] or that "[i]t is consistent with the maintenance of religious liberty for the State to restrain actions and courses of conduct which are inconsistent with the maintenance of civil government or prejudicial to the continued existence of the community" [67 CLR at 131]. Those statements are undoubtedly correct. However, they do not state the criterion of invalidity selected by s 116. It is purpose, not the **[133]** continued existence of society, which that provision selects as the mechanism by which "to reconcile religious freedom with ordered government" [67 CLR at 132] ...

It is convenient now to turn to the Commonwealth's plea that the purpose of the Ordinance was "the protection and preservation of persons of the Aboriginal race" ... Clearly, a law may have more than one purpose. Similarly, a particular purpose may be subsumed in a larger or more general purpose. That latter proposition is well illustrated by the present case. It is clear from the terms of the Ordinance that one of its purposes ... was to remove Aboriginal and half-caste people to and keep them in Aboriginal reserves and institutions. That purpose is not necessarily inconsistent with the more general purpose which the Commonwealth asserts. And neither purpose is necessarily inconsistent with the purpose of removing Aboriginal children from their families and communities, thereby preventing them from participating in community practices. Indeed, in the absence of some overriding social or humanitarian need – and none is asserted – it might well be concluded that one purpose of the power conferred by ... the Ordinance was to remove Aboriginal and half-caste children from their communities and, thus, prevent their participation in community practices. And if those practices included religious practices, that purpose necessarily extended to prohibiting the free exercise of religion ...

[A] law will not be a **[134]** law for "prohibiting the free exercise of any religion", notwithstanding that, in terms, it does just that or that it operates directly with that consequence, if it is necessary to attain some overriding public purpose or to satisfy some pressing social need. Nor will it have that purpose if it is a law for some specific purpose unconnected with the free exercise of religion and only incidentally affects that freedom. It is not pleaded in the present case either that the Ordinance was necessary for the protection or preservation of Aboriginal people or that its purpose was a purpose unconnected with the free exercise of religion. The plea is, thus, no answer to the plaintiffs' claim that the Ordinance was invalid by reason that it infringed s 116.

Were the Commonwealth to further amend its Defence to assert that the purpose of protecting and preserving Aboriginal people was unconnected with the purpose of prohibiting the free exercise of religion, a question might arise, if the plea were to be made good, whether the inter-ference with religious freedom, if any, effected by the Ordinance was appropriate and adapted or, which is the same thing, proportionate to the protection and preservation of those people. And as the purpose of a law is to be determined by reference to "the facts with which it deals", that question would necessarily have to be answered by reference to the conditions of the time in which it operated. However, the answer to the question depends on an analysis of the law's operation, not on subjective views and perceptions.

Toohey J: [86] The real problem for the plaintiffs in this aspect of their claim lies in demonstrating that the Ordinance is a law "for prohibiting the free exercise of any religion". Section 116 "is directed to the *making* of law. It is not dealing with the administration of a law" [146 CLR at 580-1]. The use of the word "for" indicates that "the purpose of the legislation in question may properly be taken into account in determining whether or not it is a law of the prohibited character" [67 CLR at 132]. "Purpose" in this context "refers to an end or object which legislation may serve ... it is the Court which must decide whether the measure possesses the requisite character" [*Australian Communist Party v Commonwealth* (1951) 83 CLR 1 at 273]. It does not follow that there is only one purpose to be discerned in a law; there may be more than one. The question should therefore be asked: was a purpose of the Ordinance to prohibit the free exercise of the religion of the Aboriginals, to whom the Ordinance was directed? It may well be that an effect of the Ordinance was to impair, even prohibit the spiritual beliefs and practices of the Aboriginal people in the Northern Territory, though this is something that could only be demonstrated by evidence. But I am unable to discern in the language of the Ordinance such a purpose.

Krygger, Jehovah's Witnesses and *Kruger* all concerned the "free exercise" clause of s 116. By contrast, *Attorney-General (Vic); Ex rel Black v Commonwealth* (*DOGS Case*) (1981) 146 CLR 559 focused on the "establishment" clause. The argument was that government funding of church schools amounted to an "establishment" of religion. The argument was rejected 6:1, with Murphy J dissenting.

Attorney-General (Vic); Ex rel Black v Commonwealth (*DOGS Case*)
(1981) 146 CLR 559

Wilson J: [653] I accept that the word "establishment" has no fixed connotation, but having regard to the other clauses which are contained in s 116, and to the precise manner of their expression, I infer a legislative intent to adopt a narrow notion of establishment, namely, that which requires statutory recognition of a religion as a national institution. The precise status, responsibility and privileges that attend such establishment may vary a good deal, and it is not necessary to consider its features in detail; the point to be made is that establishment involves the deliberate selection of one to be preferred from among others, resulting in a reciprocal relationship between church and state which confers and imposes rights and duties upon both parties. The nature of the responsibility of the state towards an established church is clearly exposed in the judgments of their Lordships in the House of Lords' decision in *General Assembly of Free Church of Scotland v Lord Overtoun* [[1904] AC 515] where the basic principle of "establishment" is asserted as "the right and duty of the civil magistrate to maintain and support an establishment of religion in accordance with God's Word" [[1904] AC at 646, 656, 677]. It identifies a relationship which goes much deeper than financial assistance, whether casual or regular, from time to time, because it is expressive of a duty to maintain and support, or, in other words, a duty to "promote religion" as embodied in the doctrine and standards of the Church [[1904] AC at 694]. Conversely, correlative to the right in the church to the protection and patronage of the state, the church is under a duty to pray for the civil magistrate and faithfully to conform to the church's doctrine and standards.

If it seems remote from reality to be speaking in terms such as these about a constitutional provision, it must be remembered **[654]** that the eighty years that have elapsed since federation have witnessed a marked change in the status and role of the church in the Australian community with a corresponding diminution of the sense of authority that formerly attached to the ecclesiastical realm.

Furthermore, it may be thought to be surprising that a prohibition of the kind that I have described was included in the absence of any express legislative power whereby the Parliament could ever have pursued such an objective. It may be that the explanation for any such incongruity is to be found in the chequered history of the clause in the constitutional conventions in the eighteen-nineties, and in an anxiety lest an inference of power was to be drawn from the acknowledgment of Almighty God in the preamble to the Commonwealth of Australia Constitution Act. While on present authority it is not permissible to seek the meaning of s 116 in the convention debates, I may say that I find it interesting that in the course of the conventions the religion clause began as a denial of power to the States, then was re-addressed to both the States and the Commonwealth, and finally took its present form. The separationist view of establishment, for which the plaintiffs contend, does not sit well with the form of s 116, addressed as it is only to the Commonwealth Parliament. The objective sought to be achieved by a clause construed consistently with the plaintiffs' contention could so easily be subverted by any of the State legislatures, which remain[ed] free to give such aid or support to religious bodies as they wished. But no State legislature could establish a national religion, and hence the prohibition was rightly directed to the Commonwealth.

Mason J took an even narrower view.

Mason J: [612] Why it was considered necessary to include in the Constitution s 116 or its first clause is not altogether clear. Mr HB Higgins thought that the reference to Almighty God in the preamble might have yielded by implication a power in the Commonwealth Parliament to legislate upon the topics mentioned in the section. Quick and Garran considered that it may have been inserted to forestall any possibility of amending the Constitution by providing for any of the matters prohibited. To others it may have seemed that there was a need to place some restraint upon the exercise of the legislative power with respect to marriage conferred by s 51(xxi). Reflection upon the question is speculative and it does not assist in the resolution of the problems which now arise.

I agree with Wilson J that the first clause in the section forbids the establishment or recognition of a religion (and by this term I would include a branch of a religion or church) as a national institution. Quick and Garran in *Annotated Constitution of the Australian Commonwealth* say of s 116 (p 951): "by the establishment of religion is meant the erection and recognition of a State Church, or the concession of special favours, titles, and advantages to one church which are denied to others." With one qualification, I agree with this statement. The qualification is that to constitute "establishment" of a "religion" the concession to one church of favours, titles and advantages must be of so special a kind that it enables us to say that by virtue of the concession the religion has become established as a national institution, as, for example, by becoming the official religion of the State.

Gibbs J also confined the "establishment" clause to requiring that the Commonwealth "**[604]** not make any law for conferring on a particular religion or religious body the position of a state (or national) religion or church". Similarly, Barwick CJ argued that "**[582]** establishing a religion involves the entrenchment of a religion as a feature of and identified with the body politic … It involves the identification of the religion with the civil authority so as to involve the citizen in a duty to maintain it and the obligation of [government]… to patronize, protect and promote the established religion … Establishing a religion involves its adoption as an institution of the Commonwealth, part of the Commonwealth 'establishment' ". Among the majority, only Stephen J took a more flexible view, extending s 116 not only to the establishment of a national church but at least to "**[610]** the favouring of one church over another".

The dissent of Murphy J relied on decisions of the United States Supreme Court on the "establishment" clause in the First Amendment to the United States Constitution. All of the majority judges denied that those decisions were relevant, in part because of the difference in wording between the American and Australian provisions: "Congress shall make no law *respecting* an establishment of religion" as against "The Commonwealth shall not make any law *for* establishing any religion".

> **Barwick CJ: [579]** The divergence in language to which I have earlier referred is apparent from the use of the word "respecting" in the American text and the word "for" in s 116. What the former may fairly embrace, quite clearly the latter cannot: and that is so, in my opinion, even without placing critical significance on the purposive nature of the Australian expression and the lack of such an element in the American text.
>
> However, in the interpretation and application of s 116, the establishment of religion must be found to be the object of the making of the law. Further, because the whole expression is "*for* establishing any religion", the law … must have that objective as its express and, as I think, single purpose. Indeed, a law establishing a religion could scarcely do so as an incident of some other and principal objective. In my opinion, a law which establishes a religion will inevitably do so expressly and directly and not, as it were, constructively.

Murphy J described the arguments for departing from the United States decisions on the "establishment" clause as "**[632]** based on the trifles of differences in wording between the United States and the Australian establishment clauses"; as "hair-splitting, and not consistent with the broad approach which should be taken to constitutional guarantees of freedom". Mason J linked this issue explicitly with the suggestion that grants of power should be broadly construed and limitations on power strictly construed.

> **Mason J: [614]** Although in some circumstances it is permissible to construe a grant of legislative power so as to apply it to things and events coming into existence and unforeseen at the time of the making of the Constitution, so that the operation of the relevant grant of power in the Constitution enlarges or expands, a constitutional **[615]** prohibition must be applied in accordance with the meaning which it had in 1900. As a prohibition is a restriction on the exercise of power there is no reason for enlarging its scope of operation beyond the mischief to which it was directed ascertained in accordance with the meaning of the prohibition at the time when the Constitution was enacted. Consequently, the content of the prohibition against establishment of religion should not be expanded by reference to a more extensive interpretation given to similar words in the First Amendment by judicial decisions pronounced since 1900, assuming, without deciding, that those decisions have such an effect.

On this basis, Mason J rejected the plaintiffs' attempt to read "establishing" in s 116 more widely than "establishment" in the First Amendment. He added:

> **Mason J: [615]** There is a second distinction between the language of s 116 and the First Amendment. We speak of any "law *for* establishing" any religion. The Americans speak of a law "*respecting* an establishment" of religion. In *Lamshed v Lake* [(1958) 99 CLR 132 at 141], Dixon CJ, when referring to s 122, equated "for" with "with respect to" in its application to the government of the Territory. Here, however, we are dealing, not with a grant of legislative power, but with a prohibition against the exercise of legislative power. In such a context "for" is more limiting than "respecting"; "for" connotes a connexion by way of purpose or result with the subject matter which is not satisfied **[616]** by the mere circumstance that the law is one which touches or relates to the subject matter. In this respect the first prohibition in s 116 is narrower than its American counterpart.

Wilson J distinguished s 116 from the First Amendment on a similar basis. Barwick CJ also narrowly construed the reference to "any law for establishing any religion", but rejected the idea that, in general, restrictions on power should be strictly interpreted.

> **Barwick CJ: [577]** It was submitted for the Commonwealth that s 116, not being a provision granting legislative power but, on the contrary, a provision denying it, ought not to be read as largely as a facultative provision should be read. This submission was based on the view expressed by Sir Owen Dixon in *Wragg v New South Wales* [(1953) 88 CLR 353]. With the greatest respect to an opinion of Sir Owen, I am unable to accept this submission. I can find no reason why the words of the Constitution should not be given their full effect, whether they be expressed in a

facultative or prohibitory provision. In particular, in this case, the emphatic universality of the language of s 116 seems to me to brook no restraint sought to be imposed by any such doctrine as the submission propounds. The control of the legislature by the Constitution is of the essence of its text.

A 1988 referendum proposal sought to amend s 116 to confer protection against State and Territory legislation. It was also proposed to eliminate the word "for" so that the section would provide in part: "The Commonwealth, a State or a Territory shall not establish any religion". This was attacked on the ground that it would undermine the reasoning in the *DOGS Case* and thereby reopen the issue of government funding of religious schools. The referendum failed in all States.

5. Rights of Out-of-State Residents

Until 1989, another example of an express guarantee rendered "illusory" by judicial interpretation was that contained in s 117 of the Constitution. Its judicial history needs to be read against that of the related provisions in ss 51(ii) and 99, which concern, respectively, discrimination and preference between the States; but there is an important difference. The latter provisions explicitly limit legislative power, while the focus of s 117 is on the individual whom the section protects.

Despite its convoluted syntax, and its focus on "subjects of the Queen", the purpose of s 117 is clear: it is designed to prevent a State from imposing any "disability or discrimination" on residents of another State by reason of their interstate residence. Thus, State A cannot impose any disability on residents of State B that is not equally applicable to residents of State A.

The Court's initial approach to s 117 in *Davies and Jones v Western Australia* (1904) 2 CLR 29 was extremely restrictive. Alfred Davies was resident in Queensland, while his father had been resident in Western Australia. When his father died, the will was proved in Western Australia. Estate duty was assessed at 9 per cent of the beneficial interests passing to the son. Had the son lived in Western Australia, the duty would have been assessed at half that rate because s 86 of the *Administration Act 1903* (WA) provided that "in so far as beneficial interests pass to persons *bonâ fide* residents of and domiciled in Western Australia ... duty shall be calculated so as to charge only one half of the percentage on the property acquired by such person". The criterion of operation of s 86 was thus residence *and domicile*. The challenge based on s 117 failed because the Court held that s 117 applies only when the criterion is residence alone.

The section was invoked again in *Henry v Boehm* (1973) 128 CLR 482, which involved a challenge to the residence requirements of the *Rules of Court Regulating the Admission of Practitioners* (SA). Rule 27(1) required a person previously admitted in another State to "reside for at least three calendar months" in South Australia before filing for admission. Under r 28, the person would then be admitted conditionally for one year, and could only be granted absolute admission by showing at the end of that time that, throughout the period of conditional admission, he or she had "continuously resided in the State". An attack on these requirements by a Victorian solicitor seeking admission in South Australia was rejected by Barwick CJ, McTiernan, Menzies and Gibbs JJ, with Stephen J dissenting.

Henry v Boehm
(1973) 128 CLR 482

Menzies J: [490] Section 117 of the Australian Constitution denies that a subject of the Queen resident in one Australian State can be subjected to any disability or discrimination in another State because he does not reside there. The section does not give a person an advantage in a State because he resides in another State; it merely prevents such a person from being put at a disadvantage by reason of his non-residence. For instance, he cannot be taxed at a higher rate than would be applicable to him were he a resident. He cannot be by law excluded from attendance at a State university because he is not a resident of the State. The section would not, however, invalidate, in relation to a person resident in another State, every State law requiring residence at a particular place for certain purposes. Thus a non-resident could not complain of a State law requiring the holder of a victualler's licence to reside at his licensed premises. If a person resident in another State were to accept a licence on such terms he would run the risk of losing his licence by non-compliance with its terms. Such a law would operate exactly in the same way upon any **[491]** licensed victualler in the State in which his hotel is situated regardless of where he resided before becoming a licensed victualler. It is the operation of the law to which attention must be paid, not to the remoter consequence of complying with the law that operates uniformly regardless of the State in which a person happens to be resident at a particular time …

Accordingly, a State law requiring the presence in a State of some person seeking an advantage in that State is not inevitably in conflict with s 117 …

It seems to me that the plaintiff would be subject to exactly the same restrictions of which he now complains were he a resident **[492]** of South Australia but not domiciled there. He would still have to reside in South Australia continuously for the three months prior to his application and he would not be absolutely admitted except upon the fulfilment of the conditions already stated …

The critical questions are then whether the requirements of continuous residence in South Australia are different when applied to him as a resident of Victoria than they would be if applied to him as a resident of South Australia and whether such difference as there is amounts to discrimination. As has already been stated, the requirement is, in each case, for continuous residence in South Australia for the periods mentioned: resident or non-resident he must stay in South Australia.

It is true that the restrictions do put those seeking admission as barristers of the Supreme Court of South Australia, by virtue of admission elsewhere wherever they reside, under disabilities not shared by those who qualify for admission on other grounds, but the restrictions operate uniformly upon those subject to them wherever their residence.

The contention to which counsel for the plaintiff returned again and again in the course of argument is that the rules would require the plaintiff, a resident of Victoria, to go to South Australia and reside there, whereas they would operate differently if he were already a resident of South Australia. It is not, however, any part of the operation of the rules that a person seeking admission must give up his residence in another State and go to South Australia, notwithstanding that, in certain circumstances, a remote consequence of the rules would mean a change of residence. A resident of Victoria might, for instance, have lived in South Australia for a month before he decided to make an application for admission there. In such a case, although still a resident of Victoria, the applicant would be in exactly the same position as if he were a resident of South Australia.

Stephen J: [501] The practical effect of these requirements of residence in South Australia will no doubt be, in all but very exceptional cases, to compel an inter-State practitioner to give up his practice in that other State if he is to be admitted to practice in South Australia.

How then does s 117 bear upon the requirements of these rules; do they subject the plaintiff to any disability or discrimination which would not be equally applicable to him if he were resident in South Australia? To answer this question the process of comparison which the section calls for must be undertaken, the plaintiff's actual situation must be contrasted with a hypothetical one which differs from actuality only because it assumes the plaintiff to be a resident of South Australia; in making the comparison called for by s 117 no departure from actuality is to be made other than this one, relating to the plaintiff's residence. Being thus resident in South Australia but having previously been admitted to practice in Victoria, his position when wishing to use **[502]** that qualification in order to gain admission to practice in South Australia is to be contrasted with his position as it is in fact.

The obvious difference between that hypothetical situation and the situation with which the plaintiff is in fact confronted is that were he already resident in South Australia he would not have to abandon his existing Victorian abode so as to reside continuously in South Australia, first for three months and then for a further twelve months. This difference arises because of the express requirements of the rules. If this may be said to be a "disability or discrimination" to which the plaintiff is subject by reason of his being "resident" in Victoria, using these words in the sense which they bear in s 117, then that section will apply.

It is, I think, no objection to the application of s 117 that residents of South Australia seeking to be admitted to practice there in reliance upon the same inter-State qualifications as the plaintiff will be equally subject to the operation of rr 27 and 28; nor that some such South Australian permanent residents might, when they wish to seek admission, happen to be absent from that State so that they, like the plaintiff, will have to journey to South Australia and may have to then live there for lengthy periods … If the comparison called for by the section is faithfully adhered to the possible situations of other persons [are] seen to be wholly irrelevant, the comparison to be made will ignore all actual residents (in whatever sense that term be used) of South Australia. This is because s 117 does not concern itself with the making of any comparison between the situation of the plaintiff were he a resident of South Australia and the situation of other residents of that State. What s 117 calls for is, instead, a comparison between the plaintiff's situation as it is in fact and as it would be were he a resident of South Australia.

In *Street v Queensland Bar Association* (1989) 168 CLR 461, *Henry v Boehm* was unanimously overruled and the dissenting judgment of Stephen J adopted. Rule 15(4) of the *Rules of the Supreme Court* (Qld) provided for the admission in Queensland of barristers from other Australian States. However, by r 38(d), any such applicant had to make an affidavit as set out in Form 10, stating in para (6): "That I ceased to practise as a barrister in *(here set forth the dates when the applicant ceased to practise in the various courts to which he has been admitted, and the nature of his employment hereafter.)*" In para (7), the applicant was to state the day on which he or she "arrived" in Queensland. On 2 July 1987, the Queensland admission rules were amended. Paragraphs (6) and (7) of Form 10 were deleted and a new para (6) required an applicant to state that: "It is my intention to practise principally in the State of Queensland commencing on *(here set forth any relevant date)*". A new r 15B also imposed a one-year period of conditional admission upon out-of-State applicants, during which the applicant had to show that "he has practised principally in Queensland".

Alexander Whistler Street was a New South Wales barrister who sought also to practise in Queensland. He argued that the practical effect of these requirements was to limit admissibility to residents of Queensland and that this infringed s 117. His claim was upheld, with the High Court deciding that s 117 requires an assessment of the actual effect of the impugned rule on the out-of-State resident: if his or her personal situation is in fact more onerous than it would be if he resided within the State, s 117 applies.

Street v Queensland Bar Association
(1989) 168 CLR 461

Mason CJ: [485] The very object of federation was to bring into existence one nation and one people. This section is one of the comparatively few provisions in the Constitution which was designed to enhance national unity and a real sense of national identity by eliminating disability or discrimination on account of residence in another State. In this respect the section should be seen as a counterpart to other provisions in the Constitution which prohibit discrimination between the States in matters of taxation, trade and finance (ss 51(ii), 92 and 99). In *James v Commonwealth* [[1936] AC 578 at 614] Lord Wright regarded the section as analogous to s 92 and referred to it as providing a constitutional guarantee of equal rights of all residents in all States. And, although the language of s 117 differs from that of Art IV, s 2 of the United States Constitution, there can be no doubt that the American model had an influential impact on the framers of our Constitution, at least to the extent of illustrating the need for a provision which, by guaranteeing to out-of-State residents who were British subjects an individual right to non-discriminatory treatment, would bring into existence a national unity and a national sense of identity transcending colonial and State loyalties …

Section 117 is contained in Ch V of the Constitution, which is entitled "The States". Chapter V contains a miscellany of provisions, all of which, except s 116, relate to the States. Some of these sections (ss 114, 115, 116) expressly prohibit the States or the Commonwealth from doing certain things. Others (ss 119, 120) impose duties upon the States. Section 117 is strikingly different. It

[486] is not expressed in terms similar to those of the surrounding sections. Notably, it relates not to a State or the Commonwealth, but to a "subject of the Queen". Its form and language indicate that s 117 is directed towards individuals and their protection from disability or discrimination of the kind contemplated by the section, and that it is not, except to that extent, a restriction on State or Commonwealth legislative power. So a person not subjected to any relevant disability or discrimination by a particular law could not have that law held invalid by establishing that it subjects a third person to such a disability or discrimination; that circumstance would not lead to a striking down of the offending law. Conversely, a person who would, but for s 117, be so affected by the law is immune from its operation in so far as it subjects him to impermissible disability or discrimination, though the law itself remains valid in its application to persons who would not be so affected. Perhaps an enactment might be rendered wholly invalid by s 117 if it depended for its operation upon the imposition of a prohibited form of disability or discrimination, but that is not a question which I need to examine. Its only significance in the present case is that it may serve to explain references to the validity of the State legislation in *Davies and Jones*. These remarks are explicable on the basis that, had the Court equated domicile with residence or otherwise regarded domicile as within the province of s 117, the result would possibly have been to deny the validity of the offending enactment because it enacted a prohibited form of discrimination.

The preponderant weight of opinion denies the individual focus which Stephen J gives to s 117. With the exception of his Honour's dissenting judgment in *Henry v Boehm*, all the judgments in *Davies and Jones* and *Henry v Boehm* insist on comparing the way in which the non-resident of the legislating State is affected by the law of that State with the way in which residents of that State are affected ... This approach denies the individual focus of the section by addressing itself to the general range of circumstances in which the State law applies.

However, as Stephen J points out, the terms of the section invite a comparison of the actual situation of the out-of-State resident with what it would be if he were a resident of the legislating State. The [487] section does not invite a comparison between his actual situation and that of other residents of the legislating State. Such a comparison poses the question whether or not the law necessarily applies differently to residents of the legislating State. The answer to that question will almost invariably be in the negative due to the range of persons in differing situations within the legislating State and the fact that some of those persons will probably be affected by the law in the same manner as the out-of-State resident. Thus, the mode of comparison adopted in the decided cases, though not suggested by the terms of the section, has confined the operation of the constitutional guarantee. When that mode of comparison is combined with the assimilation of "resident" to "permanent resident", the effect has been to deprive the section of any significant utility.

Another difficulty with the existing interpretation of s 117 is that it appears to proceed according to a narrow view of what amounts to a disability or discrimination. The statement of Griffith CJ in *Davies and Jones* [2 CLR at 39] ... suggests that, in order to bring the section into operation, the State law must make the fact of being a resident in another State the criterion of the disability or discrimination. Again, this seems to be an unduly limiting notion. In terms, the section applies when a subject of the Queen, being an out-of-State resident, is subject to a disability or discrimination under State law. The section is not concerned with the form in which that law subjects the individual to the disability or discrimination. It is enough that the individual is subject to either of the two detriments, whatever the means by which this is brought about by State law. This approach to the interpretation of the section accords with the approach generally adopted in connexion with statutes proscribing particular kinds of discrimination. They are either expressed or construed as proscribing an act or a law the effect of which is relevantly discriminatory ... It would be surprising if it were otherwise, especially since such statutes are generally intended to provide relief from discrimination rather than to punish the discriminator ... It would make little sense to deal with laws [488] which have a discriminatory purpose and leave untouched laws which have a discriminatory effect.

Once this is recognized, it becomes all the more difficult to accept that the fact that a requirement as to residence is universal in its application is necessarily an answer to the operation of s 117. Such a requirement may have a discriminatory effect in relation to an out-of-State resident for the simple reason that it may apply unequally by subjecting him to a greater burden or disadvantage than that imposed on a resident of the legislating State. So to forbid all persons from wearing a turban is on its face a prohibition applicable to all persons without distinction, but in effect is a discrimination based upon religious grounds because its only impact will fall upon adherents of a creed or religion which requires the wearing of turbans: *Mandla v Dowell Lee* [[1983] 2 AC 548]; *Bhinder v Canadian National Railway Co* [[1985] 2 SCR 561; (1985) 23 DLR (4th) 481]. An examination of the effect of the relevant law is both necessary to avoid depriving s 117 of practical effect and consistent with its emphasis upon the position of the individual.

It seems to me that for s 117 to apply it must appear that, were the person a resident of the legislating State, that different circumstance would of itself either effectively remove the disability or discrimination or, for practical purposes in all the circumstances, mitigate its effect to the point where it would be rendered illusory …

[489] Needless to say I am reluctant to depart from an earlier decision of this Court. However, two of the factors relied upon by the Court in *John v Commissioner of Taxation* [(1989) 166 CLR 417 at 438-40], for overruling the earlier decision in *Curran v Federal Commissioner of Taxation* [(1974) 131 CLR 409] are present in this case. The earlier decisions do not rest upon a principle gradually worked out in a significant succession of cases. And the decisions have not been independently acted upon in a manner or to an extent that works against reconsideration of them. Furthermore, there is in the present case an additional factor. The question at issue relates to an important provision in the Constitution dealing with individual rights central to federation. The earlier decisions placed an incorrect interpretation upon it. The Court has a responsibility to set the matter right.

Mason CJ argued that s 117 is not primarily, and perhaps not at all, a constraint on legislative power. He accepted the view of Stephen J in *Henry v Boehm* that, in applying s 117, the focus must be on the out-of-State resident. On this basis, Mason CJ held that, where s 117 applies, its effect is to confer *on an individual* an immunity against "**[486]** impermissible disability or discrimination", thereby leaving the law valid but its operation *in the individual case* averted by a personal cloak of immunity. Brennan J took a similar view. Street had relied on s 92 as well as on s 117, but most judges preferred to dispose of the case on the basis of s 117, and for Brennan J this flowed from the difference he perceived in the operation of the two sections.

Brennan J: [502] The argument founded on s 92, if successful, would lead to a different conclusion from that to which the argument founded on s 117, if successful, would lead. The s 92 argument, if successful, would lead to the conclusion that particular provisions of the 1975 rules are invalid because their purpose or their substantial effect is such that they are to be characterized as discriminatory against interstate trade or commerce in a protectionist sense … Section 92 restricts legislative power, so that a purported law which offends s 92 is to that extent made without power. Therefore, a law which is invalidated by s 92 binds nobody: any person is free to ignore the invalid law, whether or not that person is engaged in interstate trade or commerce. Conversely, s 92 gives no relief to a person who is engaged in interstate trade or commerce and whose trade or commerce is adversely affected by a law unless the purpose or substantial effect of the law is such that it is to be characterized as discriminatory against interstate trade or commerce in a protectionist sense. By contrast, s 117 does not restrict legislative or other power; it does not operate by invalidating the law or the governmental act by or under which the disability or discrimination **[503]** is imposed. It confers an immunity on individuals or, if we choose to employ the rhetoric of rights, confers a constitutional right not to be subjected to a certain disability or discrimination. The object of s 92 is to secure the freedom of markets; the object of s 117 is to secure equal treatment for the individuals whom it protects.

The idea that the operation of s 117 results only in "**[503]** individual protection rather than general invalidity of a law" was spelt out only by Mason CJ and Brennan J; but the final order of the Court was couched in those terms. What Street had asked for was an order that the relevant provisions of the Queensland Supreme Court Rules were invalid. What he got was an order that they "**[592]** are inapplicable to the plaintiff to the extent that they would require him, on any fresh application for admission, to have an intention of practising principally in Queensland or so to practise during the period between conditional and absolute admission".

Does s 117 mean that free hospital services in Queensland must be extended to out-of-State residents, or that all Australians are entitled to vote in a Queensland State election? Or (as Menzies J suggested in *Henry v Boehm*) that all Australian universities must be open to students from every State? So long as the operation of s 117 was confined by the older decisions, these questions had no practical relevance. But, when the section was given new scope and force by the *Street* case, all judges agreed that there must be some exceptions or limitations to its operation. The most obvious example related to elections for each State Parliament and for each State's representation in the federal Senate: clearly residents from other States could not demand to participate in those processes. But as to the rationale for such exceptions, and how wide the range of exceptions might be, the suggestions in *Street* varied widely. The narrowest concession was that of Brennan J.

Brennan J: [512] The s 117 guarantee of equality of treatment is not expressed to be subject to any qualification or exception. Nor is there any firm constitutional foothold for an implication that s 117 should be read down to permit discrimination in favour of in-State residents in order to foster local sentiment or to advance local interests. Yet it is clear that there must be some exception to a general application of its terms. Section 117 is drawn on the assumption that out-of-State residence can never be a ground for denying to a protected person any right to which that person would be entitled if she or he were resident in the relevant State. Yet s 7 of the Constitution demonstrates that the assumption is ill-founded: a subject of the Queen, resident in one State, must be denied a vote for the senators for another State voting as one electorate. In my opinion, the guarantee of equality of treatment is qualified only by necessary implication from the Constitution itself. No such necessity can be found in the constitutional conferring of powers on the institutions of government or in the constitutional recognition of the powers of government. Although governments (in each of their branches) may exercise their powers as they see fit within the limits of the law, the very purpose of s 117 is to ensure – and in terms it ensures – that the exercise of power by the institutions of government is ineffective when it reaches the borders of the Alsatia created by s 117. The necessity to treat a protected person differently on the **[513]** ground of out-of-State residence must therefore be found not in the powers vested in the institutions of government but in the existence of those institutions and in the protection of their functions. The necessity to preserve the institutions of government and their ability to function is an unspoken premise of all constitutional interpretation (see *Commonwealth v Tasmania; Tasmanian Dam Case* [(1983) 158 CLR 1 at 214]) for it is the necessity to preserve the Constitution itself. But that necessity does not require or authorize a qualification of the constitutional text in order to maintain what might be thought to be a convenient fund of power or a desirable distribution of power. Nothing less than the need to preserve the institutions of government and their ability to function can justify the erection by a government of a barrier to the legal and social unity of the Australian people.

The necessity to preserve the institutions of government or their ability to function demands that electoral laws providing for a franchise based on residence in a State be given full effect. It may require giving full effect to laws which impose a requirement of in-State residence in order to ensure the attendance of members of the three branches of government at their respective places of duty or to ensure their familiarity with conditions within the State in which those duties are performed. It may justify other laws in the same way. Future cases will tell … However, even if discrimination based on local residence within a State were to attract the application of s 117 in the generality of cases, it could not do so in the case of an electoral law creating a parliamentary franchise based on local residence. In such a case, the necessity of preserving the means of electing the members of the Parliament would necessitate the exclusion of non-local residents from the poll and the case would fall outside the purview of s 117.

The exception of necessity is narrowly confined: indeed, it may not amount to discrimination at all. When it is necessary to treat a protected person differently on the ground of out-of-State residence (as in the case of voting in an election of senators for another State), **[514]** that ground reflects the fact that the protected person is in a position which is relevantly and necessarily different from the position she or he would be in if she or he were an in-State resident. It is precisely because she or he is not an in-State resident that the Constitution requires her or him to be differently treated. Such different treatment is not truly discriminatory. However, as s 117 comprehends disabilities as well as discriminations, an exception of necessity must be recognized ...

[521] The law, which today pushes open the doors of the Supreme Court of Queensland for entry by suitably qualified barristers admitted and practising in other States, opens too the doors of State universities, hospitals and other institutions for entry by subjects of the Queen resident in other States on the same terms as residents of the relevant State. If a State were able to grant preference to its own residents in its own institutions there could be no valid objection to Queensland's grant of preference in its Courts to its resident Bar. Section 117 precludes that preference.

In identifying exceptions to s 117, Brennan J focused on the constitutional imperatives of each State as an autonomous government, that is, on its institutions of government and their ability to function. He spoke of "**[513]** the three branches of government", evidently referring to the "separation of powers" doctrine that identifies executive, legislative and judicial institutions as the essential components of government. McHugh J also spoke of "**[584]** necessary implication from ... the Constitution". However, his focus was on the implications of the distribution of powers between Commonwealth and States, that is, on "federalism" rather than "separation of powers".

McHugh J: [583] [T]he "structural logic" of the Constitution indicates that there are some subject-matters in respect of which an interstate resident is not entitled to equality of treatment with State residents in identical circumstances. The object of s 117 was to make federation fully effective by ensuring that subjects of the Queen who were residents of Australia and in comparable circumstances received equality of treatment within the boundaries of any State. But the existence of a federal system of government, composed of a union of independent States each continuing to govern its own people, necessarily requires the conclusion that some subject-matters are the concern only of the people of each State. And since the residents of a State and its **[584]** people are basically interchangeable concepts, it follows that laws dealing with these particular subject-matters may exclude interstate residents from participation either generally or subject to conditions. The exclusion of these subject-matters from the scope of s 117 is the necessary consequence of a federal system in which each State exercises independent powers and functions within its territory for the peace, order and good government of that territory.

Matters which are the concern only of a State and its people and are not within the scope of s 117 would seem to include the franchise, the qualifications and conditions for holding public office in the State, and conduct which threatens the safety of the State or its people. No doubt there are [other examples] ... But since all exceptions to the terms of that section arise by necessary implication from the assumptions and structure of the Constitution, they must be confined to the extent of the need for them. The question is not whether a particular subject-matter serves the object of s 117; it is whether, by necessary implication, the matter is so exclusively the concern of the State and its people that an interstate resident is not entitled to equality of treatment in respect of it.

Toohey J also saw "**[559]** the federal system contemplated by the Constitution" as the relevant context. He held that the scope of s 117 must be limited by "**[560]** implications to be drawn from the Constitution, in particular the capacity of the States to regulate their own affairs within a federal system", so that s 117 would not be offended by differential treatment as "a natural consequence of legislation aimed at protecting the legitimate interests of the 'State community'."

Mason CJ, Deane and Dawson JJ all envisaged a broader area in which State legislation might apply residential criteria without infringing s 117. In part, this more flexible approach depended on analogies with the American "privileges and immunities" clause in Art IV, §2, cl 1 of the United States Constitution, which provides: "The citizens of each State shall be entitled to all privileges and immunities of citizens in the several States". Brennan, McHugh and Toohey JJ on the other hand held that decisions on this provision by the United States Supreme Court were of little assistance in interpreting s 117.

Mason CJ: [491] Broadly speaking, the test adopted [in regard to Art IV, §2] consists of two stages. First, the Court decides whether or not the interest violated is a "fundamental right" basic to national unity: *Baldwin v Montana Fish and Game Commission* [436 US 371 (1978)]. If it is, then the second question is whether the legislating State can demonstrate a substantial reason for the discrimination. This involves showing that the discrimination against persons in their capacity as non-residents is justified, not merely that the law as a whole is justified: *Hicklin v Orbeck* [437 US 518 at 525-6 (1978)]; *Supreme Court of New Hampshire v Piper* [470 US 274 at 284 (1985)].

Both constitutional provisions broadly serve the same purpose … However, there is not the same foundation for saying that s 117 was intended to protect fundamental rights as there is in the case of Art IV, s 2. The Australian Constitution contains very few provisions guaranteeing fundamental rights. The consequence is that s 117 must be understood as providing protection in relation to rights generally …

The second limb of the United States test is a recognition that some limit must be placed upon the application of the general principle. In my view it is necessary to adopt a similar approach when considering whether or not a particular disability or discrimination is prohibited by s 117. To allow the section an unlimited scope would give it a reach extending beyond the object which it was designed to serve by trenching upon the autonomy of the States to a far-reaching degree …

[492] The preservation of the autonomy of the States demands that the exclusion of out-of-State residents from the enjoyment of rights naturally and exclusively associated with residence in a State must be recognized as standing outside the operation of s 117. Take, for example, the exclusion of out-of-State residents from the right to enjoy welfare benefits provided by a State under a scheme to assist the indigent, the aged or the ill. Generally speaking, I doubt that such an exclusion would amount to a disability or discrimination within the section. The exclusion would not seem to detract from the concept of Australian nationhood or national unity which it is the object of the section to ensure, because it would offend accepted notions of State autonomy and financial independence and a due sense of a State's responsibility to the people of the State to say that the Constitution required the State to extend the range of persons entitled under the scheme to out-of-State residents. The same comment might be made about a requirement that a person is not eligible to be the licensee of an hotel unless he resides on the premises.

On the other hand, the same comments could not be made about the exclusion of out-of-State residents from participation in professional activities open to residents of the legislating State or the imposition of discriminating burdens on such out-of-State residents, unless the exclusion could be justified as a proper and necessary discharge of the State's responsibility to the people of that State, which includes its responsibility to protect the interests of the public. Such an action against out-of-State residents would be inconsistent with the constitutional object of Australian nationhood **[493]** and national unity, unless the State were able to demonstrate that the interests of the State in maintaining its autonomy, over and above such interest it might have in giving an advantage to its residents over non-residents, required such action to be taken.

Deane J: [528] The words of s 117 must, of course, be construed in their context in a constitution which is founded upon the existence of the various States as distinct entities under the federation. So construed, s 117 does not require that no distinction at all be drawn in a State between non-resident and resident. Section 117 only applies when a non-resident is "subject to … disability or discrimination". Those words, construed in their constitutional context, convey the notion of some superimposed incapacity or disadvantage in the sense that the incapacity or disadvantage, regardless of whether it be direct or indirect, does not flow naturally from the structure of the particular State, the limited scope of its legislative powers or the nature of the particular right, privilege, immunity or other advantage or power to which it relates. Thus, a provision in a State constitution conferring particular voting rights in State elections upon residents of the State as a whole or upon persons resident in particular electorates in the State will have the effect of precluding non-residents from voting. The incapacity of the non-resident to vote flows, however, not from some superimposed disqualification or qualification but from the nature of the franchise in a political system based, to a significant extent, on residential divisions and representation. A similar comment could be made of a federal law precluding a person resident in Victoria who happened to be present in New South Wales from voting in the election of New South Wales senators. Again, State financial assistance to a particular class of its residents (eg a rental subsidy to disadvantaged tenants) could place an ineligible visitor who was resident (and a tenant) in another State at a comparable disadvantage if that other State provided no such subsidy. The disadvantage would, however, not flow from the subjection of the non-resident to a disability or discrimination. It **[529]** would flow naturally from the nature of the subsidy and the scope of State powers and responsibility under the constitutional division of governmental authority.

Gaudron J had a different approach. For her, it was not a question of exceptions to s 117 or limitations upon it, but simply of defining the "discrimination" to which it refers. The relevant conceptual framework was to be derived from experience with contemporary legislation prohibiting discrimination on grounds of race or sex (see, for example, the *Sex Discrimination Act 1984* (Cth) and her joint judgment with Deane J in *Australian Iron & Steel Pty Ltd v Banovic* (1989) 168 CLR 165). On that basis, she argued that every law is "discriminatory" in the sense that it singles out a class of cases for differential treatment. It is only when this differentiation is not justified, that is, when there are not legitimate and relevant reasons for confining the operation of the law to the specified class, that we speak of "discrimination" in an adverse sense.

Gaudron J: [571] Where protection is given by anti-discrimination legislation, the legislation usually proceeds by reference to an unexpressed declaration that certain characteristics are irrelevant within the areas in which discrimination is proscribed. Even so, the legislation frequently allows for an exception in cases where the characteristic has a relevant bearing on the matter in issue. Thus, for example, the *Anti-Discrimination Act* 1977 (NSW), whilst proscribing discrimination in employment on the grounds of race and sex, allows in ss 14 and 31 that discrimination is not unlawful if sex or race is a genuine occupational qualification.

The framework of anti-discrimination legislation has, to a considerable extent, shaped our understanding of what is involved in discrimination. Because most anti-discrimination legislation tends to proceed by reference to an unexpressed declaration that a particular characteristic is irrelevant it is largely unnecessary to note that discrimination is confined to different treatment that is not appropriate to a relevant difference. It is often equally unnecessary to note that, if there is a relevant difference, a failure to accord different treatment appropriate to that difference also constitutes discrimination ...

[572] The reference to "disability" in s 117 must be construed in the context of the expression "disability or discrimination". Just as the legal concept of discrimination does not extend to different treatment appropriate to a relevant difference, so too, the absence of a right or entitlement does not constitute a disability if the right or entitlement is appropriate to a relevant difference ...

The more difficult question is whether, there being a relevant difference, the different treatment accorded to that difference is appropriate to it. Although I have expressed the issue in terms of the appropriateness of the different treatment, it seems to me that the considerations thereby raised are similar to those which arise in application of the "privileges and immunities" clause of the United **[573]** States Constitution. In *Toomer v Witsell* [334 US 385 at 396 (1948)], the relevant enquiry in relation to the "privileges and immunities" clause was identified as one "concerned with whether [reasons for discrimination] do exist and whether the degree of discrimination bears a close relation to them". Similarly, in *Supreme Court of New Hampshire v Piper* [470 US 274 at 284 (1985)] Powell J, delivering the opinion of the Court, said that "[t]he Clause does not preclude discrimination against nonresidents where: (i) there is a substantial reason for the difference in treatment; and (ii) the discrimination practiced against nonresidents bears a substantial relationship to the State's objective" and added that "[i]n deciding whether the discrimination bears a close or substantial relationship to the State's objective, the Court has considered the availability of less restrictive means" ...

The question whether different treatment assigned by reason of a relevant difference is appropriate to that difference is one which is peculiarly apt to attract different answers according to the alternatives available at different times. It is also a question which, as the United States Supreme Court recognized in *Supreme Court of Virginia v Friedman* [487 US 59 at 69 (1988)], cannot be answered by the dictation of "specific legislative choices to the State" ... The question of appropriateness may be answered by reference to the test applied to determine the validity of legislation enacted to secure a constitutional purpose, namely, whether it is reasonably capable of being seen as appropriate and adapted to that purpose ... **[574]** For present purposes the issue may be expressed as whether the different treatment is reasonably capable of being seen as appropriate and adapted to a relevant difference.

McHugh J rejected this attempt to approach the problem by seeking criteria of "legitimate" discrimination. In his view, the word "discrimination" could not be confined to illegitimate or unjustified discrimination since the phrase used in s 117 is "disability or discrimination": since "disability" did not sensibly lend itself to qualification, it would be "[582] incongruous" to qualify its companion word "discrimination". "[583] Indeed, in many cases a restriction might be classified as both a disability and a discrimination".

The wider operation given to s 117 by the *Street* case makes it anomalous that the provision is confined to those out-of-State residents who are "subjects of the Queen". Toohey J explained this odd form of words as reflecting a deliberate choice by delegates to the 1890s Conventions to avoid the word "citizen" because of its "[553] distinctly republican flavour". Citing *Nolan v Minister for Immigration and Ethnic Affairs* (1988) 165 CLR 178, Toohey J held that: "[554] 'Subject of the Queen' is now to be understood as referring to the Queen in right of Australia". Deane and Dawson JJ similarly relied on *Nolan* to conclude that s 117 would now extend to any Australian citizen. This transformational reading of the phrase "a subject of the Queen" was later to be described by McHugh J, in *Re Patterson; Ex parte Taylor* (2001) 207 CLR 391, as "[434] one of the most radical propositions in the constitutional jurisprudence of the Court".

The *Street* decision was applied in *Goryl v Greyhound Australia Pty Ltd* (1994) 179 CLR 463. The plaintiff, a New South Wales resident, was injured in New South Wales during a bus journey from Brisbane to Wyong. She sued the bus owner in Queensland for damages. Section 20 of the *Motor Vehicles Insurance Act 1936* (Qld) restricted her, as a New South Wales resident, to the damages she could have recovered under the law of that State. A resident of Queensland would have been entitled to higher damages under Queensland law. The Court held that s 20 infringed s 117 and was thereby rendered inapplicable to the plaintiff.

Goryl v Greyhound Australia Pty Ltd
(1994) 179 CLR 463

Dawson and Toohey JJ: [485] In *Street v Queensland Bar Association* [(1989) 168 CLR 461] all members of the Court were of the view that not every kind of differential treatment by a State of a resident of another State amounts to the imposition of a disability or to discrimination within the meaning of s 117. Whether this is because the very nature of the federation, predicated as it is upon government State by State with the inevitable consequence that laws will differ from State to State, requires limits to be placed upon s 117 or whether it is because some kinds of differential treatment, properly viewed, cannot be described as imposing a disability or a discrimination, is probably a difference in approach rather than principle ... The most obvious example of differential treatment which lies **[486]** outside s 117 is the exclusion of non-residents from voting in a State election. Clearly, that is something which would not be prohibited by s 117 even if it did amount to the imposition of a disability upon non-residents or discrimination against them. But it might also be said that there is no disability or discrimination because the very nature of a State election, which is to elect representatives for the residents of the State, dictates that residence be a qualification of voters. Non-residents have no part to play in the election of representatives for residents.

No doubt difficulties may be encountered when one proceeds beyond the more obvious examples of differential treatment which are not prohibited by s 117. Guidance is then to be found in the object of s 117 which is to foster the concept of Australian nationhood, recognizing at the same time the capacity of the States to govern their own communities which is an essential feature of the federation. A similar approach to the privileges and immunities clause in the United States Constitution has been found necessary ...

[488] In applying s 117, the comparison to be made is between a non-resident in the position of the plaintiff and the position she would be in if she were resident in Queensland. Quite clearly the plaintiff is, upon such a comparison, subject both to a disability and to discrimination. She can only recover damages at a lesser rate than if she were resident in Queensland. And there is no difference in the plaintiff's position which would justify the distinction which is drawn. It is not because she claims the benefit of any welfare or insurance scheme established for and financed by Queensland residents. The disability imposed upon the plaintiff is imposed regardless of any indemnity available to the respondent under the statutory insurance scheme. It is simply a case of a non-resident being afforded under Queensland law different and less advantageous treatment than she would be afforded if she were a resident of Queensland. In our view, s 117 applies to relieve the plaintiff from that disability or discrimination so that she is entitled to recover the full amount of damages recoverable in Queensland at common law.

6. Further References

Blackshield, T, "Religion and Australian Constitutional Law" in Radan, P, Meyerson, D, and Croucher, RE (eds), *Law and Religion: God, the State and the Common Law* (Routledge, 2005), 81.

Brooks, A, "A Paragon of Democratic Virtues? The Development of the Commonwealth Franchise" (1993) 12 *University of Tasmania Law Review* 208.

Charlesworth, H, "Individual Rights and the Australian High Court" (1986) 4 *Law in Context* 52.

Coper, M, *Encounters with the Australian Constitution* (CCH, 1987), Ch 8.

Ebbeck, G, "Section 117: The Obscure Provision" (1991) 13 *Adelaide Law Review* 23.

Ebbeck, G, "The Future for Section 117 as a Constitutional Guarantee" (1993) 4 *Public Law Review* 89.

Ely, R, *Unto God and Caesar: Religious Issues in the Emerging Commonwealth 1891-1906* (Melbourne University Press, 1976).

Galligan, B, and Sampford, C (eds), *Rethinking Human Rights* (Federation Press, 1997).

Hanks, P, "Constitutional Guarantees" in Lee, HP, and Winterton, G (eds), *Australian Constitutional Perspectives* (Law Book Co, 1992), 92.

Kaye, S, and Piotrowicz, R, *Human Rights in International and Australian Law* (Butterworths, 2000).

Lee, HP, and Paterson, J, "Australian Nationhood in the Constitutional Interpretation of Section 117" (2000) 8 *Asia Pacific Law Review* 169.

Kinley, D (ed), *Human Rights in Australian Law* (Federation Press, 1998).

Mathieson, M, "Section 117 of the Constitution: The Unfinished Rehabilitation" (1999) 27 *Federal Law Review* 393.

McConvill, J, and Joy, M, "Approaching Constitutional Trial by Jury: *Brownlee v The Queen*" (2001) 6 *Deakin Law Review* 344.

McLeish, S, "Making Sense of Religion and the Constitution: A Fresh Start for Section 116" (1992) 18 *Monash University Law Review* 207.

Meagher, D, "New Day Rising? Non-originalism, Justice Kirby and Section 80 of the Constitution" (2002) 24 *Sydney Law Review* 141.

O'Neill, N, "Constitutional Human Rights in Australia" (1987) 17 *Federal Law Review* 85.

O'Neill, N, Rice, S, and Douglas, R, *Retreat from Injustice: Human Rights in Australian Law* (Federation Press, 2nd ed 2004).

Pannam, C, "Discrimination on the Basis of State Residence in Australia and the United States" (1967) 6 *Melbourne University Law Review* 105.

Pannam, C, "Travelling Section 116 with a US Road Map" (1963) 4 *Melbourne University Law Review* 41.

Pannam, C, "Trial by Jury and Section 80 of the Australian Constitution" (1968) 6 *Sydney Law Review* 1.

Simpson, A, and Wood, M, "A Puny Thing Indeed – *Cheng v The Queen* and the Constitutional Right to Trial by Jury" (2001) 29 *Federal Law Review* 95.

Stellios, J, "The Constitutional Jury – 'A Bulwark of Liberty'?" (2005) 27 *Sydney Law Review* 113.

Stellios, J, "The High Court's Recent Encounters with Section 80 Jury Trials" (2005) 29 *Criminal Law Journal* 139.

Stone, A, "Australia's Constitutional Rights and the Problem of Interpretive Disagreement" (2005) 27 *Sydney Law Review* 29.

Taylor, G, "Citizenship Rights and the Australian Constitution" (2001) 12 *Public Law Review* 205.

Williams, G, *Human Rights under the Australian Constitution* (Oxford University Press, 1999), Ch 5.

Zines, L, *The High Court and the Constitution* (Butterworths, 4th ed 1997), Ch 16.

Zines, L, and Lindell, GJ, "Form and Substance: 'Discrimination' in Modern Constitutional Law" (1992) 21 *Federal Law Review* 136.

Chapter 27

Economic Freedoms

1. Freedom of Interstate Trade, Commerce and Intercourse

The guarantee in s 92 of the Constitution that trade, commerce and intercourse among the States shall be "absolutely free" was regarded as one of the essential conditions of Australian federation; but by 1988, the number of decided cases in the High Court and the Privy Council on its meaning was estimated at over 140. The resulting maze of conflicting precedents was largely swept away by the joint unanimous judgment in *Cole v Whitfield* (1988) 165 CLR 360.

(a)   Isaacs, Dixon and Barwick

The cases before *Cole v Whitfield* can be seen as reflecting the influence of three dominant individuals: Sir Isaac Isaacs, Sir Owen Dixon and Sir Garfield Barwick. Dixon adopted, but reinterpreted, the doctrines laid down by Isaacs, and Barwick adopted, but reinterpreted, the doctrines laid down by Dixon. However, while Dixon's interpretations sought to rationalise and depoliticise the vigorous rhetorical approach of Isaacs, Barwick's interpretations sought to reinstate an underlying ideological vision. The common theme was an understanding of s 92 as conferring a personal right, often summarised as an "individual rights" approach to s 92.

In argument in *James v Commonwealth* [1936] AC 578 at 597, the Commonwealth Attorney-General, Robert Menzies KC, listed six possible meanings of the command that interstate trade, commerce and intercourse be "absolutely free":

1.   Free from all laws of every description.
2.   Free of any restrictions imposed upon trade and commerce by reason of its interstate character. That is, free of any discriminating trade law.
3.   Free as trade and commerce of all interference whether specially directed to it or not.
4.   Free of all laws the pith and substance of which is a regulation of interstate trade or commerce.
5.   Free in the sense of freedom attaching to trade and commerce regarded as a whole and not distributively. Individuals are not guaranteed freedom in relation to their trade and commerce so long as trade and commerce as a whole is not impaired.
6.   Free from pecuniary imposts.

What Isaacs J insisted on was meaning 3. In the words of his joint majority judgment in *W & A McArthur Ltd v Queensland* (1920) 28 CLR 530, interstate trade and commerce were to be

"**[550]** 'absolutely free' from all governmental control by every governmental authority". The only qualification was that "absolutely free" means "**[550]** 'free' *as* 'trade, commerce, and intercourse', and does not extend beyond the subject matter spoken of". Thus, although some of his rhetoric may have seemed closer to meaning 1, he did not suggest that acts of interstate trade and commerce were immune from *all* laws, but rather from all interference with them as *acts of trade and commerce*. On the other hand, he envisaged immunity not only from *laws* impeding interstate trade, but from *any* governmental action interfering with trade "as such".

Initially one might suppose that the purpose of s 92 is simply to eliminate customs duties at State borders; but the very first case on s 92 showed that this simple view was unsustainable. In *Fox v Robbins* (1909) 8 CLR 115, Western Australia had imposed a liquor retail licensing scheme. For retailers selling Western Australian liquor, the licence fee was £2. For retailers selling interstate liquor, the fee was £50. The scheme was held to infringe s 92. Clearly, this was just the kind of discrimination against interstate products that s 92 was designed to prevent; yet it was not achieved by a customs duty and did not operate at the State border. However, once we accept that s 92 must extend beyond border customs duties, a difficulty arises. It is easy to say that s 92 is intended to protect interstate traders against any special disadvantage; but why should it give them a special advantage?

Suppose that Victoria makes a general law which can be said to regulate trade and commerce "as such". Obviously, Victorian traders whose business lies wholly within Victoria will be bound by such a law. But what of their interstate competitors trading within Victoria in a way that amounts to "interstate" trade? And what of the Victorian traders themselves, when they sell their goods interstate? Can either of these groups claim to be exempt from the normal operation of the Victorian law simply because they are engaged in interstate trade? So long as the law in question was applicable to trade and commerce "as such", Isaacs J insisted that the answer must be "Yes". It was this claim which underlay the uncertainties arising from a series of cases beginning with *New South Wales v Commonwealth* (*Wheat Case*) (1915) 20 CLR 54.

The *Wheat Acquisition Act 1914* (NSW) was one of a wide range of wartime measures for control of essential foodstuffs enacted by both State and Commonwealth governments during World War I, primarily to ensure adequate wartime food supplies to the United Kingdom, but also to prevent local profiteering. The Act was challenged on the basis that it infringed s 92.

The *Wheat Case* was first heard by the Inter-State Commission, the body envisaged by s 101 of the Constitution, but not established by legislation until 1912 and not appointed until 1913. Its first Chief Commissioner was Albert Piddington, "the High Court judge who never sat"; he had been appointed to the High Court by Prime Minister Billy Hughes in 1913 but resigned amidst public controversy. (Before offering the appointment, Hughes had cabled to seek Piddington's views on "Commonwealth versus State Rights", and Piddington had replied: "In sympathy with supremacy of Commonwealth powers".) The Constitution had apparently envisaged that the Inter-State Commission, and not the High Court, should be responsible for "the execution and maintenance ... of the provisions of the Constitution relating to trade and commerce", including s 92. However, the *Wheat Case* held that the vesting of judicial power in the Inter-State Commission was invalid – even though s 101 spoke of "an Inter-State Commission, with such powers of adjudication ... as the Parliament deems necessary" (see Chapter 14, §1).

In the Inter-State Commission, the *Wheat Acquisition Act* was held invalid by 2:1, with Chief Commissioner Piddington dissenting. The arguments put to the Inter-State Commission introduced a question that has haunted s 92 ever since: what, if anything, is the ideological purpose of the provision? Is it merely intended to assert the colonial policy of "free trade" against that of "protectionism"? Or is it intended to guarantee "free trade" in a wider sense, reflecting 19th century ideals of economic laissez faire and serving as a constraint on any kind of governmental intervention in the free market economy?

The Seizure of Wheat Case
Parliamentary Papers No 69 of 1914-1915 (Session 1914-17, Vol 2, 1113)

Chief Commissioner Piddington: [28] The one inflexible guarantee of the exchange of natural products is not the system of individual trading, but the human motive of self-preservation ... [It] is an open question whether Inter-State commerce would be better carried on ... if the State is the only seller ... What is certain is that the new economic organization of wealth could only take place in a state of public opinion ...that has not yet been reached in Australia, and, if it ever is reached, will in all probability be reached simultaneously in all the States by that natural law of the human mind which brings about the uniform development of political opinion on vital questions in the same country. To the extent to which the Commonwealth or the States ever conceive the desire of using their own resources as State institutions, inter-State commerce carried on by individual citizens, will give place to inter-State commerce carried on by Governments, and this, in the condition of public thought postulated ..., will be simply carrying out the steadfast, mature, and rounded public opinion of the nation in its various Legislatures. Is such public opinion in the Commonwealth or in all or **[29]** any of the States, deprived of the right to translate itself into public law?

When the Constitution was framed one of the great political parties in every State had ... for its avowed programme, "The nationalization of the means of production, distribution, and exchange" ... Is it reasonable to suppose that in section 92 there is latent an indelible proscription against the realization of this or any similar political creed by the electors in their Commonwealth Parliament ..., or in their State Legislatures in respect of matters left to them? ...

If it is necessary for the decision in this case to pass judgment on an argument so far removed from those into which Courts ordinarily enter, it may well be thought that no calamity to private inter-State free trade under the recognised economic system ... can compare in extent with the calamity of discovering that a known economic creed, which has divided the political thought of all civilized countries for more than a century, has been barred out from practical politics in Australia by a section of the Constitution which speaks the language of liberty ... Section 92 was never, in my opinion, destined to carry such a burden of opprobrium or to bind the body electoral hand and foot so that it can neither strike for defence nor move where it thinks is the line of progress. It was a law for freedom of trade, not against freedom of thought. It would still operate, under the circumstances of nationalization of industries held out as an argument *in terrorem* by the plaintiff Commonwealth, to insure that no one State should put any burden or discrimination or impediment on the citizens of another State, having trade, commerce, or intercourse with the former State. The Constitution of Australia is distinguished from that of the United States of America by the very fact that no attempt has been made anywhere to bind the electors to any prescribed course of economic action ...

No such definitions of the path along which economic and social legislation must move in Australia are to be found in our Constitution. There is only one political creed recognised in it, and that is a creed of complete political liberty, and the Constitution cannot be so slavishly construed, nor can, by any incantation, the sanctity of private inter-State commerce be so invoked that the laws of Bismarck against Socialism would be mere whips compared to the scorpion that is lurking, according to the present argument, in section 92. If ever any Legislature in Australia, whether it is the Parliament of the Commonwealth for national purposes, or the Parliament of a State for the residue of self-government confided to it by the Constitution, adopts in its legislation the policy of "Socialism in our time", I do not believe it will be incumbent upon the Courts to point to section 92 as saying "Never, in this Commonwealth."

On appeal, the High Court held that s 92 had not been infringed, since compulsory State acquisition of an entire commodity operated on "ownership" and not on "trade". The resulting assumption that compulsory acquisition may be compatible with freedom of trade was later heavily qualified – notably in *James v Cowan* [1932] AC 542 – but never wholly abandoned.

New South Wales v Commonwealth (*Wheat Case*)
(1915) 20 CLR 54

Isaacs J: [100] The key to the matter lies, in my opinion, in the fact that *trade and commerce consists of acts not things*. The things themselves are indispensable, just as the human actors are; but they do not form part of the trade and commerce itself ...

Therefore, when a State deals with property on the basis of property and regulates its ownership irrespective of any element of inter-State trade, there is no abridgment of absolute freedom of trade. The State cannot know what contracts exist at a given moment, or what movement of property towards another State has begun, and if it proceeds to exercise its own lawful powers of legislation without reference in any way to and perfectly independent and irrespective of such inter-State operations, it is not an unlawful exercise of legislative power. It cannot do indirectly what it cannot do directly; but here it is not directly or indirectly interfering with commerce at all ...

When the State without reference to inter-State contracts as a criterion, or as influencing the operation of its enactment, proceeds to acquire wheat to feed its citizens, it merely changes ownership. It does not assume to govern the duties of the contracting parties to each other, or regulate in any way the interchange of goods belonging to the vendor. It would be strange indeed if sec 92 enabled individuals, by merely passing goods to and fro between States from one end of Australia to the other, to prevent any of the States, and even the Commonwealth, from exercising the most **[101]** vital and elementary function of an organized society in the protection and safety of its members.

I am clearly of opinion that sec 92 has no such function, and that while neither States nor Commonwealth can detract from the absolute freedom of trade and commerce between Australian citizens in the property they possess, there is nothing to prevent either States or Commonwealth, for their own lawful purposes, from becoming themselves owners of that property.

In *Foggitt Jones & Co Ltd v New South Wales* (1916) 21 CLR 357, the *Wheat Case* was distinguished. Again, the legislation had authorised compulsory acquisition; but in this case, before any acquisition order was made, the legislation froze any movement of stock and meat and required that they "shall be kept for the disposal of His Majesty's Imperial Government". Thus, the legislation, unlike that in the *Wheat Case*, prevented commercial movement, including inter-state movement, without first interfering with "ownership". On that basis, the legislation was held to infringe s 92; but six months later, in *Duncan v Queensland* (1916) 22 CLR 556, that decision was reversed and *Foggitt Jones* was overruled. Griffith CJ and Rich J had changed their minds, leaving Isaacs J in passionate dissent.

Duncan v Queensland
(1916) 22 CLR 556

Isaacs J: [605] This is one of the most important cases, if indeed it be not the most important of all the cases, that have ever occupied the attention of this Court. It concerns what I regard as one of the fundamental pacts of the Constitution under which we live, the absolute right of freedom of trade and intercourse between the States. The result of any decision as to that right is so momentous as to impose upon any Judge having to determine it as a permanent feature of the organic law of Australia an enormous weight of responsibility. That sense of responsibility, however, is naturally lightened by the reflection that, whatever decision we come to, **[606]** this is one of those instances which are still under our Constitution reviewable by the ultimate tribunal of the Empire ... I may say at once that I am quite unable to concur in the conclusion arrived at by the majority of my learned brethren, which, I hope I may add without disrespect, is arrived at for reasons so divergent as to require separate examination at my hands.

The real question we are called upon to decide may be thus succinctly stated: "Is the constitutional declaration of inter-State freedom of trade a reality or a sham?" The Queensland *Meat Supply for Imperial Uses Act* has been pronounced valid notwithstanding that declaration, and even assuming that on the true construction of the State Act it authorizes all that is complained of. That pronouncement ... necessarily reduces the Constitution, so far as it purports to guarantee to the people of Australia free trade between the States, to a worthless scrap of paper ...

[620] The effect of sec 92 of our Constitution may ... be seen by an illustration. A man in one State has goods belonging to him which he wishes to sell; and in another State a man desires to buy those goods, and has money which he is ready to offer in exchange for them. Sec 92 says that the man with the goods is to be absolutely free to sell and deliver his goods to his inter-State neighbour, unhindered by any interference of Commonwealth or State, and the other man is to be equally free to purchase those goods and receive them and pay for them. The States singly or combined cannot lawfully prevent the owner of the goods or the owner of the money from so acting in respect of what they possess ... It is no detraction from the right of trade and commerce that regulations are permitted which are laws of "police and order" ... A citizen in his relation to the society in which he lives has many rights, duties and obligations. He may be viewed in many capacities, and it is impossible to draw exclusive lines of demarcation between the multitudinous aspects of the civic life ... If, for instance, he has meat and wishes to sell it inter-State, he may sell it unhindered by the State, so far as trade and commerce is concerned; but, if it is poisoned meat, the meat may be seized, not because sale is directed to be prevented, but because an antecedent fact, viz, the existence of such meat in the hands of the owner, is a step towards endangering the lives of others. If he is a carrier he is free to pass across the border, but if he owes a debt to the [621] Government or to a private individual his vehicle or his horse may be taken by legal process to satisfy his obligations to pay his debts. If he has committed a crime he himself may be taken to expiate it. If the State needs his property it may take it, and, at its will and tempered only by its sense of justice, may take it with or without compensation. But in those cases "trade and commerce" are untouched; remotely and even necessarily they are affected, but this is the effect of maintaining social order as such and not of prohibiting or assuming to prohibit trade in any way. It is on these grounds that inspection laws are not forbidden. But the moment the State says "You may keep but shall not sell your merchantable goods, not because they are deleterious but because they are not," then trade and commerce are directly prohibited; and though this is still perfectly competent to the State so far as relates to its purely internal trade, it is, in my clear opinion, invalid if sec 92 is to have any operation at all – as to inter-State trade. I have put a clear case, because that is the exact position here. But it must not be understood that I think the State may directly prohibit the sale inter-State even of what, according to some standard it creates, it regards as deleterious goods. It may make the production or the possession of them in the State an offence, and it may seize them or punish the offender. But if it passes by its own territorial powers ..., and assumes to deal simply and directly with trade inter-State, it equally in my opinion offends against sec 92.

And that is so, with whatever object the interference with trade as such takes place – the *thing* is prohibited, and the object is immaterial. Otherwise, a State needs only preface an Act with an object of internal concern, and every barrier of inter-State trade is valid.

Duncan v Queensland was in turn overruled in *W & A McArthur Ltd v Queensland* (1920) 28 CLR 530, which held that *Foggitt Jones* had been right after all. By 5:1 (Gavan Duffy J dissenting), the Court upheld a challenge to s 12(1) of the *Profiteering Prevention Act 1920* (Qld), which provided that: "It is unlawful for any trader, whether as principal or agent or whether by himself or by an agent, (a) to sell or agree to sell or offer for sale any commodity at a price higher than the declared price". By a notification gazetted on 10 July 1920, the Commissioner for Prices under the Act had fixed the maximum prices for "calico, sheeting, or sheets" and for "men's felt hats" as "the actual cost ... to the wholesale trade" plus 22.5 per cent.

Knox CJ and Starke JJ joined with Isaacs J in a joint judgment, protesting that if interstate trade were to be subjected to compulsory price-fixing, it could not be "absolutely free". Rich J (changing his mind again) agreed in a separate judgment. Higgins J declined to overrule *Duncan v Queensland*, but agreed that s 92 was infringed by the price-fixing scheme.

W & A McArthur Ltd v Queensland
(1920) 28 CLR 530

Knox CJ, Isaacs and Starke JJ: [543] It is not, and cannot, be denied by the defendants that sec 92, whatever it means, binds the State of Queensland to leave the plaintiff's inter-State commerce with Queenslanders "absolutely free"; but, say the defendants, that **[544]** does not prevent the State from passing a law rendering the plaintiff liable to fine and imprisonment merely because it engages in that commerce on terms voluntarily and mutually agreed on, but at a price higher than that dictated by the State. The punishment is incurred, not because incidentally in the course of engaging in inter-State commerce some State law made on an entirely different subject is infringed, but because the State insists on the inter-State commerce itself, unconnected with any other subject, being conducted not according to the free will of the respective citizens of Queensland and New South Wales but according to the limitations imposed on it by the State of Queensland. If not so conducted, it must be abstained from altogether, under pain of fine and imprisonment. Nevertheless, say the defendants, they have left that trade "absolutely free" within the meaning of sec 92. Can it be said that a State, when it penalizes persons engaging in inter-State trade and commerce by fine and imprisonment if it is carried on contrary to restrictions directly prescribed, at the same time leaves it "absolutely free"? ...

[550] The primary meaning of these words used as they are with reference to governmental control, is that the subject matter of which they are predicated is to be "absolutely free" from all governmental control by every governmental authority to whom the command contained in the section is addressed. The expression "absolutely free" naturally means "free" *as* "trade, commerce, and intercourse," and does not extend beyond the subject matter spoken of. It is not said of "goods" or "persons," but of the *acts* which constitute "trade, commerce, and intercourse." In the *Wheat Case* [(1915) 20 CLR 54 at 100] *Isaacs J* observed that trade, commerce and intercourse consist of acts not things. "Absolute freedom" in respect of "trade, commerce, and intercourse," does not connote privilege to break all other laws. Liberty is not equivalent to anarchy or licence. Though there is "absolute freedom" in every **[551]** Victorian to cross into New South Wales ..., it is his "intercourse" only which is unfettered, not the man himself under all circumstances. If the man, while in New South Wales, steals or cheats or begs, or injures persons or property, or disturbs the public peace, or is in such a condition as to constitute a danger to his fellows – matters wholly distinct from "intercourse" – he is as amenable to the laws of the State *on those subjects*, so far as they are unaffected by sec 109 of the Constitution, as any permanent resident of the State. If he brings goods into the State, he is free to do so, and to pass through the State with them (say) to Queensland, equally without hindrance or condition by State law, so far as regards the passage through. But if, for instance, the goods are dangerous, as gunpowder or wild cattle or a mad dog, or are stolen or offensive, he cannot deny his obligation to submit in respect of them to whatever laws are in force in the State on those subjects. The constitutional freedom predicated begins and ends with respect to the act of "trade, commerce, and intercourse."

A recurring problem for "the Isaacs view" was that s 51(i) of the Constitution explicitly authorises the Commonwealth to regulate "[t]rade and commerce ... among the States". How, then, could it be "absolutely free"? In *McArthur v Queensland* Isaacs J persuaded the other majority judges to avoid this dilemma by holding that s 92 *did not bind the Commonwealth*; its restraint on legislative and executive power was directed only to the States. The argument was textually weak, since all Commonwealth powers under s 51 are expressed to be "subject to this Constitution" (and thus to s 92). Pragmatically, it was attractive, but only because a wholesale denial of State legislative power over interstate trade would create a legislative vacuum unless the Commonwealth could fill it under s 51(i). In short, an inherently unsatisfying conclusion was required as a way of avoiding the unacceptable consequences of the Isaacs approach.

In *Duncan v Queensland*, Isaacs J had seemed to concede that ordinary "**[620]** police and order" laws were compatible with "freedom" of interstate trade; and that laws aimed at "**[621]** deleterious goods", such as "**[620]** poisoned meat", might also be valid. However, in *McArthur v Queensland*, the joint judgment seemed to say that importation into a State of "**[551]** dangerous" or "offensive" goods must be "absolutely free" – although, once imported, such goods must conform to the general laws of the State. When the issue came to a head in *Ex parte Nelson (No 1)* (1928) 42 CLR 209, the Court was evenly divided. Knox CJ, Gavan Duffy and Starke JJ held that an attempt by New South Wales to protect itself against the droving of tick-infested cattle from Queensland was valid; Higgins and Powers JJ joined Isaacs J in dissent. However, since the Court divided 3:3, the case had no value as a precedent.

Ex parte Nelson (No 1)
(1928) 42 CLR 209

Isaacs J: [225] [T]he State's contention … is, and needs must be, this: that "absolutely" does not mean absolutely, and "free" does not mean free. "Absolutely," it is said, means "conditionally" or "provisionally" or "partially" or "subject to exceptions" or "unless the State in its own adverse interests or for its own single purpose thinks fit to restrict or prohibit." "Free," it is said, includes partial or total prevention, and may be accompanied with fine, penalty and punishment. The contention sounds like an aspersion on the English language. It has neither logic nor etymology to support it. It is opposed to the general understanding of the words. There is not a syllable in the Constitution or elsewhere that countenances it. If it were possible, then by force of the *lex talionis* sec 92 would speedily find itself between the hammer and the anvil in six diverging policies, and would before long be battered out of recognition. For there is nothing whatever in the Constitution that draws any distinction **[226]** with respect to sec 92 between the State's legislative power in respect to health or fraud or morals or agriculture or internal trade or labour questions, or any other of the myriad unnamed but included subjects contained in its own Constitution. If it has the power of exclusion at its own unchallengeable will in respect of imaginary ticks in cattle, it surely has the same power … for the general welfare of those within its territory. The welfare of a people is not confined to protection from the possibility of disease in cattle. In a greater degree it consists in protection from human disease and human vice, often productive of physical disease or worse, and protection from everything which the accredited representatives of the people consider inimical to its present happiness or future progress, even in relation to the trade or industrial competition of its neighbours. No Court can, consistently with British precedent, embark on such an inquiry, or place in pre-eminence any of the departments of social economy, or choose which is the most important, or say which is deserving of exception from the express and precise words of sec 92 of the Constitution, and which is not. This Court has formally renounced that unauthorized and hopeless task, but in this case has been virtually asked to resume it.

Higgins J was not prepared to say that *any* State interference with trade was incompatible with "absolute freedom". He joined Isaacs J in dissent because *this* interference was "**[246]** pointed directly at" the interstate movement of cattle, or "aimed straight at" their interstate importation.

The unresolved tensions came to a head in litigation in the 1920s and 1930s involving Frederick James. After World War I, many ex-soldiers went to the Murray River region to produce dried fruits. The supply of dried fruits expanded so rapidly that by 1924 only 20 per cent could be sold in Australia. The rest went overseas. As a result, overseas prices fell and many ex-soldiers faced disaster. Both the Commonwealth and the States offered rescue schemes. The Commonwealth first offered financial aid, then passed the *Dried Fruits Export Control Act 1924* (Cth) which regulated the total volume of dried fruit for export. With the Commonwealth controlling overseas marketing, the States tried to control the domestic market.

Frederick James was not an ex-soldier. His dried fruit business at Berri in South Australia dated from 1914. He saw the restrictions on sale of dried fruits in Australia as an unwarranted obstruction of his thriving interstate business. The five main *James* cases were as follows:

1. The *Dried Fruits Act 1924* (SA) set up a Dried Fruits Board. By s 20, the Board could set marketing quotas, to be enforced by "whatever action the Board thinks proper". Section 28 provided that, "subject to" s 92 of the Constitution, "for the purposes of this Act or of any contract made by the Board, the Minister may … acquire compulsorily any dried fruits in South Australia grown and dried in Australia" without a Commonwealth export licence. When James sold dried fruits interstate in excess of quotas set under s 20, his premises were raided and his stock was seized under s 28. In *James v South Australia* (1927) 40 CLR 1, the Court held 5:0 that s 28 was *not* invalid, because it was expressed to be "subject to" s 92. By 3:2, Isaacs ACJ and Powers J dissenting, it was further held that the seizures of James' dried fruits had been validly authorised by s 28. However, the quota provision in s 20 was unanimously held to infringe s 92.

2. In response to *James v South Australia*, the Commonwealth passed the *Dried Fruits Act 1928* (Cth). Section 3 prohibited all carriage of dried fruits interstate without a licence, but added that "prescribed authorities may issue licences". Regulations under the Act provided that "'prescribed authority' means the Dried Fruits Board of the State of Victoria, New South Wales, South Australia or Western Australia, as the case may be". No provision was made for a "prescribed authority" in Tasmania or Queensland, since they produced no dried fruits. In *James v Commonwealth* (1928) 41 CLR 442, the High Court applied *McArthur v Queensland* to hold that the Commonwealth legislation was (in principle) valid, since s 92 did not bind the Commonwealth. However, the scheme was held to be invalid under s 99 of the Constitution, since by making administrative arrangements for only four States, the scheme had "discriminated" against the other two States.

3. In *James v Cowan* [1932] AC 542, the Privy Council affirmed that aspect of the High Court decision in *James v South Australia* which held that a quota scheme restricting participation in the interstate market infringed s 92. However, the Privy Council overruled that aspect of the decision which treated compulsory acquisition as valid. Compulsory acquisition might be valid, but not if its "**[558]** real object" was a restriction of interstate trade.

4. In *James v Commonwealth* [1936] AC 578, the Privy Council overruled that aspect of *McArthur v Queensland* which held that s 92 did not bind the Commonwealth. The Privy Council went on to hold that the Commonwealth dried fruits scheme was invalid as a "**[631]** burden" on, or "interference" with, freedom of interstate trade.

5. In *James v Commonwealth* (1939) 62 CLR 339, Dixon J, sitting alone, denied that the various seizures of James' dried fruits had given rise to a constitutional cause of action for damages, but held that they did give rise to an action in tort. Legislation authorising the seizures would normally be a defence against this tort, but when s 92 operated to invalidate the legislation, it deprived the Commonwealth of its defence (see Chapter 13, §6(a)).

In *James v Cowan* the Privy Council effectively upheld the view that Isaacs J, in sole dissent, had taken in the High Court (*James v Cowan* (1930) 43 CLR 386). In that judgment – his last on s 92 – Isaacs J had given a new twist to his *Wheat Case* formula of "acts not things":

James v Cowan
(1930) 43 CLR 386

Isaacs J: [418] [O]nce it is fully apprehended that commerce includes "intercourse for the purposes of trade in any and all its forms, including the transportation, purchase, sale and exchange of commodities," the true concept emerges. As already formulated, it consists of *acts*. But acts are attributes not of property but of persons. The right of inter-State trade and commerce protected by sec 92 from State interference and regulation is *a personal right attaching to the individual and not attaching to the goods*. To think that there can be no infringement of sec 92 when and in whatever circumstances a State expropriates property, is entirely to misconceive the nature of the situation. To say that on expropriation the new owner, the Government, is free to dispose of the property, and so the power of disposition of the property is not interfered with, is nothing to the point. The question is, how has the personal right of trading inter-State by the former owner been interfered with? … The right is not an adjunct of the goods: it is the possession of the individual Australian, protected from State interference by sec 92, and it is not a sufficient answer to him, when deprived of his goods in order to prevent him from exercising that right, that the new owner, the depriving State, can **[419]** trade as it pleases with the goods. As well might it be said that to take a loaf of bread from A and give it to B does not affect A's personal right to eat, because B has the right, if he pleases, to eat the bread.

As early as *Duncan v Queensland*, Isaacs J had hinted that the meaning of s 92 might be clarified by the Privy Council. Disagreements within the High Court on the meaning of s 92 had become so pervasive that it seemed that only an authoritative statement from the Privy Council could resolve the issue. This was certainly the view of Rich J in *James v Cowan*.

Rich J: [422] The rhetorical affirmation of sec 92 that trade, commerce and intercourse between the States shall be absolutely free has a terseness and elevation of style which doubtless befits the expression of a sentiment so inspiring. But inspiring sentiments are often vague and grandiloquence is sometimes obscure. If this declaration of liberty had not stopped short at the high-sounding words "absolutely free," the pith and force of its diction might have been sadly diminished. But even if it was impossible to define precisely what it was from which inter-State trade was to be free, either because a commonplace definition forms such a pedestrian conclusion or because it needs an exactness of conception seldom achieved where constitutions are projected, yet obmutescence was both unnecessary and unsafe. Some hint at least might have been dropped, some distant allusion made, from which the nature of the immunity intended could afterwards have been deduced by those whose lot it is to explain the elliptical and expound the unexpressed. As soon as the section was brought down from the lofty clouds whence constitutional precepts are fulminated and came to be applied to **[423]** the everyday practice of trade and commerce and the sordid intercourse of human affairs, the necessity of knowing and so determining precisely what impediments and hindrances were no longer to obstruct inter-State trade obliged this Court to attempt the impossible task of supplying an exclusive and inclusive definition of a conception to be discovered only in the silences of the Constitution. The evils from which sec 92 meant to free inter-State trade were evidently particular. Universal freedom from all laws both natural and human was not in contemplation. It was plain that the Constitution was not dealing with the physical restraints which nature still inflicts on travellers who journey across this Continent … Still less possible was it to believe that sec 92 meant to free inter-State trade of all legal regulation whatever. The operation of the criminal law which is supposed to preserve property could scarcely have been excluded from inter-State trade. However much reliance in and before 1900 may have been placed upon the eighth commandment, sec 92 can scarcely have been framed to put an absconding thief at his legal ease so long as his destination was over the boundary … But, if inter-State trade is not to be free of all legal regulation, what kind of regulation is forbidden? At an early stage of the long controversy as to the true meaning of what sec 92 omits to say, I joined with my brother *Gavan Duffy* in thinking that the immunity was confined to legal restrictions imposed upon trade and commerce in virtue of its inter-State character. The justification for this view, if any there be, is set out **[424]** at length in *Duncan v Queensland* [(1916) 22 CLR 556]. One demerit was found in this view which was sufficient to make it untenable, namely, a majority of the Court steadfastly refused to adhere to it. It must be confessed that it supplied a criterion which was difficult of application, but it may also be claimed that no criterion which is easier of application has hitherto been revealed … After many years of exploration into the dark recesses of this subject I am content to take the decided cases as sailing directions upon which I may set some course, however unexpected may be the destination to which it brings me; and await with a patience not entirely hopeless the powerful beacon light of complete authoritative exposition from those who can speak with finality.

From this viewpoint, the Privy Council's pronouncements in *James v Cowan* and *James v Commonwealth* were a disappointment. The judgments were given respectively by Lord Atkin and Lord Wright, two of the greatest English judges of the time. But while both served to vindicate James, neither of them resolved the uncertainties plaguing the High Court. The criteria used by their Lordships in *James v Cowan* – "**[555]** directed at inter-State commerce as such", "**[558]** real object", "**[559]** direct object" and "object and intention" – seemed only to perpetuate the ambiguities of the High Court decisions, especially since in *James v Commonwealth* the notion of trade and commerce "as such" was said not to be helpful after all.

James v Commonwealth
[1936] AC 578

Lord Wright (for their Lordships): [627] The first question is what is meant by "absolutely free" in s 92. It may be that the word "absolutely" adds nothing. The trade is either free or it is not free. "Absolutely" may perhaps be regarded as merely inserted to add emphasis. The expression "absolutely free" is generally described as popular or rhetorical. On the other hand, "absolutely" may have been added with the object of excluding the risk of partial or veiled infringements. In any case, the use of the language involves the fallacy that a word completely general and undefined is most effective. A good draftsman would realize that the mere generality of the word must compel limitation in its interpretation. "Free" in itself is vague and indeterminate. It must take its colour from the context. Compare, for instance, its use in free speech, free love, free dinner and free trade. Free speech does not mean free speech; it means speech hedged in by all the laws against defamation, blasphemy, sedition and so forth; it means freedom governed by law, as was pointed out in *McArthur's* case [(1920) 28 CLR 530]. Free love, on the contrary, means licence or libertinage, though, even so, there are limitations based on public decency and so forth. Free dinner generally means free of expense, and sometimes a meal open to any one who comes, subject, however, to his condition or behaviour not being objectionable. Free trade means, in ordinary parlance, freedom from tariffs.

"Free" in s 92 cannot be limited to freedom in the last mentioned sense. There may at first sight appear to be some plausibility in that idea, because of the starting-point **[628]** in time specified in the section, because of the sections which surround s 92, and because the proviso to s 92 relates to customs duties. But it is clear that much more is included in the term; customs duties and other like matters constitute a merely pecuniary burden; there may be different and perhaps more drastic ways of interfering with freedom, as by restriction or partial or complete prohibition of passing into or out of the State.

Nor does "free" necessarily connote absence of discrimination between inter-State and intra-State trade. No doubt conditions restrictive of freedom of trade among the States will frequently involve a discrimination; but that is not essential or decisive. An Act may contravene s 92 though it operates in restriction both of intra-State and of inter-State trade. A compulsory seizure of goods, such as that in *James v Cowan* [[1932] AC 542], may include indifferently goods intended for intra-State trade and goods intended for trade among the States. Nor can freedom be limited to freedom from legislative control; it must equally include executive control …

[629] [I]f freedom is to be found in practice the line must be drawn somewhere. If no help is to be got from the formula "trade and commerce as such," neither can it be found by saying that freedom under s 92 is applied to acts not **[630]** persons. For instance, it is said, a man may be arrested for crime while about to cross the frontier in the course of a trade operation, and that is no infringement of s 92. That is true enough, but not very helpful: trade no doubt consists of acts (including documents), but acts imply persons who perform or create them even if only to work the necessary machines. Nor is much help to be got by reflecting that trade may still be free, though the trader has to pay for the different operations, such as tolls, railway rates, freight and so-forth …

The true criterion seems to be that what is meant is freedom as at the frontier or, to use the words of s 112, in respect of "goods passing into or out of the State." What is meant by that needs explanation. The idea starts with the admitted fact that federation in Australia was intended (inter alia) to abolish the frontiers between the different States and create one Australia. That conception involved freedom from customs duties, imports, border prohibitions and restrictions of every kind: the people of Australia were to be free to trade with each other, and to pass to and fro among the States, without any burden, hindrance or restriction based merely on the fact that they were not members of the same State. But it has become clear from the various decisions already cited that such burdens and hindrances may take diverse forms, and indeed appear under various disguises. One form may be a compulsory acquisition of goods, as in *James v Cowan* or the *Peanut* case [(1933) 48 CLR 266], if in truth the expropriation is directed wholly or partially against inter-State trade in the goods, that is, against selling them out of the State. Another form may be that of placing a special burden on the goods in the **[631]** State to which they have come, simply because they have come from the other State, as in the *Vacuum Oil* case [(1934) 51 CLR 108]: more obvious cases are those of undisguised restrictions on passing from State to State. The actual restraint or burden may operate while the goods are still in the State of origin, as in the case of a compulsory expropriation or a standstill order, or it may operate after they have arrived in the other State, as in the *Vacuum Oil* case. In every case it must be a question of fact whether there is an interference with this freedom of passage.

But the disquisition on "[627] free love" and "free speech" offered more by way of literary flourish than by way of constitutional principle; and the new test of "[630] freedom as at the frontier", like so much else in this tangled area, did not mean what it said.

Nor was it responsive to the new divisions which had by this time emerged in the High Court. In February 1929, Sir Owen Dixon had joined the Court. His distinctive approach to s 92 first emerged in the *Transport Cases* of the 1930s, beginning with *Willard v Rawson* (1933) 48 CLR 316. The State Parliaments, to protect their State government railways against competition from interstate road transport, had imposed a variety of licensing schemes and "transport coordination" requirements by which they sought to restrict the commercial carriage of goods by road. Throughout the 1930s the High Court consistently upheld these schemes as not infringing s 92, and Dixon J consistently dissented. In these early dissenting judgments, "the Dixon view" was a more schematic and intellectually elegant version of "the Isaacs view".

O Gilpin Ltd v Commissioner for Road Transport & Tramways (NSW)
(1935) 52 CLR 189

Dixon J: [204] Any act or transaction for which protection is claimed under sec 92 must be a part of trade, commerce or intercourse among the States, that is to say, it must be something done as preparatory to, or in the course of, or as a result of, inter-State movement of persons and things or inter-State communication. There can be no doubt that the use of motor vehicles for the carriage of goods from one State to another for the purpose of sale fulfils this requirement. But it does not follow … that the act of transportation is entirely free from Government control. The question whether sec 92 applies to a given case involves one or more of several considerations which are susceptible of separate examination. First, the nature and operation of the interference or of the exertion of power complained of, must be considered in order to determine whether it amounts to a restriction of or burden upon the acts or transactions for which immunity is claimed … Second, the nature of the acts or transactions found to be restricted or burdened must be examined in order to ascertain whether they are part of inter-State trade, commerce, or intercourse. Third, the nature and incidence of the restriction or burden must be examined in order to determine whether it belongs to that class freedom from which is secured by sec 92. For acts or transactions which in fact occur in the course of inter-State trade may be restrained or burdened in consequence of the intervention by the State in the [205] affairs of the citizen for causes which have no relation or relevance to trade, commerce and intercourse among the States. The expression "trade, commerce, and intercourse among the States" describes a section of social activity by reference to special characteristics. The freedom it gives plainly relates to those characteristics. It is only where they are present that the activity is to be absolutely free. It appears to me to be natural to understand a freedom that is so given as referring to restrictions or burdens imposed in virtue of those characteristics upon the presence of which the grant of immunity is based. It is, perhaps, upon some such reasoning that the interpretation of sec 92 proceeds which confines it to discriminatory laws, that is to forbidding discrimination against inter-State transactions in favour of domestic trade. But that interpretation overlooks the fact that a restriction conditioned on any one of the characteristics which are connoted by the description "trade commerce and intercourse among the States" discriminates against such transactions in favour of transactions from which that characteristic is absent. There is no reason why the freedom should be limited to restrictions based upon the inter-State character of the activity so described. Its character of trade or intercourse is just as essential to the description. "Free" must at least mean free of a restriction or burden placed upon an act because it is commerce, or trade, or intercourse, or because it involves movement into or out of the State. By this I mean that the application of the restriction or burden to the act cannot be made the consequence of that act's being of a commercial or trading character, or of its involving intercourse between two places, or of its involving movement of persons or things into or out of the State.

Very many of the difficulties which have been felt as to a logical application of the words "absolutely free" to inter-State trade, commerce and intercourse, disappear, I think, if it is recognized that it is a freedom from restrictions or burdens which have reference to one or other of the distinguishing features which form the basis of the immunity. Thus a deserting husband might be arrested under a law of a State notwithstanding that his destination lay over the border. But if the State law made his liability to arrest depend not on the fact of desertion but upon his attempting to **[206]** leave the State, I should think that sec 92 would invalidate it. In the first case, his inter-State journey might be interrupted but only as a consequence produced by a law which had no reference to any aspect of trade, commerce and intercourse among the States. In the other case, the State boundary is adopted by the law as the limit of the deserting husband's movement; the inter-State character of his flight is made the reason for his detention.

A law of a State forbidding the mixing of straw chaff with hay chaff would be perfectly good even if such a mixture were desired or required for an inter-State commercial dealing; but, if the law simply penalized the sale of such a mixture, it could not extend to sales made for delivery across the inter-State boundary. The first law applies independently of any quality which goes to constitute inter-State trade, the second depends for its application upon an essential ingredient of commerce, sale ...

Further, it is not every regulation of commerce or of movement that involves a restriction or burden constituting an impairment of freedom. Traffic regulations affecting the lighting and speed of vehicles, tolls for the use of a bridge, prohibition of fraudulent descriptions upon goods, and provisions for the safe carriage of dangerous things, supply examples.

But, given an act or transaction which falls within the conception of trade, commerce, or intercourse among the States and a restriction or burden operating upon that act or transaction, it appears to me that it must be an infringement upon the absolute freedom guaranteed by sec 92 unless the restriction or burden is imposed in virtue of or in reference to none of the essential qualities which are connoted by the description "trade, commerce, and intercourse among the States."

In essence, Dixon J was posing two questions:

1. What is the "criterion of liability" on which the operation of the statute is expressed to depend? That is, what factual element provides the "hook" to which the statute attaches itself, or the "trigger" for its operation? If it is the "interstate" character of a transaction *or* its character as "trade", "commerce" or "intercourse", then s 92 is potentially infringed.

2. Does the law impose a "restriction" or "burden" on the interstate trading activities to which it applies? Or does it merely regulate those activities in a way that does not entail a "restriction" or "burden"? In the latter event, "freedom" is not impaired and s 92 is not infringed.

Evatt J, appointed in 1930, proposed an alternative view. He argued that freedom under s 92 attaches to trade and commerce regarded as a whole and not distributively, so that individuals are not guaranteed freedom for their own particular trade and commerce so long as trade and commerce as a whole remain unimpaired. Evatt J stated his theory most fully in 1933.

R v Vizzard; Ex parte Hill
(1933) 50 CLR 30

Evatt J: [86] The predominant object of sec 92 was to secure free trade and free intercourse among what had formerly been self-governing colonies ... To assert freedom of trade between such organized communities was to lay down in formal expression a well-known economic doctrine and ideal, which was one of the chief motive forces of Federation. Neither the words used, nor the underlying doctrine they declare would seem to warrant an interpretation by which, first, "trade, commerce, and intercourse" is resolved into the infinite number of acts, transactions and operations which must occur in the course of it, secondly, from this infinite aggregation there is subtracted that infinite number of acts, transactions and operations into which "purely domestic" trade can similarly be resolved, and, thirdly, each and every one of the acts, transactions and operations, still infinite in number, which comprise the remainder, the States are rendered unable to touch or regulate in any way whatsoever. Such a test seems to be incapable of satisfactory application. The advance of a criminal towards the border of a State, considered by itself, is as much an "operation" or "act" of intercourse among the States, as the advance of an inter-State traveller from one train to another at a border town. The holding up of a vehicle travelling inter-State and the arrest of its driver because its speed endangers safety or its lights are defective may interfere as much with a "transaction" or "act" of inter-State trade as a decision of a State market authority to postpone the sale of goods simply because their place of origin is another State.

[87] The declaration of sec 92 loses much of its significance if parts of it are analysed separately and the results of the analysis are subsequently put together again. The section, if read as a whole, postulates the free flow of goods inter-State, so that goods produced in any State may be freely marketed in every other State, and so that nothing can lawfully be done to obstruct or prevent such marketing. The section may be infringed by hostile action within the State of origin of the goods, as was attempted to be done in the Dried Fruits legislation of South Australia, or at the border by means of prohibitions upon exit or entry, or by laws preventing or prohibiting sale or exchange within that State to the markets of which the commodities are destined. The declaration of sec 92 covers goods which are consigned to the market as well as goods which have been already sold, and are in the course of delivery, in this sense, that consignment and delivery, being part of commercial intercourse, cannot be prevented or obstructed by State legislation. But this does not necessarily mean that either the common or contract carrier, who is engaged in the business of transport, or the owner, if such there be, who himself carries his goods inter-State in order to sell or deliver, or the agent or servant who is the selected instrument for selling the commodities at the market place, or the person who acts as intermediary in receiving the proceeds of sale and remitting them to the owner in another State – are, each and all of them, at liberty to ignore the general laws of a State which regulate how and when and where goods must be carried, delivered, sold and accounted for ...

[94] Sec 92 does not guarantee that, in each and every part of a transaction which includes the inter-State carriage of commodities, the owner of the commodities, together with his servant and agent and each and every independent contractor co-operating in the delivery and marketing of the commodities, and each of his servants and agents, possesses, until delivery and marketing are completed, a right to ignore State transport or marketing regulations, and to choose how, when and where each of them will transport and market the commodities.

This last paragraph was quoted with approval by the Privy Council in *James v Commonwealth* [1936] AC 578, with the general comment: "[621] The elaborate judgment of Evatt J in that case is of great importance". The "Evatt view", already a major strand in the *Transport Cases*, then became even more influential. In particular, it was reflected in the judgment of Latham CJ in *Milk Board (NSW) v Metropolitan Cream Pty Ltd* (1939) 62 CLR 116, where a 4:1 majority, with Starke J dissenting, held that a compulsory marketing scheme for milk was valid. In that case Latham CJ asserted that it was at least clear "[127] that simple legislative prohibition ..., as distinct from regulation, of inter-State trade and commerce is invalid".

The distinction between "regulation" and "prohibition" was a basis for the decisions in *Australian National Airways Pty Ltd v Commonwealth* (*ANA Case*) (1945) 71 CLR 29 and the *Bank Nationalisation Case* (*Bank of NSW v Commonwealth* (1948) 76 CLR 1 (High Court) and *Commonwealth v Bank of New South Wales* [1950] AC 235 (Privy Council)). Both cases were personal forensic triumphs for Garfield Barwick KC. Moreover, both cases were crucial landmarks in the gradual shift within the High Court towards the dominance of "the Dixon view" of s 92. Dr HV Evatt, as Attorney-General for the Chifley government, may have miscalculated in not realising how far the balance of opinion in the Court had shifted since he had left the bench in 1940. The theory behind the *Australian National Airlines Act 1945* (Cth) was that, so long as adequate services for interstate movement by air were ensured, any relevant requirement of s 92 was thereby satisfied and it did not matter that the means by which it was satisfied was a Commonwealth government monopoly. Similarly, the theory behind the *Banking Act 1947* (Cth) was that, so long as the pre-existing volume and variety of interstate banking services were ensured, s 92 was satisfied, and it did not matter that the services would be rendered only by the Commonwealth Bank. On "the Evatt view" of s 92, with its emphasis on the "free flow" of trade as a whole, these theories might have been justified. However, the High Court was moving inexorably away from "the Evatt view".

The first issue in the *ANA Case* involved the use of s 51(i) of the Constitution to establish the Australian National Airlines Commission. The Commission was to operate a government-owned airline serving interstate routes, in reliance on s 51(i), and flights in and out of the Territories, in reliance on s 122. The High Court held that these provisions were valid. However, the legislation was also designed to give the airline a monopoly over the interstate air carriage of passengers. Holding that the carriage of passengers was itself "trade and commerce" – and thus incidentally undermining the rationale of the *Transport Cases* – the High Court ruled that the exclusion of private competitors was incompatible with s 92.

Australian National Airways Pty Ltd v Commonwealth (*ANA Case*)
(1945) 71 CLR 29

Dixon J: [87] The short effect of these provisions … appears to me to be … to require the Commission, on obtaining a licence, to supply an adequate service for the route licensed and then, when and so long as that is done, to exclude any other inter-State air carrier from the same stopping places by preventing his holding a licence effective for any of them. The principle upon which they proceed evidently is that facilities for the carriage by air for reward of persons and things should be assured, so far as may be, but that, so long as that is done, they should be an exclusively governmental function.

It is not material to inquire why this principle was adopted. It may have been adopted as a matter of policy. On the other hand, it may have been adopted because it was thought that it would involve less inconsistency with the constitutional freedom of trade, commerce and intercourse among the States by internal carriage than if the exclusion from inter-State air routes of all but government airlines were absolute. Some ground for such a view might be found if two assumptions were justified. The first is that trade, commerce and intercourse among the States is nothing but the interchange of goods and the movement of people. The second is that s 92 may be confined by interpretation to a denial to the various governments only of legislative or executive authority to obstruct the flow or reduce the volume in which the people move or the traffic in goods proceeds. If these assumptions were made out, it is, perhaps, not difficult to see in them a basis for a contention that a law establishing a monopoly of a form of transport might be compatible with s 92, provided that it contained sure stipulations for the furnishing of transport or of that form of transport, adequate to the flow or volume …

[89] It is, I think, unnecessary to transcribe once more the passage from the judgment of *Rich* J [in *R v Vizzard; Ex parte Hill* (1933) 50 CLR 30 at 50-1]. But it makes the following points: (1) The State legislation then in question was directed at (*a*) an ordered system of transportation (*b*) without irrational competition tending to its mutual destruction. (2) The operation of the legislation in no way depended upon the inter-State character of the traffic, but applied uniformly to intra-State and inter-State traffic. (3) "A law of that character which did differentiate between the two kinds of traffic might well be held directly to restrain inter-State trade." (4) The legislation regulated and did not suppress transport and it regulated it with a view in the long run to facilitate it by ensuring that a super-abundance of transport at one time did not lead to a deficiency at another. (5) It did not affect actual commercial dealings, the transfer of goods from one place to another, and the actual movement of individuals. (6) It dealt with motor vehicles as a means to trade, commerce and intercourse inter-State and intra-State, "but they are aids or implements to effect the thing, they are not the thing itself."

The last two of these reasons or observations, which I take to be adopted by the majority of the Court as explaining the decisions, have in the past appeared to me to mean that the use of motor vehicles in the carriage of goods from one State to another is an incident of trade, commerce and intercourse, but is not itself protected by s 92. The actual decisions in and the full reasoning of the Transport Cases are plainly shown to be inapplicable by the emphasis placed on the first four of the foregoing points. They have no analogy in the statute now under consideration. But to my mind the feature of the Transport Cases which is material is the sharp differentiation between commercial dealings, or perhaps commercial and other intercourse, on the one hand, and, on the other hand, motor vehicles as means or implements used for that purpose and no more.

We are here concerned with the trade or business of carrying men and goods over inter-State air routes, a thing which I should have thought intrinsically as much inter-State commerce as the sale and delivery of goods from one State to another and, therefore, necessarily **[90]** within the protection of s 92. But does the contrast made in the passage to which I have referred in the judgment of *Rich* J amount to a decision that the trade or business of providing inter-State carriage of men and things does not itself lie within the concept of trade, commerce and intercourse among the States; that it forms no part of the denotation of commerce because it has not the attributes required by the definition though, because it is conducive to commerce, it may in some respects be regulated under the commerce power? After a full study of the Transport Cases I have come to the conclusion that they do not decide this proposition. In the pragmatical solution which those cases gave to a problem which they approach as a complex the essential features of the legislation were examined for the purpose [of] determining its practical operation upon inter-State commerce and intercourse regarded as a sum of activities: to see whether it obstructed, restricted, retarded or impaired, not some operations of commerce considered separately or in isolation, but the commerce between New South Wales and Victoria considered as a whole. The legislation was, in effect, treated as part of an attempt to make the internal transport of the State a planned structure, a framework within which the freedom guaranteed by s 92 subsisted and even by which that freedom was secured. The reasons given for the solution necessarily comprised much that was really directed to denying that in the character and operation of the legislation factors or features could be found to which s 92 was inimical. It is, I think, in the course of this demonstration that, among other things, any adverse effect upon the flow of trade is excluded and the relation in fact which transport has to trade in goods is emphasized. It is to be noticed that it is not the business of inter-State carrying but motor trucks themselves which *Rich* J describes as aids or implements to commerce and intercourse but not the thing itself. The decision was, I think, based upon a combination of all the considerations mentioned in the passage, negative and positive, particularly the fact that it was the undifferentiated road transport of the State that was regulated on a non-discriminatory basis.

The *Airlines Act*, however, appears to me to raise quite a different question. It is whether the elimination by governmental action, legislative and executive, of the business of inter-State transportation as such in favour of a State undertaking is consistent with s 92. If the test laid down by Lord *Wright* in *James v Commonwealth* [[1936] AC 578 at 639], freedom at the frontier, be applied, it is plain that it is because the business involves crossing the frontier that it is eliminated. It is **[91]** not like the post office, something which undertakes an exclusive function independently of State boundaries. Nor, may it be added, does it resemble the post office in being a traditional function of government, dealt with as such in the Constitution, and nowhere forming a business. It is no answer to the application of Lord *Wright's* test to say that, because the general exclusion in time and place of the business of air transport in favour of a government undertaking could only be accomplished under the commerce power, the freedom infringed must necessarily be related to State boundaries. If, on the other hand, the answer is offered that the transmutation of the business into a government undertaking means that the function is still freely carried on, it is met by the proposition, so often enunciated by *Isaacs* J, that in s 92 "free" means free from governmental restriction or obstruction, whether legislative or executive … It comes back, in my opinion, to the position of the business of inter-State transportation as part of commerce and intercourse. If it is part of the denotation of that expression in s 92, as I think it clearly must be, then I see no escape from the conclusion that Part IV is inconsistent with that constitutional restraint. If, on the other hand, carrying on inter-State transportation were held to be outside the protection of s 92, it would be hard indeed to bring it directly under s 51(i).

The *Banking Act 1947* (Cth) envisaged the progressive exclusion of private banks from the business of banking. In the *Bank Nationalisation Case*, the High Court held by 4:2, Latham CJ and McTiernan J dissenting, that this was incompatible with the "freedom" to conduct such business interstate. The result was a high point in the "individual rights" approach to s 92.

Bank of NSW v Commonwealth (Bank Nationalisation Case)
(1948) 76 CLR 1

Rich and Williams JJ: [283] [T]he freedom guaranteed by s 92 is a personal right attaching to the individual … [In *James v Cowan* (1930) 43 CLR 386 at 418] *Isaacs* J referring to the expropriation of goods by a State, said: "The question is, how has the personal right of trading inter-State by the former owner been interfered with? That is a personal right, not a property right." In the *Peanut Case* [48 CLR at 288] *Dixon* J said: "The provisions operate directly upon the individual grower's liberty of disposing of the peanuts he produces for sale." In *O Gilpin Ltd v Commissioner for Road Transport and Tramways* (NSW) [(1935) 52 CLR 189 at 211] *Dixon* J said: "Trade, commerce and intercourse among the States is an expression which describes the activities of individuals. The object of s 92 is to enable individuals to conduct their commercial dealings and their personal intercourse with one another independently of State boundaries." In *James v Commonwealth* [[1936] AC 578 at 614], Lord *Wright*, in delivering the judgment of the Privy Council, said section 92 may seem to be, "a constitutional guarantee of rights, analogous to the guarantee of religious freedom in s 116, or of equal rights of all residents in all States in s 117." … It is to be noted that His Lordship groups with s 92 ss 116 and 117, that the provision in s 116 that no religious test **[284]** shall be required as a qualification for any office or public trust under the Commonwealth is an express personal guarantee, and that s 117 is also an express personal guarantee. His Lordship would appear therefore also to have been of opinion that the freedom guaranteed by s 92 is a personal right.

The infringement of s 92 was only one of several constitutional grounds for the High Court decision. Nevertheless, it was only as to s 92 that the Commonwealth appealed to the Privy Council. The appeal was brought under s 74 of the Constitution on the theory that s 92 did not involve an "inter se question", that is, it did not affect the distribution of legislative powers between the Commonwealth and the States. In the Privy Council, however, their Lordships held that decision of the s 92 issue might inevitably lead them into discussion of the inter se questions, and hence that they had no jurisdiction. Nevertheless, they went on to express their opinion on s 92 in a massive obiter dictum affirming Dixon J's "individual rights" approach to s 92. The argument had occupied 37 sitting days, during which two of their Lordships, Lord Uthwatt and Lord du Parcq, died. Much of this time was devoted to submissions made by Evatt as Attorney-General. His opening argument alone took 14 days.

Commonwealth v Bank of New South Wales (Bank Nationalisation Case)
[1950] AC 235

Lord Porter (for their Lordships): [299] The view which their Lordships have expressed that no appeal lies to them without a certificate from the High Court of Australia is conclusive of the case and in normal circumstances they would not give any opinion upon the many other matters argued before them … But for two reasons they think it right to state their views upon the question to which so large a part of the argument of the appellants was directed, viz whether s 46 of the Act offends against s 92 of the Constitution; first, because it might yet be possible to apply for, and if the High Court should think fit to grant it, to obtain a certificate which would enable the appellants to reargue a case already fully argued, and, secondly, because it appears to them that a large part of the appellants' argument was based upon a misapprehension of two cases already decided by this Board which it is their Lordships' duty so far as they can to correct …

[302] The view which at one time appeared to be put forward in argument, that the words in s 92 "whether by means of internal carriage or ocean navigation" restricted its operation **[303]** to such things and persons as are carried by land or sea, has long since been rejected and cannot be entertained. The business of banking, consisting of the creation and transfer of credit, the making of loans, the purchase and disposal of investments and other kindred activities, is a part of the trade, commerce and intercourse of a modern society and, in so far as it is carried on by means of inter-State transactions, is within the ambit of s 92. On this part of the case they respectfully adopt the language and reasoning of Dixon J, to which they can add nothing.

The business of banking being an activity of which the freedom is protected by s 92, the next question is whether the Act offends that section, and their Lordships turn at once to the cases of *James v Cowan* [[1932] AC 542] and *James v Commonwealth* [[1936] AC 578] ...

[305] The necessary implications of these decisions are important. First may be mentioned an argument strenuously maintained on this appeal that s 92 ... does not guarantee the freedom of individuals. Yet James was an individual and James vindicated his freedom in hard won fights. Clearly there is here a misconception. It is true, as has been said more than once in the High Court, that s 92 does not create any new juristic rights, but it does give the citizen of State or Common-wealth, as the case may be, the right to ignore, and, if necessary, to call on the judicial power to help him to resist, legislative or executive action which offends against the section. And this is just what James successfully did ...

[309] [T]he Act now under consideration operate[s] to restrict the freedom of inter-State trade, commerce and intercourse not remotely or incidentally, but directly. On this, and on a cognate matter, the distinction between restrictions which are regulatory and do not offend against s 92 and those which are something more than regulatory and do so offend, their Lordships think it proper to make certain further observations. It is generally recognized that the expression "free" in s 92 though **[310]** emphasized by the accompanying "absolutely," yet must receive some qualification ... As long ago as 1916 in *Duncan v Queensland* [22 CLR at 573], Sir Samuel Griffith CJ said: "But the word 'free' does not mean extra legem any more than freedom means anarchy. We boast of being an absolutely free people, but that does not mean that we are not subject to law," and through all the subsequent cases in which s 92 has been discussed, the problem has been to define the qualification of that which in the Constitution is left unqualified. In this labyrinth there is no golden thread. But it seems that two general propositions may be accepted: (1) that regulation of trade, commerce and intercourse among the States is compatible with its absolute freedom, and (2) that s 92 is violated only when a legislative or executive act operates to restrict such trade, com-merce and intercourse directly and immediately as distinct from creating some indirect or consequential impediment which may fairly be regarded as remote. In the application of these general propositions ..., there cannot fail to be differences of opinion. The problem to be solved will often be not so much legal as political, social, or economic, yet it must be solved by a court of law. For where the dispute is, as here, not only between Commonwealth and citizen but between Commonwealth and intervening States on the one hand and citizens and States on the other, it is only the court that can decide the issue. It is vain to invoke the voice of Parliament.

Difficult as the application of these general propositions must be in the infinite variety of situations that in peace or in war confront a nation, it appears to their Lordships that this further guidance may be given. In the recent case of *Australian National Airways Proprietary Ltd v Commonwealth* [(1945) 71 CLR 29 at 61], the learned Chief Justice used these words: "I venture to repeat what I said in the former case [viz, the '*Milk*' case' [(1939) 62 CLR 116 at 127]]: 'One proposition which I regard as established is that simple legislative prohibition (Federal **[311]** or State), as distinct from regulation, of inter-State trade and commerce is invalid. Further, a law which is "directed against" inter-State trade and commerce is invalid. Such a law does not regulate such trade, it merely prevents it. But a law prescribing rules as to the manner in which trade (including transport) is to be conducted is not a mere prohibition and may be valid in its application to inter-State trade, notwithstanding s 92.'" With this statement, which both repeats the general proposition and precisely states that simple prohibition is not regulation, their Lordships agree. And it is, as they think, a test which must have led the Chief Justice to a different conclusion in this case had he decided that the business of banking was within the ambit of s 92. They do not doubt that it led him to a correct decision in the *Airways* case [71 CLR at 61]. There he said: "In the present case the Act is directed against all competition with the inter-State services of the Commission. The exclusion of other services is based simply upon the fact that the competing services are themselves inter-State services ... The exclusion of competition with the Commission is not a system of regula-tion and is, in my opinion, a violation of s 92 ...". Mutatis mutandis these words may be applied to the Act now impugned, for it is an irrelevant factor that the prohibition prohibits inter-State and intra-State activities at the same time.

Yet about this, as about every other proposition in this field, a reservation must be made. For their Lordships do not intend to lay it down that in no circumstances could the exclusion of competition so as to create a monopoly either in a State or Commonwealth agency or in some other body be justified. Every case must be judged on its own facts and in its own setting of time and circumstance, and it may be that in regard to some economic activities and at some stage of social development it might be maintained that prohibition with a view to State monopoly was the only practical and reasonable manner of regulation, and that inter-State trade, commerce and intercourse thus prohibited and thus monopolized remained absolutely free.

Nor can one further aspect of prohibition be ignored. It was urged by the appellants that prohibitory measures must be permissible, for otherwise lunatics, infants and bankrupts could without restraint embark on inter-State trade, and **[312]** diseased cattle or noxious drugs could freely be taken across State frontiers. Their Lordships must therefore add, what, but for this argument so strenuously urged, they would have thought it unnecessary to add, that regulation of trade may clearly take the form of denying certain activities to persons by age or circumstances unfit to perform them, or of excluding from passage across the frontier of a State creatures or things calculated to injure its citizens. Here again a question of fact and degree is involved …

The same difficulty arises in applying the other discriminatory test, that between a restriction which is direct and one that is too remote. Yet the distinction is a real one, and their Lordships have no doubt on which side of the boundary the present case falls. It is the direct and immediate result of the Act to restrict the freedom of trade, commerce and intercourse among the States.

Their Lordships will not attempt to define this boundary. An analogous difficulty in one section of constitutional law, namely, in the determination of the question where legislative power resides, has led to the use of such phrases as "pith and substance" in relation to a particular enactment. These phrases … [may] serve a useful purpose in the process of deciding whether an enactment which works some interference with trade, commerce **[313]** and intercourse among the States is, nevertheless, untouched by s 92 as being essentially regulatory in character. But where, as here, no question of regulatory legislation can fairly be said to arise, they do not help in solving the problems which s 92 presents. Used as they have been to advance the argument of the appellants they but illustrate the way in which the human mind tries, and vainly tries, to give to a particular subject-matter a higher degree of definition than it will admit. In the field of constitutional law – and particularly in relation to a federal constitution – this is conspicuously true, and it applies equally to the use of the words "direct" and "remote" as to "pith and substance." But it appears to their Lordships that, if these two tests are applied: first, whether the effect of the Act is in a particular respect direct or remote; and, secondly, whether in its true character it is regulatory, the area of dispute may be considerably narrower. It is beyond hope that it should be eliminated.

The *ANA Case* and the *Bank Nationalisation Case* had obviously undermined the reasoning of the 1930s *Transport Cases*. *McCarter v Brodie* (1950) 80 CLR 432 was an attempt to persuade the High Court, in light of the *Bank Nationalisation Case*, that the *Transport Cases* should be overruled. The attempt failed by 4:2, with Dixon and Fullagar JJ dissenting.

McCarter v Brodie
(1950) 80 CLR 432

Dixon J: [465] I do not think that there is any room for doubting that their Lordships have rejected as erroneous three propositions that have often been put forward. The first is "that sec 92 of the Constitution does not guarantee the freedom of individuals." The second is "that, if the same volume of trade flowed from State to State before as after the interference with the individual trader … then the freedom of trade among the States remained unimpaired." The third relates to the relevance of absence of discrimination. As I understand it their Lordships have rejected the theory that because a law applies alike to inter-State commerce and to the domestic commerce of a State, it may escape objection notwithstanding that it prohibits restricts or burdens inter-State commerce …

There are two further matters settled by the decision of their Lordships that are relevant to the basis upon which the *Transport* **[466]** *Cases* appear to me to rest. One is that the object or purpose of an Act challenged as contrary to s 92 is to be ascertained from what is enacted and consists in the necessary legal effect of the law itself and not in its ulterior effect socially or economically. The other is that the question what is the pith and substance of the impugned law, though possibly of help in considering whether it is nothing but a regulation of a class of transactions forming part of trade and commerce, is beside the point when the law amounts to a prohibition or the question of regulation cannot fairly arise. Now I think that every one of these five errors will be found to have a place in what in the passage I have quoted I ventured to call the pragmatical solution which the *Transport Cases* gave to a problem they approached as a complex ...

The combination of ideas upon which, according to my **[467]** view, the *Transport Cases* are based, consists therefore of no element which can survive.

A further attempt to reopen the *Transport Cases* was made in *Hughes and Vale Pty Ltd v New South Wales* (1953) 87 CLR 49. By this time, Sir Owen Dixon was Chief Justice. The rest of the Court divided 3:3, with Fullagar, Kitto and Taylor JJ adopting "the Dixon view" and McTiernan, Williams and Webb JJ reaffirming the *Transport Cases*. In these circumstances, Dixon CJ voted against his own view, electing to reaffirm the decision in *McCarter v Brodie*.

Hughes and Vale Pty Ltd v New South Wales
(1953) 87 CLR 49

Dixon CJ: [70] The strength of the considerations against refusing to follow that decision is very great. It is a recent decision of this Court dealing with the very question of the authority of the *Transport Cases*. It was fully considered and, whether many of the reasons and the conclusion of those cases are, as I think, or are not, at variance with the principles expounded in the *Banking Case* [[1950] AC 235], nothing has occurred since this Court decided *McCarter v Brodie* [(1950) 80 CLR 432] adding to or altering the considerations then before the Court. These circumstances, in my opinion, make it right to decline to enter upon a reconsideration of *McCarter v Brodie* unless independent reasons exist for overruling it which appear to be imperative.

I do not waiver [*sic*] at all in my belief that the transport cases cannot be reconciled with principle or in the opinion that the grounds on which they were in fact decided have for the most part been expressly rejected in the judgment of the Privy Council in the *Banking Case*, but I do not regard that as enough. I believe, however, that I would regard it as an imperative judicial necessity to overrule *McCarter v Brodie* if it appeared inevitable that the consequences of the decision would extend beyond the subject of commercial transport by road and would make it necessary to hold that over the whole area of inter-State trade commerce and intercourse a power existed in every legislature to impose a prohibition subject to a licence to be granted or refused at the discretion of the Executive. At first sight it may seem that these consequences ought logically to ensue, if the decision is allowed to stand. Nevertheless, after a full re-examination of the *Transport Cases* in the light of the reasons of the majority of the Court in *McCarter v Brodie*, I have come to the con[c]lusion that the application of these cases may be confined to the particular conditions or considerations which arise from the fact that the railways and the roads form facilities for the carriage of goods (and presumably of passengers) for the provision and maintenance of which the State is responsible.

This led to an immediate appeal to the Privy Council. In *Hughes and Vale Pty Ltd v New South Wales* [1955] AC 241, the Privy Council held that "the Dixon view" of s 92 was correct. Their Lordships' judgment consisted mainly of long quotations from earlier judgments, including passages from the judgments of Dixon and Fullagar JJ in *McCarter v Brodie* and from the judgment of Dixon CJ in *Hughes & Vale* itself. The Dixon view had prevailed.

The mature "Dixon view", as vindicated by the Privy Council in *Hughes & Vale*, was a combination of elements from Dixon J's original *O Gilpin* dissent with the "two general propositions" identified by the Privy Council in the *Bank Nationalisation Case*. The resulting combination had a number of distinctive features:

1. Plaintiffs were protected only in respect of activity forming part of interstate trade, and the boundaries of interstate activity were narrowly drawn.

2. The validity of legislation was to be determined by its "direct" legal effect and not by its practical or economic effect. Whether legislation had a "direct effect" on interstate trade was

to be determined legalistically by looking to its "criterion of operation" in the manner foreshadowed in Dixon J's *O Gilpin* dissent.

3.   There was a willingness to take a pragmatic view of what constituted permissible "regulation" of interstate trade. The Dixon Court was also pragmatic in another sense. In cases which might have been expected to raise the issue of "regulation", a solution was frequently found by applying the points referred to in 1 and 2 above. As a result, the Court's definition of permissible "regulation" remained relatively undeveloped.

The first point above was reflected in *Grannall v Marrickville Margarine Pty Ltd* (1955) 93 CLR 55, where it was held that, although manufacture or production may be an essential preliminary condition of interstate trade, it is nevertheless not part of interstate trade. The defendant was prosecuted under s 22A of the *Dairy Industry Act 1915* (NSW), which prohibited the manufacture of margarine without a licence. A substantial proportion of the defendant's margarine was to be sold interstate. The Court held that s 22A was valid.

Grannall v Marrickville Margarine Pty Ltd
(1955) 93 CLR 55

Dixon CJ, McTiernan, Webb and Kitto JJ: [79] Two tendencies have grown manifest of late. One is to press the operation of s 92 beyond the subject matter of trade, commerce and intercourse among the States so that it denies to the legislatures of this country the power to impose any prohibition, restriction or burden if its consequences could be seen in what was done or not done in the course of inter-State commerce. The other is to seek to extend the freedom which s 92 guarantees to trade, commerce and intercourse among the States to antecedent or subsequent transactions on the plea that they are incidental, ancillary or conducive to inter-State transactions or necessarily consequential upon them. There is in truth nothing to justify such notions which would go far to exclude legislative power the existence of which has never been doubted.

These criticisms were directed specifically at submissions put to the Court by Barwick QC; and when in 1964 Barwick succeeded Dixon as Chief Justice, his attempts to extend the degree of immunity conferred by s 92 – either by reinterpreting "the Dixon view", or by criticising it as an unwarranted modification of what the Privy Council had said in the *Bank Nationalisation Case* – proved increasingly divisive. Three main issues were involved.

First, the Dixon Court had set strict limits on the extent of interstate trade at both ends of the interstate transaction. As to activities in the exporting State, *Grannall v Marrickville Margarine* had established that acts "preparatory or antecedent" to interstate trade did not form part of such trade. As to activities in the importing State, *Wragg v New South Wales* (1953) 88 CLR 353 had held that "the first sale across the border" was not part of interstate trade either. At both ends, the activity thus excluded from the continuum of "interstate trade" was not protected by s 92. Barwick CJ sought to extend the ambit of "interstate trade" at both ends. As to the "first sale across the border" his view ultimately prevailed, probably as early as *SOS (Mowbray) Pty Ltd v Mead* (1972) 124 CLR 529, and certainly by the time of *North Eastern Dairy Co Ltd v Dairy Industry Authority of NSW* (1975) 134 CLR 559 – either because the first sale across the border was part of interstate trade, or at least because it was, in the language of *Fergusson v Stevenson* (1951) 84 CLR 421, "**[435]** an inseparable concomitant or consequence" of interstate trade. However, as to processes of manufacture or production preparatory to interstate trade, the Dixon view prevailed.

Secondly, Kitto J (in particular) continued to insist that the "direct effect" of a law must be appraised by reference to its "direct legal effect" as ascertained from its "express terms". The "direct effect" could not include – indeed, such a formula was designed to exclude – "**[31]** the commercial or economic or practical consequences" of legislation. By contrast, Barwick CJ insisted that the "direct effect" on interstate trade was a matter of substance and included direct economic effects. On both these issues, the attempt to limit the authority of cases like *Grannall v Marrickville Margarine* provoked an anguished protest from Kitto J.

Samuels v Readers' Digest Association Pty Ltd
(1969) 120 CLR 1

Kitto J: [30] The *Margarine Cases* were cases of manufacture, but the principle for which they are authorities is missed if they are thought of as having been decided as they were because of some consideration applying exclusively to manufacture. The ratio decidendi had to do, not with anything peculiar to manufacture, but with the distinction between laws which impose by their own force restrictions or burdens upon the very things which s 92 protects, namely inter-State trade, commerce and intercourse themselves, and laws which impose restrictions or burdens upon things antecedent or preparatory or collateral to inter-State trade, commerce or intercourse and affect such trade, commerce and intercourse as a matter only of economic or practical consequence. The application of that ratio decidendi to cases other than cases of manufacture is not an extension or development of the law as laid down in the *Margarine Cases* and the long line of cases from which they extract the essence. It is not open to be condemned as resulting rather from a pursuit of logic than upon the actual provisions of the Constitution. The purpose of the test which Dixon J propounded is the exact opposite. **[31]** It is to bring thought on the subject back to the very terms of the Constitution, and to insist that since s 92 decrees freedom for nothing but trade, commerce and intercourse among the States no considerations of logic or supposed reasonableness should be allowed to extend the freedom beyond that concept to facts, events or things which, though incidental or ancillary or conducive to or necessarily consequential upon some activity of trade, commerce or intercourse neither form part and parcel of it nor give it the quality of inter-Stateness. It seems to me that when such a precisely-worded statement of principle has been worked out by strenuous thought over a long period of years, and has been made the basis of the Court's decisions in a succession of cases on the ground of its exactness in defining a complicated concept which the Constitution expresses with economy of language, the national interest is well served by a continuing acknowledgment that to that extent certainty as to the meaning of the Constitution has been achieved.

Insofar as Barwick CJ was trying to move beyond formalist or legalist constraints by taking account of what Kitto J called "**[31]** commercial or economic or practical consequences", he was sounding a theme to which a new generation of High Court judges were responsive. In *North Eastern Dairy Co Ltd v Dairy Industry Authority of NSW* (1975) 134 CLR 559, Mason and Jacobs JJ were notably alert to the "**[606]** practical effect" of laws. On this flank, the attack by Barwick CJ on "the Dixon view" largely succeeded. Yet, by shifting the focus to greater awareness of economic realities, he undermined some of the pragmatic compromises which had helped to maintain the broad consensus of the Dixon years. The very judges most likely to accept the call for awareness of economic realities were also the ones most likely to resist any drastic extension of the impact of s 92 on legislative control of the economy.

Thirdly, while widening the concepts of "interstateness" and of "direct effect", Barwick CJ sought to narrow the concept of permissible "regulation". Again, the effect was to widen the scope of s 92. Barwick CJ spelled out his approach in a series of cases beginning with *Harper v Victoria* (1966) 114 CLR 361 and culminating in the *Readers' Digest Case*.

Barwick CJ: [14] I feel it appropriate to observe at the outset that a constitutional provision to prevent at least the members of a federation, which in relation to trade and commerce is what we would now call a common market, from making or so operating laws as to inhibit the freedom of trade and commerce between them is necessary and indeed indispensable … [I]t is clearly not enough to prevent customs barriers at the territorial margins of the constituent integers of the federation. This in the Australian Constitution is done by s 90. The inhibition of the freedom of trade and commerce can take such multifarious and at times seemingly innocent forms and its prevention is so vital to the commercial life of the members of the federation as well as of the federation as a whole that only sweeping and absolute language is appropriate to express the necessary constitutional provision. The ingenuity of the present as well as of the near and distant future must be securely guarded against. Also, the unintended as well as the intended interference with the freedom of inter-State trade and commerce must be covered. This is particularly so where, as in Australia, we are not a federation of separate and distinct peoples. The advantages of the freedom of national trade [are] for this reason of peculiar advantage to all Australians wherever they may chance to reside.

Perhaps there is no need in the nature of a common market to deny to the central Government or authority any power to inhibit such freedom, though in the market set up by the Treaty of Rome which has a provision to protect the freedom of trade and commerce between the members, the common market authorities themselves have in fact no such power, not because it is expressly denied but because it is not given. But the founders of the Australian Constitution were emphatic that no government in the [15] federation should have the power to inhibit the freedom of trade, commerce or intercourse between the constituent members. Thus the Commonwealth as well as the States is bound by s 92. This creates the gap in legislative power to which reference has been made.

Yet it is the freedom of trade and commerce which is to be maintained. This of its nature, in my opinion, involves laws regulating the relationships of free men to each other and to their institutions within a society. It is not, in my opinion, that freedom is qualified by such laws. It is not really that there is a freedom "from" something. It is a freedom of – and therefore to – trade. It is the concept of freedom in a civilized society, in contrast with unbridled licence in a lawless state which itself involves the necessity for laws of the kind which accommodate one man's activities to those of another so that each is free to trade within the society organized under and controlled by law.

The limitations upon s 92, in my opinion, are thus to be found in the concept of freedom and not in qualifications imposed on that concept. The constitutional provision remains the text to be applied to the circumstances of each case as it arises rather than tests or formulae. No gloss upon it and no test for its enforcement can rise above it or qualify it. Of its nature it demands a liberal construction and application and does not warrant any judicial attempt to restrict its connotation or to limit its operation. On the other hand, failure to observe and effectuate the limitation inherent in the concept of freedom of trade and commerce ... can well result in unwarranted restrictions upon the ability of the legislatures to secure the society and its members against practices and activities which are incompatible with the maintenance of freedom of trade and commerce in a civilized society. There is thus a need in each case closely to observe a nicety of balance between freedom of trade and commerce and the permissible restrictive legislation of a free and civilized society which is compatible with that freedom.

In this passage Barwick CJ adopted an extremely narrow view of "regulation". He argued that laws are "regulatory" in a way which is compatible with freedom of trade and commerce only if what they regulate is the freedom of trade and commerce itself. Thus, trade practices legislation would be compatible with "freedom" of trade and commerce because it promotes competition (see *Mikasa (NSW) Pty Ltd v Festival Stores* (1972) 127 CLR 617), whereas laws restrictive of competition are unlikely to be compatible with "freedom" of interstate trade. However, this notion of "regulation" gained little judicial support. If anything, it provoked a counter-reaction towards a wider view of permissible "regulation" based on the public interest.

North Eastern Dairy Co Ltd v Dairy Industry Authority of NSW (1975) 134 CLR 559 concerned regulations made under the *Pure Food Act 1908* (NSW) to prohibit the supply or sale in New South Wales of pasteurised milk for human consumption unless the pasteurisation was authorised under the *Dairy Industry Authority Act 1970* (NSW). The practical effect was to prohibit the sale of milk in New South Wales unless it was pasteurised in New South Wales.

The Court held that since the scheme applied to "the first sale across the border" it affected interstate trade, and that its practical effect was to burden the interstate trade in milk. Its public health rationale did not save it because the restrictions went beyond what was reasonably necessary. However, the judgments reaffirmed strongly that a law appropriately tailored to protection of public health would be valid as reasonable regulation, even if it directly burdened interstate trade. Even Barwick CJ conceded that laws ensuring public health (and limited to what was reasonably necessary for that purpose) might not infringe s 92.

Permewan Wright Consolidated Pty Ltd v Trewhitt (1979) 145 CLR 1 involved a marketing scheme for Victorian eggs administered by the Egg Marketing Board under the *Marketing of Primary Products Act 1958* (Vic). In order to ensure the quality of eggs sold by retail in Victoria, s 41D of the Act made it an offence to sell by retail any eggs not graded and tested for quality by the Board, and marked or stamped to that effect under the Act. By s 41C, the Board could charge fees to cover the cost of its activities. The Permewan Wright company was charged with selling eggs by retail without complying with s 41D. The eggs were produced by a New South Wales consortium, Bartters Enterprises, which had appointed Permewan Wright as the agent for the sale of its eggs in Victoria. Since the eggs had already been tested and graded under New South Wales law, it was argued that the expense, inconvenience and delay arising from further testing in Victoria would amount to a burden on interstate trade.

All six judges held that the sale of the eggs in Victoria was part of interstate trade. Gibbs J cited the *North Eastern Dairy Case* to hold that the sale "[17] was an inseparable concomitant of Bartters' interstate trade". However, the legislation was held to constitute permissible regulation, with Barwick CJ and Aickin J dissenting. The point was made most fully by Stephen J.

Permewan Wright Consolidated Pty Ltd v Trewhitt
(1979) 145 CLR 1

Stephen J: [25] The reason why public health has had such ready judicial acceptance as a proper area for valid legislative intervention, despite s 92, is, perhaps, because with it is associated a relatively long history of legislative intervention in the past, the fruits of which have led to a general acceptance by the community of the need for such legislation. Whether by a conscious use of judicial notice or by some less conscious absorption of community acceptance, there has at all events been a quite general judicial recognition of such laws as ones which may validly bear upon and restrict interstate trade.

The law in question in the present case is not simply a general public health measure; it has two distinct aspects, one relates to that area of public health concerned with the fixing and enforcement of standards for perishable foodstuffs, the other to an elementary form of consumer protection and fair dealing in trade, requiring fair weights and measures and accurate labelling as to weights and quantities. This latter aspect, no less than that of public health, possesses a long history of legislative intervention and accompanying public acceptance and, in terms of permissible regulation for the purposes of s 92, can, I think, stand in no different position from public health …

[26] Interstate trade and those engaged in it cannot in my view be treated in total isolation from the activities of the community as a whole. The existence of areas of anarchy, beyond the reach of the law, in a community is as injurious to that whole community, including the part of it which is concerned with interstate trade, as is such a state of anarchy if confined to interstate trade itself. Neither is, in my view, predicated by the existence in our Constitution of s 92. It is well established that, consistently with s 92, the guaranteed freedom of interstate trade must be qualified in the interests of those engaged in that trade, so that there may be a mutual accommodation of their rights and actions, each being free in respect of that trade though none has licence in it. It cannot be any less consistent with s 92 that its guaranteed freedom should also be qualified in the interests of the community at large …

[27] The boundaries of permissible regulation extend, in my view, at least as far as to include such traditional areas of legislative intervention as the protection of standards of public health by ensuring the purity and wholesomeness of foodstuffs and the prohibition of deceptive or fraudulent practices engaged in by traders to the detriment of the public …

For a law to be valid as permissible regulation for the purposes of s 92 its effect upon interstate trade must be no more restrictive than is reasonably necessary in all the circumstances and if it is shown to discriminate against that trade it will forfeit its claim to be no more than regulatory …

[29] There is, in my view, no element of discrimination present in this legislation, nor in the evidence adduced as to its administration … Nor can I regard as unreasonably restrictive of interstate trade a legislative requirement, in the case of a commodity such as eggs, that it should be made subject to the sort of impartial testing and grading which the present Act and regulations contemplate, processes which the legislature may well have concluded should not be entrusted to producers generally but only to a government agency and to those whom that agency authorizes and whose operations it can supervise. Eggs are so notoriously perishable a foodstuff that in their deteriorated state they have much enriched the English language in a number of picturesque phrases. There are, perhaps, few other foodstuffs which combine the qualities of being so dependent for their wholesomeness upon freshness, of being so prone to deterioration and the freshness of which at the time of purchase it is so difficult for the consumer to determine from outward appearance. They are not merely perishable but are enigmatic to the ordinary shopper; nor is this quality confined to their state of freshness, it can be no easy matter to distinguish by eye alone between the various weight-related grades of egg.

Another source of instability undermining the Barwick view of s 92 was the view of Murphy J, first spelled out in *Buck v Bavone* (1976) 135 CLR 110, that only "discriminatory fiscal burdens" on interstate trade were prohibited by s 92. The argument relied in part on the extra-judicial afterthoughts of Lord Wright, who delivered the Privy Council judgment in *James v Commonwealth* [1936] AC 578. Writing in retirement 18 years later ("Section 92 – A Problem Piece" (1954) 1 *Sydney Law Review* 145), Lord Wright concluded that *James v Commonwealth* had been wrongly decided, and that the extended reading of s 92 had been "**[156]** very detrimental to the idea of freedom under the rule of law". Instead, he now argued, s 92 should be understood as "so limited that it cannot affect the general law, except on the narrow topic of fiscal affairs. Its scope is exhausted when it has excluded any operation of a fiscal character … **[157]** The idea of s 92 as a power in the air brooding and ready in the name of freedom to crush and destroy social and industrial or political experiments in Australian life ought, I think, to be exploded. In truth, as I said, s 92 is both pedestrian and humble".

The disarray to which diverging tendencies on the High Court had reduced the Court's view of s 92 was starkly revealed in *Clark King & Co Pty Ltd v Australian Wheat Board* (1978) 140 CLR 120 and *Uebergang v Australian Wheat Board* (1980) 145 CLR 266. Both cases involved a challenge to the Australian Wheat Board, which, under the *Wheat Industry Stabilization Acts* of the Commonwealth and of the States, compulsorily acquired all wheat in Australia at a fixed price. The Board then marketed that wheat in Australia and overseas, with any profits going into a stabilisation fund used to maintain the price paid to growers in years in which a loss was made. In both cases the focus was on the Privy Council's curious "**[311]** reservation" in the *Bank Nationalisation Case* [1950] AC 235 to the effect that "prohibition with a view to State monopoly" might sometimes be "the only practicable and reasonable manner of regulation".

In *Clark King*, Mason and Jacobs JJ held that the wheat stabilisation scheme was "**[188]** the only practical and reasonable manner of regulation". Barwick CJ and Stephen J held that it was not and that s 92 was infringed. Murphy J agreed with Mason and Jacobs JJ that s 92 was not infringed, but did so on the basis of his *Buck v Bavone* argument that no "discriminatory fiscal burden" was involved. The result was a 3:2 decision that rested on no majority principle.

The judgments in *Uebergang* arose from a preliminary application for directions and again concerned the validity of the *Wheat Industry Stabilization Acts*. The question was: what facts, if any, might be adduced in evidence as bearing on the question of validity under s 92? Barwick CJ and Aickin J held that no evidence could affect the outcome, since the wheat scheme was clearly invalid. Murphy J held that no evidence could affect the outcome, since the scheme was clearly valid. Gibbs and Wilson JJ formulated a stringent test of validity that could only be satisfied "**[301]** in exceptional circumstances". They argued that what would need to be shown would be "that a monopoly covering both intrastate and interstate trade is the only practicable and reasonable course open in present circumstances". Stephen and Mason JJ developed a more moderate test, arguing that what was needed was "**[306]** such material as would enable the Court to determine whether or not the restrictions which the legislation imposes upon interstate trade are no greater than are reasonably necessary in all the circumstances". *Uebergang* never came on for hearing on its merits.

In *Miller v TCN Channel Nine Pty Ltd* (1986) 161 CLR 556, Channel Nine had been prosecuted for use of an unauthorised television transmitter in a network link between Sydney and Brisbane. In *Buck v Bavone* Murphy J had offset his constricted reading of s 92 by asserting that the Constitution embodied an *implied* guarantee of interstate freedom of movement. In later cases he had extended this conception to a general freedom of movement and communication, including interstate communication (see Chapter 28, §2; and see especially *McGraw-Hinds (Aust) Pty Ltd v Smith* (1979) 144 CLR 633 at 670). The *TCN Nine* case was devised in part to test this conception; and Murphy J, in his last High Court judgment, upheld Channel Nine's appeal on that basis. The other six judges rejected any such "implied guarantee", and turned to s 92. For them, new difficulties arose as to the "antecedents" or "inseparable concomitants" of interstate transmission. A clear majority held that s 92 protected Channel Nine's *use* of its transmitter, but that the original *erection* of the transmitter was not protected since this was merely "antecedent" to interstate transmission. As to the intermediate issue of *maintenance* of the transmitter, no clear view emerged. Further complications arose as to whether the different prohibitions, of establishing, erecting, maintaining or using an unauthorised transmitter, were "severable" under s 15A of the *Acts Interpretation Act 1901* (Cth). In the end Gibbs CJ, Mason, Deane and Dawson JJ held that, even though the *use* of the transmitter was protected by s 92, the channel could validly be prosecuted for its erection. Brennan J agreed on the basis that the whole scheme was only "regulatory" and thus did not infringe s 92. Only two judges decided in favour of the channel: Murphy J (on the basis of an implied guarantee) and Wilson J (on the basis that the prohibitions were inseverable).

Miller v TCN Channel Nine Pty Ltd
(1986) 161 CLR 556

Deane J: [615] This is another case about the operation and effect of s 92 of the Constitution. Both sides argued with apparent conviction on the basis of existing authority to support diametrically opposed conclusions. Perhaps that should not be seen as surprising **[616]** since the more one becomes immersed in the decisions of the Privy Council and this Court on the subject of s 92, the plainer the impression becomes that one has entered an area where the ordinary processes of legal reasoning have had but a small part to play and where judicial exegesis has tended to confuse rather than elucidate. Indeed, it is as if many voices of authority have been speaking differently at the same time with the result that, putting to one side some basic propositions, it is all but impossible to comprehend precisely what it is that authority has said …

[618] [F]ew would deny that, somewhere along the line, things have gone wrong. The simple words of s 92 have, in an unsuccessful search for certainty in the law, been overlaid by formulae which have given rise to many problems while solving almost none. The section was, plainly enough, intended to serve the essential function of reinforcing the economic and social unity of an emerging nation by removing the barriers to commerce, trade and intercourse which the frontiers between the federating colonies had previously represented. It has been converted into a form of constitutional guarantee of the economics of laissez-faire and the politics of "small government". The importance of the notion of "freedom as at the frontier" which was recognized even in *James v Commonwealth* [(1936) 55 CLR 1 at 58] as lying at the heart of s 92 has been progressively discounted and disregarded. In the result, interstate trade, commerce and intercourse has been placed in a position of significant and preferential immunity from non-discriminatory laws which the courts have, for reasons which still await currently authoritative identification, judged to be inconsistent with s 92. Where s 92 has been held to preclude the application of such non-discriminatory laws to interstate trade and commerce leaving them to apply to intrastate trade and commerce, the section, which was intended to preclude inequality between the treatment of the trade and commerce of the interstate trader and the treatment of the trade and commerce of the local trader, has become an actual source of such inequality of treatment to the detriment of the local trader …

[619] [T]he present case does not seem to me to provide the occasion for considering whether the difficulties in the current state of authority about the nature and scope of s 92 are such as to make it incumbent upon the Court yet again to embark upon a consideration of fundamental questions which so many past cases have failed satisfactorily to resolve. It follows that I shall seek to consider the present case on the basis of my understanding of current authority and leave for another day the question of the extent (if at all) to which that authority should be reopened and reviewed.

(b)   The Whitfield Thunderbolt

In *Cole v Whitfield*, the High Court cast aside much of the existing case law on s 92 and laid down in a joint unanimous judgment a new approach to s 92. The *Sea Fisheries Regulations* (Tas), made under the *Fisheries Act 1959* (Tas), had by reg 31(1)(d) prohibited any person from taking, buying, selling, offering or exposing for sale or having possession or control of crayfish of less than a minimum size. The minimum size was set at a carapace length of 105mm for females and 110mm for males so as to maintain a breeding stock for a stable crayfish population. Similar restrictions were in place in South Australia, but given different breeding requirements in warmer waters, crayfish could be caught younger (and hence smaller). Accordingly, there was a lower minimum size of 98.55mm.

David Whitfield imported South Australian crayfish into Tasmania that were above the South Australian minimum size but below the Tasmanian minimum size. He was prosecuted for having undersized crayfish, but pleaded that reg 31(1)(d) was invalid by reason of s 92. The High Court unanimously held that the regulation did not infringe s 92.

Cole v Whitfield
(1988) 165 CLR 360

The Court: [383] No provision of the Constitution has been the source of greater **[384]** judicial concern or the subject of greater judicial effort than s 92. That notwithstanding, judicial exegesis of the section has yielded neither clarity of meaning nor certainty of operation. Over the years the Court has moved uneasily between one interpretation and another in its endeavours to solve the problems thrown up by the necessity to apply the very general language of the section to a wide variety of legislative and factual situations. Indeed, these shifts have been such as to make it difficult to speak of the section as having achieved a settled or accepted interpretation at any time since federation. The interpretation which came closest to achieving that degree of acceptance was that embodying the criterion of operation formula which we shall subsequently examine in some detail. That formula appeared to have the advantage of certainty, but that advantage proved to be illusory. Its disadvantage was that it was concerned only with the formal structure of an impugned law and ignored its real or substantive effect. It was in vogue during the twenty-five years that began with *Hospital Provident Fund Pty Ltd v Victoria* [(1953) 87 CLR 1] … [but more recently] various members of the Court have declined to accept and apply the criterion of operation formula. This process culminated in the two decisions on the Wheat Stabilization Scheme – *Clark King & Co Pty Ltd v Australian Wheat Board* [(1978) 140 CLR 120] and *Uebergang v Australian Wheat Board* [(1980) 145 CLR 266] – in which the members of the Court were unable to agree upon a common or a majority approach.

Accordingly, the Court made a fresh attempt to ascertain the meaning and purpose of s 92 by looking to the 1890s Convention Debates.

The Court: [385] Reference to the history of s 92 may be made, not for the purpose of substituting for the meaning of the words used the scope and effect – if such could be established – which the founding fathers subjectively intended the section to have, but for the purpose of identifying the contemporary meaning of language used, the subject to which that language was directed and the nature and objectives of the movement towards federation from which the compact of the Constitution finally emerged.

The differences in the external tariffs which were imposed by the several Australian colonies inevitably resulted in the imposition of restrictions on the import and export of goods between them. That was foreseen by a report of the Privy Council Committee for Trade and Plantations in 1849 which recommended that "there should be one tariff common to them all, so that goods might be carried from the one into the other with the same absolute freedom as between any two adjacent counties in England" … **[386]** However, after the late 1850s, when David Syme, founder of the Melbourne *Age*, began his campaign for tariff protection in Victoria, protection became an important issue in Australian politics. In the last three decades of the nineteenth century, parties supporting either free trade or protection dominated the colonial Parliaments ...

To create a free trade area embracing the Australian colonies it was necessary for agreement to be reached about a uniform external tariff. Differing fiscal policies represented a formidable barrier to such agreement ... In particular, the Victorian tariff appeared to have the purpose of protecting local industry, whereas the tariff of New South Wales, which favoured free trade, was fixed for the purpose of satisfying budgetary requirements ... As the 1891 Report of the South Australian Royal Commission on Intercolonial Free Trade shows (p vi), "intercolonial free trade, on the basis of a uniform tariff", was a commonly accepted ideal. Subsequently, the first report of a Victorian Board of Inquiry in 1894 expressed the belief "that the people of Victoria are practically unanimously in favour of free-trade between the colonies" ... **[387]** Notwithstanding this popular support, concrete proposals for the implementation of free trade between the separate Australian colonies languished outside the growing movement towards federation.

In that movement, the problem of intercolonial free trade within a uniform external tariff was, from the outset, a central question and problem: the "lion in the path", as Mr James Service (a former Premier of Victoria) described it in 1890, which federalists must either slay or be slain by (Quick and Garran, p 119). Professor JA LaNauze has traced the development of the debate which led to the framing of s 92, the provision which was to slay the lion, in his essay "A Little Bit of Lawyers' Language: The History of 'Absolutely Free' 1890-1900" in Martin ed, *Essays in Australian Federation* (1969), p 57 ("LaNauze, 'Absolutely Free'"). Before the 1891 Convention assembled, Parkes proposed to a preliminary meeting of New South Wales delegates a number of resolutions, the first of which read:

"That the trade and intercourse between the Federated Colonies, whether by means of land carriage or coastal navigation shall be free from the payment of Customs duties, and from all restrictions whatsoever, except such regulations as may be necessary for the conduct of business." (Parkes, *Fifty Years in the Making of Australian History* (1892), vol II, at p 359.)

When the resolution was formally proposed to the Convention, its wording was changed:

"That the trade and intercourse between the Federated Colonies, whether by means of land carriage or coastal navigation, shall be absolutely free." ...

[W]e note that "intercourse" appeared in the words of the provision as a distinct and independent concept the freedom of which was guaranteed from the very beginning. It was not, as has sometimes been suggested: see, eg, per Dixon J, *Bank of NSW v Commonwealth* ("the *Banking Case*") [(1948) 76 CLR 1 at 381], added as some kind of afterthought to "trade" and "commerce". As will be seen, it was the word "commerce" which was last added to complete the phrase "trade, commerce and intercourse" in the section. The relevance of that for present purposes is that it precludes the approach that the content of the guarantee of freedom of interstate intercourse must be governed by the pre-existing content of a **[388]** guarantee of freedom of interstate trade and commerce into which it was introduced. The notions of absolutely free trade and commerce and absolutely free intercourse are quite distinct and neither the history of the clause nor the ordinary meaning of its words require that the content of the guarantee of freedom of trade and commerce be seen as governing or governed by the content of the guarantee of freedom of intercourse. We shall return to the topic of intercourse and the question of its relationship with trade and commerce later in these reasons ...

In the draft Bill adopted by the Convention in April 1891, the clause emerged as cl 8 of Ch IV:

"So soon as the Parliament of the Commonwealth has imposed uniform duties of Customs, trade and intercourse throughout the Commonwealth, whether by means of internal carriage or ocean navigation, shall be absolutely free."...

Prior to that adoption the delegates had agreed that the federal Parliament should have power to make laws with respect to "The regulation of Trade and Commerce with other Countries, and among the several States": ibid, Ch I, cl 52(1). Professor FR Beasley has commented that:

"It did not occur to any of the delegates that there might be an antinomy between clause 52(1) and clause 8 of Chapter IV simply because to them clause 8 contained a guarantee of interstate free-trade and nothing more; subject to the observance of that principle the federal parliament was to control interstate trade and commerce." ...

Professor LaNauze conjectures that the phrase *absolutely* free trade was understood in 1891 and for some time thereafter to connote not only freedom from border customs duties to protect local industry but also freedom from border customs duties which were not **[389]** protectionist in purpose and were thought to be compatible with free trade: LaNauze, "Absolutely Free", pp 76-77. Whether that was so or not, it is clear that all border customs duties were to be abolished. Beyond that, the records of the movement towards federation, to some of which we now refer, do not establish that the notion of absolutely free trade and commerce had any precise settled contemporary content.

At the Adelaide meeting of the Federal Convention in early 1897, the 1891 clause was inserted virtually unaltered as cl 89 of a draft Bill. Barton, as Leader of the Convention, expressed the view that the 1891 clause "should be as absolute in its terms as possible. If there is to be any exception to absolute freedom of trade and intercourse from end to end of the Commonwealth it should be expressed by way of exception": ibid, pp 80-81 … O'Connor had no doubts about the necessity for the clause. But Isaacs said that the clause "goes much further than it is intended, and there are some expressions which, taken in connection with other portions of the Bill, are extremely large and alarming" … "Taken literally", he said, "it means 'free of everything, even of a licence'" …

Before the 1897 Convention resumed its sitting in September of that year, Griffith, by now Chief Justice of Queensland, prepared some notes on the draft constitution for the Queensland Government. Apparently accepting the misgivings which Isaacs had expressed as to the breadth of the clause, he wrote:

> "I venture, before passing from this subject, to suggest a doubt whether the words of s 89 (which are the same as in the Draft Bill of 1891) are, in their modern sense, quite apt to express the *meaning intended to be conveyed*." (LaNauze, "Absolutely Free", p 84 … (emphasis added).)

[Griffith] went on to explain that "intended" meaning:

> "It is, clearly, not proposed to interfere with the internal regulation of trade by means of licenses, nor to prevent the imposition of reasonable rates on State Railways. I apprehend that the real meaning is that the *free course of trade and commerce* between the different parts of the Commonwealth *is not to be restricted or interfered with* by any taxes, charges, or imposts. Would it not be better to use these or similar words? If it is also intended to prohibit such interference by the imposition of preferential or differential rates on railways or rivers suitable words should be added. The following are submitted for consideration …" (Ibid (emphasis original).)

[390] When the Convention resumed, Isaacs again pointed to the width of cl 89, and Barton and O'Connor accepted that the words of the clause were too general. That seems to have been the view also of Higgins. When one of the delegates expressed a fear that the clause as drafted might prevent laws prohibiting the passing of cattle across State borders or the introduction of diseased vines into South Australia, Barton undertook to redraft the clause to read:

> "So soon as uniform duties of customs have been imposed, trade and intercourse throughout the commonwealth is not to be restricted or interfered with by any taxes, charges, or imposts." …

In the event this amendment was not made, but Isaacs was able to secure the substitution of the words "between the States" for "throughout the Commonwealth". The purpose of the amendment was to ensure that the guarantee to be given by s 92 did not extend beyond interstate free trade. Thus Dr Cockburn (of the South Australian delegation) supported the insertion of some limitation in the clause:

> "not only with the view of seeing that the clause goes no further than is desirable in the restriction of the states, but also in order that it shall not tie the hands of the Commonwealth itself, but shall allow it to impose such restrictions and regulations of trade throughout the Commonwealth as may, from time to time, in the interests of the people, appear to be necessary." …

Dr Quick thought the amendment necessary lest the wider words prohibited local licensing provisions which "are reasonable regulations of trade upon the arrival of goods, wares, and merchandise within the state territories": *Convention Debates* (Melbourne, 1898), vol I, p 1017. Barton agreed, saying that what was wanted was "Free passage across the frontier and freedom from all preferences" (ibid). However, when Isaacs moved to add after the word "free" the words "from taxation or restriction", the amendment was defeated, Reid observing that "the moment we begin to define we have to define what the definition means, and then we involve everything in the necessary amount of confusion": *Convention Debates* (Melbourne, 1898), vol II, p 2367. Deakin shared the misgivings of Isaacs. Noting that the clause had no counterpart in the United States Constitution, he said:

> "So far as [the words of cl 89] imply the removal of everything in the nature of an obstruction placed in the way of intercolonial trade by any state they have our hearty approval. The only question is whether the words in their present connexion **[391]** and novel combination do not go further than the removal of obstructions, and imply the power to interfere in regard to matters which may be considered to affect absolute freedom of trade and intercourse." (Ibid, p 2373.)

Deakin secured Barton's agreement to examine the language of cl 89 again, but it seems that the rhetoric of the provision, which Barton acknowledged to be "the language of three lawyers", proved so powerful that it passed virtually unchanged into the Constitution. In the course of making drafting amendments the word "commerce" was inserted after "trade" in cl 89 by a drafting committee, but that amendment was not debated before acceptance. That cl 89 was intended to eliminate all border customs duties is undoubted. That it might create other immunities from government control was foreseen, though there is no suggestion that it was intended to prevent the enactment of what Parkes had described in his original draft as regulations "necessary for the conduct of business". Indeed, before Barton undertook to limit cl 89 to restriction or interference with trade throughout the Commonwealth by "any taxes, charges or imposts", he had expressed concern that the Commonwealth Parliament should not be "denuded of the powers it would otherwise have" ... Higgins was anxious lest the clause should deprive the States of power to prohibit the introduction of diseased animals and plants ... But the Conventions did not define what regulations were to be permitted and what regulations were to be forbidden. Subject to an immaterial variation of the introductory words, the amended cl 89 was adopted, without further elucidation or qualification to deal with its acknowledged obscurity and foreseen difficulty of application, as s 92 of the Constitution. The delimitation of the precise scope and effect of the guarantee was left as an unresolved task for the future.

Against this background, the Court stated:

The Court: [391] The purpose of the section is clear enough: to create a free trade area throughout the Commonwealth and to deny to Commonwealth and States alike a power to prevent or obstruct the free movement of people, goods and communications across State boundaries. Free trade was understood to give "equality of trade", which Mr McMillan (of the New South Wales delegation) asserted to be "one grand principle involved in the whole of our federation": *Convention Debates* (Melbourne, 1898), vol II, p 2345. The enemies of free trade were border taxes, discrimination, especially in railway freight rates, and preferences. Higgins pointed out: "what will be the use of talking about free-trade between the states, and diminishing the friction upon the borders, if we do not provide against a war of **[392]** railway rates?" (Ibid, p 1268.) To complement the s 92 prohibition against discriminatory laws which prevented the free flow of trade, ss 99 and 102 were introduced to prohibit preferences.

The difficulties which inhere in s 92 flow from its origin as a rallying call for federationists who wanted to be rid of discriminatory burdens and benefits in trade and who would not suffer that call to be muffled by nice qualifications. By refraining from defining any limitation on the freedom guaranteed by s 92, the Conventions and the Constitution which they framed passed to the courts the task of defining what aspects of interstate trade, commerce and intercourse were excluded from legislative or executive control or regulation. Rich J in *James v Cowan* [(1930) 43 CLR 386 at 422] lamented:

> "Some hint at least might have been dropped, some distant allusion made, from which the nature of the immunity intended could afterwards have been deduced by those whose lot it is to explain the elliptical and expound the unexpressed."

The creation of a limitation where none was expressed and where no words of limitation were acceptable was a task which, having regard to the diverse and changing nature of interstate trade, commerce and intercourse, was likely to produce a variety of propositions. And so it has. Sir

Robert Garran contemplated that a student of the first fifty years of case law on s 92 might under-standably "close his notebook, sell his law books, and resolve to take up some easy study, like nuclear physics or higher mathematics": LaNauze, "Absolutely Free", p 58 (quoting Garran, *Prosper the Commonwealth* (1958), p 415). Some thirty years on, the student who is confronted with the heightened confusion arising from the additional case law ending with *Miller v TCN Channel Nine* [(1986) 161 CLR 556] would be even more encouraged to despair of identifying the effect of the constitutional guarantee ...

The expression "free trade" commonly signified in the nineteenth century, as it does today, an absence of protectionism, ie, the **[393]** protection of domestic industries against foreign competi-tion. Such protection may be achieved by a variety of different measures – eg, tariffs that increase the price of foreign goods, non-tariff barriers such as quotas on imports, differential railway rates, subsidies on goods produced and discriminatory burdens on dealings with imports – which, alone or in combination, make importing and dealings with imports difficult or impossible. Sections 92, 99 and 102 were apt to eliminate these measures and thereby to ensure that the Australian States should be a free trade area in which legislative or executive discrimination against interstate trade and commerce should be prohibited. Section 92 precluded the imposition of protectionist burdens: not only interstate border customs duties but also burdens, whether fiscal or non-fiscal, which discriminated against interstate trade and commerce ...

The two elements in s 92 which provide an arguable foundation for giving the section a wider operation with respect to trade and commerce than that foreshadowed by its history are the reference to "intercourse" and the emphatic words "absolutely free". A constitutional guarantee of freedom of interstate intercourse, if it is to have substantial content, extends to a guarantee of personal freedom "to pass to and fro among the States without burden, hindrance or restriction": *Gratwick v Johnson* [(1945) 70 CLR 1 at 17]. If s 92 were to be viewed in isolation from its history, the attachment of the guarantee to trade and commerce along with intercourse might suggest that interstate trade and commerce must also be left without any restriction or even regulatory burden or hindrance. That is not to suggest that every form of intercourse must be left without any restriction or regulation in order to satisfy the guarantee of freedom. For example, although personal movement across a border cannot, generally speaking, be impeded, it is legitimate to restrict a pedestrian's use of a highway for the purpose of his crossing or to authorize the arrest of a fugitive offender from one State at the moment of his departure into another State. It is not necessary now to consider the content of the guarantee of freedom of various forms of inter-state intercourse. Much will depend on the form and circumstance of the intercourse involved. But it is clear that some forms of intercourse are so immune from legislative or executive interference that, if a like immunity were accorded to trade and commerce, anarchy would result. However, it has always been accepted that s 92 does not guarantee freedom in this sense, ie in **[394]** the sense of anarchy ... Once this is accepted, as it must be, there is no reason in logic or commonsense for insisting on a strict correspondence between the freedom guaranteed to interstate trade and com-merce and that guaranteed to interstate intercourse.

What we have just said is likewise an answer to the objection that the words "absolutely free" are inconsistent with any interpretation of the section that concedes to interstate trade no more than a freedom from burdens of a limited kind, whether discriminatory or otherwise. Implicit in the rejection of the notion that the words "absolutely free" are to be read in the abstract as a guarantee of anarchy is recognition of the need to identify the kinds or classes of legal burdens, restrictions, controls or standards from which the section guarantees the absolute freedom of interstate trade and commerce. As we have seen, the failure of the section to define expressly what interstate trade and commerce was to be immune from is to be explained by reference to the dictates of political expediency, not by reference to a purpose of prohibiting all legal burdens, restrictions, controls or standards. In that context, to construe s 92 as requiring that interstate trade and commerce be immune only from discriminatory burdens of a protectionist kind does not involve inconsistency with the words "absolutely free": it is simply to identify the kinds or classes of burdens, restrictions, controls and standards from which the section guarantees absolute freedom ...

[398] The impact that the interpretation favoured by history and context would have on the Commonwealth's legislative power under s 51(i) was not closely explored in argument in the present case. For this reason alone we would be reluctant to attempt to express an exhaustive opinion upon that topic, even if it were possible to do so, or to identify the precise effects of the interaction between ss 51(i), 90, 92, 99 and 102, a matter that has not been examined in the decided cases. It is, however, necessary for present purposes that we make some general reference to the relationship between s 51(i) and s 92 for the reason that the guarantee of the absolute freedom of interstate trade and commerce contained in s 92 must be read in the context of the express conferral of legislative power with respect to such trade and commerce which is contained in s 51(i).

We do not accept the explanation suggested in *Grannall v Marrickville Margarine Pty Ltd* [(1955) 93 CLR 55 at 77-8], that the key to the relationship between s 51(i) and s 92 is to be found in the presence of the words "with respect to" in the opening words of s 51(i). The consequence of reconciling the two constitutional provisions in that way is to treat the legislative power conferred by s 51(i) as essentially peripheral in character. In our view, any acceptable appreciation of the interrelationship between the two sections must recognize that s 51(i) is a plenary power on a topic of fundamental importance. That being so, the express conferral of legislative power with respect to interstate trade and commerce lends some support for the view that s 92 should not be construed as precluding an exercise of legislative power which would impose any burden or restriction on interstate trade and commerce or on an essential attribute of that trade and commerce. Obviously, the provision conferring legislative power (s 51(i)) and the provision restricting the exercise of legislative power (s 92) sit more easily together if the latter is construed as being concerned with precluding particular types of burdens, such as discriminatory burdens of a protectionist kind ...

[399] [The] concept of discrimination commonly involves the notion of a departure from equality of treatment. It does not follow that every departure from equality of treatment imposes a burden or would infringe a constitutional guarantee of the freedom of interstate trade and commerce from discriminatory burdens. Nor does it follow that to construe s 92 as guaranteeing the freedom of interstate trade and commerce from discriminatory burdens would mean that interstate trade and commerce was rendered immune from any regulation which did not affect like intrastate trade. Such regulation might not constitute a burden at all. Even if it did, it might not be discriminatory in the sense to which we have referred. In that regard, experience teaches that Commonwealth legislation is often directed to the regulation of all trade within the Commonwealth's legislative reach (eg, the *Trade Practices Act* 1974 (Cth)) or to the regulation of a particular trade to the extent that it is within that reach. There is far less likelihood that such regulatory legislation will properly be characterized as imposing a discriminatory burden on the trade and commerce with which it deals than is the case with State legislation which singles out interstate trade and commerce for particular treatment. That is not to deny that a Commonwealth law which is regulatory on its face may operate so as to discriminate against interstate trade and commerce. Even a law which applies indiscriminately to all trade and commerce within the reach of Commonwealth legislative power might, in some circumstances, impose a discriminatory burden upon interstate trade and commerce. Plainly, however, the construction which treats s 92 as being concerned to guarantee the freedom of interstate trade and commerce from discriminatory burdens does not involve the consequence that the grant of legislative power with respect to interstate trade and commerce is deprived of its essential content.

The concept of discrimination in its application to interstate trade and commerce necessarily embraces factual discrimination as well as legal operation. A law will discriminate against interstate trade or commerce if the law on its face subjects that trade or commerce to a disability or disadvantage or if the factual operation of the law produces such a result. A majority of the Court (Barwick CJ, Stephen, Mason and Jacobs JJ) so held in *North Eastern Dairy*. And the more recent decisions proceed upon that footing. The Court **[400]** looks to the practical operation of the law in order to determine its validity. Once this is recognized, it is difficult, indeed impossible, to deny that a Commonwealth law dealing with interstate trade could operate in such a way as to work an impermissible discrimination against interstate trade, in particular the trade across State borders originating in a particular [State]. For reasons already given, we should not venture into this topic in any depth. However, we would add two comments. The first is that the possibility of factual discrimination by a s 51(i) law applying only in respect of interstate trade or commerce may well be eliminated in the context of a national scheme constituted by complementary Commonwealth and State law applying, by virtue of their combined operation, to all trade or commerce of the relevant kind. The second is that s 92 will obviously operate to preclude discriminatory burdens being imposed upon interstate trade or commerce by Commonwealth laws enacted pursuant to other general heads of legislative power (eg, trading corporations).

With reference to "the Dixon view", the Court said:

The Court: [401] The doctrine is highly artificial. It depends on the formal and obscure distinction between the essential attributes of trade and commerce and those facts, events or things which are inessential, incidental, or, indeed, antecedent or preparatory to that trade and commerce. This distinction mirrors another distinction, equally unsatisfactory, between burdens which are direct and immediate (proscribed) and those that are indirect, consequential and remote (not proscribed). What is more, the first limb of the doctrine as enunciated looks to the legal operation of the law rather than to its practical operation or its economic consequences. The emphasis on the legal operation of the law gave rise to a concern that the way was open to circumvention by means of legislative device. To counter this possibility the doctrine was expressed to extend to circuitous devices but this extension of the doctrine seems itself to have turned on the legal operation of the law. At any rate, no law has been held not to apply to interstate trade on the ground that it burdened the trade by means of a circuitous device: see *Miller v TCN Channel Nine* [161 CLR at 575-6] …

[403] The second major reason for rejecting the doctrine as an acceptable interpretation of s 92 is that it fails to make any accommodation for the need for laws genuinely regulating intrastate and interstate trade. The history of the movement for abolition of colonial protection and for the achievement of intercolonial free trade does not indicate that it was intended to prohibit genuine non-protective regulation of intercolonial or interstate trade. The criterion of operation makes no concession to this aspect of the section's history. In the result there has been a continuing tension between the general application of the formula and the validity of laws which are purely regulatory in character. Judged by reference to the doctrine, the validity of a regulatory law hinged on whether it imposed a burden on an essential attribute or on a mere incident of trade or commerce. To say the least of it, this was not an appropriate criterion of validity of a regulatory law divorced, as it is, from considerations of the protectionist purpose or effect of the impugned law. It is not surprising that the Court found it necessary to develop a concept of a permissible "burden" which was associated with a somewhat ill-defined notion of what is legitimate regulation in an ordered society … **[404]** The problems which have arisen in this area culminating in *Clark King* and *Uebergang* are the inevitable consequence of any interpretation of s 92 which offers protection to interstate trade going beyond immunity from discriminatory burdens having a protectionist purpose or effect.

Accordingly, the Court concluded:

The Court: [407] Departing now from the doctrine which has failed to retain general acceptance, we adopt the interpretation which, as we have shown, is favoured by history and context. In doing so, we must say something about the resolution of cases in which no impermissible purpose appears on the face of the impugned law, but its effect is discriminatory in that it discriminates against interstate trade and commerce and thereby protects intrastate trade and commerce of the same kind. We mention first Commonwealth laws enacted under s 51(i) which govern the conduct of interstate trade and commerce. Such laws will commonly not appear to discriminate in a relevant sense if they apply to all transactions of a given kind within the reach of the Parliament. It is, however, possible for a general law enacted under s 51(i) to offend s 92 if its effect is discriminatory and the discrimination is upon protectionist grounds. Whether such a law is discriminatory in effect and whether the discrimination is of a protectionist character are questions raising issues of fact and **[408]** degree. The answer to those questions may, in the ultimate, depend upon judicial impression. That is, however, merely a reflection of the absence from the text of s 92 of any criterion by reference to which "such regulations as may be necessary for the conduct of business" (to recall Parkes' original phrase) might be distinguished from laws which infringe the guarantee of free trade and the absence of protection. Indeed, the principal reason why so much past judicial effort to elucidate and settle the content of the guarantee given by s 92 was foredoomed to fail was the impossibility of extracting from an intended guarantee of freedom from discriminatory protectionism a formula which was capable of automatic application by reference to the formal operation of a law.

In the case of a State law, the resolution of the case must start with a consideration of the nature of the law impugned. If it applies to all trade and commerce, interstate and intrastate alike, it is less likely to be protectionist than if there is discrimination appearing on the face of the law. But where the law in effect, if not in form, discriminates in favour of intrastate trade, it will nevertheless offend against s 92 if the discrimination is of a protectionist character. A law which has as its real object the prescription of a standard for a product or a service or a norm of commercial conduct will not ordinarily be grounded in protectionism and will not be prohibited by s 92. But if a law, which may be otherwise justified by reference to an object which is not protectionist, discriminates against interstate trade or commerce in pursuit of that object in a way or to an extent which warrants characterization of the law as protectionist, a court will be justified in concluding that it nonetheless offends s 92 ...

[409] The question which we must now determine is whether reg 31(1)(d) of the Sea Fisheries Regulations which reveals no discriminatory purpose on its face is impermissibly discriminatory in effect. In other words, whether the burden which the regulation imposes on interstate trade in crayfish goes beyond the prescription of a reasonable standard to be observed in all crayfish trading and, if so, whether the substantial effect of that regulation is to impose a burden which so disadvantages interstate trade in crayfish as to raise a protective barrier around Tasmanian trade in crayfish. The latter questions are questions of fact and degree on which minds might legitimately differ.

The regulation neither operates at the border or frontier nor distinguishes between local and interstate trade or produce. However, the limitation on the size of crayfish that may be sold or possessed in Tasmania is unquestionably a burden on the interstate trade and commerce in crayfish caught in South Australian waters and sold in Tasmania. But does it bear the character of being discriminatory against that interstate trade and commerce? The prohibitions against the sale and possession of undersized crayfish apply alike to crayfish caught in Tasmanian waters and to those that are imported. In that respect no discriminatory protectionist purpose appears on the face of the law. Furthermore, the object of the prohibitions, in conjunction with the prohibition against catching undersized crayfish, is to assist in the protection and conservation of an important and valuable natural resource, the stock of Tasmanian crayfish. Although the legislation operates in this way to protect the Tasmanian crayfish industry, it is not a form of protection that gives Tasmanian crayfish production or intrastate trade and commerce a competitive or market advantage over imported crayfish or the trade in such crayfish. And, even if the legislation were to give an advantage to the local trade by improving the competitive qualities of mature Tasmanian crayfish by eliminating undersized imported crayfish from the local market, the agreed facts make it clear that the extension of the prohibitions against sale and possession to imported crayfish is a necessary means of enforcing the prohibition against the catching of undersized crayfish in Tasmanian waters. The State cannot undertake inspections other than random inspections and the local crayfish are indistinguishable from those **[410]** imported from South Australia. On the materials before the Court, the legislation and the burden which it imposes on interstate trade and commerce are not properly to be described as relevantly discriminatory and protectionist.

Cole v Whitfield established that a law offends s 92 if it imposes "discriminatory burdens of a protectionist kind" or if its effect is "**[394]** discriminatory against interstate trade and commerce in that protectionist sense" or "**[407]** if its effect is discriminatory and the discrimination is upon protectionist grounds". In some passages, "discriminatory" is used alone, but this is clearly intended only as shorthand.

There are two possible ways of understanding the test of "**[394]** discriminatory burdens of a protectionist kind". One is to see "discrimination" and "protectionism" as two separate elements which must both be present to infringe s 92. "Discrimination" would provide a threshold criterion. If a law does not "discriminate" against interstate trade, it will be valid with no need for further inquiry. If it does "discriminate", it will still be valid unless the discrimination has a "protectionist" purpose or effect.

Alternatively, the Court may have established only one form of infringement of s 92, with a double-barrelled verbal formula used to identify it. On this view, a law would offend s 92 if its purpose or effect is to benefit local traders within one State by placing their interstate competitors at a competitive disadvantage. Such a law might be described as "discriminatory" and as "protectionist". However, the word "discriminatory" alone would not suffice as it might lead back to a Dixonian focus on the "direct legal effect" of the impugned legislation. The word "protectionist" alone would also not suffice as it carries a strong connotation of action *by a State* to raise protectionist barriers against competition from other States; and this might lead back to the heresy of *McArthur v Queensland* that s 92 does not bind the Commonwealth.

The following further points may be made:

1. The application of *Cole v Whitfield* to Commonwealth laws is not easy. The Court was, however, clearly anxious that the possibility should not be excluded in principle. When the source of power for a Commonwealth law is s 51(i), it will often necessarily be directed to interstate rather than intrastate trade. In that sense, it may necessarily differentiate or "discriminate" between the two. However, the kind of discrimination identified in *Cole v Whitfield* as unacceptable will not arise simply because a Commonwealth law does not apply uniformly to all trade and commerce of the relevant type. In particular, where the "trade and commerce" power is combined with other heads of power so as to suggest that the Commonwealth has endeavoured to regulate the relevant sector of trade and commerce as extensively and uniformly as lies within Commonwealth power, there will be "**[399]** far less likelihood" that such a law will be characterised as "discriminatory". The Court also suggested that, where State and Commonwealth laws combine to produce co-operatively a uniform regime for all trade and commerce in an area, this will virtually eliminate any possibility that the Commonwealth's contribution to the package will be seen as "discriminatory" because it is confined to interstate trade.

2. It is often said that *Cole v Whitfield* adopted the "free trade" approach to s 92 advocated by Michael Coper in *Freedom of Interstate Trade under the Australian Constitution* (Butterworths, 1983). While this is not inaccurate, it requires a more complex understanding both of Coper's argument and of *Cole v Whitfield* than the simple rubric "free trade" would suggest. Coper identified three broad approaches to s 92: the "fiscal burdens" approach advocated by Murphy J; the "free trade" approach which Coper himself preferred; and the "individual rights" approach adopted by Sir Isaac Isaacs, Sir Owen Dixon and Sir Garfield Barwick. However, Coper also identified three different versions of the "free trade" approach which he favoured, focusing respectively on "discrimination", on "protectionism" and on the free flow of the total volume of trade. Of these three possibilities, Coper argued for a focus on "protectionism" and not on "discrimination". On the face of it, therefore, *Cole v Whitfield* reunited the two concepts that Coper had endeavoured to set apart.

3. *Cole v Whitfield* incorporated one enduring legacy of "the Barwick view", namely, that the question of whether a law has infringed s 92 must be judged by its actual economic effects and not merely by its formal legal effects.

4. *Cole v Whitfield* dealt only with interstate "trade" and "commerce" and not with interstate "intercourse". The Court made it clear that "absolute freedom" in relation to intercourse, that is, primarily, freedom of personal movement and freedom of communication, may mean something different from the "absolute freedom" of trading and commercial activity. Indeed, the Court suggested that for some forms of personal intercourse, "freedom" from legislative or executive interference may truly be absolute.

5. The reasoning in most of the cases since *McArthur v Queensland* was swept aside in *Cole v Whitfield*. Many of the decisions in the older cases may still be "correct" in the sense that an analysis based on *Cole v Whitfield* would produce the same result. But any cases in which the outcome cannot be reconciled with the new approach must be regarded as overruled. It appears that this includes the *Bank Nationalisation Case* [1950] AC 235.

In 1989, Sir Garfield Barwick was asked if he had read *Cole v Whitfield*. He replied:

"Interview with Sir Garfield Barwick"
New South Wales Bar Association, *Bar News* (Summer 1989), 9

[17] Yes, I have read it. They've got a magnificent remark in it that the Constitution might provide the text but not the test, so then they proceed to say that what they were worried about at Federation

was protection for free trade and what they were intending is that interstate trade should be relatively free …, but they said absolutely free so you don't take any notice of the text. You find the test is whether the law is passed from a protectionist point of view. It's really laughable. I'd have great fun appealing from that with the Privy Council. Dear me, it's terrible tosh, you know.

That is a remarkable sentence when you analyse it; the Constitution might provide the text but not the test. Very sad.

(c)   Cole's New World

Bath v Alston Holdings Pty Ltd (1988) 165 CLR 411 was argued together with *Cole v Whitfield*. Judgment was handed down a month later. The *Business Franchise (Tobacco) Act 1974* (Vic) provided for retail tobacconist's licences. Under s 10(1)(c) and (d), the licence fees included an ad valorem fee of 25 per cent of the value of tobacco sold in the relevant period "other than tobacco purchased in Victoria from the holder of a wholesale tobacco merchant's licence or a group wholesale tobacco merchant's licence". The exception was made because Victorian wholesalers had already paid wholesale licence fees with an ad valorem component. The scheme was designed to ensure that each lot of tobacco incurred an ad valorem charge only once.

The Court, which had been unanimous in *Cole v Whitfield*, now divided 4:3 on what the new approach meant, or, rather, as to whether the facts gave rise to a measure that was "discriminatory in a protectionist sense". The majority, Mason CJ, Brennan, Deane and Gaudron JJ, held that s 10(1)(c) and (d) infringed s 92. Wilson, Dawson and Toohey JJ dissented.

Bath v Alston Holdings
(1988) 165 CLR 411

Mason CJ, Brennan, Deane and Gaudron JJ: [424] If the Act imposed the ad valorem licence fee by reference to the value of all tobacco products sold by a retailer in the relevant period, the imposition of the fee would not contravene s 92 since it would not differentiate between tobacco purchased in Victoria and tobacco purchased outside Victoria; a **[425]** fortiori it would not discriminate in a protectionist sense against the purchase of tobacco outside Victoria. The exclusion of tobacco purchased in Victoria from a licensed wholesaler from the total sale value of tobacco used as the basis of the calculation of the ad valorem licence fee does, however, involve an element of differentiation and at least prima facie discrimination. Since the effect of the Act is to require all Victorian wholesalers selling tobacco products in Victoria to be licensed, the tobacco products purchased by the ordinary Victorian retailer from a local wholesaler will, for practical purposes, be all purchased from the holder of a wholesaler's licence under the Act. That being so, the exclusion of tobacco purchased in Victoria from the holder of a wholesaler's licence from the value of tobacco sold in the relevant preceding period has the effect that, for practical purposes, the licence fee paid by a Victorian retailer will ordinarily consist of the flat fee of $50 (for an indefinite licence: s 10(1)(c)) or $10 (for a monthly licence: s 10(1)(d)) together with an amount equal to 25 per cent of the value of any tobacco purchased from an interstate wholesaler. In other words, the retailer who sells only tobacco products purchased by him from a Victorian wholesaler will pay the appropriate flat fee for his licence, while a retailer who sells only tobacco products purchased from an interstate wholesaler will pay that flat fee plus 25 per cent of the value of tobacco sold in the preceding relevant period. It follows that, if they be viewed in isolation, the provisions of the Act imposing the obligation to pay a retail tobacconist's licence fee of $50 or $10 plus an amount calculated by reference to the value of tobacco sold which has not been purchased in Victoria from a licensed wholesaler, discriminate against interstate purchases of tobacco in favour of purchases in Victoria. If it be viewed in isolation, that discrimination is undeniably protectionist both in form and substance. In form, the provisions of s 10(1)(c) and (d) select the fact that tobacco was "purchased in Victoria" from a licensed wholesaler as the qualifying condition for exemption from inclusion in the products by reference to which liability to ad valorem tax is calculated. In substance, those provisions protect local wholesalers and the tobacco products they sell from the competition of an out of State wholesaler whose products might be cheaper in some other

Australian market place for a variety of possible reasons, eg, that the laws of the State in which he carries on his business as a wholesaler either do not require that he hold a licence at all or exact a licence fee comparatively lower than the fee exacted from a Victorian wholesaler.

Even when the provisions of the Act imposing the liability to pay the retail tobacconist's licence fee are read in the context of the Act **[426]** as a whole, they retain their discriminatory and protectionist character. Such a reading reveals the explanation for the exclusion from the basis of calculation of the retailer's licence fee of tobacco products purchased within Victoria from a licensed wholesaler. That explanation is that the licence fee which the Act requires Victorian wholesalers to pay to the Victorian Government will not have been paid to the Victorian Government by an out of State wholesaler who does not carry on business in Victoria and therefore does not require a licence in that State. The explanation tends, however, to underline, rather than remove, the protectionist character of the discrimination at the retail level effected by the provisions imposing the tax. If wholesalers of tobacco products in another State already pay taxes and bear other costs which are reflected in wholesale prices equal to or higher than those charged by Victorian wholesalers, the practical effects of the discrimination involved in the calculation of the retailer's licence fee would be likely to be that the out of State wholesalers would be excluded from selling into Victoria and that the products which they would otherwise sell in interstate trade would be effectively excluded from the Victorian market. On the other hand, if out of State wholesalers pay less taxes and other costs than their Victorian counterparts, and in particular if they pay no (or a lower) wholesale licence fee, the effect of the discriminatory tax upon retailers will be to protect the Victorian wholesalers and the Victorian products from the competition of the wholesalers operating in the State with the lower cost structure. Either way, the operation and effect of the provisions of the Act imposing the retail tobacconist's licence fee are discriminatory against interstate trade in a protectionist sense ...

[427] The fact that taxes paid by a wholesaler in one State are higher than the taxes paid by a wholesaler in a second State may provide an inducement for the first State to protect local goods and local wholesalers by the imposition of an "equalizing" tax upon its retailers in respect of their purchases of products from that other State. The most that such notions of economic equalization can do, however, is to provide some local justification for the imposition of a protectionist tax in respect of interstate goods at the later retail stage of distribution. They do not alter the character of the tax as such or remove it from the ambit of s 92. Indeed, to hold that a law which protects local goods by imposing a discriminatory tax on interstate goods at the retail level is consistent with s 92 because the law equalizes in favour of the local goods an advantage which the interstate goods enjoy in their State of origin in the course of manufacture or distribution would be to disregard the critical constitutional purpose which the section is designed to serve ...

[429] A tax upon retailers in respect of their trading in goods may burden their trade in interstate goods consistently with the guarantee of s 92 only if it applies equally to the interstate and local goods which the retailers sell; it cannot lawfully discriminate between them so as to protect the local goods. Again to quote the words of Barton J in *Fox v Robbins* [(1909) 8 CLR 115 at 124]:

> "When the interstate transit is over and they have become part of the mass of property within the State, any goods may be taxed, no matter whence they have come. But they must be taxed alike with all other such goods in the State. The tax must be general, and laid equally on all goods of the kind to be taxed, whether their State of origin be the taxing State or another."

Wilson, Dawson and Toohey JJ: [431] [T]he argument remains that the manner in which licence fees are calculated and imposed under the Act discriminates against interstate trade in tobacco by protecting Victorian trade in that product.

That argument has a superficial plausibility in that tobacco purchased from another State is purchased from a person who is not the holder of a wholesale licence under the Act and the purchaser in Victoria, when he sells that tobacco, is therefore subject to the ad valorem component of the fee in relation to it. But to put the matter **[432]** thus is to present an incomplete picture of the practical operation of the Act and, as was observed in *Cole v Whitfield*, it is the practical operation of the legislation which will largely determine whether there is discrimination upon protectionist grounds. What the argument put in that way leaves out of account is the fact that an interstate wholesaler is not subject to any franchise fee under the legislation and is able to sell tobacco to the Victorian retailer at a price which will reflect the absence of this expense. This advantage which the interstate wholesaler has is, however, balanced by the fact that the Victorian retailer who imports the tobacco will bear a fee calculated by reference to its value when it is sold in Victoria and this fee will be reflected in the price of the product to the ultimate consumer. The legislation does not seek to operate to the advantage or disadvantage of the retailer according to whether he obtains his tobacco within or outside the State.

It is obvious that the reason why the legislation imposes the fee at the wholesale level where it is possible to do so is because there is only a small number of wholesalers but many retailers and it is easier for that reason to collect the tax from the former rather than from the latter. But that does not suggest protectionism. The plain fact of the matter is that the object of the legislation is not to favour Victorian trade at the expense of interstate trade in the product. All trade in tobacco in Victoria is subjected to the expense of the franchise fee at one point or another and the economic effect of the tax is the same, whether the tobacco is acquired by the retailer from within or outside the State.

The judgments in *Bath v Alston Holdings* appear to reflect a two-tiered approach to the *Cole v Whitfield* test. The application of the ad valorem fee to purchases of tobacco from interstate but not to purchases from Victorian wholesalers was "[425] at least prima facie discrimination". Both judgments treat this obvious discrimination on the face of the statute as sufficient to put the Court on inquiry as to whether the effect is "protectionist". It is only in response to this "second tier" question that the two judgments take opposite views.

By contrast, in *Castlemaine Tooheys Ltd v South Australia* (1990) 169 CLR 436 there was no overt "discrimination" between interstate and intrastate trade. The *Beverage Container Act 1975* (SA), as amended by the *Beverage Container Act Amendment Act 1986* (SA), was intended to render the sale of beer in non-refillable bottles commercially disadvantageous. It just happened that the major marketer of non-refillable bottles was the Bond Brewing Group, which consisted of three breweries producing beer in New South Wales, Western Australia and Queensland. Beginning from the premise of factual disadvantage to non-refillable bottles, the Court went straight to the question of whether this factual disadvantage was "protectionist" of South Australian brewers against interstate competition, and unanimously found that it was.

Castlemaine Tooheys Ltd v South Australia
(1990) 169 CLR 436

Mason CJ, Brennan, Deane, Dawson and Toohey JJ: [464] The practical effect of the 1986 Act and regulations and the notice under s 5b was to prevent the Bond brewing companies obtaining a market share in packaged beer in South Australia in excess of 1 per cent whilst their competitors used refillable beer bottles. It is uneconomic for the Bond brewing companies to convert their existing interstate plants to use refillable bottles.

It is common ground between the parties that the object and effect of the 1986 Act was to make the sale of beer in non-refillable bottles commercially disadvantageous. The plaintiffs go further and assert that the effect … was to discriminate against the sale in South Australia of packaged beer brewed interstate and to protect the beer brewed in South Australia from interstate competition …

[T]he defendant claims that the 1986 Act and regulations promoted litter control and conserved energy and resources. According to the defendant, this effect was achieved by the imposition of a deposit on non-refillable containers in an amount judged sufficient to ensure their return and discourage their use and by providing a refund point – in practice any place of sale – to encourage return and to discourage manufacturers from using such containers. Thus the defendant contends that the objects of the legislation were: (1) to promote litter control by forcing non-glass containers and non-refillable bottles into a return system by encouraging return; and (2) to promote energy and resource conservation by discouraging the use of non-refillable containers by imposing a higher deposit and by requiring acceptance of returns at the point of sale (thus discouraging retailers from handling them). The special case mentions that the use, return and refilling of refillable bottles generally results in a proportionate reduction in the release into the atmosphere of carbon dioxide from the burning of natural gas in the production of glass containers. However, the defendant does not claim that this is an independent object of the legislation …

[472] The particular question in the present case is: how should the Court approach the determination of the validity of State legislation which attempts on its face to solve pressing social problems by imposing a solution which disadvantages the trade in beer brewed outside the State as against the trade in beer brewed within the State? The central problems addressed by the legislation are the litter problem and the need to conserve energy resources. If the South Australian legislation were not attempting to provide a solution to these problems, the burden on interstate trade would be discriminatory in a protectionist sense because its operation would be discriminatory and protectionist in effect, even though the legislation on its face would treat interstate and intrastate trade evenhandedly. What difference then does it make that the burden is imposed by legislation which on its face appears to be directed to the solution of social and economic problems, not being the uncompetitive quality or character of domestic trade or industry? …

In determining what is relevantly discriminatory in the context of s 92, we must take account of the fundamental consideration that, subject to the Constitution, the legislature of a State has power to enact legislation for the well-being of the people of that State. In that context, the freedom from discriminatory burdens of a protectionist kind postulated by s 92 does not deny to the legislature of a State power to enact legislation for the well-being of the people of that State unless the legislation is relevantly discriminatory. Accordingly, interstate trade, as well as intrastate trade, must submit to such regulation as may be necessary or appropriate and adapted either to the protection of the community from a real danger or threat to its welfare or to the enhancement of its welfare.

It would extend the immunity conferred by s 92 beyond all reason if the Court were to hold that the section invalidated any **[473]** burden on interstate trade which disadvantaged that trade in competition with intrastate trade, notwithstanding that the imposition of the burden was necessary or appropriate and adapted to the protection of the people of the State from a real danger or threat to its well-being. And it would place the Court in an invidious position if the Court were to hold that only such regulation of interstate trade as is in fact necessary for the protection of the community is consistent with the freedom ordained by s 92. The question whether a particular legislative enactment is a necessary or even a desirable solution to a particular problem is in large measure a political question best left for resolution to the political process. The resolution of that problem by the Court would require it to sit in judgment on the legislative decision, without having access to all the political considerations that played a part in the making of that decision, thereby giving a new and unacceptable dimension to the relationship between the Court and the legislature of the State. An analogous field is the legislative implementation of treaty obligations under s 51(xxix) of the Constitution. The true object of the law in such a case is critical to its validity. The Court has upheld the validity of legislative provisions if they are appropriate and adapted to the implementation of the provisions of the treaty … But if the means which the law adopts are disproportionate to the object to be achieved, the law has not been considered to be appropriate to the achievement of the object … There is a compelling case for taking a similar approach to the problem now under consideration.

If we accept, as we must, that the legislature had rational and legitimate grounds for apprehending that the sale of beer in non-refillable bottles generates or contributes to the litter problem and decreases the State's finite energy resources, legislative measures which are appropriate and adapted to the resolution of those problems would be consistent with s 92 so long as any burden imposed on interstate trade was incidental and not disproportionate to their achievement. Accordingly, the validity of the 1986 legislation rests on the proposition that the legislative regime is **[474]** appropriate and adapted to the protection of the environment in South Australia from the litter problem and to the conservation of the State's finite energy resources and that its impact on interstate trade is incidental and not disproportionate to the achievement of those objects.

The first objection to this proposition is that the discrepancy between the 15 cents refund amount prescribed by reg 7(d) for non-refillable beer bottles and the 4 cents refund amount prescribed by reg 7(c) for refillable bottles goes beyond what is necessary to ensure the return of non-refillable bottles at the same rate as refillable bottles. The discrepancy means that the "bottle cost" of the Bond brewing companies' product is 26 cents per bottle as against a "bottle cost" of

16.65 cents for the [South Australian] product. The defendant's acknowledgment that a refund amount of 6 cents per non-refillable bottle for the first twelve months, reducing to 4 cents thereafter, would have been sufficient to achieve that purpose is significant. The magnitude of the discrepancy indicates that the object of fixing the 15 cents refund amount went further than ensuring the same rate of return of non-refillable and refillable bottles and that the object was to disadvantage the sale of beer in non-refillable bottles as against the sale of beer in refillable bottles.

If, in order to protect the environment from the litter problem presented by the sale of beer in non-refillable bottles, the legislature had enacted a law whose object and effect was simply to discourage the sale of beer in such bottles, the fact that the law had a more adverse impact on interstate brewers than domestic brewers because interstate brewers sell beer in such bottles would not make the law a discriminatory or protectionist law, if that impact was incidental and not disproportionate to the resolution of the litter problem. In such a case the competitive disadvantage sustained by the interstate brewer would be merely incidental to and consequential upon a regulatory measure whose object and effect was not discriminatory in a protectionist sense.

However, this is not a case in which it is possible to characterize the legislative regime simply and comprehensively as one designed to discourage the sale of beer in non-refillable bottles. The legislative regime is one which has as its immediate purpose the return and collection of containers generally, including refillable and non-refillable bottles. The solution to the litter problem sought to be achieved by the legislature lies in the successful operation of the scheme for the return and collection of containers and it is by reference to that scheme that the validity of the law must be determined. And that is how the defendant has presented its case ...

[477] It follows that neither the need to protect the environment from the litter problem nor the need to conserve energy resources offers an acceptable explanation or justification for the differential treatment given to the products of the Bond brewing companies. Accordingly, in our view, that treatment amounted to discrimination in a protectionist sense in relation to their interstate trade.

In a separate judgment, Gaudron and McHugh JJ reached the same result. They tied their exposition more closely to the general analysis of "discriminatory" laws which Gaudron J had offered in *Street v Queensland Bar Association* (1989) 168 CLR 461 (see Chapter 26, §5). The assumed starting point was that the South Australian law was "protectionist". The crucial issue was whether it was also "discriminatory".

Gaudron and McHugh JJ: [478] A law is discriminatory if it operates by reference to a distinction which some overriding law decrees to be irrelevant or by reference to a distinction which is in fact irrelevant to the object to be attained; a law is discriminatory if, although it operates by reference to a relevant distinction, the different treatment thereby assigned is not appropriate and adapted to the difference or differences which support that distinction. A law is also discriminatory if, although there is a relevant difference, it proceeds as though there is no such difference, or, in other words, if it treats equally things that are unequal – unless, perhaps, there is no practical basis for differentiation.

So far as concerns the present case, the legislative regime for beverage containers operates by reference to a distinction between refillable and non-refillable beer bottles ... **[479]** [T]he defendant sought to justify that distinction as relevant to two objectives, namely, the conservation of energy resources and the amelioration of litter problems.

To justify a distinction as relevant to an objective it is necessary to show that the distinction made is a real distinction. That involves the identification of a difference or differences explaining the distinction. It also involves showing a connexion between the distinction and the objective such that the object is reasonably capable of being seen as likely to be achieved – other than to an extent that is trifling or insignificant – by different treatment based on that distinction.

The first step in establishing that the distinction between refillable and non-refillable beer bottles is a relevant distinction supported by the objectives of conserving energy and of ameliorating litter problems is to show, in the case of each objective, that the problems referable to non-refillable beer bottles are greater than those referable to refillable beer bottles ...

[480] In the present case the questions posed in the joint judgment of Mason CJ, Brennan, Deane, Dawson and Toohey JJ reveal, for the reasons given by their Honours, that neither the objective of litter control nor the objective of energy conservation provides an acceptable explanation or justification for the different treatment assigned in the legislative regime for beverage containers.

(d) "Intercourse" among the States

Cole v Whitfield foreshadowed a separate, wider guarantee of freedom of interstate "intercourse". However, the Court has been reluctant to develop this and later statements suggest that the protection of "intercourse" might be more limited than *Cole v Whitfield* implied.

In *Street v Queensland Bar Association* (1989) 168 CLR 461, barristers from New South Wales challenged the validity of residence requirements which effectively prevented them from practising in Queensland. The challenge succeeded on the basis of s 117 of the Constitution. Only Dawson J considered an alternative argument based on s 92. He held that s 92 was inapplicable as he treated the case as one of interstate "trade" and not of "intercourse", and held that a barrister is engaged in a "profession", not in a "trade". He conceded that when a barrister crosses interstate boundaries "**[540]** his passage will constitute intercourse among the States", but added that "what is done by him upon arrival can scarcely do so. It is he, and not the case which he argues, who travels interstate … It can hardly be contended as a general proposition that the restriction of a purely intrastate activity of itself constitutes an interference with the freedom of intercourse of any person from another State who wishes to engage in it".

In *Nationwide News Pty Ltd v Wills* (1992) 177 CLR 1, the publishers of *The Australian* challenged the validity of statutory restrictions on public criticism of the Industrial Relations Commission. The restrictions were held invalid either because they were "beyond power", or because they infringed an implied guarantee of free political communication. In addition, because *The Australian* was published in every State, the plaintiffs invoked s 92 as a guarantee of interstate "intercourse". Although Deane and Toohey JJ thought it "**[82]** appropriate to make some general observations" on the topic, only Brennan J considered the argument fully. He held that s 92 had no relevant application.

Nationwide News Pty Ltd v Wills
(1992) 177 CLR 1

Brennan J: [55] The characteristic of every phenomenon falling within the section … is geographical movement. Each of the terms "trade, commerce and intercourse" in s 92 is qualified by the phrase "among the States" and that qualification is essential to attract the operation of the section. There must be some border crossing involved before any phenomenon of trade, commerce or intercourse comes within the reach of the section. The protection of s 92 is given to the movement of people, the transport of goods, the transmission of communications, the passage of signals of any kind and any other means by which "interchange, converse and dealings between States in the affairs of life" are carried on across State boundaries. The protection is given to the movement of persons and things across the border or, in the case of intangibles, to the means **[56]** by which their movement is effected. The means of movement will vary with what is moved; it is not essential that the means of movement be physically perceptible. But it is essential that something (or some person) be moved. Ideas cannot be moved. They have no geographical location. The expression of ideas, whether in literary or other form, can be moved and a movement of that kind across State borders is capable of attracting the operation of s 92 …

[57] The general criterion of invalidity of a law which places a burden on interstate intercourse is that the law is enacted for the purpose of burdening interstate intercourse. If the law is enacted for some other purpose then, provided the law is appropriate and adapted to the fulfilment of that other purpose, an incidental burdening of interstate intercourse may not be held to invalidate the law. A law may be found to be enacted for the prohibited purpose by reference to its meaning or by reference to its effect. If a law imposes a burden by reason of the crossing of the border, as in *R v Smithers; Ex parte Benson* [(1912) 16 CLR 99] and in *Gratwick v Johnson* [(1945) 70 CLR 1], the law offends s 92 unless it falls into one of the exceptional categories presently to be mentioned.

Similarly, a law which has the effect of preventing or impeding the crossing of the border will be held invalid if the circumstances are such as to show that that is its only or chief purpose. There are exceptions to these propositions.

Cases prior to *Cole v Whitfield* admitted the validity of laws for **[58]** the protection of a State against the introduction into the State of animal and plant diseases, noxious drugs, gambling materials and pornography. The Privy Council said that permissible regulation of trade might take the form "of excluding from passage across the frontier of a State creatures or things calculated to injure its citizens" [*Commonwealth v Bank of New South Wales* [1950] AC 235 at 312]. Where the true character of a law ... is to protect the State or its residents from injury, a law which expressly prohibits or impedes movement of the apprehended source of injury across the border into the State may yet be valid. After *Cole v Whitfield*, these cases need not be seen as exceptions to a general invalidation of laws impairing the guaranteed freedom of interstate trade and commerce, but the reasoning in these cases is material to the scope of the guaranteed freedom of interstate intercourse.

Although State borders are not to be regarded "as in themselves possible barriers to intercourse between Australians" [16 CLR at 117], they do mark the territorial end of one area of legislative competence and the territorial beginning of another. Since State legislative competence is maintained by ss 106 and 107 of the Constitution, s 92 cannot transform a mere change in legal regime applicable to a person, thing or intangible that is moved across a State boundary into an impermissible burden on that movement. The change in the legal regime on one side of the border may impose a burden that is not imposed on the other, but that is not enough in itself to amount to an impermissible burden. Nor does s 92 purport to place interstate intercourse in a position where it is immune from the operation of laws of general application which are not aimed at interstate intercourse. The object of s 92 is to preclude the crossing of the **[59]** border from attracting a burden which the transaction would not otherwise have to bear; its object is not to remove a burden which the transaction would otherwise have to bear if there were no border crossing. Section 92 does not invalidate laws that do not select a movement across a State border as a criterion of the imposition of the burden but do have the effect of burdening interstate intercourse provided (1) the law is enacted chiefly for a purpose other than preventing or impeding a crossing of a State border, (2) the imposition of the burden is appropriate and adapted to the fulfilment of the other purpose and (3) the prevention or impediment to border crossing is an incidental and necessary consequence of the law's operation ...

[60] In this case, s 299(1)(d)(ii) imposes no discriminatory burden on any interstate communication. Therefore it does not infringe the freedom of interstate trade and commerce. The *movement* of the article (or the *movement* of the expression of the article) was not burdened in any way by s 299(1)(d)(ii) of the Act ... The purpose of s 299(1)(d)(ii) is wholly unrelated to the placing of any burden on any movement across State boundaries.

In *Australian Capital Television Pty Ltd v Commonwealth* (1992) 177 CLR 106, Dawson J also held that the protected intercourse "**[192]** is confined to movement or activity across State borders" – so that laws with the object of restricting such movement will be invalid, but laws which restrict it only incidentally "**[195]** will not offend s 92, provided that the means adopted to achieve the object are neither inappropriate nor disproportionate".

Brennan and Dawson JJ repeated their views in *Cunliffe v Commonwealth* (1994) 182 CLR 272. On the other hand, in *Nationwide News*, the joint judgment of Deane and Toohey JJ (at 81-4) stressed that these issues were still unresolved.

The extent to which s 92 guarantees freedom of movement was considered in *AMS v AIF* (1999) 199 CLR 160. The parents of a child separated, with the mother having custody. The mother wished to move with the child from Perth, where the father also lived, to Darwin. Under the *Family Court Act 1975* (WA) the Family Court of Western Australia granted the father an injunction restraining the mother from changing the child's permanent place of residence from Perth unless she had "compelling reasons" to do so.

Since s 92 extends to "trade, commerce, and intercourse *among the States*" it could not itself apply to the movement of the child between Perth and Darwin. However, s 49 of the *Northern*

Territory (Self-Government) Act 1978 (Cth) reproduced the effect of s 92 in the Territory by providing "Trade, commerce and intercourse between the Territory and the States ... shall be absolutely free". The High Court gave s 49 the same meaning as that given to s 92. As a federal enactment, s 49 was capable of overriding any inconsistent operation of the 1975 Western Australian Act by virtue of s 109 of the Constitution.

The High Court, with Callinan J dissenting, overturned the injunction on the basis that it was not warranted under the *Family Court Act*. While this meant that consideration of s 49 was unnecessary, members of the Court nevertheless commented on its scope. The principal judgment was delivered by Gleeson CJ, McHugh and Gummow JJ, with whom Hayne J concurred as to the application of s 92.

AMS v AIF
(1999) 199 CLR 160

Gleeson CJ, McHugh and Gummow JJ: [175] Since *North Eastern Dairy Co Ltd v Dairy Industry Authority of NSW* [(1975) 134 CLR 559], it has been settled doctrine that, where a claim is made that a law interferes with the freedom guaranteed by s 92 of the Constitution, "[t]he Court looks to the practical operation of the law in order to determine its validity" [*Cole v Whitfield* (1988) 165 CLR 360 at 399-400]. In those circumstances, to invite the Court to determine this appeal on the footing that, in substance, if not necessarily in legal form, the orders do not place a significant restraint upon the freedom of movement of the mother is to seek a contemporary judgment of Solomon ...

[178] The formulations of principle by the members of the Court in *Cunliffe v Commonwealth* [(1994) 182 CLR 272] differ, but those by Mason CJ, Deane J, Dawson J, McHugh J and, perhaps, Toohey J, reflect reasoning akin to that adopted by the Privy Council in the *Bank Nationalisation Case* [[1950] AC 235], with respect to what came to be known under the former dispensation respecting s 92 as "reasonable regulation". In the working out of the measure of freedom from legislative, executive or curial interference which s 92 now is to be taken to provide in respect of interstate intercourse, each case should be decided "so far as may be, on the specific considerations or features which it presents" [*Gratwick v Johnson* (1945) 70 CLR 1 at 19] ...

[179] The 1975 WA Act did not in terms apply to impose a burden or restriction upon movement across the borders of Western Australia ... In the present case, the order of which the mother complains does not enjoin movement as such from the State to the Northern Territory. However, its practical operation is to hinder or restrict such movement by the mother by reason of the requirement that she not change the principal place of residence of the child. This, of itself, would not be fatal to validity. The question becomes whether the impediment so imposed is greater than that reasonably required to achieve the objects of the 1975 WA Act ...

When the matter is heard again, it will be for the State Family Court **[180]** to take into account, upon the evidence then before it and in framing any orders it may make, the need not to impose upon the freedom of intercourse of either party between Western Australia and the Northern Territory, or between that State and any other State, an impediment greater than that reasonably required to achieve the objects of the applicable legislation.

In *APLA Ltd v Legal Services Commissioner (NSW)* (2005) 219 ALR 403 this judgment was treated as establishing a test of whether the impediment to interstate intercourse is "greater than reasonably required to achieve the object of the legislation". As one aspect of a challenge to restrictions on legal professional advertising in New South Wales, the plaintiffs had argued that s 92 was infringed by the application of the restrictions to advertisements by lawyers in other States, or by lawyers in New South Wales whose advertisements were published or disseminated from websites in other States. Those members of the Court who considered the issue held that s 92 did not apply.

APLA Ltd v Legal Services Commissioner (NSW)
(2005) 219 ALR 403

Gleeson CJ and Heydon J: [414] The regulations should be understood as dealing with advertising in relation to the providing of legal services in New South Wales. They are not aimed at interstate communications, and they certainly do not discriminate against them. Even so, their effect would extend to advertising by way of interstate communications. Indeed, if it were not so, evasion of the regulations, especially by means of electronic communications, would be simple.

[415] The form of question (1)(c) directs primary attention to that part of s 92 which concerns intercourse, and then to the part that concerns trade and commerce. The reasoning in *Cole v Whitfield* [(1988) 165 CLR 360] denied that the guarantees of freedom of intercourse and of freedom of trade and commerce were co-extensive, raising the problem of where that leaves intercourse which is part of trade and commerce. In the present case, there being nothing discriminatory or protectionist about the regulations, if it is the test applicable to trade and commerce that operates then the argument for the plaintiffs clearly fails. It is unnecessary to decide whether, as the Commonwealth submitted, the provision of legal services for reward is trade and commerce. It is sufficient to accept the alternative submission that the promotion of legal services by way of paid advertising is trade and commerce for the purposes of s 92. The application to such trade and commerce of the *Cole v Whitfield* test does not lead to a conclusion of invalidity.

The regulations would also prohibit advertising of legal services which may not be part of trade and commerce. Communication is intercourse, and covers advertising which is not part of trade and commerce. Let it be assumed that at least some of the advertising covered by the regulations is in that category. The object of the regulations is not to impede interstate intercourse. The test to be applied therefore is whether the impediment to such intercourse imposed by the regulations is greater than is reasonably required to achieve the object of the regulations. The object of the regulations is to restrict the advertising of legal services to be provided in New South Wales. That object can only be achieved by a general restriction on the advertising of such services. The impediment to interstate intercourse is no greater than is reasonably required to achieve the object of the regulations.

This is not a case in which the application of one test would produce a result different from that produced by the application of another. The Commonwealth argued that where a law burdens interstate intercourse that occurs in or in relation to interstate trade or commerce, the trade and commerce limb of s 92 applies and the validity of the law is to be tested by reference to *Cole v Whitfield*. This may be correct, but it is unnecessary to decide the point.

Gummow J: [446] [T]here are some difficulties … in dealing with the consequences of *Cole v Whitfield*. In *Nationwide News Pty Ltd v Wills* [(1992) 177 CLR 1 at 83], Deane and Toohey JJ said that there was "obvious force" in a submission which they described as follows:

> "[O]nce it was recognized that the guarantee of interstate intercourse was not confined by the construction given to the guarantee of freedom of interstate trade and commerce, it is necessary to construe it as inapplicable to any intercourse in the course of trade or commerce. Otherwise, it was said, the Court's insistence, in *Cole v Whitfield*, that s 92 was not intended to operate and did not operate as a source of unfair and potentially divisive preference of interstate trade over intrastate trade would be unavailing."

Their Honours went on to say that the submission went too far and that the true resolution of the tension within s 92 was to be found "in the relevant characterization of the particular law" [177 CLR at 84].

However …, the solution proposed by Deane and Toohey JJ assumes a result from the process of characterisation which places the challenged law in one or the other, but not both, limbs of s 92. Yet it is readily apparent that in applying the Constitution a single law can possess more than one character.

The solution which should be accepted is that proposed by the interveners and adopted by the State. This is that, in determining the validity of a law relating to activities which have the character of "trade, commerce … among the States" in s 92 which also involve "intercourse among the States", validity is to be assessed exclusively by reference to the first-mentioned character of that law. In this way there is supported the Court's insistence in *Cole v Whitfield* that s 92 does not operate as a source of unfair and potentially divisive preference of interstate trade over intrastate trade.

It is convenient now to consider the application to the Regulation of what might be called the first limb of s 92. It yet has to be settled by this Court whether either or both the expressions "trade and commerce" in s 51(i) of the Constitution and "trade, commerce" in s 92 apply to the provision of legal services ...

[447] The present case ... presents the question not whether the provision of legal services has the character of engagement in trade or commerce, but whether the advertising ... of those services is an activity in trade or commerce. To that the answer must be in the affirmative ... However, this conclusion ... does not sufficiently assist the plaintiffs to support any case on the first limb of s 92. That is because Pt 14 cannot be characterised as a protectionist measure within the sense established by *Cole v Whitfield* and *Bath v Alston Holdings Pty Ltd* [(1988) 165 CLR 411].

There remains the reliance by the plaintiffs upon the second limb ... [E]arlier in these reasons ... it was explained that a particular advertisement might still fall within the prohibition imposed by Pt 14 where there was some degree of interstate communication, although the legal services in question would be provided in New South Wales. For example, the proposed communications by the plaintiffs include website material uploaded in Victoria but accessible in New South Wales.

In *Bank of NSW v The Commonwealth* [(1948) 76 CLR 1 at 381] Dixon J, when dealing with what then was seen as the composite expression "trade, commerce, and intercourse", said that it covers the transmission of electric current as an obvious extension of the movement of physical goods and that it covers communication by such means as broadcasting and visual signals. In the present case, there was no real dispute that the "intercourse" referred to in s 92 includes communication by means of the Internet and other electronic methods. However, the intercourse in which the plaintiffs ... wish to engage through the provision of website material is advertising in the nature of "trade, commerce" identified in the first limb of s 92. The circumstance that intercourse also would be involved does not displace the primary and exclusive operation of the first limb of s 92.

There is nothing in the definition of "advertising" in Pt 14 which limits to services for reward the provision of legal services by a barrister or solicitor and excludes the provision of gratuitous services by such persons or by non-profit organisations employing them. In those circumstances, counsel for the *amici* emphasised that the prohibition imposed in Pt 14 may apply to activities outside the potential operation of the first limb of s 92; that being so, those non-trading and non-commercial activities might nevertheless, given the necessary interstate element, attract the operation of the second limb of s 92 as involving "intercourse" ...

[449] It is apparent, particularly from the remarks of Brennan J in *Nationwide News* [177 CLR at 57], that, in speaking in this context of the object or purpose of the law in question, what is posited is an objective inquiry answered by reference to the meaning of the law or to its effect. Moreover, in speaking of an effect which imposes an impediment upon freedom of intercourse which is greater than reasonably required to achieve that object or purpose, no conundrum is presented. It is true that, at one level of analysis, an object or purpose of all legislation is that it operate according to its terms. But it does not follow that any law which has an adverse operation or effect upon interstate intercourse necessarily fails the constitutional criterion of validity under s 92. The level of characterisation required by the constitutional criterion of object or purpose is closer to that employed when seeking to identify the mischief to redress of which a law is directed or when speaking of "the objects of the legislation" ...

In the present case, on the assumption that the prohibition imposed by Pt 14 may apply to interstate communication which answers the description of "intercourse" in s 92, nevertheless, in that operation, Pt 14 is not invalid. This is because the effect of the prohibition on interstate communications is no greater than is reasonably required to achieve the object of Pt 14. That object could not be fully achieved if legal practitioners were permitted to direct from outside New South Wales to persons in New South Wales advertisements promoting the provision in New South Wales of the particular legal services with which the legislation is concerned.

Hayne J: [502] The text of s 92 does not readily yield a distinction between interstate trade and commerce, and interstate intercourse. The constitutional expression is "trade, commerce, and intercourse among the States, whether by means of internal carriage or ocean navigation". "[T]rade" and "commerce" may be grouped together and distinguished from "intercourse" if some economic criterion is adopted. But such a distinction can have purpose and utility only if it leads to some different content being given to the freedom for which s 92 provides in relation to interstate trade and commerce from that for which it provides in relation to interstate intercourse.

Nothing in the text of s 92 reveals why that should be so. In particular, the text does not readily reveal any basis for treating one of the three elements of a composite expression ("trade, commerce, and intercourse among the States") which forms the subject of an imperative ("shall be absolutely free") as connoting, let alone requiring, the application of some different test from the test to be applied to the other elements. Yet that is the accepted premise from which the determination of the present case must proceed.

How, then, is the distinction between interstate trade and commerce, and interstate intercourse to be drawn?

Like Gummow J, Hayne J queried the utility of the suggestion by Deane and Toohey JJ in *Nationwide News* that the solution lay in characterisation of the impugned law. He said:

Hayne J: [503] Characterising a law as one with respect to interstate intercourse rather than interstate trade and commerce may be thought to assume that the relevant law can be assigned only one character and that the two categories of reference which are to be considered are distinct. Such an assumption, if made, would not be well founded. And even if the underlying assumption were not cast in absolute terms but depended instead upon assigning a "principal" or "chief" character to the law, an assumption of that kind would not fit easily with the recognition that many transactions that constitute interstate trade and commerce equally constitute interstate intercourse.

Moreover, if the character of a law turns upon the rights, duties, powers and privileges which it changes, regulates or abolishes, to take the character of the law, identified in this way, as the starting point for subsequent analysis would be at odds with two critical steps that underpin the decision in *Cole v Whitfield*. First [165 CLR at 399-400], the Court said that the concept of discrimination (with which the constitutional guarantee of freedom of interstate trade and commerce is centrally concerned) embraces factual discrimination as well as legal discrimination. Secondly [165 CLR at 400-7], the Court rejected the criterion of operation test developed and applied in cases like … *Hospital Provident Fund Pty Ltd v State of Victoria* [(1953) 87 CLR 1] …

If, as *Cole v Whitfield* holds, the practical effect of a law is relevant in deciding whether it impermissibly discriminates against interstate trade or commerce, how is the law's character (or principal or chief character) to be determined? The particular facts of a case may reveal that the law does have a practical consequence in the circumstances of that case. But if the inquiry is how is that law to be characterised, what is the nature of the process being undertaken? In particular, how is practical effect to be measured?

If a distinction is to be drawn between interstate trade and commerce and interstate intercourse, the distinction cannot be found by assigning a single character to the impugned law. A law may have more than a single legal character. Its practical effects will ordinarily be many and varied. Rather, the distinction must lie elsewhere than in an exercise in characterisation which is **[504]** founded on a classification into two wholly separate categories. And if that is so, the only candidate for consideration in drawing a distinction between interstate trade and commerce and interstate intercourse is an economic criterion. That is, trade and commerce is to be understood as referring to transactions having a commercial content or purpose, and intercourse is to be understood as referring to other interstate movements or transactions. Any law dealing with interstate intercourse that is a part of interstate trade or commerce would fall to be determined according to whether the law discriminated against trade and commerce in a protectionist sense.

As pointed out earlier, the drawing of a distinction between two separate limbs or applications of s 92 can have purpose and utility only if different tests are engaged. The content of those different tests must be related to the distinction that is drawn and it is, therefore, useful to turn now to the examination of what has been said about the relevant test for laws affecting interstate intercourse …

[505] It is clear that a law which has no purpose or effect other than to impede interstate intercourse is contrary to s 92 … It is no less evident, however, that the interstate intercourse limb has not been understood as confined to striking down laws *aimed* at impeding intercourse (whether that "aim" is to be deduced by reference only to legal operation or by reference to the practical operation and effect of the law) …

[506] In *AMS v AIF* [199 CLR at 179], Gleeson CJ, McHugh and Gummow JJ said that where a law, by its practical operation rather than by its terms, imposes a burden or restriction on interstate intercourse, the law will be valid if the burden or restriction imposed is not greater than that reasonably required to achieve the *law's* objects. Leaving aside, then, laws which are specifically aimed at interstate intercourse, the test stated in the joint reasons in *AMS v AIF* invites attention to consideration of the objects of the law in question. And as Gummow J concludes in his reasons in the present matter, the principles stated in *AMS v AIF* should now be accepted as the applicable doctrine …

There is then one consequence of the conclusions reached in *AMS v AIF* which should be noticed. Expressing the relevant test by reference to consideration of what is necessary or appropriate and adapted to fulfilment of the purposes of the *law* in question, entails that few laws not directly aimed at interstate intercourse would fail such a test. And if that is so, the utility of distinguishing between interstate trade and commerce on the one hand, and interstate intercourse on the other, is much reduced.

Since *Cole v Whitfield* the freedom of trade and commerce between the States is to be understood as freedom from a particular kind of law aimed at that activity – protectionist laws. Likewise, the freedom of interstate intercourse is a freedom from laws aimed at that activity. The qualification to the freedom with respect to interstate intercourse (which would strike down laws not aimed at that activity but travelling beyond what is necessary, or appropriate and adapted, to the purposes exhibited by the law in question) is, however, an amplification whose content is problematic. That is because the ambit of the qualification is governed by the purpose of the impugned law. No matter whether practical effect or legal operation is considered, the purpose of the impugned law will include a purpose of regulating the activity in question. To explain why that is so, it is necessary to say something further about what is meant by the expression "the purpose of a law".

[507] To attribute "purpose" to a law runs the risk of eliding a useful legal concept expressed in the metaphor of "intention", and the results of some attempted exercise in psychoanalysis of those associated with the making of the law. In the familiar language of the law, there is a risk that an objective concept is turned into a subjective inquiry about the purpose of an individual or the purposes of some group of individuals. Identifying the purpose of a law is an exercise in construction. That task must begin with the words in which the law is expressed but, as has been repeatedly noticed, that is a task that requires more than sitting with the words of the Act in one hand and a dictionary in the other … Although the inquiry must begin and end with the words that are used, account must be taken of the whole of the context in which those words were and are used and, in appropriate cases, account must be taken of the various extrinsic sources to which relevant interpretation legislation permits, and in some cases requires, recourse.

[R]eferences to legislative intention or purpose must never be permitted to obscure the essentially objective nature of the inquiry. Especially is that so when it is recognised that often, perhaps too often, the search for a single legislative purpose must fail because the relevant statutory formula represents a compromise between competing considerations or competing pressures. But in the end, a court called on to construe the legislation must choose the meaning and operation that the words are to be given in the particular case. And one aspect of the "purpose" of the law in question must be to give effect to that particular operation of the law.

Thus, when an appeal is made, as it has been in connection with the freedom of interstate intercourse, to any consideration of what is necessary or appropriate and adapted to the purpose of the impugned law, the test becomes one which, at least in large measure, is self-defining in its operation. By hypothesis, the impugned law is one which has an adverse effect (either legally or in its practical operation) on interstate intercourse. Yet equally, it follows from the task of construction which the court has necessarily had to undertake, that a part of the purpose of the law that is challenged is to have that effect. The ordering of society for which the law provides includes the relevant adverse effect on interstate intercourse.

The corollary of these conclusions may very well be that the step taken in *Cole v Whitfield* to undo the law which had developed in relation to s 92 confines the operation of s 92 in connection with interstate intercourse rather more closely than may be thought to have been anticipated … Whether or not that is so is not a question that needs to be determined. It is sufficient to say that the impugned regulations, in their effect on interstate trade, commerce, and intercourse do not contravene s 92.

Several points should be noted. One is the point made by Gleeson CJ and Heydon J at 415 that any difference between the tests for "intercourse" and for "trade and commerce" would in this case produce no difference in result. Another is the view taken by Gummow and Hayne JJ at 446 and 504 respectively, but left open by Gleeson CJ and Heydon J at 415, that where an activity can be characterised both as "trade and commerce" and as "intercourse", the test appropriate to the former characterisation is exclusively to be applied. Finally, there is the suggestion advanced by Hayne J at 507, but rejected by Gummow J at 449, that the question whether a law goes beyond what is reasonably necessary for the attainment of its objects must invariably receive a negative answer, since its "objects" must necessarily include the very operation of the law that is impugned. In the light of these holdings, it may seem doubtful whether the wider freedom of "intercourse" foreshadowed in *Cole v Whitfield* now has any practical future.

2. Acquisition of Property on Just Terms

The language of s 51(xxxi) was adapted, with significant variations, from the final words of the Fifth Amendment to the United States Constitution. The American provision is formulated as a limitation on power: "nor shall private property be taken … without just compensation". By contrast, the Australian provision is expressed as a grant of power: the Commonwealth Parliament *may* make laws with respect to "the acquisition of property on just terms from any State or person for any purpose in respect of which the Parliament has power to make laws". In this form, s 51(xxxi) is both a head of power and a guarantee.

Usually, s 51 is approached on the assumption that each head of power is construed independently so that one grant of power cannot be used to justify the "reading down" of another. The major exception is that, where a grant of power is circumscribed by a specific limitation, the Court will not allow another grant of power to be read so as to circumvent that limitation (see the discussion in Chapter 16, §3). For example, on normal principles of construction, the legislative power as to "lighthouses" in s 51(vii) would imply as one of its incidents the power to legislate for the acquisition of land on which to erect a lighthouse. However, consistently with the notion that grants of power should not be construed to permit circumvention of specific limitations, the Court has concluded that this normal "incident" is *excluded* from the head of power. In other words, any acquisition of property for any of the legislative purposes set out in s 51 must find its source of power exclusively in s 51(xxxi).

(a)   "Property"

In contrast to the guarantees of civil and political rights examined in Chapter 26, the High Court has given a broad construction to the protection offered by s 51(xxxi). In particular, it has taken a wide view of the concept of "property". *Minister of State for the Army v Dalziel* (1944) 68 CLR 261 concerned reg 54 of the *National Security (General) Regulations* (Cth), which authorised the Commonwealth, in the interests of "public safety, the defence of the Commonwealth, or the efficient prosecution of the war or for maintaining supplies and services essential to the life of the community", to take possession of any land for an indefinite period. On that basis the Commonwealth took possession of vacant land in Sydney being used by a weekly tenant, Arthur Dalziel, as a commercial car park. The Court, with Latham CJ dissenting, held that there had been an "acquisition of property" under s 51(xxxi). As McTiernan J put it: "**[295]** The word 'property' in s 51(xxxi) is a general term. It means any tangible or intangible thing which the law protects under the name of property. The acquisition of the possession of land is an instance of the acquisition of property".

Minister of State for the Army v Dalziel
(1944) 68 CLR 261

Rich J: [284] What we are concerned with is not a private document **[285]** creating rights *inter partes*, but a Constitution containing a provision of a fundamental character designed to protect citizens from being deprived of their property by the Sovereign State except upon just terms. The meaning of property in such a connection must be determined upon general principles of jurisprudence, not by the artificial refinements of any particular legal system or by reference to *Sheppard's Touchstone*. The language used is perfectly general. It says the acquisition of property. It is not restricted to acquisition by particular methods or of particular types of interests, or to particular types of property. It extends to any acquisition of any interest in any property … In the case now before us, the Minister has, *in adversum*, assumed possession of land of which Dalziel was weekly tenant. With all respect to the argument which has been addressed to us to the contrary, I am quite unable to understand how this can be said not to be an acquisition of property from Dalziel within the meaning of the placitum. Property, in relation to land, is a bundle of rights exercisable with respect to the land. The tenant of an unencumbered estate in fee simple in possession has the largest possible bundle. But there is nothing in the placitum to suggest that the legislature was intended to be at liberty to free itself from the restrictive provisions of the placitum by taking care to seize something short of the whole bundle owned by the person whom it was expropriating. *Possession vaut titre* in more senses than one. Not only is a right to possession a right of property, but where the object of proprietary rights is a tangible thing it is the most characteristic and essential of those rights …

[286] It would, in my opinion, be wholly inconsistent with the language of the placitum to hold that, whilst preventing the legislature from authorizing the acquisition of a citizen's full title except upon just terms, it leaves it open to the legislature to seize possession and enjoy the full fruits of possession, indefinitely, on any terms it chooses, or upon no terms at all. In the case now before us, the Minister has seized and taken away from Dalziel everything that made his weekly tenancy worth having, and has left him with the empty husk of tenancy. In such circumstances, he may well say:–

"You take my house, when you do take the prop
That doth sustain my house; you take my life,
When you do take the means whereby I live."

In *Bank of NSW v Commonwealth* (*Bank Nationalisation Case*) (1948) 76 CLR 1, it was argued that the *Banking Act 1947* (Cth) was invalid because it infringed s 51(xxxi). The Act empowered the Commonwealth Bank to acquire shares in the private banks and the Commonwealth to acquire the assets or the business of a private bank, both with provision for compensation. However, the Act also empowered the government to appoint its own directors to the Board of a private bank in lieu of those elected by shareholders. The question was whether this involved an "acquisition of property". The Court held that it did. Dixon J stated that "property" "**[349]** is not to be confined pedantically to the taking of title by the Commonwealth to some specific estate or interest in land recognized at law or in equity and to some specific form of property in a chattel or chose in action similarly recognized … [I]t extends to innominate and anomalous interests and includes the assumption and indefinite continuance of exclusive possession and control for the purposes of the Commonwealth of any subject of property". The meaning to be given to "property" is examined further below in the context of cases considering whether a law gives rise to an "acquisition" under s 51(xxxi).

(b)   "Acquisition"

Despite the breadth of the meaning given to "property", several recurrent themes have limited the protection conferred by s 51(xxxi). In the first place, the Fifth Amendment to the United States Constitution speaks of property being "taken". It is thus enough that the holder of property has been deprived of it; its destination thereafter does not matter. By contrast, s 51(xxxi) speaks of "acquisition". Accordingly, the property must have been acquired by somebody; and the acquisition must be for a Commonwealth purpose.

In *PJ Magennis Pty Ltd v Commonwealth* (1949) 80 CLR 382, it was held that the property need not be acquired by the Commonwealth itself: the *War Service Land Settlement Agreements Act 1945* (Cth), establishing a co-operative scheme for soldier resettlement, was held to be invalid as a law with respect to the acquisition of property without just terms, even though the actual acquisition of land was by the State. Williams J stated that: "**[423]** It is immaterial whether the acquisition is to be made by the Commonwealth or some body authorized to acquire property by the Commonwealth or by a State by agreement with the Commonwealth" (see also *Trade Practices Commission v Tooth & Co Ltd* (1979) 142 CLR 397). However, the *Magennis* decision was readily circumvented: the co-operative scheme involved was restructured so that the acquisition depended wholly on State legislation, with the only formal Commonwealth role being a contribution to the cost of acquisition, effected by grants under s 96 of the Constitution. In *Pye v Renshaw* (1951) 84 CLR 58, this restructured scheme was held to be valid.

Secondly, there are some "acquisitions of property" to which s 51(xxxi) does not apply. An obvious example is taxation, which involves the compulsory taking for Commonwealth purposes of a form of property. Because this taking is the very essence of taxation, the express power with respect to taxation in s 51(ii) must obviously extend to this kind of taking; and it follows that such a taking will not be characterised as an "acquisition of property" within the meaning of s 51(xxxi). This was explained by Dixon CJ, with whom the other members of the Court agreed, in *Attorney-General (Commonwealth) v Schmidt* (1961) 105 CLR 361.

Attorney-General (Commonwealth) v Schmidt
(1961) 105 CLR 361

Dixon CJ: [371] It is hardly necessary to say that when you have, as you do in par (xxxi), an express power, subject to a safeguard, restriction or qualification, to legislate on a particular subject or to a particular effect, it is in accordance with the soundest principles of interpretation to treat that as inconsistent with any construction of other powers conferred in the context which would mean that they **[372]** included the same subject or produced the same effect and so authorized the same kind of legislation but without the safeguard, restriction or qualification. But two observations must be made. First, it is necessary to take care against an application of this doctrine to the various powers contained in s 51 in a too sweeping and undiscriminating way. For it cannot have much to do with some of the subject matters of power upon the very terms in which they are conferred. The other observation is that the principle does not apply except with respect to the ground actually covered by par (xxxi) of s 51. For example, no one would doubt that, under the power to make laws with respect to bankruptcy, property of the bankrupt may be sequestrated and property of others which has been left in his order and disposition may be vested in the Official Receiver and that s 51(xxxi) has no bearing on the matter. At the same time, if a law was made under which a piece of land was acquired for a Bankruptcy Office, s 51(xxxi) would govern the legislation and not s 51(xvii). It must be borne in mind that s 51(xxxi) confers a legislative power and it is that power only which is subject to the condition that the acquisitions provided for must be on just terms.

Similarly, in *Burton v Honan* (1952) 86 CLR 169, Dixon CJ held that the forfeiture of prohibited imports under the *Customs Act 1901* (Cth) "**[180]** is not an acquisition of property for any purpose in respect of which Parliament has **[181]** power to make laws. It is nothing but forfeiture … imposed as part of the incidental power for the purpose of vindicating the Customs laws. It has no more to do with the acquisition of property … within s 51(xxxi) than has the imposition of taxation itself".

In five cases decided in 1994, the notion that some forms of acquisition lie outside the scope of s 51(xxxi) was strongly reaffirmed. Perhaps the simplest examples were *Re Director of Public Prosecutions; Ex parte Lawler* (1994) 179 CLR 270, which confirmed that a provision for the forfeiture of a foreign commercial fishing boat found to be fishing unlawfully was not a law with respect to the acquisition of property; and *Nintendo Co Ltd v Centronics Systems Pty Ltd* (1994) 181 CLR 134, which took a similar view of the *Circuit Layouts Act 1989* (Cth) in its application to silicon chips used in video game machines. The practical effect of that Act was to enable Nintendo Co Ltd to claim that sales by Centronics Systems Pty Ltd of video games imported from Taiwan had infringed its intellectual property rights. In the High Court, Centronics argued that the impact of the legislation on their previously legitimate commercial operations amounted to an "acquisition of property", entitling them to "just terms". The Court rejected this argument.

Nintendo Co Ltd v Centronics Systems Pty Ltd
(1994) 181 CLR 134

Mason CJ, Brennan, Deane, Toohey, Gaudron and McHugh JJ: [160] [The] operation of s 51(xxxi) to confine the content of other grants of legislative power, being indirect through a rule of construction, is subject to a contrary intention either expressed or made manifest in those other grants. In particular, some of the other grants of legislative power clearly encompass the making of laws providing for the acquisition of property unaccompanied by any quid pro quo of just terms. Where that is so, the other grant of legislative power manifests a contrary intention which precludes the abstraction from it of the legislative power to make such a law.

The grant of Commonwealth legislative power which sustains the Act is that contained in s 51(xviii) of the Constitution with respect to "Copyrights, patents of inventions and designs, and trade marks". It is of the essence of that grant of legislative power that it authorises the making of laws which create, confer, and provide for the enforcement of, intellectual property rights in original compositions, inventions, designs, trade marks and other products of intellectual effort. It is of the nature of such laws that they confer such rights on authors, inventors and designers, other originators and assignees and that they conversely limit and detract from the proprietary rights which would otherwise be enjoyed by the owners of affected property. Inevitably, such laws may, at their commencement, impact upon existing proprietary rights. To the **[161]** extent that such laws involve an acquisition of property from those adversely affected by the intellectual property rights which they create and confer, the grant of legislative power contained in s 51(xviii) manifests a contrary intention which precludes the operation of s 51(xxxi).

The cases also establish that a law which is not directed towards the acquisition of property as such but which is concerned with the adjustment of the competing rights, claims or obligations of persons in a particular relationship or area of activity is unlikely to be susceptible of legitimate characterisation as a law with respect to the acquisition of property for the purposes of s 51 of the Constitution. The Act is a law of that nature. It cannot properly, either in whole or in part, be characterized as a law with respect to the acquisition of property for the purposes of that section. Its relevant character is that of a law for the adjustment and regulation of the competing claims, rights and liabilities of the designers or first makers of original circuit layouts and those who take advantage of, or benefit from, their work. Consequently, it is beyond the reach of s 51(xxxi)'s guarantee of just terms.

This second principle was spelled out most clearly in *Mutual Pools & Staff Pty Ltd v Common-wealth* (1994) 179 CLR 155. In an earlier decision (*Mutual Pools & Staff Pty Ltd v Federal Commissioner of Taxation* (1992) 173 CLR 450), the High Court had held that a statute levying a tax on swimming pools constructed inground was invalid by reason of failure to comply with s 55 of the Constitution. In 1990, while the litigation on the s 55 issue was pending, the Swimming Pool and Spa Association of Australia, an association of pool supplier companies, had made an agreement on behalf of its members with the Commissioner of Taxation to the effect that the companies would continue to pay the tax, but that if the High Court action succeeded each company would receive a refund (with interest) of the whole amount paid by it. By the *Swimming Pools Tax Refund Act 1992* (Cth), the Commonwealth purported to override that agreement. Under s 4(2), the tax would be refunded to the company only if it had not been passed on to the purchaser or if the purchaser had later received a refund from the company. In cases where a purchaser had borne the burden, s 4(3) and (4) enabled him or her to claim a refund, rather than the company. Thus, the Commonwealth did not seek to deny its obligation to pay a refund, but only to ensure that refunds were equitably allocated. However, the effect was to deprive the supplier company of its contractual right to a refund under the 1990 agreement. The High Court held that this did not involve a breach of s 51(xxxi).

Mutual Pools & Staff Pty Ltd v Commonwealth
(1994) 179 CLR 155

Deane and Gaudron JJ: [184] [T]he word "acquisition" is not to be pedantically or legalistically restricted to a physical taking of title or possession. Once it is appreciated that "property" in s 51(xxxi) extends to all **[185]** types of "innominate and anomalous interests" [*Bank of NSW v Commonwealth* (1948) 76 CLR 1 at 349], it is apparent that the meaning of the phrase "acquisition of property" is not to be confined by reference to traditional conveyancing principles and procedures. None the less, the fact remains that s 51(xxxi) is directed to "acquisition" as distinct from deprivation. The extinguishment, modification or deprivation of rights in relation to property does not of itself constitute an acquisition of property. For there to be an "acquisition of property", there must be an obtaining of at least some identifiable benefit or advantage relating to the ownership or use of property. On the other hand, it is possible to envisage circumstances in which an extinguishment, modification or deprivation of the proprietary rights of one person would involve an acquisition of property by another by reason of some identifiable and measurable countervailing benefit or advantage accruing to that other person as a result. Indeed, the extinguishment of a chose in action could, depending upon the circumstances, assume the substance of an acquisition of the chose in action by the obligee ...

[187] There are some kinds of acquisition which are of their nature antithetical to the notion of just terms but which were plainly intended to be permissible under laws made pursuant to one or more of the grants of power contained in s 51. An example of those kinds of acquisition is the compulsory forfeiture to the Commonwealth of money or specific property as punishment for breach of some general rule of conduct prescribed by a valid law of the Commonwealth. Such an acquisition stands apart from the kinds of "acquisition of property" which constitute the subject matter of s 51(xxxi) and such laws are beyond the reach of the paragraph's guarantee of just terms. Indeed, a law providing for an acquisition of property of a kind which is inconsistent or incongruous with the notion of just terms could validly be enacted pursuant to par (xxxi) itself. An example is a law providing for the payment of a pecuniary penalty for a corrupt breach of a statutory duty imposed by a valid law with respect to the acquisition of property on just terms ...

[188] [T]he indirect operation of par (xxxi) does not extend beyond abstracting from other grants of legislative power authority to make laws which can properly be characterized as laws with respect to the acquisition of property for a purpose in respect of which the Parliament has power to make laws. That does not, of course, mean that a law will be outside the reach of par (xxxi) unless that is its sole or dominant character. For the purposes of s 51, a law can have a number of characters and be, at the one time, a law with respect to the subject matter of a number of different grants of legislative power. However, unless a law can be fairly characterized, for the purposes of par (xxxi), as a law with respect to the acquisition of property, that paragraph cannot indirectly operate to exclude its enactment from the prima facie scope of another grant of legislative power ...

[189] As has been said, the limitations overlap. A law which is clearly authorised under some other grant of legislative power or which necessarily involves an acquisition of property unrestricted by any requirement of just terms, such as a law imposing a penalty for unlawful conduct, may well not be susceptible of independent characterization as a law with respect to the acquisition of property. While there is no set test or formula for determining whether a particular law can or cannot properly be characterized [in that way] ... , it is possible to identify in general terms some categories of laws which are unlikely to bear the character of a law with respect to the acquisition of property notwithstanding the fact that an acquisition of property may be an incident of their operation or application. One such category consists of laws which provide for the creation, modification, extinguishment or transfer of rights and liabilities as an incident of, or a means for enforcing, some general regulation of the conduct, rights and obligations of citizens in **[190]** relationships or areas which need to be regulated in the common interest. Another category consists of laws defining and altering rights and liabilities under a government scheme involving the expenditure of government funds to provide social security benefits or for other public purposes. A law falling within either of those categories may, as an incident of its operation or enforcement, adjust, modify or extinguish rights in a way which involves an "acquisition of property" within the wide meaning which that phrase bears for the purposes of s 51(xxxi). Yet, if such a law is of general operation, it is unlikely that it will be susceptible of being properly characterized, for the purposes of s 51 of the Constitution, as a law with respect to the acquisition of property for a purpose in respect of which the Parliament has power to make laws. The reason why that is so is that, even though an "acquisition of property" may be an incident or a consequence of the operation of such a law, it is unlikely that it will constitute an element or aspect which is capable of imparting to it the character of a law with respect to the subject matter of s 51(xxxi).

The concept spelled out in this final paragraph was further developed in *Health Insurance Commission v Peverill* (1994) 179 CLR 226, decided on the same day. By s 20A of the *Health Insurance Act 1973* (Cth), a patient entitled to Medicare benefits may assign that entitlement to a doctor or pathologist if the latter will "bulk bill", that is, accept the assignment of Medicare benefits as payment in full. Dr Richard Peverill was a pathologist testing for rubella by Enzyme-Linked Immunosorbent Assay (the ELISA test). He "bulk billed" in respect of ELISA tests administered from 3 December 1984 to 31 July 1989. For each test he claimed a fee of $34.50 under Item 1345 of the Schedule to the *Health Insurance Act*. However, the Health Insurance Commission ruled that the ELISA test came under Item 2294, which set a fee of $4.60. Peverill successfully challenged that ruling in the Federal Court. Thereupon, Parliament enacted the *Health Insurance (Pathology Services) Amendment Act 1991* (Cth), which retrospectively excluded the ELISA test from Item 1345 and included it under new Items 2294 and 2295, which prescribed a smaller fee. In a challenge to the *Amendment Act*, the whole Court held, though with different approaches and emphases, either that the benefit entitlement did not constitute "property", or that the retrospective reduction in the amount of benefits payable was not an "acquisition of property" within the meaning of s 51(xxxi).

Health Insurance Commission v Peverill
(1994) 179 CLR 226

Mason CJ, Deane and Gaudron JJ: [237] It is significant that the rights that have been terminated or diminished are statutory entitlements to receive payments from consolidated revenue which were not based on antecedent proprietary rights recognized by the general law. Rights of that kind are rights which, as a general rule, are inherently susceptible of variation. That is particularly so in the case of both the nature and quantum of welfare benefits, such as the provision of medicare benefits in respect of medical services. Whether a particular medicare benefit should be provided and, if so, in what amount, calls for a carefully considered assessment of what services should be covered and what is reasonable remuneration for the service provided, the nature and the amount of the medicare benefit having regard to the community's need for assistance, the capacity of government to pay and the future of health services in Australia. All these factors are susceptible of change so that it is to be expected that the level of benefits will change from time to time. Where such change is effected by a law which operates retrospectively to adjust competing claims or to overcome distortion, anomaly or unintended consequences in the working of the particular scheme, variations in outstanding entitlements to receive payments under the scheme may result. In such a case, what is involved is a variation of a right which is inherently susceptible of variation and the mere fact that a particular variation involves a reduction in entitlement and is retrospective does not convert it into an acquisition of property. More importantly, any incidental diminution in an individual's entitlement to payment in such a case does not suffice to invest the law adjusting entitlements under the relevant statutory scheme with the distinct character of a law with respect to the acquisition of property for the purposes of s 51(xxxi) of the Constitution.

Brennan J: [243] The right so conferred on assignee practitioners is not property: not only because the right is not assignable ... but, more fundamentally, because a right to receive a benefit to be paid by a statutory authority in discharge of a statutory duty is not susceptible of any form of repetitive or continuing enjoyment and cannot be exchanged for or converted into any kind of property ... **[244]** It does not have any degree of permanence or stability. That is not a right of a proprietary nature.

By contrast, in *Georgiadis v Australian and Overseas Telecommunications Corporation* (1994) 179 CLR 297, the Court held by 4:3, with Dawson, Toohey and McHugh JJ dissenting, that there was an "acquisition of property" under s 51(xxxi). The offending legislation was therefore rendered invalid by its failure to provide "just terms". Constantinos Georgiadis was a Telecom employee who sought to sue Telecom, and thus the Commonwealth, in respect of back injuries sustained in 1985 and 1986. The *Compensation (Commonwealth Employees) Act 1971* (Cth) had given Georgiadis the option of claiming workers' compensation or suing for damages at common law. However, s 44 of the *Commonwealth Employees' Rehabilitation and Compensation Act 1988* (Cth) (since renamed the *Safety Rehabilitation and Compensation Act 1988* (Cth)) extinguished any claim he might have had for common law damages.

Mason CJ, Deane and Gaudron JJ, with Brennan J concurring, held that a vested cause of action under the general law is a form of "property". They also held that there had been an "acquisition of property" under s 51(xxxi) because, although Georgiadis' cause of action was not "acquired" by anyone, the Commonwealth did acquire a direct benefit or financial gain in the form of a release from liability for damages. Dawson and Toohey JJ dissented – holding, as they had done in *Mutual Pools* and *Peverill*, that a mere claim to money or financial benefits is not "property" and that a release from liability to such a claim is not an "acquisition" of property. McHugh J agreed with the majority that Georgiadis had been deprived of "property" and that Telecom had "acquired" a commensurate benefit. However, he held that there was no "acquisition of property" "**[325]** because the right of the plaintiff to bring his action was dependent upon federal law and was always liable to be revoked by federal law. A right which can be extinguished by a federal law enacted under a power other than s 51(xxxi) is not a law which falls within the terms of that paragraph".

Georgiadis v Australian and Overseas Telecommunications Corporation
(1994) 179 CLR 297

Mason CJ, Deane and Gaudron JJ: [303] It is well established that s 51(xxxi) operates as a constitutional guarantee and that, for that reason, "acquisition" and "property" as used in that paragraph are to be construed liberally. In particular, s 51(xxxi) is "not to be confined pedantically to the taking of title ... to some specific estate or interest in land recognized at law or in equity ... but ... extends to innominate and anomalous interests" [*Bank of NSW v Commonwealth* (1948) 76 CLR 1 at 349]. And "property" as used in s 51(xxxi) extends to "every species of valuable right and interest including ... choses in action" [*Minister for the Army v Dalziel* (1944) 68 CLR 261 at 290], "money and the right to receive a payment of **[304]** money" [*Australian Tape Manufacturers Association Ltd v Commonwealth* (1993) 176 CLR 480 at 509; *Mutual Pools & Staff Ltd v Commonwealth* (1994) 179 CLR 155 at 172-3, 184-5]. Clearly, a right to bring an action for damages for negligence is a valuable right. Thus, the question in this case is whether s 44 is a law with respect to the acquisition of that right for a purpose in respect of which the Parliament has power to make laws within s 51(xxxi) ...

[305] It is often said in relation to constitutional guarantees and prohibitions that "you cannot do indirectly what you are forbidden to do directly" [*Wragg v New South Wales* (1953) 88 CLR 353 at 387-8]. That maxim is, in fact, an important guide to construction, indicating that guarantees and prohibitions are concerned with substance not form. Within that context, it is relevant to consider, by way of example, a vested cause of action against the Commonwealth for goods sold and delivered. If legislation extinguished that cause of action, it would, in substance, effect its acquisition, for the Commonwealth, having obtained the goods in exchange for its promise to pay, would be freed from its liability on that promise. Accordingly, "acquisition" in s 51(xxxi) extends to the extinguishment of a vested cause of action, at least where the extinguishment results in a direct benefit or financial gain (which, of course, includes liability being brought to an end without payment or other satisfaction) and the cause of action is one that arises under the general law. The position may be different in a case involving the extinguishment or modification of a right that has no existence apart from statute. That is because, prima facie at least and in the absence of a recognized legal relationship giving rise to **[306]** some like right, a right which has no existence apart from statute is one that, of its nature, is susceptible of modification or extinguishment. There is no acquisition of property involved in the modification or extinguishment of a right which has no basis in the general law and which, of its nature, is susceptible to that course. A law which effected the modification or extinguishment of a right of that kind would not have the character of a law with respect to the acquisition of property within s 51(xxxi) of the Constitution.

So far as the issues in this case are concerned, the effect of s 44, if valid, is to extinguish a vested cause of action that arose under the general law. That is so even if the right to proceed against the Commonwealth is properly identified as a statutory right. And its effect is to confer a distinct financial benefit on the Commonwealth and its agencies in respect of their pre-existing liability for employment injuries falling outside s 45 of the Act. In our view, the position is no different from that involved in the extinguishment of a vested cause of action against the Commonwealth for goods sold and delivered. Doubtless, Mr Georgiadis and other workers provided their skill and labour on the basis that they were entitled to damages at common law as well as workers' compensation benefits if injured as a result of Telecom's negligence. In that context, the right to damages can realistically be seen as part of the overall quid pro quo for the work performed. Thus and so far as it bears on the issues in this case, s 44 is, in substance, if not in form, a law for the acquisition of causes of action against the Commonwealth and its agencies which vested in employees before s 44 came into operation but which now fall outside s 45 of the Act.

Not every Commonwealth law with respect to the acquisition of property falls within s 51(xxxi) of the Constitution. It may be outside that paragraph because, although it effects an acquisition of property, it is a law of a kind that is clearly within some other head of legislative power. That is the case with a law imposing taxation or a law providing for the sequestration of the estate of a bankrupt. Or it may be outside s 51(xxxi) because it effects an acquisition of a kind that does not permit of just terms, as in the case of a law imposing a penalty by way of forfeiture. And, it may fall outside s 51(xxxi) because it cannot fairly be characterized **[307]** as a law for the acquisition of property for a purpose in respect of which the Parliament has power to make laws. That will generally be the case with laws directed to resolving competing claims or providing for "the creation, modification, extinguishment or transfer of rights and liabilities as an incident of, or a means for enforcing, some general regulation of the conduct, rights and obligations of citizens in relationships or areas which need to be regulated in the common interest" [*Mutual Pools & Staff Ltd v Commonwealth* (1994) 179 CLR at 189-90, 171-2] ...

One consequence of s 51(xxxi)'s operation through characterization and concern with substance is that there will inevitably be borderline cases in which the question whether a law bears the distinct character of a law with respect to the acquisition of property for a s 51(xxxi) purpose is finely balanced. The present is such a case. On balance, we have reached the conclusion that s 44 does possess such a distinct character.

It may well be that, if s 44 appeared in legislation establishing a compensation scheme applying to employers and employees generally (assuming power to enact a scheme of that kind), it would not fairly be characterized as a law for the acquisition of property for a purpose for which the Parliament has power to make laws. But when s 44 is viewed in the context of a scheme which applies only to Commonwealth employees, it may be fairly characterized as a law for the acquisition of the causes of action which vested in those employees prior to the commencement of the new scheme. That acquisition is for the purposes of that scheme, that is to say, it is for a purpose for which the Parliament has power to make laws. It is true that s 44 may be susceptible of other characterizations for other purposes. For the purposes of s 51(xxxi) of the Constitution, however, it bears a distinct character as a law with respect to the acquisition of property within that paragraph.

In *Commonwealth v Mewett* (1997) 191 CLR 471, the Commonwealth mounted an attack on *Georgiadis*. The respondents, three former members of the Royal Australian Navy, began actions against the Commonwealth in 1994. The actions sought damages under the common law of contract and tort for injuries sustained in 1979 and 1985. Under State legislation, the respondents' actions were statute barred unless they could gain an extension of time, which they duly sought. However, the Commonwealth argued that each of the proceedings should be struck out as a result of s 44 of the *Safety, Rehabilitation and Compensation Act*. As in *Georgiadis*, the respondents argued that s 44 was invalid in its application to a claim which had arisen before the commencement of s 44, since it effected an acquisition of property. The Commonwealth responded by challenging the correctness of *Georgiadis*. It argued that the rights which the respondents claimed against the Commonwealth arose under a Commonwealth statute, the *Judiciary Act 1903* (Cth), and were therefore inherently susceptible of modification or extinguishment. The High Court unanimously rejected this argument and upheld *Georgiadis*, again holding that s 44 contravened s 51(xxxi).

The law considered in *Smith v ANL Ltd* (2000) 204 CLR 493 combined elements of the legislation in *Georgiadis* with elements of that in *Mewett*, but in separate complementary statutes: the *Seafarers Rehabilitation and Compensation Act 1992* (Cth) and the *Seafarers Rehabilitation and Compensation (Transitional Provisions and Consequential Amendments) Act 1992* (Cth). By s 54 of the former Act and s 13 of the latter, existing common law rights of action were prospectively extinguished, but could still be asserted for six months after the legislation commenced. Thus, the practical effect was to impose a new limitation period. McHugh and Hayne JJ held that there was no "acquisition of property", because (as Hayne J put it): "**[533]** Neither the Rehabilitation Act nor the Transitional Provisions Act effected any acquisition of property on the day on which those Acts came into force". This, however, was a dissenting view; the other five judges held that *Georgiadis* and *Mewett* applied.

In *Teori Tau v Commonwealth* (1969) 119 CLR 564, an Indigenous kinship group in the Territory of Papua and New Guinea asserted a claim to land occupied by the Bougainville copper mine, arguing that successive Ordinances since 1922 had been invalid for want of just terms. The claim was dismissed *ex tempore* on the ground that laws passed under the Territories power (s 122 of the Constitution) are not subject to s 51(xxxi). Barwick CJ, speaking for the Court, stated: "**[570]** The grant of legislative power by s 122 is plenary in quality and unlimited and unqualified in point of subject matter. In particular, it is not limited or qualified by s 51(xxxi) or, for that matter, by any other paragraph of that section".

The effect of that decision was qualified in *Newcrest Mining (WA) Ltd v Commonwealth* (1997) 190 CLR 513. Between 1947 and 1974, 25 mining tenements were granted under the *Mining Ordinance 1939* (NT) in the Coronation Hill area in the Northern Territory. They came to be sold to Newcrest Mining (WA) Ltd. In 1989, the federal Cabinet decided that Stage 3 of the Kakadu National Park should be significantly increased to include the Coronation Hill area. In 1989 and 1991, proclamations were made to this effect under the *National Parks and Wildlife Conservation Act 1975* (Cth). Under s 10(1A) of the Act: "No operations for the recovery of minerals shall be carried on in Kakadu National Park". The result was to prohibit Newcrest from exploiting the 25 mining tenements. Section 7 of the *National Parks and Wildlife Conservation Amendment Act 1987* (Cth) further provided: "Notwithstanding any law of the Commonwealth or of the Northern Territory, the Commonwealth is not liable to pay compensation to any person by reason of the enactment of this Act".

Newcrest brought an action in the High Court claiming that the 1989 and 1991 proclamations were invalid because they effected an "acquisition of property". Four judges, Toohey, Gaudron, Gummow and Kirby JJ, held that there was an "acquisition of property" for the purposes of s 51(xxxi), and that s 51(xxxi) applied because (quite apart from the position under s 122) there was an acquisition for Commonwealth purposes under a s 51 head of power. Specifically, the *Conservation Act* could be characterised as a valid law under the Commonwealth's "external affairs" power in s 51(xxix). Three of these judges, Gaudron, Gummow and Kirby JJ, were also prepared to overrule *Teori Tau* by holding that s 51(xxxi) applies to laws made under s 122.

Brennan CJ, Dawson and McHugh JJ dissented. Although Brennan CJ held and Dawson J assumed that there was an "acquisition of property", they applied *Teori Tau* to hold that s 51(xxxi) does not apply to the Territories. McHugh J also applied *Teori Tau*, but in any event held (in sole dissent on this point) that there was no "acquisition of property" since "**[573]** even if there was effectively a diminution or extinguishment of all or part of Newcrest's interests, there was no gain by the Commonwealth".

Newcrest Mining (WA) Ltd v Commonwealth
(1997) 190 CLR 513

Gummow J: [633] None of the provisions relied upon by the appellants is expressed in direct language as effecting an acquisition of any property. However, the question is whether, even if not formally, the appellants effectively have been deprived of "the reality of proprietorship" by the indirect acquisition, through the collective operation of the provisions of the Conservation Act, of "the substance of a proprietary interest" …

[634] The appellants say that, in substance, the Commonwealth and the Director [of National Parks and Wildlife] acquired identifiable and measurable advantages. In the case of the Director, those advantages were the acquisition of the land freed from the rights of Newcrest to occupy and conduct mining operations thereon and, in the case of the Commonwealth, the minerals freed from the rights of Newcrest to mine them. In accordance with the authorities, that is sufficient derivation of an identifiable and measurable advantage to satisfy the constitutional requirement of an acquisition.

There is no reason why the identifiable benefit or advantage relating to the ownership or use of property, which is acquired, should correspond precisely to that which was taken. This is not a case in the category considered in *Health Insurance Commission v Peverill* [(1994) 179 CLR 226] where what was in issue were rights derived purely from statute and of their very nature inherently susceptible to the variation or extinguishment which had come to pass …

Further, the history of the [Northern] Territory, beginning with the surrender and acceptance effected pursuant to s 111 of the Constitution, shows **[635]** that the Commonwealth (or the Crown in right of the Commonwealth) acquired a radical title in the sense known to the common law and thereafter the Commonwealth dealt with the subject land in exercise of its rights of dominion over it. This involved the use of statute to carve out interests from the particular species of ownership enjoyed by the Commonwealth and, after self-government, by the Territory in the manner identified earlier in these reasons. It is not correct, for the purposes of the application of s 51(xxxi), to identify the property held by Newcrest as no more than a statutory privilege under a licensing system …

Nor is this a case where there was merely an impairment of the bundle of rights constituting the property of Newcrest. An example of such impairment is found in *Waterhouse v Minister for the Arts and Territories* [(1993) 119 ALR 89]. There, the prohibition on export of the painting in question left the owner free to retain, enjoy, display or otherwise make use of the painting and left him free to sell, mortgage or otherwise turn it to advantage subject to the requirement of an export permit if the owner or any other person desired to take it out of Australia. Here, there was an effective sterilisation of the rights constituting the property in question. That this is so is only emphasised upon a consideration of the contrary submission made by the Commonwealth and the Director. It is true, as they submit, that the mining tenements were not, in terms, extinguished. It is true also that Kakadu extended only 1,000 m beneath the surface. But, on the surface and to that depth, s 10(1A) of the Conservation Act forbade the carrying out of operations for the recovery of minerals. The vesting in the Commonwealth of the minerals to that depth and the vesting of the surface and balance of the relevant segments of the subterranean land in the Director had the effect, as a legal and practical matter, of denying to Newcrest the exercise of its rights under the mining tenements.

It was held that the Commonwealth had acquired property from Newcrest other than on just terms. This conclusion was based on the fact that the tenements were not just a creation of statute, but a modification of the Commonwealth's pre-existing common law title to the land. By contrast, in *Commonwealth v WMC Resources Ltd* (1998) 194 CLR 1 a majority of the Court, with Toohey and Kirby JJ dissenting, found no "acquisition of property" where a Commonwealth law extinguished an exploration permit over part of the continental shelf between Australia and East Timor. This situation was distinguishable from that in *Newcrest* because the Commonwealth had no underlying common law interest in the Timor Gap continental shelf. According to Gaudron J, the Commonwealth Act "**[38]** simply modified a statutory right which had no basis in the general law and which was inherently susceptible to that course".

In *Newcrest*, Gaudron J spelt out most fully the interpretive approach on which the 4:3 decision finally depended. This was that the *Conservation Act* was expressed to give effect to Australia's obligations under the 1972 Convention for the Protection of the World Cultural and Natural Heritage. It was therefore subject to s 51(xxxi) because it could be characterised as a law with respect to "external affairs", even if it could also be characterised as a law under s 122. Toohey, Gummow and Kirby JJ also accepted this analysis.

> **Gaudron J: [568]** It is clear, as the respondents contend in this case, that a law may have more than one purpose. Even if s 51(xxxi) is construed as referring to "any purpose in respect of which the Parliament has power to make laws [under this section]", a law which has a purpose of that kind clearly falls within its terms whether or not it is also a law "for the government of [a] territory" (s 122).
>
> It is one thing to read down s 51(xxxi) so that it does not apply to a law enacted pursuant to s 122 of the Constitution. It is another to treat it as not applying to a law which has two purposes, one of which falls within the terms of s 51(xxxi) and the other of which is for the government of a Territory. That is to rewrite the terms of s 51(xxxi), not to read them down. Neither course is permissible. Rather, the proper approach is to construe constitutional guarantees as liberally as their terms will allow.
>
> However, it is not necessary to take a liberal approach in this case. On the assumption that par (xxxi) is to be read down so that it applies only to laws enacted under s 51, its terms, even when strictly construed, extend to a law a purpose of which is one "in respect of which the Parliament has power to make laws [under s 51]". In *PJ Magennis Pty Ltd v Commonwealth* [(1949) 80 CLR 382 at 423] Williams J said of par (xxxi):
>
>> "In my opinion the paragraph applies to all Commonwealth legislation the object of which is to acquire property for a purpose in respect of which the Commonwealth Parliament has power to make laws."
>
> A purpose of the Conservation Act is the performance of Australia's international obligations; that is a purpose in respect of which the Parliament has power to make laws under s 51(xxix); para (xxxi) operates to fetter the implementation of that purpose by means of a **[569]** law with respect to the acquisition of property. The Commonwealth cannot enact laws for a purpose which falls within s 51 without the condition which attaches by para (xxxi).

Brennan CJ, Dawson and McHugh JJ rejected this approach.

> **Brennan CJ: [534]** When a law is supportable by a constitutional power, it is immaterial to its validity that, if some particular requirement were met, it would also be supported by a second constitutional power. So long as the Parliament has power to enact a law, from whatever provision of the Constitution that power be derived, the law is valid. As Starke J said in *Ex parte Walsh and Johnson; Re Yates* [(1925) 37 CLR 36 at 135]:

"A law enacted by a Parliament with power to enact it, cannot be unlawful. The question is not one of intention but of power, *from whatever source derived*. [The section under challenge] can be justified, in my opinion, if it is competent under any of the powers vested in Parliament, whatever the title of the Act, and whatever indications there are in the Act as to the precise power under which it may be suggested that Parliament purported to act." (Emphasis added.)

It follows that, unless there be some reason for denying the sufficiency of the power conferred by s 122 to support the Conservation Amendment Act, the Conservation Amendment Act is valid.

The refusal to find an "acquisition of property" in *Nintendo*, *Mutual Pools* and *Peverill*, combined with the willingness to do so in *Georgiadis*, *Mewett* and *Newcrest*, has resulted in difficult questions of judgment dependent on subtle distinctions, and exacerbated by the judicial differences in emphasis and approach. The judgments in *Airservices Australia v Canadian Airlines International Ltd* (1999) 202 CLR 133 are further evidence of the lack of a common interpretation of s 51(xxxi).

The *Civil Aviation Act 1988* (Cth) enabled the Civil Aviation Authority to impose charges upon aircraft operators to recoup the cost of providing certain services (such as air traffic and rescue services). Charges were levied against Compass Airlines and, when Compass went into liquidation, a lien was imposed under the Act on aircraft used by Compass. The statutory lien enabled the Authority to sell the aircraft to recoup the cost of the charges. However, the aircraft had been leased by Compass, and their owners challenged the Act on the basis, first, that the charges were a tax and not a fee for services and, secondly, that the lien effected an acquisition of property without providing just terms. Both arguments failed. Gleeson CJ, McHugh, Gummow, Kirby and Hayne JJ held that the provision imposing the lien was not a law with respect to the acquisition of property. Gaudron and Callinan JJ dissented.

Airservices Australia v Canadian Airlines International Ltd
(1999) 202 CLR 133

Gleeson CJ and Kirby J: [179] The rationale underlying [the lien] provisions is not difficult to see. Aircraft operators, who may incur liability for charges and penalties, may have few assets within a particular jurisdiction at any given time except aircraft, and aircraft may leave a jurisdiction very quickly. As the facts of the present case show, charges in large sums can accumulate in a short time. The charges are for services related to the safety of aircraft, and those with a proprietary interest in aircraft, as well as the operators, receive a benefit from those services. They are in some respects akin to necessaries supplied to a ship. The regulatory regimes which apply in various jurisdictions are likely to be widely known to owners of aircraft who may be assumed to enter into transactions affecting title to aircraft in the light of such knowledge. It is not to the point that it is possible to imagine other steps which might be taken to provide security for payment of charges and penalties. The Parliament has decided upon this regime for Australia …

[180] The principles which determine whether a law providing for a statutory lien, with the incidents specified in the Act, in support of a scheme of charging for services and facilities, is within the reach of the requirement of just terms stipulated by s 51(xxxi) have been considered in many recent cases. In *Mutual Pools & Staff Pty Ltd v The Commonwealth* [(1994) 179 CLR 155] Brennan J, referring to earlier authority, pointed out that a grant of legislative power comprehends a power to enact provisions appropriate and adapted to the fulfilment of any objective falling within the power, and that s 51(xxxi) does not abstract the power to prescribe the means appropriate and adapted to the achievement of an objective falling within another head of power where the acquisition of property without just terms is a necessary or characteristic feature of the means prescribed …

In *Re Director of Public Prosecutions; Ex parte Lawler* [(1994) 179 CLR 270 at 281] a law providing for the forfeiture of a fishing vessel operating illegally in Australian waters was held not to contravene s 51(xxxi), even though the owner of the vessel was not complicit in the offence. The considerations relevant to whether the forfeiture of property of an innocent third party, where such property has been used in the commission of an offence, is "appropriate and adapted to the **[181]** enforcement of the offence-creating provision", are not identical to those relevant to whether the creating of a statutory lien over an aircraft is appropriate and adapted to the provision, on a commercial basis, of services and facilities such as those provided by the CAA. However, the test is the same.

Having regard to the relationship between the services provided by the CAA and the safety of the aircraft concerned, the reasonableness of a system which provides that those who operate aircraft must pay charges which, in totality, will defray the cost of providing the services, the possibility that operators will have few assets in the jurisdiction apart from aircraft, the mobility of aircraft, and the desirability of providing adequate security for liabilities incurred, it is at least as easy to draw a conclusion supportive of the legislation as it was in *Ex parte Lawler*.

Concepts of "innocence", lack of "complicity" or "culpability" are difficult to relate to the present issue. However, the position of the respondents was not isolated from the conduct of Compass. They had leased or sub-leased aircraft to Compass. By inference, they did so knowing that such aircraft would be flown on routes to, from and within Australia, attracting charges for services and facilities provided to all airline operators. They could be taken to know that such charges were not insubstantial. Unpaid, they would accumulate to very large sums. They could readily have ascertained that provision for statutory liens existed under Australian law as under the laws of other jurisdictions involved in civil aviation of a comparable kind. By inference, it would have been open to them to protect themselves (by contract, insurance, or facilities for auditing and reporting) against the kind of result that ensued. Without the provision of their aircraft to Compass, that company would not have been in a position to accumulate the very substantial charges which it did. We accept that s 51(xxxi) of the Constitution must not, in accordance with the authority of this Court, be given a pedantic or narrow construction. We also accept that the taking of property under a federal law is not removed from "acquisition" simply because it is described as "forfeiture". It is not the name, but the character of the taking, that controls the outcome of constitutional characterization. But, in this case, the statutory liens are valid … They were provided to secure the effectiveness of charges relating to aircraft which, of their very nature, could otherwise leave Australia with substantial debts unpaid and with no effective means for their recovery.

McHugh J: [250] Where the inquiry is whether an acquisition of property is within federal power but outside s 51(xxxi), a two-stage process must be undertaken. First, is the impugned law a law within s 51(xxxi)? Second, if no, is the law otherwise within the legislative power of the Commonwealth as a law with respect to another head of federal power? It is incorrect to seek to answer the second question and treat it as determining the answer to the first. Section 51(xxxi) doctrine holds that, where that paragraph applies, the power of acquisition is abstracted from all other heads of Commonwealth power. The first question must always be answered, therefore, before resort is had to the second question.

I discussed the first question in *Mutual Pools* [179 CLR at 219-20] where I said:

> "The compound conception of an 'acquisition of property on just terms' predicates a compulsory transfer of property from a State or person in circumstances which require that the acquirer should pay fair compensation to the transferor. When, by a law of the Parliament, the Commonwealth or someone on its behalf compulsorily acquires property in circumstances which make the notion of fair compensation to the transferor irrelevant or incongruous, s 51(xxxi) has no operation."

In that passage, I gave content to the first question in a manner which is independent of the answer to the second. If the law effects an acquisition of property and the notion of compensation is not incongruous or irrelevant, the law is within s 51(xxxi) and its validity will depend on whether it provides just terms for the acquisition, nothing more. Of course, the notions of incongruity and irrelevance necessarily assume that the subject matter or the purpose of the acquisition is one that, but for s 51(xxxi), would prima facie fall within another head of federal power such as taxation, bankruptcy or defence. But that is different from treating s 51(xxxi) as if, in some circumstances at least, its content is the residue of other federal **[251]** powers. Where the Commonwealth acquires property, s 51(xxxi) must be addressed at the beginning and not at the end of the inquiry.

If the circumstances are such that the notion of fair compensation to the transferor is irrelevant or incongruous, the law is not a law with respect to s 51(xxxi). Its validity will then depend on whether it can be supported under another head of federal power …

[252] [T]he debt secured by the lien was the quid pro quo accruing to the Authority as the result of its prior supply of valuable services to the aircraft operator. The lien was used to secure an existing indebtedness and it was only in force until that indebtedness was discharged. The subject matter of the lien is one that is arguably within the power conferred on the Parliament by s 51(i) and s 51(xxix) of the Constitution. If "fair **[253]** compensation" were to be paid to those having a proprietary interest in an aircraft upon the imposition of a lien, it would mean that the Authority would have an interest in the aircraft which on sale could be realised to satisfy the operator's previously incurred debt to the Authority, but on the other hand the Authority would incur a liability to pay "fair compensation" to those having a proprietary interest in the aircraft. The amount of this liability for "fair compensation" would be at least equal to the amount secured by the lien (as the "fair value" of the lien in the sense of the amount required to be paid before it will be discharged), and may be greater than the amount secured by the lien (if fair compensation involved an amount for loss of profits consequent upon the loss of use of the aircraft). Thus, the entire purpose of the lien would be frustrated as the Authority would be no better off, and indeed may be worse off, in terms of net recovery of the charges levied as a quid pro quo for the provision of the services. Accordingly, in my opinion, the imposition of a statutory lien in these circumstances is irrelevant to or incongruous with the notion of fair compensation in the sense adverted to by me in *Mutual Pools*. Fair compensation would not be incongruous or irrelevant if there were no services provided. But that is not this case.

Gummow J also saw the notion of fair compensation as irrelevant or incongruous in this context, so that s 51(xxxi) had no operation. He reached the same result by holding, as did Hayne J, that the lien provisions were not directed towards the acquisition of property as such, but were concerned with the adjustment of competing rights, claims or obligations.

Gummow J: [300] The statutory lien provisions are part of the regulatory scheme for civil aviation safety created by the Act. The lien provisions adjust the respective interests of those who own, lease or operate the aircraft and of the provider of services necessary for commercial operations of the aircraft in Australia. The interests of security holders are … not displaced. The services were provided by the Authority to the aircraft, in the sense that it was particular operations using the aircraft which provided the incident for the attraction of the charges.

It would be an error to classify the relationship to which the statutory scheme gave rise as if all that were involved was an obligation in the nature of a contract between Compass and the Authority to which the respondents were strangers who might rely upon some mutation of the doctrine of privity. The "price" which had to be provided or suffered to acquire from the Authority services to the aircraft was the indebtedness of Compass. This was supplemented by the remedies available to the Authority, recourse, or threat of recourse, to which provided a strong incentive to the respondents to see that the charges and penalties were met.

The bundle of rights and remedies held by the Authority constituted the exchange for the provision of the services. In the events that occurred, the services were provided, but the charges and penalties were not recouped to the Authority. For the Authority then to assert its rights and remedies against the respondents is not to compulsorily acquire property from the respondents with an attendant obligation of fair compensation to the respondents from the Authority. The lien provisions are not invalid as laws which must answer the condition imposed by s 51(xxxi) of the Constitution in order to be valid.

It was on this point that Gaudron J dissented.

Gaudron J: [196] So far as concerns aircraft owned by persons or corporations who or which have incurred charges and penalties giving rise to a statutory lien … , the liens provisions are … properly to be characterised as laws adjusting the competing rights and claims of their existing and future creditors, rather than laws "directed **[197]** towards the acquisition of property as such" [*Nintendo Co Ltd v Centronics Systems Pty Ltd* (1994) 181 CLR 134 at 161]. However, that is not the case with persons or corporations who or which have not incurred the charges or penalties concerned ...

[A] law which operates to acquire a security interest in the property of a person to satisfy charges or penalties incurred by another is not, itself, adjusting competing claims or interests. At least that is so when there is no relationship between the former and the person or body to whom the charges or penalties are payable, as, for example, would be the case if the former had guaranteed payment of those charges or penalties. Absent a relationship of that kind, a law acquiring a security interest in the property of a person who did not incur the charges or penalties is not adjusting any interest of or claim by that person, or any obligation owed by him or her. It is simply appropriating a security interest in that person's property. The fact that, once appropriated, that interest may be utilised to adjust the competing claims and interests of creditors, of which that person may be one, cannot alter the fact that it is primarily a law for the acquisition of property and is properly characterised as such.

Callinan J based his dissent on a critical examination of the "forfeiture" cases, *Burton v Honan* and *Re Director of Public Prosecutions; Ex parte Lawler*. They held that a forfeiture of goods was not an "acquisition of property" within s 51(xxxi) where it was incidental to the enforcement of a valid penal law under another head of power. Callinan J questioned the use of the word "forfeiture" in relation to "**[309]** the extinction of all proprietary rights of innocent as opposed to complicit third parties". He held that *Burton v Honan* and *Lawler* did not extend to a statute providing, as the lien provisions did, for the forfeiture of property of "innocent" third parties in circumstances where the statute had created no criminal offence.

(c) "Just terms"

The Fifth Amendment to the United States Constitution requires "just compensation", whereas s 51(xxxi) merely requires "just terms". While "just compensation" may import equivalence of market value, the phrase "just terms" imports no such thing. The arrangements offered must be "fair", or such that a legislature could reasonably regard them as "fair" (*Nelungaloo Pty Ltd v Commonwealth* (1947) 75 CLR 495). This judgment of "fairness" must take account of all the interests affected, not just those of the dispossessed owner. In *Grace Bros Pty Ltd v Commonwealth* (1946) 72 CLR 269, a department store in Sydney was initially occupied by the Commonwealth during World War II and then permanently taken over pursuant to a statutory scheme that provided for compensation based on valuation as at "the first day of January last preceding the date of acquisition". Garfield Barwick KC argued that: "**[271]** Just terms necessarily involve the payment to the owner of the value of his property as at the date when it is taken from him". By 4:1, the High Court rejected this argument.

Grace Bros Pty Ltd v Commonwealth
(1946) 72 CLR 269

Dixon J: [290] The legislative power given by s 51(xxxi) is to make laws with respect to a compound conception, namely, "acquisition-on-just-terms." "Just terms" doubtless forms a part of the definition of the subject matter, and in that sense amounts to a condition which the law must satisfy. But the question for the Court when validity is in issue is whether the legislation answers the description of a law with respect to acquisition upon just terms. In considering such a matter much assistance may be derived from American judicial decisions and juridical writings dealing with analogous difficulties, but they must be used with care and, in my opinion, cannot be applied directly to s 51(xxxi). Under that paragraph the validity of any general law cannot, I think, be tested by inquiring whether it will be certain to operate in every individual case to place the owner in a situation in which in all respects he will be as well off as if the acquisition had not taken place. The inquiry rather must be whether the law amounts to a true attempt to provide fair and just standards of compensating or rehabilitating the individual considered as an owner of property, fair and just as between him and the government of the country. I say "the individual" because what is just as between the Commonwealth and a State, two Governments, may depend on special considerations not applicable to an individual.

The power conferred by s 51(xxxi) is express, and it was introduced as a specific power, not, like the Fifth Amendment, for the purpose of protecting the subject or citizen, but primarily to make certain that the Commonwealth possessed a power compulsorily to **[291]** acquire property, particularly from the States. The condition "on just terms" was included to prevent arbitrary exercise of the power at the expense of a State or the subject.

In deciding whether any given law is within the power the Court must, of course, examine the justice of the terms provided. But it is a legislative function to provide the terms, and the Constitution does not mean to deprive the legislature of all discretion in determining what is just. Nor does justice to the subject or to the State demand a disregard of the interests of the public or of the Commonwealth.

"Just terms" does not necessarily require that a compensation package be presented as part of the acquisition scheme. It is sufficient that the scheme provides adequate procedures for determining fair compensation. However, the Court may scrutinise such procedures to ensure their adequacy. This, for example, was the ground on which Deane J, in *Commonwealth v Tasmania* (*Tasmanian Dam Case*) (1983) 158 CLR 1, held that insofar as the laws in that case effected an "acquisition of property" they failed to satisfy s 51(xxxi). Other judges did not consider this argument because they held that there had been no "acquisition of property"; the Commonwealth legislation merely prevented the use of land for specified purposes and did not vest or divest any possessory or proprietary rights.

Section 17 of the *World Heritage Properties Conservation Act 1983* (Cth) provided a scheme for the fixing of compensation in respect of any acquisition of property. Claims under $5,000,000 were to be heard by the Federal Court, while for claims over $5,000,000 there was to be a six-month waiting period, during which compensation might be agreed to, followed by a Commission of Inquiry which was to recommend, within 12 months of its formation, "fair and just" compensation. For Deane J, these procedures were insufficient.

Commonwealth v Tasmania (*Tasmanian Dam Case*)
(1983) 158 CLR 1

Deane J: [290] The provisions of s 17 do not confer any immediate right to be paid compensation upon the acquisition of property. All they confer is a right to set a procedure in chain. If the Minister contests that there has been an acquisition, the Commonwealth is under no obligation to pay compensation unless and until the claimant has instituted proceedings in the High Court and obtained a declaration that there has been an acquisition. Inevitably, the obtaining of such a declaration will involve the passage of time. If such a declaration is obtained and the amount claimed is in excess of $5,000,000, the claimant is still not entitled to enforce payment of any amount of compensation. He is only entitled to have a Committee of Inquiry established. It is instructive to consider the situation which exists if he obtains a favourable recommendation from that Committee of Inquiry. At that stage, the Act envisages that more than eighteen months plus whatever time may be involved in obtaining a declaration in the High Court may have expired. The claimant is still not entitled to be paid an ascertained amount of compensation or to apply to have a binding determination of such an amount. He **[291]** has to wait for the next step which is for the Governor-General to determine what the Governor-General considers to be "fair and just" compensation in respect of the acquisition. The Governor-General will, of course, act on the advice of the relevant Minister of the Commonwealth. He is not obliged to accept the recommendations of the Committee of Inquiry. It is only after the Governor-General has determined what he considers to be "fair and just" compensation that the claimant has the right to seek compensation in a tribunal which has authority to make a binding decision.

There is not, of course, anything intrinsically unfair in the Parliament providing a procedure for determining the quantum of compensation outside the ordinary judicial process. There is, however, something intrinsically unfair in a procedure which, in effect, ensures that, unless a claimant agrees to accept the terms which the Commonwealth is prepared to offer, he will be forced to wait years before he is allowed even access to a court, tribunal or other body which can authoritatively determine the amount of the compensation which the Commonwealth must pay. In the case of s 17 of the Act, this intrinsic unfairness is heightened by a failure to make any provision in respect of the payment of interest during the period between the time when the acquisition is made and the time when the person whose property is acquired can finally institute an effective claim for compensation. In my view, the system established by s 17 … is quite unacceptable and unfair according to the ordinary standards of "fair dealing between the Australian nation and an Australian State or individual in relation to the acquisition of property for a purpose within the national legislative competence": *Nelungaloo Pty Ltd v Commonwealth* [(1952) 85 CLR 545 at 600].

3. Further References

Arch, AM, and Fisher, WW (eds), *Agricultural Marketing: Section 92 of the Commonwealth Constitution* (Australian Agricultural Economics Society, Victorian Branch, 1988).

Beasley, FR, "The Commonwealth Constitution: Section 92 – Its History in the Federal Conventions" (1948-1950) 1 *University of Western Australia Annual Law Review* 97, 273, 433.

Bell, A, "Section 92, Factual Discrimination and the High Court" (1991) 20 *Federal Law Review* 240.

Brennan, S, "Native Title and the 'Acquisition of Property' under the *Australian Constitution*" (2004) 28 *Melbourne University Law Review* 28.

Carney, G, "The Re-interpretation of Section 92: The Decline of Free Enterprise and the Rise of Free Trade" (1991) 3 *Bond Law Review* 149.

Coper, M, *Encounters with the Australian Constitution* (CCH, 1987), Ch 7.

Coper, M, *Freedom of Interstate Trade under the Australian Constitution* (Butterworths, 1983).

Coper, M, "Constitutional Obstacles to Organised Marketing in Australia" (1978) 46 *Review of Marketing and Agricultural Economics* 71.

Cowen, Z, *Isaac Isaacs* (Oxford University Press, 1967), 179-89.

Dixon, R, "Overriding Guarantee of Just Terms or Supplementary Source of Power?: Rethinking s51(xxxi) of the Constitution" (2005) 27 *Sydney Law Review* 639.

Evans, S, "When is an Acquisition of Property not an Acquisition of Property?" (2000) 11 *Public Law Review* 183.

La Nauze, JA, "A Little Bit of Lawyers' Language: The History of 'Absolutely Free', 1890-1900" in Martin, AW (ed), *Essays in Australian Federation* (Melbourne University Press, 1969), 57.

Lane, PH, "The Present Test for Invalidity under Section 92 of the Constitution" (1988) 62 *Australian Law Journal* 604.

Marr, D, *Barwick* (Allen & Unwin, 1980), Ch 7.

O'Brien, B, "Inchoate Rights to Interstate Communications under Section 92" (1982) 13 *Melbourne University Law Review* 198.

Puig, GV, "Free Movement of Goods: The European Experience in the Australian Context" (2001) 75 *Australian Law Journal* 639.

Rose, D, "*Cole v Whitfield*: 'Absolutely Free' Trade?" in Lee, HP, and Winterton, G (eds), *Australian Constitutional Landmarks* (Cambridge University Press, 2003), 335.

Simpson, A, "Grounding the High Court's Modern Section 92 Jurisprudence: The Case for Improper Purpose as the Touchstone" (2005) 33 *Federal Law Review* 445.

Sonter, D, "Intention or Effect? Commonwealth and State Legislation after *Cole v Whitfield*" (1995) 69 *Australian Law Journal* 332.

Staker, C, "Section 92 of the Constitution and the European Court of Justice" (1990) 19 *Federal Law Review* 322.

Starke, JG, "The *Cole v Whitfield* Test for Section 92 Explained and Applied: The Demise of the Theory of 'Individual Rights'" (1991) 65 *Australian Law Journal* 123.

Starke, JG, "The Inter-State Commission and Section 92 of the Constitution" (1988) 62 *Australian Law Journal* 586.

Temby, I, "'In this Labyrinth There is No Golden Thread': Section 92 and the Impressionistic Approach" (1984) 58 *Australian Law Journal* 86.

Williams, G, *Human Rights under the Australian Constitution* (Oxford University Press, 1999), Ch 6.

Zines, L, *The High Court and the Constitution* (Butterworths, 4th ed 1997), Chs 6-8.

Chapter 28

Freedom of Political Communication

1. Introduction

In the early 1990s the High Court began to explore the idea that the Constitution contains, by implication, a commitment to certain fundamental freedoms or democratic values operating as judicially enforceable limits on the legislative powers of the Commonwealth, and perhaps on those of the States as well. Although such implications had been foreshadowed in the judgments of Murphy J, no clear unambiguous example emerged until 1992, when a majority of the High Court recognised, in *Nationwide News Pty Ltd v Wills* (1992) 177 CLR 1 and *Australian Capital Television Pty Ltd v Commonwealth* (1992) 177 CLR 106, that the Constitution implies a commitment to freedom of political communication. The impact of this implication on the law of defamation, initially explored in *Theophanous v Herald & Weekly Times Ltd* (1994) 182 CLR 104 and *Stephens v West Australian Newspapers Ltd* (1994) 182 CLR 211, was secured (though restated) by the unanimous decision in *Lange v Australian Broadcasting Corporation* (1997) 189 CLR 520.

Initially, there were suggestions that the requirement of free political communication could be derived from a general conception of representative government inherent in the Constitution. What has now prevailed is a narrower rationale but also a more secure one: namely, that the freedom is derived from the text of the Constitution, particularly ss 7 and 24, which provide respectively that the Senate and the House of Representatives shall be "directly chosen by the people" (see Chapter 10, §4(a)). The initial decisions had engendered considerable controversy: it was said that they were inconsistent with the decision in *Amalgamated Society of Engineers v Adelaide Steamship Co Ltd* (*Engineers' Case*) (1920) 28 CLR 129, or at least that they marked a constitutional turning point potentially as significant as the *Engineers' Case* itself. However that may be, the existence of such an implication was reaffirmed in *Lange* by a unanimous Court.

2. The Murphy Catalyst

There is an early example of the High Court recognising and applying an individual freedom implied from the Constitution. In *R v Smithers; Ex parte Benson* (1912) 16 CLR 99, Griffith CJ and Barton J recognised an implied right of access to government and to the seat of government. Barton J stated that "**[109]** the creation of a federal union with one government and one legislature in respect of national affairs assures to every free citizen the **[110]** right of access to the institutions, and of due participation in the activities of the nation" (see also *Pioneer Express Pty Ltd v Hotchkiss* (1958) 101 CLR 536 at 550 per Dixon CJ).

However, it was not until the appointment of Murphy J in 1975 that further suggestions were made that the Constitution embodies a range of implied freedoms. The first of these suggestions came towards the end of Murphy J's first year on the Court. In *R v Director-General of Social Welfare (Vic); Ex parte Henry* (1975) 133 CLR 369, the whole Court upheld, but sought to confine, a statutory provision vesting guardianship of immigrant children in the Minister for Immigration. The limit proposed by Murphy J was that guardianship should cease when the child turned 18, since it "**[388]** would not be within the scope of the immigration power" for migrants "to be left in a state of guardianship indefinitely". He explained that because ours "is a Constitution for a free society", laws permitting "slavery or serfdom", or any other "subordinate role inconsistent with the status of a free person", would be "incompatible with a fundamental basis of our Constitution". Similarly, in *General Practitioners Society v Commonwealth* (1980) 145 CLR 532, he argued that: "**[565]** The Constitution makes no reference to different classes of society and its terms are inconsistent with slavery, serfdom or similar vestiges of a feudal society. It contains an implication of a free society which limits Parliament's authority to impose civil conscription".

Murphy J made many other similar suggestions. In *Ansett Transport Industries (Operations) Pty Ltd v Wardley* (1980) 142 CLR 237, he suggested that the industrial arbitration power (s 51(xxxv)) might not extend to "**[267]** awards or agreements which provide for unjustifiable sex discrimination". He said that since the Constitution itself "makes no discrimination between the sexes", it might give rise to an implication "that the Parliament's legislative powers do not extend to authorizing arbitrary discrimination between the sexes". In *Sillery v The Queen* (1981) 180 CLR 353 he held that the *Crimes (Hijacking of Aircraft) Act 1972* (Cth) should not be construed as imposing a mandatory sentence of life imprisonment regardless of mitigating circumstances. He based this conclusion on a presumption against interpreting legislation to impose "**[362]** cruel and unusual punishment". He further argued that, if necessary, this presumption should be regarded as a constitutional premise that could not be overridden by the Parliament.

In a series of cases on s 92 beginning with *Buck v Bavone* (1976) 135 CLR 110, Murphy J argued that s 92 was not applicable, but balanced his narrow view of s 92 with a broad conception of a personal right of interstate freedom of movement and communication, implied in the Constitution as "**[137]** a fundamental right arising from the union of the people in an indissoluble Commonwealth". He saw this right as "so fundamental that it is not likely it would be hidden away in s 92". In *Ansett Transport Industries (Operations) Pty Ltd v Commonwealth* (1977) 139 CLR 54, he argued for an implied right of communication similar to that later recognised in *Nationwide News* and *Australian Capital Television*.

Ansett Transport Industries (Operations) Pty Ltd v Commonwealth
(1977) 139 CLR 54

Murphy J: [88] Elections of federal Parliament provided for in the Constitution require freedom of movement, speech and other communication, not only between the States, but in and between every part of the Commonwealth. The proper operation of the system of representative government requires the same freedoms between elections. These are also necessary for the proper operation of the Constitutions of the States (which now derive their authority from Ch V of the Constitution[)]. From these provisions and from the concept of the Commonwealth arises an implication of a constitutional guarantee of such freedoms, freedoms so elementary that it was not necessary to mention them in the Constitution.

Miller v TCN Channel Nine Pty Ltd (1986) 161 CLR 556 raised a s 92 issue, but was also planned in part as a test of the implied guarantee of freedom of communication advocated by Murphy J. In 1984, when Murphy J stood aside from the High Court to answer criminal charges (see Chapter 13, §2(b)), the case was kept out of the list awaiting his return. In 1986, the case was restored to the list. By coincidence, it came on for hearing in the one week in August 1986 that Murphy J returned to the Court. He heard two cases during that week. Judgments were handed down in both cases on 21 October 1986, an hour before he died. Predictably, Murphy J rejected the s 92 claim but accepted the argument based on freedom of communication.

Miller v TCN Channel Nine Pty Ltd
(1986) 161 CLR 556

Murphy J: [581] The Australian Constitution must be interpreted against a background of responsible government and democratic principles generally. Implications should be made which would promote such principles rather than those of arbitrary government and tyranny. In *Commonwealth v Kreglinger & Fernau Ltd* [(1926) 37 CLR 393 at 413], this point is made by Isaacs J:

> "Constitutions made, not for a single occasion, but for the continued life and progress of the community may and, indeed, must be affected in their general meaning and effect by what Lord Watson in *Cooper v Stuart* [(1889) 14 App Cas 286 at 293] calls 'the silent operation of constitutional principles'. 'Responsible government', ... is part of the fabric on which the written words of the Constitution are superimposed."

In *Australian Communist Party v Commonwealth* [(1951) 83 CLR 1 at 193], Dixon J said:

> "... it is government under the Constitution and that is an instrument framed in accordance with many traditional conceptions, to some of which it gives effect, as, for example, in separating the judicial power from other functions of government, others of which are simply assumed. Among these I think that it may fairly be said that the rule of law forms an assumption."

Other "traditional conceptions ... simply assumed" include, in my view, a prohibition on slavery or serfdom (*R v Director-General of Social Welfare (Vic); Ex parte Henry* [(1975) 133 CLR 369 at 388]), a prohibition on the infliction of cruel and unusual punishments (*Sillery v The Queen* [(1981) 180 CLR 353]) and a prohibition upon persons being tried and declared guilty of criminal offences by nonjudicial bodies: *Victoria v Australian Building Construction Employees' and Builders Labourers' Federation* [(1982) 152 CLR 25].

The Constitution also contains implied guarantees of freedom of speech and other communications and freedom of movement not **[582]** only between the States and the States and the Territories but in and between every part of the Commonwealth. Such freedoms are fundamental to a democratic society. They are necessary for the proper operation of the system of representative government at the federal level. They are also necessary for the proper operation of the Constitutions of the States (which derive their authority from Ch V of the Constitution). They are a necessary corollary of the concept of the Commonwealth of Australia. The implication is not merely for the protection of individual freedom; it also serves a fundamental societal or public interest ...

[583] In relation to the drawing of implications generally, Dixon J in *Australian National Airways Pty Ltd v Commonwealth* [(1945) 71 CLR 29 at 85] said:

> "We should avoid pedantic and narrow constructions in dealing with an instrument of government and I do not see why we should be fearful about making implications." ...

The implied freedom of communication is not absolute but is subject to necessary regulation. The question arises whether the **[584]** statutory scheme under the Act conforms to the concept of necessary regulation.

The parties accepted that if there were an implied guarantee of freedom of communication, the test of whether particular regulation was compatible with that freedom should be judged by tests analogous to those of reasonable regulation presently applied to s 92.

The other judges in *Miller v TCN-Nine* rejected the implied guarantee relied upon by Murphy J, although only on the basis that s 92's express guarantee of interstate freedom of communication left no room for an implied guarantee to the same effect. Mason J said: "**[579]** It is sufficient to say that I cannot find any basis for implying a new s 92A into the Constitution". While these judges rejected the supposedly implied guarantee in this instance, they expressly or tacitly left open the broader question of whether such implications are possible.

3. A Freedom of Political Communication

Nationwide News and *Australian Capital Television* established that the Constitution embodies an implied freedom of political communication. In *Nationwide News*, the publisher of *The*

Australian had been prosecuted under s 299(1)(d)(ii) of the *Industrial Relations Act 1988* (Cth), which provided that: "A person shall not ... by writing or speech use words calculated ... to bring a member of the [Industrial Relations] Commission or the Commission into disrepute". The prosecution related to an article by Maxwell Newton published in *The Australian* on 14 November 1989, which stated in part: "[18] The right to work has been taken away from ordinary Australian workers. Their work is regulated by a mass of official controls, imposed by a vast bureaucracy in the ministry of labour and enforced by a corrupt and compliant 'judiciary' in the official Soviet-style Arbitration Commission". He also referred to the law as being enforced by "corrupt" and "pliant" judges.

The Court unanimously held that s 299(1)(d)(ii) was invalid. Mason CJ, Dawson and McHugh JJ did so on the ground that it was not within the scope of the implied incidental power attaching to s 51(xxxv) (see Chapter 16, §8). They therefore found it unnecessary to deal with the argument based upon freedom of political discussion. Brennan, Deane, Toohey and Gaudron JJ adopted a different course. They held that, even if s 299(1)(d)(ii) was within power (as both Brennan and Gaudron JJ thought that it was), it was nevertheless invalid as infringing an implied freedom of political discussion.

Nationwide News Pty Ltd v Wills
(1992) 177 CLR 1

Deane and Toohey JJ: [69] There are at least three main general doctrines of government which underlie the Constitution and are implemented by its **[70]** provisions. One of them is the doctrine or concept of a federal system under which the content of legislative, executive and judicial powers is divided between a central (or Commonwealth) government and regional (or state) governments. Another is the doctrine of a separation of legislative, executive and judicial powers. The fundamental implications of the Constitution to which attention has been directed in past cases have, in the main, been related to one or both of those doctrines. Thus, for example, the cases establish that it is a fundamental implication to be derived from the nature of the federal system established by the written terms of the Constitution that the legislative and executive powers conferred upon the Commonwealth are confined to the extent necessary to preclude their use in a manner which would be inconsistent with either the continued existence of the States as independent entities or their capacity to function as such. Again, the judgments in past cases establish that it is a fundamental implication of the Constitution's doctrine of the separation of powers that, while it allows for the adoption of the Cabinet or Westminster system of government with its merging of legislative power and executive responsibility, no part of the judicial power of the Commonwealth can be exercised either by a body which is not a Ch III court or in a manner which is inconsistent with our traditional judicial process. The implication of the Constitution which is of central importance in the resolution of the present case flows from the third of those general doctrines of government which underlie the Constitution and form part of its structure. That doctrine can conveniently be described as the doctrine of representative government, that is to say, of government by representatives directly or indirectly elected or appointed by, and ultimately responsible to, the people of the Commonwealth. The rational basis of that doctrine is the thesis that all powers of government ultimately belong to, and are derived from, the governed ...

[71] In implementing the doctrine of representative government, the Constitution reserves to the people of the Commonwealth the ultimate power of governmental control. It provides for the exercise of that ultimate power by two electoral processes. The first is the election of the members of the Parliament in which is vested the legislative power of the Commonwealth and which, under the Cabinet system of government which the Constitution assumes, sustains and directly or indirectly controls the exercise of the executive power which the Constitution formally vests in the Crown. The second is that to which reference has already been made, namely, the amendment of the Constitution itself. Under the Constitution, those ultimate powers which the Constitution reserves to the people of the Commonwealth are exercisable by direct vote **[72]** (ss 7, 24, 128). While one can point to qualifications and exceptions, such as those concerned with the protection of the position of the less populous States, the general effect of the Constitution is, at least since the adoption of full adult suffrage by all the States, that all citizens of the Commonwealth who are not under some special disability are entitled to share equally in the exercise of those ultimate powers of governmental control.

The people of the Commonwealth would be unable responsibly to discharge and exercise the powers of governmental control which the Constitution reserves to them if each person was an island, unable to communicate with any other person. The actual discharge of the very function of voting in an election or referendum involves communication. An ability to vote intelligently can exist only if the identity of the candidates for election or the content of a proposed law submitted for the decision of the people at a referendum can be communicated to the voter. The ability to cast a fully informed vote in an election of members of the Parliament depends upon the ability to acquire information about the background, qualifications and policies of the candidates for election and about the countless number of other circumstances and considerations, both factual and theoretical, which are relevant to a consideration of what is in the interests of the nation as a whole or of particular localities, communities or individuals within it. Moreover, the doctrine of representative government which the Constitution incorporates is not concerned merely with electoral processes. As has been said, the central thesis of the doctrine is that the powers of government belong to, and are derived from, the governed, that is to say, the people of the Commonwealth. The repositories of governmental power under the Constitution hold them as representatives of the people under a relationship, between representatives and represented, which is a continuing one. The doctrine presupposes an ability of represented and representatives to communicate information, needs, views, explanations and advice. It also presupposes an ability of the people of the Commonwealth as a whole to communicate, among themselves, information and opinions about matters relevant to the exercise and discharge of governmental powers and functions on their behalf.

It follows from what has been said above that there is to be **[73]** discerned in the doctrine of representative government which the Constitution incorporates an implication of freedom of communication of information and opinions about matters relating to the government of the Commonwealth ... [That implication] operates at two levels. The first is the level of communication and discussion between the represented and their representatives, that is to say, the level of communication and discussion between the people of the Commonwealth on the one hand and the Parliament and its members and other Commonwealth instrumentalities and institutions on the other ...

[74] The second level at which the implication of freedom of communication and discussion operates is the level of communication between the people of the Commonwealth. Inherent in the Constitution's doctrine of representative government is an implication of the freedom of the people of the Commonwealth to communicate information, opinions and ideas about all aspects of the government of the Commonwealth, including the qualifications, conduct and performance of those entrusted (or who seek to be entrusted) with the exercise of any part of the legislative, executive or judicial powers of government which are ultimately derived from the people themselves.

Australian Capital Television involved a challenge to the validity of the *Political Broadcasts and Political Disclosures Act 1991* (Cth), which added a new Pt IIID dealing with "Political Broadcasts" to the *Broadcasting Act 1942* (Cth). Section 95B imposed a blanket prohibition on political advertisements on radio or television during federal election periods. There were similar bans for Territory elections under s 95C and for State and local government elections under s 95D. Exceptions to the ban were made for policy launches, news and current affairs items, talkback radio programs and advertisements for charities that did not "explicitly advocate" a vote for one candidate or party.

Division 3 of Pt IIID established a scheme of "free time" for political advertising. This time was to be allocated to political parties by the Australian Broadcasting Tribunal. Of the total time available, 90 per cent was reserved for parties represented in the previous Parliament and fielding at least a prescribed number of candidates in the current election. Units of "free time" could be used for a two-minute telecast or one-minute radio broadcast by a single speaker, "without dramatic enactment or impersonation", accompanied in a telecast by a picture of the speaker's head and shoulders. The speaker had to be a candidate or a sitting member and there had to be "no other vocal sounds" and no other picture except a "static background image".

It was accepted that Pt IIID was within power under s 51(v) of the Constitution or under the Commonwealth's various powers with respect to federal elections. The question before the Court was whether Pt IIID was invalid because it infringed a constitutionally guaranteed freedom of political discussion. Mason CJ, Deane, Toohey and Gaudron JJ held that Pt IIID was wholly invalid on that basis. McHugh J held that Pt IIID was invalid except in relation to s 95C, which concerned Territory elections. All five majority judges committed themselves to an implied constitutional protection for freedom of political discussion. Only Dawson J rejected that conception. Brennan J agreed that there was such an implication, but held that the provisions were valid as a reasonable restriction on the protected freedom.

Australian Capital Television Pty Ltd v Commonwealth
(1992) 177 CLR 106

Mason CJ: [133] *Constitutional implications*
Sir Owen Dixon noted that, following the decision in *Amalgamated Society of Engineers v Adelaide Steamship Co Ltd* ("the *Engineers' Case*") [(1920) 28 CLR 129], the notion seemed to gain currency that no implications could be made in interpreting the Constitution. The *Engineers' Case* certainly did not support such a **[134]** Draconian and unthinking approach to constitutional interpretation. Sir Owen expressed his own opposition to that approach when he said [*West v Commissioner of Taxation (NSW)* (1937) 56 CLR 657 at 681]:
> "Such a method of construction would defeat the intention of any instrument, but of all instruments a written constitution seems the last to which it could be applied."

Later, he was to say [*Australian National Airways Pty Ltd v Commonwealth* (1945) 71 CLR 29 at 85]:
> "We should avoid pedantic and narrow constructions in dealing with an instrument of government and I do not see why we should be fearful about making implications."

Subsequently, Windeyer J ... remarked [*Victoria v Commonwealth* (*Payroll Tax Case*) (1971) 122 CLR 353 at 401-2] "implications have a place in the interpretation of the Constitution" and "our avowed task is simply the revealing or uncovering of implications that are already there".

In conformity with this approach, the Court has drawn implications from the federal structure prohibiting the Commonwealth from exercising its legislative and executive powers in such a way as to impose upon a State some special disability or burden unless the relevant power authorized that imposition or in such a way as to threaten the continued existence of a State as an independent entity or its capacity to function as such. But there is no reason to limit the process of constitutional implication to that particular source.

Of course, any implication must be securely based. Thus, it has been said that "ordinary principles of construction are applied so as to discover *in the actual terms* of the instrument their expressed or necessarily implied meaning" (emphasis added). This statement is too restrictive because, if taken literally, it would deny the very basis – the federal nature of the Constitution – from which the Court has implied restrictions on Commonwealth and State legislative powers. That the statement is too restrictive is **[135]** evident from the remarks of Dixon J in *Melbourne Corporation v Commonwealth* [(1947) 74 CLR 31 at 83] where his Honour stated that "the efficacy of the system logically demands" the restriction which has been implied and that "an intention of this sort is ... to be plainly seen in the very frame of the Constitution".

It may not be right to say that no implication will be made unless it is necessary. In cases where the implication is sought to be derived from the actual terms of the Constitution it may be sufficient that the relevant intention is manifested according to the accepted principles of interpretation. However, where the implication is structural rather than textual it is no doubt correct to say that the term sought to be implied must be logically or practically necessary for the preservation of the integrity of that structure.

It is essential to keep steadily in mind the critical difference between an implication and an unexpressed assumption upon which the framers proceeded in drafting the Constitution. The former is a term or concept which inheres in the instrument and as such operates as part of the instrument, whereas an assumption stands outside the instrument. Thus, the founders assumed that the Senate would protect the States but in the result it did not do so. On the other hand, the principle of responsible government – the system of government by which the executive is responsible to the legislature – is not merely an assumption upon which the actual provisions are based; it is an integral element in the Constitution. In the words of Isaacs J in *Commonwealth v Kreglinger & Fernau Ltd and Bardsley* [(1926) 37 CLR 393 at 413]: "It is part of the fabric on which the written words of the Constitution are superimposed."

Mason CJ acknowledged that the framers of the Constitution had rejected the United States model of constitutional enshrinement of judicially enforceable rights, preferring to leave the protection of personal liberty to the processes of responsible government and the common law.

Mason CJ: [136] In the light of this well recognized background, it is difficult, if not impossible, to establish a foundation for the implication of general guarantees of fundamental rights and freedoms. To make such an implication would run counter to the prevailing sentiment of the framers that there was no need to incorporate a comprehensive Bill of Rights in order to protect the rights and freedoms of citizens. That sentiment was one of the unexpressed assumptions on which the Constitution was drafted.

However, the existence of that sentiment when the Constitution was adopted and the influence which it had on the shaping of the Constitution are no answer to the case which the plaintiffs now present. Their case is that a guarantee of freedom of expression in relation to public and political affairs must necessarily be implied from the provision which the Constitution makes for a system of representative government. The plaintiffs say that, because such a freedom is an essential concomitant of representative government, it is necessarily implied in the prescription of that system.

Mason CJ accepted the plaintiffs' argument.

Mason CJ: [137] *Representative government*
The Constitution provided for representative government by creating the Parliament, consisting of the Queen, a House of Representatives and a Senate, in which legislative power is vested (s 1), the members of each House being elected by popular vote, and by vesting the executive power in the Queen and making it exercisable by the Governor-General on the advice of the Federal Executive Council (ss 61, 62), consisting of the Queen's Ministers of State drawn, subject to a minor qualification, from the House of Representatives and the Senate. In the case of the Senate, s 7 provides that it "shall be composed of senators for each State, directly chosen by the people of the State, voting, until the Parliament otherwise provides, as one electorate". In the case of the House of Representatives, s 24 provides that it "shall be composed of members directly chosen by the people of the Commonwealth". Although s 24 contains no reference to voting, s 25 makes it clear that "chosen" means "chosen by vote at an election".

In *Attorney-General (Cth) (Ex rel McKinlay) v Commonwealth* [(1975) 135 CLR 1 at 55-6], Stephen J discerned in these two provisions the principles of representative democracy ... and direct popular election. The correctness of his Honour's view is incontestable, notwithstanding that the Constitution does not prescribe universal adult suffrage ... Although prescription of the qualifications of electors was left for the ultimate determination of the Parliament (ss 8, 30), the Constitution nonetheless brought into existence a system of representative government in which those who exercise legislative and executive power are directly chosen by the people ...

The very concept of representative government and representative democracy signifies government by the people through their representatives. Translated into constitutional terms, it denotes that the sovereign power which resides in the people is exercised on their behalf by their representatives. In the case of the Australian **[138]** Constitution, one obstacle to the acceptance of that view is that the Constitution owes its legal force to its character as a statute of the Imperial Parliament enacted in the exercise of its legal sovereignty; the Constitution was not a supreme law proceeding from the people's inherent authority to constitute a government, notwithstanding that it was adopted, subject to minor amendments, by the representatives of the Australian colonies at a Convention and approved by a majority of the electors in each of the colonies at the several referenda. Despite its initial character as a statute of the Imperial Parliament, the Constitution brought into existence a system of representative government for Australia in which the elected representatives exercise sovereign power on behalf of the Australian people. Hence, the prescribed procedure for amendment of the Constitution hinges upon a referendum at which the proposed amendment is approved by a majority of electors and a majority of electors in a majority of the States (s 128). And, most recently, the *Australia Act* 1986 (UK) marked the end of the legal sovereignty of the Imperial Parliament and recognized that ultimate sovereignty resided in the Australian people. The point is that the representatives who are members of Parliament and Ministers of State are not only chosen by the people but exercise their legislative and executive powers as representatives of the people. And in the exercise of those powers the representatives of necessity are accountable to the people for what they do and have a responsibility to take account of the views of the people on whose behalf they act.

Freedom of communication as an indispensable element in representative government

Indispensable to that accountability and that responsibility is freedom of communication, at least in relation to public affairs and political discussion. Only by exercising that freedom can the citizen communicate his or her views on the wide range of matters that may call for, or are relevant to, political action or decision. Only by exercising that freedom can the citizen criticize government decisions and actions, seek to bring about change, call for action where none has been taken and in this way influence the elected representatives. By these means the elected representatives are equipped to discharge their role so that they may take account of **[139]** and respond to the will of the people. Communication in the exercise of the freedom is by no means a one-way traffic, for the elected representatives have a responsibility not only to ascertain the views of the electorate but also to explain and account for their decisions and actions in government and to inform the people so that they may make informed judgments on relevant matters. Absent such a freedom of communication, representative government would fail to achieve its purpose, namely, government by the people through their elected representatives; government would cease to be responsive to the needs and wishes of the people and, in that sense, would cease to be truly representative.

Freedom of communication in relation to public affairs and political discussion cannot be confined to communications between elected representatives and candidates for election on the one hand and the electorate on the other. The efficacy of representative government depends also upon free communication on such matters between all persons, groups and other bodies in the community. That is because individual judgment, whether that of the elector, the representative or the candidate, on so many issues turns upon free public discussion in the media of the views of all interested persons, groups and bodies and on public participation in, and access to, that discussion. In truth, in a representative democracy, public participation in political discussion is a central element of the political process.

Archibald Cox made a similar point when he said:

> "Only by uninhibited publication can the flow of information be secured and the people informed concerning men, measures, and the conduct of government ... Only by freedom of speech, of the press, and of association can people build and assert political power, including the power to change the men who govern them."

The last sentence in the passage just quoted is a striking comment on Professor Harrison Moore's statement that "[t]he great underlying principle" of the Constitution was that the rights of individuals were sufficiently secured by ensuring each an equal share **[140]** in political power. Absent freedom of communication, there would be scant prospect of the exercise of that power ...

[142] *The indivisibility of freedom of communication in relation to public affairs and political discussion*

The concept of freedom to communicate with respect to public affairs and political discussion does not lend itself to subdivision. Public affairs and political discussion are indivisible and cannot be subdivided into compartments that correspond with, or relate to, the various tiers of government in Australia. Unlike the legislative powers of the Commonwealth Parliament, there are no limits to the range of matters that may be relevant to debate in the Commonwealth Parliament or to its workings. The consequence is that the implied freedom of communication extends to all matters of public affairs and political discussion, notwithstanding that a particular matter at a given time might appear to have a primary or immediate connection with the affairs of a State, a local authority or a Territory and little or no connection with Commonwealth affairs. Furthermore, there is a continuing inter-relationship between the various tiers of government. To take one example, the Parliament provides funding for the State governments, Territory governments and local governing bodies and enterprises. That continuing inter-relationship makes it inevitable that matters of local concern have the potential to become matters of national concern. That potential is in turn enhanced by the predominant financial power which the Commonwealth Parliament and the Commonwealth government enjoy in the Australian federal system.

Infringement: the test to be applied ...

[T]he concept of freedom of communication is not an absolute. The guarantee does not postulate that the freedom must always and necessarily prevail over competing interests of the public. Thus, to take an example, Parliament may regulate the conduct of persons with regard to elections so as to prevent intimidation and undue influence, even though that regulation may fetter what otherwise would be free **[143]** communication. And, in the United States, despite the First Amendment, the media is subject to laws of general application.

A distinction should perhaps be made between restrictions on communication which target ideas or information and those which restrict an activity or mode of communication by which ideas or information are transmitted. In the first class of case, only a compelling justification will warrant the imposition of a burden on free communication by way of restriction and the restriction must be no more than is reasonably necessary to achieve the protection of the competing public interest which is invoked to justify the burden on communication. Generally speaking, it will be extremely difficult to justify restrictions imposed on free communication which operate by reference to the character of the ideas or information. But, even in these cases, it will be necessary to weigh the competing public interests, though ordinarily paramount weight would be given to the public interest in freedom of communication. So, in the area of public affairs and political discussion, restrictions of the relevant kind will ordinarily amount to an unacceptable form of political censorship.

On the other hand, restrictions imposed on an activity or mode of communication by which ideas or information are transmitted are more susceptible of justification. The regulation of radio and television broadcasting in the public interest generally involves some restrictions on the flow and dissemination of ideas and information. Whether those restrictions are justified calls for a balancing of the public interest in free communication against the competing public interest which the restriction is designed to serve, and for a determination whether the restriction is reasonably necessary to achieve the competing public interest. If the restriction imposes a burden on free communication that is disproportionate to the attainment of the competing public interest, then the existence of **[144]** the disproportionate burden indicates that the purpose and effect of the restriction is in fact to impair freedom of communication.

In weighing the respective interests involved and in assessing the necessity for the restriction imposed, the Court will give weight to the legislative judgment on these issues. But, in the ultimate analysis, it is for the Court to determine whether the constitutional guarantee has been infringed in a given case. And the Court must scrutinize with scrupulous care restrictions affecting free communication in the conduct of elections for political office for it is in that area that the guarantee fulfils its primary purpose.

Is Pt IIID valid?

The restrictions imposed in the present case are expressed so as to appear to fall into the second, rather than the first, class of case discussed above. The restrictions are imposed upon television and radio broadcasting. But the law which imposes the restrictions is not one of general application; the law is specifically directed at, and prohibits, the broadcasting, in connection with the electoral process, of matters relating to public affairs and political discussion, including political advertisements. So, in conformity with what I have already said, notwithstanding the legislative judgment that the restrictions are necessary for achieving the ends identified earlier in these reasons, the Court must scrutinize the validity of Pt IIID with scrupulous care.

In approaching the respective interests in this case, I am prepared to assume that the purpose of Pt IIID is to safeguard the integrity of the political process by reducing pressure on parties and candidates to raise substantial sums of money, thus lessening the risk of corruption and undue influence. I am prepared also to assume that other purposes of Pt IIID are to terminate (a) the advantage enjoyed by wealthy persons and groups in gaining access to use of the airwaves; and (b) the "trivialising" of political debate resulting from very brief political advertisements. Moreover, I am prepared to accept that the need to raise substantial funds in order to conduct a campaign for election to political office does generate a risk of **[145]** corruption and undue influence, that in such a campaign the rich have an advantage over the poor and that brief political advertisements may "trivialise" political debate.

Given the existence of these shortcomings or possible shortcomings in the political process, it may well be that some restrictions on the broadcasting of political advertisements and messages could be justified, notwithstanding that the impact of the restrictions would be to impair freedom of communication to some extent. In other words, a comparison or balancing of the public interest in freedom of communication and the public interest in the integrity of the political process might well justify some burdens on freedom of communication. But it is essential that the competition between the two interests be seen in perspective. The raison d'être of freedom of communication in relation to public affairs and political discussion is to enhance the political process (which embraces the electoral process and the workings of Parliament), thus making representative government efficacious.

The enhancement of the political process and the integrity of that process are by no means opposing or conflicting interests and that is one reason why the Court should scrutinize very carefully any claim that freedom of communication must be restricted in order to protect the integrity of the political process. Experience has demonstrated on so many occasions in the past that, although freedom of communication may have some detrimental consequences for society, the manifest benefits it brings to an open society generally outweigh the detriments. All too often attempts to restrict the freedom in the name of some imagined necessity have tended to stifle public discussion and criticism of government. The Court should be astute not to accept at face value claims by the legislature and the Executive that freedom of communication will, unless curtailed, bring about corruption and distortion of the political process ...

Pt IIID severely restricts freedom of communication in relation to the political process, particularly the electoral process, in such a way as to discriminate against potential participants in that process. The sweeping prohibitions against broadcasting directly exclude potential participants in the electoral process from access to an extremely important mode of communication with the electorate. Actual and potential participants include not only the candidates and established political parties but also the electors, individuals, groups and bodies who wish to present their views to the community. In the case of referenda, or at least some of them, the States would have important interests at stake and would be participants in the process.

[146] It is said that the restrictions leave unimpaired the access of potential participants during an election period to other modes of communication with the electorate. The statement serves only to underscore the magnitude of the deprivation inflicted on those who are excluded from access to the electronic media. They must make do with other modes of communication which do not have the same striking impact in the short span of an election campaign when the electors are consciously making their judgments as to how they will vote.

It is also said that the protection given by s 95A to items of news, current affairs and comments on such items, and talkback radio programmes will preserve communication on the electronic media about public and political affairs during election periods. But access on the part of those excluded is not preserved, except possibly at the invitation of the powerful interests which control and conduct the electronic media. Those who are excluded are exposed to the risk that the protection given by s 95A may result in the broadcasting of material damaging to the cause or causes they support without their being afforded an opportunity to reply.

The replacement regime, which rests substantially on the provisions relating to the grant of free time, is weighted in favour of the established political parties represented in the legislature immediately before the election and the candidates of those parties; it discriminates against new and independent candidates. By limiting their access to a maximum of ten per cent of the free time available for allocation, Pt IIID denies them meaningful access on a non-discriminatory basis. As for persons, bodies and groups who are not candidates, they are excluded from radio and television broadcasting during election periods. The consequence is that the severe restriction of freedom of communication plainly fails to preserve or enhance fair access to the mode of communication which is the subject of the restriction. The replacement regime, though it reduces the expenses of political campaigning and the risks of trivialisation of political debate, does not introduce a "level playing field". It is discriminatory in the respects already mentioned.

Deane and Toohey JJ based their decision on their joint judgment in *Nationwide News*. They held that Pt IIID was invalid in that its provisions infringed the implied freedom. In doing so, they held that the guarantee extended to political discussion at both the Commonwealth and State levels. Gaudron J substantially agreed with them. As in *Nationwide News*, she held that the implied freedom could not be limited to discussion of political matters at the Commonwealth level, but did acknowledge that it must be subject to reasonable limits, the nature of which might be indicated by "[217] the general law". Hence, "the laws which have developed to regulate speech, including the laws with respect to defamation, sedition, blasphemy, obscenity and offensive language, will indicate the kind of regulation that is consistent with the freedom of political discourse". Gaudron J concluded that Pt IIID was invalid, since it was not "reasonably and appropriately adapted" to the regulation of broadcasting under s 51(v). Like Mason CJ, she took particular account of the lack of "free time" available to persons who were not candidates and to organisations that were not political parties.

McHugh J also discerned the implication of a protected freedom. Indeed, he was the only judge to speak of "[227] constitutional *rights* of freedom of participation, association and communication in relation to federal elections" (emphasis added). However, he conceived of these "rights" as operating only in relation to federal elections. This was because, in identifying the source of the implication, he focused narrowly on the textual requirement in ss 7 and 24 that the Senate and the House of Representatives be "directly chosen by the people". Although he too invoked a broader conception of "representative government", he used it only to flesh out his conception of ss 7 and 24 of the Constitution.

McHugh J: [229] The words "directly chosen by the people" in ss 7 and 24 of the **[230]** Constitution have to be interpreted against the background of the institutions of representative government and responsible government to which the Constitution gives effect but does not specifically mention. The words of ss 7 and 24 must be construed by reference to the conceptions of representative government and responsible government as understood by informed people in Australia at the time of federation. In *Commonwealth v Kreglinger & Fernau Ltd and Bardsley* [37 CLR at 411-12], Isaacs J said:

> "it is the duty of this Court, as the chief judicial organ of the Commonwealth, to take judicial notice, in interpreting the Australian Constitution, of every fundamental constitutional doctrine existing and fully recognised at the time the Constitution was passed, and therefore to be taken as influencing the meaning in which its words were used by the Imperial Legislature".

His Honour went on to say in that case [37 CLR at 413] that the principle of responsible government is "part of the fabric on which the written words of the Constitution are superimposed".

Representative government involves the conception of a legislative chamber whose members are elected by the people. But, as Birch points out, to have a full understanding of the concept of representative government, "we need to add that the chamber must occupy a powerful position in the political system and that the elections to it must be free, with all that this implies in the way of freedom of speech and political organization". Furthermore, responsible government involves the conception of a legislative chamber where the Ministers of State are answerable ultimately to the electorate for their policies. As Sir Samuel Griffith pointed out in his *Notes on Australian Federation*, the effect of responsible government "is that the actual government of the State is conducted by officers who enjoy the confidence of the people".

It is not to be supposed, therefore, that, in conferring the right to choose their representatives by voting at periodic elections, the Constitution intended to confer on the people of Australia no more than the right to mark a ballot paper with a number, a cross or a tick, as the case may be. The "share in the government which the Constitution ensures" would be but a pious aspiration unless ss 7 **[231]** and 24 carried with them more than the right to cast a vote. The guarantees embodied in ss 7 and 24 could not be satisfied by the Parliament requiring the people to select their representatives from a list of names drawn up by government officers.

If the institutions of representative and responsible government are to operate effectively and as the Constitution intended, the business of government must be examinable and the subject of scrutiny, debate and ultimate accountability at the ballot box. The electors must be able to ascertain and examine the performances of their elected representatives and the capabilities and policies of all candidates for election. Before they can cast an effective vote at election time, they must have access to the information, ideas and arguments which are necessary to make an informed judgment as to how they have been governed and as to what policies are in the interests of themselves, their communities and the nation. As the Supreme Court of the United States pointed out in *Buckley v Valeo* 424 US 1 (1976)], the ability of the people to make informed choices among candidates for political office is fundamental because the identity of those who are elected will shape the nation's destiny.

It follows that the electors must be able to communicate with the candidates for election concerning election issues and must be able to communicate their own arguments and opinions to other members of the community concerning those issues. Only by the spread of information, opinions and arguments can electors make an effective and responsible choice in determining whether or not they should vote for a particular candidate or the party which that person represents. Few voters have the time or the capacity to make their own examination of the raw material concerning the business of government, the policies of candidates or the issues in elections even if they have access to that material ...

The words "directly chosen by the people" in ss 7 and 24 interpreted against the background of the institutions of representative government and responsible government, are to be read, therefore, as referring to a process – the process which commences **[232]** when an election is called and ends with the declaration of the poll. The process includes all those steps which are directed to the people electing their representatives – nominating, campaigning, advertising, debating, criticising and voting. In respect of such steps, the people possess the right to participate, the right to associate and the right to communicate. That means that, subject to necessary exceptions, the people have a constitutional right to convey and receive opinions, arguments and information concerning matter intended or likely to affect voting in an election for the Senate or the House of Representatives. Moreover, that right must extend to the use of all forms and methods of communication which are lawfully available for general use in the community. To fail to give effect to the rights of participation, association and communication identifiable in ss 7 and 24 would be to sap and undermine the foundations of the Constitution.

It may be that the rights to convey and receive opinions, arguments and information conferred by ss 7 and 24 are not confined to the period of an election for the Senate and House of Representatives. It may be that the rights inherent in those sections are simply part of a general right of freedom of communication in respect of the business of government of the Commonwealth. In that connection it is significant that it was recognised early on that, by necessary implication, the Constitution gave rights of access to federal officials and records ...

Furthermore, one of the conceptions of representative government is that members of Parliament have an obligation to listen to **[233]** and ascertain the views of their constituents during the life of the Parliament. This conception strengthens the case for concluding that, by implication, the Constitution gives a general right of freedom of communication in respect of the business of government of the Commonwealth. But it is unnecessary for the purposes of this case to decide whether, by implication, the Constitution gives to the people of the Commonwealth such a general right of freedom of communication.

Thus, McHugh J did not necessarily exclude the wider range of political freedoms that the other majority judgments envisaged, but confined his decision in this case to a narrower electoral context. (Later, in *Theophanous v Herald & Weekly Times Ltd* (1994) 182 CLR 104, he repudiated any broader conception of "representative government" as a source of implied limitations, emphasising the precise and narrow focus of his own reasoning in *Australian Capital Television*.) Like Mason CJ, McHugh J distinguished between laws "**[234]** which restrict the freedom of electoral communications by **[235]** prohibiting or regulating their contents", and those "which incidentally limit that freedom by regulating the time, place or manner of communication". Since Pt IIID was a law of the former kind, it could "only be upheld on grounds of compelling justification". Accordingly, he held it invalid – except for s 95C, for which he found support in the Territories power (s 122).

By contrast Dawson J, in a carefully reasoned plea for adherence to the Court's traditional role, rejected the whole idea of judicially enforceable guarantees of political freedoms.

Dawson J: [180] The Constitution is contained in an Act of the Imperial Parliament: the *Commonwealth of Australia Constitution Act* (63 & 64 Vic c 12). Notwithstanding that this Act was preceded by the agreement of the people of New South Wales, Victoria, South Australia, **[181]** Queensland and Tasmania "to unite in one indissoluble Federal Commonwealth", the legal foundation of the Constitution is the Act itself which was passed and came into force in accordance with antecedent law. And the Constitution is itself a law declared by the Imperial Parliament to be "binding on the courts, judges, and people of every State and of every part of the Commonwealth". It does not purport to obtain its force from any power residing in the people to constitute a government, nor does it involve any notion of the delegation of power by the people such as forms part of American constitutional doctrine. The words in the United States Constitution "We the People of the United States ... do ordain and establish this Constitution for the United States of America" find no counterpart in the Australian Constitution; indeed, such words would entirely belie the manner of its foundation. No doubt it may be said as an abstract proposition of political theory that the Constitution ultimately depends for its continuing validity upon the acceptance of the people, but the same may be said of any form of government which is not arbitrary. The legal foundation of the Australian Constitution is an exercise of sovereign power by the Imperial Parliament. The significance of this in the interpretation of the Constitution is that the Constitution is to be construed as a law passed pursuant to the legislative power to do so. If implications are to be drawn, they must appear from the terms of the instrument itself and not from extrinsic circumstances.

He recalled the rejection in the *Engineers' Case* of implications drawn from "**[145]** a vague, individual conception of the spirit of the compact", and its insistence that abuse of legislative power must be "**[151]** guarded against by the constituencies and not by the Courts". He went on:

Dawson J: [182] Thus the Australian Constitution, unlike the Constitution of the United States, does little to confer upon individuals by way of positive rights those basic freedoms which exist in a free and democratic society. They exist, not because they are provided for, but in the absence of any curtailment of them. Freedom of speech, for example, which is guaranteed in the United States by the First Amendment to the Constitution, is a concept which finds no expression in our Constitution, notwithstanding that it is as much the foundation of a free society here as it is there. The right to freedom of speech exists here because there is nothing to prevent its exercise and because governments recognize that if they attempt to **[183]** limit it, save in accepted areas such as defamation or sedition, they must do so at their peril. Not only that, but courts recognize the importance of the basic immunities and require the clearest expression of intention before construing legislation in such a way as to interfere with them. The fact, however, remains that in this country the guarantee of fundamental freedoms does not lie in any constitutional mandate but in the capacity of a democratic society to preserve for itself its own shared values ...

[186] [I]t is clear that Murphy J based the implication which he asserted [in *Miller v TCN Channel Nine Pty Ltd* (1986) 161 CLR 556], not upon the text of the Constitution, but upon "the nature of our society" [*McGraw-Hinds (Aust) Pty Ltd v Smith* (1979) 144 CLR 633 at 670]. In doing so, he failed, in my view, to recognize the true character of the Australian Constitution which, as I have endeavoured to explain, limits the implications which can be drawn to those which appear from the terms of the instrument itself. Indeed, those responsible for the drafting of the Constitution saw constitutional guarantees of freedoms as exhibiting a distrust of the democratic process. They preferred to place their trust in Parliament to preserve the nature of our society and regarded as undemocratic guarantees which fettered its powers. Their model in this respect was, not the United States Constitution, but the British Parliament, the supremacy of which was by then settled constitutional doctrine. Not only that, but the heresy of importing into the Constitution, by way of implication, preconceptions having their origin outside the Constitution has been exposed and decisively rejected in the *Engineers' Case*. The nature of the society or, more precisely and accurately, the nature of the federation which the Constitution established, is to be found within its four corners and not elsewhere. To say as much is not for one moment to express disagreement with the view expressed by Murphy J that freedom of movement and freedom of communication are indispensable to any free society. It is merely to differ as to the institutions in which the founding fathers placed their faith for the protection of those freedoms.

Despite this, Dawson J's final formulation of the question that the Court had to decide was very close to that of McHugh J.

Dawson J: [186] Having said that, it must nevertheless be recognized that the Constitution provides for a Parliament the members of which are to **[187]** be directly chosen by the people … Thus the Constitution provides for a choice and that must mean a true choice. It may be said – at all events in the context of an election – that a choice is not a true choice when it is made without an appreciation of the available alternatives or, at least, without an opportunity to gain an appreciation of the available alternatives. As Windeyer J observed in *Australian Consolidated Press Ltd v Uren* [(1966) 117 CLR 185 at 210]: "[f]reedom at election time to praise the merits and policies of some candidates and to dispute and decry those of others is an essential of parliamentary democracy". Perhaps the freedom is one which must extend beyond the election time to the period between elections, but that is something which it is unnecessary to consider in this case. It is enough to recognize, as this Court did in *Evans v Crichton-Browne* [(1981) 147 CLR 169 at 206], the importance of ensuring that freedom of speech is not unduly restricted during an election period. Thus an election in which the electors are denied access to the information necessary for the exercise of a true choice is not the kind of election envisaged by the Constitution. Legislation which would have the effect of denying access to that information by the electors would therefore be incompatible with the Constitution.

Dawson J held that Pt IIID of the Act did not breach this requirement.

Dawson J: [188] [I]t is for Parliament, within the limits prescribed by the Constitution, to provide the form of representative democracy which we are to have and in so doing it may adopt measures about which there may be a considerable variation of opinion. For example, the qualifications of electors are to be provided for by the Parliament under ss 8 and 30 and may amount to something less than universal adult suffrage. Today anything less than universal adult suffrage would be politically unacceptable, but at federation it was clearly envisaged. Indeed, until Parliament otherwise provided, the position was to be as it was in the States and, at federation, only South Australia had universal adult suffrage …

[191] In my view, it cannot be said that those sections of the Act which provide for the grant of free election broadcasting time are inconsistent with the requirement of the Constitution that there be a direct choice of members of Parliament by the people. Serious difficulties have been experienced in the provision of broadcasting time in accordance with capacity to pay. Free access to the airwaves by all who wish to put a point of view during an election period is an impracticality and, if there is to be free time, there must be some method by which it is to be granted. The method adopted by the Act is, I think, supportable as a means of allocating available free time in order to assist in informing electors about election issues. Whether or not it be regarded as ideal, it is within the ambit of parliamentary power to determine the circumstances in which the electoral choice is to be made.

Brennan J accepted the implication of a protected freedom; he had said as much in *Nationwide News*. However, like Dawson J, he saw nothing objectionable in the present legislation.

Brennan J: [154] By eliminating the opportunity, s 95B eliminates the practical need to engage in the most expensive form of media advertising available to influence voter opinion in an election campaign. The restriction on political advertising as a means of reducing the expenditure on election campaigns is not a novel experiment unique to Australia. The Senate examined the position in other liberal democracies and found that the position was "complex", being affected by the regime governing broadcasting in each country. In some countries, no advertising is permitted; in others no political advertising is permitted, or none during specified periods. It appears that, for one reason or another, paid political advertising is not permitted during election times in the United

Kingdom, Ireland, France, Norway, Sweden, Denmark, Austria, The Netherlands, Israel or Japan. Paid political advertising is permitted during election periods in Germany, Canada (for twenty-eight days only), the United States and New Zealand. It is also permitted in Switzerland but "there is little advertising by political parties on the electronic media due to the high costs involved". Many of the countries which ban paid political advertising during election times have constitutions guaranteeing the right to freedom of expression. Although Art 10 of the European Convention for the Protection of Human Rights and Fundamental Freedoms guarantees a freedom to "impart information and ideas", a challenge to the ban on political advertising on British television failed [*X and the Association of Z v United Kingdom* (1971) 38 CD 86]. The European Commission of Human Rights held it to be evident that the freedom guaranteed by Art 10 "cannot be taken to include a general and unfettered right for any private citizen or organisation [155] to have access to broadcasting time on radio and television in order to forward its opinion" [38 CD at 88]. It held that the recognition of a State's power to license broadcasting and television permitted the granting of licences which excluded political advertising.

It can hardly be doubted that reduction in the cost of effective participation in an election campaign reduces one of the chief impediments to political democracy ...

Of course, a prohibition on political advertising by means of the electronic media is not the only way of minimizing the risk of corruption or of reducing the untoward advantage of wealth on the formation of political opinion. A more direct way of achieving that result is to limit the expenditure which an individual or an organization is permitted to make on political advertising. Until 1980, Pt XVI of the *Commonwealth Electoral Act* 1918 had limited the electoral expenditure of candidates, but the provisions of Pt XVI [156] "proved to be unworkable". If the limiting of expenditure incurred by or on behalf of candidates has proved to be unworkable in this country, the elimination of an opportunity for political parties, interest groups or individuals to engage in costly advertising on the electronic media is easily seen as an alternative means of minimizing the risk of corruption or of reducing the untoward advantage of wealth on the formation of political opinion. Section 95B is appropriate and adapted to that end. The Parliament chosen by the people – not the Courts, not the Executive Government – bears the chief responsibility for maintaining representative democracy in the Australian Commonwealth. Representative democracy, as a principle or institution of our Constitution, can be protected to some extent by decree of the Courts and can be fostered by Executive action but, if performance of the duties of members of the Parliament were to be subverted by obligations to large benefactors or if the parties to which they belong were to trade their commitment to published policies in exchange for funds to conduct expensive campaigns, no curial decree could, and no executive action would, restore representative democracy to the Australian people.

Brennan J held that the test of proportionality was satisfied, given that, as the European Court of Human Rights had put it in *The Observer and the Guardian v United Kingdom* (1991) 14 EHHR 153, the Parliament must be allowed a "[178] margin of appreciation".

Brennan J: [159] It is both simplistic and erroneous to regard any limitation on political advertising as offensive to the Constitution. If that were not so, there could be no blackout on advertising on polling day; indeed, even advertising in the polling booth would have to be allowed unless the demands of peace, order and decorum in the polling booth qualify the limitation. Though freedom of political communication is essential to the maintenance of a representative democracy, it is not so transcendent a value as to override all interests which the law would otherwise protect. For example, it is a substantial restriction on freedom of political communication to make the publication of matter defamatory of a public figure unlawful unless the defamer can plead and prove justification or a defence of qualified privilege. Yet our law has not exposed public figures to the risk of defamation to the same extent as the Bill of Rights has been thought to expose them in the United States.

Freedom of political discussion is essential to the democratic process, chiefly for two reasons: it is a stimulus to performance in public office and it is conducive to the flow of information needed or desired for the formation of political opinions. But the salutary effect of freedom of political discussion on performance in public office can be neutralized by covert influences, particularly by the obligations which flow from financial dependence. The financial dependence of a political party on those whose interests can be served by the favours of government could cynically turn public debate into a cloak for bartering away the public interest. If Pt IIID tangibly minimizes the risk of political corruption, the restrictions it imposes on political advertising are clearly proportionate to that object of the law. Whether Pt IIID would tangibly minimize the risk **[160]** of corruption was a political assessment. It was for the Parliament to make that assessment; it is for the Court to say whether the assessment could be reasonably made.

In reviewing the assessment made by the Parliament, it is necessary to form some estimate of the effect of the restrictions imposed by Pt IIID on the flow of information needed or desired by electors to form their political judgments. If those restrictions effectively deny electors the opportunity to form political judgments or substantially impair their ability to do so, the restrictions are invalid. There would be no proportionality between restrictions having so stifling an effect on political discussion on the one hand and the apprehended risk of corruption or the untoward advantages flowing from wealth on the other. But the restrictions do not block the flow of information. All news, current affairs and talk-back programmes are unaffected by the restrictions. The print media are unaffected. The other methods of disseminating political views such as public meetings, door knocks and the distribution of handbills are unaffected.

The principal advertisements affected by Pt IIID are television advertisements. It is not necessary to determine finally the contribution made by television advertising to the mass of information needed or desired by electors to form their political judgments, but it is impossible to conclude that the Parliament could not reasonably make an adverse assessment of the information value of television advertising. Television advertising is brief; its brevity tends to trivialize the subject; it cannot deal in any depth with the complex issues of government. Its appeal is therefore directed more to the emotions than to the intellect ...

[161] No doubt it is true to say that the formation of political judgment is not solely an intellectual exercise. Aspirations and ideals are the stuff of statesmanship. But the articulation of aspirations and ideals and the conveying of information can be distinguished from many forms of political advertising. It was open to the Parliament to make a low assessment of the contribution made by electronic advertising to the formation of political judgments. It was open to the Parliament to conclude, as the experience of the majority of liberal democracies has demonstrated, that representative government can survive and flourish without paid political advertising on the electronic media during election periods. The restrictions imposed by s 95B are comfortably proportionate to the important objects which it seeks to obtain. The obtaining of those objects would go far to ensuring an open and equal democracy.

4. Defamation: The Constitutional Solution

The freedom of political communication was explored in a second series of cases in 1994, *Theophanous v Herald & Weekly Times Ltd* (1994) 182 CLR 104, *Stephens v West Australian Newspapers Ltd* (1994) 182 CLR 211 and *Cunliffe v Commonwealth* (1994) 182 CLR 272.

In *Cunliffe*, a new Pt 2A of the *Migration Act 1958* (Cth), substantially prohibiting advice or assistance to aliens except by registered migration agents, was unsuccessfully challenged. The plaintiffs, solicitors whose practice included the giving of such advice, contended that both their advice to their clients, and their representations to government on behalf of their clients, fell within the protected realm of political communication. This extension of the scope of the constitutional freedom was *accepted* by Mason CJ, Deane, Toohey and Gaudron JJ, and *rejected* by Brennan, Dawson and McHugh JJ. Mason CJ, for example, held that the "**[298]** freedom necessarily extends to the workings of the courts and tribunals which administer and enforce the laws of this country. The provision of advice and information, particularly by lawyers, to, and the receipt of that advice and information by, aliens in relation to **[299]** matters and issues arising under the Act falls clearly within the potential scope of the freedom". However, the fragility of the majority was emphasised when Toohey J joined with Brennan, Dawson and McHugh JJ in dismissing the plaintiffs' claim. For him, although the plaintiffs' communications with and on behalf of their clients were within the realm of constitutionally protected political communication, the new statutory regime of registration and restricted advice was "**[383]** not disproportionate to the legitimate aim to be achieved".

Theophanous and *Stephens* tested a question that had arisen from the earlier decisions: if the Australian Constitution was now to be read as impliedly protecting a freedom of political communication, did this mean that there was now to be (at least in political contexts) a "constitutional defence" to actions for defamation? And would this defence be similar to that which the Supreme Court of the United States derived in *New York Times Co v Sullivan*, 376 US 254 (1964), from the guarantee of "freedom of speech" in the First Amendment to the United States Constitution?

For the High Court this issue presented a strategic choice that had not been available to the United States Supreme Court. That Court is not a general court of appeal from the States in common law matters. In the circumstances of the actions for defamation in the courts of Alabama that were at issue in the *Sullivan* case, the argument for Supreme Court intervention was a compelling one (see Anthony Lewis, *Make No Law: The Sullivan Case and the First Amendment* (Random House, 1991)). Yet if it was to intervene at all, it could do so only on constitutional grounds. By contrast, while that was one option available to the High Court, there was also an alternative option: since the High Court is a general court of appeal from the States in common law matters, it might also take the simpler course of "developing" the common law rules in a manner consistent with the considerations that underlay the decisions in *Nationwide News* and *Australian Capital Television*. Which of these two options the High Court should take, and how far either of them was consistent with previous understandings of the relation between the common law and the Constitution, were among the more fundamental issues in the controversy that erupted around *Theophanous* and *Stephens*.

Both cases were decided by a 4:3 majority, with Mason CJ, Deane, Toohey and Gaudron JJ in the majority and Brennan, Dawson and McHugh JJ in dissent. The essence of the majority view in *Theophanous* was that, in respect of Commonwealth political matters, the implied freedom operates not only to invalidate Commonwealth statutes insofar as they unreasonably impair that freedom, but also to impose a similar limit on the law of defamation, whether embodied in the common law or in the statute law of the States. In respect of the State political matters considered in *Stephens*, a similar consequence followed – either due to the implication arising out of the Commonwealth Constitution, or because an equivalent implication could be derived from the *Constitution Act 1889* (WA). While all of these propositions were reaffirmed in *Lange v Australian Broadcasting Corporation* (1997) 189 CLR 520, the reasoning in *Theophanous* and *Stephens* should now be seen as merely a first (and ultimately abortive) attempt at their fuller elaboration.

In *Theophanous*, a member of the Commonwealth Parliament and the former chairman of its Joint Parliamentary Committee on Migration, Dr Andrew Theophanous, sued for defamation in Victoria following the publication in a newspaper of a letter to the editor written by Bruce Ruxton. The letter attacked Theophanous' immigration policies and accused him of bias arising from his own ethnic background. The defendant newspaper argued that Australian defamation law should be modified by a "public figure" defence analogous to that in *Sullivan*.

Theophanous v Herald & Weekly Times Ltd
(1994) 182 CLR 104

Mason CJ, Toohey and Gaudron JJ: [122] *Is the freedom confined to discussion of matters relating to the Parliament and government of the Commonwealth and Commonwealth public affairs?*

The concept of "political discussion" is not limited to matters relating to the government of the Commonwealth, using that expression in its broadest sense so as to include the public affairs of the Commonwealth. In *Australian Capital Television* [(1992) 177 CLR 106], Mason CJ, Deane and Toohey JJ and Gaudron J rejected that limitation. The interrelationship of Commonwealth and State powers and the interaction between the various tiers of government in Australia, the constant flow of political information, ideas and debate across the tiers of government and the absence of any limit capable of definition to the range of matters that may be relevant to debate in the Commonwealth Parliament and to its workings make unrealistic any attempt to confine the freedom to matters relating to the Commonwealth government. That said, the question is of little importance in the present case. The publication complained of relates to the views, performance and capacity of the plaintiff as a member of the Commonwealth Parliament, in particular as **[123]** chairperson of a Parliamentary Committee on Migration Regulations and as chairperson of the Australian Labor Party's Federal Caucus Immigration Committee. The publication questions his fitness to hold office as a member of Parliament. What is more, the comments made about the plaintiff all relate to views which he is alleged to hold on migration matters, matters which fall within the responsibilities allocated to the Commonwealth under the division of powers allocated by the Constitution (s 51(xix), (xxvii)).

As such, the publication clearly falls within the concept of "political discussion". Indeed, criticism of the views, performance and capacity of a member of Parliament and of the member's fitness for public office, particularly when an election is in the offing, is at the very centre of the freedom of political discussion. For the purposes of the present case, that is all that needs to be said on that topic.

But it is desirable to consider the question what is the content of the expression "political discussion", bearing in mind that the underlying purpose of the freedom is to ensure the efficacious working of representative democracy ... [T]he fact that it is not possible to fix a limit to the range of matters that may be relevant to debate in the Commonwealth Parliament is again a relevant consideration. That consideration prompted Mason CJ to remark in *Australian Capital Television* [177 CLR at 141] that the questions "[w]hether freedom of communication in relation to public affairs and political discussion is substantially different from an unlimited freedom of communication and, if so, what is the extent of the difference" did not call for decision in that case. Notwithstanding that consideration and the difficulty of drawing a satisfactory and workable distinction between political discussion and other forms of expression, it should be possible to develop, by means of decisions in particular cases, an acceptable limit to the type of discussion which falls within the constitutional protection.

To take an example. There is a difference between entertainment and politics, though there may be occasions when one may merge into the other. Hence, comment by a television entertainer would not ordinarily attract the constitutional protection because the comment would not, in the ordinary course, constitute political speech. But, if the television personality were engaging in comment on the legislative, executive or judicial process and the defamatory publication related to that comment, then the defamatory **[124]** publication might well, depending upon the particular circumstances, amount to political discussion. And, if an actor were seeking election, or even appointment, to a public office, discussion not only of his or her policies but also of his or her conduct, though not of his or her acting ability, would constitute political discussion if that conduct were relevant to fitness for public office.

For present purposes, it is sufficient to say that "political discussion" includes discussion of the conduct, policies or fitness for office of government, political parties, public bodies, public officers and those seeking public office. The concept also includes discussion of the political views and public conduct of persons who are engaged in activities that have become the subject of political debate, eg, trade union leaders, Aboriginal political leaders, political and economic commentators. Indeed, in our view, the concept is not exhausted by political publications and addresses which are calculated to influence choices. Barendt states that:

> "'political speech' refers to all speech relevant to the development of public opinion on the whole range of issues which an intelligent citizen should think about" ...

A similar view has been advocated by Alexander Meiklejohn. He says freedom of speech:

> "is assured only to speech which bears, directly or indirectly, upon issues with which voters have to deal – only, therefore, to the consideration of matters of public interest. Private speech, or private interest in speech, on the other hand, has no claim whatsoever to the protection of the First Amendment".

Thus he distinguishes between commercial speech – "a merchant advertising his wares" – and speech on matters of public concern. The problem is, of course, that what is ordinarily private speech may develop into speech on a matter of public concern with a change in content, emphasis or context. That conclusion is not inconsistent with the proposition that speech which is simply aimed at selling goods and services and enhancing profit-making activities will ordinarily fall outside the area of constitutional protection. Commercial speech without political content "says **[125]** nothing about how people are governed or how they should govern themselves" [*Re Klein and Law Society of Upper Canada* (1985) 16 DLR (4th) 489 at 539].

It is necessary to treat with some caution Canadian and United States judicial decisions dealing with general guarantees of freedom of speech. Their constitutional provisions are not the same as ours. In our case, not all speech can claim the protection of the constitutional implication of freedom we have identified in order to ensure the efficacious working of representative democracy and government. The foregoing examination of the freedom implied by the Australian Constitution indicates that there is a significant difference between that freedom and an unlimited freedom of expression and that the difference, though it does not lend itself to precise definition, is capable of being ascertained when the occasion to do so arises …

The relationship between the implied freedom and the common law of defamation

The decisions in *Nationwide News* [(1992) 177 CLR 1] and *Australian Capital Television* establish that the implied freedom is a restriction on legislative and executive power. Whether the implied freedom could also conceivably constitute a source of positive rights was not a question which arose for decision in those cases and it is unnecessary to decide it in this case. For that reason we shall refer **[126]** to the freedom of communication as an implication rather than as a guarantee of freedom, notwithstanding the use of the latter expression in some judgments in the two cases.

It is also clear that the implied freedom is one that shapes and controls the common law. At the very least, development in the common law must accord with its content. And, though it may not have been apparent in 1901 or, indeed, at any time prior to the decisions in *Nationwide News* and *Australian Capital Television*, if the content of the freedom so required, the common law must be taken to have adapted to it in 1901.

The question in this case is whether the nature of the implied freedom is such that that freedom impinges on the existing laws of defamation. The plaintiff argued that the limit of Australian defamation law is a matter for the proper extent of the common law only, and that it does not raise any constitutional issue. It was also argued, relying on an extra-judicial statement of Sir Owen Dixon, that as the Constitution was introduced into a pre-existing system of common law jurisprudence then this system forms the underlying basis for the Constitution such that the Constitution recognizes the common law and the common law remains in force until changed. By this argument constitutional freedoms are not absolute and therefore must be read subject to the balancing restraints imposed by the common law.

However, Sir Owen Dixon was not suggesting that the common law is superior or inferior to the Constitution. He was, we think, doing no more than setting the scene in which the Constitution operates. If the Constitution, expressly or by implication, is at variance with a doctrine of the common law, the latter must yield to the former. It will not always be easy to determine whether and to what extent there is a variance, but it is clear that the Constitution must prevail.

It is of course true, as the plaintiff argued, that constitutional freedoms are not absolute. Likewise, it is true that the common law is an antecedent system of jurisprudence to the Constitution. But the limits to constitutional freedoms are to be determined by evaluating what is necessary for the working of the Constitution and its principles. The antecedent common law can at most be a guide in this analysis. This, surely, is what Sir Owen Dixon intended when he concluded that: "constitutional questions should be considered **[127]** and resolved in the context of the whole law, of which the common law, including in that expression the doctrines of equity, forms not the least essential part." Hence, the common law forms part of the context by reference to which the question is to be decided; the question is not to be decided by reference to the common law alone …

[128] The point is then made that the framers of the Constitution did not think that the common law of defamation was inimical to the then existing system of democratic representative government. So much may be acknowledged. The framers of the Constitution, influenced by the writings of Professor Dicey on Parliament and sovereignty, no doubt considered that the ultimate protection of freedom of expression, along with other important rights, might be found in the common law and in the exercise by the legislatures of the powers which they possessed. But what the framers of the Constitution thought, but did not provide in the Constitution, 100 years ago, is hardly a sure guide in the very different circumstances which prevail today. If the purpose of the implied freedom were merely to safeguard the interests of individuals, there might be something to commend this approach. But, when the purpose of the implication is to protect the efficacious working of the system of representative government mandated by the Constitution, the freedom which is implied should be understood as being capable of extending to freedom from restraints imposed by law, whether statute law or common law …

[129] *Do the existing laws of defamation inhibit freedom of communication?* …

[130] [I]n Canada, it has been decided that the freedom of expression guaranteed by s 32 of the Charter of Rights and Freedoms does not confer upon a person any right or immunity beyond that accorded by the relevant laws of defamation … However, that is not the approach which was taken by the Supreme Court of the United States in the celebrated case of *New York Times Co v Sullivan* [376 US 254 (1964)]. In that case, the Supreme Court held that the guarantee of free speech contained in the First Amendment protected even false defamatory speech unless the plaintiff could prove actual malice or reckless disregard for truth or falsity on the part of the defendant. This approach does not limit the protection to protection against government conduct …

To our minds, it is incontrovertible that an implication of freedom of communication, the purpose of which is to ensure the efficacy of representative democracy, must extend to protect political discussion from exposure to onerous criminal and civil liability if the implication is to be effective in achieving its purpose. The correctness of that proposition has repeatedly been affirmed. In the United States, in *City of Chicago v Tribune Co* [139 NE 86 at 90 (1923)] Thompson CJ said:

> "While in the early history of the struggle for freedom of speech the restrictions were enforced by criminal prosecutions, **[131]** it is clear that a civil action is as great, if not a greater, restriction than a criminal prosecution. If the right to criticize the government is a privilege which … cannot be restricted, then all civil as well as criminal actions are forbidden. A despotic or corrupt government can more easily stifle opposition by a series of civil actions than by criminal prosecutions".

That statement, along with others to the same effect, was endorsed by the Supreme Court of the United States in *Sullivan*.

Subsequently, in *Derbyshire County Council v Times Newspapers Ltd* [[1993] AC 534 at 548], Lord Keith cited those statements and the endorsement of them in *Sullivan* and went on to say:

> "While these decisions were related most directly to the provisions of the American Constitution concerned with securing freedom of speech, the public interest considerations which underlaid them are no less valid in this country. What has been described as 'the chilling effect' induced by the threat of civil actions for libel is very important. Quite often the facts which would justify a defamatory publication are known to be true, but admissible evidence capable of proving those facts is not available." …

The statements quoted above, as well as the decision in *Sullivan*, speak eloquently of the tendency of the law of defamation to inhibit the exercise of the freedom of communication – "the chilling effect" – in the United States and the United Kingdom. In Australia also the existence of that tendency has been noted. Nonetheless, there is an argument that, despite that tendency of the law of defamation, it does not amount to an infringement of the freedom because the common law of defamation has endeavoured to achieve an acceptable balance between the public interest in giving effect to freedom of speech and the competing public interest in protecting the reputation of individuals who are defamed. The defences of truth, privilege and fair comment have been developed with a view to resolving the tension which exists between recognition of freedom of speech and the necessity of protecting the individual from injury to reputation. Thus, it may be said that, because the **[132]** common law of defamation has been moulded by the judges with that end in view, the law has arrived at an appropriate balance of the competing interests so that freedom of communication is not infringed. The answer to this argument, so it seems to us, is that, in reaching that balance, the courts have not taken account of the fact that there is an implied freedom of communication … It follows, in our view, that the Court is not justified in concluding that the balance achieved by the common law … necessarily means that there is no inconsistency between common law principles and the freedom.

Furthermore, the acknowledged tendency of the existing law of defamation to inhibit the exercise of the freedom tells strongly against the absence of such inconsistency. In *Sullivan*, Brennan J, who delivered the opinion of the Court, pointed out that a rule compelling the critic of official conduct to prove truth as a defence to actions in which punitive damages may be awarded does not deter false speech only. It is often difficult to prove the truth of the alleged libel in all its particulars. And the necessity of proving truth as a defence may well deter a critic from voicing criticism, even if it be true, because of doubt whether it can be proved or fear of the expense of having to do so …

[133] The common law defences of fair comment and qualified privilege are not always available. Fair comment is available only for the expression of opinion and, then, only if the comment is based on facts which are notorious or truly stated. Qualified privilege depends on the absence of malice and on the person who makes the communication having an interest or duty in its making and on the recipient having a corresponding interest or duty in receiving it … [Thus it] is usually not available where the information has been disseminated to the public generally …

In these circumstances, the common law defences which protect the reputation of persons who are the subject of defamatory publications do so at the price of significantly inhibiting free communication. To that extent, the balance is tilted too far against free communication and the need to protect the efficacious working of representative democracy and government in favour of the protection of individual reputation.

However, the joint judgment did not adopt the full extent of the "public figure" defence in *New York Times v Sullivan*, let alone the view of Justice Black in that case that the freedom of the press "**[296]** to criticize officials and discuss public affairs with impunity" must be absolute. Even the majority view in *Sullivan* was rejected because it "**[134]** tilts the balance unduly in favour of free speech against protection of individual reputation". Instead, the joint judgment adopted a modified version of the *Sullivan* test:

Mason CJ, Toohey and Gaudron JJ: [137] [T]he defendant should be required to establish that the circumstances were such as to make it reasonable to publish the impugned material without ascertaining whether it was true or false. The publisher should be required to show that, in the circumstances which prevailed, it acted reasonably, either by taking some steps to check the accuracy of the impugned material or by establishing that it was otherwise justified in publishing without taking such steps or steps which were adequate. To require more of those wishing to participate in political discussion would impose impractical and, sometimes, severe restraint on commentators and others who participate in discussion of public affairs. Such a restraint would severely cramp that freedom of political discussion which is so essential to the effective and open working of modern government …

In other words, if a defendant publishes false and defamatory matter about a plaintiff, the defendant should be liable in damages unless it can establish that it was unaware of the falsity, that it did not publish recklessly (ie, not caring whether the matter was true or false), and that the publication was reasonable in the sense described. These requirements will redress the balance and give the publisher protection, consistently with the implied freedom, whether or not the material is accurate …

It will be noted from the preceding paragraphs that we do not consider that the plaintiff should bear the onus of proving that the publication is not protected. In our view, it is for the defendant to establish that the publication falls within the constitutional protection.

On the basis of these last two paragraphs, Mason CJ, Toohey and Gaudron JJ held that the "constitutional defence" relied upon by the defendant was good in law. However, the precise juristic mechanism by which the new defence was to operate remained unclear. The underlying concept apparently was that, to the extent that the practical operation of the law of defamation would be inconsistent with the level of freedom required by the Constitution, that body of law was not to be *operable*, so that to that extent defamation was not to be *actionable*. Though formulated as a defence, the constitutional rule was more appropriately to be understood as charting the limits within which the courts (themselves bound by the Constitution by virtue of covering clause 5) could entertain suits for defamation.

The fourth member of the majority, Deane J, took a more expansive view. He reaffirmed strongly that the implied freedom, as derived from the Commonwealth Constitution, could restrict the constitutional powers of the States as well as those of the Commonwealth, since the States are "[165] subjugated to the Constitution as a whole by s 106". He was equally emphatic in rejecting the argument that the absence from the Constitution of any systematic list of guaranteed "rights" should inhibit today's Court from giving effect to "[171] rights, privileges and immunities [implied] from either the Constitution's express terms or the fundamental doctrines upon which it was structured and which it incorporated as part of its very fabric". As he and Toohey J had done in *Nationwide News v Wills*, he argued that: "The present legitimacy of the Constitution as the compact and highest law of our nation lies exclusively in the original adoption (by referenda) and subsequent maintenance (by acquiescence) of its provisions by the people". Accordingly, "to construe the Constitution on the basis that the dead hands of those who framed it reached from their graves to negate or constrict the natural implications of its express provisions or fundamental doctrines would deprive what was intended to be a living instrument of its vitality and its adaptability to serve succeeding generations". In support of this view of the Constitution as an adaptable "living instrument", he quoted a passage from Andrew Inglis Clark, *Studies in Australian Constitutional Law* (Charles Maxwell, 1901; repr Legal Books, 1997), 21-2 (see Chapter 8, §3). At one stage, Inglis Clark implied that, as the Constitution evolves, its judicial interpretation would acquire the same degree of authority as the original text itself; Deane J demurred from that implication. Otherwise, he adopted Inglis Clark's approach as the basis for an emphatic refutation of any form of "originalism".

Consistently with this evolutionary view of the Constitution as a "living instrument", the approach of Deane J to its effect on the common law of defamation differed from that of Mason CJ, Toohey and Gaudron JJ. Their joint judgment had argued that "[126] if the implied freedom so required, the common law must be taken to have adapted to it in 1901". By contrast, Deane J argued that both the understanding of the Constitution, and the practical uses of resort to common law defamation proceedings, had *changed* since 1901.

Deane J: [173] Since 1901, a variety of important developments have combined to transform the nature and extent of political communication and discussion in this country and to do much to translate the Constitution's theoretical doctrine of representative government with its thesis of popular sovereignty into practical reality. The more important of those developments include: the introduction of both **[174]** universal adult franchise and compulsory voting; the extraordinary development and increased utilization of the means of mass communication; advances in general education; and, the increasing appreciation and assertion of the intrinsic equality of all human beings. These developments have greatly enhanced the need to ensure that there be unrestricted public access to political information and to all political points of view. Yet, in the same period, the use of defamation proceedings in relation to political communication and discussion has expanded to the stage where there is a widespread public perception that such proceedings represent a valued source of tax-free profit for the holder of high public office who is defamed and an effective way to "stop" political criticism, particularly at election times. That widespread perception may well be exaggerated or unjustified. Its effect is, however, to intensify the chilling effect of a threat or perceived risk of defamation proceedings. In the context of those dramatic changes since 1901, there is manifest wisdom in Inglis Clark's instruction that, in its application to contemporary conditions and exigencies, the Constitution must be treated as "a living force" and not as "a declaration of the will and intentions of men long since dead". In following that instruction in the present case, the Court must take full account of contemporary social and political circumstances and perceptions in determining whether an unqualified application of State defamation laws to political communication and discussion is consistent with the constitutional implication of freedom.

Against this background, Deane J proceeded to assess the impact of State defamation laws on freedom of political discussion. He held not only that the existing law of defamation was "[185] inconsistent with the implication and precluded by the Constitution", but that simple adoption of the *New York Times* rule would be equally unacceptable. "It is true that such a confinement of the applicability of State defamation laws would mitigate the violation of the constitutional implication. It would not, however, eliminate it". Instead, he held that the constitutional implication should "preclude completely" the application of State defamation laws to statements about "[186] the official conduct of those entrusted with the powers of government". In response to the objection that such an absolute rule would enure to the benefit of large media corporations rather than individuals, he added:

> **Deane J: [186]** It is true that the proprietors of media outlets are commonly large and powerful corporations and that there are some special arguments which can be advanced to support the full application of the ordinary laws of defamation to the political communications and discussions which they publish for profit to themselves. Ultimately, however, the authors of such communications and discussions published through the mass media are individuals and publication of them is the means of communication of the political statements or views of an individual, namely, the immediate author or the individual who directs or influences what the immediate author writes or says. More important, and notwithstanding the potential for abuse, the freedom of the citizen to engage in significant political communication and discussion is largely dependent upon the freedom of the media.

In an "[187] Addendum" to his judgment, Deane J indicated that, for the sake of arriving at a clear majority decision, he would agree to the more limited modification to the law of defamation proposed by Mason CJ, Toohey and Gaudron JJ.

> **Deane J: [187]** The overall effect of the various judgments in this case is that four Justices, Mason CJ, Toohey J, Gaudron J and I, have reached the conclusion that an unqualified application of the defamation laws of Victoria to impose liability in damages in respect of political communications and discussion is precluded by the constitutional implication of political communication and discussion. There is, however, disagreement … about what flows from that conclusion for the purposes of the present case. Mason CJ, Toohey and Gaudron JJ would hold that the implication precludes the application of State defamation laws to impose liability in damages for the publication of a statement about the official conduct or suitability of a member of the Parliament [188] only if the defendant establishes that "it was unaware of the falsity of the material published", that "it did not publish the material recklessly, that is, not caring whether the material was true or false" and that "the publication was reasonable in the circumstances". For the reasons which I have given, I am quite unable to accept that the freedom which the constitutional implication protects is … conditioned upon the ability of the citizen or other publisher to satisfy a court of matters such as absence of recklessness or reasonableness. Nonetheless, I necessarily agree with their Honours that the constitutional implication precludes the imposition of liability in damages under State defamation laws to the extent which they would exclude it in a case such as the present. That means that majority support for the operation of the implication in a case such as the present exists for, but is limited to, that attributed to it by Mason CJ, Toohey and Gaudron JJ. In these circumstances, the appropriate course for me to follow is to lend my support for the answers which their Honours give to the questions reserved by the stated case.

Brennan, Dawson and McHugh JJ dissented. Brennan J had already indicated in *Nationwide News* and *Australian Capital Television* that in his view the implied constitutional freedom of political communication was derived from, and therefore also limited by, the common law.

> **Brennan J: [141]** The Constitution and the common law are bound in a symbiotic relationship: though the Constitution itself and laws enacted under the powers it confers may abrogate or alter rules of the common law, the common law is the matrix in which the Constitution came into being and which informs its text. "It is well settled", this Court declared in *Cheatle v The Queen* [(1993) 177 CLR 541 at 552], "that the interpretation of a constitution such as ours is necessarily influenced by the [142] fact that its provisions are framed in the language of the English common

law, and are to be read in the light of the common law's history". Whether the interpretation and operation of the Constitution might be affected by the development of common law doctrines is an interesting though hitherto hypothetical question which need not detain us in this case ...

Common law is amenable to development by judicial decision, subject to the Constitution and to statute. What is permissible development of the common law by the courts and what amounts to impermissible change is an issue on which minds differ most sharply. Respect for precedent and the general structure of law, assessment of the justice and efficiency of existing rules, their conformity with underlying principle, appreciation of contemporary values, the implications of change, the capacity of the legal system and of society to absorb change and, importantly, the just resolution of the instant case, all have a part to play when a proposition of the common law is reviewed by a court in which (to adopt the words of Barwick CJ) "no authority binds or current of acceptable decision compels" [*Mutual Life & Citizens' Assurance Co Ltd v Evatt* (1968) 122 CLR 556 at 563]. Some judges find unanswerable the approach of Judge Learned Hand:

> "The respect all men feel in some measure for customary law lies deep in their nature; we accept the verdict of the past until the need for change cries out loudly enough to force upon us a **[143]** choice between the comforts of further inertia and the irksomeness of action."

Other judges find the call to reform more urgent.

Whatever may be the scope of judicial power to reform the common law ..., it is clear that judicial development of the common law is a function different from judicial interpretation of statutes and of the Constitution. In the development of the common law, judicial policy has a role to perform, albeit the role is limited; in the interpretation of statutes, judicial policy is alien to the task of exegesis. The policy of the legislature, if it can be discovered, guides the Court in the interpretation of a statute where the text is ambiguous or obscure or its ordinary meaning is absurd or unreasonable. In other respects, the text itself governs the exercise of judicial power ...

In *Australian Capital Television*, Dawson J had conceded that the Constitution does imply some commitment to a system of parliamentary democracy in which the elected representatives are "directly chosen by the people", and hence to the conditions necessary for the exercise of a true choice. McHugh J, while joining in the majority result in that case, had confined himself more narrowly than the other majority judges to the implications necessarily entailed in the voting requirements of ss 7 and 24 of the Constitution. Both of them now emphasised these respective aspects of their earlier judgments, and insisted that the law of defamation was unaffected by any implied freedom.

McHugh J: [197] If this Court is to retain the confidence of the nation as the final arbiter of what the Constitution means, no interpretation of the Constitution by the Court can depart from the text of the Constitution and what is implied by the text and the structure of the Constitution. To determine what are the implied meanings of a legal instrument is seldom an easy task. But it must be done. The search for implications in the language of a legal text is a necessary part of the task of legal interpretation whether the text be a contract or a Constitution. As Windeyer J pointed out in *Victoria v Commonwealth* [(1971) 122 CLR 353 at 402] in interpreting the Constitution "our avowed task is simply the revealing or uncovering of implications that are already there" ...

[198] Since the decision in the *Engineers' Case* ... , this Court has consistently held that it is not legitimate to construe the Constitution by reference to political principles or theories that find no support in the text of the Constitution. The theory of constitutional interpretation that has prevailed since the *Engineers' Case* is that one starts with the text and not with some theory of federalism, politics or political economy. The *Engineers' Case* made it plain that the Constitution is not to be interpreted by using such theories to control, modify or organize the meaning of the Constitution unless those theories can be deduced from the terms or structure of the Constitution itself ...

A constitutional doctrine is unacceptable, therefore, unless it is based on some premise or premises that is or are contained in the Constitution itself. That is not to deny that theories of federalism, politics and economics or the principles of the common law may be used to interpret particular provisions of the Constitution. But it is legitimate to use them only when there are grounds for concluding that the meaning of the constitutional provision was intended to be understood by reference to such a theory or principle. Those grounds may arise from the very terms of particular constitutional provisions … [or] from what was said and done at the Conventions leading up to the enactment of the Constitution … **[199]** They may arise from the history of the nation and its institutions. The Commonwealth of Australia was not born into a vacuum, as Latham CJ once pointed out. It was created against the background of a system of constitutional conventions and common law rules and principles that governed the relationship between the Crown and the citizen. Those common law rules and principles are "the source of the legal conceptions that govern us in determining [the Constitution's] effect".

An examination of the Constitution shows that the terms "representative government" and "representative democracy" are not mentioned. That, of course, is not decisive: one or other of those concepts or some part of them may be implied by some term or terms in the Constitution or may be regarded as part of the express meaning of one of those terms. But with great respect to those who have reached the opposite conclusion, I can find no support in the Constitution for an implication that the institution of representative government or representative democracy is part of the Constitution independently of the terms of ss 1, 7, 24, 30 and 41 of the Constitution. I think that all that can fairly be said is that those sections of the Constitution give effect to the political institution of representative government. But neither logic nor the efficacy of those sections or the federal system itself implies that independently of those sections the institution of representative government or representative democracy is itself part of the Constitution.

It follows in my respectful view that the Constitution does not adopt or guarantee the maintenance of the institution of representative government or representative democracy except to the extent that certain sections of the Constitution embody it.

Although some of the judgments in *Australian Capital Television* and the majority judgments in the present case tend to equate representative government with the concept of representative democracy, I do not think that the concepts are interchangeable. Representative democracy is the wider concept of the two, certainly in modern times. It is commonly used to describe a society which provides for equality of rights and privileges. In his *Introduction to* **[200]** *Democratic Theory*, HB Mayo thought that the four essential principles of a democracy were: (1) popular control of policy makers through elections held at regular intervals; (2) political equality; (3) political freedoms; and (4) when the representatives are divided, the decision of the majority prevails. Even wider definitions can be found, particularly in socialist societies where it is defined to include the economic and social spheres as well as the political sphere. Although informed persons in Australia probably agree on the central tenets of representative democracy, the term is nevertheless descriptive of a wide spectrum of political institutions and processes. Moreover, the conceptions of representative democracy have been evolving for a very long period of time. The course of that evolution does not seem to be spent. The essence of representative government, on the other hand, is a political system where the people in free elections elect their representatives to the political chamber which occupies the most powerful position in the political system … Representative government is a narrower concept than representative democracy …

[201] It is likely that the makers of the Constitution saw representative government as encompassing no more than a system under which the people were governed by representatives elected in free elections by those eligible to vote. The terms of ss 7 and 24 give effect to this view. The absence of a Bill of Rights or any guarantee of universal suffrage or political equality in the Constitution is also consistent with the view that the makers of the Constitution did not intend, and the Constitution does not give effect, to any general doctrine of representative democracy…

[202] With great respect, it seems to me that those judgments in *Australian Capital Television* and *Nationwide News Pty Ltd v Wills* that hold that the institution of representative government is part of the Constitution independently of the terms of certain sections of the Constitution unintentionally depart from the method of constitutional interpretation that has existed in this country since the time of the *Engineers' Case*. Those judgments hold that, because the makers of the Constitution intended that the Commonwealth should have a representative government and that certain sections of the Constitution give effect to that intention, the institution itself is part of the Constitution. From that premise the conclusion is reached that the rights of the people inherent in that institution are constitutionally entrenched and extend to all tiers of government in Australia. The majority judgments seek to imply a general concept **[203]** of representative government with a wide meaning from the terms of the Constitution – ss 7 and 24 in particular. But those sections do not support that implication. Even if the concept of representative government has a wide meaning akin to that of representative democracy, ss 7 and 24 simply give effect to one aspect of the institution of representative government ... Those sections deal with elections, not general political rights. To give them the efficacy that their purpose requires, it is legitimate to imply other freedoms during the course of elections, as I sought to show in *Australian Capital Television*. But with great respect, I do not see how there can be implied into the Constitution from the terms of those sections – whether by necessity or otherwise – the whole apparatus of representative government in the sense used in the majority judgments, with consequential restraints on the powers of the Commonwealth, State and Territory governments and the common law, when no federal election is pending ...

[204] Having read and re-read on many occasions those judgments in *Australian Capital Television* and *Nationwide* that hold that the institution of representative government is a part of the Constitution, I have concluded that the reasoning that has led to that holding should not be followed. In *Australian Capital Television* and *Nationwide*, I agreed that the relevant legislation was invalid. But I did not do so on the ground that representative government was itself part of the Constitution independently of ss 7 and 24. In *Australian Capital Television*, I accepted that the Constitution gave effect to the institutions of representative government and responsible government. However, I used those concepts not as enactments of the Constitution but as tools for interpreting the full meaning of ss 7 and 24 of the Constitution ...

[206] In *Australian Capital Television* [177 CLR at 232], I left open the question whether the Constitution contained "a general right of freedom of communication in respect of the business of government of the Commonwealth". But having considered the matter again, I am unable to see any proper basis for inferring a *general* right of freedom of communication in the Constitution any more than I can see a proper basis for inferring a principle of representative government or representative democracy.

In *Stephens v West Australian Newspapers Ltd*, articles in the *West Australian* newspaper had alleged that six members of the Western Australian Legislative Council had wasted public money by taking an overseas trip to investigate matters which, it was said, could have been investigated in Western Australia. The trip was described as "a junket of mammoth proportions". The six Legislative Councillors sued for defamation. The alleged defamation thus related to State politicians in connection with a State political issue. Again, the defendants pleaded a defence based upon the implied freedom of political discussion.

The way in which the defence was pleaded did not precisely correspond to the specifications laid down in *Theophanous*. Accordingly, the *Theophanous* decision meant that the plea was not good in law, so that the result must depend on an alternative plea of qualified privilege. In principle, however, Mason CJ, Deane, Toohey and Gaudron JJ held that a constitutional defence was available. Once again, Brennan, Dawson and McHugh JJ dissented.

Stephens v West Australian Newspapers Ltd
(1994) 182 CLR 211

Mason CJ, Toohey and Gaudron JJ: [232] First, we consider that the freedom of communication implied in the Commonwealth Constitution extends to public discussion of the performance, conduct and fitness for office of members of a State legislature.

A majority of the justices in *Nationwide News Pty Ltd v Wills* [(1992) 177 CLR 1] and *Australian Capital Television Pty Ltd v Commonwealth* [(1992) 177 CLR 106] was of opinion that the freedom of communication as to political matters implied in the Commonwealth Constitution extended to all political discussion, including discussion of political matters relating to government at State level. The reasons for that conclusion are set out in the judgments in those cases and in our judgment in *Theophanous* [(1994) 182 CLR 104] ...

The basis of that implication has its counterpart in the Constitution of Western Australia ...

[233] Section 73 of the *Constitution Act* 1889 (WA) provides that the legislature of the State "shall have full power and authority, from time to time, by any Act, to repeal or alter any of the provisions of this Act". However, it is not lawful to present to the Governor for assent by the Queen:

"any Bill by which any change in the Constitution of the Legislative Council or of the Legislative Assembly shall be effected, unless the second and third readings of such Bill shall have been passed with the concurrence of an absolute majority of the whole number of the members for the time being of the Legislative Council and the Legislative Assembly respectively".

Section 73(2) was inserted into the Constitution … in 1978. That sub-section further restricts the capacity of the legislature to enact a Bill which expressly or impliedly provides for the abolition of either the Council or the Assembly (s 73(2)(b)) or provides that either House "shall be composed of members other than members chosen directly by the people" (s 73(2)(c)). The sub-section requires that such a Bill should not be presented for assent unless "the second and third readings of the Bill shall have been passed with the concurrence of an absolute majority of the whole number of the members for the time being of the Legislative Council and the Legislative Assembly, respectively" (s 73(2)(f)) and the Bill has been approved by a majority of electors of the State at a referendum …

[Section] 73(2) was plainly enacted with the object of reinforcing representative democracy and placing a further constitutional impediment in the way of any attempt to weaken representative democracy. And, so long, at least, as the Western Australian Constitution continues to provide for a representative democracy in which the members of the legislature are "directly chosen by the **[234]** people", a freedom of communication must necessarily be implied in that Constitution, just as it is implied in the Commonwealth Constitution, in order to protect the efficacious working of representative democracy and government.

Deane J held that a constitutional defence could be derived from the Commonwealth Constitution. Brennan J found a relevant implication both in the State Constitution and in the Commonwealth Constitution, but did not regard the implication at Commonwealth level as extending to discussion of State political matters. In any event, he adhered to his view that no such constitutional implication, whether at State or Commonwealth level, could alter the common law. Dawson and McHugh JJ denied that any relevant implication arose at either level.

The actual result in *Stephens* did not depend on the "constitutional defence" that the majority found to be available, but only on a modified version of the existing common law defences. As between the *Sullivan* option of choosing to "constitutionalise" the law of defamation by modelling a new "constitutional defence", and the lesser option of developing the common law by adapting the existing defence of qualified privilege, the joint judgment of Mason CJ, Toohey and Gaudron JJ in *Theophanous* had in fact done both.

Under the existing common law rules, the main doubt as to whether "qualified privilege" could be claimed for a newspaper story had arisen from the requirement for what is called "reciprocity of interest". As Lord Atkinson expressed the common law rule in *Adam v Ward* [1917] AC 309, this category of "privilege" to speak freely arises on "**[334]** an occasion where the person who makes a communication has an interest or a duty, legal, social or moral, to make it to the person to whom it is made, and the person to whom it is so made has a corresponding interest or duty to receive it". This formulation recognises clearly that the interests or duties giving rise to the privilege may be "legal, social or moral"; and other English judges had repeatedly emphasised that these criteria were to be broadly applied. In particular, in *Toogood v Spyring* (1834) 1 CM & R 181; 149 ER 1044, Parke B had said: "**[193]** If fairly warranted by any reasonable occasion or exigency, and honestly made, such communications are protected for the common convenience and welfare of society; and the law has not restricted the right to make them within any narrow limits".

Despite these frequently reiterated dicta, any claim by a newspaper to qualified privilege remained at best uncertain. It was not clear that a newspaper had sufficient interest or duty to publish a story, and in any event it was said that the readership of a newspaper extends far beyond the range of people with sufficient interest or duty in being made aware of a story (see especially *Morosi v Mirror Newspapers Ltd* [1977] 2 NSWLR 749 at 775-80).

Clearly, the constitutional implications spelled out in *Nationwide News* and *Australian Capital Television* had altered the assumptions on which such doubts depended. If the working of the Constitution *requires* an unrestricted involvement in political discussion by all persons in Australia – not only electors but their friends, children or visitors who might help to formulate political attitudes – then it follows that every person who reads a newspaper is doing so in the exercise of a legitimate constitutional role, and correspondingly that whatever a newspaper does to assist that role is done in the privileged exercise of a public responsibility. The joint judgment in *Theophanous* effectively accepted this reasoning.

Theophanous v Herald & Weekly Times Ltd
(1994) 182 CLR 104

Mason CJ, Toohey and Gaudron JJ: [140] Common law qualified privilege must now be viewed in the light of the implied constitutional freedom … The public at large has an interest in the discussion of political matters such that each and every person has an interest, of the kind contemplated by the common law, in communicating his or her views on those matters and each and every person has an interest in receiving information on those matters. It is an interest which exists at all times; it is not confined to situations where it is publicly anticipated that a federal election will be called. It follows that the discussion of political matters is an occasion of qualified privilege.

The joint judgment went on to say that "**[140]** [even] in this light, the common law defence does not conform to the constitutional freedom" – but gave no clear explanation of why such a defence would fall short of the level of protection which the Constitution requires, nor of why a further process of common law development would not overcome any such shortfalls.

The joint judgment in *Theophanous* also suggested that, in view of the constitutional defence which that judgment had formulated, the widening of the common law defence would have "**[140]** little, if any, practical significance". Yet in *Stephens*, the *Theophanous* dicta about the scope of qualified privilege became the ratio decidendi on which the Court's final order was based. In that case it was held that the "constitutional defence" had *not* been acceptably pleaded (since the pleader had failed to anticipate the requirements spelled out in *Theophanous*); and accordingly the crucial question was whether the defendant newspaper could rely on a defence of qualified privilege. The joint judgment in *Stephens* held that it could. Indeed, by asserting a *duty* to publish, the pleader had done more than was needed.

Stephens v West Australian Newspapers Ltd
(1994) 182 CLR 211

Mason CJ, Toohey and Gaudron JJ: [234] There is no need for us to do more than refer to our discussion in *Theophanous* of the relationship between the constitutional implication and the common law defence of qualified privilege. In the light of that discussion it is unnecessary to allege a *duty* on the part of the defendant to publish the matter complained of to its readers. However, that does not mean that the defence pleaded is not a good defence in law. It merely means that the defendant has alleged something which is unnecessary or irrelevant.

Thus, the actual result in *Stephens* was that the defence of qualified privilege had been acceptably pleaded, though the "constitutional defence" had not. The dissenters, Brennan, Dawson and McHugh JJ, held not only that no "constitutional defence" was possible, but that, on the basis of the actual pleadings, a defence of qualified privilege was not available either. However, this did not mean that they rejected the possibility of expanding that defence. Dawson and McHugh JJ excluded it only because, on the facts, they saw the relevant common law defence (if any) as "fair comment" rather than "qualified privilege". Brennan J was able to avoid that conclusion by finding "**[237]** a significant allegation of fact" in the allegation that the six plaintiffs had gone overseas "without the knowledge of Parliament"; and both he and McHugh J took the opportunity to spell out in detail their own conceptions of how the defence of qualified privilege might now be developed. The essential point for McHugh J was that the underlying common law requirement of "reciprocity of interest" must now be adapted to modern conditions:

McHugh J: [264] It is not surprising that successive generations of common law judges have been loath to extend the categories of qualified privilege to protect publications in the general media. Although the tort of defamation became established at an early stage in the history of common law, the defence of qualified privilege, as we know it, was not recognized until the first part of the last century. New legal doctrines take time to win general acceptance in the legal profession, and the low quality and sensational nature of significant parts of the late nineteenth century and twentieth century media have not been conducive to the extension of a defence that protects the publication of untrue defamatory material. However, as Cockburn CJ is reported to have said [*Wason v Walter* (1868) LR 4 QB 73 at 93] "those who administer [the law of qualified privilege] must adapt it to the varying conditions of society".

In the last decade of the twentieth century, the quality of life and the freedom of the ordinary individual in Australia are highly dependent on the exercise of functions and powers vested in public representatives and officials by a vast legal and bureaucratic apparatus funded by public moneys. How, when, why and where those functions and powers are or are not exercised are matters that are of real and legitimate interest to every member of the community. Information concerning the exercise of those functions and powers is of vital concern to the community. So is the performance of the public representatives and officials who are invested with them. It follows in my opinion that the general public has a legitimate interest in receiving information concerning matters relevant to the exercise of public functions and powers vested in public representatives and officials. Moreover, a narrow view should not be taken of the matters about which the general public has an interest in receiving information. With the increasing integration of the social, economic and political life of Australia, it is difficult to contend that the exercise or failure to exercise public functions or powers at any particular level of government or administration, or in any part of the country, is not of relevant interest to the public of Australia generally.

Accordingly, both he and Brennan J were prepared to agree that the concept of "qualified privilege" must now be stated more widely, though their formulations differed in points of detail from each other, as well as from the simpler version in the joint majority judgment. Dawson J did not necessarily dissent from these suggested developments, holding only that since *this* case raised issues of "fair comment" rather than "qualified privilege", it was "**[258]** unnecessary to consider further the scope of [the latter] defence in the present proceedings".

Despite the disagreements, *Theophanous* and *Stephens* were authority for two propositions: the availability of a new constitutional defence, and an expansion of the existing common law defence of qualified privilege. The latter, in differing versions, was supported by Mason CJ, Brennan, Toohey, Gaudron and McHugh JJ, with neither Deane J nor Dawson J dissenting.

5. Defamation: The Common Law Solution

The trilogy of 4:3 decisions in *Theophanous*, *Stephens* and *Cunliffe* ushered in a period of doubt and controversy both within and outside the Court. Changes in the composition of the bench, and the prospect of further impending changes, added to the sense of uncertainty. Mason CJ, Deane, Toohey and Gaudron JJ had formed the majority in *Theophanous* and *Stephens*; but in 1995 Mason CJ retired and Deane J resigned to become Governor-General. Thus, when a case involving the implications of "representative government" next came before the Court, only two judges from the majority in *Theophanous* and *Stephens* remained.

That next case was *McGinty v Western Australia* (1996) 186 CLR 140. The issue was whether an implication of equality of voting power could be derived from either the Commonwealth or the Western Australian Constitutions (see Chapter 10, §4(c)). By a 4:2 majority, the Court rejected the possibility of any such implication in the State Constitution. As to whether such an implication could be ascribed to the federal Constitution, the result was inconclusive; but the issue evoked a strong reassessment of the earlier decisions concerning the freedom of political communication, and of the constitutional premises on which those decisions were founded. In particular, McHugh J emphatically dissociated himself from any conception of "**[234]** a freestanding principle" of representative democracy to be discerned in the Constitution. He concluded that the use of the implied freedom of political discussion to override the common law in *Theophanous* should be reconsidered.

McGinty v Western Australia
(1996) 186 CLR 140

McHugh J: [231] I cannot accept ... that a constitutional implication can arise from a particular doctrine that "underlies the Constitution". Underlying or overarching doctrines may explain or illuminate the meaning of the text or structure of the **[232]** Constitution but such doctrines are not independent sources of the powers, authorities, immunities and obligations conferred by the Constitution. Top-down reasoning is not a legitimate method of interpreting the Constitution. As I pointed out in *Theophanous v Herald and Weekly Times Ltd* [(1994) 182 CLR 104], after the decision of this Court in the *Engineers' Case* [(1920) 28 CLR 129], the Court had consistently held, prior to *Nationwide News* [(1992) 177 CLR 1] and *Australian Capital Television Pty Ltd v Commonwealth* [(1992) 177 CLR 106], that it is not legitimate to construe the Constitution by reference to political principles or theories that are not anchored in the text of the Constitution or are not necessary implications from its structure. I pointed out that the *Engineers' Case* had made it plain that the Constitution was not to be interpreted by using such theories to control or modify the meaning of the Constitution unless those theories could be deduced from the terms or structure of the Constitution itself. It is the text and the implications to be drawn from the text and structure that contain the meaning of the Constitution. With all due respect to the judges of this Court who have held that there is a free-standing principle of representative democracy in the Constitution, their conclusion necessarily involves a rejection of the principles of interpretation laid down in the *Engineers' Case* although perhaps not the philosophy that lies behind that decision ...

[234] The result seems to be that the Constitution contains by implication a principle of representative democracy that is not confined to restricting the powers of the federal or State legislatures, nor does it necessarily confer any rights on individuals. It appears to be a free-standing principle, just as if the Constitution contained a Ch IX with a s 129 which read:

> "Subject to this Constitution, representative democracy is the law of Australia, notwith-standing any law to the contrary."

That does not mean, of course, that the implied principle of representative democracy trumps all other rights and obligations. Because the principle arises by implication, it must be subject to the express terms of the Constitution and be weighed in appropriate cases against other implications drawn from the text and structure of the Constitution. Nevertheless, when it is seen as the equivalent of the hypothetical s 129, it is plain that it is not an implication contained in the text of the Constitution, nor is it an implication "logically or practically necessary for the preservation of the integrity of [the] structure" of the Constitution [177 CLR at 135]. The "implication" has become a premise from which other implications are drawn. Thus, in *Theophanous* and *Stephens* the majority held that the preservation of representative democracy required that the common law of defamation should be restricted in its application to federal and State politicians and certain other persons. By that stage the text and structure of the Constitution have receded into the background and it is the concept of representative democracy, not the text or structure of the Constitution, that governs the application of the Constitution in such cases ...

[235] I regard the reasoning in *Nationwide News*, *Australian Capital Television*, *Theophanous* and *Stephens* [(1994) 182 CLR 211] in so far as it invokes an implied principle of representative democracy as fundamentally wrong **[236]** and as an alteration of the Constitution without the authority of the people under s 128 of the Constitution. Moreover, as much as I admire the noble vision of the justices who have found, contrary to what the overwhelming majority of lawyers had always thought, that the Constitution contains a free-standing principle of representative democracy, the principles of constitutional interpretation compel me to reject their reasoning. It may be that ultimately the representative democracy line of reasoning in *Nationwide News* and subsequent cases will be so widely followed and applied that, however erroneous one may think that reasoning is, it must be taken to reflect the meaning of the Constitution. But until that time arrives, I conceive that I have no option but to reject the authority of that reasoning.

To decide cases by reference to what the principles of representative democracy currently require is to give this Court a jurisdiction which the Constitution does not contemplate and which the Australian people have never authorised. Interpreting the Constitution is a difficult task at any time. It is not made easier by asking the justices of this Court to determine what representative democracy requires. That is a political question and, unless the Constitution turns it into a constitutional question for the judiciary, it should be left to be answered by the people and their elected representatives acting within the limits of their powers as prescribed by the Constitution.

McHugh J's charge that the implied freedom as developed in *Theophanous* and *Stephens* rests upon "[234] a free-standing principle, just as if the Constitution contained a Ch IX with a s 129" was intended as ironic (and perhaps also as a reminder of Mason CJ's gibe in *Miller v TCN Channel Nine Pty Ltd* (1986) 161 CLR 556 that Murphy J had sought to imply a new s 92A). Yet among the sections of the Constitution considered in *McGinty*, the headnote at (1996) 134 ALR 289 lists s 129!

At the hearing of *Levy v Victoria* (1997) 189 CLR 579 on 6 August 1996, Dawson J suggested that "[i]t would seem that there is now not a majority of the Court which would support" the decisions in *Theophanous* and *Stephens*. The hint was taken, and in March 1997 the High Court heard argument on whether *Theophanous* and *Stephens* should be overruled. *Levy* was heard together with *Lange v Australian Broadcasting Corporation* (1997) 189 CLR 520. In the end it was in *Lange* rather than in *Levy* that the Court chose to resolve the issue.

David Lange, a former Prime Minister of New Zealand, had sued the Australian Broadcasting Corporation for alleged defamatory statements in a *Four Corners* television program. The ABC's response asserted a "constitutional defence" (modelled upon the defence outlined by the joint judgment in *Theophanous*), and also a common law defence of qualified privilege. The Court, consisting of Brennan CJ, Dawson, Toohey, Gaudron, McHugh, Gummow and Kirby JJ, handed down a joint unanimous judgment in which it held that the "constitutional defence" was *not* available, since the constitutional implication cannot operate directly to alter private rights and immunities. This result necessarily meant that the actual decision in *Theophanous* was overruled, though the Court did not expressly say so. However, the Court also developed the common law defence of qualified privilege broadly (though not in precise detail) along the lines suggested by Brennan and McHugh JJ in *Stephens*. While the particulars set out by the ABC in its pleadings did not conform to the requirements of this (expanded) defence of qualified privilege, the Court left open the possibility that by suitably drafted particulars the ABC could bring itself within the new expanded defence. In fact, however, the matter was subsequently settled.

The unanimous judgment of the Court began by suggesting that neither *Theophanous* nor *Stephens* had laid down any binding statement of constitutional principle.

Lange v Australian Broadcasting Corporation
(1997) 189 CLR 520

The Court: [555] Although Deane J may have intended his concurrence with the answers in *Theophanous* [[(1994) 182 CLR 104]] to extend to the explanation of them in the joint judgment, the absence of an express agreement with the reasons in that judgment raises a question as to the extent to which he concurred with the terms of the answers. But, assuming that his Honour intended to agree with those answers as read in the light of the joint judgment, nevertheless the reasoning which gave rise to the answers in *Theophanous* had the direct support of only three of the seven Justices.

In *Stephens* [[(1994) 182 CLR 211]], an identical division of opinion among the Justices **[556]** occurred. Once again Deane J agreed with the answers proposed by Mason CJ, Toohey and Gaudron JJ in the case stated. He said [182 CLR at 257]:

"In view of the division between the other members of the Court, it would, to that extent, be inappropriate for me to adhere to [my views] for the purposes of this case."

Accordingly his Honour expressed his "concurrence in the answers which Mason CJ, Toohey and Gaudron JJ propose to the questions stated" [182 CLR at 257]. In these circumstances,

Theophanous and *Stephens* do not have the same authority which they would have if Deane J had agreed with the reasoning of Mason CJ, Toohey and Gaudron JJ in each case.

However, for the reasons set out below, *Theophanous* and *Stephens* should be accepted as deciding that in Australia the common law rules of defamation must conform to the requirements of the Constitution. Those cases should also be accepted as deciding that, at least by 1992, the constitutional implication precluded an unqualified application in Australia of the English common law of defamation in so far as it continued to provide no defence for the mistaken publication of defamatory matter concerning government and political matters to a wide audience. The full argument we heard in the present case and the illumination and insights gained from the subsequent cases of *McGinty v Western Australia* [(1996) 186 CLR 140], *Langer v Commonwealth* [(1996) 186 CLR 302] and *Muldowney v South Australia* [(1996) 186 CLR 352] now satisfy us, however, that some of the expressions and reasoning in the various judgments in *Theophanous* and *Stephens* should be further considered in order to settle both constitutional doctrine and the contemporary common law of Australia governing the defence of qualified privilege in actions of libel and slander.

Having regard to the foregoing discussion, the appropriate course is to examine the correctness of the defences pleaded in the present case as a matter of principle and not of authority. The starting point of that examination must be the terms of the Constitution illuminated by the assistance which is to be obtained from *Theophanous* and the other authorities which have dealt with the question of "implied freedoms" under the Constitution.

Despite the doubt thus cast on the authority of *Theophanous* and *Stephens*, and the consequent reconsideration of the matter as one "**[556]** of principle and not of authority", the Court had already made it clear in the course of this preamble that the main conclusion of those cases was to stand: that is, that the constitutional implication "precluded" the continued unrestricted operation of the law of defamation. Moreover, this was conceived of as resulting from an evolutionary process ("at least by 1992"). To that extent the preferred analysis was that of Deane J in *Theophanous*, rather than the postulate in the *Theophanous* joint judgment that the law of defamation must be taken to have changed in 1901. The Court went on to make it clear that the underlying conception of "representative government" was also to be retained.

The Court: [557] Sections 7 and 24 of the Constitution, read in context, require the members of the Senate and the House of Representatives to be directly chosen at periodic elections by the people of the States and of the Commonwealth respectively. This requirement embraces all that is necessary to effectuate the free election of representatives at periodic elections. What is involved in the people directly choosing their representatives at periodic elections, however, can be understood only by reference to the system of representative and responsible government to which ss 7 and 24 and other sections of the Constitution give effect.

That the Constitution intended to provide for the institutions of representative and responsible government is made clear both by the Convention Debates and by the terms of the Constitution itself. Thus, at the Second Australasian Convention held in Adelaide in 1897, the Convention, on the motion of Mr Edmund Barton, resolved that the purpose of the Constitution was "to enlarge the powers of self-government of the people of Australia".

Sections 1, 7, 8, 13, 24, 25, 28 and 30 of the Constitution give effect to the purpose of self-government by providing for the fundamental features of representative government. As Isaacs J put it [*Federal Commissioner of Taxation v Munro* (1926) 38 CLR 153 at 178]:

"[T]he Constitution is for the advancement of representative government." ...

[558] Other sections of the Constitution establish a formal relationship between the Executive Government and the Parliament and provide for a system of responsible ministerial government, a system of government which, "prior to the establishment of the Commonwealth of Australia in 1901 ... had become one of the central characteristics of our polity" [*Victorian Stevedoring and General Contracting Co Pty Ltd and Meakes v Dignan* (1931) 46 CLR 73 at 114]. Thus, s 6 of the Constitution requires that there be a session of the Parliament at least once in every year ... Section 83 ensures that the legislature controls supply. It does so by requiring parliamentary authority for the expenditure by the Executive Government of any fund or sum of money standing to the credit of the Crown in right of the Commonwealth, irrespective of source. Sections 62 and 64 of the

Constitution combine to provide for the executive power of the Commonwealth, which is vested in the Queen and exercisable by the Governor-General, to be exercised "on the initiative and advice" of Ministers [*Theodore v Duncan* [1919] AC 696 at 706] and limit to three months the period in which a Minister of State may hold office without being or becoming a senator or member of the House of Representatives. Section 49 of the Constitution, in dealing with the powers, privileges and immunities of the Senate and of the House of Representatives, secures the freedom of speech in debate which, in England, historically was a potent instrument by which the House of Commons defended its right to consider and express opinions on the conduct of affairs of State by the Sovereign and the Ministers, advisers and servants of the Crown. Section 49 also provides the source of coercive authority for each **[559]** chamber of the Parliament to summon witnesses, or to require the production of documents, under pain of punishment for contempt.

The requirement that the Parliament meet at least annually, the provision for control of supply by the legislature, the requirement that Ministers be members of the legislature, the privilege of freedom of speech in debate, and the power to coerce the provision of information provide the means for enforcing the responsibility of the Executive to the organs of representative government. In his *Notes on Australian Federation: Its Nature and Probable Effects*, Sir Samuel Griffith pointed out that the effect of responsible government "is that the actual government of the State is conducted by officers who enjoy the confidence of the people". That confidence is ultimately expressed or denied by the operation of the electoral process, and the attitudes of electors to the conduct of the Executive may be a significant determinant of the contemporary practice of responsible government.

Note the reaffirmation here of the constitutional commitment not only to "representative government" but also to "responsible government" – that is, to the principle that the executive government is ultimately responsible to the elected legislature.

Consistently with the views expressed in *McGinty*, the joint judgment reaffirmed that the doctrines thus spelled out were confined to what could properly be deduced from the "text and structure" of the Constitution. Neither "representative government" nor freedom of political communication was to be treated as "a free-standing principle". Hence, "**[567]** [u]nder the Constitution, the relevant question is not, 'What is required by representative and responsible government?' It is, 'What do the terms and structure of the Constitution prohibit, authorise or require?'" However, this did not mean that the scope of the freedom had been narrowed from its conception in *Australian Capital Television* and *Theophanous*. In *Levy v Victoria* (1997) 189 CLR 579 McHugh J took care to point out that "**[622 n 148]** as the decision in *Lange* shows, the scope of the freedom is at least as great as that recognised in the two earlier cases".

The Court proceeded to reformulate the scope and operation of the constitutional freedom.

The Court: [559] Freedom of communication on matters of government and politics is an indispensable incident of that system of representative government which the Constitution creates by directing that the members of the House of Representatives and the Senate shall be "directly chosen by the people" of the Commonwealth and the States, respectively. At federation, representative government was understood to mean a system of government where the people in free elections elected their representatives to the legislative chamber which occupies the most powerful position in the political system. As Birch points out, "it is the manner of choice of members of the legislative assembly, rather than their characteristics or their behaviour, which is generally taken to be the criterion of a representative form of government". However, to have a full understanding of the concept of representative government, Birch also states that:

> "we need to add that the chamber must occupy a powerful position **[560]** in the political system and that the elections to it must be free, with all that this implies in the way of freedom of speech and political organization."

Communications concerning political or government matters between the electors and the elected representatives, between the electors and the candidates for election and between the electors themselves were central to the system of representative government, as it was understood at federation. While the system of representative government for which the Constitution provides does not expressly mention freedom of communication, it can hardly be doubted, given the history of representative government and the holding of elections under that system in Australia prior to federation, that the elections for which the Constitution provides were intended to be free elections in the sense explained by Birch. Furthermore, because the choice given by ss 7 and 24 must be a true choice with "an opportunity to gain an appreciation of the available alternatives", as Dawson J pointed out in *Australian Capital Television Pty Ltd v Commonwealth* [(1992) 177 CLR 106 at 187], legislative power cannot support an absolute denial of access by the people to relevant information about the functioning of government in Australia and about the policies of political parties and candidates for election.

That being so, ss 7 and 24 and the related sections of the Constitution necessarily protect that freedom of communication between the people concerning political or government matters which enables the people to exercise a free and informed choice as electors. Those sections do not confer personal rights on individuals. Rather they preclude the curtailment of the protected freedom by the exercise of legislative or executive power. As Deane J said in *Theophanous* [182 CLR at 168], they are "a limitation or confinement of laws and powers [which] gives rise to a pro tanto immunity on the part of the citizen from being adversely affected by those laws or by the exercise of those powers rather than to a 'right' in the strict sense". In *Cunliffe v Commonwealth* [(1994) 182 CLR 272 at 326-7], Brennan J pointed out that the freedom confers no rights on individuals and, to the extent that the freedom rests upon implication, that implication defines the nature and extent of the freedom. His Honour said:

> "The implication is negative in nature: it invalidates laws and consequently creates an area of immunity from legal control, particularly from legislative control."

It was essentially because of this analysis that the "constitutional defence" established by *Theophanous* was destined to fail. A defendant could not invoke the constitutional freedom directly – so as to claim a personal immunity from suit – because that is not the way that a constitutional restriction on legislative and governmental power works. Suppose, however, that the above statement as to preclusion of curtailment "**[560]** by the exercise of legislative or executive power" were extended to the exercise of legislative or executive *or judicial* power. And suppose the *Theophanous* defence were reconceptualised as a limit, not on the ability of plaintiffs to sue for damages, but on the ability of courts to award them. Might not that provide a basis for a "constitutional defence", as distinct from an expanded common law defence?

In any event, the *Lange* judgment went on in other respects to state the effect of the implied freedom broadly. In particular, it rejected any suggestion that the freedom was to operate only at election time: "**[561]** Most of the matters necessary to enable 'the people' to make an informed choice will occur during the period between the holding of one, and the calling of the next, election. If the freedom to receive and disseminate information were confined to election periods, the electors would be deprived of the greater part of the information necessary to make an effective choice at the election". Besides, the judgment added, the implication did not arise solely from ss 7 and 24, but from other parts of the Constitution as well: in particular, both the referendum procedure prescribed by s 128, and the vesting of Commonwealth executive power in a parliamentary ministry by Ch II, gave rise to their own implications that the public "receipt and dissemination of information" must be unfettered in those contexts also. Against this background, the Court analysed the symbiotic relationship between Constitution and common law.

The Court: [564] The Constitution, the federal, State and territorial laws, and the common law in Australia together constitute the law of this country and form "one system of jurisprudence" [*McArthur v Williams* (1936) 55 CLR 324 at 347]. Covering cl 5 of the Constitution renders the Constitution "binding on the courts, judges, and people of every State and of every part of the Commonwealth, notwithstanding anything in the laws of any State". Within that single system of jurisprudence, the basic law of the Constitution provides the authority for the enactment of valid statute law and may have effect on the content of the common law.

Conversely, the Constitution itself is informed by the common law. This was explained extra-judicially by Sir Owen Dixon:

> "We do not of course treat the common law as a transcendental body of legal doctrine, but we do treat it as antecedent in operation to the constitutional instruments which first divided

Australia into separate colonies and then united her in a federal Commonwealth. We therefore regard Australian law as a unit. Its content comprises besides legislation the general common law which it is the duty of the courts to ascertain as best they may ... The anterior operation of the common law in Australia is not just a dogma of our legal system, an abstraction of our constitutional reasoning. It is a fact of legal history."

And in *Cheatle v The Queen* [(1993) 177 CLR 541 at 552], this Court said:

"It is well settled that the interpretation of a constitution such as ours is necessarily influenced by the fact that its provisions are framed in the language of the English common law, and are to be read in the light of the common law's history." ...

The issue raised by the Constitution in relation to an action for defamation is whether the immunity conferred by the common law, as it has traditionally been perceived, or, where there is statute law on the subject the immunity conferred by statute, conforms with the freedom required by the Constitution. In 1901, when the Constitution of the Commonwealth took effect and when the Judicial Committee was the ultimate Court in the judicial hierarchy, the English common law defined the scope of the torts of libel and slander. At that time, the balance that was struck by the common law between freedom of communication about government and political matters and the protection of personal reputation was thought to be consistent with the freedom that was essential and incidental to the holding of the elections and referenda for which the Constitution provided. Since 1901, the common law – now the common law of Australia – has had to be developed in response to changing conditions. The expansion of the franchise, the increase in literacy, the growth of modern political structures operating at both federal and State levels and the modern development in mass communications, especially the electronic media, now demand the striking of a different balance from that which was struck in 1901 ...

[566] Of necessity, the common law must conform with the Constitution. The development of the common law in Australia cannot run counter to constitutional imperatives. The common law and the requirements of the Constitution cannot be at odds. The common law of libel and slander could not be developed inconsistently with the Constitution, for the common law's protection of personal reputation must admit as an exception that qualified freedom to discuss government and politics which is required by the Constitution.

In any particular case, the question whether a publication of defamatory matter is protected by the Constitution or is within a common law exception to actionable defamation yields the same answer. But the answer to the common law question has a different significance from the answer to the constitutional law question. The answer to the common law question prima facie defines the existence and scope of the personal right of the person defamed against the person who published the defamatory matter; the answer to the constitutional law question defines the area of immunity which cannot be infringed by a law of the Commonwealth, a law of a State or a law of those Territories whose residents are entitled to exercise the federal franchise. That is because the requirement of freedom of communication operates as a restriction on legislative power. Statutory regimes cannot trespass upon the constitutionally required freedom.

However, a statute which diminishes the rights or remedies of persons defamed and correspondingly enlarges the freedom to discuss government and political matters is not contrary to the constitutional implication. The common law rights of persons defamed may be diminished by statute but they cannot be enlarged so as to restrict the freedom required by the Constitution. Statutes which purport to define the law of defamation are construed, if possible, conformably with the Constitution. But, if their provisions are intractably inconsistent with the Constitution, they must yield to the constitutional norm.

The common law may be developed to confer a head or heads of privilege in terms broader than those which conform to the constitutionally required freedom, but those terms cannot be any narrower. Laws made by Commonwealth or State Parliaments or the legislatures of self-governing territories which are otherwise within power may therefore extend a head of privilege, but they cannot derogate from the common law to produce a result which diminishes the extent of the immunity conferred by the Constitution.

These last three paragraphs contain the essence of the *Lange* solution. As between a constitutional limit on the law of defamation, and an expanded common law defence of qualified privilege, the

Court chose both. The available defence is a common law defence, but the Constitution imposes overriding requirements to which any such defence must conform. One objection to a common law solution had been that it might be vulnerable to restrictions or encumbrances imposed by State legislation. However, the overriding constitutional ceiling spelled out in *Lange* ensures that no such statutory intervention is possible. Both statute and common law may provide for a *wider* degree of protection of political discourse than the Constitution requires, but they cannot provide for less.

Earlier in the judgment, the Court had declined to distinguish in principle between a "proportionality" test and that of whether a law is "reasonably appropriate and adapted" to a legitimate object. Now the Court offered a formulation of precisely how, in assessing the effect of implied limitations on legislative power, such tests were to operate.

The Court: [567] When a law of a State or federal Parliament or a Territory legislature is alleged to infringe the requirement of freedom of communication imposed by ss 7, 24, 64 or 128 of the Constitution, two questions must be answered before the validity of the law can be determined. First, does the law effectively burden freedom of communication about government or political matters either in its terms, operation or effect? Second, if the law effectively burdens that freedom, is the law reasonably appropriate and adapted to serve a legitimate end the fulfilment of which is compatible with the maintenance of the constitutionally prescribed system of representative and responsible government and the procedure prescribed by s 128 for submitting a proposed amendment of the Constitution to the informed decision of the people (hereafter collectively "the system of government prescribed by the Constitution"). If the first question is **[568]** answered "yes" and the second is answered "no", the law is invalid. In *ACTV*, for example, a majority of this Court held that a law seriously impeding discussion during the course of a federal election was invalid because there were other less drastic means by which the objectives of the law could be achieved. And the common law rules, as they have traditionally been understood, must be examined by reference to the same considerations. If it is necessary, they must be developed to ensure that the protection given to personal reputation does not unnecessarily or unreasonably impair the freedom of communication about government and political matters which the Constitution requires.

In *Coleman v Power* (2004) 220 CLR 1 a majority of the High Court recast the second limb of this test to inquire whether the impugned law is "reasonably appropriate and adapted to serve a legitimate end *in a manner* which is compatible with" representative and responsible government (see Chapter 29, §2 and §5).

Within the constitutional framework thus established, the joint judgment finally turned to its restatement of the expanded common law defence of qualified privilege.

The Court: [568] The purpose of the law of defamation is to strike a balance between the right to reputation and freedom of speech. It is not to be supposed that the protection of reputation is a purpose that is incompatible with the requirement of freedom of communication imposed by the Constitution. The protection of the reputations of those who take part in the government and political life of this country from false and defamatory statements is conducive to the public good. The constitutionally prescribed system of government does not require – to the contrary, it would be adversely affected by – an unqualified freedom to publish defamatory matter damaging the reputations of individuals involved in government or politics. The question then is whether the common law of defamation, as it has traditionally been understood, and the statute law regulating the publication of defamatory matter are reasonably appropriate and adapted to the protection of reputation having regard to the **[569]** requirement of freedom of communication about government and political matters required by the Constitution ...

[571] Because the Constitution requires "the people" to be able to communicate with each other with respect to matters that could affect their choice in federal elections or constitutional referenda or that could throw light on the performance of Ministers of State and the conduct of the executive branch of government, the common law rules concerning privileged communications, as understood before the decision in *Theophanous*, had reached the point where they failed to meet that requirement. However, the common law of defamation can and ought to be developed to take into account the varied conditions to which McHugh J referred [in *Stephens*, 182 CLR at 264]. The common law rules of qualified privilege will then properly reflect the requirements of ss 7, 24, 64, 128 and related sections of the Constitution.

Accordingly, this Court should now declare that each member of the Australian community has an interest in disseminating and receiving information, opinions and arguments concerning government and political matters that affect the people of Australia. The duty to disseminate such information is simply the correlative of the interest in receiving it. The common convenience and welfare of Australian society are advanced by discussion – the giving and receiving of information – about government and political matters. The interest that each member of the Australian community has in such a discussion extends the categories of qualified privilege. Consequently, those categories now must be recognised as protecting a communication made to the public on a government or political matter. It may be that, in some respects, the common law defence as so extended goes beyond what is required for the common law of defamation to be compatible with the freedom of communication required by the Constitution. For example, discussion of matters concerning the United Nations or other countries may be protected by the extended defence of qualified privilege, even if those discussions cannot illuminate the choice for electors at federal elections or in amending the Constitution or cannot throw light on the administration of federal government.

Similarly, discussion of government or politics at State or Territory level and even at local government level is amenable to protection by the extended category of qualified privilege, whether or not it bears on matters at the federal level. Of course, the discussion of matters at State, Territory or local level might bear on the choice that the people have to make in federal elections or in voting to amend the Constitution, and on their evaluation of the performance of federal ministers and their departments. The existence of national political [572] parties operating at federal, State, Territory and local government levels, the financial dependence of State, Territory and local governments on federal funding and policies, and the increasing integration of social, economic and political matters in Australia make this conclusion inevitable. Thus, the extended category of common law qualified privilege ensures conformity with the requirements of the Constitution. The real question is as to the conditions upon which this extended category of common law qualified privilege should depend.

At common law, once an occasion of qualified privilege is found to exist, the privilege traditionally protects a communication made on that occasion unless the [defendant] is actuated by malice in making the communication. But, apart from a few exceptional cases, the common law categories of qualified privilege protect only occasions where defamatory matter is published to a limited number of recipients. If a publication is made to a large audience, a claim of qualified privilege at common law is rejected unless, exceptionally, the members of the audience all have an interest in knowing the truth. Publication beyond what was reasonably sufficient for the occasion of qualified privilege is unprotected. Because privileged occasions are ordinarily occasions of limited publication – more often than not occasions of publication to a single person – the common law has seen honesty of purpose in the publisher as the appropriate protection for individual reputation. As long as the publisher honestly and without malice uses the occasion for the purpose for which it is given, that person escapes liability even though the publication is false and defamatory. But a test devised for situations where usually only one person receives the publication is unlikely to be appropriate when the publication is to tens of thousands, or more, of readers, listeners or viewers.

No doubt it is arguable that, because qualified privilege applies only when the communication is for the common convenience and welfare of society, a person publishing to tens of thousands should be able to do so under the same conditions as those that apply to any person publishing on an occasion of qualified privilege. But the damage that can be done when there are thousands of recipients of a communication is obviously so much greater than when there are only a few recipients. Because the damage from the former class of publication is likely to be so much greater than from the latter class, a requirement of reasonableness as contained in s 22 of the *Defamation Act*, which goes beyond mere honesty, is properly to be seen as reasonably appropriate [573] and adapted to the protection of reputation and, thus, not inconsistent with the freedom of communication which the Constitution requires.

Reasonableness of conduct is the basic criterion in s 22 of the *Defamation Act* which gives a statutory defence of qualified privilege. It is a concept invoked in one of the defences of qualified protection under the Defamation Codes of Queensland and Tasmania. And it was the test of reasonableness that was invoked in the joint judgment in *Theophanous*. Given these considerations and given, also, that the requirement of honesty of purpose was developed in relation to more limited publications, reasonableness of conduct seems the appropriate criterion to apply when the occasion of the publication of defamatory matter is said to be an occasion of qualified privilege solely by reason of the relevance of the matter published to the discussion of government or political matters. But reasonableness of conduct is imported as an element only when the extended category of qualified privilege is invoked to protect a publication that would otherwise be held to have been made to too wide an audience. For example, reasonableness of conduct is not an element of that qualified privilege which protects a member of the public who makes a complaint to a Minister concerning the administration of his or her department. Reasonableness of conduct is an element for the judge to consider only when a publication concerning a government or political matter is made in circumstances that, under the English common law, would have failed to attract a defence of qualified privilege …

In *Theophanous*, the joint judgment also required the defendant to prove that it was unaware of the falsity of the matter published and that it did not publish the matter recklessly. That is a requirement that has little practical significance. The defendant must establish that its conduct in making the publication was reasonable in all the circumstances of the case. In all but exceptional cases, the proof of reasonableness will fail as a matter of fact unless the publisher establishes that it was unaware of the falsity of the matter and did not act recklessly in making the publication.

It may be that, if a statutory provision were to require the additional elements of want of knowledge of falsity and absence of recklessness, as required by *Theophanous*, it would not, on that account, infringe the freedom of communication which the Constitution requires. For present purposes, it is necessary only to state that their absence from s 22 of the *Defamation Act* cannot have the consequence that the provisions of that Act infringe the constitutional freedom. Moreover, these are not requirements of the common law, as it has traditionally been understood, and there is no reason why they should be engrafted on the expanded common law defence of qualified privilege.

[574] Having regard to the interest that the members of the Australian community have in receiving information on government and political matters that affect them, the reputations of those defamed by widespread publications will be adequately protected by requiring the publisher to prove reasonableness of conduct. The protection of those reputations will be further enhanced by the requirement that the defence will be defeated if the person defamed proves that the publication was actuated by common law malice to the extent that the elements of malice are not covered under the rubric of reasonableness. In the context of the extended defence of qualified privilege in its application to communications with respect to political matters, "actuated by malice" is to be understood as signifying a publication made not for the purpose of communicating government or political information or ideas, but for some improper purpose.

In *Theophanous*, the Court held that, once the publisher proved it was unaware of the falsity of the material, had not acted recklessly, and had acted reasonably, malice could not defeat the constitutional defence. But once the concept of actuating malice is understood in its application to government and political communications, in the sense indicated, we see no reason why a publisher who has used the occasion to give vent to its ill will or other improper motive should escape liability for the publication of false and defamatory statements. As we have explained, the existence of ill will or other improper motive will not itself defeat the privilege. The plaintiff must prove that the publication of the defamatory matter was *actuated* by that ill will or other improper motive. Furthermore, having regard to the subject matter of government and politics, the motive of causing political damage to the plaintiff or his or her party cannot be regarded as improper. Nor can the vigour of an attack or the pungency of a defamatory statement, without more, discharge the plaintiff's onus of proof of this issue.

Whether the making of a publication was reasonable must depend upon all the circumstances of the case. But, as a general rule, a defendant's conduct in publishing material giving rise to a defamatory imputation will not be reasonable unless the defendant had reasonable grounds for believing that the imputation was true, took proper steps, so far as they were reasonably open, to verify the accuracy of the material and did not believe the imputation to be untrue. Furthermore, the defendant's conduct will not be reasonable unless the defendant has sought a response from the person defamed and published the response made (if any) except in cases where the seeking or publication of a response was not practicable or it was unnecessary to give the plaintiff an opportunity to respond.

[575] Once the common law is developed in this manner, the New South Wales law of defamation cannot be said to place an undue burden on those communications that are necessary to give effect to the choice in federal elections given by ss 7 and 24 and the freedom of communication implied by those sections and ss 64 and 128 of the Constitution. It is true that the law of defamation in that State effectively places a burden on those communications although it does not prohibit them. Nevertheless, having regard to the necessity to protect reputation, the law of New South Wales goes no further than is reasonably appropriate and adapted to achieve the protection of reputation once it provides for the extended application of the law of qualified privilege. Moreover, even without the common law extension, s 22 of the *Defamation Act* ensures that the New South Wales law of defamation does not place an undue burden on communications falling within the protection of the Constitution. That is because s 22 protects matter published to any person where the recipient had an interest or apparent interest in having information on a subject, the matter was published in the course of giving information on that subject to the recipient, and the conduct of the publisher in publishing the matter was reasonable in the circumstances.

In practice, the effect of this version of the expanded common law defence may prove to be both broader and narrower than the various versions proposed in *Theophanous*. In one respect bearing directly on the *Lange* litigation, the expanded qualified privilege is likely to be wider than the *Theophanous* "constitutional defence", as the Court makes clear. In *Lange*, the ABC had pleaded a defence which sought to extend its freedom of political communication to material "of and concerning members of the parliament and government of New Zealand". It may well be doubtful whether the *constitutional* protection extends so far, especially if it is closely tied to the requirements of the Australian federal political system. But the joint judgment makes it clear that the new expanded common law defence is not so restricted. On the other hand, the new defence does not *simply* expand the traditional categories of qualified privilege. Instead, it appends an additional test of "reasonableness" that will still not apply to the older common law categories.

The *Theophanous* "constitutional defence" was liable to be defeated by any one of three factors: known falsehood, "reckless disregard" of truth or falsehood, and want of "reasonableness". The newly expanded common law defence takes up only the third of these. But the joint judgment in *Theophanous* had explained its conception of "reasonableness" in a way that largely overlapped with the absence of known falsehood or of "reckless disregard"; and the *Lange* joint judgment, for most practical purposes, envisages a similar overlap: "[573] In all but exceptional cases, the proof of reasonableness will fail as a matter of fact unless the publisher establishes that it was unaware of the falsity of the matter and did not act recklessly in making the publication". Thus the "reasonableness" requirement incorporates the absence of known falsehood or of "reckless disregard". The question is what additional requirements it may turn out to import. The main additional requirement explicitly added by the *Lange* joint judgment is one proposed by Brennan J in his *Stephens* dissent: that is, that the person defamed be given an opportunity to respond, and that any response be published promptly.

The *Theophanous* joint judgment had treated its test of "reasonableness" as obviating the need for any stipulation that the defence be defeated by "malice". The *Lange* defence, which proceeds by expanding the common law of qualified privilege, carries such a stipulation with it. But the relevance of "malice" is narrowly defined: for example, "[574] the motive of causing political damage to the plaintiff or his or her party" will not defeat the privilege.

Whether the degree of protection afforded by *Lange* is significantly less than that afforded by *Theophanous* may depend on whether the latter's disapprobation of "reckless disregard" of the truth is watered down to require "reasonable care" in ensuring the accuracy of what is published. A publication that *is* protected unless it shows "reckless disregard" has clearly much greater freedom than a publication which is *not* protected unless it shows "reasonable care". The mere use of the word "reasonable" may perhaps import the latter requirement; and the close association between the new test and that prescribed by s 22 of the *Defamation Act 1974* (NSW) may suggest that the degree of care demanded of journalists is still excessively onerous. But the current requirement of "reasonable care" as an element in the statutory defence provided by s 22 depends primarily on the Privy Council's interpretation of that section in *Austin v Mirror Newspapers Ltd* [1986] AC 299, where the Sydney *Daily Mirror* was held *not* to be protected by s 22 because a column written by the radio personality Ron Casey had failed to exercise "reasonable care". It seems possible that the facts of that case would equally have failed to meet the more stringent test of "reckless disregard". Besides, the High Court is no longer bound by Privy Council decisions, and if a restrictive reading of *Austin* were to be engrafted onto the defence expounded in *Lange* it would be arguable that the *Lange* defence, as thus modified by *Austin*, would still fail to meet the benchmark imposed by the *Lange* judgment's exposition of what the Constitution requires.

In any event, the references to the New South Wales legislation were unavoidable: what had to be determined was precisely whether the law of that State conformed to constitutional requirements. An addendum to the joint judgment made it clear that the law of defamation in other States might need further evaluation. The Court also made it clear that its rejection of the constitutional and common law defences thus far pleaded did not necessarily mean that the ABC had no defence available to it. It was stated that, although "**[575]** [t]he particulars which have been provided do not, in our view, bring the publication within the extended defence", "**[576]** it may be that further and better particulars can be provided" which would do so. "We express no view as to whether the publication can be brought within that defence, but the possibility should not be regarded as foreclosed by the orders that the Court now makes".

In later decisions on s 22 of the New South Wales *Defamation Act*, findings of a lack of "reasonableness" have depended primarily on a "reckless" failure to make adequate further inquiries. In *Rogers v Nationwide News Pty Ltd* (2003) 216 CLR 327 a journalist, who in 1996 reported (and wrongly embroidered) the facts of *Rogers v Whitaker* (1992) 175 CLR 479, had relied on a brief and incomplete summary of the case in a Federal Court judgment (*Whitaker v Federal Commissioner of Taxation* (1996) 140 ALR 257) instead of consulting the Commonwealth Law Reports, or indeed the back issues of her own newspaper. (Callinan J expressed the opinion that: "**[370]** A moderately diligent, well-motivated publisher has nothing to fear from the current legal regime".) In *Amalgamated Television Services Pty Ltd v Marsden* [2002] NSWCA 419, a finding of "reckless indifference" was contrasted with "**[1235]** [m]ere carelessness, impulsiveness or irrationality", none of which would have defeated the privilege. Another factor negating "reasonableness" was the failure to give the person defamed an adequate opportunity to respond. In this respect both the trial judge and the New South Wales Court of Appeal relied on the emphasis given to that factor in *Lange*; and the absence of "reasonableness" for the purposes of s 22 was treated as determining that issue for the purposes of a *Lange* defence as well. Indeed, although the Court of Appeal continued to deal separately with qualified privilege under s 22, under *Lange*, and under the common law principles enunciated in *Adam v Ward*, it also noted that the distinctions between different versions of qualified privilege may be breaking down. That observation was based in particular on High Court dicta in *Roberts v Bass* (2002) 212 CLR 1.

The facts of *Roberts v Bass* arose from the 1997 election for the South Australian Parliament. Throughout the election period, Geoffrey Roberts had campaigned against the re-election of Rodney Bass, the Liberal candidate for the seat of Florey. Roberts was not himself a candidate and did not represent a political party, though he claimed to speak on behalf of a "Clean Government Coalition". His grievances related to the privatisation of a local hospital. His campaign involved the distribution, in letter boxes throughout the electorate, of a simulated postcard supposedly mailed from Nauru and a "Free Travel" pamphlet (including a fictitious Frequent Flyer Statement) designed to suggest (falsely) that Bass made a practice of self-indulgent overseas travel. In addition, a how-to-vote card given out on polling day accused Bass of "numerous junkets *at your expense*" to overseas countries. After the election, Bass sued Roberts for defamation. He also sued Kenneth Case, who had handed out the how-to-vote card at one of the polling booths.

In the District Court of South Australia the trial judge (sitting without a jury) ordered Case (who had merely distributed the how-to-vote card) to pay damages of $5000, and Roberts to pay damages of $60,000, including $5000 as exemplary damages. He found that both Roberts and Case had been actuated by malice, and that this defeated their claim to qualified privilege at common law. He distinguished that "traditional" claim from what he called "the extended form of qualified privilege" arising from *Lange*, but held that any claim to the latter form of protection must also fail. The Supreme Court of South Australia dismissed an appeal, and increased the damages payable by Roberts to $100,000 (*Roberts v Bass* (2000) 78 SASR 302). From that decision Roberts and Case appealed to the High Court.

Callinan J (in dissent) would simply have dismissed the appeal. In his view the appellants' conduct was clearly unreasonable so that, even if a *Lange* defence had been available, it must have failed. The other six justices allowed Case's appeal, holding that, as against him, the finding of malice could not be sustained. As to Roberts, however, the Court divided 4:3. Gleeson CJ and Hayne J (to this extent joining Callinan J in dissent) would have dismissed his appeal, while Gaudron, McHugh, Gummow and Kirby JJ held that there must be a new trial. They insisted that, while lack of belief in the truth of a published statement may sometimes be *evidence* of malice, the common law concept of "malice" in this context cannot be *reduced* to mere absence of belief; "malice" is a separate concept, to be satisfied only by evidence that an occasion of qualified privilege has been used for an improper *purpose*.

Despite the distinction drawn by the trial judge between the "traditional" and "extended" versions of qualified privilege, the defendants had not expressly invoked the latter "extended" form of defence; and in the Supreme Court they had expressly disavowed it. Gleeson CJ assumed that this was because their conduct could not satisfy the *Lange* requirement of "reasonableness". Accordingly, the three dissenting judges held that the constitutional issues arising from *Lange* could not now be introduced in the High Court. They therefore decided the matter solely on the basis of the common law. The four majority judges also relied on the common law conceptions of "qualified privilege" and "malice", but insisted that, despite the earlier course of the litigation, it was necessary to take account of the modification of those conceptions by the implied constitutional freedom of political communication.

Central to the disposition of the case on a common law basis was the view that the common law concept of "qualified privilege" could extend to electioneering contexts. The English Court of Appeal in *Braddock v Bevins* [1948] 1 KB 580 had held that it could so extend. The actual result in the High Court in *Lang v Willis* (1934) 52 CLR 637 had also allowed a wide latitude to electioneering statements, though dicta in that case (especially those of Dixon J in dissent) had found it "[667] untenable [to suggest] that election speeches made to a large audience of unidentified persons are privileged because the speaker deals with matters in which the electors have an interest". For the four majority judges in *Roberts v Bass*, these dicta could not avail against the implied constitutional freedom.

Roberts v Bass
(2002) 212 CLR 1

Gaudron, McHugh and Gummow JJ: [29] It is a serious mistake to think that *Lange* exhaustively defined the constitutional freedom's impact on the law of defamation. *Lange* dealt with publications to the general public by the general media concerning "government and political matters". It was not concerned with statements made by electors or candidates or those working for a candidate, during an election, to electors in a State electorate, concerning the record and suitability of a candidate for election to a State Parliament. Such statements are at the heart of the freedom of communication protected by the Constitution. They are published to a comparatively small audience, most of whom have an immediate and direct interest in receiving information, arguments, facts and opinions concerning the candidates and their policies. In that context and constitutional framework, the application of traditional qualified privilege requires a holding that qualified privilege attaches to statements by electors, candidates and their helpers published to the electors of a State electorate on matters relevant to the record and suitability of candidates for the election. Nothing in *Lang v Willis* [(1934) 52 CLR 637] generally, and nothing in the judgment of Dixon J in that case in particular, requires a contrary finding. All that Dixon J said in *Lang* [52 CLR at 667] is that election speeches made to a large audience of unidentified persons are not privileged even though "the speaker deals with matters in which the electors have an interest". Those remarks were made nearly sixty years before this Court recognised the impact that the Constitution has on the law of defamation in respect of governmental and political matters. And the remarks were not directed to statements made by electors, candidates or their helpers to electors in a State **[30]** electorate concerning the record and suitability of a candidate for election …

[39] In a case like the present, persons handing out how-to-vote cards may honestly believe that they are informing the electorate of their **[40]** candidate's views and may not themselves have thought about whether much or any of the content of the how-to-vote card is true. Such persons will not lose the protection of the occasion because they had no positive belief in the truth of any defamatory matter in the how-to-vote card. It is proper for them to communicate their candidate's views to voters, and they do not lose their protection because, although acting for the purpose of the privileged occasion, they had no positive belief in the truth of the defamatory matter.

If the common law did hold that lack of belief or lack of honest belief in the truth of the defamatory matter was equivalent to knowledge of falsity or malice, it would have to be developed in respect of electoral communications to accord with the freedom of communication in respect of political matters that the Constitution protects …

The first question posed by *Lange* is answered affirmatively in cases like the present because the law of defamation … has a chilling effect on freedom of communication on political matters. The second question would have to be answered negatively if lack of belief or lack of honest belief in defamatory electoral material would destroy a defence of qualified privilege. The Australian electoral process works, and can only effectively work, with the help of the thousands of volunteers who at election time, and sometimes earlier, provide services to the candidates and political parties. Distributing election material in the form of posters, pamphlets and how-to-vote cards is one of the most important of those services … In many cases, the volunteers although honestly believing that they are providing information on electoral matters to the voters in the electorate, have no positive belief in the truth of what they are distributing. Often enough, they are persons, brought in from outside the electorate, to assist a candidate or political party and are unfamiliar with the particular issues that concern the electorate. In many cases, they will be handing out material they have not even read. To hold such persons liable in damages for untrue defamatory statements in that material because they had no positive belief in their truth would be to impose a burden **[41]** that is incompatible with the constitutional freedom of communication. If, contrary to our view, the common law made a positive belief in the truth of electoral statements a condition of the defence of qualified privilege, it would be inconsistent with the Constitution and would have to be developed to accord with the Constitution's requirements …

[42] Publishing material with the intention of injuring a candidate's political reputation and causing him or her to lose office is central to the electoral and democratic process. There is nothing improper about publishing *relevant* material with such a motive as long as the defendant is using the occasion to express his or her views about a candidate for election. That purpose is not foreign to the occasion that gives qualified privilege to such publications. The Constitution's protection of freedom of communication on political and governmental matters would be of little effect if an elector was liable in damages because he or she had the motive of injuring the political reputation of a candidate for election to the legislature. The imputations made against Bass concerned the performance of his duties as a parliamentarian. The publications were aimed at lowering his reputation as a politician and parliamentarian. They were not directed to matters **[43]** foreign to his political or parliamentary reputation. Roberts' and Case's motives in publishing the material … were not improper motives given the occasion of the publication …

The learned trial judge also held that the evidence established "that the defendants published the defamatory material without 'considering or caring whether it be true or not'". His Honour said … that, "when asked whether it had occurred to him that [Bass] might not have been a member of the frequent flyer program in preparing the [Free Travel Times] pamphlet, [Roberts'] answer was that 'it was not something I drew my mind to'". But to hold this answer to be recklessness in any relevant sense would be to equate it with carelessness or failure to check material. Roberts' evidence shows that he did not seek independent confirmation for his beliefs, that he jumped to conclusions from inadequate material and that his reasoning was often illogical. But these matters are insufficient to justify a finding that he used the occasion for an improper purpose …

[44] Roberts' reasoning process is open to serious criticism and led him to an unfair conclusion concerning the nature of Bass' trip to Nauru. But no matter how irrational his reasoning might seem to a judge, it is unfortunately typical of "reasoning" that is often found in political discussions. If Roberts' conduct on this matter was held to constitute malice sufficient to destroy the privilege of communicating electoral material to voters, the freedom of communication protected by the Constitution would be little more than a grand idea of no practical importance.

6. Further References

Aroney, N, *Freedom of Speech in the Constitution* (Centre for Independent Studies, 1998).

Blackshield, AR, "The Implied Freedom of Communication" in Lindell, G (ed), *Future Directions in Australian Constitutional Law* (Federation Press, 1994), 232.

Carney, G, "The Implied Freedom of Political Discussion – Its Impact on State Constitutions" (1995) 23 *Federal Law Review* 180.

Chesterman, M, *Freedom of Speech in Australian Law: A Delicate Plant* (Ashgate, 2000).

Chisholm, H, "The Stuff of Which Political Debate is Made: *Roberts v Bass*" (2003) 31 *Federal Law Review* 225.

Fischer, SF, "Rethinking *Sullivan*: New Approaches in Australia, New Zealand, and England" (2002) 34 *George Washington International Law Review* 101.

Glass, A, "*Australian Capital Television* and the Application of Constitutional Rights" (1995) 17 *Sydney Law Review* 29.

Kenyon, A, "Defamation and Critique: Political Speech and *New York Times v Sullivan* in Australia and England" (2001) 25 *Melbourne University Law Review* 522.

Kenyon, A, "*Lange* and *Reynolds* Qualified Privilege: Australian and English Defamation Law and Practice" (2004) 28 *Melbourne University Law Review* 406.

Kirk, J, "Constitutional Implications from Representative Democracy" (1995) 23 *Federal Law Review* 37.

Lee, HP, "The Implied Freedom of Political Communication" in Lee, HP, and Winterton, G (eds), *Australian Constitutional Landmarks* (Cambridge University Press, 2003), 383.

Lindell, G, "Expansion or Contraction? Some Reflections about the Recent Judicial Developments on Representative Democracy" (1998) 20 *Adelaide Law Review* 111.

Loveland, I, *Political Libels: A Comparative Study* (Hart Publishing, 2000).

Magnusson, R, "Freedom of Speech in Australian Defamation Law: Ridicule, Satire and Other Challenges" (2001) 9 *Torts Law Journal* 269.

Mason, K, "What is Wrong with Top-Down Legal Reasoning?" (2004) 78 *Australian Law Journal* 574.

McDonald, L, "The Denizens of Democracy: The High Court and the 'Free Speech' Cases" (1994) 5 *Public Law Review* 160.

Meagher, D, "What is 'Political Communication'? The Rationale of the Implied Freedom of Political Communication" (2004) 28 *Melbourne University Law Review* 438.

Sedgwick, D, "The Implied Freedom of Political Communication: An Empty Promise?" (2003) 7 *University of Western Sydney Law Review* 35.

Stone, A, "Freedom of Political Communication, the Constitution and the Common Law" (1998) 26 *Federal Law Review* 219.

Stone, A, "Rights, Personal Rights and Freedoms: The Nature of the Freedom of Political Communication" (2001) 25 *Melbourne University Law Review* 374.

Stone, A, and Williams, G, "Freedom of Speech and Defamation: Developments in the Common Law World" (2000) 26 *Monash University Law Review* 362.

Symposium, "Constitutional Rights for Australia?" (1994) 16 *Sydney Law Review* 145.

Weaver, RL, and Partlett, DF, "Defamation, the Media, and Free Speech: Australia's Experiment with Expanded Qualified Privilege" (2004) 36 *George Washington Law Review* 377.

Williams, G, "*Engineers* is Dead, Long Live the Engineers!" (1995) 17 *Sydney Law Review* 62.

Williams, G, "Lionel Murphy and Democracy and Rights" in Coper, M, and Williams, G (eds), *Justice Lionel Murphy – Influential or Merely Prescient?* (Federation Press, 1997), 50.

Williams, G, *Human Rights under the Australian Constitution* (Oxford University Press, 1999), Ch 7.

Zines, L, *The High Court and the Constitution* (Butterworths, 4th ed 1997), Ch 15.

Chapter 29

Freedom of Political Communication Applied and Extended

1. Expressive Conduct

Levy v Victoria (1997) 189 CLR 579 was decided three weeks later than *Lange v Australian Broadcasting Corporation* (1997) 189 CLR 520, although the two cases had been argued together. In *Levy v Victoria* the plaintiff failed; but the recognition that his claim fell within the protected area of political communication represented a significant expansion of the freedom.

At the opening of the 1994 Victorian duck shooting season Laurence Levy, an animal rights activist, sought to enter the shooting area and retrieve the bodies of dead and injured game birds, which he hoped to display for the television cameras as a protest against the continued allowance of duck shooting by the Victorian government. In March 1994, apparently in response to previous similar protests, the Victorian government promulgated the *Wildlife (Game) (Hunting Season) Regulations* (Vic), made under the *Wildlife Act 1975* (Vic) and the *Conservation, Forests and Lands Act 1987* (Vic).

Wildlife (Game) (Hunting Season) Regulations
(Statutory Rules No 27 of 1994 (Vic))

1 *Objectives*
The objectives of these Regulations are to –
  (*a*) ensure a greater degree of safety of persons in hunting areas during the open season for duck in 1994 …

5 *Entry to permitted hunting area prohibited to certain persons*
  (1) A person must not enter into or upon any permitted hunting area at any time between the hours of –
    (*a*) 5 pm on Friday, 18 March 1994 and 10.00 am on Saturday, 19 March 1994; or
    (*b*) 5 pm on Saturday, 19 March 1994 and 10.00 am on Sunday, 20 March 1994.
  Penalty: 10 penalty units
  (2) Sub-regulation (1) does not apply to a person who is the holder of a valid game licence authorised for the hunting or taking of game birds (including duck).

6 *Proximity of persons to hunters restricted in permitted hunting areas*
  (1) A person must not, at any time during the open season for duck in 1994, approach within a distance of less than 5 metres, any person who is the holder of a valid game licence authorised for

the hunting or taking of game birds (including duck) who is hunting or taking game birds, in any permitted hunting area.

Penalty: 10 penalty units

(2) Sub-regulation (1) does not apply to a person who is the holder of a valid game licence authorised for the hunting or taking of game birds (including duck) who is hunting or taking game birds from the same boat or from the same hide as another person.

When Levy sought to enter the duck-shooting area he was prevented from doing so under reg 5. Because he was thereby prevented from carrying out his intended protest, he sued in the High Court for a declaration that reg 5 was invalid by reason of its interference with his constitutionally protected freedom of political communication.

An earlier attempt to suggest that the *purpose* of the 1994 regulations was the stifling of political protest, rather than the protection of human safety, had been abandoned by the time the case reached the High Court. In the absence of any suggestion of that kind, the whole Court held that reg 5 was valid as a reasonable restriction in the interests of public safety as it was "proportionate" or "appropriate and adapted" to the objective stated in reg 1(a). At the same time, in accepting this as the applicable test of validity, the Court also accepted that the graphic televised images that Levy had hoped to present were within the constitutionally protected realm of political communication, as a form of what has been categorised by the Supreme Court of the United States as "expressive conduct" or "symbolic speech".

This extension of constitutional protection to graphic non-verbal demonstration is less problematic in Australia than in the United States. In Australia the relevant category is "*communication* about government or political matters"; while in the United States the governing category is the First Amendment's protection of freedom of "*speech*". It is easier to classify Levy's intended demonstration as "communicative action" than to classify it as "speech"; but either classification is perhaps a matter of degree. The Supreme Court of the United States, while recognising "expressive conduct" as a form of "speech", has tended to limit the degree of protection extended to such conduct – in part by distinguishing between its "speech" and "non-speech" elements, so that regulations directed primarily at the "non-speech" element may well be valid. For example, in *United States v O'Brien*, 391 US 367 (1968), the Supreme Court upheld the validity of a 1965 amendment making it a criminal offence knowingly to destroy a draft card (a "Selective Service Registration Certificate"), in a case where the card had been publicly burned as a protest against the Vietnam war. Though *assuming* that "[376] the alleged communicative element" attracted the First Amendment, the Court held that when an activity has "speech" and "nonspeech" elements, the need to regulate the "nonspeech" element may justify an incidental limitation on freedom of speech, provided that (1) the limitation is within power; (2) it [377] "furthers an important or substantial governmental interest"; (3) that interest "is unrelated to the suppression of free expression"; and (4) the incidental burden "is no greater than is essential to the furtherance of that interest".

In *Clark v Community for Creative Non-Violence*, 468 US 288 (1984), the respondent organisation planned to draw attention to the plight of the homeless by establishing "tent cities" in Washington DC – one in Lafayette Park (immediately opposite the White House) and one in "the Mall" (the corridor extending from the Capitol Building to the Lincoln Memorial, including the Washington Monument and a series of reflecting pools). The National Park Service granted permits for the demonstrations but refused to allow sleeping in the tents, citing regulations that prohibited camping in National Parks except in designated areas, and defined "camping" to include the use of land "for living accommodation purposes such as sleeping activities". The respondents argued that the proposal to sleep in the tents had been integral to the proposed demonstration, and that the refusal to allow it violated the First Amendment. By 7:2 the Supreme Court rejected the claim. Again the majority assumed, without deciding, that overnight sleeping in such a case "[293] is expressive conduct protected to some extent by the First Amendment". However, the regulation was upheld as a content-neutral regulation of the time, place and manner of expression. Justices Brennan and Marshall dissented, the latter stressing poignantly that while

"**[306]** [s]itting or standing in a library" would not normally be expressive conduct, "for Negroes to stand or sit in a 'whites only' library in Louisiana in 1965 was powerfully expressive; in that particular context, those acts became 'monuments of protest' against segregation" (see *Brown v Louisiana*, 383 US 131 at 139 (1966)).

At an "adult entertainment centre" in South Bend, Indiana, patrons inserting coins into a timing device could watch women dancing nude or semi-nude in a glass booth. At the nearby Kitty Kat Lounge, patrons could watch "go-go dancers" while drinking. In both establishments dancers were required to wear "pasties" and "G-strings" because of a statutory prohibition on nudity in public places. In *Barnes v Glen Theatre, Inc*, 501 US 560 (1991) the owners of the two establishments, joined by individual dancers, argued that nude dancing was "expressive conduct", and that the requirement of pasties and G-strings violated the First Amendment. By 5:4 the claim was rejected. The opinion of the Court conceded that there were precedents for treating nude dancing as "**[566]** expressive conduct within the outer perimeters of the First Amendment, though … only marginally so". However, it concluded that the wearing of pasties and G-strings "**[571]** does not deprive the dance of whatever erotic message it conveys; it simply makes the message slightly less graphic". In a separate opinion Justice Scalia insisted that no First Amendment issue arose at all. A later attempt to distinguish the ruling, and thereby give nude erotic dancing the full protection of the First Amendment, was overturned in *Erie v Pap's AM*, 529 US 277 (2000).

Under the implications to be drawn from the Australian Constitution, the dancing in *Barnes* and *Erie* would not be protected because it was not "political". (Contrast the sleeping in *Clark v Community for Creative Non-Violence*.) However, both dancing and public sleeping could readily be understood as "communication". In *Levy*, regardless of whether the intended protest against duck shooting was a form of "speech", most of the High Court judgments strongly affirmed that it was within the protected realm of political "communication".

Levy v Victoria
(1997) 189 CLR 579

Brennan CJ: [594] American decisions on the protection of "expressive activity" under the First Amendment must be viewed with caution in the context of our Constitution. The freedom of discussion implied in the Constitution of the Commonwealth, unlike the subject of protection under the First Amendment of the United States Constitution, does not require consideration of the connotation of "speech" or of the conduct which might be thought to constitute a form of "speech". The implication denies legislative or executive power to restrict the freedom of communication about the government or politics of the Commonwealth, whatever be the form of communication, unless the restriction is imposed to fulfil a legitimate purpose and the restriction is appropriate and adapted to the fulfilment of that purpose. In **[595]** principle, therefore, non-verbal conduct which is capable of communicating an idea about the government or politics of the Commonwealth and which is intended to do so may be immune from legislative or executive restriction so far as that immunity is needed to preserve the system of representative and responsible government that the Constitution prescribes.

Televised protests by non-verbal conduct are today a commonplace of political expression. A law which simply denied an opportunity to make such a protest about an issue relevant to the government or politics of the Commonwealth would be as offensive to the constitutionally implied freedom as a law which banned political speech-making on that issue. However, while the speaking of words is not inherently dangerous or productive of a tangible effect that might warrant prohibition or control in the public interest, non-verbal conduct may, according to its nature and effect, demand legislative or executive prohibition or control even though it conveys a political message. Bonfires may have to be banned to prevent the outbreak of bushfires, and the lighting of a bonfire does not escape such a ban by the hoisting of a political effigy as its centrepiece. A law which prohibits non-verbal conduct for a legitimate purpose other than the suppressing of its political message is unaffected by the implied freedom if the prohibition is appropriate and adapted to the fulfilment of that purpose.

McHugh J: [622] For the purpose of the Constitution, freedom of communication is not limited to verbal utterances. Signs, symbols, gestures and images **[623]** are perceived by all and used by many to communicate information, ideas and opinions. Indeed, in an appropriate context any form of expressive conduct is capable of communicating a political or government message to those who witness it. Thus, in *Brown v Louisiana* [383 US 131 (1966)], the United States Supreme Court held that a silent demonstration on the premises of a public library was constitutionally protected speech for the purpose of the First Amendment. Similarly, that Court has held that peaceful picketing to publicise a labour dispute was constitutionally protected speech [*Thornhill v Alabama*, 310 US 88 (1940)].

Moreover, the constitutional implication does more than protect rational argument and peaceful conduct that conveys political or government messages. It also protects false, unreasoned and emotional communications as well as true, reasoned and detached communications. To many people, appeals to emotions in political and government matters are deplorable or worse. That people should take this view is understandable, for history, ancient and modern, is full of examples of the use of appeals to the emotions to achieve evil ends. However, the use of such appeals to achieve political and government goals has been so widespread for so long in Western history that such appeals cannot be outside the protection of the constitutional implication ...

Furthermore, the constitutional implication ... is not confined to invalidating laws that prohibit or regulate communications. In appropriate situations, the implication will invalidate laws that effectively burden communications by denying the members of the Australian community the opportunity to communicate with each other on political and government matters relating to the Commonwealth. Thus, a law that prevents citizens from having access to the media may infringe the constitutional zone of freedom. The use of the print and electronic media to publicise political and government matters is so widespread in Australia and other Western countries that today it must be regarded as indispensable to freedom of communication. That is particularly true of television which is probably the most effective medium in the modern world for communicating with large masses of people.

In arguing that the constitutional implication will invalidate laws **[624]** that prevent access to the television media, Mr Castan QC, who appeared for the plaintiff, pointed out that:

"The impact of television depiction of the actual perpetration of cruelty, whether to humans or to other living creatures, has a dramatic impact that is totally different [from] saying, 'This is not a good idea'."

Not much experience of television is needed to accept the truth of this observation. No one could fail to understand the impact of the war in Vietnam on the civilian population after seeing the picture of a terror-stricken, naked child running away from her burning village. Such an image probably had more to do with influencing United States public opinion against the war in Vietnam than any editorial of *The New York Times* or *Washington Post*. It can send a more persuasive message to the public than any reasoned argument. Without the opportunity to use the medium of television, the citizen cannot make use of its unique communicative powers. Because that is so, the constitutional implication protecting freedom of communication also protects *the opportunity* to make use of the medium of television.

However, the freedom from laws that would burden constitutionally protected communications or the opportunity to make or send them is not absolute. The freedom is limited to what is necessary to the effective working of the Constitution's system of representative and responsible government. Consequently, a law that is reasonably appropriate and adapted to serving an end that is compatible with the maintenance of the constitutionally prescribed system of government will not infringe the constitutional implication.

Kirby J: [631] The plaintiff submitted that political communication in Australia today necessarily engages the mass media of communication. The political debates in Canada concerning prohibition of the slaughter of cub seals [were] given great impetus by the confrontational conduct of protesters and the presence of media pictures showing the act of clubbing and seal blood on the ice. Similarly, [it was submitted that] Australian (and specifically Victorian) political communication about duck shooting required the facility of observation and confrontation by protesters and the presence of the mass media bringing their statements and other actions to the attention of fellow citizens ...

[637] A threshold question arises as to whether, upon any view, conduct of the kind pleaded by the plaintiff could amount to constitutionally protected communication. Was it the kind of activity which this Court has held to be necessarily implicit in the text and structure of the Australian Constitution? Could conduct, as distinct from words, ever amount to the kind of "communication" which an implied restriction on law-making would protect?

The plaintiff relied upon the inhibition which the regulation placed upon his *words*, namely dialogue with opponents, supporters, the media and, through them, the members of Parliament and electors of Victoria. But beyond that he relied on the limitations which the regulation imposed on his *actions*. These were not only limitations upon his movement within the Commonwealth. They also extended to limitations upon protest, assembly, demonstration, agitation and the other activities which exclusion from the proclaimed area would totally prevent in the critical first days of the open season for duck shooting.

The conceptual foundation for the constitutional freedom of communication in Australia is different from that derived from the First Amendment to the United States Constitution, as it has been interpreted. Nevertheless, both sides and the interveners took this Court to United States authority. It was suggested by the plaintiff that this would establish that communication on political and governmental matters included non-verbal communication of the kind relied on by him. United States authority was also propounded to support the proposition that legislative derogations from such a constitutional freedom must be proportional to, or otherwise permissible for, the [638] purposes of the derogation taking into account the importance of upholding the freedom of political communication by limiting the power of a Parliament to make laws inconsistent with it.

A rudimentary knowledge of human behaviour teaches that people communicate ideas and opinions by means other than words spoken or written. Lifting a flag in battle, raising a hand against advancing tanks, wearing symbols of dissent, participating in a silent vigil, public prayer and meditation, turning away from a speaker, or even boycotting a big public event clearly constitutes political communication although not a single word is uttered. The constitutionally protected freedom of communication in Australia must therefore go beyond words.

Kirby J also derived assistance from American cases on a separate issue. In *Barnes v Glen Theatre, Inc*, Chief Justice Rehnquist noted that the Supreme Court's tolerance of reasonable restrictions on the "time, place and manner" of political protests had developed in the context of "[566] restrictions on expression taking place on public property which had been dedicated as a 'public forum'." In the *Levy* case the licences given to duck-shooters, and the regulatory exclusion of other persons, related entirely to Victorian Crown land. Accordingly, counsel for New South Wales submitted that the relevant American cases were those concerned with the use of public property or public facilities for political action. *Clark v Community for Creative Non-Violence* was one such case. Kirby J reviewed several others – including *Schenck v Pro Choice Network of Western New York*, 519 US 357 (1997), where the Supreme Court upheld the creation of "fixed buffer zones" outside abortion clinics to protect the clinics' staff and patients against harassment by anti-abortion protesters.

In those cases the Supreme Court has developed an elaborate classification of different kinds of "public property" to which different restrictive regimes might reasonably be applied. The protection of freedom of speech or demonstration is strongest in "quintessential public forums"; weaker in places made available by the State as places of expressive activity; and weaker again for other public property or government premises. Accepting the broad thrust of these distinctions, Kirby J considered it relevant that the area involved in the *Levy* case "[642] was not a traditional, or designated, forum for public communication. It was no 'Hyde Park'." In the end, however, what he primarily drew from these cases was a reaffirmation of the general point that "expressive conduct" may be a protected form of political communication.

Toohey and Gummow JJ also conceded "[613] that the constitutional freedom is not confined to verbal activity", but may extend to conduct "where that conduct is a means of communicating a message within the scope of the freedom"; and that, even though the television coverage sought by the plaintiff "would portray or stimulate appeals to emotion rather than to reason", "[t]he appeal to reason cannot be said to be, or ever to have been, an essential ingredient of political communication or discussion". By contrast, Gaudron J was inclined to see the decisive issue as one of interference with Levy's freedom of movement.

2. The Politics of Protest

The consensus manifested in *Lange* did not survive changes to the Court's composition. In *Australian Broadcasting Corporation v Lenah Game Meats Pty Ltd* (2001) 208 CLR 199, Callinan J (appointed in 1998) forcefully argued that *Lange* had been incorrectly decided. The case was one in which Lenah Game Meats, a company engaged in the processing and export of game meat, had obtained an interlocutory injunction in the Supreme Court of Tasmania to restrain the broadcasting of a film of its "brush tail possum processing facility". The film had been made by Animal Liberation Limited without the permission of the company, which argued that the injunction was properly granted to protect its common law right to privacy. The Australian Broadcasting Corporation disputed the existence of such a right, but argued that, if it did exist, it must be limited by the implied freedom of political communication.

Allowing the appeal against the grant of the interim injunction, a majority of the High Court held that the processing company's reliance on a tort of invasion of privacy was misplaced. The joint judgment of Gummow and Hayne JJ took care to insist that the High Court's decision in *Victoria Park Racing and Recreation Grounds Co Ltd v Taylor* (1937) 58 CLR 479 "**[249]** does not stand for any proposition respecting the existence or otherwise of a tort identified as unjustified invasion of privacy", but held that "**[258]** [w]hatever development may take place in that field will be to the benefit of natural, not artificial, persons". Gleeson CJ and Kirby J, while similarly leaving open the possibility of a developing common law protection of privacy, agreed that it could have no relevance in the present case. Accordingly, while it was recognised (in the language of Gleeson CJ) that "**[220]** because the common law of Australia conforms to the Constitution, [the implied freedom of political communication] has an important role in the formulation of common law principle", it was not necessary for most of the Court to pursue this line of argument.

Kirby J did deal with the constitutional argument, and held that the implied freedom applies not only to the common law, but also to principles of equity and to the exercise of judicial discretion – which must therefore be "**[285]** exercised in a way consistent with the relevant constitutional principle". He held that the content of the film was encompassed by the concept of "political communication", since "**[287]** concerns about animal welfare are clearly legitimate matters of public debate across the nation". The *power* to grant interlocutory injunctions did not breach the freedom, since it was not "**[282]** inconsistent with the representative democracy created by, or implied in, the Constitution". Nevertheless, he held that the *actual decision* to grant the injunction had miscarried: the Full Court had failed to give sufficient weight "**[288]** to the constitutional consideration favouring discussion in the appellant's television programme of animal welfare as a legitimate matter of governmental and political concern".

Callinan J dissented. In his view the appeal should have been dismissed, since there was "**[341]** no reason ... why the respondent should not have its injunction continued". He challenged the whole notion of the implied freedom.

Australian Broadcasting Corporation v Lenah Game Meats Pty Ltd
(2001) 208 CLR 199

Callinan J: [331] With the greatest of respect to the very experienced Court ... which unanimously put beyond doubt in *Lange* [(1997) 189 CLR 520] that there was an implied constitutional freedom of communication which would serve as a defence in some defamation cases, I would not myself have reached the same conclusion. In my opinion, modern conditions to which the Justices referred but did not identify in *Theophanous* [(1994) 182 CLR 104] did not require it. Additionally, the authors of the Constitution were well aware of the First Amendment to the Constitution of the

United States and most deliberately must have chosen not to incorporate such a provision in our Constitution ...

[332] The system of government enshrined by the Constitution ... was chosen by the Founders who were well acquainted with the law of privilege and qualified privilege. They saw no need for a constitutional provision to ensure freedom of political discourse. There was nothing novel in 1901 about democratically elected Parliaments. There are no features of the Australian Constitution requiring any special arrangements (implied or express) to ensure the accountability of Parliament or that of the State legislatures and executives. In short, responsible and representative government is no more under threat from any inhibitions upon freedom of political expression today than it was 100 years ago ...

The defamation law, both statutory and common, with respect to defences of qualified privilege had functioned very well throughout the ninety-six years that had elapsed since Federation. A defence of qualified privilege is a very difficult defence for plaintiffs to overcome ... Those who practised, particularly, in turn, for plaintiffs and publishers in defamation cases, were generally satisfied that that body of law was sensitive both to the need for free speech and to defamed plaintiffs ... [The decisions in *Australian Capital Television*], **[333]** *Theophanous* and *Lange* had the impact of the detonation of a hydrogen bomb upon practitioners practising at the defamation bar ...

In my respectful opinion, factors currently operating ... strongly argue against a significant addition to the armoury of defences, indeed armadillo-like defences [already] available to the media ... The fact is that publishers who act honestly and with ordinary diligence in the compilation and dissemination of matter of public interest have nothing to fear from the law of defamation as it existed before the discovery of the constitutional implication ... **[334]** [T]here are [reasons] which militate against the tilting any further of the balance in favour of publishers, including measures both curial and otherwise, unheard of in earlier times: the availability of the modern remedy provided by legislation for freedom of information; the expansion of remedies for the review of administrative action; the greater willingness of the courts to accord status to those who seek the intervention of the court in public affairs; recourse to ombudsmen under ombudsmen legislation throughout the country; the influence that can be exerted by media owners whose interests span international borders and all or most forms of communication; the work of boards and tribunals which regulate, inquire into, or supervise industrial and professional conduct; the advent and proliferation of "cheque book journalism" and the payment of "cash for comment"; the extensive use of commissions of inquiry armed with significant powers to inquire into and report on misconduct by government and officials; and the huge resources deployable by major media organisations enabling them to probe more deeply and to have more time and opportunity to avoid error than in the past. There has been, moreover, in recent times a reinvigoration of the committee system of the Parliament of the Commonwealth for the continuing scrutiny of Executive activity ... **[335]** Nor should s 75(iii) and (v) of the Constitution, which enable citizens and others to challenge and correct misbehaviour by Commonwealth bureaucracies and officers in various respects by prerogative writs, be left out of the equation. Furthermore, almost always the media have the advantage of resources, money and endurance over those who would seek vindication by proceeding against their members ...

[336] There are, in my opinion, very great difficulties involved in making constitutional implications. They are not readily susceptible to the tests that the law imposes with respect to the implication of contractual terms. Indeed, if those tests were to be applied so far as they could be, in constitutional discourse, then they could never satisfy the test of the hypothetical officious bystander. In asking of the Framers of the Constitution whether a term should be implied, the question is what the parties would have inserted had attention been drawn to a matter for which they had made no provision *at the time when they made their constitution*. What question would the bystander have asked: "What about free speech in a federal democracy? Have you, the draftsmen, in writing the Constitution, thought about that?" The draftsmen's response would have been: "Of course we have. This is not a matter with which the Constitution should be concerned. The law of qualified privilege, common or as articulated in the Colonies' enactments, deals with that." If an implication may be made long after the composition of the instrument into which it is to be implied, the question arises as to when, and at what intervals, the implication can be made or amended thereafter. How does this Court know when the time has arrived for the making of an implication? What proof is [337] required of the circumstances which make the implication, suddenly, to use the language of Mason CJ, "necessary" [177 CLR at 135]?

If the necessity is thought to arise because, for example, of an impression formed by judges about the powers and activities of unidentified bureaucracies, those who have an interest in contradicting the consequences of the formation of that impression should be given an opportunity to bring forward facts and other materials to demonstrate that it might be a flawed and incorrect impression. The fact that a debate of that kind would have the appearance of a parliamentary debate rather than one of a kind customarily conducted in judicial proceedings, is in itself an indication of the inadvisability of a court's drawing implications from a written constitution.

[338] [E]ven if implications may be inferred from the Constitution, the occasions for doing so could only be ones of the greatest necessity ... I do not for myself think that any such necessity dictated the implication which the Court found in *Lange*, or the other earlier cases to which I have [339] referred ... I would certainly at least resist any expansion of the doctrine for which *Lange* stands.

A controversial example in the Federal Court was *Brown v Classification Review Board* (*Rabelais Case*) (1998) 154 ALR 67. *Rabelais*, a student newspaper at La Trobe University, had published an article entitled "The Art of Shoplifting", which after "[69] a brief introductory critique on the deficiencies of capitalism" proceeded to give what was described as "a step by step guide to shoplifting". In response to a complaint by the Retail Trades Association of Victoria, the Commonwealth Office of Film and Literature Classification decided that *Rabelais* should be refused classification, thus effectively prohibiting its distribution. The decision relied on s 19(4) of the National Classification Code, which directed that classification be refused to a publication "[t]hat promotes, incites or instructs in matters of crime or violence". Pursuant to an exercise in co-operative federalism, Commonwealth decisions under the Code were effective in every State. The decision was confirmed (by majority) by the Classification Review Board, and by Merkel J under the *Administrative Decisions (Judicial Review) Act 1977* (Cth). The editors of *Rabelais* then appealed to the Full Federal Court, which dismissed the appeal.

The first issue was whether the refusal of classification effectively burdened political communication. Although most of the content of the relevant issue of *Rabelais* was rebarbatively "political", the discussion focused on whether the article on shoplifting could be so characterised. That is, instead of asking whether the refusal of classification to *Rabelais* could be characterised as burdening political communication, the Court focused on whether the particular communication that had triggered the refusal could be characterised as "political". Heerey and Sundberg JJ held that it could not be.

Brown v Classification Review Board (Rabelais Case)
(1998) 154 ALR 67

Heerey J: [87] In the present case, the article does not concern "political or government matters". The author is not advocating the repeal of the law of theft, either generally or in respect of theft from shops owned by large corporations. The article says nothing, expressly or by implication, about the conduct of holders of elected or appointed public office or the policies which should be followed by them. The article is not addressed to readers in their capacity as fellow-citizens and voters. The article does not even advocate breaking one law as a means of securing the repeal of another law perceived as bad, as with draft card burning in protest against conscription for Vietnam. (I do not express any view as to whether such conduct would or would not fall within the Constitutional freedom ...)

The appellants' counsel pointed out in their submissions that writers have from time to time advocated theft as an appropriate means of reallocation of resources (Oscar Wilde in *The Soul of Man under Socialism*), or of political dissent ("On Maoism: An Interview with Jean-Paul Sartre" in Telos, Summer 1973), or as a central tenet of Anarchist theory (Proudhon, "Qu'est-ce que la propriété?").

However, it should be noted that anarchist theory extended from non-violent writers and political leaders like Tolstoy, Thoreau and [Gandhi] to Proudhon ("property is theft"), Bakunin, who declared that "the passion for destruction is also a creative urge", and the anarcho-syndicalists whose creed was that unions should become militant organisations dedicated to the destruction of capitalism and the State.

All this may be in one sense politics, but the constitutional freedom of political communication assumes – indeed exists to support, foster and protect – **[88]** representative democracy and the rule of law. The advocacy of law breaking falls outside this protection and is antithetical to it.

It follows that in my opinion United States decisions like *Brandenburg v Ohio* 395 US 444 (1969) and the line of cases which follow it are not applicable to the implied freedom under the Australian Constitution. There is no constitutional protection for speech which is "mere advocacy" or abstract teaching of the necessity or propriety of criminal or violent conduct. The reason is simple. Such conduct is not part of the system of representative and responsible government or of the political and democratic process. In constitutional terms those who advocate, or engage in, such conduct are in the same position as they were before 1992.

Sundberg J: [98] [T]he article is not within the ambit of the freedom. That is so for two reasons. One is that it is not a communication concerning a political or government matter. Although its opening "redistribution" paragraph is "political" in one sense of the word, its true character is not political because it is overwhelmingly a manual about how successfully to steal. The other reason is that the article does not relate to the exercise by the people of a free and informed choice as electors.

Is Heerey J suggesting that advocacy of anarcho-syndicalism, as he defines it, would not be "political" in the relevant sense? If so, he might appear to imply that, instead of asking whether the impugned legislative or administrative action is compatible with the system of representative and responsible government, a court is entitled to ask whether the political viewpoints seeking expression are compatible with that system. His assumption that "the political process" is "**[87]** a synonym" for "the democratic process" might also give that impression.

The third member of the Court, French J, did not finally decide this issue, since he held that in any event the National Classification Code was compatible with the protected freedom.

French J: [80] There is much to be said for the conclusion that "The Art of Shoplifting" falls outside the scope of political discussion. But, inelegant, awkward and unconvincing as is its attempt to justify its practical message about shoplifting by reference to the evils of capitalism, it is arguable that in some aspects it would fall within a broad understanding of political discussion. That characterisation, however, will not invalidate the effective operation upon it of a law which is enacted for a legitimate end, is compatible with representative and responsible government and is reasonably appropriate and adapted to achieving that end ...

The law in question in this case is the National Classification Code and the supporting provisions of the Classification (Publications, Films and Computer Games) Act 1995 (Cth). It is the construction of that law paying due regard to the common law value of freedom of expression, Australia's international obligations under [the International Covenant for Civil and Political Rights] and the implied constitutional freedom that is the court's primary task. In my opinion properly construed ... the relevant provisions of the Classifications Code and the supporting provisions of the Act are enacted for a legitimate end, are compatible with representative and responsible government and are reasonably appropriate and adapted to achieving that end.

French J held that the Classification Code, when construed in conformity to the *Classification (Publications, Films and Computer Games) Act 1995* (Cth), was compatible with the constitutional freedom because of its "**[80]** positive recognition of freedom of expression", and because its specific criteria for refusing classification must be construed in a manner "informed by the principle that recognises the freedom". Heerey J indicated that, if necessary, he would agree that the Code "**[88]** is, in this respect, enacted for a legitimate end (the prevention of crime), is compatible with representative and responsible government and [is adapted] to achieving that end". Sundberg J also agreed, saying: "**[99]** It is open to the legislature to conclude that furnishing people with information about how to commit a crime in a manner which encourages them to do so is conduct which it is proper to proscribe". Ironically, a "Schedule" to the judgment of Heerey J reproduced the "shoplifting" article in full (154 ALR at 88-92), thus making it available to a wider readership than the original publication in *Rabelais*. No one has suggested that the *Australian Law Reports* should be refused classification.

A different kind of student activism was at issue in *Coleman v Power* (2004) 220 CLR 1. The appellant Patrick Coleman, a student of law and politics at James Cook University, was distributing a pamphlet in Townsville criticising the conduct of local police, particularly in previous incidents involving the arrest of protesters. The pamphlet bore the heading "GET TO KNOW YOUR LOCAL CORRUPT TYPE COPS". It included an allegation referring to Constable Brendan Power, and invited the police to "KISS MY ARSE YOU SLIMY LYING BASTARDS".

On being shown a copy of the pamphlet by another police officer, Constable Power approached Coleman and asked to be given a copy, whereupon Coleman cried out: "This is Constable Brendan Power, a corrupt police officer". Those words became the basis of a charge under s 7(1)(d) of the *Vagrants, Gaming and Other Offences Act 1931* (Qld), which imposes a penalty of $100 or six months' imprisonment on any person who "uses any threatening, abusive or insulting words to any person", and who does so "in any public place or so near to any public place that any person who might be therein, and whether any person is therein or not, could view or hear".

Coleman was convicted by a magistrate on this and other charges, including a charge, under s 7A(1)(c) of the Act, for distributing printed matter containing "threatening, abusive, or insulting words" likely to injure a person's reputation "or by which other persons are likely to be induced to shun, or avoid, or ridicule, or despise the person". The Queensland Court of Appeal in *Power v Coleman* [2002] 2 Qd R 620 quashed the conviction under s 7A(1)(c) on the ground that its application in such a case was inconsistent with the implied freedom of political communication. However, that Court (by 2:1) affirmed the conviction under s 7(1)(d).

The Queensland Court of Appeal held that the first limb of the *Lange* test was satisfied: that is, that the operation of s 7(1)(d) did "burden" the implied freedom of political communication. In the High Court, the respondents *conceded* that this holding had been correct. Thus the constitutional issue was confined to the second limb of *Lange*: that is, whether the burden thus imposed was "reasonably appropriate and adapted to serve a legitimate end ... compatible with ... representative and responsible government".

Coleman's appeal was allowed by a 4:3 majority (McHugh, Gummow, Kirby and Hayne JJ, with Gleeson CJ, Callinan and Heydon JJ dissenting). However, only McHugh J fully reached the constitutional issue. The other majority judges disposed of the case by interpreting s 7(1)(d) as applicable only when the words used "**[74]** are directed to hurting an identified person and are ... provocative, in the sense that either they are intended to provoke unlawful physical retaliation, or they are reasonably likely to" do so. On that reading, the use of insulting words to a police officer would not attract the provision, since "**[79]** [b]y their training and temperament police officers must be expected to resist the sting of insults directed to them".

The joint judgment of Gummow and Hayne JJ derived this interpretation primarily from "**[74]** the context provided by the section as a whole", in the light of judicial responses to similar provisions in other statutes. But they also relied on constitutional considerations to "reinforce" their conclusions. These considerations included decisions in the United States Supreme Court, such as *Cantwell v Connecticut*, 310 US 296 (1940) and *Chaplinsky v New Hampshire*, 315 US 568 (1942), which had recognised a category of "fighting words" as lying outside the First Amendment's protection of freedom of speech. By analogy, it was said that, if s 7(1)(d) were confined to "provocative" insults, it might similarly lie outside the area of traditional common law freedoms on which Parliament would be presumed to intend no encroachment. Another consideration was that, given this limited operation, s 7(1)(d) could be treated as satisfying the second limb of the test in *Lange* (as "**[78]** reasonably appropriate and adapted to serve the legitimate public end of keeping public places free from violence"), whereas, if the provision were read as extending to a wider category of "insults", it would necessarily be invalid. Its purpose would then be simply that of "**[79]** ensuring the civility of discourse"; and *Lange* itself, by concluding that the law of defamation needed modification, had demonstrated that, in the absence of further qualifications, a purpose of that kind "could not satisfy the second of the tests articulated in *Lange*".

Of the majority judges, only McHugh J did not accept a narrow reading of s 7(1)(d) as sufficient to dispose of the case. He agreed that its application could be confined to cases where the words complained of were shown to have "**[40]** a personal effect on the person or persons who heard them"; but he did not think it could otherwise be limited by construction. He therefore turned to what he called "**[46]** the real issue": that is, the constitutional issue. He began by reviewing the criticisms of *Lange* advanced by Adrienne Stone, "The Limits of Constitutional Text and Structure: Standards of Review and the Freedom of Political Communication" (1999) 23 *Melbourne University Law Review* 688. He summarised her contentions as being that tests like "proportionality" or "reasonably appropriate and adapted" "**[46]** involve an 'ad hoc balancing' process without criteria or rules for measuring the value of the means (the burden of the provision) against the value of the end (the legitimate purpose)", and that such tests "**[47]** increase the likelihood of a value-laden process being disguised in value-neutral language". He also noted similar criticisms by Elisa Arcioni, "Politics, Police and Proportionality – An Opportunity to Explore the *Lange* Test: *Coleman v Power*" (2003) 25 *Sydney Law Review* 379.

Coleman v Power
(2004) 220 CLR 1

McHugh J: [48] The above criticisms overlook two matters concerning the "reasonably appropriate and adapted" test formulated in *Lange* [(1996) 189 CLR 520]. Those matters show that freedom of communication under the Commonwealth Constitution is different from freedom of speech provisions in other Constitutions and that ideas relating to or arising out of other Constitutions have little relevance to the freedom of communication under the Commonwealth Constitution. Those matters also show that no question of ad hoc balancing is involved in the two-pronged test formulated in *Lange* and that the text and structure of the Constitution enable the Court to determine whether the freedom has been infringed without resort to political or other theories external to the Constitution.

First, freedom of political communication under the Constitution arises only by necessary implication from the system of representative and responsible government set up by the Constitution. It is not the product of an express grant. It arises because the system of representative and responsible government cannot operate without the people and their representatives communicating with each other about government and political matters … If the system is to operate effectively …, of necessity it must be free from laws whose burdens interfere or have a tendency to interfere with its effectiveness. Thus, it is a necessary implication of the system that no legislature or government within the **[49]** federation can act in a way that interferes with the effective operation of that system. But since the implication arises by necessity, it has effect only to the extent that it is necessary to effectively maintain the system of representative and responsible government that gives rise to it. "It is", said the Court in *Lange* [189 CLR at 561], "limited to what is necessary for the effective operation of that system of representative and responsible government provided for by the Constitution."

Second, the legislative powers conferred on the Commonwealth by ss 51 and 52 of the Constitution are conferred "subject to this Constitution". So is the continuance of the Constitution of each State under s 106. And the powers of a State continued under s 107 do not extend to those "withdrawn from the Parliament of the State". Those withdrawn from the State include not only those powers expressly withdrawn from the States such as those referred to in ss 51 and 90 but those powers which would entrench on the zone of immunity conferred by s 92 and the implied freedom of communication on political and governmental matters. Consequently, the powers of the Commonwealth, the States and Territories must be read subject to the Constitution's implication of freedom of communication on matters of government and politics. The constitutional immunity is the leading provision; the sections conferring powers on the federal, State and Territory legislatures are subordinate provisions that must give way to the constitutional immunity. To the extent that the exercise of legislative or executive powers, conferred or saved by the Constitution, interferes with the effective operation of the freedom, the exercise of those powers is invalid.

In determining whether a law is invalid because it is inconsistent with freedom of political communication, it is not a question of giving special weight in particular circumstances to that freedom. Nor is it a question of balancing a legislative or executive end or purpose against that freedom. Freedom of communication always trumps federal, State and Territorial powers when they conflict with the freedom. The question is not one of weight or balance but whether the federal, State or Territorial [law] is so framed that it impairs or tends to impair the effective operation of the constitutional system of representative and responsible government by impermissibly burdening communications on political or governmental matters. In all but exceptional cases, a law will not burden such communications unless, by its operation or practical effect, it directly and not remotely restricts or limits the content of those communications or the time, place, manner or conditions of their occurrence. And a law will not impermissibly burden those communications unless its object and the **[50]** manner of achieving it is incompatible with the maintenance of the system of representative and responsible government established by the Constitution.

In the two-limb test formulated in *Lange*, the adjectival phrase "compatible with the maintenance of the constitutionally prescribed system of representative and responsible government" does not merely qualify the expression "legitimate end". It qualifies the compound conception of the fulfilment of such an end, and the emphasis of the qualification is on the term "fulfilment" rather than "end". That is to say, *it is the manner of achieving* the end as much as the end itself that must be compatible with the maintenance of the constitutionally prescribed system of representative and responsible government. Of course, the end itself may be incompatible with the system of representative and responsible government. It will be incompatible, for example, if it is designed to undermine that system.

No doubt the Court would have made the meaning of the second limb in *Lange* clearer if it had used the phrase "in a manner" instead of the phrase "the fulfilment of" in that limb. The second limb would then have read "is the law reasonably appropriate and adapted to serve a legitimate end [in a manner] which is compatible with the maintenance of the constitutionally prescribed system of representative and responsible government?". However, it is clear that the Court did intend the second limb to be read in a way that requires that both the end and the manner of its achievement be compatible with the system of representative and responsible government.

He maintained that this was made clear by the reference in *Lange* to *Australian Capital Television Pty Ltd v Commonwealth* (1992) 177 CLR 106, where the object of the legislative controls on political advertising was one "**[51]** that enhanced representative government". Nevertheless, the legislation failed because of the incompatibility of the means adopted with the communicative needs of the system.

McHugh J: [51] The true test was clearly expressed by Kirby J in his judgment in *Levy v Victoria* [(1997) 189 CLR 579 at 646]. After discussing a number of tests that have been used to determine whether a law is consistent with the freedom, his Honour said:

> "A universally accepted criterion is elusive. In Australia, without the express conferral of rights which individuals may enforce, it is necessary to come back to the rather more restricted question. This is: does the law which is impugned have the effect of preventing or controlling communication upon political and governmental matters *in a manner which is inconsistent* with the system of representative government for which the Constitution provides?" (emphasis added)

In my view, this formulation accurately states the second limb of the *Lange* test …

When, then, is a law not reasonably appropriate and adapted to achieving an end in a manner that is compatible with the system of representative government enshrined in the Constitution? In my opinion, it will not be reasonably appropriate and adapted to achieving an end in such a manner whenever the burden is such that communication on political or governmental matters is no longer "free". Freedom of communication under the Constitution does not mean free of all restrictions.

The freedom is not absolute or equivalent to licence. The zone of freedom conferred by the constitutional immunity is not, as Higgins J said, in discussing s 52 of the Constitution [*Commonwealth v New South Wales* (*Royal Metals Case*) (1923) 33 CLR 1 at 59], an "Alsatia for Jack Sheppards", where law does not **[52]** run. Communications on political and governmental matters are part of the system of representative and responsible government, and they may be regulated in ways that enhance or protect the communication of those matters. Regulations that have that effect do not detract from the freedom. On the contrary, they enhance it.

Hence, a law that imposes a burden on the communication of political and governmental matter may yet leave the communication free in the relevant sense. Thus, laws which promote or protect the communications or which protect those who participate in the prescribed system, for example, will often impose burdens on communication yet leave the communications free. On the other hand, laws that burden such a communication by seeking to achieve a social objective unrelated to the system of representative and responsible government will be invalid, *pro tanto*, unless the objective of the law can be restrictively interpreted in a way that is compatible with the constitutional freedom. Thus, a law that sought to ban all political communications in the interest of national security would be invalid unless it could be demonstrated that at the time such a prohibition was the only way that the system of representative government could be protected. In such a case, the issue would not be whether the needs of national security require the prohibition of communication on political and governmental matters. It would be whether, at that time, the system of representative government is so threatened by an external or internal threat that prohibiting all communication on political and governmental matters is a reasonably appropriate and adapted means of maintaining the system. A total prohibition would not be reasonable unless there was no other way in which the system of representative government could be protected. Ordinarily, the complete prohibition on, or serious interference with, political communication would itself point to the inconsistency of the objective of the law with the system of representative government.

It follows then that not all laws burdening communications on political and governmental matters are impermissible laws. They will be permissible as long as they do no more than promote or protect such communications and those who participate in representative and responsible government from practices and activities which are incompatible with that system of government. Thus, although defamation law burdens communications on political and government matters, the law of defamation, as developed in *Lange*, is now a reasonably appropriate and adapted means of protecting the reputation of those participating in political and governmental matters.

As the reasoning in *Lange* shows, the reasonably appropriate and adapted test gives legislatures within the federation a margin of choice **[53]** as to how a legitimate end may be achieved at all events in cases where there is not a total ban on such communications. The constitutional test does not call for nice judgments as to whether one course is slightly preferable to another. But the Constitution's tolerance of the legislative judgment ends once it is apparent that the selected course unreasonably burdens the communication given the availability of other alternatives. The communication will not remain free in the relevant sense if the burden is unreasonably greater than is achievable by other means. Whether the burden leaves the communication free is, of course, a matter of judgment. But there is nothing novel about courts making judgments when they are asked *to apply* a principle or rule of law. Much of the daily work of courts requires them to make judgments as to whether a particular set of facts or circumstances is or is not within a rule or principle of law.

Applying these principles to s 7(1)(d) of the Queensland legislation, McHugh J concluded:

McHugh J: [53] In this case, the Solicitor-General of Queensland proffered two purposes to justify the enactment of s 7(1)(d) in so far as it burdened the communication of political and governmental matters. The first was that the object of the paragraph was to avoid breaches of the peace. The second was that the paragraph protected free political communication by removing threats, abuses and insults from the arena of public discussion, so that persons would not be intimidated into silence.

Breach of the peace

Regulating political statements for the purpose of preventing breaches of the peace by those provoked by the statements is an end that is compatible with the system of representative government established by the Constitution. However, in the case of insulting words, great care has to be taken in designing the means of achieving that end if infringement of the constitutional freedom is to be avoided. In so far as insulting words are used in the course of political discussion, an unqualified prohibition on their use cannot be justified as compatible with the constitutional freedom. An unqualified prohibition goes beyond anything that could be regarded as reasonably appropriate and adapted for preventing breaches of the peace in a manner compatible with the prescribed system. Without seeking to state exhaustively the qualifications needed to prevent an infringement of the freedom of communication, the law would have to make proof of a breach of the peace and the intention to commit the breach elements of the offence. It may well be the case that, in the context of political communications, further qualifications would be required before a law making it an offence to utter insulting words would be **[54]** valid. In the present case, it is enough to say that s 7(1)(d) infringed the constitutional freedom by simply making it an offence to utter insulting words in or near a public place whether or not a person hears those words even when they were used in the discussion of political and governmental matters …

Intimidating participants in the discussion

Regulating political statements for the purpose of preventing the intimidation of participants in debates on political and governmental matters is an end that is compatible with the system of representative government laid down by the Constitution. However, as in the case of preventing breaches of the peace, great care has to be taken in designing the means of achieving that end if infringement of the constitutional freedom is to be avoided.

The use of insulting words is a common enough technique in political discussion and debates. No doubt speakers and writers sometimes use them as weapons of intimidation. And whether insulting words are or are not used for the purpose of intimidation, fear of insult may have a chilling effect on political debate. However …, insults are a legitimate part of the political discussion protected by the Constitution. An unqualified prohibition on their use cannot be justified as compatible with the constitutional freedom. Such a prohibition goes beyond anything that could be regarded as reasonably appropriate and adapted to maintaining the system of representative government.

It followed for McHugh J not only that the conviction under s 7(1)(d) must be quashed, but that the Court should also quash the appellant's convictions for obstructing and assaulting the police in the performance of their duty, since it is no part of a police officer's duty to enforce a non-existent law. The arrest was unlawful, and the appellant was lawfully entitled to resist it. This conclusion was not to be averted even by s 351(1) of the *Police Powers and Responsibilities Act 1997* (Qld), which provides that it is lawful for a police officer to arrest a person whom the police officer "reasonably suspects" of committing an offence. As to this, McHugh J relied on *Hazelton v Potter* (1907) 5 CLR 445, where Griffith CJ held that in order for such a reasonable suspicion to arise, there must at least "**[460]** be some Statute in force under which the act complained of could under some circumstances have been lawful".

Although the approach taken in their joint judgment did not require them to discuss the constitutional issue in detail, Gummow and Hayne JJ expressly agreed that the second limb of the *Lange* test should be reformulated in the manner proposed by McHugh J: that is, that it should ask whether the impugned law is "reasonably appropriate and adapted to serve a legitimate end *in a manner* which is compatible with" representative and responsible government. Further, they agreed with him that the test should not be watered down as the Commonwealth and New South Wales had suggested, by requiring only that the law be "reasonably capable of being seen as appropriate and adapted". On this point Gleeson CJ also agreed, while Heydon J, in a footnote to his judgment, left the issue open. Kirby J expressly agreed on both points, but protested strongly against the continued use of the expression "appropriate and adapted" (see §5 below).

Gleeson CJ, Callinan and Heydon JJ dissented. They rejected the attempt to limit the concept of "insulting words" to those intended to provoke physical retaliation or likely to do so, finding no practical difference between this and a requirement that the words be intended or likely to provoke a "breach of the peace". They pointed out that this latter requirement, though included in the older legislation which s 7(1)(d) had replaced, had deliberately been omitted when s 7(1)(d) was enacted in 1931. Thus the narrower construction now proposed effectively involved the reversal of a deliberate legislative choice. Gleeson CJ conceded that some limit must be imposed on the operation of the provision, perhaps by reference to degree of departure from "**[26]** contemporary standards of behaviour"; but in any event he agreed with the other dissenters that the provision was constitutionally valid.

In part, these dissenting views depended on willingness to accept the wider prohibition of "insulting" words as reflecting a legitimate legislative policy. For example, Gleeson CJ said:

> **Gleeson CJ: [24]** It is open to Parliament to form the view that threatening, abusive or insulting speech and behaviour may in some circumstances constitute a serious interference with public order, even where there is no intention, and no realistic possibility, that the person threatened, abused or insulted, or some third person, might respond in such a manner that a breach of the peace will occur. A group of thugs who intimidate or humiliate someone in a public place may possess such an obvious capacity to overpower their victim, or any third person who comes to the aid of the victim, that a forceful response to their conduct is neither intended nor likely. Yet the conduct may seriously disturb public order, and affront community standards of tolerable behaviour. It requires little imagination to think of situations in which, by reason of the characteristics of those who engage in threatening, abusive or insulting behaviour, or the characteristics of those towards whom their conduct is aimed, or the circumstances in which the conduct occurs, there is no possibility of forceful retaliation. A mother who takes her children to play in a park might encounter threats, abuse or insults from some rowdy group. She may be quite unlikely to respond, physically or at all. She may be more likely simply to leave the park. There may be any number of reasons why people who are threatened, abused or insulted do not respond physically. It may be (as with police officers) that they themselves are responsible for keeping the peace. It may be that they are self-disciplined. It may be simply that they are afraid.

Turning to the constitutional issue, he said:

> **Gleeson CJ: [30]** It was accepted by the Attorney-General of Queensland that s 7(1)(d) is capable of having a practical operation that, in some circumstances, may burden communication about governmental or political matters … That is true in the sense that threatening, abusive, or insulting words might be used in the course of communicating about any subject, including governmental or political matters. The same could be said about all, or most, of the other forms of conduct referred to in s 7. However, the object of the law is not the regulation of discussion of governmental or political matters; its effect on such discussion is incidental, and its practical operation in most cases will have nothing to do with such matters. The debate concentrated on the question whether the law, in its application to this case, is reasonably appropriate and adapted to achieving its object.
>
> The facts of the case illustrate the vagueness of concepts such as "political debate", and words spoken "in the course of communication about governmental or political matters". The appellant was carrying on what the magistrate described as a personal campaign against some individual police officers, including the first respondent. Let it be accepted that his conduct was, in the broadest sense, "political". It was not party political, and it had nothing to do with any laws, or government policy. Because the constitutional freedom identified in *Lange* does not extend to speech generally, but is limited to speech of a certain kind, many cases will arise, of which the present is an example, where there may be a degree of artificiality involved in characterising conduct for the purpose of deciding whether a law, in its application to such conduct, imposes an impermissible burden upon **[31]** the protected kind of communication. The conduct prohibited by the relevant law in its application to the present case involved what the magistrate was entitled to regard as a serious disturbance of public order with personal acrimony and physical confrontation of a kind that could well have caused alarm and distress to people in a public place … [A]lmost any conduct of the kind prohibited by s 7, including indecency, obscenity, profanity, threats, abuse, insults, and offensiveness, is capable of occurring in a "political" context … Reconciling freedom of political expression with the reasonable requirements of public order becomes increasingly difficult when one is operating at the margins of the term "political".

Gleeson CJ noted that, in *Levy v Victoria* (1997) 189 CLR 579, Brennan CJ had posed the question "**[598]** whether the means adopted *could reasonably be considered* to be appropriate and adapted to the fulfilment of the purpose", while Gaudron J had asserted that a law that restricts political communication only incidentally "**[619]** is valid if it *is* reasonably appropriate and adapted to that other purpose" (emphases added). Gleeson CJ expressed his preference for the latter, more rigorous criterion, but emphasised that both versions stopped short of requiring that the chosen means be "necessary" for achievement of the legislative purpose.

Gleeson CJ: [31] [T]he standard of judicial review proposed by Gaudron J, with which I respectfully agree, is rather more strict than that proposed by Brennan CJ, but it involves the same proposition, that is to say, that the Court will not strike down a law restricting conduct which may incidentally burden freedom of political speech simply because it can be shown that some more limited restriction "could suffice to achieve a legitimate purpose". This is consistent with the respective roles of the legislature and the judiciary in a representative democracy.

[32] Legislation creating public order offences provides a good example of the reason for this difference in functions. The object of such legislation is generally the same: the preservation of order in public places in the interests of the amenity and security of citizens, and so that they may exercise, without undue disturbance, the rights and freedoms involved in the use and enjoyment of such places. The right of one person to ventilate personal grievances may collide with the right of others to a peaceful enjoyment of public space. Earlier, I gave an example of a mother who takes her children to play in a public park. Suppose that she and her children are exposed to threats, abuse and insults. Suppose, further, that the mother is an immigrant, that the basis of such threats, abuse and insults includes, either centrally or at the margin, an objection to the Federal Government's immigration policy, and that the language used is an expression, albeit an ugly expression, of an opinion on that matter. Why should the family's right to the quiet enjoyment of a public place necessarily be regarded as subordinate to the abusers' right to free expression of what might generously be described as a political opinion? The answer necessarily involves striking a balance between competing interests, both of which may properly be described as rights or freedoms. As the Solicitor-General of Queensland pointed out in the course of argument, it is often the case that one person's freedom ends where another person's right begins. The forms of conduct covered by s 7 all constitute an interference with the right of citizens to the use and enjoyment of public places. As the survey of legislation made earlier in these reasons shows, the balance struck by the Queensland Parliament is not unusual, and I am unable to conclude that the legislation, in its application to this case, is not suitable to the end of maintaining public order in a manner consistent with an appropriate balance of all the various rights, freedoms, and interests, which require consideration.

In thus emphasising that the *legislative* function in this area requires a "balance of interests", Gleeson CJ was presumably implying (in agreement with McHugh J) that the *judicial* function in such cases does not require such a balance.

Gleeson CJ emphasised that the present appeal did not involve a law directly concerned to restrict political communications, and that all parties to the appeal had assumed both that *Lange* was authoritative, and that the relevant test was "reasonably appropriate and adapted" rather than "proportionality". These comments were necessary because Kirby J had taken the opportunity to advocate a criterion of "proportionality" (rather than "appropriate and adapted") and because Callinan J had hinted once again at his disinclination to follow *Lange*.

Callinan J quoted at length from the observations of Barwick CJ in *Queensland v Commonwealth* (1977) 139 CLR 585 and of Deane J in *Stevens v Head* (1993) 176 CLR 433 to the effect that, since judges are ultimately bound to uphold the Constitution, a judge who holds a firm conviction that an earlier judicial interpretation of the Constitution is wrong should adhere to that conviction notwithstanding the normal operation of the doctrine of precedent (see Chapter 13, §7). Moreover, he emphasised that this might be so even though no party had argued that the relevant precedent should not be followed. However, he concluded that since s 7(1)(d) "**[114]** offends no principle for which *Lange* may stand", it was "unnecessary for me to decide whether I should follow [that] path".

For his part, Heydon J also held that s 7(1)(d) was valid:

Heydon J: [121] Insulting statements give rise to a risk of acrimony leading to breaches of the peace, disorder and violence, and the first legitimate end of s 7(1)(d) is to diminish that risk. A second legitimate end is to forestall the wounding effect on the person publicly insulted. A third legitimate end is to prevent other persons who hear the insults from feeling intimidated or otherwise upset: they have an interest in public peace and an interest in feeling secure, and one specific consequence of those interests being invaded is that they may withdraw from public debate or desist from contributing to it. Insulting words are a form of uncivilised violence and intimidation. It is true that the violence is verbal, not physical, but it is violence which, in its outrage to self-respect, desire for security and like human feelings, may be as damaging and unpredictable in its consequences as **[122]** other forms of violence. And while the harm that insulting words cause may not be intended, what matters in all instances is the possible effect – the victim of the insult driven to a breach of the peace, the victim of the insult wounded in feelings, other hearers of the insult upset.

The goals of s 7(1)(d) are directed to "the preservation of an ordered and democratic society" [*Australian Capital Television Pty Ltd v Commonwealth* (1992) 177 CLR 106 at 169] and "the protection or vindication of the legitimate claims of individuals to live peacefully and with dignity within such a society" [*Cunliffe v Commonwealth* (1994) 182 CLR 272 at 339]. Insulting words are inconsistent with that society and those claims because they are inconsistent with civilised standards. A legislative attempt to increase the standards of civilisation to which citizens must conform in public is legitimate. In promoting civilised standards, s 7(1)(d) not only improves the quality of communication on government and political matters by those who might otherwise descend to insults, but it also increases the chance that those who might otherwise have been insulted, and those who might otherwise have heard the insults, will respond to the communications they have heard in a like manner and thereby enhance the quantity and quality of debate. It is correct that the constitutional implication protects not only true, rational and detached communications, but also false, unreasoned and emotional ones. But there is no reason to assume that it automatically protects insulting words by characterising the goal of proscribing them as an illegitimate one.

Are the legitimate ends compatible with the maintenance of constitutional government? The legitimate ends described are "compatible with the maintenance" of the system of government prescribed by the Commonwealth Constitution. Indeed, those ends would tend to enhance that system to the extent that they foster conduct in Queensland in relation to political communication, both during federal election campaigns and at all other times, which is free of insulting behaviour. If the inquiry is shifted from the ends of s 7(1)(d) considered by themselves to the extent of their practical success, the system of government prescribed by the Constitution has worked extremely effectively in Queensland since 1931, notwithstanding the existence of s 7(1)(d), and it has worked extremely effectively in other places from earlier times, notwithstanding the existence of provisions like s 7(1)(d).

Is s 7(1)(d) reasonably appropriate and adapted to serve its legitimate ends? Section 7(1)(d) in its relevant operation is **[123]** limited in three respects. It is limited geographically to conduct in or near public places. It is limited in its application only to "insulting words". And it is limited in its requirement that the words be addressed to a person. Hence it leaves a very wide field for the discussion of government and political matters by non-insulting words, and it leaves a wide field for the use of insulting words (in private, or to persons other than those insulted or persons associated with them). In short, it leaves citizens free to use insults in private, and to debate in public any subject they choose so long as they abstain from insults. Even if s 7(1)(d) does create an effective burden on communication on government and political matters, that is not its purpose; it is not directed at political speech as such. Its purpose is to control the various harms which flow from that kind of contemptuous speech which is "insulting". Its impact on communications about government and political matters is therefore incidental only ...

Further, a law curtailing political discussion may be valid if it operates in an area in which discussion has traditionally been curtailed in the public interest, or as part of the general law. Insulting words are within a field of verbal communication which has traditionally, since well before federation, been curtailed in the public interest as part of the general law.

The inquiry into whether a law is reasonably appropriate and **[124]** adapted to achieving a legitimate end does not call for a judicial conclusion that the law is the sole or best means of achieving that end. Apart from the fact that that would be an almost impossible task for which the judiciary is not equipped, this Court has not said anything of the kind either in *Lange v Australian Broadcasting Corporation* or in any other case. This Court has only called for an inquiry into whether the law was reasonably appropriate and adapted to serve a legitimate end. This implies that, in a given instance, there may be several ways of achieving that end. It also implies that reasonable minds may differ about which is the most satisfactory. In particular, differences amongst reasonable minds can readily arise where several distinct factors – here, the preservation of the peace, the protection of feelings, the avoidance of upset, the liberty to communicate – have to be borne in mind. Other arms of government – here, the executive which introduced the Bill containing s 7(1)(d) and the legislature which enacted it – are better placed than the judiciary to assess the difficulties and merits of particular solutions to the problems at which the provision is aimed … The question is not "Is this provision the best?", but "Is this provision a reasonably adequate attempt at solving the problem?" …

It does not follow from the fact that some communications on government and political matters are insulting that those communications form a significant part of the whole field. It is possible, and indeed quite easy, to communicate the substance of what is habitually communicated about government and political matters without recourse to insulting words. The fact that in the past some **[125]** communications about government and political matters have been couched in insulting words does not establish that that element is a necessary characteristic of those communications. Nor is it a beneficial one. Insulting words do very little to further the benefits which political debate brings. Indeed, by stimulating anger or embarrassment or fear, they create obstacles to the exchange of useful communications. It is difficult speedily to overcome their effect by reasoned persuasion: commonly the method resorted to is an equally irrational counter-insult. The range of non-insulting human communication is vast and the range of non-insulting political communication is also very wide. There are almost infinite methods of conveying ideas, information and arguments on government and political matters which are not insulting. Section 7(1)(d) imposes no restrictions on subject matter, no time limitations and no area limitations on government and political communications. It does not prevent full, compelling, trenchant, robust, passionate, indecorous, acrimonious and even rancorous debate, so long as the words used are not insulting. If it can be said to burden the relevant freedom at all, that burden is very slight …

[126] Insulting words, considered as a class, are generally so unreasonable, so irrational, so much an abuse of the occasion on which they are employed, and so reckless, that they do not assist the electors to an "informed" or "true" choice. Insulting words damage, rather than enhance, any process which might lead to voter appreciation of the available alternatives. Insulting words cannot be characterised as "information" …, but they are not "opinions and arguments" either. Insulting words are therefore not "matters" which are "necessary" to enable the people to make an informed choice. The terms of insulting words are usually so offensive and violent that they do not carry any reasonable possibility of throwing "light on government or political matters". Insulting words do not advance, but rather retard, the "common convenience and welfare of society". To address insulting words to persons in a public place is conduct sufficiently alien to the virtues of free and informed debate on which the constitutional freedom rests that it falls outside it.

The appellant submitted that the strength of the implied freedom of political communication could be gauged from the fact that it reflects "the importance that our society places on open discussion and the search for truth, the need for diversified opinions to be known and for the strengths and weaknesses of those opinions to be identified, the right to criticize, the value of tolerance of the opinions of others, and the social commitment to the value of individual autonomy, all being vital to the health of any democratic system of open government". Let that be admitted. The fact is that insulting words are not truly part of "open discussion" or "the search for truth". They do not really express "opinions" or enable the strengths and weaknesses of what genuinely are opinions to be identified. They form no part of criticism which rises above abuse. They reflect the vices of intolerance rather than the virtues of tolerance. They can crush individual autonomy rather than vindicating it.

These observations on the nature of political debate provoked a strong rejoinder from Kirby J.

Kirby J: [91] Reading the description of civilised interchange about governmental and political matters in the reasons of Heydon J, I had difficulty in recognising the Australian political system as I know it. His Honour's chronicle appears more like a description of an intellectual salon where civility always (or usually) prevails. It is not, with respect, an accurate description of the Australian governmental and political system in action.

One might wish for more rationality, less superficiality, diminished invective and increased logic and persuasion in political discourse. But those of that view must find another homeland. From its earliest history, Australian politics has regularly included insult and emotion, calumny and invective, in its armoury of persuasion. They are part and parcel of the struggle of ideas. Anyone in doubt should listen for an hour or two to the broadcasts that bring debates of the Federal Parliament to the living rooms of the nation. This is the way present and potential elected representatives have long campaigned in Australia for the votes of constituents and the support of their policies. It is unlikely to change … [T]he Constitution addresses the nation's representative government as it is practised. It does not protect only the whispered civilities of intellectual discourse.

The view that freedom of expression requires civility is an old one, as is the contrary view.

John Stuart Mill, *On Liberty*
(1st ed, Parker, 1859; 4th ed, Longmans, 1869);
reprinted in JM Robson (ed), *Essays on Politics and Society by John Stuart Mill*
(*Collected Works of John Stuart Mill*, vol 18, University of Toronto Press, 1977), 213

[258] Before quitting the subject of freedom of opinion, it is fit to take some notice of those who say, that the free expression of all opinions should be permitted, on condition that the manner be temperate, and do not pass the bounds of fair discussion. Much might be said on the impossibility of fixing where these supposed bounds are to be placed; for if the test be offence to those whose opinion is attacked, I think experience testifies that this offence is given whenever the attack is telling and powerful, and that every opponent who pushes them hard, and whom they find it difficult to answer, appears to them, if he shows any strong feeling on the subject, an intemperate opponent. But this, though an important consideration in a practical point of view, merges in a more fundamental objection. Undoubtedly the manner of asserting an opinion, even though it be a true one, may be very objectionable, and may justly incur severe censure. But the principal offences of the kind are such as it is mostly impossible, unless by accidental self-betrayal, to bring home to conviction. The gravest of them is, to argue sophistically, to suppress facts or arguments, to misstate the elements of the case, or misrepresent the opposite opinion. But all this, even to the most aggravated degree, is so continually done in perfect good faith, by persons who are not considered, and in many other respects may not deserve to be considered, ignorant or incompetent, that it is rarely possible on adequate grounds conscientiously to stamp the misrepresentation as morally culpable; and still less could law presume to interfere with this kind of controversial misconduct. With regard to what is commonly meant by intemperate discussion, namely invective, sarcasm, personality, and the like, the **[259]** denunciation of these weapons would deserve more sympathy if it were ever proposed to interdict them equally to both sides; but it is only desired to restrain the employment of them against the prevailing opinion: against the unprevailing they may not only be used without general disapproval, but will be likely to obtain for him who uses them the praise of honest zeal and righteous indignation. Yet whatever mischief arises from their use, is greatest when they are employed against the comparatively defenceless; and whatever unfair advantage can be derived by any opinion from this mode of asserting it, accrues almost exclusively to received opinions. The worst offence of this kind which can be committed by a polemic, is to stigmatize those who hold the contrary opinion as bad and immoral men. To calumny of this sort, those who hold any unpopular opinion are peculiarly exposed, because they are in general few and uninfluential, and nobody but themselves feels much interested in seeing justice done them; but this weapon is, from the nature of the case, denied to those who attack a prevailing opinion: they can neither use it with safety to themselves, nor, if they could, would it do anything but recoil on their own cause. In general, opinions contrary to those commonly received can only obtain a hearing by studied moderation of language, and the most cautious avoidance of unnecessary offence, from which they hardly ever deviate even in a slight degree without losing ground: while unmeasured vituperation employed on the side of the prevailing opinion, really does deter people from professing contrary opinions, and from listening to those who profess them. For the interest, therefore, of truth and justice, it is far more important to restrain this employment of vituperative language than the other; and, for example, if it were necessary to choose, there would be much more need to discourage offensive attacks on infidelity, than on religion. It is, however, obvious that law and authority have no business with restraining either, while opinion ought, in every instance, to determine its verdict by the circumstances of the individual case; condemning every one, on whichever side of the argument he places himself, in whose mode of advocacy either want of candour, or malignity, bigotry or intolerance of feeling manifest themselves; but not inferring these vices from the side which a person takes, though it be the contrary side of the question to our own.

3. Electoral Matters

Even in cases directly relating to parliamentary or electoral matters, attempts to invoke the protection of the implied freedom have usually failed. In *Langer v Commonwealth* (1996) 186 CLR 302, the implied freedom was narrowly construed, and indeed was applied only by Dawson J (see the extract in Chapter 10, §4(a)). In *Muldowney v South Australia* (1996) 186 CLR 352, it was argued that an implied freedom of political communication could be derived from the *Constitution Act 1934* (SA), and indeed the Solicitor-General for South Australia, Bradley Selway QC, *conceded* that this was so. As in *Langer*, however, provisions in the *Electoral Act 1985* (SA), designed to protect the prescribed method of voting by prohibiting any public advocacy of departure from that method, were held to be consistent with the constitutional implication because, as Gaudron J put it, the implication "**[376]** does not operate to strike down a law which curtails freedom of communication in those limited circumstances where that curtailment is reasonably capable of being viewed as appropriate and adapted to furthering or enhancing the democratic processes of the States".

In *Mulholland v Australian Electoral Commission* (2004) 220 CLR 181, the Democratic Labor Party (DLP) challenged the party registration provisions in Pt XI of the *Commonwealth Electoral Act 1918* (Cth), thereby seeking to preserve the Party's entitlements to identification of its candidates on federal ballot papers as DLP candidates, and to listing "above the line" on Senate ballot papers for the purpose of the simplified system of voting in Senate elections introduced in 1983. The challenge was directed particularly to the requirements that, in order to secure registration, a party not actually represented in Parliament must be able to demonstrate a membership of at least 500 persons ("the 500 rule"); and that the persons relied on for this purpose must not also be members of another political party ("the no overlap rule"). One unsuccessful argument was based on limitations arising from the words "chosen by the people" in ss 7 and 24 of the Constitution (see Chapter 10, §4(d)).

The DLP also argued that party identification of candidates on federal ballot papers was protected by the implied freedom of political communication. However, this argument was unanimously rejected by the High Court. The reason for rejection attracting most judicial support was the idea that the constitutional freedom can only be used as a "shield", and not as a "sword": that is, that where pre-existing "rights" are threatened by the operation of legislation (or of the common law), the constitutional implication can be invoked to protect those "rights"; but the freedom cannot be invoked to generate enforceable "rights" or "freedoms" not already cognisable by law. One version of this idea had been stated in *Lange*, where the joint judgment explained that ss 7 and 24 of the Constitution "**[560]** do not confer personal rights on individuals. Rather they preclude the curtailment of the protected freedom by the exercise of legislative or executive power". Another version was spelled out by McHugh J in *Levy v Victoria* (1997) 189 CLR 579: "**[622]** Unlike the Constitution of the United States, our Constitution does not create rights of communication. It gives immunity from the operation of laws that inhibit a right or privilege to communicate political and government matters. But, as *Lange* shows, that right or privilege must exist under the general law".

The relevant passage from *Lange* was taken up by Hayne J, sitting alone, in *McClure v Australian Electoral Commission* (1999) 163 ALR 734. Malcolm McClure, an unsuccessful candidate at the 1998 Senate election, had appeared before Hayne J in person to complain of being disadvantaged – first, by the fact that candidates from registered parties could have their parties identified on the ballot paper and listed "above the line" and, second, by the failure of the mass media to give adequate publicity to his campaign. He apparently believed "[738] that the Court should 'informally instruct' the chiefs of staff of media bodies about how they should act in the future". His complaint about the Senate voting system was put simply as one of "unfairness" and Hayne J rejected it by explaining that the reference in s 364 of the *Commonwealth Electoral Act* to "substantial merits and good conscience" "[742] does not give the Court some power to rewrite the Act to accord with some abstract standard of fairness". It was only in response to the second complaint, about lack of publicity in the mass media, that McClure invoked the constitutional freedom of political communication, to which Hayne J responded: "[740] The short answer ... is that the *freedom* of communication implied in the Constitution is not an *obligation* to publicise. The freedom is a freedom from governmental action; it is not a right to require others [741] to provide a means of communication. The petitioner's case depends upon him having some right to require others to disseminate his views". It was this point that was taken up in response to the DLP's claim in *Mulholland*.

Mulholland v Australian Electoral Commission
(2004) 220 CLR 181

Callinan J: [298] The appellant has no constitutional right to have his party affiliation included on the ballot paper. Nor does any other candidate. The rights are entirely statutory. The Act could be repealed or amended so as to allow no right of inclusion of a party on the ballot paper at all. The appellant has no relevant rights other than such rights as may be conferred on him by the Act. In argument, McHugh J drew an analogy: protestors cannot complain about an interference with, or the prevention of their doing what they have no right to do anyway, for example, to communicate a protest on land on which their presence is a trespass. As the appellant has no relevant *right* to the imposition of an obligation upon another, to communicate a particular matter, he has no right which is capable of being burdened. The appellant is seeking a privilege, not to vindicate or avail himself of a right. He can communicate his affiliation with the DLP as a candidate in any way and at any time that he wishes. What he cannot do is compel the respondent to do so in a way which would effectively discriminate in his favour, and would be tantamount to treatment of him as having a relevant *right*.

For Heydon J, the need to point to some previously established "right" or "freedom" was only the first of several obstacles that the appellant's argument failed to surmount.

Heydon J: [303] First, there is no interference with any implied freedom of political communi-cation ... because it is necessary that there be some relevant "right or privilege ... under the general law" to be interfered with [*Levy v Victoria* (1997) 189 CLR 579 at 622]. In the absence of legislation permitting it, there is no right in any political party or candidate to have party affiliation indicated on the ballot paper. Indeed, the appellant conceded that a legislative prohibition on the appearance of any party affiliation on the ballot paper would not contravene the implied freedom. It follows that to legislate for a mixture of permissions and prohibitions, so as to permit the party affiliations of some candidates but not others to appear on the ballot paper, cannot [304] interfere with the implied freedom. The Full Federal Court saw the challenged statutory provisions as conferring "a limited privilege on registered political parties in relation to their communication with the voters", which was "a burden on all those seeking election that do not enjoy it" [198 ALR at 286]. It would be paradoxical, however, if a complete prohibition was incontestably valid while a partial prohibition was not. It would also be paradoxical if an implied freedom created a right in individuals to have their party affiliation identified in the ballot paper, and created a correlative obligation on the Commission to include it there. Indeed, it would be contrary to principle, for "the *freedom* of communication implied in the Constitution is not an *obligation* to publicise … [I]t is not a right to require others to provide a means of communication" [*McClure*, 163 ALR at 740-1] …

Secondly, what appears on the ballot paper is not political communication in the sense used in *Lange v Australian Broadcasting Corporation*, namely communications between the electors and the elected representatives, the electors and the candidates, and the electors themselves – that is, between the people. What is on the ballot paper is a communication only between the executive government and the electors. The ballot paper is the medium by which a vote is cast. It is integral to the election machinery. It is not part of the process of communicating information with a view to influencing electors to vote for one candidate or another. "It is for the electors and the candidates to choose which forms of otherwise lawful communication they prefer to use to disseminate political information, ideas and argument. Their choices are a matter of private, not public, **[305]** interest. Their choices are outside the zone of governmental control" [*Australian Capital Television Pty Ltd v Commonwealth* (1992) 177 CLR 106 at 236]. But the conduct of the election itself is a matter of public interest and is within the zone of governmental control. That is particularly true of the form of the ballot paper.

Thirdly, [the impugned provisions] … do not create a burden on the implied freedom of political communication in that there is no restraint on any activity which candidates or parties may engage in apart from the legislative system of registration. All opportunities for communication that existed before the impugned provisions were enacted continue to exist.

Fourthly, even if there were a relevant right to communicate party affiliation, even if the ballot paper is a form of exercising it, and even if there were a burden on the implied freedom of political communication, the requirements of the legislation are reasonably appropriate and adapted to serve legitimate ends, the fulfilment of which is compatible with the maintenance of the constitutionally prescribed system of representative and responsible government …

Much of the appellant's argument analysed the structure and history of the legislation to support numerous detailed criticisms of its merits and … suggestions as to how the ends of the legislation could have been more effectively achieved by other means. However, the question is not whether the impugned provisions have established the most desirable or least burdensome regime to carry out the legitimate ends. The question is only whether the legislation is reasonably appropriate and adapted to the achievement of the legislative purpose, and weight is to be given to the legislative judgment.

[306] The appellant's argument depended to some extent on an analogy with *Australian Capital Television Pty Ltd v Commonwealth*. There is no analogy between the legislation struck down in that case and the legislation challenged in this case. The legislation in that case was characterised as constituting a prohibition on a traditional category of political communications being conducted through ordinarily available media. It thus burdened an ordinary mode of communication in such a way as seriously to impede discussion about elections. This is quite distinct from the enactment of a statutory scheme regulating the content of the official ballot paper, at issue in this case.

The second point made by Heydon J – that the case could not be said to involve "political communication" at all – was rejected by Gleeson CJ, McHugh and Kirby JJ.

McHugh J: [219] In my opinion, the Full Court correctly held that the ballot-paper is a communication on political and government matters. For the purposes of the Constitution, communications on political and government matters include communications between the executive government and the people. Representative government and responsible government are the pillars upon which the constitutional implication of freedom of communication rests. Communications between the executive government and public servants and the people are as necessary to the effective working of those institutions as communications between the people and their elected representatives. As Deane J pointed out in *Cunliffe v Commonwealth* [(1994) 182 CLR 272 at 336], freedom of communication on political and government matters "extends to the broad national environment in which the individual citizen exists and in which representative government must operate."

Admittedly, in so far as a ballot-paper is a communication on political and government matters for the purpose of the constitutional freedom, it is a communication of a special kind. Freedom of communication on political and government matters is a necessary implication of the Constitution because "the business of government must be examinable and the subject of scrutiny, debate and ultimate accountability at the ballot box" [*Australian Capital Television* 177 CLR at 231]. The electors must be able to ascertain and examine the performance of their elected representatives and the capabilities and policies of candidates for election. For that purpose, the electors must have access to all the information, ideas, opinions and arguments that may enable them "to make an informed [220] judgment as to how they have been governed and as to what policies are in the interests of themselves, their communities and the nation" [177 CLR at 231].

The primary purpose of a ballot-paper, however, is to record the voter's preferences among the candidates standing for election to Parliament in the voter's electorate. It is part of a process for the casting, counting and recording of votes to elect Parliamentary representatives which is the end to which the Constitution's implication of freedom of communication is directed. It does not convey information, ideas, opinions and arguments that may enable *other voters* to make an informed judgment as to how they should vote. Nor does it seek to persuade *candidates* in the election to modify or adjust their policies. The delivery of a ballot-paper to an elector is primarily a communication by the Commission to that elector that informs the elector what candidates are standing for election and what parties, if any, they represent. It also informs the elector of the manner in which an elector may record a valid vote. In so far as the elector makes a communication by marking the ballot-paper and lodging it in the ballot-box, the elector's primary purpose is to inform the Commission – the body charged with conducting the election – which candidate or candidates the elector wishes to have elected.

But, although the ballot-paper has little resemblance to traditional communications on political and government matters, it is still properly characterised as a communication on those matters. Although the ballot-paper is printed and distributed by the Executive (the Commission), party endorsement of candidates is included only at the request of the party … The Commission determines the form and format of the ballot-paper, but the candidates and parties essentially provide the "content". The ballot-paper is thus the record of the communication. Accordingly, the endorsement details on ballot-papers constitute a communication on political and government matters between candidates and electors. In *Figueroa* [*v Canada (Attorney General)* [2003] 1 SCR 912 at 947-8; (2002) 227 DLR(4th) 1 at 31-2], the Supreme Court of Canada pointed out that the inclusion of such endorsement details on the ballot-paper is an important way in which parties and endorsed candidates communicate to voters. Implicit in the Court's reasoning … was that the ballot-paper is a medium of communication between parties and voters. In addition, the marked ballot-paper, when lodged in the ballot-box, is also a communication on such matters. That is because the marked ballot-paper contains a statement – anonymous though it is – that this candidate or these candidates should be elected to Parliament. In that respect, such a statement is no different from a statement made by an [221] elector in the course of an election meeting claiming that X is the person who should represent the electorate.

Accordingly, a ballot-paper is a communication on political and government matters.

However, in a variant of the point relied on in other judgments, McHugh J held that because there was no pre-existing "right" to party identification on the ballot paper, the only such "right" was created by the very provisions under challenge, which could therefore hardly be said to "burden" the very rights that they created.

McHugh J: [223] The short answer to the claim that the challenged provisions burden political communications by the DLP to electors is that the restrictions are the conditions of the entitlement to have a party's name placed on the ballot-paper. The restrictions do not burden rights of communication on political and government matters that exist independently of the entitlement. Any political communication that is involved in the delivery and lodging of a ballot-paper results solely from the Commission's statutory obligation to hold elections and deliver ballot-papers in the prescribed form, and from the rights of parties and candidates to have their identities marked on the ballot-paper. However, the right of a registered political party to make, or have the Commission make on its behalf, a political communication on the ballot-paper is subject to the conditions imposed by the Act.

Only registered political parties may request the Commission to include endorsement details on ballot-papers. Registration requires the party to meet other statutory requirements, such as appointing officers, having a constitution and complying with reporting obligations. Unregistered political parties do not have a statutory entitlement under the Act to request the Commission to include the party's name or abbreviation next to the names of the candidates whom the party has endorsed. Nor do they have an entitlement to request the Commission to include the party's name or abbreviation next to the "above the line" box on Senate ballot-papers, in circumstances where the party has lodged a group voting ticket with the Commission. Thus, the content of the freedom in respect of any political communication by means of a ballot-paper is commensurate with the scope of the entitlements granted by the provisions of the Act which regulate the making of the communication.

Because the DLP has no right to make communications on political matters by means of the ballot-paper other than what the Act gives, Mr Mulholland's claim that the Act burdens the DLP's freedom of political communication fails. Proof of a burden on the implied constitutional freedom requires proof that the challenged law burdens a freedom that exists independently of that law.

After quoting what he said in *Levy* and what Hayne J said in *McClure*, McHugh J concluded:

McHugh J: [224] No political party or its candidates have any right under the common law or the statute law of the Commonwealth or the States other than the Act to have the party's name printed above the line or on the ballot-paper. The only rights concerning ballot-papers which political parties and their candidates have are those rights that the Act confers on them.

The insistence on a need for pre-existing "rights" was rejected most firmly by Kirby J:

Kirby J: [267] There is one characterisation of the impugned provisions of the Act, presented as an answer to the appellant's complaints, that, with respect, I would firmly reject. It was expressed in *McClure v Australian Electoral Commission* [(1999) 163 ALR 734 at 740-1] and invoked by the AEC in this appeal. It was stated in the form of an aphorism: "the **[268]** *freedom* of communication implied in the Constitution is not an *obligation* to publicise".

Without casting doubt on the correctness of the decision in *McClure*, I question the accuracy of the propounded dichotomy, at least if it is presented as one of general application. The appellant's attack in this case was on the "500 rule" and the "no overlap rule", and the particular provisions of the Act permitting their enforcement by the AEC. He sought to show that those provisions were invalid by reference both to express and implied constitutional requirements. If he could establish his contentions, and support severance of the offending provisions (as the AEC and the appellant both urged would occur if constitutional invalidity of the provisions were shown), those provisions would be excised. That would leave the Act in the position it was before the provisions were inserted.

Such severance would leave standing provisions for registered political parties and for "above the line" voting with identification of the affiliation of those belonging to any such "eligible political party". Doing this would not cast on the AEC any duty that could fairly be characterised as an "obligation to publicise". It would simply restore the position of allowing candidates who are members of political parties, without *discriminatory* preconditions, to nominate such parties for inclusion in the Senate ballot paper absent the requirements which the appellant claimed discriminated against the DLP and in favour of incumbent parties.

According to the appellant, the DLP was not seeking the conferral of any special rights of publicity. It was simply claiming protection from this Court to delete from the Act amendments that were inconsistent with the constitutional prescription. I agree with the appellant's argument to this extent. It follows that, in this respect, I disagree with the analysis on this point contained in the reasons of Gummow and Hayne JJ.

This passage might appear to suggest that, for Kirby J, the pre-existing "rights" were those created by the original registration scheme introduced in 1984. The issue would then be whether those rights were "burdened" by the new conditions introduced before the 2001 election. That analysis might be persuasive in relation to the "no overlap" rule, introduced in the year 2000; but not for the "500 rule", which dated from 1984. Be that as it may, a later passage made it clear that Kirby J flatly rejected the idea that the constitutional freedom of communication "[276] is limited to 'rights' sustained by the common law or statutory provisions existing outside the Constitution itself". He protested that: "This approach, pushed to extremes, could effectively neuter the implied freedom of communication". Far from allowing existing common law rights to limit the operation of the Constitution, he pointed out that, under *Lange*, the common law "adapts to the Constitution". If the common law did not already embody adequate protections for the implied freedom, it would have to develop them.

In the end, only Gleeson CJ and Kirby J accepted that the case involved a "burden".

Kirby J: [274] The first question is whether the provisions of the Act introducing the "500 rule" and the "no overlap rule" and the sections providing for their enforcement burden the freedom of communication about government or political matters implied from ss 7, 24, 64 and 128 of the Constitution. If the provisions do effectively burden that freedom, a second question arises as to whether the burden in question is constitutionally permissible, in the sense of proportionate to the achievement of all of the purposes of the Constitution …

[275] The existence of a burden on political communication could only be denied by the adoption of self-fulfilling criteria as to what constitutes a "burden" or by the application of a constitutional sleight of hand. The provisions enforcing the "500 rule" place a restriction on the highly valuable ballot identification of the association of certain candidates with a named political party. They do so … [in ways] that may tend to favour larger, incumbent political parties and to disadvantage smaller, less well-organised ones which nonetheless exist and are entitled to compete for political support.

The enforcement against the DLP of laws restricting inclusion on the ballot paper of the party's name in conjunction with party candidates would inferentially have negative consequences for those candidates. Under the Act, they could still appear as a group "above the line". However, they would be politically anonymous. They would be denied ballot association with the DLP party name. For those electors who did not know the candidates personally, but knew and supported the perceived objectives of the DLP, the absence of that name from the ballot paper would frequently prove decisive. Unless electors had some other means of knowing the identity of any DLP candidates, they would effectively be deprived of the opportunity of voting for candidates of that political persuasion. It would take a great deal of political naivety to fail to see the electoral disadvantage to the DLP and its candidates of the omission of its name from the Senate ballot paper in conjunction with the candidates whom it supported and who wished to be so identified.

Proof of this particular pudding may be found in the strenuous efforts of the DLP in these proceedings to win that right without having to comply with the requirements that the Act now extracts. Whatever might be the position in respect of other, new, imaginary or unknown political parties, I consider it unarguable that the name **[276]** recognition of the DLP with electors has a practical value that would be measured in votes.

Even so, both Gleeson CJ and Kirby J joined in the unanimous result, since each of them held that the appellant had failed to show that the "burden" was unacceptable.

Gleeson CJ: [200] The circumstance that the appellant's challenge is not to the entire registration system for political parties, but to two particular aspects of that system, should not divert attention from the legislative context, which is in furtherance of, not derogation from, political communication. **[201]** The idea behind the printing of party affiliations on ballot papers, as appears from the September 1983 report of the Joint Select Committee on Electoral Reform, was to "assist voters in casting their vote in accordance with their intentions". Public funding of political parties for election campaigns, and the adoption of the list system for Senate elections, were also measures in aid of political communication and the political process. Parliament took the view that those measures necessitated provision for the registration of political parties. That view was clearly open and reasonable. Parliament then took the view that some minimum level of public support was required for registration as a party and that 500 members was a reasonable figure for that purpose. It also, later, took the view that, to guard against obvious possibilities for abuse of the registration system, the no overlap rule should be introduced. Bearing in mind the context in which the two rules operate there is justification for them which this Court ought to accept as compelling. There is no reasonable basis on which this Court could legitimately form and substitute a different opinion. Furthermore, bearing in mind that the two rules under challenge are in furtherance and support of a system that facilitates, rather than impedes, political communication and the democratic process, there is no warrant for denying their reasonable necessity.

4. The Separation of Judicial Power

Clearly, legislative or executive action that affects the judicial process will normally be of a political or governmental nature, so that comments on such action will be protected by the implied constitutional freedom. However, it seems that the judicial process itself is not judicially perceived as "political or governmental", so that criticism of the courts will be given no such protection – perhaps because "strict and complete legalism" (see Chapter 7, §4) entails an acceptance of Baron de Montesquieu's assertion (*The Spirit of the Laws*, transl T Nugent, Hafner Press, 1949) that "**[159]** judges are no more than the mouth that pronounces the words of the law, mere passive beings, incapable of moderating either its force or [its] rigor".

In *John Fairfax Publications Pty Ltd v Attorney-General (NSW)* (2000) 181 ALR 694, the New South Wales Court of Appeal struck down certain provisions of s 101A of the *Supreme Court Act 1970* (NSW), which provided that, where a person has been charged with contempt of court and acquitted, the Attorney-General may appeal on questions of law without disturbing the acquittal. The offending provisions required that the appellate proceedings be held in camera and prohibited publication of the identity of the alleged contemnor or of the arguments addressed to the Court. Spigelman CJ, with Priestley JA agreeing and Meagher JA dissenting, held that these provisions attracted the constitutional freedom because the law of contempt "**[712]** applies to a wide range of conduct including communications about matters of major social and political significance at a Commonwealth level". (The particular case involved allegations about the importation of heroin: see *Attorney-General (NSW) v X* (2000) 49 NSWLR 653.) However, Spigelman CJ rejected certain more general arguments, including a claim "**[709]** that judges and courts are within the sphere of public officials and bodies about whom the freedom could be exercised" because their conduct "was itself a legitimate matter of public interest". Whatever significance these claims might have for a common law defence of qualified privilege, he insisted that the common law defence "is not coextensive" with the constitutional freedom, since the latter is "derived from the text and structure of the Constitution insofar as it makes provision for representative government. The conduct of courts is not, of itself, a manifestation of any of the provisions relating to representative government upon which the freedom is based". He stressed that the adjectives "governmental or political" were used in *Lange* "**[710]** to confine the scope of the constitutional freedom".

In *Herald & Weekly Times Ltd v Popovic* (2003) 9 VR 1, a newspaper column criticising a Victorian magistrate was held to be defamatory. It was held that neither of the basic requirements for a *Lange* defence was satisfied. The columnist's selective use of court transcripts had not been "reasonable", and in any event his criticisms did not relate to "government or political matters".

Herald & Weekly Times Ltd v Popovic
(2003) 9 VR 1

Winneke ACJ: [10] It is apparent from the authorities … that the question whether a defamatory publication is published on an occasion of "extended" qualified privilege (on account of it being a discussion of political or government matters) will depend very much upon the nature of the published matter in question … Each case will depend upon its own circumstances, and the limits of the freedom will be worked out on a case by case basis. However ..., I do not consider that a criticism of the performance of a magistrate in the management of an isolated proceeding in his or her court is a discussion of political or government matters in the sense that such discussion is necessary for the effective operation of representative and responsible government. Quite apart from the fact that – as Spigelman CJ pointed out (in a different context) in *John Fairfax Pty Ltd v Attorney-General (NSW)* [(2000) 181 ALR 694 at 709] – the conduct of courts "is not, of itself, a manifestation of any of the provisions relating to representative government upon which the freedom is based", the conduct of individual judicial officers is carried out independently of the legislative and executive branches of government, and is not to be described, in my view, as an exercise of power at a government or administrative level. It can be conceded that judicial officers are "public figures" appointed, or recommended for appointment, by the executive branch of government. It can also be conceded that the executive branch of government has a strong interest in the due administration of justice. However those concessions, at least to my mind, do not carry with them the implication that a discussion about the discharge by a judicial officer of his or her function in a particular case is a discussion concerning political or government matters in the relevant sense. It is true that, when discharging their functions, judicial officers are performing a public role; one which is to be performed in the "public gaze" and, thus, open to public scrutiny and comment. It is also true that the discharge of functions by judicial officers in particular cases will attract comment by the media; some of it strongly critical of the judicial officer's handling and disposition of the case. However, that is not to say that such comment assumes the status of a communication concerning political or government matters which are relevant to the system of representative and responsible government ... Such comment and criticism could, in my view, have no impact or influence upon the choice of their representatives by the people of Australia.

That does not mean that there can never be a discussion about a judicial officer which will, or might, be relevant to the system of representative and responsible government. It is not difficult to conceive of circumstances where discussion of the character and/or conduct (whether in or out of court) of a judicial officer is capable of amounting to a discussion on government or political matters in the relevant sense. This would particularly be so where the discussion impacts **[11]** directly or indirectly on the executive government itself; whether in the exercise of its powers to appoint the officer, or in exercising or failing to exercise its powers to initiate the officer's removal. Such a discussion may well bear the characteristics of one which is capable of informing and shaping the views of the electors about the performance of their elected representatives. However, that is not the type of discussion which is involved in this case. There seems to me to be a discrete difference between the type of discussion to which I have referred and an opinion piece about the manner in which a judicial officer has handled individual curial proceedings ... The fact that it can be inferred from the published article that the author thinks that the respondent should be removed from office does not, in my view, make the discussion any more or less relevant to [representative government].

Warren AJA drew a similar conclusion from the separation of powers. She saw judicial power as "**[103]** quintessentially different from the other powers".

Gillard AJA, whose approach has since been followed by Gray J in *Peek v Channel Seven Adelaide Pty Ltd* (2004) 90 SASR 522, took a different view. He noted that the trial judge had been influenced by the judgment of Deane and Toohey JJ in *Nationwide News Pty Ltd v Wills* (1992) 177 CLR 1, which extended to "**[74]** the qualifications, conduct and performance of those entrusted ... with the exercise of any part of the legislative, executive or *judicial powers of government* which are ultimately derived from the people themselves" (emphasis added).

Gillard AJA: [51] If a narrow approach is taken to the question what are government or political matters, it would seriously rob the defence of content ... The High Court in *Lange* [*v Australian Broadcasting Corporation* (1997) 189 CLR 520] emphasised that the Court was broadening the common law rules of qualified privilege. The High Court quoted with approval what McHugh J said in the *Stephens* case [(1994) 182 CLR 211 at 264]. His Honour provided a broad definition of the types of matters that members of the community have a real and legitimate interest to know about and stated that a narrow view should not be taken of these matters ...

[52] At the outset, it is my opinion that the article does not refer to a political matter; the question is whether the article is disseminating information concerning a government matter? His Honour considered the article and formed the opinion that the article did discuss the behaviour of Ms Popovic whilst sitting as a magistrate in the court, and did contemplate or advocate her removal which is a matter at the initiation of the Attorney-General ... His Honour was of the view that it was that connection between the magistrate's office and the government which led to the conclusion that any discussion advocating the removal of a magistrate was a government or political matter ...

In my respectful opinion, his Honour's decision was correct but I do not think the government matter content is confined to comments which advocate the removal of a judicial officer.

A judicial officer is independent of government. Judicial officers are performing a public service. They are not public servants but they are servants of the public. The government of the day, elected by the people, has the responsibility of making and enforcing the law and establishing a judicial system to interpret and apply the law. A judicial officer, although independent of government, is performing the very important public service of construing and applying the law, enforcing it and above all, ensuring that the rule of law is upheld. It is the obligation of the government to provide and fund the judicial system. The judicial officer performs the task entrusted to him or her by the government.

The English Oxford Dictionary defines the word "government" as, inter alia, "the form or kind of polity, the governing power in a state, the body of persons **[53]** charged with the duty of government". The judicial arm of government is independent of the Legislature and the Executive but the fact is, the judicial system is established and funded by the government of the day ...

The administration of justice ... is a vital and essential ingredient in the system of government. The government in this State since the establishment of the Colony of Victoria has recognised this and established and maintained the various courts in the judicial system. The magistrates are appointed by the government of the day, and they are paid out of the public purse. The way they behave in court, their fitness for office and their conduct as magistrates are all matters which in my view every member of the Victorian community has a real and legitimate interest in knowing about.

In my opinion, a discussion of the conduct of a judicial officer and the way the officer behaves in court is a government matter. Paraphrasing what McHugh J said in *Stephens*, the quality of life and freedom of the ordinary individuals in this State are dependent on the exercise of functions and powers vested in the public representatives by a vast legal apparatus funded by public moneys. How they perform are matters that are of a real and legitimate interest to every member of the community.

Conservation Council of SA Inc v Chapman (2003) 87 SASR 62 – one of many defamation actions arising from the *Hindmarsh Island Bridge Case* (see Chapter 21, §4) – related to the regular bulletins on the affair that the Conservation Council had published in its journal *Environment South Australia*. The trial judge, Williams J, found that three of those bulletins were defamatory; but as to two of them his finding was set aside on appeal (because he had erred in finding "malice"). It was clear that the substantive issues in the Hindmarsh Island controversy related to "government or political matters" at both State and federal levels. However, Doyle CJ and Besanko J held, with Gray J dissenting, that the constitutional freedom thus attracted did not extend to comments on proceedings in the Federal Court. As Doyle CJ put it, the "**[70]** particular publication" must relate to governmental or political matters: for example, if during the Hindmarsh Island debate it had been "alleged that the bridge was unsafely designed due to incompetence by a structural engineer", that defamatory statement "would not attract the constitutional protection". Similarly, comments on Federal Court litigation, though made in the context of the wider debate, were not in themselves sufficiently "political" in nature to attract the protection: "the fact that the publication refers to the Federal Court and to court orders is not of itself enough".

John Fairfax Publications Pty Ltd v O'Shane [2005] NSWCA 164 was concerned, like *Popovic*, with a newspaper column criticising a magistrate. The trial judge, Smart JA, accepted that some aspects of the column touched on "government or political matters", but refused to extend the *Lange* defence to discussion of judicial performance. He also rejected an alternative argument that, by analogy with *Lange*, a separate extension of the common law defence of qualified privilege should be moulded for publications about the conduct of judicial officers. The New South Wales Court of Appeal was primarily concerned to reject the latter argument.

John Fairfax Publications Pty Ltd v O'Shane
[2005] NSWCA 164

Giles JA: [91] The privilege for which the appellant contended was fairly remotely analogous to the *Lange* privilege. It was also an extended common law privilege, outflanking the traditional need for reciprocity of duty and interest between publisher and recipient and resting upon an interest or duty to publish matter to the general public. But it was frankly accepted that it was not justified by constitutional considerations of freedom of communication concerning government and political matters.

[92] The appellant submitted that the administration of justice was vital to the ordered protection of persons and property, and that it was of legitimate interest to the general public to receive information on the discharge of the judicial function; and that there was a correlative duty to disseminate information and opinions on that subject. The well recognised public policy favouring the conduct of judicial proceedings in open court, and the protection given to fair reports of judicial proceedings, attested to the importance of public knowledge of judicial activity. Although not founded on the freedom of communication which the Constitution required, affording qualified privilege to discussion of the conduct of judicial officers was for "the common convenience and welfare of society" in like manner to affording the *Lange* privilege. And the defence was limited not by reasonableness, but by the law of contempt, since non-contemptuous discussion was not considered punishable.

[93] So the argument ran; accepting it would be a major development in the law ...

[94] Had interest in the general public in receiving information on the discharge of the functions of those exercising functions and powers affecting members of the community been sufficient for extension of qualified privilege, the High Court would not have tied the *Lange* privilege to constitutional provisions relating to representative government ...

[95] While there can be found reference to the "judicial branch of government" (*D'Orta-Ekenaike v Victorian Legal Aid* [(2005) 214 ALR 92 at 99-100]), judicial officers occupy a place in the exercise of functions and powers affecting members of the community unlike the position of ... public representatives and officials. Judicial officers are not elected representatives, and are not subject to the control of parliament or the executive in the exercise of their functions, short of removal from office by parliamentary act in extreme circumstances. This independence of the judiciary exists for sound reasons, was historically hard won, and serves a vital constitutional and social purpose in the impartial dispensation of justice.

[96] Apparently as a substitute for the constitutional provisions relating to representative government, the appellant submitted that discussion of the conduct of judicial officers was for the benefit of the community because it provided a form of "accountability", apart from removal in the limited circumstances when that might come about ...

[97] What was meant by accountability was, with respect, rather unclear. It is of the first importance that judicial officers decides cases brought before them according to law, uninfluenced by ephemeral public opinion and giving decisions which may be unpopular but which are necessary for the protection of legally recognised individual rights. The appellate system exists to ensure, within human frailty, that error is corrected. Interest in what judges do, during hearings and in their reasons, is commendable, but it is not an accountability mechanism, because what people think and say about the conduct of judicial officers does not and should not mould judicial decision-making ...

[98] In a form of reverse engineering, the appellant put a submission to the effect that defamatory comments about judicial officers were not uncommon, they were nowadays generally tolerated if falling short of contempt, and therefore judicial officers should be unable to sue for defamation short of contemptuous defamation. That tolerance is generally shown is not a reason to create a defence whereby judicial officers are less able to sue for defamation than other members of the community, including politicians who have the benefit of reasonableness under the *Lange* privilege. Judicial officers have reputations, like all persons, to protect and vindicate if they wish. Further, a limitation by the law of contempt would be erroneous. The law of defamation protects an individual's reputation. The law of contempt serves the different purpose of protecting the judicial institution ...

[99] I am not persuaded that there is a need or occasion for the law to develop in the manner suggested. The defences of publication of a fair protected report ... and of comment are available to the mass media, and within their bounds the desirable interest in what judicial officers do can appropriately be satisfied. Licence for ill-based publications detrimental to confidence in judicial institutions would be against the interests of the community.

The general trend of these decisions may appear to be confirmed by the High Court's decision in *APLA Ltd v Legal Services Commissioner (NSW)* (2005) 219 ALR 403. By cl 139 in Pt 14 of the *Legal Profession Amendment (Personal Injury) Regulation* (NSW), the general provisions of the *Legal Profession Act 1987* (NSW) permitting legal practitioners to advertise were restricted by prohibiting any advertisement relating to the recovery of compensation for personal injury, or making any reference to personal injury or to "any circumstance in which personal injury might occur, or any activity, event or circumstance that suggests or could suggest the possibility of personal injury, or any connection to or association with personal injury or a cause of personal injury". The restrictions were designed to counteract what New South Wales Premier Bob Carr described as a contemporary "trend to excessive litigation".

In holding that cl 139 was valid, the Court declined to take the view that the *Lange* principle was attracted either by the general impact of the clause on litigation, or by its particular impact on litigation in federal jurisdiction (for example, on potential claims under the *Trade Practices Act 1974* (Cth)). The five majority judges, Gleeson CJ, Gummow, Hayne, Callinan and Heydon JJ, held that *Lange* had no application. McHugh J, though dissenting in the result, agreed with that view, but accepted an analogous implication relating specifically to information that might assist potential litigants. Kirby J, who also dissented, was prepared to hold that "**[486]** the extremely wide prohibition expressed in the Regulation, and the broad net that it casts, amount to a burden to some degree upon the freedom of communication about government or political matters", but he too on this aspect of the case relied primarily on an analogous implication from Ch III of the Constitution.

The five majority judges did not specifically consider whether the *Lange* principle could extend to comment on the work of the courts. Nor did they make any reference to the cases in which that question had been considered in the State Supreme Courts. This question and the correctness of those decisions therefore remain open.

Instead, the relevance of *Lange* was denied on more fundamental grounds.

APLA Ltd v Legal Services Commissioner (NSW)
(2005) 219 ALR 403

Gleeson CJ and Heydon J: [412] Restrictions on the advertising of goods and services limit freedom of communication. Such restrictions are not unfamiliar. Advertising of tobacco, therapeutic goods and films of certain kinds, for example, is restricted by Commonwealth legislation. In *Cunliffe v Commonwealth* [(1994) 182 CLR 272], this Court upheld the validity of restrictions imposed by the *Migration Act 1958* (Cth) upon the giving of immigration assistance to aliens or the making of representations on their behalf ... The restrictions in question included a restriction on advertising services by way of immigration assistance ...

[413] The possibility that an advertisement of the kind prohibited by the regulations might mention some political or governmental issue, or might name some politician, does not mean that the regulations infringe the constitutional requirement. The regulations do not, in their terms, prohibit communications about government or political matters. They prohibit communication between lawyers and people who, by hypothesis, are not their clients, aimed at encouraging the recipients of the communications to engage the services of lawyers. Such communications are an essentially commercial activity. The regulations are not aimed at preventing discussion of, say, "tort law reform", or some other such issue of public policy. They restrict the marketing of professional services.

Restrictions on the marketing of legal services are not incompatible with a system of representative and responsible government, or with the requirements of ss 7, 24, 64 and 128 of the Constitution. If they were, such incompatibility has passed unnoticed for most of the time since Federation ... In recent years, legislatures decided that it was in the public interest that lawyers should be encouraged to adopt a more mercantile approach to the provision of their services. Some lawyers responded with enthusiasm. Authorities appear to have been surprised to discover that, when lawyers promote their services, litigation increases. Some lawyers may be aggrieved at the recent cooling of official mercantilist ardour. They are, however, drawing a long bow when they claim that restricting their capacity to advertise for business is incompatible with the requirements of responsible and representative government established by the Constitution.

Hayne J emphasised that, leaving aside "**[497]** extraordinary circumstances", the rights and remedies to which prospective clients might be entitled would normally be "rights and remedies existing under the law as it stood at the time an injury was sustained". He did not consider that *Lange* extended to communications about the existing state of the law, nor to communications about the underlying events which might give rise to such rights or remedies:

Hayne J: [497] As Brennan J pointed out in *Cunliffe v Commonwealth* [182 CLR at 329], it is necessary to distinguish between laws controlling an activity and laws restricting political discussion about whether that activity should be controlled. The impugned regulations are of the former type, not the latter. They control an activity – lawyers' advertising. They are directed at communications about events (actual or hypothetical) and about rights and remedies. They are not directed at communications about whether the happening of events should be regulated differently or whether available rights and remedies should be changed.

Callinan J dismissed the plaintiffs' argument in more peremptory terms: "**[520]** None of the communications proposed, or indeed anything like them, answer any acceptable practical description or definition of a government or political matter. It would be fanciful to suggest otherwise. It is unimaginable that they could possibly interfere with electors, free elections or an open referendum, or the legitimate exercise of elected politicians' rights and powers".

Accordingly, only McHugh J held that discussion of judicial matters lay outside the protection of *Lange*.

McHugh J: [421] *Lange* refers to "political or government matters". But those words must be read in the context of the decision. That context leaves no doubt that the term "government" is used to describe acts and omissions of the kind that fall within Chs I, II and VIII of the Constitution. It refers to representative and responsible government. In a broad sense, "government" includes the actions of the judiciary as the third branch of government established by the Constitution. But the freedom of communication recognised by *Lange* does not include the exercise of the judicial power of the Commonwealth by courts invested with federal jurisdiction or, for that matter, the judicial power of the States.

Nothing in *Lange* or the subsequent decision of this Court in *Coleman v Power* [(2004) 220 CLR 1] supports the proposition that the exercise of judicial power is within the freedom recognised by *Lange*. *Lange* concerned the conduct of a politician. *Coleman* concerned criticism of a police officer who was alleged to be corrupt. That case was determined on the basis, conceded by the respondents, that the criticism was a communication on a political or governmental matter. That concession was correct because the police officer was part of the Executive Government of Queensland. But the mere fact that communications concerning the conduct of police officers are within the scope of the *Lange* freedom does not mean that communications concerning the courts or judges or the exercise of judicial power are also within the scope of that freedom.

There is a difference between a communication concerning legislative and executive acts or omissions concerned with the administration of justice and communications concerning that subject that do not involve, expressly or inferentially, acts or omissions of the legislature or the Executive Government. Discussion of the appointment or removal of judges, the prosecution of offences, the withdrawal of charges, the provision of legal aid and the funding of courts, for example, are communications that attract the *Lange* freedom. That is because they concern, expressly or inferentially, acts or omissions of the legislature or the Executive Government. They do not lose the freedom recognised in *Lange* because they also deal with the administration of justice in federal jurisdiction. However, communications concerning the results of cases or the reasoning or conduct of the judges who decide them are not ordinarily within the *Lange* freedom. In some exceptional cases, they may be. But when they are, it will be because in some way such communications also concern the acts or omissions of the legislature or the Executive Government.

The distinction between communications concerning the administration of justice that are within the *Lange* freedom and those that are not may sometimes appear to be artificial. But it is a distinction that arises from the origins of the constitutional implication concerning freedom of communication on political and government matters. The *Lange* freedom arises from the necessity to promote and protect representative and responsible government. Because it arises by **[422]** necessity, the freedom is limited to "the extent of the need" [*Board of Fire Commissioners (NSW) v Ardouin* (1961) 109 CLR 105 at 118]. Courts and judges and the exercise of judicial power are not themselves subjects that are involved in representative or responsible government in the constitutional sense. Accordingly, the advertisements that the Regulation prohibits are not themselves communications concerning *government* for the purpose of the freedom identified in *Lange*.

Nor are they communications concerning "political" matters in the sense referred to in *Lange* ... It may be impossible to formulate an exhaustive definition of the term "political" for the purpose of the constitutional freedom. Indeed, the plaintiffs did not attempt to do so. But the methodology employed by the Court in *Lange* assists in determining whether a communication is "political" for the purposes of the Constitution ...

[*Lange* required] a relationship of necessity between the provisions giving rise to the freedom and the communication to be protected. The provisions that the Court identified as giving rise to an implied freedom of communication necessitate some level of communicative freedom in Australian society about matters relevant to executive responsibility and an informed electoral choice ... The requirement of necessity indicates that the communication must bear a close relationship to the Ch I, II and VIII sections from which the protection flows ...

No doubt communications about the desirability of regulations prohibiting or curtailing the ability of lawyers to advertise their services ensure that voters are informed about government policies that affect their access to such information. They are communications for the purpose of the *Lange* doctrine. So also are communications that inform the public about government policies affecting the capacity and opportunity of individuals to enforce their legal rights ... But so far as the communications relied on in this case are concerned, only that part of the advertisement referring to "Premier Bob Carr and Senator Helen Coonan" **[423]** concerns political or governmental matters within the meaning of *Lange*. The rest of that advertisement concerns matters that fall outside the protection of *Lange*. That part of the advertisement which concerns political matter is not so intertwined with non-protected matter that it cannot be severed from it.

Both McHugh and Kirby JJ accepted the plaintiffs' alternative argument based on Ch III of the Constitution: namely, that Ch III "**[423]** requires for its effective operation that the people of the Commonwealth have the capacity, ability or freedom to ascertain their legal rights and to assert those legal rights before the courts there mentioned", and hence that they have "the capacity or ability or freedom ... to receive such information or assistance as they may reasonably require for that to occur". The five majority judges rejected this argument also. In doing so, however, they focused narrowly on whether Ch III gives rise to an implication specifically protecting the freedom of lawyers to advertise their services to prospective clients. Analytically, the rejection of an implication framed in those terms says nothing about the validity or otherwise of an implication like that considered (and rejected) by the New South Wales Court of Appeal in *John Fairfax Publications Pty Ltd v O'Shane*.

Gleeson CJ and Heydon J: [413] The rule of law is one of the assumptions upon which the Constitution is based. It is an assumption upon which the Constitution depends for its efficacy. Chapter III of the Constitution ... gives practical effect to that assumption. The effective exercise of judicial power, and the maintenance of the rule of law, depend upon the providing of professional legal services so that citizens may know their rights and obligations, and have the capacity to invoke judicial power. [However, the] regulations in question are not directed towards the providing by lawyers of services to their clients. They are directed towards the marketing of their services by lawyers to people who, by hypothesis, are not their clients.

The question for this Court is not whether the uninhibited promotion of legal services will increase what is sometimes described as access to justice. **[414]** There are policy arguments for and against allowing lawyers to advertise. One argument in favour of such advertising is that it makes legal services more accessible to some citizens, and thereby increases awareness of rights and assists enforcement of rights. We are concerned, however, not with such questions of policy, but with a legal question which is to be resolved, not as a matter of opinion or personal preference, but as a matter of judgment upon a defined issue.

State and Territory schemes of regulation of the legal profession form part of the context in which federal jurisdiction is exercised, and have an impact upon the practical circumstances in which the rule of law is maintained ... The justification for such regulation is that it is in the public interest. The primary responsibility for deciding where the public interest lies is with the State and Territory legislatures. It is not self-evident that the public interest requires an unrestricted capacity on the part of lawyers to promote their services. More to the point, it is not required by the Constitution. It is a topic on which the Constitution has nothing to say in express terms. If it is said to be a matter of implication, then it is necessary to identify, with reasonable precision, the suggested implication. This has not been done.

There is nothing in the text or structure of the Constitution, or in the nature of judicial power, which requires that lawyers must be able to advertise their services. It may or may not be thought desirable, but it is not necessary.

The regulations in question do not impede communications between lawyers and their clients. Nor do they restrain or inhibit the provision of legal services, or require lawyers to conceal their existence or their identities. Professional directories, and telephone books, inform the public of the availability of legal services.

The effective exercise of the judicial power conferred by Ch III of the Constitution does not depend upon unrestricted communication between the public and anyone willing to provide advice or assistance in enforcing claims or rights. If it did, the laws which confer upon lawyers what amounts to a practical monopoly in the provision of legal services would be invalid. The practitioners who now complain that they cannot advertise as freely as they wish appear to overlook the fact that the regulatory system, of which the advertising restrictions are a part, imposes much wider restrictions on the providing of advice and assistance by people (who may or may not be lawyers) who are not legal practitioners. If Ch III required unrestricted communication, then people like the migration agents considered in *Cunliffe* would also be able to advertise, and provide, legal services.

The judgments of Gummow, Hayne and Callinan JJ all explored the methodology by which constitutional implications may legitimately be drawn. For example, Callinan J insisted that any legitimate implication must be "necessary", by analogy with the rules laid down in *Codelfa Construction Pty Ltd v State Rail Authority of NSW* (1982) 149 CLR 337 for finding implied terms in a contract. In that case Mason J, citing cases like *The Moorcock* (1889) 14 PD 64, had said that "**[346]** it is not enough that it is reasonable to imply a term; it must be *necessary* to do so to give business efficacy to the contract" (emphasis added). On that basis Callinan J said:

Callinan J: [524] There is no express provision of Ch III of the Constitution which in any way deals with, or even remotely touches upon advertising by lawyers (whether engaged in practice for profit or upon a non-profit basis) to solicit clients.

In construing Ch III of the Constitution, and in particular, in accepting invitations from parties before it to search for implications from the Chapter it is as well for this Court to keep these matters in mind. The objects of Ch III are essentially these and these only: to establish this Court as a

Federal Supreme Court; to ensure the independence and security of tenure of federal judges; to define the original and appellate jurisdiction of this Court; to recognise and necessarily thereby to "constitutionalise" the continued existence of, the State Supreme Courts; to confine appeals to the Privy Council; to empower the Parliament to make laws conferring rights to proceed in federal matters in the State and other federal courts; and to entrench trial by jury for federal indictable offences. The provisions of Ch III are, on their face, ample, explicit, concrete and clear, complete, and not such as to *necessitate* amplification by implication or otherwise. In *Kable v Director of Public Prosecutions (NSW)* [(1996) 189 CLR 51] this Court took the view that legislation detracting from the integrity, independence and impartiality of the Supreme **[525]** Court of New South Wales as a court invested with federal jurisdiction, was incompatible with Ch III. That was tantamount to a holding that there should be inferred from Ch III an implication that non-judicial powers of a particular kind could not be exercised by any court which might exercise federal jurisdiction. That seems to me, with respect, to require the drawing of a very long bow. I would be unwilling to stretch the bow any further ...

The particular, indeed rigorous, application of the "necessity rule" to the Australian Constitution is required by reason of a number of features unique to our Constitution and its composition: the prolonged and fully recorded debates and deliberations preceding it to which modern lawyers have ready access and which show clearly, in most instances, why proposals were adopted or discarded; the substantial public acceptance in Australia of the Constitution before its passage through the Parliament of the United Kingdom; its generally comprehensive and explicit language; the availability of one, and one only **[526]** mechanism for its amendment, a referendum under s 128; the reluctance, in many referenda of the people of Australia to change it; and, despite the last its enduring efficacy.

A case of this kind, in which the question posed [is], among other things, as to the expansiveness of the power of the Court itself, and the impact of its decisions upon the respective polities of the Federation, is an occasion for especial caution and restraint.

In substance, the plaintiffs seek to set up in respect of Ch III an implication of the kind found by this Court in *Lange*. When it came to the point they had even more difficulty in formulating the implication contended for and in defining the sorts of circumstances attracting its application, than the courts have had in the cases since *Lange* ...

I cannot imagine that the prohibition of advertisements or letters of the kind proposed could in any way impair or inhibit the effective operation of Ch III of the Constitution. Restriction upon them does nothing to prevent the recognition and enforcement of rights under federal law or against the Commonwealth Executive. The contested provisions deal with a different topic, the banning or regulation of a particular form of advertising by particular people. They apply to barristers and solicitors only. Absent the prohibited communications the work of the courts will continue to be done in an uninhibited way and in the ordinary course. People with federal claims will remain free to pursue them and to engage whom they wish to do so on their behalf. The contested provisions do nothing to detract from the effective operation of Ch III of the Constitution.

By contrast, both Gummow and Hayne JJ were initially inclined to reject any rigid test of "necessity", though Hayne J seemed later to revert to that test. Nor did either of them accept a rigid dichotomy between "text" and "structure" as alternative sources of implications. Instead, Gummow J (at 462) adopted a test proposed in the *Boilermakers' Case* (1956) 94 CLR 254: "**[278]** What belongs to the judicial power or is incidental or ancillary to it cannot be determined except by ascertaining if it has a *sufficient relation* to the principal or judicial function or purpose to which it may be thought to be accessory" (emphasis added).

Similarly, Hayne J (at 499) was initially content to work with the formulation by Mason CJ, in *Australian Capital Television v Commonwealth* (1992) 177 CLR 106, that "**[134]** any implication must be securely based". Later, however, he said:

Hayne J: [500] The implication alleged ... concerns what is said to be a *freedom* to *receive* advice or information about the *possible* exercise of the judicial power of the Commonwealth; it is not an implication concerned with the invocation or exercise of that judicial power.

The way in which the alleged implication is described is important. It is said to be a freedom to receive advice or information. The subject of the advice or information which it is said that the legislatures may not inhibit is advice or information which may lead the recipient to engage the judicial power of the Commonwealth. There is, therefore, a wide gap between the subject of the alleged freedom and the matters with which Ch III of the Constitution deals …

The implication which the plaintiffs seek to have drawn in this case is one which was said to be *necessary* to permit the "effective" exercise of resort to federal jurisdiction. The plaintiffs submitted that only if citizens were informed of the possibility that they may have rights which could be vindicated in federal jurisdiction would they seek to enforce those rights. And, so the argument proceeded, because the avowed aim of the impugned regulations was to "counteract the trend to excessive litigation", the impugned regulations interfered with or inhibited the vindication of rights by resort to federal jurisdiction.

If the premise for this argument is valid, the subsequent steps in reasoning may follow. But these subsequent steps would follow just as much from a premise expressed in terms of what is *desirable*, as distinct from *necessary*, to permit "*effective*" exercise of federal jurisdiction. What must be tested is the validity of the premise from which the argument proceeds, namely, that the implication is necessary. What aspect of constitutional text or structure supports the asserted implication of a freedom to *receive* advice or information which *may* lead the recipient to engage the judicial power of the Commonwealth? The plaintiffs point only to matters that may make the asserted freedom desirable. They point to no matter making it a necessary consequence of constitutional text or structure.

That is most easily demonstrated by pointing to what the impugned regulations do *not* do. The impugned regulations do not preclude the seeking of advice or information about whether to invoke the judicial power of the Commonwealth. They concern only a prior step of conveying information (which is either unsolicited or not addressed to any particular recipient) which may provoke a recipient to seek advice or information …

[501] The impugned regulations focus on steps that are at least one step removed from seeking to engage the judicial power of the Commonwealth. The implication which it is sought to draw from the Constitution, and Ch III in particular, must, therefore, be one that is itself removed a similar distance from the subject-matter of Ch III. That is why it is expressed as an implied freedom to *receive* (as distinct from give) advice or information that may (but need not) lead a recipient to engage the judicial power of the Commonwealth. But that mode of expression reveals the distance that lies between the content of Ch III and the content of the asserted implication. There is no basis in constitutional text or structure to bridge that gap.

The apparent conflict of views in these judgments as to whether a proposed implication must satisfy a test of "necessity" may to some extent reflect semantic cross-purposes. In *McCulloch v Maryland*, 17 US (4 Wheat) 316 (1819), Marshall CJ had argued that, in the context of the "necessary and proper" clause of the United States Constitution (Art I, §8, cl 18), the word "necessary" did not mean "absolutely necessary", but was used in the weaker sense suggested by its association with the word "proper" (see Chapter 7, §6); and in *Mulholland v Australian Electoral Commission* Gleeson CJ suggested that, throughout the history of Australian constitutional discourse, the word "necessary" had always been used in a correspondingly weaker sense (see §5 below). At least some of the uses of "necessary" in *APLA* should be read with that suggestion in mind.

In any event, the argument that an implication from Ch III could protect the plaintiffs' advertisements was accepted only by the dissenting judgments of McHugh and Kirby JJ.

McHugh J: [425] The plaintiffs pointed out that their advertisements and communications are not confined to matters of State law. They concern "matters" that arise under federal law … As a result, cl 139 prohibits advertisements concerning causes of action – "matters" – that involve or could involve the exercise of federal jurisdiction and the exercise of federal judicial power. Indeed, the argument for New South Wales candidly conceded that the Regulation was part of a package of legislative reforms whose object was to reduce litigation in respect of personal injury.

So the questions of constitutional principle that arise in this part of the case are whether, consistently with Ch III, a State can legislate to reduce litigation in federal jurisdiction or legislate to impair the capacity or opportunity of a person to receive offers of legal assistance concerning the availability or enforcement of causes of action in federal jurisdiction ...

[426] In accordance with its powers under ss 75, 76 and 77 of the Constitution, the Parliament of the Commonwealth has legislated for causes of action, advertising in respect of which the Regulation prohibits. That is to say, the State of New South Wales seeks to prohibit certain communications concerning the existence or potential existence of certain classes of federal causes of action with the object of reducing litigation in respect of personal injury. In my view, a State has no more power to interfere with such communications – with or without that object – than it has to prevent newspapers reporting cases in federal courts or lawyers acting for parties in federal jurisdiction or to abolish legal professional privilege in respect of federal matters ...[T]he provision of legal advice and information concerning federal law should be seen as indispensable to the exercise of the judicial power of the Commonwealth and protected by Ch III rather than the freedom identified in *Lange* ...

[427] Communications between legal practitioner and client, between legal practitioners, and between judges and practitioners, are critical to the administration of justice in Australia. They make up part of the essential elements of judicial processes required under the Constitution, without which proceedings in federal jurisdiction would become a mockery of the judicial system contemplated by Ch III. And, without communications between legal practitioners and potential litigants, the number of actions brought in federal jurisdiction would be greatly reduced. It is impossible to accept therefore that Ch III raises no barrier to State legislation interfering with or impairing such communications. The argument of New South Wales and others appeared to accept that the States could not interfere with these communications. But they contended that the Regulation operated before any relationship of practitioner and client had formed and Ch III had been engaged.

This was an argument that might have appealed 40 years ago when this Court tested constitutional validity by examining only the legal operation of impugned legislation and ignoring its social and practical effect. But at least since the decision in *North Eastern Dairy Co Ltd v Dairy Industry Authority of NSW* [(1975) 134 CLR 559] the Court has consistently rejected that approach ... **[428]** The legal criteria of liability expressed in impugned legislation do not determine its constitutional validity. Validity is determined after examining "the nature and quality of the restriction in the light of the known and proved economic social and other circumstances of its imposition and of the community in which it is imposed" [134 CLR at 624].

To hold that Ch III protects a communication between a lawyer and a lay person immediately after the lawyer was retained to act but not one made immediately before the formal retainer was created would allow form to triumph over substance. Moreover, in practice the formal client-lawyer relationship is frequently created only after the lawyer has had a preliminary consultation with the client. The protection that Ch III gives to communications between litigants and potential litigants and lawyers does not depend on the existence of retainers but on communications made by lawyers to persons with potential federal rights or obligations. Nor does it depend on the lay person seeking out the lawyer. The communications protected by Ch III are not limited to those made after a retainer has been created or the lay person has consulted the lawyer.

Clause 139 prevents potential litigants from obtaining information about their rights in respect of certain federal causes of action and about the legal practitioners who might provide appropriate advice and representation (even on a *pro bono* basis) concerning those rights. It thus impairs the capacity of courts exercising federal jurisdiction to hear and determine "matters" that Ch III authorises and for which the Parliament has legislated in the expectation that those "matters" will be determined in federal jurisdiction ... Clause 139 therefore violates the principles that inhere in Ch III. It also violates the principle inherent in Ch III that persons who have rights under federal law may enforce them in federal jurisdiction with the advice and assistance of qualified legal practitioners in accordance with the traditional judicial process. It does so because cl 139 impairs the capacity of persons with federal rights in respect of certain matters to obtain legal advice and representation in respect of those rights, if indeed it does not prevent them from doing so ... Moreover, the object and the effect of the Regulation is to reduce litigation in respect of personal injury. The Regulation does not differentiate between litigation in State jurisdiction and litigation in federal jurisdiction. Its object and its effect is to reduce litigation in respect of personal injury whatever the source of the right to sue for such injury and whatever the court that has jurisdiction to enforce the right. Thus the Regulation has the object and the effect of reducing litigation in federal jurisdiction. In my opinion, the implications to be drawn from Ch III make it clear that the States have no power to interfere in federal jurisdiction by legislation that has the effect or the object of reducing **[429]** litigation in that jurisdiction ...

It is no answer to the plaintiffs' case on Ch III that, for a long period and until comparatively recently, State laws prohibited legal practitioners from advertising *any of* their services. Perhaps, State legislation having that effect could validly have applied to advertising concerning the availability of legal services in respect of federal matters on the ground that it was a general law necessary to protect State residents and that it only incidentally had an impact on federal jurisdiction. But, however that may be, a blanket prohibition on lawyers' advertising in respect of all causes of action and legal matters stands in a different category to legislation that permits advertising by lawyers but prohibits the advertising of services in respect of a narrow class of federal and State rights. A narrow law of that type has an impact only on some available federal causes, is intended to have an impact on them and cannot be justified on the basis that the community needs protection from all advertising by lawyers. No doubt the Parliament of the Commonwealth, acting under the powers conferred by Ch III and s 51(xxxix), may regulate advertising by lawyers in respect of "matters" arising in federal jurisdiction. But what is open to the Parliament under powers expressly granted to it is not open to the States so far as federal jurisdiction is concerned.

Kirby J: **[488]** *Lange* is not a constitutional add-on, limited to the law of defamation or political speech. It is not a looseleaf supplement to those legal topics. It is a decision that states a constitutional implication and a methodology for its application. By its nature, that application could not be confined to protecting Chs I and II of the Constitution. Necessarily, the principle – and the holding – in *Lange* also extend to protecting Ch III and the Judicature for which it provides ... Communication about access to courts is communication about governmental and political matters. The courts are part of government. They resolve issues that are, in the broad sense, political ...

A high level of unimpeded communication is essential to the contemplated operation of Ch I and Ch II of the Constitution. But it is also essential, and for the same reasons, to the contemplated operation of Ch III. In principle, there can be no distinction in the applicable constitutional rule.

[I]t would be inconsistent with the operation of Ch III of the Constitution for a State law to be enacted that **[489]** prohibited, or disproportionately impeded, the publication or availability of federal statutory or subordinate legislation. Similarly, a State law attempting to interfere with, or restrict, the availability of judicial reasons of federal courts or rulings of federal tribunals would trigger the twofold test. So would a State law purporting to impose restrictions on the open performance by the courts of their functions, or on communications by news media, civil society organisations and individuals of information on all such courts (or tribunals) and their doings. In every case, laws of such a kind, to the extent that they effectively burdened freedom of communication about the Judicature, its performance and the laws it applies, would have to run the dual constitutional gauntlet ...

[T]he constitutional hypothesis of the rule of law ... lies at the heart of the Judicature provided for in the Constitution. Attempts by law to alter, impair or detract from that hypothesis immediately invite consideration of the prescriptions necessarily implied in Ch III of the Constitution. In short, just as lawmakers (including judges expressing the common law) cannot impede communication disproportionately so as to undermine the contemplated operations of a representative democracy and accountable executive expressed and implied in the institutions referred to in Ch I and Ch II of the Constitution, so they cannot impede the level of communication essential to the operation of the Judicature provided for in Ch III. Even if this Court were to confine *Lange* to a principle protective of communications about the legislature and the executive, a separate implication of similar or identical scope would arise to protect communications necessary to the operation of the Judicature provided for in Ch III of the Constitution ...

[492] Clearly, the Regulation ... burdens the freedom of communication about the integrated Australian Judicature in ways relevant to the purpose, functions and utility of the courts in

Australia ... By placing obstacles in the way of communications concerning the existence of federal causes of action, their availability in particular cases, how advice might be obtained about their application and support given to render them a reality, the lawmaker has impermissibly intruded into communications essential to the operation of federal courts and tribunals. This has been done in a way that limits the freedom of communication essential to the operation of the judicial branch of government. In this way, the first of the tests adapted from this Court's decision in *Lange* is satisfied.

When it comes to the re-worded second test in *Lange*, the answer is also clear. The impugned law is not "reasonably appropriate and adapted" to serve a legitimate end in a manner which is compatible with the maintenance of the constitutionally prescribed system of courts, nor proportional to the operation of such courts as Ch III implies they will operate. Part 14 of the Regulation is undiscriminating as between federal and State causes. It overreaches what might have been reasonably appropriate and adapted to serve the declared end of this particular State lawmaking. It is seriously disproportionate to any legitimate purposes of State law. It accepts that causes of action exist, including under federal law, affording individuals rights, privileges and remedies including in respect of personal injuries. It then attempts to forbid the defined legal **[493]** practitioners and others from telling those affected about such entitlements and how, in proper cases, they can be pursued in courts of the Australian Judicature, or in federal tribunals ... It deliberately attempts to prevent, or reduce, access to such courts (and tribunals). To this end, it imposes a special burden on the poor, the disadvantaged and the vulnerable who rely on a level of freedom of communication for knowledge and pursuit of their legal rights. It is all very well for corporations and the wealthy to see a lawyer if they wish to ascertain their legal rights. Many Australians cannot afford to do this. They do not know where to start.

APLA v Legal Services Commissioner was decided on 1 September 2005. Three days earlier, at Monash University, Justice Ronald Sackville of the Federal Court of Australia delivered the 13th annual Lucinda Lecture (which is published each year in the *Monash University Law Review*).

Ronald Sackville, "How Fragile are the Courts? Freedom of Speech and Criticism of the Judiciary"
(Speech delivered at Monash University, 29 August 2005)

[24] The current trend of authority reflects the longstanding belief that the judiciary requires special protection, when compared with other institutions of government, in order to maintain public confidence in the legal system. That belief, however, has always rested on dubious assumptions rather than solid empirical evidence. Other jurisdictions, like Canada, the European Union and South Africa, while not adopting the First Amendment jurisprudence of the United States, have modified common law or traditional principles in the interests of protecting freedom of speech. Their actions do not seem to have prompted any crises of community confidence in the judiciary of those countries.

[25] The fact is that judicial power is 'an element of the government of society' and the judicial branch is the 'third great department of government'. Although the court in *John Fairfax v O'Shane* appeared to doubt whether freedom of the press is a means of making the court accountable to the broader community, the proposition is hard to dispute. It is true that mechanisms adopted by the courts themselves, such as the appellate process and the concept of open justice, are extremely important for ensuring that the Judiciary is 'accountable'. But these are not the only mechanisms appropriate to a democratic society. Criticism of the courts often goes beyond matters that can be tested on an appeal. In any event, the perspectives informing the approach of an appellate court are not the only ones deserving of a public airing.

The work of the courts may be as relevant to the informed judgment of electors as the actions of elected representatives or public officials. This is so notwithstanding that the courts are and must remain independent of other branches of government. Unlike elected representatives, judicial officers are not answerable to the electors for their decisions in particular cases. Yet judicial decisions are not only frequently based on policy considerations in respect of which members of the community will have strongly divergent views, but they may impinge directly upon the program of the elected government of the day. Court decisions may also be intensely controversial and generate proposals for responses or changes through the political process. Even the day-to-day work of the courts can be of profound political importance. Criminal sentencing, for example, is frequently the subject of passionate community discussion and debate. More specifically, criticism of individual decisions or of the conduct of particular judicial officers, may directly bear on the appointments made by the executive government or the selection procedures followed by the government ...

[26] The ambivalent position of the judiciary under the *Lange* principle is a consequence of the limited nature of the implied freedom of political communication recognised by the High Court. Yet it is very difficult, from a policy perspective, to justify placing courts in a separate and privileged category so far as protection from unjustified criticism is concerned. Moreover, if the High Court endorses the current trend of authority, the courts will be open to the charge that they have awarded themselves an immunity that is difficult to justify and is likely to prove counter-productive to the values they have repeatedly espoused.

This is not to say the courts should be bereft of powers that are capable of being used in the rare cases misconceived verbal attacks pose a genuine threat to the standing of the judiciary. These powers ... might involve the High Court relying on the *Lange* principle to set a much higher threshold for conduct amounting to scandalising contempt. Similarly, there is no reason in principle why individual judges should enjoy fewer avenues for redress of unjustified attacks on their reputation than elected representatives or public officials. But the independence of the judiciary does not justify conferring on judges greater protection than that enjoyed by elected representatives or public officials.

It is to be hoped that the High Court will interpret the scope of the implied freedom of communication more broadly than recent decisions might suggest. If the High Court does not do so, there is a strong case for legislation to bring the principles governing criticism of the Australian judiciary into line with those of other liberal democracies.

The possibility that public discussion of judicial processes, decisions and institutions might be constitutionally protected, whether by the *Lange* principle or by an analogous implication from Ch III, was not specifically addressed (and is therefore not specifically excluded) by the majority judgments in *APLA*. Nevertheless, those who share the hopes expressed by Sackville J in his Lucinda lecture are unlikely to find those judgments encouraging.

5. The Test for Invalidity

Lange posed two questions in determining whether a law is invalid due to the implied freedom:

1. "[567] First, does the law effectively burden freedom of communication about government or political matters either in its terms, operation or effect?"

2. "Second, if the law effectively burdens that freedom, is the law reasonably appropriate and adapted to serve a legitimate end *in a manner* which is compatible with the maintenance of the constitutionally prescribed system of representative and responsible government and the procedure prescribed by s 128 for submitting a proposed amendment of the Constitution to the informed decision of the people"? The words in italics give effect to the modification accepted by a majority of the High Court in *Coleman v Power*.

Uncertainty remains about several aspects of this test. For example, as the recent cases reviewed in this chapter suggest, the precise scope of "government or political matters" is likely to be worked out progressively over time on a case-by-case basis. However, it is the second question that continues to provoke the greatest doubt.

In the earlier cases, judges contemplated that different legislative purposes might attract different levels of scrutiny. In particular, Mason CJ distinguished in *Australian Capital Television Pty Ltd v Commonwealth* (1992) 177 CLR 106 between "[143] restrictions on communication which target ideas or information and those which restrict an activity or mode of communication by which ideas or information are transmitted", while McHugh J distinguished "[234] between laws which restrict the freedom of electoral communications by **[235]** prohibiting or regulating their contents and laws which incidentally limit that freedom". Each judge suggested that laws in the former category required a "compelling justification".

On one view, such distinctions were swept away by the *Lange* formulation, which is therefore to be understood as a general all-purpose test. On another view, laws that directly target "ideas or information" or restrict the "contents" of communication are covered by the rider to the second limb of the *Lange* test, in a way which the modification in *Coleman v Power* might perhaps seem to obscure: namely, the requirement in *Lange* that the legislative purpose, as well as the means, must be "**[567]** compatible with the maintenance of the constitutionally prescribed system of representative and responsible government". For laws that directly seek to restrict the "contents" of political communication, this compatibility might be difficult to establish.

On another view, the *Lange* test might be understood merely as supplanting or explaining the "proportionality" test that Mason CJ considered appropriate for laws in his second category. On that view, the higher level of scrutiny required for laws in the first category remains untouched by *Lange*. Passages in *Levy v Victoria* (1997) 189 CLR 579 appear to assume that this view is correct. For example, after quoting from *Australian Capital Television*, Gaudron J reasserted her own conception of two distinct levels of scrutiny: a law whose "**[619]** direct purpose ... is to restrict political communication" will be "valid only if necessary for the attainment of some overriding public purpose", while for laws directed to some other purpose whose attainment "incidentally restricts political communication" she used the "appropriate and adapted" test. Again, after reciting the *Lange* test as "**[647]** the test to be applied", Kirby J noted that *Levy* was not "a case where the legislation has, by its terms, specifically targeted the idea or message so as to require a 'compelling justification'." In *Mulholland v Australian Electoral Commission* (2004) 220 CLR 181, Gleeson CJ also accepted that for such a law there must be "**[200]** close scrutiny, congruent with a search for 'compelling justification'."

Amidst the uncertainty as to the proper occasion for use of the "proportionality" test, its precise operation and its difference (if any) from the test of "appropriate and adapted", the distinction drawn by Mason CJ and Gaudron J in *Cunliffe v Commonwealth* (1994) 182 CLR 272 continues to offer useful guidance. As Gaudron J put it, when "proportionality" is invoked as an aid to characterisation (that is, as a test of whether an impugned law has a sufficient purposive connection with the positive grant of legislative power relied on), the test is "**[388]** whether the law *is reasonably capable of being viewed as* appropriate and adapted to achieving the purpose in question" (emphasis added). By contrast, when the Court is policing an express or implied constitutional limitation on the exercise of legislative power, the test of validity for a law encroaching on the constitutionally protected area is "whether the law *is* reasonably appropriate and adapted to the relevant purpose" (emphasis in original). The former test, conformably to the High Court's general approach to questions of characterisation, allows for deference to the legislative judgment so long as that judgment "is reasonably capable of being viewed as appropriate". The latter test asserts that the Court itself must be satisfied that the test of "reasonably appropriate and adapted" has been met.

One virtue of this distinction is its clear differentiation between the use of such tests as an aid to characterisation, and their use in the context of judicial protection for express or implied constitutional freedoms. In practice, however, this differentiation is repeatedly blurred. For example, in several cases on the freedom of political communication, Commonwealth and State Solicitors-General have attempted to persuade the Court that the test should be framed in the more permissive terms used by Gaudron J in the context of characterisation. We have seen in §2 above that in *Coleman v Power* Gleeson CJ, McHugh, Gummow, Kirby and Hayne JJ all rejected this attempt, though Heydon J, in a footnote to his judgment at 122n, left the issue open.

When the argument was advanced again in *Mulholland*, Heydon J again asserted in a footnote that the preferable formulation did not need to be determined, "**[305 n453]** since, on any available construction of the test, and on any available way of applying it, the appellant must fail". He noted, however, that in *Street v Queensland Bar Association* (1989) 168 CLR 461, in the context of identifying the "discrimination" forbidden by s 117 of the Constitution, Gaudron J had suggested that the test was, as Heydon J put it, "**[303]** whether the different treatment is reasonably capable of being seen as appropriate and adapted to a relevant difference".

On the other hand, Kirby J, while renewing in *Mulholland* the attack on the expression "appropriate and adapted" that he had mounted in *Coleman v Power*, spoke of "reasonably capable of being regarded by the Parliament as appropriate and adapted" as an "**[251]** even more ungainly phrase", and added: "[T]hat criterion has never been adopted by a majority of this Court. We should not do so now. It involves an impermissible transference to legislatures of the power, in effect, to define the limits of legislative powers. This is contrary to the basic design of the Australian Constitution, which reserves such questions, ultimately, to **[252]** this Court. It is also disharmonious with the rule of law implicit in the Constitution".

The appellant in *Mulholland* had argued *both* that the impugned provisions of the *Commonwealth Electoral Act 1918* (Cth) were not within power, *and* that they impermissibly impaired the implied constitutional freedom. Kirby J applied the same test of "proportionality" to both of these issues as a single all-purpose test.

Mulholland v Australian Electoral Commission
(2004) 220 CLR 181

Kirby J: [252] The Full Court confined itself to the cumbrous obscurity of verbal variations on the theme of "appropriate and adapted". Unpleasant and formulaic as it may be for judges subject to this Court's authority to have to use such expressions to explain the existence of an essential connection between a constitutional source of power and the law propounded under it, it is understandable that they invoke that formula. For ourselves, we should strive to do better: adopting an explanation of constitutional connection that is clearer and more informative ...

[266] The ungainly and unedifying phrase "appropriate and adapted", used to explain the essential link between an impugned law and its constitutional source of power, appears to have had its origin in the reasons of Marshall CJ in *McCulloch v Maryland* [17 US (4 Wheat) 316 at 421 (1819)] It is a phrase inappropriate and ill-adapted to perform the constitutional function repeatedly assigned to it by members of this Court.

The word "appropriate" is inapt because, within a given constitutional remit, it is for the Parliament (and not a court) to say whether a law is "appropriate" or "inappropriate". Appropriateness, of its nature, imports notions of political degree and judgment which normally belong to legislators, not to judges. Similarly, "adapted" is a verb signifying modification and adjustment in detail: also usually the business of legislators. In so far as the composite phrase is made still further obscure by prefacing it with a description of the law as one "capable of being reasonably considered to be" appropriate and adapted, it is subject to added objections. That phrase risks diverting judgment from the particular law and surrendering the constitutional mandate with which the courts are charged to the assessment of the Parliament or the Executive. I will continue to protest against the continued use by this Court of such an unsatisfactory and ugly expression to explain what it is doing in the cases where the issue of constitutional power is invoked.

A more accurate explanation of the constitutional connection in such cases is found in the word "proportionality". That word has long been used by individual judges. Some have used it as an explanation of the limits of the "appropriate and adapted" test. For example, in *McKinlay* [(1975) 135 CLR 1 at 61] Mason J was prepared to accept that it was "perhaps conceivable that variations in the numbers of electors or people in single member electorates could become so grossly *disproportionate* as to raise a question whether an election held on boundaries so drawn would produce a House of Representatives composed of members directly chosen by the people of the Commonwealth" as the Constitution requires. The word was there used in a context that acknowledged the limits of the constitutional phrase in imposing a requirement of practical equality of electors in federal electorates. Mason J was addressing the extreme perimeter of constitutional power. "Disproportionate" was taken as a description of a law that exceeded **[267]** the permissible boundary ...

Mason J and Deane J were the progenitors in this Court of the more general use of "proportionality" in constitutional discourse. Following their lead, other judges have treated the notion as equivalent to the "appropriate and adapted" test, at least in certain circumstances. I mentioned these developments in *Levy v Victoria* [(1997) 189 CLR 579 at 645], suggesting that proportionality represented a useful description of the actual process of constitutional reasoning. I remain of that view.

In its unanimous decision in *Lange* [(1997) 189 CLR 520 at 567n] this Court noted that, in the context there considered, "there is little difference between the test of 'reasonably appropriate and adapted' and the test of proportionality". No word or phrase exists that fully explains the evaluative function of judgment involved in constitutional characterisation where a court is deciding the limits of constitutional power having regard to the competing considerations of the text and implications that lend scope to, or impose restrictions on the ambit of the power in question. Nevertheless, the notion of proportionality has important advantages over other formulae. This is especially so where (as here) the constitutional powers in issue are of a purposive character, namely powers afforded for the purpose of providing for the conduct of elections to the Federal Parliament.

On all of these terminological issues, Gleeson CJ was more permissive.

Gleeson CJ: [197] Whichever expression is used, what is important is the substance of the idea it is intended to convey. Judicial review of legislative action, for the purpose of deciding whether it conforms to the limitations on power imposed by the Constitution, does not involve the substitution of the opinions of judges for those of legislators upon contestable issues of policy. When this Court declares legislation to be beyond power, or to infringe some freedom required by the Constitution to be respected, it applies an external standard. Individual judgments as to the application of that standard may differ, but differences of judicial opinion about the application of a constitutional standard do not imply that the Constitution means what judges want it to mean, or that the Constitution says what judges would prefer it to say.

There are criticisms that can be made of both expressions, "reasonably appropriate and adapted", and "proportionality". It is to be noted, however, that ... the test stated [in *Lange*] included the question whether the impugned law served "a legitimate end the fulfilment of which is compatible with the maintenance of the constitutionally prescribed system of representative and responsible government". Identification of the end served by a law, and deciding its compatibility with a system of representative government, is a familiar kind of judicial function. To the extent to which the word "legitimate" means more than "lawful" or "within the scope of the powers of the Parliament" it may not add anything to the requirement of compatibility. For a court to describe a law as reasonably appropriate and adapted to a legitimate end is to use a formula which is intended, among other things, to express the limits between legitimate judicial scrutiny, and illegitimate judicial encroachment upon an area of legislative power.

The concept of proportionality has both the advantage that it is commonly used in other jurisdictions in similar fields of discourse, and the disadvantage that, in the course of such use, it has taken on elaborations that vary in content, and that may be imported *sub silentio* **[198]** into a different context without explanation ...

Human rights legislation, which declares fundamental rights or freedoms but, recognising that they are rarely absolute, permits limits or restrictions provided they can be "demonstrably justified in a free and democratic society", is the context in which current jurisprudence on proportionality is most likely to be seen at work. In *R (Daly) v Secretary of State for the Home Department* [[2001] 2 AC 532 at 547], Lord Steyn said that "[t]he contours of the principle of proportionality are familiar", and ... applied a three-stage test, by which the court should ask itself:

> "whether: (i) the legislative objective is sufficiently important to justify limiting a fundamental right; (ii) the measures designed to **[199]** meet the legislative objective are rationally connected to it; and (iii) the means used to impair the right or freedom are no more than is necessary to accomplish the objective." ...

If the use, in the present context, of a test of "proportionality" were intended to pick up all that content, then it would be important to remember, and allow for the fact, that it has been developed and applied in a significantly different constitutional context ...

There is, in Australia, a long history of judicial and **[200]** legislative use of the term "necessary", not as meaning essential or indispensable, but as meaning reasonably appropriate and adapted. The High Court originally took that from *McCulloch v Maryland*. There is, therefore, also a long history of judicial application of the phrase "reasonably appropriate and adapted". It follows that, when the concept of necessity is invoked in this area of discourse, it may be important to make clear the sense in which it is used, especially if that sense is thought to differ from reasonably appropriate and adapted. Different degrees of scrutiny may be implied by the term "necessary". I have no objection to the use of the term proportionality, provided its meaning is sufficiently explained, and provided such use does not bring with it considerations relevant only to a different constitutional context. Equally, I have no objection to the expression "reasonably appropriate and adapted", which has a long history of application in many aspects of Australian jurisprudence.

6. Movement and Association

Although in *Lange* the freedom of political communication was reaffirmed by a unanimous Court, it was reaffirmed in a version closely tied to the "text or structure" of the Constitution. Consistently with dicta in *McGinty v Western Australia* (1996) 186 CLR 140, it was made clear that neither the Constitution's commitment to freedom of political communication, nor the system of representative government that was said to require that freedom, could be used as a "free-standing principle" (that is, an independent premise for legal reasoning unconfined by reference to what specific provisions of the Constitution are necessarily thought to require).

A similar restriction may confine the development of any other limitations on legislative power thought to be required for the effective operation of "free political discussion" or of "representative government". In *Australian Capital Television*, Gaudron J suggested: "[212] The notion of a free society governed in accordance with the principles of representative parliamentary democracy may entail freedom of movement, freedom of association and, perhaps, freedom of speech generally". Her suggestions as to freedom of movement and of association were grounded in what Murphy J had said in *McGraw-Hinds (Aust) Pty Ltd v Smith* (1979) 144 CLR 633 and in *Miller v TCN Channel Nine Pty Ltd* (1986) 161 CLR 556 (see Chapter 28, §2). However, when these propositions were put to the test in *Kruger v Commonwealth* (*Stolen Generations Case*) (1997) 190 CLR 1, it appeared to be common ground that any implied constitutional protection for freedom of movement or association must be merely ancillary to, and therefore parasitic upon, the freedom of political communication.

On that basis, Gaudron J felt able to hold that the powers conferred by the *Aboriginals Ordinance 1918* (NT), which had authorised the forced removal and institutional detention of Aboriginal children, were unconstitutional. Toohey J, while he did not feel able to determine such an issue on the pleadings, agreed that there was a powerful argument which should go to trial. No other judge took a similar view.

Kruger v Commonwealth (*Stolen Generations Case*)
(1997) 190 CLR 1

Gaudron J: [115] It is clear, and it has been so held, that the fundamental elements of the system of government mandated by the Constitution require that there be freedom of political communication between citizens and their elected representatives and also between citizen and citizen. However, just as communication would be impossible if "each person was an island" [*Nationwide News Pty Ltd v Wills* (1992) 177 CLR 1 at 72], so too it is substantially impeded if citizens are held in enclaves, no matter how large the enclave or congenial its composition. Freedom of political communication depends on human contact and entails at least a significant measure of freedom to associate with others. And freedom of association necessarily entails freedom of movement.

Modern means of communication notwithstanding, freedom of political communication between citizen and citizen and between citizens and their elected representatives entails, at the very least, **[116]** freedom on the part of citizens to associate with those who wish to communicate information and ideas with respect to political matters and those who wish to listen. It also entails the right to communicate with elected representatives who "have a responsibility not only to ascertain the views of the electorate but also to explain and account for their decisions and actions in government and to inform the people so that they may make informed judgments on relevant matters" [*Australian Capital Television v Commonwealth* (1992) 177 CLR 106 at 139].

Again modern methods of communication notwithstanding, freedom of political communication between citizen and citizen and between citizens and their elected representatives entails, at the very least, freedom to move within society, freedom of access to the institutions of government and, as was early recognised in *R v Smithers; Ex parte Benson* [(1912) 16 CLR 99], freedom of access to the seat of government ...

[The power conferred by] s 51 of the Constitution is limited by and subject to the implied freedom of political communication necessary for the maintenance of the system of government for which the Constitution provides. And because freedom of movement and freedom of association are, at least in the respects mentioned, aspects of freedom of political communication, they, too, are implicit in the Constitution and constrain the power conferred by s 51.

Gaudron J conceded that these constraints were not necessarily applicable to laws made for the Territories under s 122, especially since "[117] the system of representative government which the Constitution requires has no application to the Territories". However, she thought that this argument was outweighed by other considerations, including a recognition that "[120] the proper discharge of the responsibility which the people of Australia ultimately bear for the government of the Territories depends on freedom of political communication between them and persons resident in those Territories". On the other hand, she also held that the relevant freedoms were not "absolute", and that ultimately the question must be whether the purpose of the *Aboriginals Ordinance* was "[128] to prohibit or restrict political communication". The Commonwealth had claimed that the Ordinance was valid because it was made "for the purpose of the protection and preservation of persons of the Aboriginal race", and the issue before the Court was whether that plea had constituted an adequate answer to the plaintiffs' claims. Gaudron J held that it had not.

Gaudron J: [126] I have earlier described the freedoms of movement and of association as subsidiary to the freedom of political communication required for the maintenance of the system of representative government for which the Constitution provides. They are subsidiary only in the sense that they support and supplement that latter freedom and not in the sense that they are inferior to or less robust than it. On the contrary, their nature is such that, although ... the test which determines whether or not they have been infringed is the same as that applicable in the case of the implied freedom of political discussion, the circumstances in which a law may validly restrict freedom of movement and discussion are, to some extent, more circumscribed than is the case with the implied freedom of political discussion ... [N]ot every restriction on communication is a restriction on the communication of political ideas and information. On the other hand, any abridgment of the right to move in society and to associate with one's fellow citizens necessarily **[127]** restricts the opportunity to obtain and impart information and ideas with respect to political matters ...

[128] The various formulations in *Australian Capital Television* and in *Nationwide News* point to but one test of a law which restricts political communication; namely, whether the purpose of the law in question is to prohibit or restrict political communication. Questions directed to compelling justification, necessity and proportionality are, at base, questions directed to ascertaining the purpose of the law in question ...

In ascertaining that purpose, a law which is, in terms, a prohibition or restriction on political communication or which operates directly to prevent or curtail discussion of political matters is, in my view, to be taken to have that purpose unless the prohibition or restriction is necessary for the attainment of some overriding public purpose (for example, to prevent criminal conspiracies) or, in terms used by Deane J in *Cunliffe v Commonwealth* [(1994) 182 CLR 272 at 340], to satisfy some "pressing social need" (for example, to prevent sedition). Whether a law is necessary for some such purpose depends on whether it is "no more than is proportionate to the legitimate aim pursued". That in turn depends on whether less drastic measures are available. On the other hand, a law with respect to some subject matter unconnected with the discussion of political matters and which only incidentally impinges on the freedom of that discussion, is not to be taken to be a law for the purpose of restricting that freedom if it is reasonably appropriate and adapted or, which is the same thing, proportionate to some legitimate purpose connected with that other subject matter.

In my view, the test applicable in the case of the implied freedom of political communication is equally applicable to the subsidiary freedoms of movement and association which support that freedom ... Although the test is the same, it may involve different considerations in the sense that the matters of public importance or pressing social need which will justify a law restricting freedom of movement or of association will ordinarily be of a different nature from those which justify a law restricting political communication. **[129]** Similarly, different considerations may be brought into play where the question is one of proportionality.

It is necessary now to turn to the terms and operation of the Ordinance. Sections 6 and 16 conferred powers on the Chief Protector and, later, the Director which, if exercised, operated directly to prevent freedom of movement and of association. Moreover, they were couched in terms directly contrary to those freedoms, s 6 conferring a power to take people into custody and s 16 conferring power to cause Aboriginal people to be "kept within the boundaries of ... reserve[s] or Aboriginal institution[s]". Similarly, the power conferred by s 67(1)(c) to make regulations "enabling any Aboriginal or half-caste child to be sent to and detained in an Aboriginal Institution or Industrial School" permitted regulations which directly prevented freedom of movement and of association. Indeed, it only permitted regulations of that kind. Accordingly, in my view, s 6 (to the extent that it authorised the taking of people into custody), and ss 16 and 67(1)(c) were only valid if necessary for the attainment of some overriding public purpose or for the satisfaction of some pressing social need ...

If it could be said that the Ordinance was necessary for the preservation or protection of Aboriginal people, it would follow that it was valid in its entirety. However, the Commonwealth asserts no such necessity. Moreover, there is no basis on which it could be said that those provisions of the Ordinance which authorised action impairing the rights of Aboriginal people to move in society and to associate with their fellow citizens, including their fellow Aboriginal Australians, were in any way necessary for the protection or preservation of Aboriginal people or, indeed, those Aboriginal people whose rights in that regard were, in fact, curtailed. Certainly, the powers conferred on the Chief Protector and, later, the Director by ss 6 and 16 were not conditioned on any necessity to take Aboriginal people into custody or to keep and detain them in reserves and institutions for their protection or preservation.

Nor were the powers conferred by ss 6 and 16 of the Ordinance conditioned on the formation of an opinion that their exercise was necessary to protect or preserve Aboriginal people. On the contrary, the power conferred by s 16 extended to all Aboriginals, except those falling within the limited categories specified in sub-s (3), and was entirely at large; the exercise of the power conferred by s 6(1) to take people into custody was subject only to the formation of an opinion by the Chief Protector and, later, the Director that it was "necessary or **[130]** desirable in the interests of the Aboriginal or half-caste for him to do so". Interesting questions might have arisen had the power been conditioned on the formation of an opinion that it was necessary to undertake the custody of the person concerned for his or her welfare. However s 6(1) cannot be read in that way. Nor can it be read down to operate in that way: that would be to give it an entirely different operation ...

It follows in my view that s 6, so far as it conferred authority to take people into custody, and ss 16 and 67(1)(c) were at all times invalid.

Toohey J also treated freedom of association as "**[91]** an essential ingredient of political communication", which "necessarily extends to all the people of the Commonwealth". However, he felt unable to make any final assessment of the validity of the *Aboriginals Ordinance* because of the limited nature of the factual materials before the Court.

No other judge thought the issue was open even to this extent. For Dawson J it was sufficient that the freedom of communication, and "**[69]** such other rights to freedom of movement and association as may be suggested", were anchored in "the system of representative government for which the Constitution specifically provides". Accordingly, no such implications could arise for the Territories at all, since "[n]o system of government, elected or otherwise, is prescribed for the

[70] territories". McHugh J held more affirmatively that freedoms of association and travel were necessarily entailed in the operation of the political processes which the Constitution prescribes. However, he agreed with Dawson J that no such implication arose in relation to the Territories.

Brennan CJ and Gummow J held that, even if there were such a limitation on legislative power, the ostensible purposes of the *Aboriginals Ordinance* were not incompatible with it. Accordingly, the question whether such an implication existed was one that neither of them needed to decide. However, both of them made it clear that they would be very cautious about such a conclusion. Brennan CJ observed that: "**[45]** No such right has hitherto been held to be implied in the Constitution and no textual or structural foundation for the implication has been demonstrated in this case". Gummow J held that, despite the acceptance of "**[157]** a system of responsible government and representative government" as "essential elements" of "the structure established by the Constitution", the "logical or practical necessity for the preservation of the integrity of that structure" did not give rise to any implied restriction of federal legislative power relating to freedom of association "in any general sense of that expression".

A claim to a constitutionally protected "freedom of association" (at least for political purposes) was also raised in *Mulholland v Australian Electoral Commission* (2004) 220 CLR 181, where the Democratic Labor Party (DLP) challenged the statutory provisions under which the Australian Electoral Commission could demand to scrutinise its membership lists. Such scrutiny, it was said, impermissibly burdened the freedom of association in its most directly relevant form – namely, the freedom of individuals to form or join a political party. In particular, it would intrude unacceptably on the privacy both of the Party and of its individual members. That privacy was seen as an essential element in the freedom of association, itself seen as a necessary corollary of the implied constitutional freedom of political communication. As to this last-mentioned freedom, however, the Court was unanimous in holding either that it was not "burdened" by the impugned statutory provisions, or that the burden was justified. It followed that any argument based on the freedom or privacy of association met a similar fate.

Mulholland v Australian Electoral Commission
(2004) 220 CLR 181

McHugh J: [225] [In *Australian Capital Television Pty Ltd v Commonwealth* (1992) 177 CLR 106 at 232], I said that the Constitution contains "rights of participation, association and communication" in relation to federal elections but that these rights extend only in so far as they are "identifiable in ss 7 and 24" of the Constitution. In *Kruger v Commonwealth* [(1997) 190 CLR 1], Toohey and Gaudron JJ and I each recognised an implied constitutional freedom of association. Toohey J regarded the freedom of association as "an essential ingredient of political communication" [190 CLR at 91]. Gaudron J said that freedom of association was an aspect of the freedom of political communication that is protected to the extent "necessary for the maintenance of the system of government for which the Constitution provides" [190 CLR at 116]. I said that the Constitution recognises a freedom of association at least for the purposes of the constitutionally prescribed system of government and the referendum procedure.

However, disclosure to the Commission of the names of the members of political parties … does not breach the implied freedom of association. Disclosure of the names of members is simply a condition of entitlement to registration and continued registration as a political party for the purposes of the Act. It is up to the political party which seeks to obtain or maintain registration to decide whether or not to disclose the names of its members. If, for privacy reasons, it does not **[226]** wish to do so, the party is not entitled to the benefits of registration. A political party is not compelled to disclose to the Commission the names and addresses of its members. Accordingly, disclosure of the names of the members of a political party which seeks to obtain or maintain registration under the Act is not a breach of the constitutionally implied freedom of association.

In any event, upon the facts of this case, there appears to be no prospect that the names of members would become available to the general public. Although the Register is open to public inspection under s 139 of the Act, the Register does not disclose the names or other identifying characteristics of members of registered political parties. The Act requires public disclosure of the name and address of the person who is nominated as the registered officer of the party: s 126(2). It does not require public disclosure of the personal details of other members of that party. Nor is the supply to the Commission of the details of membership of the DLP likely to breach the implied freedom of association of those members. The *Privacy Act 1988* (Cth) imposes restraints on the Commission such that the prospect of public disclosure is slight. Furthermore, in so far as the Commission obtains information concerning membership under its statutory powers, the information is of a confidential nature. Equity would restrain any attempt to disclose it.

The claim based on the implied constitutional freedom of political association therefore fails.

Gummow and Hayne JJ agreed. As to the freedom of association, they said: "**[234]** There is no such 'free-standing' right to be implied from the Constitution. A freedom of association to some degree may be a corollary of the freedom of communication formulated in *Lange v Australian Broadcasting Corporation* ... But that gives [it] ... no additional life to that which it may have from a consideration ... of *Lange*". As to the right to privacy, they gave the same answer as McHugh J: the confidentiality provisions would ensure that disclosure of the names of party members to the Electoral Commission did not mean that they would be made public.

Kirby J: [277] [I am] prepared to accept ... that there is implied in ss 7 and 24 of the Constitution a freedom of association and a freedom to participate in federal elections extending to the formation of political parties, community debate about their policies and programmes, the selection of party candidates and the substantially uncontrolled right of association enjoyed by electors to associate with political parties and to communicate about such matters with other electors.

Especially given the express recognition in the amended terms of s 15 of the Constitution of the existence of "particular political part[ies]" in the context of filling casual vacancies in the Senate, it is **[278]** impossible to deny an implication of free association to some degree. At the very least, such a freedom exists in this context to the extent that it is essential to make such "political part[ies]" in s 15 a practical reality.

In so far as the Full Court expressed doubts about the existence of a freedom of association for such purposes, implied in the text of the Constitution, I consider that their Honours were unduly cautious. The logic of this Court's decision upholding freedom of political communication obliges acceptance of protected political association, at least to some extent, so that the constitutional system of representative democracy will be attained as envisaged by Ch I.

Less certain is the scope of any implication of a zone of constitutionally protected privacy in the fulfilment of popular participation in the form of representative government established by the Constitution. Opinions suggesting that the secrecy of the ballot in Australia is not protected by a constitutional implication should not, in my view, be accepted. Given the history of voting privacy in this country, reaching back to colonial times, it is unthinkable that a federal electoral law could now introduce provisions obliging electors to reveal their voting preferences. The experience of other countries where this has occurred suggests that it would constitute a most serious impediment to "direct choice" by the people of their parliamentary representatives.

Voting privacy and privacy in membership of a political party are, however, different in kind. To the extent that an elector takes part, as a member, in the organisation of a "particular political party" of the kind mentioned in the Constitution he or she, to some degree, steps outside the anonymity of citizenship into a more active involvement in the organised electoral system of the nation ...

[O]ne can accept the existence of an implied freedom of political association. Even a measure of implied political privacy, essential to fulfil the constitutional design in voting in federal elections, may be accepted. However, such implications would not necessitate treating those requirements as absolutes ... In each case where a court faces a challenge to infringements of implied constitutional "freedoms", it remains for that court to evaluate whether the burdens imposed by the impugned laws upon the achievement of those freedoms are disproportionate to the attainment of legitimate ends of electoral law, the fulfilment of **[279]** which is compatible with the maintenance of the constitutionally prescribed system of representative government ...

Accepting, as I would, that the provisions of the Act challenged by the appellant burden, to some degree, the implied freedom of political communication and the implied freedom of political association essential for the fulfilment of the constitutional system of representative government, I am unconvinced that such burdens are constitutionally impermissible. They are not disproportionate to the attainment of all of the constitutional objectives operating in this context.

Similarly, to the extent to which there is inherent in the necessity of political association within "particular political part[ies]", as envisaged by the Constitution, any implied constitutional guarantee of privacy (the existence of which I would not finally decide), I reach the same conclusion. The requirements, restrictions and disadvantages imposed on the DLP by the impugned provisions of the Act are real but proportionate to the attainment of legitimate ends chosen by the Parliament. Those ends are compatible with the Constitution.

7. Further References

Arcioni, E, "Developments in Free Speech Law in Australia: Coleman and Mulholland" (2005) 33 *Federal Law Review* 333.

Arcioni, E, "Politics, Police and Proportionality: An Opportunity to Explore the *Lange* Test: *Coleman v Power*" (2003) 25 *Sydney Law Review* 379.

Bronitt, S, and Williams, G, "Political Freedom as an Outlaw: Republican Theory and Political Protest" (1996) 18 *Adelaide Law Review* 289.

Douglas, R, "The Constitutional Freedom to Insult: The Insignificance of *Coleman v Power*" (2005) 16 *Public Law Review* 23.

"Freedom of Speech: Contemporary Issues", Forum (2005) 28 *University of New South Wales Law Journal*.

Lee, HP, "The 'Reasonably Appropriate and Adapted' Test and the Implied Freedom of Political Communication" in Groves, M (ed), *Law and Government in Australia* (Federation Press, 2005), 59.

Meagher, D, "The Protection of Political Communication under the Australian Constitution" (2005) 28 *University of New South Wales Law Journal* 30.

Stone, A, "The Freedom of Political Communication since *Lange*" in Stone, A, and Williams, G (eds), *The High Court at the Crossroads*: *Essays in Constitutional Law* (Federation Press, 2000), 1.

Stone, A, "*Lange*, *Levy* and the Direction of the Freedom of Political Communication under the Australian Constitution" (1998) 21 *University of New South Wales Law Journal* 117.

Stone, A, "The Limits of Constitutional Text and Structure: Standards of Review and the Freedom of Political Communication" (1999) 23 *Melbourne University Law Review* 668.

Twomey, A, "Dead Ducks and Endangered Political Communication – *Levy v State of Victoria* and *Lange v Australian Broadcasting Corporation*" (1997) 19 *Sydney Law Review* 76.

Chapter 30

Constitutional Change

1. Introduction

There have been moves to amend the Australian Constitution almost from its inception. Indeed, the Constitution itself incorporates, in s 128, the referendum mechanism by which it may be changed. However, achieving reform has proved difficult, with the political and other obstacles often proving insurmountable. Since 1901, 44 proposals have been put to the people, with only eight (or 18 per cent) succeeding.

The result is that the Constitution remains almost completely as it was enacted in 1901. By contrast, over 56 per cent of the member States of the United Nations made major changes to their constitutions between 1989 and 1999. Remarkably, of the States making such changes, over 70 per cent adopted a completely new constitution (Heinz Klug, *Constituting Democracy: Law, Globalism and South Africa's Political Reconstruction* (Cambridge University Press, 2000), 12). It is not surprising then that Australia was described even in 1967 as "**[208]** constitutionally speaking ... the frozen continent" (Geoffrey Sawer, *Australian Federalism in the Courts* (Melbourne University Press, 1967)). This is even more applicable today. The last successful vote to change the Constitution was in 1977, when it was amended, among other things, to set a retirement age of 70 years for High Court judges. A further eight, unsuccessful proposals have been put to the people since that time. The period since 1977 is now the longest that Australia has gone without any change to the Constitution (the next longest period was between 1946 and 1967). The political party most often associated with constitutional reform, the Australian Labor Party, has itself not succeeded in having the people support a referendum since 1946.

Despite the difficulty of achieving change, Australians continue to debate a wide array of proposals for constitutional reform, including the ideas of an Australian republic and an Australian Bill of Rights.

2. Amending the Constitution

In "A Government of Laws, and Not of Men?" (1993) 4 *Public Law Review* 158, Justice John Toohey of the High Court referred to the argument that written constitutions create a "**[172]** two-track lawmaking system". Under such a system, "the normal lawmaking path" lies through Parliament, but changes to the Constitution, that is – to "**[173]** the judgments previously made in the higher law accents of We the People" – must go down "a higher lawmaking track". In Australia, this means a referendum under s 128.

Toohey also argued that, where there is "a written constitution which is susceptible to popular amendment", the judicial enforcement of such a constitution, even against an elected legislature, serves the popular will. Where tensions arise, "**[174]** it is the people voting at a referendum who become the ultimate reconcilers". In this way, he sought to counter the argument that the Court, as an unelected, unrepresentative and unaccountable body, should not usurp the popular will by declaring legislation passed by the people's representatives in Parliament to be invalid.

Toohey's answer is only persuasive, however, if the people are able to exercise their ultimate power over the instrument effectively. The insistence in s 128 that "This Constitution shall not be altered except in the following manner" may indeed support a conceptual model of popular sovereignty (see Chapter 4, §9). But if the model does not work, or if "the people" are reluctant or unable to use it, what then?

Amendment of the Constitution is provided for by s 128. To be successful, a proposed law for the alteration of the Constitution must be:

1. passed by an absolute majority of both Houses of the Federal Parliament, or by one House twice; and

2. at a referendum, passed by a majority of the people as a whole, and by a majority of the people in a majority of the states (that is, in at least four of the six States).

If a proposal is passed twice by a Senate not controlled by the government, it need only be put to referendum if the Prime Minister instructs the Governor-General to do so.

Section 128 provides: "When a proposed law is submitted to the electors the vote shall be taken in such manner as the Parliament prescribes". Accordingly, in addition to the requirements in s 128, the referendum procedure is regulated by the *Referendum (Machinery Provisions) Act 1984* (Cth). Section 45 provides that "It is the duty of every elector to vote at a referendum", with a penalty for failing to do so. The Act specifies information to be given to voters: under s 11, the Electoral Commissioner must send each elector a pamphlet showing the proposed amendment to the Constitution, with arguments for and against the proposal of not more than 2000 words each, authorised by members of Parliament on each side of the debate.

The table in the Appendix gives the voting outcomes for each of the 44 proposals to change the Constitution. The figures are difficult to interpret. It might be plausible to suggest that when informal votes exceeded 10 per cent, a rare occurrence, the proposed amendment had been inadequately explained. In some decades, it seems possible to single out particular States as distinctively willing or unwilling to vote "Yes", but some of the State voting patterns have changed over time. For example, New South Wales voted against all but three of the 19 proposals put to 1946, but since then has voted for a majority of the proposed changes (14 out of 25), the only State to do so.

It is sometimes suggested that a difficulty arises from the "majority of States" requirement in s 128, that is, that a majority in a majority of the States must support the proposal. Thus, a proposal at the referendum of 18 May 1974 sought (unsuccessfully) to water this down to a requirement of a majority in only half of the States: that is, in three out of six instead of four out of six. However, it was only in three instances, two on 28 September 1946 and one on 21 May 1977, that this would have made any difference. In fact, in every case where a "Yes" vote prevailed, with the exception of the referendum in 1910 amending s 105, the national majority was accompanied by a "Yes" vote in every State. Rather than the s 128 mechanism itself being the primary source of difficulty, it appears that other factors may be more relevant, including issues of politics, leadership and community education.

Scott Bennett, *The Politics of Constitutional Amendment*
(Parliamentary Research Service, Commonwealth Parliament, Research Paper No 11 2002-03)

[17] The Labor Urge to Reform ...
Labor people were uncertain of the Constitution even before it became law. Federalism was seen as a barrier to social change, hindering central governmental intervention, and making uniform solutions to social problems difficult to achieve. Many would have preferred the creation of a unitary system. As this seemed unlikely to occur, for many decades after Federation Labor politicians called for a marked increase in Commonwealth Government powers ...

[18] From the first years of Federation, then, Labor politicians saw constitutional repair as an important priority, and ALP governments have rarely been prepared to leave the Constitution as they found it. The Fisher Government made eight attempts, in April 1911 and May 1913, the Curtin and Chifley Governments sponsored five attempts between 1944 and 1948, and the Whitlam and Hawke Governments proposed 12 amendments between 1973 and 1988. Labor has been in power for about one-third of the time since 1901, yet has sponsored 57 per cent of the constitutional referenda that have been held.

Significantly, Labor efforts to amend the Constitution have generally sought to bring about major changes, especially in altering the federal balance created by the Founders. This has enabled their opponents to portray the party as Constitution-wreckers ... The consequence of this has been Labor's near-failure to institute constitutional change: just a single success in 25 attempts (four per cent), compared with the conservative parties' successes in seven of 19 attempts (36 per cent). The latter figure has presumably been aided by a general Labor preparedness to support non-Labor proposals ...

Liberal Protection of the Constitution

By contrast, the Liberal Party has projected itself as the protector of a fundamental document that 'has maintained our liberties, national unity in war and depression, the federation and our national independence'. Accordingly, there has been a Liberal determination to preserve the federal system, the British connection and the basic principles of responsible government ... [19] Liberals have usually been opposed to Labor's efforts to amend the Constitution, particularly if such efforts threatened what Menzies called 'the nature and significance of federalism as the dominant factor in the Constitution'.

Politically, the conservative parties have long realised that protection of the Constitution could be used as 'a useful stick with which to beat the socialists'. This view has produced a tendency to warn of the threat posed by Labor to the very nature of government in Australia ... During the 1940s Menzies spoke of Labor's 'contempt for the basic Constitutional instrument', and portrayed the *Rents and Prices* (1948) proposal as one part of Labor's plan of complete socialisation of government and the undermining of the Australian way of life. Labor attempts to alter the Constitution have also been described by their opponents as a 'grab' for power. As former Liberal MP, Peter Shack, put it when criticising the 1988 proposals, 'The hidden agenda is a grab for power by the Federal Government for more power to interfere with our democratic rights, the rights of State and Local Governments and with our rights as individuals'.

Such a tough approach was seen particularly in the Liberal Party's response to the Whitlam Government's reforming urge. At that time the Liberals described the Constitution as an historical compact and charter which formed a fundamental law that ought not lightly be altered. This was not to say that it could not be altered, but changes ought not be rushed, a failing claimed to be common on the Labor side.

This attitude to the Constitution has also seen a conservative party reluctance over the years to propose constitutional amendments. Most notably, during Menzies' record term as Prime Minister, only the security-related issue of *Communists and Communism* (1951) was proposed. Prime Minister Howard's flagging in 2003 of a proposed alteration to the Constitution involving the Senate therefore surprised many observers who believed he shared Menzies' reluctance to tamper with the Constitution ...

[20] Short-Term Views

At various times the parties have seemed to assume that voters have no memories of previous amendment attempts. In regard to Commonwealth control over monopolies, for instance, despite having tried to gain this power in 1911 and 1913, Labor opposed a similar attempt by their Nationalist opponents in 1919. Similarly, Labor attempted to gain power to legislate in respect of trusts in 1913, but opposed their opponents' 1919 attempt, despite the provision that the new power was to remain in force for a maximum of three years.

A more recent example occurred in relation to the different efforts to introduce simultaneous elections for the House of Representatives and the Senate. In 1974 the Coalition opposed Labor's attempt to do so, claiming that the Government's real plan was the weakening and eventual abolition of the upper house. Despite this, the Fraser Government attempted to introduce simultaneous elections in 1977, earning accusations of hypocrisy from within its own ranks. With this second attempt also being defeated, Labor tried again in 1984, and once again the Coalition opposed the attempt.

Similarly, John Howard's raising of the question of Senate 'obstruction' seemed to fly in the face of previous Liberal determination to protect the Senate from Labor 'wreckers' ...

Exaggerated Claims

The assumption of voter ignorance has led to a general opportunism and the seeking of short-term victories over opponents, rather than a careful consideration of the questions under discussion. Former South Australian MLA Robin Millhouse has lamented that 'it's a sad fact that not enough of us [politicians] care sufficiently about constitutional reform to avoid party politics'. This means that a great deal of exaggeration and distortion is standard fare, leading academic Don Aitkin to complain that 'the intellectual level of referendum debates is often appalling'.

In 1937, for instance, opponents of the Commonwealth having power to make laws with regard to aviation predicted that the proposal would wreck state railway systems and spoke of a substantial increase in the price of food. In 1948, the Country Party leader alleged that centralised price control would be used to destroy private enterprise and establish a socialist state. In 1967 the Coalition Government's effort to remove the nexus between the House and the Senate was motivated by a desire to avoid establishing new Senate seats (which could only be done in multiples of six) when population increases dictated small additions to the House of Representatives. Despite this, the NO case relied largely on the populist cry of 'no more politicians'. In 1988 Liberal Senator Richard Alston reportedly warned that the passage of the *Rights and Freedoms* amendment could see the banning of corporal punishment in schools written into the Constitution. In 1999, Liberal MP Tony Abbott spoke of 'ethnic cleansing' in regard to British migrants' right to vote, while the NO [21] case campaign director asserted that an Australian republic was comparable with Nazi Germany ...

Trying To Do Too Much

Parties have also indicated their poor view of the voters by attempting too much at the one time. In 1911 and 1913 the ALP put eight questions – six of which were submitted in 1913 ... None of the amendments was ratified, though the six 1913 proposals only failed narrowly, with all achieving a 49 per cent vote as well as the votes of three States ...

In 1988 the *Parliamentary Terms* referendum effectively dealt with five separate matters: a longer term for the House, a shorter term for the Senate, ending the continuous nature of Senate terms, Senate terms to be no longer fixed and compulsory simultaneous elections for both houses ...

[22] Leadership

There have been some referenda in which it has been claimed that the leadership of particular individuals has been important in explaining the outcome – typically a defeat of a particular amendment proposal. In 1951 the leadership of the NO case in the *Communists and Communism* campaign fell to new Labor leader, HV Evatt, a development that some of his party were uncomfortable with. The margin by which the proposal failed was narrow, and some wondered if the strong fight led by Evatt had played an important role in its defeat. Even the hostile *Bulletin* acknowledged the strength of his efforts:

> Immediately the referendum was launched he took the initiative in the fight; he held it to the end, vigorously campaigning in every State, and by sheer personal earnestness and force making the other side's effort in general look careless and lethargic.

In the *Establishment of Republic* (1999) case, it has been suggested by Professor Clive Bean that the efforts of Kerry Jones, of the Australians for Constitutional Democracy, strengthened the NO case, whereas those of Malcolm Turnbull weakened the YES case. [23] Bean's work suggests that the combination of the two leadership effects may have cost the YES vote about 1.5 per cent, 'not an inconsequential slice of the margin'. A rather more subtle example was that of John Howard whose government sponsored the 1999 amendment legislation through the Parliament, yet who, according to Higley and McAllister, then 'used his position to undermine' its chances. Although many prime ministers have seen their hopes dashed in constitutional referenda, there is little doubt that the opposition of a prime minister would doom any attempt to amend the Constitution ...

[24] State Activity …

When looking at the 1999 referenda, Mr Justice Kirby has drawn attention to what he called the 'small State error'. He suggests that a major factor in the defeat of these two referenda was the strong disinclination of the smaller States to support them. We can extend this to previous cases … Tasmania has said YES to only 10 of the 44 amendment attempts, and the States of Queensland, Western Australia and South Australia have not looked very favourably on referenda over the last 50 years …

[25] Ignorance?

Crisp is one writer who has criticised the voters for their 'ignorance' and their 'conservatism':

> objective assessment of constitutional problems as such is an abstract, complex, technical business for which the average citizen is usually ill-equipped and disinclined, while the problems may be so complicated as to be ill-suited to a simple and satisfying 'Yes' or 'No' vote. The temptation, therefore, is to 'play safe' and 'let things be'.

[26] This view portrays the voters as puzzled by the wording of referenda, often confused by the complexity of the issue under discussion, and unable to make sense of the loud arguments and counter-arguments that swirl about them. Is it any wonder, asks Aitkin, that many 'shrug their shoulders and vote no'?

Opinion poll figures suggest that ignorance and uncertainty were important in 1999. Polling by ANOP uncovered an underlying 'ignorance of system of government, particularly about low profile and less newsworthy aspects – head of state, GG's role, the constitution'. ANOP noted that such a lack of knowledge meant that it was difficult for many people to comprehend 'the nature and extent of change under a republic' – and this applied even when an accurate description was given them …

For writers with a different perspective, such criticisms tell us more about the views of those who see the Constitution as out-of-date and in need of major reform, than of the voters they criticise. For Professor Mark Cooray, it indicates that the constitutional reformists possess an elitist perspective – 'that they, and they alone, know what is best', and that voters are well able to judge things for themselves. This point was seen to have been very much a feature in the outcome of the two referenda in 1999 when there was a view that the republic issue, in particular, was simply a fad of the 'chardonnay-swilling elites' …

[27] A Federal Document

It may be misleading to consider only the total YES and NO results across the 44 national votes. If the 44 cases are analysed a different picture emerges.

The Constitution is a federal document, drawn up by regional politicians determined to protect the position of the States in their federal scheme. Voters in the Federation referenda were spoken to incessantly about the need to protect the place of their colony in the future union, and in the years since, Premiers have often warned voters of the need to protect their State's rights from Commonwealth incursion. Voters have often been asked to show support for their State, most notably in regard to constitutional amendments proposing to increase central government power. Their response has been spectacular – all 17 attempts to increase Commonwealth economic power have been rejected, as have four others dealing with non-economic powers. Two referenda suggesting Commonwealth involvement with local government (1974, 1988) have also failed. Constitutional amendment can thus be difficult if it strays outside the federal parameters that seem to apply as much today as they did in the late 1890s …

[28] If we look at different categories of amendment, however, the picture alters. There have been other questions dealing with the federal system, not just the type seeking to give more power to the Commonwealth. Two of three referenda trying to tidy up Commonwealth-State financial relations have been passed (1910, 1928), though a proposal to alter arrangements for the inter-change of powers was defeated (1984). The only amendments seeking to increase Commonwealth power that have been passed were not typical of such questions. If we classify the *Social Services* (1946) and *Aboriginals* (1967) referenda as 'social', then we note that, together with the *Judges* (1977) example that dealt with retirement ages, three of five such 'social' referenda have been carried. The two that missed out were *Communism* (1951) and *Rights and Freedoms* (1988).

The other major type of alteration has dealt with what might be called 'machinery' amendments. In 1999, of course, the biggest 'machinery' amendment of them all, proposing to establish an Australian republic, was trounced. Just one of four dealing with electoral or referenda arrangements has passed – that giving Territorians the right to vote in constitutional referenda, though the issue of 'fairness' distorts this. The Senate has been the focus of seven attempts, six of them occurring in the past three decades. The *Senate elections* amendment (1906) and the *Senate Casual Vacancies* amendment (1977), were both passed comfortably. By contrast, five proposals that seemed to have been designed 'to reduce the unpredictability of the Senate in the affairs of the Government' (1967, 1974, 1977, 1984, 1988) have been defeated. It is likely that the upper house will remain free from constitutional change in the future.

In summary, amendments perceived to weaken the federal system – such as perceived attacks on the Senate – are likely to receive short shrift, whereas attempts to repair the perennially-flawed finance chapter have been received sympathetically. Questions dealing with societal relations are considered closely ...

[30] Voter Satisfaction?

Referendum returns may have also reflected a general acceptance of the political system, and a suspicion of efforts to alter it ... [I]n the eleven referenda that were held before 1914, we find that in the 66 separate State votes there were 34 (51.5 per cent) that were YES votes. In the seven between-wars referenda, the YES tally fell to 42.9 per cent of the State tallies. In the 24 referenda held since 1944, fewer than one-third (32.7 per cent) of the State totals have registered YES votes ... **[31]** Some see this as voter conservatism; equally it may represent voter satisfaction with the Australian political system coupled with a growing cynicism with politicians.

In December 1985, the Hawke Government established a Constitutional Commission to undertake a comprehensive review of the Constitution. The Commission's two-volume *Final Report* was presented in June 1988. Its recommendations on s 128 included the idea that State Parliaments, as well as the federal Parliament, should be able to initiate referendum proposals, but rejected other suggestions for ways in which such proposals could be initiated independently of parliamentary action. In particular, a majority of the Commission rejected a proposal, made by its Advisory Committee on Individual and Democratic Rights, that referendums might be initiated by a petition signed by not less than 500,000 electors.

Constitutional Commission, *Final Report of the Constitutional Commission*
(AGPS, 1988), Vol 2

[856] 13.19 We *recommend* that the Constitution be altered to allow constitutional referendums to be initiated not only by the Federal Parliament but also by State Parliaments. A proposal to alter the Constitution would be required to come from Parliaments of not fewer than half the States. There should be an additional requirement that the State Parliaments concerned represent a majority of Australians overall. It would be a requirement that the proposed alteration be passed in identical terms by the State Parliaments concerned within a 12 month period. The proposed alteration would be required to be put to a referendum not less than two months and not more than six months after this requirement was satisfied ...

[862] 13.43 We *recommend* against commission or convention initiation of proposed alterations ...

[864] *Reasons for recommendation*

13.55 If convention initiative were adopted, depending on how the convention or commission was comprised, it may be that:

    (a) more ideas would be brought into the alteration process;

    (b) more people could be involved in the alteration process;

    (c) States or State Parliaments would be more directly involved in the alteration process;

    (d) there would be more thorough debate of proposals over sufficient time; and

    (e) more alterations would be approved by voters at referendum.

13.56 On the other hand, a convention initiative would:

(a) bypass the democratically elected Parliaments; and

(b) be more expensive than States' initiative.

13.57 In light of our recommendation for States' initiative we see commission or convention initiative as being unnecessary and inappropriate, at least for the time being.

Electors' initiative

Recommendations

13.58 (i) By majority, we do *not recommend* an alteration to the Constitution to provide for the initiation by electors of referendums to alter the Constitution.

(ii) We unanimously do *not recommend* an alteration to the Constitution to provide for initiation by electors of referendums with respect to ordinary legislation.

13.59 Electors' initiative would allow a fixed number or percentage of electors to procure a referendum on proposals for alteration to the Constitution or proposals for ordinary legislation without the participation of any Parliament ...

[866] *Submissions*

13.69 The proposal for an electors' initiative for altering the Constitution attracted approximately 250 submissions. A majority of these submissions supported the idea of increasing involvement in the democratic process by means of some form of electors' initiative. Approximately 80 asserted support for such a provision without giving reasons. Three main arguments were advanced in more detailed submissions:

(a) It would reduce voter apathy and alienation from the political process by giving electors a direct role in determining the shape of constitutional change. This argument was often associated with the view that government in Australia today is not sufficiently democratic, largely as a result of a rigid party **[867]** system. A few of the submissions went so far as to maintain that, while in theory Australia is a democracy, in practice the rigid party system has resulted in 'elected dictatorship'.

(b) It would lead to more acceptance of constitutional change and a wider range of alterations being proposed. The Queensland Government stated: 'As long as the sole power to initiate reform lies with the Federal Parliament, there will not be the range and type of constitutional reform proposals that are necessary in any true Federal democracy.'

(c) It would play a useful educative role ...

[868] *Reasons for recommendations: the majority view ...*

13.75 *Responsible government.* In our political tradition, good government is associated with responsible government. This involves regular and free elections at which the electors choose between contending political parties on the basis of alternative and coherent sets of policies which reflect genuinely different views on a wide range of economic, social and political matters. Fundamental to the system is the notion of accountability. At election time, governmental decisions are subject to review by the electors.

13.76 Under the present system, any proposal to alter the Constitution must first be deliberated in Parliament, with due regard for the proposal's consistency with the existing and foreshadowed legislation of the Government of the day. With the electors' initiative it is not inconceivable that a proposal for altering the Constitution could be put to referendum which, if passed, would undermine a vital part of the Government's platform thus compromising its authority. In practical terms, the Government of the day would be left to deal with the consequences of the decision, even though it contradicted a central part of its philosophy. The principle of accountability would be weakened.

13.77 A healthy pluralism, with vigorous interest group activity, is essential to democracy. Its proper functioning is to be welcomed. The problem inherent in the electors' initiative is that it would encourage sectionalism. There are a number of facets to the argument. First, there is the danger that the electors' initiative would allow extremist groups an opportunity to parade their proposals before the public with an apparent legitimacy they could not otherwise command. Secondly, there is the possibility that, through the control of the media, the opinions of some groups may gain unwarranted publicity. Thirdly, the cause of a single issue could be furthered without regard to its wider implications for national welfare, or without due consideration for Government policy, the results of which may only be apparent in the long-term. In short, the electors' initiative is potentially divisive and is inconsistent with the purposes and principles of responsible government.

13.78 Referendums are useful devices. In Australia they are essential to constitutional reform. But they are not an alternative to responsible government. There is in this country ample opportunity for the citizen to engage in interest group activity, or in the advocacy of a single issue. Moreover, citizens can and do petition Parliament on matters they consider especially pressing. Where there is genuine, wide-spread and sustained support for a particular constitutional change it is very likely that one of the political parties would propose a law to alter the Constitution. So long as these aspects of the democratic process function properly, they will serve the interests of the people within a system of responsible government. The direct action of a group of electors should not be seen as an alternative to it.

13.79 *Representative democracy.* In our system, responsible government is based on representative democracy, that is, a popularly elected Parliament represents the various groups and interests within the community. The concerns of individual voters and interest groups alike are channelled through their Parliamentary representatives. The system is not perfect. Yet, in our view it has proved a sound model of government. Within it, a satisfactory balance has been effected between the democratic ideals of pluralism, accountability and participation.

13.80 In the majority's view, there are in Australia sufficient and reasonable avenues through which the citizen can participate in the processes of representative democracy. An individual can join a political party and work from within to influence its policies and structures. Blunt and crude solutions are not adequate alternatives to this kind of **[869]** committed engagement with political matters. Indeed, one danger inherent in the initiative proposal is that, while it purports to generate popular involvement in politics, in fact it may be taken up by a new breed of professionals, such as have appeared in California. Real involvement may be limited to these professionals. Meanwhile the participation of the majority of those signing the petition may be quite perfunctory. In this respect, the purported educational benefits of the electors' initiative may well be illusory.

13.81 *Responsible government and the protection of minorities.* In a system of responsible government and representative democracy, legislation should have the support of the majority of the people. Nevertheless, there are times when Governments and politicians have a duty to make decisions which are contrary to popular prejudice. Representatives have a certain discretion. They are not mere delegates or agents of their constituents, since they are expected to exercise their judgement in enacting legislation. Thus, while those in authority should be responsive to the felt interests of the electorate, they also have other duties and responsibilities. In particular, Governments have a duty to guard against the persecution of an unpopular minority ...

[870] *Reasons for recommendation: the minority view*

13.87 Sir Rupert Hamer and Professor Zines agree broadly with the Advisory Committee's recommendation to increase popular participation in the political process by the use of an electors' initiative for constitutional reform.

13.88 Such a provision, they believe, would help to alleviate the feeling of remoteness and impotence with respect to political affairs that is felt by many people in the community. Compulsory voting conceals the extent of alienation felt by many people. There is a sense that politicians are out of touch with the views of the voters. Also, it is thought that party political arrangements do not allow real scope for Parliament to operate as a truly representative and deliberative assembly. The minority of the Commission believes we should address these issues directly.

13.89 This is not to suggest that the electors' initiative is a panacea for our political problems. Nor does the minority agree with the more extreme formulation of these problems as expressed in some of the submissions. Nevertheless, they recognise that the electors' initiative is a mechanism which has been used successfully elsewhere. In their view there are no compelling arguments against giving to the Australian electors the opportunity of voting at referendum on whether or not they support a proposal of this kind.

However s 128 might be amended, the Constitution must embody a workable referendum mechanism if it is to reflect Justice Toohey's conception of a Constitution susceptible to popular amendment. Indeed, it has often been suggested that it is the very failure of the formal amendment procedure to keep up with changes in popular opinion and contemporary needs that has led to pressure for shifts in the interpretation of the existing text by the High Court.

3. An Australian Republic?

One issue has dominated the agenda for change since the early 1990s: should Australia become a republic? The Constitution establishes Australia as a constitutional monarchy. The preamble to the *Commonwealth of Australia Constitution Act 1900* (Imp) records that the people of the colonies "have agreed to unite in one indissoluble Federal Commonwealth under the Crown of the United Kingdom of Great Britain and Ireland", while s 2 of the Constitution provides that the Governor-General is "Her Majesty's representative". Section 59 also provides that the Queen "may disallow any law within one year from the Governor-General's assent". Although this power has never been used and is now obsolete, its presence is a reminder of the initially limited scope of Australian independence (see Chapter 4, §§5-8).

Although the *Australia Act 1986* (Cth) marked the end of the power of the British Parliament to legislate for Australia, the Constitution has never been formally "repatriated", as was done for Canada in 1982. That is, the Constitution remains an enactment of the former Imperial Parliament. Despite this, members of the High Court have made it clear that the source of the sovereignty, or "basic norm", legitimating the Constitution now lies with the Australian people, and that Australia is therefore now a fully independent nation. In *Sue v Hill* (1999) 199 CLR 462, a majority of the Court even held that, for the purposes of s 44 of the Constitution, the United Kingdom should now be considered a "foreign power" (see Chapter 4, §8). The decision acknowledged the reality of Australia's political and legal independence. Accordingly, the contemporary debate about a republic is *not* about whether Australia should amend its Constitution to become an independent nation. The debate is about whether the Constitution should be altered to reflect the existing reality of independence, and whether the nation should take a final symbolic step of replacing the Queen with an Australian President.

While there is significant popular support for an Australian republic (as there is for retaining the monarchy), there is less agreement on what republicanism means. It has been argued that the Australia is already a republic in its essential features ("a crowned republic"), despite the Queen being the nation's Head of State. (It has also been argued that the Governor-General, as the Queen's representative in Australia, is *effectively* Australia's Head of State.) Division has also emerged between those seeking to replace the Queen with an Australian resident while ensuring that any constitutional change is otherwise minimal ("minimalist republicans") and those seeking to bring about a fundamentally revised system of government that might include greater participation by citizens in the institutions of government.

George Williams, "A Republican Tradition for Australia?"
(1995) 23 *Federal Law Review* 133

[141] Pettit, writing in an Australian context, has characterised republicanism as incorporating the following themes:
1. an anti-monarchical motif;
2. republics must embody the rule of law and a rule of check and balance (that is, "the authorities who hold power under the law are institutionally constrained so that they cannot easily abuse their position"); and
3. the rule of virtue expressed both in a politically active citizenry and public officers able to stand against corruption and willing to perform their duties to the best of their ability.

Republicanism has been put forward as an alternative to a minimalist republic ... For the proponents of republicanism, the achievement of a minimalist republic would represent nothing more than "cosmetic constitutional change" that may not amount to a "genuinely *republican* movement at all" ...

The semantics of the minimalist versus republican debate can hamper understanding. The minimalist approach to an Australian republic focuses upon Pettit's first theme, the removal of the monarch of the United Kingdom as Australia's Head of State, without seeking to disturb the existing political structures in a manner consistent with Pettit's third and, to a lesser extent, second theme. Minimalists are concerned to maintain the existing facets of the Westminster system of **[142]** government to the extent possible after the sovereign has been deposed and the formal transfer of sovereign power recognised.

For ... proponents of republicanism, significance lies not only in establishing the formalities of a republic or simply changing the Head of State from a foreigner to an Australian. The aim is to alter the Australian constitutional and political structure so that it embodies some of the themes of republicanism, particularly ... Pettit's third theme ... [T]his would involve enhancing "the capacity of ordinary citizens to participate in the exercise of constitutional authority and political power". This might mean citizen-initiated referenda or the creation of a new political body, such as an elected constituent assembly, to carry out the task of transforming Australia into a republic. Such a republic might recognise not only governments, but also "business corporations and professional associations as essential constituent elements" so as to enable the people to act as citizens of the republic in everyday life.

The minimalist and republican paths offer very different terrain. Republicans argue for an agenda potentially encompassing radical constitutional and political change aimed at enhancing the citizenship of the people in a way they argue is not provided for by existing Australian traditions, such as those based upon the Westminster form of government. The minimalist position is characterised by an enduring faith in exactly those traditions.

In 1993, Prime Minister Paul Keating established a Republic Advisory Committee to report on the minimum constitutional changes required to bring about a republic.

Republic Advisory Committee, *An Australian Republic: The Options*
(AGPS, The Report of the Republic Advisory Committee, 1993), vol 1

[39] A republic is a state in which sovereignty is derived from the people, and in which all public offices are filled by persons ultimately deriving their authority from the people. The Macquarie Dictionary gives the following relevant definitions of a republic:

1. a state in which the supreme power rests in the body of citizens entitled to vote and is exercised by representatives chosen directly or indirectly by them ... 3. a state, especially a democratic state, in which the head of government is an elected or nominated president, not a hereditary monarch.

Since the Commonwealth Constitution can be amended only by the people pursuant to a referendum under section 128 of the Constitution, ultimate sovereignty in Australia vests in the Australian people, even though the Commonwealth Constitution at least initially derived its legal authority from an Act of the United Kingdom Parliament. As Chief Justice Mason recently remarked [*Australian Capital Television Pty Ltd v Commonwealth* (1992) 177 CLR 106 at 138]:

The Australia Act 1986 (UK) marked the end of the legal sovereignty of the Imperial Parliament and recognised that *ultimate sovereignty resided in the Australian people*.

Australia is, therefore, a state in which sovereignty resides in its people, and in which all public offices, except that at the very apex of the system, are filled by persons deriving authority directly or indirectly from the people. It may be appropriate to regard Australia as a 'crowned republic', a view favoured by some monarchists, in that the only Australian office incompatible with a republic is the monarchy. It follows that all that is required to make Australia completely republican is to remove the monarch; no other constitutional change is required.

The Committee outlined the options for change.

[2] Appointment of the head of state

In considering the many and varied options for appointing and removing (if necessary) the head of state, the Committee took into account the view commonly expressed that the office should be 'above politics' and that the occupant be, and be seen to be, impartial.

The Committee concluded that there are four main methods of selecting the head of state, with a number of options within these. The methods are outlined below.

Appointment by the Prime Minister

Leaving the appointment of the head of state to the Government of [the] day is the option which most closely reflects the current practice. Although Prime Ministers would no doubt continue to appoint appropriately qualified individuals, and those appointees would similarly carry out the functions of the office in an even-handed fashion, the process of appointment may be viewed as a partisan one if left to the Prime Minister alone.

Appointment by Parliament

Involving the people in the appointment process through their parliamentary representatives is a democratic process and, depending on the particular method **[3]** selected, can ensure that the person selected has the support of all major parties. Moreover, it would, through the Senate, reflect the federal nature of the Commonwealth.

There are a number of issues to be resolved. These include:

- whether the Houses should vote separately, thereby risking deadlock, or whether the members should vote in a joint sitting;
- whether the vote should require a simple majority of members or whether a 'special majority' should be required to ensure that the person selected would have not only the support of the Government members, but also of a substantial number of non-Government members; and
- whether a single nomination by the Prime Minister or a bipartisan nominating panel should be considered, or a number of nominations from other sources.

A joint sitting of the Houses would be in keeping with the importance of the occasion and could provide a symbol of unity appropriate for the appointment of a head of state who would represent the nation as a whole.

Requiring only a simple majority in each House, or indeed of members of both Houses in a joint sitting could, depending on the relative size of the Government's majority in the House of Representatives and its representation in the Senate, see the Government determine the outcome without the support of any other party, or with the support of a small number of non-Government Senators.

Adopting a voting procedure which would necessarily require the support of members of more than one political party would discourage the nomination of individuals who were not likely to gain that support and would encourage prior consultation on nominees.

A single nomination by the Government would have the advantage of avoiding parliamentary discussion on the relative merits of the candidates which could be seen as divisive and detrimental to the office. Moreover, if a two-thirds majority were required, prior consultation with other parties could be expected. An alternative to a Government nomination would be nomination by an independent commission or group of eminent people with membership on an *ex officio* basis (such as the Chief Justice of the High Court, the Prime Minister and the Leader of the Opposition) or made up of Australians outside the political process.

If having only a single nomination was considered too restrictive, multiple nominations could be allowed, possibly by a specified number of members of Parliament or by a nominating commission. A two-thirds majority requirement would ensure a bipartisan result in the end.

[4] *Popular election*

The head of state could be elected by the people in a direct election. The argument in favour of such a method is that it is entirely democratic and would give Australians a direct voice in the process.

Another argument made to the Committee is that a direct election would prevent a political appointment, as could occur if the matter was left to politicians. This may not turn out to be the case in practice – indeed a direct election could ensure that the person elected is the nominee of one or other of the major political parties which have the expertise and resources to mount nation-wide political campaigns. A popular election might ensure that the head of state is not a 'political' appointment, but it may well result in the person elected being a 'politician'.

The Committee considered two options to reduce the partisan nature of a popular election – a ban on political parties endorsing candidates for the head of state and excluding former politicians. It is doubtful whether such provisions would be effective in freeing the election from political campaigning and they may be seen as unduly restricting political freedoms.

The Committee considered that, while the option of popular election of the head of state is one which appears to have significant public support, it should be recognised that it would be expensive (particularly if held separately from a parliamentary election), would almost certainly involve political parties in the endorsement of candidates, and by its nature could discourage suitable candidates from standing. Moreover, the process of popular election may encourage the head of state to believe that he or she has a popular mandate to exercise the powers of that office, including the ability to make public statements and speeches, in a manner which could bring the head of state into conflict with the elected Government.

The Committee is therefore of the view that if popular election is selected as the appropriate method of selecting the head of state, then, if the effect of our current conventions and principles of government is to be maintained, the Constitution should be amended so as clearly to define and delimit the powers of the head of state so that the Australian people know precisely the powers and duties of the head of state they are being called upon to elect.

Appointment by electoral college

Several federal nations with non-executive heads of state establish electoral colleges to appoint their heads of state. Typically, the electoral college is made up of representatives from the national and State parliaments. The case for including representatives of the States and Territories in the process for selecting the Commonwealth head of state this way is not, in the view of the Committee, a compelling one.

[5] It would be possible to design a special body with representatives drawn from outside the Commonwealth, State and Territory Parliaments with the task of electing the head of state. Reaching a consensus in the community as to which groups or individuals should participate in such an electoral college would, to say the least, not be a straightforward task …

[6] Powers of the head of state

Options which 'maintain the effect of our current conventions and principles of government' would see a new head of state continue to exercise the same kind of 'governmental' functions on the advice of the Government of the day as are presently exercised by the Governor-General. In order to eliminate any uncertainty, the Constitution should provide that in the exercise of these powers the head of state acts on ministerial advice.

Options which eliminate the 'reserve powers' might be regarded as a substantial change to our way of government, which leaves for consideration the issue of how the reserve powers, and the unwritten constitutional conventions which govern the exercise of those powers, should be dealt with in the Constitution so as to maintain the effect of those conventions.

[7] The Committee considered the following options for dealing with the issue of the reserve powers:

- leaving the powers in the same form as are presently set out in the Constitution, but stating in the Constitution that the existing constitutional conventions will continue to apply to the exercise of those powers;
- leaving the powers in the same form as are presently set out in the Constitution with the constitutional conventions formulated in an authoritative written form, but not as part of the Constitution;
- leaving the powers in the same form as are presently set out in the Constitution and providing that Parliament can make laws (possibly by a two-thirds majority) to formulate the relevant constitutional conventions in a legislative form; and
- 'codifying' the relevant constitutional conventions by setting out in the Constitution the circumstances in which the head of state can exercise the reserve powers.

The last option can be done in one of two ways:

- by setting out the most important (and generally agreed) conventions and providing that the remaining (unwritten) conventions are otherwise to continue (ie partial codification); or
- by setting out in the Constitution all the circumstances in which the head of state can exercise a reserve power and stating expressly that in all other circumstances the head of state is to act on ministerial advice (ie full codification).

In a speech delivered on 7 June 1995, Keating responded to the Republic Advisory Committee by indicating the Government's preferred model for a republic.

Prime Minister Paul Keating, *An Australian Republic: The Way Forward*
(AGPS, 7 June 1995)

[9] The advantage of codifying the conventions, whether in whole or in part, would be to bring a degree of clarity and certainty to the options open to a Head of State in different situations.

However, after careful consideration, the Government has formed the view that it is probably impossible to write down or codify these powers in a way that would both find general community acceptance *and* cover every possible contingency. As the system evolves there needs to be some capacity to respond to circumstances quite unforeseen today. Tightly defined rules can themselves have unforeseen consequences.

Were we to try, by Constitutional amendment, to set down precisely how the reserve powers should be exercised by the Head of State, those amendments, even if intended to be otherwise, could well become justiciable – that is capable of being adjudicated by the High Court of Australia and required to be adjudicated by the High Court.

Hence, codification would be likely to result in fundamental change to our system of government and alter the status of the High Court in relation to the Executive and the Parliament. Over time, Justices of the Court could well be drawn into arbitrating purely political disputes whose resolution should ultimately be in the hands of the electorate. The Court would thus be exposed to public pressure and, in the inevitable event that a party to a dispute was unhappy with its resolution, the standing and impartiality of the Court could be called into question.

For these reasons the Government believes that, on balance, whatever the immediate attraction of this course might be, it would not be desirable to attempt to codify the reserve powers; and that the design, processes and conventions at present governing their exercise by the Governor-General should be transferred to the Australian Head of State without alteration ...

[11] Popular election guarantees that the Head of State will *not be* above politics – indeed it guarantees that the Head of State will be a politician. As Sir Zelman Cowen pointed out in his speech last week, a "direct election of a President would ensure political outcomes"; and he went on to say that people like himself and another former Governor-General, Sir Ninian Stephen, "would not have the resources or inclination to contest such an election". We cannot have a Head of State who is "above politics" if we subject candidates to popular elections – we will get instead politicians, political parties and political campaigns. And we will get a Head of State with an authority unheard of in our political system and discordant with some of the basic principles on which that system rests.

We therefore propose ... that the Head of State be elected by a two-thirds majority vote in a joint sitting of both Houses of the Commonwealth Parliament on the nomination of the Prime Minister and the Cabinet. Such a joint sitting would be a unique occasion, bringing together all the political parties, and both Houses of Parliament, in a spirit of bi-partisanship and cooperation. Obviously, before the vote was taken the non-government parties would have to be consulted to ensure that the candidate had their support.

Keating stated that his vision for an Australian republic from 2001, the centenary of Federation, would be put to the people in a referendum. However, he lost the March 1996 election to the Liberal-National Party Coalition led by John Howard, a staunch supporter of the existing monarchist Constitution. The Coalition fought the election on the basis that it would establish a Convention to debate the issue. That Convention, comprised of 152 delegates (half were elected and half were parliamentary representatives and Government appointees), was held over ten days in February 1998 (see *Report of the Constitutional Convention, Old Parliament House, Canberra, 2–13 February 1998* (1998), 4 vols).

George Williams, "Why Australia Kept the Queen"
(2000) 63 *Saskatchewan Law Review* 477

[485] The business of the Convention was defined by the Prime Minister. The Convention was asked to resolve three broad issues:
1. whether or not Australia should become a republic;
2. which republican model should be put to the electorate to consider against the status quo; and
3. in what time frame and under what circumstances might any change be considered.

The Convention was premised on a narrow view of what it means to be a republic. The boundaries set by the Prime Minister were rigorously enforced by the Chair and Deputy Chair. It was even deemed to be beyond the scope of the Convention to discuss the Australian Flag or the Coat of Arms. Although some delegates had been elected with a mandate to push for wider change to the Constitution as part of a republic, such as through the incorporation of a Bill of Rights, it became clear from the first day of the Convention that such aims would be frustrated.

On the first issue put by the Prime Minister, the Convention voted by 89 to 52 to support "in principle" Australia becoming a republic. On the third issue, the Convention resolved that a referendum be held in 1999 to allow Australians to decide whether to make the move to a republic or to maintain the status quo, and that if the referendum was in favour of a republic, the new republic would come into effect by January 1, 2001.

The second issue dominated the Convention. By the middle of the second week, four models had emerged. The most important difference between them lay in the method of choosing the President. The first model was the *Direct Election Model*, a blend of popular and parliamentary involvement in the selection of an Australian President. Under this Model, any Australian could nominate a person to be Head of State. A joint sitting of the Senate and House of Representatives would then, by at least a two-thirds majority, choose no fewer than three candidates from those nominated to stand for election by the people. The second model was proposed by Bill Hayden, a former Governor-General and federal leader of the Labor Party. The *Hayden Model* also allowed a popular election for the President. A person could stand for the office if he or she had been nominated by one per cent of voters, or around 120,000 people. The third model was that put forward by Richard McGarvie, a former Governor of Victoria. The *McGarvie Model* proposed that the President be chosen by the Prime Minister and appointed or dismissed by a [486] Constitutional Council bound to act as the Prime Minister advised. This Constitutional Council was to consist of three "elders", determined automatically by constitutional formula, with places going first to former Governors-General and Presidents, with priority to the most recently retired and in turn, unfilled places going on the same basis to former State Governors, Lieutenant-Governors (or equivalent), and High Court and Federal Court judges. The final model was the *Bi-Partisan Appointment of the President Model*, which was developed from a model brought to the Convention by the Australian Republican Movement. It allowed any person to nominate someone to be President, with the names of nominees being vetted by a Committee established by Parliament and a short-list then being passed onto the Prime Minister. The Prime Minister would then present a single nomination for the office of President, seconded by the Leader of the Opposition, for approval by a Joint Sitting of both Houses of the federal Parliament. A two thirds majority would be required to approve the choice of President.

The delegates considered the four models through a process whereby the model receiving the lowest vote in each round of voting was knocked out until only one model remained. The first model eliminated was the Hayden Model. In the second round of voting, the Direct Election Model was eliminated, receiving 30 votes as against the 31 votes for the McGarvie Model. In the third round, the McGarvie Model was eliminated with 32 votes as against the 73 votes for the Bi-Partisan Appointment of the President Model, leaving the latter as the Convention's preferred republican option.

These rounds of voting laid the seeds for the bitter disputes that would follow between supporters of the Bi-Partisan Model and proponents of direct election. The fact that only half of the delegates were elected, and the other half were parliamentary representatives and appointees of the Howard Government, had a significant impact. In general, the people appointed by the Government were supportive of either the current monarchical system or of very minimal change. This led to the strong popular support for the Direct Election Model not being reflected in the voting at the Convention, while support for the McGarvie Model was exaggerated. Of the 32 delegates who voted for the McGarvie Model in the last round of voting, 30 were appointed. The appointed delegates were successful in skewing the Convention toward a more conservative outcome and away from direct election.

The Bi-Partisan Model had achieved a pyrrhic victory. The makeup of the Convention enabled it to gain more votes than any other proposal and prevented a real challenge from the proponents of **[487]** direct election. However, the effect was to alienate many direct election supporters, leading them to advocate a "No" vote at the subsequent referendum. The split in republican ranks was evident when the following question was put to the Convention on its final day: Does this Convention support the adoption of a republican system of government on the Bi-Partisan Appointment of the President Model in preference to there being no change to the Constitution? Only 73 delegates, less than half of the Convention, voted "Yes", 57 delegates votes "No", and 22 delegates, including many of the supporters of direct election, abstained …

On the last day of the 1998 Constitutional Convention, Prime Minister Howard indicated that he would put the Bi-Partisan Model to the Australian people to allow them to determine whether to make this change to the Constitution.

A Women's Constitutional Convention held in January 1998 reached a different set of outcomes. A majority of the Convention considered that Australia should become a republic provided that certain principles were adhered to. These included "full recognition of indigenous Australians", "gender equity in all processes of change" and "respect for diversity including cultural, religious, and sexual diversity". The Convention also concluded that the "selection/appointment process for the Head of State must involve women at least to the same extent as men" and "must guarantee that women's chances of occupying the position are substantively equal to those of men". The Convention also supported wider reforms including a Bill of Rights and a process to ensure that more women are appointed to the High Court.

Following the 1998 Convention, legislation to implement a republic was introduced into the federal Parliament and passed by both Houses. It proposed the following changes:

Constitution Alteration (Establishment of Republic) 1999

59 Executive power

The executive power of the Commonwealth is vested in the President, and extends to the execution and maintenance of this Constitution, and of the laws of the Commonwealth. The President shall be the head of state of the Commonwealth.

There shall be a Federal Executive Council to advise the President in the government of the Commonwealth, and the members of the Council shall be chosen and summoned by the President and sworn as Executive Councillors, and shall hold office during the pleasure of the President.

The President shall act on the advice of the Federal Executive Council, the Prime Minister or another Minister of State; but the President may exercise a power that was a reserve power of the Governor-General in accordance with the constitutional conventions relating to the exercise of that power.

60 The President

After considering the report of a committee established and operating as the Parliament provides to invite and consider nominations for appointment as President, the Prime Minister may, in a joint sitting of the members of the Senate and the House of Representatives, move that a named Australian citizen be chosen as the President.

If the Prime Minister's motion is seconded by the leader of the Opposition in the House of Representatives, and affirmed by a two-thirds majority of the total number of the members of the Senate and the House of Representatives, the named Australian citizen is chosen as the President.

The person named in the Prime Minister's motion is qualified to be chosen as President if, when the motion is moved and affirmed:

(i) the person is qualified to be, and capable of being chosen as, a member of the House of Representatives; and

(ii) the person is not a member of the Commonwealth Parliament or a State Parliament or Territory legislature, or a member of a political party.

The actions of a person otherwise duly chosen as President under this section are not invalidated only because the person was not qualified to be chosen as President.

Each person chosen as President shall, before the term of office begins, make and subscribe before a Justice of the High Court an oath or affirmation of office in the form set forth in Schedule 1 to this Constitution.

61 Term of office and remuneration of President

The term of office of a President begins at the end of the term of office of the previous President.

But if the office of President falls vacant, or the term of office of the outgoing President ends, before the day on which the incoming President makes the oath or affirmation of office, the incoming President's term of office begins on the day after that day.

The President holds office for five years but if, at the end of the term, a new President does not take office, the office of President does not thereby fall vacant and the outgoing President continues as President until the term of office of the next President begins.

A person may serve more than one term as President.

The President may resign by signed notice delivered to the Prime Minister.

The President shall receive such remuneration as the Parliament fixes. The remuneration of a President payable during a term of office shall not be altered during that term of office.

62 Removal of President

The Prime Minister may, by instrument signed by the Prime Minister, remove the President with effect immediately.

A Prime Minister who removes a President must seek the approval of the House of Representatives for the removal of the President within thirty days after the removal, unless:

(i) within that period, the House expires or is dissolved; or

(ii) before the removal, the House had expired or been dissolved, but a general election of members of the House had not taken place.

The failure of the House of Representatives to approve the removal of the President does not operate to reinstate the President who was removed.

It was also proposed to insert transitional provisions into the Constitution as a new Sch 2:

5 The States

A State that has not altered its laws to sever its links with the Crown by the time the office of Governor-General ceases to exist retains its links with the Crown until it has so altered its laws.

6 Unified federal system

The alterations of this Constitution made by the *Constitution Alteration (Establishment of Republic) 1999* do not affect the continuity of the federal system, including the unified system of law, under this Constitution.

7 Constitutional conventions

The enactment of the *Constitution Alteration (Establishment of Republic) 1999* does not prevent the evolution of the constitutional conventions, including those relating to the exercise of the reserve powers referred to in section 59 of this Constitution.

8 Justiciability

The enactment of the *Constitution Alteration (Establishment of Republic) 1999* does not make justiciable the exercise by the President of a reserve power referred to in section 59 of this Constitution if the exercise by the Governor-General of that power was not justiciable.

Notice that, under clause 5, the successful passage of the referendum would not of itself have effected any change in the States' constitutional position. However, if the referendum had carried, the changes at Commonwealth level would not have taken effect until 1 January 2001, which would have left time for those States that wished to do so to effect their own constitutional changes before that date. Presumably, in any State where a majority of the electors had voted for the change at Commonwealth level, there would have been strong political pressure for an equivalent change at State level. However, this would still have left open the possibility of the Commonwealth and some of the States adopting a republican form of government with one or more States still retaining the Queen. Some argued that this would be a logical impossibility: the citizens of a State which retained the monarchy would simultaneously owe allegiance to the Queen (as citizens of their State) while having renounced any such allegiance (as citizens of Australia). Others, while conceding that this would be anomalous, saw no logical barrier to such an outcome.

It might have been possible for the changes to the Commonwealth Constitution to be expressed in such a way as to eliminate the Crown from the State constitutions as well. There were, however, powerful political objections to such a course and it was thought better to leave the consequential issues at State level to be worked out by each State for itself. There was also an argument that a proposal for a single comprehensive change would have faced an additional hurdle. At the least, s 128 requires an affirmative vote in a majority of States, as well as a national majority. On one view, however, any attempt to change the States' constitutional arrangements would have made it necessary to secure an affirmative vote in all six States. This was because s 128 provides that certain constitutional changes affecting a State shall not become law unless approved by "the majority of the electors in that State". On one reading of the section, the relevant changes fall into three categories:

1. Changes "diminishing the proportionate representation of any State in either House of the Parliament, or the minimum number of representatives of a State in the House of Representatives";
2. Changes "increasing, diminishing, or otherwise altering the limits of the State";
3. Changes "in any manner affecting the provisions of the Constitution in relation thereto" (that is, in relation to the State).

On an alternative reading, there are only two relevant categories: (2) and (3) above should be read together, so that the words "in relation thereto" mean only "in relation to the limits of the State". On that reading, this provision would have no bearing on the republic issue. However, if the provision is read as requiring approval by the people of a State for any change "in any manner affecting the provisions of the Constitution in relation to [that State]", it would apply to any proposal affecting the constitutional position of the Queen in any State.

Although the provision remains ambiguous, this broader interpretation has received support. McHugh J stated in *McGinty v Western Australia* (1996) 186 CLR 140 that "**[237]** where an alteration of the Constitution would in any manner affect the provisions of the Constitution in relation to a State, s 128 of the Constitution provides that the alteration shall not be valid unless the majority of electors in the State concerned approved the proposed alteration" (compare Anne Twomey, "State Constitutions in an Australian Republic" (1997) 23 *Monash University Law Review* 312 at 320-2).

Arguments for the proposed change to the Constitution were contained in a pamphlet distributed to electors in accordance with the *Referendum (Machinery Provisions) Act 1984* (Cth).

YES/NO Referendum '99
(Australian Electoral Commission, 1999)
[8] The case for voting 'YES'

An Australian Republic – it's all about our future
Australia has evolved and matured as an independent nation.

All Australians should be proud of our country and committed to its values.

Our Head of State should be chosen on merit and not by the privilege of birth.

Every Australian child should be able to aspire to be our Head of State.

As it stands today, no Australian, no matter how talented they are or how hard they work will ever be Australia's Head of State.

The past has served us well, but as a vibrant growing nation it's time to move on.

Our pride and stature as a truly independent nation are a vital part of our national unity.

An Australian President will represent our uniquely Australian identity as we face the world into the future.

Becoming a Republic simply means having an Australian as Head of State instead of the Queen

It's time to have our own Head of State.

Britain and the British monarchy have served us well and will always be part of our history.

However, the British monarchy is no longer relevant to our daily lives as Australians.

Now we need someone who will proudly promote Australia and our interests – someone who is one of us.

We should stand on our own two feet

From our beginnings as an ancient land and a British colony, we have progressed and grown.

We now come from many backgrounds and nationalities – our Head of State should represent all Australians.

Only an Australian can do that.

[9] The case for voting 'NO'

Vote 'NO' to the politicians' republic

This referendum is not just about whether Australia should become a republic. It is about the type of republic.

And the republic model being proposed is seriously flawed – it is untried, unworkable, undemocratic and elitist. The politicians will appoint the President, not the people. It removes the checks and balances from the current system.

Different people will be voting 'NO' for many different reasons:

Don't know? – Vote 'NO'

Those who don't know – should vote 'NO' – because that is the only safe way to go.

No say! – No way! – Vote 'NO'

Those who want to elect their President – should vote 'NO' – because under the proposed model, they will have no say in who their President will be.

A puppet for President! – Vote 'NO'

Those who want an appointed President – should vote 'NO' – because the proposed model is fatally flawed. The President will be a Prime Minister's puppet, subject to instant dismissal.

Keep the status quo! – Vote 'NO'

Those who value the certainty and stability of our current Constitution – should vote 'NO' – because any alternative has to be as good as or better than the current system. This proposal fails that fundamental test.

The republic was not the only change put to the people at the 1999 referendum. A second question, recommended by the 1998 Convention, proposed that a new preamble be added.

Mark McKenna, Amelia Simpson and George Williams, "With Hope in God, the Prime Minister and the Poet: Lessons from the 1999 Referendum on the Preamble"

(2001) 24 *University of New South Wales Law Journal* 401

[406] Howard announced in early March [1999] that he would 'have a chat' to poet Les Murray and that he would seek Murray's assistance in drafting a preamble …

The Howard-Murray Preamble

With hope in God, the Commonwealth of Australia is constituted by the equal sovereignty of all its citizens.

The Australian nation is woven together of people from many ancestries and arrivals.

Our vast island continent has helped to shape the destiny of our Commonwealth and the spirit of its people.

Since time immemorial our land has been inhabited by Aborigines and Torres Strait Islanders, who are honoured for their ancient and continuing cultures.

In every generation immigrants have brought great enrichment to our nation's life.

Australians are free to be proud of their country and heritage, free to realise themselves as individuals, and free to pursue their hopes and ideals.

We value excellence as well as fairness, independence as dearly as mateship.

Australia's democratic and federal system of government exists under law to preserve and protect all Australians in equal dignity which may never be infringed by prejudice or fashion or ideology nor invoked against achievement.

In this spirit we, the Australian people, commit ourselves to this Constitution …

The Howard-Murray preamble …was immediately opposed by the non-Government parties. It also attracted widespread public and media criticism …

[409] During the first two weeks of August 1999 … the Government and the Australian Democrats worked on achieving agreement on a revised version of the Howard-Murray preamble. Leading republicans such as Opposition leader Kim Beazley and Malcolm Turnbull wanted one referendum question only, believing that any additional question on a preamble would increase the likelihood of defeat on the republic question. On 11 August, one day before the republic legislation was due to be passed by Parliament …, the final version of the revised preamble was released with the introduction in the House of Representatives of the Constitution Alteration (Preamble) 1999 (Cth). With the support of the Democrats, its passage through the Senate was now certain.

The proposal put to the people read:

Constitution Alteration (Preamble) 1999

With hope in God, the Commonwealth of Australia is constituted as a democracy with a federal system of government to serve the common good.

We the Australian people commit ourselves to this Constitution:

proud that our national unity has been forged by Australians from many ancestries;

never forgetting the sacrifices of all who defended our country and our liberty in time of war;

upholding freedom, tolerance, individual dignity and the rule of law;

honouring Aborigines and Torres Strait Islanders, the nation's first people, for their deep kinship with their lands and for their ancient and continuing cultures which enrich the life of our country;

recognising the nation-building contribution of generations of immigrants;

mindful of our responsibility to protect our unique natural environment;

supportive of achievement as well as equality of opportunity for all;

and valuing independence as dearly as the national spirit which binds us together in both adversity and success.

This proposal would also have inserted a new s 125A into the Constitution, providing: "The preamble to this Constitution has no legal force and shall not be considered in interpreting this Constitution or the law in force in the Commonwealth or any part of the Commonwealth".

The new preamble was to be inserted at the beginning of the Constitution, rather than at the head of the *Commonwealth of Australia Constitution Act*. The preamble that currently prefaces that Act, and the covering clauses that precede the Constitution, would not have been changed by either the republic or the preamble proposal, in part because of concerns that the amendment mechanism in s 128 may be incapable of effecting such change. Although s 128 begins "This Constitution shall not be altered except in the following manner", it was thought to be arguable that "This Constitution" refers only to the document set out in s 9 of the *Commonwealth of Australia Constitution Act* and not to the other covering clauses, nor to the preamble.

On 6 November 1999, Australians were asked to mark their ballot papers "Yes" or "No" to:

- "A PROPOSED LAW: To alter the Constitution to establish the Commonwealth of Australia as a republic with the Queen and Governor-General being replaced by a President appointed by a two-thirds majority of the members of the Commonwealth Parliament"; and

- "A PROPOSED LAW: To alter the Constitution to insert a preamble".

Australians answered a resounding "No" to both questions.

Helen Irving, "The Republic Referendum of 6 November 1999"
(2000) 35 *Australian Journal of Political Science* 111

[111] The failure of both referendum questions … was widely predicted prior to the event. Opinion polls had shown a steady decline in the support base for the republic over the preceding weeks. The *Australian*'s Newspoll conducted on 22–24 October, for example, revealed the 'No' case leading comfortably and support for the 'Yes' case falling over the previous month. When coupled with Australia's poor record on producing affirmative referendum outcomes, such polling led many to consider a negative outcome to be inevitable. The result was, however, even worse than most had predicted. Majorities in every State rejected both questions, as had happened nine times before in referendums. The national count of just over 45% in favour put the republic question in among the lowest third of all referendum results. The national vote for the preamble question, at just over 42%, was the tenth worst out of the 44 questions this century …

[112] The consensus appears to have narrowed in on three (not incompatible) explanations for the defeat. One hypothesis is that referendums have no chance of succeeding if they do not have wide, cross-party support and particularly the support of the Prime Minister. A second hypothesis holds that this particular referendum failed because it represented the aspirations of an 'elite' and it alienated the 'people', especially the 'battlers'. A third hypothesis points at insufficient voter knowledge, with the apparent correlation between higher levels of formal education and a greater propensity to support the republic, and the complete failure of both questions in rural electorates, held up in demonstration of this explanation.

From what we know about referendum results this century, the first hypothesis is probably right, although it tells us, in fact, relatively little. No referendum, indeed, has ever succeeded without the support of the Prime Minister, but no referendum has succeeded without bipartisan support, and this has always included the Prime Minister. But bipartisan support is, as is widely known, not sufficient; at least three referendums have failed this century despite having bipartisan support. In addition, the Prime Minister's support for the preamble was in itself insufficient to ensure success (except, perhaps, in his own electorate).

The second hypothesis seems intuitively correct, although its conclusion cannot be separated from questions about the campaign itself. The 'No' campaign, indeed, ran very strongly along populist 'anti-elite' lines with, however, a confusion between several versions of 'elites': there were the alleged 'elites' ('Chardonnay drinkers') at the heart of the republican movement, those classed as 'elites' merely by being residents of Sydney, Melbourne and Canberra, and another version of 'elites' meaning simply Federal politicians. Furthermore, it is unclear whether the 'battlers' wanted no change to the Constitution, or opposed the model on offer because they preferred a direct election method of choosing the head of state.

The third (related) hypothesis, concerning levels of education, has **[113]** greater credibility. A positive correlation between formal education and support for a republic has existed over a number of years … But the value of such a finding remains to be explored, since it does not in itself reveal why people with lower levels of education reject constitutional change of the type proposed in the 1999 republic referendum. And it leaves unexplained the preamble result, with, for example, both ACT electorates, where high concentrations of tertiary educated voters are to be found, rejecting the preamble.

Justice Michael Kirby has suggested 10 reasons why the proposal for an Australian republic was defeated. One reason was what he termed "model error".

Michael Kirby, "The Australian Referendum on a Republic – Ten Lessons"
(2000) 46 *Australian Journal of Politics & History* 510

[528] This is not the occasion to canvass all of the criticisms of the republican model which was put to the 1999 referendum. Critics certainly raised many false issues. The opponents played on fear about some of these. The notion that Australia would, as a republic, not be invited to rejoin the Commonwealth of Nations (of which the Queen is the Head) was absurd. The Commonwealth Secretary-General made this plain in a statement issued at the last stages of the referendum campaign. Equally absurd was the suggestion that, upon the removal of the Queen, Crown land in Australia would revert to Aboriginal Australians. A similar distraction, in my view, was the argument that the Governor-General was actually the Head of State of Australia. Ultimately Howard stated accurately that the Governor-General was virtually the Head of State, performing as he does the functions common to that kind of office in other countries when the Queen is absent from Australia, which is most of the time.

However, if these matters are put to one side, there remained genuine concerns about the proposed amendments to the Constitution. They worried some electors. Probably the chief of these was the fear about the ease with which, under the proposed changes, the Prime Minister could dismiss the proposed President. Although the Prime Minister would be obliged to seek endorsement of such action by an affirmative vote in the House of Representatives within a short time, the provision, as drafted, contained obvious defects. These grew out of a compromise struck at the Constitutional Convention. Following such dismissal of the President, an affirmative vote was required of the House of Representatives. But that chamber would ordinarily be in the control of the Government party from which the Prime Minister was elected. No effective constitutional sanction was imposed if, remarkably, the vote of the House of **[529]** Representatives went against the Prime Minister. In particular, an adverse vote would not have meant the restoration of the ousted President to office. In Australia, these were not theoretical points, given the events surrounding the dismissal of Prime Minister Whitlam in November 1975. They therefore received a measure of attention. They could not be brushed aside.

To those who urged acceptance of the model, even if defective, on the promise of later amendment and improvement – to codify the powers of the Governor-General; to provide ultimately for direct election; to control further the dismissal of the President – the spectre of the difficulty of securing later change loomed large. Even electors generally sympathetic to the idea of a republic could therefore rationally reject the proposed model.

Despite the decisive result in the 1999 referendum, the republic issue has not left the reform agenda. Debate continues among republicans on the best way forward, and particularly on the workability of models based upon popular election of an Australian President. The federal Parliament has also examined the issue.

Senate Legal and Constitutional References Committee, *The Road to a Republic*

(Parliamentary Paper No 222 of 2004)

[133] Education, Engagement and Inclusion

8.5 The Committee received a considerable amount of evidence which suggested that lack of "ownership" was one of the problems associated with the 1999 referendum. The Committee acknowledges this evidence and considers that the Australian people should be fully consulted and involved in any process leading towards a future Australian republic …

8.6 However, the Committee recognises that, in order for the process to be fully democratic, informed participation is required. The Committee considers that constitutional awareness and education is the key to effective participation in any proposed constitutional reform, including reforms leading towards an Australian republic. The Committee heard evidence from all sides of the republic debate of the importance of constitutional education and awareness, particularly in the context of proposed constitutional change.

8.7 The Committee also received a considerable amount of evidence of a general lack of understanding in the Australian community of the Australian Constitution and [134] system of government. The Committee also notes the recent experience of the Consultative Group on Constitutional Change which was formed to consult with the public on possible reforms to section 57 of the Australian Constitution. This Group found that 'in a substantial segment of our society there is a lack of knowledge and confidence to express informed views on constitutional questions'.

8.8 The Committee therefore considers that there is a need for an ongoing and extensive information and education program to ensure Australians can make an informed choice in relation to constitutional reform, including the options that may be put to them relating to an Australian republic. The Committee strongly believes that constitutional education and awareness should be an on-going and continuous priority, not just in relation to any proposed move towards an Australian republic.

8.9 In this context, the Committee considers that there is a need for a standing body to facilitate and oversee on-going education and awareness programs to improve the level of awareness and understanding of the Australian Constitution. The Committee recommends that a parliamentary committee should be established and fully resourced to undertake this responsibility. Such a Committee would also facilitate and oversee the on-going education, involvement and engagement of the Australian people throughout any proposed process of moving towards a republic …

[136] A process

8.23 The process by which Australia would move towards a republic was a key focus of the Committee's inquiry. The Committee is of the view that Australians have a fundamental entitlement to be fully involved in any future process. It fully supports the compelling evidence of the crucial importance of engaging the Australian people and giving them ownership of their Constitution, and in the course of events, their republic …

[137] 8.26 The Committee is in favour of a three-stage consultative process, involving two plebiscites and a drafting convention, followed by the fourth and final stage of a constitutional referendum to amend the Constitution. The Committee believes that before initiating any process, it is vitally important to lay out the intended steps in the process, so that Australians have a clear picture of the opportunities they will have for involvement …

8.29 The Committee believes it is essential that the first step in the process should be to seek from Australians their view on the fundamental question of whether Australia should become a republic. The Committee notes evidence that opinion polls show[ ] majority support for an Australian republic, but supports the argument that before expending substantial resources it is important to first test this proposition in a full national non-binding plebiscite …

[139] 8.43 If the result of the initial threshold plebiscite is a majority vote for becoming a republic, the Committee is strongly of the view that Australians have a right to participate in any decision regarding what type of republic Australia may become, before reaching the stage of a constitutional referendum. The Committee considers that the optimum way to achieve this participation is through a second non-binding plebiscite, giving Australians a choice of models …

[140] 8.54 Following the second plebiscite, Australians will have had the opportunity to express their views about whether they want a republic, and what they want that republic to look like. At this point it will be necessary to refine the details of the republic model that has emerged as the preferred option, and to make preparations for **[141]** amending the Constitution, in readiness for the final, and binding, constitutional referendum.

8.55 The Committee considered options for this third, refining stage, and is of the view that the most effective means for achieving optimum outcomes would be the convening of a Drafting Convention comprising Australians who are expert in constitutional law or who have recognised relevant skills and abilities. The Committee noted evidence supporting an elected constitutional convention, but considers that the task of fleshing out the finer details of the necessary amendments to the Constitution requires the expertise of Australia's significant body of capable and skilled constitutional experts.

4. A Bill of Rights?

Another area of ongoing debate is whether Australia should have a Bill of Rights. The Bill of Rights in the United States Constitution is the classic example of express provision for judicially enforceable limitations on the powers of government. The United States Constitution was adopted in 1789, with the Bill of Rights added as the first 10 amendments in 1791.

The Constitution of the United States of America

Amendment I

Congress shall make no law respecting an establishment of religion, or prohibiting the free exercise thereof; or abridging the freedom of speech, or of the press; or the right of the people peaceably to assemble, and to petition the Government for a redress of grievances.

Amendment II

A well-regulated Militia, being necessary to the security of a free State, the right of the people to keep and bear Arms, shall not be infringed.

Amendment III

No Soldier shall, in time of peace be quartered in any house, without the consent of the Owner, nor in time of war, but in a manner to be prescribed by law.

Amendment IV

The right of the people to be secure in their persons, houses, papers, and effects, against unreasonable searches and seizures, shall not be violated, and no Warrants shall issue, but upon probable cause, supported by Oath or affirmation, and particularly describing the place to be searched, and the persons or things to be seized.

Amendment V

No person shall be held to answer for a capital, or other infamous crime, unless on a presentment or indictment of a Grand Jury, except in cases arising in the land or naval forces, or in the Militia, when in actual service, in time of War or public danger; nor shall any person be subject for the same offense to be twice put in jeopardy of life or limb; nor shall be compelled in any criminal case to be a witness against himself; nor be deprived of life, liberty, or property, without due process of law; nor shall private property be taken for public use, without just compensation.

Amendment VI

In all criminal prosecutions, the accused shall enjoy the right to a speedy and public trial, by an impartial jury of the State and district wherein the crime shall have been committed, which district shall have been previously ascertained by law, and to be informed of the nature and cause of the accusation; to be confronted with the witnesses against him; to have compulsory process for obtaining witnesses in his favor, and to have the Assistance of Counsel for his defense.

Amendment VII

In Suits at common law, where the value in controversy shall exceed twenty dollars, the right of trial by jury shall be preserved, and no fact tried by a jury shall be otherwise re-examined in any court of the United States, than according to the rules of the common law.

Amendment VIII

Excessive bail shall not be required, nor excessive fines imposed, nor cruel and unusual punishments inflicted.

Amendment IX

The enumeration in the Constitution, of certain rights, shall not be construed to deny or disparage others retained by the people.

Amendment X

The powers not delegated to the United States by the Constitution, nor prohibited by it to the States, are reserved to the States respectively, or to the people.

The guarantees in the First Amendment, and by implication those in the other amendments, apply only at the federal level. However, in 1868 after the American Civil War the Fourteenth Amendment was added to provide the same kind of protection against action by the States. Section 1 of that Amendment provides:

Amendment XIV

1. All persons born or naturalized in the United States, and subject to the jurisdiction thereof, are citizens of the United States and of the State wherein they reside. No State shall make or enforce any law which shall abridge the privileges or immunities of citizens of the United States; nor shall any State deprive any person of life, liberty, or property, without due process of law; nor deny to any person within its jurisdiction the equal protection of the laws.

The second sentence is in three parts, commonly referred to as "the privileges and immunities clause", "the due process clause" and "the equal protection clause".

In the United States, the combination of these guarantees with the practice of judicial review has meant that legislation enacted by the federal Congress but judicially perceived as infringing a Bill of Rights provision is automatically struck down by the courts. Since the adoption of the Fourteenth Amendment, the same has been true of State legislation (and other forms of "State action"). Whether these consequences of judicial enforcement are a *necessary* feature of any Bill of Rights worth having is a matter for continuing debate. The fact that the United States model does entail such consequences has been a major source of concerns about the merits and dangers of judicial "activism" (see Chapter 8, §2) and about the "democratic deficit" of allowing an elected legislature to be overridden by an unelected judiciary.

A particular focus for these concerns has been the absence of any definition of the word "liberty" in the "due process" clause of the Fourteenth Amendment. Its content has been supplied partly by reference to the first 10 Amendments, and partly by reference to societal values "**[105]** so rooted in the traditions and conscience of our people as to be ranked as fundamental" (*Snyder v Massachusetts*, 291 US 97 (1934)). Where such fundamental "liberty interests" are involved, the requirement of "due process" has been construed as requiring not only procedural fairness in judicial or executive action, but appropriate weighting in legislative action. A statute that impinges on such an interest without a sufficient countervailing reason, or without according due weight to the protected "liberty interest", may be struck down as arbitrary (that is, as failing to render "substantive due process").

Thus, while the Fourteenth Amendment is formulated as an express guarantee, it has also proved to be in effect a fertile source of implied guarantees. A recent example is *Lawrence v Texas*, 539 US 558 (2003), holding that a criminal conviction for consensual sexual activity between male homosexuals in their home infringed Fourteenth Amendment liberty "**[562]** both in its spatial and more transcendent dimensions". The contrary decision in *Bowers v Hardwick*, 478 US 186 (1986) was overruled by a 6:3 majority. The Court affirmed in *Lawrence v Texas* that: "**[567]** When sexuality finds overt expression in intimate conduct with another person, the conduct can be but one element in a personal bond that is more enduring. The liberty protected by the Constitution allows homosexual persons the right to make this choice".

Earlier examples include *Planned Parenthood of Southeastern Pennsylvania v Casey*, 505 US 833 (1992) (reaffirming the decision in *Roe v Wade*, 410 US 113 (1973) that a pregnant woman has a "liberty" interest in choosing physician-assisted abortion) and *Washington v Glucksberg*, 521 US 702 (1997) (declining to hold that a terminally ill patient has a "liberty interest" in choosing physician-assisted suicide). Such decisions are invariably controversial. They may only be possible in the context of a constitutional culture that routinely accepts the judicial enforcement of express constitutional rights. Even then, the controversies over particular issues are often intensified by claims that the Court is exceeding its legitimate role.

While the current controversies focus on issues like those in *Roe v Wade* and *Lawrence v Texas*, any debate about the merits and dangers of direct judicial enforcement of a Bill of Rights must also take account of an earlier phase of the United States Supreme Court's history. Since the 1930s, the Court has given more vigorous protection to civil and political rights (especially those set out in the First Amendment) than to economic rights. What makes this especially intriguing is that until then the Court's apparent priorities had been the opposite: "personal rights" had appeared to be subordinate to "property rights". Among the more infamous examples were *Dred Scott v Sandford*, 60 US (19 Howard) 393 (1857), which denied the personal rights of slaves and affirmed the property rights of their masters, and *Plessy v Ferguson*, 163 US 537 (1896), which upheld southern segregation laws on the basis that separate but equal is still equal.

The shift since the 1930s to "personal rights" rather than "property rights" is manifest not only in the importance attached to provisions like the First Amendment, but also in the identification of the "liberty interests" against which legislation is tested for "substantive due process". The recent examples of "liberty interests" given above relate to intimate personal matters. By contrast, when the concept of "substantive due process" was first developed a century ago, the "liberty" that it was used to defend was "liberty of contract".

The judicial enforcement of the Bill of Rights had been slow to develop. However, over a 60-year period beginning with the *Slaughterhouse Cases*, 83 US (16 Wallace) 36 (1873), those provisions in the Bill of Rights and the Fourteenth Amendment that were capable of being construed as protecting economic rights were vigorously exploited. It was in this context that the references to "liberty" in the Fifth and Fourteenth Amendments were understood almost exclusively as protecting freedom of contract.

An extreme example came in *Lochner v New York*, 198 US 45 (1905), which invalidated by 5:4 a New York law prohibiting employment in bakeries for more than 60 hours a week. The opinion of the Court, written by Justice Peckham, argued for "[54] the right of the individual to labor for such time as he may choose". It protested that "[57] bakers as a class" were "equal in intelligence and capacity to men in other trades or manual occupations" and were equally "able to assert their rights and care for themselves without the protecting arm of the state". It argued that legislative attempts to regulate working conditions denied "substantive due process" because they were "[61] mere meddlesome interferences with the rights of the individual". Justice Oliver Wendell Holmes Jr delivered a famous dissent: "[75] The Fourteenth Amendment does not enact Mr Herbert Spencer's Social Statics ... [A] constitution is not intended to embody a particular economic theory, whether of paternalism and the organic relation of the citizen to the State or of *laissez faire*". Despite persistent dissents, a majority extended the *Lochner* version of "substantive due process" to other cases, notably in *Adkins v Children's Hospital*, 261 US 525 (1923), to invalidate a law prescribing minimum wages for women.

Among the nine Justices of the United States Supreme Court in 1933 when Franklin Delano Roosevelt was inaugurated as President, there were four who staunchly adhered to the approach of *Lochner v New York*: Justices Van Devanter, McReynolds, Sutherland and Butler ("the Four Horsemen of the Apocalypse"). A dissenting position was maintained by Justices Brandeis, Stone and Cardozo. Chief Justice Hughes and Justice Roberts were swinging voters. When legislation was challenged the results were uneven and often unpredictable.

From 1934 onwards there came a dramatic series of decisions that invalidated United States statutes, especially those associated with President Roosevelt's "New Deal". Some of the most controversial cases were decided by 6:3 or 5:4 majorities, with Justices Van Devanter, McReynolds, Sutherland and Butler consistently in the majority. In *Railroad Retirement Board v*

Alton Railroad Co, 295 US 330 (1935), for example, the Court held by 5:4 that the *Railroad Retirement Act 1934* (US), which established a compulsory pension scheme for retired railroad workers, violated the "due process" clause of the Fifth Amendment.

Whatever the merits or demerits of such decisions, they provoked a constitutional crisis. In February 1937, as President Roosevelt entered on his second four-year term, he announced a plan to "pack" the Supreme Court by increasing the size of the bench from nine judges to 15 (so that issues which had formerly evoked a 5:4 decision against the validity of "New Deal" legislation might now evoke a 10:5 decision in its favour). After much controversy, the "court-packing" plan was defeated on 24 May 1937 by a Senate majority of 70:20. However, the conventional wisdom was that the threat had been averted only because the Supreme Court itself had changed its mind, or, rather, that Justice Roberts and perhaps Chief Justice Hughes had swung their support away from the "Four Horsemen" so as to leave them in ineffectual dissent. The turning point was Justice Roberts' vote in *West Coast Hotel Co v Parrish*, 300 US 379 (1937) ("the switch in time that saved nine"), the result of which was that *Lochner v New York* and *Adkins v Children's Hospital* were overruled.

As it happened, Roosevelt had the opportunity to reshape the Court in any event. Within four years of the "court-packing" plan, he was able to appoint six new Justices. Three of them (the "activists" Hugo Black and William O Douglas, and the more cautious Felix Frankfurter) were to dominate the Court's judicial philosophy for decades. The effect was fundamental. In the economic sphere, the Court shifted its ground to repudiate activism, asserting, in the language of *Nebbia v New York*, 291 US 502 (1934), that "**[537]** a state is free to adopt whatever economic policy may reasonably be deemed to promote public welfare" and that so long as laws "have a reasonable relation to a proper legislative purpose" the Court will not interfere. However, on issues of civil and political rights, the Court's activism in the 1950s and 1960s came to attract worldwide attention – most dramatically in *Brown v Board of Education*, 347 US 483 (1954), where racially segregated education in public schools was held to be unconstitutional and the "separate-but-equal" doctrine of *Plessy v Ferguson* was overruled.

More recently, Supreme Court "activism" has again taken different directions. From 1967 onwards the majority of new appointments to the Court have been made by Republican Presidents, and the changing composition of the Court is generally thought to have put an end to the "liberal" initiatives of the mid-century decades. If this has not resulted in a major reversal of decisions already established, that has largely reflected the influence of "moderate" conservatives like Sandra Day O'Connor, appointed in 1981. Her retirement in 2005 may have shifted the balance again. Current controversy centres on speculation about a possible overruling of *Roe v Wade*, and even about a possible return to *Lochner v New York*.

Despite the mixed signals emerging from political debates in the United States about the Supreme Court's role, many nations have adopted a Bill of Rights on the full United States model: that is, an instrument in which rights are constitutionally entrenched and used by the judiciary to strike down inconsistent laws and government actions. A notable example in 1950 was the Constitution of India. Part III of that Constitution, headed "Fundamental Rights", not only expanded the coverage and detail of the guaranteed rights and freedoms, but included in Art 32, as itself a fundamental right, a new simplified procedure for direct access to the Supreme Court of India "for the enforcement of the rights conferred by this Part". (However, the Indian draftsmen did accept the advice they received from Justice Felix Frankfurter of the United States Supreme Court to avoid any reference to the concept of "due process of law".)

In addition, a separate Pt IV, entitled "Directive Principles of State Policy", sought to give constitutional status to other important social aspirations and values, stipulating (in Art 37) that: "The provisions contained in this Part shall not be enforceable by any court, but the principles therein laid down are nevertheless fundamental in the governance of the country and it shall be the duty of the State to apply these principles in making laws".

The tension between judicial review and parliamentary sovereignty was particularly acute in the Indian case, since the Constitution is fully amendable by the Indian Parliament – sometimes by a special majority, but mostly by ordinary legislation. In the first two decades after Independence, the "fundamental rights" provisions – particularly the right to property – were repeatedly amended by Parliament. A series of cases grappling with whether such amendments were possible reached a climax in *Kesavananda v State of Kerala*, AIR 1973 SC 1461, where the Supreme Court of India held that Parliament could amend the whole of the Constitution, including the "fundamental rights", but not if it affects the "essential features" or "basic structure" of the Constitution. Surprisingly, the Court based its reasoning on the language used by the High Court of Australia in *Victoria v Commonwealth* (*Payroll Tax Case*) (1971) 122 CLR 353. Whether a particular right or freedom (or the aspect or application of it affected by an amendment) is an "essential feature" of the Constitution, or part of its "basic structure", is a question determined by the Supreme Court on a case-by-case basis.

Since 1950 many countries have built on the Indian model, most notably in the 1996 Constitution of post-apartheid South Africa. That Constitution goes significantly further than the Indian model by including in its "Bill of Rights" social aspirations and values of the kind that the Indian model had relegated to "Directive Principles", usually in the form of provisions adapted from the 1966 International Covenant on Economic, Social and Cultural Rights.

Constitution of the Republic of South Africa

26 Housing

(1) Everyone has the right to have access to adequate housing.

(2) The state must take reasonable legislative and other measures, within its available resources, to achieve the progressive realisation of this right.

(3) No one may be evicted from their home, or have their home demolished, without an order of court made after considering all the relevant circumstances. No legislation may permit arbitrary evictions.

27 Health care, food, water and social security

(1) Everyone has the right to have access to –

   (a) health care services, including reproductive health care;

   (b) sufficient food and water; and

   (c) social security, including, if they are unable to support themselves and their dependants, appropriate social assistance.

(2) The state must take reasonable legislative and other measures, within its available resources, to achieve the progressive realisation of each of these rights.

(3) No one may be refused emergency medical treatment.

29 Education

(1) Everyone has the right –

   (a) to a basic education, including adult basic education; and

   (b) to further education, which the state, through reasonable measures, must make progressively available and accessible.

Other countries have sought to give significant recognition and public commitment to the protection of human rights, while avoiding or modifying the consequences of direct judicial enforcement on the United States model. Thus, Canada experimented in 1960 with a statutory Bill of Rights, the *Canadian Bill of Rights 1960* (Can). Its effective operation depended on s 2, which provided: "Every law of Canada shall, unless it is expressly declared by an Act of the Parliament of Canada that it shall operate notwithstanding the Canadian Bill of Rights, be so construed and applied as not to abrogate, abridge or infringe ... any of the rights or freedoms herein declared and recognized and declared". The doubts as to the effectiveness of this device were settled in *R v Drybones* [1970] SCR 282, (1969) 9 DLR(3d) 473. The Supreme Court of Canada held that s 2 was effective not only against earlier statutes but also against later statutes – not merely as a guide to statutory construction, nor on the other hand as affecting the *validity* of the later statute, but as a mandatory directive to judges faced with two inconsistent but valid statutes that the Bill of Rights, rather than the offending statute, was to be *operative*. Whether an Australian court would take a similar view is not certain. On the one hand, the express declaration required by s 2 was the kind of "magic formula" dismissed by the High Court in *South-Eastern Drainage Board (SA) v Savings Bank of South Australia* (1939) 62 CLR 603; on the other hand, that case is of doubtful authority (see Chapter 11, §3).

In any event, the Canadian Bill of Rights was superseded in 1982 by the *Canadian Charter of Rights and Freedoms*, introduced as a new Pt I of the repatriated *Constitution Act 1982* (Can). Section 33 of the Charter develops the earlier statutory device as a so-called "override" clause. Parliament or the legislature of a province may, for a renewable five-year period, "expressly declare in an Act of Parliament or of the legislature, as the case may be, that the Act or a provision thereof shall operate notwithstanding a provision included in section 2 or sections 7 to 15 of this Charter". This means that a Canadian parliament can override rights such as "the right not to be arbitrarily detained or imprisoned" in s 8 or even the right to equality under the law in s 15, but that rights like that to vote in federal elections in s 3 are beyond its reach. Despite vigorous judicial application of the Charter, legislatures have been reluctant to make use of the "override" clause. Perhaps a more significant feature of the Charter, widely adopted or adapted elsewhere – for example, by Deane and Toohey JJ in *Nationwide News Pty Ltd v Wills* (1992) 177 CLR 1 at 77 – is the balancing formula in s 1: the protected rights and freedoms are "subject only to such reasonable limits prescribed by law as can be demonstrably justified in a free and democratic society".

If a Bill of Rights is enacted in statutory form, either as an alternative to constitutional entrenchment or as a prelude to it, it may be more easy to change. Thus, the unsuccessful proposal for an Australian Bill of Rights advanced in 1983 by Senator Gareth Evans as Attorney-General envisaged a statutory enactment, which could be amended in the light of judicial decisions and other experience over a period of perhaps a decade, after which the amended form might be put to referendum for entrenchment in the Constitution. Again, a statutory Bill of Rights may stop short of empowering the courts to override legislation, either by offering a lesser remedy or by limiting its effect to exhortatory and educative functions. In this form, a Bill of Rights is often viewed as less of a threat to parliamentary sovereignty, since the final say on any conflict of rights is left not to the judiciary but to Parliament. One example is the *New Zealand Bill of Rights Act 1990* (NZ); another is the *Human Rights Act 1998* (UK), which incorporated the 1950 European Convention for the Protection of Human Rights and Fundamental Freedoms into British law.

Human Rights Act 1998 (UK)

3 Interpretation of Legislation

(1) So far as it is possible to do so, primary legislation and subordinate legislation must be read and given effect in a way which is compatible with the Convention rights.

(2) This section –

   (a)   applies to primary legislation and subordinate legislation whenever enacted;
   (b)   does not affect the validity, continuing operation or enforcement of any incompatible primary legislation; and
   (c)   does not affect the validity, continuing operation or enforcement of any incompatible subordinate legislation if (disregarding any possibility of revocation) primary legislation prevents removal of the incompatibility.

4 Declaration of Incompatibility

(1) Subsection (2) applies in any proceedings in which a court determines whether a provision of primary legislation is compatible with a Convention right.

(2) If the court is satisfied that the provision is incompatible with a Convention right, it may make a declaration of that incompatibility.

(3) Subsection (4) applies in any proceedings in which a court determines whether a provision of subordinate legislation, made in the exercise of a power conferred by primary legislation, is compatible with a Convention right.

(4) If the court is satisfied-

    (a)   that the provision is incompatible with a Convention right, and

    (b)   that (disregarding any possibility of revocation) the primary legislation concerned prevents removal of the incompatibility,

it may make a declaration of that incompatibility ...

(6) A declaration under this section ("a declaration of incompatibility") –

    (a)   does not affect the validity, continuing operation or enforcement of the provision in respect of which it is given; and

    (b)   is not binding on the parties to the proceedings in which it is made.

As s 4 makes clear, a declaration of incompatibility by a court does not affect the validity of a law even though it has been found to be inconsistent with a protected right. The conflict will continue unless there is a response from a different arm of government. That is, the legislature may respond by amending the offending provision; or in an urgent case the amendment may be made by executive order under s 10(2), which provides that, after a declaration of incompatibility has been made, "If a Minister of the Crown considers that there are compelling reasons for proceeding under this section, he may by order make such amendments to the legislation as he considers necessary to remove the incompatibility".

Australia is now the only democratic country without a national Bill of Rights. Indeed, among all nations, democratic or not, only a few – Brunei and Burma, for example – lack a Bill of Rights in some form (see Gareth Griffith, *The Protection of Human Rights: A Review of Selected Jurisdictions* (Parliament of New South Wales, Briefing Paper 3/2000)). Of course, the fact that nations like Afghanistan or China have a Bill of Rights does not necessarily mean that human rights are better protected there than in Australia. The 1936 Constitution of the Soviet Union was notorious for the contrast between its ringing declarations of rights and freedoms, and their systematic violation in practice (see Giovanni Sartori's comments on "façade constitutions" and "fake constitutions" in Chapter 1, §1).

Nations such as Canada, New Zealand and the United Kingdom, all of which had traditionally placed their reliance on the common law tradition and parliamentary sovereignty for the protection of basic freedoms, now have Bills of Rights. By contrast, traditional conceptions of parliamentary sovereignty and the separation of powers continue to be invoked in Australia as arguments against such proposals, as illustrated by the report in 2001 of the Standing Committee on Law and Justice of the New South Wales Parliament.

Standing Committee on Law and Justice, *A NSW Bill of Rights*
(New South Wales Parliament, Report No 17, October 2001)

[110] 7.3 The Committee believes that some of the arguments put forward by advocates of a Bill of Rights have merit. During this inquiry there have been examples given where human rights of individuals or of minority groups have been neglected. Some of the examples occurred in other jurisdictions, but there have also been failures by NSW governments to address individual and at times systemic problems. The Committee agrees that the common law is not a sufficient protection of individual rights in the absence of legislative action ...

7.5 Despite these arguments in favour of a Bill of Rights, the Committee does not support the solution proposed. A statutory Bill could lead to some improvement in human rights protections in some instances. However the cost of this uncertain marginal improvement is a fundamental change in the relationship between representative democracy, through an elected Parliament, and the judicial system. The independence of the Judiciary and the supremacy of Parliament are the foundations of the current system; both begin to alter under a Bill of Rights. A Bill of Rights would increase the responsibility of the Judiciary to protect human rights, giving it a role that should primarily be the responsibility of Parliament.

7.6 Advocates of a minimalist statutory Bill … argue that parliamentary supremacy can be maintained in a Bill by its statutory **[111]** nature and by preserving the power of parliamentary override. However a number of participants in this inquiry believe that judges could undertake this task of human rights protection more effectively than its elected representatives have done to date. Regardless of whether this is correct, the Committee believes it is ultimately against the public interest for Parliament to hand over such decisions to an unelected Judiciary who are not directly accountable to the community for the consequences of their decisions. The Committee believes an increased politicisation of the Judiciary is an inevitable consequence of the introduction of a Bill of Rights.

7.7 The Committee acknowledges that the notion of representative democracy is modified by influences such as party politics and the development of a complex bureaucracy. However it believes the contrast made by some witnesses of principled, reasoned decisions made by judges compared to politically expedient decisions made by parliamentarians underestimates the very different roles that the institutions of the Courts and Parliament undertake.

7.8 The Judiciary is already subject to unprecedented, and frequently unwarranted, public criticism. This will only increase if a Bill of Rights increases the scope for judicial decision making into an area of broadly defined rights. Much of the public pressure and criticism directed at elected representatives will then also be directed to the Judiciary. It is true that, not being elected, the Judiciary is better able to make unpopular decisions without making compromises to accommodate majority opinions. However in a democracy this public pressure will still seek an outlet, with greater scrutiny of individual judges and much greater public pressure regarding appointment of judges the most likely outcomes. Executive governments will be increasingly likely to make appointments based upon judges' political views rather than their legal skills. Ultimately this tendency undermines the independence and quality of the Judiciary …

[113] 7.18 Inadequacies in the protection of human rights may exist in New South Wales but the Committee believes the Bill of Rights as a solution raises more problems than it resolves. It is preferable that Parliament become a more effective guardian of human rights rather than handing this role over to an unelected Judiciary.

Attempts to achieve a Bill of Rights for Australia, or better constitutional protection for the human rights of Australians, date back to the efforts of Inglis Clark at the first Australasian Federal Convention in 1891 (see Chapter 4, §4). His impassioned but unsuccessful attempt was the first of many failures.

George Williams, *The Case for an Australian Bill of Rights:*
Freedom in the War on Terror
(University of New South Wales Press, 2004)

[56] 1944 referendum

In 1942, at the constitutional convention held in wartime Canberra, it was proposed that the Commonwealth be given a series of new powers, including the power to make laws to guarantee "the four freedoms": "freedom of speech and expression," "religious freedom," "freedom from want," and "freedom from fear." This proposal would not have amounted to a guarantee of rights, but it would have given the Commonwealth the power to legislate to guarantee such rights against state legislation.

In the event, this provision was not included in the proposal put to the people in the referendum held on 19 August 1944. Instead it was proposed that the constitution be amended to grant the Commonwealth fourteen new powers over postwar reconstruction. The proposal also sought to insert guarantees of free speech and expression and extend to the states the guarantee of religious freedom contained in section 116 of the constitution. These powers and guarantees would only have operated for a period of five years. The referendum was lost on the national vote with a 45.39 per cent "yes" vote to a 53.30 per cent "no" vote. It received a majority "yes" vote in only two states …

[58] Human Rights Bill 1973 …

[T]he next two attempts to bring about greater protection for fundamental freedoms came in the form of statutory Bills of Rights – Bills of Rights passed by the federal parliament but not incorporated in the constitution. In 1973, Senator Lionel Murphy, attorney-general in the Whitlam Labor government, introduced the Human Rights Bill into the federal parliament. The bill would have implemented the International Covenant on Civil and Political Rights in Australia by protecting a range of rights, including freedom of expression and movement, and the right to marry. Murphy promoted the bill on the basis that the constitution provides scant protection for rights, arguing that "although we believe these rights to be basic to our democratic society, they now receive remarkably little legal protection in Australia." He went on:

> What protection is given by the Australian Constitution is minimal and does not touch the most significant of these rights... Ideally, in my view, a Bill of Rights should be written into the Australian Constitution... [T]he enactment of this legislation will be a significant milestone in the political maturity of Australia. It will help to make Australian society more free and more just.

[59] Under section 109 of the constitution, the rights listed in Murphy's legislation would have overridden inconsistent state legislation. It also provided that Commonwealth legislation would be ineffective if it breached any of the rights listed in the bill, unless the statute included an express exemption from its operation. The bill went further than subsequent attempts at statutory Bills of Rights by declaring that the listed rights could be enforced not only against governments but also against the private sector. The Human Rights Bill met strong opposition. Because the International Covenant on Civil and Political Rights had not yet received the necessary number of ratifications to come into force, the government did not press the bill and it lapsed in early 1974.

Australian Human Rights Bill 1985

The failure of Murphy's Human Rights Bill did not end attempts by Labor governments to protect rights by implementing international treaties and covenants. The Whitlam government, for example, was successful in enacting the *Racial Discrimination Act 1975*, while the Hawke government enacted the *Sex Discrimination Act 1984*. Senator Gareth Evans, attorney-general in the Hawke government, sought to take up where Murphy had left off in promoting a statutory Bill of Rights. In 1983 he prepared a Bill of Rights that, like its 1973 predecessor, would have implemented rights recognised in international law. But the 1983 model was weaker in several ways, the most significant being that it would only have applied to governmental action. Although the bill was given cabinet support, it was not introduced into parliament. Lionel Bowen, who replaced Evans as attorney-general after the 1984 federal election, introduced a redrafted and watered-down bill, the Australian Human Rights Bill, into federal parliament in November 1985. Although it was passed by the House of Representatives, it was withdrawn on 28 November 1986. Gough Whitlam has suggested that the bill was abandoned because of a deal between Prime Minister Hawke and the Western Australian [60] Labor premier, Brian Burke, because the "one vote, one value" provision could have affected electoral boundaries in that state, with potential electoral implications for the Burke government.

The constitutional commission and 1988 referendum

The legislation promoted by Murphy, Evans and Bowen sought to enact statutory Bills of Rights. In the face of the opposition to the Australian Human Rights Bill, the Hawke government changed tack. It established a constitutional commission in December 1985 to recommend a revision of the Australian constitution in order, among other things, to "ensure that democratic rights are guaranteed." The commission responded in an interim report in April 1987, in which it recommended that the scope of the express rights in the constitution should be expanded, but also foreshadowed the need for wider change.

The commission's final report of June 1988 was far more ambitious. It recommended that a new chapter ("Chapter VIA – Rights and Freedoms") be inserted into the constitution, containing a wide range of fundamental rights drawn heavily from the Canadian Charter of Rights and Freedoms 1982. It proposed that a person whose rights were breached should be able to gain an appropriate remedy in the courts and rejected the idea of allowing the Commonwealth or the states to pass legislation "notwithstanding" a guarantee of rights in the constitution. A majority of the commission argued that a power to "opt out" or override constitutional guarantees "is inconsistent with the whole process of entrenching rights in the Constitution."

Bowen had requested that the commission provide an interim report so that a referendum to amend the constitution could be held in 1988, the bicentenary of the white settlement of Australia. So, after the interim report but before the commission's final report, the Hawke government announced that it would initiate constitutional change. Four proposals were put to the people on 3 September 1988, derived, with some variations, from the recom-**[61]**-mendations in the commission's interim report. The first and third proposals, respectively, concerned four-year maximum terms for federal parliament and constitutional recognition of local government. The second proposal sought to guarantee "one vote, one value" by requiring that the population of each electorate could not deviate by more than 20 per cent from any other electorate. This proposal would also have inserted a right to vote into the constitution. The fourth proposal also sought to guarantee basic freedoms, but only by extending the operation of existing guarantees in the constitution. Section 80 would have been repealed and replaced with a provision guaranteeing trial by jury for offences under Commonwealth, state and territory laws in cases "where the accused is liable to imprisonment for more than two years or any form of corporal punishment." New sections 115A and 115B would have extended the guarantee of "just terms" for any "acquisition of property" to state laws and laws made for the territories by the Commonwealth. Finally, section 116 would have been deleted and replaced with a section guaranteeing the religious freedom already spelt out in section 116 but extended to laws passed by a state or territory.

Each of the four proposals was defeated nationally and in every state – a dismal result for the proponents of change. The highest national "yes" vote was 37.10 per cent for the proposal on "one vote, one value." The fourth proposal received an astonishingly low vote: nationally, 30.33 per cent of voters registered a "yes" vote and 68.19 per cent voted "no" – the lowest "yes" vote ever recorded in Australia. In South Australia the "yes" vote was only 25.53 per cent; in Tasmania it was 25.10 per cent. Unfortunately, the poor result undermined any move to insert other rights into the constitution or to implement the final report of the constitutional commission.

The failure of the 1988 referendum can be attributed to such factors as the strong campaign mounted by opponents of change and a lack of community understanding of the proposals. It also demonstrated how bipartisan support can be essential for success-**[62]**-ful constitutional change. A lacklustre "yes" case by the Hawke government was pitted against determined opposition. In such a climate, the support of the Australian people cannot be assumed – even for a proposal that would better protect their rights against government …

[65] [To] achieve reform in the area of constitutional rights it will be necessary to build a broad political and popular base for change underpinned by understanding of the issues and proposals. It was only in 2004 in the Australian Capital Territory that this was achieved for the first time.

The Labor government of Chief Minister Jon Stanhope came to power in the Australian Capital Territory in October 2001 having promised to seek the views of the Canberra community on the idea of a Bill or Charter of Rights. Once elected, the government established an ACT Bill of Rights Consultative Committee. The Committee sought submissions from the public and held many "town meetings" and other consultations with community and expert groups. In total, 49 public forums were held on the issue, or around one forum for every 6500 people. The Committee also commissioned a deliberative poll of residents: over a weekend, 200 people had the chance to hear different sides of the argument and discuss the issues among themselves. Both the submissions to the Committee and the deliberative poll showed majority community support for an ACT Bill of Rights. Of the submissions received, 61 per cent supported a Bill of Rights; at the deliberative poll, 59 per cent did so. Given this, the Committee recommended in favour of a Bill of Rights for the ACT.

Report of the ACT Bill of Rights Consultative Committee,
Towards an ACT Human Rights Act
(May 2003)

[2] 1. After extensive community consultations, the Bill of Rights Consultative Committee considers that some form of bill of rights is appropriate and desirable in the ACT. While highly visible abuses of human rights are not commonplace in the ACT, rights are currently protected in a partial and piecemeal manner under Commonwealth and ACT law. A bill of rights would improve the protection of rights and also provide an accessible statement of the rights that are fundamental to a life of dignity and value.

2. The Committee believes the bill of rights ought to take the form of an ACT *Human Rights Act*, an ordinary piece of legislation, rather than an entrenched bill of rights or a declaration of the Legislative Assembly. The legislation should be designed to encourage a dialogue among the branches of government and the community about the protection of human rights, rather than to allow a judicial or legislative monologue on rights. While such a document would have legal force, its primary purpose would be to encourage the development of a human rights-conscious culture in ACT public life and in the community.

3. However, the dialogue about rights proposed by the Consultative Committee cannot be an open-ended one. After debate, the legislature should still be assigned the 'last say' in relation to human rights issues. The judiciary should not be able to invalidate legislation. Rather, it should be able to give its opinion that a law is incompatible with the *Human Rights Act*. It should then be a matter for the legislature to determine whether or not to amend the legislation so that it conforms with the *Human Rights Act* …

[3] 6. The Committee proposes that the rights set out in the two major human rights treaties to which Australia is a party – the International Covenant on Economic, Social and Cultural Rights and the International Covenant on Civil and Political Rights – should be protected by the *Human Rights Act*.

The Stanhope government accepted the recommendation and the Legislative Assembly proceeded to enact the *Human Rights Act 2004* (ACT), Australia's first Bill of Rights. It came into force on 1 July 2004.

Human Rights Act 2004 (ACT)

Preamble

1 Human rights are necessary for individuals to live lives of dignity and value.

2 Respecting, protecting and promoting the rights of individuals improves the welfare of the whole community.

3 Human rights are set out in this Act so that individuals know what their rights are.

4 Setting out these human rights also makes it easier for them to be taken into consideration in the development and interpretation of legislation.

5 This Act encourages individuals to see themselves, and each other, as the holders of rights, and as responsible for upholding the human rights of others.

6 Few rights are absolute. Human rights may be subject only to the reasonable limits in law that can be demonstrably justified in a free and democratic society. One individual's rights may also need to be weighed against another individual's rights.

7 Although human rights belong to all individuals, they have special significance for Indigenous people – the first owners of this land, members of its most enduring cultures, and individuals for whom the issue of rights protection has great and continuing importance.

The Act protects a range of rights and freedoms adapted from the International Covenant on Civil and Political Rights, including:

8 Recognition and equality before the law

(1) Everyone has the right to recognition as a person before the law.

(2) Everyone has the right to enjoy his or her human rights without distinction or discrimination of any kind.

(3) Everyone is equal before the law and is entitled to the equal protection of the law without discrimination. In particular, everyone has the right to equal and effective protection against discrimination on any ground.

9 Right to life

(1) Everyone has the right to life. In particular, no-one may be arbitrarily deprived of life.

(2) This section applies to a person from the time of birth.

16 Freedom of expression

(1) Everyone has the right to hold opinions without interference.

(2) Everyone has the right to freedom of expression. This right includes the freedom to seek, receive and impart information and ideas of all kinds, regardless of borders, whether orally, in writing or in print, by way of art, or in another way chosen by him or her.

21 Fair trial

(1) Everyone has the right to have criminal charges, and rights and obligations recognised by law, decided by a competent, independent and impartial court or tribunal after a fair and public hearing.

27 Rights of minorities

Anyone who belongs to an ethnic, religious or linguistic minority must not be denied the right, with other members of the minority, to enjoy his or her culture, to declare and practise his or her religion, or to use his or her language.

The ACT government did not adopt the Consultative Committee's recommendation that the Act should also protect a range of economic, social and cultural rights, such as the rights to adequate food, clothing and housing. While the government supported such rights "in principle", it did not include them because it was felt that they could raise difficult questions about the allocation of scarce government resources.

Section 37 of the ACT Act provides that when a bill is introduced into the ACT Legislative Assembly the Attorney-General must prepare a written statement (a "compatibility statement") about whether it is consistent with the protected rights. Under s 38, a parliamentary committee must then report on any human rights issues raised by the law. In this process it is accepted that the rights in the Act are not absolute. In language modelled on s 1 of the *Canadian Charter of Rights and Freedoms*, s 28 of the ACT Act declares: "Human rights may be subject only to reasonable limits set by Territory laws that can be demonstrably justified in a free and democratic society". The Act makes no provision for Territory laws that infringe its provisions to be struck down as invalid. Instead, its legal significance is, first, as a basis for statutory interpretation: "In working out the meaning of a Territory law, an interpretation that is consistent with human rights is as far as possible to be preferred". (That provision, in s 30(1) of the Act, is itself declared to be subject to s 139 of the *Legislation Act 2001* (ACT), which states that in construing legislation, an interpretation is to be preferred that will "best achieve the purpose of the Act".)

In cases where an interpretive solution is not found to be possible – that is, where a court is unable to interpret a law as consistent with the *Human Rights Act* – the ACT Supreme Court can make a "declaration of incompatibility" similar to that envisaged by s 4 of the UK legislation. The Legislative Assembly may then amend the law, or can decide to leave it as enacted.

In short, the range of models now available for legislative protection of fundamental rights and freedoms gives rise to significant choices of policy and strategy that any Australian proposal for a Bill of Rights must make.

First, should such a Bill be limited to protecting the community against legislative and executive interferences *by government* with individual rights? Or should it reach out into the community, to protect individuals against abuses *by other individuals* – as most anti-discrimination statutes have done, and as Senator Murphy's 1973 Human Rights Bill proposed to do? Or should there be a middle course, with a primary focus on infringements by laws and government actions, but with the courts having the ability (as the United States Supreme Court has been able to do with the Fourteenth Amendment) to extend the application of the provisions to individual or community practices where these have been sufficiently sanctioned or condoned by governments in a way that involves "State action"?

Second, should a Bill of Rights be constitutionally entrenched, so that any limitations it turns out to impose on legislative or executive action can only be overcome by constitutional amendment – that is, in the Commonwealth of Australia, by referendum under s 128? Or should it be confined to what Justice Toohey referred to (in the 1993 article with which this chapter began) as "**[172]** the normal lawmaking path" – with the consequence that the declarations of rights are freely amendable by Parliament? Or here, too, should there be a middle course, as in the Canadian compromise of constitutionally entrenched provisions that are nevertheless potentially subject to legislative "override"?

Third, should a Bill of Rights be the basis for judicial remedies, or should it merely be used for educative or inspirational purposes (and also perhaps as an explicit aid to statutory interpretation)? If there are to be judicial remedies, what form should they take? Is the appropriate judicial result a declaration of *invalidity*, as in the United States model; or merely of *inoperability*, as in the early Canadian model; or even merely of *incompatibility*, as in the UK and ACT models?

Fourth, what should be the role of the other arms of government? Should the Bill of Rights require, as occurs in Canada, New Zealand and the United Kingdom, that the introduction of new legislation be accompanied by an executive statement as to whether it complies with the protected rights? And should contentious bills then be reviewed by a special parliamentary committee, like the Joint Committee on Human Rights of the United Kingdom Parliament?

Finally, should the guarantees be limited to those of the kind in the International Covenant on Civil and Political Rights? Or should they extend also to rights of the kind in the International Covenant on Economic, Social and Cultural Rights? If the legislative or constitutional protection is limited, as it is in the ACT model, to "rights" of the former kind, does that prioritise a selective range of "rights" on the basis of an outmoded ideology of classical liberalism? Or does it merely reflect the functional recognition, spelled out in the International Covenants themselves, that "economic, social and cultural rights" may not be amenable to judicial remedies, but only to achievement "progressively" by legislative measures tailored "to the maximum of ... available resources" (see Chapter 26, §1)?

It is questions like these that those who consider an Australian Bill of Rights must resolve. In 2005 they were also considered in a process to determine whether Victoria should have the first Bill of Rights to be enacted by an Australian State. Over a seven-month period the Victorian Human Rights Consultation Committee, an independent panel appointed by the government, took part in 55 community forums and had 75 other meetings with government and community bodies. It also received 2524 written submissions, of which 84 per cent (or 94 per cent if petitions and group submissions are included) were in favour of change. The Committee recommended (*Rights, Responsibilities and Respect: The Report of the Human Rights Consultation Committee* (State of Victoria, November 2005)) that the Victorian Parliament enact a Charter of Human Rights and Responsibilities similar to the human rights laws in the ACT, New Zealand and the United Kingdom. In December 2005, the Victorian government announced that it would seek to enact such a Charter in 2006.

5. Further References

Alston, P, *Promoting Human Rights through Bills of Rights: Comparative Perspectives* (Oxford University Press, 1999).

Bennett, A, "Can the Constitution be Amended Without a Referendum?" (1982) 56 *Australian Law Journal* 358.

Brennan, F, *Legislating Liberty: A Bill of Rights for Australia?* (University of Queensland Press, 1998).

Campbell, E, "Fashioning and Refashioning the Constitution" (2001) 24 *University of New South Wales Law Journal* 620.

Charlesworth, H, *Writing in Rights: Australia and the Protection of Human Rights* (UNSW Press, 2002).

Constitutional Centenary Foundation, '*We the people of Australia...*': Ideas for a New Preamble to the Australian Constitution (1999).

Coper, M, *Encounters With the Australian Constitution* (CCH, 1988), Ch 9.

Coper, M, "The People and the Judges: Constitutional Referendums and Judicial Interpretation" in Lindell, G (ed), *Future Directions in Australian Constitutional Law* (Federation Press, 1994), 73.

Craven, G, "Would the Abolition of the States be an Alteration of the Constitution under Section 128?" (1988) 18 *Federal Law Review* 85.

Craven, G, *Conversations with the Constitution: Not Just a Piece of Paper* (University of New South Wales Press, 2004).

Debeljak, J, "The *Human Rights Act 2004* (ACT): A Significant, Yet Incomplete, Step toward the Domestic Protection and Promotion of Human Rights" (2004) 15 *Public Law Review* 169.

Evans, C, "Responsibility for Rights: The ACT *Human Rights Act*" (2004) 32 *Federal Law Review* 291.

Gageler, S, and Leeming, M, "An Australian Republic: Is a Referendum Enough?" (1996) 7 *Public Law Review* 143.

Galligan, B, and Nethercote, JR, *The Constitutional Commission and the 1988 Referendums* (Centre for Research on Federal Financial Relations, Australian National University, 1989).

Harris, B, *A New Constitution for Australia* (Cavendish Publishing, 2002).

Kostakidis-Lianos, L, and Williams, G, "Bills of Responsibilities" (2005) 30 *Alternative Law Journal* 58.

Lindell, G, and Rose, D, "A Response to Gageler and Leeming: 'An Australian Republic: Is a Referendum Enough?'" (1996) 7 *Public Law Review* 155.

Mason, A, "A Bill of Rights for Australia?" (1989) 5 *Australian Bar Review* 79.

McKenna, M, *The Captive Republic: A History of Republicanism in Australia 1788-1996* (Cambridge University Press, 1996).

Orr, G, "The Conduct of Referenda and Plebiscites in Australia: A Legal Perspective" (2000) 11 *Public Law Review* 117.

Patmore, G (ed), *The Big Makeover: A New Australian Constitution* (Pluto Press, 2002).

Pettit, P, *Republicanism: A Theory of Freedom and Government* (Oxford University Press, 1997).

"Planning a New Republic", Symposium (2001) 3 *University of Notre Dame Law Review* 1.

Reilly, A, "Preparing a Preamble: The Timorous Approach of the Convention to the Inclusion of Civic Values" (1998) 21 *University of New South Wales Law Journal* 903.

Saunders, C, "Future Prospects for the Australian Constitution" in French, R, Lindell, G, and Saunders, C (eds), *Reflections on the Australian Constitution* (Federation Press, 2003), 212.

Sawer, G, "Some Legal Assumptions of Constitutional Change" (1957) 4 *University of Western Australia Annual Law Review* 1.

Thomson, JA, "Altering the Constitution: Some Aspects of Section 128" (1983) 13 *Federal Law Review* 323.

Thomson, JA, "An Australian Bill of Rights: Glorious Promises, Concealed Dangers" (1994) 19 *Melbourne University Law Review* 1020.

Tomkins, A, *Our Republican Constitution* (Hart Publishing, 2005).

Uhr, J, "After the Referendum: The Future of Constitutional Change" (2000) 11 *Public Law Review* 7.

Walker, G, *Initiative and Referendum: The People's Law* (Centre for Independent Studies, 1987).

Webber, J, "Constitutional Poetry: The Tension between Symbolic and Functional Aims in Constitutional Reform" (1999) 21 *Sydney Law Review* 260.

Williams, G, "The Australian States and an Australian Republic" (1996) 70 *Australian Law Journal* 890.

Williams, J, "The Republican Preamble: Back to the Drawing Board?" (1999) 10 *Public Law Review* 69.

Winterton, G, *Monarchy to Republic: Australian Republican Government* (Oxford University Press, rev ed 1994).

Winterton, G, *The Resurrection of the Republic* (Federation Press and Centre for International and Public Law, Law and Policy Paper 15, 2001).

Winterton, G, "The States and the Republic: A Constitutional Accord?" (1995) 6 *Public Law Review* 107.

Zines, L, "Preamble to a Republican Constitution" (1999) 10 *Public Law Review* 67.

Appendix

1. Australian Constitution

Commonwealth of Australia Constitution Act 1900

with alterations to the Constitution made by

Constitution Alteration (Senate Elections) 1906 (No 1 of 1907)
Constitution Alteration (State Debts) 1909 (No 3 of 1910)
Constitution Alteration (State Debts) 1928 (No 1 of 1929)
Constitution Alteration (Social Services) 1946 (No 81 of 1946)
Constitution Alteration (Aboriginals) 1967 (No 55 of 1967)
Constitution Alteration (Senate Casual Vacancies) 1977 (No 82 of 1977)
Constitution Alteration (Retirement Of Judges) 1977 (No 83 of 1977)
Constitution Alteration (Referendums) 1977 (No 84 of 1977)

Commonwealth of Australia Constitution Act

(63 & 64 VICTORIA, CHAPTER 12)

An Act to constitute the Commonwealth of Australia.

[9th July 1900]

WHEREAS the people of New South Wales, Victoria, South Australia, Queensland, and Tasmania, humbly relying on the blessing of Almighty God, have agreed to unite in one indissoluble Federal Commonwealth under the Crown of the United Kingdom of Great Britain and Ireland, and under the Constitution hereby established:

And whereas it is expedient to provide for the admission into the Commonwealth of other Australasian Colonies and possessions of the Queen:

Be it therefore enacted by the Queen's most Excellent Majesty, by and with the advice and consent of the Lords Spiritual and Temporal, and Commons, in this present Parliament assembled, and by the authority of the same, as follows:

1. Short title This Act may be cited as the Commonwealth of Australia Constitution Act.

2. Act to extend to the Queen's successors The provisions of this Act referring to the Queen shall extend to Her Majesty's heirs and successors in the sovereignty of the United Kingdom.

3. Proclamation of Commonwealth It shall be lawful for the Queen, with the advice of the Privy Council, to declare by proclamation that, on and after a day therein appointed, not being later than one year after the passing of this Act, the people of New South Wales, Victoria, South Australia, Queensland, and Tasmania, and also, if Her Majesty is satisfied that the people of Western Australia have agreed thereto, of Western Australia, shall be united in a Federal Commonwealth under the name of the Commonwealth of

Australia. But the Queen may, at any time after the proclamation, appoint a Governor-General for the Commonwealth.

4. Commencement of Act The Commonwealth shall be established, and the Constitution of the Commonwealth shall take effect, on and after the day so appointed. But the Parliaments of the several colonies may at any time after the passing of this Act make any such laws, to come into operation on the day so appointed, as they might have made if the Constitution had taken effect at the passing of this Act.

5. Operation of the constitution and laws This Act, and all laws made by the Parliament of the Commonwealth under the Constitution, shall be binding on the courts, judges, and people of every State and of every part of the Commonwealth, notwithstanding anything in the laws of any State; and the laws of the Commonwealth shall be in force on all British ships, the Queen's ships of war excepted, whose first port of clearance and whose port of destination are in the Commonwealth.

6. Definitions "The Commonwealth" shall mean the Commonwealth of Australia as established under this Act.

"The States" shall mean such of the colonies of New South Wales, New Zealand, Queensland, Tasmania, Victoria, Western Australia, and South Australia, including the northern territory of South Australia, as for the time being are parts of the Commonwealth, and such colonies or territories as may be admitted into or established by the Commonwealth as States; and each of such parts of the Commonwealth shall be called "a State."

"Original States" shall mean such States as are parts of the Commonwealth at its establishment.

7. Repeal of Federal Council Act 48 & 49 Vict c 60 The Federal Council of Australasia Act, 1885, is hereby repealed, but so as not to affect any laws passed by the Federal Council of Australasia and in force at the establishment of the Commonwealth.

Any such law may be repealed as to any State by the Parliament of the Commonwealth, or as to any colony not being a State by the Parliament thereof.

8. Application of Colonial Boundaries Act 58 & 59 Vict c 34 After the passing of this Act the Colonial Boundaries Act, 1895, shall not apply to any colony which becomes a State of the Commonwealth; but the Commonwealth shall be taken to be a self-governing colony for the purposes of that Act.

9. Constitution The Constitution of the Commonwealth shall be as follows:

The Constitution

___

This Constitution is divided as follows:

Chapter I	–	The Parliament
Part I	–	General
Part I	–	The Senate
Part III	–	The House of Representative
Part IV	–	Both Houses of the Parliament
Part V	–	Powers of the Parliament
Chapter II	–	The Executive Government
Chapter III	–	The Judicature
Chapter IV	–	Finance and Trade
Chapter V	–	The States
Chapter VI	–	New States
Chapter VII	–	Miscellaneous
Chapter VIII	–	Alteration of the Constitution
The Schedule		

CHAPTER I

THE PARLIAMENT

Part I – General

1. Legislative Power The legislative power of the Commonwealth shall be vested in a Federal Parliament, which shall consist of the Queen, a Senate, and a House of Representatives, and which is herein-after called "The Parliament," or "The Parliament of the Commonwealth."

2. Governor-General A Governor-General appointed by the Queen shall be Her Majesty's representative in the Commonwealth, and shall have and may exercise in the Commonwealth during the Queen's pleasure, but subject to this Constitution, such powers and functions of the Queen as Her Majesty may be pleased to assign to him.

3. Salary of Governor-General There shall be payable to the Queen out of the Consolidated Revenue fund of the Commonwealth, for the salary of the Governor-General, an annual sum which, until the Parliament otherwise provides, shall be ten thousand pounds.

The salary of a Governor-General shall not be altered during his continuance in office.

4. Provisions relating to Governor-General The provisions of this Constitution relating to the Governor-General extend and apply to the Governor-General for the time being, or such person as the Queen may appoint to administer the Government of the Commonwealth; but no such person shall be entitled to receive any salary from the Commonwealth in respect of any other office during his administration of the Government of the Commonwealth.

5. Sessions of Parliament. Prorogation and dissolution The Governor-General may appoint such times for holding the sessions of the Parliament as he thinks fit, and may also from time to time, by Proclamation or otherwise, prorogue the Parliament, and may in like manner dissolve the House of Representatives.

After any general election the Parliament shall be summoned to meet not later than thirty days after the day appointed for the return of the writs.

The Parliament shall be summoned to meet not later than six months after the establishment of the Commonwealth.

6. Yearly session of Parliament There shall be a session of the Parliament once at least in every year, so that twelve months shall not intervene between the last sitting of the Parliament in one session and its first sitting in the next session.

Part II – The Senate

7. The Senate The Senate shall be composed of senators for each State, directly chosen by the people of the State, voting, until the Parliament otherwise provides, as one electorate.

But until the Parliament of the Commonwealth otherwise provides, the Parliament of the State of Queensland, if that State be an Original State, may make laws dividing the State into divisions and determining the number of senators to be chosen for each division, and in the absence of such provision the State shall be one electorate.

Until the Parliament otherwise provides there shall be six senators for each Original State. The Parliament may make laws increasing or diminishing the number of senators for each State, but so that equal representation of the several Original States shall be maintained and that no Original State shall have less than six senators.

The senators shall be chosen for a term of six years, and the names of the senators chosen for each State shall be certified by the Governor to the Governor-General.

8. Qualification of electors The qualification of electors of senators shall be in each State that which is prescribed by this Constitution, or by the Parliament, as the qualification for electors of members of the House of Representatives; but in the choosing of senators each elector shall vote only once.

9. Method of election of senators The Parliament of the Commonwealth may make laws prescribing the method of choosing senators, but so that the method shall be uniform for all States. Subject to any such law, the Parliament of each State may make laws prescribing the method of choosing the senators for that State.

Times and places The Parliament of a State may make laws for determining the times and places of elections of senators for the State.

10. Application of State laws Until the Parliament otherwise provides, but subject to this Constitution, the laws in force in each State, for the time being, relating to elections for the more numerous House of the Parliament of the State shall, as nearly as practicable, apply to elections of senators for the State.

11. Failure to choose senators The Senate may proceed to the despatch of business, notwithstanding the failure of any State to provide for its representation in the Senate.

12. Issue of writs The Governor of any State may cause writs to be issued for elections of senators for the State. In case of the dissolution of the Senate the writs shall be issued within ten days from the proclamation of such dissolution.

13. Rotation of senators [altered by No 1, 1907, s 2] As soon as may be after the Senate first meets, and after each first meeting of the Senate following a dissolution thereof, the Senate shall divide the senators chosen for each State into two classes, as nearly equal in number as practicable; and the places of the senators of the first class shall become vacant at the expiration of ~~the third year~~ **three years,** and the places of those of the second class at the expiration of ~~the sixth year~~ **six years,** from the beginning of their term of service; and afterwards the places of senators shall become vacant at the expiration of six years from the beginning of their term of service.

The election to fill vacant places shall be made ~~in the year at the expiration of which~~ **within one year before** the places are to become vacant.

For the purposes of this section the term of service of a senator shall be taken to begin on the first day of ~~January~~ **July** following the day of his election, except in the cases of the first election and of the election next after any dissolution of the Senate, when it shall be taken to begin on the first day of ~~January~~ **July** preceding the day of his election.

14. Further provision for rotation Whenever the number of senators for a State is increased or diminished, the Parliament of the Commonwealth may make such provision for the vacating of the places of senators for the State as it deems necessary to maintain regularity in the rotation.

15. Casual vacancies [substituted by No 82, 1977, s 2] If the place of a senator becomes vacant before the expiration of his term of service, the Houses of Parliament of the State for which he was chosen, sitting and voting together, or, if there is only one House of that Parliament, that House, shall choose a person to hold the place until the expiration of the term. But if the Parliament of the State is not in session when the vacancy is notified, the Governor of the State, with the advice of the Executive Council thereof, may appoint a person to hold the place until the expiration of fourteen days from the beginning of the next session of the Parliament of the State or the expiration of the term, whichever first happens.

Where a vacancy has at any time occurred in the place of a senator chosen by the people of a State and, at the time when he was so chosen, he was publicly recognized by a particular political party as being an endorsed candidate of that party and publicly represented himself to be such a candidate, a person chosen or appointed under this section in consequence of that vacancy, or in consequence of that vacancy and a subsequent vacancy or vacancies, shall, unless there is no member of that party available to be chosen or appointed, be a member of that party.

Where:

(a) in accordance with the last preceding paragraph, a member of a particular political party is chosen or appointed to hold the place of a senator whose place had become vacant; and

(b) before taking his seat he ceases to be a member of that party (otherwise than by reason of the party having ceased to exist),

he shall be deemed not to have been so chosen or appointed and the vacancy shall be again notified in accordance with section twenty-one of this Constitution.

The name of any senator chosen or appointed under this section shall be certified by the Governor of the State to the Governor-General.

If the place of a senator chosen by the people of a State at the election of senators last held before the commencement of the *Constitution Alteration (Senate Casual Vacancies)* 1977 became vacant before that commencement and, at that commencement, no person chosen by the House or Houses of Parliament of the State, or appointed by the Governor of the State, in consequence of that vacancy, or in consequence of that vacancy and a subsequent vacancy or vacancies, held office, this section applies as if the place of the senator chosen by the people of the State had become vacant after that commencement.

A senator holding office at the commencement of the *Constitution Alteration (Senate Casual Vacancies)* 1977, being a senator appointed by the Governor of a State in consequence of a vacancy that had at any time occurred in the place of a senator chosen by the people of the State, shall be deemed to have been appointed to hold the place until the expiration of fourteen days after the beginning of the next session of the Parliament of the State that commenced or commences after he was appointed and further action under this section shall be taken as if the vacancy in the place of the senator chosen by the people of the State had occurred after that commencement.

Subject to the next succeeding paragraph, a senator holding office at the commencement of the *Constitution Alteration (Senate Casual Vacancies)* 1977 who was chosen by the House or Houses of Parliament of a State in consequence of a vacancy that had at any time occurred in the place of a senator chosen by the people of the State shall be deemed to have been chosen to hold office until the expiration of the term of service of the senator elected by the people of the State.

If, at or before the commencement of the *Constitution Alteration (Senate Casual Vacancies)* 1977, a law to alter the Constitution entitled "*Constitution Alteration (Simultaneous Elections)* 1977" came into operation, a senator holding office at the commencement of that law who was chosen by the House or Houses of Parliament of a State in consequence of a vacancy that had at any time occurred in the place of a Senator chosen by the people of the State shall be deemed to have been chosen to hold office:

(a) if the senator elected by the people of the State had a term of service expiring on the thirtieth day of June, One thousand nine hundred and seventy-eight – until the expiration or dissolution of the first House of Representatives to expire or be dissolved after that law came into operation; or

(b) if the senator elected by the people of the State had a term of service expiring on the thirtieth day of June, One thousand nine hundred and eighty-one – until the expiration or dissolution of the second House of Representatives to expire or be dissolved after that law came into operation or, if there is an earlier dissolution of the Senate, until that dissolution.

16. Qualifications of senator The qualifications of a senator shall be the same as those of a member of the House of Representatives.

17. Election of President The Senate shall, before proceeding to the despatch of any other business, choose a senator to be the President of the Senate; and as often as the office of President becomes vacant the Senate shall again choose a senator to be the President.

The President shall cease to hold his office if he ceases to be a senator. He may be removed from office by a vote of the Senate, or he may resign his office or his seat by writing addressed to the Governor-General.

18. Absence of President Before or during any absence of the President, the Senate may choose a senator to perform his duties in his absence.

19. Resignation of senator A senator may, by writing addressed to the President, or to the Governor-General if there is no President or if the President is absent from the Commonwealth, resign his place, which thereupon shall become vacant.

20. Vacancy by absence The place of a senator shall become vacant if for two consecutive months of any session of the Parliament he, without the permission of the Senate, fails to attend the Senate.

21. Vacancy to be notified Whenever a vacancy happens in the Senate, the President, or if there is no President or if the President is absent from the Commonwealth the Governor-General, shall notify the same to the Governor of the State in the representation of which the vacancy has happened.

22. Quorum Until the Parliament otherwise provides, the presence of at least one-third of the whole number of the senators shall be necessary to constitute a meeting of the Senate for the exercise of its powers.

23. Voting in the Senate Questions arising in the Senate shall be determined by a majority of votes, and each senator shall have one vote. The President shall in all cases be entitled to a vote; and when the votes are equal the question shall pass in the negative.

Part III – The House of Representatives

24. Constitution of House of Representatives The House of Representatives shall be composed of members directly chosen by the people of the Commonwealth, and the number of such members shall be, as nearly as practicable, twice the number of the senators.

The number of members chosen in the several States shall be in proportion to the respective numbers of their people, and shall, until the Parliament otherwise provides, be determined, whenever necessary, in the following manner:

(i) A quota shall be ascertained by dividing the number of the people of the Commonwealth, as shown by the latest statistics of the Commonwealth, by twice the number of the senators;

(ii) The number of members to be chosen in each State shall be determined by dividing the number of the people of the State, as shown by the latest statistics of the Commonwealth, by the quota; and if on such division there is a remainder greater than one-half of the quota, one more member shall be chosen in the State.

But notwithstanding anything in this section, five members at least shall be chosen in each Original State.

25. Provision as to races disqualified from voting For the purposes of the last section, if by the law of any State all persons of any race are disqualified from voting at elections for the more numerous House of the Parliament of the State, then, in reckoning the number of the people of the State or of the Commonwealth, persons of that race resident in that State shall not be counted.

26. Representatives in first Parliament Notwithstanding anything in section twenty-four, the number of members to be chosen in each State at the first election shall be as follows:

New South Wales.......... twenty-three;
Victoria .... twenty;
Queensland .... eight;
South Australia.............. six;
Tasmania...................... five;

Provided that if Western Australia is an Original State, the numbers shall be as follows:

New South Wales.......... twenty-six;
Victoria .... twenty-three;
Queensland.................... nine;
South Australia.............. seven;
Western Australia.......... five;
Tasmania...................... five.

27. Alteration of number of members Subject to this Constitution, the Parliament may make laws for increasing or diminishing the number of the members of the House of Representatives.

28. Duration of House of Representatives Every House of Representatives shall continue for three years from the first meeting of the House, and no longer, but may be sooner dissolved by the Governor-General.

29. Electoral divisions Until the Parliament of the Commonwealth otherwise provides, the Parliament of any State may make laws for determining the divisions in each State for which members of the House of Representatives may be chosen, and the number of members to be chosen for each division. A division shall not be formed out of parts of different States.

In the absence of other provision, each State shall be one electorate.

30. Qualification of electors Until the Parliament otherwise provides, the qualification of electors of members of the House of Representatives shall be in each State that which is prescribed by the law of the State as the qualification of electors of the more numerous House of Parliament of the State; but in the choosing of members each elector shall vote only once.

31. Application of State laws Until the Parliament otherwise provides, but subject to this Constitution, the laws in force in each State for the time being relating to elections for the more numerous House of the Parliament of the State shall, as nearly as practicable, apply to elections in the State of members of the House of Representatives.

32. Writs for general election The Governor-General in Council may cause writs to be issued for general elections of members of the House of Representatives.

After the first general election, the writs shall be issued within ten days from the expiry of a House of Representatives or from the proclamation of a dissolution thereof.

33. Writs for vacancies Whenever a vacancy happens in the House of Representatives, the Speaker shall issue his writ for the election of a new member, or if there is no Speaker or if he is absent from the Commonwealth the Governor-General in Council may issue the writ.

34. Qualifications of members Until the Parliament otherwise provides, the qualifications of a member of the House of Representatives shall be as follows:

(i) He must be of the full age of twenty-one years, and must be an elector entitled to vote at the election of members of the House of Representatives, or a person qualified to become such elector, and must have been for three years at the least a resident within the limits of the Commonwealth as existing at the time when he is chosen;

(ii) He must be a subject of the Queen, either natural-born or for at least five years naturalized under a law of the United Kingdom, or of a Colony which has become or becomes a State, or of the Commonwealth, or of a State.

35. Election of speaker The House of Representatives shall, before proceeding to the despatch of any other business, choose a member to be the Speaker of the House, and as often as the office of Speaker becomes vacant the House shall again choose a member to be the Speaker.

The Speaker shall cease to hold his office if he ceases to be a member. He may be removed from office by a vote of the House, or he may resign his office or his seat by writing addressed to the Governor-General.

36. Absence of Speaker Before or during any absence of the Speaker, the House of Representatives may choose a member to perform his duties in his absence.

37. Resignation of member A member may by writing addressed to the Speaker, or to the Governor-General if there is no Speaker or if the Speaker is absent from the Commonwealth, resign his place, which thereupon shall become vacant.

38. Vacancy by absence The place of a member shall become vacant if for two consecutive months of any session of the Parliament he, without the permission of the House, fails to attend the House.

39. Quorum Until the Parliament otherwise provides, the presence of at least one-third of the whole number of the members of the House of Representatives shall be necessary to constitute a meeting of the House for the exercise of its powers.

40. Voting in House of Representatives Questions arising in the House of Representatives shall be determined by a majority of votes other than that of the Speaker. The Speaker shall not vote unless the numbers are equal, and then he shall have a casting vote.

Part IV – Both Houses of the Parliament

41. Right of electors of States No adult person who has or acquires a right to vote at elections for the more numerous House of the Parliament of a State shall, while the right continues, be prevented by any law of the Commonwealth from voting at elections for either House of the Parliament of the Commonwealth.

42. Oath or affirmation of allegiance Every senator and every member of the House of Representatives shall before taking his seat make and subscribe before the Governor-General, or some person authorised by him, an oath or affirmation of allegiance in the form set forth in the schedule to this Constitution.

43. Member of one House ineligible for other A member of either House of the Parliament shall be incapable of being chosen or of sitting as a member of the other House.

44. Disqualification Any person who:
- (i) Is under any acknowledgment of allegiance, obedience, or adherence to a foreign power, or is a subject or a citizen or entitled to the rights or privileges of a subject or a citizen of a foreign power; or
- (ii) Is attainted of treason, or has been convicted and is under sentence, or subject to be sentenced, for any offence punishable under the law of the Commonwealth or of a State by imprisonment for one year or longer; or
- (iii) Is an undischarged bankrupt or insolvent; or
- (iv) Holds any office of profit under the Crown, or any pension payable during the pleasure of the Crown out of any of the revenues of the Commonwealth; or
- (v) Has any direct or indirect pecuniary interest in any agreement with the Public Service of the Commonwealth otherwise than as a member and in common with the other members of an incorporated company consisting of more than twenty-five persons;

shall be incapable of being chosen or of sitting as a senator or a member of the House of Representatives.

But sub-section iv. does not apply to the office of any of the Queen's Ministers of State for the Commonwealth, or of any of the Queen's Ministers for a State, or to the receipt of pay, half pay, or a pension, by any person as an officer or member of the Queen's navy or army, or to the receipt of pay as an officer or member of the naval or military forces of the Commonwealth by any person whose services are not wholly employed by the Commonwealth.

45. Vacancy on happening of disqualification If a senator or member of the House of Representatives:
- (i) Becomes subject to any of the disabilities mentioned in the last preceding section; or
- (ii) Takes the benefit, whether by assignment, composition, or otherwise, of any law relating to bankrupt or insolvent debtors; or
- (iii) Directly or indirectly takes or agrees to take any fee or honorarium for services rendered to the Commonwealth, or for services rendered in the Parliament to any person or State;

his place shall thereupon become vacant.

46. Penalty for sitting when disqualified Until the Parliament otherwise provides, any person declared by this Constitution to be incapable of sitting as a senator or as a member of the House of Representatives shall, for every day on which he so sits, be liable to pay the sum of one hundred pounds to any person who sues for it in any court of competent jurisdiction.

47. Disputed elections Until the Parliament otherwise provides, any question respecting the qualification of a senator or of a member of the House of Representatives, or respecting a vacancy in either

House of the Parliament, and any question of a disputed election to either House, shall be determined by the House in which the question arises.

48. Allowance to members Until the Parliament otherwise provides, each senator and each member of the House of Representatives shall receive an allowance of four hundred pounds a year, to be reckoned from the day on which he takes his seat.

49. Privileges, &c of Houses The powers, privileges, and immunities of the Senate and of the House of Representatives, and of the members and the committees of each House, shall be such as are declared by the Parliament, and until declared shall be those of the Commons House of Parliament of the United Kingdom, and of its members and committees, at the establishment of the Commonwealth.

50. Rules and orders Each House of the Parliament may make rules and orders with respect to:

- (i) The mode in which its powers, privileges, and immunities may be exercised and upheld;
- (ii) The order and conduct of its business and proceedings either separately or jointly with the other House.

Part V – Powers of the Parliament

51. Legislative powers of the Parliament The Parliament shall, subject to this Constitution, have power to make laws for the peace, order, and good government of the Commonwealth with respect to:

- (i) Trade and commerce with other countries, and among the States;
- (ii) Taxation; but so as not to discriminate between States or parts of States;
- (iii) Bounties on the production or export of goods, but so that such bounties shall be uniform throughout the Commonwealth;
- (iv) Borrowing money on the public credit of the Commonwealth;
- (v) Postal, telegraphic, telephonic, and other like services;
- (vi) The naval and military defence of the Commonwealth and of the several States, and the control of the forces to execute and maintain the laws of the Commonwealth;
- (vii) Lighthouses, lightships, beacons and buoys;
- (viii) Astronomical and meteorological observations;
- (ix) Quarantine;
- (x) Fisheries in Australian waters beyond territorial limits;
- (xi) Census and statistics;
- (xii) Currency, coinage, and legal tender;
- (xiii) Banking, other than State banking; also State banking extending beyond the limits of the State concerned, the incorporation of banks, and the issue of paper money;
- (xiv) Insurance, other than State insurance; also State insurance extending beyond the limits of the State concerned;
- (xv) Weights and measures;
- (xvi) Bills of exchange and promissory notes;
- (xvii) Bankruptcy and insolvency;
- (xviii) Copyrights, patents of inventions and designs, and trade marks;
- (xix) Naturalization and aliens;
- (xx) Foreign corporations, and trading or financial corporations formed within the limits of the Commonwealth;
- (xxi) Marriage;
- (xxii) Divorce and matrimonial causes; and in relation thereto, parental rights, and the custody and guardianship of infants;
- (xxiii) Invalid and old-age pensions;
- (xxiiiA) **[inserted by No 81, 1946, s 2]** The provision of maternity allowances, widows' pensions, child endowment, unemployment, pharmaceutical, sickness and hospital benefits, medical and dental services (but not so as to authorize any form of civil conscription), benefits to students and family allowances;
- (xxiv) The service and execution throughout the Commonwealth of the civil and criminal process and the judgments of the courts of the States;
- (xxv) The recognition throughout the Commonwealth of the laws, the public Acts and records, and the judicial proceedings of the States;
- (xxvi) **[altered by No 55, 1967, s 2]** The people of any race, ~~other than the aboriginal race in any State,~~ for whom it is deemed necessary to make special laws;

(xxvii)	Immigration and emigration;
(xxviii)	The influx of criminals;
(xxix)	External affairs;
(xxx)	The relations of the Commonwealth with the islands of the Pacific;
(xxxi)	The acquisition of property on just terms from any State or person for any purpose in respect of which the Parliament has power to make laws;
(xxxii)	The control of railways with respect to transport for the naval and military purposes of the Commonwealth;
(xxxiii)	The acquisition, with the consent of a State, of any railways of the State on terms arranged between the Commonwealth and the State;
(xxxiv)	Railway construction and extension in any State with the consent of that State;
(xxxv)	Conciliation and arbitration for the prevention and settlement of industrial disputes extending beyond the limits of any one State;
(xxxvi)	Matters in respect of which this Constitution makes provision until the Parliament otherwise provides;
(xxxvii)	Matters referred to the Parliament of the Commonwealth by the Parliament or Parliaments of any State or States, but so that the law shall extend only to States by whose Parliaments the matter is referred, or which afterwards adopt the law;
(xxxviii)	The exercise within the Commonwealth, at the request or with the concurrence of the Parliaments of all the States directly concerned, of any power which can at the establishment of this Constitution be exercised only by the Parliament of the United Kingdom or by the Federal Council of Australasia;
(xxxix)	Matters incidental to the execution of any power vested by this Constitution in the Parliament or in either House thereof, or in the Government of the Commonwealth, or in the Federal Judicature, or in any department or officer of the Commonwealth.

52. Exclusive powers of the Parliament The Parliament shall, subject to this Constitution, have exclusive power to make laws for the peace, order, and good government of the Commonwealth with respect to:

(i)	The seat of government of the Commonwealth, and all places acquired by the Commonwealth for public purposes;
(ii)	Matters relating to any department of the public service the control of which is by this Constitution transferred to the Executive Government of the Commonwealth;
(iii)	Other matters declared by this Constitution to be within the exclusive power of the Parliament.

53. Powers of the Houses in respect of legislation Proposed laws appropriating revenue or moneys, or imposing taxation, shall not originate in the Senate. But a proposed law shall not be taken to appropriate revenue or moneys, or to impose taxation, by reason only of its containing provisions for the imposition or appropriation of fines or other pecuniary penalties, or for the demand or payment or appropriation of fees for licenses, or fees for services under the proposed law.

The Senate may not amend proposed laws imposing taxation, or proposed laws appropriating revenue or moneys for the ordinary annual services of the Government.

The Senate may not amend any proposed law so as to increase any proposed charge or burden on the people.

The Senate may at any stage return to the House of Representatives any proposed law which the Senate may not amend, requesting, by message, the omission or amendment of any items or provisions therein. And the House of Representatives may, if it thinks fit, make any of such omissions or amendments, with or without modifications.

Except as provided in this section, the Senate shall have equal power with the House of Representatives in respect of all proposed laws.

54. Appropriation Bills The proposed law which appropriates revenue or moneys for the ordinary annual services of the Government shall deal only with such appropriation.

55. Tax Bill Laws imposing taxation shall deal only with the imposition of taxation, and any provision therein dealing with any other matter shall be of no effect.

Laws imposing taxation, except laws imposing duties of customs or of excise, shall deal with one subject of taxation only; but laws imposing duties of customs shall deal with duties of customs only, and laws imposing duties of excise shall deal with duties of excise only.

56. Recommendation of money votes A vote, resolution, or proposed law for the appropriation of revenue or moneys shall not be passed unless the purpose of the appropriation has in the same session been recommended by message of the Governor-General to the House in which the proposal originated.

57. Disagreement between the Houses If the House of Representatives passes any proposed law, and the Senate rejects or fails to pass it, or passes it with amendments to which the House of Representatives will not agree, and if after an interval of three months the House of Representatives, in the same or the next session, again passes the proposed law with or without any amendments which have been made, suggested, or agreed to by the Senate, and the Senate rejects or fails to pass it, or passes it with amendments to which the House of Representatives will not agree, the Governor-General may dissolve the Senate and the House of Representatives simultaneously. But such dissolution shall not take place within six months before the date of the expiry of the House of Representatives by effluxion of time.

If after such dissolution the House of Representatives again passes the proposed law, with or without any amendments which have been made, suggested, or agreed to by the Senate, and the Senate rejects or fails to pass it, or passes it with amendments to which the House of Representatives will not agree, the Governor-General may convene a joint sitting of the members of the Senate and of the House of Representatives.

The members present at the joint sitting may deliberate and shall vote together upon the proposed law as last proposed by the House of Representatives, and upon amendments, if any, which have been made therein by one House and not agreed to by the other, and any such amendments which are affirmed by an absolute majority of the total number of the members of the Senate and House of Representatives shall be taken to have been carried, and if the proposed law, with the amendments, if any, so carried is affirmed by an absolute majority of the total number of the members of the Senate and House of Representatives, it shall be taken to have been duly passed by both Houses of the Parliament, and shall be presented to the Governor-General for the Queen's assent.

58. Royal assent to Bills When a proposed law passed by both Houses of the Parliament is presented to the Governor-General for the Queen's assent, he shall declare, according to his discretion, but subject to this Constitution, that he assents in the Queen's name, or that he withholds assent, or that he reserves the law for the Queen's pleasure.

Recommendations by Governor-General The Governor-General may return to the house in which it originated any proposed law so presented to him, and may transmit therewith any amendments which he may recommend, and the Houses may deal with the recommendation.

59. Disallowance by the Queen The Queen may disallow any law within one year from the Governor-General's assent, and such disallowance on being made known by the Governor-General by speech or message to each of the Houses of the Parliament, or by Proclamation, shall annul the law from the day when the disallowance is so made known.

60. Signification of Queen's pleasure on Bills reserved A proposed law reserved for the Queen's pleasure shall not have any force unless and until within two years from the day on which it was presented to the Governor-General for the Queen's assent the Governor-General makes known, by speech or message to each of the Houses of the Parliament, or by Proclamation, that it has received the Queen's assent.

CHAPTER II

THE EXECUTIVE GOVERNMENT

61. Executive power The executive power of the Commonwealth is vested in the Queen and is exercisable by the Governor-General as the Queen's representative, and extends to the execution and maintenance of this Constitution, and of the laws of the Commonwealth.

62. Federal Executive Council There shall be a Federal Executive Council to advise the Governor-General in the government of the Commonwealth, and the members of the Council shall be chosen and summoned by the Governor-General and sworn as Executive Councillors, and shall hold office during his pleasure.

63. Provisions referring to Governor-General The provisions of this Constitution referring to the Governor-General in Council shall be construed as referring to the Governor-General acting with the advice of the Federal Executive Council.

64. Ministers of State The Governor-General may appoint officers to administer such departments of State of the Commonwealth as the Governor-General in Council may establish.

Such officers shall hold office during the pleasure of the Governor-General. They shall be members of the Federal Executive Council, and shall be the Queen's Ministers of State for the Commonwealth.

Ministers to sit in Parliament After the first general election no Minister of State shall hold office for a longer period than three months unless he is or becomes a senator or a member of the House of Representatives.

65. Number of Ministers Until the Parliament otherwise provides, the Ministers of State shall not exceed seven in number, and shall hold such offices as the Parliament prescribes, or, in the absence of provision, as the Governor-General directs.

66. Salaries of Ministers There shall be payable to the Queen, out of the Consolidated Revenue Fund of the Commonwealth, for the salaries of the Ministers of State, an annual sum which, until the Parliament otherwise provides, shall not exceed twelve thousand pounds a year.

67. Appointment of civil servants Until the Parliament otherwise provides, the appointment and removal of all other officers of the Executive Government of the Commonwealth shall be vested in the Governor-General in Council, unless the appointment is delegated by the Governor-General in Council or by a law of the Commonwealth to some other authority.

68. Command of naval and military forces The command in chief of the naval and military forces of the Commonwealth is vested in the Governor-General as the Queen's representative.

69. Transfer of certain departments On a date or dates to be proclaimed by the Governor-General after the establishment of the Commonwealth the following departments of the public service in each State shall become transferred to the Commonwealth:

Posts, telegraphs, and telephones;
Naval and military defence;
Lighthouses, lightships, beacons, and buoys;
Quarantine.

But the departments of customs and of excise in each State shall become transferred to the Commonwealth on its establishment.

70. Certain powers of Governors to vest in Governor-General In respect of matters which, under this Constitution, pass to the Executive Government of the Commonwealth, all powers and functions which at the establishment of the Commonwealth are vested in the Governor of a Colony, or in the Governor of a Colony with the advice of his Executive Council, or in any authority of a Colony, shall vest in the Governor-General, or in the Governor-General in Council, or in the authority exercising similar powers under the Commonwealth, as the case requires.

CHAPTER III
THE JUDICATURE

71. Judicial power and Courts The judicial power of the Commonwealth shall be vested in a Federal Supreme Court, to be called the High Court of Australia, and in such other federal courts as the Parliament creates, and in such other courts as it invests with federal jurisdiction. The High Court shall consist of a Chief Justice, and so many other Justices, not less than two, as the Parliament prescribes.

72. Judges' appointment, tenure and remuneration The Justices of the High Court and of the other courts created by the Parliament:

(i) Shall be appointed by the Governor-General in Council;
(ii) Shall not be removed except by the Governor-General in Council, on an address from both Houses of the Parliament in the same session, praying for such removal on the ground of proved misbehaviour or incapacity;
(iii) Shall receive such remuneration as the Parliament may fix; but the remuneration shall not be diminished during their continuance in office.

[this and the following paragraphs added by No 83, 1977, s 2] The appointment of a Justice of the High Court shall be for a term expiring upon his attaining the age of seventy years, and a person shall not be appointed as a Justice of the High Court if he has attained that age.

The appointment of a Justice of a court created by the Parliament shall be for a term expiring upon his attaining the age that is, at the time of his appointment, the maximum age for Justices of that court and a person shall not be appointed as a Justice of such a court if he has attained the age that is for the time being the maximum age for Justices of that court.

Subject to this section, the maximum age for Justices of any court created by the Parliament is seventy years.

The Parliament may make a law fixing an age that is less than seventy years as the maximum age for Justices of a court created by the Parliament and may at any time repeal or amend such a law, but any such repeal or amendment does not affect the term of office of a Justice under an appointment made before the repeal or amendment.

A Justice of the High Court or of a court created by the Parliament may resign his office by writing under his hand delivered to the Governor-General.

Nothing in the provisions added to this section by the *Constitution Alteration (Retirement of Judges)* 1977 affects the continuance of a person in office as a Justice of a court under an appointment made before the commencement of those provisions.

A reference in this section to the appointment of a Justice of the High Court or of a court created by the Parliament shall be read as including a reference to the appointment of a person who holds office as a Justice of the High Court or of a court created by the Parliament to another office of Justice of the same court having a different status or designation.

73. Appellate jurisdiction of High Court The High Court shall have jurisdiction, with such exceptions and subject to such regulations as the Parliament prescribes, to hear and determine appeals from all judgments, decrees, orders, and sentences:

- (i) Of any Justice or Justices exercising the original jurisdiction of the High Court;
- (ii) Of any other federal court, or court exercising federal jurisdiction; or of the Supreme Court of any State, or of any other court of any State from which at the establishment of the Commonwealth an appeal lies to the Queen in Council;
- (iii) Of the Inter-State Commission, but as to questions of law only;

and the judgment of the High Court in all such cases shall be final and conclusive.

But no exception or regulation prescribed by the Parliament shall prevent the High Court from hearing and determining any appeal from the Supreme Court of a State in any matter in which at the establishment of the Commonwealth an appeal lies from such Supreme Court to the Queen in Council.

Until the Parliament otherwise provides, the conditions of and restrictions on appeals to the Queen in Council from the Supreme Courts of the several States shall be applicable to appeals from them to the High Court.

74. Appeal to Queen in Council No appeal shall be permitted to the Queen in Council from a decision of the High Court upon any question, howsoever arising, as to the limits inter se of the Constitutional powers of the Commonwealth and those of any State or States, or as to the limits inter se of the Constitutional powers of any two or more States, unless the High Court shall certify that the question is one which ought to be determined by Her Majesty in Council.

The High Court may so certify if satisfied that for any special reason the certificate should be granted, and thereupon an appeal shall lie to Her Majesty in Council on the question without further leave.

Except as provided in this section, this Constitution shall not impair any right which the Queen may be pleased to exercise by virtue of Her Royal prerogative to grant special leave of appeal from the High Court to Her Majesty in Council. The Parliament may make laws limiting the matters in which such leave may be asked, but proposed laws containing any such limitation shall be reserved by the Governor-General for Her Majesty's pleasure.

75. Original jurisdiction of High Court In all matters:

- (i) Arising under any treaty;
- (ii) Affecting consuls or other representatives of other countries;
- (iii) In which the Commonwealth, or a person suing or being sued on behalf of the Commonwealth, is a party;
- (iv) Between States, or between residents of different States, or between a State and a resident of another State;
- (v) In which a writ of Mandamus or prohibition or an injunction is sought against an officer of the Commonwealth;

the High Court shall have original jurisdiction.

76. Additional original jurisdiction The Parliament may make laws conferring original jurisdiction on the High Court in any matter:

- (i) Arising under this Constitution, or involving its interpretation;
- (ii) Arising under any laws made by the Parliament;
- (iii) Of Admiralty and maritime jurisdiction;
- (iv) Relating to the same subject-matter claimed under the laws of different States.

77. Power to define jurisdiction With respect to any of the matters mentioned in the last two sections the Parliament may make laws:

    (i)   Defining the jurisdiction of any federal court other than the High Court;

    (ii)   Defining the extent to which the jurisdiction of any federal court shall be exclusive of that which belongs to or is invested in the courts of the States;

    (iii) Investing any court of a State with federal jurisdiction.

78. Proceedings against Commonwealth or State The Parliament may make laws conferring rights to proceed against the Commonwealth or a State in respect of matters within the limits of the judicial power.

79. Number of judges The federal jurisdiction of any court may be exercised by such number of judges as the Parliament prescribes.

80. Trial by jury The trial on indictment of any offence against any law of the Commonwealth shall be by jury, and every such trial shall be held in the State where the offence was committed, and if the offence was not committed within any State the trial shall be held at such place or places as the Parliament prescribes.

CHAPTER IV

FINANCE AND TRADE

81. Consolidated Revenue Fund All revenue or moneys raised or received by the Executive Government of the Commonwealth shall form one Consolidated Revenue Fund, to be appropriated for the purposes of the Commonwealth in the manner and subject to the charges and liabilities imposed by this Constitution.

82. Expenditure charged thereon The costs, charges, and expenses incident to the collection, management, and receipt of the Consolidated Revenue Fund shall form the first charge thereon; and the revenue of the Commonwealth shall in the first instance be applied to the payment of the expenditure of the Commonwealth.

83. Money to be appropriated by law No money shall be drawn from the Treasury of the Commonwealth except under appropriation made by law.

But until the expiration of one month after the first meeting of the Parliament the Governor-General in Council may draw from the Treasury and expend such moneys as may be necessary for the maintenance of any department transferred to the Commonwealth and for the holding of the first elections for the Parliament.

84. Transfer of officers When any department of the public service of a State becomes transferred to the Commonwealth, all officers of the department shall become subject to the control of the Executive Government of the Commonwealth.

Any such officer who is not retained in the service of the Commonwealth shall, unless he is appointed to some other office of equal emolument in the public service of the State, be entitled to receive from the State any pension, gratuity, or other compensation, payable under the law of the State on the abolition of his office.

Any such officer who is retained in the service of the Commonwealth shall preserve all his existing and accruing rights, and shall be entitled to retire from office at the time, and on the pension or retiring allowance, which would be permitted by the law of the State if his service with the Commonwealth were a continuation of his service with the State. Such pension or retiring allowance shall be paid to him by the Commonwealth; but the State shall pay to the Commonwealth a part thereof, to be calculated on the proportion which his term of service with the State bears to his whole term of service, and for the purpose of the calculation his salary shall be taken to be that paid to him by the State at the time of the transfer.

Any officer who is, at the establishment of the Commonwealth, in the public service of a State, and who is, by consent of the Governor of the State with the advice of the Executive Council thereof, transferred to the public service of the Commonwealth, shall have the same rights as if he had been an officer of a department transferred to the Commonwealth and were retained in the service of the Commonwealth.

85. Transfer of property of State When any department of the public service of a State is transferred to the Commonwealth:

    (i)   All property of the State of any kind, used exclusively in connexion with the department, shall become vested in the Commonwealth; but, in the case of the departments controlling customs and excise and bounties, for such time only as the Governor-General in Council may declare to be necessary;

(ii)   The Commonwealth may acquire any property of the State, of any kind used, but not exclusively used in connexion with the department; the value thereof shall, if no agreement can be made, be ascertained in, as nearly as may be, the manner in which the value of land, or of an interest in land, taken by the State for public purposes is ascertained under the law of the State in force at the establishment of the Commonwealth;

(iii)   The Commonwealth shall compensate the State for the value of any property passing to the Commonwealth under this section; if no agreement can be made as to the mode of compensation, it shall be determined under laws to be made by the Parliament;

(iv)   The Commonwealth shall, at the date of the transfer, assume the current obligations of the State in respect of the department transferred.

86. On the establishment of the Commonwealth, the collection and control of duties of customs and of excise, and the control of the payment of bounties, shall pass to the Executive Government of the Commonwealth.

87. During a period of ten years after the establishment of the Commonwealth and thereafter until the Parliament otherwise provides, of the net revenue of the Commonwealth from duties of customs and of excise not more than one-fourth shall be applied annually by the Commonwealth towards its expenditure.

The balance shall, in accordance with this Constitution, be paid to the several States, or applied towards the payment of interest on debts of the several States taken over by the Commonwealth.

88. Uniform duties of customs Uniform duties of customs shall be imposed within two years after the establishment of the Commonwealth.

89. Payment to States before uniform duties Until the imposition of uniform duties of customs:

(i)   The Commonwealth shall credit to each State the revenues collected therein by the Commonwealth.

(ii)   The Commonwealth shall debit to each State:

(a)   The expenditure therein of the Commonwealth incurred solely for the maintenance or continuance, as at the time of transfer, of any department transferred from the State to the Commonwealth;

(b)   The proportion of the State, according to the number of its people, in the other expenditure of the Commonwealth.

(iii)   The Commonwealth shall pay to each State month by month the balance (if any) in favour of the State.

90. Exclusive power over customs, excise, and bounties On the imposition of uniform duties of customs the power of the Parliament to impose duties of customs and of excise, and to grant bounties on the production or export of goods, shall become exclusive.

On the imposition of uniform duties of customs all laws of the several States imposing duties of customs or of excise, or offering bounties on the production or export of goods, shall cease to have effect, but any grant of or agreement for any such bounty lawfully made by or under the authority of the Government of any State shall be taken to be good if made before the thirtieth day of June, one thousand eight hundred and ninety-eight, and not otherwise.

91. Exceptions as to bounties Nothing in this Constitution prohibits a State from granting any aid to or bounty on mining for gold, silver, or other metals, nor from granting, with the consent of both Houses of the Parliament of the Commonwealth expressed by resolution, any aid to or bounty on the production or export of goods.

92. Trade within the Commonwealth to be free On the imposition of uniform duties of customs, trade, commerce, and intercourse among the States, whether by means of internal carriage or ocean navigation, shall be absolutely free.

But notwithstanding anything in this Constitution, goods imported before the imposition of uniform duties of customs into any State, or into any Colony which, whilst the goods remain therein, becomes a State, shall, on thence passing into another State within two years after the imposition of such duties, be liable to any duty chargeable on the importation of such goods into the Commonwealth, less any duty paid in respect of the goods on their importation.

93. Payment to States for five years after uniform tariffs During the first five years after the imposition of uniform duties of customs, and thereafter until the Parliament otherwise provides:

(i)   The duties of customs chargeable on goods imported into a State and afterwards passing into another State for consumption, and the duties of excise paid on goods produced or

> manufactured in a State and afterwards passing into another State for consumption, shall be taken to have been collected not in the former but in the latter State;

    (ii)   Subject to the last subsection, the Commonwealth shall credit revenue, debit expenditure, and pay balances to the several States as prescribed for the period preceding the imposition of uniform duties of customs.

94. Distribution of surplus After five years from the imposition of uniform duties of customs, the Parliament may provide, on such basis as it deems fair, for the monthly payment to the several States of all surplus revenue of the Commonwealth.

95. Customs duties of Western Australia Notwithstanding anything in this Constitution, the Parliament of the State of Western Australia, if that State be an Original State, may, during the first five years after the imposition of uniform duties of customs, impose duties of customs on goods passing into that State and not originally imported from beyond the limits of the Commonwealth; and such duties shall be collected by the Commonwealth.

But any duty so imposed on any goods shall not exceed during the first of such years the duty chargeable on the goods under the law of Western Australia in force at the imposition of uniform duties, and shall not exceed during the second, third, fourth, and fifth of such years respectively, four-fifths, three-fifths, two-fifths, and one-fifth of such latter duty, and all duties imposed under this section shall cease at the expiration of the fifth year after the imposition of uniform duties.

If at any time during the five years the duty on any goods under this section is higher than the duty imposed by the Commonwealth on the importation of the like goods, then such higher duty shall be collected on the goods when imported into Western Australia from beyond the limits of the Commonwealth.

96. Financial assistance to States During a period of ten years after the establishment of the Commonwealth and thereafter until the Parliament otherwise provides, the Parliament may grant financial assistance to any State on such terms and conditions as the Parliament thinks fit.

97. Audit Until the Parliament otherwise provides, the laws in force in any Colony which has become or becomes a State with respect to the receipt of revenue and the expenditure of money on account of the Government of the Colony, and the review and audit of such receipt and expenditure, shall apply to the receipt of revenue and the expenditure of money on account of the Commonwealth in the State in the same manner as if the Commonwealth, or the Government or an officer of the Commonwealth, were mentioned whenever the Colony, or the Government or an officer of the Colony, is mentioned.

98. Trade and commerce includes navigation and State railways The power of the Parliament to make laws with respect to trade and commerce extends to navigation and shipping, and to railways the property of any State.

99. Commonwealth not to give preference The Commonwealth shall not, by any law or regulation of trade, commerce, or revenue, give preference to one State or any part thereof over another State or any part thereof.

100. Nor abridge right to use water The Commonwealth shall not, by any law or regulation of trade or commerce, abridge the right of a State or of the residents therein to the reasonable use of the waters of rivers for conservation or irrigation.

101. Inter-State Commission There shall be an Inter-State Commission, with such powers of adjudication and administration as the Parliament deems necessary for the execution and maintenance, within the Commonwealth, of the provisions of this Constitution relating to trade and commerce, and of all laws made thereunder.

102. Parliament may forbid preferences by State The Parliament may by any law with respect to trade or commerce forbid, as to railways, any preference or discrimination by any State, or by any authority constituted under a State, if such preference or discrimination is undue and unreasonable, or unjust to any State; due regard being had to the financial responsibilities incurred by any State in connexion with the construction and maintenance of its railways. But no preference or discrimination shall, within the meaning of this section, be taken to be undue and unreasonable, or unjust to any State, unless so adjudged by the Inter-State Commission.

103. Commissioners' appointment, tenure, and remuneration The members of the Inter-State Commission:

    (i)   Shall be appointed by the Governor-General in Council;

(ii)   Shall hold office for seven years, but may be removed within that time by the Governor-General in Council, on an address from both Houses of the Parliament in the same session praying for such removal on the ground of proved misbehaviour or incapacity;

(iii)   Shall receive such remuneration as the Parliament may fix; but such remuneration shall not be diminished during their continuance in office.

104. Saving of certain rates Nothing in this Constitution shall render unlawful any rate for the carriage of goods upon a railway, the property of a State, if the rate is deemed by the Inter-State Commission to be necessary for the development of the territory of the State, and if the rate applies equally to goods within the State and to goods passing into the State from other States.

105. Taking over public debts of States [altered by No 3, 1910, s 2] The Parliament may take over from the States their public debts as existing at the establishment of the Commonwealth, or a proportion thereof according to the respective numbers of their people as shown by the latest statistics of the Commonwealth, and may convert, renew, or consolidate such debts, or any part thereof; and the States shall indemnify the Commonwealth in respect of the debts taken over, and thereafter the interest payable in respect of the debts shall be deducted and retained from the portions of the surplus revenue of the Commonwealth payable to the several States, or if such surplus is insufficient, or if there is no surplus, then the deficiency or the whole amount shall be paid by the several States.

105A. Agreements with respect to State debts [inserted by No 1, 1929, s 2] (1) The Commonwealth may make agreements with the States with respect to the public debts of the States, including:

(a)   the taking over of such debts by the Commonwealth;

(b)   the management of such debts;

(c)   the payment of interest and the provision and management of sinking funds in respect of such debts;

(d)   the consolidation, renewal, conversion, and redemption of such debts;

(e)   the indemnification of the Commonwealth by the States in respect of debts taken over by the Commonwealth; and

(f)   the borrowing of money by the States or by the Commonwealth, or by the Commonwealth for the States.

(2)   The Parliament may make laws for validating any such agreement made before the commencement of this section.

(3)   The Parliament may make laws for the carrying out by the parties thereto of any such agreement.

(4)   Any such agreement may be varied or rescinded by the parties thereto.

(5)   Every such agreement and any such variation thereof shall be binding upon the Commonwealth and the States parties thereto notwithstanding anything contained in this Constitution or the Constitution of the several States or in any law of the Parliament of the Commonwealth or of any State.

(6)   The powers conferred by this section shall not be construed as being limited in any way by the provisions of section one hundred and five of this Constitution.

CHAPTER V

THE STATES

106. Saving of Constitutions The Constitution of each State of the Commonwealth shall, subject to this Constitution, continue as at the establishment of the Commonwealth, or as at the admission or establishment of the State, as the case may be, until altered in accordance with the Constitution of the State.

107. Saving of Power of State Parliaments Every power of the Parliament of a Colony which has become or becomes a State, shall, unless it is by this Constitution exclusively vested in the Parliament of the Commonwealth or withdrawn from the Parliament of the State, continue as at the establishment of the Commonwealth, or as at the admission or establishment of the State, as the case may be.

108. Saving of State laws Every law in force in a Colony which has become or becomes a State, and relating to any matter within the powers of the Parliament of the Commonwealth, shall, subject to this Constitution, continue in force in the State; and, until provision is made in that behalf by the Parliament of the Commonwealth, the Parliament of the State shall have such powers of alteration and of repeal in respect of any such law as the Parliament of the Colony had until the Colony became a State.

109. Inconsistency of laws When a law of a State is inconsistent with a law of the Commonwealth, the latter shall prevail, and the former shall, to the extent of the inconsistency, be invalid.

110. Provisions referring to Governor The provisions of this Constitution relating to the Governor of a State extend and apply to the Governor for the time being of the State, or other chief executive officer or administrator of the government of the State.

111. States may surrender territory The Parliament of a State may surrender any part of the State to the Commonwealth; and upon such surrender, and the acceptance thereof by the Commonwealth, such part of the State shall become subject to the exclusive jurisdiction of the Commonwealth.

112. States may levy charges for inspection laws After uniform duties of customs have been imposed, a State may levy on imports or exports, or on goods passing into or out of the State, such charges as may be necessary for executing the inspection laws of the State; but the net produce of all charges so levied shall be for the use of the Commonwealth; and any such inspection laws may be annulled by the Parliament of the Commonwealth.

113. Intoxicating liquids All fermented, distilled, or other intoxicating liquids passing into any State or remaining therein for use, consumption, sale, or storage, shall be subject to the laws of the State as if such liquids had been produced in the State.

114. States may not raise forces. Taxation of property of Commonwealth or State A State shall not, without the consent of the Parliament of the Commonwealth, raise or maintain any naval or military force, or impose any tax on property of any kind belonging to the Commonwealth, nor shall the Commonwealth impose any tax on property of any kind belonging to a State.

115. States not to coin money A State shall not coin money, nor make anything but gold and silver coin a legal tender in payment of debts.

116. Commonwealth not to legislate in respect of religion The Commonwealth shall not make any law for establishing any religion, or for imposing any religious observance, or for prohibiting the free exercise of any religion, and no religious test shall be required as a qualification for any office or public trust under the Commonwealth.

117. Rights of residents in States A subject of the Queen, resident in any State, shall not be subject in any other State to any disability or discrimination which would not be equally applicable to him if he were a subject of the Queen resident in such other State.

118. Recognition of laws, &c of States Full faith and credit shall be given, throughout the Commonwealth to the laws, the public Acts and records, and the judicial proceedings of every State.

119. Protection of States from invasion and violence The Commonwealth shall protect every State against invasion and, on the application of the Executive Government of the State, against domestic violence.

120. Custody of offenders against laws of the Commonwealth Every State shall make provision for the detention in its prisons of persons accused or convicted of offences against the laws of the Commonwealth, and for the punishment of persons convicted of such offences, and the Parliament of the Commonwealth may make laws to give effect to this provision.

CHAPTER VI

NEW STATES

121. New States may be admitted or established The Parliament may admit to the Commonwealth or establish new States, and may upon such admission or establishment make or impose such terms and conditions, including the extent of representation in either House of the Parliament, as it thinks fit.

122. Government of territories The Parliament may make laws for the government of any territory surrendered by any State to and accepted by the Commonwealth, or of any territory placed by the Queen under the authority of and accepted by the Commonwealth, or otherwise acquired by the Commonwealth, and may allow the representation of such territory in either House of the Parliament to the extent and on the terms which it thinks fit.

123. Alteration of limits of States The Parliament of the Commonwealth may, with the consent of the Parliament of a State, and the approval of the majority of the electors of the State voting upon the question, increase, diminish, or otherwise alter the limits of the State, upon such terms and conditions as may be agreed on, and may with the like consent, make provision respecting the effect and operation of any increase or diminution or alteration of territory in relation to any State affected.

124. Formation of new States A new State may be formed by separation of territory from a State, but only with the consent of the Parliament thereof, and a new State may be formed by the union of two or more States or parts of States, but only with the consent of the Parliaments of the States affected.

CHAPTER VII

MISCELLANEOUS

125. Seat of Government The seat of Government of the Commonwealth shall be determined by the Parliament, and shall be within territory which shall have been granted to or acquired by the Commonwealth, and shall be vested in and belong to the Commonwealth, and shall be in the State of New South Wales, and be distant not less than one hundred miles from Sydney.

Such territory shall contain an area of not less than one hundred square miles, and such portion thereof as shall consist of Crown lands shall be granted to the Commonwealth without any payment therefor.

The Parliament shall sit at Melbourne until it meet at the seat of Government.

126. Power to Her Majesty to authorise Governor-General to appoint deputies The Queen may authorise the Governor-General to appoint any person, or any persons jointly or severally, to be his deputy or deputies within any part of the Commonwealth, and in that capacity to exercise during the pleasure of the Governor-General such powers and functions of the Governor-General as he thinks fit to assign to such deputy or deputies, subject to any limitations expressed or directions given by the Queen; but the appointment of such deputy or deputies shall not affect the exercise by the Governor-General himself of any power or function.

127. [repealed by No 55, 1967, s 3] ~~Aborigines not to be counted in reckoning population~~ ~~In reckoning the numbers of the people of the Commonwealth, or of a State or other part of the Commonwealth, aboriginal natives shall not be counted.~~

CHAPTER VIII

ALTERATION OF THE CONSTITUTION

128. Mode of altering the Constitution This Constitution shall not be altered except in the following manner:

[this paragraph altered by No 84, 1977, s 2] The proposed law for the alteration thereof must be passed by an absolute majority of each House of the Parliament, and not less than two nor more than six months after its passage through both Houses the proposed law shall be submitted in each State **and Territory** to the electors qualified to vote for the election of members of the House of Representatives.

[this paragraph altered by No 84, 1977, s 2] But if either House passes any such proposed law by an absolute majority, and the other House rejects or fails to pass it, or passes it with any amendment to which the first-mentioned House will not agree, and if after an interval of three months the first-mentioned House in the same or the next session again passes the proposed law by an absolute majority with or without any amendment which has been made or agreed to by the other House, and such other House rejects or fails to pass it or passes it with any amendment to which the first-mentioned House will not agree, the Governor-General may submit the proposed law as last proposed by the first-mentioned House, and either with or without any amendments subsequently agreed to by both Houses, to the electors in each State **and Territory** qualified to vote for the election of the House of Representatives.

When a proposed law is submitted to the electors the vote shall be taken in such manner as the Parliament prescribes. But until the qualification of electors of members of the House of Representatives becomes uniform throughout the Commonwealth, only one-half the electors voting for and against the proposed law shall be counted in any State in which adult suffrage prevails.

And if in a majority of the States a majority of the electors voting approve the proposed law, and if a majority of all the electors voting also approve the proposed law, it shall be presented to the Governor-General for the Queen's assent.

No alteration diminishing the proportionate representation of any State in either House of the Parliament, or the minimum number of representatives of a State in the House of Representatives, or increasing, diminishing, or otherwise altering the limits of the State, or in any manner affecting the provisions of the Constitution in relation thereto, shall become law unless the majority of the electors voting in that State approve the proposed law.

[this paragraph added by No 84, 1977, s 2] In this section, "Territory" means any territory referred to in section one hundred and twenty-two of this Constitution in respect of which there is in force a law allowing its representation in the House of Representatives.

SCHEDULE

Oath

I, *A.B.*, do swear that I will be faithful and bear true allegiance to Her Majesty Queen Victoria, Her heirs and successors according to law. SO HELP ME GOD!

Affirmation

I, *A.B.*, do solemnly and sincerely affirm and declare that I will be faithful and bear true allegiance to Her Majesty Queen Victoria, Her heirs and successors according to law.

(NOTE – *The name of the King or Queen of the United Kingdom of Great Britain and Ireland for the time being is to be substituted from time to time.*)

---

2. *The Colonial Laws Validity Act 1865* (Imp)

The Colonial Laws Validity Act 1865 (Imp)

(28 & 29 Vict c 63)

An Act to remove Doubts as to the Validity of Colonial Laws.

Whereas Doubts have been entertained respecting the Validity of divers Laws enacted or purporting to have been enacted by the Legislatures of Certain of Her Majesty's Colonies, and respecting the Powers of such Legislatures, and it is expedient that such Doubts should be removed:

Be it hereby enacted by the Queen's most Excellent Majesty, by and with the Advice and Consent of the Lords Spiritual and Temporal, and Commons, in this present Parliament assembled, and by the Authority of the same, as follows:

1. The Term 'Colony' shall in this Act include all of Her Majesty's Possessions abroad in which there shall exist a Legislature, as hereinafter defined, except the Channel Islands, the *Isle of Man,* and such Territories as may for the Time being be vested in Her Majesty under or by virtue of any Act of Parliament for the Government of *India*:

The Terms 'Legislature' and 'Colonial Legislature' shall severally signify the Authority, other than the Imperial Parliament or Her Majesty in Council, competent to make Laws for any Colony:

The Term 'Representative Legislature' shall signify any Colonial Legislature which shall comprise a Legislative Body of which One Half are elected by Inhabitants of the Colony:

The Term 'Colonial Law' shall include Laws made for any Colony either by such Legislature as aforesaid or by Her Majesty in Council:

An Act of Parliament, or any Provision thereof, shall, in construing this Act, be said to extend to any Colony when it is made applicable to such Colony by the express Words or necessary Intendment of any Act of Parliament:

The Term 'Governor' shall mean the Officer lawfully administering the Government of any Colony:

The Term 'Letters Patent' shall mean Letters Patent under the Great Seal of the United Kingdom of *Great Britain* and *Ireland*.

2. Any Colonial Law which is or shall be in any respect repugnant to the Provisions of any Act of Parliament extending to the Colony to which such Law may relate, or repugnant to any Order or Regulation made under Authority of such Act of Parliament, or having in the Colony the Force and Effect of such Act, shall be read subject to such Act, Order or Regulation, and shall, to the Extent of such Repugnancy, but not otherwise, be and remain absolutely void and inoperative.

3. No Colonial Law shall be or be deemed to have been void or inoperative on the Ground of Repugnancy to the Law of *England*, unless the same shall be repugnant to the Provisions of some such Act of Parliament, Order or Regulation as aforesaid.

4. No Colonial Law, passed with the Concurrence of or assented to by the Governor of any Colony, or to be hereafter so passed or assented to, shall be or be deemed to have been void or inoperative by reason only of any Instructions with reference to such Law or the Subject thereof which may have been given to such Governor by or on behalf of Her Majesty, by any Instrument other than the Letters Patent or Instrument authorizing such Governor to concur in passing or to assent to Laws for the Peace, Order, and good Government of such Colony, even though such Instructions may be referred to in such Letters Patent or last-mentioned Instrument.

5. Every Colonial Legislature shall have, and be deemed at all Times to have had, full Power within its Jurisdiction to establish Courts of Judicature, and to abolish and reconstitute the same, and to alter the Constitution thereof, and to make Provision for the Administration of Justice therein; and every Representative Legislature shall, in respect to the Colony under its Jurisdiction, have, and be deemed at all Times to have had, full Power to make Laws respecting the Constitution, Powers, and Procedure of such Legislature; provided that such Laws shall have been passed in such Manner and Form as may from Time to Time be required by any Act of Parliament, Letters Patent, Order in Council, or Colonial Law for the Time being in force in the said Colony.

6. The Certificate of the Clerk or other proper Officer of a Legislative Body in any Colony to the Effect that the Document to which it is attached is a true Copy of any Colonial Law assented to by the Governor of such Colony, or of any Bill reserved for the Signification of Her Majesty's Pleasure by the said Governor, shall be *primâ facie* Evidence that the Document so certified is a true Copy of such Law or Bill, and, as the Case may be, that such Law has been duly and properly passed and presented to the Governor; and any Proclamation purporting to be published by Authority of the Governor in any Newspaper in the Colony to which such Law or Bill shall relate, and signifying Her Majesty's Disallowance of any such Colonial Law, or Her Majesty's Assent to any such reserved Bill as aforesaid shall be *primâ facie* Evidence of such Disallowance or Assent.

And whereas Doubts are entertained respecting the Validity of certain Acts enacted or reputed to be enacted by the Legislature of *South Australia:* Be it further enacted as follows:

7. All Laws or reputed Laws enacted or purporting to have been enacted by the said Legislature, or by Persons or Bodies of Persons for the Time being acting as such Legislature, which have received the Assent of Her Majesty in Council, or which have received the Assent of the Governor of the said Colony in the Name and on behalf of Her Majesty, shall be and be deemed to have been valid and effectual from the Date of such Assent for all Purposes whatever; provided that nothing herein contained shall be deemed to give Effect to any Law or reputed Law which has been disallowed by Her Majesty or has expired, or has been lawfully repealed, or to prevent the lawful Disallowance or Repeal of any Law.

---

3. *Statute of Westminster 1931* (Imp)

Statute of Westminster 1931 (Imp)

An Act to give effect to certain resolutions passed by Imperial Conferences held in the years 1926 and 1930.

[11th December 1931]

WHEREAS the delegates of His Majesty's Governments in the United Kingdom, the Dominion of Canada, the Commonwealth of Australia, the Dominion of New Zealand, the Union of South Africa, the Irish Free State and Newfoundland, at Imperial Conferences holden at Westminster in the years of our Lord nineteen hundred and twenty-six and nineteen hundred and thirty did concur in making the declarations and resolutions set forth in the Reports of the said Conferences:

AND WHEREAS it is meet and proper to set out by way of preamble to this Act that, inasmuch as the Crown is the symbol of the free association of the members of the British Commonwealth of Nations, and as they are united by a common allegiance to the Crown, it would be in accord with the established constitutional position of all the members of the Commonwealth in relation to one another that any alteration in the law touching the Succession to the Throne or the Royal Style and Titles shall hereafter require the assent as well of the Parliaments of all the Dominions as of the Parliament of the United Kingdom:

AND WHEREAS it is in accord with the established constitutional position that no law hereafter made by the Parliament of the United Kingdom shall extend to any of the said Dominions as part of the law of that Dominion otherwise than at the request and with the consent of that Dominion:

AND WHEREAS it is necessary for the ratifying, confirming and establishing of certain of the said declarations and resolutions of the said Conferences that a law be made and enacted in due form by authority of the Parliament of the United Kingdom:

AND WHEREAS the Dominion of Canada, the Commonwealth of Australia, the Dominion of New Zealand, the Union of South Africa, the Irish Free State and Newfoundland have severally requested and consented to the submission of a measure to the Parliament of the United Kingdom for making such provision with regard to the matters aforesaid as is hereafter in this Act contained:

NOW, THEREFORE, be it enacted by the King's most Excellent Majesty by and with the advice and consent of the Lords Spiritual and Temporal, and Commons, in this present Parliament assembled, and by the authority of the same as follows: –

1. Meaning of "Dominion" in this Act In this Act the expression 'Dominion' means any of the following Dominions, that is to say, the Dominion of Canada, the Commonwealth of Australia, the Dominion of New Zealand, the Union of South Africa, the Irish Free State and Newfoundland.

2. Validity of laws made by Parliament of a Dominion 28 and 29 Vict c 63 – (1) The Colonial Laws Validity Act, 1865, shall not apply to any law made after the commencement of this Act by the Parliament of a Dominion.

(2) No law and no provision of any law made after the commencement of this Act by the Parliament of a Dominion shall be void or inoperative on the ground that it is repugnant to the law of England, or to the provisions of any existing or future Act of Parliament of the United Kingdom, or to any order, rule or regulation made under any such Act, and the powers of the Parliament of a Dominion shall include the power to repeal or amend any such Act, order, rule or regulation in so far as the same is part of the law of the Dominion.

3. Power of Parliament of Dominion to legislate extra-territorially It is hereby declared and enacted that the Parliament of a Dominion has full power to make laws having extraterritorial operation.

4. Parliament of the United Kingdom not to legislate for Dominion except by consent No Act of Parliament of the United Kingdom passed after the commencement of this Act shall extend, or be deemed to extend, to a Dominion as part of the law of that Dominion, unless it is expressly declared in that Act that that Dominion has requested, and consented to, the enactment thereof.

5. Powers of Dominion Parliaments in relation to merchant shipping 57 & 58 Vict c 60 Without prejudice to the generality of the foregoing provisions of this Act, sections seven hundred and thirty-five and seven hundred and thirty-six of the Merchant Shipping Act, 1894, shall be construed as though reference therein to the Legislature of a British possession did not include reference to the Parliament of a Dominion.

6. Powers of Dominion Parliaments in relation to Courts of Admiralty 53 & 54 Vict c 27 Without prejudice to the generality of the foregoing provisions of this Act, section four of the Colonial Courts of Admiralty Act, 1890 (which requires certain laws to be reserved for the signification of His Majesty's pleasure or to contain a suspending clause), and so much of section seven of that Act as requires the approval of His Majesty in Council to any rules of Court for regulating the practice and procedure of a Colonial Court of Admiralty, shall cease to have effect in any Dominion as from the commencement of this Act.

7. Saving for British and North America Acts and application of the Act to Canada – (1) Nothing in this Act shall be deemed to apply to the repeal, amendment or alteration of the British North America Acts, 1867 to 1930, or any order, rule or regulation made thereunder.

(2) The provisions of section two of this Act shall extend to laws made by any of the Provinces of Canada and to the powers of the legislatures of such Provinces.

(3) The powers conferred by this Act upon the Parliament of Canada or upon the legislatures of the Provinces shall be restricted to the enactment of laws in relation to matters within the competence of the Parliament of Canada or of any of the legislatures of the Provinces respectively.

8. Saving for Constitution Acts of Australia and New Zealand Nothing in this Act shall be deemed to confer any power to repeal or alter the Constitution or the Constitution Act of the Commonwealth of Australia or the Constitution Act of the Dominion of New Zealand otherwise than in accordance with the law existing before the commencement of this Act.

9. Saving with respect to States of Australia – (1) Nothing in this Act shall be deemed to authorize the Parliament of the Commonwealth of Australia to make laws on any matter within the authority of the

States of Australia, not being a matter within the authority of the Parliament or Government of the Commonwealth of Australia.

(2) Nothing in this Act shall be deemed to require the concurrence of the Parliament or Government of the Commonwealth of Australia in any law made by the Parliament of the United Kingdom with respect to any matter within the authority of the States of Australia, not being a matter within the authority of the Parliament or Government of the Commonwealth of Australia, in any case where it would have been in accordance with the constitutional practice existing before the commencement of this Act that the Parliament of the United Kingdom should make that law without such concurrence.

(3) In the application of this Act to the Commonwealth of Australia the request and consent referred to in section four shall mean the request and consent of the Parliament and Government of the Commonwealth.

10. Certain sections of Act not to apply to Australia, New Zealand or Newfoundland unless adopted – (1) None of the following sections of this Act, that is to say, sections two, three, four, five and six, shall extend to a Dominion to which this section applies as part of the law of that Dominion unless that section is adopted by the Parliament of the Dominion, and any Act of that Parliament adopting any section of this Act may provide that the adoption shall have effect either from the commencement of this Act or from such later date as is specified in the adopting Act.

(2) The Parliament of any such Dominion as aforesaid may at any time revoke the adoption of any section referred to in subsection (1) of this section.

(3) The Dominions to which this section applies are the Commonwealth of Australia, the Dominion of New Zealand and Newfoundland.

11. Meaning of "Colony" in future Acts 52 and 53 Vict c 63 Notwithstanding anything in the Interpretation Act, 1889, the expression "Colony", shall not, in any Act of the Parliament of the United Kingdom passed after the commencement of this Act, include a Dominion or any Province or State forming part of a Dominion.

12. Short Title This Act may be cited as the Statute of Westminster, 1931.

---

4. *Australia Act 1986* (Cth)

Australia Act 1986 (Cth)

An Act to bring constitutional arrangements affecting the Commonwealth and the States into conformity with the status of the Commonwealth of Australia as a sovereign, independent and federal nation

[Assented to 4 December 1985]

WHEREAS the Prime Minister of the Commonwealth and the Premiers of the States at conferences held in Canberra on 24 and 25 June 1982 and 21 June 1984 agreed on the taking of certain measures to bring constitutional arrangements affecting the Commonwealth and the States into conformity with the status of the Commonwealth of Australia as a sovereign, independent and federal nation:

AND WHEREAS in pursuance of paragraph 51(xxxviii) of the Constitution the Parliaments of all the States have requested the Parliament of the Commonwealth to enact an Act in the terms of this Act:

BE IT THEREFORE ENACTED by the Queen, and the Senate and the House of Representatives of the Commonwealth of Australia, as follows:

1. Termination of power of Parliament of United Kingdom to legislate for Australia No Act of the Parliament of the United Kingdom passed after the commencement of this Act shall extend, or be deemed to extend, to the Commonwealth, to a State or to a Territory as part of the law of the Commonwealth, of the State or of the Territory.

2. Legislative powers of Parliaments of States (1) It is hereby declared and enacted that the legislative powers of the Parliament of each State include full power to make laws for the peace, order and good government of that State that have extra-territorial operation.

(2) It is hereby further declared and enacted that the legislative powers of the Parliament of each State include all legislative powers that the Parliament of the United Kingdom might have exercised before the commencement of this Act for the peace, order and good government of that State but nothing in this subsection confers on a State any capacity that the State did not have immediately before the commencement of this Act to engage in relations with countries outside Australia.

3. Terminations of restrictions on legislative powers of Parliaments of States (1) The Act of the Parliament of the United Kingdom known as the Colonial Laws Validity Act 1865 shall not apply to any law made after the commencement of this Act by the Parliament of a State.

(2) No law and no provision of any law made after the commencement of this Act by the Parliament of a State shall be void or inoperative on the ground that it is repugnant to the law of England, or to the provisions of any existing or future Act of the Parliament of the United Kingdom, or to any order, rule or regulation made under any such Act, and the powers of the Parliament of a State shall include the power to repeal or amend any such Act, order, rule or regulation in so far as it is part of the law of the State.

4. Powers of State Parliaments in relation to merchant shipping Sections 735 and 736 of the Act of the Parliament of the United Kingdom known as the Merchant Shipping Act 1894, in so far as they are part of the law of a State, are hereby repealed.

5. Commonwealth Constitution, Constitution Act and Statute of Westminster not affected Sections 2 and 3(2) above –

(a) are subject to the Commonwealth of Australia Constitution Act and to the Constitution of the Commonwealth; and

(b) do not operate so as to give any force or effect to a provision of an Act of the Parliament of a State that would repeal, amend or be repugnant to this Act, the Commonwealth of Australia Constitution Act, the Constitution of the Commonwealth or the Statute of Westminster 1931 as amended and in force from time to time.

6. Manner and form of making certain State laws Notwithstanding sections 2 and 3(2) above, a law made after the commencement of this Act by the Parliament of a State respecting the constitution, powers or procedure of the Parliament of the State shall be of no force or effect unless it is made in such manner and form as may from time to time be required by a law made by that Parliament, whether made before or after the commencement of this Act.

7. Powers and functions of Her Majesty's Governors in respect of States (1) Her Majesty's representative in each State shall be the Governor.

(2) Subject to subsections (3) and (4) below, all powers and functions of Her Majesty in respect of a State are exercisable only by the Governor of the State.

(3) Subsection (2) above does not apply in relation to the power to appoint, and the power to terminate the appointment of, the Governor of a State.

(4) While Her Majesty is personally present in a State, Her Majesty is not precluded from exercising any of Her powers and functions in respect of the State that are the subject of subsection (2) above.

(5) The advice to Her Majesty in relation to the exercise of the powers and functions of Her Majesty in respect of a State shall be tendered by the Premier of the State.

8. State laws not subject to disallowance or suspension of operation An Act of the Parliament of a State that has been assented to by the Governor of the State shall not, after the commencement of this Act, be subject to disallowance by Her Majesty, nor shall its operation be suspended pending the signification of Her Majesty's pleasure thereon.

9. State laws not subject to withholding of assent or reservation (1) No law or instrument shall be of any force or effect in so far as it purports to require the Governor of a State to withhold assent from any Bill for an Act of the State that has been passed in such manner and form as may from time to time be required by a law made by the Parliament of the State.

(2) No law or instrument shall be of any force or effect in so far as it purports to require the reservation of any Bill for an Act of a State for the signification of Her Majesty's pleasure thereon.

10. Termination of responsibility of United Kingdom Government in relation to State matters After the commencement of this Act Her Majesty's Government in the United Kingdom shall have no responsibility for the government of any State.

11. Termination of appeals to Her Majesty in Council (1) Subject to subsection (4) below, no appeal to Her Majesty in Council lies or shall be brought, whether by leave or special leave of any court or of Her Majesty in Council or otherwise, and whether by virtue of any Act of the Parliament of the United Kingdom, the Royal Prerogative or otherwise, from or in respect of any decision of an Australian court.

(2) Subject to subsection (4) below –

(a) the enactments specified in subsection (3) below and any orders, rules, regulations or other instruments made under, or for the purposes of, those enactments; and

(b) any other provisions of Acts of the Parliament of the United Kingdom in force immediately before the commencement of this Act that make provision for or in relation to appeals to Her Majesty in Council from or in respect of decisions of courts, and any orders, rules, regulations or other instruments made under, or for the purposes of, any such provisions,

in so far as they are part of the law of the Commonwealth, of a State or of a Territory, are hereby repealed.

(3) The enactments referred to in subsection (2)(a) above are the following Acts of the Parliament of the United Kingdom or provisions of such Acts:

The Australian Courts Act 1828, section 15

The Judicial Committee Act 1833

The Judicial Committee Act 1844

The Australian Constitutions Act 1850, section 28

The Colonial Courts of Admiralty Act 1890, section 6.

(4) Nothing in the foregoing provisions of this section –

(a) affects an appeal instituted before the commencement of this Act to Her Majesty in Council from or in respect of a decision of an Australian court; or

(b) precludes the institution after that commencement of an appeal to Her Majesty in Council from or in respect of such a decision where the appeal is instituted –

(i) pursuant to leave granted by an Australian court on an application made before that commencement; or

(ii) pursuant to special leave granted by Her Majesty in Council on a petition presented before that commencement,

but this subsection shall not be construed as permitting or enabling an appeal to Her Majesty in Council to be instituted or continued that could not have been instituted or continued if this section had not been enacted.

12. Amendment of Statute of Westminster Sections 4, 9 (2) and (3) and 10(2) of the Statute of Westminster 1931, in so far as they are part of the law of the Commonwealth, of a State or of a territory, are hereby repealed.

13. Amendment of Constitution Act of Queensland (1) The Constitution Act 1867-1978 of the State of Queensland is in this section referred to as the Principal Act.

(2) Section 11A of the Principal Act is amended in subsection (3) –

(a) by omitting from paragraph (a) –

(i) "and Signet"; and

(ii) "constituted under Letters Patent under the Great Seal of the United Kingdom"; and

(b) by omitting from paragraph (b) –

(i) "and Signet"; and

(ii) "whenever and so long as the office of Governor is vacant or the Governor is incapable of discharging the duties of administration or has departed from Queensland".

(3) Section 11B of the Principal Act is amended –

(a) by omitting "Governor to conform to instructions" and substituting "Definition of Royal Sign Manual";

(b) by omitting subsection (1); and

(c) by omitting from subsection (2) –

(i) "(2)";

(ii) "this section and in"; and

(iii) "and the expression 'Signet' means the seal commonly used for the sign manual of the Sovereign or the seal with which documents are sealed by the Secretary of State in the United Kingdom on behalf of the Sovereign".

(4) Section 14 of the Principal Act is amended in subsection (2) by omitting ", subject to his performing his duty prescribed by section 11B,".

14. Amendment of Constitution Act of Western Australia (1) The Constitution Act 1889 of the State of Western Australia is in this section referred to as the Principal Act.

(2) Section 50 of the Principal Act is amended in subsection (3) –

(a) by omitting from paragraph (a) –

(i) "and Signet"; and

    (ii) "constituted under Letters Patent under the Great Seal of the United Kingdom";

(b) by omitting from paragraph (b) –
    (i) "and Signet"; and
    (ii) "whenever and so long as the office of Governor is vacant or the Governor is incapable of discharging the duties of administration or has departed from Western Australia"; and

(c) by omitting from paragraph (c) –
 (i) "under the Great Seal of the United Kingdom"; and
 (ii) "during a temporary absence of the Governor for a short period from the seat of Government or from the State".

(3) Section 51 of the Principal Act is amended –

(a) by omitting subsection (1); and

(b) by omitting from subsection (2) –
    (i) "(2)";
    (ii) "this section and in"; and
    (iii) "and the expression 'Signet' means the seal commonly used for the sign manual of the Sovereign or the seal with which documents are sealed by the Secretary of State in the United Kingdom on behalf of the Sovereign".

15. Method of repeal or amendment of this Act or Statute of Westminster (1) This Act or the Statute of Westminster 1931, as amended and in force from time to time, in so far as it is part of the law of the Commonwealth, of a State or of a Territory, may be repealed or amended by an Act of the Parliament of the Commonwealth passed at the request or with the concurrence of the Parliaments of all the States and, subject to subsection (3) below, only in that manner.

(2) For the purposes of subsection (1) above, an Act of the Parliament of the Commonwealth that is repugnant to this Act or the Statute of Westminster 1931, as amended and in force from time to time, or to any provision of this Act or of that Statute as so amended and in force, shall, to the extent of the repugnancy, be deemed an Act to repeal or amend the Act, Statute or provision to which it is repugnant.

(3) Nothing in subsection (1) above limits or prevents the exercise by the Parliament of the Commonwealth of any powers that may be conferred upon that Parliament by any alteration of the Constitution of the Commonwealth made in accordance with section 128 of the Constitution of the Commonwealth after the commencement of this Act.

16. Interpretation (1) In this Act, unless the contrary intention appears –
"appeal" includes a petition of appeal, and a complaint in the nature of an appeal;
"appeal to Her Majesty in Council" includes any appeal to Her Majesty;
"Australian court" means a court of a State or any other court of Australia or of a Territory other than the High Court;
"court" includes a judge, judicial officer or other person acting judicially;
"decision" includes a determination, judgement, decree, order or sentence;
"Governor", in relation to a State, includes any person for the time being administering the government of the State;
"State" means a State of the Commonwealth and includes a new State;
"the Commonwealth of Australia Constitution Act" means the Act of the Parliament of the United Kingdom known as the Commonwealth of Australia Constitution Act;
"the Constitution of the Commonwealth" means the Constitution of the Commonwealth set forth in section 9 of the Commonwealth of Australia Constitution Act, being that Constitution as altered and in force from time to time;
"the Statute of Westminster 1931" means the Act of Parliament of the United Kingdom known as the Statute of Westminster 1931.

(2) The expression "a law made by that Parliament" in section 6 above and the expression "a law made by the Parliament" in section 9 above include, in relation to the State of Western Australia, the Constitution Act 1889 of that State.

(3) A reference in this Act to the Parliament of a State includes, in relation to the State of New South Wales, a reference to the legislature of that State as constituted from time to time in accordance with the Constitution Act, 1902, or any other Act of that State, whether or not, in relation to any particular legislative act, the consent of the Legislative Council of that State is necessary.

17. Short title and commencement (1) This Act may be cited as the Australia Act 1986.

(2) This Act shall come into operation on a day and at a time to be fixed by Proclamation.

5. Justices of the High Court of Australia

(a) The Justices

Adapted from Tony Blackshield, Michael Coper and George Williams (eds), *The Oxford Companion to the High Court of Australia* (Oxford University Press, 2001), 20.

Name	Born	Died	Period in office	Age on Court	Government at time of appointment	State of residence
Samuel Griffith	1845	1920	CJ 1903–19	58–74	Protectionist	Qld
Edmund Barton	1849	1920	1903–20	54–70	Protectionist	NSW
Richard O'Connor	1851	1912	1903–12	52–61	Protectionist	NSW
Isaac Isaacs	1855	1948	1906–30; CJ 1930–31	51–75	Protectionist	Vic
Henry Higgins	1851	1929	1906–29	55–77	Protectionist	Vic
Frank Gavan Duffy	1852	1936	1913–31; CJ 1931–35	60–83	ALP	Vic
Charles Powers	1853	1939	1913–29	60–76	ALP	Qld
Albert Piddington	1862	1945	1913	50	ALP	NSW
George Rich	1863	1956	1913–50	49–87	ALP	NSW
Adrian Knox	1863	1932	CJ 1919–30	55–66	Nationalist	NSW
Hayden Starke	1871	1958	1920–50	48–78	Nationalist	Vic
Owen Dixon	1886	1972	1929–52; CJ 1952–64	42–77	Nationalist-CP Coalition	Vic
Herbert Vere Evatt	1894	1965	1930–40	36–46	ALP	NSW
Edward McTiernan	1892	1990	1930–76	38–84	ALP	NSW
John Latham	1877	1964	CJ 1935–52	58–74	UAP-CP Coalition	Vic
Dudley Williams	1889	1963	1940–58	50–68	UAP-CP Coalition	NSW
William Webb	1887	1972	1946–58	59–71	ALP	Qld
Wilfred Fullagar	1892	1961	1950–61	57–68	Liberal-CP Coalition	Vic
Frank Kitto	1903	1994	1950–70	46–67	Liberal-CP Coalition	NSW
Alan Taylor	1901	1969	1952–69	50–67	Liberal-CP Coalition	NSW
Douglas Menzies	1907	1974	1958–74	50–67	Liberal-CP Coalition	Vic
Victor Windeyer	1900	1987	1958–72	58–71	Liberal-CP Coalition	NSW
William Owen	1899	1972	1961–72	61–72	Liberal-CP Coalition	NSW
Garfield Barwick	1903	1997	CJ 1964–81	60–77	Liberal-CP Coalition	NSW
Cyril Walsh	1909	1973	1969–73	60–64	Liberal-CP Coalition	NSW
Harry Gibbs	1917	2005	1970–81; CJ 1981–87	53–69	Liberal-CP Coalition	Qld
Ninian Stephen	1923		1972–82	48–58	Liberal-CP Coalition	Vic
Anthony Mason	1925		1972–87; CJ 1987–95	47–69	Liberal-CP Coalition	NSW
Kenneth Jacobs	1917		1974–79	56–61	ALP	NSW
Lionel Murphy	1922	1986	1975–86	52–64	ALP	NSW

Keith Aickin	1916	1982	1976–82	60–66	Liberal-NCP Coalition	Vic
Ronald Wilson	1922	2005	1979–89	56–66	Liberal-NCP Coalition	WA
Gerard Brennan	1928		1981–95; CJ 1995–98	52–69	Liberal-NCP Coalition	Qld
William Deane	1931		1982–95	51–64	Liberal-NCP Coalition	NSW
Daryl Dawson	1933		1982–97	48–63	Liberal-NCP Coalition	Vic
John Toohey	1930		1987–98	56–67	ALP	WA
Mary Gaudron	1943		1987–2003	44–60	ALP	NSW
Michael McHugh	1935		1989–2005	53–70	ALP	NSW
William Gummow	1942		1995–	52–	ALP	NSW
Michael Kirby	1939		1996–	56–	ALP	NSW
Kenneth Hayne	1945		1997–	52–	Liberal-NPA Coalition	Vic
Ian Callinan	1937		1998–	60–	Liberal-NPA Coalition	Qld
Murray Gleeson	1938		CJ 1998–	59–	Liberal-NPA Coalition	NSW
John Dyson Heydon	1943		2003–	59–	Liberal-NPA Coalition	NSW
Susan Crennan	1945		2005–	60–	Liberal-NPA Coalition	Vic

(b)   Composition of the Court

On 5 October 1903 Samuel Walker **Griffith**, Edmund **Barton** and Richard Edwin **O'Connor** were appointed as the first three judges of the High Court of Australia. Hence, from 1903 until 1906, the Court comprised:

1903-1906: GRIFFITH BARTON O'CONNOR

On 12 and 13 October 1906, Isaac Alfred **Isaacs** and Henry Bournes **Higgins** were appointed, increasing the number of judges to five:

1906-1912: GRIFFITH BARTON O'CONNOR ISAACS HIGGINS

On 18 November 1912, Mr Justice O'Connor *died*. On 11 February 1913, he was replaced by Frank **Gavan Duffy**. The appointments of Charles **Powers** (5 March 1913), and George Edward **Rich** (5 April 1913), then increased the size of the Court to seven. It comprised:

1913-1919: GRIFFITH BARTON ISAACS HIGGINS GAVAN DUFFY POWERS RICH

On 17 October 1919, Sir Samuel Griffith *retired*; on 7 January 1920, Sir Edmund Barton *died*. Griffith had been replaced as Chief Justice by Adrian **Knox** on 18 October 1919; Barton was replaced by Hayden Erskine **Starke** on 5 February 1920. The Court comprised:

1920-1929: KNOX ISAACS HIGGINS GAVAN DUFFY POWERS RICH STARKE

On 13 January 1929, Mr Justice Higgins *died*; on 22 July 1929, Sir Charles Powers *resigned*; on 31 March 1930, Sir Adrian Knox *resigned*. Higgins had been replaced by Owen **Dixon** on 4 February 1929; Sir Isaac **Isaacs** replaced Knox as Chief Justice on 2 April 1930. At that stage, the Court comprised:

1930: ISAACS GAVAN DUFFY RICH STARKE DIXON

On 19 and 20 December 1930, the two vacancies were filled by Herbert Vere **Evatt** and Edward Aloysius **McTiernan**. A month later (21 January 1931) Sir Isaac Isaacs *resigned* to become the first Australian-born Governor-General; on 22 January 1931 Sir Frank **Gavan Duffy** replaced him as Chief Justice. In a time of economic depression (and controversy over the Evatt-McTiernan appointments), the Labor government left the new vacancy unfilled. Thus, from 1931 until 1935, the Court comprised:

1931-1935: GAVAN DUFFY RICH STARKE DIXON EVATT McTIERNAN

On 1 October 1935, Sir Frank Gavan Duffy *retired*; on 11 October 1935 he was replaced as Chief Justice by John Greig **Latham**. The Court comprised:

1935-1940: LATHAM RICH STARKE DIXON EVATT McTIERNAN

On 2 September 1940 Dr HV Evatt *resigned* to re-enter federal politics; on 15 October 1940, Dudley **Williams** replaced him. The Court comprised:

1940-1946: LATHAM RICH STARKE DIXON McTIERNAN WILLIAMS

On 16 May 1946, William Flood **Webb** became the Australian president of the International Military Tribunal for the Far East, with the status of a High Court judge. His appointment restored the number of judges to seven, though he did not sit as a High Court judge until 1948. The Court comprised:

1946-1950: LATHAM RICH STARKE DIXON McTIERNAN WILLIAMS WEBB

After the election of the Menzies government, Sir Hayden Starke *resigned* on 31 January 1950 at the age of 79 (after 30 years on the Court) and Sir George Rich *resigned* on 3 May 1950 at the age of 87 after 37 years on the Court. Starke was replaced by Wilfred Kelsham **Fullagar** on 8 February 1950 and Rich by Frank Walters **Kitto** on 10 May 1950. The Court now comprised:

1950-1952: LATHAM DIXON McTIERNAN WILLIAMS WEBB FULLAGAR KITTO

After a long illness, Sir John Latham *retired* on 7 April 1952. Sir Owen **Dixon** replaced him as Chief Justice on 18 April; the new vacancy was filled by Alan Russell **Taylor** on 3 September 1952. The Court comprised:

1952-1958: DIXON McTIERNAN WILLIAMS WEBB FULLAGAR KITTO TAYLOR

Sir William Webb *resigned* on 16 May 1958; Sir Dudley Williams on 31 July 1958. Webb was replaced by Douglas Ian **Menzies** on 12 June 1958; Williams by William John Victor **Windeyer** on 8 September 1958. The Court comprised:

1958-1961: DIXON McTIERNAN FULLAGAR KITTO TAYLOR MENZIES WINDEYER

Sir Wilfred Fullagar *died* on 9 July 1961, and was replaced by William Francis Langer **Owen**, on 22 September 1961. The Court comprised:

1961-1964: DIXON McTIERNAN KITTO TAYLOR MENZIES WINDEYER OWEN

Sir Owen Dixon *retired* on 13 April 1964 after 35 years on the Court, including 12 years as Chief Justice. Garfield Edward John **Barwick** replaced him as Chief Justice on 27 April 1964, and the Court comprised:

1964-1969: BARWICK McTIERNAN KITTO TAYLOR MENZIES WINDEYER OWEN

Sir Alan Taylor *died* on 3 August 1969; Cyril Ambrose **Walsh** replaced him on 20 September. Sir Frank Kitto *resigned* on 1 August 1970; Harry Talbot **Gibbs** replaced him on 4 August, and the Court comprised:

1970-1972: BARWICK McTIERNAN MENZIES WINDEYER OWEN WALSH GIBBS

Sir Victor Windeyer *retired* on 29 February 1972; and Sir William Owen *died* on 31 March 1972. Windeyer was replaced by Ninian Martin **Stephen** on 1 March 1972; Owen by Anthony Frank **Mason** on 21 September 1972. The Court comprised:

1972-1973: BARWICK McTIERNAN MENZIES WALSH GIBBS STEPHEN MASON

Sir Cyril Walsh *died* on 29 November 1973, and was replaced by Kenneth Sydney **Jacobs** on 8 February 1974. The Court comprised:

1974: BARWICK McTIERNAN MENZIES GIBBS STEPHEN MASON JACOBS

Sir Douglas Menzies *died* on 29 November 1974, and was replaced by Lionel Keith **Murphy** on 10 February 1975. The Court comprised:

1975-1976: BARWICK McTIERNAN GIBBS STEPHEN MASON JACOBS MURPHY

Sir Edward McTiernan *retired* on 12 September 1976, at the age of 84, after 46 years on the Court. He was replaced by Keith Arthur **Aickin** on 20 September 1976, and the Court comprised:

1976-1979: BARWICK GIBBS STEPHEN MASON JACOBS MURPHY AICKIN

Sir Kenneth Jacobs *resigned* on 6 April 1979, and was replaced by Ronald Darling **Wilson** on 19 May 1979. The Court comprised:

1979-1980: BARWICK GIBBS STEPHEN MASON MURPHY AICKIN WILSON

Sir Garfield Barwick *retired* on 11 February 1981, and was replaced as Chief Justice by Sir Harry **Gibbs** on 12 February 1981. The vacancy was filled by Francis Gerard **Brennan** (also on 12 February 1981), and the Court comprised:

1981-1982: GIBBS STEPHEN MASON MURPHY AICKIN WILSON BRENNAN

Sir Ninian Stephen *resigned* (to become Governor-General) on 11 May 1982; Sir Keith Aickin *died* on 18 June 1982. Stephen was replaced by William Patrick **Deane** on 27 July 1982, and Aickin by Daryl Michael **Dawson** on 16 August 1982. The Court comprised:

1982-1986: GIBBS MASON MURPHY WILSON BRENNAN DEANE DAWSON

Mr Justice Murphy *died* on 21 October 1986; Sir Harry Gibbs *retired* on 5 February 1987. On 6 February Sir Anthony **Mason** replaced Gibbs as Chief Justice, and the vacancies were filled by John Leslie **Toohey** and Mary Genevieve **Gaudron**. The Court comprised:

1987-1989: MASON WILSON BRENNAN DEANE DAWSON TOOHEY GAUDRON

Sir Ronald Wilson *resigned* on 13 February 1989, and was replaced by Michael Hudson **McHugh** on 14 February 1989. The Court comprised:

1989-1995: MASON BRENNAN DEANE DAWSON TOOHEY GAUDRON McHUGH

Sir Anthony Mason *retired* on 20 April 1995. On 21 April Sir Gerard **Brennan** replaced him as Chief Justice; the resulting vacancy was filled by William Montague Charles **Gummow**. The Court comprised:

1995: BRENNAN DEANE DAWSON TOOHEY GAUDRON McHUGH GUMMOW

Sir William Deane *resigned* (to become Governor-General) on 10 November 1995, and was replaced by Michael Donald **Kirby** on 6 February 1996. The Court comprised:

1996-1997: BRENNAN DAWSON TOOHEY GAUDRON McHUGH GUMMOW KIRBY

Sir Daryl Dawson *resigned* as from 15 August 1997; Justice Toohey *resigned* as from 2 February 1998; and Sir Gerard Brennan *retired* on 21 May 1998. Sir Daryl Dawson was replaced by Kenneth Madison **Hayne** on 22 September 1997; Toohey by Ian David Francis **Callinan** on 3 February 1998, and Sir Gerard Brennan by Anthony Murray **Gleeson**, appointed as Chief Justice on 22 May 1998. The Court comprised:

1998- 2003: GLEESON GAUDRON McHUGH GUMMOW KIRBY HAYNE CALLINAN

Justice Gaudron *resigned* on 10 February 2003, and was replaced by John Dyson **Heydon** on 11 February 2003. The Court comprised:

2003-2005 : GLEESON McHUGH GUMMOW KIRBY HAYNE CALLINAN HEYDON

Justice McHugh *retired* on 31 October 2005, and was replaced by Susan Marie **Crennan** on 8 November 2005. The Court now comprises:

2005- : GLEESON GUMMOW KIRBY HAYNE CALLINAN HEYDON CRENNAN

6. Outcomes in Constitutional Referenda

Forty-four proposals to change the Constitution have been put to the Australian people over 19 referendum days. One of the successful amendments in 1977 altered s 128 to enable people in the Territories to vote in referenda (although only for the purpose of calculating the national vote). Section 128 states that a proposal is passed only if "in a majority of the States a majority of the electors voting approve the proposed law, and if a majority of all the electors voting also approve the proposed law". If an informal vote is a "vote" for the purposes of s 128, a matter not yet determined by the High Court, a referendum will only succeed where more than half of the votes, including informal ballots, are "Yes".

12 December 1906

Amendment of s 13 to facilitate concurrent elections for Senate and House of Representatives

	Yes	No	Informal
Total	73.81%	15.49%	10.70%
New South Wales	75.48%	14.54%	9.98%
Victoria	74.57%	15.16%	10.27%
Queensland	67.12%	20.23%	12.65%
South Australia	77.23%	11.55%	11.22%
Western Australia	69.03%	18.43%	12.54%
Tasmania	71.48%	16.42%	12.09%

CARRIED (nationally and in all States)

13 April 1910

(1) Amendment of s 105 to enable the Commonwealth to take over State debts

	Yes	No	Informal
Total	51.17%	41.95%	6.88%
New South Wales	31.12%	62.22%	6.65%
Victoria	59.91%	32.84%	7.25%
Queensland	60.76%	33.34%	5.90%
South Australia	66.36%	24.32%	9.32%
Western Australia	69.01%	25.79%	5.20%
Tasmania	75.63%	17.78%	6.59%

CARRIED (nationally and in five States)

(2) Proposed amendment of s 87: immediate substitution of per capita grants to States

	Yes	No	Informal
Total	46.15%	47.96%	5.89%
New South Wales	44.45%	49.42%	6.13%
Victoria	42.90%	51.89%	5.21%
Queensland	51.52%	42.87%	5.61%
South Australia	44.75%	46.47%	8.78%
Western Australia	58.86%	36.47%	4.67%
Tasmania	56.15%	37.45%	6.40%

Not carried nationally (but in three States)

26 April 1911

(1) More Commonwealth powers over trade and commerce, corporations, industrial relations and trade practices

	Yes	No	Informal
Total	38.76%	59.56%	1.67%
New South Wales	35.41%	62.66%	1.93%
Victoria	37.99%	60.32%	1.69%
Queensland	42.94%	55.21%	1.85%
South Australia	37.68%	61.29%	1.03%
Western Australia	54.08%	44.49%	1.42%
Tasmania	41.62%	57.22%	1.16%

Not carried nationally (but in one State)

(2) Commonwealth power to nationalise any industry declared to be a monopoly by both Houses of Parliament

	Yes	No	Informal
Total	39.19%	59.06%	1.75%
New South Wales	36.00%	62.02%	1.98%
Victoria	38.25%	59.96%	1.79%
Queensland	43.39%	54.64%	1.98%
South Australia	38.03%	60.96%	1.01%
Western Australia	55.02%	43.51%	1.47%
Tasmania	41.88%	56.82%	1.30%

Not carried nationally (but in one State)

31 May 1913

(1) The 1911 proposal for an expanded Commonwealth trade and commerce power – now put separately

	Yes	No	Informal
Total	47.19%	48.39%	4.42%
New South Wales	44.36%	50.16%	5.49%
Victoria	47.45%	49.16%	3.39%
Queensland	52.15%	43.81%	4.03%
South Australia	49.21%	46.68%	4.11%
Western Australia	50.33%	44.90%	4.77%
Tasmania	43.18%	52.43%	4.40%

Not carried nationally (but in three States)

(2) The 1911 proposal for an expanded Commonwealth corporations power – now put separately

	Yes	No	Informal
Total	47.31%	48.59%	4.10%
New South Wales	44.33%	50.41%	5.26%
Victoria	47.64%	49.31%	3.05%
Queensland	52.42%	44.11%	3.47%
South Australia	49.33%	46.75%	3.93%
Western Australia	50.52%	45.10%	4.38%
Tasmania	43.26%	52.70%	4.04%

Not carried nationally (but in three States)

(3) The 1911 proposal for an expanded Commonwealth industrial relations power – now put separately

	Yes	No	Informal
Total	47.35%	48.63%	4.02%
New South Wales	44.46%	50.38%	5.15%
Victoria	47.55%	49.45%	3.01%
Queensland	52.50%	44.08%	3.42%
South Australia	49.49%	46.79%	3.72%
Western Australia	50.41%	45.22%	4.36%
Tasmania	43.40%	52.62%	3.98%

Not carried nationally (but in three States)

(4) The 1911 proposal for an expanded Commonwealth trade practices power – now put separately

	Yes	No	Informal
Total	47.63%	48.06%	4.31%
New South Wales	44.54%	49.98%	5.48%
Victoria	48.16%	48.72%	3.12%
Queensland	52.75%	43.56%	3.69%
South Australia	49.37%	46.19%	4.44%
Western Australia	51.09%	44.24%	4.67%
Tasmania	43.40%	52.24%	4.36%

Not carried nationally (but in three States)

(5) The 1911 proposal for nationalisation of monopolies

	Yes	No	Informal
Total	45.16%	46.38%	8.45%
New South Wales	42.03%	47.69%	10.28%
Victoria	45.87%	47.62%	6.52%
Queensland	49.60%	41.96%	8.45%
South Australia	46.82%	44.52%	8.67%
Western Australia	49.30%	43.38%	7.32%
Tasmania	41.33%	50.07%	8.60%

Not carried nationally (but in three States)

(6) An attempt to override the *Railway Servants' Case* (1906) 4 CLR 488 (see Chapter 7) by extending Commonwealth arbitration to State railways

	Yes	No	Informal
Total	47.09%	48.75%	4.15%
New South Wales	44.23%	50.48%	5.29%
Victoria	47.28%	49.63%	3.09%
Queensland	52.27%	44.19%	3.54%
South Australia	49.21%	46.74%	4.05%
Western Australia	50.04%	45.49%	4.47%
Tasmania	43.13%	52.69%	4.17%

Not carried nationally (but in three States)

13 December 1919

(1) Temporary extension of Commonwealth power over trade and commerce, corporations, industrial relations and trusts

	Yes	No	Informal
Total	44.87%	45.50%	9.62%
New South Wales	36.21%	54.43%	9.36%
Victoria	57.93%	31.68%	10.39%
Queensland	53.11%	39.49%	7.39%
South Australia	22.77%	67.31%	9.92%
Western Australia	46.79%	43.63%	9.58%
Tasmania	28.26%	56.28%	15.46%

Not carried nationally (but in three States)

(2) Another attempt at nationalisation of monopolies

	Yes	No	Informal
Total	40.07%	42.32%	17.61%
New South Wales	31.67%	51.00%	17.33%
Victoria	50.89%	29.52%	19.59%
Queensland	49.12%	37.18%	13.70%
South Australia	21.64%	63.08%	15.29%
Western Australia	44.01%	37.50%	18.49%
Tasmania	25.24%	48.83%	25.93%

Not carried nationally (but in three States)

4 September 1926

(1) Regulation of industrial employment through parallel Commonwealth and State authorities; and a trade practices power for the Commonwealth

	Yes	No	Informal
Total	42.07%	54.64%	3.29%
New South Wales	50.10%	47.12%	2.77%
Victoria	34.91%	61.46%	3.63%
Queensland	50.72%	46.63%	2.65%
South Australia	28.06%	67.64%	4.30%
Western Australia	28.24%	68.17%	3.59%
Tasmania	42.41%	52.14%	5.46%

Not carried nationally (but in two States)

(2) Commonwealth power to protect essential services

	Yes	No	Informal
Total	40.33%	53.90%	5.77%
New South Wales	48.18%	47.43%	4.39%
Victoria	33.37%	60.49%	6.14%
Queensland	47.16%	46.12%	6.72%
South Australia	29.12%	63.85%	7.03%
Western Australia	24.04%	68.80%	7.15%
Tasmania	44.41%	46.99%	8.60%

Not carried nationally (but in two States)

17 November 1928

Adding s 105A to authorise the Financial Agreement

	Yes	No	Informal
Total	69.39%	24.00%	6.61%
New South Wales	60.60%	33.40%	5.99%
Victoria	83.00%	11.55%	5.44%
Queensland	84.37%	10.85%	4.78%
South Australia	54.66%	32.54%	12.79%
Western Australia	52.82%	39.00%	8.18%
Tasmania	59.09%	29.24%	11.67%

CARRIED (nationally and in all six States)

6 March 1937

(1) An attempt to override *R v Burgess; Ex parte Henry* (1936) 55 CLR 608 (see Chapter 18) by giving the Commonwealth power over air navigation and aircraft

	Yes	No	Informal
Total	51.41%	44.58%	4.02%
New South Wales	45.46%	50.75%	3.79%
Victoria	62.88%	33.71%	3.41%
Queensland	59.69%	36.78%	3.53%
South Australia	37.66%	56.18%	6.16%
Western Australia	45.23%	49.83%	4.95%
Tasmania	36.49%	57.21%	6.30%

Not carried (national majority but only two States)

(2) An attempt to override *James v Commonwealth* [1936] AC 578 (see Chapter 25) by freeing the Commonwealth from s 92 in respect of marketing laws

	Yes	No	Informal
Total	33.65%	59.14%	7.22%
New South Wales	31.25%	61.32%	7.43%
Victoria	43.59%	49.99%	6.41%
Queensland	36.10%	56.99%	6.91%
South Australia	19.14%	72.78%	8.08%
Western Australia	25.71%	66.86%	7.44%
Tasmania	19.68%	70.23%	10.10%

Not carried nationally or in any State

19 August 1944

The "Fourteen Powers" Bill: 14 new heads of Commonwealth power plus guarantees of rights, as a package deal

	Yes	No	Informal
Total	45.39%	53.30%	1.31%
New South Wales	44.81%	53.81%	1.37%
Victoria	48.70%	50.06%	1.24%
Queensland	36.07%	62.69%	1.24%
South Australia	50.02%	48.75%	1.23%
Western Australia	51.55%	47.11%	1.34%
Tasmania	38.29%	60.09%	1.62%

Not carried nationally (but in two States)

28 September 1946

(1) Insertion of s 51(xxiiiA): additional Commonwealth social services powers

	Yes	No	Informal
Total	51.59%	43.27%	5.14%
New South Wales	51.10%	43.52%	5.38%
Victoria	53.27%	41.89%	4.83%
Queensland	48.88%	46.47%	4.66%
South Australia	49.44%	46.12%	4.44%
Western Australia	58.77%	35.62%	5.60%
Tasmania	46.56%	45.50%	7.93%

CARRIED (nationally and in all six States)

(2) Exclusion of cooperative marketing schemes from s 92

	Yes	No	Informal
Total	47.51%	46.43%	6.05%
New South Wales	48.67%	45.24%	6.09%
Victoria	49.50%	45.02%	5.48%
Queensland	41.11%	52.87%	6.01%
South Australia	46.00%	48.38%	5.62%
Western Australia	52.24%	40.69%	7.07%
Tasmania	38.35%	51.78%	9.87%

Not carried (national majority but only three States)

(3) Additional Commonwealth power over industrial employment

	Yes	No	Informal
Total	46.26%	45.71%	8.03%
New South Wales	47.45%	44.29%	8.25%
Victoria	48.31%	44.46%	7.23%
Queensland	39.73%	51.78%	8.49%
South Australia	44.87%	48.21%	6.92%
Western Australia	50.95%	40.45%	8.60%
Tasmania	36.25%	51.38%	12.37%

Not carried (national majority but only three States)

29 May 1948

Rents and prices: permanent postwar Commonwealth control

	Yes	No	Informal
Total	40.07%	58.49%	1.43%
New South Wales	41.04%	57.47%	1.49%
Victoria	44.04%	54.64%	1.32%
Queensland	30.43%	68.36%	1.21%
South Australia	41.50%	56.96%	1.53%
Western Australia	37.95%	60.40%	1.65%
Tasmania	34.75%	63.28%	1.97%

Not carried nationally or in any State

22 September 1951

Overriding the *Communist Party Case* (1951) 83 CLR 1 (see Chapter 17) by enshrining the *Communist Party Dissolution Act* 1950 (Cth) in the Constitution and giving Commonwealth power over communism

	Yes	No	Informal
Total	48.75%	49.85%	1.40%
New South Wales	46.52%	52.11%	1.37%
Victoria	48.02%	50.57%	1.41%
Queensland	55.21%	43.80%	1.00%
South Australia	46.57%	51.90%	1.53%
Western Australia	53.98%	44.00%	2.02%
Tasmania	49.28%	48.77%	1.95%

Not carried nationally (but in three States)

27 May 1967

(1) Breaking the nexus between the number of members of the House of Representatives and of the Senate

	Yes	No	Informal
Total	39.62%	58.81%	1.57%
New South Wales	50.20%	48.21%	1.59%
Victoria	30.47%	68.23%	1.30%
Queensland	43.62%	55.22%	1.16%
South Australia	33.23%	64.75%	2.03%
Western Australia	28.31%	69.15%	2.54%
Tasmania	22.60%	75.38%	2.02%

Not carried nationally (but in one State)

(2) Aborigines: amending s 51(xxvi) and deleting s 127

	Yes	No	Informal
Total	89.34%	9.08%	1.58%
New South Wales	89.96%	8.40%	1.64%
Victoria	93.53%	5.25%	1.22%
Queensland	88.20%	10.67%	1.12%
South Australia	84.42%	13.44%	2.14%
Western Australia	78.84%	18.56%	2.60%
Tasmania	88.34%	9.58%	2.08%

CARRIED (nationally and in all six States)

8 December 1973

(1) Commonwealth control over prices

	Yes	No	Informal
Total	43.22%	55.43%	1.35%
New South Wales	48.02%	50.88%	1.10%
Victoria	44.51%	54.00%	1.48%
Queensland	38.14%	61.00%	0.86%
South Australia	40.37%	57.71%	1.91%
Western Australia	31.29%	66.80%	1.92%
Tasmania	37.39%	60.44%	2.17%

Not carried nationally or in any State

(2) Commonwealth control over incomes

	Yes	No	Informal
Total	33.86%	64.53%	1.61%
New South Wales	39.77%	58.89%	1.34%
Victoria	32.86%	65.40%	1.74%
Queensland	31.38%	67.62%	1.00%
South Australia	27.60%	70.10%	2.30%
Western Australia	24.63%	73.08%	2.29%
Tasmania	27.57%	69.80%	2.63%

Not carried nationally or in any State

18 May 1974

(1) Simultaneous elections for both Houses of Parliament

	Yes	No	Informal
Total	47.50%	50.84%	1.67%
New South Wales	50.30%	48.21%	1.49%
Victoria	48.34%	49.93%	1.73%
Queensland	43.80%	55.03%	1.17%
South Australia	46.01%	51.58%	2.41%
Western Australia	43.06%	54.64%	2.31%
Tasmania	40.69%	57.65%	1.66%

Not carried nationally (but in one State)

(2) Amendment of s 128 to require a national majority plus a majority in only half the States and to permit Territory residents to vote in referenda

	Yes	No	Informal
Total	47.20%	51.14%	1.66%
New South Wales	50.59%	47.93%	1.47%
Victoria	48.37%	49.91%	1.72%
Queensland	43.78%	55.06%	1.15%
South Australia	43.18%	54.38%	2.43%
Western Australia	41.55%	56.13%	2.32%
Tasmania	40.05%	58.29%	1.66%

Not carried nationally (but in one State)

(3) "One vote one value": average size of electorates to be determined on basis of population

	Yes	No	Informal
Total	46.41%	51.91%	1.68%
New South Wales	49.80%	48.72%	1.48%
Victoria	46.88%	51.38%	1.74%
Queensland	43.18%	55.64%	1.18%
South Australia	43.03%	54.52%	2.46%
Western Australia	41.86%	55.81%	2.33%
Tasmania	40.13%	58.19%	1.68%

Not carried nationally (but in one State)

(4) Commonwealth financial assistance to local government

	Yes	No	Informal
Total	45.97%	52.15%	1.88%
New South Wales	49.96%	48.39%	1.65%
Victoria	46.44%	51.58%	1.99%
Queensland	43.10%	55.58%	1.31%
South Australia	41.32%	55.85%	2.83%
Western Australia	39.68%	57.88%	2.44%
Tasmania	39.30%	58.88%	1.82%

Not carried nationally (but in one State)

21 May 1977

(1) Simultaneous elections for both Houses of Parliament

	Yes	No	Informal
Total	61.12%	37.11%	1.77%
New South Wales	69.63%	28.85%	1.52%
Victoria	63.64%	34.27%	2.09%
Queensland	46.97%	51.89%	1.14%
South Australia	64.45%	33.21%	2.33%
Western Australia	47.35%	50.33%	2.32%
Tasmania	33.64%	64.54%	1.81%

Not carried (national majority but only three States)

(2) Amendment of s 15 to re-establish State parliamentary conventions broken in 1975

	Yes	No	Informal
Total	72.02%	26.20%	1.78%
New South Wales	80.39%	18.10%	1.51%
Victoria	74.53%	23.37%	2.10%
Queensland	58.19%	40.67%	1.14%
South Australia	74.79%	22.86%	2.35%
Western Australia	55.77%	41.89%	2.34%
Tasmania	52.80%	45.37%	1.83%

CARRIED (nationally and in all six States)

(3) Amendment of s 128 to allow Territory residents to vote

	Yes	No	Informal
Total	76.33%	21.88%	1.79%
New South Wales	82.64%	15.83%	1.53%
Victoria	79.07%	18.81%	2.12%
Queensland	58.90%	39.96%	1.14%
South Australia	81.33%	16.32%	2.34%
Western Australia	70.90%	26.73%	2.37%
Tasmania	61.10%	37.06%	1.84%

CARRIED (nationally and in all six States)

(4) Amendment of s 72: High Court judges to retire at 70 and other federal judges at 70 or lower statutory retirement age

	Yes	No	Informal
Total	78.63%	19.53%	1.84%
New South Wales	83.51%	14.92%	1.56%
Victoria	79.65%	18.17%	2.18%
Queensland	64.47%	34.35%	1.18%
South Australia	83.48%	14.07%	2.45%
Western Australia	76.48%	21.10%	2.42%
Tasmania	71.10%	27.02%	1.88%

CARRIED (nationally and in all six States)

1 December 1984

(1) Simultaneous elections for both Houses of Parliament

	Yes	No	Informal
Total	48.21%	47.00%	4.78%
New South Wales	50.43%	44.96%	4.61%
Victoria	50.26%	44.22%	5.52%
Queensland	44.41%	52.88%	2.71%
South Australia	46.50%	46.54%	6.96%
Western Australia	44.44%	51.20%	4.36%
Tasmania	37.08%	57.30%	5.62%
ACT	54.55%	41.68%	3.77%
Northern Territory	48.25%	44.77%	6.98%

Not carried (national majority but only two States)

(2) "Interchange of powers": provision for cooperative referral of powers by Commonwealth and States to each other

	Yes	No	Informal
Total	43.91%	49.39%	6.70%
New South Wales	45.89%	47.69%	6.42%
Victoria	46.03%	46.29%	7.68%
Queensland	39.98%	55.92%	5.68%
South Australia	41.53%	48.87%	9.60%
Western Australia	41.68%	52.44%	5.88%
Tasmania	31.73%	59.86%	8.40%
ACT	53.01%	41.49%	5.50%
Northern Territory	43.78%	47.84%	8.38%

Not carried nationally or in any State

3 September 1988

(1) Four-year maximum terms in both Houses of Parliament

	Yes	No	Informal
Total	32.49%	66.23%	1.27%
New South Wales	31.32%	67.59%	1.10%
Victoria	35.57%	62.69%	1.74%
Queensland	34.93%	64.44%	0.63%
South Australia	26.32%	72.06%	1.62%
Western Australia	30.24%	68.33%	1.43%
Tasmania	25.00%	73.66%	1.34%
ACT	43.22%	55.88%	0.90%
Northern Territory	37.42%	60.71%	1.87%

Not carried nationally or in any State

(2) "One vote one value": electorates on population basis deviating no more than 10%, and a guaranteed right to vote

	Yes	No	Informal
Total	37.10%	61.59%	1.30%
New South Wales	35.17%	63.71%	1.12%
Victoria	39.40%	58.81%	1.79%
Queensland	44.53%	54.84%	0.63%
South Australia	30.11%	68.24%	1.65%
Western Australia	31.55%	66.98%	1.47%
Tasmania	28.51%	70.15%	1.35%
ACT	51.51%	47.57%	0.92%
Northern Territory	42.16%	55.90%	1.94%

Not carried nationally or in any State

(3) A new s 119A: "Each State shall provide for the establishment and continuance of a system of local government"

	Yes	No	Informal
Total	33.17%	65.51%	1.32%
New South Wales	31.34%	67.53%	1.13%
Victoria	35.41%	62.78%	1.81%
Queensland	38.06%	61.29%	0.65%
South Australia	29.36%	68.97%	1.67%
Western Australia	29.32%	69.20%	1.48%
Tasmania	27.13%	71.51%	1.37%
ACT	39.40%	59.64%	0.96%
Northern Territory	38.05%	60.01%	1.94%

Not carried nationally or in any State

(4) Guarantees of trial by jury, religious freedom and "just terms" for acquisition of property (see Chapter 26) clarified and extended to the States

	Yes	No	Informal
Total	30.33%	68.19%	1.48%
New South Wales	29.27%	69.44%	1.29%
Victoria	32.76%	65.25%	1.99%
Queensland	32.63%	66.60%	0.77%
South Australia	25.53%	72.63%	1.84%
Western Australia	27.68%	70.67%	1.65%
Tasmania	25.10%	73.37%	1.52%
ACT	40.28%	58.05%	1.08%
Northern Territory	36.37%	61.56%	2.07%

Not carried nationally or in any State

6 November 1999

(1) An Australian republic

	Yes	No	Informal
Total	44.74%	54.40%	0.86%
New South Wales	46.02%	53.09%	0.88%
Victoria	49.38%	49.69%	0.93%
Queensland	37.18%	62.12%	0.69%
South Australia	43.17%	55.92%	0.91%
Western Australia	41.13%	58.02%	0.85%
Tasmania	40.00%	59.09%	0.91%
ACT	62.78%	36.45%	0.77%
Northern Territory	48.31%	50.76%	0.93%

Not carried nationally or in any State

(2) A new preamble to the Constitution

	Yes	No	Informal
Total	38.96%	60.08%	0.95%
New South Wales	41.72%	57.28%	0.99%
Victoria	42.03%	56.96%	1.01%
Queensland	32.56%	66.67%	0.77%
South Australia	37.70%	61.25%	1.05%
Western Australia	34.41%	64.65%	0.94%
Tasmania	35.30%	63.65%	1.06%
ACT	43.25%	55.91%	0.84%
Northern Territory	38.09%	60.80%	1.10%

Not carried nationally or in any State

Index